Sports Illustrated
1999
Sports Almanac

By the Editors of Sports Illustrated

LITTLE, BROWN AND COMPANY

Boston   New York   London

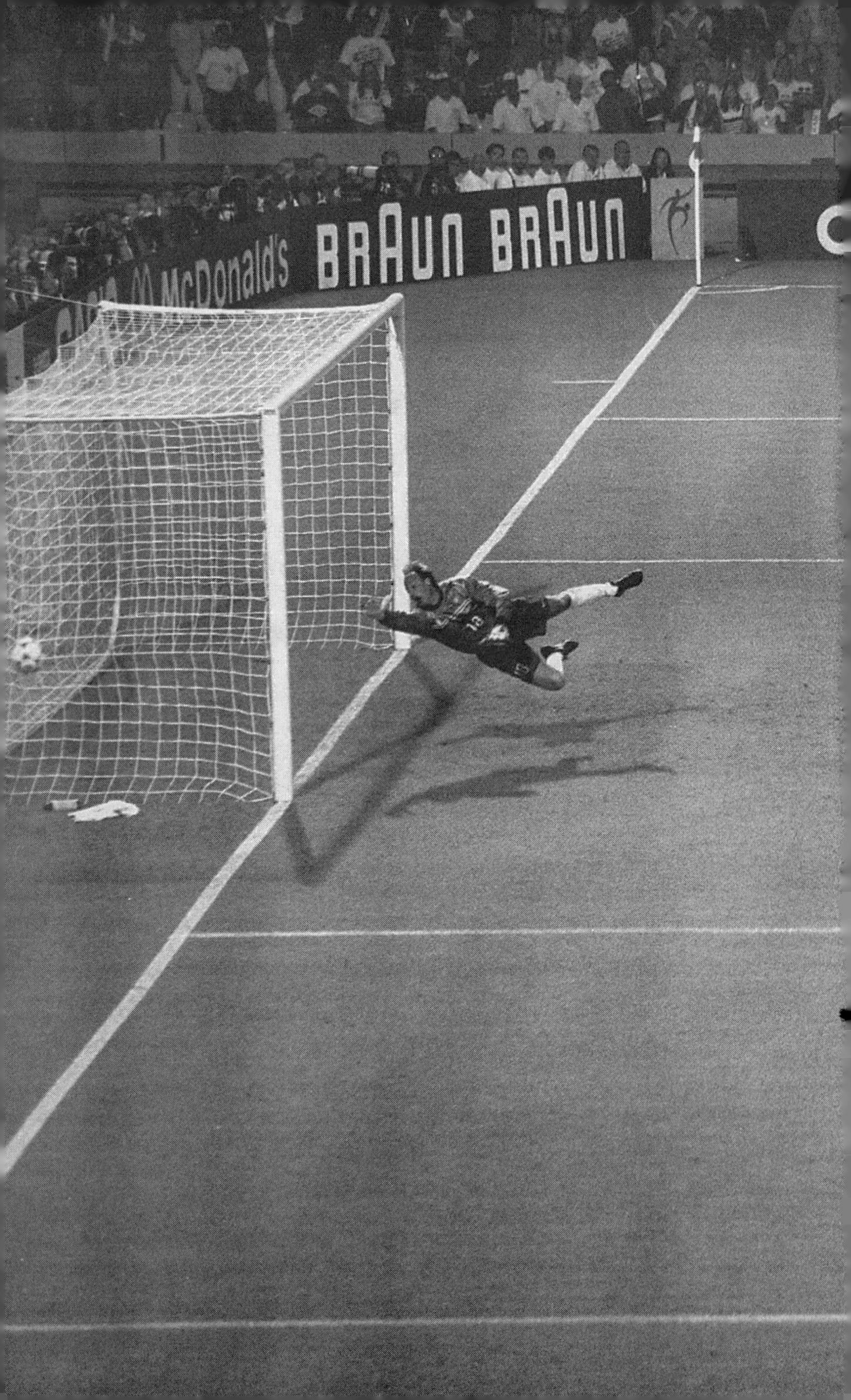

McDonald's
BRAUN BRAUN

Sports Illustrated
1999
Sports
Almanac

First Edition
ISBN 0-316-80694-3

Sports Illustrated 1999 Sports Almanac was produced by
Bishop Books of New York City.

Sports Illustrated Editorial Director for Books: Joe Marshall
Sports Illustrated Director of Development: Stanley Weil

Paperback edition front cover photography credits (clockwise from top left):
Venus Williams: Ron Angle
Mark McGwire: John Iacono
Mark O'Meara: Chris Cole/TGPL

Paperback edition back cover photography credits (clockwise from left):
John Elway: Damian Strohmeyer
Jeff Gordon: George Tiedemann
Dominik Hasek: Bill Wippert

Hardcover edition front cover photography credits (left to right):
Brett Favre: Al Tielemans
Mark McGwire: John Iacono

Hardcover edition back cover photography credits (clockwise from top right):
Jeff Gordon: George Tiedemann
Dominik Hasek: Bill Wippert
Mark O'Meara: Chris Cole/TGPL

Title page photography credit: Simon Bruty

10 9 8 7 6 5 4 3 2 1
COM

PRINTED IN THE UNITED STATES OF AMERICA

CONTENTS

Expanded Contents

Expanded Contents *(Cont.)*

SOURCES

In compiling the *Sports Illustrated 1999 Sports Almanac*, the editors would again like to thank the staff of the *Sports Illustrated* library for its invaluable assistance. They would also like to extend their gratitude to the media relations offices of the following organizations for their help in providing information and materials relating to their sports: Major League Baseball; the Canadian Football League; the National Football League; the National Collegiate Athletic Association; the National Basketball Association; the National Hockey League; the Association of Tennis Professionals; the World Tennis Association; the U.S. Tennis Association; the U.S. Golf Association; the Ladies Professional Golf Association; the Professional Golfers Association; Thoroughbred Racing Communications, Inc.; the U.S. Trotting Association; the Breeders' Cup; Churchill Downs; the New York Racing Association, Inc.; the Maryland Jockey Club; Championship Auto Racing Teams; the National Hot Rod Association; the International Motor Sports Association; the National Association for Stock Car Auto Racing; the Professional Bowlers Association; the Ladies Professional Bowlers Tour; the American Professional Soccer League; the National Professional Soccer League; the *Fédération Internationale de Football Association*; the U.S. Soccer Federation; the U.S. Olympic Committee; USA Track & Field; U.S. Swimming; U.S. Diving; U.S. Skiing; U.S. Skating; the U.S. Chess Federation; U.S. Curling; the Iditarod Trail Committee; the International Game Fish Association; the U.S. Gymnastics Federation; U.S. Handball Association; the Lacrosse Foundation; the American Power Boat Association; the Hydroplane Racing Association; the Professional Rodeo Cowboys Association; U.S. Rowing; the American Softball Association; the U.S. Speed Skating Association; U.S. Rugby Football Union; the Triathlon Federation USA; the National Archery Association; USA Wrestling; the U.S. Squash Racquets Association; the U.S. Polo Association; ABC Sports and the U.S. Volleyball Association.

The following sources were consulted in gathering information:

Baseball *The Baseball Encyclopedia*, Macmillan Publishing Co., 1990; *Total Baseball*, Viking Penguin, 1995; *Baseballistics*, St. Martin's Press, 1990; *The Book of Baseball Records*, Seymour Siwoff, publisher, 1991; *The Complete Baseball Record Book*, The Sporting News Publishing Co., 1992; *The Sporting News Baseball Guide*, The Sporting News Publishing Co., 1996; *The Sporting News Official Baseball Register*, The Sporting News Publishing Co., 1996; *National League Green Book—1994*, The Sporting News Publishing Co., 1993; *American League Red Book—1994*, The Sporting News Publishing Co., 1993; *The Scouting Report: 1996*, Harper Perennial, 1996.

Pro Football *The Official 1997 National Football League Record & Fact Book*, The National Football League, 1997; *The Official National Football League Encyclopedia*, New American Library, 1990; *The Sporting News Football Guide*, The Sporting News Publishing Co., 1996; *The Sporting News Football Register*, The Sporting News Publishing Co., 1996; *The 1993 National Football League Record & Fact Book*, Workman Publishing, 1993; *The Football Encyclopedia*, David Neft and Richard Cohen, St. Martin's Press, 1991.

College Football *1997 NCAA Football*, The National Collegiate Athletic Association, 1997.

Pro Basketball *The Official NBA Basketball Encyclopedia*, Villard Books, 1994; *The Sporting News Official NBA Guide*, The Sporting News Publishing Co., 1996; *The Sporting News Official NBA Register*, The Sporting News Publishing Co., 1996.

College Basketball *1997 NCAA Basketball*, The National Collegiate Athletic Association, 1996.

Hockey *The National Hockey League Official Guide & Record Book 1997–98*, The National Hockey League, 1997; *The Sporting News Complete Hockey Book,* The Sporting News Publishing Co., 1993; *The Complete Encyclopedia of Hockey,* Visible Ink Press, 1993.

Tennis *1997 Official USTA Tennis Yearbook*, H.O. Zimman, Inc., 1997; *IBM/ATP Tour 1997 Player Guide*, Association of Tennis Professionals, 1997; *1997 Corel WTA Tour Media Guide*, Corel WTA Tour, 1997.

Golf *PGA Tour Book 1997*, PGA Tour Creative Services, 1997; *LPGA 1997 Player Guide*, LPGA Communications Department, 1997; *Senior PGA Tour Book 1997*, PGA Tour Creative Services, 1997; *USGA Yearbook 1997*, U.S. Golf Association, 1997.

Boxing *The Ring 1986–87 Record Book and Boxing Encyclopedia*, The Ring Publishing Corp., 1987. (To subscribe to *The Ring* magazine, write to P.O. Box 768, Rockville Centre, New York 11571-9905; or call (516) 678-7464); *Computer Boxing Update*, Ralph Citro, Inc., 1992; Bob Yalen, boxing statistician at ESPN.

Horse Racing *The American Racing Manual 1994*, Daily Racing Form, Inc., 1994; *1994 Directory and Record Book*, The Thoroughbred Racing Association, 1994; *The Trotting and Pacing Guide 1994*, United States Trotting Association, 1994; *Breeders' Cup 1993 Statistics*, Breeders' Cup Limited, 1993; *NYRA Media Guide 1993*, The New York Racing Association, 1994; *The 120th Kentucky Derby Media Guide, 1994*, Churchill Downs Public Relations Dept., 1994; *The 120th Preakness Press Guide, 1994*, Maryland Jockey Club, 1994; *Harness Racing News,* Harness Racing Communications.

Motor Sports *The Official NASCAR Yearbook and Press Guide 1997*, UMI Publications, Inc., 1997; *1994 Indianapolis 500 Media Fact Book*, Indy 500 Publications, 1994; *IMSA Yearbook 1995 Season Review*, International Motor Sports Association, 1995; *1994 Winston Drag Racing Series Media Guide*, Sports Marketing Enterprises, 1994.

Bowling *1994 Professional Bowlers Association Press, Radio and Television Guide*, Professional Bowlers Association, Inc., 1994; *The Professional Women's Bowling Association Tour Guide 1997*.

Soccer *Rothmans Football Yearbook 1993–94*, Headline Book Publishing, 1993; *American Professional Soccer League 1992 Media Guide*, APSL Media Relations Department, 1992; *The European Football Yearbook*, Facer Publications Limited, 1988; *Soccer America,* Burling Communications; Dan Goldstein, editor of *Football Europe.*

NCAA Sports *1997–98 National Collegiate Championships*, The National Collegiate Athletic Association, 1998; *1993–94 National Directory of College Athletics,* Collegiate Directories Inc., 1993.

Olympics *The Complete Book of the Olympics*, Little, Brown and Co., 1991; *The Complete Book of the Summer Olympics,* Little, Brown and Co., 1996

Track and Field *American Athletics Annual 1996*, The Athletics Congress/USA, 1996.

Swimming *6th World Swimming Championships Media Guide*, The World Swimming Championships Organizing Committee, 1991.

Skiing *U.S. Ski Team 1994 Media Guide / USSA Directory*, U.S. Ski Association, 1993; *Ski Racing Annual Competition Guide 1993–94*, Ski Racing International, 1993; *Ski Magazine's Encyclopedia of Skiing*, Harper & Row, 1974; *Caffe Lavazza Ski World Cup Press Kit*, Biorama, 1991.

Scorecard

Sports Illustrated

Ripken
Takes a Seat

Sosa and McGwire
Down the Stretch

Flo-Jo
Remembered

Riddell

30

BRONCOS

30

Storybook Run

Terrell Davis's remarkable rise to NFL stardom

SEPTEMBER 28, 1998
www.cnnsi.com

MICKEY PFLEGER

A summary of Fall 1998 events

CLIVE MASON/ALLSPORT

Hakkinen dueled Schumacher down to the wire in Formula One.

AUTO RACING

Despite his domination of the Winston Cup circuit the past few years, Jeff Gordon has acquired a reputation for late-season swoons. Gordon went a long way towards living that down when he held off hard-charging Bobby Labonte to win the Pepsi 400 in Daytona Beach on Oct. 17 and all but wrap up his third Winston Cup championship in four years. It was Gordon's 11th win of the season—his 40th in six years on the circuit—and it underscored a run of amazing consistency: In 17 races since mid-June, he never finished out of the top five and in 13 of those races, he finished first or second. "He makes the difference," marveled his crew chief, Ray Evernham. "Somebody else could win in that car, but not the way he does it."

Alex Zanardi of Italy, who gave up Formula One racing for the CART circuit, showed no sign of letting up after claiming his second straight series title in September. On Oct. 18, Zanardi won his seventh CART race of the year, holding off Scotland's Dario Franchitti in the wreck-filled Australian IndyCarnival at Surfers Paradise. "This circuit seems to be designed for my driving," said the ebullient Italian, though the same could be said of many of the circuits in the series. Zanardi plans to return to Formula One for the 1999 season.

Fans of the star-starved Indy Racing League

are hoping that a heartening victory in Las Vegas on Oct. 11 will steer Arie Luyendyk's thoughts away from retirement. But the 45-year-old Dutchman, who had not finished higher than fourth all season or won a race in 16 months, remained non-committal even in the flush of victory. "If I sit at home from November through December, I might want to get ready to go racing again in January," he said. "It might not be a full year. It might be limited to a couple of races that are good races for me. That would include Indianapolis. For me, that would be the race if I had to run one race."

Mika Hakkinen moved closer to his first Formula One championship by beating his only rival for the title, Michael Schumacher, in the Luxembourg Grand Prix at Nurburgring, Germany, on Sept. 27. It was Hakkinen's seventh win of the season, and gave him a 90–86 lead over Schumacher going into the season's final race, in Suzuka, Japan, on Nov. 1.

PRO BASKETBALL

On Oct. 13, NBA commissioner David Stern announced he was canceling the first two weeks of the 1998–99 season—99 games in all—marking the first such stoppage in league history. "It's evident we're not going to be making a deal anytime soon, so we are reluctantly canceling the first two weeks," said deputy commissioner Russ Granik. Stern added that he would cancel the season in two-week increments if time continues to pass with no resolution.

Until this season, the NBA had staged 35,001 games in 52 seasons with no labor-related interruptions, surviving owner-imposed lockouts in the summers of 1995 and '96. This latest lockout, which commenced on July 1, stems from a dispute over the so-called Larry Bird exemption to the salary cap. The exemption, which allows teams to exceed the cap in order to re-sign their free agents, is a sacred cow to the players' union.

For fans, it's tough deciding who the good guys are in this dispute. Last year, the average NBA salary was $2.24 million, and 36 players made more than $5 million. The owners, meanwhile, have raised ticket prices 56% over seven years, according to *Team Marketing Report*, despite television deals worth a total of $2.24 billion over the next four years.

The fact that the 1998–99 season was in real jeopardy made the ongoing speculation over Michael Jordan's retirement look rather unimportant. In mid-October, Jordan was making noises that suggested he was seriously considering returning to play. He insisted that if he wants to play neither Bulls general manager Jerry Krause nor new coach Tim Floyd would stop him and that when the lockout ends, he would "look deep inside."

In contrast to its brother league, the WNBA wrapped up a second encouraging season on Sept. 1, when the Houston Comets beat the Phoenix Mercury 80–71 in the deciding game of their three-game series to win their second straight WNBA title. The Comets, 27–3 in the regular season, were led by Sheryl Swoopes, who scored 10 of the team's final 17 points, and by Cynthia Cooper, who paced the team with 23 points. Cooper won a second straight championship series MVP award to go with the regular season MVP award she had already received.

BOXING

It is not like Mike Tyson to need backup—at least not the Mike Tyson of old. But when the IRS is hounding you for $18 million in back taxes and your self control is a tenuous thing, you welcome all the help you can get.

Banned from boxing for the 16 months since that awful night when his concentration slipped and he allowed himself an uninvited nosh on Evander Holyfield's ear, the former heavyweight champ appeared before the Nevada State Athletic Commission with a retinue of psychiatrists and heavyweight do-gooders Muhammed Ali and Magic Johnson. "I'm not going to kill anybody," he reassured the commission. "I'm not a mass murderer." No doubt relieved to hear that, they voted 4 to 1 to restore Tyson's license, with James Nave casting the lone dissenting vote.

But chairman Elias Ghanem left no doubt that Tyson was running out of chances. "If Mike has another problem like this, he'll never fight again in Nevada," said Ghanem. "This is his one chance."

At times during the hearing there were disturbing signs that Tyson still doesn't get it, or at least that his notion of humor is a bit different from the rest of the world's. Waiting for the hearing to start, Tyson leaned over to his wife, Monica, and pretended to bite her ear. Later, perhaps disappointed that this first joke did not get a bigger reaction, he turned to the row of psychiatrists sitting behind him and rolled his eyes in mock lunacy.

With his license restored, Tyson did not know who his next opponent would be or, indeed, when his next fight would take place or who would promote it. But since he is already

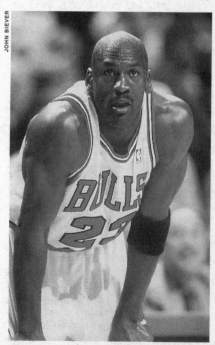

Would '98 be the last hurrah for Jordan?

32 and his last, brief stint as a fighter was unimpressive, one hopes he doesn't wait too long. For his sake as well as ours.

Then again, Tyson returns to a heavyweight division that gets older and older with no sign of new blood anywhere on the horizon. On Sept. 19, fighting before a hometown crowd in the Georgia Dome in Atlanta, WBA/IBF champion Holyfield claimed a unanimous decision over Vaughn Bean but looked bored and listless doing so. He knocked Vaughn down just once, in the 10th round. That's hardly the dominating performance you expect from the division's class act, especially when he's up against a slow, overweight fighter like Bean, whose nickname is Shake 'n' Bake and whose favorite food is not a piece of steak but a bowl of Fruity Pebbles.

Next up for Holyfield seems to be Henry Akinwande, in a rescheduling of their June fight which fell through when Akinwande came down with hepatitis. After that, Holyfield and promoter Don King have set their sights on Englishman Lennox Lewis. "We're gonna destroy Lennox Lewis in 1999," huffed and puffed the tonsorially challenged one. "We're gonna do it the same way the 13 colonies beat King George in 1776."

For more honest pugilism you still have to look at the smaller divisions. On Sept. 18 in Las Vegas, Oscar De La Hoya beat Julio César Chávez so badly in their welterweight title fight that Chávez failed to answer the bell for the 9th round. The fight revealed two things: At 36, Chávez is old enough to know when he's had more than enough. At 25, De La Hoya is immature enough not to have learned yet that magnanimity is a trait of a true champion. After the battered Chávez shook his head and the horribly bloodied lip that somehow still hung from it, De La Hoya chastised him. "That's a no-no," he said. "Quitting. That's the worst that can happen to any fighter." Either that or turning into a less-than-gracious winner.

Stern (right) and Granik faced unprecedented labor strife.

COLLEGE FOOTBALL

Grown men wept and hugged each other in an unashamed display of deep feeling. Others merely shook their heads in disbelief.

No, the occasion wasn't the announcement of Ohio State linebacker Andy Katzenmoyer's summer school grades, upon which the hopes of the No. 1 Buckeyes seemed to ride. It was the conclusion of Prairie View A&M's 14–12 victory over Langston on Sept. 26, which brought to an end the Panthers' NCAA-record losing streak of 80 games. Prairie View's last win came on Oct. 28, 1989, when it beat Mississippi Valley State 21–12.

It was that kind of season in college football. There were surprises everywhere: For the first time in 10 years, the Michigan Wolverines, national co-champions last year, lost the first two games of a season; No. 2 Florida State was stunned by unranked North Carolina State 24–7; two weeks after whupping No. 8 Washington 55–7 and picking up a number of first place votes, Nebraska lost to Texas A&M 28–21, ending the Huskers' 19-game win streak; and winless Temple shocked undefeated, tenth-ranked Virginia Tech, 28–24.

Meanwhile, at the top of the national polls, the announcement that Katzenmoyer had indeed passed his summer school courses meant that long-suffering Ohio State fans were free to entertain hopes that the Buckeyes might win the national championship 30 years after they last did so, under legendary Woody Hayes. Led by quarterback Joe Germaine, running back Michael Wiley and a rock solid defense anchored by Katzenmoyer, the Buckeyes won their first six games with ease. Even Penn State bowed easily to the Buckeyes, losing 28–9.

Other teams that remained undefeated midway through the season were Kansas State, which was 6–0 a decade after an 0–11 season; Tennessee, 6–0 after beating the Florida Gators for the first time in five years; and UCLA, which ran its record to 6–0 with a 41–38 overtime defeat of Oregon. In that game Bruin quarterback Cade McNown, who was fighting a stomach virus, completed 20 of 36 passes for 395 yards and three touchdowns.

McNown was one of several players making this the most crowded Heisman Trophy chase in years. Along with McNown, who through six games had completed 81 of 149 passes for 1,425 yards and 10 TDs, there were fellow quarterbacks Tim Couch of Kentucky and Donovan McNabb of Syracuse. Of the three Couch had the gaudiest numbers: 252 completions in 353 attempts for 2,782 yards and 25 touchdowns. McNabb had completed 71% of his passes (96 of 136) and had a touchdown-to-interception ratio of 13–2.

Of the running backs, big Ron Dayne had rushed for 834 yards in Wisconsin's seven straight wins, but it was Ricky Williams of Texas who owned the most eye-popping numbers of all: a national-best 1,225 rushing yards for an average of 6.5 yards per carry and 22 touchdowns in just six games. The only problem with Williams's candidacy was that the 4–2 Longhorns had slipped from the national rankings. The last player on an unranked team to win the Heisman was running back George

Rogers of South Carolina 18 years ago.

PRO FOOTBALL

They say a rolling stone gathers no moss, but the Minnesota Vikings, who rolled through the first half of the 1998–99 season with boulder-like momentum, picked up Moss in April at the NFL draft in New York City. That's Randy Moss, WR, Marshall. Twenty NFL teams passed on the 6' 4" 205-pound receiver before the Vikings drafted him and spent the first half of the season passing *to* him. In his NFL debut Moss made his first answer to skeptics (all 20 teams' worth of them) who thought he was a risky prospect because of his history of discipline problems in college. He caught four passes for 95 yards and two touchdowns, including a 48-yarder, to lead the Vikings to a 31–7 upset of Tampa Bay. He appeared to have answered any questions about whether or not he could translate

At 35, Cunningham was having his best season ever.

JOHN BIEVER

his dominance at Division I-AA Marshall (where he ended up after being expelled from FSU) to the rigors of the NFL.

If there were any lingering doubts, Moss removed them in Week 5 against the defending NFC champion Packers in a nationally televised Monday night battle of unbeatens. In a driving rain at Lambeau Field he caught five passes for 190 yards and two touchdowns as Minnesota ended Green Bay's 25-game home winning streak and ran its record to 5–0. Suddenly, experts were calling the Vikings Super Bowl contenders. And quarterback Randall Cunningham was enjoying a rebirth at age 35. Against Green Bay, in what he called the best game of his career, he passed for a whopping 442 yards and four touchdowns.

Another experienced QB, John Elway, was doing all right for himself in Denver. The Broncos had not missed a beat since winning Super Bowl XXXII. Their 21–16 win over Seattle on Oct. 11—in which Terrell Davis rushed for 208 yards—ran their record to 6–0.

On the opposite end of the NFL—and the quarterback—spectrum were the Carolina Panthers, the Washington Redskins and the Philadelphia Eagles. Especially Carolina. While all three teams were winless through five games, the Panthers had to contend with the unprecedented crisis of having their starting quarterback, Kerry Collins, walk into Dom Capers's office on Oct. 7 and tell his coach "my heart's not in it … I don't feel like I can play right now." Collins was released from the team on Oct. 13—he was picked up by the New Orleans Saints the next day—but cutting him did little for Carolina's fortunes. They lost to Tampa Bay 16–13 the following Sunday to run their record to 0–6. The Eagles and the Redskins met on Oct. 11, each vying for their first win of the year. Rodney Peete, who had battled Bobby Hoying for the starting quarterback spot, passed for one touchdown and ran for another as the Eagles won 17–12. The victory did not create a habit, however, as the Eagles fell to San Diego 13–10 in their next game. Washington also lost, 41–7 to Minnesota, to go 0–7, its worst start since 1961.

GOLF

It might well have been a friendly match at their local club, the kind they've played on countless occasions over the last few years. But it was the World Match Play Championship. In the first all-U.S. final since 1975, when Hale Irwin beat Al Geiberger, Mark O'Meara beat his neighbor Tiger Woods by draining a 15-foot birdie putt from just off the fringe of the 36th hole at the Wentworth Club in Virginia Water, England, on Oct. 18. O'Meara trailed by four holes after they had played five, and by three holes after 18.

O'Meara, 41, credits Woods, 23, with rekindling his passion for the game and pushing him to win both the Masters and the British Open this year, and the spirited play between the two friends delighted spectators. On the 11th hole, Woods somewhat sheepishly refused to concede an 18-inch putt, prompting O'Meara to shout across the green, "I'm going to remember that next week."

Their good humor was in marked contrast to the grim visages they had worn the previous week during competition for the Dunhill Cup, which was contested at the Old Course in St. Andrews. For part of the week, the weather was as atrocious as Scottish weather gets, with high winds and low temperatures forcing the golfers to bundle up as if for a trip up Everest and pushing many scores into the 80s. A knockout tournament pitting 16 three-man teams from a wide variety of golfing nations, the Cup was won this year by the South African team of Ernie Els, David Frost and Retief Goosen, which beat Spain in the final 3–0.

The U.S. team of Woods, O'Meara and John Daly lost to Spain 2–1 in the semifinals. After Daly had beaten Miguel Angel Jimenez by two strokes and O'Meara had lost to José Maria Olazabal by one, it was up to Tiger Woods to decide the match. Needing to sink a four-foot putt on the final hole to send his match with Santiago Luna into extra holes, Woods knocked it three feet past. "I pulled it and gave him the match," moaned Woods, who at one point in the 18-hole match had been up by four strokes. The one cause for celebration was the brave performance of Daly, a recovering alcoholic who had suffered a bad case of the shakes at the Greater Van-

Vanbiesbrouck and his new team, the Flyers, led the NHL out of the gate in '98–99.

be my mom and dad instead of me being your business?" If a judge rules in her favor, making her an adult in the eyes of the law, Moceanu will be able to demand an accounting of her financial affairs. "As much as she's made since age 10, to have little or nothing doesn't seem right to me," said Roy W. Moore, Moceanu's lawyer.

ICE HOCKEY

A year removed from one of the worst seasons in league history, full of drab, neutral-zone-trap nonaction, anemic scoring and abysmal TV ratings, the NHL ... added a new franchise. In Nashville. That's right, Hockey, er, Music City. But if early returns were any indication, the extra electricity needed to keep

couver Open six weeks earlier, prompting calls for him to quit the team.

GYMNASTICS

On Oct. 19, in a move that said a great deal about the strange pressures faced by the child stars of the gymnastics world, 17-year-old Dominique Moceanu filed suit in a Houston court seeking independence from her parents, Dumitru and Camelia. Charging them with squandering most of the $1 million she has earned before and after the 1996 Olympics, where she won a gold medal as part of the U.S. women's team, the suit asks that she be declared an adult. Moceanu also was granted a temporary restraining order requiring her parents to stay away from her and reportedly was hiding in the Houston area as she awaited a Nov. 11 hearing.

In an interview with the *Houston Chronicle*, Moceanu said that she "never had a childhood," that her parents screamed at her, and that her father had even hit her several times. She told the *Chronicle* she had often wanted to tell her parents, "Can't you

the ice solid in sunny Tennessee would prove worth it. Some 2,000 newly-minted Nashville Predators fans lined the sidewalk outside Nashville Arena three hours before the first puck dropped in Tennessee, and the new franchise sold more than 12,000 season tickets. Predators owner Craig Leipold worked the crowd, shaking hands and accepting thanks, and inside the arena, Gary Chapman, host of TNN's *Prime Time Country*, revved up the capacity crowd of 17,500. Chapman did his job well: The fans started performing the wave 30 minutes before game time. Duly inspired, the Predators performed admirably but lost, 1–0, to the Florida Panthers on a power-play goal by Ray Whitney in the third period. Nashville secured its first win in its next game, at home on Oct. 13, exploding for three goals in the first 12:18 and holding on for a 3–2 win over the Carolina Hurricanes.

Other early returns in the 1998–99 season found the '96 champion Colorado Avalanche stumbling to its worst start ever at 0-4-1. Joining the Avalanche in the doldrums were the Tampa Bay Lightning, who carried a 15-game winless streak from the previous season into their sixth game of '98–99, when they broke through with a 5–0 win over Pittsburgh. The troubled Lightning dismissed general manager Phil Esposito and his brother Tony, the assistant GM, in the first week of the season. The Philadelphia Flyers, with newly acquired goalie John Vanbiesbrouck, jumped out to a league-best 4-0-1 record, while Dallas welcomed free agent Brett Hull, who scored seven points in five games as the Stars went 3-1-1. Also impressive in the early season was two-time defending champion Detroit, which went 4-1-0 in its first five games.

MARATHON

After a decade of stagnation, marathon times began to tumble once more in the fall of 1998. In the 10 years that had passed since Belayneh Dinsamo of Ethiopia set the world record of 2:06:50, no one had really threatened it. But that changed dramatically on Sept. 20, when Ronaldo da Costa, a 28-year-old Brazilian, chopped more than three minutes off his previous marathon best by clocking a stunning 2:06:05 at the Berlin Marathon.

What made da Costa's run all the more amazing is that he ran the second half of the race faster than the first (1:04:42/1:01:23), contrary to conventional marathon pacing. Judging at the halfway point that the pace makers were going too slow, da Costa ran the next 5,000 meters in 14:20, a move that left the field 40 seconds behind and stunned onlookers. "When I saw him take off like that, so far from the finish, I thought, 'Too bad. He looked like he had a good marathon in him,' " says Don Paul, a San Francisco–based sports agent. But the amazing Brazilian kept going, averaging 4:42 per mile for the second half of the race.

Da Costa's challenge to the African domination of distance running seems certain to revitalize the sport. Maybe the Africans are supermen, but they aren't the only ones on the planet. Unlike most of the Africans, da Costa grew up and still trains at an altitude close to sea level, just north of Rio de Janeiro. He also supports an extended family of 20 and often pays his nephews to pace him and carry water on their bicycles during his training runs. For the win and the record, da Costa took home some $200,000 in prize and bonus money, which ought to buy him quite bit of water and pacing.

With the spell cast by Dinsamo's ancient record finally broken, marathon fans expected big things from the Chicago Marathon, where the field included defending champion Khalid Khannouchi of Morocco. Last year Khannouchi ran the fastest time of the year at Chicago, in his first attempt at the distance, and until the closing miles of this year's race it looked as if he would again win in a very fast time. But with just one kilometer remaining, as he passed Soldier Field, the Moroccan was overhauled by Ondoro Osoro of Kenya who won handily in 2:06:54, 24 seconds ahead of Khannouchi. Gert Thys of South Africa and Joseph Kahugu of Kenya finished third and fourth, respectively, in 2:07:45 and 2:07:59, making the race the first in which four runners have broken 2:08 for the distance. The women's race was won by Joyce Chepchmba of Kenya, who overhauled early leader Colleen deReuck of South Africa in the 22nd mile and finished in 2:23:57.

For Osoro, running his first marathon, the win was particularly sweet: Not only had he been deemed unworthy to receive an appearance fee, but three years earlier a car he was riding in back home in Kenya was hit by a 12-ton truck, causing him months of agony and threatening an end to his running career.

TRIATHLON

After finishing fourth the last two years, 29-year-old Peter Reid of Canada won the Hawaiian Ironman Triathlon with a time of 8 hours, 24 minutes, 20 seconds. Reid took the lead for good about two miles into the marathon, the third and last of the 140.6-mile event's three legs. But Reid's fiancée, Lori Bowden, failed to make it a sweetheart sweep, as she finished second, in 9:27:19, to Natashca Badmann of Switzerland, who beat her by 3 minutes and 3 seconds. It was a disappointing year for Americans at Kailua-Kona: In a record field of 1,486 entrants, the first American man was Timothy DeBoom of Boulder, Colo., who finished 10th in 8:48:54, while the top American woman was Joanna Zieger of Baltimore, who finished sixth in 9:46:30.

The Year in Sport

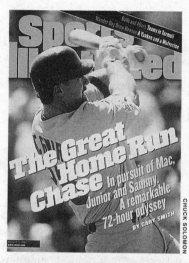

CHUCK SOLOMON

JOHN W. McDONOUGH

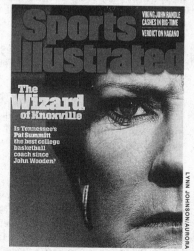

LYNN JOHNSON/AURORA

JOHN BIEVER

Flawed Gem

While 1998 will be remembered as a sports year for the ages, and rightly so, it was not without its share of lowlights

BY JACK McCALLUM

THE CATALOG, *Heroes of 1998*, lies tantalizingly on the magazine rack, just out of reach. You're dying to pick it up and start leafing through it, aren't you? You can see McGwire and Sosa on the cover and you catch a glimpse of Jordan on the gatefold inside. But you must wait. You must crawl through the muck before you can find the glory of your times. That was the message of *Saving Private Ryan*. Or perhaps it was *There's Something About Mary*.

Anyway, 1998 presented us with heroics of such lapidary magnitude—RECORD-BREAKING HOME RUNS! MJ'S LAST-SECOND HEROICS! VICTORY AT LAST FOR ELWAY! CAL SITS DOWN!—that we may have forgotten, temporarily, that sports is sometimes a cesspool. So put on your nose plugs for a minute and, I promise, we shall resurface soon and peruse that catalog of heroes.

Our tour guide for this descent into the muck is Green Bay Packers defensive lineman Reggie White, who should go into the Pro Football Hall of Fame on the first ballot

and with a piece of tape over his mouth. In one March speech that dropped the collective jaw of the Wisconsin state legislature the length of a good-sized bratwurst, White insulted practically every segment of the United States save for Bible-spouting homophobic defensive linemen. Say this for Albert Belle of the Chicago White Sox: He's not going to grab a soapbox and bowl you over with words. He may, however, bowl you over. In July his otherwise fine (and explosionless) season was marred when he was arrested for allegedly hitting a woman and ripping the phone from the wall when she called for help. Belle was charged with domestic battery; the charges were dropped on Oct. 20.

The paternal responsibilities—or lack thereof—of dozens of pro athletes was called into question in an SI story in May. Almost as disappointing was the reaction of the NBA hierarchy, which, rather than address the problem, chose to castigate the messenger and claim that the story had a racial bias. Another league, the NHL, saw,

JOHN BIEVER

McGwire captivated the nation with his pursuit of Roger Maris's home run record.

heard, or spoke no evil in regard to the embarrassing, room-wrecking behavior of some members of the U.S. Olympic hockey team in Nagano, Japan. Speaking of embarrassing, the fold-arama staged by the

NHL-dominated U.S. team was one of the lowest on-ice moments of the year.

It was not, in fact, a banner year for Olympic sports, some of the glories of Nagano *(page 601)* notwithstanding. The Tour de France was exposed as something of a rave on wheels, with drug use (performance-enhancing rather than recreational)

appearing to be the norm rather than the exception. The scandal that put seven teams out of the race only confirmed long-standing suspicions that drug-free pedalers are the exception, rather than the rule; and the Tour must do a massive public relations job if it is to reclaim credibility in 1999. Track and field, meanwhile, had to endure the drug-related suspensions of sprinter Dennis Mitchell and shot-putter Randy Barnes.

To make matters worse, the sport's most famous drug casualty, Canadian sprinter Ben Johnson, the pesky fly that just won't go away, first said he was attempting a comeback, then settled for a race against a car and two horses on Oct. 15. He came in third. We shudder to think where and when in '99 Carl Lewis will surface, what he'll be wearing and what he'll choose to sing.

Rumors of drug use continued to follow Irish swimmer Michelle Smith, who was

Gutting it out: Katzenmoyer passed golf, music and AIDS awareness to stay eligible.

suspended for four years when officials ruled she had tampered with a urine sample. Sadly, rumors of drug use also followed Florence Griffith Joyner to the grave. The most memorable female sprinter of her era died early on Sept. 21 of apparent heart failure at age 38, leaving behind the world record times of 10.49 in the 100 and 21.34 in the 200, which in 1988 gave rise to the suspicions.

Baseball had no drug suspensions, but that's just because the national pastime doesn't acknowledge performance-enhancing substances, not even androstenedione, a steroid that raises the body's level of testosterone. In late August an AP reporter spotted a bottle of andro, the same substance that had gotten Barnes suspended, in Mark McGwire's locker. McGwire freely admitted he took it and said that several of his teammates did, too. The andro issue, not to mention the game's widespread and open embrace of creatine, was largely forgotten in the Great Home Run Chase, but baseball might have to address it in the off-season. Then again,

ROBERT BECK

MANNY MILLAN

Jordan topped himself in what might have been his last performance.

knowing baseball, perhaps it won't.

By contrast, executives at the PGA and NASCAR spent entirely too much time talking about Casey Martin's golf cart and Jeff Gordon's tires, respectively.

Good news: No one has ever accused the U.S. World Cup soccer team of taking performance-enhancing drugs. The squad remained immune from that charge after their play in the World Cup, which conjured up neither performance nor enhancing. Losing to Germany is one thing; falling to Iran is quite another; and after that defeat, the exit of Steve Sampson as coach was a virtual fait accompli. Soccer continued to

RONALD C. MODRA

offs and looking quite confused in the process, and another L.A. team, the Dodgers, being gutted at midseason. Gee, what a coincidence—Murdoch owns the Dodgers, too.

There's Mike Tyson, looking like a human firecracker ready to detonate, at his reinstatement hearings. There's Evander Holyfield, a kind of Reggie White in Everlast, admitting to fathering two children with two different women, neither of them his wife. (That gives Holyfield a career total of nine kids with five women.) There's Don King blithely fending off lawsuits and taking juries that cleared him to the Bahamas. There's Oscar De La Hoya, one of the sport's saviors, taking entirely too much joy in pummeling Julio César Chávez for the WBC welterweight title. Hey, we must be at the bottom. We're talking about boxing!

So, pick up that catalog, America. How do you like your heroes? Study the order form carefully, for in this glorious 1998—neither a leap year nor a Sprewell year—there are all kinds to choose from.

Do you like them sandy-haired, rugged and wizened? Take John Elway. Do you favor one who speaks of faith (no, not Reggie), walks with a limp and suffers from an affliction (Klippel-Trenaunay-Weber syndrome) you can never remember unless you work for the PGA? Take Martin. Do you like the cocky kid who can wisecrack with Letterman one day and snake his way around a patch of oil and through a crack in the pack the next? Take

thrive elsewhere, though, particularly in London, where BSkyB, a satellite-television company controlled by Rupert Murdoch's News Corp., paid $1 billion for English Premier League club Manchester United. A cynic might suggest that Murdoch just needs programming for his stations.

O.K., we're almost at the bottom of the cesspool. There's Andy Katzenmoyer, Ohio State's bullyboy linebacker, taking three summer gut courses (golf, music and AIDS awareness) to stay eligible. There are the star-studded Los Angeles Lakers bowing out early in the NBA play-

Gordon. Or do you like the old-time pit bird, the driver's driver, the man of the masses? Well, ol' Dale Earnhardt is yours.

Do you like your female heroes cold-weather tough? Take a U.S. hockey player, perhaps forward Cammi Granato, who was chosen to carry the American flag in the closing ceremonies at Nagano after the U.S. won the gold medal over Canada. Or would you rather see a fancy costume on your skater? Surya Bonaly of France wouldn't be a bad choice. She's the figure skater who nailed a backflip in Nagano because—surprise, surprise—she wanted "to please the crowd, not the judges."

You may prefer to see your women athletes strolling along a fairway in a pair of shorts and a big, big smile. Put Jenny Chuasiriporn—who seemed to be having a joyous time even as she lost a 20-hole playoff to the frighteningly talented Se Ri Pak in the U.S. Women's Open—on your order form. Or you might like them tall, brazen, breezy and braided. We've got a Venus or a Serena for you. If the Williams sisters are too flashy, you can choose someone who's as stern and taciturn as a New England winter: Cindy Blodgett. The University of Maine's high-scoring point guard was the best thing to happen to the state since a lobster crawled into a pool of drawn butter.

You like heroes who court danger? Don't forget about these baseball players who escaped their native Cuba in a harrowing raft trip: first baseman Jorge Luis Toca, catcher Angel Lopez, second baseman Jorge Diaz, shortstop Michael Jova and pitching coach Orlando Chinea. Or do you like an older fellow whose idea of danger is pulling out a three-wood to carry a creek

Pak took the women's Tour by storm, winning the LPGA and the U.S. Women's Open.

from 220 yards? Forty-one-year-old Mark O'Meara is a candidate, as is 48-year-old Tom Watson.

The baseball section of the catalog is expanded this year. Take an Atlanta Braves pitcher, maybe. Greg Maddux might be your righty, Tom Glavine your lefty and John Smoltz your comeback guy. Or if you prefer youth, take the kid who looks like he should be playing air guitar in the basement on *Wayne's World*: the one-hit man, Kerry Wood, whose strikeout total against the Houston Astros on May 6 matched his age, 20. There are so many members of the 114-win New York Yankees to choose from that it's all but impossible to single out one, unless you're still under the perfect-game spell that David Wells cast on a Sunday afternoon in May against the Minnesota Twins. Understandable, but, for a pinstriped long shot, think about Jim Bouton, whose pen (not his bullpen) was once mightier than his right arm, and who, after years of being spurned for his tell-all baseball book *Ball Four*, was finally invited back to Old-Timers' Day at Yankee Stadium.

Finally, you'll come to the classics section of the catalog, the one that lists Ath-

JIM GUND

Sosa's year—.308, 66 HRs, 158 RBI—was arguably the best in Cubs history.

age 29, ending 12 years of frustration. And she did it on the grass of Wimbledon, the site of her most memorable gag (in '93 against Steffi Graf). The Duchess of Kent, who had embraced Novotna after her grinding defeat to Graf, couldn't have been happier.

Happy is how all of Daytona felt (except the Gordonites) when Earnhardt finally broke through and won the 500 after 19 unsuccessful runs at NASCAR's version of the Super Bowl. Princeton's basketball team, which featured a 1950s-looking backdoor offense run by 1950s-looking players, was ranked as high as eighth during the season, and at one point during its first-round NCAA tournament game against UNLV ran off 20 straight points to win easily. The Tigers' heart-of-the-country counterpart, little-known Valparaiso, used a Merriwell ending by the coach's son, Bryce Drew, to make it to the Sweet 16. You like old school? At Valpo, they raise money with a Hug Homer program, in which five bucks will earn you a hug—and nothing else, mind you—from coach Homer Drew.

O'Meara won his first major, a little tourney down in Georgia called the Masters, at age 41. He got some first-round competition from Gay Brewer, who's 66, and some fourth-round heat from Jack Nicklaus, who was playing in his 40th Masters and who, days earlier, had been touched when a plaque in his honor had been affixed to a fountain between the 16th and 17th greens. It's a wonder they didn't distribute Viagra at the turn. So you're a little bored by the low-key (and reportedly penurious) O'Meara? You'd rather see his fishing buddy, Tiger Woods,

letes for the Ages. Mark and Sammy are there. Available swinging a bat separately or hugging together. Cal is there. Available playing or sitting, which he finally did on Sept. 20 after 2,632 games. And Michael is there. Again. Available on either offense or defense.

Yes, though the year may have opened with the image of Latrell (I Didn't Choke Nobody) Sprewell fresh in everyone's mind, it was quickly replaced by another image that set the feel-good tone for 1998. See the Denver Broncos quarterback. See him elevate (well, only a foot or so). See him give up his 37-year-old body to get an important first down in the Super Bowl. See the Denver Broncos beat the favored Green Bay Packers. Old school was in. Underdog was in. Redemption was in.

Nebraska coach Tom Osborne walked away from the Orange Bowl with a 42–17 rout of Tennessee, one half of a national championship (the coaches voted for him, naturally, while the writers went with Michigan), 255 career wins and the grudging respect of sportswriters who never much cared for him. A guy who looks like a stork, Petr Korda, won his first Grand Slam title (the Australian Open) at age 30. Jana Novotna won her first Grand Slam at

on the victory stand? Tough. O'Meara went out and won the British Open, too, beating Woods by one stroke and taking a playoff from Brian Watts. O'Meara was only 24 years older than one of the contenders who was hot on his trail, 17-year-old Justin Rose of Great Britain. Tom Watson won a perfectly titled tournament for a 48-year-old—the MasterCard Colonial—though we expect that the veteran can flash a platinum.

The Utah Jazz, led by old-school players Karl Malone and John Stockton running an old-school pick-and-roll, made it to the Finals for the second straight year. Can we call Dan O'Brien old school, too, even though he's only 32? Sure we can. It seems like he's been around forever, but after missing all of '97 with injuries, he won the decathlon at the Goodwill Games in July. An old-school NHL coach named Scotty Bowman won the Cup in a sweep with the Detroit Red Wings, the eighth time he has kissed Lord Stanley, suggesting that, as an NHL coach, he may be the best there ever was.

That's what Marv Albert might be in his field, too. Albert's redemption came nearly a year after a humiliating series of revelations about his sex life was ended by his plea bargain in an assault case in Virginia. Albert returned to the microphone to do a nightly highlight show on the Madison Square Garden network, and he is scheduled to do the Knicks' games on radio, too. Can his return as lead play-by-play man on NBC be far behind?

The return that matters most, however, was not decided at press time. When Jordan stole the ball from Malone in Game 6 of the NBA Finals, then hit the winning jumper seconds later to give the Bulls their sixth title of the decade, he left viewers able to draw only one conclusion: His domination of his sport is not only unprecedented, it's ridiculous. Even though he was 35 when he was named MVP of the '98 Finals, the same gulf that existed between Jordan and the rest of the NBA a half-dozen years earlier is still there. He may be better than anyone else in a different way—his favorite weapon

MANNY MILLAN

The greatest sportswriter of his time, Murray will be sorely missed.

now, for example, is an unblockable fallaway jumper instead of an acrobatic sashay to the hoop—but he's still better.

The bold, nay, mythic stamp that Jordan put on the year in June was enhanced by the McGwire-Sosa home run race. It wasn't just the titanic home runs. It was the way the two players handled themselves: McGwire the bashful big lug who couldn't seem to believe his own success, Sosa the carefree, free-swinger who—to mask a burning competitiveness—liked to pretend he was just along for the ride. They were a sitcom, *The Mark and Sammy Show*, that America tuned in to daily and, like *Seinfeld*, they almost never disappointed.

One of the few journalists with the grace, the wit and the knowledge to capture the splendor of Jordan and the drama of the home run race died in August, before Jordan made up his mind about returning to the NBA, and before McGwire and Sosa finished their home run barrage. Jim Murray, like Jordan, was the best there ever was.

The Year in Sport Calendar

compiled by John Bolster and Anthony Zumpano

Baseball

Nov 4, 1997—Red Sox shortstop Nomar Garciaparra, who batted .306 with 30 home runs and 98 RBIs, is the unanimous choice as AL Rookie of the Year.

Nov 4—Phillies third baseman Scott Rolen, who batted .283 with 92 RBIs, is unanimously named NL Rookie of the Year, breaking the five-year streak of Dodgers rookies winning the award.

Nov 5—In the first league shift this century, Milwaukee becomes a National League city for the first time since 1965 when baseball's Executive Council unanimously approves the Brewers' shift from the AL as part of baseball's first phase of realignment.

Nov 5—Davey Johnson, who led the Orioles to a first-place finish in the AL East before resigning after a feud with owner Peter Angelos, is voted AL Manager of the Year. The following day Dusty Baker, who guided the San Francisco Giants from a worst-to-first NL West title, is named NL Manager of the Year for the second time.

Nov 10—Toronto's Roger Clemens, winner of the pitching triple crown for leading the AL in victories, ERA and strikeouts, wins his fourth Cy Young award.

Nov 11—Montreal's Pedro Martinez, the first ERA leader (1.90) with 300 strikeouts since Steve Carlton in 1972, easily wins the NL Cy Young award.

Nov 11—The Florida Marlins begin dismantling their world champion roster by trading slugger Moises Alou to the Astros for three minor-league pitchers.

Nov 11—Orioles pitching coach Ray Miller replaces Davey Johnson as Baltimore manager.

Nov 12—Mariners superstar Ken Griffey Jr., who led the league in home runs, RBIs, total bases and slugging percentage, is the unanimous choice for AL MVP.

Nov 13—Larry Walker of the Colorado Rockies wins the NL MVP award, receiving 22 of 28 first-place votes. He is the first Canadian to win the MVP.

Nov 18—The first two picks of the expansion draft are lefthanders who played in the World Series: Florida's Tony Saunders (by Tampa Bay) and Cleveland's Brian Anderson (by Arizona). Moments after the final selection in the expansion draft, several big-name trades are executed. The Expos deal Cy Young Award–winner Pedro Martinez to the Red Sox for pitching prospect Carl Pavano and a player to be named later; the Devil Rays acquire first baseman Fred McGriff from Atlanta and sign free-agent closer Roberto Hernandez; the Diamondbacks acquire Detroit third baseman Travis Fryman; and Florida trades closer Robb Nen to the Giants for three pitching prospects.

Nov 20—The Florida Marlins continue to dismantle their roster as they trade first baseman Jeff Conine to Kansas City shortly after dealing pitcher Ed Vosberg to San Diego. Other '97 Marlins no longer with the

CHUCK SOLOMON

In Martinez, the Red Sox got the ace they needed to replace Clemens.

team include Devon White, who was traded to Arizona, and Darren Daulton, who became a free agent. Pitcher Kevin Brown and outfielder Gary Sheffield are reportedly on the trading block.

Nov 20—The Braves sign free-agent first baseman Andres Galarraga, the only active player to lead the league in home runs, RBIs and batting average (although not all in the same year), to a three-year, $24.75 million deal.

Nov 24—Minor league manager Tim Johnson, a former Blue Jays shortstop, is named Toronto's manager.

Dec 1—Third baseman Matt Williams is traded from the Indians to the Diamondbacks for third baseman Travis Fryman, reliever Tom Martin and $3 million. Two days later Tampa Bay signs pitcher Wilson Alvarez to a five-year, $35 million deal.

Dec 4—The Chicago White Sox hire Florida bench coach Jerry Manuel as manager.

Dec 8—Leadoff man Kenny Lofton returns to the Indians as Cleveland signs him along with pitcher Dwight Gooden. The Indians also trade outfielder Marquis Grissom and pitcher Jeff Juden to the Brewers for three pitchers.

Dec 11—The Red Sox and pitcher Pedro Martinez agree to a six-year contract worth a record $75 million.

Dec 15—The Marlins deal ace righthander Kevin Brown to San Diego for three prospects.

Jan 5, 1998—In his fifth year of eligibility, Don Sutton, who had 324 wins and 3,574 strikeouts in 23 major league seasons, is elected to the baseball Hall of Fame. Tony Perez narrowly misses election.

Jan 13—The New York Mets sign Japanese pitcher Masato Yoshii, a former teammate of Dodgers pitcher Hideo Nomo in Japan's Pacific League.

Jan 14—Baseball's Executive Council approves a 2-2-1 plan for the Division Series, replacing the 2–3 plan that gave home-field advantage to the host team for the final three games. In the new arrangement, the higher-finishing team hosts Games 1, 2 and 5.

Feb 4—Righthander Andy Benes, whose five-year, $30 million contract to return to the Cardinals was voided because it was reached after the Dec. 7 deadline for free agents to re-sign with their teams, signs a three-year, $18 million deal with the Diamondbacks.

Feb 18—The Yankees and Bernie Williams avoid arbitration by agreeing to a one-year, $8.25 million contract.

March 3—The Hall of Fame Veterans Committee elects Larry Doby, the AL's first black player, Lee MacPhail, a former AL president, Joe (Bullet) Rogan, a former Negro League star, and turn-of-the-century shortstop George Davis.

March 8—Cuban defector Orlando (El Duque) Hernandez, the former ace of the Cuban national team and half-brother of 1997 World Series MVP Livan Hernandez, signs a four-year, $6.6 million contract with the Yankees.

March 10—Nomar Garciaparra, the '97 AL Rookie of the Year, re-signs with the Red Sox for five years and $23.25 million.

March 31—Opening Day features a grand slam by Mark McGwire as the Cardinals blank the Dodgers 4–0. Wilson Alvarez delivers the first ever Tampa Bay Devil Rays regular-season pitch, a ball, to Detroit's Brian Hunter. He also earns the franchise's first loss as the Devil Rays lose to the Tigers 11–6. The Arizona Diamondbacks also lose their inaugural game, 9–2 to the Rockies. The Brewers, who moved to the NL in the off season, lose their debut on the senior circuit 2–1 to the Braves, a team that played in Milwaukee from 1953–65. Cincinnati's Pokey Reese ties a record for errors by a shortstop in a season opener with four in the first three innings of a 10–2 loss to San Diego.

April 4—Mark McGwire ties Willie Mays's record for home runs to start a season, hitting one in each of the Cardinals' first four games.

April 13—Seattle outfielder Ken Griffey Jr., at 28 years, 143 days, becomes the second-youngest player to hit 300 home runs as he hits No. 300 in a 6–5 loss to Cleveland. Jimmie Foxx was 27 years, 328 days old when he reached the milestone.

April 13—The Yankees are forced to play their series against the Angels at Shea Stadium, home of the Mets, when a 500-pound steel joint collapses into the stands at Yankee Stadium. Two days later the Yankees–Angels game at 12:05 is followed by a Mets–Cubs game at 7:30.

May 6—Cubs rookie Kerry Wood, a 20-year-old making his fifth major league start, sets an NL record and ties Roger Clemens' major league record when he strikes out 20 Astros in a 2–0 one-hit victory.

May 8—In a Cardinals–Mets game at Shea Stadium, St. Louis's Mark McGwire hits his 400th career home run in the third inning. Atlanta first baseman Andres Galarraga cracks the 300th of his career in the seventh inning of a 3–2 Braves loss to the Padres.

May 12—Cubs pitcher Kerry Wood strikes out 13 Arizona Diamondbacks in a 4–2 Chicago win. His 33 strikeouts in consecutive starts, are a major-league record.

May 15—In a blockbuster trade, the Los Angeles Dodgers send Mike Piazza and Todd Zeile to Florida for Gary Sheffield, Bobby Bonilla and Charles Johnson. The 1997 world champions also give up Jim Eisenreich and Manuel Barrios. Piazza and his mammoth contract are not expected to remain with the cost-cutting Marlins for long.

May 17—Yankees lefthander David Wells, who begins the day with a 5.23 ERA, retires 27 consecutive Minnesota batters in a 4–0 victory at Yankee Stadium. It is the 13th perfect game in modern baseball history, and the second in Yankees' history, after Don Larsen's 1956 World Series gem. Incredibly, Wells and Larsen went to the same high school, Point Loma in San Diego.

May 18—Oakland infielder Mike Blowers, who hits an average of one triple per year, hits for the cycle in a 14–0 win against the White Sox.

May 19—At Yankee Stadium, New York beats the Orioles 9–5 in a game marred by a 10-minute brawl. After Bernie Williams hits a three-run homer to put the Yanks ahead 7–5, Armando Benitez drills Tino Martinez in the back with his next pitch. Several players are fined and suspended for their roles in the fight that follows. When play resumes, Tim Raines hits the first pitch from Bobby Munoz over the rightfield fence.

May 22—One week after being traded to the Marlins, catcher Mike Piazza is dealt to the Mets for outfielder Preston Wilson and pitching prospect Ed Yarnall.

June 3—Pitcher Orlando Hernandez, makes his major-league debut at Yankee Stadium, and receives a warm welcome from the fans, many of them waving Cuban flags. Hernandez scatters five hits, strikes out seven and walks two in seven innings in New York's 7–1 victory over Tampa Bay.

June 4—In their second big deal in two weeks, the Mets acquire Dodgers pitcher Hideo Nomo and reliever Brad Clontz for righthanders Dave Mlicki and Greg McMichael.

June 10—The owners' committee unanimously approves the sale of the Rangers from a group that includes Texas Gov. George W. Bush to media mogul Tom Hicks for $250 million.

June 11—Tim Raines steals the 800th base of his career in the Yankees' 6–2 win over the Expos. He is the fifth player to reach the milestone.

June 18—Yankees pitcher Mike Stanton is suspended for five games for hitting Baltimore's Eric Davis with a pitch. The action comes a month after Orioles reliever Armando Benitez hit New York's Tino Martinez.

June 21—In the latest change to the Los Angeles Dodgers since Rupert Murdoch's Fox News Corp.

purchased the team, manager Bill Russell and general manager Fred Claire are fired and replaced by Glenn Hoffman and Tommy Lasorda, respectively.

June 26—Cubs outfielder Sammy Sosa hits his 19th homer in June, breaking the major league record for home runs in one month. He will hit one more before the month is over.

July 7—The American League defeats the National League in a 13–8 All-Star slugfest at homer-friendly Coors Field in Denver. Roberto Alomar gets three of the game's record-tying 31 hits and wins the MVP award a year after his brother, Cleveland catcher Sandy Alomar, earned the honor.

July 9—Baseball owners unanimously elect Allan H. (Bud) Selig the ninth commissioner of Major League Baseball and the first since Fay Vincent was fired on Sept. 7, 1992. Selig had served as interim commissioner since Sept. 9, 1992.

July 13—Cardinals first baseman Mark McGwire continues his record home run pace with his 39th and 40th homers in a 6–4 win over Houston.

July 31—A flurry of player exchanges occurs before the trading deadline, the most surprising

Sosa set a major-league record with 20 taters in June.

JOHN BIEVER

of which is the trade of disgruntled Seattle ace Randy Johnson to Houston for three little-known players. In his Astros debut two days later, Johnson fans 12 Pirates in a 6–2 victory.

Aug 2—Oakland starter Mike Oquist becomes the first pitcher since 1977 to give up 14 earned runs as he is blown out 14–1 by the Yankees. With the teams scheduled to play a doubleheader the next day, A's manager Art Howe saves his bullpen by leaving Oquist in the game. In five innings of work, he gives up 16 hits and four home runs.

Aug 16—Eric Davis, a year removed from colon-cancer surgery, goes 0 for 3 in the Orioles' 5–3 loss to the Indians, ending his 30-game hitting streak, the longest in the majors this season.

Aug 23—In the Giants' 10–9 win over Florida, Barry Bonds hits his 400th career home run. He also has 438 career steals, making him the only player in major league history to hit 400 home runs and steal 400 bases.

Aug 23—The home run chase heats up as the Cardinals' Mark McGwire belts No. 53 and Chicago's Sammy Sosa hits Nos. 50 and 51, only the second time two NL players have reached 50 in the same season.

Sept 1—In a 7–1 Cardinals victory against Florida, Mark McGwire ties and breaks Hack Wilson's NL home run record with Nos. 56 and 57.

Sept 1—Yankee David Wells, who tossed a perfect game on May 17, retires the first 20 Athletics he faces before Jason Giambi hits a breaking ball softly into centerfield for a single; Wells finishes with a two-hitter.

Sept 1—The Detroit Tigers fire manager Buddy Bell, replacing him with coach Larry Parrish.

Sept 8—Facing Cubs pitcher Steve Trachsel in the fourth inning at Busch Stadium in St. Louis, Mark McGwire hits his 62nd and shortest home run of the season—341 feet—just over the left-field fence. The line drive roundtripper, which comes in McGwire's 144th game of the season, breaks the single-season home run record, held for 37 years by Roger Maris. A 10-minute celebration ensues as McGwire hugs his 10-year-old son, Matt, as well as members of the Maris family, sitting in the stands along the first-base line. In right field, Sammy Sosa, who has 58 homers and has chased McGwire most of the season, applauds before running over to embrace McGwire.

Sept 13—It's Sammy Sosa's turn to lower Maris a notch in the record book as he hits home runs Nos. 61 and 62, off Bronswell Patrick and Eric Plunk, respectively, at Wrigley Field against the Brewers.

Sept 14—With a 4–2 win against the Phillies, the Atlanta Braves win an unprecedented seventh straight division title.

Sept 20—Announcing that "the time is right," Cal Ripken Jr. removes himself from the lineup in the

JOHN GILLIS/AP

After 17 years and 2,632 consecutive games, Ripken decided it was time for a day off.

Orioles' final home game, against the Yankees, ending his streak of consecutive games at 2,632.

Sept 27—Mark McGwire of St. Louis finishes his season with a bang, hitting his 70th home run, the new major league record, in his last at bat.

Sept 28—The Cubs and Giants meet in a one-game playoff for the NL wild-card spot, and Chicago wins 5–3. Sammy Sosa goes homerless in the extra game, which counts toward his regular-season statistics, leaving his season HR total at 66.

Oct 1—Yankees outfielder Darryl Strawberry's season ends when he is diagnosed with colon cancer. He undergoes surgery on Oct. 3.

Oct 3—The Indians defeat the Red Sox 2–1 to win their divisional playoff, 3–1. They advance to the ALCS to face the Yankees, who sweep the Rangers in the other divisional playoff.

Oct 4—Houston fireballer Randy Johnson loses for the second time in the Astros–Padres divisional series, falling 6–1, as San Diego wins the series 3–1 and advances to the NLCS to face the Braves, who sweep the Cubs, in the other division series.

Oct 13—The Yankees rebound from a 2–1

series deficit, and win three games in a row against Cleveland in the ALCS to advance to the World Series for the 35th time in franchise history. They will meet the Padres, who knocked off the seven-time NL East champion Braves in the NLCS, four games to two.

Oct 21—The Yankees, who won 114 regular-season games, take a place as one of the best teams in major-league baseball history with a 3–0 win over the San Diego Padres to complete a sweep of the World Series. Scott Brosius, who homered twice in Game 3, is named MVP.

Boxing

Nov 8, 1997—In a wild fight in Las Vegas, Evander Holyfield drops Michael Moorer once in the fifth round, twice in the seventh and twice in the eighth, after which the bout is halted. With the victory, Holyfield wins the IBF heavyweight title to go with the WBA belt he already owns.

Nov 22—Forty-eight-year-old George Foreman, who held the unified heavyweight title in 1973 and the WBA and IBF belts in 1994 (at the age of 45, the oldest heavyweight champion ever), squares off against 25-year-old Shannon Briggs in Atlantic City. Briggs wins a disputed majority decision and Foreman speculates that this fight—probably—is his last.

Dec 19—Flamboyant WBO featherweight champion Naseem Hamed, who is 29–0 with 27 knockouts, and has multimillion-dollar deals with HBO and Britain's Sky TV, makes his U.S. debut in Madison Square Garden against Kevin Kelley of New York. With cable TV executives no doubt

holding their breath, Hamed goes down three times in the first three rounds—but puts Kelley on the canvas three times as well. In the fourth round Hamed knocks Kelley out with a left hook.

Jan 13, 1998—Trainer Eddie Futch, 86, who handled such heavyweight champions as Joe Frazier, Ken Norton, Larry Holmes and Michael Spinks, announces his retirement.

March 5—Former heavyweight champion Mike Tyson files a $100 million lawsuit in U.S. District Court seeking to end his business relationship with promoter Don King, whom Tyson claims defrauded and financially gouged him.

March 28—Lennox Lewis retains his WBC heavyweight title with a fifth round TKO of challenger Shannon Briggs in Atlantic City.

April 1—Citing episodes of memory loss, former heavyweight champion Floyd Patterson, 63, resigns as New York State athletic commission chairman.

April 18—WBO featherweight champion Naseem Hamed of England stops former WBA

For the second time in his career De La Hoya (right) battered his idol Chavez.

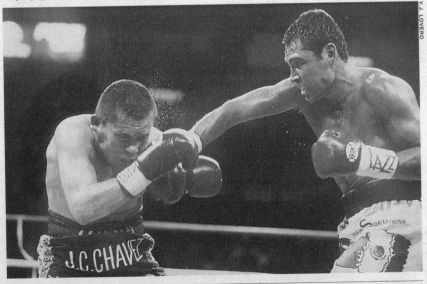

V.J. LOVERO

title holder Wilfredo Vasquez, 37, in the seventh round in Manchester, England.

April 26—Roy Jones Jr. stops Virgil Hill with a powerful body punch in the fourth round of their light-heavyweight non-title fight in Biloxi, Miss.

May 9—IBF Lightweight champion Shane Mosley stops Juan Molina in the eighth round of their title bout in Atlantic City. On the undercard, former Olympic gold medalist David Reid KOs Nick Rupa in the second round.

June 5—A scheduled WBA/IBF heavyweight title fight in New York between Evander Holyfield and Henry Akinwande is canceled when Akinwande tests positive for hepatitis B during his prefight physical. Incredibly, another fighter on the program, heavyweight Ray Mercer, also tests positive for hepatitis B and withdraws from his scheduled bout with Jerry Ballard.

June 13—Oscar De La Hoya scores a third-round TKO over Patrick Carpentier in El Paso to retain his WBC welterweight title.

June 27—The busiest fighter in the division,

lightweight Shane Mosley defends his IBF title with a fifth round KO of Wilfredo Ruiz in Philadelphia.

July 18—Roy Jones Jr. decisions Lou Del Valle in New York City to win the WBA and WBC light heavyweight titles.

Aug 28—No más—por favor—no más: William Joppy Jr. scores a TKO over 47-year-old Roberto Duran in Las Vegas to retain his WBA middleweight title.

Sept 18—Oscar De La Hoya batters Julio César Chávez in Las Vegas, stopping the 36-year-old former champion in the eighth round to retain his WBC welterweight title.

Sept 19—Evander Holyfield has all he can handle in his WBA/IBF title bout with the lightly regarded heavyweight Vaughn Bean in Atlanta. Fighting before a crowd of 41,357, the largest audience for a heavyweight fight since the 1978 Muhammad Ali–Leon Spinks rematch, Holyfield struggles but finally wins a unanimous decision after flooring Bean in the tenth round.

College Basketball

Nov 23, 1997—The third-ranked Stanford women suffer their second loss in three days, falling to unranked Purdue 78–68.

Nov 25—In a rematch of the 1997 NCAA championship, No. 1 Arizona defeats No. 7 Kentucky 89–74. Arizona's Mike Bibby and A.J. Bramlett combine for 36 points. Kentucky commits 18 turnovers.

Nov 26—LIU blows out Division III Medgar Evers 179–62. LIU leads 81–30 at halftime and its 117-point victory margin, 76 field goals and 39 steals are NCAA records. The Blackbirds shoot 61% from the field and Charles Jones scores a school-record 53 points.

Nov 30—North Carolina wins its third Great Alaska Shootout title, beating Purdue 73–69 in Anchorage. The Tar Heels rise to No. 2 behind Duke, which secured the top ranking after defeating Arizona in the Maui Invitational.

Dec 5—Former Arizona State guards Stevin Smith and Isaac Burton Jr. plead guilty to conspiracy charges, admitting they took bribes for fixing games during the 1993–94 season.

Dec 7—Maryland hands No. 2 Kansas its first loss of the season, 86–83. The 8–1 Jayhawks fall to No. 3 in the rankings. Maryland which moves to No. 19 with the Kansas victory, is upset 70–66 the following day by George Washington.

Dec 14—Eighteenth-ranked Stanford, powered by Olympia Scott's 26 points, defeats No. 5 Illinois 91–78 to avoid going 1–4, which would

PATRICK MURPHY-RACEY

Only John Wooden has more NCAA titles than Tennessee coach Summitt's six.

have been its worst start in 10 years.

Dec 18—Citing a personality conflict with coach Bob Knight, Indiana's Jason Collier announces he will transfer. The 7-foot sophomore accuses the coach of physical and verbal abuse.

Dec 24-25—No. 12 Arizona finds coal in its stocking when it suffers its first defeats of the season, losing 64-59 to Division II American-Puerto Rico on Christmas Eve and falling to Murray State, 94-83, on Christmas Day.

Jan 12, 1998—In women's hoops, Arizona breaks Stanford's 48-game Pac-10 winning streak, 91-90, on a last-second shot by Reshea Bristol.

Jan 14—Maryland delivers another blow to an undefeated team, this time knocking off top-ranked North Carolina 89-83 in overtime. The loss is the first for the Tar Heels (17-1) under coach Bill Guthridge, who replaced Dean Smith shortly before the season began.

Feb 18—Jeff Clement, a junior at Division III Grinnell (IA), breaks his all-division NCAA record by sinking 17 three-pointers in a 149-144 victory over Illinois College. His 77 points are a Division III record.

Feb 22—Indiana suffers its second-worst loss of the Bob Knight era, a 112-64 drubbing by Michigan. The 112 points are the most allowed by a Knight-coached team at Indiana.

Feb 24—Connecticut's Nykesha Sales, hobbling on a ruptured Achilles' tendon, breaks the school scoring record when she makes an uncontested layup in a ceremony arranged by her coach Geno Auriemma and Villanova coach Harry Perretta. Connecticut then calls timeout and deliberately leaves the huddle late so Villanova can match the basket.

March 14—In the women's NCAA tournament, Harvard upsets Stanford, which had been to the last three Final Fours, 71-67, to become the first No. 16 seed—men's or women's—to defeat a No. 1 seed.

March 15—Controversy mars the UCLA–Alabama game in the second round of the women's Midwest Regional. With 1.8 seconds left, UCLA's Maylana Martin is fouled and makes her first free throw, giving the Bruins a 74-73 lead. She misses the second, Alabama gets the rebound and calls a timeout with the clock at 0.8 seconds. After the break, official Jack Riordan tells Alabama guard Brittney Ezell that she can run the baseline on the inbounds pass, a ruling he later admits was incorrect—players can only run the baseline after a basket or made free throw. Ezell runs the baseline and throws a pass three quarters of the court, where it is tipped by two players before being caught by UCLA's Erica Gomez and Alabama's Dominique Canty. Canty's deflection goes to teammate LaToya

Caudle, who banks in a jumper from the top of the key for the winning points.

March 17—Two Fresno State players, Avondre Jones and Kenny Brunner, are arrested for assault with a deadly weapon and grand theft after allegedly holding handguns in an acquaintance's face and stealing money and a camera from him.

March 23—Top-ranked Tennessee avoids an upset, defeating North Carolina 76-70 to reach the women's Final Four and rack up its 43rd consecutive win. The Lady Vols trail 61-49 with 7:35 left. Chamique Holdsclaw, who scores 14 of her 29 points in the final 7:06, leads the rally.

March 26—As the men's Final Four nears tip-off in San Antonio, federal indictments are handed down in Chicago charging former Northwestern players Kenneth Dion Lee and Dewey Williams and two others with fixing the outcomes of three 1995 games.

March 26—Kevin Clark scores 28 points and Sam Jacobson 21 as Minnesota beats Penn State 79-72 in an all-Big 10 NIT final.

March 28—Kentucky gets by Stanford 86-85 in overtime in the NCAA semifinals. The Wildcats miss seven of their first eight shots, trail by 10 points twice and don't take the lead until the middle of the second half, during which they force 11 second-half turnovers. In the other semifinal, No. 3-seed Utah, from the WAC, which hasn't had a Final Four representative since 1966, never trails en route to a 65-59 defeat of top-ranked North Carolina.

March 29—Tennessee rolls to a third consecutive women's championship by defeating Louisiana Tech 93-75. The Lady Vols, who won their games by an average of 30 points, complete a 39-0 season and a 45-game winning streak stretching back to the 1996-97 season. It is the sixth national title for coach Pat Summitt.

March 30—Despite leading 41-31 at halftime, Utah falls 78-69 to Kentucky in the national title game. Guard Jeff Sheppard, who finishes with 16 points and makes crucial shots throughout the second half, is named most outstanding player of the Final Four.

April 20—Kenneth Dion Lee, a former Northwestern basketball player, pleads guilty to a sports bribery charge. He admits accepting or agreeing to accept cash bribes totaling $12,000 from former Notre Dame kicker Kevin Pendergast to fix three games in 1995.

April 30—The NCAA places the UCLA basketball program on probation for three years for recruiting violations and other improprieties involving its athletes from 1993-95. Former coach Jim Harrick, who was dismissed before the 1996 season and is currently coaching Rhode Island, is cited for unethical conduct for lying to school officials during an investigation.

May 4—A federal court rules that the NCAA must pay nearly $67 million in damages to assistant basketball coaches whose earnings were unlawfully restricted.

May 13—St. John's coach Fran Fraschilla, who in 1998 led the Red Storm to a 22–10 record and an NCAA tournament appearance, is fired. He is replaced on June 11 by former George Washington coach Mike Jarvis.

July 6—Carolyn Peck, who coached the Purdue women to a 23–10 record and the Big Ten championship in '98, announces that she will take over as coach and general manager of Orlando's still unnamed WNBA expansion franchise.

Sept 22—The Louisville men's basketball team is banned from the 1999 postseason and the school is placed on three years' probation for violations committed by former assistant coach Scooter McCray. In 1996 McCray made efforts to keep Louisville player Nate Johnson's father from being evicted from his home.

College Football

Oct 25, 1997—Boston University announces that its football program is being eliminated after the 1997 season due in part to a mere four wins in the Terriers' last 29 games and a loss in revenue of more than $2 million in 1996.

Oct 27—Texas Christian coach Pat Sullivan, whose team has suffered disciplinary upheaval and controversy since 1996 and is 0–7 in '97, announces that he will resign after the season.

Nov 1—Heisman hopeful Ryan Leaf is sacked six times and fumbles twice as Washington State is upset 44–31 by Arizona State. The Cougars fall from No. 10 to No. 16 in the AP poll.

Nov 15—Rutgers is blown out by Miami 51–23, ending an 0–11 season, the worst in its 128-year football history.

Nov 19—Attorney Richard Barrett, a self-proclaimed white supremacist, sues the University of Mississippi over its ban on flag sticks at Ole Miss football games. Barrett contends that the ban interferes with free speech rights by keeping Confederate flags from the stadium.

Nov 22—With a 20–14 victory over Ohio State, Michigan (11–0) wins the Big Ten championship and clinches a berth in the Rose Bowl, where it will face Washington State (10–1).

Nov 24—Louisville, which suffered through a 1–10 season, hires Utah State coach John L. Smith to replace fired coach Ron Cooper.

Nov 29—Grambling's Eddie Robinson coaches the 588th and final game of his 57-year career, a 30–7 loss to Southern. Former Super Bowl MVP and Grambling alum Doug Williams is selected to replace Robinson, who retires with 408 wins, the most of all time.

Dec 4—Quarterback Peyton Manning throws for 373 yards and four touchdowns in a 30–29 Tennessee victory over Auburn in the Southeastern Conference championship. In the Big 12 championship, Nebraska back Ahman Green rushes for 179 yards and three touchdowns as the Cornhuskers cap a 12–0 season by crushing Texas A&M 41–15. No. 2 Nebraska and No. 3 Tennessee will meet in the Orange Bowl.

Dec 10—Nebraska coach Tom Osborne, citing health concerns, announces his retirement, effective after the Orange Bowl. He will be replaced by longtime assistant Frank Solich.

Dec 14—Michigan defensive back Charles Woodson, with 1,815 votes, becomes the first predominantly defensive player to win the Heisman Trophy, edging quarterbacks Peyton Manning of Tennessee (1,543) and Ryan Leaf of

HEINZ KLUETMEIER

Texas's Ricky Williams was the early favorite for the '98 Heisman.

Washington State (861). A two-way player, Woodson also caught 11 passes for two touchdowns and returned a punt 78 yards for a touchdown in the Wolverines' 21–16 Rose Bowl win over Washington State.

Dec 16—Southern Cal coach John Robinson learns of his dismissal through a message Athletic Director Mike Garrett leaves on his home answering machine, hours after hearing reports that Kansas City Chiefs offensive coordinator Paul Hackett has agreed to take the USC coaching position. The following day at a press conference Garrett and USC president Steven B. Sample claim that Robinson voluntarily stepped down. An embarrassed Sample later admits he was wrong.

Dec 20—College football's postseason gets underway as unranked Oregon, which at 7–5 barely has enough wins to qualify for a bowl, triumphs over No. 21 Air Force 41–13 in the Las Vegas Bowl.

Dec 23—Penn State junior running back Curtis Enis is banned from the Citrus Bowl against Florida because he lied about a sports agent buying him a suit. He later announces that he will enter the NFL draft.

Dec 25—Rashaan Shehee, returning to the Washington lineup after missing the last three games with a knee injury, rushes for 193 yards and two touchdowns as the Huskies crush Michigan State 51–23 in the Aloha Bowl.

Dec 28—No. 15 Louisiana State tops Notre Dame 29–9 in the Independence Bowl to finish 9–3 and avenge an earlier 24–6 loss to the Irish.

Dec 29—No. 17 Colorado State (11–2) wins its ninth consecutive game, defeating No. 20 Missouri (7–5) 35–24 in the Holiday Bowl.

Dec 31—In the Fiesta Bowl, Kansas State quarterback Michael Bishop outguns Syracuse's Donovan McNabb, passing for four TDs and and running for another as the No. 9 Wildcats down the Orangemen 35–18.

Jan 1, 1998—Staking their claim for the national championship, Michigan shuts down the vaunted Washington State offense and quarterback Ryan Leaf in the Rose Bowl, defeating the Cougars 21–16. The Wolverines (12–0) battle back from deficits twice in the game, and quarterback Brian Griese (son of NFL legend Bob) hits Tai Sheets with a 58-yard scoring pass to provide the decisive score.

Jan 1—Fourth-ranked Florida State gives coach Bobby Bowden his 16th bowl victory as the Seminoles trounce No. 10 Ohio State 31–14 in the Sugar Bowl. In the Gator Bowl, No. 5 North Carolina routs Virginia Tech 42–3. Florida's Fred Taylor rushes for a Citrus Bowl–record 243 yards on 43 carries in the Gators' 21–6 defeat of Penn State. In the Cotton Bowl, No. 6 UCLA overcomes a 16-point deficit to beat No. 19 Texas A&M 29–23.

Jan 2—Nebraska Coach Tom Osborne retires on a winning note as the Huskers roll over Tennessee 42–17 in the Orange Bowl. With the victory, Nebraska completes a 13–0 season and stakes a claim for the No. 1 ranking along with Michigan. Ahman Green, Nebraska's junior running back, rushes for an Orange Bowl–record 206 yards.

Jan 6—For the third time in seven years, two teams split the national championship: 13–0 Nebraska is No. 1 in the *USA Today*/ESPN poll while 12–0 Michigan tops the Associated Press poll. For retiring coach Tom Osborne and the Huskers it is the third national title in four years.

June 9—Roy Kramer, coordinator of college football's new Bowl Championship Series (formerly the Bowl Alliance) announces the criteria under which teams will be selected for the series' national championship game. The Bowl Championship Series will attempt to "rate and identify the teams best qualified to play in a national title game." The system assigns points in each of the four categories and the teams with the lowest point totals will play in the Fiesta Bowl on Jan. 4, 1999. The new formula will use computer rankings published by *The New York Times* and the *Seattle Times*, as well as ratings compiled by Jeff Sagarin and a complex strength-of-schedule analysis.

July 2—When Florida State junior quarterback Dan Kendra announces that an anterior cruciate ligament tear in his right knee has not healed sufficiently enough to let him play, the Seminoles promote 26-year-old sophomore Chris Weinke, who is older than 10 starting NFL quarterbacks, to the starting position.

Aug 13—The College Football Hall of Fame inducts several new members, including former Grambling coach Eddie Robinson and Danny White, who quarterbacked the Arizona Sun Devils before spending 13 seasons with the Dallas Cowboys.

Aug 29—No. 4 Nebraska wins its first game under new coach Frank Solich, beating Louisiana Tech 56–27 in the Eddie Robinson Classic despite a record-setting day by the losing team. LSU wide receiver Troy Edwards breaks the NCAA all-division record for receiving yards with 21 receptions for 405 yards, including touchdown catches of 94, 80 and 52 yards. Quarterback Tim Rattay completes 46 of 68 passes for 590 yards in the losing effort.

Sept 6—Ohio State begins its season by justifying its No. 1 ranking, winning 34–17 on the road against No. 11 West Virginia. Buckeyes quarterback Joe Germaine passes for 301 yards.

Sept 26—Nebraska (4–0) remains No. 2 behind Ohio State (3–0) but picks up eight more first-place votes after routing Washington 55–7.

Sept 26—Prairie View breaks its NCAA-record

80-game losing streak by beating NAIA school Langston (OK) 14–12. The win is the Panthers' first since Oct. 28, 1989.

Oct 10—Texas A&M cornerback Sedrick Curry's interception with 59 seconds left stops Nebraska's final drive as the second-ranked Cornhuskers end their 19-game winning streak with a shocking 28–21 defeat. The loss, which drops the Huskers to No. 8 in the polls, is their first regular-season conference defeat since 1992. Nebraska recovers the following week with a 41–0 whipping of Kansas.

Oct 10—Texas tailback Ricky Williams continues his strong run for the Heisman Trophy, rushing for 139 yards in a 34–3 win over Oklahoma. His 5,380 career yards are third on the alltime NCAA Division I-A list. He is averaging 204.2 yards per game as he closes in on Tony Dorsett's career record of 6,082 yards.

Oct 17—Ohio State rolls over Minnesota 45–15 in Columbus to run its record to 6–0 and retain the top spot in the polls. Second-ranked UCLA remains undefeated, getting by No. 12 Oregon at home 41–38 in OT. Kansas State, ranked third, remains unbeaten with a 52–20 drubbing of Oklahoma State, and undefeated fourth-ranked Tennessee is idle.

Golf

Oct 26, 1997—Bill Glasson, who thought his career was over after missing most of 1996 due to forearm surgery, wins the Las Vegas Invitational. The victory, his first in three years, adds $324,000 to the $426,551 he won during the season.

Nov 2—David Duval wins his third straight tournament, edging Davis Love III for the $720,000 Tour Championship in Houston, and knocking Love out of the race with Tiger Woods for the season money title.

Nov 9—Gil Morgan wins his sixth title on the Senior PGA Tour, the Senior Tour Championship in Myrtle Beach, S.C., denying runner-up Hale Irwin a record 10th victory. Irwin finishes with $2,343,364, more than any golfer in history.

Nov 23—Winning the LPGA Tour Championship in Las Vegas, Annika Sörenstam finishes the season with an LPGA-record $1,236,789. In addition to winning the money title, Sörenstam is also named player of the year.

Dec 7—Nick Price sinks a 12-foot putt to save par and win the Million Dollar Challenge at Sun City, South Africa.

Jan 4, 1998—European champ Colin Montgomerie defeats Davis Love III of the U.S. 2-up to win the Andersen Consulting World Championship in Scottsdale, Ariz., and earn $1 million.

Jan 11—The 1998 PGA Tour season opens in Carlsbad, Calif., where Phil Mickelson bogeys the final hole but still wins by a stroke over Tiger Woods and Mark O'Meara in the Mercedes Championships.

Jan 18—Kelly Robbins, who shot a first-round 76, follows with a 67 and final-round 6-par-under 66 to win the LPGA-opening HealthSouth Inaugural in Orlando. Robbins makes 15 birdies in the last two rounds.

Jan 24—F. Morgan Taylor Jr. replaces Judy Bell as president of the USGA.

Jan 25—Tiger Woods completes his greatest professional comeback, overcoming an eight-stroke deficit to win the Johnnie Walker Classic in Phuket, Thailand. He defeats Ernie Els with a 14-foot putt on the second playoff hole.

Feb 11—A U.S. magistrate judge rules that the PGA must accommodate Casey Martin—who has a circulatory ailment that affects his lower right leg and limits his ability to walk without pain—by allowing him to use a motorized golf cart for Tour events.

Feb 15—In Honolulu, John Huston breaks one of the oldest PGA Tour records when he

BOB MARTIN

Woods didn't win any majors in '98, but he was an improved all-around player.

Golf (Cont.)

shoots an unprecedented 28-under-par at the Hawaiian Open.

March 1—Billy Mayfair edges Tiger Woods in a playoff at the Nissan Open in Valencia, Calif. On the LPGA Tour, Katie Webb wins the Australian Ladies Masters.

March 29—Justin Leonard rallies from a five-stroke deficit to win The Players Championship in Ponte Vedra Beach, Fla.

April 12—Mark O'Meara wins the Masters by one stroke over David Duval and Fred Couples, making birdie putts on three of the last four holes, including a 20-footer on 18 to clinch the victory.

April 19—Hale Irwin wins his third consecutive PGA Seniors' Championship in Palm Beach Gardens, Fla., with a 13-under-par 275.

May 8—Nike Tour player Notah Begay III shoots a 59 in the second round of The Dominion Open, tying the 18-hole record, He finishes tied for sixth with rounds of 70-59-74-74.

May 10—Ending his longest victory drought as a pro, Tiger Woods shoots a 17-under 271 to win the BellSouth Classic in Duluth, Ga.

May 17—Leading from start to finish, 20-year-old rookie Se Ri Pak of South Korea wins the LGPA Championship.

May 18—The World Golf Hall of Fame opens in St. Augustine, Fla., combining the Hall of Fame of the LGPA and the PGA World Golf Hall of Fame, which had closed in 1993 due to a lack of funds. Ben Hogan, Gene Sarazen, Gary Player, Nancy Lopez and Arnold Palmer are among the 73 golfers reinducted from other halls of fame.

June 21—For the second time in six years, Lee Janzen overtakes Payne Stewart for the U.S. Open title. Janzen shoots a final-round 68 to finish at 280, while Stewart, who was 3-under for the first three rounds, shoots 74 to score 281.

July 6—Se Ri Pak defeats 20-year-old amateur Jenny Chuasiriporn, after an unprecedented 20-hole playoff to win the U.S. Women's Open. Pak, also 20, becomes the youngest Open champion ever.

July 8—Hip problems force Jack Nicklaus out of the British Open, ending his streak of playing in 154 consecutive majors. Five days later he announces that the four majors in 2000 will be his last.

July 19—Mark O'Meara defeats Brian Watts in a two-hole playoff to win the British Open in Southport, England.

Aug 16—Vijay Singh of Fiji wins his first major, the PGA Championship, in Redmond, Wash. Tiger Woods shoots a first-round, 4-under-par 66, a course record. Singh follows up his victory with a win at the Sprint International on Aug. 23. He earns $900,000 from the two wins.

Oct 18—Mark O'Meara captures the World Matchplay Championship in Virginia Water, England, rallying from four holes down against Tiger Woods to win the 36-hole final 1-up. Woods winds down his season with no majors, but maintains a 69.06 average, second only to David Duval's 69.02.

Oct 18—Jim Furyk holds off Mark Calcavecchia to win the Las Vegas Invitational.

Hockey

Oct 19, 1997—Pittsburgh goalie Tom Barrasso nets his 300th career victory in a 4–1 win over Florida. He becomes the first American-born goalie and the 14th in NHL history to reach the milestone.

Oct 26—With two assists in a 3–3 tie against Anaheim, the Rangers' Wayne Gretzky now has more assists than any other NHL player has points. His assists total of 1,851 is more than the overall point total of Gordie Howe, who is No. 2 behind Gretzky on the alltime scoring list.

Nov 4—The NHL suspends Florida Panthers coach Doug MacLean for two games and fines him $5,000 for an on-ice confrontation with referee Dennis LaRue during a 4–3 overtime loss to Buffalo on Nov. 1. His team has a 7-12-14 record when he is fired on Nov. 24.

Nov 4—Mired in an 0–7 slump, the Vancouver Canucks fire 10-year general manager Pat Quinn.

Nov 11—Washington's Chris Simon, an Ojibwa Indian, is suspended for three games for directing an obscenity and a racial epithet at Edmonton's Mike Grier. Simon's teammate, Craig Berube, who is a member of the Cree tribe, receives a one-game suspension on Dec. 1 for directing a racial slur at Florida's Peter Worrell in a Nov. 23 game.

Nov 13—Mike Keenan, who was fired on Dec. 19, 1997, as GM/coach of St. Louis, is hired as coach of the Vancouver Canucks.

Nov 13—The Canucks' Mark Messier is left off Canada's 1998 Olympic hockey team.

Nov 17—Former Penguins star Mario Lemieux is inducted into the Hall of Fame with ex-Islander Bryan Trottier, and Glen Sather, current GM and former coach of the Oilers.

Dec 2—The NHL Board of Governors approves a plan for Toronto to join Boston, Buffalo, Montreal and Ottawa in the new Northeast Division as the NHL moves to a six-division format in 1998–99.

Dec 11—Colorado's Jarri Kurri scores the 600th goal of his career, becoming the first European and eighth player in NHL history to reach the milestone. He also becomes the sixth player with 600 goals and 800 assists.

Dec 11—Paul Kariya ends a 10-week holdout with Anaheim by agreeing to a two-year contract worth $5.5 million in 1997–98 and $8.5 million the following season.

Dec 14—Mike Gartner of the Phoenix Coyotes becomes the fifth player in NHL history with 700 career goals when he scores the first of his two goals in a 3–3 tie with Detroit.

Dec 30—Roman Hamrlik of the Tampa Bay Lightning is traded to Edmonton for centers Steve Kelly and Jason Bonsignore and defenseman Bryan Marchment.

Jan 1, 1998—Northrup Knox, cofounder of the Buffalo Sabres in 1970, steps down as chairman of the team. John Rigas, who owns the cable company that broadcasts Sabres games, is named interim chairman.

Jan 4—Bill Guerin and Valeri Zelepukin of the Devils are traded to Edmonton for Jason Arnott and Bryan Muir.

Jan 10—Mark Messier records his 1,000th assist in the Canucks' 2–2 tie with Florida. He is the sixth player in NHL history to reach that mark. Two days later, when Messier records an assist against the Blackhawks, he passes Phil Esposito to move into fourth place on the alltime points list with 1,591.

Jan 12—Wayne Gretzky is named the top hockey player of all time in a poll conducted by *Hockey News*.

Jan 19—The NHL All-Star game pits North Americans against World players. The North Americans rally from a three-goal deficit to win 8–7 on Mark Messier's third-period goal. Teemu Selanne of the World squad scores a hat trick and is named MVP.

Feb 8—The NHL begins a 17-day hiatus for the Olympic Games in Nagano, Japan. For the first time, Olympic hockey teams are stocked with NHL players. The Czech Republic, led by the Penguins' Jaromir Jagr and Buffalo's Dominik Hasek, wins the gold medal on Feb. 21.

Feb 18—The Rangers dismiss three-year coach Colin Campbell. John Muckler replaces him.

Feb 26—The Red Wings match the Hurricanes' six-year, $38 million offer to Sergei Federov, who has sat out the season thus far. The contract is structured to pay him $28 million if Detroit reaches the Eastern Conference Finals.

March 1—The Buffalo Sabres make Dominik Hasek the NHL's highest-paid goaltender with a $18.5 million extension, the biggest two-year deal in league history.

March 16—New York Rangers center Pat LaFontaine suffers the sixth concussion of his career when he collides with teammate Mike Keane during a game against the Senators.

LaFontaine announces his retirement on Aug. 11.

March 22—During his team's 1000th win, a 4–3 victory over Philadelphia, Pittsburgh's Ron Francis becomes the seventh NHL player with 1,000 assists.

March 25—Alan Eagleson, the former head of the NHL Players Association who is serving an 18-month sentence for defrauding players, resigns from the Hockey Hall of Fame, six days before the Hall's board was to hold a vote on whether or not to expel him. Eagleson was inducted in 1989 as one of the game's builders.

April 28—The Chicago Blackhawks, who failed to make the playoffs for the first time since

Sergei Fedorov and the Red Wings won another title.

1968–69, fire coach Craig Hartsburg and two assistants.

May 2—The Ottawa Senators defeat top-seeded New Jersey 3–1 to eliminate the Devils in the Eastern Conference quarterfinals, 4–2, and capture their first-ever playoff series. Devils coach Jacques Lemaire, who led the team to the Stanley Cup championship in 1995, resigns six days later.

May 4—The Oilers become the 14th team in NHL playoff history to come back from a three-games-to-one deficit, shocking the Avalanche, 4–0, in Game 7 of the Western Conference quarterfinals.

May 14—With a sweep of the Montreal Canadiens, the Sabres reach the Eastern Conference finals for the first time since 1980.

May 18—Art Williams, a retired insurance magnate, buys the Tampa Bay Lightning and the lease to the team's arena for $117 million.

May 27—Colorado coach Marc Crawford, who led the Avalanche to the 1996 Stanley Cup championship and a 165-88-41 record in four years, stuns his team by resigning with one year left on his contract. He is replaced by minor league coach Bob Hartley.

May 30—With 30 saves, Washington goalie Olaf Kolzig notches his record-tying fourth playoff shutout in one season.

June 4—The Capitals advance to the Stanley Cup finals for the first time in the team's 24-year history when Joe Juneau scores at 6:24 of overtime to give Washington a 3–2 win over the Sabres in Game 6 of the Eastern Conference finals. Washington won all three overtime games in the series.

June 13—Down two goals in the third period of Game 2, the Red Wings rally for a 5–4 overtime win to take a 2–0 finals lead over the Capitals. Kris Draper scores the winning goal on Detroit's 60th shot with 4:36 left in the first overtime period. Two minutes after Detroit's Martin Lapointe cuts the Capitals' lead to 4–3 in the third period, Washington's Esa Tikkanen misses an open-net opportunity that could have put Detroit away. Doug Brown ties the game for Detroit with 4:14 left in regulation.

June 16—The Capitals hardly put up a fight in Game 4 as the Red Wings complete back-to-back sweeps of the Stanley Cup finals. It is the NHL's fourth consecutive finals sweep. Coach Scotty Bowman ties Toe Blake's record with eight Stanley Cup championships as a coach. Captain and playoff-MVP Steve Yzerman hands the Cup to former Wings defenseman Vladimir Konstantinov, who is wheelchair-bound as a result of injuries sustained in an auto accident after winning the Stanley Cup last season. Carrying the Cup on his lap, Konstantinov is wheeled around the ice on an emotional victory lap.

June 23—The Maple Leafs fire coach Mike Murphy, who failed to lead the team to the playoffs for the second year in a row. The expansion Atlanta Thrashers hire Don Waddell, formerly Detroit's assistant GM, as general manager.

June 25—Sabres goalie Dominik Hasek is awarded his second consecutive Hart Trophy as the regular-season MVP. He also wins his fourth Vezina trophy as the league's top goalie.

June 29—Chicago hires former Blackhawks captain Dirk Graham as coach.

July 7—The free-agent goalie carousel begins as Florida's John Vanbiesbrouck signs with the Flyers. The following week, Mike Richter re-signs with the Rangers, and the Oilers' Curtis Joseph lands a deal with Toronto.

July 20—Colin Campbell replaces Brian Burke, who became GM of Vancouver, as NHL senior vice president and director of operations.

Aug 26—Mike Gartner, who has scored 708 career goals with five teams, announces his retirement. In 19 seasons, he did not play for a Stanley Cup-winning team.

Oct 10—Pro hockey debuts in Nashville as the expansion Predators are shut out by Florida 1–0. They defeat Carolina in their next game 3–2.

Oct 13—In a rematch of the '98 Stanley Cup finalists, the Red Wings down the Capitals 3–2, but do so without coach Scotty Bowman, who is recovering from an angioplasty he underwent in July. He returns on Oct. 22.

Horse Racing

Nov 8, 1997—At the Breeders' Cup in Hollywood Park, Horse of the Year candidates Skip Away and Favorite Trick boost their claims for the honor by winning the Classic and the Juvenile, respectively, but owner Allen Paulson has the most rewarding day of anyone at the track as five of his horses finish in the money. His Ajina wins the Distaff, Geri places in the Mile and Escena, Flag Down and Dowty each show, in the Distaff, Turf and Classic, respectively. Other winners at the Breeders' Cup include Countess Diana (Juvenile Fillies), Elmhurst (Sprint), Spinning World (Mile) and Chief Bearhart (Turf).

Nov 23—Pilsudski, the winner of the 1996 Breeders' Cup Turf, wins the $2.7 million Japan Cup in Tokyo with Mike Kinane up.

Dec 14—Ridden by Kent Desormeaux, Real Quiet wins the 470,000 Hollywood Futurity at Hollywood Park.

Dec 31—Hall of Fame jockey Jorge Velasquez, 51, who has won 6,795 races in his career, announces his retirement at Miami's Calder Race Course.

Feb 10, 1998—Favorite Trick becomes the first 2-year-old since Secretariat in 1972 to win the Eclipse Award as Horse of the Year.

Feb 28—Skip Away, narrowly defeated by Favorite Trick in the voting for 1997 horse of the year, wins the $500,000 Gulfstream Park Handicap. The 5-year-old, with Jerry Bailey up, has won two consecutive races to start the '98 season.

March 7—Alex Solis rides Malek to victory in the $1,000,000 Santa Anita Handicap.

March 28—Ridden by Gary Stevens, Silver Charm, who won the first two legs of the Triple Crown in 1997 before finishing a close second in the Belmont, wins the world's richest horse race, the $4,000,000 Dubai World Cup in Nad Al Sheba, United Arab Emirates.

April 11—Victory Gallop enters the field of Kentucky Derby contenders by holding off Hanuman Highway and Favorite Trick to win the

Horse Racing (Cont.)

BILL FRAKES

Arkansas Derby. Coronado's Quest wins the $500,000 Wood Memorial at Aqueduct.

May 2—For the second consecutive year, a Bob Baffert-trained horse wins the Kentucky Derby as Real Quiet, with Kent Desormeaux in

Baffert challenged for the Triple Crown for an unprecedented second year in a row.

the saddle, takes the 124th Run for the Roses.

May 16—Real Quiet wins the Preakness, giving him and, for the second straight year, trainer Bob Baffert, two thirds of the Triple Crown. Baffert is the first trainer in history to achieve such a double.

June 6—Real Quiet's Triple Crown bid falls short when Victory Gallop, who lost to Real Quiet by half a length in the Derby, charges down the stretch and wins the Belmont Stakes by a nose.

Aug 8—With alltime leading money-winner John Campbell in the sulky, Muscles Yankee wins harness racing's $1,000,000 Hambletonian at the Meadowlands.

Sept 24—Having won the Cane Pace on Sept. 5, Shady Character, with Ron Pierce in the sulky, seizes a wire-to-wire victory at the Little Brown Jug in Delaware, Ohio, to earn a chance at the pacing triple crown. The final leg is the Messenger Stakes on Oct. 16.

Oct 16—After a strong start, Shady Character fades to sixth at the Messenger Stakes, won by Fit For Life.

Motor Sports

Oct 26, 1997—Jacques Villeneuve finishes third at the Grand Prix in Jerez, Spain, a performance good enough to secure his first F1 season title. Michael Shumacher, who needed to finish ahead of Villeneuve at Jerez to win his third F1 championship, collides with his rival on lap 48 and spins off the track.

Nov 16—Overcoming a succession of prerace snafus, including a crash that totaled his No. 1 car, Jeff Gordon finishes 17th at the season-ending Atlanta 500, to clinch the second NASCAR season title of his career.

Jan 24, 1998—The Indy Racing League opens its third season as Tony Stewart wins the Indy 200 in Orlando. There are 10 caution flags in the race and only 15 of 28 cars finish the race running.

Feb 1—Gianpiero Moretti and teammates Arie Luyendyk, Didier Theys and Mauro Baldi win the 24 Hours of Daytona. Moretti, 57, announces his retirement after the race.

Feb 15—Famously jinxed at Daytona for losing leads in a variety of ways in 19 years of competing there, Dale Earnhardt finally wins the Daytona 500 on his 20th attempt.

March 9—Bobby Labonte wins the Atlanta 500 for the second year in a row.

March 29—Team McLaren sweeps in Formula One for the second straight week as Mika Hakkinen and David Coulthard finish 1–2 at the Brazilian Grand Prix.

April 5—Defending CART champion Alex Zanardi wins his first race of 1998, charging from one lap behind to pass pole winner Bryan Herta two laps from the finish at the Grand Prix of Long Beach.

April 12—Michael Schumacher seizes his first F1 victory of the '98 season at the Argentine Grand Prix in Buenos Aires.

April 26—In a race marred by a 20-car wreck which saw NASCAR veteran Dale Earnhardt suffer second-degree burns, polesitter Bobby Labonte holds on to win the Talladega 500.

May 10—Mika Hakkinen and David Coulthard score another 1–2 finish for Team McLaren, taking the Spanish Grand Prix in Barcelona.

May 24—Passing Bobby Labonte with 12 laps to go, Jeff Gordon wins the World 600 at Charlotte Motor Speedway for the third time in his career.

May 24—Eddie Cheever, 40, who had competed in 133 Formula One races and 81 CART events without a victory, wins the 82nd Indy 500.

June 6—Terry Labonte wins a controversial Richmond 400 when he bumps Dale Jarrett off the lead on the 398th lap. Officials then decide to halt the race because of a multicar incident which occurred on lap 394.

June 28—At the Sonoma 350, on a newly-configured, 11-turn road course, Jeff Gordon falls back from the pole then charges from 20th place to win, edging Bobby Hamilton by 2.75 seconds.

July 12—Michael Schumacher wins the Grand Prix of Great Britain, his third F1 victory in a row.

July 19—Alex Zanardi races to a fourth straight CART victory, taking the lead at the Indy Toronto on the 93rd of 95 laps and holding on to tie Al Unser Jr.'s series-record for consecutive wins.

Aug 1—Having won the World 600 on May 24, Jeff Gordon earns a $1 million bonus—to go with the $637,625 winner's purse—for winning the Brickyard 400, his sixth NASCAR victory of the year.

Aug 16—Jeff Gordon ties a NASCAR record as he wins his fourth consecutive race, edging Bobby Labonte at the Michigan 400. He fails in his bid for a record fifth successive win as Mark Martin takes the Bristol 500 the following week.

Sept 6—Dario Franchitti wins for the second week in a row on the CART circuit, taking the Indy Vancouver with an average speed of 77.081 mph.

Sept 27—Answering Michael Schumacher's victory in the Grand Prix of Italy on Sept. 13, Mika Hakkinen storms to victory in the Luxembourg Grand Prix. He has a four-point lead over Schumacher with one race, the Nov. 1 Grand Prix in Suzuka, remaining. A second place finish at Suzuka will clinch the title for Hakkinen regardless of what Schumacher does. If Hakkinen finishes out of the top six, Schumacher can win his third F1 title with a first- or second-place finish.

Oct 11—Dale Jarrett wins the Talladega 500 and a $1 million corporate-sponsored bonus, holding off a pack of eight drivers behind him. It is Jarrett's third win of the year. Jeff Gordon finishes second in the race to extend his season-points lead to 288 over runner-up Mark Martin with four races remaining.

Olympics

Nov 3, 1997—Team USA general manager Lou Lamoriello announces the roster for U.S. Olympic men's hockey team. For the first time in the history of the Games, professionals will be allowed to compete, and the U.S. lineup features such NHL All-Stars as defenseman Chris Chelios of the Chicago Blackhawks, center Jeremy Roenick of the Phoenix Coyotes and center Brett Hull of the St. Louis Blues.

Nov 23—Chris Witty of the U.S. and Lee Kyu Hyuk of South Korea set speed skating world records at the World Cup Sprints in Calgary. Lee wins the men's 1,000 meters in 1:10.42, while Witty takes the women's 1,000 in 1:15.43.

Nov 31—The U.S. bobsled team of Brian Shimer, Chip Minton, Randy Jones and Garrett Hines wins the World Cup race in Winterberg, Germany, defeating Germany by 0.02 seconds.

Dec 2—After five years of dispute, Nagano Olympic organizers and the International Ski Federation (FIS) reach a compromise on the Nagano Olympic downhill course. FIS wanted to raise the starting line to 5,906 feet but Nagano organizers, who wanted the course to begin at 5,512, objected to the move because it would have infringed on protected land. The compromise, which puts the starting line at an altitude of 5,791, is deemed adequate by FIS president Marc Hodler.

Dec 14—U.S. luger Duncan Kennedy, who has been inactive for five weeks due to a non-cancerous lesion on his brain stem, announces his retirement. He leaves the sport as the most decorated racer in U.S. luge history.

Jan 25, 1998—The U.S. doubles luge team of Mark Grimmette and Brian Martin win the World Cup event in Winterberg, Germany, thereby clinching the overall World Cup season title.

Feb 7—The 1998 Winter Olympics begin. Two-time Olympic silver medalist speed skater Eric Flaim leads the U.S. athletes into Nagano's Minami Stadium for the opening ceremony.

Feb 9—Ekaterina Dafovska of Bulgaria wins her country's first-ever Winter Olympics gold medal, taking the 15-kilometer biathlon at the Nagano Games in a time of 54:52.0. In other events on the first full day of competition, skier Mario Reiter of Austria wins the men's combined slalom, Larissa Lazutina of Russia wins the gold medal in the women's 5k Classical Nordic skiing event, and George Hackl of Germany wins the third gold medal of his career, taking the men's singles luge.

Feb 10—Hiroyasu Shimizu of Japan wins the host country's first gold medal of the Nagano Olympics, finishing first in the 500-meter speed skating event in an Olympic-record time of 35.59.

Feb 11—Freestyle skier Jonny Moseley of the U.S. wins his country's first gold medal at the Nagano Games, seizing the freestyle moguls with a 360-degree-Mute-Grab jump in his final run.

Feb 11—One year after undergoing reconstructive knee surgery, skier Picabo Street of the U.S. wins the women's Olympic super-G gold medal in Hakuba.

Feb 11—The International Olympic Committee announces that snowboarder Ross Rebagliati, who won the giant slalom on Feb. 8, has tested positive for marijuana and will have to return his gold medal pending appeal by the Canadian delegation. Two days later the appeal proves successful and Rebagliati's medal is reinstated.

Feb 12—Cross-country skier Bjørn Dæhlie of Norway wins the men's 10 kilometer classical in Hakuba. The victory brings Dæhlie the sixth gold medal of his career, a Winter Olympics record.

Feb 12—Austria's Hermann Maier suffers a frightening crash in his second run in the downhill at Nagano, soaring off the course and tumbling through two safety nets. He emerges relatively unscathed, with bruises and a strained right knee. Three days later Maier wins the super-G gold medal.

Feb 12—Jean-Luc Cretier of France wins the men's downhill.

Feb 13—Sweden gets two goals from defenseman Daniel Alfredsson and defeats the U.S. 4–2 in a Group D matchup in men's ice hockey.

Feb 14—Russia's Ilya Kulik wins the gold medal in men's figure skating. Canada's Elvis Stojko wins the silver and Philippe Candeloro of France takes the bronze. Todd Eldredge of the U.S. finishes fourth.

Feb 15—The Netherlands scores a 1–2 finish in the men's 1,000-meter speed skating at Nagano as Ids Postma wins in an Olympic-record time of 1:10.64, and his countryman Jan Bos finishes second in 1:10.71. The Netherlands has won six of the 12 speed skating medals contested thus far at Nagano.

Feb 16—Germany's Katja Seizinger takes the women's downhill to become the first Alpine skier to win the event in consecutive Olympics. She also has a gold in the combined. In speed skating, Marainne Timmer of the Netherlands wins the women's 1,500-meters setting a new world record of 1:57.58.

Feb 16—Canada downs the U.S. 4–1 in men's ice hockey to win Group D and relegate the Americans to third place. The U.S. will face the Czech Republic in the quarterfinals.

Feb 17—Led by Kazuyoshi Funaki, who won the gold medal in the large-hill ski jumping competition on Feb.14, Japan wins the team jumping gold medal. The victory brings redemption for Japan's Masahiko Harada, who had botched his team's chance for a medal with a poor final jump in Lillehammer in 1994. He makes the longest jump of the day in the team competition at Nagano, and earlier won the bronze in the large-hill individual jump.

Feb 17—The U.S. women's ice hockey team defeats Canada 3–1 in a thrilling gold medal game to win the first women's ice hockey competition in Olympic history.

Feb 17—Speed skater Gianni Romme of the Netherlands wins the men's 10,000 meters, clocking 13:15.33 to shatter the world record by

15.22 seconds. The Dutch sweep the event as Bob De Jong finishes second and Rintje Risma wins the bronze, with both men also surpassing the previous world record of 13:30.55, held by their countryman Johann Olav Koss. Romme also won the 5,000 meters on Feb. 8.

Feb 18—Eric Bergoust of the U.S. sets a world record en route to winning the men's freestyle skiing aerials, while his countrywoman Nikki Stone takes the women's event for a U.S. sweep.

Feb 18—Skier Hermann Maier of Austria wins the giant slalom, his second gold of the Games following a terrifying crash in the downhill on Feb. 12.

Feb 19—The Czech Republic defeats the U.S. 4–1 in the quarterfinals of the men's ice hockey competition at Nagano. The loss eliminates the Americans, who had been one of the favorites, from the tournament. In other quarterfinal games, Canada defeats Kazakhstan 4–1, Russia downs Belarus 4–1 and Finland upsets Sweden 2–1.

Feb 20—Italy's Deborah Campagnoni becomes the first Alpine skier ever to win gold medals in three consecutive Olympics when she takes the giant slalom at Shiga Kogen. She won the super-G in Albertville and the giant slalom in Lillehammer.

Feb 20—Julija Tchepalova wins the 30-kilometer freestyle to complete a Russian sweep of the five women's cross-country gold medals at Nagano. Larissa Lazutina finishes with three golds and five medals overall.

Feb 20—U.S. Olympic officials announce that players on the U.S. men's ice hockey team vandalized two apartments in the Nagano Olympic Village, causing about $1,000 worth of damage. The incident occurred in the early morning hours following Team USA's loss to the Czech Republic.

Feb 20—Fifteen-year-old Tara Lipinski of the U.S. wins the gold medal in women's figure skating, and displaces Sonja Henie—who was two months older than Lipinski when she won the first of her three Olympic golds in 1928—as the youngest woman ever to win an Olympic figure skating title. Michelle Kwan of the U.S. wins the silver medal and China's Lu Chen takes the bronze.

Feb 20—In a thrilling semifinal game decided by a shootout, the Czech Republic upsets Canada 2–1 in men's ice hockey. Russia defeats Finland 7–4 in the other semifinal.

Feb 21—Defenseman Petr Svoboda scores at 8:08 of the third period to give the Czech Republic a 1–0 victory over Russia in the men's ice hockey gold medal game. Goalie Dominik Hasek, the MVP of the National Hockey League in 1997, stops 20 shots to lead the Czech Republic to its first Olympic hockey title. Hasek gave up six goals in six Olympic hockey games. In the bronze medal game, Finland surprises Canada 3–2.

Feb 21—Japan's Takafumi Nishitani wins the gold medal in the men's 500-meter short track speed skating event.

Feb 22—Norway's Bjørn Dæhlie wins the 50-kilometer cross-country ski race in Hakuba. The victory brings Dæhlie a Winter Olympic-record eighth career gold medal. Dæhlie has won three golds and a silver at the Nagano Games, giving him 12 medals overall, also a Winter Olympic record.

Feb 22—The curtain falls on the 18th Winter Olympics with the closing ceremonies in Nagano's Minami Stadium. International Olympic Committee president Juan Antonio Samaranch calls the Nagano Games the "best organized" Olympics in history.

Pro Basketball

Oct 12, 1997—The American Basketball League, a circuit for women, tips off its second season as the the New England Blizzard buries the Atlanta Glory 86–66 in Hartford.

Oct 23—Forward Dennis Rodman agrees to an incentive-laden one-year, $4.5 million contract with the Chicago Bulls.

Oct 26—Houston Rockets forward Charles Barkley is arrested after allegedly throwing Jorge Lugo, 20, through the window of an Orlando, Fla., bar. Barkley is charged with aggravated battery and resisting arrest without violence and is released on a $6,000 bond.

Oct 31—Violet Palmer becomes the first female in league history to officiate a regular-season NBA game when she acts as the third referee in a season-opening matchup between the Dallas Mavericks and the Vancouver Grizzlies in Vancouver.

Nov 11—The NBC and Turner television networks announce that they have extended their TV contracts with the NBA for four additional years. Beginning with the 1998–99 season, NBC will pay roughly $425 million a year and Turner will pony up approximately $200 million per season for the exclusive rights to televise NBA games.

Nov 20—With his former Los Angeles Lakers teammate Magic Johnson and baseball iron man Cal Ripken of the Baltimore Orioles looking on, Dallas Mavericks forward A.C. Green sets an NBA record of 907 consecutive games-played when he suits up against the Golden State Warriors in Dallas's Reunion Arena.

Nov 20—The Atlanta Hawks, who began the season with 11 straight victories, lose their first game of the year, falling to the New York Knicks 100–79.

Nov 24—Hakeem Olajuwon of the Houston Rockets undergoes arthroscopic surgery on his left knee and is expected to be out until early February.

Nov 25—The Lakers are the last team to fall from the ranks o f the unbeaten as they lose to the Miami Heat on the road, 103–86. Los Angeles equals Atlanta's 11–0 start, something only eight teams in NBA history have done, but remains four wins short of the league record for the best start to a season, held by Houston (1993) and Washington (1948).

Dec 1—Golden State forward Latrell Sprewell attacks his coach, P.J. Carlesimo, twice during a Warriors practice session. Sprewell reportedly grabbed Carlesimo's neck, was pulled off the coach by teammates and dismissed from practice, but then returned about 15 minutes later and went after Carlesimo again. Golden State (1–13) announces that Sprewell is suspended indefinitely from the team.

Dec 3—In an unprecedented decision, the Golden State Warriors announce that they have terminated the contract of leading scorer Latrell Sprewell on the grounds that the star forward's assault on coach P.J. Carlesimo violated Section 16 of the uniform player contract, which states that players must conform to standards of good citizenship and good moral character.

Dec 4—The NBA announces it is suspending Golden State forward Latrell Sprewell from the league for one year following the player's attack on Warriors coach P.J. Carlesimo.

Dec 9—Michael Jordan moves past Moses Malone and into third place on the NBA's alltime career scoring list when he banks in a shot in the first quarter of the Bulls' game against the Knicks. The bucket gives Jordan 27,411 career points to Malone's 27,409. Jordan scores 29 points in the Bulls' 100–82 victory over New York.

Dec 18—The 76ers trade guard Jerry Stackhouse and center Eric Montross to the Detroit Pistons for center Theo Raliff and guard Aaron McKie.

Dec 20—New York center Patrick Ewing dislocates a bone and tears ligaments in his right wrist during the Knicks' 98–78 loss to Milwaukee. Ewing, who suffered the injury trying to break his fall after being knocked to the floor by Bucks forward Andrew Lang, undergoes surgery the following day and is expected to miss the rest of the season.

Dec 23—Stephon Marbury scores 35 points to

lead the Minnesota Timberwolves over the Seattle SuperSonics 112–103. The victory ends Minnesota's NBA-record streak of 26 straight losses to Seattle over six seasons.

Dec 23—Chicago defeats the Los Angeles Clippers 94–89 to give Bulls coach Phil Jackson his 500th career coaching victory. Jackson has reached the milestone in 682 games, surpassing Pat Riley's previous record of 684.

Jan 11, 1998—Hall of Famer Nancy Lieberman-Cline announces she will coach the WNBA expansion team the Detroit Shock, which will begin play in the summer of '98.

Jan 18—Former Celtics great Larry Bird returns to the Boston Garden for the first time as coach of the Indiana Pacers and guides the visitors to a 103–96 victory.

Jan 24—The Denver Nuggets lose to the Phoenix Suns 93–77 and tie the NBA record of 23 straight losses set by Vancouver (1995–96). The following day the Nuggets secure their first win since Dec. 9, defeating the Clippers 99–81.

Feb 3—Hakeem Olajuwon returns to the Houston lineup after missing 33 games due to knee surgery, scoring 10 points to help the Rockets to a 110–97 win over Vancouver.

Feb 8—The East defeats the West 135–114 in the NBA All-Star Game. Michael Jordan, who scores 23 points, makes eight assists and three steals, is named MVP of the game.

Feb 16—During the Rockets' 121–99 win over the Clippers, swingman Clyde Drexler scores 25 points and dishes off for five assists to join Hall of Famers John Havlicek, Jerry West and Oscar Robertson as the only players in NBA history with 6,000 career assists and 20,000 career points.

Feb 18—With the trade deadline looming, two NBA deals are derailed as Orlando Magic center Rony Seikaly refuses to report to Utah, where he had been sent in exchange for center Greg Foster and guard Chris Morris, and Portland guard Kenny Anderson refuses to go to Toronto, where he had been dealt for guard Damon Stoudamire. Anderson requests, and receives, a trade to Boston, which sends guard Chauncey Billups to Toronto in a transaction that involves seven players and ships Stoudamire to Portland. Seikaly, whose decision forces Utah to void its trade with Orlando, is traded to the New Jersey Nets along with forward Brian Evans. The Magic receive forward David Benoit, guard Kevin Edwards, center Yinka Dare and a 1998 lottery pick.

March 3—The Portland (OR) Power's Lin Dunn is named ABL coach of the year. Portland center Natalie Williams, the ABL's top scorer (21.9) and rebounder (11.6), wins the MVP award.

March 4—Arbiter John Feerick rules on a grievance filed by Warriors swingman Latrell Sprewell, who, after twice attacking Golden State coach P.J. Carlesimo on Dec. 1, had his contract terminated by the Warriors and was suspended for a year by the NBA. Stating that violence must "be dealt with severely but always with due regard to fairness," Feerick reinstates Sprewell's contract with Golden State and reduces the player's suspension from the league to seven months.

March 15—After dropping the first two games at Long Beach, the Columbus Quest win three in a row at home, including a 86–81 victory in Game 5, to win their second straight ABL championship. Columbus's Valerie Still scores 25 points and is named series MVP for the second year in a row.

March 18—Houston Rockets swingman Clyde Drexler announces he will retire from the NBA following the season to become the head basketball coach at the University of Houston, his alma mater.

March 29—The Indiana Pacers set an NBA record for fewest points in a game since the inception of the shot clock when they lose to the San Antonio Spurs 74–55.

April 19—The New Jersey Nets secure the final NBA playoff berth by defeating the Detroit Pistons 114–101 on the final day of the regular season. In Chicago, Michael Jordan scores 44 points to lead the Bulls over the Knicks 111–109 and secure his record 10th NBA scoring title with a 28.7 average.

April 23—Forward Danny Manning of the Phoenix Suns wins the NBA's Sixth Man Award.

April 27—Receiving 113 of a possible 116 votes, San Antonio forward Tim Duncan is named NBA rookie of the year.

May 2—For the second year in a row, fisticuffs break out in a playoff game between the Knicks and the Miami Heat, as Miami center Alonzo Mourning squares off with New York forward Larry Johnson in the closing seconds of Game 4 of their first-round series. Both players, along with Knicks forward Chris Mills, who stepped off the New York bench during the fight, are suspended for the fifth and deciding game of the series, which the Knicks win, 98–81.

May 3—Led by Karl Malone, who scores 31 points and pulls down 15 rebounds, the Utah Jazz eliminate the Rockets in Game 5 of their hotly contested first-round playoff series, 84–70. The loss ends the 15-year career of Rockets star Clyde Drexler.

May 7—Patrick Ewing returns to the Knicks lineup for the first time since dislocating his wrist on Dec. 20, facing Indiana in Game 2 of Eastern Conference semifinal series. Ewing looks rusty and the Knicks lose 85–77 to fall behind 2–0 in the best-of-seven series.

May 12—Pacers coach Larry Bird is named NBA coach of the year.

May 13—The Washington Wizards trade forward Chris Webber to the Sacramento Kings in exchange for guard Mitch Richmond and forward Otis Thorpe.

May 18—Bulls guard Michael Jordan is named MVP of the league for the fifth time in his career. Jordan, 35, who averaged 28.7 points per game and made the NBA all-defensive first team, is the oldest player in league history to be named MVP.

May 24—Led by forward Karl Malone, who scores 32 points and grabs 14 rebounds, Utah defeats the Lakers 96–92 in Los Angeles to complete a surprising four-game sweep of the Western Conference finals and advance to the NBA championship for the second year in a row.

May 26—The Seattle SuperSonics dismiss George Karl, their coach of the past six seasons. On June 17 Seattle hires former Suns coach Paul Westphal to replace Karl.

May 31—Chicago guard Michael Jordan holds Pacers guard Reggie Miller scoreless in the fourth quarter to lead the Bulls to an 88–83 victory in Game 7 of the Eastern Conference finals. The Bulls advance to the NBA finals for the third straight year.

June 7—Ruthie Bolton-Holifield nails two three-pointers in the final two minutes to lead the U.S. to a 71–65 victory over Russia in the finals of the Women's World Championship.

June 7—The Bulls defeat Utah 96–54 in Game 3 of the NBA finals, sending the Jazz to the most lopsided defeat in finals history and holding Utah to the lowest point total in any game, regular-season or playoffs, since the inception of the 24-second shot clock.

June 11—The WNBA season tips off in Cleveland as the hometown Rockers defeat the New York Liberty 78–71.

June 14—The incomparable Michael Jordan takes over Game 6 of the NBA finals with 41.9 seconds remaining. His team trailing by three following a John Stockton three-pointer, Jordan scores a quick bucket off the inbounds pass, then strips Utah's Karl Malone of the ball at the defensive end before hitting a 20-foot jump shot over Utah's Bryon Russell with 5.2 seconds to play. The basket proves to be the game-winner and Jordan, who finishes with 45 points, is named MVP of the series, which delivers the Bulls their sixth title of the 1990s.

June 22—Lenny Wilkens is selected for induction to the basketball Hall of Fame as a coach, making him and former UCLA coach John Wooden the only men inducted to the Hall as both players and coaches.

June 23—Phil Jackson resigns as coach of the six-time NBA champion Bulls, with whom he compiled the highest winning percentage of any coach in regular-season (.738) and playoff (.730) history.

June 24—The Clippers select Michael Olowokandi, a 7-foot center from the University of the Pacific who didn't start playing basketball until 1995, with the No. 1 pick in the NBA draft. Arizona guard Mike Bibby goes to Vancouver as the No. 2 selection.

July 1—The NBA enters its third player lockout in four years as league owners impose the freeze on any business involving players after they are unable to reach an agreement with the players association.

Sept 1—The Houston Comets win a second consecutive WNBA title, defeating the Phoenix Mercury 80–71 in Game 3 of the final series. Cynthia Cooper scores 23 points and is named MVP of the finals for the second straight year.

Sept 24—The NBA lockout stretches into its 13th week, delaying the opening of training camps and postponing 24 of 114 preseason games. It is the first time in league history that competition has been affected by labor difficulties. The start of the regular season, scheduled for Nov. 3, is in jeopardy.

Oct 13—The NBA—after 35,001 games over 52 seasons—cancels the first two weeks of the 1998–99 regular season when collective bargaining talks between owners and players break down. The NBA had been the only major American professional sports league never to have lost a game to a labor dispute. A total of 99 games from Nov. 3–16 will be eliminated from the schedule.

Pro Football

Oct 19, 1997—Thirty five-year-old Herschel Walker of Dallas moves past Kansas City's Marcus Allen and into second place on the NFL's alltime combined-yardage list when he gains 89 all-purpose yards, including a game-winning 64-yard touchdown reception, in the Cowboys' 26–22 win over the Jacksonville Jaguars.

Oct 20—In a 9–6 Monday night victory over Indianapolis, two Buffalo Bills achieve NFL milestones. Running back Thurman Thomas rushes for 42 yards to push his career total to 11,021 and move into 10th place on the alltime rushing list. Wide receiver Andre Reed catches four passes to run his career receptions total to 802, fourth-best alltime.

Oct 27—For just the second time ever, there are

two games played on a Monday night in the NFL. The doubleheader occurs because Game 7 of the Florida Marlins–Atlanta Braves World Series bumps the Dolphins–Bears game out of Miami's Pro Player Stadium on Oct. 26. In the originally scheduled game, Green Bay downs New England 28–10, and in the additional game Chicago rallies to beat Miami in overtime, 36–33.

Nov 16—Emmitt Smith of the Cowboys becomes the 11th player in league history to rush for 11,000 career yards when he runs for 99 yards in Dallas's 17–14 win over the Washington Redskins.

Nov 16—The 49ers win their 10th straight game, defeating the Carolina Panthers 27–19 in San Francisco. With the victory the Niners run their record to 10–1 and clinch the AFC West title. In Indianapolis, the Colts upset Green Bay 41–38 for their first win of the season, against 10 losses; and in Baltimore, the Ravens and the Eagles play through 15 minutes of overtime to a 10–10 tie, the first such NFL deadlock since 1989.

Nov 20—Citing poor performance, the St. Louis Rams release running back Lawrence Phillips. Phillips, the sixth pick in the 1996 draft, has had a series of off-field troubles since 1995, including arrests for drunken driving, violating probation and an assault charge involving his ex-girlfriend at the University of Nebraska.

Nov 23—Detroit's Barry Sanders becomes the first NFL rusher to gain at least 100 yards in 10 straight games in a single season when he rambles for 216 in the Lions' 32–10 win over the Colts. At Washington's new Jack Kent Cooke Stadium, the Redskins tie the Giants 7–7 after overtime. Washington QB Gus Frerotte leaves the game with a sprained neck suffered while head-butting the end zone wall in celebration of a first-half touchdown.

Nov 27—Barry Sanders of the Lions ties Marcus Allen's NFL record, set over two seasons, of 11 consecutive 100-yard games. Sanders rushes for 167 yards in Detroit's 55–20 rout of Chicago, and also moves past Eric Dickerson into the No. 2 spot on the alltime NFL rushing list. He now has 13,319 yards, 3,407 fewer than alltime leader Walter Payton.

Dec 2—Amid rumors that he will be indicted, along with former Louisiana Governor Edwin Edwards, on federal gambling fraud charges stemming from a New Orleans casino deal, 49ers owner Edward DeBartolo Jr. turns control of the team over to his sister, Denise DeBartolo York.

Dec 2—The Miami Dolphins sign troubled running back Lawrence Phillips, who was released on Nov. 20 by the Rams.

Dec 4—Bengals running back Corey Dillon breaks Jim Brown's 40-year-old single-game

rookie rushing record when he gains 246 yards in Cincinnati's 41–14 romp over the Tennessee Oilers. Brown rushed for 237 yards as a rookie against the L.A. Rams in 1957.

Dec 7—Behind Kordell Stewart's three touchdown passes and two touchdown runs, the Steelers upend Denver 35–24 in a late-season AFC showdown in Pittsburgh.

Dec 8—For the first time since 1990, the last year they failed to make the playoffs, the Cowboys lose a third consecutive game, falling 23–13 to Carolina, and dropping to 6–8 on the season.

Dec 14—The Baltimore Ravens and the Tennessee Oilers play the final game in Baltimore's Memorial Stadium, and the Ravens win, 21–19. Following the game, a group of former Baltimore Colts, including John Unitas, Art Donovan and Lenny Moore, run a ceremonial last play in the hallowed stadium. In Minneapolis, the Lions' Barry Sanders rushes for over 100 yards for a record 13th time this season, gaining 138 yards in Detroit's 14–13 win over the Vikings.

Dec 15—Just 15 weeks after reconstructive surgery to repair torn ligaments in his left knee, San Francisco's Jerry Rice returns to the Niners lineup for a Monday night game against Denver. It's a big night for the 49ers, who retire former star QB Joe Montana's jersey No. 16 at halftime. Rice catches a touchdown pass in the second quarter but bruises

BILL HABER/AP

The Big Easy was anything but for DeBartolo.

DAMIAN STROHMEYER

Levy retired after 11 years and four Super Bowl appearances with the Bills.

his left knee on the play and sits out the remainder of the game.

Dec 16—X-rays reveal that Jerry Rice suffered a transverse fracture of the kneecap on Dec. 15, in his first game since injuring the same knee in the season opener. He undergoes more surgery and will miss the rest of the season.

Dec 21—Detroit's Barry Sanders becomes the third back in league history, and the first since Eric Dickerson in 1984, to top 2,000 yards rushing in a season. Sanders runs for 184 yards in the Lions' year-ending 13–10 victory over the Jets, pushing his season total to 2,053. His season average of 6.1 yards per carry is the second-highest alltime, behind Jim Brown's 6.4 in 1963.

Dec 21—The New York Giants knock off Dallas 20–7 in the season finale, sending the Cowboys to a 6–10 record, their worst record since 1989. The victory gives the Giants a 7-0-1 record within their division, making them the first team ever to go unbeaten in the NFC East since division rivals began playing one another twice a season.

Dec 22—Linebacker Reggie Brown of the Lions emerges from successful surgery in Detroit's Henry Ford Hospital to fuse his first and second vertebrae. The procedure is designed to maintain stability following Brown's career-ending bruising of his spinal cord in Detroit's 13–10 win over the Jets the previous day.

Dec 22—Tied atop the AFC East with 9–6 records, the Dolphins and the Patriots meet in Miami to settle the division title and determine which team will host the wild-card playoff game between the two teams the following week. New England ekes out a 14–12 victory.

Dec 22—Following a 3–13 season, the Indianapolis Colts dismiss coach Lindy Infante and director of operations Bill Tobin. Indianapolis

then exchanges a draft pick with Carolina for GM Bill Polian, who will replace Tobin.

Dec 27—The Minnesota Vikings score 10 points in the final 90 seconds to upend the New York Giants 23–22 in the first round of the playoffs at Giants Stadium. The following day Tampa Bay, in the playoffs for the first time since 1983, limits Barry Sanders to 65 yards rushing and knocks Detroit out of the playoffs with a 20–10 win.

Dec 27—Denver avenges its bitter playoff loss of 1996 and earns its first postseason victory since '91 by trouncing Jacksonville 42–17 at Mile High Stadium. In the other AFC playoff game, the Patriots defeat Miami for the second week in a row, rolling to a 17–3 victory in Foxboro.

Dec 31—Marv Levy, who led the Buffalo Bills to four consecutive Super Bowls during his 11 years as their coach, announces his retirement. At 72 years-old, he was the oldest NFL head coach.

Jan 4, 1998—The NFL's final four is set as the Green Bay Packers flatten Tampa Bay 21–7 and advance to the NFC title game, where they will meet the 49ers, 38–22 winners over Minnesota. In the AFC, Denver, which beat Kansas City 14–10, will meet the Steelers, 7–6 winners over New England, for the conference championship.

Jan 11—The Packers defeat San Francisco 23–10 to return to the Super Bowl. Green Bay running back Dorsey Levens rushes for 114 yards and a touchdown. The following day in Pittsburgh the Broncos get 139 rushing yards from Terrell Davis and defeat the Steelers 24-21 to become the fifth wild-card to reach the Super Bowl. The Packers are installed as 14-point favorites in Super Bowl XXXII.

Jan 25—Shaking off the onset of a migraine headache in the second quarter, Denver's Terrell Davis runs for 157 yards and three touchdowns to lead the Broncos to a 31–24 upset of the defending champion Packers in perhaps the greatest of the 32 Super Bowls to date. Davis is named MVP of the game, which ends the AFC's 13-year Super-Bowl losing streak, and quarterback John Elway, who had been to three previous Super Bowls without a victory, finally wins the big one.

Feb 3—A group led by writer Tom Clancy purchases the Minnesota Vikings for slightly more than $200 million. Two weeks later the Vikings sign defensive end John Randle to a five-year, $32.5 million contract, making him the highest-paid defensive player in league history.

Feb 2—The AFC defeats the NFC 29–24 in the Pro Bowl. Seattle Seahawks quarterback

Warren Moon, 41, is named MVP of the game.

Feb 11—The Dallas Cowboys hire Pittsburgh Steelers offensive coordinator Chan Gailey to replace Barry Switzer, who was dismissed after the 1997–98 season.

Feb 23—Free agent defensive tackle Dana Stubblefield leaves the 49ers and signs a six-year, $36 million contract with Washington.

March 25—At the winter meetings in Orlando, Fla., owners vote down the reinstatement of instant replay as an officiating tool in the NFL.

April 9—Kansas City Chiefs running back Marcus Allen, 38, the NFL's alltime leader in rushing touchdowns with 123, announces his retirement.

April 18—The Indianapolis Colts select Tennessee quarterback Peyton Manning with the No. 1 pick in the NFL draft. Washington State QB Ryan Leaf goes to the Chargers as the No. 2 pick.

June 1—Denver QB John Elway announces that he will return to the Broncos for one more season.

July 22—Minnesota wide receiver Cris Carter signs a four-year, $23.5 million contract extension with the Vikings to become the highest-paid player at his position.

Aug 1—Five former NFL stars—safety Paul Krause of Minnesota, Bears linebacker Mike Singletary, center Dwight Stephenson of Miami, wide receiver Tommy McDonald of the Eagles and Cincinnati offensive tackle Anthony Munoz—are inducted to the Pro Football Hall of Fame in Canton, Ohio.

Aug 2—The New York Jets sign linebacker Bryan Cox, who had been released by the Bears, to replace the injured Marvin Jones.

Sept 6–7—The 1998–99 NFL season kicks off as John Elway passes for 257 yards and a TD to lead the Broncos past the Patriots 27–21; Vikings rookie receiver Randy Moss catches two TD passes in Minnesota's surprising 31–7 rout of Tampa Bay and the Jets take the 49ers to OT before falling 36–30.

Oct 5—In a battle of unbeaten teams, quarterback Randall Cunningham leads the Vikings to a 37–24 walloping of Green Bay, throwing for 442 yards and four TDs. With the victory, Minnesota runs its record to 5–0, tops in the NFC.

Oct 12—Jacksonville defeats Miami 28–21 to run its record to 5–0 and join the 6–0 Broncos 21–16 winners over Seattle, as the only undefeated teams in the AFC. Idle Minnesota is the NFC's only unbeaten franchise.

Soccer

MARK LENNIHAN/AP

Sampson resigned after the U.S. disaster in France.

Nov 2, 1997—The U.S. national team ties Mexico 0–0 in a World Cup qualifier in front of 114,000 fans in Mexico City's Guillermo Canedo Stadium, where Mexico has not lost since 1981.

Nov 9—The U.S. defeats Canada 3–0 in Burnaby, B.C., to clinch a spot in the 1998 World Cup finals.

Dec 2—U.S. Soccer announces that Steve Sampson will remain as national team coach at least through the 1998 World Cup.

Dec 4—The balls don't bounce the U.S.'s way at the World Cup draw in Marseille's Velodrome Stadium: the Americans land in Group F along with world power Germany, highly touted Yugoslavia and Iran, a bitter political rival.

Jan 12, 1998—Former Portugal coach Carlos Quieroz signs with U.S. Soccer to evaluate the country's youth programs and submit formal recommendations for improvements.

Jan 14—Alfonso Mondelo, who led the Long Island Rough Riders to the 1997 A-League title, is hired to coach the NY/NJ MetroStars. He is the team's fourth coach in three seasons.

Jan 27—The Los Angeles Galaxy of MLS trade goalkeeper Jorge Campos and midfielder Chris Armas to the Chicago Fire in exchange for defender Danny Pena goalkeeper Kevin Hartman, and a player to be named later.

Feb 1—The Gold Cup opens in Oakland as the U.S. knocks off lightly regarded Cuba 3–0.

Feb 4—In a three-way deal, the MetroStars acquire defender Alexi Lalas from the New England Revolution while New England receives striker Raul Diaz Arce from D.C. United. D.C. receives favorable draft picks, including New England's top selection in '99.

Feb 10—In one of the biggest upsets in modern soccer history, the U.S. stuns Brazil 1–0 in the semifinals of the Gold Cup in Los Angeles.

Feb 15—Mexico wins the Gold Cup final in front of 91,000 fans in the Los Angeles Coliseum, defeating the U.S. 1–0.

Feb 27—Jamar Beasley, 18, a striker at South Side High in Fort Wayne, Ind., signs with the New England Revolution of MLS, making him the youngest player in the league.

March 15—MLS opens its third season in Fort Lauderdale's Lockhart Stadium, where a sellout crowd of 20,450 watches D.C. United defeat the expansion Miami Fusion 2–0.

April 14—Coach Steve Sampson drops a bombshell: he announces he is cutting captain John Harkes, a veteran of two World Cups and 90 appearances for the U.S., from the national team.

April 22—The U.S. scores a resounding 3–0 defeat over Austria in Vienna.

May 24—Midfielder Tab Ramos, who underwent reconstructive knee surgery in November 1997, returns to the lineup as the U.S. defeats Kuwait 2–0 in Portland, Ore. The game is also the debut of David Regis, a defender from France who became a U.S. citizen on May 20.

May 27—Carlos Hermosillo, the alltime leading scorer for Mexico's national team, signs a two-year contract with MLS and will be assigned to the Los Angeles Galaxy.

June 10—The 1998 World Cup kicks off in Montpelier as defending champion Brazil defeats Scotland 2–1.

June 15—The U.S. opens France '98 with a timid performance, losing 2–0 to Germany in Paris.

June 21—Before a sellout crowd of 44,000 in Lyon, the U.S. is eliminated from the World Cup when it loses to Iran 2–1.

June 23—Norway capitalizes on a controversial late penalty kick to defeat Group A winners Brazil, 2–1, and advance to the second round.

June 25—The U.S. plays its final game in France '98, losing to Yugoslavia 1–0 in Nantes.

June 27—Brazil advances to the World Cup quarterfinals with a 4–1 victory over Chile in Paris. The following day Denmark surprises Group D winner Nigeria 4–1 in Saint Denis.

June 29—Steve Sampson announces his resignation as U.S. coach. His record of 26-22-14 is the best of any U.S. coach ever.

July 4—Dennis Bergkamp scores a spectacular late goal to lift the Netherlands to a 2–1 victory over Argentina and into the World Cup semifinals, where they will face Brazil, 3–2 winners over Denmark. In Lyon, Croatia, playing in its first World Cup, surprises Germany 3–0 to advance to the semifinals against host nation France, which beat Italy on penalty kicks.

July 7—In perhaps the best game of the tournament, Brazil advances past the Netherlands on penalty kicks after the teams play to a 1–1 tie in Marseille. In Saint Denis, France gets two goals from defender Lilian Thuram to defeat Croatia 2–1 and advance to the World Cup final against Brazil.

July 12—Midfielder Zinedine Zidane scores twice in the first half and striker Emmanuel Petit adds a late goal as France stuns Brazil 3–0 to win the World Cup final in Saint-Denis.

Aug 16—D.C. United wins the CONCACAF Champions Cup, a tournament featuring the top club teams in North and Central America and the Caribbean. United defeats Toluca of Mexico 1–0 in the final to become the first ever U.S.-based continental club champion.

Aug 24—Thomas Rongen steps down as coach of the New England Revolution. He is replaced by Walter Zenga, the Revs goalkeeper in '97.

Oct 4—Trailing Dallas 2–0 with 10 minutes to play in Game 2 of their first-round playoff series, Los Angeles explodes for three goals to eliminate the Burn from the playoffs.

Oct 16—In front of 32,744 fans at Soldier Field, the Chicago Fire upsets the Los Angeles Galaxy 2–1 in a shootout to win the Western Conference final two games to one and advance to the MLS championship in its first year as a franchise.

Oct 18—Brian McBride scores two goals as the Crew defeats D.C. 4–2 in a driving rain in Columbus to force a deciding Game 3 in the Eastern Conference final.

Oct 21—MLS Cup '98 is set as D.C. United defeats Columbus 3–0 to advance to the championship game for the third time in the three-year history of the league. United gets its goals from defender Jeff Agoos and striker Roy Lassiter, who scores twice, including the clincher in the 85th minute.

Nov 2, 1997—Pete Sampras wins the Paris Open, defeating Jonas Bjorkman of Sweden 6–3, 4–6, 6–3, 6–1 in the final to all but lock up the No. 1 ranking in men's tennis for the fifth consecutive year, a feat equaled only by Jimmy Connors.

Nov 9—With a 6–0, 7–5 victory over Nathalie Tauziat in the final of the Ameritech Cup in Chicago, Lindsay Davenport picks up her sixth tournament victory of the season and moves from No. 5 in the women's rankings to No. 3, a career high.

Nov 16—Top-ranked Pete Sampras rolls over Yevgeny Kafelnikov 6–3, 6–2, 6–2 to win the season-ending ATP Tour World Championship in Hanover, Germany.

MANNY MILLAN

Rafter downed Philippoussis to repeat as U.S. Open champ.

Nov 23—In the final of the women's season-ending tournament, the Chase Championships at Madison Square Garden, second-seeded Jana Novotna defeats No. 7 seed Mary Pierce 7–6 (7–4), 6–2, 6–3.

Nov 29—Sweden blanks the U.S. 5–0 to win the Davis Cup in Göteborg. Michael Chang of the U.S. loses two matches and his teammate Pete Sampras defaults against Magnus Larsson due to a calf injury. It is the first time the U.S. has been shut out in Davis Cup play since 1973.

Dec 29—Saying she needs more time to recover from knee surgery, Steffi Graf, who hasn't played since June '97, decides to withdraw from the '98 Australian Open.

Jan 12, 1998—Lleyton Hewitt, a 16-year-old high school student from Australia who is ranked No. 550 in the world, wins the Australian Men's Hardcourt Championship, defeating countryman Jason Stoltenberg 3–6, 6–3, 7–6 (7–4) in the final.

Jan 31—Martina Hingis defends her Australian Open title with a 6–3, 6–3 defeat of Conchita Martinez in Melbourne. The following day, Petr Korda defeats Marcelo Ríos 6–2, 6–2, 6–2 to win the men's title.

Mar 15—Top-ranked Martina Hingis defeats No. 2 Lindsay Davenport 6–3, 6–4 to win the Evert Cup in Indian Wells, Calif. In the men's tournament, known as the Champion's Cup, Marcelo Ríos downs Greg Rusedski 6–3, 6–7, 7–6, 6–4 in the final.

March 28—Seventeen-year-old Venus Williams defeats 16-year-old Anna Kournikova 2–6, 6–4, 6–1 to win the Lipton Championships. To reach the final, Williams defeated world-No. 1 Martina Hingis while Kournikova knocked off a record four top-10 players, including No. 2 Lindsay

Davenport and No. 5 Monica Seles.

March 29—Chile's Marcelo Ríos beats Andre Agassi 7–5, 6–3, 6–4 to win the Lipton Championships and become the first South American ever to claim the No. 1 ranking.

April 6—Jim Courier guts out a 0–6, 6–4, 4–6, 6–1, 6–4 victory over Marat Safin to clinch a 3-2 victory for the U.S. over Russia in the first round of the Davis Cup in Stone Mountain, Ga.

April 19—Monica Seles and Lindsay Davenport score convincing victories in their singles matches to lead the U.S. to a 5–0 blanking of the Netherlands in first-round Fed Cup play.

May 27—Paraguay's Ramon Delgado, ranked No. 97 in the world, upsets No. 1 Pete Sampras 7–6 (8–6), 6–3, 6–4 in the second round of the French Open.

June 6—Arantxa Sánchez Vicario defeats Monica Seles 7–6 (7–5), 0–6, 6–2 to win the French Open for the third time in her career.

June 7—With members of Spain's royal family looking on, Spaniard Carlos Moya defeats countryman Alex Corretja in the French Open final, 6–3, 7–5, 6–3.

June 5—The mixed doubles team of Justin Gimelstob and Venus Williams wins the French Open final 6–4, 6–4 over Serena Williams and Luis Lobo. Coupled with their Australian Open triumph, the victory gives Williams and Gimelstob two legs of a mixed doubles Grand Slam.

June 22—Returning to Wimbledon for the first time since 1996, Steffi Graf, who has won the tournament seven times, defeats Gala Leon Garcia 6–4, 6–1 in a first-round match.

June 24—World No. 2 Marcelo Ríos tumbles out of Wimbledon in the first round, losing to

Francisco Clavet 6–3, 3–6, 7–5, 3–6, 6–3.

June 29—England's Tim Henman thrills the Centre Court fans by upsetting No. 6 seed Pat Rafter 6–3, 6–7 (3–7), 6–3, 6–2 to reach the quarterfinals of Wimbledon for the third straight year.

July 4—Jana Novotna wins her first Grand Slam singles title, defeating Nathalie Tauziat 6–4, 7–6 (7–2) in the Wimbledon final.

July 5—Outlasting Goran Ivanisevic 6–7 (2–7), 7–6 (11–9), 6–4, 3–6, 6–2 in a two hour, 52 minute final, Pete Sampras wins his fifth Wimbledon and 11th grand slam title. He is now tied with Bjorn Borg and Rod Laver in career grand slams and within one of alltime leader Roy Emerson.

July 11—Jimmy Connors is inducted into the International Tennis Hall of Fame.

Aug 16—Patrick Rafter wins the ATP Championship, defeating Pete Sampras 1–6, 7–6 (7–2), 6–4 in the final in Cincinnati.

Aug 16—With a 4–6, 6–4, 6–3 victory over Martina Hingis in the final of the Acura Classic in Los Angeles, Lindsay Davenport claims her third straight WTA Tour title. She beat Venus Williams to take the Bank of the West Classic in Palo Alto on Aug. 2, and won the Toshiba Classic in San Diego the following week, routing Mary Pierce 6–3, 6–1 in the final.

Aug 23—Monica Seles wins her fourth consecutive du Maurier Open title with a 6–3, 6–2 victory over Arantxa Sánchez Vicario.

Sept 10—Patrick Rafter defeats Pete Sampras for the second time in less than a month,

knocking off the No. 1 seed in the semifinals of the U.S. Open 6–7 (8–10), 6–4, 2–6, 6–4, 6–3. Sampras strains a hip flexor after the second set.

Sept 12—Announcing, "I am a threat for No. 1," world No. 2 Lindsay Davenport edges top-ranked Martina Hingis 6–3, 7–5 to win the U.S. Open, her fourth title in the past five tournaments and her first Grand Slam title.

Sept 13—Martina Hingis becomes the fourth player in tennis history to win a doubles Grand Slam. Hingis and Jana Novotna, who won the French Open and Wimbledon doubles titles together, down Lindsay Davenport and Natasha Zvereva 6–3, 6–3 to win the U.S. Open doubles championship. Hingis had teamed with Mirjana Lucic to win the Australian Open doubles title in January.

Sept 13—Patrick Rafter wins the U.S. Open for the second year in a row with a 6–3, 3–6, 6–2, 6–0 victory over fellow Australian and former doubles partner Mark Philipoussis.

Sept 27—With Michael Chang, Andre Agassi and Pete Sampras begging off, and Jim Courier sidelined by injury, the U.S. fields a second-string Davis Cup team and loses its semifinal tie with Italy 4–1.

Sept 20—Led by Conchita Martinez and Arantxa Sánchez Vicario, Spain defeats Switzerland 3–2 in the Federation Cup final.

Oct 12—U.S. Open champ Lindsay Davenport takes over the women's No. 1 ranking from Martina Hingis, who had held it for 80 weeks.

Other Sports

Thompson savored four golds in Perth.

Oct 25, 1997—In the first Olympic tuneup of the figure skating season, the Skate America at Detroit's Joe Louis Arena, Michelle Kwan takes the women's title, scoring all 5.9s (out of 6.0) on both her long and short program. Tara Lipinski finishes second.

Nov 1—Kenya's John Kagwe wins the the New York City marathon in 2 hours, 8 minutes, 12 seconds, despite having to stop twice during the race to retie his shoelaces. At about 23 miles, with his right lace undone again and flapping with each stride, Kagwe pulls away from the field to win by more than a minute over countryman Joseph Chebet. Franziska Rochat-Moser of Switzerland wins the women's race with a time of 2 hours, 28 minutes, 43 seconds.

Nov 12—Steve Hoskins defeats Danny Wiseman 233–184 to win bowling's Touring Players Championship in Harmarville, Pa.

Nov 22—Kim Adlear defeats Carolyn Dorin-Ballard 257–206 to win the Sam's Town

MARK THOMPSON/ALLSPORT

Gebrselassie broke two world records in '98.

Invitational bowling tournament in Las Vegas.

Nov 23—Zali Steggall scores the first victory ever by an Australian woman on the skiing World Cup circuit, taking the slalom in Park City, Utah, with a two-run time of 1:36.30. Kristina Koznick of the U.S. finishes fourth, a career best for her and the only top-10 finish by a U.S. skier, man or woman, of the season.

Dec 4—At the U.S. Open Swimming Championships in Indianapolis, Diana Munz, a 15-year-old high school sophomore from Chagrin Falls, Ohio, wins the women's 800-meter free, catching defending champion Brooke Bennett in the final 50 meters and clocking 8:36.23. Another teenager scores an upset as Robert Margalis, 15, of Clearwater, Fla., defeats world record holder and Olympic gold medalist Tom Dolan in the men's 400-meter individual medley.

Dec 7—Extending one of the greatest dynasties in NCAA sports, the North Carolina women's soccer team defeats the University of Connecticut 2–0 in Greensboro, N.C., to claim the national title for the 14th time in 16 years.

Dec 8—Masahiko Harada of Japan wins his fifth World Cup title in ski jumping, landing jumps of 90.5 and 95 meters to take the competition in Villach, Austria.

Dec 14—At the National Finals Rodeo in Las Vegas, Dan Mortensen of Manhattan, Mont., wins his first All-Around world title, unseating two-time defending champion Joe Beaver. Mortensen also claims the saddle bronc world championship, his fourth.

Dec 14—Led by striker Seth George, who scores two goals in a three-minute span, and goalkeeper Matt Reis, who makes several outstanding saves in the first half, the UCLA men's soccer team downs Virginia 2–0 to win the national title before 20,143 fans in Richmond, Va.

Dec 18—Germany's Katja Seizinger wins her sixth consecutive World Cup title, seizing the super-G in Val d'Isere, France with a time of 1:07.09.

Dec 21—Tara Lipinski wins the women's title at the Champions Series Final figure skating competition in Munich. Tanja Szewczenko of Germany finishes second and Russia's Maria Butyrskaya is third. Michelle Kwan of the U.S. skips the event to rest a stress fracture in her toe.

Jan 8, 1998—Attempting a quadruple toe loop—a maneuver never completed in competition—in his long program, Todd Eldredge wins his fifth U.S. figure skating title at the CoreStates Center in Philadelphia. Eldredge doesn't land the jump, but the judges reward his effort with marks of 5.8 and 5.9.

Jan 10—Michelle Kwan, who has battled injuries all season long, turns in two nearly flawless performances to win the second U.S. figure skating title of her career. She earns eight perfect scores from nine judges for her long program. Tara Lipinski recovers from a subpar short program to place second, and veteran Nicole Bobek finishes third.

Jan 12—At the world championships in Perth, Australia, U.S. swimmer Jenny Thompson wins the 100-meter freestyle to claim her first individual gold medal in international competition. Thompson, who wins with a time of 54.95, has five Olympic gold medals and one other world championship gold, but won them all as part of a relay team.

Jan 13—Newcomer Kristy Kowal of the U.S. wins the 100-meter breaststroke at the swimming world championships in Perth, Australia, upsetting defending Olympic champ and world record–holder Penny Heyns of South Africa. In the men's 400 individual medley, Tom Dolan of the U.S. defends his world title, comfortably beating Marcel Wouda of the Netherlands.

Jan 14—Four members of China's national swimming team are suspended from the world championships after testing positive for the banned diuretic triamterene, which dilutes urine and masks the use of steroids. Swimming's governing body, FINA, also announces it is suspending Chinese breaststroker Yuan Yuan for four years and her coach, Zhou Zhewen, for 15 years. The pair were found to be in possession of 13 vials of human growth hormone as they entered Australia for the world championships. Twenty-seven swimmers from China have tested positive for banned substances since 1990.

Jan 15—The U.S. wins three gold medals at the swimming world championships as Lenny Krayzelburg takes the 100-meter backstroke in 55.0, Jenny Thompson wins the 100-meter butterfly, clocking 58.46, and the men's 4 x 100-meter freestyle relay team of Scott Tucker, Neil Walker, Jon Olsen and Gary Hall Jr., touches first in 3:16.69.

Jan 18—Bill Pilczuk of the U.S. scores a major upset at the swimming world championships, beating Olympic champion Aleksandr Popov of Russia in the 50-meter freestyle. Pilczuk clocks 22.29 and Popov, who had not lost in the event since 1991, finishes in 22.43.

Jan 29—In the last skiing event before the Nagano Games, Kristina Koznick of Burnsville, Minn., wins the slalom in Are, Sweden, for the first World Cup victory of her career and the first by a U.S. Alpine skier this season.

Feb 3—After predicting he would do so two days earlier, U.S. sprinter Maurice Greene breaks the world indoor record in the 60-meter dash, clocking 6.39 in Madrid.

Feb 16—New York's Marty Clark defeats Mark Lewis of Boston 9–1, 9–4, 9–1 to retain his U.S. squash title at the national championships in Los Angeles.

March 1—Tanzania's Zebedayo Bayo wins the Los Angeles Marathon in 2:11:21. Bayo, 21, had run just two marathons prior to his victory.

March 8—Kraig Welborn of DeRidder, La., hauls in a 14-pound, 11-ounce largemouth bass near Anacoco, La., to break the world record by three ounces.

March 17—Jeff King wins his third Iditarod Trail Sled Dog Race, battling swirling snow and poor visibility to finish the 1,100-mile race in nine days, five hours, 52 minutes.

April 5—At the World Cup of Freestyle Wrestling in Stillwater, Okla., Andrei Shumilin of Russia edges the U.S.'s Tom Eriksen 1–0 in the heavyweight final, giving Russia a 16–15, double-tiebreaker win, and the team title.

April 11—Bowler Walter Ray Williams Jr. captures the first major of his career, winning the U.S. Open in Fairfield, CT. Aleta Sill wins the women's event, rolling a 276 in the final.

April 20—Kenya's Moses Tanui wins the Boston Marathon in a time of 2 hours, 7 minutes

34 seconds, the third-fastest in the 102-year history of the race. His countryman and training partner Joseph Chebet finishes three seconds behind him. Fatuma Roba of Ethiopia repeats as women's champion, clocking 2 hours, 23 minutes, 21 seconds.

May 12—Marion Jones of the U.S. runs the second-fastest women's 100 meters ever, winning in 10.71 in Chengdu, China.

May 25—Scoring five unanswered goals to break a 3–3 tie after halftime, Princeton buries Maryland 15–5, and wins its third consecutive men's NCAA lacrosse title and fifth of the decade.

June 1—Haile Gebrselassie of Ethiopia breaks Kenyan Paul Tergat's 10,000-meter world record by 5.1 seconds in Hengelo, the Netherlands, finishing in 26:22.75.

June 13—Ethiopia's Haile Gebrselassie breaks the world record in the 5,000 meters—the 14th world record of his career—clocking 12:39.36 in Helsinki.

June 21—At the U.S. outdoor track and field championships in New Orleans, Marion Jones cruises to a triple no one has accomplished in 50 years: She easily wins the 200 meters to follow her victories the previous day in the 100 and the long jump.

July 14—Morocco's Hicham El Guerrouj shatters the 1,500-meter world record by more than a second, clocking 3:26.0 in Rome.

July 27—The International Amateur Athletic Federation announces that it is suspending sprinter Dennis Mitchell and shot-putter Randy Barnes, both of the U.S., indefinitely for failing out-of-competition drug tests.

Aug 2—Marco Pantani becomes the first rider from Italy to win the Tour de France since Felice Gimondi did so in 1965. Bobby Julich of the U.S. finishes third in the race, which is marred by drug scandals that cause seven teams to depart the competition.

Aug 6—Ireland's Michelle Smith, who won three gold medals and one bronze in swimming at the 1996 Olympics, is suspended for four years by FINA for tampering with a urine sample.

Sept 12—Inching ever closer to Florence-Griffith Joyner's 10-year-old 100-meter record of 10.49, Marion Jones of the U.S. clocks 10.65 at the World Cup in Johannesburg.

Sept 20—Ronaldo da Costa of Brazil wins the Berlin Marathon in a world-record time of 2:06:05.

Oct 7—U.S. cyclist Lance Armstrong, competing again after battling testicular cancer, finishes fourth in the elite time trial at the World Championships in Valkenburg, Netherlands.

Baseball

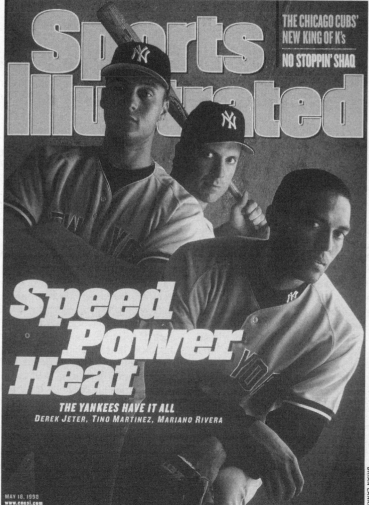

Sports Illustrated

THE CHICAGO CUBS'
NEW KING OF K's

NO STOPPIN' SHAQ

**Speed
Power
Heat**

THE YANKEES HAVE IT ALL
DEREK JETER, TINO MARTINEZ, MARIANO RIVERA

MAY 18, 1998
www.cnnsi.com

BRIAN LANKER

45

Yankee Dandy

A season for the ages ended, fittingly, with another title for baseball's most storied franchise

BY TIM CROTHERS

WHY NOT? Why shouldn't the greatest baseball season anybody can remember conclude with a World Series dominated by the greatest team anyone can remember? The New York Yankees swept the awestruck San Diego Padres in the World Series to finish the season with a breathtaking overall record of 125–50, the most victories by any team in baseball history. "When you win more games than anybody and win the World Series in four straight games," Yankees shortstop Derek Jeter said, "you have to be considered one of the best teams that ever played the game."

While it is foolhardy at best to try to compare baseball teams from different eras, the '98 Yankees certainly proved that they belong in that barroom conversation. These Yankees not only won the team's second World Series title in the last three seasons and the 24th in franchise history, a record for American sports, they reinvented the image of the Bronx Bombers. These guys didn't have a Babe Ruth or a Mickey Mantle or a Reggie Jackson or a fancy nickname like Murderer's Row. These Yankees were a true team, a ballclub without a single legitimate candidate for the league MVP, but instead a variety of overachievers playing the roles of Mr. April, Mr. July and Mr. October. While cornerstones like Jeter, Chuck Knoblauch, David Cone and Mariano Rivera provided stability, there was always room for an unlikely hero like minor league lifer Shane Spencer to step in and carry the team for a week. It spoke volumes about this team, for instance, that its best hitter, American League batting champion Bernie Williams, produced just one hit in 16 at bats in the World Series and nobody even noticed. Williams was picked up by Scott Brosius, a journeyman who hit .203 in Oakland in '97 but was rescued by the Yankees and won the World Series MVP in '98.

In what had already become a season full of uplifting stories, the Yankees' World Series sweep acted as a poignant Get Well card to a fallen teammate, Darryl Strawberry, who learned just before the playoffs that he suffered from colon cancer. The Yankees wore Strawberry's No. 39 on the backs of

Series MVP Brosius had plenty to shout about, including two HRs in Game 3.

their caps and during the championship celebration each of Strawberry's teammates took time to credit him for providing some inspiration. "We wouldn't have accomplished this without Darryl," Tino Martinez said. "This championship isn't about a bunch of good players, but about our entire team."

The Yankees exquisite teamwork provided an incongruous backdrop to a season that was otherwise characterized by dozens of incredible individual accomplishments, most notably the unprecedented home run chase. What baseball fan will ever forget where he or she was on Sept. 8 at 8:18 p.m. CDT? At that precise moment Mark McGwire launched his 62nd home run, breaking the sacred record that Roger Maris had owned for the last 37 years. Ironically McGwire's 341-foot laser down the leftfield line off Chicago's Steve Trachsel would turn out to be the shortest homer Big Mac would hit all season. During his exuberant trot around the diamond, McGwire nearly neglected to touch first base. He was congratulated by each of the Cubs infielders as he passed by and was embraced finally at home plate by the Cardinals batboy who also happened to be his son, Matt. McGwire briefly basked in the adulation of his teammates and the sellout crowd before climbing into the stands to share the moment with several members of Maris's family who were on hand to witness the passing of the torch. True to the pattern he had followed all season, McGwire reacted to the homer humbly by saying, "I can't believe I did it."

While No. 62 was clearly the most notable homer of the season, it was only one thrust in a memorable home run duel between McGwire and the Cubs' Sammy Sosa. The chase was so competitive that one or both players hit a home run on 26 of the final 40 days of the season, and during that span no more than two days elapsed without a homer from either Sosa or McGwire. On two occasions during the season Sosa actually wrested the homer lead away from McGwire, but McGwire displayed the best finishing kick. He cracked five homers in the final three games of the season to finish with 70, four

STEPHEN GREEN

Rodriguez, 22, became the third member of baseball's 40–40 club.

the overwhelming national pride enveloping the exploits of "Mike McGwire" and "Sammy Sooser."

McGwire and Sosa became symbols of a baseball revival. Perhaps the movement's definitive moment occurred on the baseball season's final Sunday when the crowd at a St. Louis Rams football game, being played just a few blocks from Busch Stadium, created such a clamor before a third-and-nine play that the disoriented Rams took an illegal motion penalty. The error was caused by the uproar over McGwire's 69th homer. "As far as I'm concerned it's the best season ever," Montreal manager Felipe Alou said. "The game has emerged from the grave with thunder. You don't hear about the strike anymore. Sometimes something has to almost die, like baseball did, for the miracle to take place."

As if the long-ball heroics of McGwire and Sosa weren't enough, Seattle's Ken Griffey Jr. hit 56 homers and San Diego's Greg Vaughn cracked his 50th in his last at bat to round out the largest fraternity ever to hit at least 50 in a single season. Barry Bonds hit 37 homers and became the first player with 400 homers and 400 stolen bases in a career. In fact, Bonds's mere presence was so intimidating that on May 28, in the season's most outrageous managerial move, Arizona skipper Buck Showalter intentionally walked Bonds with the bases loaded and the Diamondbacks ahead by two runs in the ninth inning. (Showalter's pusillanimous plot worked when Gregg Olson induced the next Giants batter, Brent Mayne, to line out.)

Seattle's wunderkind Alex Rodriguez joined Bonds and Jose Canseco as the only players to hit 40 homers and steal 40 bases in a season. Houston's Craig Biggio rekindled interest in a long-forgotten 50–50 category: He matched Tris Speaker as the only other player to hit 50 doubles and steal 50 bases in the same season. For much of the summer

ahead of Sosa's 66, and establish the new home run record, which could easily stand as long as Maris's did (unless McGwire sees more strikes next season). "Obviously it's a huge number," McGwire said after the final game of the season. "I think the magnitude of the number won't be understood for a while. I'm in awe of myself."

The breakdown of McGwire's power numbers is staggering. One out of every five balls he put into play landed over the outfield fence. His homers traveled a combined 29,598 feet, a distance greater than the height of the world's tallest mountain. In his last 40 games McGwire launched 23 homers, a total that would have led the Cardinals' team in 22 of the previous 32 seasons. Fascination over his awesome accomplishment extended well beyond the sport. McGwire received personal congratulations from the President of the United States and the Prime Minister of Japan, and during one infamous speech Senator Ted Kennedy acknowledged

Texas's Juan Gonzalez kept pace with Hack Wilson's major league record of 190 RBIs. Gonzalez had 101 at the All-Star break but finished with 157 and was eventually overtaken by Sosa, who knocked in 158 runs, the most in the majors in nearly 50 years.

The '98 season was also blessed with the emergence of a particularly stellar breed of young hitter, such as Toronto's Shawn Green, Anaheim's Darin Erstad, Colorado's Todd Helton, Arizona's Travis Lee, Oakland's Ben Grieve and Minnesota's Todd Walker. The sport even grudgingly welcomed the notorious rookie J.D. Drew. Drew conducted 13 months of high-profile haggling with the Phillies and then the Cardinals before finally signing a four-year, $7 million guaranteed contract with St. Louis. His Cardinals teammate Brian Jordan said the lucrative pact for the unproven youngster was "outrageous." But Drew then suggested he might be worth it by hitting five homers in 36 at bats during a September call-up.

On May 15 baseball was stunned by the most titanic trade in the history of the game,

Clemens joined exclusive company with his second straight pitching Triple Crown.

a seven-player swap between Los Angeles and Florida that involved a total of $108.1 million worth of contracts. The Dodgers gave up their best player, catcher Mike Piazza, in a move indicative of the instability of a franchise that would change its ownership, general manager, manager and most of its roster in one chaotic year. For their part, the defending champion Marlins completed their monumental purge of talent by sending the Dodgers three World Series starters: Bobby Bonilla, Charles Johnson and Gary Sheffield. By the end of the season only two players, Edgar Renteria and Craig Counsell, remained from Florida's starting lineup for Game 7 of the '97 World Series.

Florida thus became the first team ever to plummet from being World Series champs to having the worst record in baseball. The disarray caused manager Jim Leyland to exercise his right to flee the sinking ship, but not before a memorable July game at the Astrodome that summed up Leyland's comic misery. On that evening Marlins starting pitcher Brian Meadows allowed five Houston runs on his first *eight* pitches, including two home runs, two singles and a hit batsman. The beleaguered Leyland walked to

the mound and asked his catcher Mike Redmond, "How's he throwing?"

Redmond looked at Leyland and said, "I don't know. I haven't caught one yet."

Only the Marlins fire sale kept the two expansion teams, Arizona and Tampa Bay, out of the major league cellar. As in any expansion season, the quality of the added pitching did not match that of the added hitting, causing overall pitching statistics to soar. Going resolutely against this trend on May 17, however, was portly New York Yankees southpaw David Wells, who retired 27 consecutive Minnesota Twins to fire the 13th perfect game in major league history. After the game Wells received a phone call from Don Larsen, who had thrown the only other perfecto in Yankees history in the '56 World Series. In one of baseball's more legendary coincidences the two pitchers confirmed that they had both graduated from the high school, Point Loma in San Diego.

On May 6 Cubs rookie Kerry Wood nearly matched Wells's feat against Houston in just his fifth major league start, allowing just one questionable infield hit and no walks while tying the major league record with 20 strikeouts. Pitching his first complete game since high school, Wood produced one of the most dominant performances in baseball history. After the game he said, "It felt like a game of catch out there." The next morning Wood received congratulations from his boyhood idol and fellow Texan, Roger Clemens, who would rack up some rather dominant numbers himself in 1998. Clemens joined Grover Cleveland Alexander, Lefty Grove and Sandy Koufax as the only pitchers to win back-to-back pitching Triple Crowns (leading the league in wins, ERA and strikeouts). Pedro Martinez rekindled memories of Clemens's halcyon days at Fenway Park, earning his massive contract with 19 victories and a 2.89 ERA and sending throngs of Dominican fans into a flag-waving frenzy. Another Latin hero, Orlando (El Duque) Hernandez, defected from Cuba with seven companions on a makeshift raft and five months later found himself pitching in Yankee Stadium. After an 18-month pitching hiatus, Hernandez won 12 games and had a 3.13 ERA in 21 starts. He also admitted he was motivated by his hatred for Cuban dictator Fidel Castro. Said Hernandez, "I hope he watches me and is pulling the hair out of his beard."

Philadephia's Curt Schilling became just the fifth pitcher to strike out 300 batters in consecutive seasons. San Diego closer Trevor Hoffman led the majors with 53 saves, and the Cubs' Rod Beck had 51, the first time two relievers have reached 50 in one season. Atlanta's Mark Wohlers

BOB ROSATO

One year after cancer surgery, Davis, 36, led the Orioles with a .327 average.

Hoffman went 53 for 54 in save opportunities to lead the National League.

DARREN CARROLL

was no threat to join them, contracting Steve Blass disease midway through the season and getting shipped to the minors.

The '98 season also celebrated the power of perseverance. Oakland's Rickey Henderson, 39 years young, led the majors with 66 stolen bases, the oldest player ever to swipe more than 50 bases. Boston's Dennis Eckersley quietly made his 1,071st appearance to nudge past Hoyt Wilhelm atop the alltime list. Eric Davis, 36, who underwent surgery for colon cancer in '97, batted .327 with 28 homers and led the Orioles on a furious, yet unsuccessful, pennant drive after the All-Star break. In Baltimore's final home game of the season, Davis's teammate Cal Ripken Jr. voluntarily halted what had become known as The Streak after playing 2,632 games in a row over 17 seasons. During that time 524 shortstops started for all the other major league teams before Ripken moved to third base in '96. Seven Orioles managers came and went, each penciling Ripken's name into the lineup on a daily basis. Therefore it was almost surreal when Ripken didn't take his position for the first time since '82. After the well-deserved rest, Ripken said, "So that's what an off day feels like, huh?" Naturally, he was back in the Baltimore lineup the following day.

Beginning in early April the Yankees dominated the regular-season standings, winning 61 games by the All-Star break and chasing the 1906 Cubs' major league victory record of 116. The Yankees "slumped" in September and ended up with 114 wins to set a new American League record. The Bronx Bombers faced Texas in the Division Series and allowed the robust Rangers lineup a total of one run in a three-game sweep. That set up a confrontation with the Cleveland Indians, who had lost their playoff opener to the wild-card Boston Red Sox, 11–3, before rallying to win the next three games and extend Boston's streak without a championship to 80 years. The Yankees were favored to defeat Cleveland easily, but New York's lumber slumbered, and they needed a pair of victories from Wells—and a clutch Game 4 performance from El Duque—to finish the series in six games.

The Padres won a World Series date with the Yankees by battling through a tough Division Series against the Houston Astros, beating Astros ace Randy Johnson twice.

Houston had acquired Johnson at the trade deadline with the postseason in mind. The Padres advanced to face the mighty Atlanta Braves, who had swept three straight from the Cubs in their Division Series. The Cubs had survived a one-game playoff with the San Francisco Giants to get into the playoffs. The Braves reached the NLCS for the seventh straight season but once again failed to capture a World Series title; they have won just one championship in the '90s. The Padres stunned them by grabbing a quick 3–0 lead in the series. In a classic Game 5, San Diego manager Bruce Bochy, looking to close out the Braves, brought his ace starter, Kevin Brown, into the game with a 4–2 lead in the seventh inning. The move did not pay off as Brown gave up a dramatic eighth-inning, three-run homer to the Braves' No. 8 hitter, Michael Tucker. Braves manager Bobby Cox matched Bochy's unorthodox move by calling upon his ace, four-time Cy Young award winner Greg Maddux, to hold

Maddux made a rare relief appearance in Game 5 of the NLCS, picking up the save.

a 7–6 lead in the ninth inning. Maddux, in the fifth relief appearance of his 13-year career, earned his first save. Alas, despite becoming the first team in baseball ever to lose the first three games of a playoff series and then force a Game 6, the Braves were shut out 5–0 in the sixth game and left cursing yet another postseason stumble.

Every team eventually came to realize that the World Series trophy truly belonged in the Bronx. However, despite the Yankees' sublime dominance in October, this is one season that will not be remembered primarily for its World Series. Years from now when historians hark back on the '98 season they will dwell more on the dog days of summer when McGwire and Sosa chased history together. Three days before McGwire would break Maris's record, the dynamic duo sat together at a press conference in St. Louis and joked about their magical season. Finally, Sosa smiled broadly, leaned into the microphone and performed an impression of the legendary Chico Escuela. Said Sosa, "Baseball been bery, bery good to me."

To all of us, Sammy.

Final Standings

National League

EASTERN DIVISION

Team	Won	Lost	Pct	GB	Home	Away
Atlanta	106	56	.654	—	56–25	50–31
New York	88	74	.543	18	47–34	41–40
Philadelphia	75	87	.463	31	40–41	35–46
Montreal	65	97	.401	41	39–42	26–55
Florida	54	108	.333	52	31–50	23–58

CENTRAL DIVISION

Team	Won	Lost	Pct	GB	Home	Away
Houston	102	60	.630	—	55–26	47–34
†*Chicago	90	73	.552	12½	51–31	39–42
St. Louis	83	79	.512	19	48–34	35–45
Cincinnati	77	85	.475	25	39–42	38–43
Milwaukee	74	88	.457	28	38–43	36–45
Pittsburgh	69	93	.426	33	40–40	29–54

WESTERN DIVISION

Team	Won	Lost	Pct	GB	Home	Away
San Diego	98	64	.605	—	54–27	44–37
San Francisco	89	74	.546	9½	49–32	40–42
Los Angeles	83	79	.512	15	48–33	35–46
Colorado	77	85	.475	21	42–39	35–46
Arizona	65	97	.401	33	34–47	31–50

†Wild-card team. *Won one-game playoff.

American League

EASTERN DIVISION

Team	Won	Lost	Pct	GB	Home	Away
New York	114	48	.704	—	62–19	52–29
†Boston	92	70	.568	22	51–30	41–40
Toronto	88	74	.543	26	51–30	37–44
Baltimore	79	83	.488	35	42–39	37–44
Tampa Bay	63	99	.389	51	33–48	30–51

CENTRAL DIVISION

Team	Won	Lost	Pct	GB	Home	Away
Cleveland	89	73	.549	—	46–35	43–38
Chicago	80	82	.494	9	44–37	36–45
Kansas City	72	89	.447	16½	29–51	43–38
Minnesota	70	92	.432	19	35–46	35–46
Detroit	65	97	.401	24	32–49	33–48

WESTERN DIVISION

Team	Won	Lost	Pct	GB	Home	Away
Texas	88	74	.543	—	48–33	40–41
Anaheim	85	77	.525	3	42–39	43–38
Seattle	76	85	.472	11½	42–39	34–46
Oakland	74	88	.457	14	39–42	35–46

1998 Playoffs

National League Divisional Playoffs

Sept 29 .... San Diego 2 at Houston 1
Oct 1 .... San Diego 4 at Houston 5
Oct 3 .... Houston 1 at San Diego 2
Oct 4 .... Houston 1 at San Diego 6

(San Diego won series 3–1.)

Sept 30 .... Chicago 1 at Atlanta 7
Oct 3 .... Chicago 1 at Atlanta 2 (10 innings)
Oct 5 .... Atlanta 6 at Chicago 2

(Atlanta won series 3–0.)

National League Championship Series

Oct 7 .... San Diego 3 at Atlanta 2 (10 innings)
Oct 8 .... San Diego 3 at Atlanta 0
Oct 10 .... Atlanta 1 at San Diego 4
Oct 11 .... Atlanta 8 at San Diego 3
Oct 12 .... Atlanta 7 at San Diego 6
Oct 14 .... San Diego 5 at Atlanta 0

(San Diego won series 4–2.)

GAME 1

San Diego	0	0	0		0	1	0		0	1	0	1—3
Atlanta	0	0	1		0	0	0		0	0	1	0—2

WP—Hoffman. **LP**—Ligtenberg. **Save**—Wall. **E**—Atlanta: Smoltz (1); Galarraga (2). **LOB**—San Diego 10, Atlanta 8. **2B**—San Diego: Rivera (1); Atlanta: Tucker (1); Lockhart (1). **HR**—San Diego: Caminiti (1); Atlanta: A. Jones (1). **Sac**—San Diego: Atlanta: A. Jones (fly). **GIDP**—San Diego: Gomez 2; Atlanta: C. Jones. **T**—3:27. **A**—44,117.
Recap: After Padres closer Trevor Hoffman, who led the majors in saves with 53, uncharacteristically let the Braves back in it in the bottom of the ninth, Ken Caminiti bailed him out with a home run in the tenth.

GAME 2

San Diego	0	0	0		0	0	1		0	0	2	—3
Atlanta	0	0	0		0	0	0		0	0	0	—0

GAME 2 (CONT.)

WP—Brown. **LP**—Glavine. **E**—Atlanta: Lopez (1). **LOB**—San Diego 13, Atlanta 5. **2B**—San Diego: Veras (1), Gomez (1). **Sac**—Gwynn (bunt). **GIDP**—San Diego, Gwynn; Atlanta: Lopez. **T**—2:54. **A**—43,083.
Recap: Kevin Brown, who beat the Braves twice in the '97 postseason while with Florida, continues his mastery of Atlanta with an 11-strikeout, three-hit gem. He also contributes to the offense with a pair of singles.

GAME 3

Atlanta	0	0	1		0	0	0		0	0	0	—1
San Diego	0	0	0		0	2	0		0	2	x	—4

WP—Hitchcock. **LP**—Maddux. **Save**—Hoffman. **E**—Atlanta: Galarraga (3); Klesko (1). **LOB**—Atlanta 12, San Diego 7. **2B**—San Diego: Finley (2), Hernandez (1). **CS**—San Diego: Veras (1).

National League Championship Series (Cont.)

GAME 3 (CONT.)

SB—Atlanta: Weiss (1); San Diego: Rivera (1). **Sac**—Atlanta: Maddux (bunt), E. Perez (bunt). **GIDP**—Atlanta: C. Jones; San Diego: Gomez. **T**—3:00. **A**—62,799.
Recap: Sterling Hitchcock pitched five clutch innings and Steve Finley and Ken Caminiti both ran-scoring singles in the fifth inning to put the Braves in a 3–0 hole in the NLCS. Atlanta loaded the bases three times but scored just one run. Braves ace Greg Maddux fell to 9–8 in the postseason.

GAME 4

| Atlanta | 0 0 0 | 1 0 1 | 6 0 0 | —8 |
| San Diego | 0 0 2 | 0 0 1 | 0 0 0 | —3 |

WP—Martinez. **LP**—Hamilton.
LOB—Atlanta 8, San Diego 7. **2B**—Atlanta: C. Jones (1); San Diego: Gwynn (3), Rivera (2). **3B**—Atlanta: Lockhart (1). **HR**—Atlanta: Lopez (2), Galarraga (1); San Diego: Leyritz (4). **GIDP**—Atlanta: Galarraga; San Diego: Hernandez. **T**—2:58. **A**—65,042.
Recap: Andres Galarraga's grand slam was the highlight of Atlanta's six-run seventh inning as the Braves, who scored just three runs in the first three games of the series, avoided a sweep.

GAME 5

| Atlanta | 0 0 0 | 1 0 1 | 0 5 0 | —7 |
| San Diego | 2 0 0 | 0 0 2 | 0 0 2 | —6 |

GAME 5 (CONT.)

WP—Rocker. **LP**—Brown. **Save**—Maddux.
E—Atlanta: Galarraga (4); San Diego: Gomez. **LOB**—Atlanta 10, San Diego 6. **2B**—Atlanta: Graffanino (1). **3B**—Atlanta: Lofton (1). **HR**—Atlanta: Tucker (2); San Diego: Caminiti (2), Vander Wal (1), G. Myers (1). **CS**—Atlanta: A. Jones (2). **SB**—Atlanta: A. Jones (3). **T**—3:17. **A**—58,988.
Recap: Michael Tucker's homer off Kevin Brown, pitching in relief, capped a five-RBI game and a late comeback by the Braves, who refused to die. After the Padres came within one in the ninth on a home run by Greg Myers off Kerry Ligtenberg, Greg Maddux made his first relief appearance in 11 years, shutting down San Diego and picking up his first career save.

GAME 6

| San Diego | 0 0 0 | 0 0 5 | 0 0 0 | —5 |
| Atlanta | 0 0 0 | 0 0 0 | 0 0 0 | —0 |

WP—Hitchcock. **LP**—Glavine.
E—Atlanta: Bautista (1). **LOB**—San Diego 9, Atlanta 7. **CS**—San Diego: Johnson (1). **SB**—Atlanta: Williams (1). **GIDP**—San Diego: Gwynn. **T**—3:10. **A**—50,988.
Recap: With the bases loaded and a 2–0 lead, NLCS MVP Sterling Hitchcock hit a low liner that bounced off the glove of leftfielder Danny Bautista; the error enabled two more runs to score, propelling the Padres to their second World Series and first since 1984.

American League Divisional Playoffs

Sept 29............Texas 0 at New York 2
Sept 30............Texas 1 at New York 3

Oct 2 ....New York 4 at Texas 0

(New York won series 3–0.)

Sept 29............Boston 11 at Cleveland 3
Sept 30............Boston 5 at Cleveland 9

Oct 2 ....Cleveland 4 at Boston 2
Oct 3 ....Cleveland 2 at Boston 1

(Cleveland won series 3–1.)

American League Championship Series

Oct 6 ....Cleveland 2 at New York 7
Oct 7 ....Cleveland 4 at New York 1 (12 innings)
Oct 9 ....New York 1 at Cleveland 6

Oct 10 ....New York 4 at Cleveland 0
Oct 11 ....New York 5 at Cleveland 3
Oct 13.............Cleveland 5 at New York 9

(New York won series 4–2.)

GAME 1

| Cleveland | 0 0 0 | 0 0 0 | 0 0 2 | —2 |
| New York | 5 0 0 | 0 1 1 | 0 0 x | —7 |

WP—Wells. **LP**—Wright.
LOB—Cleveland 4, New York 10. **2B**—New York: O'Neill (3), Williams (1). **HR**—Cleveland: Ramirez (3); New York: Posada (1). **SB**—Cleveland: Vizquel (1); New York: Martinez (1), Jeter (1). **GIDP**—Cleveland: Justice. **T**—3:31. **A**—57,138.
Recap: A five-run Yankee first inning quickly chased pitcher Jaret Wright, who beat New York twice in Cleveland's five-game Division Series victory last fall. David Wells, who had 23 consecutive shutout innings in the postseason before Manny Ramirez homered with one out in the ninth, struck out seven and walked one.

GAME 2

| Cleveland | 0 0 0 | 1 0 0 | 0 0 0 | 3 | —4 |
| New York | 0 0 0 | 0 0 0 | 1 0 0 | 0 | —1 |

WP—Burba. **LP**—Nelson. **Save**—Jackson.
E—Cleveland: Fryman (1); New York: Martinez (1).
LOB—Cleveland 7, New York 10. **2B**—New York:

GAME 2 (CONT.)

Jeter (1), O'Neill (4), Brosius (1). **3B**—Cleveland: Vizquel (1). **HR**—Cleveland: Justice (2). **SB**—New York: Jeter (2), Bush (2). **GIDP**—Cleveland: Ramirez; New York: Posada. **T**—4:28. **A**—57,128.
Recap: Enrique Wilson scored from first base in the 12th inning when Travis Fryman bunted down the first-base line. First baseman Tino Martinez fielded, then threw to Chuck Knoblauch, who was covering the base. The throw hit Fryman, who was running inside the base line, in the back just before he reached the bag. The ball caromed off Fryman and to the edge of the right-field grass as Knoblauch chose to argue instead of chasing the ball.

GAME 3

| New York | 1 0 0 | 0 0 0 | 0 0 0 | —1 |
| Cleveland | 0 2 0 | 0 4 0 | 0 0 x | —6 |

WP—Colon. **LP**—Pettitte.
LOB—New York 4, Cleveland 10. **2B**—Cleveland: Whiten (1), Ramirez (3). **HR**—Cleveland: Thome 2 (4), Ramirez (4), Whiten (1). **Sac**—New York: Jeter (bunt).

American League Championship Series *(Cont.)*

GAME 3 *(CONT.)*

GIDP—New York: Williams, Spencer, Jeter. **T**—2:53. **A**—44,904.

Recap: Manny Ramirez, Jim Thome and Mark Whiten tagged Andy Pettitte for home runs during a four-run fifth inning. Thome homered again later and Bartolo Colon fired a four-hit complete game as Cleveland took a 2–1 ACLS lead.

GAME 4

New York	1	0	0	2	0	0	0	0	1	—4
Cleveland	0	0	0	0	0	0	0	0	0	—0

WP—Hernandez. **LP**—Gooden.

E—Cleveland: Alomar 2 (3), Lofton (1). **LOB**—New York 6, Cleveland 6. **2B**—New York: Davis (1), Martinez (3); Cleveland: Lofton 2 (2). **HR**—New York: O'Neill (2). **SB**—New York: Martinez (2), O'Neill (1), Jeter (3); Cleveland: Vizquel 2 (3). **Sac**—New York: Martinez (fly), Brosius (fly); Cleveland: Vizquel (bunt), Seitzer (bunt). **GIDP**—New York: Curtis; Cleveland: Justice. **T**—3:31. **A**—44,981.

Recap: Orlando Hernandez pitched seven shutout innings as Dwight Gooden continued his winless postseason streak. Paul O'Neill homered and Chili Davis added a run-scoring double.

GAME 5

New York	3	1	0	1	0	1	0	0	0	—5
Cleveland	2	0	0	0	0	1	0	0	0	—3

WP—Wells. **LP**—Ogea. **Save**—Rivera.

GAME 5 *(CONT.)*

E—Cleveland: Williams (2). **LOB**— New York 11, Cleveland 6. **HR**—New York: Davis (1); Cleveland: Lofton (3), Thome (5). **CS**—New York: Posada (1); Cleveland: Vizquel (1). **SB**—New York: O'Neill (2); Cleveland: Vizquel (4), Fryman (2). **Sac**—New York: Jeter (bunt), Brosius (bunt); Cleveland: Ramirez (fly). **GIDP**—New York: Davis, Raines; Cleveland: Sexson, Whiten. **T**—3:33. **A**—44,966.

Recap: David Wells pitched another gem, striking out 11 and walking just three, while Chili Davis homered and had three RBIs.

GAME 6

Cleveland	3	1	0	1	0	1	0	0	0	—5
New York	2	0	0	0	0	1	0	0	0	—3

WP—Cone. **LP**—Nagy.

E—Cleveland: Giles (1), Wilson (1), Vizquel (1); New York: Brosius (1). **LOB**—Cleveland 6, New York 7. **2B**—New York: Knoblauch (1). **3B**—New York: Jeter (1). **HR**—Cleveland: Thome (6), New York: Brosius (2). **CS**—New York: Williams (1). **SB**—Cleveland: Lofton (3). **Sac**—New York: Davis (fly). **T**—3:31. **A**—57,142.

Recap: The Yanks built a six-run lead that was reduced to one in the fifth inning after David Cone walked David Justice with the bases loaded then gave up a grand slam to the next batter, Jim Thome. Ramiro Mendoza replaced Cone in the sixth and pitched one-hit ball until the ninth, when Mariano Rivera shut down Cleveland as the Yankees won their 35th pennant.

Composite Box Scores

National League Championship Series

SAN DIEGO

BATTING	AB	R	H	HR	RBI	Avg
G. Myers	1	1	1	1	2	1.000
Brown	4	1	2	0	0	.500
Vander Wal	7	1	3	1	2	.429
Finley	21	3	7	0	2	.333
Hernandez	18	2	6	0	0	.333
Joyner	16	3	5	0	2	.313
Caminiti	22	3	6	2	4	.273
Veras	24	2	6	0	2	.250
Vaughn	8	1	2	0	0	.250
Gwynn	26	1	6	0	0	.231
Rivera	13	1	3	0	0	.231
Hitchcock	5	1	1	0	0	.200
Leyritz	12	1	2	1	4	.167
Gomez	20	2	3	0	0	.150
4 others	11	1	0	0	0	.000
Totals	208	24	53	5	20	.255

PITCHING	G	IP	H	BB	SO	ERA
Boehringer	3	3	3	1	1	0.00
Langston	3	1⅓	1	0	1	0.00
Hitchcock	3	16	14	9	16	0.90
Ashby	1	7	5	1	3	1.29
Hoffman	3	4⅓	2	2	7	2.08
Brown	2	10⅓	5	4	12	2.61
Wall	3	3	3	4	4	3.00
Hamilton	2	7⅓	7	3	6	4.91
R. Myers	4	2	3	2	3	13.50
Miceli	3	⅔	4	0	1	13.50
Totals	6	55	47	26	54	2.78

ATLANTA

BATTING	AB	R	H	HR	RBI	Avg
E. Perez	4	0	3	0	0	.750
Guillen	12	1	5	0	1	.417
Tucker	13	1	5	1	5	.385
Colbrunn	6	0	2	0	0	.333
Graffanino	3	2	1	0	1	.333
Lopez	20	2	6	1	1	.300
A. Jones	22	3	6	1	2	.273
Glavine	4	0	1	0	0	.250
Lockhart	17	2	4	0	0	.235
C. Jones	24	2	5	0	1	.208
Weiss	15	0	3	0	1	.200
Smoltz	5	0	1	0	0	.200
Williams	13	0	2	0	0	.154
Galarraga	21	1	2	1	4	.095
Klesko	12	2	1	0	0	.083
5 others	9	2	0	0	0	.000
Totals	200	18	47	4	17	.235

PITCHING	G	IP	H	BB	SO	ERA
Rocker	6	4⅔	3	1	5	0.00
Martinez	4	3⅓	1	1	0	0.00
Glavine	2	11⅔	13	9	8	2.31
Maddux	2	6	5	3	4	3.00
Neagle	2	7⅔	8	2	9	3.52
Smoltz	2	13¾	13	6	13	3.95
Seanez	4	3	2	1	4	6.00
Ligtenberg	4	3⅔	3	2	5	7.36
O. Perez	2	⅓	5	2	0	54.00
Totals	6	54	53	27	48	3.50

American League Championship Series

CLEVELAND

BATTING	AB	R	H	HR	RBI	Avg
Vizquel	25	2	11	0	0	.440
M. Ramirez	21	2	7	2	4	.333
Thome	23	4	7	4	8	.304
Whiten	7	2	2	1	1	.286
E. Wilson	14	2	3	0	1	.214
Lofton	27	2	5	1	3	.185
Fryman	23	2	4	0	0	.174
Justice	19	2	3	1	2	.158
Cora	7	1	1	0	0	.143
Giles	12	0	1	0	0	.083
S. Alomar	16	1	1	0	0	.063
3 others	11	0	0	0	0	.000
Totals	205	20	45	9	19	.220

PITCHING	G	IP	H	BB	SO	ERA
Shuey	5	6	4	7	7	0.00
Assenmacher	3	2	0	0	3	0.00
Reed	3	1⅓	0	1	0	0.00
Poole	4	1⅓	1	1	2	0.00
Jackson	1	1	0	0	2	0.00
Colon	1	9	4	4	3	1.00
Burba	3	6	3	5	8	3.00
Nagy	2	9⅔	13	1	6	3.72
Gooden	1	4⅔	3	3	3	5.79
Ogea	2	6⅔	9	5	4	8.10
Wright	2	6⅔	7	8	4	8.10
Totals	6	55	43	35	42	3.60

NEW YORK

BATTING	AB	R	H	HR	RBI	Avg
Williams	21	4	8	0	5	.381
Brosius	20	2	6	1	6	.300
Davis	14	2	4	1	5	.286
O'Neill	25	6	7	1	3	.280
Girardi	8	2	2	0	0	.250
Jeter	25	3	5	0	2	.200
Knoblauch	25	4	5	0	0	.200
Posada	11	1	2	1	2	.182
Martinez	19	1	2	0	1	.105
Raines	10	0	1	0	1	.100
Spencer	10	1	1	0	0	.100
Curtis	4	0	0	0	0	.000
Ledee	5	0	0	0	0	.000
Bush	0	1	0	0	0	—
Totals	197	19	54	4	25	.248

PITCHING	G	IP	H	BB	SO	ERA
Hernandez	2	7⅓	3	2	6	0.00
Rivera	4	5⅓	0	1	5	0.00
Mendoza	2	4⅓	4	0	1	0.00
Stanton	3	3⅔	2	1	4	0.00
Lloyd	1	⅔	1	0	0	0.00
Wells	2	15⅔	12	1	18	2.87
Cone	2	13	12	6	13	4.15
Pettitte	1	4⅔	8	3	1	11.57
Nelson	3	1⅓	3	1	3	20.26
Totals	6	56	45	16	51	3.21

1998 World Series

Oct 17 .... San Diego 6 at New York 9
Oct 18 .... San Diego 3 at New York 9
Oct 20 .... New York 4 at San Diego 5
Oct 21 .... New York 3 at San Diego 0

(New York won series 4–0.)

GAME 1

San Diego	0 0 2	0 3 0	0 1 0	—6
New York	0 2 0	0 0 0	7 0 x	—9

WP—Wells. **LP**—Wall. **Save**—M. Rivera.
E—San Diego: Vaughn (1), New York: Knoblauch (1).
LOB—San Diego 4, New York 7. **2B**—San Diego:
Finley (1); New York: Ledee (1). **HR**—San Diego:
Vaughn 2 (2); New York: Knoblauch (1), Martinez (1).
GIDP—San Diego: Vaughn.
T—3:29. **A**—56,712.
Recap: Yankees Chuck Knoblauch and Tino
Martinez atoned for fielding gaffes that cost New York
Game 2 of the ACLS with home runs during a seven-
run seventh inning. In the fifth inning, when Tony
Gwynn followed Greg Vaughn's second homer of the
night with a tater of his own, the Padres enjoyed a
5–2 lead and threatened Yanks pitcher David Wells
with his first loss of the postseason. But Knoblauch's
three-run homer off Donne Wall, relieving San Diego
starter Kevin Brown, tied the game. Derek Jeter
singled off Mark Langston, who replaced Wall. Jeter
moved to second after a wild pitch followed Paul
O'Neill's flyout, forcing Langston to intentionally walk
Bernie Williams. After Chili Davis walked to load the
bases, Martinez, who had struggled throughout the
postseason, came to the plate. Martinez took a close
2–2 pitch for a ball, then belted the next pitch into the
right upper deck for a grand slam.

GAME 2

San Diego	0 0 0	0 1 0	0 2 0	—3
New York	3 3 1	0 2 0	0 0 x	—9

WP—O. Hernandez. **LP**—Ashby.
E—San Diego: Caminiti (1). **LOB**—San Diego 10,
New York 11. **2B**—San Diego: Veras (1), Vander Wal
(1), Caminiti (1), R. Rivera (1). New York: Ledee (2).
3B—San Diego: Gomez (1). **HR**—New York:
Williams (1), Posada (1). **SB**—New York: Knoblauch
(1). **CS**—New York: Ledee (1). **GIDP**—New York:
Posada, Brosius, Jeter.
T—3:31. **A**—56,692.
Recap: The Padres did not retire two straight batters
until the fourth inning; by then, starter Andy Ashby was
out of the game and the Yankees had a 7–0 lead. The
damage began when Chuck Knoblauch, leading off for
the Yanks in the first, hit a pop foul that was dropped
by sliding catcher Greg Myers. Knoblauch then walked
and stole second. One out later, Paul O'Neill, who
earlier crashed into the wall to rob Wally Joyner of a hit
with two men on, slapped a grounder at third baseman
Ken Caminiti. The three-time Gold Glove fielder rushed
his throw and launched it too high for first baseman
Joyner, enabling Knoblauch to score. Bernie Williams
and Jorge Posada padded the lead with two-run
homers in the second and fifth innings, respectively,
while Orlando (El Duque) Hernandez scattered six hits,
gave up one run and struck out seven in seven innings.

GAME 3

| New York | 0 0 0 | 0 0 0 | 2 3 0 | —5 |
| San Diego | 0 0 0 | 0 0 3 | 0 1 0 | —4 |

WP—Mendoza. **LP**—Hoffman. **Save**—M. Rivera.
E—New York: O'Neill (1); San Diego: Caminiti (2).
LOB—New York 7, San Diego 5. **2B**—New York:
Spencer (1); San Diego: Veras (2). **HR**—New York:
Brosius 2 (2). **CS**—San Diego: Giles (1). **SB**—San
Diego: Finley (1). **Sac**—San Diego: Caminiti (fly),
Vaughn (fly). **GIDP**—New York: O'Neill.
T—3:14. **A**—64,667.
Recap: In the first World Series game in San Diego
since 1984, fans enjoyed a pitching duel for the first
half. The Padres finally drew blood in the sixth, when
pitcher Sterling Hitchcock, a career .120 hitter, ended
David Cone's no-hitter with a single to right center. After
a walk to Quilvio Veras, Gwynn singled to right field and
Hitchcock scored. O'Neill retrieved the ball but made a
wild throw that went into the Yankees dugout for an
error that allowed another run to score. Ken Caminiti's
sacrifice fly scored Gwynn to make it 3–0, and the
Padres, backed by towel-waving fans at Qualcomm
Stadium, seemed poised to win their first game of the
series. The best closer in baseball, Trevor Hoffman,
took to the mound in the eighth to protect a 3–2 lead
with no outs and Paul O'Neill at first base. One out and
a Tino Martinez walk later, Hoffman faced Scott
Brosius, who had already homered in the seventh off
Hitchcock. The odds seemed to favor Hoffman, who
blew just one save in 54 chances during the regular
season, but Brosius homered to center for a 5–3 lead.

GAME 4

| New York | 0 0 0 | 0 1 0 | 0 2 0 | —3 |
| San Diego | 0 0 0 | 0 0 0 | 0 0 0 | —0 |

WP—Pettitte. **LP**—Brown. **Save**—M. Rivera.
LOB—New York 9, San Diego 8. **2B**—New York:
Ledee (2), O'Neill (1); San Diego: R. Rivera (2).
Sac—New York, Pettitte (bunt), Ledee (fly). **GIDP**—
San Diego: Caminiti, C. Hernandez.
T—2:58. **A**—65,427.
Recap: In finishing their season with a World Series
sweep and a 125–50 record, the New York Yankees
made their case for being the best team in baseball
history. Andy Pettitte, supposedly the weak link on
the New York pitching staff, pitched 7⅓ scoreless
innings. Bernie Williams broke a scoreless tie with an
RBI chopper off Padres starter Kevin Brown in the
sixth. In the seventh inning Series MVP Scott Brosius
singled home a run and rookie Ricky Ledee, who
batted .600 with three doubles and four RBIs in three
starts, hit a sacrifice fly. San Diego tried to rally in the
eighth when Jim Leyritz—a former Yankees
postseason hero—faced Mariano Rivera with two
outs and the bases loaded. He flied out to center
field, and the Padres, who beat 100-game winners
Houston and Atlanta in the NL playoffs, were unable
to prevent a Series sweep, the first since Cincinnati
upset Oakland in 1990 and the first by the Yankees
since they blanked Philadelphia in 1950. With their
24th World Series title, the Yankees broke a tie with
the NHL's Montreal Canadiens for most
championships by a major league franchise.

1998 World Series Composite Box Score

SAN DIEGO

BATTING	AB	R	H	HR	RBI	Avg
R. Rivera	5	1	4	0	1	.800
Sweeney	3	0	2	0	1	.667
Gwynn	16	2	8	1	3	.500
Brown	2	0	1	0	0	.500
Hitchcock	2	1	1	0	0	.500
Vander Wall	5	0	2	0	0	.400
Gomez	11	2	4	0	0	.364
Veras	15	3	3	0	1	.200
C. Hernandez	10	0	2	0	0	.200
Caminiti	14	1	2	0	1	.143
Vaughn	15	3	2	2	4	.133
Finley	12	0	1	0	0	.083
Sheets	2	0	0	0	0	.000
G. Myers	4	0	0	0	0	.000
Joyner	8	0	0	0	0	.000
Leyritz	10	0	0	0	0	.000
Totals	134	13	32	3	11	.239

PITCHING	G	IP	H	BB	SO	ERA
Miceli	2	1⅓	2	2	1	0.00
Hamilton	1	1	0	1	1	0.00
Hitchcock	1	6	7	1	7	1.50
Brown	2	14⅓	14	6	13	4.40
Wall	2	2⅔	3	3	1	6.75
Boehringer	2	2	4	2	3	9.00
Hoffman	1	2	2	1	0	9.00
R. Myers	3	1	0	1	2	9.00
Ashby	1	2⅔	10	1	1	13.50
Langston	1	⅔	1	2	0	40.50
Totals	4	34	43	20	29	5.82

NEW YORK

BATTING	AB	R	H	HR	RBI	Avg
Ledee	10	1	6	0	4	.600
Cone	2	0	1	0	0	.500
Brosius	17	3	8	2	6	.471
Martinez	13	4	5	1	4	.385
Knoblauch	16	3	6	1	3	.375
Jeter	17	4	6	0	1	.353
Posada	9	2	3	1	2	.333
Spencer	3	1	1	0	0	.333
Davis	7	3	2	0	2	.286
O'Neill	19	3	4	0	0	.211
Williams	16	2	1	1	3	.063
M. Rivera	1	0	0	0	0	.000
Mendoza	1	0	0	0	0	.000
Pettitte	2	0	0	0	0	.000
Girardi	6	0	0	0	0	.000
Totals	139	26	43	6	25	.309

PITCHING	G	IP	H	BB	SO	ERA
Pettitte	1	7⅓	5	3	4	0.00
M. Rivera	3	4⅓	5	0	4	0.00
Nelson	3	2⅓	2	1	4	0.00
Lloyd	1	⅓	0	0	0	0.00
O. Hernandez	1	7	6	3	7	1.29
Cone	1	6	2	3	4	3.00
Wells	1	7	7	2	4	6.43
Mendoza	1	1	2	0	1	9.00
Stanton	1	⅔	3	0	1	27.00
Totals	4	36	32	13	29	2.75

1998 Individual Leaders

National League Batting

BATTING AVERAGE

Larry Walker, Col .... .363
John Olerud, NY .... .354
Dante Bichette, Col. .... .331
Mike Piazza, LA-Fla-NY ..... .328
Jason Kendall, Pitt .... .327
Craig Biggio, Hou .... .325
Vladimir Guerrero, Mtl .... .324
Jeff Cirillo, Mil .... .321
Tony Gwynn, SD .... .321
Vinny Castilla, Col. .... .318

HITS

Dante Bichette, Col. 219
Craig Biggio, Hou 210
Vinny Castilla, Col. 206
Vladimir Guerrero, Mtl. 202
Derek Bell, Hou. 198
Sammy Sosa, Chi 198
Fernando Vina, Mil. 198
John Olerud, NY 197
Jeff Cirillo, Mil 194
Doug Glanville, Phil 189

DOUBLES

Craig Biggio, Hou 51
Dante Bichette, Col. 48
Dmitri Young, Cin. 48
Larry Walker, Col 46
Cliff Floyd, Fla 45
Scott Rolen, Phil. 45

TRIPLES

Dave Dellucci, Ariz 12
Barry Larkin, Cin 10
Neifi Perez, Col 9
Wilton Guerrero, Mtl. 9
Andruw Jones, Atl. 8
Delino DeShields, StL. 8
Karim Garcia, Ariz 8

EARNED RUN AVERAGE

Greg Maddux, Atl 1.98
Kevin Brown, SD 2.41
Al Leiter, NY 2.47
Omar Daal, Ariz 2.55
Tom Glavine, Atl 2.61
Andy Ashby, SD 3.09
Francisco Cordova, Pitt 3.17
Dustin Hermanson, Mtl 3.22
Curt Schilling, Phil. 3.24
Rick Reed, NY 3.27

SAVES

Trevor Hoffman, SD 53
Rod Beck, Chi. 51
Jeff Shaw, LA. 48
Robb Nen, SF 40
John Franco, NY 38
Ugueth Urbina, Mtl 34
Kerry Ligtenberg, Atl 30
Greg Olson, Ariz 30
Billy Wagner, Hou 30
Bob Wickman, Mil. 25

HOME RUNS

Mark McGwire, StL 70
Sammy Sosa, Chi 66
Greg Vaughn, SD 50
Vinny Castilla, Col. 46
Andres Galarraga, Atl. 44
Moises Alou, Hou. 38
Jeromy Burnitz, Mil 38
Vladimir Guerrero, Mtl. 38
Barry Bonds, SF. 37
Jeff Bagwell, Hou. 34
Chipper Jones, Atl 34
Javier Lopez, Atl 34

RUNS SCORED

Sammy Sosa, Chi 134
Mark McGwire, StL 130
Jeff Bagwell, Hou. 124
Craig Biggio, Hou 123
Chipper Jones, Atl 123
Barry Bonds, SF. 120
Scott Rolen, Phil. 120
Larry Walker, Col 113
Greg Vaughn, SD 112
Derek Bell, Hou. 111

TOTAL BASES

Sammy Sosa, Chi 416
Mark McGwire, StL 383
Vinny Castilla, Col. 380
Vladimir Guerrero, Mtl. 367
Greg Vaughn, SD 342

STOLEN BASES

Tony Womack, Pitt 58
Craig Biggio, Hou 50
Eric Young, LA. 42
Edgar Renteria, Fla. 41
Barry Bonds, SF. 28

National League Pitching

WINS

Tom Glavine, Atl 20
Shane Reynolds, Hou 19
Kevin Tapani, Chi 19
Kevin Brown, SD 18
Greg Maddux, Atl 18
Andy Ashby, SD 17
Al Leiter, NY 17
Kevin Millwood, Atl 17
John Smoltz, Atl 17
Four tied with 16.

GAMES PITCHED

Rod Beck, Chi. 81
Steve Kline, Mtl 78
Chuck McElroy, Col 78
Robb Nen, SF 77
Anthony Telford, Mtl. 75

INNINGS PITCHED

Curt Schilling, Phil 268⅔
Kevin Brown, SD 257
Greg Maddux, Atl 251
Carlos Perez, LA. 241
Livan Hernandez, Fla 234⅓

RUNS BATTED IN

Sammy Sosa, Chi 158
Mark McGwire, StL 147
Vinny Castilla, Col. 144
Jeff Kent, SF 128
Jeromy Burnitz, Mil 125
Moises Alou, Hou. 124
Dante Bichette, Col. 122
Barry Bonds, SF. 122
Andres Galarraga, Atl 121
Greg Vaughn, SD 119

SLUGGING PERCENTAGE

Mark McGwire, StL .... .752
Sammy Sosa, Chi .... .647
Larry Walker, Col .... .630
Barry Bonds, SF. .... .609
Greg Vaughn, SD .... .597

ON-BASE PERCENTAGE

Mark McGwire, StL .... .470
John Olerud, NY .... .447
Larry Walker, Col .... .445
Barry Bonds, SF. .... .438
Gary Sheffield, LA. .... .428

BASES ON BALLS

Mark McGwire, StL 162
Barry Bonds, SF. 130
Jeff Bagwell, Hou. 109
Chipper Jones, Atl 96
John Olerud, NY 96

STRIKEOUTS

Curt Schilling, Phil. 300
Kevin Brown, SD 257
Kerry Wood, Chi 233
Shane Reynolds, Hou 209
Greg Maddux, Atl 204
Chan Ho Park, LA. 191
Al Leiter, NY 174
John Smoltz, Atl 173
Pedro Astacio, Col. 170
Jose Lima, Hou. 169

COMPLETE GAMES

Curt Schilling, Phil. 15
Livan Hernandez, Fla. 9
Greg Maddux, Atl 9
Kevin Brown, SD 7
Carlos Perez, Mtl 7

SHUTOUTS

Greg Maddux, Atl 5
Randy Johnson, Hou 4
Kevin Brown, SD 3
Tom Glavine, Atl 3
Nine tied with two.

American League Batting

BATTING AVERAGE

Bernie Williams, NY	.339
Mo Vaughn, Bos	.337
Albert Belle, Chi	.328
Eric Davis, Balt	.327
Derek Jeter, NY	.324
Nomar Garciaparra, Bos	.323
Edgar Martinez, Sea	.322
Ivan Rodriguez, Tex	.321
Tony Fernandez, Tor	.321
Juan Gonzalez, Tex	.318

HITS

Alex Rodriguez, Sea	213
Mo Vaughn, Bos	205
Derek Jeter, NY	203
Albert Belle, Chi	200
Nomar Garciaparra, Bos	195
Juan Gonzalez, Tex	193
Jose Offerman, KC	191
Paul O'Neill, NY	191
Ivan Rodriguez, Tex	186
Jim Edmonds, Ana	184

DOUBLES

Juan Gonzalez, Tex	50
Albert Belle, Chi	48
Edgar Martinez, Sea	46
John Valentin, Bos	44
Carlos Delgado, Tor	43

TRIPLES

Jose Offerman, KC	13
Johnny Damon, KC	10
Randy Winn, TB	9
Ray Durham, Chi	8
Derek Jeter, NY	8
Nomar Garciaparra, Bos	8
Troy O'Leary, Bos	8

HOME RUNS

Ken Griffey Jr., Sea	56
Albert Belle, Chi	49
Jose Canseco, Tor	46
Juan Gonzalez, Tex	45
Manny Ramirez, Clev	45
Rafael Palmeiro, Balt	43
Alex Rodriguez, Sea	42
Mo Vaughn, Bos	40
Carlos Delgado, Tor	38
Nomar Garciaparra, Bos	35
Shawn Green, Tor	35

RUNS SCORED

Derek Jeter, NY	127
Ray Durham, Chi	126
Alex Rodriguez, Sea	123
Ken Griffey Jr., Sea	120
Chuck Knoblauch, NY	117
Jim Edmonds, Ana	115
Albert Belle, Chi	113
John Valentin, Bos	113
Joey Cora, Clev	111
Nomar Garciaparra, Bos	111

TOTAL BASES

Albert Belle, Chi	399
Ken Griffey Jr., Sea	387
Alex Rodriguez, Sea	384
Juan Gonzalez, Tex	382
Mo Vaughn, Bos	360

STOLEN BASES

Rickey Henderson, Oak	66
Kenny Lofton, Clev	54
Shannon Stewart, Tor	51
Alex Rodriguez, Sea	46
Jose Offerman, KC	45

RUNS BATTED IN

Juan Gonzalez, Tex	157
Albert Belle, Chi	152
Ken Griffey Jr., Sea	146
Manny Ramirez, Clev	145
Alex Rodriguez, Sea	124
Tino Martinez, NY	123
Nomar Garciaparra, Bos	122
Rafael Palmeiro, Balt	121
Dean Palmer, KC	119
Paul O'Neill, NY	116

SLUGGING PERCENTAGE

Albert Belle, Chi	.655
Juan Gonzalez, Tex	.630
Ken Griffey Jr., Sea	.611
Manny Ramirez, Clev	.599
Carlos Delgado, Tor	.592

ON-BASE PERCENTAGE

Edgar Martinez, Sea	.429
Bernie Williams, NY	.422
Jim Thome, Clev	.413
Tim Salmon, Ana	.410
Jose Offerman, KC	.403

BASES ON BALLS

Rickey Henderson, Oak	118
Frank Thomas, Chi	110
Edgar Martinez, Sea	106
Tim Salmon, Ana	90
Jim Thome, Clev	90

American League Pitching

EARNED RUN AVERAGE

Roger Clemens, Tor	2.64
Pedro Martinez, Bos	2.67
Chuck Finley, Ana	3.20
Kenny Rogers, Oak	3.22
David Wells, NY	3.22
Bartolo Colon, Clev	3.32
Mike Mussina, Balt	3.51
Rolando Arrojo, TB	3.58
Jamie Moyer, Sea	3.64
David Cone, NY	3.67

SAVES

Tom Gordon, Bos	46
Troy Percival, Ana	42
John Wetteland, Tex	42
Mike Jackson, Clev	40
Rick Aguilera, Minn	38
Mariano Rivera, NY	36
Jeff Montgomery, KC	36
Bill Taylor, Oak	33
Todd Jones, Det	28
Randy Myers, Balt	28

WINS

Roger Clemens, Tor	20
David Cone, NY	20
Rick Helling, Tex	20
Pedro Martinez, Bos	19
Aaron Sele, Tex	19
David Wells, NY	18
Tim Wakefield, Bos	17
Scott Erickson, Balt	16
Andy Pettitte, NY	16
Kenny Rogers, Oak	16

GAMES PITCHED

Sean Runyan, Det	88
Paul Quantrill, Tor	82
Greg Swindell, Bos	81
Eddie Guardado, Minn	79
Dan Plesac, Tor	78

INNINGS PITCHED

Scott Erickson, Balt	251⅓
Kenny Rogers, Oak	238⅔
Roger Clemens, Tor	234⅔
Jamie Moyer, Sea	234⅓
Tim Belcher, KC	234

STRIKEOUTS

Roger Clemens, Tor	271
Pedro Martinez, Bos	251
Randy Johnson, Sea	213
Chuck Finley, Ana	212
David Cone, NY	209
Scott Erickson, Balt	186
Jeff Fassero, Sea	176
Mike Mussina, Balt	175
Tony Saunders, TB	172
Juan Guzman, Balt	168

COMPLETE GAMES

Scott Erickson, Balt	11
David Wells, NY	8
Jeff Fassero, Sea	7
Kenny Rogers, Oak	7
Bartolo Colon, Clev	6
Randy Johnson, Sea	6

SHUTOUTS

David Wells, NY	5
Roger Clemens, Tor	3
Brian Moehler, Det	3
Jamie Moyer, Sea	3
Eight tied with two.	

1998 Team Statistics

National League

TEAM BATTING

TEAM BATTING	BA	AB	R	H	TB	2B	3B	HR	RBI	SB	BB	SO
Colorado	.291	5632	826	1640	2594	333	36	183	791	67	469	949
Houston	.280	5641	874	1578	2458	326	28	166	818	155	621	1122
San Francisco	.274	5628	845	1540	2367	292	26	161	800	102	678	1040
Atlanta	.272	5484	826	1489	2484	296	27	215	794	98	548	1062
Chicago	.264	5649	831	1494	2448	250	34	212	788	65	601	1223
Philadelphia	.264	5617	713	1482	2218	286	36	126	672	97	508	1080
Cincinnati	.262	5496	750	1441	2209	298	28	138	723	95	608	1107
Milwaukee	.260	5541	707	1439	2195	266	17	152	673	81	532	1039
New York	.259	5510	706	1425	2170	289	24	136	671	62	572	1049
St. Louis	.258	5593	810	1444	2465	292	30	223	781	133	676	1179
Pittsburgh	.254	5493	650	1395	2057	271	35	107	613	159	393	1060
San Diego	.253	5490	749	1390	2243	292	30	167	715	79	604	1072
Los Angeles	.252	5461	669	1374	2114	209	27	159	630	137	447	1057
Montreal	.249	5417	644	1348	2133	280	32	147	602	91	439	1057
Florida	.248	5558	667	1381	2072	277	36	114	621	115	525	1120
Arizona	.246	5491	665	1353	2156	235	46	159	621	73	489	1239

TEAM PITCHING

TEAM PITCHING	ERA	W	L	Sho	CG	SV	Inn	H	R	ER	BB	SO
Atlanta	3.25	106	56	23	24	45	1438⅔	1291	581	520	467	1232
Houston	3.50	102	60	11	12	44	1471⅓	1435	620	572	465	1187
San Diego	3.63	98	64	11	14	59	1454⅔	1384	635	587	501	1217
New York	3.77	88	74	16	9	46	1458	1381	645	611	532	1129
Los Angeles	3.81	83	79	10	16	47	1447⅓	1332	678	612	587	1178
Pittsburgh	3.91	69	93	10	7	41	1449	1433	718	629	530	1112
San Francisco	4.19	89	74	6	6	44	1477	1457	739	687	562	1089
St. Louis	4.32	83	79	10	6	44	1469⅔	1513	782	706	558	972
Montreal	4.38	65	97	5	4	39	1427	1448	783	696	533	1017
Cincinnati	4.44	77	85	8	6	42	1441⅓	1400	760	711	573	1098
Chicago	4.50	90	73	7	7	56	1477⅓	1528	792	738	575	1207
Milwaukee	4.63	74	88	2	2	39	1451	1538	812	746	550	1063
Arizona	4.64	65	97	6	7	37	1432⅓	1463	812	738	489	908
Philadelphia	4.64	75	87	10	21	32	1463	1476	808	754	544	1176
Colorado	5.00	77	85	5	9	36	1432⅔	1583	855	796	562	951
Florida	5.20	54	108	3	11	24	1449⅔	1617	923	838	715	1016

American League

TEAM BATTING

TEAM BATTING	BA	AB	R	H	TB	2B	3B	HR	RBI	SB	BB	SO
Texas	.289	5672	940	1637	2618	314	32	201	894	82	595	1045
New York	.288	5643	965	1625	2598	290	31	207	907	153	653	1025
Boston	.280	5601	876	1568	2591	338	35	205	827	72	541	1049
Seattle	.276	5628	859	1553	2632	321	28	234	822	115	558	1081
Baltimore	.273	5565	817	1520	2487	303	11	214	783	86	593	903
Anaheim	.272	5630	787	1530	2339	314	27	147	739	143	510	1028
Cleveland	.272	5616	850	1530	2518	334	30	198	811	93	631	1061
Chicago	.271	5585	861	1516	2477	291	38	198	806	127	551	916
Minnesota	.266	5641	734	1499	2193	285	32	115	691	112	506	915
Toronto	.266	5580	816	1482	2500	317	19	221	776	184	564	1132
Detroit	.264	5664	722	1494	2353	306	29	165	691	122	455	1070
Kansas City	.263	5543	715	1459	2215	274	40	134	686	135	475	982
Tampa Bay	.261	5559	620	1450	2136	267	43	111	579	120	473	1109
Oakland	.257	5490	803	1413	2181	295	13	149	755	131	633	1122

TEAM PITCHING

TEAM PITCHING	ERA	W	L	Sho	CG	SV	Inn	H	R	ER	BB	SO
New York	3.82	114	48	16	22	48	1456⅔	1357	656	619	466	1080
Boston	4.19	92	70	8	5	53	1436	1406	729	667	504	1025
Toronto	4.29	88	74	11	10	47	1465	1443	768	697	587	1154
Tampa Bay	4.35	63	99	7	7	28	1443	1425	751	698	643	1008
Cleveland	4.45	89	73	4	9	47	1460	1552	779	721	563	1037
Anaheim	4.49	85	77	5	3	52	1444	1481	783	720	630	1091
Baltimore	4.73	79	83	10	16	37	1431⅓	1505	785	754	535	1065
Minnesota	4.76	70	92	8	7	42	1447⅓	1622	818	764	458	952
Oakland	4.83	74	88	4	12	39	1434	1555	866	766	529	922
Detroit	4.93	65	97	4	9	32	1446⅓	1551	863	792	595	947
Seattle	4.95	76	85	7	17	31	1424⅓	1530	855	781	528	1156
Texas	5.00	88	74	8	10	46	1431⅓	1624	871	794	519	994
Kansas City	5.16	72	89	5	6	46	1436½	1590	899	823	568	999
Chicago	5.24	80	82	4	8	42	1438⅔	1569	931	835	580	911

National League Team-by-Team Statistical Leaders

Arizona Diamondbacks

BATTING	BA	G	AB	R	H	TB	2B	3B	HR	RBI	SB	BB	SO
Miller, Damian	.286	57	168	17	48	75	14	2	3	14	1	11	43
White, Devon	.279	146	563	84	157	257	32	1	22	85	22	42	102
Fox, Andy	.277	139	502	67	139	199	21	6	9	44	14	43	97
Batista, Tony	.273	106	293	46	80	152	16	1	18	41	1	18	52
Lee, Travis	.269	146	562	71	151	240	20	2	22	72	8	67	123
Williams, Matt	.267	135	510	72	136	224	26	1	20	71	5	43	102
Dellucci, David	.260	124	416	43	108	166	19	12	5	51	3	33	103
Stinnett, Kelly	.259	92	274	35	71	120	14	1	11	34	0	35	74
Bell, Jay	.251	155	549	79	138	237	29	5	20	67	3	81	129
Gilkey, Bernard	.233	111	365	41	85	115	15	0	5	33	9	43	80
Brede, Brent	.226	98	212	23	48	69	9	3	2	17	1	24	43
Garcia, Karim	.222	113	333	39	74	127	10	8	9	43	5	18	78

PITCHING	ERA	W	L	G	GS	CG	SV	INN	H	R	ER	BB	SO
Daal, Omar	2.88	8	12	33	23	3	0	162⅔	146	60	52	51	132
Olson, Gregg	3.01	3	4	64	0	0	30	68⅔	56	25	23	25	55
Banks, Willie	3.09	1	2	33	0	0	1	43⅔	34	21	15	25	32
Small, Aaron	3.69	3	1	23	0	0	0	31⅔	32	14	13	8	14
Telemaco, Amaury	3.93	7	10	41	18	0	0	148⅔	150	75	65	46	78
Benes, Andy	3.97	14	13	34	34	1	0	231⅓	221	111	102	74	164
Chouinard, Bobby	4.14	0	2	27	2	0	0	41⅓	46	24	19	11	27
Embree, Alan	4.19	4	2	55	0	0	1	53⅔	56	32	25	23	43
Anderson, Brian	4.33	12	13	32	32	2	0	208	221	109	100	24	95
Sodowsky, Clint	5.68	3	6	45	6	0	0	77⅔	86	56	49	39	42

Atlanta Braves

BATTING	BA	G	AB	R	H	TB	2B	3B	HR	RBI	SB	BB	SO
Perez, Eddie	.336	61	149	18	50	80	12	0	6	32	1	15	28
Jones, Chipper	.313	160	601	123	188	329	29	5	34	107	16	96	93
Colbrunn, George	.307	90	166	18	51	75	11	2	3	23	4	10	34
Williams, Gerald	.305	129	266	46	81	135	18	3	10	44	11	17	48
Galarraga, Andres	.305	153	555	103	169	330	27	1	44	121	7	63	146
Lopez, Javier	.284	133	489	73	139	264	21	1	34	106	5	30	85
Weiss, Walt	.280	96	347	64	97	119	18	2	0	27	7	59	53
Guillen, Ozzie	.277	83	264	35	73	93	15	1	1	22	1	24	25
Klesko, Ryan	.274	129	427	69	117	202	29	1	18	70	5	56	66
Jones, Andruw	.271	159	582	89	158	300	33	8	31	90	27	40	129
Lockhart, Keith	.257	109	366	50	94	142	21	0	9	37	2	29	37
Pride, Curtis	.252	70	107	19	27	44	6	1	3	9	4	9	29
Bautista, Danny	.250	82	144	17	36	56	11	0	3	17	1	7	21
Tucker, Michael	.244	130	414	54	101	173	27	3	13	46	8	49	112

PITCHING	ERA	W	L	G	GS	CG	SV	INN	H	R	ER	BB	SO
Charlton, Norm	1.38	0	0	13	0	0	1	13	7	2	2	8	6
Rocker, John	2.13	1	3	47	0	0	2	38	22	10	9	22	42
Maddux, Greg	2.22	18	9	34	34	9	0	251	201	75	62	45	204
Glavine, Tom	2.47	20	6	33	33	4	0	229⅓	202	67	63	74	157
Ligtenberg, Kerry	2.71	3	2	75	0	0	30	73	51	24	22	24	79
Seanez, Rudy	2.75	4	1	34	0	0	2	36	25	13	11	16	50
Smoltz, John	2.90	17	3	26	26	2	0	167⅔	145	58	54	44	173
Neagle, Denny	3.55	16	11	32	31	5	0	210⅓	196	91	83	60	165
Cather, Mike	3.92	2	2	36	0	0	0	41⅓	39	21	18	12	33
Millwood, Kevin	4.08	17	8	31	29	3	0	174⅓	175	86	79	56	163
Wohlers, Mark	10.18	0	1	27	0	0	8	20⅓	18	23	23	33	22

Chicago Cubs

BATTING	BA	G	AB	R	H	TB	2B	3B	HR	RBI	SB	BB	SO
Grace, Mark	.309	158	595	92	184	280	39	3	17	89	4	93	56
Sosa, Sammy	.308	159	643	134	198	416	20	0	66	158	18	73	171
Morandini, Mickey	.296	154	582	93	172	224	20	4	8	53	13	72	84
Brown, Brant	.291	123	347	56	101	174	17	7	14	48	4	30	95
Gaetti, Gary	.281	128	434	60	122	215	34	4	19	70	1	43	62
Johnson, Lance	.280	85	304	51	85	107	8	4	2	21	10	26	22
Martinez, Sandy	.264	45	87	7	23	34	9	1	0	7	1	13	21
Houston, Tyler	.255	95	255	26	65	101	7	1	9	33	2	13	53
Hernandez, Jose	.254	149	488	76	124	230	23	7	23	75	4	40	140
Rodriguez, Henry	.251	128	415	56	104	220	21	1	31	85	1	54	113

National League Team-by-Team Statistical Leaders *(Cont.)*

Chicago Cubs *(Cont.)*

PITCHING	ERA	W	L	G	GS	CG	SV	INN	H	R	ER	BB	SO
Mulholland, Terry	2.89	6	5	70	6	0	3	112	100	49	36	39	72
Beck, Rod	3.02	3	4	81	0	0	51	80⅓	86	33	27	20	81
Wood, Kerry	3.04	13	6	26	26	1	0	166⅔	117	69	63	85	233
Pisciotta, Marc	4.09	1	2	43	0	0	0	44	44	21	20	32	31
Adams, Terry	4.33	7	7	63	0	0	1	72⅔	72	39	35	41	73
Trachsel, Steve	4.46	15	8	33	33	1	0	208	204	107	103	84	149
Stevens, Dave	4.74	1	2	31	0	0	0	38	42	20	20	17	31
Clark, Mark	4.84	9	14	33	33	2	0	213⅔	236	116	115	48	161
Tapani, Kevin	4.85	19	9	35	34	2	0	219	244	120	118	62	136
Heredia, Felix	5.06	3	3	71	2	0	2	58⅔	57	39	33	38	54

Cincinnati Reds

BATTING	BA	G	AB	R	H	TB	2B	3B	HR	RBI	SB	BB	SO
Young, Dmitri	.310	144	536	81	166	258	48	1	14	83	2	47	94
Larkin, Barry	.309	145	538	93	166	271	34	10	17	72	26	79	69
Hammonds, Jeffrey	.302	26	86	14	26	32	4	1	0	11	1	13	18
Boone, Aaron	.282	58	181	24	51	74	13	2	2	28	6	15	36
Taubensee, Eddie	.278	130	431	61	120	180	27	0	11	72	1	52	93
Casey, Sean	.272	96	302	44	82	126	21	1	7	52	1	43	45
Sanders, Reggie	.268	135	481	83	129	201	18	6	14	59	20	51	137
Boone, Bret	.266	157	583	76	155	267	38	1	24	95	6	48	104
Watkins, Pat	.265	83	147	11	39	55	8	1	2	15	1	8	26
Reese, Pokey	.256	59	133	20	34	43	2	2	1	16	3	14	28
Stynes, Chris	.254	123	347	52	88	118	10	1	6	27	15	32	36
Fordyce, Brook	.253	57	146	8	37	55	9	0	3	14	0	11	28
Nieves, Melvin	.252	83	119	8	30	40	4	0	2	17	0	26	42

PITCHING	ERA	W	L	G	GS	CG	SV	INN	H	R	ER	BB	SO
Hudek, John	3.09	5	6	58	0	0	0	64	50	27	22	47	68
Harnisch, Pete	3.14	14	7	32	32	2	0	209	176	79	73	64	157
Belinda, Stan	3.23	4	8	40	0	0	1	61⅓	46	23	22	28	57
Graves, Danny	3.32	2	1	62	0	0	8	81⅓	76	31	30	28	44
Parris, Steve	3.73	6	5	18	16	1	0	99	89	44	41	32	77
White, Gabe	4.01	5	5	69	3	0	9	98⅔	86	46	44	27	83
Bere, Jason	4.12	3	2	9	7	0	0	43⅔	39	20	20	20	31
Tomko, Brett	4.44	13	12	34	34	1	0	210⅔	198	111	104	64	162
Reyes, Dennis	4.54	3	5	19	10	0	0	67⅓	62	36	34	47	77
Remlinger, Mike	4.82	8	15	35	28	1	0	164⅓	164	96	88	87	144

Colorado Rockies

BATTING	BA	G	AB	R	H	TB	2B	3B	HR	RBI	SB	BB	SO
Walker, Larry	.363	130	454	113	165	286	46	3	23	67	14	64	61
Bichette, Dante	.331	161	662	97	219	337	48	2	22	122	14	28	76
Castilla, Vinny	.319	162	645	108	206	380	28	4	46	144	5	40	89
Helton, Todd	.315	152	530	78	167	281	37	1	25	97	3	53	54
Hamilton, Darryl	.308	148	561	95	173	225	28	3	6	51	13	82	73
Reed, Jeff	.290	113	259	43	75	121	17	1	9	39	0	37	57
Lansing, Mike	.276	153	584	73	161	240	39	2	12	66	10	39	88
Perez, Neifi	.274	162	647	80	177	247	25	9	9	59	5	38	70
Abbott, Kurt	.254	42	71	9	18	33	6	0	3	15	0	2	19
Manwaring, Kirt	.247	110	291	30	72	96	12	3	2	26	1	38	49
Goodwin, Curtis	.245	119	159	27	39	49	7	0	1	6	5	16	40

PITCHING	ERA	W	L	G	GS	CG	SV	INN	H	R	ER	BB	SO
Veres, Dave	2.83	3	1	63	0	0	8	76⅓	67	26	24	27	74
McElroy Chuck	2.90	6	4	78	0	0	2	68⅓	68	23	22	24	61
DeJean, Mike	3.03	3	1	59	1	0	2	74⅓	78	29	25	24	27
DiPoto, Jerry	3.53	3	4	68	0	0	19	71⅓	61	31	28	25	49
Leskanic, Curt	4.40	6	4	66	0	0	2	75⅔	75	37	37	40	55
Thomson, John	4.81	8	11	26	26	2	0	161	174	86	86	49	106
Kile, Darryl	5.20	13	17	36	35	4	0	230	257	141	133	96	158
Jones, Bobby	5.22	7	8	35	20	1	0	141⅓	153	87	82	66	109
Munoz, Mike	5.66	2	2	40	0	0	3	41⅓	53	32	26	16	24
Wright, Jamey	5.67	9	14	34	34	1	0	206⅓	235	143	130	95	86
Astacio, Pedro	6.23	13	14	35	34	0	0	209⅓	245	160	145	74	170

Florida Marlins

BATTING	BA	G	AB	R	H	TB	2B	3B	HR	RBI	SB	BB	SO
Redmond, Mike	.331	37	118	10	39	54	9	0	2	12	0	5	16
Berg, Dave	.313	81	182	18	57	74	11	0	2	21	3	26	46
Floyd, Cliff	.282	153	588	85	166	283	45	3	22	90	41	47	112
Renteria, Edgar	.282	133	517	79	146	177	18	2	3	31	27	48	78
Kotsay, Mark	.279	154	578	72	161	233	25	7	11	68	10	34	61
Zeile, Todd	.276	106	392	59	108	169	18	2	13	66	3	41	58
Cangelosi, John	.251	104	171	19	43	54	8	0	1	10	2	30	23
Dunwoody, Todd	.251	116	434	53	109	165	27	7	5	28	5	21	113
Counsell, Craig	.251	107	335	43	84	125	19	5	4	40	3	51	47
Jackson, Ryan	.250	111	260	26	65	97	15	1	5	31	1	20	73
Lee, Derrek	.233	141	454	62	106	188	29	1	17	74	5	47	120
Wehner, John	.227	53	88	10	20	22	2	0	0	5	1	7	12
Orie, Kevin	.219	112	379	47	83	131	22	1	8	38	2	32	59

PITCHING	ERA	W	L	G	GS	CG	SV	INN	H	R	ER	BB	SO
Mantei, Matt	2.96	3	4	42	0	0	9	54⅔	38	19	18	23	63
Darensbourg, Vic	3.68	0	7	59	0	0	1	71	52	29	29	30	74
Edmondson, Brian	3.91	4	4	53	0	0	0	76	76	38	33	37	40
Alfonseca, Antonio	4.08	4	6	58	0	0	8	70⅔	75	36	32	33	46
Ojala, Kirt	4.25	2	7	41	13	1	0	125	128	71	59	59	75
Sanchez, Jesus	4.47	7	9	35	29	0	0	173	178	98	86	91	137
Hernandez, Livan	4.72	10	12	33	33	9	0	234	265	133	123	104	162
Pall, Donn	5.13	0	1	23	0	0	0	33⅓	42	19	19	7	26
Meadows, Brian	5.21	11	13	31	31	1	0	174½	222	106	101	46	88
Stanifer, Robby	5.63	2	4	38	0	0	1	48	54	33	30	22	30

Houston Astros

BATTING	BA	G	AB	R	H	TB	2B	3B	HR	RBI	SB	BB	SO
Biggio, Craig	.325	160	646	123	210	325	51	2	20	88	50	64	113
Berry, Sean	.314	102	299	48	94	152	17	1	13	52	3	31	50
Bell, Derek	.314	156	630	111	198	309	41	2	22	108	13	51	126
Alou, Moises	.312	159	584	104	182	340	34	5	38	124	11	84	87
Bagwell, Jeff	.304	147	540	124	164	301	33	1	34	111	19	109	90
Hidalgo, Richard	.303	74	211	31	64	100	15	0	7	35	3	17	37
Everett, Carl	.296	133	467	72	138	225	34	4	15	76	14	44	102
Howell, Jack	.289	24	38	4	11	19	5	0	1	7	0	4	12
Spiers, Bill	.273	123	384	66	105	152	27	4	4	43	11	45	62
Ausmus, Brad	.269	128	412	62	111	147	10	4	6	45	10	53	60
Gutierrez, Ricky	.261	141	491	55	128	164	24	3	2	46	13	54	84
Eusebio, Tony	.253	66	182	13	46	57	6	1	1	36	1	18	31

PITCHING	ERA	W	L	G	GS	CG	SV	INN	H	R	ER	BB	SO
Johnson, Randy	1.28	10	1	11	11	4	0	84½	57	12	12	26	116
Wagner, Billy	2.70	4	3	58	0	0	30	60	46	19	18	25	97
Miller, Trever	3.04	2	0	37	1	0	1	53⅓	57	21	18	20	30
Henry, Doug	3.04	8	2	59	0	0	2	71	55	25	24	35	59
Elarton, Scott	3.32	2	1	28	2	0	2	57	40	21	21	20	56
Powell, Jay	3.33	7	7	62	0	0	7	70⅓	58	28	26	37	62
Hampton, Mike	3.36	11	7	32	32	1	0	211⅔	227	92	79	81	137
Reynolds, Shane	3.51	19	8	35	35	3	0	233⅓	257	99	91	53	209
Lima, Jose	3.70	16	8	33	33	3	0	233⅓	229	100	96	32	169
Bergman, Sean	3.72	12	9	31	27	1	0	172	183	81	71	42	100

Los Angeles Dodgers

BATTING	BA	G	AB	R	H	TB	2B	3B	HR	RBI	SB	BB	SO
Sheffield, Gary	.302	130	437	73	132	229	27	2	22	85	22	95	46
Hubbard, Trenidad	.298	94	208	29	62	94	9	1	7	18	9	18	46
Karros, Eric	.296	139	507	59	150	241	20	1	23	87	7	47	93
Young, Eric	.285	117	452	78	129	179	24	1	8	43	42	45	32
Mondesi, Raul	.279	148	580	85	162	288	26	5	30	90	16	30	112
Grudzielanek, Mark	.272	156	589	62	160	213	29	1	10	62	18	26	73
Hollandsworth, Todd	.269	54	175	23	47	70	6	4	3	20	4	9	42
Vizcaino, Jose	.262	67	237	30	62	80	9	0	3	29	7	17	35
Bonilla, Bobby	.249	100	333	39	83	129	11	1	11	45	1	41	59
Cedeno, Roger	.242	105	240	33	58	77	11	1	2	17	8	27	57
Luke, Matt	.236	102	237	34	56	106	12	1	12	34	2	17	60
Johnson, Charles	.218	133	459	44	100	175	18	0	19	58	0	45	12

Los Angeles Dodgers (Cont.)

PITCHING	ERA	W	L	G	GS	CG	SV	INN	H	R	ER	BB	SO
Shaw, Jeff	2.12	3	8	73	0	0	48	85	75	22	20	19	55
Radinsky, Scott	2.63	6	6	62	0	0	13	61⅔	63	21	18	20	45
Bohanon, Brian	2.67	7	11	39	18	2	0	151¾	121	56	45	57	111
Martinez, Ramon	2.83	7	3	15	15	1	0	101⅓	76	41	32	41	91
Osuna, Antonio	3.06	7	1	54	0	0	6	64⅔	50	26	22	32	72
Guthrie, Mark	3.50	2	1	53	0	0	0	54	56	26	21	24	45
Perez, Carlos	3.59	11	14	34	34	7	0	241	244	109	96	63	128
Park, Chan Ho	3.71	15	9	34	34	2	0	220⅔	199	101	91	97	191
Valdes, Ismael	3.98	11	10	27	27	2	0	174	171	82	77	66	122
Dreifort, Darren	4.00	8	12	32	26	1	0	180	171	84	80	57	168
Mlicki, Dave	4.57	8	7	30	30	3	0	181⅓	188	102	92	63	117

Milwaukee Brewers

BATTING	BA	G	AB	R	H	TB	2B	3B	HR	RBI	SB	BB	SO
Levis, Jesse	.351	22	37	4	13	13	0	0	0	4	1	7	6
Cirillo, Jeff	.321	156	604	97	194	269	31	1	14	68	10	79	88
Loretta, Mark	.316	140	434	55	137	184	29	0	6	54	9	42	47
Vina, Fernando	.311	159	637	101	198	272	39	7	7	45	22	54	46
Grissom, Marquis	.271	142	542	57	147	207	28	1	10	60	13	24	78
Nilsson, Dave	.269	102	309	39	83	135	14	1	12	56	2	33	48
Burnitz, Jeromy	.263	161	609	92	160	304	28	1	38	125	7	70	158
Jackson, Darrin	.240	114	204	20	49	76	13	1	4	20	1	9	37
Matheny Mike	.238	108	320	24	76	107	13	0	6	27	1	12	63
Newfield, Marc	.237	93	186	15	44	60	7	0	3	25	0	19	29
Jenkins, Geoff	.229	84	262	33	60	101	12	1	9	28	1	20	61
Hughes, Bobby	.229	85	218	28	50	88	7	2	9	29	1	16	54
Valentin, Jose	.224	151	428	65	96	168	24	6	16	49	10	62	105
Hamelin, Bob	.219	108	146	15	32	59	6	0	7	22	0	16	30
Jaha, John	.208	73	216	29	45	74	6	1	7	38	1	49	66

PITCHING	ERA	W	L	G	GS	CG	SV	INN	H	R	ER	BB	SO
Myers, Mike	2.70	2	2	70	0	0	1	50	44	19	15	22	40
Plunk, Eric	3.69	1	2	26	0	0	1	31⅔	33	14	13	15	36
Wickman, Bob	3.72	6	9	72	0	0	25	82⅓	79	38	34	39	71
Fox, Chad	3.95	1	4	49	0	0	0	57	56	27	25	20	64
Reyes, Al	3.95	5	1	50	0	0	0	57	55	26	25	31	58
Woodard, Steve	4.18	10	12	34	26	0	0	165⅓	170	83	77	33	135
Karl, Scott	4.40	10	11	33	33	0	0	192¾	219	104	94	66	102
Patrick, Bronswell	4.69	4	1	32	3	0	0	78⅔	83	43	41	29	49
Eldred, Cal	4.80	4	8	23	23	0	0	133	157	82	71	61	86
Weathers, Dave	4.91	6	5	44	9	0	0	110	130	69	60	41	94
Woodall, Brad	4.96	7	9	31	20	0	0	138	145	81	76	47	85

Montreal Expos

BATTING	BA	G	AB	R	H	TB	2B	3B	HR	RBI	SB	BB	SO
Guerrero, Vladimir	.324	159	623	108	202	367	37	7	38	109	11	42	95
Henley, Bob	.304	41	115	16	35	54	8	1	3	18	3	11	26
White, Rondell	.300	97	357	54	107	183	21	2	17	58	16	30	57
Guerrero, Wilton	.284	116	402	50	114	152	14	9	2	27	8	14	63
Cabrera, Orlando	.280	79	261	44	73	108	16	5	3	22	6	18	27
Fullmer, Brad	.273	140	505	58	138	225	44	2	13	73	6	39	70
Seguignol, Fernando	.262	16	42	6	11	21	4	0	2	3	0	3	15
May, Derrick	.239	85	180	13	43	66	8	0	5	15	0	11	24
Andrews, Shane	.238	150	492	48	117	224	30	1	25	69	1	58	137
Perez, Robert	.236	52	106	9	25	29	1	0	1	8	0	2	23
Widger, Chris	.233	125	417	36	97	162	18	1	15	53	6	29	85
Vidro, Jose	.220	83	205	24	45	57	12	0	0	18	2	27	33
Jones, Terry	.217	60	212	30	46	60	7	2	1	15	16	21	46
Santangelo, F.P.	.214	122	383	53	82	112	18	0	4	23	7	44	72

PITCHING	ERA	W	L	G	GS	CG	SV	INN	H	R	ER	BB	SO
Urbina, Ugueth	1.30	6	3	64	0	0	34	69⅓	37	11	10	33	94
Kline, Steve	2.76	3	6	78	0	0	1	71⅓	62	25	22	41	76
Hermanson, Dustin	3.13	14	11	32	30	1	0	187	163	80	65	56	154
Maddux, Mike	3.72	3	4	51	0	0	1	55¾	50	24	23	15	33
Batista, Miguel	3.80	3	5	56	13	0	0	135	141	66	57	65	92
Telford, Anthony	3.86	3	6	77	0	0	1	91	85	45	39	36	59

Montreal Expos (Cont.)

PITCHING (Cont.)	ERA	W	L	G	GS	CG	SV	INN	H	R	ER	BB	SO
Pavano, Carl	4.21	6	9	24	23	0	0	134⅔	130	70	63	43	83
Thurman, Mike	4.70	4	5	14	13	0	0	67	60	38	35	26	32
DeHart, Rick	4.82	0	0	26	0	0	1	28	34	22	15	13	14
Bennett, Shayne	5.50	5	5	62	0	0	1	91⅓	97	61	56	45	59
Vazquez, Javier	6.06	5	15	33	32	0	0	172⅓	196	121	116	68	139

New York Mets

BATTING	BA	G	AB	R	H	TB	2B	3B	HR	RBI	SB	BB	SO
Olerud, John	.354	160	557	91	197	307	36	4	22	93	2	96	73
Piazza, Mike	.328	151	561	88	184	320	38	1	32	111	1	58	80
Allensworth, Jermaine	.289	103	287	39	83	119	15	3	5	28	8	19	59
Alfonzo, Edgardo	.278	144	557	94	155	238	28	2	17	78	8	65	77
Franco, Matt	.273	103	161	20	44	58	7	2	1	13	0	23	26
Baerga, Carlos	.266	147	511	46	136	186	27	1	7	53	0	24	55
McRae, Brian	.264	159	552	79	146	255	36	5	21	79	20	80	90
Harris, Lenny	.259	132	290	30	75	108	15	0	6	27	6	17	21
Huskey, Butch	.252	113	369	43	93	150	18	0	13	59	7	26	66
Lopez, Luis	.252	117	266	37	67	90	13	2	2	22	2	20	60
Ordonez, Rey	.246	153	505	46	124	151	20	2	1	42	3	23	60
Phillips, Tony	.223	52	188	25	42	62	11	0	3	14	1	38	44
Hundley, Todd	.161	53	124	8	20	33	4	0	3	12	1	16	55

PITCHING	ERA	W	L	G	GS	CG	SV	INN	H	R	ER	BB	SO
Cook, Dennis	2.38	8	4	73	0	0	18	68	60	21	18	27	79
Leiter, Al	2.47	17	6	28	28	4	0	193	151	55	53	71	174
Wendell, Turk	2.93	5	1	66	0	0	17	76⅔	62	25	25	33	58
Reed, Rick	3.48	16	11	31	31	2	0	212⅓	208	84	82	29	153
Franco, John	3.62	0	8	0	0	0	54	64⅔	66	28	26	29	59
Reynoso, Armando	3.82	7	3	11	11	0	0	68⅓	64	31	29	32	40
Yoshii, Masato	3.93	6	8	29	29	1	0	171⅓	166	79	75	53	117
Jones, Bobby	4.05	9	9	30	30	0	0	195⅓	192	94	88	53	115
McMichael, Greg	4.10	5	4	0	0	0	19	68	81	39	31	35	55
Nomo, Hideo	4.92	6	12	28	28	3	0	157⅓	130	88	86	94	167
Blair, Willie	4.98	5	16	25	25	0	2	175⅓	188	101	97	61	92

Philadelphia Philies

BATTING	BA	G	AB	R	H	TB	2B	3B	HR	RBI	SB	BB	SO
Anderson, Marlon	.326	17	43	4	104	20	3	0	1	4	2	1	6
Sefcik, Kevin	.314	104	169	27	53	73	7	2	3	20	4	25	32
Abreu, Bobby	.312	151	497	68	155	247	29	6	17	74	19	84	133
Jeffries, Greg	.294	125	483	65	142	194	22	3	8	48	11	29	27
Arias, Alex	.293	56	133	17	39	50	8	0	1	16	0	13	18
Magee, Wendell	.293	20	75	9	22	33	6	1	1	11	2	7	11
Rolen, Scott	.290	160	601	120	174	320	45	4	31	110	14	93	141
Glanville, Doug	.279	158	678	106	189	255	28	7	8	49	23	42	89
Jordan, Kevin	.276	112	250	23	69	88	13	0	2	27	0	8	30
Brogna, Rico	.265	153	565	77	150	252	36	3	20	104	7	49	125
Lieberthal, Mike	.256	86	313	39	80	125	15	3	8	45	2	17	44
Lewis, Mark	.249	142	518	52	129	181	21	2	9	54	3	48	111
Relaford, Desi	.245	142	494	45	121	167	25	3	5	41	9	33	87

PITCHING	ERA	W	L	G	GS	CG	SV	INN	H	R	ER	BB	SO
Schilling, Curt	3.25	15	14	35	35	15	0	268⅔	236	101	97	61	300
Spradlin, Jerry	3.53	4	4	69	0	0	1	81⅓	63	34	32	20	76
Leiter, Mark	3.55	7	5	69	0	0	23	88⅓	67	36	35	47	84
Perez, Yorkis	3.81	0	2	57	0	0	0	52	40	23	22	25	42
Gomes, Wayne	4.24	9	6	71	0	0	1	93⅓	94	48	44	35	86
Portugal, Mark	4.44	10	5	26	26	3	0	166⅓	186	88	82	32	104
Green, Tyler	5.03	6	12	27	27	0	0	159⅓	142	97	89	85	113
Beech, Matt	5.15	3	9	21	21	0	0	117	126	78	67	63	113
Grace, Mike	5.48	4	7	21	15	0	0	90⅓	116	61	55	30	46
Loewer, Carlton	6.09	7	8	21	21	1	0	122⅔	154	86	83	39	58

Pittsburgh Pirates

BATTING	BA	G	AB	R	H	TB	2B	3B	HR	RBI	SB	BB	SO
Kendall, Jason	.327	149	535	95	175	253	36	3	12	75	26	51	51
Brown, Adrian	.283	41	152	20	43	49	4	1	0	5	4	9	18
Womack, Tony	.282	159	655	85	185	234	26	7	3	45	58	38	94
Young, Kevin	.270	159	592	88	160	285	40	2	27	108	15	44	127
Guillen, Jose	.267	153	573	60	153	237	38	2	14	84	3	21	100
Ward, Turner	.262	123	282	33	74	120	13	3	9	46	5	27	40
Brown, Emil	.256	13	39	2	10	11	1	0	0	3	0	1	11
Garcia, Freddy	.256	56	172	27	44	84	11	1	9	26	0	18	45
Martinez, Manny	.250	73	180	21	45	78	11	2	6	24	0	9	44
Collier, Lou	.246	110	334	30	82	113	13	6	2	34	2	31	70
Martin, Al	.239	125	440	57	105	160	15	2	12	47	20	32	91
Ramirez, Aramis	.235	72	251	23	59	88	9	1	6	24	0	18	72

PITCHING	ERA	W	L	G	GS	CG	SV	INN	H	R	ER	BB	SO
Williams, Mike	1.94	4	2	37	1	0	0	51	39	12	11	16	59
Christiansen, Jason	2.51	3	3	60	0	0	6	64⅔	51	22	18	27	71
Rincon, Ricardo	2.91	0	2	60	0	0	14	65	50	31	21	29	64
Tabaka, Jeff	3.02	2	2	37	0	0	0	50⅔	37	19	17	22	40
Cordova, Francisco	3.31	13	14	33	33	3	0	220⅓	204	91	81	69	157
Loiselle, Rich	3.44	2	7	54	0	0	19	55	56	26	21	36	48
Peters, Chris	3.47	8	10	39	21	1	1	148	142	63	57	55	103
Schmidt, Jason	4.07	11	14	33	33	0	0	214⅓	228	106	97	71	158
Lieber, Jon	4.11	8	14	29	28	2	1	171	182	93	78	40	138
Silva, Jose	4.40	6	7	18	18	1	0	100⅓	104	55	49	30	64
Loaiza, Esteban	4.52	6	5	21	14	0	0	91⅔	96	50	46	30	53

St. Louis Cardinals

BATTING	BA	G	AB	R	H	TB	2B	3B	HR	RBI	SB	BB	SO
Drew, J.D.	.417	14	36	9	15	35	3	1	5	13	0	4	10
Jordan, Brian	.316	150	564	100	178	301	34	7	25	91	17	40	66
McGwire, Mark	.299	155	509	130	152	383	21	0	70	147	1	162	155
Lankford, Ray	.293	154	533	94	156	288	37	1	31	105	26	86	151
DeShields, Delino	.290	117	420	74	122	180	21	8	7	44	26	56	61
Tatis, Fernando	.287	55	202	28	58	102	16	2	8	26	7	24	57
Polanco, Placido	.254	45	114	10	29	39	3	2	1	11	2	5	9
McGee, Willie	.253	120	269	27	68	89	10	1	3	34	7	14	49
Mabry, John	.249	141	377	41	94	143	22	0	9	46	0	30	76
Howard, David	.245	46	102	15	25	34	1	1	2	12	0	12	22
Marrero, Eli	.244	83	254	28	62	94	18	1	4	20	6	28	42
Gant, Ron	.240	121	383	60	92	189	17	1	26	67	8	51	92
Clayton, Royce	.234	90	355	59	83	116	19	1	4	29	19	40	51
Lampkin, Tom	.231	93	216	25	50	82	12	1	6	28	3	24	32
Pagnozzi, Tom	.219	51	160	735	47	9	0	0	1	10	0	14	37

PITCHING	ERA	W	L	G	GS	CG	SV	INN	H	R	ER	BB	SO
Morris, Matt	2.53	7	5	17	17	2	0	113⅔	101	37	32	42	79
Acevedo, Juan	2.56	8	3	50	9	0	15	98⅓	83	30	28	29	56
Stottlemyre, Todd	3.51	9	9	23	23	3	0	161⅓	146	74	63	51	147
King, Curtis	3.53	2	0	36	0	0	2	51	50	20	20	20	28
Painter, Lance	3.99	4	0	65	0	0	1	47⅓	42	24	21	28	39
Osborne, Donovan	4.09	5	4	14	14	1	0	83.2	84	42	38	22	60
Frascatore, John	4.14	3	4	69	0	0	0	95.2	95	48	44	36	49
Oliver, Darren	4.26	4	4	10	10	0	0	57	64	31	27	23	29
Brantley, Jeff	4.44	0	5	48	0	0	14	50⅔	40	26	25	18	48
Bottenfield, Kent	4.44	4	6	44	17	0	4	133⅔	128	72	66	57	98
Busby, Mike	4.50	5	2	26	2	0	0	46	45	23	23	15	33
Petkovsek, Mark	4.77	7	4	48	10	0	0	105.2	131	63	56	36	55
Witt, Bobby	4.94	2	5	17	5	0	0	47⅓	55	32	26	20	28
Mercker, Kent	5.07	11	11	30	29	0	0	161⅓	199	99	91	53	72

San Diego Padres

BATTING	BA	G	AB	R	H	TB	2B	3B	HR	RBI	SB	BB	SO
Gwynn, Tony	.321	127	461	65	148	231	35	0	16	69	3	35	18
Joyner, Wally	.298	131	439	58	131	199	30	1	12	80	1	51	44
Vander Wal, John	.279	109	129	21	36	66	13	1	5	20	0	22	34
Vaughn, Greg	.272	158	573	112	156	342	28	4	50	119	11	79	121
Gomez, Chris	.267	145	449	55	120	170	32	3	4	39	1	51	87
Veras, Quilvio	.267	138	517	79	138	184	24	2	6	45	24	84	78
Leyritz, Jim	.266	62	143	17	38	60	10	0	4	18	0	21	40
Hernandez, Carlos	.262	129	390	34	102	144	15	0	9	52	2	16	54
Caminiti, Ken	.252	131	452	87	114	230	29	0	29	82	6	71	108
Finley, Steve	.249	159	619	92	154	248	40	6	14	67	12	45	103
Myers, Greg	.246	69	171	19	42	64	10	0	4	20	0	17	36
Sheets, Andy	.242	88	194	31	47	79	5	3	7	29	7	21	62
Sweeney, Mark	.234	122	192	17	45	65	8	3	2	15	1	26	37
Giovanola Ed	.230	92	139	19	32	44	3	3	1	9	1	22	22

PITCHING	ERA	W	L	G	GS	CG	SV	INN	H	R	ER	BB	SO
Hoffman, Trevor	1.48	4	2	66	0	0	53	73	41	12	12	21	86
Brown, Kevin	2.38	18	7	36	35	7	0	257	225	77	68	49	257
Wall, Donne	2.43	5	4	46	1	0	1	70⅓	50	20	19	32	56
Miceli, Dan	3.22	10	5	67	0	0	2	72⅔	64	28	26	27	70
Ashby, Andy	3.34	17	9	33	33	5	0	226⅔	223	90	84	58	151
Bruske, Jim	3.53	3	0	39	0	0	1	51	57	22	20	23	35
Hitchcock, Sterling	3.93	9	7	39	27	2	1	176½	169	83	77	48	158
Sanders, Scott	4.11	3	1	23	0	0	0	30⅔	33	20	14	5	26
Hamilton, Joey	4.27	13	13	34	34	0	0	217⅓	220	113	103	106	147
Boehringer, Brian	4.36	5	2	56	1	0	0	76⅓	75	38	37	45	67
Smith, Pete	4.78	3	2	10	8	0	0	43⅓	45	23	23	18	36

San Francisco Giants

BATTING	BA	G	AB	R	H	TB	2B	3B	HR	RBI	SB	BB	SO
Benard, Marvin	.322	121	286	41	92	124	21	1	3	36	11	34	39
Martinez, Ramon	.316	19	19	4	6	7	1	0	0	0	0	4	2
Bonds, Barry	.303	156	552	120	167	336	44	7	37	122	28	130	92
Kent, Jeff	.297	137	526	94	156	292	37	3	31	128	9	48	110
Carter, Joe	.295	41	105	15	31	59	7	0	7	29	1	6	13
Mueller, Bill	.294	145	534	93	157	211	27	0	9	59	3	79	83
Burks, Ellis	.292	142	504	76	147	250	28	6	21	76	11	58	111
Javier, Stan	.290	135	417	63	121	156	13	5	4	49	21	65	63
Hayes, Charlie	.286	111	329	39	94	138	8	0	12	62	2	34	61
Sanchez, Rey	.285	109	316	44	90	114	14	2	2	30	0	16	47
Mayne, Brent	.273	94	275	26	75	99	15	0	3	32	2	37	47
Aurilia, Rich	.266	122	413	54	110	168	27	2	9	49	3	31	62
Snow, J.T.	.248	138	435	65	108	184	29	1	15	79	1	58	84
Johnson, Brian	.237	99	308	34	73	122	8	1	13	34	0	28	67

PITCHING	ERA	W	L	G	GS	CG	SV	INN	H	R	ER	BB	SO
Reed, Steve	1.48	2	1	50	0	0	1	54⅔	30	10	9	19	50
Nen, Robb	1.52	7	7	78	0	0	40	88⅔	59	21	15	25	110
Johnstone, John	3.07	6	5	70	0	0	0	88	72	32	30	38	86
Mesa, Jose	3.52	5	3	32	0	0	0	30⅔	30	14	12	18	28
Rodriguez, Rich	3.70	4	0	68	0	0	2	65⅔	69	28	27	20	44
Tavarez, Julian	3.80	5	3	60	0	0	1	85½	96	41	36	36	52
Gardner, Mark	4.33	13	6	33	33	4	0	212	203	106	102	65	151
Rueter, Kirk	4.36	16	9	33	33	1	0	187⅔	193	100	91	57	102
Hershiser, Orel	4.41	11	10	34	34	0	0	202	200	105	99	85	126
Ortiz, Russ	4.99	4	4	22	13	0	0	88½	90	51	49	46	75
Estes, Shawn	5.06	7	12	25	25	1	0	149⅓	150	89	84	80	136
Poole, Jim	5.29	1	3	26	0	0	0	32½	38	20	19	9	16
Darwin, Danny	5.51	8	10	33	25	0	0	148⅔	176	97	91	49	81

American League Team-by-Team Statistical Leaders

Anaheim Angels

BATTING	BA	G	AB	R	H	TB	2B	3B	HR	RBI	SB	BB	SO
Palmeiro, Orlando	.321	75	165	28	53	64	7	2	0	21	5	20	11
Edmonds, Jim	.307	154	599	115	184	303	42	1	25	91	7	57	114
Salmon, Tim	.300	136	463	84	139	247	28	1	26	88	0	90	100
Erstad, Darin	.296	133	537	84	159	261	39	3	19	82	20	43	77
Anderson, Garret	.294	156	622	62	183	283	41	7	15	79	8	29	80
Pritchett, Chris	.288	31	80	12	23	33	2	1	2	8	2	4	16
DiSarcina, Gary	.287	157	551	73	158	212	39	3	3	56	11	21	51
Velarde, Randy	.261	51	188	29	49	76	13	1	4	26	7	34	42
Shipley, Craig	.259	77	147	18	38	53	7	1	2	17	0	5	22
Walbeck, Matt	.257	108	338	41	87	124	15	2	6	46	1	30	68
O'Brien, Charlie	.257	62	175	13	45	66	9	0	4	18	0	10	33
Baughman, Justin	.255	63	196	24	50	64	9	1	1	20	10	6	36
Greene, Todd	.254	29	71	3	18	25	4	0	1	7	0	2	20
Kreuter, Chad	.250	96	252	27	63	81	10	1	2	33	1	33	49
Hollins, Dave	.242	101	363	60	88	141	16	2	11	39	11	44	69

PITCHING	ERA	W	L	G	GS	CG	SV	INN	H	R	ER	BB	SO
Hasegawa, Shigetoshi	3.14	8	3	61	0	0	5	97⅓	86	37	34	32	73
Finley, Chuck	3.39	11	9	34	34	1	0	223⅓	210	97	84	109	212
Percival, Troy	3.65	2	7	67	0	0	42	66⅔	45	31	27	37	81
Olivares, Omar	4.03	9	9	37	26	1	0	183	189	92	82	91	112
DeLucia, Rich	4.27	2	6	61	0	0	3	71⅓	56	36	34	46	73
Fetters, Mike	4.30	2	8	60	0	0	5	58⅔	62	34	28	25	43
Sparks, Steve	4.34	9	4	22	20	0	0	128⅔	130	66	62	58	90
Harris, Pep	4.35	3	1	49	0	0	0	60	55	32	29	23	34
Washburn, Jarrod	4.62	6	3	15	11	0	0	74	70	40	38	27	48
Hill, Ken	4.98	9	6	19	19	0	0	103	123	60	57	47	57
McDowell, Jack	5.09	5	3	14	14	0	0	76	96	45	43	19	45
Watson, Allen	6.04	6	7	28	14	1	0	92½	122	67	62	34	64
Dickson, Jason	6.05	10	10	27	18	0	0	122	147	89	82	41	61

Baltimore Orioles

BATTING	BA	G	AB	R	H	TB	2B	3B	HR	RBI	SB	BB	SO
Davis, Eric	.327	131	452	81	148	263	29	1	28	89	7	44	108
Baines, Harold	.300	104	293	40	88	132	17	0	9	57	0	32	40
Palmeiro, Rafael	.296	162	619	98	183	350	36	1	43	121	11	79	91
Webster, Lenny	.285	108	309	37	88	134	16	0	10	46	0	15	38
Alomar, Roberto	.282	147	588	86	166	246	36	1	14	56	18	59	70
Surhoff, B.J.	.279	162	573	79	160	262	34	1	22	92	9	49	81
Ripken, Cal Jr.	.271	161	601	65	163	234	27	1	14	61	0	51	68
Hoiles, Chris	.262	97	267	36	70	127	12	0	15	56	0	38	50
Bordick, Mike	.260	151	465	59	121	191	29	1	13	51	6	39	65
Reboulet, Jeff	.246	79	126	20	31	40	6	0	1	8	0	19	34
Anderson, Brady	.236	133	479	84	113	201	28	3	18	51	21	75	78
Becker, Rich	.204	79	113	22	23	33	1	0	3	11	2	22	34

PITCHING	ERA	W	L	G	GS	CG	SV	INN	H	R	ER	BB	SO
Orosco, Jesse	3.18	4	1	69	0	0	7	56⅔	46	20	20	28	50
Mussina, Mike	3.49	13	10	29	29	4	0	206½	189	85	80	41	175
Rhodes, Arthur	3.51	4	4	45	0	0	4	77	65	30	30	34	83
Mills, Allen	3.74	3	4	72	0	0	2	77	55	32	32	50	57
Benitez, Armando	3.82	5	6	71	0	0	22	68½	48	29	29	39	87
Erickson, Scott	4.01	16	13	36	36	11	0	251⅓	284	125	112	69	186
Key, Jimmy	4.20	6	3	25	11	0	0	79⅓	77	39	37	23	53
Guzman, Juan	4.35	10	16	33	33	2	0	211	193	117	102	98	168
Johns, Doug	4.57	3	3	31	10	0	1	86⅔	108	46	44	32	34
Ponson, Sidney	5.27	8	9	31	20	0	1	135	157	82	79	42	85
Kamieniecki, Scott	6.75	2	6	12	11	0	0	54⅔	67	41	41	26	25
Drabek, Doug	7.29	6	11	23	21	1	0	108⅔	138	90	88	29	55

Boston Red Sox

BATTING	BA	G	AB	R	H	TB	2B	3B	HR	RBI	SB	BB	SO
Vaughn, Mo	.337	154	609	107	205	360	31	2	40	115	0	61	144
Garciaparra, Nomar	.323	143	604	111	195	353	37	8	35	122	12	33	62
Jefferson, Reggie	.306	62	196	24	60	102	16	1	8	31	0	21	40
Cummings, Midre	.283	67	120	20	34	57	8	0	5	15	3	17	19
Buford, Damon	.282	86	216	37	61	113	14	4	10	42	5	22	43
Merloni, Lou	.281	39	96	10	27	36	6	0	1	15	1	7	20
Bragg, Darren	.279	129	409	51	114	173	29	3	8	57	5	42	99
Hatteberg, Scott	.276	112	359	46	99	160	23	1	12	43	0	43	58
Benjamin, Mike	.272	124	349	46	95	130	23	0	4	39	3	15	73
O'Leary, Troy	.270	156	611	95	165	286	36	8	23	83	2	36	108
Lewis, Darren	.268	155	585	95	157	212	25	3	8	63	29	70	94
Stanley, Mike	.256	145	497	74	127	239	25	0	29	79	3	82	129
Varitek, Jason	.253	86	221	31	56	90	13	0	7	33	2	17	45
Valentin, John	.247	153	588	113	145	260	44	1	23	73	4	77	82

PITCHING	ERA	W	L	G	GS	CG	SV	INN	H	R	ER	BB	SO
Corsi, Jim	2.59	3	2	59	0	0	0	66	58	23	19	23	49
Gordon, Tom	2.72	7	4	73	0	0	46	79⅓	55	24	24	25	78
Martinez, Pedro	2.89	19	7	33	33	3	0	233⅔	188	82	75	67	251
Garces, Rich	3.33	1	1	30	0	0	1	46	36	19	17	27	34
Reyes, Carlos	3.52	1	1	24	0	0	0	38⅓	35	15	15	14	23
Swindell, Greg	3.59	5	6	81	0	0	2	90⅓	92	40	36	31	63
Saberhagen, Bret	3.96	15	8	31	31	0	0	175	181	82	77	29	100
Lowe, Derek	4.02	3	9	63	10	0	4	123	126	65	55	42	77
Schourek, Pete	4.30	1	3	10	8	0	0	44	45	21	21	14	36
Wakefield, Tim	4.58	17	8	36	33	2	0	216	211	123	110	79	146
Eckersley, Dennis	4.76	4	1	50	0	0	1	39⅔	46	21	21	8	22
Avery, Steve	5.25	10	7	34	23	0	0	123⅔	128	74	69	64	57
Wasdin, John	5.02	6	4	47	8	0	0	96	111	57	56	27	59

Chicago White Sox

BATTING	BA	G	AB	R	H	TB	2B	3B	HR	RBI	SB	BB	SO
Belle, Albert	.328	163	609	113	200	399	48	2	49	152	6	81	84
Caruso, Mike	.306	133	523	81	160	204	17	6	5	55	22	14	38
Durham, Ray	.285	158	635	126	181	289	35	8	19	67	36	73	105
Ordonez, Magglio	.282	145	636	70	151	222	25	2	14	65	9	28	53
Abbott, Jeff	.279	89	244	33	68	120	14	1	12	41	3	9	28
Codero, Wil	.267	96	341	58	91	152	18	2	13	49	2	22	66
Thomas, Frank	.265	160	585	109	155	281	35	2	29	109	7	110	93
Ventura, Robin	.263	161	590	84	155	257	31	4	21	91	1	79	111
Norton, Greg	.237	105	299	38	71	119	17	2	9	36	3	26	77
Cameron, Mike	.210	141	396	53	83	133	16	5	8	43	27	37	101
Muchado, Robert	.207	34	111	14	23	38	6	0	3	15	0	7	22

PITCHING	ERA	W	L	G	GS	CG	SV	INN	H	R	ER	BB	SO
Howry, Bob	3.15	0	3	44	0	0	9	54⅓	37	20	19	19	51
Bradford, Chad	3.23	2	1	29	0	0	1	30⅔	27	16	11	7	11
Ward, Bryan	3.33	1	2	28	0	0	1	27	30	13	10	7	17
Simas, Bill	3.57	4	3	60	0	0	18	70⅔	54	29	28	22	56
Foulke, Keith	4.13	3	2	54	0	0	1	65⅓	51	31	30	20	57
Abbott, Jim	4.55	5	0	5	5	0	0	31⅓	35	16	16	12	14
Snyder, John	4.80	7	2	15	14	1	0	86⅓	96	49	46	23	52
Sirotka, Mike	5.06	14	*15	33	33	5	0	211⅓	255	137	119	47	128
Parque, Jim	5.10	7	5	21	21	0	0	113	135	72	64	49	77
Castillo, Carlos	5.11	6	4	54	2	0	0	100⅓	94	61	57	35	64
Baldwin, James	5.32	13	6	37	24	1	0	159	176	103	94	60	108
Eyre, Scott	5.38	3	8	33	17	0	0	107	114	78	64	64	73
Navarro, Jaime	6.36	8	16	37	27	1	1	172⅔	223	135	122	77	71

Cleveland Indians

BATTING

BATTING	BA	G	AB	R	H	TB	2B	3B	HR	RBI	SB	BB	SO
Wilson, Enrique	.322	32	90	13	29	41	6	0	2	12	2	4	8
Sexson, Richie	.310	49	174	28	54	103	14	1	11	35	1	6	42
Ramirez, Manny	.294	150	571	108	168	342	35	2	45	145	5	76	121
Thome, Jim	.293	123	440	89	129	257	34	2	30	85	1	90	141
Vizquel, Omar	.288	151	576	86	166	214	30	6	2	50	37	62	64
Fryman, Travis	.287	146	557	74	160	281	33	2	28	96	10	44	125
Whiten, Mark	.283	88	226	31	64	96	14	0	6	29	2	29	60
Lofton, Kenny	.282	154	600	101	169	248	31	6	12	64	54	87	80
Justice, David	.280	146	540	94	151	257	39	2	21	88	9	76	98
Cora, Joey	.276	155	602	111	166	223	27	6	6	32	15	73	59
Giles, Brian	.269	112	350	56	94	161	19	0	16	66	10	73	75
Manto, Jeff	.239	31	67	14	16	28	3	0	3	9	1	5	21
Borders, Pat	.238	54	160	12	38	44	6	0	0	6	0	10	40
Alomar, Sandy	.235	117	409	45	96	144	26	2	6	44	0	18	45
Branson, Jeff	.200	63	100	6	20	29	4	1	1	9	0	3	21

PITCHING

PITCHING	ERA	W	L	G	GS	CG	SV	INN	H	R	ER	BB	SO
Jackson, Mike	1.55	1	1	69	0	0	40	64	43	11	11	13	55
Shuey, Paul	3.00	5	4	43	0	0	2	51	44	19	17	25	58
Assenmacher, Paul	3.26	2	5	69	0	0	3	47	54	22	17	19	43
Jones, Doug	3.45	1	2	23	0	0	1	31⅓	34	12	12	6	28
Colon, Bartolo	3.71	14	9	31	31	6	0	204	205	91	84	79	158
Gooden, Dwight	3.76	8	6	23	23	0	0	134	135	59	56	51	83
Burba, Dave	4.11	15	10	32	31	0	0	203⅔	210	100	93	69	132
Wright, Jaret	4.72	12	10	32	32	1	0	192⅔	207	109	101	87	143
Nagy, Charles	5.22	15	10	33	33	2	0	210⅓	250	139	122	66	120
Ogea, Chad	5.61	5	4	19	9	0	0	69	74	44	43	25	43

Detroit Tigers

BATTING

BATTING	BA	G	AB	R	H	TB	2B	3B	HR	RBI	SB	BB	SO
Encarnacion, Juan	.329	40	164	30	54	92	9	4	7	21	7	7	31
Clark, Tony	.291	157	602	84	175	314	37	0	34	103	3	63	128
Higginson, Bob	.284	157	612	92	174	294	37	4	25	85	3	63	101
Catalanotto, Frank	.282	89	213	23	60	95	13	2	6	25	3	12	39
Bako, Paul	.272	96	305	23	83	106	12	1	3	30	1	23	82
Easley, Damion	.271	153	594	84	161	284	38	2	27	100	15	39	112
Gonzalez, Luis	.267	154	547	84	146	260	35	5	23	71	12	57	62
Cruz, Deivi	.260	135	454	52	118	161	22	3	5	45	8	13	55
Randa, Joe	.254	138	460	56	117	169	21	2	9	50	8	41	70
Hunter, Brian	.254	142	595	67	151	198	29	3	4	36	42	36	94
Alvarez, Gabe	.231	58	199	16	46	72	11	0	5	29	1	18	65
Berroa, Geronimo	.225	72	191	23	43	57	7	2	1	13	1	24	44

PITCHING

PITCHING	ERA	W	L	G	GS	CG	SV	INN	H	R	ER	BB	SO
Brocail, Doug	2.73	5	2	60	0	0	0	62⅔	47	23	19	18	55
Anderson, Matt	3.27	5	1	42	0	0	0	44	38	16	16	31	44
Runyan, Sean	3.58	1	4	88	0	0	1	50⅓	47	23	20	28	39
Moehler, Brian	3.90	14	13	33	33	4	0	221⅓	220	103	96	56	123
Thompson, Justin	4.05	11	15	34	34	5	0	222	227	114	100	79	149
Florie, Bryce	4.80	8	9	42	16	0	0	133	141	80	71	59	97
Jones, Todd	4.97	1	4	65	0	0	28	63⅓	58	38	35	36	57
Greisinger, Scott	5.12	6	9	21	21	0	0	130	142	79	74	48	66
Bochtler, Doug	6.15	0	2	51	0	0	0	67⅓	73	48	46	42	45
Powell, Brian	6.35	3	8	18	16	0	0	83⅔	101	67	59	36	46
Sager, A.J.	6.52	4	2	31	3	0	2	59⅓	79	47	43	23	23
Castillo, Frank	6.83	3	9	27	19	0	1	116	150	91	88	44	81

Kansas City Royals

BATTING	BA	G	AB	R	H	TB	2B	3B	HR	RBI	SB	BB	SO
Offerman, Jose	.315	158	607	102	191	266	28	13	7	66	45	89	96
Morris, Hal	.309	127	472	50	146	180	27	2	1	40	1	32	52
Palmer, Dean	.278	152	572	84	159	292	27	2	34	119	8	48	134
Mack, Shane	.278	69	209	31	58	93	15	1	6	29	8	15	36
Damon, Johnny	.277	161	642	104	178	282	30	10	18	66	26	58	84
King, Jeff	.263	131	486	83	128	219	17	1	24	93	10	42	73
Sweeney, Mike	.259	92	282	32	73	115	18	0	8	35	2	24	38
Pendleton, Terry	.257	79	237	17	61	80	10	0	3	29	1	15	49
Conine, Jeff	.256	93	309	30	79	129	26	0	8	43	3	26	68
Sutton, Larry	.245	111	310	29	76	109	14	2	5	42	3	29	46
Lopez, Mendy	.243	74	206	18	50	67	10	2	1	15	5	12	40
Dye, Jermaine	.234	60	214	24	50	72	5	1	5	23	2	11	46
Fasano, Sal	.227	74	216	21	49	83	10	0	8	31	1	10	56
Giambi, Jeremy	.224	18	58	6	13	23	4	0	2	8	0	11	9
Halter, Shane	.221	86	204	17	45	63	12	0	2	13	2	12	38

PITCHING	ERA	W	L	G	GS	CG	SV	INN	H	R	ER	BB	SO
Bones, Ricky	3.04	2	2	32	0	0	1	53⅓	49	18	18	24	38
Service, Scott	3.48	6	4	73	0	0	4	82⅔	70	35	32	34	95
Belcher, Tim	4.27	14	14	34	34	2	0	234	247	127	111	73	130
Rosado, Jose	4.69	8	11	38	25	2	1	174⅔	180	106	91	57	135
Whisenant, Matt	4.90	2	1	70	0	0	2	60⅔	61	37	33	33	45
Montgomery, Jeff	4.98	2	5	56	0	0	36	56	58	35	31	22	54
Pichardo, Hipolito	5.13	7	8	27	18	0	1	112½	126	73	64	43	55
Rapp, Pat	5.30	12	13	32	32	1	0	188⅓	208	117	111	107	132
Rusch, Glendon	5.88	6	15	29	24	1	1	154⅔	191	104	101	50	94
Pittsley, Jim	6.59	1	1	39	2	0	0	68½	88	56	50	37	44
Appier, Kevin	7.80	1	2	3	3	0	0	15	21	13	13	5	9

Minnesota Twins

BATTING	BA	G	AB	R	H	TB	2B	3B	HR	RBI	SB	BB	SO
Walker, Todd	.316	143	528	85	167	250	41	3	12	62	19	47	65
Nixon, Otis	.297	110	448	71	133	154	6	6	1	20	37	44	56
Molitor, Paul	.281	126	502	75	141	192	29	5	4	69	9	45	41
Lawton, Matt	.278	152	557	91	155	266	36	6	21	77	16	86	64
Ortiz, David	.277	86	278	47	77	124	20	0	9	46	1	39	72
Coomer, Ron	.276	137	529	54	146	215	22	1	15	72	2	18	72
Meares, Pat	.260	149	543	56	141	200	26	3	9	70	7	24	86
Ochoa, Alex	.257	94	249	35	64	88	14	2	2	25	6	10	35
Cordova, Marty	.253	119	438	52	111	165	20	2	10	69	3	50	103
Gates, Brent	.249	107	333	31	83	107	15	0	3	42	3	36	46
Steinbach, Terry	.242	124	422	45	102	173	25	2	14	54	0	38	89
Hocking, Denny	.202	110	198	32	40	57	6	1	3	15	2	16	44

PITCHING	ERA	W	L	G	GS	CG	SV	INN	H	R	ER	BB	SO
Trombley, Mike	3.63	6	5	77	1	0	1	96⅔	90	41	39	41	89
Miller, Travis	3.86	0	2	14	0	0	0	23⅓	25	10	10	11	23
Aguilera, Rick	4.24	4	9	68	0	0	38	74½	75	35	35	15	57
Radke, Brad	4.30	12	14	32	32	5	0	213⅔	238	109	102	43	146
Carrasco, Hector	4.38	4	2	63	0	0	1	61⅔	75	30	30	31	46
Guardado, Eddie	4.52	3	1	79	0	0	0	65⅔	66	34	33	28	53
Tewksbury, Bob	4.79	7	13	26	25	1	0	148½	174	82	79	20	60
Hawkins, LaTroy	5.25	7	14	33	33	0	0	190½	227	126	111	61	105
Milton, Eric	5.64	8	14	32	32	1	0	172½	195	113	108	70	107
Baptist, Travis	5.67	0	1	13	0	0	0	27	34	18	17	11	11
Serafini, Dan	6.48	7	4	28	9	0	0	75	95	58	54	29	46
Rodriguez, Frank	6.56	4	6	20	11	0	0	70	88	58	51	30	62

New York Yankees

BATTING	BA	G	AB	R	H	TB	2B	3B	HR	RBI	SB	BB	SO
Bush, Homer	.380	45	71	17	27	33	3	0	1	5	6	5	19
Spencer, Shane	.373	27	67	18	25	61	6	0	10	27	0	5	12
Williams, Bernie	.339	128	499	101	169	287	30	5	26	97	15	74	81
Jeter, Derek	.324	149	626	127	203	307	25	8	19	84	30	57	119
O'Neill, Paul	.317	152	602	95	191	307	40	2	24	116	15	57	103
Brosius, Scott	.300	152	530	86	159	250	34	0	19	98	11	52	97
Davis, Chili	.291	35	103	11	30	46	7	0	3	9	0	14	18
Raines, Tim	.290	109	321	53	93	123	13	1	5	47	8	55	49
Martinez, Tino	.281	142	531	92	149	268	33	1	28	123	2	61	83
Girardi, Joe	.276	78	254	31	70	98	11	4	3	31	2	14	38
Posada, Jorge	.268	111	358	56	96	170	23	0	17	63	0	47	92
Knoblauch, Chuck	.265	150	603	117	160	244	25	4	17	64	31	76	70
Strawberry, Darryl	.247	101	295	44	73	160	11	2	24	57	8	46	90
Curtis, Chad	.243	151	456	79	111	164	21	1	10	56	21	75	80

PITCHING	ERA	W	L	G	GS	CG	SV	INN	H	R	ER	BB	SO
Lloyd, Graeme	1.67	3	0	50	0	0	0	37⅔	26	10	7	6	20
Rivera, Mariano	1.91	3	0	54	0	0	36	61⅓	48	13	13	17	36
Hernandez, Orlando	3.13	12	4	21	21	3	0	141	113	53	49	52	131
Mendoza, Ramiro	3.25	10	2	41	14	1	1	130⅓	131	50	47	30	56
Holmes, Darren	3.33	0	3	34	0	0	2	51⅓	53	19	19	14	31
Wells, David	3.49	18	4	30	30	8	0	214⅓	195	86	83	29	163
Cone, David	3.55	20	7	31	31	3	0	207⅔	186	89	82	59	209
Nelson, Jeff	3.79	5	3	45	0	0	3	40⅓	44	18	17	22	35
Irabu, Hideki	4.06	13	9	29	28	2	0	173	148	79	78	76	126
Pettitte, Andy	4.24	16	11	33	32	5	0	216⅓	226	110	102	87	146
Stanton, Mike	5.47	4	1	67	0	0	6	79	71	51	48	26	69

Oakland Athletics

BATTING	BA	G	AB	R	H	TB	2B	3B	HR	RBI	SB	BB	SO
Magadan, Dave	.321	35	109	12	35	46	8	0	1	13	0	13	12
Giambi, Jason	.295	153	562	92	166	275	28	0	27	110	2	81	102
Stairs, Matt	.294	149	523	88	154	267	33	1	26	106	8	59	93
Grieve, Ben	.288	155	583	94	168	267	41	2	18	89	2	85	123
Roberts, Bip	.268	95	295	45	79	99	17	0	1	24	16	31	38
Spiezio, Scott	.259	114	406	54	105	153	19	1	9	50	1	44	56
Christenson, Ryan	.257	117	370	56	95	136	22	2	5	40	5	36	106
McDonald, Jason	.251	70	175	25	44	56	9	0	1	16	10	27	33
Macfarlane, Mike	.243	81	218	29	53	86	12	0	7	34	1	12	36
Blowers, Mike	.237	129	409	56	97	158	24	2	11	71	1	39	116
Henderson, Rickey	.236	152	542	101	128	188	16	1	14	57	66	118	114
Tejada, Miguel	.233	105	365	53	85	140	20	1	11	45	5	28	86
Hinch, A.J.	.231	120	337	34	78	115	10	0	9	35	3	30	89
Bournigal, Rafael	.225	85	209	23	47	61	11	0	1	19	6	10	11
Sprague, Ed	.221	132	469	57	104	189	25	0	20	58	1	26	90

PITCHING	ERA	W	L	G	GS	CG	SV	INN	H	R	ER	BB	SO
Heredia, Gil	2.74	3	3	8	6	0	0	42⅔	43	14	13	3	27
Rogers, Kenny	3.17	16	8	34	34	7	0	238⅔	215	96	84	67	138
Taylor, Billy	3.58	4	9	70	0	0	33	73	71	37	29	22	58
Telgheder, Dave	3.60	0	1	8	2	0	0	20	19	12	8	6	5
Groom, Buddy	4.24	3	1	75	0	0	0	57⅓	62	30	27	20	36
Mathews, T.J.	4.58	7	4	66	0	0	1	72⅔	71	44	37	29	53
Candiotti, Tom	4.84	11	16	33	33	3	0	201	222	124	108	63	98
Haynes, Jimmy	5.09	11	9	33	33	1	0	194⅓	229	124	110	88	134
Mohler, Mike	5.16	3	3	57	0	0	0	61	70	38	35	26	42
Worrell, Tim	5.24	2	7	43	9	0	0	103	106	62	60	29	82
Oquist, Mike	6.22	7	11	31	29	0	0	175	210	125	121	57	112
Stein, Blake	6.37	5	9	24	20	1	0	117⅓	117	92	83	71	89

Seattle Mariners

BATTING	BA	G	AB	R	H	TB	2B	3B	HR	RBI	SB	BB	SO
Martinez, Edgar	.322	154	556	86	179	314	46	1	29	102	1	106	96
Rodriguez, Alex	.310	161	686	123	213	384	35	5	42	124	46	45	121
Segui, David	.305	143	522	79	159	254	36	1	19	84	3	49	80
Griffey, Ken Jr.	.284	161	633	120	180	387	33	3	56	146	20	76	121
Amaral, Rich	.276	73	134	25	37	46	6	0	1	4	11	13	24
Bell, David	.274	128	420	48	115	178	29	2	10	49	0	27	62
Davis, Russ	.259	141	502	68	130	222	30	1	20	82	4	34	134
Ibanez, Raul	.255	37	98	12	25	40	7	1	2	12	0	5	22
Wilson, Dan	.252	96	325	39	82	128	17	1	9	44	2	24	56
Buhner, Jay	.242	72	244	33	59	113	7	1	15	45	0	38	71
Monahan, Shane	.242	62	211	17	51	73	8	1	4	28	1	8	53
Ducey, Rob	.240	97	217	30	52	89	18	2	5	23	4	23	61
Gipson, Charles	.235	44	51	11	12	13	1	0	0	2	2	5	9
Marzano, John	.233	50	133	13	31	52	7	1	4	12	0	9	24

PITCHING	ERA	W	L	G	GS	CG	SV	INN	H	R	ER	BB	SO
Timlin, Mike	2.95	3	3	70	0	0	0	79⅓	78	26	26	16	60
Moyer, Jamie	3.53	15	9	34	34	4	19	234⅓	234	99	92	42	158
Fassero, Jeff	3.97	13	12	32	32	7	0	224⅔	223	115	99	66	176
Johnson, Randy	4.33	9	10	23	23	6	0	160	146	90	77	60	213
McCarthy, Greg	5.01	1	2	29	0	0	0	23⅔	18	13	13	17	25
Slocumb, Heathcliff	5.32	2	5	57	0	0	6	67⅔	72	40	40	44	51
Swift, Bill	5.85	11	9	29	26	0	0	144⅔	183	103	94	51	77
Wells, Bob	6.10	2	2	30	0	0	0	51⅔	54	38	35	16	29
Cloude, Ken	6.37	8	10	30	30	0	0	155⅓	187	116	110	80	114
Spoljaric, Paul	6.48	4	6	53	6	0	0	83⅓	85	67	60	55	89
Ayala, Bobby	7.29	1	10	62	0	0	8	75⅓	100	66	61	26	68

Tampa Bay Devil Rays

BATTING	BA	G	AB	R	H	TB	2B	3B	HR	RBI	SB	BB	SO
Ledesma, Aaron	.324	95	299	30	97	119	16	3	0	29	9	9	9
McCracken, Quinton	.292	155	614	77	179	252	38	7	7	59	19	41	19
Trammell, Bubba	.286	59	199	28	57	113	18	1	12	35	0	16	0
McGriff, Fred	.284	151	564	73	160	250	33	0	19	81	7	79	7
Boggs, Wade	.280	123	435	51	122	174	23	4	7	52	3	46	3
Winn, Randy	.278	109	338	51	94	124	9	9	1	17	26	29	26
Smith, Bobby	.276	117	370	44	102	156	15	3	11	55	5	34	5
Cairo, Miguel	.268	150	515	49	138	189	26	5	5	46	19	24	19
Martinez, Dave	.256	90	309	31	79	99	11	0	3	20	8	35	8
Kelly, Mike	.240	106	279	39	67	112	11	2	10	33	13	22	13
DiFelice, Mike	.230	84	248	17	57	84	12	3	3	23	0	15	0
Butler, Rich	.226	72	217	25	49	79	3	3	7	20	4	15	4
Sorrento, Paul	.225	137	435	40	98	176	27	0	17	57	2	54	2

PITCHING	ERA	W	L	G	GS	CG	SV	INN	H	R	ER	BB	SO
Lopez, Albie	2.60	7	4	54	0	0	1	79⅔	73	31	23	32	62
Mecir, Jim	3.11	7	2	68	0	0	0	84	68	30	29	33	77
Arrojo, Rolando	3.56	14	12	32	32	2	0	202	195	84	80	65	152
Aldred, Scott	3.73	0	0	48	0	0	0	31⅔	33	13	13	12	21
White, Rick	3.80	2	6	38	3	0	0	68⅔	66	32	29	23	39
Yan, Esteban	3.86	5	4	64	0	0	1	88⅔	78	41	38	41	77
Hernandez, Roberto	4.04	2	6	67	0	0	26	71⅓	55	33	32	41	55
Saunders, Tony	4.12	6	15	31	31	2	0	192⅓	191	95	88	111	172
Santana, Julio	4.39	5	6	35	19	1	0	145⅔	151	77	71	62	61
Alvarez, Wilson	4.73	6	14	25	25	0	0	142⅔	130	78	75	68	107
Rekar, Bryan	4.98	2	8	16	15	1	0	86⅔	95	56	48	21	55
Springer, Dennis	5.45	3	11	29	17	1	0	115⅔	120	77	70	60	46

Texas Rangers

BATTING	BA	G	AB	R	H	TB	2B	3B	HR	RBI	SB	BB	SO
Kelly, Roberto	.323	75	257	48	83	144	7	3	16	46	0	8	46
Rodriguez, Ivan	.321	145	579	88	186	297	40	4	21	91	9	32	88
Gonzalez, Juan	.318	154	606	110	193	382	50	2	45	157	2	46	126
Haselman, Bill	.314	40	105	11	33	57	6	0	6	17	0	3	17
Greer, Rusty	.306	155	598	107	183	272	31	5	16	108	2	80	93
Clark, Will	.305	149	554	98	169	281	41	1	23	102	1	72	97
Simms, Mike	.296	86	186	36	55	114	11	0	16	46	0	24	47
Goodwin, Tom	.290	154	520	102	151	176	13	3	2	33	38	73	90
Clayton, Royce	.285	52	186	30	53	82	12	1	5	24	5	13	32
Alicea, Luis	.274	101	259	51	71	110	15	3	6	33	4	37	40
Stevens, Lee	.265	120	344	52	91	176	17	4	20	59	0	31	93
Cedeno, Domingo	.262	61	141	19	37	54	9	1	2	21	2	10	32
Zeile, Todd	.261	52	180	26	47	81	14	1	6	28	1	28	32
McLemore, Mark	.247	126	461	79	114	146	15	1	5	53	12	89	64

PITCHING	ERA	W	L	G	GS	CG	SV	INN	H	R	ER	BB	SO
Wetteland, John	2.03	3	1	63	0	0	42	62	47	17	14	14	72
Hernandez, Xavier	3.57	6	6	46	0	0	1	58	43	27	23	30	41
Crabtree, Tim	3.59	6	1	64	0	0	0	85½	86	40	34	35	60
Cadaret, Craig	4.23	1	2	50	0	0	1	44⅔	49	21	21	18	42
Sele, Aaron	4.23	19	11	33	33	3	0	212⅔	239	116	100	84	167
Stottlemyre, Todd	4.33	5	4	10	10	0	0	60½	68	33	29	30	57
Helling, Rick	4.41	20	7	33	33	4	0	216½	209	109	106	78	164
Patterson, Danny	4.45	2	5	56	0	0	2	60⅔	64	31	30	19	33
Levine, Al	4.50	0	1	30	0	0	0	58	68	30	29	16	19
Gunderson, Eric	5.19	0	3	68	1	0	0	67	88	43	39	19	41
Burkett, John	5.68	9	13	32	32	0	0	195	230	131	123	46	131

Toronto Blue Jays

BATTING	BA	G	AB	R	H	TB	2B	3B	HR	RBI	SB	BB	SO
Fernandez, Tony	.321	138	486	71	156	223	36	2	9	72	13	45	53
Santiago, Benito	.310	15	29	3	9	14	5	0	0	4	0	1	6
Dalesandro, Mark	.299	32	67	8	20	31	5	0	2	14	0	1	6
Delgado, Carlos	.292	142	530	94	155	314	43	1	38	115	3	73	139
Fletcher, Darrin	.283	124	407	37	115	167	23	1	9	52	0	25	39
Stewart, Shannon	.279	144	516	90	144	215	29	3	12	55	51	67	77
Green, Shawn	.278	158	630	106	175	321	33	4	35	100	35	50	142
Brown, Kevin	.264	52	110	17	29	44	7	1	2	15	0	9	31
Crespo, Felipe	.262	66	130	11	34	47	8	1	1	15	4	15	27
Grebeck, Craig	.256	102	301	33	77	104	17	2	2	27	2	29	42
Cruz, Jose Jr.	.253	105	352	55	89	142	14	3	11	42	11	57	99
Gonzalez, Juan	.239	158	568	70	136	205	28	1	13	51	21	28	121
Canseco, Jose	.237	151	583	98	138	302	26	0	46	107	29	65	159
Samuel, Juan	.180	43	50	14	9	14	2	0	1	2	13	7	13

PITCHING	ERA	W	L	G	GS	CG	SV	INN	H	R	ER	BB	SO
Quantrill, Paul	2.59	3	4	82	0	0	7	80	88	26	23	22	59
Clemens, Roger	2.65	20	6	33	33	5	0	234⅔	169	78	69	88	271
Escobar, Kelvim	3.73	7	3	22	10	0	0	79⅓	72	37	33	35	72
Plesac, Dan	3.78	4	3	78	0	0	4	50	41	23	21	16	55
Carpenter, Chris	4.37	12	7	33	24	1	0	175	177	97	85	61	136
Williams, Woody	4.46	10	9	32	32	1	0	209⅔	196	112	104	81	151
Steib, Dave	4.83	1	2	19	3	0	2	50⅓	58	31	27	17	27
Hentgen, Pat	5.17	12	11	29	29	0	0	177⅔	208	109	102	69	94
Risley, Bill	5.27	3	4	44	0	0	0	54⅔	52	37	32	34	42
Almanzar, Carlos	5.34	2	2	25	0	0	0	28⅓	34	18	17	8	20
Person, Robert	7.04	3	1	27	0	0	6	38⅓	45	31	30	22	31

FOR THE RECORD·Year by Year

The World Series

Results

1903	Boston (A) 5, Pittsburgh (N) 3
1904	No series
1905	New York (N) 4, Philadelphia (A) 1
1906	Chicago (A) 4, Chicago (N) 2
1907	Chicago (N) 4, Detroit (A) 0; 1 tie
1908	Chicago (N) 4, Detroit (A) 1
1909	Pittsburgh (N) 4, Detroit (A) 3
1910	Philadelphia (A) 4, Chicago (N) 1
1911	Philadelphia (A) 4, New York (N) 2
1912	Boston (A) 4, New York (N) 3; 1 tie
1913	Philadelphia (A) 4, New York (N) 1
1914	Boston (N) 4, Philadelphia (A) 0
1915	Boston (A) 4, Philadelphia (N) 1
1916	Boston (A) 4, Brooklyn (N) 1
1917	Chicago (A) 4, New York (N) 2
1918	Boston (A) 4, Chicago (N) 2
1919	Cincinnati (N) 5, Chicago (A) 3
1920	Cleveland (A) 5, Brooklyn (N) 2
1921	New York (N) 5, New York (A) 3
1922	New York (N) 4, New York (A) 0; 1 tie
1923	New York (A) 4, New York (N) 2
1924	Washington (A) 4, New York (N) 3
1925	Pittsburgh (N) 4, Washington (A) 3
1926	St. Louis (N) 4, New York (A) 3
1927	New York (A) 4, Pittsburgh (N) 0
1928	New York (A) 4, St. Louis (N) 0
1929	Philadelphia (A) 4, Chicago (N) 1
1930	Philadelphia (A) 4, St. Louis (N) 2
1931	St. Louis (N) 4, Philadelphia (A) 3
1932	New York (A) 4, Chicago (N) 0
1933	New York (N) 4, Washington (A) 1
1934	St. Louis (N) 4, Detroit (A) 3
1935	Detroit (A) 4, Chicago (N) 2
1936	New York (A) 4, New York (N) 2
1937	New York (A) 4, New York (N) 1
1938	New York (A) 4, Chicago (N) 0
1939	New York (A) 4, Cincinnati (N) 0
1940	Cincinnati (N) 4, Detroit (A) 3
1941	New York (A) 4, Brooklyn (N) 1
1942	St. Louis (N) 4, New York (A) 1
1943	New York (A) 4, St. Louis (N) 1
1944	St. Louis (N) 4, St. Louis (A) 2
1945	Detroit (A) 4, Chicago (N) 3
1946	St. Louis (N) 4, Boston (A) 3
1947	New York (A) 4, Brooklyn (N) 3
1948	Cleveland (A) 4, Boston (N) 2
1949	New York (A) 4, Brooklyn (N) 1
1950	New York (A) 4, Philadelphia (N) 0
1951	New York (A) 4, New York (N) 2
1952	New York (A) 4, Brooklyn (N) 3
1953	New York (A) 4, Brooklyn (N) 2
1954	New York (N) 4, Cleveland (A) 0
1955	Brooklyn (N) 4, New York (A) 3
1956	New York (A) 4, Brooklyn (N) 3
1957	Milwaukee (N) 4, New York (A) 3
1958	New York (A) 4, Milwaukee (N) 3
1959	Los Angeles (N) 4, Chicago (A) 2
1960	Pittsburgh (N) 4, New York (A) 3
1961	New York (A) 4, Cincinnati (N) 1
1962	New York (A) 4, San Francisco (N) 3
1963	Los Angeles (N) 4, New York (A) 0
1964	St. Louis (N) 4, New York (A) 3
1965	Los Angeles (N) 4, Minnesota (A) 3
1966	Baltimore (A) 4, Los Angeles (N) 0
1967	St. Louis (N) 4, Boston (A) 3
1968	Detroit (A) 4, St. Louis (N) 3
1969	New York (N) 4, Baltimore (A) 1
1970	Baltimore (A) 4, Cincinnati (N) 1
1971	Pittsburgh (N) 4, Baltimore (A) 3
1972	Oakland (A) 4, Cincinnati (N) 3
1973	Oakland (A) 4, New York (N) 3
1974	Oakland (A) 4, Los Angeles (N) 1
1975	Cincinnati (N) 4, Boston (A) 3
1976	Cincinnati (N) 4, New York (A) 0
1977	New York (A) 4, Los Angeles (N) 2
1978	New York (A) 4, Los Angeles (N) 2
1979	Pittsburgh (N) 4, Baltimore (A) 3
1980	Philadelphia (N) 4, Kansas City (A) 2
1981	Los Angeles (N) 4, New York (A) 2
1982	St. Louis (N) 4, Milwaukee (A) 3
1983	Baltimore (A) 4, Philadelphia (N) 1
1984	Detroit (A) 4, San Diego (N) 1
1985	Kansas City (A) 4, St. Louis (N) 3
1986	New York (N) 4, Boston (A) 3
1987	Minnesota (A) 4, St. Louis (N) 3
1988	Los Angeles (N) 4, Oakland (A) 1
1989	Oakland (A) 4, San Francisco (N) 0
1990	Cincinnati (N) 4, Oakland (A) 0
1991	Minnesota (A) 4, Atlanta (N) 3
1992	Toronto (A) 4, Atlanta (N) 2
1993	Toronto (A) 4, Philadelphia (N) 2
1994	Series canceled due to players' strike
1995	Atlanta (N) 4, Cleveland (A) 2
1996	New York (A) 4, Atlanta (N) 2
1997	Florida (N) 4, Cleveland (A) 3
1998	New York (A) 4, San Diego (N) 0

THEY SAID IT

Tommy Lasorda, Los Angeles Dodgers general manager, explaining during an appearance before the U.S. Senate in support of a constitutional amendment to ban flag burning why that act of protest is not protected by the First Amendment:
"Freedom of speech is when you talk."

Most Valuable Players

1955	Johnny Podres, Bklyn
1956	Don Larsen, NY (A)
1957	Lew Burdette, Mil
1958	Bob Turley, NY (A)
1959	Larry Sherry, LA
1960	Bobby Richardson, NY (A)
1961	Whitey Ford, NY (A)
1962	Ralph Terry, NY (A)
1963	Sandy Koufax, LA
1964	Bob Gibson, StL
1965	Sandy Koufax, LA
1966	Frank Robinson, Balt
1967	Bob Gibson, StL
1968	Mickey Lolich, Det
1969	Donn Clendenon, NY (N)
1970	Brooks Robinson, Balt
1971	Roberto Clemente, Pitt
1972	Gene Tenace, Oak
1973	Reggie Jackson, Oak
1974	Rollie Fingers, Oak
1975	Pete Rose, Cin
1976	Johnny Bench, Cin
1977	Reggie Jackson, NY (A)

1978	Bucky Dent, NY (A)
1979	Willie Stargell, Pitt
1980	Mike Schmidt, Phil
1981	Ron Cey, LA
	Pedro Guerrero, LA
	Steve Yeager, LA
1982	Darrell Porter, StL
1983	Rick Dempsey, Balt
1984	Alan Trammell, Det
1985	Bret Saberhagen, KC
1986	Ray Knight, NY (N)
1987	Frank Viola, Minn
1988	Orel Hershiser, LA
1989	Dave Stewart, Oak
1990	Jose Rijo, Cin
1991	Jack Morris, Minn
1992	Pat Borders, Tor
1993	Paul Molitor, Tor
1994	Series canceled due to strike
1995	Tom Glavine, Atl
1996	John Wetteland, NY (A)
1997	Livan Hernandez, Fla
1998	Scott Brosius, NY (A)

Career Batting Leaders (Minimum 50 at bats)

GAMES

Pogi Berra	75
Mickey Mantle	65
Elston Howard	54
Hank Bauer	53
Gil McDougald	53
Phil Rizzuto	52
Joe DiMaggio	51
Frankie Frisch	50
Pee Wee Reese	44
Roger Maris	41
Babe Ruth	41

AT BATS

Yogi Berra	259
Mickey Mantle	230
Joe DiMaggio	199
Frankie Frisch	197
Gil McDougald	190
Hank Bauer	188
Phil Rizzuto	183
Elston Howard	171
Pee Wee Reese	169
Roger Maris	152

HITS

Yogi Berra	71
Mickey Mantle	59
Frankie Frisch	58
Joe DiMaggio	54
Pee Wee Reese	46
Hank Bauer	46
Phil Rizzuto	45
Gil McDougald	45
Lou Gehrig	43
Eddie Collins	42
Babe Ruth	42
Elston Howard	42

BATTING AVERAGE

Pepper Martin	.418
Paul Molitor	.418
Lou Brock	.391
Marquis Grissom	.390
Thurman Munson	.373
George Brett	.373
Hank Aaron	.364
Frank Baker	.363
Roberto Clemente	.362
Lou Gehrig	.361

HOME RUNS

Mickey Mantle	18
Babe Ruth	15
Yogi Berra	12
Duke Snider	11
Reggie Jackson	10
Lou Gehrig	10
Frank Robinson	8
Bill Skowron	8
Joe DiMaggio	8
Goose Goslin	7
Hank Bauer	7
Gil McDougald	7

RUNS BATTED IN

Mickey Mantle	40
Yogi Berra	39
Lou Gehrig	35
Babe Ruth	33
Joe DiMaggio	30
Bill Skowron	29
Duke Snider	26
Reggie Jackson	24
Bill Dickey	24
Hank Bauer	24
Gil McDougald	24

RUNS

Mickey Mantle	42
Yogi Berra	41
Babe Ruth	37
Lou Gehrig	30
Joe DiMaggio	27
Roger Maris	26
Elston Howard	25
Gil McDougald	23
Jackie Robinson	22
Gene Woodling	21
Reggie Jackson	21
Duke Snider	21
Phil Rizzuto	21
Hank Bauer	21

STOLEN BASES

Lou Brock	14
Eddie Collins	14
Frank Chance	10
Davey Lopes	10
Phil Rizzuto	10
Honus Wagner	9
Frankie Frisch	9
Johnny Evers	8
Pepper Martin	7
Joe Morgan	7
Rickey Henderson	7

TOTAL BASES

Mickey Mantle	123
Yogi Berra	117
Babe Ruth	96
Lou Gehrig	87
Joe DiMaggio	84
Duke Snider	79
Hank Bauer	75
Reggie Jackson	74
Frankie Frisch	74
Gil McDougald	72

Career Batting Leaders (Cont.)

SLUGGING AVERAGE

Reggie Jackson	.755
Babe Ruth	.744
Lou Gehrig	.731
Al Simmons	.658
Lou Brock	.655
Paul Molitor	.636
Pepper Martin	.636
Hank Greenberg	.624
Charlie Keller	.611
Jimmie Foxx	.609
Dave Henderson	.606

STRIKEOUTS

Mickey Mantle	54
Elston Howard	37
Duke Snider	33
Babe Ruth	30
Gil McDougald	29
Bill Skowron	26
Hank Bauer	25
Reggie Jackson	24
Bob Meusel	24
Frank Robinson	23
George Kelly	23
Tony Kubek	23
Joe DiMaggio	23

Career Pitching Leaders

GAMES

Whitey Ford	22
Rollie Fingers	16
Allie Reynolds	15
Bob Turley	15
Clay Carroll	14
Clem Labine	13
Waite Hoyt	12
Catfish Hunter	12
Art Nehf	12
Paul Derringer	11
Carl Erskine	11
Rube Marquard	11
Christy Mathewson	11
Vic Raschi	11

INNINGS PITCHED

Whitey Ford	146
Christy Mathewson	101⅔
Red Ruffing	85⅔
Chief Bender	85
Waite Hoyt	83⅔
Bob Gibson	81
Art Nehf	79
Allie Reynolds	77
Jim Palmer	65
Catfish Hunter	63

WINS

Whitey Ford	10
Bob Gibson	7
Red Ruffing	7
Allie Reynolds	7
Lefty Gomez	6
Chief Bender	6
Waite Hoyt	6
Jack Coombs	5
Three Finger Brown	5
Herb Pennock	5
Christy Mathewson	5
Vic Raschi	5
Catfish Hunter	5

LOSSES

Whitey Ford	8
Eddie Plank	5
Schoolboy Rowe	5
Joe Bush	5
Rube Marquard	5
Christy Mathewson	5

SAVES

Rollie Fingers	6
Allie Reynolds	4
Johnny Murphy	4
John Wetteland	4
Roy Face	3
Herb Pennock	3
Kent Tekulve	3
Firpo Marberry	3
Will McEnaney	3
Todd Worrell	3
Tug McGraw	3

*EARNED RUN AVERAGE

Jack Billingham	.36
Harry Brecheen	.83
Babe Ruth	.87
Sherry Smith	.89
Sandy Koufax	.95
Hippo Vaughn	1.00
Monte Pearson	1.01
Christy Mathewson	1.15
Babe Adams	1.29
Eddie Plank	1.32

SHUTOUTS

Christy Mathewson	4
Three Finger Brown	3
Whitey Ford	3
Bill Hallahan	2
Lew Burdette	2
Bill Dinneen	2
Sandy Koufax	2
Allie Reynolds	2
Art Nehf	2
Bob Gibson	2

COMPLETE GAMES

Christy Mathewson	10
Chief Bender	9
Bob Gibson	8
Red Ruffing	7
Whitey Ford	7
George Mullin	6
Eddie Plank	6
Art Nehf	6
Waite Hoyt	6

STRIKEOUTS

Whitey Ford	94
Bob Gibson	92
Allie Reynolds	62
Sandy Koufax	61
Red Ruffing	61
Chief Bender	59
George Earnshaw	56
Waite Hoyt	49
Christy Mathewson	48
Bob Turley	46

BASES ON BALLS

Whitey Ford	34
Allie Reynolds	32
Art Nehf	32
Jim Palmer	31
Bob Turley	29
Paul Derringer	27
Red Ruffing	27
Don Gullett	26
Burleigh Grimes	26
Vic Raschi	25

*Minimum 25 innings pitched.

Alltime Team Rankings (by championships)

Team	W	L	Appearances	Pct.	Most Recent	Last Championship
New York Yankees	24	11	35	.686	1998	1998
Phil/K.C./Oakland Athletics	9	5	14	.643	1990	1989
St. Louis Cardinals	9	6	15	.600	1987	1982
Brooklyn/L.A. Dodgers	6	12	18	.333	1988	1988
Pittsburgh Pirates	5	2	7	.714	1979	1979
Cincinnati Reds	5	4	9	.556	1990	1990
Boston Red Sox	5	4	9	.556	1986	1918
New York/San Francisco Giants	5	11	16	.313	1989	1954
Detroit Tigers	4	5	9	.444	1984	1984
Washington/Minnesota Twins	3	3	6	.500	1991	1991
St. Louis/Baltimore Orioles	3	4	7	.429	1983	1983
Boston/Milwaukee/Atlanta Braves	3	5	8	.375	1996	1995
Toronto Blue Jays	2	0	2	1.000	1993	1993
New York Mets	2	1	3	.667	1986	1986
Chicago White Sox	2	2	4	.500	1959	1917
Cleveland Indians	2	3	5	.400	1997	1948
Chicago Cubs	2	8	10	.200	1945	1908
Florida Marlins	1	0	1	1.000	1997	1997
Kansas City Royals	1	1	2	.500	1985	1985
Philadelphia Phillies	1	4	5	.200	1993	1980
Seattle/Milwaukee Brewers	0	1	1	.000	1982	—
San Diego Padres	0	2	2	.000	1998	—

League Championship Series

National League

1969 .... New York (E) 3, Atlanta (W) 0
1970 .... Cincinnati (W) 3, Pittsburgh (E) 0
1971 .... Pittsburgh (E) 3, San Francisco (W) 1
1972 .... Cincinnati (W) 3, Pittsburgh (E) 2
1973 .... New York (E) 3, Cincinnati (W) 2
1974 .... Los Angeles (W) 3, Pittsburgh (E) 1
1975 .... Cincinnati (W) 3, Pittsburgh (E) 0
1976 .... Cincinnati (W) 3, Philadelphia (E) 0
1977 .... Los Angeles (W) 3, Philadelphia (E) 1
1978 .... Los Angeles (W) 3, Philadelphia (E) 1
1979 .... Pittsburgh (E) 3, Cincinnati (W) 0
1980 .... Philadelphia (E) 3, Houston (W) 2
1981 .... Los Angeles (W) 3, Montreal (E) 2
1982 .... St. Louis (E) 3, Atlanta (W) 0
1983 .... Philadelphia (E) 3, Los Angeles (W) 1
1984 .... San Diego (W) 3, Chicago (E) 2
1985 .... St. Louis (E) 4, Los Angeles (W) 2
1986 .... New York (E) 4, Houston (W) 2
1987 .... St. Louis (E) 4, San Francisco (W) 3
1988 .... Los Angeles (W) 4, New York (E) 3
1989 .... San Francisco (W) 4, Chicago (E) 1
1990 .... Cincinnati (W) 4, Pittsburgh (E) 2
1991 .... Atlanta (W) 4, Pittsburgh (E) 3
1992 .... Atlanta (W) 4, Pittsburgh (E) 3
1993 .... Philadelphia (E) 4, Atlanta (W) 2
1994 .... Playoffs canceled due to players' strike
1995 .... Atlanta (E) 4, Cincinnati (C) 0
1996 .... Atlanta (E) 4, St. Louis (C) 3
1997 .... Florida (wc) 4, Atlanta (E) 2
1998 .... San Diego (W) 4, Atlanta (E) 2

American League

1969 .... Baltimore (E) 3, Minnesota (W) 0
1970 .... Baltimore (E) 3, Minnesota (W) 0
1971 .... Baltimore (E) 3, Oakland (W) 0
1972 .... Oakland (W) 3, Detroit (E) 2
1973 .... Oakland (W) 3, Baltimore (E) 2
1974 .... Oakland (W) 3, Baltimore (E) 1
1975 .... Boston (E) 3, Oakland (W) 0
1976 .... New York (E) 3, Kansas City (W) 2
1977 .... New York (E) 3, Kansas City (W) 2
1978 .... New York (E) 3, Kansas City (W) 1
1979 .... Baltimore (E) 3, California (W) 1
1980 .... Kansas City (W) 3, New York (E) 0
1981 .... New York (E) 3, Oakland (W) 0
1982 .... Milwaukee (E) 3, California (W) 2
1983 .... Baltimore (E) 3, Chicago (W) 1
1984 .... Detroit (E) 3, Kansas City (W) 0
1985 .... Kansas City (W) 4, Toronto (E) 3
1986 .... Boston (E) 4, California (W) 3
1987 .... Minnesota (W) 4, Detroit (E) 1
1988 .... Oakland (W) 4, Boston (E) 0
1989 .... Oakland (W) 4, Toronto (E) 1
1990 .... Oakland (W) 4, Boston (E) 0
1991 .... Minnesota (W) 4, Toronto (E) 1
1992 .... Toronto (E) 4, Oakland (W) 2
1993 .... Toronto (E) 4, Chicago (W) 2
1994 .... Playoffs canceled due to players' strike
1995 .... Cleveland (C) 4, Seattle (W) 2
1996 .... New York (E) 4, Baltimore (wc) 1
1997 .... Cleveland (C) 4, Baltimore (E) 2
1998 .... New York (E) 4, Cleveland (C) 2

NLCS Most Valuable Player

1977 .... Dusty Baker, LA
1978 .... Steve Garvey, LA
1979 .... Willie Stargell, Pitt
1980 .... Manny Trillo, Phil
1981 .... Burt Hooton, LA
1982 .... Darrell Porter, StL
1983 .... Gary Matthews, Phil
1984 .... Steve Garvey, SD

1985 .... Ozzie Smith, StL
1986 .... Mike Scott, Hou
1987 .... Jeffrey Leonard, SF
1988 .... Orel Hershiser, LA
1989 .... Will Clark, SF
1990 .... Randy Myers, Cin
            Rob Dibble, Cin
1991 .... Steve Avery, Atl

1992 .... John Smoltz, Atl
1993 .... Curt Schilling, Phil
1994 .... Playoffs canceled
1995 .... Mike Devereaux, Atl
1996 .... Javier Lopez, Atl
1997 .... Livan Hernandez, Fla
1998 .... Sterling Hitchcock, SD

ALCS Most Valuable Player

1980.......Frank White, KC	1987.......Gary Gaetti, Minn	1994.......Playoffs canceled
1981.......Graig Nettles, NY	1988.......Dennis Eckersley, Oak	1995.......Orel Hershiser, Clev
1982.......Fred Lynn, Calif	1989.......Rickey Henderson, Oak	1996.......Bernie Williams, NY
1983.......Mike Boddicker, Balt	1990.......Dave Stewart, Oak	1997.......Marquis Grissom, Clev
1984.......Kirk Gibson, Det	1991.......Kirby Puckett, Minn	1998.......David Wells, NY
1985.......George Brett, KC	1992.......Roberto Alomar, Tor	
1986.......Marty Barrett, Bos	1993.......Dave Stewart, Tor	

Divisional Playoffs

National League

1995 ....Atlanta (E) 3, Colorado (wc) 1	
	Cincinnati (C) 3, Los Angeles (W) 0
1996 ....St. Louis (C) 3, San Diego (W) 0	
	Atlanta (E) 3, Los Angeles (wc) 0
1997 ....Atlanta (E) 3, Houston (C) 0	
	Florida (wc) 3, San Francisco (W) 0
1998 ....San Diego (W) 3, Houston (C) 1	
	Atlanta (E) 3, Chicago (wc) 0

American League

1995 ....Cleveland (C) 3, Boston (E) 0	
	Seattle (W) 3, New York (wc) 2
1996 ....Baltimore (wc) 3, Cleveland (C) 1	
	New York (E) 3, Texas (W) 1
1997 ....Baltimore 3, Seattle (W) 1	
	Cleveland (C) 3, New York (wc) 2
1998 ....New York (E) 3, Texas (W) 0	
	Cleveland (C) 3, Boston (wc) 1

The All Star Game

Results

Date	Winner	Score	Site	Date	Winner	Score	Site
7-6-33	American	4–2	Comiskey Park, Chi	7-8-52	National	3–2	Shibe Park, Phil
7-10-34	American	9–7	Polo Grounds, NY	7-14-53	National	5–1	Crosley Field, Cin
7-8-35	American	4–1	Municipal Stadium, Clev	7-13-54	American	11–9	Municipal Stadium, Clev
7-7-36	National	4–3	Braves Field, Bos	7-12-55	National	6–5	County Stadium, Mil
7-7-37	American	8–3	Griffith Stadium, Wash	7-10-56	National	7–3	Griffith Stadium, Wash
7-6-38	National	4–1	Crosley Field, Cin	7-9-57	American	6–5	Busch Stadium, StL
7-11-39	American	3–1	Yankee Stadium, NY	7-8-58	American	4–3	Memorial Stadium, Balt
7-10-40	National	4–0	Sportsman's Park, StL	7-7-59	National	5–4	Forbes Field, Pitt
7-8-41	American	7–5	Briggs Stadium, Det	8-3-59	American	5–3	Memorial Coliseum, LA
7-6-42	American	3–1	Polo Grounds, NY	7-11-60	National	5–3	Municipal Stadium, KC
7-13-43	American	5–3	Shibe Park, Phil	7-13-60	National	6–0	Yankee Stadium, NY
7-11-44	National	7–1	Forbes Field, Pitt	7-11-61	National	5–4	Candlestick Park, SF
1945	No game due to wartime travel restrictions			7-31-61	Tie*	1–1	Fenway Park, Bos
7-9-46	American	12–0	Fenway Park, Bos	7-10-62	National	3–1	D.C. Stadium, Wash
7-8-47	American	2–1	Wrigley Field, Chi	7-30-62	American	9–4	Wrigley Field, Chi
7-13-48	American	5–2	Sportsman's Park, StL	7-9-63	National	5–3	Municipal Stadium, Clev
7-12-49	American	11–7	Ebbets Field, Bklyn	7-7-64	National	7–4	Shea Stadium, NY
7-11-50	National	4–3	Comiskey Park, Chi	7-13-65	National	6–5	Metropolitan Stadium, Minn
7-10-51	National	8–3	Briggs Stadium, Det				

*Game called because of rain after 9 innings.

Endgame

Even iron has a melting point. Morning newspapers landed a little harder on America's doorsteps on Sept. 21, 1998, with the affirmation of the scientific reality one man kept suspended for more than 16 years. It was there in the Baltimore Orioles' boxscore, the first one since the second game of a May 29, 1982, doubleheader that didn't include Cal Ripken Jr. An elegy in agate.

In perfect health except for a weariness of what he has called "the management" of his remarkable record of consecutive games,

Ripken chose on Sunday, Sept. 20, to sit out the Orioles' last home game of the season. Calibrate Ripken Jr.: 2,632 is baseball's newest magic number.

The Streak was a triumph more of his will than his considerable skill. DiMaggio's 56-game hitting streak, by comparison, was more artful. But like DiMaggio, the Iron Man carried himself with unfailing class, even when the temperature around him soared to 1,535°C. What greater legacy can a ballplayer leave than that?

Results *(Cont.)*

Date	Winner	Score	Site	Date	Winner	Score	Site
7-12-66	National	2–1	Busch Stadium, StL	7-6-83	American	13–3	Comiskey Park, Chi
7-11-67	National	2–1	Anaheim Stadium, Cal	7-10-84	National	3–1	Candlestick Park, SF
7-9-68	National	1–0	Astrodome, Hou	7-16-85	National	6–1	Metrodome, Minn
7-23-69	National	9–3	R.F.K. Memorial	7-15-86	American	3–2	Astrodome, Hou
			Stadium, Wash	7-14-87	National	2–0	Oakland Coliseum, Oak
7-14-70	National	5–4	Riverfront Stadium, Cin	7-12-88	American	2–1	Riverfront Stadium, Cin
7-13-71	American	6–4	Tiger Stadium, Det	7-11-89	American	5–3	Anaheim Stadium, Cal
7-25-72	National	4–3	Atlanta Stadium, Atl	7-10-90	American	2–0	Wrigley Field, Chi
7-24-73	National	7–1	Royals Stadium, KC	7-9-91	American	4–2	SkyDome, Tor
7-23-74	National	7–2	Three Rivers Stadium, Pitt	7-14-92	American	13–6	Jack Murphy Stadium, SD
7-15-75	National	6–3	County Stadium, Mil	7-13-93	American	9–3	Camden Yards, Balt
7-13-76	National	7–1	Veterans Stadium, Phil	7-12-94	National	8–7	Three Rivers Stadium, Pitt
7-19-77	National	7–5	Yankee Stadium, NY	7-11-95	National	3–2	The Ballpark in
7-11-78	National	7–3	Jack Murphy Stadium, SD				Arlington, Tex
7-17-79	National	7–6	Kingdome, Sea	7-9-96	National	6–0	Veterans Stadium, Phil
7-8-80	National	4–2	Dodger Stadium, LA	7-8-97	American	3–1	Jacobs Field, Clev
8-9-81	National	5–4	Municipal Stadium, Clev	7-7-98	American	13–8	Coors Field, Col
7-13-82	National	4–1	Olympic Stadium, Mtl				

Most Valuable Players

1962	Maury Wills, LA	NL	1974	Steve Garvey, LA	NL	1986	Roger Clemens, Bos	AL
	Leon Wagner, LA	AL	1975	Bill Madlock, Chi	NL	1987	Tim Raines, Mtl	NL
1963	Willie Mays, SF	NL		Jon Matlack, NY	NL	1988	Terry Steinbach, Oak	AL
1964	Johnny Callison, Phil	NL	1976	George Foster, Cin	NL	1989	Bo Jackson, KC	AL
1965	Juan Marichal, SF	NL	1977	Don Sutton, LA	NL	1990	Julio Franco, Tex	AL
1966	Brooks Robinson, Balt	AL	1978	Steve Garvey, LA	NL	1991	Cal Ripken Jr, Balt	AL
1967	Tony Perez, Cin	NL	1979	Dave Parker, Pitt	NL	1992	Ken Griffey Jr, Sea	AL
1968	Willie Mays, SF	NL	1980	Ken Griffey, Cin	NL	1993	Kirby Puckett, Minn	AL
1969	Willie McCovey, SF	NL	1981	Gary Carter, Mtl	NL	1994	Fred McGriff, Atl	NL
1970	Carl Yastrzemski, Bos	AL	1982	Dave Concepcion, Cin	NL	1995	Jeff Conine, Fla	NL
1971	Frank Robinson, Balt	AL	1983	Fred Lynn, Calif	AL	1996	Mike Piazza, LA	NL
1972	Joe Morgan, Cin	NL	1984	Gary Carter, Mtl	NL	1997	Sandy Alomar, Clev	AL
1973	Bobby Bonds, SF	NL	1985	LaMarr Hoyt, SD	NL	1998	Roberto Alomar, Balt	AL

The Regular Season

Most Valuable Players

NATIONAL LEAGUE

Year	Name and Team	Position	Noteworthy
1911	Wildfire Schulte, Chi	Outfield	21 HR†, 121 RBI†, .300
1912	*Larry Doyle, NY	Second base	10 HR, 90 RBI, .330
1913	Jake Daubert, Bklyn	First base	52 RBI, .350†
1914	*Johnny Evers, Bos	Second base	F.A. .976†, .279
1915–23	No selection		
1924	Dazzy Vance, Bklyn	Pitcher	28†–6, 2.16 ERA†, 262 K†
1925	Rogers Hornsby, StL	Second base, Manager	39 HR†, 143 RBI†, .403†
1926	*Bob O'Farrell, StL	Catcher	7 HR, 68 RBI, .293
1927	*Paul Waner, Pitt	Outfield	237 hits†, 131 RBI†, .380†
1928	*Jim Bottomley, StL	First base	31 HR†, 136 RBI†, .325
1929	*Rogers Hornsby, Chi	Second base	39 HR, 149 RBI, 156 runs†, .380
1930	No selection		
1931	*Frankie Frisch, StL	Second base	4 HR, 82 RBI, 28 SB†, .311
1932	Chuck Klein, Phil	Outfield	38 HR†, 137 RBI, 226 hits†, .348
1933	*Carl Hubbell, NY	Pitcher	23†–12, 1.66 ERA†, 10 SO†
1934	*Dizzy Dean, StL	Pitcher	30†–7, 2.66 ERA, 195 K†
1935	*Gabby Hartnett, Chi	Catcher	13 HR, 91 RBI, .344
1936	*Carl Hubbell, NY	Pitcher	26†–6, 2.31 ERA†
1937	Joe Medwick, StL	Outfield	31 HR†, 154 RBI†, 111 runs†, .374†
1938	Ernie Lombardi, Cin	Catcher	19 HR, 95 RBI, .342†

*Played for pennant or, after 1968, division winner. †Led league. ‡Tied for league lead.

Most Valuable Players *(Cont.)*

NATIONAL LEAGUE *(Cont.)*

Year	Name and Team	Position	Noteworthy
1939	*Bucky Walters, Cin	Pitcher	27†–11, 2.29 ERA†, 137 K‡
1940	*Frank McCormick, Cin	First base	19 HR, 127 RBI, 191 hits†, .309
1941	*Dolph Camilli, Bklyn	First base	34 HR†, 120 RBI†, .285
1942	*Mort Cooper, StL	Pitcher	22†–7, 1.78 ERA†, 10 SO†
1943	*Stan Musial, StL	Outfield	13 HR, 81 RBI, 220 hits†, .357†
1944	*Marty Marion, StL	Shortstop	F.A. .972†, 63 RBI
1945	*Phil Cavarretta, Chi	First base	6 HR, 97 RBI, .355†
1946	*Stan Musial, StL	First base, Outfield	103 RBI, 124 runs†, 228 hits†, .365†
1947	Bob Elliott, Bos	Third base	22 HR, 113 RBI, .317
1948	Stan Musial, StL	Outfield	39 HR, 131 RBI†, .376†
1949	*Jackie Robinson, Bklyn	Second base	16 HR, 124 RBI, 37 SB†, .342†
1950	*Jim Konstanty, Phil	Pitcher	16–7, 22 saves†, 2.66 ERA
1951	Roy Campanella, Bklyn	Catcher	33 HR, 108 RBI, .325
1952	Hank Sauer, Chi	Outfield	37 HR‡, 121 RBI†, .270
1953	*Roy Campanella, Bklyn	Catcher	41 HR, 142 RBI†, .312
1954	*Willie Mays, NY	Outfield	41 HR, 110 RBI, 13 3B†, .345†
1955	*Roy Campanella, Bklyn	Catcher	32 HR, 107 RBI, .318
1956	*Don Newcombe, Bklyn	Pitcher	27†–7, 3.06 ERA
1957	*Hank Aaron, Mil	Outfield	44 HR†, 132 RBI†, .322
1958	Ernie Banks, Chi	Shortstop	47 HR†, 129 RBI†, .313
1959	Ernie Banks, Chi	Shortstop	45 HR, 143 RBI†, .304
1960	*Dick Groat, Pitt	Shortstop	2 HR, 50 RBI, .325†
1961	*Frank Robinson, Cin	Outfield	37 HR, 124 RBI, .323
1962	Maury Wills, LA	Shortstop	104 SB†, 208 hits, .299, GG
1963	*Sandy Koufax, LA	Pitcher	25‡–5, 1.88 ERA†, 306 K†
1964	*Ken Boyer, StL	Third Base	24 HR, 119 RBI†, .295
1965	Willie Mays, SF	Outfield	52 HR†, 112 RBI, .317, GG
1966	Roberto Clemente, Pitt	Outfield	29 HR, 119 RBI, 202 hits, .317, GG
1967	*Orlando Cepeda, StL	First base	25 HR, 111 RBI†, .325
1968	*Bob Gibson, StL	Pitcher	22–9, 1.12 ERA†, 268 K†, 13 SO†, GG
1969	Willie McCovey, SF	First base	45 HR†, 126 RBI†, .320
1970	*Johnny Bench, Cin	Catcher	45 HR†, 148 RBI†, .293, GG
1971	Joe Torre, StL	Third base	24 HR, 137 RBI†, .363†
1972	*Johnny Bench, Cin	Catcher	40 HR†, 125 RBI†, .270, GG
1973	*Pete Rose, Cin	Outfield	5 HR, 64 RBI, .338†, 230 hits†
1974	*Steve Garvey, LA	First base	21 HR, 111 RBI, 200 hits, .312, GG
1975	*Joe Morgan, Cin	Second base	17 HR, 94 RBI, 67 SB, .327, GG
1976	*Joe Morgan, Cin	Second base	27 HR, 111 RBI, 60 SB, .320, GG
1977	George Foster, Cin	Outfield	52 HR†, 149 RBI†, .320
1978	Dave Parker, Pitt	Outfield	30 HR, 117 RBI, .334†, GG
1979	Keith Hernandez, StL	First base	11 HR, 105 RBI, 210 hits, .344†, GG
	*Willie Stargell, Pitt	First base	32 HR, 82 RBI, .281
1980	*Mike Schmidt, Phil	Third base	48 HR†, 121 RBI†, .286, GG
1981	Mike Schmidt, Phil	Third base	31 HR†, 91 RBI†, 78 runs†, .316, GG
1982	*Dale Murphy, Atl	Outfield	36 HR, 109 RBI‡, .281, GG
1983	Dale Murphy, Atl	Outfield	36 HR, 121 RBI†, .302, GG
1984	*Ryne Sandberg, Chi	Second base	19 HR, 84 RBI, 114 runs†, .314, GG
1985	*Willie McGee, StL	Outfield	10 HR, 82 RBI, 18 3B†, .353†, GG
1986	Mike Schmidt, Phil	Third base	37 HR†, 119 RBI†, .290, GG
1987	Andre Dawson, Chi	Outfield	49 HR†, 137 RBI†, .287, GG
1988	*Kirk Gibson, LA	Outfield	25 HR, 76 RBI, 106 runs, .290
1989	*Kevin Mitchell, SF	Outfield	47 HR†, 125 RBI†, .291
1990	*Barry Bonds, Pitt	Outfield	33 HR, 114 RBI; .301
1991	*Terry Pendleton, Atl	Third base	23 HR, 86 RBI, .319†
1992	Barry Bonds, SF	Outfield	34 HR, 103 RBI, .311
1993	Barry Bonds, SF	Outfield	46 HR†, 123 RBI†, .336
1994	Jeff Bagwell, Hou	First base	39 HR, 116 RBI†, .368
1995	*Barry Larkin, Cin	Shortstop	15 HR, 66 RBI, 51 SB, .319
1996	*Ken Caminiti, SD	Third base	40 HR, 130 RBI, .326
1997	Larry Walker, Col	Outfield	49 HR†, 130 RBI, .452 OBA†, .366, GG

*Played for pennant or, after 1968, division winner. †Led league. ‡Tied for league lead.

Most Valuable Players *(Cont.)*

AMERICAN LEAGUE

Year	Name and Team	Position	Noteworthy
1911	Ty Cobb, Det	Outfield	8 HR, 144 RBI†, 24 3B†, .420†
1912	*Tris Speaker, Bos	Outfield	10 HR‡, 98 RBI, 53 2B†, .383
1913	Walter Johnson, Wash	Pitcher	36†–7, 1.09 ERA†, 11 SO†, 243 K†
1914	*Eddie Collins, Phil	Second base	2 HR, 85 RBI, 122 runs†, .344
1915-21	No selection		
1922	George Sisler, StL	First base	8 HR, 105 RBI, 246 hits†, .420†
1923	*Babe Ruth, NY	Outfield	41 HR†, 131 RBI†, .393
1924	*Walter Johnson, Wash	Pitcher	23†–7, 2.72 ERA†, 158 K†
1925	*Roger Peckinpaugh, Wash	Shortstop	4 HR, 64 RBI, .294
1926	George Burns, Clev	First base	114 RBI, 216 hits†, 64 2B†, .358
1927	*Lou Gehrig, NY	First base	47 HR, 175 RBI†, 52 2B†, .373
1928	Mickey Cochrane, Phil	Catcher	10 HR, 57 RBI, .293
1929	No selection		
1930	No selection		
1931	*Lefty Grove, Phil	Pitcher	31†–4, 2.06 ERA†, 175 K†
1932	Jimmie Foxx, Phil	First base	58 HR†, 169 RBI†, 151 runs†, .364
1933	Jimmie Foxx, Phil	First base	48 HR†, 163 RBI†, .356†
1934	*Mickey Cochrane, Det	Catcher	2 HR, 76 RBI, .320
1935	*Hank Greenberg, Det	First base	36 HR†, 170 RBI†, 203 hits, .328
1936	*Lou Gehrig, NY	First base	49 HR†, 152 RBI, 167 runs†, .354
1937	Charlie Gehringer, Det	Second base	14 HR, 96 RBI, 133 runs, .371†
1938	Jimmie Foxx, Bos	First base	50 HR, 175 RBI†, .349†
1939	*Joe DiMaggio, NY	Outfield	30 HR, 126 RBI, .381†
1940	*Hank Greenberg, Det	Outfield	41 HR†, 150 RBI†, 50 2B†, .340
1941	*Joe DiMaggio, NY	Outfield	30 HR, 125 RBI†, .357
1942	*Joe Gordon, NY	Second base	18 HR, 103 RBI, .322
1943	*Spud Chandler, NY	Pitcher	20†–4, 1.64 ERA†, 5 SO‡
1944	Hal Newhouser, Det	Pitcher	29†–9, 2.22 ERA†, 187 K†
1945	*Hal Newhouser, Det	Pitcher	25†–9, 1.81 ERA†, 8 SO†, 212 K†
1946	*Ted Williams, Bos	Outfield	38 HR, 123 RBI, 142 runs†, .342
1947	*Joe DiMaggio, NY	Outfield	20 HR, 97 RBI, .315
1948	*Lou Boudreau, Clev	Shortstop	18 HR, 106 RBI, .355
1949	Ted Williams, Bos	Outfield	43 HR†, 159 RBI‡, 150 runs†, .343
1950	*Phil Rizzuto, NY	Shortstop	125 runs, 200 hits, .324
1951	*Yogi Berra, NY	Catcher	27 HR, 88 RBI, .294
1952	Bobby Shantz, Phil	Pitcher	24†–7, 2.48 ERA
1953	Al Rosen, Clev	Third base	43 HR†, 145 RBI†, 115 runs†, .336
1954	Yogi Berra, NY	Catcher	22 HR, 125 RBI, .307
1955	*Yogi Berra, NY	Catcher	27 HR, 108 RBI, .272
1956	*Mickey Mantle, NY	Outfield	52 HR†, 130 RBI†, 132 runs†, .353†
1957	*Mickey Mantle, NY	Outfield	34 HR, 94 RBI, 121 runs†, .365
1958	Jackie Jensen, Bos	Outfield	35 HR, 122 RBI†, .286
1959	*Nellie Fox, Chi	Second base	2 HR, 70 RBI, .306, GG
1960	*Roger Maris, NY	Outfield	39 HR, 112 RBI†, .283, GG
1961	*Roger Maris, NY	Outfield	61 HR†, 142 RBI†, .269
1962	*Mickey Mantle, NY	Outfield	30 HR, 89 RBI, .321, GG
1963	*Elston Howard, NY	Catcher	28 HR, 85 RBI, .287, GG
1964	Brooks Robinson, Balt	Third base	28 HR, 118 RBI†, .317, GG
1965	*Zoilo Versalles, Minn	Shortstop	126 runs†, 45 2B‡, 12 3B‡, GG
1966	*Frank Robinson, Balt	Outfield	49 HR†, 122 RBI†, 122 runs†, .316†
1967	*Carl Yastrzemski, Bos	Outfield	44 HR†, 121 RBI†, 112 runs†, .326†, GG
1968	*Denny McLain, Det	Pitcher	31†–6, 1.96 ERA, 280 K
1969	*Harmon Killebrew, Minn	Third base, First base	49 HR†, 140 RBI†, .276
1970	*Boog Powell, Balt	First base	35 HR, 114 RBI, .297
1971	*Vida Blue, Oak	Pitcher	24–8, 1.82 ERA†, 8 SO†, 301 K
1972	Dick Allen, Chi	First base	37 HR†, 113 RBI†, .308
1973	*Reggie Jackson, Oak	Outfield	32 HR†, 117 RBI†, 99 runs†, .293
1974	Jeff Burroughs, Tex	Outfield	25 HR, 118 RBI†, .301
1975	*Fred Lynn, Bos	Outfield	21 HR, 105 RBI, 103 runs†, .331, GG
1976	*Thurman Munson, NY	Catcher	17 HR, 105 RBI, .302
1977	Rod Carew, Minn	First base	100 RBI, 128 runs†, 239 hits†, .388†
1978	Jim Rice, Bos	Outfield, DH	46 HR†, 139 RBI†, 213 hits†, .315
1979	*Don Baylor, Calif	Outfield, DH	36 HR, 139 RBI†, 120 runs†, .296

Most Valuable Players (Cont.)

AMERICAN LEAGUE (Cont.)

Year	Name and Team	Position	Noteworthy
1980	*George Brett, KC	Third base	24 HR, 118 RBI, .390†
1981	*Rollie Fingers, Mil	Pitcher	6–3, 28 saves†, 1.04 ERA
1982	*Robin Yount, Mil	Shortstop	29 HR, 114 RBI, 210 hits†, .331, GG
1983	*Cal Ripken, Balt	Shortstop	27 HR, 102 RBI, 211 hits†, .318
1984	*Willie Hernandez, Det	Pitcher	9–3, 32 saves, 1.92 ERA
1985	Don Mattingly, NY	First base	35 HR, 145 RBI†, 48 2B†, .324, GG
1986	*Roger Clemens, Bos	Pitcher	24†–4, 2.48 ERA†, 238 K
1987	George Bell, Tor	Outfield	47 HR, 134 RBI†, .308
1988	*Jose Canseco, Oak	Outfield	42 HR†, 124 RBI†, 40 SB, .307
1989	Robin Yount, Mil	Outfield	21 HR, 103 RBI, 101 runs, .318
1990	*Rickey Henderson, Oak	Outfield	28 HR, 119 runs†, 65 SB†, .325
1991	Cal Ripken Jr., Balt	Shortstop	34 HR, 114 RBI, .323
1992	Dennis Eckersley, Oak	Pitcher	7–1, 1.91 ERA, 51 saves
1993	Frank Thomas, Chi	First base	41 HR, 128 RBI, .317
1994	Frank Thomas, Chi	First base	38 HR, 101 RBI, .353
1995	*Mo Vaughn, Bos	First base	39 HR, 126 RBI, .300
1996	*Juan Gonzalez, Tex	Outfield	47 HR, 144 RBI, .314
1997	*Ken Griffey Jr., Sea	Outfield	56 HR†, 125 runs†, 393 TB†, 147 RBI†, .304

*Played for pennant or, after 1968, division winner. †Led league. ‡Tied for league lead.

Notes: 2B=doubles; 3B=triples; F.A.=fielding average; GG=won Gold Glove, award begun in 1957; K=strikeouts; SO=shutouts; SB=stolen bases; TB=total bases.

Rookies of the Year

NATIONAL LEAGUE

1947*	Jackie Robinson, Bklyn (1B)
1948*	Alvin Dark, Bos (SS)
1949	Don Newcombe, Bklyn (P)
1950	Sam Jethroe, Bos (OF)
1951	Willie Mays, NY (OF)
1952	Joe Black, Bklyn (P)
1953	Junior Gilliam, Bklyn (2B)
1954	Wally Moon, StL (OF)
1955	Bill Virdon, StL (OF)
1956	Frank Robinson, Cin (OF)
1957	Jack Sanford, Phil (P)
1958	Orlando Cepeda, SF (1B)
1959	Willie McCovey, SF (1B)
1960	Frank Howard, LA (OF)
1961	Billy Williams, Chi (OF)
1962	Ken Hubbs, Chi (2B)
1963	Pete Rose, Cin (2B)
1964	Dick Allen, Phil (3B)
1965	Jim Lefebvre, LA (2B)
1966	Tommy Helms, Cin (2B)
1967	Tom Seaver, NY (P)
1968	Johnny Bench, Cin (C)
1969	Ted Sizemore, LA (2B)
1970	Carl Morton, Mtl(P)
1971	Earl Williams, Atl (C)
1972	Jon Matlack, NY (P)
1973	Gary Matthews, SF (OF)
1974	Bake McBride, StL (OF)
1975	John Montefusco, SF (P)
1976	Pat Zachry, Cin (P)
	Butch Metzger, SD (P)
1977	Andre Dawson, Mtl (OF)
1978	Bob Horner, Atl (3B)
1979	Rick Sutcliffe, LA (P)
1980	Steve Howe, LA (P)
1981	Fernando Valenzuela, LA (P)

AMERICAN LEAGUE

1949	Roy Sievers, StL (OF)
1950	Walt Dropo, Bos (1B)
1951	Gil McDougald, NY (3B)
1952	Harry Byrd, Phil (P)
1953	Harvey Kuenn, Det (SS)
1954	Bob Grim, NY (P)
1955	Herb Score, Clev (P)
1956	Luis Aparicio, Chi (SS)
1957	Tony Kubek, NY (OF, SS)
1958	Albie Pearson, Wash (OF)
1959	Bob Allison, Wash (OF)
1960	Ron Hansen, Balt (SS)
1961	Don Schwall, Bos (P)
1962	Tom Tresh, NY (SS)
1963	Gary Peters, Chi (P)
1964	Tony Oliva, Minn (OF)
1965	Curt Blefary, Balt (OF)
1966	Tommie Agee, Chi (OF)
1967	Rod Carew, Minn (2B)
1968	Stan Bahnsen, NY (P)
1969	Lou Piniella, KC (OF)
1970	Thurman Munson, NY (C)
1971	Chris Chambliss, Clev (1B)
1972	Carlton Fisk, Bos (C)
1973	Al Bumbry, Balt (OF)
1974	Mike Hargrove, Tex (1B)
1975	Fred Lynn, Bos (OF)
1976	Mark Fidrych, Det (P)
1977	Eddie Murray, Balt (DH)
1978	Lou Whitaker, Det (2B)
1979	Alfredo Griffin, Tor (SS)
	John Castino, Minn (3B)
1980	Joe Charboneau, Clev (OF)
1981	Dave Righetti, NY (P)
1982	Cal Ripken, Balt (SS)
1983	Ron Kittle, Chi (OF)

*Just one selection for both leagues.

Rookies of the Year (Cont.)

NATIONAL LEAGUE (Cont.)

1982 ....Steve Sax, LA (2B)
1983 ....Darryl Strawberry, NY (OF)
1984 ....Dwight Gooden, NY (P)
1985 ....Vince Coleman, StL (OF)
1986 ....Todd Worrell, StL (P)
1987 ....Benito Santiago, SD (C)
1988 ....Chris Sabo, Cin (3B)
1989 ....Jerome Walton, Chi (OF)
1990 ....Dave Justice, Atl (OF)
1991 ....Jeff Bagwell, Hou (3B)
1992 ....Eric Karros, LA (1B)
1993 ....Mike Piazza, LA (C)
1994 ....Raul Mondesi, LA (OF)
1995 ....Hideo Nomo, LA (P)
1996 ....Todd Hollandsworth, LA (OF)
1997 ....Scott Rolen, Phil (3B)

AMERICAN LEAGUE (Cont.)

1984 ....Alvin Davis, Sea (1B)
1985 ....Ozzie Guillen, Chi (SS)
1986 ....Jose Canseco, Oak (OF)
1987 ....Mark McGwire, Oak (1B)
1988 ....Walt Weiss, Oak (SS)
1989 ....Gregg Olson, Balt (P)
1990 ....Sandy Alomar Jr., Clev (C)
1991 ....Chuck Knoblauch, Minn (2B)
1992 ....Pat Listach, Mil (SS)
1993 ....Tim Salmon, Calif (OF)
1994 ....Bob Hamelin, Minn (DH)
1995 ....Marty Cordova, Minn (OF)
1996 ....Derek Jeter, NY (SS)
1997 ....Nomar Garciaparra, Bos (SS)

Cy Young Award

Year		W–L	Sv	ERA	Year		W–L	Sv	ERA
1956	*Don Newcombe, Bklyn (NL)	27–7	0	3.06	1962	Don Drysdale, LA (NL)	25–9	1	2.83
1957	Warren Spahn, Mil (NL)	21–11	3	2.69	1963	*Sandy Koufax, LA (NL)	25–5	0	1.88
1958	Bob Turley, NY (AL)	21–7	1	2.97	1964	Dean Chance, LA (AL)	20–9	4	1.65
1959	Early Wynn, Chi (AL)	22–10	0	3.17	1965	Sandy Koufax, LA (NL)	26–8	2	2.04
1960	Vernon Law, Pitt (NL)	20–9	0	3.08	1966	Sandy Koufax, LA (NL)	27–9	0	1.73
1961	Whitey Ford, NY (AL)	25–4	0	3.21					

NATIONAL LEAGUE

Year		W–L	Sv	ERA
1967	Mike McCormick, SF	22–10	0	2.85
1968	*Bob Gibson, StL	22–9	0	1.12
1969	Tom Seaver, NY	25–7	0	2.21
1970	Bob Gibson, StL	23–7	0	3.12
1971	Ferguson Jenkins, Chi	24–13	0	2.77
1972	Steve Carlton, Phil	27–10	0	1.97
1973	Tom Seaver, NY	19–10	0	2.08
1974	Mike Marshall, LA	15–12	21	2.42
1975	Tom Seaver, NY	22–9	0	2.38
1976	Randy Jones, SD	22–14	0	2.74
1977	Steve Carlton, Phil	23–10	0	2.64
1978	Gaylord Perry, SD	21–6	0	2.72
1979	Bruce Sutter, Chi	6–6	37	2.23
1980	Steve Carlton, Phil	24–9	0	2.34
1981	Fernando Valenzuela, LA	13–7	0	2.48
1982	Steve Carlton, Phil	23–11	0	3.10
1983	John Denny, Phil	19–6	0	2.37
1984	†Rick Sutcliffe, Chi	16–1	0	2.69
1985	Dwight Gooden, NY	24–4	0	1.53
1986	Mike Scott, Hou	18–10	0	2.22
1987	Steve Bedrosian, Phil	5–3	40	2.83
1988	Orel Hershiser, LA	23–8	1	2.26
1989	Mark Davis, SD	4–3	44	1.85
1990	Doug Drabek, Pitt	22–6	0	2.76
1991	Tom Glavine, Atl	20–11	0	2.55
1992	Greg Maddux, Chi	20–11	0	2.18
1993	Greg Maddux, Atl	20–10	0	2.36
1994	Greg Maddux, Atl	16–6	0	1.56
1995	Greg Maddux, Atl	19–2	0	1.63
1996	John Smoltz, Atl	24–8	0	2.94
1997	Pedro Martinez, Mtl	17–8	0	1.90

AMERICAN LEAGUE

Year		W–L	Sv	ERA
1967	Jim Lonborg, Bos	22–9	0	3.16
1968	*Denny McLain, Det	31–6	0	1.96
1969	Denny McLain, Det	24–9	0	2.80
	Mike Cuellar, Balt	23–11	0	2.38
1970	Jim Perry, Minn	24–12	0	3.03
1971	*Vida Blue, Oak	24–8	0	1.82
1972	Gaylord Perry, Clev	24–16	1	1.92
1973	Jim Palmer, Balt	22–9	1	2.40
1974	Catfish Hunter, Oak	25–12	0	2.49
1975	Jim Palmer, Balt	23–11	1	2.09
1976	Jim Palmer, Balt	22–13	0	2.51
1977	Sparky Lyle, NY	13–5	26	2.17
1978	Ron Guidry, NY	25–3	0	1.74
1979	Mike Flanagan, Balt	23–9	0	3.08
1980	Steve Stone, Balt	25–7	0	3.23
1981	*Rollie Fingers, Mil	6–3	28	1.04
1982	Pete Vuckovich, Mil	18–6	0	3.34
1983	LaMarr Hoyt, Chi	24–10	0	3.66
1984	*Willie Hernandez, Det	9–3	32	1.92
1985	Bret Saberhagen, KC	20–6	0	2.87
1986	*Roger Clemens, Bos	24–4	0	2.48
1987	Roger Clemens, Bos	20–9	0	2.97
1988	Frank Viola, Minn	24–7	0	2.64
1989	Bret Saberhagen, KC	23–6	0	2.16
1990	Bob Welch, Oak	27–6	0	2.95
1991	Roger Clemens, Bos	18–10	0	2.62
1992	*Dennis Eckersley, Oak	7–1	51	1.91
1993	Jack McDowell, Chi	22–10	0	3.37
1994	David Cone, KC	16–4	0	2.94
1995	Randy Johnson, Sea	18–2	0	2.48
1996	Pat Hentgen, Tor	20–10	0	3.22
1997	Roger Clemens, Tor	21–7	0	2.05

*Pitchers who won the MVP and Cy Young awards in the same season.

†NL games only. Sutcliffe pitched 15 games with Cleveland before being traded to the Cubs.

Career Individual Batting

GAMES

Pete Rose	3562
Carl Yastrzemski	3308
Hank Aaron	3298
Ty Cobb	3035
Stan Musial	3026
Eddie Murray	3026
Willie Mays	2992
Dave Winfield	2973
Rusty Staub	2951
Brooks Robinson	2896
Robin Yount	2856
Al Kaline	2834
Eddie Collins	2826
Reggie Jackson	2820
Frank Robinson	2808
Honus Wagner	2792
Tris Speaker	2789
Tony Perez	2777
Mel Ott	2730
George Brett	2707

AT BATS

Pete Rose	14053
Hank Aaron	12364
Carl Yastrzemski	11988
Ty Cobb	11434
Eddie Murray	11336
Robin Yount	11008
Dave Winfield	11003
Stan Musial	10972
Willie Mays	10881
Paul Molitor	10835
Brooks Robinson	10654
Cal Ripken Jr.	10433
Honus Wagner	10430
George Brett	10349
Lou Brock	10332
Luis Aparicio	10230
Tris Speaker	10195
Al Kaline	10116
Rabbit Maranville	10078
Frank Robinson	10006

HOME RUNS

Hank Aaron	755
Babe Ruth	714
Willie Mays	660
Frank Robinson	586
Harmon Killebrew	573
Reggie Jackson	563
Mike Schmidt	548
Mickey Mantle	536
Jimmie Foxx	534
Ted Williams	521
Willie McCovey	521
Eddie Mathews	512
Ernie Banks	512
Mel Ott	511
Eddie Murray	504
Lou Gehrig	493
Willie Stargell	475
Stan Musial	475
Dave Winfield	465
Mark McGwire	457

HITS

Pete Rose	4256
Ty Cobb	4189
Hank Aaron	3771
Stan Musial	3630
Tris Speaker	3514
Carl Yastrzemski	3419
Honus Wagner	3415
Paul Molitor	3319
Eddie Collins	3312
Willie Mays	3283
Eddie Murray	3255
Nap Lajoie	3242
George Brett	3154
Paul Waner	3152
Robin Yount	3142
Dave Winfield	3110
Rod Carew	3053
Lou Brock	3023
Al Kaline	3007
Roberto Clemente	3000

BATTING AVERAGE

Ty Cobb	.366
Rogers Hornsby	.358
Joe Jackson	.356
Ed Delahanty	.346
Tris Speaker	.345
Ted Williams	.344
Billy Hamilton	.344
Dan Brouthers	.342
Babe Ruth	.342
Harry Heilmann	.342
Pete Browning	.341
Willie Keeler	.341
Bill Terry	.341
George Sisler	.340
Lou Gehrig	.340
Tony Gwynn	.339
Jesse Burkett	.338
Nap Lajoie	.338
Riggs Stephenson	.336
Al Simmons	.334

RUNS

Ty Cobb	2246
Babe Ruth	2174
Hank Aaron	2174
Pete Rose	2165
Willie Mays	2062
Rickey Henderson	2014
Stan Musial	1949
Lou Gehrig	1888
Tris Speaker	1882
Mel Ott	1859
Frank Robinson	1829
Eddie Collins	1821
Carl Yastrzemski	1816
Ted Williams	1798
Paul Molitor	1782
Charlie Gehringer	1774
Jimmie Foxx	1751
Honus Wagner	1736
Jesse Burkett	1720
Cap Anson	1719
Willie Keeler	1719

DOUBLES

Tris Speaker	792
Pete Rose	746
Stan Musial	725
Ty Cobb	724
George Brett	665
Nap Lajoie	657
Carl Yastrzemski	646
Honus Wagner	640
Hank Aaron	624
Paul Waner	605
Paul Molitor	605
Robin Yount	583
Charlie Gehringer	574
Wade Boggs	564
Eddie Murray	560
Cal Ripken, Jr.	544
Harry Heilmann	542
Rogers Hornsby	541
Joe Medwick	540
Dave Winfield	540

TRIPLES

Sam Crawford	309
Ty Cobb	295
Honus Wagner	252
Jake Beckley	243
Roger Connor	233
Tris Speaker	222
Fred Clarke	220
Dan Brouthers	205
Joe Kelley	194
Paul Waner	191
Bid McPhee	188
Eddie Collins	186
Ed Delahanty	185
Sam Rice	184
Jesse Burkett	182
Edd Roush	182
Ed Konetchy	181
Buck Ewing	178
Rabbit Maranville	177
Stan Musial	177

BASES ON BALLS

Babe Ruth	2056
Ted Williams	2019
Rickey Henderson	1890
Joe Morgan	1865
Carl Yastrzemski	1845
Mickey Mantle	1733
Mel Ott	1708
Eddie Yost	1614
Darrell Evans	1605
Stan Musial	1599
Pete Rose	1566
Harmon Killebrew	1559
Lou Gehrig	1508
Mike Schmidt	1507
Eddie Collins	1499
Willie Mays	1464
Jimmie Foxx	1452
Eddie Mathews	1444
Frank Robinson	1420
Hank Aaron	1402

Career Individual Batting *(Cont.)*

RUNS BATTED IN

Hank Aaron	2297
Babe Ruth	2213
Lou Gehrig	1995
Stan Musial	1951
Ty Cobb	1937
Jimmie Foxx	1922
Eddie Murray	1917
Willie Mays	1903
Cap Anson	1879
Mel Ott	1860
Carl Yastrzemski	1844
Ted Williams	1839
Dave Winfield	1833
Al Simmons	1827
Frank Robinson	1812
Honus Wagner	1732
Reggie Jackson	1702
Tony Perez	1652
Ernie Banks	1636
Goose Goslin	1609

STOLEN BASES

Rickey Henderson	1297
Lou Brock	938
Billy Hamilton	912
Ty Cobb	892
Tim Raines	803
Vince Coleman	752
Eddie Collins	744
Arlie Latham	739
Max Carey	738
Honus Wagner	722
Joe Morgan	689
Willie Wilson	668
Tom Brown	657
Bert Campaneris	649
George Davis	616
Dummy Hoy	594
Otis Nixon	594
Maury Wills	586
George Van Haltren	583
Ozzie Smith	580

TOTAL BASES

Hank Aaron	6856
Stan Musial	6134
Willie Mays	6066
Ty Cobb	5854
Babe Ruth	5793
Pete Rose	5752
Carl Yastrzemski	5539
Eddie Murray	5397
Frank Robinson	5373
Dave Winfield	5221
Tris Speaker	5101
Lou Gehrig	5060
George Brett	5044
Mel Ott	5041
Jimmie Foxx	4956
Ted Williams	4884
Honus Wagner	4862
Paul Molitor	4854
Al Kaline	4852
Reggie Jackson	4834

SLUGGING AVERAGE

Babe Ruth	.690
Ted Williams	.634
Lou Gehrig	.632
Jimmie Foxx	.609
Hank Greenberg	.605
Frank Thomas	.584
Joe DiMaggio	.579
Albert Belle	.577
Rogers Hornsby	.577
Mark McGwire	.576
Mike Piazza	.575
Ken Griffey Jr.	.568
Juan Gonzalez	.568
Johnny Mize	.562
Stan Musial	.559
Willie Mays	.557
Mickey Mantle	.557
Barry Bonds	.556
Hank Aaron	.555
Larry Walker	.549

PINCH HITS

Manny Mota	150
Smoky Burgess	145
Greg Gross	143
Jose Morales	123
Jerry Lynch	116
Red Lucas	114
Steve Braun	113
Terry Crowley	108
Denny Walling	108
Gates Brown	107
Mike Lum	103
Jim Dwyer	102
Rusty Staub	100
Larry Biittner	95
Vic Davalillo	95
Jerry Hairston	94
Dave Philley	93
Joel Youngblood	93
Jay Johnstone	92
Ed Kranepool	90
Elmer Valo	90

STRIKEOUTS

Reggie Jackson	2597
Willie Stargell	1936
Mike Schmidt	1883
Tony Perez	1867
Dave Kingman	1816
Bobby Bonds	1757
Dale Murphy	1748
Lou Brock	1730
Mickey Mantle	1710
Harmon Killebrew	1699
Dwight Evans	1697
Dave Winfield	1686
Jose Canseco	1630
Andres Galarraga	1615
Chili Davis	1598
Lee May	1570
Dick Allen	1556
Willie McCovey	1550
Gary Gaetti	1548
Dave Parker	1537

The 30–30 Club (30 HR, 30 SB in single season)

NATIONAL LEAGUE

Year		HR	SB	Year		HR	SB
1956	Willie Mays, NYG	36	40	1991	Howard Johnson, NY	38	30
1957	Willie Mays, NYG	35	38	1992	Barry Bonds, Pitt	34	39
1963	Hank Aaron, Mil	44	31	1993	Sammy Sosa, Chi	33	36
1969	Bobby Bonds, SF	32	45	1995	Barry Bonds, SF	33	31
1973	Bobby Bonds, SF	39	43	1995	Sammy Sosa, Chi	36	34
1983	Dale Murphy, Atl	36	30	1996	Barry Bonds, SF	42	40
1987	Eric Davis, Cin	37	50	1996	Ellis Burks, Col	40	32
1987	Darryl Strawberry, NYM	39	36	1996	Barry Larkin, Cin	33	36
1987	Howard Johnson, NYM	36	32	1996	Dante Bichette, Col	31	31
1989	Howard Johnson, NYM	36	41	1997	Larry Walker, Col	49	33
1990	Ron Gant, Atl	32	33	1997	Jeff Bagwell, Hou	43	31
1990	Barry Bonds, Pitt	33	52	1997	Raul Mondesi, LA	30	32
1991	Ron Gant, Atl	32	34	1997	Barry Bonds, SF	40	37

AMERICAN LEAGUE

Year		HR	SB	Year		HR	SB
1922	Kenny Williams, StL	39	37	1987	Joe Carter, Clev	32	31
1970	Tommy Harper, Mil	31	38	1988	Jose Canseco, Oak	42	40
1975	Bobby Bonds, NY	32	30	1998	Alex Rodriguez, Sea	42	46
1977	Bobby Bonds, Cal	37	41	1998	Shawn Green, Tor	35	35
1978	Bobby Bonds, Chi/Tex	31	43				

Career Individual Pitching

GAMES

Dennis Eckersley	1071
Hoyt Wilhelm	1070
Kent Tekulve	1050
Jesse Orosco	1025
Lee Smith	1022
Goose Gossage	1002
Lindy McDaniel	987
Rollie Fingers	944
Gene Garber	931
Cy Young	906
Sparky Lyle	899
Jim Kaat	898
Jeff Reardon	880
Don McMahon	874
Phil Niekro	864
Charlie Hough	858
Roy Face	848
John Franco	832
Paul Assenmacher	829
Tug McGraw	824

LOSSES

Cy Young	316
Pud Galvin	308
Nolan Ryan	292
Walter Johnson	279
Phil Niekro	274
Gaylord Perry	265
Don Sutton	256
Jack Powell	254
Eppa Rixey	251
Bert Blyleven	250
Robin Roberts	245
Warren Spahn	245
Steve Carlton	244
Early Wynn	244
Jim Kaat	237
Frank Tanana	236
Gus Weyhing	232
Tommy John	231
Bob Friend	230
Ted Lyons	230

EARNED RUN AVERAGE

Ed Walsh	1.82
Addie Joss	1.89
Three Finger Brown	2.06
John Ward	2.10
Christy Mathewson	2.13
Rube Waddell	2.16
Walter Johnson	2.17
Orval Overall	2.23
Tommy Bond	2.25
Ed Reulbach	2.28
Will White	2.28
Jim Scott	2.30
Eddie Plank	2.35
Larry Corcoran	2.36
Eddie Cicotte	2.38
Ed Killian	2.38
George McQuillan	2.38
Doc White	2.39
Nap Rucker	2.42
Terry Larkin	2.43
Jim McCormick	2.43
Jeff Tesreau	2.43

INNINGS PITCHED

Cy Young	7356.2
Pud Galvin	5941.1
Walter Johnson	5914.2
Phil Niekro	5404.1
Nolan Ryan	5386.0
Gaylord Perry	5350.1
Don Sutton	5282.1
Warren Spahn	5243.2
Steve Carlton	5217.1
Grover Alexander	5190.0
Kid Nichols	5056.1
Tim Keefe	5047.1
Bert Blyleven	4970.0
Mickey Welch	4802.0
Tom Seaver	4782.2
Christy Mathewson	4780.2
Tommy John	4710.1
Robin Roberts	4688.2
Early Wynn	4564.0
John Clarkson	4536.1

WINNING PERCENTAGE

Dave Foutz	.690
Whitey Ford	.690
Bob Caruthers	.688
Lefty Grove	.680
Vic Raschi	.667
Mike Mussina	.667
Larry Corcoran	.665
Christy Mathewson	.665
Sam Leever	.660
Sal Maglie	.657
Sandy Koufax	.655
Johnny Allen	.654
Roger Clemens	.653
Ron Guidry	.651
Lefty Gomez	.649
John Clarkson	.648
Three Finger Brown	.648
Randy Johnson	.644
David Cone	.644
Dizzy Dean	.644

SHUTOUTS

Walter Johnson	110
Grover Alexander	90
Christy Mathewson	79
Cy Young	76
Eddie Plank	69
Warren Spahn	63
Nolan Ryan	61
Tom Seaver	61
Bert Blyleven	60
Don Sutton	58
Pud Galvin	57
Ed Walsh	57
Bob Gibson	56
Three Finger Brown	55
Steve Carlton	55
Jim Palmer	53
Gaylord Perry	53
Juan Marichal	52
Rube Waddell	50
Vic Willis	50

WINS

Cy Young	511
Walter Johnson	417
Grover Alexander	373
Christy Mathewson	373
Warren Spahn	363
Kid Nichols	361
Pud Galvin	360
Tim Keefe	342
Steve Carlton	329
John Clarkson	328
Eddie Plank	326
Nolan Ryan	324
Don Sutton	324
Phil Niekro	318
Gaylord Perry	314
Tom Seaver	311
Charley Radbourn	309
Mickey Welch	307
Lefty Grove	300
Early Wynn	300

SAVES

Lee Smith	478
John Franco	397
Dennis Eckersley	390
Jeff Reardon	367
Randy Myers	347
Rollie Fingers	341
Tom Henke	311
Goose Gossage	310
Bruce Sutter	300
Doug Jones	291
Rick Aguilera	275
Jeff Montgomery	256
John Wetteland	253
Dave Righetti	252
Todd Worrell	252
Rod Beck	250
Dan Quisenberry	244
Doug Jones	242
Sparky Lyle	238
Hoyt Wilhelm	227

COMPLETE GAMES

Cy Young	749
Pud Galvin	639
Tim Keefe	554
Walter Johnson	531
Kid Nichols	531
Mickey Welch	525
Charley Radbourn	489
John Clarkson	485
Tony Mullane	468
Jim McCormick	466
Gus Weyhing	448
Grover Alexander	437
Christy Mathewson	434
Jack Powell	422
Eddie Plank	410
Will White	394
Amos Rusie	392
Vic Willis	388
Warren Spahn	382
Jim Whitney	377

Career Individual Pitching (Cont.)

<table>
<tr><td colspan="2">STRIKEOUTS</td><td colspan="2">BASES ON BALLS</td></tr>
<tr><td>Nolan Ryan</td><td>5714</td><td>Nolan Ryan</td><td>2795</td></tr>
<tr><td>Steve Carlton</td><td>4136</td><td>Steve Carlton</td><td>1833</td></tr>
<tr><td>Bert Blyleven</td><td>3701</td><td>Phil Niekro</td><td>1809</td></tr>
<tr><td>Tom Seaver</td><td>3640</td><td>Early Wynn</td><td>1775</td></tr>
<tr><td>Don Sutton</td><td>3574</td><td>Bob Feller</td><td>1764</td></tr>
<tr><td>Gaylord Perry</td><td>3534</td><td>Bobo Newsom</td><td>1732</td></tr>
<tr><td>Walter Johnson</td><td>3509</td><td>Amos Rusie</td><td>1704</td></tr>
<tr><td>Phil Niekro</td><td>3342</td><td>Charlie Hough</td><td>1665</td></tr>
<tr><td>Ferguson Jenkins</td><td>3192</td><td>Gus Weyhing</td><td>1566</td></tr>
<tr><td>Roger Clemens</td><td>3153</td><td>Red Ruffing</td><td>1541</td></tr>
<tr><td>Bob Gibson</td><td>3117</td><td>Bump Hadley</td><td>1442</td></tr>
<tr><td>Jim Bunning</td><td>2855</td><td>Warren Spahn</td><td>1434</td></tr>
<tr><td>Mickey Lolich</td><td>2832</td><td>Earl Whitehill</td><td>1431</td></tr>
<tr><td>Cy Young</td><td>2803</td><td>Tony Mullane</td><td>1408</td></tr>
<tr><td>Frank Tanana</td><td>2773</td><td>Sad Sam Jones</td><td>1396</td></tr>
<tr><td>Warren Spahn</td><td>2583</td><td>Jack Morris</td><td>1390</td></tr>
<tr><td>Bob Feller</td><td>2581</td><td>Tom Seaver</td><td>1390</td></tr>
<tr><td>Jerry Koosman</td><td>2556</td><td>Gaylord Perry</td><td>1379</td></tr>
<tr><td>Tim Keefe</td><td>2543</td><td>Mike Torrez</td><td>1371</td></tr>
<tr><td>Christy Mathewson</td><td>2502</td><td>Walter Johnson</td><td>1363</td></tr>
</table>

Alltime Winningest Managers

CAREER

	W	L	Pct	Yrs		W	L	Pct	Yrs
Connie Mack	3755	3967	.486	53	Ralph Houk	1627	1539	.514	20
John McGraw	2810	1987	.586	33	Fred Clarke	1609	1189	.575	19
Sparky Anderson	2238	1855	.547	26	Dick Williams	1592	1474	.519	21
Bucky Harris	2168	2228	.493	29	Tommy Lasorda	1589	1434	.526	20
Joe McCarthy	2155	1346	.616	24	Tony LaRussa	1587	1446	.523	20
Walter Alston	2063	1634	.558	23	Earl Weaver	1506	1080	.582	17
Leo Durocher	2015	1717	.540	24	Clark Griffith	1491	1367	.522	20
Casey Stengel	1942	1868	.510	25	Bobby Cox	1466	1176	.555	17
Gene Mauch	1907	2044	.483	26	Miller Huggins	1431	1149	.555	17
Bill McKechnie	1904	1737	.523	25	Al Lopez	1412	1012	.583	17

REGULAR SEASON

	W	L	Pct	Yrs		W	L	Pct	Yrs
Connie Mack	3731	3948	.486	53	Ralph Houk	1619	1531	.514	20
John McGraw	2784	1959	.587	33	Fred Clarke	1602	1181	.576	19
Sparky Anderson	2194	1834	.545	26	Dick Williams	1571	1451	.520	21
Bucky Harris	2157	2218	.493	29	Tommy Lasorda	1558	1404	.526	20
Joe McCarthy	2125	1333	.615	24	Tony LaRussa	1564	1425	.523	20
Walter Alston	2040	1613	.558	23	Clark Griffith	1491	1367	.522	20
Leo Durocher	2008	1709	.540	24	Earl Weaver	1480	1060	.583	17
Casey Stengel	1905	1842	.508	25	Bobby Cox	1418	1145	.553	17
Gene Mauch	1902	2037	.483	26	Miller Huggins	1413	1134	.555	17
Bill McKechnie	1896	1723	.524	25	Al Lopez	1410	1004	.584	17

WORLD SERIES

	W	L	T	Pct	App	WS		W	L	T	Pct	App	WS
Casey Stengel	37	26	0	.587	10	7	Billy Southworth	11	11	0	.500	4	2
Joe McCarthy	30	13	0	.698	9	7	Earl Weaver	11	13	0	.458	4	1
John McGraw	26	28	2	.482	9	2	Bobby Cox	11	14	0	.440	4	1
Connie Mack	24	19	0	.558	8	5	Whitey Herzog	10	11	0	.476	3	1
Walter Alston	20	20	0	.500	7	4	Bill Carrigan	8	2	0	.800	2	2
Miller Huggins	18	15	1	.544	6	3	Cito Gaston	8	4	0	.667	2	2
Sparky Anderson	16	12	0	.571	5	3	Danny Murtaugh	8	6	0	.571	2	2
Tommy Lasorda	12	11	0	.522	4	2	Tom Kelly	8	6	0	.571	2	2
Dick Williams	12	14	0	.462	4	2	Ralph Houk	8	8	0	.500	3	2
Frank Chance	11	9	1	.548	4	2	Bill McKechnie	8	14	0	.364	4	2
Bucky Harris	11	10	0	.524	3	2							

Individual Batting (Single Season)

HITS

George Sisler, 1920............257
Lefty O'Doul, 1929.............254
Bill Terry, 1930..................254
Al Simmons, 1925...............253
Rogers Hornsby, 1922.........250
Chuck Klein, 1930 250
Ty Cobb, 1911.....................248
George Sisler, 1922.............246
Heinie Manush, 1928...........241
Babe Herman, 1930 241

BATTING AVERAGE

Hugh Duffy, 1894................440
Tip O'Neill, 1887 435
Ross Barnes, 1876 429
Nap Lajoie, 1901.................426
Willie Keeler, 1897...............424
Rogers Hornsby, 1924........424
George Sisler, 1922.............420
Ty Cobb, 1911.....................420
Fred Dunlap, 1884...............412
Ed Delahanty, 1899 410

DOUBLES

Earl Webb, 1931....................67
George Burns, 1926..............64
Joe Medwick, 1936...............64
Hank Greenberg, 1934..........63
Paul Waner, 1932..................62
Charlie Gehringer, 1936........60
Tris Speaker, 1923................59
Chuck Klein, 1930 59
Billy Herman, 1936................57
Billy Herman, 1935 57

TOTAL BASES

Babe Ruth, 1921..................457
Rogers Hornsby, 1922.........450
Lou Gehrig, 1927.................447
Chuck Klein, 1930 445
Jimmie Foxx, 1932...............438
Stan Musial, 1948................429
Hack Wilson, 1930...............423
Chuck Klein, 1932 420
Lou Gehrig, 1930.................419
Joe DiMaggio, 1937 418

TRIPLES

Chief Wilson, 1912.................36
Dave Orr, 1886......................31
Heinie Reitz, 1894.................31
Perry Werden, 1893..............29
Harry Davis, 1897..................28
George Davis, 1893...............27
Sam Thompson, 1894...........27
Jimmy Williams, 1899............27
John Reilly, 1890 26
George Treadway, 1894........26
Joe Jackson, 1912................26
Sam Crawford, 1914.............26
Kiki Cuyler, 1925...................26

HOME RUNS

Mark McGwire, 1998 70
Sammy Sosa, 1998................66
Roger Maris, 1961 61
Babe Ruth, 1927...................60
Babe Ruth, 1921...................59
Jimmie Foxx, 1932................58
Hank Greenberg, 1938..........58
Mark McGwire, 1997 58
Hack Wilson, 1930................56
Ken Griffey Jr., 1997..............56
Ken Griffey Jr., 1998...........56

RUNS BATTED IN

Hack Wilson, 1930...............190
Lou Gehrig, 1931.................184
Hank Greenberg, 1937........183
Lou Gehrig, 1927.................175
Jimmie Foxx, 1938...............175
Lou Gehrig, 1930.................174
Babe Ruth, 1921..................171
Chuck Klein, 1930 170
Hank Greenberg, 1935........170
Jimmie Foxx, 1932...............169

STRIKEOUTS

Bobby Bonds, 1970.............189
Bobby Bonds, 1969..............187
Rob Deer, 1987 186
Pete Incaviglia, 1986...........185
Cecil Fielder, 1990...............182
Mike Schmidt, 1975..............180
Rob Deer, 1986 179
Dave Nicholson, 1963 175
Gorman Thomas, 1979.........175
Jose Canseco, 1986.............175
Rob Deer, 1991 175
Jay Buhner, 1997.................175

RUNS

Billy Hamilton, 1894 192
Tom Brown, 1891.................177
Babe Ruth, 1921..................177
Tip O'Neill, 1887 167
Lou Gehrig, 1936.................167
Billy Hamilton, 1895.............166
Willie Keeler, 1894...............165
Joe Kelley, 1894..................165
Arlie Latham, 1887...............163
Babe Ruth, 1928..................163
Lou Gehrig, 1931.................163

STOLEN BASES

Hugh Nicol, 1887.................138
Rickey Henderson, 1982 130
Arlie Latham, 1887...............129
Lou Brock, 1974..................118
Charlie Comiskey, 1887.......117
John Ward, 1887..................111
Billy Hamilton, 1889.............111
Billy Hamilton, 1891.............111
Vince Coleman, 1985 110
Arlie Latham, 1888...............109
Vince Coleman, 1987 109

BASES ON BALLS

Babe Ruth, 1923..................170
Ted Williams, 1947...............162
Ted Williams, 1949 162
Mark McGwire, 1998 162
Ted Williams, 1946...............156
Eddie Yost, 1956 151
Eddie Joost, 1949................149
Babe Ruth, 1920..................148
Eddie Stanky, 1945..............148
Jimmy Wynn, 1969 148

SLUGGING AVERAGE

Babe Ruth, 1920.................847
Babe Ruth, 1921.................846
Babe Ruth, 1927.................772
Lou Gehrig, 1927................765
Babe Ruth, 1923.................764
Rogers Hornsby, 1925........756
Mark McGwire, 1998 752
Jeff Bagwell, 1994..............750
Jimmie Foxx, 1932..............749
Babe Ruth, 1924................739

Individual Pitching (Single Season)

GAMES

Mike Marshall, 1974	106
Kent Tekulve, 1979	94
Mike Marshall, 1973	92
Kent Tekulve, 1978	91
Wayne Granger, 1969	90
Mike Marshall, 1979	90
Kent Tekulve, 1987	90
Mark Eichhorn, 1987	89
Wilbur Wood, 1968	88
Mike Myers, 1997	88

GAMES STARTED

Will White, 1879	75
Jim Galvin, 1883	75
Jim McCormick, 1880	74
Charley Radbourn, 1884	73
Guy Hecker, 1884	73
Jim Galvin, 1884	72
John Clarkson, 1889	72
Bill Hutchison, 1892	71
John Clarkson, 1885	70
Matt Kilroy, 1887	69

INNINGS PITCHED

Will White, 1878	680.0
Charley Radbourn, 1884	678.2
Guy Hecker, 1884	670.2
Jim McCormick, 1880	657.2
Jim Galvin, 1883	656.1
Jim Galvin, 1884	636.1
Charley Radbourn, 1883	632.1
Bill Hutchison, 1892	627.0
John Clarkson, 1885	623.0
Jim Devlin, 1876	622.0

WINS

Charley Radbourn, 1884	59
John Clarkson, 1885	53
Guy Hecker, 1884	52
John Clarkson, 1889	49
Charley Radbourn, 1883	48
Charlie Buffinton, 1884	48
Al Spalding, 1876	47
John Ward, 1879	47
Jim Galvin, 1883	46
Jim Galvin, 1884	46
Matt Kilroy, 1887	46

LOSSES

John Coleman, 1883	48
Will White, 1880	42
Larry McKeon, 1884	41
George Bradley, 1879	40
Jim McCormick, 1879	40
Henry Porter, 1888	37
Kid Carsey, 1891	37
George Cobb, 1892	37
Stump Weidman, 1886	36
Bill Hutchison, 1892	36

WINNING PERCENTAGE

Roy Face, 1959	.947
Johnny Allen, 1937	.938
Greg Maddux, 1995	.905
Randy Johnson, 1995	.900
Ron Guidry, 1978	.893
Freddie Fitzsimmons, 1940	.889
Lefty Grove, 1931	.886
Bob Stanley, 1978	.882
Preacher Roe, 1951	.880
Fred Goldsmith, 1880	.875
Tom Seaver, 1981	.875

SAVES

Bobby Thigpen, 1990	57
Randy Myers, 1993	53
Trevor Hoffman, 1998	53
Dennis Eckersley, 1992	51
Rod Beck, 1998	51
Dennis Eckersley, 1990	48
Rod Beck, 1993	48
Jeff Shaw, 1998	48
Lee Smith, 1991	47
Lee Smith, 1993	46
Dave Righetti, 1986	46
Bryan Harvey, 1991	46
Jose Mesa, 1995	46
Tom Gordon, 1998	46

EARNED RUN AVERAGE

Tim Keefe, 1880	0.86
Dutch Leonard, 1914	0.96
Three Finger Brown, 1906	1.04
Bob Gibson, 1968	1.12
Christy Mathewson, 1909	1.14
Walter Johnson, 1913	1.14
Jack Pfiester, 1907	1.15
Addie Joss, 1908	1.16
Carl Lundgren, 1907	1.17
Denny Driscoll, 1882	1.21

SHUTOUTS

George Bradley, 1876	16
Grover Alexander, 1916	16
Jack Coombs, 1910	13
Bob Gibson, 1968	13
Jim Galvin, 1884	12
Ed Morris, 1886	12
Grover Alexander, 1915	12
Tommy Bond, 1879	11
Charley Radbourn, 1884	11
Dave Foutz, 1886	11
Christy Mathewson, 1908	11
Ed Walsh, 1908	11
Walter Johnson, 1913	11
Sandy Koufax, 1963	11
Dean Chance, 1964	11

COMPLETE GAMES

Will White, 1879	75
Charley Radbourn, 1884	73
Jim McCormick, 1880	72
Jim Galvin, 1883	72
Guy Hecker, 1884	72
Jim Galvin, 1884	71
Tim Keefe, 1883	68
John Clarkson, 1885	68
John Clarkson, 1889	68
Bill Hutchison, 1892	67

STRIKEOUTS

Matt Kilroy, 1886	513
Toad Ramsey, 1886	499
Hugh Daily, 1884	483
Dupee Shaw, 1884	451
Charley Radbourn, 1884	441
Charlie Buffinton, 1884	417
Guy Hecker, 1884	385
Nolan Ryan, 1973	383
Sandy Koufax, 1965	382
Bill Sweeney, 1884	374

BASES ON BALLS

Amos Rusie, 1890	289
Mark Baldwin, 1889	274
Amos Rusie, 1892	267
Amos Rusie, 1891	262
Mark Baldwin, 1890	249
Jack Stivetts, 1891	232
Mark Baldwin, 1891	227
Phil Knell, 1891	226
Bob Barr, 1890	219
Amos Rusie 1893	218

The Regular Season *(Cont.)*

Manager of the Year

NATIONAL LEAGUE

1983	Tommy Lasorda, LA
1984	Jim Frey, Chi
1985	Whitey Herzog, StL
1986	Hal Lanier, Hou
1987	Buck Rodgers, Mtl
1988	Tommy Lasorda, LA
1989	Don Zimmer, Chi
1990	Jim Leyland, Pitt
1991	Bobby Cox, Atl
1992	Jim Leyland, Pitt
1993	Dusty Baker, SF
1994	Felipe Alou, Mtl
1995	Don Baylor, Col
1996	Bruce Bochy, SD
1997	Dusty Baker, SF

AMERICAN LEAGUE

1983	Tony La Russa, Chi
1984	Sparky Anderson, Det
1985	Bobby Cox, Tor
1986	John McNamara, Bos
1987	Sparky Anderson, Det
1988	Tony La Russa, Oak
1989	Frank Robinson, Balt
1990	Jeff Torborg, Chi
1991	Tom Kelly, Minn
1992	Tony La Russa, Oak
1993	Gene Lamont, Chi
1994	Buck Showalter, NY
1995	Lou Piniella, Sea
1996	Joe Torre, NY
	Johnny Oates, Tex
1997	Davey Johnson, Balt

Individual Batting (Single Game)

MOST RUNS

7 ....Guy Hecker, Lou   Aug 15, 1886

MOST HITS

7 ....Wilbert Robinson, Balt   June 10, 1892
Rennie Stennett, Pitt   Sept 16, 1975

MOST HOME RUNS

4 ....Bobby Lowe, Bos (N)   May 30, 1894
Ed Delahanty, Phil   July 13, 1896
Lou Gehrig, NY (A)   June 3, 1932
Gil Hodges, Bklyn   Aug 31, 1950
Joe Adcock, Mil (N)   July 31, 1954
Rocky Colavito, Clev   June 10, 1959
Willie Mays, SF   April 30, 1961
Bob Horner, Atl   July 6, 1986
Mark Whiten, StL   Sept 7, 1993

MOST GRAND SLAMS

2 ....Tony Lazzeri, NY (A)   May 24, 1936
Jim Tabor, Bos (A)   July 4, 1939
Rudy York, Bos (A)   July 27, 1946
Jim Gentile, Balt   May 9, 1961
Tony Cloninger, Atl   July 3, 1966
Jim Northrup, Det   June 24, 1968
Frank Robinson, Balt   June 26, 1970
Robin Ventura, Chi (A)   Sept 4, 1995

MOST RBI

12 .....Jim Bottomley, StL   Sept 16, 1924
Mark Whiten, StL   Sept 7, 1993

Individual Batting (Single Inning)

MOST RUNS

3 ....Tommy Burns, Chi (N) Sept 6, 1883, 7th inning
Ned Williamson, Chi (N) Sept 6, 1883, 7th inning
Sammy White, Bos (A) June 18, 1953, 7th inning

MOST HITS

3 ....Tommy Burns, Chi (N) Sept 6, 1883, 7th inning
Fred Pfeiffer, Chi (N) Sept 6, 1883, 7th inning
Ned Williamson, Chi (N) Sept 6, 1883, 7th inning
Gene Stephens, Bos (A) June 18, 1953, 7th inning

Note: All single-game hitting records for nine-inning game.

MOST RBI

6 ....Fred Merkle, NY (N)   May 13, 1911 (RBI not officially adopted until 1920)
Bob Johnson, Phil (A)   Aug 29, 1937
Tom McBride, Bos (A)   Aug 4, 1945
Joe Astroth, Phil (A)   Sept 23, 1950
Gil McDougald, NY (A)   May 3, 1951
Sam Mele, Chi (A)   June 10, 1952
Jim Lemon, Wash   Sept 5, 1959
Jim Ray Hart, SF   July 8, 1970
Andre Dawson, Mtl   Sept 24, 1985
Dale Murphy, Atl   July 27, 1989
Carlos Quintana, Bos (A)   July 30, 1991

The Regular Season (Cont.)

Individual Pitching (Single Game)

MOST INNINGS PITCHED

26 .....Leon Cadore, Bklyn   May 1, 1920, tie 1–1
       Joe Oeschger, Bos (N)   May 1, 1920, tie 1–1

MOST RUNS ALLOWED

24 .....Al Travers, Det   May 18, 1912

MOST HITS ALLOWED

36 .....Jack Wadsworth, Lou   Aug 17, 1894

MOST STRIKEOUTS

20 .....Roger Clemens, Bos (A)   April 29, 1986
20 .....Roger Clemens, Bos (A)   Sept 18, 1996
20 .....Kerry Wood, Chi (N)   May 6, 1998

MOST WALKS ALLOWED

16 .....Bill George, NY (N)   May 30, 1887
       George Van Haltren, June 27, 1887
       Chi (N)
       Henry Gruber, Clev   Apr 19, 1890
       Bruno Haas, Phil (A) June 2, 1915

MOST WILD PITCHES

6 .......J.R. Richard, Hou   April 10, 1979
      Phil Niekro, Atl   Aug 14, 1979
      Bill Gullickson, Mtl April 10, 1982

Individual Pitching (Single Inning)

MOST RUNS ALLOWED

13 .....Lefty O'Doul, Bos (A)   July 7, 1923

MOST WALKS ALLOWED

8 ....Dolly Gray, Wash   Aug 28, 1909

MOST WILD PITCHES

4 ....Walter Johnson, Wash   Sept 21, 1914
      Phil Niekro, Atl   Aug 14, 1979

Miscellaneous

LONGEST GAME, BY INNINGS

26 .....Brooklyn 1, Boston 1   May 1, 1920

LONGEST NINE-INNING GAME, BY TIME

4:21...New York 13, Baltimore 10   April 30, 1996

Baseball Hall of Fame

Players

	Position	Career	Selected
Hank Aaron	OF	1954–76	1982
Grover Alexander	P	1911–30	1938
Cap Anson	1B	1876–97	1939
Luis Aparicio	SS	1956–73	1984
Luke Appling	SS	1930–50	1964
Richie Ashburn	OF	1948–62	1995
Earl Averill	OF	1929–41	1975
Frank Baker	3B	1908–22	1955
Dave Bancroft	SS	1915–30	1971
Ernie Banks	SS-1B	1953–71	1977
Jake Beckley	1B	1888–1907	1971
Cool Papa Bell*	OF		1974
Johnny Bench	C	1967–83	1989
Chief Bender	P	1903–25	1953
Yogi Berra	C	1946–65	1972
Jim Bottomley	1B	1922–37	1974
Lou Boudreau	SS	1938–52	1970
Roger Bresnahan	C	1897–1915	1945
Lou Brock	OF	1961–79	1985
Dan Brouthers	1B	1879–1904	1945
Three Finger Brown	P	1903–16	1949
Jim Bunning	P	1955–1971	1996
Jesse Burkett	OF	1890–1905	1946
Roy Campanella	C	1948–57	1969
Rod Carew	1B-2B	1967–85	1991
Max Carey	OF	1910–29	1961
Steve Carlton	P	1965–88	1994
Frank Chance	1B	1898–1914	1946
Oscar Charleston*	OF		1976

	Position	Career	Selected
Jack Chesbro	P	1899–1909	1946
Fred Clarke	OF	1894–1915	1945
John Clarkson	P	1882–94	1963
Roberto Clemente	OF	1955–72	1973
Ty Cobb	OF	1905–28	1936
Mickey Cochrane	C	1925–37	1947
Eddie Collins	2B	1906–30	1939
Jimmy Collins	3B	1895–1908	1945
Earle Combs	OF	1924–35	1970
Roger Connor	1B	1880–97	1976
Stan Coveleski	P	1912–28	1969
Sam Crawford	OF	1899–1917	1957
Joe Cronin	SS	1926–45	1956
Candy Cummings	P	1872–77	1939
Kiki Cuyler	OF	1921–38	1968
Ray Dandridge*	3B		1987
George Davis	SS	1890–1909	1998
Leon Day*	P		1995
Dizzy Dean	P	1930–47	1953
Ed Delahanty	OF	1888–1903	1945
Bill Dickey	C	1928–46	1954
Martin Dihigo*	P-OF		1977
Joe DiMaggio	OF	1936–51	1955
Larry Doby	OF	1947–59	1998
Bobby Doerr	2B	1937–51	1986
Don Drysdale	P	1956–69	1984
Hugh Duffy	OF	1888–1906	1945
Johnny Evers	2B	1902–29	1939
Buck Ewing	C	1880–97	1946

Note: Career dates indicate first and last appearances in the majors.
*Elected on the basis of his career in the Negro leagues.

Players *(Cont.)*

	Position	Career	Selected
Red Faber	P	1914–33	1964
Bob Feller	P	1936–56	1962
Rick Ferrell	C	1929–47	1984
Rollie Fingers	P	1968–85	1992
Elmer Flick	OF	1898–1910	1963
Whitey Ford	P	1950–67	1974
Bill Foster*	P		1996
Nellie Fox	2B	1947–65	1997
Jimmie Foxx	1B	1925–45	1951
Frankie Frisch	2B	1919–37	1947
Pud Galvin	P	1879–92	1965
Lou Gehrig	1B	1923–39	1939
Charlie Gehringer	2B	1924–42	1949
Bob Gibson	P	1959–75	1981
Josh Gibson*	C		1972
Lefty Gomez	P	1930–43	1972
Goose Goslin	OF	1921–38	1968
Hank Greenberg	1B	1930–47	1956
Burleigh Grimes	P	1916–34	1964
Lefty Grove	P	1925–41	1947
Chick Hafey	OF	1924–37	1971
Jesse Haines	P	1918–37	1970
Billy Hamilton	OF	1888–1901	1961
Gabby Hartnett	C	1922–41	1955
Harry Heilmann	OF	1914–32	1952
Billy Herman	2B	1931–47	1975
Harry Hooper	OF	1909–25	1971
Rogers Hornsby	2B	1915–37	1942
Waite Hoyt	P	1918–38	1969
Carl Hubbell	P	1928–43	1947
Catfish Hunter	P	1965–79	1987
Monte Irvin*	OF	1949–56	1973
Reggie Jackson	OF	1967–87	1993
Travis Jackson	SS	1922–36	1982
Ferguson Jenkins	P	1965–83	1991
Hugh Jennings	SS	1891–1918	1945
Judy Johnson*	3B		1975
Walter Johnson	P	1907–27	1936
Addie Joss	P	1902–10	1978
Al Kaline	OF	1953–74	1980
Tim Keefe	P	1880–93	1964
Willie Keeler	OF	1892–1910	1939
George Kell	3B	1943–57	1983
Joe Kelley	OF	1891–1908	1971
George Kelly	1B	1915–32	1973
King Kelly	C	1878–93	1945
Harmon Killebrew	1B-3B	1954–75	1984
Ralph Kiner	OF	1946–55	1975
Chuck Klein	OF	1928–44	1980
Sandy Koufax	P	1955–66	1972
Nap Lajoie	2B	1896–1916	1937
Tony Lazzeri	2B	1926–39	1991
Bob Lemon	P	1941–58	1976
Buck Leonard*	1B		1977
Fred Lindstrom	3B	1924–36	1976
Pop Lloyd*	SS-1B		1977
Ernie Lombardi	C	1931–47	1986
Ted Lyons	P	1923–46	1955
Mickey Mantle	OF	1951–68	1974
Heinie Manush	OF	1923–39	1964
Rabbit Maranville	SS-2B	1912–35	1954
Juan Marichal	P	1960–75	1983
Rube Marquard	P	1908–25	1971
Eddie Mathews	3B	1952–68	1978
Christy Mathewson	P	1900–16	1936
Willie Mays	OF	1951–73	1979

	Position	Career	Selected
Tommy McCarthy	OF	1884–96	1946
Willie McCovey	1B	1959–80	1986
Joe McGinnity	P	1899–1908	1946
Joe Medwick	OF	1932–48	1968
Johnny Mize	1B	1936–53	1981
Joe Morgan	2B	1963–84	1990
Stan Musial	OF-1B	1941–63	1969
Hal Newhouser	P	1939–55	1992
Kid Nichols	P	1890–1906	1949
Phil Niekro	P	1964–87	1997
Jim O'Rourke	OF	1876–1904	1945
Mel Ott	OF	1926–47	1951
Satchel Paige*	P	1948–65	1971
Jim Palmer	P	1965–84	1990
Herb Pennock	P	1912–34	1948
Gaylord Perry	P	1962–83	1991
Eddie Plank	P	1901–17	1946
Charley Radbourn	P	1880–91	1939
Pee Wee Reese	SS	1940–58	1984
Sam Rice	OF	1915–35	1963
Eppa Rixey	P	1912–33	1963
Phil Rizzuto	SS	1941–56	1994
Robin Roberts	P	1948–66	1976
Brooks Robinson	3B	1955–77	1983
Frank Robinson	OF	1956–76	1982
Jackie Robinson	2B	1947–56	1962
Joe (Bullet) Rogan*	P		1998
Edd Roush	OF	1913–31	1962
Red Ruffing	P	1924–47	1967
Amos Rusie	P	1889–1901	1977
Babe Ruth	OF	1914–35	1936
Ray Schalk	C	1912–29	1955
Mike Schmidt	3B	1972–89	1995
Red Schoendienst	2B	1945–63	1989
Tom Seaver	P	1967–86	1992
Joe Sewell	SS	1920–33	1977
Al Simmons	OF	1924–44	1953
George Sisler	1B	1915–30	1939
Enos Slaughter	OF	1938–59	1985
Duke Snider	OF	1947–64	1980
Warren Spahn	P	1942–65	1973
Al Spalding	P	1871–78	1939
Tris Speaker	OF	1907–28	1937
Willie Stargell	OF-1B	1962–82	1988
Don Sutton	P	1966–88	1998
Bill Terry	1B	1923–36	1954
Sam Thompson	OF	1885–1906	1974
Joe Tinker	SS	1902–16	1946
Pie Traynor	3B	1920–37	1948
Dazzy Vance	P	1915–35	1955
Arky Vaughan	SS	1932–48	1985
Rube Waddell	P	1897–1910	1946
Honus Wagner	SS	1897–1917	1936
Bobby Wallace	SS	1894–1918	1953
Ed Walsh	P	1904–17	1946
Lloyd Waner	OF	1927–45	1967
Paul Waner	OF	1926–45	1952
John Ward	2B-P	1878–94	1964
Mickey Welch	P	1880–92	1973
Willie Wells*	SS	1924–49	1997
Zach Wheat	OF	1909–27	1959
Hoyt Wilhelm	P	1952–72	1985
Billy Williams	OF	1959–76	1987
Ted Williams	OF	1939–60	1966
Vic Willis	P	1898–1910	1995
Hack Wilson	OF	1923–34	1979

Players (Cont.)

	Position	Career	Selected
Early Wynn	P	1939–63	1972
Carl Yastrzemski	OF	1961–83	1989
Cy Young	P	1890–1911	1937
Ross Youngs	OF	1917–26	1972

Umpires

	Year Selected
Al Barlick	1989
Jocko Conlan	1974
Tom Connolly	1953
Billy Evans	1973
Cal Hubbard	1976
Bill Klem	1953
Bill McGowan	1992

Pioneers/Executives

	Year Selected
Ed Barrow (manager-executive)	1953
Morgan Bulkeley (executive)	1937
Alexander Cartwright (executive)	1938
Henry Chadwick (writer-executive)	1938
Happy Chandler (commissioner)	1982
Charles Comiskey (manager-executive)	1939
Rube Foster (player–manager–executive)	1981
Ford Frick (commissioner-executive)	1970
Warren Giles (executive)	1979
Will Harridge (executive)	1972
William Hulbert (executive)	1995

Pioneers/Executives (Cont.)

	Year Selected
Ban Johnson (executive)	1937
Kenesaw M. Landis (commissioner)	1944
Larry MacPhail (executive)	1978
Lee MacPhail Jr (executive)	1998
Branch Rickey (manager–executive)	1967
Al Spalding (player–executive)	1939
Bill Veeck (owner)	1991
George Weiss (executive)	1971
George Wright (player–manager)	1937
Harry Wright (player–manager–executive)	1953
Tom Yawkey (executive)	1980

Managers

	Years Managed	Year Selected
Walt Alston	1954–76	1983
Leo Durocher	1939–73	1994
Clark Griffith	1901–20	1946
Bucky Harris	1924–56	1975
Ned Hanlon	1899–1907	1996
Miller Huggins	1913–29	1964
Tom Lasorda	1977–96	1997
Al Lopez	1951–69	1977
Connie Mack	1894–1950	1937
Joe McCarthy	1926–50	1957
John McGraw	1899–1932	1937
Bill McKechnie	1915–46	1962
Wilbert Robinson	1902–31	1945
Casey Stengel	1934–65	1966
Earl Weaver	1968–82, 85–86	1996

Notable Achievements

No-Hit Games, 9 Innings or More
NATIONAL LEAGUE

Date	Pitcher and Game
1876......July 15	George Bradley, StL vs Hart 2–0
1880......June 12	John Richmond, Wor vs Clev 1–0 (perfect game)
June 17	Monte Ward, Prov vs Buff 5–0 (perfect game)
Aug 19	Larry Corcoran, Chi vs Bos 6–0
Aug 20	Pud Galvin, Buff at Wor 1–0
1882......Sept 20	Larry Corcoran, Chi vs Wor 5–0
Sept 22	Tim Lovett, Bklyn vs NY 4–0
1883......July 25	Hoss Radbourn, Prov at Clev 8–0
Sept 13	Hugh Daily, Clev at Phil 1–0
1884......June 27	Larry Corcoran, Chi vs Prov 6–0
Aug 4	Pud Galvin, Buff at Det 18–0
1885......July 27	John Clarkson, Chi at Prov 4–0
Aug 29	Charles Ferguson, Phil vs Prov 1–0
1891......July 31	Amos Rusie, NY vs Bklyn 6–0
June 22	Tom Lovett, Bklyn vs NY 4–0
1892......Aug 6	Jack Stivetts, Bos vs Bklyn 11–0
Aug 22	Alex Sanders, Lou vs Balt 6–2
Oct 15	Bumpus Jones, Cin vs Pitt 7–1 (first major league game)
1893......Aug 16	Bill Hawke, Balt vs Wash 5–0

Date	Pitcher and Game
1897......Sept 18	Cy Young, Clev vs Cin 6–0
1898......Apr 22	Ted Breitenstein, Cin vs Pitt 11–0
Apr 22	Jim Hughes, Balt vs Bos 8–0
July 8	Frank Donahue, Phil vs Bos 5–0
Aug 21	Walter Thornton, Chi vs Bklyn 2–0
1899......May 25	Deacon Phillippe, Lou vs NY 7–0
Aug 7	Vic Willis, Bos vs Wash 7–1
1900......July 12	Noodles Hahn, Cin vs Phil 4–0
1901......July 15	Christy Mathewson, NY at StL 5–0
1903......Sept 18	Chick Fraser, Phil at Chi 10–0
1904......June 11	Bob Wicker, Chi at NY 1–0 (hit in 10th; won in 12th)
1905......June 13	Christy Mathewson, NY at Chi 1–0
1906......May 1	John Lush, Phil at Bklyn 6–0
July 20	Mal Eason, Bklyn at StL 2–0
Aug 1	Harry McIntire, Bklyn vs Pitt 0–1 (hit in 11th; lost in 13th)
1907......May 8	Frank Pfeffer, Bos vs Cin 6–0
Sept 20	Nick Maddox, Pitt vs Bklyn 2–1
1908......July 4	George Wiltse, NY vs Phil 1–0 (10 innings)
Sept 5	Nap Rucker, Bklyn vs Bos 6–0

No-Hit Games, 9 Innings or More *(Cont.)*

NATIONAL LEAGUE *(Cont.)*

Date	Pitcher and Game	Date	Pitcher and Game
1909......Apr 15	Leon Ames, NY vs Bklyn 0–3 (hit in 10th; lost in 13th)	1967......June 18	Don Wilson, Hou vs Atl 2–0
1912......Sept 6	Jeff Tesreau, NY at Phil 3–0	1968......July 29	George Culver, Cin at Phil 6–1
1914......Sept 9	George Davis, Bos vs Phil 7–0	Sept 17	Gaylord Perry, SF vs StL 1–0
1915......Apr 15	Rube Marquard, NY vs Bklyn 2–0	Sept 18	Ray Washburn, StL at SF 2–0
Aug 31	Jimmy Lavender, Chi at NY 2–0	1969......Apr 17	Bill Stoneman, Mtl at Phil 7–0
1916......June 16	Tom Hughes, Bos vs Pitt 2–0	Apr 30	Jim Maloney, Cin vs Hou 10–0
1917......May 2	Jim Vaughn, Chi vs Cin 0–1 (hit in 10th; lost in 10th)	May 1	Don Wilson, Hou at Cin 4–0
		Aug 19	Ken Holtzman, Chi vs Atl 3–0
May 2	Fred Toney, Cin at Chi 1–0 (10 innings)	Sept 20	Bob Moose, Pitt at NY 4–0
1919......May 11	Hod Eller, Cin vs StL 6–0	1970......June 12	Dock Ellis, Pitt at SD 2–0
1922......May 7	Jesse Barnes, NY vs Phil 6–0	July 20	Bill Singer, LA vs Phil 5–0
1924......July 17	Jesse Haines, StL vs Bos 5–0	1971......June 3	Ken Holtzman, Chi at Cin 1–0
1925......Sept 13	Dazzy Vance, Bklyn vs Phil 10–1	June 23	Rick Wise, Phil at Cin 4–0
1929......May 8	Carl Hubbell, NY vs Pitt 11–0	Aug 14	Bob Gibson, StL at Pitt 11–0
1934......Sept 21	Paul Dean, StL vs Bklyn 3–0	1972......Apr 16	Burt Hooton, Chi vs Phil 4–0
1938 June 11	Johnny Vander Meer, Cin vs Bos 3–0	Sept 2	Milt Pappas, Chi vs SD 8–0
		Oct 2	Bill Stoneman, Mtl vs NY 7–0
June 15	Johnny Vander Meer, Cin at Bklyn 6–0	1973......Aug 5	Phil Niekro, Atl vs SD 9–0
		1975......Aug 24	Ed Halicki, SF vs NY 6–0
1940......Apr 30	Tex Carleton, Bklyn at Cin, 3–0	1976......July 9	Larry Dierker, Hou vs Mtl 6–0
1941......Aug 30	Lon Warneke, StL at Cin 2–0	Aug 9	John Candelaria, Pitt vs LA 2–0
1944......Apr 27	Jim Tobin, Bos vs Bklyn 2–0	Sept 29	John Mtlefusco, SF at Atl 9–0
May 15	Clyde Shoun, Cin vs Bos 1–0	1978......Apr 16	Bob Forsch, StL vs Phil 5–0
1946......Apr 23	Ed Head, Bklyn vs Bos 5–0	June 16	Tom Seaver, Cin vs StL 4–0
1947......June 18	Ewell Blackwell, Cin vs Bos 6–0	1979......Apr 7	Ken Forsch, Hou vs Atl 6–0
1948......Sept 9	Rex Barney, Bklyn at NY 2–0	1980......June 27	Jerry Reuss, LA at SF 8–0
1950......Aug 11	Vern Bickford, Bos vs Bklyn 7–0	1981......May 10	Charlie Lea, Mtl vs SF 4–0
1951......May 6	Cliff Chambers, Pitt at Bos 3–0	Sept 26	Nolan Ryan, Hou vs LA 5–0
1952......June 19	Carl Erskine, Bklyn vs Chi 5–0	1983......Sept 26	Bob Forsch, StL vs Mtl 3–0
1954......June 12	Jim Wilson, Mil vs Phil 2–0	1986......Sept 25	Mike Scott, Hou vs SF 2–0
1955......May 12	Sam Jones, Chi vs Pitt 4–0	1988......Sept 16	Tom Browning, Cin vs LA 1–0 (perfect game)
1956......May 12	Carl Erskine, Bklyn vs NY 3–0		
Sept 25	Sal Maglie, Bklyn vs Phil 5–0	1990 June 29	Fernando Valenzuela, LA vs StL 6–0
1959......May 26	Harvey Haddix, Pitt at Mil 0–1 (hit in 13th; lost in 13th)	1990......Aug 15	Terry Mulholland, Phil vs SF 6–0
1960......May 15	Don Cardwell, Chi vs StL 4–0	1991......May 23	Tommy Greene, Phil at Mtl 2–0
Aug 18	Lew Burdette, Mil vs Phil 1–0	July 26	Mark Gardner, Mtl at LA 0–1 (hit in 10th, lost in 10th)
Sept 16	Warren Spahn, Mil vs Phil 4–0		
1961......Apr 28	Warren Spahn, Mil vs SF 1–0	July 28	Dennis Martinez, Mtl at LA 2–0 (perfect game)
1962......June 30	Sandy Koufax, LA vs NY 5–0		
1963......May 11	Sandy Koufax, LA vs SF 8–0	Sept 11	Kent Mercker (6), Mark Wohlers (2), and Alejandro Pena (1), Atl at SD 1–0
May 17	Don Nottebart, Hou vs Phil 4–1		
June 15	Juan Marichal, SF vs Hou 1–0	1992......Aug 17	Kevin Gross, LA vs SF 2–0
1964......Apr 23	Ken Johnson, Hou vs Cin 0–1	1993......Sept 8	Darryl Kile, Hou vs NY 7–1
June 4	Sandy Koufax, LA at Phil 3–0	1994......Apr 8	Kent Mercker, Atl vs LA 6–0
June 21	Jim Bunning, Phil at NY 6–0 (perfect game)	1995......June 3	Pedro Martinez, Mtl vs SD 1–0 (perfect through 9, hit in 10th)
1965......June 14	Jim Maloney, Cin vs NY 0–1 (hit in 11th; lost in 11th)	July 14	Ramon Martinez, LA vs Fla 7–0
		1996......May 11	Al Leiter, Fla vs Colorado 11–0
Aug 19	Jim Maloney, Cin at Chi 1–0 (10 innings)	Sept 17	Hideo Nomo, LA at Colorado 9–0
		1997......June 10	Kevin Brown, Fla vs SF 9–0
Sept 9	Sandy Koufax, LA vs Chi 1–0 (perfect game)	July 12	Francisco Cordova (9) and Ricardo Rincon (1), Pittsburgh vs Colorado 3–0

Note: Includes the games struck from the record book on September 4, 1991, when baseball's committee on statistical accuracy voted to define no-hitters as games of 9 innings or more that end with a team getting no hits.

AMERICAN LEAGUE

Date	Pitcher and Game	Date	Pitcher and Game
1901......May 9	Earl Moore, Clev vs Chi 2–4 (hit in 10th; lost in 10th)	1905......July 22	Weldon Henley, Phil at StL 6–0
		Sept 6	Frank Smith, Chi at Det 15–0
1902......Sept 20	Jimmy Callahan, Chi vs Det 3–0	Sept 27	Bill Dinneen, Bos vs Chi 2–0
1904......May 5	Cy Young, Bos vs Phil 3–0 (perfect game)	1908......June 30	Cy Young, NY vs NY 8–0
		Sept 18	Bob Rhoades, Clev vs Bos 2–1
Aug 17	Jesse Tannehill, Bos at Chi 6–0	Sept 20	Frank Smith, Chi vs Phil 1–0

No-Hit Games, 9 Innings or More *(Cont.)*

AMERICAN LEAGUE *(Cont.)*

Date		Pitcher and Game	Date		Pitcher and Game
1908	Oct 2	Addie Joss, Clev vs Chi 1–0 (perfect game)	1965	Sept 16	Dave Morehead, Bos vs Clev 2–0
			1966	June 10	Sonny Siebert, Clev vs Wash 2–0
1910	Apr 20	Addie Joss, Clev at Chi 1–0	1967	Apr 30	Steve Barber (8⅔) and Stu Miller (⅓), Balt vs Det 1–2
	May 12	Chief Bender, Phil vs Clev 4–0			
	Aug 30	Tom Hughes, NY vs Clev 0–5 (hit in 10th; lost in 11th)		Aug 25	Dean Chance, Minn at Clev 2–1
				Sept 10	Joel Horlen, Chi vs Det 6–0
1911	July 29	Joe Wood, Bos vs StL 5–0	1968	Apr 27	Tom Phoebus, Balt vs Bos 6–0
	Aug 27	Ed Walsh, Chi vs Bos 5–0		May 8	Catfish Hunter, Oak vs Minn 4–0 (perfect game)
1912	July 4	George Mullin, Det vs StL 7–0			
	Aug 30	Earl Hamilton, StL at Det 5–1	1969	Aug 13	Jim Palmer, Balt vs Oak 8–0
1914	May 14	Jim Scott, Chi at Wash 0–1 (hit in 10th; lost in 10th)	1970	July 3	Clyde Wright, Cal vs Oak 4–0
				Sept 21	Vida Blue, Oak vs Minn 6–0
	May 31	Joe Benz, Chi vs Clev 6–1	1973	Apr 27	Steve Busby, KC at Det 3–0
1916	June 21	George Foster, Bos vs NY 2–0		May 15	Nolan Ryan, Cal at KC 3–0
	Aug 26	Joe Bush, Phil vs Clev 5–0		July 15	Nolan Ryan, Cal at Det 6–0
	Aug 30	Dutch Leonard, Bos vs StL 4–0		July 30	Jim Bibby, Tex at Oak 6–0
1917	Apr 14	Ed Cicotte, Chi at StL 11–0	1974	June 19	Steve Busby, KC at Mil 2–0
	Apr 24	George Mogridge, NY at Bos 2–1		July 19	Dick Bosman, Clev vs Oak 4–0
	May 5	Ernie Koob, StL vs Chi 1–0		Sept 28	Nolan Ryan, Cal vs Minn 4–0
	May 6	Bob Groom, StL vs Chi 3–0	1975	June 1	Nolan Ryan, Cal vs Balt 1–0
	June 23	Ernie Shore, Bos vs Wash 4–0 (perfect game)		Sept 28	Vida Blue (5), Glenn Abbott and Paul Lindblad (1), Rollie Fingers (2), Oak vs Cal 5–0
1918	June 3	Dutch Leonard, Bos at Det 5–0			
1919	Sept 10	Ray Caldwell, Clev at NY 3–0	1976	July 28	John Odom (5) and Francisco Barrios (4), Chi at Oak 2–1
1920	July 1	Walter Johnson, Wash at Bos 1–0			
1922	Apr 30	Charlie Robertson, Chi at Det 2–0 (perfect game)	1977	May 14	Jim Colborn, KC vs Tex 6–0
				May 30	Dennis Eckersley, Clev vs Cal 1–0
1923	Sept 4	Sam Jones, NY at Phil 2–0			
	Sept 7	Howard Ehmke, Bos at Phil 4–0		Sept 22	Bert Blyleven, Tex at Cal 6–0
1926	Aug 21	Ted Lyons, Chi at Bos 6–0	1981	May 15	Len Barker, Clev vs Tor 3–0 (perfect game)
1931	Apr 29	Wes Ferrell, Clev vs StL 9–0			
	Aug 8	Bob Burke, Wash vs Bos 5–0	1983	July 4	Dave Righetti, NY vs Bos 4–0
1934	Sept 18	Bobo Newsom, StL vs Bos 1–2 (hit in 10th; lost in 10th)		Sept 29	Mike Warren, Oak vs Chi 3–0
			1984	Apr 7	Jack Morris, Det at Chi 4–0
1935	Aug 31	Vern Kennedy, Chi vs Clev 5–0		Sept 30	Mike Witt, Cal at Tex 1–0 (perfect game)
1937	June 1	Bill Dietrich, Chi vs StL 8–0			
1938	Aug 27	Mtle Pearson, NY vs Clev 13–0	1986	Sept 19	Joe Cowley, Chi at Cal 7–1
1940	Apr 16	Bob Feller, Clev at Chi 1–0 (opening day)	1987	Apr 15	Juan Nieves, Mil at Balt 7–0
			1990	Apr 11	Mark Langston (7), Mike Witt (2), Cal vs Sea 1–0
1945	Sept 9	Dick Fowler, Phil vs StL 1–0			
1946	Apr 30	Bob Feller, Clev at NY 1–0		June 2	Randy Johnson, Sea vs Det 2–0
1947	July 10	Don Black, Clev vs Phil 3–0		June 11	Nolan Ryan, Tex at Oak 5–0
	Sep 3	Bill McCahan, Phil vs Wash 3–0		June 29	Dave Stewart, Oak at Tor 5–0
1948	June 30	Bob Lemon, Clev at Det 2–0	1990	July 1	Andy Hawkins, NY at Chi 0–4 (pitched 8 innings of 9-inning game)
1951	July 1	Bob Feller, Clev vs Det 2–1			
	July 12	Allie Reynolds, NY at Clev 1–0		Sept 2	Dave Stieb, Tor at Clev 3–0
	Sept 28	Allie Reynolds, NY vs Bos 8–0	1991	May 1	Nolan Ryan, Tex vs Tor 3–0
1952	May 15	Virgil Trucks, Det vs Wash 1–0		July 13	Bob Milacki (6), Mike Flanagan (1), Mark Williamson (1), and Gregg Olson (1), Balt at Oak 2–0
	Aug 25	Virgil Trucks, Det at NY 1–0			
1953	May 6	Bobo Holloman, StL vs Phil 6–0 (first major league start)		Aug 11	Wilson Alvarez, Chi at Balt 7–0
				Aug 26	Bret Saberhagen, KC vs Chi 7–0
1956	July 14	Mel Parnell, Bos vs Chi 4–0	1993	Apr 22	Chris Bosio, Sea vs Bos 7–0
1966	Oct 8	Don Larsen, NY (A) vs Bklyn (N) 2–0 (World Series) (perfect game)		Sept 4	Jim Abbott, NY vs Clev 4–0
			1994	Apr 27	Scott Erickson, Minn vs Mil 6–0
1957	Aug 20	Bob Keegan, Chi vs Wash 6–0		July 28	Kenny Rogers, Texas vs Cal 4–0 (perfect game)
1958	July 20	Jim Bunning, Det at Bos 3–0			
	Sept 20	Hoyt Wilhelm, Balt vs NY 1–0	1996	May 14	Dwight Gooden, NY vs Sea 2–0
1962	May 5	Bo Belinsky, LA vs Balt 2–0	1998	May 17	David Wells, NY vs Minn 4–0 (perfect game)
	June 26	Earl Wilson, Bos vs LA 2–0			
	Aug 1	Bill Monbouquette, Bos at Chi 1–0			
	Aug 26	Jack Kralick, Minn vs KC 1–0			

Longest Hitting Streaks

NATIONAL LEAGUE			AMERICAN LEAGUE		
Player and Team	**Year**	**G**	**Player and Team**	**Year**	**G**
Willie Keeler, Balt	1897	44	Joe DiMaggio, NY	1941	56
Pete Rose, Cin	1978	44	George Sisler, StL	1922	41
Bill Dahlen, Chi	1894	42	Ty Cobb, Det	1911	40
Tommy Holmes, Bos	1945	37	Paul Molitor, Mil	1987	39
Billy Hamilton, Phil	1894	36	Ty Cobb, Det	1917	35
Fred Clarke, Lou	1895	35	Ty Cobb, Det	1912	34
Benito Santiago, SD	1987	34	George Sisler, StL	1925	34
George Davis, NY	1893	33	John Stone, Det	1930	34
Rogers Hornsby, StL	1922	32	George McQuinn, StL	1938	34
Ed Delahanty, Phil	1899	31	Dom DiMaggio, Bos	1949	34
Willie Davis, LA	1969	31	Hal Chase, NY	1907	33
Rico Carty, Atl	1970	31	Heinie Manush, Wash	1933	33
			Nap Lajoie, Clev	1906	31
			Sam Rice, Wash	1924	31
			Ken Landreaux, Minn	1980	31

Triple Crown Hitters

NATIONAL LEAGUE				AMERICAN LEAGUE			
Player and Team	**Year**	**HR**	**RBI**	**BA**			
Paul Hines, Prov	1878	4	50	.358			
Hugh Duffy, Bos	1894	18	145	.438			
Heinie Zimmerman*, Chi	1912	14	103	.372			
Rogers Hornsby, StL	1922	42	152	.401			
	1925	39	143	.403			
Chuck Klein, Phil	1933	28	120	.368			
Joe Medwick, StL	1937	31	154	.374			

Player and Team	**Year**	**HR**	**RBI**	**BA**
Nap Lajoie, Phil	1901	14	125	.422
Ty Cobb, Det	1909	9	115	.377
Jimmie Foxx, Phil	1933	48	163	.356
Lou Gehrig, NY	1934	49	165	.363
Ted Williams, Bos	1942	36	137	.356
	1947	32	114	.343
Mickey Mantle, NY	1956	52	130	.353
Frank Robinson, Balt	1966	49	122	.316
Carl Yastrzemski, Bos	1967	44	121	.326

*Zimmerman ranked first in RBIs as calculated by Ernie Lanigan, but only third as calculated by Information Concepts Inc.

Triple Crown Pitchers

NATIONAL LEAGUE					
Player and Team	**Year**	**W**	**L**	**SO**	**ERA**
Tommy Bond, Bos	1877	40	17	170	2.11
Hoss Radbourn, Prov	1884	60	12	441	1.38
Tim Keefe, NY	1888	35	12	333	1.74
John Clarkson, Bos	1889	49	19	284	2.73
Amos Rusie, NY	1894	36	13	195	2.78
Christy Mathewson, NY	1905	31	8	206	1.27
	1908	37	11	259	1.43
Grover Alexander, Phil	1915	31	10	241	1.22
	1916	33	12	167	1.55
	1917	30	13	201	1.86
Hippo Vaughn, Chi	1918	22	10	148	1.74
Grover Alexander, Chi	1920	27	14	173	1.91
Dazzy Vance, Bklyn	1924	28	6	262	2.16
Bucky Walters, Cin	1939	27	11	137	2.29
Sandy Koufax, LA	1963	25	5	306	1.88
	1965	26	8	382	2.04
	1966	27	9	317	1.73
Steve Carlton, Phil	1972	27	10	310	1.97
Dwight Gooden, NY	1985	24	4	268	1.53

AMERICAN LEAGUE					
Player and Team	**Year**	**W**	**L**	**SO**	**ERA**
Cy Young, Bos	1901	33	10	158	1.62
Rube Waddell, Phil	1905	26	11	287	1.48
Walter Johnson, Wash	1913	36	7	303	1.09
	1918	23	13	162	1.27
	1924	23	7	158	2.72
Lefty Grove, Phil	1930	28	5	209	2.54
	1931	31	4	175	2.06
Lefty Gomez, NY	1934	26	5	158	2.33
	1937	21	11	194	2.33
Hal Newhouser, Det	1945	25	9	212	1.81
Roger Clemens, Tor	1997	21	7	292	2.05
	1998	20	6	271	2.64

Consecutive Games Played, 500 or More Games

Cal Ripken Jr.	2,632	Frank McCormick	652
Lou Gehrig	2,130	Sandy Alomar Sr.	648
Everett Scott	1,307	Eddie Brown	618
Steve Garvey	1,207	Roy McMillan	585
Billy Williams	1,117	George Pinckney	577
Joe Sewell	1,103	Steve Brodie	574
Stan Musial	895	Aaron Ward	565
Eddie Yost	829	Candy LaChance	540
Gus Suhr	822	Buck Freeman	535
Nellie Fox	798	Fred Luderus	533
Pete Rose	745	Clyde Milan	511
Dale Murphy	740	Charlie Gehringer	511
Richie Ashburn	730	Vada Pinson	508
Ernie Banks	717	Tony Cuccinello	504
Earl Averill	673	Charlie Gehringer	504
Pete Rose	678	Omar Moreno	503

Unassisted Triple Plays

Player and Team	Date	Pos	Opp	Opp Batter
Neal Ball, Clev	7-19-09	SS	Bos	Amby McConnell
Bill Wambsganss, Clev	10-10-20	2B	Bklyn	Clarence Mitchell
George Burns, Bos	9-14-23	1B	Clev	Frank Brower
Ernie Padgett, Bos	10-6-23	SS	Phil	Walter Holke
Glenn Wright, Pitt	5-7-25	SS	StL	Jim Bottomley
Jimmy Cooney, Chi	5-30-27	SS	Pitt	Paul Waner
Johnny Neun, Det	5-31-27	1B	Clev	Homer Summa
Ron Hansen, Wash	7-30-68	SS	Clev	Joe Azcue
Mickey Morandini, Phil	9-20-92	2B	Pitt	Jeff King
John Valentin, Bos	7-15-94	SS	Minn	Marc Newfield

National League

Pennant Winners

Year	Team	Manager	W	L	Pct	GA
1900	Brooklyn	Ned Hanlon	82	54	.603	4½
1901	Pittsburgh	Fred Clarke	90	49	.647	7½
1902	Pittsburgh	Fred Clarke	103	36	.741	27½
1903	Pittsburgh	Fred Clarke	91	49	.650	6½
1904	New York	John McGraw	106	47	.693	13
1905	New York	John McGraw	105	48	.686	9
1906	Chicago	Frank Chance	116	36	.763	20
1907	Chicago	Frank Chance	107	45	.704	17
1908	Chicago	Frank Chance	99	55	.643	1
1909	Pittsburgh	Fred Clarke	110	42	.724	6½
1910	Chicago	Frank Chance	104	50	.675	13
1911	New York	John McGraw	99	54	.647	7½
1912	New York	John McGraw	103	48	.682	10
1913	New York	John McGraw	101	51	.664	12½
1914	Boston	George Stallings	94	59	.614	10½
1915	Philadelphia	Pat Moran	90	62	.592	7
1916	Brooklyn	Wilbert Robinson	94	60	.610	2½
1917	New York	John McGraw	98	56	.636	10
1918	Chicago	Fred Mitchell	84	45	.651	10½
1919	Cincinnati	Pat Moran	96	44	.686	9
1920	Brooklyn	Wilbert Robinson	93	61	.604	7
1921	New York	John McGraw	94	59	.614	4
1922	New York	John McGraw	93	61	.604	7
1923	New York	John McGraw	95	58	.621	4½
1924	New York	John McGraw	93	60	.608	1½

Pennant Winners *(Cont.)*

Year	Team	Manager	W	L	Pct	GA
1925	Pittsburgh	Bill McKechnie	95	58	.621	8½
1926	St. Louis	Rogers Hornsby	89	65	.578	2
1927	Pittsburgh	Donie Bush	94	60	.610	1½
1928	St. Louis	Bill McKechnie	95	59	.617	2
1929	Chicago	Joe McCarthy	98	54	.645	10½
1930	St. Louis	Gabby Street	92	62	.597	2
1931	St. Louis	Gabby Street	101	53	.656	13
1932	Chicago	Charlie Grimm	90	64	.584	4
1933	New York	Bill Terry	91	61	.599	5
1934	St. Louis	Frankie Frisch	95	58	.621	2
1935	Chicago	Charlie Grimm	100	54	.649	4
1936	New York	Bill Terry	92	62	.597	5
1937	New York	Bill Terry	95	57	.625	3
1938	Chicago	Gabby Hartnett	89	63	.586	2
1939	Cincinnati	Bill McKechnie	97	57	.630	4½
1940	Cincinnati	Bill McKechnie	100	53	.654	12
1941	Brooklyn	Leo Durocher	100	54	.649	2½
1942	St. Louis	Billy Southworth	106	48	.688	2
1943	St. Louis	Billy Southworth	105	49	.682	18
1944	St. Louis	Billy Southworth	105	49	.682	14½
1945	Chicago	Charlie Grimm	98	56	.636	3
1946	St. Louis*	Eddie Dyer	98	58	.628	2
1947	Brooklyn	Burt Shotton	94	60	.610	5
1948	Boston	Billy Southworth	91	62	.595	6½
1949	Brooklyn	Burt Shotton	97	57	.630	1
1950	Philadelphia	Eddie Sawyer	91	63	.591	2
1951	New York†	Leo Durocher	98	59	.624	1
1952	Brooklyn	Chuck Dressen	96	57	.627	4½
1953	Brooklyn	Chuck Dressen	105	49	.682	13
1954	New York	Leo Durocher	97	57	.630	5
1955	Brooklyn	Walt Alston	98	55	.641	13½
1956	Brooklyn	Walt Alston	93	61	.604	1
1957	Milwaukee	Fred Haney	95	59	.617	8
1958	Milwaukee	Fred Haney	92	62	.597	8
1959	Los Angeles‡	Walt Alston	88	68	.564	2
1960	Pittsburgh	Danny Murtaugh	95	59	.617	7
1961	Cincinnati	Fred Hutchinson	93	61	.604	4
1962	San Francisco#	Al Dark	103	62	.624	1
1963	Los Angeles	Walt Alston	99	63	.611	6
1964	St. Louis	Johnny Keane	93	69	.574	1
1965	Los Angeles	Walt Alston	97	65	.599	2
1966	Los Angeles	Walt Alston	95	67	.586	1½
1967	St. Louis	Red Schoendienst	101	60	.627	10½
1968	St. Louis	Red Schoendienst	97	65	.599	9
1969	New York (E)††	Gil Hodges	100	62	.617	8
1970	Cincinnati (W)††	Sparky Anderson	102	60	.630	14½
1971	Pittsburgh (E)††	Danny Murtaugh	97	65	.599	7
1972	Cincinnati (W)††	Sparky Anderson	95	59	.617	10½
1973	New York (E)††	Yogi Berra	82	79	.509	1½
1974	Los Angeles (W)††	Walt Alston	102	60	.630	4
1975	Cincinnati (W)††	Sparky Anderson	108	54	.667	20
1976	Cincinnati (W)††	Sparky Anderson	102	60	.630	10
1977	Los Angeles (W)††	Tommy Lasorda	98	64	.605	10
1978	Los Angeles (W)††	Tommy Lasorda	95	67	.586	2½
1979	Pittsburgh (E)††	Chuck Tanner	98	64	.605	2
1980	Philadelphia (E)††	Dallas Green	91	71	.562	1
1981	Los Angeles (W)††	Tommy Lasorda	63	47	.573	**
1982	St. Louis	Whitey Herzog	92	70	.568	3
1983	Philadelphia (E)††	Pat Corrales/Paul Owens	90	72	.556	6
1984	San Diego (W)††	Dick Williams	92	70	.568	12

*Defeated Brooklyn, two games to none, in playoff for pennant. †Defeated Brooklyn, two games to one, in playoff for pennant. ‡Defeated Milwaukee, two games to none, in playoff for pennant. #Defeated Los Angeles, two games to one, in playoff for pennant. ††Won Championship Series. **First half 36–21; second half 27–26, in season split by strike; defeated Houston in playoff for Western Division title.

Pennant Winners (Cont.)

Year	Team	Manager	W	L	Pct	GA
1985	St. Louis (E)††	Whitey Herzog	101	61	.623	3
1986	New York (E)††	Dave Johnson	108	54	.667	21½
1987	St. Louis (E)††	Whitey Herzog	95	67	.586	3
1988	Los Angeles (W)††	Tommy Lasorda	94	67	.584	7
1989	San Francisco (W)††	Roger Craig	92	70	.568	3
1990	Cincinnati (W)††	Lou Piniella	91	71	.562	5
1991	Atlanta (W)††	Bobby Cox	94	68	.580	1
1992	Atlanta (W)††	Bobby Cox	98	64	.605	8
1993	Philadelphia (E)††	Jim Fregosi	97	65	.599	3
1994	Season ended Aug. 11 due to players' strike					
1995	Atlanta (E)††	Bobby Cox	90	54	.625	21
1996	Atlanta (E)††	Bobby Cox	96	66	.593	8
1997	Florida (wc)††	Jim Leyland	92	70	.568	—
1998	San Diego (W)††	Bruce Bochy	98	64	.605	9½

††Won Championship Series.

Leading Batsmen

Year	Player and Team	BA	Year	Player and Team	BA
1900	Honus Wagner, Pitt	.381	1935	Arky Vaughan, Pitt	.385
1901	Jesse Burkett, StL	.382	1936	Paul Waner, Pitt	.373
1902	Ginger Beaumtl, Pitt	.357	1937	Joe Medwick, StL	.374
1903	Honus Wagner, Pitt	.355	1938	Ernie Lombardi, Cin	.342
1904	Honus Wagner, Pitt	.349	1939	Johnny Mize, StL	.349
1905	Cy Seymour, Cin	.377	1940	Debs Garms, Pitt	.355
1906	Honus Wagner, Pitt	.339	1941	Pete Reiser, Bklyn	.343
1907	Honus Wagner, Pitt	.350	1942	Ernie Lombardi, Bos	.330
1908	Honus Wagner, Pitt	.354	1943	Stan Musial, StL	.357
1909	Honus Wagner, Pitt	.339	1944	Dixie Walker, Bklyn	.357
1910	Sherry Magee, Phil	.331	1945	Phil Cavarretta, Chi	.355
1911	Honus Wagner, Pitt	.334	1946	Stan Musial, StL	.365
1912	Heinie Zimmerman, Chi	.372	1947	Harry Walker, StL-Phil	.363
1913	Jake Daubert, Bklyn	.350	1948	Stan Musial, StL	.376
1914	Jake Daubert, Bklyn	.329	1949	Jackie Robinson, Bklyn	.342
1915	Larry Doyle, NY	.320	1950	Stan Musial, StL	.346
1916	Hal Chase, Cin	.339	1951	Stan Musial, StL	.355
1917	Edd Roush, Cin	.341	1952	Stan Musial, StL	.336
1918	Zach Wheat, Bklyn	.335	1953	Carl Furillo, Bklyn	.344
1919	Edd Roush, Cin	.321	1954	Willie Mays, NY	.345
1920	Rogers Hornsby, StL	.370	1955	Richie Ashburn, Phil	.338
1921	Rogers Hornsby, StL	.397	1956	Hank Aaron, Mil	.328
1922	Rogers Hornsby, StL	.401	1957	Stan Musial, StL	.351
1923	Rogers Hornsby, StL	.384	1958	Richie Ashburn, Phil	.350
1924	Rogers Hornsby, StL	.424	1959	Hank Aaron, Mil	.355
1925	Rogers Hornsby, StL	.403	1960	Dick Groat, Pitt	.325
1926	Bubbles Hargrave, Cin	.353	1961	Roberto Clemente, Pitt	.351
1927	Paul Waner, Pitt	.380	1962	Tommy Davis, LA	.346
1928	Rogers Hornsby, Bos	.387	1963	Tommy Davis, LA	.326
1929	Lefty O'Doul, Phil	.398	1964	Roberto Clemente, Pitt	.339
1930	Bill Terry, NY	.401	1965	Roberto Clemente, Pitt	.329
1931	Chick Hafey, StL	.349	1966	Matty Alou, Pitt	.342
1932	Lefty O'Doul, Bklyn	.368	1967	Roberto Clemente, Pitt	.357
1933	Chuck Klein, Phil	.368	1968	Pete Rose, Cin	.335
1934	Paul Waner, Pitt	.362	1969	Pete Rose, Cin	.348

What Was He Thinking?

In the first inning of a May 12, 1998, game in Tampa Bay, Cleveland Indians second baseman David Bell fielded a double play grounder and flipped the ball to shortstop Omar Vizquel, who stepped on second—but neglected to catch the ball. It was Vizquel's first error in 71 games, which ended the longest active errorless streak by a shortstop in the majors. Vizquel later explained that when he had come to bat in the top of the first, he had seen out of the corner of his eye a note about his streak on the scoreboard. "It was something about Omar and 70," Vizquel said. "I figured it must be 70 straight games without an error. The first ball I handled after that was the error. I can't believe I missed it."

Leading Batsmen *(Cont.)*

Year	Player and Team	BA	Year	Player and Team	BA
1970	Rico Carty, Atl	.366	1985	Willie McGee, StL	.353
1971	Joe Torre, StL	.363	1986	Tim Raines, Mtl	.334
1972	Billy Williams, Chi	.333	1987	Tony Gwynn, SD	.370
1973	Pete Rose, Cin	.338	1988	Tony Gwynn, SD	.313
1974	Ralph Garr, Atl	.353	1989	Tony Gwynn, SD	.336
1975	Bill Madlock, Chi	.354	1990	Willie McGee, StL	.335
1976	Bill Madlock, Chi	.339	1991	Terry Pendleton, Atl	.319
1977	Dave Parker, Pitt	.338	1992	Gary Sheffield, SD	.330
1978	Dave Parker, Pitt	.334	1993	Andres Galarraga, Col	.370
1979	Keith Hernandez, StL	.344	1994	Tony Gwynn, SD	.394
1980	Bill Buckner, Chi	.324	1995	Tony Gwynn, SD	.368
1981	Bill Madlock, Pitt	.341	1996	Tony Gwynn, SD	.353
1982	Al Oliver, Mtl	.331	1997	Tony Gwynn, SD	.372
1983	Bill Madlock, Pitt	.323	1998	Larry Walker, Col	.363
1984	Tony Gwynn, SD	.351			

Leaders in Runs Scored

Year	Player and Team	Runs	Year	Player and Team	Runs
1900	Roy Thomas, Phil	131	1941	Pete Reiser, Bklyn	117
1901	Jesse Burkett, StL	139	1942	Mel Ott, NY	118
1902	Honus Wagner, Pitt	105	1943	Arky Vaughan, Bklyn	112
1903	Ginger Beaumont, Pitt	137	1944	Bill Nicholson, Chi	116
1904	George Browne, NY	99	1945	Eddie Stanky, Bklyn	128
1905	Mike Donlin, NY	124	1946	Stan Musial, StL	124
1906	Honus Wagner, Pitt	103	1947	Johnny Mize, NY	137
	Frank Chance, Chi	103	1948	Stan Musial, StL	135
1907	Spike Shannon, NY	104	1949	Pee Wee Reese, Bklyn	132
1908	Fred Tenney, NY	101	1950	Earl Torgeson, Bos	120
1909	Tommy Leach, Pitt	126	1951	Stan Musial, StL	124
1910	Sherry Magee, Phil	110		Ralph Kiner, Pitt	124
1911	Jimmy Sheckard, Chi	121	1952	Stan Musial, StL	105
1912	Bob Bescher, Cin	120		Solly Hemus, StL	105
1913	Tommy Leach, Chi	99	1953	Duke Snider, Bklyn	132
	Max Carey, Pitt	99	1954	Stan Musial, StL	120
1914	George Burns, NY	100		Duke Snider, Bklyn	120
1915	Gavvy Cravath, Phil	89	1955	Duke Snider, Bklyn	126
1916	George Burns, NY	105	1956	Frank Robinson, Cin	122
1917	George Burns, NY	103	1957	Hank Aaron, Mil	118
1918	Heinie Groh, Cin	88	1958	Willie Mays, SF	121
1919	George Burns, NY	86	1959	Vada Pinson, Cin	131
1920	George Burns, NY	115	1960	Bill Bruton, Mil	112
1921	Rogers Hornsby, StL	131	1961	Willie Mays, SF	129
1922	Rogers Hornsby, StL	141	1962	Frank Robinson, Cin	134
1923	Ross Youngs, NY	121	1963	Hank Aaron, Mil	121
1924	Frankie Frisch, NY	121	1964	Dick Allen, Phil	125
	Rogers Hornsby, StL	121	1965	Tommy Harper, Cin	126
1925	Kiki Cuyler, Pitt	144	1966	Felipe Alou, Atl	122
1926	Kiki Cuyler, Pitt	113	1967	Hank Aaron, Atl	113
1927	Lloyd Waner, Pitt	133		Lou Brock, StL	113
	Rogers Hornsby, NY	133	1968	Glenn Beckert, Chi	98
1928	Paul Waner, Pitt	142	1969	Bobby Bonds, SF	120
1929	Rogers Hornsby, Chi	156		Pete Rose, Cin	120
1930	Chuck Klein, Phil	158	1970	Billy Williams, Chi	137
1931	Bill Terry, NY	121	1971	Lou Brock, StL	126
	Chuck Klein, Phil	121	1972	Joe Morgan, Cin	122
1932	Chuck Klein, Phil	152	1973	Bobby Bonds, SF	131
1933	Pepper Martin, StL	122	1974	Pete Rose, Cin	110
1934	Paul Waner, Pitt	122	1975	Pete Rose, Cin	112
1935	Augie Galan, Chi	133	1976	Pete Rose, Cin	130
1936	Arky Vaughan, Pitt	122	1977	George Foster, Cin	124
1937	Joe Medwick, StL	111	1978	Ivan DeJesus, Chi	104
1938	Mel Ott, NY	116	1979	Keith Hernandez, StL	116
1939	Billy Werber, Cin	115	1980	Keith Hernandez, StL	111
1940	Arky Vaughan, Pitt	113	1981	Mike Schmidt, Phil	78

Leader in Runs Scored (Cont.)

Year	Player and Team	Runs	Year	Player and Team	Runs
1982	Lonnie Smith, StL	120	1990	Ryne Sandberg, Chi	116
1983	Tim Raines, Mtl	133	1991	Brett Butler, LA	112
1984	Ryne Sandberg, Chi	114	1992	Barry Bonds, Pitt	109
1985	Dale Murphy, Atl	118	1993	Lenny Dykstra, Phil	143
1986	Von Hayes, Phil	107	1994	Jeff Bagwell, Hou	104
	Tony Gwynn, SD	107	1995	Craig Biggio, Hou	123
1987	Tim Raines, Mtl	123	1996	Ellis Burks, Col	142
1988	Brett Butler, SF	109	1997	Craig Biggio, Hou	146
1989	Howard Johnson, NY	104	1998	Sammy Sosa, Chi	134
	Will Clark, SF	104			
	Ryne Sandberg, Chi	104			

Leaders in Hits

Year	Player and Team	Hits	Year	Player and Team	Hits
1900	Willie Keeler, Bklyn	208	1948	Stan Musial, StL	230
1901	Jesse Burkett, StL	228	1949	Stan Musial, StL	207
1902	Ginger Beaumont, Pitt	194	1950	Duke Snider, Bklyn	199
1903	Ginger Beaumont, Pitt	209	1951	Richie Ashburn, Phil	221
1904	Ginger Beaumont, Pitt	185	1952	Stan Musial, StL	194
1905	Cy Seymour, Cin	219	1953	Richie Ashburn, Phil	205
1906	Harry Steinfeldt, Chi	176	1954	Don Mueller, NY	212
1907	Ginger Beaumont, Bos	187	1955	Ted Kluszewski, Cin	192
1908	Honus Wagner, Pitt	201	1956	Hank Aaron, Mil	200
1909	Larry Doyle, NY	172	1957	Red Schoendienst, NY-Mil	200
1910	Honus Wagner, Pitt	178	1958	Richie Ashburn, Phil	215
	Bobby Byrne, Pitt	178	1959	Hank Aaron, Mil	223
1911	Doc Miller, Bos	192	1960	Willie Mays, SF	190
1912	Heinie Zimmerman, Chi	207	1961	Vada Pinson, Cin	208
1913	Gavvy Cravath, Phil	179	1962	Tommy Davis, LA	230
1914	Sherry Magee, Phil	171	1963	Vada Pinson, Cin	204
1915	Larry Doyle, NY	189	1964	Roberto Clemente, Pitt	211
1916	Hal Chase, Cin	184		Curt Flood, StL	211
1917	Heinie Groh, Cin	182	1965	Pete Rose, Cin	209
1918	Charlie Hollocher, Chi	161	1966	Felipe Alou, Atl	218
1919	Ivy Olson, Bklyn	164	1967	Roberto Clemente, Pitt	209
1920	Rogers Hornsby, StL	218	1968	Felipe Alou, Atl	210
1921	Rogers Hornsby, StL	235		Pete Rose, Cin	210
1922	Rogers Hornsby, StL	250	1969	Matty Alou, Pitt	231
1923	Frankie Frisch, NY	223	1970	Pete Rose, Cin	205
1924	Rogers Hornsby, StL	227		Billy Williams, Chi	205
1925	Jim Bottomley, StL	227	1971	Joe Torre, StL	230
1926	Eddie Brown, Bos	201	1972	Pete Rose, Cin	198
1927	Paul Waner, Pitt	237	1973	Pete Rose, Cin	230
1928	Freddy Lindstrom, NY	231	1974	Ralph Garr, Atl	214
1929	Lefty O'Doul, Phil	254	1975	Dave Cash, Phil	213
1930	Bill Terry, NY	254	1976	Pete Rose, Cin	215
1931	Lloyd Waner, Pitt	214	1977	Dave Parker, Pitt	215
1932	Chuck Klein, Phil	226	1978	Steve Garvey, LA	202
1933	Chuck Klein, Phil	223	1979	Garry Templeton, StL	211
1934	Paul Waner, Pitt	217	1980	Steve Garvey, LA	200
1935	Billy Herman, Chi	227	1981	Pete Rose, Phil	140
1936	Joe Medwick, StL	223	1982	Al Oliver, Mtl	204
1937	Joe Medwick, StL	237	1983	Jose Cruz, Hou	189
1938	Frank McCormick, Cin	209		Andre Dawson, Mtl	189
1939	Frank McCormick, Cin	209	1984	Tony Gwynn, SD	213
1940	Stan Hack, Chi	191	1985	Willie McGee, StL	216
	Frank McCormick, Cin	191	1986	Tony Gwynn, SD	211
1941	Stan Hack, Chi	186	1987	Tony Gwynn, SD	218
1942	Enos Slaughter, StL	188	1988	Andres Galarraga, Mtl	184
1943	Stan Musial, StL	220	1989	Tony Gwynn, SD	203
1944	Stan Musial, StL	197	1990	Brett Butler, SF	192
	Phil Cavarretta, Chi	197		Lenny Dykstra, Phil	192
1945	Tommy Holmes, Bos	224	1991	Terry Pendleton, Atl	187
1946	Stan Musial, StL	228	1992	Terry Pendleton, Atl	199
1947	Tommy Holmes, Bos	191		Andy Van Slyke, Pitt	199

Leaders in Hits (Cont.)

Year	Player and Team	Hits	Year	Player and Team	Hits
1993	Lenny Dykstra, Phil	194	1996	Lance Johnson, NY	227
1994	Tony Gwynn, SD	165	1997	Tony Gwynn, SD	220
1995	Dante Bichette, Col	197	1998	Dante Bichette, Col	219
	Tony Gwynn, SD	197			

Home Run Leaders

Year	Player and Team	HR	Year	Player and Team	HR
1900	Herman Long, Bos	12	1948	Ralph Kiner, Pitt	40
1901	Sam Crawford, Cin	16		Johnny Mize, NY	40
1902	Tommy Leach, Pitt	6	1949	Ralph Kiner, Pitt	54
1903	Jimmy Sheckard, Bklyn	9	1950	Ralph Kiner, Pitt	47
1904	Harry Lumley, Bklyn	9	1951	Ralph Kiner, Pitt	42
1905	Fred Odwell, Cin	9	1952	Ralph Kiner, Pitt	37
1906	Tim Jordan, Bklyn	12		Hank Sauer, Chi	37
1907	Dave Brain, Bos	10	1953	Eddie Mathews, Mil	47
1908	Tim Jordan, Bklyn	12	1954	Ted Kluszewski, Cin	49
1909	Red Murray, NY	7	1955	Willie Mays, NY	51
1910	Fred Beck, Bos	10	1956	Duke Snider, Bklyn	43
	Wildfire Schulte, Chi	10	1957	Hank Aaron, Mil	44
1911	Wildfire Schulte, Chi	21	1958	Ernie Banks, Chi	47
1912	Heinie Zimmerman, Chi	14	1959	Eddie Mathews, Mil	46
1913	Gavvy Cravath, Phil	19	1960	Ernie Banks, Chi	41
1914	Gavvy Cravath, Phil	19	1961	Orlando Cepeda, SF	46
1915	Gavvy Cravath, Phil	24	1962	Willie Mays, SF	49
1916	Dave Robertson, NY	12	1963	Hank Aaron, Mil	44
	Cy Williams, Chi	12		Willie McCovey, SF	44
1917	Dave Robertson, NY	12	1964	Willie Mays, SF	47
	Gavvy Cravath, Phil	12	1965	Willie Mays, SF	52
1918	Gavvy Cravath, Phil	8	1966	Hank Aaron, Atl	44
1919	Gavvy Cravath, Phil	12	1967	Hank Aaron, Atl	39
1920	Cy Williams, Phil	15	1968	Willie McCovey, SF	36
1921	George Kelly, NY	23	1969	Willie McCovey, SF	45
1922	Rogers Hornsby, StL	42	1970	Johnny Bench, Cin	45
1923	Cy Williams, Phil	41	1971	Willie Stargell, Pitt	48
1924	Jack Fournier, Bklyn	27	1972	Johnny Bench, Cin	40
1925	Rogers Hornsby, StL	39	1973	Willie Stargell, Pitt	44
1926	Hack Wilson, Chi	21	1974	Mike Schmidt, Phil	36
1927	Hack Wilson, Chi	30	1975	Mike Schmidt, Phil	38
	Cy Williams, Phil	30	1976	Mike Schmidt, Phil	38
1928	Hack Wilson, Chi	31	1977	George Foster, Cin	52
	Jim Bottomley, StL	31	1978	George Foster, Cin	40
1929	Chuck Klein, Phil	43	1979	Dave Kingman, Chi	48
1930	Hack Wilson, Chi	56	1980	Mike Schmidt, Phil	48
1931	Chuck Klein, Phil	31	1981	Mike Schmidt, Phil	31
1932	Chuck Klein, Phil	38	1982	Dave Kingman, NY	37
	Mel Ott, NY	38	1983	Mike Schmidt, Phil	40
1933	Chuck Klein, Phil	28	1984	Dale Murphy, Atl	36
1934	Ripper Collins, StL	35		Mike Schmidt, Phil	36
	Mel Ott, NY	35	1985	Dale Murphy, Atl	37
1935	Wally Berger, Bos	34	1986	Mike Schmidt, Phil	37
1936	Mel Ott, NY	33	1987	Andre Dawson, Chi	49
1937	Mel Ott, NY	31	1988	Darryl Strawberry, NY	39
	Joe Medwick, StL	31	1989	Kevin Mitchell, SF	47
1938	Mel Ott, NY	36	1990	Ryne Sandberg, Chi	40
1939	Johnny Mize, StL	28	1991	Howard Johnson, NY	38
1940	Johnny Mize, StL	43	1992	Fred McGriff, SD	35
1941	Dolph Camilli, Bklyn	34	1993	Barry Bonds, SF	46
1942	Mel Ott, NY	30	1994	Matt Williams, SF	43
1943	Bill Nicholson, Chi	29	1995	Dante Bichette, Col	40
1944	Bill Nicholson, Chi	33	1996	Andres Galarraga, Col	47
1945	Tommy Holmes, Bos	28	1997	Larry Walker, Col	49
1946	Ralph Kiner, Pitt	23	1998	Mark McGwire, StL	70
1947	Ralph Kiner, Pitt	51			
	Johnny Mize, NY	51			

Runs Batted In Leaders

Year	Player and Team	RBI	Year	Player and Team	RBI
1900	Elmer Flick, Phil	110	1950	Del Ennis, Phil	126
1901	Honus Wagner, Pitt	126	1951	Monte Irvin, NY	121
1902	Honus Wagner, Pitt	91	1952	Hank Sauer, Chi	121
1903	Sam Mertes, NY	104	1953	Roy Campanella, Bklyn	142
1904	Bill Dahlen, NY	80	1954	Ted Kluszewski, Cin	141
1905	Cy Seymour, Cin	121	1955	Duke Snider, Bklyn	136
1906	Jim Nealon, Pitt	83	1956	Stan Musial, StL	109
	Harry Steinfeldt, Chi	83	1957	Hank Aaron, Mil	132
1907	Sherry Magee, Phil	85	1958	Ernie Banks, Chi	129
1908	Honus Wagner, Pitt	109	1959	Ernie Banks, Chi	143
1909	Honus Wagner, Pitt	100	1960	Hank Aaron, Mil	126
1910	Sherry Magee, Phil	123	1961	Orlando Cepeda, SF	142
1911	Wildfire Schulte, Chi	121	1962	Tommy Davis, LA	153
1912	Heinie Zimmerman, Chi	103	1963	Hank Aaron, Mil	130
1913	Gavvy Cravath, Phil	128	1964	Ken Boyer, StL	119
1914	Sherry Magee, Phil	103	1965	Deron Johnson, Cin	130
1915	Gavvy Cravath, Phil	115	1966	Hank Aaron, Atl	127
1916	Heinie Zimmerman, Chi-NY	83	1967	Orlando Cepeda, StL	111
1917	Heinie Zimmerman, NY	102	1968	Willie McCovey, SF	105
1918	Sherry Magee, Phil	76	1969	Willie McCovey, SF	126
1919	Hi Myers, Bklyn	73	1970	Johnny Bench, Cin	148
1920	George Kelly, NY	94	1971	Joe Torre, StL	137
	Rogers Hornsby, StL	94	1972	Johnny Bench, Cin	125
1921	Rogers Hornsby, StL	126	1973	Willie Stargell, Pitt	119
1922	Rogers Hornsby, StL	152	1974	Johnny Bench, Cin	129
1923	Irish Meusel, NY	125	1975	Greg Luzinski, Phil	120
1924	George Kelly, NY	136	1976	George Foster, Cin	121
1925	Rogers Hornsby, StL	143	1977	George Foster, Cin	149
1926	Jim Bottomley, StL	120	1978	George Foster, Cin	120
1927	Paul Waner, Pitt	131	1979	Dave Winfield, SD	118
1928	Jim Bottomley, StL	136	1980	Mike Schmidt, Phil	121
1929	Hack Wilson, Chi	159	1981	Mike Schmidt, Phil	91
1930	Hack Wilson, Chi	190	1982	Dale Murphy, Atl	109
1931	Chuck Klein, Phil	121		Al Oliver, Mtl	109
1932	Don Hurst, Phil	143	1983	Dale Murphy, Atl	121
1933	Chuck Klein, Phil	120	1984	Gary Carter, Mtl	106
1934	Mel Ott, NY	135		Mike Schmidt, Phil	106
1935	Wally Berger, Bos	130	1985	Dave Parker, Cin	125
1936	Joe Medwick, StL	138	1986	Mike Schmidt, Phil	119
1937	Joe Medwick, StL	154	1987	Andre Dawson, Chi	137
1938	Joe Medwick, StL	122	1988	Will Clark, SF	109
1939	Frank McCormick, Cin	128	1989	Kevin Mitchell, SF	125
1940	Johnny Mize, StL	137	1990	Matt Williams, SF	122
1941	Dolph Camilli, Bklyn	120	1991	Howard Johnson, NY	117
1942	Johnny Mize, NY	110	1992	Darren Daulton, Phil	109
1943	Bill Nicholson, Chi	128	1993	Barry Bonds, SF	123
1944	Bill Nicholson, Chi	122	1994	Jeff Bagwell, Hou	116
1945	Dixie Walker, Bklyn	124	1995	Dante Bichette, Col	128
1946	Enos Slaughter, StL	130	1996	Andres Galarraga, Col	150
1947	Johnny Mize, NY	138	1997	Andres Galarraga, Col	140
1948	Stan Musial, StL	131	1998	Sammy Sosa, Chi	158
1949	Ralph Kiner, Pitt	127			

THEY SAID IT

Terry Francona, Philadelphia Phillies manager, on San Francisco Giants outfielder Marvin Berard, who was 12 for 18 against the Phils in a recent series: "If he goes to arbitration, he should take us with him."

Leading Base Stealers

Year	Player and Team	SB	Year	Player and Team	SB
1900	George Van Haltren, NY	45	1954	Bill Bruton, Mil	34
	Patsy Donovan, StL	45	1955	Bill Bruton, Mil	35
1901	Honus Wagner, Pitt	48	1956	Willie Mays, NY	40
1902	Honus Wagner, Pitt	43	1957	Willie Mays, NY	38
1903	Jimmy Sheckard, Bklyn	67	1958	Willie Mays, SF	31
	Frank Chance, Chi	67	1959	Willie Mays, SF	27
1904	Honus Wagner, Pitt	53	1960	Maury Wills, LA	50
1905	Billy Maloney, Chi	59	1961	Maury Wills, LA	35
	Art Devlin, NY	59	1962	Maury Wills, LA	104
1906	Frank Chance, Chi	57	1963	Maury Wills, LA	40
1907	Honus Wagner, Pitt	61	1964	Maury Wills, LA	53
1908	Honus Wagner, Pitt	53	1965	Maury Wills, LA	94
1909	Bob Bescher, Cin	54	1966	Lou Brock, StL	74
1910	Bob Bescher, Cin	70	1967	Lou Brock, StL	52
1911	Bob Bescher, Cin	80	1968	Lou Brock, StL	62
1912	Bob Bescher, Cin	67	1969	Lou Brock, StL	53
1913	Max Carey, Pitt	61	1970	Bobby Tolan, Cin	57
1914	George Burns, NY	62	1971	Lou Brock, StL	64
1915	Max Carey, Pitt	36	1972	Lou Brock, StL	63
1916	Max Carey, Pitt	63	1973	Lou Brock, StL	70
1917	Max Carey, Pitt	46	1974	Lou Brock, StL	118
1918	Max Carey, Pitt	58	1975	Davey Lopes, LA	77
1919	George Burns, NY	40	1976	Davey Lopes, LA	63
1920	Max Carey, Pitt	52	1977	Frank Taveras, Pitt	70
1921	Frankie Frisch, NY	49	1978	Omar Moreno, Pitt	71
1922	Max Carey, Pitt	51	1979	Omar Moreno, Pitt	77
1923	Max Carey, Pitt	51	1980	Ron LeFlore, Mtl	97
1924	Max Carey, Pitt	49	1981	Tim Raines, Mtl	71
1925	Max Carey, Pitt	46	1982	Tim Raines, Mtl	78
1926	Kiki Cuyler, Pitt	35	1983	Tim Raines, Mtl	90
1927	Frankie Frisch, StL	48	1984	Tim Raines, Mtl	75
1928	Kiki Cuyler, Chi	37	1985	Vince Coleman, StL	110
1929	Kiki Cuyler, Chi	43	1986	Vince Coleman, StL	107
1930	Kiki Cuyler, Chi	37	1987	Vince Coleman, StL	109
1931	Frankie Frisch, StL	28	1988	Vince Coleman, StL	81
1932	Chuck Klein, Phil	20	1989	Vince Coleman, StL	65
1933	Pepper Martin, StL	26	1990	Vince Coleman, StL	77
1934	Pepper Martin, StL	23	1991	Marquis Grissom, Mtl	76
1935	Augie Galan, Chi	22	1992	Marquis Grissom, Mtl	78
1936	Pepper Martin, StL	23	1993	Chuck Carr, Flor	58
1937	Augie Galan, Chi	23	1994	Craig Biggio, Hou	39
1938	Stan Hack, Chi	16	1995	Quilvio Veras, Fla	56
1939	Stan Hack, Chi	17	1996	Eric Young, Col	53
	Lee Handley, Pitt	17	1997	Tony Womack, Pitt	60
1940	Lonny Frey, Cin	22	1998	Tony Womack, Pitt	58
1941	Danny Murtaugh, Phil	18			
1942	Pete Reiser, Bklyn	20			
1943	Arky Vaughan, Bklyn	20			
1944	Johnny Barrett, Pitt	28			
1945	Red Schoendienst, StL	26			
1946	Pete Reiser, Bklyn	34			
1947	Jackie Robinson, Bklyn	29			
1948	Richie Ashburn, Phil	32			
1949	Jackie Robinson, Bklyn	37			
1950	Sam Jethroe, Bos	35			
1951	Sam Jethroe, Bos	35			
1952	Pee Wee Reese, Bklyn	30			
1953	Bill Bruton, Mil	26			

THEY SAID IT

Rod Beck, Chicago Cubs closer, contending that his far-less-than-buff physique doesn't make him injury-prone: "I've never seen anyone on the DL with pulled fat."

Leading Pitchers—Winning Percentage

Year	Pitcher and Team	W	L	Pct	Year	Pitcher and Team	W	L	Pct
1900	Jesse Tannehill, Pitt	20	6	.769	1950	Sal Maglie, NY	18	4	.818
1901	Jack Chesbro, Pitt	21	10	.677	1951	Preacher Roe, Bklyn	22	3	.880
1902	Jack Chesbro, Pitt	28	6	.824	1952	Hoyt Wilhelm, NY	15	3	.833
1903	Sam Leever, Pitt	25	7	.781	1953	Carl Erskine, Bklyn	20	6	.769
1904	Joe McGinnity, NY	35	8	.814	1954	Johnny Antonelli, NY	21	7	.750
1905	Sam Leever, Pitt	20	5	.800	1955	Don Newcombe, Bklyn	20	5	.800
1906	Ed Reulbach, Chi	19	4	.826	1956	Don Newcombe, Bklyn	27	7	.794
1907	Ed Reulbach, Chi	17	4	.810	1957	Bob Buhl, Mil	18	7	.720
1908	Ed Reulbach, Chi	24	7	.774	1958	Warren Spahn, Mil	22	11	.667
1909	Christy Mathewson, NY	25	6	.806		Lew Burdette, Mil	20	10	.667
	Howie Camnitz, Pitt	25	6	.806	1959	Roy Face, Pitt	18	1	.947
1910	King Cole, Chi	20	4	.833	1960	Ernie Broglio, StL	21	9	.700
1911	Rube Marquard, NY	24	7	.774	1961	Johnny Podres, LA	18	5	.783
1912	Claude Hendrix, Pitt	24	9	.727	1962	Bob Purkey, Cin	23	5	.821
1913	Bert Humphries, Chi	16	4	.800	1963	Ron Perranoski, LA	16	3	.842
1914	Bill James, Bos	26	7	.788	1964	Sandy Koufax, LA	19	5	.792
1915	Grover Alexander, Phil	31	10	.756	1965	Sandy Koufax, LA	26	8	.765
1916	Tom Hughes, Bos	16	3	.842	1966	Juan Marichal, SF	25	6	.806
1917	Ferdie Schupp, NY	21	7	.750	1967	Dick Hughes, StL	16	6	.727
1918	Claude Hendrix, Chi	19	7	.731	1968	Steve Blass, Pitt	18	6	.750
1919	Dutch Ruether, Cin	19	6	.760	1969	Tom Seaver, NY	25	7	.781
1920	Burleigh Grimes, Bklyn	23	11	.676	1970	Bob Gibson, StL	23	7	.767
1921	Bill Doak, StL	15	6	.714	1971	Don Gullett, Cin	16	6	.727
1922	Pete Donohue, Cin	18	9	.667	1972	Gary Nolan, Cin	15	5	.750
1923	Dolf Luque, Cin	27	8	.771	1973	Tommy John, LA	16	7	.696
1924	Emil Yde, Pitt	16	3	.842	1974	Andy Messersmith, LA	20	6	.769
1925	Bill Sherdel, StL	15	6	.714	1975	Don Gullett, Cin	15	4	.789
1926	Ray Kremer, Pitt	20	6	.769	1976	Steve Carlton, Phil	20	7	.741
1927	Larry Benton, Bos-NY	17	7	.708	1977	John Candelaria, Pitt	20	5	.800
1928	Larry Benton, NY	25	9	.735	1978	Gaylord Perry, SD	21	6	.778
1929	Charlie Root, Chi	19	6	.760	1979	Tom Seaver, Cin	16	6	.727
1930	Freddie Fitzsimmons, NY	19	7	.731	1980	Jim Bibby, Pitt	19	6	.760
1931*	Paul Derringer, StL	18	8	.692	1981*	Tom Seaver, Cin	14	2	.875
1932	Lon Warneke, Chi	22	6	.786	1982	Phil Niekro, Atl	17	4	.810
1933	Ben Cantwell, Bos	20	10	.667	1983	John Denny, Phil	19	6	.760
1934	Dizzy Dean, StL	30	7	.811	1984	Rick Sutcliffe, Chi	16	1	.941
1935	Bill Lee, Chi	20	6	.769	1985	Orel Hershiser, LA	19	3	.864
1936	Carl Hubbell, NY	26	6	.813	1986	Bob Ojeda, NY	18	5	.783
1937	Carl Hubbell, NY	22	8	.733	1987	Dwight Gooden, NY	15	7	.682
1938	Bill Lee, Chi	22	9	.710	1988	David Cone, NY	20	3	.870
1939	Paul Derringer, Cin	25	7	.781	1989	Mike Bielecki, Chi	18	7	.720
1940	Freddie Fitzsimmons, Bklyn	16	2	.889	1990	Doug Drabeck, Pitt	22	6	.786
1941	Elmer Riddle, Cin	19	4	.826	1991	John Smiley, Pitt	20	8	.714
1942	Larry French, Bklyn	15	4	.789		Jose Rijo, Cin	15	6	.714
1943	Mort Cooper, StL	21	8	.724	1992	Bob Tewksbury, StL	16	5	.762
1944	Ted Wilks, StL	17	4	.810	1993	Tom Glavine, Atl	22	6	.786
1945	Harry Brecheen, StL	15	4	.789	1994	Ken Hill, Mtl	16	5	.762
1946	Murray Dickson, StL	15	6	.714	1995	Greg Maddux, Atl	19	2	.905
1947	Larry Jansen, NY	21	5	.808	1996	John Smoltz, Atl	24	8	.750
1948	Harry Brecheen, StL	20	7	.741	1997	Denny Neagle, Atl	20	5	.800
1949	Preacher Roe, Bklyn	15	6	.714	1998	John Smoltz, Atl	17	3	.850

*1981 percentages based on 10 or more victories. Note: Percentages based on 15 or more victories in all other years.

Leading Pitchers—Earned-Run Average

Year	Player and Team	ERA	Year	Player and Team	ERA
1900	Rube Waddell, Pitt	2.37	1910	George McQuillan, Phil	1.60
1901	Jesse Tannehill, Pitt	2.18	1911	Christy Mathewson, NY	1.99
1902	Jack Taylor, Chi	1.33	1912	Jeff Tesreau, NY	1.96
1903	Sam Leever, Pitt	2.06	1913	Christy Mathewson, NY	2.06
1904	Joe McGinnity, NY	1.61	1914	Bill Doak, StL	1.72
1905	Christy Mathewson, NY	1.27	1915	Grover Alexander, Phil	1.22
1906	Three Finger Brown, Chi	1.04	1916	Grover Alexander, Phil	1.55
1907	Jack Pfiester, Chi	1.15	1917	Grover Alexander, Phil	1.83
1908	Christy Mathewson, NY	1.43	1918	Hippo Vaughn, Chi	1.74
1909	Christy Mathewson, NY	1.14	1919	Grover Alexander, Chi	1.72

Leading Pitchers—Earned-Run Average *(Cont.)*

Year	Player and Team	ERA	Year	Player and Team	ERA
1920	Grover Alexander, Chi	1.91	1960	Mike McCormick, SF	2.70
1921	Bill Doak, StL	2.58	1961	Warren Spahn, Mil	3.01
1922	Rosy Ryan, NY	3.00	1962	Sandy Koufax, LA	2.54
1923	Dolf Luque, Cin	1.93	1963	Sandy Koufax, LA	1.88
1924	Dazzy Vance, Bklyn	2.16	1964	Sandy Koufax, LA	1.74
1925	Dolf Luque, Cin	2.63	1965	Sandy Koufax, LA	2.04
1926	Ray Kremer, Pitt	2.61	1966	Sandy Koufax, LA	1.73
1927	Ray Kremer, Pitt	2.47	1967	Phil Niekro, Atl	1.87
1928	Dazzy Vance, Bklyn	2.09	1968	Bob Gibson, StL	1.12
1929	Bill Walker, NY	3.08	1969	Juan Marichal, SF	2.10
1930	Dazzy Vance, Bklyn	2.61	1970	Tom Seaver, NY	2.81
1931	Bill Walker, NY	2.26	1971	Tom Seaver, NY	1.76
1932	Lon Warneke, Chi	2.37	1972	Steve Carlton, Phil	1.98
1933	Carl Hubbell, NY	1.66	1973	Tom Seaver, NY	2.08
1934	Carl Hubbell, NY	2.30	1974	Buzz Capra, Atl	2.28
1935	Cy Blanton, Pitt	2.59	1975	Randy Jones, SD	2.24
1936	Carl Hubbell, NY	2.31	1976	John Denny, StL	2.52
1937	Jim Turner, Bos	2.38	1977	John Candelaria, Pitt	2.34
1938	Bill Lee, Chi	2.66	1978	Craig Swan, NY	2.43
1939	Bucky Walters, Cin	2.29	1979	J.R. Richard, Hou	2.71
1940	Bucky Walters, Cin	2.48	1980	Don Sutton, LA	2.21
1941	Elmer Riddle, Cin	2.24	1981	Nolan Ryan, Hou	1.69
1942	Mort Cooper, StL	1.77	1982	Steve Rogers, Mtl	2.40
1943	Howie Pollet, StL	1.75	1983	Atlee Hammaker, SF	2.25
1944	Ed Heusser, Cin	2.38	1984	Alejandro Pena, LA	2.48
1945	Hank Borowy, Chi	2.14	1985	Dwight Gooden, NY	1.53
1946	Howie Pollet, StL	2.10	1986	Mike Scott, Hou	2.22
1947	Warren Spahn, Bos	2.33	1987	Nolan Ryan, Hou	2.76
1948	Harry Brecheen, StL	2.24	1988	Joe Magrane, StL	2.18
1949	Dave Koslo, NY	2.50	1989	Scott Garrelts, SF	2.28
1950	Jim Hearn, StL-NY	2.49	1990	Danny Darwin, Hou	2.21
1951	Chet Nichols, Bos	2.88	1991	Dennis Martinez, Mtl	2.39
1952	Hoyt Wilhelm, NY	2.43	1992	Bill Swift, SF	2.08
1953	Warren Spahn, Mil	2.10	1993	Greg Maddux, Atl	2.36
1954	Johnny Antonelli, NY	2.29	1994	Greg Maddux, Atl	1.56
1955	Bob Friend, Pitt	2.84	1995	Greg Maddux, Atl	1.63
1956	Lew Burdette, Mil	2.71	1996	Kevin Brown, Fla	1.89
1957	Johnny Podres, Bklyn	2.66	1997	Pedro Martinez, Mtl	1.90
1958	Stu Miller, SF	2.47	1998	Greg Maddux, Atl	1.98
1959	Sam Jones, SF	2.82			

Note: Based on 10 complete games through 1950, then 154 innings until National League expanded in 1962, when it became 162 innings. In strike-shortened 1981, one inning per game required.

Leading Pitchers—Strikeouts

Year	Player and Team	SO	Year	Player and Team	SO
1900	Rube Waddell, Pitt	133	1919	Hippo Vaughn, Chi	141
1901	Noodles Hahn, Cin	233	1920	Grover Alexander, Chi	173
1902	Vic Willis, Bos	226	1921	Burleigh Grimes, Bklyn	136
1903	Christy Mathewson, NY	267	1922	Dazzy Vance, Bklyn	134
1904	Christy Mathewson, NY	212	1923	Dazzy Vance, Bklyn	197
1905	Christy Mathewson, NY	206	1924	Dazzy Vance, Bklyn	262
1906	Fred Beebe, Chi-StL	171	1925	Dazzy Vance, Bklyn	221
1907	Christy Mathewson, NY	178	1926	Dazzy Vance, Bklyn	140
1908	Christy Mathewson, NY	259	1927	Dazzy Vance, Bklyn	184
1909	Orval Overall, Chi	205	1928	Dazzy Vance, Bklyn	200
1910	Christy Mathewson, NY	190	1929	Pat Malone, Chi	166
1911	Rube Marquard, NY	237	1930	Bill Hallahan, StL	177
1912	Grover Alexander, Phil	195	1931	Bill Hallahan, StL	159
1913	Tom Seaton, Phil	168	1932	Dizzy Dean, StL	191
1914	Grover Alexander, Phil	214	1933	Dizzy Dean, StL	199
1915	Grover Alexander, Phil	241	1934	Dizzy Dean, StL	195
1916	Grover Alexander, Phil	167	1935	Dizzy Dean, StL	182
1917	Grover Alexander, Phil	200	1936	Van Lingle Mungo, Bklyn	238
1918	Hippo Vaughn, Chi	148	1937	Carl Hubbell, NY	159

Leading Pitchers—Strikeouts *(Cont.)*

Year	Player and Team	SO	Year	Player and Team	SO
1938	Clay Bryant, Chi	135	1968	Bob Gibson, StL	268
1939	Claude Passeau, Phil-Chi	137	1969	Ferguson Jenkins, Chi	273
	Bucky Walters, Cin	137	1970	Tom Seaver, NY	283
1940	Kirby Higbe, Phil	137	1971	Tom Seaver, NY	289
1941	Johnny Vander Meer, Cin	202	1972	Steve Carlton, Phil	310
1942	Johnny Vander Meer, Cin	186	1973	Tom Seaver, NY	251
1943	Johnny Vander Meer, Cin	174	1974	Steve Carlton, Phil	240
1944	Bill Voiselle, NY	161	1975	Tom Seaver, NY	243
1945	Preacher Roe, Pitt	148	1976	Tom Seaver, NY	235
1946	Johnny Schmitz, Chi	135	1977	Phil Niekro, Atl	262
1947	Ewell Blackwell, Cin	193	1978	J.R. Richard, Hou	303
1948	Harry Brecheen, StL	149	1979	J.R. Richard, Hou	313
1949	Warren Spahn, Bos	151	1980	Steve Carlton, Phil	286
1950	Warren Spahn, Bos	191	1981	Fernando Valenzuela, LA	180
1951	Warren Spahn, Bos	164	1982	Steve Carlton, Phil	286
	Don Newcombe, Bklyn	164	1983	Steve Carlton, Phil	275
1952	Warren Spahn, Bos	183	1984	Dwight Gooden, NY	276
1953	Robin Roberts, Phil	198	1985	Dwight Gooden, NY	268
1954	Robin Roberts, Phil	185	1986	Mike Scott, Hou	306
1955	Sam Jones, Chi	198	1987	Nolan Ryan, Hou	270
1956	Sam Jones, Chi	176	1988	Nolan Ryan, Hou	228
1957	Jack Sanford, Phil	188	1989	Jose DeLeon, StL	201
1958	Sam Jones, StL	225	1990	David Cone, NY	233
1959	Don Drysdale, LA	242	1991	David Cone, NY	241
1960	Don Drysdale, LA	246	1992	John Smoltz, Atl	215
1961	Sandy Koufax, LA	269	1993	Jose Rijo, Cin	227
1962	Don Drysdale, LA	232	1994	Andy Benes, SD	189
1963	Sandy Koufax, LA	306	1995	Hideo Nomo, LA	236
1964	Bob Veale, Pitt	250	1996	John Smoltz, Atl	276
1965	Sandy Koufax, LA	382	1997	Curt Schilling, Phil	319
1966	Sandy Koufax, LA	317	1998	Curt Schilling, Phil	300
1967	Jim Bunning, Phil	253			

Leading Pitchers—Saves

Year	Player and Team	SV	Year	Player and Team	SV
1947	Hugh Casey, Bklyn	18	1973	Mike Marshall, Mtl	13
1948	Harry Gumpert, Cin	17	1974	Mike Marshall, LA	21
1949	Ted Wilks, StL	9	1975	Al Hrabosky, StL	22
1950	Jim Konstanty, Phil	22		Rawly Eastwick, Cin	22
1951	Ted Wilks, StL, Pitt	13	1976	Rawly Eastwick, Cin	26
1952	Al Brazle, StL	16	1977	Rollie Fingers, SD	35
1953	Al Brazle, StL	18	1978	Rollie Fingers, SD	37
1954	Jim Hughes, Bklyn	24	1979	Bruce Sutter, Chi	37
1955	Jack Meyer, Phil	16	1980	Bruce Sutter, Chi	28
1956	Clem Labine, Bklyn	19	1981	Bruce Sutter, StL	25
1957	Clem Labine, Bklyn	17	1982	Bruce Sutter, StL	36
1958	Roy Face, Pitt	20	1983	Lee Smith, Chi	29
1959	Lindy McDaniel, StL	15	1984	Bruce Sutter, StL	45
	Don McMahon, Mil	15	1985	Jeff Reardon, Mtl	41
1960	Lindy McDaniel, StL	26	1986	Todd Worrell, StL	36
1961	Stu Miller, SF	17	1987	Steve Bedrosian, Phil	40
	Roy Face, Pitt	17	1988	John Franco, Cin	39
1962	Roy Face, Pitt	28	1989	Mark Davis, SD	44
1963	Lindy McDaniel, Chi	22	1990	John Franco, NY	33
1964	Hal Woodeshick, Hou	23	1991	Lee Smith, StL	47
1965	Ted Abernathy, Chi	31	1992	Lee Smith, StL	42
1966	Phil Regan, LA	21	1993	Randy Myers, Chi	53
1967	Ted Abernathy, Cin	28	1994	John Franco, NY	30
1968	Phil Regan, Chi, LA	25	1995	Randy Myers, Chi	38
1969	Fred Gladding, Hou	29	1996	Jeff Brantley, Cin	44
1970	Wayne Granger, Cin	35		Todd Worrell, LA	44
1971	Dave Giusti, Pitt	30	1997	Jeff Shaw, Cin	42
1972	Clay Carroll, Cin	37	1998	Trevor Hoffman, SD	53

American League

Pennant Winners

Year	Team	Manager	W	L	Pct	GA
1901	Chicago	Clark Griffith	83	53	.610	4
1902	Philadelphia	Connie Mack	83	53	.610	5
1903	Boston	Jimmy Collins	91	47	.659	14½
1904	Boston	Jimmy Collins	95	59	.617	1½
1905	Philadelphia	Connie Mack	92	56	.622	2
1906	Chicago	Fielder Jones	93	58	.616	3
1907	Detroit	Hughie Jennings	92	58	.613	1½
1908	Detroit	Hughie Jennings	90	63	.588	½
1909	Detroit	Hughie Jennings	98	54	.645	3½
1910	Philadelphia	Connie Mack	102	48	.680	14½
1911	Philadelphia	Connie Mack	101	50	.669	13½
1912	Boston	Jake Stahl	105	47	.691	14
1913	Philadelphia	Connie Mack	96	57	.627	6½
1914	Philadelphia	Connie Mack	99	53	.651	8½
1915	Boston	Bill Carrigan	101	50	.669	2½
1916	Boston	Bill Carrigan	91	63	.591	2
1917	Chicago	Pants Rowland	100	54	.649	9
1918	Boston	Ed Barrow	75	51	.595	2½
1919	Chicago	Kid Gleason	88	52	.629	3½
1920	Cleveland	Tris Speaker	98	56	.636	2
1921	New York	Miller Huggins	98	55	.641	4½
1922	New York	Miller Huggins	94	60	.610	1
1923	New York	Miller Huggins	98	54	.645	16
1924	Washington	Bucky Harris	92	62	.597	2
1925	Washington	Bucky Harris	96	55	.636	8½
1926	New York	Miller Huggins	91	63	.591	3
1927	New York	Miller Huggins	110	44	.714	19
1928	New York	Miller Huggins	101	53	.656	2½
1929	Philadelphia	Connie Mack	104	46	.693	18
1930	Philadelphia	Connie Mack	102	52	.662	8
1931	Philadelphia	Connie Mack	107	45	.704	13½
1932	New York	Joe McCarthy	107	47	.695	13
1933	Washington	Joe Cronin	99	53	.651	7
1934	Detroit	Mickey Cochrane	101	53	.656	7
1935	Detroit	Mickey Cochrane	93	58	.616	3
1936	New York	Joe McCarthy	102	51	.667	19½
1937	New York	Joe McCarthy	102	52	.662	13
1938	New York	Joe McCarthy	99	53	.651	9½
1939	New York	Joe McCarthy	106	45	.702	17
1940	Detroit	Del Baker	90	64	.584	1
1941	New York	Joe McCarthy	101	53	.656	17
1942	New York	Joe McCarthy	103	51	.669	9
1943	New York	Joe McCarthy	98	56	.636	13½
1944	St. Louis	Luke Sewell	89	65	.578	1
1945	Detroit	Steve O'Neill	88	65	.575	1½
1946	Boston	Joe Cronin	104	50	.675	12
1947	New York	Bucky Harris	97	57	.630	12
1948	Cleveland†	Lou Boudreau	97	58	.626	1
1949	New York	Casey Stengel	97	57	.630	1
1950	New York	Casey Stengel	98	56	.636	3
1951	New York	Casey Stengel	98	56	.636	5
1952	New York	Casey Stengel	95	59	.617	2
1953	New York	Casey Stengel	99	52	.656	8½
1954	Cleveland	Al Lopez	111	43	.721	8
1955	New York	Casey Stengel	96	58	.623	3
1956	New York	Casey Stengel	97	57	.630	9
1957	New York	Casey Stengel	98	56	.636	8
1958	New York	Casey Stengel	92	62	.597	10
1959	Chicago	Al Lopez	94	60	.610	5
1960	New York	Casey Stengel	97	57	.630	8
1961	New York	Ralph Houk	109	53	.673	8
1962	New York	Ralph Houk	96	66	.593	5
1963	New York	Ralph Houk	104	57	.646	10½
1964	New York	Yogi Berra	99	63	.611	1
1965	Minnesota	Sam Mele	102	60	.630	7
1966	Baltimore	Hank Bauer	97	63	.606	9

Pennant Winners *(Cont.)*

Year	Team	Manager	W	L	Pct	GA
1967	Boston	Dick Williams	92	70	.568	1
1968	Detroit	Mayo Smith	103	59	.636	12
1969	Baltimore (E)‡	Earl Weaver	109	53	.673	19
1970	Baltimore (E)‡	Earl Weaver	108	54	.667	15
1971	Baltimore (E)‡	Earl Weaver	101	57	.639	12
1972	Oakland (W)‡	Dick Williams	93	62	.600	5½
1973	Oakland (W)‡	Dick Williams	94	68	.580	6
1974	Oakland (W)‡	Al Dark	90	72	.556	5
1975	Boston (E)‡	Darrell Johnson	95	65	.594	4½
1976	New York (E)‡	Billy Martin	97	62	.610	10½
1977	New York (E)‡	Billy Martin	100	62	.617	2½
1978	New York (E)†‡	Billy Martin, Bob Lemon	100	63	.613	1
1979	Baltimore (E)‡	Earl Weaver	102	57	.642	8
1980	Kansas City (W)‡	Jim Frey	97	65	.599	14
1981	New York (E)‡	Gene Michael, Bob Lemon	59	48	.551	#
1982	Milwaukee (E)‡	Buck Rodgers, Harvey Kuenn	95	67	.586	1
1983	Baltimore (E)‡	Joe Altobelli	98	64	.605	6
1984	Detroit (E)‡	Sparky Anderson	104	58	.642	15
1985	Kansas City (W)‡	Dick Howser	91	71	.562	1
1986	Boston (E)‡	John McNamara	95	66	.590	5½
1987	Minnesota (W)‡	Tom Kelly	85	77	.525	2
1988	Oakland (W)‡	Tony La Russa	104	58	.642	13
1989	Oakland (W)‡	Tony La Russa	99	63	.611	7
1990	Oakland (W)‡	Tony La Russa	103	59	.636	9
1991	Minnesota (W)‡	Tom Kelly	95	67	.586	8
1992	Toronto‡	Cito Gaston	96	66	.593	4
1993	Toronto‡	Cito Gaston	95	67	.586	7
1994	Season ended Aug. 11 due to players' strike					
1995	Cleveland (C)‡	Mike Hargrove	100	44	.694	30
1996	New York (E)‡	Joe Torre	92	70	.568	4
1997	Cleveland (C)‡	Mike Hargrove	86	75	.534	6
1998	New York (E)‡	Joe Torre	114	48	.704	22

†Defeated Boston in one-game playoff. ‡Won championship series.
#First half 34–22; second 25–26, in season split by strike; defeated Milwaukee in playoff for Eastern Division title.

Leading Batsmen

Year	Player and Team	BA	Year	Player and Team	BA
1901	Nap Lajoie, Phil	.422	1925	Harry Heilmann, Det	.393
1902	Ed Delahanty, Wash	.376	1926	Heinie Manush, Det	.378
1903	Nap Lajoie, Clev	.355	1927	Harry Heilmann, Det	.398
1904	Nap Lajoie, Clev	.381	1928	Goose Goslin, Wash	.379
1905	Elmer Flick, Clev	.306	1929	Lew Fonseca, Clev	.369
1906	George Stone, StL	.358	1930	Al Simmons, Phil	.381
1907	Ty Cobb, Det	.350	1931	Al Simmons, Phil	.390
1908	Ty Cobb, Det	.324	1932	Dale Alexander, Det-Bos	.367
1909	Ty Cobb, Det	.377	1933	Jimmie Foxx, Phil	.356
1910	Nap Lajoie, Clev*	.383	1934	Lou Gehrig, NY	.363
1911	Ty Cobb, Det	.420	1935	Buddy Myer, Wash	.349
1912	Ty Cobb, Det	.410	1936	Luke Appling, Chi	.388
1913	Ty Cobb, Det	.390	1937	Charlie Gehringer, Det	.371
1914	Ty Cobb, Det	.368	1938	Jimmie Foxx, Bos	.349
1915	Ty Cobb, Det	.369	1939	Joe DiMaggio, NY	.381
1916	Tris Speaker, Clev	.386	1940	Joe DiMaggio, NY	.352
1917	Ty Cobb, Det	.383	1941	Ted Williams, Bos	.406
1918	Ty Cobb, Det	.382	1942	Ted Williams, Bos	.356
1919	Ty Cobb, Det	.384	1943	Luke Appling, Chi	.328
1920	George Sisler, StL	.407	1944	Lou Boudreau, Clev	.327
1921	Harry Heilmann, Det	.394	1945	Snuffy Stirnweiss, NY	.309
1922	George Sisler, StL	.420	1946	Mickey Vernon, Wash	.353
1923	Harry Heilmann, Det	.403	1947	Ted Williams, Bos	.343
1924	Babe Ruth, NY	.378	1948	Ted Williams, Bos	.369

*League president Ban Johnson declared Ty Cobb batting champion with a .385 average, beating Lajoie's .384. However, subsequent research has led to the revision of Lajoie's average to .383 and Cobb's to .382.

Leading Batsmen *(Cont.)*

Year	Player and Team	BA	Year	Player and Team	BA
1949	George Kell, Det	.343	1974	Rod Carew, Minn	.364
1950	Billy Goodman, Bos	.354	1975	Rod Carew, Minn	.359
1951	Ferris Fain, Phil	.344	1976	George Brett, KC	.333
1952	Ferris Fain, Phil	.327	1977	Rod Carew, Minn	.388
1953	Mickey Vernon, Wash	.337	1978	Rod Carew, Minn	.333
1954	Bobby Avila, Clev	.341	1979	Fred Lynn, Bos	.333
1955	Al Kaline, Det	.340	1980	George Brett, KC	.390
1956	Mickey Mantle, NY	.353	1981	Carney Lansford, Bos	.336
1957	Ted Williams, Bos	.388	1982	Willie Wilson, KC	.332
1958	Ted Williams, Bos	.328	1983	Wade Boggs, Bos	.361
1959	Harvey Kuenn, Det	.353	1984	Don Mattingly, NY	.343
1960	Pete Runnels, Bos	.320	1985	Wade Boggs, Bos	.368
1961	Norm Cash, Det	.361	1986	Wade Boggs, Bos	.357
1962	Pete Runnels, Bos	.326	1987	Wade Boggs, Bos	.363
1963	Carl Yastrzemski, Bos	.321	1988	Wade Boggs, Bos	.366
1964	Tony Oliva, Minn	.323	1989	Kirby Puckett, Minn	.339
1965	Tony Oliva, Minn	.321	1990	George Brett, KC	.329
1966	Frank Robinson, Balt	.316	1991	Julio Franco, Tex	.341
1967	Carl Yastrzemski, Bos	.326	1992	Edgar Martinez, Sea	.343
1968	Carl Yastrzemski, Bos	.301	1993	John Olerud, Tor	.363
1969	Rod Carew, Minn	.332	1994	Paul O'Neill, NY	.359
1970	Alex Johnson, Cal	.329	1995	Edgar Martinez, Sea	.356
1971	Tony Oliva, Minn	.337	1996	Alex Rodriguez, Sea	.358
1972	Rod Carew, Minn	.318	1997	Frank Thomas, Chi	.347
1973	Rod Carew, Minn	.350	1998	Bernie Williams, NY	.339

Leaders in Runs Scored

Year	Player and Team	Runs	Year	Player and Team	Runs
1901	Nap Lajoie, Phil	145	1939	Red Rolfe, NY	139
1902	Dave Fultz, Phil	110	1940	Ted Williams, Bos	134
1903	Patsy Dougherty, Bos	108	1941	Ted Williams, Bos	135
1904	Patsy Dougherty, Bos-NY	113	1942	Ted Williams, Bos	141
1905	Harry Davis, Phil	92	1943	George Case, Wash	102
1906	Elmer Flick, Clev	98	1944	Snuffy Stirnweiss, NY	125
1907	Sam Crawford, Det	102	1945	Snuffy Stirnweiss, NY	107
1908	Matty McIntyre, Det	105	1946	Ted Williams, Bos	142
1909	Ty Cobb, Det	116	1947	Ted Williams, Bos	125
1910	Ty Cobb, Det	106	1948	Tommy Henrich, NY	138
1911	Ty Cobb, Det	147	1949	Ted Williams, Bos	150
1912	Eddie Collins, Phil	137	1950	Dom DiMaggio, Bos	131
1913	Eddie Collins, Phil	125	1951	Dom DiMaggio, Bos	113
1914	Eddie Collins, Phil	122	1952	Larry Doby, Clev	104
1915	Ty Cobb, Det	144	1953	Al Rosen, Clev	115
1916	Ty Cobb, Det	113	1954	Mickey Mantle, NY	129
1917	Donie Bush, Det	112	1955	Al Smith, Clev	123
1918	Ray Chapman, Clev	84	1956	Mickey Mantle, NY	132
1919	Babe Ruth, Bos	103	1957	Mickey Mantle, NY	121
1920	Babe Ruth, NY	158	1958	Mickey Mantle, NY	127
1921	Babe Ruth, NY	177	1959	Eddie Yost, Det	115
1922	George Sisler, StL	134	1960	Mickey Mantle, NY	119
1923	Babe Ruth, NY	151	1961	Mickey Mantle, NY	132
1924	Babe Ruth, NY	143		Roger Maris, NY	132
1925	Johnny Mostil, Chi	135	1962	Albie Pearson, LA	115
1926	Babe Ruth, NY	139	1963	Bob Allison, Minn	99
1927	Babe Ruth, NY	158	1964	Tony Oliva, Minn	109
1928	Babe Ruth, NY	163	1965	Zoilo Versalles, Minn	126
1929	Charlie Gehringer, Det	131	1966	Frank Robinson, Balt	122
1930	Al Simmons, Phil	152	1967	Carl Yastrzemski, Bos	112
1931	Lou Gehrig, NY	163	1968	Dick McAuliffe, Det	95
1932	Jimmie Foxx, Phil	151	1969	Reggie Jackson, Oak	123
1933	Lou Gehrig, NY	138	1970	Carl Yastrzemski, Bos	125
1934	Charlie Gehringer, Det	134	1971	Don Buford, Balt	99
1935	Lou Gehrig, NY	125	1972	Bobby Murcer, NY	102
1936	Lou Gehrig, NY	167	1973	Reggie Jackson, Oak	99
1937	Joe DiMaggio, NY	151	1974	Carl Yastrzemski, Bos	93
1938	Hank Greenberg, Det	144	1975	Fred Lynn, Bos	103

Leaders in Runs Scored (Cont.)

Year	Player and Team	Runs	Year	Player and Team	Runs
1976	Roy White, NY	104	1989	Rickey Henderson, NY-Oak	113
1977	Rod Carew, Minn	128		Wade Boggs, Bos	113
1978	Ron LeFlore, Det	126	1990	Rickey Henderson, Oak	119
1979	Don Baylor, Cal	120	1991	Paul Molitor, Mil	133
1980	Willie Wilson, KC	133	1992	Tony Phillips, Det	114
1981	Rickey Henderson, Oak	89	1993	Rafael Palmeiro, Tex	124
1982	Paul Molitor, Mil	136	1994	Frank Thomas, Chi	106
1983	Cal Ripken, Balt	121	1995	Albert Belle, Clev	121
1984	Dwight Evans, Bos	121		Edgar Martinez, Sea	121
1985	Rickey Henderson, NY	146	1996	Alex Rodriguez, Sea	141
1986	Rickey Henderson, NY	130	1997	Ken Griffey Jr., Sea	125
1987	Paul Molitor, Mil	114	1998	Derek Jeter, NY	127
1988	Wade Boggs, Bos	128			

Leaders in Hits

Year	Player and Team	Hits	Year	Player and Team	Hits
1901	Nap Lajoie, Phil	229	1944	Snuffy Stirnweiss, NY	205
1902	Piano Legs Hickman, Bos-Clev	194	1945	Snuffy Stirnweiss, NY	195
1903	Patsy Dougherty, Bos	195	1946	Johnny Pesky, Bos	208
1904	Nap Lajoie, Clev	211	1947	Johnny Pesky, Bos	207
1905	George Stone, StL	187	1948	Bob Dillinger, StL	207
1906	Nap Lajoie, Clev	214	1949	Dale Mitchell, Clev	203
1907	Ty Cobb, Det	212	1950	George Kell, Det	218
1908	Ty Cobb, Det	188	1951	George Kell, Det	191
1909	Ty Cobb, Det	216	1952	Nellie Fox, Chi	192
1910	Nap Lajoie, Clev	227	1953	Harvey Kuenn, Det	209
1911	Ty Cobb, Det	248	1954	Nellie Fox, Chi	201
1912	Ty Cobb, Det	227		Harvey Kuenn, Det	201
1913	Joe Jackson, Clev	197	1955	Al Kaline, Det	200
1914	Tris Speaker, Bos	193	1956	Harvey Kuenn, Det	196
1915	Ty Cobb, Det	208	1957	Nellie Fox, Chi	196
1916	Tris Speaker, Clev	211	1958	Nellie Fox, Chi	187
1917	Ty Cobb, Det	225	1959	Harvey Kuenn, Det	198
1918	George Burns, Phil	178	1960	Minnie Minoso, Chi	184
1919	Ty Cobb, Det	191	1961	Norm Cash, Det	193
	Bobby Veach, Det	191	1962	Bobby Richardson, NY	209
1920	George Sisler, StL	257	1963	Carl Yastrzemski, Bos	183
1921	Harry Heilmann, Det	237	1964	Tony Oliva, Minn	217
1922	George Sisler, StL	246	1965	Tony Oliva, Minn	185
1923	Charlie Jamieson, Clev	222	1966	Tony Oliva, Minn	191
1924	Sam Rice, Wash	216	1967	Carl Yastrzemski, Bos	189
1925	Al Simmons, Phil	253	1968	Bert Campaneris, Oak	177
1926	George Burns, Clev	216	1969	Tony Oliva, Minn	197
	Sam Rice, Wash	216	1970	Tony Oliva, Minn	204
1927	Earle Combs, NY	231	1971	Cesar Tovar, Minn	204
1928	Heinie Manush, StL	241	1972	Joe Rudi, Oak	181
1929	Dale Alexander, Det	215	1973	Rod Carew, Minn	203
	Charlie Gehringer, Det	215	1974	Rod Carew, Minn	218
1930	Johnny Hodapp, Clev	225	1975	George Brett, KC	195
1931	Lou Gehrig, NY	211	1976	George Brett, KC	215
1932	Al Simmons, Phil	216	1977	Rod Carew, Minn	239
1933	Heinie Manush, Wash	221	1978	Jim Rice, Bos	213
1934	Charlie Gehringer, Det	214	1979	George Brett, KC	212
1935	Joe Vosmik, Clev	216	1980	Willie Wilson, KC	230
1936	Earl Averill, Clev	232	1981	Rickey Henderson, Oak	135
1937	Beau Bell, StL	218	1982	Robin Yount, Mil	210
1938	Joe Vosmik, Bos	201	1983	Cal Ripken, Balt	211
1939	Red Rolfe, NY	213	1984	Don Mattingly, NY	207
1940	Rip Radcliff, StL	200	1985	Wade Boggs, Bos	240
	Barney McCosky, Det	200	1986	Don Mattingly, NY	238
	Doc Cramer, Bos	200	1987	Kirby Puckett, Minn	207
1941	Cecil Travis, Wash	218		Kevin Seitzer, KC	207
1942	Johnny Pesky, Bos	205	1988	Kirby Puckett, Minn	234
1943	Dick Wakefield, Det	200	1989	Kirby Puckett, Minn	215

Leaders in Hits (Cont.)

Year	Player and Team	Hits	Year	Player and Team	Hits
1990	Rafael Palmeiro, Tex	191	1995	Lance Johnson, Chi	186
1991	Paul Molitor, Mil	216	1996	Paul Molitor, Minn	225
1992	Kirby Puckett, Minn	210	1997	Nomar Garciaparra, Bos	209
1993	Paul Molitor, Tor	211	1998	Alex Rodriguez, Sea	213
1994	Kenny Lofton, Clev	160			

Home Run Leaders

Year	Player and Team	HR	Year	Player and Team	HR
1901	Nap Lajoie, Phil	13	1953	Al Rosen, Clev	43
1902	Socks Seybold, Phil	16	1954	Larry Doby, Clev	32
1903	Buck Freeman, Bos	13	1955	Mickey Mantle, NY	37
1904	Harry Davis, Phil	10	1956	Mickey Mantle, NY	52
1905	Harry Davis, Phil	8	1957	Roy Sievers, Wash	42
1906	Harry Davis, Phil	12	1958	Mickey Mantle, NY	42
1907	Harry Davis, Phil	8	1959	Rocky Colavito, Clev	42
1908	Sam Crawford, Det	7		Harmon Killebrew, Wash	42
1909	Ty Cobb, Det	9	1960	Mickey Mantle, NY	40
1910	Jake Stahl, Bos	10	1961	Roger Maris, NY	61
1911	Frank Baker, Phil	9	1962	Harmon Killebrew, Minn	48
1912	Frank Baker, Phil	10	1963	Harmon Killebrew, Minn	45
	Tris Speaker, Bos	10	1964	Harmon Killebrew, Minn	49
1913	Frank Baker, Phil	13	1965	Tony Conigliaro, Bos	32
1914	Frank Baker, Phil	9	1966	Frank Robinson, Balt	49
1915	Braggo Roth, Chi-Clev	7	1967	Harmon Killebrew, Minn	44
1916	Wally Pipp, NY	12		Carl Yastrzemski, Bos	44
1917	Wally Pipp, NY	9	1968	Frank Howard, Wash	44
1918	Babe Ruth, Bos	11	1969	Harmon Killebrew, Minn	49
	Tilly Walker, Phil	11	1970	Frank Howard, Wash	44
1919	Babe Ruth, Bos	29	1971	Bill Melton, Chi	33
1920	Babe Ruth, NY	54	1972	Dick Allen, Chi	37
1921	Babe Ruth, NY	59	1973	Reggie Jackson, Oak	32
1922	Ken Williams, StL	39	1974	Dick Allen, Chi	32
1923	Babe Ruth, NY	41	1975	Reggie Jackson, Oak	36
1924	Babe Ruth, NY	46		George Scott, Mil	36
1925	Bob Meusel, NY	33	1976	Graig Nettles, NY	32
1926	Babe Ruth, NY	47	1977	Jim Rice, Bos	39
1927	Babe Ruth, NY	60	1978	Jim Rice, Bos	46
1928	Babe Ruth, NY	54	1979	Gorman Thomas, Mil	45
1929	Babe Ruth, NY	46	1980	Reggie Jackson, NY	41
1930	Babe Ruth, NY	49		Ben Oglivie, Mil	41
1931	Babe Ruth, NY	46	1981	Tony Armas, Oak	22
	Lou Gehrig, NY	46	1981	Dwight Evans, Bos	22
1932	Jimmie Foxx, Phil	58		Bobby Grich, Cal	22
1933	Jimmie Foxx, Phil	48		Eddie Murray, Balt	22
1934	Lou Gehrig, NY	49	1982	Reggie Jackson, Cal	39
1935	Jimmie Foxx, Phil	36		Gorman Thomas, Mil	39
	Hank Greenberg, Det	36	1983	Jim Rice, Bos	39
1936	Lou Gehrig, NY	49	1984	Tony Armas, Bos	43
1937	Joe DiMaggio, NY	46	1985	Darrell Evans, Det	40
1938	Hank Greenberg, Det	58	1986	Jesse Barfield, Tor	40
1939	Jimmie Foxx, Bos	35	1987	Mark McGwire, Oak	49
1940	Hank Greenberg, Det	41	1988	Jose Canseco, Oak	42
1941	Ted Williams, Bos	37	1989	Fred McGriff, Tor	36
1942	Ted Williams, Bos	36	1990	Cecil Fielder, Det	51
1943	Rudy York, Det	34	1991	Jose Canseco, Oak	44
1944	Nick Etten, NY	22		Cecil Fielder, Det	44
1945	Vern Stephens, StL	24	1992	Juan Gonzalez, Tex	43
1946	Hank Greenberg, Det	44	1993	Juan Gonzalez, Tex	46
1947	Ted Williams, Bos	32	1994	Ken Griffey Jr., Sea	40
1948	Joe DiMaggio, NY	39	1995	Albert Belle, Clev	50
1949	Ted Williams, Bos	43	1996	Mark McGwire, Oak	52
1950	Al Rosen, Clev	37	1997	Ken Griffey Jr., Sea	56
1951	Gus Zernial, Chi-Phil	33	1998	Ken Griffey Jr., Sea	56
1952	Larry Doby, Clev	32			

Runs Batted In Leaders

Year	Player and Team	RBI	Year	Player and Team	RBI
1907	Ty Cobb, Det	116	1953	Al Rosen, Clev	145
1908	Ty Cobb, Det	108	1954	Larry Doby, Clev	126
1909	Ty Cobb, Det	107	1955	Ray Boone, Det	116
1910	Sam Crawford, Det	120		Jackie Jensen, Bos	116
1911	Ty Cobb, Det	144	1956	Mickey Mantle, NY	130
1912	Frank Baker, Phil	133	1957	Roy Sievers, Wash	114
1913	Frank Baker, Phil	126	1958	Jackie Jensen, NY	122
1914	Sam Crawford, Det	104	1959	Jackie Jensen, Bos	112
1915	Sam Crawford, Det	112	1960	Roger Maris, NY	112
	Bobby Veach, Det	112	1961	Roger Maris, NY	142
1916	Del Pratt, StL	103	1962	Harmon Killebrew, Minn	126
1917	Bobby Veach, Det	103	1963	Dick Stuart, Bos	118
1918	Bobby Veach, Det	78	1964	Brooks Robinson, Balt	118
1919	Babe Ruth, Bos	114	1965	Rocky Colavito, Clev	108
1920	Babe Ruth, NY	137	1966	Frank Robinson, Balt	122
1921	Babe Ruth, NY	171	1967	Carl Yastrzemski, Bos	121
1922	Ken Williams, StL	155	1968	Ken Harrelson, Bos	109
1923	Babe Ruth, NY	131	1969	Harmon Killebrew, Minn	140
1924	Goose Goslin, Wash	129	1970	Frank Howard, Wash	126
1925	Bob Meusel, NY	138	1971	Harmon Killebrew, Minn	119
1926	Babe Ruth, NY	145	1972	Dick Allen, Chi	113
1927	Lou Gehrig, NY	175	1973	Reggie Jackson, Oak	117
1928	Babe Ruth, NY	142	1974	Jeff Burroughs, Tex	118
	Lou Gehrig, NY	142	1975	George Scott, Mil	109
1929	Al Simmons, Phil	157	1976	Lee May, Balt	109
1930	Lou Gehrig, NY	174	1977	Larry Hisle, Minn	119
1931	Lou Gehrig, NY	184	1978	Jim Rice, Bos	139
1932	Jimmie Foxx, Phil	169	1979	Don Baylor, Cal	139
1933	Jimmie Foxx, Phil	163	1980	Cecil Cooper, Mil	122
1934	Lou Gehrig, NY	165	1981	Eddie Murray, Balt	78
1935	Hank Greenberg, Det	170	1982	Hal McRae, KC	133
1936	Hal Trosky, Clev	162	1983	Cecil Cooper, Mil	126
1937	Hank Greenberg, Det	183		Jim Rice, Bos	126
1938	Jimmie Foxx, Bos	175	1984	Tony Armas, Bos	123
1939	Ted Williams, Bos	145	1985	Don Mattingly, NY	145
1940	Hank Greenberg, Det	150	1986	Joe Carter, Clev	121
1941	Joe DiMaggio, NY	125	1987	George Bell, Tor	134
1942	Ted Williams, Bos	137	1988	Jose Canseco, Oak	124
1943	Rudy York, Det	118	1989	Ruben Sierra, Tex	119
1944	Vern Stephens, StL	109	1990	Cecil Fielder, Det	132
1945	Nick Etten, NY	111	1991	Cecil Fielder, Det	133
1946	Hank Greenberg, Det	127	1992	Cecil Fielder, Det	124
1947	Ted Williams, Bos	114	1993	Albert Belle, Clev	129
1948	Joe DiMaggio, NY	155	1994	Kirby Puckett, Minn	112
1949	Ted Williams, Bos	159	1995	Albert Belle, Clev	126
	Vern Stephens, Bos	159		Mo Vaughn, Bos	126
1950	Walt Dropo, Bos	144	1996	Albert Belle, Clev	148
	Vern Stephens, Bos	144	1997	Ken Griffey Jr., Sea	147
1951	Gus Zernial, Chi-Phil	129	1998	Juan Gonzales, Tex	157
1952	Al Rosen, Clev	105			

Note: Runs Batted In not compiled before 1907; officially adopted in 1920.

Leading Base Stealers

Year	Player and Team	SB	Year	Player and Team	SB
1901	Frank Isbell, Chi	48	1911	Ty Cobb, Det	83
1902	Topsy Hartsel, Phil	54	1912	Clyde Milan, Wash	88
1903	Harry Bay, Clev	46	1913	Clyde Milan, Wash	75
1904	Elmer Flick, Clev	42	1914	Fritz Maisel, NY	74
	Harry Bay, Clev	42	1915	Ty Cobb, Det	96
1905	Danny Hoffman, Phil	46	1916	Ty Cobb, Det	68
1906	Elmer Flick, Clev	39	1917	Ty Cobb, Det	55
	John Anderson, Wash	39	1918	George Sisler, StL	45
1907	Ty Cobb, Det	49	1919	Eddie Collins, Chi	33
1908	Patsy Dougherty, Chi	47	1920	Sam Rice, Wash	63
1909	Ty Cobb, Det	76	1921	George Sisler, StL	35
1910	Eddie Collins, Phil	81	1922	George Sisler, StL	51

Leading Base Stealers *(Cont.)*

Year	Player and Team	SB	Year	Player and Team	SB
1923	Eddie Collins, Chi	49	1961	Luis Aparicio, Chi	53
1924	Eddie Collins, Chi	42	1962	Luis Aparicio, Chi	31
1925	John Mostil, Chi	43	1963	Luis Aparicio, Balt	40
1926	John Mostil, Chi	35	1964	Luis Aparicio, Balt	57
1927	George Sisler, StL	27	1965	Bert Campaneris, KC	51
1928	Buddy Myer, Bos	30	1966	Bert Campaneris, KC	52
1929	Charlie Gehringer, Det	27	1967	Bert Campaneris, KC	55
1930	Marty McManus, Det	23	1968	Bert Campaneris, Oak	62
1931	Ben Chapman, NY	61	1969	Tommy Harper, Sea	73
1932	Ben Chapman, NY	38	1970	Bert Campaneris, Oak	42
1933	Ben Chapman, NY	27	1971	Amos Otis, KC	52
1934	Bill Werber, Bos	40	1972	Bert Campaneris, Oak	52
1935	Bill Werber, Bos	29	1973	Tommy Harper, Bos	54
1936	Lyn Lary, StL	37	1974	Bill North, Oak	54
1937	Bill Werber, Phil	35	1975	Mickey Rivers, Cal	70
	Ben Chapman, Wash-Bos	35	1976	Bill North, Oak	75
1938	Frank Crosetti, NY	27	1977	Freddie Patek, KC	53
1939	George Case, Wash	51	1978	Ron LeFlore, Det	68
1940	George Case, Wash	35	1979	Willie Wilson, KC	83
1941	George Case, Wash	33	1980	Rickey Henderson, Oak	100
1942	George Case, Wash	44	1981	Rickey Henderson, Oak	56
1943	George Case, Wash	61	1982	Rickey Henderson, Oak	130
1944	Snuffy Stirnweiss, NY	55	1983	Rickey Henderson, Oak	108
1945	Snuffy Stirnweiss, NY	33	1984	Rickey Henderson, Oak	66
1946	George Case, Clev	28	1985	Rickey Henderson, NY	80
1947	Bob Dillinger, StL	34	1986	Rickey Henderson, NY	87
1948	Bob Dillinger, StL	28	1987	Harold Reynolds, Sea	60
1949	Bob Dillinger, StL	20	1988	Rickey Henderson, NY	93
1950	Dom DiMaggio, Bos	15	1989	Rickey Henderson, NY-Oak	77
1951	Minnie Minoso, Clev-Chi	31	1990	Rickey Henderson, Oak	65
1952	Minnie Minoso, Chi	22	1991	Rickey Henderson, Oak	58
1953	Minnie Minoso, Chi	25	1992	Kenny Lofton, Clev	66
1954	Jackie Jensen, Bos	22	1993	Kenny Lofton, Clev	70
1955	Jim Rivera, Chi	25	1994	Kenny Lofton, Clev	60
1956	Luis Aparicio, Chi	21	1995	Kenny Lofton, Clev	54
1957	Luis Aparicio, Chi	28	1996	Kenny Lofton, Clev	75
1958	Luis Aparicio, Chi	29	1997	Brian Hunter, Det	74
1959	Luis Aparicio, Chi	56	1998	Rickey Henderson, Oak	66
1960	Luis Aparicio, Chi	51			

Leading Pitchers—Winning Percentage

Year	Pitcher and Team	W	L	Pct	Year	Pitcher and Team	W	L	Pct
1901	Clark Griffith, Chi	24	7	.774	1924	Walter Johnson, Wash	23	7	.767
1902	Bill Bernhard, Phil-Clev	18	5	.783	1925	Stan Coveleski, Wash	20	5	.800
1903	Earl Moore, Clev	22	7	.759	1926	George Uhle, Clev	27	11	.711
1904	Jack Chesbro, NY	41	12	.774	1927	Waite Hoyt, NY	22	7	.759
1905	Jess Tannehill, Bos	22	9	.710	1928	General Crowder, StL	21	5	.808
1906	Eddie Plank, Phil	19	6	.760	1929	Lefty Grove, Phil	20	6	.769
1907	Wild Bill Donovan, Det	25	4	.862	1930	Lefty Grove, Phil	28	5	.848
1908	Ed Walsh, Chi	40	15	.727	1931	Lefty Grove, Phil	31	4	.886
1909	George Mullin, Det	29	8	.784	1932	Johnny Allen, NY	17	4	.810
1910	Chief Bender, Phil	23	5	.821	1933	Lefty Grove, Phil	24	8	.750
1911	Chief Bender, Phil	17	5	.773	1934	Lefty Gomez, NY	26	5	.839
1912	Smoky Joe Wood, Bos	34	5	.872	1935	Eldon Auker, Det	18	7	.720
1913	Walter Johnson, Wash	36	7	.837	1936	Monte Pearson, NY	19	7	.731
1914	Chief Bender, Phil	17	3	.850	1937	Johnny Allen, Clev	15	1	.938
1915	Smoky Joe Wood, Bos	15	5	.750	1938	Red Ruffing, NY	21	7	.750
1916	Eddie Cicotte, Chi	15	7	.682	1939	Lefty Grove, Bos	15	4	.789
1917	Reb Russell, Chi	15	5	.750	1940	Schoolboy Rowe, Det	16	3	.842
1918	Sad Sam Jones, Bos	16	5	.762	1941	Lefty Gomez, NY	15	5	.750
1919	Eddie Cicotte, Chi	29	7	.806	1942	Ernie Bonham, NY	21	5	.808
1920	Jim Bagby, Clev	31	12	.721	1943	Spud Chandler, NY	20	4	.833
1921	Carl Mays, NY	27	9	.750	1944	Tex Hughson, Bos	18	5	.783
1922	Joe Bush, NY	26	7	.788	1945	Hal Newhouser, Det	25	9	.735
1923	Herb Pennock, NY	19	6	.760	1946	Boo Ferriss, Bos	25	6	.806

Leading Pitchers—Winning Percentage *(Cont.)*

Year	Pitcher and Team	W	L	Pct	Year	Pitcher and Team	W	L	Pct
1947	Allie Reynolds, NY	19	8	.704	1973	Catfish Hunter, Oak	21	5	.808
1948	Jack Kramer, Bos	18	5	.783	1974	Mike Cuellar, Balt	22	10	.688
1949	Ellis Kinder, Bos	23	6	.793	1975	Mike Torrez, Balt	20	9	.690
1950	Vic Raschi, NY	21	8	.724	1976	Bill Campbell, Minn	17	5	.773
1951	Bob Feller, Clev	22	8	.733	1977	Paul Splittorff, KC	16	6	.727
1952	Bobby Shantz, Phil	24	7	.774	1978	Ron Guidry, NY	25	3	.893
1953	Ed Lopat, NY	16	4	.800	1979	Mike Caldwell, Mil	16	6	.727
1954	Sandy Consuegra, Chi	16	3	.842	1980	Steve Stone, Balt	25	7	.781
1955	Tommy Byrne, NY	16	5	.762	1981*	Pete Vuckovich, Mil	14	4	.778
1956	Whitey Ford, NY	19	6	.760	1982	Pete Vuckovich, Mil	18	6	.750
1957	Dick Donovan, Chi	16	6	.727		Jim Palmer, Balt	15	5	.750
	Tom Sturdivant, NY	16	6	.727	1983	Richard Dotson, Chi	22	7	.759
1958	Bob Turley, NY	21	7	.750	1984	Doyle Alexander, Tor	17	6	.739
1959	Bob Shaw, Chi	18	6	.750	1985	Ron Guidry, NY	22	6	.786
1960	Jim Perry, Clev	18	10	.643	1986	Roger Clemens, Bos	24	4	.857
1961	Whitey Ford, NY	25	4	.862	1987	Roger Clemens, Bos	20	9	.690
1962	Ray Herbert, Chi	20	9	.690	1988	Frank Viola, Minn	24	7	.774
1963	Whitey Ford, NY	24	7	.774	1989	Bret Saberhagen, KC	23	6	.793
1964	Wally Bunker, Balt	19	5	.792	1990	Bob Welch, Oak	27	6	.818
1965	Mudcat Grant, Minn	21	7	.750	1991	Scott Erickson, Minn	20	8	.714
1966	Sonny Siebert, Clev	16	8	.667	1992	Mike Mussina, Balt	18	5	.783
1967	Joel Horlen, Chi	19	7	.731	1993	Jimmy Key, NY	18	6	.750
1968	Denny McLain, Det	31	6	.838	1994	Jimmy Key, NY	17	4	.810
1969	Jim Palmer, Balt	16	4	.800	1995	Randy Johnson, Sea	18	2	.900
1970	Mike Cuellar, Balt	24	8	.750	1996	Charles Nagy, Clev	17	5	.773
1971	Dave McNally, Balt	21	5	.808	1997	Randy Johnson, Sea	20	4	.833
1972	Catfish Hunter, Oak	21	7	.750	1998	David Wells, NY	18	4	.818

*1981 percentages based on 10 or more victories. Note: Percentages based on 15 or more victories in all other years.

Leading Pitchers—Earned-Run Average

Year	Player and Team	ERA	Year	Player and Team	ERA
1913	Walter Johnson, Wash	1.14	1947	Spud Chandler, NY	2.46
1914	Dutch Leonard, Bos	1.01	1948	Gene Bearden, Clev	2.43
1915	Smoky Joe Wood, Bos	1.49	1949	Mel Parnell, Bos	2.78
1916	Babe Ruth, Bos	1.75	1950	Early Wynn, Clev	3.20
1917	Eddie Cicotte, Chi	1.53	1951	Saul Rogovin, Det-Chi	2.78
1918	Walter Johnson, Wash	1.27	1952	Allie Reynolds, NY	2.07
1919	Walter Johnson, Wash	1.49	1953	Ed Lopat, NY	2.43
1920	Bob Shawkey, NY	2.46	1954	Mike Garcia, Clev	2.64
1921	Red Faber, Chi	2.47	1955	Billy Pierce, Chi	1.97
1922	Red Faber, Chi	2.80	1956	Whitey Ford, NY	2.47
1923	Stan Coveleski, Clev	2.76	1957	Bobby Shantz, NY	2.45
1924	Walter Johnson, Wash	2.72	1958	Whitey Ford, NY	2.01
1925	Stan Coveleski, Wash	2.84	1959	Hoyt Wilhelm, Balt	2.19
1926	Lefty Grove, Phil	2.51	1960	Frank Baumann, Chi	2.68
1927	Wilcy Moore, NY#	2.28	1961	Dick Donovan, Wash	2.40
1928	Garland Braxton, Wash	2.52	1962	Hank Aguirre, Det	2.21
1929	Lefty Grove, Phil	2.81	1963	Gary Peters, Chi	2.33
1930	Lefty Grove, Phil	2.54	1964	Dean Chance, LA	1.65
1931	Lefty Grove, Phil	2.06	1965	Sam McDowell, Clev	2.18
1932	Lefty Grove, Phil	2.84	1966	Gary Peters, Chi	1.98
1933	Monte Pearson, Clev	2.33	1967	Joe Horlen, Chi	2.06
1934	Lefty Gomez, NY	2.33	1968	Luis Tiant, Clev	1.60
1935	Lefty Grove, Bos	2.70	1969	Dick Bosman, Wash	2.19
1936	Lefty Grove, Bos	2.81	1970	Diego Segui, Oak	2.56
1937	Lefty Gomez, NY	2.33	1971	Vida Blue, Oak	1.82
1938	Lefty Grove, Bos	3.07	1972	Luis Tiant, Bos	1.91
1939	Lefty Grove, Bos	2.54	1973	Jim Palmer, Balt	2.40
1940	Bob Feller, Clev†	2.62	1974	Catfish Hunter, Oak	2.49
1941	Thornton Lee, Chi	2.37	1975	Jim Palmer, Balt	2.09
1942	Ted Lyons, Chi	2.10	1976	Mark Fidrych, Det	2.34
1943	Spud Chandler, NY	1.64	1977	Frank Tanana, Cal	2.54
1944	Dizzy Trout, Det	2.12	1978	Ron Guidry, NY	1.74
1945	Hal Newhouser, Det	1.81	1979	Ron Guidry, NY	2.78
1946	Hal Newhouser, Det	1.94	1980	Rudy May, NY	2.47

Leading Pitchers—Earned-Run Average (Cont.)

Year	Player and Team	ERA	Year	Player and Team	ERA
1981	Steve McCatty, Oak	2.32	1990	Roger Clemens, Bos	1.93
1982	Rick Sutcliffe, Clev	2.96	1991	Roger Clemens, Bos	2.62
1983	Rick Honeycutt, Tex	2.42	1992	Roger Clemens, Bos	2.41
1984	Mike Boddicker, Balt	2.79	1993	Kevin Appier, KC	2.56
1985	Dave Stieb, Tor	2.48	1994	Steve Ontiveros, Oak	2.65
1986	Roger Clemens, Bos	2.48	1995	Randy Johnson, Sea	2.48
1987	Jimmy Key, Tor	2.76	1996	Juan Guzman, Tor	2.93
1988	Allan Anderson, Minn	2.45	1997	Roger Clemens, Tor	2.05
1989	Bret Saberhagen, KC	2.16	1998	Roger Clemens, Tor	2.64

Note: Based on 10 complete games through 1950, then, 154 innings until the American League expanded in 1961, when it became 162 innings. In strike-shortened 1981, one inning per game required. Earned runs not tabulated in American League prior to 1913.

#Wilcy Moore pitched only six complete games—he started 12—in 1927, but was recognized as leader because of 213 innings pitched. †Ernie Bonham, New York, had 1.91 ERA and 10 complete games in 1940, but appeared in only 12 games and 99 innings, and Bob Feller was recognized as leader.

Leading Pitchers—Strikeouts

Year	Player and Team	SO	Year	Player and Team	SO
1901	Cy Young, Bos	159	1947	Bob Feller, Clev	196
1902	Rube Waddell, Phil	210	1948	Bob Feller, Clev	164
1903	Rube Waddell, Phil	301	1949	Virgil Trucks, Det	153
1904	Rube Waddell, Phil	349	1950	Bob Lemon, Clev	170
1905	Rube Waddell, Phil	286	1951	Vic Raschi, NY	164
1906	Rube Waddell, Phil	203	1952	Allie Reynolds, NY	160
1907	Rube Waddell, Phil	226	1953	Billy Pierce, Chi	186
1908	Ed Walsh, Chi	269	1954	Bob Turley, Balt	185
1909	Frank Smith, Chi	177	1955	Herb Score, Clev	245
1910	Walter Johnson, Wash	313	1956	Herb Score, Clev	263
1911	Ed Walsh, Chi	255	1957	Early Wynn, Clev	184
1912	Walter Johnson, Wash	303	1958	Early Wynn, Chi	179
1913	Walter Johnson, Wash	243	1959	Jim Bunning, Det	201
1914	Walter Johnson, Wash	225	1960	Jim Bunning, Det	201
1915	Walter Johnson, Wash	203	1961	Camilo Pascual, Minn	221
1916	Walter Johnson, Wash	228	1962	Camilo Pascual, Minn	206
1917	Walter Johnson, Wash	188	1963	Camilo Pascual, Minn	202
1918	Walter Johnson, Wash	162	1964	Al Downing, NY	217
1919	Walter Johnson, Wash	147	1965	Sam McDowell, Clev	325
1920	Stan Coveleski, Clev	133	1966	Sam McDowell, Clev	225
1921	Walter Johnson, Wash	143	1967	Jim Lonborg, Bos	246
1922	Urban Shocker, StL	149	1968	Sam McDowell, Clev	283
1923	Walter Johnson, Wash	130	1969	Sam McDowell, Clev	279
1924	Walter Johnson, Wash	158	1970	Sam McDowell, Clev	304
1925	Lefty Grove, Phil	116	1971	Mickey Lolich, Det	308
1926	Lefty Grove, Phil	194	1972	Nolan Ryan, Cal	329
1927	Lefty Grove, Phil	174	1973	Nolan Ryan, Cal	383
1928	Lefty Grove, Phil	183	1974	Nolan Ryan, Cal	367
1929	Lefty Grove, Phil	170	1975	Frank Tanana, Cal	269
1930	Lefty Grove, Phil	209	1976	Nolan Ryan, Cal	327
1931	Lefty Grove, Phil	175	1977	Nolan Ryan, Cal	341
1932	Red Ruffing, NY	190	1978	Nolan Ryan, Cal	260
1933	Lefty Gomez, NY	163	1979	Nolan Ryan, Cal	223
1934	Lefty Gomez, NY	158	1980	Len Barker, Clev	187
1935	Tommy Bridges, Det	163	1981	Len Barker, Clev	127
1936	Tommy Bridges, Det	175	1982	Floyd Bannister, Sea	209
1937	Lefty Gomez, NY	194	1983	Jack Morris, Det	232
1938	Bob Feller, Clev	240	1984	Mark Langston, Sea	204
1939	Bob Feller, Clev	246	1985	Bert Blyleven, Clev-Minn	206
1940	Bob Feller, Clev	261	1986	Mark Langston, Sea	245
1941	Bob Feller, Clev	260	1987	Mark Langston, Sea	262
1942	Bobo Newsom, Wash		1988	Roger Clemens, Bos	291
	Tex Hughson, Bos	113	1989	Nolan Ryan, Tex	301
1943	Allie Reynolds, Clev	151	1990	Nolan Ryan, Tex	232
1944	Hal Newhouser, Det	187	1991	Roger Clemens, Bos	241
1945	Hal Newhouser, Det	212	1992	Randy Johnson, Sea	241
1946	Bob Feller, Clev	348	1993	Randy Johnson, Sea	308

Leading Pitchers—Strikeouts (Cont.)

1994	Randy Johnson, Sea	204	1997	Roger Clemens, Tor	292
1995	Randy Johnson, Sea	294	1998	Roger Clemens, Tor	271
1996	Roger Clemens, Bos	257			

Leading Pitchers—Saves

Year	Player and Team	SV	Year	Player and Team	SV
1947	Joe Page, NY	17	1973	John Hiller, Det	38
1948	Russ Christopher, Clev	17	1974	Terry Forster, Chi	24
1949	Joe Page, NY	29	1975	Goose Gossage, Chi	26
1950	Mickey Harris, Wash	15	1976	Sparky Lyle, NY	23
1951	Ellis Kinder, Bos	14	1977	Bill Campbell, Bos	31
1952	Harry Dorish, Chi	11	1978	Goose Gossage, NY	27
1953	Ellis Kinder, Bos	27	1979	Mike Marshall, Minn	32
1954	Johnny Sain, NY	22	1980	Dan Quisenberry, KC	33
1955	Ray Narleski, Clev	19	1981	Rollie Fingers, Mil	28
1956	George Zuverink, Bal	16	1982	Dan Quisenberry, KC	35
1957	Bob Grim, NY	19	1983	Dan Quisenberry, KC	35
1958	Ryne Duren, NY	20	1984	Dan Quisenberry, KC	44
1959	Turk Lown, Chi	15	1985	Dan Quisenberry, KC	37
1960	Mike Fornieles, Bos	14	1986	Dave Righetti, NY	46
	Johnny Klippstein, Clev	14	1987	Tom Henke, Tor	34
1961	Luis Arroyo, NY	29	1988	Dennis Eckersley, Oak	45
1962	Dick Radatz, Bos	24	1989	Jeff Russell, Tex	38
1963	Stu Miller, Bal	27	1990	Bobby Thigpen, Chi	57
1964	Dick Radatz, Bos	29	1991	Bryan Harvey, Cal	46
1965	Ron Kline, Wash	29	1992	Dennis Eckersley, Oak	51
1966	Jack Aker, KC	32	1993	Jeff Montgomery, KC	45
1967	Minnie Rojas, Cal	27		Duane Ward, Tor	45
1968	Al Worthington, Minn	18	1994	Lee Smith, Bal	33
1969	Ron Perranoski, Minn	31	1995	Jose Mesa, Clev	46
1970	Ron Perranoski, Minn	34	1996	John Wetteland, NY	43
1971	Ken Sanders, Mil	31	1997	Randy Myers, Balt	45
1972	Sparky Lyle, NY	35	1998	Tom Gordon, Bos	46

The Commissioners of Baseball

Kenesaw Mountain Landis	Elected November 12, 1920. Served until his death on November 25, 1944.
Happy Chandler	Elected April 24, 1945. Served until July 15, 1951.
Ford Frick	Elected September 20, 1951. Served until November 16, 1965.
William Eckert	Elected November 17, 1965. Served until December 20, 1968.
Bowie Kuhn	Elected February 8, 1969. Served until September 30, 1984.
Peter Ueberroth	Elected March 3, 1984. Took office October 1, 1984. Served through March 31, 1989.
A. Bartlett Giamatti	Elected September 8, 1988. Took office April 1, 1989. Served until his death on September 1, 1989.
Francis Vincent Jr.	Appointed Acting Commissioner September 2, 1989. Elected Commissioner September 13, 1989. Served through September 7, 1992.
Allan H. (Bud) Selig	Elected chairman of the executive council and given the powers of interim commissioner on September 9, 1992. Unanimously elected Commissioner July 9, 1998.

Vizquel's First-Class Act

Flying to the All-Star game in Denver from Kansas City, Mo., Cleveland Indians shortstop Omar Vizquel, snug in first class, glanced back into coach. There he noticed Rachel Dando, 15, struggling to get settled in her seat while wearing a large brace on her knee. Rachel, who plays on a Denver girls' softball team, had hurt the knee in a Kansas City tournament and was headed home with her teammates. Vizquel—in a move that coming from a pro athlete was only slightly less astounding than, say, jumping out of the plane and flying on to Denver by flapping his arms—walked back and invited Rachel to swap seats. Rachel, initially reluctant, gave in to her teammates' urgings and hobbled up front, leaving Vizquel in coach.

"I've been on the disabled list twice with torn ligaments, so I felt sorry for her," Vizquel said later, explaining the upgrade. "I never told her who I was."

Pro Football

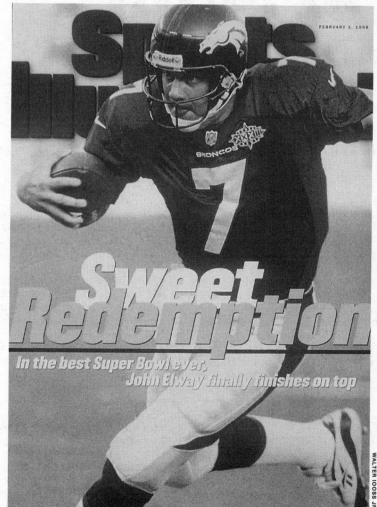

FEBRUARY 2, 1998

Sweet Redemption

In the best Super Bowl ever, John Elway finally finishes on top

WALTER IOOSS JR.

This One's For John

The triumph of John Elway's Broncos was a boost for the NFL in a season short on feel-good stories

BY PETER KING

IN A YEAR in which the margin between good and bad in the NFL got as minute as the pro football world has ever seen, it was fitting that a decided underdog won the Super Bowl, that the AFC Super Bowl jinx died and that John Elway's 15-year quest for the Holy Grail surprisingly and justly ended.

When Denver's 31–24 Super Bowl win over the NFL's latest King Kong team, the Green Bay Packers, was over, the first words America heard from any Bronco came from the lips of team owner Pat Bowlen. "Just four words," Bowlen yelled to the crowd at San Diego's Qualcomm Stadium and a worldwide TV audience: "This one's for John!"

How ironic. In one of the worst games he's ever played—a game won by the smallest offensive line in football blocking for the game's new superback, Terrell Davis, who rushed for 157 yards and three touchdowns—Elway basically spent the Super Bowl handing the ball off and getting out of the way. But that figured in this season and

in the off-season that followed. The most predictable thing that happened in the NFL in 1997–98 was that the TV networks obscenely overpaid for rights to NFL games into the millenium.

In the list of the 10 Significant Events of the NFL year, let's start right there. Off the field. In a negotiation. With angry people. With networks vastly overpaying because the NFL is the most popular sport in the country right now. (By a 2-to-1 count, according to a recent poll. When asked which pro sport was their favorite, one quarter of all poll respondents said pro football; an eighth each said baseball and the NBA.)

Here's what made NFL headlines as the 1998–99 season dawned:

1. TV OR NOT TV, THAT IS THE QUESTION. Don't ever say NFL owners aren't profit-magnets. The prestigious TV committee of the NFL figured out perfectly how to play one network against another, and the result was NBC being out of the pro football business

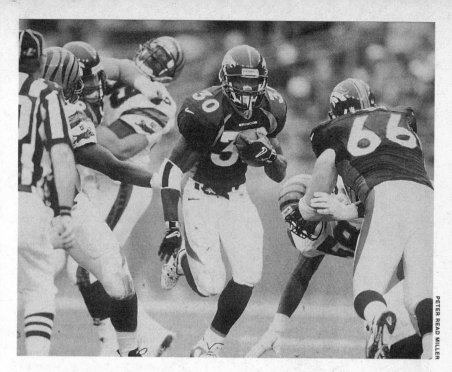

Super Bowl MVP Davis found the holes all year, gaining 1,750 yards to lead the AFC.

for the first time in 33 years, ESPN winning the entire cable package, and CBS getting back into the game after a four-year absence. For $17.6 billion over eight years, the TV cartel was set. ABC kept *Monday Night Football*, and its cable partner ESPN won the Sunday night games. CBS won AFC games, while Fox kept the more popular NFC package. In the end, NBC may have been the smartest company of all. "We're not in the money-losing business," said NBC Sports president Dick Ebersol, who privately was bitter at the NFL for conducting an auction that betrayed loyalty. "And there's no question that this package will lose money." He wasn't the only bitter man after these talks. Fox is the network that set the bar remarkably high in the 1994 negotiations by paying $395 million per year for NFC rights, and the league made Fox, which lost money on that first deal, pay $550 million a year this time around. One

Fox executive felt the league did it no favors by taking advantage of its 1994 payment to leverage the 1998 price, then asking Fox to pay more than CBS this time. The money, by all accounts, is insane. NBC felt it would lose a few bucks offering $340 million a year for the AFC games, but for prestige's sake it would be worth it. Honda made a deal to buy four 30-second, in-game commercials per week from CBS for about $125,000 apiece. This figure is still far short of what the network needs to break even in 1998. But the NFL is laughing all the way to the bank, getting a 100 percent increase in TV rights fees while the ratings are flat. What a great country. Right, Jerry Jones?

2. THE SUN SETS ON THE COWBOYS. What a shame. We won't have Barry Switzer to kick around anymore. Cowboys owner Jones is approaching his 10th anniversary of team ownership, and when he reflects on his first decade—if he's really honest with himself—he'll look in the mirror and say, "Jerry, you really screwed up when you

JOHN IACONO

The great Rice may have rushed his comeback.

rushed Emmitt Smith. Malcolm Glazer outmanaged Jerry Jones. Gailey had better bring salary-cap relief and an offensive fountain of youth to this tarnished team.

3. BABY, THEY WERE BORN TO RUN. Trend of the year: running rules. Rushing average was up over 1996 (4.0 per carry to 3.8), and pass completion percentage down (from 57.6 percent last year to 56.2). Coaches, revamp your engines.

4. RICE-A-GROANIE. Jerry Rice played long enough in the season opener at Tampa Bay to catch four passes and get his left knee wrenched awkwardly, forcing him to undergo what should have been season-ending knee surgery. His astonishing comeback, 15 weeks later, lasted nine plays and ended in a muddy end zone at 3Com Park. Rice, the leading receiver in NFL history, cracked his left kneecap in his Dec. 15 return against Denver. Coincidence, Niners say. Came back too soon, everyone else says. By late spring, though, Rice was running full speed and planned to return for the start of the '98 season.

5. BIG APPLE COMEBACK. The Giants and Jets, a combined 7–25 in 1996, went a stunning 19-12-1 in '97. And the Giants win the pennant! The Giants win the pennant! But after taking the NFC East crown, they were bounced out of the playoffs in an excruciating loss to Minnesota. "I'm looking for pioneers, not historians," rookie coach Jim Fassel said. He got them, plus the best young defense in football. The Giants' co-

hired Switzer." In four years under Switzer, the most star-studded team in football's one Super Bowl was vastly overshadowed by a host of off-field headlines, including those generated by Switzer's attempt to bring a loaded gun onto a commercial airline flight in August 1997. By February '98, Jones had hired a conservative and disciplined man with a wide-open offensive philosophy, Pittsburgh offensive coordinator Chan Gailey, as his third head coach. Good call. Bad '97 for the 6–10 Cowboys. The Jets outwon them. Chris Chandler outplayed Troy Aikman. Corey Dillon out-

tenants at the Meadowlands, the Jets, got a total mental and football makeover from despotic coach Bill Parcells, and went 9–7, compared with 1–15 the season before.

6. UP WAS DOWN. The season's essence was captured in the Green Bay–Indianapolis game at the RCA Dome in November. Here were the playing-out-the-string 0–10 Colts facing the defending Super Bowl champion Packers, who hadn't lost in two months. The final score from the 1997 Parity Bowl: Colts 41, Packers 38.

There's more. The Oilers looked playoff-ready when they met the Bengals in early December. The Bengals looked like they'd packed it in. Second-quarter score: Cincinnati 28, Tennessee 0. The Dolphins could have clinched the AFC East with a win over the 2–12 Colts in the second-to-last week of the season. The envelope please: Indianapolis 41, Miami 0. The Saints won six, the Falcons seven, the Jets nine, the Bucs 10.

"No longer will San Francisco's third team be better than most teams' first teams," Denver coach Mike Shanahan said. "It's impossible. The salary cap's caught up to everybody now." In the Green Bay–Indy game, Packer stalwarts Reggie White, Gilbert Brown and Robert Brooks missed some or all of the game with injuries, and in their places were Darius Holland, Bob Kuberski and Derrick Mayes. "No matter what you say about your backups, it ain't the same," Green Bay quarterback Brett Favre said. "The quality of player drops off when you lose a Reggie, a Gilbert, a Robert. It's happening to all of us. I bet the 49ers had 20 big-time guys in the '80s. Today, no way."

7. HOPE SPRINGS ETERNAL. Only twice since 1970 had quarterbacks gone one-two in the NFL draft. It happened once in 1971, when Jim Plunkett and Archie Manning were the top picks, going to New England and New Orleans, respectively. Archie's kid Peyton, of Tennessee, was the No. 1 pick this time. He went to Indianapolis, and raw Washington State product Ryan Leaf went No. 2 to San Diego. But they weren't the only new passers on the block on draft day. Bob Griese's son, Michigan quarterback Brian Griese, was selected in the third round by Denver, where, if no-name Jeff Lewis fails to grab the Broncos' reins, Griese could be the heir to Elway. In the second round Detroit traded three picks to grab the man whom the Lions hope will pressure Scott Mitchell into being a reliable player. He is Eastern Michigan's Charlie Batch. He is also Detroit's future at quarterback.

8. THE BIGGEST RACIAL INEQUITY IN SPORTS. A group of African-American NFL coaches and executives, rightfully outraged

AL TIELEMANS

Fassel oversaw the Giants' run to the NFC East title.

that the last 16 NFL head coaching hires have been white—in a league in which 67% of the players are black—held a May job seminar. They broke bread with most of the 30 NFL owners and built an employment data base to better promote minority coaching candidates. Their work was funded by the NFL, which has egg on its face because of its unenlightened hiring practices. The most recent embarrassment was Dallas's slight of Green Bay offensive coordinator Sherm Lewis after he wowed Cowboys staff and players during a two-day interview. "But Sherm Lewis can't be Colin Powell, our only hope," said Jacksonville vice president Michael Huyghue, who heads this ad hoc committee. "It's not a one-candidate issue." One of the other top black candidates, Stanford coach Tyrone Willingham, may be out of the mix for a while, having taken himself out of the running for the Colts job this year. It's getting old to say this, but the NFL has to stop the lip service and do the right thing.

9. JUNKING A JINX. Maybe it was the sight of Richard Simmons at the Media Center that unnerved them, or the rumor that Jerry Mathers, of *Leave It to Beaver* fame, was in town looking for Brett Favre's autograph. Surely that would be too much for the Packers to bear and still keep their game faces on, wouldn't it? But the NFC finally lost a Super Bowl, for the first time since Paul Tagliabue was a Washington lawyer no one ever heard of. Since January 22, 1984, to be precise. Raiders 38, Redskins 9. This was never a story with much rhyme or reason to it, but the AFC Super Bowl representative had year after year been the team with butterfingers in the Big Game, the team that turned the ball over, the team whose running game always got steamrollered. This year, Denver was the steamroller, not the steamrollee, and Green Bay had the slippery fingers and the tight throats.

10. TAMPA BAY GOT GOOD. That's no misprint. After scaring Green Bay in the playoffs ("Tampa Bay" and "playoffs" can now fit comfortably in the same sentence), the Bucs spent an off-season securing their current talent and collecting more youth-

Flake Ditka

PETER READ MILLER

When they unearth the 1997 sports journalism time capsule decades from now, those gathered will have a two-stage reaction. First, their brows will furrow in confusion. Then they will fill the air around them with the sounds of cackling laughter.

Mike Ditka, back in coaching after a five-year hiatus doing TV commentary, got a poor New Orleans Saints team to overachieve and finish 6–10. He also said enough of the darndest things to fill a book by Art Linkletter. Herewith, the Official Ditka Quotes of the Year:

Week 5. Minutes after a Saints loss to the Giants: "We are wandering through the desert looking for ourselves. We had no emotion going into that game. We could have been going down Fifth Avenue on a shopping spree as well as playing the Giants. No difference. We were like,

Quotable notable : Ditka made good copy.

The youthful and talented Dunn (28) typified the up-and-coming Buccaneers.

JOHN IACONO

ful booty. They signed coach Tony Dungy, general manager Rich McKay and defensive leader Warren Sapp to rich and lengthy contract extensions. They bought free-agent wideout Bert Emanuel from Atlanta. They drafted speedy receiver Jacquez Green from the University of Florida. They now have a young and dangerous offense, one that's going to be terrific in the future if quarterback Trent Dilfer improves 10% more. The great thing about the offense? The average age of the skill players set to play major roles (Dilfer, Warrick Dunn, Mike Alstott, Green, Emanuel, Reidel Anthony, Dave Moore) is 24. Add that youth to a rising-star defense, and what you have is a team no one wants to see on the schedule anytime soon.

• • •

There were other highlights of the season, some surprising, some less so. Detroit's Barry Sanders became the third NFL player to crack the 2,000-yard mark for rushing in a

'Cabbie, over here. I'm going over there.' That's the way it looked.

"If we think we're going to go in with three-button suits on and *The Wall Street Journal* under our arm and sit down and conduct a businesslike game with somebody, we're crazy."

Week 13. Minutes after New Orleans's 20–3 loss to Atlanta: "I'm probably the wrong guy for the job. I don't think I have it anymore. They are probably better off getting somebdy else."

The following day: "I plan to fulfill my contract and, the good lord willing, beyond that contract. There's nowhere else I want to be or anything else I want to do than to be here. I said some very stupid things, but that's me."

Week 14. Ditka dissects his personality: "I'm a flake. Just write that. I'm a flake. I

got a lot of split personality and stuff like that. Some night, if you're at the right place at the right time, you'll probably see me in a dress."

Week 15. Sullenly, after loss to Rams: "I'm not going to get excited anymore. That's finished. It doesn't matter. It's only a football game. Six billion people don't care about it in this world. Do you know that? And that's only this world. What about the other worlds? I don't know. There must be one out there somewhere. They keep making movies about it."

In the off-season Ditka issued the 4,567th pronouncement of his coaching career, saying he was entering 1998 with a No-More-Mr.-Nice-Guy attitude.

Mike Ditka might be the only man in sports who makes you long for his next press conference.

ROBERT ROGERS

The incomparable Sanders moved into second place on the alltime rushing list.

season. He gained 163 yards in the last 16 minutes of the regular season against the Jets. Sanders and Favre split the MVP award. The Oilers limped through their inaugural season in Memphis (the Liberty Bowl was 28% full on a sunny, 73° day for the Oilers' second home game, a 36–10 loss to Baltimore) and moved, as planned, to Nashville after the season. It was clear that the rivalry between the two cities would doom the Oilers' ticket-selling fortunes in Memphis. A freak 26-inch blizzard hit Denver in October, the day the Broncos were to leave for a game at Buffalo, and snowbound kicker Jason Elam had to be rescued from I-25 by the state police. Elam rescued the Broncos with a game-winning overtime field goal the next day at Buffalo. Colts quarterback Jim Harbaugh attacked Buffalo-QB-turned-TV-guy Jim Kelly after Kelly called him a baby. Harbaugh was fined $145,000 by his team for missing a game with a broken hand suffered in the attack. The injury report should have read: Harbaugh, out (macho act). On Nov. 13, Patriots Drew Bledsoe and Max Lane (a 302-pounder)

leaped from the stage of a Boston nightclub into the mosh pit during a concert by the grunge band Everclear. Asked why he wasn't there, African-American New England tackle Bruce Armstrong said, "Black men can't jump." An injured concertgoer filed suit after the pair of Patriot missiles landed on her. Inmates continue to run the asylum that is the Oakland Raiders franchise, as most pointedly evidenced against Seattle on Dec. 14. When the second half began, the Raiders burned a timeout waiting for safety James Trapp to come out of the locker room. Seattle won the game 22–21. For grabbing 49ers wideout J.J. Stokes's crotch and spitting in his face in Denver's loss at San Francisco, the Broncos' Bill Romanowski was fined $7,500 by the NFL. Stokes seethed. "I have something for him the next time I see him—a good stiff one to the jaw," Stokes said.

But this was our personal favorite highlight of the year: In Green Bay, a limited edition sculpture of Mike Holmgren riding a Harley went on sale for $395.

It's a good thing we had the Elway story, to give the NFL a feel-good story for the year. Otherwise—surprise!—money ruled the day in America's biggest game.

FOR THE RECORD·1997-1998

1997 NFL Final Standings

American Football Conference

EASTERN DIVISION

	W	L	T	Pct	Pts	OP
New England	10	6	0	.625	369	289
†Miami	9	7	0	.562	339	327
NY Jets	9	7	0	.562	348	287
Buffalo	6	10	0	.375	255	367
Indianapolis	3	13	0	.188	313	401

CENTRAL DIVISION

	W	L	T	Pct	Pts	OP
Pittsburgh	11	5	0	.689	372	307
†Jacksonville	11	5	0	.689	394	318
Tennessee	8	8	0	.500	333	310
Cincinnati	7	9	0	.438	355	405
Baltimore	6	9	1	.406	326	345

WESTERN DIVISION

	W	L	T	Pct	Pts	OP
Kansas City	13	3	0	.813	375	232
†Denver	12	4	0	.750	472	287
Seattle	8	8	0	.500	365	362
Oakland	4	12	0	.250	324	419
San Diego	4	12	0	.250	266	425

National Football Conference

EASTERN DIVISION

	W	L	T	Pct	Pts	OP
NY Giants	10	5	1	.656	307	265
Washington	8	7	1	.531	327	289
Philadelphia	6	9	1	.406	317	372
Dallas	6	10	0	.375	304	314
Arizona	4	12	0	.250	283	379

CENTRAL DIVISION

	W	L	T	Pct	Pts	OP
Green Bay	13	3	0	.813	422	282
†Tampa Bay	10	6	0	.625	299	263
†Detroit	9	7	0	.562	379	306
†Minnesota	9	7	0	.562	354	359
Chicago	4	12	0	.250	263	421

WESTERN DIVISION

	W	L	T	Pct	Pts	OP
San Francisco	13	3	0	.813	375	265
Carolina	7	9	0	.438	265	314
Atlanta	7	9	0	.438	320	361
New Orleans	6	10	0	.375	237	327
St. Louis	5	11	0	.313	299	359

† Wild-card team.

1997-98 NFL Playoffs

AFC FIRST ROUND	AFC DIVISIONAL PLAYOFF	AFC CHAMPIONSHIP	NFC CHAMPIONSHIP	NFC DIVISIONAL PLAYOFF	NFC FIRST ROUND

SUPER BOWL XXXII
January 25, 1998

Jacksonville 17
Denver 42

Denver 14

Denver 24

Kansas City 10

Minnesota 22

San Francisco 10

San Francisco 38

Minnesota 23
NY Giants 22

**DENVER 31
Green Bay 24**

Miami 3
New England 17

New England 6

Pittsburgh 21

Pittsburgh 7

Tampa Bay 7

Green Bay 23

Green Bay 21

Detroit 10
Tampa Bay 20

NFL Playoff Box Scores

AFC Wild-card Games

```
Jacksonville...........0    7   10    0—17
Denver.................14    7    0   21—42
```

FIRST QUARTER

Denver: Davis 2 run (Elam kick), 7:21. Drive: 73 yards, 15 plays.
Denver: R. Smith 43 pass from Elway (Elam kick), 12:23. Drive: 60 yards, 6 plays.

SECOND QUARTER

Denver: Davis 5 run (Elam kick), 4:14. Drive: 92 yards, 11 plays.
Jacksonville: Means 2 run (Hollis kick), 9:51. Drive: 79 yards, 9 plays.

THIRD QUARTER

Jacksonville: FG Hollis 38, 1:27. Drive: 7 yards, 4 plays.
Jacksonville: Davis 29 return of blocked punt (Hollis kick), 5:44.

FOURTH QUARTER

Denver: Loville 25 run (Elam kick), 1:39. Drive: 48 yards, 2 plays.
Denver: Loville 8 run (Elam kick), 11:17. Drive: 80 yards, 10 plays.
Denver: Hebron 6 run (Elam kick), 13:49. Drive: 15 yards, 4 plays.
A: 74,481; T: 3:02.

```
Miami ......................0    0    0    3— 3
New England...........0    7   10    0—17
```

SECOND QUARTER

New England: Brown 24 pass from Bledsoe (Vinatieri kick), 4:33. Drive: 29 yards, 3 plays.

THIRD QUARTER

New England: Collins 40 interception return (Vinatieri kick), 0:55.
New England: FG Vinatieri 22, 13:02. Drive: 66 yards, 15 plays.

FOURTH QUARTER

Miami: FG Mare 38, 0:09. Drive: 23 yards, 8 plays.
A: 60,041; T: 3:00.

THEY SAID IT

John Elway, Denver Broncos quarterback, on the repeated diagramming in Denver newspapers of his ruptured biceps tendon: "I just hope I never get kicked in the groin."

NFC Wild-card Games

```
Minnesota ..............0    3    7   13—23
NY Giants...............6   13    0    3—22
```

FIRST QUARTER

New York: FG Daluiso 43, 8:25. Drive: -3 yards, 4 plays.
New York: FG Daluiso 22, 12:40. Drive: 42 yards, 7 plays.

SECOND QUARTER

New York: Pierce 2 pass from Kanell (Daluiso kick), 3:27. Drive: 56 yards, 7 plays.
New York: FG Daluiso 41, 10:06. Drive: 23 yards, 6 plays.
Minnesota: FG Murray 26, 13:13. Drive: 19 yards, 5 plays.
New York: FG Daluiso 51, 14:47. Drive: 26 yards, 10 plays.

THIRD QUARTER

Minnesota: Hoard 4 run (Murray kick), 4:34. Drive: 4 yards, 1 play.

FOURTH QUARTER

Minnesota: FG Murray 26, 0:15. Drive: 52 yards, 11 plays.
New York: FG Daluiso 22, 7:57. Drive: 74 yards, 13 plays.
Minnesota: Reed 30 pass from Cunningham (Murray kick), 13:30. Drive: 49 yards, 4 plays.
Minnesota: FG Murray 24, 14:50. Drive: 56 yards, 7 plays.
A: 77,710; T: 3:08.

```
Detroit .....................0    0    3    7—10
Tampa Bay..............3   10    7    0—20
```

FIRST QUARTER

Tampa Bay: FG Husted 22, 9:36. Drive: 40 yards, 7 plays.

SECOND QUARTER

Tampa Bay: Copeland 9 pass from Dilfer (Husted kick), 4:36. Drive: 89 yards, 17 plays.
Tampa Bay: FG Husted 42, 8:11. Drive: -4 yards, 4 plays.

THIRD QUARTER

Tampa Bay: Alstott 31 run (Husted kick), 3:54. Drive: 53 yards, 6 plays.
Detroit: FG Hanson 33, 14:32. Drive: 46 yards, 10 plays.

FOURTH QUARTER

Detroit: Vardell 1 run (Hanson kick), 7:12. Drive: 82 yards, 9 plays.
A: 73,361; T: 3:10.

AFC Divisional Games

Denver	0	7	0	7—14
Kansas City	0	0	10	0—10

SECOND QUARTER

Denver: Davis 1 run (Elam kick), 13:04. Drive: 65 yards, 8 plays.

THIRD QUARTER

Kansas City: FG Stoyanovich 20, 5:18. Drive: 57 yards, 11 plays.
Kansas City: Gonzalez 12 pass from Grbac (Stoyanovich kick), 14:50. Drive: 65 yards, 4 plays.

FOURTH QUARTER

Denver: Davis 1 run (Elam kick), 2:28. Drive: 49 yards, 6 plays.
A: 76,956; T: 2:59.

New England	0	3	0	3— 6
Pittsburgh	7	0	0	0— 7

FIRST QUARTER

Pittsburgh: Stewart 40 run (N. Johnson kick), 5:11. Drive: 62 yards, 8 plays.

SECOND QUARTER

New England: FG Vinatieri 31, 7:20. Drive: 65 yards, 10 plays.

FOURTH QUARTER

New England: FG Vinatieri 46, 2:44. Drive: 52 yards, 10 plays.
A: 61,228; T: 3:08.

NFC Divisional Games

Tampa Bay	0	0	7	0— 7
Green Bay	7	6	0	8—21

FIRST QUARTER

Green Bay: Chmura 3 pass from Favre (Longwell kick), 9:24. Drive: 67 yards, 7 plays.

SECOND QUARTER

Green Bay: FG Longwell 21, 13:08. Drive: 27 yards, 5 plays.
Green Bay: FG Longwell 32, 14:58. Drive: 13 yards, 7 plays.

THIRD QUARTER

Tampa Bay: Alstott 6 run (Husted kick), 8:43. Drive: 94 yards, 8 plays.

FOURTH QUARTER

Green Bay: Levens 2 run (Favre run for two-point conversion), 1:23. Drive: 54 yards, 9 plays.
A: 60,327; T: 2:57.

Minnesota	7	0	7	8—22
San Francisco	7	14	10	7—38

FIRST QUARTER

San Francisco: Floyd 1 run (Anderson kick), 6:57. Drive: 26 yards, 4 plays.
Minnesota: Carter 66 pass from Cunningham (Murray kick), 7:34. Drive: 61 yards, 1 play.

SECOND QUARTER

San Francisco: Kirby 1 run (Anderson kick), 8:32. Drive: 61 yards, 4 plays.
San Francisco: Norton 23 interception return (Anderson kick), 9:19.

THIRD QUARTER

San Francisco: FG Anderson 34, 6:43. Drive: 46 yards, 14 plays.
Minnesota: Carter 3 pass from Cunningham (Murray kick), 9:47. Drive: 76 yards, 5 plays.
San Francisco: Owens 15 pass from Young (Anderson kick), 13:00. Drive: 75 yards, 7 plays.

FOURTH QUARTER

San Francisco: Kirby 1 run (Anderson kick), 7:28. Drive: 79 yards, 10 plays.
Minnesota: Hatchette 13 pass from Cunningham (Cunningham pass to Walsh for two-point conversion), 11:13. Drive: 73 yards, 12 plays.
A: 65,013; T: 3:10.

NFL Playoff Box Scores *(Cont.)*

AFC Championship

Denver	7	17	0	0—24
Pittsburgh	7	7	0	7—21

FIRST QUARTER

Denver: Davis 8 run (Elam kick), 5:42. Drive: 72 yards, 6 plays.
Pittsburgh: Stewart 33 run (N. Johnson kick), 8:44. Drive: 65 yards, 6 plays.

SECOND QUARTER

Pittsburgh: Bettis 1 run (N. Johnson kick), 2:18. Drive: 68 yards, 11 plays.
Denver: FG Elam 43, 6:40. Drive: 45 yards, 11 plays.
Denver: Griffith 16 pass from Elway (Elam kick), 13:13. Drive: 80 yards, 5 plays.
Denver: McCaffrey 1 pass from Elway (Elam kick), 14:47. Drive: 54 yards, 4 plays.

FOURTH QUARTER

Pittsburgh: C. Johnson 15 pass from Stewart (N. Johnson kick), 12:14. Drive: 79 yards, 10 plays.
A: 61,382; T: 2:59.

NFC Championship

Green Bay	3	10	0	10—23
San Francisco	0	3	0	7—10

FIRST QUARTER

Green Bay: FG Longwell 19, 12:12. Drive: 76 yards, 10 plays.

SECOND QUARTER

Green Bay: Freeman 27 pass from Favre (Longwell kick), 3:30. Drive: 28 yards, 2 plays.
San Francisco: FG Anderson 28, 14:02. Drive: 52 yards, 10 plays.
Green Bay: FG Longwell 43, 15:00. Drive: 47 yards, 3 plays.

FOURTH QUARTER

Green Bay: FG Longwell 25, 9:56. Drive: 28 yards, 9 plays.
Green Bay: Levens 5 run (Longwell kick), 11:50. Drive: 11 yards, 2 plays.
San Francisco: Levy 95 kickoff return (Anderson kick), 12:08.
A: 68,987; T: 3:00.

Super Bowl Box Score

Green Bay	7	7	3	7—24
Denver	7	10	7	7—31

FIRST QUARTER

Green Bay: Freeman 22 pass from Favre (Longwell kick), 4:02. Drive: 76 yards, 8 plays. Key plays: Freeman 13 pass from Favre; Levens 11 and 13 runs. **Green Bay 7–0**.
Denver: Davis 1 run (Elam kick), 9:21. Drive: 58 yards, 10 plays. Key plays: Davis 27 run; Elway 10 run. **7–7**.

SECOND QUARTER

Denver: Elway 1 run (Elam kick), :05. Drive: 45 yards, 8 plays. Key play: Davis 16 run. **Denver 14–7**.
Denver: FG Elam 51, 2:39. Drive: 0 yards, 4 plays. Key play: Favre fumbles when sacked by Atwater, recovered by N. Smith. **Denver 17–7**.
Green Bay: Chmura 6 pass from Favre (Longwell kick), 14:48. Drive: 95 yards, 17 plays. Key play: Chmura 21 pass from Favre. **Denver 17–14**.

THIRD QUARTER

Green Bay: FG Longwell 27, 3:01. Drive: 77 yards, 10 plays. Key play: Levens 16 run. **17–17**.
Denver: Davis 1 run (Elam kick), 14:26. Drive: 92 yards, 13 plays. Key plays: McCaffrey 36 pass from Elway; Elway 8 run. **Denver 24–17**.

FOURTH QUARTER

Green Bay: Freeman 13 pass from Favre (Longwell kick), 1:28. Drive: 85 yards, 4 plays. Key plays: Robinson interception of Elway pass in end zone; Freeman 26 pass from Favre; 25-yard pass interference penalty on Gordon; Freeman 17 pass from Favre. **24–24**.
Denver: Davis 1 run (Elam kick), 13:15. Drive: 49 yards, 5 plays. Key plays: Davis 2 run plus 15-yard face mask penalty; Griffith 23 pass from Elway; Davis 17 run. **Denver 31–24**.
A: 68,912; T: 3:25.

Team Statistics

	Green Bay	Denver
FIRST DOWNS	21	21
Rushing	4	14
Passing	14	5
Penalty	3	2
THIRD DOWN EFF	5–14	5–10
FOURTH DOWN EFF	0–1	0–0
TOTAL NET YARDS	350	302
Total plays	63	61
Avg gain	5.6	5.0
NET YARDS RUSHING	95	179
Rushes	20	39
Avg per rush	4.8	4.6
NET YARDS PASSING	255	123
Completed–Att	25–42	12–22
Yards per pass	5.9	5.6
Sacked–yards lost	1–1	0–0
Had intercepted	1	1
PUNTS–Avg	4–35.5	4–36.5
TOTAL RETURN YARDS	121	95
Punt returns	0–0	0–0
Kickoff returns	6–104	5–105
Interceptions	1–17	1–0
PENALTIES–Yds	9–59	7–65
FUMBLES–Lost	2–2	1–1
TIME OF POSSESSION	27:35	32:25

Passing

GREEN BAY

	Comp	Att	Yds	Int	TD
Favre	25	42	256	1	3

DENVER

	Comp	Att	Yds	Int	TD
Elway	12	22	123	1	0

Rushing

GREEN BAY

	No.	Yds	Lg	TD
Levens	19	90	16	0
R. Brooks	1	5	5	0

DENVER

	No.	Yds	Lg	TD
Davis	30	157	27	3
Elway	5	17	10	1
Hebron	3	3	2	0
Griffith	1	2	2	0

Receiving

GREEN BAY

	No.	Yds	Lg	TD
Freeman	9	126	27	2
Levens	6	56	22	0
Chmura	4	43	21	1
R. Brooks	3	16	10	0
W. Henderson	2	9	7	0
T. Mickens	1	6	6	0

DENVER

	No.	Yds	Lg	TD
Sharpe	5	38	12	0
McCaffrey	2	45	36	0
Davis	2	8	4	0
Griffith	1	23	23	0
Hebron	1	5	5	0
Carswell	1	4	4	0

Defense

GREEN BAY

	Tck	Ast	Int	Sack
Butler	7	2	0	0
E. Robinson	6	2	1	0
Harris	6	1	0	0
S. Dotson	6	0	0	0
T. Williams	6	0	0	0
B. Williams	5	0	0	0
Brown	3	1	0	0
Joyner	3	0	0	0
Evans	2	1	0	0
Mullen	2	0	0	0
R. White	1	0	0	0
Chmura	1	0	0	0
Darkins	1	0	0	0
T. Mickens	1	0	0	0
Thomason	1	0	0	0

DENVER

	Tck	Ast	Int	Sack
Braxton	6	1	1	0
Atwater	6	0	0	0
Crockett	6	0	0	0
Mobley	6	0	0	0
Romanowski	4	1	0	0
Aldrige	4	0	0	0
Gordon	3	0	0	0
Dodge	2	0	0	0
Lodish	2	0	0	0
Traylor	2	0	0	0
Loville	2	0	0	0
A. Williams	1	1	0	0
Hasselbach	1	0	0	0
D. Johnson	1	0	0	0
Tanuvasa	1	0	0	0
Burns	1	0	0	0
Sharpe	1	0	0	0

1997 Associated Press All-Pro Team

OFFENSE

Rob Moore, Arizona	Wide Receiver
Herman Moore, Detroit	Wide Receiver
Shannon Sharpe, Denver	Tight End
Jonathan Ogden, Baltimore	Tackle
Tony Boselli, Jacksonville	Tackle
David Szott, Kansas City	Guard
Larry Allen, Dallas	Guard
Dermontti Dawson, Pittsburgh	Center
Brett Favre, Green Bay	Quarterback
Terrell Davis, Denver	Running Back
Barry Sanders, Detroit	Running Back
Mike Alstott, Tampa Bay	Fullback

DEFENSE

Bruce Smith, Buffalo	Defensive End
Michael Strahan, NY Giants	Defensive End
Dana Stubblefield, San Francisco	Tackle
John Randle, Minnesota	Tackle
Jessie Armstead, NY Giants	Outside Linebacker
John Mobley, Denver	Outside Linebacker
Hardy Nickerson, Tampa Bay	Inside Linebacker
Levon Kirkland, Pittsburgh	Inside Linebacker
Deion Sanders, Dallas	Cornerback
Aeneas Williams, Arizona	Cornerback
LeRoy Butler, Green Bay	Safety
Carnell Lake, Pittsburgh	Safety

SPECIALISTS

Richie Cunningham, Dallas	Kicker
Bryan Barker, Jacksonville	Punter
Eric Metcalf, San Diego	Kick Returner

1997 AFC Team-by-Team Results

BALTIMORE RAVENS (6-9-1)		
27	JACKSONVILLE	28
23	CINCINNATI	10
24	at NY Giants	23
36	at Tennessee	10
17	at San Diego	21
34	PITTSBURGH	42
	OPEN DATE	
13	MIAMI	24
20	at Washington	17
16	at NY Jets (OT)	19
0	at Pittsburgh	37
10	PHILADELPHIA (OT)	10
13	ARIZONA	16
27	at Jacksonville	29
31	SEATTLE	24
21	TENNESSEE	19
14	at Cincinnati	16
326		345

BUFFALO BILLS (6-10)		
13	MINNESOTA	34
28	at NY Jets	22
16	at Kansas City	22
37	INDIANAPOLIS	35
	OPEN DATE	
22	DETROIT	13
6	at New England	33
9	at Indianapolis	6
20	DENVER (OT)	23
9	MIAMI	6
10	NEW ENGLAND	31
13	at Miami	30
14	at Tennessee	31
20	NY Jets	10
3	at Chicago	20
14	JACKSONVILLE	20
21	at Green Bay	31
255		367

CINCINNATI BENGALS (7-9)		
24	ARIZONA	21
10	at Baltimore	23
	OPEN DATE	
20	at Denver	38
14	NY JETS	31
13	at Jacksonville	21
7	at Tennessee	30
10	PITTSBURGH	26
27	at NY Giants	29
38	SAN DIEGO	31
28	at Indianapolis	13
3	at Pittsburgh	20
31	JACKSONVILLE	26
42	at Philadelphia	44
41	TENNESSEE	14
31	DALLAS	24
16	BALTIMORE	14
355		405

DENVER BRONCOS (12–4)

19	KANSAS CITY	3
35	at Seattle	14
35	ST LOUIS	14
38	CINCINNATI	20
29	at Atlanta	21
34	NEW ENGLAND	13
	OPEN DATE	
25	at Oakland	28
23	at Buffalo (OT)	20
30	SEATTLE	27
34	CAROLINA	0
22	at Kansas City	24
31	OAKLAND	3
38	at San Diego	28
24	at Pittsburgh	35
17	at San Francisco	34
38	SAN DIEGO	3
472		**287**

INDIANAPOLIS COLTS (3–13)

10	at Miami	16
6	NEW ENGLAND	31
3	SEATTLE	31
35	at Buffalo	37
	OPEN DATE	
12	NY JETS	16
22	at Pittsburgh	24
6	BUFFALO	9
19	at San Diego	35
28	TAMPA BAY	31
13	CINCINNATI	28
41	GREEN BAY	38
10	at Detroit	32
17	at New England	20
22	at NY Jets	14
41	MIAMI	0
28	at Minnesota	39
313		**401**

JACKSONVILLE JAGUARS (11–5)

28	BALTIMORE	27
40	NY GIANTS	13
	OPEN DATE	
30	PITTSBURGH	21
12	at Washington	24
21	CINCINNATI	13
38	PHILADELPHIA	21
22	at Dallas	26
17	PITTSBURGH	23
30	at Tennessee	24
24	KANSAS CITY	10
17	TENNESSEE	9
26	at Cincinnati	31
29	BALTIMORE	27
20	NEW ENGLAND	26
20	at Buffalo	14
20	at Oakland	9
394		**318**

KANSAS CITY CHIEFS (13–3)

3	at Denver	19
28	at Oakland	27
22	BUFFALO	16
35	at Carolina	14
20	SEATTLE (OT)	17
14	at Miami	17
	OPEN DATE	
31	SAN DIEGO	3
28	at St Louis	20
13	PITTSBURGH	10
10	at Jacksonville	24
24	DENVER	22
19	at Seattle	14
44	SAN FRANCISCO	9
30	OAKLAND	0
29	at San Diego	7
25	NEW ORLEANS	13
375		**232**

MIAMI DOLPHINS (9–7)

16	INDIANAPOLIS	10
16	TENNESSEE (OT)	13
18	at Green Bay	23
21	at Tampa Bay	31
	OPEN DATE	
17	KANSAS CITY	14
31	at NY Jets	20
24	at Baltimore	13
33	CHICAGO (OT)	36
6	at Buffalo	9
24	NY JETS	17
30	BUFFALO	13
24	at New England	27
34	at Oakland	16
33	DETROIT	30
0	at Indianapolis	41
12	NEW ENGLAND	14
339		**327**

NEW ENGLAND PATRIOTS (10–6)

41	SAN DIEGO	7
31	at Indianapolis	6
27	NY JETS (OT)	24
31	CHICAGO	3
	OPEN DATE	
13	at Denver	34
33	BUFFALO	6
19	at NY Jets	24
10	GREEN BAY	28
18	at Minnesota	23
31	at Buffalo	10
7	at Tampa Bay	27
27	MIAMI	24
20	INDIANAPOLIS	17
26	at Jacksonville	20
21	PITTSBURGH (OT)	24
14	at Miami	12
369		**289**

NEW YORK JETS (9–7)

41	at Seattle	3
22	BUFFALO	28
24	at New England (OT)	27
23	OAKLAND	22
31	at Cincinnati	14
16	at Indianapolis	12
20	MIAMI	31
24	NEW ENGLAND	19
	OPEN DATE	
19	BALTIMORE (OT)	16
17	at Miami	24
23	at Chicago	15
23	MINNESOTA	21
10	at Buffalo	20
14	INDIANAPOLIS	22
31	TAMPA BAY	0
10	at Detroit	13
348		**287**

OAKLAND RAIDERS (4–12)

21	at Tennessee (OT)	24
27	KANSAS CITY	28
36	at Atlanta	31
22	at NY Jets	23
35	ST LOUIS	17
10	SAN DIEGO	25
	OPEN DATE	
28	DENVER	25
34	at Seattle	45
14	at Carolina	38
10	NEW ORLEANS	13
38	at San Diego	13
3	at Denver	31
16	MIAMI	34
0	at Kansas City	30
21	SEATTLE	22
9	JACKSONVILLE	20
324		**419**

PITTSBURGH STEELERS (11–5)

7	DALLAS	37
14	WASHINGTON	13
	OPEN DATE	
21	at Jacksonville	30
37	TENNESSEE	24
42	at Baltimore	34
24	INDIANAPOLIS	22
26	at Cincinnati	10
23	JACKSONVILLE	17
10	at Kansas City	13
37	BALTIMORE	0
20	CINCINNATI	3
20	at Philadelphia	23
26	at Arizona (OT)	20
35	DENVER	24
24	at New England (OT)	21
6	at Tennessee	16
372		**307**

SAN DIEGO CHARGERS (4–12)

7	at New England	41
20	at New Orleans	6
7	CAROLINA	26
22	at Seattle	26
21	BALTIMORE	17
25	at Oakland	10
	OPEN DATE	
3	at Kansas City	31
35	INDIANAPOLIS	19
31	at Cincinnati	38
31	SEATTLE	37
13	OAKLAND	38
10	at San Francisco	17
28	DENVER	38
3	ATLANTA	14
7	KANSAS CITY	29
3	at Denver	38
266		425

SEATTLE SEAHAWKS (8–8)

3	NY JETS	41
14	DENVER	35
31	at Indianapolis	3
26	SAN DIEGO	22
17	at Kansas City (OT)	20
16	TENNESSEE	13
	OPEN DATE	
17	at St Louis	9
45	OAKLAND	34
27	at Denver	30
37	at San Diego	31
17	at New Orleans (OT)	20
14	KANSAS CITY	19
17	ATLANTA	24
24	at Baltimore	31
22	at Oakland	21
38	SAN FRANCISCO	9
365		362

TENNESSEE OILERS (8–8)

24	OAKLAND (OT)	21
13	at Miami (OT)	16
	OPEN DATE	
10	BALTIMORE	36
24	at Pittsburgh	37
13	at Seattle	16
30	CINCINNATI	7
28	WASHINGTON	14
41	at Arizona	14
24	JACKSONVILLE	30
10	NY JETS	6
9	at Jacksonville	17
31	BUFFALO	14
27	at Dallas	14
14	at Cincinnati	41
19	at Baltimore	21
16	PITTSBURGH	6
333		310

ARIZONA CARDINALS (4–12)

21	at Cincinnati	24
25	DALLAS (OT)	22
13	at Washington (OT)	19
	OPEN DATE	
18	at Tampa Bay	19
19	MINNESOTA	20
13	NY GIANTS	27
10	at Philadelphia (OT)	13
14	TENNESSEE	41
31	PHILADELPHIA	21
6	at Dallas	24
10	at NY Giants	19
16	at Baltimore	13
20	PITTSBURGH (OT)	26
28	WASHINGTON	38
10	at New Orleans	27
29	ATLANTA	26
283		379

ATLANTA FALCONS (7–9)

17	at Detroit	28
6	CAROLINA	9
31	OAKLAND	36
7	at San Francisco	34
21	DENVER	29
	OPEN DATE	
23	at New Orleans	17
28	SAN FRANCISCO	35
12	at Carolina	21
34	ST LOUIS	31
10	TAMPA BAY	31
27	at St Louis	21
20	NEW ORLEANS	3
24	at Seattle	17
14	at San Diego	3
20	PHILADELPHIA	17
26	at Arizona	29
320		361

CAROLINA PANTHERS (7–9)

10	WASHINGTON	24
9	at Atlanta	6
26	at San Diego	7
14	KANSAS CITY	35
21	SAN FRANCISCO	34
	OPEN DATE	
14	at Minnesota	21
13	at New Orleans	0
21	ATLANTA	12
38	OAKLAND	14
0	at Denver	34
19	at San Francisco	27
16	at St Louis	10
13	NEW ORLEANS	16
23	at Dallas	13
10	GREEN BAY	31
18	ST LOUIS	30
265		314

CHICAGO BEARS (4–12)

24	at Green Bay	38
24	MINNESOTA	27
7	DETROIT	32
3	at New England	31
3	DALLAS	27
17	NEW ORLEANS	20
23	GREEN BAY	24
	OPEN DATE	
36	at Miami (OT)	33
8	WASHINGTON	31
22	at Minnesota	29
15	NY JETS	23
13	TAMPA BAY	7
20	at Detroit	55
20	BUFFALO	3
13	at St Louis	10
15	at Tampa Bay	31
263		421

DALLAS COWBOYS (6–10)

37	at Pittsburgh	7
22	at Arizona (OT)	25
21	PHILADELPHIA	20
	OPEN DATE	
27	CHICAGO	3
17	at NY Giants	20
16	at Washington	21
26	JACKSONVILLE	22
12	at Philadelphia	13
10	at San Francisco	17
24	ARIZONA	6
17	WASHINGTON	14
17	at Green Bay	45
14	TENNESSEE	27
13	CAROLINA	23
24	at Cincinnati	31
7	NY GIANTS	20
304		314

DETROIT LIONS (9–7)

28	ATLANTA	17
17	TAMPA BAY	24
32	at Chicago	7
17	at New Orleans	35
26	GREEN BAY	15
13	at Buffalo	22
27	at Tampa Bay	9
20	NY GIANTS (OT)	26
	OPEN DATE	
10	at Green Bay	20
7	at Washington	30
38	MINNESOTA	15
32	INDIANAPOLIS	10
55	CHICAGO	20
30	MIAMI	33
14	at Minnesota	13
13	NY JETS	10
379		306

GREEN BAY PACKERS (13–3)

38	CHICAGO	24
9	at Philadelphia	10
23	MIAMI	18
38	MINNESOTA	32
15	at Detroit	26
21	TAMPA BAY	16
24	at Chicago	23
	OPEN DATE	
28	at New England	10
20	DETROIT	10
17	ST LOUIS	7
38	at Indianapolis	41
45	DALLAS	17
27	at Minnesota	11
17	at Tampa Bay	6
31	at Carolina	10
31	BUFFALO	21
422		**282**

MINNESOTA VIKINGS (9–7)

34	at Buffalo	13
27	at Chicago	24
14	TAMPA BAY	28
32	at Green Bay	38
28	PHILADELPHIA	19
20	at Arizona	19
21	CAROLINA	14
	OPEN DATE	
10	at Tampa Bay	6
23	NEW ENGLAND	18
29	CHICAGO	22
15	at Detroit	38
21	at NY Jets	23
11	GREEN BAY	27
17	at San Francisco	28
13	DETROIT	14
39	INDIANAPOLIS	28
354		**359**

NEW ORLEANS SAINTS (6–10)

24	at St Louis	38
6	SAN DIEGO	20
7	at San Francisco	33
35	DETROIT	17
9	at NY Giants	14
20	at Chicago	17
17	ATLANTA	23
0	CAROLINA	13
0	SAN FRANCISCO	23
	OPEN DATE	
13	at Oakland	10
20	SEATTLE	17
3	at Atlanta	20
16	at Carolina	13
27	ST LOUIS	34
27	ARIZONA	10
13	at Kansas City	25
237		**327**

NEW YORK GIANTS (10-5-1)

31	PHILADELPHIA	17
13	at Jacksonville	40
23	BALTIMORE	24
3	at St Louis	13
14	NEW ORLEANS	9
20	DALLAS	17
27	at Arizona	13
26	at Detroit (OT)	20
29	CINCINNATI	27
	OPEN DATE	
6	at Tennessee	10
19	ARIZONA	10
7	at Washington (OT)	7
8	TAMPA BAY	20
31	at Philadelphia	21
30	WASHINGTON	10
20	at Dallas	7
307		**265**

PHILADELPHIA EAGLES (6-9-1)

17	at NY Giants	31
10	GREEN BAY	9
20	at Dallas	21
	OPEN DATE	
19	at Minnesota	28
24	WASHINGTON	10
21	at Jacksonville	38
13	ARIZONA (OT)	10
13	DALLAS	12
21	at Arizona	31
12	SAN FRANCISCO	24
10	at Baltimore (OT)	10
23	PITTSBURGH	20
44	CINCINNATI	42
21	NY GIANTS	31
17	at Atlanta	20
32	at Washington	35
317		**372**

ST. LOUIS RAMS (5–11)

38	NEW ORLEANS	24
12	SAN FRANCISCO	15
14	at Denver	35
13	NY GIANTS	3
17	at Oakland	35
	OPEN DATE	
10	at San Francisco	30
20	SEATTLE	17
20	KANSAS CITY	28
31	at Atlanta	34
7	at Green Bay	17
21	ATLANTA	27
10	CAROLINA	16
23	at Washington	20
34	at New Orleans	27
10	CHICAGO	13
30	at Carolina	18
299		**359**

SAN FRANCISCO 49ERS (13–3)

6	at Tampa Bay	13
15	at St Louis	12
33	NEW ORLEANS	7
34	ATLANTA	7
34	at Carolina	21
	OPEN DATE	
30	ST LOUIS	10
35	at Atlanta	28
23	at New Orleans	0
17	DALLAS	10
24	at Philadelphia	12
27	CAROLINA	19
17	SAN DIEGO	10
9	at Kansas City	44
28	MINNESOTA	17
34	DENVER	17
9	at Seattle	38
375		**265**

TAMPA BAY BUCCANEERS (10–6)

13	SAN FRANCISCO	6
24	at Detroit	17
28	at Minnesota	14
31	MIAMI	21
19	ARIZONA	18
16	at Green Bay	21
9	DETROIT	27
	OPEN DATE	
6	MINNESOTA	10
31	at Indianapolis	28
31	at Atlanta	10
27	NEW ENGLAND	7
7	at Chicago	13
20	at NY Giants	8
6	GREEN BAY	17
0	at NY Jets	31
31	CHICAGO	15
299		**263**

WASHINGTON REDSKINS (8-7-1)

24	at Carolina	10
13	at Pittsburgh	14
19	ARIZONA	13
	OPEN DATE	
24	JACKSONVILLE	12
10	at Philadelphia	24
21	DALLAS	16
14	at Tennessee	28
17	BALTIMORE	20
31	at Chicago	8
30	DETROIT	7
14	at Dallas	17
7	NY GIANTS (OT)	7
20	ST LOUIS	23
38	at Arizona	28
10	at NY Giants	30
35	PHILADELPHIA	32
327		**289**

American Football Conference

Scoring

TOUCHDOWNS	TD	Rush	Rec	Ret	Pts
Abdul-Jabbar, Mia	16	15	1	0	96
Davis, Den	15	15	0	0	96
Gallway, Sea	12	0	12	0	72
Jett, Oak	12	0	12	0	72
R. Smith, Den	12	0	12	0	72
Allen, KC	11	11	0	0	66
Stewart, Pitt	11	11	0	0	66
Dillon, Cin	10	10	0	0	60

Four tied with nine.

KICKING	PAT	FG	Lg	Pts
Hollis, Jax	41/41	31/36	52	134
Elam, Den	46/46	26/36	53	124
Hall, NYJ	36/36	28/41	55	120
Blanchard, Ind	21/21	32/41	50	117
Mare, Mia	33/33	28/36	50	117
Vinatieri, NE	40/40	25/29	52	115
Del Greco, Tenn	32/32	27/35	52	113
Stoyanovich, KC	35/36	26/27	54	113
Stover, Balt	32/32	26/34	49	110
Davis, SD	31/32	26/34	45	109

Passing

	Att	Comp	Pct Comp	Yds	Avg Gain	TD	Pct TD	Int	Pct Int	Lg	Rating Pts
Brunell, Jax	435	264	60.7	3281	7.54	18	4.1	7	1.6	75	91.2
George, Oak	521	290	55.7	3917	7.52	29	5.6	9	1.7	76	91.2
Bledsoe, NE	522	314	60.2	3706	7.10	28	5.4	15	2.9	76	87.7
Elway, Den	502	280	55.8	3635	7.24	27	5.4	11	2.2	78	87.5
Harbaugh, Ind	309	189	61.2	2060	6.67	10	3.2	4	1.3	58	86.2
Moon, Sea	528	313	59.3	3678	6.97	25	4.7	16	3.0	t60	83.7
Marino, Mia	548	319	58.2	3780	6.90	16	2.9	11	2.0	55	80.7
O'Donnell, NYJ	460	259	56.3	2796	6.08	17	3.7	7	1.5	79	80.3
Grbac, KC	314	179	57.0	1943	6.19	11	3.5	6	1.9	t55	79.1
Blake, Cin	317	184	58.0	2125	6.70	8	2.5	7	2.2	t50	77.6

Pass Receiving

RECEPTIONS	No.	Yds	Avg	Lg	TD
T. Brown, Oak	104	1408	13.5	t59	5
McCardell, Jax	85	1164	13.7	60	5
Smith, Jax	82	1324	16.1	75	4
Thigpen, Pitt	79	1398	17.7	t69	7
McDuffie, Mia	76	943	12.4	55	1
Harrison, Ind	73	866	11.9	44	6
Sharpe, Den	72	1107	15.4	t68	3
Rison, KC	72	1092	15.2	45	7
Galloway, Sea	72	1049	14.6	t53	12
R. Smith, Den	70	1180	16.9	78	12
K. Johnson, NYJ	70	963	13.8	39	5

YARDS	Yds	No.	Avg	Lg	TD
Brown, Oak	1408	104	13.5	t59	5
Thigpen, Pitt	1398	79	17.7	t69	7
J. Smith, Jax	1324	82	16.1	75	4
R. Smith, Den	1180	70	16.9	78	12
McCardell, Jax	1164	85	13.7	60	5
Sharpe, Den	1107	72	15.4	t68	3
Rison, KC	1092	72	15.2	45	7
Galloway, Sea	1049	72	14.6	t53	12
Alexander, Balt	1009	65	15.5	92	9
K. Johnson, NYJ	963	70	13.8	39	5

Rushing

	Att	Yds	Avg	Lg	TD
Davis, Den	369	1750	4.7	t50	15
Bettis, Pitt	375	1665	4.4	34	7
George, Hou	357	1399	3.9	30	6
Kaufman, Oak	272	1294	4.8	t83	6
Martin, NE	274	1160	4.2	t70	4
Watters, Phil	233	1129	4.8	t71	10
Murrell, NYJ	300	1086	3.6	t43	7
Faulk, Ind	264	1054	4.0	45	7
Brown, SD	253	945	3.7	32	4
Abdul-Jabbar, Mia	283	892	3.2	22	15

Total Yards from Scrimmage

	Total	Rush	Rec
Davis, Den	2037	1750	287
Bettis, Pitt	1775	1665	110
Kaufman, Oak	1697	1294	403
Faulk, Ind	1525	1054	471
George, Tenn	1443	1399	44
Brown, Oak	1427	19	1408
Thigpen, Pitt	1401	3	1398
Dillon, Cin	1388	1129	259
J. Smith, Jax	1324	0	1324
R. Smith, Den	1196	16	1180

Interceptions

	No.	Yds	Lg	TD
McMillian, KC	8	274	t87	3
D. Williams, Sea	8	172	t44	1
Clay, NE	6	109	t53	1
Smith, NYJ	6	158	t51	3

Three tied with five.

Sacks

B. Smith, Buff	14.0
Sinclair, Sea	12.0
Boulware, Balt	11.5
Footman, Ind	10.5
Williams, KC	10.5
Paup, Buff	9.5
Thomas, KC	9.5

American Football Conference *(Cont.)*
Punting

	No.	Yds	Avg	Net Avg	TB	In 20	Lg	Blk	Ret	Ret Yds
Tupa, NE	78	3569	45.8	36.1	14	24	73	1	38	437
Gardocki, Ind	67	3034	45.3	36.2	6	18	72	0	43	491
Araguz, Oak	93	4189	45.0	39.1	6	28	63	0	52	431
Barker, Jax	66	2964	44.9	38.8	8	27	64	0	29	241
Bennett, SD	89	3972	44.6	37.7	8	26	66	1	39	416

Punt Returns

	No.	Yds	Avg	Lg	TD
J. Lewis, Balt	28	437	15.6	t89	2
Gordon, Den	40	543	13.6	t94	3
L. Johnson, NYJ	51	619	12.1	t66	1
Barlow, Jax	36	412	11.4	52	0
Vanover, KC	35	383	10.9	t82	1

Kickoff Returns

	No.	Yds	Avg	Lg	TD
Glenn, NYJ	28	741	26.5	t96	1
Vanover, KC	50	1283	25.7	t94	1
Meggett, NE	33	816	24.7	61	0
Blackwell, Pitt	32	791	24.7	t97	1
Spikes, Mia	24	565	23.5	48	0

National Football Conference
Scoring

TOUCHDOWNS	TD	Rush	Rec	Ret	Pts	KICKING	PAT	FG	Lg	Pts
Sanders, Det	14	11	3	0	84	Cunningham, Dall	24/24	34/37	53	126
Carter, Minn	13	0	13	0	84	Anderson, SF	38/38	29/36	51	125
Levens, GB	12	7	5	0	74	Longwell, GB	48/48	24/30	50	120
Freeman, GB	12	0	12	0	72	Hanson, Det	39/40	26/29	55	117
Alstott, TB	10	7	3	0	60	Wilkins, StL	32/32	25/37	52	107
Anderson, Atl	10	7	3	0	60	Andersen, Atl	35/35	23/27	55	104
R. Harris, Chi	10	10	0	0	60	Boniol, Phil	33/33	22/31	49	99
Emanuel, Atl	9	0	9	0	54	Daluiso, NYG	27/29	22/32	52	93
Irvin, Dall	9	0	9	0	54	Brien, NO	22/22	23/27	53	91
Five tied with eight.						Kasay, Car	25/25	22/26	54	91

Passing

	Att	Comp	Pct Comp	Yds	Avg Gain	TD	Pct TD	Int	Pct Int	Lg	Rating Pts
S. Young, SF	356	241	67.7	3029	8.51	19	5.3	6	1.7	82	104.7
Chandler, Atl	342	202	59.1	2692	7.87	20	5.8	7	2.0	56	95.1
Favre, GB	513	304	59.3	3867	7.54	35	6.8	16	3.1	74	92.6
Johnson, Minn	452	275	60.8	3036	6.72	20	4.4	12	2.7	56	84.5
Hoying, Phil	225	128	56.9	1573	6.99	11	4.9	6	2.7	t72	83.8
Dilfer, TB	386	217	56.2	2555	6.62	21	5.4	11	2.8	t59	82.8
Mitchell, Det	509	293	57.6	3484	6.84	19	3.7	14	2.8	79	79.6
Aikman, Dall	518	292	56.4	3283	6.34	19	3.7	12	2.3	t64	78.0
Kramer, Chi	477	275	57.7	3011	6.31	14	2.9	14	2.9	t78	74.0
T. Detmer, Phil	244	134	54.9	1567	6.42	7	2.9	6	2.5	57	73.9

Pass Receiving

RECEPTIONS	No.	Yds	Avg	Lg	TD
Moore, Det	104	1293	12.4	79	8
Rob Moore, Ariz	97	1584	16.3	t47	8
Carter, Minn	89	1069	12.0	43	13
Fryar, Phil	86	1316	15.3	t72	6
Freeman, GB	81	1243	15.3	t58	12
Morton, Det	80	1057	13.2	t73	6
Irvin, Phil	75	1180	15.7	55	9
Sanders, Ariz	75	1017	13.6	t70	4
Reed, Minn	68	1138	16.7	56	6
Emanuel, Atl	65	991	15.2	56	9

YARDS	Yds	No.	Avg	Lg	TD
Rob Moore, Ariz	1584	97	16.3	t47	8
Fryar, Phil	1316	86	15.3	t72	6
Moore, Det	1293	104	12.4	79	8
Freeman, GB	1243	81	15.3	t58	12
Irvin, Dall	1180	75	15.7	55	9
Reed, Minn	1138	68	16.7	56	6
Carter, Minn	1069	89	12.0	43	13
Morton, Det	1057	80	13.2	t73	6
Sanders, Ariz	1017	75	13.6	t70	4
R. Brooks, GB	1010	60	16.8	48	7

National Football Conference *(Cont.)*

Rushing

	Att	Yds	Avg	Lg	TD
Sanders, Det	335	2053	6.1	t82	11
Levens, GB	329	1435	4.4	t52	7
R. Smith, Minn	232	1266	5.5	t78	6
Watters, Phil	285	1110	3.9	28	7
E. Smith, Dall	261	1074	4.1	44	4
R. Harris, Chi	275	1033	3.8	t68	10
Hearst, SF	234	1019	4.4	51	4
Anderson, Atl	290	1002	3.5	39	7
Dunn, TB	224	978	4.4	76	4
Lane, Car	182	809	4.4	50	7

Total Yards from Scrimmage

	Total	Rush	Rec
Sanders, Det	2358	2053	305
Levens, GB	1805	1435	370
Rob Moore, Ariz	1584	0	1584
Watters, Phil	1550	1110	440
R. Smith, Minn	1463	1266	197
Martin, NE	1456	1160	296
Dunn, TB	1440	978	462
Fryar, Phil	1316	0	1316
E. Smith, Dall	1308	1074	234
Moore, Det	1293	0	1293

Interceptions

	No.	Yds	Lg	TD
McNeil, StL	9	127	t75	1
Lyle, StL	8	102	39	0
Hanks, SF	6	103	t55	1
Williams, Ariz	6	95	t42	2
Sehorn, NYG	6	74	41	1

Ten tied with five.

Sacks

Randle, Minn	15.5
Stubblefield, SF	15.0
Strahan, NYG	14.0
Porcher, Det	12.5
Doleman, SF	12.0
Smith, Atl	12.0

Punting

	No.	Yds	Avg	Net Avg	TB	In 20	Lg	Blk	Ret	Ret Yds
Royals, NO	88	4038	45.9	34.9	13	21	66	0	50	706
M. Turk, Wash	84	3788	45.1	39.2	11	32	62	1	33	237
Hentrich, GB	75	3378	45.0	36.0	21	26	65	0	32	255
Feagles, Ariz	91	4028	44.3	36.8	10	24	62	1	40	441
Berger, Minn	73	3133	42.9	34.1	5	22	65	0	46	545
Horan, StL	53	2272	42.9	36.3	4	10	60	0	33	266

Punt Returns

	No.	Yds	Avg	Lg	TD
Palmer, Minn	34	444	13.1	57	0
Williams, TB	46	597	13.0	63	1
Sanders, Dall	33	407	12.3	t83	1
Mitchell, Wash	38	442	11.6	t63	1
Williams, Ariz	40	462	11.6	50	0

Kickoff Returns

	No.	Yds	Avg	Lg	TD
Bates, Car	47	1281	27.3	56	0
Guilford, NO	43	1128	26.2	t102	1
K. Williams, Ariz	59	1458	24.7	63	0
Hanspard, Atl	40	987	24.7	t99	2
Staley, Phil	57	1139	24.2	57	0

1997 NFL Team Leaders

AFC Total Offense

	Total Yds	Yds Rush	Yds Pass	Time of Poss	Avg Pts/Game
Denver	5872	2378	3494	32:07	29.5
Seattle	5759	1800	3959	30:47	22.7
Pittsburgh	5542	2479	3063	32:05	23.3
Jacksonville	5424	1720	3704	29:40	24.6
Baltimore	5291	1589	3702	28:30	20.4
Cincinnati	5282	1966	3316	27:56	22.2
Miami	5125	1343	3782	30:29	21.2
Oakland	5102	1588	3514	26:24	20.3
Kansas City	5064	2171	2893	31:16	23.4
New England	5014	1464	3550	28:08	23.0
Tennessee	4919	2414	2505	31:27	20.8
Indianapolis	4869	1727	3142	32:56	19.6
NY Jets	4727	1485	3242	29:42	21.8
Buffalo	4657	1782	2875	27:59	15.9
San Diego	4505	1416	3089	29:22	16.6

AFC Total Defense

	Opp Total Yds	Opp Yds Rush	Opp Yds Pass	Avg PA/Game
Denver	4671	1803	2868	17.9
Pittsburgh	4705	1318	3387	19.2
Seattle	4849	1731	3118	22.5
Buffalo	4853	1792	3061	22.9
Indianapolis	4854	2034	2820	25.1
Kansas City	4880	1621	3259	14.5
New England	5075	1616	3459	18.1
San Diego	5166	1698	3468	26.6
Tennessee	5231	1573	3658	19.4
Jacksonville	5238	1734	3504	19.9
NY Jets	5320	1899	3421	17.9
Baltimore	5363	1690	3673	21.6
Miami	5364	1813	3551	20.4
Cincinnati	5682	2223	3459	25.3
Oakland	6116	2246	3870	26.2

NFC Total Offense

	Total Yds	Yds Rush	Yds Pass	Time of Poss	Avg Pts/Game
Detroit	5798	2464	3334	28:37	23.7
Green Bay	5614	1909	3705	30:05	26.4
Philadelphia	5590	1943	3647	31:09	19.8
Minnesota	5354	2041	3313	29:46	22.1
San Francisco	5112	1969	3143	32:28	23.4
Washington	4998	1615	3383	29:27	20.4
Chicago	4987	1746	3241	33:08	16.4
Dallas	4778	1637	3141	29:53	19.0
St. Louis	4761	1563	3198	29:47	18.7
Atlanta	4716	1643	3073	31:29	20.0
Arizona	4713	1255	3458	29:02	17.7
Carolina	4604	1759	2845	29:43	16.6
NY Giants	4513	1988	2525	29:27	19.2
Tampa Bay	4376	1934	2542	29:22	18.7
New Orleans	4045	1461	2584	27:47	14.8

NFC Total Defense

	Opp Total Yds	Opp Yds Rush	Opp Yds Pass	Avg PA/Game
San Francisco	4013	1366	2647	16.6
Dallas	4516	1994	2522	19.6
Tampa Bay	4625	1617	3008	16.4
New Orleans	4645	1764	2881	20.4
Green Bay	4827	1876	2951	17.6
Chicago	4888	1858	3030	26.3
Philadelphia	4932	2009	2923	23.3
Detroit	4947	1833	3114	19.1
Carolina	4980	1973	3007	19.6
Washington	5030	2212	2818	18.1
St. Louis	5055	1676	3379	22.4
NY Giants	5067	1451	3616	16.6
Atlanta	5106	1666	3440	22.6
Arizona	5426	2180	3246	23.7
Minnesota	5687	1983	3704	22.4

Takeaways/Giveaways

American Football Conference

	Takeaways Int	Fum	Total	Giveaways Int	Fum	Total	Net Diff
Kansas City	21	13	34	10	10	20	14
Denver	18	13	31	11	10	21	10
New England	19	13	32	15	7	22	10
Jacksonville	14	15	29	9	11	20	9
Miami	10	17	27	12	8	20	7
Tennessee	14	17	31	13	13	26	5
NY Jets	18	7	25	10	12	22	3
Cincinnati	13	10	23	9	13	22	1
Pittsburgh	20	14	34	19	14	33	1
Oakland	10	12	22	10	14	24	-2
Indianapolis	12	13	25	17	11	28	-3
Seattle	13	16	29	21	11	32	-3
Baltimore	17	11	28	16	16	32	-4
San Diego	15	11	26	21	14	35	-9
Buffalo	15	7	22	25	17	42	-20

National Football Conference

	Takeaways Int	Fum	Total	Giveaways Int	Fum	Total	Net Diff
NY Giants	27	17	44	12	7	19	25
San Francisco	25	16	41	11	9	20	21
St. Louis	25	14	39	15	15	30	9
Minnesota	12	15	27	16	6	22	5
Atlanta	18	10	28	11	13	24	4
Tampa Bay	13	13	26	12	11	23	3
Washington	16	14	30	22	7	29	1
Green Bay	21	11	32	16	16	32	0
Detroit	17	8	25	17	11	28	-3
Dallas	7	12	19	12	11	23	-4
Philadelphia	14	12	26	16	16	32	-6
Chicago	13	17	30	22	19	41	-11
Carolina	11	11	22	24	15	39	-17
Arizona	15	5	20	22	20	42	-22
New Orleans	16	15	31	33	22	55	-24

Conference Rankings

American Football Conference

	Offense Total	Rush	Pass	Defense Total	Rush	Pass
Baltimore	5	10	4	12	5	14
Buffalo	14	7	14	4	9	3
Cincinnati	6	5	8	14	14	9
Denver	1	3	7	1	10	2
Indianapolis	12	8	10	5	13	1
Jacksonville	4	9	3	10	8	11
Kansas City	9	4	13	6	4	5
Miami	7	15	2	13	11	12
New England	10	13	5	7	3	8
NY Jets	13	12	9	11	12	7
Oakland	8	11	6	15	15	15
Pittsburgh	3	1	12	2	1	6
San Diego	15	14	11	8	6	10
Seattle	2	6	1	3	7	4
Tennessee	11	2	15	9	2	13

National Football Conference

	Offense Total	Rush	Pass	Defense Total	Rush	Pass
Arizona	11	15	3	14	14	11
Atlanta	10	10	11	13	4	13
Carolina	12	8	12	9	10	7
Chicago	7	9	7	6	8	9
Dallas	8	11	10	2	12	1
Detroit	1	1	5	8	7	10
Green Bay	2	7	1	5	9	6
Minnesota	4	2	6	15	11	15
New Orleans	15	14	13	4	6	4
NY Giants	13	3	14	12	2	14
Philadelphia	3	5	2	7	13	5
St. Louis	9	13	8	11	5	12
San Francisco	5	4	9	1	1	2
Tampa Bay	14	6	15	3	3	8
Washington	6	12	4	10	15	3

Baltimore Ravens

SCORING	Rush	Rec	Ret	PAT	FG	S	Pts
Stover	0	0	0	32/32	26/34	0	110
Alexander	0	9	0	0/0	0/0	0	54
J. Lewis	0	6	2	0/0	0/0	0	48
Green	0	5	0	0/0	0/0	0	30
Jackson	0	4	0	0/0	0/0	0	26
Morris	4	0	0	0/0	0/0	0	24

RUSHING	No.	Yds	Avg	Lg	TD
Morris	204	774	3.8	25	4
Byner	84	313	3.7	19	0
Graham	81	299	3.7	19	2
Testaverde	34	138	4.1	16	0

PASSING	Att	Comp	Pct Comp	Yds	Avg Gain	TD	Int	Rating Pts
T'verde	470	271	57.7	2971	6.32	18	15	75.9
Zeier	116	67	57.8	958	8.26	7	1	101.1

RECEIVING	No.	Yds	Avg	Lg	TD
Jackson	69	918	13.3	t54	4
Alexander	65	1009	15.5	92	9
Green	65	601	9.2	t37	5
J. Lewis	42	648	15.4	t42	6

INTERCEPTIONS: Moore, 4

PUNTING	No.	Yds	Avg	Net Avg	TB	In 20	Lg	Blk
M'gomery	83	3540	42.7	36.6	2	24	60	0

SACKS: Boulware, 11.5

Buffalo Bills

SCORING	Rush	Rec	Ret	PAT	FG	S	Pts
Christie	0	0	0	21/21	24/30	0	93
A. Smith	8	0	0	0/0	0/0	0	48
Early	0	5	0	0/0	0/0	0	30
Reed	0	5	0	0/0	0/0	0	30
Riemersma	0	2	0	0/0	0/0	0	14

RUSHING	No.	Yds	Avg	Lg	TD
A. Smith	194	840	4.3	t56	8
Thomas	154	643	4.2	24	1

PASSING	Att	Comp	Pct Comp	Yds	Avg Gain	TD	Int	Rating Pts
Collins	391	215	55.0	2367	6.05	12	13	69.5
Van Pelt	124	60	48.4	684	5.52	2	10	37.2

RECEIVING	No.	Yds	Avg	Lg	TD
Reed	60	880	14.7	t77	5
Early	60	853	14.2	45	5
Johnson	41	340	8.3	t62	2
Thomas	30	208	6.9	30	0
Moulds	29	294	10.1	32	0

INTERCEPTIONS: Five tied with 2.

PUNTING	No.	Yds	Avg	Net Avg	TB	In 20	Lg	Blk
Mohr	90	3764	41.8	36.0	6	24	59	1

SACKS: B. Smith, 14

Cincinnati Bengals

SCORING	Rush	Rec	Ret	PAT	FG	S	Pts
Pelfrey	0	0	0	41/43	12/16	0	77
Dillon	10	0	0	0/0	0/0	0	60
Carter	7	0	0	0/0	0/0	0	42
McGee	0	6	0	0/0	0/0	0	38
Scott	0	5	0	0/0	0/0	0	30
Pickens	0	5	0	0/0	0/0	0	30

RUSHING	No.	Yds	Avg	Lg	TD
Dillon	233	1129	4.8	t71	10
Carter	128	464	3.6	t79	7
Blake	45	234	5.2	16	3

PASSING	Att	Comp	Pct Comp	Yds	Avg Gain	TD	Int	Rating Pts
Blake	317	184	58.0	2125	6.70	8	7	77.6
Esiason	186	118	63.4	1478	7.95	13	2	106.9

RECEIVING	No.	Yds	Avg	Lg	TD
Scott	54	797	14.8	t77	5
Pickens	52	695	13.4	t50	5
McGee	34	414	12.2	37	6
Bieniemy	31	249	8.0	21	0
Dunn	27	414	15.3	t39	2
Dillon	27	259	9.6	28	0

INTERCEPTIONS: Sawyer, 4

PUNTING	No.	Yds	Avg	Net Avg	TB	In 20	Lg	Blk
Johnson	81	3471	42.9	35.9	8	26	66	0

SACKS: Dixon, 8

Denver Broncos

SCORING	Rush	Rec	Ret	PAT	FG	S	Pts
Elam	0	0	0	46/46	26/36	0	124
Davis	15	0	0	0/0	0/0	0	96
R. Smith	0	12	0	0/0	0/0	0	72
McCaffrey	0	8	0	0/0	0/0	0	48
Gordon	0	0	4	0/0	0/0	0	24
Sharpe	0	3	0	0/0	0/0	0	20

RUSHING	No.	Yds	Avg	Lg	TD
Davis	369	1750	4.7	t50	15
Hebron	49	222	4.5	46	1
Elway	50	218	4.4	23	1
Loville	25	124	5.0	17	1

PASSING	Att	Comp	Pct Comp	Yds	Avg Gain	TD	Int	Rating Pts
Elway	502	280	55.8	3635	7.24	27	11	87.5

RECEIVING	No.	Yds	Avg	Lg	TD
Sharpe	72	1107	15.4	t68	3
R. Smith	70	1180	16.9	78	12
McCaffrey	45	590	13.1	35	8
Davis	42	287	6.8	25	0
Green	19	240	12.6	31	2

INTERCEPTIONS: Three tied with 4.

PUNTING	No.	Yds	Avg	Net Avg	TB	In 20	Lg	Blk
Rouen	60	2598	43.3	38.1	4	22	57	0

SACKS: N. Smith and Tanuvasa, 8.5

Indianapolis Colts

SCORING	TD Rush	Rec	Ret	PAT	FG	S	Pts
Blanchard 0	0	0	21/21	32/41	0	117
Faulk 7	1	0	0/0	0/0	0	48
Harrison 0	6	0	0/0	0/0	0	40
Dilger 0	3	0	0/0	0/0	0	18
Bailey 0	3	0	0/0	0/0	0	18

RUSHING	No.	Yds	Avg	Lg	TD
Faulk.......................264	1054	4.0	45	7
Crockett....................95	300	3.2	20	1
Harbaugh.................36	206	5.7	18	0
Warren......................28	80	2.9	11	2
Groce 10	66	6.6	29	0

PASSING	Att	Comp	Pct Comp	Yds	Avg Gain	TD	Int	Rating Pts
H'baugh...309	189	61.2	2060	6.67	10	4	86.2
Justin.......140	83	59.3	1046	7.47	5	5	79.6

RECEIVING	No.	Yds	Avg	Lg	TD
Harrison...................73	866	11.9	44	6
Dawkins...................68	804	11.8	51	2
Faulk.......................47	471	10.0	58	1
Dilger.......................27	380	14.1	43	3
Bailey 26	329	12.7	22	3

INTERCEPTIONS: Three tied with 2.

PUNTING	No.	Yds	Avg	Net Avg	TB	In 20	Lg	Blk
Gardocki...67	3034	45.3	36.2	6	18	72	0

SACKS: Footman, 10.5

Kansas City Chiefs

SCORING	TD Rush	Rec	Ret	PAT	FG	S	Pts
Stoyanovich 0	0	0	35/36	26/27	0	113
Allen 11	0	0	0/0	0/0	0	66
Rison 0	7	0	0/0	0/0	0	42
Three tied with 18.						

RUSHING	No.	Yds	Avg	Lg	TD
Hill 157	550	3.5	38	0
Allen 124	505	4.1	30	11
Anders.......................79	397	5.0	43	0
Bennett......................94	369	3.9	14	1

PASSING	Att	Comp	Pct Comp	Yds	Avg Gain	TD	Int	Rating Pts
Grbac 314	179	57.0	1943	6.19	11	6	79.1
Gannon ...175	98	56.0	1144	6.54	7	4	79.8

RECEIVING	No.	Yds	Avg	Lg	TD
Rison 72	1092	15.2	45	7
Anders......................59	453	7.7	t55	2
Popson 35	320	9.1	21	2
Gonzalez...................33	368	11.2	30	2
Dawson 21	273	13.0	27	2

INTERCEPTIONS: McMillian, 8

PUNTING	No.	Yds	Avg	Net Avg	TB	In 20	Lg	Blk
Aguiar 81	3433	42.4	38.2	4	28	65	0

SACKS: Williams, 10.5

Jacksonville Jaguars

SCORING	TD Rush	Rec	Ret	PAT	FG	S	Pts
Hollis 0	0	0	41/41	31/36	0	134
Means 9	0	0	0/0	0/0	0	54
Stewart 8	1	0	0/0	0/0	0	54
McCardell 0	5	0	0/0	0/0	0	30

RUSHING	No.	Yds	Avg	Lg	TD
Means........................244	823	3.4	20	9
Stewart 136	555	4.1	33	8
Brunell 48	257	5.4	15	2

PASSING	Att	Comp	Pct Comp	Yds	Avg Gain	TD	Int	Rating
Brunell 435	264	60.7	3281	7.54	18	7	91.2
Johnson.....28	22	78.6	344	12.29	2	2	112.8
Matthews....40	26	65.0	275	6.88	0	0	84.9

RECEIVING	No.	Yds	Avg	Lg	TD
McCardell...................85	1164	13.7	60	5
Smith 82	1324	16.1	75	4
Stewart 41	336	8.2	40	1
Mitchell......................35	380	10.9	33	4
Hallock 18	131	7.3	23	1

INTERCEPTIONS: Figures, 5

PUNTING	No.	Yds	Avg	Net Avg	TB	In 20	Lg	Blk
Barker 66	2964	44.9	38.8	8	27	64	0

SACKS: Simmons, 8.5

Miami Dolphins

SCORING	TD Rush	Rec	Ret	PAT	FG	S	Pts
Mare...................0	0	0	33/33	28/36	0	117
Abdul-Jabbar.....15	1	0	0/0	0/0	0	96
Drayton 0	4	0	0/0	0/0	0	24
Jordan.................0	3	0	0/0	0/0	0	18
Four tied with 12.						

RUSHING	No.	Yds	Avg	Lg	TD
Abdul-Jabbar 283	892	3.2	22	15
Spikes.......................63	180	2.9	14	2

PASSING	Att	Comp	Pct Comp	Yds	Avg Gain	TD	Int	Rating Pts
Marino 548	319	58.2	3780	6.90	16	11	80.7
Erickson ...28	13	46.4	165	5.89	0	1	50.4

RECEIVING	No.	Yds	Avg	Lg	TD
McDuffie...................76	943	12.4	55	1
Drayton.....................39	558	14.3	t30	4
McPhail.....................34	262	7.7	19	1
Abdul-Jabbar...........29	261	9.0	t36	1
L. Thomas 28	402	14.4	26	2
Parmalee 28	301	10.8	29	1
Jordan......................27	471	17.4	t44	3

INTERCEPTIONS: Buckley, 4

PUNTING	No.	Yds	Avg	Net Avg	TB	In 20	Lg	Blk
Kidd 52	2247	43.2	37.0	4	13	58	0

SACKS: Armstrong, 5.5

New England Patriots

SCORING	Rush	TD Rec	Ret	PAT	FG	S	Pts
Vinatieri	0	0	0	40/40	25/29	0	115
Coates	0	8	0	0/0	0/0	0	48
T. Brown	0	6	0	0/0	0/0	0	36
Martin	4	1	0	0/0	0/0	0	30

RUSHING	No.	Yds	Avg	Lg	TD
Martin	274	1160	4.2	t70	4
Cullors	22	101	4.6	24	0
Grier	33	75	2.3	12	1

PASSING	Att	Comp	Pct Comp	Yds	Avg Gain	TD	Int	Rating Pts
Bledsoe	522	314	60.2	3706	7.10	28	15	87.7

RECEIVING	No.	Yds	Avg	Lg	TD
Coates	66	737	11.2	35	8
Jefferson	54	841	15.6	76	2
T. Brown	41	607	14.8	67	6
Martin	41	296	7.2	22	1
Glenn	27	431	16.0	50	2
Brisby	23	276	12.0	31	2

INTERCEPTIONS: Clay, 6

PUNTING	No.	Yds	Avg	Net Avg	TB	In 20	Lg	Blk
Tupa	78	3569	45.8	36.1	14	24	73	1

SACKS: Slade, 9

New York Jets

SCORING	Rush	TD Rec	Ret	PAT	FG	S	Pts
Hall	0	0	0	36/36	28/41	0	120
Murrell	7	0	0	0/0	0/0	0	42
K. Johnson	0	5	0	0/0	0/0	0	30
L. Johnson	2	0	2	0/0	0/0	0	24

Three tied with 18.

RUSHING	No.	Yds	Avg	Lg	TD
Murrell	30	1086	3.6	t43	7
L. Johnson	48	158	3.3	20	2
Anderson	21	70	3.3	19	0

PASSING	Att	Comp	Pct Comp	Yds	Avg Gain	TD	Int	Rating Pts
O'Donnell	460	259	56.3	2796	6.08	17	7	80.3
Foley	97	56	57.7	705	7.27	3	1	86.5

RECEIVING	No.	Yds	Avg	Lg	TD
K. Johnson	70	963	13.8	39	5
Chrebet	58	799	13.8	70	3
Graham	42	542	12.9	t47	2
Baxter	27	276	10.2	37	3
Murrell	27	106	3.9	23	0

INTERCEPTIONS: Smith, 6

PUNTING	No.	Yds	Avg	Net Avg	TB	In 20	Lg	Blk
Hansen	71	3068	43.2	35.3	5	20	58	1

SACKS: Lewis, 8

Oakland Raiders

SCORING	Rush	TD Rec	Ret	PAT	FG	S	Pts
Ford	0	0	0	33/35	13/22	0	72
Jett	0	12	0	0/0	0/0	0	72
Kaufman	6	2	0	0/0	0/0	0	48
Dudley	0	7	0	0/0	0/0	0	42
T. Brown	0	5	0	0/0	0/0	0	32
Williams	3	2	0	0/0	0/0	0	32

RUSHING	No.	Yds	Avg	Lg	TD
Kaufman	272	1294	4.8	t83	6
Hall	23	120	5.2	15	0
Williams	18	70	3.9	13	3
George	17	44	2.6	12	0

PASSING	Att	Comp	Pct Comp	Yds	Avg Gain	TD	Int	Rating Pts
George	521	290	55.7	3917	7.52	29	9	91.2

RECEIVING	No.	Yds	Avg	Lg	TD
T. Brown	104	1408	13.5	t59	5
Dudley	48	787	16.4	76	7
Jett	46	804	17.5	t56	12
Kaufman	40	403	10.1	t70	2
Williams	16	147	9.2	t32	2

INTERCEPTIONS: Four tied with two.

PUNTING	No.	Yds	Avg	Net Avg	TB	In 20	Lg	Blk
Araguz	93	4189	45.0	39.1	6	28	63	0

SACKS: Smith, 6.5

Pittsburgh Steelers

SCORING	Rush	TD Rec	Ret	PAT	FG	S	Pts
N. Johnson	0	0	0	40/40	22/25	0	106
Stewart	11	0	0	0/0	0/0	0	66
Bettis	7	2	0	0/0	0/0	0	54
Thigpen	0	7	0	0/0	0/0	0	44
Bruener	0	6	0	0/0	0/0	0	36

RUSHING	No.	Yds	Avg	Lg	TD
Bettis	375	1665	4.4	34	7
Stewart	88	476	5.4	t74	11
G. Jones	72	235	3.3	32	1
McAfee	13	41	3.2	9	0

PASSING	Att	Comp	Pct Comp	Yds	Avg Gain	TD	Int	Rating Pts
Stewart	440	236	53.6	3020	6.86	21	17	75.2
Tomczak	24	16	66.7	185	7.71	1	2	68.9

RECEIVING	No.	Yds	Avg	Lg	TD
Thigpen	79	1398	17.7	t69	7
C. Johnson	46	568	12.3	49	2
Hawkins	45	555	12.3	t44	3
Bruener	18	117	6.5	t18	6
G. Jones	16	96	6.0	25	1

INTERCEPTIONS: Wooford and Perry, 4

PUNTING	No.	Yds	Avg	Net Avg	TB	In 20	Lg	Blk
Jo. Miller	64	2729	42.6	35.0	11	17	72	0

SACKS: Lake, 6

San Diego Chargers

SCORING	TD Rush	Rec	Ret	PAT	FG	S	Pts
G. Davis	0	0	0	31/32	26/34	0	109
Martin	0	6	0	0/0	0/0	0	36
Metcalf	0	2	3	0/0	0/0	0	30
Brown	4	0	0	0/0	0/0	0	24
Harrison	0	0	3	0/0	0/0	0	18

RUSHING	No.	Yds	Avg	Lg	TD
Brown	253	945	3.7	32	4
Fletcher	51	161	3.2	13	0
Bynum	30	97	3.2	19	0

PASSING	Att	Comp	Pct Comp	Yds	Avg Gain	TD	Int	Rating Pts
Whelihan	237	118	49.8	1357	5.73	6	10	58.3
Humphries	225	121	53.8	1488	6.61	5	6	70.8

RECEIVING	No.	Yds	Avg	Lg	TD
Martin	63	904	14.3	t72	6
F. Jones	41	505	12.3	62	2
Metcalf	40	576	14.4	62	2
Fletcher	39	292	7.5	25	0
C. Jones	32	423	13.2	t44	1

INTERCEPTIONS: Five tied with 2.

PUNTING	No.	Yds	Avg	Net Avg	TB	In 20	Lg	Blk
Bennett	89	3972	44.6	37.7	8	26	66	1

SACKS: Seau, 7

Seattle Seahawks

SCORING	TD Rush	Rec	Ret	PAT	FG	S	Pts
Peterson	0	0	0	37/37	22/28	0	103
Galloway	0	12	0	0/0	0/0	0	72
McKnight	0	6	0	0/0	0/0	0	36
Broussard	5	1	0	0/0	0/0	0	36
Warren	4	0	0	0/0	0/0	0	24

RUSHING	No.	Yds	Avg	Lg	TD
Warren	200	847	4.2	t36	4
Broussard	70	418	6.0	t77	5
Smith	91	392	4.3	35	2

PASSING	Att	Comp	Pct Comp	Yds	Avg Gain	TD	Int	Rating Pts
Moon	528	313	59.3	3678	6.97	25	16	83.7
Kitna	45	31	68.9	371	8.24	1	2	82.7

RECEIVING	No.	Yds	Avg	Lg	TD
Galloway	72	1049	14.6	t53	12
Pritchard	64	843	13.2	61	2
Warren	45	257	5.7	20	0
McKnight	34	637	18.7	t60	6

INTERCEPTIONS: D. Williams, 8

PUNTING	No.	Yds	Avg	Net Avg	TB	In 20	Lg	Blk
Tuten	48	2007	41.8	36.4	5	15	65	0
Stark	20	813	40.7	26.9	2	7	52	0

SACKS: Sinclair, 12

Tennessee Oilers

SCORING	TD Rush	Rec	Ret	PAT	FG	S	Pts
Del Greco	0	0	0	32/32	27/35	0	113
McNair	8	0	0	0/0	0/0	0	48
E. George	6	1	0	0/0	0/0	0	44
Wycheck	0	4	0	0/0	0/0	0	26
Davis	0	4	0	0/0	0/0	0	24

RUSHING	No.	Yds	Avg	Lg	TD
E. George	357	1399	3.9	30	6
McNair	101	674	6.7	47	8
Thomas	67	310	4.6	t25	3

PASSING	Att	Comp	Pct Comp	Yds	Avg Gain	TD	Int	Rating Pts
McNair	415	216	52.0	2665	6.42	14	13	70.4

RECEIVING	No.	Yds	Avg	Lg	TD
Wycheck	63	748	11.9	42	4
Davis	43	564	13.1	46	4
Sanders	31	498	16.1	t55	3
Harmon	16	189	11.8	27	0
Mason	14	186	13.3	38	0
Thomas	14	111	7.9	22	0

INTERCEPTIONS: Robertson and D. Lewis, 5

PUNTING	No.	Yds	Avg	Net Avg	TB	In 20	Lg	Blk
Roby	73	3049	41.8	35.6	1	25	59	0

SACKS: Holmes and G. Walker, 7

Arizona Cardinals

SCORING	Rush	Rec	Ret	PAT	FG	S	Pts
Nedney 0		0	0	19/19	11/17	0	52
Rob Moore 0		8	0	0/0	0/0	0	50
Butler...................0		0	0	9/10	8/12	0	33
Sanders................0		4	0	0/0	0/0	0	26
Gedney 0		4	0	0/0	0/0	0	24
Plummer...............2		0	0	0/0	0/0	0	14

RUSHING	No.	Yds	Avg	Lg	TD
McElroy 135	424	3.1	18	2
Centers 101	276	2.7	14	1
Ron Moore 81	278	3.4	t27	1

PASSING	Att	Comp	Pct Comp	Yds	Avg Gain	TD	Int	Rating Pts
Plummer.....296	457	53.0	2203	7.44	15	15	73.1
K. Graham ...250	130	52.0	1408	5.63	4	5	65.9

RECEIVING	No.	Yds	Avg	Lg	TD
Rob Moore 97	1584	16.3	t47	8
Sanders...................75	1017	13.6	t70	4
Centers....................54	409	7.6	29	1
Gedney 23	261	11.3	t37	4
K. Williams...............20	273	13.7	t31	1
Edwards...................20	203	10.2	33	0

INTERCEPTIONS: A. Williams, 6

PUNTING	No.	Yds	Avg	Net Avg	TB	In 20	Lg	Blk
Feagles 91	4028	44.3	36.8	10	24	62	1

SACKS: Swann, 7.5

Carolina Panthers

SCORING	Rush	Rec	Ret	PAT	FG	S	Pts
Kasay 0		0	0	25/25	22/26	0	91
Lane 7		0	0	0/0	0/0	0	42
Walls.....................0		6	0	0/0	0/0	0	36
Carruth 0		4	0	0/0	0/0	0	24

Four tied with 12.

RUSHING	No.	Yds	Avg	Lg	TD
Lane 182	809	4.4	50	7
Johnson.......................97	358	3.7	20	0
Biakabutuka 75	299	4.0	t26	2

PASSING	Att	Comp	Pct Comp	Yds	Avg Gain	TD	Int	Rating Pts
Collins.........381	200	52.5	2124	5.57	11	21	55.7
Beuerlein.....153	89	58.2	1032	6.75	6	3	83.6

RECEIVING	No.	Yds	Avg	Lg	TD
Walls.........................58	746	12.9	52	6
Carruth 44	545	12.4	52	4
S. Greene 40	277	6.9	25	1
Ismail.......................36	419	11.6	t59	2
Carrier 33	436	13.2	36	2
Muhammad 27	317	11.7	38	0

INTERCEPTIONS: Davis, 5

PUNTING	No.	Yds	Avg	Net Avg	TB	In 20	Lg	Blk
Walter.......85	3604	42.4	36.4	4	29	62	0

SACKS: Barrow, 8.5

Atlanta Falcons

SCORING	Rush	Rec	Ret	PAT	FG	S	Pts
Andersen 0		0	0	35/35	23/27	0	104
Anderson 7		3	0	0/0	0/0	0	60
Emanuel 0		9	0	0/0	0/0	0	54
Mathis 0		6	0	0/0	0/0	0	36
Hanspard 0		1	2	0/0	0/0	0	18
Santiago 0		2	0	0/0	0/0	0	12

RUSHING	No.	Yds	Avg	Lg	TD
Anderson...................290	1002	3.5	39	7
Hanspard 53	335	6.3	77	0
Chandler....................43	158	3.7	19	0

PASSING	Att	Comp	Pct Comp	Yds	Avg Gain	TD	Int	Rating Pts
Chandler.....342	202	59.1	2692	7.87	20	7	95.1
Tolliver 115	63	54.8	685	5.16	5	1	83.4

RECEIVING	No.	Yds	Avg	Lg	TD
Emanuel 65	991	15.2	56	9
Mathis.......................62	802	12.9	49	6
Green 29	360	12.4	47	0
Anderson...................29	284	9.8	t47	3
Christian 22	154	7.0	19	1

INTERCEPTIONS: Buchanan, 5

PUNTING	No.	Yds	Avg	Net Avg	TB	In 20	Lg	Blk
Stryzinski...89	3498	39.3	36.7	9	20	57	0

SACKS: C. Smith, 12

Chicago Bears

SCORING	Rush	Rec	Ret	PAT	FG	S	Pts
Jaeger...................0		0	0	20/20	21/26	0	83
R. Harris 10		0	0	0/0	0/0	0	60
Proehl...................0		7	0	0/0	0/0	0	44
Penn.....................0		3	0	0/0	0/0	0	18
Engram 0		2	0	0/0	0/0	0	14
Kramer 2		0	0	0/0	0/0	0	12

RUSHING	No.	Yds	Avg	Lg	TD
R. Harris 275	1033	3.8	t68	10
Autry 112	319	2.8	17	1

PASSING	Att	Comp	Pct Comp	Yds	Avg Gain	TD	Int	Rating Pts
Kramer 477	275	57.7	3011	6.31	14	14	74.0
Mirer..........103	53	51.5	420	4.08	0	6	37.7

RECEIVING	No.	Yds	Avg	Lg	TD
Proehl.......................58	753	13.0	t78	7
Penn.........................47	576	12.3	33	3
Wetnight...................46	464	10.1	34	1
Engram.....................45	399	8.9	23	2
Conway 30	476	15.9	t55	1

INTERCEPTIONS: W. Harris, 5

PUNTING	No.	Yds	Avg	Net Avg	TB	In 20	Lg	Blk
Sauerbrun..95	4059	42.7	32.8	11	26	67	0

SACKS: Flanigan and Minter, 6

Dallas Cowboys

SCORING	Rush	Rec	Ret	PAT	FG	S	Pts
		TD					
Cunningham	0	0	0	24/24	34/37	0	126
Irvin	0	9	0	0/0	0/0	0	54
E. Smith	4	0	0	0/0	0/0	0	26
Miller	0	4	0	0/0	0/0	0	24
Four tied with 12.							

RUSHING	No.	Yds	Avg	Lg	TD
E. Smith	261	1074	4.1	44	4
Sh. Williams	121	468	3.9	18	2
Aikman	25	79	3.2	13	0

PASSING	Att	Comp	Pct Comp	Yds	Avg Gain	TD	Int	Rating Pts
Aikman	518	292	56.4	3283	6.34	19	12	78.0

RECEIVING	No.	Yds	Avg	Lg	TD
Irvin	75	1180	15.7	55	9
Bjornson	47	442	9.4	32	0
Miller	46	645	14.0	54	4
E. Smith	40	234	5.9	24	0
St. Williams	30	308	10.3	20	1
Sh. Williams	21	159	7.6	18	0

INTERCEPTIONS: Sanders and Stoutmire, 2

PUNTING	No.	Yds	Avg	Net Avg	TB	In 20	Lg	Blk
Gowin	86	3592	41.8	35.4	9	26	72	0

SACKS: Carver, 6

Detroit Lions

SCORING	Rush	Rec	Ret	PAT	FG	S	Pts
		TD					
Hanson	0	0	0	39/40	26/29	0	117
Sanders	11	3	0	0/0	0/0	0	84
Moore	0	8	0	0/0	0/0	0	50
Morton	0	6	0	0/0	0/0	0	36
Vardell	6	0	0	0/0	0/0	0	36

RUSHING	No.	Yds	Avg	Lg	TD
Sanders	335	2053	6.1	t82	11
Rivers	29	166	5.7	31	1
Vardell	32	122	3.8	41	0

PASSING	Att	Comp	Pct Comp	Yds	Avg Gain	TD	Int	Rating Pts
Mitchell	509	293	57.6	3484	6.84	19	14	79.6
Reich	30	11	36.7	121	4.03	0	2	21.7

RECEIVING	No.	Yds	Avg	Lg	TD
Moore	104	1293	12.4	79	8
Morton	80	1057	13.2	t73	6
Sanders	33	305	9.2	t66	3
Sloan	29	264	9.1	25	0
Metzelaars	17	144	8.5	22	0

INTERCEPTIONS: Carrier, 5

PUNTING	No.	Yds	Avg	Net Avg	TB	In 20	Lg	Blk
Jett	84	3576	42.6	35.6	4	24	60	2

SACKS: Porcher, 12.5

Green Bay Packers

SCORING	Rush	Rec	Ret	PAT	FG	S	Pts
		TD					
Longwell	0	0	0	48/48	24/30	0	120
Levens	7	5	0	0/0	0/0	0	74
Freeman	0	12	0	0/0	0/0	0	72
R. Brooks	0	7	0	0/0	0/0	0	42
Chmura	0	6	0	0/0	0/0	0	36

RUSHING	No.	Yds	Avg	Lg	TD
Levens	329	1435	4.4	t52	7
Favre	58	187	3.2	16	1
Hayden	32	148	4.6	21	1
Henderson	31	113	3.6	15	0

PASSING	Att	Comp	Pct Comp	Yds	Avg Gain	TD	Int	Rating Pts
Favre	513	304	59.3	3867	7.54	35	16	92.6

RECEIVING	No.	Yds	Avg	Lg	TD
Freeman	81	1243	15.3	t58	12
R. Brooks	60	1010	16.8	48	7
Levens	53	370	7.0	56	5
Henderson	41	367	9.0	25	1
Chmura	38	417	11.0	t32	6

INTERCEPTIONS: Butler, 5

PUNTING	No.	Yds	Avg	Net Avg	TB	In 20	Lg	Blk
Hentrich	75	3378	45.0	36.0	21	26	65	0

SACKS: White, 11

Minnesota Vikings

SCORING	Rush	Rec	Ret	PAT	FG	S	Pts
		TD					
Carter	0	13	0	0/0	0/0	0	84
Murray	0	0	0	23/24	12/17	0	59
R. Smith	6	1	0	0/0	0/0	0	42
Reed	0	6	0	0/0	0/0	0	36
Hoard	4	0	0	0/0	0/0	0	24
Glover	0	3	0	0/0	0/0	0	18

RUSHING	No.	Yds	Avg	Lg	TD
R. Smith	232	1266	5.5	t78	6
Hoard	80	235	2.9	20	4
Evans	43	157	3.7	13	2
Johnson	35	139	4.0	28	0

PASSING	Att	Comp	Pct Comp	Yds	Avg Gain	TD	Int	Rating Pts
Johnson	452	275	60.8	3036	6.72	20	12	84.5
Cunningham	88	44	50.0	501	5.69	6	4	71.3

RECEIVING	No.	Yds	Avg	Lg	TD
Carter	89	1069	12.0	43	13
Reed	68	1138	16.7	56	6
R. Smith	37	197	5.3	20	1
Glover	32	378	11.8	43	3
Palmer	26	193	7.4	23	1

INTERCEPTIONS: Washington, 4

PUNTING	No.	Yds	Avg	Net Avg	TB	In 20	Lg	Blk
Berger	73	3133	42.9	34.1	5	22	65	0

SACKS: Randle, 15.5

New Orleans Saints

SCORING

SCORING	Rush	TD Rec	Ret	PAT	FG	S	Pts
Brien	0	0	0	22/22	23/27	0	91
Hastings	0	5	0	0/0	0/0	0	32
Bates	4	0	0	0/0	0/0	0	24
Zellars	4	0	0	0/0	0/0	0	24
Hill	0	2	0	0/0	0/0	0	12
Poole	0	2	0	0/0	0/0	0	12
Guilford	0	1	1	0/0	0/0	0	12

RUSHING

RUSHING	No.	Yds	Avg	Lg	TD
Zellars	156	552	3.5	27	4
Bates	119	440	3.7	t74	4

PASSING

PASSING	Att	Comp	Pct Comp	Yds	Avg Gain	TD	Int	Rating Pts
Shuler	203	106	52.2	1288	6.34	2	14	46.6
Hobert	131	61	46.6	891	6.80	6	8	59.0

RECEIVING

RECEIVING	No.	Yds	Avg	Lg	TD
Hill	55	761	13.8	t89	2
Hastings	48	722	15.0	39	5
Zellars	31	263	8.5	38	0
Guilford	27	362	13.4	47	1
Farquhar	17	253	14.9	42	1

INTERCEPTIONS: Knight, 5

PUNTING

PUNTING	No.	Yds	Avg	Net Avg	TB	In 20	Lg	Blk
Royals	88	4038	45.9	34.9	13	21	66	0

SACKS: Martin, 10.5

New York Giants

SCORING

SCORING	Rush	TD Rec	Ret	PAT	FG	S	Pts
Daluiso	0	0	0	27/29	22/32	0	93
Calloway	0	8	0	0/0	0/0	0	48
Way	4	1	0	0/0	0/0	0	30
Barber	3	1	0	0/0	0/0	0	26
Wheatley	4	0	0	0/0	0/0	0	24

RUSHING

RUSHING	No.	Yds	Avg	Lg	TD
Way	151	698	4.6	42	4
Wheatley	152	583	3.8	38	4
Barber	136	511	3.8	42	3

PASSING

PASSING	Att	Comp	Pct Comp	Yds	Avg Gain	TD	Int	Rating Pts
Kanell	294	156	53.1	1740	5.92	11	9	70.7
Brown	180	93	51.7	1023	5.68	5	3	71.1

RECEIVING

RECEIVING	No.	Yds	Avg	Lg	TD
Calloway	58	849	14.6	t68	8
Way	37	304	8.2	62	1
Barber	34	299	8.8	29	1
Cross	21	150	7.1	26	2

INTERCEPTIONS: Sehorn, 6

PUNTING

PUNTING	No.	Yds	Avg	Net Avg	TB	In 20	Lg	Blk
Maynard	111	4531	40.8	34.6	14	33	57	1

SACKS: Strahan, 14

Philadelphia Eagles

SCORING

SCORING	Rush	TD Rec	Ret	PAT	FG	S	Pts
Boniol	0	0	0	33/33	22/31	0	99
Watters	7	0	0	0/0	0/0	0	42
Fryar	0	4	0	0/0	0/0	0	36
Lewis	0	3	0	0/0	0/0	0	24
Solomon	0	3	0	0/0	0/0	0	20

RUSHING

RUSHING	No.	Yds	Avg	Lg	TD
Watters	285	1110	3.9	52	17
Garner	116	547	4.7	69	5

PASSING

PASSING	Att	Comp	Pct Comp	Yds	Avg Gain	TD	Int	Rating Pts
T. Detmer	244	134	54.9	1567	6.42	7	6	73.9
Hoying	225	128	56.9	1573	6.99	11	6	83.8
Peete	118	68	57.6	869	7.36	4	4	78.0

RECEIVING

RECEIVING	No.	Yds	Avg	Lg	TD
Fryar	86	1316	15.3	t72	6
Turner	48	443	9.2	36	3
Watters	48	440	9.2	37	0
Timpson	42	484	11.5	26	2
Solomon	29	455	15.7	56	3

INTERCEPTIONS: Dawkins and Vincent, 3

PUNTING

PUNTING	No.	Yds	Avg	Net Avg	TB	In 20	Lg	Blk
Hutton	87	3660	42.1	34.6	5	19	61	1

SACKS: Hall, 8

St. Louis Rams

SCORING

SCORING	Rush	TD Rec	Ret	PAT	FG	S	Pts
Wilkins	0	0	0	32/32	25/37	0	107
Phillips	8	0	0	0	0	0	48
Bruce	0	5	0	0/0	0/0	0	30
Conwell	0	4	0	0/0	0/0	0	24

RUSHING

RUSHING	No.	Yds	Avg	Lg	TD
Phillips	183	633	3.5	28	8
J. Moore	104	380	3.7	26	3
Banks	47	186	4.0	23	1
Lee	28	104	3.7	14	0
R. Moore	24	103	4.3	t27	1

PASSING

PASSING	Att	Comp	Pct Comp	Yds	Avg Gain	TD	Int	Rating Pts
Banks	487	252	51.7	3524	6.68	14	13	71.5
Rypien	39	19	48.7	270	6.92	0	2	50.2

RECEIVING

RECEIVING	No.	Yds	Avg	Lg	TD
Lee	61	825	13.5	62	3
Bruce	56	815	14.6	59	5
Conwell	38	404	10.6	t46	4
Small	32	488	15.3	46	1

INTERCEPTIONS: McNeil, 9

PUNTING

PUNTING	No.	Yds	Avg	Net Avg	TB	In 20	Lg	Blk
Brice	41	1713	41.8	30.5	4	6	61	1
Horan	53	2272	42.9	36.3	4	10	60	0

SACKS: O'Neal, 10

San Francisco 49ers

SCORING

SCORING	Rush	TD Rec	Ret	PAT	FG	S	Pts
Anderson	0	0	0	38/38	29/36	0	125
Kirby	6	1	1	0/0	0/0	0	52
Owens	0	8	0	0/0	0/0	0	48
Hearst	4	2	0	0/0	0/0	0	36
Stokes	0	4	0	0/0	0/0	0	24
Floyd	3	1	0	0/0	0/0	0	24

RUSHING	No.	Yds	Avg	Lg	TD
Hearst	234	1019	4.4	51	4
Kirby	125	418	3.3	38	6
Floyd	78	231	3.0	22	3

PASSING	Att	Comp	Pct Comp	Yds	Avg Gain	TD	Int	Rating Pts
S. Young	356	241	67.7	3029	8.51	19	6	104.7
Druckenmiller	52	21	40.4	239	4.60	1	4	29.2

RECEIVING	No.	Yds	Avg	Lg	TD
Owens	60	936	15.6	t56	8
Stokes	58	733	12.6	36	4
Floyd	37	321	8.7	t44	1
Jones	29	383	13.2	33	2
Kirby	23	279	12.1	82	1
Hearst	21	194	9.2	69	2

INTERCEPTIONS: Hanks, 6

PUNTING	No.	Yds	Avg	Net Avg	TB	In 20	Lg	Blk
Thompson	78	3182	40.8	34.6	7	22	55	1

SACKS: Stubblefield, 15

Tampa Bay Buccaneers

SCORING

SCORING	Rush	TD Rec	Ret	PAT	FG	S	Pts
Husted	0	0	0	32/35	13/17	0	71
Alstott	7	3	0	0/0	0/0	0	60
Dunn	4	3	0	0/0	0/0	0	42
Williams	0	4	1	0/0	0/0	0	30
Moore	0	4	0	0/0	0/0	0	24
Anthony	0	4	0	0/0	0/0	0	24

RUSHING	No.	Yds	Avg	Lg	TD
Dunn	224	978	4.4	76	4
Alstott	176	665	3.8	t47	7

PASSING	Att	Comp	Pct Comp	Yds	Avg Gain	TD	Int	Rating Pts
Dilfer	386	217	56.2	2555	6.62	21	11	82.8

RECEIVING	No.	Yds	Avg	Lg	TD
Dunn	39	462	11.8	t59	3
Anthony	35	448	12.8	t38	4
Williams	33	486	14.7	55	4
Copeland	33	431	13.1	49	1
Alstott	23	178	7.1	26	3

INTERCEPTIONS: Abraham, 5

PUNTING	No.	Yds	Avg	Net Avg	TB	In 20	Lg	Blk
Barnhardt	29	1304	45.0	39.1	3	12	61	0
Landeta	54	2274	42.1	34.1	6	15	74	1

SACKS: Sapp, 10.5

Washington Redskins

SCORING

SCORING	Rush	TD Rec	Ret	PAT	FG	S	Pts
Blanton	0	0	0	34/34	16/24	0	82
Allen	4	1	0	0/0	0/0	0	30
Shepherd	0	5	0	0/0	0/0	0	30
Three tied with 24.							

RUSHING	No.	Yds	Avg	Lg	TD
Allen	210	724	3.4	34	4
Davis	141	567	4.0	18	3
Mitchell	23	107	4.7	26	1

PASSING	Att	Comp	Pct Comp	Yds	Avg Gain	TD	Int	Rating Pts
Frerotte	402	204	50.7	2682	6.67	17	12	73.8
Hostetler	144	79	54.9	899	6.24	5	10	56.5

RECEIVING	No.	Yds	Avg	Lg	TD
Asher	49	474	9.7	24	1
Mitchell	36	438	12.2	69	1
Westbrook	34	559	16.4	t40	3
Bowie	34	388	11.4	t39	2
Ellard	32	485	15.2	27	4

INTERCEPTIONS: Dishman, 4

PUNTING	No.	Yds	Avg	Net Avg	TB	In 20	Lg	Blk
M. Turk	84	3788	45.1	39.2	11	32	62	1

SACKS: Harvey, 9.5

1998 NFL Draft

First two rounds of the 63rd annual NFL Draft held April 18–19 in New York City.

First Round

Team	Selection	Position
1. ....Indianapolis	Peyton Manning, Tennessee	QB
2. ....San Diego	Ryan Leaf, Wash St	QB
3. ....Arizona	Andre Wadsworth, Fla St	DL
4. ....Oakland	Charles Woodson, Michigan	DB
5. ....Chicago	Curtis Enis, Penn St	RB
6. ....St. Louis	Grant Wistrom, Nebraska	DL
7. ....New Orleans	Kyle Turkey, San Diego St	OL
8. ......Dallas	Greg Ellis, N Carolina	DL
9. ......Jacksonville	Fred Taylor, Florida	RB
10. ......Baltimore	Duane Starks, Miami (FL)	DB
11. ......Philadelphia	Tra Thomas, Florida St	OL
12. ......Tampa Bay	Keith Brooking, Georgia Tech	LB
13. ......Cincinnati	Takeo Spikes, Auburn	LB
14. ......Carolina	Jason Peter, Nebraska	DL
15. ......Seattle	Anthony Simmons, Clemson	LB
16. ......Tennessee	Kevin Dyson, Utah	WR
17. ......Cincinnati	Brian Simmons, N Carolina	LB
18. ......New England	Robert Edwards, Georgia	RB
19. ......Green Bay	Vonnie Holliday, N Carolina	DL
20. ......Detroit	Terry Fair, Tennessee	DB
21. ......Minnesota	Randy Moss, Marshall	WR
22. ......New England	Tebucky Jones, Syracuse	DB
23. ......Oakland	Damon Collins, Florida	OL
24. ......NY Giants	Shaun Williams, UCLA	DB
25. ......Jacksonville	Donovin Darius, Syracuse	DB
26. ......Pittsburgh	Alan Faneca, Louisiana St	OL
27 ......Kansas City	Victor Riley, Auburn	OL
28. ......San Francisco	R.W. McQuarters, Oklahoma St	DB
29. ......Miami	John Avery, Mississippi	RB
30. ......Denver	Marcus Nash, Tennessee	WR

Second Round

Team	Selection	Position
31. ......Oakland	Leon Bender, Wash St	DL
32. ......Indianapolis	Jerome Pathon, Washington	WR
33. ......Arizona	Corey Chavous, Vanderbilt	DB
34. ......Tampa Bay	Jacquez Green, Florida	WR
35. ......Chicago	Tony Parrish, Washington	DB
36. ......Arizona	Anthony Clement, SW Louisiana	OL
37. ......St. Louis	Robert Holcombe, Illinois	RB
38. ......Dallas	Flozell Adams, Mich St	OL
39. ......Buffalo	Sam Cowart, Florida St	LB
40. ......New Orleans	Cameron Cleeland, Washington	TE
41. ......Pittsburgh	Jeremy Staat, Arizona St	DL
42. ......Baltimore	Pat Johnson, Oregon	WR
43. ......Cincinnati	Artrell Hawkins, Cincinnati	DB
44. ......Miami	Patrick Surtain, Southern Mississippi	DB
45. ......Tampa Bay	Brian Kelly, USC	DB
46. ......Tennessee	Samari Rolle, Florida St	DB
47. ......Seattle	Todd Weiner, Kansas St	OL
48. ......Washington	Steven Alexander, Oklahoma	TE
49. ......Miami	Kenny Mixon, Louisiana St	DL
50. ......Detroit	Germane Crowell, Virginia	WR
51. ......Minnesota	Kailee Wong, Stanford	LB
52. ......New England	Tony Simmons, Wisconsin	WR
53. ......Atlanta	Bob Hallen, Kent St	OL
54. ......New England	Rod Rutledge, Alabama	TE
55. ......NY Giants	Joe Jurevicius, Penn St	WR
56. ......NY Jets	Dorian Boose, Wash St	DL
57. ......Jacksonville	Cordell Taylor, Hampton (Va.)	DB
58. ......San Francisco	Jeremy Newberry, California	OL
59. ......San Diego	Mikhael Ricks, Stephen F. Austin	WR
60. ......Detroit	Charlie Batch, Eastern Michigan	QB
61. ......Denver	Eric Brown, Miss St	DB

A Piece of the Pack

The Green Bay Packers' ballyhooed offering, on Nov. 14, 1997, of 400,000 shares of common stock as a way of raising $80 million for the Pack's building fund has stirred the interest of cheeseheads everywhere. While certificates for the $200-per-share issue were hot gift items for Packers fans during the '97 holiday season, buyers might have wanted to check the fine print.

According to the offering, purchasers receive no dividends, get nothing for the stock if the Packers are liquidated or sold, cannot sell the stock in any market, receive just 2.5 cents per share if the team chooses to buy back the stock and could even be assessed $200 per share if Green Bay for some reason can't meet its payroll.

What's more, as part owners, shareholders come under the jurisdiction of the NFL's "detrimental conduct" clause, meaning that should the proud owner of a $200 share in the Packers publicly criticize any team or referee, said proud owner could find himself or herself fined as much as $500,000 by the league. Any wager on a game could draw a $5,000 fine. And, of course, the NFL is authorized to run credit and background checks on an owner.

Don't worry, cheeseheads. Painting yourself green and gold and drinking too much of what made Milwaukee famous isn't considered detrimental conduct.

1998 NFL Europe†

Final Standings

	W	L	T	Pct	Pts/ Tm	Pts/ Opp
Frankfurt*	7	3	0	.700	167	164
Rhein*	7	3	0	.700	198	142
Amsterdam	7	3	0	.700	205	174
Barcelona	4	6	0	.400	185	200
London	3	7	0	.300	161	200
Scotland	2	8	0	.200	153	182

†Formerly World League of American Football.
*Clinched World Bowl '98 berth.

1998 World Bowl

June 14, 1998, in Frankfurt

Rhein Fire	10	7	7	10—34
Frankfurt Galaxy	0	7	3	0—10

FIRST QUARTER

Rhein: FG Burgsmuller 29, 4:13.
Rhein: Burks 15 pass from Arellanes (Burgsmuller kick), 12:29.

SECOND QUARTER

Frankfurt: Chaney 3 run (Kleinmann kick), 4:13.
Rhein: Burks 20 pass from Arellanes (Burgsmuller kick), 11:24.

THIRD QUARTER

Frankfurt: FG Kleinmann 41, 2:22.
Rhein: Robinson 74 pass from Arellanes (Burgsmuller kick), 3:52.

FOURTH QUARTER

Rhein: FG Burgsmuller 20, 11:01.
Rhein: Vaughn 15 run (Burgsmuller kick), 13:07.

A: 42,846.

NFL Europe Individual Leaders

PASSING

	Att	Comp	Pct Comp	Yds	Avg Gain	TD	Pct TD	Int	Pct Int	Lg	Rating Pts
M. Quinn, Rhein	264	133	50.4	1997	7.56	13	4.9	3	1.1	68	87.3
K. Warner, Amsterdam	326	165	50.6	2101	6.44	15	4.6	6	1.8	t47	78.8
D. Huard, Frankfurt	290	159	54.8	1857	6.40	12	4.1	7	2.4	72	78.2
J. LaRocca, England	257	122	47.5	1641	6.39	14	5.4	11	4.2	t74	68.6
J. Ballard, Scotland	212	113	53.3	1425	6.72	4	1.8	8	3.7	44	65.1

RECEIVING

RECEPTIONS	No.	Yds	Avg	Lg	TD
J. Shelley, Amsterdam	42	559	13.3	46	2
M. Robinson, Rhein	39	811	20.8	68	5
M. Bailey, Frankfurt	38	544	14.3	72	6
J. Douglass, Amsterdam	38	499	13.1	t47	5
R. Jones, England	36	649	18.0	t74	7
D. Branch, Frankfurt	36	468	13.0	t63	4

YARDS	Yds	No.	Avg	Lg	TD
M. Robinson, Rhein	811	39	20.8	68	5
R. Jones, England	649	36	18.0	t74	7
J. Shelley, Amsterdam	559	42	13.3	46	2
M. Bailey, Frankfurt	544	38	14.3	72	6
C. Miller, Scotland	527	34	15.5	53	1

RUSHING

	Att	Yds	Avg	Lg	TD
D. Clark, Rhein	177	739	4.2	44	6
M. Thomas, Amsterdam	150	664	4.4	33	5
J. Chaney, Frankfurt	137	491	3.6	24	2
C. Bender, Scotland	108	441	4.1	44	0
R. Dawkins, Amsterdam	104	435	4.2	23	2

Other Statistical Leaders

Points (TDs)	R. Jones, England	42
Points (Kicking)	M. Burgsmuller, Rhein	57
Yards from Scrimmage	D. Clark, Rhein	889
Interceptions	R. Jones, Rhein	4
	K. Branscomb, Frankfurt	4
Sacks	E. Philion, Rhein	9
	J. Taves, Barcelona	9
Punting Avg.	B. Greenfield, England	45.2
Punt Return Avg.	K. McEntyre, Frankfurt	12.7
Kickoff Return Avg.	J. Vaughn, Rhein	21.8

1997 Canadian Football League

EASTERN DIVISION

	W	L	T	Pts	Pct	PF	PA
Toronto	15	3	0	30	.833	660	327
Montreal	13	5	0	26	.722	509	532
Winnipeg	4	14	0	8	.222	443	548
Hamilton	2	16	0	4	.111	362	549

WESTERN DIVISION

	W	L	T	Pts	Pct	PF	PA
Edmonton	12	6	0	24	.666	479	400
Calgary	10	10	0	20	.500	522	442
British Columbia	8	10	0	16	.444	429	536
Saskatchewan	8	10	0	16	.444	413	479

Regular Season Statistical Leaders

Points (TDs)	Robert Drummond, Toronto	108
Points (Kicking)	Mike Vanderjagt, Toronto	190
Yards (Rushing)	Michael Pringle, Saskatch	1775
Yards (Passing)	Doug Flutie, Toronto	5505
Yards (Receiving)	Milt Stegall, Winnipeg	1616
Receptions	Mike Clemons, Toronto	122

1997 Playoff Results

DIVISION SEMIFINALS

East: MONTREAL 45, BC 35
West: SASKATCHEWAN 33, Calgary 30

DIVISION FINALS

East: TORONTO 37, Montreal 30
West: SASKATCHEWAN 31, Edmonton 30

1997 Grey Cup Championship

Nov. 16, 1997, at Commonwealth Stadium, Edmonton

Saskatch Roughriders	3	6	0	14—23
Toronto Argonauts	7	13	21	6—47

A: 60,431.

Just Desserts for Switzer

The Barry Switzer who should be remembered by Dallas Cowboys fans isn't the coach who went 29–9 in his first two seasons and won Super Bowl XXX in January 1996, but the coach who in his last two seasons went 17–17 and won only one postseason game. He's the coach who brought zero innovations to the Cowboys even after they began slumping last season. He's the coach who, aside from an unsuccessful fourth-down gamble against the Philadelphia Eagles in 1995, made no memorable calls. He's the coach who deserved to be "allowed to resign," as Cowboys owner Jerry Jones put it at a press conference announcing Switzer's departure.

Switzer outdid other NFL coaches in two respects: a cavalier attitude toward his job and a lax approach to team discipline. He missed important team meetings on more than one Saturday, not only to watch his son Doug play quarterback for Missouri Southern but also to have dinner with old friends like David Boren, a former U.S. senator from Oklahoma. He allowed Dallas offensive linemen to get grossly overweight in the weeks before Super Bowl XXX because, according to at least one Cowboy, he stopped mandatory weigh-ins late in the season. And in the early morning hours of the Saturday before that game, Switzer was partying hard in his hotel suite.

The championship Dallas won under Switzer came about more because of astute scouting and drafting before he got there than Switzer's coaching. By and large Switzer relaxed in the off-season; unlike predecessor Jimmy Johnson, he rarely went on scouting missions.

Switzer talked of wanting to smell the roses in his retirement. Well, that's pretty much what he's been doing for the last four years.

The Super Bowl

Results

Date	Winner (Share)	Loser (Share)	Score	Site (Attendance)
I 1-15-67	Green Bay ($15,000)	Kansas City ($7,500)	35–10	Los Angeles (61,946)
II 1-14-68	Green Bay ($15,000)	Oakland ($7,500)	33–14	Miami (75,546)
III 1-12-69	NY Jets ($15,000)	Baltimore ($7,500)	16–7	Miami (75,389)
IV 1-11-70	Kansas City ($15,000)	Minnesota ($7,500)	23–7	New Orleans (80,562)
V 1-17-71	Baltimore ($15,000)	Dallas ($7,500)	16–13	Miami (79,204)
VI 1-16-72	Dallas ($15,000)	Miami ($7,500)	24–3	New Orleans (81,023)
VII 1-14-73	Miami ($15,000)	Washington ($7,500)	14–7	Los Angeles (90,182)
VIII 1-13-74	Miami ($15,000)	Minnesota ($7,500)	24–7	Houston (71,882)
IX 1-12-75	Pittsburgh ($15,000)	Minnesota ($7,500)	16–6	New Orleans (80,997)
X 1-18-76	Pittsburgh ($15,000)	Dallas ($7,500)	21–17	Miami (80,187)
XI 1-9-77	Oakland ($15,000)	Minnesota ($7,500)	32–14	Pasadena (103,438)
XII 1-15-78	Dallas ($18,000)	Denver ($9,000)	27–10	New Orleans (75,583)
XIII 1-21-79	Pittsburgh ($18,000)	Dallas ($9,000)	35–31	Miami (79,484)
XIV 1-20-80	Pittsburgh ($18,000)	Los Angeles ($9,000)	31–19	Pasadena (103,985)
XV 1-25-81	Oakland ($18,000)	Philadelphia ($9,000)	27–10	New Orleans (76,135)
XVI 1-24-82	San Francisco ($18,000)	Cincinnati ($9,000)	26–21	Pontiac, MI (81,270)
XVII 1-30-83	Washington ($36,000)	Miami ($18,000)	27–17	Pasadena (103,667)
XVIII 1-22-84	LA Raiders ($36,000)	Washington ($18,000)	38–9	Tampa (72,920)
XIX 1-20-85	San Francisco ($36,000)	Miami ($18,000)	38–16	Stanford (84,059)
XX 1-26-86	Chicago ($36,000)	New England ($18,000)	46–10	New Orleans (73,818)
XXI 1-25-87	NY Giants ($36,000)	Denver ($18,000)	39–20	Pasadena (101,063)
XXII 1-31-88	Washington ($36,000)	Denver ($18,000)	42–10	San Diego (73,302)
XXIII 1-22-89	San Francisco ($36,000)	Cincinnati ($18,000)	20–16	Miami (75,129)
XXIV 1-28-90	San Francisco ($36,000)	Denver ($18,000)	55–10	New Orleans (72,919)
XXV 1-27-91	NY Giants ($36,000)	Buffalo ($18,000)	20–19	Tampa (73,813)
XXVI 1-26-92	Washington ($36,000)	Buffalo ($18,000)	37–24	Minneapolis (63,130)
XXVII 1-31-93	Dallas ($36,000)	Buffalo ($18,000)	52–17	Pasadena (98,374)
XXVIII 1-30-94	Dallas ($38,000)	Buffalo ($23,500)	30–13	Atlanta (72,817)
XXIX 1-29-95	San Francisco ($42,000)	San Diego ($26,000)	49–26	Miami (74,107)
XXX 1-28-96	Dallas ($42,000)	Pittsburgh ($27,000)	27–17	Tempe, AZ (76,347)
XXXI 1-26-97	Green Bay ($48,000)	New England ($29,000)	35–21	New Orleans (72,301)
XXXII 1-25-98	Denver ($48,000)	Green Bay ($27,500)	31–24	San Diego (68,912)

Most Valuable Players

		Position
I ....Bart Starr, GB		QB
II ....Bart Starr, GB		QB
III ....Joe Namath, NYJ		QB
IV ....Len Dawson, KC		QB
V ....Chuck Howley, Dall		LB
VI ....Roger Staubach, Dall		QB
VII ....Jake Scott, Mia		S
VIII ....Larry Csonka, Mia		RB
IX ....Franco Harris, Pitt		RB
X ....Lynn Swann, Pitt		WR
XI ....Fred Biletnikoff, Oak		WR
XII ....Randy White, Dall		DT
Harvey Martin, Dall		DE
XIII ....Terry Bradshaw, Pitt		QB
XIV ....Terry Bradshaw, Pitt		QB
XV ....Jim Plunkett, Oak		QB
XVI ....Joe Montana, SF		QB
XVII ....John Riggins, Wash		RB
XVIII ....Marcus Allen, Rai		RB
XIX ....Joe Montana, SF		QB
XX ....Richard Dent, Chi		DE
XXI ....Phil Simms, NYG		QB
XXII ....Doug Williams, Wash		QB
XXIII ....Jerry Rice, SF		WR
XXIV ....Joe Montana, SF		QB
XXV ....Ottis Anderson, NYG		RB
XXVI ....Mark Rypien, Wash		QB
XXVII ....Troy Aikman, Dall		QB

Most Valuable Players (Cont.)

		Position
XXVIII ....Emmitt Smith, Dall		RB
XXIX ....Steve Young, SF		QB
XXX ....Larry Brown, Dall		DB
XXXI ....Desmond Howard, GB		KR
XXXII ....Terrell Davis, Den		RB

Composite Standings

	W	L	Pct	Pts	Opp Pts
San Francisco 49ers......5	5	0	1.000	188	89
NY Giants.....................2	2	0	1.000	59	39
Chicago Bears...............1	1	0	1.000	46	10
NY Jets 1	1	0	1.000	16	7
Pittsburgh Steelers 4	4	1	.800	120	100
Green Bay Packers 3	3	1	.750	127	76
Oakland/LA Raiders 3	3	1	.750	111	66
Dallas Cowboys 5	5	3	.625	221	132
Washington Redskins 3	3	2	.600	122	103
Baltimore Colts 1	1	1	.500	23	29
Kansas City Chiefs 1	1	1	.500	33	42
Miami Dolphins 2	2	3	.400	74	103
Denver Broncos.............1	1	4	.200	81	187
LA Rams 0	0	1	.000	19	31
Philadelphia Eagles 0	0	1	.000	10	27
San Diego Chargers 0	0	1	.000	26	49
Cincinnati Bengals.........0	0	2	.000	37	46
New England Patriots 0	0	2	.000	31	81
Buffalo Bills 0	0	4	.000	73	139
Minnesota Vikings..........0	0	4	.000	34	95

Career Leaders

Passing

	GP	Att	Comp	Pct Comp	Yds	Avg Gain	TD	Pct TD	Int	Pct Int	Lg	Rating Pts
Joe Montana, SF	4	122	83	68.0	1142	9.36	11	9.0	0	0.0	44	127.8
Jim Plunkett, Rai	2	46	29	63.0	433	9.41	4	8.7	0	0.0	t80	122.8
Terry Bradshaw, Pitt	4	84	49	58.3	932	11.10	9	10.7	4	4.8	t75	112.8
Troy Aikman, Dall	3	80	56	70.0	689	8.61	5	6.3	1	1.3	t56	111.9
Bart Starr, GB	2	47	29	61.7	452	9.62	3	6.4	1	2.1	t62	106.0
Brett Favre, GB	2	69	39	56.5	502	7.28	5	7.2	1	1.4	t81	97.7
Roger Staubach, Dall	4	98	61	62.2	734	7.49	8	8.2	4	4.1	t45	95.4
Len Dawson, KC	2	44	28	63.6	353	8.02	2	4.5	2	4.5	t46	84.8
Bob Griese, Mia	3	41	26	63.4	295	7.20	1	2.4	2	4.9	t28	72.7
Dan Marino, Mia	1	50	29	58.0	318	6.36	1	2.0	2	4.0	30	66.9

Note: Minimum 40 attempts.

Rushing

	GP	Yds	Att	Avg	Lg	TD
Franco Harris, Pitt	4	354	101	3.5	25	4
Larry Csonka, Mia	3	297	57	5.2	9	2
Emmitt Smith, Dall	3	289	70	4.1	38	5
John Riggins, Wash	2	230	64	3.6	43	2
Timmy Smith, Wash	1	204	22	9.3	58	2
Thurman Thomas, Buff	4	204	52	3.9	31	4
Roger Craig, SF	3	198	52	3.8	18	2
Marcus Allen, Rai	1	191	20	9.6	t74	2
Tony Dorsett, Dall	2	162	31	5.2	29	1
Terrell Davis, Den	1	157	30	5.2	27	3

Receiving

	GP	No.	Yds	Avg	Lg	TD
Jerry Rice, SF	3	28	512	18.3	t44	7
Andre Reed, Buff	4	27	323	11.9	40	0
Roger Craig, SF	3	20	212	10.6	40	2
Thurman Thomas, Buff	4	20	144	7.2	24	0
Tom Novacek, Dall	3	17	178	10.5	23	2
Lynn Swann, Pitt	4	16	364	22.8	t64	3
Michael Irvin, Dall	3	16	256	16.0	25	2
Chuck Foreman, Minn	3	15	139	9.3	26	0
Cliff Branch, Rai	3	14	181	12.9	50	3
Preston Pearson, Balt-Pitt-Dall	5	12	105	8.8	14	0
Don Beebe, Buff-GB	5	12	171	14.3	43	2
Kenneth Davis, Buff	4	12	72	6.0	19	0
Antonio Freeman, GB	2	12	231	19.3	t81	3

Single-Game Leaders

Scoring

	Pts
Roger Craig: XIX, San Francisco vs Miami (1 R, 2 P)	18
Jerry Rice: XXIV, San Francisco vs Denver (3 P); XXIX, SF vs San Diego (3 P)	18
Ricky Watters: XXIX, San Francisco vs San Diego (1 R, 2 P)	18
Terrell Davis: XXXII, Denver vs Green Bay (3 R)	18

Rushing Yards

	Yds
Timmy Smith: XXII, Washington vs Denver	204
Marcus Allen: XVIII, LA Raiders vs Washington	191
John Riggins: XVII, Washington vs Miami	166
Franco Harris: IX, Pittsburgh vs Minnesota	158
Terrell Davis: XXXII, Denver vs Green Bay	157
Larry Csonka: VIII, Miami vs Minnesota	145
Clarence Davis: XI, Oakland vs Minnesota	137
Thurman Thomas: XXV, Buffalo vs NY Giants	135
Emmitt Smith: XXVIII, Dallas vs Buffalo	132
Matt Snell: III, New York Jets vs Baltimore Colts	121

Receptions

	No.
Dan Ross: XVI, Cincinnati vs San Francisco	11
Jerry Rice: XXIII, San Francisco vs Cincinnati	11
Tony Nathan: XIX, Miami vs San Francisco	10
Jerry Rice: XXIX, San Francisco vs San Diego	10
Andre Hastings: XXX, Pittsburgh vs Dallas	10
Ricky Sanders: XXII, Washington vs Denver	9
Antonio Freeman: XXXII, Green Bay vs Denver	9

Six tied with 8.

Touchdown Passes

	No.
Steve Young: XXIX, San Francisco vs San Diego	6
Joe Montana: XXIV, San Francisco vs Denver	5
Terry Bradshaw: XIII, Pittsburgh vs Dallas	4
Doug Williams: XXII, Washington vs Denver	4
Troy Aikman: XXVII, Dallas vs Buffalo	4

Five tied with 3.

Receiving Yards

	Yds
Jerry Rice: XXIII, San Francisco vs Cincinnati	215
Ricky Sanders: XXII, Washington vs Denver	193
Lynn Swann: X, Pittsburgh vs Dallas	161
Andre Reed: XXVII, Buffalo vs Dallas	152
Jerry Rice: XXIX, San Francisco vs San Diego	149
Jerry Rice: XXIV, San Francisco vs Denver	148
Max McGee: I, Green Bay vs Kansas City	138
George Sauer: III, NY Jets vs Baltimore	133

Passing Yards

	Yds
Joe Montana: XXIII, San Francisco vs Cincinnati	357
Doug Williams: XXII, Washington vs Denver	340
Joe Montana: XIX, San Francisco vs Miami	331
Steve Young: XXIX, San Francisco vs San Diego	325
Terry Bradshaw: XIII, Pittsburgh vs Dallas	318
Dan Marino: XIX, Miami vs San Francisco	318
Terry Bradshaw: XIV, Pittsburgh vs LA Rams	309
John Elway: XXI, Denver vs NY Giants	304

1933
NFL championship   Chicago Bears 23, NY Giants 21

1934
NFL championship   NY Giants 30, Chicago Bears 13

1935
NFL championship   Detroit 26, NY Giants 7

1936
NFL championship   Green Bay 21, Boston 6

1937
NFL championship   Washington 28, Chicago Bears 21

1938
NFL championship   NY Giants 23, Green Bay 17

1939
NFL championship   Green Bay 27, NY Giants 0

1940
NFL championship   Chicago Bears 73, Washington 0

1941
W. div. playoff   Chicago Bears 33, Green Bay 14
NFL championship   Chicago Bears 37, NY Giants 9

1942
NFL championship   Washington 14, Chicago Bears 6

1943
E. div. playoff   Washington 28, NY Giants 0
NFL championship   Chicago Bears 41, Washington 21

1944
NFL championship   Green Bay 14, NY Giants 7

1945
NFL championship   Cleveland 15, Washington 14

1946
NFL championship   Chicago Bears 24, NY Giants 14

1947
E. div. playoff   Philadelphia 21, Pittsburgh 0
NFL championship   Chi Cardinals 28, Philadelphia 21

1948
NFL championship   Philadelphia 7, Chi Cardinals 0

1949
NFL championship   Philadelphia 14, Los Angeles 0

1950
Am. Conf. playoff   Cleveland 8, NY Giants 3
Nat. Conf. playoff   Los Angeles 24, Chicago Bears 14
NFL championship   Cleveland 30, Los Angeles 28

1951
NFL championship   Los Angeles 24, Cleveland 17

1952
Nat. Conf. playoff   Detroit 31, Los Angeles 21
NFL championship   Detroit 17, Cleveland 7

1953
NFL championship   Detroit 17, Cleveland 16

1954
NFL championship   Cleveland 56, Detroit 10

1955
NFL championship   Cleveland 38, Los Angeles 14

1956
NFL championship   NY Giants 47, Chicago Bears 7

1957
W. Conf. playoff   Detroit 31, San Francisco 27
NFL championship   Detroit 59, Cleveland 14

1958
E. Conf. playoff   NY Giants 10, Cleveland 0
NFL championship   Baltimore 23, NY Giants 17

1959
NFL championship   Baltimore 31, NY Giants 16

1960
NFL championship   Philadelphia 17, Green Bay 13
AFL championship   Houston 24, LA Chargers 16

1961
NFL championship   Green Bay 37, NY Giants 0
AFL championship   Houston 10, San Diego 3

1962
NFL championship   Green Bay 16, NY Giants 7
AFL championship   Dallas Texans 20, Houston 17

1963
NFL championship   Chicago 14, NY Giants 10
AFL E. div. playoff Boston 26, Buffalo 8
AFL championship   San Diego 51, Boston 10

1964
NFL championship   Cleveland 27, Baltimore 0
AFL championship   Buffalo 20, San Diego 7

1965
NFL W. Conf.   Green Bay 13, Baltimore 10
playoff
NFL championship   Green Bay 23, Cleveland 12
AFL championship   Buffalo 23, San Diego 0

1966
NFL championship   Green Bay 34, Dallas 27
AFL championship   Kansas City 31, Buffalo 7

1967
NFL E. Conf.   Dallas 52, Cleveland 14
championship
NFL W. Conf.   Green Bay 28, Los Angeles 7
championship
NFL championship   Green Bay 21, Dallas 17
AFL championship   Oakland 40, Houston 7

1968
NFL E. Conf.   Cleveland 31, Dallas 20
championship
NFL W. Conf.   Baltimore 24, Minnesota 14
championship
NFL championship   Baltimore 34, Cleveland 0
AFL W. div. playoff Oakland 41, Kansas City 6
AFL championship   NY Jets 27, Oakland 23

1969
NFL E. Conf.   Cleveland 38, Dallas 14
championship
NFL W. Conf.   Minnesota 23, Los Angeles 20
championship
NFL championship   Minnesota 27, Cleveland 7
AFL div. playoffs   Kansas City 13, NY Jets 6
                            Oakland 56, Houston 7
AFL championship   Kansas City 17, Oakland 7

1970

AFC div. playoffs	Baltimore 17, Cincinnati 0
	Oakland 21, Miami 14
AFC championship	Baltimore 27, Oakland 17
NFC div. playoffs	Dallas 5, Detroit 0
	San Francisco 17, Minnesota 14
NFC championship	Dallas 17, San Francisco 10

1971

AFC div. playoffs	Miami 27, Kansas City 24
	Baltimore 20, Cleveland 3
AFC championship	Miami 21, Baltimore 0
NFC div. playoffs	Dallas 20, Minnesota 12
	San Francisco 24, Washington 20
NFC championship	Dallas 14, San Francisco 3

1972

AFC div. playoffs	Pittsburgh 13, Oakland 7
	Miami 20, Cleveland 14
AFC championship	Miami 21, Pittsburgh 17
NFC div. playoffs	Dallas 30, San Francisco 28
	Washington 16, Green Bay 3
NFC championship	Washington 26, Dallas 3

1973

AFC div. playoffs	Oakland 33, Pittsburgh 14
	Miami 34, Cincinnati 16
AFC championship	Miami 27, Oakland 10
NFC div. playoffs	Minnesota 27, Washington 20
	Dallas 27, Los Angeles 16
NFC championship	Minnesota 27, Dallas 10

1974

AFC div. playoffs	Oakland 28, Miami 26
	Pittsburgh 32, Buffalo 14
AFC championship	Pittsburgh 24, Oakland 13
NFC div. playoffs	Minnesota 30, St Louis 14
	Los Angeles 19, Washington 10
NFC championship	Minnesota 14, Los Angeles 10

1975

AFC div. playoffs	Pittsburgh 28, Baltimore 10
	Oakland 31, Cincinnati 28
AFC championship	Pittsburgh 16, Oakland 10
NFC div. playoffs	Los Angeles 35, St Louis 23
	Dallas 17, Minnesota 14
NFC championship	Dallas 37, Los Angeles 7

1976

AFC div. playoffs	Oakland 24, New England 21
	Pittsburgh 40, Baltimore 14
AFC championship	Oakland 24, Pittsburgh 7
NFC div. playoffs	Minnesota 35, Washington 20
	Los Angeles 14, Dallas 12
NFC championship	Minnesota 24, Los Angeles 13

1977

AFC div. playoffs	Denver 34, Pittsburgh 21
	Oakland 37, Baltimore 31
AFC championship	Denver 20, Oakland 17
NFC div. playoffs	Dallas 37, Chicago 7
	Minnesota 14, Los Angeles 7
NFC championship	Dallas 23, Minnesota 6

1978

AFC 1st-rd. playoff	Houston 17, Miami 9
AFC div. playoffs	Houston 31, New England 14
	Pittsburgh 33, Denver 10
AFC championship	Pittsburgh 34, Houston 5

1978 *(Cont.)*

NFC 1st-rd. playoff	Atlanta 14, Philadelphia 13
NFC div. playoffs	Dallas 27, Atlanta 20
	Los Angeles 34, Minnesota 10
NFC championship	Dallas 28, Los Angeles 0

1979

AFC 1st-rd. playoff	Houston 13, Denver 7
AFC div. playoffs	Houston 17, San Diego 14
	Pittsburgh 34, Miami 14
AFC championship	Pittsburgh 27, Houston 13
NFC 1st-rd. playoff	Philadelphia 27, Chicago 17
NFC div. playoffs	Tampa Bay 24, Philadelphia 17
	Los Angeles 21, Dallas 19
NFC championship	Los Angeles 9, Tampa Bay 0

1980

AFC 1st-rd. playoff	Oakland 27, Houston 7
AFC div. playoffs	San Diego 20, Buffalo 14
	Oakland 14, Cleveland 12
AFC championship	Oakland 34, San Diego 27
NFC 1st-rd. playoff	Dallas 34, Los Angeles 13
NFC div. playoffs	Philadelphia 31, Minnesota 16
	Dallas 30, Atlanta 27
NFC championship	Philadelphia 20, Dallas 7

1981

AFC 1st-rd. playoff	Buffalo 31, NY Jets 27
AFC div. playoffs	San Diego 41, Miami 38
	Cincinnati 28, Buffalo 21
AFC championship	Cincinnati 27, San Diego 7
NFC 1st-rd. playoff	NY Giants 27, Philadelphia 21
NFC div. playoffs	Dallas 38, Tampa Bay 0
	San Francisco 38, NY Giants 24
NFC championship	San Francisco 28, Dallas 27

1982

AFC 1st-rd. playoffs	Miami 28, New England 13
	LA Raiders 27, Cleveland 10
	NY Jets 44, Cincinnati 17
	San Diego 31, Pittsburgh 28
AFC div. playoffs	NY Jets 17, LA Raiders 14
	Miami 34, San Diego 13
AFC championship	Miami 14, NY Jets 0
NFC 1st-rd. playoffs	Washington 31, Detroit 7
	Green Bay 41, St Louis 16
	Minnesota 30, Atlanta 24
	Dallas 30, Tampa Bay 17
NFC div. playoffs	Washington 21, Minnesota 7
	Dallas 37, Green Bay 26
NFC championship	Washington 31, Dallas 17

1983

AFC 1st-rd. playoff	Seattle 31, Denver 7
AFC div. playoffs	Seattle 27, Miami 20
	LA Raiders 38, Pittsburgh 10
AFC championship	LA Raiders 30, Seattle 14
NFC 1st-rd. playoff	LA Rams 24, Dallas 17
NFC div. playoffs	San Francisco 24, Detroit 23
	Washington 51, LA Rams 7
NFC championship	Washington 24, San Francisco 21

1984

AFC 1st-rd. playoff	Seattle 13, LA Raiders 7
AFC div. playoffs	Miami 31, Seattle 10
	Pittsburgh 24, Denver 17
AFC championship	Miami 45, Pittsburgh 28
NFC 1st-rd. playoff	NY Giants 16, LA Rams 13
NFC div. playoffs	San Francisco 21, NY Giants 10
	Chicago 23, Washington 19
NFC championship	San Francisco 23, Chicago 0

1985

AFC 1st-rd. playoff	New England 26, NY Jets 14
AFC div. playoffs	Miami 24, Cleveland 21
	New England 27, LA Raiders 20
AFC championship	New England 31, Miami 14
NFC 1st-rd. playoff	NY Giants 17, San Francisco 3
NFC div. playoffs	LA Rams 20, Dallas 0
	Chicago 21, NY Giants 0
NFC championship	Chicago 24, LA Rams 0

1986

AFC 1st-rd. playoff	NY Jets 35, Kansas City 15
AFC div. playoffs	Cleveland 23, NY Jets 20
	Denver 22, New England 17
AFC championship	Denver 23, Cleveland 20
NFC 1st-rd. playoff	Washington 19, LA Rams 7
NFC div playoffs	Washington 27, Chicago 13
	NY Giants 49, San Francisco 3
NFC championship	NY Giants 17, Washington 0

1987

AFC div. playoffs	Cleveland 38, Indianapolis 21
	Denver 34, Houston 10
AFC championship	Denver 38, Cleveland 33
NFC 1st-rd. playoff	Minnesota 44, New Orleans 10
NFC div playoffs	Minnesota 36, San Francisco 24
	Washington 21, Chicago 17
NFC championship	Washington 17, Minnesota 10

1988

AFC 1st-rd. playoff	Houston 24, Cleveland 23
AFC div. playoffs	Cincinnati 21, Seattle 13
	Buffalo 17, Houston 10
AFC championship	Cincinnati 21, Buffalo 10
NFC 1st-rd. playoff	Minnesota 28, LA Rams 17
NFC div. playoffs	Chicago 20, Philadelphia 12
	San Francisco 34, Minnesota 9
NFC championship	San Francisco 28, Chicago 3

1989

AFC 1st-rd. playoff	Pittsburgh 26, Houston 23
AFC div. playoffs	Cleveland 34, Buffalo 30
	Denver 24, Pittsburgh 23
AFC championship	Denver 37, Cleveland 21
NFC 1st-rd. playoff	LA Rams 21, Philadelphia 7
NFC div. playoffs	LA Rams 19, NY Giants 13
	San Francisco 41, Minnesota 13
NFC championship	San Francisco 30, LA Rams 3

1990

AFC 1st-rd. playoffs	Miami 17, Kansas City 16
	Cincinnati 41, Houston 14
AFC div. playoffs	Buffalo 44, Miami 34
	LA Raiders 20, Cincinnati 10
AFC championship	Buffalo 51, LA Raiders 3
NFC 1st-rd. playoffs	Chicago 16, New Orleans 6
	Washington 20, Philadelphia 6
NFC div. playoffs	NY Giants 31, Chicago 3
	San Francisco 28, Washington 10
NFC championship	NY Giants 15, San Francisco 13

1991

AFC 1st-rd. playoffs	Houston 17, NY Jets 10
	Kansas City 10, LA Raiders 6
AFC div. playoffs	Denver 26, Houston 24
	Buffalo 37, Kansas City 14
AFC championship	Buffalo 10, Denver 7
NFC 1st-rd. playoffs	Atlanta 27, New Orleans 20
	Dallas 17, Chicago 13
NFC div. playoffs	Washington 24, Atlanta 7
	Detroit 38, Dallas 6
NFC championship	Washington 41, Detroit 10

1992

AFC 1st-rd. playoffs	San Diego 17, Kansas City 0
	Buffalo 41, Houston 38 (OT)
AFC div. playoffs	Buffalo 24, Pittsburgh 3
	Miami 31, San Diego 0
AFC championship	Buffalo 29, Miami 10
NFC 1st-rd. playoffs	Washington 24, Minnesota 7
	Philadelphia 36, New Orleans 20
NFC div. playoffs	San Francisco 20, Washington 13
	Dallas 34, Philadelphia 10
NFC championship	Dallas 30, San Francisco 20

1993

AFC 1st-rd. playoffs	LA Raiders 42, Denver 24
	Kansas City 27, Pittsburgh 24 (OT)
AFC div. playoffs	Buffalo 29, LA Raiders 23
	Kansas City 28, Houston 20
AFC championship	Buffalo 30, Kansas City 13
NFC 1st-rd. playoffs	NY Giants 17, Minnesota 10
	Green Bay 28, Detroit 24
NFC div. playoffs	San Francisco 44, NY Giants 3
	Dallas 27, Green Bay 17
NFC championship	Dallas 38, San Francisco 21

1994

AFC 1st-rd. playoffs	Miami 27, Kansas City 17
	Cleveland 20, New England 13
AFC div. playoffs	San Diego 22, Miami 21
	Pittsburgh 29, Cleveland 9
AFC championship	San Diego 17, Pittsburgh 13
NFC 1st-rd. playoffs	Green Bay 16, Detroit 12
	Chicago 35, Minnesota 18
NFC div. playoffs	Dallas 35, Green Bay 9
	San Francisco 44, Chicago 15
NFC championship	San Francisco 38, Dallas 28

1995

AFC 1st-rd. playoffs	Buffalo 37, Miami 22
	Indianapolis 35, San Diego 20
AFC div. playoffs	Pittsburgh 40, Buffalo 21
	Indianapolis 10, Kansas City 7
AFC championship	Pittsburgh 20, Indianapolis 16
NFC 1st-rd. playoffs	Philadelphia 58, Detroit 37
	Green Bay 37, Atlanta 20
NFC div. playoffs	Dallas 30, Philadelphia 11
	Green Bay 27, San Francisco 17
NFC championship	Dallas 38, Green Bay 27

1996

AFC 1st-rd. playoffs	Jacksonville 30, Buffalo 27
	Pittsburgh 42, Indianapolis 14
AFC div. playoffs	Jacksonville 30, Denver 27
	New England 28, Pittsburgh 3
AFC championship	New England 20, Jacksonville 6
NFC 1st-rd. playoffs	Dallas 40, Minnesota 15
	San Francisco 14, Philadelphia 0
NFC div. playoffs	Green Bay 35, San Francisco 14
	Carolina 26, Dallas 17
NFC championship	Green Bay 30, Carolina 13

1997

AFC 1st-rd. playoffs	Denver 42, Jacksonville 17
	New England 17, Miami 3
AFC div. playoffs	Denver 14, Kansas City 0
	Pittsburgh 7, New England 6
AFC championship	Denver 24, Pittsburgh 21
NFC 1st-rd. playoffs	Minnesota 23, NY Giants 22
	Tampa Bay 20, Detroit 10
NFC div. playoffs	Green Bay 21, Tampa Bay 7
	San Francisco 38, Minnesota 22
NFC championship	Green Bay 23, San Francisco 10

Career Leaders

Scoring

	Yrs	TD	FG	PAT	Pts
George Blanda	26	9	335	943	2002
Nick Lowery	18	0	383	562	1711
Jan Stenerud	19	0	373	580	1699
†Gary Anderson	16	0	385	526	1681
†Morten Andersen	16	0	378	507	1641
†Norm Johnson	16	0	322	592	1558
Eddie Murray	17	0	325	498	1473
Pat Leahy	18	0	304	558	1470
Jim Turner	16	1	304	521	1439
Matt Bahr	17	0	300	522	1422
Mark Moseley	16	0	300	482	1382
Jim Bakken	17	0	282	534	1380
Fred Cox	15	0	282	519	1365
Lou Groza	17	1	234	641	1349
Jim Breech	14	0	243	517	1246
†Al Del Greco	14	0	263	435	1224
Chris Bahr	14	0	241	490	1213
Kevin Butler	13	0	265	426	1208
Gino Cappelletti	11	42	176	350	1130
Ray Wersching	15	0	222	456	1122

Cappelletti's total includes four two-point conversions.

Rushing

	Yrs	Att	Yds	Avg	Lg	TD
Walter Payton	13	3,838	16,726	4.4	76	110
†Barry Sanders	9	2,719	13,778	5.1	85	95
Eric Dickerson	11	2,996	13,259	4.4	85	90
Tony Dorsett	12	2,936	12,739	4.3	99	77
Jim Brown	9	2,359	12,312	5.2	80	106
Marcus Allen	16	3,022	12,243	4.1	61	123
Franco Harris	13	2,949	12,120	4.1	75	91
†Thurman Thomas	10	2,720	11,445	4.2	80	63
John Riggins	14	2,916	11,352	3.9	66	104
O.J. Simpson	11	2,404	11,236	4.7	94	61
†Emmitt Smith	8	2,595	11,234	4.3	75	112
Ottis Anderson	14	2,562	10,273	4.0	76	81
Earl Campbell	8	2,187	9,407	4.3	81	74
Jim Taylor	10	1,941	8,597	4.4	84	83
Joe Perry	14	1,737	8,378	4.8	78	53
†Earnest Byner	14	2,095	8,261	3.9	54	56
†Herschel Walker	12	1,954	8,225	4.2	91	61
Roger Craig	11	1,991	8,189	4.1	71	56
Gerald Riggs	10	1,989	8,188	4.1	58	69
Larry Csonka	11	1,891	8,081	4.3	54	64

Touchdowns

	Yrs	Rush	Pass Rec	Ret	Total TD
†Jerry Rice	13	10	155	1	166
Marcus Allen	16	123	21	0	145
Jim Brown	9	106	20	0	126
Walter Payton	13	110	15	0	125
†Emmitt Smith	8	112	7	0	119
John Riggins	14	104	12	0	116
Lenny Moore	12	63	48	2	113
Don Hutson	11	3	99	3	105
†Barry Sanders	9	95	10	0	105
Steve Largent	14	1	100	0	101
Franco Harris	13	91	9	0	100

	Yrs	Rush	Pass Rec	Ret	Total TD
Eric Dickerson	11	90	6	0	96
Jim Taylor	10	83	10	0	93
Tony Dorsett	12	77	13	1	91
Bobby Mitchell	11	18	65	8	91
Leroy Kelly	10	74	13	3	90
Charley Taylor	13	11	79	0	90
Don Maynard	15	0	88	0	88
Lance Alworth	11	2	85	0	87
Ottis Anderson	14	81	5	0	86
Paul Warfield	13	1	85	0	86

Combined Yards Gained

	Yrs	Total	Rush	Rec	Int Ret	Punt Ret	Kickoff Ret	Fum Ret
Walter Payton	13	21,803	16,726	4,538	0	0	539	0
†Herschel Walker	12	18,168	8,225	4,859	0	0	5,084	0
Marcus Allen	16	17,562	12,243	5,325	0	0	0	-6
†Jerry Rice	13	17,075	614	16,455	0	0	6	0
†Barry Sanders	9	16,528	13,778	2,632	0	0	118	0
Tony Dorsett	12	16,326	12,739	3,554	0	0	0	33
†Henry Ellard	15	15,603	50	13,662	0	1,527	364	0
†Thurman Thomas	10	15,489	11,405	4,084	0	0	0	0
Jim Brown	9	15,459	12,312	2,499	0	0	648	0
Eric Dickerson	11	15,411	13,259	2,137	0	0	0	15
James Brooks	12	14,910	7,962	3,621	0	565	2,762	0
Franco Harris	13	14,622	12,120	2,287	0	0	233	-18
O.J. Simpson	11	14,368	11,236	2,142	0	0	990	0
James Lofton	16	14,277	246	14,004	0	0	0	27
Bobby Mitchell	11	14,078	2,735	7,954	0	699	2,690	0
John Riggins	14	13,435	11,352	2,090	0	0	0	-7
Steve Largent	14	13,396	83	13,089	0	68	156	0
Ottis Anderson	14	13,364	10,273	3,062	0	0	0	29
Drew Hill	14	13,337	19	9,831	0	22	3,460	5
Greg Pruitt	12	13,262	5,672	3,069	0	2,007	2,514	0

† Active player.

Career Leaders (Cont.)

Passing

PASSING EFFICIENCY*

	Yrs	Att	Comp	Pct Comp	Yds	Avg Gain	TD	Pct TD	Int	Pct Int	Rating Pts
†Steve Young	13	3,548	2,300	64.8	28,508	8.03	193	5.4	91	2.6	97.0
Joe Montana	15	5,391	3,409	63.2	40,551	7.52	273	5.1	139	2.6	92.3
†Brett Favre	7	3,206	1,971	61.5	22,591	7.05	182	5.2	95	3.0	89.3
†Dan Marino	15	7,452	4,453	59.8	55,416	7.44	385	5.2	211	3.0	87.8
Jim Kelly	11	4,779	2,874	60.1	35,467	7.42	237	5.0	175	3.7	84.3
Roger Staubach	11	2,958	1,685	57.0	22,700	7.67	153	5.2	109	3.7	83.4
Neil Lomax	8	3,153	1,817	57.6	22,771	7.22	136	4.3	90	2.9	82.7
Sonny Jurgensen	18	4,262	2,433	57.1	32,224	7.56	255	6.0	189	4.4	82.6
Len Dawson	19	3,741	2,136	57.1	28,711	7.67	239	6.4	183	4.9	82.6
†Troy Aikman	9	3,696	2,292	62.0	26,016	7.03	129	3.5	110	3.0	82.3
Bernie Kosar	12	3,365	1,994	59.3	23,301	6.93	124	3.7	87	2.6	81.9
Ken Anderson	16	4,475	2,654	59.3	32,838	7.34	197	4.4	160	3.6	81.9
Danny White	13	2,950	1,761	59.7	21,959	7.44	155	5.3	132	4.5	81.7
†Dave Krieg	18	5,290	3,093	58.5	37,948	7.17	261	4.9	199	3.8	81.5
†Warren Moon	14	6,528	3,827	58.6	47,465	7.27	279	4.3	224	3.4	81.2
Boomer Esiason	14	5,205	2,969	57.0	37,920	7.29	247	4.7	181	3.5	81.1
†Jeff Hostetler	12	2,338	1,357	58.0	16,430	7.03	94	4.0	71	3.0	80.5
†Neil O'Donnell	7	2,519	1,438	57.1	16,810	6.67	89	3.5	53	2.1	80.5
Bart Starr	16	3,149	1,808	57.4	24,718	7.85	152	4.8	138	4.4	80.5
Ken O'Brien	10	3,602	2,110	58.6	25,094	6.97	128	3.6	98	2.7	80.4
Fran Tarkenton	18	6,467	3,686	57.0	47,003	7.27	342	5.3	266	4.1	80.4

*1,500 or more attempts. The passer ratings are based on performance standards established for completion percentage, interception percentage, touchdown percentage and average gain. Passers are allocated points according to how their marks compare with those standards.

YARDS

	Yrs	Att	Comp	Pct Comp	Yds		Yrs	Att	Comp	Pct Comp	Yds
†Dan Marino	15	7,452	4,453	59.8	55,416	Jim Everett	12	4,923	2,841	57.7	34,837
†John Elway	15	6,894	3,913	56.8	48,669	Jim Hart	19	5,076	2,593	51.1	34,665
†Warren Moon	14	6,528	3,827	58.6	47,465	Steve DeBerg	16	4,965	2,844	57.3	33,872
Fran Tarkenton	18	6,467	3,686	57.0	47,003	John Hadl	16	4,687	2,363	50.4	33,503
Dan Fouts	15	5,604	3,297	58.8	43,040	Phil Simms	14	4,647	2,576	55.4	33,462
Joe Montana	15	5,391	3,409	63.2	40,551	Ken Anderson	16	4,475	2,654	59.3	32,838
Johnny Unitas	18	5,186	2,830	54.6	40,239	Sonny Jurgensen	18	4,262	2,433	57.1	32,224
†Dave Krieg	18	5,290	3,093	58.5	37,948	John Brodie	17	4,491	2,469	55.0	31,548
Boomer Esiason	14	5,205	2,969	57.0	37,920	Norm Snead	15	4,353	2,276	52.3	30,797
Jim Kelly	11	4,779	2,874	60.1	35,467	Joe Ferguson	18	4,519	2,369	52.4	29,817

TOUCHDOWNS

	No.		No.		No.
†Dan Marino	385	John Hadl	244	Phil Simms	199
Fran Tarkenton	342	Len Dawson	239	Ken Anderson	197
Johnny Unitas	290	Jim Kelly	237	Joe Ferguson	196
†Warren Moon	279	George Blanda	236	Bobby Layne	196
†John Elway	278	John Brodie	214	Norm Snead	196
Joe Montana	273	Terry Bradshaw	212	Ken Stabler	194
†Dave Krieg	261	Y.A. Tittle	212	Steve DeBerg	193
Sonny Jurgensen	255	Jim Hart	209	†Steve Young	193
Dan Fouts	254	Jim Everett	203	Bob Griese	192
Boomer Esiason	247	Roman Gabriel	201	Sammy Baugh	187

† Active player.

Career Leaders *(Cont.)*

Receiving

RECEPTIONS

	Yrs	No.	Yds	Avg	Lg	TD		Yrs	No.	Yds	Avg	Lg	TD
†Jerry Rice	13	1057	16,455	15.6	96	155	†Michael Irvin	10	666	10,680	16.0	87	61
Art Monk	16	940	12,721	13.5	79	68	Ozzie Newsome	13	662	7,980	12.1	74	47
†Andre Reed	13	826	11,764	14.2	83	80	Charley Taylor	13	649	9,110	14.0	88	79
Steve Largent	14	819	13,089	16.0	74	100	†Andre Rison	9	641	8,839	13.8	75	73
†Henry Ellard	15	807	13,662	16.9	81	65	Drew Hill	14	634	9,831	15.5	81	60
James Lofton	16	764	14,004	18.3	80	75	Don Maynard	15	633	11,834	18.7	87	88
†Cris Carter	11	756	9,436	12.5	80	89	Raymond Berry	13	631	9,275	14.7	70	68
Charlie Joiner	18	750	12,146	16.2	87	65	†Anthony Miller	10	595	9,148	15.4	76	63
†Irving Fryar	14	736	11,427	15.5	80	75	Sterling Sharpe	7	595	8,134	13.7	79	65
Gary Clark	11	699	10,856	15.5	84	65	Harold Carmichael	14	590	8,985	15.2	85	79

YARDS

	No.		No.		No.
†Jerry Rice	16,455	†Andre Reed	11,764	Drew Hill	9,831
James Lofton	14,004	†Irving Fryar	11,427	†Cris Carter	9,436
†Henry Ellard	13,662	Gary Clark	10,856	Raymond Berry	9,275
Steve Largent	13,089	Stanley Morgan	10,716	†Anthony Miller	9,148
Art Monk	12,721	†Michael Irvin	10,680	Charley Taylor	9,110
Charlie Joiner	12,146	Harold Jackson	10,372	Harold Carmichael	8,985
Don Maynard	11,834	Lance Alworth	10,266		

Sacks

†Reggie White	176.5	Lawrence Taylor	132.5
†Bruce Smith	154.0	Rickey Jackson	128.0
†Richard Dent	137.5		

Note: Officially compiled since 1982.

Interceptions

	Yrs	No.	Yds	Avg	Lg	TD
Paul Krause	16	81	1185	14.6	81	3
Emlen Tunnell	14	79	1282	16.2	55	4
Dick (Night Train) Lane	14	68	1207	17.8	80	5
Ken Riley	15	65	596	9.2	66	5
Ronnie Lott	14	63	730	11.3	83	5

Punt Returns

	Yrs	No.	Yds	Avg	Lg	TD
†Darrien Gordon	4	103	1407	13.7	90	3
George McAfee	8	112	1431	12.8	74	2
Jack Christiansen	8	85	1084	12.8	89	8
Claude Gibson	5	110	1381	12.6	85	3
Bill Dudley	9	124	1515	12.2	96	3

Note: 75 or more returns.

Punting

	Yrs	No.	Yds	Avg	Lg	Blk
Sammy Baugh	16	338	15,245	45.1	85	9
Tommy Davis	11	511	22,833	44.7	82	2
Yale Lary	11	503	22,279	44.3	74	4
Bob Scarpitto	8	283	12,408	43.8	87	4
Horace Gillom	7	385	16,872	43.8	80	5
Jerry Norton	11	358	15,671	43.8	78	2

Note: 250 or more punts.

Kickoff Returns

	Yrs	No.	Yds	Avg	Lg	TD
Gale Sayers	7	91	2781	30.6	103	6
Lynn Chandnois	7	92	2720	29.6	93	3
Abe Woodson	9	193	5538	28.7	105	5
Claude (Buddy) Young	6	90	2514	27.9	104	2
Travis Williams	5	102	2801	27.5	105	6

Note: 75 or more returns.

† Active player.

THEY SAID IT

Mike Shanahan, coach of the Denver Broncos, when asked whether he was surprised at any of the Broncos' final roster cuts: "No. I made them."

Single-Season Leaders
Scoring

POINTS

	Year	TD	PAT	FG	Pts
Paul Hornung, GB	1960	15	41	15	176
Mark Moseley, Wash	1983	0	62	33	161
Gino Cappelletti, Bos	1964	7	38	25	155
Emmitt Smith, Dall	1995	25	0	0	150
Chip Lohmiller, Wash	1991	0	56	31	149
Gino Cappelletti, Bos	1961	8	48	17	147
Paul Hornung, GB	1961	10	41	15	146
Jim Turner, NYJ	1968	0	43	34	145
John Kasay, Car	1996	0	34	37	145
John Riggins, Wash	1983	24	0	0	144
Kevin Butler, Chi	1985	0	51	31	144

Note: Cappelletti's 1964 total includes a two-point conversion.

TOUCHDOWNS

	Year	Rush	Rec	Ret	Total
Emmitt Smith, Dall	1995	25	0	0	25
John Riggins, Wash	1983	24	0	0	24
O.J. Simpson, Buff	1975	16	7	0	23
Jerry Rice, SF	1987	1	22	0	23
Gale Sayers, Chi	1965	14	6	2	22
Emmitt Smith, Dall	1994	21	1	0	22

FIELD GOALS

	Year	Att	No.
John Kasay, Car	1996	45	37
Cary Blanchard, Ind	1996	40	36
Jeff Jaeger, LA Raiders	1993	44	35
Ali Haji-Sheikh, NYG	1983	42	35
Jim Turner, NYJ	1968	46	34
Jason Hanson, Det	1993	43	34
John Carney, SD	1994	38	34
Fuad Reveiz, Minn	1994	39	34
Norm Johnson, Pitt	1995	41	34
Richie Cunningham, Dall	1997	37	34

Rushing

YARDS GAINED

	Year	Att	Yds	Avg
Eric Dickerson, LA Rams	1984	379	2105	5.6
Barry Sanders, Det	1997	335	2053	6.1
O.J. Simpson, Buff	1973	332	2003	6.0
Earl Campbell, Hou	1980	373	1934	5.2
Jim Brown, Clev	1963	291	1883	6.4
Barry Sanders, Det	1994	331	1883	5.7
Walter Payton, Chi	1977	339	1852	5.5
Eric Dickerson, LA Rams	1986	404	1821	4.5
O.J. Simpson, Buff	1975	329	1817	5.5
Eric Dickerson, LA Rams	1983	390	1808	4.6

AVERAGE GAIN

	Year	Avg
Beattie Feathers, Chi	1934	8.44
Randall Cunningham, Phil	1990	7.98
Bobby Douglass, Chi	1972	6.87

TOUCHDOWNS

	Year	No.
Emmitt Smith, Dall	1995	25
John Riggins, Wash	1983	24
Emmitt Smith, Dall	1994	21
Joe Morris, NYG	1985	21
Terry Allen, Wash	1996	21

Passing

YARDS GAINED

	Year	Att	Comp	Pct	Yds
Dan Marino, Mia	1984	564	362	64.2	5084
Dan Fouts, SD	1981	609	360	59.1	4802
Dan Marino, Mia	1986	623	378	60.7	4746
Dan Fouts, SD	1980	589	348	59.1	4715
Warren Moon, Hou	1991	655	404	61.7	4690
Warren Moon, Hou	1990	584	362	62.0	4689
Neil Lomax, StL Cards	1984	560	345	61.6	4614
Drew Bledsoe, NE	1994	691	400	57.9	4555
Lynn Dickey, GB	1983	484	289	59.7	4458
Dan Marino, Mia	1994	615	385	62.6	4453

PASSER RATING

	Year	Rat.
Steve Young, SF	1994	112.8
Joe Montana, SF	1989	112.4
Milt Plum, Clev	1960	110.4
Sammy Baugh, Wash	1945	109.9
Dan Marino, Mia	1984	108.9

TOUCHDOWNS

	Year	No.
Dan Marino, Mia	1984	48
Dan Marino, Mia	1986	44
Brett Favre, GB	1995	38
George Blanda, Hou	1961	36
Y.A. Tittle, NYG	1963	36

Single-Season Leaders *(Cont.)*

Receiving

RECEPTIONS

	Year	No.	Yds
Herman Moore, Det	1995	123	1686
Cris Carter, Minn	1994	122	1256
Jerry Rice, SF	1995	122	1848
Cris Carter, Minn	1995	122	1371
Isaac Bruce, StL Rams	1995	119	1781
Sterling Sharpe, GB	1993	112	1274
Jerry Rice, SF	1994	112	1499
Terance Mathis, Atl	1994	111	1342
Michael Irvin, Dall	1995	111	1603
Sterling Sharpe, GB	1992	108	1461
Brett Perriman, Det	1995	108	1488
Jerry Rice, SF	1996	108	1254

YARDS GAINED

	Year	Yds
Jerry Rice, SF	1995	1848
Isaac Bruce, StL Rams	1995	1781
Charley Hennigan, Hou	1961	1746
Herman Moore, Det	1995	1686
Michael Irvin, Dall	1995	1603

TOUCHDOWNS

	Year	No.
Jerry Rice, SF	1987	22
Mark Clayton, Mia	1984	18
Sterling Sharpe, GB	1994	18

Six tied with 17.

All-Purpose Yards

	Year	Run	Rec	Ret	Total
Lionel James, SD	1985	516	1027	992	2535
Terry Metcalf, StL Cards	1975	816	378	1268	2462
Mack Herron, NE	1974	824	474	1146	2444
Gale Sayers, Chi	1966	1231	447	762	2440
Timmy Brown, Phil	1963	841	487	1100	2428
Barry Sanders, Det	1997	2053	305	0	2358
Tim Brown, LA Rai	1988	50	725	1542	2317
Marcus Allen, LA Rai	1985	1759	555	−6	2308
Timmy Brown, Phil	1962	545	849	912	2306
Gale Sayers, Chi	1965	867	507	898	2272
Eric Dickerson, LA Rams	1984	2105	139	15	2259
O.J. Simpson, Buff	1975	1817	426	0	2243

Punting

	Year	No.	Yds	Avg
Sammy Baugh, Wash	1940	35	1799	51.4
Yale Lary, Det	1963	35	1713	48.9
Sammy Baugh, Wash	1941	30	1462	48.7
Yale Lary, Det	1961	52	2516	48.4
Sammy Baugh, Wash	1942	37	1783	48.2

Sacks

	Year	No.
Mark Gastineau, NYJ	1984	22
Reggie White, Phil	1987	21
Chris Doleman, Minn	1989	21
Lawrence Taylor, NYG	1986	20.5

Interceptions

	Year	No.
Dick (Night Train) Lane, LA Rams	1952	14
Dan Sandifer, Wash	1948	13
Spec Sanders, NY Yanks	1950	13
Lester Hayes, Oak	1980	13

Nine tied with 12.

Kickoff Returns

	Year	Avg
Travis Williams, GB	1967	41.1
Gale Sayers, Chi	1967	37.7
Ollie Matson, Chi Cards	1958	35.5
Jim Duncan, Balt Colts	1970	35.4
Lynn Chandnois, Pitt	1952	35.2

Punt Returns

	Year	Avg
Herb Rich, Balt Colts	1950	23.0
Jack Christiansen, Det	1952	21.5
Dick Christy, NY Titans	1961	21.3
Bob Hayes, Dall	1968	20.8

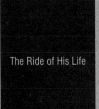

The Ride of His Life

The problem with being on the losing end of three Super Bowls, John Elway and his family discovered after Super Bowl XXXII, is not knowing what to do when you finally win one. John kept looking for his championship hat, only to be told he was carrying it in his hand. He had refused to watch tapes of the other three Super Bowl blowouts, but he couldn't wait to get the popcorn out for this one, only, "I don't think anybody taped it." His wife, Janet, her makeup running, was flummoxed. "I know how to handle a loss in these," she said. "I'm not sure how to handle a win."

Jack, John's father, knew. The Broncos' director of pro scouting found his favorite pro person and put a hug on him that might've killed a polar bear. For two guys who usually talk until dawn at these things, they sure didn't say much. "Just that we loved each other," the son says. *So this is what the other side on these feels like.*

Single-Game Leaders

Scoring

POINTS

	Date	Pts
Ernie Nevers, Chi Cards vs Chi	11-28-29	40
Dub Jones, Clev vs Chi	11-25-51	36
Gale Sayers, Chi vs SF	12-12-65	36
Paul Hornung, GB vs Balt Colts	10-8-61	33

On Thanksgiving Day, 1929, Nevers scored all the Cardinals' points on six rushing TDs and four PATs. The Cards defeated Red Grange and the Bears, 40-6. Jones and Sayers each rushed for four touchdowns and scored two more on returns in their teams' victories. Hornung scored four touchdowns and kicked 6 PATs and a field goal in a 45-7 win over the Colts.

FIELD GOALS

	Date	No.
Jim Bakken, StL Cards vs Pitt	9-24-67	7
Rich Karlis, Minn vs LA Rams	11-5-89	7
Chris Boniol, Dall vs GB	11-18-96	7

Thirteen players tied with 6 FGs each.

Bakken was 7 for 9, Karlis and Boniol 7 for 7.

TOUCHDOWNS

	Date	No.
Ernie Nevers, Chi Cards vs Chi	11-28-29	6
Dub Jones, Clev vs Chi	11-25-51	6
Gale Sayers, Chi vs SF	12-12-65	6
Bob Shaw, Chi Cards vs Balt Colts	10-2-50	5
Jim Brown, Clev vs Balt Colts	11-1-59	5
Abner Haynes, Dall Texans vs Oak	11-26-61	5
Billy Cannon, Hou vs NY Titans	12-10-61	5
Cookie Gilchrist, Buff vs NYJ	12-8-63	5
Paul Hornung, GB vs Balt Colts	12-12-65	5
Kellen Winslow, SD vs Oak	11-22-81	5
Jerry Rice, SF vs Atl	10-14-90	5
James Stewart, Jax vs Phil	10-12-97	5

Rushing

YARDS GAINED

	Date	Yds
Walter Payton, Chi vs Minn	11-20-77	275
O.J. Simpson, Buff vs Det	11-25-76	273
O.J. Simpson, Buff vs NE	9-16-73	250
Willie Ellison, LA Rams vs NO	12-5-71	247
Corey Dillon, Cin vs Tenn	12-4-97	246

TOUCHDOWNS

	Date	No.
Ernie Nevers, Chi Cards vs Chi	11-28-29	6
Jim Brown, Clev vs Balt Colts	11-1-59	5
Cookie Gilchrist, Buff vs NYJ	12-8-63	5
James Stewart, Jax vs Phil	10-12-97	5

CARRIES

	Date	No.
Jamie Morris, Wash vs Cin	12-17-88	45
Butch Woolfolk, NYG vs Phil	11-20-83	43
James Wilder, TB vs GB	9-30-84	43
James Wilder, TB vs Pitt	10-30-83	42
Franco Harris, Pitt vs Cin	10-17-76	41
Gerald Riggs, Atl vs LA Rams	11-17-85	41

Passing

YARDS GAINED

	Date	Yds
N. Van Brocklin, LA Rams vs NY Yanks	9-28-51	554
Warren Moon, Hou vs KC	12-16-90	527
Boomer Esiason, Ariz vs Wash	11-10-96	522
Dan Marino, Mia vs NYJ	10-23-88	521
Phil Simms, NYG vs Cin	10-13-85	513

COMPLETIONS

	Date	No.
Drew Bledsoe, NE vs Minn	11-13-94	45
Richard Todd, NYJ vs SF	9-21-80	42
Warren Moon, Hou vs Dall	11-10-91	41
Ken Anderson, Cin vs SD	12-20-82	40
Phil Simms, NYG vs Cin	10-13-85	40
Dan Marino, Mia vs Buff	11-16-86	39

TOUCHDOWNS

	Date	No.
Sid Luckman, Chi vs NYG	11-14-43	7
Adrian Burk, Phil vs Wash	10-17-54	7
George Blanda, Hou vs NY Titans	11-19-61	7
Y. A. Tittle, NYG vs Wash	10-28-62	7
Joe Kapp, Minn vs Balt Colts	9-28-69	7

Single-Game Leaders *(Cont.)*
Receiving

YARDS GAINED

	Date	Yds
Flipper Anderson, LA Rams vs NO	11-26-89	336
Stephone Paige, KC vs SD	12-22-85	309
Jim Benton, Clev vs Det	11-22-45	303
Cloyce Box, Det vs Balt Colts	12-3-50	302
Jerry Rice, SF vs Minn	12-18-95	289

TOUCHDOWNS

	Date	No.
Bob Shaw, Chi Cards vs Balt Colts	10-2-50	5
Kellen Winslow, SD vs Oak	11-22-81	5
Jerry Rice, SF vs Atl	10-14-90	5

RECEPTIONS

	Date	No.
Tom Fears, LA Rams vs GB	12-3-50	18
Clark Gaines, NYJ vs SF	9-21-80	17
Sonny Randle, StL Cards vs NYG	11-4-62	16
Jerry Rice, SF vs LA Rams	11-20-94	16
Keenan McCardell, Jax vs StL Rams	10-20-96	16
Rickey Young, Minn vs NE	12-16-79	15
William Andrews, Atl vs Pitt	11-15-81	15
Andre Reed, Buff vs GB	11-20-94	15
Isaac Bruce, StL Rams vs Mia	12-24-95	15

All-Purpose Yards

	Date	Yds
Glyn Milburn, Den vs Sea	12-10-95	404
Billy Cannon, Hou vs NY Titans	12-10-61	373
Tyrone Hughes, NO vs LA Rams	10-23-94	347
Lionel James, SD vs LA Rai	11-10-85	345
Timmy Brown, Phil vs StL Cards	12-16-62	341

Longest Plays

RUSHING

	Opponent	Year	Yds
Tony Dorsett, Dall	Minn	1983	99
Andy Uram, GB	Chi Cards	1939	97
Bob Gage, Pitt	Chi	1949	97
Jim Spitival, Balt Colts	GB	1950	96
Bob Hoernschemeyer, Det	NY Yanks	1950	96

PASSING

	Opponent	Year	Yds
Frank Filchock to Andy Farkas, Wash	Pitt	1939	99
George Izo to Bobby Mitchell, Wash	Clev	1963	99
Karl Sweetan to Pat Studstill, Det	Balt Colts	1966	99
Sonny Jurgensen to Gerry Allen, Wash	Chi	1968	99
Jim Plunkett to Cliff Branch, LA Rai	Wash	1983	99
Ron Jaworski to Mike Quick, Phil	Atl	1985	99
Stan Humphries to Tony Martin, SD	Sea	1994	99
Brett Favre to Robert Brooks, GB	Chi	1995	99

FIELD GOALS

	Opponent	Year	Yds
Tom Dempsey, NO	Det	1970	63
Steve Cox, Clev	Cin	1984	60
Morten Andersen, NO	Chi	1991	60

PUNTS

	Opponent	Year	Yds
Steve O'Neal, NYJ	Den	1969	98
Joe Lintzenich, Chi	NYG	1931	94
Shawn McCarthy, NE	Buff	1991	93
Randall Cunningham, Phil	NYG	1989	91

INTERCEPTION RETURNS

	Opponent	Year	Yds
Vencie Glenn, SD	Den	1987	103
Louis Oliver, Mia	Buff	1992	103
Six players tied at 102.			

KICKOFF RETURNS

	Opponent	Year	Yds
Al Carmichael, GB	Chi	1956	106
Noland Smith, KC	Den	1967	106
Roy Green, StL Cards	Dall	1979	106

PUNT RETURNS

	Opponent	Year	Yds
Robert Bailey, LA Rams	NO	1994	103
Gil LeFebvre, Cin	Brooklyn	1933	98
Charlie West, Minn	Wash	1968	98
Dennis Morgan, Dall	StL Cards	1974	98
Terance Mathis, NYJ	Dall	1990	98

Rushing

Year	Player, Team	Att.	Yards	Avg.	TD
1932	Cliff Battles, Bos	148	576	3.9	3
1933	Jim Musick, Bos	173	809	4.7	5
1934	Beattie Feathers, Chi	101	1004	9.9	8
1935	Doug Russell, Chi Cards	140	499	3.6	0
1936	Alphonse Leemans, NY	206	830	4.0	2
1937	Cliff Battles, Wash	216	874	4.0	5
1938	Byron White, Pitt	152	567	3.7	4
1939	Bill Osmanski, Chi	121	699	5.8	7
1940	Byron White, Det	146	514	3.5	5
1941	Clarence Manders, Bklyn	111	486	4.4	5
1942	Bill Dudley, Pitt	162	696	4.3	5
1943	Bill Paschal, NY	147	572	3.9	10
1944	Bill Paschal, NY	196	737	3.8	9
1945	Steve Van Buren, Phil	143	832	5.8	15
1946	Bill Dudley, Pitt	146	604	4.1	3
1947	Steve Van Buren, Phil	217	1008	4.6	13
1948	Steve Van Buren, Phil	201	945	4.7	10
1949	Steve Van Buren, Phil	263	1146	4.4	11
1950	Marion Motley, Clev	140	810	5.8	3
1951	Eddie Price, NY	271	971	3.6	7
1952	Dan Towler, LA	156	894	5.7	10
1953	Joe Perry, SF	192	1018	5.3	10
1954	Joe Perry, SF	173	1049	6.1	8
1955	Alan Ameche, Balt	213	961	4.5	9
1956	Rick Casares, Chi	234	1126	4.8	12
1957	Jim Brown, Clev	202	942	4.7	9
1958	Jim Brown, Clev	257	1527	5.9	17
1959	Jim Brown, Clev	290	1329	4.6	14
1960	Jim Brown, Clev, NFL	215	1257	5.8	9
	Abner Haynes, Dall Texans, AFL	156	875	5.6	9
1961	Jim Brown, Clev, NFL	305	1408	4.6	8
	Billy Cannon, Hou, AFL	200	948	4.7	6
1962	Jim Taylor, GB, NFL	272	1474	5.4	19
	Cookie Gilchrist, Buff, AFL	214	1096	5.1	13
1963	Jim Brown, Clev, NFL	291	1863	6.4	12
	Clem Daniels, Oak, AFL	215	1099	5.1	3
1964	Jim Brown, Clev, NFL	280	1446	5.2	7
	Cookie Gilchrist, Buff, AFL	230	981	4.3	6
1965	Jim Brown, Clev, NFL	289	1544	5.3	17
	Paul Lowe, SD, AFL	222	1121	5.0	7
1966	Jim Nance, Bos, AFL	299	1458	4.9	11
	Gale Sayers, Chi, NFL	229	1231	5.4	8
1967	Jim Nance, Bos, AFL	269	1216	4.5	7
	Leroy Kelly, Clev, NFL	235	1205	5.1	11
1968	Leroy Kelly, Clev, NFL	248	1239	5.0	16
	Paul Robinson, Cin, AFL	238	1023	4.3	8
1969	Gale Sayers, Chi, NFL	236	1032	4.4	8
	Dickie Post, SD, AFL	182	873	4.8	6
1970	Larry Brown, Wash, NFC	237	1125	4.7	5
	Floyd Little, Den, AFC	209	901	4.3	3
1971	Floyd Little, Den, AFC	284	1133	4.0	6
	John Brockington, GB, NFC	216	1105	5.1	4
1972	O.J. Simpson, Buff, AFC	292	1251	4.3	6
	Larry Brown, Wash, NFC	285	1216	4.3	8
1973	O.J. Simpson, Buff, AFC	332	2003	6.0	12
	John Brockington, GB, NFC	265	1144	4.3	3

Year	Player, Team	Att.	Yards	Avg.	TD
1974	Otis Armstrong, Den, AFC	263	1407	5.3	9
	Lawrence McCutcheon, LA, NFC	236	1109	4.7	3
1975	O.J. Simpson, Buff, AFC	329	1817	5.5	16
	Jim Otis, StL, NFC	269	1076	4.0	5
1976	O.J. Simpson, Buff, AFC	290	1503	5.2	8
	Walter Payton, Chi, NFC	311	1390	4.5	13
1977	Walter Payton, Chi, NFC	339	1852	5.5	14
	Mark van Eeghen, Oak, AFC	324	1273	3.9	7
1978	Earl Campbell, Hou, AFC	302	1450	4.8	13
	Walter Payton, Chi, NFC	333	1395	4.2	11
1979	Earl Campbell, Hou, AFC	368	1697	4.6	19
	Walter Payton, Chi, NFC	369	1610	4.4	14
1980	Earl Campbell, Hou, AFC	373	1934	5.2	13
	Walter Payton, Chi, NFC	317	1460	4.6	6
1981	George Rogers, NO, NFC	378	1674	4.4	13
	Earl Campbell, Hou, AFC	361	1376	3.8	10
1982	Freeman McNeil, NY Jets, AFC	151	786	5.2	6
	Tony Dorsett, Dall, NFC	177	745	4.2	5
1983	Eric Dickerson, LA Rams, NFC	390	1808	4.6	18
	Curt Warner, Sea, AFC	335	1449	4.3	13
1984	Eric Dickerson, LA Rams, NFC	379	2105	5.6	14
	Earnest Jackson, SD, AFC	296	1179	4.0	8
1985	Marcus Allen, LA Raiders, AFC	380	1759	4.6	11
	Gerald Riggs, Atl, NFC	397	1719	4.3	10
1986	Eric Dickerson, LA Rams, NFC	404	1821	4.5	11
	Curt Warner, Sea, AFC	319	1481	4.6	13
1987	Charles White, LA Rams, NFC	324	1374	4.2	11
	Eric Dickerson, Ind, AFC	223	1011	4.5	5
1988	Eric Dickerson, Ind, AFC	388	1659	4.3	14
	Herschel Walker, Dall, NFC	361	1514	4.2	5
1989	Christian Okoye, KC, AFC	370	1480	4.0	12
	Barry Sanders, Det, NFC	280	1470	5.3	14
1990	Barry Sanders, Det, NFC	255	1304	5.1	13
	Thurman Thomas, Buff, AFC	271	1297	4.8	11
1991	Emmitt Smith, Dall, NFC	365	1563	4.3	12
	Thurman Thomas, Buff, AFC	288	1407	4.9	7
1992	Emmitt Smith, Dall, NFC	373	1713	4.6	18
	Barry Foster, Pitt, AFC	390	1690	4.3	11
1993	Emmitt Smith, Dall, NFC	283	1486	5.3	9
	Thurman Thomas, Buff, AFC	355	1315	3.7	6
1994	Barry Sanders, Det, NFC	331	1883	5.7	7
	Chris Warren, Sea, AFC	333	1545	4.6	9
1995	Emmitt Smith, Dall, NFC	377	1773	4.7	25
	Curtis Martin, NE, AFC	368	1487	4.0	14
1996	Barry Sanders, Det, NFC	307	1553	5.1	11
	Terrell Davis, Den, AFC	345	1538	4.5	13
1997	Barry Sanders, Det, NFC	335	2053	6.1	11
	Terrell Davis, Den, AFC	369	1730	4.7	15

Passing*

Year	Player, Team	Att.	Comp	Yards	TD	Int
1932	Arnie Herber, GB	101	37	639	9	9
1933	Harry Newman, NY	136	53	973	11	17
1934	Arnie Herber, GB	115	42	799	8	12
1935	Ed Danowski, NY	113	57	794	10	9
1936	Arnie Herber, GB	173	77	1239	11	13
1937	Sammy Baugh, Wash	171	81	1127	8	14
1938	Ed Danowski, NY	129	70	848	7	8
1939	Parker Hall, Clev	208	106	1227	9	13
1940	Sammy Baugh, Wash	177	111	1367	12	10
1941	Cecil Isbell, GB	206	117	1479	15	11
1942	Cecil Isbell, GB	268	146	2021	24	14
1943	Sammy Baugh, Wash	239	133	1754	23	19
1944	Frank Filchock, Wash	147	84	1139	13	9
1945	Sammy Baugh, Wash	182	128	1669	11	4
	Sid Luckman, Chi	217	117	1725	14	10
1946	Bob Waterfield, LA	251	127	1747	18	17
1947	Sammy Baugh, Wash	354	210	2938	25	15
1948	Tommy Thompson, Phil	246	141	1965	25	11
1949	Sammy Baugh, Wash	255	145	1903	18	14
1950	Norm Van Brocklin, LA	233	127	2061	18	14
1951	Bob Waterfield, LA	176	88	1566	13	10
1952	Norm Van Brocklin, LA	205	113	1736	14	17
1953	Otto Graham, Clev	258	167	2722	11	9
1954	Norm Van Brocklin, LA	260	139	2637	13	21
1955	Otto Graham, Clev	185	98	1721	15	8
1956	Ed Brown, Chi	168	96	1667	11	12
1957	Tommy O'Connell, Clev	110	63	1229	9	8
1958	Eddie LeBaron, Wash	145	79	1365	11	10
1959	Charlie Conerly, NY	194	113	1706	14	4
1960	Milt Plum, Clev, NFL	250	151	2297	21	5
	Jack Kemp, LA, AFL	406	211	3018	20	25
1961	George Blanda, Hou, AFL	362	187	3330	36	22
	Milt Plum, Clev, NFL	302	177	2416	18	10
1962	Len Dawson, Dall, AFL	310	189	2759	29	17
	Bart Starr, GB, NFL	285	178	2438	12	9
1963	Y.A. Tittle, NY, NFL	367	221	3145	36	14
	Tobin Rote, SD, AFL	286	170	2510	20	17
1964	Len Dawson, KC, AFL	354	199	2879	30	18
	Bart Starr, GB, NFL	272	163	2144	15	4
1965	Rudy Bukich, Chi, NFL	312	176	2641	20	9
	John Hadl, SD, AFL	348	174	2798	20	21
1966	Bart Starr, GB, NFL	251	156	2257	14	3
	Len Dawson, KC, AFL	284	159	2527	26	10
1967	Sonny Jurgensen, Wash, NFL	508	288	3747	31	16
	Daryle Lamonica, Oakland, AFL	425	220	3228	30	20
1968	Len Dawson, KC, AFL	224	131	2109	17	9
	Earl Morrall, Balt, NFL	317	182	2909	26	17
1969	Sonny Jurgensen, Wash, NFL	442	274	3102	22	15
	Greg Cook, Cin, AFL	197	106	1854	15	11
1970	John Brodie, SF, NFC	378	223	2941	24	10
	Daryle Lamonica, Oak, AFC	356	179	2516	22	15
1971	Roger Staubach, Dall, NFC	211	126	1882	15	4
	Bob Griese, Mia, AFC	263	145	2089	19	9
1972	Norm Snead, NY, NFC	325	196	2307	17	12
	Earl Morrall, Mia, AFC	150	83	1360	11	7
1973	Roger Staubach, Dall, NFC	286	179	2428	23	15
	Ken Stabler, Oak, AFC	260	163	1997	14	10
1974	Ken Anderson, Cin, AFC	328	213	2667	18	10
	Sonny Jurgensen, Wash, NFC	167	107	1185	11	5
1975	Ken Anderson, Cin, AFC	377	228	3169	21	11
	Fran Tarkenton, Minn, NFC	425	273	2994	25	13
1976	Ken Stabler, Oak, AFC	291	194	2737	27	17
	James Harris, LA, NFC	158	91	1460	8	6
1977	Bob Griese, Mia, AFC	307	180	2252	22	13
	Roger Staubach, Dall, NFC	361	210	2620	18	9
1978	Roger Staubach, Dall, NFC	413	231	3190	25	16
	Terry Bradshaw, Pitt, AFC	368	207	2915	28	20
1979	Roger Staubach, Dall, NFC	461	267	3586	27	11
	Dan Fouts, SD, AFC	530	332	4082	24	24
1980	Brian Sipe, Clev, AFC	554	337	4132	30	14
	Ron Jaworski, Phi, NFC	451	257	3529	27	12
1981	Ken Anderson, Cin, AFC	479	300	3754	29	10
	Joe Montana, SF, NFC	488	311	3565	19	12
1982	Ken Anderson, Cin, AFC	309	218	2495	12	9
	Joe Theismann, Wash, NFC	252	161	2033	13	9
1983	Steve Bartkowski, Atl, NFC	432	274	3167	22	5
	Dan Marino, Mia AFC	296	173	2210	20	6
1984	Dan Marino, Mia, AFC	564	362	5084	48	17
	Joe Montana, SF, NFC	432	279	3630	28	10
1985	Ken O'Brien, NY, AFC	488	297	3888	25	8
	Joe Montana, SF, NFC	494	303	3653	27	13
1986	Tommy Kramer, Minn, NFC	372	208	3000	24	10
	Dan Marino, Mia, AFC	623	378	4746	44	23
1987	Joe Montana, SF, NFC	398	266	3054	31	13
	Bernie Kosar, Clev, AFC	389	241	3033	22	9
1988	Boomer Esiason, Cin, AFC	388	223	3572	28	14
	Wade Wilson, Minn, NFC	332	204	2746	15	9
1989	Joe Montana, SF, NFC	386	271	3521	26	8
	Boomer Esiason, Cin, AFC	455	258	3525	28	11
1990	Jim Kelly, Buffalo, AFC	346	219	2829	24	9
	Phil Simms, NY, NFC	311	184	2284	15	4
1991	Steve Young, SF, NFC	279	180	2517	17	8
	Jim Kelly, Buff, AFC	474	304	3844	33	17

*Since 1973, the annual passing leaders have been determined by a passer rating system that compares individual performances to a fixed performance standard.

Passing *(Cont.)*

Year	Player, Team	Att.	Comp	Yards	TD	Int
1992	Steve Young, SF, NFC	402	268	3465	25	7
	Warren Moon, Hou, AFC	346	224	2521	18	12
1993	Steve Young, SF, NFC	462	314	4023	29	16
	John Elway, Den, AFC	551	348	4030	25	10
1994	Steve Young, SF, NFC	461	324	3969	35	10
	Dan Marino, Mia, AFC	615	385	4453	30	17
1995	Brett Favre, GB, NFC	570	359	4413	38	13
	Jeff Blake, Cin, AFC	567	326	3822	28	17
1996	Vinny Testaverde, Balt, AFC	549	325	4177	33	19
	Brett Favre, GB, NFC	543	325	3899	39	13
1997	Steve Young, SF, NFC	356	241	3029	19	6
	Mark Brunell, Jax, AFC	435	264	3281	18	7

Pass Receiving*

Year	Player, Team	No.	Yds	Avg	TD
1932	Ray Flaherty, NY	21	350	16.7	3
1933	John Kelly, Brooklyn	22	246	11.2	3
1934	Joe Carter, Phil	16	238	14.9	4
	Morris Badgro, NY	16	206	12.9	1
1935	Tod Goodwin, NY	26	432	16.6	4
1936	Don Hutson, GB	34	536	15.8	8
1937	Don Hutson, GB	41	552	13.5	7
1938	Gaynell Tinsley, Chi Cards	41	516	12.6	1
1939	Don Hutson, GB	34	846	24.9	6
1940	Don Looney, Phil	58	707	12.2	4
1941	Don Hutson, GB	58	738	12.7	10
1942	Don Hutson, GB	74	1211	16.4	17
1943	Don Hutson, GB	47	776	16.5	11
1944	Don Hutson, GB	58	866	14.9	9
1945	Don Hutson, GB	47	834	17.7	9
1946	Jim Benton, LA	63	981	15.6	6
1947	Jim Keane, Chi	64	910	14.2	10
1948	Tom Fears, LA	51	698	13.7	4
1949	Tom Fears, LA	77	1013	13.2	9
1950	Tom Fears, LA	84	1116	13.3	7
1951	Elroy Hirsch, LA	66	1495	22.7	17
1952	Mac Speedie, Clev	62	911	14.7	5
1953	Pete Pihos, Phil	63	1049	16.7	10
1954	Pete Pihos, Phil	60	872	14.5	10
	Billy Wilson, SF	60	830	13.8	5
1955	Pete Pihos, Phil	62	864	13.9	7
1956	Billy Wilson, SF	60	889	14.8	5
1957	Billy Wilson, SF	52	757	14.6	6
1958	Raymond Berry, Balt	56	794	14.2	9
	Pete Retzlaff, Phil	56	766	13.7	2
1959	Raymond Berry, Balt	66	959	14.5	14
1960	Lionel Taylor, Den, AFL	92	1235	13.4	12
	Raymond Berry, Balt, NFL	74	1298	17.5	10
1961	Lionel Taylor, Den, AFL	100	1176	11.8	4
	Jim Phillips, LA, NFL	78	1092	14.0	5
1962	Lionel Taylor, Den, AFL	77	908	11.8	4
	Bobby Mitchell, Wash, NFL	72	1384	19.2	11
1963	Lionel Taylor, Den, AFL	78	1101	14.1	10
	Bobby Joe Conrad, St. Louis, NFL	73	967	13.2	10
1964	Charley Hennigan, Houston, AFL	101	1546	15.3	8
	Johnny Morris, Chi, NFL	93	1200	12.9	10
1965	Lionel Taylor, Den, AFL	85	1131	13.3	6
	Dave Parks, SF, NFL	80	1344	16.8	12
1966	Lance Alworth, SD, AFL	73	1383	18.9	13
	Charley Taylor, Wash, NFL	72	1119	15.5	12
1967	George Sauer, NY, AFL	75	1189	15.9	6
	Charley Taylor, Wash, NFL	70	990	14.1	9
1968	Clifton McNeil, SF, NFL	71	994	14.0	7
	Lance Alworth, SD, AFL	68	1312	19.3	10
1969	Dan Abramowicz, NO, NFL	73	1015	13.9	7
	Lance Alworth, SD, AFL	64	1003	15.7	4
1970	Dick Gordon, Chi, NFC	71	1026	14.5	13
	Marlin Briscoe, Buff, AFC	57	1036	18.2	8
1971	Fred Biletnikoff, Oak, AFC	61	929	15.2	9
	Bob Tucker, NY, NFC	59	791	13.4	4
1972	Harold Jackson, Phil, NFC	62	1048	16.9	4
	Fred Biletnikoff, Oak, AFC	58	802	13.8	7
1973	Harold Carmichael, Phil, NFC	67	1116	16.7	9
	Fred Willis, Hou, AFC	57	371	6.5	1
1974	Lydell Mitchell, Balt, AFC	72	544	7.6	2
	Charles Young, Phil, NFC	63	696	11.0	3
1975	Chuck Foreman, Minn, NFC	73	691	9.5	9
	Reggie Rucker, Clev, AFC	60	770	12.8	3
	Lydell Mitchell, Balt, AFC	60	544	9.1	4
1976	MacArthur Lane, KC, AFC	66	686	10.4	1
	Drew Pearson, Dall, NFC	58	806	13.9	6
1977	Lydell Mitchell, Balt, AFC	71	620	8.7	4
	Ahmad Rashad, Minn, NFC	51	681	13.4	2
1978	Rickey Young, Minn, NFC	88	704	8.0	5
	Steve Largent, Sea, AFC	71	1168	16.5	8
1979	Joe Washington, Balt, AFC	82	750	9.1	3
	Ahmad Rashad, Minn, NFC	80	1156	14.5	9
1980	Kellen Winslow, SD, AFC	89	1290	14.5	9
	Earl Cooper, SF, NFC	83	567	6.8	4
1981	Kellen Winslow, SD, AFC	88	1075	12.2	10
	Dwight Clark, SF, NFC	85	1105	13.0	4
1982	Dwight Clark, SF, NFC	60	913	15.2	5
	Kellen Winslow, SD, AFC	54	721	13.4	6
1983	Todd Christensen, LA, AFC	92	1247	13.6	12
	Roy Green, StL, NFC	78	1227	15.7	14
	Charlie Brown, Wash, NFC	78	1225	15.7	8
	Earnest Gray, NY, NFC	78	1139	14.6	5
1984	Art Monk, Wash, NFC	106	1372	12.9	7
	Ozzie Newsome, Clev, AFC	89	1001	11.2	5
1985	Roger Craig, SF, NFC	92	1016	11.0	6
	Lionel James, SD, AFC	86	1027	11.9	6
1986	Todd Christensen, LA Rai, AFC	95	1153	12.1	8
	Jerry Rice, SF, NFC	86	1570	18.3	15

*Most catches.

Pass Receiving *(Cont.)*

Year	Player, Team	No.	Yds	Avg	TD
1987	J.T. Smith, StL Card, NFC	91	1117	12.3	8
	Al Toon, NY, AFC	68	976	14.4	5
1988	Al Toon, NY, AFC	93	1067	11.5	5
	Henry Ellard, LA Rams, NFC	86	1414	16.4	10
1989	Sterling Sharpe, GB, NFC	90	1423	15.8	12
	Andre Reed, Buff, AFC	88	1312	14.9	9
1990	Jerry Rice, SF, NFC	100	1502	15.0	13
	Haywood Jeffires, Hou, AFC	74	1048	14.2	8
	Drew Hill, Hou, AFC	74	1019	13.8	5
1991	Haywood Jeffires, Hou, AFC	100	1181	11.8	7
	Michael Irvin, Dall, NFC	93	1523	16.4	8
1992	Sterling Sharpe, GB, NFC	108	1461	13.5	13
	Haywood Jeffires, Hou, AFC	90	913	10.1	9
1993	Sterling Sharpe, GB, NFC	112	1274	11.4	11
	Reggie Langhorne, Ind, AFC	85	1038	12.2	3
1994	Cris Carter, Minn, NFC	122	1256	10.3	7
	Ben Coates, NE, AFC	96	1174	12.2	7
1995	Herman Moore, Det, NFC	123	1686	13.7	14
	Carl Pickens, Cin, AFC	99	1234	12.5	17
1996	Jerry Rice, SF, NFC	108	1254	11.6	8
	Carl Pickens, Cin, AFC	100	1180	11.8	12
1997	Herman Moore, Det, NFC	104	1293	12.4	8
	Tim Brown, Oak, AFC	104	1408	13.5	5

Scoring

Year	Player, Team	TD	FG	PAT	TP
1932	Earl Clark, Portsmouth	6	3	10	55
1933	Ken Strong, NY	6	5	13	64
	Glenn Presnell, Ports	6	6	10	64
1934	Jack Manders, Chi	3	10	31	79
1935	Earl Clark, Det	6	1	16	55
1936	Earl Clark, Det	7	4	19	73
1937	Jack Manders, Chi	5	18	15	69
1938	Clarke Hinkle, GB	7	3	7	58
1939	Andy Farkas, Wash	11	0	2	68
1940	Don Hutson, GB	7	0	15	57
1941	Don Hutson, GB	12	1	20	95
1942	Don Hutson, GB	17	1	33	138
1943	Don Hutson, GB	12	3	36	117
1944	Don Hutson, GB	9	0	31	85
1945	Steve Van Buren, Phil	18	0	2	110
1946	Ted Fritsch, GB	10	9	13	100
1947	Pat Harder, Chicago Cards	7	7	39	102
1948	Pat Harder, Chicago Cards	6	7	53	110
1949	Pat Harder, Chicago Cards	8	3	45	102
	Gene Roberts, NY	17	0	0	102
1950	Doak Walker, Det	11	8	38	128
1951	Elroy Hirsch, LA	17	0	0	102
1952	Gordy Soltau, SF	7	6	34	94
1953	Gordy Soltau, SF	6	10	48	114
1954	Bobby Walston, Phil	11	4	36	114
1955	Doak Walker, Det	7	9	27	96
1956	Bobby Layne, Det	5	12	33	99
1957	Sam Baker, Wash	1	14	29	77
	Lou Groza, Clev	0	15	32	77
1958	Jim Brown, Clev	18	0	0	108
1959	Paul Hornung, GB	7	7	31	94
1960	Paul Hornung, GB, NFL	15	15	41	176
	Gene Mingo, Den, AFL	6	18	33	123
1961	Gino Cappelletti, Bos, AFL	8	17	48	147
	Paul Hornung, GB, NFL	10	15	41	146
1962	Gene Mingo, Den, AFL	4	27	32	137
	Jim Taylor, GB, NFL	19	0	0	114
1963	Gino Cappelletti, Bos, AFL	2	22	35	113
	Don Chandler, NY, NFL	0	18	52	106
1964	Gino Cappelletti, Bos, AFL	7	25	36	155
	Lenny Moore, Balt, NFL	20	0	0	120
1965	Gale Sayers, Chi, NFL	22	0	0	132
	Gino Cappelletti, Bos, AFL	9	17	27	132
1966	Gino Cappelletti, Bos, AFL	6	16	35	119
	Bruce Gossett, LA, NFL	0	28	29	113
1967	Jim Bakken, StL, NFL	0	27	36	117
	George Blanda, Oak, AFL	0	20	56	116
1968	Jim Turner, NY, AFL	0	34	43	145
	Leroy Kelly, Clev, NFL	20	0	0	120
1969	Jim Turner, NY, AFL	0	32	33	129
	Fred Cox, Minn, NFL	0	26	43	121
1970	Fred Cox, Minn, NFC	0	30	35	125
	Jan Stenerud, KC, AFC	0	30	26	116
1971	Garo Yepremian, Mia, AFC	0	28	33	117
	Curt Knight, Wash, NFC	0	29	27	114
1972	Chester Marcol, GB, NFC	0	33	29	128
	Bobby Howfield, NY AFC	0	27	40	121
1973	David Ray, LA, NFC	0	30	40	130
	Roy Gerela, Pitt, AFC	0	29	36	123
1974	Chester Marcol, GB, NFC	0	25	19	94
	Roy Gerela, Pitt, AFC	0	20	33	93
1975	O.J. Simpson, Buff, AFC	23	0	0	138
	Chuck Foreman, Minn, NFC	22	0	0	132
1976	Toni Linhart, Balt, AFC	0	20	49	109
	Mark Moseley, Wash, NFC	0	22	31	97
1977	Errol Mann, Oak, AFC	0	20	39	99
	Walter Payton, Chi, NFC	16	0	0	96
1978	Frank Corral, LA, NFC	0	29	31	118
	Pat Leahy, NY, AFC	0	22	41	107
1979	John Smith, NE, AFC	0	23	46	115
	Mark Moseley, Wash, NFC	0	25	39	114
1980	John Smith, NE, AFC	0	26	51	129
	Ed Murray, Det, NFC	0	27	35	116
1981	Ed Murray, Det, NFC	0	25	46	121
	Rafael Septien, Dall, NFC	0	27	40	121
	Jim Breech, Cin, AFC	0	22	49	115
	Nick Lowery, KC, AFC	0	26	37	115
1982	Marcus Allen, LA, AFC	14	0	0	84
	Wendell Tyler, LA, NFC	13	0	0	78
1983	Mark Moseley, Wash, NFC	0	33	62	161
	Gary Anderson, Pitt, AFC	0	27	38	119
1984	Ray Wersching, SF, NFC	0	25	56	131
	Gary Anderson, Pitt, AFC	0	24	45	117
1985	Kevin Butler, Chi, NFC	0	31	51	144
	Gary Anderson, Pitt, AFC	0	33	40	139

Scoring (Cont.)

Year	Player, Team	TD	FG	PAT	TP	Year	Player, Team	TD	FG	PAT	TP
1986	Tony Franklin, NE, AFC	0	32	44	140	1993	Jeff Jaeger, Rai, AFC	0	35	27	132
	Kevin Butler, Chi, NFC	0	28	36	120		Jason Hanson, Det, NFC	0	34	28	130
1987	Jerry Rice, SF, NFC	23	0	0	138	1994	John Carney, SD, AFC	0	34	33	135
	Jim Breech, Cin, AFC	0	24	25	97		Fuad Reveiz, Minn, NFC	0	34	30	132
1988	Scott Norwood, Buff, AFC	0	32	33	129		Emmitt Smith, Dall, NFC	22	0	0	132
	Mike Cofer, SF, NFC	0	27	40	121	1995	Emmitt Smith, Dall, NFC	25	0	0	150
1989	Mike Cofer, SF, NFC	0	29	49	136		Norm Johnson, Pitt, AFC	0	34	39	141
	David Treadwell, Den, AFC	0	27	39	120	1996	John Kasay, Car, NFC	0	37	34	145
1990	Nick Lowery, KC, AFC	0	34	37	139		Cary Blanchard, Ind, AFC	0	36	27	135
	Chip Lohmiller, Wash, NFC	0	30	41	131	1997	Richie Cunningham,				
1991	Chip Lohmiller, Wash, NFC	0	31	56	149		Dall, NFC	0	34	24	126
	Pete Stoyanovich, Mia, AFC	0	31	28	121		Mike Holl's, Jax, AFC	0	41	31	134
1992	Pete Stoyanovich, Mia, AFC	0	30	34	124						
	Morten Anderson, NO, NFC	0	29	33	120						
	Chip Lohmiller, Wash, NFC	0	30	30	120						

Pro Bowl Alltime Results

Date	Result	Date	Result	Date	Result
1-15-39	NY Giants 13, Pro All-Stars 10	1-13-63	AFL West 21, East 14	1-17-77	AFC 24, NFC 14
1-14-40	Green Bay 16, NFL All-Stars 7	1-13-63	NFL East 30, West 20	1-23-78	NFC 14, AFC 13
12-29-40	Chi Bears 28, NFL All-Stars 14	1-12-64	NFL West 31, East 17	1-29-79	NFC 13, AFC 7
1-4-42	Chi Bears 35, NFL All-Stars 24	1-19-64	AFL West 27, East 24	1-27-80	NFC 37, AFC 27
12-27-42	NFL All-Stars 17, Washington 14	1-10-65	NFL West 34, East 14	2-1-81	NFC 21, AFC 7
1-14-51	A Conf 28, N Conf 27	1-16-65	AFL West 38, East 14	1-31-82	AFC 16, NFC 13
1-12-52	N Conf 30, A Conf 13	1-15-66	AFL All-Stars 30, Buffalo 19	2-6-83	NFC 20, AFC 19
1-10-53	N Conf 27, A Conf 7	1-15-66	NFL East 36, West 7	1-29-84	NFC 45, AFC 3
1-17-54	East 20, West 9	1-21-67	AFL East 30, West 23	1-27-85	AFC 22, NFC 14
1-16-55	West 26, East 19	1-22-67	NFL East 20, West 10	2-2-86	NFC 28, AFC 24
1-15-56	East 31, West 30	1-21-68	AFL East 25, West 24	2-1-87	AFC 10, NFC 6
1-13-57	West 19, East 10	1-21-68	NFL West 38, East 20	2-7-88	AFC 15, NFC 6
1-12-58	West 26, East 7	1-19-69	AFL West 38, East 25	1-29-89	NFC 34, AFC 3
1-11-59	East 28, West 21	1-19-69	NFL West 10, East 7	2-4-90	NFC 27, AFC 21
1-17-60	West 38, East 21	1-17-70	AFL West 26, East 3	2-3-91	AFC 23, NFC 21
1-15-61	West 35, East 31	1-18-70	NFL West 16, East 13	2-2-92	NFC 21, AFC 15
1-7-62	AFL West 47, East 27	1-24-71	NFC 27, AFC 6	2-7-93	AFC 23, NFC 20
1-14-62	NFL West 31, East 30	1-23-72	AFC 26, NFC 13	2-6-94	NFC 17, AFC 3
		1-21-73	AFC 33, NFC 28	2-5-95	AFC 41, NFC 13
		1-20-74	AFC 15, NFC 13	2-4-96	NFC 20, AFC 13
		1-20-75	NFC 17, AFC 10	2-2-97	AFC 26, NFC 23
		1-26-76	NFC 23, AFC 20	2-1-98	AFC 29, NFC 24

The Thinking Man's Coach

The NFL didn't just lose its 10th-winningest coach or the only man to guide a team to four straight Super Bowls when Marv Levy, 72, retired in January 1998 from the Buffalo Bills. It also lost one of the league's few true intellectuals. Levy quoted Byron to his players; in fact, he lifted some of Byron's poem *To Thomas Moore* for his farewell: "Here's a sigh to those who love me, a smile to those who hate. To whatever sky's above me, here's a heart for every fate." When Dallas Cowboys coach Jimmy Johnson gloated after Levy's fourth Super Bowl loss, a 30–13 thrashing at the hands of the Cowboys, that "my players are belly-laughing to *The Flintstones* while he's reading his guys Shakespeare," Levy said, "There should never be any shame in intelligence."

If not the father of special teams, Levy was at least their uncle, having been among the first in pro football to exclusively coach them, when he was an assistant with the Philadelphia Eagles in 1969. In Buffalo he brought unprecedented sophistication to special-teams play. He never met an innovation he didn't like; quarterback Jim Kelly became a genius at running the no-huddle offense because Levy gave him the freedom to try it. For these reasons and a hundred others, it would be a shame if Levy was remembered only because he went 0 for 4 in Super Bowls.

Chicago All-Star Game Results

Date	Result (Attendance)
8-31-34	Chi Bears 0, All-Stars 0 (79,432)
8-29-35	Chi Bears 5, All-Stars 0 (77,450)
9-3-36	All-Stars 7, Detroit 7 (76,000)
9-1-37	All-Stars 6, Green Bay 0 (84,560)
8-31-38	All-Stars 28, Washington 16 (74,250)
8-30-39	NY Giants 9, All-Stars 0 (81,456)
8-29-40	Green Bay 45, All-Stars 28 (84,567)
8-28-41	Chi Bears 37, All-Stars 13 (98,203)
8-28-42	Chi Bears 21, All-Stars 0 (101,100)
8-25-43	All-Stars 27, Washington 7 (48,471)
8-30-44	Chi Bears 24, All-Stars 21 (48,769)
8-30-45	Green Bay 19, All-Stars 7 (92,753)
8-23-46	All-Stars 16, Los Angeles 0 (97,380)
8-22-47	All-Stars 16, Chi Bears 0 (105,840)
8-20-48	Chi Cardinals 28, All-Stars 0 (101,220)
8-12-49	Philadelphia 38, All-Stars 0 (93,780)
8-11-50	All-Stars 17, Philadelphia 7 (88,885)
8-17-51	Cleveland 33, All-Stars 0 (92,180)
8-15-52	Los Angeles 10, All-Stars 7 (88,316)
8-14-53	Detroit 24, All-Stars 10 (93,818)
8-13-54	Detroit 31, All-Stars 6 (93,470)
8-12-55	All-Stars 30, Cleveland 27 (75,000)

Date	Result (Attendance)
8-10-56	Cleveland 26, All-Stars 0 (75,000)
8-9-57	NY Giants 22, All-Stars 12 (75,000)
8-15-58	All-Stars 35, Detroit 19 (70,000)
8-14-59	Baltimore 29, All-Stars 0 (70,000)
8-12-60	Baltimore 32, All-Stars 7 (70,000)
8-4-61	Philadelphia 28, All-Stars 14 (66,000)
8-3-62	Green Bay 42, All-Stars 20 (65,000)
8-2-63	All-Stars 20, Green Bay 17 (65,000)
8-7-64	Chicago 28, All-Stars 17 (65,000)
8-6-65	Cleveland 24, All-Stars 16 (68,000)
8-5-66	Green Bay 38, All-Stars 0 (72,000)
8-4-67	Green Bay 27, All-Stars 0 (70,934)
8-2-68	Green Bay 34, All-Stars 17 (69,917)
8-1-69	NY Jets 26, All-Stars 24 (74,208)
7-31-70	Kansas City 24, All-Stars 3 (69,940)
7-30-71	Baltimore 24, All-Stars 17 (52,289)
7-28-72	Dallas 20, All-Stars 7 (54,162)
7-27-73	Miami 14, All-Stars 3 (54,103)
1974	No game
8-1-75	Pittsburgh 21, All-Stars 14 (54,103)
7-23-76	Pittsburgh 24, All-Stars 0 (52,895)

Alltime Winningest NFL Coaches

Most Career Wins

Coach	Yrs	Teams	Regular Season				Career			
			W	L	T	Pct	W	L	T	Pct
Don Shula	33	Colts, Dolphins	328	156	6	.676	347	173	6	.665
George Halas	40	Bears	318	148	31	.671	324	151	31	.671
Tom Landry	29	Cowboys	250	162	6	.605	270	178	6	.601
Curly Lambeau	33	Packers, Cardinals, Redskins	226	132	22	.624	229	134	22	.623
Chuck Noll	23	Steelers	193	148	1	.566	209	156	1	.572
Chuck Knox	22	Rams, Bills, Seahawks	186	147	1	.558	193	158	1	.550
Paul Brown	21	Browns, Bengals	166	100	6	.621	170	108	6	.609
Bud Grant	18	Vikings	158	96	5	.620	168	108	5	.607
†Dan Reeves	17	Broncos, Giants, Falcons	148	115	1	.559	156	122	1	.561
Marv Levy	17	Chiefs, Bills	143	112	0	.561	154	120	0	.562
Steve Owen	23	Giants	151	100	17	.595	153	108	17	.581
†M. Schottenheimer	14	Browns, Chiefs	138	76	1	.644	143	87	1	.621
Joe Gibbs	12	Redskins	124	60	0	.674	140	65	0	.683
Hank Stram	17	Chiefs, Saints	131	97	10	.571	136	100	10	.573
Weeb Ewbank	20	Colts, Jets	130	129	7	.502	134	130	7	.507
†Bill Parcells	13	Giants, Patriots, Jets	118	88	1	.572	128	93	1	.579
Sid Gillman	18	Rams, Chargers, Oilers	122	99	7	.550	123	104	7	.541
George Allen	12	Rams, Redskins	116	47	5	.705	118	54	5	.681
†Mike Ditka	12	Bears, Saints	112	72	0	.609	118	78	0	.602
Don Coryell	14	Cardinals, Chargers	111	83	1	.572	114	89	1	.561

Top Winning Percentages

	W	L	T	Pct		W	L	T	Pct
George Seifert	108	35	0	.755	George Halas	324	151	31	.671
Vince Lombardi	105	35	6	.740	Don Shula	347	173	6	.665
John Madden	112	39	7	.731	Curly Lambeau	229	134	22	.623
Joe Gibbs	140	65	0	.683	†M. Schottenheimer	143	87	1	.621
George Allen	118	54	5	.681	Bill Walsh	102	63	1	.617

Note: Minimum 100 victories.

†Active coach.

Alltime Number-One Draft Choices

Year	Team	Selection	Position
1936	Philadelphia	Jay Berwanger, Chicago	HB
1937	Philadelphia	Sam Francis, Nebraska	FB
1938	Cleveland	Corbett Davis, Indiana	FB
1939	Chicago Cardinals	Ki Aldrich, Texas Christian	C
1940	Chicago Cardinals	George Cafego, Tennessee	HB
1941	Chicago Bears	Tom Harmon, Michigan	HB
1942	Pittsburgh	Bill Dudley, Virginia	HB
1943	Detroit	Frank Sinkwich, Georgia	HB
1944	Boston	Angelo Bertelli, Notre Dame	QB
1945	Chicago Cardinals	Charley Trippi, Georgia	HB
1946	Boston	Frank Dancewicz, Notre Dame	QB
1947	Chicago Bears	Bob Fenimore, Oklahoma A&M	HB
1948	Washington	Harry Gilmer, Alabama	QB
1949	Philadelphia	Chuck Bednarik, Pennsylvania	C
1950	Detroit	Leon Hart, Notre Dame	E
1951	New York Giants	Kyle Rote, Southern Methodist	HB
1952	Los Angeles	Bill Wade, Vanderbilt	QB
1953	San Francisco	Harry Babcock, Georgia	E
1954	Cleveland	Bobby Garrett, Stanford	QB
1955	Baltimore	George Shaw, Oregon	QB
1956	Pittsburgh	Gary Glick, Colorado A&M	DB
1957	Green Bay	Paul Hornung, Notre Dame	HB
1958	Chicago Cardinals	King Hill, Rice	QB
1959	Green Bay	Randy Duncan, Iowa	QB
1960	Los Angeles	Billy Cannon, Louisiana State	RB
1961	Minnesota	Tommy Mason, Tulane	RB
	Buffalo (AFL)	Ken Rice, Auburn	G
1968	Minnesota	Ron Yary, Southern California	T
1969	Buffalo (AFL)	O.J. Simpson, Southern California	RB
1970	Pittsburgh	Terry Bradshaw, Louisiana Tech	QB
1971	New England	Jim Plunkett, Stanford	QB
1972	Buffalo	Walt Patulski, Notre Dame	DE
1973	Houston	John Matuszak, Tampa	DE
1974	Dallas	Ed Jones, Tennessee State	DE
1975	Atlanta	Steve Bartkowski, California	QB
1976	Tampa Bay	Lee Roy Selmon, Oklahoma	DE
1977	Tampa Bay	Ricky Bell, Southern California	RB
1978	Houston	Earl Campbell, Texas	RB
1979	Buffalo	Tom Cousineau, Ohio State	LB
1980	Detroit	Billy Sims, Oklahoma	RB
1981	New Orleans	George Rogers, South Carolina	RB
1982	New England	Kenneth Sims, Texas	DT
1983	Baltimore	John Elway, Stanford	QB
1984	New England	Irving Fryar, Nebraska	WR
1985	Buffalo	Bruce Smith, Virginia Tech	DE
1986	Tampa Bay	Bo Jackson, Auburn	RB
1987	Tampa Bay	Vinny Testaverde, Miami (FL)	QB
1988	Atlanta	Aundray Bruce, Auburn	LB
1989	Dallas	Troy Aikman, UCLA	QB
1990	Indianapolis	Jeff George, Illinois	QB
1991	Dallas	Russell Maryland, Miami (FL)	DT
1992	Indianapolis	Steve Emtman, Washington	DT
1993	New England	Drew Bledsoe, Washington State	QB
1994	Cincinnati	Dan Wilkinson, Ohio State	DT
1995	Cincinnati	Ki-Jana Carter, Penn State	RB
1996	New York Jets	Keyshawn Johnson, Southern California	WR
1997	St Louis	Orlando Pace, Ohio State	OT
1998	Indianapolis	Peyton Manning, Tennessee	QB

From 1947 through 1958, the first selection in the draft was a bonus pick, awarded to the winner of a random draw. That club, in turn, forfeited its last-round draft choice. The winner of the bonus choice was eliminated from future draws. The system was abolished after 1958, by which time all clubs had received a bonus choice.

Herb Adderley
Lance Alworth
Doug Atkins
Morris (Red) Badgro
Lem Barney
Cliff Battles
Sammy Baugh
Chuck Bednarik
Bert Bell
Bobby Bell
Raymond Berry
Charles W. Bidwill, Sr.
Fred Biletnikoff
George Blanda
Mel Blount
Terry Bradshaw
Jim Brown
Paul Brown
Roosevelt Brown
Willie Brown
Buck Buchanan
Dick Butkus
Earl Campbell
Tony Canadeo
Joe Carr
Guy Chamberlin
Jack Christiansen
Earl (Dutch) Clark
George Connor
Jimmy Conzelman
Lou Creekmur
Larry Csonka
Al Davis
Willie Davis
Len Dawson
Dan Dierdorf
Mike Ditka
Art Donovan
Tony Dorsett
John (Paddy) Driscoll
Bill Dudley
Albert Glen (Turk) Edwards
Weeb Ewbank
Tom Fears
Jim Finks
Ray Flaherty
Len Ford
Dan Fortmann
Dan Fouts
Frank Gatski
Bill George
Joe Gibbs
Frank Gifford
Sid Gillman
Otto Graham
Harold (Red) Grange
Bud Grant
Joe Greene
Forrest Gregg
Bob Griese
Lou Groza
Joe Guyon
George Halas
Jack Ham
John Hannah

Franco Harris
Mike Haynes
Ed Healey
Mel Hein
Ted Hendricks
Wilbur (Pete) Henry
Arnie Herber
Bill Hewitt
Clarke Hinkle
Elroy (Crazylegs) Hirsch
Paul Hornung
Ken Houston
Cal Hubbard
Sam Huff
Lamar Hunt
Don Hutson
Jimmy Johnson
John Henry Johnson
Charlie Joiner
David (Deacon) Jones
Stan Jones
Henry Jordan
Sonny Jurgensen
Leroy Kelly
Walt Kiesling
Frank (Bruiser) Kinard
Paul Krause
Earl (Curly) Lambeau
Jack Lambert
Tom Landry
Dick (Night Train) Lane
Jim Langer
Willie Lanier
Steve Largent
Yale Lary
Dante Lavelli
Bobby Layne
Alphonse (Tuffy) Leemans
Bob Lilly
Larry Little
Vince Lombardi
Sid Luckman
William Roy (Link) Lyman
John Mackey
Tim Mara
Wellington Mara
Gino Marchetti
George Preston Marshall
Ollie Matson
Don Maynard
George McAfee
Mike McCormack
Tommy McDonald
Hugh McElhenny
Johnny (Blood) McNally
Mike Michalske
Wayne Millner
Bobby Mitchell
Ron Mix
Lenny Moore
Marion Motley
Anthony Munoz
George Musso
Bronko Nagurski
Joe Namath

Earle (Greasy) Neale
Ernie Nevers
Ray Nitschke
Chuck Noll
Leo Nomellini
Merlin Olsen
Jim Otto
Steve Owen
Alan Page
Clarence (Ace) Parker
Jim Parker
Walter Payton
Joe Perry
Pete Pihos
Hugh (Shorty) Ray
Dan Reeves
Mel Renfro
John Riggins
Jim Ringo
Andy Robustelli
Art Rooney
Pete Rozelle
Bob St. Clair
Gale Sayers
Joe Schmidt
Tex Schramm
Lee Roy Selmon
Art Shell
Don Shula
O.J. Simpson
Mike Singletary
Jackie Smith
Bart Starr
Roger Staubach
Ernie Stautner
Jan Stenerud
Dwight Stephenson
Ken Strong
Joe Stydahar
Fran Tarkenton
Charley Taylor
Jim Taylor
Jim Thorpe
Y.A. Tittle
George Trafton
Charley Trippi
Emlen Tunnell
Clyde (Bulldog) Turner
Johnny Unitas
Gene Upshaw
Norm Van Brocklin
Steve Van Buren
Doak Walker
Bill Walsh
Paul Warfield
Bob Waterfield
Mike Webster
Arnie Weinmeister
Randy White
Bill Willis
Larry Wilson
Kellen Winslow
Alex Wojciechowicz
Willie Wood

Canadian Football League Grey Cup

Year	Results	Site	Attendance
1909	U of Toronto 26, Parkdale 6	Toronto	3,807
1910	U of Toronto 16, Hamilton Tigers 7	Hamilton	12,000
1911	U of Toronto 14, Toronto 7	Toronto	13,687
1912	Hamilton Alerts 11, Toronto 4	Hamilton	5,337
1913	Hamilton Tigers 44, Parkdale 2	Hamilton	2,100
1914	Toronto 14, U of Toronto 2	Toronto	10,500
1915	Hamilton Tigers 13, Toronto RAA 7	Toronto	2,808
1916-19	No game		
1920	U of Toronto 16, Toronto 3	Toronto	10,088
1921	Toronto 23, Edmonton 0	Toronto	9,558
1922	Queen's U 13, Edmonton 1	Kingston	4,700
1923	Queen's U 54, Regina 0	Toronto	8,629
1924	Queen's U 11, Balmy Beach 3	Toronto	5,978
1925	Ottawa Senators 24, Winnipeg 1	Ottawa	6,900
1926	Ottawa Senators 10, Toronto U 7	Toronto	8,276
1927	Balmy Beach 9, Hamilton Tigers 6	Toronto	13,676
1928	Hamilton Tigers 30, Regina 0	Hamilton	4,767
1929	Hamilton Tigers 14, Regina 3	Hamilton	1,906
1930	Balmy Beach 11, Regina 6	Toronto	3,914
1931	Montreal AAA 22, Regina 0	Montreal	5,112
1932	Hamilton Tigers 25, Regina 6	Hamilton	4,806
1933	Toronto 4, Sarnia 3	Sarnia	2,751
1934	Sarnia 20, Regina 12	Toronto	8,900
1935	Winnipeg 18, Hamilton Tigers 12	Hamilton	6,405
1936	Sarnia 26, Ottawa RR 20	Toronto	5,883
1937	Toronto 4, Winnipeg 3	Toronto	11,522
1938	Toronto 30, Winnipeg 7	Toronto	18,778
1939	Winnipeg 8, Ottawa 7	Ottawa	11,738
1940	Ottawa 12, Balmy Beach 5	Ottawa	1,700
1940	Ottawa 8, Balmy Beach 2	Toronto	4,998
1941	Winnipeg 18, Ottawa 16	Toronto	19,065
1942	Toronto RCAF 8, Winnipeg RCAF 5	Toronto	12,455
1943	Hamilton F Wild 23, Winnipeg RCAF 14	Toronto	16,423
1944	Montreal St H-D Navy 7, Hamilton F Wild 6	Hamilton	3,871
1945	Toronto 35, Winnipeg 0	Toronto	18,660
1946	Toronto 28, Winnipeg 6	Toronto	18,960
1947	Toronto 10, Winnipeg 9	Toronto	18,885
1948	Calgary 12, Ottawa 7	Toronto	20,013
1949	Montreal Als 28, Calgary 15	Toronto	20,087
1950	Toronto 13, Winnipeg 0	Toronto	27,101
1951	Ottawa 21, Saskatchewan 14	Toronto	27,341
1952	Toronto 21, Edmonton 11	Toronto	27,391
1953	Hamilton Ticats 12, Winnipeg 6	Toronto	27,313
1954	Edmonton 26, Montreal 25	Toronto	27,321
1955	Edmonton 34, Montreal 19	Vancouver	39,417
1956	Edmonton 50, Montreal 27	Toronto	27,425
1957	Hamilton 32, Winnipeg 7	Toronto	27,051
1958	Winnipeg 35, Hamilton 28	Vancouver	36,567
1959	Winnipeg 21, Hamilton 7	Toronto	33,133
1960	Ottawa 16, Edmonton 6	Vancouver	38,102
1961	Winnipeg 21, Hamilton 14	Toronto	32,651
1962	Winnipeg 28, Hamilton 27	Toronto	32,655
1963	Hamilton 21, British Columbia 10	Vancouver	36,545
1964	British Columbia 34, Hamilton 24	Toronto	32,655
1965	Hamilton 22, Winnipeg 16	Toronto	32,655
1966	Saskatchewan 29, Ottawa 14	Vancouver	36,553
1967	Hamilton 24, Saskatchewan 1	Ottawa	31,358
1968	Ottawa 24, Calgary 21	Toronto	32,655
1969	Ottawa 29, Saskatchewan 11	Montreal	33,172
1970	Montreal 23, Calgary 10	Toronto	32,669
1971	Calgary 14, Toronto 11	Vancouver	34,484
1972	Hamilton 13, Saskatchewan 10	Hamilton	33,993
1973	Ottawa 22, Edmonton 18	Toronto	36,653
1974	Montreal 20, Edmonton 7	Vancouver	34,450
1975	Edmonton 9, Montreal 8	Calgary	32,454

Canadian Football League Grey Cup (Cont.)

Year	Results	Site	Attendance
1976	Ottawa 23, Saskatchewan 20	Toronto	53,467
1977	Montreal 41, Edmonton 6	Montreal	68,318
1978	Edmonton 20, Montreal 13	Toronto	54,695
1979	Edmonton 17, Montreal 9	Montreal	65,113
1980	Edmonton 48, Hamilton 10	Toronto	54,661
1981	Edmonton 26, Ottawa 23	Montreal	52,478
1982	Edmonton 32, Toronto 16	Toronto	54,741
1983	Toronto 18, British Columbia 17	Vancouver	59,345
1984	Winnipeg 47, Hamilton 17	Edmonton	60,081
1985	British Columbia 37, Hamilton 24	Montreal	56,723
1986	Hamilton 39, Edmonton 15	Vancouver	59,621
1987	Edmonton 38, Toronto 36	Vancouver	59,478
1988	Winnipeg 22, British Columbia 21	Ottawa	50,604
1989	Saskatchewan 43, Hamilton 40	Toronto	54,088
1990	Winnipeg 50, Edmonton 11	Vancouver	46,968
1991	Toronto 36, Calgary 21	Winnipeg	51,985
1992	Calgary 24, Winnipeg 10	Toronto	45,863
1993	Edmonton 33, Winnipeg 23	Calgary	50,035
1994	British Columbia 26, Baltimore 23	Vancouver	55,097
1995	Baltimore 37, Calgary 20	Regina, Saskatchewan	52,564
1996	Toronto 43, Edmonton 37	Hamilton, Ontario	38,595
1997	Toronto 47, Saskatchewan 23	Edmonton	60,431

In 1909, Earl Grey, the Governor-General of Canada, donated a trophy for the Rugby Football Championship of Canada. The trophy, which subsequently became known as the Grey Cup, was originally open only to teams registered with the Canada Rugby Union. Since 1954, it has been awarded to the winner of the Canadian Football League's championship game.

AMERICAN FOOTBALL LEAGUE I

Year	Champion	Record
1926	Philadelphia Quakers	7-2

AMERICAN FOOTBALL LEAGUE II

Year	Champion	Record
1936	Boston Shamrocks	8-3
1937	LA Bulldogs	8-0

AMERICAN FOOTBALL LEAGUE III

Year	Champion	Record
1940	Columbus Bullies	8-1-1
1941	Columbus Bullies	5-1-2

ALL-AMERICAN FOOTBALL CONFERENCE

Year	Championship Game
1946	Cleveland 14, NY Yankees 9
1947	Cleveland 14, NY Yankees 3
1948	Cleveland 49, Buffalo 7
1949	Cleveland 21, San Francisco 7

WORLD FOOTBALL LEAGUE

Year	World Bowl Championship
1974	Birmingham 22, Florida 21
1975	Disbanded midseason

UNITED STATES FOOTBALL LEAGUE

Year	Championship Game
1983	Michigan 24, Philadelphia 22, at Denver
1984	Philadelphia 23, Arizona 3, at Tampa
1985	Baltimore 28, Oakland 24, at East Rutherford

NFL EUROPE

Year	Champion	Record
1992	Sacramento	8-2-0
1995	Frankfurt	6-4-0
1996	Scotland	7-3-0
1997	Barcelona	5-5-0
1998	Rhein	7-3-0

Known as World League of American Football until 1998.

College Football

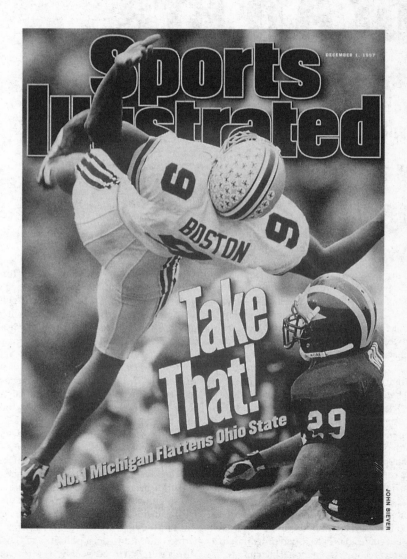

Sports Illustrated

DECEMBER 1, 1997

Take That!

No. 1 Michigan Flattens Ohio State

JOHN BIEVER

The End of An Era

With the expanded bowl alliance set to take hold in 1998, the '97 season was the last for college football's imperfect poll system

BY TIM LAYDEN

SOME WOULD SAY the beauty of college football lies in its imperfection. Power teams are lodged in disparate geographic pockets, scattering allegiances and preventing the type of national focus that drives the NFL on Sundays. The players are unfinished athletes, prone to mistakes and unreliable from week to week. And at the end, on a January morning when the bowl games are over and the polls tallied, the identity of the national champion sometimes remains open to debate. All of this, you either love or hate.

The rules are soon to change. Jumping the millennium by a year, college football will have entered a new era with the 1998 season, flush with the increased possibility of crowning an undisputed champion. The bowl alliance will be refined to include the Rose Bowl, and thus the champions of the Big Ten and the Pac-10 conferences. This move, which should put an end to postseason poll debate, made the 1997 season a perfect close to the age of sweet confusion. Two storied programs, two perfect records, two national champions.

The stalemate developed quite by surprise in the wee hours of Jan. 3. Entering the bowl season, Michigan held a commanding lead over Nebraska and retiring coach Tom Osborne in both the Associated Press media poll and the *USA Today*/ESPN coaches' poll. It seemed certain that the Wolverines needed only to defeat eighth-ranked Washington State in the Rose Bowl—by any margin—to secure their first title in 50 years. However, when Michigan escaped Pasadena with only a 21–16 victory over the Cougars, the door was left slightly ajar. A little more than 24 hours later Nebraska sent Osborne into the sunset with a dominating 42–17 whipping of No. 3 Tennessee. Voila! Dual champions, for the third time in the '90s (Colorado and Georgia Tech in 1990 and Miami [FL] and Washington in '91 were the others).

For Michigan, the championship restored the splendor of traditional greatness that had been eroded in recent years. "The block 'M' in Michigan stands for 'mediocre,'" wrote one Midwestern pundit, and those words were parroted weekly, as Michigan

RICHARD MACKSON

struggled through four consecutive four-loss seasons from 1993 to '96. Following the second of those, in 1994, five-year head coach Gary Moeller was fired after an embarrassing drunken incident at a suburban Detroit restaurant. His replacement was Lloyd Carr, an earnest foot soldier who had apprenticed under both longtime Wolverine coach Bo Schembechler and Moeller. Carr's first two teams went a combined 17–8 and in each of those years gained a measure of satisfaction from the season only by upsetting Ohio State in the teams' annual year-ending grudge match. Mediocre, indeed. In a college football universe overrun with parity, there was little to separate Michigan from many other teams.

But that changed dramatically in the fall of '97. Fueled by a new defense, piloted by an unlikely hero at quarterback and inspired by Carr's relentless, passionate motivation, Michigan was reborn.

Carr gave the season a theme: climbing Everest. He implored his team to attack the season like a mountain climber went after a summit, concentrating fully on each step. To enrich what might otherwise have been a shallow ploy, he brought in Bloomfield Hills, Mich., businessman Lou Kasischke, who had participated in the tragic 1996 Everest expedition chronicled in Jon Krakauer's bestseller *Into Thin Air*. Each player was given an ice axe inscribed with his name and position. "They symbolize our struggle to get to the top, the importance of playing as a

team," said senior tailback Chris Howard.

Michigan reeled off 11 wins against a schedule that included Colorado, Notre Dame, Penn State and Ohio State. The Wolverines' backbone was their defense, an attacking, aggressive scheme devised by first-year defensive coordinator Jim Herrmann. Michigan led the nation in total defense and yielded just 8.9 points per game during the regular season. Like Carr, Herrmann urged his team in ways that can't be taught on the practice field. Most pointedly, he hung a large cardboard key in the defensive meeting room, near a small maize-and-blue box. The key had 12 notches, one for each of the starters and the last for everybody else on the defense. "All of the notches have to be intact or we can't open the door to our season," Herrmann told his unit. "If one notch gets

A lethal two-way threat, Woodson tucked the Heisman away and ran to the NFL.

broken, the key doesn't work." In the box was a fresh rose, a reminder of where the Wolverines' season could end, and each defender had a key to open it.

Carr and Herrmann shared something else: Charles Woodson, the 6'1", 198-pound junior who played defensive back and wide receiver and returned punts. Woodson's excellence and versatility won him the Heisman Trophy in a stirring three-way race with quarterbacks Peyton Manning of Tennessee and Ryan Leaf of Washington State. All Woodson did was intercept seven passes, break up five others, blitz frequently and turn his side of the field into a no-passing zone on defense, while catching 11 passes for 231 yards and two touchdowns on offense. He also brought back 32 punts, including a key 78-yard touchdown romp against Ohio State.

But it was neither Woodson, who would leave for the NFL in April, nor the Michigan defense that won a piece of the national title. That honor belonged to fifth-year senior quarterback Brian Griese. Nearly dropped from the Wolverines' program after a late-night incident two years earlier, Griese steadily, if unspectacularly, guided the Wolverines through the regular season. In the Rose Bowl, however, Pac-10 champion Washington State denied Michigan its running game and challenged Griese. He responded by throwing touchdown passes of 53 and 58 yards to Tai Streets and a game-winning 23-yarder to Jerame Tuman, and was named MVP of the Wolverines' victory. "I've been a college football fan my whole life," he said at a family party after the game. "I've seen Rose Bowls, Orange Bowls; I can name the MVPs. I never thought of myself in that class."

Michigan's players celebrated on the lush Rose Bowl grass that night, certain that a national championship was theirs and theirs alone. One night later and a continent away, Osborne stood in front of his Nebraska team in the belly of Miami's Pro Player Stadium and told them that they could still get a piece of the title. "The door is still open at least a crack," Osborne said. "It's open, and we've got to take advantage."

Any words at all from Osborne would have shaken his players to their souls. It was his last game after 25 years at the helm of a modern college football dynasty. His early teams were an easy target: too big, too slow, too unimaginative to succeed. He didn't win his first national championship until 1994–95, but then he won another the following season, as his Cornhuskers put aside a season of controversy and crushed Florida 62–24 in a performance that ranks with the most devastating in college football history. As he headed into his final game with 254 wins, more than any college coach over the same span, his program's steamroller efficiency was the envy of every coach in the country. But there was one more duty to perform, one more title to win.

Unlike the dominant '94 and '95 teams, or even the '96 squad that was upset early by Arizona State and later by Texas, the Cornhuskers were not expected to be so close to another title. Quarterback Scott Frost, a native Nebraskan who couldn't seem to live up to the legacy of Tommie Frazier, was seen by many as the weak link in an otherwise typical Husker offense. This team needed overtime to secure a controversial victory over Missouri on the first Saturday in November.

In the Orange Bowl, however, Nebraska was a force of nature. Frost, fully developed into a tough, mature option quarterback, pushed the throttle wide open. Junior I-back Ahman Green rushed for 206 yards, and Tennessee, which had beaten Auburn to win the Southeastern Conference championship, was overwhelmed. When Frost scored to put the Cornhuskers ahead 21–3 in the third quarter, Osborne implored his team to score again for the polls. "We've got to score some more points," he screamed on the sideline. After the victory, Nebraska players dared voters not to elect them champions. "If you had to play one game with your job on the line," Frost asked, "who would you rather play, Nebraska or Michigan?" Senior defensive end Grant Wistrom said, "If anybody can honestly find it in their heart not to vote us No. 1, that's their problem."

The issue was resolved by early the next morning, when each team was voted national champion. There is a footnote to Nebraska's third national title—shared or won outright—in four years. After the 1993 season Nebraska lost the national championship game to Florida State only when Byron Bennett's field goal attempt sailed wide left on the final snap of the game. In '96, despite the early loss in the Arizona desert, the Cornhuskers were one game away from playing Florida State for the national title in the Sugar Bowl, when Texas upset them in the inaugural Big 12 championship game, a victory that was secured by a brave, fourth-down pass completion by the Longhorns from deep in their own territory. Think of it this way: It could be argued that Nebraska ended the Osborne era exactly two plays short of five consecutive national championships. That is truly a dynasty.

The shared title reignited the simmering debate over the method college football uses to decide its national champion. Purists embrace the tradition of the bowl system and the seasonlong march to judgment, in which every weekend is precious to a team in the hunt for the title. Yet there remains a public thirst for some type of playoff system, a January Madness built along the lines of the NCAA basketball tournament. Clearly such an event would bring a huge financial windfall to the NCAA, but at a cost. The most meaningful regular season in mainstream American sport would be lost. (Consider: Florida State lost its shot at a national title when it was upset by Florida 32–29 in late November. Under a playoff system, the Seminoles could shrug off such a loss and simply begin preparing for their first-round playoff game.) In any case, the page is turned for '98. The No. 1– and No. 2–ranked teams in the nation will always meet in the ultimate college bowl game. One element of imperfection, however, will remain, that of the polls themselves.

The ranks of contenders for the '97 title was thinned through the customary elimination process. Ohio State, still unable to

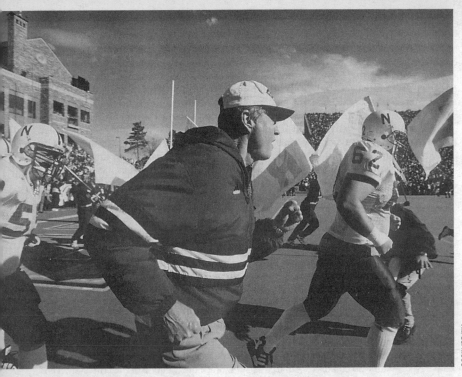

Tom Terrific: Osborne retired with 255 wins and three national titles.

choose between quarterbacks Stanley Jackson and Joe Germaine, was beaten in October at Penn State, which in turn was crushed by Michigan on the second Saturday in November. Later that same day, Florida State ended North Carolina's hopes of winning its first national title in football with a 20–3 pasting that deflated the biggest crowd in Tar Heel history. The Seminoles' run at the crown didn't make it out of November, as Florida won their annual blood match. That victory was the highlight of the season for the defending national champions—who dashed the title hopes of Tennessee and Manning in September—but without '96 Heisman Trophy winner Danny Wuerffel and receivers Ike Hilliard and Reidel Anthony, the Gators subsequently lost at both LSU and Georgia.

In the far West, Washington State beat UCLA on the first Saturday of the season,

37–34, and both developed into teams that were among the best in the country. The Cougars, led by Leaf, reached the Rose Bowl for the first time in 67 years. The game in Pasadena against Michigan might have been a battle for the national title had the Cougars not lost at Arizona State 44–31, on Nov. 1. For their part, the Bruins followed their opening loss with another defeat, at home to Tennessee, but didn't lose again all season, as quarterback Cade McNown engineered a 9–2 record and a Cotton Bowl victory over Texas A&M.

There were surprising performances from Purdue, which went 8–3 in the regular season under first-year coach Joe Tiller, including a 4–0 start in the Big Ten; and from Oklahoma State, which also went 8–3, behind two-way star R.W. McQuarters, the poor man's Woodson. These two teams met in the Alamo Bowl, with Purdue winning the battle of upstarts 33–20. LSU not only beat Florida, but also finished 9–3 and narrowly lost the SEC West title to Auburn.

There were disappointments as well, most of them involving traditional powerhouses. Under first-year coach Bob Davie, who replaced Lou Holtz, Notre Dame started 2–5 but rallied to finish 7–6, including an Independence Bowl loss to LSU. Colorado, which had been picked by some experts to contend for the national title, opened the season with a 27–3 loss at Michigan and never recovered, finishing 5–6 under third-year coach Rick Neuheisel. The most spectacular collapse of all belonged to Texas, once one of the proudest programs in the country. Just one year after head coach John Mackovic seemed to get the Longhorns on solid ground with that Big 12 title game upset of Nebraska, they fell completely apart. The low point, and the game that probably ensured that Mackovic would be fired at the end of the season, was a humiliating 66–3 loss to UCLA at Memorial Stadium in Austin in the second game of the season. Junior running back Ricky Williams, who finished fifth in the Heisman voting, was the lone bright spot in the Lonhorns' dismal season. North Carolina's Mack Brown will coach the team in '98.

Penn State seemed poised not only to contend for the national title, but also to give legendary coach Joe Paterno his 300th career win, a milestone achieved only by Bear Bryant, Pop Warner and Amos Alonzo Stagg. But in addition to losing to Michigan, the Nittany Lions were crushed by Michigan State in the regular-season finale and by Florida in the Florida Citrus Bowl, leaving Paterno with 298 victories at season's end.

The Heisman Trophy race that was eventually won by Woodson was one of the hottest in recent years. It featured not only Woodson, Leaf and Manning, but also

Leaf led the Cougars to their first Rose Bowl appearance in 67 years.

wide receiver Randy Moss of Marshall, a Division I-A neophyte from the Mid-American Conference whose combination of stunning athletic skills and unsteady off-field behavior made him a natural foil to the Big Three.

It was Manning who was practically given the Heisman before the start of the season. The son of a southern football legend, Archie Manning, Peyton had carved a niche in Tennessee history in his first three years as a starter. In the spring of 1997 he was all but promised that the New York Jets would make him the No. 1 pick in the NFL draft. But Manning stunned most people by

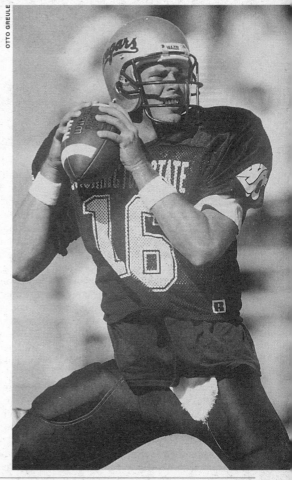

OTTO GREULE

DAVID E. KLUTHO

the televised ceremony, by beating out a trio of talented running backs: Williams of Texas, Curtis Enis of Penn State and the Cornhuskers' Green. Williams, given the nickname "Little Earl," for his resemblance to former Texas star Earl Campbell, led the nation with a school-record 1,893 yards and 25 rushing touchdowns. He will enter 1998 as the leading Heisman candidate and needs only 289 yards to break Campbell's Texas career record. ("After that," said Williams, "He's Little Ricky.") Green and Enis each made himself available for the NFL draft, and each

returning to Tennessee and, despite the disappointing loss to Florida (Manning went 0–4 in his career against Gators coach Steve Spurrier, who once recruited him), put together a brilliant final college season and won the conference title that had eluded his father. He left in possession of 33 school and two NCAA passing records.

Yet even as Manning piled up numbers and victories, his status as the top quarterback—never mind the top player—in the college game was challenged. Leaf, Washington State's 6' 5", 240-pound gunslinger, caught the attention of pro scouts and fans alike. Leaf threw for 3,637 yards and 33 touchdowns and led the Cougars to the Rose Bowl with his unique brand of confidence and bravado.

Those latter two qualities bring to mind Moss, a cocky, gifted 6' 3" wide receiver who might have gone to Notre Dame and did briefly go to Florida State, but wound up at Marshall because of discipline problems. Moss finished fourth in the Heisman voting, and earned a trip to New York for

was drafted, Enis by the Chicago Bears as the fifth pick of the draft and Green by the Seattle Seahawks in the third round.

Heisman-worthy talent wasn't limited to offense. Ohio State sophomore Andy Katzenmoyer emerged as one of the most dominant players in the game without touching the ball on offense (though he did play blocking back in certain goal line situations), and won the Butkus Award as the nation's top linebacker. Florida State senior defensive lineman Andre Wadsworth symbolized the possibilities of the college game. A 6' 2", 217-pound walk-on in the fall of 1992, Wadsworth grew to 6' 4", 282, and was the third player selected in the NFL draft. But neither Katzenmoyer nor Wadsworth was more remarkable than Arizona State's Pat Tillman, a 5' 11", 195-pound linebacker who through sheer hard work and aggression became the Pac-10's defensive player of the year. It would be hard to find a more appropriate poster boy for a season defined by imperfection, framed by passion.

Final Polls

Associated Press

		Record	Pts	Head Coach	SI Preseason Rank
1.	Michigan (51½)	12–0	1731½	Lloyd Carr	18
2.	Nebraska (18½)	13–0	1698½	Tom Osborne	8
3.	Florida St	11–1	1599	Bobby Bowden	6
4.	Florida	10–2	1455	Steve Spurrier	4
5.	UCLA	10–2	1413	Bob Toledo	23
6.	North Carolina	11–1	1397	Mack Brown	7
7.	Tennessee	11–2	1320	Phillip Fulmer	2
8.	Kansas St	11–1	1302	Bill Snyder	27
9.	Washington St	10–2	1259	Mike Price	38
10.	Georgia	10–2	1121	Jim Donnan	36
11.	Auburn	10–3	1025	Terry Bowden	20
12.	Ohio St	10–3	975	John Cooper	11
13.	Louisiana St	9–3	856	Gerry DiNardo	10
14.	Arizona St	8–3	773	Bruce Snyder	35
15.	Purdue	9–3	715	Joe Tiller	70
16.	Penn St	9–3	706	Joe Paterno	1
17.	Colorado St	11–2	673	Sonny Lubick	25
18.	Washington	8–4	617	Jim Lambright	3
19.	Southern Mississippi	9–3	490	Jeff Bower	48
20.	Texas A&M	9–4	421	R. C. Slocum	30
21.	Syracuse	9–4	331	Paul Pasqualoni	17
22.	Mississippi	8–4	255	Tommy Tuberville	71
23.	Missouri	7–5	175	Larry Smith	56
24.	Oklahoma St	8–4	72	Bob Simmons	63
25.	Georgia Tech	7–5	64	George O'Leary	33

Note: As voted by a panel of 70 sportswriters and broadcasters following bowl games (1st-place votes in parentheses).

USA Today/ESPN

		Pts	Prev Rank			Pts	Prev Rank
1.	Nebraska	1520 (32)	2	14.	Arizona St	667	18
2.	Michigan	1516 (30)	1	15.	Purdue	666	16
3.	Florida St	1414	4	16.	Colorado St	646	17
4.	N Carolina	1292	5	17.	Penn St	585	12
5.	UCLA	1239	6	18.	Washington	512	23
6.	Florida	1209	8	19.	Southern Mississ	462	22
7.	Kansas St	1192	9	20.	Syracuse	380	14
8.	Tennessee	1122	3	21.	Texas A&M	359	19
9.	Washington St	1076	7	22.	Mississippi	188	—
10.	Georgia	1007	11	23.	Missouri	114	20
11.	Auburn	854	13	24.	Oklahoma St	103	24
12.	Ohio St	826	10	25.	Air Force	74	21
13.	Louisiana St	786	15				

Note: As voted by a panel of 62 Division I-A head coaches; 25 points for 1st, 24 for 2nd, etc. (1st-place votes in parentheses).

Bowls and Playoffs

NCAA Division I-A Bowl Results

Date	Bowl	Result	Payout/Team ($)	Attendance
12-20-97	Las Vegas	Oregon 41, Air Force 13	800,000	21,514
12-25-97	Aloha	Washington 51, Michigan St 23	750,000	44,598
12-26-96	Motor City	Mississippi 34, Marshall 31	750,000	43,340
12-27-97	Insight. com	Arizona 20, New Mexico 14	750,000	49,385
12-28-97	Independence	Louisiana St 27, Notre Dame 9	800,000	50,549
12-29-97	Humanitarian	Cincinnati 35, Utah St 19	750,000	16,131
12-29-97	Carquest	Georgia Tech 35, W Virginia 30	750,000	28,262
12-29-97	Holiday	Colorado St 35, Missouri 24	1.35 million	50,761

NCAA Division I-A Bowl Results (*Cont.*)

Date	Bowl	Result	Payout/Team ($)	Attendance
12-31-97	Liberty	Southern Mississippi 41, Pittsburgh 7	800,000	50,209
12-31-97	Fiesta	Kansas St 35, Syracuse 18	8.225 million	65,106
1-1-98	Outback	Georgia 33, Wisconsin 6	1.65 million	56,186
1-1-98	Gator	N Carolina 42, Virginia Tech 3	1.3 million	54,116
1-1-98	Florida Citrus	Florida 21, Penn St 6	3.5 million	72,940
1-1-98	Cotton	UCLA 29, Texas A&M 23	2.5 million	59,215
1-1-98	Rose	Michigan 21, Washington St 16	9.5 million	101,219
1-1-98	Sugar	Florida St 31, Ohio St 14	8.225 million	67,289
1-2-98	Peach	Auburn 21, Clemson 17	1.5 million	71,212
1-2-98	Orange	Nebraska 42, Tennessee 17	8.475 million	72,385

NCAA Division I-AA Championship Boxscore

Youngstown St	0	3	0	7—10
McNeese St	3	0	6	0— 9

FIRST QUARTER
McNeese St: FG LaFrenz 22, 9:30.

SECOND QUARTER
Youngstown St: FG Mark Griffith 21, 12:41.

THIRD QUARTER
McNeese St: FG LaFrenz 37, 6:52.
McNeese St: FG LaFrenz 46, 14:09.

FOURTH QUARTER
Youngstown St: Ray 9 pass from Tidwell (Griffith kick), 6:52.

	Youngstown St	McNeese St
First downs	12	11
Rushing yardage	73	58
Passing yardage	127	143
Return yardage	42	23
Passes (comp-att-int)	12-21-0	14-28-1
Punts (no.–avg)	9-33.1	5-36.6
Fumbles (no.–lost)	0–0	0–0
Penalties (no.–yards)	3–20	3–35

Att: 14,771.

Small College Championship Summaries

NCAA DIVISION II

First round: New Haven 47, Glenville St 7; Slippery Rock 30, Ashland 20; NW Missouri St 39, N Dakota St 28; Northern Colorado 24, Pittsburgh St 16; Carson-Newman 21, N Alabama 7; Albany St (GA) 10, Southern Arkansas 0; UC-Davis 37, Texas A&M-Kingsville 33; Angelo St 46, Western St 12.
Quarterfinals: UC-Davis 50, Angelo St 33; New Haven 49, Slippery Rock 21; Northern Colorado 35, NW Missouri St 19; Carson-Newman 23, Albany St 22.
Semifinals: New Haven 27, UC-Davis 25; Northern Colorado 30, Carson-Newman 29.

Championship: 12-13-97 Florence, AL

New Haven	0	0	0	0— 0
Northern Colorado	14	21	2	14—51

NCAA DIVISION III

First round: Mount Union 34, Allegheny 20; John Carroll 30, Hanover 20; Lycoming 27, Western Maryland 13; Trinity (TX) 44, Catholic 33; Rowan 43, Coast Guard 0; College of New Jersey 34, Cortland St 30; Augsburg 34, Concordia-Moorhead 22.
Quarterfinals: Mount Union 59, John Carroll 7; Simpson 61, Augsburg 21; Lycoming 46, Trinity 26; Rowan 13, College of New Jersey 7.
Semifinals: Mount Union 54, Simpson 7; Lycoming 28, Rowan 20.

Championship: 12-6-97 Salem, VA

Lycoming	0	6	0	6—12
Mount Union	14	14	21	12—61

NAIA PLAYOFFS

First round: Geneva (PA) 34, Cambellsville (KY) 14; Findlay (OH) 40, Westminster (PA) 0; Evangel (MO) 46, McKendree (ILL) 6; Doane (NB) 53, Southwestern (KS) 28; Sioux Falls (SD) 57, Ottawa (KS) 14; Jamestown (ND) 55, Benedictine (KS) 30; Montana Tech 51, Minnesota-Crookston 10; Willamette (OR) 26, Western Oregon 20 (ot).
Quarterfinals: Findlay 28, Geneva 7; Doane 28, Evangel 20; Sioux Falls 29, Jamestown 6; Willamette 17, Montana Tech 24.
Semifinals: Findlay 26, Doane 25; Willamette 17, Sioux Falls 7

Championship: 12-13-97 Hardin County, TN

Willamette	0	7	0	0— 7
Findlay	0	7	7	0—14

Awards

Heisman Memorial Trophy

Player, School	Class	Pos	1st	2nd	3rd	Total
Charles Woodson, Michigan	Jr	DB	433	209	98	1815
Peyton Manning, Tennessee	Sr	QB	281	263	174	1543
Ryan Leaf, Washington St	Jr	QB	70	205	241	861
Randy Moss, Marshall	Jr	WR	17	56	90	253
Ricky Williams, Texas	Jr	RB	4	31	61	135
Curtis Enis, Penn St	Jr	TB	3	18	20	65
Tim Dwight, Iowa	Sr	KR	5	3	11	32
Cade McNown, UCLA	Jr	QB	0	7	12	26
Tim Couch, Kentucky	Sr	QB	0	5	12	22
Amos Zereoue, W Virginia	So	RB	3	1	10	21

Note: Former Heisman winners and the media vote, with ballots allowing for three names (3 points for 1st, 2 for 2nd, 1 for 3rd).

Offensive Players of the Year

Maxwell Award (Player) ....Peyton Manning, Tennessee, QB
Walter Camp Player of the Year (Back) .....Charles Woodson, Michigan, CB
Davey O'Brien Award (QB) ....Peyton Manning, Tennessee, QB
Doak Walker Award (RB) ....Ricky Williams, Texas, RB
Biletnikoff Award (WR) ....Randy Moss, Marshall, WR

Other Awards

Vince Lombardi/Rotary Award (Lineman) ...Grant Wistrom, Nebraska, DE
Outland Trophy (Interior lineman) ....Aaron Taylor, Nebraska, OG
Butkus Award (Linebacker) ....Andy Katzenmoyer, Ohio St, LB
Jim Thorpe Award (Defensive back) ....Charles Woodson, Michigan, CB
Sporting News Player of the Year ....Charles Woodson, Michigan, CB/WR
Walter Payton Award (Div I-AA Player) ......Brian Finneran, Villanova, WR
Harlon Hill Trophy (Div II Player) ....Irvin Sigler, Bloomsburg, RB

Coaches' Awards

Walter Camp Award ....Lloyd Carr, Michigan
Eddie Robinson Award (Div I-AA) ....Mike Price, Washington St
Bobby Dodd Award ....Mike Price, Washington St
Bear Bryant Award ....Lloyd Carr, Michigan

AFCA COACHES OF THE YEAR

Division I-A ....Lloyd Carr, Michigan
Division I-AA ....Andy Talley, Villanova
Division II and NAIA Division I....................Joe Glenn, Northern Colorado
Division III and NAIA Division II.................Larry Kehres, Mount Union

Football Writers Association of America All-America Team

OFFENSE		DEFENSE	
Randy Moss, Marshall, So	Wide receiver	Grant Wistrom, Nebraska, Sr	DL
Jacquez Green, Florida, Jr	Wide receiver	Lamanzer Williams, Minnesota, Sr	DL
Aaron Taylor, Nebraska, Sr	OL	Jason Peter, Nebraska, Sr	DL
Kyle Turley, San Diego St, Sr	OL	Jeremy Staat, Arizona St, Sr	DL
Chad Overhauser, UCLA, Sr	OL	Sam Cowart, Florida St, Sr	Linebacker
Alan Feneca, Louisiana St, Sr	OL	Andy Katzenmoyer, Ohio St, So	Linebacker
Ben Fricke, Houston, Sr	Center	Jamie Duncan, Vanderbilt, Sr	Linebacker
Peyton Manning, Tennessee, Sr	Quarterback	Brian Lee, Wyoming, Sr	Defensive back
Alonzo Mayes, Oklahoma St, Sr	Tight end	Antoine Winfield, Ohio St, Jr	Defensive back
Ricky Williams, Texas, Jr	Running back	Dre' Bly, N Carolina, So	Defensive back
Curtis Enis, Penn St, Jr	Running back	Charles Woodson, Michigan, Jr	Defensive back
Martin Gramatica, Kansas St, Jr	Placekicker	Chris Sailer, UCLA, Jr	Punter
Tim Dwight, Iowa, Sr	Kick returner		

1997 NCAA Conference Standings

Division I-A

ATLANTIC COAST CONFERENCE

	Conference		Full Season		
	W	L	W	L	Pct
Florida St	8	0	11	1	.917
N Carolina	7	1	11	1	.917
Virginia	5	3	7	4	.636
Georgia Tech	5	3	7	5	.583
Clemson	4	4	7	5	.583
N Carolina St	3	5	6	5	.545
Wake Forest	3	5	5	6	.454
Maryland	1	7	2	9	.182
Duke	0	8	2	9	.182

BIG EAST CONFERENCE

	Conference		Full Season		
	W	L	W	L	Pct
Syracuse	6	1	9	4	.692
Virginia Tech	5	2	7	5	.583
W Virginia	4	3	7	5	.583
Pittsburgh	4	3	6	5	.545
Miami (FL)	3	4	5	6	.454
Boston College	3	4	4	7	.364
Temple	3	4	3	8	.273
Rutgers	0	7	0	11	.000

BIG TEN CONFERENCE

	Conference		Full Season		
	W	L	W	L	Pct
Michigan	8	0	12	0	1.000
Ohio St	6	2	10	3	.770
Penn St	6	2	9	3	.750
Purdue	6	2	9	3	.750
Wisconsin	5	3	8	5	.615
Iowa	4	4	7	5	.583
Michigan St	4	4	7	5	.583
Northwestern	3	5	5	7	.417
Minnesota	1	7	3	9	.250
Indiana	1	7	2	9	.182
Illinois	0	8	0	11	.000

BIG 12 CONFERENCE

	Conference		Full Season		
NORTH	W	L	W	L	Pct
*Nebraska	9	0	13	0	1.000
Kansas St	7	1	11	1	.917
Missouri	5	3	7	5	.583
Colorado	3	5	5	6	.455
Kansas	3	5	5	6	.455
Iowa St	1	7	1	10	.090
SOUTH					
*Texas A&M	6	3	9	4	.692
Oklahoma St	5	3	8	4	.667
Texas Tech	5	3	6	5	.546
Texas	2	6	4	7	.364
Oklahoma	2	6	4	8	.333
Baylor	1	7	2	9	.182

*Full season record includes Big 12 Championship Game in which Nebraska defeated Texas A&M 54–15, on Dec. 6.

BIG WEST CONFERENCE

	Conference		Full Season		
	W	L	W	L	Pct
Utah St	4	1	6	6	.500
Nevada	4	1	5	6	.455
Boise St	3	2	4	7	.364
Idaho	2	3	5	6	.455
N Texas	2	3	4	7	.364
New Mexico St	0	5	2	9	.182

Division I-A (Cont.)

CONFERENCE USA

	Conference		Full Season		
	W	L	W	L	Pct
Southern Mississippi	6	0	9	3	.750
Tulane	5	1	7	4	.636
E Carolina	4	2	5	6	.455
Cincinnati	2	4	8	4	.666
Memphis	2	4	4	7	.364
Houston	2	4	3	8	.273
Louisville	0	6	1	10	.090

MID-AMERICAN ATHLETIC CONFERENCE

	Conference		Full Season		
EAST	W	L	W	L	Pct
*Marshall	8	1	10	3	.770
Miami (OH)	6	2	8	3	.727
Ohio	6	2	8	3	.727
Bowling Green	3	5	3	8	.273
Kent	3	5	3	8	.273
Akron	2	7	2	9	.182
WEST					
*Toledo	7	2	9	3	.750
Western Michigan	6	2	8	3	.727
Ball St	4	4	5	6	.455
Eastern Michigan	4	5	4	7	.364
Central Michigan	1	7	2	9	.182
Northern Illinois	0	8	0	11	.000

*Full season record includes MAC Championship Game in which Marshall defeated Toledo 34–14, on Dec. 5.

PACIFIC-10 CONFERENCE

	Conference		Full Season		
	W	L	W	L	Pct
Washington St	7	1	10	2	.833
UCLA	7	1	10	2	.833
Arizona St	6	2	9	3	.750
Washington	5	3	8	4	.666
Arizona	4	4	7	5	.583
Southern Cal	4	4	6	5	.545
Oregon	3	5	7	5	.583
Stanford	3	5	5	6	.455
California	1	7	3	8	.273
Oregon St	0	8	3	8	.273

SOUTHEASTERN CONFERENCE

	Conference		Full Season		
EAST	W	L	W	L	Pct
*Tennessee	8	1	11	2	.846
Florida	6	2	10	2	.833
Georgia	6	2	10	2	.833
S Carolina	3	5	5	6	.455
Kentucky	2	6	5	6	.455
Vanderbilt	0	8	3	8	.273
WEST					
Louisiana St	6	2	9	3	.750
*Auburn	6	3	10	3	.769
Mississippi	4	4	8	4	.666
Mississippi St	4	4	7	4	.636
Alabama	2	6	4	7	.364
Arkansas	2	6	4	7	.364

*Full season record includes SEC Championship Game in which Tennessee defeated Auburn 30–29, on Dec. 6.

Division I-A (Cont.)

WESTERN ATHLETIC CONFERENCE

	Conference		Full Season		
PACIFIC	**W**	**L**	**W**	**L**	**Pct**
*Colorado St	8	1	11	2	.846
Air Force	6	2	10	3	.769
Fresno St	5	3	6	6	.500
Wyoming	4	4	7	6	.538
San Diego St	4	4	5	7	.417
San Jose St	4	4	4	7	.364
UNLV	2	6	3	8	.273
Hawaii	1	7	3	9	.250
MOUNTAIN					
*New Mexico	6	3	9	4	.692
Rice	5	3	7	4	.636
Southern Methodist	5	3	6	5	.545
Utah	5	3	6	5	.545
Brigham Young	4	4	6	5	.545
UTEP	3	5	4	7	.571
Tulsa	2	6	2	9	.182
Texas Christian	1	7	1	10	.090

*Full season record includes WAC Championship Game in which Colorado St defeated New Mexico 41–13, on Dec. 6.

INDEPENDENTS

	Full Season		
	W	**L**	**Pct**
Louisiana Tech	9	2	.818
Navy	7	4	.636
Notre Dame	7	5	.583
AL-Birmingham	5	6	.455
Central Florida	5	6	.455
NE Louisiana	5	7	.416
Army	4	7	.364
Arkansas St	2	9	.182
SW Louisiana	1	10	.090

Division I-AA

BIG SKY CONFERENCE

	Conference		Full Season		
	W	**L**	**W**	**L**	**Pct**
Eastern Washington	7	1	12	1	.923
Montana	6	2	8	4	.750
Montana St	5	3	6	5	.545
Northern Arizona	4	4	6	5	.545
Weber St	4	4	6	5	.545
Cal St-Northridge	4	4	6	6	.500
*Portland St	3	5	4	7	.364
Idaho St	2	6	3	8	.273
Cal St-Sacramento	1	7	1	10	.090

*Portland State is in Division II and not eligible for a league title.

GATEWAY COLLEGIATE ATHLETIC CONFERENCE

	Conference		Full Season		
	W	**L**	**W**	**L**	**Pct**
Western Illinois	6	0	11	2	.846
Northern Iowa	5	1	7	4	.636
Youngstown St	4	2	11	2	.846
SW Missouri St	3	3	5	6	.455
Indiana St	2	4	3	8	.273
Southern Illinois	1	5	3	8	.273
Illinois St	0	6	2	9	.182

Division I-AA *(Cont.)*

IVY GROUP

	Conference		Full Season		
	W	L	W	L	Pct
Harvard	7	0	9	1	.900
Dartmouth	6	1	8	2	.800
Pennsylvania	5	2	6	4	.600
Brown	3	4	6	4	.600
Cornell	3	4	5	5	.500
Princeton	2	5	5	5	.500
Columbia	2	5	3	7	.300
Yale	0	7	1	9	.100

METRO ATLANTIC ATHLETIC CONFERENCE

	Conference		Full Season		
	W	L	W	L	Pct
Georgetown	7	0	8	3	.727
Duquesne	6	1	7	3	.700
Fairfield	4	3	7	3	.700
Siena	4	3	6	3	.666
Marist	4	3	6	4	.600
Canisius	2	5	4	6	.400
St. Peter's	1	6	1	9	.100
*St. John's	—	—	8	3	.727
Iona	0	7	0	10	.000

*St. John's was not eligible for the league title.

PIONEER FOOTBALL LEAGUE

	Conference		Full Season		
	W	L	W	L	Pct
Dayton	5	0	9	1	.900
San Diego	4	1	8	3	.727
Drake	2	3	8	3	.727
Butler	2	3	6	4	.600
Valparaiso	2	3	3	7	.300
Evansville	0	5	2	8	.200

SOUTHERN CONFERENCE

	Conference		Full Season		
	W	L	W	L	Pct
Georgia Southern	7	1	10	3	.769
Appalachian St	6	2	7	4	.636
E Tennessee St	5	3	7	4	.636
Furman	5	3	7	4	.636
TN-Chattanooga	4	4	7	4	.636
The Citadel	4	4	6	5	.545
Western Carolina	3	5	3	8	.273
Wofford	2	6	3	7	.300
Virginia Military	0	8	0	11	.000

SOUTHLAND CONFERENCE

	Conference		Full Season		
	W	L	W	L	Pct
McNeese St	6	1	12	1	.923
Northwestern St	6	1	8	4	.666
Stephen F. Austin St	5	2	8	3	.727
Nicholls St	3	4	5	6	.455
Sam Houston St	3	4	5	6	.455
SW Texas St	2	5	5	6	.455
Troy St	2	5	5	6	.455
Jacksonville St	1	6	1	10	.090

Division I-AA *(Cont.)*

SOUTHWESTERN

	Conference		Full Season		
	W	L	W	L	Pct
Southern	8	0	10	1	.909
Jackson St	7	1	9	2	.818
*AR-Pine Bluff	6	2	8	3	.727
Texas Southern	4	4	5	6	.455
Alcorn St	4	4	4	7	.364
Mississippi Valley St	3	5	4	6	.400
Alabama St	2	6	3	8	.273
Grambling	2	6	3	8	.273
Prairie View	0	8	0	9	.000

*Arkansas-Pine Bluff was not eligible for the league title.

ATLANTIC TEN

	Conference		Full Season		
NEW ENGLAND	W	L	W	L	Pct
New Hampshire	5	3	5	6	.455
Connecticut	4	4	7	4	.636
Maine	4	4	5	6	.455
Rhode Island	2	6	2	9	.182
Massachusetts	1	7	2	9	.182
Boston University	1	7	1	10	.090
MID ATLANTIC					
Villanova	8	0	12	1	.923
Delaware	7	1	12	1	.923
Northeastern	5	3	8	3	.727
William & Mary	4	4	7	4	.636
Richmond	4	4	6	5	.545
James Madison	3	5	5	6	.455

INDEPENDENTS

	Full Season		
	W	L	Pct
Cal Poly-San Luis Obispo	10	1	.909
Western Kentucky	10	2	.833
Liberty	9	2	.818
Hofstra	9	3	.750
Morehead St	7	3	.700
Elon College	7	4	.636
Samford	7	4	.636
S Florida	5	6	.455
Southern Utah	5	6	.455
St. Mary's	4	6	.400
Norfolk St	3	7	.300
Buffalo	2	9	.182
Davidson	2	9	.182
La Salle	1	8	.111
Charleston Southern	1	9	.100
Austin Peay	0	10	.000

Division I-A

SCORING

	Class	GP	TD	XP	FG	Pts	Pts/Game
Ricky Williams, Texas	Jr	11	25	2	0	152	13.82
Skip Hicks, UCLA	Sr	11	25	0	0	150	13.64
Travis Prentice, Miami (OH)	So	11	25	0	0	150	13.64
Randy Moss, Marshall	So	12	25	2	0	152	12.67
Curtis Enis, Penn St	Jr	11	20	2	0	122	11.09
Ahman Green, Nebraska	Jr	12	22	0	0	132	11.00
Chris McCoy, Navy	Sr	11	20	0	0	120	10.91
Tavian Banks, Iowa	Sr	11	19	0	0	114	10.36
Chris Lemon, Nevada	Jr	11	19	0	0	114	10.36
Eugene Baker, Kent	Jr	11	18	0	0	110	10.00

FIELD GOALS

	Class	GP	FGA	FG	Pct	FG/Game
Brad Palazzo, Tulane	Jr	11	28	23	.821	2.09
Colby Carson, New Mexico	Sr	12	30	21	.700	1.75
Martin Gramatica, Kansas St	Jr	11	20	19	.950	1.73
Shayne Graham, Virginia Tech	So	11	23	19	.826	1.73
Chris Sailer, UCLA	Jr	11	24	19	.792	1.73
Brian Gowins, Northwestern	Sr	12	27	20	.741	1.67
Kris Brown, Nebraska	Jr	12	21	18	.857	1.50
Kyle Bryant, Texas A&M	Sr	12	22	18	.818	1.50

TOTAL OFFENSE

			Rushing		Passing		Total Offense			
	Class	GP	Car	Net	Att	Yds	Yds	Yds/Play	TDR*	Yds/Game
Tim Rattay, Louisiana Tech	So	11	64	87	477	3881	3968	7.33	35	360.73
Tim Couch, Kentucky	Sr	11	66	-125	547	3884	3759	6.13	40	341.73
Ryan Leaf, Washington St	Sr	11	72	-54	375	3637	3583	8.02	39	325.73
Daunte Culpepper, Central Fla	Fr	12	136	438	381	3086	3524	6.82	30	320.36
John Dutton, Nevada	Sr	11	44	-4	367	3526	3522	8.57	21	320.18
Peyton Manning, Tennessee	Sr	12	49	-30	477	3819	3789	7.20	39	315.75
Charlie Batch, Eastern Mich	Sr	11	85	110	434	3280	3390	6.53	24	308.18
Thad Busby, Florida St	Jr	11	57	-16	390	3317	3301	7.38	27	300.09
Jose Davis, Kent	Sr	11	50	176	365	2707	2883	6.95	35	288.30
Jon Denton, UNLV	Sr	14	64	5	374	2586	2591	5.92	21	287.89
Chad Pennington, Marshall	Sr	14	55	-59	428	3480	3421	7.08	40	285.08
Billy Dicken, Purdue	Sr	14	89	308	373	2811	3119	6.75	24	283.55

*Touchdowns responsible for are TDs scored and passed for.

RUSHING

	Class	GP	Car	Yds	Avg	TD	Yds/Game
Ricky Williams, Texas	Jr	11	279	1893	6.8	25	172.09
Ahman Green, Nebraska	Jr	12	278	1877	6.8	22	156.42
Amos Zereoue, W Virginia	So	10	264	1505	5.7	16	150.50
Tavion Banks, Iowa	Sr	11	246	1639	6.7	17	149.00
Ron Dayne, Wisconsin	So	10	249	1421	5.7	15	142.10
Travis Prentice, Miami (OH)	So	11	296	1549	5.2	25	140.82
Dwayne Harris, Toledo	Jr	10	254	1278	5.0	10	127.80
Kevin Faulk, Louisiana St	Jr	9	205	1144	5.6	15	127.11
Demond Parker, Oklahoma	So	9	194	1143	5.9	6	127.00
Chris McCoy, Navy	Sr	11	246	1370	5.6	20	124.55
Curtis Enis, Penn St	Jr	11	228	1363	6.0	19	123.91

Division I-A (Cont.)

PASSING EFFICIENCY

	Class	GP	Att	Comp	Pct Comp	Yds	Yds/Att	TD	Int	Rating Pts
Cade McNown, UCLA	Jr	11	283	173	61.13	2877	10.17	22	5	168.6
Ryan Leaf, Washington St	Jr	11	375	210	56.00	3637	9.70	33	10	161.2
Joe Germaine, Ohio St	Sr	12	184	119	64.67	1674	9.10	15	7	160.4
John Dutton, Nevada	Sr	11	367	255	61.31	3526	9.61	20	6	156.7
Brock Huard, Washington	So	10	244	146	59.84	2140	8.77	23	10	156.4
Mike Bobo, Georgia	Sr	11	306	199	65.03	2751	8.99	19	8	155.8
Donovan McNabb, Syracuse	Jr	12	265	145	54.72	2488	9.39	20	6	154.0
Graham Leigh, New Mexico	Jr	12	276	166	60.14	2318	8.40	24	8	153.6
Moses Moreno, Colorado St	Sr	12	257	157	61.09	2257	8.78	20	9	153.5
Chad Pennington, Marshall	So	12	428	253	59.11	3480	8.13	39	12	151.9

Note: Minimum 15 attempts per game.

RECEPTIONS PER GAME

	Class	GP	No.	Yds	TD	R/Game
Eugene Baker, Kent	Jr	11	103	1549	18	9.36
Troy Edwards, Louisiana Tech	Jr	11	102	1707	13	9.27
Troy Walters, Stanford	Jr	11	86	1206	8	7.82
Geoff Noisy, Nevada	Jr	11	86	1184	5	7.82
Randy Moss, Marshall	So	12	90	1647	25	7.50

RECEIVING YARDS PER GAME

	Class	GP	No.	Yds	TD	Yds/Game
Troy Edwards, Louisiana Tech	Jr	11	102	1707	13	155.18
Eugene Baker, Kent	Jr	11	103	1549	18	140.82
Randy Moss, Marshall	So	12	90	1647	25	137.25
Jerome Pathon, Washington	Sr	11	69	1245	8	113.18
Troy Walters, Stanford	Jr	11	86	1206	8	109.64

ALL-PURPOSE RUNNERS

	Class	GP	Rush	Rec	PR	KOR	Yds	Yds/Game
Troy Edwards, Louisiana Tech	Jr	11	190	1707	6	241	2144	194.91
Ricky Williams, Texas	Jr	11	1893	150	0	0	2043	185.73
Kevin Faulk, Louisiana St	Jr	9	1144	93	192	217	1646	182.89
Randy Moss, Marshall	So	12	2	1647	266	263	2178	181.50
Michael Perry, Rice	Jr	10	1034	44	26	680	1784	178.40

INTERCEPTIONS

	Class	GP	No.	Yds	TD	Int/Game
Brian Lee, Wyoming	Sr	11	8	103	1	.73
Cedric Donaldson, Louisiana St	Sr	11	7	192	2	.64
John Noel, Louisiana Tech	Sr	11	7	93	0	.64
Omarr Smith, San Jose St	Jr	11	7	80	0	.64
Tevell Jones, Ohio	Sr	11	7	36	0	.64
Samari Rolle, Florida St	Sr	11	7	32	0	.64
Charles Woodson, Michigan	Jr	11	7	7	0	.64

PUNTING

	Class	No.	Avg
Chad Kessler, Louisiana St	Sr	39	50.28
John Baker, N Texas	So	62	47.18
Shane Lechler, Texas A&M	So	56	46.98
Brad Hill, Tulane	Sr	42	46.19
Chad Shrout, Hawaii	So	68	46.07

Note: Minimum of 3.6 per game.

PUNT RETURNS

	Class	No.	Yds	TD	Avg
Tim Dwight, Iowa	Sr	19	367	3	19.32
R.W. McQuarters, OK St	Jr	32	521	1	16.28
Steve Smith, Utah St	Sr	22	344	2	15.64
Nod Washington, Miami (OH)	Jr	12	185	0	15.42
Geoff Turner, Colorado St	Sr	20	304	1	15.20

Note: Minimum 1.2 per game.

Division I-A (Cont.)

KICKOFF RETURNS

	Class	No.	Yds	TD	Avg
Eric Booth, Southern Mississippi...........Sr		22	766	2	34.82
Ben Kelly, Colorado...............................Fr		25	777	1	31.08
Pat McGrew, Navy................................Sr		15	441	0	29.40
Boo Williams, S Carolina......................So		18	527	2	29.28
Pat Johnson, Oregon............................Sr		16	462	0	28.88

Note: Minimum of 1.2 per game.

Division I-A Single-Game Highs

RUSHING AND PASSING

Rushing and passing plays: 74—Tim Couch, Kentucky, Nov 1 (vs Louisiana St).
Rushing and passing yards: 568—John Dutton, Nevada, Nov 8 (vs Boise St).
Rushing plays: 43—Ivory Bryant, Northern Illinois Oct 25 (vs Ball St).
Net rushing yards: 373—Astron Whatley, Kent, Sept 20 (vs Eastern Michigan).
Passes attempted: 66—Tim Couch, Kentucky, Nov 1 (vs Louisiana St).
Passes completed: 41—Tim Couch, Kentucky, Oct 25 (vs Georgia); Nov 1
(vs Louisiana St).
Passing yards: 557—John Dutton, Nevada, Nov 8 (vs Boise St).

RECEIVING AND RETURNS

Passes caught: 18—Geoff Noisy, Nevada, Sept 13 (vs Oregon).
Receiving yards: 284—Lennie Johnson, Arkansas St, Nov 8 (vs SW Missouri St).
Punt return yards: 168—Nate Terry, W Virginia, Oct 4 (vs Rutgers).
Kickoff return yards: 248—Tyrone Watley, Iowa St, Nov 15 (vs Nebraska).

Division I-AA

SCORING

	Class	GP	TD	XP	FG	Pts	Pts/Game
Aaron Stecker, Western Illinois ....Jr		11	25	0	0	150	13.64
Reggie Greene, Siena.......................Sr		9	18	2	0	110	12.22
Sean Bennett, Evansville....................Jr		10	20	2	0	122	12.20
Stan House, Central Connecticut St...Sr		10	18	2	0	110	11.10
Rabih Abdullah, Lehigh.....................Sr		10	18	0	0	108	10.80

FIELD GOALS

	Class	GP	FGA	FG	Pct	FG/Game
Travis Brawner, SW Missouri St ....So		11	28	21	.750	1.91
Alex Sierk, Princeton ....Jr		10	21	18	.857	1.80
Ron Torro, Florida A&M......................Jr		11	21	17	.810	1.55
Dave Ettinger, Hofstra.......................Sr		11	22	17	.773	1.55
Scott Shields, Weber St.....................Jr		11	25	17	.680	1.55

TOTAL OFFENSE

			Rushing				Passing		Total Offense		
	Class	GP	Car	Gain	Loss	Net	Att	Yds	Yds	Yds/Play	TDR*	Yds/Game
A. Flowers, Cal St-N'ridge....Sr		9	52	76	170	-94	404	3226	3132	6.87	26	348.00
Giovanni Carmazzi, Hofstra...Jr		11	116	351	198	153	408	3554	3707	7.07	36	337.00
Oteman Sampson, FL A&M...Sr		11	113	551	216	335	379	3290	3625	7.37	27	329.55
Travis Brown, Northern AZ ....So		11	49	98	130	-32	474	3395	3363	6.43	23	305.73
James Perry, Brown..............So		10	50	181	114	67	397	2873	2940	6.58	25	294.00

*Touchdowns responsible for are TDs scored and passed for.

RUSHING

	Class	GP	Car	Yds	Avg	TD	Yds/Game
Reggie Greene, Siena ....Sr		9	265	1778	6.9	18	197.56
Aaron Stecker, Western Illinois ....Jr		11	298	1957	6.6	24	177.91
Sean Bennett, Evansville..........................Jr		10	235	1668	7.1	16	166.80
Rex Prescott, Eastern Washington ....Sr		10	212	1494	7.0	12	149.40
Claude Mathis, SW Texas St ....Sr		11	311	1595	5.1	14	145.00

Division I-AA *(Cont.)*

PASSING EFFICIENCY

	Class	GP	Att	Comp	Pct Comp	Yds	Yds/Att	TD	Int	Rating Pts
Alli Abrew, Cal Poly-SL Obispo	Sr	11	191	130	68.06	1961	10.27	17	4	179.5
Doug Turner, Morehead St	Sr	10	290	190	65.52	2869	9.89	29	6	177.5
Chris Boden, Villanova	So	11	345	231	66.96	3079	8.92	36	4	174.0
Harry Leons, Eastern Wash	Sr	10	257	159	61.87	2588	10.07	21	5	169.5
Simon Fuentes, Eastern KY	Sr	11	189	116	61.38	1932	10.22	13	2	167.8

Note: Minimum 15 attempts per game.

RECEPTIONS PER GAME

	Class	GP	No.	Yds	TD	R/Game
Eric Krawczyk, Cornell	Sr	10	89	1042	11	8.90
Rameek Wright, Maine	Sr	11	88	1176	7	8.00
Mike Furrey, Northern Iowa	Jr	11	82	1291	7	7.45
Bryan Kish, Hofstra	Sr	11	82	1084	7	7.45
Sean Morey, Brown	Jr	10	72	832	6	7.20

RECEIVING YARDS PER GAME

	Class	GP	No.	Yds	TD	Yds/Game
Sean Morey, Brown	Jr	10	73	1427	15	142.70
B.J. Adigun, E Tennessee St	Sr	11	68	1389	12	126.27
Mikhael Ricks, Stephen F. Austin St	Sr	11	47	1358	13	123.45
Mike Furrey, Northern Iowa	Jr	11	82	1291	7	117.36
Carl Bond, Connecticut	Sr	11	51	1178	6	107.09

ALL-PURPOSE RUNNERS

	Class	GP	Rush	Rec	PR	KOR	Yds*	Yds/Game
Reggie Greene, Siena	Sr	9	1778	73	0	158	2009	223.22
Sean Bennett, Evansville	Jr	10	1668	260	81	34	2043	204.30
Aaron Stecker, Western Illinois	Jr	11	1957	288	0	0	2245	204.09
Jerry Azumah, New Hampshire	Jr	11	1572	297	0	351	2220	201.82
Sean Morey, Brown	Jr	10	15	1427	15	465	1922	192.20

*Includes interception return yards.

INTERCEPTIONS

	Class	GP	No.	Yds	TD	Int/Game
Roderic Parson, Brown	Sr	8	8	93	0	1.00
Tony Booth, James Madison	Jr	10	8	77	1	.80
Paul Serie, Siena	Jr	9	7	36	1	.78
Trevor Bell, Idaho St	Sr	11	8	148	0	.73
Derek Carter, Maine	Sr	11	8	137	0	.73

PUNTING

	Class	No.	Avg
Barry Cantrell, Fordham	Sr	65	45.85
Chad Stanley, Stephen F. Austin	Jr	62	44.69
Brad Costello, Boston University	Sr	73	44.37
Ken Hinsley, Western Carolina	Jr	46	44.17
Steve Thorns, Cal St-Sacramento	Jr	66	44.05

Note: Minimum 3.6 per game.

Division II

SCORING

	Class	GP	TD	XP	FG	Pts	Pts/Game
Brian Shay, Emporia St	Jr	11	32	6	0	198	18.0
Travis Walch, Winona St	Sr	11	30	2	0	182	16.5
Wimont Perry, Livingstone	Jr	10	21	2	0	128	12.8
Irvin Sigler, Bloomsburg	Sr	10	20	0	0	120	12.0
Carlos Ferralls, Glenville St	Jr	10	20	0	0	120	12.0

FIELD GOALS

	Class	GP	FGA	FG	Pct	FG/Game
Shane Meyer, C Missouri St	Sr	11	25	18	72.0	1.64
Tim Seder, Ashland	Sr	10	19	14	73.7	1.40
John Sedely, W Alabama	Sr	10	17	13	76.5	1.30
Dave Purnell, NW Missouri St	So	11	16	14	87.5	1.27
Lao Loiacano, Saginaw Valley	Jr	11	18	14	77.8	1.27

TOTAL OFFENSE

	Class	GP	Yds	Yds/Game
Wilke Perez, Glenville St	Jr	11	4301	391.0
Erik Hartman, Angelo St	Sr	10	2744	274.4
Jeff Fox, Grand Valley St	Jr	11	2904	264.0
Damian Poalucci, E Stroudsburg	Sr	10	2635	263.5
Mike Lazo, Concord	Jr	10	2504	250.4

RUSHING

	Class	GP	Car	Yds	TD	Yds/Game
Anthony Gray, Western New Mexico	Jr	10	277	2220	12	222.0
Irvin Sigler, Bloomsburg	Sr	10	299	2038	20	203.8
Phillip Moore, N Dakota	Jr	10	293	1771	14	177.1
Willmont Perry, Livingstone	Jr	10	195	1770	20	177.0
Brian Shay, Emporia St	Jr	11	269	1912	29	173.8

PASSING EFFICIENCY

	Class	GP	Att	Comp	Pct Comp	Yds	TD	Int	Rating Pts
Wilkie Perez, Glenville St	Jr	11	425	280	65.8	4189	45	12	178.0
Jake Goettl, Winona St	Jr	11	259	153	59.0	2504	23	13	159.6
Joe Savino, Albany (NY)	Sr	12	256	150	58.5	2377	22	11	156.4
Justin Coleman, Nebraska-Kearny	Fr	11	309	177	57.2	2804	29	13	156.0
Chris Greisen, NW Missouri St	Jr	11	272	155	56.9	2456	23	7	155.6

Note: Minimum 15 attempts per game.

RECEPTIONS PER GAME

	Class	GP	No.	Yds	TD	Rec/Game
Carlos Ferralls, Glenville St	Sr	10	94	1566	19	9.4
Jamar Nailor, NM Highlands	Sr	10	82	1149	9	8.2
Shon King, Wayne St (NB)	Sr	9	72	1166	9	8.0
Ryan Bartemeyer, W Virginia Wesleyan	Sr	9	70	1243	16	7.8
Chad Gomarko, Augustana (SD)	Sr	11	78	1037	8	7.1

RECEIVING YARDS PER GAME

	Class	GP	No.	Yds	TD	Yds/Game
Carlos Ferralls, Greenville St	Sr	10	94	1566	19	156.6
Ryan Bartemeyer, W Virginia Wesleyan	Sr	9	70	1243	16	138.1
Shon King, Wayne St (NB)	Sr	9	72	1166	9	129.6
Jamor Nailor, NM Highlands	Sr	10	82	1149	9	114.9
Mark DeBrito, Bentley	So	9	60	1013	13	112.6

Division II *(Cont.)*

INTERCEPTIONS

	Class	GP	No.	Yds	Int/ Game
Jamey Hutchinson, Winona St	Jr	11	11	125	1.0
Tim Bednarski, Mercyhurst	Jr	9	9	59	1.0
Victor Burke, Abilene Christian	Sr	11	10	229	.9
Jarvis Davis, Fayetteville St	So	10	8	84	.8
Marcus Dover, Kentucky St	Sr	9	7	83	.8

PUNTING

	Class	No.	Avg
Brian Moorman, Pittsburg St	Jr	36	46.0
Tom O'Brien, S Dakota St	Jr	50	44.8
Jason Van Dyke, Adams St	Jr	71	43.6
Jeff Works, Quachita Baptist	So	60	43.3
Caleb Lewis, Missouri Southern St	Jr	37	42.4

Note: Minimum 3.6 per game.

Division III

SCORING

	Class	GP	TD	XP	FG	Pts	Pts/Game
James Regan, Pomona-Pitzer	Jr	8	21	34	2	166	20.8
Chad Hoiska, WI-Eau Claire	Sr	10	29	2	0	176	17.6
Jim Mormino, Allegheny	Sr	10	29	0	0	174	17.4
Doug Steiner, Grove City	Sr	10	29	0	0	174	17.4
Cory Christiansen, Simpson	Sr	10	25	0	0	150	15.0

FIELD GOALS

	Class	GP	FGA	FG	Pct	FG/Game
Ryan Boutwell, Gustavus Adolphus	Jr	10	18	13	72.2	1.30
Paul Morrris, Trinity (TX)	So	9	14	11	78.6	1.22
Rick Brands, Alma	Jr	9	19	11	57.9	1.22
Paul Boehms, Wheaton	Sr	9	13	10	76.9	1.11
Chase Young, Buena Vista	Fr	9	18	10	55.6	1.11

TOTAL OFFENSE

	Class	GP	Yds	Yds/Game
Matt Bunyan, WI-Stout	Jr	10	3216	321.6
Chris Stormer, Hanover	Jr	8	2563	320.4
Kevin Ricca, Catholic	Sr	10	3200	320.0
Sidney Chappell, Randolph-Macon	Sr	10	3149	314.9
Sean Hoolihan, WI-Eau Claire	Jr	10	3148	314.8

RUSHING

	Class	GP	Car	Yds	TD	Yds/Game
Jamie Lee, MacMurray	Sr	8	207	1639	11	204.9
Shane Davis, Loras	Sr	10	267	1774	18	177.4
Brandon Graham, Hope	Sr	9	275	1516	20	168.4
Ray Neosh, Coe	Jr	9	183	1447	14	160.8
Jason Scott, Concordia	Sr	10	254	1593	17	159.3

PASSING EFFICIENCY

	Class	GP	Att	Comp	Pct Comp	Yds	TD	Int	Rating Pts
Bill Borchert, Mount Union	Sr	10	272	190	69.8	2933	47	1	216.7
Greg Lister, Rowan	Sr	9	162	111	68.5	1688	20	4	191.9
Kevin Ricca, Catholic	Sr	10	306	208	67.9	2990	35	6	183.9
Jack Ramirez, Pomona-Pitzer	Sr	8	196	109	55.6	2013	20	9	166.4
Bryan Snyder, Albright	Sr	9	315	207	65.7	2808	26	6	164.0

Note: Minimum 15 attempts per game.

Division III (Cont.)

RECEPTIONS PER GAME

	Class	GP	No.	Yds	TD	Rec/Game
Jeff Clay, Catholic	Sr	10	112	1625	20	11.2
Scott Pingel, Westminster (MO)	So	10	98	1420	17	9.8
Eric Nemec, Albright	Jr	9	86	1147	15	9.6
Felix Brooks-Church, Oberlin	Jr	8	68	698	8	8.5
Fred Rau, McMurry	So	9	76	775	5	8.4

RECEIVING YARDS PER GAME

	Class	GP	No.	Yds	TD	Yds/Game
Jeff Clay, Catholic	Sr	10	112	1625	20	162.5
Scott Pingel, Westminster, (MO)	So	10	98	1420	17	142.0
Jeremy Snyder, Whittier	Jr	9	71	1237	15	137.4
Scott Hvistendahl, Augsburg	Jr	10	84	1329	15	132.9
Craig Carreiro, Hartwick	Sr	9	67	1166	9	129.6

INTERCEPTIONS

	Class	GP	No.	Yds	Int/Game
Joel Feuerstahler, Martin Luther	Sr	9	10	222	1.1
Duane Stevens, MIT	Sr	9	9	69	1.0
Tom Massey, Brockport St	Jr	10	9	99	.9

Five tied with eight.

PUNTING

	Class	No.	Avg
Justin Shively, Anderson (IN)	Jr	55	45.5
Jeff Shea, Cal Lutheran	Sr	43	44.4
Matt George, Chapman	Sr	38	43.8
Jeff Floyd, Centre	Sr	48	42.8
Richard Harr, Ferrum	So	66	42.5

Note: Minimum 3.6 per game.

1997 NCAA Division I-A Team Leaders

Offense

SCORING

	GP	Pts	Avg
Nebraska	12	565	47.1
Washington St	11	467	42.5
UCLA	11	448	40.7
Florida St	11	437	39.7
Marshall	12	453	37.8
Miami (OH)	11	412	37.5
Florida	11	409	37.2
Colorado St	12	442	36.8
Iowa	11	404	36.7
Navy	11	398	36.2

RUSHING

	GP	Car	Yds	Avg	TD	Yds/Game
Nebraska	12	755	4711	6.2	66	392.6
Rice	11	690	3660	5.3	38	332.7
Navy	11	618	3370	5.5	36	306.4
Ohio	11	649	3321	5.1	32	301.9
Army	11	670	3247	4.8	44	295.2
Missouri	11	592	2899	4.9	35	263.5
Louisiana St	11	521	2823	5.4	34	256.6
Iowa	11	492	2585	5.3	25	235.9
Air Force	12	688	2791	4.1	22	232.6
Oklahoma St	11	592	2486	4.2	25	226.0

TOTAL OFFENSE

	GP	Plays	Yds	Avg	TD*	Yds/Game
Nebraska	12	937	6164	6.6	71	513.67
Washington St	11	808	5524	6.8	60	502.18
Louisiana Tech	11	813	5456	6.7	48	496.00
Tennessee	12	890	5794	6.5	50	482.83
Nevada	11	796	5272	6.6	45	479.27
Kentucky	11	876	5214	6.0	45	474.00
Purdue	11	794	5056	6.4	42	459.64
Florida St	11	784	4973	6.3	49	452.09
Utah St	11	835	4933	5.9	45	448.45
Marshall	12	832	5339	6.4	58	444.92

*Defensive and special teams TDs not included.

Offense (Cont.)

PASSING

	GP	Att	Comp	Yds	Pct Comp	Yds/Att	TD	Int	Yds/Game
Nevada	11	443	265	4072	59.8	9.2	21	11	370.2
Kentucky	11	562	374	4019	66.5	7.2	37	19	365.4
Louisiana Tech	11	495	301	3965	60.8	8.0	34	11	360.5
Florida St.	11	440	262	3740	59.5	8.5	30	11	340.0
Tennessee	12	492	296	3981	60.2	8.1	37	12	331.8
Marshall	12	450	264	3688	58.7	8.2	41	13	307.3
Eastern Michigan	11	438	250	3314	57.1	7.6	23	11	301.3
Louisville	11	473	276	3282	58.4	6.9	19	14	298.4
Kent	11	451	235	3243	52.1	7.2	35	16	294.8
Central Florida	11	394	243	3187	61.7	8.1	26	10	289.7

Single-Game Highs

Points scored: 82—Florida, Sept 6 (vs Central Michigan).
Net rushing yards: 612—Ohio, Oct 4 (vs Eastern Michigan).
Passing yards: 557—Nevada, Nov 8 (vs Boise St.).
Rushing and passing yards: 708—Florida, Sept 6
    (vs Central Michigan).
Fewest rushing and passing yards allowed: 48—Nebraska,
    Oct 25 (vs Kansas).

Defense

SCORING

	GP	Pts	Avg
Michigan	11	98	8.9
Ohio St.	12	139	11.6
Air Force	12	149	12.4
Iowa	11	142	12.9
N Carolina	11	143	13.0
Kansas St	11	159	14.5
Colorado St	12	179	14.9
Florida St	11	167	15.2
Syracuse	12	191	15.9
Ohio	11	177	16.1

TOTAL DEFENSE

	GP	Plays	Yds	Avg	Yds/Game
Michigan	11	660	2276	3.4	206.9
N Carolina	11	693	2302	3.3	209.3
Florida St	11	717	2655	3.7	241.4
Kansas St	11	702	2825	4.0	256.8
Nebraska	12	717	3088	4.3	257.3
Navy	11	642	2863	4.5	260.3
Iowa	11	733	2927	4.0	266.1
Ohio St	12	820	3215	3.9	267.9
Vanderbilt	11	704	3026	4.3	275.1
Air Force	12	756	3471	4.6	289.3

RUSHING

	GP	Car	Yds	Avg	TD	Yds/Game
Florida St	11	379	571	1.5	10	51.9
Florida	11	362	778	2.1	12	70.7
Nebraska	12	407	881	2.2	12	73.4
N Carolina	11	371	857	2.3	5	77.9
Cincinnati	11	338	930	2.8	10	84.5
Clemson	11	362	971	2.7	10	88.3
Michigan	11	368	1001	2.7	6	91.0
Tennessee	12	382	1119	2.9	11	93.3
Southern Cal	11	381	1032	2.7	12	93.8
Wake Forest	11	364	1057	2.9	11	96.1

TURNOVER MARGIN

		Turnovers Gained			Turnovers Lost			Margin/
	GP	Fum	Int	Total	Fum	Int	Total	Game
Colorado St	12	20	18	38	4	9	13	2.08
UCLA	11	18	21	39	14	5	19	1.82
Texas A&M	12	22	11	33	11	4	15	1.50
Florida St	11	10	22	32	6	11	17	1.36
Tulane	11	8	26	34	6	14	20	1.27
SMU	11	12	15	27	7	7	14	1.18
Oklahoma St	11	14	15	29	8	8	16	1.18
Navy	11	13	14	27	6	8	14	1.18

PASSING EFFICIENCY

	GP	Att	Comp	Yds	Pct Comp	Yds/Att	TD	Pct TD	Int	Pct Int	Rating Pts
Michigan	11	292	145	1275	49.66	4.37	4	1.37	22	7.53	75.79
Ohio St	12	360	160	1724	44.44	4.79	6	1.67	19	5.28	79.62
N Carolina	11	322	148	1445	45.96	4.49	7	2.17	15	4.66	81.52
Iowa	11	325	146	1766	44.92	5.43	12	3.69	22	6.77	89.21
Kansas St	11	239	99	1396	41.42	5.84	4	1.67	5	2.09	91.83
Wyoming	13	374	169	2358	45.19	6.30	11	2.94	24	6.42	95.02
Marshall	12	322	146	1948	45.34	6.05	8	2.48	15	4.66	95.04
New Mexico	12	333	153	1989	45.95	5.97	10	3.00	16	4.80	96.42
AL-Birmingham	11	337	159	1912	47.18	5.67	12	3.56	17	5.04	96.50
Florida St	11	338	164	2084	48.52	6.17	12	3.55	22	6.51	99.01

FOR THE RECORD·Year by Year

National Champions

Year	Champion	Record	Bowl Game	Head Coach
1883	Yale	8-0-0	No bowl	Ray Tompkins (Captain)
1884	Yale	9-0-0	No bowl	Eugene L. Richards (Captain)
1885	Princeton	9-0-0	No bowl	Charles DeCamp (Captain)
1886	Yale	9-0-1	No bowl	Robert N. Corwin (Captain)
1887	Yale	9-0-0	No bowl	Harry W. Beecher (Captain)
1888	Yale	13-0-0	No bowl	Walter Camp
1889	Princeton	10-0-0	No bowl	Edgar Poe (Captain)
1890	Harvard	11-0-0	No bowl	George A. Stewart/George C. Adams
1891	Yale	13-0-0	No bowl	Walter Camp
1892	Yale	13-0-0	No bowl	Walter Camp
1893	Princeton	11-0-0	No bowl	Tom Trenchard (Captain)
1894	Yale	16-0-0	No bowl	William C. Rhodes
1895	Pennsylvania	14-0-0	No bowl	George Woodruff
1896	Princeton	10-0-1	No bowl	Garrett Cochran
1897	Pennsylvania	15-0-0	No bowl	George Woodruff
1898	Harvard	11-0-0	No bowl	W. Cameron Forbes
1899	Harvard	10-0-1	No bowl	Benjamin H. Dibblee
1900	Yale	12-0-0	No bowl	Malcolm McBride
1901	Michigan	11-0-0	Won Rose	Fielding Yost
1902	Michigan	11-0-0	No bowl	Fielding Yost
1903	Princeton	11-0-0	No bowl	Art Hillebrand
1904	Pennsylvania	12-0-0	No bowl	Carl Williams
1905	Chicago	11-0-0	No bowl	Amos Alonzo Stagg
1906	Princeton	9-0-1	No bowl	Bill Roper
1907	Yale	9-0-1	No bowl	Bill Knox
1908	Pennsylvania	11-0-1	No bowl	Sol Metzger
1909	Yale	10-0-0	No bowl	Howard Jones
1910	Harvard	8-0-1	No bowl	Percy Houghton
1911	Princeton	8-0-2	No bowl	Bill Roper
1912	Harvard	9-0-0	No bowl	Percy Houghton
1913	Harvard	9-0-0	No bowl	Percy Houghton
1914	Army	9-0-0	No bowl	Charley Daly
1915	Cornell	9-0-0	No bowl	Al Sharpe
1916	Pittsburgh	8-0-0	No bowl	Pop Warner
1917	Georgia Tech	9-0-0	No bowl	John Heisman
1918	Pittsburgh	4-1-0	No bowl	Pop Warner
1919	Harvard	9-0-1	Won Rose	Bob Fisher
1920	California	9-0-0	Won Rose	Andy Smith
1921	Cornell	8-0-0	No bowl	Gil Dobie
1922	Cornell	8-0-0	No bowl	Gil Dobie
1923	Illinois	8-0-0	No bowl	Bob Zuppke
1924	Notre Dame	10-0-0	Won Rose	Knute Rockne
1925	Alabama (H)	10-0-0	Won Rose	Wallace Wade
	Dartmouth (D)	8-0-0	No bowl	Jesse Hawley
1926	Alabama (H)	9-0-1	Tied Rose	Wallace Wade
	Stanford (D)(H)	10-0-1	Tied Rose	Pop Warner
1927	Illinois	7-0-1	No bowl	Bob Zuppke
1928	Georgia Tech (H)	10-0-0	Won Rose	Bill Alexander
	Southern Cal (D)	9-0-1	No bowl	Howard Jones
1929	Notre Dame	9-0-0	No bowl	Knute Rockne
1930	Notre Dame	10-0-0	No bowl	Knute Rockne
1931	Southern Cal	10-1-0	Won Rose	Howard Jones
1932	Southern Cal (H)	10-0-0	Won Rose	Howard Jones
	Michigan (D)	8-0-0	No bowl	Harry Kipke
1933	Michigan	7-0-1	No bowl	Harry Kipke
1934	Minnesota	8-0-0	No bowl	Bernie Bierman
1935	Minnesota (H)	8-0-0	No bowl	Bernie Bierman
	Southern Methodist (D)	12-1-0	Lost Rose	Matty Bell
1936	Minnesota	7-1-0	No bowl	Bernie Bierman
1937	Pittsburgh	9-0-1	No bowl	Jock Sutherland
1938	Texas Christian (AP)	11-0-0	Won Sugar	Dutch Meyer
	Notre Dame (D)	8-1-0	No bowl	Elmer Layden
1939	Southern Cal (D)	8-0-2	Won Rose	Howard Jones
	Texas A&M (AP)	11-0-0	Won Sugar	Homer Norton
1940	Minnesota	8-0-0	No bowl	Bernie Bierman
1941	Minnesota	8-0-0	No bowl	Bernie Bierman
1942	Ohio St	9-1-0	No bowl	Paul Brown

Year	Champion	Record	Bowl Game	Head Coach
1943	Notre Dame	9-1-0	No bowl	Frank Leahy
1944	Army	9-0-0	No bowl	Red Blaik
1945	Army	9-0-0	No bowl	Red Blaik
1946	Notre Dame	8-0-1	No bowl	Frank Leahy
1947	Notre Dame	9-0-0	No bowl	Frank Leahy
	Michigan*	10-0-0	Won Rose	Fritz Crisler
1948	Michigan	9-0-0	No bowl	Bennie Oosterbaan
1949	Notre Dame	10-0-0	No bowl	Frank Leahy
1950	Oklahoma	10-1-0	Lost Sugar	Bud Wilkinson
1951	Tennessee	10-1-0	Lost Sugar	Bob Neyland
1952	Michigan St	9-0-0	No bowl	Biggie Munn
1953	Maryland	10-1-0	Lost Orange	Jim Tatum
1954	Ohio St	10-0-0	Won Rose	Woody Hayes
	UCLA (UPI)	9-0-0	No bowl	Red Sanders
1955	Oklahoma	11-0-0	Won Orange	Bud Wilkinson
1956	Oklahoma	10-0-0	No bowl	Bud Wilkinson
1957	Auburn	10-0-0	No bowl	Shug Jordan
	Ohio St (UPI)	9-1-0	Won Rose	Woody Hayes
1958	Louisiana St	11-0-0	Won Sugar	Paul Dietzel
1959	Syracuse	11-0-0	Won Cotton	Ben Schwartzwalder
1960	Minnesota	8-2-0	Lost Rose	Murray Warmath
1961	Alabama	11-0-0	Won Sugar	Bear Bryant
1962	Southern Cal	11-0-0	Won Rose	John McKay
1963	Texas	11-0-0	Won Cotton	Darrell Royal
1964	Alabama	10-1-0	Lost Orange	Bear Bryant
1965	Alabama	9-1-1	Won Orange	Bear Bryant
	Michigan St (UPI)	10-1-0	Lost Rose	Duffy Daugherty
1966	Notre Dame	9-0-1	No bowl	Ara Parseghian
1967	Southern Cal	10-1-0	Won Rose	John McKay
1968	Ohio St	10-0-0	Won Rose	Woody Hayes
1969	Texas	11-0-0	Won Cotton	Darrell Royal
1970	Nebraska	11-0-1	Won Orange	Bob Devaney
	Texas (UPI)	10-1-0	Lost Cotton	Darrell Royal
1971	Nebraska	13-0-0	Won Orange	Bob Devaney
1972	Southern Cal	12-0-0	Won Rose	John McKay
1973	Notre Dame	11-0-0	Won Sugar	Ara Parseghian
	Alabama (UPI)	11-1-0	Lost Sugar	Bear Bryant
1974	Oklahoma	11-0-0	No bowl	Barry Switzer
	Southern Cal (UPI)	10-1-1	Won Rose	John McKay
1975	Oklahoma	11-1-0	Won Orange	Barry Switzer
1976	Pittsburgh	12-0-0	Won Sugar	Johnny Majors
1977	Notre Dame	11-1-0	Won Cotton	Dan Devine
1978	Alabama	11-1-0	Won Sugar	Bear Bryant
	Southern Cal (UPI)	12-1-0	Won Rose	John Robinson
1979	Alabama	12-0-0	Won Sugar	Bear Bryant
1980	Georgia	12-0-0	Won Sugar	Vince Dooley
1981	Clemson	12-0-0	Won Orange	Danny Ford
1982	Penn St	11-1-0	Won Sugar	Joe Paterno
1983	Miami (FL)	11-1-0	Won Orange	Howard Schnellenberger
1984	Brigham Young	13-0-0	Won Holiday	LaVell Edwards
1985	Oklahoma	11-1-0	Won Orange	Barry Switzer
1986	Penn St	12-0-0	Won Fiesta	Joe Paterno
1987	Miami (FL)	12-0-0	Won Orange	Jimmy Johnson
1988	Notre Dame	12-0-0	Won Fiesta	Lou Holtz
1989	Miami (FL)	11-1-0	Won Sugar	Dennis Erickson
1990	Colorado	11-1-1	Won Orange	Bill McCartney
	Georgia Tech (UPI)	11-0-1	Won Citrus	Bobby Ross
1991	Miami (FL)	12-0-0	Won Orange	Dennis Erickson
	Washington (CNN)	12-0-0	Won Rose	Don James
1992	Alabama	13-0-0	Won Sugar	Gene Stallings
1993	Florida St	12-1-0	Won Orange	Bobby Bowden
1994	Nebraska	13-0-0	Won Orange	Tom Osborne
1995	Nebraska	12-0-0	Won Fiesta	Tom Osborne
1996	Florida	12-1-0	Won Sugar	Steve Spurrier
1997	Michigan	12-0-0	Won Rose	Lloyd Carr
	Nebraska (ESPN)	13-0-0	Won Orange	Tom Osborne

*The AP, which had voted Notre Dame No. 1, took a second vote, giving the national title to Michigan after its 49–0 win over Southern Cal in the Rose Bowl.   Note: Selectors: Helms Athletic Foundation (H) 1883–1935, The Dickinson System (D) 1924–40, The Associated Press (AP) 1936–present, United Press International (UPI) 1958–90, *USA Today*/CNN (CNN) 1991–96, and *USA Today*/ESPN (ESPN) 1997–present.

Results of Major Bowl Games

Rose Bowl

1-1-02	Michigan 49, Stanford 0
1-1-16	Washington St 14, Brown 0
1-1-17	Oregon 14, Pennsylvania 0
1-1-18	Mare Island 19, Camp Lewis 7
1-1-19	Great Lakes 17, Mare Island 0
1-1-20	Harvard 7, Oregon 6
1-1-21	California 28, Ohio St 0
1-2-22	Washington & Jefferson 0, California 0
1-1-23	Southern Cal 14, Penn St 3
1-1-24	Navy 14, Washington 14
1-1-25	Notre Dame 27, Stanford 10
1-1-26	Alabama 20, Washington 19
1-1-27	Alabama 7, Stanford 7
1-2-28	Stanford 7, Pittsburgh 6
1-1-29	Georgia Tech 8, California 7
1-1-30	Southern Cal 47, Pittsburgh 14
1-1-31	Alabama 24, Washington St 0
1-1-32	Southern Cal 21, Tulane 12
1-2-33	Southern Cal 35, Pittsburgh 0
1-1-34	Columbia 7, Stanford 0
1-1-35	Alabama 29, Stanford 13
1-1-36	Stanford 7, Southern Methodist 0
1-1-37	Pittsburgh 21, Washington 0
1-1-38	California 13, Alabama 0
1-2-39	Southern Cal 7, Duke 3
1-1-40	Southern Cal 14, Tennessee 0
1-1-41	Stanford 21, Nebraska 13
1-1-42	Oregon St 20, Duke 16
1-1-43	Georgia 9, UCLA 0
1-1-44	Southern Cal 29, Washington 0
1-1-45	Southern Cal 25, Tennessee 0
1-1-46	Alabama 34, Southern Cal 14
1-1-47	Illinois 45, UCLA 14
1-1-48	Michigan 49, Southern Cal 0
1-1-49	Northwestern 20, California 14
1-2-50	Ohio St 17, California 14
1-1-51	Michigan 14, California 6
1-1-52	Illinois 40, Stanford 7
1-1-53	Southern Cal 7, Wisconsin 0
1-1-54	Michigan St 28, UCLA 20
1-1-55	Ohio St 20, Southern Cal 7
1-2-56	Michigan St 17, UCLA 14
1-1-57	Iowa 35, Oregon St 19
1-1-58	Ohio St 10, Oregon 7
1-1-59	Iowa 38, California 12
1-1-60	Washington 44, Wisconsin 8
1-2-61	Washington 17, Minnesota 7
1-1-62	Minnesota 21, UCLA 3
1-1-63	Southern Cal 42, Wisconsin 37
1-1-64	Illinois 17, Washington 7
1-1-65	Michigan 34, Oregon St 7
1-1-66	UCLA 14, Michigan St 12
1-2-67	Purdue 14, Southern Cal 13
1-1-68	Southern Cal 14, Indiana 3
1-1-69	Ohio St 27, Southern Cal 16
1-1-70	Southern Cal 10, Michigan 3
1-1-71	Stanford 27, Ohio St 17
1-1-72	Stanford 13, Michigan 12
1-1-73	Southern Cal 42, Ohio St 17
1-1-74	Ohio St 42, Southern Cal 21
1-1-75	Southern Cal 18, Ohio St 17
1-1-76	UCLA 23, Ohio St 10
1-1-77	Southern Cal 14, Michigan 6

1-2-78	Washington 27, Michigan 20
1-1-79	Southern Cal 17, Michigan 10
1-1-80	Southern Cal 17, Ohio St 16
1-1-81	Michigan 23, Washington 6
1-1-82	Washington 28, Iowa 0
1-1-83	UCLA 24, Michigan 14
1-2-84	UCLA 45, Illinois 9
1-1-85	Southern Cal 20, Ohio St 17
1-1-86	UCLA 45, Iowa 28
1-1-87	Arizona St 22, Michigan 15
1-1-88	Michigan St 20, Southern Cal 17
1-2-89	Michigan 22, Southern Cal 14
1-1-90	Southern Cal 17, Michigan 10
1-1-91	Washington 46, Iowa 34
1-1-92	Washington 34, Michigan 14
1-1-93	Michigan 38, Washington 31
1-1-94	Wisconsin 21, UCLA 16
1-2-95	Penn St 38, Oregon 20
1-1-96	Southern Cal 41, Northwestern 32
1-1-97	Ohio St 20, Arizona St 17
1-1-98	Michigan 21, Washington St 16

City: Pasadena. Stadium: Rose Bowl, capacity 102,083.
Playing Sites: Tournament Park (1902, 1916-22), Rose Bowl (1923-41, since 1943), Duke Stadium, Durham, NC (1942).

Orange Bowl

1-1-35	Bucknell 26, Miami (FL) 0
1-1-36	Catholic 20, Mississippi 19
1-1-37	Duquesne 13, Mississippi St 12
1-1-38	Auburn 6, Michigan St 0
1-2-39	Tennessee 17, Oklahoma 0
1-1-40	Georgia Tech 21, Missouri 7
1-1-41	Mississippi St 14, Georgetown 7
1-1-42	Georgia 40, Texas Christian 26
1-1-43	Alabama 37, Boston College 21
1-1-44	Louisiana St 19, Texas A&M 14
1-1-45	Tulsa 26, Georgia Tech 12
1-1-46	Miami (FL) 13, Holy Cross 6
1-1-47	Rice 8, Tennessee 0
1-1-48	Georgia Tech 20, Kansas 14
1-1-49	Texas 41, Georgia 28
1-2-50	Santa Clara 21, Kentucky 13
1-1-51	Clemson 15, Miami (FL) 14
1-1-52	Georgia Tech 17, Baylor 14
1-1-53	Alabama 61, Syracuse 6
1-1-54	Oklahoma 7, Maryland 0
1-1-55	Duke 34, Nebraska 7
1-2-56	Oklahoma 20, Maryland 6
1-1-57	Colorado 27, Clemson 21
1-1-58	Oklahoma 48, Duke 21
1-1-59	Oklahoma 21, Syracuse 6
1-1-60	Georgia 14, Missouri 0
1-2-61	Missouri 21, Navy 14
1-1-62	Louisiana St 25, Colorado 7
1-1-63	Alabama 17, Oklahoma 0
1-1-64	Nebraska 13, Auburn 7
1-1-65	Texas 21, Alabama 17
1-1-66	Alabama 39, Nebraska 28
1-2-67	Florida 27, Georgia Tech 12
1-1-68	Oklahoma 26, Tennessee 24
1-1-69	Penn St 15, Kansas 14

Note: The Fiesta, Orange and Sugar Bowls constitute the Bowl Alliance, formed in 1995. The Alliance holds six berths: one each for the champions of the SEC, Big 12, Big East and ACC, and two at-large, one of which is guaranteed to Notre Dame if it is ranked in the top 10 in one of the two final regular-season polls. Of the six teams, the two highest-ranked go to the Fiesta Bowl in 1996, the Sugar Bowl in 1997, and the Orange Bowl in 1998. The champions of the Big Ten and Pac-10 go to the Rose Bowl, which will join the alliance after the 1998 season. Once these four matches have been set conferences may place the remaining qualified teams in the other bowls. Teams that have won at least six games against Division I-A teams qualify.

Orange Bowl *(Cont.)*

1-1-70 ....Penn St 10, Missouri 3
1-1-71 ....Nebraska 17, Louisiana St 12
1-1-72 ....Nebraska 38, Alabama 6
1-1-73 ....Nebraska 40, Notre Dame 6
1-1-74 ....Penn St 16, Louisiana St 9
1-1-75 ....Notre Dame 13, Alabama 11
1-1-76 ....Oklahoma 14, Michigan 6
1-1-77 ....Ohio St 27, Colorado 10
1-2-78 ....Arkansas 31, Oklahoma 6
1-1-79 ....Oklahoma 31, Nebraska 24
1-1-80 ....Oklahoma 24, Florida St 7
1-1-81 ....Oklahoma 18, Florida St 17
1-1-82 ....Clemson 22, Nebraska 15
1-1-83 ....Nebraska 21, Louisiana St 20
1-2-84 ....Miami (FL) 31, Nebraska 30
1-1-85 ....Washington 28, Oklahoma 17
1-1-86 ....Oklahoma 25, Penn St 10
1-1-87 ....Oklahoma 42, Arkansas 8
1-1-88 ....Miami (FL) 20, Oklahoma 14
1-2-89 ....Miami (FL) 23, Nebraska 3
1-1-90 ....Notre Dame 21, Colorado 6
1-1-91 ....Colorado 10, Notre Dame 9
1-1-92 ....Miami (FL) 22, Nebraska 0
1-1-93 ....Florida St 27, Nebraska 14
1-1-94 ....Florida St 18, Nebraska 16
1-1-95 ....Nebraska 24, Miami (FL) 17
1-1-96 ....Florida St 31, Notre Dame 26
12-31-96 ....Nebraska 41, Virginia Tech 21
1-2-98 ....Nebraska 42, Tennessee 17

City: Miami. Stadium: Pro Player Stadium, capacity 75,192.
Playing Sites: Orange Bowl (1935-96), Pro Player Stadium
(since 1996).

Sugar Bowl

1-1-35 ....Tulane 20, Temple 14
1-1-36 ....Texas Christian 3, Louisiana St 2
1-1-37 ....Santa Clara 21, Louisiana St 14
1-1-38 ....Santa Clara 6, Louisiana St 0
1-2-39 ....Texas Christian 15, Carnegie Tech 7
1-1-40 ....Texas A&M 14, Tulane 13
1-1-41 ....Boston Col 19, Tennessee 13
1-1-42 ....Fordham 2, Missouri 0
1-1-43 ....Tennessee 14, Tulsa 7
1-1-44 ....Georgia Tech 20, Tulsa 18
1-1-45 ....Duke 29, Alabama 26
1-1-46 ....Oklahoma St 33, St Mary's (CA) 13
1-1-47 ....Georgia 20, N Carolina 10
1-1-48 ....Texas 27, Alabama 7
1-1-49 ....Oklahoma 14, N Carolina 6
1-2-50 ....Oklahoma 35, Louisiana St 0
1-1-51 ....Kentucky 13, Oklahoma 7
1-1-52 ....Maryland 28, Tennessee 13
1-1-53 ....Georgia Tech 24, Mississippi 7
1-1-54 ....Georgia Tech 42, W Virginia 19
1-1-55 ....Navy 21, Mississippi 0
1-2-56 ....Georgia Tech 7, Pittsburgh 0
1-1-57 ....Baylor 13, Tennessee 7
1-1-58 ....Mississippi 39, Texas 7
1-1-59 ....Louisiana St 7, Clemson 0
1-1-60 ....Mississippi 21, Louisiana St 0
1-2-61 ....Mississippi 14, Rice 6
1-1-62 ....Alabama 10, Arkansas 3
1-1-63 ....Mississippi 17, Arkansas 13
1-1-64 ....Alabama 12, Mississippi 7
1-1-65 ....Louisiana St 13, Syracuse 10
1-1-66 ....Missouri 20, Florida 18
1-2-67 ....Alabama 34, Nebraska 7
1-1-68 ....Louisiana St 20, Wyoming 13

Sugar Bowl *(Cont.)*

1-1-69 ....Arkansas 16, Georgia 2
1-1-70 ....Mississippi 27, Arkansas 22
1-1-71 ....Tennessee 34, Air Force 13
1-1-72 ....Oklahoma 40, Auburn 22
12-31-72 ....Oklahoma 14, Penn St 0
12-31-73 ....Notre Dame 24, Alabama 23
12-31-74 ....Nebraska 13, Florida 10
12-31-75 ....Alabama 13, Penn St 6
1-1-77 ....Pittsburgh 27, Georgia 3
1-2-78 ....Alabama 35, Ohio St 6
1-1-79 ....Alabama 14, Penn St 7
1-1-80 ....Alabama 24, Arkansas 9
1-1-81 ....Georgia 17, Notre Dame 10
1-1-82 ....Pittsburgh 24, Georgia 20
1-1-83 ....Penn St 27, Georgia 23
1-2-84 ....Auburn 9, Michigan 7
1-1-85 ....Nebraska 28, Louisiana St 10
1-1-86 ....Tennessee 35, Miami (FL) 7
1-1-87 ....Nebraska 30, Louisiana St 15
1-1-88 ....Syracuse 16, Auburn 16
1-2-89 ....Florida St 13, Auburn 7
1-1-90 ....Miami (FL) 33, Alabama 25
1-1-91 ....Tennessee 23, Virginia 22
1-1-92 ....Notre Dame 39, Florida 28
1-1-93 ....Alabama 34, Miami (FL) 13
1-1-94 ....Florida 41, West Virginia 7
1-2-95 ....Florida St 23, Florida 17
12-31-95 ....Virginia Tech 28, Texas 10
1-2-97 ....Florida 52, Florida St 20
1-1-98 ....Florida St 31, Ohio St 14

City: New Orleans. Stadium: Louisiana Superdome,
capacity 76,791.

Playing Sites: Tulane Stadium (1935-74), Louisiana
Superdome (since 1975).

Cotton Bowl

1-1-37 ....Texas Christian 16, Marquette 6
1-1-38 ....Rice 28, Colorado 14
1-2-39 ....St. Mary's (CA) 20, Texas Tech 13
1-1-40 ....Clemson 6, Boston Col 3
1-1-41 ....Texas A&M 13, Fordham 12
1-1-42 ....Alabama 29, Texas A&M 21
1-1-43 ....Texas 14, Georgia Tech 7
1-1-44 ....Texas 7, Randolph Field 7
1-1-45 ....Oklahoma St 34, Texas Christian 0
1-1-46 ....Texas 40, Missouri 27
1-1-47 ....Arkansas 0, Louisiana St 0
1-1-48 ....SMU 13, Penn St 13
1-1-49 ....SMU 21, Oregon 13
1-2-50 ....Rice 27, N Carolina 13
1-1-51 ....Tennessee 20, Texas 14
1-1-52 ....Kentucky 20, Texas Christian 7
1-1-53 ....Texas 16, Tennessee 0
1-1-54 ....Rice 28, Alabama 6
1-1-55 ....Georgia Tech 14, Arkansas 6
1-2-56 ....Mississippi 14, Texas Christian 13
1-1-57 ....Texas Christian 28, Syracuse 27
1-1-58 ....Navy 20, Rice 7
1-1-59 ....Texas Christian 0, Air Force 0
1-1-60 ....Syracuse 23, Texas 14
1-2-61 ....Duke 7, Arkansas 6
1-1-62 ....Texas 12, Mississippi 7
1-1-63 ....Louisiana St 13, Texas 0
1-1-64 ....Texas 28, Navy 6
1-1-65 ....Arkansas 10, Nebraska 7
1-1-66 ....Louisiana St 14, Arkansas 7
12-31-66 ....Georgia 24, SMU 9

Cotton Bowl *(Cont.)*

1-1-68 ....Texas A&M 20, Alabama 16
1-1-69 ....Texas 36, Tennessee 13
1-1-70 ....Texas 21, Notre Dame 17
1-1-71 ....Notre Dame 24, Texas 11
1-1-72 ....Penn St 30, Texas 6
1-1-73 ....Texas 17, Alabama 13
1-1-74 ....Nebraska 19, Texas 3
1-1-75 ....Penn St 41, Baylor 20
1-1-76 ....Arkansas 31, Georgia 10
1-1-77 ....Houston 30, Maryland 21
1-2-78 ....Notre Dame 38, Texas 10
1-1-79 ....Notre Dame 35, Houston 34
1-1-80 ....Houston 17, Nebraska 14
1-1-81 ....Alabama 30, Baylor 2
1-1-82 ....Texas 14, Alabama 12
1-1-83 ....SMU 7, Pittsburgh 3
1-2-84 ....Georgia 10, Texas 9
1-1-85 ....Boston Col 45, Houston 28
1-1-86 ....Texas A&M 36, Auburn 16
1-1-87 ....Ohio St 28, Texas A&M 12
1-1-88 ....Texas A&M 35, Notre Dame 10
1-2-89 ....UCLA 17, Arkansas 3
1-1-90 ....Tennessee 31, Arkansas 27
1-1-91 ....Miami (FL) 46, Texas 3
1-1-92 ....Florida St 10, Texas A&M 2
1-1-93 ....Notre Dame 28, Texas A&M 3
1-1-94 ....Notre Dame 24, Texas A&M 21
1-2-95 ....Southern Cal 55, Texas Tech 14
1-1-96 ....Colorado 38, Oregon 6
1-1-97 ....Brigham Young 19, Kansas St 15
1-1-98 ....UCLA 29, Texas A&M 23

City: Dallas. Stadium: Cotton Bowl, capacity 68,252.

Sun Bowl

1-1-36 ....Hardin-Simmons 14, New Mexico St 14
1-1-37 ....Hardin-Simmons 34, UTEP 6
1-1-38 ....W Virginia 7, Texas Tech 6
1-2-39 ....Utah 26, New Mexico 0
1-1-40 ....Catholic 0, Arizona St 0
1-1-41 ....Case Reserve 26, Arizona St 13
1-1-42 ....Tulsa 6, Texas Tech 0
1-1-43 ....2nd Air Force 13, Hardin-Simmons 7
1-1-44 ....Southwestern (TX) 7, New Mexico 0
1-1-45 ....Southwestern (TX) 35, New Mexico 0
1-1-46 ....New Mexico 34, Denver 24
1-1-47 ....Cincinnati 18, Virginia Tech 6
1-1-48 ....Miami (OH) 13, Texas Tech 12
1-1-49 ....W Virginia 21, UTEP 12
1-2-50 ....UTEP 33, Georgetown 20
1-1-51 ....West Texas St 14, Cincinnati 13
1-1-52 ....Texas Tech 25, Pacific 14
1-1-53 ....Pacific 26, Southern Miss 7
1-1-54 ....UTEP 37, Southern Miss 14
1-1-55 ....UTEP 47, Florida St 20
1-2-56 ....Wyoming 21, Texas Tech 14
1-1-57 ....George Washington 13, UTEP 0
1-1-58 ....Louisville 34, Drake 20
12-31-58 ....Wyoming 14, Hardin-Simmons 6
12-31-59 ....New Mexico St 28, N Texas 8
12-31-60 ....New Mexico St 20, Utah St 13
12-30-61 ....Villanova 17, Wichita St 9
12-31-62 ....W Texas St 15, Ohio 14
12-31-63 ....Oregon 21, SMU 14
12-26-64 ....Georgia 7, Texas Tech 0
12-31-65 ....UTEP 13, Texas Christian 12
12-24-66 ....Wyoming 28, Florida St 20
12-30-67 ....UTEP 14, Mississippi 7
12-28-68 ....Auburn 34, Arizona 10

Sun Bowl *(Cont.)*

12-20-69 ....Nebraska 45, Georgia 6
12-19-70 ....Georgia Tech 17, Texas Tech 9
12-18-71 ....Louisiana St 33, Iowa St 15
12-30-72 ....N Carolina 32, Texas Tech 28
12-29-73 ....Missouri 34, Auburn 17
12-28-74 ....Mississippi St 26, N Carolina 24
12-26-75 ....Pittsburgh 33, Kansas 19
1-2-77 ....Texas A&M 37, Florida 14
12-31-77 ....Stanford 24, Louisiana St 14
12-23-78 ....Texas 42, Maryland 0
12-22-79 ....Washington 14, Texas 7
12-27-80 ....Nebraska 31, Mississippi St 17
12-26-81 ....Oklahoma 40, Houston 14
12-25-82 ....N Carolina 26, Texas 10
12-24-83 ....Alabama 28, SMU 7
12-22-84 ....Maryland 28, Tennessee 27
12-28-85 ....Georgia 13, Arizona 13
12-25-86 ....Alabama 28, Washington 6
12-25-87 ....Oklahoma St 35, W Virginia 33
12-24-88 ....Alabama 29, Army 28
12-30-89 ....Pittsburgh 31, Texas A&M 28
12-31-90 ....Michigan St 17, Southern Cal 16
12-31-91 ....UCLA 6, Illinois 3
12-31-92 ....Baylor 20, Arizona 15
12-24-93 ....Oklahoma 41, Texas Tech 10
12-30-94 ....Texas 35, N Carolina 31
12-29-95 ....Iowa 38, Washington 18
12-31-96 ....Stanford 38, Michigan St 0
12-31-97 ....Arizona 17, Iowa 7

City: El Paso. Stadium: Sun Bowl, capacity 52,000.

Name Changes: Sun Bowl (1936-86; 94-), John Hancock Sun Bowl (1987-88), John Hancock Bowl (1989-93).

Playing Sites: Kidd Field (1936-62), Sun Bowl (since 1963).

Gator Bowl

1-1-46 ....Wake Forest 26, S Carolina 14
1-1-47 ....Oklahoma 34, N Carolina St 13
1-1-48 ....Maryland 20, Georgia 20
1-1-49 ....Clemson 24, Missouri 23
1-2-50 ....Maryland 20, Missouri 7
1-1-51 ....Wyoming 20, Washington & Lee 7
1-1-52 ....Miami (FL) 14, Clemson 0
1-1-53 ....Florida 14, Tulsa 13
1-1-54 ....Texas Tech 35, Auburn 13
12-31-54 ....Auburn 33, Baylor 13
12-31-55 ....Vanderbilt 25, Auburn 13
12-29-56 ....Georgia Tech 21, Pittsburgh 14
12-28-57 ....Tennessee 3, Texas A&M 0
12-27-58 ....Mississippi 7, Florida 3
1-2-60 ....Arkansas 14, Georgia Tech 7
12-31-60 ....Florida 13, Baylor 12
12-30-61 ....Penn St 30, Georgia Tech 15
12-29-62 ....Florida 17, Penn St 7
12-28-63 ....N Carolina 35, Air Force 0
1-2-65 ....Florida St 36, Oklahoma 19
12-31-65 ....Georgia Tech 31, Texas Tech 21
12-31-66 ....Tennessee 18, Syracuse 12
12-30-67 ....Penn St 17, Florida St 17
12-28-68 ....Missouri 35, Alabama 10
12-27-69 ....Florida 14, Tennessee 13
1-2-71 ....Auburn 35, Mississippi 28
12-31-71 ....Georgia 7, N Carolina 3
12-30-72 ....Auburn 24, Colorado 3
12-29-73 ....Texas Tech 28, Tennessee 19
12-30-74 ....Auburn 27, Texas 3
12-29-75 ....Maryland 13, Florida 0
12-27-76 ....Notre Dame 20, Penn St 9
12-30-77 ....Pittsburgh 34, Clemson 3
12-29-78 ....Clemson 17, Ohio St 15

Gator Bowl *(Cont.)*

12-28-79.........N Carolina 17, Michigan 15
12-29-80.........Pittsburgh 37, S Carolina 9
12-28-81.........N Carolina 31, Arkansas 27
12-30-82.........Florida St 31, W Virginia 12
12-30-83.........Florida 14, Iowa 6
12-28-84.........Oklahoma St 21, S Carolina 14
12-30-85.........Florida St 34, Oklahoma St 23
12-27-86.........Clemson 27, Stanford 21
12-31-87.........Louisiana St 30, S Carolina 13
1-1-89.............Georgia 34, Michigan St 27
12-30-89.........Clemson 27, W Virginia 7
1-1-91.............Michigan 35, Mississippi 3
12-29-91.........Oklahoma 48, Virginia 14
12-31-92.........Florida 27, N Carolina St 10
12-31-93.........Alabama 24, North Carolina 10
12-30-94.........Tennessee 45, Virginia Tech 23
1-1-96.............Syracuse 41, Clemson 0
1-1-97.............N Carolina 20, W Virginia 13
1-1-98.............N Carolina 42, Viginia Tech 13

City: Jacksonville, FL. Stadium: Jacksonville Municipal Stadium, capacity 73,000.

Florida Citrus Bowl

1-1-47.............Catawba 31, Maryville (TN) 6
1-1-48.............Catawba 7, Marshall 0
1-1-49.............Murray St 21, Sul Ross St 21
1-2-50.............St Vincent 7, Emory & Henry 6
1-1-51.............Morris Harvey 35, Emory & Henry 14
1-1-52.............Stetson 35, Arkansas St 20
1-1-53.............E Texas St 33, Tennessee Tech 0
1-1-54.............E Texas St 7, Arkansas St 7
1-1-55.............NE-Omaha 7, Eastern Kentucky 6
1-2-56.............Juniata 6, Missouri Valley 6
1-1-57.............W Texas St 20, Southern Miss 13
1-1-58.............E Texas St 10, Southern Miss 9
12-27-58.........E Texas St 26, Missouri Valley 7
1-1-60.............Middle Tennessee St 21, Presbyterian 12
12-30-60.........Citadel 27, Tennessee Tech 0
12-29-61.........Lamar 21, Middle Tennessee St 14
12-22-62.........Houston 49, Miami (OH) 21
12-28-63.........Western Kentucky 27, Coast Guard 0
12-12-64.........E Carolina 14, Massachusetts 13
12-11-65.........E Carolina 31, Maine 0
12-10-66.........Morgan St 14, West Chester 6
12-16-67.........TN-Martin 25, West Chester 8
12-27-68.........Richmond 49, Ohio 42
12-26-69.........Toledo 56, Davidson 33
12-28-70.........Toledo 40, William & Mary 12
12-28-71.........Toledo 28, Richmond 3
12-29-72.........Tampa 21, Kent St 18
12-22-73.........Miami (OH) 16, Florida 7
12-21-74.........Miami (OH) 21, Georgia 10
12-20-75.........Miami (OH) 20, S Carolina 7
12-18-76.........Oklahoma St 49, Brigham Young 21
12-23-77.........Florida St 40, Texas Tech 17
12-23-78.........N Carolina St 30, Pittsburgh 17
12-22-79.........Louisiana St 34, Wake Forest 10
12-20-80.........Florida 35, Maryland 20
12-19-81.........Missouri 19, Southern Miss 17
12-18-82.........Auburn 33, Boston Col 26
12-17-83.........Tennessee 30, Maryland 23
12-22-84.........Georgia 17, Florida St 17
12-28-85.........Ohio St 10, Brigham Young 7
1-1-87.............Auburn 16, Southern Cal 7
1-1-88.............Clemson 35, Penn St 10
1-2-89.............Clemson 13, Oklahoma 6
1-1-90.............Illinois 31, Virginia 21
1-1-91.............Georgia Tech 45, Nebraska 21

Florida Citrus Bowl *(Cont.)*

1-1-92.............California 37, Clemson 13
1-1-93.............Georgia 21, Ohio State 14
1-1-94.............Penn State 31, Tennessee 13
1-2-95.............Alabama 24, Ohio St 17
1-1-96.............Tennessee 20, Ohio St 14
1-1-97.............Tennessee 48, Northwestern 28
1-1-98.............Florida 21, Penn St 6

City: Orlando, FL. Stadium: Florida Citrus Bowl, capacity 72,000.

Name Change: Tangerine Bowl (1947-82).

Playing Sites: Tangerine Bowl (1947-72, 1974-82); Florida Field, Gainesville (1973); Orlando Stadium (1983-85); Florida Citrus Bowl-Orlando (since 1986). Tangerine Bowl, Orlando Stadium and Florida Citrus Bowl-Orlando are identical site.

Liberty Bowl

12-19-59.........Penn St 7, Alabama 0
12-17-60.........Penn St 41, Oregon 12
12-16-61.........Syracuse 15, Miami (FL) 14
12-15-62.........Oregon St 6, Villanova 0
12-21-63.........Mississippi St 16, N Carolina St 12
12-19-64.........Utah 32, W Virginia 6
12-18-65.........Mississippi 13, Auburn 7
12-10-66.........Miami (FL) 14, Virginia Tech 7
12-16-67.........N Carolina St 14, Georgia 7
12-14-68.........Mississippi 34, Virginia Tech 17
12-13-69.........Colorado 47, Alabama 33
12-12-70.........Tulane 17, Colorado 3
12-20-71.........Tennessee 14, Arkansas 13
12-18-72.........Georgia Tech 31, Iowa St 30
12-17-73.........N Carolina St 31, Kansas 18
12-16-74.........Tennessee 7, Maryland 3
12-22-75.........Southern Cal 20, Texas A&M 0
12-20-76.........Alabama 36, UCLA 6
12-19-77.........Nebraska 21, N Carolina 17
12-23-78.........Missouri 20, Louisiana St 15
12-22-79.........Penn St 9, Tulane 6
12-27-80.........Purdue 28, Missouri 25
12-30-81.........Ohio St 31, Navy 28
12-29-82.........Alabama 21, Illinois 15
12-29-83.........Notre Dame 19, Boston Col 18
12-27-84.........Auburn 21, Arkansas 15
12-27-85.........Baylor 21, Louisiana St 7
12-29-86.........Tennessee 21, Minnesota 14
12-29-87.........Georgia 20, Arkansas 17
12-28-88.........Indiana 34, S Carolina 10
12-28-89.........Mississippi 42, Air Force 29
12-27-90.........Air Force 23, Ohio St 11
12-29-91.........Air Force 38, Mississippi St 15
12-31-92.........Mississippi 13, Air Force 0
12-28-93.........Louisville 18, Michigan St 7
12-31-94.........Illinois 30, E Carolina 0
12-30-95.........East Carolina 19, Stanford 13
12-27-96.........Syracuse 30, Houston 17
12-31-97.........Southern Missipi 41, Pittsburgh 7

City: Memphis (since 1965). Stadium: Liberty Bowl Memorial Stadium, capacity 62,380.

Playing Sites: Philadelphia (Municipal Stadium, 1959-63), Atlantic City (Convention Center, 1964).

Bluebonnet Bowl (Discontinued)

12-19-59.........Clemson 23, Texas Christian 7
12-17-60.........Texas 3, Alabama 3
12-16-61.........Kansas 33, Rice 7
12-22-62.........Missouri 14, Georgia Tech 10
12-21-63.........Baylor 14, LSU 7

Bluebonnet Bowl *(Cont.)*

12-19-64..........Tulsa 14, Mississippi 7
12-18-65..........Tennessee 27, Tulsa 6
12-17-66..........Texas 19, Mississippi 0
12-23-67..........Colorado 31, Miami (FL) 21
12-31-68..........SMU 28, Oklahoma 27
12-31-69..........Houston 36, Auburn 7
12-31-70..........Alabama 24, Oklahoma 24
12-31-71..........Colorado 29, Houston 17
12-30-72..........Tennessee 24, Louisiana St 17
12-29-73..........Houston 47, Tulane 7
12-23-74..........N Carolina St 31, Houston 31
12-27-75..........Texas 38, Colorado 21
12-31-76..........Nebraska 27, Texas Tech 24
12-31-77..........Southern Cal 47, Texas A&M 28
12-31-78..........Stanford 25, Georgia 22
12-31-79..........Purdue 27, Tennessee 22
12-31-80..........N Carolina 16, Texas 7
12-31-81..........Michigan 33, UCLA 14
12-31-82..........Arkansas 28, Florida 24
12-31-83..........Oklahoma 24, Baylor 14
12-31-84..........W Virginia 31, Texas Christian 14
12-31-85..........Air Force 24, Texas 16
12-31-86..........Baylor 21, Colorado 9
12-31-87..........Texas 32, Pittsburgh 27

City: Houston. Playing sites: Rice Stadium (1959-67; 1985-86), Astrodome (1968-84, 1987).

Name change: Astro-Bluebonnet Bowl (1968-76).

Peach Bowl

12-30-68..........Louisiana St 31, Florida St 27
12-30-69..........W Virginia 14, S Carolina 3
12-30-70..........Arizona St 48, N Carolina 26
12-30-71..........Mississippi 41, Georgia Tech 18
12-29-72..........N Carolina St 49, W Virginia 13
12-28-73..........Georgia 17, Maryland 16
12-28-74..........Vanderbilt 6, Texas Tech 6
12-31-75..........W Virginia 13, N Carolina St 10
12-31-76..........Kentucky 21, N Carolina 0
12-31-77..........N Carolina St 24, Iowa St 14
12-25-78..........Purdue 41, Georgia Tech 21
12-31-79..........Baylor 24, Clemson 18
1-2-81............Miami (FL) 20, Virginia Tech 10
12-31-81..........W Virginia 26, Florida 6
12-31-82..........Iowa 28, Tennessee 22
12-30-83..........Florida St 28, N Carolina 3
12-31-84..........Virginia 27, Purdue 24
12-31-85..........Army 31, Illinois 29
12-31-86..........Virginia Tech 25, N Carolina St 24
1-2-88............Tennessee 27, Indiana 22
12-31-88..........N Carolina St 28, Iowa 23
12-30-89..........Syracuse 19, Georgia 18
12-29-90..........Auburn 27, Indiana 23
1-1-92............E Carolina 37, N Carolina St 34
1-2-93............North Carolina 21, Mississippi St 17
12-31-93..........Clemson 14, Kentucky 13
1-1-95............N Carolina St 28, Mississippi St 24
12-30-95..........Virginia 34, Georgia 27
12-28-96..........Louisiana St 10, Clemson 7
1-2-98............Auburn 21, Clemson 17

City: Atlanta. Stadium: Georgia Dome, capacity 71,228.
Playing Sites: Grant Field (1968-70), Atlanta-Fulton County Stadium (1971-92), Georgia Dome (since 1993).

Fiesta Bowl

12-27-71..........Arizona St 45, Florida St 38
12-23-72..........Arizona St 49, Missouri 35
12-21-73..........Arizona St 28, Pittsburgh 7
12-28-74..........Oklahoma St 16, Brigham Young 6

Fiesta Bowl *(Cont.)*

12-26-75..........Arizona St 17, Nebraska 14
12-25-76..........Oklahoma 41, Wyoming 7
12-25-77..........Penn St 42, Arizona St 30
12-25-78..........Arkansas 10, UCLA 10
12-25-79..........Pittsburgh 16, Arizona 10
12-26-80..........Penn St 31, Ohio St 19
1-1-82............Penn St 26, Southern Cal 10
1-1-83............Arizona St 32, Oklahoma 21
1-2-84............Ohio St 28, Pittsburgh 23
1-1-85............UCLA 39, Miami (FL) 37
1-1-86............Michigan 27, Nebraska 23
1-2-87............Penn St 14, Miami (FL) 10
1-1-88............Florida St 31, Nebraska 28
1-2-89............Notre Dame 34, W Virginia 21
1-1-90............Florida St 41, Nebraska 17
1-1-91............Louisville 34, Alabama 7
1-1-92............Penn St 42, Tennessee 17
1-1-93............Syracuse 26, Colorado 22
1-1-94............Arizona 29, Miami (FL) 0
1-2-95............Colorado 41, Notre Dame 24
1-2-96............Nebraska 62, Florida 24
1-1-97............Penn St 38, Texas 15
12-31-97..........Kansas St 35, Syracuse 18

City: Tempe, AZ. Stadium: Sun Devil Stadium, capacity 73,656.

Independence Bowl

12-13-76..........McNeese St 20, Tulsa 16
12-17-77..........Louisiana Tech 24, Louisville 14
12-16-78..........E Carolina 35, Louisiana Tech 13
12-15-79..........Syracuse 31, McNeese St 7
12-13-80..........Southern Miss 16, McNeese St 14
12-12-81..........Texas A&M 33, Oklahoma St 16
12-11-82..........Wisconsin 14, Kansas St 3
12-10-83..........Air Force 9, Mississippi 3
12-15-84..........Air Force 23, Virginia Tech 7
12-21-85..........Minnesota 20, Clemson 13
12-20-86..........Mississippi 20, Texas Tech 17
12-19-87..........Washington 24, Tulane 12
12-23-88..........Southern Miss 38, UTEP 18
12-16-89..........Oregon 27, Tulsa 24
12-15-90..........Louisiana Tech 34, Maryland 34
12-29-91..........Georgia 24, Arkansas 15
12-31-92..........Wake Forest 39, Oregon 35
12-31-93..........Virginia Tech 45, Indiana 20
12-28-94..........Virginia 20, Texas Christian 10
12-29-95..........Louisiana St 45, Michigan St 26
12-31-96..........Auburn 32, Army 29
12-28-97..........Louisiana St 27, Notre Dame 9

City: Shreveport, LA. Stadium: Independence Stadium, capacity 50,832.

All-American Bowl (Discontinued)

12-22-77..........Maryland 17, Minnesota 7
12-20-78..........Texas A&M 28, Iowa St 12
12-29-79..........Missouri 24, S Carolina 14
12-27-80..........Arkansas 34, Tulane 15
12-31-81..........Mississippi St 10, Kansas 0
12-31-82..........Air Force 36, Vanderbilt 28
12-22-83..........W Virginia 20, Kentucky 16
12-29-84..........Kentucky 20, Wisconsin 19
12-31-85..........Georgia Tech 17, Michigan St 14
12-31-86..........Florida St 27, Indiana 13
12-22-87..........Virginia 22, Brigham Young 16
12-29-88..........Florida 14, Illinois 10
12-28-89..........Texas Tech 49, Duke 21
12-28-90..........N Carolina St 31, S Mississippi 27

City: Birmingham, AL. Stadium: Legion Field.
Name Change: Hall of Fame Classic (1977-84).

Holiday Bowl

12-22-78 ....Navy 23, Brigham Young 16
12-21-79 ....Indiana 38, Brigham Young 37
12-19-80 ....Brigham Young 46, SMU 45
12-18-81 ....Brigham Young 38, Washington St 36
12-17-82 ....Ohio St 47, Brigham Young 17
12-23-83 ....Brigham Young 21, Missouri 17
12-21-84 ....Brigham Young 24, Michigan 17
12-22-85 ....Arkansas 18, Arizona St 17
12-30-86 ....Iowa 39, San Diego St 38
12-30-87 ....Iowa 20, Wyoming 19
12-30-88 ....Oklahoma St 62, Wyoming 14
12-29-89 ....Penn St 50, Brigham Young 39
12-29-90 ....Texas A&M 65, Brigham Young 14
12-30-91 ....Iowa 13, Brigham Young 13
12-30-92 ....Hawaii 27, Illinois 17
12-30-93 ....Ohio St 28, Brigham Young 21
12-30-94 ....Michigan 24, Colorado St 14
12-29-95 ....Kansas St 54, Colorado St 21
12-30-96 ....Colorado 33, Washington 21
12-29-97 ....Colorado St 35, Missouri 24

City: San Diego. Stadium: San Diego Jack Murphy Stadium, capacity 60,000.

Las Vegas Bowl

12-19-81 ....Toledo 27, San Jose St 25
12-18-82 ....Fresno St 29, Bowling Green 28
12-17-83 ....Northern Illinois 20, Cal St-Fullerton 13
12-15-84 ....UNLV 30, Toledo 13*
12-14-85 ....Fresno St 51, Bowling Green 7
12-13-86 ....San Jose St 37, Miami (OH) 7
12-12-87 ....Eastern Michigan 30, San Jose St 27
12-10-88 ....Fresno St 35, Western Michigan 30
12-9-89 ....Fresno St 27, Ball St 6
12-8-90 ....San Jose St 48, Central Michigan 24
12-14-91 ....Bowling Green 28, Fresno St 21
12-18-92 ....Bowling Green 35, Nevada 34
12-17-93 ....Utah St 42, Ball St 33
12-15-94 ....UNLV 52, Central Michigan 24
12-14-95 ....Toledo 40, Nevada 37
12-19-96 ....Nevada 18, Ball St 15
12-19-97 ....Oregon 41, Air Force 13

* Toledo won later by forfeit.
City: Las Vegas (since 1992). Stadium: Sam Boyd Silver Bowl Stadium, capacity 32,000.
Name change: California Bowl (1981-91).
Playing sites: Fresno, CA (Bulldog Stadium, 1981-91), Las Vegas.

Aloha Bowl

12-25-82 ....Washington 21, Maryland 20
12-26-83 ....Penn St 13, Washington 10
12-29-84 ....SMU 27, Notre Dame 20
12-28-85 ....Alabama 24, Southern Cal 3
12-27-86 ....Arizona 30, N Carolina 21
12-25-87 ....UCLA 20, Florida 16
12-25-88 ....Washington St 24, Houston 22
12-25-89 ....Michigan St 33, Hawaii 13
12-25-90 ....Syracuse 28, Arizona 0
12-25-91 ....Georgia Tech 18, Stanford 17
12-25-92 ....Kansas 23, Brigham Young 20
12-25-93 ....Colorado 41, Fresno St 30
12-25-94 ....Boston College 12, Kansas St 7
12-25-95 ....Kansas 51, UCLA 30
12-25-96 ....Navy 42, California 38
12-25-97 ....Washington 51, Michigan St 23

City: Honolulu. Stadium: Aloha Stadium, capacity 50,000.

Freedom Bowl (Discontinued)

12-16-84 ....Iowa 55, Texas 17
12-30-85 ....Washington 20, Colorado 17
12-30-86 ....UCLA 31, Brigham Young 10
12-30-87 ....Arizona St 33, Air Force 28
12-29-88 ....Brigham Young 20, Colorado 17
12-30-89 ....Washington 34, Florida 7
12-29-90 ....Colorado St 32, Oregon 31
12-30-91 ....Tulsa 28, San Diego St 17
12-29-92 ....Fresno St 24, Southern Cal 7
12-30-93 ....Southern Cal 28, Utah 21
12-29-94 ....Utah 16, Arizona 13

City: Anaheim. Stadium: Anaheim Stadium.

Outback Bowl

12-23-86 ....Boston College 27, Georgia 24
1-2-88 ....Michigan 28, Alabama 24
1-2-89 ....Syracuse 23, Louisiana St 10
1-1-90 ....Auburn 31, Ohio St 14
1-1-91 ....Clemson 30, Illinois 0
1-1-92 ....Syracuse 24, Ohio St 17
1-1-93 ....Tennessee 38, Boston College 23
1-1-94 ....Michigan 42, N Carolina St 7
1-2-95 ....Wisconsin 34, Duke 20
1-1-96 ....Penn St 43, Auburn 14
1-1-97 ....Alabama 17, Michigan 14
1-1-98 ....Georgia 33, Wisconsin 6

Name change: Hall of Fame Bowl (1986-95).

Copper Bowl

12-31-89 ....Arizona 17, N Carolina St 10
12-31-90 ....California 17, Wyoming 15
12-31-91 ....Indiana 24, Baylor 0
12-29-92 ....Washington St 31, Utah 28
12-29-93 ....Kansas St 52, Wyoming 17
12-29-94 ....Brigham Young 31, Oklahoma 6
12-27-95 ....Texas Tech 55, Air Force 41
12-27-96 ....Wisconsin 38, Utah 10
12-27-97 ....Arizona 20, New Mexico 14

City: Tucson. Stadium: Arizona Stadium, capacity 56,167.

Carquest Bowl

12-28-90 ....Florida St 24, Penn St 17
12-28-91 ....Alabama 30, Colorado 25
1-1-93 ....Stanford 24, Penn St 3
1-1-94 ....Boston College 31, Virginia 13
1-2-95 ....S Carolina 24, W Virginia 21
12-30-95 ....N Carolina 20, Arkansas 10
12-27-96 ....Miami (FL) 31, Virginia 21
12-29-97 ....Georgia Tech 35, West Virginia 30

City: Miami. Stadium: Pro Player Stadium, capacity 75,192.
Name Change: Blockbuster Bowl (1990-93).

Alamo Bowl

12-31-93 ....California 37, Iowa 3
12-31-94 ....Washington St 10, Baylor 3
12-28-95 ....Texas A&M 22, Michigan 20
12-29-96 ....Iowa 27, Texas Tech 0
12-30-97 ....Purdue 33, Oklahoma St 20

City: San Antonio, TX. Stadium: Alamodome, capacity 65,000.

1936

		Record	Coach
1.	Minnesota	7-1-0	Bernie Bierman
2.	Louisiana St	9-0-1	Bernie Moore
3.	Pittsburgh	7-1-1	Jack Sutherland
4.	Alabama	8-0-1	Frank Thomas
5.	Washington	7-1-1	Jimmy Phelan
6.	Santa Clara	7-1-0	Buck Shaw
7.	Northwestern	7-1-0	Pappy Waldorf
8.	Notre Dame	6-2-1	Elmer Layden
9.	Nebraska	7-2-0	Dana X. Bible
10.	Pennsylvania	7-1-0	Harvey Harman
11.	Duke	9-1-0	Wallace Wade
12.	Yale	7-1-0	Ducky Pond
13.	Dartmouth	7-1-1	Red Blaik
14.	Duquesne	7-2-0	John Smith
15.	Fordham	5-1-2	Jim Crowley
16.	Texas Christian	8-2-2	Dutch Meyer
17.	Tennessee	6-2-2	Bob Neyland
18.	Arkansas	7-3-0	Fred Thomsen
19.	Navy	6-3-0	Tom Hamilton
20.	Marquette	7-1-0	Frank Murray

1937

		Record	Coach
1.	Pittsburgh	9-0-1	Jack Sutherland
2.	California	9-0-1	Stub Allison
3.	Fordham	7-0-1	Jim Crowley
4.	Alabama	9-0-0	Frank Thomas
5.	Minnesota	6-2-0	Bernie Bierman
6.	Villanova	8-0-1	Clipper Smith
7.	Dartmouth	7-0-2	Red Blaik
8.	Louisiana St	9-1-0	Bernie Moore
9.	Notre Dame	6-2-1	Elmer Layden
	Santa Clara	8-0-0	Buck Shaw
11.	Nebraska	6-1-2	Biff Jones
12.	Yale	6-1-1	Ducky Pond
13.	Ohio St	6-2-0	Francis Schmidt
14.	Holy Cross	8-0-2	Eddie Anderson
	Arkansas	6-2-2	Fred Thomsen
16.	Texas Christian	4-2-2	Dutch Meyer
17.	Colorado	8-0-0	Bunnie Oakes
18.	Rice	5-3-2	Jimmy Kitts
19.	N Carolina	7-1-1	Ray Wolf
20.	Duke	7-2-1	Wallace Wade

1938

		Record	Coach
1.	Texas Christian	10-0-0	Dutch Meyer
2.	Tennessee	10-0-0	Bob Neyland
3.	Duke	9-0-0	Wallace Wade
4.	Oklahoma	10-0-0	Tom Stidham
5.	#Notre Dame	8-1-0	Elmer Layden
6.	Carnegie Tech	7-1-0	Bill Kern
7.	Southern Cal	8-2-0	Howard Jones
8.	Pittsburgh	8-2-0	Jack Sutherland
9.	Holy Cross	8-1-0	Eddie Anderson
10.	Minnesota	6-2-0	Bernie Bierman
11.	Texas Tech	10-0-0	Pete Cawthon
12.	Cornell	5-1-1	Carl Snavely
13.	Alabama	7-1-1	Frank Thomas
14.	California	10-1-0	Stub Allison

#Selected No. 1 by the Dickinson System.

1938 (Cont.)

		Record	Coach
15.	Fordham	6-1-2	Jim Crowley
16.	Michigan	6-1-1	Fritz Crisler
17.	Northwestern	4-2-2	Pappy Waldorf
18.	Villanova	8-0-1	Clipper Smith
19.	Tulane	7-2-1	Red Dawson
20.	Dartmouth	7-2-0	Red Blaik

1939

		Record	Coach
1.	Texas A&M	10-0-0	Homer Norton
2.	Tennessee	10-0-0	Bob Neyland
3.	#Southern Cal	7-0-2	Howard Jones
4.	Cornell	8-0-0	Carl Snavely
5.	Tulane	8-0-1	Red Dawson
6.	Missouri	8-1-0	Don Faurot
7.	UCLA	6-0-4	Babe Horrell
8.	Duke	8-1-0	Wallace Wade
9.	Iowa	6-1-1	Eddie Anderson
10.	Duquesne	8-0-1	Buff Donelli
11.	Boston College	9-1-0	Frank Leahy
12.	Clemson	8-1-0	Jess Neely
13.	Notre Dame	7-2-0	Elmer Layden
14.	Santa Clara	5-1-3	Buck Shaw
15.	Ohio St	6-2-0	Francis Schmidt
16.	Georgia Tech	7-2-0	Bill Alexander
17.	Fordham	6-2-0	Jim Crowley
18.	Nebraska	7-1-1	Biff Jones
19.	Oklahoma	6-2-1	Tom Stidham
20.	Michigan	6-2-0	Fritz Crisler

#Selected No. 1 by the Dickinson System.

1940

		Record	Coach
1.	Minnesota	8-0-0	Bernie Bierman
2.	Stanford	9-0-0	C. Shaughnessy
3.	Michigan	7-1-0	Fritz Crisler
4.	Tennessee	10-0-0	Bob Neyland
5.	Boston College	10-0-0	Frank Leahy
6.	Texas A&M	8-1-0	Homer Norton
7.	Nebraska	8-1-0	Biff Jones
8.	Northwestern	6-2-0	Pappy Waldorf
9.	Mississippi St	9-0-1	Allyn McKeen
10.	Washington	7-2-0	Jimmy Phelan
11.	Santa Clara	6-1-1	Buck Shaw
12.	Fordham	7-1-0	Jim Crowley
13.	Georgetown	8-1-0	Jack Hagerty
14.	Pennsylvania	6-1-1	George Munger
15.	Cornell	6-2-0	Carl Snavely
16.	SMU	8-1-1	Matty Bell
17.	Hard.-Simmons	9-0-0	Abe Woodson
18.	Duke	7-2-0	Wallace Wade
19.	Lafayette	9-0-0	Hooks Mylin
20.	—		

Only 19 teams selected.

Note: Except where indicated with an asterisk, the polls from 1936 through 1964 were taken before the bowl games and those from 1965 through the present were taken after the bowl games.

1941

		Record	Coach
1.	Minnesota	8-0-0	Bernie Bierman
2.	Duke	9-0-0	Wallace Wade
3.	Notre Dame	8-0-1	Frank Leahy
4.	Texas	8-1-1	Dana X. Bible
5.	Michigan	6-1-1	Fritz Crisler
6.	Fordham	7-1-0	Jim Crowley
7.	Missouri	8-1-0	Don Faurot
8.	Duquesne	8-0-0	Buff Donelli
9.	Texas A&M	9-1-0	Homer Norton
10.	Navy	7-1-1	Swede Larson
11.	Northwestern	5-3-0	Pappy Waldorf
12.	Oregon St.	7-2-0	Lon Stiner
13.	Ohio St	6-1-1	Paul Brown
14.	Georgia	8-1-1	Wally Butts
15.	Pennsylvania	7-1-1	George Munger
16.	Mississippi St	8-1-1	Allyn McKeen
17.	Mississippi	6-2-1	Harry Mehre
18.	Tennessee	8-2-0	John Barnhill
19.	Washington St	6-4-0	Babe Hollingbery
20.	Alabama	8-2-0	Frank Thomas

1942

		Record	Coach
1.	Ohio St	9-1-0	Paul Brown
2.	Georgia	10-1-0	Wally Butts
3.	Wisconsin	8-1-1	H. Stuhldreher
4.	Tulsa	10-0-0	Henry Frnka
5.	Georgia Tech	9-1-0	Bill Alexander
6.	Notre Dame	7-2-2	Frank Leahy
7.	Tennessee	8-1-1	John Barnhill
8.	Boston College	8-1-0	Denny Myers
9.	Michigan	7-3-0	Fritz Crisler
10.	Alabama	7-3-0	Frank Thomas
11.	Texas	8-2-0	Dana X. Bible
12.	Stanford	6-4-0	Marchie Schwartz
13.	UCLA	7-3-0	Babe Horrell
14.	William & Mary	9-1-1	Carl Voyles
15.	Santa Clara	7-2-0	Buck Shaw
16.	Auburn	6-4-1	Jack Meagher
17.	Washington St	6-2-2	Babe Hollingbery
18.	Mississippi St	8-2-0	Allyn McKeen
19.	Minnesota	5-4-0	George Hauser
	Holy Cross	5-4-1	Ank Scanlon
	Penn St	6-1-1	Bob Higgins

1943

		Record	Coach
1.	Notre Dame	9-1-0	Frank Leahy
2.	Iowa Pre-Flight	9-1-0	Don Faurot
3.	Michigan	8-1-0	Fritz Crisler
4.	Navy	8-1-0	Billick Whelchel
5.	Purdue	9-0-0	Elmer Burnham
6.	Great Lakes	10-2-0	Tony Hinkle
7.	Duke	8-1-0	Eddie Cameron
8.	Del Monte P-F	7-1-0	Bill Kern
9.	Northwestern	6-2-0	Pappy Waldorf
10.	March Field	9-1-0	Paul Schissler
11.	Army	7-2-1	Red Blaik
12.	Washington	4-0-0	Ralph Welch
13.	Georgia Tech	7-3-0	Bill Alexander
14.	Texas	7-1-0	Dana X. Bible
15.	Tulsa	6-0-1	Henry Frnka
16.	Dartmouth	6-1-0	Earl Brown

1943 (Cont.)

		Record	Coach
17.	Bainbridge NTS	7-0-0	Joe Maniaci
18.	Colorado College	7-0-0	Hal White
19.	Pacific	7-2-0	Amos A. Stagg
20.	Pennsylvania	6-2-1	George Munger

1944

		Record	Coach
1.	Army	9-0-0	Red Blaik
2.	Ohio St	9-0-0	Carroll Widdoes
3.	Randolph Field	11-0-0	Frank Tritico
4.	Navy	6-3-0	Oscar Hagberg
5.	Bainbridge NTS	9-0-0	Joe Maniaci
6.	Iowa Pre-Flight	10-1-0	Jack Meagher
7.	Southern Cal	7-0-2	Jeff Cravath
8.	Michigan	8-2-0	Fritz Crisler
9.	Notre Dame	8-2-0	Ed McKeever
10.	March Field	7-1-2	Paul Schissler
11.	Duke	5-4-0	Eddie Cameron
12.	Tennessee	8-0-1	John Barnhill
13.	Georgia Tech	8-2-0	Bill Alexander
	Norman P-F	6-0-0	John Gregg
15.	Illinois	5-4-1	Ray Eliot
16.	El Toro Marines	8-1-0	Dick Hanley
17.	Great Lakes	9-2-1	Paul Brown
18.	Fort Pierce	9-0-0	Hamp Pool
19.	St. Mary's P-F	4-4-0	Jules Sikes
20.	2nd Air Force	7-2-1	Bill Reese

1945

		Record	Coach
1.	Army	9-0-0	Red Blaik
2.	Alabama	9-0-0	Frank Thomas
3.	Navy	7-1-1	Oscar Hagberg
4.	Indiana	9-0-1	Bo McMillan
5.	Oklahoma A&M	8-0-0	Jim Lookabaugh
6.	Michigan	7-3-0	Fritz Crisler
7.	St. Mary's (CA)	7-1-0	Jimmy Phelan
8.	Pennsylvania	6-2-0	George Munger
9.	Notre Dame	7-2-1	Hugh Devore
10.	Texas	9-1-0	Dana X. Bible
11.	Southern Cal	7-3-0	Jeff Cravath
12.	Ohio St	7-2-0	Carroll Widdoes
13.	Duke	6-2-0	Eddie Cameron
14.	Tennessee	8-1-0	John Barnhill
15.	Louisiana St	7-2-0	Bernie Moore
16.	Holy Cross	8-1-0	John DeGrosa
17.	Tulsa	8-2-0	Henry Frnka
18.	Georgia	8-2-0	Wally Butts
19.	Wake Forest	4-3-1	Peahead Walker
20.	Columbia	8-1-0	Lou Little

1946

		Record	Coach
1.	Notre Dame	8-0-1	Frank Leahy
2.	Army	9-0-1	Red Blaik
3.	Georgia	10-0-0	Wally Butts
4.	UCLA	10-0-0	B. LaBrucherie
5.	Illinois	7-2-0	Ray Eliot
6.	Michigan	6-2-1	Fritz Crisler
7.	Tennessee	9-1-0	Bob Neyland
8.	Louisiana St	9-1-0	Bernie Moore
9.	N Carolina	8-1-1	Carl Snavely
10.	Rice	8-2-0	Jess Neely
11.	Georgia Tech	8-2-0	Bobby Dodd

1946 (Cont.)

	Record	Coach
12. Yale	7-1-1	Howard Odell
13. Pennsylvania	6-2-0	George Munger
14. Oklahoma	7-3-0	Jim Tatum
15. Texas	8-2-0	Dana X. Bible
16. Arkansas	6-3-1	John Barnhill
17. Tulsa	9-1-0	J.O. Brothers
18. N Carolina St	8-2-0	Beattie Feathers
19. Delaware	9-0-0	Bill Murray
20. Indiana	6-3-0	Bo McMillan

1947

	Record	Coach
1. Notre Dame	9-0-0	Frank Leahy
2. #Michigan	9-0-0	Fritz Crisler
3. SMU	9-0-1	Matty Bell
4. Penn St	9-0-0	Bob Higgins
5. Texas	9-1-0	Blair Cherry
6. Alabama	8-2-0	Red Drew
7. Pennsylvania	7-0-1	George Munger
8. Southern Cal	7-1-1	Jeff Cravath
9. N Carolina	8-2-0	Carl Snavely
10. Georgia Tech	9-1-0	Bobby Dodd
11. Army	5-2-2	Red Blaik
12. Kansas	8-0-2	George Sauer
13. Mississippi	8-2-0	Johnny Vaught
14. William & Mary	9-1-0	Rube McCray
15. California	9-1-0	Pappy Waldorf
16. Oklahoma	7-2-1	Bud Wilkinson
17. N Carolina St	5-3-1	Beattie Feathers
18. Rice	6-3-1	Jess Neely
19. Duke	4-3-2	Wallace Wade
20. Columbia	7-2-0	Lou Little

#The AP, which had voted Notre Dame No. 1 before the bowl games, took a second vote, giving the title to Michigan after its 49-0 win over Southern Cal in the Rose Bowl.

1948

	Record	Coach
1. Michigan	9-0-0	Bennie Oosterbaan
2. Notre Dame	9-0-1	Frank Leahy
3. N Carolina	9-0-1	Carl Snavely
4. California	10-0-0	Pappy Waldorf
5. Oklahoma	9-1-0	Bud Wilkinson
6. Army	8-0-1	Red Blaik
7. Northwestern	7-2-0	Bob Voigts
8. Georgia	9-1-0	Wally Butts
9. Oregon	9-1-0	Jim Aiken
10. SMU	8-1-1	Matty Bell
11. Clemson	10-0-0	Frank Howard
12. Vanderbilt	8-2-1	Red Sanders
13. Tulane	9-1-0	Henry Frnka
14. Michigan St	6-2-2	Biggie Munn
15. Mississippi	8-1-0	Johnny Vaught
16. Minnesota	7-2-0	Bernie Bierman
17. William & Mary	6-2-2	Rube McCray
18. Penn St	7-1-1	Bob Higgins
19. Cornell	8-1-0	Lefty James
20. Wake Forest	6-3-0	Peahead Walker

1949

	Record	Coach
1. Notre Dame	10-0-0	Frank Leahy
2. Oklahoma	10-0-0	Bud Wilkinson
3. California	10-0-0	Pappy Waldorf
4. Army	9-0-0	Red Blaik

1949 (Cont.)

	Record	Coach
5. Rice	9-1-0	Jess Neely
6. Ohio St	6-1-2	Wes Fesler
7. Michigan	6-2-1	Bennie Oosterbaan
8. Minnesota	7-2-0	Bernie Bierman
9. Louisiana St	8-2-0	Gaynell Tinsley
10. Pacific	11-0-0	Larry Siemering
11. Kentucky	9-2-0	Bear Bryant
12. Cornell	8-1-0	Lefty James
13. Villanova	8-1-0	Jim Leonard
14. Maryland	8-1-0	Jim Tatum
15. Santa Clara	7-2-1	Len Casanova
16. N Carolina	7-3-0	Carl Snavely
17. Tennessee	7-2-1	Bob Neyland
18. Princeton	6-3-0	Charlie Caldwell
19. Michigan St	6-3-0	Biggie Munn
20. Missouri	7-3-0	Don Faurot
Baylor	8-2-0	Bob Woodruff

1950

	Record	Coach
1. Oklahoma	10-0-0	Bud Wilkinson
2. Army	8-1-0	Red Blaik
3. Texas	9-1-0	Blair Cherry
4. Tennessee	10-1-0	Bob Neyland
5. California	9-0-1	Pappy Waldorf
6. Princeton	9-0-0	Charlie Caldwell
7. Kentucky	10-1-0	Bear Bryant
8. Michigan St	8-1-0	Biggie Munn
9. Michigan	5-3-1	Bennie Oosterhaan
10. Clemson	8-0-1	Frank Howard
11. Washington	8-2-0	Howard Odell
12. Wyoming	9-0-0	Bowden Wyatt
13. Illinois	7-2-0	Ray Eliot
14. Ohio St	6-3-0	Wes Fesler
15. Miami (FL)	9-0-1	Andy Gustafson
16. Alabama	9-2-0	Red Drew
17. Nebraska	6-2-1	Bill Glassford
18. Wash & Lee	8-2-0	George Barclay
19. Tulsa	9-1-1	J.O. Brothers
20. Tulane	6-2-1	Henry Frnka

1951

	Record	Coach
1. Tennessee	10-0-0	Bob Neyland
2. Michigan St	9-0-0	Biggie Munn
3. Maryland	9-0-0	Jim Tatum
4. Illinois	8-0-1	Ray Eliot
5. Georgia Tech	10-0-1	Bobby Dodd
6. Princeton	9-0-0	Charlie Caldwell
7. Stanford	9-1-0	Chuck Taylor
8. Wisconsin	7-1-1	Ivy Williamson
9. Baylor	8-1-1	George Sauer
10. Oklahoma	8-2-0	Bud Wilkinson
11. Texas Christian	6-4-0	Dutch Meyer
12. California	8-2-0	Pappy Waldorf
13. Virginia	8-1-0	Art Guepe
14. San Francisco	9-0-0	Joe Kuharich
15. Kentucky	7-4-0	Bear Bryant
16. Boston Univ	6-4-0	Buff Donelli
17. UCLA	5-3-1	Red Sanders
18. Washington St	7-3-0	Forest Evashevski
19. Holy Cross	8-2-0	Eddie Anderson
20. Clemson	7-2-0	Frank Howard

1952

		Record	Coach
1.	Michigan St	9-0-0	Biggie Munn
2.	Georgia Tech	11-0-0	Bobby Dodd
3.	Notre Dame	7-2-1	Frank Leahy
4.	Oklahoma	8-1-1	Bud Wilkinson
5.	Southern Cal	9-1-0	Jess Hill
6.	UCLA	8-1-0	Red Sanders
7.	Mississippi	8-0-2	Johnny Vaught
8.	Tennessee	8-1-1	Bob Neyland
9.	Alabama	9-2-0	Red Drew
10.	Texas	8-2-0	Ed Price
11.	Wisconsin	6-2-1	Ivy Williamson
12.	Tulsa	8-1-1	J.O. Brothers
13.	Maryland	7-2-0	Jim Tatum
14.	Syracuse	7-2-0	Ben Schwartzwalder
15.	Florida	7-3-0	Bob Woodruff
16.	Duke	8-2-0	Bill Murray
17.	Ohio St	6-3-0	Woody Hayes
18.	Purdue	4-3-2	Stu Holcomb
19.	Princeton	8-1-0	Charlie Caldwell
20.	Kentucky	5-4-2	Bear Bryant

1953

		Record	Coach
1.	Maryland	10-0-0	Jim Tatum
2.	Notre Dame	9-0-1	Frank Leahy
3.	Michigan St	8-1-0	Biggie Munn
4.	Oklahoma	8-1-1	Bud Wilkinson
5.	UCLA	8-1-0	Red Sanders
6.	Rice	8-2-0	Jess Neely
7.	Illinois	7-1-1	Ray Eliot
8.	Georgia Tech	8-2-1	Bobby Dodd
9.	Iowa	5-3-1	Forest Evashevski
10.	West Virginia	8-1-0	Art Lewis
11.	Texas	7-3-0	Ed Price
12.	Texas Tech	10-1-0	DeWitt Weaver
13.	Alabama	6-2-3	Red Drew
14.	Army	7-1-1	Red Blaik
15.	Wisconsin	6-2-1	Ivy Williamson
16.	Kentucky	7-2-1	Bear Bryant
17.	Auburn	7-2-1	Shug Jordan
18.	Duke	7-2-1	Bill Murray
19.	Stanford	6-3-1	Chuck Taylor
20.	Michigan	6-3-0	Bennie Oosterbaan

1954

		Record	Coach
1.	Ohio St	9-0-0	Woody Hayes
2.	#UCLA	9-0-0	Red Sanders
3.	Oklahoma	10-0-0	Bud Wilkinson
4.	Notre Dame	9-1-0	Terry Brennan
5.	Navy	7-2-0	Eddie Erdelatz
6.	Mississippi	9-1-0	Johnny Vaught
7.	Army	7-2-0	Red Blaik
8.	Maryland	7-2-1	Jim Tatum
9.	Wisconsin	7-2-0	Ivy Williamson
10.	Arkansas	8-2-0	Bowden Wyatt

1954 (Cont.)

		Record	Coach
11.	Miami (FL)	8-1-0	Andy Gustafson
12.	West Virginia	8-1-0	Art Lewis
13.	Auburn	7-3-0	Shug Jordan
14.	Duke	7-2-1	Bill Murray
15.	Michigan	6-3-0	Bennie Oosterbaan
16.	Virginia Tech	8-0-1	Frank Moseley
17.	Southern Cal	8-3-0	Jess Hill
18.	Baylor	7-3-0	George Sauer
19.	Rice	7-3-0	Jess Neely
20.	Penn St	7-2-0	Rip Engle

#Selected No. 1 by UP.

1955

		Record	Coach
1.	Oklahoma	10-0-0	Bud Wilkinson
2.	Michigan St	8-1-0	Duffy Daugherty
3.	Maryland	10-0-0	Jim Tatum
4.	UCLA	9-1-0	Red Sanders
5.	Ohio St	7-2-0	Woody Hayes
6.	Texas Christian	9-1-0	Abe Martin
7.	Georgia Tech	8-1-1	Bobby Dodd
8.	Auburn	8-1-1	Shug Jordan
9.	Notre Dame	8-2-0	Terry Brennan
10.	Mississippi	9-1-0	Johnny Vaught
11.	Pittsburgh	7-3-0	John Michelosen
12.	Michigan	7-2-0	Bennie Oosterbaan
13.	Southern Cal	6-4-0	Jess Hill
14.	Miami (FL)	6-3-0	Andy Gustafson
15.	Miami (OH)	9-0-0	Ara Parseghian
16.	Stanford	6-3-1	Chuck Taylor
17.	Texas A&M	7-2-1	Bear Bryant
18.	Navy	6-2-1	Eddie Erdelatz
19.	West Virginia	8-2-0	Art Lewis
20.	Army	6-3-0	Red Blaik

1956

		Record	Coach
1.	Oklahoma	10-0-0	Bud Wilkinson
2.	Tennessee	10-0-0	Bowden Wyatt
3.	Iowa	8-1-0	Forest Evashevski
4.	Georgia Tech.	9-1-0	Bobby Dodd
5.	Texas A&M	9-0-1	Bear Bryant
6.	Miami (FL)	8-1-1	Andy Gustafson
7.	Michigan	7-2-0	Bennie Oosterbaan
8.	Syracuse	7-1-0	Ben Schwartzwalder
9.	Michigan St	7-2-0	Duffy Daugherty
10.	Oregon St	7-2-1	Tommy Prothro
11.	Baylor	8-2-0	Sam Boyd
12.	Minnesota	6-1-2	Murray Warmath
13.	Pittsburgh	7-2-1	John Michelosen
14.	Texas Christian	7-3-0	Abe Martin
15.	Ohio St	6-3-0	Woody Hayes
16.	Navy	6-1-2	Eddie Erdelatz
17.	Geo Washington	7-1-1	Gene Sherman
18.	Southern Cal	8-2-0	Jess Hill
19.	Clemson	7-1-2	Frank Howard
20.	Colorado	7-2-1	Dallas Ward
	Penn St	6-2-1	Rip Engle

1957

		Record	Coach
1.	Auburn	10-0-0	Shug Jordan
2.	#Ohio St	8-1-0	Woody Hayes
3.	Michigan St	8-1-0	Duffy Daugherty
4.	Oklahoma	9-1-0	Bud Wilkinson
5.	Navy	8-1-1	Eddie Erdelatz
6.	Iowa	7-1-1	Forest Evashevski
7.	Mississippi	8-1-1	Johnny Vaught
8.	Rice	7-3-0	Jess Neely
9.	Texas A&M	8-2-0	Bear Bryant
10.	Notre Dame	7-3-0	Terry Brennan
11.	Texas	6-3-1	Darrell Royal
12.	Arizona St	10-0-0	Dan Devine
13.	Tennessee	7-3-0	Bowden Wyatt
14.	Mississippi St	6-2-1	Wade Walker
15.	N Carolina St	7-1-2	Earle Edwards
16.	Duke	6-2-2	Bill Murray
17.	Florida	6-2-1	Bob Woodruff
18.	Army	7-2-0	Red Blaik
19.	Wisconsin	6-3-0	Milt Brunt
20.	VMI	9-0-1	John McKenna

#Selected No. 1 by UP.

1958

		Record	Coach
1.	Louisiana St	10-0-0	Paul Dietzel
2.	Iowa	7-1-1	Forest Evashevski
3.	Army	8-0-1	Red Blaik
4.	Auburn	9-0-1	Shug Jordan
5.	Oklahoma	9-1-0	Bud Wilkinson
6.	Air Force	9-0-1	Ben Martin
7.	Wisconsin	7-1-1	Milt Bruhn
8.	Ohio St	6-1-2	Woody Hayes
9.	Syracuse	8-1-0	Ben Schwartzwalder
10.	Texas Christian	8-2-0	Abe Martin
11.	Mississippi	8-2-0	Johnny Vaught
12.	Clemson	8-2-0	Frank Howard
13.	Purdue	6-1-2	Jack Mollenkopf
14.	Florida	6-3-1	Bob Woodruff
15.	S Carolina	7-3-0	Warren Giese
16.	California	7-3-0	Pete Elliott
17.	Notre Dame	6-4-0	Terry Brennan
18.	SMU	6-4-0	Bill Meek
19.	Oklahoma St	7-3-0	Cliff Speegle
20.	Rutgers	8-1-0	John Stiegman

1959

		Record	Coach
1.	Syracuse	10-0-0	Ben Schwartzwalder
2.	Mississippi	9-1-0	Johnny Vaught
3.	Louisiana St	9-1-0	Paul Dietzel
4.	Texas	9-1-0	Darrell Royal
5.	Georgia	9-1-0	Wally Butts
6.	Wisconsin	7-2-0	Milt Bruhn
7.	Texas Christian	8-2-0	Abe Martin
8.	Washington	9-1-0	Jim Owens
9.	Arkansas	8-2-0	Frank Broyles
10.	Alabama	7-1-2	Bear Bryant

1959 *(Cont.)*

		Record	Coach
11.	Clemson	8-2-0	Frank Howard
12.	Penn St	8-2-0	Rip Engle
13.	Illinois	5-3-1	Ray Eliot
14.	Southern Cal	8-2-0	Don Clark
15.	Oklahoma	7-3-0	Bud Wilkinson
16.	Wyoming	9-1-0	Bob Devaney
17.	Notre Dame	5-5-0	Joe Kuharich
18.	Missouri	6-4-0	Dan Devine
19.	Florida	5-4-1	Bob Woodruff
20.	Pittsburgh	6-4-0	John Michelosen

1960

		Record	Coach
1.	Minnesota	8-1-0	Murray Warmath
2.	Mississippi	9-0-1	Johnny Vaught
3.	Iowa	8-1-0	Forest Evashevski
4.	Navy	9-1-0	Wayne Hardin
5.	Missouri	9-1-0	Dan Devine
6.	Washington	9-1-0	Jim Owens
7.	Arkansas	8-2-0	Frank Broyles
8.	Ohio St	7-2-0	Woody Hayes
9.	Alabama	8-1-1	Bear Bryant
10.	Duke	7-3-0	Bill Murray
11.	Kansas	7-2-1	Jack Mitchell
12.	Baylor	8-2-0	John Bridgers
13.	Auburn	8-2-0	Shug Jordan
14.	Yale	9-0-0	Jordan Oliver
15.	Michigan St	6-2-1	Duffy Daugherty
16.	Penn St	6-3-0	Rip Engle
17.	New Mexico St	10-0-0	Warren Woodson
18.	Florida	8-2-0	Ray Graves
19.	Syracuse	7-2-0	Ben Schwartzwalder
	Purdue	4-4-1	Jack Mollenkopf

1961

		Record	Coach
1.	Alabama	10-0-0	Bear Bryant
2.	Ohio St	8-0-1	Woody Hayes
3.	Texas	9-1-0	Darrell Royal
4.	Louisiana St	9-1-0	Paul Dietzel
5.	Mississippi	9-1-0	Johnny Vaught
6.	Minnesota	7-2-0	Murray Warmath
7.	Colorado	9-1-0	Sonny Grandelius
8.	Michigan St	7-2-0	Duffy Daugherty
9.	Arkansas	8-2-0	Frank Broyles
10.	Utah St	9-0-1	John Ralston
11.	Missouri	7-2-1	Dan Devine
12.	Purdue	6-3-0	Jack Mollenkopf
13.	Georgia Tech	7-3-0	Bobby Dodd
14.	Syracuse	7-3-0	Ben Schwartzwalder
15.	Rutgers	9-0-0	John Bateman
16.	UCLA	7-3-0	Bill Barnes
17.	Rice	7-3-0	Jess Neely
	Penn St	7-3-0	Rip Engle
	Arizona	8-1-1	Jim LaRue
20.	Duke	7-3-0	Bill Murray

1962

		Record	Coach
1.	Southern Cal	10-0-0	John McKay
2.	Wisconsin	8-1-0	Milt Bruhn
3.	Mississippi	9-0-0	Johnny Vaught
4.	Texas	9-0-1	Darrell Royal
5.	Alabama	9-1-0	Bear Bryant
6.	Arkansas	9-1-0	Frank Broyles
7.	Louisiana St	8-1-1	Charlie McClendon
8.	Oklahoma	8-2-0	Bud Wilkinson
9.	Penn St	9-1-0	Rip Engle
10.	Minnesota	6-2-1	Murray Warmath

11-20: UPI

11.	Georgia Tech	7-2-1	Bobby Dodd
12.	Missouri	7-1-2	Dan Devine
13.	Ohio St	6-3-0	Woody Hayes
14.	Duke	8-2-0	Bill Murray
	Washington	7-1-2	Jim Owens
16.	Northwestern	7-2-0	Ara Parseghian
	Oregon St	8-2-0	Tommy Prothro
18.	Arizona St	7-2-1	Frank Kush
	Miami (FL)	7-3-0	Andy Gustafson
	Illinois	2-7-0	Pete Elliott

1963

		Record	Coach
1.	Texas	10-0-0	Darrell Royal
2.	Navy	9-1-0	Wayne Hardin
3.	Illinois	7-1-1	Pete Elliott
4.	Pittsburgh	9-1-0	John Michelosen
5.	Auburn	9-1-0	Shug Jordan
6.	Nebraska	9-1-0	Bob Devaney
7.	Mississippi	7-0-2	Johnny Vaught
8.	Alabama	8-2-0	Bear Bryant
9.	Oklahoma	8-2-0	Bud Wilkinson
10.	Michigan St	6-2-1	Duffy Daugherty

11-20: UPI

11.	Mississippi St	6-2-2	Paul Davis
12.	Syracuse	8-2-0	Ben Schwartzwalder
13.	Arizona St	8-1-0	Frank Kush
14.	Memphis St	9-0-1	Billy J. Murphy
15.	Washington	6-4-0	Jim Owens
16.	Penn St	7-3-0	Rip Engle
	Southern Cal	7-3-0	John McKay
	Missouri	7-3-0	Dan Devine
19.	N Carolina	8-2-0	Jim Hickey
20.	Baylor	7-3-0	John Bridgers

1964

		Record	Coach
1.	Alabama	10-0-0	Bear Bryant
2.	Arkansas	10-0-0	Frank Broyles
3.	Notre Dame	9-1-0	Ara Parseghian
4.	Michigan	8-1-0	Bump Elliott
5.	Texas	9-1-0	Darrell Royal
6.	Nebraska	9-1-0	Bob Devaney
7.	Louisiana St	7-2-1	Charlie McClendon
8.	Oregon St	8-2-0	Tommy Prothro
9.	Ohio St	7-2-0	Woody Hayes
10.	Southern Cal	7-3-0	John McKay

1964 (Cont.)

11-20: UPI

		Record	Coach
11.	Florida St	8-1-1	Bill Peterson
12.	Syracuse	7-3-0	Ben Schwartzwalder
13.	Princeton	9-0-0	Dick Colman
14.	Penn St	6-4-0	Rip Engle
	Utah	8-2-0	Ray Nagel
16.	Illinois	6-3-0	Pete Elliott
	New Mexico	9-2-0	Bill Weeks
18.	Tulsa	8-2-0	Glenn Dobbs
19.	Missouri	6-3-1	Dan Devine
20.	Mississippi	5-4-1	Johnny Vaught
	Michigan St	4-5-1	Duffy Daugherty

1965

		Record	Coach
1.	Alabama	9-1-1	Bear Bryant
2.	#Michigan St	10-1-0	Duffy Daugherty
3.	Arkansas	10-1-0	Frank Broyles
4.	UCLA	8-2-1	Tommy Prothro
5.	Nebraska	10-1-0	Bob Devaney
6.	Missouri	8-2-1	Dan Devine
7.	Tennessee	8-1-2	Doug Dickey
8.	Louisiana St	8-3-0	Charlie McClendon
9.	Notre Dame	7-2-1	Ara Parseghian
10.	Southern Cal	7-2-1	John McKay

11-20: UPI

11.	Texas Tech	8-2-0	J.T. King
12.	Ohio St	7-2-0	Woody Hayes
13.	Florida	7-3-0	Ray Graves
14.	Purdue	7-2-1	Jack Mollenkopf
15.	Georgia	6-4-0	Vince Dooley
16.	Tulsa	8-2-0	Glenn Dobbs
17.	Mississippi	6-4-0	Johnny Vaught
18.	Kentucky	6-4-0	Charlie Bradshaw
19.	Syracuse	7-3-0	Ben Schwartzwalder
20.	Colorado	6-2-2	Eddie Crowder

#Selected No. 1 by UPI.

1966*

		Record	Coach
1.	Notre Dame	9-0-1	Ara Parseghian
2.	Michigan St	9-0-1	Duffy Daugherty
3.	Alabama	10-0-0	Bear Bryant
4.	Georgia	9-1-0	Vince Dooley
5.	UCLA	9-1-0	Tommy Prothro
6.	Nebraska	9-1-0	Bob Devaney
7.	Purdue	8-2-0	Jack Mollenkopf
8.	Georgia Tech	9-1-0	Bobby Dodd
9.	Miami (FL)	7-2-1	Charlie Tate
10.	SMU	8-2-0	Hayden Fry

11-20: UPI

11.	Florida	8-2-0	Ray Graves
12.	Mississippi	8-2-0	Johnny Vaught
13.	Arkansas	8-2-0	Frank Broyles
14.	Tennessee	7-3-0	Doug Dickey
15.	Wyoming	9-1-0	Lloyd Eaton
16.	Syracuse	8-2-0	Ben Schwartzwalder
17.	Houston	8-2-0	Bill Yeoman
18.	Southern Cal	7-3-0	John McKay
19.	Oregon St	7-3-0	Dee Andros
20.	Virginia Tech	8-1-1	Jerry Claiborne

Note: Except where indicated with an asterisk, the polls from 1936 through 1964 were taken before the bowl games and those from 1965 through the present were taken after the bowl games. Additionally, the AP ranked only ten teams in its polls from 1962–67; positions 11–20 from those years are from the UPI poll.

1967*

		Record	Coach
1.	Southern Cal	9-1-0	John McKay
2.	Tennessee	9-1-0	Doug Dickey
3.	Oklahoma	9-1-0	Chuck Fairbanks
4.	Indiana	9-1-0	John Pont
5.	Notre Dame	8-2-0	Ara Parseghian
6.	Wyoming	10-0-0	Lloyd Eaton
7.	Oregon St	7-2-1	Dee Andros
8.	Alabama	8-1-1	Bear Bryant
9.	Purdue	8-2-0	Jack Mollenkopf
10.	Penn St	8-2-0	Joe Paterno

11-20: UPI†

		Record	Coach
11.	UCLA	7-2-1	Tommy Prothro
12.	Syracuse	8-2-0	Ben Schwartzwalder
13.	Colorado	8-2-0	Eddie Crowder
14.	Minnesota	8-2-0	Murray Warmath
15.	Florida St	7-2-1	Bill Peterson
16.	Miami (FL)	7-3-0	Charlie Tate
17.	N Carolina St	8-2-0	Earle Edwards
18.	Georgia	7-3-0	Vince Dooley
19.	Houston	9-2-0	Bill Yeoman
20.	Arizona St	8-2-0	Frank Kush

†UPI ranked Penn St 11th and did not rank Alabama, which was on probation.

1968

		Record	Coach
1.	Ohio St	10-0-0	Woody Hayes
2.	Penn St	11-0-0	Joe Paterno
3.	Texas	9-1-1	Darrell Royal
4.	Southern Cal	9-1-1	John McKay
5.	Notre Dame	7-2-1	Ara Parseghian
6.	Arkansas	10-1-0	Frank Broyles
7.	Kansas	9-2-0	Pepper Rodgers
8.	Georgia	8-1-2	Vince Dooley
9.	Missouri	8-3-0	Dan Devine
10.	Purdue	8-2-0	Jack Mollenkopf
11.	Oklahoma	7-4-0	Chuck Fairbanks
12.	Michigan	8-2-0	Bump Elliott
13.	Tennessee	8-2-1	Doug Dickey
14.	SMU	8-3-0	Hayden Fry
15.	Oregon St	7-3-0	Dee Andros
16.	Auburn	7-4-0	Shug Jordan
17.	Alabama	8-3-0	Bear Bryant
18.	Houston	6-2-2	Bill Yeoman
19.	Louisiana St	8-3-0	Charlie McClendon
20.	Ohio	10-1-0	Bill Hess

1969

		Record	Coach
1.	Texas	11-0-0	Darrell Royal
2.	Penn St	11-0-0	Joe Paterno
3.	Southern Cal	10-0-1	John McKay
4.	Ohio St	8-1-0	Woody Hayes
5.	Notre Dame	8-2-1	Ara Parseghian
6.	Missouri	9-2-0	Dan Devine
7.	Arkansas	9-2-0	Frank Broyles
8.	Mississippi	8-3-0	Johnny Vaught
9.	Michigan	8-3-0	Bo Schembechler
10.	Louisiana St	9-1-0	Charlie McClendon

1969 (Cont.)

		Record	Coach
11.	Nebraska	9-2-0	Bob Devaney
12.	Houston	9-2-0	Bill Yeoman
13.	UCLA	8-1-1	Tommy Prothro
14.	Florida	9-1-1	Ray Graves
15.	Tennessee	9-2-0	Doug Dickey
16.	Colorado	8-3-0	Eddie Crowder
17.	West Virginia	10-0-1	Jim Carlen
18.	Purdue	8-2-0	Jack Mollenkopf
19.	Stanford	7-2-1	John Ralston
20.	Auburn	8-3-0	Shug Jordan

1970

		Record	Coach
1.	Nebraska	11-0-1	Bob Devaney
2.	Notre Dame	10-1-0	Ara Parseghian
3.	#Texas	10-1-0	Darrell Royal
4.	Tennessee	11-0-1	Bill Battle
5.	Ohio St	9-1-0	Woody Hayes
6.	Arizona St	11-0-0	Frank Kush
7.	Louisiana St	9-3-0	Charlie McClendon
8.	Stanford	9-3-0	John Ralston
9.	Michigan	9-1-0	Bo Schembechler
10.	Auburn	9-2-0	Shug Jordan
11.	Arkansas	9-2-0	Frank Broyles
12.	Toledo	12-0-0	Frank Lauterbur
13.	Georgia Tech	9-3-0	Bud Carson
14.	Dartmouth	9-0-0	Bob Blackman
15.	Southern Cal	6-4-1	John McKay
16.	Air Force	9-3-0	Ben Martin
17.	Tulane	8-4-0	Jim Pittman
18.	Penn St	7-3-0	Joe Paterno
19.	Houston	8-3-0	Bill Yeoman
20.	Oklahoma	7-4-1	Chuck Fairbanks
	Mississippi	7-4-0	Johnny Vaught

#Selected No. 1 by UPI.

1971

		Record	Coach
1.	Nebraska	13-0-0	Bob Devaney
2.	Oklahoma	11-1-0	Chuck Fairbanks
3.	Colorado	10-2-0	Eddie Crowder
4.	Alabama	11-1-0	Bear Bryant
5.	Penn St	11-1-0	Joe Paterno
6.	Michigan	11-1-0	Bo Schembechler
7.	Georgia	11-1-0	Vince Dooley
8.	Arizona St	11-1-0	Frank Kush
9.	Tennessee	10-2-0	Bill Battle
10.	Stanford	9-3-0	John Ralston
11.	Louisiana St	9-3-0	Charlie McClendon
12.	Auburn	9-2-0	Shug Jordan
13.	Notre Dame	8-2-0	Ara Parseghian
14.	Toledo	12-0-0	John Murphy
15.	Mississippi	10-2-0	Billy Kinard
16.	Arkansas	8-3-1	Frank Broyles
17.	Houston	9-3-0	Bill Yeoman
18.	Texas	8-3-0	Darrell Royal
19.	Washington	8-3-0	Jim Owens
20.	Southern Cal	6-4-1	John McKay

1972

		Record	Coach
1.	Southern Cal	12-0-0	John McKay
2.	Oklahoma	11-1-0	Chuck Fairbanks
3.	Texas	10-1-0	Darrell Royal
4.	Nebraska	9-2-1	Bob Devaney
5.	Auburn	10-1-0	Shug Jordan
6.	Michigan	10-1-0	Bo Schembechler
7.	Alabama	10-2-0	Bear Bryant
8.	Tennessee	10-2-0	Bill Battle
9.	Ohio St	9-2-0	Woody Hayes
10.	Penn St	10-2-0	Joe Paterno
11.	Louisiana St	9-2-1	Charlie McClendon
12.	N Carolina	11-1-0	Bill Dooley
13.	Arizona St	10-2-0	Frank Kush
14.	Notre Dame	8-3-0	Ara Parseghian
15.	UCLA	8-3-0	Pepper Rodgers
16.	Colorado	8-4-0	Eddie Crowder
17.	N Carolina St	8-3-1	Lou Holtz
18.	Louisville	9-1-0	Lee Corso
19.	Washington St	7-4-0	Jim Sweeney
20.	Georgia Tech	7-4-1	Bill Fulcher

1973

		Record	Coach
1.	Notre Dame	11-0-0	Ara Parseghian
2.	Ohio St	10-0-1	Woody Hayes
3.	Oklahoma	10-0-1	Barry Switzer
4.	#Alabama	11-1-0	Bear Bryant
5.	Penn St	12-0-0	Joe Paterno
6.	Michigan	10-0-1	Bo Schembechler
7.	Nebraska	9-2-1	Tom Osborne
8.	Southern Cal	9-2-1	John McKay
9.	Arizona St	11-1-0	Frank Kush
	Houston	11-1-0	Bill Yeoman
11.	Texas Tech	11-1-0	Jim Carlen
12.	UCLA	9-2-0	Pepper Rodgers
13.	Louisiana St	9-3-0	Charlie McClendon
14.	Texas	8-3-0	Darrell Royal
15.	Miami (OH)	11-0-0	Bill Mallory
16.	N Carolina St	9-3-0	Lou Holtz
17.	Missouri	8-4-0	Al Onofrio
18.	Kansas	7-4-1	Don Fambrough
19.	Tennessee	8-4-0	Bill Battle
20.	Maryland	8-4-0	Jerry Claiborne
	Tulane	9-3-0	Bennie Ellender

#Selected No. 1 by UPI.

1974

		Record	Coach
1.	Oklahoma	11-0-0	Barry Switzer
2.	#Southern Cal	10-1-1	John McKay
3.	Michigan	10-1-0	Bo Schembechler
4.	Ohio St	10-2-0	Woody Hayes
5.	Alabama	11-1-0	Bear Bryant
6.	Notre Dame	10-2-0	Ara Parseghian
7.	Penn St	10-2-0	Joe Paterno
8.	Auburn	10-2-0	Shug Jordan
9.	Nebraska	9-3-0	Tom Osborne
10.	Miami (OH)	10-0-1	Dick Crum
11.	N Carolina St	9-2-1	Lou Holtz
12.	Michigan St	7-3-1	Denny Stolz
13.	Maryland	8-4-0	Jerry Claiborne
14.	Baylor	8-4-0	Grant Teaff
15.	Florida	8-4-0	Doug Dickey
16.	Texas A&M	8-3-0	Emory Ballard

1974 *(Cont.)*

		Record	Coach
17.	Mississippi St	9-3-0	Bob Tyler
	Texas	8-4-0	Darrell Royal
19.	Houston	8-3-1	Bill Yeoman
20.	Tennessee	7-3-2	Bill Battle

#Selected No. 1 by UPI.

1975

		Record	Coach
1.	Oklahoma	11-1-0	Barry Switzer
2.	Arizona St	12-0-0	Frank Kush
3.	Alabama	11-1-0	Bear Bryant
4.	Ohio St	11-1-0	Woody Hayes
5.	UCLA	9-2-1	Dick Vermeil
6.	Texas	10-2-0	Darrell Royal
7.	Arkansas	10-2-0	Frank Broyles
8.	Michigan	8-2-2	Bo Schembechler
9.	Nebraska	10-2-0	Tom Osborne
10.	Penn St	9-3-0	Joe Paterno
11.	Texas A&M	10-2-0	Emory Bellard
12.	Miami (OH)	11-1-0	Dick Crum
13.	Maryland	9-2-1	Jerry Claiborne
14.	California	8-3-0	Mike White
15.	Pittsburgh	8-4-0	Johnny Majors
16.	Colorado	9-3-0	Bill Mallory
17.	Southern Cal	8-4-0	John McKay
18.	Arizona	9-2-0	Jim Young
19.	Georgia	9-3-0	Vince Dooley
20.	West Virginia	9-3-0	Bobby Bowden

1976

		Record	Coach
1.	Pittsburgh	12-0-0	Johnny Majors
2.	Southern Cal	11-1-0	John Robinson
3.	Michigan	10-2-0	Bo Schembechler
4.	Houston	10-2-0	Bill Yeoman
5.	Oklahoma	9-2-1	Barry Switzer
6.	Ohio St	9-2-1	Woody Hayes
7.	Texas A&M	10-2-0	Emory Bellard
8.	Maryland	11-1-0	Jerry Claiborne
9.	Nebraska	9-3-1	Tom Osborne
10.	Georgia	10-2-0	Vince Dooley
11.	Alabama	9-3-0	Bear Bryant
12.	Notre Dame	9-3-0	Dan Devine
13.	Texas Tech	10-2-0	Steve Sloan
14.	Oklahoma St	9-3-0	Jim Stanley
15.	UCLA	9-2-1	Terry Donahue
16.	Colorado	8-4-0	Bill Mallory
17.	Rutgers	11-0-0	Frank Burns
18.	Kentucky	9-3-0	Fran Curci
19.	Iowa St	8-3-0	Earle Bruce
20.	Mississippi St	9-2-0	Bob Tyler

1977

		Record	Coach
1.	Notre Dame	11-1-0	Dan Devine
2.	Alabama	11-1-0	Bear Bryant
3.	Arkansas	11-1-0	Lou Holtz
4.	Texas	11-1-0	Fred Akers
5.	Penn St	11-1-0	Joe Paterno
6.	Kentucky	10-1-0	Fran Curci
7.	Oklahoma	10-2-0	Barry Switzer
8.	Pittsburgh	9-2-1	Jackie Sherrill
9.	Michigan	10-2-0	Bo Schembechler
10.	Washington	10-2-0	Don James

1977 *(Cont.)*

		Record	Coach
11.	Ohio St	9-3-0	Woody Hayes
12.	Nebraska	9-3-0	Tom Osborne
13.	Southern Cal	8-4-0	John Robinson
14.	Florida St	10-2-0	Bobby Bowden
15.	Stanford	9-3-0	Bill Walsh
16.	San Diego St	10-1-0	Claude Gilbert
17.	N Carolina	8-3-1	Bill Dooley
18.	Arizona St	9-3-0	Frank Kush
19.	Clemson	8-3-1	Charley Pell
20.	Brigham Young	9-2-0	LaVell Edwards

1978

		Record	Coach
1.	Alabama	11-1-0	Bear Bryant
2.	#Southern Cal	12-1-0	John Robinson
3.	Oklahoma	11-1-0	Barry Switzer
4.	Penn St	11-1-0	Joe Paterno
5.	Michigan	10-2-0	Bo Schembechler
6.	Clemson	11-1-0	Charley Pell
7.	Notre Dame	9-3-0	Dan Devine
8.	Nebraska	9-3-0	Tom Osborne
9.	Texas	9-3-0	Fred Akers
10.	Houston	9-3-0	Bill Yeoman
11.	Arkansas	9-2-1	Lou Holtz
12.	Michigan St	8-3-0	Darryl Rogers
13.	Purdue	9-2-1	Jim Young
14.	UCLA	8-3-1	Terry Donahue
15.	Missouri	8-4-0	Warren Powers
16.	Georgia	9-2-1	Vince Dooley
17.	Stanford	8-4-0	Bill Walsh
18.	N Carolina St	9-3-0	Bo Rein
19.	Texas A&M	8-4-0	Emory Bellard (4-2)
			Tom Wilson (4-2)
20.	Maryland	9-3-0	Jerry Claiborne

#Selected No. 1 by UPI.

1979

		Record	Coach
1.	Alabama	12-0-0	Bear Bryant
2.	Southern Cal	11-0-1	John Robinson
3.	Oklahoma	11-1-0	Barry Switzer
4.	Ohio St	11-1-0	Earle Bruce
5.	Houston	11-1-0	Bill Yeoman
6.	Florida St	11-1-0	Bobby Bowden
7.	Pittsburgh	11-1-0	Jackie Sherrill
8.	Arkansas	10-2-0	Lou Holtz
9.	Nebraska	10-2-0	Tom Osborne
10.	Purdue	10-2-0	Jim Young
11.	Washington	10-1-0	Don James
12.	Texas	9-3-0	Fred Akers
13.	Brigham Young	11-1-0	LaVell Edwards
14.	Baylor	8-4-0	Grant Teaff
15.	N Carolina	8-3-1	Dick Crum
16.	Auburn	8-3-0	Doug Barfield
17.	Temple	10-2-0	Wayne Hardin
18.	Michigan	8-4-0	Bo Schembechler
19.	Indiana	8-4-0	Lee Corso
20.	Penn St	8-4-0	Joe Paterno

1980

		Record	Coach
1.	Georgia	12-0-0	Vince Dooley
2.	Pittsburgh	11-1-0	Jackie Sherrill
3.	Oklahoma	10-2-0	Barry Switzer
4.	Michigan	10-2-0	Bo Schembechler
5.	Florida St	10-2-0	Bobby Bowden

1980 *(Cont.)*

		Record	Coach
6.	Alabama	10-2-0	Bear Bryant
7.	Nebraska	10-2-0	Tom Osborne
8.	Penn St	10-2-0	Joe Paterno
9.	Notre Dame	9-2-1	Dan Devine
10.	N Carolina	11-1-0	Dick Crum
11.	Southern Cal	8-2-1	John Robinson
12.	Brigham Young	12-1-0	LaVell Edwards
13.	UCLA	9-2-0	Terry Donahue
14.	Baylor	10-2-0	Grant Teaff
15.	Ohio St	9-3-0	Earle Bruce
16.	Washington	9-3-0	Don James
17.	Purdue	9-3-0	Jim Young
18.	Miami (FL)	9-3-0	H. Schnellenberger
19.	Mississippi St	9-3-0	Emory Bellard
20.	SMU	8-4-0	Ron Meyer

1981

		Record	Coach
1.	Clemson	12-0-0	Danny Ford
2.	Texas	10-1-1	Fred Akers
3.	Penn St	10-2-0	Joe Paterno
4.	Pittsburgh	11-1-0	Jackie Sherrill
5.	SMU	10-1-0	Ron Meyer
6.	Georgia	10-2-0	Vince Dooley
7.	Alabama	9-2-1	Bear Bryant
8.	Miami (FL)	9-2-0	H. Schnellenberger
9.	N Carolina	10-2-0	Dick Crum
10.	Washington	10-2-0	Don James
11.	Nebraska	9-3-0	Tom Osborne
12.	Michigan	9-3-0	Bo Schembechler
13.	Brigham Young	11-2-0	LaVell Edwards
14.	Southern Cal	9-3-0	John Robinson
15.	Ohio St	9-3-0	Earle Bruce
16.	Arizona St	9-2-0	Darryl Rogers
17.	West Virginia	9-3-0	Don Nehlen
18.	Iowa	8-4-0	Hayden Fry
19.	Missouri	8-4-0	Warren Powers
20.	Oklahoma	7-4-1	Barry Switzer

1982

		Record	Coach
1.	Penn St	11-1-0	Joe Paterno
2.	SMU	11-0-1	Bobby Collins
3.	Nebraska	12-1-0	Tom Osborne
4.	Georgia	11-1-0	Vince Dooley
5.	UCLA	10-1-1	Terry Donahue
6.	Arizona St	10-2-0	Darryl Rogers
7.	Washington	10-2-0	Don James
8.	Clemson	9-1-1	Danny Ford
9.	Arkansas	9-2-1	Lou Holtz
10.	Pittsburgh	9-3-0	Foge Fazio
11.	Louisiana St	8-3-1	Jerry Stovall
12.	Ohio St	9-3-0	Earle Bruce
13.	Florida St	9-3-0	Bobby Bowden
14.	Auburn	9-3-0	Pat Dye
15.	Southern Cal	8-3-0	John Robinson
16.	Oklahoma	8-4-0	Barry Switzer
17.	Texas	9-3-0	Fred Akers
18.	N Carolina	8-4-0	Dick Crum
19.	West Virginia	9-3-0	Don Nehlen
20.	Maryland	8-4-0	Bobby Ross

1983

		Record	Coach
1.	Miami (FL)	11-1-0	H. Schnellenberger
2.	Nebraska	12-1-0	Tom Osborne
3.	Auburn	11-1-0	Pat Dye
4.	Georgia	10-1-1	Vince Dooley
5.	Texas	11-1-0	Fred Akers
6.	Florida	9-2-1	Charlie Pell
7.	Brigham Young	11-1-0	LaVell Edwards
8.	Michigan	9-3-0	Bo Schembechler
9.	Ohio St	9-3-0	Earle Bruce
10.	Illinois	10-2-0	Mike White
11.	Clemson	9-1-1	Danny Ford
12.	SMU	10-2-0	Bobby Collins
13.	Air Force	10-2-0	Ken Hatfield
14.	Iowa	9-3-0	Hayden Fry
15.	Alabama	8-4-0	Ray Perkins
16.	West Virginia	9-3-0	Don Nehlen
17.	UCLA	7-4-1	Terry Donahue
18.	Pittsburgh	8-3-1	Foge Fazio
19.	Boston College	9-3-0	Jack Bicknell
20.	E Carolina	8-3-0	Ed Emory

1984

		Record	Coach
1.	Brigham Young	13-0-0	LaVell Edwards
2.	Washington	11-1-0	Don James
3.	Florida	9-1-1	Chas Pell (0-1-1) Galen Hall (9-0)
4.	Nebraska	10-2-0	Tom Osborne
5.	Boston College	10-2-0	Jack Bicknell
6.	Oklahoma	9-2-1	Barry Switzer
7.	Oklahoma St	10-2-0	Pat Jones
8.	SMU	10-2-0	Bobby Collins
9.	UCLA	9-3-0	Terry Donahue
10.	Southern Cal	10-3-0	Ted Tollner
11.	South Carolina	10-2-0	Joe Morrison
12.	Maryland	9-3-0	Bobby Ross
13.	Ohio St	9-3-0	Earle Bruce
14.	Auburn	9-4-0	Pat Dye
15.	Louisiana St	8-3-1	Bill Arnsparger
16.	Iowa	8-4-1	Hayden Fry
17.	Florida St	7-3-2	Bobby Bowden
18.	Miami (FL)	8-5-0	Jimmy Johnson
19.	Kentucky	9-3-0	Jerry Claiborne
20.	Virginia	8-2-2	George Welsh

1985

		Record	Coach
1.	Oklahoma	11-1-0	Barry Switzer
2.	Michigan	10-1-1	Bo Schembechler
3.	Penn St	11-1-0	Joe Paterno
4.	Tennessee	9-1-2	Johnny Majors
5.	Florida	9-1-1	Galen Hall
6.	Texas A&M	10-2-0	Jackie Sherrill
7.	UCLA	9-2-1	Terry Donahue
8.	Air Force	12-1-0	Fisher DeBerry
9.	Miami (FL)	10-2-0	Jimmy Johnson
10.	Iowa	10-2-0	Hayden Fry
11.	Nebraska	9-3-0	Tom Osborne
12.	Arkansas	10-2-0	Ken Hatfield
13.	Alabama	9-2-1	Ray Perkins
14.	Ohio St	9-3-0	Earle Bruce
15.	Florida St	9-3-0	Bobby Bowden
16.	Brigham Young	11-3-0	LaVell Edwards
17.	Baylor	9-3-0	Grant Teaff
18.	Maryland	9-3-0	Bobby Ross
19.	Georgia Tech	9-2-1	Bill Curry
20.	Louisiana St	9-2-1	Bill Arnsparger

1986

		Record	Coach
1.	Penn St	12-0-0	Joe Paterno
2.	Miami (FL)	11-1-0	Jimmy Johnson
3.	Oklahoma	11-1-0	Barry Switzer
4.	Arizona St	10-1-1	John Cooper
5.	Nebraska	10-2-0	Tom Osborne
6.	Auburn	10-2-0	Pat Dye
7.	Ohio St	10-3-0	Earle Bruce
8.	Michigan	11-2-0	Bo Schembechler
9.	Alabama	10-3-0	Ray Perkins
10.	Louisiana St	9-3-0	Bill Arnsparger
11.	Arizona	9-3-0	Larry Smith
12.	Baylor	9-3-0	Grant Teaff
13.	Texas A&M	9-3-0	Jackie Sherrill
14.	UCLA	8-3-1	Terry Donahue
15.	Arkansas	9-3-0	Ken Hatfield
16.	Iowa	9-3-0	Hayden Fry
17.	Clemson	8-2-2	Danny Ford
18.	Washington	8-3-1	Don James
19.	Boston College	9-3-0	Jack Bicknell
20.	Virginia Tech.	9-2-1	Bill Dooley

1987

		Record	Coach
1.	Miami (FL)	12-0-0	Jimmy Johnson
2.	Florida St	11-1-0	Bobby Bowden
3.	Oklahoma	11-1-0	Barry Switzer
4.	Syracuse	11-0-1	Dick MacPherson
5.	Louisiana St	10-1-1	Mike Archer
6.	Nebraska	10-2-0	Tom Osborne
7.	Auburn	9-1-2	Pat Dye
8.	Michigan St	9-2-1	George Perles
9.	UCLA	10-2-0	Terry Donahue
10.	Texas A&M	10-2-0	Jackie Sherrill
11.	Oklahoma St	10-2-0	Pat Jones
12.	Clemson	10-2-0	Danny Ford
13.	Georgia	9-3-0	Vince Dooley
14.	Tennessee	10-2-1	Johnny Majors
15.	S Carolina	8-4-0	Joe Morrison
16.	Iowa	10-3-0	Hayden Fry
17.	Notre Dame	8-4-0	Lou Holtz
18.	Southern Cal	8-4-0	Larry Smith
19.	Michigan	8-4-0	Bo Schembechler
20.	Arizona St	7-4-1	John Cooper

1988

		Record	Coach
1.	Notre Dame	12-0-0	Lou Holtz
2.	Miami (FL)	11-1-0	Jimmy Johnson
3.	Florida St	11-1-0	Bobby Bowden
4.	Michigan	9-2-1	Bo Schembechler
5.	West Virginia	11-1-0	Don Nehlen
6.	UCLA	10-2-0	Terry Donahue
7.	Southern Cal	10-2-0	Larry Smith
8.	Auburn	10-2-0	Pat Dye
9.	Clemson	10-2-0	Danny Ford
10.	Nebraska	11-2-0	Tom Osborne
11.	Oklahoma St	10-2-0	Pat Jones
12.	Arkansas	10-2-0	Ken Hatfield
13.	Syracuse	10-2-0	Dick MacPherson
14.	Oklahoma	9-3-0	Barry Switzer
15.	Georgia	9-3-0	Vince Dooley
16.	Washington St	9-3-0	Dennis Erickson
17.	Alabama	9-3-0	Bill Curry
18.	Houston	9-3-0	Jack Pardee
19.	Louisiana St	8-4-0	Mike Archer
20.	Indiana	8-3-1	Bill Mallory

1989

		Record	Coach
1.	Miami (FL)	11-1-0	Dennis Erickson
2.	Notre Dame	12-1-0	Lou Holtz
3.	Florida St.	10-2-0	Bobby Bowden
4.	Colorado	11-1-0	Bill McCartney
5.	Tennessee	11-1-0	Johnny Majors
6.	Auburn	10-2-0	Pat Dye
7.	Michigan	10-2-0	Bo Schembechler
8.	Southern Cal	9-2-1	Larry Smith
9.	Alabama	10-2-0	Bill Curry
10.	Illinois	10-2-0	John Mackovic
11.	Nebraska	10-2-0	Tom Osborne
12.	Clemson	10-2-0	Danny Ford
13.	Arkansas	10-2-0	Ken Hatfield
14.	Houston	9-2-0	Jack Pardee
15.	Penn St.	8-3-1	Joe Paterno
16.	Michigan St	8-4-0	George Perles
17.	Pittsburgh	8-3-1	Mike Gottfried
18.	Virginia	10-3-0	George Welsh
19.	Texas Tech	9-3-0	Spike Dykes
20.	Texas A&M	8-4-0	R.C. Slocum
21.	West Virginia	8-3-1	Don Nehlen
22.	Brigham Young	10-3-0	LaVell Edwards
23.	Washington	8-4-0	Don James
24.	Ohio St	8-4-0	John Cooper
25.	Arizona	8-4-0	Dick Tomey

1990

		Record	Coach
1.	Colorado	11-1-1	Bill McCartney
2.	#Georgia Tech	11-0-1	Bobby Ross
3.	Miami (FL)	10-2-0	Dennis Erickson
4.	Florida St.	10-2-0	Bobby Bowden
5.	Washington	10-2-0	Don James
6.	Notre Dame	9-3-0	Lou Holtz
7.	Michigan	9-3-0	Gary Moeller
8.	Tennessee	9-2-2	Johnny Majors
9.	Clemson	10-2-0	Ken Hatfield
10.	Houston	10-1-0	John Jenkins
11.	Penn St.	9-3-0	Joe Paterno
12.	Texas	10-2-0	David McWilliams
13.	Florida	9-2-0	Steve Spurrier
14.	Louisville	10-1-1	H. Schnellenberger
15.	Texas A&M	9-3-1	R.C. Slocum
16.	Michigan St	8-3-1	George Perles
17.	Oklahoma	8-3-0	Gary Gibbs
18.	Iowa	8-4-0	Hayden Fry
19.	Auburn	8-3-1	Pat Dye
20.	Southern Cal	8-4-1	Larry Smith
21.	Mississippi	9-3-0	Billy Brewer
22.	Brigham Young	10-3-0	LaVell Edwards
23.	Virginia	8-4-0	George Welsh
24.	Nebraska	9-3-0	Tom Osborne
25.	Illinois	8-4-0	John Mackovic

#Selected No. 1 by UPI.

1991

		Record	Coach
1.	Miami (FL)	12-0-0	Dennis Erickson
2.	#Washington	12-0-0	Don James
3.	Penn St.	11-2-0	Joe Paterno
4.	Florida St.	11-2-0	Bobby Bowden
5.	Alabama	11-1-0	Gene Stallings
6.	Michigan	10-2-0	Gary Moeller
7.	Florida	10-2-0	Steve Spurrier
8.	California	10-2-0	Bruce Snyder

1991 (Cont.)

		Record	Coach
9.	E Carolina	11-1-0	Bill Lewis
10.	Iowa	10-1-1	Hayden Fry
11.	Syracuse	10-2-0	Paul Pasqualoni
12.	Texas A&M	10-2-0	R.C. Slocum
13.	Notre Dame	10-3-0	Lou Holtz
14.	Tennessee	9-3-0	Johnny Majors
15.	Nebraska	9-2-1	Tom Osborne
16.	Oklahoma	9-3-0	Gary Gibbs
17.	Georgia	9-3-0	Ray Goff
18.	Clemson	9-2-1	Ken Hatfield
19.	UCLA	9-3-0	Terry Donahue
20.	Colorado	8-3-1	Bill McCartney
21.	Tulsa	10-2-0	David Rader
22.	Stanford	8-4-0	Dennis Green
23.	Brigham Young	8-3-2	LaVell Edwards
24.	N Carolina St.	9-3-0	Dick Sheridan
25.	Air Force	10-3-0	Fisher DeBerry

#Selected No. 1 by USA Today/ CNN.

1992

		Record	Coach
1.	Alabama	13-0-0	Gene Stallings
2.	Florida St.	11-1-0	Bobby Bowden
3.	Miami	11-1-0	Dennis Erickson
4.	Notre Dame	10-1-1	Lou Holtz
5.	Michigan	9-0-3	Gary Moeller
6.	Syracuse	10-2-0	Paul Pasqualoni
7.	Texas A&M	12-1-0	R.C. Slocum
8.	Georgia	10-2-0	Ray Goff
9.	Stanford	10-3-0	Bill Walsh
10.	Florida	9-4-0	Steve Spurrier
11.	Washington	9-3-0	Don James
12.	Tennessee	9-3-0	Johnny Majors
13.	Colorado	9-2-1	Bill McCartney
14.	Nebraska	9-3-0	Tom Osborne
15.	Washington St	9-3-0	Mike Price
16.	Mississippi	9-3-0	Billy Brewer
17.	N Carolina St.	9-3-1	Dick Sheridan
18.	Ohio St	8-3-1	John Cooper
19.	N Carolina	9-3-0	Mack Brown
20.	Hawaii	11-2-0	Bob Wagner
21.	Boston College	8-3-1	Tom Coughlin
22.	Kansas	8-4-0	Glen Mason
23.	Mississippi St	7-5-0	Jackie Sherrill
24.	Fresno St	9-4-0	Jim Sweeney
25.	Wake Forest	8-4-0	Bill Dooley

1993

		Record	Coach
1.	Florida St.	12-1-0	Bobby Bowden
2.	Notre Dame	11-1-0	Lou Holtz
3.	Nebraska	11-1-0	Tom Osborne
4.	Auburn	11-0-0	Terry Bowden
5.	Florida	11-2-0	Steve Spurrier
6.	Wisconsin	10-1-1	Barry Alvarez
7.	West Virginia	11-1-0	Don Nehlen
8.	Penn St.	10-2-0	Joe Paterno
9.	Texas A&M	10-2-0	R.C. Slocum
10.	Arizona	10-2-0	Dick Tomey
11.	Ohio St	10-1-1	John Cooper
12.	Tennessee	9-2-1	Phil Fulmer
13.	Boston College	9-3-0	Tom Coughlin
14.	Alabama	9-3-1	Gene Stallings
15.	Miami	9-3-0	Dennis Erickson

†Beginning in 1989, the Associated Press expanded its final poll to 25 teams.

1993 *(Cont.)*

		Record	Coach
16.	Colorado	8-3-1	Bill McCartney
17.	Oklahoma	9-3-0	Gary Gibbs
18.	UCLA	8-4-0	Terry Donahue
19.	N Carolina	10-3-0	Mack Brown
20.	Kansas St	9-2-1	Bill Snyder
21.	Michigan	8-4-0	Gary Moeller
22.	Virginia Tech	9-3-0	Frank Beamer
23.	Clemson	9-3-0	Ken Hatfield
24.	Louisville	9-3-0	H. Schnellenberger
25.	California	9-4-0	Keith Gilbertson

1994

		Record	Coach
1.	Nebraska	13-0-0	Tom Osborne
2.	Penn St	12-0-0	Joe Paterno
3.	Colorado	11-1-0	Bill McCartney
4.	Florida St	10-1-1	Bobby Bowden
5.	Alabama	12-1-0	Gene Stallings
6.	Miami (FL)	10-2-0	Dennis Erickson
7.	Florida	10-2-1	Steve Spurrier
8.	Texas A&M	10-0-1	R.C. Slocum
9.	Auburn	9-1-1	Terry Bowden
10.	Utah	10-2-0	Ron McBride
11.	Oregon	9-4-0	Rich Brooks
12.	Michigan	8-4-0	Gary Moeller
13.	Southern Cal	8-3-1	John Robinson
14.	Ohio St	9-4-0	John Cooper
15.	Virginia	9-3-0	George Welsh
16.	Colorado St	10-2-0	Sonny Lubick
17.	N Carolina St	9-3-0	Mike O'Cain
18.	Brigham Young	10-3-0	LaVell Edwards
19.	Kansas St	9-3-0	Bill Snyder
20.	Arizona	8-4-0	Dick Tomey
21.	Washington St	8-4-0	Mike Price
22.	Tennessee	8-4-0	Phillip Fulmer
23.	Boston College	7-4-1	Dan Henning
24.	Mississippi St	8-4-0	Jackie Sherrill
25.	Texas	8-4-0	John Mackovic

1995

		Record	Coach
1.	Nebraska	12-0-0	Tom Osborne
2.	Florida	12-1-0	Steve Spurrier
3.	Tennessee	11-1-0	Phillip Fulmer
4.	Florida St	10-2-0	Bobby Bowden
5.	Colorado	10-2-0	Rick Neuheisel
6.	Ohio St	11-2-0	John Cooper
7.	Kansas St	10-2-0	Bill Snyder
8.	Northwestern	10-2-0	Gary Barnett
9.	Kansas	10-2-0	Glen Mason
10.	Virginia Tech	10-2-0	Frank Beamer
11.	Notre Dame	9-3-0	Lou Holtz
12.	Southern Cal	9-2-1	John Robinson
13.	Penn St	9-3-0	Joe Paterno
14.	Texas	10-2-1	John Mackovic
15.	Texas A&M	9-3-0	S.C. Slocum
16.	Virginia	9-4-0	George Welsh
17.	Michigan	9-4-0	Lloyd Carr
18.	Oregon	9-3-0	Mike Bellotti
19.	Syracuse	9-3-0	Paul Pasqualoni
20.	Miami (FL)	8-3-0	Butch Davis
21.	Alabama	8-3-0	Gene Stallings
22.	Auburn	8-4-0	Terry Bowden
23.	Texas Tech	9-3-0	Spike Dykes
24.	Toledo	11-0-1	Gary Pinkel
25.	Iowa	8-4-0	Hayden Fry

1996

		Record*	Coach
1.	Florida	12–1	Steve Spurrier
2.	Ohio St	11–1	John Cooper
3.	Florida St	11–1	Bobby Bowden
4.	Arizona St	11–1	Bruce Snyder
5.	Brigham Young	14–1	LaVell Edwards
6.	Nebraska	11–2	Tom Osborne
7.	Penn St	11–2	Joe Paterno
8.	Colorado	10–2	Rick Neuheisel
9.	Tennessee	10–2	Phillip Fulmer
10.	North Carolina	10–2	Mack Brown
11.	Alabama	10–3	Gene Stallings
12.	Louisiana St	10–2	Gerry DiNardo
13.	Virginia Tech	10–2	Frank Beamer
14.	Miami (FL)	9–3	Butch Davis
15.	Northwestern	9–3	Gary Barnett
16.	Washington	9–3	Jim Lambright
17.	Kansas St	9–3	Bill Snyder
18.	Iowa	9–3	Hayden Fry
19.	Notre Dame	8–3	Lou Holtz
20.	Michigan	8–4	Lloyd Carr
21.	Syracuse	9–3	Paul Pasqualoni
22.	Wyoming	10–2	Joe Tiller
23.	Texas	8–5	John Mackovic
24.	Auburn	8–4	Terry Bowden
25.	Army	10–2	Bob Sutton

1997

		Record	Coach
1.	Michigan	12–0	Lloyd Carr
2.	Nebraska	13–0	Tom Osborne
3.	Florida St	11–1	Bobby Bowden
4.	Florida	10–2	Steve Spurrier
5.	UCLA	10–2	Bob Toledo
6.	N Carolina	11–1	Mack Brown
7.	Tennessee	11–2	Phillip Fulmer
8.	Kansas St	11–1	Bill Snyder
9.	Washington St	10–2	Mike Price
10.	Georgia	10–2	Jim Donnan
11.	Auburn	10–3	Terry Bowden
12.	Ohio St	10–3	John Cooper
13.	Louisiana St	9–3	Gerry DiNardo
14.	Arizona St	8–3	Bruce Snyder
15.	Purdue	9–3	Joe Tiller
16.	Penn St	9–3	Joe Paterno
17.	Colorado St	11–2	Sonny Lubick
18.	Washington	8–4	Jim Lambright
19.	Southern Mississippi	9–3	Jeff Bower
20.	Texas A&M	9–4	R. C. Slocum
21.	Syracuse	9–4	Paul Pasqualoni
22.	Mississippi	8–4	Tommy Tuberville
23.	Missouri	7–5	Larry Smith
24.	Oklahoma St	8–4	Bob Simmons
25.	Georgia Tech	7–5	George O'Leary

*In 1996 the NCAA introduced overtime to break ties.

NCAA Divisional Championships

Division I-AA

Year	Winner	Runner-Up	Score
1978	Florida A&M	Massachusetts	35–28
1979	Eastern Kentucky	Lehigh	30–7
1980	Boise St	Eastern Kentucky	31–29
1981	Idaho St	Eastern Kentucky	34–23
1982	Eastern Kentucky	Delaware	17–14
1983	Southern Illinois	Western Carolina	43–7
1984	Montana St	Louisiana Tech	19–6
1985	Georgia Southern	Furman	44–42
1986	Georgia Southern	Arkansas St	48–21
1987	NE Louisiana	Marshall	43–42
1988	Furman	Georgia Southern	17–12
1989	Georgia Southern	SF Austin St	37–34
1990	Georgia Southern	NV-Reno	36–13
1991	Youngstown St	Marshall	25–17
1992	Marshall	Youngstown St	31–28
1993	Youngstown St	Marshall	17–5
1994	Youngstown St	Boise St	28–14
1995	Montana	Marshall	22–20
1996	Marshall	Montana	49–29
1997	Youngstown St	McNesse St	10–9

Division II

Year	Winner	Runner-Up	Score
1973	Louisiana Tech	Western Kentucky	34–0
1974	Central Michigan	Delaware	54–14
1975	Northern Michigan	Western Kentucky	16–14
1976	Montana St	Akron	24–13
1977	Lehigh	Jacksonville St	33–0
1978	Eastern Illinois	Delaware	10–9
1979	Delaware	Youngstown St	38–21
1980	Cal Poly SLO	Eastern Illinois	21–13
1981	SW Texas St	N Dakota St	42–13
1982	SW Texas St	UC-Davis	34–9
1983	N Dakota St	Central St (OH)	41–21
1984	Troy St	N Dakota St	18–17
1985	N Dakota St	N Alabama	35–7
1986	N Dakota St	S Dakota	27–7
1987	Troy St	Portland St	31–17
1988	N Dakota St	Portland St	35–21
1989	Mississippi College	Jacksonville St	3–0
1990	N Dakota St	Indiana (PA)	51–11
1991	Pittsburg St	Jacksonville St	23–6
1992	Jacksonville St	Pittsburg St	17–13
1993	N Alabama	Indiana (PA)	41–34
1994	N Alabama	Texas A&M-Kingsville	16–10
1995	N Alabama	Pittsburg St	27–7
1996	Northern Colorado	Carson-Newman	23–14
1997	Northern Colorado	New Haven	51–0

Division III

Year	Winner	Runner-Up	Score
1973	Wittenberg	Juniata	41–0
1974	Central (IA)	Ithaca	10–8
1975	Wittenberg	Ithaca	28–0
1976	St John's (MN)	Towson St	31–28
1977	Widener	Wabash	39–36
1978	Baldwin-Wallace	Wittenberg	24–10
1979	Ithaca	Wittenberg	14–10
1980	Dayton	Ithaca	63–0
1981	Widener	Dayton	17–10
1982	W Georgia	Augustana (IL)	14–0
1983	Augustana (IL)	Union (NY)	21–17
1984	Augustana (IL)	Central (IA)	21–12
1985	Augustana (IL)	Ithaca	20–7
1986	Augustana (IL)	Salisbury St	31–3
1987	Wagner	Dayton	19–3
1988	Ithaca	Central (IA)	39–24
1989	Dayton	Union (NY)	17–7

Division III *(Cont.)*

Year	Winner	Runner-Up	Score
1990	Allegheny	Lycoming	21–14 (OT)
1991	Ithaca	Dayton	34–20
1992	WI-LaCrosse	Washington & Jefferson	16–12
1993	Mount Union	Rowan	34–24
1994	Albion	Washington & Jefferson	38–15
1995	WI-LaCrosse	Rowan	36–7
1996	Mount Union	Rowan	56–24
1997	Mount Union	Lycoming	61–12

NAIA Divisional Championships†

Division I

Year	Winner	Runner-Up	Score
1956	St Joseph's (IN)/ Montana St		0–0
1957	Pittsburg St (KS)	Hillsdale (MI)	27–26
1958	NE Oklahoma	Northern Arizona	19–13
1959	Texas A&I	Lenoir-Rhyne (NC)	20–7
1960	Lenoir-Rhyne (NC)	Humboldt St (CA)	15–14
1961	Pittsburg St (KS)	Linfield (OR)	12–7
1962	Central St (OK)	Lenoir-Rhyne (NC)	28–13
1963	St John's (MN)	Prairie View (TX)	33–27
1964	Concordia-Moorhead/ Sam Houston		7–7
1965	St John's (MN)	Linfield (OR)	33–0
1966	Waynesburg (PA)	WI-Whitewater	42–21
1967	Fairmont St (WV)	Eastern Washington	28–21
1968	Troy St (MI)	Texas A&I	43–35
1969	Texas A&I	Concordia-Moorhead (MN)	32–7
1970	Texas A&I	Wofford (SC)	48–7
1971	Livingston (AL)	Arkansas Tech	14–12
1972	E Texas St	Carson-Newman (TN)	21–18
1973	Abilene Christian	Elon (NC)	42–14
1974	Texas A&I	Henderson St (AR)	34–23
1975	Texas A&I	Salem (WV)	37–0
1976	Texas A&I	Central Arkansas	26–0
1977	Abilene Christian	SW Oklahoma	24–7
1978	Angelo St (TX)	Elon (NC)	34–14
1979	Texas A&I	Central St (OK)	20–14
1980	Elon (NC)	NE Oklahoma	17–10
1981	Elon (NC)	Pittsburg St	3–0
1982	Central St (OK)	Mesa (CO)	14–11
1983	Carson-Newman (TN)	Mesa (CO)	36–28
1984	Carson-Newman (TN)/ Central Arkansas		19–19
1985	Central Arkansas/ Hillsdale (MI)		10–10
1986	Carson-Newman (TN)	Cameron (OK)	17–0
1987	Cameron (OK)	Carson-Newman (TN)	30–2
1988	Carson-Newman (TN)	Adams St (CO)	56–21
1989	Carson-Newman (TN)	Emporia St (KS)	34–20
1990	Central St (OH)	Mesa St (CO)	38–16
1991	Central Arkansas	Central St (OH)	19–16
1992	Central St (OH)	Gardner-Webb (NC)	19–16
1993	East Central (OK)	Glenville St (WV)	49–35
1994	Northeastern St (OK)	Arkansas-Pine Bluff	13–12
1995	Central St (OH)	Northeastern St (OK)	37–7
1996	SW Oklahoma St	Montana Tech	33–31
1997	Findlay (OH)	Willamette (OR)	14–7

† In 1997 the NAIA consolidated its two divisions into one.

Division II

Year	Winner	Runner-Up	Score
1970	Westminster (PA)	Anderson (IN)	21–16
1971	California Lutheran	Westminster (PA)	30–14
1972	Missouri Southern	Northwestern (IA)	21–14
1973	Northwestern (IA)	Glenville St (WV)	10–3
1974	Texas Lutheran	Missouri Valley	42–0
1975	Texas Lutheran	California Lutheran	34–8
1976	Westminster (PA)	Redlands (CA)	20–13
1977	Westminster (PA)	California Lutheran	17–9
1978	Concordia-Moorhead (MN)	Findlay (OH)	7–0
1979	Findlay (OH)	Northwestern (IA)	51–6
1980	Pacific Lutheran	Wilmington (OH)	38–10
1981	Austin Coll./ Conc.-Moorhead (MN)		24–24
1982	Linfield (OR)	William Jewell (MO)	33–15
1983	Northwestern (IA)	Pacific Lutheran	25–21
1984	Linfield (OR)	Northwestern (IA)	33–22
1985	WI-La Crosse	Pacific Lutheran	24–7
1986	Linfield (OR)	Baker (KS)	17–0
1987	Pacific Lutheran	WI-Stevens Point*	16–16
1988	Westminster (PA)	WI-La Crosse	21–14
1989	Westminster (PA)	WI-La Crosse	51–30
1990	Peru St (NE)	Westminster (PA)	17–7
1991	Georgetown (KY)	Pacific Lutheran	28–20
1992	Findlay (OH)	Linfield (OR)	26–13
1993	Pacific Lutheran (WA)	Westminster (PA)	50–20
1994	Westminster (PA)	Pacific Lutheran	27–7
1995	Findlay (OH)/ Central Washington		21–21
1996	Sioux Falls (SD)	Western Washington	47–25

*Forfeited 1987 season due to use of an ineligible player.   †In 1997 the NAIA consolidated its two divisions into one.

Awards

Heisman Memorial Trophy

Awarded to the best college player by the Downtown Athletic Club of New York City. The trophy is named after John W. Heisman, who coached Georgia Tech to the national championship in 1917 and later served as DAC athletic director.

Year	Winner, College, Position	Winner's Season Statistics	Runner-Up, College
1935	Jay Berwanger, Chicago, HB	Rush:119 Yds: 577 TD: 6	Monk Meyer, Army
1936	Larry Kelley, Yale, E	Rec: 17 Yds: 372 TD: 6	Sam Francis, Nebraska
1937	Clint Frank, Yale, HB	Rush: 157 Yds: 667 TD: 11	Byron White, Colorado
1938	†Davey O'Brien, Texas Christian, QB	Att/Comp: 194/110 Yds: 1733 TD: 19	Marshall Goldberg, Pittsburgh
1939	Nile Kinnick, Iowa, HB	Rush: 106 Yds: 374 TD: 5	Tom Harmon, Michigan
1940	Tom Harmon, Michigan, HB	Rush: 191 Yds: 852 TD: 16	John Kimbrough, Texas A&M
1941	†Bruce Smith, Minnesota, HB	Rush: 98 Yds: 480 TD: 6	Angelo Bertelli, Notre Dame
1942	Frank Sinkwich, Georgia, HB	Att/Comp: 166/84 Yds: 1392 TD: 10	Paul Governali, Columbia
1943	Angelo Bertelli, Notre Dame, QB	Att/Comp: 36/25 Yds: 511 TD: 10	Bob Odell, Pennsylvania
1944	Les Horvath, Ohio State, QB	Rush: 163 Yds: 924 TD: 12	Glenn Davis, Army
1945	*†Doc Blanchard, Army, FB	Rush: 101 Yds: 718 TD: 13	Glenn Davis, Army
1946	Glenn Davis, Army, HB	Rush: 123 Yds: 712 TD: 7	Charley Trippi, Georgia
1947	†John Lujack, Notre Dame, QB	Att/Comp: 109/61 Yds: 777 TD: 9	Bob Chappius, Michigan
1948	*Doak Walker, Southern Methodist, HB	Rush: 108 Yds: 532 TD: 8	Charlie Justice, N Carolina
1949	†Leon Hart, Notre Dame, E	Rec: 19 Yds: 257 TD: 5	Charlie Justice, N Carolina
1950	*Vic Janowicz, Ohio St, HB	Att/Comp: 77/32 Yds: 561 TD: 12	Kyle Rote, Southern Methodist
1951	Dick Kazmaier, Princeton, HB	Rush: 149 Yds: 861 TD: 9	Hank Lauricella, Tennessee
1952	Billy Vessels, Oklahoma, HB	Rush: 167 Yds: 1072 TD: 17	Jack Scarbath, Maryland
1953	John Lattner, Notre Dame, HB	Rush: 134 Yds: 651 TD: 6	Paul Giel, Minnesota
1954	Alan Ameche, Wisconsin, FB	Rush: 146 Yds: 641 TD: 9	Kurt Burris, Oklahoma
1955	Howard Cassady, Ohio St, HB	Rush: 161 Yds: 958 TD: 15	Jim Swink, Texas Christian
1956	Paul Hornung, Notre Dame, QB	Att/Comp: 111/59 Yds: 917 TD: 3	Johnny Majors, Tennessee

Heisman Memorial Trophy (Cont.)

Year	Winner, College, Position	Winner's Season Statistics	Runner-Up, College
1957	John David Crow, Texas A&M, HB	Rush: 129 Yds: 562 TD: 10	Alex Karras, Iowa
1958	Pete Dawkins, Army, HB	Rush: 78 Yds: 428 TD: 6	Randy Duncan, Iowa
1959	Billy Cannon, Louisiana St, HB	Rush: 139 Yds: 598 TD: 6	Rich Lucas, Penn St
1960	Joe Bellino, Navy, HB	Rush: 168 Yds: 834 TD: 18	Tom Brown, Minnesota
1961	Ernie Davis, Syracuse, HB	Rush: 150 Yds: 823 TD: 15	Bob Ferguson, Ohio St
1962	Terry Baker, Oregon St, QB	Att/Comp: 203/112 Yds: 1738 TD: 15	Jerry Stovall, Louisiana St
1963	*Roger Staubach, Navy, QB	Att/Comp: 161/107 Yds: 1474 TD: 7	Billy Lothridge, Georgia Tech
1964	John Huarte, Notre Dame, QB	Att/Comp: 205/114 Yds: 2062 TD: 16	Jerry Rhome, Tulsa
1965	Mike Garrett, Southern Cal, HB	Rush: 267 Yds: 1440 TD: 16	Howard Twilley, Tulsa
1966	Steve Spurrier, Florida, QB	Att/Comp: 291/179 Yds: 2012 TD: 16	Bob Griese, Purdue
1967	Gary Beban, UCLA, QB	Att/Comp: 156/87 Yds: 1359 TD: 8	O.J. Simpson, Southern Cal
1968	O.J. Simpson, Southern Cal, HB	Rush: 383 Yds: 1880 TD: 23	Leroy Keyes, Purdue
1969	Steve Owens, Oklahoma, FB	Rush: 358 Yds: 1523 TD: 23	Mike Phipps, Purdue
1970	Jim Plunkett, Stanford, QB	Att/Comp: 358/191 Yds: 2715 TD: 18	Joe Theismann, Notre Dame
1971	Pat Sullivan, Auburn, QB	Att/Comp: 281/162 Yds: 2012 TD: 20	Ed Marinaro, Cornell
1972	Johnny Rodgers, Nebraska, FL	Rec: 55 Yds: 942 TD: 17	Greg Pruitt, Oklahoma
1973	John Cappelletti, Penn St, HB	Rush: 286 Yds: 1522 TD: 17	John Hicks, Ohio St
1974	*Archie Griffin, Ohio St, HB	Rush: 256 Yds: 1695 TD: 12	Anthony Davis, Southern Cal
1975	Archie Griffin, Ohio St, HB	Rush: 262 Yds: 1450 TD: 4	Chuck Muncie, California
1976	†Tony Dorsett, Pittsburgh, HB	Rush: 370 Yds: 2150 TD: 23	Ricky Bell, Southern Cal
1977	Earl Campbell, Texas, FB	Rush: 267 Yds: 1744 TD: 19	Terry Miller, Oklahoma St
1978	*Billy Sims, Oklahoma, HB	Rush: 231 Yds: 1762 TD: 20	Chuck Fusina, Penn St
1979	Charles White, Southern Cal, HB	Rush: 332 Yds: 1803 TD: 19	Billy Sims, Oklahoma
1980	George Rogers, S Carolina, HB	Rush: 324 Yds: 1894 TD: 14	Hugh Green, Pittsburgh
1981	Marcus Allen, Southern Cal, HB	Rush: 433 Yds: 2427 TD: 23	Herschel Walker, Georgia
1982	*Herschel Walker, Georgia, HB	Rush: 335 Yds: 1752 TD: 17	John Elway, Stanford
1983	Mike Rozier, Nebraska, HB	Rush: 275 Yds: 2148 TD: 29	Steve Young, Brigham Young
1984	Doug Flutie, Boston College, QB	Att/Comp: 396/233 Yds: 3454 TD: 27	Keith Byars, Ohio St
1985	Bo Jackson, Auburn, HB	Rush: 278 Yds: 1786 TD: 17	Chuck Long, Iowa
1986	Vinny Testaverde, Miami (FL), QB	Att/Comp: 276/175 Yds: 2557 TD: 26	Paul Palmer, Temple
1987	Tim Brown, Notre Dame, WR	Rec: 39 Yds: 846 TD: 7	Don McPherson, Syracuse
1988	*Barry Sanders, Oklahoma St, RB	Rush: 344 Yds: 2628 TD: 39	Rodney Peete, Southern Cal
1989	*Andre Ware, Houston, QB	Att/Comp: 578/365 Yds: 4699 TD: 46	Anthony Thompson, Indiana
1990	*Ty Detmer, Brigham Young, QB	Att/Comp: 562/361 Yds: 5188 TD: 41	Raghib Ismail, Notre Dame
1991	*Desmond Howard, Michigan, WR	Rec: 61 Yds: 950 TD: 23	Casey Weldon, Florida St
1992	Gino Torretta, Miami (FL), QB	Att/Comp: 402/228 Yds: 3060 TD: 19	Marshall Faulk, San Diego St
1993	†Charlie Ward, Florida St, QB	Att/Comp: 380/264 Yds: 3032 TD: 27	Heath Shuler, Tennessee
1994	Rashaan Salaam, Colorado, RB	Rush: 298 Yds: 2055 TD: 24	Ki-Jana Carter, Penn St
1995	Eddie George, Ohio State, RB	Rush: 303 Yds: 1826 TD: 23	Tommie Frazier, Nebraska
1996	†Danny Wuerffel, Florida, QB	Att/Comp: 360/207 Yds: 3625 TD: 39	Troy Davis, Iowa St
1997	†Charles Woodson, Michigan, CB/WR	7 interceptions; Rec: 11 Yds: 231 TD: 4	Peyton Manning, Tennessee

*Juniors (all others seniors). †Winners who played for national championship teams the same year.

Note: Former Heisman winners and national media cast votes, with ballots allowing for three names (3 points for first, 2 for second and 1 for third).

Maxwell Award

Given to the nation's outstanding college football player by the Maxwell Football Club of Philadelphia.

Year	Player, College, Position	Year	Player, College, Position
1937	Clint Frank, Yale, HB	1967	Gary Beban, UCLA, QB
1938	Davey O'Brien, Texas Christian, QB	1968	O.J. Simpson, Southern Cal, RB
1939	Nile Kinnick, Iowa, HB	1969	Mike Reid, Penn St, DT
1940	Tom Harmon, Michigan, HB	1970	Jim Plunkett, Stanford, QB
1941	Bill Dudley, Virginia, HB	1971	Ed Marinaro, Cornell, RB
1942	Paul Governali, Columbia, QB	1972	Brad Van Pelt, Michigan St, DB
1943	Bob Odell, Pennsylvania, HB	1973	John Cappelletti, Penn St, RB
1944	Glenn Davis, Army, HB	1974	Steve Joachim, Temple, QB
1945	Doc Blanchard, Army, FB	1975	Archie Griffin, Ohio St, RB
1946	Charley Trippi, Georgia, HB	1976	Tony Dorsett, Pittsburgh, RB
1947	Doak Walker, Southern Meth, HB	1977	Ross Browner, Notre Dame, DE
1948	Chuck Bednarik, Pennsylvania, C	1978	Chuck Fusina, Penn St, QB
1949	Leon Hart, Notre Dame, E	1979	Charles White, Southern Cal, RB
1950	Reds Bagnell, Pennsylvania, HB	1980	Hugh Green, Pittsburgh, DE
1951	Dick Kazmaier, Princeton, HB	1981	Marcus Allen, Southern Cal, RB
1952	John Lattner, Notre Dame, HB	1982	Herschel Walker, Georgia, RB
1953	John Lattner, Notre Dame, HB	1983	Mike Rozier, Nebraska, RB
1954	Ron Beagle, Navy, E	1984	Doug Flutie, Boston College, QB
1955	Howard Cassady, Ohio St, HB	1985	Chuck Long, Iowa, QB
1956	Tommy McDonald, Oklahoma, HB	1986	Vinny Testaverde, Miami (FL), QB
1957	Bob Reifsnyder, Navy, T	1987	Don McPherson, Syracuse, QB
1958	Pete Dawkins, Army, HB	1988	Barry Sanders, Oklahoma St, RB
1959	Rich Lucas, Penn St, QB	1989	Anthony Thompson, Indiana, RB
1960	Joe Bellino, Navy, HB	1990	Ty Detmer, Brigham Young, QB
1961	Bob Ferguson, Ohio St, FB	1991	Desmond Howard, Michigan, WR
1962	Terry Baker, Oregon St, QB	1992	Gino Torretta, Miami (FL), QB
1963	Roger Staubach, Navy, QB	1993	Charlie Ward, Florida St, QB
1964	Glenn Ressler, Penn St, C	1994	Kerry Collins, Penn St, QB
1965	Tommy Nobis, Texas, LB	1995	Eddie George, Ohio St, RB
1966	Jim Lynch, Notre Dame, LB	1996	Danny Wuerffel, Florida, QB
		1997	Peyton Manning, Tennessee, QB

Davey O'Brien National Quarterback Award

Given to the top quarterback in the nation by the Davey O'Brien Educational and Charitable Trust of Fort Worth. Named for Texas Christian Hall of Fame quarterback Davey O'Brien (1936-38).

Year	Player, College	Year	Player, College
1981	Jim McMahon, Brigham Young	1990	Ty Detmer, Brigham Young
1982	Todd Blackledge, Penn St	1991	Ty Detmer, Brigham Young
1983	Steve Young, Brigham Young	1992	Gino Torretta, Miami (FL)
1984	Doug Flutie, Boston College	1993	Charlie Ward, Florida St
1985	Chuck Long, Iowa	1994	Kerry Collins, Penn St
1986	Vinny Testaverde, Miami (FL)	1995	Danny Wuerffel, Florida
1987	Don McPherson, Syracuse	1996	Danny Wuerffel, Florida
1988	Troy Aikman, UCLA	1997	Peyton Manning, Tennessee
1989	Andre Ware, Houston		

Note: Originally known as the Davey O'Brien Memorial Trophy, honoring the outstanding football player in the Southwest as follows: 1977—Earl Campbell, Texas, RB; 1978—Billy Sims, Oklahoma, RB; 1979—Mike Singletary, Baylor, LB; 1980—Mike Singletary, Baylor, LB.

Vince Lombardi/Rotary Award

Given to the outstanding college lineman of the year, the award is sponsored by the Rotary Club of Houston.

Year	Player, College, Position	Year	Player, College, Position
1970	Jim Stillwagon, Ohio St, MG	1984	Tony Degrate, Texas, DT
1971	Walt Patulski, Notre Dame, DE	1985	Tony Casillas, Oklahoma, NG
1972	Rich Glover, Nebraska, MG	1986	Cornelius Bennett, Alabama, LB
1973	John Hicks, Ohio St, OT	1987	Chris Spielman, Ohio St, LB
1974	Randy White, Maryland, DT	1988	Tracy Rocker, Auburn, DT
1975	Lee Roy Selmon, Oklahoma, DT	1989	Percy Snow, Michigan St, LB
1976	Wilson Whitley, Houston, DT	1990	Chris Zorich, Notre Dame, NG
1977	Ross Browner, Notre Dame, DE	1991	Steve Emtman, Washington, DT
1978	Bruce Clark, Penn St, DT	1992	Marvin Jones, Florida St, LB
1979	Brad Budde, Southern Cal, G	1993	Aaron Taylor, Notre Dame, OT
1980	Hugh Green, Pittsburgh, DE	1994	Warren Sapp, Miami (FL), DT
1981	Kenneth Sims, Texas, DT	1995	Orlando Pace, Ohio St, OT
1982	Dave Rimington, Nebraska, C	1996	Orlando Pace, Ohio St, OT
1983	Dean Steinkuhler, Nebraska, G	1997	Grant Wistrom, Nebraska, DE

Outland Trophy

Given to the outstanding interior lineman, selected by the Football Writers Association of America.

Year	Player, College, Position	Year	Player, College, Position
1946	George Connor, Notre Dame, T	1972	Rich Glover, Nebraska, MG
1947	Joe Steffy, Army, G	1973	John Hicks, Ohio St, OT
1948	Bill Fischer, Notre Dame, G	1974	Randy White, Maryland, DE
1949	Ed Bagdon, Michigan St, G	1975	Lee Roy Selmon, Oklahoma, DT
1950	Bob Gain, Kentucky, T	1976	*Ross Browner, Notre Dame, DE
1951	Jim Weatherall, Oklahoma, T	1977	Brad Shearer, Texas, DT
1952	Dick Modzelewski, Maryland, T	1978	Greg Roberts, Oklahoma, G
1953	J.D. Roberts, Oklahoma, G	1979	Jim Ritcher, N Carolina St, C
1954	Bill Brooks, Arkansas, G	1980	Mark May, Pittsburgh, OT
1955	Calvin Jones, Iowa, G	1981	*Dave Rimington, Nebraska, C
1956	Jim Parker, Ohio St, G	1982	Dave Rimington, Nebraska, C
1957	Alex Karras, Iowa, T	1983	Dean Steinkuhler, Nebraska, G
1958	Zeke Smith, Auburn, G	1984	Bruce Smith, Virginia Tech, DT
1959	Mike McGee, Duke, T	1985	Mike Ruth, Boston Col, NG
1960	Tom Brown, Minnesota, G	1986	Jason Buck, Brigham Young, DT
1961	Merlin Olsen, Utah St, T	1987	Chad Hennings, Air Force, DT
1962	Bobby Bell, Minnesota, T	1988	Tracy Rocker, Auburn, DT
1963	Scott Appleton, Texas, T	1989	Mohammed Elewonibi, Brigham Young, G
1964	Steve DeLong, Tennessee, T	1990	Russell Maryland, Miami (FL), DT
1965	Tommy Nobis, Texas, G	1991	*Steve Emtman, Washington, DT
1966	Loyd Phillips, Arkansas, T	1992	Will Shields, Nebraska, G
1967	Ron Yary, Southern Cal, T	1993	Rob Waldrop, Arizona, NG
1968	Bill Stanfill, Georgia, T	1994	Zach Wiegert, Nebraska, G
1969	Mike Reid, Penn St, DT	1995	Jonathan Ogden, UCLA, OT
1970	Jim Stillwagon, Ohio St, MG	1996	*Orlando Pace, Ohio St, OT
1971	Larry Jacobson, Nebraska, DT	1997	Aaron Taylor, Nebraska, G

*Juniors (all others seniors).

Butkus Award

Given to the top collegiate linebacker, the award was established by the Downtown Athletic Club of Orlando and named for college Hall of Famer Dick Butkus of Illinois.

Year	Player, College	Year	Player, College
1985	Brian Bosworth, Oklahoma	1992	Marvin Jones, Florida St
1986	Brian Bosworth, Oklahoma	1993	Trev Alberts, Nebraska
1987	Paul McGowan, Florida St	1994	Dana Howard, Illinois
1988	Derrick Thomas, Alabama	1995	Kevin Hardy, Illinois
1989	Percy Snow, Michigan St	1996	Matt Russell, Colorado
1990	Alfred Williams, Colorado	1997	Andy Katzenmoyer, Ohio St
1991	Erick Anderson, Michigan		

Jim Thorpe Award

Given to the best defensive back of the year, the award is presented by the Jim Thorpe Athletic Club of Oklahoma City.

Year	Player, College	Year	Player, College
1986	Thomas Everett, Baylor	1992	Deon Figures, Colorado
1987	Bennie Blades, Miami (FL)	1993	Antonio Langham, Alabama
	Rickey Dixon, Oklahoma	1994	Chris Hudson, Colorado
1988	Deion Sanders, Florida St	1995	Greg Myers, Colorado St
1989	Mark Carrier, Southern Cal	1996	Lawrence Wright, Florida
1990	Darryl Lewis, Arizona	1997	Charles Woodson, Michigan
1991	Terrell Buckley, Florida St		

Walter Payton Player of the Year Award

Given to the top Division I-AA football player, the award is sponsored by Sports Network and voted on by Division I-AA sports information directors.

Year	Player, College, Position
1987	Kenny Gamble, Colgate, RB
1988	Dave Meggett, Towson St, RB
1989	John Friesz, Idaho, QB
1990	Walter Dean, Grambling, RB
1991	Jamie Martin, Weber St, QB
1992	Michael Payton, Marshall, QB
1993	Doug Nussmeier, Idaho, QB
1994	Steve McNair, Alcorn St, QB
1995	Dave Dickenson, Montana, QB
1996	Archie Amerson, Northern Arizona, RB
1997	Brian Finneran, Villanova, WR

The Harlon Hill Trophy

Given to the outstanding NCAA Division II college football player, the award is sponsored by the National Harlon Hill Awards Committee, Florence, AL.

Year	Player, College, Position
1986	Jeff Bentrim, N Dakota St, QB
1987	Johnny Bailey, Texas A&I, RB
1988	Johnny Bailey, Texas A&I, RB
1989	Johnny Bailey, Texas A&I, RB
1990	Chris Simdorn, N Dakota St, QB
1991	Ronnie West, Pittsburg St, WR
1992	Ronald Moore, Pittsburg St, RB
1993	Roger Graham, New Haven, RB
1994	Chris Hatcher, Valdosta St, QB
1995	Ronald McKinnon, N Alabama, LB
1996	Jarrett Anderson, Truman St, RB
1997	Irvin Sigler, Bloomsburg, RB

NCAA Division I-A Individual Records

Career

SCORING

Most Points Scored: 423 — Roman Anderson, Houston, 1988-91
Most Points Scored per Game: 12.1 — Marshall Faulk, San Diego St, 1991-93
Most Touchdowns Scored: 65 — Anthony Thompson, Indiana, 1986-89
Most Touchdowns Scored per Game: 2.0 — Marshall Faulk, San Diego St, 1991-93
Most Touchdowns Scored, Rushing: 64 — Anthony Thompson, Indiana, 1986-89
Most Touchdowns Scored, Passing: 121 — Ty Detmer, Brigham Young, 1988-91
Most Touchdowns Scored, Receiving: 43 — Aaron Turner, Pacific, 1989-92
Most Touchdowns Scored, Interception Returns: 5 — Ken Thomas, San Jose St, 1979-82; Jackie Walker, Tennessee, 1969-71
Most Touchdowns Scored, Punt Returns: 7 — Johnny Rodgers, Nebraska, 1970-72; Jack Mitchell, Oklahoma, 1946-48
Most Touchdowns Scored, Kickoff Returns: 6 — Anthony Davis, Southern Cal, 1972-74

TOTAL OFFENSE

Most Plays: 1795 — Ty Detmer, Brigham Young, 1988-91
Most Plays per Game: 48.5 — Doug Gaynor, Long Beach St, 1984-85
Most Yards Gained: 14,665 — Ty Detmer, Brigham Young, 1988-91 (15,031 passing, -366 rushing)
Most Yards Gained per Game: 320.9 — Chris Vargas, Nevada, 1992-93
Most 300+ Yard Games: 33 —Ty Detmer, Brigham Young, 1988-91

RUSHING

Most Rushes: 1,215 — Steve Bartalo, Colorado St, 1983-86 (4813 yds)
Most Rushes per Game: 34.0 — Ed Marinaro, Cornell, 1969-71
Most Yards Gained: 6,082 — Tony Dorsett, Pittsburgh, 1973-76
Most Yards Gained per Game: 174.6 — Ed Marinaro, Cornell, 1969-71
Most 100+ Yard Games: 33 — Tony Dorsett, Pittsburgh, 1973-76; Archie Griffin, Ohio St, 1972-75
Most 200+ Yard Games: 11 — Marcus Allen, Southern Cal, 1978-81

PASSING

Highest Passing Efficiency Rating: 163.6 — Danny Wuerffel, Florida, 1993-96 (1,170 attempts, 708 completions, 42 interceptions, 10,875 yards, 114 touchdown passes)
Most Passes Attempted: 1,530 — Ty Detmer, Brigham Young, 1988-91
Most Passes Attempted per Game: 39.6 — Mike Perez, San Jose St, 1986-87
Most Passes Completed: 958 — Ty Detmer, Brigham Young, 1988-91
Most Passes Completed per Game: 25.9 — Doug Gaynor, Long Beach St, 1984-85
***Highest Completion Percentage:** 63.9 — Jack Trudeau, Illinois, 1981, 1983-85
Most Yards Gained: 15,031 — Ty Detmer, Brigham Young, 1988-91
Most Yards Gained per Game: 326.8 — Ty Detmer, Brigham Young, 1988-91

RECEIVING

Most Passes Caught: 266 — Aaron Turner, Pacific, 1989-92
Most Passes Caught per Game: 10.5 — Emmanuel Hazard, Houston, 1989-90
Most Yards Gained: 4,518 — Marcus Harris, Wyoming, 1993-96
Most Yards Gained per Game: 140.9 — Alex Van Dyke, Nevada, 1994-95
Highest Average Gain per Reception: 25.7 — Wesley Walker, California, 1973-75

*Minimum 1100 attempts.

Career *(Cont.)*

ALL-PURPOSE RUNNING

Most Plays: 1347 — Steve Bartalo, Colorado St, 1983-86 (1215 rushes, 132 receptions)
Most Yards Gained: 7172 — Napoleon McCallum, Navy, 1981-85 (4179 rushing, 796 receiving, 858 punt returns, 1339 kickoff returns)
Most Yards Gained per Game: 237.8 — Ryan Benjamin, Pacific, 1990-92
Highest Average Gain per Play: 17.4 — Anthony Carter, Michigan, 1979-82

INTERCEPTIONS

Most Passes Intercepted: 29 — Al Brosky, Illinois, 1950-52
Most Passes Intercepted per Game: 1.1 — Al Brosky, Illinois, 1950-52
Most Yards on Interception Returns: 501 — Terrell Buckley, Florida St, 1989-91
Highest Average Gain per Interception: 26.5 — Tom Pridemore, W Virginia, 1975-77

SPECIAL TEAMS

Highest Punt Return Average: 23.6 — Jack Mitchell, Oklahoma, 1946-48
Highest Kickoff Return Average: 36.2 — Forrest Hall, San Francisco, 1946-47
Highest Average Yards per Punt: 46.3 — Todd Sauerbrun, West Virginia, 1991-94

Single Season

SCORING

Most Points Scored: 234 — Barry Sanders, Oklahoma St, 1988
Most Points Scored per Game: 21.27 — Barry Sanders, Oklahoma St, 1988
Most Touchdowns Scored: 39 — Barry Sanders, Oklahoma St, 1988
Most Touchdowns Scored, Rushing: 37 — Barry Sanders, Oklahoma St, 1988
Most Touchdowns Scored, Passing: 54 — David Klingler, Houston, 1990
Most Touchdowns Scored, Receiving: 25 — Randy Moss, Marshall, 25
Most Touchdowns Scored, Interception Returns: 3 — by many players
Most Touchdowns Scored, Punt Returns: 4 — Quinton Spotwood, Syracuse, 1997; Tinker Keck, Cincinnati, 1997; James Henry, Southern Miss, 1987; Golden Richards, Brigham Young, 1971; Cliff Branch, Colorado, 1971
Most Touchdowns Scored, Kickoff Returns: 3 — Leland McElroy, Texas A&M, 1993; Terance Mathis, New Mexico, 1989; Willie Gault, Tennessee, 1980; Anthony Davis, Southern Cal, 1974; Stan Brown, Purdue, 1970; Forrest Hall, San Francisco, 1946

TOTAL OFFENSE

Most Plays: 704 — David Klingler, Houston, 1990
Most Yards Gained: 5,221 — David Klingler, Houston, 1990
Most Yards Gained per Game: 474.6 — David Klingler, Houston, 1990
Most 300+ Yard Games: 12 — Ty Detmer, Brigham Young, 1990

RUSHING

Most Rushes: 403 — Marcus Allen, Southern Cal, 1981
Most Rushes per Game: 39.6 — Ed Marinaro, Cornell, 1971
Most Yards Gained: 2628 — Barry Sanders, Oklahoma St, 1988
Most Yards Gained per Game: 238.9 — Barry Sanders, Oklahoma St, 1988
Most 100+ Yard Games: 11 — By 13 players, most recently Troy Davis, Iowa St, 1996

PASSING

Highest Passing Efficiency Rating: 178.4 — Danny Wuerffel, Florida, 1995 (325 attempts, 210 completions, 10 interceptions, 3266 yards, 35 TD passes)
Most Passes Attempted: 643 — David Klingler, Houston, 1990
Most Passes Attempted per Game: 58.5 — David Klingler, Houston, 1990
Most Passes Completed: 374 — David Klingler, Houston, 1990
Most Passes Completed per Game: 34.0 — David Klingler, Houston, 1990
Highest Completion Percentage: 71.3 — Steve Young, Brigham Young, 1983
Most Yards Gained: (12 games) 5188 — Ty Detmer, Brigham Young, 1990; (11 games) 5140 — David Klingler, Houston, 1990
Most Yards Gained per Game: 467.3 — David Klingler, Houston, 1990

RECEIVING

Most Passes Caught: 142 — Emmanuel Hazard, Houston, 1989
Most Passes Caught per Game: 13.4 — Howard Twilley, Tulsa, 1965
Most Yards Gained: 1854 — Alex Van Dyke, Nevada, 1995.
Most Yards Gained per Game: 177.9 — Howard Twilley, Tulsa, 1965
Highest Average Gain per Reception: 27.9 — Elmo Wright, Houston, 1968 (min. 30 receptions)

ALL-PURPOSE RUNNING

Most Plays: 432 — Marcus Allen, Southern Cal, 1981
Most Yards Gained: 3250 — Barry Sanders, Oklahoma St, 1988
Most Yards Gained per Game: 295.5 — Barry Sanders, Oklahoma St, 1988
Highest Average Gain per Play: 18.5 — Henry Bailey, UNLV, 1992

Single Season *(Cont.)*

INTERCEPTIONS

Most Passes Intercepted: 14 — Al Worley, Washington, 1968
Most Yards on Interception Returns: 302 — Charles Phillips, Southern Cal, 1974
Highest Average Gain per Interception: 50.6 — Norm Thompson, Utah, 1969

SPECIAL TEAMS

Highest Punt Return Average: 25.9 — Bill Blackstock, Tennessee, 1951
Highest Kickoff Return Average: 40.1 — Paul Allen, Brigham Young, 1961
Highest Average Yards per Punt: 50.3 — Chad Kessler, Louisiana St, 1997

Single Game

SCORING

Most Points Scored: 48 — Howard Griffith, Illinois, 1990 (vs Southern Illinois)
Most Field Goals: 7 — Dale Klein, Nebraska, 1985 (vs Missouri); Mike Prindle, Western Michigan, 1984 (vs Marshall)
Most Extra Points (Kick): 13 — Derek Mahoney, Fresno St, 1991 (vs New Mexico); Terry Leiweke, Houston, 1968 (vs Tulsa)
Most Extra Points (2-Pts): 6 — Jim Pilot, New Mexico St, 1961 (vs Hardin-Simmons)

TOTAL OFFENSE

Most Yards Gained: 732 — David Klingler, Houston, 1990 (vs Arizona St)

RUSHING

Most Yards Gained: 396 — Tony Sands, Kansas, 1991 (vs Missouri)
Most Touchdowns Rushed: 8 — Howard Griffith, Illinois, 1990 (vs Southern Illinois)

PASSING

Most Passes Completed: 55 — Rusty LaRue, Wake Forest, 1995 (vs Duke)
Most Yards Gained: 716 — David Klingler, Houston, 1990 (vs Arizona St)
Most Touchdowns Passed: 11 — David Klingler, Houston, 1990 [vs Eastern Washington (I-AA)]

RECEIVING

Most Passes Caught: 23 — Randy Gatewood, UNLV, 1994 (vs Idaho)
Most Yards Gained: 363 — Randy Gatewood, UNLV, 1994 (vs Idaho)
Most Touchdown Catches: 6 — Tim Delaney, San Diego St, 1969 (vs New Mexico St)

NCAA Division I-AA Individual Records

Career

SCORING

Most Points Scored: 385 — Marty Zendejas, NV-Reno, 1984-87
Most Touchdowns Scored: 61 — Sherriden May, Idaho, 1992-94
Most Touchdowns Scored, Rushing: 55 — Kenny Gamble, Colgate, 1984-87
Most Touchdowns Scored, Passing: 139 — Willie Totten, Mississippi Valley, 1982-85
Most Touchdowns Scored, Receiving: 50 — Jerry Rice, Mississippi Valley, 1981-84

RUSHING

Most Rushes: 1,027 — Erik Marsh, Lafayette, 1991-94
Most Rushes per Game: 38.2 — Arnold Mickens, Butler, 1994-95
Most Yards Gained: 5,415 — Reggie Greene, Siena, 1994-97
Most Yards Gained per Game: 150.4 — Reggie Greene, Siena, 1994-97

PASSING

Highest Passing Efficiency Rating: 170.8 — Shawn Knight, William & Mary, 1991-94
Most Passes Attempted: 1,680 — Steve McNair, Alcorn St, 1991-94
Most Passes Completed: 934 — Jamie Martin, Weber St, 1989-92
Most Passes Completed per Game: 25.1 — Aaron Flowers, Cal St-Northridge, 1996-97
Highest Completion Percentage: 67.3 — Dave Dickenson, Montana, 1992-95
Most Yards Gained: 14,496 — Steve McNair, Alcorn St, 1991-94
Most Yards Gained per Game: 350 — Neil Lomax, Portland St, 1978-80

RECEIVING

Most Passes Caught: 301 — Jerry Rice, Mississippi Valley, 1981-84
Most Yards Gained: 4,693 — Jerry Rice, Mississippi Valley, 1981-84
Most Yards Gained per Game: 114.5 — Jerry Rice, Mississippi Valley, 1981-84
Highest Average Gain per Reception: 24.3 — John Taylor, Delaware St, 1982-85

Single Season

SCORING

Most Points Scored: 170 — Geoff Mitchell, Weber St, 1991
Most Touchdowns Scored: 28 — Geoff Mitchell, Weber St, 1991
Most Touchdowns Scored, Rushing: 25 — Archie Amerson, Northern Arizona, 1996
Most Touchdowns Scored, Passing: 56 — Willie Totten, Mississippi Valley, 1984
Most Touchdowns Scored, Receiving: 27 — Jerry Rice, Mississippi Valley, 1984

RUSHING

Most Rushes: 409 — Arnold Mickens, Butler, 1994
Most Rushes per Game: 40.9 — Arnold Mickens, Butler, 1994
Most Yards Gained: 2255 — Arnold Mickens, Butler, 1994
Most Yards Gained per Game: 225.5 — Arnold Mickens, Butler, 1994

PASSING

Highest Passing Efficiency Rating: 204.6 — Shawn Knight, William & Mary, 1993
Most Passes Attempted: 530 — Steve McNair, Alcorn St, 1994
Most Passes Completed: 324 — Willie Totten, Mississippi Valley, 1984
Most Passes Completed per Game: 32.4 — Willie Totten, Mississippi Valley, 1984
Highest Completion Percentage: 70.6 — Giovanni Carmazzi, Hofstra, 1997
Most Yards Gained: 4,863 — Steve McNair, Alcorn St, 1994
Most Yards Gained per Game: 455.7 — Willie Totten, Mississippi Valley, 1984

RECEIVING

Most Passes Caught: 115 — Brian Forster, Rhode Island, 1985
Most Yards Gained: 1,682 — Jerry Rice, Mississippi Valley, 1984
Most Yards Gained per Game: 168.2 — Jerry Rice, Mississippi Valley, 1984
Highest Average Gain per Reception: 28.9 — Mikhael Ricks, Stephen F. Austin, 1997; (min. 35 receptions)

Single Game

SCORING

Most Points Scored: 42 — Archie Amerson, Northern Arizona, 1996 (vs Weber St)
Most Field Goals: 8 — Goran Lingmerth, Northern Arizona, 1986 (vs Idaho)

RUSHING

Most Yards Gained: 379 — Reggie Green, Siena, 1996 (vs St John's [NY])
Most Touchdowns Rushed: 7 — Archie Amerson, Northern Arizona, 1996 (vs Weber St)

PASSING

Most Passes Completed: 48 — Clayton Millis, Cal St-Northridge, 1995 (vs St Mary's [CA])
Most Yards Gained: 649 — Steve McNair, Alcorn St, 1994 (vs Southern-BR)
Most Touchdowns Passed: 9 — Willie Totten, Mississippi Valley, 1984 (vs Kentucky St)

RECEIVING

Most Passes Caught: 24 — Jerry Rice, Mississippi Valley, 1983 (vs Southern-BR)
Most Yards Gained: 370 — Michael Lerch, Princeton, 1991 (vs Brown)
Most Touchdown Catches: 5 — Four players, most recently by Rod Marshall, Northern Arizona, 1995 (vs Abilene Christian)

NCAA Division II Individual Records

Career

SCORING

Most Points Scored: 464 — Walter Payton, Jackson St, 1971-74
Most Touchdowns Scored: 73 — Jarrett Anderson, Truman St, 1993-96
Most Touchdowns Scored, Rushing: 72 — Shawn Graves, Wofford, 1989-92
Most Touchdowns Scored, Passing: 116 — Chris Hatcher, Valdosta St, 1991-94
Most Touchdowns Scored, Receiving: 53 — Carlos Ferralls, Glenville St, 1994-97

RUSHING

Most Rushes: 1,072 — Bernie Peeters, Luther, 1968-71
Most Rushes per Game: 29.8 — Bernie Peeters, Luther, 1968-71
Most Yards Gained: 6,320 — Johnny Bailey, Texas A&I*, 1986-89
Most Yards Gained per Game: 162.1 — Johnny Bailey, Texas A&I*, 1986-89

*Became Texas A&M-Kingsville in 1993

Career *(Cont.)*

PASSING

Highest Passing Efficiency Rating: 164.0 — Chris Petersen, UC-Davis, 1985-86
Most Passes Attempted: 1,719 — Bob McLaughlin, Lock Haven, 1992-95
Most Passes Completed: 1,001 — Chris Hatcher, Valdosta St, 1991-94
Most Passes Completed per Game: 25.7 — Chris Hatcher, Valdosta St, 1991-94
Highest Completion Percentage: 69.6 — Chris Peterson, UC-Davis, 1985-86
Most Yards Gained: 10,878 — Chris Hatcher, Valdosta St, 1991-94
Most Yards Gained per Game: 312.1 — Grady Benton, West Texas A&M, 1994-95

RECEIVING

Most Passes Caught: 282 — Carlos Ferralls, Glenville St, 1994-97
Most Yards Gained: 4,468 — James Roe, Norfolk St, 1992-95
Most Yards Gained per Game: 160.8 — Chris George, Glenville St, 1993-94
Highest Average Gain per Reception: 22.8 — Tyrone Johnson, Western St (CO), 1990-93

Single Season

SCORING

Most Points Scored: 198 — Brian Shay, Emporia St, 1997
Most Touchdowns Scored: 32 — Brian Shay, Emporia St, 1997
Most Touchdowns Scored, Rushing: 29 — Brian Shay, Emporia St, 1997
Most Touchdowns Scored, Passing: 50 — Chris Hatcher, Valdosta St, 1994
Most Touchdowns Scored, Receiving: 21 — Chris Perry, Adams St, 1995

RUSHING

Most Rushes: 385 — Joe Gough, Wayne St (MI), 1994
Most Rushes per Game: 38.6 — Mark Perkins, Hobart, 1968
Most Yards Gained: 2,220 — Anthony Gray, Western New Mexico, 1997
Most Yards Gained per Game: 222.0 — Anthony Gray, Western New Mexico, 1997

PASSING

Highest Passing Efficiency Rating: 210.1 — Boyd Crawford, College of Idaho, 1953
Most Passes Attempted: 544 — Lance Funderburk, Valdosta St, 1995
Most Passes Completed: 356 — Lance Funderburk, Valdosta St, 1995
Most Passes Completed per Game: 32.4 — Lance Funderburk, Valdosta St, 1995
Highest Completion Percentage: 74.6 — Chris Hatcher, Valdosta St, 1994
Most Yards Gained: 4,189 — Wilkie Perez, Glenville St, 1997
Most Yards Gained per Game: 393.4 — Grady Benton, W Texas A&M, 1994

RECEIVING

Most Passes Caught: 119 — Brad Bailey, W Texas A&M, 1994
Most Yards Gained: 1,876 — Chris George, Glenville St, 1993
Most Yards Gained per Game: 187.6 — Chris George, Glenville St, 1993
Highest Average Gain per Reception: 32.5 — Tyrone Johnson, Western St, 1991 (min. 30 receptions)

Single Game

SCORING

Most Points Scored: 48 — Paul Zaeske, N Park, 1968 (vs N Central); Junior Wolf, Panhandle St, 1958 (vs St Mary [KS])
Most Field Goals: 6 — Steve Huff, Central Missouri St, 1985 (vs SE Missouri St)

RUSHING

Most Yards Gained: 382 — Kelly Ellis, Northern Iowa, 1979 (vs Western Illinois)
Most Touchdowns Rushed: 8 — Junior Wolf, Panhandle St, 1958 (vs St Mary [KS])

PASSING

Most Passes Completed: 56 — Jarrod DeGeorgia, Wayne St (NE), 1996 (vs Drake)
Most Yards Gained: 642 — Wilkie Perez, Glenville St, 1997, (vs Concord)
Most Touchdowns Passed: 10 — Bruce Swanson, N Park, 1968 (vs N Central)

RECEIVING

Most Passes Caught: 23 — Chris George, Glenville St, 1994 (vs W VA Wesleyan); Barry Wagner, Alabama A&M, 1989 (vs Clark Atlanta)
Most Yards Gained: 370 — Barry Wagner, Alabama A&M, 1989 (vs Clark Atlanta)
Most Touchdown Catches: 8 — Paul Zaeske, N Park, 1968 (vs N Central)

NCAA Division III Individual Records

Career

SCORING

Most Points Scored: 528 — Carey Bender, Coe, 1991-94
Most Touchdowns Scored: 86 — Carey Bender, Coe, 1991-94
Most Touchdowns Scored, Rushing: 76 — Joe Dudek, Plymouth St, 1982-85
Most Touchdowns Scored, Passing: 141 — Bill Borchert, Mt Union, 1994-97
Most Touchdowns Scored, Receiving: 55 — Chris Bisaillon, Illinois Wesleyan, 1989-92

RUSHING

Most Rushes: 1,112 — Mike Birosak, Dickinson, 1986-89
Most Rushes per Game: 32.7 — Chris Sizemore, Bridgewater (VA), 1972-74
Most Yards Gained: 6,125 — Carey Bender, Coe, 1991-94
Most Yards Gained per Game: 175.1 — Ricky Gales, Simpson, 1988-89

PASSING

Highest Passing Efficiency Rating: 194.2 — Bill Borchert, Mt Union, 1994-97
Most Passes Attempted: 1,696 — Kirk Baumgartner, WI-Stevens Point, 1986-89
Most Passes Completed: 883 — Kirk Baumgartner, WI-Stevens Point, 1986-89
Most Passes Completed per Game: 24.9 — Keith Bishop, Illinois Wesleyan, 1981, Wheaton (IL), 1983-85
Highest Completion Percentage: 66.5 — Bill Borchert, Mt Union (OH) 1994-97
Most Yards Gained: 13,028 — Kirk Baumgartner, WI-Stevens Point, 1986-89
Most Yards Gained per Game: 317.8 — Kirk Baumgartner, WI-Stevens Point, 1986-89

RECEIVING

Most Passes Caught: 287 — Matt Newton, Principia (IL), 1990-93
Most Yards Gained: 4,311 — Kurt Barth, Eureka, 1994-97
Most Yards Gained per Game: 110.5 — Kurt Barth, Eureka, 1994-97
Highest Average Gain per Reception: 21.7 — R. J. Hoppe, Carroll (WI), 1993-96

Single Season

SCORING

Most Points Scored: 194 — Carey Bender, Coe, 1994
Most Points Scored per Game: 20.8 — James Regan, Pomona-Pitzer, 1997
Most Touchdowns Scored: 32 — Carey Bender, Coe, 1994
Most Touchdowns Scored, Rushing: 29 — Carey Bender, Coe, 1994
Most Touchdowns Scored, Passing: 47 — Bill Borchert, Mt Union, 1997
Most Touchdowns Scored, Receiving: 20 — Jeff Clay, Catholic, 1997; John Aromando, Trenton St, 1983

RUSHING

Most Rushes: 380 — Mike Birosak, Dickinson, 1989
Most Rushes per Game: 38.0 — Mike Birosak, Dickinson, 1989
Most Yards Gained: 2,385 — Dante Brown, Marietta, 1996
Most Yards Gained per Game: 238.5 — Dante Brown, Marietta, 1996

PASSING

Highest Passing Efficiency Rating: 225.0 — Mike Simpson, Eureka, 1994
Most Passes Attempted: 527 — Kirk Baumgartner, WI-Stevens Point, 1988
Most Passes Completed: 283 — Terry Peebles, Hanover, 1995
Most Passes Completed per Game: 29.1 — Keith Bishop, Illinois Wesleyan, 1985
Highest Completion Percentage: 73.4 — Mike Simpson, Eureka, 1994
Most Yards Gained: 3,828 — Kirk Baumgartner, WI-Stevens Point, 1988
Most Yards Gained per Game: 369.2 — Kirk Baumgartner, WI-Stevens Point, 1989

RECEIVING

Most Passes Caught: 112 — Jeff Clay, Catholic, 1997
Most Yards Gained: 1,693 — Sean Munroe, Mass-Boston, 1992
Most Yards Gained per Game: 188.1 — Sean Munroe, Mass-Boston 1992
Highest Average Gain per Reception: 26.9 — Marty Redlawsk, Concordia (IL), 1985

Single Game

SCORING

Most Field Goals: 6 — Jim Hever, Rhodes, 1984 (vs Millsaps)

PASSING

Most Passes Completed: 50 — Tim Lynch, Hofstra, 1991 (vs Fordham)
Most Yards Gained: 602 — Tom Stallings, St. Thomas (MN), 1993 (vs Bethel)
Most Touchdowns Passed: 8 — Steve Austin, Mass-Boston, 1992 (vs Framingham St); Kirk Baumgartner, WI-Stevens Point, 1989 (vs WI-Superior); John Koz, Baldwin-Wallace, 1993 (vs Ohio Northern)

RUSHING

Most Yards Gained: 441 — Dante Brown, Marietta, 1996 (vs Baldwin-Wallace)
Most Touchdowns Rushed: 8 — Carey Bender, Coe, 1994 (vs Beloit)

RECEIVING

Most Passes Caught: 23 — Sean Munroe, Mass-Boston, 1992 (vs Mass-Maritime)
Most Yards Gained: 364 — Jeff Clay, Catholic, 1996 (vs Albright)
Most Touchdown Catches: 5 — 12 players, most recently V. Roques, Claremont MS, 1995 (vs Occidental)

NCAA Division I-A Alltime Individual Leaders

Career

Scoring

POINTS (KICKERS)

	Years	Pts
Roman Anderson, Houston	1988-91	423
Carlos Huerta, Miami (FL)	1988-91	397
Jason Elam, Hawaii	1988-92	395
Derek Schmidt, Florida St	1984-87	393
Luis Zendejas, Arizona St	1981-84	368

POINTS (NON-KICKERS)

	Years	Pts
Anthony Thompson, Indiana	1986-89	394
Marshall Faulk, San Diego St	1991-93	376
Tony Dorsett, Pittsburgh	1973-76	356
Glenn Davis, Army	1943-46	354
Art Luppino, Arizona	1953-56	337

POINTS PER GAME (NON-KICKERS)

	Years	Pts/Game
Marshall Faulk, San Diego St	1991-93	12.1
Ed Marinaro, Cornell	1969-71	11.8
Bill Burnett, Arkansas	1968-70	11.3
Steve Owens, Oklahoma	1967-69	11.2
Eddie Talboom, Wyoming	1948-50	10.8

Total Offense

YARDS GAINED

	Years	Yds
Ty Detmer, Brigham Young	1988-91	14,665
Doug Flutie, Boston Col	1981-84	11,317
Peyton Manning, Tennessee	1994-97	11,020
Eric Zeier, Georgia	1991-94	10,841
Alex Van Pelt, Pittsburgh	1989-92	10,814

YARDS PER GAME

	Years	Yds/Game
Chris Vargas, Nevada	1992-93	320.9
Ty Detmer, Brigham Young	1988-91	318.8
Mike Perez, San Jose St	1986-87	309.1
Josh Wallwork, Wyoming	1995-96	307.0
Doug Gaynor, Long Beach St	1984-85	305.0

Rushing

YARDS GAINED

	Years	Yds
Tony Dorsett, Pittsburgh	1973-76	6,082
Charles White, Southern Cal	1976-79	5,598
Herschel Walker, Georgia	1980-82	5,259
Archie Griffin, Ohio St	1972-75	5,177
Darren Lewis, Texas A&M	1987-90	5,012

YARDS PER GAME

	Years	Yds/Game
Ed Marinaro, Cornell	1969-71	174.6
O.J. Simpson, Southern Cal	1967-68	164.4
Herschel Walker, Georgia	1980-82	159.4
LeShon Johnson, N Illinois	1992-93	150.6
Marshall Faulk, San Diego St	1991-93	148.0

TOUCHDOWNS RUSHING

	Years	TD
Anthony Thompson, Indiana	1986-89	64
Marshall Faulk, San Diego St	1991-93	57
Steve Owens, Oklahoma	1967-69	56
Tony Dorsett, Pittsburgh	1973-76	55
Pete Johnson, Ohio St	1973-76	51

Passing

PASSING EFFICIENCY

	Years	Rating
Danny Wuerffel, Florida	1993-96	163.6
Ty Detmer, Brigham Young	1988-91	162.7
Steve Sarkisian, Brigham Young	1995-96	162.0
Billy Blanton, San Diego St	1993-96	157.1
Jim McMahon, Brigham Young	1977-78, 80-81	156.9

Note: Minimum 500 completions.

YARDS GAINED

	Years	Yds
Ty Detmer, Brigham Young	1988-91	15,031
Todd Santos, San Diego St	1984-87	11,425
Peyton Manning, Tennessee	1994-97	11,201
Eric Zeier, Georgia	1991-94	11,153
Alex Van Pelt, Pittsburgh	1989-92	10,913

Note: Minimum 500 completions.

COMPLETIONS

	Years	Comp
Ty Detmer, Brigham Young	1988-91	958
Todd Santos, San Diego St	1984-87	910
Brian McClure, Bowling Green	1982-85	900
Eric Wilhelm, Oregon St	1989-92	870
Peyton Manning, Tennessee	1994-97	863

Note: Minimum 500 completions.

TOUCHDOWNS PASSING

	Years	TD
Ty Detmer, Brigham Young	1988-91	121
Danny Wuerffel, Florida	1993-96	114
David Klingler, Houston	1988-91	92
Peyton Manning, Tennessee	1994-97	89
Troy Kopp, Pacific	1989-92	87

Receiving

CATCHES

	Years	No.
Aaron Turner, Pacific	1989-92	266
Chad Mackey, Louisiana Tech	1993-96	264
Terance Mathis, New Mexico	1985-87, 89	263
Mark Templeton, Long Beach St	1983-86	262
Howard Twilley, Tulsa	1963-65	261

CATCHES PER GAME

	Years	No./Game
Emmanuel Hazard, Houston	1989-90	10.5
Alex Van Dyke, Nevada	1994-95	10.3
Howard Twilley, Tulsa	1963-65	10.0
Jason Phillips, Houston	1987-88	9.4
Bryan Reeves, Nevada	1992-93	8.2

YARDS GAINED

	Years	Yds
Marcus Harris, Wyoming	1993-96	4,518
Ryan Yarborough, Wyoming	1990-93	4,357
Aaron Turner, Pacific	1989-92	4,345
Terance Mathis, New Mexico	1985-87, 89	4,254
Chad Macke, Louisiana Tech	1993-96	3,789

TOUCHDOWN CATCHES

	Years	TD
Aaron Turner, Pacific	1989-92	43
Ryan Yarborough, Wyoming	1990-93	42
Marcus Harris, Wyoming	1993-96	38
Clarkston Hines, Duke	1986-89	38
Terance Mathis, New Mexico	1985-87, 89	36

Career (Cont.)

All-Purpose Running

YARDS GAINED	Years	Yds
Napoleon McCallum, Navy	1981-85	7172
Darrin Nelson, Stanford	1977-78, 80-81	6885
Terance Mathis, New Mexico	1985-87, 89	6691
Tony Dorsett, Pittsburgh	1973-76	6615
Paul Palmer, Temple	1983-86	6609

YARDS PER GAME	Years	Yds/Game
Ryan Benjamin, Pacific	1990-92	237.8
Sheldon Canley, San Jose St	1988-90	205.8
Howard Stevens, Louisville	1971-72	193.7
O.J. Simpson, Southern Cal	1967-68	192.9
Alex Van Dyke, Nevada	1994-95	188.5

THEY SAID IT

Woody Widenhofer, Vanderbilt football coach, on what he wanted his team to show against Alabama: "The kind of confidence that the 82-year-old man had when he married a 25-year-old woman and bought a five-bedroom house next to an elementary school."

Interceptions

PLAYER/SCHOOL	Years	Int
Al Brosky, Illinois	1950-52	29
John Provost, Holy Cross	1972-74	27
Martin Bayless, Bowling Green	1980-83	27
Tom Curtis, Michigan	1967-69	25
Tony Thurman, Boston Col	1981-84	25
Tracy Saul, Texas Tech	1989-92	25

Punting Average

PLAYER/SCHOOL	Years	Avg
Todd Sauerbrun, W Virginia	1991-94	46.3
Reggie Roby, Iowa	1979-82	45.6
Greg Montgomery, Michigan St	1985-87	45.4
Tom Tupa, Ohio St	1984-87	45.2
Barry Helton, Colorado	1984-87	44.9

Note: At least 150 punts kicked.

Punt Return Average

PLAYER/SCHOOL	Years	Avg
Jack Mitchell, Oklahoma	1946-48	23.6
Gene Gibson, Cincinnati	1949-50	20.5
Eddie Macon, Pacific	1949-51	18.9
Jackie Robinson, UCLA	1939-40	18.8
Mike Fuller, Auburn	1972-74	17.7
Bobby Dillon, Texas	1949-51	17.7

Note: At least 1.2 punt returns per game.

Kickoff Return Average

PLAYER/SCHOOL	Years	Avg
Anthony Davis, Southern Cal	1972-74	35.1
Eric Booth, Southern Miss	1994-97	32.4
Overton Curtis, Utah St	1957-58	31.0
Fred Montgomery, New Mexico St	1991-92	30.5
Altie Taylor, Utah St	1966-68	29.3
Stan Brown, Purdue	1968-70	28.8

Note: At least 1.2 kickoff returns per game. Min. 30 returns.

Single Season

Scoring

POINTS	Year	Pts
Barry Sanders, Oklahoma St	1988	234
Mike Rozier, Nebraska	1983	174
Lydell Mitchell, Penn St	1971	174
Art Luppino, Arizona	1954	166
Bobby Reynolds, Nebraska	1950	157

FIELD GOALS	Year	FG
John Lee, UCLA	1984	29
Paul Woodside, W Virginia	1982	28
Luis Zendejas, Arizona St	1983	28
Fuad Reveiz, Tennessee	1982	27

Four tied with 25.

All-Purpose Running

YARDS GAINED	Year	Yds
Barry Sanders, Oklahoma St	1988	3250
Ryan Benjamin, Pacific	1991	2995
Mike Pringle, Fullerton St	1989	2690
Paul Palmer, Temple	1986	2633
Ryan Benjamin, Pacific	1992	2597

All-Purpose Running (Cont.)

YARDS PER GAME	Year	Yds/Game
Barry Sanders, Oklahoma St	1988	295.5
Ryan Benjamin, Pacific	1991	249.6
Byron (Whizzer) White, Colorado	1937	246.3
Mike Pringle, Fullerton St	1989	244.6
Paul Palmer, Temple	1986	239.4

Total Offense

YARDS GAINED	Year	Yds
David Klingler, Houston	1990	5221
Ty Detmer, Brigham Young	1990	5022
Andre Ware, Houston	1989	4661
Jim McMahon, Brigham Young	1980	4627
Ty Detmer, Brigham Young	1989	4433

YARDS PER GAME	Year	Yds/Game
David Klingler, Houston	1990	474.6
Andre Ware, Houston	1989	423.7
Ty Detmer, Brigham Young	1990	418.5
Mike Maxwell, Nevada	1995	402.6
Steve Young, Brigham Young	1983	395.1

Single Season (Cont.)

Rushing

YARDS GAINED

	Year	Yds
Barry Sanders, Oklahoma St	1988	2628
Marcus Allen, Southern Cal	1981	2342
Troy Davis, Iowa St	1996	2185
Mike Rozier, Nebraska	1983	2148
Byron Hanspard, Texas Tech	1996	2084

YARDS PER GAME

	Year	Yds/Game
Barry Sanders, Oklahoma St	1988	238.9
Marcus Allen, Southern Cal	1981	212.9
Ed Marinaro, Cornell	1971	209.0
Troy Davis, Iowa St	1996	198.6
Byron Hanspard, Texas Tech	1996	189.5

TOUCHDOWNS RUSHING

	Year	TD
Barry Sanders, Oklahoma St	1988	37
Mike Rozier, Nebraska	1983	29
Ed Marinaro, Cornell	1971	24
Anthony Thompson, Indiana	1988	24
Anthony Thompson, Indiana	1989	24
Rashaan Salaam, Colorado	1994	24

Passing

PASSING EFFICIENCY

	Year	Rating
Danny Wuerffel, Florida	1995	178.4
Jim McMahon, Brigham Young	1980	176.9
Ty Detmer, Brigham Young	1989	175.6
Steve Sarkisian, Brigham Young	1996	173.6
Trent Dilfer, Fresno St	1993	173.1

YARDS GAINED

	Year	Yds
Ty Detmer, Brigham Young	1990	5188
David Klingler, Houston	1990	5140
Andre Ware, Houston	1989	4699
Jim McMahon, Brigham Young	1980	4571
Ty Detmer, Brigham Young	1989	4560

COMPLETIONS

	Year	Att	Comp
David Klingler, Houston	1990	643	374
Andre Ware, Houston	1989	578	365
Tim Couch, Kentucky	1997	547	363
Ty Detmer, Brigham Young	1990	562	361
Robbie Bosco, Brigham Young	1985	511	338

TOUCHDOWNS PASSING

	Year	TD
David Klingler, Houston	1990	54
Jim McMahon, Brigham Young	1980	47
Andre Ware, Houston	1989	46
Ty Detmer, Brigham Young	1990	41
Dennis Shaw, San Diego St	1969	39
Danny Wuerffel, Florida	1996	39

Receiving

CATCHES

	Year	GP	No.
Emmanuel Hazard, Houston	1989	11	142
Howard Twilley, Tulsa	1965	10	134
Alex Van Dyke, Nevada	1995	11	129
Damond Wilkins, Nevada	1996	11	114
Marcus Harris, Wyoming	1996	12	109

CATCHES PER GAME

	Year	No.	No./Game
Howard Twilley, Tulsa	1965	134	13.4
Emmanuel Hazard, Houston	1989	142	12.9
Alex Van Dyke, Nevada	1995	129	11.7
Damond Wilkins, Nevada	1996	114	10.4
Jason Phillips, Houston	1988	108	9.8

YARDS GAINED

	Year	Yds
Alex Van Dyke, Nevada	1995	1854
Howard Twilley, Tulsa	1965	1779
Troy Edwards, Louisiana Tech	1997	1707
Emmanuel Hazard, Houston	1989	1689
Marcus Harris, Wyoming	1996	1650

TOUCHDOWN CATCHES

	Year	TD
Randy Moss, Marshall	1997	25
Emmanuel Hazard, Houston	1989	22
Desmond Howard, Michigan	1991	19
Eugene Baker, Kentucky	1997	18
Reidel Anthony, Florida	1996	18
Tom Reynolds, San Diego St	1969	18
Dennis Smith, Utah	1989	18
Aaron Turner, Pacific	1991	18

Single Game

Scoring

POINTS

	Opponent	Year	Pts
Howard Griffith, Illinois	Southern Illinois	1990	48
Marshall Faulk, San Diego St	Pacific	1991	44
Jim Brown, Syracuse	Colgate	1956	43
Showboat Boykin, Mississippi	Mississippi St	1951	42
Fred Wendt, UTEP*	New Mexico St	1948	42

*UTEP was Texas Mines in 1948.

FIELD GOALS

	Opponent	Year	FG
Dale Klein, Nebraska	Missouri	1985	7
Mike Prindle, Western Michigan	Marshall	1984	7

Note: Klein's distances were 32-22-43-44-29-43-43.
Prindle's distances were 32-44-42-23-48-41-27.

Single Game (Cont.)

Total Offense

YARDS GAINED	Opponent	Year	Yds
David Klingler, Houston	Arizona St	1990	732
Matt Vogler, Texas Christian	Houston	1990	696
David Klingler, Houston	Texas Christian	1990	625
Scott Mitchell, Utah	Air Force	1988	625
Jimmy Klingler, Houston	Rice	1992	612

Passing

YARDS GAINED	Opponent	Year	Yds
David Klingler, Houston	Arizona St	1990	716
Matt Vogler, Texas Christian	Houston	1990	690
Scott Mitchell, Utah	Air Force	1988	631
Jeremy Leach, New Mexico	Utah	1989	622
Dave Wilson, Illinois	Ohio St	1980	621

COMPLETIONS	Opponent	Year	Comp
Rusty LaRue, Wake Forest	Duke	1995	55
Rusty LaRue, Wake Forest	NC St	1995	50
David Klingler, Houston	SMU	1990	48
Jimmy Klingler, Houston	Rice	1992	46
Scott Milanovich, Maryland	Florida St	1995	46

TOUCHDOWNS PASSING	Opponent	Year	TD
David Klingler, Houston	E. Wash	1990	11

Note: Klingler's TD passes were 5-48-29-7-3-7-40-10-7-8-51.

Rushing

YARDS GAINED	Opponent	Year	Yds
Tony Sands, Kansas	Missouri	1991	396
Marshall Faulk, San Diego St	Pacific	1991	386
Troy Davis, Iowa St	Missouri	1996	378
Anthony Thompson, Indiana	Wisconsin	1989	377
Mike Pringle, California St-Fullerton	New Mex St	1989	357
Rueben Mayes, Washington St	Oregon	1984	357

TOUCHDOWNS RUSHING	Opponent	Year	TD
Howard Griffith, Illinois	Southern Illinois	1990	8

Note: Griffith's TD runs were 5-51-7-41-5-18-5-3.

Receiving

CATCHES	Opponent	Year	No.
Randy Gatewood, UNLV	Idaho	1994	23
Jay Miller, Brigham Young	New Mexico	1973	22
Rick Eber, Tulsa	Idaho St	1967	20
Emmanuel Hazard, Hou	Texas Christian	1989	19
Emmanuel Hazard, Hou	Texas	1989	19
Ron Fair, Arizona St	Washington St	1989	19
Howard Twilley, Tulsa	Colorado St	1965	19

YARDS GAINED	Opponent	Year	Yds
Randy Gatewood, UNLV	Idaho	1994	363
Chuck Hughes, UTEP*	N Texas St	1965	349
Rick Eber, Tulsa	Idaho St	1967	322
Harry Wood, Tulsa	Idaho St	1967	318
Jeff Evans, New Mexico St	Southern IL	1978	316

*UTEP was Texas Western in 1965.

TOUCHDOWN CATCHES	Opponent	Year	TD
Tim Delaney, San Diego St	New Mexico St	1969	6

Note: Delaney's TD catches were 2-22-34-31-30-9.

Longest Plays (since 1941)

PASSING	Opponent	Year	Yds
Fred Owens to Jack Ford, Portland	St Mary's (CA)	1947	99
Bo Burris to Warren McVea, Houston	Washington St	1966	99
Colin Clapton to Eddie Jenkins, Holy Cross	Boston U	1970	99
Terry Peel to Robert Ford, Houston	Syracuse	1970	99
Terry Peel to Robert Ford, Houston	San Diego St	1972	99
Cris Collinsworth to Derrick Gaffney, Florida	Rice	1977	99
Scott Ankrom to James Maness, Texas Christian	Rice	1984	99
Gino Toretta to Horace Copeland, Miami	Arkansas	1991	99
John Paci to Thomas Lewis, Indiana	Penn St	1993	99
Troy DeGar to Wes Caswell, Tulsa	Oklahoma	1996	99

RUSHING	Opponent	Year	Yds
Gale Sayers, Kansas	Nebraska	1963	99
Max Anderson, Arizona St	Wyoming	1967	99
Ralph Thompson, W Texas St	Wichita St	1970	99
Kelsey Finch, Tennessee	Florida	1977	99

FIELD GOALS	Opponent	Year	Yds
Steve Little, Arkansas	Texas	1977	67
Russell Erxleben, Texas	Rice	1977	67
Joe Williams, Wichita St	Southern IL	1978	67
Tony Franklin, Texas A&M	Baylor	1976	65
Tony Franklin, Texas A&M	Baylor	1976	64
Russell Erxleben, Texas	Oklahoma	1977	64

PUNTS	Opponent	Year	Yds
Pat Brady, Nevada*	Loyola (CA)	1950	99
George O'Brien, Wisconsin	Iowa	1952	96
John Hadl, Kansas	Oklahoma	1959	94
Carl Knox, Texas Christian	Oklahoma St	1947	94
Preston Johnson, SMU	Pittsburgh	1940	94

*Nevada was Nevada-Reno in 1950.

DIVISION I-A WINNINGEST TEAMS
Alltime Winning Percentage

	Yrs	W	L	T	Pct	GP	Bowl Record
Notre Dame	109	753	228	42	.757	1,023	13-9-0
Michigan	118	776	254	36	.745	1,054	13-15-0
Alabama	103	717	260	43	.724	1,020	28-17-3
Ohio St	108	699	276	53	.706	1,028	13-17-0
Oklahoma	103	677	267	53	.706	997	20-11-1
Texas	105	717	291	33	.705	1,041	17-18-2
Nebraska	108	722	292	40	.704	1,054	18-18-0
Southern Cal	105	659	270	54	.698	983	25-13-0
Penn St	111	715	299	41	.697	1,055	21-11-2
Tennessee	101	677	285	52	.693	1,014	21-17-0
Florida St	51	358	181	17	.659	556	16-8-2
Boise St	30	225	119	2	.653	346	0-0-0
Washington	108	593	325	50	.638	968	13-10-1
Central Michigan	97	500	280	36	.635	816	0-2-0
Miami (OH)	109	574	322	44	.634	940	5-2-0
Louisiana St	104	603	341	47	.632	991	14-16-1
Arizona St	85	473	272	24	.631	769	10-6-1
Army	108	611	348	51	.630	1,010	2-2-0
Georgia	104	616	351	54	.630	1,021	16-14-3
Auburn	105	593	347	47	.625	987	14-10-2
Colorado	108	593	359	36	.618	988	9-12-0
Miami (FL)	71	443	274	19	.615	736	11-11-0
Florida	91	535	338	40	.608	913	12-13-0
Texas A&M	103	583	374	48	.604	1005	12-11-0
Syracuse	108	617	397	49	.603	1063	10-7-1

Note: Includes bowl games.

Alltime Victories

Michigan 776	Syracuse 617	Pittsburgh.........................582
Notre Dame....................753	Georgia 616	Georgia Tech 574
Nebraska 722	Army..................................611	Miami (OH) 574
Alabama..........................717	Louisiana St 603	Arkansas 571
Texas 717	Auburn 593	Navy...................................570
Penn St............................715	Colorado 593	Minnesota 568
Ohio St 699	Washington 593	Clemson............................553
Oklahoma........................677	N Carolina 584	Viriginia Tech 548
Tennessee 677	W Virginia 584	California 546
Southern Cal 659	Texas A&M........................583	Rutgers 541

NUMBER ONE VS NUMBER TWO

The No. 1 and No. 2 teams, according to the Associated Press Poll, have met 31 times, including 11 bowl games, since the poll's inception in 1936. The No. 1 teams have a 18-11-2 record in these matchups. Notre Dame (4-3-2) has played in nine of the games.

Date	Results	Stadium
10-9-43 ....No. 1 Notre Dame 35, No. 2 Michigan 12		Michigan (Ann Arbor)
11-20-43 ....No. 1 Notre Dame 14, No. 2 Iowa Pre-Flight 13		Notre Dame (South Bend)
12-2-44 ....No. 1 Army 23, No. 2 Navy 7		Municipal (Baltimore)
11-10-45 ....No. 1 Army 48, No. 2 Notre Dame 0		Yankee (New York)
12-1-45 ....No. 1 Army 32, No. 2 Navy 13		Municipal (Philadelphia)
11-9-46 ....No. 1 Army 0, No. 2 Notre Dame 0		Yankee (New York)
1-1-63 ....No. 1 Southern Cal 42, No. 2 Wisconsin 37 (Rose Bowl)		Rose Bowl (Pasadena)
10-12-63 ....No. 2 Texas 28, No. 1 Oklahoma 7		Cotton Bowl (Dallas)
1-1-64 ....No. 1 Texas 28, No. 2 Navy 6 (Cotton Bowl)		Cotton Bowl (Dallas)
11-19-66 ....No. 1 Notre Dame 10, No. 2 Michigan St 10		Spartan (East Lansing)
9-28-68 ....No. 1 Purdue 37, No. 2 Notre Dame 22		Notre Dame (South Bend)
1-1-69 ....No. 1 Ohio St 27, No. 2 Southern Cal 16 (Rose Bowl)		Rose Bowl (Pasadena)
12-6-69 ....No. 1 Texas 15, No. 2 Arkansas 14		Razorback (Fayetteville)
11-25-71 ....No. 1 Nebraska 35, No. 2 Oklahoma 31		Owen Field (Norman)
1-1-72 ....No. 1 Nebraska 38, No. 2 Alabama 6 (Orange Bowl)		Orange Bowl (Miami)
1-1-79 ....No. 2 Alabama 14, No. 1 Penn St 7 (Sugar Bowl)		Sugar Bowl (New Orleans)
9-26-81 ....No. 1 Southern Cal 28, No. 2 Oklahoma 24		Coliseum (Los Angeles)
1-1-83 ....No. 2 Penn St 27, No. 1 Georgia 23 (Sugar Bowl)		Sugar Bowl (New Orleans)

NUMBER ONE VS NUMBER TWO *(Cont.)*

Date	Results	Stadium
10-19-85	No. 1 Iowa 12, No. 2 Michigan 10	Kinnick (Iowa City)
9-27-86	No. 2 Miami (FL) 28, No. 1 Oklahoma 16	Orange Bowl (Miami)
1-2-87	No. 2 Penn St 14, No. 1 Miami (FL) 10 (Fiesta Bowl)	Fiesta Bowl (Tempe)
11-21-87	No. 2 Oklahoma 17, No. 1 Nebraska 7	Memorial (Lincoln)
1-1-88	No. 2 Miami (FL) 20, No. 1 Oklahoma 14 (Orange Bowl)	Orange Bowl (Miami)
11-26-88	No. 1 Notre Dame 27, No. 2 Southern Cal 10	Coliseum (Los Angeles)
9-16-89	No. 1 Notre Dame 24, No. 2 Michigan 19	Michigan (Ann Arbor)
11-16-91	No. 2 Miami (FL) 17, No. 1 Florida St 16	Campbell (Tallahassee)
1-1-93	No. 2 Alabama 34, No. 1 Miami (FL) 13	Superdome (New Orleans)
11-13-93	No. 2 Notre Dame 31, No. 1 Florida St 24	Notre Dame (South Bend)
1-1-94	No. 1 Florida St 18, No. 2 Nebraska 16 (Orange Bowl)	Orange Bowl (Miami)
1-2-96	No. 1 Nebraska 62, No. 2 Florida 24 (Fiesta Bowl)	Sun Devil (Tempe)
1-2-96	No. 1 Nebraska 62, No. 2 Florida 24 (Fiesta Bowl)	Sun Devil (Tempe)
11-30-96	No. 2 Florida St 24, No. 1 Florida 21	Campbell (Tallahassee)

LONGEST DIVISION I-A WINNING STREAKS

Wins	Team	Yrs	Ended by	Score
47	Oklahoma	1953-57	Notre Dame	7–0
39	Washington	1908-14	Oregon St	0–0
37	Yale	1890-93	Princeton	6–0
37	Yale	1887-89	Princeton	10–0
35	Toledo	1969-71	Tampa	21–0
34	Pennsylvania	1894-96	Lafayette	6–4
31	Oklahoma	1948-50	Kentucky	13–7
31	Pittsburgh	1914-18	Cleveland Naval Reserve	10–9
31	Pennsylvania	1896-98	Harvard	10–0
30	Texas	1968-70	Notre Dame	24–11
29	Miami (FL)	1990-93	Alabama	34–13
29	Michigan	1901-03	Minnesota	6–6

LONGEST DIVISION I-A UNBEATEN STREAKS

No.	W	T	Team	Yrs	Ended by	Score
63	59	4	Washington	1907-17	California	27–0
56	55	1	Michigan	1901-05	Chicago	2–0
50	46	4	California	1920-25	Olympic Club	15–0
48	47	1	Oklahoma	1953-57	Notre Dame	7–0
48	47	1	Yale	1885-89	Princeton	10–0
47	42	5	Yale	1879-85	Princeton	6–5
44	42	2	Yale	1894-96	Princeton	24–6
42	39	3	Yale	1904-08	Harvard	4–0
39	37	2	Notre Dame	1946-50	Purdue	28–14
37	36	1	Oklahoma	1972-75	Kansas	23–3
37	37	0	Yale	1890-93	Princeton	6–0
35	35	0	Toledo	1969-71	Tampa	21–0
35	34	1	Minnesota	1903-05	Wisconsin	16–12
34	33	1	Nebraska	1912-16	Kansas	7–3
34	34	0	Pennsylvania	1894-96	Lafayette	6–4
34	32	2	Princeton	1884-87	Harvard	12–0
34	29	5	Princeton	1877-82	Harvard	1–0
33	30	3	Tennessee	1926-30	Alabama	18–6
33	31	2	Georgia Tech	1914-18	Pittsburgh	32–0
33	30	3	Harvard	1911-15	Cornell	10–0
32	31	1	Nebraska	1969-71	UCLA	20–17
32	30	2	Army	1944-47	Columbia	21–20
32	31	1	Harvard	1898-1900	Yale	28–0
31	30	1	Alabama	1991-93	Louisiana St	17–13
31	30	1	Penn St	1967-70	Colorado	41–13
31	30	1	San Diego St	1967-70	Long Beach St	27–11
31	29	2	Georgia Tech	1950-53	Notre Dame	27–14
31	31	0	Oklahoma	1948-50	Kentucky	13–7
31	31	0	Pittsburgh	1919-22	Cleveland Naval	10–9
31	31	0	Pennsylvania	1896-98	Harvard	10–0

Note: Includes bowl games.

LONGEST DIVISION I-A LOSING STREAKS

Losses		Seasons	Ended Against	Score
34	Northwestern	1979-82	Northern Illinois	31–6
28	Virginia	1958-61	William & Mary	21–6
28	Kansas St	1945-48	Arkansas St	37–6
27	New Mexico St	1988-90	Cal St-Fullerton	43-9
27	Eastern Michigan	1980-82	Kent St	9–7

MOST-PLAYED DIVISION I-A RIVALRIES

GP	Opponents (Series Leader Listed First)	Record	First Game	GP	Opponents (Series Leader Listed First)	Record	First Game
107	Minnesota-Wisconsin	57-42-8	1890	100	Stanford-California	50-39-11	1892
106	Missouri-Kansas	49-48-9	1891	98	Army-Navy	47-44-7	1890
104	Nebraska-Kansas	80-21-3	1892	95	Utah-Utah St	62-29-4	1892
104	Texas-Texas A&M	66-33-5	1894	95	Clemson-S Carolina	56-35-4	1896
103	Baylor-Texas Christian*	49-47-7	1899	95	Kansas-Kansas St	61-29-5	1902
102	Miami (OH)-Cincinnati	54-41-7	1888	95	Oklahoma-Kansas	62-27-6	1903
102	N Carolina-Virginia	55-44-4	1892	94	N Carolina-Wake Forest	63-29-2	1888
101	Auburn-Georgia	48-45-8	1892	94	Michigan-Ohio St	54-34-6	1897
101	Oregon-Oregon St	51-40-10	1894	94	Mississippi-Miss St	54-34-6	1901
100	Purdue-Indiana	60-34-6	1891		*Did not meet in 1997.		

NCAA Coaches' Records

ALLTIME WINNINGEST DIVISION I-A COACHES

By Percentage

Coach (Alma Mater)	Colleges Coached	Yrs	W	L	T	Pct
Knute Rockne (Notre Dame '14)†	Notre Dame 1918-30	13	105	12	5	.881
Frank W. Leahy (Notre Dame '31)†	Boston Col 1939-40; Notre Dame 1941-43, 1946-53	13	107	13	9	.864
George W. Woodruff (Yale 1889)†	Pennsylvania 1892-01; Illinois 1903; Carlisle 1905	12	142	25	2	.846
Barry Switzer (Arkansas '60)	Oklahoma 1973-88	16	157	29	4	.837
Tom Osborne (Hastings '59)†	Nebraska 1973-98	25	255	49	3	.836
Percy D. Haughton (Harvard 1899)†	Cornell 1899-1900; Harvard 1908-16; Columbia 1923-24	13	96	17	6	.832
Bob Neyland (Army '16)†	Tennessee 1926-34, 1936-40, 1946-52	21	173	31	12	.829
Fielding (Hurry Up) Yost (West Virginia 1895)†	Ohio Wesleyan 1897; Nebraska 1898; Kansas 1899; Stanford 1900; Michigan 1901-23, 1925-26	29	196	36	12	.828
Bud Wilkinson (Minnesota '37)†	Oklahoma 1947-63	17	145	29	4	.826
Jock Sutherland (Pittsburgh '18)†	Lafayette 1919-23; Pittsburgh 1924-38	20	144	28	14	.812
Bob Devaney (Alma, MI '39)†	Wyoming 1957-61; Nebraska 1962-72	16	136	30	7	.806
Frank W. Thomas (Notre Dame '23)†	Tenn.-Chattanooga 1925-28; Alabama 1931-42, 1944-46	19	141	33	9	.795
Joe Paterno (Brown '50)*	Penn St 1966-present	31	298	77	3	.792
Henry L. Williams (Yale 1891)†	Army 1891; Minnesota 1900-21	23	141	34	12	.786
Gil Dobie (Minnesota '02)†	N Dakota St 1906-07; Washington 1908-16; Navy 1917-19; Cornell 1920-35; Boston College 1936-38	33	180	45	15	.781

*Active coach. †Hall of Fame member.

Note: Minimum 10 years as head coach at Division I institutions; record at four-year colleges only; bowl games included; ties computed as half won, half lost.

ALLTIME WINNINGEST DIVISION I-A COACHES (Cont.)

By Victories

	Yrs	W	L	T	Pct		Yrs	W	L	T	Pct
Paul (Bear) Bryant	38	323	85	17	.780	*LaVell Edwards	26	234	86	3	.729
Glenn (Pop) Warner	44	319	106	32	.733	*Hayden Fry	36	229	170	10	.572
Amos Alonzo Stagg	57	314	199	35	.605	Lou Holtz	27	216	95	7	.690
*Joe Paterno	32	298	74	3	.792	Jess Neely	40	207	176	19	.539
*Bobby Bowden	32	281	83	4	.769	Warren Woodson	31	203	95	14	.673
Tom Osborne	25	255	49	3	.836	Vince Dooley	25	201	77	10	.715
Woody Hayes	33	238	72	10	.759	Eddie Anderson	39	201	128	15	.606
Bo Schembechler	27	234	65	8	.775						

*Active coach.

Most Bowl Victories

	W	L	T		W	L	T
*Joe Paterno	18	9	1	Barry Switzer	8	5	0
*Bobby Bowden	16	4	1	Darrell Royal	8	7	1
Paul (Bear) Bryant	15	12	2	Vince Dooley	8	10	2
Jim Wacker	13	2	0	John Robinson	7	1	0
Tom Osborne	12	13	0	Bob Devaney	7	3	0
Don James	10	5	0	Dan Devine	7	3	0
Lou Holtz	10	8	2	Earle Bruce	7	5	0
John Vaught	10	8	0	Charlie McClendon	7	6	0
Bobby Dodd	9	4	0	*Hayden Fry	7	9	1
Johnny Majors	9	7	0	*LaVell Edwards	7	9	1
Terry Donahue	8	4	1	Pat Dye	7	2	1

*Active coach.

WINNINGEST ACTIVE DIVISION I-A COACHES
By Percentage

Coach, College	Yrs	W	L	T	Pct#	Bowls W	L	T
Phillip Fulmer, Tennessee	6	54	11	0	.831	4	2	0
Joe Paterno, Penn St	32	298	77	3	.793	18	9	1
Steve Spurrier, Florida	11	103	29	2	.776	4	4	0
Bobby Bowden, Florida St	32	281	83	4	.769	16	4	1
R. C. Slocum, Texas A&M	9	83	25	2	.764	2	5	0
LaVell Edwards, Brigham Young	26	234	86	3	.729	7	12	1
Paul Pasqualoni, Syracuse	12	94	39	1	.705	*4	2	0
Terry Bowden, Auburn	14	110	48	2	.694	*4	5	0
John Cooper, Ohio St	21	167	73	6	.691	4	8	0
Dennis Franchione, Texas Christian	15	113	55	2	.671	*6	6	0

#Bowl games included in overall record. Ties computed as half win, half loss. *Includes record in NCAA and/or NAIA championships.
Note: Minimum five years as Division I-A head coach; record at four-year colleges only.

You Know Who You Is	Florida coach Steve Spurrier is a tough man to please, so it's nice to see that he accepted some of the blame when asked about the Gators' poor special teams play in the 1997–98 season. Said Spurrier in November '97, "We've got some mentally slow guys on our team, but we keep putting them out there."

WINNINGEST ACTIVE DIVISION I-A COACHES *(Cont.)*
By Victories

Joe Paterno, Penn St	298	Dick Tomey, Arizona	135
Bobby Bowden, Florida St	281	Ken Hatfield, Rice	134
LaVell Edwards, Brigham Young	234	Larry Smith, Missouri	128
Hayden Fry, Iowa	229	Dennis Franchione, Texas Christian	113
Don Nehlen, West Virginia	183	Terry Bowden, Auburn	110
John Cooper, Ohio St	167	Frank Beamer, Virginia Tech	110
George Welsh, Virginia	167	Fisher DeBerry, Air Force	108
Jackie Sherrill, Mississippi St	146		

WINNINGEST ACTIVE DIVISION I-AA COACHES
By Percentage

Coach, College	Yrs	W	L	T	Pct*
Mike Kelly, Dayton	17	165	28	1	.853
Al Bagnoli, Pennsylvania	16	125	39	0	.762
Pete Richardson, Southern	10	87	27	1	.761
Larry Blakeney, Troy St	7	63	21	1	.747
John Lyons, Dartmouth	6	44	15	1	.742
Roy Kidd, Eastern Kentucky	34	280	103	8	.726
Walt Hamelin, Wagner	17	129	48	2	.726
Tubby Raymond, Delaware	32	270	103	3	.722
Joe Gardi, Hofstra	8	62	24	2	.716
Greg Gattuso, Duquesne	5	37	15	0	.712

*Playoff games included.

Note: Minimum five years as a Division I-A and/or Division I-AA head coach; record at four-year colleges only.

By Victories

Roy Kidd, Eastern Kentucky	280	Willie Jeffries, S Carolina St	161
Tubby Raymond, Delaware	270	Bill Hayes, N Carolina A&T	156
Ron Randleman, Sam Houston St	175	James (Boots) Donnelly, Middle Tennessee St	149
Bill Bowes, New Hampshire	171	Walt Hamelin, Wagner	129
Mike Kelly, Dayton	165	Bob Ricca, St. John's	127

WINNINGEST ACTIVE DIVISION II COACHES
By Percentage

Coach, College	Yrs	W	L	T	Pct*
Chuck Broyles, Pittsburg St	8	86	13	2	.861
Ken Sparks, Carson-Newman	18	172	43	2	.797
Gene Nicholson, Westminster (PA)	7	61	17	2	.775
Peter Yetten, Bentley	10	72	21	1	.771
Danny Hale, Bloomsburg	10	80	27	1	.745
Brian Kelly, Grand Valley St	7	56	21	2	.722
Gene Carpenter, Millersville	29	197	81	6	.704
Connie Driscoll, Stonehill	5	35	15	0	.700
Frank Cignetti, Indiana (PA)	16	130	56	1	.698
Rob Smith, Western Washington	9	61	28	1	.683

*Ties computed as half win, half loss. Playoff games included.

Note: Minimum five years as a college head coach; record at four-year colleges only.

By Victories

Jim Malosky, MN-Duluth	255	Claire Boroff, NE-Kearney	157
Ron Harms, Texas A&M-Kingsville*	203	Robert Ford, Albany (NY)	157
Gene Carpenter, Millersville	197	Bud Elliott, Eastern New Mexico	157
Ken Sparks, Carson-Newman	172	Jimmy Parker, Ouachita Baptist	153
Willard Bailey, Virginia Union	167	Dennis Douds, E Stroudsburg	143

*Formerly Texas A&I.

WINNINGEST ACTIVE DIVISION III COACHES
By Percentage

Coach, College	Yrs	W	L	T	Pct*
Larry Kehres, Mt Union	12	124	16	3	.878
Dick Farley, Williams	11	73	12	3	.847
Tom Coen, Salve Regina	5	36	9	0	.800
John Luckhardt, Washington & Jefferson	16	132	33	2	.796
K.C. Keeler, Rowan	5	48	12	7	.795
Roger Harring, WI-LaCrosse	29	250	66	7	.785
Bob Packard, Baldwin-Wallace	17	130	40	2	.762
John Gagliardi, St John's (MN)	49	342	104	11	.760
Tony DeCarlo, John Carroll	11	82	25	4	.757
Rich Lackner, Carnegie Mellon	12	88	29	2	.748

*Ties computed as half won, half lost. Playoff games included.

Note: Minimum five years as a college head coach; record at four-year colleges only.

By Victories

John Gagliardi, St John's (MN)	342	Peter Mazzaferro, Bridgewater (MA)	163
Roger Harring, WI-LaCrosse	250	Tom Gilburg, Franklin & Marshall	149
Jim Christopherson, Concordia-M'head	203	John Luckhardt, Washington & Jefferson	132
Frank Girardi, Lycoming	192	Eric Hamilton, College of New Jersey	131
Don Miller, Trinity (CT)	172	Bob Packard, Baldwin-Wallace	130

WINNINGEST ACTIVE NAIA COACHES
By Percentage

Coach, College	Yrs	W	L	T	Pct*
Ted Kessinger, Bethany (KS)	22	179	41	1	.812
Frosty Westering, Pacific Lutheran	34	256	81	7	.754
Hank Biesiot, Dickinson State (ND)	22	156	52	1	.749
Dick Strahm, Findlay (OH)	23	178	59	5	.746
Rob Smith, Western Washington	9	61	28	1	.683
Carl Poelker, McKendree (IL)	17	99	47	1	.677
Keith Barefield, Evangel College (MO)	9	61	29	2	.674
Bob Petrino, Carroll (MT)	27	162	79	1	.671
Bob Young, Sioux Falls (SD)	15	104	54	3	.655
Vic Wallace, Lambuth (TN)	17	117	61	4	.654

*Playoff games included.

Note: Minimum five years as a collegiate head coach and includes record against four-year institutions only.

By Victories

Frosty Westering, Pacific Lutheran	256	Hank Biesiot, Dickinson State (ND)	156
Ted Kessinger, Bethany (KS)	179	Larry Wilcox, Benedictine (KS)	123
Dick Strahm, Findlay (OH)	178	Vic Wallace, Lambuth (TN)	117
Bob Petrino, Carroll (MT)	162	Bob Young, Sioux Falls (SD)	104
Bill Ramseyer, Clinch Valley (VA)	157	Jim Dennison, Walsh (OH)	100

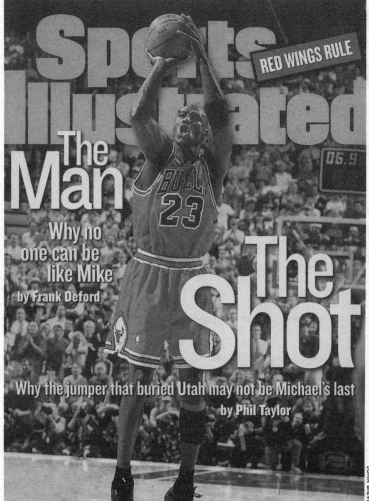

RED WINGS RULE

Sports Illustrated

The Man

Why no one can be like Mike

by Frank Deford

The Shot

Why the jumper that buried Utah may not be Michael's last

by Phil Taylor

JOHN BIEVER

Shifting Sands

Michael Jordan's excellence was the only certainty in a year that raised more questions than it answered

BY PHIL TAYLOR

THEY WERE BOTH stunning, in very different ways. One event was fairy-tale perfect, a final flourish by an incomparable artist. The other was a cardinal sin, an act that went outside the lines of sport and outraged a nation. Together, Michael Jordan's clutch shot and Latrell Sprewell clutching his coach's neck formed the upper and lower extremes of the NBA's year. Nothing else on the league's calendar—not the extraordinarily awful Denver Nuggets, not the rise and fall of Los Angeles Laker phenom Kobe Bryant, not the brilliant rookie seasons of Tim Duncan as a player and Larry Bird as a coach, not even the ominous labor dispute that brought league business to a halt in July—was as awe-inspiring as Jordan's heroics in the Finals against the Utah Jazz or as heinous as Sprewell's attack on Golden State Warrior head coach P.J. Carlesimo.

In the end, Jordan, the MVP of the regular season and the Finals, made everything all right. His performance throughout the year—culminating in the steal and winning

shot in Game 6 of the Finals, which sealed the Chicago Bulls' sixth championship of the decade—helped overcome the foul memory of Sprewell's act. The Bulls had never seemed so vulnerable entering a Finals, and after they lost Game 1 in Utah, the end of their dynasty appeared imminent. But Chicago came back to edge the Jazz 93–88 in Game 2, thanks in part to a horrid shooting night by Utah forward Karl Malone, who missed 11 of his 16 shots. The series then moved to Chicago, where the Bulls administered a whipping for the record books, 96–54. The Jazz's feeble output in Game 3 was the lowest total in an NBA game since the introduction of the 24-second clock in 1954. Suddenly the Chicago dynasty didn't look so vulnerable anymore. And when the Bulls eked out Game 4, 86–82, the predictions of doom for Chicago looked wildly premature; the Bulls led 3–1 and were headed back to the United Center for Game 5. But with his team on the brink, Malone finally rose to the occasion, redeeming his Game 2 debacle with 39 points in Utah's 83–81 victory.

One man show: Jordan stripped Malone, then hit the series-winner.

The teams returned to Utah for Game 6, and the Jazz might well have forced a seventh and deciding game if not for Jordan. With Chicago trailing by a point, he sneaked up from behind Malone and stripped him of the ball, then took it down to the other end and hit a jump shot that gave the Bulls an 87–86 lead with 5.2 seconds left. When Utah's John Stockton missed a desperation jump shot at the buzzer, the Bulls had won their third straight title, and the peerless Jordan had once again topped himself.

It was a thrilling ending to a season that at one time seemed to be irreparably damaged by Sprewell, the Warriors' 6'5" All-Star guard who put his hands around Carlesimo's throat and threatened to kill him in an altercation during a Dec. 1, 1997, practice. Carlesimo was only a month into his first season with Golden State when his relationship with Sprewell reached the boiling point, but it came as no surprise to anyone who had been following the team. During the second week of the season Carlesimo had pulled his star guard out of a game against the Los Angeles Lakers when he saw Sprewell laughing in the huddle during a timeout even though the Warriors were being blown out. Sprewell's response to

Sprewell's attack on Carlesimo marred the season and left the Warriors in a bind.

being benched was to call Carlesimo "a f------ joke" in front of the rest of the team, and Carlesimo held him out of the starting lineup in the following game, against the Detroit Pistons. Three days before the choking incident, Sprewell was fined after missing the team flight to Salt Lake City for a game against the Jazz.

All that set the stage for the ill-fated workout. During a drill, Carlesimo told Sprewell to "put a little mustard on those passes," to which Sprewell replied, according to witnesses, "I don't want to hear it today." More words were exchanged, and what initially seemed like a minor disagreement escalated into a confrontation that will follow both men for the rest of their careers. Sprewell eventually grabbed Carlesimo by the throat, dragging him to the ground and choking him for 10 to 15 seconds before other players pulled Sprewell away. After being thrown out of practice, Sprewell went to the locker room but returned roughly 20 minutes later and went after Carlesimo again. Several Warrior

players said Sprewell landed a glancing blow on Carlesimo before he was dragged away for good, but Sprewell insisted he was never close enough to the coach during the second incident to land a punch.

The scuffle quickly became a national topic for discussion. Barbershops and boardrooms were buzzing, and callers jammed the lines of talk-radio shows. Some pointed to Carlesimo's reputation for being hard on his players, but even those who placed some of the blame on the coach made it clear that they thought Sprewell's actions were inexcusable. Even his fellow players gave him only qualified support. "The players are concerned about what led up to this," said New York Knicks forward Buck Williams, a former president of the players' association. "They are angry that Sprewell has not had the chance to tell his side of the story. They're not taking Sprewell's side, because nobody in his right mind can really take his side. He was totally wrong."

The Warriors acted swiftly, first suspending Sprewell for 10 games, then, two days later, terminating his four-year, $32 million contract, which had nearly three years and about $25 million remaining. The club cited the conduct clause in the basic player agreement that says players must conform to standards of good citizenship. After the Warriors kicked Sprewell out the door, commissioner David Stern locked it behind him by suspending him for a year. But the players' association appealed the punishments on Sprewell's behalf, sending the matter to binding arbitration, and on March 4 arbitrator John Feerick overturned part of the penalty. He reduced Sprewell's suspension without pay to the remainder of the season, costing the player $6.4 million, and reinstated the final two years of his contract. The decision left the team as the biggest loser, with a player they wanted nothing more to do with still on their roster. The Warriors headed into the off-season—and the lockout—still desperately trying to solicit a decent trade offer for Sprewell.

But no team began the off-season with more uncertainty than the champion Bulls. After polishing off the Jazz in six games, no one knew whether their dynasty would be dismantled or not, least of all the Bulls themselves. Coach Phil Jackson answered one question when he resigned eight days after the Finals ended, but the future of the Bulls' three stars, Jordan, Scottie Pippen and Dennis Rodman, was still undecided. When the lockout arrived, Jordan was seriously considering retirement; Pippen, a free agent, had not decided whether to re-sign with Chicago; and Rodman, also a free agent, was too busy making a spectacle of himself in pro wrestling to worry a great deal about whether or not he would be asked to return.

The only certainties were that the Bulls had once again established themselves as the class of the league and that the Chicago dynasty would go down as the second greatest in NBA history, behind the Boston Celtics of the '50s and '60s, who won 11 titles, including eight in a row. Chicago's '98 championship was its sixth title in eight years, and it was certainly the most hard-won of those six. The Bulls nearly sputtered to a halt in the Eastern Conference finals against the Indiana Pacers, who en-

joyed a surprising rebirth in Bird's first season as a coach. Many observers expected Bird, the former Boston Celtics great who was voted into the Hall of Fame following the season, to further prove the theory that great players do not become great coaches. The conventional wisdom was that Bird would be frustrated working with players who were not as gifted as he was, and that he would become disenchanted when he discovered that they didn't have his legendary work habits.

On the contrary, it quickly became apparent that relating to his players was Bird's biggest strength. His approach was simple: He tried to be the kind of coach he would have wanted to play for. He didn't like coaches who put players in the doghouse, so he didn't have one. "If you screw up one night, it doesn't necessarily mean you're going to screw up the next," he said, using a characteristic piece of logic. "Guys on my roster are getting paid to play, so I'm going to play them." He had no use for coaches who yelled at players, so he spoke in a normal tone of voice even when he was being critical. He asked only that his players be on time, act like professionals away from the court and give him their best effort on it.

Bird also felt no need to impress anyone with his ability as a strategist. He hired only two assistants, Dick Harter for defense and Rick Carlisle for offense—"I don't see how there would be enough work for more than two," he said—and he let them do their work. "For a guy who was one of the greatest players ever, he has remarkably little ego," said Indiana point guard Mark Jackson. "He doesn't just say he has faith in his players and his staff, he proves it. He gives us the freedom to do the things we do well, and you want to reward him for having that faith. That's why he's been so effective as a coach." Bird was effective enough to be voted coach of the year, which made him the first man to win that award as well as the MVP and rookie of the year trophies.

With Bird at the controls, the Pacers transformed themselves from a 39–43 team in 1996–97, under Larry Brown, into a 58–24 team in '97–98. Before the season

they were considered an over-the-hill, former contender. By the time they reached the conference finals against the Bulls, the Pacers were considered a serious threat to Chicago's dominance. Indiana lived up to its billing by extending the Bulls to seven games in the best series of the playoffs. The series also provided one of the more memorable images of the postseason after Indiana guard Reggie Miller hit the winning shot in the final seconds of Game 4. While Pacer fans rejoiced, and Miller himself became apoplectic with joy, leaping ecstatically around the backcourt, Bird stood on the sideline, impassive as a rock.

Another rookie who had success similar to Bird's was Duncan, the San Antonio Spurs' smooth, 7-foot forward. The No. 1 pick of the draft, Duncan proved to be even better than advertised, with averages of 21.1 points and 11.9 rebounds per game. He was remarkably consistent throughout the year, winning the rookie of the month award every month of the season and finishing as one of only four players with at least 20 points and 10 rebounds per game.

O'Neal and the Lakers thudded back to earth in the Western Conference finals.

"He was sensational from start to finish," said Spurs coach and general manager Gregg Popovich after San Antonio was eliminated in the second round of the playoffs by Utah. "I don't know if there's been a rookie since Bird and Magic [Johnson] who has come into the league and instantly been a star the way Tim has. He's exceeded all expectations." Others shared Popovich's opinion. Duncan was named to the first-team All-NBA squad, the first rookie since Bird in 1980 to receive that honor.

Duncan's consistent excellence was in marked contrast to the peaks and valleys of another young, talented player, the 19-year-old Bryant. Bryant began the season in spectacular fashion, coming off the bench to give Los Angeles not only scoring punch but also plenty of flash and charisma. Television cameras and fans adored the explosive guard in equal measure. He became the latest player to be anointed the second coming of Jordan, and even though he wasn't a starter on his own team, the fans made him a starter in the All-Star game. He was the youngest All-Star starter in league history.

Bryant took all of the hype in stride, particularly during the All-Star break in New York, where he was one of four Lakers—center Shaquille O'Neal and guards Eddie Jones and Nick Van Exel were the others—on the All-Star team. With the ease of a veteran, Bryant gave time to every media outlet from MTV to *Meet the Press*. He was as entertaining as ever in the game itself, and brashly took Jordan to the hole in a one-on-one confrontation. But in retrospect, the All-Star Game looks like the turning point in Bryant's season, and the turn was for the worse. The second-year guard had the temerity to wave off Utah's Malone when he tried to set a pick for Bryant during the game, and Malone complained about it publicly, saying that he wasn't used to being ordered around by such a young player. That was the beginning of a forgettable second half of the season for Bryant. He went into a shooting slump immediately after the All-Star break and never really recovered. While he had been creative and acrobatic in the first half of the season, he became a raw, one-on-one-type of player, oblivious to the finer points of team basketball.

The low point of Bryant's season came in the playoffs, when, stricken by the flu, he missed the second two games of the Lakers' series against the Seattle Super-Sonics. Los Angeles played exceptionally well, especially in Game 2, and Laker coach Del Harris, not wanting to change a player rotation that was working well, limited Bryant's minutes for the rest of the series. The Lakers went on to dominate Seattle, winning the series in five games, mostly without Bryant. He got more playing time in the following series, against Utah, but the Lakers suffered a complete collapse, losing to the Jazz in a sweep and prompting grave questions about the team that had been built to contend for the title around center O'Neal. When the year was over, it looked less like a breakthrough for Bryant than an indication of how much work he had to do to become an NBA star.

The Denver Nuggets would have gladly settled for an up-and-down season like Bryant's. The Nuggets' season was all down. Beset by injuries to key players like Eric Williams and LaPhonso Ellis, and sorely missing former star guards Mark Jackson and Jalen Rose, whom the team had let go in questionable trades, Denver threatened to set new standards for ineptitude. The Nuggets narrowly averting finishing with the worst record in NBA history. It wasn't until they won their 10th game on April 9 that the Nuggets were assured of a better record than the 9–73 effort turned in by the Philadelphia 76ers in 1972–73. Denver won one more game after that indignity-averting 10th victory and finished at 11–71, but it was not enough to save the jobs of general manager Allan Bristow or first-year coach Bill Hanzlik. The Nuggets hired Dan Issel, a former coach and star center for Denver, to lead the team out of the wilderness as its new general manager.

Bristow and Hanzlik had lots of company among the ranks of the NBA's unemployed, although some weren't jobless for long. Detroit fired coach Doug Collins in February, and Collins quickly found a spot as a television analyst with NBC's top announcing team of Bob Costas and Isiah Thomas. Dallas Mavericks general manager Don Nelson fired coach Jim Cleamons in December and took over the coaching reins himself. Toronto coach Darrell Walker resigned in February, immediately after the Raptors, faced with the likelihood of losing star guard Damon Stoudamire to free agency after the season, traded Stoudamire to the Portland Trail Blazers in a six-player deal. The Sonics fired coach George Karl after Seattle was eliminated from the playoffs in May and replaced him with ex–Phoenix coach Paul Westphal. And Chicago's Jackson went through with his avowed plans to leave the Bulls after the season. Soon after the Finals Jackson packed up his things and rode away from the Bulls' practice facility on a Harley-Davidson motorcycle autographed by his players.

Miller and the Pacers pushed the Bulls to the limit in the Eastern Conference finals.

All the movement left plenty of jobs to be filled and questions to be answered before the start of the '98–99 season, but when the lockout went into effect on July 1, the biggest questions of all were, Will there even be a '98–99 season? And if so, when will it start? No one knew the answers as the off-season moved forward with little progress in negotiations. It was clear, however, that both sides were prepared to hold their ground, even if it meant a work stoppage that extended into the season.

The basic dispute between the owners and the players' association was simple even if the solution was not. The owners wanted to do away with the loopholes in the salary cap, particularly the provision that allowed teams to re-sign their own free agents for any amount regardless of how much or how little space the club had under the cap. The rule has led to contracts in excess of $100 million for players such as Miami Heat center Alonzo Mourning and Washington Wizards forward Juwan Howard, as well as several other deals for more than $80 million. The owners argued that the league could not continue to prosper if salaries continued to escalate at that rate. The union's response was that the league's revenues were still growing steadily, and as evidence they pointed to the $2.6 billion television contract that was to go into effect for the '98–99 season, whether or not it started on time, or at all. High-salaried players, the union maintained, were just earning what the market would bear.

Although the two sides had different perspectives, they had at least one common goal—to maintain the public's affection for the league. Jordan's heroic flourish in the Finals might have been enough to make most fans forget the ugly Sprewell affair, but the last thing the NBA needed was a long work stoppage to give its image yet another blow. With the '98–99 season looming (or not), two essential truths should have been in the minds of both players and owners: Fan loyalty has its limits, and so does the playing career of the magical Michael Jordan.

FOR THE RECORD·1997–1998

NBA Final Standings

Eastern Conference

ATLANTIC DIVISION

Team	W	L	Pct	GB
Miami	55	27	.671	—
New York	43	39	.524	12
New Jersey	43	39	.524	12
Washington	42	40	.512	13
Orlando	41	41	.500	14
Boston	36	46	.439	19
Philadelphia	31	51	.378	24

CENTRAL DIVISION

Team	W	L	Pct	GB
Chicago	62	20	.756	—
Indiana	58	24	.707	4
Charlotte	51	31	.622	11
Atlanta	50	32	.610	12
Cleveland	47	35	.573	15
Detroit	37	45	.451	25
Milwaukee	36	46	.439	26
Toronto	16	66	.195	46

Western Conference

MIDWEST DIVISION

Team	W	L	Pct	GB
Utah	62	20	.756	—
San Antonio	56	26	.683	6
Minnesota	45	37	.549	17
Houston	41	41	.500	21
Dallas	20	62	.244	42
Vancouver	19	63	.232	43
Denver	11	71	.134	51

PACIFIC DIVISION

Team	W	L	Pct	GB
Seattle	61	21	.744	—
LA Lakers	61	21	.744	—
Phoenix	56	26	.683	5
Portland	46	36	.561	15
Sacramento	27	55	.329	34
Golden State	19	63	.232	42
LA Clippers	17	65	.207	44

1998 NBA Playoffs

EASTERN CONFERENCE

1st ROUND | SEMIFINALS | FINALS

Chicago
New Jersey — Chicago (3–0)
Charlotte
Atlanta — Charlotte (3–1)
Indiana
Cleveland — Indiana (3–1)
Miami
New York — New York (3–2)

Chicago (4–1)
Chicago (4–3)
Indiana (4–1)

NBA FINALS

CHICAGO (4–2)

WESTERN CONFERENCE

FINALS | SEMIFINALS | 1st ROUND

Utah (3–2) — Utah
Houston
Utah (4–1)
San Antonio (3–1) — Phoenix
San Antonio
Utah (4–0)
Seattle (3–2) — Seattle
Minnesota
LA Lakers (4–1)
LA Lakers (3–1) — LA Lakers
Portland

1998 NBA Playoff Results

Eastern Conference First Round

Apr 24	New York	79	at Miami	94
Apr 26	New York	96	at Miami	86
Apr 28	Miami	91	at New York	85
Apr 30	Miami	86	at New York	90
May 3	New York	98	at Miami	91

New York won series 3–2.

Apr 24	New Jersey	93	at Chicago	96*
Apr 26	New Jersey	91	at Chicago	96
Apr 29	Chicago	116	at New Jersey	101

Chicago won series 3–0.

Apr 23	Atlanta	87	at Charlotte	97
Apr 25	Atlanta	85	at Charlotte	92
Apr 28	Charlotte	64	at Atlanta	96
May 1	Charlotte	91	at Atlanta	82

Charlotte won series 3–1.

Apr 25	Cleveland	77	at Indiana	106
Apr 27	Cleveland	86	at Indiana	92
Apr 29	Indiana	77	at Cleveland	86
May 2	Indiana	80	at Cleveland	74

Indiana won series 3–1.

Western Conference First Round

Apr 24	Portland	102	at LA Lakers	104
Apr 26	Portland	99	at LA Lakers	108
Apr 28	LA Lakers	94	at Portland	99
Apr 30	LA Lakers	110	at Portland	99

LA Lakers won series 3–1.

Apr 24	Minnesota	83	at Seattle	108
Apr 26	Minnesota	98	at Seattle	93
Apr 28	Seattle	90	at Minnesota	98
Apr 30	Seattle	92	at Minnesota	88
May 2	Minnesota	84	at Seattle	116

Seattle won series 3–2.

Apr 23	San Antonio	102	at Phoenix	96
Apr 25	San Antonio	101	at Phoenix	108
Apr 27	Phoenix	88	at San Antonio	100
Apr 29	Phoenix	80	at San Antonio	99

San Antonio won series 3–1.

Apr 23	Houston	103	at Utah	90
Apr 25	Houston	90	at Utah	105
Apr 29	Utah	85	at Houston	89
May 1	Utah	93	at Houston	71
May 3	Houston	70	at Utah	84

Utah won series 3–2.

Eastern Conference Semifinals

May 3	Charlotte	70	at Chicago	83
May 6	Charlotte	78	at Chicago	76
May 8	Chicago	103	at Charlotte	89
May 10	Chicago	94	at Charlotte	80
May 13	Charlotte	84	at Chicago	93

Chicago won series 4–1.

May 5	New York	83	at Indiana	93
May 7	New York	77	at Indiana	85
May 9	Indiana	76	at New York	83
May 10	Indiana	118	at New York	107*
May 13	New York	88	at Indiana	91

Indiana won series 4–1.

Western Conference Semifinals

May 5	San Antonio	82	at Utah	83
May 7	San Antonio	106	at Utah	109*
May 9	Utah	64	at San Antonio	86
May 10	Utah	82	at San Antonio	73
May 12	San Antonio	77	at Utah	87

Utah won series 4–1.

May 4	LA Lakers	92	at Seattle	106
May 6	LA Lakers	92	at Seattle	68
May 8	Seattle	103	at LA Lakers	119
May 10	Seattle	100	at LA Lakers	112
May 12	LA Lakers	110	at Seattle	95

LA Lakers won series 4–1.

Eastern Conference Finals

May 17	Indiana	79	at Chicago	85
May 19	Indiana	98	at Chicago	104
May 23	Chicago	105	at Indiana	107
May 25	Chicago	94	at Indiana	96
May 27	Indiana	87	at Chicago	106
May 29	Chicago	89	at Indiana	92
May 31	Indiana	83	at Chicago	88

Chicago won series 4–3.

Western Conference Finals

May 16	LA Lakers	77	at Utah	112
May 18	LA Lakers	95	at Utah	99
May 22	Utah	109	at LA Lakers	98
May 24	Utah	96	at LA Lakers	92

Utah won series 4–0.

Finals

June 3	Chicago	85	at Utah	88*
June 5	Chicago	93	at Utah	88
June 7	Utah	54	at Chicago	96
June 10	Utah	82	at Chicago	86

June 12	Utah	83	at Chicago	81
June 14	Chicago	87	at Utah	86

Chicago won series 4–2.

*Overtime game.

NBA Finals Composite Box Score

CHICAGO BULLS

Player	GP	Field Goals FGM	Pct	3-Pt FG FGM	FGA	Free Throws FTM	Pct	Rebounds Off	Total	A	Stl	TO	BS	Avg	Hi
Jordan	6	70	42.7	4	13	57	81.4	9	24	14	11	10	4	33.5	45
Pippen	6	34	41.0	6	26	20	83.3	17	41	29	10	16	5	15.7	28
Kukoc	6	38	50.0	7	23	8	61.5	10	28	16	7	10	4	15.2	30
Harper	6	12	36.4	1	6	7	58.3	3	27	17	9	7	4	5.3	8
Longley	6	12	44.4	0	0	6	75.0	11	29	9	5	11	5	5.0	10
Kerr	6	7	35.0	5	13	4	100.0	1	2	15	2	3	0	3.8	7
Burrell	6	9	40.9	1	4	2	66.7	0	15	0	7	3	1	3.5	10
Rodman	6	6	46.2	0	0	8	66.7	20	50	6	7	6	2	3.3	7
Buechler	6	3	60.0	2	3	0	—	1	2	2	1	1	1	1.3	6
Wennington	3	2	33.3	0	0	0	—	0	3	1	0	2	1	1.3	2
Simpkins	2	1	50.0	0	0	0	0.0	1	3	1	0	1	1	1.0	2
Brown	2	1	33.3	0	0	0	—	0	2	0	1	2	0	1.0	2
Total	**6**	**195**	**43.0**	**26**	**88**	**112**	**75.7**	**73**	**226**	**110**	**60**	**72**	**28**	**88.0**	**96**

UTAH JAZZ

Player	GP	Field Goals FGM	Pct	3-Pt FG FGM	FGA	Free Throws FTM	Pct	Rebounds Off	Total	A	Stl	TO	BS	Avg	Hi
Malone	6	60	50.4	0	1	30	78.9	21	63	23	6	23	7	25.0	39
Hornacek	6	23	41.1	3	9	15	83.3	1	16	16	5	11	1	10.7	20
Stockton	6	24	49.0	2	9	8	72.7	1	15	52	12	18	0	9.7	24
Russell	6	18	40.9	6	21	11	68.8	4	30	8	7	9	1	8.8	15
Anderson	6	17	50.0	1	3	9	81.8	6	16	2	1	11	1	7.3	12
Eisley	6	12	37.5	1	7	3	100.0	2	12	23	2	10	1	4.7	9
Morris	6	11	39.3	0	9	4	66.7	2	5	3	2	2	1	4.3	9
Carr	6	11	50.0	0	0	3	75.0	5	12	0	1	4	1	4.2	12
Keefe	5	6	42.9	0	0	2	50.0	9	17	1	2	3	0	2.8	6
Ostertag	5	5	41.7	0	0	1	100.0	5	16	0	0	2	1	1.8	7
Foster	6	4	26.7	0	1	0	—	5	14	0	0	4	1	1.3	4
Vaughn	1	0	0.0	0	0	0	—	0	2	0	0	1	0	0.0	0
Total	**6**	**191**	**44.3**	**13**	**60**	**86**	**76.8**	**61**	**228**	**128**	**38**	**98**	**15**	**80.2**	**88**

NBA Finals Box Scores

Game 1

CHICAGO 85

CHICAGO	Min	FG M–A	FT M–A	Reb O–T	A	PF	S	TO	TP
Pippen	44	7–19	6–6	2–8	1	1	1	5	21
Kukoc	31	4–12	0–0	1–3	2	4	0	1	9
Longley	28	4–7	2–2	3–8	1	2	2	3	10
Jordan	46	13–29	6–8	1–3	2	3	0	0	33
Harper	24	2–4	0–0	0–6	1	0	1	0	4
Rodman	40	0–2	0–0	2–10	2	0	2	1	0
Kerr	27	2–3	0–0	0–0	5	1	0	1	4
Buechler	10	0–1	0–0	0–2	0	1	0	0	0
Simpkins	7	0–0	0–0	0–2	0	2	0	1	0
Burrell	6	2–5	0–0	0–0	0	2	0	4	4
Brown	2	0–0	0–0	0–1	0	2	0	2	0
Totals	240	34–82	14–16	9–32	14	17	8	14	85

Percentages: FG—.415, FT—.875. 3-pt goals: 3–16, .188 (Pippen 1–7, Kukoc 1–5, Jordan 1–2, Harper 0–1, Burrell 0–1). Team rebounds: 8. Blocked shots: 8 (Pippen, Kukoc 2, Longley, Jordan 2, Simpkins, Rodman).

UTAH 88 (OT)

UTAH	Min	FG M–A	FT M–A	Reb O–T	A	PF	S	TO	TP
Russell	48	6–12	3–4	1–8	2	3	1	1	15
Malone	43	9–25	3–4	1–14	2	3	2	2	21
Foster	15	1–5	0–0	2–3	0	1	0	0	2
Hornacek	35	2–10	0–0	0–4	3	2	1	2	4
Stockton	35	9–12	6–7	1–2	8	1	2	3	24
Eisley	23	4–6	0–0	0–1	6	2	1	1	8
Morris	20	3–6	0–0	1–3	1	1	1	0	6
Ostertag	17	1–1	0–0	1–3	0	3	0	0	2
Anderson	16	3–5	0–0	1–3	1	3	0	3	6
Carr	13	0–3	0–0	1–1	0	2	0	1	0
Totals	240	38–85	12–15	9–42	23	21	8	13	88

Percentages: FG—.447, FT—.800. 3-pt goals: 0–8, .000 (Russell 0–4, Hornacek 0–1, Eisley 0–1, Morris 0–2). Team rebounds: 9. Blocked shots: 3 (Malone 2, Foster).

A: 19,911. Officials: Javie, Garretson, Salvatore.

Game 2

CHIGAGO 93

CHICAGO	Min	FG M–A	FT M–A	Reb O–T	A	PF	S	TO	TP
Kukoc	43	6–16	0–2	5–9	2	1	2	3	13
Pippen	41	7–13	7–7	3–6	4	3	1	2	21
Longley	17	2–2	0–0	0–2	2	6	1	0	4
Jordan	40	14–33	9–10	3–5	3	2	1	0	37
Harper	24	1–4	1–2	1–2	2	3	1	2	3
Kerr	27	1–5	4–4	1–1	2	1	0	1	7
Rodman	27	1–1	1–2	5–9	1	5	2	1	3
Burrell	15	2–5	0–0	0–1	0	1	1	0	5
Wennington	4	0–1	0–0	0–1	0	0	0	0	0
Buechler	2	0–0	0–0	0–0	1	0	0	0	0
Totals	240	34–80	22–27	18–36	17	21	10	7	93

Percentages: FG—.425, FT—.815. 3-pt goals: 3–16, .188 (Kukoc 1–6, Pippen 0–1, Jordan 0–2, Harper 0–1, Kerr 1–4, Burrell 1–2). Team rebounds: 7. Blocked shots: 3 (Pippen, Jordan, Wennington).

UTAH 88

UTAH	Min	FG M–A	FT M–A	Reb O–T	A	PF	S	TO	TP
Malone	39	5–16	6–9	5–12	4	5	0	4	16
Russell	37	4–7	0–0	1–5	1	2	1	3	11
Foster	13	0–1	0–0	0–3	0	2	0	0	0
Hornacek	32	7–11	4–4	0–1	2	6	0	3	20
Stockton	31	4–5	0–0	0–3	7	5	2	3	9
Anderson	24	4–7	4–5	0–2	0	1	0	1	12
Eisley	24	4–10	0–0	1–2	7	3	0	3	9
Morris	15	1–2	0–0	1–4	0	3	0	0	2
Carr	9	1–2	0–0	0–1	0	0	0	0	2
Keefe	9	0–2	0–0	1–2	1	1	0	2	0
Ostertag	7	3–4	1–1	0–3	0	0	0	0	7
Totals	240	33–67	15–19	9–38	22	28	3	19	88

Percentages: FG—.493, FT—.789. 3-pt goals: 7–13, .538 (Russell 3–5, Hornacek 2–3, Stockton 1–2, Eisley 1–2). Team rebounds: 8. Blocked shots: 5 (Malone 3, Eisley, Morris).
A: 19,911. Officials: J. Crawford, D. Crawford, Oakes.

Game 3

UTAH 54

UTAH	Min	FG M–A	FT M–A	Reb O–T	A	PF	S	TO	TP
Malone	31	8–11	6–6	0–3	1	4	1	7	22
Russell	29	1–7	3–4	0–4	2	1	2	4	5
Ostertag	24	1–7	0–0	4–9	0	3	0	1	2
Hornacek	27	3–8	0–0	0–3	4	2	1	2	6
Stockton	26	1–4	0–0	0–2	7	3	1	5	2
Anderson	21	3–6	1–2	1–3	0	4	0	2	8
Morris	19	2–9	1–2	0–2	0	1	0	2	5
Foster	17	0–2	0–0	1–4	0	3	0	1	0
Eisley	15	0–6	0–0	1–1	2	3	1	0	0
Carr	12	0–2	0–0	0–2	0	1	0	1	0
Keefe	12	2–2	0–0	2–3	0	1	1	0	4
Vaughn	7	0–6	0–0	0–2	0	0	0	1	0
Totals	240	21–70	11–14	9–38	16	26	7	26	54

Percentages: FG—.300, FT—.786. 3-pt goals: 1–9, .111 (Russell 0–2, Hornacek 0–1, Anderson 1–1, Morris 0–3, Eisley 0–2). Team rebounds: 7. Blocked shots: 3 (Malone, Ostertag, Carr).

CHICAGO 96

CHICAGO	Min	FG M–A	FT M–A	Reb O–T	A	PF	S	TO	TP
Pippen	35	5–10	0–1	1–4	4	3	2	2	10
Kukoc	34	7–12	2–2	3–6	4	3	4	4	16
Longley	25	3–8	2–4	2–7	3	4	1	3	8
Jordan	32	7–14	10–11	1–3	2	1	1	2	24
Harper	30	3–8	2–4	1–10	7	2	1	3	8
Burrell	25	4–5	2–2	0–9	0	4	2	0	10
Rodman	23	1–5	0–0	2–6	0	2	0	2	2
Kerr	12	2–5	0–0	0–1	2	0	0	0	6
Buechler	9	2–3	0–0	0–0	1	0	1	1	6
Brown	5	1–3	0–0	0–1	0	0	1	0	2
Simpkins	5	1–2	0–2	1–1	1	0	0	0	2
Wennington	5	1–3	0–0	0–2	1	0	0	0	2
Totals	240	37–76	18–26	11–50	25	19	13	17	96

Percentages: FG—.467, FT—.692. 3-pt goals: 4–11, .364 (Pippen 0–1, Kukoc 0–2, Harper 0–1, Kerr 2–4, Buechler 2–3). Team rebounds: 4. Blocked shots: 6 (Pippen, Longley, Jordan, Harper, Burrell, Buechler).
A: 23,844. Officials: Bavetta, Nunn, Hollins.

Game 4

UTAH 82

UTAH	Min	FG M–A	FT M–A	Reb O–T	A	PF	S	TO	TP
Malone	43	10–21	1–2	6–14	4	3	1	4	21
Russell	31	3–7	2–4	0–3	0	4	2	0	10
Keefe	20	2–4	2–4	3–7	0	4	0	1	6
Hornacek	35	3–8	2–2	0–0	2	5	0	0	8
Stockton	31	3–11	1–2	0–1	13	4	2	2	7
Anderson	26	2–5	3–3	1–5	0	5	1	2	7
Morris	18	4–7	1–2	0–3	3	0	0	0	9
Eisley	17	3–8	2–2	0–3	5	1	0	1	8
Foster	9	2–5	0–0	2–2	0	2	0	0	4
Carr	5	1–2	0–0	1–1	0	1	0	0	2
Ostertag	5	0–0	0–0	0–1	0	3	0	0	0
Totals	240	33–78	14–21	13–40	24	32	6	10	82

Percentages: FG—.423, FT—.667. 3-pt goals: 2–15, .133 (Russell 2–5, Stockton 0–3, Anderson 0–1, Morris 0–3, Eisley 0–2, Foster 0–1). Team rebounds: 10. Blocked shots: 1 (Anderson).

CHICAGO 86

CHICAGO	Min	FG M–A	FT M–A	Reb O–T	A	PF	S	TO	TP
Pippen	46	9–18	5–8	5–9	5	2	1	1	28
Kukoc	29	3–9	2–2	0–1	4	3	0	0	8
Longley	23	0–1	2–2	1–3	2	3	0	0	2
Jordan	43	12–27	10–15	3–8	2	1	2	2	34
Harper	34	2–7	2–4	1–4	2	4	3	3	6
Rodman	30	0–3	6–8	7–14	2	3	0	0	6
Burrell	18	1–5	0–1	0–5	0	1	0	0	2
Kerr	16	1–3	0–0	0–0	1	2	1	1	0
Buechler	1	0–0	0–0	0–0	0	0	0	0	0
Totals	240	27–73	27–40	17–44	18	19	7	9	86

Percentages: FG—.370, FT—.675. 3-pt goals: 5–15, .333 (Pippen 5–10, Kukoc 0–2, Harper 0–1, Kerr 0–2). Team rebounds: 17. Blocked shots: 2 (Kukoc, Longley).
A: 23,844. Officials: Evans, Javie, Nies.

Game 5

UTAH 83

UTAH	Min	FG M–A	FT M–A	Reb O–T	A	PF	S	TO	TP
Malone	44	17–27	5–6	4–9	5	2	1	1	39
Russell	34	2–6	0–0	1–6	1	3	1	0	5
Keefe	5	1–3	0–0	2–4	0	3	0	0	2
Hornacek	39	2–7	5–8	0–2	5	3	2	1	9
Stockton	38	3–7	0–0	0–4	12	2	5	2	6
Anderson	23	3–7	0–0	2–2	0	2	0	3	6
Carr	21	5–6	2–2	2–4	0	3	0	2	12
Morris	17	0–1	2–2	0–1	1	5	1	0	2
Eisley	11	0–1	0–0	0–3	0	0	0	5	0
Foster	6	1–2	0–0	0–2	0	1	0	1	2
Ostertag	2	0–0	0–0	0–0	0	0	0	1	0
Totals	240	34–67	14–18	11–37	24	24	10	16	83

Percentages: FG—.507, FT—.778. 3-pt goals: 1–5, .200 (Malone 0–1, Russell 1–3, Hornacek 0–1). Team rebounds: 7. Blocked shots: 3 (Malone, Russell, Hornacek).

CHICAGO 81

CHICAGO	Min	FG M–A	FT M–A	Reb O–T	A	PF	S	TO	TP
Pippen	45	2–16	2–2	6–11	11	6	3	4	6
Kukoc	43	11–13	4–7	1–6	0	2	1	2	30
Longley	23	3–8	0–0	5–7	1	4	0	3	6
Jordan	45	9–26	10–11	1–4	4	4	3	4	28
Harper	31	1–6	0–0	0–2	1	2	1	1	3
Rodman	24	1–1	0–0	0–3	0	5	1	0	2
Kerr	18	2–4	0–0	0–0	2	1	0	0	6
Burrell	10	0–1	0–0	0–0	0	1	2	2	0
Buechler	1	0–0	0–0	0–0	0	0	0	0	0
Totals	240	29–75	16–20	13–33	19	25	11	16	81

Percentages: FG—.387, FT—.800. 3-pt goals: 7–20, .350 (Pippen 0–8, Kukoc 4–6, Jordan 0–2, Harper 1–1, Kerr 2–3, Burrell 0–1). Team rebounds: 10. Blocked shots: 5 (Pippen, Kukoc, Longley 2, Harper).

A: 23,844. Officials: Salvatore, J. Crawford, Oakes.

Game 6

CHICAGO 87

CHICAGO	Min	FG M–A	FT M–A	Reb O–T	A	PF	S	TO	TP
Kukoc	42	7–14	0–0	0–3	4	3	0	0	15
Pippen	26	4–7	0–0	0–3	4	2	2	2	8
Longley	14	0–1	0–0	0–2	0	4	1	0	0
Jordan	44	15–35	12–15	0–1	1	2	4	1	45
Harper	29	3–4	2–2	0–3	3	2	1	1	8
Rodman	39	3–3	1–2	4–8	1	5	2	2	7
Kerr	24	0–0	0–0	0–0	3	3	1	1	0
Burrell	10	0–1	0–0	0–0	0	0	0	0	0
Buechler	8	1–1	0–0	1–2	1	1	0	2	2
Wennington	4	1–1	0–0	0–0	0	1	0	2	2
Totals	240	34–67	15–19	5–22	17	23	11	9	87

Percentages: FG—.507, FT—.789. 3-pt goals: 4–10, .400 (Kukoc 1–2, Jordan 3–7, Harper 0–1). Team rebounds: 13. Blocked shots: 4 (Pippen, Harper 2, Rodman).

UTAH 86

UTAH	Min	FG M–A	FT M–A	Reb O–T	A	PF	S	TO	TP
Malone	43	11–19	9–11	5–11	7	2	1	5	31
Russell	37	2–5	3–4	1–4	2	2	0	1	7
Keefe	14	1–3	0–0	1–1	0	1	1	0	2
Hornacek	37	6–12	4–4	1–6	0	0	1	3	17
Stockton	33	4–10	1–2	0–3	5	4	0	3	10
Carr	26	4–7	1–2	1–3	0	4	0	0	9
Anderson	16	2–4	1–1	1–1	1	0	0	0	5
Morris	16	1–3	0–0	0–2	1	4	0	0	2
Eisley	5	1–1	1–1	0–2	3	1	0	0	3
Foster	3	0–0	0–0	0–0	0	1	1	2	0
Totals	240	32–64	20–25	10–33	19	19	4	14	86

Percentages: FG—.500, FT—.800. 3-pt goals: 2–10, .200 (Russell 0–2, Hornacek 1–3, Stockton 1–4, Morris 0–1). Team rebounds: 6. Blocked shots: none.

A: 19,911. Officials: Bavetta, Hollins, D. Crawford.

NBA Awards

All-NBA Teams

FIRST TEAM	SECOND TEAM	THIRD TEAM
G Michael Jordan, Chicago	Tim Hardaway, Miami	Mitch Richmond, Sacramento
G Gary Payton, Seattle	Rod Strickland, Washington	Reggie Miller, Indiana
C Shaquille O'Neal, LA Lakers	David Robinson, San Antonio	Dikembe Mutombo, Atlanta
F Karl Malone, Utah	Grant Hill, Detroit	Scottie Pippen, Chicago
F Tim Duncan, San Antonio	Vin Baker, Seattle	Glen Rice, Charlotte

NBA All-Defensive Teams

FIRST TEAM	SECOND TEAM
G Michael Jordan, Chicago	Mookie Blaylock, Atlanta
G Gary Payton, Seattle	Eddie Jones, LA Lakers
C Dikembe Mutombo, Atlanta	David Robinson, San Antonio
F Scottie Pippen, Chicago	Tim Duncan, San Antonio
F Karl Malone, Utah	Charles Oakley, New York

NBA Awards *(Cont.)*

All-Rookie Teams
(Chosen Without Regard to Position)

FIRST TEAM	SECOND TEAM
Tim Duncan, San Antonio	Tim Thomas, Philadelphia
Keith Van Horn, New Jersey	Cedric Henderson, Cleveland
Brevin Knight, Cleveland	Derek Anderson, Cleveland
Zydrunas Ilgauskas, Cleveland	Maurice Taylor, LA Clippers
Ron Mercer, Boston	Bobby Jackson, Denver

NBA Individual Leaders

Scoring

	GP	Pts	Avg
Michael Jordan, Chi	82	2357	28.7
Shaquille O'Neal, LA Lakers	60	1699	28.3
Karl Malone, Utah	81	2190	27.0
Mitch Richmond, Sac	70	1623	25.9
Antoine Walker, Bos	82	1840	22.4
Sharif Abdur-Rahim, Van	82	1829	22.3
Glen Rice, Char	82	1826	22.3
Allen Iverson, Phil	80	1758	22.0
Chris Webber, Wash	71	1555	21.9
David Robinson, SA	73	1574	21.6

Rebounds

	GP	Reb	Avg
Dennis Rodman, Chi	80	1201	15.0
Jayson Williams, NJ	65	883	13.6
Tim Duncan, SA	82	977	11.9
Dikembe Mutombo, Den	82	932	11.4
David Robinson, SA	73	775	10.6
Karl Malone, Utah	81	834	10.3
Anthony Mason, Char	81	826	10.2
Antoine Walker, Bos	82	836	10.2
Arvydas Sabonis, Port	73	729	10.0
Kevin Garnett, Minn	82	786	9.6

Assists

	GP	Assists	Avg
Rod Strickland, Wash	76	801	10.5
Jason Kidd, Phoe	82	745	9.1
Mark Jackson, Ind	82	713	8.7
Stephon Marbury, Minn	82	704	8.6
John Stockton, Utah	64	543	8.5
Tim Hardaway, Mia	81	672	8.3
Gary Payton, Sea	82	679	8.3
Brevin Knight, Clev	80	656	8.2
Damon Stoudamire, Tor-Port	71	580	8.2
Sam Cassell, NJ	75	603	8.0

Field-Goal Percentage

	FGA	FGM	Pct
Shaquille O'Neal, LA Lakers	1147	670	.584
Charles Outlaw, Orl	543	301	.554
Alonzo Mourning, Mia	732	403	.551
Tim Duncan, SA	1287	706	.549
Vin Baker, Sea	1164	631	.542
Dikembe Mutombo, Atl	743	399	.537
Antonio McDyess, Phoe	927	497	.536
Rasheed Wallace, Port	875	466	.533
Karl Malone, Utah	1472	780	.530
Bryant Reeves, Van	941	492	.523

Free-Throw Percentage

	FTA	FTM	Pct
Chris Mullin, Ind	164	154	.939
Jeff Hornacek, Utah	322	285	.885
Ray Allen, Mil	391	342	.875
Derek Anderson, Clev	315	275	.873
Kevin Johnson, Phoe	186	162	.871
Tracy Murray, Wash	209	182	.871
Hersey Hawkins, Sea	204	177	.868
Reggie Miller, Ind	440	382	.868
Christian Laettner, Atl	354	306	.864
Mitch Richmond, Sac	471	407	.864

Three-Point Field-Goal Percentage

	FGA	FGM	Pct
Dale Ellis, Sea	276	127	.460
Jeff Hornacek, Utah	127	56	.441
Chris Mullin, Ind	243	107	.440
Hubert Davis, Dall	260	101	.439
Steve Kerr, Chi	130	57	.438
Glen Rice, Char	300	130	.433
Wesley Person, Clev	447	192	.430
Reggie Miller, Ind	382	164	.429
Dell Curry, Char	145	61	.421
Kerry Kittles, NJ	263	110	.418

Steals

	GP	Steals	Avg
Mookie Blaylock, Atl	70	183	2.61
Brevin Knight, Clev	80	196	2.45
Doug Christie, Tor	78	190	2.44
Gary Payton, Sea	82	185	2.26
Allen Iverson, Phil	80	176	2.20
Eddie Jones, LA Lakers	80	160	2.00
Jason Kidd, Phoe	82	162	1.98
Kendall Gill, NJ	81	156	1.93
Clyde Drexler, Hou	70	126	1.80
Hersey Hawkins, Sea	82	148	1.80

Blocked Shots

	GP	BS	Avg
Marcus Camby, Tor	63	230	3.65
Dikembe Mutombo, Atl	82	277	3.38
Shawn Bradley, Dall	64	214	3.34
Theo Ratliff, Phil	82	258	3.15
David Robinson, SA	73	192	2.63
Tim Duncan, SA	82	206	2.51
Michael Stewart, Sac	81	195	2.41
Shaquille O'Neal, LA Lakers	60	144	2.40
Alonzo Mourning, Mia	58	130	2.24
Charles Outlaw, Orl	82	181	2.21

NBA Team Statistics

Offense

Team	Field Goals		3-Pt Field Goals		Free Throws		Rebounds				Scoring
	FGM	Pct	3FGM	Pct	FTM	Pct	Off	Total	A	Stl	Avg
LA Lakers	3146	48.1	497	35.0	1863	68.0	1079	3550	2009	734	105.5
Minnesota	3157	46.1	303	34.7	1673	73.9	1063	3492	2068	639	101.1
Utah	2993	49.0	249	37.2	2044	77.3	962	3367	2070	648	101.0
Seattle	3052	47.3	621	39.5	1521	72.1	932	3157	1983	804	100.6
New Jersey	3055	44.1	310	33.1	1750	74.4	1344	3481	1685	777	99.6
Phoenix	3138	46.8	431	35.6	1459	74.9	991	3443	2123	757	99.6
Houston	2946	45.2	573	34.3	1634	77.1	987	3337	1799	686	98.8
Washington	3080	45.2	320	33.9	1489	69.1	1119	3457	1900	689	97.2
Chicago	3064	45.1	311	32.3	1492	74.3	1243	3681	1952	695	96.7
Charlotte	2968	46.8	346	38.3	1641	75.1	985	3326	1944	692	96.6
Vancouver	3006	45.8	325	36.2	1586	73.9	1081	3394	1960	614	96.6
Indiana	2921	46.9	401	39.0	1631	76.4	874	3222	1787	645	96.0
Boston	3012	43.5	415	33.2	1425	72.6	1196	3240	1811	987	95.9
LA Clippers	2930	43.8	525	35.8	1480	72.3	1039	3316	1525	625	95.9
Atlanta	2887	45.5	337	33.2	1749	75.6	1107	3523	1569	648	95.8
Miami	2850	45.0	548	35.4	1539	73.9	1023	3442	1759	664	95.0
Toronto	2965	43.5	372	34.3	1479	71.8	1187	3336	1746	769	94.9
Milwaukee	2918	45.6	249	35.3	1663	76.7	1035	3271	1650	733	94.5
Portland	2885	45.1	324	30.9	1640	73.7	1086	3607	1766	585	94.3
Detroit	2862	44.9	293	31.2	1704	74.5	1045	3382	1597	678	94.2
Philadelphia	2837	44.3	243	30.0	1734	73.7	1126	3420	1729	729	93.3
Sacramento	2957	44.2	283	35.1	1440	68.7	1093	3398	1836	596	93.1
Cleveland	2817	45.4	298	37.2	1653	75.6	954	3285	1894	814	92.5
San Antonio	2898	46.8	302	35.0	1489	68.8	984	3622	1839	517	92.5
New York	2864	44.7	382	33.5	1399	77.2	978	3412	1787	634	91.6
Dallas	2882	42.7	422	35.7	1308	75.2	1007	3288	1535	646	91.4
Orlando	2771	42.9	293	32.2	1552	72.6	1178	3381	1694	649	90.1
Denver	2677	41.7	288	32.3	1658	77.2	1040	3197	1552	664	89.0
Golden State	2845	41.3	189	27.2	1358	71.0	1288	3763	1760	620	88.3

Defense (Opponent's Statistics)

Team	Field Goals		3-Pt Field Goals		Free Throws		Rebounds			Scoring	
	FGM	Pct	3FGM	Pct	FTM	Pct	Off	Total	Stl	Avg	Diff
San Antonio	2737	41.1	338	32.8	1448	74.0	1017	3253	730	88.5	+4.0
New York	2624	42.8	331	31.7	1728	75.0	854	3195	653	89.1	+2.5
Chicago	2797	43.1	329	32.2	1425	72.9	1016	3255	652	89.6	+7.1
Cleveland	2689	43.3	341	34.4	1642	75.5	950	3178	707	89.8	+2.7
Indiana	2788	43.2	274	31.6	1525	72.8	1114	3368	644	89.9	+6.1
Miami	2723	42.9	305	33.1	1632	74.4	1058	3290	637	90.0	+5.0
Orlando	2930	45.4	313	32.4	1302	73.6	1089	3357	747	91.2	-1.1
Atlanta	2961	44.2	348	34.2	1302	73.5	1081	3233	616	92.3	+3.5
Detroit	2840	44.5	363	33.0	1549	74.6	991	3325	648	92.6	+1.6
Portland	2810	43.1	373	34.3	1626	72.2	1011	3212	770	92.9	+1.4
Seattle	2896	44.6	417	32.4	1449	72.4	1141	3455	640	93.4	+7.2
Phoenix	2923	44.2	394	36.1	1501	73.2	1051	3394	720	94.4	+5.2
Utah	2806	43.9	401	35.7	1730	75.7	983	2995	645	94.4	+6.7
Charlotte	2977	46.4	369	34.7	1436	72.8	962	3219	582	94.6	+2.0
Philadelphia	2906	45.1	384	34.4	1651	73.0	1115	3456	766	95.7	-2.4
Milwaukee	2911	46.1	304	32.7	1779	74.3	1001	3263	764	96.4	-1.9
Washington	2975	45.5	348	35.6	1623	74.7	1029	3497	632	96.6	+0.6
Golden State	2992	44.4	334	34.6	1667	72.9	1134	3669	757	97.4	-9.1
Dallas	3138	46.0	386	34.2	1333	71.4	1222	3867	658	97.5	-6.1
LA Lakers	2984	43.9	380	35.4	1669	73.1	1123	3462	660	97.8	+7.7
New Jersey	3016	47.1	356	34.5	1653	74.8	1079	3395	616	98.1	+1.5
Boston	2864	47.9	299	31.8	2052	74.4	1015	3461	696	98.5	-2.6
Sacramento	3095	45.7	345	35.6	1560	74.3	1157	3690	694	98.7	-5.6
Houston	3173	46.9	409	36.5	1406	74.4	1041	3367	733	99.5	-0.7
Minnesota	3076	44.8	432	35.8	1648	74.2	1116	3527	609	100.4	+0.7
Denver	3015	47.3	419	37.9	1817	75.4	1095	3496	662	100.8	-11.8
LA Clippers	3236	47.4	334	36.0	1663	73.4	1167	3633	727	103.3	-7.4
Vancouver	3230	47.5	428	38.5	1634	73.2	1144	3503	836	103.9	-7.3
Toronto	3271	47.9	396	38.3	1603	70.0	1270	3775	737	104.2	-9.3

NBA Team-by-Team Statistical Leaders

Atlanta Hawks

Player	GP	Min	Field Goals		3-Pt FG		Free Throws		Rebounds		A	Stl	TO	BS	Avg
			FGM	Pct	FGA	FGM	FTM	Pct	Off	Total					
Smith	73	2857	489	44.4	276	97	389	85.5	133	309	292	75	176	29	20.1
Henderson	69	2000	365	48.5	6	3	253	65.2	199	442	73	42	110	36	14.3
Laettner	74	2282	354	48.5	27	6	306	86.4	142	487	190	71	183	73	13.8
Mutombo	82	2917	399	53.7	0	0	303	67.0	276	932	82	34	168	277	13.4
Blaylock	70	2700	368	39.2	334	90	95	70.9	81	341	469	183	176	21	13.2
Corbin	79	2699	328	43.9	141	49	101	78.9	78	62	173	105	86	7	10.2
Recasner	59	1454	206	45.6	148	62	74	93.7	32	142	117	41	91	1	9.3
Gray	30	472	77	38.1	46	18	55	84.6	9	45	34	15	30	11	7.6
Brown	77	1202	161	43.3	8	2	63	72.4	57	183	55	23	51	13	5.0
Crawford	40	256	46	41.8	3	1	57	83.8	20	41	9	12	18	7	3.8
Miller	37	228	29	55.8	0	0	21	53.8	30	70	3	15	14	3	2.1
Barry	27	256	18	47.4	21	9	11	84.6	5	35	49	10	30	1	2.1
Anderson	50	398	36	44.4	5	0	16	39.0	39	118	15	19	17	10	1.8
Hawks	82	19,880	2,887	45.5	1,016	337	1,749	75.6	1,107	3,523	1,569	648	1,214	489	95.8
Opponents	82	19,880	2,961	44.2	1,017	348	1,302	73.5	1,081	3,233	1,753	616	1,118	378	92.3

Boston Celtics

Player	GP	Min	Field Goals		3-Pt FG		Free Throws		Rebounds		A	Stl	TO	BS	Avg
			FGM	Pct	FGA	FGM	FTM	Pct	Off	Total					
Walker	82	3268	722	42.3	292	91	305	64.5	270	836	273	142	292	60	22.4
Mercer	80	2662	515	45.0	28	3	188	83.9	109	280	176	125	132	17	15.3
Anderson	61	1858	268	39.8	160	57	153	78.9	39	173	345	87	143	1	12.2
Barros	80	1686	281	46.1	246	100	122	84.7	28	153	286	83	107	6	9.8
McCarty	82	2340	295	40.4	175	54	144	74.2	141	364	177	110	141	44	9.6
P. Jones	14	352	52	40.9	3	2	14	73.7	50	102	18	10	16	3	8.6
Knight	74	1503	193	44.1	55	15	81	78.6	146	365	104	54	87	82	6.5
Bowen	61	1305	122	40.9	59	20	76	62.3	79	174	81	87	52	29	5.6
DeClerq	81	1523	169	49.7	1	0	101	60.1	180	392	59	85	84	49	5.4
Tabak	57	984	142	46.7	1	0	23	37.7	84	212	48	20	61	38	5.4
Edney	52	623	93	43.1	10	3	88	79.3	20	55	139	51	66	1	5.3
Minor	69	1126	140	43.6	31	6	59	68.6	55	150	88	53	43	11	5.0
Ellison	33	447	40	57.1	0	0	20	58.8	52	109	31	20	28	31	3.0
D. Jones	15	91	19	33.3	23	6	0	—	3	9	5	2	11	3	2.9
Celtics	82	19,730	3,012	43.5	1,249	415	1,964	72.6	1,196	3,240	1,811	987	1,330	366	95.9
Opponents	82	19,730	2864	47.9	940	299	2,052	74.4	1,015	3,461	1,815	696	1,691	406	98.5

Charlotte Hornets

Player	GP	Min	Field Goals		3-Pt FG		Free Throws		Rebounds		A	Stl	TO	BS	Avg
			FGM	Pct	FGA	FGM	FTM	Pct	Off	Total					
Rice	82	3295	634	45.7	300	130	428	84.9	89	353	182	77	182	22	22.3
Wesley	81	2845	383	44.3	170	59	229	79.5	49	213	529	140	226	30	13.0
Mason	81	3148	389	50.9	4	0	261	64.9	177	826	342	68	146	18	12.8
Geiger	78	1839	358	50.5	11	1	168	71.2	196	521	78	68	111	87	11.3
Divac	64	1805	267	49.8	14	3	130	69.1	183	518	172	83	114	94	10.4
Phills	62	1887	246	44.6	114	44	106	75.7	59	216	187	81	108	18	10.4
Curry	52	971	194	44.7	145	61	41	78.8	26	101	69	31	54	4	9.4
Maxwell	42	636	103	39.9	112	37	48	80.0	14	57	52	16	40	4	6.9
Reid	79	1109	146	45.9	8	3	89	73.0	72	210	51	35	65	19	4.9
Armstrong	66	831	105	49.3	35	9	42	84.0	16	76	150	29	42	0	4.0
Williams	39	365	56	47.1	1	0	24	52.2	53	92	20	18	30	5	3.5
Beck	59	738	73	45.9	4	2	43	72.9	27	90	98	33	70	7	3.2
Royal	31	323	25	36.2	0	0	29	87.9	18	41	17	7	10	1	2.5
Farmer	27	169	17	32.1	9	2	31	79.5	16	32	5	10	9	4	2.5
Hornets	82	19,780	2,968	46.8	904	346	1,641	75.1	985	2,215	1,944	692	1,247	320	96.6
Opponents	82	19,780	2,977	46.4	1,063	369	1,436	72.8	962	3,219	1,806	582	1,241	372	94.6

Chicago Bulls

Player	GP	Min	Field Goals FGM	Pct	3-Pt FG FGA	FGM	Free Throws FTM	Pct	Rebounds Off	Total	A	Stl	TO	BS	Avg
Jordan	82	3181	881	46.5	126	30	565	78.4	130	475	283	141	185	45	28.7
Pippen	44	1652	315	44.7	192	61	150	77.7	53	227	254	79	109	43	19.1
Kukoc	17	2235	383	45.5	174	63	1555	70.7	121	327	314	76	154	37	13.3
Longley	58	1703	277	45.5	0	0	109	73.6	113	341	161	34	130	62	11.4
Harper	82	2284	293	44.1	84	16	162	75.0	107	290	241	108	91	48	9.3
Kerr	50	1119	137	45.4	130	57	45	91.8	14	77	96	26	27	5	7.5
Burrell	80	1096	159	42.4	144	51	47	73.4	80	198	65	64	50	37	5.2
Rodman	80	2856	155	43.1	23	4	61	55.0	421	1201	230	47	147	18	4.7
Brown	71	1149	116	38.4	5	0	56	71.8	34	94	151	71	63	12	4.1
LaRue	14	140	20	40.8	16	4	5	62.5	1	8	5	3	6	1	3.5
Wennington	48	467	75	45.6	0	0	17	81.0	32	80	19	4	16	5	3.5
Simpkins	40	433	48	53.9	2	0	36	51.4	27	77	33	9	32	5	3.3
Buechler	74	608	85	48.3	65	25	3	50.0	24	77	49	22	21	15	2.7
Kleine	46	397	39	36.8	0	0	15	83.3	27	77	30	4	28	5	2.0
Bulls	**82**	**19,855**	**3,064**	**45.1**	**962**	**311**	**1,492**	**74.3**	**1,243**	**3,681**	**1,952**	**695**	**1,178**	**353**	**96.7**
Opponents	**82**	**19,855**	**2,797**	**43.1**	**1,022**	**329**	**1,425**	**72.9**	**1,016**	**3,255**	**1,595**	**652**	**1,268**	**356**	**89.6**

Cleveland Cavaliers

Player	GP	Min	Field Goals FGM	Pct	3-Pt FG FGA	FGM	Free Throws FTM	Pct	Rebounds Off	Total	A	Stl	TO	BS	Avg
Kemp	80	2769	518	44.5	8	2	404	72.7	219	745	197	108	271	90	18.0
Person	82	3198	440	46.0	447	192	132	77.6	65	363	188	129	110	49	14.7
Ilgauskas	82	2379	454	51.8	4	1	230	76.2	279	723	71	52	146	135	13.9
Anderson	66	1839	239	40.8	84	17	275	87.3	55	187	227	86	128	13	11.7
Henderson	82	2527	348	48.0	4	0	136	71.6	71	325	168	96	165	45	10.1
Knight	80	2483	261	44.1	7	0	201	80.1	67	253	656	196	194	18	9.0
Potapenko	80	1412	234	48.0	1	0	102	70.8	110	313	57	27	132	28	7.1
Sura	46	942	87	37.7	60	19	74	56.5	25	94	171	44	93	7	5.8
Ferry	69	1034	113	39.5	99	33	32	80.0	23	114	59	26	53	17	4.2
Thomas	43	426	56	40.0	59	20	16	64.0	10	47	19	21	18	7	3.4
James	28	166	24	40.7	25	11	21	95.5	2	15	5	1	12	1	2.9
Graham	6	56	7	58.3	3	0	2	100.0	0	1	6	1	10	0	2.7
Butler	18	206	15	31.9	6	1	6	60.0	1	22	18	8	8	0	2.1
Dumas	7	47	6	50.0	4	2	0	0.0	1	5	5	0	5	0	2.0
Brooks	43	312	28	42.4	11	5	18	90.0	6	30	49	18	12	3	1.8
Scott	41	188	16	44.4	0	0	12	66.7	20	59	8	6	10	8	1.1
Cavs	**82**	**19,830**	**2,817**	**45.4**	**801**	**298**	**1,353**	**75.6**	**954**	**3,285**	**1,894**	**814**	**1,420**	**419**	**92.5**
Opponents	**82**	**19,830**	**2,689**	**43.3**	**992**	**341**	**1,642**	**75.5**	**950**	**3,178**	**1,794**	**707**	**1,444**	**455**	**89.8**

Dallas Mavericks

Player	GP	Min	Field Goals FGM	Pct	3-Pt FG FGA	FGM	Free Throws FTM	Pct	Rebounds Off	Total	A	Stl	TO	BS	Avg
Finley	82	3394	675	44.9	244	87	326	78.4	149	438	405	132	219	30	21.5
Bradley	64	1822	300	42.2	3	1	130	72.2	164	518	60	51	96	214	11.4
Ceballos	47	990	204	49.2	70	21	107	73.8	75	221	60	33	72	16	11.4
Davis	81	2378	350	45.6	230	101	97	83.6	34	169	157	43	88	5	11.1
Walker	41	1027	156	48.6	1	0	53	54.6	96	302	24	30	61	40	8.9
Reeves	82	1950	248	41.8	152	56	165	77.4	54	185	230	80	130	10	8.7
Pack	12	292	33	33.7	6	3	25	69.4	8	34	42	20	38	1	7.8
Strickland	67	1505	199	35.7	63	48	65	77.4	35	161	167	56	106	8	7.6
Thomas	5	73	17	37.8	0	0	3	100.0	8	24	3	1	10	0	7.4
Green	82	2649	242	45.3	4	0	116	71.62	19	668	123	78	68	27	7.3
Respert	82	911	130	44.4	93	31	48	78.7	37	100	61	34	48	1	5.9
Anstey	82	680	92	39.8	16	3	53	71.6	53	157	35	31	41	27	5.9
Muursepp	41	603	83	43.5	38	16	51	76.1	46	114	30	29	29	14	5.7
Riley	39	544	56	41.5	1	0	27	75.0	43	133	22	15	37	46	3.6
Wells	39	395	48	41.4	6	1	31	72.1	22	68	34	15	31	4	3.3
Mavericks	**82**	**19,905**	**2,882**	**42.7**	**1,183**	**422**	**1,308**	**75.2**	**1,007**	**3,288**	**1,535**	**646**	**1,182**	**460**	**91.4**
Opponents	**82**	**19,905**	**3,138**	**46.0**	**1,130**	**386**	**1,333**	**71.4**	**1,222**	**3867**	**1882**	**658**	**1,240**	**373**	**97.5**

Denver Nuggets

Player	GP	Min	FGM	Pct	FGA	FGM	FTM	Pct	Off	Total	A	Stl	TO	BS	Avg
			Field Goals		3-Pt FG		Free Throws		Rebounds						
Williams	4	145	24	39.3	0	0	31	68.9	10	21	12	4	9	0	19.8
Newman	74	2176	344	43.1	105	36	365	82.0	50	141	138	77	147	24	14.7
L. Ellis	76	2575	410	40.7	201	57	206	80.5	146	544	213	65	173	49	14.3
Jackson	68	2042	310	39.2	81	21	149	81.4	78	302	317	105	184	11	11.6
Fortson	80	1811	276	45.2	3	1	263	77.6	182	448	76	44	157	30	10.2
Goldwire	82	2212	269	42.3	164	63	150	80.6	40	147	277	86	85	7	9.2
Battie	65	1506	234	44.6	14	3	73	70.2	138	351	60	54	98	69	8.4
Alexander	60	1298	171	42.8	176	66	80	78.4	17	146	209	70	112	11	8.1
Washington	66	1539	201	40.4	137	44	65	78.3	47	127	78	53	72	25	7.7
Stith	31	718	75	33.3	48	10	75	87.2	15	65	50	21	35	8	7.6
Garrett	82	2632	242	42.8	0	0	114	64.8	227	644	90	57	84	133	7.3
H. Ellis	27	344	62	55.9	4	0	40	63.5	27	50	18	19	19	4	6.1
Lauderdale	39	345	53	41.7	0	0	38	55.1	27	100	21	7	46	17	3.7
Garris	28	225	22	33.8	14	5	19	76.0	3	19	28	7	15	1	2.4
Wolf	57	621	40	33.1	10	2	5	50.0	56	126	30	20	22	7	1.5
Nuggets	**82**	**19,730**	**2,677**	**41.7**	**893**	**288**	**1,658**	**77.2**	**1,040**	**3,197**	**1,552**	**664**	**1,312**	**389**	**89.0**
Opponents	**82**	**19,730**	**3,015**	**47.3**	**1,105**	**419**	**1,817**	**75.4**	**1,095**	**3,496**	**1,983**	**662**	**1,243**	**532**	**100.8**

Detroit Pistons

Player	GP	Min	FGM	Pct	FGA	FGM	FTM	Pct	Off	Total	A	Stl	TO	BS	Avg
			Field Goals		3-Pt FG		Free Throws		Rebounds						
Hill	81	3294	615	45.2	21	3	479	74.0	93	623	551	143	285	53	21.1
B. Williams	78	2619	531	51.1	3	1	198	70.7	223	695	94	67	181	55	16.2
Stackhouse	79	2545	424	43.5	195	47	354	78.7	105	266	241	89	224	59	15.8
Dumars	72	2326	329	41.6	426	158	128	82.5	14	104	253	4	84	2	13.1
Hunter	71	2505	316	38.3	265	85	145	74.0	61	247	224	123	110	10	12.1
Sealy	77	1641	216	42.8	41	9	150	82.4	48	219	100	65	79	20	7.7
J. Williams	77	1305	151	52.4	1	0	108	65.1	170	379	48	51	60	10	5.3
Long	40	739	50	42.7	4	0	41	71.9	57	150	25	29	22	12	3.5
Reid	68	994	94	53.4	0	0	50	70.4	77	175	26	25	28	55	3.5
Montross	48	691	61	42.4	0	0	16	40.0	69	199	11	13	29	27	2.9
Pollard	33	317	35	50.0	0	0	19	28.6	34	74	9	8	12	10	2.7
Mahorn	59	707	59	45.7	0	0	23	67.6	65	195	15	14	37	7	2.4
O'Bannon	30	234	26	37.7	3	0	12	80.0	14	33	17	9	9	1	2.1
Henson	23	65	13	50.0	8	3	7	100.0	0	2	4	1	6	0	1.6
Pistons	**82**	**19,955**	**2,862**	**44.9**	**938**	**293**	**1,704**	**74.5**	**1,045**	**3,382**	**1,597**	**678**	**1,198**	**344**	**94.2**
Opponents	**82**	**19,955**	**2,840**	**44.5**	**1,100**	**363**	**1,549**	**74.6**	**991**	**3,325**	**1,753**	**648**	**1,263**	**382**	**92.6**

Golden State Warriors

Player	GP	Min	FGM	Pct	FGA	FGM	FTM	Pct	Off	Total	A	Stl	TO	BS	Avg
			Field Goals		3-Pt FG		Free Throws		Rebounds						
Sprewell	14	547	110	397	48	9	70	74.5	7	51	68	19	44	5	21.4
Jackson	79	3046	476	430	191	61	229	81.2	130	400	381	79	263	8	15.7
Marshall	73	2611	451	413	201	63	158	73.1	210	628	159	95	147	73	15.4
Dampier	82	2656	352	445	2	0	267	66.9	272	715	94	39	175	139	11.8
Delk	77	1681	314	393	157	42	111	73.5	38	172	172	73	109	12	10.1
Weatherspoon	79	2325	268	441	0	0	200	72.2	198	594	89	85	119	74	9.3
Coles	53	1471	166	379	57	13	78	88.6	17	123	248	51	89	13	8.0
Caffey	80	1423	226	485	2	0	131	65.5	160		67	25	105	20	7.3
Bogues	61	1570	141	437	16	4	61	89.7	30	132	331	67	105	3	5.7
Williams	9	140	16	320	9	3	2	50.0	4	15	3	6	9	3	4.1
Fuller	57	613	86	420	4	0	55	68.8	61	196	10	6	37	16	4.0
Foyle	55	656	69	406	1	0	27	43.5	73	184	14	13	50	52	3.0
Spencer	68	813	59	457	0	0	44	55.7	93	226	17	23	49	37	2.4
Grayer	5	34	4	364	6	2	0	—	0	4	2	2	4	0	2.0
Madkins	19	243	13	382	15	6	5	71.4	2	15	45	13	13	1	1.9
Ferrell	50	461	41	369	6	0	12	54.5	25	47	26	21	18	6	1.9
Warriors	**82**	**19,8304**	**2,845**	**41.3**	**696**	**189**	**1,358**	**71.0**	**1,288**	**3,763**	**1,706**	**620**	**1,370**	**452**	**88.3**
Opponents	**82**	**19,830**	**2,992**	**44.4**	**965**	**334**	**1,667**	**72.9**	**1,134**	**3,669**	**2,012**	**757**	**1,168**	**477**	**97.4**

Houston Rockets

Player	GP	Min	Field Goals		3-Pt FG		Free Throws		Rebounds		A	Stl	TO	BS	Avg
			FGM	Pct	FGA	FGM	FTM	Pct	Off	Total					
Drexler	70	2473	452	42.7	334	106	277	80.1	105	346	382	126	189	42	18.4
Olajuwon	47	1633	306	48.3	3	0	160	75.5	116	460	143	84	126	96	16.4
Willis	81	2528	531	51.0	7	1	242	79.3	232	679	78	55	170	38	16.1
Barkley	68	2243	361	48.5	84	18	296	47.6	241	794	217	71	147	28	15.2
Maloney	78	2217	239	40.8	346	126	65	83.3	16	142	219	62	107	5	8.6
Johnson	75	1490	227	41.7	198	66	113	83.1	50	153	88	32	62	3	8.4
Elie	73	1988	206	45.2	189	55	145	83.3	39	156	221	81	100	8	8.4
Bullard	67	1190	175	45.0	231	96	20	74.1	25	146	60	31	39	24	7.0
Harrington	58	903	129	48.5	1	0	92	75.4	73	207	24	10	47	27	6.0
Rhodes	58	1070	112	36.7	8	2	111	61.7	28	7	110	62	97	10	5.8
Price	72	1332	128	41.3	77	78	77	78.6	37	107	192	52	111	4	5.6
Davis	45	599	63	44.4	72	27	31	83.8	10	47	59	17	52	3	4.1
Stepens	7	37	10	35.7	10	3	4	66.7	3	6	1	2	2	0	3.9
Jones	24	127	7	70.0	0	0	1	50.0	12	24	5	1	4	6	0.6
Rockets	**82**	**19,830**	**2,946**	**45.2**	**1,640**	**573**	**1,634**	**77.1**	**987**	**3,337**	**1,799**	**686**	**1,298**	**318**	**98.8**
Opponents	**82**	**19,830**	**3,173**	**46.9**	**1,122**	**409**	**1,406**	**74.4**	**1,041**	**3,367**	**1,914**	**733**	**1,170**	**362**	**99.5**

Indiana Pacers

Player	GP	Min	Field Goals		3-Pt FG		Free Throws		Rebounds		A	Stl	TO	BS	Avg
			FGM	Pct	FGA	FGM	FTM	Pct	Off	Total					
Miller	81	2795	516	47.7	382	164	382	86.8	46	232	171	78	128	11	19.5
Smits	73	2085	514	49.5	3	0	188	78.3	127	505	101	40	134	88	16.7
Mullin	82	2177	333	48.1	243	107	154	93.9	38	249	186	95	117	39	11.3
A. Davis	82	2191	254	48.1	3	0	277	69.6	192	560	61	45	103	72	9.6
Rose	82	1706	290	47.8	73	25	166	72.8	28	195	155	56	132	14	9.4
Jackson	82	2413	249	41.6	137	43	137	76.1	67	322	713	84	174	2	8.3
D. Davis	78	2174	273	54.8	0	0	80	46.5	233	611	70	51	73	87	8.0
Best	82	1547	201	41.9	70	21	112	85.5	28	122	281	85	111	5	6.5
McKey	57	1316	150	45.9	17	4	55	71.4	74	211	88	57	79	30	6.3
Hoiberg	65	874	85	38.3	85	32	59	85.5	14	123	45	40	22	3	4.0
Croshere	26	243	32	37.2	13	4	8	57.1	10	45	8	9	13	5	2.9
West	15	105	10	47.6	0	0	3	50.0	6	15	2	2	8	4	1.5
Pope	28	193	14	34.1	3	1	10	58.8	9	26	7	3	10	6	1.4
Pacers	**82**	**19,930**	**2,921**	**46.9**	**1,029**	**401**	**1,631**	**76.4**	**874**	**3,222**	**1,878**	**645**	**1,168**	**374**	**96.0**
Opponents	**82**	**19,930**	**2,788**	**43.2**	**868**	**274**	**1,525**	**72.8**	**1,114**	**3,368**	**1,586**	**644**	**1,239**	**366**	**89.9**

Los Angeles Clippers

Player	GP	Min	Field Goals		3-Pt FG		Free Throws		Rebounds		A	Stl	TO	BS	Avg
			FGM	Pct	FGA	FGM	FTM	Pct	Off	Total					
Murray	79	2579	473	48.1	153	54	220	74.8	172	484	142	118	171	54	15.4
Rogers	76	2499	426	45.6	212	72	225	68.6	155	424	202	93	193	38	15.1
Austin	78	2266	406	46.6	8	0	243	66.9	199	557	175	61	206	56	13.5
Taylor	71	1513	321	47.6	1	0	173	70.9	118	296	53	34	107	40	11.5
Piatkowski	67	1740	257	45.2	259	106	140	82.4	70	236	85	51	0	12	11.3
Martin	82	2299	275	37.7	293	107	184	84.8	19	164	331	82	154	10	10.3
Wright	69	2067	241	44.5	2	0	141	65.9	180	606	55	55	81	87	9.0
Robinson	70	1231	195	38.9	225	74	77	72.0	37	111	135	37	97	10	7.7
Vaught	10	265	36	42.9	2	0	3	37.5	16	65	7	4	13	2	7.5
Richardson	69	1252	124	37.2	57	11	30	69.8	17	96	226	44	54	3	4.2
Closs	58	740	93	44.9	0	0	46	59.7	63	168	19	12	38	81	4.0
Smith	34	292	49	39.2	47	15	6	54.5	13	27	21	12	27	6	3.5
Vrankovic	65	996	79	42.5	0	0	37	56.9	71	263	36	11	46	66	3.0
Collins	23	103	21	38.2	20	9	8	57.1	7	14	3	6	8	3	2.6
Clippers	**82**	**19,780**	**2,930**	**43.8**	**1,468**	**525**	**1,480**	**72.3**	**1,039**	**3,316**	**1,525**	**625**	**1,323**	**452**	**95.9**
Opponents	**82**	**19,780**	**3,236**	**47.4**	**928**	**334**	**1,663**	**73.4**	**1,167**	**3,633**	**1,822**	**727**	**1,158**	**412**	**103.3**

Los Angeles Lakers

Player	GP	Min	FGM	Pct	FGA	FGM	FTM	Pct	Off	Total	A	Stl	TO	BS	Avg
			Field Goals		3-Pt FG		Free Throws		Rebounds						
O'Neal	60	2175	670	58.4	0	0	359	52.7	208	681	142	39	175	144	28.3
Jones	80	2910	486	48.4	368	143	234	76.5	85	302	246	160	146	55	16.9
Bryant	79	2056	391	42.8	220	75	363	79.4	79	242	199	74	157	40	15.4
Van Exel	64	2053	311	41.9	316	123	136	79.1	31	194	442	64	104	6	13.8
Fox	82	2709	363	47.1	265	86	71	74.3	78	358	276	100	201	48	12.0
Campbell	81	1784	289	46.3	2	1	237	69.3	143	455	78	35	115	102	10.1
Horry	72	2192	200	47.6	93	19	117	69.2	186	542	163	112	99	94	7.4
Fisher	82	1760	164	43.4	81	31	115	75.7	38	193	333	75	119	5	5.8
Bennett	45	354	80	59.3	2	1	16	36.4	60	126	18	19	21	11	3.9
Blount	70	1029	107	57.2	4	0	39	50.0	114	298	37	29	51	25	3.6
Rooks	41	425	46	45.5	0	0	47	59.5	46	118	24	2	19	23	3.4
Barry	49	374	38	36.5	61	18	27	93.1	8	37	51	24	22	3	2.5
Lakers	**82**	**19,830**	**3,146**	**48.1**	**1,418**	**497**	**1,863**	**68.0**	**1,079**	**3,550**	**2,009**	**734**	**1,256**	**556**	**105.5**
Opponents	**82**	**19,830**	**2,984**	**43.9**	**1,073**	**380**	**1,669**	**73.1**	**1,123**	**3,462**	**1,841**	**660**	**1,280**	**423**	**97.8**

Miami Heat

Player	GP	Min	FGM	Pct	FGA	FGM	FTM	Pct	Off	Total	A	Stl	TO	BS	Avg
			Field Goals		3-Pt FG		Free Throws		Rebounds						
Mourning	58	1939	403	55.1	0	0	309	66.5	193	558	52	40	179	130	19.2
Hardaway	81	3031	558	43.1	442	155	257	78.1	48	299	672	136	224	16	18.9
Mashburn	48	1729	251	43.5	122	37	184	79.7	72	236	132	43	108	14	15.1
Lenard	81	2621	363	42.5	378	153	141	78.8	72	292	180	58	99	16	12.6
Barry	58	1600	213	42.1	229	90	115	85.8	29	171	153	64	104	27	10.9
Brown	74	2362	278	47.1	0	0	151	76.6	235	635	103	66	97	98	9.6
Majerle	72	1928	184	41.9	295	111	40	78.4	48	268	157	68	65	15	7.2
Strickland	51	847	145	53.9	1	0	59	72.0	80	213	26	18	47	34	6.8
Murdock	82	1395	177	42.2	91	28	125	80.1	39	156	219	103	104	13	6.2
Day	5	69	11	35.5	12	2	6	66.7	4	6	7	7	3	0	6.0
Conlon	18	209	28	45.2	0	0	32	72.7	16	46	12	9	11	5	4.9
Mills	50	782	81	39.3	81	25	25	75.8	34	152	39	19	45	9	4.2
Askins	46	681	39	32.0	74	21	12	63.2	28	101	29	27	26	12	2.4
Causwell	37	363	37	41.6	0	0	15	57.7	29	99	5	7	18	27	2.4
Walters	38	235	24	45.6	22	6	26	92.9	5	24	35	8	27	1	2.1
Lang	6	29	3	60.0	0	0	6	75.0	2	5	1	2	4	0	2.0
Heat	**82**	**19,755**	**2,850**	**45.0**	**1,547**	**548**	**1,539**	**73.9**	**1,023**	**3,442**	**1,759**	**664**	**1,226**	**429**	**95.0**
Opponents	**82**	**19,755**	**2,723**	**42.9**	**921**	**305**	**1,632**	**74.4**	**1,058**	**3,290**	**1,630**	**637**	**1,213**	**370**	**90.0**

Milwaukee Bucks

Player	GP	Min	FGM	Pct	FGA	FGM	FTM	Pct	Off	Total	A	Stl	TO	BS	Avg
			Field Goals		3-Pt FG		Free Throws		Rebounds						
Robinson	56	2294	534	47.0	65	25	215	80.8	82	307	158	69	200	34	23.4
Allen	82	3287	563	42.8	368	134	342	87.5	127	405	356	111	263	12	19.5
Brandon	50	1784	339	46.4	93	31	132	84.6	23	176	387	111	145	17	16.8
Gilliam	82	2114	327	48.4	4	0	267	80.2	146	439	104	65	148	37	11.2
Hill	57	2064	208	49.8	1	0	155	60.8	212	608	88	67	106	30	10.0
Johnson	81	2261	253	53.7	0	0	143	60.1	242	685	59	79	117	158	8.0
Perry	81	1752	241	43.0	50	17	92	84.4	21	108	230	90	128	2	7.3
Curry	82	1978	196	46.9	9	4	147	83.5	26	98	137	56	77	14	6.6
Honeycutt	38	530	90	40.7	77	29	36	62.1	27	93	33	20	49	6	6.4
Pierce	39	442	52	36.4	13	4	43	82.7	19	45	34	9	21	0	3.9
Smith	7	80	8	33.3	4	0	3	75.0	4	7	10	5	9	2	2.7
Lang	57	692	54	37.8	1	0	44	77.2	56	153	16	18	33	27	2.7
Feick	45	450	39	43.3	13	4	20	48.8	45	124	16	25	21	17	2.3
Breaux	6	30	4	36.4	3	1	1	50.0	0	2	2	1	1	1	1.7
Nordgaard	13	48	5	27.8	0	0	8	88.9	4	14	3	2	3	0	1.4
Gilliam	21	124	5	21.7	2	0	15	75.0	1	7	16	4	8	0	1.2
Bucks	**82**	**19,930**	**2,918**	**45.6**	**706**	**249**	**1,663**	**76.7**	**1,035**	**3,271**	**1,650**	**733**	**1,382**	**355**	**94.5**
Opponents	**82**	**19,930**	**2,911**	**46.1**	**929**	**304**	**1,779**	**74.3**	**1,001**	**3,263**	**1,744**	**764**	**1,349**	**396**	**96.4**

Minnesota Timberwolves

Player	GP	Min	FGM	Pct	FGA	FGM	FTM	Pct	Off	Total	A	Stl	TO	BS	Avg
			Field Goals		**3-Pt FG**		**Free Throws**		**Rebounds**						
Gugliotta	41	1582	319	50.2	17	2	183	82.1	106	356	167	61	109	22	20.1
Garnett	82	3222	635	49.1	16	3	245	73.8	222	786	348	139	192	150	18.5
Marbury	82	3112	513	41.5	304	95	329	73.1	58	230	704	104	256	7	17.7
Mitchell	81	2239	371	46.4	43	15	243	83.2	118	385	107	64	66	22	12.3
Peeler	38	1193	190	45.2	125	53	36	76.6	37	123	137	61	51	6	12.3
Carr	51	1165	190	42.0	127	40	84	84.8	43	155	85	17	69	11	9.9
Porter	82	1786	259	44.9	233	92	167	85.6	37	168	271	63	104	16	9.5
Parks	79	1703	224	49.9	1	0	110	65.1	140	437	53	36	66	86	7.1
Roberts	74	1328	191	49.5	0	0	75	48.1	109	363	27	24	70	72	6.2
Hammonds	57	1140	127	51.6	1	0	92	69.7	10	71	36	15	48	17	6.1
Curley	11	146	16	48.5	1	0	2	66.7	11	28	4	3	3	1	3.1
Jordan	57	487	54	47.8	1	0	41	56.9	57	97	50	35	30	9	2.6
Williams	25	161	16	33.3	4	0	32	97.0	2	14	32	9	16	2	2.6
Wheat	34	150	20	40.0	17	8	9	60.0	3	11	25	6	9	1	1.7
T'wolves	**82**	**19,930**	**3,157**	**46.1**	**873**	**303**	**1,673**	**73.9**	**1,063**	**3,492**	**2,068**	**639**	**1,138**	**427**	**101.1**
Opponents	**82**	**19,930**	**3,076**	**44.8**	**1,206**	**432**	**1,648**	**74.2**	**1,116**	**3,527**	**1,914**	**609**	**1,228**	**414**	**100.4**

New Jersey Nets

Player	GP	Min	FGM	Pct	FGA	FGM	FTM	Pct	Off	Total	A	Stl	TO	BS	Avg
			Field Goals		**3-Pt FG**		**Free Throws**		**Rebounds**						
Van Horn	62	2325	446	42.6	224	69	258	84.6	142	408	106	64	14	25	19.7
Cassell	75	2606	510	44.1	80	15	436	86.0	73	228	603	121	269	20	19.6
Kittles	77	2814	508	44.0	263	110	202	80.8	132	362	176	132	106	37	17.2
Gill	81	2733	418	42.9	101	26	225	68.8	112	391	200	156	124	64	13.4
Seikaly	56	1636	250	43.2	2	0	246	74.1	146	393	77	28	146	43	13.3
Williams	65	2343	321	49.8	4	0	195	66.6	443	883	67	45	95	49	12.9
Gatling	57	1359	248	45.5	4	1	159	60.0	118	334	53	52	99	29	11.5
Douglas	80	1699	255	49.5	46	14	115	66.9	52	135	319	55	110	7	8.0
Evans	72	893	123	39.4	87	29	46	80.7	49	137	55	29	38	13	4.5
Vaughn	40	489	66	44.6	1	0	30	63.8	53	152	20	15	40	10	4.1
Harris	50	671	69	39.0	39	12	41	74.5	21	52	42	42	21	5	3.8
Haley	16	51	5	27.8	1	0	12	57.1	5	15	0	0	4	1	1.4
Cage	79	1201	43	51.2	1	0	20	55.6	115	308	32	45	23	44	1.3
McDaniel	20	180	10	33.3	0	0	5	62.5	12	31	9	3	8	2	1.3
Dare	10	60	4	22.2	0	0	4	50.0	10	17	1	0	2	2	1.2
Nets	**82**	**19,980**	**3,055**	**44.1**	**937**	**310**	**1,750**	**74.4**	**1,344**	**3,481**	**1,685**	**777**	**1,180**	**314**	**99.6**
Opponents	**82**	**19,980**	**3,016**	**47.1**	**1,031**	**356**	**1,653**	**74.8**	**1,079**	**3,395**	**1,771**	**616**	**1,482**	**515**	**98.1**

New York Knickerbockers

Player	GP	Min	FGM	Pct	FGA	FGM	FTM	Pct	Off	Total	A	Stl	TO	BS	Avg
			Field Goals		**3-Pt FG**		**Free Throws**		**Rebounds**						
Ewing	26	848	203	50.4	2	0	134	72.0	59	265	28	16	77	58	20.8
Houston	82	2848	571	44.7	213	82	285	85.1	43	274	212	63	200	24	18.4
Johnson	70	2412	429	48.5	63	15	214	75.6	175	401	150	40	127	13	15.5
Starks	82	2188	372	39.3	398	130	185	78.7	48	230	219	78	143	5	12.9
Mills	80	2183	292	43.3	137	40	152	80.4	120	408	133	45	107	30	9.7
Oakley	79	2734	307	44.0	6	0	97	85.1	218	724	201	123	126	22	9.0
Ward	82	2317	235	45.5	215	81	91	80.5	32	274	466	144	175	37	7.8
Cummings	74	1185	200	46.7	1	0	67	68.4	97	283	47	38	51	10	6.3
Childs	68	1599	149	42.1	87	27	104	82.5	29	162	268	56	103	6	6.3
B. Williams	41	738	75	50.3	0	0	52	73.2	78	183	21	17	38	15	4.9
Dudley	51	858	58	40.6	0	0	41	44.6	108	275	21	13	44	51	3.1
Bowie	27	224	32	54.2	4	3	8	88.9	9	26	11	6	7	2	2.8
Thompson	30	167	23	41.1	30	9	4	50.0	1	15	27	10	16	1	2.0
Myers	9	40	5	50.0	0	0	4	66.7	5	10	3	4	4	0	1.6
H. Williams	27	178	18	41.9	0	0	1	12.5	6	29	4	6	5	9	1.4
Knicks	**82**	**19,830**	**2,864**	**44.7**	**1,139**	**382**	**1,399**	**77.2**	**978**	**3,412**	**1,787**	**634**	**1,247**	**278**	**91.6**
Opponents	**82**	**19,830**	**2,624**	**42.8**	**1,045**	**331**	**1,728**	**75.0**	**854**	**3,195**	**1,585**	**653**	**1,234**	**319**	**89.1**

Orlando Magic

Player	GP	Min	Field Goals		3-Pt FG		Free Throws		Rebounds		A	Stl	TO	BS	Avg
			FGM	Pct	FGA	FGM	FTM	Pct	Off	Total					
Hardaway	19	625	103	37.7	50	15	90	76.3	8	76	68	28	46	15	16.4
Anderson	58	1701	343	45.5	214	77	127	63.8	98	297	119	72	85	23	15.3
Strong	58	1638	259	42.0	4	0	218	78.1	152	427	51	31	74	24	12.7
Grant	76	2803	393	45.9	7	0	135	67.8	228	618	172	81	88	79	12.1
Outlaw	82	2953	301	55.4	4	1	180	57.5	255	637	216	107	175	181	9.5
Price	63	1430	229	43.1	155	52	87	84.5	24	129	297	53	162	5	9.5
Armstrong	48	1236	156	41.1	65	25	105	85.4	65	159	236	58	112	5	9.2
Harper	66	1761	226	41.7	164	59	55	69.6	23	103	233	72	101	10	8.6
Schayes	74	1272	155	41.8	0	0	96	80.7	97	242	44	34	61	33	5.5
Benoit	77	1123	152	37.3	170	55	61	82.4	60	203	25	35	52	20	5.5
Wilkins	72	1252	141	32.5	109	29	69	70.4	16	90	78	34	79	6	5.3
Edwards	39	487	57	34.5	15	6	30	85.7	20	54	39	26	30	1	3.8
Ollie	35	430	37	37.8	1	0	49	70.0	9	39	65	13	44	0	3.5
Taylor	12	108	13	35.1	2	1	11	68.8	4	13	1	3	8	2	3.2
Lawson	17	80	9	60.0	0	0	8	80.0	8	27	5	4	2	4	1.5
Magic	82	19,830	2,771	42.9	909	293	1,552	72.6	1,178	3381	1,694	649	1,258	440	90.1
Opponents	82	19,830	2,930	45.4	967	313	1,302	73.6	1,089	3357	1,740	747	1,259	388	91.2

Philadelphia 76ers

Player	GP	Min	Field Goals		3-Pt FG		Free Throws		Rebounds		A	Stl	TO	BS	Avg
			FGM	Pct	FGA	FGM	FTM	Pct	Off	Total					
Iverson	80	3150	649	46.1	235	70	390	72.9	86	296	494	176	244	25	22.0
Coleman	59	2135	356	41.1	98	26	302	77.2	149	587	145	46	157	68	17.6
Smith	79	2344	464	43.4	8	0	227	77.5	199	471	94	62	158	51	14.6
Thomas	77	1779	306	44.7	17	62	171	74.0	107	288	90	54	118	17	11.0
Ratliff	82	2447	306	51.3	0	0	197	70.1	221	547	57	50	116	258	9.9
Shaw	59	1530	154	34.5	95	28	36	69.2	37	215	261	49	99	17	6.3
Benjamin	14	197	22	53.7	0	0	19	63.3	18	53	3	4	12	4	4.5
McKie	81	1813	139	36.5	63	12	42	76.4	58	231	175	101	76	13	4.1
Williams	58	801	93	43.7	5	0	51	81.0	87	211	29	17	30	21	4.1
Davis	71	906	109	44.7	6	0	64	63.4	64	158	73	49	91	18	4.0
Snow	64	918	79	42.9	17	2	49	69.0	19	81	177	60	63	5	3.3
Overton	23	277	24	38.1	3	0	14	87.5	2	14	37	8	23	1	2.7
Stewart	15	110	12	46.2	0	0	16	64.0	9	31	2	5	8	2	2.7
Parker	37	196	25	39.7	28	9	13	65.0	8	26	19	11	11	3	1.9
76ers	82	19,755	2,837	44.3	810	243	1,734	73.7	1,126	3,420	1,729	729	1,356	490	93.3
Opponents	82	19,755	2,906	45.1	1,115	384	1,651	73.0	1,115	3,456	1,927	766	1,317	508	95.7

Phoenix Suns

Player	GP	Min	Field Goals		3-Pt FG		Free Throws		Rebounds		A	Stl	TO	BS	Avg
			FGM	Pct	FGA	FGM	FTM	Pct	Off	Total					
Chapman	68	2263	408	24.7	311	120	146	78.1	30	173	203	71	116	14	15.9
McDyess	81	2441	497	53.6	2	0	231	70.2	206	613	106	100	142	135	15.1
Robinson	80	2359	429	47.9	84	27	248	68.9	152	410	170	92	140	90	14.2
Manning	70	1764	390	51.6	7	0	167	73.9	110	392	139	71	100	46	13.5
Kidd	82	3118	357	41.6	233	73	167	79.9	108	510	745	162	261	26	11.6
Scott	81	2290	329	39.7	342	125	105	80.8	47	247	153	53	104	39	11.0
Johnson	50	1290	155	44.7	26	4	162	87.1	35	164	245	27	101	8	9.5
Nash	76	1664	268	45.9	195	81	74	86.0	32	160	262	63	98	4	9.1
McCloud	63	1213	173	40.5	208	71	39	76.5	45	218	84	54	63	13	7.2
Bryant	70	1110	109	48.4	1	0	73	76.8	92	244	46	36	58	15	4.2
Williams	71	1333	95	47.0	0	0	65	69.9	107	312	49	33	29	60	3.6
Llamas	8	42	8	38.1	3	1	7	70.0	4	18	1	1	9	3	3.0
Milic	33	163	39	60.9	6	3	11	64.7	10	25	12	10	21	0	2.8
Suns	82	19,955	3,138	46.8	1,211	431	1,459	74.9	991	3,443	2,123	757	1,236	429	99.6
Opponents	82	19,955	2,923	44.2	1,091	394	1,501	73.2	1,051	3,394	1,803	720	1,363	320	94.4

Portland Trail Blazers

Player	GP	Min	FGM	Pct	FGA	FGM	FTM	Pct	Off	Total	A	Stl	TO	BS	Avg
			Field Goals		3-Pt FG		Free Throws		Rebounds						
Rider	74	2786	551	42.3	420	135	221	82.8	99	346	231	55	187	19	19.7
Stoudamire	71	2839	448	41.1	304	91	238	82.9	87	298	580	113	223	7	17.3
Sabonis	73	2333	407	49.3	115	30	323	79.8	149	729	218	65	190	80	16.0
Wallace	77	2896	466	53.3	39	8	184	66.2	132	478	195	75	167	88	14.6
B. Grant	61	1921	283	50.8	1	0	171	75.0	197	555	86	44	110	45	12.1
W. Williams	59	1470	210	38.6	219	80	108	86.4	50	200	122	59	92	35	10.3
Augmon	71	1445	154	41.4	7	1	94	60.3	104	235	88	57	81	32	5.7
Rogers	21	376	47	51.6	2	0	18	56.3	35	67	18	10	14	8	5.3
G. Grant	22	359	43	46.2	19	7	12	85.7	8	48	84	17	24	2	4.8
O'Neal	60	808	112	48.5	2	0	45	50.6	80	201	17	15	55	58	4.5
Brunson	38	622	49	34.8	61	22	42	67.7	14	56	100	25	52	3	4.3
Cato	74	1007	98	42.8	3	0	86	68.8	91	252	23	29	44	94	3.8
Crotty	26	379	29	32.2	20	6	32	94.1	4	32	63	10	42	1	3.7
Askew	30	443	19	35.2	2	0	28	71.8	21	68	38	19	35	5	2.2
Trail Blazers	82	19,830	2,885	45.1	1,047	324	1,640	73.7	1,086	3,607	1,766	585	1,383	471	94.3
Opponents	82	19,830	2,810	43.1	1,087	373	1,626	72.2	1,011	3,212	1,764	770	1,160	445	92.9

Sacramento Kings

Player	GP	Min	FGM	Pct	FGA	FGM	FTM	Pct	Off	Total	A	Stl	TO	BS	Avg
			Field Goals		3-Pt FG		Free Throws		Rebounds						
Richmond	70	2569	543	44.5	334	130	407	86.4	50	229	279	88	181	15	23.2
Williamson	79	2819	561	49.5	9	0	279	63.0	162	446	230	76	199	48	17.7
Owens	78	2348	338	46.4	70	27	116	58.9	170	582	219	93	153	38	10.5
Thorpe	74	2197	294	47.1	5	0	164	68.3	151	537	222	48	152	30	10.2
Funderburke	52	1094	191	49.0	7	1	110	67.9	80	234	63	19	62	15	9.5
Polynice	70	1458	249	45.9	1	0	52	45.2	173	439	107	37	98	45	7.9
Johnson	77	2266	226	37.1	128	42	80	72.7	51	171	329	64	120	6	7.5
Abdul-Rauf	31	530	103	37.7	31	5	16	100.0	6	37	58	16	19	1	7.3
Abdul-Wahad	59	959	144	40.3	19	4	84	67.2	44	116	51	35	65	13	6.4
Dehere	77	1410	180	39.9	132	50	79	79.8	21	106	196	52	96	4	6.4
Stewart	81	1761	155	48.0	0	0	65	45.8	197	536	61	29	85	195	4.6
Robinson	35	414	65	37.4	66	24	8	50.0	9	46	39	19	33	4	4.6
Hendrickson	48	737	58	38.9	5	0	47	82.5	33	143	41	26	31	9	3.4
Kings	82	19,730	2,957	44.2	806	283	1,440	68.7	1,093	3,398	1,836	596	1,271	420	93.1
Opponents	82	19,730	3,095	45.7	968	345	1,560	74.3	1,157	3,690	1,824	694	1,255	483	98.7

San Antonio Spurs

Player	GP	Min	FGM	Pct	FGA	FGM	FTM	Pct	Off	Total	A	Stl	TO	BS	Avg
			Field Goals		3-Pt FG		Free Throws		Rebounds						
Robinson	73	2457	544	51.1	4	0	485	73.5	239	775	199	64	202	192	21.6
Duncan	82	3204	706	54.9	10	0	319	66.2	274	977	224	55	279	206	21.1
Johnson	75	2674	321	47.8	13	2	122	72.6	30	150	591	84	165	18	10.2
Del Negro	54	1721	211	44.1	39	17	74	79.6	13	152	183	39	53	6	9.5
Elliott	36	1012	122	40.3	90	34	56	71.8	16	124	62	24	57	14	9.3
Jackson	82	2226	258	39.4	297	112	94	79.7	55	210	156	60	104	8	8.8
Person	61	1455	143	35.9	276	95	28	75.7	17	204	86	29	67	10	6.7
Williams	72	1314	165	44.8	2	1	122	67.0	67	179	89	34	82	24	6.3
Perdue	79	1491	162	54.9	1	0	70	52.6	177	535	57	22	81	50	5.0
Rose	53	429	59	43.4	3	1	39	63.9	40	90	19	21	44	7	3.0
Herrera	58	516	76	43.4	1	0	18	40.9	24	91	22	19	38	12	2.9
Geary	62	685	56	33.1	40	12	28	50.0	19	67	74	37	42	12	2.5
Lohaus	9	102	7	33.3	14	4	1	33.3	3	12	5	1	3	2	2.1
Burton	13	43	8	38.1	9	3	8	66.7	3	9	1	2	1	2	2.1
Spurs	82	19,830	2,898	46.8	863	302	1,489	68.8	984	3,622	1,839	517	1,318	568	92.5
Opponents	82	19,830	2,737	41.1	1,029	338	1,448	74.0	1,017	3,253	1,556	730	1,046	378	88.5

Seattle SuperSonics

Player	GP	Min	FGM	Pct	FGA	FGM	FTM	Pct	Off	Total	A	Stl	TO	BS	Avg
Baker	82	2944	631	54.2	7	1	311	59.1	286	656	152	91	174	86	19.2
Payton	82	3145	579	45.3	397	134	279	74.4	77	376	679	185	229	18	19.2
Schrempf	78	2742	437	48.7	147	61	297	84.4	135	554	341	60	168	19	15.8
Ellis	79	1939	348	49.7	274	127	111	78.2	51	184	89	60	74	5	11.8
Hawkins	82	2597	280	44.0	301	125	177	86.8	71	334	221	148	102	17	10.5
Perkins	81	1675	196	41.6	222	87	101	78.9	53	255	113	62	62	29	7.2
Kersey	37	717	97	41.6	10	1	39	60.0	56	135	44	52	36	14	6.3
Anthony	80	1021	150	43.0	159	66	53	66.3	18	111	205	64	91	3	5.2
Williams	65	757	115	52.3	1	0	66	77.6	48	147	14	19	50	38	4.6
McMillan	18	279	23	34.3	34	15	1	100.0	13	4	55	14	12	4	3.4
McIlvaine	78	1211	101	45.3	3	0	45	55.6	96	259	19	24	54	137	3.2
Cotton	9	33	8	38.1	4	0	8	88.9	2	6	0	1	6	1	2.7
Wingate	58	546	66	47.1	7	3	15	51.7	19	79	37	21	37	3	2.6
Zidek	12	64	7	24.1	2	1	14	87.5	4	17	2	0	4	2	2.4
Howard	13	53	8	38.1	0	0	9	50.0	6	12	3	3	6	1	1.9
SuperSonics	**82**	**19,755**	**3,052**	**47.3**	**1,571**	**621**	**1,521**	**72.1**	**932**	**3,157**	**1,983**	**804**	**1,159**	**374**	**100.6**
Opponents	**82**	**19,755**	**2,896**	**44.6**	**1,287**	**417**	**1,449**	**72.4**	**1,141**	**3,455**	**1,817**	**640**	**1,395**	**410**	**93.4**

Toronto Raptors

Player	GP	Min	FGM	Pct	FGA	FGM	FTM	Pct	Off	Total	A	Stl	TO	BS	Avg
Christie	78	2939	458	42.8	307	100	271	82.9	94	404	282	190	228	57	16.5
Wallace	82	2361	468	47.8	2	1	210	71.7	117	373	110	62	172	101	14.0
Camby	63	2002	308	41.2	2	0	149	61.1	203	466	111	68	134	230	12.1
Trent	54	1360	241	47.7	12	4	144	67.9	123	338	72	35	94	27	11.7
Billups	80	2216	280	37.4	325	107	226	85.0	62	190	314	107	174	4	11.2
Brown	72	1719	246	43.8	271	108	58	81.7	24	152	154	82	73	23	9.1
Slater	78	1662	211	46.0	0	0	203	63.0	134	305	74	45	102	30	8.0
McGrady	64	1179	179	45.0	41	14	79	71.2	105	269	98	49	66	61	7.0
Miller	64	1628	170	46.1	4	0	61	60.4	146	400	196	58	131	72	6.3
A.Williams	54	1071	125	44.3	28	9	65	72.2	24	81	103	38	58	3	6.0
Thomas	54	535	55	48.7	0	0	41	75.9	48	106	17	22	46	12	2.8
Wright	7	44	7	50.0	0	0	2	50.0	1	9	4	0	2	0	2.3
Garner	38	293	23	32.9	14	4	3	42.9	7	24	45	21	25	4	1.4
R. Rogers	15	106	9	36.0	0	0	2	33.3	8	17	3	5	8		1.3
Raptors	**82**	**19,330**	**2,965**	**43.5**	**1,086**	**372**	**1,479**	**71.8**	**1,187**	**3,336**	**1,746**	**769**	**1,371**	**662**	**94.9**
Opponents	**82**	**19,330**	**3,271**	**47.9**	**1,034**	**396**	**1,603**	**70.0**	**1,270**	**3,775**	**2,219**	**737**	**1,370**	**514**	**104.2**

Utah Jazz

Player	GP	Min	FGM	Pct	FGA	FGM	FTM	Pct	Off	Total	A	Stl	TO	BS	Avg
Malone	81	3030	780	53.0	6	2	628	76.1	189	834	316	96	247	70	27.0
Hornacek	80	2460	399	48.2	127	56	285	88.5	65	270	349	109	132	15	14.2
Stockton	64	1858	270	52.8	91	39	191	82.7	35	166	543	89	161	10	12.0
Russell	82	2219	226	43.0	214	73	213	76.6	78	326	101	90	81	31	9.0
Anderson	82	1602	269	53.8	32	2	136	73.5	86	227	89	66	92	18	8.3
Keefe	80	2047	229	54.0	0	0	162	81.0	179	438	89	52	71	24	7.8
Eisley	82	1726	229	44.1	118	48	127	85.2	25	166	346	54	160	13	7.7
Carr	66	1086	151	46.5	0	0	76	77.6	42	131	48	11	48	53	5.7
Foster	78	1446	186	44.5	9	2	67	77.0	85	273	51	15	68	28	5.7
Ostertag	63	1288	115	48.1	0	0	67	47.9	134	374	25	28	74	122	4.7
Morris	54	538	85	41.1	62	19	44	72.1	35	114	24	25	33	17	4.3
Vaughn	45	419	44	36.1	8	3	48	70.6	4	38	84	9	56	1	3.1
Jazz	**82**	**19,780**	**2,993**	**49.0**	**670**	**249**	**2,044**	**77.3**	**962**	**3,367**	**2,070**	**648**	**1,260**	**412**	**101.0**
Opponents	**82**	**19,780**	**2,806**	**43.9**	**1,122**	**401**	**1,730**	**75.7**	**983**	**2,995**	**1,690**	**645**	**1,157**	**422**	**94.4**

Vancouver Grizzlies

Player	GP	Min	Field Goals		3-Pt FG		Free Throws		Rebounds		A	Stl	TO	BS	Avg
			FGM	Pct	FGA	FGM	FTM	Pct	Off	Total					
Abdur-Rahim	82	2950	1347	48.5	51	21	502	78.4	227	581	213	89	257	76	22.3
Reeves	74	2527	941	52.3	4	0	223	70.6	196	585	155	39	156	80	16.3
Mack	57	1414	559	39.7	269	110	62	80.5	30	133	101	41	69	11	10.8
B. Edwards	81	1968	742	43.9	120	40	180	83.7	61	217	201	86	134	27	10.8
Daniels	74	1956	548	41.6	52	11	112	65.9	22	143	334	55	164	10	7.8
Lynch	82	1493	516	48.1	30	9	111	70.3	147	362	122	65	104	41	7.5
Masenburg	61	894	309	47.9	0	0	100	73.0	80	232	21	25	60	24	6.5
Smith	48	1053	194	47.9	1	0	65	63.1	120	306	88	41	51	15	5.2
Chilcutt	82	1420	359	43.5	130	54	39	66.1	77	306	104	53	62	37	4.9
Mayberry	79	1835	349	37.5	180	63	38	74.5	19	114	349	65	113	10	4.6
West	38	688	171	37.4	2	0	29	72.5	23	82	45	11	21	5	4.1
Hurley	61	875	238	39.1	22	5	59	77.6	12	66	177	23	86	0	4.1
Newbill	28	249	20	35.1	1	1	17	56.7	24	69	9	10	17	3	2.1
Grizzlies	**82**	**19,830**	**3,006**	**45.8**	**899**	**325**	**1,586**	**73.9**	**1,081**	**3,394**	**1,960**	**614**	**1,404**	**349**	**96.6**
Opponents	**82**	**19,730**	**3,230**	**47.5**	**1,111**	**428**	**1,634**	**73.2**	**1,144**	**3,503**	**2,101**	**836**	**1,163**	**536**	**103.9**

Washington Wizards

Player	GP	Min	Field Goals		3-Pt FG		Free Throws		Rebounds		A	Stl	TO	BS	Avg
			FGM	Pct	FGA	FGM	FTM	Pct	Off	Total					
Webber	71	2809	647	48.2	205	65	196	58.9	176	674	273	111	185	124	21.9
Howard	64	2559	463	46.7	2	0	258	72.1	161	449	208	82	185	23	18.5
Strickland	76	3020	490	43.4	48	12	357	72.6	112	405	801	126	266	25	17.8
Murray	82	2227	449	44.6	403	158	182	87.1	75	277	84	67	102	25	15.1
Cheaney	82	2841	448	45.7	53	15	139	64.7	82	324	173	96	104	36	12.8
Eackles	42	547	75	42.9	46	16	52	88.1	25	75	16	17	29	0	5.2
Whitney	82	1073	126	35.5	169	52	118	91.5	16	115	196	34	65	6	5.1
Davis	74	1705	127	49.6	1	0	69	58.0	209	480	30	41	56	24	4.4
Wallace	67	1124	85	51.8	0	0	35	35.7	112	324	18	61	28	72	3.1
Shammgod	20	146	19	32.8	2	0	23	76.7	2	7	36	7	21	1	3.1
Grant	65	895	75	38.3	6	1	19	63.3	60	168	39	23	26	15	2.6
Ham	71	635	55	52.9	0	0	35	47.3	72	131	16	21	37	25	2.0
Williams	14	111	13	76.5	0	0	0	0.0	16	26	3	2	2	3	1.9
Wizards	**82**	**19,805**	**3,080**	**45.2**	**944**	**320**	**1,489**	**69.1**	**1,119**	**3,457**	**1,900**	**689**	**1,157**	**379**	**97.2**
Opponents	**82**	**19,805**	**2,975**	**45.5**	**977**	**348**	**1,623**	**74.7**	**1,029**	**3,497**	**1,725**	**632**	**1,328**	**377**	**96.6**

1998 NBA Draft

The 1998 NBA Draft was held on June 24 in Vancouver.

First Round

1. Michael Olowokandi, LA Clippers
2. Mike Bibby, Vancouver
3. Raef LaFrentz, Denver
4. Antawn Jamison, Toronto (to Golden State)
5. Vince Carter, Golden State (to Toronto)
6. Robert Traylor, Dallas (to Milwaukee)
7. Jason Williams, Sacramento
8. Larry Hughes, Philadelphia
9. Dirk Nowitzki, Milwaukee (to Dallas)
10. Paul Pierce, Boston
11. Bonzi Wells, Detroit
12. Michael Doleac, Orlando
13. Keon Clark, Orlando
14. Michael Dickerson, Houston
15. Matt Harping, Orlando
16. Bryce Drew, Houston
17. Radoslav Nesterovic, Minnesota
18. Mirsad Turkcan, Houston
19. Pat Garrity (to Dallas, then Phoenix)
20. Roshown McLeod, Atlanta
21. Ricky Davis, Charlotte
22. Brian Skinner, LA Clippers
23. Tyronn Lue, Denver (to LA Lakers)
24. Felipe Lopez, San Antonio (to Vancouver)
25. Al Harrington, Indiana
26. Sam Jacobson, LA Lakers
27. Vladimir Stepania, Seattle
28. Corey Benjamin, Chicago
29. Nazr Mohammed, Utah (to Philadelphia)

Second Round

30. Ansu Sesay, Dallas
31. Ruben Patterson, LA Lakers
32. Rashard Lewis, Seattle
33. Jelani McCoy, Seattle
34. Shammond Williams, Chicago (to Atlanta)
35. Bruno Sundov, Dallas
36. Jerome James, Sacramento
37. Casey Shaw, Philadelphia
38. DeMarco Johnson, New York
39. Rafer Alston, Milwaukee
40. Korleone Young, Detroit
41. Cuttino Mobley, Houston
42. Miles Simon, Orlando
43. Jahidi White, Washington
44. Sean Marks, New York
45. Toby Bailey, LA Lakers
46. Andrae Patterson, Minnesota
47. Tyson Wheeler, Toronto
48. Ryan Stack, Cleveland
49. Cory Carr, Atlanta (to Chicago)
50. Andrew Betts, Charlotte
51. Corey Brewer, Miami
52. Derrick Dial, San Antonio
53. Greg Buckner, Dallas
54. Tremaine Fowlkes, Denver
55. Ryan Bowen, Denver
56. J.R. Henderson, Vancouver
57. Torrayne Braggs, Utah
58. Maceo Baston, Chicago

American Basketball League

Final Standings

WEST DIVISION

Team	W	L	Pct	GB
Portland	27	17	.613	—
Long Beach	26	18	.591	1
San Jose	21	23	.477	6
Colorado	21	23	.477	6
Seattle	15	29	.340	12

EAST DIVISION

Team	W	L	Pct	GB
Columbus	36	8	.818	—
New England	24	20	.545	12
Atlanta	15	29	.340	21
Philadelphia	13	31	.295	23

1998 Playoffs

FIRST ROUND

Feb 20	San Jose	80	at New England	78
Feb 22	New England	71	at San Jose	83

New England won series 2–0.

Feb 21	Colorado	72	at Long Beach	96
Feb 22	Long Beach	68	at Colorado	88
Feb 25	Colorado	61	at Long Beach	92

Long Beach won series 2–1.

SEMI-FINALS

Feb 27	Portland	62	at Long Beach	72
March 1	Long Beach	70	at Portland	69

Long Beach won series 2–0.

Feb 28	San Jose	88	at Columbus	94
March 9	Columbus	74	at San Jose	62

Columbus won series 2–0.

CHAMPIONSHIP SERIES

March 8	Columbus	62	at Long Beach	65
March 9	Columbus	61	at Long Beach	71
March 11	Long Beach	61	at Columbus	70

March 13	Long Beach	53	at Columbus	68
March 15	Long Beach	81	at Columbus	86

Columbus won series 3–2.

Women's National Basketball Association

Final Standings

EASTERN CONFERENCE

Team	W	L	Pct	GB
Cleveland	20	10	.667	—
Charlotte	18	12	.600	2
New York	18	12	.600	2
Detroit	17	13	.567	3
Washington	3	27	.100	17

WESTERN CONFERENCE

Team	W	L	Pct	GB
Houston	27	3	.900	—
Phoenix	19	11	.633	8
Los Angeles	12	18	.400	15
Sacramento	8	22	.267	19
Utah	8	22	.267	19

1998 Playoffs

SEMI-FINALS

Aug 22	Houston	85	at Charlotte	71
Aug 24	Charlotte	61	at Houston	77

Aug 22	Cleveland	68	at Phoenix	78
Aug 24	Phoenix	66	at Cleveland	67
Aug 25	Phoenix	71	at Cleveland	60

WNBA CHAMPIONSHIP

Aug. 27	Houston	51	at Phoenix	54
Aug. 29	Phoenix	69	at Houston	74
Sept. 1	Phoenix	71	at Houston	80

The New Cradle of Coaches?

When Frank Layden retired as coach of the Utah Jazz in 1988, the rotund clown prince of basketball figured two things were certain: He would never again be able to squeeze into an airplane seat, and he would never again coach in the pros.

Yet there was Layden on July 27, 1998, guiding the Utah Starzz to a 90–80 victory over the Phoenix Mercury in his WNBA coaching debut. Layden, 66, had been hired to replace the fired Denise Taylor. "I like teaching basketball, and I wanted to help the women's game grow," says Layden, who will remain the Jazz's president.

Layden isn't the only high-profile NBA figure in women's hoops. Four days later, the WNBA's Los Angeles Sparks elevated assistant coach and former NBA star Orlando Woolridge to replace fired coach Julie Rousseau. Erstwhile Dallas Mavericks coach Jim Cleamons has signed on to guide the Chicago Condors of the ABL in 1998–99, joining Boston Celtics legend and New England Blizzard coach K.C. Jones in that league.

Unlike Cleamons and Woolridge, Layden has no interest in coaching in the NBA. He lost 175 pounds since his non-salad days in the Show, and his goal is to transform the Starzz, who began the season losing 13 of 19 games, in similarly dramatic fashion. "One of the reasons I quit coaching in the NBA was because much of the fun had gone out of the game," Layden says. "I don't see that in this league."

NBA Champions

Season	Winner	Series	Runner-Up	Winning Coach
1946–47	Philadelphia	4–1	Chicago	Eddie Gottlieb
1947–48	Baltimore	4–2	Philadelphia	Buddy Jeannette
1948–49	Minneapolis	4–2	Washington	John Kundla
1949–50	Minneapolis	4–2	Syracuse	John Kundla
1950–51	Rochester	4–3	New York	Les Harrison
1951–52	Minneapolis	4–3	New York	John Kundla
1952–53	Minneapolis	4–1	New York	John Kundla
1953–54	Minneapolis	4–3	Syracuse	John Kundla
1954–55	Syracuse	4–3	Ft Wayne	Al Cervi
1955–56	Philadelphia	4–1	Ft Wayne	George Senesky
1956–57	Boston	4–3	St Louis	Red Auerbach
1957–58	St Louis	4–2	Boston	Alex Hannum
1958–59	Boston	4–0	Minneapolis	Red Auerbach
1959–60	Boston	4–3	St Louis	Red Auerbach
1960–61	Boston	4–1	St Louis	Red Auerbach
1961–62	Boston	4–3	LA Lakers	Red Auerbach
1962–63	Boston	4–2	LA Lakers	Red Auerbach
1963–64	Boston	4–1	San Francisco	Red Auerbach
1964–65	Boston	4–1	LA Lakers	Red Auerbach
1965–66	Boston	4–3	LA Lakers	Red Auerbach
1966–67	Philadelphia	4–2	San Francisco	Alex Hannum
1967–68	Boston	4–2	LA Lakers	Bill Russell
1968–69	Boston	4–3	LA Lakers	Bill Russell
1969–70	New York	4–3	LA Lakers	Red Holzman
1970–71	Milwaukee	4–0	Baltimore	Larry Costello
1971–72	LA Lakers	4–1	New York	Bill Sharman
1972–73	New York	4–1	LA Lakers	Red Holzman
1973–74	Boston	4–3	Milwaukee	Tommy Heinsohn
1974–75	Golden State	4–0	Washington	Al Attles
1975–76	Boston	4–2	Phoenix	Tommy Heinsohn
1976–77	Portland	4–2	Philadelphia	Jack Ramsay
1977–78	Washington	4–3	Seattle	Dick Motta
1978–79	Seattle	4–1	Washington	Lenny Wilkens
1979–80	LA Lakers	4–2	Philadelphia	Paul Westhead
1980–81	Boston	4–2	Houston	Bill Fitch
1981–82	LA Lakers	4–2	Philadelphia	Pat Riley
1982–83	Philadelphia	4–0	LA Lakers	Billy Cunningham
1983–84	Boston	4–3	LA Lakers	K.C. Jones
1984–85	LA Lakers	4–2	Boston	Pat Riley
1985–86	Boston	4–2	Houston	K.C. Jones
1986–87	LA Lakers	4–2	Boston	Pat Riley
1987–88	LA Lakers	4–3	Detroit	Pat Riley
1988–89	Detroit	4–0	LA Lakers	Chuck Daly
1989–90	Detroit	4–1	Portland	Chuck Daly
1990–91	Chicago	4–1	LA Lakers	Phil Jackson
1991–92	Chicago	4–2	Portland	Phil Jackson
1992–93	Chicago	4–2	Phoenix	Phil Jackson
1993–94	Houston	4–3	New York	Rudy Tomjanovich
1994–95	Houston	4–0	Orlando	Rudy Tomjanovich
1995–96	Chicago	4–2	Seattle	Phil Jackson
1996–97	Chicago	4–2	Utah	Phil Jackson
1997–98	Chicago	4–2	Utah	Phil Jackson

NBA Finals Most Valuable Player

1969.....Jerry West, LA	1980.....Magic Johnson, LA	1990.....Isiah Thomas, Det
1970.....Willis Reed, NY	1981.....Cedric Maxwell, Bos	1991.....Michael Jordan, Chi
1971.....Kareem Abdul-Jabbar, Mil	1982.....Magic Johnson, LA	1992.....Michael Jordan, Chi
1972.....Wilt Chamberlain, LA	1983.....Moses Malone, Phil	1993.....Michael Jordan, Chi
1973.....Willis Reed, NY	1984.....Larry Bird, Bos	1994.....Hakeem Olajuwon, Hou
1974.....John Havlicek, Bos	1985.....K. Abdul-Jabbar,	1995.....Hakeem Olajuwon, Hou
1975.....Rick Barry, GS	LA Lakers	1996.....Michael Jordan, Chi
1976.....JoJo White, Bos	1986.....Larry Bird, Bos	1997.....Michael Jordan, Chi
1977.....Bill Walton, Port	1987.....Magic Johnson, LA Lakers	1998.....Michael Jordan, Chi
1978.....Wes Unseld, Wash	1988.....James Worthy, LA Lakers	
1979.....Dennis Johnson, Sea	1989.....Joe Dumars, Det	

Most Valuable Player: Maurice Podoloff Trophy

Season	Player, Team	GP	Field Goals		3-Pt FG		Free Throws		Rebounds		A	Stl	BS	Avg
			FGM	Pct	FGM	Pct	FTM	Pct	Off	Total				
1955–56	Bob Pettit, StL	72	646	42.9	–	–	557	73.6	–	1,164	189	–	–	25.7
1956–57	Bob Cousy, Bos	64	478	37.8	–	–	363	82.1	–	309	478	–	–	20.6
1957–58	Bill Russell, Bos	69	456	44.2	–	–	230	51.9	–	1,564	202	–	–	16.6
1958–59	Bob Pettit, StL	72	719	43.8	–	–	667	75.9	–	1,182	221	–	–	29.2
1959–60	Wilt Chamberlain, Phil	72	1,065	46.1	–	–	577	58.2	–	1,941	168	–	–	37.6
1960–61	Bill Russell, Bos	78	532	42.6	–	–	258	55.0	–	1,868	264	–	–	16.9
1961–62	Bill Russell, Bos	76	575	45.7	–	–	286	59.5	–	1,891	341	–	–	18.9
1962–63	Bill Russell, Bos	78	511	43.2	–	–	287	55.5	–	1,843	348	–	–	16.8
1963–64	Oscar Robertson, Cin	79	840	48.3	–	–	800	85.3	–	783	868	–	–	31.4
1964–65	Bill Russell, Bos	78	429	43.8	–	–	244	57.3	–	1,878	410	–	–	14.1
1965–66	Wilt Chamberlain, Phil	79	1,074	54.0	–	–	501	51.3	–	1,943	414	–	–	33.5
1966–67	Wilt Chamberlain, Phil	81	785	68.3	–	–	386	44.1	–	1,957	630	–	–	24.1
1967–68	Wilt Chamberlain, Phil	82	819	59.5	–	–	354	38.0	–	1,952	702	–	–	24.3
1968–69	Wes Unseld, Balt	82	427	47.6	–	–	277	60.5	–	1,491	213	–	–	13.8
1969–70	Willis Reed, NY	81	702	50.7	–	–	351	75.6	–	1,126	161	–	–	21.7
1970–71	Kareem Abdul-Jabbar, Mil	82	1,063	57.7	–	–	470	69.0	–	1,311	272	–	–	31.7
1971–72	Kareem Abdul-Jabbar, Mil	81	1,159	57.4	–	–	504	68.9	–	1,346	370	–	–	34.8
1972–73	Dave Cowens, Bos	82	740	45.2	–	–	204	77.9	–	1,329	333	–	–	20.5
1973–74	Kareem Abdul-Jabbar, Mil	81	948	53.9	–	–	295	70.2	287	1,178	386	112	283	27.0
1974–75	Bob McAdoo, Buff	82	1,095	51.2	–	–	641	80.5	307	1,155	179	92	174	34.5
1975–76	Kareem Abdul-Jabbar, LA	82	914	52.9	–	–	447	70.3	272	1,383	413	119	338	37.7
1976–77	Kareem Abdul-Jabbar, LA	82	888	57.9	–	–	376	70.1	266	1,090	319	101	261	26.2
1977–78	Bill Walton, Port	58	460	52.2	–	–	177	72.0	118	766	291	60	146	18.9
1978–79	Moses Malone, Hou	82	716	54.0	–	–	599	73.9	587	1,444	147	79	119	24.8
1979–80	Kareem Abdul-Jabbar, LA	82	835	60.4	0	00.0	364	76.5	190	886	371	81	280	24.8
1980–81	Julius Erving, Phil	82	794	52.1	4	22.2	422	78.7	244	657	364	173	147	24.6
1981–82	Moses Malone, Hou	81	945	51.9	0	00.0	630	76.2	558	1,188	142	76	125	31.1
1982–83	Moses Malone, Phil	78	654	50.1	0	00.0	600	76.1	445	1,194	101	89	157	24.5
1983–84	Larry Bird, Bos	79	758	49.2	18	24.7	374	88.8	181	796	520	144	69	24.2
1984–85	Larry Bird, Bos	80	918	52.2	56	42.7	403	88.2	164	842	531	129	98	28.7
1985–86	Larry Bird, Bos	82	796	49.6	82	42.3	441	89.6	190	805	557	166	51	25.8
1986–87	Magic Johnson, LA Lakers	80	683	52.2	8	20.5	535	84.8	122	504	977	138	36	23.9
1987–88	Michael Jordan, Chi	82	1,069	53.5	7	13.2	723	84.1	139	449	485	259	131	35.0
1988–89	Magic Johnson, LA Lakers	77	579	50.9	59	31.4	513	91.1	111	607	988	138	22	22.5
1989–90	Magic Johnson, LA Lakers	79	546	48.0	106	38.4	567	89.0	128	522	907	132	34	22.3
1990–91	Michael Jordan, Chi	82	990	53.9	29	31.2	571	85.1	118	492	453	223	83	31.5
1991–92	Michael Jordan, Chi	80	943	51.9	27	27.0	491	83.2	91	511	489	182	75	30.1
1992–93	Charles Barkley, Phoe	76	716	52.0	67	30.5	445	76.5	237	928	385	119	74	25.6
1993–94	Hakeem Olajuwon, Hou	80	894	52.8	8	42.1	388	71.6	229	955	287	128	297	27.3
1994–95	David Robinson, SA	81	788	53.0	6	30.0	656	77.4	234	877	236	134	262	27.6
1995–96	Michael Jordan, Chi	82	916	49.5	111	42.7	548	83.4	148	543	352	180	42	30.4
1996–97	Karl Malone, Utah	82	864	55.0	0	00.0	521	75.5	193	809	368	113	48	27.4
1997–98	Michael Jordan, Chi	82	881	46.5	30	23.8	565	78.4	130	475	283	141	45	28.7

Coach of the Year: Arnold "Red" Auerbach Trophy

1962–63	Harry Gallatin, StL	1980–81	Jack McKinney, Ind
1963–64	Alex Hannum, SF	1981–82	Gene Shue, Wash
1964–65	Red Auerbach, Bos	1982–83	Don Nelson, Mil
1965–66	Dolph Schayes, Phil	1983–84	Frank Layden, Utah
1966–67	Johnny Kerr, Chi	1984–85	Don Nelson, Mil
1967–68	Richie Guerin, StL	1985–86	Mike Fratello, Atl
1968–69	Gene Shue, Balt	1986–87	Mike Schuler, Port
1969–70	Red Holzman, NY	1987–88	Doug Moe, Den
1970–71	Dick Motta, Chi	1988–89	Cotton Fitzsimmons, Phoe
1971–72	Bill Sharman, LA	1989–90	Pat Riley, LA Lakers
1972–73	Tom Heinsohn, Bos	1990–91	Don Chaney, Hou
1973–74	Ray Scott, Det	1991–92	Don Nelson, GS
1974–75	Phil Johnson, KC-Oma	1992–93	Pat Riley, NY
1975–76	Bill Fitch, Clev	1993–94	Lenny Wilkens, Atl
1976–77	Tom Nissalke, Hou	1994–95	Del Harris, LA Lakers
1977–78	Hubie Brown, Atl	1995–96	Phil Jackson, Chi
1978–79	Cotton Fitzsimmons, KC	1996–97	Pat Riley, Mia
1979–80	Bill Fitch, Bos	1997–98	Larry Bird, Ind

Note: Award named after Auerbach in 1986.

Rookie of the Year: Eddie Gottlieb Trophy

1952–53...Don Meineke, FW
1953–54...Ray Felix, Balt
1954–55...Bob Pettit, Mil
1955–56...Maurice Stokes, Roch
1956–57...Tom Heinsohn, Bos
1957–58...Woody Sauldsberry, Phil
1958–59...Elgin Baylor, Minn
1959–60...Wilt Chamberlain, Phil
1960–61...Oscar Robertson, Cin
1961–62...Walt Bellamy, Chi
1962–63...Terry Dischinger, Chi
1963–64...Jerry Lucas, Cin
1964–65...Willis Reed, NY
1965–66...Rick Barry, SF
1966–67...Dave Bing, Det
1967–68...Earl Monroe, Balt
1968–69...Wes Unseld, Balt

1969–70...K. Abdul-Jabbar, Mil
1970–71...Dave Cowens, Bos
           Geoff Petrie, Port
1971–72...Sidney Wicks, Port
1972–73...Bob McAdoo, Buff
1973–74...Ernie DiGregorio, Buff
1974–75...Keith Wilkes, GS
1975–76...Alvan Adams, Phoe
1976–77...Adrian Dantley, Buff
1977–78...Walter Davis, Phoe
1978–79...Phil Ford, KC
1979–80...Larry Bird, Bos
1980–81...Darrell Griffith, Utah
1981–82...Buck Williams, NJ
1982–83...Terry Cummings, SD
1983–84...Ralph Sampson, Hou
1984–85...Michael Jordan, Chi

1985–86...Patrick Ewing, NY
1986–87...Chuck Person, Ind
1987–88...Mark Jackson, NY
1988–89...Mitch Richmond, GS
1989–90...David Robinson, SA
1990–91...Derrick Coleman, NJ
1991–92...Larry Johnson, Char
1992–93...Shaquille O'Neal, Orl
1993–94...Chris Webber, GS
1994–95...Jason Kidd, Dal
           Grant Hill, Det
1995–96...Damon Stoudamire, Tor
1996–97...Allen Iverson, Phil
1997–98...Tim Duncan, SA

Defensive Player of the Year

1982–83...Sidney Moncrief, Mil
1983–84...Sidney Moncrief, Mil
1984–85...Mark Eaton, Utah
1985–86...Alvin Robertson, SA
1986–87...Michael Cooper, LA
           Lakers

1987–88...Michael Jordan, Chi
1988–89...Mark Eaton, Utah
1989–90...Dennis Rodman, Det
1990–91...Dennis Rodman, Det
1991–92...David Robinson, SA
1992–93...Hakeem Olajuwon, Hou

1993–94...Hakeem Olajuwon, Hou
1994–95...Dikembe Mutombo, Den
1995–96...Gary Payton, Sea
1996–97...Dikembe Mutombo, Den
1997–98...Dikembe Mutombo, Atl

Sixth Man Award

1982–83...Bobby Jones, Phil
1983–84...Kevin McHale, Bos
1984–85...Kevin McHale, Bos
1985–86...Bill Walton, Bos
1986–87...Ricky Pierce, Mil
1987–88...Roy Tarpley, Dall

1988–89...Eddie Johnson, Phoe
1989–90...Ricky Pierce, Mil
1990–91...Detlef Schrempf, Ind
1991–92...Detlef Schrempf, Ind
1992–93...Cliff Robinson, Port
1993–94...Dell Curry, Char

1994–95...Anthony Mason, NY
1995–96...Toni Kukoc, Chi
1996–97...John Starks, NY
1997–98...Danny Manning, Phoe

J. Walter Kennedy Citizenship Award

1974–75...Wes Unseld, Wash
1975–76...Slick Watts, Sea
1976–77...Dave Bing, Wash
1977–78...Bob Lanier, Det
1978–79...Calvin Murphy, Hou
1979–80...Austin Carr, Clev
1980–81...Mike Glenn, NY
1981–82...Kent Benson, Det
1982–83...Julius Erving, Phil

1983–84...Frank Layden, Utah
1984–85...Dan Issel, Den
1985–86...Michael Cooper, LA
           Lakers
           Rory Sparrow, NY
1986–87...Isiah Thomas, Det
1987–88...Alex English, Den
1988–89...Thurl Bailey, Utah
1989–90...Glenn Rivers, Atl

1990–91...Kevin Johnson, Phoe
1991–92...Magic Johnson, LA
           Lakers
1992–93...Terry Porter, Port
1993–94...Joe Dumars, Det
1994–95...Joe O'Toole, Atl
1995–96...Chris Dudley, Port
1996–97...P.J. Brown, Mia
1997–98...Steve Smith, Atl

Most Improved Player

1985–86...Alvin Robertson, SA
1986–87...Dale Ellis, Sea
1987–88...Kevin Duckworth, Port
1988–89...Kevin Johnson, Phoe
1989–90...Rony Seikaly, Mia

1990–91...Scott Skiles, Orl
1991–92...Pervis Ellison, Wash
1992–93...Chris Jackson, Den
1993–94...Don MacLean, Wash
1994–95...Dana Barros, Phil

1995–96...Gheorghe Muresan,
           Wash
1996–97...Isaac Austin, Mia
1997–98...Alan Henderson, Atl

Executive of the Year

1972–73...Joe Axelson, KC-Oma
1973–74...Eddie Donovan, Buff
1974–75...Dick Vertlieb, GS
1975–76...Jerry Colangelo, Phoe
1976–77...Ray Patterson, Hou
1977–78...Angelo Drossos, SA
1978–79...Bob Ferry, Wash
1979–80...Red Auerbach, Bos
1980–81...Jerry Colangelo, Phoe
1981–82...Bob Ferry, Wash

1982–83...Zollie Volchok, Sea
1983–84...Frank Layden, Utah
1984–85...Vince Boryla, Den
1985–86...Stan Kasten, Atl
1986–87...Stan Kasten, Atl
1987–88...Jerry Krause, Chi
1988–89...Jerry Colangelo, Phoe
1989–90...Bob Bass, SA
1990–91...Bucky Buckwalter, Port
1991–92...Wayne Embry, Clev

1992–93...Jerry Colangelo, Phoe
1993–94...Bob Whitsitt, Sea
1994–95...Jerry West, LA Lakers
1995–96...Jerry Krause, Chi
1996–97...Bob Bass, Char
1997–98...Wayne Embry, Clev

Selected by *The Sporting News.*

Scoring

MOST POINTS, CAREER

	Pts	Avg
Kareem Abdul-Jabbar	38,387	24.6
Wilt Chamberlain	31,419	30.1
Michael Jordan	29,277	31.5
Karl Malone	27,782	26.2
Moses Malone	27,409	20.6
Elvin Hayes	27,313	21.0
Oscar Robertson	26,710	25.7
Dominique Wilkins	26,534	25.3
John Havlicek	26,395	20.8
Alex English	25,613	21.5

MOST POINTS, SEASON

Wilt Chamberlain, Phil	4,029	1961–62
Wilt Chamberlain, SF	3,586	1962–63
Michael Jordan, Chi	3,041	1986–87
Wilt Chamberlain, Phil	3,033	1960–61
Wilt Chamberlain, SF	2,948	1963–64
Michael Jordan, Chi	2,868	1987–88
Bob McAdoo, Buff	2,831	1974–75
Rick Barry, SF	2,775	1966–67
Michael Jordan, Chi	2,753	1989–90
Elgin Baylor, LA	2,719	1962–63

HIGHEST SCORING AVERAGE, CAREER

Michael Jordan	31.5	930 games
Wilt Chamberlain	30.1	1,045 games
Elgin Baylor	27.4	846 games
Shaquille O'Neal	27.2	406 games
Jerry West	27.0	932 games
Bob Pettit	26.4	792 games
Karl Malone	26.2	1,061 games
George Gervin	26.2	791 games
Oscar Robertson	25.7	1,040 games
Dominique Wilkins	25.3	1,047 games

HIGHEST SCORING AVERAGE, SEASON

Wilt Chamberlain, Phil	50.4	1961–62
Wilt Chamberlain, SF	44.8	1962–63
Wilt Chamberlain, Phil	38.4	1960–61
Wilt Chamberlain, Phil	37.6	1959–60
Michael Jordan, Chi	37.1	1986–87
Wilt Chamberlain, SF	36.9	1963–64
Rick Barry, SF	35.6	1966–67
Michael Jordan, Chi	35.0	1987–88
Elgin Baylor, LA	34.8	1960–61

Note: Minimum 70 games.

MOST POINTS, GAME

Player, Team		Opp	Date
100	Wilt Chamberlain, Phil	NY	3/2/62
78	Wilt Chamberlain, Phil	LA	12/8/61
73	Wilt Chamberlain, Phil	Chi	1/13/62
73	Wilt Chamberlain, SF	NY	11/16/62
73	David Thompson, Den	Det	4/9/78
72	Wilt Chamberlain, SF	LA	11/3/62
71	David Robinson, SA	LAC	4/24/94
71	Elgin Baylor, LA	NY	11/15/60
70	Wilt Chamberlain, SF	Syr	3/10/63
69	Michael Jordan, Chi	Clev	3/28/90

Field-Goal Percentage

Highest Field-Goal Percentage, Career: .599—Artis Gilmore

Highest Field-Goal Percentage, Season: .727—Wilt Chamberlain, LA Lakers, 1972–73 (426/586)

Free Throws

HIGHEST FREE-THROW PERCENTAGE, CAREER

Mark Price	.907
Rick Barry	.900
Calvin Murphy	.892
Scott Skiles	.890
Larry Bird	.886

Note: Minimum 1200 free throws made.

HIGHEST FREE-THROW PERCENTAGE, SEASON

Calvin Murphy, Hou	.958	1980–81
Mahmoud Abdul-Rauf, Den	.956	1993–94
Mark Price, Clev	.948	1992–93
Mark Price, Clev	.947	1991–92
Rick Barry, Hou	.946	1978–79

MOST FREE THROWS MADE, CAREER

	No.	Yrs	Pct
Moses Malone	8,531	19	.769
Oscar Robertson	7,694	14	.838
Jerry West	7,160	14	.814
Karl Malone	7,133	13	.727
Dolph Schayes	6,979	16	.844

Three-Point Field Goals

Most Three-Point Field-Goals, Career: 1,596—Reggie Miller

Highest Three-Point Field-Goal Percentage, Career: .473—Steve Kerr

Most Three-Point Field Goals, Season: 267—Dennis Scott, Orl, 1995–96

Highest Three-Point Field-Goal Percentage, Season: .524—Steve Kerr, Chi, 1994–95

Most Three-Point Field Goals, Game: 11—Dennis Scott, Orlando vs Atlanta, 4/18/96

Note: First year of shot: 1979–80.

Steals

Most Steals, Career: 2,620—John Stockton

Most Steals, Season: 301—Alvin Robertson, San Antonio, 1985–86

Most Steals, Game: 11—Larry Kenon, San Antonio vs Kansas City, 12/26/76

Rebounds

MOST REBOUNDS, CAREER

	No.	Yrs	Avg
Wilt Chamberlain	23,924	14	22.9
Bill Russell	21,620	13	22.5
Kareem Abdul-Jabbar	17,440	20	11.4
Elvin Hayes	16,279	16	12.5
Moses Malone	16,212	19	12.2
Robert Parish	14,715	21	9.1
Nate Thurmond	14,464	14	15.0
Walt Bellamy	14,241	14	13.7
Wes Unseld	13,769	13	14.0
Jerry Lucas	12,942	11	15.6

MOST REBOUNDS, SEASON

Wilt Chamberlain, Phil	2,149	1960–61
Wilt Chamberlain, Phil	2,052	1961–62
Wilt Chamberlain, Phil	1,957	1966–67
Wilt Chamberlain, Phil	1,952	1967–68
Wilt Chamberlain, SF	1,946	1962–63
Wilt Chamberlain, Phil	1,943	1965–66
Wilt Chamberlain, Phil	1,941	1959–60
Bill Russell, Bos	1,930	1963–64
Bill Russell, Bos	1,878	1964–65
Bill Russell, Bos	1,868	1960–61

MOST REBOUNDS, GAME

	Player, Team	Opp	Date
55	Wilt Chamberlain, Phi	Bos	11/24/60
51	Bill Russell, Bos	Syr	2/5/60
49	Bill Russell, Bos	Phi	11/16/57
49	Bill Russell, Bos	Det	3/11/65
45	Wilt Chamberlain, Phil	Syr	2/6/60
45	Wilt Chamberlain, Phil	LA	1/21/61

Assists

MOST ASSISTS, CAREER

John Stockton	12,713
Magic Johnson	10,141
Oscar Robertson	9,887
Isiah Thomas	9,061
Mark Jackson	7,538

MOST ASSISTS, SEASON

John Stockton, Utah	1,164	1990–91
John Stockton, Utah	1,134	1989–90
John Stockton, Utah	1,128	1987–88
John Stockton, Utah	1,126	1991–92
Isiah Thomas, Det	1,123	1984–85

MOST ASSISTS, GAME: 30—Scott Skiles, Orlando vs Denver, 12/30/90

Blocked Shots

MOST BLOCKED SHOTS, CAREER

Hakeem Olajuwon	3,459
Kareem Abdul-Jabbar	3,189
Mark Eaton	3,064
Wayne (Tree) Rollins	2,542

MOST BLOCKED SHOTS, SEASON

Mark Eaton, Utah	456	1984–85
Manute Bol, Wash	397	1985–86
Elmore Smith, LA	393	1973–74

MOST BLOCKED SHOTS, GAME: 17—Elmore Smith, LA Lakers vs Portland, 10/28/73

NBA Alltime Playoff Leaders

Scoring

MOST POINTS, CAREER

	Pts	Yrs	Avg
Michael Jordan	5,987	13	33.4
Kareem Abdul-Jabbar	5,762	18	24.3
Jerry West	4,457	13	29.1
Larry Bird	3,897	12	23.8
John Havlicek	3,776	13	22.0
Magic Johnson	3,701	13	19.5
Karl Malone	3,691	13	26.9
Hakeem Olajuwon	3,674	13	27.0
Elgin Baylor	3,623	12	27.0
Wilt Chamberlain	3,607	13	22.5

*HIGHEST SCORING AVERAGE, CAREER

	Avg	Games
Michael Jordan	33.4	179
Jerry West	29.1	153
Hakeem Olajuwon	27.0	136
Elgin Baylor	27.0	134
George Gervin	27.0	59
Karl Malone	26.9	137
Shaquille O'Neal	26.7	58

HIGHEST SCORING AVERAGE, CAREER (Cont.)

	Avg	Games
Dominique Wilkins	25.8	55
Bob Pettit	25.5	88
Rick Barry	24.8	74

*Minimum of 25 games.

MOST POINTS, GAME

	Player, Team	Opp	Date
†63	Michael Jordan, Chi	Bos	4/20/86
61	Elgin Baylor, LA	Bos	4/14/62
56	Wilt Chamberlain, Phil	Syr	3/22/62
56	Michael Jordan, Chi	Mia	4/29/92
56	Charles Barkley, Phoe	GS	5/4/94
55	Rick Barry, SF	Phil	4/18/67
55	Michael Jordan, Chi	Clev	5/1/88
55	Michael Jordan, Chi	Phoe	4/16/95
55	Michael Jordan, Chi	Wash	4/27/97

†Double overtime game.

NBA Alltime Playoff Leaders (Cont.)

Rebounds

MOST REBOUNDS, CAREER

	No.	Yrs	Avg
Bill Russell	4,104	13	24.9
Wilt Chamberlain	3,913	13	24.5
Kareem Abdul-Jabbar	2,481	18	10.5
Wes Unseld	1,777	12	14.9
Robert Parish	1,765	16	9.6

MOST REBOUNDS, GAME

Player, Team	Opp	Date
41 .... Wilt Chamberlain, Phil	Bos	4/5/67
40 .... Bill Russell, Bos	Phi	3/23/58
40 .... Bill Russell, Bos	StL	3/29/60
*40 .... Bill Russell, Bos	LA	4/18/62

Three tied at 39.

*Overtime game.

Games played

Kareem Abdul-Jabbar	237
Danny Ainge	193
Magic Johnson	190
Robert Parish	184
Byron Scott	183

Assists

MOST ASSISTS, CAREER

	No.	Games
Magic Johnson	2,346	190
John Stockton	1,521	147
Larry Bird	1,062	164
Dennis Johnson	1,006	180
Isiah Thomas	987	111

MOST ASSISTS, GAME

Player, Team	Opp	Date
24 .... Magic Johnson, LA	Pho	5/15/84
24 .... John Stockton, Utah	LAL	5/17/88
23 .... Magic Johnson, LA	Port	5/3/85
22 .... Doc Rivers, Atl	Bos	5/16/88

Four tied at 21.

Appearances

Kareem Abdul-Jabbar	18
Robert Parish	16
Dolph Schayes	15
Clyde Drexler	15
Paul Silas	14
John Stockton	14
Buck Williams	14

NBA Season Leaders

Scoring

1946–47	Joe Fulks, Phil	1389	1972–73	Nate Archibald, KC-Oma	34.0
1947–48	Max Zaslofsky, Chi	1007	1973–74	Bob McAdoo, Buff	30.6
1948–49	George Mikan, Minn	1698	1974–75	Bob McAdoo, Buff	34.5
1949–50	George Mikan, Minn	1865	1975–76	Bob McAdoo, Buff	31.1
1950–51	George Mikan, Minn	1932	1976–77	Pete Maravich, NO	31.1
1951–52	Paul Arizin, Phil	1674	1977–78	George Gervin, SA	27.2
1952–53	Neil Johnston, Phil	1564	1978–79	George Gervin, SA	29.6
1953–54	Neil Johnston, Phil	1759	1979–80	George Gervin, SA	33.1
1954–55	Neil Johnston, Phil	1631	1980–81	Adrian Dantley, Utah	30.7
1955–56	Bob Pettit, StL	1849	1981–82	George Gervin, SA	32.3
1956–57	Paul Arizin, Phil	1817	1982–83	Alex English, Den	28.4
1957–58	George Yardley, Det	2001	1983–84	Adrian Dantley, Utah	30.6
1958–59	Bob Pettit, StL	2105	1984–85	Bernard King, NY	32.9
1959–60	Wilt Chamberlain, Phil	2707	1985–86	Dominique Wilkins, Atl	30.3
1960–61	Wilt Chamberlain, Phil	3033	1986–87	Michael Jordan, Chi	37.1
1961–62	Wilt Chamberlain, Phil	4029	1987–88	Michael Jordan, Chi	35.0
1962–63	Wilt Chamberlain, SF	3586	1988–89	Michael Jordan, Chi	32.5
1963–64	Wilt Chamberlain, SF	2948	1989–90	Michael Jordan, Chi	33.6
1964–65	Wilt Chamberlain, SF-Phil	2534	1990–91	Michael Jordan, Chi	31.5
1965–66	Wilt Chamberlain, Phil	2649	1991–92	Michael Jordan, Chi	30.1
1966–67	Rick Barry, SF	2775	1992–93	Michael Jordan, Chi	32.6
1967–68	Dave Bing, Det	2142	1993–94	David Robinson, SA	29.8
1968–69	Elvin Hayes, SD	2327	1994–95	Shaquille O'Neal, Orl	29.3
1969–70	Jerry West, LA	*31.2	1995–96	Michael Jordan, Chi	30.4
1970–71	Kareem Abdul-Jabbar, Mil	31.7	1996–97	Michael Jordan, Chi	29.6
1971–72	Kareem Abdul-Jabbar, Mil	34.8	1997–98	Michael Jordan, Chi	28.7

*Based on per game average since 1969–70.

Rebounding

1950–51	Dolph Schayes, Syr	1080	1955–56	Bob Pettit, StL	1164
1951–52	Larry Foust, FW	880	1956–57	Maurice Stokes, Roch	1256
	Mel Hutchins, Mil	880	1957–58	Bill Russell, Bos	1564
1952–53	George Mikan, Minn	1007	1958–59	Bill Russell, Bos	1612
1953–54	Harry Gallatin, NY	1098	1959–60	Wilt Chamberlain, Phil	1941
1954–55	Neil Johnston, Phil	1085	1960–61	Wilt Chamberlain, Phil	2149

Rebounding (Cont.)

1961–62	Wilt Chamberlain, Phil	2052	1980–81	Moses Malone, Hou	14.8
1962–63	Wilt Chamberlain, SF	1946	1981–82	Moses Malone, Hou	14.7
1963–64	Bill Russell, Bos	1930	1982–83	Moses Malone, Phil	15.3
1964–65	Bill Russell, Bos	1878	1983–84	Moses Malone, Phil	13.4
1965–66	Wilt Chamberlain, Phil	1943	1984–85	Moses Malone, Phil	13.1
1966–67	Wilt Chamberlain, Phil	1957	1985–86	Bill Laimbeer, Det	13.1
1967–68	Wilt Chamberlain, Phil	1952	1986–87	Charles Barkley, Phil	14.6
1968–69	Wilt Chamberlain, LA	1712	1987–88	Michael Cage, LA Clippers	13.0
1969–70	Elvin Hayes, SD	*16.9	1988–89	Hakeem Olajuwon, Hou	13.5
1970–71	Wilt Chamberlain, LA	18.2	1989–90	Hakeem Olajuwon, Hou	14.0
1971–72	Wilt Chamberlain, LA	19.2	1990–91	David Robinson, SA	13.0
1972–73	Wilt Chamberlain, LA	18.6	1991–92	Dennis Rodman, Det	18.7
1973–74	Elvin Hayes, Capital	18.1	1992–93	Dennis Rodman, Det	18.3
1974–75	Wes Unseld, Wash	14.8	1993–94	Dennis Rodman, SA	17.3
1975–76	Kareem Abdul-Jabbar, LA	16.9	1994–95	Dennis Rodman, SA	16.8
1976–77	Bill Walton, Port	14.4	1995–96	Dennis Rodman, Chi	14.9
1977–78	Len Robinson, NO	15.7	1996–97	Dennis Rodman, Chi	16.1
1978–79	Moses Malone, Hou	17.6	1997–98	Dennis Rodman, Chi	15.0
1979–80	Swen Nater, SD	15.0			

*Based on per game average since 1969–70.

Assists

1946–47	Ernie Calverly, Prov	202	1972–73	Nate Archibald, KC-Oma	11.4
1947–48	Howie Dallmar, Phil	120	1973–74	Ernie DiGregorio, Buff	8.2
1948–49	Bob Davies, Roch	321	1974–75	Kevin Porter, Wash	8.0
1949–50	Dick McGuire, NY	386	1975–76	Don Watts, Sea	8.1
1950–51	Andy Phillip, Phil	414	1976–77	Don Buse, Ind	8.5
1951–52	Andy Phillip, Phil	539	1977–78	Kevin Porter, NJ-Det	10.2
1952–53	Bob Cousy, Bos	547	1978–79	Kevin Porter, Det	13.4
1953–54	Bob Cousy, Bos	578	1979–80	Micheal Richardson, NY	10.1
1954–55	Bob Cousy, Bos	557	1980–81	Kevin Porter, Wash	9.1
1955–56	Bob Cousy, Bos	642	1981–82	Johnny Moore, SA	9.6
1956–57	Bob Cousy, Bos	478	1982–83	Magic Johnson, LA	10.5
1957–58	Bob Cousy, Bos	463	1983–84	Magic Johnson, LA	13.1
1958–59	Bob Cousy, Bos	557	1984–85	Isiah Thomas, Det	13.9
1959–60	Bob Cousy, Bos	715	1985–86	Magic Johnson, LA Lakers	12.6
1960–61	Oscar Robertson, Cin	690	1986–87	Magic Johnson, LA Lakers	12.2
1961–62	Oscar Robertson, Cin	899	1987–88	John Stockton, Utah	13.8
1962–63	Guy Rodgers, SF	825	1988–89	John Stockton, Utah	13.6
1963–64	Oscar Robertson, Cin	868	1989–90	John Stockton, Utah	14.5
1964–65	Oscar Robertson, Cin	861	1990–91	John Stockton, Utah	14.2
1965–66	Oscar Robertson, Cin	847	1991–92	John Stockton, Utah	13.7
1966–67	Guy Rodgers, Chi	908	1992–93	John Stockton, Utah	12.0
1967–68	Wilt Chamberlain, Phil	702	1993–94	John Stockton, Utah	12.6
1968–69	Oscar Robertson, Cin	772	1994–95	John Stockton, Utah	12.3
1969–70	Len Wilkens, Sea	*9.1	1995–96	John Stockton, Utah	11.2
1970–71	Norm Van Lier, Cin	10.1	1996–97	Mark Jackson, Ind	11.4
1971–72	Jerry West, LA	9.7	1997–98	Rod Strickland, Wash	10.1

*Based on per game average since 1969–70.

Field-Goal Percentage

1946–47	Bob Feerick, Wash	40.1	1962–63	Wilt Chamberlain, SF	52.8
1947–48	Bob Feerick, Wash	34.0	1963–64	Jerry Lucas, Cin	52.7
1948–49	Arnie Risen, Roch	42.3	1964–65	Wilt Chamberlain, SF-Phil	51.0
1949–50	Alex Groza, Ind	47.8	1965–66	Wilt Chamberlain, Phil	54.0
1950–51	Alex Groza, Ind	47.0	1966–67	Wilt Chamberlain, Phil	68.3
1951–52	Paul Arizin, Phil	44.8	1967–68	Wilt Chamberlain, Phil	59.5
1952–53	Neil Johnston, Phil	45.2	1968–69	Wilt Chamberlain, LA	58.3
1953–54	Ed Macauley, Bos	48.6	1969–70	Johnny Green, Cin	55.9
1954–55	Larry Foust, FW	48.7	1970–71	Johnny Green, Cin	58.7
1955–56	Neil Johnston, Phil	45.7	1971–72	Wilt Chamberlain, LA	64.9
1956–57	Neil Johnston, Phil	44.7	1972–73	Wilt Chamberlain, LA	72.7
1957–58	Jack Twyman, Cin	45.2	1973–74	Bob McAdoo, Buff	54.7
1958–59	Ken Sears, NY	49.0	1974–75	Don Nelson, Bos	53.9
1959–60	Ken Sears, NY	47.7	1975–76	Wes Unseld, Wash	56.1
1960–61	Wilt Chamberlain, Phil	50.9	1976–77	Kareem Abdul-Jabbar, LA	57.9
1961–62	Walt Bellamy, Chi	51.9	1977–78	Bobby Jones, Den	57.8

Field-Goal Percentage *(Cont.)*

1978–79	Cedric Maxwell, Bos	58.4		1988–89	Dennis Rodman, Det	59.5
1979–80	Cedric Maxwell, Bos	60.9		1989–90	Mark West, Phoe	62.5
1980–81	Artis Gilmore, Chi	67.0		1990–91	Buck Williams, Port	60.2
1981–82	Artis Gilmore, Chi	65.2		1991–92	Buck Williams, Port	60.4
1982–83	Artis Gilmore, SA	62.6		1992–93	Cedric Ceballos, Phoe	57.6
1983–84	Artis Gilmore, SA	63.1		1993–94	Shaquille O'Neal, Orl	59.9
1984–85	James Donaldson, LA Clippers	63.7		1994–95	Chris Gatling, GS	63.3
1985–86	Steve Johnson, SA	63.2		1995–96	Gheorghe Muresan, Wash	58.4
1986–87	Kevin McHale, Bos	60.4		1996–97	Gheorghe Muresan, Wash	60.4
1987–88	Kevin McHale, Bos	60.4		1997–98	Shaquille O'Neal, LA Lakers	58.4

Free-Throw Percentage

1946–47	Fred Scolari, Wash	81.1		1972–73	Rick Barry, GS	90.2
1947–48	Bob Feerick, Wash	78.8		1973–74	Ernie DiGregorio, Buff	90.2
1948–49	Bob Feerick, Wash	85.9		1974–75	Rick Barry, GS	90.4
1949–50	Max Zaslofsky, Chi	84.3		1975–76	Rick Barry, GS	92.3
1950–51	Joe Fulks, Phil	85.5		1976–77	Ernie DiGregorio, Buff	94.5
1951–52	Bob Wanzer, Roch	90.4		1977–78	Rick Barry, GS	92.4
1952–53	Bill Sharman, Bos	85.0		1978–79	Rick Barry, Hou	94.7
1953–54	Bill Sharman, Bos	84.4		1979–80	Rick Barry, Hou	93.5
1954–55	Bill Sharman, Bos	89.7		1980–81	Calvin Murphy, Hou	95.8
1955–56	Bill Sharman, Bos	86.7		1981–82	Kyle Macy, Phoe	89.9
1956–57	Bill Sharman, Bos	90.5		1982–83	Calvin Murphy, Hou	92.0
1957–58	Dolph Schayes, Syr	90.4		1983–84	Larry Bird, Bos	88.8
1958–59	Bill Sharman, Bos	93.2		1984–85	Kyle Macy, Phoe	90.7
1959–60	Dolph Schayes, Syr	89.2		1985–86	Larry Bird, Bos	89.6
1960–61	Bill Sharman, Bos	92.1		1986–87	Larry Bird, Bos	91.0
1961–62	Dolph Schayes, Syr	89.6		1987–88	Jack Sikma, Mil	92.2
1962–63	Larry Costello, Syr	88.1		1988–89	Magic Johnson, LA Lakers	91.1
1963–64	Oscar Robertson, Cin	85.3		1989–90	Larry Bird, Bos	93.0
1964–65	Larry Costello, Phil	87.7		1990–91	Reggie Miller, Ind	91.8
1965–66	Larry Siegfried, Bos	88.1		1991–92	Mark Price, Clev	94.7
1966–67	Adrian Smith, Cin	90.3		1992–93	Mark Price, Clev	94.8
1967–68	Oscar Robertson, Cin	87.3		1993–94	Mahmoud Abdul-Rauf, Den	95.6
1968–69	Larry Siegfried, Bos	86.4		1994–95	Spud Webb, Sac	93.4
1969–70	Flynn Robinson, Mil	89.8		1995–96	Mahmoud Abdul-Rauf, Den	93.0
1970–71	Chet Walker, Chi	85.9		1996–97	Mark Price, GS	90.6
1971–72	Jack Marin, Balt	89.4		1997–98	Chris Mullin, Ind	93.9

Three-Point Field-Goal Percentage

1979–80	Fred Brown, Sea	44.3		1989–90	Steve Kerr, Clev	50.7
1980–81	Brian Taylor, SD	38.3		1990–91	Jim Les, Sac	46.1
1981–82	Campy Russell, NY	43.9		1991–92	Dana Barros, Sea	44.6
1982–83	Mike Dunleavy, SA	34.5		1992–93	B.J. Armstrong, Chi	45.3
1983–84	Darrell Griffith, Utah	36.1		1993–94	Tracy Murray, Por	45.9
1984–85	Byron Scott, LA Lakers	43.3		1994–95	Steve Kerr, Chi	52.4
1985–86	Craig Hodges, Mil	45.1		1995–96	Tim Legler, Wash	52.2
1986–87	Kiki Vandeweghe, Por	48.1		1996–97	Kevin Gamble, Sac	48.2
1987–88	Craig Hodges, Mil-Phoe	49.1		1997–98	Dale Ellis, Sea	46.0
1988–89	Jon Sundvold, Mia	52.2				

Steals

1973–74	Larry Steele, Por	2.68		1986–87	Alvin Robertson, SA	3.21
1974–75	Rick Barry, GS	2.85		1987–88	Michael Jordan, Chi	3.16
1975–76	Don Watts, Sea	3.18		1988–89	John Stockton, Utah	3.21
1976–77	Don Buse, Ind	3.47		1989–90	Michael Jordan, Chi	2.77
1977–78	Ron Lee, Phoe	2.74		1990–91	Alvin Robertson, Mil	3.04
1978–79	M.L. Carr, Det	2.46		1991–92	John Stockton, Utah	2.98
1979–80	Micheal Richardson, NY	3.23		1992–93	Michael Jordan, Chi	2.83
1980–81	Magic Johnson, LA	3.43		1993–94	Nate McMillan, Sea	2.96
1981–82	Magic Johnson, LA	2.67		1994–95	Scottie Pippen, Chi	2.94
1982–83	Micheal Richardson, GS-NJ	2.84		1995–96	Gary Payton, Sea	2.85
1983–84	Rickey Green, Utah	2.65		1996–97	Mookie Blaylock, Atl	2.72
1984–85	Micheal Richardson, NJ	2.96		1997–98	Mookie Blaylock, Atl	2.61
1985–86	Alvin Robertson, SA	3.67				

Blocked Shots

1973–74	Elmore Smith, LA	4.85	1986–87	Mark Eaton, Utah	4.06
1974–75	Kareem Abdul-Jabbar, Mil	3.26	1987–88	Mark Eaton, Utah	3.71
1975–76	Kareem Abdul-Jabbar, LA	4.12	1988–89	Manute Bol, GS	4.31
1976–77	Bill Walton, Port	3.25	1989–90	Hakeem Olajuwon, Hou	4.59
1977–78	George Johnson, NJ	3.38	1990–91	Hakeem Olajuwon, Hou	3.95
1978–79	Kareem Abdul-Jabbar, LA	3.95	1991–92	David Robinson, SA	4.49
1979–80	Kareem Abdul-Jabbar, LA	3.41	1992–93	Hakeem Olajuwon, Hou	4.17
1980–81	George Johnson, SA	3.39	1993–94	Dikembe Mutombo, Den	4.10
1981–82	George Johnson, SA	3.12	1994–95	Dikembe Mutombo, Den	3.91
1982–83	Wayne Rollins, Atl	4.29	1995–96	Dikembe Mutombo, Den	4.49
1983–84	Mark Eaton, Utah	4.28	1996–97	Shawn Bradley, NJ	3.40
1984–85	Mark Eaton, Utah	5.56	1997–98	Marcus Camby, Tor	3.65
1985–86	Manute Bol, Wash	4.96			

NBA All-Star Game Results

Year	Result	Site	Winning Coach	Most Valuable Player
1951	East 111, West 94	Boston	Joe Lapchick	Ed Macauley, Bos
1952	East 108, West 91	Boston	Al Cervi	Paul Arizin, Phil
1953	West 79, East 75	Ft Wayne	John Kundla	George Mikan, Minn
1954	East 98, West 93 (OT)	New York	Joe Lapchick	Bob Cousy, Bos
1955	East 100, West 91	New York	Al Cervi	Bill Sharman, Bos
1956	West 108, East 94	Rochester	Charley Eckman	Bob Pettit, StL
1957	East 109, West 97	Boston	Red Auerbach	Bob Cousy, Bos
1958	East 130, West 118	St Louis	Red Auerbach	Bob Pettit, StL
1959	West 124, East 108	Detroit	Ed Macauley	Bob Pettit, StL
				Elgin Baylor, Minn
1960	East 125, West 115	Philadelphia	Red Auerbach	Wilt Chamberlain, Phil
1961	West 153, East 131	Syracuse	Paul Seymour	Oscar Robertson, Cin
1962	West 150, East 130	St Louis	Fred Schaus	Bob Pettit, StL
1963	East 115, West 108	Los Angeles	Red Auerbach	Bill Russell, Bos
1964	East 111, West 107	Boston	Red Auerbach	Oscar Robertson, Cin
1965	East 124, West 123	St Louis	Red Auerbach	Jerry Lucas, Cin
1966	East 137, West 94	Cincinnati	Red Auerbach	Adrian Smith, Cin
1967	West 135, East 120	San Francisco	Fred Schaus	Rick Barry, SF
1968	East 144, West 124	New York	Alex Hannum	Hal Greer, Phil
1969	East 123, West 112	Baltimore	Gene Shue	Oscar Robertson, Cin
1970	East 142, West 135	Philadelphia	Red Holzman	Willis Reed, NY
1971	West 108, East 107	San Diego	Larry Costello	Lenny Wilkens, Sea
1972	West 112, East 110	Los Angeles	Bill Sharman	Jerry West, LA
1973	East 104, West 84	Chicago	Tom Heinsohn	Dave Cowens, Bos
1974	West 134, East 123	Seattle	Larry Costello	Bob Lanier, Det
1975	East 108, West 102	Phoenix	K.C. Jones	Walt Frazier, NY
1976	East 123, West 109	Philadelphia	Tom Heinsohn	Dave Bing, Wash
1977	West 125, East 124	Milwaukee	Larry Brown	Julius Erving, Phil
1978	East 133, West 125	Atlanta	Billy Cunningham	Randy Smith, Buff
1979	West 134, East 129	Detroit	Lenny Wilkens	David Thompson, Den
1980	East 144, West 135 (OT)	Washington	Billy Cunningham	George Gervin, SA
1981	East 123, West 120	Cleveland	Billy Cunningham	Nate Archibald, Bos
1982	East 120, West 118	New Jersey	Bill Fitch	Larry Bird, Bos
1983	East 132, West 123	Los Angeles	Billy Cunningham	Julius Erving, Phil
1984	East 154, West 145 (OT)	Denver	K.C. Jones	Isiah Thomas, Det
1985	West 140, East 129	Indiana	Pat Riley	Ralph Sampson, Hou
1986	East 139, West 132	Dallas	K.C. Jones	Isiah Thomas, Det
1987	West 154, East 149 (OT)	Seattle	Pat Riley	Tom Chambers, Sea
1988	East 138, West 133	Chicago	Mike Fratello	Michael Jordan, Chi
1989	West 143, East 134	Houston	Pat Riley	Karl Malone, Utah
1990	East 130, West 113	Miami	Chuck Daly	Magic Johnson, LA Lakers
1991	East 116, West 114	Charlotte	Chris Ford	Charles Barkley, Phil
1992	West 153, East 113	Orlando	Don Nelson	Magic Johnson, LA Lakers
1993	West 135, East 132	Salt Lake City	Paul Westphal	Karl Malone, Utah
				John Stockton, Utah
1994	East 127, West 118	Minneapolis	Lenny Wilkens	Scottie Pippen, Chi
1995	West 139, East 112	Phoenix	Paul Westphal	Mitch Richmond, Sac
1996	East 129, West 118	San Antonio	Phil Jackson	Michael Jordan, Chi
1997	East 132, West 120	Cleveland	Doug Collins	Glen Rice, Char
1998	East 135, West 114	New York	Larry Bird	Michael Jordan, Chi

Members of the Basketball Hall of Fame

Contributors

Senda Abbott (1984)
Forest C. (Phog) Allen (1959)
Clair F. Bee (1967)
Walter A. Brown (1965)
John W. Bunn (1964)
Bob Douglas (1971)
Al Duer (1981)
Clifford Fagan (1983)
Harry A. Fisher (1973)
Larry Fleisher (1991)
Edward Gottlieb (1971)
Luther H. Gulick (1959)
Lester Harrison (1979)
Ferenc Hepp (1980)
Edward J. Hickox (1959)

Paul D. (Tony) Hinkle (1965)
Ned Irish (1964)
R. William Jones (1964)
J. Walter Kennedy (1980)
Emil S. Liston (1974)
John B. McLendon (1978)
Bill Mokray (1965)
Ralph Morgan (1959)
Frank Morgenweck (1962)
James Naismith (1959)
Peter F. Newell (1978)
John J. O'Brien (1961)
Larry O'Brien (1991)
Harold G. Olsen (1959)
Maurice Podoloff (1973)

H. V. Porter (1960)
William A. Reid (1963)
Elmer Ripley (1972)
Lynn W. St. John (1962)
Abe Saperstein (1970)
Arthur A. Schabinger (1961)
Amos Alonzo Stagg (1959)
Boris Stankovic (1991)
Edward Steitz (1983)
Chuck Taylor (1968)
Oswald Tower (1959)
Arthur L. Trester (1961)
Clifford Wells (1971)
Lou Wilke (1982)

Players

Kareem Abdul-Jabbar (1995)
Nate (Tiny) Archibald (1991)
Paul J. Arizin (1977)
Thomas B. Barlow (1980)
Rick Barry (1987)
Elgin Baylor (1976)
John Beckman (1972)
Walt Bellamy (1993)
Sergei Belov (1992)
Dave Bing (1990)
Larry Bird (1998)
Carol Blazejowski (1994)
Bennie Borgmann (1961)
Bill Bradley (1982)
Joseph Brennan (1974)
Al Cervi (1984)
Wilt Chamberlain (1978)
Charles (Tarzan) Cooper (1976)
Kresimir Cosic (1996)
Bob Cousy (1970)
Dave Cowens (1991)
Joan Crawford (1997)
Billy Cunningham (1986)
Denise Curry (1997)
Bob Davies (1969)
Forrest S. DeBernardi (1961)
Dave DeBusschere (1982)
H.G. (Dutch) Dehnert (1968)
Anne Donovan (1995)
Paul Endacott (1971)
Alex English (1997)
Julius Erving (1993)
Harold (Bud) Foster (1964)
Walter (Clyde) Frazier (1987)
Max (Marty) Friedman (1971)
Joe Fulks (1977)
Lauren (Laddie) Gale (1976)
Harry (the Horse) Gallatin (1991)
William Gates (1989)

George Gervin (1996)
Tom Gola (1975)
Gail Goodrich (1996)
Hal Greer (1981)
Robert (Ace) Gruenig (1963)
Clifford O. Hagan (1977)
Victor Hanson (1960)
John Havlicek (1983)
Connie Hawkins (1992)
Elvin Hayes (1990)
Marques Haynes (1998)
Tom Heinsohn (1986)
Nat Holman (1964)
Robert J. Houbregs (1987)
Bailey Howell (1997)
Chuck Hyatt (1959)
Dan Issel (1993)
Harry (Buddy) Jeannette (1994)
William C. Johnson (1976)
D. Neil Johnston (1990)
K.C. Jones (1989)
Sam Jones (1983)
Edward (Moose) Krause (1975)
Bob Kurland (1961)
Bob Lanier (1992)
Joe Lapchick (1966)
Nancy Lieberman-Cline (1996)
Clyde Lovellette (1988)
Jerry Lucas (1979)
Angelo (Hank) Luisetti (1959)
C. Edward Macauley (1960)
Peter P. Maravich (1987)
Slater Martin (1981)
Branch McCracken (1960)
Jack McCracken (1962)
Bobby McDermott (1988)
Dick McGuire (1993)
Ann Meyers (1993)
George L. Mikan (1959)

Vern Mikkelsen (1995)
Cheryl Miller (1995)
Earl Monroe (1990)
Calvin Murphy (1993)
Charles (Stretch) Murphy (1960)
H. O. (Pat) Page (1962)
Bob Pettit (1970)
Andy Phillip (1961)
Jim Pollard (1977)
Frank Ramsey (1981)
Willis Reed (1981)
Arnie Risen (1998)
Oscar Robertson (1979)
John S. Roosma (1961)
Bill Russell (1974)
John (Honey) Russell (1964)
Adolph Schayes (1972)
Ernest J. Schmidt (1973)
John J. Schommer (1959)
Barney Sedran (1962)
Uljana Semjonova (1993)
Bill Sharman (1975)
Christian Steinmetz (1961)
Lusia Harris Stewart (1992)
David Thompson (1996)
John A. (Cat) Thompson (1962)
Nate Thurmond (1984)
Jack Twyman (1982)
Wes Unseld (1988)
Robert (Fuzzy) Vandivier (1974)
Edward A. Wachter (1961)
Bill Walton (1993)
Robert F. Wanzer (1987)
Jerry West (1979)
Nera White (1992)
Lenny Wilkens (1989)
John R. Wooden (1960)
George (Bird) Yardley (1996)

Coaches

Harold Anderson (1984)
Red Auerbach (1968)
Sam Barry (1978)
Ernest A. Blood (1960)
Howard G. Cann (1967)
H. Clifford Carlson (1959)

Lou Carnesecca (1992)
Ben Carnevale (1969)
Pete Carril (1997)
Everett Case (1981)
Jody Conradt (1998)
Denny Crum (1994)

Chuck Daly (1994)
Everett S. Dean (1966)
Antonio Diaz-Miguel (1997)
Edgar A. Diddle (1971)
Bruce Drake (1972)
Clarence Gaines (1981)

Note: Year of election in parentheses.

Coaches *(Cont.)*

Jack Gardner (1983)
Amory T. (Slats) Gill (1967)
Aleksandr Gomelsky (1995)
Alex Hannum (1998)
Marv Harshman (1984)
Don Haskins (1997)
Edgar S. Hickey (1978)
Howard A. Hobson (1965)
Red Holzman (1986)
Hank Iba (1968)
Alvin F. (Doggie) Julian (1967)
Frank W. Keaney (1960)
George E. Keogan (1961)

Bob Knight (1991)
John Kundla (1995)
Ward L. Lambert (1960)
Harry Litwack (1975)
Kenneth D. Loeffler (1964)
A.C. (Dutch) Lonborg (1972)
Arad A. McCutchan (1980)
Al McGuire (1992)
Frank McGuire (1976)
Walter E. Meanwell (1959)
Raymond J. Meyer (1978)
Ralph Miller (1988)
Aleksandar Nikolic (1998)

Jack Ramsay (1992)
Cesare Rubini (1994)
Adolph F. Rupp (1968)
Leonard D. Sachs (1961)
Everett F. Shelton (1979)
Dean Smith (1982)
Fred R. Taylor (1985)
Bertha Teague (1984)
Margaret Wade (1984)
Stanley H. Watts (1985)
Lenny Wilkens (1998)
John R. Wooden (1972)
Phil Woolpert (1992)

Referees

James E. Enright (1978)
George T. Hepbron (1960)
George Hoyt (1961)
Matthew P. Kennedy (1959)
Lloyd Leith (1982)
Zigmund J. Mihalik (1985)

John P. Nucatola (1977)
Ernest C. Quigley (1961)
J. Dallas Shirley (1979)
Earl Strom (1995)
David Tobey (1961)
David H. Walsh (1961)

Teams

Buffalo Germans (1961)
First Team (1959)
Original Celtics (1959)
Renaissance (1963)

Note: Year of election in parentheses.

ABA Champions

Year	Champion	Series	Loser	Winning Coach
1968	Pittsburgh Pipers	4–3	New Orleans Bucs	Vince Cazetta
1969	Oakland Oaks	4–1	Indiana Pacers	Alex Hannum
1970	Indiana Pacers	4–2	Los Angeles Stars	Bob Leonard
1971	Utah Stars	4–3	Kentucky Colonels	Bill Sharman
1972	Indiana Pacers	4–2	New York Nets	Bob Leonard
1973	Indiana Pacers	4–3	Kentucky Colonels	Bob Leonard
1974	New York Nets	4–1	Utah Stars	Kevin Loughery
1975	Kentucky Colonels	4–1	Indiana Pacers	Hubie Brown
1976	New York Nets	4–2	Denver Nuggets	Kevin Loughery

ABA Postseason Awards

Most Valuable Player

1967–68	Connie Hawkins, Pitt
1968–69	Mel Daniels, Ind
1969–70	Spencer Haywood, Den
1970–71	Mel Daniels, Ind
1971–72	Artis Gilmore, Ken
1972–73	Billy Cunningham, Car
1973–74	Julius Erving, NY
1974–75	Julius Erving, NY
	George McGinnis, Ind
1975–76	Julius Erving, NY

Rookie of the Year

1967–68	Mel Daniels, Minn
1968–69	Warren Armstrong, Oak
1969–70	Spencer Haywood, Den
1970–71	Charlie Scott, Vir
	Dan Issel, Ken
1971–72	Artis Gilmore, Ken
1972–73	Brian Taylor, NY
1973–74	Swen Nater, SA
1974–75	Marvin Barnes, StL
1975–76	David Thompson, Den

Coach of the Year

1967–68	Vince Cazetta, Pitt
1968–69	Alex Hannum, Oak
1969–70	Bill Sharman, LA
	Joe Belmont, Den
1970–71	Al Bianchi, Vir
1971–72	Tom Nissalke, Dall
1972–73	Larry Brown, Car
1973–74	Babe McCarthy, Ken
	Joe Mullaney, Utah
1974–75	Larry Brown, Den
1975–76	Larry Brown, Den

ABA Season Leaders

Scoring

	GP	Pts	Avg
1967–68...Connie Hawkins, Pitt	70	1875	26.8
1968–69...Rick Barry, Oak	35	1190	34.0
1969–70...Spencer Haywood, Den	84	2519	30.0
1970–71...Dan Issel, Ken	83	2480	29.4
1971–72...Charlie Scott, Vir	73	2524	34.6
1972–73...Julius Erving, Vir	71	2268	31.9
1973–74...Julius Erving, NY	84	2299	27.4
1974–75...George McGinnis, Ind	79	2353	29.8
1975–76...Julius Erving, NY	84	2462	29.3

Rebounds

1967–68................Mel Daniels, Minn	15.6
1968–69................Mel Daniels, Ind	16.5
1969–70................Spencer Haywood, Den	19.5
1970–71................Mel Daniels, Ind	18.0
1971–72................Artis Gilmore, Ken	17.8
1972–73................Artis Gilmore, Ken	17.5
1973–74................Artis Gilmore, Ken	18.3
1974–75................Swen Nater, SA	16.4
1975–76................Artis Gilmore, Ken	15.5

Assists

1967–68................Larry Brown, NO	6.5
1968–69................Larry Brown, Oak	7.1
1969–70................Larry Brown, Wash	7.1
1970–71................Bill Melchionni, NY	8.3
1971–72................Bill Melchionni, NY	8.4
1972–73................Bill Melchionni, NY	7.5
1973–74................Al Smith, Den	8.2
1974–75................Mack Calvin, Den	7.7
1975–76................Don Buse, Ind	8.2

Steals

1973–74................Ted McClain, Car	2.98
1974–75................Brian Taylor, NY	2.80
1975–76................Don Buse, Ind	4.12

Blocked Shots

1973–74................Caldwell Jones, SD	4.00
1974–75................Caldwell Jones, SD	3.24
1975–76................Billy Paultz, SA	3.05

World Championship of Basketball

Year	Winner	Runner-Up	Score	Site
1950 ....Argentina	United States	†	Rio de Janeiro
1954 ....United States	Brazil	†	Rio de Janeiro
1959 ....Brazil	United States	†	Santiago, Chile
1963 ....Brazil	Yugoslavia	†	Rio de Janeiro
1967 ....Soviet Union	Yugoslavia	†	Montevideo, Uruguay
1970 ....Yugoslavia	Brazil	†	Ljubljana, Yugoslavia
1974 ....Soviet Union	Yugoslavia	†	San Juan
1978 ....Yugoslavia	Soviet Union	82–81 (OT)	Manila
1982 ....Soviet Union	United States	95–94	Cali, Colombia
1986 ....United States	Soviet Union	87–85	Madrid
1990 ....Yugoslavia	Soviet Union	92–75	Buenos Aires
1994* ....United States	Russia	137–91	Toronto
1998 ....Yugoslavia	Russia	64–62	Athens

*U.S. professionals began competing in 1994. In 1998, the NBA labor dispute resulted in a boycott of the World Championship by NBA stars; the U.S. roster was filled by members of the CBA and European professional leagues and college players.
†Result determined by overall record in final round of competition.

THEY SAID IT

Clyde Drexler, Houston Rockets guard and, beginning in 1998, University of Houston basketball coach, after Michael Jordan asked if there was anything he could do to help Drexler in his new job:
"Send me your kids."

College Basketball

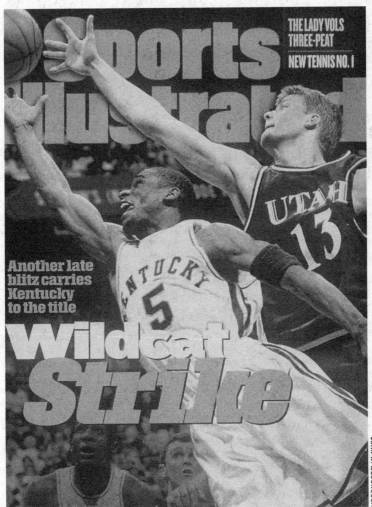

THE LADY VOLS THREE-PEAT

NEW TENNIS NO. 1

Another late blitz carries Kentucky to the title

Sports Illustrated

Wildcat Strike

JOHN W. MCDONOUGH

Rally Cats

A series of dramatic late-game comebacks propelled Kentucky to its second title in three years

BY KELLI ANDERSON

NOW IS THE time to praise the uniform designer who saw to it that the Kentucky Wildcats had *Kentucky* stitched on the seat of their pants this year, for the word's placement there provided both team identification and, so it seemed at times, modus operandi. By what method other than seat-of-the-pants could a team put itself in position to overcome double-digit deficits in three straight games on the way to its second NCAA title in three years? However they pulled off their tournament wins, the Wildcats were fun to watch; indeed, their backside billboard provided one other service, a clue to where we'd all be perched as we watched them play their final three games—on the edge of our seats.

The most remarkable thing about the Comeback Cats' rallies was that they hardly stood out in this year's surpassingly entertaining NCAA tournament. March Madness lived up to its name as never before as office pool sheets around the nation were quickly regretted and shredded. It didn't matter when or how often one clicked on the show, there was always a cliffhanger in progress; it was as though CBS was televising a *Perils of Pauline* marathon. Only the greedy could ask for

more thrills than these: Eight double-digit seeds beat their first-round opponents, and three—No. 13 Valparaiso, No. 11 Washington and No. 10 West Virginia—made it to the Sweet 16. Eleven games were decided by three points or less, five by a single point. There were four overtimes, and three players—Valparaiso's Bryce Drew, West Virginia's Jarrod West and Syracuse's Marius Janulis—who became instant legends by launching game-winning, buzzer-beating three pointers. And that was just in the first weekend.

What did all the early upsets tell us about the state of the game? "The only dividing line now is at one and two," said Purdue coach Gene Keady after his second-seeded Boilermakers escaped rounds 1 and 2 unthreatened by an upset. "You can take everyone three and up and throw 'em in a hat. They're all the same." As the tournament wore on, it became clear that Nos. 1 and 2 had been thrown into the hat as well. Though a two seed won the whole thing, it had to overcome two very tough threes to do it.

By the time the tournament boiled down to four teams, all led by coaches making their first appearance in the Final Four, it was clear that the alarmists who had been itching to write col-

Drew made his buzzer-beater in front of his father and coach, Homer (left).

lege basketball's obituary had it wrong. The absence of superstars, wrought largely by the lure of the NBA, had not diminished the game at all. Only one team at the Final Four had an All-America on its roster, and that team, North Carolina, would not be around for the final. The other three squads had all adjusted to the loss of a first-round NBA draft pick—Stanford's Brevin Knight, Utah's Keith Van Horn and Kentucky's Ron Mercer—by becoming consummatxe teams: fundamentally sound, unselfish, tight-knit and star-free.

Though the Final Four's surprise guests, Utah and Stanford, both began their seasons with 18 straight wins, there was little else in the regular season that predicted the unpredictable NCAA tournament that followed it. The top of the polls were dominated, as usual, by the eventual top seeds, Arizona, North Carolina, Kansas and Duke, which also happened to be the teams with all the first-team All-Americas and most of the other well-known talent.

Which is not to suggest that the 1997–98 season was ordinary. For one thing, it was bracketed by indictments in two point-shaving scandals. In December, four people involved in a point-shaving scheme at Arizona State in 1994 were indicted (two others pleaded guilty); in March, four people, including two former Northwestern players, were charged with conspiracy to commit sports bribery during Northwestern's 1994–95 season.

Like Northwestern and ASU, the

Player of the year Holdsclaw (23) led the Vols to a 39–0 season.

NCAA took a few public relations hits in the spring. One month after the organization made a $2.5 million settlement with Fresno State coach Jerry Tarkanian for a lawsuit he had filed in 1992 claiming persecution and harassment, it lost a five-year antitrust lawsuit and a whopping $67 million judgment to 1,900 assistant college coaches whose salaries had been found to be illegally restricted.

Two other landmark decisions worth noting: For the first time ever, there was a black head coach pacing Kentucky's sidelines, and for the first time in 37 years, there was no Dean Smith patrolling North Carolina's. After two NCAA titles, a record 879 wins and numerous coaching alcolytes launched into the basketball world, Smith retired in October; among the things he said he'd like to see happen to the game in the wake of his departure was the reinstatement of the freshman ineligibility rule. Mr. Smith's pronouncement aside, this season would have been a very different and less entertaining one without the prodigiously talented and confident rookies who ran teams from UCLA to Connecticut. Indiana, St. Louis and Tennessee made it to the NCAAs largely on the backs of their freshman stars, Luke Recker, Larry Hughes and Tony Harris, respectively.

Freshman Khalid El-Amin pushed UConn to the Elite Eight, the goal UCLA fell just short of when first-year star Baron Davis injured his knee.

Freshmen were also a big part of the biggest story—make that the only story—of the women's season. Two-time defending champion Tennessee entered the season with two-time All-America junior forward Chamique Holdsclaw and the top recruiting class in the nation, and they emerged four months later with a perfect 39–0 season, a third consecutive title and the consensus nod for greatest women's team of all time. Led by "the Three Meeks"—player of

PATRICK MURPHY-RACEY

the year Holdsclaw and precociously talented freshmen guard Semeka Randall and forward Tamika Catchings—the Lady Vols shredded a schedule that might have been the toughest in history. The Lady Vols won their 39 games by an average of 30.1 points, and 17 of their opponents were in the Top 25. They beat other Top 5 teams by an average of 17.8 points and crushed No. 17 Georgia by 59 points.

What distinguished this team from coach Pat Summitt's five previous championship teams—indeed from most past women's teams—was its speed and athleticism at every position. By employing a withering press, the Lady Vols forced 26.6 turnovers a game. Said Summitt, who had never relied on the full-court press in her 23 years at Tennessee, "I never knew the press could be so much fun."

Fun, of course, was not the primary experience of Lady Vols opponents, most of whom were just grateful to be done with the ordeal. "I haven't seen anyone who can beat them," said Florida coach Carol Ross after her team lost to the Big Orange by a big 39 points, "and I sure hope we don't have to play the team that can."

During the season, the Lady Vols had a few minor scares—they twice beat Alabama by less than 10 points—but they didn't create any real suspense for their fans until they met up with the equally quick North Carolina Tar Heels in the Mideast Regional finals in Nashville. With 7:35 left in the game, the Lady Vols were down by 12, the deepest hole they had been in that late in a game all season. Then a struggling Holdsclaw demonstrated why she is considered the most dominant player of any era: In those final minutes, she made all 10 of her free throws, hit two baskets from the field and made a crucial steal that led to the go-ahead bucket. "I didn't want to be the kind of player who chokes," said Holdsclaw after Tennessee's 76–70 win. "I was praying, Please let us get something done."

The Lady Vols got it all done at an anticlimactic Final Four in Kansas City, where they tore apart Arkansas 86–58 and beat by 93–75 a Louisiana Tech team that had begun the season as SI's top-ranked team. "We got beat by the best women's team I've personally ever seen," said 16-year Lady Techster coach Leon Barmore after his team folded. "Whatever they needed, they got it done."

If other coaches had harbored some small hope that the Tennessee juggernaut would be dismantled after the '98 season, it was crushed in Kansas City when Holdsclaw confirmed that she was not planning to become the first woman to challenge the professional leagues' no underclassmen rule. "We all get along great, we're winning," said Holdsclaw. "If we have the team that's considered the best this year, it's going to be better next year. We've got some recruits coming in."

Though Tennessee may well dominate the women's game for years to come, there will always be room for sideshows, as there was this year. When Connecticut's senior star Nykesha Sales continued a dubious tradition of sports gimmes by hobbling out on a ruptured Achilles tendon at the start of a game against Villanova on Feb. 24 to score a pre-arranged, uncontested layup and her school-record 2,178th point, she thought she was getting "a gift" from her coach, Geno Auriemma. Much to Sales's and Auriemma's surprise, a firestorm of protest broke out from all quarters, with every media outlet from the sports-radio station WFAN to *Time* magazine weighing in on whether this was simply "a nice gesture" by Auriemma or evidence that women don't compete as seriously as men.

The commentary, which ranged from thoughtful to insulting—Big East commissioner Mike Tranghese said he had approved Auriemma's plot because "men compete, get along and move on with few emotions, but women break down, get emotional"—didn't die down until about three weeks later, when another controversy broke out, after a women's second-round NCAA game between Alabama and UCLA. With .8 of a second remaining in the game and UCLA leading 74–73 at Alabama, officials started the clock late on the Tide's inbounds pass under their own basket. Addi-

BOB ROSATO

History maker: Smith delivered the goods in his first year at Kentucky.

about my desire for a national championship," Williams said after his latest disappointment. "I know one thing. I'm tired of grading these kinds of effects, these hurts."

Unlike Kansas, Kentucky was relatively unburdened by high expectations this year. In fact, rumor had it that former coach Rick Pitino left for the Celtics job after last season partly because he didn't think the Wildcats, who had sent six players to the NBA over the last two years but didn't currently have a sure lottery pick among them, had little chance to win this year. It did seem like a tall order, particularly for a new coach, Tubby Smith, who was under the microscope as the first black coach to run a team that hadn't welcomed its first black player until 1971.

Most of his best players had some hurdles to clear as well. Junior center Nazr Mohammed had come into the Kentucky program as an overweight freshman project and shed 75 pounds since; Scott Padgett had to sit out the '96 championship season after flunking out his freshman year; guard Jeff Sheppard had to sit out last season because of a glut of future lottery picks at his position; and Allen Edwards would lose his mother to breast cancer in February. "Every player on our team endured some kind of hardship," Mohammed would say later. That was part of the bond that knitted them into a group so tight they rotated roommates on road trips. There was also the rocky season they endured.

From the start, this didn't appear to be Kentucky's year. Smith abandoned Pitino's hallmark full-court defense early in the season and adopted a basic half-court, man-to-man "ball-line" approach

tionally, Alabama's Brittney Ezell violated the rules by running along the baseline before making her entry pass. Alabama got off a game-winning shot downcourt as a result. Though the NCAA admitted the officials blew it and banned them from the rest of the tournament, the tainted result stood. (The Tide went on to lose in the next round to Louisiana Tech.) Amid all the fist pounding, 16th-seed Harvard's 71–67 win over top-seeded but injury-riddled Stanford, the first such upset in the history of either the men's or women's tournament, caused barely a ripple.

No single upset in the men's tournament was historic; indeed a few of them were shocking mostly because of the way they echoed previous stunners. For the second year in a row, a highly seeded South Carolina team was knocked out in the first round; and No. 1–seed Kansas—a team loaded with two first-team All-Americas, Paul Pierce and Raef LaFrentz—departed in the second. It was the fourth time Roy Williams had failed to take a top-seeded Kansas team to the final eight. Was the program cursed, or had coach Williams just wanted an NCAA title too much? "I told the players I was sorry if I caused them problems by openly talking

because he recognized that these Wildcats weren't as athletic as last year's team—a diagnosis that was seconded at the November Maui Invitational by 1997 Final Four MVP Miles Simon after Arizona beat Kentucky 89–74 in a rematch of the '97 NCAA final. "Last year's [Kentucky] team was probably better than this year," observed Simon. "I think they've lost some quickness."

There would be other losses. For the first time since the 1988–89 season, the Cats were defeated three times at home—by lowly, 3–6 Louisville on Dec. 27, by Florida on Feb. 1 and by Mississippi—a team that hadn't won in Lexington since 1927—on Feb. 14. After that Valentine's Day heartbreak, Smith introduced a curfew and added 6 a.m. practices to the team's afternoon sessions. The Wildcats responded well, winning their next 10 games by an average of 20.7 points.

In the South Regional final, the second–seeded Cats met up with No. 1-seed Duke in a rematch of the storied 1992 East Regional final that the Blue Devils won, 104–103, on a last-second shot by center Christian Laettner. Like that Duke team, this one had much to recommend it, including a group of seasoned upperclassmen, the nation's most heralded freshman class, a 32–3 record and the nation's largest average margin of victory in the regular season (25.4 points). Most daunting of all, with 9:38 remaining in the game on March 22, the Dookies had a 17-point lead.

But Smith had instituted a practice drill for just such an occasion. Called "24 in two," the drill gives the Wildcats two minutes to make two dozen three-point shots. "It teaches our kids that they're never out of a game," Smith would say. With the coach hollering "24 in two" on the sideline, Kentucky whittled Duke's lead down to one in less than four minutes. The Wildcats took their first lead with 2:15 left to play, and when Duke's last-second shot bounced off the backboard, Kentucky had rallied and held on for an 86–84 win.

As thrilling as that comeback was, it paled next to the one Stanford pulled off in the last two minutes of the Midwest Regional final against Rhode Island. With the Cardinal down by eight and 2:05 on the clock, Arthur Lee, a former backup to NBAer Brevin Knight, sank two three-pointers, a lay-up and a free throw, then stripped the ball from the hands of Rhode Island's Cuttino Mobley and redirected it into those of Stanford's Mark Madsen, who made a dunk that put Stanford ahead for good in their stunning 79–77 win.

Still, few people expected the Cardinal, a team that hadn't been to a Final Four in 56 years, to give the Wildcats much trouble in San Antonio. Though Stanford had 10 players who logged at least 12 minutes a game, eight who were 6'7" or taller and five who could shoot 40% or better from beyond the arc, Kentucky had frontcourt depth to match, as well as an edge in rebounding and overall team agility.

So guess who was trailing by 10 with two and a half minutes gone in the second half? Even after the Wildcats had mounted their trademark comeback and pulled ahead of Stanford by four points with 1:10 remaining, they needed every second of overtime to squeeze out an 86–85 win. As both teams left the floor exhausted, they got a standing ovation from the coaches' section. "I thought we were going to come back and win," said Stanford's Lee, who made 26 points and a highlight-reel full of heroic plays. "It felt like it was happening all over again. It was so close. We just ran out of time."

Kentucky would find the going just as tough in the Final against Utah, a team that had saved its most overwhelming tournament victories for its most daunting opponents. After fairly pedestrian wins over San Francisco, Arkansas and West Virginia, the Utes shocked the nation by annihilating defending champion Arizona 76–51 in the Elite Eight using a triangle-and-two defense called "66."

Led by Andre Miller, a point guard from South Central L. A. who had had to endure his friends teasing him for going to, as he put it, "Mormonville, where everybody rides bikes and dresses in black suits and acts like Jehovah's Witnesses and stuff," the Utes continued their tear in San Antonio by dis-

locker room at halftime down by 10, outrebounded by 18 and unable to hit a three-point shot, it appeared that all that band-wagon-jumping had been justified, and that Utah, which had been knocked out of the previous two tournaments by Kentucky—first in the Sweet 16 and then in the Elite Eight—was about to enjoy some very sweet revenge.

But the Wildcats hadn't used up all their magic. Four minutes into the second half, they began to chip away at the Utes' lead by hitting threes and by putting so much pressure on Miller, one of only nine Utes to play in the game, that in the end the guard looked, according to Majerus, "like a punch-drunk fighter." As the Utes wilted—they made just eight baskets in the second half, and missed 15 of 18 in the last 11 minutes—Kentucky gained confidence, and the lead.

JOHN W. McDONOUGH

patching top-seeded North Carolina and player of the year Antawn Jamison, 65–59. Suddenly solid and stodgy Utah, a team that had stayed undefeated longer than any other but had remained off the national radar screen largely because of its repeated failure to make the nightly highlight shows—"What are they gonna say?" asked Utah coach Rick Majerus. 'Here's a down-screen and jump shot?'"—was on the brink of winning it all. Now they were considered one of the canniest, best prepared and most indomitable teams around.

And when the Wildcats went into the

The Cats dispensed with the nail-biting down the stretch this time, winning comfortably, 78–69, but their 10-point deficit after 20 minutes was the largest halftime lead any team had overcome to win a title game. "In '96 everyone knew we were going to win it," said Final Four MVP Sheppard, who added 16 points to his career-best 27 against Stanford. "We had so much talent, it was more of a relief when we won it. This year, it's pure joy."

As for next year? "I think," said Sheppard, "the guys need to work on not getting down by so much."

FOR THE RECORD · 1997-1998

NCAA Championship Game Box Score

Utah 69

UTAH	Min	FG M–A	FT M–A	Reb O–T	A	PF	TP
Mottola	28	4–10	6–6	4–8	0	4	15
Jensen	35	5–6	3–3	0–2	2	2	14
Doleac	34	5–12	4–6	5–10	1	2	15
Miller	37	6–15	4–7	2–6	5	5	16
Hansen	32	1–6	0–0	1–5	1	2	2
Johnsen	16	3–4	0–0	0–4	0	0	7
McTavish	3	0–0	0–0	0–0	2	1	0
Jackson	10	0–1	0–0	0–0	1	2	0
Caton	5	0–1	0–0	0–0	0	0	0
Totals	200	24–55	17–22	12–35	12	18	69

Percentages: FG—.436, FT—.773. 3-pt goals: 4–14, .286 (Mottola 1–3, Jensen 1–1, Doleac 1–1, Miller 0–3, Hansen 0–2, Johnsen 1–2, Jackson 0–1, Caton 0–1). Team rebounds: 4. Blocked shots: 2 (Doleac 2). Turnovers: 18 (Miller 8, Johnsen 3, Mottola 3, Hansen 2, Doleac, Jensen). Steals: 8 (Doleac 3, Hansen 3, Miller 2).
Halftime: Utah 41, Kentucky 31.   A: 40,509.
Officials: Burr, Gray, Sanzere.

Kentucky 78

KENTUCKY	Min	FG M–A	FT M–A	Reb O–T	A	PF	TP
Edwards	24	2–7	0–0	0–1	5	0	4
Padgett	33	6–11	4–4	2–5	1	4	17
Mohammed	13	5–9	0–0	0–2	0	4	10
Turner	27	2–5	2–4	0–2	4	0	6
Sheppard	34	7–14	2–2	2–4	3	1	16
Magloire	22	2–3	3–3	0–2	1	4	7
Evans	23	3–4	2–2	1–6	0	1	10
Mills	12	2–4	2–2	0–0	1	0	8
Smith	7	0–0	0–0	0–0	0	0	0
Bradley	5	0–0	0–0	0–1	0	1	0
Totals	200	29–57	15–17	5–23	15	15	78

Percentages: FG—.509, FT—.882. 3-pt goals: 5–17, .294 (Edwards 0–3, Padgett 1–5, Turner 0–1, Sheppard 0–2, Evans 2–2, Mills 2–4). Team rebounds: 1. Blocked shots: 6 (Magloire 3, Mohammed 2, Evans). 11 (Turner 5, Evans 3, Sheppard 2, Mohammed). Steals: 7 (Turner 3, Sheppard 2, Edwards, Evans).

Final AP Top 25

Poll taken before NCAA Tournament.

1. N Carolina	30–3	
2. Kansas	24–3	
3. Duke	29–3	
4. Arizona	26–3	
5. Kentucky	29–4	
6. Connecticut	29–4	
7. Utah	25–3	
8. Princeton	26–1	
9. Cincinnati	26–5	
10. Stanford	26–4	
11. Purdue	26–7	
12. Michigan	24–8	
13. Ole Miss	22–6	
14. S Carolina	23–7	
15. Texas Christian	27–5	
16. Michigan St	20–7	
17. Arkansas	23–8	
18. New Mexico	23–7	
19. UCLA	22–8	
20. Maryland	19–10	
21. Syracuse	24–8	
22. Illinois	22–9	
23. Xavier (OH)	22–7	
24. Temple	21–8	
25. Murray St	29–3	

National Invitation Tournament Scores

First round: Fresno St 73, Pacific 70; Memphis 90, Ball State 67; Hawaii 90, Arizona St 73; Georgia 100, Iowa 93; N Carolina St 59, Kansas St 39; Vanderbilt 73, St. Bonaventure 61; Wake Forest 56, NC-Wilmington 52; Minnesota 77, Colorado St 65; AL-Birmingham 93, Missouri 86; Marquette 80, Creighton 68; Auburn 77, Southern Miss 62; Penn St 82, Rider 68; Dayton 95, LIU-Brooklyn 92; Georgia Tech 88, Seton Hall 78; Georgetown 71, Florida 69; Gonzaga 69, Wyoming 55.
Second round: Fresno St 83, Memphis 80; Hawaii 78, Gonzaga 70; Georgia 61, N Carolina St 55; Vanderbilt 72, Wake Forest 68; Minnesota 79, AL-Birmingham 66; Marquette 75, Auburn 60; Penn St 77, Dayton 74; Georgia Tech 80, Georgetown 79.
Third round: Fresno St 85, Hawaii 83; Georgia 79, Vanderbilt 65; Minnesota 73, Marquette 71; Penn St 75, Georgia Tech 70.
Semifinals: Penn St 66, Georgia 60; Minnesota 91, Fresno St 89.
Championship: Minnesota 79, Penn St 72.
Consolation game: Georgia 95, Fresno St 79.

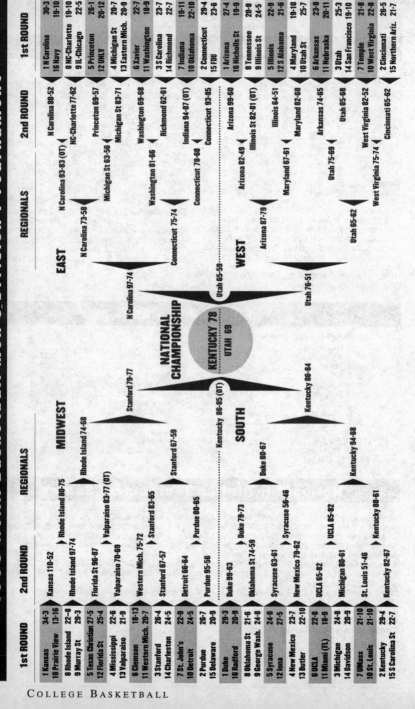

1998 NCAA Basketball Men's Division I Tournament

EAST

1st ROUND

1 N Carolina	30-3	
16 Navy	19-10	
8 NC-Charlotte	19-10	
9 IL-Chicago	22-5	
5 Princeton	26-1	
12 UNLV	20-12	
4 Michigan St.	20-7	
13 Eastern Mich.	20-9	
6 Xavier	22-7	
11 Washington	18-9	
3 S Carolina	23-7	
14 Richmond	22-7	
7 Indiana	19-11	
10 Oklahoma	22-10	
2 Connecticut	29-4	
15 FIU	23-6	

2nd ROUND

N Carolina 88-52
NC-Charlotte 77-62
Princeton 69-57
Michigan St 83-71
Washington 69-68
Richmond 62-61
Indiana 94-87 (OT)
Connecticut 93-85

REGIONALS

N Carolina 93-83 (OT)

Michigan St 63-56

N Carolina 73-58

Washington 81-66

Connecticut 75-74

Connecticut 78-68

N Carolina 97-74

Utah 65-59

WEST

1st ROUND

1 Arizona	27-4	
16 Nicholls St	19-9	
8 Tennessee	20-8	
9 Illinois St	24-5	
5 Illinois	22-9	
12 S Alabama	21-6	
4 Maryland	19-10	
10 Utah St	25-7	
6 Arkansas	23-8	
11 Nebraska	20-11	
3 Utah	25-3	
14 San Francisco	19-10	
7 Temple	21-8	
10 West Virginia	22-8	
2 Cincinnati	26-5	
15 Northern Ariz.	21-7	

2nd ROUND

Arizona 99-60
Illinois St 82-81 (OT)
Illinois 64-51
Maryland 82-68
Arkansas 74-65
Utah 85-68
West Virginia 82-52
Cincinnati 65-62

REGIONALS

Arizona 82-49

Maryland 67-61

Arizona 87-79

Utah 75-69

Utah 65-62

West Virginia 75-74

Utah 76-51

NATIONAL CHAMPIONSHIP

KENTUCKY 78
UTAH 69

MIDWEST

REGIONALS

Rhode Island 80-75

Rhode Island 74-68

Valparaiso 83-77 (OT)

Stanford 83-65

Stanford 67-59

Stanford 79-77

2nd ROUND

Kansas 110-52
Rhode Island 97-74
Florida St 96-87
Valparaiso 70-69
Western Mich. 75-72
Stanford 67-57
Detroit 66-64
Purdue 95-56

1st ROUND

1 Kansas	34-3	
16 Prairie View	13-16	
8 Rhode Island	22-8	
9 Murray St	29-3	
5 Texas Christian	27-5	
12 Florida St	25-4	
4 Mississippi	22-6	
13 Valparaiso	21-9	
6 Clemson	18-13	
11 Western Mich.	20-7	
3 Stanford	26-4	
14 Charleston	24-5	
7 St. John's	22-9	
10 Detroit	24-5	
2 Purdue	26-7	
15 Delaware	20-9	

SOUTH

REGIONALS

Duke 79-73

Stanford 67-57

Duke 80-67

Syracuse 56-46

UCLA 85-82

Kentucky 94-68

Kentucky 88-61

Kentucky 86-85 (OT)

Kentucky 86-84

2nd ROUND

Duke 99-63
Oklahoma St 74-59
Syracuse 63-61
New Mexico 79-62
UCLA 65-82
Michigan 80-61
St. Louis 51-46
Kentucky 82-67

1st ROUND

1 Duke	29-3	
16 Radford	20-9	
8 Oklahoma St	21-6	
9 George Wash.	24-8	
5 Syracuse	24-8	
12 Iona	27-5	
4 New Mexico	23-7	
13 Butler	22-10	
6 UCLA	22-8	
11 Miami (FL)	18-9	
3 Michigan	24-8	
14 Davidson	20-9	
7 UMass	21-10	
10 St. Louis	21-10	
2 Kentucky	29-4	
15 S Carolina St	22-7	

America East

	Conference			All Games		
	W	L	Pct	W	L	Pct
†Delaware	12	6	.667	20	10	.667
Boston University	12	6	.667	19	11	.633
Hofstra	11	7	.611	19	12	.613
Vermont	11	7	.611	16	11	.593
Hartford	11	7	.611	15	12	.556
Drexel	10	8	.588	13	15	.464
Northeastern	9	9	.500	14	14	.500
New Hampshire	6	12	.333	10	17	.370
Towson St	4	14	.222	8	20	.286
Maine	4	14	.222	7	20	.259

Atlantic Coast

	Conference			All Games		
	W	L	Pct	W	L	Pct
Duke	15	1	.938	32	4	.889
†N Carolina	13	3	.813	34	4	.895
Maryland	10	6	.625	21	11	.656
Clemson	7	9	.438	18	14	.563
Wake Forest	7	9	.438	16	14	.533
Georgia Tech	6	10	.375	19	14	.576
Florida St	6	10	.375	18	14	.563
N Carolina St	5	11	.313	17	15	.531
Virginia	3	13	.188	11	19	.367

Atlantic 10

	Conference			All Games		
EAST	W	L	Pct	W	L	Pct
Temple	13	3	.813	21	9	.700
Rhode Island	12	4	.750	25	9	.735
Massachusetts	12	4	.750	21	11	.656
St. Bonaventure	6	10	.375	17	15	.531
St. Joseph's (PA)	3	13	.188	11	17	.393
Fordham	2	14	.125	6	21	.222
WEST						
†Xavier (OH)	11	5	.688	22	8	.733
George Washington	11	5	.688	24	9	.727
Dayton	11	5	.688	21	12	.636
Virginia Tech	5	11	.313	10	17	.370
Duquesne	5	11	.313	11	19	.367
La Salle	5	11	.313	9	18	.333

Big East

	Conference			All Games		
BIG EAST 7	W	L	Pct	W	L	Pct
Syracuse	12	6	.667	26	9	.743
Miami (FL)	11	7	.611	18	10	.643
Seton Hall	9	9	.500	15	15	.500
Providence	7	11	.389	13	16	.448
Georgetown	6	12	.333	16	15	.516
Rutgers	6	12	.333	14	15	.483
Pittsburgh	6	12	.333	11	16	.407
BIG EAST 6						
†Connecticut	15	3	.833	32	5	.865
St. John's (NY)	13	5	.722	22	10	.688
West Virginia	11	7	.611	24	9	.727
Villanova	8	10	.444	12	17	.414
Notre Dame	7	11	.389	13	14	.481
Boston College	6	12	.333	15	16	.484

Big Sky

	Conference			All Games		
	W	L	Pct	W	L	Pct
†Northern Arizona	13	3	.813	21	8	.724
Weber St	12	4	.750	14	13	.519
Eastern Washington	10	6	.625	16	11	.593
*Portland St	10	6	.625	15	12	.556
Montana St	9	7	.563	19	11	.633
Montana	9	7	.563	16	14	.533
Cal St-Northridge	7	9	.438	12	16	.429
Idaho St	2	14	.125	6	20	.231
Cal St-Sacramento	0	16	.000	1	25	.038

Big South

	Conference			All Games		
	W	L	Pct	W	L	Pct
NC-Asheville	11	1	.917	19	9	.679
†Radford	10	2	.833	20	10	.667
MD-Balt. County	6	6	.500	14	14	.500
Liberty	5	7	.417	11	17	.393
Coastal Carolina	4	8	.333	8	19	.296
Winthrop	4	8	.333	7	20	.259
Charleston So.	2	10	.167	5	22	.185

Big Ten

	Conference			All Games		
	W	L	Pct	W	L	Pct
Michigan St	13	3	.813	22	8	.733
Illinois	13	3	.813	23	10	.697
Purdue	12	4	.750	28	8	.778
†Michigan	11	5	.688	25	9	.735
Iowa	9	7	.563	20	11	.645
Indiana	9	7	.563	20	12	.625
Penn St	8	8	.500	19	13	.594
Minnesota	6	10	.375	20	15	.571
Wisconsin	3	13	.188	12	19	.387
Northwestern	3	13	.188	10	17	.370
Ohio St	1	15	.063	8	22	.267

Big 12

	Conference			All Games		
	W	L	Pct	W	L	Pct
†Kansas	15	1	.938	35	4	.897
Oklahoma St	11	5	.688	22	7	.759
Oklahoma	11	5	.688	22	11	.667
Nebraska	10	6	.625	20	12	.625
Missouri	8	8	.500	17	15	.531
Baylor	8	8	.500	14	14	.500
Kansas St	7	9	.438	17	12	.586
Colorado	7	9	.438	13	14	.481
Texas Tech	7	9	.438	13	14	.481
Texas	6	10	.375	14	17	.452
Iowa St	5	11	.313	12	18	.400
Texas A&M	1	15	.063	7	20	.259

†Conference tourney winner. *Not Division I.
Note: Standings based on regular-season conference play only; overall records include all tournament play.

Big West

EASTERN	Conference			All Games		
	W	L	Pct	W	L	Pct
†Utah St	13	3	.813	25	8	.758
Nevada	11	5	.688	16	12	.571
Boise St	9	7	.563	17	13	.567
Idaho	9	7	.563	15	12	.556
New Mexico St	8	8	.500	18	12	.600
North Texas	4	12	.250	5	21	.192
WESTERN						
Pacific (CA)	14	2	.875	23	10	.697
Cal Poly SLO	7	9	.438	14	14	.500
Cal St-Fullerton	6	10	.375	12	16	.429
UC-Irvine	6	10	.375	9	18	.333
Long Beach St	5	11	.313	10	19	.345
UC-Santa Barbara	4	12	.250	7	19	.269

Colonial Athletic

	Conference			All Games		
	W	L	Pct	W	L	Pct
William & Mary	13	3	.813	20	7	.741
NC-Wilmington	13	3	.813	20	11	.645
†Richmond	12	4	.750	23	8	.742
Old Dominion	8	8	.500	12	16	.429
James Madison	6	10	.375	11	16	.407
George Mason	6	10	.375	9	18	.333
E Carolina	5	11	.313	10	17	.370
American	5	11	.313	9	19	.321
VCU	4	12	.250	9	19	.321

Conference USA

AMERICAN	Conference			All Games		
	W	L	Pct	W	L	Pct
†Cincinnati	14	2	.875	27	6	.818
NC-Charlotte	13	3	.813	20	11	.645
St. Louis	11	5	.688	22	11	.667
Marquette	8	8	.500	20	11	.645
Louisville	5	11	.313	12	20	.375
DePaul	3	13	.188	7	23	.233
NATIONAL						
Memphis	12	4	.750	17	12	.586
AL-Birmingham	10	6	.625	21	12	.636
Southern Mississippi	9	7	.563	22	11	.667
S Florida	7	9	.438	17	13	.567
Houston	2	14	.125	9	20	.310
Tulane	2	14	.125	7	22	.241

Ivy League

	Conference			All Games		
	W	L	Pct	W	L	Pct
Princeton	13	0	1.000	27	2	.931
Pennsylvania	10	3	.769	17	12	.586
Yale	7	7	.500	12	14	.462
Harvard	6	8	.429	13	13	.500
Columbia	6	8	.429	11	15	.423
Cornell	6	8	.429	9	17	.346
Dartmouth	4	10	.286	7	19	.269
Brown	3	11	.214	6	20	.231

Metro Atlantic Athletic

	Conference			All Games		
	W	L	Pct	W	L	Pct
†Iona	15	3	.833	27	6	.818
Rider	12	6	.667	18	10	.643
Siena	10	8	.556	17	12	.586
Niagara	10	8	.556	14	13	.519
Canisius	9	9	.500	13	14	.481
Loyola (MD)	9	9	.500	12	16	.429
Fairfield	7	11	.389	12	15	.444
Manhattan	7	11	.389	12	17	.414
Marist	7	11	.389	11	17	.393
St. Peter's	4	14	.222	8	19	.296

Mid-American

EAST	Conference			All Games		
	W	L	Pct	W	L	Pct
Akron	13	5	.722	17	10	.630
Miami (OH)	9	9	.500	17	12	.586
Kent	9	9	.500	13	17	.433
Marshall	7	11	.389	11	16	.407
Bowling Green	7	11	.389	10	16	.385
Ohio	3	15	.167	5	21	.192
WEST						
Ball St	14	4	.778	21	8	.724
Western Michigan	14	4	.778	21	8	.724
†Eastern Michigan	13	5	.722	20	10	.667
Toledo	10	8	.556	15	12	.556
Northern Illinois	6	12	.333	10	16	.385
Central Michigan	3	15	.167	5	21	.192

Mid-Continent

	Conference			All Games		
	W	L	Pct	W	L	Pct
†Valparaiso	13	3	.813	23	10	.697
Oral Roberts	12	4	.750	19	12	.613
Youngstown St	11	5	.688	20	9	.690
Western Ill.	11	5	.688	16	11	.593
Buffalo	9	7	.563	15	13	.536
Troy St	7	9	.438	9	18	.333
MO-Kansas City	4	12	.250	7	20	.259
Northeastern Ill.	3	13	.188	6	19	.240
Chicago St	2	14	.125	2	25	.074

Mid-Eastern Athletic

	Conference			All Games		
	W	L	Pct	W	L	Pct
Coppin St	17	1	.944	21	8	.724
†S Carolina St	16	2	.889	22	8	.733
Hampton	11	7	.611	14	12	.538
Morgan St	11	7	.611	12	16	.429
Florida A&M	8	10	.444	11	17	.393
Delaware St	7	11	.389	9	18	.333
MD-Eastern Shore	7	11	.389	9	18	.333
N Carolina A&T	7	11	.389	8	19	.296
Howard	5	13	.278	8	20	.286
Bethune-Cookman	1	17	.056	1	26	.037
Norfolk St	—	—	—	6	21	.222

†Conference tourney winner.

Midwestern Collegiate

	Conference			All Games		
	W	L	Pct	W	L	Pct
Detroit	12	2	.857	25	6	.806
IL-Chicago	12	2	.857	22	6	.786
†Butler	8	6	.571	22	11	.667
WI-Green Bay	7	7	.500	17	12	.586
Loyola (IL)	6	8	.429	15	15	.500
Cleveland St	6	8	.429	12	15	.444
Wright St	3	11	.214	10	18	.357
WI-Milwaukee	2	12	.143	3	24	.111

Missouri Valley

	Conference			All Games		
	W	L	Pct	W	L	Pct
†Illinois St	16	2	.889	25	6	.806
Creighton	12	6	.667	18	10	.643
Wichita St	11	7	.611	16	15	.516
SW Missouri St	11	7	.611	16	16	.500
Indiana St	10	8	.556	16	11	.593
Bradley	9	9	.500	15	14	.517
Evansville	9	9	.500	15	15	.500
Southern Illinois	8	10	.444	14	18	.438
Northern Iowa	4	14	.222	10	17	.370
Drake	0	18	.000	3	24	.111

Northeast

	Conference			All Games		
	W	L	Pct	W	L	Pct
LIU-Brooklyn	14	2	.875	21	11	.656
†Fairleigh Dickinson	13	3	.813	23	7	.767
Robert Morris	10	6	.625	17	10	.630
St. Francis (PA)	10	6	.625	15	12	.556
St. Francis (NY)	8	8	.500	13	15	.464
Mt. St. Mary's (MD)	7	9	.438	13	16	.448
Wagner	4	12	.250	8	19	.296
Central Conn. St	3	13	.188	4	22	.154
Monmouth (NJ)	3	13	.188	4	23	.148

Ohio Valley

	Conference			All Games		
	W	L	Pct	W	L	Pct
†Murray St	16	2	.889	29	4	.879
Eastern Illinois	13	5	.722	16	11	.593
Middle Tenn. St	12	6	.667	19	9	.679
Austin Peay	11	7	.611	17	11	.607
SE Missouri St	10	8	.556	14	13	.519
Tennessee St	8	10	.444	13	16	.448
Eastern Kentucky	8	10	.444	10	17	.370
Tennessee Tech	5	13	.278	9	21	.300
TN-Martin	5	13	.278	7	20	.259
Morehead St	2	16	.111	3	23	.115

Pacific-10

	Conference			All Games		
	W	L	Pct	W	L	Pct
Arizona	17	1	.944	30	5	.857
Stanford	15	3	.833	30	5	.857
UCLA	12	6	.667	24	9	.727
Washington	11	7	.611	20	10	.667
Arizona St	8	10	.444	18	14	.563
Oregon	8	10	.444	13	14	.481
California	8	10	.444	12	15	.444
Southern Cal	5	13	.278	9	19	.321
Oregon St	3	15	.167	13	17	.433
Washington St	3	15	.167	10	19	.345

Patriot League

	Conference			All Games		
	W	L	Pct	W	L	Pct
Lafayette	10	2	.833	19	9	.679
†Navy	10	2	.833	19	11	.633
Bucknell	8	4	.667	13	15	.464
Colgate	5	7	.417	10	18	.357
Lehigh	4	8	.333	10	17	.370
Holy Cross	3	9	.250	7	20	.259
Army	2	10	.167	8	19	.296

Southeastern

	Conference			All Games		
EASTERN	W	L	Pct	W	L	Pct
†Kentucky	14	2	.875	35	4	.897
S Carolina	11	5	.688	23	8	.742
Tennessee	9	7	.563	20	9	.690
Vanderbilt	7	9	.438	20	13	.606
Georgia	7	9	.438	20	15	.571
Florida	6	10	.375	14	15	.483
WESTERN						
Mississippi	12	4	.750	22	7	.759
Arkansas	11	5	.688	24	9	.727
Auburn	7	9	.438	16	14	.533
Alabama	6	10	.375	15	16	.484
Mississippi St	4	12	.250	15	15	.500
Louisiana St	2	14	.125	9	18	.333

Southern

	Conference			All Games		
NORTH	W	L	Pct	W	L	Pct
Appalachian St	13	2	.867	21	8	.724
†Davidson	13	2	.867	20	10	.667
VMI	8	7	.533	14	13	.519
Western Carolina	6	9	.400	12	15	.444
E Tennessee St	6	9	.400	11	16	.407
NC-Greensboro	6	9	.400	9	19	.321
SOUTH						
Chattanooga	7	7	.500	13	15	.464
Citadel	6	8	.429	15	13	.536
Wofford	6	8	.429	9	18	.333
Furman	5	9	.357	9	20	.310
Georgia Southern	4	10	.286	10	18	.357

†Conference tourney winner.

Southland

	Conference			All Games		
	W	L	Pct	W	L	Pct
†Nicholls St	15	1	.938	19	10	.655
SW Texas St	10	6	.625	17	11	.607
TX-San Antonio	10	6	.625	16	11	.593
Northwestern St	10	6	.625	13	14	.481
NE Louisiana	8	8	.500	13	16	.448
TX-Arlington	8	8	.500	13	16	.448
Sam Houston St	7	9	.438	9	17	.346
Stephen F. Austin	6	10	.375	10	16	.385
McNeese St	4	12	.250	7	19	.269
Southeastern LA	2	14	.125	6	20	.231

Southwestern Athletic

	Conference			All Games		
	W	L	Pct	W	L	Pct
Texas Southern	12	4	.750	15	16	.484
Jackson St	11	5	.688	14	13	.519
Grambling	10	6	.625	16	12	.571
Southern University	10	6	.625	14	13	.519
Alcorn St	8	8	.500	12	15	.444
†Prairie View	6	10	.375	13	17	.433
Alabama St	6	10	.375	11	17	.393
Mississippi Valley	6	10	.375	6	21	.222
*AR-Pine Bluff	3	13	.188	4	23	.148

Sun Belt

	Conference			All Games		
	W	L	Pct	W	L	Pct
†S Alabama	14	4	.778	21	7	.750
Arkansas St	14	4	.778	20	9	.690
Southwestern LA	12	6	.667	18	13	.581
AR-Little Rock	10	8	.556	15	13	.536
New Orleans	9	9	.500	15	12	.556
Louisiana Tech	9	9	.500	12	15	.444
Lamar	7	11	.389	15	14	.517
Western Kentucky	6	12	.333	10	19	.345
Jacksonville	6	12	.333	8	19	.296
TX-Pan American	3	15	.167	3	24	.111

Trans America Athletic

	Conference			All Games		
EAST	W	L	Pct	W	L	Pct
†Coll. of Charleston	14	2	.875	24	6	.800
Florida Int'l	13	3	.813	21	8	.724
Central Florida	11	5	.688	17	11	.607
Stetson	8	8	.500	11	15	.423
Florida Atlantic	5	11	.313	5	22	.185
Campbell	4	12	.250	10	17	.370
WEST						
Georgia St	11	5	.688	16	12	.571
Samford	9	7	.563	14	13	.519
Centenary (LA)	8	8	.500	10	20	.333
Jacksonville St	6	10	.375	12	14	.462
Troy St	5	11	.313	7	20	.259
Mercer	2	14	.125	5	21	.192

West Coast

	Conference			All Games		
	W	L	Pct	W	L	Pct
Gonzaga	10	4	.714	24	10	.706
Pepperdine	9	5	.643	17	10	.630
Santa Clara	8	6	.571	18	10	.643
†San Francisco	7	7	.500	19	11	.633
Portland	7	7	.500	14	13	.519
St. Mary's (CA)	7	7	.500	11	15	.423
San Diego	5	9	.357	14	14	.500
Loyola Marymount	3	11	.214	7	20	.259

Western Athletic

	Conference			All Games		
PACIFIC	W	L	Pct	W	L	Pct
Texas Christian	14	0	1.000	27	6	.818
Fresno St	10	4	.714	21	13	.618
Tulsa	9	5	.643	19	12	.613
Hawaii	8	6	.571	21	9	.700
Southern Methodist	6	8	.429	18	10	.643
San Diego St	5	9	.357	13	15	.464
Rice	3	11	.214	6	22	.214
San Jose St	1	13	.071	3	23	.115
MOUNTAIN						
Utah	12	2	.857	30	4	.882
New Mexico	11	3	.786	24	8	.750
Wyoming	9	5	.643	19	9	.679
Colorado St	8	6	.571	20	9	.690
†UNLV	7	7	.500	20	13	.606
Brigham Young	4	10	.286	9	21	.300
UTEP	3	11	.214	12	14	.462
Air Force	2	12	.143	10	16	.385

†Conference tourney winner. *Not Division I.

Scoring

	Class	GP	Field Goals			3-Pt FG		Free Throws			Reb	Pts	Avg
			FGA	FG	Pct	FGA	FG	FTA	FT	Pct			
Charles Jones, LIU-Brooklyn	Sr	30	720	326	45.3	337	116	158	101	63.9	156	869	29.0
Earl Boykins, Eastern Michigan	Sr	29	563	266	47.2	209	85	158	129	81.6	66	746	25.7
Lee Nailon, Texas Christian	Jr	32	594	329	55.4	2	1	184	137	74.5	285	796	24.9
Brett Eppehimer, Lehigh	Jr	27	488	195	40.0	231	92	211	185	87.7	60	667	24.7
Cory Carr, Texas Tech	Sr	27	494	209	42.3	198	67	166	143	86.1	131	628	23.3
Pat Garrity, Notre Dame	Sr	27	445	214	48.1	108	40	212	159	75.0	225	627	23.2
Mike Powell, Loyola (MD)	Sr	28	444	197	44.4	140	46	255	207	81.2	137	647	23.1
Bonzi Wells, Ball St	Sr	29	486	238	49.0	142	53	193	133	68.9	184	662	22.8
Xavier Singletary, Howard	So	23	443	158	35.7	197	71	165	127	77.0	141	514	22.3
Michael Olowokandi, Pacific (CA)	Sr	33	509	310	60.9	0	0	235	114	48.5	369	734	22.2
Antawn Jamison, N Carolina	Jr	37	546	316	57.9	15	6	276	184	66.7	389	822	22.2
Michael Redd, Ohio St	Fr	30	550	241	43.8	152	46	211	130	61.6	194	658	21.9
Evan Eschmeyer, Northwestern	Sr	27	328	200	61.0	0	0	302	185	61.3	290	585	21.7
Matt Harping, Georgia Tech	Sr	32	504	230	45.6	168	52	221	179	81.0	302	691	21.6
Saddi Washington, Western Michigan	Sr	29	469	208	44.3	158	57	189	153	81.0	123	626	21.6
De'Teri Mayes, Murray St	Sr	33	524	246	45.9	234	103	148	116	78.4	143	711	21.5
Richard Hamilton, Connecticut	So	37	614	270	44.0	245	99	185	153	84.3	163	795	21.5
Mike Jones, Texas Christian	Sr	33	548	263	48.0	164	62	142	114	80.3	188	702	21.3
Tyronn Lue, Nebraska	Jr	32	547	240	43.9	209	78	145	120	82.8	137	678	21.2
Rick Kaye, Eastern Illinois	Sr	27	454	196	43.2	148	44	183	134	73.2	123	570	21.1
DeMarco Johnson, NC-Charlotte	Sr	31	475	238	50.1	50	18	204	159	77.9	280	653	21.1
Norman Nolan, Virginia	Sr	30	490	257	52.4	2	0	179	116	64.8	276	630	21.0
Larry Hughes, St. Louis	Fr	32	540	224	41.5	145	42	260	180	69.2	162	670	20.9
Derrick Dial, Eastern Michigan	Sr	29	459	222	48.4	198	79	107	84	78.5	195	607	20.9
Tywan Meadows, Idaho St	Jr	22	353	156	44.2	97	30	168	117	69.6	136	459	20.9
Omar Sneed, Memphis	Jr	29	395	231	58.5	21	5	207	138	66.7	266	605	20.9
Jeremy Veal, Arizona St	Sr	32	529	244	46.1	133	56	155	122	78.7	135	666	20.8
Corey Brewer, Oklahoma	Sr	33	499	214	42.9	192	72	233	186	79.8	186	686	20.8
Mark Jones, Central Florida	Sr	28	446	220	49.3	85	30	165	111	67.3	201	581	20.8
Roderick Blakney, S Carolina St	Sr	30	458	197	43.0	147	56	212	171	80.7	152	621	20.7

FIELD-GOAL PERCENTAGE

	Class	GP	FGA	FG	Pct
Todd MacCulloch, Washington	Jr	30	346	225	65.0
Ryan Moss, AR-Little Rock	Jr	28	257	167	65.0
Jarrett Stephens, Penn St	Jr	31	258	165	64.0
Isaac Spencer, Murray St	So	33	270	171	63.3
Brad Miller, Purdue	Sr	34	302	191	63.2
Zoran Viskovic, Valparaiso	Jr	33	280	176	62.9
Kareem Livingston, Appalachian St	Sr	29	231	145	62.8
	Jr	27	227	141	62.1
David Montgomery, SE Missouri St	Jr	27	227	141	62.1
Travis Lyons, Manhattan	Jr	29	277	172	62.1
Leon Watson, TX-San Antonio	So	27	245	151	61.6

Note: Minimum 5 made per game.

REBOUNDS

	Class	GP	Reb	Avg
Ryan Perryman, Dayton	Sr	33	412	12.5
Eric Taylor, St. Francis (PA)	Sr	27	321	11.9
Raef LaFrentz, Kansas	Sr	30	342	11.4
Tremaine Fowlkes, Fresno St	Jr	32	359	11.2
Michael Olowokandi, Pacific (CA)	Sr	33	359	11.2
T.J. Lux, Northern Illinois	Jr	26	289	11.1
Thad Burton, Wright St	Sr	28	305	10.9
Allen Ledbetter, Maine	Jr	27	294	10.9
Rashon Turner, Fairleigh Dickinson	Sr	29	313	10.8
Kenyon Ross, Mississippi Valley	Sr	27	291	10.8

FREE-THROW PERCENTAGE

	Class	GP	FTA	FT	Pct
Matt Sundblad, Lamar	Jr	27	104	96	92.3
Louis Bullock, Michigan	Jr	34	135	123	91.1
Shammond Williams, N Carolina	Sr	38	146	133	91.1
Kevin Ault, SW Missouri St	So	32	110	99	90.0
Clifton Ellis, SW Texas	Jr	28	80	72	90.0
Pete Lisicky, Penn St	Sr	32	119	106	89.1
Danny Sprinkle, Montana St	Jr	29	82	73	89.0
Mike Wozniak, Cal Poly SLO	So	27	145	129	89.0
Garrett Davis, Stetson	Jr	26	98	87	88.8
Arthur Lee, Stanford	Jr	35	185	164	88.6

Note: Minimum 2.5 made per game.

ASSISTS

	Class	GP	A	Avg
Ahlon Lewis, Arizona St	Sr	32	294	9.2
Chico Fletcher, Arkansas St	So	29	240	8.3
Sean Colson, NC-Charlotte	Sr	29	231	8.0
Ed Cota, N Carolina	So	37	274	7.4
Charles Jones, LIU-Brooklyn	Sr	30	221	7.4
Anthony Carter, Hawaii	Sr	29	212	7.3
Rafer Alston, Fresno St	Jr	33	240	7.3
Mateen Cleaves, Michigan St	So	30	217	7.2
Craig Claxton, Hofstra	So	31	224	7.2
Michael Wheeler, Wagner	Jr	28	197	7.0

*Includes games played in tournaments.

THREE-POINT FIELD-GOAL PERCENTAGE

	Class	GP	FGA	FG	Pct
Jim Cantamessa, Siena	So	29	117	66	56.4
Coby Turner, Dayton	Jr	33	118	61	51.7
Royce Olney, New Mexico	Sr	25	156	80	51.3
Mike Beam, Harvard	Jr	25	80	41	51.3
Kenyan Weeks, Florida	So	26	120	61	50.8
Jaraan Cornell, Purdue	So	28	122	61	50.0
Matt Langel, Pennsylvania	So	26	90	45	50.0
Justin Jones, Utah St	Sr	33	121	60	49.6
Mike Warhank, Montana	So	30	105	52	49.5
Rico Hill, Illinois St	Jr	30	91	45	49.5

Note: Minimum 1.5 made per game.

THREE-POINT FIELD GOALS MADE PER GAME

	Class	GP	FG	Avg
Curtis Staples, Virginia	Sr	30	130	4.3
Cedric Foster, Mississippi Valley	Sr	22	86	3.9
Charles Jones, LIU-Brooklyn	Sr	30	116	3.9
Demond Mallet, McNeese St	So	26	94	3.6
Cory Johnson, SE Missouri St	Jr	27	95	3.5
Denmark Reid, New Mexico St	Sr	30	104	3.5
Brett Eppehimer, Lehigh	Jr	27	92	3.4
Ronnie McCollum, Centenary (LA)	Fr	30	101	3.4
Kenny Price, Colorado	Jr	27	90	3.3
Seth Schaeffer, Colgate	Sr	28	93	3.3

BLOCKED SHOTS

	Class	GP	BS	Avg
Jerome James, Florida A&M	Sr	27	125	4.6
Calvin Booth, Penn St	Jr	32	140	4.4
Alvin Jones, Georgia Tech	Fr	33	141	4.3
Etan Thomas, Syracuse	So	35	138	3.9
Brian Skinner, Baylor	Sr	28	98	3.5
Tarvis Williams, Hampton	So	26	83	3.2
Caswell Cyrus, St. Bonaventure	So	32	99	3.1
Chris Mihm, Texas	Fr	31	90	2.9
Michael Olowokandi, Pacific (CA)	Sr	33	95	2.9
Erik Nelson, Vermont	Sr	27	76	2.8

STEALS

	Class	GP	S	Avg
Bonzi Wells, Ball St	Sr	29	103	3.6
Pepe Sanchez, Temple	So	27	93	3.4
Willie Coleman, DePaul	Jr	30	100	3.3
J.R. Camel, Montana	Jr	29	90	3.1
Jason Rowe, Loyola (MD)	So	28	86	3.1
Damian Owens, West Virginia	Sr	32	97	3.0
Jason Bell, VMI	Jr	27	79	2.9
Mike Jones, Texas Christian	Sr	33	96	2.9
Charles Jones, LIU-Brooklyn	Sr	30	87	2.9
Mike Campbell, LIU-Brooklyn	Sr	32	89	2.8

Single-Game Highs

POINTS

53 ....Charles Jones, LIU-Brooklyn, Nov 26 (vs Medgar Evers)
53 ....Lee Nailon, Texas Christian, Dec 12 (vs Mississippi Valley)
52 ....Roderic Hall, TX-San Antonio, Dec 6 (vs Maine)

REBOUNDS

23 ....Nick Davis, Arkansas, Nov 21 (vs Jackson St)
23 ....Kenyon Martin, Cincinnati, Feb 21 (vs DePaul)
Four tied with 22.

ASSISTS

18 ....Michael Johnson, Oklahoma, Dec 22 (vs N Texas)
18 ....Sean Colson, NC-Charlotte, Feb 28 (vs Houston)
17 ....Jason Williams, Florida, Dec 3 (vs Duquesne)
17 ....Rafer Alston, Fresno St, Dec 22 (vs N Florida)

THREE-POINT FIELD GOALS

10 ....Melvin Levett, Cincinnati, Dec 20 (vs Eastern Kentucky)
10 ....Mike Martinho, Buffalo, Feb 3 (vs Rochester)
Eleven tied with nine.

STEALS

11 ....Ali Ton, Davidson, Nov 26 (vs Tufts)
10 ....Todd Burgan, Syracuse, Nov 30 (vs Colgate)
10 ....Antrone Lee, Long Beach St, Feb 19 (vs UC-Irvine)

BLOCKED SHOTS

11 ....Alvin Jones, Georgia Tech, Nov 24 (vs Winthrop)
10 ....Rashon Turner, Fairleigh Dickinson, Nov 22 (vs Hartford)
10 ....Brian Skinner, Baylor, Nov 29 (vs Eastern Washington)
10 ....Calvin Booth, Penn St, Dec 8 (vs George Mason)
10 ....Kenyon Martin, Cincinnati, Feb 21 (vs DePaul)

SCORING OFFENSE

	GP	W	L	Pts	Avg		GP	W	L	Pts	Avg
Texas Christian	33	27	6	3209	97.2	Southern	27	14	13	2333	86.4
LIU-Brooklyn	32	27	5	3102	96.9	Duke	36	32	4	3082	85.6
Arizona	35	30	5	3177	90.8	Kansas	39	35	4	3300	84.6
Florida International	29	21	8	2533	87.3	Cal Poly SLO	28	14	14	2367	84.5
Murray St	33	29	4	2862	86.7	Arizona St	32	18	14	2703	84.5

SCORING DEFENSE

	GP	W	L	Pts	Avg		GP	W	L	Pts	Avg
Princeton	29	27	2	1491	51.4	WI-Green Bay	29	17	12	1737	59.9
S Alabama	28	21	7	1526	54.5	Marquette	31	20	11	1860	60.0
College of Charleston	30	24	6	1662	55.4	Temple	30	21	9	1820	60.7
Utah	34	30	4	1959	57.6	Bradley	29	15	14	1772	61.1
Wyoming	28	19	9	1656	59.1	NC-Wilmington	31	20	11	1905	61.5

SCORING MARGIN

	Off	Def	Mar		Off	Def	Mar
Duke	85.6	64.1	21.5	Murray St	86.7	70.7	16.0
Texas Christian	97.2	77.9	19.4	Princeton	66.5	51.4	15.1
Kansas	84.6	67.4	17.2	Xavier	83.5	68.8	14.7
N Carolina	81.9	65.6	16.3	College of Charleston	70.1	55.4	14.7
Arizona	90.8	74.6	16.2	Kentucky	80.1	67.0	13.1

FIELD-GOAL PERCENTAGE

	FGA	FG	Pct		FGA	FG	Pct
N Carolina	2184	1131	51.8	Texas Christian	2463	1220	49.5
Northern Arizona	1577	806	51.1	Kansas	2536	1249	49.3
Murray St	2070	1037	50.1	Indiana	1792	879	49.1
Princeton	1374	684	49.8	UCLA	2011	985	49.0
Pacific (CA)	1692	841	49.7	Michigan	1907	932	48.9

FIELD-GOAL PERCENTAGE DEFENSE

	FGA	FG	Pct		FGA	FG	Pct
Miami (FL)	1672	634	37.9	Utah	1729	668	38.6
Bradley	1614	617	38.2	College of Charleston	1591	616	38.7
Kentucky	2324	892	38.4	Temple	1599	620	38.8
N Carolina	2403	923	38.4	Marquette	1729	672	38.9
Wyoming	1405	541	38.5	Colorado St	1570	612	39.0

FREE-THROW PERCENTAGE

	FTA	FT	Pct		FTA	FT	Pct
Siena	715	574	80.3	Evansville	600	454	75.7
Montana St	570	437	76.7	WI-Green Bay	625	470	75.2
Purdue	864	657	76.0	Western Michigan	639	477	74.6
Montana	621	472	76.0	Arizona St	661	493	74.6
New Mexico	568	460	75.7	Hartford	730	541	74.1

THREE-POINT FIELD GOALS MADE PER GAME

	GP	FG	Avg		GP	FG	Avg
Florida	29	285	9.8	Cal Poly SLO	28	246	8.8
LIU-Brooklyn	32	310	9.7	Northern Arizona	29	254	8.8
N Texas	26	250	9.6	Southeastern Louisiana	26	227	8.7
New Mexico	32	301	9.4	Jacksonville St	26	225	8.7
Princeton	29	265	9.1	Oral Roberts	31	268	8.6

THREE-POINT FIELD-GOAL PERCENTAGE

	GP	FGA	FG	Pct		GP	FGA	FG	Pct
Northern Arizona	29	591	254	43.0	IL-Chicago	28	460	192	41.7
Utah St	33	324	139	42.9	Western Michigan	29	511	509	40.9
Pennsylvania	29	526	223	42.4	Stanford	35	642	262	40.8
Harvard	26	448	188	42.0	Gonzaga	34	678	274	40.4
Michigan	34	621	260	41.9	New Mexico	32	748	301	40.2

Note: Minimum 3.0 made per game.

NCAA Women's Championship Game Box Score

Louisiana Tech 75

Louisiana Tech	Min	FG M-A	FT M-A	Reb O-T	A	PF	TP
Maxwell	39	7-12	0-1	3-8	1	3	15
Wilson	31	2-6	0-1	1-5	0	4	4
Burras	34	9-16	1-5	5-10	0	3	19
Stallworth	30	0-6	2-2	0-1	9	0	2
Jackson	37	11-25	0-0	0-4	5	2	26
Cochran	1	0-0	0-0	0-0	0	0	0
Scheppmann	15	1-5	0-0	0-0	2	2	3
Gilmore	8	0-0	2-2	1-1	0	0	2
Bowman	7	2-3	0-1	0-0	0	2	4
Totals	200	32-73	5-10	10-29	17	16	75

Percentages: FG—.438, FT—.500. 3-pt goals: 6-18, .333 (Maxwell 1-3, Stallworth 0-1, Jackson 4-12, Scheppmann 1-2). Team rebounds: 5. Blocked shots: 7 (Burras 2, Bowman 2, Maxwell, Jackson, Gilmore). Turnovers: 20 (Stallworth 5, Jackson 4, Maxwell 3, Wilson 3, Burras 2, Scheppmann 2, Bowman) Steals: 11 (Wilson 3, Burras 2, Jackson 2, Maxwell 2, Stallworth 2).

Tennessee 93

Tennessee	Min	FG M-A	FT M-A	Reb O-T	A	PF	TP
Holdsclaw	36	11-25	3-4	4-10	6	0	25
Catchings	34	8-16	11-13	3-7	2	3	27
Stephens	8	0-2	0-0	1-2	0	2	0
Jolly	34	7-10	2-2	0-4	3	2	20
Randall	34	4-9	2-4	2-8	2	2	10
Butts	1	1-1	0-0	1-1	0	0	2
Elzy	1	0-1	0-0	0-0	0	0	0
Milligan	1	0-0	0-0	0-0	0	0	0
Greene	1	0-0	0-0	0-0	0	0	0
Laxton	1	0-0	0-0	0-1	0	0	0
Clement	15	3-4	0-0	0-1	2	1	6
Geter	34	1-1	1-2	2-7	0	3	3
Totals	200	35-69	19-25	13-41	15	13	93

Percentages: FG—.507, FT—.760. 3-pt goals: 4-9, .444 (Catchings 0-4, Jolly 4-5). Team rebounds: 6. Blocked shots: 5 (Geter 4, Jolly). Turnovers: 19 (Catchings 4, Randall 4, Clement 3, Holdsclaw 2, Jolly 2, Elzy, Geter, Laxton, Stephens). Steals: 11 (Catchings 4, Jolly 3, Randall 2, Geter, Holdsclaw).

Halftime: Tennessee 55, Louisiana Tech 32. A: 17,976. Officials: Bell, Trammell, Dean.

Defining a Double Standard

Some advocates of women's basketball believe that their college season should start and end one month sooner. The women's NCAA tournament might thus avoid being rendered nearly invisible by the men's. Indeed, startling news from a 1998 women's tournament site didn't draw much attention.

Replays of the finish of a Midwest Regional game clearly showed that UCLA got jobbed—twice—in its 75–74 second-round loss to Alabama. With .8 of a second left and the Bruins leading 74–73, the Crimson Tide's Britney Ezell ran along the baseline before throwing a long inbounds pass downcourt. That was a clear violation; only after a basket may an inbounder move. But no violation was called.

Ezell's pass went to Dominique Canty, who tipped it to LaToya Caudle, who caught it and shot a 15-foot jump shot that went in as the buzzer sounded. Replays showed that the clock didn't start when Canty touched the ball. The three referees left the floor immediately, officially ending the game. NCAA officials later reviewed the tape and, although they could do nothing about the result, they banned the refs from working the rest of the tournament. The referees were from neutral conferences. The timer, however, was from Alabama. In the women's tournament, the top four seeds in each region play at home for the first two rounds, and the UCLA–Alabama game was in Tuscaloosa.

It's hard to believe that two blatant errors would have been allowed to stand in a men's game. The outcry would have been too great.

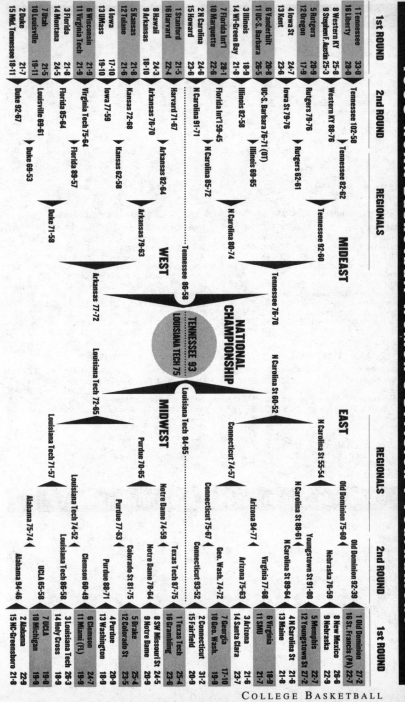

1998 NCAA Basketball Women's Division I Tournament

MIDEAST

1st ROUND

1 Tennessee	33-0
16 Liberty	28-0
8 Western KY	25-8
9 Stephen F. Austin	25-3
5 Rutgers	20-9
12 Oregon	17-9
4 Iowa St.	24-7
13 Kent	23-6
6 Vanderbilt	20-8
11 UC-S. Barbara	26-5
3 Illinois	18-9
14 WI-Green Bay	19-8
7 Florida Int'l	28-1
10 Marquette	22-6
2 N Carolina	24-6
15 Howard	23-6

2nd ROUND

Tennessee 102-58
Tennessee 82-62
Western KY 88-76
Rutgers 79-76
Rutgers 62-61
Iowa St. 79-76
UC-S. Barbara 76-71 (OT)
Illinois 82-58
Illinois 69-65
Florida Int'l 59-45
N Carolina 85-72
N Carolina 91-71

REGIONALS

Tennessee 92-60
Tennessee 86-58

WEST

1st ROUND

1 Stanford	21-5
16 Harvard	22-4
8 Harvard	24-3
9 Arkansas	18-10
5 Kansas	21-8
12 Tulane	21-8
4 Iowa	17-10
13 UMass	19-10
6 Wisconsin	21-9
11 Virginia Tech	21-9
3 Florida	21-8
14 Montana	24-5
7 Utah	21-5
10 Louisville	19-11
2 Duke	21-7
15 Mid. Tennessee	18-11

2nd ROUND

Harvard 71-67
Arkansas 76-70
Kansas 72-68
Virginia Tech 75-64
Iowa 77-59
Florida 85-64
Louisville 69-61
Duke 92-67

REGIONALS

Arkansas 82-64
Kansas 62-58
Florida 89-57
Duke 69-53

Arkansas 79-63
Duke 71-58

Arkansas 77-72

NATIONAL CHAMPIONSHIP

TENNESSEE 93
LOUISIANA TECH 75

Tennessee 76-70
Louisiana Tech 72-65

EAST

REGIONALS

N Carolina St 55-54

N Carolina St 60-52

Connecticut 74-57

2nd ROUND

Old Dominion 92-39
N Carolina St 88-61
Youngstown St 91-80
Arizona 94-77
Virginia 77-68
Geo. Wash. 74-72
Connecticut 93-52

Old Dominion 75-60
N Carolina St 89-64
Arizona 75-63
Connecticut 75-67

1st ROUND

1 Old Dominion	27-2
16 St. Francis (PA)	22-7
8 New Mexico	26-6
9 Nebraska	22-9
5 Memphis	22-7
12 Youngstown St	27-2
4 N Carolina St	21-6
13 Maine	21-8
6 Virginia	18-9
11 SMU	21-7
3 Arizona	21-6
14 Santa Clara	23-7
7 Georgia	17-10
10 Geo. Wash.	19-9
2 Connecticut	31-2
15 Fairfield	20-9

MIDWEST

REGIONALS

Louisiana Tech 84-65

Louisiana Tech 71-57

Purdue 70-65

2nd ROUND

Notre Dame 74-59
Texas Tech 87-75
Arizona St 81-75
Clemson 60-43
Purdue 88-71
Louisiana Tech 86-58
UCLA 65-58
Alabama 94-46

Notre Dame 78-64
Purdue 77-63
Louisiana Tech 74-52
Alabama 75-74

1st ROUND

1 Texas Tech	25-4
16 Grambling	23-6
8 SW Missouri St.	24-5
9 Notre Dame	20-9
5 Drake	25-4
12 Colorado St	23-5
4 Purdue	20-9
13 Washington	18-9
6 Clemson	24-7
11 Miami (FL)	19-9
3 Louisiana Tech	26-3
14 Holy Cross	18-9
7 UCLA	19-8
10 Michigan	19-9
2 Alabama	22-9
15 NC-Greensboro	21-8

NCAA Women's Division I Individual Leaders

SCORING

Player and Team	Class	GP	TFG	3FG	FT	Pts	Avg
Allison Feaster, Harvard	Sr	28	272	58	195	797	28.5
Cindy Blodgett, Maine	Sr	26	237	54	176	704	27.1
Korie Hlede, Duquesne	Sr	28	294	64	106	758	27.1
Amy O'Brien, Holy Cross	Jr	30	295	15	177	782	26.1
Tamika Whitmore, Memphis	Jr	29	300	3	151	754	26.0
Karalyn Church, Vermont	So	29	280	5	147	712	24.6
Becky Hammon, Colorado St	Jr	30	238	80	148	704	23.5
Chamique Holdsclaw, Tennessee	Sr	39	370	9	166	915	23.5
Alicia Thompson, Texas Tech	Sr	31	299	4	117	719	23.2
Marlene Stollings, Ohio	Sr	28	200	87	155	642	22.9
Delores Jones, Northeastern Illinois	Sr	26	231	0	129	591	22.7
Myndee Larsen, Southern Utah	Sr	28	249	0	120	618	22.1
Kristina Divjak, Nortwestern	Jr	31	243	82	116	684	22.1
Katrina Price, Stephen F. Austin	Sr	28	218	50	130	616	22.0
Kim Knuth, Texas Tech	Jr	31	254	57	116	681	22.0

FIELD-GOAL PERCENTAGE

Player and Team	Class	GP	FGA	FG	Pct
Myndee Larsen, Southern Utah	Sr	28	344	249	72.4
Barbara Farris, Tulane	Sr	27	210	151	71.9
Tammi Blackstone, Drake	So	30	266	173	65.0
Tamika Whitmore, Memphis	Jr	29	464	300	64.7
Sharon Mitchell, Georgia Southern	So	29	251	160	63.7
Nyree Roberts, Old Dominion	Sr	32	416	263	63.2
Diane Seng, Tennessee Tech	So	28	304	190	62.5
Pollyanna Johns, Michigan	Sr	28	283	176	62.2
Gergana Branzova, Florida Int'l	Sr	31	355	220	62.0
Amanda Wilson, Louisiana Tech	Jr	34	464	287	61.9

Note: Minimum 5 made per game.

FREE-THROW PERCENTAGE

Player and Team	Class	GP	FTA	FT	Pct
Kristi Green, Indiana	Jr	33	109	99	90.8
Ann Marie Martin, Y'ngstown St	Sr	31	118	107	90.7
Amy Towne, Arkansas St	Sr	30	116	105	90.5
Chrissy Roberts, Eastern KY	Sr	28	102	91	89.2
Becky Hammon, Colorado St	Jr	30	167	148	88.6
Jennifer Marlow, Butler	Jr	31	124	109	87.9
Rebecca Viverette, NC-Greensboro	Sr	30	114	100	87.7
Dawn Zerman, Kent	So	30	202	177	87.6
Amy Geren, Clemson	Jr	33	105	92	87.6
Nicole Erickson, Duke	Jr	32	105	92	87.6

Note: Minimum 2.5 made per game.

REBOUNDS

Player and Team	Class	GP	Reb	Avg
Alisha Hill, Howard	Sr	30	297	13.2
Murriel Page, Florida	Sr	32	402	12.6
Jessica Zinobile, St. Francis (PA)	So	30	365	12.2
Nyree Roberts, Old Dominion	Sr	32	384	12.0
Leticia Oseguara, Cal St-Irvine	Sr	22	262	11.9
Mfon Udoka, DePaul	Sr	24	281	11.7
Amy O'Brien, Holy Cross	Jr	30	344	11.5
Elise James, Robert Morris	So	26	291	11.2
Amber Hall, Washington	Jr	28	313	11.2
Kristina Bohnfeldt, Marshall	Jr	29	324	11.2

ASSISTS

Player and Team	Class	GP	A	Avg
Dalma Ivanyi, Florida Int'l	Jr	31	294	9.5
Alli Bills, Utah	Sr	27	212	7.9
Ticha Penicheiro, Old Dominion	Sr	32	239	7.5
Nicki Taggart, Marquette	Sr	29	215	7.4
Gina Graziani, Miami (FL)	So	29	210	7.2
Joyce Howard, TX-San Antonio	Sr	28	201	7.2
Lisa Witherspoon, Virginia Tech	Jr	31	219	7.1
Keisha Cox, Drake	Sr	30	209	7.0
Tori Boudreaux, Northeastern Illinois	Sr	26	181	7.0
Amber DeWall, Northwestern	Sr	30	205	6.8

NCAA Men's Division II Individual Leaders

SCORING

Player and Team	Class	GP	TFG	3FG	FT	Pts	Avg
Carlos Knox, IN-Purdue-Indianapolis	Sr	26	238	96	209	781	30.0
Joe Newton, Central Oklahoma	Sr	32	298	82	187	865	27.0
Danny Sancomb, Wheeling Jesuit	Sr	28	282	23	141	728	26.0
Sean Hampton, Alderson-Broaddus	Sr	29	300	6	94	700	24.1
Troy Nesmith, Gannon	Sr	27	225	49	146	645	23.9
Durville Patton, Morningside	Sr	27	230	47	131	638	23.6
Titus Warmsley, Montana St-Billings	Jr	27	177	77	190	621	23.0
Rodney Horton, Indiana (PA)	Sr	28	240	32	126	638	22.8
Ryan Miller, Northern St	Sr	32	244	101	137	726	22.7
Shawn Wilson, St. Leo	Sr	26	237	22	91	587	22.6

REBOUNDS

Player and Team	Class	GP	Reb	Avg
Antonio Garcia, Kentucky Wesleyan	Jr	33	457	13.8
James Spears, Shaw	Jr	26	339	13.0
Soce Faye, Queens (NC)	Sr	30	335	11.2
Cameron Mack, W Virginia Wesleyan	Sr	27	299	11.1
Anthony Russell, W Florida	Sr	28	310	11.1
Donald Cunningham, Tuskegee	Jr	26	278	10.7
Marvin Wells, Clarion	Jr	26	273	10.5
Ian Morris, Kutztown	So	25	261	10.4
Anthony Rollins, St. Andrews	So	28	290	10.4
Chris Sykes, Delta St	Jr	31	321	10.4

ASSISTS

Player and Team	Class	GP	A	Avg
Emanuel Richardson, Pitt.-Johnstown	Sr	29	260	9.0
Art Ford, Tuskegee	Sr	23	194	8.4
Adam Kaufman, Edinboro	Fr	34	273	8.0
Gus Abellar, Colorado Christian	Jr	26	208	8.0
Larry Coates, Columbus St	Sr	33	261	7.9
Brian Norberg, S Dakota St	Sr	29	225	7.8
Keith Moyer, Le Moyne	Sr	28	215	7.7
James Vitrano, Florida Tech	So	28	195	7.0
Steve Amenta, Queens (NY)	Sr	26	180	6.9
Tyler Johnson, Wayne St (NE)	Jr	27	184	6.8

FIELD-GOAL PERCENTAGE

Player and Team	Class	GP	FGA	FG	Pct
Anthony Russell, W Florida	Sr	28	284	191	67.3
Julian Pitt, St. Augustine's	Jr	23	176	118	67.0
Josh Quigley, Henderson	So	27	262	173	66.0
Mike Vig, Mesa St	Jr	22	238	157	66.0
Devin Baker, Central Oklahoma	Sr	32	252	166	65.9
Cliff Clinton, Northern Kentucky	Sr	28	267	173	64.8
Stuart Love, Oakland City	Sr	23	268	171	63.8
Matt Olson, Missouri Southern St	Jr	26	238	150	63.0
Kevin Coduti, Northern Michigan	So	27	302	189	62.6
Kurt Hold, Assumption	Sr	33	272	170	62.5

Note: Minimum 5 made per game.

FREE-THROW PERCENTAGE

Player and Team	Class	GP	FTA	FT	Pct
Troy Nesmith, Gannon	Sr	27	158	145	92.4
Junior Allen, Florida Tech	Jr	29	95	86	90.5
Chris Jackson, Mankato St	So	27	87	77	88.5
Blaine Joerger, Mankato St	So	27	87	77	88.5
Travis Starns, Colorado Mines	Jr	26	95	84	88.4
T.J. Trimboli, Southern Conn. St	So	31	143	126	88.1
Bryan Lentz, Lenoir-Rhyne	So	26	89	78	87.6
Marcus Moss, Cal St-Bakersfield	Sr	27	104	91	87.5
Kevin Hamilton, Gannon	So	27	96	84	87.5
James Wade, Kennesaw St	Sr	29	102	89	87.3

Note: Minimum 2.5 made per game.

NCAA Women's Division II Individual Leaders

SCORING

Player and Team	Class	GP	TFG	3FG	FT	Pts	Avg
Konecka Drakeford, Johnson Smith	Jr	27	339	19	146	843	31.2
Karen Curtis, High Point	Sr	27	250	30	132	662	24.5
Serita Gauldin, N Alabama	Jr	25	241	1	129	612	24.5
Mary Randall, Grand Valley St	So	28	265	0	142	672	24.0
Tammy Brown, Fayetteville St	Sr	26	211	75	103	600	23.1
Brenda Begnaud, AR-Monticello	Jr	28	210	0	219	639	22.8
Tanisha Rickman, W Florida	Jr	30	225	70	158	678	22.6
Amber Kirk, W Virginia St	Sr	27	206	44	121	577	21.4
Lashonda Albert, Central Missouri St	Sr	29	241	15	120	617	21.3
Sharon Kukal, NJ Institute of Technology	Jr	24	184	0	140	508	21.2

REBOUNDS

Player and Team	Class	GP	Reb	Avg
Latriesha Moon, Alabama A&M	Sr	27	403	14.9
Sheneeka Watkins, Miles	Sr	25	360	14.4
Loarie Hanna, W Virginia Tech	So	26	351	13.5
Tracy Sprolden, Valdosta St	Fr	26	324	12.5
Nicole Allman, New Mex. Highlands	Sr	27	335	12.4
Konecka Drakeford, Johnson Smith	Jr	27	328	12.1
Farrah Magee, Metro St	Sr	30	361	12.0
Kelly Borch, St. Michael's	Jr	24	283	11.8
Devonyalle Tedford, Livingstone	Sr	28	326	11.6
Ashley Totedo, Shippensburg	Jr	32	370	11.6

ASSISTS

Player and Team	Class	GP	A	Avg
Pam Cummings, NW Missouri St	Sr	27	234	8.7
Isabel Gonzalez, Lincoln Memorial	Jr	27	220	8.1
Hayley Blue, Charleston (WV)	Jr	30	239	8.0
Simons Gilliam, Shaw	Jr	27	193	7.1
Kris Manske, Northern Michigan	Sr	32	223	7.0
Becky Stoner, Millersville	Jr	21	140	6.7
Debbie Miller, Seattle Pacific	Sr	30	198	6.6
Angie Schmitt, AK-Fairbanks	Jr	26	169	6.5
Alisa DiBonaventura, Slippery Rock	Fr	27	174	6.4
Kelly Kohn, St. Leo	Jr	28	180	6.4

NCAA Women's Division II Individual Leaders *(Cont.)*

FIELD-GOAL PERCENTAGE

Player and Team	Class	GP	FGA	FG	Pct
Jenny Crouse, N Dakota	Jr	32	345	236	68.4
Trina Davis, Delta St	Sr	32	349	232	66.5
Evija Azace, St. Rose	Jr	34	280	185	66.1
Keisha Allison, Cal St-San Bernadino	Sr	29	270	176	65.2
Brandy Brown, Lincoln Memorial	Sr	27	254	165	65.0
Temeshia Dawkins, Wingate	Fr	26	212	133	62.7
Krista Jabdere, St. Rose	Sr	34	317	198	62.5
Tarra Blackwell, Fla. Southern	Sr	29	348	216	62.1
Serita Gauldin, N Alabama	Jr	25	393	241	61.3
Shari Grady, SW Baptist	So	26	247	151	61.1

Note: Minimum 5 made per game.

FREE-THROW PERCENTAGE

Player and Team	Class	GP	FTA	FT	Pct
Becky Mauck, N Alabama	So	25	107	94	87.9
Nikki Olberding, Washburn	Sr	27	161	141	87.6
Carrie Dykstra, Northern Mich.	So	32	154	133	86.4
Jill Razor, Rollins	Fr	29	183	158	86.3
Lori Morth, Mercyhurst	Sr	26	130	112	86.2
Monica Sortino, Phila. Textile	Jr	33	131	111	84.7
Jessica Wollaston, Rollins	Jr	29	137	116	84.7
Christy Heavin, Central Okla.	Sr	26	78	66	84.6
Shatonya Fort, LeMoyne-Owen	Sr	23	101	85	84.2
Heather Kearney, Slippery Rock	Jr	27	226	190	84.1

Note: Minimum 2.5 made per game.

NCAA Men's Division III Individual Leaders

SCORING

Player and Team	Class	GP	TFG	3FG	FT	Pts	Avg
Jeff Clement, Grinnell	Jr	22	238	186	84	746	33.9
John Patraitis, Anna Maria	Sr	25	284	15	165	748	29.9
Darrel Lewis, Lincoln (PA)	Jr	18	169	48	98	484	26.9
Henry Shannon, Maryville (MO)	Jr	26	253	31	149	686	26.4
Verdel Baskin, Colorado College	Jr	25	236	19	160	651	26.0
Eric Joldersma, Bethel (MN)	Jr	23	212	41	126	591	25.7
Devean George, Augsburg	Jr	26	218	43	185	664	25.5
Andrew Panko, Lebanon Valley	Jr	28	240	35	200	715	25.5
Demarcus Morrison, Averett	So	25	204	31	167	606	24.2
Eric Nelson, Hobart	Sr	25	240	4	122	606	24.2

REBOUNDS

Player and Team	Class	GP	Reb	Avg
Adam Doll, Simpson	Jr	25	366	14.6
Jeff Leclerc, Rivier	Sr	26	341	13.1
Jason Crockett, Albertus Magnus	Sr	25	326	13.0
Tyler Field, UC San Diego	Fr	19	239	12.6
Jon Schmiegel, Hamilton	Jr	27	329	12.2
Ben Turk, Cal Tech	Sr	23	279	12.1
Michael Schantz, Hamilton	Jr	27	321	11.9
Rich Williamson, Thiel	Jr	26	298	11.5
Tarron Richardson, Lincoln (PA)	Jr	24	275	11.5
Tirek Gayle, Vassar	Fr	25	283	11.3

FIELD-GOAL PERCENTAGE

Player and Team	Class	GP	FGA	FG	Pct
Lonnie Walker, Alvernia	Jr	27	237	165	69.6
Stephen Hodges, Centre	So	25	205	136	66.3
Terrell Dozier, Colby-Sawyer	Jr	29	256	169	66.0
Nate Thomas, Neb. Wesleyan	Sr	26	272	179	65.8
Adnan Krupalija, Rockford	So	19	216	142	65.7
Tyree Jones, Delaware Valley	Fr	24	233	152	65.2
Tony Higgins, Castleton St	Sr	27	230	150	65.2
Johnny Nicholson, York (NY)	Jr	30	282	181	64.2
Brent Niebrugge, Ill. Wesleyan	Sr	27	326	208	63.8
Matt Bell, Carroll (WI)	Sr	22	214	136	63.6

Note: Minimum 5 made per game.

ASSISTS

Player and Team	Class	GP	A	Avg
David Rubin, Hobart	Sr	25	237	9.5
Mitch Mosser, Nebraska Wesleyan	Sr	26	211	8.1
Chris Ballerini, Binghamton	Jr	27	217	8.0
David Love, Mary Washington	Jr	25	190	7.6
Alex Morrison, Daniel Webster	So	26	184	7.1
Greg Dunne, Nazareth	Jr	27	190	7.0
Verdel Baskin, Colorado College	Jr	25	174	7.0
Eric Prendeville, Salisbury St	Jr	24	160	6.7
Ryan Patton, Washington (MO)	Fr	24	160	6.7
Mike Holland, Chris. Newport	Jr	28	186	6.6

FREE-THROW PERCENTAGE

Player and Team	Class	GP	FTA	FT	Pct
Chanse Young, Manchester	Sr	25	68	65	95.6
Brett Davis, WI-Oshkosh	Sr	27	76	72	94.7
Johnny Baer, York (PA)	Sr	25	89	82	92.1
C.J. Wurster, RIT	Jr	25	89	81	91.0
Wade Vander Molen, Central (IA)	So	25	86	78	90.7
Josh Estelle, Wabash	So	27	106	96	90.6
Joel Kauffman, Eastern Mennonite	Fr	25	83	75	90.4
Ryan Ankstitus, Nichols	Fr	25	102	92	90.2
Korey Coon, Illinois Wesleyan	So	27	117	105	89.7
Bryan Bates, Centre	Sr	25	83	74	89.2

Note: Minimum 2.5 made per game.

NCAA Women's Division III Individual Leaders

SCORING

Player and Team	Class	GP	TFG	3FG	FT	Pts	Avg
Glenda Gileud, Stillman	Sr	25	291	69	98	749	30.0
Ronda Jo Miller, Gallaudet	So	25	289	7	132	717	28.7
Laura Haynes, Guilford	Sr	26	256	2	165	679	26.1
Stacy Manfredi, St. Joseph's (CT)	Sr	26	207	26	199	639	24.6
Staci Brown, Rockford	Sr	25	211	0	188	610	24.4
Misty Hart, Christopher Newport	Sr	28	238	64	120	660	23.6
Melissa Posse, Cabrini	Jr	26	249	0	109	607	23.3
Deb Hughes, Elmhurst	Jr	25	221	0	128	570	22.8
Danielle Moore, St. Joseph's (NY)	Sr	24	209	0	120	538	22.4
Deann Trapp, Clarke	Jr	22	191	1	110	493	22.4

REBOUNDS

Player and Team	Class	GP	Reb	Avg
Heather Stewart, New Rochelle	So	24	494	20.6
Sayunara Lopez, Lehman	Sr	25	442	17.7
Melissa Posse, Cabrini	Jr	26	425	16.3
Ronda Jo Miller, Gallaudet	So	25	402	16.1
Helen Libby, Hood	Jr	18	281	15.6
Molly Zahr, Emerson-MCA	Fr	18	250	13.9
Tehesha Parsons, Johnson & Wales	Fr	22	293	13.3
Deann Trapp, Clarke	Jr	22	291	13.2
Kelly McCandlish, Lynchburg	So	24	303	12.6
Jen Joyce, Framingham St	Fr	25	310	12.4

ASSISTS

Player and Team	Class	GP	A	Avg
Suzy Venet, Mount Union	Sr	32	303	9.5
Amy Cooke Salisbury St	Jr	26	205	7.9
Sheryl Ferguson, Oneonta St	Sr	28	206	7.4
Liz Londergan, Curry	So	25	175	7.0
Colleen McCrave, Bates	Jr	26	177	6.8
Artina Trader, N Carolina Wesleyan	Jr	24	160	6.7
Debbie Rinaldi, Mt. St. Mary's (NY)	Sr	27	177	6.6
Heidi Stevens, Endicott	So	25	161	6.4
Cristie Ansbach, Alvernia	Sr	28	178	6.4
Shannon Galbraith, Thomas More	Sr	23	145	6.3

FIELD-GOAL PERCENTAGE

Player and Team	Class	GP	FGA	FG	Pct
Kirsten Vipond, St. Thomas (MN)	Sr	28	297	212	71.4
Beth Goodale, Meredith	So	23	253	160	63.2
Rachel Lachecki, WI-Oshkosh	Jr	26	240	148	61.7
Karyn Kern, Susquehanna	So	24	237	146	61.6
Alia Fischer, Washington (MO)	So	30	389	237	60.9
Melissa Posse, Cabrini	Jr	26	410	249	60.7
Jayme Anderson, Beloit	Fr	25	281	170	60.5
Amy Todd, Methodist	Jr	25	284	169	59.5
Gretchen MacColl, Trinity (CT)	So	25	278	165	59.4
Joanne Polakoski, King's (PA)	So	27	314	186	59.2

Note: Minimum 5 made per game.

FREE-THROW PERCENTAGE

Player and Team	Class	GP	FTA	FT	Pct
Holly Spee, WI-Oshkosh	Sr	28	81	72	88.9
Paige Olson, St. Thomas (MN)	Jr	24	85	75	88.2
Jeanne Waznak, Delaware Valley	So	22	92	81	88.0
Christina Page, Beloit	Sr	25	91	80	87.9
Jill Schultz, Montclair St	Sr	27	88	76	86.4
Kerry Cole, Wheaton (IL)	Jr	21	103	88	85.4
Megan Stoll, Luther	So	26	91	77	84.6
Anika Egli, Eastern Mennonite	Jr	24	113	95	84.1
Alison Grubbs, Lake Forest	Fr	24	81	68	84.0
Deb Hughes, Elmhurst	Jr	25	153	125	83.7

Note: Minimum 2.5 made per game.

A Presidential Abdication

In the three years that Jerry Tarkanian has coached basketball at Fresno State, the school's president, John Welty, has been for the most part the model of accommodation for Tark's give-'em-another-chance-and-then-maybe-another-one philosophy. As Tarkanian peopled his roster with criminals and drug abusers, Welty stood behind him, and on March 9, 1998, even extended his $95,000-a-year contract through the 1998–99 season with options to renew through 2000–01. After a March 15, 1998, segment on 60 Minutes about the Bulldogs' basketball program that was mostly negative—John Welty appeared briefly on the program and spoke about his being a member of the Society for Values in higher Education—Welty joined Tark in criticizing the report.

After another ugly incident two days after that report—Bulldogs starter Avondre Jones, a senior center, and transfer Kenny Brunner, a freshman guard, were arrested after allegedly robbing an acquaintance and assaulting him with a gun and two samurai swords—Welty suddenly developed a sense of outrage. (While the players were not immediately charged, according to a Fresno Bee article, on July 7, 1998, Jones was ordered to stand trial on felony assault and robbery charges; no preliminary hearing has been held for Brunner, who is fighting attempted-murder charges in a Los Angeles case.) "With each shameful incident, the institutional damage is compounded," he said. "My patience and the patience of others throughout this university are at an end." Still, Welty wasn't that outraged. He accepted the Tark-imposed penalties. Tarkanian dismissed Jones, whose eligibility was up only a couple of weeks after the incident, but only "indefinitely suspended" Brunner, who had 2½ years of eligibility remaining. And he did not pull Fresno State from the NIT. That would've been a real statement.

FOR THE RECORD·Year by Year

NCAA Final Four Results

Year	Winner	Score	Runner-up	Third Place	Fourth Place	Winning Coach
1939	Oregon	46–33	Ohio St	*Oklahoma	*Villanova	Howard Hobson
1940	Indiana	60–42	Kansas	*Duquesne	*Southern Cal	Branch McCracken
1941	Wisconsin	39–34	Washington St	*Pittsburgh	*Arkansas	Harold Foster
1942	Stanford	53–38	Dartmouth	*Colorado	*Kentucky	Everett Dean
1943	Wyoming	46–34	Georgetown	*Texas	*DePaul	Everett Shelton
1944	Utah	42–40 (OT)	Dartmouth	*Iowa St	*Ohio St	Vadal Peterson
1945	Oklahoma St	49–45	NYU	*Arkansas	*Ohio St	Hank Iba
1946	Oklahoma St	43–40	N Carolina	Ohio St	California	Hank Iba
1947	Holy Cross	58–47	Oklahoma	Texas	CCNY	Alvin Julian
1948	Kentucky	58–42	Baylor	Holy Cross	Kansas St	Adolph Rupp
1949	Kentucky	46–36	Oklahoma St	Illinois	Oregon St	Adolph Rupp
1950	CCNY	71–68	Bradley	N Carolina St	Baylor	Nat Holman
1951	Kentucky	68–58	Kansas St	Illinois	Oklahoma St	Adolph Rupp
1952	Kansas	80–63	St. John's (NY)	Illinois	Santa Clara	Forrest Allen
1953	Indiana	69–68	Kansas	Washington	Louisiana St	Branch McCracken
1954	La Salle	92–76	Bradley	Penn St	Southern Cal	Kenneth Loeffler
1955	San Francisco	77–63	La Salle	Colorado	Iowa	Phil Woolpert
1956	San Francisco	83–71	Iowa	Temple	Southern Meth	Phil Woolpert
1957	N Carolina	54–53 (3OT)	Kansas	San Francisco	Michigan St	Frank McGuire
1958	Kentucky	84–72	Seattle	Temple	Kansas St	Adolph Rupp
1959	California	71–70	W Virginia	Cincinnati	Louisville	Pete Newell
1960	Ohio St	75–55	California	Cincinnati	NYU	Fred Taylor
1961	Cincinnati	70–65 (OT)	Ohio St	Vacated‡	Utah	Edwin Jucker
1962	Cincinnati	71–59	Ohio St	Wake Forest	UCLA	Edwin Jucker
1963	Loyola (IL)	60–58 (OT)	Cincinnati	Duke	Oregon St	George Ireland
1964	UCLA	98–83	Duke	Michigan	Kansas St	John Wooden
1965	UCLA	91–80	Michigan	Princeton	Wichita St	John Wooden
1966	UTEP	72–65	Kentucky	Duke	Utah	Don Haskins
1967	UCLA	79–64	Dayton	Houston	N Carolina	John Wooden
1968	UCLA	78–55	N Carolina	Ohio St	Houston	John Wooden
1969	UCLA	92–72	Purdue	Drake	N Carolina	John Wooden
1970	UCLA	80–69	Jacksonville	New Mexico St	St. Bonaventure	John Wooden
1971	UCLA	68–62	Vacated‡	Vacated‡	Kansas	John Wooden
1972	UCLA	81–76	Florida St	N Carolina	Louisville	John Wooden
1973	UCLA	87–66	Memphis St	Indiana	Providence	John Wooden
1974	N Carolina St	76–64	Marquette	UCLA	Kansas	Norm Sloan
1975	UCLA	92–85	Kentucky	Louisville	Syracuse	John Wooden
1976	Indiana	86–68	Michigan	UCLA	Rutgers	Bob Knight
1977	Marquette	67–59	N Carolina	UNLV	NC-Charlotte	Al McGuire
1978	Kentucky	94–88	Duke	Arkansas	Notre Dame	Joe Hall
1979	Michigan St	75–64	Indiana St	DePaul	Penn	Jud Heathcote
1980	Louisville	59–54	Vacated‡	Purdue	Iowa	Denny Crum
1981	Indiana	63–50	N Carolina	Virginia	Louisiana St	Bob Knight
1982	N Carolina	63–62	Georgetown	*Houston	*Louisville	Dean Smith
1983	N Carolina St	54–52	Houston	*Georgia	*Louisville	Jim Valvano
1984	Georgetown	84–75	Houston	*Kentucky	*Virginia	John Thompson
1985	Villanova	66–64	Georgetown	St. John's (NY)	Vacated‡	Rollie Massimino
1986	Louisville	72–69	Duke	*Kansas	*Louisiana St	Denny Crum
1987	Indiana	74–73	Syracuse	*UNLV	*Providence	Bob Knight
1988	Kansas	83–79	Oklahoma	*Arizona	*Duke	Larry Brown
1989	Michigan	80–79 (OT)	Seton Hall	*Duke	*Illinois	Steve Fisher
1990	UNLV	103–73	Duke	*Arkansas	*Georgia Tech	Jerry Tarkanian
1991	Duke	72–65	Kansas	*UNLV	*N Carolina	Mike Krzyzewski
1992	Duke	71–51	Michigan	*Cincinnati	*Indiana	Mike Krzyzewski
1993	N Carolina	77–71	Michigan	*Kansas	*Kentucky	Dean Smith
1994	Arkansas	76–72	Duke	*Arizona	*Florida	Nolan Richardson
1995	UCLA	89–78	Arkansas	*N Carolina	*Oklahoma St	Jim Harrick
1996	Kentucky	76–67	Syracuse	Vacated‡	Mississippi St	Rick Pitino
1997	Arizona	84–79	Kentucky	*Minnesota	*N Carolina	Lute Olson
1998	Kentucky	78–69	Utah	*Stanford	*N Carolina	Tubby Smith

*Tied for third place. ‡Student-athletes representing St. Joseph's (PA) in 1961, Villanova in 1971, Western Kentucky in 1971, UCLA in 1980, Memphis State in 1985 and Massachusetts in 1996 were declared ineligible subsequent to the tournament. Under NCAA rules, the teams' and ineligible student-athletes' records were deleted, and the teams' places in the standings were vacated.

NCAA Final Four MVPs

Year	Winner, School	GP	Field Goals FGM	Pct	3-Pt FG FGA	FGM	Free Throws FTM	Pct	Reb	A	Stl	BS	Avg
1939	....None selected												
1940	....Marv Huffman, Indiana	2	7	—	—	—	4	—	—	—	—	—	9.0
1941	....John Kotz, Wisconsin	2	8	—	—	—	6	—	—	—	—	—	11.0
1942	....Howard Dallmar, Stanford	2	8	—	—	—	4	66.7	—	—	—	—	10.0
1943	....Ken Sailors, Wyoming	2	10	—	—	—	8	72.7	—	—	—	—	14.0
1944	....Arnie Ferrin, Utah	2	11	—	—	—	6	—	—	—	—	—	14.0
1945	....Bob Kurland, Oklahoma St	2	16	—	—	—	5	—	—	—	—	—	18.5
1946	....Bob Kurland, Oklahoma St	2	21	—	—	—	10	66.7	—	—	—	—	26.0
1947	....George Kaftan, Holy Cross	2	18	—	—	—	12	70.6	—	—	—	—	24.0
1948	....Alex Groza, Kentucky	2	16	—	—	—	5	—	—	—	—	—	18.5
1949	....Alex Groza, Kentucky	2	19	—	—	—	14	—	—	—	—	—	26.0
1950	....Irwin Dambrot, CCNY	2	12	42.9	—	—	4	50.0	—	—	—	—	14.0
1951	....None selected												
1952	....Clyde Lovellette, Kansas	2	24	—	—	—	18	—	—	—	—	—	33.0
1953	....*B.H. Horn, Kansas	2	17	—	—	—	17	—	—	—	—	—	25.5
1954	....Tom Gola, La Salle	2	12	—	—	—	14	—	—	—	—	—	19.0
1955	....Bill Russell, San Francisco	2	19	—	—	—	9	—	—	—	—	—	23.5
1956	....*Hal Lear, Temple	2	32	—	—	—	16	—	—	—	—	—	40.0
1957	....*Wilt Chamberlain, Kansas	2	18	51.4	—	—	19	70.4	25	—	—	—	32.5
1958	....*Elgin Baylor, Seattle	2	18	34.0	—	—	12	75.0	41	—	—	—	24.0
1959	....*Jerry West, West Virginia	2	22	66.7	—	—	22	68.8	25	—	—	—	33.0
1960	....Jerry Lucas, Ohio State	2	16	66.7	—	—	3	100.0	23	—	—	—	17.5
1961	....*Jerry Lucas, Ohio State	2	20	71.4	—	—	16	94.1	25	—	—	—	28.0
1962	....Paul Hogue, Cincinnati	2	23	63.9	—	—	12	63.2	38	—	—	—	29.0
1963	....Art Heyman, Duke	2	18	41.0	—	—	15	68.2	19	—	—	—	25.5
1964	....Walt Hazzard, UCLA	2	11	55.0	—	—	8	66.7	10	—	—	—	15.0
1965	....*Bill Bradley, Princeton	2	34	63.0	—	—	19	95.0	24	—	—	—	43.5
1966	....*Jerry Chambers, Utah	2	25	53.2	—	—	20	83.3	35	—	—	—	35.0
1967	....Lew Alcindor, UCLA	2	14	60.9	—	—	11	45.8	38	—	—	—	19.5
1968	....Lew Alcindor, UCLA	2	22	62.9	—	—	9	90.0	34	—	—	—	26.5
1969	....Lew Alcindor, UCLA	2	23	67.7	—	—	16	64.0	41	—	—	—	31.0
1970	....Sidney Wicks, UCLA	2	15	71.4	—	—	9	60.0	34	—	—	—	19.5
1971	....*†Howard Porter, Villanova	2	20	48.8	—	—	7	77.8	24	—	—	—	23.5
1972	....Bill Walton, UCLA	2	20	69.0	—	—	17	73.9	41	—	—	—	28.5
1973	....Bill Walton, UCLA	2	28	82.4	—	—	2	40.0	30	—	—	—	29.0
1974	....David Thompson, NC State	2	19	51.4	—	—	11	78.6	17	—	—	—	24.5
1975	....Richard Washington, UCLA	2	23	54.8	—	—	8	72.7	20	—	—	—	27.0
1976	....Kent Benson, Indiana	2	17	50.0	—	—	7	63.6	18	—	—	—	20.5
1977	....Butch Lee, Marquette	2	11	34.4	—	—	8	100.0	6	2	1	1	15.0
1978	....Jack Givens, Kentucky	2	28	65.1	—	—	8	66.7	17	4	1	3	32.0
1979	....Earvin Johnson, Michigan St	2	17	68.0	—	—	19	86.4	17	3	0	2	26.5
1980	....Darrell Griffith, Louisville	2	23	62.2	—	—	11	68.8	7	15	0	2	28.5
1981	....Isiah Thomas, Indiana	2	14	56.0	—	—	9	81.8	4	9	3	4	18.5
1982	....James Worthy, N Carolina	2	20	74.1	—	—	2	28.6	8	9	0	4	21.0
1983	....*Akeem Olajuwon, Houston	2	16	55.2	—	—	9	64.3	40	3	2	5	20.5
1984	....Patrick Ewing, Georgetown	2	8	57.1	—	—	2	100.0	18	1	1	15	9.0
1985	....Ed Pinckney, Villanova	2	8	57.1	—	—	12	75.0	15	6	3	0	14.0
1986	....Pervis Ellison, Louisville	2	15	60.0	—	—	6	75.0	24	2	3	1	18.0
1987	....Keith Smart, Indiana	2	14	63.6	1	0	7	77.8	7	7	0	2	17.5
1988	....Danny Manning, Kansas	2	25	55.6	1	0	6	66.7	17	4	8	9	28.0
1989	....Glen Rice, Michigan	2	24	49.0	16	7	4	100.0	16	1	0	3	29.5
1990	....Anderson Hunt, UNLV	2	19	61.3	16	9	2	50.0	4	9	1	1	24.5
1991	....Christian Laettner, Duke	2	12	54.5	1	1	21	91.3	17	2	1	2	23.0
1992	....Bobby Hurley, Duke	2	10	41.7	12	7	8	80.0	3	11	0	3	17.5
1993	....Donald Williams, N Carolina	2	15	65.2	14	10	10	100.0	4	2	2	0	25.0
1994	....Corliss Williamson, Arkansas	2	21	50.0	0	0	10	71.4	21	8	4	3	26.0
1995	....Ed O'Bannon, UCLA	2	16	45.7	8	3	10	76.9	25	3	7	1	22.5
1996	....Tony Delk, Kentucky	2	15	41.7	16	8	6	54.6	9	2	3	2	22.0
1997	....Miles Simon, Arizona	2	17	45.9	10	3	17	77.3	8	6	0	1	27.0
1998	....Jeff Sheppard, Kentucky	2	16	55.2	10	4	7	77.8	10	7	4	0	21.5

*Not a member of the championship-winning team.   †Record later vacated.

Best NCAA Tournament Single-Game Scoring Performances

Player and Team	Year	Round	FG	3FG	FT	TP
Austin Carr, Notre Dame vs Ohio	1970	1st	25	—	11	61
Bill Bradley, Princeton vs Wichita St	1965	C*	22	—	14	58
Oscar Robertson, Cincinnati vs Arkansas	1958	C	21	—	14	56
Austin Carr, Notre Dame vs Kentucky	1970	2nd	22	—	8	52
Austin Carr, Notre Dame vs Texas Christian	1971	1st	20	—	12	52
David Robinson, Navy vs Michigan	1987	1st	22	0	6	50
Elvin Hayes, Houston vs Loyola (IL)	1968	1st	20	—	9	49
Hal Lear, Temple vs SMU	1956	C*	17	—	14	48
Austin Carr, Notre Dame vs Houston	1971	C	17	—	13	47
Dave Corzine, DePaul vs Louisville	1978	2nd	18	—	10	46

C regional third place; C* third-place game.

NIT Championship Results

Year	Winner	Score	Runner-up	Year	Winner	Score	Runner-up
1938	Temple	60–36	Colorado	1969	Temple	89–76	Boston College
1939	Long Island U	44–32	Loyola (IL)	1970	Marquette	65–53	St. John's (NY)
1940	Colorado	51–40	Duquesne	1971	N Carolina	84–66	Georgia Tech
1941	Long Island U	56–42	Ohio U	1972	Maryland	100–69	Niagara
1942	W Virginia	47–45	W Kentucky	1973	Virginia Tech	92–91 (OT)	Notre Dame
1943	St. John's (NY)	48–27	Toledo	1974	Purdue	97–81	Utah
1944	St. John's (NY)	47–39	DePaul	1975	Princeton	80–69	Providence
1945	DePaul	71–54	Bowling Green	1976	Kentucky	71–67	NC-Charlotte
1946	Kentucky	46–45	Rhode Island	1977	St. Bonaventure	94–91	Houston
1947	Utah	49–45	Kentucky	1978	Texas	101–93	N Carolina St
1948	St. Louis	65–52	NYU	1979	Indiana	53–52	Purdue
1949	San Francisco	48–47	Loyola (IL)	1980	Virginia	58–55	Minnesota
1950	CCNY	69–61	Bradley	1981	Tulsa	86–84 (OT)	Syracuse
1951	BYU	62–43	Dayton	1982	Bradley	67–58	Purdue
1952	La Salle	75–64	Dayton	1983	Fresno St	69–60	DePaul
1953	Seton Hall	58–46	St. John's (NY)	1984	Michigan	83–63	Notre Dame
1954	Holy Cross	71–62	Duquesne	1985	UCLA	65–62	Indiana
1955	Duquesne	70–58	Dayton	1986	Ohio St	73–63	Wyoming
1956	Louisville	93–80	Dayton	1987	Southern Miss	84–80	La Salle
1957	Bradley	84–83	Memphis St	1988	Connecticut	72–67	Ohio St
1958	Xavier (OH)	78–74 (OT)	Dayton	1989	St. John's (NY)	73–65	St. Louis
1959	St. John's (NY)	76–71 (OT)	Bradley	1990	Vanderbilt	74–72	St. Louis
1960	Bradley	88–72	Providence	1991	Stanford	78–72	Oklahoma
1961	Providence	62–59	St. Louis	1992	Virginia	81–76	Notre Dame
1962	Dayton	73–67	St. John's (NY)	1993	Minnesota	62–61	Georgetown
1963	Providence	81–66	Canisius	1994	Villanova	80–73	Vanderbilt
1964	Bradley	86–54	New Mexico	1995	Virginia Tech	65–64 (OT)	Marquette
1965	St. John's (NY)	55–51	Villanova	1996	Nebraska	60–56	St. Joseph's
1966	BYU	97–84	NYU	1997	Michigan	82–73	Florida St
1967	Southern Illinois	71–56	Marquette	1998	Minnesota	79–72	Penn St
1968	Dayton	61–48	Kansas				

NCAA Men's Division I Season Leaders

Scoring Average

Year	Player and Team	Ht	Class	GP	FG	3FG	FT	Pts	Avg
1948	Murray Wier, Iowa	5-9	Sr	19	152	—	95	399	21.0
1949	Tony Lavelli, Yale	6-3	Sr	30	228	—	215	671	22.4
1950	Paul Arizin, Villanova	6-3	Sr	29	260	—	215	735	25.3
1951	Bill Mlkvy, Temple	6-4	Sr	25	303	—	125	731	29.2
1952	Clyde Lovellette, Kansas	6-9	Sr	28	315	—	165	795	28.4
1953	Frank Selvy, Furman	6-3	Jr	25	272	—	194	738	29.5
1954	Frank Selvy, Furman	6-3	Sr	29	427	—	355	1209	41.7
1955	Darrell Floyd, Furman	6-1	Jr	25	344	—	209	897	35.9
1956	Darrell Floyd, Furman	6-1	Sr	28	339	—	268	946	33.8
1957	Grady Wallace, S Carolina	6-4	Sr	29	336	—	234	906	31.2
1958	Oscar Robertson, Cincinnati	6-5	So	28	352	—	280	984	35.1
1959	Oscar Robertson, Cincinnati	6-5	Jr	30	331	—	316	978	32.6
1960	Oscar Robertson, Cincinnati	6-5	Sr	30	369	—	273	1011	33.7
1961	Frank Burgess, Gonzaga	6-1	Sr	26	304	—	234	842	32.4
1962	Billy McGill, Utah	6-9	Sr	26	394	—	221	1009	38.8

Scoring Average *(Cont.)*

Year	Player and Team	Ht	Class	GP	FG	3FG	FT	Pts	Avg
1963	Nick Werkman, Seton Hall	6-3	Jr	22	221	—	208	650	29.5
1964	Howard Komives, Bowling Green	6-1	Sr	23	292	—	260	844	36.7
1965	Rick Barry, Miami (FL)	6-7	Sr	26	340	—	293	973	37.4
1966	Dave Schellhase, Purdue	6-4	Sr	24	284	—	213	781	32.5
1967	Jim Walker, Providence	6-3	Sr	28	323	—	205	851	30.4
1968	Pete Maravich, Louisiana St	6-5	So	26	432	—	274	1138	43.8
1969	Pete Maravich, Louisiana St	6-5	Jr	26	433	—	282	1148	44.2
1970	Pete Maravich, Louisiana St	6-5	Sr	31	522	—	337	1381	44.5
1971	Johnny Neumann, Mississippi	6-6	So	23	366	—	191	923	40.1
1972	Dwight Lamar, Southwestern Louisiana	6-1	Jr	29	429	—	196	1054	36.3
1973	William Averitt, Pepperdine	6-1	Sr	25	352	—	144	848	33.9
1974	Larry Fogle, Canisius	6-5	So	25	326	—	183	835	33.4
1975	Bob McCurdy, Richmond	6-7	Sr	26	321	—	213	855	32.9
1976	Marshall Rodgers, TX-Pan American	6-2	Sr	25	361	—	197	919	36.8
1977	Freeman Williams, Portland St	6-4	Jr	26	417	—	176	1010	38.8
1978	Freeman Williams, Portland St	6-4	Sr	27	410	—	149	969	35.9
1979	Lawrence Butler, Idaho St	6-3	Sr	27	310	—	192	812	30.1
1980	Tony Murphy, Southern-BR	6-3	Sr	29	377	—	178	932	32.1
1981	Zam Fredrick, S Carolina	6-2	Sr	27	300	—	181	781	28.9
1982	Harry Kelly, Texas Southern	6-7	Jr	29	336	—	190	862	29.7
1983	Harry Kelly, Texas Southern	6-7	Sr	29	333	—	169	835	28.8
1984	Joe Jakubick, Akron	6-5	Sr	27	304	—	206	814	30.1
1985	Xavier McDaniel, Wichita St	6-8	Sr	31	351	—	142	844	27.2
1986	Terrance Bailey, Wagner	6-2	Jr	29	321	—	212	854	29.4
1987	Kevin Houston, Army	5-11	Sr	29	311	63	268	953	32.9
1988	Hersey Hawkins, Bradley	6-3	Sr	31	377	87	284	1125	36.3
1989	Hank Gathers, Loyola Marymount	6-7	Jr	31	419	0	177	1015	32.7
1990	Bo Kimble, Loyola Marymount	6-5	Sr	32	404	92	231	1131	35.3
1991	Kevin Bradshaw, U.S. Int'l	6-6	Sr	28	358	60	278	1054	37.6
1992	Brett Roberts, Morehead St	6-8	Sr	29	278	66	193	815	28.1
1993	Greg Guy, TX-Pan American	6-1	Jr	19	189	67	111	556	29.3
1994	Glenn Robinson, Purdue	6-8	Jr	34	368	79	215	1030	30.3
1995	Kurt Thomas, Texas Christian	6-9	Sr	27	288	3	202	781	28.9
1996	Kevin Granger, Texas Southern	6-3	Sr	24	194	30	230	648	27.0
1997	Charles Jones, LIU-Brooklyn	6-3	Jr	30	338	109	118	903	30.1
1998	Charles Jones, LIU-Brooklyn	6-3	Sr	30	326	116	101	869	29.0

Rebounds

Year	Player and Team	Ht	Class	GP	Reb	Avg
1951	Ernie Beck, Pennsylvania	6-4	So	27	556	20.6
1952	Bill Hannon, Army	6-3	So	17	355	20.9
1953	Ed Conlin, Fordham	6-5	So	26	612	23.5
1954	Art Quimby, Connecticut	6-5	Jr	26	588	22.6
1955	Charlie Slack, Marshall	6-5	Jr	21	538	25.6
1956	Joe Holup, George Washington	6-6	Sr	26	604	†.256
1957	Elgin Baylor, Seattle	6-6	Jr	25	508	†.235
1958	Alex Ellis, Niagara	6-5	Sr	25	536	†.262
1959	Leroy Wright, Pacific	6-8	Jr	26	652	†.238
1960	Leroy Wright, Pacific	6-8	Sr	17	380	†.234
1961	Jerry Lucas, Ohio St	6-8	Jr	27	470	†.198
1962	Jerry Lucas, Ohio St	6-8	Sr	28	499	†.211
1963	Paul Silas, Creighton	6-7	Sr	27	557	20.6
1964	Bob Pelkington, Xavier (OH)	6-7	Sr	26	567	21.8
1965	Toby Kimball, Connecticut	6-8	Sr	23	483	21.0
1966	Jim Ware, Oklahoma City	6-8	Sr	29	607	20.9
1967	Dick Cunningham, Murray St	6-10	Jr	22	479	21.8
1968	Neal Walk, Florida	6-10	Jr	25	494	19.8
1969	Spencer Haywood, Detroit	6-8	So	22	472	21.5
1970	Artis Gilmore, Jacksonville	7-2	Jr	28	621	22.2
1971	Artis Gilmore, Jacksonville	7-2	Sr	26	603	23.2
1972	Kermit Washington, American	6-8	Jr	23	455	19.8
1973	Kermit Washington, American	6-8	Sr	22	439	20.0
1974	Marvin Barnes, Providence	6-9	Sr	32	597	18.7
1975	John Irving, Hofstra	6-9	So	21	323	15.4
1976	Sam Pellom, Buffalo	6-8	So	26	420	16.2
1977	Glenn Mosley, Seton Hall	6-8	Sr	29	473	16.3
1978	Ken Williams, N Texas St	6-7	Sr	28	411	14.7

†From 1956-1962, title was based on highest individual recoveries out of total by both teams in all games.

Rebounds (Cont.)

Year	Player and Team	Ht	Class	GP	Reb	Avg
1979	Monti Davis, Tennessee St	6-7	Jr	26	421	16.2
1980	Larry Smith, Alcorn St	6-8	Sr	26	392	15.1
1981	Darryl Watson, Miss Valley	6-7	Sr	27	379	14.0
1982	LaSalle Thompson, Texas	6-10	Jr	27	365	13.5
1983	Xavier McDaniel, Wichita St	6-7	So	28	403	14.4
1984	Akeem Olajuwon, Houston	7-0	Jr	37	500	13.5
1985	Xavier McDaniel, Wichita St	6-8	Sr	31	460	14.8
1986	David Robinson, Navy	6-11	Jr	35	455	13.0
1987	Jerome Lane, Pittsburgh	6-6	So	33	444	13.5
1988	Kenny Miller, Loyola (IL)	6-9	Fr	29	395	13.6
1989	Hank Gathers, Loyola (CA)	6-7	Jr	31	426	13.7
1990	Anthony Bonner, St. Louis	6-8	Sr	33	456	13.8
1991	Shaquille O'Neal, Louisiana St	7-1	So	28	411	14.7
1992	Popeye Jones, Murray St	6-8	Sr	30	431	14.4
1993	Warren Kidd, Middle Tenn St	6-9	Sr	26	386	14.8
1994	Jerome Lambert, Baylor	6-8	Jr	24	355	14.8
1995	Kurt Thomas, Texas Christian	6-9	Sr	27	393	14.6
1996	Marcus Mann, Mississippi Valley	6-8	Sr	29	394	13.6
1997	Tim Duncan, Wake Forest	6-11	Sr	31	457	14.7
1998	Ryan Perryman, Dayton	6-7	Sr	33	412	12.5

Assists

Year	Player and Team	Class	GP	A	Avg
1984	Craig Lathen, IL-Chicago	Jr	29	274	9.45
1985	Rob Weingard, Hofstra	Sr	24	228	9.50
1986	Mark Jackson, St. John's (NY)	Jr	36	328	9.11
1987	Avery Johnson, Southern-BR	Jr	31	333	10.74
1988	Avery Johnson, Southern-BR	Sr	30	399	13.30
1989	Glenn Williams, Holy Cross	Sr	28	278	9.93
1990	Todd Lehmann, Drexel	Sr	28	260	9.29
1991	Chris Corchiani, N Carolina St	Sr	31	299	9.65
1992	Van Usher, Tennessee Tech	Sr	29	254	8.76
1993	Sam Crawford, New Mex St	Sr	34	310	9.12
1994	Jason Kidd, California	So	30	272	9.06
1995	Nelson Haggerty, Baylor	Sr	28	284	10.10
1996	Raimonds Miglinieks, UC-Irvine	Sr	27	230	8.52
1997	Kenny Mitchell, Dartmouth	Sr	26	203	7.81
1998	Ahlon Lewis, Arizona St	Sr	32	294	9.19

Blocked Shots

Year	Player and Team	Class	GP	BS	Avg
1986	David Robinson, Navy	Jr	35	207	5.91
1987	David Robinson, Navy	Sr	32	144	4.50
1988	Rodney Blake, St. Joseph's (PA)	Sr	29	116	4.00
1989	Alonzo Mourning, Georgetown	Fr	34	169	4.97
1990	Kenny Green, Rhode Island	Sr	26	124	4.77
1991	Shawn Bradley, Brigham Young	Fr	34	177	5.21
1992	Shaquille O'Neal, Louisiana St	Jr	30	157	5.23
1993	Theo Ratliff, Wyoming	Jr	28	124	4.43
1994	Grady Livingston, Howard	Jr	26	115	4.42
1995	Keith Closs, Central Conn St	Fr	26	139	5.35
1996	Keith Closs, Central Conn St	So	28	178	6.36
1997	Adonal Foyle, Colgate	Jr	28	180	6.43
1998	Jerome James, Florida A&M	Sr	27	125	4.63

Steals

Year	Player and Team	Class	GP	S	Avg
1986	Darron Brittman, Chicago St	Sr	28	139	4.96
1987	Tony Fairley, Charleston Sou	Sr	28	114	4.07
1988	Aldwin Ware, Florida A&M	Sr	29	142	4.90
1989	Kenny Robertson, Cleveland St	Jr	28	111	3.96
1990	Ronn McMahon, E Washington	Sr	29	130	4.48
1991	Van Usher, Tennessee Tech	Jr	28	104	3.71
1992	Victor Snipes, NE Illinois	So	25	86	3.44
1993	Jason Kidd, California	Fr	29	110	3.80
1994	Shawn Griggs, SW Louisiana	Sr	30	120	4.00
1995	Roderick Anderson, Texas	Sr	30	101	3.37
1996	Pointer Williams, McNeese St	Sr	27	118	4.37
1997	Joel Hoover, MD-Eastern Shore	Fr	28	90	3.21
1998	Bonzi Wells, Ball St	Sr	29	103	3.55

Single Game Records

SCORING HIGHS VS DIVISION I OPPONENT

Pts	Player and Team vs Opponent	Date
72	Kevin Bradshaw, U.S. Int'l vs Loyola Marymount	1-5-91
69	Pete Maravich, Louisiana St vs Alabama	2-7-70
68	Calvin Murphy, Niagara vs Syracuse	12-7-68
66	Jay Handlan, Washington & Lee vs Furman	2-17-51
66	Pete Maravich, Louisiana St vs Tulane	2-10-69
66	Anthony Roberts, Oral Roberts vs N Carolina A&T	2-19-77
65	Anthony Roberts, Oral Roberts vs Oregon	3-9-77
65	Scott Haffner, Evansville vs Dayton	2-18-89
64	Pete Maravich, Louisiana St vs Kentucky	2-21-70
63	Johnny Neumann, Mississippi vs Louisiana St	1-30-71
63	Hersey Hawkins, Bradley vs Detroit	2-22-88

SCORING HIGHS VS NON-DIVISION I OPPONENT

Pts	Player and Team vs Opponent	Date
100	Frank Selvy, Furman vs Newberry	2-13-54
85	Paul Arizin, Villanova vs Philadelphia NAMC	2-12-49
81	Freeman Williams, Portland St vs Rocky Mountain	2-3-78
73	Bill Mlkvy, Temple vs Wilkes	3-3-51
71	Freeman Williams, Portland St vs Southern Oregon	2-9-77

REBOUNDING HIGHS BEFORE 1973

Reb	Player and Team vs Opponent	Date
51	Bill Chambers, William & Mary vs Virginia	2-14-53
43	Charlie Slack, Marshall vs Morris Harvey	1-12-54
42	Tom Heinsohn, Holy Cross vs Boston College	3-1-55
40	Art Quimby, Connecticut vs Boston U	1-11-55
39	Maurice Stokes, St. Francis (PA) vs John Carroll	1-28-55
39	Dave DeBusschere, Detroit vs Central Michigan	1-30-60
39	Keith Swagerty, Pacific vs UC-Santa Barbara	3-5-65

REBOUNDING HIGHS SINCE 1973*

Reb	Player and Team vs Opponent	Date
34	David Vaughn, Oral Roberts vs Brandeis	1-8-73
33	Robert Parish, Centenary vs Southern Miss	1-22-73
32	Jervaughn Scales, Southern-BR vs Grambling	2-7-94
32	Durand Macklin, Louisiana St vs Tulane	11-26-76
31	Jim Bradley, Northern Illinois vs WI-Milwaukee	2-19-73
31	Calvin Natt, NE Louisiana vs Georgia Southern	12-29-76

ASSISTS

A	Player and Team vs Opponent	Date
22	Tony Fairley, Baptist vs Armstrong St	2-9-87
22	Avery Johnson, Southern-BR vs Texas Southern	1-25-88
22	Sherman Douglas, Syracuse vs Providence	1-28-89
21	Mark Wade, UNLV vs Navy	12-29-86
21	Kelvin Scarborough, New Mexico vs Hawaii	2-13-87
21	Anthony Manuel, Bradley vs UC-Irvine	12-19-87
21	Avery Johnson, Southern-BR vs Alabama St	1-16-88

STEALS

S	Player and Team vs Opponent	Date
13	Mookie Blaylock, Oklahoma vs Centenary	12-12-87
13	Mookie Blaylock, Oklahoma vs Loyola Marymount	12-17-88
12	Kenny Robertson, Cleveland St vs Wagner	12-3-88
12	Terry Evans, Oklahoma vs Florida A&M	1-27-93

Nine tied with 11, most recently Philip Huler, Fla. Atlantic vs Campbell, 1-18-97.

*Freshmen became eligible for varsity play in 1973.

Single Game Records *(Cont.)*

BLOCKED SHOTS

BS	Player and Team vs Opponent	Date
14	David Robinson, Navy vs NC-Wilmington	1-4-86
14	Shawn Bradley, Brigham Young vs Eastern Kentucky	12-7-90
14	Roy Rogers, Alabama vs Georgia	2-10-96
13	Kevin Roberson, Vermont vs New Hampshire	1-9-92
13	Jim McIlvaine, Marquette vs Northeastern (IL)	12-9-92
13	Keith Closs, Central Conn. St vs St. Francis (PA)	12-21-94

Single Season Records

POINTS

Player and Team	Year	GP	FG	3FG	FT	Pts
Pete Maravich, Louisiana St	1970	31	522	—	337	1381
Elvin Hayes, Houston	1968	33	519	—	176	1214
Frank Selvy, Furman	1954	29	427	—	355	1209
Pete Maravich, Louisiana St	1969	26	433	—	282	1148
Pete Maravich, Louisiana St	1968	26	432	—	274	1138
Bo Kimble, Loyola Marymount	1990	32	404	92	231	1131
Hersey Hawkins, Bradley	1988	31	377	87	284	1125
Austin Carr, Notre Dame	1970	29	444	—	218	1106
Austin Carr, Notre Dame	1971	29	430	—	241	1101
Otis Birdsong, Houston	1977	36	452	—	186	1090

SCORING AVERAGE

Player and Team	Year	GP	FG	3FG	FT	Pts
Pete Maravich, Louisiana St	1970	31	522	337	1381	44.5
Pete Maravich, Louisiana St	1969	26	433	282	1148	44.2
Pete Maravich, Louisiana St	1968	26	432	274	1138	43.8
Frank Selvy, Furman	1954	29	427	355	1209	41.7
Johnny Neumann, Mississippi	1971	23	366	191	923	40.1
Freeman Williams, Portland St	1977	26	417	176	1010	38.8
Billy McGill, Utah	1962	26	394	221	1009	38.8
Calvin Murphy, Niagara	1968	24	337	242	916	38.2
Austin Carr, Notre Dame	1970	29	444	218	1106	38.1
Austin Carr, Notre Dame	1971	29	430	241	1101	38.0

REBOUNDS

Player and Team	Year	GP	Reb	Player and Team	Year	GP	Reb
Walt Dukes, Seton Hall	1953	33	734	Artis Gilmore, Jacksonville	1970	28	621
Leroy Wright, Pacific	1959	26	652	Tom Gola, La Salle	1955	31	618
Tom Gola, La Salle	1954	30	652	Ed Conlin, Fordham	1953	26	612
Charlie Tyra, Louisville	1956	29	645	Art Quimby, Connecticut	1955	25	611
Paul Silas, Creighton	1964	29	631	Bill Russell, San Francisco	1956	29	609
Elvin Hayes, Houston	1968	33	624	Jim Ware, Oklahoma City	1966	29	607

REBOUND AVERAGE BEFORE 1973

Player and Team	Year	GP	Reb	Avg
Charlie Slack, Marshall	1955	21	538	25.6
Leroy Wright, Pacific	1959	26	652	25.1
Art Quimby, Connecticut	1955	25	611	24.4
Charlie Slack, Marshall	1956	22	520	23.6
Ed Conlin, Fordham	1953	26	612	23.5

REBOUND AVERAGE SINCE 1973*

Player and Team	Year	GP	Reb	Avg
Kermit Washington, American	1973	22	439	20.0
Marvin Barnes, Providence	1973	30	571	19.0
Marvin Barnes, Providence	1974	32	597	18.7
Pete Padgett, NV-Reno	1973	26	462	17.8
Jim Bradley, Northern Illinois	1973	24	426	17.8

*Freshmen became eligible for varsity play in 1973.

Single Season Records (Cont.)

ASSISTS

Player and Team	Year	GP	A	Player and Team	Year	GP	A
Mark Wade, UNLV	1987	38	406	Sherman Douglas, Syracuse	1989	38	326
Avery Johnson, Southern-BR	1988	30	399	Sam Crawford, New Mex. St	1993	34	310
Anthony Manuel, Bradley	1988	31	373	Greg Anthony, UNLV	1991	35	310
Avery Johnson, Southern-BR	1987	31	333	Reid Gettys, Houston	1984	37	309
Mark Jackson, St. John's (NY)	1986	32	328	Carl Golston, Loyola (IL)	1985	33	305

ASSIST AVERAGE

Player and Team	Year	GP	A	Avg	Player and Team	Year	GP	A	Avg
Avery Johnson, Southern-BR	1988	30	399	13.3	Chris Corchiani, N Carolina St	1991	31	299	9.6
Anthony Manuel, Bradley	1988	31	373	12.0	Tony Fairley, Charleston S'thern*	1987	28	270	9.6
Avery Johnson, Southern-BR	1987	31	333	10.7	Tyrone Bogues, Wake Forest	1987	29	276	9.5
Mark Wade, UNLV	1987	38	406	10.7	Ron Weingard, Hofstra	1985	24	228	9.5
Nelson Haggerty, Baylor	1995	28	284	10.1	Craig Neal, Georgia Tech	1988	32	303	9.5
Glenn Williams, Holy Cross	1989	28	278	9.9	*Formerly Baptist.				

FIELD-GOAL PERCENTAGE

Player and Team	Year	GP	FG	FGA	Pct
Steve Johnson, Oregon St	1981	28	235	315	74.6
Dwayne Davis, Florida	1989	33	179	248	72.2
Keith Walker, Utica	1985	27	154	216	71.3
Steve Johnson, Oregon St	1980	30	211	297	71.0
Oliver Miller, Arkansas	1991	38	254	361	70.4
Alan Williams, Princeton	1987	25	163	232	70.3
Mark McNamara, California	1982	27	231	329	70.2
Warren Kidd, Middle Tennessee St	1991	30	173	247	70.0
Pete Freeman, Akron	1991	28	175	250	70.0
Joe Senser, West Chester	1977	25	130	186	69.9

Based on qualifiers for annual championship.

FREE-THROW PERCENTAGE

Player and Team	Year	GP	FT	FTA	Pct
Craig Collins, Penn St	1985	27	94	98	95.9
Rod Foster, UCLA	1982	27	95	100	95.0
Danny Basile, Marist	1994	27	84	89	94.4
Carlos Gibson, Marshall	1978	28	84	89	94.4
Jim Barton, Dartmouth	1986	26	65	69	94.2
Jack Moore, Nebraska	1982	27	123	131	93.9
Dandrea Evans, Troy St	1994	27	72	77	93.5
Rob Robbins, New Mexico	1990	34	101	108	93.5
Tommy Boyer, Arkansas	1962	23	125	134	93.3
Damon Goodwin, Dayton	1986	30	95	102	93.1

Based on qualifiers for annual championship.

THREE-POINT FIELD-GOAL PERCENTAGE

Player and Team	Year	GP	3FG	3FGA	Pct
Glenn Tropf, Holy Cross	1988	29	52	82	63.4
Sean Wightman, Western Michigan	1992	30	48	76	63.2
Keith Jennings, E Tennessee St	1991	33	84	142	59.2
Dave Calloway, Monmouth (NJ)	1989	28	48	82	58.5
Steve Kerr, Arizona	1988	38	114	199	57.3
Reginald Jones, Prairie View	1987	28	64	112	57.1
Jim Cantamessa, Siena	1998	29	66	117	56.4
Joel Tribelhorn, Colorado St	1989	33	76	135	56.3
Mike Joseph, Bucknell	1988	28	65	116	56.0
Brian Jackson, Evansville	1995	27	53	95	55.8

Based on qualifiers for annual championship.

Single Season Records (Cont.)

STEALS

Player and Team	Year	GP	S
Mookie Blaylock, Oklahoma	1988	39	150
Aldwin Ware, Florida A&M	1988	29	142
Darron Brittman, Chicago St	1986	28	139
Nadav Henefeld, Connecticut	1990	37	138
Mookie Blaylock, Oklahoma	1989	35	131

BLOCKED SHOTS

Player and Team	Year	GP	BS
David Robinson, Navy	1986	35	207
Adonal Foyle, Colgate	1997	28	180
Keith Closs, Central Conn St	1996	28	178
Shawn Bradley, BYU	1991	34	177
Alonzo Mourning, Georgetown	1989	34	169

STEAL AVERAGE

Player and Team	Year	GP	S	Avg
Darron Brittman, Chicago St	1986	28	139	4.96
Aldwin Ware, Florida A&M	1988	29	142	4.90
Ronn McMahon, E Washington	1990	29	130	4.48
Pointer Williams, McNeese St	1996	27	118	4.37
Jim Paguaga, St Francis (NY)	1986	28	120	4.29

BLOCKED-SHOT AVERAGE

Player and Team	Year	GP	BS	Avg
Adonal Foyle, Colgate	1997	28	180	6.43
Keith Closs, Central Conn St	1996	28	178	6.36
David Robinson, Navy	1986	35	207	5.91
Adonal Foyle, Colgate	1996	29	165	5.69
Keith Closs, Central Conn St	1995	26	139	5.34

Career Records

POINTS

Player and Team	Ht	Final Year	GP	FG	3FG*	FT	Pts
Pete Maravich, Louisiana St	6-5	1970	83	1387	—	893	3667
Freeman Williams, Portland St	6-4	1978	106	1369	—	511	3249
Lionel Simmons, La Salle	6-7	1990	131	1244	56	673	3217
Alphonso Ford, Mississippi Valley	6-2	1993	109	1121	333	590	3165
Harry Kelly, Texas Southern	6-7	1983	110	1234	—	598	3066
Hersey Hawkins, Bradley	6-3	1988	125	1100	118	690	3008
Oscar Robertson, Cincinnati	6-5	1960	88	1052	—	869	2973
Danny Manning, Kansas	6-10	1988	147	1216	10	509	2951
Alfredrick Hughes, Loyola (IL)	6-5	1985	120	1226	—	462	2914
Elvin Hayes, Houston	6-8	1968	93	1215	—	454	2884
Larry Bird, Indiana St	6-9	1979	94	1154	—	542	2850
Otis Birdsong, Houston	6-4	1977	116	1176	—	480	2832
Kevin Bradshaw, Bethune-Cookman, U.S. Int'l	6-6	1991	111	1027	132	618	2804
Allan Houston, Tennessee	6-6	1993	128	902	346	651	2801
Hank Gathers, Southern Cal, Loyola Marymount	6-7	1990	117	1127	0	469	2723
Reggie Lewis, Northeastern	6-7	1987	122	1043	30 (1)	592	2708
Daren Queenan, Lehigh	6-5	1988	118	1024	29	626	2703
Byron Larkin, Xavier (OH)	6-3	1988	121	1022	51	601	2696
David Robinson, Navy	7-1	1987	127	1032	1	604	2669
Wayman Tisdale, Oklahoma	6-9	1985	104	1077	—	507	2661

*Listed is the number of three-pointers scored since it became the national rule in 1987; the number in the parentheses is number scored prior to 1987—these counted as three points in the game but counted as two-pointers in the national rankings. The three-pointers in the parentheses are not included in total points.

Career Records (Cont.)
SCORING AVERAGE

Player and Team	Final Year	GP	FG	FT	Pts	Avg
Pete Maravich, Louisiana St	1968	83	1387	893	3667	44.2
Austin Carr, Notre Dame	1971	74	1017	526	2560	34.6
Oscar Robertson, Cincinnati	1960	88	1052	869	2973	33.8
Calvin Murphy, Niagara	1970	77	947	654	2548	33.1
Dwight Lamar, Southwestern Louisiana	1973	57	768	326	1862	32.7
Frank Selvy, Furman	1954	78	922	694	2538	32.5
Rick Mount, Purdue	1970	72	910	503	2323	32.3
Darrell Floyd, Furman	1956	71	868	545	2281	32.1
Nick Werkman, Seton Hall	1964	71	812	649	2273	32.0
Willie Humes, Idaho St	1971	48	565	380	1510	31.5
William Averitt, Pepperdine	1973	49	615	311	1541	31.4
Elgin Baylor, Coll. of Idaho, Seattle	1958	80	956	588	2500	31.3
Elvin Hayes, Houston	1968	93	1215	454	2884	31.0
Freeman Williams, Portland St	1978	106	1369	511	3249	30.7
Larry Bird, Indiana St	1979	94	1154	542	2850	30.3

REBOUNDS BEFORE 1973

Player and Team	Final Year	GP	Reb
Tom Gola, La Salle	1955	118	2201
Joe Holup, George Washington	1956	104	2030
Charlie Slack, Marshall	1956	88	1916
Ed Conlin, Fordham	1955	102	1884
Dickie Hemric, Wake Forest	1955	104	1802

REBOUNDS SINCE 1973*

Player and Team	Final Year	GP	Reb
Tim Duncan, Wake Forest	1997	128	1570
Derrick Coleman, Syracuse	1990	143	1537
Malik Rose, Drexel	1996	120	1514
Ralph Sampson, Virginia	1983	132	1511
Pete Padgett, NV-Reno	1976	104	1464

ASSISTS

Player and Team	Final Year	GP	A
Bobby Hurley, Duke	1993	140	1076
Chris Corchiani, N Carolina St	1991	124	1038
Keith Jennings, E Tennessee St	1991	127	983
Sherman Douglas, Syracuse	1989	138	960
Tony Miller, Marquette	1995	123	956

FIELD-GOAL PERCENTAGE

Player and Team	Final Year	FG	FGA	Pct
Ricky Nedd, Appalachian St	1994	412	597	69.0
Stephen Scheffler, Purdue	1990	408	596	68.5
Steve Johnson, Oregon St	1981	828	1222	67.8
Murray Brown, Florida St	1980	566	847	66.8
Lee Campbell, SW Missouri St	1990	411	618	66.5

Note: Minimum 400 field goals.

FREE-THROW PERCENTAGE

Player and Team	Final Year	FT	FTA	Pct
Greg Starrick, Kentucky, Southern Illinois	1972	341	375	90.9
Jack Moore, Nebraska	1982	446	495	90.1
Steve Henson, Kansas St	1990	361	401	90.0
Steve Alford, Indiana	1987	535	596	89.8
Bob Lloyd, Rutgers	1967	543	605	89.8

Note: Minimum 300 free throws.

*Freshmen became eligible for varsity play in 1973.

Career Records *(Cont.)*

THREE-POINT FIELD GOALS MADE

Player and Team	Final Year	GP	3FG
Curtis Staples, Virginia	1998	122	413
Keith Veney, Lamar; Marshall	1997	111	409
Doug Day, Radford	1993	117	401
Ronnie Schmitz, MO-Kansas City	1993	112	378
Mark Alberts, Akron	1993	103	375

THREE-POINT FIELD-GOAL PERCENTAGE

Player and Team	Final Year	3FG	3FGA	Pct
Tony Bennett, WI-Green Bay	1992	290	584	49.7
Keith Jennings, E Tennessee St	1991	223	452	49.3
Kirk Manns, Michigan St.	1990	212	446	47.5
Tim Locum, Wisconsin	1991	227	481	47.2
David Olson, Eastern Illinois	1992	262	562	46.6

Note: Minimum 200 3-point field goals.

STEALS

Player and Team	Final Year	GP	S
Eric Murdock, Providence	1991	117	376
Bonzi Wells, Ball St	1998	116	347
Gerald Walker, San Francisco	1996	111	344
Johnny Rhodes, Maryland	1996	122	344
Michael Anderson, Drexel	1988	115	341
Kenny Robertson, New Mexico; Clev. St	1990	119	341

BLOCKED SHOTS

Player and Team	Final Year	GP	BS
Adonal Foyle, Colgate	1997	87	492
Tim Duncan, Wake Forest	1997	128	481
Alonzo Mourning, Georgetown	1992	120	453
Lorenzo Coleman, Tennessee Tech	1997	113	437
Theo Ratliff, Wyoming	1995	111	425

NCAA Men's Division I Team Leaders

Division I Team Alltime Wins

Team	First Year	Yrs	W	L	T
Kentucky	1903	95	1720	529	1
N Carolina	1911	88	1709	599	0
Kansas	1899	100	1665	714	0
St. John's (NY)	1908	91	1554	706	0
Duke	1906	93	1548	753	0
Temple	1895	102	1496	813	0
Syracuse	1901	97	1477	692	0
Oregon St	1902	97	1456	985	0
Pennsylvania	1897	98	1454	832	2
Indiana	1901	98	1430	767	0
Notre Dame	1898	93	1427	776	1
UCLA	1920	79	1423	612	0
Princeton	1901	98	1386	843	0
Washington	1896	96	1386	893	0
Purdue	1897	100	1383	758	0

Note: Minimum of 25 years in Division I.

Division I Alltime Winning Percentage

Team	First Year	Yrs	W	L	T	Pct
Kentucky	1903	95	1720	529	1	.765
N Carolina	1911	88	1709	599	0	.740
UNLV	1959	40	831	307	0	.730
Kansas	1899	100	1665	714	0	.700
UCLA	1920	79	1423	612	0	.699
St. John's (NY)	1908	91	1554	706	0	.688
Syracuse	1901	97	1477	692	0	.681
Duke	1906	93	1548	753	0	.673
Western Kentucky	1915	79	1366	669	0	.671
Arkansas	1924	75	1292	671	0	.658
Utah	1909	90	1376	732	0	.653
Indiana	1901	98	1430	767	0	.651
Louisville	1912	84	1337	716	0	.651
Temple	1895	102	1496	813	0	.648
Notre Dame	1898	93	1427	776	1	.648

Note: Minimum of 25 years in Division I.

NCAA Men's Division I Winning Streaks

Longest—Full Season

Team	Games	Years	Ended by
UCLA	88	1971–74	Notre Dame (71–70)
San Francisco	60	1955–57	Illinois (62–33)
UCLA	47	1966–68	Houston (71–69)
UNLV	45	1990–91	Duke (79–77)
Texas	44	1913–17	Rice (24–18)
Seton Hall	43	1939–41	LIU-Brooklyn (49–26)
LIU-Brooklyn	43	1935–37	Stanford (45–31)
UCLA	41	1968–69	Southern Cal (46–44)
Marquette	39	1970–71	Ohio St (60–59)
Cincinnati	37	1962–63	Wichita St (65–64)
N Carolina	37	1957–58	W Virginia (75–64)

Longest—Regular Season

Team	Games	Years	Ended by
UCLA	76	1971–74	Notre Dame (71–70)
Indiana	57	1975–77	Toledo (59–57)
Marquette	56	1970–72	Detroit (70–49)
Kentucky	54	1952–55	Georgia Tech (59–58)
San Francisco	51	1955–57	Illinois (62–33)
Pennsylvania	48	1970–72	Temple (57–52)
Ohio State	47	1960–62	Wisconsin (86–67)
Texas	44	1913–17	Rice (24–18)
UCLA	43	1966–68	Houston (71–69)
LIU-Brooklyn	43	1935–37	Stanford (45–31)
Seton Hall	42	1939–41	LIU-Brooklyn (49–26)

Longest—Home Court

Team	Games	Years		Team	Games	Years
Kentucky	129	1943–55		Lamar	80	1978–84
St. Bonaventure	99	1948–61		Long Beach St	75	1968–74
UCLA	98	1970–76		UNLV	72	1974–78
Cincinnati	86	1957–64		Arizona	71	1987–92
Marquette	81	1967–73		Cincinnati	68	1972–78
Arizona	81	1945–51		Western Kentucky	67	1949–55

NCAA Men's Division I Winningest Coaches

Active Coaches

WINS

Coach and Team	W
James Phelan, Mt. St. Mary's (MD)	785
Bob Knight, Indiana	720
Norm Stewart, Missouri	711
Don Haskins, UTEP	703
Lefty Driesell, James Madison	699
Jerry Tarkanian, Fresno St	688
Lou Henson, New Mexico St	681
Denny Crum, Louisville	625
Eddie Sutton, Oklahoma St	609
John Thompson, Georgetown	589

Note: Minimum 5 years as a Division I head coach; includes record at 4-year colleges only.

WINNING PERCENTAGE

Coach and Team	Yrs	W	L	Pct
Jerry Tarkanian, Fresno St	28	688	158	.813
Roy Williams, Kansas	10	282	62	.820
John Kresse, Coll. of Charleston	18	441	112	.798
Jim Boeheim, Syracuse	22	528	181	.745
Nolan Richardson, Arkansas	18	433	155	.736
John Chaney, Temple	26	581	208	.736
Rick Majerus, Utah	14	309	111	.736
Lute Olson, Arizona	25	564	206	.732
Denny Crum, Louisville	27	625	233	.728
Bob Knight, Indiana	33	720	270	.727

Note: Minimum 5 years as a Division I head coach; includes record at 4-year colleges only.

Alltime Winningest Men's Division I Coaches

WINS

Coach (Team)	W
Dean Smith (N Carolina)	879
Adolph Rupp (Kentucky)	876
Hank Iba (NW Missouri St, Colorado, Oklahoma St)	767
Ed Diddle (Western Kentucky)	759
Phog Allen (Baker, Kansas, Haskell, Central Missouri St, Kansas)	746
Ray Meyer (DePaul)	724
Bob Knight (Army, Indiana)	720
Don Haskins (UTEP)	703
Lefty Driesell (Davidson, Maryland, James Madison)	699
Norm Stewart (Missouri)	694
Jerry Tarkanian (Long Beach St, UNLV, Fresno St)	688
Lou Henson (Hardin-Simmons, New Mexico St, Illinois)	681
John Wooden (Indiana St, UCLA)	664
Ralph Miller (Wichita St, Iowa, Oregon St)	657
Marv Harshman (Pacific Lutheran, Washington St, Washington)	654

Note: Minimum 10 head coaching seasons in Division I.

Alltime Winningest Men's Division I Coaches (Cont.)

WINNING PERCENTAGE

Coach (Team)	Yrs	W	L	Pct
Clair Bee (Rider 29–31, LIU-Brooklyn 32–45, 46–51)	21	412	87	.826
Adolph Rupp (Kentucky 31–72)	41	876	190	.822
Roy Williams (Kansas 89–)	10	282	62	.820
Jerry Tarkanian (Long Beach St 69–73, UNLV 74–92, Fresno St 95–)	27	688	158	.813
John Wooden (Indiana St 47–48, UCLA 49–75)	29	664	162	.804
Dean Smith (N Carolina 62–97)	36	879	254	.776
Harry Fisher (Columbia 07–16, Army 22–23, 25)	13	147	44	.770
Frank Keaney (Rhode Island 21–48)	27	387	117	.768
George Keogan (St. Louis 16, Allegheny 19, Valparaiso 20–21, Notre Dame 24–43)	24	385	117	.767
Jack Ramsay (St. Joseph's [PA] 56–66)	11	231	71	.765
Vic Bubas (Duke 60–69)	10	213	67	.761
Charles (Chick) Davies (Duquesne 25–43, 47–48)	21	314	106	.748
Ray Mears (Wittenberg 57–62, Tennessee 63–77)	21	399	135	.747
Jim Boeheim (Syracuse 77–)	22	528	181	.745
Al McGuire (Belmont Abbey 58–64, Marquette 65–77)	20	405	143	.739
Rick Pitino (Boston 79–83, Providence 86–87, Kentucky 90–97)	15	352	124	.739
Phog Allen (Baker 06–08, Kansas 08–09, Haskell 09, Cent MO St 13–19, Kansas 20–56)	48	746	264	.739
Everett Case (N Carolina St 47–64)	18	376	133	.739
Nolan Richardson (Tulsa 81–85, Arkansas 86–)	18	433	155	.736
John Chaney (Cheyney 73–82, Temple 83–)	26	581	208	.736

Note: Minimum 10 head coaching seasons in Division I.

NCAA Women's Division I Championship Results

Year	Winner	Score	Runner-up	Winning Coach
1982	Louisiana Tech	76–62	Cheyney	Sonja Hogg
1983	Southern Cal	69–67	Louisiana Tech	Linda Sharp
1984	Southern Cal	72–61	Tennessee	Linda Sharp
1985	Old Dominion	70–65	Georgia	Marianne Stanley
1986	Texas	97–81	Southern Cal	Jody Conradt
1987	Tennessee	67–44	Louisiana Tech	Pat Summitt
1988	Louisiana Tech	56–54	Auburn	Leon Barmore
1989	Tennessee	76–60	Auburn	Pat Summitt
1990	Stanford	88–81	Auburn	Tara VanDerveer
1991	Tennessee	70–67 (OT)	Virginia	Pat Summitt
1992	Stanford	78–62	Western Kentucky	Tara VanDerveer
1993	Texas Tech	84–82	Ohio State	Marsha Sharp
1994	N Carolina	60–59	Louisiana Tech	Sylvia Hatchell
1995	Connecticut	70–64	Tennessee	Geno Auriemma
1996	Tennessee	83–65	Georgia	Pat Summitt
1997	Tennessee	68–59	Old Dominion	Pat Summitt
1998	Tennessee	93–75	Louisiana Tech	Pat Summitt

NCAA Women's Division I Alltime Individual Leaders

Single-Game Records

SCORING HIGHS

Pts	Player and Team vs Opponent	Year
60	Cindy Brown, Long Beach St vs San Jose St	1987
58	Kim Perrot, SW Louisiana vs SE Louisiana	1990
58	Lorri Bauman, Drake vs SW Missouri St	1984
55	Patricia Hoskins, Mississippi Valley vs Southern-BR	1989
55	Patricia Hoskins, Mississippi Valley vs Alabama St	1989
54	Anjinea Hopson, Grambling vs Jackson St	1994
54	Mary Lowry, Baylor vs Texas	1994
54	Wanda Ford, Drake vs SW Missouri St	1986
53	Felisha Edwards, NE Louisiana vs Southern Mississippi	1991
53	Chris Starr, NV-Reno vs Cal St-Sacramento	1983
53	Sheryl Swoopes, Texas Tech vs Texas	1993

Single-Game Records *(Cont.)*

REBOUNDING HIGHS

Reb	Player and Team vs Opponent	Year
40	Deborah Temple, Delta St vs AL-Birmingham	1983
37	Rosina Pearson, Bethune-Cookman vs Florida Memorial	1985
33	Maureen Formico, Pepperdine vs Loyola (CA)	1985
31	Darlene Beale, Howard vs S Carolina St	1987
30	Cindy Bonforte, Wagner vs Queens (NY)	1983
30	Kayone Hankins, New Orleans vs. Nicholls St	1994
29	Wanda Ford, Drake vs Eastern Illinois	1985
29	Gail Norris, Alabama St vs Texas Southern	1992
29	Joy Kellogg, Oklahoma City vs Oklahoma Christian	1984
29	Joy Kellogg, Oklahoma City vs UTEP	1984

ASSISTS

A	Player and Team vs Opponent	Year
23	Michelle Burden, Kent St vs Ball St	1991
22	Shawn Monday, Tennessee Tech vs Morehead St	1988
22	Veronica Pettry, Loyola (IL) vs Detroit	1989
22	Tine Freil, Pacific vs Wichita St	1991
21	Tine Freil, Pacific vs Fresno St	1992
21	Amy Bauer, Wisconsin vs Detroit	1989
21	Neacole Hall, Alabama St vs Southern-BR	1989

Five tied with 20.

POINTS

Season Records

Player and Team	Year	GP	FG	3FG	FT	Pts
Cindy Brown, Long Beach St	1987	35	362	—	250	974
Genia Miller, Cal St-Fullerton	1991	33	376	0	217	969
Sheryl Swoopes, Texas Tech	1993	34	356	32	211	955
Andrea Congreaves, Mercer	1992	28	353	77	142	925
Wanda Ford, Drake	1986	30	390	—	139	919
Chamique Holdsclaw, Tennessee	1998	39	370	9	166	915
Barbara Kennedy, Clemson	1982	31	392	—	124	908
Patricia Hoskins, Mississippi Valley	1989	27	345	13	205	908
LaTaunya Pollard, Long Beach St	1983	31	376	—	155	907
Tina Hutchinson, San Diego St	1984	30	383	—	132	898

SEASON SCORING AVERAGE

Player and Team	Year	GP	FG	3FG	FT	Pts	Avg
Patricia Hoskins, Mississippi Valley	1989	27	345	13	205	908	33.6
Andrea Congreaves, Mercer	1992	28	353	77	142	925	33.0
Deborah Temple, Delta St	1984	28	373	—	127	873	31.2
Andrea Congreaves, Mercer	1993	26	302	51	150	805	31.0
Wanda Ford, Drake	1986	30	390	—	139	919	30.6
Anucha Browne, Northwestern	1985	28	341	—	173	855	30.5
LeChandra LeDay, Grambling	1988	28	334	36	146	850	30.4
Kim Perrot, Southwestern Louisiana	1990	28	308	95	128	839	30.0
Tina Hutchinson, San Diego St	1984	30	383	—	132	898	29.9
Jan Jensen, Drake	1991	30	358	6	166	888	29.6
Genia Miller, Cal St-Fullerton	1991	33	376	0	217	969	29.4
Barbara Kennedy, Clemson	1982	31	392	—	124	908	29.3
LaTaunya Pollard, Long Beach St	1983	31	376	—	155	907	29.3
Lisa McMullen, Alabama St	1991	28	285	126	119	815	29.1
Tresa Spaulding, BYU	1987	28	347	—	116	810	28.9
Hope Linthicum, Central Conn. St	1987	23	282	—	101	665	28.9

Season Records (Cont.)

REBOUNDS

Player and Team	Year	GP	Reb	Player and Team	Year	GP	Reb
Wanda Ford, Drake	1985	30	534	Rosina Pearson, Beth.-Cookman	1985	26	480
Wanda Ford, Drake	1986	30	506	Patricia Hoskins, Miss Valley	1987	28	476
Anne Donovan, Old Dominion	1983	35	504	Cheryl Miller, Southern Cal	1985	30	474
Darlene Jones, Miss Valley	1983	31	487	Darlene Beale, Howard	1987	29	459
Melanie Simpson, Okla. City	1982	37	481	Olivia Bradley, W Virginia	1985	30	458

REBOUND AVERAGE

Player and Team	Year	GP	Reb	Avg
Rosina Pearson, Bethune-Cookman	1985	26	480	18.5
Wanda Ford, Drake	1985	30	534	17.8
Katie Beck, E Tennessee St	1988	25	441	17.6
DeShawne Blocker, E Tenn. St	1994	26	450	17.3
Patricia Hoskins, Mississippi Valley	1987	28	476	17.0
Wanda Ford, Drake	1986	30	506	16.9
Patricia Hoskins, Mississippi Valley	1989	27	440	16.3
Joy Kellogg, Oklahoma City	1984	23	373	16.2
Deborah Mitchell, Mississippi Coll.	1983	28	447	16.0

FIELD-GOAL PERCENTAGE

Player and Team	Year	GP	FG	FGA	Pct
Myndee Larsen, Southern Utah	1998	28	249	344	72.4
Deneka Knowles, Southeastern La.	1996	26	199	276	72.1
Barbara Farris, Tulane	1998	27	151	210	71.9
Renay Adams, Tennessee Tech	1991	30	185	258	71.7
Regina Days, Georgia Southern	1986	27	234	332	70.5
Kim Wood, WI-Green Bay	1994	27	188	271	69.4
Kelly Lyons, Old Dominion	1990	31	308	444	69.4
Alisha Hill, Howard	1995	28	194	281	69.0
Trina Roberts, Georgia Southern	1982	31	189	277	68.2
Lidiya Varbanova, Boise St	1991	22	128	188	68.1
Diane Seng, Tennessee Tech	1997	29	257	379	67.8

Based on qualifiers for annual championship.

FREE-THROW PERCENTAGE

Player and Team	Year	GP	FT	FTA	Pct
Ginny Doyle, Richmond	1992	29	96	101	95.0
Linda Cyborski, Delaware	1991	29	74	79	93.7
Jennifer Howard, N Carolina St	1994	27	118	127	92.9
Keely Feeman, Cincinnati	1986	30	76	82	92.7
Amy Slowikowski, Kent St	1989	27	112	121	92.6
Lea Ann Parsley, Marshall	1990	28	96	104	92.3
Chris Starr, NV-Reno	1986	25	119	129	92.2
DeAnn Craft, Central Florida	1987	24	94	102	92.2
Kristin Mattox, Louisville	1996	27	116	126	92.1

Based on qualifiers for annual championship.

Career Records

POINTS

Player and Team	Yrs	GP	Pts
Patricia Hoskins, Mississippi Valley	1985–89	110	3122
Lorri Bauman, Drake	1981–84	120	3115
Cheryl Miller, Southern Cal	1983–86	128	3018
Cindy Blodgett, Maine	1994–98	118	3005
Valorie Whiteside, Appalachian St	1984–88	116	2944
Joyce Walker, Louisiana St	1981–84	117	2906
Sandra Hodge, New Orleans	1981–84	107	2860
Andrea Congreaves, Mercer	1989–93	108	2796
Karen Pelphrey, Marshall	1983–86	114	2746
Cindy Brown, Long Beach St	1983–87	128	2696
Carolyn Thompson, Texas Tech	1981–84	121	2655

SCORING AVERAGE

Player and Team	Yrs	GP	FG	3FG	FT	Pts	Avg
Patricia Hoskins, Mississippi Valley	1985–89	110	1196	24	706	3122	28.4
Sandra Hodge, New Orleans	1981–84	107	1194	—	472	2860	26.7
Lorri Bauman, Drake	1981–84	120	1104	—	907	3115	26.0
Andrea Congreaves, Mercer	1989–93	108	1107	153	429	2796	25.9
Cindy Blodgett, Maine	1994–98	118	1055	219	676	3005	25.5
Valorie Whiteside, Appalachian St	1984–88	116	1153	0	638	2944	25.4
Joyce Walker, Louisiana St	1981–84	117	1259	—	388	2906	24.8
Tarcha Hollis, Grambling	1988–91	85	904	3	247	2058	24.2
Korie Hlede, Duquesne	1994–98	109	1045	162	379	2631	24.1
Karen Pelphrey, Marshall	1983–86	114	1175	—	396	2746	24.1
Erma Jones, Bethune-Cookman	1982–84	87	961	—	173	2095	24.1

NCAA Men's Division II Championship Results

Year	Winner	Score	Runner-up	Third Place	Fourth Place
1957	Wheaton (IL)	89–65	Kentucky Wesleyan	Mount St Mary's (MD)	Cal St-Los Angeles
1958	S Dakota	75–53	St. Michael's	Evansville	Wheaton (IL)
1959	Evansville	83–67	SW Missouri St	N Carolina A&T	Cal St-Los Angeles
1960	Evansville	90–69	Chapman	Kentucky Wesleyan	Cornell College
1961	Wittenberg	42–38	SE Missouri St	S Dakota St	Mount St Mary's (MD)
1962	Mount St Mary's (MD)	58–57 (OT)	Cal St-Sacramento	Southern Illinois	Nebraska Wesleyan
1963	S Dakota St	44–42	Wittenberg	Oglethorpe	Southern Illinois
1964	Evansville	72–59	Akron	N Carolina A&T	Northern Iowa
1965	Evansville	85–82 (OT)	Southern Illinois	N Dakota	St Michael's
1966	Kentucky Wesleyan	54–51	Southern Illinois	Akron	N Dakota
1967	Winston-Salem	77–74	SW Missouri St	Kentucky Wesleyan	Illinois St
1968	Kentucky Wesleyan	63–52	Indiana St	Trinity (TX)	Ashland
1969	Kentucky Wesleyan	75–71	SW Missouri St	†Vacated	Ashland
1970	Philadelphia Textile	76–65	Tennessee St	UC-Riverside	Buffalo St
1971	Evansville	97–82	Old Dominion	†Vacated	Kentucky Wesleyan
1972	Roanoke	84–72	Akron	Tennessee St	Eastern Mich
1973	Kentucky Wesleyan	78–76 (OT)	Tennessee St	Assumption	Brockport St
1974	Morgan St	67–52	SW Missouri St	Assumption	New Orleans
1975	Old Dominion	76–74	New Orleans	Assumption	TN-Chattanooga
1976	Puget Sound	83–74	TN-Chattanooga	Eastern Illinois	Old Dominion
1977	TN-Chattanooga	71–62	Randolph-Macon	N Alabama	Sacred Heart
1978	Cheyney	47–40	WI-Green Bay	Eastern Illinois	Central Florida
1979	N Alabama	64–50	WI-Green Bay	Cheyney	Bridgeport
1980	Virginia Union	80–74	New York Tech	Florida Southern	N Alabama
1981	Florida Southern	73–68	Mount St Mary's (MD)	Cal Poly-SLO	WI-Green Bay
1982	District of Columbia	73–63	Florida Southern	Kentucky Wesleyan	Cal St-Bakersfield
1983	Wright St	92–73	District of Columbia	*Cal St-Bakersfield	*Morningside
1984	Central Missouri St	81–77	St. Augustine's	*Kentucky Wesleyan	*N Alabama
1985	Jacksonville St	74–73	S Dakota St	*Kentucky Wesleyan	*Mount St. Mary's (MD)
1986	Sacred Heart	93–87	SE Missouri St	*Cheyney	*Florida Southern
1987	Kentucky Wesleyan	92–74	Gannon	*Delta St	*Eastern Montana

*Indicates tied for third. †Student-athletes representing American International in 1969 and Southwestern Louisiana in 1971 were declared ineligible subsequent to the tournament. Under NCAA rules, the teams' and ineligible student-athletes' records were deleted, and the teams' places in the final standings were vacated.

Year	Winner	Score	Runner-up	Third Place	Fourth Place
1988	Lowell	75–72	AK-Anchorage	Florida Southern	Troy St
1989	N Carolina Central	73–46	SE Missouri St	UC-Riverside	Jacksonville St
1990	Kentucky Wesleyan	93–79	Cal St-Bakersfield	N Dakota	Morehouse
1991	N Alabama	79–72	Bridgeport (CT)	*Cal St-Bakersfield	*Virginia Union
1992	Virginia Union	100–75	Bridgeport (CT)	*Cal St-Bakersfield	*California (PA)
1993	Cal St-Bakersfield	85–72	Troy St (AL)	*New Hampshire Coll	*Wayne St (MI)
1994	Cal St-Bakersfield	92–86	Southern Indiana	*New Hampshire Coll	*Washburn
1995	Southern Indiana	71–63	UC-Riverside	*Norfolk St	*Indiana (PA)
1996	Fort Hays St	70–63	Northern Kentucky	*California (PA)	*Virginia Union
1997	Cal St-Bakersfield	57–56	Northern Kentucky	*Lynn	*Salem-Teikyo
1998	UC-Davis	83–77	Kentucky Wesleyan	*St. Rose	*Virginia Union

NCAA Men's Division II Alltime Individual Leaders

SINGLE-GAME SCORING HIGHS

Pts	Player and Team vs Opponent	Date
113	Bevo Francis, Rio Grande vs Hillsdale	1954
84	Bevo Francis, Rio Grande vs Alliance	1954
82	Bevo Francis, Rio Grande vs Bluffton	1954
80	Paul Crissman, Southern Cal Col vs Pacific Christian	1966
77	William English, Winston-Salem vs Fayetteville St	1968

Season Records

SCORING AVERAGE

Player and Team	Year	GP	FG	FT	Pts	Avg
Bevo Francis, Rio Grande	1954	27	444	367	1255	46.5
Earl Glass, Mississippi Industrial	1963	19	322	171	815	42.9
Earl Monroe, Winston-Salem	1967	32	509	311	1329	41.5
John Rinka, Kenyon	1970	23	354	234	942	41.0
Willie Shaw, Lane	1964	18	303	121	727	40.4

REBOUND AVERAGE

Player and Team	Year	GP	Reb	Avg
Tom Hart, Middlebury	1956	21	620	29.5
Tom Hart, Middlebury	1955	22	649	29.5
Frank Stronczek, American Int'l	1966	26	717	27.6
R.C. Owens, College of Idaho	1954	25	677	27.1
Maurice Stokes, St Francis (PA)	1954	26	689	26.5

ASSISTS

Player and Team	Year	GP	A
Steve Ray, Bridgeport	1989	32	400
Steve Ray, Bridgeport	1990	33	385
Tony Smith, Pfeiffer	1992	35	349
Jim Ferrer, Bentley	1989	31	309
Rob Paternostro, New Hamp. Coll	1995	33	309

ASSIST AVERAGE

Player and Team	Year	GP	A	Avg
Steve Ray, Bridgeport	1989	32	400	12.5
Steve Ray, Bridgeport	1990	33	385	11.7
Demetri Beekman, Assumption	1993	23	264	11.5
Ernest Jenkins, NM Highlands	1995	27	291	10.8
Brian Gregory, Oakland	1989	28	300	10.7

FIELD-GOAL PERCENTAGE

Player and Team	Year	Pct
Todd Linder, Tampa	1987	75.2
Maurice Stafford, N Alabama	1984	75.0
Matthew Cornegay, Tuskegee	1982	74.8
Brian Moten, W Georgia	1992	73.4
Ed Phillips, Alabama A&M	1968	73.3

FREE-THROW PERCENTAGE

Player and Team	Year	Pct
Paul Cluxton, Northern Kentucky	1997	100.0
Tomas Rimkus, Pace	1997	95.6
Billy Newton, Morgan St	1976	94.4
Kent Andrews, McNeese St	1968	94.4
Mike Sanders, Northern Colorado	1987	94.3

Career Records

POINTS

Player and Team	Yrs	Pts
Travis Grant, Kentucky St	1969-72	4045
Bob Hopkins, Grambling	1953-56	3759
Tony Smith, Pfeiffer	1989-92	3350
Earnest Lee, Clark Atlanta	1984-87	3298
Joe Miller, Alderson-Broaddus	1954-57	3294

Career Records *(Cont.)*

CAREER SCORING AVERAGE

Player and Team	Yrs	GP	Pts	Avg
Travis Grant, Kentucky St	1969–72	121	4045	33.4
John Rinka, Kenyon	1967–70	99	3251	32.8
Florindo Vieira, Quinnipiac	1954–57	69	2263	32.8
Willie Shaw, Lane	1961–64	76	2379	31.3
Mike Davis, Virginia Union	1966–69	89	2758	31.0

REBOUND AVERAGE

Player and Team	Yrs	GP	Reb	Avg
Tom Hart, Middlebury	1953, 55–56	63	1738	27.6
Maurice Stokes, St. Francis (PA)	1953–55	72	1812	25.2
Frank Stronczek, American Int'l	1965–67	62	1549	25.0
Bill Thieben, Hofstra	1954–56	76	1837	24.2
Hank Brown, Lowell Tech	1965–67	49	1129	23.0

ASSISTS

Player and Team	Yrs	A
Demetri Beekman, Assumption	1990–93	1044
Rob Paternostro, New Hamp. Coll.	1992–95	919
Gallagher Driscoll, St. Rose	1989–92	878
Tony Smith, Pfeiffer	1989–92	828
Steve Ray, Bridgeport	1989–90	785

ASSIST AVERAGE

Player and Team	Yrs	GP	A	Avg
Steve Ray, Bridgeport	1989–90	65	785	12.1
Demetri Beekman, Assumption	1990–93	119	1044	8.8
Ernest Jenkins, NM Highlands	1992–95	84	699	8.3
Mark Benson, Texas A&I	1989–91	86	674	7.8
Pat Madden, Jacksonville St	1989–91	88	688	7.8

Note: Minimum 550 Assists.

FIELD-GOAL PERCENTAGE

Player and Team	Yrs	Pct
Todd Linder, Tampa	1984–87	70.8
Tom Schurfranz, Bellarmine	1989–92	70.2
Chad Scott, California (PA)	1991–94	70.0
Ed Phillips, Alabama, A&M	1968–71	68.9
Ulysses Hackett, SC-Spartanburg	1990–92	67.9

Note: Minimum 400 FGM.

FREE-THROW PERCENTAGE

Player and Team	Yrs	Pct
Paul Cluxton, Northern Kentucky	1994–97	93.5
Kent Andrews, McNeese St	1967–69	91.6
Jon Hagen, Mankato St	1963–65	90.0
Dave Reynolds, Davis & Elkins	1986–89	89.3
Michael Shue, Lock Haven	1994–97	88.5

Note: Minimum 250 FTM.

NCAA Men's Division III Championship Results

Year	Winner	Score	Runner-up	Third Place	Fourth Place
1975	LeMoyne-Owen	57–54	Glassboro St	Augustana (IL)	Brockport St
1976	Scranton	60–57	Wittenberg	Augustana (IL)	Plattsburgh St
1977	Wittenberg	79–66	Oneonta St	Scranton	Hamline
1978	North Park	69–57	Widener	Albion	Stony Brook
1979	North Park	66–62	Potsdam St	Franklin & Marshall	Centre
1980	North Park	83–76	Upsala	Wittenberg	Longwood
1981	Potsdam St	67–65 (OT)	Augustana (IL)	Ursinus	Otterbein
1982	Wabash	83–62	Potsdam St	Brooklyn	Cal St-Stanislaus
1983	Scranton	64–63	Wittenberg	Roanoke	WI-Whitewater
1984	WI-Whitewater	103–86	Clark (MA)	DePauw	Upsala
1985	North Park	72–71	Potsdam St	Nebraska Wesleyan	Widener
1986	Potsdam St	76–73	LeMoyne-Owen	Nebraska Wesleyan	Jersey City St
1987	North Park	106–100	Clark (MA)	Wittenberg	Stockton St
1988	Ohio Wesleyan	92–70	Scranton	Nebraska Wesleyan	Hartwick
1989	WI-Whitewater	94–86	Trenton St	Southern Maine	Centre
1990	Rochester	43–42	DePauw	Washington (MD)	Calvin
1991	WI-Platteville	81–74	Franklin & Marshall	Otterbein	Ramapo (NJ)
1992	Calvin	62–49	Rochester	WI-Platteville	Jersey City St
1993	Ohio Northern	71–68	Augustana	Mass-Dartmouth	Rowan
1994	Lebanon Valley Coll	66–59 (OT)	New York University	Wittenberg	St Thomas (MN)
1995	WI-Platteville	69–55	Manchester	Rowan	Trinity (CT)
1996	Rowan	100–93	Hope (MI)	Illinois Wesleyan	Franklin & Marshall
1997	Illinois Wesleyan	89–86	Nebraska Wesleyan	Williams	Alvernia
1998	WI-Platteville	69–56	Hope (MI)	Williams	Wilkes

NCAA Men's Division III Alltime Individual Leaders

SINGLE-GAME SCORING HIGHS

Pts	Player and Team vs Opponent	Year
77	Jeff Clement, Grinnell vs Illinois College	1998
69	Steve Diekmann, Grinnell vs Simpson	1995
63	Joe DeRoche, Thomas vs St. Joseph's (ME)	1988
62	Shannon Lilly, Bishop vs Southwest Assembly of God	1983
61	Steve Honderd, Calvin vs Kalamazoo	1993
61	Dana Wilson, Husson vs Ricker	1974

Season Records

SCORING AVERAGE

Player and Team	Year	GP	FG	FT	Pts	Avg
Steve Diekmann, Grinnell	1995	20	223	162	745	37.3
Rickey Sutton, Lyndon St	1976	14	207	93	507	36.2
Shannon Lilly, Bishop	1983	26	345	218	908	34.9
Dana Wilson, Husson	1974	20	288	122	698	34.9
Rickey Sutton, Lyndon St	1977	16	223	112	558	34.9

REBOUND AVERAGE

Player and Team	Year	GP	Reb	Avg
Joe Manley, Bowie St	1976	29	579	20.0
Fred Petty, New Hampshire College	1974	22	436	19.8
Larry Williams, Pratt	1977	24	457	19.0
Charles Greer, Thomas	1977	17	318	18.7
Larry Parker, Plattsburgh St	1975	23	430	18.7

ASSISTS

Player and Team	Year	GP	A
Robert James, Kean	1989	29	391
Ricky Spicer, WI-Whitewater	1989	31	295
Joe Marcotte, New Jersey Tech	1995	30	292
Andre Bolton, Chris. Newport	1996	30	289
Ron Torgalski, Hamilton	1989	26	275

ASSIST AVERAGE

Player and Team	Year	GP	A	Avg
Robert James, Kean	1989	29	391	13.5
Albert Kirchner, Mt. St. Vincent	1990	24	267	11.1
Ron Torgalski, Hamilton	1989	26	275	10.6
Louis Adams, Rust	1989	22	227	10.3
Eric Johnson, Coe	1991	24	238	9.9

FIELD-GOAL PERCENTAGE

Player and Team	Year	Pct
Travis Weiss, St. John's (MN)	1994	76.6
Pete Metzelaars, Wabash	1982	75.3
Tony Rychlec, Mass. Maritime	1981	74.9
Tony Rychlec, Mass. Maritime	1982	73.1
Russ Newnan, Menlo	1991	73.0

FREE-THROW PERCENTAGE

Player and Team	Year	Pct
Chanse Young, Manchester	1998	95.6
Andy Enfield, Johns Hopkins	1991	95.3
Chris Carideo, Widener	1992	95.2
Yudi Teichman, Yeshiva	1989	95.2
Brett Davis, WI-Oshkosh	1998	94.7

Career Records

POINTS

Player and Team	Yrs	Pts
Andre Foreman, Salisbury St	1989–92	2940
Lamont Strothers, Chris. Newport	1988–91	2709
Matt Hancock, Colby	1987–90	2678
Scott Fitch, Geneseo St	1990–94	2634
Greg Grant, Trenton St	1987–89	2611

CAREER SCORING AVERAGE

Player and Team	Yrs	GP	Avg
Dwain Govan, Bishop	1974–75	55	32.8
Dave Russell, Shepherd	1974–75	60	30.6
Rickey Sutton, Lyndon St	1976–79	60	29.7
John Atkins, Knoxville	1976–78	70	28.7
Steve Peknik, Windham	1974–77	76	27.6

REBOUND AVERAGE

Player and Team	Yrs	GP	Reb	Avg
Larry Parker, Plattsburgh St	1975–78	85	1482	17.4
Charles Greer, Thomas	1975–77	58	926	16.0
Willie Parr, LeMoyne-Owen	1974–76	76	1182	15.6
Michael Smith, Hamilton	1989–92	107	1632	15.2
Dave Kufeld, Yeshiva	1977–80	81	1222	15.1
Ed Owens, Hampden-Sydney	1977–80	77	1160	15.1

ASSIST AVERAGE

Player and Team	Yrs	Avg
Phil Dixon, Shenandoah	1993–96	8.6
Steve Artis, Chris. Newport	1990–93	8.1
David Genovese, Mt. St. Vincent	1992–95	7.5
Kevin Root, Eureka	1989–91	7.1
Dennis Jacobi, Bowdoin	1989–92	7.1

Hockey

A League in Crisis

After a drab season of holdouts, injuries, low scoring and lower TV ratings, the NHL looked for ways to cure its ailing game

BY MICHAEL FARBER

WHEN THE DETROIT Red Wings and the Washington Capitals skated out for Game 1 of the 1998 Stanley Cup finals, they didn't line up at their blue lines for the traditional introductions. Not that it mattered in Detroit, a city that knows its hockey (nor would it have mattered in hockey-challenged Washington, where the three favorite sports are football, political football and, at World Cup time, *futbol*), but the absence of bells and whistles underscored the lack of festivity that characterizes the National Hockey League. Maybe skipping the intros was a time-saving measure, but a glance at a calendar would have told you it was way too late for that: Although the Red Wings won their second straight Stanley Cup in a brisk four games, the season ended on June 16 and lasted a record 253 days.

If the missing introductions were cheap symbolism, then they were the only thing cheap about hockey in 1997–98 other than the chairs the American players broke in the Olympic Village.

Everything was dear, from Sergei Fedorov's $12 million bonus to the loss of marquee players, from elusive TV ratings points to, most notably, goals, which were rarer than they had been in 42 years. After Game 1 of the Stanley Cup finals, a 2–1 yawner, a senior NHL official conceded that there was a "malaise" hanging over the game this season, one that probably can be dated to June 13, 1997, when Red Wings defenseman Vladimir Konstantinov suffered a severe head injury in a limousine accident. Three hundred and sixty-eight days later Konstantinov took a joyride in his wheelchair on the ice, with the Cup in his lap, a moving, bittersweet moment that will live in Stanley Cup lore but also an image that unintentionally highlighted the extraordinary toll the season exacted on the players and the game.

Paul Kariya of the Mighty Ducks of Anaheim could serve as the poster boy for 1997–98. He was a major talent ready to take over hockey with his speed and verve, but he didn't play until mid-December

because of a contract dispute—one of six star players who missed the beginning of the year while their agents were haggling. Seven weeks later he was out for the season with a severe concussion from an ugly and unnecessary cross-check to the jaw by Chicago's Gary Suter. Philadelphia's Eric Lindros, the only other young player with Kariya's magnetism and potential widespread appeal, also missed 18 games late in the season with a concussion. To its credit, the NHL introduced baseline neuropsychological testing in training camp in an effort to ensure players don't return to the ice when they are still at risk, but the concussion contagion showed no signs of slowing. More than 60 players—roughly one of every 10 NHLers—missed games because of postconcussion syndrome, including an incredible nine on the Calgary Flames.

The NHL vowed to further crack down on elbows to the head for 1998–99, but its concern about concussions didn't get the proper attention because of its more highly publicized attempts to address another

Kariya rifled home 17 goals in 22 games before being felled by a cheap shot.

issue: the dearth of goals. In an effort to open up the game the NHL—with seven weeks left in the season—ordered referees to enforce rules against obstruction, a well-intentioned edict but one as curious as Major League Baseball deciding on, say, Aug. 15, to have umpires call the high strike. The timing made the league seem more capricious than decisive, but it didn't back down as it had after halfhearted attempts in previous years. Commissioner Gary Bettman attended the referees' training camp after the Olympics, telling officials that anyone who wouldn't enforce the new guidelines might consider another line of work. He wasn't kidding. During the Dallas–Edmonton second-round playoff series, Stars defenseman Darryl Sydor found himself in the penalty box for the most minor of interferences.

"What's up with that?" Sydor asked an official in the box.

LOU CAPOZZOLA

Though Gretzky was still great at 37, the NHL needs a superstar to take his place.

"The Big Guy"—Bettman—"is in the stands," came the reply. "They got to call it tight."

The NHL had been bound and gagged and kidnapped by defensive systems, trapped by cautious coaches and victimized by a shallow talent pool that will only continue to diminish with the expansion to Nashville in 1998–99 and with three more teams joining in the following two seasons. After scoring a tick below seven goals a game in 1991–92, NHL teams averaged 5.28 a game in 1997–98. (If you are unfamiliar with .28 of a goal, you weren't watching the Tampa Bay Lightning.) There were only four 50-goal scorers—Washington's Peter Bondra and Anaheim's Teemu Selanne topped the league with 52—and the 102 points by Pittsburgh's Jaromir Jagr was the lowest to lead the league over a full season in the past 30 years. The leading scorer on 15 of the 26 teams didn't average a point a game; Paul Ysebaert led the execrable Lightning with 40 points, which used to be a decent month for Wayne Gretzky. Gretzky, who, at the advanced age of 37, produced 90 points for a mediocre New York Rangers team and finished tied for third in scoring, set the league record of 215 points with Edmonton in 1985–86. In 1997–98 the entire Oilers team had 215 goals.

The NHL hoped to revive offenses with additional rule changes for 1998–99. Prior to Game 4 of the finals in Washington, general managers approved changes that included shrinking neutral ice by four feet and adding space behind the nets and reconfiguring the crease by reducing its width from 12 feet to eight feet. The league also planned to experiment with two referees in a limited number of games, a move designed to create more flow in the same way cops speed traffic at busy intersections. After the recommendations to the board of governors were announced, most general managers bolted for flights home, not bothering to stick around to see Detroit win the most glorious trophy in North American sports.

The exodus begged the question: If NHL general managers didn't seem to care, why should anyone else?

Answer: No one else seemed to.

Bettman scoffed at the validity of the television ratings, noting the fragmentation of the TV universe and the absence of big-market teams in the conference finals. He was spinning the numbers like a top. But until some other system comes along, the NHL doesn't have much wiggle room. The TV ratings were abysmal. Fox, which four years ago signed a landmark agreement with a league that for almost two decades was shut out of a regular over-the-air deal in the United States, saw its numbers dip 27% in the regular season and then about 22% in the playoffs. The figures for the finals were down from a year ago by 37% on ESPN and 33% on CBC's *Hockey Night in Canada*. The nadir might have been a Detroit–St. Louis second-round playoff game on Fox, which should have held at least a modicum of interest for fans in Southern California, considering that the area has two NHL teams—the Kings and the Ducks. The game finished last in its time slot, trailing PBS's *America's Favorite Trails* with Tom Bodett, who is best known for his commercials for a discount lodging chain. The score: Motel 6, NHL 0.

Theories abounded to explain the general ennui. Sports marketers focused on the absence of fresh North American stars, an accepted fact although nothing most hockey fans view with alarm. (Buffalo goalie Dominik Hasek of the Czech Republic won his second straight MVP award, beating out two Europeans, Jagr and Selanne; Dallas winger Jere Lehtinen of Finland was named the best defensive forward; and Boston's Sergei Samsonov of Russia won the rookie of the year award over a pair of Europeans, the Vancouver Canucks' Mattias Ohlund and Patrik Elias of the New Jersey Devils.) But for those who had neither a financial nor a direct rooting interest in the games, the most common complaint was that the season simply was too long.

The NHL scheduled a 17-day hiatus in February to send its players to the Olympics in Nagano, a welcome break from its past as an inward-looking National House League. League officials privately called it "a dress rehearsal" for the 2002 Games in Salt Lake City because they knew full well that the time difference between Japan and North America, which meant middle-of-the-night matches back in New York, wouldn't exactly give the league optimum exposure. Initially, the prospect of the NHL at the Games produced a strong buzz. Certainly it was the talk of every dressing room, especially after Team Canada general manager Bob Clarke decided to leave the venerable Mark Messier off his roster. Before a Senators–Blackhawks game on Nov. 29 in Ottawa, with spotlights shining and *Fanfare for the Common Man* blaring and several networks going live, Clarke introduced a squad that included Tampa Bay left wing Rob Zamuner, who had played in as many career playoff games, six, as Messier had won Stanley Cups. This explained *Fanfare for the Common Man*, but it didn't assuage a nation that has come to regard Messier much the way Linus views his blanket. Indeed the Olympic hype almost seemed to put the league on hold for the first 4½ months of the season, which, considering the goal drought and the high-profile holdouts, might not have been a bad thing.

The Olympics *should* be remembered for the brilliant penalty-shot victory by Hasek and the Czech Republic over Canada in the semifinals—one of the top 20 games of all-time on almost everybody's list—and the massive celebration in Prague's Wenceslas Square after the Czechs beat Russia for the gold medal. This was a Prague winter. Unfortunately, the Games *will* be recalled for the most publicized act of vandalism by Americans since the Boston Tea Party. Two or three U.S. players damaged fire extinguishers and broke some chairs, causing damage estimated at $3,000. The monetary value was a pittance compared to the embarrassing nature of the acts themselves, especially in a nation as rooted in civility as

Bettman did his best to put a positive spin on the NHL's problems.

The Dallas Stars had dominated the year with 109 points in the regular season. Led by Mike Modano, who has evolved into a superb all-around player, and goalie Ed Belfour, the Stars played with purpose and intelligence, like a team on which everybody had scored 1,300 on his SATs. But they were also old, a little slow and plain unlucky. Modano separated his shoulder against Phoenix in March, and while he recovered in time for the playoffs, Joe Nieuwendyk suffered a season-ending knee injury in Game 1 of the opening round against San Jose. Without Nieuwendyk, the offensive burden fell more heavily on Modano. He might have been able to carry it, too, if other supporting forwards, such as Greg Adams and Lehtinen, didn't have injuries of their own. The Stars made it to the western conference finals, but it was clear that they would not limp their way to a title. In Game 2 of their second-round series against Edmonton, the Stars didn't put a shot on goal in the first period.

Colorado also appeared frail. The Avalanche, which sent coach Marc Crawford and an NHL-high nine players to Nagano, cruised in the final weeks of the season knowing it couldn't overtake the Stars and assured that the Kings couldn't catch it in the Pacific Division. But Colorado's 95 points and comfortable position in the standings masked the team's profound indifference. The Avalanche had looked like a potential dynasty after winning the 1996 Stanley Cup, but while general manager Pierre Lacroix was able to keep the core of the team together, he lost important players on the fringes. Colorado kept its skill but lost its enthusiasm, incredibly mailing in a 4–0 loss in Game 7 at home to the swift-skating Oilers in the first round. Although Lacroix belatedly offered Crawford a contract extension, neither seemed enthralled with the other. Three weeks after his season ended prematurely, Crawford resigned.

Edmonton had exposed the lack of speed along the Dallas blue line in the second round, and Detroit exploited that weakness in its six-game Western Conference finals

Japan. None of the culprits fessed up, teammates closed ranks, and an incident that could have been cleared up immediately with a sincere apology by the miscreants and a check for less than what some of them spend on a suit festered until it was a malignancy that scarred the players, their country, their game, their league. Instead of leaving Nagano with a higher profile, the NHL limped back to North America shaken. Hockey had caught the Asian flu.

Steve Yzerman, the Red Wings' captain, was one of the few who seemed immune to the bug. The Olympics actually rejuvenated him. He fed off the energy of the high-tempo games and the companionship of Nagano flatmates Gretzky, Martin Brodeur of New Jersey and Philadelphia's Rod Brind'Amour. Yzerman was shunned by Canada when he was a 50-goal sniper—he didn't make its 1991 Canada Cup team—but now as an occasional goal scorer (24 in 1997–98), two-way player and quiet leader, he was considered indispensable. Certainly the Wings wouldn't have made it through the difficult Western Conference competition without him.

against the Stars. The series wouldn't have lasted quite so long if Red Wings goalie Chris Osgood hadn't developed a brain cramp each time the puck was shot from outside the blue line. He gave up one long-distance goal in every round: to Jeremy Roenick of Phoenix, Al MacInnis of St. Louis and to the Stars' Jamie Langenbrunner in the first minute of overtime in Game 5, a shocker that sent the series back to Detroit. Twenty minutes before Game 6, Detroit coach Scotty Bowman barged into the locker room and announced he was switching his lines. He would play Yzerman at left wing and Brendan Shanahan at right wing with Fedorov, the former holdout who had been brilliant in the first two rounds. (Coincidentally, Fedorov earned a lump-sum $12 million bonus for reaching the conference finals, part of his deal when Detroit matched the Carolina Hurricane's

Hasek won an Olympic gold medal and a second straight league MVP award.

offer sheet during the Olympics.) "With any other coach you'd think, What the hell is he doing? This could cost us the series," said Shanahan, who hadn't played right wing in nine years. "With Scotty, I don't think anybody even popped his head up. I was thinking that if Scotty thinks it's a good idea, I think it's a good idea." The Wings won 2–0, Fedorov scored once, and Osgood was impeccable.

The New Jersey Devils, who had 107 points during the regular season and appeared to be every bit as deep and balanced as Detroit, should have been waiting for the Red Wings in the finals, but they were long gone, shocked in the first round by Ottawa. The Senators got a stellar performance from goalie Damian Rhodes, a bottle blond with a history of self-doubt, and their quicksilver if not noticeably skilled forwards. New Jersey was eliminated in six games—coach Jacques Lemaire would quit six days after the humiliation—and when it was over, all

RICHARD MACKSON

Konstantinov (16) provided a dramatic, bittersweet close to the season.

Buffalo's "average" team produced more offense than anticipated, but Hasek couldn't maintain the impossibly high standards he set at Nagano, which provided the opening the Capitals needed to advance to the Stanley Cup finals. The NHL's oldest team, which improved 17 points in coach Ron Wilson's first year, didn't discourage easily. If an opponent let them hang around, the Capitals usually would find a way to win. They out-loitered Buffalo in six games, although compared to the quality of the hockey in the Western Conference, this clearly was the jayvee series.

In contrast to the keenly anticipated Philadelphia-Detroit finals in 1997, the Detroit-Washington matchup lacked luster. The series promptly lived down to its billing, the fourth straight sweep in the NHL's showcase. The Red Wings were so superior that they violated every axiom of playoff hockey: Their goaltending wasn't as solid as Washington's, their power play was shut out for three games, they turned their game on and off like a spigot. Only Game 2 was compelling. Detroit rallied twice from two-goal deficits after lollygagging through the second period. Center Esa Tikkanen could have given the Capitals a third two-goal advantage with less than 10 minutes remaining in the game. He came in alone on Osgood, faked a slap shot, which drew the goalie out of position, and then incredibly steered the puck wide past the empty net. Wings center Kris Draper, alone in the high slot, scored in overtime. Game 2 was the only time Detroit was sorely tested in the series.

Indeed the most dramatic Cup moment occurred with 17 minutes left in the clincher when Konstantinov rose from his wheelchair to acknowledge the chants and applause at the MCI Center. This was a grand prologue to his Stanley Cup "skate," a display of courage and hope that recalled the tragedy of the previous summer but hinted at better things ahead.

Let's hope so. The 1997–98 NHL season couldn't have been much worse.

Senators winger Shawn McEachern had to say was, "I'm just surprised it took six games."

This was a short spring for the Eastern Conference heavyweights. Pittsburgh was bumped in the first round by Montreal. And Philadelphia looked flustered while going out in five to Buffalo, not a shock considering that the Flyers were on their third head coach in less than a year. With 21 games remaining in the regular season, Flyers general manager Clarke demoted Wayne Cashman to assistant coach and hired Roger Neilson. Clarke also traded for Sean Burke, a slight upgrade in goal over the incumbent, Ron Hextall, but hardly the answer for a team that tried to finesse another Cup run without a topflight goalie.

Buffalo was assessed during the second round by Canadiens winger Martin Rucinsky, who called the Sabres an average team with a great goalie. Yet Rucinsky and Montreal were gone in four games.

FOR THE RECORD·1997–1998

Western Conference

CENTRAL DIVISION

	GP	W	L	T	GF	GA	Pts
Dallas	82	49	22	11	242	167	109
Detroit	82	44	23	15	250	196	103
St. Louis	82	45	29	8	256	204	98
Phoenix	82	35	35	12	224	227	82
Chicago	82	30	39	13	192	199	73
Toronto	82	30	43	9	194	237	69

PACIFIC DIVISION

	GP	W	L	T	GF	GA	Pts
Colorado	82	39	26	17	231	205	95
Los Angeles	82	38	33	11	227	225	87
Edmonton	82	35	37	10	215	224	80
San Jose	82	34	38	10	210	216	78
Calgary	82	26	41	15	217	252	67
Anaheim	82	26	43	13	205	261	65
Vancouver	82	25	43	14	224	273	64

Eastern Conference

NORTHEAST DIVISION

	GP	W	L	T	GF	GA	Pts
Pittsburgh	82	40	24	18	228	188	98
Boston	82	39	30	13	221	194	91
Buffalo	82	36	29	17	211	187	89
Montreal	82	37	32	13	235	208	87
Ottawa	82	34	33	15	193	200	83
Carolina	82	33	41	8	200	219	74

ATLANTIC DIVISION

	GP	W	L	T	GF	GA	Pts
New Jersey	82	48	23	11	225	166	107
Philadelphia	82	42	29	11	242	193	95
Washington	82	40	30	12	220	201	92
NY Islanders	82	30	41	11	212	225	71
NY Rangers	82	25	39	18	197	231	68
Florida	82	24	43	15	203	256	63
Tampa Bay	82	17	55	10	151	269	44

1998 Stanley Cup Playoffs

EASTERN CONFERENCE

QUARTERFINALS SEMIFINALS CONFERENCE FINAL

Ottawa
New Jersey → Ottawa (4–2)
Boston
Washington → Washington (4–2) → Washington (4–1)
Pittsburgh
Montreal → Montreal (4–2) → Washington (4–2)
Philadelphia
Buffalo → Buffalo (4–1) → Buffalo (4–0)

STANLEY CUP

Detroit (4–0)

WESTERN CONFERENCE

CONFERENCE FINAL SEMIFINALS QUARTERFINALS

San Jose
Dallas → Dallas (4–2)
Edmonton
Colorado → Edmonton (4–3) → Dallas (4–1)
Phoenix
Detroit → Detroit (4–2) → Detroit (4–2)
Los Angeles
St. Louis → St. Louis (4–0) → Detroit (4–2)

Stanley Cup Playoff Results

Conference Quarterfinals

EASTERN CONFERENCE

April 22	Ottawa	2	at New Jersey	1
April 24	Ottawa	1	at New Jersey	3
April 26	New Jersey	1	at Ottawa	2*
April 28	New Jersey	3	at Ottawa	4
April 30	Ottawa	1	at New Jersey	3
May 2	New Jersey	1	at Ottawa	3

Ottawa won series 4–2.

April 23	Montreal	3	at Pittsburgh	2
April 25	Montreal	1	at Pittsburgh	4
April 27	Pittsburgh	1	at Montreal	3
April 29	Pittsburgh	6	at Montreal	3
May 1	Montreal	5	at Pittsburgh	2
May 3	Pittsburgh	0	at Montreal	3

Montreal won series 4–2.

Conference Quarterfinals (Cont.)

EASTERN CONFERENCE (Cont.)

April 23	Buffalo	3	at Philadelphia	2	April 22	Boston	1	at Washington	3
April 25	Buffalo	2	at Philadelphia	3	April 24	Boston	4	at Washington	3†
April 27	Philadelphia	1	at Buffalo	6	April 26	Washington	3	at Boston	2†
April 29	Philadelphia	1	at Buffalo	4	April 28	Washington	3	at Boston	0
May 1	Buffalo	3	at Philadelphia	2*	May 1	Boston	4	at Washington	0
	Buffalo won series 4–1.				May 3	Washington	3	at Boston	2*
						Washington won series 4–2.			

WESTERN CONFERENCE

April 22	San Jose	1	at Dallas	4	April 22	Phoenix	3	at Detroit	6
April 24	San Jose	2	at Dallas	5	April 24	Phoenix	7	at Detroit	4
April 26	Dallas	1	at San Jose	4	April 26	Detroit	2	at Phoenix	3
April 28	Dallas	0	at San Jose	1*	April 28	Detroit	4	at Phoenix	2
April 30	San Jose	2	at Dallas	3	April 30	Phoenix	1	at Detroit	3
May 2	Dallas	3	at San Jose	2*	May 3	Detroit	5	at Phoenix	2
	Dallas won series 4–2.					Detroit won series 4–2.			
April 22	Edmonton	3	at Colorado	2	April 23	Los Angeles	3	at St. Louis	8
April 24	Edmonton	2	at Colorado	5	April 25	Los Angeles	1	at St. Louis	2
April 26	Colorado	5	at Edmonton	4*	April 27	St. Louis	4	at Los Angeles	3
April 28	Colorado	3	at Edmonton	1	April 29	St. Louis	2	at Los Angeles	1
April 30	Edmonton	3	at Colorado	1		St. Louis won series 4–0.			
May 2	Colorado	0	at Edmonton	2					
May 4	Edmonton	4	at Colorado	0					
	Edmonton won series 4–3.								

Conference Semifinals

EASTERN CONFERENCE

May 7	Ottawa	2	at Washington	4	May 7	Edmonton	1	at Dallas	3
May 9	Ottawa	1	at Washington	6	May 9	Edmonton	2	at Dallas	0
May 11	Washington	3	at Ottawa	4	May 11	Dallas	1	at Edmonton	0
May 13	Washington	2	at Ottawa	0	May 13	Dallas	3	at Edmonton	1
May 15	Ottawa	0	at Washington	3	May 16	Edmonton	1	at Dallas	2
	Washington won series 4–1.					Dallas won series 4–1.			
May 8	Montreal	2	at Buffalo	3*	May 8	St. Louis	4	at Detroit	2
May 10	Montreal	3	at Buffalo	6	May 10	St. Louis	1	at Detroit	6
May 12	Buffalo	5	at Montreal	4†	May 12	Detroit	3	at St. Louis	2†
May 14	Buffalo	3	at Montreal	1	May 14	Detroit	5	at St. Louis	2
	Buffalo won series 4–0.				May 17	St. Louis	3	at Detroit	1
					May 19	Detroit	6	at St. Louis	1
						Detroit won series 4–2.			

WESTERN CONFERENCE

Eastern Finals

May 23	Buffalo	2	at Washington	0	May 24	Detroit	2	at Dallas	0
May 25	Buffalo	2	at Washington	3*	May 26	Detroit	1	at Dallas	3
May 28	Washington	4	at Buffalo	3*	May 29	Dallas	3	at Detroit	5
May 30	Washington	2	at Buffalo	0	May 31	Dallas	2	at Detroit	3
June 2	Buffalo	2	at Washington	1	June 3	Detroit	2	at Dallas	3*
June 2	Buffalo	2	at Washington	3*	June 5	Dallas	0	at Detroit	2
	Washington won series 4–2.					Detroit won series 4–2.			

Western Finals

Stanley Cup Finals

June 9	Washington	1	at Detroit	2	June 13	Detroit	2	at Washington	1
June 11	Washington	4	at Detroit	5*	June 16	Detroit	4	at Washington	1
						Detroit won series 4–0.			

*Overtime game. †Double overtime game.

Stanley Cup Championship Box Scores

Game 1

Washington......0	1	0—1
Detroit.............2	0	0—2

FIRST PERIOD

Scoring: 1, Det, Kocur 4 (Brown, Holmstrom), 14:04. 2, Det, Lidstrom 6 (Yzerman, Holmstrom), 16:18. Penalties: Lapointe, Det (tripping), 4:21; Tinordi, Wash (interference), 17:22.

SECOND PERIOD

Scoring: 3, Wash, Zednik 7 (Nikolishin, Bondra), 15:57. Penalties: Detroit bench, served by Kozlov (too many men on the ice), 5:48; Yzerman, Det (slashing), 8:51; Simon, Wash (roughing), 18:06.

THIRD PERIOD

Scoring: None. Penalties: Nikolishin, Wash (interference), 0:38; Kocur, Det (roughing), 4:19.

Shots on goal: Wash—6-4-7—17. Det10-9-12—31. Power-play opportunities: Wash 0-of-4; Det 0-of-3. Goalies: Wash, Kolzig (31 shots, 29 saves). Det, Osgood (17 shots, 16 saves). A: 19,983. Referee: McCreary. Linesmen: Scapinello, Schachte.

Game 2

Washington......0	3	1	0—4
Detroit.............1	0	3	1—5

FIRST PERIOD

Scoring: 1, Det, Yzerman 5 (Holmstrom, Lidstrom), 7:49. Penalties: Reekie, Wash (obstruction holding),13:05; Bondra, Wash (hooking), 15:22.

SECOND PERIOD

Scoring: 2, Wash, Bondra 7 (Nikolishin, Brown), 1:51. 3, Wash, Simon 1 (Brown, Hunter), 6:11. 4, Wash, Oates 6 (Juneau, C Johansson), 11:03. Penalties: Maltby, Det (high sticking), 3:09; Zednik, Wash (obstruction hooking), 7:12; Simon, Wash (roughing), 14:11; Osgood, Det served by Kocur (unsportsmanlike conduct), 14:11; Maltby, Det (slashing), 16:20.

THIRD PERIOD

Scoring: 5, Det, Yzerman 6 (shorthanded) (Fetisov, McCarty), 6:37. 6, Wash, Juneau 7 (power play) (Gonchar, Bellows), 7:05. 7, Det, Lapointe 8 (Larionov, Fetisov), 8:08. 8, Det, Brown 2 (unassisted), 15:46. Penalties: Lidstrom, Det (interference), 6:23; Zednik, Wash (cross checking), 10:18; Lapointe, Det (interference), 11:40.

OVERTIME

Scoring: 9, Det, Draper 1 (Lapointe, Shanahan), 15:24. Penalties: Tikkanen, Wash (roughing), 5:24; Kocur, Det (roughing), 5:24.

Shots on goal: Wash—8-15-7-3—28. Det—14-14-20-12—60. Power-play opportunities: Wash 1-of-4; Det 0-of-4. Goalies: Wash, Kolzig (60 shots, 55 saves). Det, Osgood (33 shots, 29 saves). A: 19,983. Referee: Koharski. Linesmen: Collins, Broseker.

Game 3

Detroit.............1	0	1—2
Washington......0	0	1—1

FIRST PERIOD

Scoring: 1, Det, Holmstrom 7 (Yzerman, McCarty), 0:35. Penalties: Simon, Wash (slashing), 2:48; Hunter, Wash (charging), 8:10; Housley, Wash (elbowing), 12:29; Holmstrom, Det (goalie interference), 13:11; Lapointe, Det (interference), 17:01.

SECOND PERIOD

Scoring: None. Penalties: Krygier, Wash (roughing), 2:05; Eriksson, Det (obstruction holding), 7:29; Larionov, Det (obstruction tripping), 10:17; Draper, Det (roughing), 15:23; Gonchar, Wash (roughing),15:23.

THIRD PERIOD

Scoring: 2, Wash, Bellows 5 (power play) (Oates, Juneau), 10:35. 3, Det, Fedorov 10 (Brown, Fetisov), 15:09. Penalties: Gonchar, Wash (roughing), 5:50; McCarty, Det (tripping), 9:22.

Shots on goal: Det—13-11-10—34. Power-play opportunities: Det 0-of-5; Wash 1-of-5. Goalies: Det, Osgood (18 shots, 17 saves). Wash, Kolzig (34 shots, 32 saves). A: 19,740. Referee: Gregson. Linesmen: Scapinello, Schachte.

Game 4

Detroit..............1	2	1——4	
Washington......0	1	0——1	

FIRST PERIOD

Scoring: 1, Det, Brown 3 (power play) (Fedorov, Murphy), 10:30. Penalties: Eriksson, Det (interference), 7:17; Bondra, Wash (interference), 9:12; Johansson, Wash (roughing), 11:01.

SECOND PERIOD

Scoring: 2, Det, Lapointe 9 (Larionov, Rouse), 2:26. 3, Washington, Bellows 6 (Oates, Juneau), 7:49. 4, Detroit, Murphy 3 (power play) (Holmstrom, Fedorov), 11:46. Penalties: Maltby, Det (roughing), 9:13; Tinordi, Wash (roughing), 9:13; Tikkanen, Wash (goalie interference), 11:02; Larionov, Det (hooking), 12:41; Rouse, Det (high sticking), 16:07; Tinordi, Wash (slashing), 19:53.

THIRD PERIOD

Scoring: 5, Det, Brown 4 (power play) (Kozlov, Eriksson), 1:32. Penalties: Fetisov, Det (interference), 13:08.

Shots on goal: Det—14-12-12—38. Wash—6-14-11—31. Power-play opportunities: Det 3-of-4; Wash 0-of-4. Goalies: Det, Osgood (31 shots, 30 saves); Wash, Kolzig (38 shots, 34 saves). A: 19,740.
Referee: McCreary. Linesmen: Broseker, Collins.

Individual Playoff Leaders

Scoring

POINTS

Player and Team	GP	G	A	Pts	+/–	PM	Player and Team	GP	G	A	Pts	+/–	PM
Steve Yzerman, Det....22		6	18	24	10	22	Igor Larionov, Det........22		3	10	13	5	12
Sergei Fedorov, Det....22		10	10	20	0	12	Matthew Barnaby, Buff...15		7	6	13	6	22
Nicklas Lidstrom, Det....22		6	13	19	12	8	Donald Audette, Buff.....15		5	8	13	-4	10
Tomas Holmstrom, Det..22		7	12	19	9	16	Peter Bondra, Wash......17		7	5	12	4	12
Joe Juneau, Wash.......21		7	10	17	6	8	Mark Recci, Mtl...........10		4	8	12	2	6
Adam Oates, Wash.......21		6	11	17	8	8	Brian Holzinger, Buff......15		4	7	11	-2	18
Larry Murphy, Det........22		3	12	15	12	2	Darren McCarty, Det......22		3	8	11	9	34
Martin Lapointe, Det......21		9	6	15	6	20	Sergei Gonchar, Wash....21		7	4	11	2	30
Vyacheslav Kozlov, Det...22		6	8	14	4	10	Jason Woolley, Buff.......15		2	9	11	8	12
Mike Modano, Dall.......17		4	10	14	4	12	Dixon Ward, Buff...........15		3	8	11	8	6
Andrei Nikolishin, Wash...21		1	13	13	4	12	Peter Forsberg, Col.......7		6	5	11	3	12
Brian Bellows, Wash........21		6	7	13	6	6	Michal Grosek, Buff.......15		6	4	10	5	28

GOALS

Player and Team	GP	G
Sergei Fedorov, Det 22		10
Martin Lapointe, Det......21		9
Jim Campbell, StL...........10		7
Daniel Alfredsson, Ott.....11		7
Bill Guerin, Edm..............12		7
Matthew Barnaby, Buff.....15		7
Peter Bondra, Wash........17		7
Richard Zednik, Wash......17		7
Sergei Gonchar, Wash 21		7
Joe Juneau, Wash...........21		7
Tomas Holmstrom, Det....22		7

POWER PLAY GOALS

Player and Team	GP	PP
Jim Campbell, StL............10		4
Bill Guerin, Edm..............12		4
Miroslav Satan, Buff........14		4
Nine tied with three.		

GAME-WINNING GOALS

Player and Team	GP	GW
Joe Juneau, Wash...........21		4
Vyacheslav Kozlov, Det...22		4
Michal Grosek, Buff.........15		3
Thirteen tied with two.		

SHORT-HANDED GOALS

Player and Team	GP	SH
Jeremy Roenick, Phoe.......6		2
Larry Murphy, Det............22		2
Eighteen tied with one.		

ASSISTS

Player and Team	GP	A
Steve Yzerman, Det 22		18
Nicklas Lidstrom, Det......22		13
Andrei Nikolishin, Wash ...21		12
Tomas Holmstrom, Det....22		12
Larry Murphy, Det 22		12

PLUS/MINUS

Player and Team	GP	+/–
Nicklas Lidstrom, Det......22		12
Larry Murphy, Det 22		12
Steve Yzerman, Det........22		10
Tomas Holmstrom, Det....22		9
Darren McCarty, Det 22		9
Bob Boughner, Buff.........14		9

Goaltending (Minimum 420 minutes)

GOALS AGAINST AVERAGE

Player and Team	GP	Mins	GA	Avg
Ed Belfour, Dall 17		1039	31	1.79
Curtis Joseph, Edm 12		714	23	1.93
Olaf Kolzig, Wash 21		1352	44	1.95
Byron Dafoe, Bos..............6		422	14	1.99

SAVE PERCENTAGE

Player and Team	GP	Mins	GA	SA	Pct	W	L
Olaf Kolzig, Wash.........21		1352	44	740	.941	12	9
Dominik Hasek, Buff.......15		949	32	514	.938	10	5
Curtis Joseph, Edm........12		714	23	319	.928	5	7
Ed Belfour, Dall..........17		1039	31	399	.922	10	7

NHL Awards

Award	Player and Team	Award	Player and Team
Hart Trophy (MVP)	Dominik Hasek, Buff	Selke Trophy (top defensive forward)	Jere Lehtinen, Dall
Calder Trophy (top rookie)	Sergei Samsonov, Bos	Adams Award (top coach)	Pat Burns, Bos
Vezina Trophy (top goaltender)	Dominik Hasek, Buff	Jennings Trophy (goaltender on club allowing fewest goals)	Martin Brodeur, NJ
Norris Trophy (top defenseman)	Rob Blake, LA		Michael Dunham, NJ
Lady Byng Trophy (for gentlemanly play)	Ron Francis, Pitt	Conn Smythe Trophy (playoff MVP)	Steve Yzerman, Det

NHL Individual Leaders

Scoring

POINTS

Player and Team	GP	G	A	Pts	+/–	PM	Player and Team	GP	G	A	Pts	+/–	PM
Jaromir Jagr, Pitt	77	35	67	102	17	64	Peter Bondra, Wash	76	52	26	78	14	44
Peter Forsberg, Col	72	25	66	91	6	94	Theoren Fleury, Cal	82	27	51	78	0	197
Pavel Bure, Van	82	51	39	90	5	48	Adam Oates, Wash	82	18	58	76	6	36
Wayne Gretzky, NYR	82	23	67	90	-11	28	Rod Brind'amour, Phil	82	36	38	74	-2	54
John LeClair, Phil	82	51	36	87	30	32	Mats Sundin, Tor	82	33	41	74	-3	49
Zigmund Palffy, NYI	82	45	42	87	-2	34	Mark Recci, Mtl	82	32	42	74	11	51
Ron Francis, Pitt	81	25	62	87	12	20	Tony Amonte, Chi	82	31	42	73	21	66
Teemu Selanne, Ana	73	52	34	86	12	30	Alexei Yashin, Ott	82	33	39	72	6	24
Jason Allison, Bos	81	33	50	83	33	60	Brett Hull, StL	66	27	45	72	-1	26
Jozef Stumpel, LA	77	21	58	79	17	53	Eric Lindros, Phil	63	30	41	71	14	134

GOALS

Player and Team	GP	G
Teemu Selanne, Ana	73	52
Peter Bondra, Wash	76	52
John LeClair, Phil	82	51
Pavel Bure, Van	82	51
Zigmund Palffy, NYI	82	45

GAME-WINNING GOALS

Player and Team	GP	GW
Peter Bondra, Wash	76	13
Joe Nieuwendyk, Dall	73	11
Teemu Selanne, Ana	73	10
Brendan Shanahan, Det	75	9
John LeClair, Phil	82	9

ASSISTS

Player and Team	GP	A
Jaromir Jagr, Pitt	77	67
Wayne Gretzky, NYR	82	67
Peter Forsberg, Col	72	66
Ron Francis, Pitt	81	62
Jozef Stumpel, LA	77	58
Adam Oates, Wash	82	58

POWER PLAY GOALS

Player and Team	GP	PP
Zigmund Palffy, NYI	82	17
John LeClair, Phil	82	16
Brendan Shanahan, Det	75	15
Stu Barnes, Pitt	78	15
Shayne Corson, Mtl	62	14
Joe Nieuwendyk, Dall	73	14

SHORT-HANDED GOALS

Player and Team	GP	SHG
Jeff Friesen, SJ	79	6
Pavel Bure, Van	82	6
Mike Modano, Dall	52	5
Michael Peca, Buff	61	5
Peter Bondra, Wash	76	5
Bob Corkum, Phoe	76	5

PLUS/MINUS

Player and Team	GP	+/–
Chris Pronger, StL	81	47
Larry Murphy, Det	82	35
Jason Allison, Bos	81	33
Randy McKay, NJ	74	30
John LeClair, Phil	82	30

Goaltending
(Minimum 25 games)

GOALS AGAINST AVERAGE

Player and Team	GP	Mins	GA	Avg
Ed Belfour, Dall	61	3581	112	1.88
Martin Brodeur, NJ	70	4128	130	1.89
Tom Barrasso, Pitt	63	3542	122	2.07
Dominik Hasek, Buff	72	4220	147	2.09
Ron Hextall, Phil	46	2688	97	2.17
Trevor Kidd, Car	47	2685	97	2.17
Jamie McLennan, StL	30	1658	60	2.17

WINS

Player and Team	GP	Mins	W	L	T
Martin Brodeur, NJ	70	4128	43	17	8
Ed Belfour, Dall	61	3581	37	12	10
Olaf Kolzig, Wash	64	3788	33	18	10
Chris Osgood, Det	64	3807	33	20	11
Dominik Hasek, Buff	72	4220	33	23	13

SAVE PERCENTAGE

Player and Team	GP	GA	SA	Pct	W	L	T
Dominik Hasek, Buff	72	147	2149	.932	33	23	13
Tom Barrasso, Pitt	63	122	1556	.922	31	14	13
Trevor Kidd, Car	47	97	1238	.922	21	21	3
Olaf Kolzig, Wash	64	139	1729	.920	33	18	10
Martin Brodeur, NJ	70	130	1569	.917	43	17	8
Jeff Hackett, Chi	58	126	1520	.917	21	25	11

SHUTOUTS

Player and Team	GP	Mins	SO	W	L	T
Dominik Hasek, Buff	72	4220	13	33	23	13
Martin Brodeur, NJ	70	4128	10	43	17	8
Ed Belfour, Dall	61	3581	9	37	12	10
Jeff Hackett, Chi	58	3441	8	21	25	11
Curtis Joseph, Edm	71	4132	8	29	31	9
Tom Barrasso, Pitt	63	3542	7	31	14	13
Byron Dafoe, Bos	65	3693	6	30	25	9
Chris Osgood, Det	64	3807	6	33	20	11

NHL Team-by-Team Statistical Leaders

Anaheim Mighty Ducks

SCORING

Player	GP	G	A	Pts	+/-	PM
Teemu Selanne, R.........73	73	52	34	86	12	30
Steve Rucchin, C.........72	72	17	36	53	8	13
Travis Green, C.........76	76	19	23	42	-29	82
Scott Young, R.........73	73	13	20	33	-13	22
Paul Kariya, L.........22	22	17	14	31	12	23
*Matt Cullen, C.........61	61	6	21	27	-4	23
*Josef Marha, C.........23	23	9	9	18	4	4
Tomas Sandstrom, R.....77	77	9	8	17	-25	64
Ted Drury, C.........73	73	6	10	16	-10	82
Ruslan Salei, D.........66	66	5	10	15	7	70
Dave Karpa, D.........78	78	1	11	12	-3	217
*Frank Banham, R.........21	21	9	2	11	-6	12
Kevin Todd, C.........27	27	4	7	11	-5	12
*Jeff Nielsen, R.........32	32	4	5	9	-1	16
Jason Marshall, D.........72	72	3	6	9	-8	189
Jamie Pushor, D.........64	64	2	7	9	3	81
*Jeremy Stevenson, L...45	45	3	5	8	-4	101
Drew Bannister, D.........61	61	0	8	8	-9	89
*Pavel Trnka, D.........48	48	3	4	7	-4	40
Doug Houda, D.........55	55	2	4	6	-11	99
*Mike Crowley, D.........8	8	2	2	4	0	8

GOALTENDING

Player	GP	Mins	Avg	W	L	T	SO
*Tom Askey.........7	7	273	2.64	0	1	2	0
Guy Hebert.........46	46	2660	2.93	13	24	6	3
M. Shtalenkov.........40	40	2049	3.22	13	18	5	1
Team total.........82	82	5007	3.13	26	43	13	4

*Rookie.

Boston Bruins

SCORING

Player	GP	G	A	Pts	+/-	PM
Jason Allison, C.........81	81	33	50	83	33	60
Dmitri Khristich, R.........82	82	29	37	66	25	42
Ray Bourque, D.........82	82	13	35	48	2	80
*Sergei Samsonov, L...81	81	22	25	47	9	8
Steve Heinze, R.........61	61	26	20	46	8	54
Anson Carter, C.........78	78	16	27	43	7	31
Ted Donato, C.........67	67	25	26	51	-9	37
Tim Taylor, C.........79	79	16	23	39	6	54
Rob Dimaio, R.........79	79	20	11	31	-16	57
*Per Axelsson, R.........82	82	8	19	27	-14	38
Kyle McLaren, D.........66	66	5	20	25	13	56
Grant Ledyard, D.........71	71	4	20	24	-4	20
Dave Ellett, D.........82	82	3	20	23	3	67
Mike Sullivan, L.........77	77	5	13	18	-1	34
Don Sweeney, D.........59	59	1	15	16	12	24
Darren Van Impe, D.....69	69	3	11	14	-6	40
*Joe Thornton, C.........55	55	3	4	7	-6	19
*Hal Gill, D.........68	68	2	4	6	4	47
Landon Wilson, R.........28	28	1	5	6	3	7

GOALTENDING

Player	GP	Mins	Avg	W	L	T	SO
Robbie Tallas.........14	14	788	1.83	6	3	3	1
Byron Dafoe.........65	65	3693	2.24	30	25	9	6
Jim Carey.........10	10	496	2.90	3	2	1	2
Team total.........82	82	4995	2.33	39	30	13	9

Younger and Younger

Already 6'3" and 175 pounds, Tony Williams of Saint Thomas, Ont., is one of the best 15-year-old hockey players in Canada. He's also at the center of a debate over whether agents should be recruiting players at increasingly younger ages in hopes of cashing in when the players turn pro.

In August 1997, after fielding inquiries from five other agents, Tony and his family spent a week at the Cape Cod vacation house of Hall of Famer Bobby Orr, one of the game's most powerful agents. While at Orr's, Williams, then 14, met NHL stars and played golf with his host. By that time, the Williams family and Orr had entered into an oral agreement: If all goes well and Tony is drafted by an NHL team, Orr will be his paid representative. "Bobby Orr is not an agent to us; he's an adviser," says Tony's uncle and guardian, Winston Williams, a 53-year-old police constable, who emphasizes that no money changed hands and that Tony needs someone like Orr to counsel him on decisions involving school and training.

Toronto Maple Leafs general manager Ken Dryden disagrees. "There are various ways of getting that information—it doesn't have to come from an agent," Dryden says. "Having an agent is an immense distraction for a 14-year-old." Adds NHL Players' Association (NHLPA) executive director Bob Goodenow, "Hockey players don't make decisions that require the assistance of an agent until they're 16." Canada's junior leagues draft players as young as 16, though a player must be 18 to be taken in the NHL draft. Anyone planning to suit up at an NCAA school would forfeit his eligibility by agreeing to let an agent represent him in the future.

Orr isn't alone in recruiting 14-year-olds. Since January 1996, when the NHLPA began requiring agents to register, their number has nearly doubled, from 125 to 240. And agents are snapping up younger and younger players. "I've seen people who call themselves representatives standing in the hallways of rinks waiting to meet a 14-year-old after a game," says David Branch, commissioner of the Ontario Hockey League, one of the main sources of talent for the NHL.

Orr would not comment, but Jay Fee, the hockey director at Orr's Boston-based Woolf Associates agency, argues that the dramatic increase in NHL salaries has prompted parents of young players to seek more help in structuring their children's career paths. "Someone like Bobby can share his experiences," Fee says. "If that's recruiting, fine. We're in the business of giving advice, so that's what we're going to do."

For now, Goodenow says that the NHLPA has no plans to introduce rules forbidding contact between agents and players in their early teens. But Dryden maintains that it's up to the players' association to take action. "Set a standard, and if complaints rise, then that's the risk an agent takes."

Buffalo Sabres

SCORING

Player	GP	G	A	Pts	+/–	PM
Miroslav Satan, L	79	22	24	46	2	34
Alexei Zhitnik, D	78	15	30	45	19	102
Donald Audette, R	75	24	20	44	10	59
Mike Peca, C	61	18	22	40	12	57
Brian Holzinger, C	69	14	21	35	-2	36
Jason Woolley, D	71	9	26	35	8	35
Derek Plante, C	72	13	21	34	8	26
Michal Grosek, L	67	10	20	30	9	60
Geoff Sanderson, L	75	11	18	29	1	38
Matthew Barnaby, L	72	5	20	25	8	289
Jason Dawe, L	81	22	26	48	14	32
Curtis Brown, L	63	12	12	24	11	34
Dixon Ward, R	71	10	13	23	9	42
Darryl Shannon, D	76	3	19	22	26	56
Richard Smehlik, D	72	3	17	20	11	62
Jay McKee, D	56	1	13	14	-1	42
Wayne Primeau, C	69	6	6	12	9	87
*Vaclav Varada, R	27	5	6	11	0	15
Randy Burridge, L	30	4	6	10	0	0
Paul Kruse, L	74	7	2	9	-11	187
Mike Wilson, D	66	4	4	8	13	48
Rob Ray, R	63	2	4	6	2	234

GOALTENDING

Player	GP	Mins	Avg	W	L	T	SO
Dominik Hasek	72	4220	2.09	33	23	13	13
*Steve Shields	16	785	2.83	3	6	4	0
Team total	82	5029	2.24	36	29	17	13

Carolina Hurricanes

SCORING

Player	GP	G	A	Pts	+/–	PM
Keith Primeau, C	81	26	37	63	19	110
Sami Kapanen, R	81	26	37	63	9	16
Gary Roberts, L	61	20	29	49	3	103
Nelson Emerson, R	81	21	24	45	-17	50
Jeff O'Neill, C	74	19	20	39	-8	67
Ray Sheppard, R	71	18	19	37	-11	23
Robert Kron, R	81	16	20	36	-8	12
Martin Gelinas, L	64	16	18	34	-5	40
Steve Chiasson, D	66	7	27	34	-2	65
Glen Wesley, D	82	6	19	25	7	36
Kevin Dineen, R	54	7	16	23	-7	105
Paul Ranheim, L	73	5	9	14	-11	28
Curtis Leschyshyn, D	73	2	10	12	-2	45
Adam Burt, D	76	1	11	12	-6	106
Steve Leach, R	45	4	5	9	-19	42
Kent Manderville, C	77	4	4	8	-6	31
Kevin Haller, D	65	3	5	8	-5	94
Stu Grimson, L	82	3	4	7	0	204
Sean Hill, D	55	1	6	7	-5	54
*John Battaglia, L	33	2	4	6	-1	10
Steven Rice, R	47	2	4	6	-16	38

GOALTENDING

Player	GP	Mins	Avg	W	L	T	SO
Trevor Kidd	47	2685	2.17	21	21	3	3
Sean Burke	25	1415	2.80	7	11	5	1
Pat Jablonski	5	279	3.01	1	4	0	0
Kirk McLean	8	401	3.29	4	2	0	0
*Michael Fountain	3	163	3.68	0	3	0	0
Team total	82	4973	2.64	33	41	8	4

Calgary Flames

SCORING

Player	GP	G	A	Pts	+/–	PM
Theoren Fleury, R	82	27	51	78	0	197
Cory Stillman, C	72	27	22	49	-9	40
Marty McInnis, L	75	19	25	44	1	34
Andrew Cassels, C	81	17	27	44	-7	32
German Titov, C	68	18	22	40	-1	38
Valeri Bure, R	66	12	26	38	-5	35
Michael Nylander, C	65	13	23	36	10	24
Jarome Iginla, R	70	13	19	32	-10	29
*Derek Morris, D	82	9	20	29	1	88
Cale Hulse, D	79	5	22	27	1	169
Jason Wiemer, L	79	10	10	22	-10	160
Tommy Albelin, D	69	2	17	19	9	32
James Patrick, D	60	6	11	17	-2	26
*Hnat Domenichelli, C	31	9	7	16	4	6
Jim Dowd, C	48	6	8	14	10	12
Joel Bouchard, D	44	5	7	12	0	57
*Jamie Allison, D	43	3	8	11	3	104
Ed Ward, R	64	4	5	9	-1	122
*Chris Dingman, L	70	3	3	6	-11	149
Todd Simpson, D	53	1	5	6	-10	109

GOALTENDING

Player	GP	Mins	Avg	W	L	T	SO
Rick Tabaracci	42	2419	2.88	13	22	2	0
Dwayne Roloson	39	2205	2.99	11	16	4	0
*Tyler Moss	6	367	3.27	2	3	0	0
Team total	82	5016	3.01	26	41	6	0

*Rookie.

THEY SAID IT

*Roman Hamrlik, Tampa Bay
Lightning defenseman, when asked
the difference between his level of
performance and that of Metallica,
his heavy-metal heroes:
"They play great every night."*

Chicago Blackhawks

SCORING

Player	GP	G	A	Pts	+/-	PM
Tony Amonte, R	82	31	42	73	21	66
Alexei Zhamnov, C	70	21	28	49	16	61
Eric Daze, L	80	31	11	42	4	22
Gary Suter, D	73	14	28	42	1	74
Chris Chelios, D	81	3	39	42	-7	151
Greg Johnson, C	74	12	22	34	-2	40
Jeff Shantz, C	61	11	20	31	0	36
Sergei Krivokrasov, R	58	10	13	23	-1	33
Eric Weinrich, D	82	2	21	23	10	106
Ethan Moreau, L	54	9	9	18	0	73
Steve Dubinsky, C	82	5	13	18	-6	57
James Black, L	52	10	5	15	-8	8
*Jean-Yves Leroux, L	66	6	7	13	-2	55
Jay More, D	58	5	7	12	7	61
Chad Kilger, C	32	3	9	12	0	10
*Dmitri Nabokov, C	25	7	4	11	-1	10
Jarrod Skalde, C	30	4	7	11	-2	18
Kevin Miller, R	37	4	7	11	-4	8
Christian Laflamme, D	72	0	11	11	14	59
Brent Sutter, C	52	2	6	8	-6	28
Reid Simpson, L	44	3	2	5	-3	118
*Brian Felsner, L	12	1	3	4	0	12

GOALTENDING

Player	GP	Mins	Avg	W	L	T	SO
Jeff Hackett	58	3441	2.20	21	25	11	8
Chris Terreri	21	1222	2.41	8	10	2	2
Andrei Trefilov	6	299	3.41	1	4	0	0
Team total	82	4999	2.39	30	39	13	10

Colorado Avalanche

SCORING

Player	GP	G	A	Pts	+/-	PM
Peter Forsberg, C	72	25	66	91	6	94
Valeri Kamensky, L	75	26	40	66	-2	60
Joe Sakic, C	64	27	36	63	0	50
Claude Lemieux, R	78	26	27	53	-7	115
Sandis Ozolinsh, D	66	13	38	51	-12	65
Adam Deadmarsh, R	73	22	21	43	0	125
Eric Lacroix, L	82	16	15	31	0	84
Uwe Krupp, D	78	9	22	31	21	38
Rene Corbet, L	68	16	12	28	8	133
Stephane Yelle, C	81	7	15	22	-10	48
Jari Kurri, C	70	5	17	22	6	12
Tom Fitzgerald, R	80	12	6	18	-4	79
Shean Donovan, R	67	8	10	18	6	70
Adam Foote, D	77	3	14	17	-3	124
*Eric Messier, D	62	4	12	16	4	20
Jon Klemm, D	67	6	8	14	-3	30
Alexei Gusarov, D	72	4	10	14	9	42
Jeff Odgers, R	68	5	8	13	5	213
Warren Rychel, L	71	5	6	11	-11	221
Keith Jones, R	23	3	7	10	-4	22
Sylvain Lefebvre, D	81	0	10	10	2	48

GOALTENDING

Player	GP	Mins	Avg	W	L	T	SO
Craig Billington	23	1162	2.32	8	7	4	1
Patrick Roy	65	3835	2.39	31	19	13	4
Team total	82	5017	2.45	39	26	17	5

Dallas Stars

SCORING

Player	GP	G	A	Pts	+/-	PM
Joe Nieuwendyk, C	73	39	30	69	16	30
Mike Modano, C	52	21	38	59	25	32
Pat Verbeek, R	82	31	26	57	15	170
Sergei Zubov, D	73	10	47	57	16	16
Jamie Langenbrunner, C	81	23	29	52	9	61
Darryl Sydor, D	79	11	35	46	17	51
Jere Lehtinen, R	72	23	19	42	19	20
Greg Adams, L	49	14	18	32	11	20
Derian Hatcher, D	70	6	25	31	9	132
Guy Carbonneau, C	77	7	17	24	3	40
Shawn Chambers, D	57	2	22	24	11	26
Mike Keane, R	83	10	13	23	-12	52
Benoit Hogue, L	53	6	16	22	7	35
Todd Harvey, C	59	9	10	19	5	104
Grant Marshall, R	72	9	10	19	-2	96
Dave Reid, L	65	6	12	18	-15	14
Richard Matvichuck, D	74	3	15	18	7	63
Brian Skrudland, C	72	7	6	13	-6	49
Bob Bassen, C	58	3	4	7	-4	57
Craig Ludwig, D	80	0	7	7	21	131
*Jamie Wright, L	21	4	2	6	8	2
*Juha Lind, L	39	2	3	5	4	6

GOALTENDING

Player	GP	Mins	Avg	W	L	T	SO
*Emmanuel Ferande	2	69	1.74	1	0	0	0
Ed Belfour	61	3581	1.88	37	12	10	9
Roman Turek	23	1324	2.22	11	10	1	1
Team total	82	4986	2.01	49	22	11	10

Detroit Red Wings

SCORING

Player	GP	G	A	Pts	+/-	PM
Steve Yzerman, C	75	24	45	69	3	46
Nicklas Lidstrom, D	80	17	42	59	22	18
Brendan Shanahan, L	75	28	29	57	6	15
Vyacheslav Kozlov, L	80	25	27	52	14	46
Larry Murphy, D	82	11	41	52	35	37
Igor Larionov, C	69	8	39	47	14	40
Dmitri Mironov, D	77	8	35	43	-7	119
Doug Brown, R	80	19	23	42	17	12
Darren McCarty, R	71	15	22	37	0	157
Martin LaPointe, R	79	15	19	34	0	106
Brent Gilchrist, C	61	13	14	27	4	40
Kirk Maltby, L	65	14	9	23	11	89
Kris Draper, C	64	13	10	23	5	45
Tomas Holmstrom, L	57	5	17	22	6	44
*Anders Eriksson, D	66	7	14	21	21	32
Sergei Fedorov, C	21	6	11	17	10	25
Mathieu Dandenault, R	68	5	12	17	5	43
Viacheslav Fetisov, D	58	2	12	14	4	72
*Michael Knuble, R	53	7	6	13	2	16
Bob Rouse, D	71	1	11	12	-9	57
Joey Kocur, R	63	6	5	11	7	92
Aaron Ward, D	52	5	5	10	-1	47

GOALTENDING

Player	GP	Mins	Avg	W	L	T	S
Chris Osgood	64	3807	2.21	33	20	11	6
*Kevin Hodson	21	988	2.67	9	3	3	2
Team total	82	4995	2.35	44	23	15	9

Note: Osgood and Hodson shared a shutout on 4-1-98.

* Rookie.

Edmonton Oilers

SCORING

Player	GP	G	A	Pts	+/-	PM
Doug Weight, C	79	26	44	70	1	69
Dean McAmmond, L	77	19	31	50	9	46
Boris Mironov, D	81	16	30	46	-8	100
Janne Niinimaa, D	77	4	39	43	-13	62
Roman Hamrlik, D	78	9	32	41	-15	70
Bill Guerin, R	59	18	21	39	1	93
Todd Marchant, L	76	14	21	35	9	71
Ryan Smyth, L	65	20	13	33	-24	44
Tony Hrkac, C	49	13	14	27	3	10
Mats Lindgren, C	82	13	13	26	0	42
*Scott Fraser, C	29	12	11	23	6	6
Andrei Kovalenko, L	9	6	17	23	-14	28
Kelly Buchberger, R	82	6	17	23	-10	122
Valeri Zelepukin, L	68	4	18	22	-2	89
Rem Murray, L	61	9	9	18	-9	39
Mike Grier, R	66	9	6	15	-3	73
Greg DeVries, D	65	7	4	11	-17	80
Bobby Dollas, D	52	2	6	8	-6	49
Drake Berehowsky, D	67	1	6	7	1	169
*Boyd Devereaux, C	38	1	4	5	-5	6
*Craig Millar, D	11	4	0	4	-3	8
*Joe Hulbig, L	17	2	2	4	-1	2

GOALTENDING

Player	GP	Mins	Avg	W	L	T	SO
Bob Essensa	16	825	2.55	6	6	1	0
Curtis Joseph	71	4132	2.63	29	31	9	8
Team total	82	4980	2.70	35	37	10	8

Florida Panthers

SCORING

Player	GP	G	A	Pts	+/-	PM
Ray Whitney, L	77	33	32	65	9	28
Dave Gagner, C	78	20	28	48	-21	55
Robert Svehla, D	79	9	34	43	-3	113
Scott Mellanby, R	79	15	24	39	-14	127
Radek Dvorak, L	64	12	24	36	-1	33
Dino Ciccarelli, R	62	16	17	33	-16	70
Viktor Kozlov, C	64	17	13	30	-3	16
Kirk Muller, C	70	8	21	29	-14	54
Bill Lindsay, L	82	12	16	28	-2	80
Ed Jovanovski, D	81	9	14	23	-12	158
David Nemirovsky, R	41	9	12	21	-3	8
*Steve Washburn, C	58	11	8	19	-6	32
Gord Murphy, D	79	6	11	17	-3	46
Jeff Norton, D	56	4	13	17	-32	44
Rob Niedermayer, C	33	8	7	15	-9	41
Chris Wells, C	61	5	10	15	4	47
Paul Laus, D	77	0	11	11	-5	293
Terry Carkner, D	74	1	7	8	6	63
Johan Garpenlov, L	39	2	3	5	-6	8
Rhett Warrener, D	79	0	4	4	-16	99

GOALTENDING

Player	GP	Mins	Avg	W	L	T	SO
J. Vanbiesbrouck	60	3451	2.87	18	29	11	4
Mark Fitzpatrick	12	640	3.00	2	7	2	1
Kirk McLean	7	406	3.25	4	2	1	0
*Kevin Weekes	11	485	3.96	0	5	1	0
Team total	82	5009	3.07	24	43	15	5

Los Angeles Kings

SCORING

Player	GP	G	A	Pts	+/-	PM
Jozef Stumpel, C	77	21	58	79	17	53
Glen Murray, R	81	29	31	60	6	54
Vladimir Tsyplakov, L	73	18	34	52	15	18
Rob Blake, D	81	23	27	50	-3	94
Yanic Perreault, C	79	28	20	48	6	32
Luc Robitaille, L	57	16	24	40	5	66
Craig Johnson, L	74	17	21	38	9	42
Garry Galley, D	74	9	28	37	-5	63
Sandy Moger, R	62	11	13	24	4	70
Ian Laperriere, C	77	6	15	21	0	131
Russ Courtnall, R	58	12	6	18	-2	27
Sean O'Donnell, D	80	2	15	17	7	179
Philippe Boucher, D	45	6	10	16	6	49
Ray Ferraro, C	40	6	9	15	-10	42
Mattias Nordstrom, D	73	1	12	13	14	90
Dan Bylsma, L	65	3	9	12	9	33
Nathan Lafayette, C	34	5	3	8	2	32
*Steve McKenna, L	62	4	4	8	-9	150
Doug Zmolek, D	46	0	8	8	0	111
Aki Berg, D	72	0	8	8	3	61
*Donald MacLean, C	22	5	2	7	-1	4
Matt Johnson, L	66	2	4	6	-8	249
Jan Vopat, D	21	1	5	6	8	10
Roman Vopat, C	25	0	3	3	-7	55

GOALTENDING

Player	GP	Mins	Avg	W	L	T	SO
*Jamie Storr	17	920	2.22	9	5	1	2
Stephane Fiset	60	3497	2.71	26	25	8	2
Frederic Chabot	12	554	3.14	3	3	2	0
Team total	82	4990	2.71	38	33	11	4

* Rookie.

THEY SAID IT

Matthew Barnaby, Buffalo Sabres right wing, on his team's response to Washington Capitals coach Ron Wilson's attempt to goad the Sabres by calling them "chicken": "I don't think anyone is smart enough to fall for that."

Montreal Canadiens

SCORING

Player	GP	G	A	Pts	+/–	PM
Mark Recchi, R	82	32	42	74	11	51
V. Damphousse, C	76	18	41	59	14	58
Saku Koivu, L	69	14	43	57	8	48
Shayne Corson, L	62	21	34	55	2	108
Martin Rucinsky, L	78	21	32	53	13	84
Vladimir Malakhov, D	74	13	31	44	16	70
Brian Savage, L	64	26	17	43	11	36
Patrice Brisebois, D	79	10	27	37	16	67
Dave Manson, D	81	4	30	34	22	122
Benoit Brunet, L	68	12	20	32	11	61
Jonas Hoglund, L	8	12	13	25	-7	22
Marc Bureau, C	74	13	6	19	0	12
Patrick Poulin, L	78	6	13	19	-4	27
Stephane Quintal, D	71	6	10	16	13	97
Scott Thornton, C	67	6	9	15	0	158
Zarley Zalapski, D	63	3	12	15	-13	63
Sebastien Bordeleau, C	53	6	8	14	5	36
Turner Stevenson, R	63	4	6	10	-8	110
Igor Ulanov, D	49	2	8	10	-7	97
Peter Popovic, D	69	2	6	8	-6	38

GOALTENDING

Player	GP	Mins	Avg	W	L	T	SO
Jocelyn Thibault	47	2652	2.47	19	15	8	2
Andy Moog	42	2337	2.49	18	14	5	3
Team total	82	5009	2.49	37	32	13	5

New Jersey Devils

SCORING

Player	GP	G	A	Pts	+/–	PM
Bobby Holik, C	82	29	36	65	23	100
Scott Niedermayer, D	81	14	43	57	5	27
Doug Gilmour, C	63	13	40	53	10	68
Randy McKay, R	74	24	24	48	30	86
Dave Andreychuk, L	75	14	34	48	19	26
*Patrik Elias, R	74	18	19	37	18	28
Petr Sykora, C	58	16	20	36	0	22
Jason Arnott, C	70	10	23	33	-24	99
Brian Rolston, L	76	16	14	30	7	16
Scott Stevens, D	80	4	22	26	19	80
Steve Thomas, L	55	14	10	24	4	32
Lyle Odelein, D	79	4	19	23	11	171
Doug Bodger, D	77	9	11	20	-1	57
Bob Carpenter, C	66	9	9	18	-4	22
*Sheldon Souray, D	60	3	7	10	18	85
*Brendan Morrison, C	11	5	4	9	3	0
Kevin Dean, D	50	1	8	9	12	12
*Brad Bombardir, D	43	1	5	6	11	8
Sergei Brylin, C	18	2	3	5	4	0
*Krzysztof Oliwa, L	73	2	3	5	3	295

GOALTENDING

Player	GP	Mins	Avg	W	L	T	SO
Martin Brodeur	70	4128	1.89	43	17	8	10
Rich Shulmistra	1	62	1.94	0	1	0	0
Mike Dunham	15	773	2.25	5	5	3	1
Jeff Reese	1	20	3.00	0	0	0	0
Team total	82	4991	2.00	48	23	11	11

New York Islanders

SCORING

Player	GP	G	A	Pts	+/–	PM
Zigmund Palffy, R	82	45	42	87	-2	34
Robert Reichel, C	82	25	40	65	-11	32
Bryan Berard, C	75	14	32	46	-32	59
Bryan Smolinski, C	81	13	30	43	-16	34
Kenny Jonsson, D	81	14	26	40	-2	58
Jason Dawe, R	81	20	19	39	8	42
Trevor Linden, C	67	17	21	38	-14	82
Tom Chorske, L	82	12	23	35	7	39
Sergei Nemchinov, C	74	10	19	29	3	24
Mariusz Czerkawski, C	68	12	13	25	11	23
Joe Sacco, R	80	11	14	25	0	34
J.J Daigneault, D	71	2	21	23	-9	49
Claude Lapointe, C	78	10	10	20	-9	47
Scott Lachance, D	63	2	11	13	-11	45
Mike Hough, L	74	5	7	12	-4	27
Richard Pilon, D	76	0	7	7	1	291
Gino Odjick, L	48	3	2	5	-2	212
Ken Belanger, L	37	3	1	4	1	101
Kip Miller, C	9	1	3	4	-2	2
Dennis Vaske, D	19	0	3	3	2	12

GOALTENDING

Player	GP	Mins	Avg	W	L	T	SO
Wade Flaherty	16	694	1.99	4	4	3	3
Tommy Salo	62	3461	2.64	23	29	5	4
Eric Fichaud	17	807	2.97	3	8	3	0
Team total	82	4982	2.71	30	41	11	8

Note: Flaherty and Salo shared a shutout on 4-4-98.

* Rookie.

Gretzky to Gartner

Until Dec. 14, 1997, Mike Gartner of the Phoenix Coyotes was known primarily as one of the NHL's fastest skaters—he won the fastest-skater competition at the 1990 and '93 All-Star Games—and for being president of the NHL players' union. But when he wristed in a goal at 10:41 of the first period against the Detroit Red Wings, he became known as something else: an immortal.

Well, maybe that's a little strong. But only four other players in NHL history have scored 700, and their names are Wayne Gretzky, Gordie Howe, Marcel Dionne and Phil Esposito. But Gartner would trade it all for one sip from the Stanley Cup—he has appeared in more games without winning a championship than any other active player.

New York Rangers

SCORING

Player	GP	G	A	Pts	+/–	PM
Wayne Gretzky, C	82	23	67	90	-11	28
Pat Lafontaine, C	67	23	39	62	-16	36
Alexei Kovalev, R	73	23	30	53	-22	44
Brian Leetch, D	76	17	33	50	-36	32
Niklas Sundstrom, R	70	19	28	47	0	24
Kevin Stevens, L	80	14	27	41	-7	130
Adam Graves, L	72	23	12	35	-30	41
Tim Sweeney, R	56	11	18	29	7	26
Bruce Driver, D	75	5	15	20	-3	46
Ulf Samuelsson, D	73	3	9	12	1	122
Bob Errey, L	71	2	9	11	2	53
Harry York, C	60	4	6	10	-1	31
A. Karpovtsev, D	47	3	7	10	-1	38
Bill Berg, L	67	1	9	10	-15	55
*Peter Ferraro, R	30	3	4	7	-4	14
Jeff Finley, D	63	1	6	7	-3	55
Darren Langdon, L	70	3	3	6	0	197
*Marc Savard, C	28	1	5	6	-4	4
*P.J. Stock, C	38	2	3	5	4	114
Jeff Beukeboom, D	63	0	5	5	-25	195
*Vladimir Vorobiev, R	15	2	2	4	-10	6
Brad Smyth, R	10	1	3	4	-1	4
Johan Lindbom, L	38	1	3	4	4	28

GOALTENDING

Player	GP	Mins	Avg	W	L	T	SO
*Dan Cloutier	12	551	2.50	4	5	1	0
Mike Richter	72	4143	2.66	21	31	15	0
Jason Muzzatti	6	313	3.26	0	3	2	0
Team total	82	5028	2.76	25	39	18	0

Philadelphia Flyers

SCORING

Player	GP	G	A	Pts	+/–	PM
John LeClair, L	82	51	36	87	30	32
Rod Brind'Amour, L	82	38	74	-2	54	
Eric Lindros, C	63	30	41	71	14	134
Chris Gratton, C	82	22	40	62	11	159
Alexandre Daigle, R	75	16	26	42	-8	14
Trent Klatt, R	82	14	28	42	2	16
Mike Sillinger, C7	5	21	20	41	-11	50
Dainius Zubrus, C	69	8	25	33	29	42
Eric Desjardins, D	77	6	27	33	11	36
Daniel McGillis, D	80	11	20	31	-21	109
Paul Coffey, D	57	2	27	29	3	30
Shjon Podein, L	82	11	13	24	8	53
*Colin Forbes, L	63	12	7	19	2	59
Chris Therien, D	78	3	16	19	5	80
Petr Svoboda, D	56	3	15	18	19	83
Dave Babych, D	53	0	9	9	-9	49
Joel Otto, C	68	3	4	7	-2	78
Luke Richardson, D	81	2	3	5	7	139
Daniel Lacroix, C	56	1	4	5	0	135
John Druce, R	23	1	2	3	0	2
Kjell Samuelsson, D	49	0	3	3	9	28

GOALTENDING

Player	GP	Mins	Avg	W	L	T	SO
Ron Hextall	46	2688	2.17	21	17	7	4
Garth Snow	29	1651	2.43	14	9	4	1
Sean Burke	11	632	2.56	7	3	0	1
Team total	82	4988	2.32	42	29	11	6

Ottawa Senators

SCORING

Player	GP	G	A	Pts	+/–	PM
Alexei Yashin, C	82	33	39	72	6	24
Shawn McEachern, L	81	24	24	48	1	42
Daniel Alfredsson, R	55	17	28	45	7	18
Igor Kravchuk, D	81	8	27	35	-19	8
Andreas Dackell, R	82	15	18	33	-11	24
*Magnus Arvedson, L	61	11	15	26	2	36
*Vaclav Prospal, C	56	6	19	25	-11	21
Sergei Zholtok, C	78	10	13	23	-7	16
Wade Redden, D	80	8	14	22	17	27
Janne Laukkanen, D	60	4	17	21	-15	64
Denny Lambert, C	72	9	10	19	4	250
Shaun Van Allen, C	80	4	15	19	4	48
Pat Falloon, C	58	8	10	18	-8	16
Bruce Gardiner, C	55	7	11	18	2	50
Radek Bonk, C	65	7	9	16	-13	16
*Chris Phillips, D	72	5	11	16	2	38
Jason York, D	73	3	13	16	8	62
Randy Cunneyworth, L	71	2	11	13	-14	63
Chris Murray, R	53	5	4	9	3	118
Lance Pitlick, D	69	2	7	9	8	50

GOALTENDING

Player	GP	Mins	Avg	W	L	T	SO
Ron Tugnutt	42	2236	2.25	15	14	8	3
Damian Rhodes	50	2743	2.34	19	19	7	5
Team total	82	5002	2.40	34	33	15	8

Phoenix Coyotes

SCORING

Player	GP	G	A	Pts	+/–	PM
Keith Tkachuk, L	69	40	26	66	9	147
Jeremy Roenick, C	79	24	32	56	5	103
Cliff Ronning, C	80	11	44	55	5	36
Craig Janney, C	68	10	43	53	5	12
Teppo Numminen, D	82	11	40	51	25	30
Rick Tocchet, R	68	26	19	45	1	157
Dallas Drake, C	60	11	29	40	17	71
Mike Gartner, R	60	12	15	27	-4	24
Keith Carney, D	80	3	19	22	-2	91
Bob Corkum, C	76	12	9	21	-7	28
Oleg Tverdovsky, D	46	7	12	19	1	12
Gerald Diduck, D	78	8	10	18	14	118
*Brad Isbister, R	66	9	8	17	4	102
John Slaney, D	55	3	14	17	-3	24
Darrin Shannon, L	58	2	12	14	4	26
Mark Janssens, C	74	5	7	12	-21	154
*Juha Ylonen, C	55	1	11	12	-3	10
Shane Doan, R	33	5	6	11	-3	35
Deron Quint, D	32	4	7	11	-6	16
Mike Stapleton, C	64	5	5	10	-4	36
Norm Maciver, D	41	2	6	8	-11	38

GOALTENDING

Player	GP	Mins	Avg	W	L	T	SO
Jim Waite	17	793	2.12	5	6	1	1
N. Khabibulin	70	4026	2.74	30	28	10	4
*Scott Langkow	3	137	4.38	0	1	0	0
Team total	82	4985	2.73	35	35	12	5

* Rookie.

Pittsburgh Penguins

SCORING

Player	GP	G	A	Pts	+/−	PM
Jaromir Jagr, R	77	35	67	102	17	64
Ron Francis, C	81	25	62	87	12	20
Stu Barnes, C	78	30	35	65	15	30
Kevin Hatcher, D	74	19	29	48	-3	66
Martin Straka, C	75	19	23	42	-1	28
Rob Brown, R	82	15	25	40	-1	59
Fredrik Olausson, D	76	6	27	33	13	42
*Alexei Morozov, R	76	13	13	26	-4	8
Ed Olczyk, L	56	11	11	22	-9	35
Robert Lang, C	54	9	13	22	7	16
Sean Pronger, C	67	6	15	21	-10	32
Alex Hicks, C	58	7	13	20	4	54
Brad Werenka, D	71	3	15	18	15	46
Jiri Slegr, D	73	5	12	17	10	109
Andreas Johansson, C	50	5	10	15	4	20
Darius Kasparaitis, D	81	4	8	12	3	127
*Robert Dome, C	30	5	2	7	-1	12
*Chris Ferraro, R	46	3	4	7	-2	43
Tyler Wright, C	82	3	4	7	-3	112
Ian Moran, R	37	1	6	7	0	19
Chris Tamer, D	79	0	7	7	4	181
Neil Wilkinson, D	34	2	4	6	0	24

GOALTENDING

Player	GP	Mins	Avg	W	L	T	SO
*Peter Skudra	17	851	1.83	6	4	3	0
Tom Barrasso	63	3542	2.07	31	14	13	7
Ken Wregget	15	611	2.75	3	6	2	0
Team total	82	5022	2.25	40	24	18	7

St. Louis Blues

SCORING

Player	GP	G	A	Pts	+/−	PM
Brett Hull, R	66	27	45	72	-1	26
Pierre Turgeon, C	60	22	46	68	13	24
Geoff Courtnall, L	79	31	31	62	12	94
Steve Duchesne, D	80	14	42	56	9	32
Pavol Demitra, L	61	22	30	52	11	22
Al MacInnis, D	71	19	30	49	6	80
Craig Conroy, C	81	14	29	43	20	46
Jim Campbell, C	76	22	19	41	0	55
Chris Pronger, D	81	9	27	36	47	180
Todd Gill, D	75	13	17	30	-11	41
Scott Pellerin, L	80	8	21	29	14	62
Blair Atcheynum, R	61	11	15	26	5	10
Terry Yake, R	65	10	15	25	1	38
Darren Turcotte, C	62	12	6	18	6	26
*Pascal Rheaume, L	48	6	9	15	4	35
Mike Eastwood, C	58	6	5	11	-2	22
Chris McAlpine, D	54	3	7	10	14	36
Marc Bergevin, D	81	3	7	10	-2	90
Michel Picard, L	16	1	8	9	3	29
Kelly Chase, R	67	4	3	7	10	231
*Jamie Rivers, D	59	2	4	6	5	36
Tony Twist, L	60	1	1	2	-4	105

GOALTENDING

Player	GP	Mins	Avg	W	L	T	SO
Jamie McLennan	30	1658	2.17	16	8	2	2
Grant Fuhr	58	3274	2.53	29	21	6	3
Team total	82	4970	2.46	45	29	8	5

San Jose Sharks

SCORING

Player	GP	G	A	Pts	+/−	PM
Jeff Friesen, L	79	31	32	63	8	40
John Maclean, R	77	16	27	43	-6	42
Owen Nolan, R	75	14	27	41	-2	144
*Patrick Marleau, C	74	13	19	32	5	14
Bill Houlder, D	82	7	25	32	13	48
*Marco Sturm, C	74	10	20	30	-2	40
Stephane Matteau, L	73	15	14	29	4	60
Murray Craven, C	67	12	17	29	4	25
Bernie Nicholls, C	60	6	22	28	-4	26
Mike Ricci, L	65	9	18	27	-4	32
Tony Granato, L	59	16	9	25	3	70
Marcus Ragnarsson, D	79	5	20	25	-11	65
Joe Murphy, R	37	9	13	22	9	36
Mike Rathje, D	81	3	12	15	-4	59
*Andrei Zyuzin, D	56	6	7	13	8	66
Bryan Marchment, D	61	2	11	13	-3	144

Player	GP	G	A	Pts	+/−	PM
Shawn Burr, L	42	6	6	12	2	50
Marty McSorley, D	56	2	10	12	10	140
Al Iafrate, D	21	2	7	9	-1	28
Ron Sutter, C	57	2	7	9	-2	22
Dave Lowry, L	57	4	4	8	-1	53
*Alexander Korolyuk, C	19	2	3	5	-5	6
*Richard Brennan, D	11	1	2	3	-4	2

GOALTENDING

Player	GP	Mins	Avg	W	L	T	SO
Mike Vernon	62	3564	2.46	30	22	8	5
Kelly Hrudey	28	1360	2.74	4	16	2	1
Jason Muzzatti	1	27	4.44	0	0	0	0
Team total	82	4973	2.61	34	38	10	7

Note: Hrudey and Vernon shared a shutout on 4-7-98.

* Rookie.

Gold, Silver, Bronze and Wood

The Americans left their marks on the 1998 Winter Olympics after bowing out to Dominik Hasek and the Czechs 4-1 in the quarterfinals. According to the Nagano Olympic Organizing Committee (NAOC), the marks were about $3,000 worth. The vandalism in three apartments occupied by U.S. players in the Olympic Village, the NAOC said, included an eight-inch hole in a door as well as damage to one desk, two beds (one smashed into two pieces) three fire extinguishers (one tossed over a fifth-floor balcony) and 10 folding chairs (three tossed over the balcony), although contrary to initial reports, none of those chairs beat U.S. goalie Mike Richter through the five hole.

Tampa Bay Lightning

SCORING

Player	GP	G	A	Pts	+/-	PM
Paul Ysebaert, L	82	13	27	40	-43	32
Mikael Renberg	68	16	22	38	-37	34
Alexander Selivanov, R	70	16	19	35	-38	85
Stephane Richer, L	40	14	15	29	-6	41
Rob Zamuner, L	77	14	12	26	-3	41
Daymond Langkow, C	68	8	14	22	-9	62
Darcy Tucker, C	74	7	13	20	-14	146
Sandy McCarthy, R	66	8	10	18	-19	241
Mikael Andersson, R	72	6	11	17	-4	29
Karl Dykhuis, D	78	5	9	14	-8	110
*Jason Bonsignore, C	35	2	8	10	-11	22
Cory Cross, D	74	3	6	9	-24	77
Jody Hull, R	49	4	4	8	3	8
Yves Racine, D	60	0	8	8	-23	41
Brian Bradley, C	14	2	5	7	-9	6
David Wilkie, D	34	2	5	7	-22	21
Vladamir Vujtek, C	30	2	4	6	-2	16
*Brent Peterson, L	19	5	0	5	-2	2
*Steve Kelly, C	43	2	3	5	-13	23
Andrei Nazarov, R	54	2	2	4	-13	170
Enrico Ciccone, D	39	0	4	4	-2	175

GOALTENDING

Player	GP	Mins	Avg	W	L	T	SO
Daren Puppa	26	1456	2.72	5	14	6	0
Corey Schwab	16	821	2.92	2	9	1	1
Mark Fitzpatrick	34	1938	3.16	7	24	1	1
*Derek Wilkinson	8	311	3.28	2	4	1	0
*Zac Bierk	13	433	4.16	1	4	1	0
Team total	82	4978	3.24	17	55	10	3

Note: Schwab and Wilkinson shared a shutout on 12-31-97.

Toronto Maple Leafs

SCORING

Player	GP	G	A	Pts	+/-	PM
Mats Sundin, C	82	33	41	74	-3	49
*Mike Johnson, R	82	15	32	47	-4	24
Igor Korolev, C	77	21	25	46	-7	43
Mathieu Schneider, D	76	11	26	37	-12	44
Fredrik Modin, L	74	16	16	32	-5	32
Sergei Berezin, R	68	16	15	31	-3	10
Steve Sullivan, C	63	10	18	28	-8	40
Sylvain Cote, D	71	4	21	25	-3	42
Wendel Clark, L	47	12	7	19	-21	80
*Alyn McCauley, C	60	6	10	16	-7	6
Jason Smith, D	81	3	13	16	-5	100
Tie Domi, R	80	4	10	14	-5	365
Todd Warriner, L	45	5	8	13	5	20
Darby Hendrickson, C	80	8	4	12	-20	67
Dimitri Yushkevich, D	72	0	12	12	-13	78
Lonny Bohonos, R	37	5	4	9	-8	8
*Daniil Markov, D	25	2	5	7	0	28
Rob Zettler, D	59	0	7	7	-8	108
Kris King, L	82	3	3	6	-13	199
*Martin Prochazka, L	29	2	4	6	-1	8
*Yannick Tremblay, D	38	2	4	6	-6	6
Jamie Baker, C	13	0	5	5	1	10

GOALTENDING

Player	GP	Mins	Avg	W	L	T	SO
*M. Cousineau	2	17	0.00	0	0	0	0
Felix Potvin	67	3864	2.73	26	33	7	5
Glenn Healy	21	1068	2.98	4	10	2	0
Team total	82	4970	2.86	30	43	9	6

Note: Healy and Cousineau shared a shutout on 11-4-97.

Vancouver Canucks

SCORING

Player	GP	G	A	Pts	+/-	PM
Pavel Bure, R	82	51	39	90	5	48
Mark Messier, C	82	22	38	60	-10	58
Alexander Mogilny, R	51	18	27	45	-6	36
Markus Naslund, L	76	14	20	34	5	56
Todd Bertuzzi, L	74	13	20	33	-17	121
Jyrki Lumme, D	74	9	21	30	-25	34
*Mattias Ohlund, D	77	7	23	30	3	76
Bret Hedican, D	71	3	24	27	3	79
Brian Noonan, R	82	10	15	25	-19	62
*Dave Scatchard, C	76	13	11	24	-4	165
Bryan McCabe, D	82	4	20	24	19	209
Brad May, L	63	13	10	23	2	154
Peter Zezel, C	30	5	15	20	15	2
Donald Brashear, L	77	9	9	18	-9	372
Scott Walker, R	59	3	10	13	-8	164
Dana Murzyn, D	31	5	2	7	-3	42
Steve Staios, D	77	3	4	7	-3	134
Adrian Aucoin, D	35	3	3	6	-4	21
*Bert Robertsson, D	30	2	4	6	2	24
Jamie Huscroft, D	51	0	4	4	-2	177
*Chris McAllister, D	36	1	2	3	-12	106

GOALTENDING

Player	GP	Mins	Avg	W	L	T	SO
Arturs Irbe	41	1999	2.73	14	11	6	2
Garth Snow	12	504	3.10	3	6	0	0
Sean Burke	16	838	3.51	2	9	4	0
Kirk McLean	29	1583	3.68	6	17	4	1
Corey Hirsch	1	50	6.00	0	0	0	0
Team total	82	4996	3.28	25	43	14	3

* Rookie.

Washington Capitals

SCORING

Player	GP	G	A	Pts	+/–	PM	Player	GP	G	A	Pts	+/–	PM
Peter Bondra, R	76	52	26	78	14	44	Craig Berube, L	74	6	9	15	-3	189
Adam Oates, C	82	18	58	76	6	36	Kelly Miller, L	76	7	7	14	-2	41
Calle Johansson, D	73	15	20	35	-11	30	Todd Krygier, L	45	2	12	14	-3	30
Steve Konowalchuk, C	80	10	24	34	9	80	Jeff Toms, L	46	4	6	10	-17	15
Joe Juneau, C	56	9	22	31	8	26	Joe Reekie, D	68	2	8	10	15	70
Phil Housley, D	64	6	25	31	-10	24	Brian Bellows, L	11	6	3	9	-3	6
Jeff Brown, D	60	4	24	28	5	32	Michal Pivonka, C	33	3	6	9	5	20
*Richard Zednik, L	65	17	9	26	-2	28	Brendan Witt, D	64	1	7	8	-11	112
Dale Hunter, C	82	8	18	26	1	103	Ken Klee, D	51	4	2	6	-3	46
Andrew Brunette, L	28	11	12	23	2	12	*Jaroslav Svejkovsky, L	17	4	1	5	-5	10
Sergei Gonchar, D	72	5	16	21	2	66							
Esa Tikkanen, L	48	3	18	21	-11	18							
Mark Tinordi, D	47	8	9	17	9	39							

GOALTENDING

Player	GP	Mins	Avg	W	L	T	SO
Chris Simon, L	28	7	10	17	-1	38	Olaf Kolzig	64	3788	2.20	33	18	10	5
Andre Nikolishin, C	38	6	10	16	1	14	Bill Ranford	22	1183	2.79	7	12	2	0
*Jan Bulis, C	48	5	11	16	-5	18	Team total	82	4997	2.43	40	30	12	5

* Rookie.

1998 NHL Draft

First Round

The opening round of the 1998 NHL draft was held on June 27 in Buffalo.

	Team	Selection	Position		Team	Selection	Position
1.	Tampa Bay	Vincent Lecavalier	C	15.	Ottawa	Mathieu Chouinard	G
2.	Nashville	David Legwand	C	16.	Montreal	Eric Chouinard	C
3.	San Jose	Brad Stuart	D	17.	Colorado	Martin Skoula	D
4.	Vancouver	Bryan Allen	D	18.	Buffalo	Dmitri Kalinin	D
5.	Anaheim	Vitali Vishnevsky	D	19.	Colorado	Robyn Regehr	D
6.	Calgary	Rico Fata	C	20.	Colorado	Scott Parker	RW
7.	NY Rangers	Manny Halhotra	C	21.	Los Angeles	Mathieu Biron	D
8.	Chicago	Mark Bell	C	22.	Philadelphia	Simon Gagne	C
9.	NY Islanders	Michael Rupp	LW	23.	Pittsburgh	Milan Kraft	C
10.	Toronto	Nikolai Antropov	C	24.	St. Louis	Christian Backman	D
11.	Carolina	Jeff Heerema	RW	25.	Detroit	Jiri Fischer	D
12.	Colorado	Alex Tanguay	C	26.	New Jersey	Mike Van Ryn	D
13.	Edmonton	Michael Henrich	RW	27.	New Jersey	Scott Gomez	C
14.	Phoenix	Patrick DesRochers	G				

Jury Red-lights the Case

The most controversial—and expensive—goal in the 10-year history of the Miami Arena was not scored by the Florida Panthers or any of their NHL opponents. It came off the stick of Randy Giunto, 40, of Hollywood, Fla., who on April 17, 1998, was awarded $1 million in a court case stemming from a promotional contest.

Giunto took the $1 million shot, a 118-footer from the far blue line, during the second intermission of a March '94 game. The contest rules that Giunto had picked up at a local Blockbuster called for him to shoot a puck "through" a 3½-inch wide, 1½-inch high slot. A form he was given minutes before he took the shot said it had to go "completely through."

Giunto's shot appeared to enter the opening partway, but Panthers officials say the puck deflected off an edge of the slot. Giunto went home with only a year's supply of Coke and videos. A few weeks later he attended another Panthers game, at which, he says, he was told by a team employee that he had gotten "screwed." Giunto studied a videotape, determined that the puck had gone at least partway through the slot and hired a lawyer. That's how a six-member Miami–Dade County District Court came to be goal judges.

"I have no idea how something that doesn't go in counts as going in," says David Carlisle, lawyer for the contest's sponsors (the Panthers, Blockbuster Entertainment and Coca-Cola), who claim that Giunto's shot never even entered the slot and may appeal the verdict. But Giunto's lawyer, Richard Diaz, persuaded the jury not only that the puck did enter the slot but also that, as he says, "*through* and *completely through* are two different things." Adds Diaz: "There's no question this was a trial of semantics."

FOR THE RECORD·Year by Year

The Stanley Cup

Awarded annually to the team that wins the NHL's best-of-seven final-round playoffs. The Stanley Cup is the oldest trophy competed for by professional athletes in North America. It was donated in 1893 by Frederick Arthur, Lord Stanley of Preston.

Results

WINNERS PRIOR TO FORMATION OF NHL IN 1917

1892–93 ....Montreal A.A.A.	1904–05 ....Ottawa Silver Seven
1893–94 ....Montreal A.A.A.	1905–06 ....Ottawa Silver Seven (Feb)
1894–95 ....Montreal Victorias	1905–06 ....Montreal Wanderers (Mar)
1895–96 ....Winnipeg Victorias (Feb)	1906–07 ....Kenora Thistles (Jan)
1895–96 ....Montreal Victorias (Dec)	1906–07 ....Montreal Wanderers (Mar)
1896–97 ....Montreal Victorias	1907–08 ....Montreal Wanderers
1897–98 ....Montreal Victorias	1908–09 ....Ottawa Senators
1898–99 ....Montreal Victorias (Feb)	1909–10 ....Montreal Wanderers
1898–99 ....Montreal Shamrocks (Mar)	1910–11 ....Ottawa Senators
1899–1900 ....Montreal Shamrocks	1911–12 ....Quebec Bulldogs
1900–01 ....Winnipeg Victorias	1912–13 ....Quebec Bulldogs
1901–02 ....Winnipeg Victorias (Jan)	1913–14 ....Toronto Blueshirts
1901–02 ....Montreal A.A.A. (Mar)	1914–15 ....Vancouver Millionaires
1902–03 ....Montreal A.A.A. (Feb)	1915–16 ....Montreal Canadiens
1902–03 ....Ottawa Silver Seven (Mar)	1916–17 ....Seattle Metropolitans
1903–04 ....Ottawa Silver Seven	

NHL WINNERS AND FINALISTS

Season	Champion	Finalist	GP in Final
1917–18	Toronto Arenas	Vancouver Millionaires	5
1918–19	No decision*	No decision*	5
1919–20	Ottawa Senators	Seattle Metropolitans	5
1920–21	Ottawa Senators	Vancouver Millionaires	5
1921–22	Toronto St Pats	Vancouver Millionaires	5
1922–23	Ottawa Senators	Vancouver Maroons, Edmonton Eskimos	2, 4
1923–24	Montreal Canadiens	Vancouver Maroons, Calgary Tigers	2, 2
1924–25	Victoria Cougars	Montreal Canadiens	4
1925–26	Montreal Maroons	Victoria Cougars	4
1926–27	Ottawa Senators	Boston Bruins	4
1927–28	New York Rangers	Montreal Maroons	5
1928–29	Boston Bruins	New York Rangers	2
1929–30	Montreal Canadiens	Boston Bruins	2
1930–31	Montreal Canadiens	Chicago Blackhawks	5
1931–32	Toronto Maple Leafs	New York Rangers	3
1932–33	New York Rangers	Toronto Maple Leafs	4
1933–34	Chicago Blackhawks	Detroit Red Wings	4
1934–35	Montreal Maroons	Toronto Maple Leafs	3
1935–36	Detroit Red Wings	Toronto Maple Leafs	4
1936–37	Detroit Red Wings	New York Rangers	5
1937–38	Chicago Blackhawks	Toronto Maple Leafs	4
1938–39	Boston Bruins	Toronto Maple Leafs	5
1939–40	New York Rangers	Toronto Maple Leafs	6
1940–41	Boston Bruins	Detroit Red Wings	4
1941–42	Toronto Maple Leafs	Detroit Red Wings	7
1942–43	Detroit Red Wings	Boston Bruins	4
1943–44	Montreal Canadiens	Chicago Blackhawks	4
1944–45	Toronto Maple Leafs	Detroit Red Wings	7
1945–46	Montreal Canadiens	Boston Bruins	5
1946–47	Toronto Maple Leafs	Montreal Canadiens	6
1947–48	Toronto Maple Leafs	Detroit Red Wings	4
1948–49	Toronto Maple Leafs	Detroit Red Wings	4
1949–50	Detroit Red Wings	New York Rangers	7
1950–51	Toronto Maple Leafs	Montreal Canadiens	5
1951–52	Detroit Red Wings	Montreal Canadiens	4
1952–53	Montreal Canadiens	Boston Bruins	5
1953–54	Detroit Red Wings	Montreal Canadiens	7
1954–55	Detroit Red Wings	Montreal Canadiens	7
1955–56	Montreal Canadiens	Detroit Red Wings	5

NHL WINNERS AND FINALISTS (Cont.)

Season	Champion	Finalist	GP in Final
1956–57	Montreal Canadiens	Boston Bruins	5
1957–58	Montreal Canadiens	Boston Bruins	6
1958–59	Montreal Canadiens	Toronto Maple Leafs	5
1959–60	Montreal Canadiens	Toronto Maple Leafs	4
1960–61	Chicago Blackhawks	Detroit Red Wings	6
1961–62	Toronto Maple Leafs	Chicago Blackhawks	6
1962–63	Toronto Maple Leafs	Detroit Red Wings	5
1963–64	Toronto Maple Leafs	Detroit Red Wings	7
1964–65	Montreal Canadiens	Chicago Blackhawks	7
1965–66	Montreal Canadiens	Detroit Red Wings	6
1966–67	Toronto Maple Leafs	Montreal Canadiens	6
1967–68	Montreal Canadiens	St. Louis Blues	4
1968–69	Montreal Canadiens	St. Louis Blues	4
1969–70	Boston Bruins	St. Louis Blues	4
1970–71	Montreal Canadiens	Chicago Blackhawks	7
1971–72	Boston Bruins	New York Rangers	6
1972–73	Montreal Canadiens	Chicago Blackhawks	6
1973–74	Philadelphia Flyers	Boston Bruins	6
1974–75	Philadelphia Flyers	Buffalo Sabres	6
1975–76	Montreal Canadiens	Philadelphia Flyers	4
1976–77	Montreal Canadiens	Boston Bruins	4
1977–78	Montreal Canadiens	Boston Bruins	6
1978–79	Montreal Canadiens	New York Rangers	5
1979–80	New York Islanders	Philadelphia Flyers	6
1980–81	New York Islanders	Minnesota North Stars	5
1981–82	New York Islanders	Vancouver Canucks	4
1982–83	New York Islanders	Edmonton Oilers	4
1983–84	Edmonton Oilers	New York Islanders	5
1984–85	Edmonton Oilers	Philadelphia Flyers	5
1985–86	Montreal Canadiens	Calgary Flames	6
1986–87	Edmonton Oilers	Philadelphia Flyers	7
1987–88	Edmonton Oilers	Boston Bruins	4
1988–89	Calgary Flames	Montreal Canadiens	6
1989–90	Edmonton Oilers	Boston Bruins	5
1990–91	Pittsburgh Penguins	Minnesota North Stars	6
1991–92	Pittsburgh Penguins	Chicago Blackhawks	4
1992–93	Montreal Canadiens	Los Angeles Kings	5
1993–94	New York Rangers	Vancouver Canucks	7
1994–95	New Jersey Devils	Detroit Red Wings	4
1995–96	Colorado Avalanche	Florida Panthers	4
1996–97	Detroit Red Wings	Philadelphia Flyers	4
1997–98	Detroit Red Wings	Washington Capitals	4

*In 1919 the Montreal Canadiens traveled to meet Seattle, the PCHL champions. After 5 games had been played—the teams were tied at 2 wins and 1 tie—the series was called off by the local Department of Health because of the influenza epidemic and the death of Canadian defenseman Joe Hall from influenza.

Conn Smythe Trophy

Awarded to the Most Valuable Player of the Stanley Cup playoffs, as selected by the Professional Hockey Writers Association. The trophy is named after the former coach, general manager, president and owner of the Toronto Maple Leafs.

1965	Jean Beliveau, Mtl
1966	Roger Crozier, Det
1967	Dave Keon, Tor
1968	Glenn Hall, StL
1969	Serge Savard, Mtl
1970	Bobby Orr, Bos
1971	Ken Dryden, Mtl
1972	Bobby Orr, Bos
1973	Yvan Cournoyer, Mtl
1974	Bernie Parent, Phil
1975	Bernie Parent, Phil
1976	Reggie Leach, Phil
1977	Guy Lafleur, Mtl
1978	Larry Robinson, Mtl
1979	Bob Gainey, Mtl
1980	Bryan Trottier, NYI
1981	Butch Goring, NYI
1982	Mike Bossy, NYI
1983	Bill Smith, NYI
1984	Mark Messier, Edm
1985	Wayne Gretzky, Edm
1986	Patrick Roy, Mtl
1987	Ron Hextall, Phil
1988	Wayne Gretzky, Edm
1989	Al MacInnis, Cgy
1990	Bill Ranford, Edm
1991	Mario Lemieux, Pitt
1992	Mario Lemieux, Pitt
1993	Patrick Roy, Mtl
1994	Brian Leetch, NYR
1995	Claude Lemieux, NJ
1996	Joe Sakic, Col
1997	Mike Vernon, Det
1998	Steve Yzerman, Det

Alltime Stanley Cup Playoff Leaders

Points

	Yrs	GP	G	A	Pts		Yrs	GP	G	A	Pts
*Wayne Gretzky, four teams	17	208	122	260	382	Mike Bossy, NYI	10	129	85	75	160
*Mark Messier, Edm, NYR	17	236	109	186	295	Gordie Howe, Det, Hart	20	157	68	92	160
*Jari Kurri, four teams	15	200	106	127	233	Bobby Smith, Minn, Mtl	13	184	64	96	160
Glenn Anderson, four teams	15	225	93	121	214	Mario Lemieux, Pitt	7	89	70	85	155
*Paul Coffey, five teams	15	193	59	136	195	*Ray Bourque, Bos	18	168	36	115	151
Bryan Trottier, NYI, Pitt	17	221	71	113	184	Stan Mikita, Chi	18	155	59	91	150
Jean Beliveau, Mtl	17	162	79	97	176	Brian Propp, Phil, Bos, Minn	13	160	64	84	148
Denis Savard, Chi, Mtl	16	169	66	109	175	Larry Robinson, Mtl, LA	20	227	28	116	144
*Doug Gilmour, four teams	14	152	54	117	171	*Larry Murphy, six teams	17	190	35	109	144
Denis Potvin, NYI	14	185	56	108	164	Jacques Lemaire, Mtl	11	145	61	78	139

*Active player.

Goals

	Yrs	GP	G
*Wayne Gretzky, four teams	17	208	122
*Mark Messier, Edm, NYR	17	236	109
*Jari Kurri, five teams	15	200	106
Glenn Anderson, four teams	15	225	93
Mike Bossy, NYI	10	129	85
Maurice Richard, Mtl	15	133	82
Jean Beliveau, Mtl	17	162	79
*Dino Ciccarelli, five teams	14	141	73
*Esa Tikkanen, six teams	13	186	72
Bryan Trottier, NYI, Pitt	17	221	71

*Active player.

Assists

	Yrs	GP	A
*Wayne Gretzky, four teams	17	208	260
*Mark Messier, Edm, NYR	17	236	186
*Paul Coffey, five teams	16	193	136
*Jari Kurri, five teams	15	196	127
Glenn Anderson, four teams	15	225	121
*Doug Gilmour, four teams	14	152	117
Larry Robinson, Mtl, LA	20	227	116
*Ray Bourque, Bos	18	168	115
Bryan Trottier, NYI, Pitt	17	221	113
Denis Savard, Chi, Mtl	16	169	109

*Active player.

Goaltending

WINS	W	L	Pct
*Patrick Roy, Mtl, Col	99	59	.627
Billy Smith, LA, NYI	88	36	.710
*Grant Fuhr, five teams	86	44	.662
Ken Dryden, Mtl	80	32	.714
*Mike Vernon, Cgy, Det, SJ	75	49	.605
Jacques Plante, five teams	71	37	.657
*Andy Moog, four teams	68	57	.544
Turk Broda, Tor	58	42	.580
Terry Sawchuk, five teams	54	48	.529
*Tom Barrasso, Buff, Pitt	53	43	.552

*Active player.

SHUTOUTS	GP	W	SO
Clint Benedict, Ott, Mtl M	48	25	15
Jacques Plante, five teams	112	71	14
Turk Broda, Tor	101	58	13
Terry Sawchuk, five teams	106	54	12
*Patrick Roy, Mtl, Col	160	99	11

GOALS AGAINST AVG			Avg
*Martin Brodeur, NJ			1.84
George Hainsworth, Mtl, Tor			1.93
Turk Broda, Tor			1.98
Jacques Plante, five teams			2.17
*Ed Belfour, Chi, Dall			2.35

Note: At least 50 games played.

Alltime Stanley Cup Standings

TEAM	W	L	Pct	TEAM	W	L	Pct
Montreal	381	249	.605	Calgary*	69	87	.442
Boston	230	246	.483	Colorado**	64	62	.508
Detroit	222	207	.517	Washington	64	73	.467
Toronto	210	230	.477	Los Angeles	55	91	.376
Chicago	187	214	.467	Vancouver	54	70	.435
NY Rangers	183	195	.484	New Jersey†	54	49	.574
Philadelphia	145	129	.529	Phoenix††	23	51	.311
Edmonton	130	74	.637	Carolina§	18	31	.367
NY Islanders	128	90	.587	Florida	13	14	.481
St. Louis	111	135	.451	San Jose	13	18	.419
Dallas#	99	105	.485	Ottawa	8	10	.444
Pittsburgh	88	78	.530	Anaheim	4	7	.364
Buffalo	77	93	.453	Tampa Bay	2	4	.333

*Atlanta Flames 1972–80. †Colorado Rockies 1976–82. #Minnesota North Stars 1967–93. **Quebec Nordiques 1979–95. ††Winnipeg Jets 1979–96. §Hartford Whalers 1979–97. Note: Teams ranked by playoff victories.

Stanley Cup Coaching Records

Coach	Team	Yrs	Series	Series W	Series L	Games	Games W	Games L	T	Cups	Pct
Glen Sather ....Edm		10	27	21	6	*126	89	37	0	4	.706
Toe Blake....................Mtl		13	23	18	5	119	82	37	0	8	.689
†Scott Bowman ....Five teams		24	59	43	16	305	194	111	0	8	.636
Hap Day ....Tor		9	14	10	4	80	49	31	0	5	.613
Jacques Lemaire.........Mtl, NJ		6	15	10	5	83	49	34	0	1	.590
Al Arbour ....StL, NYI		16	42	30	12	209	123	86	0	4	.589
†Mike Keenan ....five teams		11	28	18	10	160	91	69	0	1	.569
Fred Shero.................Phil, NYR		8	21	15	6	108	61	47	0	2	.565
Jacques Demers ....Que, StL, Det, Mtl		9	19	11	8	104	57	47	0	1	.548
Bob Johnson ....Cgy, Pitt		6	14	9	5	76	41	35	0	1	.539

*Does not include suspended game, May 24, 1988. †Active coach.
Note: Coaches ranked by winning percentage. Minimum: 65 games.

The 10 Longest Overtime Games

Date	Result	OT	Scorer	Series	Series Winner
3-24-36 ....Det 1 vs Mtl M 0		116:30	Mud Bruneteau	SF	Det
4-3-33 ....Tor 1 vs Bos 0		104:46	Ken Doraty	SF	Tor
4-24-96 ....Pitt 3 vs Wash 2		79:15	Petr Nedved	CQF	Pitt
3-23-43 ....Tor 3 vs Det 2		70:18	Jack McLean	SF	Det
3-28-30 ....Mtl 2 vs NYR 1		68:52	Gus Rivers	SF	Mtl
4-18-87 ....NYI 3 vs Wash 2		68:47	Pat LaFontaine	DSF	NYI
4-27-94 ....Buff 1 vs NJ 0		65:43	Dave Hannan	CQF	NJ
3-27-51 ....Mtl 3 vs Det 2		61:09	Maurice Richard	SF	Mtl
3-27-38 ....NYA 3 vs NYR 2		60:40	Lorne Carr	QF	NYA
3-26-32 ....NYR 4 vs Mtl 3		59:32	Fred Cook	SF	NYR

NHL Awards

Hart Memorial Trophy

Awarded annually "to the player adjudged to be the most valuable to his team." The original trophy was donated by Dr. David A. Hart, father of Cecil Hart, former manager-coach of the Montreal Canadiens. In the decade of the 1980s Wayne Gretzky won the award nine of 10 times.

	Winner	Key Statistics	Runner-Up
1924	Frank Nighbor, Ott	10 goals, 3 assists in 20 games	Sprague Cleghorn, Mtl
1925	Billy Burch, Ham	20 goals, 4 assists in 27 games	Howie Morenz, Mtl
1926	Nels Stewart, Mtl M	42 points in 36 games	Sprague Cleghorn, Mtl
1927	Herb Gardiner, Mtl	12 points in 44 games as defenseman	Bill Cook, NYR
1928	Howie Morenz, Mtl	33 goals, 18 assists	Roy Worters, Pitt
1929	Roy Worters, NYA	1.21 goals against, 13 shutouts	Ace Bailey, Tor
1930	Nels Stewart, Mtl M	39 goals, 16 assists	Lionel Hitchman, Bos
1931	Howie Morenz, Mtl	28 goals, 23 assists	Eddie Shore, Bos
1932	Howie Morenz, Mtl	24 goals, 25 assists	Ching Johnson, NYR
1933	Eddie Shore, Bos	27 assists in 48 games as defenseman	Bill Cook, NYR
1934	Aurel Joliat, Mtl	27 points	Lionel Conacher, Chi
1935	Eddie Shore, Bos	26 assists in 48 games as defenseman	Charlie Conacher, Tor
1936	Eddie Shore, Bos	16 assists in 46 games as defenseman	Hooley Smith, Mtl M
1937	Babe Siebert, Mtl	28 points	Lionel Conacher, Mtl M
1938	Eddie Shore, Bos	17 points in 47 games as defenseman	Paul Thompson, Chi
1939	Toe Blake, Mtl	led NHL in points (47)	Syl Apps, Tor
1940	Ebbie Goodfellow, Det	28 points	Syl Apps, Tor
1941	Bill Cowley, Bos	led NHL in assists (45) and points (62)	Dit Clapper, Bos
1942	Tom Anderson, Bos	41 points	Syl Apps, Tor
1943	Bill Cowley, Bos	led NHL in assists (45)	Doug Bentley, Chi
1944	Babe Pratt, Tor	57 points in 50 games	Bill Cowley, Bos
1945	Elmer Lach, Mtl	led NHL in assists (54) and points (80)	Maurice Richard, Mtl
1946	Max Bentley, Chi	61 points in 47 games	Gaye Stewart, Tor
1947	Maurice Richard, Mtl	led NHL in goals (45); 26 assists	Milt Schmidt, Bos
1948	Buddy O'Connor, NYR	60 points in 60 games	Frank Brimsek, Bos
1949	Sid Abel, Det	28 goals, 26 assists	Bill Durnan, Mtl

Hart Memorial Trophy (Cont.)

Winner	Key Statistics	Runner-Up
1950...............Charlie Rayner, NYR	6 shutouts	Ted Kennedy, Tor
1951...............Milt Schmidt, Bos	61 points in 62 games	Maurice Richard, Mtl
1952...............Gordie Howe, Det	led NHL in goals (47) and points (86)	Elmer Lach, Mtl
1953...............Gordie Howe, Det	led NHL in goals (49) and points (95)	Al Rollins, Chi
1954...............Al Rollins, Chi	5 shutouts	Red Kelly, Det
1955...............Ted Kennedy, Tor	52 points	Harry Lumley, Tor
1956...............Jean Beliveau, Mtl	led NHL in goals (47) and points (88)	Tod Sloan, Tor
1957...............Gordie Howe, Det	led NHL in goals (44) and points (89)	Jean Beliveau, Mtl
1959...............Andy Bathgate, NYR	74 points in 70 games	Gordie Howe, Det
1960...............Gordie Howe, Det	45 assists, 73 points	Bobby Hull, Chi
1961...............Bernie Geoffrion, Mtl	50 goals, 95 points	Johnny Bower, Tor
1962...............Jacques Plante, Mtl	42 wins, 2.37 goals against avg.	Doug Harvey, NYR
1963...............Gordie Howe, Det	47 assists, 73 points	Stan Mikita, Chi
1964...............Jean Beliveau, Mtl	50 assists, 78 points	Bobby Hull, Chi
1965...............Bobby Hull, Chi	39 goals, 32 assists	Norm Ullman, Det
1966...............Bobby Hull, Chi	led NHL in goals (54) and points (97)	Jean Beliveau, Mtl
1967...............Stan Mikita, Chi	led NHL in assists (62) and points (97)	Ed Giacomin, NYR
1968...............Stan Mikita, Chi	40 goals, 47 assists	Jean Beliveau, Mtl
1969...............Phil Esposito, Bos	led NHL in goals (77) and points (126)	Jean Beliveau, Mtl
1970...............Bobby Orr, Bos	led NHL in assists (87) and points (120)	Tony Esposito, Chi
1971...............Bobby Orr, Bos	102 assists, 139 points	Tony Esposito, Chi
1972...............Bobby Orr, Bos	80 assists, 117 points	Ken Dryden, Mtl
1973...............Bobby Clarke, Phil	67 assists, 104 points	Phil Esposito, Bos
1974...............Phil Esposito, Bos	led NHL in goals (68) and points (145)	Bernie Parent, Phil
1975...............Bobby Clarke, Phil	89 assists, 116 points	Rogatien Vachon, LA
1976...............Bobby Clarke, Phil	89 assists, 119 points	Denis Potvin, NYI
1977...............Guy Lafleur, Mtl	led NHL in assists (80) and points (136)	Bobby Clarke, Phil
1978...............Guy Lafleur, Mtl	led NHL in goals (60) and points (132)	Bryan Trottier, NYI
1979...............Bryan Trottier, NYI	led NHL in assists (87) and points (134)	Guy Lafleur, Mtl
1980...............Wayne Gretzky, Edm	51 goals, 86 assists	Marcel Dionne, LA
1981...............Wayne Gretzky, Edm	led NHL in assists (109) and points (164)	Mike Liut, StL
1982...............Wayne Gretzky, Edm	NHL-record 92 goals and 212 points	Bryan Trottier, NYI
1983...............Wayne Gretzky, Edm	led NHL in goals (71) and points (196)	Pete Peeters, Bos
1984...............Wayne Gretzky, Edm	led NHL in goals (87) and points (205)	Rod Langway, Wash
1985...............Wayne Gretzky, Edm	led NHL in goals (73) and points (208)	Dale Hawerchuk, Winn
1986...............Wayne Gretzky, Edm	NHL-record 163 assists and 215 points	Mario Lemieux, Pitt
1987...............Wayne Gretzky, Edm	led NHL in assists (121) and points (183)	Ray Bourque, Bos
1988...............Mario Lemieux, Pitt	led NHL in goals (70) and points (168)	Grant Fuhr, Edm
1989...............Wayne Gretzky, LA	114 assists, 168 points	Mario Lemieux, Pitt
1990...............Mark Messier, Edm	84 assists, 129 points	Ray Bourque, Bos
1991...............Brett Hull, StL	led NHL in goals (86); 131 points	Wayne Gretzky, LA
1992...............Mark Messier, NYR	72 assists, 107 points	Patrick Roy, Mtl
1993...............Mario Lemieux, Pitt	69 goals, 91 assists in 60 games	Doug Gilmour, Tor
1994...............Sergei Fedorov, Det	56 goals, 64 assists	Dominik Hasek, Buff
1995...............Eric Lindros, Phil	29 goals, 41 assists in 46 games	Jaromir Jagr, Pitt
1996...............Mario Lemieux, Pitt	led NHL in goals (69) and points (161)	Mark Messier, NYR
1997...............Dominik Hasek, Buff	5 shutouts, 2.27 goals against	Paul Kariya, Ana
1998...............Dominik Hasek, Buff	13 shutouts, 2.09 goals against	Jaromir Jagr, Pitt

Art Ross Trophy

Awarded annually "to the player who leads the league in scoring points at the end of the regular season." The trophy was presented to the NHL in 1947 by Arthur Howie Ross, former manager-coach of the Boston Bruins. The tie-breakers, in order, are as follows: (1) player with most goals, (2) player with fewer games played, (3) player scoring first goal of the season. Bobby Orr is the only defenseman in NHL history to win this trophy, and he won it twice (1970 and 1975).

Winner	Pts	Winner	Pts
1919...............Newsy Lalonde, Mtl	44	1929 ....Ace Bailey, Tor	51
1920...............Joe Malone, Que	30	1930 ....Cooney Weiland, Bos	32
1921...............Newsy Lalonde, Mtl	48	1931 ....Howie Morenz, Mtl	73
1922...............Punch Broadbent, Ott	41	1932 ....Harvey Jackson, Tor	51
1923...............Babe Dye, Tor	46	1933 ....Bill Cook, NYR	53
1924...............Cy Denneny, Ott	37	1934 ....Charlie Conacher, Tor	50
1925...............Babe Dye, Tor	23	1935 ....Charlie Conacher, Tor	57
1926...............Nels Stewart, Mtl M	44	1936 ....Sweeney Schriner, NYA	45
1927 ....Bill Cook, NYR	42	1937 ....Sweeney Schriner, NYA	46
1928 ....Howie Morenz, Mtl	37	1938 ....Gordie Drillon, Tor	52

Art Ross Trophy (Cont.)

Winner	Pts	Winner	Pts
1939 ....Toe Blake, Mtl	47	1969 ....Phil Esposito, Bos	126
1940 ....Milt Schmidt, Bos	52	1970 ....Bobby Orr, Bos	120
1941 ....Bill Cowley, Bos	62	1971 ....Phil Esposito, Bos	152
1942 ....Bryan Hextall, NYR	56	1972 ....Phil Esposito, Bos	133
1943 ....Doug Bentley, Chi	73	1973 ....Phil Esposito, Bos	130
1944 ....Herb Cain, Bos	82	1974 ....Phil Esposito, Bos	145
1945 ....Elmer Lach, Mtl	80	1975 ....Bobby Orr, Bos	135
1946 ....Max Bentley, Chi	61	1976 ....Guy Lafleur, Mtl	125
1947 ....*Max Bentley, Chi	72	1977 ....Guy Lafleur, Mtl	136
1948 ....Elmer Lach, Mtl	61	1978 ....Guy Lafleur, Mtl	132
1949 ....Roy Conacher, Chi	68	1979 ....Bryan Trottier, NYI	134
1950 ....Ted Lindsay, Det	78	1980 ....Marcel Dionne, LA	137
1951 ....Gordie Howe, Det	86	1981 ....Wayne Gretzky, Edm	164
1952 ....Gordie Howe, Det	86	1982 ....Wayne Gretzky, Edm	212
1953 ....Gordie Howe, Det	95	1983 ....Wayne Gretzky, Edm	196
1954 ....Gordie Howe, Det	81	1984 ....Wayne Gretzky, Edm	205
1955 ....Bernie Geoffrion, Mtl	75	1985 ....Wayne Gretzky, Edm	208
1956 ....Jean Beliveau, Mtl	88	1986 ....Wayne Gretzky, Edm	215
1957 ....Gordie Howe, Det	89	1987 ....Wayne Gretzky, Edm	183
1958 ....Dickie Moore, Mtl	84	1988 ....Mario Lemieux, Pitt	168
1959 ....Dickie Moore, Mtl	96	1989 ....Mario Lemieux, Pitt	199
1960 ....Bobby Hull, Chi	81	1990 ....Wayne Gretzky, LA	142
1961 ....Bernie Geoffrion, Mtl	95	1991 ....Wayne Gretzky, LA	163
1962 ....Bobby Hull, Chi	84	1992 ....Mario Lemieux, Pitt	131
1963 ....Gordie Howe, Det	86	1993 ....Mario Lemieux, Pitt	160
1964 ....Stan Mikita, Chi	89	1994 ....Wayne Gretzky, LA	130
1965 ....Stan Mikita, Chi	87	1995 ....Jaromir Jagr, Pitt	70
1966 ....Bobby Hull, Chi	97	1996 ....Mario Lemieux, Pitt	161
1967 ....Stan Mikita, Chi	97	1997 ....Mario Lemieux, Pitt	122
1968 ....Stan Mikita, Chi	87	1998 ....Jaromir Jagr, Pitt	102

Note: Listing includes scoring leaders prior to inception of Art Ross Trophy in 1947–48.

Lady Byng Memorial Trophy

Awarded annually "to the player adjudged to have exhibited the best type of sportsmanship and gentlemanly conduct combined with a high standard of playing ability." Lady Byng, who first presented the trophy in 1925, was the wife of Canada's Governor-General. She donated a second trophy in 1936 after the first was given permanently to Frank Boucher of the New York Rangers, who won it seven times in eight seasons. Stan Mikita, one of the league's most penalized players during his early years in the NHL, won the trophy twice late in his career (1967 and 1968).

1925..........Frank Nighbor, Ott	1950..........Edgar Laprade, NYR	1975..........Marcel Dionne, Det
1926..........Frank Nighbor, Ott	1951..........Red Kelly, Det	1976..........Jean Ratelle, NYR-Bos
1927..........Billy Burch, NYA	1952..........Sid Smith, Tor	1977..........Marcel Dionne, LA
1928..........Frank Boucher, NYR	1953..........Red Kelly, Det	1978..........Butch Goring, LA
1929..........Frank Boucher, NYR	1954..........Red Kelly, Det	1979..........Bob MacMillan, Atl
1930..........Frank Boucher, NYR	1955..........Sid Smith, Tor	1980..........Wayne Gretzky, Edm
1931..........Frank Boucher, NYR	1956..........Earl Reibel, Det	1981..........Rick Kehoe, Pitt
1932..........Joe Primeau, Tor	1957..........Andy Hebenton, NYR	1982..........Rick Middleton, Bos
1933..........Frank Boucher, NYR	1958..........Camille Henry, NYR	1983..........Mike Bossy, NYI
1934..........Frank Boucher, NYR	1959..........Alex Delvecchio, Det	1984..........Mike Bossy, NYI
1935..........Frank Boucher, NYR	1960..........Don McKenney, Bos	1985..........Jari Kurri, Edm
1936..........Doc Romnes, Chi	1961..........Red Kelly, Tor	1986..........Mike Bossy, NYI
1937..........Marty Barry, Det	1962..........Dave Keon, Tor	1987..........Joe Mullen, Cgy
1938..........Gordie Drillon, Tor	1963..........Dave Keon, Tor	1988..........Mats Naslund, Mtl
1939..........Clint Smith, NYR	1964..........Ken Wharram, Chi	1989..........Joe Mullen, Cgy
1940..........Bobby Bauer, Bos	1965..........Bobby Hull, Chi	1990..........Brett Hull, StL
1941..........Bobby Bauer, Bos	1966..........Alex Delvecchio, Det	1991..........Wayne Gretzky, LA
1942..........Syl Apps, Tor	1967..........Stan Mikita, Chi	1992..........Wayne Gretzky, LA
1943..........Max Bentley, Chi	1968..........Stan Mikita, Chi	1993..........Pierre Turgeon, NYI
1944..........Clint Smith, Chi	1969..........Alex Delvecchio, Det	1994..........Wayne Gretzky, LA
1945..........Billy Mosienko, Chi	1970..........Phil Goyette, StL	1995..........Ron Francis, Pitt
1946..........Toe Blake, Mtl	1971..........John Bucyk, Bos	1996..........Paul Kariya, Ana
1947..........Bobby Bauer, Bos	1972..........Jean Ratelle, NYR	1997..........Paul Kariya, Ana
1948..........Buddy O'Connor, NYR	1973..........Gilbert Perreault, Buff	1998..........Ron Francis, Pitt
1949..........Bill Quackenbush, Det	1974..........John Bucyk, Bos	

James Norris Memorial Trophy

Awarded annually "to the defense player who demonstrates throughout the season the greatest all-around ability in the position." James Norris was the former owner-president of the Detroit Red Wings. Bobby Orr holds the record for most consecutive times winning the award (eight, 1968–1975).

1954 ....Red Kelly, Det	1969 ....Bobby Orr, Bos	1984 ....Rod Langway, Wash
1955 ....Doug Harvey, Mtl	1970 ....Bobby Orr, Bos	1985 ....Paul Coffey, Edm
1956 ....Doug Harvey, Mtl	1971 ....Bobby Orr, Bos	1986 ....Paul Coffey, Edm
1957 ....Doug Harvey, Mtl	1972 ....Bobby Orr, Bos	1987 ....Ray Bourque, Bos
1958 ....Doug Harvey, Mtl	1973 ....Bobby Orr, Bos	1988 ....Ray Bourque, Bos
1959 ....Tom Johnson, Mtl	1974 ....Bobby Orr, Bos	1989 ....Chris Chelios, Mtl
1960 ....Doug Harvey, Mtl	1975 ....Bobby Orr, Bos	1990 ....Ray Bourque, Bos
1961 ....Doug Harvey, Mtl	1976 ....Denis Potvin, NYI	1991 ....Ray Bourque, Bos
1962 ....Doug Harvey, NYR	1977 ....Larry Robinson, Mtl	1992 ....Brian Leetch, NYR
1963 ....Pierre Pilote, Chi	1978 ....Denis Potvin, NYI	1993 ....Chris Chelios, Chi
1964 ....Pierre Pilote, Chi	1979 ....Denis Potvin, NYI	1994 ....Ray Bourque, Bos
1965 ....Pierre Pilote, Chi	1980 ....Larry Robinson, Mtl	1995 ....Paul Coffey, Det
1966 ....Jacques Laperriere, Mtl	1981 ....Randy Carlyle, Pitt	1996 ....Chris Chelios, Chi
1967 ....Harry Howell, NYR	1982 ....Doug Wilson, Chi	1997 ....Brian Leetch, NYR
1968 ....Bobby Orr, Bos	1983 ....Rod Langway, Wash	1998 ....Rob Blake, LA

Calder Memorial Trophy

Awarded annually "to the player selected as the most proficient in his first year of competition in the National Hockey League." Frank Calder was a former NHL president. Sergei Makarov, who won the award in 1989–90, was the oldest recipient of the trophy, at 31. Players are no longer eligible for the award if they are 26 or older as of September 15th of the season in question.

1933 ....Carl Voss, Det	1955 ....Ed Litzenberger, Chi	1977 ....Willi Plett, Atl
1934 ....Russ Blinko, Mtl M	1956 ....Glenn Hall, Det	1978 ....Mike Bossy, NYI
1935 ....Dave Schriner, NYA	1957 ....Larry Regan, Bos	1979 ....Bobby Smith, Minn
1936 ....Mike Karakas, Chi	1958 ....Frank Mahovlich, Tor	1980 ....Ray Bourque, Bos
1937 ....Syl Apps, Tor	1959 ....Ralph Backstrom, Mtl	1981 ....Peter Stastny, Que
1938 ....Cully Dahlstrom, Chi	1960 ....Bill Hay, Chi	1982 ....Dale Hawerchuk, Winn
1939 ....Frank Brimsek, Bos	1961 ....Dave Keon, Tor	1983 ....Steve Larmer, Chi
1940 ....Kilby MacDonald, NYR	1962 ....Bobby Rousseau, Mtl	1984 ....Tom Barrasso, Buff
1941 ....Johnny Quilty, Mtl	1963 ....Kent Douglas, Tor	1985 ....Mario Lemieux, Pitt
1942 ....Grant Warwick, NYR	1964 ....Jacques Laperriere, Mtl	1986 ....Gary Suter, Cgy
1943 ....Gaye Stewart, Tor	1965 ....Roger Crozier, Det	1987 ....Luc Robitaille, LA
1944 ....Gus Bodnar, Tor	1966 ....Brit Selby, Tor	1988 ....Joe Nieuwendyk, Cgy
1945 ....Frank McCool, Tor	1967 ....Bobby Orr, Bos	1989 ....Brian Leetch, NYR
1946 ....Edgar Laprade, NYR	1968 ....Derek Sanderson, Bos	1990 ....Sergei Makarov, Cgy
1947 ....Howie Meeker, Tor	1969 ....Danny Grant, Minn	1991 ....Ed Belfour, Chi
1948 ....Jim McFadden, Det	1970 ....Tony Esposito, Chi	1992 ....Pavel Bure, Van
1949 ....Pentti Lund, NYR	1971 ....Gilbert Perreault, Buff	1993 ....Teemu Selanne, Winn
1950 ....Jack Gelineau, Bos	1972 ....Ken Dryden, Mtl	1994 ....Martin Brodeur, NJ
1951 ....Terry Sawchuk, Det	1973 ....Steve Vickers, NYR	1995 ....Peter Forsberg, Que
1952 ....Bernie Geoffrion, Mtl	1974 ....Denis Potvin, NYI	1996 ....Daniel Alfredsson, Ott
1953 ....Gump Worsley, NYR	1975 ....Eric Vail, Atl	1997 ....Bryan Berard, NYI
1954 ....Camille Henry, NYR	1976 ....Bryan Trottier, NYI	1998 ....Sergei Samsonov, Bos

Vezina Trophy

Awarded annually "to the goalkeeper adjudged to be the best at his position." The trophy is named after Georges Vezina, an outstanding goalie for the Montreal Canadiens who collapsed during a game on November 28, 1925, and died four months later of tuberculosis. The general managers of the 21 NHL teams vote on the award.

1927 ....George Hainsworth, Mtl	1939 ....Frank Brimsek, Bos	1951 ....Al Rollins, Tor
1928 ....George Hainsworth, Mtl	1940 ....Dave Kerr, NYR	1952 ....Terry Sawchuk, Det
1929 ....George Hainsworth, Mtl	1941 ....Turk Broda, Tor	1953 ....Terry Sawchuk, Det
1930 ....Tiny Thompson, Bos	1942 ....Frank Brimsek, Bos	1954 ....Harry Lumley, Tor
1931 ....Roy Worters, NYA	1943 ....Johnny Mowers, Det	1955 ....Terry Sawchuk, Det
1932 ....Charlie Gardiner, Chi	1944 ....Bill Durnan, Mtl	1956 ....Jacques Plante, Mtl
1933 ....Tiny Thompson, Bos	1945 ....Bill Durnan, Mtl	1957 ....Jacques Plante, Mtl
1934 ....Charlie Gardiner, Chi	1946 ....Bill Durnan, Mtl	1958 ....Jacques Plante, Mtl
1935 ....Lorne Chabot, Chi	1947 ....Bill Durnan, Mtl	1959 ....Jacques Plante, Mtl
1936 ....Tiny Thompson, Bos	1948 ....Turk Broda, Tor	1960 ....Jacques Plante, Mtl
1937 ....Normie Smith, Det	1949 ....Bill Durnan, Mtl	1961 ....Johnny Bower, Tor
1938 ....Tiny Thompson, Bos	1950 ....Bill Durnan, Mtl	1962 ....Jacques Plante, Mtl

Vezina Trophy (Cont.)

1963 ....Glenn Hall, Chi		1985 ....Pelle Lindbergh, Phil
1964 ....Charlie Hodge, Mtl	Tony Esposito, Chi	1986 ....John Vanbiesbrouck,
1965 ....Terry Sawchuk, Tor	1975 ....Bernie Parent, Phil	NYR
Johnny Bower, Tor	1976 ....Ken Dryden, Mtl	1987 ....Ron Hextall, Phil
1966 ....Gump Worsley, Mtl	1977 ....Ken Dryden, Mtl	1988 ....Grant Fuhr, Edm
Charlie Hodge, Mtl	Michel Larocque, Mtl	1989 ....Patrick Roy, Mtl
1967 ....Glenn Hall, Chi	1978 ....Ken Dryden, Mtl	1990 ....Patrick Roy, Mtl
Rogie Vachon, Mtl	Michel Larocque, Mtl	1991 ....Ed Belfour, Chi
1969 ....Jacques Plante, StL	1979 ....Ken Dryden, Mtl	1992 ....Patrick Roy, Mtl
Glenn Hall, StL	Michel Larocque, Mtl	1993 ....Ed Belfour, Chi
1970 ....Tony Esposito, Chi	1980 ....Bob Sauve, Buff	1994 ....Dominik Hasek, Buff
1971 ....Ed Giacomin, NYR	Don Edwards, Buff	1995 ....Dominik Hasek, Buff
Gilles Villemure, NYR	1981 ....Richard Sevigny, Mtl	1996 ....Jim Carey, Wash
1972 ....Tony Esposito, Chi	Denis Herron, Mtl	1997 ....Dominik Hasek, Buff
Gary Smith, Chi	Michel Larocque, Mtl	1998 ....Dominik Hasek, Buff
1973 ....Ken Dryden, Mtl	1982 ....Bill Smith, NYI	
1974 ....Bernie Parent, Phil	1983 ....Pete Peeters, Bos	
	1984 ....Tom Barrasso, Buff	

Selke Trophy

Awarded annually "to the forward who best excels in the defensive aspects of the game." The trophy is named after Frank J. Selke, the architect of the Montreal Canadians dynasty that won five consecutive Stanley Cups in the late '50s. The winner is selected by a vote of the Professional Hockey Writers Association.

1978........Bob Gainey, Mtl	1985........Craig Ramsay, Buff	1992........Guy Carbonneau, Mtl
1979........Bob Gainey, Mtl	1986........Troy Murray, Chi	1993........Doug Gilmour, Tor
1980........Bob Gainey, Mtl	1987........Dave Poulin, Phil	1994........Sergei Fedorov, Det
1981........Bob Gainey, Mtl	1988........Guy Carbonneau, Mtl	1995........Ron Francis, Pitt
1982........Steve Kasper, Bos	1989........Guy Carbonneau, Mtl	1996........Sergei Fedorov, Det
1983........Bobby Clarke, Phil	1990........Rick Meagher, StL	1997........Michael Peca, Buff
1984........Doug Jarvis, Wash	1991........Dirk Graham, Chi	1998........Jere Lehtinen, Dall

Adams Award

Awarded annually "to the NHL coach adjudged to have contributed the most to his team's success." The trophy is named in honor of Jack Adams, longtime coach and general manager of the Detroit Red Wings. The winner is selected by a vote of the National Hockey League Broadcasters' Association.

1974 .....Fred Shero, Phil	1983 .....Orval Tessier, Chi	1992 .....Pat Quinn, Van
1975 .....Bob Pulford, LA	1984 .....Bryan Murray, Wash	1993 .....Pat Burns, Tor
1976 .....Don Cherry, Bos	1985 .....Mike Keenan, Phil	1994 .....Jacques Lemaire, NJ
1977 .....Scott Bowman, Mtl	1986 .....Glen Sather, Edm	1995 .....Marc Crawford, Que
1978 .....Bobby Kromm, Det	1987 .....Jacques Demers, Det	1996 .....Scotty Bowman, Det
1979 .....Al Arbour, NYI	1988 .....Jacques Demers, Det	1997 .....Ted Nolan, Buff
1980 .....Pat Quinn, Phil	1989 .....Pat Burns, Mtl	1998 .....Pat Burns, Bos
1981 .....Red Berenson, StL	1990 .....Bob Murdoch, Winn	
1982 .....Tom Watt, Winn	1991 .....Brian Sutter, StL	

Let the Stars Have the Star

Chicago, City of Big Shoulders and no Stanley Cups since the Kennedy Administration, was grumbling in early July 1998 about free agent Brett Hull. The eight-time All-Star had slipped through the Blackhawks' fingers and signed a three-year contract with the Dallas Stars for $17 million, about $1 million less than Chicago lavished a few hours later on another free agent, Doug Gilmour, also for three years. The Hull name is magic in Chicago—Brett's father, Bobby, the best left wing ever, played on the last Hawks' Cup winner 37 years ago—and Brett might have lured some fans to the United Center. The one thing Hull couldn't have done in Chicago is edge the Blackwks any closer to being a cup contender. Gilmour might.

Gilmour is simply a better and more well-rounded player than Hull, a one-way right wing who can still light up a scoreboard—he had 72 points in 66 games for the St. Louis Blues in 1997–98—but who hasn't had 50 goals in four years. Against the Detroit Red Wings in the second round of the 1998 playoffs, Hull, 33, vanished, finishing with one point in six games. Gilmour, who played with the New Jersey Devils for the last 1¼ seasons, also has been ineffective in recent springs. But during the 1993 and '94 postseasons the slender center wore himself down to Kate Moss dimensions and practically willed the Toronto Maple Leafs into the semis. Gilmour, 35, is still capable of averaging close to a point a game. Some consolation prize.

Career Records

Alltime Point Leaders

	Player	Yrs	GP	G	A	Pts	Pts/game
1.	*Wayne Gretzky, Edm, LA, StL, NYR	19	1417	885	1910	2795	1.972
2.	Gordie Howe, Det, Hart	26	1767	801	1049	1850	1.047
3.	Marcel Dionne, Det, LA, NYR	18	1348	731	1040	1771	1.314
4.	*Mark Messier, Edm, NYR, Van	19	1354	597	1015	1612	1.190
5.	Phil Esposito, Chi, Bos, NYR	18	1282	717	873	1590	1.240
6.	Mario Lemieux, Pitt	12	745	613	881	1494	2.005
7.	*Paul Coffey, Edm, Pitt, LA, Det, Hart, Phil	18	1268	383	1090	1473	1.162
8.	Stan Mikita, Chi	22	1394	541	926	1467	1.052
9.	*Ron Francis, Hart, Pitt	17	1247	428	1006	1434	1.150
10.	Bryan Trottier, NYI, Pitt	18	1279	524	901	1425	1.114
11.	*Ray Bourque, Bos	19	1372	375	1036	1411	1.028
12.	*Steve Yzerman, Det	15	1098	563	846	1409	1.283
12.	Dale Hawerchuk, Winn, Buff, StL, Phil	16	1188	518	891	1409	1.186
14.	*Jari Kurri, Edm, LA, NYR, Ana, Col	17	1251	601	797	1397	1.118
15.	John Bucyk, Det, Bos	23	1540	556	813	1369	.889

*Active player.

Alltime Goal-Scoring Leaders

	Player	Yrs	GP	G	G/game
1.	*Wayne Gretzky, Edm, LA, StL, NYR	19	1417	885	.625
2.	Gordie Howe, Det, Hart	26	1767	801	.453
3.	Marcel Dionne, Det, LA, NYR	18	1348	731	.542
4.	Phil Esposito, Chi, Bos, NYR	18	1282	717	.559
5.	*Mike Gartner, Wash, Minn, NYR, Tor, Phoe	19	1432	708	.494
6.	Mario Lemieux, Pitt	12	745	613	.823
7.	Bobby Hull, Chi, Winn, Hart	16	1063	610	.574
8.	*Dino Ciccarelli, Minn, Wash, Det, TB, Fla	18	1218	602	.494
9.	*Jari Kurri, Edm, LA, NYR, Ana, Col	17	1251	601	.480
10.	*Mark Messier, Edm, NYR, Van	19	1354	597	.441

*Active player.

Alltime Assist Leaders

	Player	Yrs	GP	A	A/game
1.	*Wayne Gretzky, Edm, LA, StL	19	1417	1910	1.348
2.	*Paul Coffey, Edm, Pitt, LA, Det, Hart, Phil	18	1268	1090	.860
3.	Gordie Howe, Det, Hart	26	1767	1049	.594
4.	Marcel Dionne, Det, LA, NYR	18	1348	1040	.771
5.	*Ray Bourque, Bos	19	1372	1036	.755
6.	*Mark Messier, Edm, NYR, Van	19	1354	1015	.750
7.	*Ron Francis, Hart, Pitt	17	1247	1006	.807
8.	Stan Mikita, Chi	22	1394	926	.664
9.	Bryan Trottier, NYI, Pitt	18	1279	901	.704
10.	Dale Hawerchuk, Winn, Buff, StL, Phil	16	1188	891	.750

*Active player.

Alltime Penalty Minutes Leaders

	Player	Yrs	GP	PIM	Min/game
1.	Dave Williams, Tor, Van, Det, LA, Hart	14	962	3966	4.12
2.	*Dale Hunter, Que, Wash	18	1345	3446	2.56
3.	*Marty McSorley, Pitt, Edm, LA, NYR, SJ	15	888	3218	3.62
4.	Tim Hunter, Calg, Que, Van, SJ	16	815	3146	3.86
5.	Chris Nilan, Mtl, NYR, Bos	13	688	3043	4.42
6.	*Bob Probert, Det, Chi	12	648	2701	4.17
7.	*Rick Tocchet, Phil, Pitt, LA, Bos, Wash, Phoe	14	909	2626	2.89
8.	Willi Plett, Atl, Calg, Minn, Bos	13	834	2572	3.08
9.	*Pat Verbeek, NJ, Hart, NYR, Dall	16	1147	2532	2.05
10.	Basil McRae, Chi, Que, Tor, Det, Minn, StL, TB	16	576	2457	4.27
10.	*Craig Berube, Phil, Tor, Cgy, Wash	12	719	2457	3.42

*Active player.

Goaltending Records

ALLTIME WIN LEADERS

Goaltender	W	L	T	Pct
Terry Sawchuk, five teams	447	330	173	.562
Jacques Plante, five teams	434	246	147	.614
Tony Esposito, Mtl, Chi	423	306	152	.566
Glenn Hall, Det, Chi, StL	407	327	163	.545
*Grant Fuhr, five teams	382	271	104	.573
*Patrick Roy, Mtl, Col	380	224	87	.613
Andy Moog, Edm, Bos, Dall, Mtl	372	209	88	.622
Rogie Vachon, Mtl, LA, Det, Bos	355	291	127	.541
Gump Worsley, NYR, Mtl, Minn	335	353	151	.489
Harry Lumley, five teams	333	326	143	.504

*Active player.

ACTIVE GOALTENDING LEADERS

Goaltender	W	L	T	Pct
Martin Brodeur, NJ	162	84	47	.633
Patrick Roy, Mtl, Col	380	224	87	.613
Mike Vernon, Cgy, Det	331	201	73	.608
Ed Belfour, Chi	241	159	66	.588
Mike Richter, NYR	203	144	49	.574
Tom Barrasso, Buff, Pitt	326	232	76	.574
Grant Fuhr, five teams	382	271	104	.573
Ron Hextall, Phil, Que, NYI	286	207	65	.571
Dominik Hasek, Chi, Buff	165	122	48	.564
Curtis Joseph, StL, Edm	213	172	54	.547

Note: Ranked by winning percentage; minimum 250 games played.

ALLTIME SHUTOUT LEADERS

Goaltender	Team	Yrs	GP	SO
Terry Sawchuk	Det, Bos, Tor, LA, NYR	21	971	103
George Hainsworth	Mtl, Tor	11	465	94
Glenn Hall	Det, Chi, StL	18	906	84
Jacques Plante	Mtl, NYR, StL, Tor, Bos	18	837	82
Tiny Thompson	Bos, Det	12	553	81
Alex Connell	Ott, Det, NYA, Mtl M	12	417	81
Tony Esposito	Mtl, Chi	16	886	76
Lorne Chabot	NYR, Tor, Mtl, Chi, Mtl M, NYA	11	411	73
Harry Lumley	Det, NYR, Chi, Tor, Bos	16	804	71
Roy Worters	Pitt Pir, NYA, *Mtl	12	484	66

*Played 1 game for Canadiens in 1929–30, not a shutout.

ALLTIME GOALS AGAINST AVERAGE LEADERS (PRE-1950)

Goaltender	Team	Yrs	GP	GA	GAA
George Hainsworth	Mtl, Tor	11	465	937	1.91
Alex Connell	Ott, Det, NYA, Mtl M	12	417	830	1.91
Chuck Gardiner	Chi	7	316	664	2.02
Lorne Chabot	NYR, Tor, Mtl, Chi, Mtl M, NYA	11	411	861	2.04
Tiny Thompson	Bos, Det	12	553	1183	2.08

ALLTIME GOALS AGAINST AVERAGE LEADERS (POST-1950)

Goaltender	Team	Yrs	GP	GA	GAA
*Martin Brodeur	NJ	6	305	627	2.16
Ken Dryden	Mtl	8	397	870	2.24
*Dominik Hasek	Chi, Buff	8	350	782	2.34
Jacques Plante	Mtl, NYR, StL, Tor, Bos	18	837	1965	2.38
Glenn Hall	Det, Chi, StL	18	906	2239	2.51

*Active player

Note: Minimum 250 games played. Goals against average equals goals against per 60 minutes played.

Coaching Records

Coach	Team	Seasons	W	L	T	Pct
Scott Bowman	five teams	1967–87, 91–	1057	483	278	.658
Toe Blake	Mtl	1955–68	500	255	159	.634
Glen Sather	Edm	1979–89, 93–94	464	268	110	.616
Fred Shero	Phil, NYR	1971–81	390	225	119	.612
Tommy Ivan	Det, Chi	1947–54, 56–58	288	174	111	.599
Mike Keenan	five teams	1984–	491	336	109	.588
Pat Burns	Mtl, Tor, Bos	1988–	346	241	96	.577
Emile Francis	NYR, StL	1965–77, 81–83	393	273	112	.577
Bryan Murray	Wash, Det	1981–93	467	337	112	.571
Billy Reay	Tor, Chi	1957–59, 63–77	542	385	175	.571

Note: Minimum 600 sregular-season games. Ranked by percentage.

Single-Season Records

Goals

Player	Season	GP	G	Player	Season	GP	G
Wayne Gretzky, Edm	1981-82	80	92	Wayne Gretzky, Edm	1982-83	80	71
Wayne Gretzky, Edm	1983-84	74	87	Brett Hull, StL	1991-92	73	70
Brett Hull, StL	1990-91	78	86	Mario Lemieux, Pitt	1987-88	77	70
Mario Lemieux, Pitt	1988-89	76	85	Bernie Nicholls, LA	1988-89	79	70
Alexander Mogilny, Buff	1992-93	77	76	Mario Lemieux, Pitt	1992-93	60	69
Phil Esposito, Bos	1970-71	78	76	Mario Lemieux, Pitt	1995-96	70	69
Teemu Selanne, Winn	1992-93	84	76	Mike Bossy, NYI	1978-79	80	69
Wayne Gretzky, Edm	1984-85	80	73	Phil Esposito, Bos	1973-74	78	68
Brett Hull, StL	1989-90	80	72	Jari Kurri, Edm	1985-86	78	68
Jari Kurri, Edm	1984-85	73	71	Mike Bossy, NYI	1980-81	79	68

Assists

Player	Season	GP	A	Player	Season	GP	A
Wayne Gretzky, Edm	1985-86	80	163	Wayne Gretzky, LA	1989-90	73	102
Wayne Gretzky, Edm	1984-85	80	135	Bobby Orr, Bos	1970-71	78	102
Wayne Gretzky, Edm	1982-83	80	125	Mario Lemieux, Pitt	1987-88	77	98
Wayne Gretzky, LA	1990-91	78	122	Adam Oates, Bos	1992-93	84	97
Wayne Gretzky, Edm	1986-87	79	121	Doug Gilmour, Tor	1992-93	83	95
Wayne Gretzky, Edm	1981-82	80	120	Pat LaFontaine, Buff	1992-93	84	95
Wayne Gretzky, Edm	1983-84	74	118	Mario Lemieux, Pitt	1985-86	79	93
Mario Lemieux, Pitt	1988-89	76	114	Peter Stastny, Que	1981-82	80	93
Wayne Gretzky, LA	1988-89	78	114	Wayne Gretzky, LA	1993-94	81	92
Wayne Gretzky, Edm	1987-88	64	109	Mario Lemieux, Pitt	1995-96	70	92
Wayne Gretzky, Edm	1980-81	80	109	Ron Francis, Pitt	1995-96	77	92

Points

Player	Season	G	A	Pts	Player	Season	G	A	Pts
Wayne Gretzky, Edm	1985-86	52	163	215	Wayne Gretzky, LA	1990-91	41	122	163
Wayne Gretzky, Edm	1981-82	92	120	212	Mario Lemieux, Pitt	1995-96	69	92	161
Wayne Gretzky, Edm	1984-85	73	135	208	Mario Lemieux, Pitt	1992-93	69	91	160
Wayne Gretzky, Edm	1983-84	87	118	205	Steve Yzerman, Det	1988-89	65	90	155
Mario Lemieux, Pitt	1988-89	85	114	199	Phil Esposito, Bos	1970-71	76	76	152
Wayne Gretzky, Edm	1982-83	71	125	196	Bernie Nicholls, LA	1988-89	70	80	150
Wayne Gretzky, Edm	1986-87	62	121	183	Wayne Gretzky, Edm	1987-88	40	109	149
Mario Lemieux, Pitt	1987-88	70	98	168	Pat LaFontaine, Buff	1992-93	53	95	148
Wayne Gretzky, LA	1988-89	54	114	168	Mike Bossy, NYI	1981-82	64	83	147
Wayne Gretzky, Edm	1980-81	55	109	164	Phil Esposito, Bos	1973-74	68	77	145

Points per Game

Player	Season	GP	Pts	Avg	Player	Season	GP	Pts	Avg
Wayne Gretzky, Edm	1983-84	74	205	2.77	Mario Lemieux, Pitt	1987-88	77	168	2.18
Wayne Gretzky, Edm	1985-86	80	215	2.69	Wayne Gretzky, LA	1988-89	78	168	2.15
Mario Lemieux, Pitt	1992-93	60	160	2.67	Wayne Gretzky, LA	1990-91	78	163	2.09
Wayne Gretzky, Edm	1981-82	80	212	2.65	Mario Lemieux, Pitt	1989-90	59	123	2.08
Mario Lemieux, Pitt	1988-89	76	199	2.62	Wayne Gretzky, Edm	1980-81	80	164	2.05
Wayne Gretzky, Edm	1984-85	80	208	2.60	Mario Lemieux, Pitt	1991-92	64	131	2.05
Wayne Gretzky, Edm	1982-83	80	196	2.45	Bill Cowley, Bos	1943-44	36	71	1.97
Wayne Gretzky, Edm	1987-88	64	149	2.33	Phil Esposito, Bos	1970-71	78	152	1.95
Wayne Gretzky, Edm	1986-87	79	183	2.32	Wayne Gretzky, LA	1989-90	73	142	1.95
Mario Lemieux, Pitt	1995-96	70	161	2.30	Steve Yzerman, Det	1988-89	80	155	1.94

Note: Minimum 50 points in one season.

Single-Season Records *(Cont.)*

Goals per Game

Player	Season	GP	G	Avg
Joe Malone, Mtl	1917–18	20	44	2.20
Cy Denneny, Ott	1917–18	22	36	1.64
Newsy Lalonde, Mtl	1917–18	14	23	1.64
Joe Malone, Que	1919–20	24	39	1.63
Newsy Lalonde, Mtl	1919–20	23	36	1.57
Joe Malone, Ham	1920–21	20	30	1.50
Babe Dye, Ham-Tor	1920–21	24	35	1.46
Cy Denneny, Ott	1920–21	24	34	1.42
Reg Noble, Tor	1917–18	20	28	1.40
Newsy Lalonde, Mtl	1920–21	24	33	1.38

Note: Minimum 20 goals in one season.

Assists per Game

Player	Season	GP	A	Avg
Wayne Gretzky, Edm	1985–86	80	163	2.04
Wayne Gretzky, Edm	1987–88	64	109	1.70
Wayne Gretzky, Edm	1984–85	80	135	1.69
Wayne Gretzky, Edm	1983–84	74	118	1.59
Wayne Gretzky, Edm	1982–83	80	125	1.56
Wayne Gretzky, LA	1990–91	78	122	1.56
Wayne Gretzky, Edm	1986–87	79	121	1.53
Mario Lemieux, Pitt	1992–93	60	91	1.52
Wayne Gretzky, Edm	1981–82	80	120	1.50
Mario Lemieux, Pitt	1988–89	76	114	1.50

Note: Minimum 35 assists in one season.

Shutout Leaders

	Season	SO	Length of Schedule		Season	SO	Length of Schedule
George Hainsworth, Mtl	1928–29	22	44	Bernie Parent, Phil	1974–75	12	80
Alex Connell, Ott	1925–26	15	36	Lorne Chabot, NYR	1927–28	11	44
Alex Connell, Ott	1927–28	15	44	Harry Holmes, Det	1927–28	11	44
Hal Winkler, Bos	1927–28	15	44	Clint Benedict, Mtl M	1928–29	11	44
Tony Esposito, Chi	1969–70	15	76	Joe Miller, Pitt Pirates	1928–29	11	44
George Hainsworth, Mtl	1926–27	14	44	Tiny Thompson, Bos	1932–33	11	48
Clint Benedict, Mtl M	1926–27	13	44	Terry Sawchuck, Det	1950–51	11	70
Alex Connell, Ott	1926–27	13	44	Lorne Chabot, NYR	1926–27	10	44
George Hainsworth, Mtl	1927–28	13	44	Roy Worters, Pitt Pirates	1927–28	10	44
John Roach, NYR	1928–29	13	44	Clarence Dolson, Det	1928–29	10	44
Roy Worters, NYA	1928–29	13	44	John Roach, Det	1932–33	10	48
Harry Lumley, Tor	1953–54	13	70	Chuck Gardiner, Chi	1933–34	10	48
Dominik Hasek, Buff	1997–98	13	82	Tiny Thompson, Bos	1935–36	10	48
Tiny Thompson, Bos	1928–29	12	44	Frank Brimsek, Bos	1938–39	10	48
Lorne Chabot, Tor	1928–29	12	44	Bill Durnan, Mtl	1948–49	10	60
Chuck Gardiner, Chi	1930–31	12	44	Gerry McNeil, Mtl	1952–53	10	70
Terry Sawchuk, Det	1951–52	12	70	Harry Lumley, Tor	1952–53	10	70
Terry Sawchuk, Det	1953–54	12	70	Tony Esposito, Chi	1973–74	10	78
Terry Sawchuk, Det	1954–55	12	70	Ken Dryden, Mtl	1976–77	10	80
Glenn Hall, Det	1955–56	12	70	Martin Brodeur, NJ	1996–97	10	82
Bernie Parent, Phil	1973–74	12	78	Martin Brodeur, NJ	1997–98	10	82

Wins

	Season	Record
Bernie Parent, Phil	1973-74	47-13-12
Bernie Parent, Phil	1974-75	44-14-9
Terry Sawchuk, Det	1950-51	44-13-13
Terry Sawchuk, Det	1951-52	44-14-12
Tom Barasso, Pitt	1992-93	43-14-5
Ed Belfour, Chi	1990-91	43-19-7
Martin Brodeur, NJ	1997-98	43-17-8
Jacques Plante, Mtl	1955-56	42-12-10
Jacques Plante, Mtl	1961-62	42-14-14
Ken Dryden, Mtl	1975-76	42-10-8
Mike Richter, NYR	1993-94	42-12-6

Goals Against Average

(PRE-1950)

	Season	GP	GAA
George Hainsworth, Mtl	1928-29	44	0.92
George Hainsworth, Mtl	1927-28	44	1.05
Alex Connell, Ott	1925-26	36	1.12
Tiny Thompson, Bos	1928-29	44	1.18
Roy Worters, NYA	1928-29	38	1.21

(POST-1950)

	Season	GP	GAA
Al Rollins, Tor	1950-51	40	1.7744
Tony Esposito, Chi	1971-72	48	1.7698
Jacques Plante, Mtl	1955-56	64	1.8594
Harry Lumley, Tor	1953-54	69	1.8551
Jacques Plante, Tor	1970-71	40	1.8806
Martin Brodeur, NJ	1996-97	67	1.8759
Ed Belfour, Dall	1997-98	61	1.8766

Single-Game Records

Goals

	Date	G
Joe Malone, Que vs Tor	1-31-20	7
Newsy Lalonde, Mtl vs Tor	1-10-20	6
Joe Malone, Que vs Ott	3-10-20	6
Corb Denneny, Tor vs Ham	1-26-21	6
Cy Denneny, Ott vs Ham	3-7-21	6
Syd Howe, Det vs NYR	2-3-44	6
Red Berenson, StL vs Phil	11-7-68	6
Darryl Sittler, Tor vs Bos	2-7-76	6

Assists

	Date	A
Billy Taylor, Det vs Chi	3-16-47	7
Wayne Gretzky, Edm vs Wash	2-15-80	7
Wayne Gretzky, Edm vs Chi	12-11-85	7
Wayne Gretzky, Edm vs Que	2-14-86	7

Note: 19 tied with 6.

Points

	Date	G	A	Pts
Darryl Sittler, Tor vs Bos	2-7-76	6	4	10
Maurice Richard, Mtl vs Det	12-28-44	5	3	8
Bert Olmstead, Mtl vs Chi	1-9-54	4	4	8
Tom Bladon, Phil vs Clev	12-11-77	4	4	8
Bryan Trottier, NYI vs NYR	12-23-78	5	3	8
Peter Stastny, Que vs Wash	2-22-81	4	4	8
Anton Stastny, Que vs Wash	2-22-81	3	5	8
Wayne Gretzky, Edm vs NJ	11-19-83	3	5	8
Wayne Gretzky, Edm vs Minn	1-4-84	4	4	8
Paul Coffey, Edm vs Det	3-14-86	2	6	8
Mario Lemieux, Pitt vs StL	10-15-88	2	6	8
Bernie Nicholls, LA vs Tor	12-1-88	2	6	8
Mario Lemieux, Pitt vs NJ	12-31-88	5	3	8

NHL Season Leaders

Points

Season	Player and Club	Pts	Season	Player and Club	Pts
1917-18	Joe Malone, Mtl	44	1952-53	Gordie Howe, Det	95
1918-19	Newsy Lalonde, Mtl	30	1953-54	Gordie Howe, Det	81
1919-20	Joe Malone, Que	48	1954-55	Bernie Geoffrion, Mtl	75
1920-21	Newsy Lalonde, Mtl	41	1955-56	Jean Beliveau, Mtl	88
1921-22	Punch Broadbent, Ott	46	1956-57	Gordie Howe, Det	89
1922-23	Babe Dye, Tor	37	1957-58	Dickie Moore, Mtl	84
1923-24	Cy Denneny, Ott	23	1958-59	Dickie Moore, Mtl	96
1924-25	Babe Dye, Tor	44	1959-60	Bobby Hull, Chi	81
1925-26	Nels Stewart, Mtl M	42	1960-61	Bernie Geoffrion, Mtl	95
1926-27	Bill Cook, NY	37	1961-62	Andy Bathgate, NY	84
1927-28	Howie Morenz, Mtl	51		Bobby Hull, Chi	84
1928-29	Ace Bailey, Tor	32	1962-63	Gordie Howe, Det	86
1929-30	Cooney Weiland, Bos	73	1963-64	Stan Mikita, Chi	89
1930-31	Howie Morenz, Mtl	51	1964-65	Stan Mikita, Chi	87
1931-32	Harvey Jackson, Tor	53	1965-66	Bobby Hull, Chi	97
1932-33	Bill Cook, NY	50	1966-67	Stan Mikita, Chi	97
1933-34	Charlie Conacher, Tor	52	1967-68	Stan Mikita, Chi	87
1934-35	Charlie Conacher, Tor	57	1968-69	Phil Esposito, Bos	126
1935-36	Sweeney Schriner, NYA	45	1969-70	Bobby Orr, Bos	120
1936-37	Sweeney Schriner, NYA	46	1970-71	Phil Esposito, Bos	152
1937-38	Gord Drillon, Tor	52	1971-72	Phil Esposito, Bos	133
1938-39	Hector Blake, Mtl	47	1972-73	Phil Esposito, Bos	130
1939-40	Milt Schmidt, Bos	52	1973-74	Phil Esposito, Bos	145
1940-41	Bill Cowley, Bos	62	1974-75	Bobby Orr, Bos	135
1941-42	Bryan Hextall, NY	54	1975-76	Guy Lafleur, Mtl	125
1942-43	Doug Bentley, Chi	73	1976-77	Guy Lafleur, Mtl	136
1943-44	Herb Cain, Bos	82	1977-78	Guy Lafleur, Mtl	132
1944-45	Elmer Lach, Mtl	80	1978-79	Bryan Trottier, NYI	134
1945-46	Max Bentley, Chi	61	1979-80	Marcel Dionne, LA	137
1946-47	Max Bentley, Chi	72		Wayne Gretzky, Edm	137
1947-48	Elmer Lach, Mtl	61	1980-81	Wayne Gretzky, Edm	164
1948-49	Roy Conacher, Chi	68	1981-82	Wayne Gretzky, Edm	212
1949-50	Ted Lindsay, Det	78	1982-83	Wayne Gretzky, Edm	196
1950-51	Gordie Howe, Det	86	1983-84	Wayne Gretzky, Edm	205
1951-52	Gordie Howe, Det	86	1984-85	Wayne Gretzky, Edm	208

NHL Season Leaders (Cont.)

Points (Cont.)

Season	Player and Club	Pts	Season	Player and Club	Pts
1985-86	Wayne Gretzky, Edm	215	1992-93	Mario Lemieux, Pitt	160
1986-87	Wayne Gretzky, Edm	183	1993-94	Wayne Gretzky, LA	130
1987-88	Mario Lemieux, Pitt	168	1994-95	Jaromir Jagr, Pitt	70
1988-89	Mario Lemieux, Pitt	199	1995-96	Mario Lemieux, Pitt	161
1989-90	Wayne Gretzky, LA	142	1996-97	Mario Lemieux, Pitt	122
1990-91	Wayne Gretzky, LA	163	1997-98	Jaromir Jagr, Pitt	102
1991-92	Mario Lemieux, Pitt	131			

Goals

Season	Player and Club	G	Season	Player and Club	G
1917-18	Joe Malone, Mtl	44	1958-59	Jean Beliveau, Mtl	45
1918-19	Odie Cleghorn, Mtl	23	1959-60	Bobby Hull, Chi	39
1919-20	Joe Malone, Que	39		Bronco Horvath, Bos	39
1920-21	Babe Dye, Ham-Tor	35	1960-61	Bernie Geoffrion, Mtl	50
1921-22	Punch Broadbent, Ott	32	1961-62	Bobby Hull, Chi	50
1922-23	Babe Dye, Tor	26	1962-63	Gordie Howe, Det	38
1923-24	Cy Denneny, Ott	22	1963-64	Bobby Hull, Chi	43
1924-25	Babe Dye, Tor	38	1964-65	Norm Ullman, Det	42
1925-26	Nels Stewart, Mtl	34	1965-66	Bobby Hull, Chi	54
1926-27	Bill Cook, NY	33	1966-67	Bobby Hull, Chi	52
1927-28	Howie Morenz, Mtl	33	1967-68	Bobby Hull, Chi	44
1928-29	Ace Bailey, Tor	22	1968-69	Bobby Hull, Chi	58
1929-30	Cooney Weiland, Bos	43	1969-70	Phil Esposito, Bos	43
1930-31	Bill Cook, NY	30	1970-71	Phil Esposito, Bos	76
1931-32	Charlie Conacher, Tor	34	1971-72	Phil Esposito, Bos	66
	Bill Cook, NY	34	1972-73	Phil Esposito, Bos	55
1932-33	Bill Cook, NY	28	1973-74	Phil Esposito, Bos	68
1933-34	Charlie Conacher, Tor	32	1974-75	Phil Esposito, Bos	61
1934-35	Charlie Conacher, Tor	36	1975-76	Guy Lafleur, Mtl	56
1935-36	Charlie Conacher, Tor	23	1976-77	Steve Shutt, Mtl	60
	Bill Thoms, Tor	23	1977-78	Guy Lafleur, Mtl	60
1936-37	Larry Aurie, Det	23	1978-79	Mike Bossy, NYI	69
	Nels Stewart, Bos-NYA	23	1979-80	Charlie Simmer, LA	56
1937-38	Gord Drill, Tor	26		Blaine Stoughton, Hart	56
1938-39	Roy Conacher, Bos	26	1980-81	Mike Bossy, NYI	68
1939-40	Bryan Hextall, NY	24	1981-82	Wayne Gretzky, Edm	92
1940-41	Bryan Hextall, NY	26	1982-83	Wayne Gretzky, Edm	71
1941-42	Lynn Patrick, NY	32	1983-84	Wayne Gretzky, Edm	87
1942-43	Doug Bentley, Chi	43	1984-85	Wayne Gretzky, Edm	73
1943-44	Doug Bentley, Chi	38	1985-86	Jari Kurri, Edm	68
1944-45	Maurice Richard, Mtl	50	1986-87	Wayne Gretzky, Edm	62
1945-46	Gaye Stewart, Tor	37	1987-88	Mario Lemieux, Pitt	70
1946-47	Maurice Richard, Mtl	50	1988-89	Mario Lemieux, Pitt	85
1947-48	Ted Lindsay, Det	33	1989-90	Brett Hull, StL	72
1948-49	Sid Abel, Det	28	1990-91	Brett Hull, StL	78
1949-50	Maurice Richard, Mtl	43	1991-92	Brett Hull, StL	70
1950-51	Gordie Howe, Det	43	1992-93	Alexander Mogilny, Buff	76
1951-52	Gordie Howe, Det	47		Teemu Selanne, Winn	76
1952-53	Gordie Howe, Det	49	1993-94	Pavel Bure, Van	60
1953-54	Maurice Richard, Mtl	37	1994-95	Peter Bondra, Wash	34
1954-55	Bernie Geoffrion, Mtl	38	1995-96	Mario Lemieux, Pitt	69
	Maurice Richard, Mtl	38	1996-97	Keith Tkachuk, Phoe	52
1955-56	Jean Beliveau, Mtl	47	1997-98	Teemu Selanne, Ana	52
1957-58	Dickie Moore, Mtl	36		Peter Bondra, Wash	52
1956-57	Gordie Howe, Det	44			

Assists

Season	Player and Club	A	Season	Player and Club	A
1917-18	statistic not kept		1960-61	Jean Beliveau, Mtl	58
1918-19	Newsy Lalonde, Mtl	9	1961-62	Andy Bathgate, NY	56
1919-20	Corbett Denneny, Tor	12	1962-63	Henri Richard, Mtl	50
1920-21	Louis Berlinquette, Mtl	9	1963-64	Andy Bathgate, NY-Tor	58
1921-22	Punch Broadbench, Ott	14	1964-65	Stan Mikita, Chi	59
1922-23	Babe Dye, Tor	11	1965-66	Stan Mikita, Chi	48
1923-24	Billy Boucher, Mtl	6		Bobby Rousseau, Mtl	48
1924-25	Cy Denneny, Ott	15		Jean Beliveau, Mtl	48
1925-26	Cy Denneny, Ott	12	1966-67	Stan Mikita, Chi	62
1926-27	Dick Irvin, Chi	18	1967-68	Phil Esposito, Bos	49
1927-28	Howie Morenz, Mtl	18	1968-69	Phil Esposito, Bos	77
1928-29	Frank Boucher, NY	16	1969-70	Bobby Orr, Bos	87
1929-30	Frank Boucher, NY	36	1970-71	Bobby Orr, Bos	102
1930-31	Joe Primeau, Tor	36	1971-72	Bobby Orr, Bos	80
1931-32	Joe Primeau, Tor	37	1972-73	Phil Esposito, Bos	75
1932-33	Frank Boucher, NY	28	1973-74	Bobby Orr, Bos	89
1933-34	Joe Primeau, Tor	32	1974-75	Bobby Clarke, Phil	89
1934-35	Art Chapman, NYA	28		Bobby Orr, Bos	89
1935-36	Art Chapman, NYA	28	1975-76	Bobby Clarke, Phil	89
1936-37	Syl Apps, Tor	29	1976-77	Guy Lafleur, Mtl	80
1937-38	Syl Apps, Tor	29	1977-78	Bryan Trottier, NYI	77
1938-39	Bill Cowley, Bos	34	1978-79	Bryan Trottier, NYI	87
1939-40	Milt Schmidt, Bos	30	1979-80	Wayne Gretzky, Edm	86
1940-41	Bill Cowley, Bos	45	1980-81	Wayne Gretzky, Edm	109
1941-42	Phil Watson, NY	37	1981-82	Wayne Gretzky, Edm	120
1942-43	Bill Cowley, Bos	45	1982-83	Wayne Gretzky, Edm	125
1943-44	Clint Smith, Chi	49	1983-84	Wayne Gretzky, Edm	118
1944-45	Elmer Lach, Mtl	54	1984-85	Wayne Gretzky, Edm	135
1945-46	Elmer Lach, Mtl	34	1985-86	Wayne Gretzky, Edm	163
1946-47	Billy Taylor, Det	46	1986-87	Wayne Gretzky, Edm	121
1947-48	Doug Bentley, Chi	37	1987-88	Wayne Gretzky, Edm	109
1948-49	Doug Bentley, Chi	43	1988-89	Wayne Gretzky, LA	114
1949-50	Ted Lindsay, Det	55		Mario Lemieux, Pitt	114
1950-51	Gordie Howe, Det	43	1989-90	Wayne Gretzky, LA	102
	Ted Kennedy, Tor	43	1990-91	Wayne Gretzky, LA	122
1951-52	Elmer Lach, Mtl	50	1991-92	Wayne Gretzky, LA	90
1952-53	Gordie Howe, Det	46	1992-93	Adam Oates, Bos	97
1953-54	Gordie Howe, Det	48	1993-94	Wayne Gretzky, LA	92
1954-55	Bert Olmstead, Mtl	48	1994-95	Ron Francis, Pitt	48
1955-56	Bert Olmstead, Mtl	56	1995-96	Mario Lemieux, Pitt	92
1956-57	Ted Lindsay, Det	55		Ron Francis, Pitt	92
1957-58	Henri Richard, Mtl	52	1996-97	Mario Lemieux, Pitt	72
1958-59	Dickie Moore, Mtl	55	1997-98	Jaromir Jagr, Pitt	67
1959-60	Bobby Hull, Chi	42		Wayne Gretzky, NYR	67

Passing into History

On Oct. 26, 1997, New York Rangers center and alltime NHL point leader Wayne Gretzky notched his 1,850th and 1,851st assists, surpassing, with assists alone, Gordie Howe's career point total of 1,850, which Howe achieved with 1,049 assists and 801 goals. That means that even if Gretzky never scored a single goal (he finished the 1997–98 season with 885), he would still have more points than anyone else in history. Here's a look at some of the Great One's assist statistics prior to his historic game. All numbers are NHL records.

• Gretzky got his first assist on Oct. 10, 1979, against the Chicago Blackhawks, when he helped set up Kevin Lowe for the first goal in Edmonton Oilers history.

• Gretzky assisted 132 players, including three—Jari Kurri, Luc Robitaille and Glenn Anderson—on more than 100 goals, and Colin Campbell, his coach that October night, on one.

• Of the 598 goals Kurri scored in his career, 364 (61%) were set up by Gretzky.

• In 1985–86, Gretzky averaged 2.04 assists a game for the Oilers, well above the next-best single-season average—Gretzky's 1.70 in 1987–88.

• In three seasons during the '80s Gretzky had more assists than any other player had points.

• Gretzky had 260 playoff assists. Only one player, Mark Messier, with 295, had more playoff *points*.

• Gretzky had 783 more assists than Paul Coffey, who was second on the list; only 22 players have had 783 assists in league history.

• Against the Vancouver Canucks, where Messier, his former Oilers and Rangers teammate, now plays, Gretzky had 161 assists, more than against any other team.

Goals Against Average

Season	Goaltender and Club	GP	Min	GA	SO	Avg
1917-18	Georges Vezina, Mtl	21	1282	84	1	3.93
1918-19	Clint Benedict, Ott	18	1113	53	2	2.86
1919-20	Clint Benedict, Ott	24	1444	64	5	2.66
1920-21	Clint Benedict, Ott	24	1457	75	2	3.09
1921-22	Clint Benedict, Ott	24	1508	84	2	3.34
1922-23	Clint Benedict, Ott	24	1478	54	4	2.19
1923-24	Georges Vezina, Mtl	24	1459	48	3	1.97
1924-25	Georges Vezina, Mtl	30	1860	56	5	1.81
1925-26	Alex Connell, Ott	36	2251	42	15	1.12
1926-27	Clint Benedict, Mtl M	43	2748	65	13	1.42
1927-28	George Hainsworth, Mtl	44	2730	48	13	1.05
1928-29	George Hainsworth, Mtl	44	2800	43	22	0.92
1929-30	Tiny Thompson, Bos	44	2680	98	3	2.19
1930-31	Roy Worters, NYA	44	2760	74	8	1.61
1931-32	Chuck Gardiner, Chi	48	2989	92	4	1.85
1932-33	Tiny Thompson, Bos	48	3000	88	11	1.76
1933-34	Wilf Cude, Det-Mtl	30	1920	47	5	1.47
1934-35	Lorne Chabot, Chi	48	2940	88	8	1.80
1935-36	Tiny Thompson, Bos	48	2930	82	10	1.68
1936-37	Normie Smith, Det	48	2980	102	6	2.05
1937-38	Tiny Thompson, Bos	48	2970	89	7	1.80
1938-39	Frank Brimsek, Bos	43	2610	68	10	1.56
1939-40	Dave Kerr, NYR	48	3000	77	8	1.54
1940-41	Turk Broda, Tor	48	2970	99	5	2.00
1941-42	Frank Brimsek, Bos	47	2930	115	3	2.35
1942-43	Johnny Mowers, Det	50	3010	124	6	2.47
1943-44	Bill Durnan, Mtl	50	3000	109	2	2.18
1944-45	Bill Durnan, Mtl	50	3000	121	1	2.42
1945-46	Bill Durnan, Mtl	40	2400	104	4	2.60
1946-47	Bill Durnan, Mtl	60	3600	138	4	2.30
1947-48	Turk Broda, Tor	60	3600	143	5	2.38
1948-49	Bill Durnan, Mtl	60	3600	126	10	2.10
1949-50	Bill Durnan, Mtl	64	3840	141	8	2.20
1950-51	Al Rollins, Tor	40	2367	70	5	1.77
1951-52	Terry Sawchuk, Det	70	4200	133	12	1.90
1952-53	Terry Sawchuk, Det	63	3780	120	9	1.90
1953-54	Harry Lumley, Tor	69	4140	128	13	1.86
1954-55	Harry Lumley, Tor	69	4140	134	8	1.94
	Terry Sawchuk, Det	68	4060	132	12	1.94
1955-56	Jacques Plante, Mtl	64	3840	119	7	1.86
1956-57	Jacques Plante, Mtl	61	3660	123	9	2.02
1957-58	Jacques Plante, Mtl	57	3386	119	9	2.11
1958-59	Jacques Plante, Mtl	67	4000	144	9	2.16
1959-60	Jacques Plante, Mtl	69	4140	175	3	2.54
1960-61	Johnny Bower, Tor	58	3480	145	2	2.50
1961-62	Jacques Plante, Mtl	70	4200	166	4	2.37
1962-63	Jacques Plante, Mtl	56	3320	138	5	2.49
1963-64	Johnny Bower, Tor	51	3009	106	5	2.11
1964-65	Johnny Bower, Tor	34	2040	81	3	2.38
1965-66	Johnny Bower, Tor	35	1998	75	3	2.25
1966-67	Glenn Hall, Chi	32	1664	66	2	2.38
1967-68	Gump Worsley, Mtl	40	2213	73	6	1.98
1968-69	Jacques Plante, StL	37	2139	70	5	1.96
1969-70	Ernie Wakely, StL	30	1651	58	4	2.11
1970-71	Jacques Plante, Tor	40	2329	73	4	1.88
1971-72	Tony Esposito, Chi	48	2780	82	9	1.77
1972-73	Ken Dryden, Mtl	54	3165	119	6	2.26
1973-74	Bernie Parent, Phil	73	4314	136	12	1.89
1974-75	Bernie Parent, Phil	68	4041	137	12	2.03
1975-76	Ken Dryden, Mtl	62	3580	121	8	2.03
1976-77	Michael Larocque, Mtl	26	1525	53	4	2.09
1977-78	Ken Dryden, Mtl	52	3071	105	5	2.05
1978-79	Ken Dryden, Mtl	47	2814	108	5	2.30

Goals Against Average (Cont.)

Season	Goaltender and Club	GP	Min	GA	SO	Avg
1979-80	Bob Sauve, Buff	32	1880	74	4	2.36
1980-81	Richard Sevigny, Mtl	33	1777	71	2	2.40
1981-82	Denis Herron, Mtl	27	1547	68	3	2.64
1982-83	Pete Peeters, Bos	62	3611	142	8	2.36
1983-84	Pat Riggin, Wash	41	2299	102	4	2.66
1984-85	Tom Barrasso, Buff	54	3248	144	5	2.66
1985-86	Bob Froese, Phil	51	2728	116	5	2.55
1986-87	Brian Hayward, Mtl	37	2178	102	1	2.81
1987-88	Pete Peeters, Wash	35	1896	88	2	2.78
1988-89	Patrick Roy, Mtl	48	2744	113	4	2.47
1989-90	Patrick Roy, Mtl	54	3173	134	3	2.53
	Mike Liut, Hart-Wash	37	2161	91	4	2.53
1990-91	Ed Belfour, Chi	74	4127	170	4	2.47
1991-92	Patrick Roy, Mtl	67	3935	155	5	2.36
1992-93	*Felix Potvin, Tor	48	2781	116	2	2.50
1993-94	Dominik Hasek, Buff	58	3358	109	7	1.95
1994-95	Dominik Hasek, Buff	41	2416	85	5	2.11
1995-96	Ron Hextall, Phil	53	3102	112	4	2.17
	Chris Osgood, Det	50	2933	106	5	2.17
1996-97	Martin Brodeur, NJ	67	3838	120	10	1.88
1997-98	Ed Belfour, Dall	61	3581	112	9	1.88

*Rookie.

Penalty Minutes

Season	Player and Club	GP	PIM	Season	Player and Club	GP	PIM
1918-19	Joe Hall, Mtl	17	85	1958-59	Ted Lindsay, Chi	70	184
1919-20	Cully Wilson, Tor	23	79	1959-60	Carl Brewer, Tor	67	150
1920-21	Bert Corbeau, Mtl	24	86	1960-61	Pierre Pilote, Chi	70	165
1921-22	Sprague Cleghorn, Mtl	24	63	1961-62	Lou Fontinato, Mtl	54	167
1922-23	Billy Boucher, Mtl	24	52	1962-63	Howie Young, Det	64	273
1923-24	Bert Corbeau, Tor	24	55	1963-64	Vic Hadfield, NYR	69	151
1924-25	Billy Boucher, Mtl	30	92	1964-65	Carl Brewer, Tor	70	177
1925-26	Bert Corbeau, Tor	36	121	1965-66	Reggie Fleming, Bos-NYR	69	166
1926-27	Nels Stewart, Mtl M	44	133	1966-67	John Ferguson, Mtl	67	177
1927-28	Eddie Shore, Bos	44	165	1967-68	Barclay Plager, StL	49	153
1928-29	Red Dutton, Mtl M	44	139	1968-69	Forbes Kennedy, Phil-Tor	77	219
1929-30	Joe Lamb, Ott	44	119	1969-70	Keith Magnuson, Chi	76	213
1930-31	Harvey Rockburn, Det	42	118	1970-71	Keith Magnuson, Chi	76	291
1931-32	Red Dutton, NYA	47	107	1971-72	Brian Watson, Pitt	75	212
1932-33	Red Horner, Tor	48	144	1972-73	Dave Schultz, Phil	76	259
1933-34	Red Horner, Tor	42	126	1973-74	Dave Schultz, Phil	73	348
1934-35	Red Horner, Tor	46	125	1974-75	Dave Schultz, Phil	76	472
1935-36	Red Horner, Tor	43	167	1975-76	Steve Durbano, Pitt-KC	69	370
1936-37	Red Horner, Tor	48	124	1976-77	Dave Williams, Tor	77	338
1937-38	Red Horner, Tor	47	82	1977-78	Dave Schultz, LA-Pitt	74	405
1938-39	Red Horner, Tor	48	85	1978-79	Dave Williams, Tor	77	298
1939-40	Red Horner, Tor	30	87	1979-80	Jimmy Mann, Winn	72	287
1940-41	Jimmy Orlando, Det	48	99	1980-81	Dave Williams, Van	77	343
1941-42	Jimmy Orlando, Det	48	81	1981-82	Paul Baxter, Pitt	76	409
1942-43	Jimmy Orlando, Det	40	89	1982-83	Randy Holt, Wash	70	275
1943-44	Mike McMahon, Mtl	42	98	1983-84	Chris Nilan, Mtl	76	338
1944-45	Pat Egan, Bos	48	86	1984-85	Chris Nilan, Mtl	77	358
1945-46	Jack Stewart, Det	47	73	1985-86	Joey Kocur, Det	59	377
1946-47	Gus Mortson, Tor	60	133	1986-87	Tim Hunter, Cgy	73	361
1947-48	Bill Barilko, Tor	57	147	1987-88	Bob Probert, Det	74	398
1948-49	Bill Ezinicki, Tor	52	145	1988-89	Tim Hunter, Cgy	75	375
1949-50	Bill Ezinicki, Tor	67	144	1989-90	Basil McRae, Minn	66	351
1950-51	Gus Mortson, Tor	60	142	1990-91	Bob Ray, Buff	66	350
1951-52	Gus Kyle, Bos	69	127	1991-92	Mike Peluso, Chi	63	408
1952-53	Maurice Richard, Mtl	70	112	1992-93	Marty McSorley, LA	81	399
1953-54	Gus Mortson, Chi	68	132	1993-94	Tie Domi, Winn	81	347
1954-55	Fern Flaman, Bos	70	150	1994-95	Enrico Ciccone, TB	41	225
1955-56	Lou Fontinato, NYR	70	202	1995-96	Matthew Barnaby, Buff	73	335
1956-57	Gus Mortson, Chi	70	147	1996-97	Gino Odjick, Van	70	371
1957-58	Lou Fontinato, NYR	70	152	1997-98	Donald Brashear, Van	77	372

NHL All-Star Game

First played in 1947, this game was scheduled before the start of the regular season and used to match the defending Stanley Cup Champions against a squad made up of the league All-stars from other teams. In 1966 the games were moved to mid-season, although there was no game that year. The format changed to a conference versus conference showdown in 1969.

Results

Year	Site	Score	MVP	Attendance
1947	Toronto	All-Stars 4, Toronto 3	None named	14,169
1948	Chicago	All-Stars 3, Toronto 1	None named	12,794
1949	Toronto	All-Stars 3, Toronto 1	None named	13,541
1950	Detroit	Detroit 7, All-Stars 1	None named	9,166
1951	Toronto	1st team 2, 2nd team 2	None named	11,469
1952	Detroit	1st team 1, 2nd team 1	None named	10,680
1953	Montreal	All-Stars 3, Montreal 1	None named	14,153
1954	Detroit	All-Stars 2, Detroit 2	None named	10,689
1955	Detroit	Detroit 3, All-Stars 1	None named	10,111
1956	Montreal	All-Stars 1, Montreal 1	None named	13,095
1957	Montreal	All-Stars 5, Montreal 3	None named	13,003
1958	Montreal	Montreal 6, All-Stars 3	None named	13,989
1959	Montreal	Montreal 6, All-Stars 1	None named	13,818
1960	Montreal	All-Stars 2, Montreal 1	None named	13,949
1961	Chicago	All-Stars 3, Chicago 1	None named	14,534
1962	Toronto	Toronto 4, All-Stars 1	Eddie Shack, Tor	14,236
1963	Toronto	All-Stars 3, Toronto 3	Frank Mahovlich, Tor	14,034
1964	Toronto	All-Stars 3, Toronto 2	Jean Beliveau, Mtl	14,232
1965	Montreal	All-Stars 5, Montreal 2	Gordie Howe, Det	13,529
1967	Montreal	Montreal 3, All-Stars 0	Henri Richard, Mtl	14,284
1968	Toronto	Toronto 4, All-Stars 3	Bruce Gamble, Tor	15,753
1969	Montreal	East 3, West 3	Frank Mahovlich, Det	16,260
1970	St Louis	East 4, West 1	Bobby Hull, Chi	16,587
1971	Boston	West 2, East 1	Bobby Hull, Chi	14,790
1972	Minnesota	East 3, West 2	Bobby Orr, Bos	15,423
1973	NY Rangers	East 5, West 4	Greg Polis, Pitt	16,986
1974	Chicago	West 6, East 4	Garry Unger, StL	16,426
1975	Montreal	Wales 7, Campbell 1	Syl Apps Jr, Pitt	16,080
1976	Philadelphia	Wales 7, Campbell 5	Pete Mahovlich, Mtl	16,436
1977	Vancouver	Wales 4, Campbell 3	Rick Martin, Buff	15,607
1978	Buffalo	Wales 3, Campbell 2 (OT)	Billy Smith, NYI	16,433
1980	Detroit	Wales 6, Campbell 3	Reg Leach, Phil	21,002
1981	Los Angeles	Campbell 4, Wales 1	Mike Liut, StL	15,761
1982	Washington	Wales 4, Campbell 2	Mike Bossy, NYI	18,130
1983	NY Islanders	Campbell 9, Wales 3	Wayne Gretzky, Edm	15,230
1984	NJ Devils	Wales 7, Campbell 6	Don Maloney, NYR	18,939
1985	Calgary	Wales 6, Campbell 4	Mario Lemieux, Pitt	16,825
1986	Hartford	Wales 4, Campbell 3 (OT)	Grant Fuhr, Edm	15,100
1988	St Louis	Wales 6, Campbell 5 (OT)	Mario Lemieux, Pitt	17,878
1989	Edmonton	Campbell 9, Wales 5	Wayne Gretzky, LA	17,503
1990	Pittsburgh	Wales 12, Campbell 7	Mario Lemieux, Pitt	16,236
1991	Chicago	Campbell 11, Wales 5	Vince Damphousse, Tor	18,472
1992	Philadelphia	Campbell 10, Wales 6	Brett Hull, StL	17,380
1993	Montreal	Wales 16, Campbell 6	Mike Gartner, NYR	17,137
1994	NY Rangers	East 9, West 8	Mike Richter, NYR	18,200
1996	Boston	East 5, West 4	Ray Bourque, Bos	17,565
1997	San Jose	East 11, West 7	Mark Recchi, Mtl	17,565
1998	Vancouver	North America 8, World 7	Teemu Selanne, Ana (World)	18,422

Note: The Challenge Cup, a series between the NHL All-Stars and the Soviet Union, was played instead of the All-Star Game in 1979. Eight years later, Rendez-Vous '87, a two-game series matching the Soviet Union and the NHL All-Stars, replaced the All-Star Game. The 1995 NHL All-Star game was cancelled due to a labor dispute. The 1998 NHL All-Star game, billed as a preview to the 1998 Winter Olympics in Nagano, Japan, matched North Amercian-born All-Stars and All-Stars born elsewhere.

Bad Apples, Good Nuts

We aren't going to let a few highly publicized bad apples at the 1998 Nagano Games spoil the experience for everybody, so we offer, as paragons of the Olympic spirit, the Canadian players. Marc Crawford, Canada's coach, scheduled team meetings at 9 p.m. on the eve of games, and after the meetings broke up, many of his players would drift into a common area for informal ice cream socials. "They have this pretty good nut bar," Crawford explained. He was referring to an ice cream flavor, not Team USA.

Hockey Hall of Fame

Located in Toronto, the Hockey Hall of Fame was officially opened on August 26, 1961. The current chairman is Ian (Scotty) Morrison, a former NHL referee. There are, at present, 303 members of the Hockey Hall of Fame—208 players, 83 "builders," and 13 on-ice officials. (One member, Alan Eagleson, resigned from the Hall 3-25-98.) To be eligible, player and referee/linesman candidates should have been out of the game for three years, but the Hall's Board of Directors can make exceptions.

Players

Sid Abel (1969)
Jack Adams (1959)
Charles (Syl) Apps (1961)
George Armstrong (1975)
Irvine (Ace) Bailey (1975)
Donald H. (Dan) Bain (1945)
Hobey Baker (1945)
Bill Barber (1990)
Marty Barry (1965)
Andy Bathgate (1978)
Bobby Bauer (1996)
Jean Beliveau (1972)
Clint Benedict (1965)
Douglas Bentley (1964)
Max Bentley (1966)
Hector (Toe) Blake (1966)
Leo Boivin (1986)
Dickie Boon (1952)
Mike Bossy (1991)
Emile (Butch) Bouchard (1966)
Frank Boucher (1958)
George (Buck) Boucher (1960)
Johnny Bower (1976)
Russell Bowie (1945)
Frank Brimsek (1966)
Harry L. (Punch) Broadbent (1962)
Walter (Turk) Broda (1967)
John Bucyk (1981)
Billy Burch (1974)
Harry Cameron (1962)
Gerry Cheevers (1985)
Francis (King) Clancy (1958)
Aubrey (Dit) Clapper (1947)
Bobby Clarke (1987)
Sprague Cleghorn (1958)
Neil Colville (1967)
Charlie Conacher (1961)
Lionel Conacher (1994)
Alex Connell (1958)
Bill Cook (1952)
Fred (Bun) Cook (1995)
Arthur Coulter (1974)
Yvan Cournoyer (1982)
Bill Cowley (1968)
Samuel (Rusty) Crawford (1962)
Jack Darragh (1962)
Allan M. (Scotty) Davidson (1950)
Clarence (Hap) Day (1961)
Alex Delvecchio (1977)
Cy Denneny (1959)
Marcel Dionne (1992)
Gordie Drillon (1975)
Charles Drinkwater (1950)
Ken Dryden (1983)

Woody Dumart (1992)
Thomas Dunderdale (1974)
Bill Durnan (1964)
Mervyn A. (Red) Dutton (1958)
Cecil (Babe) Dye (1970)
Phil Esposito (1984)
Tony Esposito (1988)
Arthur F. Farrell (1965)
Ferdinand (Fern) Flaman (1990)
Frank Foyston (1958)
Frank Frederickson (1958)
Bill Gadsby (1970)
Bob Gainey (1992)
Chuck Gardiner (1945)
Herb Gardiner (1958)
Jimmy Gardner (1962)
Bernie (Boom Boom) Geoffrion (1972)
Eddie Gerard (1945)
Ed Giacomin (1987)
Rod Gilbert (1982)
Hamilton (Billy) Gilmour (1962)
Frank (Moose) Goheen (1952)
Ebenezer R. (Ebbie) Goodfellow (1963)
Mike Grant (1950)
Wilfred (Shorty) Green (1962)
Si Griffis (1950)
George Hainsworth (1961)
Glenn Hall (1975)
Joe Hall (1961)
Doug Harvey (1973)
George Hay (1958)
William (Riley) Hern (1962)
Bryan Hextall (1969)
Harry (Hap) Holmes (1972)
Tom Hooper (1962)
George (Red) Horner (1965)
Miles (Tim) Horton (1977)
Gordie Howe (1972)
Syd Howe (1965)
Harry Howell (1979)
Bobby Hull (1983)
John (Bouse) Hutton (1962)
Harry M. Hyland (1962)
James (Dick) Irvin (1958)
Harvey (Busher) Jackson (1971)
Ernest (Moose) Johnson (1952)
Ivan (Ching) Johnson (1958)
Tom Johnson (1970)
Aurel Joliat (1947)
Gordon (Duke) Keats (1958)
Leonard (Red) Kelly (1969)
Ted (Teeder) Kennedy (1966)
Dave Keon (1986)

Elmer Lach (1966)
Guy Lafleur (1988)
Edouard (Newsy) Lalonde (1950)
Jacques Laperriere (1987)
Guy LaPointe (1993)
Edgar Laprade (1993)
Reed Larson (1996)
Jean (Jack) Laviolette (1962)
Hugh Lehman (1958)
Jacques Lemaire (1984)
Mario Lemieux (1997)
Percy LeSueur (1961)
Herbert A. Lewis (1989)
Ted Lindsay (1966)
Harry Lumley (1980)
Lanny McDonald (1992)
Frank McGee (1945)
Billy McGimsie (1962)
George McNamara (1958)
Duncan (Mickey) MacKay (1952)
Frank Mahovlich (1981)
Joe Malone (1950)
Sylvio Mantha (1960)
Jack Marshall (1965)
Fred G. (Steamer) Maxwell (1962)
Stan Mikita (1983)
Dicky Moore (1974)
Patrick (Paddy) Moran (1958)
Howie Morenz (1945)
Billy Mosienko (1965)
Frank Nighbor (1947)
Reg Noble (1962)
Herbert (Buddy) O'Connor (1988)
Harry Oliver (1967)
Bert Olmstead (1985)
Bobby Orr (1979)
Bernie Parent (1984)
Brad Park (1988)
Lester Patrick (1947)
Lynn Patrick (1980)
Gilbert Perreault (1990)
Tommy Phillips (1945)
Pierre Pilote (1975)
Didier (Pit) Pitre (1962)
Jacques Plante (1978)
Denis Potvin (1991)
Walter (Babe) Pratt (1966)
Joe Primeau (1963)
Marcel Pronovost (1978)
Bob Pulford (1991)
Harvey Pulford (1945)
Hubert (Bill) Quackenbush (1976)

Players *(Cont.)*

Frank Rankin (1961)
Jean Ratelle (1985)
Claude (Chuck) Rayner (1973)
Kenneth Reardon (1966)
Henri Richard (1979)
Maurice (Rocket) Richard (1961)
George Richardson (1950)
Gordon Roberts (1971)
Larry Robinson (1995)
Art Ross (1945)
Blair Russel (1965)
Ernest Russell (1965)
Jack Ruttan (1962)
Borje Salming (1996)
Serge Savard (1986)
Terry Sawchuk (1971)
Fred Scanlan (1965)
Milt Schmidt (1961)
Dave (Sweeney) Schriner
   (1962)
Earl Seibert (1963)
Oliver Seibert (1961)
Eddie Shore (1947)
Steve Shutt (1993)
Albert C. (Babe) Siebert (1964)
Harold (Bullet Joe) Simpson
   (1962)
Daryl Sittler (1989)
Alfred E. Smith (1962)
Billy Smith (1993)
Clint Smith (1991)
Reginald (Hooley) Smith (1972)
Thomas Smith (1973)
Allan Stanley (1981)
Russell (Barney) Stanley
   (1962)
John (Black Jack) Stewart
   (1964)
Nels Stewart (1962)
Bruce Stuart (1961)
Hod Stuart (1945)
Frederic (Cyclone) (O.B.E.)
   Taylor (1947)
Cecil R. (Tiny) Thompson
   (1959)
Vladislav Tretiak (1989)
Harry J. Trihey (1950)
Bryan Trottier (1997)
Norm Ullman (1982)
Georges Vezina (1945)
Jack Walker (1960)
Marty Walsh (1962)
Harry Watson (1994)
Harry E. Watson (1962)
Ralph (Cooney) Weiland (1971)
Harry Westwick (1962)
Fred Whitcroft (1962)
Gordon (Phat) Wilson (1962)
Lorne (Gump) Worsley (1980)
Roy Worters (1969)

Builders

Charles Adams (1960)
Weston W. Adams (1972)
Thomas (Frank) Ahearn (1962)
John (Bunny) Ahearne (1977)
Montagu Allan (C.V.O.) (1945)
Keith Allen (1992)
Al Arbour (1996)
Harold Ballard (1977)
David Bauer (1989)
John Bickell (1978)
Scott Bowman (1991)
George V. Brown (1961)
Walter A. Brown (1962)
Frank Buckland (1975)
Jack Butterfield (1980)
Frank Calder (1947)
Angus D. Campbell (1964)
Clarence Campbell (1966)
Joe Cattarinich (1977)
Bob Cole (1996)
Joseph (Leo) Dandurand
   (1963)
Francis Dilio (1964)
George S. Dudley (1958)
James A. Dunn (1968)
Robert Alan Eagleson (1989–98*)
Sergio Gambucci (1996)
Emile Francis (1982)
Jack Gibson (1976)
Tommy Gorman (1963)
Frank Griffiths (1993)
William Hanley (1986)
Charles Hay (1974)
James C. Hendy (1968)
Foster Hewitt (1965)
William Hewitt (1947)
Fred J. Hume (1962)
George (Punch) Imlach (1984)
William M. Jennings (1975)
Bob Johnson (1992)
Gordon W. Juckes (1979)
John Kilpatrick (1960)
Seymour Knox III (1993)
George Leader (1969)
Robert LeBel (1970)
Thomas F. Lockhart (1965)
Paul Loicq (1961)
Frederic McLaughlin (1963)
John Mariucci (1985)
Frank Mathers (1992)
John (Jake) Milford (1984)
Hartland Molson (1973)
Francis Nelson (1947)
Bruce A. Norris (1969)
James Norris, Sr. (1958)
James D. Norris (1962)
William M. Northey (1947)
John O'Brien (1962)
Brian O'Neill (1994)

Builders *(Cont.)*

Fred Page (1993)
Craig Patrick (1996)
Frank Patrick (1958)
Allan W. Pickard (1958)
Rudy Pilous (1985)
Norman (Bud) Poile (1990)
Samuel Pollock (1978)
Donat Raymond (1958)
John Robertson (1947)
Claude C. Robinson (1947)
Philip D. Ross (1976)
Gunther Sabetzki (1995)
Glen Sather (1997)
Frank J. Selke (1960)
Harry Sinden (1983)
Frank D. Smith (1962)
Conn Smythe (1958)
Edward M. Snider (1988)
Lord Stanley of Preston
   (G.C.B.) (1945)
James T. Sutherland (1947)
Anatoli V. Tarasov (1974)
Bill Torrey (1995)
Lloyd Turner (1958)
William Tutt (1978)
Carl Potter Voss (1974)
Fred C. Waghorn (1961)
Arthur Wirtz (1971)
Bill Wirtz (1976)
John A. Ziegler, Jr. (1987)

Referees/Linesmen

Neil Armstrong (1991)
John Ashley (1981)
William L. Chadwick (1964)
John D'Amico (1993)
Chaucer Elliott (1961)
George Hayes (1988)
Robert W. Hewitson (1963)
Fred J. (Mickey) Ion (1961)
Matt Pavelich (1987)
Mike Rodden (1962)
J. Cooper Smeaton (1961)
Roy (Red) Storey (1967)
Frank Udvari (1973)

Note: Year of election to the Hall of Fame is in parentheses after the member's name.
*Eagleson resigned from Hall 3-25-98.

Tennis

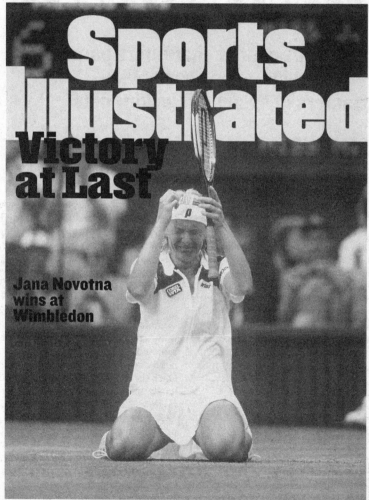

Sports Illustrated

Victory at Last

Jana Novotna wins at Wimbledon

Theater of the Absurd

A clamorous cast of characters paraded through a wide-open season like characters in a Samuel Beckett play

BY FRANZ LIDZ

A TENNIS BUFF, THE late Samuel Beckett wrote bleak comedies of the absurd in which protagonists diverted themselves with endless verbal volleying. His plays of dismal routine are relieved only by lyric effusions—poetic drop shots—as brief as they are poignant. And characters often draw laughs with smart serves and odd little lobs that knuckle barely inside the baseline.

ESTRAGON: Let us try to converse calmly, since we are incapable of keeping silent.

VLADIMIR: You're right, we're inexhaustible.

ESTRAGON: It's so we won't think.

VLADIMIR: We have that excuse.

ESTRAGON: It's so we won't hear.

VLADIMIR: We have our reasons.

ESTRAGON: All the dead voices.

VLADIMIR: They make a noise like wings.

ESTRAGON: Like leaves.

VLADIMIR: Like sand.

ESTRAGON: Like leaves.

The 1998 tennis season played out as if scripted by the Nobel Laureate himself. Incapable of keeping silent, players fumed and clamored, cried and exulted. Their rackets thrashed through the stadium air, making noises like wings, like leaves, like sand, like leaves.

MORE PRICKS THAN KICKS

A sort of baseline incarnation of *Waiting for Godot*'s Pozo, Marcelo Ríos twice replaced Wimbledon winner Pete Sampras as the world's top-ranked player. The chilly Chilean achieved a certain notoriety Down Under, not for reaching the finals of the Australian Open (he lost in straight sets to Petr Korda), but for the way he had prepared for a match in New Zealand. Before leaving the tiny locker room to go oncourt, Ríos allegedly urinated all over the toilet seat.

Haughty and vigorously hostile, Ríos bullied anyone who got in the way of his self-glorification, lobbed insults at umpires, openly mocked lesser opponents and snubbed greater ones. Kids seeking his autograph were more apt to be flipped the bird or showered with oaths better suited to

Chilly Chilean: if only Ríos's off-court manners were as admirable as his tennis.

a proctologist's office. Tired of waiting in the clubhouse lunch line at Wimbledon in 1997, Our Man from Santiago reportedly told Monica Seles, "Move your fat ass!"

Ríos's bullwhip temper is matched only by his bullwhip forehand. Once called the Andre Agassi of Chile, the 5'9", 140-pound southpaw is an aggressive baseliner who takes the ball early on the rise and punches last-second passing shots with great disguise. Against huge-serving Greg Rusedski in the Indian Wells final in March '98, Ríos moved with such prowling grace that he seemed never to reach for a ball—he merely awaited it. He kept the '97 U.S. Open finalist off balance with a parade of topspins and slices, and finished him off 6–3, 6–7 (15–17), 7–6 (7–4), 6–4 with spirit-crushing passing shots. "In this age of power, rarely do you see a player manipulate the ball like Ríos," said Ion Tiriac, the onetime coach of Boris Becker. "Without being overly romantic, talent still should play a role."

Without being underly romantic, tennis

writers at the French Open awarded Ríos his third straight Prix Citron (Lemon Prize) for noncooperation. When Ríos did cooperate, he sometimes overdid it. After winning his semifinal match at the Australian, he was asked what he would do with his two nights off before the final. "I don't know," he said. "I don't want to go to the casino. I lose so many bets."

"Will the winner's check cover the losses?" he was asked.

"I don't think so."

Though his "gambling problem" was widely reported, Ríos said he was just kidding. "Unfortunately, anybody can be a tennis journalist," he said. "They are not really smart people." He may have a point. A simpleminded tennis scribe once asked the tawny-skinned Ríos if he had "Indian blood." The terse reply: "What if I called you the son of a whore?"

NOT I

In Beckett's *Not I*, a relentless torrent of words pours forth from a woman's flaming red mouth. That pretty much sums up the women's game, where a gaggle of lip-flapping teenage sirens became the talk of tennis. Seventeen-year-old Martina Hingis won the Australian Open, made the cover of *GQ* and openly disparaged the comeback of the great Steffi Graf. Venus Williams, who's 18, had a screaming jag over a line call at Wimbledon, got fined at the U.S. Open for openly defying the WTA dress code and posed for Annie Leibovitz in *Vogue*. And when Anna Kournikova—the 17-year-old Russian who dated NHL star Sergei Fedorov and bragged to a press conference about her lack of butt fat—withdrew unexpectedly from Wimbledon, a headline in a Fleet Street tabloid screamed: NOTICE TO ALL MEN: WIMBLEDON IS OVER.

Though the teen squad got the majority of press, the old ladies won most of the major tournaments. A 26-year-old (Arantxa Sánchez Vicario) beat a 24-year-old (Seles) in the French Open finals; a 29-year-old (Jana Novotna) beat a 30-year-old (Nathalie Tauziat) in the Wimbledon finals; and a 22-year-old (Lindsay Davenport) won the U.S. Open. Davenport, a freeway-loving Southern Californian, drove from her Manhattan hotel to the National Tennis Center in Queens every day. "Normally I take the Triboro Bridge," she said. "But if I hear there's traffic on the radio, I take the Midtown Tunnel."

Thirty pounds lighter than she was in '96 and many times fitter, Davenport used power and precision to upset defending champ Hingis in the finals and become the first American-born women's U.S. Open champ since Chris Evert in 1982. Of the generation gap, she said, "I think it's kind of inspired the older players—and I'll include myself in that group—to practice harder, to maybe want it more. There's more of a sense that we don't want that 16-year-old to win a Grand Slam. It gives new life to the game."

Seles, the year's second-most talked about Monica, had the morning off on the first day of the U.S. Open. So the two-time champ accepted an offer to ring the opening bell and swat tennis balls onto the trading floor at the New York Stock Exchange. When she left, the market was up 43

The streetwise Davenport won the U.S. Open, her first major title.

points. Within a few minutes it nose-dived and finished down more than 500 points. "The chairman of the exchange told me I could come back anytime," said Seles. "After what happened, I am not so sure he wants me back."

WAITING FOR GAMBILL
Come and Go is a Beckett playlet consisting of little more than a series of symbolic exits and entrances. The most sensational entrance of an American male last year was by a 21-year-old Trekkie who lives with his parents on a ranch in that tennis hotbed Spokane, drives his Jaguars at speeds faster than his 134 mph serve, hits potent two-handed shots from both sides, and got his name from a TV actor turned soft-porn star.

Jan-Michael Gambill, whose nickname, Hollywood, derives from his box-office good looks, vaulted into the tennis consciousness last March by upending four top 50 opponents and reaching the semifinals at Indian Wells. The last-minute wild card creamed Mark Philippoussis, Francisco Clavet, Jim

Courier and Agassi before losing 6–7 (3–7), 3–6 to Ríos, the eventual winner. In the fourth round of the U.S. Open, Gambill was defeated 6–2, 3–6, 3–6, 6–3, 7–6 (7–4) by French Open champion Carlos Moya. In 10 months Gambill's ranking climbed from 227th to the mid-40s.

Diane Gambill named her only son after *Airwolf* heartthrob Jan-Michael Vincent, the hard-living actor best known these days—when known at all—for such soft-core features as *Jurassic Woman* and *Sins of the Flesh*. "My mom just liked the name," says the 6′3″, 195-pound Gambill, whose father, Chuck, a retired stockbroker, is now his coach. Chuck taught Jan-Michael the two-handed forehand, a shot that leaves him vulnerable on wide-ranging returns. Jan-Michael compensates by wielding a racket two inches longer than conventional models.

As a kid Gambill idolized Captain Kirk and Graf. "I used to love the way Steffi would crush an opponent, then gracefully leave the court," he recalls. "To me she was a superhero who had special abilities far above other women." Gambill's own abilities earned him a scholarship to the University of Washington, an offer he turned down in 1996 to turn pro. He orbited aimlessly in the satellites and lost in the finals of the qualifiers in six ATP events. His breakthrough came in '97, when he made the quarterfinals in Auckland. Five months later he won his first pro title.

The tennis life has been tough on Gambill's gamboling. "I broke up with my girlfriend in Spokane after six months," he says. "The long-distance thing just doesn't work for me." Nor does the low-percentage thing. "Hollywood's shot selection could be improved," says veteran Courier. "He'll be a serious threat when he learns to manage his game better." In other words, Gambill needs to take fewer gambles.

ENDGAME

Like Nagg and Nell, the ash can–residing coots in Beckett's *Endgame*, former world-beaters Courier and Agassi entered 1998 on the scrap heap. Since surrendering his No. 1 ranking in 1993, Courier has been hampered by shoulder, arm and racket problems. He was a bust at last year's Grand Slams, and his ranking hovered in the 60s. Exclude a victorious run in April at his hometown tournament in Orlando, and Courier won just six matches through August. Yet, at the advanced age of 28, Courier is not a man going gentle into his sunset years. As stubbornly persistent as ever, he metamorphosed into America's foremost Davis Cup patriot in '98. His most heroic performance came in Stone Mountain, Ga., during the rubber match of a tie with Russia. After dropping the first eight games, Courier spared America the shame of an opening-round defeat by outlasting Marat Safin 0–6, 6–4, 4–6, 6–1, 6–4. The U.S. has never lost in a series when Courier has played, going 12–0. "I have nothing to say about that," deadpanned Courier. "You don't talk about a no-hitter when you're in the dugout."

The fade of 28-year-old Agassi has been more dramatic. Ranked No. 1 briefly in early '96, he won only 12 matches and no titles in '97. By November of that year he had plunged to No. 141. Embarrassed by his ponderous play, Agassi lost 20 pounds and found his stroke by dropping down to the Challenger circuit, the tennis equivalent of Triple A. He made the final of the first tournament and won the second.

Revitalized, Agassi sailed through a February tournament in San Jose, brutalizing Sampras from the baseline 6–2, 6–4 in the final. A month later in Scottsdale, he won again. And the week after that, in Indian Wells, he crushed U.S. Open king Patrick Rafter. But after losing in the finals of the Lipton and Munich, Agassi's sizzling season fizzled. He pulled up lame during an opening-round defeat to Marat Safin at the French Open and played lamely in a second-round loss to Tommy Haas at Wimbledon. Agassi rebounded by winning consecutive hardcourt titles in Washington and Los Angeles and reaching the finals of Indianapolis. But he stumbled again at the U.S. Open, looking ash can–old in a fourth-round drubbing by Karol Kucera.

"Is Andre conditioned enough to win a

BOB MARTIN

Agassi's advancing age and offcourt distractions could be draining his motivation.

final to Hingis after pulling up lame with a two-game lead in the third set.

The term choke artist implies a unifying vision in conception and execution—as if the athlete has made a conscious effort to self-destruct. In Novotna's case, when a situation called for instinct and simplicity, she often got gummed up in thinking and complexity. "I don't think I'm a choker," she said, "but I've got a label on my back that says, 'At the most important point of a big match, Jana will choke.' The label is almost impossible to get rid of. I could win three straight tournaments, and people would still say, 'Yes, she's playing well. But remember the Wimbledon final when she choked?'"

People will remember the '98 Wimbledon final as the one in which Novotna stopped choking. Ahead 6–4, 6–6 (6–2), she hit a forehand past Tauziat, fell to her knees, raised her arms and then, overwhelmed, covered her face as her shoulders shook with joy. Alas, the monkey didn't stay off Novotna's back long. In the semis of the U.S. Open, she blew a huge third-set lead and lost 3–6, 6–1, 6–4 to Hingis. Novotna was up 4–1 in the final set, just six points from winning the match and ending her doubles partner's 76-week reign as No. 1 in the world, when her game collapsed. She missed several easy shots and won just four of the final 22 points. After her 50th unforced error settled into the net on match point, Novotna stood with hands on hips at the baseline in disbelief. The result called to mind a Beckett couplet:

On entre, on crie,
Et c'est la vie.
On crie, on sort,
Et c'est la mort.

(One enters, one screams,/And that's life./ One screams, one leaves,/ And that's death.)

tournament of five-setters?" asked John McEnroe. "Best-of-three matches, he can get away with. But in best-of-five-setters you have to contend with fatigue, both physical and mental. The older you get, the tougher it is to stay focused." Especially when you're taking home $14 million a year in endorsements—$6 million more than Sampras. "It's hard to quit when you're making that much dough," McEnroe says. "Maybe it's also hard to keep motivated, but Pete figured out how this year at Wimbledon."

HAPPY DAYS

The aging Winnie of Beckett's *Happy Days* is embedded in a mound of earth. Until now, Novotna played Grand Slams as if in a similar state of immobility. While no one disputed Novotna's artistry—the athletic Czech is the last pure serve-and-volleyer in the women's game—she was best known for her choke artistry. Novotna had worn a choke collar since the 1993 Wimbledon finals, when she had Graf within a point of 1–5 in the third set, only to double-fault her way out of victory. At the '95 French Open, Novotna lost to Chanda Rubin after having a match point and a 5–0 lead in the third set. And she dropped the '97 Wimbledon

1998 Grand Slam Champions

Australian Open
Men's Singles

	Winner	Finalist	Score
Quarterfinals	Karol Kucera ....Pete Sampras (1)		6-4, 6-2, 6-7 (5-7), 6-3
	Petr Korda (6)..........................Jonas Bjorkman (4)		3-6, 5-7, 6-3, 6-4, 6-2
	Marcelo Ríos (9).......................Alberto Berasategui		6-7 (6-8), 6-4, 6-4, 6-0
	Nicolas Escude ....Nicolas Kiefer		4-6, 3-6, 6-4, 6-1, 6-2
Semifinals	Petr Korda ....Karol Kucera		7-5, 6-2, 6-4
	Marcelo Ríos ....Nicolas Escude		6-1, 6-4, 1-6, 6-2
Final	Petr Korda ....Marcelo Ríos		6-2, 6-2, 6-2

Women's Singles

	Winner	Finalist	Score
Quarterfinals	Lindsay Davenport (2) ....Venus Williams		1-6, 7-5, 6-3
	Conchita Martinez (8)..............Sandrine Testud (9)		6-3, 6-2
	Martina Hingis (1)...................Mary Pierce (5)		6-2, 6-3
	Anke Huber (10).....................Arantxa Sánchez Vicario (7)		7-6 (9-7), 7-5
Semifinals	Martina Hingis ....Anke Huber		6-1, 2-6, 6-1
	Conchita Martinez ....Lindsay Davenport		4-6, 6-3, 6-3
Final	Martina Hingis ....Conchita Martinez		6-3, 6-3

Doubles

	Winner	Finalist	Score
Men's Final	Jonas Bjorkman/ Jacco Eltingh (5)	Mark Woodforde/ Todd Woodbridge (1)	6-2, 5-7, 2-6, 6-4, 6-3
Women's Final	Martina Hingis/ Mirjana Zvereva.........................	Lindsay Davenport/ Natasha Zvereva (1)	6-4, 2-6, 6-3
Mixed Final	Venus Williams/ Justin Gimelstob	Helena Sukova/ Cyril Suk (5)	6-2, 6-1

French Open
Men's Singles

	Winner	Finalist	Score
Quarterfinals	Felix Mantilla (15)...................Thomas Muster		6-4, 6-2, 4-6, 6-3
	Carlos Moya (12)....................Marcelo Ríos (3)		6-1, 2-6, 6-2, 6-4
	Alex Corretja (14) ....Filip DeWulf		7-5, 6-4, 6-3
	Cedric Pioline...........................Hicham Arazi		3-6, 6-2, 7-6 (8-6), 4-6, 6-3
Semifinals	Carlos Moya ....Felix Mantilla		5-7, 6-2, 6-4, 6-2
	Alex Corretja ....Cedric Pioline		6-3, 6-4, 6-2
Final	Carlos Moya ....Alex Corretja		6-3, 7-5, 6-3

Women's Singles

	Winner	Finalist	Score
Quarterfinals	Arantxa Sánchez Vicario (4) ...Patty Schnyder		6-2, 6-7 (5-7), 6-0
	Lindsay Davenport (2) ....Iva Majoli (10)		6-1, 5-7, 6-3
	Martina Hingis (1)...................Venus Williams (8)		6-3, 6-4
	Monica Seles (6) ....Jana Novotna (3)		4-6, 6-3, 6-3
Semifinals	Arantxa Sánchez Vicario ....Lindsay Davenport		6-3, 7-6 (7-5)
	Monica Seles..........................Martina Hingis		6-3, 6-2
Final	Arantxa Sánchez Vicario ....Monica Seles		7-6 (7-5), 0-6, 6-2

Note: Seedings in parentheses.

French Open *(Cont.)*

Doubles

	Winner	Finalist	Score
Men's Final	Jacco Eltingh/ Paul Haarhuis (1)	Mark Knowles/ Daniel Nestor	6–3, 3–6, 6–3
Women's Final	Martina Hingis/ Jana Novotna (2)	Lindsay Davenport/ Natasha Zvereva (1)	6–1, 7–6 (7–4)
Mixed Final	Venus Williams/ Justin Gimelstob	Serena Williams/ Luis Lobo	6–4, 6–4

Wimbledon

Men's Singles

	Winner	Finalist	Score
Quarterfinals	Pete Sampras (1)	Mark Philippoussis	7–6 (7–5), 6–4, 6–4
	Tim Henman (12)	Nicolas Kiefer	6–3, 6–4, 6–2
	Richard Krajicek (9)	Tim Henman (14)	6–2, 6–3, 6–4
	Goran Ivanisevic (14)	Greg Rusedski	7–6 (12–10), 7–6
Semifinals	Pete Sampras	Tim Henman	6–3, 4–6, 7–5, 6–3 (7–5), 7–6 (8–6)
	Goran Ivanisevic	Richard Krajicek	6–3, 5–7, 6–7 (5–7), 15–13
Final	Pete Sampras	Goran Ivanisevic	6–7 (2–7), 7–6 (11–9), 6–4, 3–6, 6–2

Women's Singles

	Winner	Finalist	Score
Quarterfinals	Martina Hingis (1)	Arantxa Sánchez Vicario (5)	6–3, 3–6, 6–3
	Nathalie Tauziat (16)	Lindsay Davenport (2)	6–3, 6–3
	Jana Novotna (3)	Venus Williams (7)	7–5, 7–6 (7–2)
	Natasha Zvereva	Monica Seles (6)	7–6 (7–4), 6–2
Semifinals	Jana Novotna	Martina Hingis	6–4, 6–4
	Nathalie Tauziat	Natasha Zvereva	1–6, 7–6 (7–1), 6–3
Final	Jana Novotna	Nathalie Tauziat	6–4, 7–6 (7–2)

Doubles

	Winner	Finalist	Score
Men's Final	Jacco Eltingh/ Paul Haarhuis (1)	Todd Woodbridge/ Mark Woodforde (2)	2–6, 6–4, 7–6 (7–3), 5–7, 10–8
Women's Final	Martina Hingis/ Jana Novotna (1)	Lindsay Davenport/ Natasha Zvereva (2)	6–3, 3–6, 8–6
Mixed Final	Serena Williams/ Max Mirnyi	Mirjana Lucic/ Mahesh Bhupathi (5)	6–4, 6–4

U.S. Open

Men's Singles

	Winner	Finalist	Score
Quarterfinals	Pete Sampras (1)	Karol Kucera (9)	6–3, 7–5, 6–4
	Patrick Rafter (3)	Jonas Bjorkman (12)	6–2, 6–3, 7–5
	Carlos Moya (10)	Magnus Larsson	6–4, 6–3, 6–3
	Mark Philippoussis	Thomas Johansson	4–6, 6–3, 6–7 (3–7), 6–3, 7–6 (12–10)
Semifinals	Mark Philippoussis	Carlos Moya	6–1, 6–4, 5–7, 6–4
	Patrick Rafter	Pete Sampras	6–7 (8–10), 6–4, 2–6, 6–4, 6–3
Final	Patrick Rafter	Mark Philippoussis	6–3, 3–6, 6–2, 6–0

Note: Seedings in parentheses.

U.S. Open (Cont.)
Women's Singles

	Winner	Finalist	Score
Quarterfinals	Jana Novotna (3)	Patty Schnyder (11)	6–2, 6–3
	Martina Hingis (1)	Monica Seles (6)	6–4, 6–4
	Lindsay Davenport (2)	Amanda Coetzer (13)	6–0, 6–4
	Venus Williams (5)	Arantxa Sánchez Vicario (4)	4–6, 6–1, 6–1
Semifinals	Martina Hingis	Jana Novotna	6–2, 6–4
	Lindsay Davenport	Venus Williams	7–6 (7–5), 4–6, 7–6 (9–7)
Final	Lindsay Davenport	Martina Hingis	6–0, 6–4

Doubles

	Winner	Finalist	Score
Men's Final	Sandon Stolle/ Cyril Suk (15)	Mark Knowles/ Daniel Nestor (6)	4–6, 7–6 (10–8), 6–2
Women's Final	Martina Hingis/ Jana Novotna (1)	Lindsay Davenport/ Natasha Zvereva (2)	6–3, 6–3
Mixed Final	Serena Williams/ Max Mirnyi	Lisa Raymond/ Patrick Galbraith (3)	6–2, 6–2

Major Tournament Results

Men's Tour (late 1997)

Date	Tournament	Site	Winner	Finalist	Score
Sept 22–28	Romanian Open	Bucharest	R. Fromberg	A. Gaudenzi	6–1, 7–6 (7–2)
Oct 6–12	Heineken Open	Singapore	M. Gustafsson	Nicolas Kiefer	4–6, 6–3, 6–3
Oct 13–19	Beijing Open	Beijing	Jim Courier	M. Gustafsson	7–6 (12–10), 3–6, 6–3
Oct 13–19	Grand Prix de Tennis	Lyon, France	Fabrice Santoro	Tommy Haas	6–4, 6–4
Oct 20–26	Eurocard Open	Stuttgart, Germany	Petr Korda	R. Krajicek	7–6 (8–6), 6–2, 6–4
Oct 27–Nov 2	Paris Open	Paris	Thomas Enqvist	Yvegeny Kafelnikov	6–2, 6–4, 7–5
Nov 3–9	Stockholm Open	Stockholm	Jonas Bjorkman	J. Siemerink	3–6, 7–6 (7–2), 6–2, 6–4
Nov 10–16	ATP Tour World Championships	Hanover, Germany	Pete Sampras	Yvegeny Kafelnikov	6–3, 6–2, 6–2

Men's Tour (Through October 4, 1998)

Date	Tournament	Site	Winner	Finalist	Score
Jan 5–Feb 1	Australian Open	Melbourne	Petr Korda	Marcelo Ríos	6–2, 6–2, 6–2
Feb 2–8	Croatian Indoors	Split, Croatia	Goran Ivanisevic	Greg Rusedski	7–6 (7–3), 7–6 (7–5)
Feb 2–8	Marseille Open	Marseille, France	Thomas Enqvist	Yevgeny Kafelnikov	6–4, 6–1
Feb 9–15	Dubai Open	Dubai, United Arab Emirates	Alex Corretja	Felix Mantilla	7–6 (7–0), 6–1
Feb 16–22	European Championships	Antwerp, Belgium	Greg Rusedski	Marc Rosset	7–6 (7–3), 3–6, 6–1, 6–4
Feb 16–22	Kroger St. Jude	Memphis	M. Philippoussis	Michael Chang	6–3, 6–2
Mar 2–8	ABN/AMRO World	Rotterdam, Netherlands	Jan Siemerink	Thomas Johansson	7–6 (7–2), 6–2
Mar 9–15	Champions Cup	Indian Wells, California	Marcelo Ríos	Greg Rusedski	6–3, 6–7 (15–17), 7–6 (7–4), 6–4
Mar 16–29	Lipton Championships	Key Biscane, Florida	Marcelo Ríos	Andre Agassi	7–5, 6–3, 6–4
Apr 13–19	Japan Open	Tokyo	Andrei Pavel	Byron Black	6–3, 6–4
Apr 13–19	Barcelona Open	Barcelona	Todd Martin	Alberto Berasategui	6–2, 1–6, 6–3, 6–2
Apr 20–26	Monte Carlo Open	Monte Carlo	Carlos Moya	Cedric Pioline	6–3, 6–0, 7–5
Apr 27–May 3	German Open	Munich	Thomas Enqvist	Andre Agassi	6–7 (4–7), 7–6 (8–6), 6–3

Men's Tour (Through October 4, 1998) (Cont.)

Date	Tournament	Site	Winner	Finalist	Score
May 11–17	Italian Open	Rome	Marcelo Ríos	Albert Costa	walkover
May 25–June 7	French Open	Paris	Carlos Moya	Alex Corretja	6–3, 7–5, 6–3
June 8–14	Gerry Weber Open	Halle, Germany	Yevgeny Kafelnikov	Magnus Larsson	6–4, 6–4
June 23–July 6	Wimbledon	Wimbledon	Pete Sampras	Goran Ivanisevic	6–7 (2–7), 7–6 (11–9), 6–4, 3–6, 6–2
July 20–26	Mercedes Cup	Stuttgart, Germany	Gustavo Kuerten	Karol Kucera	4–6, 6–2, 6–4
Aug 10–16	ATP Championship	Cincinnati	Patrick Rafter	Pete Sampras	1–6, 7–6 (7–2), 6–4
Aug 17–23	RCA Championships	Indianapolis	Alex Corretja	Andre Agassi	2–6, 6–2, 6–3
Aug 17–23	Pilot Pen International	New Haven, Connecticut	Karol Kucera	Goran Ivanisevic	6–4, 5–7, 6–2
Aug 18–24	Hamlet Cup	Commack, New York	Patrick Rafter	Felix Mantilla	7–6 (7–3), 6–2
Aug 26–Sept 8	U.S. Open	New York City	Patrick Rafter	Mark Philippoussis	6–3, 3–6, 6–2, 6–0
Sept 28–Oct 4	Grand Slam Cup	Munich	Marcelo Ríos	Andre Agassi	6–4, 2–6, 7–6 (7–1), 5–7, 6–3

Women's Tour (Late 1997)

Date	Tournament	Site	Winner	Finalist	Score
Oct 6–12	Porsche Tennis Grand Prix	Filderstadt, Germany	Martina Hingis	Lisa Raymond	6–4, 6–2
Oct 13–19	European Indoors	Zurich	L. Davenport	Nathalie Tauziat	7–6 (7–3), 7–5
Nov 3–9	Ameritech Cup	Chicago	L. Davenport	Nathalie Tauziat	6–0, 7–5
Nov 3–9	Ladies Kremlin Cup	Moscow	Jana Novotna	Ai Sugiyama	6–3, 6–4
Nov 10–16	Advanta Championships	Philadelphia	Martina Hingis	Lindsay Davenport	7–5, 6–7 (7–9), 7–6 (7–4)
Nov 17–23	WTA Tour Championships	New York	Jana Novotna	Mary Pierce	7–6 (7–4), 6–2, 6–3

Women's Tour (Through October 4, 1998)

Date	Tournament	Site	Winner	Finalist	Score
Jan 12–17	Sydney International	Sydney	A. Sánchez Vicario	Venus Williams	6–1, 6–3
Jan 19–Feb 1	Australian Open	Melbourne	Martina Hingis	Conchita Martinez	6–3, 6–3
Feb 2–8	Pan Pacific Open	Tokyo	L. Davenport	Martina Hingis	6–3, 6–3
Feb 9–15	Open Gaz de France	Paris	Mary Pierce	D. van Roost	6–3, 7–5
Feb 16–22	Faber Grand Prix	Hanover, Germany	Patty Schnyder	Jana Novotna	6–0, 2–6, 7–5
Mar 2–14	Evert Cup at Indian Wells	Indian Wells, California	Martina Hingis	Lindsay Davenport	6–3, 6–4
Mar 16–28	Lipton Championships	Key Biscayne, Florida	Venus Williams	Anna Kournikova	2–6, 6–4, 6–1
Mar 30–Apr 5	Family Circle Cup	Hilton Head, S Carolina	Amanda Coetzer	Irina Spirlea	6–3, 6–4
Apr 6–12	Bausch & Lomb Championships	Amelia Island, Florida	Mary Pierce	Conchita Martinez	6–7 (8–10), 6–0, 6–2
Apr 27–May 3	Rexona Cup	Hamburg	Martina Hingis	Jana Novotna	6–3, 7–5
May 4–10	Italian Open	Rome	Martina Hingis	Venus Williams	6–3, 2–6, 6–3
May 11–17	German Open	Berlin	C. Martinez	Amelie Mauresmo	6–4, 6–4
May 18–24	Internatix de Strasbourg	Strasbourg, France	Irina Spirlea	Julie Halard-Decugis	7–6 (7–5), 6–3
May 25–June 7	French Open	Paris	Arantxa Sánchez Vicario	Monica Seles	7–6 (7–5), 0–6, 6–2
June 22–July 4	Wimbledon Championships	Wimbledon	Jana Novotna	Nathalie Tauziat	6–4, 7–6 (7–2)
July 27–Aug 2	Bank of the West Classic	Stanford	L. Davenport	Venus Williams	6–4, 5–7, 6–4
Aug 3–9	Toshiba Tennis Classic	San Diego	L. Davenport	Mary Pierce	6–3, 6–1
Aug 10–16	Acura Classic	Los Angeles	L. Davenport	Martina Hingis	4–6, 6–4, 6–3

Women's Tour (Through October 4, 1998) *(Cont.)*

Date	Tournament	Site	Winner	Finalist	Score
Aug 17–23	du Maurier Open	Montreal	Monica Seles	A. Sánchez Vicario	6–3, 6–2
Aug 31–Sept 13	U.S. Open	New York	L. Davenport	Martina Hingis	6–3, 7–5
Sept 21–27	Princess Cup	Tokyo	Monica Seles	A. Sánchez Vicario	4–6, 6–3, 6–4
Sept 28–Oct 4	Grand Slam Cup	Munich	Venus Williams	Patty Schnyder	6–2, 3–6, 6–2

1997 Singles Leaders

Men

Rank	Player	Tournament Wins	Match Record	Earnings ($)
1.	Pete Sampras	8	55–12	6,498,311
2.	Patrick Rafter	1	65–29	2,923,519
3.	Michael Chang	5	57–21	2,541,830
4.	Jonas Bjorkman	3	71–26	1,950,375
5.	Yevgeny Kafelnikov	3	55–27	3,207,757
6.	Greg Rusedski	2	53–23	1,515,473
7.	Carlos Moya	0	56–30	1,137,400
8.	Sergi Bruguera	0	49–28	1,227,428
9.	Thomas Muster	2	46–24	2,186,590
10.	Marcelo Ríos	1	60–26	1,397,445
11.	Richard Krajicek	3	49–19	1,434,584
12.	Alex Corretja	3	49–22	1,182,807
13.	Petr Korda	1	55–24	1,515,483
14.	Gustavo Kuerten	1	36–25	1,586,753
15.	Goran Ivanisevic	3	53–22	1,458,257
16.	Felix Mantilla	5	53–22	1,105,593
17.	Tim Henman	2	48–24	802,746
18.	Mark Philippoussis	3	48–21	904,211
19.	Albert Costa	2	44–22	864,684
20.	Cedric Pioline	1	36–28	999,701

Note: Compiled by the ATP Tour.

Women

Rank	Player	Tournament Wins	Match Record	Earnings ($)
1.	Martina Hingis	12	75–5	3,400,196
2.	Jana Novotna	4	54–15	1,685,115
3.	Lindsay Davenport	6	59–16	1,533,101
4.	Amanda Coetzer	2	61–26	701,994
5.	Monica Seles	3	45–13	914,020
6.	Iva Majoli	3	41–17	1,227,332
7.	Mary Pierce	1	45–15	881,639
8.	Irina Spirlea	0	47–23	720,758
9.	Arantxa Sánchez Vicario	0	47–24	890,512
10.	Mary Joe Fernandez	1	40–18	769,132
11.	Nathalie Tauziat	1	45–21	600,642
12.	Conchita Martinez	0	37–19	528,544
13.	Sandrine Testud	1	44–23	417,753
14.	Anke Huber	0	36–23	411,315
15.	Brenda Schultz-McCarthy	1	36–27	348,247
16.	Sabine Applemans	0	39–28	339,845
17.	Lisa Raymond	0	31–21	450,070
18.	Dominique Van Roost	2	44–17	274,010
19.	Ruxandra Dragomir	0	37–26	381,500
20.	Ai Sugiyama	1	32–28	307,837

Note: Compiled by the Women's Tennis Association (WTA).

Up in Arms Down Under

The U.S. Open final, pitting Pat Rafter against Mark Philippoussis, was a banner occasion for Australian tennis. It was also a flash point for controversy. Angered that Tony Roche, Australia's Davis Cup coach, watched the match from Rafter's box, Philippoussis accused Roche of favoritism and Roche, in turn, suggested he might resign from the team. Rafter, the world's No. 2 player, responded, "If Rochey goes, I go. He doesn't deserve the abuse he's gotten." With Roche coaching and Rafter playing, Australia beat Uzbekistan 5–0 in late September '98 to clinch a spot in the World Group of the 1999 Cup. Philippoussis was AWOL.

The recent contretemps is the latest in a long-running, if petty, saga that resulted in Philippoussis skipping the previous Davis Cup tie (in which the Aussies were upset by Zimbabwe) and then Rafter dumping Philippoussis as a doubles partner. "Mark and I are starting to patch things up," Rafter said a week after the U.S. Open. "But it's hard to defend him when he offends a good friend."

Rafter, normally a preternaturally mellow fellow, is also agitated that Pete Sampras wasn't more gracious in defeat the last two times they played. Sampras attributed his loss in the finals of August's ATP Championships to a questionable line call on match point. After losing to Rafter in the U.S. Open semis, Sampras noted that he was winning before pulling a quadriceps muscle. "He has become a bit of a crybaby," says Rafter, fanning the flames of a rivalry that men's tennis badly needs.

1997 Davis Cup World Group Final

Sweden d. United States 5–0, Nov. 28–30 in Göteborg, Sweden
Jonas Bjorkman (Swe) d. Michael Chang (U.S.) 7–5, 1–6, 6–3, 6–3
Magnus Larsson (Swe) d. Pete Sampras (U.S.) 3–6, 7–6 (7–1), 2–1, ret.
Jonas Bjorkman/Nicklas Kulti (Swe) d. Todd Martin/Jonathan Stark (U.S.)
6–4, 6–4, 6–4
Jonas Bjorkman (Swe) d. Jonathan Stark (U.S.) 6–1, 6–1
Magnus Larsson (Swe) def. Michael Chang (U.S.) 7–6 (7–4), 6–7 (6–8), 6–4

1998 Davis Cup World Group Tournament

FIRST ROUND

Sweden d. Slovakia 3–2
Italy d. India, 4–1
Switzerland d. Czech Republic 3–2
Belgium d. Netherlands 3–2
United States d. Russia 3–2
Germany d. South Africa 5–0
Spain d. Brazil 3–2
Zimbabwe d. Australia 3–2

QUARTERFINAL ROUND

United States d. Belgium 4–1
Sweden d. Germany 3–2
Spain d. Switzerland 4–1
Italy d. Zimbabwe 5–0

SEMIFINALS

Sweden d. Spain 4–1
Jonas Bjorkman (Swe) d. Alex Corretja (Spa)
6–3, 7–5, 6–7 (5–7), 6–3
Thomas Johansson (Swe) d. Carlos Moya (Spa)
7–5, 7–6 (7–4), 7–6 (8–6)
Jonas Bjorkman/Nicklas Kulti (Swe) d.
Javier Sanchez/Julian Alonso (Spa) 6–2, 6–2, 6–2
Julian Alonso (Spa) d.Thomas Johansson (Swe)
6–1, 7–6 (7–3)
Jonas Bjorkman (Swe) d.Carlos Moya (Spa)
6–3, 7–5

Italy d. United States 4–1
Andrea Gaudenzi (Ita) d. Jan-Michael Gambill (U.S.)
6–2, 0–6, 7–6 (7–0), 7–6 (7–4)
Davide Sanguinetti (Ita) bt Todd Martin (U.S.)
7–6 (7–0), 6–3, 7–6 (10–8)
Andrea Gaudenzi/Diego Nargiso (Ita) d.
Todd Martin/Justin Gimelstob (U.S.)
6–4, 7–6 (7–3), 5–7, 2–6, 6–3
Gianluca Pozzi (Ita) d. Justin Gimelstob (U.S.)
7–6 (7–4), 7–5
Jan-Michael Gambill (U.S.) d. Davide Sanguinetti (Ita)
4–6, 6–3, 6–3

FINAL: Italy versus Sweden to be held Dec. 4–6, in Turin, Italy.

1998 Federation Cup World Group Tournament

FIRST ROUND

United States d. Netherlands 5–0
Spain d. Germany 3–2
France d. Belgium 3–2
Switzerland d. Czech Republic 4–1

SEMIFINALS

Spain d. United States 3–2
Arantxa Sánchez Vicario (Spa) d. Lisa Raymond (U.S.)
6–7 (7–4), 6–3, 6–0
Monica Seles (U.S.) d. Conchita Martinez (Spa)
6–3, 3–6, 6–1
Monica Seles (U.S.) d. Arantxa Sánchez Vicario (Spa)
6–4, 6–0
Conchita Martinez (Spa) d. Lisa Raymond (U.S.)
7–6 (7–1), 6–4
Conchita Martinez/Arantxa Sánchez Vicario (Spa) d.
Lisa Raymond/Mary Joe Fernandez (U.S.)
6–4, 6–7 (5–7), 11–9

Switzerland d. France 5–0
Martina Hingis (Swi) d. Julie Halard-Decugis (Fra)
7–5, 6–1
Patty Schnyder (Swi) d. Amelie Mauresmo (Fra)
7–5, 2–6, 6–3
Martina Hingis (Swi) d. Amelie Mauresmo (Fra)
6–7 (6–8), 6–4, 6–2
Patty Schnyder (Swi) d. Julie Halard-Decugis (Fra)
6–3, 6–2
Patty Schnyder/Emmanuelle Gagliardi (Swi) d.
Alexandra Fusai/Nathalie Tauziat (Fra)
2–6, 6–3, 6–3

FINAL

Spain d. Switzerland 3–2, Sept. 18–20 in Geneva
Arantxa Sánchez Vicario (Spa) d. Patty Schnyder (Swi) 6–2, 3–6, 6–2
Martina Hingis (Swi) d. Conchita Martinez (Spa) 6–4, 6–4
Martina Hingis (Swi) d. Arantxa Sánchez Vicario (Spa) 7–6 (7–5), 6–3
Conchita Martinez (Spa) d. Patty Schnyder (Swi) 6–3, 2–6, 9–7
Conchita Martinez/Arantxa Sánchez Vicario (Spa) d. Martina Hingis/Patty Schnyder (Swi) 6–0, 6–2

Grand Slam Tournaments

MEN

Australian Championships

Year	Winner	Finalist	Score
1905	Rodney Heath	A. H. Curtis	4–6, 6–3, 6–4, 6–4
1906	Tony Wilding	H. A. Parker	6–0, 6–4, 6–4
1907	Horace M. Rice	H. A. Parker	6–3, 6–4, 6–4
1908	Fred Alexander	A. W. Dunlop	3–6, 3–6, 6–0, 6–2, 6–3
1909	Tony Wilding	E. F. Parker	6–1, 7–5, 6–2
1910	Rodney Heath	Horace M. Rice	6–4, 6–3, 6–2
1911	Norman Brookes	Horace M. Rice	6–1, 6–2, 6–3
1912	J. Cecil Parke	A. E. Beamish	3–6, 6–3, 1–6, 6–1, 7–5
1913	E. F. Parker	H. A. Parker	2–6, 6–1, 6–2, 6–3
1914	Pat O'Hara Wood	G. L. Patterson	6–4, 6–3, 5–7, 6–1
1915	Francis G. Lowe	Horace M. Rice	4–6, 6–1, 6–1, 6–4
1916–18	No tournament		
1919	A. R. F. Kingscote	E. O. Pockley	6–4, 6–0, 6–3
1920	Pat O'Hara Wood	Ron Thomas	6–3, 4–6, 6–8, 6–1, 6–3
1921	Rhys H. Gemmell	A. Hedeman	7–5, 6–1, 6–4
1922	Pat O'Hara Wood	Gerald Patterson	6–0, 3–6, 3–6, 6–3, 6–2
1923	Pat O'Hara Wood	C. B. St John	6–1, 6–1, 6–3
1924	James Anderson	R. E. Schlesinger	6–3, 6–4, 3–6, 5–7, 6–3
1925	James Anderson	Gerald Patterson	11–9, 2–6, 6–2, 6–3
1926	John Hawkes	J. Willard	6–1, 6–3, 6–1
1927	Gerald Patterson	John Hawkes	3–6, 6–4, 3–6, 18–16, 6–3
1928	Jean Borotra	R. O. Cummings	6–4, 6–1, 4–6, 5–7, 6–3
1929	John C. Gregory	R. E. Schlesinger	6–2, 6–2, 5–7, 7–5
1930	Gar Moon	Harry C. Hopman	6–3, 6–1, 6–3
1931	Jack Crawford	Harry C. Hopman	6–4, 6–2, 2–6, 6–1
1932	Jack Crawford	Harry C. Hopman	4–6, 6–3, 3–6, 6–3, 6–1
1933	Jack Crawford	Keith Gledhill	2–6, 7–5, 6–3, 6–2
1934	Fred Perry	Jack Crawford	6–3, 7–5, 6–1
1935	Jack Crawford	Fred Perry	2–6, 6–4, 6–4, 6–4
1936	Adrian Quist	Jack Crawford	6–2, 6–3, 4–6, 3–6, 9–7
1937	Vivian B. McGrath	John Bromwich	6–3, 1–6, 6–0, 2–6, 6–1
1938	Don Budge	John Bromwich	6–4, 6–2, 6–1
1939	John Bromwich	Adrian Quist	6–4, 6–1, 6–3
1940	Adrian Quist	Jack Crawford	6–3, 6–1, 6–2
1941–45	No tournament		
1946	John Bromwich	Dinny Pails	5–7, 6–3, 7–5, 3–6, 6–2
1947	Dinny Pails	John Bromwich	4–6, 6–4, 3–6, 7–5, 8–6
1948	Adrian Quist	John Bromwich	6–4, 3–6, 6–3, 2–6, 6–3
1949	Frank Sedgman	Ken McGregor	6–3, 6–3, 6–2
1950	Frank Sedgman	Ken McGregor	6–3, 6–4, 4–6, 6–1
1951	Richard Savitt	Ken McGregor	6–3, 2–6, 6–3, 6–1
1952	Ken McGregor	Frank Sedgman	7–5, 12–10, 2–6, 6–2
1953	Ken Rosewall	Mervyn Rose	6–0, 6–3, 6–4
1954	Mervyn Rose	Rex Hartwig	6–2, 0–6, 6–4, 6–2
1955	Ken Rosewall	Lew Hoad	9–7, 6–4, 6–4
1956	Lew Hoad	Ken Rosewall	6–4, 3–6, 6–4, 7–5
1957	Ashley Cooper	Neale Fraser	6–3, 9–11, 6–4, 6–2
1958	Ashley Cooper	Mal Anderson	7–5, 6–3, 6–4
1959	Alex Olmedo	Neale Fraser	6–1, 6–2, 3–6, 6–3
1960	Rod Laver	Neale Fraser	5–7, 3–6, 6–3, 8–6, 8–6
1961	Roy Emerson	Rod Laver	1–6, 6–3, 7–5, 6–4
1962	Rod Laver	Roy Emerson	8–6, 0–6, 6–4, 6–4
1963	Roy Emerson	Ken Fletcher	6–3, 6–3, 6–1
1964	Roy Emerson	Fred Stolle	6–3, 6–4, 6–2
1965	Roy Emerson	Fred Stolle	7–9, 2–6, 6–4, 7–5, 6–1
1966	Roy Emerson	Arthur Ashe	6–4, 6–8, 6–2, 6–3
1967	Roy Emerson	Arthur Ashe	6–4, 6–1, 6–1
1968	Bill Bowrey	Juan Gisbert	7–5, 2–6, 9–7, 6–4
1969*	Rod Laver	Andres Gimeno	6–3, 6–4, 7–5

*Became Open (amateur and professional) in 1969.

Australian Championships *(Cont.)*

Year	Winner	Finalist	Score
1970	Arthur Ashe	Dick Crealy	6–4, 9–7, 6–2
1971	Ken Rosewall	Arthur Ashe	6–1, 7–5, 6–3
1972	Ken Rosewall	Mal Anderson	7–6, 6–3, 7–5
1973	John Newcombe	Onny Parun	6–3, 6–7, 7–5, 6–1
1974	Jimmy Connors	Phil Dent	7–6, 6–4, 4–6, 6–3
1975	John Newcombe	Jimmy Connors	7–5, 3–6, 6–4, 7–5
1976	Mark Edmondson	John Newcombe	6–7, 6–3, 7–6, 6–1
1977 (Jan)	Roscoe Tanner	Guillermo Vilas	6–3, 6–3, 6–3
1977 (Dec)	Vitas Gerulaitis	John Lloyd	6–3, 7–6, 5–7, 3–6, 6–2
1978	Guillermo Vilas	John Marks	6–4, 6–4, 3–6, 6–3
1979	Guillermo Vilas	John Sadri	7–6, 6–3, 6–2
1980	Brian Teacher	Kim Warwick	7–5, 7–6, 6–3
1981	Johan Kriek	Steve Denton	6–2, 7–6, 6–7, 6–4
1982	Johan Kriek	Steve Denton	6–3, 6–3, 6–2
1983	Mats Wilander	Ivan Lendl	6–1, 6–4, 6–4
1984	Mats Wilander	Kevin Curren	6–7, 6–4, 7–6, 6–2
1985 (Dec)	Stefan Edberg	Mats Wilander	6–4, 6–3, 6–3
1987 (Jan)	Stefan Edberg	Pat Cash	6–3, 6–4, 3–6, 5–7, 6–3
1988	Mats Wilander	Pat Cash	6–3, 6–7, 3–6, 6–1, 8–6
1989	Ivan Lendl	Miloslav Mecir	6–2, 6–2, 6–2
1990	Ivan Lendl	Stefan Edberg	4–6, 7–6, 5–2, ret.
1991	Boris Becker	Ivan Lendl	1–6, 6–4, 6–4, 6–4
1992	Jim Courier	Stefan Edberg	6–3, 3–6, 6–4, 6–2
1993	Jim Courier	Stefan Edberg	6–2, 6–1, 2–6, 7–5
1994	Pete Sampras	Todd Martin	7–6 (7–4), 6–4, 6–4
1995	Andre Agassi	Pete Sampras	4–6, 6–1, 7–6 (8–6), 6–4
1996	Boris Becker	Michael Chang	6–2, 6–4, 2–6, 6–2
1997	Pete Sampras	Carlos Moya	6–2, 6–3, 6–3
1998	Petr Korda	Marcelo Rios	6–2, 6–2, 6–2

French Championships

Year	Winner	Finalist	Score
1925†	Rene Lacoste	Jean Borotra	7–5, 6–1, 6–4
1926	Henri Cochet	Rene Lacoste	6–2, 6–4, 6–3
1927	Rene Lacoste	Bill Tilden	6–4, 4–6, 5–7, 6–3, 11–9
1928	Henri Cochet	Rene Lacoste	5–7, 6–3, 6–1, 6–3
1929	Rene Lacoste	Jean Borotra	6–3, 2–6, 6–0, 2–6, 8–6
1930	Henri Cochet	Bill Tilden	3–6, 8–6, 6–3, 6–1
1931	Jean Borotra	Claude Boussus	2–6, 6–4, 7–5, 6–4
1932	Henri Cochet	Giorgio de Stefani	6–0, 6–4, 4–6, 6–3
1933	Jack Crawford	Henri Cochet	8–6, 6–1, 6–3
1934	Gottfried von Cramm	Jack Crawford	6–4, 7–9, 3–6, 7–5, 6–3
1935	Fred Perry	Gottfried von Cramm	6–3, 3–6, 6–1, 6–3
1936	Gottfried von Cramm	Fred Perry	6–0, 2–6, 6–2, 2–6, 6–0
1937	Henner Henkel	Henry Austin	6–1, 6–4, 6–3
1938	Don Budge	Roderick Menzel	6–3, 6–2, 6–4
1939	Don McNeill	Bobby Riggs	7–5, 6–0, 6–3
1940	No tournament		
1941‡	Bernard Destremau	n/a	n/a
1942‡	Bernard Destremau	n/a	n/a
1943‡	Yvon Petra	n/a	n/a
1944‡	Yvon Petra	n/a	n/a
1945‡	Yvon Petra	Bernard Destremau	7–5, 6–4, 6–2
1946	Marcel Bernard	Jaroslav Drobny	3–6, 2–6, 6–1, 6–4, 6–3
1947	Joseph Asboth	Eric Sturgess	8–6, 7–5, 6–4
1948	Frank Parker	Jaroslav Drobny	6–4, 7–5, 5–7, 8–6
1949	Frank Parker	Budge Patty	6–3, 1–6, 6–1, 6–4
1950	Budge Patty	Jaroslav Drobny	6–1, 6–2, 3–6, 5–7, 7–5
1951	Jaroslav Drobny	Eric Sturgess	6–3, 6–3, 6–3
1952	Jaroslav Drobny	Frank Sedgman	6–2, 6–0, 3–6, 6–4
1953	Ken Rosewall	Vic Seixas	6–3, 6–4, 1–6, 6–2

†1925 was the first year that entries were accepted from all countries.
‡From 1941 to 1945 the event was called Tournoi de France and was closed to all foreigners.

French Championships *(Cont.)*

Year	Winner	Finalist	Score
1954	Tony Trabert	Arthur Larsen	6–4, 7–5, 6–1
1955	Tony Trabert	Sven Davidson	2–6, 6–1, 6–4, 6–2
1956	Lew Hoad	Sven Davidson	6–4, 8–6, 6–3
1957	Sven Davidson	Herbie Flam	6–3, 6–4, 6–4
1958	Mervyn Rose	Luis Ayala	6–3, 6–4, 6–4
1959	Nicola Pietrangeli	Ian Vermaak	3–6, 6–3, 6–4, 6–1
1960	Nicola Pietrangeli	Luis Ayala	3–6, 6–3, 6–4, 4–6, 6–3
1961	Manuel Santana	Nicola Pietrangeli	4–6, 6–1, 3–6, 6–0, 6–2
1962	Rod Laver	Roy Emerson	3–6, 2–6, 6–3, 9–7, 6–2
1963	Roy Emerson	Pierre Darmon	3–6, 6–1, 6–4, 6–4
1964	Manuel Santana	Nicola Pietrangeli	6–3, 6–1, 4–6, 7–5
1965	Fred Stolle	Tony Roche	3–6, 6–0, 6–2, 6–3
1966	Tony Roche	Istvan Gulyas	6–1, 6–4, 7–5
1967	Roy Emerson	Tony Roche	6–1, 6–4, 2–6, 6–2
1968*	Ken Rosewall	Rod Laver	6–3, 6–1, 2–6, 6–2
1969	Rod Laver	Ken Rosewall	6–4, 6–3, 6–4
1970	Jan Kodes	Zeljko Franulovic	6–2, 6–4, 6–0
1971	Jan Kodes	Ilie Nastase	8–6, 6–2, 2–6, 7–5
1972	Andres Gimeno	Patrick Proisy	4–6, 6–3, 6–1, 6–1
1973	Ilie Nastase	Nikki Pilic	6–3, 6–3, 6–0
1974	Bjorn Borg	Manuel Orantes	6–7, 6–0, 6–1, 6–1
1975	Bjorn Borg	Guillermo Vilas	6–2, 6–3, 6–4
1976	Adriano Panatta	Harold Solomon	6–1, 6–4, 4–6, 7–6
1977	Guillermo Vilas	Brian Gottfried	6–0, 6–3, 6–0
1978	Bjorn Borg	Guillermo Vilas	6–1, 6–1, 6–3
1979	Bjorn Borg	Victor Pecci	6–3, 6–1, 6–7, 6–4
1980	Bjorn Borg	Vitas Gerulaitis	6–4, 6–1, 6–2
1981	Bjorn Borg	Ivan Lendl	6–1, 4–6, 6–2, 3–6, 6–1
1982	Mats Wilander	Guillermo Vilas	1–6, 7–6, 6–0, 6–4
1983	Yannick Noah	Mats Wilander	6–2, 7–5, 7–6
1984	Ivan Lendl	John McEnroe	3–6, 2–6, 6–4, 7–5, 7–5
1985	Mats Wilander	Ivan Lendl	3–6, 6–4, 6–2, 6–2
1986	Ivan Lendl	Mikael Pernfors	6–3, 6–2, 6–4
1987	Ivan Lendl	Mats Wilander	7–5, 6–2, 3–6, 7–6
1988	Mats Wilander	Henri Leconte	7–5, 6–2, 6–1
1989	Michael Chang	Stefan Edberg	6–1, 3–6, 4–6, 6–4, 6–2
1990	Andres Gomez	Andre Agassi	6–3, 2–6, 6–4, 6–4
1991	Jim Courier	Andre Agassi	3–6, 6–4, 2–6, 6–1, 6–4
1992	Jim Courier	Petr Korda	7–5, 6–2, 6–1
1993	Sergi Bruguera	Jim Courier	6–4, 2–6, 6–2, 3–6, 6–3
1994	Sergi Bruguera	Alberto Berasategui	6–3, 7–5, 2–6, 6–1
1995	Thomas Muster	Michael Chang	7–5, 6–2, 6–4
1996	Yevgeny Kafelnikov	Michael Stich	7–6 (7–4), 7–5, 7–6 (7–4)
1997	Gustavo Kuerten	Sergi Bruguera	6–3, 6–4, 6–2
1998	Carlos Moya	Alex Corretja	6–3, 7–5, 6–3

*Became Open (amateur and professional) in 1968 but closed to contract professionals in 1972.

Wimbledon Championships

Year	Winner	Finalist	Score
1877	Spencer W. Gore	William C. Marshall	6–1, 6–2, 6–4
1878	P. Frank Hadow	Spencer W. Gore	7–5, 6–1, 9–7
1879	John T. Hartley	V. St Leger Gould	6–2, 6–4, 6–2
1880	John T. Hartley	Herbert F. Lawford	6–0, 6–2, 2–6, 6–3
1881	William Renshaw	John T. Hartley	6–0, 6–2, 6–1
1882	William Renshaw	Ernest Renshaw	6–1, 2–6, 4–6, 6–2, 6–2
1883	William Renshaw	Ernest Renshaw	2–6, 6–3, 6–3, 4–6, 6–3
1884	William Renshaw	Herbert F. Lawford	6–0, 6–4, 9–7
1885	William Renshaw	Herbert F. Lawford	7–5, 6–2, 4–6, 7–5
1886	William Renshaw	Herbert F. Lawford	6–0, 5–7, 6–3, 6–4
1887	Herbert F. Lawford	Ernest Renshaw	1–6, 6–3, 3–6, 6–4, 6–4
1888	Ernest Renshaw	Herbert F. Lawford	6–3, 7–5, 6–0
1889	William Renshaw	Ernest Renshaw	6–4, 6–1, 3–6, 6–0
1890	William J. Hamilton	William Renshaw	6–8, 6–2, 3–6, 6–1, 6–1
1891	Wilfred Baddeley	Joshua Pim	6–4, 1–6, 7–5, 6–0
1892	Wilfred Baddeley	Joshua Pim	4–6, 6–3, 6–3, 6–2

Wimbledon Championship *(Cont.)*

Year	Winner	Finalist	Score
1893	Joshua Pim	Wilfred Baddeley	3–6, 6–1, 6–3, 6–2
1894	Joshua Pim	Wilfred Baddeley	10–8, 6–2, 8–6
1895	Wilfred Baddeley	Wilberforce V. Eaves	4–6, 2–6, 8–6, 6–2, 6–3
1896	Harold S. Mahoney	Wilfred Baddeley	6–2, 6–8, 5–7, 8–6, 6–3
1897	Reggie F. Doherty	Harold S. Mahoney	6–4, 6–4, 6–3
1898	Reggie F. Doherty	H. Laurie Doherty	6–3, 6–3, 2–6, 5–7, 6–1
1899	Reggie F. Doherty	Arthur W. Gore	1–6, 4–6, 6–2, 6–3, 6–3
1900	Reggie F. Doherty	Sidney H. Smith	6–8, 6–3, 6–1, 6–2
1901	Arthur W. Gore	Reggie F. Doherty	4–6, 7–5, 6–4, 6–4
1902	H. Laurie Doherty	Arthur W. Gore	6–4, 6–3, 3–6, 6–0
1903	H. Laurie Doherty	Frank L. Riseley	7–5, 6–3, 6–0
1904	H. Laurie Doherty	Frank L. Riseley	6–1, 7–5, 8–6
1905	H. Laurie Doherty	Norman E. Brookes	8–6, 6–2, 6–4
1906	H. Laurie Doherty	Frank L. Riseley	6–4, 4–6, 6–2, 6–3
1907	Norman E. Brookes	Arthur W. Gore	6–4, 6–2, 6–2
1908	Arthur W. Gore	H. Roper Barrett	6–3, 6–2, 4–6, 3–6, 6–4
1909	Arthur W. Gore	M. J. G. Ritchie	6–8, 1–6, 6–2, 6–2, 6–2
1910	Anthony F. Wilding	Arthur W. Gore	6–4, 7–5, 4–6, 6–2
1911	Anthony F. Wilding	H. Roper Barrett	6–4, 4–6, 2–6, 6–2 ret
1912	Anthony F. Wilding	Arthur W. Gore	6–4, 6–4, 4–6, 6–4
1913	Anthony F. Wilding	Maurice E. McLoughlin	8–6, 6–3, 10–8
1914	Norman E. Brookes	Anthony F. Wilding	6–4, 6–4, 7–5
1915–18	No tournament		
1919	Gerald L. Patterson	Norman E. Brookes	6–3, 7–5, 6–2
1920	Bill Tilden	Gerald L. Patterson	2–6, 6–3, 6–2, 6–4
1921	Bill Tilden	Brian I. C. Norton	4–6, 2–6, 6–1, 6–0, 7–5
1922	Gerald L. Patterson	Randolph Lycett	6–3, 6–4, 6–2
1923	Bill Johnston	Francis T. Hunter	6–0, 6–3, 6–1
1924	Jean Borotra	Rene Lacoste	6–1, 3–6, 6–1, 3–6, 6–4
1925	Rene Lacoste	Jean Borotra	6–3, 6–3, 4–6, 8–6
1926	Jean Borotra	Howard Kinsey	8–6, 6–1, 6–3
1927	Henri Cochet	Jean Borotra	4–6, 4–6, 6–3, 6–4, 7–5
1928	Rene Lacoste	Henri Cochet	6–1, 4–6, 6–4, 6–2
1929	Henri Cochet	Jean Borotra	6–4, 6–3, 6–4
1930	Bill Tilden	Wilmer Allison	6–3, 9–7, 6–4
1931	Sidney B. Wood Jr	Francis X. Shields	walkover
1932	Ellsworth Vines	Henry Austin	6–4, 6–2, 6–0
1933	Jack Crawford	Ellsworth Vines	4–6, 11–9, 6–2, 2–6, 6–4
1934	Fred Perry	Jack Crawford	6–3, 6–0, 7–5
1935	Fred Perry	Gottfried von Cramm	6–2, 6–4, 6–4
1936	Fred Perry	Gottfried von Cramm	6–1, 6–1, 6–0
1937	Don Budge	Gottfried von Cramm	6–3, 6–4, 6–2
1938	Don Budge	Henry Austin	6–1, 6–0, 6–3
1939	Bobby Riggs	Elwood Cooke	2–6, 8–6, 3–6, 6–3, 6–2
1940–45	No tournament		
1946	Yvon Petra	Geoff E. Brown	6–2, 6–4, 7–9, 5–7, 6–4
1947	Jack Kramer	Tom P. Brown	6–1, 6–3, 6–2
1948	Bob Falkenburg	John Bromwich	7–5, 0–6, 6–2, 3–6, 7–5
1949	Ted Schroeder	Jaroslav Drobny	3–6, 6–0, 6–3, 4–6, 6–4
1950	Budge Patty	Frank Sedgman	6–1, 8–10, 6–2, 6–3
1951	Dick Savitt	Ken McGregor	6–4, 6–4, 6–4
1952	Frank Sedgman	Jaroslav Drobny	4–6, 6–3, 6–2, 6–3
1953	Vic Seixas	Kurt Nielsen	9–7, 6–3, 6–4
1954	Jaroslav Drobny	Ken Rosewall	13–11, 4–6, 6–2, 9–7
1955	Tony Trabert	Kurt Nielsen	6–3, 7–5, 6–1
1956	Lew Hoad	Ken Rosewall	6–2, 4–6, 7–5, 6–4
1957	Lew Hoad	Ashley Cooper	6–2, 6–1, 6–2
1958	Ashley Cooper	Neale Fraser	3–6, 6–3, 6–4, 13–11
1959	Alex Olmedo	Rod Laver	6–4, 6–3, 6–4
1960	Neale Fraser	Rod Laver	6–4, 3–6, 9–7, 7–5
1961	Rod Laver	Chuck McKinley	6–3, 6–1, 6–4
1962	Rod Laver	Martin Mulligan	6–2, 6–2, 6–1
1963	Chuck McKinley	Fred Stolle	9–7, 6–1, 6–4
1964	Roy Emerson	Fred Stolle	6–4, 12–10, 4–6, 6–3
1965	Roy Emerson	Fred Stolle	6–2, 6–4, 6–4
1966	Manuel Santana	Dennis Ralston	6–4, 11–9, 6–4

Wimbledon Championships *(Cont.)*

Year	Winner	Finalist	Score
1967	John Newcombe	Wilhelm Bungert	6–3, 6–1, 6–1
1968*	Rod Laver	Tony Roche	6–3, 6–4, 6–2
1969	Rod Laver	John Newcombe	6–4, 5–7, 6–4, 6–4
1970	John Newcombe	Ken Rosewall	5–7, 6–3, 6–2, 3–6, 6–1
1971	John Newcombe	Stan Smith	6–3, 5–7, 2–6, 6–4, 6–4
1972	Stan Smith	Ilie Nastase	4–6, 6–3, 6–3, 4–6, 7–5
1973	Jan Kodes	Alex Metreveli	6–1, 9–8, 6–3
1974	Jimmy Connors	Ken Rosewall	6–1, 6–1, 6–4
1975	Arthur Ashe	Jimmy Connors	6–1, 6–1, 5–7, 6–4
1976	Bjorn Borg	Ilie Nastase	6–4, 6–2, 9–7
1977	Bjorn Borg	Jimmy Connors	3–6, 6–2, 6–1, 5–7, 6–4
1978	Bjorn Borg	Jimmy Connors	6–2, 6–2, 6–3
1979	Bjorn Borg	Roscoe Tanner	6–7, 6–1, 3–6, 6–3, 6–4
1980	Bjorn Borg	John McEnroe	1–6, 7–5, 6–3, 6–7, 8–6
1981	John McEnroe	Bjorn Borg	4–6, 7–6, 7–6, 6–4
1982	Jimmy Connors	John McEnroe	3–6, 6–3, 6–7, 7–6, 6–4
1983	John McEnroe	Chris Lewis	6–2, 6–2, 6–2
1984	John McEnroe	Jimmy Connors	6–1, 6–1, 6–2
1985	Boris Becker	Kevin Curren	6–3, 6–7, 7–6, 6–4
1986	Boris Becker	Ivan Lendl	6–4, 6–3, 7–5
1987	Pat Cash	Ivan Lendl	7–6, 6–2, 7–5
1988	Stefan Edberg	Boris Becker	4–6, 7–6, 6–4, 6–2
1989	Boris Becker	Stefan Edberg	6–0, 7–6, 6–4
1990	Stefan Edberg	Boris Becker	6–2, 6–2, 3–6, 3–6, 6–4
1991	Michael Stich	Boris Becker	6–4, 7–6, 6–4
1992	Andre Agassi	Goran Ivanisevic	6–7, 6–4, 6–4, 1–6, 6–4
1993	Pete Sampras	Jim Courier	7–6 (7–3), 7–6 (8–6), 3–6, 6–3
1994	Pete Sampras	Goran Ivanisevic	7–6 (7–2), 7–6 (7–5), 6–0
1995	Pete Sampras	Boris Becker	6–7 (5–7), 6–2, 6–4, 6–2
1996	Richard Krajicek	MaliVai Washington	6–3, 6–4, 6–3
1997	Pete Sampras	Cedric Pioline	6–4, 6–2, 6–4
1998	Pete Sampras	Goran Ivanisevic	6–7 (2–7), 7–6 (11–9), 6–4, 3–6, 6–2

*Became Open (amateur and professional) in 1968 but closed to contract professionals in 1972.

Note: Prior to 1922 the tournament was run on a challenge-round system. The previous year's winner "stood out" of an All Comers event, which produced a challenger to play him for the title.

United States Championships

Year	Winner	Finalist	Score
1881	Richard D. Sears	W.E. Glyn	6–0, 6–3, 6–2
1882	Richard D. Sears	C.M. Clark	6–1, 6–4, 6–0
1883	Richard D. Sears	James Dwight	6–2, 6–0, 9–7
1884	Richard D. Sears	H.A. Taylor	6–0, 1–6, 6–0, 6–2
1885	Richard D. Sears	G.M. Brinley	6–3, 4–6, 6–0, 6–3
1886	Richard D. Sears	R.L. Beeckman	4–6, 6–1, 6–3, 6–4
1887	Richard D. Sears	H.W. Slocum Jr	6–1, 6–3, 6–2
1888‡	H. W. Slocum Jr	H.A. Taylor	6–4, 6–1, 6–0
1889	H. W. Slocum Jr	Q.A. Shaw	6–3, 6–1, 4–6, 6–2
1890	Oliver S. Campbell	H.W. Slocum Jr	6–2, 4–6, 6–3, 6–1
1891	Oliver S. Campbell	Clarence Hobart	2–6, 7–5, 7–9, 6–1, 6–2
1892	Oliver S. Campbell	Frederick H. Hovey	7–5, 3–6, 6–3, 7–5
1893‡	Robert D. Wrenn	Frederick H. Hovey	6–4, 3–6, 6–4, 6–4
1894	Robert D. Wrenn	M.F. Goodbody	6–8, 6–1, 6–4, 6–4
1895	Frederick H. Hovey	Robert D. Wrenn	6–3, 6–2, 6–4
1896	Robert D. Wrenn	Frederick H. Hovey	7–5, 3–6, 6–0, 1–6, 6–1
1897‡	Robert D. Wrenn	Wilberforce V. Eaves	4–6, 8–6, 6–3, 2–6, 6–2
1898‡	Malcolm D. Whitman	Dwight F. Davis	3–6, 6–2, 6–2, 6–1
1899	Malcolm D. Whitman	J. Parmly Paret	6–1, 6–2, 3–6, 7–5
1900	Malcolm D. Whitman	William A. Larned	6–4, 1–6, 6–2, 6–2
1901‡	William A. Larned	Beals C. Wright	6–2, 6–8, 6–4, 6–4
1902	William A. Larned	Reggie F. Doherty	4–6, 6–2, 6–4, 8–6
1903	H. Laurie Doherty	William A. Larned	6–0, 6–3, 10–8
1904‡	Holcombe Ward	William J. Clothier	10–8, 6–4, 9–7
1905	Beals C. Wright	Holcombe Ward	6–2, 6–1, 11–9

‡No challenge round played.

United States Championships *(Cont.)*

Year	Winner	Finalist	Score
1906	William J. Clothier	Beals C. Wright	6–3, 6–0, 6–4
1907‡	William A. Larned	Robert LeRoy	6–2, 6–2, 6–4
1908	William A. Larned	Beals C. Wright	6–1, 6–2, 8–6
1909	William A. Larned	William J. Clothier	6–1, 6–2, 5–7, 1–6, 6–1
1910	William A. Larned	Thomas C. Bundy	6–1, 5–7, 6–0, 6–8, 6–1
1911	William A. Larned	Maurice E. McLoughlin	6–4, 6–4, 6–2
1912†	Maurice E. McLoughlin	Bill Johnson	3–6, 2–6, 6–2, 6–4, 6–2
1913	Maurice E. McLoughlin	Richard N. Williams	6–4, 5–7, 6–3, 6–1
1914	Richard N. Williams	Maurice E. McLoughlin	6–3, 8–6, 10–8
1915	Bill Johnston	Maurice E. McLoughlin	1–6, 6–0, 7–5, 10–8
1916	Richard N. Williams	Bill Johnston	4–6, 6–4, 0–6, 6–2, 6–4
1917#	R.L. Murray	N. W. Niles	5–7, 8–6, 6–3, 6–3
1918	R.L. Murray	Bill Tilden	6–3, 6–1, 7–5
1919	Bill Johnston	Bill Tilden	6–4, 6–4, 6–3
1920	Bill Tilden	Bill Johnston	6–1, 1–6, 7–5, 5–7, 6–3
1921	Bill Tilden	Wallace F. Johnson	6–1, 6–3, 6–1
1922	Bill Tilden	Bill Johnston	4–6, 3–6, 6–2, 6–3, 6–4
1923	Bill Tilden	Bill Johnston	6–4, 6–1, 6–4
1924	Bill Tilden	Bill Johnston	6–1, 9–7, 6–2
1925	Bill Tilden	Bill Johnston	4–6, 11–9, 6–3, 4–6, 6–3
1926	Rene Lacoste	Jean Borotra	6–4, 6–0, 6–4
1927	Rene Lacoste	Bill Tilden	11–9, 6–3, 11–9
1928	Henri Cochet	Francis T. Hunter	4–6, 6–4, 3–6, 7–5, 6–3
1929	Bill Tilden	Francis T. Hunter	3–6, 6–3, 4–6, 6–2, 6–4
1930	John H. Doeg	Francis X. Shields	10–8, 1–6, 6–4, 16–14
1931	Ellsworth Vines	George M. Lott Jr	7–9, 6–3, 9–7, 7–5
1932	Ellsworth Vines	Henri Cochet	6–4, 6–4, 6–4
1933	Fred Perry	Jack Crawford	6–3, 11–13, 4–6, 6–0, 6–1
1934	Fred Perry	Wilmer L. Allison	6–4, 6–3, 1–6, 8–6
1935	Wilmer L. Allison	Sidney B. Wood Jr	6–2, 6–2, 6–3
1936	Fred Perry	Don Budge	2–6, 6–2, 8–6, 1–6, 10–8
1937	Don Budge	Gottfried von Cramm	6–1, 7–9, 6–1, 3–6, 6–1
1938	Don Budge	Gene Mako	6–3, 6–8, 6–2, 6–1
1939	Bobby Riggs	Welby Van Horn	6–4, 6–2, 6–4
1940	Don McNeill	Bobby Riggs	4–6, 6–8, 6–3, 6–3, 7–5
1941	Bobby Riggs	Francis Kovacs II	5–7, 6–1, 6–3, 6–3
1942	Ted Schroeder	Frank Parker	8–6, 7–5, 3–6, 4–6, 6–2
1943	Joseph R. Hunt	Jack Kramer	6–3, 6–8, 10–8, 6–0
1944	Frank Parker	William F. Talbert	6–4, 3–6, 6–3, 6–3
1945	Frank Parker	William F. Talbert	14–12, 6–1, 6–2
1946	Jack Kramer	Tom P. Brown	9–7, 6–3, 6–0
1947	Jack Kramer	Frank Parker	4–6, 2–6, 6–1, 6–0, 6–3
1948	Pancho Gonzales	Eric W. Sturgess	6–2, 6–3, 14–12
1949	Pancho Gonzales	Ted Schroeder	16–18, 2–6, 6–1, 6–2, 6–4
1950	Arthur Larsen	Herbie Flam	6–3, 4–6, 5–7, 6–4, 6–3
1951	Frank Sedgman	Vic Seixas	6–4, 6–1, 6–1
1952	Frank Sedgman	Gardnar Mulloy	6–1, 6–2, 6–3
1953	Tony Trabert	Vic Seixas	6–3, 6–2, 6–3
1954	Vic Seixas	Rex Hartwig	3–6, 6–2, 6–4, 6–4
1955	Tony Trabert	Ken Rosewall	9–7, 6–3, 6–3
1956	Ken Rosewall	Lew Hoad	4–6, 6–2, 6–3, 6–3
1957	Mal Anderson	Ashley J. Cooper	10–8, 7–5, 6–4
1958	Ashley J. Cooper	Mal Anderson	6–2, 3–6, 4–6, 10–8, 8–6
1959	Neale Fraser	Alex Olmedo	6–3, 5–7, 6–2, 6–4
1960	Neale Fraser	Rod Laver	6–4, 6–4, 9–7
1961	Roy Emerson	Rod Laver	7–5, 6–3, 6–2
1962	Rod Laver	Roy Emerson	6–2, 6–4, 5–7, 6–4
1963	Rafael Osuna	Frank Froehling III	7–5, 6–4, 6–2
1964	Roy Emerson	Fred Stolle	6–4, 6–2, 6–4
1965	Manuel Santana	Cliff Drysdale	6–2, 7–9, 7–5, 6–1
1966	Fred Stolle	John Newcombe	4–6, 12–10, 6–3, 6–4
1967	John Newcombe	Clark Graebner	6–4, 6–4, 8–6

‡No challenge round played.

United States Championships (Cont.)

Year	Winner	Finalist	Score
1968*	Arthur Ashe	Tom Okker	14–12, 5–7, 6–3, 3–6, 6–3
1968**	Arthur Ashe	Bob Lutz	4–6, 6–3, 8–10, 6–0, 6–4
1969	Rod Laver	Tony Roche	7–9, 6–1, 6–3, 6–2
1969**	Stan Smith	Bob Lutz	9–7, 6–3, 6–1
1970	Ken Rosewall	Tony Roche	2–6, 6–4, 7–6, 6–3
1971	Stan Smith	Jan Kodes	3–6, 6–3, 6–2, 7–6
1972	Ilie Nastase	Arthur Ashe	3–6, 6–3, 6–7, 6–4, 6–3
1973	John Newcombe	Jan Kodes	6–4, 1–6, 4–6, 6–2, 6–3
1974	Jimmy Connors	Ken Rosewall	6–1, 6–0, 6–1
1975	Manuel Orantes	Jimmy Connors	6–4, 6–3, 6–3
1976	Jimmy Connors	Bjorn Borg	6–4, 3–6, 7–6, 6–4
1977	Guillermo Vilas	Jimmy Connors	2–6, 6–3, 7–6, 6–0
1978	Jimmy Connors	Bjorn Borg	6–4, 6–2, 6–2
1979	John McEnroe	Vitas Gerulaitis	7–5, 6–3, 6–3
1980	John McEnroe	Bjorn Borg	7–6, 6–1, 6–7, 5–7, 6–4
1981	John McEnroe	Bjorn Borg	4–6, 6–2, 6–4, 6–3
1982	Jimmy Connors	Ivan Lendl	6–3, 6–2, 4–6, 6–4
1983	Jimmy Connors	Ivan Lendl	6–3, 6–7, 7–5, 6–0
1984	John McEnroe	Ivan Lendl	6–3, 6–4, 6–1
1985	Ivan Lendl	John McEnroe	7–6, 6–3, 6–4
1986	Ivan Lendl	Miloslav Mecir	6–4, 6–2, 6–0
1987	Ivan Lendl	Mats Wilander	6–7, 6–0, 7–6, 6–4
1988	Mats Wilander	Ivan Lendl	6–4, 4–6, 6–3, 5–7, 6–4
1989	Boris Becker	Ivan Lendl	7–6, 1–6, 6–3, 7–6
1990	Pete Sampras	Andre Agassi	6–4, 6–3, 6–2
1991	Stefan Edberg	Jim Courier	6–2, 6–4, 6–0
1992	Stefan Edberg	Pete Sampras	3–6, 6–4, 7–6, 6–2
1993	Pete Sampras	Cedric Pioline	6–4, 6–4, 6–3
1994	Andre Agassi	Michael Stich	6–1, 7–6 (7–5), 7–5
1995	Pete Sampras	Andre Agassi	6–4, 6–3, 4–6, 7–5
1996	Pete Sampras	Michael Chang	6–1, 6–4, 7–6 (7–3)
1997	Patrick Rafter	Greg Rusedski	6–3, 6–2, 4–6, 7–5
1998	Patrick Rafter	Mark Philippoussis	6–3, 3–6, 6–2, 6–0

*Became Open (amateur and professional) in 1968.

†Challenge round abolished; #National Patriotic Tournament. **Amateur event held.

WOMEN

Australian Championships

Year	Winner	Finalist	Score
1922	Margaret Molesworth	Esna Boyd	6–3, 10–8
1923	Margaret Molesworth	Esna Boyd	6–1, 7–5
1924	Sylvia Lance	Esna Boyd	6–3, 3–6, 6–4
1925	Daphne Akhurst	Esna Boyd	1–6, 8–6, 6–4
1926	Daphne Akhurst	Esna Boyd	6–1, 6–3
1927	Esna Boyd	Sylvia Harper	5–7, 6–1, 6–2
1928	Daphne Akhurst	Esna Boyd	7–5, 6–2
1929	Daphne Akhurst	Louise Bickerton	6–1, 5–7, 6–2
1930	Daphne Akhurst	Sylvia Harper	10–8, 2–6, 7–5
1931	Coral Buttsworth	Margorie Crawford	1–6, 6–3, 6–4
1932	Coral Buttsworth	Kathrine Le Messurier	9–7, 6–4
1933	Joan Hartigan	Coral Buttsworth	6–4, 6–3
1934	Joan Hartigan	Margaret Molesworth	6–1, 6–4
1935	Dorothy Round	Nancye Wynne Bolton	1–6, 6–1, 6–3
1936	Joan Hartigan	Nancye Wynne Bolton	6–4, 6–4
1937	Nancye Wynne Bolton	Emily Westacott	6–3, 5–7, 6–4
1938	Dorothy Bundy	D. Stevenson	6–3, 6–2
1939	Emily Westacott	Nell Hopman	6–1, 6–2
1940	Nancye Wynne Bolton	Thelma Coyne	5–7, 6–4, 6–0
1941–45	No tournament		
1946	Nancye Wynne Bolton	Joyce Fitch	6–4, 6–4
1947	Nancye Wynne Bolton	Nell Hopman	6–3, 6–2
1948	Nancye Wynne Bolton	Marie Toorney	6–3, 6–1

Australian Championships *(Cont.)*

Year	Winner	Finalist	Score
1949	Doris Hart	Nancye Wynne Bolton	6–3, 6–4
1950	Louise Brough	Doris Hart	6–4, 3–6, 6–4
1951	Nancye Wynne Bolton	Thelma Long	6–1, 7–5
1952	Thelma Long	H. Angwin	6–2, 6–3
1953	Maureen Connolly	Julia Sampson	6–3, 6–2
1954	Thelma Long	J. Staley	6–3, 6–4
1955	Beryl Penrose	Thelma Long	6–4, 6–3
1956	Mary Carter	Thelma Long	3–6, 6–2, 9–7
1957	Shirley Fry	Althea Gibson	6–3, 6–4
1958	Angela Mortimer	Lorraine Coghlan	6–3, 6–4
1959	Mary Carter-Reitano	Renee Schuurman	6–2, 6–3
1960	Margaret Smith	Jan Lehane	7–5, 6–2
1961	Margaret Smith	Jan Lehane	6–1, 6–4
1962	Margaret Smith	Jan Lehane	6–0, 6–2
1963	Margaret Smith	Jan Lehane	6–2, 6–2
1964	Margaret Smith	Lesley Turner	6–3, 6–2
1965	Margaret Smith	Maria Bueno	5–7, 6–4, 5–2 ret.
1966	Margaret Smith	Nancy Richey	Default
1967	Nancy Richey	Lesley Turner	6–1, 6–4
1968	Billie Jean King	Margaret Smith	6–1, 6–2
1969*	Margaret Smith Court	Billie Jean King	6–4, 6–1
1970	Margaret Smith Court	Kerry Melville Reid	6–3, 6–1
1971	Margaret Smith Court	Evonne Goolagong	2–6, 7–6, 7–5
1972	Virginia Wade	Evonne Goolagong	6–4, 6–4
1973	Margaret Smith Court	Evonne Goolagong	6–4, 7–5
1974	Evonne Goolagong	Chris Evert	7–6, 4–6, 6–0
1975	Evonne Goolagong	Martina Navratilova	6–3, 6–2
1976	Evonne Goolagong Cawley	Renata Tomanova	6–2, 6–2
1977 (Jan)	Kerry Melville Reid	Dianne Balestrat	7–5, 6–2
1977 (Dec)	Evonne Goolagong Cawley	Helen Gourlay	6–3, 6–0
1978	Chris O'Neil	Betsy Nagelsen	6–3, 7–6
1979	Barbara Jordan	Sharon Walsh	6–3, 6–3
1980	Hana Mandlikova	Wendy Turnbull	6–0, 7–5
1981	Martina Navratilova	Chris Evert Lloyd	6–7, 6–4, 7–5
1982	Chris Evert Lloyd	Martina Navratilova	6–3, 2–6, 6–3
1983	Martina Navratilova	Kathy Jordan	6–2, 7–6
1984	Chris Evert Lloyd	Helena Sukova	6–7, 6–1, 6–3
1985 (Dec)	Martina Navratilova	Chris Evert Lloyd	6–2, 4–6, 6–2
1987 (Jan)	Hana Mandlikova	Martina Navratilova	7–5, 7–6
1988	Steffi Graf	Chris Evert	6–1, 7–6
1989	Steffi Graf	Helena Sukova	6–4, 6–4
1990	Steffi Graf	Mary Joe Fernandez	6–3, 6–4
1991	Monica Seles	Jana Novotna	5–7, 6–3, 6–1
1992	Monica Seles	Mary Joe Fernandez	6–2, 6–3
1993	Monica Seles	Steffi Graf	4–6, 6–3, 6–2
1994	Steffi Graf	Arantxa Sánchez Vicario	6–0, 6–2
1995	Mary Pierce	Arantxa Sánchez Vicario	6–3, 6–2
1996	Monica Seles	Anke Huber	6–4, 6–1
1997	Martina Hingis	Mary Pierce	6–2, 6–2
1998	Martina Hingis	Conchita Martinez	6–3, 6–3

*Became Open (amateur and professional) in 1969.

French Championships

Year	Winner	Finalist	Score
1925†	Suzanne Lenglen	Kathleen McKane	6–1, 6–2
1926	Suzanne Lenglen	Mary K. Browne	6–1, 6–0
1927	Kea Bouman	Irene Peacock	6–2, 6–4
1928	Helen Wills	Eileen Bennett	6–1, 6–2
1929	Helen Wills	Simone Mathieu	6–3, 6–4
1930	Helen Wills Moody	Helen Jacobs	6–2, 6–1
1931	Cilly Aussem	Betty Nuthall	8–6, 6–1
1932	Helen Wills Moody	Simone Mathieu	7–5, 6–1
1933	Margaret Scriven	Simone Mathieu	6–2, 4–6, 6–4

†1925 was the first year that entries were accepted from all countries.

French Championships (Cont.)

Year	Winner	Finalist	Score
1934	Margaret Scriven	Helen Jacobs	7–5, 4–6, 6–1
1935	Hilde Sperling	Simone Mathieu	6–2, 6–1
1936	Hilde Sperling	Simone Mathieu	6–3, 6–4
1937	Hilde Sperling	Simone Mathieu	6–2, 6–4
1938	Simone Mathieu	Nelly Landry	6–0, 6–3
1939	Simone Mathieu	Jadwiga Jedrzejowska	6–3, 8–6
1940–45	No tournament		
1946	Margaret Osborne	Pauline Betz	1–6, 8–6, 7–5
1947	Patricia Todd	Doris Hart	6–3, 3–6, 6–4
1948	Nelly Landry	Shirley Fry	6–2, 0–6, 6–0
1949	Margaret Osborne duPont	Nelly Adamson	7–5, 6–2
1950	Doris Hart	Patricia Todd	6–4, 4–6, 6–2
1951	Shirley Fry	Doris Hart	6–3, 3–6, 6–3
1952	Doris Hart	Shirley Fry	6–4, 6–4
1953	Maureen Connolly	Doris Hart	6–2, 6–4
1954	Maureen Connolly	Ginette Bucaille	6–4, 6–1
1955	Angela Mortimer	Dorothy Knode	2–6, 7–5, 10–8
1956	Althea Gibson	Angela Mortimer	6–0, 12–10
1957	Shirley Bloomer	Dorothy Knode	6–1, 6–3
1958	Zsuzsi Kormoczi	Shirley Bloomer	6–4, 1–6, 6–2
1959	Christine Truman	Zsuzsi Kormoczi	6–4, 7–5
1960	Darlene Hard	Yola Ramirez	6–3, 6–4
1961	Ann Haydon	Yola Ramirez	6–2, 6–1
1962	Margaret Smith	Lesley Turner	6–3, 3–6, 7–5
1963	Lesley Turner	Ann Haydon Jones	2–6, 6–3, 7–5
1964	Margaret Smith	Maria Bueno	5–7, 6–1, 6–2
1965	Lesley Turner	Margaret Smith	6–3, 6–4
1966	Ann Jones	Nancy Richey	6–3, 6–1
1967	Francoise Durr	Lesley Turner	4–6, 6–3, 6–4
1968*	Nancy Richey	Ann Jones	5–7, 6–4, 6–1
1969	Margaret Smith Court	Ann Jones	6–1, 4–6, 6–3
1970	Margaret Smith Court	Helga Niessen	6–2, 6–4
1971	Evonne Goolagong	Helen Gourlay	6–3, 7–5
1972	Billie Jean King	Evonne Goolagong	6–3, 6–3
1973	Margaret Smith Court	Chris Evert	6–7, 7–6, 6–4
1974	Chris Evert	Olga Morozova	6–1, 6–2
1975	Chris Evert	Martina Navratilova	2–6, 6–2, 6–1
1976	Sue Barker	Renata Tomanova	6–2, 0–6, 6–2
1977	Mima Jausovec	Florenza Mihai	6–2, 6–7, 6–1
1978	Virginia Ruzici	Mima Jausovec	6–2, 6–2
1979	Chris Evert Lloyd	Wendy Turnbull	6–2, 6–0
1980	Chris Evert Lloyd	Virginia Ruzici	6–0, 6–3
1981	Hana Mandlikova	Sylvia Hanika	6–2, 6–4
1982	Martina Navratilova	Andrea Jaeger	7–6, 6–1
1983	Chris Evert Lloyd	Mima Jausovec	6–1, 6–2
1984	Martina Navratilova	Chris Evert Lloyd	6–3, 6–1
1985	Chris Evert Lloyd	Martina Navratilova	6–3, 6–7, 7–5
1986	Chris Evert Lloyd	Martina Navratilova	2–6, 6–3, 6–3
1987	Steffi Graf	Martina Navratilova	6–4, 4–6, 8–6
1988	Steffi Graf	Natalia Zvereva	6–0, 6–0
1989	Arantxa Sánchez Vicario	Steffi Graf	7–6, 3–6, 7–5
1990	Monica Seles	Steffi Graf	7–6, 6–4
1991	Monica Seles	Arantxa Sánchez Vicario	6–3, 6–4
1992	Monica Seles	Steffi Graf	6–2, 3–6, 10–8
1993	Steffi Graf	Mary Joe Fernandez	4–6, 6–2, 6–4
1994	Arantxa Sánchez Vicario	Mary Pierce	6–4, 6–4
1995	Steffi Graf	Arantxa Sánchez Vicario	7–5, 4–6, 6–0
1996	Steffi Graf	Arantxa Sánchez Vicario	6–3, 6–7 (4–7), 10–8
1997	Iva Majoli	Martina Hingis	6–4, 6–2
1998	Arantxa Sánchez Vicario	Monica Seles	7–6 (7–5), 0–6, 6–2

*Became Open (amateur and professional) in 1968 but closed to contract professionals in 1972.

Wimbledon Championships

Year	Winner	Finalist	Score
1884	Maud Watson	Lilian Watson	6–8, 6–3, 6–3
1885	Maud Watson	Blanche Bingley	6–1, 7–5
1886	Blanche Bingley	Maud Watson	6–3, 6–3
1887	Charlotte Dod	Blanche Bingley	6–2, 6–0
1888	Charlotte Dod	Blanche Bingley Hillyard	6–3, 6–3
1889	Blanche Bingley Hillyard	n/a	n/a
1890	Lena Rice	n/a	n/a
1891	Charlotte Dod	n/a	n/a
1892	Charlotte Dod	Blanche Bingley Hillyard	6–1, 6–1
1893	Charlotte Dod	Blanche Bingley Hillyard	6–8, 6–1, 6–4
1894	Blanche Bingley Hillyard	n/a	n/a
1895	Charlotte Cooper		
1896	Charlotte Cooper	Mrs. W. H. Pickering	6–2, 6–3
1897	Blanche Bingley Hillyard	Charlotte Cooper	5–7, 7–5, 6–2
1898	Charlotte Cooper	n/a	n/a
1899	Blanche Bingley Hillyard	Charlotte Cooper	6–2, 6–3
1900	Blanche Bingley Hillyard	Charlotte Cooper	4–6, 6–4, 6–4
1901	Charlotte Cooper Sterry	Blanche Bingley Hillyard	6–2, 6–2
1902	Muriel Robb	Charlotte Cooper Sterry	7–5, 6–1
1903	Dorothea Douglass	n/a	n/a
1904	Dorothea Douglass	Charlotte Cooper Sterry	6–0, 6–3
1905	May Sutton	Dorothea Douglass	6–3, 6–4
1906	Dorothea Douglass	May Sutton	6–3, 9–7
1907	May Sutton	Dorothea Douglass Lambert Chambers	6–1, 6–4
1908	Charlotte Cooper Sterry	n/a	n/a
1909	Dora Boothby	n/a	n/a
1910	Dorothea Douglass Lambert Chambers	Dora Boothby	6–2, 6–2
1911	Dorothea Douglass Lambert Chambers	Dora Boothby	6–0, 6–0
1912	Ethel Larcombe	n/a	n/a
1913	Dorothea Douglass Lambert Chambers		
1914	Dorothea Douglass Lambert Chambers	Ethel Larcombe	7–5, 6–4
1915–18	No tournament		
1919	Suzanne Lenglen	Dorothea Douglass Lambert Chambers	10–8, 4–6, 9–7
1920	Suzanne Lenglen	Dorothea Douglass Lambert Chambers	6–3, 6–0
1921	Suzanne Lenglen	Elizabeth Ryan	6–2, 6–0
1922	Suzanne Lenglen	Molla Mallory	6–2, 6–0
1923	Suzanne Lenglen	Kathleen McKane	6–2, 6–2
1924	Kathleen McKane	Helen Wills	4–6, 6–4, 6–2
1925	Suzanne Lenglen	Joan Fry	6–2, 6–0
1926	Kathleen McKane Godfree	Lili de Alvarez	6–2, 4–6, 6–3
1927	Helen Wills	Lili de Alvarez	6–2, 6–4
1928	Helen Wills	Lili de Alvarez	6–2, 6–3
1929	Helen Wills	Helen Jacobs	6–1, 6–2
1930	Helen Wills Moody	Elizabeth Ryan	6–2, 6–2
1931	Cilly Aussem	Hilde Kranwinkel	7–5, 7–5
1932	Helen Wills Moody	Helen Jacobs	6–3, 6–1
1933	Helen Wills Moody	Dorothy Round	6–4, 6–8, 6–3
1934	Dorothy Round	Helen Jacobs	6–2, 5–7, 6–3
1935	Helen Wills Moody	Helen Jacobs	6–3, 3–6, 7–5
1936	Helen Jacobs	Hilde Kranwinkel Sperling	6–2, 4–6, 7–5
1937	Dorothy Round	Jadwiga Jedrzejowska	6–2, 2–6, 7–5
1938	Helen Wills Moody	Helen Jacobs	6–4, 6–0
1939	Alice Marble	Kay Stammers	6–2, 6–0
1940–45	No tournament		
1946	Pauline Betz	Louise Brough	6–2, 6–4
1947	Margaret Osborne	Doris Hart	6–2, 6–4
1948	Louise Brough	Doris Hart	6–3, 8–6
1949	Louise Brough	Margaret Osborne duPont	10–8, 1–6, 10–8

Wimbledon Championships *(Cont.)*

Year	Winner	Finalist	Score
1950	Louise Brough	Margaret Osborne duPont	6–1, 3–6, 6–1
1951	Doris Hart	Shirley Fry	6–1, 6–0
1952	Maureen Connolly	Louise Brough	6–4, 6–3
1953	Maureen Connolly	Doris Hart	8–6, 7–5
1954	Maureen Connolly	Louise Brough	6–2, 7–5
1955	Louise Brough	Beverly Fleitz	7–5, 8–6
1956	Shirley Fry	Angela Buxton	6–3, 6–1
1957	Althea Gibson	Darlene Hard	6–3, 6–2
1958	Althea Gibson	Angela Mortimer	8–6, 6–2
1959	Maria Bueno	Darlene Hard	6–4, 6–3
1960	Maria Bueno	Sandra Reynolds	8–6, 6–0
1961	Angela Mortimer	Christine Truman	4–6, 6–4, 7–5
1962	Karen Hantze Susman	Vera Sukova	6–4, 6–4
1963	Margaret Smith	Billie Jean Moffitt	6–3, 6–4
1964	Maria Bueno	Margaret Smith	6–4, 7–9, 6–3
1965	Margaret Smith	Maria Bueno	6–4, 7–5
1966	Billie Jean King	Maria Bueno	6–3, 3–6, 6–1
1967	Billie Jean King	Ann Haydon Jones	6–3, 6–4
1968*	Billie Jean King	Judy Tegart	9–7, 7–5
1969	Ann Haydon Jones	Billie Jean King	3–6, 6–3, 6–2
1970	Margaret Smith Court	Billie Jean King	14–12, 11–9
1971	Evonne Goolagong	Margaret Smith Court	6–4, 6–1
1972	Billie Jean King	Evonne Goolagong	6–3, 6–3
1973	Billie Jean King	Chris Evert	6–0, 7–5
1974	Chris Evert	Olga Morozova	6–0, 6–4
1975	Billie Jean King	Evonne Goolagong Cawley	6–0, 6–1
1976	Chris Evert	Evonne Goolagong Cawley	6–3, 4–6, 8–6
1977	Virginia Wade	Betty Stove	4–6, 6–3, 6–1
1978	Martina Navratilova	Chris Evert	2–6, 6–4, 7–5
1979	Martina Navratilova	Chris Evert Lloyd	6–4, 6–4
1980	Evonne Goolagong Cawley	Chris Evert Lloyd	6–1, 7–6
1981	Chris Evert Lloyd	Hana Mandlikova	6–2, 6–2
1982	Martina Navratilova	Chris Evert Lloyd	6–1, 3–6, 6–2
1983	Martina Navratilova	Andrea Jaeger	6–0, 6–3
1984	Martina Navratilova	Chris Evert Lloyd	7–6, 6–2
1985	Martina Navratilova	Chris Evert Lloyd	4–6, 6–3, 6–2
1986	Martina Navratilova	Hana Mandlikova	7–6, 6–3
1987	Martina Navratilova	Steffi Graf	7–5, 6–3
1988	Steffi Graf	Martina Navratilova	5–7, 6–2, 6–1
1989	Steffi Graf	Martina Navratilova	6–2, 6–7, 6–1
1990	Martina Navratilova	Zina Garrison	6–4, 6–1
1991	Steffi Graf	Gabriela Sabatini	6–4, 3–6, 8–6
1992	Steffi Graf	Monica Seles	6–2, 6–1
1993	Steffi Graf	Jana Novotna	7–6 (8–6), 1–6, 6–4
1994	Conchita Martinez	Martina Navratilova	6–4, 3–6, 6–3
1995	Steffi Graf	Arantxa Sánchez Vicario	4–6, 6–1, 7–5
1996	Steffi Graf	Arantxa Sánchez Vicario	6–3, 7–5
1997	Martina Hingis	Jana Novotna	2–6, 6–3, 6–3
1998	Jana Novotna	Nathalie Tauziat	6–4, 7–6 (7–2)

*Became Open (amateur and professional) in 1968 but closed to contract professionals in 1972.

Note: Prior to 1922 the tournament was run on a challenge-round system. The previous year's winner "stood out" of an All Comers event, which produced a challenger to play her for the title.

United States Championships

Year	Winner	Finalist	Score
1887	Ellen Hansell	Laura Knight	6–1, 6–0
1888	Bertha L. Townsend	Ellen Hansell	6–3, 6–5
1889	Bertha L. Townsend	Louise Voorhes	7–5, 6–2
1890	Ellen C. Roosevelt	Bertha L. Townsend	6–2, 6–2
1891	Mabel Cahill	Ellen C. Roosevelt	6–4, 6–1, 4–6, 6–3
1892	Mabel Cahill	Elisabeth Moore	5–7, 6–3, 6–4, 4–6, 6–2
1893	Aline Terry	Alice Schultze	6–1, 6–3
1894	Helen Hellwig	Aline Terry	7–5, 3–6, 6–0, 3–6, 6–3
1895	Juliette Atkinson	Helen Hellwig	6–4, 6–2, 6–1

United States Championship *(Cont.)*

Year	Winner	Finalist	Score
1896	Elisabeth Moore	Juliette Atkinson	6–4, 4–6, 6–2, 6–2
1897	Juliette Atkinson	Elisabeth Moore	6–3, 6–3, 4–6, 3–6, 6–3
1898	Juliette Atkinson	Marion Jones	6–3, 5–7, 6–4, 2–6, 7–5
1899	Marion Jones	Maud Banks	6–1, 6–1, 7–5
1900	Myrtle McAteer	Edith Parker	6–2, 6–2, 6–0
1901	Elisabeth Moore	Myrtle McAteer	6–4, 3–6, 7–5, 2–6, 6–2
1902**	Marion Jones	Elisabeth Moore	6–1, 1–0, ret.
1903	Elisabeth Moore	Marion Jones	7–5, 8–6
1904	May Sutton	Elisabeth Moore	6–1, 6–2
1905	Elisabeth Moore	Helen Homans	6–4, 5–7, 6–1
1906	Helen Homans	Maud Barger–Wallach	6–4, 6–3
1907	Evelyn Sears	Carrie Neely	6–3, 6–2
1908	Maud Barger–Wallach	Evelyn Sears	6–3, 1–6, 6–3
1909	Hazel Hotchkiss	Maud Barger–Wallach	6–0, 6–1
1910	Hazel Hotchkiss	Louise Hammond	6–4, 6–2
1911	Hazel Hotchkiss	Florence Sutton	8–10, 6–1, 9–7
1912†	Mary K. Browne	Eleanora Sears	6–4, 6–2
1913	Mary K. Browne	Dorothy Green	6–2, 7–5
1914	Mary K. Browne	Marie Wagner	6–2, 1–6, 6–1
1915	Molla Bjurstedt	Hazel Hotchkiss Wightman	4–6, 6–2, 6–0
1916	Molla Bjurstedt	Louise Hammond Raymond	6–0, 6–1
1917‡	Molla Bjurstedt	Marion Vanderhoef	4–6, 6–0, 6–2
1918	Molla Bjurstedt	Eleanor Goss	6–4, 6–3
1919	Hazel Hotchkiss Wightman	Marion Zinderstein	6–1, 6–2
1920	Molla Bjurstedt Mallory	Marion Zinderstein	6–3, 6–1
1921	Molla Bjurstedt Mallory	Mary K. Browne	4–6, 6–4, 6–2
1922	Molla Bjurstedt Mallory	Helen Wills	6–3, 6–1
1923	Helen Wills	Molla Bjurstedt Mallory	6–2, 6–1
1924	Helen Wills	Molla Bjurstedt Mallory	6–1, 6–3
1925	Helen Wills	Kathleen McKane	3–6, 6–0, 6–2
1926	Molla Bjurstedt Mallory	Elizabeth Ryan	4–6, 6–4, 9–7
1927	Helen Wills	Betty Nuthall	6–1, 6–4
1928	Helen Wills	Helen Jacobs	6–2, 6–1
1929	Helen Wills	Phoebe Holcroft Watson	6–4, 6–2
1930	Betty Nuthall	Anna McCune Harper	6–1, 6–4
1931	Helen Wills Moody	Eileen Whitingstall	6–4, 6–1
1932	Helen Jacobs	Carolin Babcock	6–2, 6–2
1933	Helen Jacobs	Helen Wills Moody	8–6, 3–6, 3–0, ret.
1934	Helen Jacobs	Sarah Palfrey	6–1, 6–4
1935	Helen Jacobs	Sarah Palfrey Fabyan	6–2, 6–4
1936	Alice Marble	Helen Jacobs	4–6, 6–3, 6–2
1937	Anita Lizane	Jadwiga Jedrzejowska	6–4, 6–2
1938	Alice Marble	Nancye Wynne	6–0, 6–3
1939	Alice Marble	Helen Jacobs	6–0, 8–10, 6–4
1940	Alice Marble	Helen Jacobs	6–2, 6–3
1941	Sarah Palfrey Cooke	Pauline Betz	7–5, 6–2
1942	Pauline Betz	Louise Brough	4–6, 6–1, 6–4
1943	Pauline Betz	Louise Brough	6–3, 5–7, 6–3
1944	Pauline Betz	Margaret Osborne	6–3, 8–6
1945	Sarah Palfrey Cooke	Pauline Betz	3–6, 8–6, 6–4
1946	Pauline Betz	Patricia Canning	11–9, 6–3
1947	Louise Brough	Margaret Osborne	8–6, 4–6, 6–1
1948	Margaret Osborne duPont	Louise Brough	4–6, 6–4, 15–13
1949	Margaret Osborne duPont	Doris Hart	6–4, 6–1
1950	Margaret Osborne duPont	Doris Hart	6–4, 6–3
1951	Maureen Connolly	Shirley Fry	6–3, 1–6, 6–4
1952	Maureen Connolly	Doris Hart	6–3, 7–5
1953	Maureen Connolly	Doris Hart	6–2, 6–4
1954	Doris Hart	Louise Brough	6–8, 6–1, 8–6
1955	Doris Hart	Patricia Ward	6–4, 6–2
1956	Shirley Fry	Althea Gibson	6–3, 6–4
1957	Althea Gibson	Louise Brough	6–3, 6–2
1958	Althea Gibson	Darlene Hard	3–6, 6–1, 6–2
1959	Maria Bueno	Christine Truman	6–1, 6–4
1960	Darlene Hard	Maria Bueno	6–4, 10–12, 6–4

**Five-set final abolished; †Challenge round abolished.

United States Championship *(Cont.)*

Year	Winner	Finalist	Score
1961	Darlene Hard	Ann Haydon	6–3, 6–4
1962	Margaret Smith	Darlene Hard	9–7, 6–4
1963	Maria Bueno	Margaret Smith	7–5, 6–4
1964	Maria Bueno	Carole Graebner	6–1, 6–0
1965	Margaret Smith	Billie Jean Moffitt	8–6, 7–5
1966	Maria Bueno	Nancy Richey	6–3, 6–1
1967	Billie Jean King	Ann Haydon Jones	11–9, 6–4
1968*	Virginia Wade	Billie Jean King	6–4, 6–4
1968#	Margaret Smith Court	Maria Bueno	6–2, 6–2
1969	Margaret Smith Court	Nancy Richey	6–2, 6–2
1969#	Margaret Smith Court	Virginia Wade	4–6, 6–3, 6–0
1970	Margaret Smith Court	Rosie Casals	6–2, 2–6, 6–1
1971	Billie Jean King	Rosie Casals	6–4, 7–6
1972	Billie Jean King	Kerry Melville	6–3, 7–5
1973	Margaret Smith Court	Evonne Goolagong	7–6, 5–7, 6–2
1974	Billie Jean King	Evonne Goolagong	3–6, 6–3, 7–5
1975	Chris Evert	Evonne Goolagong Cawley	5–7, 6–4, 6–2
1976	Chris Evert	Evonne Goolagong Cawley	6–3, 6–0
1977	Chris Evert	Wendy Turnbull	7–6, 6–2
1978	Chris Evert	Pam Shriver	7–6, 6–4
1979	Tracy Austin	Chris Evert Lloyd	6–4, 6–3
1980	Chris Evert Lloyd	Hana Mandlikova	5–7, 6–1, 6–1
1981	Tracy Austin	Martina Navratilova	1–6, 7–6, 7–6
1982	Chris Evert Lloyd	Hana Mandlikova	6–3, 6–1
1983	Martina Navratilova	Chris Evert Lloyd	6–1, 6–3
1984	Martina Navratilova	Chris Evert Lloyd	4–6, 6–4, 6–4
1985	Hana Mandlikova	Martina Navratilova	7–6, 1–6, 7–6
1986	Martina Navratilova	Helena Sukova	6–3, 6–2
1987	Martina Navratilova	Steffi Graf	7–6, 6–1
1988	Steffi Graf	Gabriela Sabatini	6–3, 3–6, 6–1
1989	Steffi Graf	Martina Navratilova	3–6, 6–4, 6–2
1990	Gabriela Sabatini	Steffi Graf	6–2, 7–6
1991	Monica Seles	Martina Narvatilova	7–6, 6–1
1992	Monica Seles	Arantxa Sánchez Vicario	6–3, 6–2
1993	Steffi Graf	Helena Sukova	6–3, 6–3
1994	Arantxa Sánchez Vicario	Steffi Graf	1–6, 7–6 (7–3), 6–4
1995	Steffi Graf	Monica Seles	7–6 (8–6), 0–6, 6–3
1996	Steffi Graf	Monica Seles	7–5, 7–4
1997	Martina Hingis	Venus Williams	6–0, 6–4
1998	Lindsay Davenport	Martina Hingis	6–3, 7–5

*Became Open (amateur and professional) in 1968.
‡National Patriotic Tournament; #Amateur event held.

Grand Slams

Singles

Don Budge, 1938
Maureen Connolly, 1953
Rod Laver, 1962, 1969
Margaret Smith Court, 1970
Steffi Graf, 1988

Doubles

Frank Sedgman and Ken McGregor, 1951
Martina Navratilova and Pam Shriver, 1984
Maria Bueno and two partners: Christine Truman
   (Australian), Darlene Hard (French, Wimbledon
   and U.S. Championships), 1960

Mixed Doubles

Margaret Smith and Ken Fletcher, 1963
Owen Davidson and two partners: Lesley Turner
   (Australian), Billie Jean King (French, Wimbledon
   and U.S. Championships), 1967

Alltime Grand Slam Champions

MEN

Player	Aus. S-D-M	French S-D-M	Wim. S-D-M	U.S. S-D-M	Total
Roy Emerson	6-3-0	2-6-0	2-3-0	2-4-0	28
John Newcombe	2-5-0	0-3-0	3-6-0	2-3-1	25
Frank Sedgman	2-2-2	0-2-2	1-3-2	2-2-2	22
Bill Tilden	†	0-0-1	3-1-0	7-5-4	21
Rod Laver	3-4-0	2-1-1	4-1-2	2-0-0	20
John Bromwich	2-8-1	0-0-0	0-2-2	0-3-1	19
Jean Borotra	1-1-1	1-5-2	2-3-1	0-0-1	18
Fred Stolle	0-3-1	1-2-0	0-2-3	1-3-2	18
Ken Rosewall	4-3-0	2-2-0	0-2-0	2-2-1	18
Neale Fraser	0-3-1	0-3-0	1-2-0	2-3-3	18
Adrian Quist	3-10-0	0-1-0	0-2-0	0-1-0	17
John McEnroe	0-0-0	0-0-1	3-4-0	4-5-0	17
Jack Crawford	4-4-3	1-1-1	1-1-1	0-0-0	17

†Did not compete.

WOMEN

Player	Aus. S-D-M	French S-D-M	Wim. S-D-M	U.S. S-D-M	Total
Margaret Smith Court	11-8-2	5-4-4	3-2-5	5-5-8	62
Martina Navratilova	3-8-0	2-7-2	9-7-3	4-9-2	56
Billie Jean King	1-0-1	1-1-2	6-10-4	4-5-4	39
Doris Hart	1-1-2	2-5-3	1-4-5	2-4-5	35
Helen Wills Moody	†	4-2-0	8-3-1	7-4-2	31
Louise Brough	1-1-0	0-3-0	4-5-4	1-8-3	30**
Margaret Osborne duPont	†	2-3-0	1-5-1	3-8-6	29**
Elizabeth Ryan	†	0-4-0	0-12-7	0-1-2	26
*Steffi Graf	4-0-0	5-0-0	7-1-0	5-0-0	22
Pam Shriver	0-7-0	0-4-1	0-5-0	0-5-0	22
Chris Evert	2-0-0	7-2-0	3-1-0	6-0-0	21
Darlene Hard	†	1-3-2	0-4-3	2-6-0	21
Suzanne Lenglen	†	2-2-2#	6-6-3	0-0-0	21
Nancye Wynne Bolton	6-10-4	0-0-0	0-0-0	0-0-0	20
Maria Bueno	0-1-0	0-1-1	3-5-0	4-4-0	19
Thelma Coyne Long	2-12-4	0-0-1	0-0-0	0-0-0	19

*Active player. †Did not compete.
#Suzanne Lenglen also won four singles titles at the French Championships before 1925, when competition was first opened to entries from all nations
**From 1940–45, with competition in the U.S. Championships thinned due to wartime constraints, Louise Brough Clapp also won four doubles titles (1942–45) and one mixed doubles title (1942); and Margaret Osborne duPont won five doubles titles (1941–45) and three mixed doubles titles (1943–45).

Alltime Grand Slam Singles Champions

MEN

Player	Aus.	French	Wim.	U.S.	Total
Roy Emerson	6	2	2	2	12
Bjorn Borg	0	6	5	0	11
Rod Laver	3	2	4	2	11
*Pete Sampras	2	0	5	4	11
Bill Tilden	†	0	3	7	10
Jimmy Connors	1	0	2	5	8
Ivan Lendl	2	3	0	3	8
Fred Perry	1	1	3	3	8
Ken Rosewall	4	2	0	2	8
Henri Cochet	†	4	2	1	7
Rene Lacoste	†	3	2	2	7
Bill Larned	†	†	0	7	7
John McEnroe	0	0	3	4	7
John Newcombe	2	0	3	2	7
Willie Renshaw	†	†	7	†	7
Dick Sears	†	†	0	7	7

*Active player. †Did not compete.

Alltime Grand Slam Singles Champions *(Cont.)*

WOMEN

Player	Aus.	French	Wim.	U.S.	Total
Margaret Smith Court	11	5	3	5	24
*Steffi Graf	4	5	7	5	21
Helen Wills Moody	†	4	8	7	19
Chris Evert	2	7	3	6	18
Martina Navratilova	3	2	9	4	18
Billie Jean King	1	1	6	4	12
Maureen Connolly	1	2	3	3	9
*Monica Seles	4	3	0	2	9
Suzanne Lenglen	†	2#	6	0	8
Molla Bjurstedt Mallory	†	†	0	8	8
Maria Bueno	0	0	3	4	7
Evonne Goolagong	4	1	2	0	7
Dorothea D.L. Chambers	†	†	7	0	7
Nancye Wynne Bolton	6	0	0	0	6
Louise Brough	1	0	4	1	6
Margaret Osborne duPont	†	2	1	3	6
Doris Hart	1	2	1	2	6
Blanche Bingley Hillyard	†	†	6	†	6

*Active player. †Did not compete.
#Suzanne Lenglen also won four singles titles at the French Championships before 1925, when competition was first opened to entries from all nations.

National Team Competition

Davis Cup

Started in 1900 as the International Lawn Tennis Challenge Trophy by America's Dwight Davis, the runner-up in the 1898 U.S. Championships. A Davis Cup meeting between two countries is known as a tie and is a three-day event consisting of two singles matches, followed by one doubles match and then two more singles matches. The United States boasts the greatest number of wins (31), followed by Australia (20).

Year	Winner	Finalist	Site	Score
1900	United States	Great Britain	Boston	3–0
1901	No tournament			
1902	United States	Great Britain	New York	3–2
1903	Great Britain	United States	Boston	4–1
1904	Great Britain	Belgium	Wimbledon	5–0
1905	Great Britain	United States	Wimbledon	5–0
1906	Great Britain	United States	Wimbledon	5–0
1907	Australasia	Great Britain	Wimbledon	3–2
1908	Australasia	United States	Melbourne	3–2
1909	Australasia	United States	Sydney	5–0
1910	No tournament			
1911	Australasia	United States	Christchurch, NZ	5–0
1912	Great Britain	Australasia	Melbourne	3–2
1913	United States	Great Britain	Wimbledon	3–2
1914	Australasia	United States	New York	3–2
1915–18	No tournament			
1919	Australasia	Great Britain	Sydney	4–1
1920	United States	Australasia	Auckland, NZ	5–0
1921	United States	Japan	New York	5–0
1922	United States	Australasia	New York	4–1
1923	United States	Australasia	New York	4–1
1924	United States	Australia	Philadelphia	5–0
1925	United States	France	Philadelphia	5–0
1926	United States	France	Philadelphia	4–1
1927	France	United States	Philadelphia	3–2
1928	France	United States	Paris	4–1
1929	France	United States	Paris	3–2
1930	France	United States	Paris	4–1
1931	France	Great Britain	Paris	3–2

Davis Cup (Cont.)

Year	Winner	Finalist	Site	Score
1932	France	United States	Paris	3–2
1933	Great Britain	France	Paris	3–2
1934	Great Britain	United States	Wimbledon	4–1
1935	Great Britain	United States	Wimbledon	5–0
1936	Great Britain	Australia	Wimbledon	3–2
1937	United States	Great Britain	Wimbledon	4–1
1938	United States	Australia	Philadelphia	3–2
1939	Australia	United States	Philadelphia	3–2
1940–45	No tournament			
1946	United States	Australia	Melbourne	5–0
1947	United States	Australia	New York	4–1
1948	United States	Australia	New York	5–0
1949	United States	Australia	New York	4–1
1950	Australia	United States	New York	4–1
1951	Australia	United States	Sydney	3–2
1952	Australia	United States	Adelaide	4–1
1953	Australia	United States	Melbourne	3–2
1954	United States	Australia	Sydney	3–2
1955	Australia	United States	New York	5–0
1956	Australia	United States	Adelaide	5–0
1957	Australia	United States	Melbourne	3–2
1958	United States	Australia	Brisbane	3–2
1959	Australia	United States	New York	3–2
1960	Australia	Italy	Sydney	4–1
1961	Australia	Italy	Melbourne	5–0
1962	Australia	Mexico	Brisbane	5–0
1963	United States	Australia	Adelaide	3–2
1964	Australia	United States	Cleveland	3–2
1965	Australia	Spain	Sydney	4–1
1966	Australia	India	Melbourne	4–1
1967	Australia	Spain	Brisbane	4–1
1968	United States	Australia	Adelaide	4–1
1969	United States	Romania	Cleveland	5–0
1970	United States	West Germany	Cleveland	5–0
1971	United States	Romania	Charlotte, NC	3–2
1972	United States	Romania	Bucharest	3–2
1973	Australia	United States	Cleveland	5–0
1974	South Africa	India	*	walkover
1975	Sweden	Czechoslovakia	Stockholm	3–2
1976	Italy	Chile	Santiago	4–1
1977	Australia	Italy	Sydney	3–1
1978	United States	Great Britain	Palm Springs	4–1
1979	United States	Italy	San Francisco	5–0
1980	Czechoslovakia	Italy	Prague	4–1
1981	United States	Argentina	Cincinnati, Ohio	3–1
1982	United States	France	Grenoble	4–1
1983	Australia	Sweden	Melbourne	3–2
1984	Sweden	United States	Göteborg, Sweden	4–1
1985	Sweden	West Germany	Munich	3–2
1986	Australia	Sweden	Melbourne	3–2
1987	Sweden	India	Göteborg, Sweden	5–0
1988	West Germany	Sweden	Göteborg, Sweden	4–1
1989	West Germany	Sweden	Stuttgart	3–2
1990	United States	Australia	St. Petersburg	3–2
1991	France	United States	Lyon	3–1
1992	United States	Switzerland	Fort Worth, TX	3–1
1993	Germany	Australia	Dusseldorf	4–1
1994	Sweden	Russia	Moscow	4–1
1995	United States	Russia	Moscow	3–2
1996	France	Sweden	Malmö, Sweden	3–2
1997	Sweden	United States	Göteborg, Sweden	5–0

*India refused to play the final in protest over South Africa's governmental policy of apartheid.
Note: Prior to 1972 the challenge-round system was in effect, with the previous year's winner "standing out" of the competition until the finals. A straight 16-nation tournament has been held since 1981.

Federation Cup

The Federation Cup was started in 1963 by the International Lawn Tennis Federation (now the ITF). Until 1991 all entrants gathered at one site at one time for a tournament that was concluded within one week. Since 1995 the Fed Cup, as it is now called, has been contested in three rounds by a World Group of eight nations. A meeting between two countries now consists of five matches: four singles and one doubles. The United States has the most wins (15), followed by Australia (7).

Year	Winner	Finalist	Site	Score
1963	United States	Australia	London	2–1
1964	Australia	United States	Philadelphia	2–1
1965	Australia	United States	Melbourne	2–1
1966	United States	West Germany	Turin	3–0
1967	United States	Great Britain	West Berlin	2–0
1968	Australia	Netherlands	Paris	3–0
1969	United States	Australia	Athens	2–1
1970	Australia	Great Britain	Freiburg	3–0
1971	Australia	Great Britain	Perth	3–0
1972	South Africa	Great Britain	Johannesburg	2–1
1973	Australia	South Africa	Bad Homburg	3–0
1974	Australia	United States	Naples	2–1
1975	Czechoslovakia	Australia	Aix-en-Provence	3–0
1976	United States	Australia	Philadelphia	2–1
1977	United States	Australia	Eastbourne, UK	2–1
1978	United States	Australia	Melbourne	2–1
1979	United States	Australia	Madrid	3–0
1980	United States	Australia	West Berlin	3–0
1981	United States	Great Britain	Nagoya	3–0
1982	United States	West Germany	Santa Clara	3–0
1983	Czechoslovakia	West Germany	Zurich	2–1
1984	Czechoslovakia	Australia	Sao Paulo	2–1
1985	Czechoslovakia	United States	Tokyo	2–1
1986	United States	Czechoslovakia	Prague	3–0
1987	West Germany	United States	Vancouver	2–1
1988	Czechoslovakia	USSR	Melbourne	2–1
1989	United States	Spain	Tokyo	3–0
1990	United States	USSR	Atlanta	2–1
1991	Spain	United States	Nottingham	2–1
1992	Germany	Spain	Frankfurt	2–1
1993	Spain	Australia	Frankfurt	3–0
1994	Spain	United States	Frankfurt	3–0
1995	Spain	United States	Valencia, Spain	3–2
1996	United States	Spain	Atlantic City	5–0
1997	France	Netherlands	Hertogenbosch, Neth.	4–1
1998	Spain	Switzerland	Geneva	3–2

Attention, Sergei Federov

Jennifer Capriati turned pro at 13, only to burn out within a few years, to be arrested on a drug-related charge and to become a walking, talking cautionary tale. But Rick Macci, who coached Capriati as a junior, has apparently learned little from her experience. On Sept. 17 the Macci Tennis Academy in Fort Lauderdale issued a press release saying that Monique Viele, a top junior in Macci's stable, will turn pro after her 14th birthday in the first week of October 1998. "We also are exploring the possibility of legally challenging the age eligibility rule of 14 that the WTA now enforces," the release adds. "We feel it inhibits Monique from making a living."

More disturbing than this announcement is the academy's breathless characterization of Monique, who's from Colorado Springs. At a time when the WTA vows to market its players as athletes and not underage sex symbols, the Macci release says of Monique, "She rivals a champion thoroughly with her physical grace and beauty. Her long, lean, tanned, muscular legs are both an attribute to her good looks and her speed on the court. Her physique is astonishing ... she looks more like a supermodel than a tennis player." Even her "sea green eyes" don't escape mention.

Monique's results are encouraging. By 11 she had a top 40 ranking in Florida's girls' 18 division, and in '98 she became the youngest player ever to win the 18 division of the Florida Open. But those credentials hardly mandate turning pro.

Macci sees it differently. "Her intensity level is scary," he says. "I see many Grand Slam titles in her future."

Rankings

ATP Computer Year-End Top 10
MEN

1973
1 ....Ilie Nastase
2 ....John Newcombe
3 ....Jimmy Connors
4 ....Tom Okker
5 ....Stan Smith
6 ....Ken Rosewall
7 ....Manuel Orantes
8 ....Rod Laver
9 ....Jan Kodes
10 ..Arthur Ashe

1974
1 ....Jimmy Connors
2 ....John Newcombe
3 ....Bjorn Borg
4 ....Rod Laver
5 ....Guillermo Vilas
6 ....Tom Okker
7 ....Arthur Ashe
8 ....Ken Rosewall
9 ....Stan Smith
10 ..Ilie Nastase

1975
1 ....Jimmy Connors
2 ....Guillermo Vilas
3 ....Bjorn Borg
4 ....Arthur Ashe
5 ....Manuel Orantes
6 ....Ken Rosewall
7 ....Ilie Nastase
8 ....John Alexander
9 ....Roscoe Tanner
10 ..Rod Laver

1976
1 ....Jimmy Connors
2 ....Bjorn Borg
3 ....Ilie Nastase
4 ....Manuel Orantes
5 ....Raul Ramirez
6 ....Guillermo Vilas
7 ....Adriano Panatta
8 ....Harold Solomon
9 ....Eddie Dibbs
10 ..Brian Gottfried

1977
1 ....Jimmy Connors
2 ....Guillermo Vilas
3 ....Bjorn Borg
4 ....Vitas Gerulaitis
5 ....Brian Gottfried
6 ....Eddie Dibbs
7 ....Manuel Orantes
8 ....Raul Ramirez
9 ....Ilie Nastase
10 ..Dick Stockton

1978
1 ....Jimmy Connors
2 ....Bjorn Borg
3 ....Guillermo Vilas
4 ....John McEnroe
5 ....Vitas Gerulaitis
6 ....Eddie Dibbs
7 ....Brian Gottfried
8 ....Raul Ramirez
9 ....Harold Solomon
10 ..Corrado Barazzutti

1979
1 ....Bjorn Borg
2 ....Jimmy Connors
3 ....John McEnroe
4 ....Vitas Gerulaitis
5 ....Roscoe Tanner
6 ....Guillermo Vilas
7 ....Arthur Ashe
8 ....Harold Solomon
9 ....Jose Higueras
10 ..Eddie Dibbs

1980
1 ....Bjorn Borg
2 ....John McEnroe
3 ....Jimmy Connors
4 ....Gene Mayer
5 ....Guillermo Vilas
6 ....Ivan Lendl
7 ....Harold Solomon
8 ....Jose–Luis Clerc
9 ....Vitas Gerulaitis
10 ..Eliot Teltscher

1981
1 ....John McEnroe
2 ....Ivan Lendl
3 ....Jimmy Connors
4 ....Bjorn Borg
5 ....Jose–Luis Clerc
6 ....Guillermo Vilas
7 ....Gene Mayer
8 ....Eliot Teltscher
9 ....Vitas Gerulaitis
10 ..Peter McNamara

1982
1 ....John McEnroe
2 ....Jimmy Connors
3 ....Ivan Lendl
4 ....Guillermo Vilas
5 ....Vitas Gerulaitis
6 ....Jose–Luis Clerc
7 ....Mats Wilander
8 ....Gene Mayer
9 ....Yannick Noah
10 ..Peter McNamara

1983
1 ....John McEnroe
2 ....Ivan Lendl
3 ....Jimmy Connors
4 ....Mats Wilander
5 ....Yannick Noah
6 ....Jimmy Arias
7 ....Jose Higueras
8 ....Jose–Luis Clerc
9 ....Kevin Curren
10 ..Gene Mayer

1984
1 ....John McEnroe
2 ....Jimmy Connors
3 ....Ivan Lendl
4 ....Mats Wilander
5 ....Andres Gomez
6 ....Anders Jarryd
7 ....Henrik Sundstrom
8 ....Pat Cash
9 ....Eliot Teltscher
10 ..Yannick Noah

1985
1 ....Ivan Lendl
2 ....John McEnroe
3 ....Mats Wilander
4 ....Jimmy Connors
5 ....Stefan Edberg
6 ....Boris Becker
7 ....Yannick Noah
8 ....Anders Jarryd
9 ....Miloslav Mecir
10 ..Kevin Curren

1986
1 ....Ivan Lendl
2 ....Boris Becker
3 ....Mats Wilander
4 ....Yannick Noah
5 ....Stefan Edberg
6 ....Henri Leconte
7 ....Joakim Nystrom
8 ....Jimmy Connors
9 ....Miloslav Mecir
10 ..Andres Gomez

1987
1 ....Ivan Lendl
2 ....Stefan Edberg
3 ....Mats Wilander
4 ....Jimmy Connors
5 ....Boris Becker
6 ....Miloslav Mecir
7 ....Pat Cash
8 ....Yannick Noah
9 ....Tim Mayotte
10 ..John McEnroe

ATP Computer Year-End Top 10 *(Cont.)*
MEN *(CONT.)*

1988

1 ....Mats Wilander
2 ....Ivan Lendl
3 ....Andre Agassi
4 ....Boris Becker
5 ....Stefan Edberg
6 ....Kent Carlsson
7 ....Jimmy Connors
8 ....Jakob Hlasek
9 ....Henri Leconte
10...Tim Mayotte

1989

1 ....Ivan Lendl
2 ....Boris Becker
3 ....Stefan Edberg
4 ....John McEnroe
5 ....Michael Chang
6 ....Brad Gilbert
7 ....Andre Agassi
8 ....Aaron Krickstein
9 ....Alberto Mancini
10...Jay Berger

1990

1 ....Stefan Edberg
2 ....Boris Becker
3 ....Ivan Lendl
4 ....Andre Agassi
5 ....Pete Sampras
6 ....Andres Gomez
7 ....Thomas Muster
8 ....Emilio Sanchez
9 ....Goran Ivanisevic
10...Brad Gilbert

1991

1 ....Stefan Edberg
2 ....Jim Courier
3 ....Boris Becker
4 ....Michael Stich
5 ....Ivan Lendl
6 ....Pete Sampras
7 ....Guy Forget
8 ....Karel Novacek
9 ....Petr Korda
10...Andre Agassi

1992

1 ....Jim Courier
2 ....Stefan Edberg
3 ....Pete Sampras
4 ....Goran Ivanisevic
5 ....Boris Becker
6 ....Michael Chang
7 ....Petr Korda
8 ....Ivan Lendl
9 ....Andre Agassi
10...Richard Krajicek

1993

1 ....Pete Sampras
2 ....Michael Stich
3 ....Jim Courier
4 ....Sergi Bruguera
5 ....Stefan Edberg
6 ....Andrei Medvedev
7 ....Goran Ivanisevic
8 ....Michael Chang
9 ....Thomas Muster
10...Cedric Pioline

1994

1 ....Pete Sampras
2 ....Andre Agassi
3 ....Boris Becker
4 ....Sergi Bruguera
5 ....Goran Ivanisevic
6 ....Michael Chang
7 ....Stefan Edberg
8 ....Alberto Berasategui
9 ....Michael Stich
10...Todd Martin

1995

1 ....Pete Sampras
2 ....Andre Agassi
3 ....Thomas Muster
4 ....Boris Becker
5 ....Michael Chang
6 ....Yevgeny Kafelnikov
7 ....Thomas Enqvist
8 ....Jim Courier
9 ....Wayne Ferreira
10...Goran Ivanisevic

1996

1 ....Pete Sampras
2 ....Michael Chang
3 ....Yevgeny Kafelnikov
4 ....Goran Ivanisevic
5 ....Thomas Muster
6 ....Boris Becker
7 ....Richard Krajicek
8 ....Andre Agassi
9 ....Thomas Enqvist
10...Wayne Ferreira

1997

1 ....Pete Sampras
2 ....Patrick Rafter
3 ....Michael Chang
4 ....Jonas Bjorkman
5 ....Yevgeny Kafelnikov
6 ....Greg Rusedski
7 ....Carlos Moya
8 ....Sergei Bruguera
9 ....Thomas Muster
10...Marcelo Ríos

WTA Computer Year-End Top 10
WOMEN

1973

1 ....Margaret Smith Court
2 ....Billie Jean King
3 ....Evonne Goolagong
4 ....Chris Evert
5 ....Rosie Casals
6 ....Virginia Wade
7 ....Kerry Reid
8 ....Nancy Gunter
9 ....Julie Heldman
10...Helga Masthoff

1974

1 ....Billie Jean King
2 ....Evonne Goolagong
3 ....Chris Evert
4 ....Virginia Wade
5 ....Julie Heldman
6 ....Rosie Casals
7 ....Kerry Reid
8 ....Olga Morozova
9 ....Lesley Hunt
10...Francoise Durr

1975

1 ....Chris Evert
2 ....Billie Jean King
3 ....Evonne Goolagong Cawley
4 ....Martina Navratilova
5 ....Virginia Wade
6 ....Margaret Smith Court
7 ....Olga Morozova
8 ....Nancy Gunter
9 ....Francoise Durr
10...Rosie Casals

WTA Computer Year-End Top 10 (Cont.)
WOMEN (CONT.)

1976

1 ....Chris Evert
2 ....Evonne Goolagong Cawley
3 ...Virginia Wade
4 ...Martina Navratilova
5 ....Sue Barker
6 ....Betty Stove
7 ....Dianne Balestrat
8 ...Mima Jausovec
9 ...Rosie Casals
10...Francoise Durr

1977

1 ....Chris Evert
2 ....Billie Jean King
3 ....Martina Navratilova
4 ...Virginia Wade
5 ....Sue Barker
6 ....Rosie Casals
7 ....Betty Stove
8 ....Dianne Balestrat
9 ....Wendy Turnbull
10...Kerry Reid

1978

1 ....Martina Navratilova
2 ....Chris Evert
3 ....Evonne Goolagong Cawley
4 ....Virginia Wade
5 ....Billie Jean King
6 ....Tracy Austin
7 ....Wendy Turnbull
8 ....Kerry Reid
9 ....Betty Stove
10...Dianne Balestrat

1979

1 ....Martina Navratilova
2 ....Chris Evert Lloyd
3 ....Tracy Austin
4 ....Evonne Goolagong Cawley
5 ....Billie Jean King
6 ....Dianne Balestrat
7 ....Wendy Turnbull
8 ....Virginia Wade
9 ....Kerry Reid
10...Sue Barker

1980

1 ....Chris Evert Lloyd
2 ....Tracy Austin
3 ....Martina Navratilova
4 ...Hana Mandlikova
5 ....Evonne Goolagong Cawley
6 ....Billie Jean King
7 ....Andrea Jaeger
8 ....Wendy Turnbull
9 ....Pam Shriver
10...Greer Stevens

1981

1 ....Chris Evert Lloyd
2 ....Tracy Austin
3 ....Martina Navratilova
4 ....Andrea Jaeger
5 ....Hana Mandlikova
6 ....Sylvia Hanika
7 ....Pam Shriver
8 ....Wendy Turnbull
9 ....Bettina Bunge
10...Barbara Potter

1982

1 ....Martina Navratilova
2 ....Chris Evert Lloyd
3 ....Andrea Jaeger
4 ....Tracy Austin
5 ....Wendy Turnbull
6 ....Pam Shriver
7 ....Hana Mandlikova
8 ....Barbara Potter
9 ....Bettina Bunge
10...Sylvia Hanika

1983

1 ....Martina Navratilova
2 ....Chris Evert Lloyd
3 ....Andrea Jaeger
4 ....Pam Shriver
5 ....Sylvia Hanika
6 ....Jo Durie
7 ....Bettina Bunge
8 ....Wendy Turnbull
9 ....Tracy Austin
10...Zina Garrison

1984

1 ....Martina Navratilova
2 ....Chris Evert Lloyd
3 ....Hana Mandlikova
4 ....Pam Shriver
5 ....Wendy Turnbull
6 ....Manuela Maleeva
7 ....Helena Sukova
8 ....Claudia Kohde-Kilsch
9 ....Zina Garrison
10...Kathy Jordan

1985

1 ....Martina Navratilova
2 ....Chris Evert Lloyd
3 ....Hana Mandlikova
4 ....Pam Shriver
5 ....Claudia Kohde-Kilsch
6 ....Steffi Graf
7 ....Manuela Maleeva
8 ....Zina Garrison
9 ....Helena Sukova
10...Bonnie Gadusek

1986

1 ....Martina Navratilova
2 ....Chris Evert Lloyd
3 ....Pam Shriver
4 ....Hana Mandlikova
5 ....Helena Sukova
6 ....Pam Shriver
7 ....Claudia Kohde-Kilsch
8 ....Manuela Maleeva
9 ....Kathy Rinaldi
10...Gabriela Sabatini

1987

1 ....Steffi Graf
2 ....Martina Navratilova
3 ....Chris Evert
4 ....Pam Shriver
5 ....Hana Mandlikova
6 ....Gabriela Sabatini
7 ....Helena Sukova
8 ....Manuela Maleeva
9 ....Zina Garrison
10...Claudia Kohde-Kilsch

1988

1 ....Steffi Graf
2 ....Martina Navratilova
3 ....Chris Evert
4 ....Gabriela Sabatini
5 ....Pam Shriver
6 ....Manuela Maleeva-Fragniere
7 ....Natalia Zvereva
8 ....Helena Sukova
9 ....Zina Garrison
10...Barbara Potter

1989

1 ....Steffi Graf
2 ....Martina Navratilova
3 ....Gabriela Sabatini
4 ....Zina Garrison
5 ....Arantxa Sánchez Vicario
6 ....Monica Seles
7 ....Conchita Martinez
8 ....Helena Sukova
9 ....Manuela Maleeva-Fragniere
10...*Chris Evert

1990

1 ....Steffi Graf
2 ....Monica Seles
3 ....Martina Navratilova
4 ....Mary Joe Fernandez
5 ....Gabriela Sabatini
6 ....Katerina Maleeva
7 ....Arantxa Sánchez Vicario
8 ....Jennifer Capriati
9 ....Manuela Maleeva-Fragniere
10...Zina Garrison

*When Chris Evert announced her retirement at the 1989 United States Open, she was ranked fourth in the world. That was her last official series tournament.

WTA Computer Year-End Top 10 (Cont.)
WOMEN (CONT.)

1991
1 ....Monica Seles
2 ....Steffi Graf
3 ....Gabriela Sabatini
4 ....Martina Navratilova
5 ....Arantxa Sánchez Vicario
6 ....Jennifer Capriati
7 ....Jana Novotna
8 ....Mary Joe Fernandez
9 ....Conchita Martinez
10 ..Manuela Maleeva-Fragniere

1992
1 ....Monica Seles
2 ....Steffi Graf
3 ....Gabriela Sabatini
4 ....Arantxa Sánchez Vicario
5 ....Martina Navratilova
6 ....Mary Joe Fernandez
7 ....Jennifer Capriati
8 ....Conchita Martinez
9 ....Manuela Maleeva-Fragniere
10 ..Jana Novotna

1993
1 ....Steffi Graf
2 ....Arantxa Sánchez Vicario
3 ....Martina Navratilova
4 ....Conchita Martinez
5 ....Gabriela Sabatini
6 ....Jana Novotna
7 ....Mary Joe Fernandez
8 ....Monica Seles
9 ....Jennifer Capriati
10 ..Anke Huber

1994
1 ....Steffi Graf
2 ....Arantxa Sánchez Vicario
3 ....Conchita Martinez
4 ....Jana Novotna
5 ....Mary Pierce
6 ....Lindsay Davenport
7 ....Gabriela Sabatini
8 ....Martina Navratilova
9 ....Kimiko Date
10 ..Natasha Zvereva

1995
1 ....Steffi Graf (co-No. 1)
1 ....Monica Seles (co-No. 1)
2 ....Conchita Martinez
3 ....Arantxa Sánchez Vicario
4 ....Kimiko Date
5 ....Mary Pierce
6 ....Magdalena Maleeva
7 ....Gabriela Sabatini
8 ....Mary Joe Fernandez
9 ....Iva Majoli
10 ..Anke Huber

1996
1 ....Steffi Graf
2 ....Monica Seles
3 ....Jana Novotna
4 ....Lindsay Davenport
5 ....Martina Hingis
6 ....Stephanie de Ville
7 ....Tamarine Tanasugarn
8 ....Anke Huber
9 ....Conchita Martinez
10 ..Julie Halard-Decugis

1997
1 ....Martina Hingis
2 ....Jana Novotna
3 ....Lindsay Davenport
4 ....Amanda Coetzer
5 ....Monica Seles
6 ....Iva Majoli
7 ....Mary Pierce
8 ....Irina Spirlea
9 ....Arantxa Sánchez Vicario
10 ...Mary Joe Fernandez

Prize Money

Top 25 Men's Career Prize Money Leaders
Note: From arrival of Open tennis in 1968 through December 31, 1997.

	Earnings ($)
Pete Sampras	32,060,668
Boris Becker	24,515,647
Ivan Lendl	21,262,417
Stefan Edberg	20,630,941
Michael Chang	16,286,739
Goran Ivanisevic	16,208,537
Jim Courier	13,322,689
Andre Agassi	13,208,483
Michael Stich	12,628,890
John McEnroe	12,539,622
Thomas Muster	11,640,654
Sergi Bruguera	10,748,329
Yevgeny Kafelnikov	9,804,741
Petr Korda	9,039,709
Jimmy Connors	8,641,040
Mats Wilander	7,976,256
Richard Krajicek	6,835,339
Mark Woodforde	6,727,181
Todd Woodbridge	6,169,747
Wayne Ferreira	5,928,744
Jakob Hlasek	5,784,225
Guy Forget	5,657,293
Paul Haarhuis	5,618,152
Brad Gilbert	5,508,745
Anders Jarryd	5,377,067

Top 25 Women's Career Prize Money Leaders
Note: From arrival of Open tennis in 1968 through October 6, 1998.

	Earnings ($)
Martina Navratilova	20,344,061
Steffi Graf	20,330,092
Arantxa Sánchez Vicario	13,801,832
Monica Seles	10,706,249
Jana Novotna	10,077,455
Chris Evert	8,896,195
Gabriela Sabatini	8,785,850
Conchita Martinez	7,573,792
Martina Hingis	7,340,588
Natasha Zvereva	6,758,101
Helena Sukova	6,390,095
Lindsay Davenport	5,636,897
Pam Shriver	5,460,566
Mary Joe Fernandez	4,981,181
Gigi Fernandez	4,680,456
Zina Garrison Jackson	4,590,816
Larisa Neiland	3,715,204
Nathalie Tauziat	3,613,628
Mary Pierce	3,578,671
Iva Majoli	3,444,373
Lori McNeil	3,392,777
Anke Huber	3,355,232
Hana Mandlikova	3,340,959
Manuela Maleeva-Fragniere	3,244,811
Amanda Coetzer	3,077,781

Open Era Overall Wins

Men's Career Leaders—Singles Titles Won

The top tournament-winning men from the institution of Open tennis in 1968 through October 5, 1998.

	W			W
Jimmy Connors	109		Stefan Edberg	41
Ivan Lendl	94		Stan Smith	39
John McEnroe	77		Andre Agassi	38
Bjorn Borg	62		Arthur Ashe	33
Guillermo Vilas	62		Mats Wilander	33
Ilie Nastase	57		John Newcombe	32
Pete Sampras	55		Manuel Orantes	32
Boris Becker	48		Ken Rosewall	32
Rod Laver	47		Michael Chang	32
Thomas Muster	44		Tom Okker	31

Women's Career Leaders—Singles Titles Won

The top tournament-winning women from the institution of Open tennis in 1968 through October 5, 1998.

	W			W
Martina Navratilova	167		Olga Morozova	31
Chris Evert	157		Tracy Austin	29
Steffi Graf	104		Hana Mandlikova	27
Evonne Goolagong Cawley	88		Gabriela Sabatini	27
Margaret Smith Court	79		Arantxa Sánchez Vicario	26
Billie Jean King	67		Nancy Richey	25
Virginia Wade	55		Kerry Melville Reid	22
Monica Seles	43		Sue Barker	21
Helga Masthoff	37		Pam Shriver	21
Conchita Martinez	32		Julie Heldman	20

Annual ATP/WTA Champions

Men—ATP Tour World Championship

Year	Player		Year	Player
1970	Stan Smith		1985	John McEnroe
1971	Ilie Nastase		1986 (Jan)	Ivan Lendl
1972	Ilie Nastase		1986 (Dec)	Ivan Lendl
1973	Ilie Nastase		1987	Ivan Lendl
1974	Guillermo Vilas		1988	Boris Becker
1975	Ilie Nastase		1989	Stefan Edberg
1976	Manuel Orantes		1990	Andre Agassi
1977	Not held		1991	Pete Sampras
1978	Jimmy Connors		1992	Boris Becker
1979	John McEnroe		1993	Michael Stich
1980	Bjorn Borg		1994	Pete Sampras
1981	Bjorn Borg		1995	Boris Becker
1982	Ivan Lendl		1996	Pete Sampras
1983	Ivan Lendl		1997	Pete Sampras
1984	John McEnroe			

Note: Event held twice in 1986.

Women—WTA Tour Championship

Year	Player	Year	Player
1972	Chris Evert	1986 (Mar)	Martina Navratilova
1973	Chris Evert	1986 (Nov)	Martina Navratilova
1974	Evonne Goolagong	1987	Steffi Graf
1975	Chris Evert	1988	Gabriela Sabatini
1976	Evonne Goolagong Cawley	1989	Steffi Graf
1977	Chris Evert	1990	Monica Seles
1978	Martina Navratilova	1991	Monica Seles
1979	Martina Navratilova	1992	Monica Seles
1980	Tracy Austin	1993	Steffi Graf
1981	Martina Navratilova	1994	Gabriela Sabatini
1982	Sylvia Hanika	1995	Steffi Graf
1983	Martina Navratilova	1996	Steffi Graf
1984*	Martina Navratilova	1997	Jana Novotna
1985	Martina Navratilova		

*Since 1984 the final has been best-of-five sets.
Note: Event held twice in 1986.

Arrivederci, Tom

If the Brewers of Milwaukee were to bottle a beer commemorating the Sept. 26,1998, Davis Cup tie, rest assured it would be a lite. With Pete Sampras, Andre Agassi and Michael Chang all in absentia, the less-thrilling U.S. team that converged on Milwaukee Arena consisted of Todd Martin, Jan-Michael Gambill and Justin Gimelstob. The trio—one gray-templed veteran near the omega of his career and two Davis Cup neophytes ranked 50th and 100th, respectively—was something other than a murderers' row. "I guess you could call us the B team," said Martin, "but we're the guys who got the call, for better or for worse." Though their Italian counterparts were themselves no-names whom only the most fervent tennis fan could distinguish from the kitchen help in Big Night, it definitely was for worse.

You wouldn't have known it from the Italians' riotous celebrating, but their victory was diluted by the absence of the best U.S. players. Adamant about not overtaxing his creaky body, Sampras swore off the Davis Cup at the start of the year. Chang, who has never been big on the event, begged off to apply the defib paddles to his moribund career. As for Agassi, usually a loyal Cup participant, the tie coincided with a fundraiser for his charity foundation in Las Vegas. Instead of explaining the conflict and going on his black-tie way, Agassi took the opportunity to rip the U.S. Davis Cup operation. "The USTA runs it the way they want to run it, but no one who wears a tie should be making the decisions," he said, adding that if he were a fan and no top American were playing, he wouldn't buy a ticket.

All but a few thousand Wisconsinites thought likewise. (How's this for a sign of the times: The Promise Keepers' convention, held simultaneously at the adjacent Bradley Center, packed the house.) Taken aback by such indifference to la Coppa Davis, Italy's No. 1 singles player Andrea Gaudenzi said, "I would rather the whole place was filled with fans who are against me than have it be like this. In Italy, Davis Cup is the biggest event in tennis."

To make it bigger here, the USTA, ATP Tour and ITF have discussed a range of options, from rewarding participants with tour ranking points to holding the event every other year, like the Ryder Cup. The first order of business, however, should be replacing Tom Gullikson, who has played out his hand after a solid if unspectacular five-year captaincy. Gullikson is well-liked and respected, but the perception that he's a good soldier (read puppet) for the USTA is fatal to his ability to recruit the stars. "We need someone who will represent the players," says Agassi. "Someone who can light a fire."

An obvious candidate is the cantankerous proprietor of a SoHo art gallery. As he did last time there was a vacancy, John McEnroe has made it known that he's available. Although volatile and less than willing to appease sponsors, McEnroe would stand the best chance of arming a team with top guns, and his presence on the sidelines would bolster the event's popularity. "He would be good as a player's coach," says outgoing USTA president Harry Marmion, "but you have to become part of management. He's too unpredictable. I wouldn't know where he stood on any issue until I read it in the paper."

Perhaps not. But Mac would add much needed carbonation to a U.S. Davis Cup team that's more than a little flat.

—L. Jon Wertheim

Pauline Betz Addie (1965)
George T. Adee (1964)
Fred B. Alexander (1961)
Wilmer L. Allison (1963)
Manuel Alonso (1977)
Arthur Ashe (1985)
Juliette Atkinson (1974)
H.W. Bunny Austin (1997)
Tracy Austin (1992)
Lawrence A. Baker Sr. (1975)
Maud Barger–Wallach (1958)
Angela Mortimer Barrett (1993)
Karl Behr (1969)
Bjorn Borg (1987)
Jean Borotra (1976)
Lesley Turner Bowrey (1997)
Maureen Connolly Brinker(1968)
John Bromwich (1984)
Norman Everard Brookes (1977)
Mary K. Browne (1957)
Jacques Brugnon (1976)
J. Donald Budge (1964)
Maria E. Bueno (1978)
May Sutton Bundy (1956)
Mabel E. Cahill (1976)
Rosie Casals (1996)
Oliver S. Campbell (1955)
Malcolm Chace (1961)
Dorothea Douglass
  Chambers (1981)
Philippe Chatrier (1992)
Louise Brough Clapp (1967)
Clarence Clark (1983)
Joseph S. Clark (1955)
William J. Clothier (1956)
Henri Cochet (1976)
Arthur W. (Bud) Collins Jr. (1994)
Jimmy Connors (1998)
Ashley Cooper (1991)
Margaret Smith Court (1979)
Gottfried von Cramm (1977)
Jack Crawford (1979)
Joseph F. Cullman III (1990)
Allison Danzig (1968)
Sarah Palfrey Danzig (1963)
Herman David (1998)
Dwight F. Davis (1956)
Charlotte Dod (1983)
John H. Doeg (1962)
Lawrence Doherty (1980)
Reginald Doherty (1980)
Jaroslav Drobny (1983)
Margaret Osborne duPont
  (1967)
James Dwight (1955)
Roy Emerson (1982)
Pierre Etchebaster (1978)
Chris Evert (1995)
Robert Falkenburg (1974)
Neale Fraser (1984)

Shirley Fry-Irvin (1970)
Charles S. Garland (1969)
Althea Gibson (1971)
Kathleen McKane Godfree
  (1978)
Richard A. Gonzales (1968)
Evonne Goolagong Cawley
  (1988)
Bryan M. Grant Jr. (1972)
David Gray (1985)
Clarence Griffin (1970)
King Gustaf V of Sweden
  (1980)
Harold H. Hackett (1961)
Ellen Forde Hansell (1965)
Darlene R. Hard (1973)
Doris J. Hart (1969)
Gladys M. Heldman (1979)
W.E. (Slew) Hester Jr. (1981)
Bob Hewitt (1992)
Lew Hoad (1980)
Harry Hopman (1978)
Fred Hovey (1974)
Joseph R. Hunt (1966)
Lamar Hunt (1993)
Francis T. Hunter (1961)
Helen Hull Jacobs (1962)
William Johnston (1958)
Ann Haydon Jones (1985)
Perry Jones (1970)
Billie Jean King (1987)
Jan Kodes (1990)
John A. Kramer (1968)
Rene Lacoste (1976)
Al Laney (1979)
William A. Larned (1956)
Arthur D. Larsen (1969)
Rod G. Laver (1981)
Suzanne Lenglen (1978)
Dorothy Round Little (1986)
George M. Lott Jr. (1964)
Gene Mako (1973)
Molla Bjurstedt Mallory (1958)
Hana Mandlikova (1994)
Alice Marble (1964)
Alastair B. Martin (1973)
Dan Maskell (1996)
William McChesney Martin (1982)
Chuck McKinley (1986)
Maurice McLoughlin (1957)
Frew McMillan (1992)
W. Donald McNeill (1965)
Elisabeth H. Moore (1971)
Gardnar Mulloy (1972)
R. Lindley Murray (1958)
Julian S. Myrick (1963)
Ilie Nastase (1991)
John D. Newcombe (1986)
Arthur C. Nielsen Sr (1971)
Alex Olmedo (1987)

Rafael Osuna (1979)
Mary Ewing Outerbridge (1981)
Frank A. Parker (1966)
Gerald Patterson (1989)
Budge Patty (1977)
Theodore R. Pell (1966)
Fred Perry (1975)
Tom Pettitt (1982)
Nicola Pietrangeli (1986)
Adrian Quist (1984)
Dennis Ralston (1987)
Ernest Renshaw (1983)
William Renshaw (1983)
Vincent Richards (1961)
Bobby Riggs (1967)
Helen Wills Moody Roark
  (1959)
Anthony D. Roche (1986)
Ellen C. Roosevelt (1975)
Ken Rosewall (1980)
Elizabeth Ryan (1972)
Manuel Santana (1984)
Richard Savitt (1976)
Frederick R. Schroeder (1966)
Eleonora Sears (1968)
Richard D. Sears (1955)
Frank Sedgman (1979)
Pancho Segura (1984)
Vic Seixas Jr. (1971)
Francis X. Shields (1964)
Betty Nuthall Shoemaker (1977)
Henry W. Slocum Jr. (1955)
Stan Smith (1987)
Fred Stolle (1985)
William F. Talbert (1967)
Bill Tilden (1959)
Lance Tingay (1982)
Ted Tinling (1986)
Bertha Townsend Toulmin
  (1974)
Tony Trabert (1970)
James H. Van Alen (1965)
John Van Ryn (1963)
Guillermo Vilas (1991)
Ellsworth Vines (1962)
Virginia Wade (1989)
Marie Wagner (1969)
Holcombe Ward (1956)
Watson Washburn (1965)
Malcolm D. Whitman (1955)
Hazel Hotchkiss Wightman
  (1957)
Anthony Wilding (1978)
Richard Norris Williams II
  (1957)
Major Walter Clopton Wingfield
  (1997)
Sidney B. Wood (1964)
Robert D. Wrenn (1955)
Beals C. Wright (1956)

Note: Years in parentheses are dates of induction.

Golf

Redskins: Ready to Rumble
Albert Belle Coach Clyde Drexler Marv Albert

Sports Illustrated

The Unlikely
CHAMPION

MARK O'MEARA *triumphs in a brutal* BRITISH OPEN
to win his second major of the year

JULY 27, 1998
www.cnnsi.com

CHRIS COLE/TGPL

Bait and Switch

Golf promised plenty of young stars in '98, but delivered something else: a graceful stand by the old guard

BY JAIME DIAZ

AT FIRST GLANCE, it might seem that the 1998 golf season promised more than it delivered.

Tiger Woods didn't become golf's absolute ruler, nor did the PGA Tour's other 20-something princes form an all-powerful cartel. Fading stars like Greg Norman, Nick Faldo and Corey Pavin, voicing early-season determination to regain their old turf, never emerged from deep slumps. The USGA began the year dropping hints it would legislate limits on the galloping advances on equipment technology, but then blinked in its first showdown with manufacturers. And Casey Martin won a landmark court decision that paved the way for him to ride a cart on the PGA Tour, but couldn't win enough to get off the Nike Tour.

Still, 1998 made up for its letdowns with some delightful surprises. It was a year to be reminded that while golf is never predictable, it's always provocative.

First and foremost, there was Mark O'Meara, who at age 41 won the Masters and

the British Open, and nearly won the PGA. It was one of the best runs in the majors since 1953, when Ben Hogan became the first and so far only player to win three of them in a year. O'Meara's performance made him one of the important players of his era, as well as the player of the year by a mile.

There was plenty of excellence elsewhere, from the spectacular emergence of Se Ri Pak on the LPGA Tour, to the continued domination of the Senior Tour by Hale Irwin and Gil Morgan, to the 59s shot on the Nike Tour by Doug Dunakey and Notah Begay III, to Colin Montgomerie's sixth consecutive Order of Merit. A 12-year-old prodigy named Henry Liaw of Rowland Heights, Calif., shot 58 on a 5,214-yard par-70 course in a junior tournament, and 62-year-old Gary Player won a Senior Tour event and became the oldest competitor to make the cut at the Masters.

But the man who defined the year was O'Meara. Before 1998 he had 14 victories in 17 years on the PGA Tour. He had played on Ryder Cup teams, won overseas, consis-

After 16 years as a pro, Singh won his first major in '98, taking the PGA at Sahalee.

tently placed high on the money list, and won six times since 1995. But O'Meara was never considered a member of golf's elite because of his relatively poor record in the majors. His best finish in 56 tries had been ties for third in the 1985 and 1991 British Opens, and the 1988 U.S. Open.

But over the last few years, O'Meara quietly drove himself to get to the next level, working with longtime teacher Hank Haney to get a higher trajectory on both his driver and irons, and to become a better wedge player. At the same time, he knew that a perfectionist bent had made him try too hard and self destruct in the big events. "I'd always thought I had to play my very best in majors, and I'd get down on myself when I didn't," he said. "I just finally decided playing Mark O'Meara's game was good enough to win."

Helping to convince him of this was the fact that his game was very often good enough to win head-to-head matches with a certain Mr. Woods. In late 1996 Tiger Woods moved into O'Meara's neighborhood at Isleworth, an exclusive community in Orlando, and the two have been close ever since. The young superstar valued the veteran's wisdom, while O'Meara rekindled his passion and competitiveness measuring himself against the most talented player in the game. In their friendly but furious practice sessions, O'Meara was forced to find a way to offset Woods' physical advantages with savvy and finesse. When he did, it raised his confidence and increased his ambition.

Of course, going into the '98 Masters, O'Meara faced none of the crushing pressure that confronted Woods, who was expected to reprise the magic of his '97 performance. O'Meara by contrast was where

he likes to be, in the background, sneaking up on people. Even better, a strong north wind buffeted Augusta most of the week, causing the usually easy par 5s on the back nine to be virtually unreachable in two shots. It put O'Meara on equal footing with the long hitters who generally have the advantage at the Masters.

O'Meara was five strokes behind Fred Couples after two rounds, but a 68 on Saturday got him within two. Playing in the final group with Couples on Sunday, he sank long birdie putts on the 3rd and 4th holes to tie. "Freddie told me Mark makes the hole look like a basketball hoop," said O'Meara's caddie, Jerry Higgenbotham.

But David Duval played holes 7 through 15 in six under par on Sunday to take a three-stroke lead. O'Meara birdied the par five 15th, just missed a 20-footer on 16, then holed a key nine-footer for birdie on 17. He had chased down both Couples and Duval. A good drive and a 7-iron on the finishing hole put him 20 feet away, and just like that the player who had never held the lead in the entire tournament was the right man in the right place. "I told myself, "This is what it's all about," O'Meara said. "I've got it in my hands and I can finish it off." Drano. The son of the furniture salesman closed the deal. He was finally a major champion.

"Mark came in and stole it," Woods said after helping his friend into the green jacket. The 22-year-old had finished tied for 8th, scrambling all the way with a swing that never felt comfortable, scoring 15 strokes higher than the year before. The performance set the tone for an oddly frustrating year for Woods. He didn't achieve the brilliance that marked his first 11 months as a pro, when he won six times on the PGA Tour, but he was a much more balanced golfer. Though he won only once, in Atlanta, he consistently contended all year, posting 12 top 10s in 17 appearances (including a tie for third at the British Open). Woods's swing became more reliable, his iron game more controlled, and his on-course countenance more composed. "There's no doubt I'm a better player," he said. By the end of the year, his consistently high finishes had strengthened Woods's hold on the No. 1 position in the world rankings. But the year had also revealed a weakness— Woods ranked 122nd on the PGA Tour in putting, and was at times shockingly bad from short range—that he will have to overcome to be the player he and much of the golf world expect him to be.

Putting has rarely been a problem for O'Meara, especially on seaside courses. On the classic links of Royal Birkdale, where he won a European Tour event in 1987, O'Meara seemingly holed every big putt he needed to add the Claret Jug to his Green Jacket.

He also benefited from a colossal stroke of luck. In the windblown third round, O'Meara was three over par for his first five holes when he hit his second shot on the 6th hole into a tangle of tall grass and bushes. After searching for the ball for a few minutes, a dispirited O'Meara gave up and began walking back to the fairway. Just then a member of the gallery who had found the ball and innocently put it in his pocket declared that he had it. O'Meara was allowed to drop into a good lie and salvaged a bogey when it appeared he would have made much worse. He played the final 12 holes of the round two under par. "It was a tremendous break," he said.

On Sunday O'Meara birdied six of the final 15 holes to tie Brian Watts, a former NCAA champion who has won 11 events on the Japanese tour since 1994. Watts played the tournament of his life, and pulled off the shot of his life—a downhill sand shot from a deep bunker on the 72nd hole that nearly went in—but O'Meara was too much. Continuing his mistake-free play, he took the four-hole playoff by two strokes.

With the specter of Hogan lurking over him at the PGA Championship at Sahalee Country Club near Seattle, O'Meara rose to the occasion. Tee-to-green, he was better than he had been in the other majors, eventually leading the field in greens hit in regulation. But his putter never caught fire, and on Sunday, three straight bogeys on the front nine disconnected him from the leaders. O'Meara eventually finished fourth, five strokes behind Vijay Singh, the native of Fiji who won his first major.

Sandwiched between O'Meara's heroics, Lee Janzen won the U.S. Open, outlasting Payne Stewart at the Olympic Club. Janzen had also beaten Stewart for the 1993 Open at Baltusrol, and the victory in San Francisco made the 34-year-old one of 17 players who have won the world's hardest golf tournament more than once.

Indeed, conditions at Olympic made the 98th Open even more difficult than usual. The course's banked fairways were cut so short it was very difficult to keep the ball from rolling in the rough. The tournament also featured one of the worst holes in Open history, the uphill 468-yard 17th, a converted par 5 with a small green that played more over par than any U.S. Open hole in 16 years. And on Friday officials placed the hole on the severely sloped 18th green in an area where uphill putts would

JIM GUND

For the second time this decade, Janzen outdueled Stewart to win the U.S. Open.

die near the cup and then roll backward.

A player needed a break in such an environment, and Janzen got one on Sunday. He was seven strokes behind Stewart with 15 holes to play, and looked to fall farther behind when his 4-wood tee shot on the 5th hole went right and stuck high in one of Olympic's thick cypress pines. While Janzen trudged back to the tee, where a penalty stroke would have had him hitting three, a gust of win blew the ball down. He chipped back into the fairway, hit an iron past the pin, and chipped in for par. From that point on he played three under, his 68 beating Stewart by one. "There are plenty of golfers who are better than me," said a deeply satisfied Jansen. "But that's the best I can do."

Pak, a 20-year-old from South Korea, consistently demonstrated the best she can do while taking women's golf by storm in '98. Pak made her first victory on the women's tour a major, the MacDonald's LPGA Championship. Showing a powerfully grooved swing and a steely countenance, Pak made it clear that she was a talent who was going to be around for a while.

At the U.S. Women's Open at Blackwolf Run, a diabolical Pete Dye design in Kohler, Wisconsin, Pak tied with amateur Jenny Chuasiriporn, also 20, who had made a 45-footer on the 72nd hole for birdie.

It looked like Chuasiriporn would take the playoff. The Duke University senior made three quick birdies and jumped out to a four-stroke lead. But a triple bogey at the par-3 6th hole let Pak back in. Both players were remarkably steady until the 18th, where Pak drove onto the bank of a water hazard. Chuasiriporn put her approach in the right fringe, 45 feet from the cup, and it appeared certain that the Open would have its first amateur champion since Catherine Lacoste in 1967. But Pak recovered with a bogey, Chuasiriporn hit a poor chip and failed on a 12-foot putt. In the longest playoff in the history of women's golf, Pak, on the 92nd hole of the week, made an 18-footer for birdie to win it.

All four of the women's major winners are in their 20s—Pat Hurst, 28, won the Dinah Shore, and Brandie Burton, 26, took the du Maurier—and so is the best player on the LPGA Tour, 28-year-old Annika Sörenstam. She answered Pak's challenge by winning four times and finishing in the top 10 16 times in 19 appearances.

On the Senior Tour, Irwin's second monster year in a row established him as the most dominating Senior golfer ever. He won six times, giving him 19 Senior titles since he turned 50 in 1996, and again won the money title, setting a new record with $2,499,420 in earnings. Irwin's crowning achievement came at the U.S. Senior Open, where he wrested the lead away from Raymond Floyd

Smiling all the way, Kuchar finished 21st at Augusta and 14th at the U.S. Open.

in the fourth round, then made a dramatic 12-foot birdie putt on the 18th to edge Vicente Fernandez.

Gil Morgan again played a very lucrative second fiddle to Irwin, also winning six times. The two players split the four Senior majors. Meanwhile, 58-year-old Jack Nicklaus had a landmark year. At Augusta, where a bronze plaque was dedicated to him behind the 16th green before the tournament, Nicklaus worked the place into a frenzy with an early Sunday charge that got him to within two strokes of the lead on the front nine. He ultimately finished a wondrous sixth, only four behind O'Meara.

Nicklaus also made the cut at the U.S. Open. It was his 146th consecutive major championship as a pro, dating back to the 1962 Masters, and he chose to make it the last championship in a streak that will probably never be broken. "It was the right time for me to stop the streak," said Nicklaus, who will continue to play in the Masters.

At the same time, the game was being infused with new blood, as amateur golf had a banner year. Besides Chuasiriporn, several young men made their mark in big events. Justin Rose of England, 17, finished 4th in the British Open, punctuating his feat by holing a 45-yard wedge shot for a birdie on the final hole. Matt Kuchar was 21st at the Masters and 14th at the U.S. Open, and made a strong defense of his U.S. Amateur crown before losing in the quarterfinals to another promising talent, 18-year-old Sergio Garcia of Spain. Hank Kuehne, the brother of former women's national champion Kelli and '94 Amateur runner-up Trip, won the tournament.

In the end, it was a year that underscored the fact that golfers are getting better younger. Although Woods and company didn't dominate the PGA Tour as much as expected, youth was definitely served. Duval was the leading money winner, winning four times. Justin Leonard won the Players Championship. Ernie Els won at Bay Hill and was headed for a big year until back problems undermined his confidence. Phil Mickelson won twice, beginning with the season-opening Mercedes Championships and following with the strangest tournament of the year, the AT&T Pebble Beach National Pro-Am. When the final 36 holes of the event were washed out on Feb. 1 by El Niño, the tour decided that rather than declare a winner, a final 18 would be played at the beginning of March. But when the logistics became too complicated, the round was moved to ... August 17! On the Monday after the PGA ended in Seattle, some 60 players played the three courses used in the Pebble Beach, and Mickelson gained his 12th career victory.

It's just a matter of time before these kids take over. Colin Montgomerie, now the best player never to have won a major, sounded an ominous note when he said, "It's going to get that much harder to get one because Tiger Woods will be playing." But what was nice about the year was the ingenuity and will with which the old guys resisted. It made 48-year-old Tom Watson's victory at Colonial that much more impressive, just as it made more special O'Meara's feat of replacing Nicklaus as the oldest player to win two majors in one year. If 1998 was a last stand for the old guard, it was a majestic one.

Men's Majors

The Masters

Augusta National GC; Augusta, GA
(par 72; 6,925 yds) April 9–12

Player	Score	Earnings ($)
Mark O'Meara	74-70-68-67—279	576,000
David Duval	71-68-74-67—280	281,600
Fred Couples	69-70-71-70—280	281,600
Jim Furyk	76-70-67-68—281	153,600
Paul Azinger	71-72-69-70—282	128,000
Jack Nicklaus	73-72-70-68—283	111,200
David Toms	75-72-72-64—283	111,200
Darren Clarke	76-73-67-69—285	89,600
Justin Leonard	74-73-69-69—285	89,600
Colin Montgomerie	71-75-69-70—285	89,600
Tiger Woods	71-72-72-70—285	89,600
Jay Haas	72-71-71-72—286	64,800
P. Johansson	74-75-67-70—286	64,800
Phil Mickelson	74-69-69-74—286	64,800
J.M. Olazabal	70-73-71-72—286	64,800
M. Calcavecchia	74-74-69-70—287	48,000
Ernie Els	75-70-70-72—287	48,000
Scott Hoch	70-71-73-73—287	48,000
Ian Woosnam	74-71-72-70—287	48,000
Scott McCarron	73-71-72-71—287	48,000

U.S. Open

The Olympic Club; San Francisco, CA
(par 70; 6,797 yds) June 18–21

Player	Score	Earnings ($)
Lee Janzen	73-66-73-68—280	535,000
Payne Stewart	66-71-70-74—281	315,000
Bob Tway	68-70-73-73—284	201,730
Nick Price	73-68-71-73—285	140,957
Tom Lehman	68-75-68-75—286	107,392
Steve Stricker	73-71-69-73—286	107,392
David Duval	75-68-75-69—287	83,794
Jeff Maggert	69-69-75-74—287	83,794
Lee Westwood	72-74-70-71—287	83,794
Jeff Sluman	72-74-74-68—288	64,490
Phil Mickelson	71-73-74-70—288	64,490
Stuart Appleby	73-74-70-71—288	64,490
Stewart Cink	73-68-73-74—288	64,490
Paul Azinger	75-72-77-65—289	52,214
Jesper Parnevik	69-74-76-70—289	52,214
Jim Furyk	74-73-68-74—289	52,214
*Matt Kuchar	70-69-76-74—289	
Colin Montgomerie	70-74-77-69—290	41,833
Tiger Woods	74-72-71-73—290	41,833
Loren Roberts	71-76-71-72—290	41,833
Jose Maria Olazabal	68-77-71-74—290	41,833
Frank Lickliter II	73-71-72-74—290	41,833

British Open

Royal Birkdale GC; Southport, England
(par 70; 7,018 yds) July 16–19

Player	Score	Earnings ($)
†Mark O'Meara	72-68-72-68—280	492,000
Brian Watts	68-69-73-70—280	308,320
Tiger Woods	65-73-77-66—281	221,400
Jesper Parnevik	68-72-72-70—282	125,733
Jim Furyk	70-70-72-70—282	125,733
*Justin Rose	72-66-75-69—282	
Raymond Russell	68-73-75-66—282	125,733
Davis Love III	67-73-77-68—285	81,180
Costantino Rocca	72-74-70-70—286	69,994
Thomas Bjorn	68-71-76-71—286	69,994
Brad Faxon	67-74-74-72—287	54,666
David Duval	67-77-67-76—287	54,666
John Huston	65-77-73-72—287	54,666
Gordon Brand Jr	71-70-76-71—288	47,560
Greg Turner	68-75-75-71—289	38,786
Des Smyth	74-69-75-71—289	38,786
José María Olazábal	73-72-75-69—289	38,786
Peter Baker	69-72-77-71—289	38,786
Mark James	71-74-74-71—290	28,240
Sandy Lyle	71-72-75-72—290	28,240
Curtis Strange	73-73-74-70—290	28,240
Vijay Singh	67-74-78-71—290	28,240
Robert Allenby	67-76-78-69—290	28,240

PGA Championship

Sahalee CC; Redmond, WA
(par 70; 6,906 yds) August 13–16

Player	Score	Earnings ($)
Vijay Singh	70-66-67-68—271	540,000
Steve Stricker	69-68-66-70—273	324,000
Steve Elkington	69-69-69-67—274	204,000
Mark O'Meara	69-70-69-68—276	118,000
Frank Lickliter	68-71-69-68—276	118,000
Billy Mayfair	73-67-67-70—277	89,500
Davis Love III	70-68-69-70—277	89,500
John Cook	71-68-70-69—278	80,000
Tiger Woods	66-72-70-71—279	69,000
Skip Kendall	72-68-68-71—279	69,000
Brad Faxon	70-68-74-68—280	46,000
John Huston	70-71-68-71—280	46,000
Robert Allenby	72-68-69-71—280	46,000
Ernie Els	72-72-71-66—281	32,000
Per-Ulrik Johansson	69-74-71-68—282	26,000
Fred Funk	70-71-71-70—282	26,000
Greg Kraft	71-73-65-73—282	26,000
Jeff Sluman	71-73-70-69—283	20,500
Hal Sutton	72-68-72-71—283	20,500
Glen Day	68-71-75-70—284	17,100
Tom Lehman	71-71-70-72—284	17,100

* Amateur
† Won four-hole playoff

Men's Tour Results

Late 1997 PGA Tour Events

Tournament	Final Round	Winner	Score/Under Par	Earnings ($)
Las Vegas Invitational	Oct 26	Bill Glasson	340/–20	324,000
The Tour Championship	Nov 2	David Duval	273/–11	720,000
Kapalua International	Nov 9	Davis Love III	268/–22	216,000
Sarazen World Open Championship	Nov 9	Mark Calcavecchia	271/–17	360,000
World Cup of Golf	Nov 23	Padraig Harrington/Paul McGinley	545/–31	200,000 each
JC Penney Classic	Dec 7	Amy Fruhwirth/Clarence Rose	264/–20	187,500 each

1998 PGA Tour Events

Tournament	Final Round	Winner	Score/Under Par	Earnings ($)
Mercedes Championships	Jan 11	Phil Mickelson	271/–17	306,000
Bob Hope Chrysler Classic	Jan 18	Fred Couples*	332/–28	414,000
Phoenix Open	Jan 25	Jesper Parnevik	269/–15	450,000
Buick Invitational#	Feb 8	Scott Simpson*	204/–12	378,000
United Airlines Hawaiian Open	Feb 15	John Huston	260/–28	324,000
Tucson Chrysler Classic	Feb 22	David Duval	269/–19	360,000
Nissan Open	Mar 1	Billy Mayfair*	272/–12	378,000
Doral-Ryder Open	Mar 8	Michael Bradley	278/–10	360,000
Honda Classic	Mar 15	Mark Calcavecchia	270/–18	324,000
Bay Hill Invitational	Mar 21	Ernie Els	274/–14	360,000
Players Championship	Mar 29	Justin Leonard	278/–10	720,000
Entergy Classic	Apr 5	Lee Westwood	273/–15	306,000
The Masters	Apr 12	Mark O'Meara	279/–9	576,000
MCI Classic	Apr 19	Davis Love III	266/–18	342,000
Greater Greensboro Classic	Apr 26	Trevor Dodds*	276/–12	396,000
Houston Open	May 3	David Duval	276/–12	360,000
BellSouth Classic	May 10	Tiger Woods	271/–17	324,000
GTE Byron Nelson Classic	May 17	John Cook	265/–15	450,000
MasterCard Colonial	May 24	Tom Watson	265/–15	414,000
The Memorial	May 31	Fred Couples	271/–17	396,000
Kemper Open	June 7	Stuart Appleby	274/–10	360,000
Buick Classic#	June 14	J.P. Hayes*	201/–12	324,000
U.S. Open	June 21	Lee Janzen	280/even	535,000
Motorola Western Open	July 28	Joe Durant	271/–17	396,000
Canon Greater Hartford Open	July 5	Olin Browne*	266/–14	360,000
Quad City Classic	July 12	Steve Jones	263/–17	279,000
British Open	July 19	Mark O'Meara†	280/even	492,000
Deposit Guaranty Classic	July 19	Fred Funk	270/–18	216,000
CVS Charity Classic	July 26	Steve Pate	269/–15	270,000
FedEx St. Jude Classic	Aug 2	Nick Price*	268/–16	324,000
Buick Open	Aug 9	Billy Mayfair	271/–17	324,000
PGA Championship	Aug 16	Vijay Singh	271/–9	540,000
Pebble Beach Pro-Am§	Aug 17	Phil Mickelson	202/–14	450,000
Sprint International	Aug 23	Vijay Singh	47‡	360,000
NEC World Series of Golf	Aug 30	David Duval	269/–11	405,000
Greater Vancouver Open	Aug 30	Brandel Chamblee	265/–19	360,000
Greater Milwaukee Open	Sep 6	Jeff Sluman	265/–19	324,000
Bell Canadian Open	Sept 13	Billy Andrade*	275/–13	396,000
B.C. Open	Sept 20	Chris Petty	273/–15	270,000
Westin Texas Open	Sept 27	Hal Sutton	270/–18	306,000
Buick Challenge	Oct 4	Steve Elkington*	267/–21	270,000
Michelob Championship	Oct 11	David Duval	268/–16	342,000

* Won sudden-death playoff. † Won four-hole playoff. # Tournament shortened by rain. ‡ Revised Stableford scoring.
§ First rounds played Jan. 29–Feb. 1; final round postponed to Aug. 17 due to weather.

Women's Majors

Nabisco Dinah Shore
Mission Hills CC; Rancho Mirage, CA
(par 72; 6,460 yds) March 26–29

Player	Score	Earnings ($)
Pat Hurst	68-72-70-71—281	150,000
Helen Dobson	70-74-71-67—282	93,093
Laura Davies	75-70-70-68—283	60,385
Helen Alfredsson	70-73-70-70—283	60,385
Donna Andrews	71-72-71-70—284	38,998
Liselotte Neumann	69-71-71-73—284	38,998
Annika Sörensam	76-71-69-70—286	27,928
Karrie Webb	71-72-70-73—286	27,928
Dottie Pepper	73-72-74-68—287	22,393
Sherri Steinhauer	69-76-71-71—287	22,393
Amy Fruhwirth	73-71-73-71—288	18,438
Dawn Coe-Jones	70-72-74-72—288	18,438
Catriona Matthew	75-74-70-70—289	15,670
Penny Hammel	73-72-71-73—289	15,670
Nancy Lopez	71-71-73-74—289	15,670
Meg Mallon	75-69-76-70—290	13,658
*Beth Bauer	76-70-72-72—290	
Lorie Kane	76-71-74-70—291	12,147
Rosie Jones	75-66-78-72—291	12,147
JoAnne Carner	73-72-73-73—291	12,147
Muffin Spencer-Devlin	72-70-76-73—291	12,147
Lisa Hackney	71-71-73-76—291	12,147

LPGA Championship
DuPont Country Club; Wilmington, DE
(par 71; 6,386 yds) May 14–17

Player	Score	Earnings ($)
Se Ri Pak	65-68-72-68—273	195,000
Donna Andrews	71-67-69-69—276	104,666
Lisa Hackney	70-66-69-71—276	104,666
Karrie Webb	71-73-67-66—277	62,145
Wendy Ward	71-67-69-70—277	62,145
Meg Mallon	71-69-68-70—278	39,467
Chris Johnson	69-71-67-71—278	39,467
Emilee Klein	72-67-68-71—278	39,467
Catrin Nilsmark	69-73-70-67—279	29,110
Kelly Robbins	69-71-68-71—279	29,110
Joan Pitcock	69-75-70-66—280	23,180
Annette DeLuca	70-70-71-69—280	23,180
Jane Geddes	69-69-70-72—280	23,180
Tammie Green	72-68-70-71—281	19,691
Lisa Walters	66-69-73-73—281	19,691
Maria Hjorth	71-70-73-68—282	17,402
Juli Inkster	70-71-69-72—282	17,402
Michele Redman	70-71-74-68—283	15,767
Carin Koch	71-73-69-70—283	15,767
Cathy Johnston-Forbes	71-70-70-72—283	15,767

U.S. Women's Open
Blackwolf Run Golf Resort; Kohler, WI
(par 71; 6,412 yds) July 2–5

Player	Score	Earnings ($)
†Se Ri Pak	69-70-75-76—290	232,500
*Jenny Chuasiriporn	72-71-75-72—290	
Liselotte Neumann	70-70-75-76—291	137,500
Da. Ammaccapane	76-71-74-71—292	65,358
Pat Hurst	69-75-75-73—292	65,358
Chris Johnson	72-70-76-74—292	65,358
Stefania Croce	74-71-76-72—293	39,490
Tammie Green	73-71-76-73—293	39,490
Mhairi McKay	72-70-73-78—293	39,490
Trish Johnson	73-71-77-73—294	32,966
Laura Davies	68-75-78-74—295	29,513
Dottie Pepper	71-71-78-75—295	29,513
Carin Koch	72-74-77-73—296	25,927
Helen Alfredsson	75-75-73-73—296	25,927
Hollis Stacy	76-68-82-71—297	21,860
Anna Acker-Macosko	74-74-76-73—297	21,860
Dina Ammaccapane	75-70-78-74—297	21,860
Brandie Burton	74-72-77-74—297	21,860
Lorie Kane	74-72-82-70—298	16,053
Jenny Lidback	71-73-79-75—298	16,053
Akiko Fukushima	72-71-79-76—298	16,053
Rosie Jones	74-74-74-76—298	16,053
Wendy Ward	76-69-75-78—298	16,053
Donna Andrews	75-70-75-78—298	16,053
Lisa Walters	76-70-74-78—298	16,053

du Maurier Classic
Essex Golf & CC; Windsor, Ontario
(par 72; 6,359 yds) July 30–August 2

Player	Score	Earnings ($)
Brandie Burton	68-64-66-72—270	180,000
Annika Sörenstam	68-66-67-70—271	111,711
Betsy King	64-69-70-72—275	81,519
Gail Graham	70-70-68-68—276	44,804
Dawn Coe-Jones	67-70-69-70—276	44,804
Deb Richard	67-69-70-70—276	44,804
Michelle Estill	69-69-66-72—276	44,804
Meg Mallon	65-69-67-75—276	44,804
Sherri Steinhauer	70-71-69-67—277	26,871
Hiromi Kobayashi	68-70-66-73—277	26,871
Tammie Green	66-69-74-69—278	21,335
Alicia Dibos	68-68-69-73—278	21,335
Pat Hurst	67-65-71-75—278	21,335
Juli Inkster	74-68-68-69—279	15,624
Catriona Matthew	68-68-74-69—279	15,624
Michele Redman	70-70-69-70—279	15,624
Charlotta Sörenstam	69-69-71-70—279	15,624
Karrie Webb	69-69-69-72—279	15,624
Allison Finney	70-67-70-72—279	15,624
Dottie Pepper	66-70-71-72—279	15,624
Dana Dormann	68-68-70-73—279	15,624

* Amateur.

† Won on second hole of sudden death after an 18-hole playoff ended in a tie.

Women's Tour Results

Late 1997 LPGA Tour Events

Tournament	Final Round	Winner	Score/ Under Par	Earnings ($)
Japan Queens Cup	Nov 9	Liselotte Neumann	205/–11	112,500
LPGA Tour Championship	Nov 23	Annika Sörenstam	277/–11	160,000
JC Penney Classic	Dec 7	Amy Fruhwirth/Clarence Rose	264/–20	187,500 each

1998 LPGA Tour Events

Tournament	Final Round	Winner	Score/ Under Par	Earnings ($)
HEALTHSOUTH Inaugural	Jan 18	Kelly Robbins	209/–7	90,000
The Office Depot	Jan 25	Helen Alfredsson	277/–11	90,000
Los Angeles Championship#	Feb 15	Dale Eggeling*	141/–3	97,500
Hawaiian Open	Feb 21	Wendy Ward*	204/–12	97,500
Australian Masters	Mar 1	Karrie Webb	272/–16	105,000
Welch's/Circle K Championship	Mar 15	Helen Alfredsson	274/–14	75,000
Standard Register PING	Mar 22	Liselotte Neumann*	279/–13	127,500
Nabisco Dinah Shore	Mar 29	Pat Hurst	281/–7	150,000
Longs Drugs Challenge	Apr 5	Donna Andrews	278/–10	90,000
Myrtle Beach Classic	Apr 19	Karrie Webb	269/–19	90,000
Chick-fil-A Charity Championship	Apr 26	Liselotte Neumann	202/–14	105,000
Titleholders Championship	May 3	Danielle Ammaccapane	276/–12	150,000
Sara Lee Classic	May 10	Barb Mucha*	205/–11	112,500
LPGA Championship	May 17	Se Ri Pak	273/–11	195,000
LPGA Corning Classic	May 24	Tammie Green	268/–20	105,000
LPGA Skins Game	May 24	Laura Davies	10 skins	270,000
Rochester International	May 31	Rosie Jones	279/–9	105,000
Michelob Light Classic	June 7	Annika Sörenstam*	208/–8	90,000
Oldsmobile Classic	June 14	Lisa Walters	265/–23	97.500
Friendly's Classic	June 21	Amy Fruhwirth	280/–8	90,000
ShopRite Classic	June 28	Annika Sörenstam	196/–17	150,000
U.S. Women's Open	July 5	Se Ri Pak*	290/+6	232,500
Jamie Farr Kroger Classic	July 12	Se Ri Pak	261/–23	120,000
Big Apple Classic	July 19	Annika Sörenstam	265/–19	116,250
Giant Eagle Classic	July 26	Se Ri Pak	201/–15	120,000
du Maurier Classic	Aug 2	Brandie Burton	270/–14	180,000
Star Bank Classic	Aug 9	Meg Mallon*	199/–17	90,000
Women's British Open	Aug 16	Sherri Steinhauer	292/+4	162,000
Minnesota Classic	Aug 23	Hiromi Kobayashi*	206/–10	90,000
Rail Classic	Aug 30	Pearl Sinn	200/–16	105,000
Safeway Championship	Sept 6	Danielle Ammaccapane	204/–12	90,000
SAFECO Classic	Sept 13	Annika Sörenstam	273/–15	90,000
Betsy King Classic	Sept 27	Rachel Hetherington*	274/–14	97,500
LPGA Tournament of Champions	Oct 11	Kelly Robbins	276/–12	122,000

* Won sudden-death playoff. #Shortened due to rain.

Senior Men's Tour Results

Late 1997 Senior Tour Events

Tournament	Final Round	Winner	Score/ Under Par	Earnings ($)
Gold Rush Classic	Oct 26	Bob Eastwood	204/–12	135,000
Ralphs Senior Classic	Nov 2	Gil Morgan	197/–16	150,000
Senior Tour Championship	Nov 9	Gil Morgan	272/–16	328,000

1998 Senior Tour Events

Tournament	Final Round	Winner	Score/ Under Par	Earnings ($)
MasterCard Championship	Jan 18	Gil Morgan	195/–21	200,000
Royal Caribbean Classic	Feb 1	David Graham*	202/–11	127,500
LG Championship	Feb 8	Gil Morgan	210/–16	180,000
GTE Classic	Feb 16	Jim Albus	207/–6	165,000
American Express Invitational	Feb 22	Larry Nelson	203/–13	180,000

1998 Senior Tour Events (Cont.)

Tournament	Final Round	Winner	Score/ Under Par	Earnings ($)
Toshiba Classic	Mar 15	Hale Irwin	200/–13	165,000
The Dominion	Mar 29	Lee Trevino	205/–11	150,000
The Tradition	Apr 5	Gil Morgan	276/–12	210,000
PGA Seniors' Championship	Apr 19	Hale Irwin	275/–13	270,000
Las Vegas Classic	Apr 26	Hale Irwin	281/–6	210,000
Bruno's Memorial Classic	May 3	Hubert Green	203/–13	172,500
Home Depot Invitational	May 10	Jim Dent*	207/–9	165,000
St Luke's Classic	May 17	Larry Ziegler	208/–2	150,000
Bell Atlantic Classic	May 24	Jay Sigel*	205/–11	165,000
Pittsburg Classic	May 31	Larry Nelson	204/–12	165,000
Nationwide Championship	June 7	John Jacobs	206/–10	202,500
BellSouth Classic	June 14	Isao Aoki	198/–18	195,000
Canada Open	June 21	Brian Barnes	277/–11	165,000
NFL Classic	June 28	Bob Dickson*	207/–9	165,000
State Farm Classic	July 5	Bruce Summerhays	206/–10	187,500
Senior Players' Championship	July 12	Gil Morgan	267/–21	300,000
Ameritech Open	July 19	Hale Irwin	201/–15	195,000
U.S. Senior Open	July 26	Hale Irwin	285/+1	267,500
Utah Showdown	Aug 2	Gil Morgan	200/–16	150,000
Burnet Classic#	Aug 7	Leonard Thompson*	134/–10	225,000
First of America Classic	Aug 16	George Archer	199/–17	150,000
Long Island Classic	Aug 23	Gary Player	204/–12	150,000
BankBoston Classic	Aug 30	Hale Irwin	201/–15	150,000
Emerald Coast Classic	Sept 6	Dana Quigley	200/–10	165,000
Comfort Classic	Sept 13	Hugh Baiocchi	196/–20	172,500
Kroger Classic#	Sept 20	Hugh Baiocchi*	133/–7	165,000
Boone Valley Classic	Sept 27	Larry Nelson	200/–16	195,000
Vantage Championship	Oct 4	Gil Morgan	198/–12	225,000
The Transamerica	Oct 11	Jim Colbert	205/–11	150,000

*Won sudden-death playoff.

U.S. Amateur Results

Tournament	Final Round	Winner	Score	Runner-Up
Women's Amateur Public Links	June 28	Amy Spooner	2 & 1	Natalie Wong
Men's Amateur Public Links	July 18	Trevor Immelman	3 & 2	Jason Dufner
Boys' Junior Amateur	July 25	James Oh	1 up	Aaron Baddeley
Girls' Junior Amateur	Aug 9	Leigh Anne Hardin	2 up	Brittany Straza
Women's Amateur	Aug 16	Grace Park	7 & 6	Jenny Chuasiriporn
Men's Amateur	Aug 30	Hank Kuehne	2 & 1	Tom McKnight
Senior Men	Sept 17	Bill Shean Jr	5 & 3	William King
Senior Women	Sept 19	Gayle Borthwick	4 & 3	Valerie Hassett
Men's Mid-Amateur	Oct 8	John (Spider) Miller	1 up	Chip Holcombe
Women's Mid-Amateur	Oct 9	Virginia Derby Grimes	4 & 3	Robin Weiss

International Results

Tournament	Final Round	Winner	Score	Runner-Up
Curtis Cup	Aug 2	United States	10–8	GB/Ireland
Solheim Cup	Sept 20	United States	16–12	Europe

PGA Tour Final 1997 Money Leaders

Name	Events	Best Finish	Scoring Average*	Money ($)
Tiger Woods	21	1 (4)	69.10	2,066,833
David Duval	29	1 (3)	69.91	1,885,308
Davis Love III	25	1 (3)	69.47	1,635,953
Jim Furyk	27	2 (3)	69.64	1,619,480
Justin Leonard	29	1 (2)	69.76	1,587,531
Scott Hoch	22	1	69.70	1,393,788
Greg Norman	15	1 (2)	69.16	1,345,856
Steve Elkington	17	1	70.09	1,320,411
Ernie Els	19	1 (2)	69.90	1,243,008
Brad Faxon	23	1	69.97	1,233,505

*Adjusted for average score of field in each tournament entered.

LPGA Tour Final 1997 Money Leaders

Name	Events	Best Finish	Scoring Average	Money ($)
Annika Sörenstam	22	1 (7)	70.04	1,236,789
Karrie Webb	25	1 (3)	70.09	987,606
Kelly Robbins	28	1 (2)	70.35	910,907
Chris Johnson	29	1 (2)	70.84	722,330
Tammie Green	25	1 (2)	71.24	595,077
Juli Inkster	24	1	70.64	557,988
Liselotte Neumann	27	1 (2)	71.28	497,841
Laura Davies	21	1	70.86	483,571
Nancy Lopez	16	1	70.70	470,386
Betsy King	30	1	71.52	469,632

Senior Tour Final 1997 Money Leaders

Name	Events	Best Finish	Scoring Average	Money ($)
Hale Irwin	23	1 (9)	68.92	2,343,364
Gil Morgan	25	1 (6)	69.29	2,160,562
Isao Aoki	28	1	70.03	1,410,499
Jay Sigel	31	1 (2)	70.37	1,294,838
David Graham	30	1 (3)	70.40	1,173,579
John Bland	33	2 (3)	70.39	1,169,707
Graham Marsh	29	1 (2)	70.47	1,128,578
Hugh Baiocchi	25	1	70.66	906,565
Larry Gilbert	23	1	70.71	902,816
Dave Stockton	29	1	70.78	854,611

Call the Swing Doctors

The next time you hear a kid say, "I'm Tiger Woods," duck! According to a report delivered at the annual meeting of the American Association of Neurological Surgeons in April 1998, in the four months following Woods's 1997 Masters victory, doctors at Westchester Medical Center in Valhalla, N.Y., were confronted with a spate of "pediatric cranial injuries due to golf club impacts."

Explains Deborah Benzil, the associate director of neurosurgery at the center, "Kids, excited by Tiger, were taking golf clubs into their yards, swinging away and hitting each other in the head." Benzil and her colleagues dubbed the rash of accidental clubbings—four fractured skulls, all among boys aged six to nine who were watching their friends swing—the Tiger Woods Syndrome. All four underwent surgery and have recovered.

Since delivering their report, doctors have heard from other neurosurgeons of similar Woods-inspired mishaps. "We obviously don't blame Tiger for this," says Benzil. "But as golf gains in popularity, especially among youngsters, it is important to raise awareness of the safety issues.

Kids, can you say, "Fore!"

Men's Golf

THE MAJOR TOURNAMENTS
The Masters

Year	Winner	Score	Runner-Up
1934	Horton Smith	284	Craig Wood
1935	Gene Sarazen* (144)	282	Craig Wood (149) (only 36-hole playoff)
1936	Horton Smith	285	Harry Cooper
1937	Byron Nelson	283	Ralph Guldahl
1938	Henry Picard	285	Ralph Guldahl, Harry Cooper
1939	Ralph Guldahl	279	Sam Snead
1940	Jimmy Demaret	280	Lloyd Mangrum
1941	Craig Wood	280	Byron Nelson
1942	Byron Nelson* (69)	280	Ben Hogan (70)
1943–45	No tournament		
1946	Herman Keiser	282	Ben Hogan
1947	Jimmy Demaret	281	Byron Nelson, Frank Stranahan
1948	Claude Harmon	279	Cary Middlecoff
1949	Sam Snead	282	Johnny Bulla, Lloyd Mangrum
1950	Jimmy Demaret	283	Jim Ferrier
1951	Ben Hogan	280	Skee Riegel
1952	Sam Snead	286	Jack Burke Jr
1953	Ben Hogan	274	Ed Oliver Jr
1954	Sam Snead* (70)	289	Ben Hogan (71)
1955	Cary Middlecoff	279	Ben Hogan
1956	Jack Burke Jr.	289	Ken Venturi
1957	Doug Ford	282	Sam Snead
1958	Arnold Palmer	284	Doug Ford, Fred Hawkins
1959	Art Wall Jr.	284	Cary Middlecoff
1960	Arnold Palmer	282	Ken Venturi
1961	Gary Player	280	Charles R. Coe, Arnold Palmer
1962	Arnold Palmer* (68)	280	Gary Player (71), Dow Finsterwald (77)
1963	Jack Nicklaus	286	Tony Lema
1964	Arnold Palmer	276	Dave Marr, Jack Nicklaus
1965	Jack Nicklaus	271	Arnold Palmer, Gary Player
1966	Jack Nicklaus* (70)	288	Tommy Jacobs (72), Gay Brewer, Jr (78)
1967	Gay Brewer Jr.	280	Bobby Nichols
1968	Bob Goalby	277	Roberto DeVicenzo
1969	George Archer	281	Billy Casper, George Knudson, Tom Weiskopf
1970	Billy Casper* (69)	279	Gene Littler (74)
1971	Charles Coody	279	Johnny Miller, Jack Nicklaus
1972	Jack Nicklaus	286	Bruce Crampton, Bobby Mitchell, Tom Weiskopf
1973	Tommy Aaron	283	J.C. Snead
1974	Gary Player	278	Tom Weiskopf, Dave Stockton
1975	Jack Nicklaus	276	Johnny Miller, Tom Weiskopf
1976	Ray Floyd	271	Ben Crenshaw
1977	Tom Watson	276	Jack Nicklaus
1978	Gary Player	277	Hubert Green, Rod Funseth, Tom Watson
1979†	Fuzzy Zoeller* (4–3)	280	Ed Sneed (4–4), Tom Watson (4–4)
1980	Seve Ballesteros	275	Gibby Gilbert, Jack Newton
1981	Tom Watson	280	Johnny Miller, Jack Nicklaus
1982	Craig Stadler* (4)	284	Dan Pohl (5)
1983	Seve Ballesteros	280	Ben Crenshaw, Tom Kite
1984	Ben Crenshaw	277	Tom Watson
1985	Bernhard Langer	282	Curtis Strange, Seve Ballesteros, Ray Floyd
1986	Jack Nicklaus	279	Greg Norman, Tom Kite
1987	Larry Mize* (4–3)	285	Seve Ballesteros (5), Greg Norman (4-4)
1988	Sandy Lyle	281	Mark Calcavecchia
1989	Nick Faldo* (5–3)	283	Scott Hoch (5–4)
1990	Nick Faldo* (4–4)	278	Ray Floyd (4–x)
1991	Ian Woosnam	277	José María Olazábal
1992	Fred Couples	275	Ray Floyd
1993	Bernhard Langer	277	Chip Beck
1994	José María Olazábal	279	Tom Lehman
1995	Ben Crenshaw	274	Davis Love III

The Masters (Cont.)

Year	Winner	Score	Runner-Up
1996 ....Nick Faldo		276	Greg Norman
1997 ....Tiger Woods		270	Tom Kite
1998 ....Mark O'Meara		279	David Duval, Fred Couples

*Winner in playoff. Playoff scores are in parentheses. †Playoff cut from 18 holes to sudden death.
Note: Played at Augusta National Golf Club, Augusta, GA.

United States Open Championship

Year	Winner	Score	Runner-Up	Site
1895........Horace Rawlins		†173	Willie Dunn	Newport GC, Newport, RI
1896........James Foulis		†152	Horace Rawlins	Shinnecock Hills GC, Southampton, NY
1897........Joe Lloyd		†162	Willie Anderson	Chicago GC, Wheaton, IL
1898........Fred Herd		328	Alex Smith	Myopia Hunt Club, Hamilton, MA
1899........Willie Smith		315	George Low	Baltimore CC, Baltimore
			Val Fitzjohn	
			W. H. Way	
1900........Harry Vardon		313	John H. Taylor	Chicago GC, Wheaton, IL
1901........Willie Anderson* (85)		331	Alex Smith (86)	Myopia Hunt Club, Hamilton, MA
1902........Laurie Auchterlonie		307	Stewart Gardner	Garden City GC, Garden City, NY
1903........Willie Anderson* (82)		307	David Brown (84)	Baltusrol GC, Springfield, NJ
1904........Willie Anderson		303	Gil Nicholls	Glen View Club, Golf, IL
1905........Willie Anderson		314	Alex Smith	Myopia Hunt Club, Hamilton, MA
1906........Alex Smith		295	Willie Smith	Onwentsia Club, Lake Forest, IL
1907........Alex Ross		302	Gil Nicholls	Philadelphia Cricket Club, Chestnut Hill, PA
1908........Fred McLeod* (77)		322	Willie Smith (83)	Myopia Hunt Club, Hamilton, MA
1909........George Sargent		290	Tom McNamara	Englewood GC, Englewood, NJ
1910........Alex Smith* (71)		298	John McDermott (75)	Philadelphia Cricket Club, Chestnut Hill, PA
			Macdonald Smith (77)	
1911........John McDermott* (80)		307	Mike Brady (82)	Chicago GC, Wheaton, IL
			George Simpson (85)	
1912........John McDermott		294	Tom McNamara	CC of Buffalo, Buffalo
1913........Francis Ouimet* (72)		304	Harry Vardon (77)	The Country Club, Brookline, MA
			Edward Ray (78)	
1914........Walter Hagen		290	Chick Evans	Midlothian CC, Blue Island, IL
1915........Jerry Travers		297	Tom McNamara	Baltusrol GC, Springfield, NJ
1916........Chick Evans		286	Jock Hutchison	Minikahda Club, Minneapolis
1917-18 ..No tournament				
1919........Walter Hagen* (77)		301	Mike Brady (78)	Brae Burn CC, West Newton, MA
1920........Edward Ray		295	Harry Vardon	Inverness CC, Toledo
			Jack Burke	
			Leo Diegel	
			Jock Hutchison	
1921........Jim Barnes		289	Walter Hagen	Columbia CC, Chevy Chase, MD
			Fred McLeod	
1922........Gene Sarazen		288	John L. Black	Skokie CC, Glencoe, IL
			Bobby Jones	
1923........Bobby Jones* (76)		296	Bobby Cruickshank (78)	Inwood CC, Inwood, NY
1924........Cyril Walker		297	Bobby Jones	Oakland Hills CC, Birmingham, MI
1925........W. MacFarlane* (75–72)		291	Bobby Jones (75–73)	Worcester CC, Worcester, MA
1926........Bobby Jones		293	Joe Turnesa	Scioto CC, Columbus, OH
1927........Tommy Armour* (76)		301	Harry Cooper (79)	Oakmont CC, Oakmont, PA
1928........Johnny Farrell* (143)		294	Bobby Jones (144)	Olympia Fields CC, Matteson, IL
1929........Bobby Jones* (141)		294	Al Espinosa (164)	Winged Foot GC, Mamaroneck, NY
1930........Bobby Jones		287	Macdonald Smith	Interlachen CC, Hopkins, MN
1931........Billy Burke* (149–148)		292	George Von Elm (149–149)	Inverness Club, Toledo
1932........Gene Sarazen		286	Phil Perkins	Fresh Meadows CC, Flushing, NY
			Bobby Cruickshank	
1933........Johnny Goodman		287	Ralph Guldahl	North Shore CC, Glenview, IL
1934........Olin Dutra		293	Gene Sarazen	Merion Cricket Club, Ardmore, PA
1935........Sam Parks Jr.		299	Jimmy Thompson	Oakmont CC, Oakmont, PA
1936........Tony Manero		282	Harry Cooper	Baltusrol GC (Upper Course), Springfield, NJ
1937........Ralph Guldahl		281	Sam Snead	Oakland Hills CC, Birmingham, MI
1938........Ralph Guldahl		284	Dick Metz	Cherry Hills CC, Denver, CO
1939........Byron Nelson* (68–70)		284	Craig Wood (68–73)	Philadelphia CC, Philadelphia
			Denny Shute (76)	

United States Open Championship *(Cont.)*

Year	Winner	Score	Runner-Up	Site
1940	Lawson Little* (70)	287	Gene Sarazen (73)	Canterbury GC, Cleveland
1941	Craig Wood	284	Denny Shute	Colonial Club, Fort Worth
1942–45	No tournament			
1946	Lloyd Mangrum* (72–72)	284	Vic Ghezzi (72–73) Byron Nelson (72–73)	Canterbury GC, Cleveland
1947	Lew Worsham* (69)	282	Sam Snead (70)	St. Louis CC, Clayton, MO
1948	Ben Hogan	276	Jimmy Demaret	Riviera CC, Los Angeles
1949	Cary Middlecoff	286	Sam Snead Clayton Heafner	Medinah CC, Medinah, IL
1950	Ben Hogan* (69)	287	Lloyd Mangrum (73) George Fazio (75)	Merion GC, Ardmore, PA
1951	Ben Hogan	287	Clayton Heafner	Oakland Hills CC, Birmingham, MI
1952	Julius Boros	281	Ed Oliver	Northwood CC, Dallas
1953	Ben Hogan	283	Sam Snead	Oakmont CC, Oakmont, PA
1954	Ed Furgol	284	Gene Littler	Baltusrol GC (Lower Course), Springfield, NJ
1955	Jack Fleck* (69)	287	Ben Hogan (72)	Olympic Club (Lake Course), San Francisco
1956	Cary Middlecoff	281	Ben Hogan Julius Boros	Oak Hill CC, Rochester, NY
1957	Dick Mayer* (72)	282	Cary Middlecoff (79)	Inverness Club, Toledo
1958	Tommy Bolt	283	Gary Player	Southern Hills CC, Tulsa
1959	Billy Casper	282	Bob Rosburg	Winged Foot GC, Mamaroneck, NY
1960	Arnold Palmer	280	Jack Nicklaus	Cherry Hills CC, Denver
1961	Gene Littler	281	Bob Goalby Doug Sanders	Oakland Hills CC, Birmingham, MI
1962	Jack Nicklaus* (71)	283	Arnold Palmer (74)	Oakmont CC, Oakmont, PA
1963	Julius Boros* (70)	293	Jacky Cupit (73) Arnold Palmer (76)	The Country Club, Brookline, MA
1964	Ken Venturi	278	Tommy Jacobs	Congressional CC, Bethesda, MD
1965	Gary Player* (71)	282	Kel Nagle (74)	Bellerive CC, St. Louis
1966	Billy Casper* (69)	278	Arnold Palmer (73)	Olympic Club (Lake Course), San Francisco
1967	Jack Nicklaus	275	Arnold Palmer	Baltusrol GC (Lower Course), Springfield, NJ
1968	Lee Trevino	275	Jack Nicklaus	Oak Hill CC, Rochester, NY
1969	Orville Moody	281	Deane Beman Al Geiberger Bob Rosburg	Champions GC (Cypress Creek Course), Houston
1970	Tony Jacklin	281	Dave Hill	Hazeltine GC, Chaska, MN
1971	Lee Trevino* (68)	280	Jack Nicklaus (71)	Merion GC (East Course), Ardmore, PA
1972	Jack Nicklaus	290	Bruce Crampton	Pebble Beach GL, Pebble Beach, CA
1973	Johnny Miller	279	John Schlee	Oakmont CC, Oakmont, PA
1974	Hale Irwin	287	Forrest Fezler	Winged Foot GC, Mamaroneck, NY
1975	Lou Graham* (71)	287	John Mahaffey (73)	Medinah CC, Medinah, IL
1976	Jerry Pate	277	Tom Weiskopf Al Geiberger	Atlanta Athletic Club, Duluth, GA
1977	Hubert Green	278	Lou Graham	Southern Hills CC, Tulsa
1978	Andy North	285	Dave Stockton J.C. Snead	Cherry Hills CC, Denver
1979	Hale Irwin	284	Gary Player Jerry Pate	Inverness Club, Toledo
1980	Jack Nicklaus	272	Isao Aoki	Baltusrol GC (Lower Course), Springfield, NJ
1981	David Graham	273	George Burns Bill Rogers	Merion GC, Ardmore, PA
1982	Tom Watson	282	Jack Nicklaus	Pebble Beach GL, Pebble Beach, CA
1983	Larry Nelson	280	Tom Watson	Oakmont CC, Oakmont, PA
1984	Fuzzy Zoeller* (67)	276	Greg Norman (75)	Winged Foot GC, Mamaroneck, NY
1985	Andy North	279	Dave Barr T.C. Chen Denis Watson	Oakland Hills CC, Birmingham, MI
1986	Ray Floyd	279	Lanny Wadkins Chip Beck	Shinnecock Hills GC, Southampton, NY
1987	Scott Simpson	277	Tom Watson	Olympic Club (Lake Course), San Francisco
1988	Curtis Strange* (71)	278	Nick Faldo (75)	The Country Club, Brookline, MA
1989	Curtis Strange	278	Chip Beck Mark McCumber Ian Woosnam	Oak Hill CC, Rochester, NY
1990	Hale Irwin* (74) (3)	280	Mike Donald (74) (4)	Medinah CC, Medinah, IL
1991	Payne Stewart (75)	282	Scott Simpson (77)	Hazeltine GC, Chaska, MN

U.S. Open *(Cont.)*

Year	Winner	Score	Runner-Up	Site
1992	Tom Kite	285	Jeff Sluman	Pebble Beach GL, Pebble Beach, CA
1993	Lee Janzen	272	Payne Stewart	Baltusrol GC, Springfield, NJ
1994	Ernie Els*	279	Loren Roberts	Oakmont CC, Oakmont, PA
			Colin Montgomerie	
1995	Corey Pavin	280	Greg Norman	Shinnecock Hills GC, Southampton, NY
1996	Steve Jones	278	Davis Love III	Oakland Hills CC, Birmingham, MI
			Tom Lehman	
1997	Ernie Els	276	Colin Montgomerie	Congressional CC, Bethesda, MD
1998	Lee Janzen	280	Payne Stewart	The Olympic Club, San Francisco, CA

*Winner in playoff. Playoff scores are in parentheses. The 1990 playoff went to one hole of sudden death after an 18-hole playoff. In the 1994 playoff, Montgomerie was eliminated after 18 playoff holes, and Els beat Roberts on the 20th.
†Before 1898, 36 holes. From 1898 on, 72 holes.

British Open

Year	Winner	Score	Runner-Up	Site
1860†	Willie Park	174	Tom Morris Sr.	Prestwick, Scotland
1861‡	Tom Morris Sr.	163	Willie Park	Prestwick, Scotland
1862	Tom Morris Sr.	163	Willie Park	Prestwick, Scotland
1863	Willie Park	168	Tom Morris Sr.	Prestwick, Scotland
1864	Tom Morris, Sr.	160	Andrew Strath	Prestwick, Scotland
1865	Andrew Strath	162	Willie Park	Prestwick, Scotland
1866	Willie Park	169	David Park	Prestwick, Scotland
1867	Tom Morris Sr.	170	Willie Park	Prestwick, Scotland
1868	Tom Morris Jr.	154	Tom Morris Sr.	Prestwick, Scotland
1869	Tom Morris Jr.	157	Tom Morris Sr.	Prestwick, Scotland
1870	Tom Morris Jr.	149	David Strath	Prestwick, Scotland
			Bob Kirk	
1871	No tournament			
1872	Tom Morris Jr.	166	David Strath	Prestwick, Scotland
1873	Tom Kidd	179	Jamie Anderson	St. Andrews, Scotland
1874	Mungo Park	159	No record	Musselburgh, Scotland
1875	Willie Park	166	Bob Martin	Prestwick, Scotland
1876	Bob Martin#	176	David Strath	St. Andrews, Scotland
1877	Jamie Anderson	160	Bob Pringle	Musselburgh, Scotland
1878	Jamie Anderson	157	Robert Kirk	Prestwick, Scotland
1879	Jamie Anderson	169	Andrew Kirkaldy	St. Andrews, Scotland
			James Allan	
1880	Robert Ferguson	162	No record	Musselburgh, Scotland
1881	Robert Ferguson	170	Jamie Anderson	Prestwick, Scotland
1882	Robert Ferguson	171	Willie Fernie	St. Andrews, Scotland
1883	Willie Fernie*	159	Robert Ferguson	Musselburgh, Scotland
1884	Jack Simpson	160	Douglas Rolland	Prestwick, Scotland
			Willie Fernie	
1885	Bob Martin	171	Archie Simpson	St. Andrews, Scotland
1886	David Brown	157	Willie Campbell	Musselburgh, Scotland
1887	Willie Park, Jr.	161	Bob Martin	Prestwick, Scotland
1888	Jack Burns	171	Bernard Sayers	St. Andrews, Scotland
			David Anderson	
1889	Willie Park Jr.* (158)	155	Andrew Kirkaldy (163)	Musselburgh, Scotland
1890	John Ball	164	Willie Fernie	Prestwick, Scotland
1891	Hugh Kirkaldy	166	Andrew Kirkaldy	St. Andrews, Scotland
			Willie Fernie	
1892	Harold Hilton	**305	John Ball	Muirfield, Scotland
			Hugh Kirkaldy	
1893	William Auchterlonie	322	John E. Laidlay	Prestwick, Scotland
1894	John H. Taylor	326	Douglas Rolland	Royal St. George's, England
1895	John H. Taylor	322	Alexander Herd	St. Andrews, Scotland
1896	Harry Vardon* (157)	316	John H. Taylor (161)	Muirfield, Scotland
1897	Harold Hilton	314	James Braid	Hoylake, England
1898	Harry Vardon	307	Willie Park Jr.	Prestwick, Scotland
1899	Harry Vardon	310	Jack White	Royal St. George's, England
1900	John H. Taylor	309	Harry Vardon	St. Andrews, Scotland
1901	James Braid	309	Harry Vardon	Muirfield, Scotland
1902	Alexander Herd	307	Harry Vardon	Hoylake, England
1903	Harry Vardon	300	Tom Vardon	Prestwick, Scotland
1904	Jack White	296	John H. Taylor	Royal St. George's, England

British Open (Cont.)

Year	Winner	Score	Runner-Up	Site
1905	James Braid	318	John H. Taylor	St. Andrews, Scotland
			Rolland Jones	
1906	James Braid	300	John H. Taylor	Muirfield, Scotland
1907	Arnaud Massy	312	John H. Taylor	Hoylake, England
1908	James Braid	291	Tom Ball	Prestwick, Scotland
1909	John H. Taylor	295	James Braid	Deal, England
			Tom Ball	
1910	James Braid	299	Alexander Herd	St. Andrews, Scotland
1911	Harry Vardon	303	Arnaud Massy	Royal St. George's, England
1912	Ted Ray	295	Harry Vardon	Muirfield, Scotland
1913	John H. Taylor	304	Ted Ray	Hoylake, England
1914	Harry Vardon	306	John H. Taylor	Prestwick, Scotland
1915–19	No tournament			
1920	George Duncan	303	Alexander Herd	Deal, England
1921	Jock Hutchison* (150)	296	Roger Wethered (159)	St. Andrews, Scotland
1922	Walter Hagen	300	George Duncan	Royal St. George's, England
			Jim Barnes	
1923	Arthur G. Havers	295	Walter Hagen	Troon, Scotland
1924	Walter Hagen	301	Ernest Whitcombe	Hoylake, England
1925	Jim Barnes	300	Archie Compston	Prestwick, Scotland
			Ted Ray	
1926	Bobby Jones	291	Al Watrous	Royal Lytham & St. Anne's, England
1927	Bobby Jones	285	Aubrey Boomer	St. Andrews, Scotland
1928	Walter Hagen	292	Gene Sarazen	Royal St. George's, England
1929	Walter Hagen	292	Johnny Farrell	Muirfield, Scotland
1930	Bobby Jones	291	Macdonald Smith	Hoylake, England
			Leo Diegel	
1931	Tommy Armour	296	Jose Jurado	Carnoustie, Scotland
1932	Gene Sarazen	283	Macdonald Smith	Prince's, England
1933	Denny Shute* (149)	292	Craig Wood (154)	St. Andrews, Scotland
1934	Henry Cotton	283	Sidney F. Brews	Royal St. George's, England
1935	Alfred Perry	283	Alfred Padgham	Muirfield, Scotland
1936	Alfred Padgham	287	James Adams	Hoylake, England
1937	Henry Cotton	290	Reginald A. Whitcombe	Carnoustie, Scotland
1938	Reginald A. Whitcombe	295	James Adams	Royal St. George's, England
1939	Richard Burton	290	Johnny Bulla	St. Andrews, Scotland
1940–45	No tournament			
1946	Sam Snead	290	Bobby Locke	St. Andrews, Scotland
			Johnny Bulla	
1947	Fred Daly	293	Reginald W. Horne	Hoylake, England
			Frank Stranahan	
1948	Henry Cotton	294	Fred Daly	Muirfield, Scotland
1949	Bobby Locke* (135)	283	Harry Bradshaw (147)	Royal St. George's, England
1950	Bobby Locke	279	Roberto DeVicenzo	Troon, Scotland
1951	Max Faulkner	285	Tony Cerda	Portrush, Ireland
1952	Bobby Locke	287	Peter Thomson	Royal Lytham & St. Anne's, England
1953	Ben Hogan	282	Frank Stranahan	Carnoustie, Scotland
			Dai Rees	
			Peter Thomson	
			Tony Cerda	
1954	Peter Thomson	283	Sidney S. Scott	Royal Birkdale, England
			Dai Rees	
			Bobby Locke	
1955	Peter Thomson	281	John Fallon	St. Andrews, Scotland
1956	Peter Thomson	286	Flory Van Donck	Hoylake, England
1957	Bobby Locke	279	Peter Thomson	St. Andrews, Scotland
1958	Peter Thomson* (139)	278	Dave Thomas (143)	Royal Lytham & St. Anne's, England
1959	Gary Player	284	Fred Bullock	Muirfield, Scotland
			Flory Van Donck	
1960	Kel Nagle	278	Arnold Palmer	St. Andrews, Scotland
1961	Arnold Palmer	284	Dai Rees	Royal Birkdale, England
1962	Arnold Palmer	276	Kel Nagle	Troon, Scotland
1963	Bob Charles* (140)	277	Phil Rodgers (148)	Royal Lytham & St. Anne's, England
1964	Tony Lema	279	Jack Nicklaus	St. Andrews, Scotland
1965	Peter Thomson	285	Brian Huggett	Southport, England
			Christy O'Connor	

British Open (Cont.)

Year	Winner	Score	Runner-Up	Site
1966	Jack Nicklaus	282	Doug Sanders Dave Thomas	Muirfield, Scotland
1967	Robert DeVicenzo	278	Jack Nicklaus	Hoylake, England
1968	Gary Player	289	Jack Nicklaus Bob Charles	Carnoustie, Scotland
1969	Tony Jacklin	280	Bob Charles	Royal Lytham & St. Anne's, England
1970	Jack Nicklaus* (72)	283	Doug Sanders (73)	St. Andrews, Scotland
1971	Lee Trevino	278	Lu Liang Huan	Royal Birkdale, England
1972	Lee Trevino	278	Jack Nicklaus	Muirfield, Scotland
1973	Tom Weiskopf	276	Johnny Miller	Troon, Scotland
1974	Gary Player	282	Peter Oosterhuis	Royal Lytham & St. Anne's, England
1975	Tom Watson* (71)	279	Jack Newton (72)	Carnoustie, Scotland
1976	Johnny Miller	279	Jack Nicklaus Seve Ballesteros	Royal Birkdale, England
1977	Tom Watson	268	Jack Nicklaus	Turnberry, Scotland
1978	Jack Nicklaus	281	Ben Crenshaw Tom Kite Ray Floyd Simon Owen	St. Andrews, Scotland
1979	Seve Ballesteros	283	Ben Crenshaw Jack Nicklaus	Royal Lytham & St. Anne's, England
1980	Tom Watson	271	Lee Trevino	Muirfield, Scotland
1981	Bill Rogers	276	Bernhard Langer	Royal St. George's, England
1982	Tom Watson	284	Nick Price Peter Oosterhuis	Troon, Scotland
1983	Tom Watson	275	Andy Bean	Royal Birkdale, England
1984	Seve Ballesteros	276	Tom Watson Bernhard Langer	St. Andrews, Scotland
1985	Sandy Lyle	282	Payne Stewart	Royal St. George's, England
1986	Greg Norman	280	Gordon Brand	Turnberry, Scotland
1987	Nick Faldo	279	Paul Azinger Rodger Davis	Muirfield, Scotland
1988	Seve Ballesteros	273	Nick Price	Royal Lytham & St. Anne's, England
1989††	Mark Calcavecchia* (4-3-3-3)	275	Wayne Grady (4-4-4-4) Greg Norman (3-3-4-x)	Troon, Scotland
1990	Nick Faldo	270	Payne Stewart Mark McNulty	St. Andrews, Scotland
1991	Ian Baker-Finch	272	Mike Harwood	Royal Birkdale, England
1992	Nick Faldo	272	John Cook	Muirfield, Scotland
1993	Greg Norman	267	Nick Faldo	Royal St. George's, England
1994	Nick Price	268	Jesper Parnevik	Turnberry, Scotland
1995	John Daly* (4-3-4-4)	282	C. Rocca (5-4-7-3)	St. Andrews, Scotland
1996	Tom Lehman	271	Mark McCumber Ernie Els	Royal Lytham & St. Anne's, England
1997	Justin Leonard	272	Jesper Parnevik Darren Clarke	Troon, Scotland
1998	Mark O'Meara* (4-4-5-4)	280	Brian Watts (5-4-5-5)	Southport, England

*Winner in playoff. Playoff scores are in parentheses. †The first event was open only to professional golfers.
‡The second annual open was open to amateurs and pros. #Tied, but refused playoff.
**Championship extended from 36 to 72 holes. ††Playoff cut from 18 holes to 4 holes.

PGA Championship

Year	Winner	Score	Runner-Up	Site
1916	Jim Barnes	1 up	Jock Hutchison	Siwanoy CC, Bronxville, NY
1917–18	No tournament			
1919	Jim Barnes	6 & 5	Fred McLeod	Engineers CC, Roslyn, NY
1920	Jock Hutchison	1 up	J. Douglas Edgar	Flossmoor CC, Flossmoor, IL
1921	Walter Hagen	3 & 2	Jim Barnes	Inwood CC, Far Rockaway, NY
1922	Gene Sarazen	4 & 3	Emmet French	Oakmont CC, Oakmont, PA
1923	Gene Sarazen	1 up 38 holes	Walter Hagen	Pelham CC, Pelham, NY
1924	Walter Hagen	2 up	Jim Barnes	French Lick CC, French Lick, IN
1925	Walter Hagen	6 & 5	William Mehlhorn	Olympia Fields CC, Olympia Fields, IL
1926	Walter Hagen	5 & 3	Leo Diegel	Salisbury GC, Westbury, NY
1927	Walter Hagen	1 up	Joe Turnesa	Cedar Crest CC, Dallas

PGA Championship (Cont.)

Year	Winner	Score	Runner-Up	Site
1928	Leo Diegel	6 & 5	Al Espinosa	Five Farms CC, Baltimore
1929	Leo Diegel	6 & 4	Johnny Farrell	Hillcrest CC, Los Angeles
1930	Tommy Armour	1 up	Gene Sarazen	Fresh Meadow CC, Flushing, NY
1931	Tom Creavy	2 & 1	Denny Shute	Wannamoisett CC, Rumford, RI
1932	Olin Dutra	4 & 3	Frank Walsh	Keller GC, St. Paul
1933	Gene Sarazen	5 & 4	Willie Goggin	Blue Mound CC, Milwaukee
1934	Paul Runyan	1 up	Craig Wood	Park CC, Williamsville, NY
1935	Johnny Revolta	5 & 4	Tommy Armour	Twin Hills CC, Oklahoma City
		38 holes		
1936	Denny Shute	3 & 2	Jimmy Thomson	Pinehurst CC, Pinehurst, NC
1937	Denny Shute	1 up	Harold McSpaden	Pittsburgh FC, Aspinwall, PA
		37 holes		
1938	Paul Runyan	8 & 7	Sam Snead	Shawnee CC, Shawnee-on-Delaware, PA
1939	Henry Picard	1 up	Byron Nelson	Pomonok CC, Flushing, NY
		37 holes		
1940	Byron Nelson	1 up	Sam Snead	Hershey CC, Hershey, PA
1941	Vic Ghezzi	1 up	Byron Nelson	Cherry Hills CC, Denver
		38 holes		
1942	Sam Snead	2 & 1	Jim Turnesa	Seaview CC, Atlantic City
1943	No tournament			
1944	Bob Hamilton	1 up	Byron Nelson	Manito G & CC, Spokane, WA
1945	Byron Nelson	4 & 3	Sam Byrd	Morraine CC, Dayton
1946	Ben Hogan	6 & 4	Ed Oliver	Portland GC, Portland, OR
1947	Jim Ferrier	2 & 1	Chick Harbert	Plum Hollow CC, Detroit
1948	Ben Hogan	7 & 6	Mike Turnesa	Norwood Hills CC, St. Louis
1949	Sam Snead	3 & 2	Johnny Palmer	Hermitage CC, Richmond
1950	Chandler Harper	4 & 3	Henry Williams Jr.	Scioto CC, Columbus, OH
1951	Sam Snead	7 & 6	Walter Burkemo	Oakmont CC, Oakmont, PA
1952	Jim Turnesa	1 up	Chick Harbert	Big Spring CC, Louisville
1953	Walter Burkemo	2 & 1	Felice Torza	Birmingham CC, Birmingham, MI
1954	Chick Harbert	4 & 3	Walter Burkemo	Keller GC, St. Paul
1955	Doug Ford	4 & 3	Cary Middlecoff	Meadowbrook CC, Detroit
1956	Jack Burke	3 & 2	Ted Kroll	Blue Hill CC, Boston
1957	Lionel Hebert	2 & 1	Dow Finsterwald	Miami Valley CC, Dayton
1958	Dow Finsterwald	276	Billy Casper	Llanerch CC, Havertown, PA
1959	Bob Rosburg	277	Jerry Barber	Minneapolis GC, St. Louis Park, MN
			Doug Sanders	
1960	Jay Hebert	281	Jim Ferrier	Firestone CC, Akron
1961	Jerry Barber* (67)	277	Don January (68)	Olympia Fields CC, Olympia Fields, IL
1962	Gary Player	278	Bob Goalby	Aronimink GC, Newton Square, PA
1963	Jack Nicklaus	279	Dave Ragan Jr.	Dallas Athletic Club, Dallas
1964	Bobby Nichols	271	Jack Nicklaus	Columbus CC, Columbus, OH
			Arnold Palmer	
1965	Dave Marr	280	Billy Casper	Laurel Valley CC, Ligonier, PA
			Jack Nicklaus	
1966	Al Geiberger	280	Dudley Wysong	Firestone CC, Akron
1967	Don January* (69)	281	Don Massengale (71)	Columbine CC, Littleton, CO
1968	Julius Boros	281	Bob Charles	Pecan Valley CC, San Antonio
			Arnold Palmer	
1969	Ray Floyd	276	Gary Player	NCR CC, Dayton
1970	Dave Stockton	279	Arnold Palmer	Southern Hills CC, Tulsa
			Bob Murphy	
1971	Jack Nicklaus	281	Billy Casper	PGA Natl GC, Palm Beach Gardens, FL
1972	Gary Player	281	Tommy Aaron	Oakland Hills CC, Birmingham, MI
			Jim Jamieson	
1973	Jack Nicklaus	277	Bruce Crampton	Canterbury GC, Cleveland
1974	Lee Trevino	276	Jack Nicklaus	Tanglewood GC, Winston-Salem, NC
1975	Jack Nicklaus	276	Bruce Crampton	Firestone CC, Akron
1976	Dave Stockton	281	Ray Floyd	Congressional CC, Bethesda, MD
			Don January	
1977†	Lanny Wadkins* (4-4-4)	282	Gene Littler (4-4-5)	Pebble Beach GL, Pebble Beach, CA
1978	John Mahaffey* (4-3)	276	Jerry Pate (4-4)	Oakmont CC, Oakmont, PA
			Tom Watson (4-5)	
1979	David Graham* (4-4-2)	272	Ben Crenshaw (4-4-4)	Oakland Hills CC, Birmingham, MI
1980	Jack Nicklaus	274	Andy Bean	Oak Hill CC, Rochester, NY
1981	Larry Nelson	273	Fuzzy Zoeller	Atlanta Athletic Club, Duluth, GA

PGA Championship *(Cont.)*

Year	Winner	Score	Runner-Up	Site
1982	Raymond Floyd	272	Lanny Wadkins	Southern Hills CC, Tulsa
1983	Hal Sutton	274	Jack Nicklaus	Riviera CC, Pacific Palisades, CA
1984	Lee Trevino	273	Gary Player	Shoal Creek, Birmingham, AL
			Lanny Wadkins	
1985	Hubert Green	278	Lee Trevino	Cherry Hills CC, Denver
1986	Bob Tway	276	Greg Norman	Inverness CC, Toledo
1987	Larry Nelson* (4)	287	Lanny Wadkins (5)	PGA Natl GC, Palm Beach Gardens, FL
1988	Jeff Sluman	272	Paul Azinger	Oak Tree GC, Edmond, OK
1989	Payne Stewart	276	Mike Reid	Kemper Lakes GC, Hawthorn Woods, IL
1990	Wayne Grady	282	Fred Couples	Shoal Creek, Birmingham, AL
1991	John Daly	276	Bruce Lietzke	Crooked Stick GC, Carmel, IN
1992	Nick Price	278	Jim Gallagher Jr.	Bellerive CC, St. Louis
1993	Paul Azinger* (4–4)	272	Greg Norman (4–5)	Inverness CC, Toldeo, OH
1994	Nick Price	269	Corey Pavin	Southern Hills CC, Tulsa, OK
1995	Steve Elkington* (3)	267	Colin Montgomerie (4)	Riviera CC, Pacific Palisades, CA
1996	Mark Brooks* (3)	277	Kenny Perry (x)	Valhalla GC, Louisville, KY
1997	Davis Love III	269	Justin Leonard	Winged Foot GC, Mamaroneck, NY
1998	Vijay Singh	271	Steve Stricker	Sahalee CC, Redmond, WA

*Winner in playoff. Playoff scores are in parentheses. †Playoff changed from 18 holes to sudden death.

Alltime Major Championship Winners

	Masters	U.S. Open	British Open	PGA Champ.	U.S. Amateur	British Amateur	Total
†Jack Nicklaus	6	4	3	5	2	0	20
Bobby Jones	0	4	3	0	5	1	13
Walter Hagen	0	2	4	5	0	0	11
Ben Hogan	2	4	1	2	0	0	9
†Gary Player	3	1	3	2	0	0	9
John Ball	0	0	1	0	0	8	9
†Arnold Palmer	4	1	2	0	1	0	8
*Tom Watson	2	1	5	0	0	0	8
Harold Hilton	0	0	2	0	1	4	7
Gene Sarazen	1	2	1	3	0	0	7
Sam Snead	3	0	1	3	0	0	7
Harry Vardon	0	1	6	0	0	0	7

*Active PGA player. †Active Senior PGA player.

Alltime Multiple Professional Major Winners

MASTERS

Jack Nicklaus	6
Arnold Palmer	4
Jimmy Demaret	3
Nick Faldo	3
Gary Player	3
Sam Snead	3
Seve Ballesteros	2
Ben Crenshaw	2
Ben Hogan	2
Bernhard Langer	2
Byron Nelson	2
Horton Smith	2
Tom Watson	2

U.S. OPEN

Willie Anderson	4
Ben Hogan	4
Bobby Jones	4
Jack Nicklaus	4
Hale Irwin	3

U.S. OPEN *(Cont.)*

Julius Boros	2
Billy Casper	2
Ernie Els	2
Ralph Guldahl	2
Walter Hagen	2
Lee Janzen	2
John McDermott	2
Cary Middlecoff	2
Andy North	2
Gene Sarazen	2
Alex Smith	2
Curtis Strange	2
Lee Trevino	2

BRITISH OPEN

Harry Vardon	6
James Braid	5
J.H. Taylor	5
Peter Thomson	5

BRITISH OPEN *(Cont.)*

Tom Watson	5
Walter Hagen	4
Bobby Locke	4
Tom Morris Sr	4
Tom Morris Jr	4
Willie Park	4
Jamie Anderson	3
Seve Ballesteros	3
Henry Cotton	3
Nick Faldo	3
Robert Ferguson	3
Bobby Jones	3
Jack Nicklaus	3
Gary Player	3
Harold Hilton	2
Bob Martin	2
Greg Norman	2
Arnold Palmer	2
Willie Park Jr	2
Lee Trevino	2

PGA CHAMPIONSHIP

Walter Hagen	5
Jack Nicklaus	5
Gene Sarazen	3
Sam Snead	3
Jim Barnes	2
Leo Diegel	2
Raymond Floyd	2
Ben Hogan	2
Byron Nelson	2
Larry Nelson	2
Gary Player	2
Paul Runyan	2
Denny Shute	2
Dave Stockton	2
Lee Trevino	2

THE PGA TOUR

Most Career Wins

	Wins		Wins		Wins
Sam Snead	81	Billy Casper	51	Tom Watson	34
Jack Nicklaus	70	Walter Hagen	40	Horton Smith	32
Ben Hogan	63	Cary Middlecoff	40	Harry Cooper	31
Arnold Palmer	60	Gene Sarazen	38	Jimmy Demaret	31
Byron Nelson	52	Lloyd Mangrum	36	Leo Diegel	30

Season Money Leaders

		Earnings ($)			Earnings ($)
1934	Paul Runyan	6,767.00	1966	Billy Casper	121,944.92
1935	Johnny Revolta	9,543.00	1967	Jack Nicklaus	188,998.08
1936	Horton Smith	7,682.00	1968	Billy Casper	205,168.67
1937	Harry Cooper	14,138.69	1969	Frank Beard	164,707.11
1938	Sam Snead	19,534.49	1970	Lee Trevino	157,037.63
1939	Henry Picard	10,303.00	1971	Jack Nicklaus	244,490.50
1940	Ben Hogan	10,655.00	1972	Jack Nicklaus	320,542.26
1941	Ben Hogan	18,358.00	1973	Jack Nicklaus	308,362.10
1942	Ben Hogan	13,143.00	1974	Johnny Miller	353,021.59
1943	No statistics compiled		1975	Jack Nicklaus	298,149.17
1944	Byron Nelson (war bonds)	37,967.69	1976	Jack Nicklaus	266,438.57
1945	Byron Nelson (war bonds)	63,335.66	1977	Tom Watson	310,653.16
1946	Ben Hogan	42,556.16	1978	Tom Watson	362,428.93
1947	Jimmy Demaret	27,936.83	1979	Tom Watson	462,636.00
1948	Ben Hogan	32,112.00	1980	Tom Watson	530,808.33
1949	Sam Snead	31,593.83	1981	Tom Kite	375,698.84
1950	Sam Snead	35,758.83	1982	Craig Stadler	446,462.00
1951	Lloyd Mangrum	26,088.83	1983	Hal Sutton	426,668.00
1952	Julius Boros	37,032.97	1984	Tom Watson	476,260.00
1953	Lew Worsham	34,002.00	1985	Curtis Strange	542,321.00
1954	Bob Toski	65,819.81	1986	Greg Norman	653,296.00
1955	Julius Boros	63,121.55	1987	Curtis Strange	925,941.00
1956	Ted Kroll	72,835.83	1988	Curtis Strange	1,147,644.00
1957	Dick Mayer	65,835.00	1989	Tom Kite	1,395,278.00
1958	Arnold Palmer	42,607.50	1990	Greg Norman	1,165,477.00
1959	Art Wall	53,167.60	1991	Corey Pavin	979,430.00
1960	Arnold Palmer	75,262.85	1992	Fred Couples	1,344,188.00
1961	Gary Player	64,540.45	1993	Nick Price	1,478,557.00
1962	Arnold Palmer	81,448.33	1994	Nick Price	1,499,927.00
1963	Arnold Palmer	128,230.00	1995	Greg Norman	1,654,959.00
1964	Jack Nicklaus	113,284.50	1996	Tom Lehman	1,780,159.00
1965	Jack Nicklaus	140,752.14	1997	Tiger Woods	2,066,833.00

Note: Total money listed from 1968 through 1974. Official money listed from 1975 on.

Career Money Leaders‡

		Earnings ($)			Earnings ($)			Earnings ($)
1.	Greg Norman	11,936,443	18.	Jay Haas	6,901,285	35.	Jack Nicklaus	5,691,673
2.	Fred Couples	10,448,476	19.	Phil Mickelson	6,883,377	36.	Scott Simpson	5,659,927
3.	Tom Kite	10,447,472	20.	Tom Lehman	6,551,107	37.	Larry Mize	5,614,010
4.	Mark O'Meara	10,194,133	21.	David Frost	6,475,440	38.	Jeff Maggert	5,319,196
5.	Nick Price	9,749,834	22.	Lee Janzen	6,410,845	39.	Ray Floyd	5,300,595
6.	Davis Love III	9,595,601	23.	Lanny Wadkins	6,282,248	40.	Peter Jacobsen	5,297,028
7.	Payne Stewart	9,590,858	24.	David Duval	6,279,418	41.	Mark McCumber	5,290,798
8.	Tom Watson	9,204,662	25.	Bruce Lietzke	6,257,272	42.	Gil Morgan	5,259,164
9.	Scott Hoch	9,062,703	26.	Hal Sutton	6,252,978	43.	Billy Mayfair	5,254,281
10.	Mark Calcavecchia	8,700,685	27.	Brad Faxon	6,240,355	44.	Jim Gallagher Jr.	5,218,765
11.	Corey Pavin	8,294,601	28.	Jeff Sluman	6,183,939	45.	John Huston	5,145,995
12.	Paul Azinger	7,994,642	29.	Loren Roberts	6,086,908	46.	Mark Brooks	5,142,971
13.	Curtis Strange	7,226,587	30.	Chip Beck	6,000,924	47.	Justin Leonard	4,875,535
14.	Craig Stadler	7,206,768	31.	Hale Irwin	5,907,550	48.	Andrew Magee	4,790,587
15.	John Cook	7,150,666	32.	Vijay Singh	5,752,556	49.	Steve Pate	4,673,935
16.	Ben Crenshaw	7,075,996	33.	Bob Tway	5,726,772	50.	Wayne Levi	4,634,518
17.	Steve Elkington	7,023,912	34.	Fuzzy Zoeller	5,706,218			

‡ Through 10/11/98.

Year by Year Statistical Leaders

SCORING AVERAGE

1980	Lee Trevino	69.73
1981	Tom Kite	69.80
1982	Tom Kite	70.21
1983	Raymond Floyd	70.61
1984	Calvin Peete	70.56
1985	Don Pooley	70.36
1986	Scott Hoch	70.08
1987	David Frost	70.09
1988	Greg Norman	69.38
1989	Payne Stewart	69.485†
1990	Greg Norman	69.10
1991	Fred Couples	69.59
1992	Fred Couples	69.38
1993	Greg Norman	68.90
1994	Greg Norman	68.81
1995	Greg Norman	69.06
1996	Tom Lehman	69.32
1997	Nick Price	68.98

Note: Scoring average per round, with adjustments made at each round for the field's course scoring average.

DRIVING DISTANCE

		Yds
1980	Dan Pohl	274.3
1981	Dan Pohl	280.1
1982	Bill Calfee	275.3
1983	John McComish	277.4
1984	Bill Glasson	276.5
1985	Andy Bean	278.2
1986	Davis Love III	285.7
1987	John McComish	283.9
1988	Steve Thomas	284.6
1989	Ed Humenik	280.9
1990	Tom Purtzer	279.6
1991	John Daly	288.9
1992	John Daly	283.4
1993	John Daly	288.9
1994	Davis Love III	283.8
1995	John Daly	289.0
1996	John Daly	288.8
1997	John Daly	302.0

Note: Average computed by charting distance of two tee shots on a predetermined par-four or par-five hole (one on front nine, one on back nine).

DRIVING ACCURACY

1980	Mike Reid	79.5
1981	Calvin Peete	81.9
1982	Calvin Peete	84.6
1983	Calvin Peete	81.3
1984	Calvin Peete	77.5
1985	Calvin Peete	80.6
1986	Calvin Peete	81.7
1987	Calvin Peete	83.0
1988	Calvin Peete	82.5
1989	Calvin Peete	82.6
1990	Calvin Peete	83.7
1991	Hale Irwin	78.3

DRIVING ACCURACY (Cont.)

1992	Doug Tewell	82.3
1993	Doug Tewell	82.5
1994	David Edwards	81.6
1995	Fred Funk	81.3
1996	Fred Funk	78.7
1997	Allen Doyle	80.8

Note: Percentage of fairways hit on number of par-four and par-five holes played; par-three holes excluded.

GREENS IN REGULATION

1980	Jack Nicklaus	72.1
1981	Calvin Peete	73.1
1982	Calvin Peete	72.4
1983	Calvin Peete	71.4
1984	Andy Bean	72.1
1985	John Mahaffey	71.9
1986	John Mahaffey	72.0
1987	Gil Morgan	73.3
1988	John Adams	73.9
1989	Bruce Lietzke	72.6
1990	Doug Tewell	70.9
1991	Bruce Lietzke	73.3
1992	Tim Simpson	74.0
1993	Fuzzy Zoeller	73.6
1994	Bill Glasson	73.0
1995	Lenny Clements	72.3
1996	Fred Couples	71.8
	Mark O'Meara	71.8
1997	Tom Lehman	72.7

Note: Average of greens reached in regulation out of total holes played; hole is considered in regulation if any part of the ball rests on the putting surface in two shots less than the hole's par—a par-5 hit in two shots is one green in regulation.

PUTTING

1980	Jerry Pate	28.81
1981	Alan Tapie	28.70
1982	Ben Crenshaw	28.65
1983	Morris Hatalsky	27.96
1984	Gary McCord	28.57
1985	Craig Stadler	28.627†
1986	Greg Norman	1.736
1987	Ben Crenshaw	1.743
1988	Don Pooley	1.729
1989	Steve Jones	1.734
1990	Larry Rinker	1.7467†
1991	Jay Don Blake	1.7326†
1992	Mark O'Meara	1.731
1993	David Frost	1.739
1994	Loren Roberts	1.737
1995	Jim Furyk	1.708
1996	Brad Faxon	1.709
1997	Don Pooley	1.718

Note: Average number of putts taken on greens reached in regulation; prior to 1986, based on average number of putts per 18 holes.

ALL-AROUND

1987	Dan Pohl	170
1988	Payne Stewart	170
1989	Paul Azinger	250
1990	Paul Azinger	162
1991	Scott Hoch	283
1992	Fred Couples	256
1993	Gil Morgan	252
1994	Bob Estes	227
1995	Justin Leonard	323
1996	Fred Couples	214
1997	Bill Glasson	282

Note: Sum of the places of standing from the other seven statistical categories; the player with the number closest to zero leads.

SAND SAVES

1980	Bob Eastwood	65.4
1981	Tom Watson	60.1
1982	Isao Aoki	60.2
1983	Isao Aoki	62.3
1984	Peter Oosterhuis	64.7
1985	Tom Purtzer	60.8
1986	Paul Azinger	63.8
1987	Paul Azinger	63.2
1988	Greg Powers	63.5
1989	Mike Sullivan	66.0
1990	Paul Azinger	67.2
1991	Ben Crenshaw	64.9
1992	Mitch Adcock	66.9
1993	Ken Green	64.4
1994	Corey Pavin	65.4
1995	Billy Mayfair	68.6
1996	Gary Rusnak	64.0
1997	Bob Estes	70.3

Note: Percentage of up-and-down efforts from greenside sand traps only—fairway bunkers excluded.

PAR BREAKERS

1980	Tom Watson	.213
1981	Bruce Lietzke	.225
1982	Tom Kite	.2154†
1983	Tom Watson	.211
1984	Craig Stadler	.220
1985	Craig Stadler	.218
1986	Greg Norman	.248
1987	Mark Calcavecchia	.221
1988	Ken Green	.236
1989	Greg Norman	.224
1990	Greg Norman	.219

Note: Average based on total birdies and eagles scored out of total holes played. Discontinued as an official category after 1990.

† Number had to be carried to extra decimal place to determine winner.

Year by Year Statistical Leaders (Cont.)

EAGLES

1980	Dave Eichelberger	16	1985	Larry Rinker	14	1991	Andy Bean	15
1981	Bruce Lietzke	12	1986	Joey Sindelar	16	1992	Dan Forsman	18
1982	Tom Weiskopf	10	1987	Phil Blackmar	20	1993	Davis Love III	15
	J. C. Snead	10	1988	Ken Green	21	1994	Davis Love III	18
	Andy Bean	10	1989	Lon Hinkle	14	1995	Kelly Gibson	16
1983	Chip Beck	15		Duffy Waldorf	14	1996	Tom Watson	97.2
1984	Gary Hallberg	15	1990	Paul Azinger	14	1997	Tiger Woods	104.1

Note: Total of eagles scored 1980–1995. Since 1996 winner determined by number of holes played per eagle.

BIRDIES

1980	Andy Bean	388	1986	Joey Sindelar	415	1992	Jeff Sluman	417
1981	Vance Heafner	388	1987	Dan Forsman	409	1993	John Huston	426
1982	Andy Bean	392	1988	Dan Forsman	465	1994	Brad Bryant	397
1983	Hal Sutton	399	1989	Ted Schulz	415	1995	Steve Lowery	410
1984	Mark O'Meara	419	1990	Mike Donald	401	1996	Fred Couples	4.20
1985	Joey Sindelar	411	1991	Scott Hoch	446	1997	Tiger Woods	4.25

Note: Total of birdies scored 1980–95. Since 1996, winner determined by average number of birdies per round.

PGA Player of the Year Award

1948	Ben Hogan	1965	Dave Marr	1982	Tom Watson
1949	Sam Snead	1966	Billy Casper	1983	Hal Sutton
1950	Ben Hogan	1967	Jack Nicklaus	1984	Tom Watson
1951	Ben Hogan	1968	Not awarded	1985	Lanny Wadkins
1952	Julius Boros	1969	Orville Moody	1986	Bob Tway
1953	Ben Hogan	1970	Billy Casper	1987	Paul Azinger
1954	Ed Furgol	1971	Lee Trevino	1988	Curtis Strange
1955	Doug Ford	1972	Jack Nicklaus	1989	Tom Kite
1956	Jack Burke	1973	Jack Nicklaus	1990	Wayne Levi
1957	Dick Mayer	1974	Johnny Miller	1991	Fred Couples
1958	Dow Finsterwald	1975	Jack Nicklaus	1992	Fred Couples
1959	Art Wall	1976	Jack Nicklaus	1993	Nick Price
1960	Arnold Palmer	1977	Tom Watson	1994	Nick Price
1961	Jerry Barber	1978	Tom Watson	1995	Greg Norman
1962	Arnold Palmer	1979	Tom Watson	1996	Tom Lehman
1963	Julius Boros	1980	Tom Watson	1997	Tiger Woods
1964	Ken Venturi	1981	Bill Rogers		

Vardon Trophy: Scoring Average

Year	Winner	Avg	Year	Winner	Avg	Year	Winner	Avg
1937	Harry Cooper	*500	1960	Billy Casper	69.95	1979	Tom Watson	70.27
1938	Sam Snead	520	1961	Arnold Palmer	69.85	1980	Lee Trevino	69.73
1939	Byron Nelson	473	1962	Arnold Palmer	70.27	1981	Tom Kite	69.80
1940	Ben Hogan	423	1963	Billy Casper	70.58	1982	Tom Kite	70.21
1941	Ben Hogan	494	1964	Arnold Palmer	70.01	1983	Raymond Floyd	70.61
1942–46	No award		1965	Billy Casper	70.85	1984	Calvin Peete	70.56
1947	Jimmy Demaret	69.90	1966	Billy Casper	70.27	1985	Don Pooley	70.36
1948	Ben Hogan	69.30	1967	Arnold Palmer	70.18	1986	Scott Hoch	70.08
1949	Sam Snead	69.37	1968	Billy Casper	69.82	1987	Don Pohl	70.25
1950	Sam Snead	69.23	1969	Dave Hill	70.34	1988	Chip Beck	69.46
1951	Lloyd Mangrum	70.05	1970	Lee Trevino	70.64	1989	Greg Norman	69.49
1952	Jack Burke	70.54	1971	Lee Trevino	70.27	1990	Greg Norman	69.10
1953	Lloyd Mangrum	70.22	1972	Lee Trevino	70.89	1991	Fred Couples	69.59
1954	E.J. Harrison	70.41	1973	Bruce Crampton	70.57	1992	Fred Couples	69.38
1955	Sam Snead	69.86	1974	Lee Trevino	70.53	1993	Nick Price	69.11
1956	Cary Middlecoff	70.35	1975	Bruce Crampton	70.51	1994	Greg Norman	68.81
1957	Dow Finsterwald	70.30	1976	Don January	70.56	1995	Steve Elkington	69.62
1958	Bob Rosburg	70.11	1977	Tom Watson	70.32	1996	Tom Lehman	69.32
1959	Art Wall	70.35	1978	Tom Watson	70.16	1997	Nick Price	68.98

*Point system used, 1937–41.

Note: As of 1988, based on minimum of 60 rounds per year. Adjusted for average score of field in tournaments entered.

Alltime PGA Tour Records*

Scoring

90 HOLES
325—(67-67-64-65-62) by Tom Kite, at four courses, Indian Hills, CA, in winning the 1993 Bob Hope Classic (35 under par).

72 HOLES
257—(60-68-64-65) by Mike Souchak, at Brackenridge Park GC, San Antonio, to win 1955 Texas Open (27 under par).

260—(63-65-66-66) by John Huston, at Waialae CC, Honolulu, at the 1998 Hawaiian Open (28 under par).

54 HOLES, OPENING ROUNDS
189—(64-62-63) by John Cook, at the TPC at Southwind, Memphis, TN, en route to winning the 1996 St. Jude Classic.

54 HOLES, CONSECUTIVE ROUNDS
189—(63-63-63) by Chandler Harper in the last three rounds to win the 1954 Texas Open at Brackenridge Park GC, San Antonio.

189—(64-62-63) by John Cook, at the TPC at Southwind, Memphis, TN, in the first three rounds of the 1996 St. Jude Classic.

36 HOLES, OPENING ROUNDS
126—(64-62) by Tommy Bolt, at Cavalier Yacht & CC, Virginia Beach, VA, in 1954 Virginia Beach Open.

126—(64-62) by Paul Azinger, at Oak Hills CC, San Antonio, in the 1989 Texas Open.

126—(64-62) by John Cook, at the TPC at Southwind, Memphis, TN, in the 1996 St. Jude Classic.

126—(64-62) by Rick Fehr, at the Las Vegas Hilton CC/TPC at Summerlin, Las Vegas, in the 1996 Las Vegas Invitational.

126—(62-64) by Steve Jones, at the TPC, Scottsdale, AR in the 1997 Phoenix Open.

36 HOLES, CONSECUTIVE ROUNDS
125—(64-61) by Gay Brewer in the middle rounds of the 1967 Pensacola Open, which he won, at Pensacola CC, Pensacola, FL.

125—(63-62) by Ron Streck in the last two rounds to win the 1978 Texas Open at Oak Hills CC, San Antonio.

125—(62-63) by Blaine McCallister in the middle two rounds in winning the 1988 Hardee's Golf Classic at Oakwood CC, Coal Valley, IL.

125—(62-63) by John Cook, in the middle two rounds in winning the 1996 St. Jude Classic at the TPC at Southwind, Memphis, TN.

125—(62-63) by John Cook, in the fourth and fifth rounds in winning the 1997 Bob Hope Chrysler Classic at Indian Wells CC, Indian Hills, CA.

18 HOLES
59—by Al Geiberger, at Colonial Country Club, Memphis, in second round in winning the 1977 Memphis Classic.

59—by Chip Beck, at Sunrise Golf Club, Las Vegas, in third round of the 1991 Las Vegas Invitational.

9 HOLES
27—by Mike Souchak, at Brackenridge Park GC, San Antonio, on par-35 second nine of first round in the 1955 Texas Open.

27—by Andy North at En-Joie GC, Endicott, NY, on par-34 second nine of first round in the 1975 BC Open.

Scoring *(Cont.)*

MOST CONSECUTIVE ROUNDS UNDER 70
19—Byron Nelson in 1945.

MOST BIRDIES IN A ROW
8—Bob Goalby at Pasadena GC, St. Petersburg, FL, during fourth round in winning the 1961 St Petersburg Open.

8—Fuzzy Zoeller, at Oakwood CC, Coal Valley, IL, during first round of 1976 Quad Cities Open.

8—Dewey Arnette, at Warwick Hills GC, Grand Blanc, MI, during first round of the 1987 Buick Open.

MOST BIRDIES IN A ROW TO WIN
5—Jack Nicklaus to win 1978 Jackie Gleason Inverrary Classic (last 5 holes).

Wins

MOST CONSECUTIVE YEARS WINNING AT LEAST ONE TOURNAMENT
17—Jack Nicklaus, 1962–78.
17—Arnold Palmer, 1955–71.
16—Billy Casper, 1956–71.

MOST CONSECUTIVE WINS
11—Byron Nelson, from Miami Four Ball, March 8–11, 1945, through Canadian Open, August 2–4, 1945.

MOST WINS IN A SINGLE EVENT
8—Sam Snead, Greater Greensboro Open, 1938, 1946, 1949, 1950, 1955, 1956, 1960, and 1965.

MOST CONSECUTIVE WINS IN A SINGLE EVENT
4—Walter Hagen, PGA Championships, 1924-27.
4—Gene Sarazen, Miami Open, 1926, (schedule change) 1928–30.

MOST WINS IN A CALENDAR YEAR
18—Byron Nelson, 1945

MOST YEARS BETWEEN WINS
15 yrs, 5 mos—Butch Baird, 1961–76.

MOST YEARS FROM FIRST WIN TO LAST
28 yrs, 11 mos, 20 days—Raymond Floyd, 1963–92.

YOUNGEST WINNERS
19 yrs, 10 mos—John McDermott, 1911 US Open.

OLDEST WINNER
52 yrs, 10 mos—Sam Snead, 1965 Greater Greensboro Open.

WIDEST WINNING MARGIN: STROKES
16—Bobby Locke, 1948 Chicago Victory National Championship.

Putting

FEWEST PUTTS, ONE ROUND
18—Andy North, at Kingsmill GC, in second round of 1990 Anheuser Busch Golf Classic.

18—Kenny Knox, at Harbour Town GL, in first round of 1989 MCI Heritage Classic.

18—Mike McGee, at Colonial CC, in first round of 1987 Federal Express St. Jude Classic.

18—Sam Trahan, at Whitemarsh Valley CC, in final round of 1979 IVB Philadelphia Golf Classic.

18—Jim McGovern, at TPC at Southwind, in second round of 1992 Federal Express St. Jude Classic.

FEWEST PUTTS, FOUR ROUNDS
93—Kenny Knox, in 1989 MCI Heritage Classic at Harbour Town GL.

*Through 10/11/98.

THE MAJOR TOURNAMENTS
LPGA Championship

Year	Winner	Score	Runner-Up	Site
1955	Beverly Hanson† (4 and 3)	220	Louise Suggs	Orchard Ridge CC, Ft Wayne, IN
1956	Marlene Hagge*	291	Patty Berg	Forest Lake CC, Detroit
1957	Louise Suggs	285	Wiffi Smith	Churchill Valley CC, Pittsburgh
1958	Mickey Wright	288	Fay Crocker	Churchill Valley CC, Pittsburgh
1959	Betsy Rawls	288	Patty Berg	Sheraton Hotel CC, French Lick, IN
1960	Mickey Wright	292	Louise Suggs	Sheraton Hotel CC, French Lick, IN
1961	Mickey Wright	287	Louise Suggs	Stardust CC, Las Vegas
1962	Judy Kimball	282	Shirley Spork	Stardust CC, Las Vegas
1963	Mickey Wright	294	Mary Lena Faulk Mary Mills Louise Suggs	Stardust CC, Las Vegas
1964	Mary Mills	278	Mickey Wright	Stardust CC, Las Vegas
1965	Sandra Haynie	279	Clifford A. Creed	Stardust CC, Las Vegas
1966	Gloria Ehret	282	Mickey Wright	Stardust CC, Las Vegas
1967	Kathy Whitworth	284	Shirley Englehorn	Pleasant Valley CC, Sutton, MA
1968	Sandra Post* (68)	294	Kathy Whitworth (75)	Pleasant Valley CC, Sutton, MA
1969	Betsy Rawls	293	Susie Berning Carol Mann	Concord GC, Kiameshia Lake, NY
1970	Shirley Englehorn* (74)	285	Kathy Whitworth (78)	Pleasant Valley CC, Sutton, MA
1971	Kathy Whitworth	288	Kathy Ahern	Pleasant Valley CC, Sutton, MA
1972	Kathy Ahern	293	Jane Blalock	Pleasant Valley CC, Sutton, MA
1973	Mary Mills	288	Betty Burfeindt	Pleasant Valley CC, Sutton, MA
1974	Sandra Haynie	288	JoAnne Carner	Pleasant Valley CC, Sutton, MA
1975	Kathy Whitworth	288	Sandra Haynie	Pine Ridge GC, Baltimore
1976	Betty Burfeindt	287	Judy Rankin	Pine Ridge GC, Baltimore
1977	Chako Higuchi	279	Pat Bradley Sandra Post Judy Rankin	Bay Tree Golf Plantation, N. Myrtle Beach, SC
1978	Nancy Lopez	275	Amy Alcott	Jack Nicklaus GC, Kings Island, OH
1979	Donna Caponi	279	Jerilyn Britz	Jack Nicklaus GC, Kings Island, OH
1980	Sally Little	285	Jane Blalock	Jack Nicklaus GC, Kings Island, OH
1981	Donna Caponi	280	Jerilyn Britz Pat Meyers	Jack Nicklaus GC, Kings Island, OH
1982	Jan Stephenson	279	JoAnne Carner	Jack Nicklaus GC, Kings Island, OH
1983	Patty Sheehan	279	Sandra Haynie	Jack Nicklaus GC, Kings Island, OH
1984	Patty Sheehan	272	Beth Daniel Pat Bradley	Jack Nicklaus GC, Kings Island, OH
1985	Nancy Lopez	273	Alice Miller	Jack Nicklaus GC, Kings Island, OH
1986	Pat Bradley	277	Patty Sheehan	Jack Nicklaus GC, Kings Island, OH
1987	Jane Geddes	275	Betsy King	Jack Nicklaus GC, Kings Island, OH
1988	Sherri Turner	281	Amy Alcott	Jack Nicklaus GC, Kings Island, OH
1989	Nancy Lopez	274	Ayako Okamoto	Jack Nicklaus GC, Kings Island, OH
1990	Beth Daniel	280	Rosie Jones	Bethesda CC, Bethesda, MD
1991	Meg Mallon	274	Pat Bradley Ayako Okamoto	Bethesda CC, Bethesda, MD
1992	Betsy King	267	Karen Noble	Bethesda CC, Bethesda, MD
1993	Patty Sheehan	275	Lauri Merten	Bethesda CC, Bethesda, MD
1994	Laura Davies	279	Alice Ritzman	DuPont CC, Wilmington, DE
1995	Kelly Robbins	274	Laura Davies	DuPont CC, Wilmington, DE
1996	Laura Davies	213†	Julie Piers	DuPont CC, Wilmington, DE
1997	Chris Johnson*	281	Leta Lindley	DuPont CC, Wilmington, DE
1998	Se Ri Pak	273	Donna Andrews	DuPont CC, Wilmington, DE

*Won in playoff. Playoff scores are in parentheses. 1956 and 1997 were sudden death; 1968 and 1970 were 18-hole playoffs. †Won match play final. #Shortened due to rain.

U.S. Women's Open

Year	Winner	Score	Runner-Up	Site
1946	Patty Berg	5 & 4	Betty Jameson	Spokane CC, Spokane, WA
1947	Betty Jameson	295	Sally Sessions	Starmount Forest CC, Greensboro, NC
			Polly Riley	
1948	Babe Zaharias	300	Betty Hicks	Atlantic City CC, Northfield, NJ
1949	Louise Suggs	291	Babe Zaharias	Prince George's G & CC, Landover, MD
1950	Babe Zaharias	291	Betsy Rawls	Rolling Hills CC, Wichita, KS
1951	Betsy Rawls	293	Louise Suggs	Druid Hills GC, Atlanta
1952	Louise Suggs	284	Marlene Bauer	Bala GC, Philadelphia
			Betty Jameson	
1953	Betsy Rawls* (71)	302	Jackie Pung (77)	CC of Rochester, Rochester, NY
1954	Babe Zaharias	291	Betty Hicks	Salem CC, Peabody, MA
1955	Fay Crocker	299	Mary Lena Faulk	Wichita CC, Wichita, KS
			Louise Suggs	
1956	Kathy Cornelius* (75)	302	Barbara McIntire (82)	Northland CC, Duluth, MN
1957	Betsy Rawls	299	Patty Berg	Winged Foot GC, Mamaroneck, NY
1958	Mickey Wright	290	Louise Suggs	Forest Lake CC, Detroit
1959	Mickey Wright	287	Louise Suggs	Churchill Valley CC, Pittsburgh
1960	Betsy Rawls	292	Joyce Ziske	Worcester CC, Worcester, MA
1961	Mickey Wright	293	Betsy Rawls	Baltusrol GC (Lower Course), Springfield, NJ
1962	Murle Breer	301	Jo Ann Prentice	Dunes GC, Myrtle Beach, SC
			Ruth Jessen	
1963	Mary Mills	289	Sandra Haynie	Kenwood CC, Cincinnati
			Louise Suggs	
1964	Mickey Wright* (70)	290	Ruth Jessen (72)	San Diego CC, Chula Vista, CA
1965	Carol Mann	290	Kathy Cornelius	Atlantic City CC, Northfield, NJ
1966	Sandra Spuzich	297	Carol Mann	Hazeltine Natl GC, Chaska, MN
1967	Catherine LaCoste	294	Susie Berning	Hot Springs GC (Cascades Course),
			Beth Stone	Hot Springs, VA
1968	Susie Berning	289	Mickey Wright	Moslem Springs GC, Fleetwood, PA
1969	Donna Caponi	294	Peggy Wilson	Scenic Hills CC, Pensacola, FL
1970	Donna Caponi	287	Sandra Haynie	Muskogee CC, Muskogee, OK
			Sandra Spuzich	
1971	JoAnne Carner	288	Kathy Whitworth	Kahkwa CC, Erie, PA
1972	Susie Berning	299	Kathy Ahern	Winged Foot GC, Mamaroneck, NY
			Pam Barnett	
			Judy Rankin	
1973	Susie Berning	290	Gloria Ehret	CC of Rochester, Rochester, NY
			Shelley Hamlin	
1974	Sandra Haynie	295	Carol Mann	La Grange CC, La Grange, IL
			Beth Stone	
1975	Sandra Palmer	295	JoAnne Carner	Atlantic City CC, Northfield, NJ
			Sandra Post	
			Nancy Lopez	
1976	JoAnne Carner* (76)	292	Sandra Palmer (78)	Rolling Green CC, Springfield, PA
1977	Hollis Stacy	292	Nancy Lopez	Hazeltine Natl GC, Chaska, MN
1978	Hollis Stacy	289	JoAnne Carner	CC of Indianapolis, Indianapolis
			Sally Little	
1979	Jerilyn Britz	284	Debbie Massey	Brooklawn CC, Fairfield, CT
			Sandra Palmer	
1980	Amy Alcott	280	Hollis Stacy	Richland CC, Nashville
1981	Pat Bradley	279	Beth Daniel	La Grange CC, La Grange, IL
1982	Janet Anderson	283	Beth Daniel	Del Paso CC, Sacramento
			Sandra Haynie	
			Donna White	
			JoAnne Carner	
1983	Jan Stephenson	290	JoAnne Carner	Cedar Ridge CC, Tulsa
			Patty Sheehan	
1984	Hollis Stacy	290	Rosie Jones	Salem CC, Peabody, MA
1985	Kathy Baker	280	Judy Dickinson	Baltusrol GC (Upper Course), Springfield, NJ
1986	Jane Geddes* (71)	287	Sally Little (73)	NCR GC, Dayton
1987	Laura Davies* (71)	285	Ayako Okamoto (73)	Plainfield CC, Plainfield, NJ
			JoAnne Carner (74)	
1988	Liselotte Neumann	277	Patty Sheehan	Baltimore CC, Baltimore
1989	Betsy King	278	Nancy Lopez	Indianwood G & CC, Lake Orion, MI
1990	Betsy King	284	Patty Sheehan	Atlanta Athletic Club, Duluth, GA
1991	Meg Mallon	283	Pat Bradley	Colonial Club, Fort Worth

U.S. Women's Open (Cont.)

Year	Winner	Score	Runner-Up	Site
1992	Patty Sheehan* (72)	280	Juli Inkster	Oakmont CC, Oakmont, PA
1993	Lauri Merten	280	Donna Andrew	Crooked Stick, Carmel, IN
			Helen Alfredsson	
1994	Patty Sheehan	277	Tammie Green	Indianwood G & CC, Lake Orion, MI
1995	Annika Sörenstam	278	Meg Mallon	The Broadmoor GC, Colorado Springs, CO
1996	Annika Sörenstam	272	Kris Tschetter	Pine Needles GC, Southern Pines, NC
1997	Alison Nicholas	274	Nancy Lopez	Pumpkin Ridge CC, North Plains, OR
1998	Se Ri Pak†	290	Jenny Chuasiriporn	Blackwolf Run Golf Resort, Kohler, WI

* Winner in playoff; 18-hole playoff scores are in parentheses.
† Winner on second hole of sudden death after 18-hole playoff ended in a tie.

Dinah Shore

Year	Winner	Score	Runner-Up
1972	Jane Blalock	213	Carol Mann, Judy Rankin
1973	Mickey Wright	284	Joyce Kazmierski
1974	Jo Ann Prentice*	289	Jane Blalock, Sandra Haynie
1975	Sandra Palmer	283	Kathy McMullen
1976	Judy Rankin	285	Betty Burfeindt
1977	Kathy Whitworth	289	JoAnne Carner, Sally Little
1978	Sandra Post*	283	Penny Pulz
1979	Sandra Post	276	Nancy Lopez
1980	Donna Caponi	275	Amy Alcott
1981	Nancy Lopez	277	Carolyn Hill
1982	Sally Little	278	Hollis Stacy, Sandra Haynie
1983	Amy Alcott	282	Beth Daniel, Kathy Whitworth
1984	Juli Inkster*	280	Pat Bradley
1985	Alice Miller	275	Jan Stephenson
1986	Pat Bradley	280	Val Skinner
1987	Betsy King*	283	Patty Sheehan
1988	Amy Alcott	274	Colleen Walker
1989	Juli Inkster	279	Tammie Green, JoAnne Carner
1990	Betsy King	283	Kathy Postlewait, Shirley Furlong
1991	Amy Alcott	273	Dottie Mochrie
1992	Dottie Mochrie*	279	Juli Inkster
1993	Helen Alfredsson	284	Amy Benz, Tina Barrett, Betsy King
1994	Donna Andrews	276	Laura Davies
1995	Nanci Bowen	285	Susie Redman
1996	Patti Sheehan	281	Kelly Robbins, Meg Mallon, Annika Sörenstam
1997	Betsy King	276	Kris Tschetter
1998	Pat Hurst	281	Helen Dobson

*Winner in sudden-death playoff.
Note: Designated fourth major in 1983.
Played at Mission Hills CC, Rancho Mirage, CA.

du Maurier Classic

Year	Winner	Score	Runner-Up	Site
1973	Jocelyne Bourassa*	214	Sandra Haynie	Montreal GC, Montreal
			Judy Rankin	
1974	Carole Jo Callison	208	JoAnne Carner	Candiac GC, Montreal
1975	JoAnne Carner*	214	Carol Mann	St. George's CC, Toronto
1976	Donna Caponi*	212	Judy Rankin	Cedar Brae G & CC, Toronto
1977	Judy Rankin	214	Pat Meyers	Lachute G & CC, Montreal
			Sandra Palmer	
1978	JoAnne Carner	278	Hollis Stacy	St. George's CC, Toronto
1979	Amy Alcott	285	Nancy Lopez	Richelieu Valley CC, Montreal
1980	Pat Bradley	277	JoAnne Carner	St. George's CC, Toronto
1981	Jan Stephenson	278	Nancy Lopez	Summerlea CC, Dorion, Quebec
			Pat Bradley	
1982	Sandra Haynie	280	Beth Daniel	St. George's CC, Toronto
1983	Hollis Stacy	277	JoAnne Carner	Beaconsfield GC, Montreal
			Alice Miller	
1984	Juli Inkster	279	Ayako Okamoto	St. George's G & CC, Toronto
1985	Pat Bradley	278	Jane Geddes	Beaconsfield CC, Montreal
1986	Pat Bradley*	276	Ayako Okamoto	Board of Trade CC, Toronto

du Maurier Classic (Cont.)

Year	Winner	Score	Runner-Up	Site
1987	Jody Rosenthal	272	Ayako Okamoto	Islesmere GC, Laval, Quebec
1988	Sally Little	279	Laura Davies	Vancouver GC, Coquitlam, British Columbia
1989	Tammie Green	279	Pat Bradley Betsy King	Beaconsfield GC, Montreal
1990	Cathy Johnston	276	Patty Sheehan	Westmount G & CC, Kitchener, Ontario
1991	Nancy Scranton	279	Debbie Massey	Vancouver GC, Coquitlam, British Columbia
1992	Sherri Steinhauer	277	Judy Dickinson	St. Charles CC, Winnipeg, Manitoba
1993	Brandie Burton	277	Betsy King	London Hunt and CC, London, Ontario
1994	Martha Nause	279	Michelle McGann	Ottawa Hunt and GC, Ottawa, Ont.
1995	Jenny Lidback	280	Liselotte Neumann	Beaconsfield GC, Pointe-Claire, Quebec
1996	Laura Davies	277	Nancy Lopez, Karrie Webb	Edmonton CC, Edmonton, Alberta
1997	Colleen Walker	278	Liselotte Neumann	Glen Abbey GC, Oakville, Ontario
1998	Brandie Burton	270	Annika Sörenstam	Essex G & CC, Windsor, Ontario

*Winner in sudden-death playoff.
Note: Designated third major in 1979.

Alltime Major Championship Winners

	LPGA	U.S. Open	Dinah Shore	du Maurier	#Ttitleholders	†Western	U.S. Am	British Am	Total
Patty Berg	0	1	0	0	7	7	1	0	16
Mickey Wright	4	4	0	0	2	3	0	0	13
Louise Suggs	1	2	0	0	4	4	1	1	13
Babe Zaharias	0	3	0	0	3	4	1	1	12
Betsy Rawls	2	4	0	0	0	2	0	0	8
*JoAnne Carner	0	2	0	0	0	0	5	0	7
Kathy Whitworth	3	0	0	0	2	1	0	0	6
*Pat Bradley	1	1	1	3	0	0	0	0	6
*Juli Inkster	0	0	2	1	0	0	3	0	6
*Patty Sheehan	3	2	1	0	0	0	0	0	6
Glenna Vare	0	0	0	0	0	0	6	0	6
*Betsy King	1	2	3	0	0	0	0	0	6

*Active LPGA player.
#Major from 1937–1972. †Major from 1937–1967.

Alltime Multiple Professional Major Winners

LPGA

Mickey Wright	4
Nancy Lopez	3
Patty Sheehan	3
Kathy Whitworth	3
Donna Caponi	2
Sandra Haynie	2
Mary Mills	2
Betsy Rawls	2
Laura Davies	2

U.S. OPEN

Betsy Rawls	4
Mickey Wright	4
Susie Maxwell Berning	3

U.S. OPEN (Cont.)

Hollis Stacy	3
Babe Zaharias	3
JoAnne Carner	2
Donna Caponi	2
Betsy King	2
Patty Sheehan	2
Louise Suggs	2
Annika Sorenstam	2

DINAH SHORE

Amy Alcott	3
Betsy King	3
Juli Inkster	2

DU MAURIER

Pat Bradley	3
Brandie Burton	2
JoAnne Carner	2

TITLEHOLDERS

Patty Berg	7
Louise Suggs	4
Babe Zaharias	3
Dorothy Kirby	2
Marilynn Smith	2
Kathy Whitworth	2
Mickey Wright	2

WESTERN OPEN

Patty Berg	7
Louise Suggs	4
Babe Zaharias	4
Mickey Wright	3
June Beebe	2
Opal Hill	2
Betty Jameson	2
Betsy Rawls	2

THE LPGA TOUR

Most Career Wins†

	Wins		Wins		Wins
Kathy Whitworth	88	JoAnne Carner	42	Babe Zaharias	31
Mickey Wright	82	Sandra Haynie	42	*Betsy King	31
Patty Berg	57	Carol Mann	38	Amy Alcott	29
Betsy Rawls	55	*Patty Sheehan	35	Jane Blalock	29
Louise Suggs	50	*Beth Daniel	32	Judy Rankin	26
*Nancy Lopez	48	*Pat Bradley	31		

*Active LPGA player. †Through 10/12/98.

Season Money Leaders

		Earnings ($)			Earnings ($)
1950	Babe Zaharias	14,800	1974	JoAnne Carner	87,094
1951	Babe Zaharias	15,087	1975	Sandra Palmer	76,374
1952	Betsy Rawls	14,505	1976	Judy Rankin	150,734
1953	Louise Suggs	19,816	1977	Judy Rankin	122,890
1954	Patty Berg	16,011	1978	Nancy Lopez	189,814
1955	Patty Berg	16,492	1979	Nancy Lopez	197,489
1956	Marlene Hagge	20,235	1980	Beth Daniel	231,000
1957	Patty Berg	16,272	1981	Beth Daniel	206,998
1958	Beverly Hanson	12,639	1982	JoAnne Carner	310,400
1959	Betsy Rawls	26,774	1983	JoAnne Carner	291,404
1960	Louise Suggs	16,892	1984	Betsy King	266,771
1961	Mickey Wright	22,236	1985	Nancy Lopez	416,472
1962	Mickey Wright	21,641	1986	Pat Bradley	492,021
1963	Mickey Wright	31,269	1987	Ayako Okamoto	466,034
1964	Mickey Wright	29,800	1988	Sherri Turner	350,851
1965	Kathy Whitworth	28,658	1989	Betsy King	654,132
1966	Kathy Whitworth	33,517	1990	Beth Daniel	863,578
1967	Kathy Whitworth	32,937	1991	Pat Bradley	763,118
1968	Kathy Whitworth	48,379	1992	Dottie Mochrie	693,335
1969	Carol Mann	49,152	1993	Betsy King	595,992
1970	Kathy Whitworth	30,235	1994	Laura Davies	687,201
1971	Kathy Whitworth	41,181	1995	Annika Sörenstam	666,533
1972	Kathy Whitworth	65,063	1996	Karrie Webb	1,002,000
1973	Kathy Whitworth	82,864	1997	Annika Sörenstam	1,236,789

Career Money Leaders†

	Earnings ($)		Earnings ($)		Earnings ($)
1. Betsy King	6,239,378.50	11. Juli Inkster	3,556,317.23	21. Brandie Burton	2,665,820.00
2. Pat Bradley	5,591,035.03	12. Liselotte Neumann	3,411,310.00	22. Jan Stephenson	2,609,796.00
3. Patty Sheehan	5,454,161.01	13. Jane Geddes	3,409,274.30	23. Karrie Webb	2,585,308.00
4. Beth Daniel	5,332,061.80	14. Amy Alcott	3,320,754.14	24. Michelle McGann	2,514,377.00
5. Nancy Lopez	5,159,690.83	15. Tammie Green	3,142,179.00	25. Sherri Steinhauer	2,487,740.00
6. Dottie Pepper	4,446,311.00	16. Kelly Robbins	3,085,379.00	26. D. Ammaccapane	2,483,678.00
7. Laura Davies	3,910,187.00	17. Chris Johnson	3,010,435.00	27. Donna Andrews	2,431,863.00
8. Annika Sörenstam	3,838,082.00	18. JoAnne Carner	2,921,687.63	23. Hollis Stacy	2,350,974.99
9. Rosie Jones	3,643,340.97	19. Ayako Okamoto	2,743,174.85	24. Deb Richard	2,337,396.00
10. Meg Mallon	3,601,774.00	20. Colleen Walker	2,721,226.71	28. Dawn Coe-Jones	2,295,096.57

†Through 10/12/98.

LPGA Player of the Year

1966	Kathy Whitworth	1977	Judy Rankin	1988	Nancy Lopez
1967	Kathy Whitworth	1978	Nancy Lopez	1989	Betsy King
1968	Kathy Whitworth	1979	Nancy Lopez	1990	Beth Daniel
1969	Kathy Whitworth	1980	Beth Daniel	1991	Pat Bradley
1970	Sandra Haynie	1981	JoAnne Carner	1992	Dottie Mochrie
1971	Kathy Whitworth	1982	JoAnne Carner	1993	Betsy King
1972	Kathy Whitworth	1983	Patty Sheehan	1994	Beth Daniel
1973	Kathy Whitworth	1984	Betsy King	1995	Annika Sörenstam
1974	JoAnne Carner	1985	Nancy Lopez	1996	Laura Davies
1975	Sandra Palmer	1986	Pat Bradley	1997	Annika Sörenstam
1976	Judy Rankin	1987	Ayako Okamoto		

Vare Trophy: Best Scoring Average

		Avg			Avg			Avg
1953	Patty Berg	75.00	1968	Carol Mann	72.04	1983	JoAnne Carner	71.41
1954	Babe Zaharias	75.48	1969	Kathy Whitworth	72.38	1984	Patty Sheehan	71.40
1955	Patty Berg	74.47	1970	Kathy Whitworth	72.26	1985	Nancy Lopez	70.73
1956	Patty Berg	74.57	1971	Kathy Whitworth	72.88	1986	Pat Bradley	71.10
1957	Louise Suggs	74.64	1972	Kathy Whitworth	72.38	1987	Betsy King	71.14
1958	Beverly Hanson	74.92	1973	Judy Rankin	73.08	1988	Colleen Walker	71.26
1959	Betsy Rawls	74.03	1974	JoAnne Carner	72.87	1989	Beth Daniel	70.38
1960	Mickey Wright	73.25	1975	JoAnne Carner	72.40	1990	Beth Daniel	70.54
1961	Mickey Wright	73.55	1976	Judy Rankin	72.25	1991	Pat Bradley	70.76
1962	Mickey Wright	73.67	1977	Judy Rankin	72.16	1992	Dottie Mochrie	70.80
1963	Mickey Wright	72.81	1978	Nancy Lopez	71.76	1993	Nancy Lopez	70.83
1964	Mickey Wright	72.46	1979	Nancy Lopez	71.20	1994	Beth Daniel	70.90
1965	Kathy Whitworth	72.61	1980	Amy Alcott	71.51	1995	Annika Sörenstam	71.00
1966	Kathy Whitworth	72.60	1981	JoAnne Carner	71.75	1996	Annika Sörenstam	70.47
1967	Kathy Whitworth	72.74	1982	JoAnne Carner	71.49	1997	Karrie Webb	70.00

Alltime LPGA Tour Records†

Scoring

72 HOLES

261—(71-61-63-66) by Se Ri Pak to win at the Highland Meadows CC, Sylvania, OH, in the 1998 Jamie Farr Kroger Classic (23 under par).

54 HOLES

195—(66-65-64) by Wendy Ward to lead at the Peninsula CC, Charlotte, NC, in the 1997 Fieldcrest Cannon Classic (21 under par).

195—(71-61-63) by Se Ri Pak in winning at the Highland Meadows CC, Sylvania, OH, in the 1998 Jamie Farr Kroger Classic (23 under par).

36 HOLES

129—(64–65) by Judy Dickinson at Pasadena Yacht & CC, St. Petersburg, in the 1985 S&H Golf Classic (15 under par).

18 HOLES

61—by Se Ri Pak at Highland Meadows CC, Sylvania, OH, in the second round in winning 1998 Jamie Farr Kroger Classic (10 under par).

9 HOLES

28—by Mary Beth Zimmerman at Rail GC, 1984 Rail Charity Golf Classic, Springfield, IL (par 36). Zimmerman shot 64.

28—by Pat Bradley at Green Gables CC, Denver, 1984 Columbia Savings Classic (par 35). Bradley shot 65.

28—by Muffin Spencer-Devlin at Knollwood CC, Elmsford, NY, in winning the 1985 MasterCard International Pro-Am (par 35). Spencer-Devlin shot 64.

†Through 10/12/98.

Scoring (Cont.)

9 HOLES (CONT.)

28—by Peggy Kirsch at Squaw Creek CC, Vienna, OH, in the 1991 Phar-Mor (par 35).

28—by Renee Heiken at Highland Meadows CC, Sylvania, OH, in the 1996 Jamie Farr Kroger Classic (par 34).

MOST CONSECUTIVE ROUNDS UNDER 70

9—Beth Daniel, in 1990.

MOST BIRDIES IN A ROW

8—Mary Beth Zimmerman at Rail GC in Springfield, IL, in the second round of the 1984 Rail Charity Classic. Zimmerman shot 64 (8 under par).

Wins

MOST CONSECUTIVE WINS IN SCHEDULED EVENTS

4—Mickey Wright, in 1962.

4—Mickey Wright, in 1963.

4—Kathy Whitworth, in 1969.

MOST CONSECUTIVE WINS IN ENTERED TOURNAMENTS

5—Nancy Lopez, in 1987.

MOST WINS IN A CALENDAR YEAR

13—Mickey Wright, in 1963.

WIDEST WINNING MARGIN, STROKES

14—Louise Suggs, 1949 US Women's Open.

14—Cindy Mackey, 1986 MasterCard Int'l Pro-Am.

U.S. Senior Open

Year	Winner	Score	Runner-Up	Site
1980	Roberto DeVicenzo	285	William C. Campbell	Winged Foot GC, Mamaroneck, NY
1981	Arnold Palmer* (70)	289	Bob Stone (74)	Oakland Hills CC, Birmingham, MI
			Billy Casper (77)	
1982	Miller Barber	282	Gene Littler	Portland GC, Portland, OR
			Dan Sikes, Jr	
1983	Billy Casper* (75) (3)	288	Rod Funseth (75) (4)	Hazeltine GC, Chaska, MN
1984	Miller Barber	286	Arnold Palmer	Oak Hill CC, Rochester, NY
1985	Miller Barber	285	Roberto DeVicenzo	Edgewood Tahoe GC, Stateline, NV
1986	Dale Douglass	279	Gary Player	Scioto CC, Columbus, OH
1987	Gary Player	270	Doug Sanders	Brooklawn CC, Fairfield, CT
1988	Gary Player* (68)	288	Bob Charles (70)	Medinah CC, Medinah, IL
1989	Orville Moody	279	Frank Beard	Laurel Valley GC, Ligonier, PA
1990	Lee Trevino	275	Jack Nicklaus	Ridgewood CC, Paramus, NJ
1991	Jack Nicklaus (65)	282	Chi Chi Rodriguez (69)	Oakland Hills CC, Birmingham, MI
1992	Larry Laoretti	275	Jim Colbert	Saucon Valley CC, Bethlehem, PA
1993	Jack Nicklaus	278	Tom Weiskopf	Cherry Hills CC, Englewood, CO
1994	Simon Hobday	274	Jim Albus	Pinehurst Resort & CC, Pinehurst, NC
1995	Tom Weiskopf	275	Jack Nicklaus	Congressional CC, Bethesda, MD
1996	Dave Stockton	277	Hale Irwin	Canterbury GC, Beachwood, OH
1997	Graham Marsh	280	Hale Irwin	Olympia Fields CC, Olympia Fields, IL
1998	Hale Irwin	285	Vicente Fernandez	Riviera CC, Pacific Palisades, CA

*Winner in playoff. Playoff scores are in parentheses. The 1983 playoff went to one hole of sudden death after an 18-hole playoff.

SENIOR TOUR

Season Money Leaders

		Earnings ($)			Earnings ($)
1980	Don January	44,100	1989	Bob Charles	725,887
1981	Miller Barber	83,136	1990	Lee Trevino	1,190,518
1982	Miller Barber	106,890	1991	Mike Hill	1,065,657
1983	Don January	237,571	1992	Lee Trevino	1,027,002
1984	Don January	328,597	1993	Dave Stockton	1,175,944
1985	Peter Thomson	386,724	1994	Dave Stockton	1,402,519
1986	Bruce Crampton	454,299	1995	Jim Colbert	1,444,386
1987	Chi Chi Rodriguez	509,145	1996	Jim Colbert	1,627,890
1988	Bob Charles	533,929	1997	Hale Irwin	2,449,420

Career Money Leaders†

	Earnings ($)		Earnings ($)
1. Jim Colbert	8,133,838	17. J.C. Snead	4,596,468
2. Lee Trevino	8,017,077	18. Al Geiberger	4,392,948
3. Bob Charles	7,592,458	19. Jim Albus	4,326,578
4. Dave Stockton	7,573,540	20. Tom Wargo	4,312,704
5. Hale Irwin	7,257,728	21. Gil Morgan	4,221,348
6. Mike Hill	6,611,263	22. Graham Marsh	4,125,872
7. George Archer	6,246,467	23. Miller Barber	3,875,464
8. Ray Floyd	6,211,100	24. Rocky Thompson	3,780,143
9. Chi Chi Rodriguez	6,184,587	25. Gibby Gilbert	3,656,120
10. Isao Aoki	6,129,851	26. Harold Henning	3,612,410
11. Jim Dent	6,020,652	27. Simon Hobday	3,602,947
12. Dale Douglass	5,623,646	28. Charles Coody	3,531,352
13. Bob Murphy	5,111,622	29. Jimmy Powell	3,484,761
14. Gary Player	4,913,630	30. Kermit Zarley	3,309,637
15. Jay Sigel	4,674,567		
16. Bruce Crampton	4,625,106	†Through 10/11/98.	

Most Career Wins†

	Wins		Wins
Lee Trevino	27	Gary Player	19
Miller Barber	24	Hale Irwin	19
Bob Charles	22	Mike Hill	18
Don January	22	George Archer	18
Chi Chi Rodriguez	22	Jim Colbert	18
Bruce Crampton	21	Dave Stockton	15

†Through 10/16/98.

MAJOR MEN'S AMATEUR CHAMPIONSHIPS
U.S. Amateur

Year	Winner	Score	Runner-Up	Site
1895	Charles B. Macdonald	12 & 11	Charles E. Sands	Newport GC, Newport, RI
1896	H. J. Whigham	8 & 7	J.G Thorp	Shinnecock Hills GC, Southampton, NY
1897	H. J. Whigham	8 & 6	W. Rossiter Betts	Chicago GC, Wheaton, IL
1898	Findlay S. Douglas	5 & 3	Walter B. Smith	Morris County GC, Morristown, NJ
1899	H. M. Harriman	3 & 2	Findlay S. Douglas	Onwentsia Club, Lake Forest, IL
1900	Walter Travis	2 up	Findlay S. Douglas	Garden City GC, Garden City, NY
1901	Walter Travis	5 & 4	Walter E. Egan	CC of Atlantic City, NJ
1902	Louis N. James	4 & 2	Eben M. Byers	Glen View Club, Golf, IL
1903	Walter Travis	5 & 4	Eben M. Byers	Nassau CC, Glen Cove, NY
1904	H. Chandler Egan	8 & 6	Fred Herreshoff	Baltusrol GC, Springfield, NJ
1905	H. Chandler Egan	6 & 5	D.E. Sawyer	Chicago GC, Wheaton, IL
1906	Eben M. Byers	2 up	George S. Lyon	Englewood GC, Englewood, NJ
1907	Jerry Travers	6 & 5	Archibald Graham	Euclid Club, Cleveland, OH
1908	Jerry Travers	8 & 7	Max H. Behr	Garden City GC, Garden City, NY
1909	Robert A. Gardner	4 & 3	H. Chandler Egan	Chicago GC, Wheaton, IL
1910	William C. Fownes Jr.	4 & 3	Warren K. Wood	The Country Club, Brookline, MA
1911	Harold Hilton	1 up	Fred Herreshoff	The Apawamis Club, Rye, NY
1912	Jerry Travers	7 & 6	Charles Evans Jr.	Chicago GC, Wheaton, IL
1913	Jerry Travers	5 & 4	John G. Anderson	Garden City GC, Garden City, NY
1914	Francis Ouimet	6 & 5	Jerry Travers	Ekwanok CC, Manchester, VT
1915	Robert A. Gardner	5 & 4	John G. Anderson	CC of Detroit, Grosse Pt. Farms, MI
1916	Chick Evans	4 & 3	Robert A. Gardner	Merion Cricket Club, Haverford, PA
1917-18	No tournament			
1919	S. Davidson Herron	5 & 4	Bobby Jones	Oakmont CC, Oakmont, PA
1920	Chick Evans	7 & 6	Francis Ouimet	Engineers' CC, Roslyn, NY
1921	Jesse P. Guilford	7 & 6	Robert A. Gardner	St. Louis CC, Clayton, MO
1922	Jess W. Sweetser	3 & 2	Chick Evans	The Country Club, Brookline, MA
1923	Max R. Marston	1 up	Jess W. Sweetser	Flossmoor CC, Flossmoor, IL
1924	Bobby Jones	9 & 8	George Von Elm	Merion Cricket Club, Ardmore, PA
1925	Bobby Jones	8 & 7	Watts Gunn	Oakmont CC, Oakmont, PA
1926	George Von Elm	2 & 1	Bobby Jones	Baltusrol GC, Springfield, NJ
1927	Bobby Jones	8 & 7	Chick Evans	Minikahda Club, Minneapolis
1928	Bobby Jones	10 & 9	T. Phillip Perkins	Brae Burn CC, West Newton, MA
1929	Harrison R. Johnston	4 & 3	Dr. O.F. Willing	Del Monte G & CC, Pebble Beach, CA
1930	Bobby Jones	8 & 7	Eugene V. Homans	Merion Cricket Club, Ardmore, PA
1931	Francis Ouimet	6 & 5	Jack Westland	Beverly CC, Chicago, IL
1932	C. Ross Somerville	2 & 1	John Goodman	Baltimore CC, Timonium, MD
1933	George T. Dunlap Jr.	6 & 5	Max R. Marston	Kenwood CC, Cincinnati, OH
1934	Lawson Little	8 & 7	David Goldman	The Country Club, Brookline, MA
1935	Lawson Little	4 & 2	Walter Emery	The Country Club, Cleveland, OH
1936	John W. Fischer	1 up	Jack McLean	Garden City GC, Garden City, NY
1937	John Goodman	2 up	Raymond E. Billows	Alderwood CC, Portland, OR
1938	William P. Turnesa	8 & 7	B. Patrick Abbott	Oakmont CC, Oakmont, PA
1939	Marvin H. Ward	7 & 5	Raymond E. Billows	North Shore CC, Glenview, IL
1940	Richard D. Chapman	11 & 9	W. McCullough Jr.	Winged Foot GC, Mamaroneck, NY
1941	Marvin H. Ward	4 & 3	B. Patrick Abbott	Omaha Field Club, Omaha, NE
1942-45	No tournament			
1946	Ted Bishop	1 up	Smiley L. Quick	Baltusrol GC, Springfield, NJ
1947	Skee Riegel	2 & 1	John W. Dawson	Del Monte G & CC, Pebble Beach, CA
1948	William P. Turnesa	2 & 1	Raymond E. Billows	Memphis CC, Memphis, TN
1949	Charles R. Coe	11 & 10	Rufus King	Oak Hill CC, Rochester, NY
1950	Sam Urzetta	1 up	Frank Stranahan	Minneapolis GC, Minneapolis, MN
1951	Billy Maxwell	4 & 3	Joseph F. Gagliardi	Saucon Valley CC, Bethlehem, PA
1952	Jack Westland	3 & 2	Al Mengert	Seattle GC, Seattle, WA
1953	Gene Littler	1 up	Dale Morey	Oklahoma City G & CC, Oklahoma City
1954	Arnold Palmer	1 up	Robert Sweeny	CC of Detroit, Grosse Pt. Farms, MI
1955	E. Harvie Ward Jr.	9 & 8	Wm. Hyndman III	CC of Virginia, Richmond, VA
1956	E. Harvie Ward Jr.	5 & 4	Charles Kocsis	Knollwood Club, Lake Forest, IL
1957	Hillman Robbins Jr.	5 & 4	Dr. Frank M. Taylor	The Country Club, Brookline, MA
1958	Charles R. Coe	5 & 4	Tommy Aaron	Olympic Club, San Francisco, CA
1959	Jack Nicklaus	1 up	Charles R. Coe	Broadmoor CC, Colorado Springs, CO
1960	Deane Beman	6 & 4	Robert W. Gardner	St. Louis CC, Clayton, MO
1961	Jack Nicklaus	8 & 6	H. Dudley Wysong	Pebble Beach GL, Pebble Beach, CA

U.S. Amateur *(Cont.)*

Year	Winner	Score	Runner-Up	Site
1962	Labron E. Harris Jr.	1 up	Downing Gray	Pinehurst CC, Pinehurst, NC
1963	Deane Beman	2 & 1	Richard H. Sikes	Wakonda Club, Des Moines, IA
1964	William C. Campbell	1 up	Edgar M. Tutwiler	Canterbury GC, Cleveland, OH
1965	Robert J. Murphy Jr.	291	Robert B. Dickson	Southern Hills, CC, Tulsa, OK
1966	Gary Cowan	285–75	Deane Beman	Merion GC, Ardmore, PA
1967	Robert B. Dickson	285	Marvin Giles III	Broadmoor GC, Colorado Springs, CO
1968	Bruce Fleisher	284	Marvin Giles III	Scioto CC, Columbus, OH
1969	Steven N. Melnyk	286	Marvin Giles III	Oakmont CC, Oakmont, PA
1970	Lanny Wadkins	279	Tom Kite	Waverley CC, Portland, OR
1971	Gary Cowan	280	Eddie Pearce	Wilmington CC, Wilmington DE
1972	Marvin Giles III	285	two tied	Charlotte CC, Charlotte, NC
1973	Craig Stadler	6 & 5	David Strawn	Inverness Club, Toledo, OH
1974	Jerry Pate	2 & 1	John P. Grace	Ridgewood CC, Ridgewood, NJ
1975	Fred Ridley	2 up	Keith Fergus	CC of Virginia, Richmond, VA
1976	Bill Sander	8 & 6	C. Parker Moore Jr.	Bel Air CC, Los Angeles, CA
1977	John Fought	9 & 8	Doug Fischesser	Aronimink GC, Newton Square, PA
1978	John Cook	5 & 4	Scott Hoch	Plainfield CC, Plainfield, NJ
1979	Mark O'Meara	8 & 7	John Cook	Canterbury GC, Cleveland, OH
1980	Hal Sutton	9 & 8	Bob Lewis	CC of North Carolina, Pinehurst, NC
1981	Nathaniel Crosby	1 up	Brian Lindley	Olympic Club, San Francisco, CA
1982	Jay Sigel	8 & 7	David Tolley	The Country Club, Brookline, MA
1983	Jay Sigel	8 & 7	Chris Perry	North Shore CC, Glenviedw IL
1984	Scott Verplank	4 & 3	Sam Randolph	Oak Tree GC, Edmond, OK
1985	Sam Randolph	1 up	Peter Persons	Montclair GC, West Orange, NJ
1986	Buddy Alexander	5 & 3	Chris Kite	Shoal Creek, Shoal Creek AL
1987	Bill Mayfair	4 & 3	Eric Rebmann	Jupiter Hills Club, Jupiter, FL
1988	Eric Meeks	7 & 6	Danny Yates	Va. Hot Springs G & CC, VA
1989	Chris Patton	3 & 1	Danny Green	Merion GC, Ardmore, PA
1990	Phil Mickelson	5 & 4	Manny Zerman	Cherry Hills CC, Englewood, CO
1991	Mitch Voges	7 & 6	Manny Zerman	The Honors Course, Ooltewah, TN
1992	Justin Leonard	8 & 7	Tom Scherrer	Muirfield Village GC, Dublin, OH
1993	John Harris	5 & 3	Danny Ellis	Champions GC, Houston, TX
1994	Tiger Woods	2 up	Trip Kuehne	TPC-Sawgrass, Ponte Vedre, FL
1995	Tiger Woods	2 up	Buddy Marucci	Newport Country Club, Newport, RI
1996	Tiger Woods	38 holes	Steve Scott	Pumpkin Ridge GC, Cornelius, OR
1997	Matthew Kuchar	2 & 1	Joel Kribel	Cog Hill G & CC, Lemont, IL
1998	Hank Kuehne	2 & 1	Tom McKnight	Oak Hill CC, Rochester, NY

Note: All stroke play from 1965 to 1972.

U.S. Junior Amateur

1948	Dean Lind	1965	James Masserio	1982	Rich Marik
1949	Gay Brewer	1966	Gary Sanders	1983	Tim Straub
1950	Mason Rudolph	1967	John Crooks	1984	Doug Martin
1951	Tommy Jacobs	1968	Eddie Pearce	1985	Charles Rymer
1952	Don Bisplinghoff	1969	Aly Trompas	1986	Brian Montgomery
1953	Rex Baxter	1970	Gary Koch	1987	Brett Quigley
1954	Foster Bradley	1971	Mike Brannan	1988	Jason Widener
1955	William Dunn	1972	Bob Byman	1989	David Duval
1956	Harlan Stevenson	1973	Jack Renner	1990	Mathew Todd
1957	Larry Beck	1974	David Nevatt	1991	Tiger Woods
1958	Buddy Baker	1975	Brett Mullin	1992	Tiger Woods
1959	Larry Lee	1976	Madden Hatcher, III	1993	Tiger Woods
1960	Bill Tindall	1977	Willie Wood Jr	1994	Terry Noe
1961	Charles McDowell	1978	Don Hurter	1995	D. Scott Hailes
1962	Jim Wiechers	1979	Jack Larkin	1996	Shane McMenamy
1963	Gregg McHatton	1980	Eric Johnson	1997	Jason Allred
1964	Johnny Miller	1981	Scott Erickson	1998	James Oh

Note: Event is for amateur golfers younger than 18 years of age.

Mid-Amateur Championship

1981	Jim Holtgrieve	1987	Jay Sigel	1993	Jeff Thomas
1982	William Hoffer	1988	David Eger	1994	Tim Jackson
1983	Jay Sigel	1989	James Taylor	1995	Jerry Courville Jr
1984	Mike Podolak	1990	Jim Stuart	1996	John Miller
1985	Jay Sigel	1991	Jim Stuart	1997	Ken Bakst
1986	Bill Loeffler	1992	Danny Yates	1998	John Miller

Note: Event is for amateur golfers at least 25 years of age.

British Amateur

1887	H. G. Hutchinson	1926	Jess Sweetser	1966	C.R. Cole
1888	John Ball	1927	Dr. W. Tweddell	1967	R. Dickson
1889	J.E. Laidlay	1928	T.P. Perkins	1968	M. Bonallack
1890	John Ball	1929	C.J.H. Tolley	1969	M. Bonallack
1891	J.E. Laidlay	1930	Robert T. Jones Jr.	1970	M. Bonallack
1892	John Ball	1931	E. Martin Smith	1971	Steve Melnyk
1893	Peter Anderson	1932	J. DeForest	1972	Trevor Homer
1894	John Ball	1933	M. Scott	1973	R. Siderowf
1895	L.M.B. Melville	1934	W. Lawson Little	1974	Trevor Homer
1896	F.G. Tait	1935	W. Lawson Little	1975	M. Giles
1897	A.J.T. Allan	1936	H. Thomson	1976	R. Siderowf
1898	F.G. Tait	1937	R. Sweeney Jr.	1977	P. McEvoy
1899	John Ball	1938	C.R. Yates	1978	P. McEvoy
1900	H.H. Hilton	1939	A.T. Kyle	1979	J. Sigel
1901	H.H. Hilton	1940–45	not held	1980	D. Evans
1902	C. Hutchings	1946	J. Bruen	1981	P. Ploujoux
1903	R. Maxwell	1947	Willie D. Turnesa	1982	M. Thompson
1904	W.J. Travis	1948	Frank R. Stranahan	1983	A. Parkin
1905	A.G. Barry	1949	S.M. McReady	1984	J.M. Olazabal
1906	James Robb	1950	Frank R. Stranahan	1985	G. McGimpsey
1907	John Ball	1951	Richard D. Chapman	1986	D. Curry
1908	E.A. Lassen	1952	E.H. Ward	1987	P. Mayo
1909	R. Maxwell	1953	J.B. Carr	1988	C. Hardin
1910	John Ball	1954	D.W. Bachli	1989	S. Dodd
1911	H.H. Hilton	1955	J.W. Conrad	1990	R. Muntz
1912	John Ball	1956	J.C. Beharrel	1991	G. Wolstenholme
1913	H.H. Hilton	1957	R. Reid Jack	1992	S. Dundas
1914	J.L.C. Jenkins	1958	J.B. Carr	1993	I. Pyman
1915-19	not held	1959	Deane Beman	1994	L. James
1920	C.J.H. Tolley	1960	J.B. Carr	1995	G. Sherry
1921	W.I. Hunter	1961	M. Bonallack	1996	W. Bladon
1922	E.W.E. Holderness	1962	R. Davies	1997	C. Watson
1923	R.H. Wethered	1963	M. Lunt	1998	Sergio Garcia
1924	E.W.E. Holderness	1964	C. Clark		
1925	R. Harris	1965	M. Bonallack		

Amateur Public Links

1922	Edmund R. Held	1949	Kenneth J. Towns	1974	Charles Barenaba
1923	Richard J. Walsh	1950	Stanley Bielat	1975	Randy Barenaba
1924	Joseph Coble	1951	Dave Stanley	1976	Eddie Mudd
1925	Raymond J. McAuliffe	1952	Omer L. Bogan	1977	Jerry Vidovic
		1953	Ted Richards Jr.	1978	Dean Prince
1926	Lester Bolstad	1954	Gene Andrews	1979	Dennis Walsh
1927	Carl F. Kauffmann	1955	Sam D. Kocsis	1980	Jodie Mudd
1928	Carl F. Kauffmann	1956	James H. Buxbaum	1981	Jodie Mudd
1929	Carl F. Kauffmann	1957	Don Essig III	1982	Billy Tuten
1930	Robert E. Wingate	1958	Daniel D. Sikes Jr.	1983	Billy Tuten
1931	Charles Ferrera	1959	William A. Wright	1984	Bill Malley
1932	R.L. Miller	1960	Verne Callison	1985	Jim Sorenson
1933	Charles Ferrera	1961	Richard H. Sikes	1986	Bill Mayfair
1934	David A. Mitchell	1962	Richard H. Sikes	1987	Kevin Johnson
1935	Frank Strafaci	1963	Robert Lunn	1988	Ralph Howe III
1936	B. Patrick Abbott	1964	William McDonald	1989	Tim Hobby
1937	Bruce N. McCormick	1965	Arne Dokka	1990	Michael Combs
1938	Al Leach	1966	Lamont Kaser	1991	David Berganio Jr.
1939	Andrew Szwedko	1967	Verne Callison	1992	Warren Schulte
1940	Robert C. Clark	1968	Gene Towry	1993	David Berganio Jr.
1941	William M. Welch Jr.	1969	John M. Jackson Jr.	1994	Guy Yamamoto
1942–45	not held	1970	Robert Risch	1995	Chris Wollmann
1946	Smiley L. Quick	1971	Fred Haney	1996	Tim Hogarth
1947	Wilfred Crossley	1972	Bob Allard	1997	Tim Clark
1948	Michael R. Ferentz	1973	Stan Stopa	1998	Trevor Immelman

U.S. Senior Golf

1955	J. Wood Platt	1970	Gene Andrews	1985	Lewis W. Oehmig
1956	Frederick J. Wright	1971	Tom Draper	1986	Bo Williams
1957	J. Clark Espie	1972	Lewis W. Oehmig	1987	John Richardson
1958	Thomas C. Robbins	1973	William Hyndman III	1988	Clarence Moore
1959	J. Clark Espie	1974	Dale Morey	1989	Bo Williams
1960	Michael Cestone	1975	William F. Colm	1990	Jackie Cummings
1961	Dexter H. Daniels	1976	Lewis W. Oehmig	1991	Bill Bosshard
1962	Merrill L. Carlsmith	1977	Dale Morey	1992	Clarence Moore
1963	Merrill L. Carlsmith	1978	K.K. Compton	1993	Joe Ungvary
1964	William D. Higgins	1979	William C. Campbell	1994	O. Gordon Brewer
1965	Robert B. Kiersky	1980	William C. Campbell	1995	James Stahl Jr.
1966	Dexter H. Daniels	1981	Ed Updegraff	1996	O. Gordon Brewer
1967	Ray Palmer	1982	Alton Duhon	1997	Cliff Cunningham
1968	Curtis Person Sr.	1983	William Hyndman III	1998	Bill Shean Jr.
1969	Curtis Person Sr.	1984	Bob Rawlins		

Note: Event is for golfers at least 55 years of age.

MAJOR WOMEN'S AMATEUR CHAMPIONSHIPS

U.S. Women's Amateur

Year	Winner	Score	Runner-Up	Site
1895	Mrs. Charles S. Brown	132	Nellie Sargent	Meadow Brook Club, Hempstead, NY
1896	Beatrix Hoyt	2 & 1	Mrs. Arthur Turnure	Morris Couty GC, Morristown, NJ
1897	Beatrix Hoyt	5 & 4	Nellie Sargent	Essex County Club, Manchester, MA
1898	Beatrix Hoyt	5 &3	Maude Wetmore	Ardsley Club, Ardsley-on-Hudson, NY
1899	Ruth Underhill	2 & 1	Margaret Fox	Philadelphia CC, Philadelphia, PA
1900	Frances C. Griscom	6 & 5	Margaret Curtis	Shinnecock Hills GC, Shinnecock Hills, NY
1901	Genevieve Hecker	5 & 3	Lucy Herron	Baltusrol GC, Springfield, NJ
1902	Genevieve Hecker	4 & 3	Louisa A. Wells	The Country Club, Brookline, MA
1903	Bessie Anthony	7 & 6	J. Anna Carpenter	Chicago GC, Wheaton, IL
1904	Georgianna M. Bishop	5 & 3	Mrs. E.F. Sanford	Merion Cricket Club, Haverford, PA
1905	Pauline Mackay	1 up	Margaret Curtis	Morris County GC, Convent, NJ
1906	Harriot S. Curtis	2 & 1	Mary B. Adams	Brae Burn CC, West Newton, MA
1907	Margaret Curtis	7 & 6	Harriot S. Curtis	Midlothian CC, Blue Island, IL
1908	Katherine C. Harley	6 & 5	Mrs. T.H. Polhemus	Chevy Chase Club, Chevy Chase, MD
1909	Dorothy I. Campbell	3 & 2	Nonna Barlow	Merion Cricket Club, Haverford, PA
1910	Dorothy I. Campbell	2 & 1	Mrs. G.M. Martin	Homewood CC, Flossmoor, IL
1911	Margaret Curtis	5 & 3	Lillian B. Hyde	Baltusrol GC, Springfield, NJ
1912	Margaret Curtis	3 & 2	Nonna Barlow	Essex County Club, Manchester, MA
1913	Gladys Ravenscroft	2 up	Marion Hollins	Wilmington CC, Wilmington, DE
1914	Katherine Harley	1 up	Elaine V. Rosenthal	Nassau CC, Glen Cove, NY
1915	Florence Vanderbeck	3 & 2	Margaret Gavin	Onwentsia Club, Lake Forest, IL
1916	Alexa Stirling	2 & 1	Mildred Caverly	Belmont Springs CC, Waverley, MA
1917–18	No tournament			
1919	Alexa Stirling	6 & 5	Margaret Gavin	Shawnee CC, Shawnee-on-Delaware, PA
1920	Alexa Stirling	5 & 4	Dorothy Campbell	Mayfield CC, Cleveland, OH
1921	Marion Hollins	5 & 4	Alexa Stirling	Hollywood GC, Deal, NJ
1922	Glenna Collett	5 & 4	Margaret Gavin	Greenbriar GC, White Sulphur Springs, WV
1923	Edith Cummings	3 & 2	Alexa Stirling	Westchester-Biltmore CC, Rye, NY
1924	Dorothy Campbell	7 & 6	Mary K. Browne	Rhode Island CC, Nyatt, RI
1925	Glenna Collett	9 & 8	Alexa Stirling	St. Louis CC, Clayton, MO
1926	Helen Stetson	3 & 1	Elizabeth Goss	Merion Cricket Club, Ardmore, PA
1927	Miiriam Burns Horn	5 & 4	Maureen Orcutt	Cherry Valley Club, Garden City, NY
1928	Glenna Collett	13 & 12	Virginia Van Wie	Va. Hot Springs G & TC, Hot Springs, VA
1929	Glenna Collett	4 & 3	Leona Pressler	Oakland Hills CC, Birmingham, MI
1930	Glenna Collett	6 & 5	Virginia Van Wie	Los Angeles CC, Beverly Hills, CA
1931	Helen Hicks	2 & 1	Glenna Collet Vare	CC of Buffalo, Williamsville, NY
1932	Virginia Van Wie	10 & 8	Glenna Collet Vare	Salem CC, Peabody, MA
1933	Virginia Van Wie	4 & 3	Helen Hicks	Exmoor CC, Highland Park, IL
1934	Virginia Van Wie	2 & 1	Dorothy Traung	Whitemarsh Valley CC, Chestnut Hill, PA
1935	Glenna Collett Vare	3 & 2	Patty Berg	Interlachen CC, Hopkins, MN
1936	Pamela Barton	4 & 3	Maureen Orcutt	Canoe Brook CC, Summit, NJ
1937	Estelle Lawson	7 & 6	Patty Berg	Memphis CC, Memphis, TN
1938	Patty Berg	6 & 5	Estelle Lawson	Westmoreland CC, Wilmette, IL

U.S. Women's Amateur (Cont.)

Year	Winner	Score	Runner-Up	Site
1939	Betty Jameson	3 & 2	Dorothy Kirby	Wee Burn Club, Darien, CT
1940	Betty Jameson	6 & 5	Jane S. Cothran	Del Monte G & CC, Pebble Beach, CA
1941	Elizabeth Hicks	5 & 3	Helen Sigel	The Country Club, Brookline, MA
1942-45	No tournament			
1946	Babe Zaharias	11 & 9	Clara Sherman	Southern Hills CC, Tulsa, OK
1947	Louise Suggs	2 up	Dorothy Kirby	Franklin Hills CC, Franklin, MI
1948	Grace S. Lenczyk	4 & 3	Helen Sigel	Del Monte G & CC, Pebble Beach, CA
1949	Dorothy Porter	3 & 2	Dorothy Kielty	Merion GC, Ardmore, PA
1950	Beverly Hanson	6 & 4	Mae Murray	Atlanta AC, Atlanta, GA
1951	Dorothy Kirby	2 & 1	Claire Doran	Town & CC, St. Paul, MN
1952	Jacqueline Pung	2 & 1	Shirley McFedters	Waverley CC, Portland, OR
1953	Mary Lena Faulk	3 & 2	Polly Riley	Rhode Island CC, West Barrington, RI
1954	Barbara Romack	4 & 2	Mickey Wright	Allegheny CC, Sewickley, PA
1955	Patricia A. Lesser	7 & 6	Jane Nelson	Myers Park CC, Charlotte, NC
1956	Marlene Stewart	2 & 1	JoAnne Gunderson	Meridian Hills CC, Indianapolis, IN
1957	JoAnne Gunderson	8 & 6	Ann Casey Johnstone	Del Paso CC, Sacramento, CA
1958	Anne Quast	3 & 2	Barbara Romack	Wee Burn CC, Darien, CT
1959	Barbara McIntire	4 & 3	Joanne Goodwin	Congressional CC, Washington, D.C.
1960	JoAnne Gunderson	6 & 5	Jean Ashley	Tulsa CC, Tulsa, OK
1961	Anne Quast Decker	14 & 13	Phyllis Preuss	Tacoma G & CC, Tacoma, WA
1962	JoAnne Gunderson	9 & 8	Anne Baker	CC of Rochester, Rochester, NY
1963	Anne Quast Decker	2 & 1	Peggy Conley	Taconic GC, Williamstown, MA
1964	Barbara McIntire	3 & 2	JoAnne Gunderson	Prairie Dunes CC, Hutchinson, KS
1965	Jean Ashley	5 & 4	Anne Quast Decker	Lakewood CC, Denver, CO
1966	JoAnne Gunderson	1 up	Marlene Stewart Streit	Sewickley Heights GC, Sewickley, PA
1967	Mary Lou Dill	5 & 4	Jean Ashley	Annandale GC, Pasadena, CA
1968	JoAnne Gunderson Carner	5 & 4	Anne Quast Decker	Birmingham CC, Birmingham, MI
1969	Catherine Lacoste	3 & 2	Shelley Hamling	Las Colinas CC, Irving, TX
1970	Martha Wilkinson	3 & 2	Cynthia Hall	Wee Burn CC, Darien, CT
1971	Laura Baugh	1 up	Beth Barry	Atlanta CC, Atlanta, GA
1972	Mary Budke	5 & 4	Cynthia Hill	St. Louis CC, St. Louis, MO
1973	Carol Semple	1 up	Anne Quast Decker	Montclair GC, Montclair, NJ
1974	Cynthia Hill	5 & 4	Carol Semple	Broadmoor GC, Seattle, WA
1975	Beth Daniel	3 & 2	Donna Horton	Brae Burn CC, West Newton, MA
1976	Donna Horton	2 & 1	Marianne Bretton	Del Paso CC, Sacramento, CA
1977	Beth Daniel	3 & 1	Cathy Sherk	Cincinnati CC, Cincinnati, OH
1978	Cathy Sherk	4 & 3	Judith Oliver	Sunnybrook GC, Plymouth Meeting, PA
1979	Carolyn Hill	7 & 6	Patty Sheehan	Memphis CC, Memphis, TN
1980	Juli Inkster	2 up	Patti Rizzo	Prairie Dunes CC, Hutchinson, KS
1981	Juli Inkster	1 up	Lindy Goggin	Waverley CC, Portland, OR
1982	Juli Inkster	4 & 3	Cathy Hanlon	Broadmoor GC, Colorado Springs, CO
1983	Joanne Pacillo	2 & 1	Sally Quinlan	Canoe Brook CC, Summit, NJ
1984	Deb Richard	1 up	Kimberly Williams	Broadmoor GC, Seattle, WA
1985	Michiko Hattori	5 & 4	Cheryl Stacy	Fox Chapel GC, Pittsburgh, PA
1986	Kay Cockerill	9 & 7	Kathleen McCarthy	Pasatiempo GC, Santa Cruz, CA
1987	Kay Cockerill	3 & 2	Tracy Kerdyk	Rhode Island CC, Barrington, RI
1988	Pearl Sinn	6 & 5	Karen Noble	Minikahda Club, Minneapolis, MN
1989	Vicki Goetze	4 & 3	Brandie Burton	Pinehurst CC (No. 2), Pinehurst, NC
1990	Pat Hurst	37 holes	Stephanie Davis	Canoe Brook CC, Summit, NJ
1991	Amy Fruhwirth	5 & 4	Heidi Voorhees	Prairie Dunes CC, Hutchinson, KN
1992	Vicki Goetz	1-up	Annika Sorensteam	Kemper Lakes GC, Hawthorne Hills, IL
1993	Jill McGill	1-up	Sarah Ingram	San Diego CC, Chula Vista, CA
1994	Wendy Ward	2 & 1	Jill McGill	The Homestead, Hot Springs, WV
1995	Kelli Kuehne	4 & 3	Anne-Marie Knight	The Country Club, Brookline, MA
1996	Kelli Kuehne	2 & 1	Marisa Baena	Firethorn GC, Lincoln, NE
1997	Silvia Cavalleri	5 & 4	Robin Burke	Brae Burn CC, West Newton, MA
1998	Grace Park	7 & 6	Jenny Chuasiriporn	Barton Hills CC, Ann Arbor, MI

U.S. Girls' Junior Amateur

1949 ....Marlene Bauer	1967 ....Elizabeth Story	1985 ....Dana Lofland
1950 ....Patricia Lesser	1968 ....Peggy Harmon	1986 ....Pat Hurst
1951 ....Arlene Brooks	1969 ....Hollis Stacy	1987 ....Michelle McGann
1952 ....Mickey Wright	1970 ....Hollis Stacy	1988 ....Jamille Jose
1953 ....Millie Meyerson	1971 ....Hollis Stacy	1989 ....Brandie Burton
1954 ....Margaret Smith	1972 ....Nancy Lopez	1990 ....Sandrine Mendiburu
1955 ....Carole Jo Kabler	1973 ....Amy Alcott	1991 ....Emilee Klein
1956 ....JoAnne Gunderson	1974 ....Nancy Lopez	1992 ....Jamie Koizumi
1957 ....Judy Eller	1975 ....Dayna Benson	1993 ....Kellee Booth
1958 ....Judy Eller	1976 ....Pilar Dorado	1962 ....Maureen Orcutt
1959 ....Judy Rand	1977 ....Althea Tome	1963 ....Sis Choate
1960 ....Carol Sorenson	1978 ....Lori Castillo	1994 ....Kelli Kuehne
1961 ....Mary Lowell	1979 ....Penny Hammel	1995 ....Marcy Newton
1962 ....Mary Lou Daniel	1980 ....Laurie Rinker	1996 ....Dorothy Delasin
1963 ....Janis Ferraris	1981 ....Kay Cornelius	1997 ....Beth Bauer
1964 ....Peggy Conley	1982 ....Heather Farr	1998 ....Leigh Anne Hardin
1965 ....Gail Sykes	1983 ....Kim Saiki	
1966 ....Claudia Mayhew	1984 ....Cathy Mockett	

Women's British Amateur

1893 ....Lady Margaret Scott	1928 ....Miss N. Le Blan	1964 ....C. Sorenson
1894 ....Lady Margaret Scott	1929 ....Miss J. Wethered	1965 ....B. Varangot
1895 ....Lady Margaret Scott	1930 ....Miss D. Fishwick	1966 ....E. Chadwick
1896 ....Miss Pascoe	1931 ....Miss E. Wilson	1967 ....E. Chadwick
1897 ....Miss E.C. Orr	1932 ....Miss E. Wilson	1968 ....B. Varangot
1898 ....Miss L. Thomson	1933 ....Miss E. Wilson	1975 ....C. Lacoste
1899 ....Miss M. Hezlet	1934 ....Mrs. A.M. Holm	1976 ....D. Oxley
1900 ....Miss Adair	1935 ....Miss W. Morgan	1977 ....A. Uzielli
1901 ....Miss Graham	1936 ....Miss P. Barton	1978 ....E. Kennedy
1902 ....Miss M. Hezlet	1937 ....Miss J. Anderson	1979 ....M. Madill
1903 ....Miss Adair	1938 ....Mrs. A.M. Holm	1980 ....A. Quast
1904 ....Miss L. Dod	1939 ....Miss P. Barton	1981 ..............I.C. Robertson
1905 ....Miss B. Thompson	1940–45 ....not held	1982 ....K. Douglas
1906 ....Mrs. Kennon	1946 ..............G.W. Hetherington	1983 ....J. Thornhill
1907 ....Miss M. Hezlet	1947 ....B. Zaharias	1984 ....J. Rosenthal
1908 ....Miss M. Titterton	1948 ....L. Suggs	1985 ....L. Beman
1909 ....Miss D. Campbell	1949 ....F. Stephens	1986 ....M. McGuire
1910 ....Miss Grant Suttie	1950 ....Vicomtesse de Saint	1987 ....J. Collingham
1911 ....Miss D. Campbell	Sauveur	1988 ....J. Furby
1912 ....Miss G. Ravenscroft	1951 ..............P.J. MacCann	1989 ....H. Dobson
1913 ....Miss M. Dodd	1952 ....M. Paterson	1990 ....J. Hall
1914 ....Miss C. Leitch	1953 ....M. Stewart	1991 ....V. Michaud
1915–19 ....not held	1954 ....F. Stephens	1992 ....P. Pedersen
1920 ....Miss C. Leitch	1955 ....J. Valentine	1993 ....Catriona Lambert
1921 ....Miss C. Leitch	1956 ....M. Smith	1994 ....Emma Duggleby
1922 ....Miss J. Wethered	1957 ....P. Garvey	1995 ....Julie Hall
1923 ....Miss D. Chambers	1958 ....J. Valentine	1996 ....Kelli Kuehne
1924 ....Miss J. Wethered	1959 ....E. Price	1997 ....Alison Rose
1925 ....Miss J. Wethered	1960 ....B. McIntyre	1998 ....Elaine Ratcliffe
1926 ....Miss C. Leitch	1961 ....M. Spearman	
1927 ....Miss Thion de la	1962 ....M. Spearman	
Chaume	1963 ....B. Varangot	

Women's Amateur Public Links

1977 ....Kelly Fuiks	1985 ....Danielle	1992 ....Amy Fruhwirth
1978 ....Kelly Fuiks	Ammaccapane	1993 ....Connie Masterson
1979 ....Lori Castillo	1986 ....Cindy Schreyer	1994 ....Jill McGill
1980 ....Lori Castillo	1987 ....Tracy Kerdyk	1995 ....Jo Jo Robertson
1981 ....Mary Enright	1988 ....Pearl Sinn	1996 ....Heather Graff
1982 ....Nancy Taylor	1989 ....Pearl Sinn	1997 ....Jo Jo Robertson
1983 ....Kelli Antolock	1990 ....Cathy Mockett	1998 ....Amy Spooner
1984 ....Heather Farr	1991 ....Tracy Hanson	

U.S. Senior Women's Amateur

1964 ....Loma Smith	1976 ....Cecile H. Maclaurin	1988 ....Lois Hodge
1965 ....Loma Smith	1977 ....Dorothy Porter	1989 ....Anne Sander
1966 ....Maureen Orcutt	1978 ....Alice Dye	1990 ....Anne Sander
1967 ....Marge Mason	1979 ....Alice Dye	1991 ....Phyllis Preuss
1968 ....Carolyn Cudone	1980 ....Dorothy Porter	1992 ....Rosemary Thompson
1969 ....Carolyn Cudone	1981 ....Dorothy Porter	1993 ....Anne Sander
1970 ....Carolyn Cudone	1982 ....Edean Ihlanfeldt	1994 ....Marlene Streit
1971 ....Carolyn Cudone	1983 ....Dorothy Porter	1995 ....Jean Smith
1972 ....Carolyn Cudone	1984 ....Constance Guthrie	1996 ....Gayle Borthwick
1973 ....Gwen Hibbs	1985 ....Marlene Streit	1997 ....Nancy Fitzgerald
1974 ....Justine Cushing	1986 ....Connie Guthrie	1998 ....Gayle Borthwick
1975 ....Alberta Bower	1987 ....Anne Sander	

Women's Mid-Amateur Championship

1987 ....Cindy Scholefield	1991 ....Sarah LeBrun Ingram	1995 ....Ellen Port
1988 ....Martha Lang	1992 ....Marion Mamey-	1996 ....Ellen Port
1989 ....Robin Weiss	............McInerney	1997 ....Carol Semple
1990 ....Carol Semple	1993 ....Sarah Ingram	............Thompson
............Thompson	1994 ....Sarah Ingram	1998 ....Virginia Derby Grimes

International Golf

Ryder Cup Matches

Year	Results	Site
1927 ....United States 9½, Great Britain 2½		Worcester CC, Worcester, MA
1929 ....Great Britain 7, United States 5		Moortown GC, Leeds, England
1931 ....United States 9, Great Britain 3		Scioto CC, Columbus, OH
1933 ....Great Britain 6½, United States 5½		Southport and Ainsdale Courses, Southport, England
1935 ....United States 9, Great Britain 3		Ridgewood CC, Ridgewood, NJ
1937 ....United States 8, Great Britain 4		Southport and Ainsdale Courses, Southport, England
1939-1945 .....No tournament		
1947 ....United States 11, Great Britain 1		Portland GC, Portland, OR
1949 ....United States 7, Great Britain 5		Ganton GC, Scarborough, England
1951 ....United States 9½, Great Britain 2½		Pinehurst CC, Pinehurst, NC
1953 ....United States 6½, Great Britain 5½		Wentworth Club, Surrey, England
1955 ....United States 8, Great Britain 4		Thunderbird Ranch & CC, Palm Springs, CA
1957 ....Great Britain 7½, United States 4½		Lindrick GC, Yorkshire, England
1959 ....United States 8½, Great Britain 3½		Eldorado CC, Palm Desert, CA
1961 ....United States 14½, Great Britain 9½		Royal Lytham & St. Anne's GC, St Anne's-on-the-Sea, England
1963 ....United States 23, Great Britain 9		East Lake CC, Atlanta
1965 ....United States 19½, Great Britain 12½		Royal Birkdale GC, Southport, England
1967 ....United States 23½, Great Britain 8½		Champions GC, Houston
1969 ....United States 16, Great Britain 16		Royal Birkdale GC, Southport, England
1971 ....United States 18½, Great Britain 13½		Old Warson CC, St. Louis
1973 ....United States 19, Great Britain 13		Hon Co of Edinburgh Golfers, Muirfield, Scotland
1975 ....United States 21, Great Britain 11		Laurel Valley GC, Ligonier, PA
1977 ....United States 12½, Great Britain 7½		Royal Lytham & St. Anne's GC, St. Anne's-on-the-Sea, England
1979 ....United States 17, Europe 11		Greenbrier, White Sulphur Springs, WV
1981 ....United States 18½, Europe 9½		Walton Heath GC, Surrey, England
1983 ....United States 14½, Europe 13½		PGA National GC, Palm Beach Gardens, FL
1985 ....Europe 16½, United States 11½		Belfry GC, Sutton Coldfield, England
1987 ....Europe 15, United States 13		Muirfield GC, Dublin, OH
1989 ....Europe 14, United States 14		Belfry GC, Sutton Coldfield, England
1991 ....United States 14½, Europe 13½		Ocean Course, Kiawah Island, SC
1993 ....United States 15, Europe 13		Belfry GC, Sutton Coldfield, England
1995 ....Europe 14½, United States 13½		Oak Hill CC, Rochester, NY
1997 ....Europe 14½, United States 13½		Valderrama GC, Sotogrande, Spain

Team matches held every odd year between U.S. professionals and those of Great Britain/Europe (since 1979—prior to that it was U.S. vs G.B.). Team members selected on basis of finishes in PGA and European tour events.

Walker Cup Matches

Year	Results	Site
1922	..............United States 8, Great Britain 4	Nat. Golf Links of America, Southampton, NY
1923	..............United States 6, Great Britain 5	St. Andrews, Scotland
1924	..............United States 9, Great Britain 3	Garden City GC, Garden City, NY
1926	..............United States 6, Great Britain 5	St. Andrews, Scotland
1928	..............United States 11, Great Britain 1	Chicago GC, Wheaton, IL
1930	..............United States 10, Great Britain 2	Royal St. George GC, Sandwich, England
1932	..............United States 8, Great Britain 1	The Country Club, Brookline, MA
1934	..............United States 9, Great Britain 2	St. Andrews, Scotland
1936	..............United States 9, Great Britain 0	Pine Valley GC, Clementon, NJ
1938	..............Great Britain 7, United States 4	St. Andrews, Scotland
1940–46	........No tournament	
1947	..............United States 8, Great Britain 4	St. Andrews, Scotland
1949	..............United States 10, Great Britain 2	Winged Foot GC, Mamaroneck, NY
1951	..............United States 6, Great Britain 3	Birkdale GC, Southport, England
1953	..............United States 9, Great Britain 3	The Kittansett Club, Marion, MA
1955	..............United States 10, Great Britain 2	St. Andrews, Scotland
1957	..............United States 8, Great Britain 3	Minikahda Club, Minneapolis, MN
1959	..............United States 9, Great Britain 3	Muirfield, Scotland
1961	..............United States 11, Great Britain 1	Seattle GC, Seattle, WA
1963	..............United States 12, Great Britain 8	Ailsa Course, Turnberry, Scotland
1965	..............Great Britain 11, United States 11	Baltimore CC, Five Farms, Baltimore, MD
1967	..............United States 13, Great Britain 7	Royal St. George's GC, Sandwich, England
1969	..............United States 10, Great Britain 8	Milwaukee CC, Milwaukee, WI
1971	..............Great Britain 13, United States 11	St. Andrews, Scotland
1973	..............United States 14, Great Britain 10	The Country Club, Brookline, MA
1975	..............United States 15½, Great Britain 8½	St. Andrews, Scotland
1977	..............United States 16, Great Britain 8	Shinnecock Hills GC, Southampton, NY
1979	..............United States 15½, Great Britain 8½	Muirfield, Scotland
1981	..............United States 15, Great Britain 9	Cypress Point Club, Pebble Beach, CA
1983	..............United States 13½, Great Britain 10½	Royal Liverpool GC, Hoylake, England
1985	..............United States 13, Great Britain 11	Pine Valley GC, Pine Valley, NJ
1987	..............United States 16½, Great Britain 7½	Sunningdale GC, Berkshire, England
1989	..............Great Britain 12½, United States 11½	Peachtree Golf Club, Atlanta, GA
1991	..............United States 14, Great Britain 10	Portmarnock GC, Dublin, Ireland
1993	..............United States 19, Great Britain 5	Interlachen CC, Edina, MN
1995	..............Great Britain/Ireland 14, United States 10	Royal Porthcawl, Porthcawl, Wales
1997	..............United States 18, Great Britain/Ireland 6	Quaker Ridge GC, Scarsdale, NY

Men's amateur team competition every other year between United States and Great Britain/Ireland. U.S. team members selected by USGA.

Solheim Cup Matches

Year	Results	Site
1990	..............United States 11½, Europe 4½	Lake Nona GC, Orlando, FL
1992	..............Europe 11½, United States 6½	Dalmahoy Hotel GC, Edinburgh
1994	..............United States 13, Europe 7	The Greenbriar, White Sulpher Springs, WV
1996	..............United States 17, Europe 11	Marriot St Pierre Hotel & CC, Chepstow, Wales
1998	..............United States 16, Europe 12	Muirfield Village GC, Dublin, OH

Team matches held every odd year between U.S. professionals and those of Europe. Team members selected on basis of finishes in LPGA and European tour events.

Curtis Cup Matches

Year	Results	Site
1932	..............United States 5½, British Isles 3½	Wentworth GC, Wentworth, England
1934	..............United States 6½, British Isles 2½	Chevy Chase Club, Chevy Chase, MD
1936	..............United States 4½, British Isles 4½	King's Course, Gleneagles, Scotland
1938	..............United States 5½, British Isles 3½	Essex CC, Manchester, MA
1940–46	.........No tournament	
1948	..............United States 6½, British Isles 2½	Birkdale GC, Southport, England
1950	..............United States 7½, British Isles 1½	CC of Buffalo, Williamsville, NY
1952	..............British Isles 5, United States 4	Muirfield, Scotland
1954	..............United States 6, British Isles 3	Merion GC, Ardmore, PA
1956	..............British Isles 5, United States 4	Prince's GC, Sandwich Bay, England
1958	..............British Isles 4½, United States 4½	Brae Burn CC, West Newton, Mass.
1960	..............United States 6½, British Isles 2½	Lindrick GC, Worksop, England

Curtis Cup Matches *(Cont.)*

Year	Results	Site
1962	United States 8, British Isles 1	Broadmoor CG, Colorado Springs,CO
1964	United States 10½, British Isles 7½	Royal Porthcawl GC, Porthcawl, South Wales
1966	United States 13, British Isles 5	Va. Hot Springs G & TC, Hot Springs, VA
1968	United States 10½, British Isles 7½	Royal County Down GC, Newcastle, N. Ire.
1970	United States 11½, British Isles 6½	Brae Burn CC, West Newton, MA
1972	United States 10, British Isles 8	Western Gailes, Ayrshire, Scotland
1974	United States 13, British Isles 5	San Francisco GC, San Francisco, CA
1976	United States 11½, British Isles 6½	Royal Lytham & St. Anne's GC, England
1978	United States 12, British Isles 6	Apawamis Club, Rye, NY
1980	United States 13, British Isles 5	St. Pierre G & CC, Chepstow, Wales
1982	United States 14½, British Isles 3½	Denver CC, Denver, CO
1984	United States 9½, British Isles 8½	Muirfield, Scotland
1986	British Isles 13, United States 5	Prairie Dunes CC, Hutchinson, KS
1988	British Isles 11, United States 7	Royal St. George's GC, Sandwich, England
1990	United States 14, British Isles 4	Somerset Hills CC, Bernardsville, NJ
1992	Great Britain/Ireland 10, United States 8	Royal Liverpool GC, Hoylake, England
1994	Great Britain/Ireland 9, United States 9	The Honors Course, Ooltewah, TN
1996	Great Britain/Ireland 11½, United States 6½	Killarney Golf & Fishing Club, Killarney, Ireland
1998	United States 10, Great Britain/Ireland 8	The Minikahda Club, Minneapolis

Women's amateur team competition every other year between the United States and Great Britain/Ireland. U.S. team members selected by USGA.

Playing Partners

It's hard to look like Che Guevara while wearing a Ping visor, but a band of insurgent professional golfers is stirring up a quiet rebellion against one of pro sports' most conservative elites—the PGA Tour. The newly formed Tour Players Association (TPA), which claims 50 members from among the 200 or so touring pros, charges that the Tour is secretive about its more than $400 million in annual revenue, of which only about 18% goes to tournament purses. The TPA wants to know where the other 82% goes. It also wants to know why the rank-and-file pros, who make a 10th of the $2 million a year in prize money that a big star does, don't share more of the wealth.

Commissioner Tim Finchem calls the TPA's speaking out "divisive," while player Paul Azinger refers to a proposal that would pay players who miss cuts a stipend of about $2,000 for expenses as "socialist." Yet pros like Azinger, who is 12th on the career money list with $7,451,410 through Sept. 30, don't have to sweat expenses. Others do. When Mark Woodforde, who ranks 100th on the tennis tour, lost in the first round of the 1998 U.S. Open, he took home $12,000. When 100th-ranked Omar Uresti missed the cut at golf's Open, he got nothing.

The TPA leaders are Danny Edwards (201st on the career money list, with $1,212,304) and Larry Rinker (151st, $1,741,655). They question whether the four player-members of the Tour's policy board— Jay Haas, Tom Lehman, Davis Love III and Mark O'Meara, who are all among the top 20 career money winners—share their concerns. Why, the rebels ask, will only the top 64 pros be allowed into next year's three-event World Championships, the richest tournaments in history? Why will loot from those events count as official earnings, which will only widen the income gap? In a meeting with Finchem last week in San Antonio, Edwards and Rinker stood by their demands for more information, more power and more money.

Touring pros are too prosperous and too independent to support radical changes, so a strike is about as likely as a modeling career for John Daly. Yet many pros support the TPA's goals of getting the Tourocracy to open up about its finances and spread the wealth.

For Finchem there's a sure way to test the TPA's support, as well as make good on his claim that his administration has never made a decision "that wasn't in concert with the majority of the players." Let all Tour players vote on the TPA's proposed expenses stipend, and open the Tour's books.
—Kevin Cook

Boxing

Sports Illustrated

Year-in-Review
Double Issue

DEC. 29, 1997–JAN. 5, 1998

Evander
Holyfield

GEORGE LANGE

A Dread-ful Season

With Mike Tyson suspended and Don King in court, boxing struggled through a lackluster and depressing year

BY RICHARD HOFFER

WHAT'S WORSE THAN a year in which Mike Tyson loses twice to Evander Holyfield, bites part of Holyfield's ear off in one of those losses, is suspended from boxing in Nevada and is finally written off as a has-been (or, in some crueler estimations, a never-was)?

How about a year in which he doesn't fight at all?

It was another of those forgettable seasons in boxing, one without a single memorable performance, an exciting breakout talent, or even an honest and honorable matchup. The sport's stars refused to break a sweat, taking in unearned dollars for unexciting fights, and generally avoiding any opportunity to achieve greatness. It was, without the perverse presence of Tyson, an altogether lackluster year.

Yet the game had its chances. Holyfield, brought to the precipice of significance by his ballyhooed defeats of Tyson in 1997, backed away. He could have easily capitalized on his beatings of the class bully and secured immense popularity. Instead, after scheduling

one potentially challenging fight (a rematch with Michael Moorer, which he won easily), the Georgian evangelist signed for fights with Henry Akinwande and Vaughn Bean.

These were needless preoccupations; they frittered away the respect he'd just regained and quelled any interest he might have stirred in the moribund heavyweight division. Holyfield, who held the WBA and IBF belts after beating Tyson, had reserved some of his religious zeal for unifying the division. But attempts to make a fight with WBC champ Lennox Lewis—the one desirable matchup in heavyweight boxing—bogged down time after time.

There were organization problems, with the fighters having to take care of mandatory defenses (Holyfield would have to fight lightly regarded Bean, and Lewis would have to dispatch one Zeljko Marovic). There were contract problems, made all the more difficult by Lewis's ties with HBO and Holyfield's with rival Showtime. There was the problem of Don King, who retained the promotional right to Holyfield after the Tyson fights, and who many thought was loath to

JOHN IACONO

Surprisingly, Lewis's victory over Briggs (right) held appeal beyond barber shops.

risk a match that could leave Holyfield, if he lost, out of the heavyweight picture altogether. But mostly there were money problems. As important as the fight might have been, it still would not have generated enough money—Tyson-type money that is—to provoke Holyfield into combat.

So while that fight remained out in the ether, with each fighter advancing in years and the prospect gradually becoming about as attractive as the George Foreman–Larry Holmes matchup scheduled for 1999 (Foreman and Holmes will be 51 and 49, respectively), fight fans were treated to the following events:

In March, Lewis, a 32-year-old bomber whose marquee value had been sabotaged by unwilling opponents (Oliver McCall cried in the ring, Akinwande hugged Lewis, and Andrew Golota nearly died of fright), was pitted against Shannon Briggs in Atlantic City. This was a fight that appealed chiefly to barbers, as the two fighters' dreadlocks were

supposedly on the line. It turned out to be more than a battle of braids when Briggs stormed Lewis in the first round and nearly dropped him. But Lewis roared back and knocked Briggs out in the fifth round. Both men left the arena with their locks unshorn.

In June, Holyfield zipped up to New York to meet Akinwande who had earned this title shot by … well, no one could say how. The last time Akinwande had been in a big fight, hugging Lewis to distraction 11 months earlier, even his own trainer condemned him for cowardice. But Akinwande, a Don King fighter, somehow remained the WBA's top contender. The Akinwande-Holyfield fight was more of a fan-appreciation event than an actual bout, with crowds expected to fill Madison Square Garden simply to honor the Holyfield legacy.

Apparently fans didn't appreciate the Holyfield aura as much as promoters had hoped, at least not enough to pay for tickets that ranged in price from $1,000 ringside to $100. As durable and as hardworking as Holyfield has been—he trained for Akinwande as if it were Tyson III—he is simply not a draw. Though he'd been involved in most of the sport's biggest money fights, his role had often been that of foil. When he was not the counterpart to a Foreman or a Riddick Bowe or Tyson, the people stayed home in droves. That much was clear when his

MIKE DERER/AP

Tyson lost his cool before the New Jersey commission.

Moorer fight turned out to be a financial dud.

Further inhibiting Holyfield's ability to fill seats was the virtual absence of King, who was once more defending himself against federal charges of insurance fraud. It was a difficult case the government had chosen to prosecute, especially as Lloyds of London, the defendant, had been conspicuously unenthusiastic in testifying against King. The charge, going back to insurance payments for a canceled Julio César Chávez fight, was practically frivolous considering the other wrongdoings—cheating fighters and managing the rankings—King has been accused of. But it kept King in court, and, like him or not, his bombast is nearly essential in a big fight's promotion.

To the relief of almost everyone but Holyfield, who'd been guaranteed $10 million, the Akinwande-Holyfield fight was postponed indefinitely when Huggin' Henry, as he was known for the Lewis bout, tested positive for hepatitis. Holyfield was in the middle of a workout when he heard the news, and any lip reader could tell exactly what his response to it was: "What about my money?" Had the fight gone forward, that likely would have been the fans' complaint.

So it had come to this: Not only was the fight game worse off without Tyson, it also suffered without King. This logic didn't hold up entirely since it was King who made the Holyfield-Akinwande fight possible (or necessary), and it's unlikely that even he could reverse a hepatitis diagnosis. But, lackluster as it promised to be, that fight surely would have been more entertaining than its alternatives. The prospects of a Lewis-Mavrovic fight and a Holyfield-Bean bout did more for boxing abolitionists than any potential legislation could have done.

Not long after that botched promotional effort, King emerged from court, acquitted of all charges and apparently untouchable. He was free to conduct business as usual, for better or worse, and boxing would presumably be energized by the 66-year-old's determination to control the heavyweight division.

Problem was, as swimmingly as things had gone in court, King was having more and more trouble in boxing, where he supposedly wielded considerable control. The big news, after all, wasn't that the feds had sidetracked King, it was that Tyson had dumped him. There was irony in there somewhere. What was the point of being free if you weren't free to make money?

The two became estranged—violently so, according to one report—over the very issue that King can never be properly pinned down on: his ability to make more money off his fighters than the fighters make themselves. It seems that King maneuvered Tyson into a payday with the World Wrestling Federation, a $3 million bit of horseplay that appealed to both Tyson's need for money and his love of professional wrestling. Although it was widely decried at the time (this was before basketball star Karl Malone would enter the ring for the rival wrestling federation and make this burlesque acceptable for other stars), Tyson's decision to "referee" a match in Boston in March was prob-

ADAM NADEL/AP

This was an insult to Nevada's commission, which expected its punishment of Tyson to be recognized by all commissions. It was as if Tyson had decided to fight on barges, outside all jurisdiction. This was even more cynical than anything King had ever proposed. And it collapsed under the weight of Tyson's ever-erratic personality. Appearing before the New Jersey board, the fighter lost his cool, cursed into the microphone and bailed out of a prepared statement. It was not a reassuring performance.

Perhaps realizing that New Jersey might not be the slam-dunk that Finkel and Tyson first thought, they withdrew their application a month later, before New Jersey could announce a ruling, and decided to spin the wheel in Las Vegas. Anticipating a favorable ruling, Tyson went into training, finally. But not even that was without a swerve or two. Although he had dumped all vestiges of his King-promoted days—trainer Richie Giachetti was not invited back—Tyson still had trouble choosing a direction and sticking to it. Veteran trainer Jesse Reid, chosen in August, worked three days with Tyson before he left camp in confusion over his duties. Less than a week later Tyson was in the news again when he had to be restrained in an argument over a fender bender. Whenever Tyson's comeback does begin, rest assured there will be fits and starts and the usual confusion.

ably not going to damage either his credibility or his chances of being reinstated by the Nevada State Athletic Commission. It was all in fun.

But when Tyson found out how much money King was getting for such ancillary rights as T-shirt sales—or rather when Tyson's wife, Monica, found out—he snapped. There were even reports that Tyson got physical with King in a curbside set-to, but whether or not those reports were true, the partnerships that had generated $140 million in a brilliantly—if cynically and greedily—engineered comeback were suddenly over. Tyson fired his co-managers, Rory Holloway and John Horne, filed suits against everybody and got Hollywood representation in his financial matters and boxing advice from Shelly Finkel, a former rock and roll promoter who was with Holyfield at one time.

Many people in boxing cheered Tyson's breakaway from King, but they were hard pressed to understand what his new advisers had in mind for the fighter. When it came time for Tyson to apply for his license last July in Nevada, the fighter was silent. Then, in a stunning move, he went to New Jersey and applied for a license there.

With the heavyweights muddling about, you might have thought some of those stars in the lower heavens would shine. But Oscar De La Hoya, boxing's brightest, allowed the year to slip by without acquiring anything more than a new nickname. Once the Golden Boy, he was now tagged Chicken De La Hoya for his apparent refusal to meet other welterweight champions and contenders of note, such as Ike Quartey, Felix Trinidad or Jose Luis Lopez.

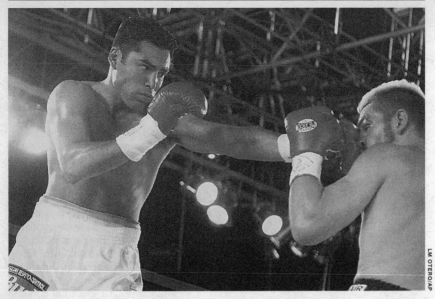

Carpentier (right) swooned before De La Hoya, as did thousands of teenage girls.

Instead, in a display of drawing power but little else, De La Hoya fought somebody named Patrick Carpentier. It happened in El Paso, and it was encouraging in the sense that the public, despite everything that's happened in boxing, is still hungry to participate in a fighter's stardom. Promoters sold more than 30,000 tickets the first day they went on sale and, in a town not known for pugilistic spectacles, filled the Sun Bowl with more than 45,000 fans by fight night.

A remarkable percentage of those fans were female. And at least some of them bought Oscar-autographed pillowcases for $14.95 apiece. If Oscarmania continues, it promises to be a unique phenomenon in the sport.

But De La Hoya will have to fight a more ambitious schedule than he did in 1998, when his only name opponent was Chávez, in a rematch of a fight that hadn't been much more competitive than the Carpentier bout. By year's end De La Hoya had told promoter Bob Arum that he was getting embarrassed by his career and wanted to be matched with his more able peers. Arum set about getting Quartey for November and possibly Trinidad

in May 1999. If those fights were to come off (there were, predictably, promotional entanglements that threatened them), with De La Hoya victorious, Oscarmania would surely spread from El Paso to the rest of North America.

Others who might have occupied more of the spotlight, and didn't, were featherweight Prince Naseem Hamed and lightweight Arturo Gatti. The Prince, who developed the ring entrance into a piece of theater that often overshadowed his fights, was scheduled to fight Wayne McCullough on Halloween. Hamed had spent a lot of time on the shelf with a hand injury and hadn't been able to turn in many persuasive performances during the year. Gatti, whose 1997 bouts were all candidates for fight of the year, was matched up with the devilish Angel Manfredy, and the popular but limited fighter's progress was finally halted in the loss. But even in defeat Gatti, a noble and fearless competitor, was able to remind fans how good boxing can be.

Unfortunately, in a year in which the only improvement over '97 was referee Mills Lane's turn as a TV judge and Mike Tyson's stab at professional wrestling, the reminders were mostly otherwise.

FOR THE RECORD·1997-1998

Current Champions

Division	Weight Limit	WBC Champion	WBA Champion	IBF Champion
Heavyweight	None	Lennox Lewis	Evander Holyfield	Evander Holyfield
Cruiserweight	190	Juan Carlos Gomez	Fabrice Tiozzo	Imamu Mayfield
Light heavyweight	175	Roy Jones	Roy Jones	Reggie Johnson
Super middleweight	168	Richie Woodhall	Frank Liles	Charles Brewer
Middleweight	160	Hassine Cherifi	William Joppy Jr.	Bernard Hopkins
Junior middleweight	154	Keith Mullings	Laurent Boudouani	Yori Boy Campas
Welterweight	147	Oscar De La Hoya	vacant	Felix Trinidad
Junior welterweight	140	vacant	Khalid Rahilou	Vincent Phillips
Lightweight	135	Cesar Bazan	Jean-Baptiste Mendy	Shane Mosley
Junior lightweight	130	Genaro Hernandez	Choi Yong-Soo	Roberto Garcia
Featherweight	126	Luisito Espinosa	Freddy Norwood	Manuel Medina
Junior featherweight	122	Erik Morales	Enrique Sanchez	Vuyani Bungu
Bantamweight	118	Joichiro Tatsuyoshi	Nana Yaw Konadu	Tim Austin
Junior bantamweight	115	Cho In-Joo	Satoshi Iida	Johnny Tapia
Flyweight	112	Chatchai Sasakul	Hugo Soto	Mark Johnson
Junior flyweight	108	Saman Sor Jaturong	Pichit Chor Siriwat	vacant
Strawweight	105	Ricardo Lopez	Rosendo Alvarez	Zolani Petelo

Note: WBC = World Boxing Council; WBA = World Boxing Association; IBF = International Boxing Federation

Championship and Major Fights of 1997 and 1998

Abbreviations: WBC=World Boxing Council; WBA= World Boxing Association; IBF=International Boxing Federation; KO=knockout; TKO=technical knockout; Dec=decision; Split=split decision; Disq=disqualification.

Heavyweight

Date	Winner	Loser	Result	Title	Site
Oct 4	Lennox Lewis	Andrew Golota	TKO 1	WBC	Atlantic City
Nov 8	Evander Holyfield	Michael Moorer	TKO 8	WBA/IBF	Las Vegas
Mar 28	Lennox Lewis	Shannon Briggs	TKO 5	WBC	Atlantic City

Cruiserweight

Date	Winner	Loser	Result	Title	Site
Nov 8	Fabrice Tiozzo	Nate Miller	Dec 12	WBA	Las Vegas
Nov 8	Imamu Mayfield	Uriah Grant	Dec 12	IBF	Las Vegas
Feb 21	Juan Carlos Gomez	Marcelo Dominguez	Dec 12	WBC	Mar Del Plata, Argentina
Mar 28	Imamu Mayfield	Terry Dunstan	KO 11	IBF	Hull, England
May 2	Fabrice Tiozzo	Terry Ray	TKO 1	WBA	Villeurbanne, France
June 5	Juan Carlos Gomez	Guy Waters	TKO 6	WBC	Hamburg, Germany

Light Heavyweight

Date	Winner	Loser	Result	Title	Site
June 13	Dariusz Michalczewski	Virgil Hill	Dec 12	WBA/IBF	Oberhausen, Germany
Sept 20	Lou Del Valle	Eddy Smulders	TKO 8	WBA	Aachen, Germany
Feb 6	Reggie Johnson	William Guthrie	KO 5	IBF	Uncasville, CT
Mar 21	Graciano Rocchigiani	Michael Nunn	Split 12	interim WBC	Berlin
May 29	Reggie Johnson	Ole Klemetsen	Dec 12	IBF	Pesaro, Italy
July 18	Roy Jones	Lou Del Valle	Dec 12	WBC/WBA	New York City

Super Middleweight

Date	Winner	Loser	Result	Title	Site
Sept 11	Robin Reid	Hassine Cherifi	Split 12	WBC	Widnes, England
Dec 2	Charles Brewer	Joey DeGrandis	Dec 12	IBF	Philadelphia
Dec 19	Thulane Malinga	Robin Reid	Dec 12	WBC	Milwall, England
Mar 27	Richie Woodhall	Thulane Malinga	Dec 12	WBC	Telford, England
Mar 28	Charles Brewer	Herol Graham	TKO 10	IBF	Atlantic City
Apr 3	Frank Liles	Andrei Shkalikov	Dec 12	WBA	Bayamon, Puerto Rico
Aug 22	Charles Brewer	Antoine Byrd	TKO 3	IBF	Leipzig, Germany

Middleweight

Date	Winner	Loser	Result	Title	Site
Oct 19	William Joppy Jr.	Julio Cesar Green	Dec 12	WBA	Tampa, FL
Nov 18	Bernard Hopkins	Andrew Council	Dec 12	IBF	Upper Marlboro, MD
Dec 5	Keith Holmes	Paul Vaden	TKO 11	WBC	Pompano Beach, FL
Jan 31	Bernard Hopkins	Simon Brown	KO 6	IBF	Atlantic City
May 2	Hassine Cherifi	Keith Holmes	Dec 12	WBC	Villeurbanne, France
Aug 22	Bernard Hopkins	Robert Allen	NC 4	IBF	Las Vegas
Aug 28	William Joppy Jr.	Roberto Duran	TKO 3	WBA	Las Vegas

Junior Middleweight (Super Welterweight)

Date	Winner	Loser	Result	Title	Site
June 5	Raul Marquez	Keith Mullings	Split 12	IBF	Las Vegas
Dec 6	Keith Mullings	Terry Norris	TKO 9	WBC	Atlantic City
Dec 6	Yori Boy Campas	Raul Marquez	TKO 8	IBF	Atlantic City
Feb 13	Laurent Boudouani	Guillermo Jones	Maj. Draw	WBA	Albuquerque
Mar 14	Keith Mullings	Davide Ciarlante	TKO 5	WBC	Atlantic City
Mar 23	Yori Boy Campas	Anthony Stephans	TKO 3	IBF	Mashantucket, CT
May 30	Laurent Boudouani	Guillermo Jones	Split 12	WBA	Las Vegas
June 5	Yori Boy Campas	Pedro Ortega	TKO 11	IBF	Tijuana, Mexico

Welterweight

Date	Winner	Loser	Result	Title	Site
Sept 13	Oscar De La Hoya	Hector Camacho	Dec 12	WBC	Las Vegas
Dec 6	Oscar De La Hoya	Wilfredo Rivera	TKO 8	WBC	Atlantic City
Oct 17	Ike Quartey	Jose Luis Lopez	Maj. Draw	WBA	Ledyard, CT
Apr 3	Felix Trinidad	Mahenge Zulu	TKO 4	IBF	Bayamon, Puerto Rico
June 13	Oscar De La Hoya	Patrick Cahrpentier	TKO 3	WBC	El Paso, TX

Junior Welterweight (Super Lightweight)

Date	Winner	Loser	Result	Title	Site
Dec 13	Vincent Phillips	Freddie Pendleton	KO 10	IBF	Pompano Beach, FL
Feb 21	Khalid Rahilou	Jean-Baptiste Mendy	Dec 12	WBA	Bercy, France
Mar 7	Julio César Chávez	Miguel Angel Gonzalez	Split Draw*	WBC	Mexico City
Dec 14	Vincent Phillips	Alfonso Sanchez	KO 1	IBF	Atlantic City

*Because the bout ended in a draw, neither boxer claimed the vacant WBC title.

Lightweight

Date	Winner	Loser	Result	Title	Site
Sept 12	Steve Johnston	Saul Duran	Dec 12	WBC	Las Vegas
Oct 19	Shane Mosley	Manuel Gomez	KO 11	IBF	El Paso, TX
Feb 6	Shane Mosley	Demitrio Ceballos	TKO 8	IBF	Uncasville, CT
Feb 28	Steve Johnston	George Scott	Dec 12	WBC	Atlantic City
May 9	Shane Mosley	Juan Molina	TKO 8	IBF	Atlantic City
May 16	Jean-Baptiste Mendy	Orzubek Nazarov	Dec 12	WBA	Paris-Bercy, France
June 13	Cesar Bazan	Steve Johnston	Split 12	WBC	El Paso, TX
June 27	Shane Mosley	Wilfrido Ruiz	KO 5	IBF	Philadelphia
Aug 23	Cesar Bazan	Hiroyuki Sakamoto	Dec 12	WBC	Yokohama, Japan

Junior Lightweight (Super Featherweight)

Date	Winner	Loser	Result	Title	Site
Oct 4	Arturo Gatti	Gabriel Ruelas	TKO 5	IBF	Atlantic City
Oct 5	Choi Yong-Soo	Takanori Hatakeyama	Split Draw	WBA	Tokyo
Nov 20	Genaro Hernandez	Carlos Hernandez	Dec 12	WBC	Los Angeles
Mar 13	Roberto Garcia	Harrold Warren	Dec 12	IBF	Miami
Apr 18	Choi Yong-Soo	Gilberto Serrano	TKO 9	WBA	Seoul
May 16	Genaro Hernandez	Carlos Gerena	Dec 12	WBC	Indio, CA

Featherweight

Date	Winner	Loser	Result	Title	Site
Dec 7	Wilfredo Vazquez	Genaro Rios	Dec 12	WBA	Las Vegas
Dec 6	Luisito Espinosa	Carlos Rios	TKO 6	WBC	Koronadal, Philippines
Dec 13	Hector Lizarraga	Welcome Ncita	TKO 10	IBF	Pompano Beach, FL
Apr 3	Freddie Norwood	Antonio Cermeno	Dec 12	WBA	Bayamon, Puerto Rico
Apr 24	Manuel Medina	Hector Lizarraga	Dec 12	IBF	San Jose, CA
June 13	Freddie Norwood	Genaro Rios	TKO 8	WBA	Atlantic City
July 10	Freddie Norwood	Luis Mendoza	Dec 12	WBA	Miami
Aug 15	Luisito Espinosa	Juan Carlos Ramirez	Spl. Tech 11	WBC	El Paso, TX

Junior Featherweight (Super Bantamweight)

Date	Winner	Loser	Result	Title	Site
Sept 6	Erik Morales	Daniel Zaragoza	KO 11	WBC	El Paso, TX
Sept 27	Antonio Cermeno	Jose Rojas	Dec 12	WBA	Caracas, Venezuela
Nov 15	Vuyani Bungu	Arnel Barotillo	Dec 12	IBF	Hammanskraal, S.A.
Dec 12	Erik Morales	John Lowey	TKO 7	WBC	Tijuana, Mexico
Feb 8	Enrique Sanchez	Rafael del Valle	Dec 12	WBA	Lake Charles, LA
Apr 4	Erik Morales	Remigio Molino	TKO 6	WBC	Tijuana, Mexico
May 16	Erik Morales	Jose Luis Bueno	TKO 2	WBC	Indio, CA
May 16	Vuyani Bungu	Ernesto Grey	Split 12	IBF	Hamanskraal, S.A.

Bantamweight

Date	Winner	Loser	Result	Title	Site
Nov 22	Joychiro Tatsuyoshi	S. Singmanassak	TKO 7	WBC	Osaka, Japan
Feb 21	Nana Yaw Konadu	Abraham Torres	KO 2	WBA	Mar Del Plata, Argentina
Mar 8	Joychiro Tatsuyoshi	Jose Rafael Sosa	Dec 12	WBC	Yokohama, Japan
Mar 28	Timothy Austin	Paul Lloyd	TKO 2	IBF	Hull, England
May 30	Timothy Austin	Andrian Kaspari	TKO 3	IBF	Las Vegas

Junior Bantamweight (Super Flyweight)

Date	Winner	Loser	Result	Title	Site
Dec 23	Satoshi Iida	Yokthai Sith-Oar	Dec 12	WBA	Nagoya, Japan
Dec 13	Johnny Tapia	Andy Agosto	Dec 12	IBF	Pompano Beach
Apr 29	Satoshi Iida	Hiroki Ioka	Maj. 12	WBA	Nagoya, Japan
July 26	Satoshi Iida	Julio Gamboa	Dec 12	WBA	Nagoya, Japan
Feb 13	Johnny Tapia	Rodolfo Blanco	Dec 12	IBF	Albuquerque, NM
Aug 29	Cho In-Joo	Gerry Penalosa	Split 12	WBC	Seoul

THEY SAID IT

*The Reverend Muhamed Siddeeq,
spiritual adviser to Mike Tyson,
testifying before the New Jersey
Athletic Control Board on why Tyson
should have his boxing license
reinstated: "I see Mike solving many
of the world's problems."*

Flyweight

Date	Winner	Loser	Result	Title	Site
Sept. 16 ...Mark Johnson		Angel Almena	Dec 12	IBF	Nashville
Nov 12 .....Chatchai Sasakul		Yuri Arbachakov	Dec 12	WBC	Sapporo, Japan
Nov 22 .....Jose Bonilla		Keiji Yamaguchi	TKO 6	WBA	Osaka, Japan
Feb 22 .....Mark Johnson		Arthur Johnson	KO 1	IBF	Washington, D.C.
Feb 27......Chatchai Sasakul		Kim Yong-Jin	Dec 12	WBC	Koh Samui, Thailand
May 1........Chatchai Sasakul		Chang Yong-Soon	KO 5	WBC	Kanchanaburi, Thailand
May 29......Hugo Soto		Jose Bonilla	Split 12	WBA	Las Vegas
July 26......Mark Johnson		Luis Rolon	Dec 12	IBF	Oneida Ind. Nation, NY

Junior Flyweight

Date	Winner	Loser	Result	Title	Site
Dec 13 ....Mauricio Pastrana		Manuel Herrera	TKO 3	IBF	Pompano Beach, FL
Mar 8 ......Saman Sor Jaturong		Shiro Yahiro	TKO 4	WBC	Yokohama, Japan
Mar 1 ......Phichit Chor Siriwat		Hadao CP Gym	Dec 12	WBA	Bangkok
Apr 30......Mauricio Pastrana		Anis Roga	KO 4	IBF	Fort Lauderdale, FL

Strawweight (Mini Flyweight)

Date	Winner	Loser	Result	Title	Site
Nov 23 .....Gerry Penalosa		Cho Young-Joo	KO 10	WBC	Songham, South Korea
Dec 27 .....Zolani Petelo		Rantanapol Sow Vorapin	TKO 4	IBF	Songkhla, Thailand
Mar 7 ....Ricardo Lopez (WBC)		Rosendo Alvarez (WBA)	Tech Draw 7*	WBC/WBA	Mexico City
Mar 21 .....Zolani Petelo		Faisol Askbar	Split 12	IBF	Hammanskraal, S.A.
Apr 25......Gerry Penalosa		Joel Luna Zarate	Tech Draw 2	WBC	Pasay City, Philippines
July 4 ....Zolani Petelo		Carmelo Caceres	TKO 7	IBF	Hammanskraal, S.A.

*Both men retained their titles after the bout was stopped due to an accidental head butt by Alvarez.

He Ain't So Heavy

For all of us who enjoy breathing the secondhand fumes of danger, the end is near. A heavyweight title fight, which used to suffocate us in the smoke of vicarious jeopardy, no longer gives off even a thin vapor. Not a whiff.

What is it about heavyweight boxing these days that produces more torpor than terror? It's not us, it's not that evolution has finally carried us beyond our appetite for natural disaster. We still watch *Scary Police Chases II* on Fox, don't we? It can't be the sport itself, which stubbornly resists all efforts to civilize it. We still have Don King, more or less.

Is it that badness, which is what heavyweight boxing is supposed to be about, is now the domain of sulking basketball players? To judge from the shoe company ads and sports drink commercials, today's gladiatorial arena is the NBA, a league ruled by an army of slammin', jammin', elbow-swinging intimidators. Meanwhile, off the court, players seem increasingly determined to give even Sonny Liston a run for his bail money. Evander Holyfield ought to inspire more than caricature. He's a rugged, hard-hitting fellow. Yet the guy you really want to stay away from is Latrell Sprewell.

Maybe it's just Holyfield, with his droning Christianity. But we don't think so. Lennox Lewis, another heavyweight champion, also fails to produce night sweats in the rest of us. Even though he hits like a sonuvabitch and never spouts Biblical quotations, Lewis evokes more gentility than he does menace. Here's the test: You're standing in front of a plate-glass window, and here comes Lewis up behind you. Are you scared? Now here comes Charles Barkley.

Maybe it's just personality. When Mike Tyson was around, well, we didn't want to run into him unless conditions were strictly controlled. It turned out he couldn't fight anymore, but the fun of his highly rigged comeback was seeing the intimidation reflected on the face of whatever boiled ham was brought into the ring that night. Of course, that only worked up to a point.

Maybe it's the talent level. Holyfield and Lewis are both in their 30s, and George Foreman, the other big draw, is 102. Everybody who has come along to try to replace this generation has failed in one spectacular fashion or another.

But those complaints have always been in play. Here's the more likely reason for the creeping irrelevancy of the heavyweight champion: He—Holyfield, Foreman, whoever—is boring and, bitten ears aside, predictable. These aren't the times for the ballet of boxing, for ritualized violence, scheduled destruction. Where's the thrill? Give us gloves thrown on the ice, set-tos in the paint, brawls on the mound. Give it to us down and dirty, give it to us raw. Give us Jerry Springer and *When Animals Attack IV*. Sad truth: The smell of a safely shared catastrophe, disaster at a remove, is a comparative perfume, overpowered these days by the stink of spontaneity.

FOR THE RECORD·Year by Year

World Champions

Sanctioning bodies: the National Boxing Association (NBA), the New York State Athletic Commission (NY), the World Boxing Association (WBA), the World Boxing Council (WBC), and the International Boxing Federation (IBF).

Heavyweights
(Weight: Unlimited)

Champion	Reign	Champion	Reign	Champion	Reign
John L. Sullivan	1885–92	Sonny Liston	1962–64	Tim Witherspoon* WBA	1986
James J. Corbett	1892–97	Muhammad Ali	1964–70	Trevor Berbick* WBC	1986
Bob Fitzsimmons	1897–99	Ernie Terrell* WBA	1965–67	Mike Tyson* WBC	1986–87
James J. Jeffries	1899–1905†	Joe Frazier* NY	1968–70	James Bonecrusher	
Marvin Hart	1905–06	Jimmy Ellis* WBA	1968–70	Smith* WBA	1986–87
Tommy Burns	1906–08	Joe Frazier	1970–73	Tony Tucker* IBF	1987
Jack Johnson	1908–15	George Foreman	1973–74	Mike Tyson	1987–90
Jess Willard	1915–19	Muhammad Ali	1974–78	Buster Douglas	1990
Jack Dempsey	1919–26	Leon Spinks	1978	Evander Holyfield	1990–92
Gene Tunney	1926–28	Ken Norton* WBC	1978	Lennox Lewis* WBC	1993–95
Max Schmeling	1930–32	Larry Holmes* WBC	1978–80	Riddick Bowe	1992–93
Jack Sharkey	1932–33	Muhammad Ali	1978–79†	Evander Holyfield	1993–94
Primo Carnera	1933–34	John Tate* WBA	1979–80	Michael Moorer	1994
Max Baer	1934–35	Mike Weaver* WBA	1980–82	George Foreman	1994–95
James J. Braddock	1935–37	Larry Holmes	1980–85	Frank Bruno* WBC	1995–96
Joe Louis	1937–49†	Michael Dokes* WBA	1982–83	Bruce Seldon* WBA	1995–96
Ezzard Charles	1949–51	Gerrie Coetzee* WBA	1983–84	Mike Tyson WBA	1996
Jersey Joe Walcott	1951–52	Tim Witherspoon* WBC	1984	Michael Moorer* IBF	1996–97
Rocky Marciano	1952–56†	Pinklon Thomas* WBC	1984–86	Lennox Lewis* WBC	1997–
Ingemar Johansson	1959–60	Greg Page* WBA	1984–85	E. Holyfield WBA/IBF	1996–
Floyd Patterson	1960–62	Michael Spinks	1985–87		

Cruiserweights
(Weight Limit: 190 pounds)

Champion	Reign	Champion	Reign	Champion	Reign
Marvin Camel* WBC	1980	Evander Holyfield* WBA	1986–88	James Pritchard* IBF	1991
Carlos De Leon* WBC	1980–82	Ricky Parkey* IBF	1986–87	James Warring* IBF	1991–92
Ossie Ocasio* WBA	1982–84	E. Holyfield* IBF/WBA	1987–88	Alfred Cole* IBF	1992–96
S.T. Gordon* WBC	1982–83	Evander Holyfield	1988†	Orlin Norris* WBA	1993–95
Carlos De Leon* WBC	1983–85	Toufik Belbouli* WBA	1989	Nate Miller* WBA	1995–97
Marvin Camel* IBF	1983–84	Robert Daniels* WBA	1989–91	Marcelo	
Lee Roy Murphy* IBF	1984–86	Carlos De Leon* WBC	1989–90	Dominguez* WBC	1996–98
Piet Crous* WBA	1984–85	Glenn McCrory* IBF	1989–90	A. Washington* IBF	1996–97
Alfonso Ratliff* WBC	1985	Jeff Lampkin* IBF	1990	Uriah Grant* IBF	1997
Dwight Braxton* WBA	1985–86	M. Duran* WBC	1990–91	Imamu Mayfield* IBF	1997–
Bernard Benton* WBC	1985–86	Bobby Czyz* WBA	1991–92†	Fabrice Tiozzo* WBA	1997–
Carlos De Leon* WBC	1986–88	Anaclet Wamba* WBC	1991–95	J.C. Gomez* WBC	1998–

Note: Division called Junior Heavyweight by the WBA.

Light Heavyweights
(Weight Limit: 175 pounds)

Champion	Reign	Champion	Reign	Champion	Reign
Jack Root	1903	George Nichols* NBA	1932	Dick Tiger	1966–68
George Gardner	1903	Bob Godwin* NBA	1933	Bob Foster	1968–74†
Bob Fitzsimmons	1903–05	Bob Olin	1934–35	Vicente Rondon* WBA	1971–72
Philadelphia Jack		John Henry Lewis	1935–38	John Conteh* WBC	1974–77
O'Brien	1905–12†	Melio Bettina	1939	Victor Galindez* WBA	1974–78
Jack Dillon	1914–16	Billy Conn	1939–40†	Miguel A. Cuello* WBC	1977–78
Battling Levinsky	1916–20	Anton Christoforidis	1941	Mate Parlov* WBC	1978
Georges Carpentier	1920–22	Gus Lesnevich	1941–48	Mike Rossman* WBA	1978–79
Battling Siki	1922–23	Freddie Mills	1948–50	Marvin Johnson* WBC	1978–79
Mike McTigue	1923–25	Joey Maxim	1950–52	Matthew Saad	
Paul Berlenbach	1925–26	Archie Moore	1952–62†	Muhammad* WBC	1979–81
Jack Delaney	1926–27†	Harold Johnson* NBA	1961	Marvin Johnson* WBA	1979–80
Jimmy Slattery* NBA	1927	Harold Johnson	1962–63	Eddie Mustapha	
Tommy Loughran	1927–29	Willie Pastrano	1963–65	Muhammad* WBA	1980–81
Maxie Rosenbloom	1930–34	Jose Torres	1965–66	Michael Spinks* WBA	1981–83

*Champion not generally recognized. †Champion retired or relinquished title.

Light Heavyweights *(Cont.)*

Champion	Reign	Champion	Reign	Champion	Reign
D. Muhammad		Virgil Hill* WBA	1987	Jeff Harding* WBC	1991–94
Qawi* WBC	1981–83	Pr Charles Williams* IBF	1987–93	Iran Barkley* WBA	1992
Michael Spinks	1983–85†	Thomas Hearns* WBC	1987†	Virgil Hill* WBA	1992–97
J. B. Williamson* WBC	1985–86	Donny Lalonde* WBC	1987–88	Henry Maske* IBF	1993–96
Slobodan Kacar* IBF	1985–86	Sugar Ray Leonard* WBC	1988	Mike McCallum* WBC	1994–95
Marvin Johnson* WBA	1986–87	Dennis Andries* WBC	1989	Fabrice Tiozzo* WBC	1995–96
Dennis Andries* WBC	1986–87	Jeff Harding* WBC	1989–90	Roy Jones WBC/WBA	1997–
Bobby Czyz* IBF	1986–87	Dennis Andries* WBC	1990–91	William Guthrie* IBF	1997–98
Leslie Stewart* WBA	1987	Thomas Hearns* WBA	1991–92	Reggie Johnson* IBF	1998–

Super Middleweights
(Weight Limit: 168 pounds)

Champion	Reign	Champion	Reign	Champion	Reign
Murray Sutherland* IBF	1984	Mauro Galvano* WBC	1990–92	Roy Jones* IBF	1994–96
Chong-Pal Park* IBF	1984–87	Victor Cordova* WBA	1991	Thulane Malinga* WBC	1996
Chong-Pal Park* WBA	1987–88	Darrin Van Horn* IBF	1991–92	V. Nardiello* WBC	1996
G. Rocchigiani* IBF	1988–89	Iran Barkley *WBA	1992	Robin Reid* WBC	1996–97
F. Obelmejias* WBA	1988–89	Nigel Benn* WBC	1992–96	Charles Brewer* IBF	1997–
Ray Leonard* WBC	1988–90†	James Toney* IBF	1992–94	Thulane Malinga* WBC	1997–98
In-Chul Baek* WBA	1989–90	Michael Nunn* WBA	1992–94	Richie Woodhall* WBC	1998–
Lindell Holmes* IBF	1990–91	Steve Little* WBA	1994		
C. Tiozzo* WBA	1990–91	Frank Liles* WBA	1994–		

Middleweights
(Weight Limit: 160 pounds)

Champion	Reign	Champion	Reign	Champion	Reign
Jack Dempsey	1884–91	Tony Zale	1948	Hugo Corro	1978–79
Bob Fitzsimmons	1891–97	Marcel Cerdan	1948–49	Vito Antuofermo	1979–80
Kid McCoy	1897–98	Jake La Motta	1949–51	Alan Minter	1980
Tommy Ryan	1898–1907	Sugar Ray Robinson	1951	Marvin Hagler	1980–87
Stanley Ketchel	1908	Randy Turpin	1951	Sugar Ray Leonard	1987
Billy Papke	1908	Sugar Ray Robinson	1951–52	Frank Tate* IBF	1987–88
Stanley Ketchel	1908–10	Bobo Olson	1953–55	Sumbu Kalambay* WBA	1987–89
Frank Klaus	1913	Sugar Ray Robinson	1955–57	Thomas Hearns* WBC	1987–88
George Chip	1913–14	Gene Fullmer	1957	Iran Barkley* WBC	1988–89
Al McCoy	1914–17	Sugar Ray Robinson	1957	Michael Nunn* IBF	1988–91
Mike O'Dowd	1917–20	Carmen Basilio	1957–58	Roberto Duran* WBC	1989–90
Johnny Wilson	1920–23	Sugar Ray Robinson	1958–60	Mike McCallum* WBA	1989–91
Harry Greb	1923–26	Gene Fullmer* NBA	1959–62	Julian Jackson* WBC	1990–93
Tiger Flowers	1926	Paul Pender	1960–61	James Toney* IBF	1991–93
Mickey Walker	1926–31†	Terry Downes	1961–62	Reggie Johnson* WBA	1992–94
Gorilla Jones	1931–32	Paul Pender	1962–63	Roy Jones* WBC	1993–95†
Marcel Thil	1932–37	Dick Tiger* WBA	1962–63	G. McClellan* WBC	1993–95†
Fred Apostoli	1937–39	Dick Tiger	1963	Jorge Castro* WBA	1994–95
Al Hostak* NBA	1938	Joey Giardello	1963–65	Shinji Takehara* WBA	1995–96
Solly Krieger* NBA	1938–39	Dick Tiger	1965–66	Jullian Jackson*WBC	1995
Al Hostak* NBA	1939–40	Emile Griffith	1966–67	Quincy Taylor* WBC	1995–96
Ceferino Garcia	1939–40	Nino Benvenuti	1967	Bernard Hopkins* IBF	1995–
Ken Overlin	1940–41	Emile Griffith	1967–68	Keith Holmes* WBC	1996–98
Tony Zale* NBA	1940–41	Nino Benvenuti	1968–70	William Joppy Jr.* WBA	1996–97
Billy Soose	1941	Carlos Monzon	1970–77†	J.C. Green* WBA	1997
Tony Zale	1941–47	Rodrigo Valdez* WBC	1974–76	William Joppy Jr.* WBA	1998–
Rocky Graziano	1947–48	Rodrigo Valdez	1977–78	Hassine Cherifi* WBC	1998–

Junior Middleweights
(Weight Limit: 154 pounds)

Champion	Reign	Champion	Reign	Champion	Reign
Emile Griffith (EBU)	1962–63	Miguel de Oliveira* WBC	1975–76	Wilfred Benitez* WBC	1981–82
Dennis Moyer	1962–63	Jae-Do Yuh	1975–76	Sugar Ray Leonard	1981–82
Ralph Dupas	1963	Elisha Obed* WBC	1975–76	Tadashi Mihara* WBA	1981–82
Sandro Mazzinghi	1963–65	Koichi Wajima	1976	Davey Moore* WBA	1982–83
Nino Benvenuti	1965–66	Jose Duran	1976	Thomas Hearns* WBC	1982–84
Ki-Soo Kim	1966–68	Eckhard Dagge* WBC	1976–77	Roberto Duran* WBA	1983–84
Sandro Mazzinghi	1968	Miguel Angel Castellini	1976–77	Mark Medal* IBF	1984
Freddie Little	1969–70	Eddie Gazo	1977–78	Thomas Hearns	1984–86
Carmelo Bossi	1970–71	Rocky Mattioli* WBC	1977–79	Mike McCallum* WBA	1984–87
Koichi Wajima	1971–74	Masashi Kudo	1978–79	Carlos Santos* IBF	1984–86
Oscar Albarado	1974–75	Maurice Hope* WBC	1979–81	Buster Drayton* IBF	1986–87
Koichi Wajima	1975	Ayub Kalule	1979–81	Duane Thomas* WBC	1986–87

*Champion not generally recognized. †Champion retired or relinquished title.

Junior Middleweights (Cont.)

Champion	Reign	Champion	Reign	Champion	Reign
Matthew Hilton* IBF	1987–88	Gianfranco Rosi* IBF	1989–94	Carl Daniels* WBA	1995
Lupe Aquino* WBC	1987	Terry Norris WBC	1990–94	Terry Norris WBC	1995–97
Gianfranco Rosi* WBC	1987–88	Gilbert Dele* WBA	1991	Terry Norris IBF	1995–96
Julian Jackson* WBA	1987–90	Vinny Pazienza* WBA	1991–92	L. Boudouani* WBA	1996–
Donald Curry* WBC	1988–89	Julio C. Vasquez* WBA	1992–95	Raul Marquez* IBF	1997
Robert Hines* IBF	1988–89	Simon Brown* WBC	1994	Keith Mullings* WBC	1997–
Darrin Van Horn* IBF	1989	Terry Norris *WBC	1994–	Yori Boy Campas* IBF	1997–
Rene Jacquot* WBC	1989	Vincent Pettway* IBF	1994–95		
John Mugabi* WBC	1989–90	Paul Vaden* IBF	1995		

Note: Division called Super Welterweight by the WBC.

Welterweights
(Weight Limit: 147 pounds)

Champion	Reign	Champion	Reign	Champion	Reign
Paddy Duffy	1888–90	Young Corbett III	1933	John H. Stracey	1975–76
Mysterious Billy Smith	1892–94	Jimmy McLarnin	1933–34	Carlos Palomino	1976–79
Tommy Ryan	1894–98	Barney Ross	1934	Pipino Cuevas* WBA	1976–80
Mysterious Billy Smith	1898–1900	Jimmy McLarnin	1934–35	Wilfredo Benitez	1979
Rube Ferns	1900	Barney Ross	1935–38	Sugar Ray Leonard	1979–80
Matty Matthews	1900–01	Henry Armstrong	1938–40	Roberto Duran	1980
Rube Ferns	1901	Fritzie Zivic	1940–41	Thomas Hearns* WBA	1980–81
Joe Walcott	1901–04	Red Cochrane	1941–46	Sugar Ray Leonard	1980–82
The Dixie Kid	1904–05	Marty Servo	1946	Donald Curry* WBA	1983–85
Honey Mellody	1906–07	Sugar Ray Robinson	1946–51†	Milton McCrory* WBC	1983–85
Twin Sullivan	1907–08	Johnny Bratton	1951	Donald Curry	1985–86
Jimmy Gardner	1908	Kid Gavilan	1951–54	Lloyd Honeyghan	1986–87
Jimmy Clabby	1910–11	Johnny Saxton	1954–55	Jorge Vaca WBC	1987–88
Waldemar Holberg	1914	Tony DeMarco	1955	Lloyd Honeyghan WBC	1988–89
Tom McCormick	1914	Carmen Basilio	1955–56	Mark Breland* WBA	1987
Matt Wells	1914–15	Johnny Saxton	1956	Marlon Starling* WBA	1987–88
Mike Glover	1915	Carmen Basilio	1956–57	Tomas Molinares* WBA	1988–89
Jack Britton	1915	Virgil Akins	1958	Simon Brown* IBF	1988–91
Ted "Kid" Lewis	1915–16	Don Jordan	1958–60	Mark Breland*	1989–90
Jack Britton	1916–17	Kid Paret	1960–61	Marlon Starling* WBC	1989–90
Ted "Kid" Lewis	1917–19	Emile Griffith	1961	Aaron Davis* WBA	1990–91
Jack Britton	1919–22	Kid Paret	1961–62	Maurice Blocker* WBC	1990–91
Mickey Walker	1922–26	Emile Griffith	1962–63	Meldrick Taylor* WBA	1991–92
Pete Latzo	1926–27	Luis Rodriguez	1963	Simon Brown* WBC	1991
Joe Dundee	1927–29	Emile Griffith	1963–66	Buddy McGirt* WBC	1991–93
Jackie Fields	1929–30	Curtis Cokes	1966–69	Felix Trinidad* IBF	1993–
Young Jack Thompson	1930	Jose Napoles	1969–70	Pernell Whitaker WBC	1993–97
Tommy Freeman	1930–31	Billy Backus	1970–71	Crisanto Espana* WBA	1992–94
Young Jack Thompson	1931	Jose Napoles	1971–75	Ike Quartey* WBA	1994–97†
Lou Brouillard	1931–32	Hedgemon Lewis* NY	1972–73	Oscar De La Hoya*, WBC	1997–
Jackie Fields	1932–33	Angel Espada* WBA	1975–76		

Junior Welterweights
(Weight Limit: 140 pounds)

Champion	Reign	Champion	Reign	Champion	Reign
Pinkey Mitchell	1922–25	Carlos Hernandez	1965–66	Leroy Haley* WBC	1982–83
Red Herring	1925	Sandro Lopopolo	1966–67	Aaron Pryor* IBF	1983–85
Mushy Callahan	1926–30	Paul Fujii	1967–68	Bruce Curry* WBC	1983–84
Jack (Kid) Berg	1930–31	Nicolino Loche	1968–72	Johnny Bumphus* WBA	1984
Tony Canzoneri	1931–32	Pedro Adigue* WBC	1968–70	Bill Costello* WBC	1984–85
Johnny Jadick	1932–33	Bruno Arcari* WBC	1970–74	Gene Hatcher* WBA	1984–85
Sammy Fuller*	1932–33	Alfonso Frazer	1972	Ubaldo Sacco* WBA	1985–86
Battling Shaw	1933	Antonio Cervantes	1972–76	Lonnie Smith* WBC	1985–86
Tony Canzoneri	1933	Perico Fernandez* WBC	1974–75	Patrizio Oliva* WBA	1986–87
Barney Ross	1933–35	S. Muangsurin* WBC	1975–76	Gary Hinton* IBF	1986
Tippy Larkin	1946	Wilfred Benitez	1976–79	Rene Arredondo* WBC	1986
Carlos Ortiz	1959–60	M. Velasquez* WBC	1976	Tsuyoshi Hamada* WBC	1986–87
Duilio Loi	1960–62	S. Muangsurin* WBC	1976–78	Joe Louis Manley* IBF	1986–87
Eddie Perkins	1962	A. Cervantes* WBA	1977–80	Terry Marsh* IBF	1987
Duilio Loi	1962–63	Sang-Hyun Kim* WBC	1978–80	Juan Coggi* WBA	1987–90
Roberto Cruz* WBA	1963	Saoul Mamby* WBC	1980–82	Rene Arredondo* WBC	1987
Eddie Perkins	1963–65	Aaron Pryor* WBA	1980–83	R. Mayweather* WBC	1987–89

*Champion not generally recognized. †Champion retired or relinquished title.

Junior Welterweights *(Cont.)*

Champion	Reign
James McGirt* IBF	1988
Meldrick Taylor* IBF	1988–90
Julio César Chávez* WBC	1989–94
Julio César Chávez* IBF	1990–91
Loreto Garza* WBA	1990–91
Juan Coggi* WBA	1991
Edwin Rosario* WBA	1991–92
Rafael Pineda* IBF	1991–92

Champion	Reign
Akinobu Hiranaka* WBA	1992
Pernell Whitaker*† IBF	1992–93
Charles Murray* IBF	1993–94
Jake Rodriguez* IBF	1994–95
Juan Coggi* WBA	1993–94
Frankie Randall* WBC	1994
Frankie Randall* WBA	1994–96
Juan Coggi* WBA	1996

Champion	Reign
Julio César Chávez WBC	1994–96
Kostya Tszyu* IBF	1995–97
Frankie Randall* WBA	1996–97
Oscar De La Hoya WBC	1996–97†
Khalid Rahilou* WBA	1997–
Vincent Phillips* IBF	1997–

Lightweights
(Weight Limit: 135 pounds)

Champion	Reign
Jack McAuliffe	1886–94
Kid Lavigne	1896–99
Frank Erne	1899–1902
Joe Gans	1902–04
Jimmy Britt	1904–05
Battling Nelson	1905–06
Joe Gans	1906–08
Battling Nelson	1908–10
Ad Wolgast	1910–12
Willie Ritchie	1912–14
Freddie Welsh	1915–17
Benny Leonard	1917–25†
Jimmy Goodrich	1925
Rocky Kansas	1925–26
Sammy Mandell	1926–30
Al Singer	1930
Tony Canzoneri	1930–33
Barney Ross	1933–35†
Tony Canzoneri	1935–36
Lou Ambers	1936–38
Henry Armstrong	1938–39
Lou Ambers	1939–40
Sammy Angott* NBA	1940–41
Lew Jenkins	1940–41
Sammy Angott	1941–42†
Beau Jack* NY	1942–43
Bob Montgomery* NY	1943
Sammy Angott* NBA	1943–44
Beau Jack* NY	1943–44
Bob Montgomery* NY	1944–47
Juan Zurita* NBA	1944–45
Ike Williams	1947–51

Champion	Reign
James Carter	1951–52
Lauro Salas	1952
James Carter	1952–54
Paddy DeMarco	1954
James Carter	1954–55
Wallace Smith	1955–56
Joe Brown	1956–62
Carlos Ortiz	1962–65
Ismael Laguna	1965
Carlos Ortiz	1965–68
Carlos Teo Cruz	1968–69
Mando Ramos	1969–70
Ismael Laguna	1970
Ken Buchanan	1970–72
Roberto Duran	1972–79†
Chango Carmona* WBC	1972
Rodolfo Gonzalez* WBC	1972–74
Ishimatsu Suzuki* WBC	1974–76
Estaban DeJesus* WBC	1976–78
Jim Watt* WBC	1979–81
Ernesto Espana* WBA	1979–80
Hilmer Kenty* WBA	1980–81
Sean O'Grady* WBA	1981
Claude Noel* WBA	1981
Alexis Arguello* WBC	1981–82
Arturo Frias* WBA	1981–82
Ray Mancini* WBA	1982–84
Alexis Arguello	1982–83
Edwin Rosario* WBC	1983–84
Choo Choo Brown* IBF	1984
L. Bramble* WBA	1984–86
Jose Luis Ramirez* WBC	1984–85

Champion	Reign
Harry Arroyo* IBF	1984–85
Jimmy Paul* IBF	1985–86
Hector Camacho* WBC	1985–86
Greg Haugen* IBF	1986–87
Edwin Rosario* WBA	1986–87
Julio César Chávez* WBA	1987–88
Jose Luis Ramirez* WBC	1987–88
Julio César Chávez	1988–89
Vinny Pazienza* IBF	1987–88
Greg Haugen* IBF	1988–89
P. Whitaker* WBC, IBF	1989–90
Edwin Rosario* WBA	1989–90
Juan Nazario* WBA	1990
P. Whitaker* WBA, WBC	1990–92
Pernell Whitaker* IBF	1991–92
Julio César Chávez* IBF	1990–91
Edwin Rosario* WBA	1991–92
Julio César Chávez* WBC	1990–92
Miguel Gonzalez* WBC	1992–95
Joey Gamache* WBA	1992–93
Dingaan Thobela* WBA	1993
Fred Pendleton* IBF	1993–94
Orzubek Nazarov* WBA	1993–98
Rafael Ruelas* IBF	1994–95
Phillip Holiday* IBF	1995–97
Jean B. Mendy* WBC	1996–97
Steve Johnston* WBC	1997–98
Shane Mosley* IBF	1997–
Jean B. Mendy* WBA	1998–
Cesar Bazan* WBC	1998–

Junior Lightweights
(Weight Limit: 130 pounds)

Champion	Reign
Johnny Dundee	1921–23
Jack Bernstein	1923
Johnny Dundee	1923–24
Steve (Kid) Sullivan	1924–25
Mike Ballerino	1925
Tod Morgan	1925–29
Benny Bass	1929–31
Kid Chocolate	1931–33
Frankie Klick	1933–34
Sandy Saddler	1949–50
Harold Gomes	1959–60
Gabriel (Flash) Elorde	1960–67
Yoshiaki Numata	1967
Hiroshi Kobayashi	1967–71
Rene Barrientos* WBC	1969–70
Yoshiaki Numata* WBC	1970–71
Alfredo Marcano	1971–72
R. Arredondo* WBC	1971–74
Ben Villaflor	1972–73
Kuniaki Shibata	1973

Champion	Reign
Ben Villaflor	1973–76
Kuniaki Shibata* WBC	1974–75
Alfredo Escalera* WBC	1975–78
Samuel Serrano	1976–80
Alexis Arguello* WBC	1978–80
Yasutsune Uehara	1980–81
Rafael Limon* WBC	1980–81
C. Boza-Edwards* WBC	1981
Samuel Serrano	1981–83
R. Navarrete* WBC	1981–82
Rafael Limon* WBC	1982
Bobby Chacon* WBC	1982–83
Roger Mayweather	1983–84
Hector Camacho* WBC	1983–84
Rocky Lockridge	1984–85
Hwan-Kil Yuh* IBF	1984–85
Julio César Chávez* WBC	1984–87
Lester Ellis* IBF	1985
Wilfredo Gomez	1985–86
Barry Michael* IBF	1985–87

Champion	Reign
Alfredo Layne* WBA	1986
Brian Mitchell* WBA	1986–91
Rocky Lockridge* IBF	1987–88
Azumah Nelson* WBC	1988–94
Tony Lopez* IBF	1988–89
Juan Molina* IBF	1989–90
Tony Lopez* IBF	1990–91
Joey Gamache WBA	1991
Brian Mitchell* IBF	1991
Genaro Hernandez* WBA	1991–95
James Leija* WBC	1994
Juan Molina* IBF	1991–95
Gabriel Ruelas* WBC	1994–95
Eddie Hopson* IBF	1995
Tracy Patterson* IBF	1995
Azumah Nelson* WBC	1995–97
Choi Yong-Soo* WBA	1995–
Arturo Gatti* IBF	1995–98†
Genaro Hernandez* WBC	1997–
Roberto Garcia* IBF	1998–

*Champion not generally recognized. †Champion retired or relinquished title.

Featherweights
(Weight Limit: 126 pounds)

Champion	Reign
Torpedo Billy Murphy	1890
Young Griffo	1890–92
George Dixon	1892–97
Solly Smith	1897–98
Dave Sullivan	1898
George Dixon	1898–1900
Terry McGovern	1900–01
Young Corbett II	1901–04
Jimmy Britt	1904
Tommy Sullivan	1904–05
Abe Attell	1906–12
Johnny Kilbane	1912–23
Eugene Criqui	1923
Johnny Dundee	1923–24
"Kid" Kaplan	1925–26
Benny Bass	1927–28
Tony Canzoneri	1928
Andre Routis	1928–29
Battling Battalino	1929–32
Tommy Paul* NBA	1932–33
Kid Chocolate* NY	1932–33
Freddie Miller* NBA	1933–36
Mike Beloise* NY	1936–37
Petey Sarron* NBA	1936–37
Maurice Holtzer	1937–38
Henry Armstrong	1937–38
Joey Archibald* NY	1938–39
Leo Rodak* NBA	1938–39
Joey Archibald	1939–40
Petey Scalzo* NBA	1940–41
Harry Jeffra	1940–41
Joey Archibald	1941

Champion	Reign
Richie Lamos* NBA	1941
Chalky Wright	1941–42
Jackie Wilson* NBA	1941–43
Willie Pep	1942–48
Jackie Callura* NBA	1943
Phil Terranova* NBA	1943–44
Sal Bartolo* NBA	1944–46
Sandy Saddler	1948–49
Willie Pep	1949–50
Sandy Saddler	1950–57†
Kid Bassey	1957–59
Davey Moore	1959–63
Sugar Ramos	1963–64
Vicente Saldivar	1964–67†
Paul Rojas* WBA	1968
Jose Legra* WBC	1968–69
Shozo Saijyo* WBA	1968–71
J. Famechon* WBC	1969–70
Vicente Saldivar WBC	1970
Kuniaki Shibata WBC	1970–72
Antonio Gomez* WBA	1971–72
C. Sanchez WBC	1972
Ernesto Marcel* WBA	1972–74
Jose Legra WBC	1972–73
Eder Jofre WBC	1973–74
Ruben Olivares* WBA	1974
Bobby Chacon* WBC	1974–75
Alexis Arguello WBA	1974–76
Ruben Olivares* WBC	1975
Poison Kotey* WBC	1975–76
Danny Lopez WBC	1976–80
Rafael Ortega* WBA	1977

Champion	Reign
Cecilio Lastra* WBA	1977–78
Eusebio Pedroza* WBA	1978–85
S. Sanchez WBC	1980–82
Juan LaPorte* WBC	1982–84
Wilfredo Gomez* WBC	1984
Min-Keun Oh* IBF	1984–85
Azumah Nelson* WBC	1984–88
Barry McGuigan* WBA	1985–86
Ki Young Chung* IBF	1985–86
Steve Cruz* WBA	1986–87
Antonio Rivera* IBF	1986–88
A. Esparragoza* WBA	1987–91
Calvin Grove* IBF	1988
Jorge Paez* IBF	1988–91
Jeff Fenech* WBC	1988–90†
Marcos Villasana* WBC	1990–91
Paul Hodkinson* WBC	1991–93
Troy Dorsey* IBF	1991
Manuel Medina* IBF	1991–93
Yung Kyun Park* WBA	1991–93
Gregorio Vargas* WBC	1993
Tom Johnson* IBF	1993–97†
Eloy Rojas* WBA	1993–96
Kevin Kelley* WBC	1993–95
A. Gonzalez* WBC	1995
Manuel Medina* WBC	1995–95
Luisito Espinosa* WBC	1995–
Wilfredo Vazquez* WBA	1996–98†
Hector Lizarraga* IBF	1997–98
Freddie Norwood* WBA	1998–
Manuel Medina* IBF	1998–

Junior Featherweights
(Weight Limit: 122 pounds)

Champion	Reign
Jack (Kid) Wolfe*	1922–23
Carl Duane*	1923–24
Rigoberto Riasco* WBC	1976
Royal	
Kobayashi* WBC	1976
Dong-Kyun Yum* WBC	1976–77
Wilfredo Gomez* WBC	1977–83
Soo-Hwan Hong* WBA	1977–78
Ricardo Cardona* WBA	1978–80
Leo Randolph* WBA	1980
Sergio Palma* WBA	1980–82
Leonardo Cruz* WBA	1982–84
Jaime Garza* WBC	1983
Bobby Berna* IBF	1983–84
Loris Stecca* WBA	1984
Seung-Il Suh* IBF	1984–85
Victor Callejas* WBA	1984–86

Champion	Reign
Juan (Kid) Meza* WBC	1984–85
Ji-Won Kim* IBF	1985–86
Lupe Pintor* WBC	1985–86
Samart	
Payakaroon* WBC	1986–87
Seung-Hoon Lee* IBF	1987–88
Louie Espinoza* WBA	1987
Jeff Fenech* WBC	1987
Julio Gervacio* WBA	1987–88
Daniel Zaragoza* WBC	1988–90
Jose Sanabria* IBF	1988–89
Bernardo	
Pinango* WBA	1988
Juan Jose	
Estrada* WBA	1988–89
Fabrice Benichou* IBF	1989–90
Jesus Salud* WBA	1989–90

Champion	Reign
Welcome Ncita* IBF	1990–92
Paul Banke* WBC	1990
Luis Mendoza* WBA	1990–91
Rual Perez* WBA	1992
Pedro Decima* WBC	1990–91
K. Hatanaka* WBC	1991
Daniel Zaragoza* WBC	1991–92
Tracy Patterson* WBC	1992–94
Kennedy McKinney* IBF	1993–94
Wilfredo Vasquez* WBA	1992–95
Vuyani Bungu* IBF	1994–
H. Acero Sanchez* WBC	1994–95
Antonio Cermeno* WBA	1995–98†
Daniel Zaragoza* WBC	1995–97
Erik Morales* WBC	1997–
Enrique Sanchez* WBA	1998–

Bantamweights
(Weight Limit: 118 pounds)

Champion	Reign
Spider Kelly	1887
Hughey Boyle	1887–88
Spider Kelly	1889
Chappie Moran	1889–90
George Dixon	1890–91
Pedlar Palmer*	1895–99
Terry McGovern	1899–1900

Champion	Reign
Harry Harris	1901–02
Harry Forbes	1902–03
Frankie Neil	1903–04
Joe Bowker	1904–05
Jimmy Walsh	1905–06
Owen Moran	1907–08
Monte Attell*	1909–10

Champion	Reign
Frankie Conley	1910–11
Johnny Coulon	1911–14
Kid Williams	1914–17
Kewpie Ertle*	1915
Pete Herman	1917–20
Joe Lynch	1920–21
Pete Herman	1921

*Champion not generally recognized. †Champion retired or relinquished title.

Bantamweights (Cont.)

Champion	Reign	Champion	Reign	Champion	Reign
Johnny Buff	1921–22	Joe Becerra	1959–60†	W. Vasquez* WBA	1987–88
Joe Lynch	1922–24	Eder Jofre	1961–65	Kevin Seabrooks* IBF	1987–88
Abe Goldstein	1924	Fighting Harada	1965–68	Kaokor Galaxy* WBA	1988
Cannonball Martin	1924–25	Lionel Rose	1968–69	Moon Sung-Kil* WBA	1988–89
Phil Rosenberg	1925–27	Ruben Olivares	1969–70	Kaokor Galaxy* WBA	1989
Bud Taylor NBA	1927–28	Chucho Castillo	1970–71	Raul Perez* WBC	1988–91
Bushy Graham* NY	1928–29	Ruben Olivares	1971–72	O. Canizales* IBF	1988–95
Panama Al Brown	1929–35	Rafael Herrera	1972	Luisito Espinosa* WBA	1989–91
Sixto Escobar* NBA	1934–35	Enrique Pinder	1972–73	Israel Contreras* WBA	1991–92
Baltazar Sangchilli	1935–36	Romeo Anaya	1973	Eddie Cook* WBA	1992–93
Lou Salica* NBA	1935	Rafael Herrera* WBC	1973–74	Greg Richardson* WBC	1991
Sixto Escobar* NBA	1935–36	Soo-Hwan Hong	1974–75	J. Tatsuyoshi, WBC	1991–92
Tony Marino	1936	Rodolfo Martinez* WBC	1974–76	Victor Rabanales* WBC	1992–93
Sixto Escobar	1936–37	Alfonso Zamora	1975–77	Jung-Il Byun* WBC	1993
Harry Jeffra	1937–38†	Carlos Zarate* WBC	1976–79	Jorge Julio WBA	1993
Sixto Escobar	1938–39	Jorge Lujan	1977–80	Yasuei Yakushiji* WBC	1993–95
Georgie Pace NBA	1939–40	Lupe Pintor* WBC	1979–83	Junior Jones WBA*	1994
Lou Salica	1940–42	Julian Solis	1980	John M. Johnson* WBA 1994	
Manuel Ortiz	1942–47	Jeff Chandler	1980–84	D. Chuvatana*WBA	1994–95
Harold Dade	1947	Albert Davila* WBC	1983–85	V. Sahaprom* WBA	1995–96
Manuel Ortiz	1947–50	Richard Sandoval	1984–86	W. McCullough* WBC	1995–96
Vic Toweel	1950–52	Satoshi Shingaki* IBF	1984–85	Harold Mestre* IBF	1995
Jimmy Carruthers	1952–54†	Jeff Fenech* IBF	1985	Mbulelo Botile* IBF	1995–97
Robert Cohen	1954–56	Daniel Zaragoza* WBC	1985	Nana Yaw Konadu* WBC	1996–
Paul Macias* NBA	1955–57	Miguel Lora* WBC	1985–88	S. Singmanassak* WBC	1996–97
Mario D'Agata	1956–57	Gaby Canizales	1986	Tim Austin* IBF	1997–
Alphonse Halimi	1957–59	Bernardo Pinango	1986–87	Joichiro Tatsuyoshi* WBC	1997–

Junior Bantamweights
(Weight Limit: 115 pounds)

Champion	Reign	Champion	Reign	Champion	Reign
Rafael Orono* WBC	1980–81	Ellyas Pical* IBF	1986	Jose Luis Bueno* WBC	1993–94
Chul-Ho Kim* WBC	1981–82	Santos Laciar* WBC	1987	Hiroshi Kawashima*WBC	1994–97
Gustavo Ballas* WBA	1981	Tae-Il Chang* IBF	1987	Harold Grey* IBF	1994–95
Rafael Pedroza* WBA	1981–82	Sugar Rojas* WBC	1987–88	Alimi Goitia* WBA	1995–96
Jiro Watanabe* WBA	1982–84	Ellyas Pical* IBF	1987–89	Yokthai Sith-Oar* WBA	1996–97
Rafael Orono* WBC	1982–83	Giberto Roman* WBC	1988–89	Carlos Salazar* IBF	1995–96
Payao Poontarat* WBC	1983–84	Juan Polo Perez* IBF	1989–90	Harold Grey* IBF	1996
Joo-Do Chun* IBF	1983–85	Nana Konadu* WBC	1989–90	Danny Romero* IBF	1996–97
Jiro Watanabe	1984–86	Sung-Kil Moon* WBC	1990–93	Gerry Penalosa* WBC	1997–98
Kaosai Galaxy* WBA	1984	Robert Quiroga* IBF	1990–93	Johnny Tapia* IBF	1997–
Ellyas Pical* IBF	1985–86	Julio Borboa* IBF	1993–94	Satoshi Iida* WBA	1997–
Cesar Polanco* IBF	1986	Katsuya Onizuka* WBA	1993–94	Cho In-Joo* WBC	1998–
Gilberto Roman* WBC	1986–87	Lee Hyung-Chul* WBA	1994–95		

Flyweights
(Weight Limit: 112 pounds)

Champion	Reign	Champion	Reign	Champion	Reign
Sid Smith	1913	Little Dado* NY	1938–40	B. Villacampo* WBA	1969–70
Bill Ladbury	1913–14	Jackie Paterson	1943–48	Chartchai Chionoi	1970
Percy Jones	1914	Rinty Monaghan	1948–50	B. Chartvanchai* WBA	1970
Joe Symonds	1914–16	Terry Allen	1950	Masao Ohba* WBA	1970–73
Jimmy Wilde	1916–23	Dado Marino	1950–52	Erbito Salavarria	1970–73
Pancho Villa	1923–25	Yoshio Shirai	1953–54	B. Gonzalez* WBA	1972
Fidel LaBarba	1925–27†	Pascual Perez	1954–60	V. Borkorsor* WBC	1972–73
Frenchy Belanger NBA	1927–28	Pone Kingpetch	1960–62	Venice Borkorsor	1973
Izzy Schwartz NY	1927–29	Masahiko Harada	1962–63	Chartchai Chionoi* WBA	1973–74
Frankie Genaro NBA	1928–29	Pone Kingpetch	1963	B. Gonzalez* WBA	1973–74
Spider Pladner NBA	1929	Hiroyuki Ebihara	1963–64	Shoji Oguma* WBC	1974–75
Frankie Genaro NBA	1929–31	Pone Kingpetch	1964–65	S. Hanagata* WBA	1974–75
Midget Wolgast* NY	1930–35	Salvatore Burrini	1965–66	Miguel Canto* WBC	1975–79
Young Perez NBA	1931–32	H. Accavallo* WBA	1966–68	Erbito Salavarria* WBA	1975–76
Jackie Brown NBA	1932–35	Walter McGowan	1966	Alfonso Lopez* WBA	1976
Benny Lynch	1935–38	Chartchai Chionoi	1966–69	G. Espadas* WBA	1976–78
Small Montana* NY	1935–37	Efren Torres	1969–70	B. Gonzalez* WBA	1978–79
Peter Kane	1938–43	Hiroyuki Ebihara* WBA	1969	Chan-Hee Park* WBC	1979–80

*Champion not generally recognized. †Champion retired or relinquished title.

Flyweights (Cont.)

Champion	Reign
Luis Ibarra* WBA	1979–80
Tae-Shik Kim* WBA	1980
Shoji Oguma* WBC	1980–81
Peter Mathebula* WBA	1980–81
Santos Laciar* WBA	1981
Antonio Avelar* WBC	1981–82
Luis Ibarra* WBA	1981
Juan Herrera* WBA	1981–82
P. Cardona* WBC	1982
Santos Laciar* WBA	1982–85
Freddie Castillo* WBC	1982
E. Mercedes* WBC	1982–83
Charlie Magri* WBC	1983
Frank Cedeno* WBC	1983–84
Soon-Chun Kwon* IBF	1983–85
Koji Kobayashi* WBC	1984

Champion	Reign
Gabriel Bernal* WBC	1984
Sot Chitalada* WBC	1984–88
Hilario Zapate* WBA	1985–87
Chong-Kwan Chung* IBF	1985–86
Bi-Won Chung* IBF	1986
Hi-Sup Shin* IBF	1986–87
Dodie Penalosa* IBF	1987
Fidel Bassa* WBA	1987–89
Choi-Chang Ho* IBF	1987–88
Rolando Bohol* IBF	1988
Yong-Kang Kim* WBC	1988–89
Duke McKenzie* IBF	1988–89
Sot Chitalada* WBC	1989–91
Dave McAuley* IBF	1989–92
Jesus Rojas* WBA	1989–90

Champion	Reign
Yul-Woo Lee* WBA	1990
L. Tamakuma* WBA	1990–91
M. Kittikasem* WBC	1991–92
Yuri Arbachakov* WBC	1992–97
Yong Kang Kim* WBA	1991–92
Rodolfo Blanco* IBF	1992–93
P. Sithbangprachan* IBF	1993–95
David Griman* WBA	1992–94
S.S. Ploenchit* WBA	1994–96
Francisco Tejedor* IBF	1995
Danny Romero* IBF	1995–96
Mark Johnson* IBF	1996–
Jose Bonilla* WBA	1996–98
Chatchai Sasakul* WBC	1997–
Hugo Soto* WBA	1998–

Junior Flyweights
(Weight Limit: 108 pounds)

Champion	Reign
Franco Udella* WBC	1975
Jaime Rios* WBA	1975–76
Luis Estaba* WBC	1975–78
Juan Guzman* WBA	1976
Yoko Gushiken* WBA	1976–81
Freddy Castillo* WBC	1978
Netrnoi Vorasingh* WBC	1978
Sung-Jun Kim* WBC	1978–80
Shigeo Nakajima* WBC	1980
Hilario Zapata* WBC	1980–82
Pedro Flores* WBA	1981
Hwan-Jin Kim* WBA	1981
Katsuo Tokashiki* WBA	1981–83
Amado Urzua* WBC	1982
Tadashi Tomori* WBC	1982
Hilario Zapata* WBC	1982–83

Champion	Reign
Jung-Koo Chang* WBC	1983–88
Lupe Madera* WBA	1983–84
Dodie Penalosa* IBF	1983–86
Francisco Quiroz* WBA	1984–85
Joey Olivo* WBA	1985
Myung-Woo Yuh* WBA	1985–91
Jum-Hwan Choi* IBF	1986–88
Tacy Macalos* IBF	1988–89
German Torres* WBC	1988–89
Yul-Woo Lee* WBC	1989
Muangchai Kittikasem* IBF	1989–90
Humberto Gonzalez* WBC	1989–90
Michael Carbajal* IBF	1990–94
R. Pascua* WBC	1990

Champion	Reign
M. C. Castro* WBC	1991
H. Gonzalez* WBC	1991–93
Hirokia Ioka* WBA	1991–92
Michael Carbajal, WBC	1993–94
Myung-Woo Yuh* WBA	1993
Leo Gamez* WBA	1993–95
H. Gonzalez* WBC, IBF	1994–95
Choi Hi-Yong* WBA	1995–96
S. Sor Jaturong* WBC, IBF	1995–96
Carlos Murillo* WBA	1996
Keiji Yamaguchi* WBA	1996
Michael Carbajal* IBF	1996–97
S. Sor Jaturong* WBC	1995–
Phichit Chor Sirlwat* WBA	1996–
Mauricio Pastrana* IBF	1997–98†

Strawweights
(Weight Limit: 105 pounds)

Champion	Reign
Franco Udella* WBC	1975
Jaime Rios* WBA	1975–76
Luis Estaba* WBC	1975–78
Juan Guzman* WBA	1976
Yoko Gushiken* WBA	1976–81
Freddy Castillo* WBC	1978
Netrnoi Vorasingh* WBC	1978
Sung-Jun Kim* WBC	1978–80
Shigeo Nakajima* WBC	1980
Hilario Zapata* WBC	1980–82
Pedro Flores* WBA	1981
Hwan-Jin Kim* WBA	1981

Champion	Reign
Katsuo Tokashiki* WBA	1981–83
Amado Urzua* WBC	1982
Tadashi Tomori* WBC	1982
Hilario Zapata* WBC	1982–83
Jung-Koo Chang* WBC	1983–88
Lupe Madera* WBA	1983–84
Dodie Penalosa* IBF	1983–86
Francisco Quiroz* WBA	1984–85
Joey Olivo* WBA	1985
Myung-Woo Yuh* WBA	1985–93
Jum-Hwan Choi* IBF	1986–88
Tacy Macalos* IBF	1988–89

Champion	Reign
German Torres* WBC	1988–89
Yul-Woo Lee* WBC	1989
M. Kittikasem* IBF	1989–90
H. Gonzalez* WBC	1989–90
Michael Carbajal* IBF	1990
Rolando Pascua* WBC	1990
M.C. Castro* WBC	1991
Ricardo Lopez* WBC	1990–
R.S. Voraphin* IBF	1992–97
Chana Porpaoin* WBA	1993–95
Rosendo Alvarez* WBA	1995–
Zolani Petelo* IBF	1997–

*Champion not generally recognized. †Champion retired or relinquished title.

Total Bouts

Name	Years Active	Bouts	Name	Years Active	Bouts
Len Wickwar	1928–47	463	Maxie Rosenbloom	1923–39	299
Jack Britton	1905–30	350	Harry Greb	1913–26	298
Johnny Dundee	1910–32	333	Young Stribling	1921–33	286
Billy Bird	1920–48	318	Battling Levinsky	1910–29	282
George Marsden	1928–46	311	Ted (Kid) Lewis	1909–29	279

Note: Based on records in *The Ring Record Book* and *Boxing Encyclopedia*.

Most Knockouts

Name	Years Active	KOs	Name	Years Active	KOs
Archie Moore	1936–63	130	Sandy Saddler	1944–56	103
Young Stribling	1921–33	126	Sam Langford	1902–26	102
Billy Bird	1920–48	125	Henry Armstrong	1931–45	100
George Odwell	1930–45	114	Jimmy Wilde	1911–23	98
Sugar Ray Robinson	1940–65	110	Len Wickwar	1928–47	93

Note: Based on records in *The Ring Record Book* and *Boxing Encyclopedia*.

World Heavyweight Championship Fights

Date	Winner	Wgt	Loser	Wgt	Result	Site
Sept 7, 1892	James J. Corbett*	178	John L. Sullivan	212	KO 21	New Orleans
Jan 25, 1894	James J. Corbett	184	Charley Mitchell	158	KO 3	Jacksonville, FL
Mar 17, 1897	Bob Fitzsimmons*	167	James J. Corbett	183	KO 14	Carson City, NV
June 9, 1899	James J. Jeffries*	206	Bob Fitzsimmons	167	KO 11	Coney Island, NY
Nov 3, 1899	James J. Jeffries	215	Tom Sharkey	183	Ref 25	Coney Island, NY
Apr 6, 1900	James J. Jeffries	n/a	Jack Finnegan	n/a	KO 1	Detroit
May 11, 1900	James J. Jeffries	218	James J. Corbett	188	KO 23	Coney Island, NY
Nov 15, 1901	James J. Jeffries	211	Gus Ruhlin	194	TKO 6	San Francisco
July 25, 1902	James J. Jeffries	219	Bob Fitzsimmons	172	KO 8	San Francisco
Aug 14, 1903	James J. Jeffries	220	James J. Corbett	190	KO 10	San Francisco
Aug 25, 1904	James J. Jeffries	219	Jack Munroe	186	TKO 2	San Francisco
July 3, 1905	Marvin Hart*	190	Jack Root	171	KO 12	Reno
Feb 23, 1906	Tommy Burns*	180	Marvin Hart	188	Ref 20	Los Angeles
Oct 2, 1906	Tommy Burns	n/a	Jim Flynn	n/a	KO 15	Los Angeles
Nov 28, 1906	Tommy Burns	172	Jack O'Brien	163½	Draw 20	Los Angeles
May 8, 1907	Tommy Burns	180	Jack O'Brien	167	Ref 20	Los Angeles
Jul 4, 1907	Tommy Burns	181	Bill Squires	180	KO 1	Colma, CA
Dec 2, 1907	Tommy Burns	177	Gunner Moir	204	KO 10	London
Feb 10, 1908	Tommy Burns	n/a	Jack Palmer	n/a	KO 4	London
Mar 17, 1908	Tommy Burns	n/a	Jem Roche	n/a	KO 1	Dublin
Apr 18, 1908	Tommy Burns	n/a	Jewey Smith	n/a	KO 5	Paris
June 13, 1908	Tommy Burns	184	Bill Squires	183	KO 8	Paris
Aug 24, 1908	Tommy Burns	181	Bill Squires	184	KO 13	Sydney
Sept 2, 1908	Tommy Burns	183	Bill Lang	187	KO 6	Melbourne
Dec 26, 1908	Jack Johnson*	192	Tommy Burns	168	TKO 14	Sydney
Mar 10, 1909	Jack Johnson	n/a	Victor McLaglen	n/a	ND 6	Vancouver
May 19, 1909	Jack Johnson	205	Jack O'Brien	161	ND 6	Philadelphia
June 30, 1909	Jack Johnson	207	Tony Ross	214	ND 6	Pittsburgh
Sept 9, 1909	Jack Johnson	209	Al Kaufman	191	ND 10	San Francisco
Oct 16, 1909	Jack Johnson	205½	Stanley Ketchel	170¼	KO 12	Colma, CA
July 4, 1910	Jack Johnson	208	James J. Jeffries	227	KO 15	Reno
July 4, 1912	Jack Johnson	195½	Jim Flynn	175	TKO 9	Las Vegas
Dec 19, 1913	Jack Johnson	n/a	Jim Johnson	n/a	Draw 10	Paris
June 27, 1914	Jack Johnson	221	Frank Moran	203	Ref 20	Paris
Apr 5, 1915	Jess Willard*	230	Jack Johnson	205½	KO 26	Havana
Mar 25, 1916	Jess Willard	225	Frank Moran	203	ND 10	New York City
July 4, 1919	Jack Dempsey*	187	Jess Willard	245	TKO 4	Toledo, OH
Sept 6, 1920	Jack Dempsey	185	Billy Miske	187	KO 3	Benton Harbor, MI
Dec 14, 1920	Jack Dempsey	188¼	Bill Brennan	197	KO 12	New York City
July 2, 1921	Jack Dempsey	188	Georges Carpentier	172	KO 4	Jersey City
July 4, 1923	Jack Dempsey	188	Tommy Givvons	175½	Ref 15	Shelby, MT
Sept 14, 1923	Jack Dempsey	192½	Luis Firpo	216½	KO 2	New York City
Sept 23, 1926	Gene Tunney*	189½	Jack Dempsey	190	UD 10	Philadelphia
Sept 22, 1927	Gene Tunney	189½	Jack Dempsey	192½	UD 10	Chicago
July 26, 1928	Gene Tunney	192	Tom Heeney	203½	TKO 11	New York City
June 12, 1930	Max Schmeling*	188	Jack Sharkey	197	DQ 4	New York City
July 3, 1931	Max Schmeling	189	Young Stribling	186½	TKO 15	Cleveland
June 21, 1932	Jack Sharkey*	205	Max Schmeling	188	Split 15	Long Island City
June 29, 1933	Primo Carnera*	260½	Jack Sharkey	201	KO 6	Long Island City
Oct 22, 1933	Primo Carnera	259½	Paulino Uzcudun	229¼	UD 15	Rome
Mar 1, 1934	Primo Carnera	270	Tommy Loughran	184	UD 15	Miami
June 14, 1934	Max Baer*	209½	Primo Carnera	263¼	TKO 11	Long Island City
June 13, 1935	James J. Braddock*	193¾	Max Baer	209½	UD 15	Long Island City
June 22, 1937	Joe Louis	197¼	James J. Braddock	197	KO 8	Chicago
Aug 30, 1937	Joe Louis	197	Tommy Farr	204¼	UD 15	New York City
Feb 23, 1938	Joe Louis	200	Nathan Mann	193½	KO 3	New York City

World Heavyweight Championship Fights (Cont.)

Date	Winner	Wgt	Loser	Wgt	Result	Site
Apr 1, 1938	Joe Louis	202½	Harry Thomas	196	KO 5	Chicago
June 22, 1938	Joe Louis	198¼	Max Schmeling	193	KO 1	New York City
Jan 25, 1939	Joe Louis	200¼	John Henry Lewis	180¾	KO 1	New York City
Apr 17, 1939	Joe Louis	201¼	Jack Roper	204¾	KO 1	Los Angeles
June 28, 1939	Joe Louis	200¾	Tony Galento	233¾	TKO 4	New York City
Sept 20, 1939	Joe Louis	200	Bob Pastor	183	KO 11	Detroit
Feb 9, 1940	Joe Louis	203	Arturo Godoy	202	Split 15	New York City
Mar 29, 1940	Joe Louis	201½	Johnny Paychek	187½	KO 2	New York City
June 20, 1940	Joe Louis	199	Arturo Godoy	201¼	TKO 8	New York City
Dec 16, 1940	Joe Louis	202¼	Al McCoy	180¾	TKO 6	Boston
Jan 31, 1941	Joe Louis	202½	Red Burman	188	KO 5	New York City
Feb 17, 1941	Joe Louis	203½	Gus Dorazio	193½	KO 2	Philadelphia
Mar 21, 1941	Joe Louis	202	Abe Simon	254½	TKO 13	Detroit
Apr 8, 1941	Joe Louis	203½	Tony Musto	199½	TKO 9	St Louis
May 23, 1941	Joe Louis	201½	Buddy Baer	237½	DQ 7	Washington, DC
June 18, 1941	Joe Louis	199½	Billy Conn	174	KO 13	New York City
Sept 29, 1941	Joe Louis	202¼	Lou Nova	202½	TKO 6	New York City
Jan 9, 1942	Joe Louis	206¾	Buddy Baer	250	KO 1	New York City
Mar 27, 1942	Joe Louis	207½	Abe Simon	255½	KO 6	New York City
June 9, 1946	Joe Louis	207	Billy Conn	187	KO 8	New York City
Sept 18, 1946	Joe Louis	211	Tami Mauriello	198½	KO 1	New York City
Dec 5, 1947	Joe Louis	211½	Jersey Joe Walcott	194½	Split 15	New York City
June 25, 1948	Joe Louis	213½	Jersey Joe Walcott	194¾	KO 11	New York City
June 22, 1949	Ezzard Charles*	181¾	Jersey Joe Walcott	195½	UD 15	Chicago
Aug 10, 1949	Ezzard Charles	180	Gus Lesnevich	182	TKO 8	New York City
Oct 14, 1949	Ezzard Charles	182	Pat Valentino	188½	KO 8	San Francisco
Aug 15, 1950	Ezzard Charles	183¼	Freddie Beshore	184½	TKO 14	Buffalo
Sept 27, 1950	Ezzard Charles	184½	Joe Louis	218	UD 15	New York City
Dec 5, 1950	Ezzard Charles	185	Nick Barone	178½	KO 11	Cincinnati
Jan 12, 1951	Ezzard Charles	185	Lee Oma	193	TKO 10	New York City
Mar 7, 1951	Ezzard Charles	186	Jersey Joe Walcott	193	UD 15	Detroit
May 30, 1951	Ezzard Charles	182	Joey Maxim	181½	UD 15	Chicago
July 18, 1951	Jersey Joe Walcott*	194	Ezzard Charles	182	KO 7	Pittsburgh
June 5, 1952	Jersey Joe Walcott	196	Ezzard Charles	191½	UD 15	Philadelphia
Sept 23, 1952	Rocky Marciano*	184	Jersey Joe Walcott	196	KO 13	Philadelphia
May 15, 1953	Rocky Marciano	184½	Jersey Joe Walcott	197¾	KO 1	Chicago
Sept 24, 1953	Rocky Marciano	185	Roland LaStarza	184¾	TKO 11	New York City
June 17, 1954	Rocky Marciano	187½	Ezzard Charles	185½	UD 15	New York City
Sept 17, 1954	Rocky Marciano	187	Ezzard Charles	192½	KO 8	New York City
May 16, 1955	Rocky Marciano	189	Don Cockell	205	TKO 9	San Francisco
Sept 21, 1955	Rocky Marciano	188¼	Archie Moore	188	KO 9	New York City
Nov 30, 1956	Floyd Patterson*	182¼	Archie Moore	187¾	KO 5	Chicago
July 29, 1957	Floyd Patterson	184	Tommy Jackson	192½	TKO 10	New York City
Aug 22, 1957	Floyd Patterson	187¼	Pete Rademacher	202	KO 6	Seattle
Aug 18, 1958	Floyd Patterson	184½	Roy Harris	194	TKO 13	Los Angeles
May 1, 1959	Floyd Patterson	182½	Brian London	206	KO 11	Indianapolis
June 26, 1959	Ingemar Johansson*	196	Floyd Patterson	182	TKO 3	New York City
June 20, 1960	Floyd Patterson	190	Ingemar Johansson	194¾	KO 5	New York City
Mar 13, 1961	Floyd Patterson	194¾	Ingemar Johansson	206½	KO 6	Miami Beach
Dec 4, 1961	Floyd Patterson	188½	Tom McNeeley	197	KO 4	Toronto
Sept 25, 1962	Sonny Liston*	214	Floyd Patterson	189	KO 1	Chicago
July 22, 1963	Sonny Liston	215	Floyd Patterson	194½	KO 1	Las Vegas
Feb 25, 1964	Cassius Clay	210½	Sonny Liston	218	TKO 7	Miami Beach
Mar 5, 1965	Ernie Terrell WBA*	199	Eddie Machen	192	UD 15	Chicago
May 25, 1965	Muhammad Ali	206	Sonny Liston	215¼	KO 1	Lewiston, ME
Nov 1, 1965	Ernie Terrell WBA*	206	George Chuvalo	209	UD 15	Toronto
Nov 22, 1965	Muhammad Ali	210	Floyd Patterson	196¾	TKO 12	Las Vegas
Mar 29, 1966	Muhammad Ali	214½	George Chuvalo	216	UD 15	Toronto
May 21, 1966	Muhammad Ali	201½	Henry Cooper	188	TKO 6	London
June 28, 1966	Ernie Terrell WBA*	209½	Doug Jones	187½	UD 15	Houston
Aug 6, 1966	Muhammad Ali	209½	Brian London	201½	KO 3	London
Sept 10, 1966	Muhammad Ali	203½	Karl Mildenberger	194¼	TKO 12	Frankfurt
Nov 14, 1966	Muhammad Ali	212¾	Cleveland Williams	210½	TKO 3	Houston
Feb 6, 1967	Muhammad Ali	212¼	Ernie Terrell WBA	212½	UD 15	Houston
Mar 22, 1967	Muhammad Ali	211½	Zora Folley	202½	KO 7	New York City
Mar 4, 1968	Joe Frazier*	204½	Buster Mathis	243½	TKO 11	New York City
Apr 27, 1968	Jimmy Ellis*	197	Jerry Quarry	195	Maj 15	Oakland
June 24, 1968	Joe Frazier NY*	203½	Manuel Ramos	208	TKO 2	New York City

Date	Winner	Wgt	Loser	Wgt	Result	Site
Aug 14, 1968	Jimmy Ellis WBA*	198	Floyd Patterson	188	Ref 15	Stockholm
Dec 10, 1968	Joe Frazier NY*	203	Oscar Bonavena	207	UD 15	Philadelphia
Apr 22, 1969	Joe Frazier NY*	204½	Dave Zyglewicz	190½	KO 1	Houston
June 23, 1969	Joe Frazier NY*	203½	Jerry Quarry	198½	TKO 8	New York City
Feb 16, 1970	Joe Frazier NY*	205	Jimmy Ellis WBA	201	TKO 5	New York City
Nov 18, 1970	Joe Frazier*	209	Bob Foster	188	KO 2	Detroit
Mar 8, 1971	Joe Frazier*	205½	Muhammad Ali	215	UD 15	New York City
Jan 15, 1972	Joe Frazier	215½	Terry Daniels	195	TKO 4	New Orleans
May 26, 1972	Joe Frazier	217½	Ron Stander	218	TKO 5	Omaha
Jan 22, 1973	George Foreman*	217½	Joe Frazier	214	TKO 2	Kingston, Jam.
Sept 1, 1973	George Foreman	219½	Jose Roman	196½	KO 1	Tokyo
Mar 26, 1974	George Foreman	224¼	Ken Norton	212¼	TKO 2	Caracas
Oct 30, 1974	Muhammad Ali*	216½	George Foreman	220	KO 8	Kinshasa, Zaire
Mar 24, 1975	Muhammad Ali	223½	Chuck Wepner	225	TKO 15	Cleveland
May 16, 1975	Muhammad Ali	224½	Ron Lyle	219	TKO 11	Las Vegas
July 1, 1975	Muhammad Ali	224½	Joe Bugner	230	UD 15	Kuala Lumpur, Malay.
Oct 1, 1975	Muhammad Ali	224½	Joe Frazier	215	TKO 15	Manila
Feb 20, 1976	Muhammad Ali	226	Jean Pierre Coopman	206	KO 5	San Juan
Apr 30, 1976	Muhammad Ali	230	Jimmy Young	209	UD 15	Landover, MD
May 24, 1976	Muhammad Ali	230	Richard Dunn	206½	TKO 5	Munich
Sept 28, 1976	Muhammad Ali	221	Ken Norton	217½	UD 15	New York City
May 16, 1977	Muhammad Ali	221¼	Alfredo Evangelista	209¼	UD 15	Landover, MD
Sept 29, 1977	Muhammad Ali	225	Earnie Shavers	211¼	UD 15	New York City
Feb 15, 1978	Leon Spinks*	197¼	Muhammad Ali	224¼	Split 15	Las Vegas
June 9, 1978	Larry Holmes*	209	Ken Norton WBC	220	Split 15	Las Vegas
Sept 15, 1978	Muhammad Ali*	221	Leon Spinks	201	UD 15	New Orleans
Nov 10, 1978	Larry Holmes WBC*	214	Alfredo Evangelista	208¼	KO 7	Las Vegas
Mar 23, 1979	Larry Holmes WBC*	214	Osvaldo Ocasio	207	TKO 7	Las Vegas
June 22, 1979	Larry Holmes WBC*	215	Mike Weaver	202	TKO 12	New York City
Sept 28, 1979	Larry Holmes WBC*	210	Earnie Shavers	211	TKO 11	Las Vegas
Oct 20, 1979	John Tate*	240	Gerrie Coetzee	222	UD 15	Pretoria
Feb 3, 1980	Larry Holmes WBC*	213½	Lorenzo Zanon	215	TKO 6	Las Vegas
Mar 31, 1980	Mike Weaver*	232	John Tate WBA	232	KO 15	Knoxville
Mar 31, 1980	Larry Holmes WBC*	211	Leroy Jones	254½	TKO 8	Las Vegas
July 7, 1980	Larry Holmes WBC*	214¼	Scott LeDoux	226	TKO 7	Minneapolis
Oct 2, 1980	Larry Holmes WBC*	211¼	Muhammad Ali	217½	TKO 11	Las Vegas
Oct 25, 1980	Mike Weaver WBA*	210	Gerrie Coetzee	226½	KO 13	Sun City, S.A.
Apr 11, 1981	Larry Holmes	215	Trevor Berbick	215½	UD 15	Las Vegas
June 12, 1981	Larry Holmes	212¼	Leon Spinks	200¼	TKO 3	Detroit
Oct 3, 1981	Mike Weaver WBA*	215	James Quick Tillis	209	UD 15	Rosemont, IL
Nov 6, 1981	Larry Holmes	213¼	Renaldo Snipes	215¾	TKO 11	Pittsburgh
June 11, 1982	Larry Holmes	212½	Gerry Cooney	225½	TKO 13	Las Vegas
Nov 26, 1982	Larry Holmes	217½	Tex Cobb	234¼	UD 15	Houston
Dec 10, 1982	Michael Dokes*	216	Mike Weaver WBA	209¾	TKO 1	Las Vegas
Mar 27, 1983	Larry Holmes	221	Lucien Rodriguez	209	UD 12	Scranton, PA
May 20, 1983	Michael Dokes WBA*	223	Mike Weaver	218½	Draw 15	Las Vegas
May 20, 1983	Larry Holmes	213	Tim Witherspoon	219½	Split 12	Las Vegas
Sept 10, 1983	Larry Holmes	223	Scott Frank	211¼	TKO 5	Atlantic City
Sept 23, 1983	Gerrie Coetzee*	215	Michael Dokes WBA	217	KO 10	Richfield, OH
Nov 25, 1983	Larry Holmes	219	Marvis Frazier	200	TKO 1	Las Vegas
Mar 9, 1984	Tim Witherspoon	220¼	Greg Page	239½	Maj 12	Las Vegas
Aug 31, 1984	Pinklon Thomas*	216	Tim Witherspoon WBC	217	Maj 12	Las Vegas
Nov 9, 1984	Larry Holmes IBF	221½	James Smith	227	TKO 12	Las Vegas
Dec 1, 1984	Greg Page*	236½	Gerrie Coetzee WBA	218	KO 8	Sun City, S.A.
Mar 15, 1985	Larry Holmes	223½	David Bey	233¼	TKO 10	Las Vegas
Apr 29, 1985	Tony Tubbs*	229	Greg Page WBA	239½	UD 15	Buffalo
May 20, 1985	Larry Holmes	224¼	Carl Williams	215	UD 15	Las Vegas
June 15, 1985	Pinklon Thomas*	220¼	Mike Weaver	221¼	KO 8	Las Vegas
Sept 21, 1985	Michael Spinks*	200	Larry Holmes IBF	221½	UD 15	Las Vegas
Jan 17, 1986	Tim Witherspoon	227	Tony Tubbs WBA	229	Maj 15	Atlanta
Mar 22, 1986	Trevor Berbick*	218½	Pinklon Thomas WBC	222¾	UD 15	Las Vegas
Apr 19, 1986	Michael Spinks	205	Larry Holmes	223	Split 15	Las Vegas
July 19, 1986	Tim Witherspoon*	234¾	Frank Bruno	228	TKO 11	Wembley, Eng.
Sept 6, 1986	Michael Spinks	201	Steffen Tangstad	214¾	TKO 4	Las Vegas
Nov 22, 1986	Mike Tyson*	221¼	Trevor Berbick WBC	218½	TKO 2	Las Vegas
Dec 12, 1986	James Smith*	228½	Tim Witherspoon WBA	233½	TKO 1	New York City
Mar 7, 1987	Mike Tyson WBC*	219	James Smith WBA	233	UD 12	Las Vegas
May 30, 1987	Mike Tyson*	218¾	Pinklon Thomas	217¾	TKO 6	Las Vegas
May 30, 1987	Tony Tucker	222¼	Buster Douglas	227¼	TKO 10	Las Vegas
June 15, 1987	Michael Spinks	208¾	Gerry Cooney	238	TKO 5	Atlantic City

Date	Winner	Wgt	Loser	Wgt	Result	Site
Aug 1, 1987	Mike Tyson*	221	Tony Tucker IBF	221	UD 12	Las Vegas
Oct 16, 1987	Mike Tyson*	216	Tyrell Biggs	228¾	TKO 7	Atlantic City
Jan 22, 1988	Mike Tyson*	215¾	Larry Holmes	225¾	TKO 4	Atlantic City
Mar 20, 1988	Mike Tyson*	216¼	Tony Tubbs	238¼	KO 2	Tokyo
June 27, 1988	Mike Tyson*	218¼	Michael Spinks	212¼	KO 1	Atlantic City
Feb 25, 1989	Mike Tyson	218	Frank Bruno	228	TKO 5	Las Vegas
July 21, 1989	Mike Tyson	219¼	Carl Williams	218	TKO 1	Atlantic City
Feb 10, 1990	Buster Douglas*	231½	Mike Tyson	220½	KO 10	Tokyo
Oct 25, 1990	Evander Holyfield	208	Buster Douglas	246	KO 3	Las Vegas
Apr 19, 1991	Evander Holyfield	212	George Foreman	257	UD 12	Atlantic City
Nov 23, 1991	Evander Holyfield	210	Bert Cooper	215	TKO 7	Atlanta
June 19, 1992	Evander Holyfield	210	Larry Holmes	233	UD 12	Las Vegas
Nov 13, 1992	Riddick Bowe	235	Evander Holyfield	205	UD 12	Las Vegas
Feb 6, 1993	Riddick Bowe	243	Michael Dokes	244	KO 1	New York City
May 8, 1993	Lennox Lewis	235	Tony Tucker	235	UD 12	Las Vegas
May 22, 1993	Riddick Bowe	244	Jesse Ferguson	224	KO 2	Washington, DC
Oct 2, 1993	Lennox Lewis	229	Frank Bruno	233	KO 7	London
Nov 6, 1993	Evander Holyfield	217	Riddick Bowe	246	Split 12	Las Vegas
Apr 22, 1994	Michael Moorer	214	Evander Holyfield	214	Split 12	Las Vegas
May 6, 1994	Lennox Lewis	235	Phil Jackson	218	TKO 8	Atlantic City
Nov 6, 1994	George Foreman	250	Michael Moorer	222	KO 10	Las Vegas
Mar 11, 1995	Riddick Bowe	241	Herbie Hide	214	KO 6	Las Vegas
Apr 8, 1995	Oliver McCall	231	Larry Holmes	236	UD 12	Las Vegas
Apr 8, 1995	Bruce Seldon	236	Tony Tucker	243	TKO 7	Las Vegas
Apr 22, 1995	George Foreman	256	Axel Schulz	221	Split 12	Las Vegas
Jun 17, 1995	Riddick Bowe	243	Jorge Luis Gonzalez	237	KO 6	Las Vegas
Aug 19, 1995	Bruce Seldon	234	Joe Hipp	233	TKO 10	Las Vegas
Sept 2, 1995	Frank Bruno	247¾	Oliver McCall	234¾	UD 12	London
Dec 9, 1995	Frans Botha	237	Axel Shulz	223	Split 12	Stuttgart
Mar 16, 1996	Mike Tyson	220	Frank Bruno	247	TKO 3	Las Vegas
June 22, 1996	Michael Moorer	222¼	Axel Shulz	222¾	Split 12	Dortmund, Ger.
Sept 7, 1996	Mike Tyson	219	Bruce Seldon	229	TKO 1	Las Vegas
Nov 9, 1996	Evander Holyfield	215	Mike Tyson	222	TKO 11	Las Vegas
Feb 7, 1997	Lennox Lewis*	251	Oliver McCall	237	TKO 5	Las Vegas
June 28, 1997	Evander Holyfield	218	Mike Tyson	218	DQ 4	Las Vegas
Oct 4, 1997	Lennox Lewis*	244	Andrew Golota	244	TKO 1	Atlantic City
Nov 8, 1997	Evander Holyfield	214	Michael Moorer	223	TKO 8	Las Vegas
Mar 28, 1998	Lennox Lewis*	243	Shannon Briggs	228	TKO 5	Atlantic City

*Champion not generally recognized. KO=knockout; TKO=technical knockout; UD=unanimous decision; Split=split decision; Ref=referee's decision; DQ=disqualification; ND=no decision.

Ring Magazine Fighter and Fight of the Year

Year	Fighter	Year	Fighter	Year	Fighter
1928	Gene Tunney	1935	Barney Ross	1940	Billy Conn
1929	Tommy Loughran	1936	Joe Louis	1941	Joe Louis
1930	Max Schmeling	1937	Henry Armstrong	1942	Ray Robinson
1932	Jack Sharkey	1938	Joe Louis	1943	Fred Apostoli
1934	T. Canzoneri/B. Ross	1939	Joe Louis	1944	Beau Jack

Note: No award in 1933; no fight of the year named until 1945

Year	Fighter	Fight	Winner	Site
1945	Willie Pep	Rocky Graziano–Freddie Cochrane	Rocky Graziano	New York City
1946	Tony Zale	Tony Zale–Rocky Graziano	Tony Zale	New York City
1947	Gus Lesnevich	Rocky Graziano–Tony Zale	Rocky Graziano	Chicago
1948	Ike Williams	Marcel Cerdan–Tony Zale	Marcel Cerdan	Jersey City
1949	Ezzard Charles	Willie Pep–Sandy Saddler	Willie Pep	New York City
1950	Ezzard Charles	Jake LaMotta–Laurent Dauthuille	Jake LaMotta	Detroit
1951	Ray Robinson	Jersey Joe Walcott–Ezzard Charles	Jersey Joe Walcott	Pittsburgh
1952	Rocky Marciano	Rocky Marciano–Jersey Joe Walcott	Rocky Marciano	Philadelphia
1953	Carl Olson	Rocky Marciano–Roland LaStarza	Rocky Marciano	New York City
1954	Rocky Marciano	Rocky Marciano–Ezzard Charles	Rocky Marciano	New York City
1955	Rocky Marciano	Carmen Basilio–Tony DeMarco	Carmen Basilio	Boston
1956	Floyd Patterson	Carmen Basilio–Johnny Saxton	Carmen Basilio	Syracuse
1957	Carmen Basilio	Carmen Basilio–Ray Robinson	Carmen Basilio	New York City
1958	Ingemar Johansson	Ray Robinson–Carmen Basilio	Ray Robinson	Chicago
1959	Ingemar Johansson	Gene Fullmer–Carmen Basilio	Gene Fullmer	San Francisco
1960	Floyd Patterson	Floyd Patterson–Ingemar Johansson	Floyd Patterson	New York City
1961	Joe Brown	Joe Brown–Dave Charnley	Joe Brown	London

Year	Fighter	Fight	Winner	Site
1962	Dick Tiger	Joey Giardello–Henry Hank	Joey Giardello	Philadelphia
1963	Cassius Clay	Cassius Clay–Doug Jones	Cassius Clay	New York City
1964	Emile Griffith	Cassius Clay–Sonny Liston	Cassius Clay	Miami Beach
1965	Dick Tiger	Floyd Patterson–George Chuvalo	Floyd Patterson	New York City
1966	No award	Jose Torres–Eddie Cotton	Jose Torres	Las Vegas
1967	Joe Frazier	Nino Benvenuti–Emile Griffith	Nino Benvenuti	New York City
1968	Nino Benvenuti	Dick Tiger–Frank DePaula	Dick Tiger	New York City
1969	Jose Napoles	Joe Frazier–Jerry Quarry	Joe Frazier	New York City
1970	Joe Frazier	Carlos Monzon–Nino Benvenuti	Carlos Monzon	Rome
1971	Joe Frazier	Joe Frazier–Muhammad Ali	Joe Frazier	New York City
1972	Muhammad Ali Carlos Monzon	Bob Foster–Chris Finnegan	Bob Foster	London
1973	George Foreman	George Foreman–Joe Frazier	George Foreman	Kingston, Jam.
1974	Muhammad Ali	Muhammad Ali–George Foreman	Muhammad Ali	Kinshasa, Zaire
1975	Muhammad Ali	Muhammad Ali–Joe Frazier	Muhammad Ali	Manila
1976	George Foreman	George Foreman–Ron Lyle	George Foreman	Las Vegas
1977	Carlos Zarate	Joe Young–George Foreman	Joe Young	San Juan
1978	Muhammad Ali	Leon Spinks–Muhammad Ali	Leon Spinks	Las Vegas
1979	Ray Leonard	Danny Lopez–Tony Ayala	Danny Lopez	San Antonio
1980	Thomas Hearns	Saad Muhammad–Danny Lopez	Saad Muhammad	McAfee, NJ
1981	Ray Leonard Salvador Sanchez	Ray Leonard–Tonny Hearns	Ray Leonard	Las Vegas
1982	Larry Holmes	Bobby Chacon–Rafael Limon	Bobby Chacon	Sacramento
1983	Marvin Hagler	Bobby Chacon–Cornelius Boza-Edwards	Bobby Chacon	Las Vegas
1984	Thomas Hearns	Jose Luis Ramirez–Edwin Rosario	Jose Luis Ramirez	San Juan
1985	Donald Curry Marvin Hagler	Marvin Hagler–Tommy Hearns	Marvin Hagler	Las Vegas
1986	Mike Tyson	Stevie Cruz–Barry McGuigan	Stevie Cruz	Las Vegas
1987	Evander Holyfield	Ray Leonard–Marvin Hagler	Ray Leonard	Las Vegas
1988	Mike Tyson	Tony Lopez–Rocky Lockridge	Tony Lopez	Inglewood, CA
1989	Pernell Whitaker	Roberto Duran–Iran Barkley	Roberto Duran	Atlantic City
1990	Julio César Chávez	Julio César Chávez–Meldrick Taylor	Julio César Chávez	Las Vegas
1991	James Toney	Robert Quiroga–Kid Akeem Anifowoshe	Robert Quiroga	San Antonio
1992	Riddick Bowe	Riddick Bowe–Evander Holyfield	Riddick Bowe	Las Vegas
1993	Michael Carbajal	Michael Carbajal–Humberto Gonzalez	Michael Carbajal	Las Vegas
1994	Roy Jones	Jorge Castro–John David Jackson	Jorge Castro	Monterrey, Mex.
1995	Oscar De La Hoya	Saman Sor Jaturong–Chiquita Gonzalez	Saman Sor Jaturong	Inglewood, CA
1996	Evander Holyfield	Evander Holyfield–Mike Tyson	Evander Holyfield	Las Vegas
1997	Evander Holyfield	Arturo Gatti–Gabriel Ruelas	Arturo Gatti	Atlantic City

U.S. Olympic Gold Medalists

LIGHT FLYWEIGHT
1984	Paul Gonzales

FLYWEIGHT
1904	George Finnegan
1920	Frank Di Gennara
1024	Fidel LaBarba
1952	Nathan Brooks
1976	Leo Randolph
1984	Steve McCrory

BANTAMWEIGHT
1904	Oliver Kirk
1988	Kennedy McKinney

FEATHERWEIGHT
1904	Oliver Kirk
1924	John Fields
1984	Meldrick Taylor

LIGHTWEIGHT
1904	Harry Spanger
1920	Samuel Mosberg
1968	Ronald W. Harris
1976	Howard Davis
1984	Pernell Whitaker
1992	Oscar De La Hoya

LIGHT WELTERWEIGHT
1952	Charles Adkins
1972	Ray Seales
1976	Ray Leonard
1984	Jerry Page

WELTERWEIGHT
1904	Albert Young
1932	Edward Flynn
1984	Mark Breland

LIGHT MIDDLEWEIGHT
1960	Wilbert McClure
1984	Frank Tate
1996	David Reid

MIDDLEWEIGHT
1904	Charles Mayer
1932	Carmen Bath
1952	Floyd Patterson
1960	Edward Crook
1976	Michael Spinks

LIGHT HEAVYWEIGHT
1920	Eddie Eagan
1952	Norvel Lee
1956	James Boyd
1960	Cassius Clay
1976	Leon Spinks
1988	Andrew Maynard

HEAVYWEIGHT
1984	Henry Tillman
1988	Ray Mercer

SUPER HEAVYWEIGHT
1904	Samuel Berger
1952	H. Edward Sanders
1956	T. Peter Rademacher
1964	Joe Frazier
1968	George Foreman
1984	Tyrell Biggs

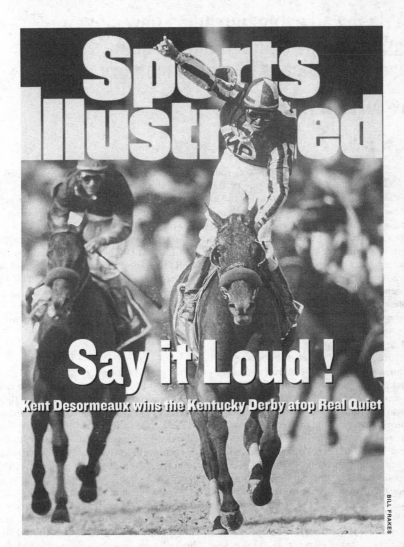

Say it Loud !

Kent Desormeaux wins the Kentucky Derby atop Real Quiet

BILL FRAKES

Go, Baby, Go!

A flashy ad campaign and a new slogan coincided with one of horse racing's most exciting seasons in recent memory

BY WILLIAM F. REED

H E GREW UP in Princeton, Ind., hanging around one of the three pool rooms in town. Owned by his dad, it was called the Palace and considered to be a classier joint than its rivals, Cricket's and the Howdy. It was the sort of place where you could get a cheeseburger for a quarter and Harry Caray's radio play-by-play of the St. Louis Cardinals baseball games for free. For those of a more intellectual bent, a copy of *The Daily Racing Form* was usually available for study.

Last year, on the first Saturday in May, Mike Pegram remembered those times as he prepared to watch a horse he had bought for a paltry $17,000 run in the Kentucky Derby. So despite the fact that he owned 22 McDonald's franchises in Washington State and was wealthy beyond his wildest dreams, Pegram decided to watch the world's most popular race from the area beside the track that's reserved for grooms and hotwalkers. "I started going to races down along the rail," said Pegram. "I thought it was very appropriate to watch that race from where I started."

With his grandson, Gator, sitting on his shoulders, that's where Pegram saw his ultimate dream come true. Down the stretch, Real Quiet, with jockey Kent Des-ormeaux bedecked in red-and-yellow silks, held off a fierce challenge by Victory Gallop to win the 124th running of the race universally known as the Run for the Roses.

When it was over, much to the chagrin of Churchill Downs racing officials and the ABC television network, Pegram held up the trophy presentation until all of his friends—around 50 of them—could be wedged into the winner's circle.

"If you ain't got your friends with you," Pegram said, "you ain't got nothing."

• • •

After years of losing ground in the battle for the sports/entertainment/gambling dollar, thoroughbred racing began to fight back in 1998. The National Thoroughbred Racing Association, a new umbrella group founded to bring unity and cohesion to the fragmented sport, launched a national advertising campaign built around the motto, "Go, baby, go!"

Not everyone in the sport liked the campaign—the TV commercials featuring a streetwise actress yelling the slogan and snapping her fingers as she rooted her horse home especially drew critics' ire—but at least the ads forced the public to

Down to earth: Pegram watched from trackside as Real Quiet ran for the roses.

Quest and Touch Gold gave horseplayers plenty of reason to shout "Go, baby, go!" or a variation thereof.

At the beginning of the year, the racing world was electrified when trainer Patrick Byrne, who had won both 1997 Breeders' Cup juvenile races, announced that he was giving up his public stable to accept a private training job with Canadian industrialist Frank Stronach. This meant saying goodbye to Favorite Trick, the colt who had capped an eight for eight year by winning the '97 Breeders' Cup Juvenile at Hollywood Park. Never before had a trainer willingly walked away from the winter-book favorite for the Kentucky Derby.

The plot thickened when Joseph LaCombe, the principal owner of Favorite Trick, decided to turn the colt over to Bill Mott, who had trained Cigar to 16 consecutive victories and back-to-back horse of the year honors in 1995 and '96. Although Mott is one of the most respected trainers in the game (he was inducted into the Racing Hall of Fame in 1998 at the age of 45), he had never shown any enthusiasm for the Triple Crown races. Instead, he had built his reputation with older horses, many of them grass specialists.

In early February, when it was announced that Favorite Trick had become the first 2-year-old since Secretariat to win horse of the year honors, Byrne and Mott both had mixed feelings because each knew that they would be subjected to a lot of second-guessing, no matter how things worked out. When Mott openly wondered if Favorite Trick was prepared to last the

take a new look at an old sport that for the first half of the century ranked behind only baseball on the list of America's favorite professional sports.

Fortunately for racing, the arrival of the NTRA and its ad campaign dovetailed nicely with a year chockful of talented horses, thrilling races and sparkling personalities. Pegram proved that a guy with a blue-collar background can reach the top of the so-called Sport of Kings. White-haired Bob Baffert became the first trainer ever to go to Belmont two years in a row with a horse that could win the Triple Crown. And jockey Laffit Pincay, 51, continued his relentless pursuit of Bill Shoemaker's alltime record of 8,833 victories.

But primarily there was the most interesting array of horses to come along in years. On the way to the XVth Breeders' Cup on Nov. 7 at Churchill Downs, such luminaries as Skip Away, Silver Charm, Real Quiet, Victory Gallop, Coronado's

Sliver Charm, shown here at the '97 Derby, won the Dubai World Cup.

Derby's mile and a quarter, Byrne bristled and a lot of observers speculated that Mott might be setting up excuses in advance.

But there was no ambivalence surrounding trainer Sonny Hine, whose Skip Away had closed out his 4-year-old season with a smashing victory in the '97 Breeders' Cup Classic. Angered that Skip Away had lost the horse of the year award to a 2-year-old, Hine accused the voters (turf writers, racing secretaries and *Racing Form* correspondents) of failing to give his roan horse the respect he had earned. It was clear that as far as Hine and his wife, Carolyn, (the horse's owner) were concerned, Skip Away's main goal in his 5-year-old season would be to prove how wrong the voters were.

While all this turmoil was roiling, Baffert was still on the magical mystery tour he had begun when his Silver Charm came only three-quarters of a length short of winning the 1997 Triple Crown. After close victories in the Derby and Preakness, Silver Charm had been overtaken by the Stronach-owned Touch Gold in the final strides of the Belmont. Nevertheless, the series established the wisecracking, fast-quipping Baffert as the sport's new media darling, not to mention one of its premier trainers.

In late March, Baffert interrupted his preparations for the 1998 Derby—he was bringing along two colts, Indian Charlie and Real Quiet—to take Silver Charm halfway around the world for the $4 million Dubai World Cup, the world's richest race, along with the Breeders' Cup Classic. On March 28, before a wildly appreciative throng at the Nad Al Sheba track, Silver Charm passed the pace-setting Behrens at the top of the stretch, then held off challenges by Loup Sauvage, Malek and Swain to win by a nose.

"It may not have been his best race," said Gary Stevens, Silver Charm's jockey, "but it was his greatest performance."

A week later Baffert watched Indian Charlie and Real Quiet finish one-two, respectively, in the Santa Anita Derby. Although he respected Real Quiet (he had been able to buy him for Pegram so cheaply because he had a modest pedigree and a crooked front end as a yearling), Baffert believed Indian Charlie, unbeaten in four starts, was a better horse. And as fate would have it in the year of "Go, baby, go!" one of Indian Charlie's owners was

John Gaines, the Kentucky breeder who was a driving force behind the NTRA, just as he had been the founder of the Breeders' Cup in the early 1980s.

Sent off as the favorite in the Derby, Indian Charlie finished third to his lesser-known stablemate. Even so, he wasn't as big a disappointment as Favorite Trick, who came into the Derby following a third-place finish to Victory Gallop in the Arkansas Derby—the first loss of his career.

Favorite Trick was never a factor in the Derby and finished eighth. Mott didn't seem too disappointed, perhaps because he had misgivings going into the race about the colt's ability to handle the classic distances. Instead of sending Favorite Trick on to the Preakness in Baltimore, Mott decided to give him a long layoff before bringing him back in shorter races more suited to his pedigree.

By the time the Preakness field sorted itself out, the race seemed to boil down to a rematch between Real Quiet and Victory Gallop—and that's exactly how it worked out, except this time Real Quiet prevailed by an authoritative 2¼ lengths. The victory was especially meaningful to Desormeaux, a Louisiana native who considers Maryland his second home because of the success he enjoyed there in the late 1980s, when he led the nation's riders in victories for three consecutive years.

"I feel indebted to Maryland," Desormeaux said, "so, I swear, coming to the wire I thought, This is for you, Maryland. This is for all those horsemen who put me on those maidens and claimers to give me the credentials I needed to take on in my career."

Alas, the race at venerable Pimlico is destined to be remembered as the Preakness from Hell. While a fire burned in an air-conditioning unit in the jockeys' room, a transformer three blocks from the track blew, knocking out power in most areas of the track.

On a day when the temperature reached 96°, the grandstand was plunged into darkness for hours, smoke poured out of heating ducts in the clubhouse, and many patrons were without air-conditioning and TV monitors. Said Pimlico senior vice president of racing Karin DeFrancis, "I sure hope it doesn't hurt our image."

But the grumbling was quickly suppressed by the euphoria over Real Quiet's chance to be racing's 12th Triple Crown winner and the first since Affirmed in 1978. As it turned out, he became the 14th Derby-Preakness winner to come up short in the Belmont.

An eighth of a mile from the finish of the 1½-mile classic, Real Quiet had put daylight between him and the rest of the field. He seemed to be a lock, a shoo-in, a cinch. But then here came Victory Gallop, mounting a late charge that cut into Real Quiet's lead with each stride. Ironically, Victory Gallop's jockey was Stevens, who, atop Silver Charm, had lost a Triple Crown bid to Touch Gold the year before.

At the finish it was too close to call. The people around Baffert slapped him on the back and told him he had won the Triple Crown. But Baffert, whose Cavonnier had lost the 1996 Derby in a photo finish with Grindstone, kept his cool. Finally the official order of finish was flashed on the infield tote board: Victory Gallop first, Real Quiet second. For the second consecutive year, Baffert had been denied the trainer's 10% share of the $5 million bonus that Visa had pledged for a Triple Crown winner.

The winning trainer, Elliott Walden, was hobbling on crutches, the result of an injury suffered while playing pickup basketball. Unlike Baffert, Walden is an old-fashioned horseman who believes in letting his horses' performances do his talking for him. Yet his work with Victory Gallop, along with the Churchill Downs training title he won in the spring of 1997, indicates that his horsemanship, if not his repartee with the press, is ready for prime time.

Earlier on the Belmont card, Coronado's Quest won the Riva Ridge Stakes, serving notice that he was finally ready to challenge the nation's best runners. As a 2-year-old,

BILL FRAKES

Victory Gallop (left) edged Real Quiet in a photo finish at the Belmont.

Coronado's Quest flashed so much potential that trainer Shug McGaughey believed he would be a serious Kentucky Derby contender. But the horse proved to be such a head case in Florida, rearing and bucking in the paddock and on the track before three races, that McGaughey decided not to risk putting him in the inferno that is Churchill Downs on Derby Day.

Even after the horse had partially redeemed himself with a win in New York's Wood Memorial, McGaughey didn't change his mind. However, he did plan on running him in the Preakness, only to scratch him the Friday before the race because of a slight foot problem. That set back his training just enough that McGaughey opted for the Riva Ridge instead of the Belmont.

The week after the Belmont, Baffert was back at Churchill Downs to saddle Silver Charm for the Stephen Foster Handicap, his first start since the virtuoso performance in Dubai. Baffert shrugged off

charges from Hine that Silver Charm was ducking Skip Away, who was drilling every field he faced.

"I don't worry about that stuff," Baffert said. "Sonny's got a good horse. I've got a lot of respect for him. But he's got it good right now. The horses he's been running against aren't very tough. He'll get his chance against Silver Charm. But he's probably not going to like the end result."

After the Stephen Foster, named for the noted composer, Baffert had to change his tune a bit. Silver Charm finished second to Awesome Again, who was one of the horses Byrne picked up when he went to work for Stronach. Another was Touch Gold. Sidelined for nearly eight months due to a chronic foot problem, the 1997 Belmont winner announced his return to competition with a blazing allowance-race win at Churchill.

While Byrne suddenly had two of the best handicap horses in the nation, justifying his decision to give up Favorite Trick and go to work for Stronach, Baffert's Midas touch was suddenly missing in action. Silver Charm finished last in the San Diego Handicap, the worst performance of his career, and Real Quiet developed a minor problem that forced him to miss the Aug. 9 Haskell Invitational, where Victory Gallop was beaten by a 1¼ lengths by the rejuvenated Coronado's Quest. At the Travers later that month, Coronado's Quest proved just how rejuvenated he was, winning by a nose over Belmont champ Victory Gallop.

Despite the gripping drama at tracks everywhere and Skip Away's marvelous campaign for vindication, the game's most enduring image at year's end was that of Pegram, erstwhile small-town pool-hall denizen, watching his horse win the Kentucky Derby, surrounded by grooms and hot-walkers and $2 bettors. No high-priced Madison Avenue advertising agency could have produced a better commercial for the NTRA or a sport that's trying to regain the fans that have drifted off to riverboat casinos or NASCAR or wherever else they've gone.

Indeed, Pegram and his friends probably would be the first to shout, with feeling, "Go, baby, go!"

FOR THE RECORD·1997–1998

THOROUGHBRED RACING

The Triple Crown

124th Kentucky Derby

May 2, 1998. Grade I, 3-year-olds; 8th race, Churchill Downs, Louisville. All 126 lbs. Distance: 1¼ miles. Stakes value: $1,038,800; Winner: $738,800; Second: $170,000; Third: $85,000; Fourth: $45,000. Track: Fast. Off: 5:29 p.m. Winner: Real Quiet (B. c, Mar, by Quiet American—Really Blue, by Believe It); Times: 0:22⅘, 0:45⅗, 1:10⅗, 1:35⅗, 2:02⅕. Won: Driving. Breeder:Little Hill Farm.

Horse	Finish-PP	Margin	Jockey/Owner
Real Quiet	1–3	½	Kent Desormeaux/Mike Pegram
Victory Gallop	2–13	2¼	Alex Solis/Prestonwood Farm, Inc.
Indian Charlie	3–8	head	Gary Stevens/Earnhardt and John R. Gaines,
Halory Hunter	4–4	1	Corey Nakatani/Celtic Pride Stable
Cape Town	5–11	8	Jerry Bailey/Overbrook Farm
Parade Ground	6–10	neck	Shane Sellers/W.S.Farish and Stephen C. Hilbert
Hanuman Highway	7–6	neck	D.R. Flores/Budget Stable
Favorite Trick	8–7	6¾	Pat Day/Joseph LaCombe
Nationalore	9–1	4¾	G.F. Almeida/Cho Myung Kwon
Old Trieste	10–14	3¾	R.J. Albarado/Cobra Farm, Inc.
Chilito	11–5	7¼	G. Boulanger/Lazy Lane Farms, Inc.
Robinwould	12–15	4½	Earlie Fires/Dee and William H. Davenport
Artax	13–12	22¾	Chris McCarron/Paraneck Stable
Rock and Roll	14–9	10¾	F.C. Torres/Jenny Craig and Madeleine Paulson
Basic Trainee	15–2	—	J.R. Velazquez/Luis Gambotto and Enrique Oceho

123rd Preakness Stakes

May 16, 1998. Grade I, 3-year-olds; 10th race, Pimlico Race Course, Baltimore. All 126 lbs. Distance: 1$\frac{3}{16}$ miles; Stakes value: $1,000,000; Winner: $650,000; Second: $200,000; Third: $100,000; Fourth: $50,000. Track: Fast. Off: 5:29 p.m. Winner: Real Quiet (B. c, Mar, by Quiet American—Really Blue, by Believe It); Times: 0:23.31, 0:46.50, 1:11.10, 1:35.84, 1:54.75. Won: Driving. Breeder: Little Hill Farm.

Horse	Finish-PP	Margin	Jockey/Owner
Real Quiet	1–10	2¼	Kent Desormeaux/Mike Pegram
Victory Gallop	2–9	¾	Gary Stevens/Prestonwood Farm
Classic Cat	3–3	3¾	Robbie Albarado/Gary M. Garber
Hot Wells	4–7	neck	Edgar Prado/Mike Warren
Black Cash	5–2	head	Shane Sellers/Frank Stronach
Spartan Cat	6–1	9¾	Rick Wilson/Peter Angelos
Baquero	7–6	7¼	Pat Day/Bob and Beverly Lewis
Basic Trainee	8–5	nose	Cornelio Velazquez/Luis A. Gambotto and Enrique Oceho
Cape Town	9–4	5	Jerry Bailey/Overbrook Farm
Silver's Prospect	10–8	—	Frank Douglas/Robert G. Sowder

130th Belmont Stakes

June 6, 1998. Grade I, 3-year-olds; 9th race, Belmont Park, Elmont, NY. All 126 lbs. Distance: 1½ miles. Stakes purse: $1,000,000; Winner: $600,000; Second: $200,000; Third: $110,000; Fourth: $50,000; Fifth: $30,000. Track: Fast. Off: 5:31 p.m. Winner: Touch Gold (Brown Bay Colt, 1994, Deputy Minister-Passing Mood by Buckpasser); Times: 0:23⅗, 49⅕, 1:13⅗, 1:38⅗, 2:04, 2:28⅘. Won: Driving. Breeder: Hill 'n Dale Farm & Holtsinger, Inc.

Horse	Finish-PP	Margin	Jockey/Owner
Victory Gallop	1–9	nose	Gary Stevens/Prestonwood Farm, Inc.
Real Quiet	2–7	6	Kent Desormeaux/Mike Pegram
Thomas Jo	3–1	1¼	Chris McCarron/Earle I. Mack and Team Valor
Parade Ground	4–4	2½	Pat Day/W.S. Farish and Stephen C. Hilbert
Raffie's Majesty	5–8	4	J. Chavez/Barrios and Lester and Prieger
Chilito	6–3	4	R. Davis/Lazy Lane Farms, Inc.
Grand Slam	7–11	neck	Jerry Bailey/R.C. Baker and D. Cornstein and W.L. Mack
Classic Cat	8–5	9½	J. Velazquez/Gary M. Garber
Limit Out	9–6	11	J. Samyn/Joseph V. Shields Jr.
Yarrow Brae	10–10	20	Mike Smith/Mrs. John Magnier and Michael Tabor
Basic Trainee	11–2	—	J. Bravo/Luis A. Gambotto and Enrique Oceho

Major Stakes Races

Late 1997

Date	Race	Track	Distance	Winner	Jockey/Trainer	Purse ($)
Sept 20 ...	Woodward Stakes	Belmont Park	1⅛ miles	Formal Gold	Kent Desormeaux/ W. Perry	500,000
Sept 20 ...	Pegasus Handicap	Meadowlands	1⅛ miles	Behrens	Jerry Bailey/ J. Bond	1,000,000
Sept 20 ...	Woodbine Mile	Woodbine	1 mile	Geri	Chris Antley/ William Mott	500,000
Sept 21 ...	Man O' War	Belmont Park	1³/₈ miles	Influent	Jerry Bailey/ H. Tesher	400,000
Sept 28 ...	Super Derby	Louisiana Downs	1¼ miles	Deputy Commander	Chris McCarron/ W. Dollase	500,000
Oct 4	Flower Bowl Invitational Handicap	Belmont Park	1¼ miles	Yashmak	Corey Nakatani/ H. Cecil	400,000
Oct 4	Queen Elizabeth II Challenge Cup	Keeneland	1⅛ miles	Ryafan	Alex Solis/ J. Gosden	400,000
Oct 11	Alcibiades Stakes	Keeneland	1¹/₁₆ miles	Countess Diana	Shane Sellers/ Patrick Byrne	430,000
Oct 12	Spinster Stakes	Keeneland	1⅛ miles	Clear Mandate	Pat Day/ G. Arnold	542,500
Oct 12	Oak Tree Turf Championship Stakes	Oak Tree	1¼ miles	Rainbow Dancer	Alex Solis/ J. Sahadi	300,000
Oct 18	The Jockey Club Gold Cup	Belmont Park	1¼ miles	Skip Away	Jerry Bailey/ S. Hine	1,000,000
Oct 18	Turf Classic Invitational	Belmont Park	1½ miles	Val's Prince	Mike Smith/ J. Picou	500,000
Oct 18	Moet Champagne Stakes	Belmont Park	1¹/₁₆ miles	Grand Slam	Gary Stevens/ D. Wayne Lukas	400,000
Oct 18	Breeders' Futurity	Keeneland	1¹/₁₆ miles	Favorite Trick	Pat Day/ Patrick Byrne	427,600
Oct 19	Beldame Stakes	Belmont Park	1⅛ miles	Hidden Lake	Richard Migliore/ J. Kimmel	400,000
Oct 19	Canadian International Stakes	Woodbine	1½ miles	Chief Bearhart	Jose Santos/ M. Frostad	1,000,000
Oct 19	Frizette Stakes	Belmont Park	1¹/₁₆ miles	Silver Maiden	Jerry Bailey/ B. McGehee	400,000
Oct 19	E.P. Taylor Stakes	Woodbine	1¼ miles	Kool Kat Katie	Olivier Peslier/ D. Lodor	344,100
Nov 2	Yellow Ribbon Stakes	Santa Anita Park	1¼ miles	Ryafan	Alex Solis/ J. Gosden	500,000
Nov 4	Foster's Melbourne Cup	Flemington, Australia	2 miles	Might and Power	Jim Cassidy/ J. Denham	1,591,665
Nov 8	Breeders' Cup Classic	Hollywood Park	1¼ miles	Skip Away	Mike Smith/ S. Hine	4,030,400
Nov 8	Breeders' Cup Turf	Hollywood Park	1½ miles	Chief Bearhart	Jose Santos/ M. Frostad	1,832,000
Nov 8	Breeders' Cup Sprint	Hollywood Park	6 furlongs	Elmhurst	Corey Nakatani/ J. Sahadi	1,080,880
Nov 8	Breeders' Cup Mile	Hollywood Park	1 mile	Spinning World	Cash Asmussen/ J. Pease	1,007,600
Nov 8	Breeders' Cup Juvenile Fillies	Hollywood Park	1¹/₁₆ miles	Countess Diana	Shane Sellers/ Patrick Byrne	1,000,000
Nov 8	Breeders' Cup Distaff	Hollywood Park	1⅛ miles	Ajina	Mike Smith/ William Mott	1,000,000
Nov 8	Breeders' Cup Juvenile	Hollywood Park	1¹/₁₆ miles	Favorite Trick	Pat Day/ Patrick Byrne	1,000,000
Nov 23	Japan Cup	Tokyo Racecourse	1½ miles	Pilsudski	Mike Kinane/ M. Stoute	2,702,743
Nov 30	Matriarch	Hollywood Park	1¼ miles	Ryafan	Alex Solis/ Robert Frankel	700,000
Nov 30	Hollywood Derby	Hollywood Park	1⅛ miles	Subordination	Jerry Bailey/ G. Sciacca	500,000
Dec 13	Hollywood Starlet	Hollywood Park	1¹/₁₆ miles	Love Lock	Kent Desormeaux/ D. Wayne Lukas	291,000
Dec 14	Hollywood Turf Cup	Hollywood Park	1½ miles	River Bay	Alex Solis/ F. Frankel	500,000
Dec 14	Hollywood Futurity	Hollywood Park	1¹/₁₆ miles	Real Quiet	Kent Desormeaux/ Bob Baffert	470,200

1998 (Through September 14)

Date	Race	Track	Distance	Winner	Jockey/Trainer	Purse ($)
Feb 7	Donn Handicap	Gulfstream Park	1⅛ miles	Skip Away	Jerry Bailey/ Hubert Hine	300,000
Feb 28	Gulfstream Park Handicap	Gulfstream Park	1¼ miles	Skip Away	Jerry Bailey/ S. Hine	500,000
Mar 7	Santa Anita Handicap	Santa Anita Park	1¼ miles	Malek	Alex Solis/ Richard Mandella	1,000,000
Mar 8	Santa Margarita Handicap	Santa Anita Park	1⅛ miles	Toda Una Dama	Concalino Almeida/ Ronald McAnally	300,000
Mar 8	New Orleans Handicap	Fair Grounds	1⅛ miles	Phantom On Tour	Larry Melancon/ L. Whiting	500,000
Mar 14	Fair Grounds Oaks	Fair Grounds	1¹⁄₁₆ miles	Lu Ravi	Willie Martinez/ C. Bowman	300,000
Mar 15	Louisiana Derby	Fair Grounds	1¹⁄₁₆ miles	Comic Strip	Shane Sellers/ Neil Howard	500,000
Mar 15	Santa Anita Oaks	Santa Anita Park	1¹⁄₁₆ miles	Hedonist	Kent Desormeaux/ Randy Bradshaw	250,000
Mar 28	Emirates Dubai World Cup	Nad Al Sheba	1¼ miles	Silver Charm	Gary Stevens/ Bob Baffert	4,000,000
Mar 29	Jim Beam Stakes	Turfway Park	1⅛ miles	Event of the Year	Russell Baze/ Jerry Hollendorfer	600,000
Apr 4	Santa Anita Derby	Santa Anita Park	1⅛ miles	Indian Charlie	Gary Stevens/ Bob Bafffert	750,000
Apr 4	Oaklawn Park Handicap	Oaklawn Park	1⅛ miles	Precocity	Carlos Gonzalez/ Bobby Barnett	750,000
Apr 4	Ashland Stakes	Keeneland	1¹⁄₁₆ miles	Well Chosen	Craig Woods/ D. Wayne Lukas	555,500
Apr 10	Apple Blossom Handicap	Oaklawn Park	1¹⁄₁₆ miles	Escena	Jerry Bailey/ William Mott	500,000
Apr 11	Arkansas Derby	Oaklawn Park	1⅛ miles	Victory Gallop	Alex Solis/ E. Walden	500,000
Apr 11	Bluegrass Stakes	Keeneland	1⅛ miles	Halory Hunter	Gary Stevens/ Nick Zito	700,000
Apr 11	Wood Memorial Stakes	Aqueduct	1⅛ miles	Coronado's Quest	Robbie Davis/ S. McGaughey	500,000
May 1	Kentucky Oaks	Churchill Downs	1⅛ miles	Keeper Hill	David Flores/ Robert Frankel	605,500
May 2	Kentucky Derby	Churchill Downs	1¼ miles	Real Quiet	Kent Desormeaux/ Bob Baffert	1,000,000
May 9	Pimlico Special Handicap	Pimlico	1³⁄₁₆ miles	Skip Away	Jerry Bailey/ Hubert Hine	750,000
May 9	Illinois Derby	Sportsman's Park	1⅛ miles	Yarrow Brae	Willie Martinez/ D. Wayne Lukas	500,000
May 16	The Preakness Stakes	Pimlico	1³⁄₁₆ miles	Real Quiet	Kent Desormeaux/ Bob Baffert	1,000,000
May 25	Metropolitan Handicap	Belmont Park	1 mile	Wild Rush	Jerry Bailey/ Richard Mandella	500,000
May 25	Hollywood Turf Handicap	Hollywood Park	1¼ miles	Storm Trooper	Kent Desormeaux/ N. Drysdale	400,000
May 30	Massachusetts Handicap	Suffolk Downs	1⅛ miles	Skip Away	Jerry Bailey/ Hubert Hine	614,000
May 31	Les Emirats Arabes Unis Prix du Jockey Club	Chantilly, France	1½ miles	Dream Well	Cash Asmussen/ P. Bary	732,830
June 6	Fleur De Lis Handicap	Churchill Downs	1⅛ miles	Escena	Shane Sellers/ William Mott	321,000
June 6	Belmont Stakes	Belmont Park	1½ miles	Victory Gallop	Gary Stevens/ E. Walden	1,000,000
June 13	Stephen Foster Stakes	Churchill Downs	1⅛ miles	Awesome Again	Pat Day/ Patrick Byrne	799,500
June 14	Shoemaker Breeders' Cup Mile	Hollywood Park	1 mile	Labeeb	Kent Desormeaux/ N. Drysdale	532,000
June 21	Queen's Plate	Woodbine	1¼ miles	Archers Bay	Kent Desormeaux/ T. Pletcher	500,000
June 27	Vanity Invitational Handicap	Hollywood Park	1⅛ miles	Escena	Jerry Bailey/ William Mott	350,000
June 28	Hollywood Gold Cup	Hollywood Park	1¼ miles	Skip Away	Jerry Bailey/ Hubert Hine	1,000,000

1998 (Through September 14) *(Cont.)*

Date	Race	Track	Distance	Winner	Jockey/Trainer	Purse ($)
June 28 ...Irish Derby		The Curragh	1½ miles	Dream Well	Cash Asmussen/ P. Bary	1,048,278
July 4 ......Suburban Handicap		Belmont Park	1¼ miles	Frisk Me Now	Ed King/ R. Durso	350,000
July 19 ....Swaps Stakes		Hollywood Park	1⅛ miles	Old Trieste	Chris McCarron/ M. Puype	500,000
July 19 ....Sunset Handicap		Hollywood Park	1½ miles	River Bay	Alex Solis/ Robert Frankel	350,000
July 25 ....King George VI Queen Elizabeth		Ascot, England	1½ miles	Swain	FrankieDettori/ Saeed bin Suroor	956,333
July 26 ....Delaware Handicap		Delaware Park	1¼ miles	Amarillo	Julie Krone/ J. Forbes	501,200
Aug 8 ......Whitney Handicap		Saratoga	1⅛ miles	Awesome Again	Pat Day/ Patrick Byrne	400,000
Aug 9 ......Haskell Invitational		Monmouth Park	1⅛ miles	Coronado's Quest	Mike Smith/ S. McGaughey	1,000,000
Aug 15 ....Pacific Classic		Del Mar	1¼ miles	Free House	Chris McCarron/ P. Gonzalez	1,000,000
Aug 28 ....Personal Ensign Handicap		Saratoga	1¼ miles	Tomisue's Delight	Pat Day/ Neil Howard	400,000
Aug 29 ....Travers Stakes		Saratoga	1¼ miles	Coronado's Quest	Mike Smith/ S. McGaughey	750,000
Aug 30 ....Philip H. Iselin Handicap		Monmouth Park	1⅛ miles	Skip Away	Jerry Bailey/ Hubert Hine	500,000
Sept 7 .....Del Mar Derby		Del Mar	1⅛ miles	Ladies Din	Kent Desormeaux/ J. Canani	300,000
Sept 13 ...Man O' War		Belmont Park	1⅜ miles	Daylami	Jerry Bailey/ Saeed bin Suroor	400,000

1997 Statistical Leaders

Horses

Horse	Starts	1st	2nd	3rd	Purses ($)	Horse	Starts	1st	2nd	3rd	Purses ($)
Skip Away..............11		4	5	2	4,089,000	Silver Charm............7		3	4	0	1,638,750
Gentlemen..............6		4	0	1	2,125,300	Touch Gold..............7		4	0	0	1,522,313
Siphon 6		2	3	0	2,021,000	Marlin....................10		4	0	2	1,521,600
Chief Bearhart 7		5	2	0	2,011,259	Free House............10		3	2	3	1,336,910
Deputy Commander...10		4	2	1	1,849,440	Favorite Trick..........8		8	0	0	1,231,998

Jockeys

Jockey	Mounts	1st	2nd	3rd	Purses ($)	Win Pct	$ Pct*
Jerry Bailey....................1,043		272	186	178	18,260,553	.26	.60
Gary Stevens 942		195	169	141	15,766,501	.21	.54
Mike Smith 1,272		239	201	160	14,703,351	.19	.47
Pat Day..........................1,217		266	207	171	14,060,954	.22	.53
Alex Solis 1,364		253	217	197	13,435,116	.19	.49
Shane Sellers.................1,383		280	259	206	13,036,256	.20	.54
Corey Nakatani.................829		169	121	125	11,306,186	.20	.50
Chris McCarron 643		128	105	91	10,628,231	.20	.50
Kent Desormeaux..........1,053		183	168	146	10,471,490	.17	.47
Jorge Chavez 1,433		258	193	190	9,067,593	.19	.45

*Percentage in the Money (1st, 2nd, and 3rd).

Trainers

Trainer	Starts	1st	2nd	3rd	Purses ($)	Win Pct	$ Pct*
D. Wayne Lukas	850	175	124	109	10,338,957	.21	.48
Richard Mandella	357	67	57	52	9,523,799	.19	.49
William Mott	618	128	116	84	9,474,680	.21	.53
Bob Baffert	427	112	77	73	8,839,328	.26	.61
Jerry Hollendorfer	933	227	152	138	5,185,374	.24	.55
Wallace Dollase	182	48	31	25	5,027,430	.26	.57
Mark Frostad	235	66	43	36	4,863,931	.28	.62
Hubert Hine	132	22	25	19	4,805,791	.17	.50
David Hofmans	292	53	43	38	4,432,542	.18	.46
John Kimmel	431	97	72	55	4,385,872	.23	.52

*Percentage in the Money (1st, 2nd, and 3rd).

Owners

Owner	Starts	1st	2nd	3rd	Purses ($)
Allen E. Paulson	307	66	49	51	5,257,917
Golden Eagle Farm	423	109	61	64	4,414,936
Carolyn Hine	26	7	5	6	4,347,895
Frank Stronach	523	117	79	66	4,239,053
John Franks	839	117	120	111	4,076,273
Sam-Son Farms	146	48	20	23	3,773,463
Robert and Beverly Lewis	222	40	39	31	3,125,776
Augustin Stable	380	87	61	70	2,689,542
Juddmonte Farms, Inc.	134	26	14	18	2,487,969
Overbrook Farm	288	66	44	35	2,347,336

HARNESS RACING

Major Stakes Races

Late 1997

Date	Race	Location	Winner	Driver/Trainer	Purse ($)
Oct 24	BC Two-year-old Filly Trot	Mohawk Raceway	My Dolly	Wally Hennessey/ Nathanial Varty	405,000
Oct 24	BC Two-year-old Colt/Gelding Trot	Mohawk Raceway	Catch As Catch Can	Wally Hennessey/ Osvaldo Formia	405,000
Oct 24	BC Two-year-old Filly Pace	Mohawk Raceway	Take Flight	Luc Ouellette/ Gene Riegle	583,200
Oct 24	BC Two-year-old Colt/Gelding Pace	Mohawk Raceway	Artiscape	Michel Lachance/ Robert McIntosh	665,145
Oct 24	BC Three-year-old Filly Trot	Mohawk Raceway	No Nonsense Woman	Jim Doherty/ Jim Doherty	438,750
Oct 24	BC Three-year-old Colt/Gelding Trot	Mohawk Raceway	Malabar Man	Malvern Burroughs/ Jimmy Takter	594,000
Oct 24	BC Three-year-old Filly Pace	Mohawk Raceway	Stienam's Place	Jack Moiseyev/ Bruce Riegle	492,750
Oct 24	BC Three-year-old Colt/Gelding Pace	Mohawk Raceway	Village Jasper	Paul MacDonell/ William Wellwood	594,000
Nov 7	Three Diamonds Pace	Garden State Park	Mybrowneyedgirl	Cat Manzi/ Noel Daley	506,700
Nov 14	Governor's Cup	Garden State Park	Sealed 'N Delivered	Ron Pierce/ Chris Ryder	590,600

1998 (Through September 24)

Date	Race	Location	Winner	Driver/Trainer	Purse ($)
May 25	New Jersey Classic	Meadowlands	Shady Character	Michel Lachance Brett Pelling	500,000
June 20	North America Cup	Woodbine	Straight Path	Michel Lachance/ Shawn Robinson	1,000,000

Major Stakes Races (Cont.)

1998 (Through September 24) *(Cont.)*

Date	Race	Location	Winner	Driver/Trainer	Purse ($)
July 11	Meadowlands Pace	Meadowlands	Day In A Life	Luc Ouellette/ Monte Gelrod	1,000,000
July 25	Beacon Course Trot	Meadowlands	Muscles Yankee	John Campbell/ Chuck Sylvester	1,000,000
Aug 1	BC Three and up Open Trot	Meadowlands	Moni Maker	Wally Hennessey/ Jimmy Takter	500,000
Aug 1	BC Three and up Mare Pace	Meadowlands	Jay's Table	John Campbell/ Nathanial Varty	282,500
Aug 1	BC Three and up Open Pace	Meadowlands	Red Bow Tie	Luc Ouellette/ Monti Gelrod	340,000
Aug 6	Sweetheart	Meadowlands	Mattaroni	John Campbell/ Robert McIntosh	517,600
Aug 7	P. Haughton Memorial	Meadowlands	Enjoy Lavec	Jimmy Takter/ Conny Stevenson	458,000
Aug 7	Woodrow Wilson	Meadowlands	Grinfromeartoear	Luc Ouellette/ Monti Gelrod	660,250
Aug 8	Hambletonian	Meadowlands	Muscles Yankee	John Campbell/ Chuck Sylvester	1,000,000
Aug 8	Hambletonian Oaks	Meadowlands	Fern	Luc Ouellette/ Arild Eggen	500,000
Sept 24	Little Brown Jug	Delaware, OH	Shady Character	Ron Pierce/ Brett Pelling	566,630

Major Races

The Hambletonian

Ran at The Meadowlands, East Rutherford, NJ, on August 8, 1998.

Horse	Driver	PP	¼	½	¾	Stretch-Margin	Finish-Margin
Muscles Yankee	John Campbell	6	4	3<	1	1-1	1-3
David Raymond	Cat Manzi	1	3	1<	3	3-1	2-3
Kick Tail	Berndt Lindstedt	8	2<	2	2<	2-1	3-3½
Conway Hall	Michel Lachance	9	9	9	9<	7-7¼	4-7¼
Confident Victory	Ron Pierce	7	8	8	7<	6-6	5-8
Giant Keeper	Luc Ouellette	10	7	7	6<	4-5¼	6-8½
Rockaroundtheclock	Wally Hennessey	4	6	5<	4<	5-5½	7-13½
Indurain	Bill O'Donnell	5	1	4	5	8-13¼	8-23
Silver Pine	George Brennan	3	5	x6x	10	10-22¼	9-23½
Armbro Rotary	J.A. Morrill Jr.	2	10	10	8	9x-19¼	10-36

Times: 0:27.4, 0:55.2, 1:24.0, 1:52.2; Fast.

The Little Brown Jug

Ran at the Delaware County Fairgrounds, in Delaware, OH, on September 24, 1998.

Horse	Driver	PP	¼	½	¾	Stretch-Margin	Finish-Margin
Shady Character	Ron Pierce	2	1	1	1	1-½	1-head
Cam Knows Best	George Brennan	1	3	2	2o	2-½	2-head
Day In A Life	Luc Oullette	8	4	3	3	3-1	3-3¾
Aristcape	Michel Lachance	4	7	7	6	4-1¼	4-1
Emergency Signal	Wally Hennessey	5	9	8	7	6-2¾	5-2
Browning Blue Chip	John Campbell	3	6	4o	4o	5-2¼	6-2¼
Givemewhatineed	Tony Morgan	9	5	5	5o	7-3¾	7-2½
Artist Stena	Peter Wrenn	7	8oX	9X	8	8-23¾	8-22
Inaugural Ball	Cat Manzi	6	2o	6o	9	9-DIS	9-31

Time: 0:25⅘, 0:55⅘, 1:23⅕, 1:52⅗; Fast

1997 Statistical Leaders

1997 Leading Moneywinners by Age, Sex and Gait

Division	Horse	Starts	1st	2nd	3rd	Earnings ($)
2-Year-Old Pacing Colts	Rustler Hanover	16	6	3	2	639,931
2-Year-Old Pacing Fillies	Take Flight	14	8	3	1	596,023
3-Year-Old Pacing Colts	Western Dreamer	29	14	7	3	1,349,401
3-Year-Old Pacing Fillies	Stienam's Place	19	14	2	0	897,033
Aged Pacing Horses	Tune Town	27	6	10	5	434,050
Aged Pacing Mares	Ooh's 'n Aah's	25	8	5	4	267,685
2-Year-Old Trotting Colts	Harry's Bar	6	4	1	1	302,332
2-Year-Old Trotting Fillies	My Dolly	12	4	1	3	366,055
3-Year-Old Trotting Colts	Malabar Man	16	13	3	0	1,679,860
3-Year-Old Trotting Fillies	No Nonsense Woman	17	14	3	0	838,563
Aged Trotting Horses	Wesgate Crown	18	7	4	4	949,416
Aged Trotting Mares	Moni Maker	19	9	5	3	942,999

Drivers

Driver	Earnings ($)	Driver	Earnings ($)
Michel Lachance	9,215,388	Ron Pierce	5,229,871
John Campbell	8,922,139	Cat Manzi	4,763,896
Luc Ouellette	6,160,861	Doug Brown	4,700,250
Jack Moiseyev	5,793,124	George Brennan	4,474,022
Tony Morgan	5,576,191	Steve Condren	4,388,081

It Is a Far, Far Bettor Place

Martin Panza, Hollywood Park's 34-year-old racing secretary, probably never had a better idea in his life. While eating dinner with two other track executives in December 1997, Panza marveled at the excitement generated by that day's paltry $73,755 carryover on the pick six, a wager on the winners of six successive races. If railbirds got that worked up over such a shallow pool, he thought, what would they do if the water were deeper?

After six months of aggressive promotion, Hollywood Park guaranteed a $1 million pick-six payout on June 14, 1998. That day a track-record $3.3 million was wagered on the pick six, the largest at Hollywood Park for an event other than a Breeders' Cup or a day that included a simulcast of a Triple Crown race. When Hollywood guaranteed a $1.5 million pool on July 18, the handle rose to $3.8 million for the pick six and nearly $19 million for the day. "It was like sharks feeding," said Hollywood marketing director Keith Chamblin. "All we had to do was throw more chum in the water."

At a time when race tracks all over the country are trying to bolster slipping attendance, Hollywood's experiment is a reminder that the prospect of a mammoth payoff is a powerful lure even for regular gamblers. Call it the Powerball phenomenon: Unlike giveaways of T-shirts or Beanie Babies, this promotion draws the hard-core fans who are more likely to return to the track. "The pick six is a cerebral bet," says William Nadler, director of promotions for the New York Racing Association. "People will spend hours and hours trying to put together a winning ticket."

No one suggests, however, that mental stimulation is the main draw. Says *Washington Post* racing columnist Andrew Beyer, "I don't think there are many things that can excite the imagination quite like a million dollars."

FOR THE RECORD · Year by Year

THOROUGHBRED RACING

Kentucky Derby

Run at Churchill Downs, Louisville, KY, on the first Saturday in May.

Year	Winner (Margin)	Jockey	Second	Third	Time
1875	Aristides (1)	Oliver Lewis	Volcano	Verdigris	2:37¾
1876	Vagrant (2)	Bobby Swim	Creedmoor	Harry Hill	2:38¼
1877	Baden-Baden (2)	William Walker	Leonard	King William	2:38
1878	Day Star (2)	Jimmie Carter	Himyar	Leveler	2:37¼
1879	Lord Murphy (1)	Charlie Shauer	Falsetto	Strathmore	2:37
1880	Fonso (1)	George Lewis	Kimball	Bancroft	2:37½
1881	Hindoo (4)	Jimmy McLaughin	Lelex	Alfambra	2:40
1882	Apollo (½)	Babe Hurd	Runnymede	Bengal	2:40¼
1883	Leonatus (3)	Billy Donohue	Drake Carter	Lord Raglan	2:43
1884	Buchanan (2)	Isaac Murphy	Loftin	Audrain	2:40¼
1885	Joe Cotton (Neck)	Erskine Henderson	Bersan	Ten Booker	2:37¼
1886	Ben Ali (½)	Paul Duffy	Blue Wing	Free Knight	2:36½
1887	Montrose (2)	Isaac Lewis	Jim Gore	Jacobin	2:39¼
1888	MacBeth II (1)	George Covington	Gallifet	White	2:38¼
1889	Spokane (Nose)	Thomas Kiley	Proctor Knott	Once Again	2:34½
1890	Riley (2)	Isaac Murphy	Bill Letcher	Robespierre	2:45
1891	Kingman (1)	Isaac Murphy	Balgowan	High Tariff	2:52¼
1892	Azra (Nose)	Alonzo Clayton	Huron	Phil Dwyer	2:41½
1893	Lookout (5)	Eddie Kunze	Plutus	Boundless	2:39¼
1894	Chant (2)	Frank Goodale	Pearl Song	Sigurd	2:41
1895	Halma (3)	Soup Perkins	Basso	Laureate	2:37½
1896	Ben Brush (Nose)	Willie Simms	Ben Eder	Semper Ego	2:07¼
1897	Typhoon II (Head)	Buttons Garner	Ornament	Dr. Catlett	2:12½
1898	Plaudit (Neck)	Willie Simms	Lieber Karl	Isabey	2:09
1899	Manuel (2)	Fred Taral	Corsini	Mazo	2:12
1900	Lieut. Gibson (4)	Jimmy Boland	Florizar	Thrive	2:06¼
1901	His Eminence (2)	Jimmy Winkfield	Sannazarro	Driscoll	2:07¾
1902	Alan-a-Dale (Nose)	Jimmy Winkfield	Inventor	The Rival	2:08¾
1903	Judge Himes (¾)	Hal Booker	Early	Bourbon	2:09
1904	Elwood (½)	Frankie Prior	Ed Tierney	Brancas	2:08½
1905	Agile (3)	Jack Martin	Ram's Horn	Layson	2:10¾
1906	Sir Huon (2)	Roscoe Troxler	Lady Navarre	James Reddick	2:08⅕
1907	Pink Star (2)	Andy Minder	Zal	Ovelando	2:12⅗
1908	Stone Street (1)	Arthur Pickens	Sir Cleges	Dunvegan	2:15⅕
1909	Wintergreen (4)	Vincent Powers	Miami	Dr. Barkley	2:08⅕
1910	Donau (½)	Fred Herbert	Joe Morris	Fighting Bob	2:06⅖
1911	Meridian (¾)	George Archibald	Governor Gray	Colston	2:05
1912	Worth (Neck)	Carroll H. Schilling	Duval	Flamma	2:09⅖
1913	Donerail (½)	Roscoe Goose	Ten Point	Gowell	2:04⅘
1914	Old Rosebud (8)	John McCabe	Hodge	Bronzewing	2:03⅖
1915	Regret (2)	Joe Notter	Pebbles	Sharpshooter	2:05⅖
1916	George Smith (Neck)	Johnny Loftus	Star Hawk	Franklin	2:04
1917	Omar Khayyam (2)	Charles Borel	Ticket	Midway	2:04⅗
1918	Exterminator (1)	William Knapp	Escoba	Viva America	2:10⅘
1919	Sir Barton (5)	Johnny Loftus	Billy Kelly	Under Fire	2:09⅘
1920	Paul Jones (Head)	Ted Rice	Upset	On Watch	2:09
1921	Behave Yourself (Head)	Charles Thompson	Black Servant	Prudery	2:04⅕
1922	Morvich (½)	Albert Johnson	Bet Mosie	John Finn	2:04⅗
1923	Zev (1½)	Earl Sande	Martingale	Vigil	2:05⅖
1924	Black Gold (½)	John Mooney	Chilhowee	Beau Butler	2:05⅕
1925	Flying Ebony (1½)	Earl Sande	Captain Hal	Son of John	2:07⅗
1926	Bubbling Over (5)	Albert Johnson	Bagenbaggage	Rock Man	2:03⅗
1927	Whiskery (Head)	Linus McAtee	Osmond	Jock	2:06
1928	Reigh Count (3)	Chick Lang	Misstep	Toro	2:10⅖
1929	Clyde Van Dusen (2)	Linus McAtee	Naishapur	Panchio	2:10⅘
1930	Gallant Fox (2)	Earl Sande	Gallant Knight	Ned O.	2:07⅗
1931	Twenty Grand (4)	Charles Kurtsinger	Sweep All	Mate	2:01⅘
1932	Burgoo King (5)	Eugene James	Economic	Stepenfetchit	2:05⅕
1933	Brokers Tip (Nose)	Don Meade	Head Play	Charley O.	2:06⅘

Kentucky Derby *(Cont.)*

Year	Winner (Margin)	Jockey	Second	Third	Time
1934	Cavalcade (2½)	Mack Garner	Discovery	Agrarian	2:04
1935	Omaha (1½)	Willie Saunders	Roman Soldier	Whiskolo	2:05
1936	Bold Venture (Head)	Ira Hanford	Brevity	Indian Broom	2:03⅗
1937	War Admiral (1¾)	Charles Kurtsinger	Pompoon	Reaping Reward	2:03⅕
1938	Lawrin (1)	Eddie Arcaro	Dauber	Can't Wait	2:04⅘
1939	Johnstown (8)	James Stout	Challedon	Heather Broom	2:03⅗
1940	Gallahadion (1½)	Carroll Bierman	Bimelech	Dit	2:05
1941	Whirlaway (8)	Eddie Arcaro	Staretor	Market Wise	2:01⅖
1942	Shut Out (2½)	Wayne Wright	Alsab	Valdina Orphan	2:04⅖
1943	Count Fleet (3)	John Longden	Blue Swords	Slide Rule	2:04
1944	Pensive (4½)	Conn McCreary	Broadcloth	Stir Up	2:04⅕
1945	Hoop Jr. (6)	Eddie Arcaro	Pot o' Luck	Darby Dieppe	2:07
1946	Assault (8)	Warren Mehrtens	Spy Song	Hampden	2:06⅗
1947	Jet Pilot (Head)	Eric Guerin	Phalanx	Faultless	2:06⅘
1948	Citation (3½)	Eddie Arcaro	Coaltown	My Request	2:05⅖
1949	Ponder (3)	Steve Brooks	Capot	Palestinian	2:04⅕
1950	Middleground (1¼)	William Boland	Hill Prince	Mr. Trouble	2:01⅗
1951	Count Turf (4)	Conn McCreary	Royal Mustang	Ruhe	2:02⅗
1952	Hill Gail (2)	Eddie Arcaro	Sub Fleet	Blue Man	2:01⅗
1953	Dark Star (Head)	Hank Moreno	Native Dancer	Invigorator	2:02
1954	Determine (1½)	Ray York	Hasty Road	Hasseyampa	2:03
1955	Swaps (1½)	Bill Shoemaker	Nashua	Summer Tan	2:01⅘
1956	Needles (¾)	Dave Erb	Fabius	Come On Red	2:03⅖
1957	Iron Liege (Nose)	Bill Hartack	Gallant Man	Round Table	2:02⅕
1958	Tim Tam (½)	Ismael Valenzuela	Lincoln Road	Noureddin	2:05
1959	Tomy Lee (Nose)	Bill Shoemaker	Sword Dancer	First Landing	2:02⅕
1960	Venetian Way (3½)	Bill Hartack	Bally Ache	Victoria Park	2:02⅖
1961	Carry Back (¾)	John Sellers	Crozier	Bass Clef	2:04
1962	Decidedly (2¼)	Bill Hartack	Roman Line	Ridan	2:00⅖
1963	Chateaugay (1¼)	Braulio Baeza	Never Bend	Candy Spots	2:01⅘
1964	Northern Dancer (Neck)	Bill Hartack	Hill Rise	The Scoundrel	2:00
1965	Lucky Debonair (Neck)	Bill Shoemaker	Dapper Dan	Tom Rolfe	2:01⅕
1966	Kauai King (½)	Don Brumfield	Advocator	Blue Skyer	2:02
1967	Proud Clarion (1)	Bobby Ussery	Barbs Delight	Damascus	2:00⅗
1968	Forward Pass (Disq.)	Ismael Valenzuela	Francie's Hat	T.V. Commercial	2:02⅕
1969	Majestic Prince (Neck)	Bill Hartack	Arts and Letters	Dike	2:01⅘
1970	Dust Commander (5)	Mike Manganello	My Dad George	High Echelon	2:03⅖
1971	Canonero II (3¾)	Gustavo Avila	Jim French	Bold Reason	2:03⅕
1972	Riva Ridge (3¼)	Ron Turcotte	No Le Hace	Hold Your Peace	2:01⅘
1973	Secretariat (2½)	Ron Turcotte	Sham	Our Native	1:59⅖
1974	Cannonade (2¼)	Angel Cordero Jr.	Hudson County	Agitate	2:04
1975	Foolish Pleasure (1¾)	Jacinto Vasquez	Avatar	Diabolo	2:02
1976	Bold Forbes (1)	Angel Cordero Jr.	Honest Pleasure	Elocutionist	2:01⅗
1977	Seattle Slew (1¾)	Jean Cruguet	Run Dusty Run	Sanhedrin	2:02⅕
1978	Affirmed (1¼)	Steve Cauthen	Alydar	Believe It	2:01⅕
1979	Spectacular Bid (2¾)	Ronald J. Franklin	General Assembly	Golden Act	2:02⅖
1980	Genuine Risk (1)	Jacinto Vasquez	Rumbo	Jaklin Klugman	2:02
1981	Pleasant Colony (¾)	Jorge Velasquez	Woodchopper	Partez	2:02
1982	Gato Del Sol (2½)	Eddie Delahoussaye	Laser Light	Reinvested	2:02⅕
1983	Sunny's Halo (2)	Eddie Delahoussaye	Desert Wine	Caveat	2:02⅕
1984	Swale (3¼)	Laffit Pincay Jr.	Coax Me Chad	At the Threshold	2:02⅖
1985	Spend A Buck (5)	Angel Cordero Jr.	Stephan's Odyssey	Chief's Crown	2:00⅕
1986	Ferdinand (2¼)	Bill Shoemaker	Bold Arrangement	Broad Brush	2:02⅘
1987	Alysheba (¾)	Chris McCarron	Bet Twice	Avies Copy	2:03⅖
1988	Winning Colors (Neck)	Gary Stevens	Forty Niner	Risen Star	2:02⅕
1989	Sunday Silence (2½)	Pat Valenzuela	Easy Goer	Awe Inspiring	2:05
1990	Unbridled (3½)	Craig Perret	Summer Squall	Pleasant Tap	2:02
1991	Strike the Gold (1¾)	Chris Antley	Best Pal	Mane Minister	2:03
1992	Lil E. Tee (1)	Pat Day	Casual Lies	Dance Floor	2:03
1993	Sea Hero (2½)	Jerry Bailey	Prairie Bayou	Wild Gale	2:02⅖
1994	Go for Gin (2½)	Chris McCarron	Strodes Creek	Blumin Affair	2:03⅗
1995	Thunder Gulch (2¼)	Gary Stevens	Tejano Run	Timber Country	2:01⅕
1996	Grindstone (Nose)	Jerry Bailey	Cavonnier	Prince of Thieves	2:01
1997	Silver Charm (Head)	Gary Stevens	Captain Bodgit	Free House	2:02⅖
1998	Real Quiet (½)	Kent Desormeaux	Victory Gallop	Indian Charlie	2:02⅒

Note: Distance: 1½ miles (1875–95), 1¼ miles (1896–present).

Preakness

Run at Pimlico Race Course, Baltimore, Md., two weeks after the Kentucky Derby.

Year	Winner (Margin)	Jockey	Second	Third	Time
1873	Survivor (10)	G. Barbee	John Boulger	Artist	2:43
1874	Culpepper (¾)	W. Donohue	King Amadeus	Scratch	2:56½
1875	Tom Ochiltree (2)	L. Hughes	Viator	Bay Final	2:43½
1876	Shirley (4)	G. Barbee	Rappahannock	Algerine	2:44¾
1877	Cloverbrook (4)	C. Holloway	Bombast	Lucifer	2:45½
1878	Duke of Magenta (6)	C. Holloway	Bayard	Albert	2:41¾
1879	Harold (3)	L. Hughes	Jericho	Rochester	2:40½
1880	Grenada (¾)	L. Hughes	Oden	Emily F.	2:40½
1881	Saunterer (½)	T. Costello	Compensation	Baltic	2:40½
1882	Vanguard (Neck)	T. Costello	Heck	Col Watson	2:44½
1883*	Jacobus (4)	G. Barbee	Parnell		2:42½
1884*	Knight of Ellerslie (2)	S. Fisher	Welcher		2:39½
1885	Tecumseh (2)	Jim McLaughlin	Wickham	John C.	2:49
1886	The Bard (3)	S. Fisher	Eurus	Elkwood	2:45
1887	Dunboyne (1)	W. Donohue	Mahoney	Raymond	2:39½
1888	Refund (3)	F. Littlefield	Judge Murray	Glendale	2:49
1889*	Buddhist (8)	W. Anderson	Japhet	*	2:17½
1890*	Montague (3)	W. Martin	Philosophy	Barrister	2:36¾
1894	Assignee (3)	Fred Taral	Potentate	Ed Kearney	1:49¼
1895	Belmar (1)	Fred Taral	April Fool	Sue Kittie	1:50½
1896	Margrave (1)	H. Griffin	Hamilton II	Intermission	1:51
1897	Paul Kauvar (1½)	C. Thorpe	Elkins	On Deck	1:51¼
1898	Sly Fox (2)	C. W. Simms	The Huguenot	Nuto	1:49⅗
1899	Half Time (1)	R. Clawson	Filigrane	Lackland	1:47
1900	Hindus (Head)	H. Spencer	Sarmation	Ten Candles	1:48⅖
1901	The Parader (2)	F. Landry	Sadie S.	Dr. Barlow	1:47⅕
1902	Old England (Nose)	L. Jackson	Major Daingerfield	Namtor	1:45⅘
1903	Flocarline (½)	W. Gannon	Mackey Dwyer	Rightful	1:44⅘
1904	Bryn Mawr (1)	E. Hildebrand	Wotan	Dolly Spanker	1:44⅕
1905	Cairngorm (Head)	W. Davis	Kiamesha	Coy Maid	1:45⅘
1906	Whimsical (4)	Walter Miller	Content	Larabie	1:45
1907	Don Enrique (1)	G. Mountain	Ethon	Zambesi	1:45⅖
1908	Royal Tourist (4)	E. Dugan	Live Wire	Robert Cooper	1:46⅖
1909	Effendi (1)	Willie Doyle	Fashion Plate	Hilltop	1:39⅘
1910	Layminster (½)	R. Estep	Dalhousie	Sager	1:40⅗
1911	Watervale (1)	E. Dugan	Zeus	The Nigger	1:51
1912	Colonel Holloway (5)	C. Turner	Bwana Tumbo	Tipsand	1:56⅗
1913	Buskin (Neck)	J. Butwell	Kleburne	Barnegat	1:53⅖
1914	Holiday (¾)	A. Schuttinger	Brave Cunarder	Defendum	1:53⅘
1915	Rhine Maiden (1½)	Douglas Hoffman	Half Rock	Runes	1:58
1916	Damrosch (1½)	Linus McAtee	Greenwood	Achievement	1:54⅘
1917	Kalitan (2)	E. Haynes	Al M. Dick	Kentucky Boy	1:54⅖
1918*	War Cloud (¾)	Johnny Loftus	Sunny Slope	Lanius	1:53⅗
1918*	Jack Hare, Jr (2)	C. Peak	The Porter	Kate Bright	1:53⅖
1919	Sir Barton (4)	Johnny Loftus	Eternal	Sweep On	1:53
1920	Man o' War (1½)	Clarence Kummer	Upset	Wildair	1:51⅗
1921	Broomspun (¾)	F. Coltiletti	Polly Ann	Jeg	1:54⅕
1922	Pillory (Head)	L. Morris	Hea	June Grass	1:51⅗
1923	Vigil (1¼)	B. Marinelli	General Thatcher	Rialto	1:53⅗
1924	Nellie Morse (1½)	J. Merimee	Transmute	Mad Play	1:57⅕
1925	Coventry (4)	Clarence Kummer	Backbone	Almadel	1:59
1926	Display (Head)	J. Maiben	Blondin	Mars	1:59⅘
1927	Bostonian (½)	A. Abel	Sir Harry	Whiskery	2:01⅗
1928	Victorian (Nose)	Sonny Workman	Toro	Solace	2:00⅕
1929	Dr. Freeland (1)	Louis Schaefer	Minotaur	African	2:01⅗
1930	Gallant Fox (¾)	Earl Sande	Crack Brigade	Snowflake	2:00⅗
1931	Mate (1½)	G. Ellis	Twenty Grand	Ladder	1:59
1932	Burgoo King (Head)	E. James	Tick On	Boatswain	1:59⅘
1933	Head Play (4)	Charles Kurtsinger	Ladysman	Utopian	2:02
1934	High Quest (Nose)	R. Jones	Cavalcade	Discovery	1:58⅕
1935	Omaha (6)	Willie Saunders	Firethorn	Psychic Bid	1:58⅖
1936	Bold Venture (Nose)	George Woolf	Granville	Jean Bart	1:59
1937	War Admiral (Head)	Charles Kurtsinger	Pompoon	Flying Scot	1:58⅖
1938	Dauber (7)	M. Peters	Cravat	Menow	1:59⅘

Preakness (Cont.)

Year	Winner (Margin)	Jockey	Second	Third	Time
1939	Challedon (1¼)	George Seabo	Gilded Knight	Volitant	1:59⅘
1940	Bimelech (3)	F. A. Smith	Mioland	Gallahadion	1:58⅗
1941	Whirlaway (5½)	Eddie Arcaro	King Cole	Our Boots	1:58⅘
1942	Alsab (1)	B. James	Requested Sun Again	(dead heat for second)	1:57
1943	Count Fleet (8)	Johnny Longden	Blue Swords	Vincentive	1:57⅖
1944	Pensive (¾)	Conn McCreary	Platter	Stir Up	1:59⅕
1945	Polynesian (2½)	W. D. Wright	Hoop Jr.	Darby Dieppe	1:58⅘
1946	Assault (Neck)	Warren Mehrtens	Lord Boswell	Hampden	2:01⅖
1947	Faultless (1¼)	Doug Dodson	On Trust	Phalanx	1:59
1948	Citation (5½)	Eddie Arcaro	Vulcan's Forge	Boyard	2:02⅖
1949	Capot (Head)	Ted Atkinson	Palestinian	Noble Impulse	1:56
1950	Hill Prince (5)	Eddie Arcaro	Middleground	Dooley	1:59⅕
1951	Bold (7)	Eddie Arcaro	Counterpoint	Alerted	1:56⅖
1952	Blue Man (3½)	Conn McCreary	Jampol	One Count	1:57⅖
1953	Native Dancer (Neck)	Eric Guerin	Jamie K.	Royal Bay Gem	1:57⅘
1954	Hasty Road (Neck)	Johnny Adams	Correlation	Hasseyampa	1:57⅖
1955	Nashua (1)	Eddie Arcaro	Saratoga	Traffic Judge	1:54⅗
1956	Fabius (¾)	Bill Hartack	Needles	No Regrets	1:58⅖
1957	Bold Ruler (2)	Eddie Arcaro	Iron Liege	Inside Tract	1:56⅕
1958	Tim Tam (1½)	I. Valenzuela	Lincoln Road	Gone Fishin'	1:57⅕
1959	Royal Orbit (4)	William Harmatz	Sword Dancer	Dunce	1:57
1960	Bally Ache (4)	Bobby Ussery	Victoria Park	Celtic Ash	1:57⅗
1961	Carry Back (¾)	Johnny Sellers	Globemaster	Crozier	1:57⅗
1962	Greek Money (Nose)	John Rotz	Ridan	Roman Line	1:56⅕
1963	Candy Spots (3½)	Bill Shoemaker	Chateaugay	Never Bend	1:56⅕
1964	Northern Dancer (2¼)	Bill Hartack	The Scoundrel	Hill Rise	1:56⅘
1965	Tom Rolfe (Neck)	Ron Turcotte	Dapper Dan	Hail to All	1:56⅕
1966	Kauai King (1¾)	Don Brumfield	Stupendous	Amberoid	1:55⅖
1967	Damascus (2¼)	Bill Shoemaker	In Reality	Proud Clarion	1:55⅕
1968	Forward Pass (6)	I. Valenzuela	Out of the Way	Nodouble	1:56⅘
1969	Majestic Prince (Head)	Bill Hartack	Arts and Letters	Jay Ray	1:55⅗
1970	Personality (Neck)	Eddie Belmonte	My Dad George	Silent Screen	1:56⅕
1971	Canonero II (1½)	Gustavo Avila	Eastern Fleet	Jim French	1:54
1972	Bee Bee Bee (1¼)	Eldon Nelson	No Le Hace	Key to the Mint	1:55⅗
1973	Secretariat (2½)	Ron Turcotte	Sham	Our Native	1:54⅖
1974	Little Current (7)	Miguel Rivera	Neapolitan Way	Cannonade	1:54⅗
1975	Master Derby (1)	Darrel McHargue	Foolish Pleasure	Diabolo	1:56⅖
1976	Elocutionist (3)	John Lively	Play the Red	Bold Forbes	1:55
1977	Seattle Slew (1½)	Jean Cruguet	Iron Constitution	Run Dusty Run	1:54⅖
1978	Affirmed (Neck)	Steve Cauthen	Alydar	Believe It	1:54⅖
1979	Spectacular Bid (5½)	Ron Franklin	Golden Act	Screen King	1:54⅕
1980	Codex (4¾)	Angel Cordero Jr.	Genuine Risk	Colonel Moran	1:54⅕
1981	Pleasant Colony (1)	Jorge Velasquez	Bold Ego	Paristo	1:54⅗
1982	Aloma's Ruler (½)	Jack Kaenel	Linkage	Cut Away	1:55⅖
1983	Deputed Testamony (2¾)	Donald Miller Jr.	Desert Wine	High Honors	1:55⅖
1984	Gate Dancer (1½)	Angel Cordero Jr.	Play On	Fight Over	1:53⅗
1985	Tank's Prospect (Head)	Pat Day	Chief's Crown	Eternal Prince	1:53⅖
1986	Snow Chief (4)	Alex Solis	Ferdinand	Broad Brush	1:54⅘
1987	Alysheba (½)	Chris McCarron	Bet Twice	Cryptoclearance	1:55⅘
1988	Risen Star (1¼)	E. Delahoussaye	Brian's Time	Winning Colors	1:56⅕
1989	Sunday Silence (Nose)	Pat Valenzuela	Easy Goer	Rock Point	1:53⅘
1990	Summer Squall (2¼)	Pat Day	Unbridled	Mister Frisky	1:53⅗
1991	Hansel (Head)	Jerry Bailey	Corporate Report	Mane Minister	1:54
1992	Pine Bluff (¾)	Chris McCarron	Alydeed	Casual Lies	1:55⅗
1993	Prairie Bayou (½)	Mike Smith	Cherokee Run	El Bakan	1:56⅗
1994	Tabasco Cat (¾)	Pat Day	Go For Gin	Concern	1:56⅖
1995	Timber Country (½)	Pat Day	Oliver's Twist	Thunder Gulch	1:54⅖
1996	Louis Quatorze (3¼)	Pat Day	Skip Away	Editor's Note	1:53⅖
1997	Silver Charm (Head)	Gary Stevens	Free House	Captain Bodgit	1:54⅖
1998	Real Quiet (2¼)	Kent Desormeaux	Victory Gallop	Classic Cat	1:54⅗

*Preakness was a two-horse race in 1883, '84 and '89. It was not run 1891–1893; and in 1918, it was run in two divisions.

Note: Distance: 1½ miles (1873–88), 1¼ miles (1889), 1½ miles (1890), 1 1/16 miles (1894–1900), 1 mile and 70 yards (1901–1907), 1 1/16 miles (1908), 1 mile (1909–10), 1⅛ miles (1911–24), 1 3/16 miles (1925–present).

Belmont

Run at Belmont Park, Elmont, NY, three weeks after the Preakness Stakes. Held previously at two locations in the Bronx, NY: Jerome Park (1867–1889) and Morris Park (1890–1904).

Year	Winner (Margin)	Jockey	Second	Third	Time
1867	Ruthless (Head)	J. Gilpatrick	De Courcy	Rivoli	3:05
1868	General Duke (2)	R. Swim	Northumberland	Fannie Ludlow	3:02
1869	Fenian (Unknown)	C. Miller	Glenelg	Invercauld	3:04¼
1870	Kingfisher (½)	E. Brown	Foster	Midday	2:59½
1871	Harry Bassett (3)	W. Miller	Stockwood	By-the-Sea	2:56
1872	Joe Daniels (¾)	James Rowe	Meteor	Shylock	2:58¼
1873	Springbok (4)	James Rowe	Count d'Orsay	Strachino	3:01¾
1874	Saxon (Neck)	G. Barbee	Grinstead	Aaron Pennington	2:39½
1875	Calvin (2)	R. Swim	Aristides	Milner	2:40¼
1876	Algerine (Head)	W. Donahue	Fiddlestick	Barricade	2:40½
1877	Cloverbrook (1)	C. Holloway	Loiterer	Baden-Baden	2:46
1878	Duke of Magenta (2)	L. Hughes	Bramble	Sparta	2:43½
1879	Spendthrift (5)	S. Evans	Monitor	Jericho	2:42¾
1880	Grenada (½)	L. Hughes	Ferncliffe	Turenne	2:47
1881	Saunterer (Neck)	T. Costello	Eole	Baltic	2:47
1882	Forester (5)	James McLaughlin	Babcock	Wyoming	2:43
1883	George Kinney (2)	James McLaughlin	Trombone	Renegade	2:42½
1884	Panique (½)	James McLaughlin	Knight of Ellerslie	Himalaya	2:42
1885	Tyrant (3½)	Paul Duffy	St. Augustine	Tecumseh	2:43
1886	Inspector B (1)	James McLaughlin	The Bard	Linden	2:41
1887	Hanover (28-32)	James McLaughlin	Oneko		2:43½
1888	Sir Dixon (12)	James McLaughlin	Prince Royal		2:40¼
1889	Eric (Head)	W. Hayward	Diable	Zephyrus	2:47
1890	Burlington (1)	S. Barnes	Devotee	Padishah	2:07¾
1891	Foxford (Neck)	E. Garrison	Montana	Laurestan	2:08¾
1892	Patron (Unknown)	W. Hayward	Shellbark		2:17
1893	Comanche (Head)(21)	Willie Simms	Dr. Rice	Rainbow	1:53¼
1894	Henry of Navarre (2-4)	Willie Simms	Prig	Assignee	1:56½
1895	Belmar (Head)	Fred Taral	Counter Tenor	Nanki Pooh	2:11½
1896	Hastings (Neck)	H. Griffin	Handspring	Hamilton II	2:24½
1897	Scottish Chieftain (1)	J. Scherrer	On Deck	Octagon	2:23¼
1898	Bowling Brook (8)	P. Littlefield	Previous	Hamburg	2:32
1899	Jean Bereaud (Head)	R. R. Clawson	Half Time	Glengar	2:23
1900	Ildrim (Head)	N. Turner	Petrucio	Missionary	2:21½
1901	Commando (½)	H. Spencer	The Parader	All Green	2:21
1902	Masterman (2)	John Bullmann	Ranald	King Hanover	2:22½
1903	Africander (2)	John Bullmann	Whorler	Red Knight	2:23⅕
1904	Delhi (3½)	George Odom	Graziallo	Rapid Water	2:06⅗
1905	Tanya (1/2)	E. Hildebrand	Blandy	Hot Shot	2:08
1906	Burgomaster (4)	L. Lyne	The Quail	Accountant	2:20
1907	Peter Pan (1)	G. Mountain	Superman	Frank Gill	Unknown
1908	Colin (Head)	Joe Notter	Fair Play	King James	Unknown
1909	Joe Madden (8)	E. Dugan	Wise Mason	Donald MacDonald	2:21⅗
1910*	Sweep (6)	J. Butwell	Duke of Ormonde		2:22
1913	Prince Eugene (½)	Roscoe Troxler	Rock View	Flying Fairy	2:18
1914	Luke McLuke (8)	M. Buxton	Gainer	Charlestonian	2:20
1915	The Finn (4)	G. Byrne	Half Rock	Pebbles	2:18⅖
1916	Friar Rock (3)	E. Haynes	Spur	Churchill	2:22
1917	Hourless (10)	J. Butwell	Skeptic	Wonderful	2:17⅘
1918	Johren (2)	Frank Robinson	War Cloud	Cum Sah	2:20⅖
1919	Sir Barton (5)	Johnny Loftus	Sweep On	Natural Bridge	2:17⅖
1920	Man o' War (20)	Clarence Kummer	Donnacona		2:14⅕
1921	Grey Lag (3)	Earl Sande	Sporting Blood	Leonardo II	2:16⅘
1922	Pillory (2)	C. H. Miller	Snob II	Hea	2:18⅘
1923	Zev (1½)	Earl Sande	Chickvale	Rialto	2:19
1924	Mad Play (2)	Earl Sande	Mr. Mutt	Modest	2:18⅘
1925	American Flag (8)	Albert Johnson	Dangerous	Swope	2:16⅘
1926	Crusader (1)	Albert Johnson	Espino	Haste	2:32⅕
1927	Chance Shot (1½)	Earl Sande	Bois de Rose	Flambino	2:32⅖
1928	Vito (3)	Clarence Kummer	Genie	Diavolo	2:33⅕

Belmont *(Cont.)*

Year	Winner (Margin)	Jockey	Second	Third	Time
1929	Blue Larkspur (¾)	Mack Garner	African	Jack High	2:32⅘
1930	Gallant Fox (3)	Earl Sande	Whichone	Questionnaire	2:31⅗
1931	Twenty Grand (10)	Charles Kurtsinger	Sun Meadow	Jamestown	2:29⅗
1932	Faireno (1½)	T. Malley	Osculator	Flag Pole	2:32⅘
1933	Hurryoff (1½)	Mack Garner	Nimbus	Union	2:32⅗
1934	Peace Chance (6)	W. D. Wright	High Quest	Good Goods	2:29⅕
1935	Omaha (1½)	Willie Saunders	Firethorn	Rosemont	2:30⅗
1936	Granville (Nose)	James Stout	Mr. Bones	Hollyrood	2:30
1937	War Admiral (3)	Charles Kurtsinger	Sceneshifter	Vamoose	2:28⅗
1938	Pasteurized (Neck)	James Stout	Dauber	Cravat	2:29⅖
1939	Johnstown (5)	James Stout	Belay	Gilded Knight	2:29⅗
1940	Bimelech (¾)	F. A. Smith	Your Chance	Andy K	2:29⅗
1941	Whirlaway (2½)	Eddie Arcaro	Robert Morris	Yankee Chance	2:31
1942	Shut Out (2)	Eddie Arcaro	Alsab	Lochinvar	2:29⅕
1943	Count Fleet (25)	Johnny Longden	Fairy Manhurst	Deseronto	2:28⅕
1944	Bounding Home (½)	G. L. Smith	Pensive	Bull Dandy	2:32⅕
1945	Pavot (5)	Eddie Arcaro	Wildlife	Jeep	2:30⅕
1946	Assault (3)	Warren Mehrtens	Natchez	Cable	2:30⅘
1947	Phalanx (5)	R. Donoso	Tide Rips	Tailspin	2:29⅖
1948	Citation (8)	Eddie Arcaro	Better Self	Escadru	2:28⅕
1949	Capot (½)	Ted Atkinson	Ponder	Palestinian	2:30⅕
1950	Middleground (1)	William Boland	Lights Up	Mr. Trouble	2:28⅗
1951	Counterpoint (4)	D. Gorman	Battlefield	Battle Morn	2:29
1952	One Count (2½)	Eddie Arcaro	Blue Man	Armageddon	2:30⅕
1953	Native Dancer (Neck)	Eric Guerin	Jamie K.	Royal Bay Gem	2:38⅗
1954	High Gun (Neck)	Eric Guerin	Fisherman	Limelight	2:30⅘
1955	Nashua (9)	Eddie Arcaro	Blazing Count	Portersville	2:29
1956	Needles (Neck)	David Erb	Career Boy	Fabius	2:29⅘
1957	Gallant Man (8)	Bill Shoemaker	Inside Tract	Bold Ruler	2:26⅗
1958	Cavan (6)	Pete Anderson	Tim Tam	Flamingo	2:30⅕
1959	Sword Dancer (¾)	Bill Shoemaker	Bagdad	Royal Orbit	2:28⅖
1960	Celtic Ash (5½)	Bill Hartack	Venetian Way	Disperse	2:29⅗
1961	Sherluck (2¼)	Braulio Baeza	Globemaster	Guadalcanal	2:29⅕
1962	Jaipur (Nose)	Bill Shoemaker	Admiral's Voyage	Crimson Satan	2:28⅘
1963	Chateaugay (2½)	Braulio Baeza	Candy Spots	Choker	2:30⅕
1964	Quadrangle (2)	Manuel Ycaza	Roman Brother	Northern Dancer	2:28⅖
1965	Hail to All (Neck)	John Sellers	Tom Rolfe	First Family	2:28⅖
1966	Amberold (2½)	William Boland	Buffle	Advocator	2:29⅗
1967	Damascus (2½)	Bill Shoemaker	Cool Reception	Gentleman James	2:28⅘
1968	Stage Door Johnny (1¼)	Hellodoro Gustines	Forward Pass	Call Me Prince	2:27⅕
1969	Arts and Letters (5½)	Braulio Baeza	Majestic Prince	Dike	2:28⅘
1970	High Echelon (¾)	John L. Rotz	Needles N Pins	Naskra	2:34
1971	Pass Catcher (¾)	Walter Blum	Jim French	Bold Reason	2:30⅖
1972	Riva Ridge (7)	Ron Turcotte	Ruritania	Cloudy Dawn	2:28
1973	Secretariat (31)	Ron Turcotte	Twice a Prince	My Gallant	2:24
1974	Little Current (7)	Miguel A. Rivera	Jolly Johu	Cannonade	2:29⅕
1975	Avatar (Neck)	Bill Shoemaker	Foolish Pleasure	Master Derby	2:28⅕
1976	Bold Forbes (Neck)	Angel Cordero Jr.	McKenzie Bridge	Great Contractor	2:29
1977	Seattle Slew (4)	Jean Cruguet	Run Dusty Run	Sanhedrin	2:29⅗
1978	Affirmed (Head)	Steve Cauthen	Alydar	Darby Creek Road	2:26⅘
1979	Coastal (3¼)	Ruben Hernandez	Golden Act	Spectacular Bid	2:28⅗
1980	Temperence Hill (2)	Eddie Maple	Genuine Risk	Rockhill Native	2:29⅘
1981	Summing (Neck)	George Martens	Highland Blade	Pleasant Colony	2:29
1982	Conquistador Cielo (14½)	Laffit Pincay, Jr.	Gato Del Sol	Illuminate	2:28⅕
1983	Caveat (3½)	Laffit Pincay Jr.	Slew o'Gold	Barberstown	2:27⅘
1984	Swale (4)	Laffit Pincay Jr.	Pine Circle	Morning Bob	2:27⅕
1985	Creme Fraiche (½)	Eddie Maple	Stephan's Odyssey	Chief's Crown	2:27
1986	Danzig Connection (1¼)	Chris McCarron	Johns Treasure	Ferdinand	2:29⅘
1987	Bet Twice (14)	Craig Perret	Cryptoclearance	Gulch	2:28⅕
1988	Risen Star (14¾)	Eddie Delahoussaye	Kingpost	Brian's Time	2:26⅖

Belmont (Cont.)

Year	Winner (Margin)	Jockey	Second	Third	Time
1989	Easy Goer (8)	Pat Day	Sunday Silence	Le Voyageur	2:26
1990	Go and Go (8¼)	Michael Kinane	Thirty Six Red	Baron de Vaux	2:27⅕
1991	Hansel (Head)	Jerry Bailey	Strike the Gold	Mane Minister	2:28
1992	A.P. Indy (¾)	Eddie Delahoussaye	My Memoirs	Pine Bluff	2:26
1993	Colonial Affair (2¼)	Julie Krone	Kissin Kris	Wild Gale	2:29⅘
1994	Tabasco Cat (2)	Pat Day	Go For Gin	Strodes Creek	2:26⅘
1995	Thunder Gulch (2)	Gary Stevens	Star Standard	Citadeed	2:32
1996	Editor's Note (1)	Rene Douglas	Skip Away	My Flag	2:28⅘
1997	Touch Gold (¾)	Chris McCarron	Silver Charm	Free House	2:28⅘
1998	Victory Gallop (Nose)	Gary Stevens	Real Quiet	Thomas Jo	2:28⅘

*Belmont was a two-horse race in 1887, 88, 92, 1910 and '20; and was not held in 1911–1912.
Note: Distance: 1 mile 5 furlongs (1867–89), 1¼ miles (1890–1905), 1⅜ miles (1906–25), 1½ miles (1926–present).

Triple Crown Winners

Year	Horse	Jockey	Owner	Trainer
1919	Sir Barton	John Loftus	J. K. L. Ross	H. G. Bedwell
1930	Gallant Fox	Earle Sande	Belair Stud	James Fitzsimmons
1935	Omaha	William Saunders	Belair Stud	James Fitzsimmons
1937	War Admiral	Charles Kurtsinger	Samuel D. Riddle	George Conway
1941	Whirlaway	Eddie Arcaro	Calumet Farm	Ben Jones
1943	Count Fleet	John Longden	Mrs J. D. Hertz	Don Cameron
1946	Assault	Warren Mehrtens	King Ranch	Max Hirsch
1948	Citation	Eddie Arcaro	Calumet Farm	Jimmy Jones
1973	Secretariat	Ron Turcotte	Meadow Stable	Lucien Laurin
1977	Seattle Slew	Jean Cruguet	Karen L. Taylor	William H. Turner Jr.
1978	Affirmed	Steve Cauthen	Harbor View Farm	Laz Barrera

Awards

Horse of the Year

Year	Horse	Owner	Trainer	Breeder
1936	Granville	Belair Stud	James Fitzsimmons	Belair Stud
1937	War Admiral	Samuel D. Riddle	George Conway	Mrs. Samuel D. Riddle
1938	Seabiscuit	Charles S. Howard	Tom Smith	Wheatley Stable
1939	Challedon	William L. Brann	Louis J. Schaefer	Branncastle Farm
1940	Challedon	William L. Brann	Louis J. Schaefer	Branncastle Farm
1941	Whirlaway	Calumet Farm	Ben Jones	Calumet Farm
1942	Whirlaway	Calumet Farm	Ben Jones	Calumet Farm
1943	Count Fleet	Mrs. John D. Hertz	Don Cameron	Mrs. John D. Hertz
1944	Twilight Tear	Calumet Farm	Ben Jones	Calumet Farm
1945	Busher	Louis B. Mayer	George Odom	Idle Hour Stock Farm
1946	Assault	King Ranch	Max Hirsch	King Ranch
1947	Armed	Calumet Farm	Jimmy Jones	Calumet Farm
1948	Citation	Calumet Farm	Jimmy Jones	Calumet Farm
1949	Capot	Greentree Stable	John M. Gaver Sr.	Greentree Stable
1950	Hill Prince	C.T. Chenery	Casey Hayes	C.T. Chenery
1951	Counterpoint	C.V. Whitney	Syl Veitch	C.V. Whitney
1952	One Count	Mrs. W. M. Jeffords	O. White	W M. Jeffords
1953	Tom Fool	Greentree Stable	John M. Gaver Sr.	D.A. Headley
1954	Native Dancer	A.G. Vanderbilt	Bill Winfrey	A.G. Vanderbilt
1955	Nashua	Belair Stud	James Fitzsimmons	Belair Stud
1956	Swaps	Ellsworth-Galbreath	Mesh Tenney	R. Ellsworth
1957	Bold Ruler	Wheatley Stable	James Fitzsimmons	Wheatley Stable
1958	Round Table	Kerr Stables	Willy Molter	Claiborne Farm
1959	Sword Dancer	Brookmeade Stable	Elliott Burch	Brookmeade Stable
1960	Kelso	Bohemia Stable	C. Hanford	Mrs. R.C. duPont
1961	Kelso	Bohemia Stable	C. Hanford	Mrs. R.C. duPont
1962	Kelso	Bohemia Stable	C. Hanford	Mrs. R.C. duPont
1963	Kelso	Bohemia Stable	C. Hanford	Mrs. R.C. duPont
1964	Kelso	Bohemia Stable	C. Hanford	Mrs. R.C. duPont
1965	Roman Brother	Harbor View Stable	Burley Parke	Ocala Stud
1966	Buckpasser	Ogden Phipps	Eddie Neloy	Ogden Phipps
1967	Damascus	Mrs. E. W. Bancroft	Frank Y. Whiteley Jr.	Mrs. E. W. Bancroft

Horse of the Year (Cont.)

Year	Horse	Owner	Trainer	Breeder
1968	Dr. Fager	Tartan Stable	John A. Nerud	Tartan Farms
1969	Arts and Letters	Rokeby Stable	Elliott Burch	Paul Mellon
1970	Fort Marcy	Rokeby Stable	Elliott Burch	Paul Mellon
1971	Ack Ack	E.E. Fogelson	Charlie Whittingham	H.F. Guggenheim
1972	Secretariat	Meadow Stable	Lucien Laurin	Meadow Stud
1973	Secretariat	Meadow Stable	Lucien Laurin	Meadow Stud
1974	Forego	Lazy F Ranch	Sherrill W. Ward	Lazy F Ranch
1975	Forego	Lazy F Ranch	Sherrill W. Ward	Lazy F Ranch
1976	Forego	Lazy F Ranch	Frank Y. Whiteley Jr.	Lazy F Ranch
1977	Seattle Slew	Karen L. Taylor	Billy Turner Jr.	B.S. Castleman
1978	Affirmed	Harbor View Farm	Laz Barrera	Harbor View Farm
1979	Affirmed	Harbor View Farm	Laz Barrera	Harbor View Farm
1980	Spectacular Bid	Hawksworth Farm	Bud Delp	Mmes. Gilmore and Jason
1981	John Henry	Dotsam Stable	Ron McAnally and Lefty Nickerson	Golden Chance Farm
1982	Conquistador Cielo	H. de Kwiatkowski	Woody Stephens	L.E. Landoli
1983	All Along	Daniel Wildenstein	P.L. Biancone	Dayton
1984	John Henry	Dotsam Stable	Ron McAnally	Golden Chance Farm
1985	Spend a Buck	Hunter Farm	Cam Gambolati	Irish Hill Farm & R.W. Harper
1986	Lady's Secret	Mr. & Mrs. Eugene Klein	D. Wayne Lukas	R.H. Spreen
1987	Ferdinand	Mrs. H.B. Keck	Charlie Whittingham	H.B. Keck
1988	Alysheba	D. & P. Scharbauer	Jack Van Berg	Preston Madden
1989	Sunday Silence	Gaillard, Hancock, & Whittingham	Charlie Whittingham	Oak Cliff Thoroughbreds
1990	Criminal Type	Calumet Farm	D. Wayne Lukas	Calumet Farm
1991	Black Tie Affair	Jeffrey Sullivan	Ernie Poulos	Stephen D. Peskoff
1992	A.P. Indy	Tomonori Tsurumaki	Neil Drysdale	W.S. Farish & W.S. Kilroy
1993	Kotashaan	La Presle Farm	Richard Mandella	La Presle Farm
1994	Holy Bull	Jimmy Croll	Jimmy Croll	Pelican Stable
1995	Cigar	Allen E. Paulson	William Mott	Allen E. Paulson
1996	Cigar	Allen E. Paulson	William Mott	Allen E. Paulson
1997	Favorite Trick	Joseph LaCombe	William Mott	Mr. & Mrs. M.L. Wood

Note: From 1936 to 1970, the *Daily Racing Form* annually selected a "Horse of the Year." In 1971 the *Daily Racing Form*, with the Thoroughbred Racing Association and the National Turf Writers Association, jointly created the Eclipse Awards.

Eclipse Award Winners

2-YEAR-OLD COLT	2-YEAR-OLD FILLY	3-YEAR-OLD COLT
1971 Riva Ridge	1971 Numbered Account	1971 Canonero II
1972 Secretariat	1972 La Prevoyante	1972 Key to the Mint
1973 Protagonist	1973 Talking Picture	1973 Secretariat
1974 Foolish Pleasure	1974 Ruffian	1974 Little Currant
1975 Honest Pleasure	1975 Dearly Precious	1975 Wajima
1976 Seattle Slew	1976 Sensational	1976 Bold Forbes
1977 Affirmed	1977 Lakeville Miss	1977 Seattle Slew
1978 Spectacular Bid	1978 Candy Eclair, It's in the Air	1978 Affirmed
1979 Rockhill Native	1979 Smart Angle	1979 Spectacular Bid
1980 Lord Avie	1980 Heavenly Cause	1980 Temperence Hill
1981 Deputy Minister	1981 Before Dawn	1981 Pleasant Colony
1982 Roving Boy	1982 Landaluce	1982 Conquistador Cielo
1983 Devil's Bag	1983 Althea	1983 Slew o' Gold
1984 Chief's Crown	1984 Outstandingly	1984 Swale
1985 Tasso	1985 Family Style	1985 Spend A Buck
1986 Capote	1986 Brave Raj	1986 Snow Chief
1987 Forty Niner	1987 Epitome	1987 Alysheba
1988 Easy Goer	1988 Open Mind	1988 Risen Star
1989 Rhythm	1989 Go for Wand	1989 Sunday Silence
1990 Fly So Free	1990 Meadow Star	1990 Unbridled
1991 Arazi	1991 Pleasant Stage	1991 Hansel
1992 Gilded Time	1992 Eliza	1992 A.P. Indy
1993 Dehere	1993 Phone Chatter	1993 Prairie Bayou
1994 Timber Country	1994 Flanders	1994 Holy Bull
1995 Maria's Mon	1995 Golden Attraction	1995 Thunder Gulch
1996 Boston Harbor	1996 Storm Song	1996 Skip Away
1997 Favorite Trick	1997 Countess Diana	1997 Silver Charm

Eclipse Award Winners (Cont.)

3-YEAR-OLD FILLY

1971 ....Turkish Trousers
1972 ....Susan's Girl
1973 ....Desert Vixen
1974 ....Chris Evert
1975 ....Ruffian
1976 ....Revidere
1977 ....Our Mims
1978 ....Tempest Queen
1979 ....Davona Dale
1980 ....Genuine Risk
1981 ....Wayward Lass
1982 ....Christmas Past
1983 ....Heartlight No. One
1984 ....Life's Magic
1985 ....Mom's Command
1986 ....Tiffany Lass
1987 ....Sacahuista
1988 ....Winning Colors
1989 ....Open Mind
1990 ....Go for Wand
1991 ....Dance Smartly
1992 ....Saratoga Dew
1993 ....Hollywood Wildcat
1994 ....Heavenly Prize
1995 ....Serena's Song
1996 ....Yank's Music
1997 ....Ajina

OLDER COLT, HORSE OR GELDING

1971 ....Ack Ack (5)
1972 ....Autobiography (4)
1973 ....Riva Ridge (4)
1974 ....Forego (4)
1975 ....Forego (5)
1976 ....Forego (6)
1977 ....Forego (7)
1978 ....Seattle Slew (4)
1979 ....Affirmed (4)
1980 ....Spectacular Bid (4)
1981 ....John Henry (6)
1982 ....Lemhi Gold (4)
1983 ....Bates Motel (4)
1984 ....Slew o'Gold (4)
1985 ....Vanlandingham (4)
1986 ....Turkoman (4)
1987 ....Ferdinand (4)
1988 ....Alysheba (4)
1989 ....Blushing John (4)
1990 ....Criminal Type (4)
1991 ....Black Tie Affair (5)
1992 ....Pleasant Tap (5)
1993 ....Bertrando (4)
1994 ....The Wicked North (5)
1995 ....Cigar (5)
1996 ....Cigar (6)
1997 ....Skip Away (4)

OLDER FILLY OR MARE

1971 ....Shuvee (5)
1972 ....Typecast (6)
1973 ....Susan's Girl (4)
1974 ....Desert Vixen (4)
1975 ....Susan's Girl (6)
1976 ....Proud Delta (4)
1977 ....Cascapedia (4)

OLDER FILLY OR MARE (Cont.)

1978 ....Late Bloomer (4)
1979 ....Waya (4)
1980 ....Glorious Song (4)
1981 ....Relaxing (5)
1982 ....Track Robbery (6)
1983 ....Ambassador of Luck (4)
1984 ....Princess Rooney (4)
1985 ....Life's Magic (4)
1986 ....Lady's Secret (4)
1987 ....North Sider (5)
1988 ....Personal Ensign (4)
1989 ....Bayakoa (5)
1990 ....Bayakoa (6)
1991 ....Queena (5)
1992 ....Paseana (5)
1993 ....Paseana (6)
1994 ....Sky Beauty (4)
1995 ....Inside Information (4)
1996 ....Jewel Princess (4)
1997 ....Hidden Lake (4)

CHAMPION TURF HORSE

1971 .....Run the Gantlet (3)
1972 .....Cougar II (6)
1973 .....Secretariat (3)
1974 .....Dahlia (4)
1975 .....Snow Knight (4)
1976 .....Youth (3)
1977 .....Johnny D (3)
1978 .....Mac Diarmida (3)

CHAMPION MALE TURF HORSE

1979 .....Bowl Game (5)
1980 .....John Henry (5)
1981 .....John Henry (6)
1982 .....Perrault (4)
1983 .....John Henry (8)
1984 .....John Henry (9)
1985 .....Cozzene (4)
1986 .....Manila (3)
1987 .....Theatrical (5)
1988 .....Sunshine Forever (3)
1989 .....Steinlen (6)
1990 .....Itsallgreektome (3)
1991 .....Tight Spot (4)
1992 .....Sky Classic (5)
1993 .....Kotashaan (5)
1994 .....Paradise Creek (5)
1995 .....Northern Spur (4)
1996 .....Singspiel (4)
1997 .....Chief Bearhart (4)

CHAMPION FEMALE TURF HORSE

1979 .....Trillion (5)
1980 .....Just a Game II (4)
1981 .....De La Rose (3)
1982 .....April Run (4)
1983 .....All Along (4)
1984 .....Royal Heroine (4)
1985 .....Pebbles (4)
1986 .....Estrapade (6)
1987 .....Miesque (3)
1988 .....Miesque (4)
1989 .....Brown Bess (7)
1990 .....Laugh and Be Merry (5)
1991 .....Miss Alleged (4)

CHAMPION FEMALE TURF HORSE (Cont.)

1992 .....Flawlessly (4)
1993 .....Flawlessly (5)
1994 .....Hatoof (5)
1995 .....Possibly Perfect (5)
1996 .....Wandesta (5)
1997 .....Ryafan (3)

STEEPLECHASE OR HURDLE HORSE

1971 .....Shadow Brook (7)
1972 .....Soothsayer (5)
1973 .....Athenian Idol (5)
1974 .....Gran Kan (8)
1975 .....Life's Illusion (4)
1976 .....Straight & True (6)
1977 .....Cafe Prince (7)
1978 .....Cafe Prince (8)
1979 .....Martie's Anger (4)
1980 .....Zaccio (4)
1981 .....Zaccio (5)
1982 .....Zaccio (6)
1983 .....Flatterer (4)
1984 .....Flatterer (5)
1985 .....Flatterer (6)
1986 .....Flatterer (7)
1987 .....Inlander (6)
1988 .....Jimmy Lorenzo (6)
1989 .....Highland Bud (4)
1990 .....Morley Street (7)
1991 .....Morley Street (8)
1992 .....Lonesome Glory (4)
1993 .....Lonesome Glory (5)
1994 .....Warm Spell (6)
1995 .....Lonesome Glory (7)
1996 .....Corregio (5)
1997 .....Lonesome Glory (9)

SPRINTER

1971 .....Ack Ack (5)
1972 .....Chou Croute (4)
1973 .....Shecky Greene (3)
1974 .....Forego (4)
1975 .....Gallant Bob (3)
1976 .....My Juliet (4)
1977 .....What a Summer (4)
1978 .....Dr. Patches (4)
           J.O. Tobin (4)
1979 .....Star de Naskra (4)
1980 .....Plugged Nickel (3)
1981 .....Guilty Conscience (5)
1982 .....Gold Beauty (3)
1983 .....Chinook Pass (4)
1984 .....Eillo (4)
1985 .....Precisionist (4)
1986 .....Smile (4)
1987 .....Groovy (4)
1988 .....Gulch (4)
1989 .....Safely Kept (3)
1990 .....Housebuster (3)
1991 .....Housebuster (4)
1992 .....Rubiano (5)
1993 .....Cardmania (7)
1994 .....Cherokee Run (4)
1995 .....Not Surprising (5)
1996 .....Lit de Justice (6)
1997 .....Smoke Glacken (3)

Note: Number in parentheses is horse's age.

Eclipse Award Winners (Cont.)

OUTSTANDING OWNER

1971.....Mr. & Mrs. E. E. Fogleson
1974.....Dan Lasater
1975.....Dan Lasater
1976.....Dan Lasater
1977.....Maxwell Gluck
1978.....Harbor View Farm
1979.....Harbor View Farm
1980.....Mr. & Mrs. Bertram
1981.....Dotsam Stable
1982.....Viola Sommer
1983.....John Franks
1984.....John Franks
1985.....Mr. & Mrs. Eugene Klein
1986.....Mr. & Mrs. Eugene Klein
1987.....Mr. & Mrs. Eugene Klein
1988.....Ogden Phipps
1989.....Ogden Phipps
1990.....Frances Genter
1991.....Sam-Son Farm
1992.....Juddmonte Farms
1993.....John Franks
1994.....John Franks
1995.....Allen E. Paulson
1996.....Allen E. Paulson
1997.....Carolyn Hine

OUTSTANDING TRAINER

1971.....Charlie Whittingham
1972.....Lucien Laurin
1973.....H. Allen Jerkens
1974.....Sherrill Ward
1975.....Steve DiMauro
1976.....Lazaro Barrera
1977.....Lazaro Barrera
1978.....Lazaro Barrera
1979.....Lazaro Barrera
1980.....Bud Delp
1981.....Ron McAnally
1982.....Charlie Whittingham
1983.....Woody Stephens
1984.....Jack Van Berg
1985.....D. Wayne Lukas
1986.....D. Wayne Lukas
1987.....D. Wayne Lukas
1988.....Claude R. McGaughey III
1989.....Charlie Whittingham
1990.....Carl Nafzger
1991.....Ron McAnally
1992.....Ron McAnally
1993.....Bobby Frankel
1994.....D. Wayne Lukas
1995.....William Mott
1996.....William Mott
1997.....Bob Baffert

OUTSTANDING JOCKEY

1971.....Laffit Pincay Jr.
1972.....Braulio Baeza
1973.....Laffit Pincay Jr.
1974.....Laffit Pincay Jr.
1975.....Braulio Baeza
1976.....Sandy Hawley
1977.....Steve Cauthen
1978.....Darrel McHargue
1979.....Laffit Pincay Jr.
1991.....Pat Day
1992.....Kent Desormeaux
1993.....Mike Smith
1994.....Mike Smith
1995.....Jerry Bailey
1996.....Jerry Bailey
1997.....Jerry Bailey

OUTSTANDING APPRENTICE JOCKEY

1971.....Gene St. Leon
1972.....Thomas Wallis
1973.....Steve Valdez
1974.....Chris McCarron
1975.....Jimmy Edwards
1976.....George Martens
1977.....Steve Cauthen
1978.....Ron Franklin
1979.....Cash Asmussen
1980.....Frank Lovato Jr.
1981.....Richard Migliore
1982.....Alberto Delgado
1983.....Declan Murphy
1984.....Wesley Ward
1985.....Art Madrid Jr.
1986.....Allen Stacy
1987.....Kent Desormeaux
1988.....Steve Capanas
1989.....Michael Luzzi
1990.....Mark Johnston
1991.....Mickey Walls
1992.....Jesus A. Bracho
1993.....Juan Umana
1994.....Dale Beckner
1995.....Ramon Perez
1996.....Neil Pozansky
1997.....Phil Teator
　　　　 Roberto Rosado

OUTSTANDING BREEDER

1974.....John W. Galbreath
1975.....Fred W. Hooper
1976.....Nelson Bunker Hunt
1977.....Edward Plunket Taylor
1978.....Harbor View Farm
1979.....Claiborne Farm
1980.....Mrs. Henry D. Paxson
1981.....Golden Chance Farm
1982.....Fred W. Hooper
1983.....Edward Plunket Taylor
1984.....Claiborne Farm
1985.....Nelson Bunker Hunt
1986.....Paul Mellon
1987.....Nelson Bunker Hunt
1988.....Ogden Phipps
1989.....North Ridge Farm
1990.....Calumet Farm
1991.....John and Betty Mabee
1992.....William S. Farish III
1993.....Allen Paulson
1994.....William T. Young
1995.....Juddmonte Farms
1996.....Fansworth Farms
1997.....Golden Eagle Farm

AWARD OF MERIT

1976.....Jack J. Dreyfus
1977.....Steve Cauthen
1978.....Ogden Phipps
1979.....Frank E. Kilroe
1980.....John D. Schapiro
1981.....Bill Shoemaker
1984.....John Gaines
1985.....Keene Daingerfield
1986.....Herman Cohen
1987.....J. B. Faulconer
1988.....John Forsythe
1989.....Michael P. Sandler
1991.....Fred W. Hooper
1994.....Alfred G. Vanderbilt
1996.....Allen E. Paulson

SPECIAL AWARD

1971.....Robert J. Kleberg
1974.....Charles Hatton
1976.....Bill Shoemaker
1980.....John T. Landry
　　　　 Pierre E. Bellocq (Peb)
1984.....C. V. Whitney
1985.....Arlington Park
1987.....Anheuser-Busch
1988.....Edward J. DeBartolo Sr.
1989.....Richard Duchossois
1994.....John Longden
　　　　 Edward Arcaro

Note: Special Award and Award of Merit not presented annually. For long-term and/or outstanding service to the industry.

Breeders' Cup

Location: Hollywood Park (CA) 1984, '87, '97; Aqueduct Racetrack (NY) 1985; Santa Anita Park (CA) 1986, '93; Churchill Downs (KY) 1988, '91; Gulfstream Park (FL) 1989, '92; Belmont Park (NY) 1990, '95; Woodbine (Toronto) 1996.

Juveniles

Year	Winner (Margin)	Jockey	Second	Third	Time
1984	Chief's Crown (¾)	Don MacBeth	Tank's Prospect	Spend a Buck	1:36⅕
1985	Tasso (Nose)	Laffit Pincay Jr.	Storm Cat	Scat Dancer	1:36⅕
1986	Capote (1¼)	Laffit Pincay Jr.	Qualify	Alysheba	1:43⅘
1987	Success Express (1¾)	Jose Santos	Regal Classic	Tejano	1:35⅕
1988	Is It True (1¼)	Laffit Pincay Jr.	Easy Goer	Tagel	1:46⅗
1989	Rhythm (2)	Craig Perret	Grand Canyon	Slavic	1:43⅗
1990	Fly So Free (3)	Jose Santos	Take Me Out	Lost Mountain	1:43⅖
1991	Arazi (4¾)	Pat Valenzuela	Bertrando	Snappy Landing	1:44⅗
1992	Gilded Time (¾)	Chris McCarron	It'sali'lknownfact	River Special	1:43⅖
1993	Brocco (5)	Gary Stevens	Blumin Affair	Tabasco Cat	1:42⅘
1994	Timber Country (½)	Pat Day	Eltish	Tejano Run	1:44⅖
1995	Unbridled's Song (Neck)	Mike Smith	Hennessy	Editor's Note	1:41⅗
1996	Boston Harbor (Neck)	Jerry Bailey	Acceptable	Ordway	1:43⅖
1997	Favorite Trick (5½)	Pat Day	Dawson's Legacy	Nationalore	1:41⅗

Note: One mile (1984–85, 87); 1 1/16 miles (1986 and since 1988).

Juvenile Fillies

Year	Winner (Margin)	Jockey	Second	Third	Time
1984	Outstandingly*	Walter Guerra	Dusty Heart	Fine Spirit	1:37⅘
1985	Twilight Ridge (1)	Jorge Velasquez	Family Style	Steal a Kiss	1:35⅘
1986	Brave Raj (5½)	Pat Valenzuela	Tappiano	Saros Brig	1:43⅕
1987	Epitome (Nose)	Pat Day	Jeanne Jones	Dream Team	1:36⅖
1988	Open Mind (1¾)	Angel Cordero Jr.	Darby Shuffle	Lea Lucinda	1:46⅗
1989	Go for Wand (2¾)	Randy Romero	Sweet Roberta	Stella Madrid	1:44⅕
1990	Meadow Star (5)	Jose Santos	Private Treasure	Dance Smartly	1:44
1991	Pleasant Stage (Neck)	Eddie Delahoussaye	La Spia	Cadillac Women	1:46⅖
1992	Eliza (1½)	Pat Valenzuela	Educated Risk	Boots 'n Jackie	1:42⅘
1993	Phone Chatter (Head)	Laffit Pincay	Sardula	Heavenly Prize	1:43
1994	Flanders (Head)	Pat Day	Serena's Song	Stormy Blues	1:45⅕
1995	My Flag (½)	Jerry Bailey	Cara Rafaela	Golden Attraction	1:42⅖
1996	Storm Song (4½)	Craig Perret	Love That Jazz	Critical Factor	1:43⅗
1997	Countess Diana (8½)	Shane Sellers	Career Collection	Primaly	1:42⅕

*In 1984, winner Fran's Valentine was disqualified for interference in the stretch and placed 10th.
Note: One mile (1984–85, 87); 1 1/16 miles (1986 and since 1988).

Sprint

Year	Winner (Margin)	Jockey	Second	Third	Time
1984	Eillo (Nose)	Craig Perret	Commemorate	Fighting Fit	1:10⅕
1985	Precisionist (¾)	Chris McCarron	Smile	Mt. Livermore	1:08⅖
1986	Smile (1¼)	Jacinto Vasquez	Pine Tree Lane	Bedside Promise	1:08⅖
1987	Very Subtle (4)	Pat Valenzuela	Groovy	Exclusive Enough	1:08⅘
1988	Gulch (¾)	Angel Cordero Jr	Play the King	Afleet	1:10⅖
1989	Dancing Spree (Neck)	Angel Cordero Jr	Safely Kept	Dispersal	1:09
1990	Safely Kept (Neck)	Craig Perret	Dayjur	Black Tie Affair	1:09⅗
1991	Sheikh Albadou (Neck)	Pat Eddery	Pleasant Tap	Robyn Dancer	1:09⅕
1992	Thirty Slews (Neck)	Eddie Delahoussaye	Meafara	Rubiano	1:08⅕
1993	Cardmania (Neck)	Eddie Delahoussaye	Meafara	Gilded Time	1:08⅗
1994	Cherokee Run (Head)	Mike Smith	Soviet Problem	Cardmania	1:09⅖
1995	Desert Stormer (Neck)	Kent Desormeaux	Mr. Greeley	Lit de Justice	1:09
1996	Lit de Justice (1¼)	Corey Nakatani	Paying Dues	Honour and Glory	1:08⅗
1997	Elmhurst (½)	Corey Nakatani	Hesabull	Bet on Sunshine	1:08

Note: Six furlongs (since 1984).

Mile

Year	Winner (Margin)	Jockey	Second	Third	Time
1984	Royal Heroine (1½)	Fernando Toro	Star Choice	Cozzene	1:32⅗
1985	Cozzene (2¼)	Walter Guerra	Al Mamoon*	Shadeed	1:35
1986	Last Tycoon (Head)	Yves St-Martin	Palace Music	Fred Astaire	1:35⅕
1987	Miesque (3½)	Freddie Head	Show Dancer	Sonic Lady	1:32⅘
1988	Miesque (4)	Freddie Head	Steinlen	Simply Majestic	1:38⅗
1989	Steinlen (¾)	Jose Santos	Sabona	Most Welcome	1:37⅕
1990	Royal Academy (Neck)	Lester Piggott	Itsallgreektome	Priolo	1:35⅕

Breeders' Cup *(Cont.)*

Mile *(Cont.)*

Year	Winner (Margin)	Jockey	Second	Third	Time
1991	Opening Verse (2¼)	Pat Valenzuela	Val de Bois	Star of Cozzene	1:37⅖
1992	Lure (3)	Mike Smith	Paradise Creek	Brief Truce	1:32⅘
1993	Lure (2¼)	Mike Smith	Ski Paradise	Fourstars Allstar	1:33⅖
1994	Barathea (Head)	Frankie Dettori	Johann Quatz	Unfinished Symph	1:34⅖
1995	Ridgewood Pearl (2)	John Murtagh	Fastness	Sayyedati	1:43⅗
1996	Da Hoss (1½)	Gary Stevens	Spinning World	Same Old Wish	1:35⅘
1997	Spinning World (2)	Cash Asmussen	Geri	Decorated Hero	1:32⅘

*2nd place finisher Palace Music was disqualified for interference and placed 9th.

Distaff

Year	Winner (Margin)	Jockey	Second	Third	Time
1984	Princess Rooney (7)	Eddie Delahoussaye	Life's Magic	Adored	2:02⅖
1985	Life's Magic (6¼)	Angel Cordero Jr.	Lady's Secret	Dontstop Themusic	2:02
1986	Lady's Secret (2½)	Pat Day	Fran's Valentine	Outstandingly	2:01⅕
1987	Sacahuista (2¼)	Randy Romero	Clabber Girl	Oueee Bebe	2:02⅘
1988	Personal Ensign (Nose)	Randy Romero	Winning Colors	Goodbye Halo	1:52
1989	Bayakoa (1½)	Laffit Pincay Jr.	Gorgeous	Open Mind	1:47⅖
1990	Bayakoa (6¾)	Laffit Pincay Jr.	Colonial Waters	Valay Maid	1:49⅕
1991	Dance Smarty (½)	Pat Day	Versailles Treaty	Brought to Mind	1:50⅘
1992	Paseana (4)	Chris McCarron	Versailles Treaty	Magical Maiden	1:48
1993	Hollywood Wildcat (Nose)	Eddie Delahoussaye	Paseana	Re Toss	1:48⅕
1994	One Dreamer (Neck)	Gary Stevens	Heavenly Prize	Miss Dominique	1:50⅗
1995	Inside Information (13½)	Mike Smith	Heavenly Prize	Lakeway	1:46
1996	Jewel Princess (1½)	Corey Nakatani	Serena's Song	Different	1:48⅖
1997	Ajina (2)	Mike Smith	Sharp Cat	Escena	1:47⅕

Note: 1¼ miles (1984–87); 1⅛ miles (since 1988).

Turf

Year	Winner (Margin)	Jockey	Second	Third	Time
1984	Lashkari (Neck)	Yves St. Martin	All Along	Raami	2:25⅕
1985	Pebbles (Neck)	Pat Eddery	Strawberry Rd II	Mourjane	2:27
1986	Manila (Neck)	Jose Santos	Theatrical	Estrapade	2:25⅖
1987	Theatrical (½)	Pat Day	Trempolino	Village Star II	2:24⅖
1988	Great Communicator (½)	Ray Sibille	Sunshine Forever	Indian Skimmer	2:35⅕
1989	Prized (Head)	Eddie Delahoussaye	Sierra Roberta	Star Lift	2:28
1990	In the Wings (½)	Gary Stevens	With Approval	El Senor	2:29⅗
1991	Miss Alleged (2)	Eric Legrix	Itsallgreektome	Quest for Fame	2:30⅘
1992	Fraise (Nose)	Pat Valenzuela	Sky Classic	Quest For Fame	2:24
1993	Kotashaan (½)	Kent Desormeaux	Bien Bien	Luazar	2:25
1994	Tikkanen (1½)	Mike Smith	Hatoof	Paradise Creek	2:26⅖
1995	Northern Spur (Neck)	Chris McCarron	Freedom Cry	Carnegie	2:42
1996	Pilsudski (1¼)	Walter Swinburn	Singspiel	Swain	2:30⅕
1997	Chief Bearhart (¾)	Jose Santos	Borgia	Flag Down	2:23⅘

Note: 1½ miles.

Classic

Year	Winner (Margin)	Jockey	Second	Third	Time
1984	Wild Again (Head)	Pat Day	Slew o' Gold*	Gate Dancer	2:03⅖
1985	Proud Truth (Head)	Jorge Velasquez	Gate Dancer	Turkoman	2:00⅘
1986	Skywalker (1¼)	Laffit Pincay Jr.	Turkoman	Precisionist	2:00⅖
1987	Ferdinand (Nose)	Bill Shoemaker	Alysheba	Judge Angelucci	2:01⅖
1988	Alysheba (Nose)	Chris McCarron	Seeking the Gold	Waquoit	2:04⅘
1989	Sunday Silence (½)	Chris McCarron	Easy Goer	Blushing John	2:00⅕
1990	Unbridled (1)	Pat Day	Ibn Bey	Thirty Six Red	2:02⅕
1991	Black Tie Affair (1¼)	Jerry Bailey	Twilight Agenda	Unbridled	2:02⅘
1992	A.P. Indy (2)	Eddie Delahoussaye	Pleasant Tap	Jolypha	2:00⅕
1993	Arcangues (2)	Jerry Bailey	Bertrando	Kissin Kris	2:00⅘
1994	Concern (Neck)	Jerry Bailey	Tabasco Cat	Dramatic Gold	2:02⅖
1995	Cigar (2½)	Jerry Bailey	L'Carriere	Unaccounted For	1:59⅖
1996	Alphabet Soup (Nose)	Chris McCarron	Louis Quatorze	Cigar	2:01
1997	Skip Away (6)	Mike Smith	Deputy Commander	Dowty	1:59⅕

*2nd place finisher Gate Dancer was disqualified for interference and placed 3rd.
Note: 1¼ miles.

England's Triple Crown Winners

England's Triple Crown consists of the Two Thousand Guineas, held at Newmarket; the Epsom Derby, held at Epsom Downs; and the St. Leger Stakes, held at Doncaster.

Year	Horse	Owner	Year	Horse	Owner
1853	West Australian	Mr. Bowes	1900	Diamond Jubilee	Prince of Wales
1865	Gladiateur	F. DeLagrange	1903	*Rock Sand	J. Miller
1866	Lord Lyon	R. Sutton	1915	Pommern	S. Joel
1886	*Ormonde	Duke of Westminster	1917	Gay Crusader	Mr. Fairie
1891	Common	†F. Johnstone	1918	Gainsborough	Lady James Douglas
1893	Isinglass	H. McCalmont	1935	*Bahram	Aga Khan
1897	Galtee More	J. Gubbins	1970	‡Nijinsky II	C. W. Engelhard
1899	Flying Fox	Duke of Westminster			

*Imported into United States. †Raced in name of Lord Alington in Two Thousand Guineas. ‡Canadian-bred.

Annual Leaders

Horse—Money Won

Year	Horse	Age	Starts	1st	2nd	3rd	Winnings ($)
1919	Sir Barton	3	13	8	3	2	88,250
1920	Man o'War	3	11	11	0	0	166,140
1921	Morvich	2	11	11	0	0	115,234
1922	Pillory	3	7	4	1	1	95,654
1923	Zev	3	14	12	1	0	272,008
1924	Sarzen	3	12	8	1	1	95,640
1925	Pompey	2	10	7	2	0	121,630
1926	Crusader	3	15	9	4	0	166,033
1927	Anita Peabody	2	7	6	0	1	111,905
1928	High Strung	2	6	5	0	0	153,590
1929	Blue Larkspur	3	6	4	1	0	153,450
1930	Gallant Fox	3	10	9	1	0	308,275
1931	Gallant Flight	2	7	7	0	0	219,000
1932	Gusto	3	16	4	3	2	145,940
1933	Singing Wood	2	9	3	2	2	88,050
1934	Cavalcade	3	7	6	1	0	111,235
1935	Omaha	3	9	6	1	2	142,255
1936	Granville	3	11	7	3	0	110,295
1937	Seabiscuit	4	15	11	2	2	168,580
1938	Stagehand	3	15	8	2	3	189,710
1939	Challedon	3	15	9	2	3	184,535
1940	Bimelech	3	7	4	2	1	110,005
1941	Whirlaway	3	20	13	5	2	272,386
1942	Shut Out	3	12	8	2	0	238,872
1943	Count Fleet	3	6	6	0	0	174,055
1944	Pavot	2	8	8	0	0	179,040
1945	Busher	3	13	10	2	1	273,735
1946	Assault	3	15	8	2	3	424,195
1947	Armed	6	17	11	4	1	376,325
1948	Citation	3	20	19	1	0	709,470
1949	Ponder	3	21	9	5	2	321,825
1950	Noor	5	12	7	4	1	346,940
1951	Counterpoint	3	15	7	2	1	250,525
1952	Crafty Admiral	4	16	9	4	1	277,225
1953	Native Dancer	3	10	9	1	0	513,425
1954	Determine	3	15	10	3	2	328,700
1955	Nashua	3	12	10	1	1	752,550
1956	Needles	3	8	4	2	0	440,850
1957	Round Table	3	22	15	1	3	600,383
1958	Round Table	4	20	14	4	0	662,780
1959	Sword Dancer	3	13	8	4	0	537,004
1960	Bally Ache	3	15	10	3	1	445,045
1961	Carry Back	3	16	9	1	3	565,349
1962	Never Bend	2	10	7	1	2	402,969
1963	Candy Spots	3	12	7	2	1	604,481
1964	Gun Bow	4	16	8	4	2	580,100
1965	Buckpasser	2	11	9	1	0	568,096

Note: Annual leaders on pages 484–488 courtesy of *The American Racing Manual*, a publication of Daily Racing Form, Inc.

Horse—Money Won (Cont.)

Year	Horse	Age	Starts	1st	2nd	3rd	Winnings ($)
1966	Buckpasser	3	14	13	1	0	669,078
1967	Damascus	3	16	12	3	1	817,941
1968	Forward Pass	3	13	7	2	0	546,674
1969	Arts and Letters	3	14	8	5	1	555,604
1970	Personality	3	18	8	2	1	444,049
1971	Riva Ridge	2	9	7	0	0	503,263
1972	Droll Role	4	19	7	3	4	471,633
1973	Secretariat	3	12	9	2	1	860,404
1974	Chris Evert	3	8	5	1	2	551,063
1975	Foolish Pleasure	3	11	5	4	1	716,278
1976	Forego	6	8	6	1	1	401,701
1977	Seattle Slew	3	7	6	0	1	641,370
1978	Affirmed	3	11	8	2	0	901,541
1979	Spectacular Bid	3	12	10	1	1	1,279,334
1980	Temperence Hill	3	17	8	3	1	1,130,452
1981	John Henry	6	10	8	0	0	1,798,030
1982	Perrault	5	8	4	1	2	1,197,400
1983	All Along	4	7	4	1	1	2,138,963
1984	Slew o'Gold	4	6	5	1	0	2,627,944
1985	Spend A Buck	3	7	5	1	1	3,552,704
1986	Snow Chief	3	9	6	1	1	1,875,200
1987	Alysheba	3	10	3	3	1	2,511,156
1988	Alysheba	4	9	7	1	0	3,808,600
1989	Sunday Silence	3	9	7	2	0	4,578,454
1990	Unbridled	3	11	4	3	2	3,718,149
1991	Dance Smartly	3	8	8	0	0	2,876,821
1992	A.P. Indy	3	7	5	0	1	2,622,560
1993	Kotashaan	3	10	6	3	0	2,619,014
1994	Paradise Creek	5	11	8	2	1	2,610,187
1995	Cigar	5	10	10	0	0	4,819,800
1996	Cigar	6	8	5	2	1	4,910,000
1997	Skip Away	4	11	4	5	2	4,089,000

Trainer—Money Won

Year	Trainer	Wins	Winnings ($)	Year	Trainer	Wins	Winnings ($)
1908	James Rowe, Sr.	50	284,335	1938	Earl Sande	15	226,495
1909	Sam Hildreth	73	123,942	1939	Sunny Jim Fitzsimmons	45	266,205
1910	Sam Hildreth	84	148,010	1940	Silent Tom Smith	14	269,200
1911	Sam Hildreth	67	49,418	1941	Plain Ben Jones	70	475,318
1912	John F. Schorr	63	58,110	1942	John M. Gaver Sr.	48	406,547
1913	James Rowe, Sr.	18	45,936	1943	Plain Ben Jones	73	267,915
1914	R. C. Benson	45	59,315	1944	Plain Ben Jones	60	601,660
1915	James Rowe, Sr.	19	75,596	1945	Silent Tom Smith	52	510,655
1916	Sam Hildreth	39	70,950	1946	Hirsch Jacobs	99	560,077
1917	Sam Hildreth	23	61,698	1947	Jimmy Jones	85	1,334,805
1918	H. Guy Bedwell	53	80,296	1948	Jimmy Jones	81	1,118,670
1919	H. Guy Bedwell	63	208,728	1949	Jimmy Jones	76	978,587
1920	L. Feustal	22	186,087	1950	Preston Burch	96	637,754
1921	Sam Hildreth	85	262,768	1951	John M. Gaver Sr.	42	616,392
1922	Sam Hildreth	74	247,014	1952	Plain Ben Jones	29	662,137
1923	Sam Hildreth	75	392,124	1953	Harry Trotsek	54	1,028,873
1924	Sam Hildreth	77	255,608	1954	Willie Molter	136	1,107,860
1925	G. R. Tompkins	30	199,245	1955	Sunny Jim Fitzsimmons	66	1,270,055
1926	Scott P. Harlan	21	205,681	1956	Willie Molter	142	1,227,402
1927	W. H. Bringloe	63	216,563	1957	Jimmy Jones	70	1,150,910
1928	John F. Schorr	65	258,425	1958	Willie Molter	69	1,116,544
1929	James Rowe, Jr.	25	314,881	1959	Willie Molter	71	847,290
1930	Sunny Jim Fitzsimmons	47	397,355	1960	Hirsch Jacobs	97	748,349
1931	Big Jim Healey	33	297,300	1961	Jimmy Jones	62	759,856
1932	Sunny Jim Fitzsimmons	68	266,650	1962	Mesh Tenney	58	1,099,474
1933	Humming Bob Smith	53	135,720	1963	Mesh Tenney	40	860,703
1934	Humming Bob Smith	43	249,938	1964	Bill Winfrey	61	1,350,534
1935	Bud Stotler	87	303,005	1965	Hirsch Jacobs	91	1,331,628
1936	Sunny Jim Fitzsimmons	42	193,415	1966	Eddie Neloy	93	2,456,250
1937	Robert McGarvey	46	209,925	1967	Eddie Neloy	72	1,776,089

Trainer—Money Won (Cont.)

Year	Trainer	Wins	Winnings ($)	Year	Trainer	Wins	Winnings ($)
1968	Eddie Neloy	52	1,233,101	1983	D. Wayne Lukas	78	4,267,261
1969	Elliott Burch	26	1,067,936	1984	D. Wayne Lukas	131	5,835,921
1970	Charlie Whittingham	82	1,302,354	1985	D. Wayne Lukas	218	11,155,188
1971	Charlie Whittingham	77	1,737,115	1986	D. Wayne Lukas	259	12,345,180
1972	Charlie Whittingham	79	1,734,020	1987	D. Wayne Lukas	343	17,502,110
1973	Charlie Whittingham	85	1,865,385	1988	D. Wayne Lukas	318	17,842,358
1974	Pancho Martin	166	2,408,419	1989	D. Wayne Lukas	305	16,103,998
1975	Charlie Whittingham	93	2,437,244	1990	D. Wayne Lukas	267	14,508,871
1976	Jack Van Berg	496	2,976,196	1991	D. Wayne Lukas	289	15,942,223
1977	Laz Barrera	127	2,715,848	1992	D. Wayne Lukas	230	9,806,436
1978	Laz Barrera	100	3,307,164	1993	Robert Frankel	79	8,883,252
1979	Laz Barrera	98	3,608,517	1994	D. Wayne Lukas	147	9,247,457
1980	Laz Barrera	99	2,969,151	1995	D. Wayne Lukas	194	12,842,865
1981	Charlie Whittingham	74	3,993,300	1996	D. Wayne Lukas	192	15,966,344
1982	Charlie Whittingham	63	4,587,457	1997	D. Wayne Lukas	175	10,338,957

Jockey—Money Won

Year	Jockey	Mts	1st	2nd	3rd	Pct	Winnings ($)
1919	John Loftus	177	65	36	24	.37	252,707
1920	Clarence Kummer	353	87	79	48	.25	292,376
1921	Earl Sande	340	112	69	59	.33	263,043
1922	Albert Johnson	297	43	57	40	.14	345,054
1923	Earl Sande	430	122	89	79	.28	569,394
1924	Ivan Parke	844	205	175	121	.24	290,395
1925	Laverne Fator	315	81	54	44	.26	305,775
1926	Laverne Fator	511	143	90	86	.28	361,435
1927	Earl Sande	179	49	33	19	.27	277,877
1928	Pony McAtee	235	55	43	25	.23	301,295
1929	Mack Garner	274	57	39	33	.21	314,975
1930	Sonny Workman	571	152	88	79	.27	420,438
1931	Charles Kurtsinger	519	93	82	79	.18	392,095
1932	Sonny Workman	378	87	48	55	.23	385,070
1933	Robert Jones	471	63	57	70	.13	226,285
1934	Wayne D. Wright	919	174	154	114	.19	287,185
1935	Silvio Coucci	749	141	125	103	.19	319,760
1936	Wayne D. Wright	670	100	102	73	.15	264,000
1937	Charles Kurtsinger	765	120	94	106	.16	384,202
1938	Nick Wall	658	97	94	82	.15	385,161
1939	Basil James	904	191	165	105	.21	353,333
1940	Eddie Arcaro	783	132	143	112	.17	343,661
1941	Don Meade	1,164	210	185	158	.18	398,627
1942	Eddie Arcaro	687	123	97	89	.18	481,949
1943	John Longden	871	173	140	121	.20	573,276
1944	Ted Atkinson	1,539	287	231	213	.19	899,101
1945	John Longden	778	180	112	100	.23	981,977
1946	Ted Atkinson	1,377	233	213	173	.17	1,036,825
1947	Douglas Dodson	646	141	100	75	.22	1,429,949
1948	Eddie Arcaro	726	188	108	98	.26	1,686,230
1949	Steve Brooks	906	209	172	110	.23	1,316,817
1950	Eddie Arcaro	888	195	153	144	.22	1,410,160
1951	Bill Shoemaker	1,161	257	197	161	.22	1,329,890
1952	Eddie Arcaro	807	188	122	109	.23	1,859,591
1953	Bill Shoemaker	1,683	485	302	210	.29	1,784,187
1954	Bill Shoemaker	1,251	380	221	142	.30	1,876,760
1955	Eddie Arcaro	820	158	126	108	.19	1,864,796
1956	Bill Hartack	1,387	347	252	184	.25	2,343,955
1957	Bill Hartack	1,238	341	208	178	.28	3,060,501
1958	Bill Shoemaker	1,133	300	185	137	.26	2,961,693
1959	Bill Shoemaker	1,285	347	230	159	.27	2,843,133
1960	Bill Shoemaker	1,227	274	196	158	.22	2,123,961
1961	Bill Shoemaker	1,256	304	186	175	.24	2,690,819
1962	Bill Shoemaker	1,126	311	156	128	.28	2,916,844
1963	Bill Shoemaker	1,203	271	193	137	.22	2,526,925
1964	Bill Shoemaker	1,056	246	147	133	.23	2,649,553

Jockey—Money Won *(Cont.)*

Year	Jockey	Mts	1st	2nd	3rd	Pct	Winnings ($)
1965	Braulio Baeza	1,245	270	200	201	.22	2,582,702
1966	Braulio Baeza	1,341	298	222	190	.22	2,951,022
1967	Braulio Baeza	1,064	256	184	127	.24	3,088,888
1968	Braulio Baeza	1,089	201	184	145	.18	2,835,108
1969	Jorge Velasquez	1,442	258	230	204	.18	2,542,315
1970	Laffit Pincay Jr.	1,328	269	208	187	.20	2,626,526
1971	Laffit Pincay Jr.	1,627	380	288	214	.23	3,784,377
1972	Laffit Pincay Jr.	1,388	289	215	205	.21	3,225,827
1973	Laffit Pincay Jr.	1,444	350	254	209	.24	4,093,492
1974	Laffit Pincay Jr.	1,278	341	227	180	.27	4,251,060
1975	Braulio Baeza	1,190	196	208	180	.16	3,674,398
1976	Angel Cordero Jr.	1,534	274	273	235	.18	4,709,500
1977	Steve Cauthen	2,075	487	345	304	.23	6,151,750
1978	Darrel McHargue	1,762	375	294	263	.21	6,188,353
1979	Laffit Pincay Jr.	1,708	420	302	261	.25	8,183,535
1980	Chris McCarron	1,964	405	318	282	.20	7,666,100
1981	Chris McCarron	1,494	326	251	207	.22	8,397,604
1982	Angel Cordero Jr.	1,838	397	338	227	.22	9,702,520
1983	Angel Cordero Jr.	1,792	362	296	237	.20	10,116,807
1984	Chris McCarron	1,565	356	276	218	.23	12,038,213
1985	Laffit Pincay Jr.	1,409	289	246	183	.21	13,415,049
1986	Jose Santos	1,636	329	237	222	.20	11,329,297
1987	Jose Santos	1,639	305	268	208	.19	12,407,355
1988	Jose Santos	1,867	370	287	265	.20	14,877,298
1989	Jose Santos	1,459	285	238	220	.20	13,847,003
1990	Gary Stevens	1,504	283	245	202	.19	13,881,198
1991	Chris McCarron	1,440	265	228	206	.18	14,441,083
1992	Kent Desormeaux	1,568	361	260	208	.23	14,193,006
1993	Mike Smith	1,510	343	235	214	.23	14,008,148
1994	Mike Smith	1,484	317	250	196	.21	15,979,820
1995	Jerry Bailey	1,265	287	193	144	.23	16,308,230
1996	Jerry Bailey	1,187	298	189	165	.25	19,465,376
1997	Jerry Bailey	1,143	272	186	178	.26	18,260,553

Jockey—Races Won

Year	Jockey	Mts	1st	2nd	3rd	Pct
1895	J. Perkins	762	192	177	129	.25
1896	J. Scherrer	1,093	271	227	172	.24
1897	H. Martin	803	173	152	116	.21
1898	T. Burns	973	277	213	149	.28
1899	T. Burns	1,064	273	173	266	.26
1900	C. Mitchell	874	195	140	139	.23
1901	W. O'Connor	1,047	253	221	192	.24
1902	J. Ranch	1,069	276	205	181	.26
1903	G.C. Fuller	918	229	152	122	.25
1904	E. Hildebrand	1,169	297	230	171	.25
1905	D. Nicol	861	221	143	136	.26
1906	W. Miller	1,384	388	300	199	.28
1907	W. Miller	1,194	334	226	170	.28
1908	V. Powers	1,260	324	204	185	.26
1909	V. Powers	704	173	121	114	.25
1910	G. Garner	947	200	188	153	.20
1911	T. Koerner	813	162	133	112	.20
1912	P. Hill	967	168	141	129	.17
1913	M. Buxton	887	146	131	136	.16
1914	J. McTaggart	787	157	132	106	.20
1915	M. Garner	775	151	118	90	.19
1916	F. Robinson	791	178	131	124	.23
1917	W. Crump	803	151	140	101	.19
1918	F. Robinson	864	185	140	108	.21
1919	C. Robinson	896	190	140	126	.21
1920	J. Butwell	721	152	129	139	.21
1921	C. Lang	696	135	110	105	.19
1922	M. Fator	859	188	153	116	.22
1923	I. Parke	718	173	105	95	.24
1924	I. Parke	844	205	175	121	.24

Jockey—Races Won *(Cont.)*

Year	Jockey	Mts	1st	2nd	3rd	Pct
1925	A. Mortensen	987	187	145	138	.19
1926	R. Jones	1,172	190	163	152	.16
1927	L. Hardy	1,130	207	192	151	.18
1928	J. Inzelone	1,052	155	152	135	.15
1929	M. Knight	871	149	132	133	.17
1930	H.R. Riley	861	177	145	123	.21
1931	H. Roble	1,174	173	173	155	.15
1932	J. Gilbert	1,050	212	144	160	.20
1933	J. Westrope	1,224	301	235	166	.25
1934	M. Peters	1,045	221	179	147	.21
1935	C. Stevenson	1,099	206	169	146	.19
1936	B. James	1,106	245	195	161	.22
1937	J. Adams	1,265	260	186	177	.21
1938	J. Longden	1,150	236	168	171	.21
1939	D. Meade	1,284	255	221	180	.20
1940	E. Dew	1,377	287	201	180	.21
1941	D. Meade	1,164	210	185	158	.18
1942	J. Adams	1,120	245	185	150	.22
1943	J. Adams	1,069	228	159	171	.21
1944	T. Atkinson	1,539	287	231	213	.19
1945	J.D. Jessop	1,085	290	182	168	.27
1946	T. Atkinson	1,377	233	213	173	.17
1947	J. Longden	1,327	316	250	195	.24
1948	J. Longden	1,197	319	233	161	.27
1949	G. Glisson	1,347	270	217	181	.20
1950	W. Shoemaker	1,640	388	266	230	.24
1951	C. Burr	1,319	310	232	192	.24
1952	A. DeSpirito	1,482	390	247	212	.26
1953	W. Shoemaker	1,683	485	302	210	.29
1954	W. Shoemaker	1,251	380	221	142	.30
1955	W. Hartack	1,702	417	298	215	.25
1956	W. Hartack	1,387	347	252	184	.25
1957	W. Hartack	1,238	341	208	178	.28
1958	W. Shoemaker	1,133	300	185	137	.26
1959	W. Shoemaker	1,285	347	230	159	.27
1960	W. Hartack	1,402	307	247	190	.22
1961	J. Sellers	1,394	328	212	227	.24
1962	R. Ferraro	1,755	352	252	226	.20
1963	W. Blum	1,704	360	286	215	.21
1964	W. Blum	1,577	324	274	170	.21
1965	J. Davidson	1,582	319	228	190	.20
1966	A. Gomez	996	318	173	142	.32
1967	J. Velasquez	1,939	438	315	270	.23
1968	A. Cordero Jr.	1,662	345	278	219	.21
1969	L. Snyder	1,645	352	290	243	.21
1970	S. Hawley	1,908	452	313	265	.24
1971	L Pincay Jr.	1,627	380	288	214	.23
1972	S. Hawley	1,381	367	269	200	.27
1973	S. Hawley	1,925	515	336	292	.27
1974	C.J. McCarron	2,199	546	392	297	.25
1975	C.J. McCarron	2,194	458	389	305	.21
1976	S. Hawley	1,637	413	245	201	.25
1977	S. Cauthen	2,075	487	345	304	.23
1978	E. Delahoussaye	1,666	384	285	238	.23
1979	D. Gall	2,146	479	396	326	.22
1980	C.J. McCarron	1,964	405	318	282	.20
1981	D. Gall	1,917	376	305	297	.20
1982	Pat Day	1,870	399	326	255	.21
1983	Pat Day	1,725	454	321	251	.26
1984	Pat Day	1,694	399	296	259	.24
1985	C.W. Antley	2,335	469	371	288	.20
1986	Pat Day	1,417	429	246	202	.30
1987	Kent Desormeaux	2,207	450	370	294	.28
1988	Kent Desmoreaux	1,897	474	295	276	.25
1989	Kent Desmoreaux	2,312	598	385	309	.25
1990	Pat Day	1,421	364	265	222	.26
1991	Pat Day	1,405	430	256	213	.31
1992	Russell Baze	1,691	433	296	237	.25

Jockey—Races Won *(Cont.)*

Year	Jockey	Mts	1st	2nd	3rd	Pct
1993	Russell Baze	1,579	410	297	225	.26
1994	Russell Baze	1,588	415	301	266	.26
1995	Russell Baze	1,531	445	310	232	.29
1996	Russell Baze	1,482	415	297	200	.28
1997	Edgar S. Prado	2,037	533	384	308	.26

Leading Jockeys—Career Records

Jockey	Years Riding	Mts	1st	2nd	3rd	Win Pct	Winnings ($)
Bill Shoemaker (1990)	42	40,350	8,833	6,136	4,987	.219	123,375,524
Laffit Pincay	32	42,875	8,573	6,957	5,915	.200	196,772,775
Dave Gall	40	40,647	7,184	6,315	5,960	.178	23,755,468
Pat Day	25	32,293	7,087	5,508	4,520	.219	188,681,842
Angel Cordero (1992)	31	38,646	7,057	6,136	5,359	.183	164,561,227
Jorge Velasquez	35	40,852	6,795	6,178	5,755	.166	125,544,379
Chris McCarron	23	31,342	6,558	5,182	4,317	.209	213,851,293
Sandy Hawley (1998)	31	31,418	6,442	4,822	4,151	.205	88,463,806
Larry Snyder (1994)	35	35,681	6,388	5,030	3,440	.179	47,207,289
Carl Gambardella (1994)	39	39,018	6,349	5,953	5,353	.163	29,389,041
Russell Baze	24	30,260	6,032	4,882	4,232	.199	83,260,899
John Longden (1966)	40	32,413	6,032	4,914	4,273	.186	24,665,800
Earlie Fires	33	40,630	5,967	5,042	4,853	.147	72,328,911
Eddie Delahoussaye	28	35,636	5,867	5,166	5,005	.165	163,300,374
Jacinto Vasquez	38	37,392	5,231	4,721	4,513	.140	80,764,853
Eddie Arcaro (1961)	31	24,092	4,779	3,807	3,302	.198	30,039,543
Ron Ardoin	25	27,890	4,622	3,775	3,310	.166	47,108,677
Don Brumfield (1989)	37	33,223	4,573	4,076	3,758	.138	43,567,861
Steve Brooks (1975)	34	30,330	4,451	4,219	3,658	.147	18,239,817
Rodolfo Baez	23	26,279	4,383	3,913	3,751	.167	26,428,227
Walter Blum (1975)	22	28,673	4,382	3,913	3,350	.153	26,497,189
Eddie Maple	30	33,696	4,367	4,480	4,303	.130	104,447,863
Bill Hartack (1974)	22	21,535	4,272	3,370	2,871	.198	26,466,758
Gary Stevens	23	24,227	4,268	3,818	3,471	.176	161,563,531

Note: Records go through January 1,1998, and include available statistics for races ridden in foreign countries. Figures in parentheses after jockey's name indicate last year in which he rode.

Leading jockeys courtesy of *The American Racing Manual*, a publication of Daily Racing Form, Inc.

National Museum of Racing Hall of Fame

HORSES

Ack Ack (1986, 1966)
Affectionately (1989, 1960)
Affirmed (1980, 1975)
All Along (1990, 1979)
Alsab (1976, 1939)
Alydar (1989, 1975)
Alysheba (1993, 1984)
American Eclipse (1970, 1814)
Armed (1963, 1941)
Artful (1956, 1902)
Arts and Letters (1994, 1966)
Assault (1964, 1943)
Battleship (1969, 1927)
Bayakoa (1998, 1984)
Bed o' Roses (1976, 1947)
Beldame (1956, 1901)
Ben Brush (1955, 1893)
Bewitch (1977, 1945)
Bimelech (1990, 1937)
Black Gold (1989, 1921)
Black Helen (1991, 1932)
Blue Larkspur (1957, 1926)

Bold 'n Determined (1997, 1977)
Bold Ruler (1973, 1954)
Bon Nouvel (1976, 1960)
Boston (1955, 1833)
Broomstick (1956, 1901)
Buckpasser (1970, 1963)
Busher (1964, 1942)
Bushranger (1967, 1930)
Cafe Prince (1985, 1970)
Carry Back (1975, 1958)
Cavalcade (1993, 1931)
Challedon (1977, 1936)
Chris Evert (1988, 1971)
Cicada (1967, 1959)
Citation (1959, 1945)
Coaltown (1983, 1945)
Colin (1956, 1905)
Commando (1956, 1898)
Count Fleet (1961, 1940)
Crusader (1995, 1923)
Dahlia (1981, 1970)
Damascus (1974, 1964)

Dark Mirage (1974, 1965)
Davona Dale (1985, 1976)
Desert Vixen (1979, 1970)
Devil Diver (1980, 1939)
Discovery (1969, 1931)
Domino (1955, 1891)
Dr. Fager (1971, 1964)
Easy Goer (1997, 1986)
Eight Thirty (1994, 1936)
Elkridge (1966, 1938)
Emperor of Norfolk (1988, 1885)
Equipoise (1957, 1928)
Exterminator (1957, 1915)
Fairmount (1985, 1921)
Fair Play (1956, 1905)
Fashion (1980, 1837)
Firenze (1981, 1884)
Flatterer (1994, 1979)
Foolish Pleasure (1995, 1972)
Forego (1979, 1970)
Fort Marcy (1998, 1964)
Gallant Bloom (1977, 1966)

Note: Years of election and foaling in parentheses.

HORSES *(Cont.)*

Gallant Fox (1957, 1927)
Gallant Man (1987, 1954)
Gallorette (1962, 1942)
Gamely (1980, 1964)
Genuine Risk (1986, 1977)
Go For Wand (1996, 1987)
Good and Plenty (1956, 1900)
Grandville (1997, 1933)
Grey Lag (1957, 1918)
Hamburg (1986, 1895)
Hanover (1955, 1884)
Henry of Navarre (1985, 1891)
Hill Prince (1991, 1947)
Hindoo (1955, 1878)
Imp (1965, 1894)
Jay Trump (1971, 1957)
John Henry (1990, 1975)
Johnstown (1992, 1936)
Jolly Roger (1965, 1922)
Kelso (1967, 1957)
Kentucky (1983, 1861)
Kingston (1955, 1884)
Lady's Secret (1992, 1982)
La Prevoyante (1995, 1970)
L'Escargot (1977, 1963)
Lexington (1955, 1850)
Longfellow (1971, 1867)
Luke Blackburn (1956, 1877)
Majestic Prince (1988, 1966)
Man o' War (1957, 1917)

Miss Woodford (1967, 1880)
Myrtlewood (1979, 1932)
Nashua (1965, 1952)
Native Dancer (1963, 1950)
Native Diver (1978, 1959)
Neji (1966, 1950)
Northern Dancer (1976, 1961)
Oedipus (1978, 1946)
Old Rosebud (1968, 1911)
Omaha (1965, 1932)
Pan Zareta (1972, 1910)
Parole (1984, 1873)
Personal Ensign (1993, 1984)
Peter Pan (1956, 1904)
Princess Doreen (1982, 1921)
Princess Rooney (1991, 1980)
Real Delight (1987, 1949)
Regret (1957, 1912)
Reigh Count (1978, 1923)
Riva Ridge (1998, 1969)
Roamer (1981, 1911)
Roseben (1956, 1901)
Round Table (1972, 1954)
Ruffian (1976, 1972)
Ruthless (1975, 1864)
Salvator (1955, 1886)
Sarazen (1957, 1921)
Seabiscuit (1958, 1933)
Searching (1978, 1952)
Seattle Slew (1981, 1974)

Secretariat (1974, 1970)
Shuvee (1975, 1966)
Silver Spoon (1978, 1956)
Sir Archy (1955, 1805)
Sir Barton (1957, 1916)
Slew o' Gold (1992, 1980)
Spectacular Bid (1982, 1976)
Stymie (1975, 1941)
Sun Beau (1996, 1925)
Sunday Silence (1996, 1986)
Susan's Girl (1976, 1969)
Swaps (1966, 1952)
Sword Dancer (1977, 1956)
Sysonby (1956, 1902)
Ta Wee (1994, 1967)
Ten Broeck (1982, 1872)
Tim Tam (1985, 1955)
Tom Fool (1960, 1949)
Top Flight (1966, 1929)
Tosmah (1984, 1961)
Twenty Grand (1957, 1928)
Twilight Tear (1963, 1941)
Two Lea (1982, 1946)
War Admiral (1958, 1934)
Whirlaway (1959, 1938)
Whisk Broom II (1979, 1907)
Zaccio (1990, 1976)
Zev (1983, 1920)

HARNESS RACING

Major Races

Hambletonian

Year	Winner	Driver	Year	Winner	Driver
1926	Guy McKinney	Nat Ray	1955	Scott Frost	Joe O'Brien
1927	Iosola's Worthy	Marvin Childs	1956	The Intruder	Ned Bower
1928	Spenser	W. H. Leese	1957	Hickory Smoke	J. Simpson Sr.
1929	Walter Dear	Walter Cox	1958	Emily's Pride	Flave Nipe
1930	Hanover's Bertha	Tom Berry	1959	Diller Hanover	Frank Ervin
1931	Calumet Butler	R. D. McMahon	1960	Blaze Hanover	Joe O'Brien
1932	The Marchioness	William Caton	1961	Harlan Dean	James Arthur
1933	Mary Reynolds	Ben White	1962	A. C.'s Viking	Sanders Russell
1934	Lord Jim	Doc Parshall	1963	Speedy Scot	Ralph Baldwin
1935	Greyhound	Sep Palin	1964	Ayres	J. Simpson Sr.
1936	Rosalind	Ben White	1965	Egyptian Candor	Del Cameron
1937	Shirley Hanover	Henry Thomas	1966	Kerry Way	Frank Ervin
1938	McLin Hanover	Henry Thomas	1967	Speedy Streak	Del Cameron
1939	Peter Astra	Doc Parshall	1968	Nevele Pride	Stanley Dancer
1940	Spencer Scott	Fred Egan	1969	Lindy's Pride	H. Beissinger
1941	Bill Gallon	Lee Smith	1970	Timothy T.	J. Simpson Jr.
1942	The Ambassador	Ben White	1971	Speedy Crown	H. Beissinger
1943	Volo Song	Ben White	1972	Super Bowl	Stanley Dancer
1944	Yankee Maid	Henry Thomas	1973	Flirth	Ralph Baldwin
1945	Titan Hanover	H. Pownall Sr.	1974	Christopher T.	Bill Haughton
1946	Chestertown	Thomas Berry	1975	Bonefish	Stanley Dancer
1947	Hoot Mon	Sep Palin	1976	Steve Lobell	Bill Haughton
1948	Demon Hanover	Harrison Hoyt	1977	Green Speed	Bill Haughton
1949	Miss Tilly	Fred Egan	1978	Speedy Somolli	H. Beissinger
1950	Lusty Song	Del Miller	1979	Legend Hanover	George Sholty
1951	Mainliner	Guy Crippen	1980	Burgomeister	Bill Haughton
1952	Sharp Note	Bion Shively	1981	Shiaway St. Pat	Ray Remmen
1953	Helicopter	Harry Harvey	1982	Speed Bowl	Tom Haughton
1954	Newport Dream	Del Cameron	1983	Duenna	Stanley Dancer

Hambletonian *(Cont.)*

Year	Winner	Driver	Year	Winner	Driver
1984	Historic Freight	Ben Webster	1992	Alf Palema	Mickey McNichol
1985	Prakas	Bill O'Donnell	1993	American Winner	Ron Pierce
1986	Nuclear Kosmos	Ulf Thoresen	1994	Victory Dream	Michel LaChance
1987	Mack Lobell	John Campbell	1995	Tagliabue	John Campbell
1988	Armbro Goal	John Campbell	1996	Continentalvictory	Michel LaChance
1989	Park Ave. Joe/ Probe*	R. Waples/B. Fahy	1997	Malabar Man	Mal Burroughs
1990	Harmonious	John Campbell	1998	Muscles Yankee	John Campbell
1991	Giant Victory	Jack Moiseyev			

*Park Avenue Joe and Probe dead-heated for win. Park Avenue finished first in the summary 2-1-1 to Probe's 1-9-1 finish.
Note: Run at 1 mile since 1947.

Little Brown Jug

Year	Winner	Driver	Year	Winner	Driver
1946	Ensign Hanover	Wayne Smart	1973	Melvin's Woe	Joe O'Brien
1947	Forbes Chief	Del Cameron	1974	Armbro Omaha	Bill Haughton
1948	Knight Dream	Frank Safford	1975	Seatrain	Ben Webster
1949	Good Time	Frank Ervin	1976	Keystone Ore	Stanley Dancer
1950	Dudley Hanover	Del Miller	1977	Governor Skipper	John Chapman
1951	Tar Heel	Del Cameron	1978	Happy Escort	William Popfinger
1952	Meadow Rice	Wayne Smart	1979	Hot Hitter	Herve Filion
1953	Keystoner	Frank Ervin	1980	Niatross	Clint Galbraith
1954	Adios Harry	Morris MacDonald	1981	Fan Hanover	Glen Garnsey
1955	Quick Chief	Bill Haughton	1982	Merger	John Campbell
1956	Noble Adios	John Simpson Sr.	1983	Ralph Hanover	Ron Waples
1957	Torpid	John Simpso Sr.	1984	Colt Fortysix	Chris Boring
1958	Shadow Wave	Joe O'Brien	1985	Nihilator	Bill O'Donnell
1959	Adios Butler	Clint Hodgins	1986	Barberry Spur	Bill O'Donnell
1960	Bullet Hanover	John Simpson Sr.	1987	Jaguar Spur	Dick Stillings
1961	Henry T. Adios	Stanley Dancer	1988	B. J. Scoot	Michel Lachance
1962	Lehigh Hanover	Stanley Dancer	1989	Goalie Jeff	Michel Lachance
1963	Overtrick	John Patterson	1990	Beach Towel	Ray Remmen
1964	Vicar Hanover	Bill Haughton	1991	Precious Bunny	Jack Moiseye
1965	Bret Hanover	Frank Ervin	1992	Fake Left	Ron Waples
1966	Romeo Hanover	George Sholty	1993	Life Sign	John Campbell
1967	Best of All	James Hackett	1994	Magical Mike	Michel Lachance
1968	Rum Customer	Bill Haughton	1995	Nick's Fantasy	John Campbell
1969	Laverne Hanover	Bill Haughton	1996	Armbro Operative	Jack Moiseyev
1970	Most Happy Fella	Stanley Dancer	1997	Western Dreamer	Michel Lachance
1971	Nansemond	Herve Filion	1998	Shady Character	Ron Pierce
1972	Strike Out	Keith Waples			

Breeders' Crown

1984

Div	Winner	Driver
2PC	Dragon's Lair	Jeff Mallet
2PF	Amneris	John Campbell
3PC	Troublemaker	Bill O'Donnell
3PF	Naughty But Nice	Tommy Haughton
2TC	Workaholic	Berndt Lindstedt
2TF	Conifer	George Sholty
3TC	Baltic Speed	Jan Nordin
3TF	Fancy Crown	Bill O'Donnell

1985

Div	Winner	Driver
2PC	Robust Hanover	John Campbell
2PF	Caressable	Herve Filion
3PC	Nihilator	Bill O'Donnell
3PF	Stienam	Buddy Gilmour
2TC	Express Ride	John Campbell
2TF	JEF's Spice	Mickey McNichol
3TC	Prakas	John Campbell
3TF	Armbro Devona	Bill O'Donnell
AP	Division Street	Michel Lachance
AT	Sandy Bowl	John Campbell

1986

Div	Winner	Driver
2PC	Sunset Warrior	Bill Gale
2PF	Halcyon	Ray Remmen
3PC	Masquerade	Richard Silverman
3PF	Glow Softly	Ron Waples
2TC	Mack Lobell	John Campbell
2TF	Super Flora	Ron Waples
3TC	Sugarcane Hanover	Ron Waples
3TF	JEF's Spice	Bill O'Donnell
APM	Samshu Bluegrass	Michel Lachance
ATM	Grades Singing	Herve Filion
APH	Forrest Skipper	Lucien Fontaine
ATH	Nearly Perfect	Mickey McNichol

1987

Div	Winner	Driver
2PC	Camtastic	Bill O'Donnell
2PF	Leah Almahurst	Bill Fahy
3PC	Call For Rain	Clint Galbraith
3PF	Pacific	Tom Harmer
2TC	Defiant One	Howard Beissinger
2TF	Nan's Catch	Berndt Lindstedt
3TC	Mack Lobell	John Campbell

Note: 2=Two-year-old; T=Trotter; C=Colt; 3=Three-year-old; P=Pacer; F=Filly; A=Aged; H=Horse; M=Mare.

Breeders' Crown *(Cont.)*

1987 *(Cont.)*

Div	Winner	Driver
3TF	Armbro Fling	George Sholty
APM	Follow My Star	John Campbell
ATM	Grades Singing	Olle Goop
APH	Armbro Emerson	Walter Whelan
ATH	Sugarcane Hanover	Ron Waples

1988

Div	Winner	Driver
2PC	Kentucky Spur	Dick Stillings
2PF	Central Park West	John Campbell
3PC	Camtastic	Bill O'Donnell
3PF	Sweet Reflection	Bill O'Donnell
2TC	Valley Victory	Bill O'Donnell
2TF	Peace Corps	John Campbell
3TC	Firm Tribute	Mark O'Mara
3TF	Nalda Hanover	Mickey McNichol
APM	Anniecrombie	Dave Magee
ATM	Armbro Flori	Larry Walker
APH	Call For Rain	Clint Galbraith
ATH	Mack Lobell	John Campbell

1989

Div	Winner	Driver
2PC	Till We Meet Again	Mickey McNichol
2PF	Town Pro	Doug Brown
3PC	Goalie Jeff	Michel LaChance
3PF	Cheery Hello	John Campbell
2TC	Royal Troubador	Carl Allen
2TF	Delphi's Lobell	Ron Waples
3TC	Esquire Spur	Dick Stillings
3TF	Pace Corps	John Campbell
APM	Armbro Feather	John Kopas
ATM	Grades Singing	Olle Goop
APH	Matt's Scooter	Michel LaChance
ATH	Delray Lobell	John Campbell

1990

Div	Winner	Driver
2PC	Artsplace	John Campbell
2PF	Miss Easy	John Campbell
3PC	Beach Towel	Ray Remmen
3PF	Town Pro	Doug Brown
2TC	Crysta's Best	Dick Richardson Jr.
2TF	Jean Bi	Jan Nordin
3TC	Embassy Lobell	Michel Lachance
3TF	Me Maggie	Berndt Lindstedt
APM	Caesar's Jackpot	Bill Fahy
ATM	Peace Corps	Stig Johansson
APH	Bay's Fella	Paul MacDonell
ATH	No Sex Please	Ron Waples

1991

Div	Winner	Driver
2PC	Digger Almahurst	Doug Brown
2PF	Hazleton Kay	John Campbell
3PC	Three Wizzards	Bill Gale
3PF	Miss Easy	John Campbell
2TC	King Conch	Bill Gale
2TF	Armbro Keepsake	John Campbell
3TC	Giant Victory	Ron Pierce
3TF	Twelve Speed	Ron Waples
APM	Delinquent Account	Bill O'Donnell
ATM	Me Maggie	Berndt Lindstedt
APH	Camluck	Michel LaChance
ATH	Billyjojimbob	Paul MacDonell

1992

Div	Winner	Driver
2PC	Village Jiffy	Ron Waples
2PF	Immortality	John Campbell

1992 *(Cont.)*

Div	Winner	Driver
3PC	Kingsbridge	Roger Mayotte
3PF	So Fresh	John Campbell
2TC	Giant Chill	John Patterson Jr.
2TF	Winky's Goal	Cat Manzi
3TC	Baltic Striker	Michel LaChance
3TF	Imperfection	Michel LaChance
APM	Shady Daisy	Ron Pierce
ATM	Peace Corps	Torbjorn Jansson
APH	Artsplace	John Campbell
ATH	No Sex Please	Ron Waples

1993

Div	Winner	Driver
2PC	Expensive Scooter	Jack Moiseyev
2PF	Electric Scooter	Mike LaChance
3PC	Life Sign	John Campbell
3PF	Immortality	John Campbell
2TC	Westgate Crown	John Campbell
2TF	Gleam	Jimmy Takter
3TC	Pine Chip	John Campbell
3TF	Expressway Hanover	Per Henriksen
APM	Swing Back	Kelly Sheppard
ATM	Lifetime Dream	Paul MacDonnell
APH	Staying Together	Bill O'Donnell
ATH	Earl	Chris Christoforou Jr.

1994

Div	Winner	Driver
2PC	Jenna's Beach Boy	Bill Fahy
2PF	Yankee Cashmere	Peter Wrenn
3PC	Magical Mike	Michel LaChance
3PF	Hardie Hanover	Tim Twaddle
2TC	Eager Seelster	Teddy Jacobs
2TF	Lookout Victory	John Patterson
3TC	Incredible Abe	Italo Tamborrino
3TF	Imageofa Clear Day	Bill O'Donnell
APM	Shady Daisy	Michel LaChance
ATM	Armbro Keepsake	Stig Johansson
APH	Village Jiffy	Paul MacDonell
ATH	Pine Chip	John Campbell

1995

Div	Winner	Driver
2PC	John Street North	Jack Moiseyev
2PF	Paige Nicole Q	John Campbell
3PC	Jenna's Beach Boy	Bill Fahy
3PF	Headline Hanover	Doug Brown
2TC	Armbro Officer	Steve Condren
2TF	Continentalvictory	Michel LaChance
3TC	Abundance	Bill O'Donnell
3TF	Lookout Victory	Sonny Patterson
APM	Ellamony	Mike Saftic
ATM	CR Kay Suzie	Rod Allen
APH	Thatll Be Me	Roger Mayotte
ATH	Panifesto	Luc Ouellette

1996

Div	Winner	Driver
2PC	His Mattjesty	Doug Brown
2PF	Before Sunrise	Steve Condren
3PC	Armbro Operative	Michel LaChance
3PF	Mystical Maddy	Michel LaChance
2TC	Malabar Man	Mal Burroughs
2TF	Armbro Prowess	Jimmy Takter
3TC	Running Sea	Wally Hennessey
3TF	Personal Banner	Peter Wrenn
APM	She's A Great Lady	John Campbell
APH	Jenna's Beach Boy	Bill Fahy
AT	CR Kay Suzie	Rod Allen

Note: 2=Two-year-old; T=Trotter; C=Colt; 3=Three-year-old; P=Pacer; F=Filly; A=Aged; H=Horse; M=Mare.

Breeders' Crown *(Cont.)*

1997 *(Cont.)*

Div	Winner	Driver	Div	Winner	Driver
2PC	His Mattjesty	Doug Brown	3TC	Running Sea	Wally Hennessey
2PF	Before Sunrise	Steve Condren	3TF	Personal Banner	Peter Wrenn
3PC	Armbro Operative	Michel LaChance	APM	She's A Great Lady	John Campbell
3PF	Mystical Maddy	Michel LaChance	APH	Jenna's Beach Boy	Bill Fahy
2TC	Malabar Man	Mal Burroughs	AT	CR Kay Suzie	Rod Allen
2TF	Armbro Prowess	Jimmy Takter			

Triple Crown Winners

Trotting

Trotting's Triple Crown consists of the Hambletonian (first run in 1926), the Kentucky Futurity (first run in 1893), and the Yonkers Trot (known as the Yonkers Futurity when it began in 1955).

Year	Horse	Owner	Breeder	Trainer & Driver
1955	Scott Frost	S.A. Camp Farms	Est of W.N. Reynolds	Joe O'Brien
1963	Speedy Scot	Castleton Farms	Castleton Farms	Ralph Baldwin
1964	Ayres	Charlotte Sheppard	Charlotte Sheppard	John Simpson Sr
1968	Nevele Pride	Nevele Acres & Lou Resnick	Mr & Mrs E.C. Quin	Stanley Dancer
1969	Lindy's Pride	Lindy Farm	Hanover Shoe Farms	Howard Beissinger
1972	Super Bowl	Rachel Dancer & Rose Hild Breeding Farm	Stoner Creek Stud	Stanley Dancer

Pacing

Pacing's Triple Crown consists of the Cane Pace (called the Cane Futurity when it began in 1955), the Little Brown Jug (first run in 1946), and the Messenger Stakes (first run in 1956).

Year	Horse	Owner	Breeder	Trainer/Driver
1959	Adios Butler	Paige West & Angelo Pellillo	R.C. Carpenter	Paige West/Clint Hodgins
1965	Bret Hanover	Richard Downing	Hanover Shoe Farms	Frank Ervin
1966	Romeo Hanover	Lucky Star Stables & Morton Finder	Hanover Shoe Farms	Jerry Silverman/ William Meyer (Cane) & George Sholty (Jug & Messenger)
1968	Rum Customer	Kennilworth Farms & L. C. Mancuso	Mr. & Mrs. R.C. Larkin	Bill Haughton
1970	Most Happy Fella	Egyptian Acres Stable	Stoner Creek Stud	Stanley Dancer
1980	Niatross	Niagara Acres, C. Galbraith & Niatross Stables	Niagara Acres	Clint Galbraith
1983	Ralph Hanover	Waples Stable, Pointsetta Stable, Grant's Direct Stable & P. J. Baugh	Hanover Shoe Farms	Stew Firlotte/Ron Waples
1997	Western Dreamer	Daniel and Matthew Daly and Patrick Daly Jr.	Kentuckiana Farms	Bill Robinson/Michel Lachance

Awards

Horse of the Year

Year	Horse	Gait	Owner	Year	Horse	Gait	Owner
1947	Victory Song	T	Castleton Farm	1957	Torpid	P	Sherwood Farm
1948	Rodney	T	R.H. Johnston	1958	Emily's Pride	T	Walnut Hall and Castleton Farms
1949	Good Time	P	William Cane	1959	Bye Bye Byrd	P	Mr. and Mrs. Rex Larkin
1950	Proximity	T	Ralph and Gordon Verhurst	1960	Adios Butler	P	Adios Butler Syndicate
1951	Pronto Don	T	Hayes Fair Acres Stable	1961	Adios Butler	P	Adios Butler Syndicate
1952	Good Time	P	William Cane	1962	Su Mac Lad	T	I.W. Berkemeyer
1953	Hi Lo's Forbes	P	Mr. and Mrs. Earl Wagner	1963	Speedy Scot	T	Castleton Farm
1954	Stenographer	T	Max Hempt	1964	Bret Hanover	P	Richard Downing
1955	Scott Frost	T	S.A. Camp Farms	1965	Bret Hanover	P	Richard Downing
1956	Scott Frost	T	S.A. Camp Farms	1966	Bret Hanover	P	Richard Downing

Horse of the Year (Cont.)

Year	Horse	Gait	Owner	Year	Horse	Gait	Owner
1967	Nevele Pride	T	Nevele Acres	1983	Cam Fella	P	JEF's Standardbred, Norm Clements, Norm Faulkner
1968	Nevele Pride	T	Nevele Acres, Louis Resnick	1984	Fancy Crown	T	Fancy Crown Stable
1969	Nevele Pride	T	Nevele Acres, Louis Resnick	1985	Nihilator	P	Wall Street-Nihilator Syndicate
1970	Fresh Yankee	T	Duncan MacDonald	1986	Forrest	P	Forrest L. Bartlett
1971	Albatross	P	Albatross Stable		Skipper		
1972	Albatross	P	Amicable Stable	1987	Mack Lobell	T	One More Time Stable and Fair Wind Farm
1973	Sir Dalrae	P	A La Carte Racing Stable	1988	Mack Lobell	T	John Erik Magnusson
1974	Delmonica Hanover	T	Delvin Miller, W. Arnold Hanger	1989	Matt's Scooter	P	Gordon and Illa Rumpel, Charles Jurasvinski
1975	Savoir	T	Allwood Stable	1990	Beach Towel	P	Uptown Stables
1976	Keystone Ore	P	Mr. and Mrs. Stanley Dancer, Rose Hild Farms, Robert Jones	1991	Precious Bunny	P	R. Peter Heffering
1977	Green Speed	T	Beverly Lloyds	1992	Artsplace	P	George Segal
1978	Abercrombie	P	Shirley Mitchell, L. Keith Bulen	1993	Staying Together	P	Robert Hamather
1979	Niatross	P	Niagara Acres, Clint Galbraith	1994	Cam's Card Shark	P	Jeffrey S. Snyder
1980	Niatross	P	Niatross Syndicate, Niagara Acres, Clint Galbraith	1995	CR Kay Suzie	T	Carl & Rod Allen Stable, Inc.
1981	Fan Hanover	P	Dr. J. Glen Brown	1996	Continental-victory	T	Continentalvictory Stables
1982	Cam Fella	P	Norm Clements, Norm Faulkner	1997	Malabar Man	T	Malvern Burroughs

Note: Balloting is conducted by the U.S Trotting Association for the U.S. Harness Writers Association.

Leading Drivers—Money Won

Year	Driver	Winnings ($)	Year	Driver	Winnings ($)
1946	Thomas Berry	121,933	1972	Herve Filion	2,473,265
1947	H.C. Fitzpatrick	133,675	1973	Herve Filion	2,233,303
1948	Ralph Baldwin	153,222	1974	Herve Filion	3,474,315
1949	Clint Hodgins	184,108	1975	Carmine Abbatiello	2,275,093
1950	Del Miller	306,813	1976	Herve Filion	2,278,634
1951	John Simpson Sr.	333,316	1977	Herve Filion	2,551,058
1952	Bill Haughton	311,728	1978	Carmine Abbatiello	3,344,457
1953	Bill Haughton	374,527	1979	John Campbell	3,308,984
1954	Bill Haughton	415,577	1980	John Campbell	3,732,306
1955	Bill Haughton	599,455	1981	Bill O'Donnell	4,065,608
1956	Bill Haughton	572,945	1982	Bill O'Donnell	5,755,067
1957	Bill Haughton	586,950	1983	John Campbell	6,104,082
1958	Bill Haughton	816,659	1984	Bill O'Donnell	9,059,184
1959	Bill Haughton	771,435	1985	Bill O'Donnell	10,207,372
1960	Del Miller	567,282	1986	John Campbell	9,515,055
1961	Stanley Dancer	674,723	1987	John Campbell	10,186,495
1962	Stanley Dancer	760,343	1988	John Campbell	11,148,565
1963	Bill Haughton	790,086	1989	John Campbell	9,738,450
1964	Stanley Dancer	1,051,538	1990	John Campbell	11,620,878
1965	Bill Haughton	889,943	1991	Jack Moiseyev	9,568,468
1966	Stanley Dancer	1,218,403	1992	John Campbell	8,202,108
1967	Bill Haughton	1,305,773	1993	John Campbell	9,926,482
1968	Bill Haughton	1,654,463	1994	John Campbell	9,834,139
1969	Del Insko	1,635,463	1995	John Campbell	9,469,797
1970	Herve Filion	1,647,837	1996	Michel Lachance	8,408,231
1971	Herve Filion	1,915,945	1997	Michel Lachance	9,215,388

Motor Sports

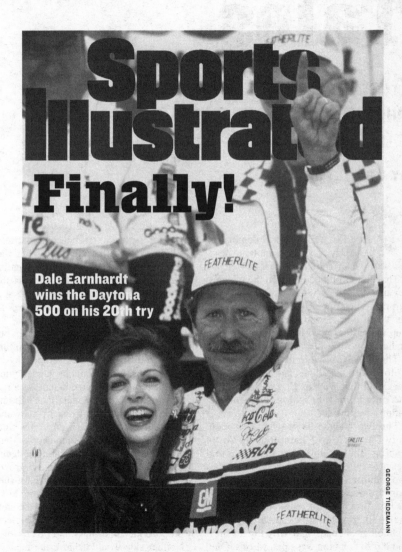

Sports Illustrated

Finally!

Dale Earnhardt wins the Daytona 500 on his 20th try

FEATHERLITE

GEORGE TIEDEMANN

Tire Tales

Frustrated by Jeff Gordon's unprecedented dominance of NASCAR, a rival leveled charges of cheating

BY ED HINTON

THAT DALE EARNHARDT dominated the Daytona 500 was nothing new; the aberration was that he won.

That Jeff Gordon dominated the remainder of the 1998 NASCAR season was no surprise. The gripping plot was his ongoing pursuit of a level of command of Winston Cup racing that no driver before him had attained.

That NASCAR dominated America's motor sports headlines and telecasts—to the extent that Winston Cup was just about the only bona fide major series in the nation—was inevitable.

The two fragments of what had been Indy Car racing—Championship Auto Racing Teams and the Indy Racing League—carried on separately, with relative stability, in the third year of their division. By mid-'98 both had privately realized the dire need for reunion. But by then they had traveled down such disparate technological roads that virtually all they had left in common was open wheels. One or both of the circuits will have to cross a

chasm for the two to reach a compromise.

While each was breathing, neither was vibrant—though CART gained a singular pizzazz in the person of Alex Zanardi, the delightful presence who breezed to his second series championship while he pondered returning to Formula One.

NASCAR didn't win only by default, but also by its people-pleasing competition that emphasized drivers over machines; by its easy-to-follow format; and by its marketing plan, the best-orchestrated in motor sports.

Outside the U.S., Formula One's drama turned from the usual one of man and machine into one of man *against* machine: the brilliant Michael Schumacher's talent (and temper) versus the brilliantly designed McLaren Mercedes's might and grace. While Schumacher's Ferrari played a supporting role to him, McLaren driver Mika Hakkinen was upstaged by his black-and-silver machine, which had the most perfectly proportioned body in Grand Prix racing.

Neither side would achieve the peak of its potential because each had a flaw. Schu-

According to one observer, Gordon and Evernham (left) are simply the best alltime.

macher had his wildness; the McLaren had its temperamental gearbox. And so neither Schumacher nor Hakkinen could break clear of the other as the world championship duel entered the homestretch.

While Earnhardt may not have been in the running for the Winston Cup title down *its* homestretch, the finish at Daytona was another matter. Time and again he had dominated the early, middle, even late stages of the 500. In the most tantalizing of several near misses, he'd commanded the 1990 race for 499 miles before running over debris and shredding a tire in Turn 3 on the final lap.

He'd won every other type of event that stock cars run at Daytona International Speedway. But he was 0 for 19 in the 500 going into its '98 running. Pre- and post-race accounts of the seven-time Winston Cup champion's misfortunes at Daytona had become perennial fodder for the media covering Daytona each February. The best NASCAR driver of his generation simply could not, it seemed, win the big one.

And this time he came in on a 59-race losing streak on the Winston Cup tour

overall, the worst of his career. Theories of his being washed-up abounded.

But 50 years to the day after NASCAR staged its first race on the sands of Daytona Beach, 40 years after the first Daytona 500 and 20 years after Earnhardt's debut in the big race (he had been a cocky rookie back then, behaving as if he would win a bunch of these in short order), his stars finally aligned.

It is unlikely that even one person among the 175,000-plus in the grandstand was surprised to see the ominous black number 3 Chevrolet Monte Carlo out front in the waning laps. It is just as unlikely that a single spectator failed to wonder what might spoil it this time.

But Earnhardt dodged bullet after bullet. With 27 laps to go, teammates Rusty Wallace and Jeremy Mayfield were preparing to draft past Earnhardt when John Andretti and Robert Pressley collided, bringing out the second caution flag of the day and leaving Earnhardt on the point. After the lead pack pitted, Earnhardt's Richard Childress Racing crew—which had absorbed as much over-the-hill talk as Earnhardt himself—got him back onto the track first.

On the restart, with 23 laps left, Earnhardt's teammate, Mike Skinner, tucked his Chevy up behind Earnhardt's and gave Earnhardt an enormous aerodynamic boost, allowing Earnhardt to jump comfortably out front. As Bobby Labonte came charging up in a Pontiac on the penultimate lap and was about to give Earnhardt his hardest test of the day, a three-car wreck brought out the yellow flag along with the white, making the final lap Earnhardt's early victory parade.

With an attention-demanding thud, Earnhardt stomped onto the platform for the winner's interview he'd coveted for so long. "I'm here," he crowed. "And I've got that goddamn *monkey* off my back!" With that he produced a stuffed toy monkey from his uniform and flung it into the crowd of reporters. Then he announced that he would go on to win a record eighth season championship in 1998.

It was not to be; not even close. Earnhardt would slip back into the doldrums, and Jeff Gordon would pick up where he left off in '97, his blistering pace taking him steadily toward the pinnacle of stock car racing. Little noted nor long remembered was the fact that Gordon had, in racers' jargon, "checked out" (taken the lead with ease) in the '98 Daytona 500, and should have won the race handily for the second straight year. But on about Lap 123—not even Gordon was sure of the moment—of the 200 laps, his Monte Carlo struck a small chunk of rubber from a disintegrated tire on the track. That dented the front-end air dam and ruined the erstwhile perfect handling of Gordon's car.

If not for this happenstance Earnhardt would still be 0 for career in the Daytona 500. At least the younger racer allowed Earnhardt one piece of glory in '98; Gordon would take all the rest. After 10-win seasons in '96 and '97, Gordon's 10th win of '98—in the Southern 500 at Darlington—made him the first driver in NASCAR's "modern era" (from 1972 forward) to achieve double-digit victory totals in three consecutive seasons.

But along with that Labor Day weekend win at Darlington came the biggest controversy of Gordon's career to date: His team

had been accused of "soaking" its tires—treating them with chemicals to make them softer for better grip—the week before by rival owner Jack Roush. Although Gordon's team appeared to be innocent from the outset of the controversy, the charges took on a life of their own.

Time was when cheating in NASCAR was greeted with winks and chuckles. That time has past. NASCAR has been pursuing an image-improvement campaign in recent years, and the squeaky-clean Gordon has helped that campaign and become a nationally recognized figure in the process. He has made Pepsi commercials with Shaquille O'Neal and is one of the few drivers who transcend motor sports. For Gordon's team to be caught cheating would, in the words of NASCAR legend Richard Petty, "be earth-shattering." Thus the allegations unfolded as *the* ongoing drama of late summer in U.S. motor sports.

The only drama CART had to offer was whether or not Zanardi, who had nothing left to prove in American open-wheel competition, would return to the series in '99. CART needed his effervescent personality and his trademark, victory-celebrating doughnuts—the marks he left on the pavement after spinning his car in tight circles each time he won. Alas, on Sept. 22 Zanardi announced he would return to Formula One racing.

The IRL was developing a hero it hadn't bargained for. Formula One dropout Kenny Brack of Sweden was exactly the sort of driver the IRL had complained was becoming too dominant in the rival CART. Supposedly the IRL's mission was to give struggling young American dirt-trackers big-time opportunities that weren't available to them in CART. There had been no greater nor louder proponent of this ideal than tough old A.J. Foyt, the four-time Indy 500 winner turned team owner. Yet it was Foyt who'd hired Brack and made him a winner.

Foyt succinctly expressed the IRL's attitude adjustment—not to mention his own worldliness—when he told Brack, "We love you, you foreigner!" after the driver took the checkered flag at Atlanta

MARK DUNCAN/AP

on Aug. 29 for his third win in a row.

International racing enthusiasts were preoccupied with the flamboyant driving and off-track outbursts of Schumacher. After he had wrecked himself out of a chance to overtake Hakkinen for the points lead in the Belgian Grand Prix on Aug. 30, Schumacher accused Hakkinen's McLaren teammate, David Coulthard, of "trying to kill me." But it was Schumacher who had plowed into the back of Coulthard's McLaren in the rain at Spa-Francorchamps. And it was the second time Schumacher had so melodramatically accused a competitor. Both times Schumacher's words had all the appearance of a ploy to deflect attention from his own potentially deadly doings on the track.

At Montreal on June 7, Schumacher leveled a similar charge at Damon Hill for a relatively minor incident that harmed neither driver. But on the same day, Schumacher had come flying out of the pits and driven right into the middle of the groove, leaving Heinz-Harald Frentzen with the sudden option of crashing alone or wrecking them both. Frentzen flew off the track. Schumacher, given what arguably amounted to a slap on the wrist for the offense—a 10-second penalty—went on to win.

It seems unlikely that Gordon's team will receive any penalty as a result of the tire brouhaha since the entire controversy, as even NASCAR president Bill France Jr. observed, is rooted in Roush's frustration. While Gordon ripped through a four-race winning streak in July and August, Mark

Out of doughnuts: Zanardi and his signature celebration departed CART.

Martin, the senior driver on Roush's five-car team, finished second to Gordon three straight times and dominated another race, at Michigan Speedway on Aug. 16, before finishing fourth to Gordon.

In Bristol, Tenn., on Aug. 22, Gordon tried for a fifth consecutive win, which would have been a modern-era record. Six racers before him—Cale Yarborough in 1976, Darrell Waltrip in '81, Earnhardt in '87, Harry Gant in '91, Bill Elliott in '92 and Martin in '93—had won four in a row, but none of those legends had won a fifth straight.

Alas, Gordon's car was fitful at Bristol, oversteering terribly, and repeated adjustments in the pits failed to cure it. He finished fifth, while Martin won his fifth race of the season. All was well at Roush Racing again—for a week. In the next race, in Loudon, N.H., Martin dominated most of the race, but Gordon took only two tires on his last pit stop while Martin took on four, and Gordon drove away with the win.

Roush cried foul, and added that he had recently received samples of a substance that, its unidentified distributor claimed, would soften tires for better grip while remaining completely undetectable.

Such softeners are illegal in NASCAR for two reasons. The lesser of the two is that the artificially enhanced grip provides an unfair advantage. The primary reason is that chemical breakdown in a tire's compound drastically increases the

Schumacher won the Hungarian Grand Prix, but few friends on the F1 circuit.

risk of tire failure at high speeds.

Due to Roush's protests, NASCAR confiscated Gordon's race tires and conducted initial field tests, both chemical and physical. The results indicated that the tires had not been tampered with. Further evidence of Gordon's innocence was that he had run the final 67 laps of the race on the tires in question. Artificially softened tires, though they would have given him a boost for four or five laps, probably would have worn out after fewer than 20 laps and would have disintegrated after fewer than 67.

To ensure that the public was convinced, NASCAR sent the tires to an independent lab to undergo tests of such scrutiny that Winston Cup director Gary Nelson called them "a DNA test for tires." Those too came back negative, and tire engineering experts said the notion that any undetectable softening agent could exist was absurd. Even if some miracle chemical disappeared entirely from the tire, they said, evidence that some chemical reaction had occurred would have been obvious in the tire's compound during analysis.

But while the sophisticated tests were ongoing, the furor climaxed at Darlington. Gordon's crew chief, Ray Evernham,

was livid at Roush's challenge to his integrity and was bent on defeating Roush in the Southern 500, where there would be no question of tire-doctoring—for that race NASCAR tire security and scrutiny would be at an alltime high. No race tires were allotted to teams by Goodyear until race morning, and after that, every tire in the event was constantly monitored by NASCAR officials, who then confiscated tires at random following pit stops.

Gordon hinted that Roush might have ignited the entire affair "to distract us" from the Winston Cup points duel with Martin. If that was so, Roush's strategy backfired: His own team's efficiency lapsed. Roush's personal specialty on his team is supervising engine preparation, and at Darlington, Martin's engine failed for the first time in more than a year. One valve, Roush admitted, had been improperly finished and/or fitted.

Another Roush driver, Jeff Burton, took up the cause and dominated for most of the Southern 500. On orders from Evernham in the pits, Gordon conserved his car and himself, challenging for the lead only in the late stages of the race. But Roush and Co. knew what was coming. With 26 laps to go, Gordon pounced. With the victory came Gordon's second Winston No Bull million-dollar race bonus of the season. The other had come in the Brickyard 400 on Aug. 1 as part of a motor sports–record winner's share of $1,637,625.

If Gordon's team wasn't cheating on tires, the question remained throughout the garages of NASCAR, then what *was* the secret that put Gordon and Evernham in a league of their own? The least popular but most likely explanation was offered by team owner Felix Sabates. "I think," he said, "that Jeff Gordon is the best stock car driver of all time. And I think he's got the best crew of all time."

The mathematical proof of that, Evernham figured, is inevitable. "Ten years from now," he said, "the numbers will be in the record books, and the truth will be in black and white."

FOR THE RECORD · 1997 – 1998

Indy Racing League

Indianapolis 500

Results of the 82nd running of the Indianapolis 500 and third round of the 1998 Indy Racing League season. Held Sunday May 24, 1998, at the 2.5-mile Indianapolis Motor Speedway in Indianapolis, IN.

Distance, 500 miles; starters, 33; time of race, 3 hours, 26 minutes, 40.524 seconds; average speed, 145.155 mph; margin of victory, 3.191 seconds; caution flags, 12 for 50 laps; lead changes, 24 among 11 drivers.

TOP 10 FINISHERS

Pos	Driver (start pos.)	Chassis-Engine	Qual. Speed	Laps	Status
1	Eddie Cheever (17)	Dallara-Aurora	217.334	200	running
2	Buddy Lazier (11)	Dallara-Aurora	218.288	200	running
3	Steve Knapp (23)	G Force-Aurora	216.445	200	running
4	Davey Hamilton (8)	G Force-Aurora	219.748	199	running
5	Robby Unser (21)	Dallara-Aurora	216.534	198	running
6	Kenny Brack (3)	Dallara-Aurora	220.982	198	running
7	John Paul Jr. (16)	Dallara-Aurora	217.351	197	running
8	Andy Michner (19)	Dallara-Aurora	216.922	197	running
9	J.J. Yeley (13)	Dallara-Aurora	218.044	197	running
10	Buzz Calkins (18)	G Force-Aurora	217.197	195	running

1998 Indy Racing League Results

Date	Race	Winner (start pos.)	Chassis-Engine	Avg Speed
Jan 24	Indy 200	Tony Stewart (1)	G Force-Aurora	95.14
Mar 22	Phoenix 200	Scott Sharp (8)	Dallara-Aurora	98.110
May 24	Indianapolis 500	Eddie Cheever (17)	Dallara-Aurora	145.155
June 6	True Value 500K	Billy Boat (2)	Dallara-Aurora	145.388
June 28	New England 200	Tony Stewart (1)	Dallara-Aurora	113.861
July 19	Pep Boys 400K	Scott Sharp (4)	Dallara-Aurora	99.318
July 25	Charlotte 500	Kenny Brack (3)	Dallara-Aurora	158.408
Aug 16	Radisson 200	Kenny Brack (5)	Dallara-Aurora	133.515
Aug 29	Atlanta 500K	Kenny Brack (6)	Dallara-Oldsmobile	140.026
Sept 20	Lone Star 500K	John Paul Jr. (14)	G Force-Aurora	109.080

Note: Distances are in miles unless followed by K (kilometers).

1996–97 Final Championship Standings

Driver	Starts	Highest Finish	Pts
Tony Stewart	10	1	278
Davey Hamilton	10	3	272
Marco Greco	10	4	230
Eddie Cheever	10	1	230
Scott Goodyear	8	2	226

Championship Auto Racing Teams

U.S. 500

Results of the 3rd running of the U.S. 500 and 12th round of the 1998 CART FedEx Series. Held Sunday, July 26, 1998 at the 2-mile Michigan International Speedway in Brooklyn, MI.

Distance, 500 miles; starters, 28; time of race, 3:00:48.785; average speed, 165.913 mph; margin of victory, .259 seconds; caution flags, eight for 55 laps; lead changes, 62 among nine drivers.

TOP 10 FINISHERS

Pos	Driver (start pos.)	Car	Qual. Speed	Laps	Status
1	Greg Moore (14)	Reynard-Mercedes	225.437	250	running
2	Jimmy Vasser (2)	Reynard-Honda	228.855	250	running
3	Alex Zanardi (7)	Reynard-Honda	227.237	250	running
4	Scott Pruett (6)	Reynard-Ford	227.316	250	running
5	Richie Hearn (3)	Swift-Ford	228.238	250	running
6	Michael Andretti (8)	Swift-Ford	227.129	250	running
7	Bobby Rahal (12)	Reynard-Ford	225.882	250	running
8	Patrick Carpentier (21)	Reynard-Mercedes	223.755	250	running
9	Paul Tracy (15)	Reynard-Honda	225.113	250	running
10	Bryan Herta (5)	Reynard-Ford	227.395	250	running

1998 CART Championship Series Results (Through September 13)

Date	Event	Winner (start pos.)	Car	Avg Speed
Mar 15	Grand Prix of Miami	Michael Andretti (8)	Swift-Ford	144.339
Mar 28	Budweiser 500	Adrian Fernandez (2)	Reynard-Ford	159.393
Apr 5	Grand Prix of Long Beach	Alex Zanardi (11)	Reynard-Honda	89.946
Apr 26	Nazareth Grand Prix	Jimmy Vasser (5)	Reynard-Honda	108.839
May 10	Rio 400	Greg Moore (7)	Reynard-Mercedes	131.251
May 23	Motorola 300	Alex Zanardi (11)	Reynard-Honda	125.725
May 31	Milwaukee 200	Jimmy Vasser (5)	Reynard-Honda	131.349
June 7	Detroit Grand Prix	Alex Zanardi (2)	Reynard-Honda	100.052
June 21	Portland 200	Alex Zanardi (5)	Reynard-Honda	101.355
July 12	Grand Prix of Cleveland	Alex Zanardi (3)	Reynard-Honda	112.449
July 19	Indy Toronto	Alex Zanardi (2)	Reynard-Honda	87.274
July 26	U.S. 500	Greg Moore (14)	Reynard-Mercedes	165.913
Aug 9	Mid-Ohio 200	Adrian Fernandez (5)	Reynard-Ford	98.428
Aug 16	Elkhart Lake 200	Dario Franchitti (6)	Reynard-Honda	127.145
Sept 6	Indy Vancouver	Dario Franchitti (1)	Reynard-Honda	77.081
Sept 13	Grand Prix of Monterey	Bryan Herta (1)	Reynard-Ford	96.726

1997 Championship Standings

Driver	Starts	Wins	Pts
Alex Zanardi	16	5	195
Gil de Ferran	17	0	162
Jimmy Vasser	17	1	144
Mauricio Gugelmin	17	1	132
Paul Tracy	16	3	121
Mark Blundell	17	3	115
Greg Moore	17	2	111
Michael Andretti	17	1	108
Scott Pruett	17	1	102
Raul Boesel	17	0	91

National Association for Stock Car Auto Racing

Daytona 500

Results of the opening round of the 1998 Winston Cup series. Held Sunday, February 15, at the 2.5-mile high-banked Daytona International Speedway.

Distance, 500 miles; starters, 43; time of race, 2:53:42; average speed, 172.712 mph; margin of victory, under caution; caution flags, 3 for 9 laps; lead changes, 13 among 8 drivers.

TOP 10 FINISHERS

Pos	Driver (start pos.)	Car	Laps	Winnings ($)
1	Dale Earnhardt (4)	Chevrolet	200	1,059,105
2	Bobby Labonte (1)	Pontiac	200	548,555
3	Jeremy Mayfield (13)	Ford	200	375,005
4	Ken Schrader (31)	Chevrolet	200	312,780
5	Rusty Wallace (12)	Ford	200	232,005
6	Ernie Irvan (10)	Pontiac	200	204,500
7	Chad Little (21)	Ford	200	126,980
8	Mike Skinner (8)	Chevrolet	200	135,005
9	Michael Waltrip (6)	Ford	200	142,005
10	Bill Elliott (19)	Ford	200	128,455

Late 1997 Winston Cup Series Results

Date	Track/Distance	Winner (start pos.)	Car	Avg Speed	Winnings ($)
Oct 6	Charlotte 500	Terry Labonte (16)	Chevrolet	143.143	133,950
Oct 12	Talladega 500	Terry Labonte (6)	Chevrolet	156.601	116,725
Oct 20	Rockingham 400	Ricky Rudd (3)	Ford	122.320	90,025
Oct 27	Phoenix 500K	Bobby Hamilton (17)	Pontiac	109.709	97,550
Nov 10	Atlanta 500	Bobby Labonte (1)	Pontiac	134.661	274,900

Note: Distances are in miles unless followed by * (laps) or K (kilometers).

1998 Winston Cup Series Results (through September 21)

Date	Track/Distance	Winner (start pos.)	Car	Avg Speed	Winnings ($)
Feb 15	Daytona 500	Dale Earnhardt (4)	Chevrolet	172.712	1,059,105
Feb 23	N Carolina 400	Jeff Gordon (4)	Chevrolet	117.065	90,090
Mar 1	Las Vegas 400	Mark Martin (7)	Ford	146.530	313,900
Mar 9	Atlanta 500	Bobby Labonte (14)	Pontiac	139.501	106,800
Mar 22	Darlington 400	Dale Jarrett (3)	Ford	127.962	110,035
Mar 29	Bristol 500*	Jeff Gordon (2)	Chevrolet	82.850	90,860
Apr 5	Texas 500	Mark Martin (7)	Ford	136.771	356,850
Apr 20	Martinsville 500*	Bobby Hamilton (1)	Chevrolet	70.709	227,025
Apr 26	Talladega 500	Bobby Labonte (1)	Pontiac	163.439	141,870
May 3	California 500	Mark Martin (3)	Ford	140.220	141,375
May 24	World 600	Jeff Gordon (1)	Chevrolet	136.424	346,500
May 31	Dover Downs 400	Dale Jarrett (4)	Ford	119.522	89,850
June 6	Richmond 400*	Terry Labonte (16)	Chevrolet	97.044	99,975
June 14	Michigan 400	Mark Martin (7)	Ford	158.695	92,375
June 21	Pocono 500	Jeremy Mayfield (3)	Ford	117.801	111,580
June 28	Sears Point 350K	Jeff Gordon (1)	Chevrolet	72.387	160,675
July 12	New Hampshire 300*	Jeff Burton (5)	Ford	102.996	128,575
July 26	Pennsylvania 500	Jeff Gordon (2)	Chevrolet	134.650	165,495
Aug 1	Indianapolis 400	Jeff Gordon (24)	Chevrolet	126.770	1,637,625
Aug 9	Watkins Glen 90*	Jeff Gordon (1)	Chevrolet	94.446	152,970
Aug 16	Michigan 400	Jeff Gordon (3)	Chevrolet	151.995	120,302
Aug 22	Bristol 500*	Mark Martin (4)	Ford	86.918	80,315
Sept 14	New Hampshire 300*	Jeff Gordon (1)	Chevrolet	112.078	205,400
Sept 6	Southern 500	Jeff Gordon (5)	Chevrolet	139.031	134,655
Sept 12	Richmond 400	Jeff Burton (3)	Ford	91.985	108,495
Sept 20	Dover 400	Mark Martin (1)	Ford	113.834	126,130
Sept 27	Martinsville 500*	Ricky Rudd (2)	Ford	73.350	102,575

Note: Distances are in miles unless followed by * (laps) or K (kilometers).

1997 Winston Cup Final Standings

Driver	Car	Starts	Wins	Pts
Jeff Gordon	Chevy	32	10	4,710
Dale Jarrett	Ford	32	7	4,696
Mark Martin	Ford	32	4	4,681
Jeff Burton	Ford	32	3	4,285
Dale Earnhardt	Chevy	32	0	4,216
Terry Labonte	Chevy	32	1	4,177
Bobby Labonte	Pontiac	32	1	4,101
Bill Elliott	Ford	32	0	3,836
Rusty Wallace	Ford	32	1	3,598
Ken Schrader	Chevy	32	0	3,576

1997 Winston Cup Driver Winnings

Driver	Winnings ($)
Jeff Gordon	6,375,658
Dale Jarrett	3,240,542
Mark Martin	2,532,484
Jeff Burton	2,296,614
Terry Labonte	2,270,144
Bobby Labonte	2,217,999
Dale Earnhardt	2,151,909
Ricky Rudd	1,975,981
Rusty Wallace	1,705,625
Ernie Irvan	1,614,281

Formula One Grand Prix Racing

1998 Formula One Results (Through September 27)

Date	Grand Prix	Winner	Car	Time
Mar 8	Australia	Mika Hakkinen	McLaren-Mercedes	1:31:45.996
Mar 29	Brazil	Mika Hakkinen	McLaren-Mercedes	1:37:11.747
Apr 12	Argentina	Michael Schumacher	Ferrari	1:48:36.175
Apr 26	San Marino	David Coulthard	McLaren-Mercedes	1:34:24.593
May 10	Spain	Mika Hakkinen	McLaren-Mercedes	1:33:37.621
May 24	Monaco	Jacques Villeneuve	Williams-Renault	1:51:23.595
June 7	Canada	Michael Schumacher	Ferrari	1:40:57.355
June 28	France	Michael Schumacher	Ferrari	1:34:45.026
July 12	Great Britain	Michael Schumacher	Scuderia-Ferrari	1:47:02.450
July 26	Austria	Mika Hakkinen	McLaren-Mercedes	1:30:44.086
Aug 2	Germany	Mika Hakkinen	McLaren-Mercedes	1:20:47.984
Aug 16	Hungary	Michael Schumacher	Ferrari	1:45:25.550
Aug 30	Belgium	Damon Hill	Jordan-Mugen Honda	1:43:47.407
Sept 13	Italy	Michael Schumacher	Ferrari	1:17:09.672
Sept 27	Luxembourg	Mika Hakkinen	McLaren-Mercedes	1:32:14.789

1997 World Championship Final Standings

Drivers compete in Grand Prix races for the title of World Driving Champion. Below are the top 10 results from the 1997 season. Points are awarded for places 1–6 as follows: 10-6-4-3-2-1.

Driver, Country	Starts	Wins	Car	Pts
Jacques Villeneuve, Canada	17	7	Williams-Renault	81
Heinz-Harald Frentzen, Germany	17	1	Williams-Renault	42
Jean Alesi, France	17	0	Benetton-Renault	36
David Coulthard, Great Britain	17	1	McLaren-Mercedes	36
Mika Häkkinen, Finland	17	1	McLaren-Mercedes	27
Gerhard Berger, Austria	17	1	Benetton-Renault	27
Eddie Irvine, Great Britain	17	0	Ferrari	24
Giancarlo Fisichella, Italy	17	0	Jordan-Peugeot	20
Olivier Panis, France	17	0	Prost-Mugen Honda	16
Johnny Herbert, Great Britain	17	0	Sauber-Petronas	15

Note: Michael Schumacher of Germany, who finished with five wins and 78 points, was stripped of his second-place standing on Nov. 11, 1997, for an "apparently deliberate but instinctive and not premeditated" collision with Villeneuve at the European Grand Prix on October 26.

Professional SportsCar Racing, Inc.

The 24 Hours of Daytona

Held at the Daytona International Speedway on January 31–February 1, 1998, the 24 Hours of Daytona annually serves as the opening round of Professional SportsCar Racing's season.

Place	Drivers	Car (Class)	Distance
1	Arie Luyendyk, Didier Theys, Mauro Baldi	Ferrari (CA)	711 laps (105.465 mph)
2	Danny Sullivan, Allan McNish, Jorg Mueller, Dirk Mueller, Uwe Alzen	Porsche (GT-1)	703 laps
3	Clark Rosenblad, Christophe Bouchut, Patrice Goueslard, André Ahrie	Porsche (GT-1)	667 laps
4	Peter Kitchak, Angelo Zadura, Toni Seller, Wido Roessler	Porsche (GT-2)	660 laps
5	John Graham, John Morton, Patrick Huisman, Duncan Huisman	Porsche (GT-2)	659 laps

1998 World SportsCar Championship Results (Through September 17)

Date	Race	Winners	Car
Jan 31–Feb 1	24 Hours of Daytona	Arie Luyendyk, Didier Theys, Mauro Baldi	Ferrari
Mar 21	12 Hours of Sebring	Didier Theys, Gianpierro Moretti, Mauro Baldi	Ferrari
Apr 26	Las Vegas Grand Prix	Wayne Taylor, Eric van de Poele	Ferrari
May 25	Lime Rock Grand Prix	Butch Leitzinger, James Weaver	Ford
June 21	Grand Prix of Atlanta	Butch Leitzinger, James Weaver	Ford
Aug 9	Mosport 500	Butch Leitzinger, James Weaver	Ford
Sept 17	Sebring Classic	James Weaver, Butch Leitzinger	Ford

1998 Supreme GTS-1 Results (Through September 17)

Date	Race	Winners	Car
Jan 31–Feb 1	24 Hours of Daytona	Danny Sullivan, Allan McNish, Jorg Mueller, Dirk Mueller, Uwe Alzen	Porsche
Mar 21	12 Hours of Sebring	Andy Wallace, David Brabham	Panoz
Apr 26	Las Vegas Grand Prix	Andy Wallace, David Brabham	Panoz
May 25	Lime Rock Grand Prix	Andy Wallace, David Brabham	Panoz
June 21	Grand Prix of Atlanta	Thierry Boutsen, Bob Wollek	Porsche
Aug 9	Mosport 500	David Brabham, Andy Wallace	Panoz
Sept 17	Sebring Classic	Andy Wallace, David Brabham	Panoz

1997 World SportsCar Championship Final Standings

Driver	Pts
Butch Leitzinger	205
Elliott Forbes-Robinson	199
James Weaver	189
Rob Morgan	179
Antonio Hermann	155
Andrea Montermini	154
Jim Pace	148
Wayne Taylor	145
Eric van de Poele	143
Jim Downing	133

24 Hours of Le Mans

Held at Le Mans, France, on June 6–7, 1998, the 24 Hours of Le Mans is the most prestigious international event in endurance racing.

Place	Drivers	Car	Distance
1	Alan McNish, Laurent Aiello, Stephane Ortelli	Porsche GT One	351 laps (2,967.9 mi)
2	Jorg Muller, Uwe Alzen, Bob Wolleck	Porsche GT One	350
3	Kazuyoshi Hoshino, Aguri Suzuki, Masahiko Kageyama	Nissan R390	347
4	Steve O'Rourke, Tim Sugden, Bill Auberlen	McLaren F1	343
5	John Nielsen, Franck Lagorce, Michael Krumm	Nissan R390 GT One	342
6	Erik Comas, Jan Lammers, Andrea Montermini	Nissan V8	342
7	David Brabham, Andy Wallace, Jamie Davies	Panoz GT-R1	335
8	Wayne Taylor, Eric van de Poele, Fermin Velez	Ferrari 333	332
9	Ukyo Katayama, Toshio Suzuki, Keichi Tsuchiya	Toyota GT One	326
10	Takuya Kurosawa, Satoshi Motoyama, Masami Kageyama	Nissan R390 GT1	319

National Hot Rod Association

1998 Results (Through September 20)

TOP FUEL

Date	Race, Site	Winner	Time	Speed
Jan 29–Feb 1	Winternationals, Pomona, CA	Larry Dixon Jr.	4.752	251.18
Feb 19–22	ATSCO Nationals, Phoenix	Cory McClenathan	4.627	319.71
Mar 13–14	Mac Tools Gatornationals, Gainesville, FL	Kenny Bernstein	4.604	318.47
Mar 20–23	Pennzoil Nationals, Houston	Cory McClenathan	4.559	320.74
Apr 3–5	Winston Invitational, Rockingham, NC	Kenny Bernstein	4.710	305.39
Apr 16–19	Fram Nationals, Atlanta	Cory McClenathan	4.756	306.12
Apr 23–26	Pennzoil Nationals, Richmond, VA	Cory McClenathan	4.723	302.01
Apr 30–May 3	Lone Star Nationals, Dallas	Joe Amato	4.695	313.58
May 14–17	Mopar Nationals, Englishtown, NJ	Joe Amato	4.614	319.90
May 28–31	Route 66 Nationals, Joliet, IL	Kenny Bernstein	5.586	265.43
June 11–14	Pontiac Nationals, Columbus, OH	Kenny Bernstein	4.687	310.66
June 25–28	Sears Nationals, Madison, IL	Gary Scelzi	4.711	300.60
July 16–19	Mile-High Nationals, Denver	Cory McClenathan	4.926	297.52
July 24–26	Autolite Nationals, Sonoma, CA	Doug Kalitta	4.802	306.43
July 31–Aug 3	Northwest Nationals, Seattle	Joe Amato	4.857	294.88
Aug 20–23	Champion Auto Nationals, Brainerd, MN	Gary Scelzi	4.829	303.23
Sept 2–7	U.S. Nationals, Indianapolis	Gary Scelzi	5.961	282.57
Sept 17–20	Keystone Nationals, Mohnton, PA	Gary Scelzi	4.637	305.39

FUNNY CAR

Date	Race, Site	Winner	Time	Speed
Jan 29–Feb 1	Winternationals, Pomona, CA	Ron Capps	6.603	211.71
Feb 19–22	ATSCO Nationals, Phoenix	Chuck Etchells	4.944	312.82
Mar 13–14	Mac Tools Gatornationals, Gainesville, FL	Cruz Pedregon	5.747	277.77
Mar 19–22	Pennzoil Nationals, Houston	Tony Pedregon	4.847	316.67
Apr 3–5	Winston Invitational, Rockingham, NC	Cruz Pedregon	4.927	312.06
Apr 16–19	Fram Nationals, Atlanta	Cruz Pedregon	5.049	303.74
Apr 23–26	Pennzoil Nationals, Richmond, VA	Chuck Etchells	6.019	238.79

1998 Results (Through September 20) *(Cont.)*

FUNNY CAR *(CONT.)*

Date	Race, Site	Winner	Time	Speed
Apr 30–May 3	Lone Star Nationals, Dallas	Ron Capps	4.960	292.39
May 14–17	Mopar Nationals, Englishtown, NJ	John Force	4.845	323.89
May 28–31	Route 66 Nationals, Joliet, IL	Whit Bazemore	5.001	297.42
June 11–14	Pontiac Nationals, Columbus, OH	Frank Pedregon	5.262	285.53
June 25–28	Sears Nationals, Madison, IL	Frank Pedregon	5.295	232.07
July 16–19	Mile-High Nationals, Denver	Tony Pedregon	5.417	282.30
July 24–26	Autolite Nationals, Sonoma, CA	Cruz Pedregon	5.073	300.80
July 31–Aug 3	Northwest Nationals, Seattle	Ron Capps	5.136	288.27
Aug 20–23	Champion Auto Nationals, Brainerd, MN	Ron Capps	5.098	291.16
Sept 2–7	U.S. Nationals, Indianapolis	John Force	4.992	306.43
Sept 17–20	Keystone Nationals, Mohnton, PA	Dean Skuza	5.039	288.55

PRO STOCK

Date	Race, Site	Winner	Time	Speed
Jan 29–Feb 1	Winternationals, Pomona, CA	Jim Yates	6.968	197.49
Feb 19–22	ATSCO Nationals, Phoenix	Warren Johnson	6.974	197.49
Mar 13–14	Mac Tools Gatornationals, Gainesville, FL	Warren Johnson	6.873	201.20
Mar 19–22	Pennzoil Nationals, Houston	Warren Johnson	6.878	201.02
Apr 3–5	Winston Invitational, Rockingham, NC	Mark Osborne	7.025	196.89
Apr 16–19	Fram Nationals, Atlanta	Mark Osborne	6.996	198.10
Apr 23–26	Pennzoil Nationals, Richmond, VA	Warren Johnson	6.952	198.50
Apr 30–May 3	Lone Star Nationals, Dallas	Mike Edwards	7.024	195.56
May 14–17	Mopar Nationals, Englishtown, NJ	Jeg Coughlin	6.932	198.52
May 28–31	Route 66 Nationals, Joliet, IL	Mike Thomas	7.024	196.39
June 11–14	Pontiac Nationals, Columbus, OH	Jeg Coughlin	7.022	196.03
June 25–28	Sears Nationals, Madison, IL	Kurt Johnson	7.056	195.31
July 16–19	Mile-High Nationals, Denver	Jeg Coughlin	7.468	184.31
July 24–26	Autolite Nationals, Sonoma, CA	Warren Johnson	7.135	196.24
July 31–Aug 3	Northwest Nationals, Seattle	Warren Johnson	6.967	198.45
Aug 20–23	Champion Auto Nationals, Brainerd, MN	Tom Martino	7.165	191.81
Sept 2–7	U.S. Nationals, Indianapolis	Mike Edwards	7.034	194.46
Sept 17–20	Keystone Nationals, Reading, PA	Kurt Johnson	6.984	196.63

1997 Standings

TOP FUEL

Driver	Wins	Pts
Gary Scelzi	5	1,837
Cory McClenathan	6	1,660
Joe Amato	5	1,597
Scott Kalitta	1	1,301
Kenny Bernstein	2	1,279
Bob Vandergriff Jr.	0	1,083
Larry Dixon	0	1,071
Mike Dunn	0	1,044
Jim Head	2	955
Shelly Anderson	0	889

FUNNY CAR

Driver	Wins	Pts
John Force	6	1,865
Tony Pedregon	2	1,411
Whit Bazemore	4	1,405
Chuck Etchells	1	1,298
Ron Capps	2	1,174
Randy Anderson	2	1,167
Cruz Pedregon	0	1,166
Dean Skuza	1	1,083
Kenji Okazaki	1	959
Gary Densham	0	924

PRO STOCK

Driver	Wins	Pts
Jim Yates	9	1,963
Warren Johnson	4	1,629
Kurt Johnson	3	1,575
Bruce Allen	0	1,110
Steve Schmidt	0	1,085
Tom Martino	2	910
George Marnell	0	895
Troy Coughlin	0	831
Larry Morgan	0	823
Scott Geoffrion	1	821

Indianapolis 500

First held in 1911, the Indianapolis 500—200 laps of the 2.5-mile Indianapolis Motor Speedway Track (called the Brickyard in honor of its original pavement)—grew to become the most famous auto race in the world. Though the Memorial Day weekend event lost participants and prestige in the mid-1990s due to feuding in the world of U.S. open-wheel racing, it annually attracts crowds of over 100,000.

Year	Winner (Start Position)	Car	Avg MPH	Pole Winner	MPH
1911	Ray Harroun (28)	Marmon Wasp	74.590	Lewis Strang	Awarded pole
1912	Joe Dawson (7)	National	78.720	Gil Anderson	Drew pole
1913	Jules Goux (7)	Peugeot	75.930	Caleb Bragg	Drew pole
1914	Rene Thomas (15)	Delage	82.470	Jean Chassagne	Drew pole
1915	Ralph DePalma (2)	Mercedes	89.840	Howard Wilcox	98.90
1916	Dario Resta (4)	Peugeot	84.000	John Aitken	96.69
1917–18	No race				
1919	Howard Wilcox (2)	Peugeot	88.050	Rene Thomas	104.78
1920	Gaston Chevrolet (6)	Monroe	88.620	Ralph DePalma	99.15
1921	Tommy Milton (20)	Frontenac	89.620	Ralph DePalma	100.75
1922	Jimmy Murphy (1)	Murphy Special	94.480	Jimmy Murphy	100.50
1923	Tommy Milton (1)	H.C.S. Special	90.950	Tommy Milton	108.17
1924	L.L. Corum	Duesenberg Special	98.230	Jimmy Murphy	108.037
	Joe Boyer (21)				
1925	Peter DePaolo (2)	Duesenberg Special	101.130	Leon Duray	113.196
1926	Frank Lockhart (20)	Miller Special	95.904	Earl Cooper	111.735
1927	George Souders (22)	Duesenberg	97.545	Frank Lockhart	120.100
1928	Louis Meyer (13)	Miller Special	99.482	Leon Duray	122.391
1929	Ray Keech (6)	Simplex Piston Ring Special	97.585	Cliff Woodbury	120.599
1930	Billy Arnold (1)	Miller Hartz Special	100.448	Billy Arnold	113.268
1931	Louis Schneider (13)	Bowes Seal-Fast Special	96.629	Russ Snowberger	112.796
1932	Fred Frame (27)	Miller Hartz Special	104.144	Lou Moore	117.363
1933	Louis Meyer (6)	Tydol Special	104.162	Bill Cummings	118.524
1934	Bill Cummings (10)	Boyle Products Special	104.863	Kelly Petillo	119.329
1935	Kelly Petillo (22)	Gilmore Speedway Special	106.240	Rex Mays	120.736
1936	Louis Meyer (28)	Ring-Free Special	109.069	Rex Mays	119.664
1937	Wilbur Shaw (2)	Shaw-Gilmore Special	113.580	Bill Cummings	123.343
1938	Floyd Roberts (1)	Burd Piston Ring Special	117.200	Floyd Roberts	125.681
1939	Wilbur Shaw (3)	Boyle Special	115.035	Jimmy Snyder	130.138
1940	Wilbur Shaw (2)	Boyle Special	114.277	Rex Mays	127.850
1941	Floyd Davis	Noc-Out Hose Clamp Special	115.117	Mauri Rose	128.691
	Mauri Rose (17)				
1942–45	No race				
1946	George Robson (15)	Thorne Engineering Special	114.820	Cliff Bergere	126.471
1947	Mauri Rose (3)	Blue Crown Spark Plug Special	116.338	Ted Horn	126.564
1948	Mauri Rose (3)	Blue Crown Spark Plug Special	119.814	Rex Mays	130.577
1949	Bill Holland (4)	Blue Crown Spark Plug Special	121.327	Duke Nalon	132.939
1950	Johnnie Parsons (5)	Wynn's Friction Proofing	124.002	Walt Faulkner	134.343
1951	Lee Wallard (2)	Belanger Special	126.244	Duke Nalon	136.498
1952	Troy Ruttman (7)	Agajanian Special	128.922	Fred Agabashian	138.010
1953	Bill Vukovich (1)	Fuel Injection Special	128.740	Bill Vukovich	138.392
1954	Bill Vukovich (19)	Fuel Injection Special	130.840	Jack McGrath	141.033
1955	Bob Sweikert (14)	John Zink Special	128.209	Jerry Hoyt	140.045
1956	Pat Flaherty (1)	John Zink Special	128.490	Pat Flaherty	145.596
1957	Sam Hanks (13)	Belond Exhaust Special	135.601	Pat O'Connor	143.948
1958	Jim Bryan (7)	Belond AP Parts Special	133.791	Dick Rathmann	145.974
1959	Rodger Ward (6)	Leader Card 500 Roadster	135.857	Johnny Thomson	145.908
1960	Jim Rathmann (2)	Ken-Paul Special	138.767	Eddie Sachs	146.592
1961	A.J. Foyt (7)	Bowes Seal-Fast Special	139.130	Eddie Sachs	147.481
1962	Rodger Ward (2)	Leader Card 500 Roadster	140.293	Parnelli Jones	150.370
1963	Parnelli Jones (1)	Agajanian-Willard Special	143.137	Parnelli Jones	151.153
1964	A.J. Foyt (5)	Sheraton-Thompson Special	147.350	Jim Clark	158.828
1965	Jim Clark (2)	Lotus Ford	150.686	A.J. Foyt	161.233
1966	Graham Hill (15)	American Red Ball Special	144.317	Mario Andretti	165.899
1967	A.J. Foyt (4)	Sheraton-Thompson Special	151.207	Mario Andretti	168.982
1968	Bobby Unser (3)	Rislone Special	152.882	Joe Leonard	171.559
1969	Mario Andretti (2)	STP Oil Treatment Special	156.867	A.J. Foyt	170.568
1970	Al Unser (1)	Johnny Lightning 500 Special	155.749	Al Unser	170.221
1971	Al Unser (5)	Johnny Lightning Special	157.735	Peter Revson	178.696
1972	Mark Donohue (3)	Sunoco McLaren	162.962	Bobby Unser	195.940
1973	Gordon Johncock (11)	STP Double Oil Filters	159.036	Johnny Rutherford	198.413
1974	Johnny Rutherford (25)	McLaren	158.589	A.J. Foyt	191.632

Indianapolis 500 (Cont.)

Year	Winner (Start Position)	Car	Avg MPH	Pole Winner	MPH
1975	Bobby Unser (3)	Jorgensen Eagle	149.213	A.J. Foyt	193.976
1976	Johnny Rutherford (1)	Hy-Gain McLaren/Goodyear	148.725	Johnny Rutherford	188.957
1977	A.J. Foyt (4)	Gilmore Racing Team	161.331	Tom Sneva	198.884
1978	Al Unser (5)	FNCTC Chaparral Lola	161.361	Tom Sneva	202.156
1979	Rick Mears (1)	The Gould Charge	158.899	Rick Mears	193.736
1980	Johnny Rutherford (1)	Pennzoil Chaparral	142.862	Johnny Rutherford	192.256
1981	Bobby Unser (1)	Norton Spirit Penske PC-9B	139.084	Bobby Unser	200.546
1982	Gordon Johncock (5)	STP Oil Treatment	162.026	Rick Mears	207.004
1983	Tom Sneva (4)	Texaco Star	162.117	Teo Fabi	207.395
1984	Rick Mears (3)	Pennzoil Z-7	163.612	Tom Sneva	210.029
1985	Danny Sullivan (8)	Miller American Special	152.982	Pancho Carter	212.583
1986	Bobby Rahal (4)	Budweiser/Truesports/March	170.722	Rick Mears	216.828
1987	Al Unser (20)	Cummins Holset Turbo	162.175	Mario Andretti	215.390
1988	Rick Mears (1)	Penske-Chevrolet	144.809	Rick Mears	219.198
1989	Emerson Fittipaldi (3)	Penske-Chevrolet	167.581	Rick Mears	223.885
1990	Arie Luyendyk (3)	Domino's Pizza Chevrolet	185.981*	Emerson Fittipaldi	225.301
1991	Rick Mears (1)	Penske-Chevrolet	176.457	Rick Mears	224.113
1992	Al Unser Jr (12)	G92-Chevrolet	134.477	Roberto Guerrero	232.482
1993	Emerson Fittipaldi (9)	Penske-Chevrolet	157.207	Arie Luyendyk	223.967
1994	Al Unser Jr (1)	Penske-Mercedes	160.872	Al Unser Jr.	228.011
1995	Jacques Villeneuve (5)	Reynard-Ford	153.616	Scott Brayton	231.616
1996	Buddy Lazier (5)	Reynard-Ford	147.956	Tony Stewart	233.100†
1997	Arie Luyendyk (1)	G Force Aurora	145.827	Arie Luyendyk	231.468
1998	Eddie Cheever (17)	Dallara Aurora	145.155	Billy Boat	223.503

*Track record, winning time. †Track record, qualifying time.

Indianapolis 500 Rookie of the Year Award

1952 ....Art Cross	1969 ....Mark Donohue*	1985 ....Arie Luyendyk*
1953 ....Jimmy Daywalt	1970 ....Donnie Allison	1986 ....Randy Lanier
1954 ....Larry Crockett	1971 ....Denny Zimmerman	1987 ....Fabrizio Barbazza
1955 ....Al Herman	1972 ....Mike Hiss	1988 ....Billy Vukovich III
1956 ....Bob Veith	1973 ....Graham McRae	1989 ....Bernard Jourdain
1957 ....Don Edmunds	1974 ....Pancho Carter	Scott Pruett
1958 ....George Amick	1975 ....Bill Puterbaugh	1990 ....Eddie Cheever
1959 ....Bobby Grim	1976 ....Vern Schuppan	1991 ....Jeff Andretti
1960 ....Jim Hurtubise	1977 ....Jerry Sneva	1992 ....Lyn St. James
1961 ....Parnelli Jones*	1978 ....Rick Mears*	1993 ....Nigel Mansell
Bobby Marshman	Larry Rice	1994 ....Jacques Villeneuve*
1962 ....Jimmy McElreath	1979 ....Howdy Holmes	1995 ....Gil de Ferran
1963 ....Jim Clark*	1980 ....Tim Richmond	1996 ....Tony Stewart
1964 ....Johnny White	1981 ....Josele Garza	1997 ....Jeff Ward
1965 ....Mario Andretti*	1982 ....Jim Hickman	1998 ....Steve Knapp
1966 ....Jackie Stewart	1983 ....Teo Fabi	*Future winner of Indy 500.
1967 ....Denis Hulme	1984 ....Michael Andretti	
1968 ....Billy Vukovich	Roberto Guerrero	

Championship Auto Racing Teams

CART Championship Series Champions

From 1909 to 1955, this championship was awarded by the American Automobile Association (AAA), and from 1956 to 1979 by the United States Auto Club (USAC). Since 1979, Championship Auto Racing Teams (CART) has conducted the championship. Known as PPG CART World Series until 1998.

1909 ....George Robertson	1919 ....Howard Wilcox	1929 ....Louis Meyer
1910 ....Ray Harroun	1920 ....Tommy Milton	1930 ....Billy Arnold
1911 ....Ralph Mulford	1921 ....Tommy Milton	1931 ....Louis Schneider
1912 ....Ralph DePalma	1922 ....Jimmy Murphy	1932 ....Bob Carey
1913 ....Earl Cooper	1923 ....Eddie Hearne	1933 ....Louis Meyer
1914 ....Ralph DePalma	1924 ....Jimmy Murphy	1934 ....Bill Cummings
1915 ....Earl Cooper	1925 ....Peter DePaolo	1935 ....Kelly Petillo
1916 ....Dario Resta	1926 ....Harry Hartz	1936 ....Mauri Rose
1917 ....Earl Cooper	1927 ....Peter DePaolo	1937 ....Wilbur Shaw
1918 ....Ralph Mulford	1928 ....Louis Meyer	1938 ....Floyd Roberts

PPG CART World Series Champions (Cont.)

1939	Wilbur Shaw	1961	A.J. Foyt	1979	Rick Mears
1940	Rex Mays	1962	Rodger Ward	1980	Johnny Rutherford
1941	Rex Mays	1963	A.J. Foyt	1981	Rick Mears
1942–45	No racing	1964	A.J. Foyt	1982	Rick Mears
1946	Ted Horn	1965	Mario Andretti	1983	Al Unser
1947	Ted Horn	1966	Mario Andretti	1984	Mario Andretti
1948	Ted Horn	1967	A.J. Foyt	1985	Al Unser
1949	Johnnie Parsons	1968	Bobby Unser	1986	Bobby Rahal
1950	Henry Banks	1969	Mario Andretti	1987	Bobby Rahal
1951	Tony Bettenhausen	1970	Al Unser	1988	Danny Sullivan
1952	Chuck Stevenson	1971	Joe Leonard	1989	Emerson Fittipaldi
1953	Sam Hanks	1972	Joe Leonard	1990	Al Unser Jr.
1954	Jimmy Bryan	1973	Roger McCluskey	1991	Michael Andretti
1955	Bob Sweikert	1974	Bobby Unser	1992	Bobby Rahal
1956	Jimmy Bryan	1975	A.J. Foyt	1993	Nigel Mansell
1957	Jimmy Bryan	1976	Gordon Johncock	1994	Al Unser Jr.
1958	Tony Bettenhausen	1977	Tom Sneva	1995	Jacques Villeneuve
1959	Rodger Ward	1978	Tom Sneva	1996	Jimmy Vasser
1960	A.J. Foyt	1979	A.J. Foyt	1997	Alex Zanardi

Alltime CART Leaders

WINS		WINNINGS ($)		POLE POSITIONS	
A.J. Foyt	67	*Al Unser Jr.	18,101,656	Mario Andretti	67
Mario Andretti	52	*Bobby Rahal	15,592,258	A.J. Foyt	53
Al Unser	39	*Michael Andretti	14,347,869	Bobby Unser	49
*Michael Andretti	37	Emerson Fittipaldi	14,293,625	Rick Mears	39
Bobby Unser	35	Mario Andretti	11,552,154	*Michael Andretti	31
*Al Unser Jr.	31	Rick Mears	11,050,807	Al Unser	27
Johnny Rutherford	27	*Arie Luyendyk	8,358,088	Johnny Rutherford	23
Rick Mears	26	Danny Sullivan	8,254,673	Gordon Johncock	20
Rodger Ward	26	*Raul Boesel	6,967,737	Rex Mays	19
Gordon Johncock	25	Al Unser	6,740,843	Danny Sullivan	19
*Bobby Rahal	24	*Jimmy Vasser	5,970,744	*Bobby Rahal	18
Ralph DePalma	24	*Eddie Cheever	5,664,226	Emerson Fittipaldi	17
Tommy Milton	23	A.J. Foyt	5,357,589	Tony Bettenhausen	14
Tony Bettenhausen	22	*Scott Goodyear	5,307,201	Don Branson	14
Emerson Fittipaldi	22	*Teo Fabi	5,045,881	Tom Sneva	14
Earl Cooper	20	*Scott Brayton	4,807,274	Parnelli Jones	12
Jimmy Bryan	19	*Roberto Guerrero	4,563,563	Danny Ongais	11
Jimmy Murphy	19	Tom Sneva	4,392,993		
Ralph Mulford	17	Johnny Rutherford	4,209,232		
Danny Sullivan	17	*Jaques Villeneuve	4,097,732		

*Active driver. Note: Leaders through September 27, 1998.

National Association for Stock Car Auto Racing

Stock Car Racing's Major Events

Winston offers a $1 million bonus to any driver to win three of NASCAR's top four events in the same season. These races are the richest (Daytona 500), the fastest (Talladega 500), the longest (World 600 at Charlotte) and the oldest (Southern 500 at Darlington). These events form the backbone of NASCAR racing. Only four drivers, Lee Roy Yarbrough (1969), David Pearson (1976), Bill Elliott (1985) and Jeff Gordon (1997) have scored the three-track hat trick.

Daytona 500

Year	Winner	Car	Avg MPH	Pole Winner	MPH
1959	Lee Petty	Oldsmobile	135.520	Cotton Owens	143.198
1960	Junior Johnson	Chevrolet	124.740	Fireball Roberts	151.556
1961	Marvin Panch	Pontiac	149.601	Fireball Roberts	155.709
1962	Fireball Roberts	Pontiac	152.529	Fireball Roberts	156.995
1963	Tiny Lund	Ford	151.566	Johnny Rutherford	165.183
1964	Richard Petty	Plymouth	154.345	Paul Goldsmith	174.910
1965	Fred Lorenzen	Ford	141.539	Darel Dieringer	171.151
1966	Richard Petty	Plymouth	160.627	Richard Petty	175.165
1967	Mario Andretti	Ford	149.926	Curtis Turner	180.831
1968	Cale Yarborough	Mercury	143.251	Cale Yarborough	189.222
1969	Lee Roy Yarbrough	Ford	157.950	David Pearson	190.029

Daytona 500 *(Cont.)*

Year	Winner	Car	Avg MPH	Pole Winner	MPH
1970	Pete Hamilton	Plymouth	149.601	Cale Yarborough	194.015
1971	Richard Petty	Plymouth	144.462	A.J. Foyt	182.744
1972	A.J. Foyt	Mercury	161.550	Bobby Isaac	186.632
1973	Richard Petty	Dodge	157.205	Buddy Baker	185.662
1974	Richard Petty	Dodge	140.894	David Pearson	185.017
1975	Benny Parsons	Chevrolet	153.649	Donnie Allison	185.827
1976	David Pearson	Mercury	152.181	A.J. Foyt	185.943
1977	Cale Yarborough	Chevrolet	153.218	Donnie Allison	188.048
1978	Bobby Allison	Ford	159.730	Cale Yarborough	187.536
1979	Richard Petty	Oldsmobile	143.977	Buddy Baker	196.049
1980	Buddy Baker	Oldsmobile	177.602*	A.J. Foyt	195.020
1981	Richard Petty	Buick	169.651	Bobby Allison	194.624
1982	Bobby Allison	Buick	153.991	Benny Parsons	196.317
1983	Cale Yarborough	Pontiac	155.979	Ricky Rudd	198.864
1984	Cale Yarborough	Chevrolet	150.994	Cale Yarborough	201.848
1985	Bill Elliott	Ford	172.265	Bill Elliott	205.114
1986	Geoff Bodine	Chevrolet	148.124	Bill Elliott	205.039
1987	Bill Elliott	Ford	176.263	Bill Elliott	210.364†
1988	Bobby Allison	Buick	137.531	Ken Schrader	193.823
1989	Darrell Waltrip	Chevrolet	148.466	Ken Schrader	196.996
1990	Derrike Cope	Chevrolet	165.761	Ken Schrader	196.515
1991	Ernie Irvan	Chevrolet	148.148	Davey Allison	195.955
1992	Davey Allison	Ford	160.256	Sterling Marlin	192.213
1993	Dale Jarrett	Chevrolet	154.972	Kyle Petty	189.426
1994	Sterling Marlin	Chevrolet	156.931	Loy Allen Jr.	190.158
1995	Sterling Marlin	Chevrolet	141.710	Dale Jarrett	193.498
1996	Dale Jarrett	Ford	154.308	Dale Earnhardt	189.510
1997	Jeff Gordon	Chevrolet	148.295	Mike Skinner	189.813
1998	Dale Earnhardt	Chevrolet	172.712	Bobby Labonte	192.415

*Track record, winning time. †Track record, qualifying time. Note: The Daytona 500, held annually in February, now opens the NASCAR season with 200 laps around the high-banked Daytona International Speedway.

World 600

Year	Winner	Car	Avg MPH	Pole Winner
1960	Joe Lee Johnson	Chevrolet	107.752	J.L. Johnson
1961	David Pearson	Pontiac	111.634	Richard Petty
1962	Nelson Stacy	Ford	125.552	Fireball Roberts
1963	Fred Lorenzen	Ford	132.418	Junior Johnson
1964	Jim Paschal	Plymouth	125.772	Junior Johnson
1965	Fred Lorenzen	Ford	121.772	Fred Lorenzon
1966	Marvin Panch	Plymouth	135.042	Paul Goldsmith
1967	Jim Paschal	Plymouth	135.832	Cale Yarborough
1968	Buddy Baker	Dodge	104.207	Donnie Allison
1969	Lee Yarbrough	Mercury	134.631	Donnie Allison
1970	Donnie Allison	Ford	129.680	Bobby Isaac
1971	Bobby Allison	Mercury	140.442	Charlie Glotzbach
1972	Buddy Baker	Dodge	142.255	Bobby Allison
1973	Buddy Baker	Dodge	134.890	Buddy Baker
1974	David Pearson	Mercury	135.720	David Pearson
1975	Richard Petty	Dodge	145.327	David Pearson
1976	David Pearson	Mercury	137.352	David Pearson
1977	Richard Petty	Dodge	137.636	David Pearson
1978	Darrell Waltrip	Chevrolet	138.355	David Pearson
1979	Darrell Waltrip	Chevrolet	136.674	Neil Bonnet
1980	Benny Parsons	Chevrolet	119.265	Cale Yarborough
1981	Bobby Allison	Buick	129.326	Neil Bonnett
1982	Neil Bonnett	Ford	130.508	David Pearson
1983	Neil Bonnett	Chevrolet	140.406	Buddy Baker
1984	Bobby Allison	Buick	129.233	Harry Gant
1985	Darrell Waltrip	Chevrolet	141.807	Bill Elliott
1986	Dale Earnhardt	Chevrolet	140.406	Geoff Bodine
1987	Kyle Petty	Ford	131.483	Bill Elliott
1988	Darrell Waltrip	Chevrolet	124.460	Davey Allison
1989	Darrell Waltrip	Chevrolet	144.077	Alan Kulwicki
1990	Rusty Wallace	Pontiac	137.650	Ken Schrader
1991	Davey Allison	Ford	138.951	Mark Martin
1992	Dale Earnhardt	Chevrolet	132.980	Bill Elliott
1993	Dale Earnhardt	Chevrolet	145.504	Ken Schrader
1994	Jeff Gordon	Chevrolet	139.445	Jeff Gordon

World 600 (Cont.)

Year	Winner	Car	Avg MPH	Pole Winner
1995	Bobby Labonte	Chevrolet	151.952	Jeff Gordon
1996	Dale Jarrett	Ford	147.581	Jeff Gordon
1997	Jeff Gordon	Chevrolet	136.745	Jeff Gordon
1998	Jeff Gordon	Chevrolet	136.424	Jeff Gordon

Note: Held at the 1.5-mile high-banked Charlotte Motor Speedway on Memorial Day weekend.

Talladega 500

Year	Winner	Car	Avg MPH	Pole Winner	MPH
1969	Richard Brickhouse	Dodge	153.778	Charlie Glotzbach	199.466
1970	Pete Hamilton	Plymouth	158.517	Bobby Isaac	186.834
1971	Bobby Allison	Mercury	145.945	Davey Allison	187.323
1972	James Hylton	Mercury	148.728	Bobby Isaac	190.677
1973	Dick Brooks	Plymouth	145.454	Bobby Allison	187.064
1974	Richard Petty	Dodge	148.637	David Pearson	184.926
1975	Buddy Baker	Ford	130.892	Dave Marcis	191.340
1976	Dave Marcis	Dodge	157.547	Dave Marcis	190.651
1977	Davey Allison	Chevrolet	162.524	Benny Parsons	192.682
1978	Lennie Pond	Olds	174.700	Cale Yarborough	192.917
1979	Darrell Waltrip	Olds	161.229	Neil Bonnet	193.600
1980	Neil Bonnett	Mercury	166.894	Buddy Baker	198.545
1981	Ron Bouchard	Buick	156.737	Harry Gant	195.897
1982	Darrell Waltrip	Buick	168.157	Geoff Bodine	199.400
1983	Dale Earnhardt	Ford	170.611	Cale Yarborough	201.744
1984	Dale Earnhardt	Chevrolet	155.485	Cale Yarborough	202.474
1985	Cale Yarborough	Ford	148.772	Bill Elliott	207.578
1986	Bobby Hillin	Buick	151.552	Bill Elliott	209.005
1987	Bill Elliott	Ford	171.293	Bill Elliott	203.827
1988	Ken Schrader	Chevrolet	154.505	Darrell Waltrip	196.274
1989	Terry Labonte	Ford	157.354	Mark Martin	194.800
1990	Dale Earnhardt	Chevrolet	174.430	Dale Earnhardt	192.513
1991	Harry Gant	Olds	165.620	Sterling Marlin	192.085
1992	Ernie Irvan	Chevrolet	176.309	Sterling Marlin	190.586
1993	Dale Earnhardt	Chevrolet	153.858	Bill Elliott	192.397
1994	Jimmy Spencer	Ford	163.217	Dale Earnhardt	193.470
1995	Sterling Marlin	Chevrolet	173.188	Sterling Marlin	194.212
1996	Jeff Gordon	Chevrolet	133.387	Jeremy Mayfield	192.370
1997	Mark Martin	Ford	188.345	John Andretti	193.627
1998	Bobby Labonte	Pontiac	163.439	Bobby Labonte	195.728

Note: Held every spring at the 2.66-mile Talladega Superspeedway.

Southern 500

Year	Winner	Car	Avg MPH	Pole Winner
1950	Johnny Mantz	Plymouth	76.260	Wally Campbell
1951	Herb Thomas	Hudson	76.900	Marshall Teague
1952	Fonty Flock	Olds	74.510	Dick Rathman
1953	Buck Baker	Olds	92.780	Fonty Flock
1954	Herb Thomas	Hudson	94.930	Buck Baker
1955	Herb Thomas	Chevrolet	92.281	Tim Flock
1956	Curtis Turner	Ford	95.067	Buck Baker
1957	Speedy Thompson	Chevrolet	100.100	Paul Goldsmith
1958	Fireball Roberts	Chevrolet	102.590	Fireball Roberts
1959	Jim Reed	Chevrolet	111.836	Fireball Roberts
1960	Buck Baker	Pontiac	105.901	Cotton Owens
1961	Nelson Stacy	Ford	117.880	Fireball Roberts
1962	Larry Frank	Ford	117.965	Fireball Roberts
1963	Fireball Roberts	Ford	129.784	Fireball Roberts
1964	Buck Baker	Dodge	117.757	Richard Petty
1965	Ned Jarrett	Ford	115.924	Junior Johnson
1966	Darel Dieringer	Mercury	114.830	Lee Yarborough
1967	Richard Petty	Plymouth	131.933	David Pearson
1968	Cale Yarborough	Mercury	126.132	Charlie Glotzbach
1969	Lee Roy Yarbrough	Ford	105.612	Cale Yarborough
1970	Buddy Baker	Dodge	128.817	David Pearson
1971	Bobby Allison	Mercury	131.398	Bobby Allison
1972	Bobby Allison	Chevrolet	128.124	David Pearson
1973	Cale Yarborough	Chevrolet	134.033	David Pearson
1974	Cale Yarborough	Chevrolet	111.075	Richard Petty

Southern 500 (Cont.)

Year	Winner	Car	Avg MPH	Pole Winner
1975	Bobby Allison	Matador	116.825	David Pearson
1976	David Pearson	Mercury	120.534	David Pearson
1977	David Pearson	Mercury	106.797	Darrell Waltrip
1978	Cale Yarborough	Olds	116.828	David Pearson
1979	David Pearson	Chevrolet	126.259	Bobby Allison
1980	Terry Labonte	Chevrolet	115.210	Darrell Waltrip
1981	Neil Bonnett	Ford	126.410	Harry Gant
1982	Cale Yarborough	Buick	126.703	David Pearson
1983	Bobby Allison	Buick	123.343	Neil Bonnett
1984	Harry Gant	Chevrolet	128.270	Harry Gant
1985	Bill Elliott	Ford	121.254	Bill Elliott
1986	Tim Richmond	Chevrolet	121.068	Tim Richmond
1987	Dale Earnhardt	Chevrolet	115.520	Davey Allison
1988	Bill Elliott	Ford	128.297	Bill Elliott
1989	Dale Earnhardt	Chevrolet	135.462	Alan Kulwicki
1990	Dale Earnhardt	Chevrolet	123.141	Dale Earnhardt
1991	Harry Gant	Olds	133.508	Davey Allison
1992	Darrell Waltrip	Chevrolet	129.114	Sterling Marlin
1993	Mark Martin	Ford	137.932	Ken Schrader
1994	Bill Elliott	Ford	127.915	Geoff Bodine
1995	Jeff Gordon	Chevrolet	121.231	John Andretti
1996	Jeff Gordon	Chevrolet	135.757	Dale Jarrett
1997	Jeff Gordon	Chevrolet	121.149	Bobby Labonte
1998	Jeff Gordon	Chevrolet	139.031	Dale Jarrett

Note: Held at the 1.366-mile Darlington (SC) Raceway on Labor Day weekend.

Winston Cup NASCAR Champions

Year	Driver	Car	Wins	Poles	Winnings ($)
1949	Red Byron	Oldsmobile	2	0	5,800
1950	Bill Rexford	Oldsmobile	1	0	6,175
1951	Herb Thomas	Hudson	7	4	18,200
1952	Tim Flock	Hudson	8	4	20,210
1953	Herb Thomas	Hudson	11	10	27,300
1954	Lee Petty	Dodge	7	3	26,706
1955	Tim Flock	Chrysler	18	19	33,750
1956	Buck Baker	Chrysler	14	12	29,790
1957	Buck Baker	Chevrolet	10	5	24,712
1958	Lee Petty	Olds	7	4	20,600
1959	Lee Petty	Plymouth	10	2	45,570
1960	Rex White	Chevrolet	6	3	45,260
1961	Ned Jarrett	Chevrolet	1	4	27,285
1962	Joe Weatherly	Pontiac	9	6	56,110
1963	Joe Weatherly	Mercury	3	6	58,110
1964	Richard Petty	Plymouth	9	8	98,810
1965	Ned Jarrett	Ford	13	9	77,966
1966	David Pearson	Dodge	14	7	59,205
1967	Richard Petty	Plymouth	27	18	130,275
1968	David Pearson	Ford	16	12	118,824
1969	David Pearson	Ford	11	14	183,700
1970	Bobby Isaac	Dodge	11	13	121,470
1971	Richard Petty	Plymouth	21	9	309,225
1972	Richard Petty	Plymouth	8	3	227,015
1973	Benny Parsons	Chevrolet	1	0	114,345
1974	Richard Petty	Dodge	10	7	299,175
1975	Richard Petty	Dodge	13	3	378,865
1976	Cale Yarborough	Chevrolet	9	2	387,173
1977	Cale Yarborough	Chevrolet	9	3	477,499
1978	Cale Yarborough	Oldsmobile	10	8	530,751
1979	Richard Petty	Chevrolet	5	1	531,292
1980	Dale Earnhardt	Chevrolet	5	0	588,926
1981	Darrell Waltrip	Buick	12	11	693,342
1982	Darrell Waltrip	Buick	12	7	873,118
1983	Bobby Allison	Buick	6	0	828,355
1984	Terry Labonte	Chevrolet	2	2	713,010
1985	Darrell Waltrip	Chevrolet	3	4	1,318,735
1986	Dale Earnhardt	Chevrolet	5	1	1,783,880
1987	Dale Earnhardt	Chevrolet	11	1	2,099,243
1988	Bill Elliott	Ford	6	6	1,574,639

Winston Cup NASCAR Champions *(Cont.)*

Year	Driver	Car	Wins	Poles	Winnings ($)
1989	Rusty Wallace	Pontiac	6	4	2,247,950
1990	Dale Earnhardt	Chevrolet	9	4	3,083,056
1991	Dale Earnhardt	Chevrolet	4	0	2,396,685
1992	Alan Kulwicki	Ford	2	6	2,322,561
1993	Dale Earnhardt	Chevrolet	6	2	3,353,789
1994	Dale Earnhardt	Chevrolet	4	2	3,400,733
1995	Jeff Gordon	Chevrolet	7	8	4,347,343
1996	Terry Labonte	Chevrolet	2	4	4,030,648
1997	Jeff Gordon	Chevrolet	10	1	4,201,227

Alltime NASCAR Leaders

WINS		WINNINGS ($)		POLE POSITIONS	
Richard Petty	200	*Dale Earnhardt	32,707,585	Richard Petty	126
David Pearson	105	*Jeff Gordon	21,187,769	David Pearson	113
Bobby Allison	84	*Bill Elliott	19,028,117	Cale Yarborough	70
*Darrell Waltrip	84	*Terry Labonte	18,293,527	*Darrell Waltrip	59
Cale Yarborough	83	*Rusty Wallace	17,853,465	Bobby Allison	57
*Dale Earnhardt	71	*Mark Martin	17,274,172	Bobby Isaac	51
Lee Petty	54	*Darrell Waltrip	16,996,400	*Bill Elliott	49
Ned Jarrett	50	*Ricky Rudd	14,827,340	Junior Johnson	47
Junior Johnson	50	*Dale Jarrett	13,222,257	Buck Baker	44
Herb Thomas	49	*Geoff Bodine	12,597,337	Buddy Baker	40
*Rusty Wallace	47	*Ken Schrader	11,619,659	Tim Flock	39
Buck Baker	46	*Sterling Marlin	11,248,942	Herb Thomas	39
*Bill Elliott	40	*Ernie Irvan	10,337,150	*Geoff Bodine	37
Tim Flock	40	*Kyle Petty	8,524,504	*Mark Martin	37
Bobby Isaac	37	Harry Grant	8,456,094	Rex White	35
				Fireball Roberts	35
				Ned Jarrett	35

*Active drivers. Note: NASCAR leaders through September 27, 1998.

Formula One Grand Prix Racing

World Driving Champions

Year	Winner	Car	Year	Winner	Car
1950	Guiseppe Farina, Italy	Alfa Romeo	1971	Jackie Stewart, Scotland	Tyrell-Ford
1951	Juan-Manuel Fangio, Argentina	Alfa Romeo	1972	Emerson Fittipaldi, Brazil	Lotus-Ford
			1973	Jackie Stewart, Scotland	Tyrell-Ford
1952	Alberto Ascari, Italy	Ferrari	1974	Emerson Fittipaldi, Brazil	McLaren-Ford
1953	Alberto Ascari, Italy	Ferrari	1975	Niki Lauda, Austria	Ferrari
1954	Juan-Manuel Fangio, Argentina	Maserati/ Mercedes	1976	James Hunt, England	McLaren-Ford
			1977	Niki Lauda, Austria	Ferrari
1955	Juan-Manuel Fangio, Argentina	Mercedes	1978	Mario Andretti, U.S.	Lotus-Ford
			1979	Jody Scheckter, S Africa	Ferrari
1956	Juan-Manuel Fangio, Argentina	Ferrari	1980	Alan Jones, Australia	Williams-Ford
			1981	Nelson Piquet, Brazil	Brabham-Ford
1957	Juan-Manuel Fangio, Argentina	Maserati	1982	Keke Rosberg, Finland	Williams-Ford
			1983	Nelson Piquet, Brazil	Brabham-BMW
1958	Mike Hawthorne, England	Ferrari	1984	Niki Lauda, Austria	McLaren-Porsche
1959	Jack Brabham, Australia	Cooper-Climax	1985	Alain Prost, France	McLaren-Porsche
1960	Jack Brabham, Australia	Cooper-Climax	1986	Alain Prost, France	McLaren-Porsche
1961	Phil Hill, United States	Ferrari	1987	Nelson Piquet, Brazil	Williams-Honda
1962	Graham Hill, England	BRM	1988	Ayrton Senna, Brazil	McLaren-Honda
1963	Jim Clark, Scotland	Lotus-Climax	1989	Alain Prost, France	McLaren-Honda
1964	John Surtees, England	Ferrari	1990	Ayrton Senna, Brazil	McLaren-Honda
1965	Jim Clark, Scotland	Lotus-Climax	1991	Ayrton Senna, Brazil	McLaren-Honda
1966	Jack Brabham, Australia	Brabham-Climax	1992	Nigel Mansell, Britain	Williams-Renault
1967	Denis Hulme, New Zealand	Brabham-Repco	1993	Alain Prost, France	Williams-Renault
			1994	Michael Schumacher, Ger	Benetton-Ford
1968	Graham Hill, England	Lotus-Ford	1995	Michael Schumacher, Ger	Benetton-Renault
1969	Jackie Stewart, Scotland	Matra-Ford	1996	Damon Hill, Great Britain	Williams-Renault
1970	Jochen Rindt, Austria*	Lotus-Ford	1997	Jacques Villeneuve	Williams-Renault

*The championship was awarded after Rindt was killed in practice for the Italian Grand Prix.

Formula One Grand Prix Racing (Cont.)

Alltime Grand Prix Winners

Driver	Wins	Driver	Wins
Alain Prost, France	51	Jim Clark, Great Britain	25
Ayrton Senna, Brazil	41	Niki Lauda, Austria	25
*Michael Schumacher, Germany	33	Juan Manuel Fangio, Argentina	24
Nigel Mansell, Great Britain	31	Nelson Piquet, Brazil	23
Jackie Stewart, Great Britain	27	*Damon Hill, Great Britain	22

*Active driver. Note: Grand Prix winners through September 27, 1998.

Alltime Grand Prix Pole Winners

Driver	Poles	Driver	Poles
Ayrton Senna, Brazil	65	Niki Lauda, Austria	24
Alain Prost, France	33	Nelson Piquet, Brazil	24
Jim Clark, Great Britain	33	*Damon Hill, Great Britain	20
Nigel Mansell, Great Britain	32	*Michael Schumacher, Germany	19
Juan Manuel Fangio, Argentina	28	Mario Andretti, United States	18
		Rene Arnoux, France	18

*Active driver. Note: Pole winners through September 27, 1998.

Professional SportsCar Racing, Inc.

The 24 Hours of Daytona

Year	Winner	Car	Avg Speed	Distance
1962	Dan Gurney	Lotus 19-Class SP11	104.101 mph	3 hrs (312.42 mi)
1963	Pedro Rodriguez	Ferrari-Class 12	102.074 mph	3 hrs (308.61 mi)
1964	Pedro Rodriguez/Phil Hill	Ferrari 250 LM	98.230 mph	2,000 km
1965	Ken Miles/Lloyd Ruby	Ford	99.944 mph	2,000 km
1966	Ken Miles/Lloyd Ruby	Ford Mark II	108.020 mph	24 hrs (2,570.63 mi)
1967	Lorenzo Bandini/Chris Amon	Ferrari 330 P4	105.688 mph	24 hrs (2,537.46 mi)
1968	Vic Elford/Jochen Neerpasch	Porsche 907	106.697 mph	24 hrs (2,565.69 mi)
1969	Mark Donohue/Chuck Parsons	Chevy Lola	99.268 mph	24 hrs (2,383.75 mi)
1970	Pedro Rodriguez/Leo Kinnunen	Porsche 917	114.866 mph	24 hrs (2,758.44 mi)
1971	Pedro Rodriguez/Jackie Oliver	Porsche 917K	109.203 mph	24 hrs (2,621.28 mi)
1972*	Mario Andretti/Jacky Ickx	Ferrari 312/P	122.573 mph	6 hrs (738.24 mi)
1973	Peter Gregg/Hurley Haywood	Porsche Carrera	106.225 mph	24 hrs (2,552.7 mi)
1974	(No race)			
1975	Peter Gregg/Hurley Haywood	Porsche Carrera	108.531 mph	24 hrs (2,606.04 mi)
1976†	Peter Gregg/Brian Redman/ John Fitzpatrick	BMW CSL	104.040 mph	24 hrs (2,092.8 mi)
1977	John Graves/Hurley Haywood/ Dave Helmick	Porsche Carrera	108.801 mph	24 hrs (2,615)
1978	Rolf Stommelen/ Antoine Hezemans/Peter Gregg	Porsche Turbo	108.743 mph	24 hrs (2,611.2 mi)
1979	Ted Field/Danny Ongais/ Hurley Haywood	Porsche Turbo	109.249 mph	24 hrs (2,626.56 mi)
1980	Volkert Meri/Rolf Stommelen/ Reinhold Joest	Porsche Turbo	114.303 mph	24 hrs
1981	Bob Garretson/Bobby Rahal/ Brian Redman	Porsche Turbo	113.153 mph	24 hrs
1982	John Paul Jr./John Paul Sr./ Rolf Stommelen	Porsche Turbo	114.794 mph	24 hrs
1983	Preston Henn/Bob Wollek/ Claude Ballot-Lena/A. J. Foyt	Porsche Turbo	98.781 mph	24 hrs
1984	Sarel van der Merwe/ Graham Duxbury/Tony Martin	Porsche March	103.119 mph	24 hrs (2,476.8 mi)
1985	A. J. Foyt/Bob Wollek/ Al Unser/Thierry Boutsen	Porsche 962	104.162 mph	24 hrs (2,502.68 mi)
1986	Al Holbert/Derek Bell/Al Unser Jr.	Porsche 962	105.484 mph	24 hrs (2,534.72 mi)
1987	Chip Robinson/Derek Bell/ Al Holbert/Al Unser Jr.	Porsche 962	111.599 mph	24 hrs (2,680.68 mi)
1988	Martin Brundle/John Nielsen/ Raul Boesel	Jaguar XJR-9	107.943 mph	24 hrs (2,591.68 mi)
1989	John Andretti/Derek Bell/ Bob Wollek	Porsche 962	92.009 mph	24 hrs (2,210.76 mi)

*Race shortened due to fuel crisis. †Course lengthened from 3.81 miles to 3.84 miles.

The 24 Hours of Daytona *(Cont.)*

Year	Winner	Car	Avg Speed	Distance
1990	Davy Jones/ Jan Lammers/ Andy Wallace	Jaguar XJR-12	112.857 mph	24 hrs (2,709.16 mi)
1991	Hurley Haywood/ John Winter/ Frank Jelinski/ Henri Pescarolo/ Bob Wollek	Porsche 962C	106.633 mph	24 hrs (2,559.64 mi)
1992	Massahiro Hasemi/ Kazuoyshi Hoshino/ Toshio Suzuki/ Anders Olofsson	Nissan R91CP	112.987 mph	24 hrs (2,712.72 mi)
1993	P.J. Jones/Mark Dismore/ Rocky Moran	Toyota Eagle MK III	103.537 mph	24 hrs (2,484.88 mi)
1994	Paul Gentilozzi/ Scott Pruett/ Butch Leitzinger/ Steve Millen	Nissan 300 ZX	104.80 mph	24 hrs (2,693.67 mi)
1995	Jurgen Lassig/ Christophe Buochut/ Giovanni Lavaggi/ Marco Werner	Porsche Spyder K8	102.28 mph	690 laps (2,456.4 mi)
1996	Wayne Taylor/ Scott Sharp/ Jim Pace	Oldsmobile Mark III	103.32 mph	697 laps (2,481.32 mi)
1997	Elliot Forbes/John Schneider/ Rob Dyson/John Paul Jr./ Butch Leitzinger/James Weaver/ Andy Wallace	Ford R & S MK III	102.292 mph	690 laps (2,456.4 mi)
1998	Arie Luyendyk/Didier Theys/ Mauro Baldi	Ferrari 333 SP	105.565 mph	711 laps (2,531.16 mi)

World SportsCar Champions*

Year	Winner	Car	Year	Winner	Car
1978	Peter Gregg	Porsche 935	1988	Geoff Brabham	Nissan GTP
1979	Peter Gregg	Porsche 935	1989	Geoff Brabham	Nissan GTP
1980	John Fitzpatrick	Porsche 935	1990	Geoff Brabham	Nissan GTP
1981	Brian Redman	Chevy Lola	1991	Geoff Brabham	Nissan NPT
1982	John Paul Jr.	Chevy Lola	1992	Juan Fangio II	Toyota EGL MKIII
1983	Al Holbert	Chevy March	1993	Juan Fangio II	Toyota EGL MKIII
1984	Randy Lanier	Chevy March	1994	Wayne Taylor	Mazda Kudzu
1985	Al Holbert	Porsche 962	1995	Fermin Velez	Ferrari 333 SP
1986	Al Holbert	Porsche 962	1996	Wayne Taylor	Mazda Kudzu
1987	Chip Robinson	Porsche 962	1997	Butch Leitzinger	Ford R&S MKIII

*1978–93 champions raced in the GT series, which in 1994 was replaced by the World SportsCar series.

Alltime SportsCar Leaders

SUPREME GT SERIES WINS

James Weaver	10
Butch Leitzinger	9
Gianpiero Moretti	6
Wayne Taylor	6
Fermin Velez	5
John Paul, Jr.	5
Jeremy Dale	4
Andy Wallace	4
Andy Evans	3
Jim Pace	3
Max Papis	3
Eliseo Salazar	3
Antonio Hermann	3
Andrea Montermini	3

SUPREME GT SERIES WINS

Al Holbert	49
Peter Gregg	41
Hurley Haywood	31
Geoff Brabham	26
Parker Johnstone	25
Jim Downing	23
Irv Hoerr	23
Jack Baldwin	22
Don Devendorf	22
Bob Earl	22
Tommy Riggins	22
Juan Fangio II	21
Roger Mandeville	21

Note: Leaders through September 28, 1998.

24 Hours of Le Mans

Year	Winning Drivers	Car
1923	André Lagache/René Léonard	Chenard & Walker
1924	John Duff/Francis Clement	Bentley
1925	Gérard de Courcelles/André Rossignol	La Lorraine
1926	Robert Bloch/André Rossignol	La Lorraine
1927	J. Dudley Benjafield/Sammy Davis	Bentley

Year	Winning Drivers	Car
1928	Woolf Barnato/Bernard Rubin	Bentley
1929	Woolf Barnato/Sir Henry Birkin	Bentley Speed 6
1930	Woolf Barnato/Glen Kidston	Bentley Speed 6
1931	Earl Howe/Sir Henry Birkin	Alfa Romeo 8C-2300 sc
1932	Raymond Sommer/Luigi Chinetti	Alfa Romeo 8C-2300 sc
1933	Raymond Sommer/Tazio Nuvolari	Alfa Romeo 8C-2300 sc
1934	Luigi Chinetti/Philippe Etancelin	Alfa Romeo 8C-2300 sc
1935	John Hindmarsh/Louis Fontés	Lagonda M45R
1936	Race cancelled	
1937	Jean-Pierre Wimille/Robert Benoist	Bugatti 57G sc
1938	Eugene Chaboud/Jean Tremoulet	Delahaye 135M
1939	Jean-Pierre Wimille/Pierre Veyron	Bugatti 57G sc
1940–48	Races cancelled	
1949	Luigi Chinetti/Lord Selsdon	Ferrari 166MM
1950	Louis Rosier/Jean-Louis Rosier	Talbot-Lago
1951	Peter Walker/Peter Whitehead	Jaguar C
1952	Hermann Lang/Fritz Reiss	Mercedes-Benz 300 SL
1953	Tony Rolt/Duncan Hamilton	Jaguar C
1954	Froilan Gonzales/Maurice Trintignant	Ferrari 375
1955	Mike Hawthorn/Ivor Bueb	Jaguar D
1956	Ron Flockhart/Ninian Sanderson	Jaguar D
1957	Ron Flockhart/Ivor Buab	Jaguar D
1958	Olivier Gendebien/Phil Hill	Ferrari 250 TR58
1959	Carroll Shelby/Roy Salvadori	Aston Martin DBR1
1960	Olivier Gendebien/Paul Fråre	Ferrari 250 TR59/60
1961	Olivier Gendebien/Phil Hill	Ferrari 250 TR61
1962	Olivier Gendebien/Phil Hill	Ferrari 250P
1963	Lodovico Scarfiotti/Lorenzo Bandini	Ferrari 250P
1964	Jean Guichel/Nino Vaccarella	Ferrari 275P
1965	Jochen Rindt/Masten Gregory	Ferrari 250LM
1966	Chris Amon/Bruce McLaren	Ford Mk2
1967	Dan Gurney/A. J. Foyt	Ford Mk4
1968	Pedro Rodriguez/Lucien Bianchi	Ford GT40
1969	Jacky Ickx/Jackie Oliver	Ford GT40
1970	Hans Herrmann/Richard Attwood	Porsche 917
1971	Helmut Marko/Gijs van Lennep	Porsche 917
1972	Henri Pescarolo/Graham Hill	Matra-Simca MS670
1973	Henri Pescarolo/Gérard Larrousse	Matra-Simca MS670B
1974	Henri Pescarolo/Gérard Larrousse	Matra-Simca MS670B
1975	Jacky Ickx/Derek Bell	Mirage-Ford MB
1976	Jacky Ickx/Gijs van Lennep	Porsche 936
1977	Jacky Ickx/Jurgen Barth/Hurley Haywood	Porsche 936
1978	Jean-Pierre Jaussaud/Didier Pironi	Renault-Alpine A442
1979	Klaus Ludwig/Bill Whittington/Don Whittington	Porsche 935
1980	Jean-Pierre Jaussaud/Jean Rondeau	Rondeau-Ford M379B
1981	Jacky Ickx/Derek Bell	Porsche 936-81
1982	Jacky Ickx/Derek Bell	Porsche 956
1983	Vern Schuppan/Hurley Haywood/Al Holbert	Porsche 956-83
1984	Klaus Ludwig/Henri Pescarolo	Porsche 956B
1985	Klaus Ludwig/Paolo Barilla/John Winter	Porsche 956B
1986	Derek Bell/Hans-Joachim Stuck/Al Holbert	Porsche 962C
1987	Derek Bell/Hans-Joachim Stuck/Al Holbert	Porsche 962C
1988	Jan Lammers/Johnny Dumfries/Andy Wallace	Jaguar XJR9LM
1989	Jochen Mass/Manuel Reuter/Stanley Dickens	Sauber-Mercedes C9-88
1990	John Nielsen/Price Cobb/Martin Brundle	TWR Jaguar XJR-12
1991	Volker Weidler/Johnny Herbert/Bertrand Gachof	Mazda 787B
1992	Derek Warwick/Yannick Dalmas/Mark Blundell	Peugeot 905B
1993	Geoff Brabham/Christophe Bouchut/Eric Helary	Peugeot 905
1994	Yannick Dalmas/Hurley Haywood/Mauro Baldi	Porsche 962
1995	Yannick Dalmas/J.J. Lehto/Masanori Sekiya	McLaren BMW
1996	Manuel Reuter/Davy Jones/Alexander Wurz	TWR Porsche
1997	Michele Alboreto/Stefan Johansson/Tom Kristensen	TWR Porsche
1998	Alan McNish, Laurent Aiello, Stephane Ortelli	Porsche GT One

Drag Racing: Milestone Performances

Top Fuel

ELAPSED TIME

Time (Sec.)	Driver	Date	Site
9.00	Jack Chrisman	Feb 18, 1961	Pomona, CA
8.97	Jack Chrisman	May 20, 1961	Empona, VA
7.96	Bobby Vodnick	May 16, 1964	Bayview, MD
6.97	Don Johnson	May 7, 1967	Carlsbad, CA
5.97	Mike Snively	Nov 17, 1972	Ontario, CA
5.78	Don Garlits	Nov 18, 1973	Ontario, CA
5.698	Gary Beck	Oct 10, 1975	Ontario, CA
5.573	Gary Beck	Oct 18, 1981	Irvine, CA
5.484	Gary Beck	Sept 6, 1982	Clermont, IN
5.391	Gary Beck	Oct 1, 1983	Fremont, CA
5.280	Darrell Gwynn	Sept 25, 1986	Ennis, TX
5.176	Darrell Gwynn	April 4, 1987	Ennis, TX
5.090	Joe Amato	Oct 1, 1987	Ennis, TX
4.990	Eddie Hill	April 9, 1988	Ennis, TX
4.881	Gary Ormsby	Sept 28, 1990	Topeka, KS
4.799	Cory McClenathan	Sept 19, 1992	Mohnton, PA
4.762	Cory McClenathan	Oct 3, 1993	Topeka, KS
4.690	Michael Brotherton	May 20, 1994	Englishtown, NJ
4.595	Joe Amato	July 5,1996	Topeka, KS
4.539	Joe Amato	Mar 21, 1998	Baytown, TX

SPEED

MPH	Driver	Date	Site
180.36	Connie Kalitta	Sept 3, 1962	Indianapolis
190.26	Don Garlits	Sept 21, 1963	East Haddam, CT
201.34	Don Garlits	Aug 1, 1964	Great Meadows, NJ
211.26	Donny Milani	May 15, 1965	Sacramento, CA
223.32	Don Cook	Apr 24, 1965	Fremont, CA
230.17	James Warren	Apr 10, 1967	Fresno, CA
243.24	Don Garlits	March 18, 1973	Gainesville, FL
250.69	Don Garlits	Oct 11, 1975	Ontario, CA
260.11	Joe Amato	March 18, 1984	Gainesville, FL
272.56	Don Garlits	March 23, 1986	Gainesville, FL
282.13	Joe Amato	Sept 5, 1987	Clermont, IN
291.54	Connie Kalitta	Feb 11, 1989	Pomona, CA
301.70	Kenny Bernstein	March 20, 1992	Gainesville, FL
311.86	Kenny Bernstein	Oct 30, 1994	Pomona, CA
319.82	Joe Amato	Mar 21, 1998	Baytown, TX
323.50	Joe Amato	May 17, 1998	Englishtown, NJ

Funny Car

ELAPSED TIME

Time (Sec.)	Driver	Date	Site
6.92	Leroy Goldstein	Sept 3, 1970	Clermont, IN
5.987	Don Prudhomme	Oct 12, 1975	Ontario, CA
5.868	Raymond Beadle	July 16, 1981	Englishtown, NJ
5.799	Tom Anderson	Sept 3, 1982	Clermont, IN
5.637	Don Prudhomme	Sept 4, 1982	Clermont, IN
5.588	Rick Johnson	Feb 3, 1985	Pomona, CA
5.425	Kenny Bernstein	Sept 26, 1986	Ennis, TX
5.397	Kenny Bernstein	April 5, 1987	Ennis, TX
5.255	Ed McCulloch	April 17, 1988	Ennis, TX
5.193	Don Prudhomme	March 2, 1989	Baytown, TX
5.077	Cruz Pedregon	Sept 20, 1992	Mohnton, PA
4.987	Chuck Etcholis	Oct 2, 1993	Topeka, KS
4.819	Cruz Pedregon	Mar 21, 1998	Baytown, TX

Funny Car (Cont.)

SPEED

MPH	Driver	Date	Site
200.44	Gene Snow	August, 1968	Houston, TX
250.00	Don Prudhomme	May 23, 1982	Baton Rouge, LA
260.11	Kenny Bernstein	March 18, 1984	Gainesville, FL
271.41	Kenny Bernstein	Aug 30, 1986	Indianapolis
280.72	Mike Dunn	Oct 2, 1987	Ennis, TX
290.13	Jim White	Oct 11, 1991	Ennis, TX
291.82	Jim White	Oct 25, 1991	Pomona, CA
300.40	Jim Epler	Oct 3, 1993	Topeka, KS
303.64	John Force	Sept 2, 1995	Indianapolis
308.74	John Force	Sept 28, 1997	Topeka, KS
317.46	John Force	Mar 21, 1998	Baytown, TX
323.89	John Force	May 17, 1998	Englishtown, NJ

Pro Stock

ELAPSED TIME

Time (Sec.)	Driver	Date	Site
7.778	Lee Shepherd	March 12, 1982	Gainesville, FL
7.655	Lee Shepherd	Oct 1, 1982	Fremont, CA
7.557	Bob Glidden	Feb 2, 1985	Pomona, CA
7.497	Bob Glidden	Sep 13, 1985	Maple Grove, PA
7.377	Bob Glidden	Aug 28, 1986	Clermont, IN
7.294	Frank Sanchez	Oct 7, 1988	Baytown, TX
7.184	Darrell Alderman	Oct 12, 1990	Ennis, TX
7.099	Scott Geoffrion	Sept 19, 1992	Mohnton, PA
6.988	Kurt Johnson	May 20, 1994	Englishtown, NJ
6.873	Warren Johnson	Mar 14, 1998	Gainesville, FL

SPEED

MPH	Driver	Date	Site
181.08	Warren Johnson	Oct 1, 1982	Fremont, CA
190.07	Warren Johnson	Aug 29, 1986	Clermont, IN
191.32	Bob Glidden	Sep 4, 1987	Clermont, IN
192.18	Warren Johnson	Oct 13, 1990	Ennis, TX
193.21	Bob Glidden	July 28, 1991	Sonoma, CA
194.51	Warren Johnson	July 31, 1992	Sonoma, CA
195.99	Warren Johnson	May 21, 1993	Englishtown, NJ
196.24	Warren Johnson	Mar 19, 1993	Gainesville, FL
197.15	Warren Johnson	Apr 23, 1994	Commerce, GA
199.15	Warren Johnson	Mar 10, 1995	Baytown, TX
201.20	Warren Johnson	Mar 14, 1998	Gainesville, FL

Alltime Drag Racing Leaders

NATIONAL EVENT WINS

*Bob Glidden	85
*John Force	69
*Warren Johnson	69
*Kenny Bernstein	51
Don Prudhomme	49
*Joe Amato	44
*David Schultz	42
Don Garlits	35
John Myers	33
*Darrell Alderman	27

BEST WON-LOST RECORD (WINNING PCT)

*Matt Hines	119–18 (.869)
John Myers	268–69 (.795)
*David Schultz	304–85 (.781)
*Gary Scelzi	84–30 (.737)
*John Force	568–205 (.735)
*Warren Johnson	626–234 (.728)
*Darrell Alderman	202–78 (.721)
*Angelle Seeling	65–26 (.714)
*Jim Yates	227–111 (.672)
*Joe Amato	458–226 (.670)

*Active driver. Note: Leaders through September 21, 1998.

Bowling

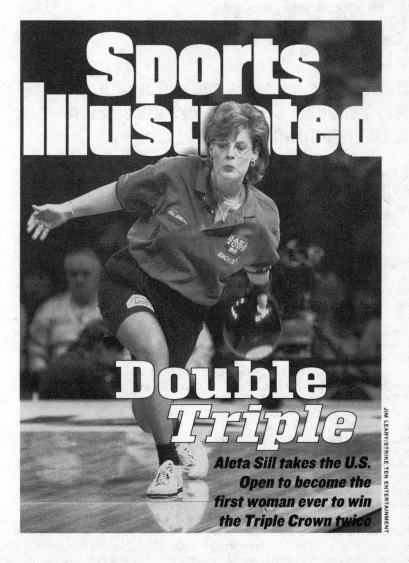

Sports Illustrated

Double Triple

Aleta Sill takes the U.S. Open to become the first woman ever to win the Triple Crown twice

JIM LEARY/STRIKE TEN ENTERTAINMENT

Kegler Caper

Bowling, which got a zany tribute from Hollywood in '98, has more in common with tinseltown than meets the eye

BY FRANZ LIDZ

EVERY SPORT DESERVES a classic screwball comedy. Football has *Horse Feathers*, in which Groucho Marx, told a college dean is outside his office "waxing wroth," says, "Is Roth out there, too? Tell Roth to wax the dean for a while!" Track and field boasts the cornball surrealism of *Million Dollar Legs*, an Olympics farce starring W.C. Fields as the president of Klopstokia. And now bowling has the Coen brothers' *The Big Lebowski*, the kookiest kegler caper ever made.

The Coens—Joel directs, Ethan produces, they cowrite—don't so much send-up or rip-off old movie genres as reimagine them. In *The Big Lebowski* they channel Raymond Chandler's *The Big Sleep* through Cheech and Chong's *Up in Smoke* by way of *Mad* magazine's Arthur the Potted Plant. Like *The Big Sleep*, *The Big Lebowski* has snarling repartee, shaky plotting and an unending succession of seedy scoundrels: blackmailers, pornographers, child molesters, gold diggers and marmot-brandishing nihilists. "Not many films portray bowling in

a positive light," said Walter Ray Williams Jr., the marquee name at the 1998 U.S. Open. "But at least *The Big Lebowski* doesn't portray it in a totally negative light."

The hero of *Lebowski* is the Dude, a glassy-eyed, grassy-eyed league bowler who chills out in his ratty bungalow by listening to audiotapes of falling pins. Williams has the Dude's drowsy panache but none of his vices. "In the movies, bowlers always smoke and drink beer and rent their shoes," said the sport's alltime leading money winner. "I don't do any of those things. Something may be wrong with me, I guess."

Coming into the Open in April 1998, the 38-year-old Williams had never won a Triple Crown event despite holding considerable leads in several of them. The tournament's No. 1 qualifier had reached three Triple Crown finals in his career and lost them all. He was beaten in the 1989 Tournament of Champions after leading by more than 200 pins, and he blew the '93 Open after being up by 430 pins. In 1996 he paced the field at the PBA National by a wide margin, but a split in the final's ninth frame cost him the tournament.

In the semis of the '98 Open at Sacred Heart University in Fairfield, Conn., Williams strung together six strikes to beat unranked Martin Letscher 245–222. His fellow finalist, Tim Criss, recorded more splits than a blue-chip stock. Criss came within a 4-pin of making a Greek church in frame 5 of the final but couldn't take advantage of Williams's unconverted 4-7-10 in frame 6. With Criss crossed-up, Williams struck out. Final score: Williams, 221; Criss, 189. Hugging the crumbling winner's trophy—a hand-painted sculpture of an eagle—to his chest, Williams smiled Dude-ishly and said, "After all the bugging I got from people this week, I'm glad I finally won." His $40,000 payday paled next to the $125,000 he made in April at a made-for-TV skins game in Lady Lake, Fla. "It was nerveracking," Williams said after outdueling Parker Bohn III on his 12th overtime attempt in sudden death. Bohn III was doubly cursed in '98. After completing only the second nationally televised perfect game in Masters history, he was mastered in the final 224–192 by Mike Aulby.

Williams's perennial foil, Pete Weber Jr., bears a slight resemblance to the Dude's chronically irate buddy, Walter Sobchak, a Vietnam-obsessed vet who enforces line calls with the semiautomatic in his ball bag. The oft-suspended Weber was banned from the tour's first three tournaments in '98 for disparaging lane conditions at a '97 event. "That pissed me off," he said. "I didn't think I did anything wrong." The pissy Weber shot back to win the PBA Nationals—defeating David Ozio 277–236 for the top seed—in just his second tournament of the year. Still, his

BILL VINT

Williams, the PBA's alltime money leader, finally won a major.

appearance at the Open amounted to a cameo— he missed the first cut and finished in 110th place.

Billed as the first "equality" Open in history, the tournament offered identical fields of 180 men and 180 women, and identical $187,500 purses. On the women's side, the unprecedented "bracket elimination" format allowed Aleta Sill to rise from the No. 12 qualifying position to the final. As willful as the cinematic trophy wife Bunny Lebowski, Sill displayed a penchant for the macabre. Better make that *pendant*—dangling from a chain around her neck was a tiny urn in which the ashes of her grandmother were interred. "I used to worry she'd get wet if I took a shower," said Sill, "but I unscrewed the urn, and it seemed airtight."

Her opponent in the semis was the top woman qualifier, Marianne DiRupo—who just happened to be her motor home roomie. A pen collector whose parents were undergrads at Penn, DiRupo keeps drawers filled with pens back home in Succasunna, N.J. "Marianne lends me Bics, but I lose them," said Sill. "Then she gets mad at me." DiRupo cried when her pin pal struck on six of the last seven throws to win 243–208. "It was awful bowling against Marianne," said Sill. "I hated it. I didn't want to bowl her. She got one bad break, and it cost her." In the final Sill rolled eight straight strikes in a 276–151 romp over No. 10 qualifier Tammy Turner to become the first woman ever to win the Triple Crown twice. "I'm glad I wasn't bowling Aleta," said Williams. "She would have run right over me."

So much for equality: If the men's and women's champions had faced each other in the final, Sill would have won by 55 pins.

FOR THE RECORD·1997–1998

MEN

1998 BPAA United States Open

CHAMPIONSHIP ROUND

Bowler	Games	Total	Earnings ($)
Walter Ray Williams Jr.	2	466	40,000
Tim Criss	2	422	25,000
*Ryan Shafer	1	193	11,000
*Niles Letscher	1	222	11,000

*Tied for third place.

Playoff Results: Criss def. Shafer, 235–193; Williams def. Letscher, 245–222; Williams def. Criss, 221–189.

Held at Sacred Heart University Fairfield, CT, April 5–11, 1998

1997 Touring Players Championship

CHAMPIONSHIP ROUND

Bowler	Games	Total	Earnings ($)
Steve Hoskins	4	932	40,000
Danny Wiseman	1	184	22,000
Brian Voss	1	214	15,000
Dave Arnold	1	183	10,000
Doug Kent	1	218	8,000

Playoff Results: Hoskins def. Kent, 232–218; Hoskins def. Arnold, 244–183; Hoskins def. Voss, 223–214; Hoskins def. Wiseman, 233–184.

Held at FunFest Entertainment Center, Harmarville, PA, November 6–12, 1997.

1998 Touring Players Championship

CHAMPIONSHIP ROUND

Bowler	Games	Total	Earnings ($)
Dennis Horan Jr.	2	481	40,000
Parker Bohn III	1	202	21,000
Mike Aulby	1	234	13,000
Pete Weber	1	212	10,000

Playoff Results: Horan def. Aulby, 236–234; Horan def. Weber, 236–212; Horan def. Bohn, 245–202.

Held at the Stonehedge Family Fun Center, Akron, OH, April 13–18, 1998.

PBA National Championship

CHAMPIONSHIP ROUND

Bowler	Games	Total	Earnings ($)
Pete Weber	1	277	28,000
David Ozio	2	506	14,500
Tom Baker	2	473	7,500
Mike Aulby	2	488	6,000
Jim Johnson Jr.	1	201	5,000

Playoff Results: Aulby defeated Johnson, 280–201; Baker defeated Aulby, 238–208; Ozio defeated Baker, 270–235; Weber defeated Ozio, 277–236

Held at Ducat's Imperial Lanes, Toledo, OH, February 14–21,1998.

MEN *(Cont.)*

ABC Masters Tounament

CHAMPIONSHIP ROUND

Bowler	Games	Total	Earnings ($)
Mike Aulby	1	224	50,600
Parker Bohn III	2	492	26,600
Chris Sand	1	246	20,600
Mike Mullin	1	191	15,500

Note: Bohn also earned $10,000 bonus for bowling 12th televised perfect game.

Playoff Results: Bohn def. Sand, 300–246; Bohn def. Mullin, 300–191; Aulby def. Bohn, 224–192.

Held at National Bowling Stadium, Reno, NV, May 5–9, 1998.

WOMEN

1998 BPAA United States Open

CHAMPIONSHIP ROUND

Bowler	Games	Total	Earnings ($)
Aleta Sill	2	518	40,000
Tammy Turner	2	350	25,000
*Marianne DiRupo	1	208	11,000
*Kim Adler	1	175	11,000

*Tied for third place.

Playoff Results: Turner def. Adler, 199–175; Sill def. DiRupo, 243–208; Sill Def. Turner, 276–151.

Held at Sacred Heart University Fairfield, CT, April 5–11, 1998

Sam's Town Invitational

CHAMPIONSHIP ROUND

Bowler	Games	Total	Earnings ($)
Kim Adler	4	953	17,000
Carolyn Dorin-Ballard	1	206	8,500
Wendy Macpherson	1	177	4,700
Carol Gianotti-Block	1	218	4,200
Jeanne Naccarato	1	204	3,700

Playoff Results: Adler def. Naccarato, 213–204; Adler def. Gianotti-Block, 235–218; Adler def. Macpherson, 248–177; Adler def. Dorin-Ballard, 257–206.

Held at Sam's Town Bowling Center, Las Vegas, NV, November 15–22, 1997.

WIBC Queens

CHAMPIONSHIP ROUND

Bowler	Games	Total	Earnings ($)
Lynda Norry	2	403	20,000
Karen Stroud	4	721	10,000
Kendra Cameron	1	148	7,500
Lisa Bishop	2	411	6,000
Tennelle Grijalva	1	205	4,500

Playoff Results: Bishop def. Grijalva, 244–205; Stroud def. Bishop, 202–167; Stroud def. Cameron, 150–148; Stroud def. Norry, 212–190; Norry def Stroud, 213–157.
Note: Stroud defeated Norry in the fourth match of the finals, but because Norry had advanced through match-play competition undefeated, Stroud needed a second victory over Norry to win the title.

Held at Miller Time Bowl, Davenport, IA, May 12–16, 1998.

WOMEN (Cont.)

AMF Gold Cup

CHAMPIONSHIP ROUND

Bowler	Games	Total	Earnings ($)
Aleta Sill	2	498	25,000
Carol Gianotti-Block	1	226	13,500
Wendy Macpherson	1	194	9,000
Carolyn Dorin-Ballard	1	195	7,000
Marianne DiRupo	1	165	6,000

Playoff Results: Macpherson def. DiRupo 191–170; Macpherson def. Dorin-Ballard, 212–182; Sill def. Macpherson, 277–172; Sill def. Gianotti-Block, 221–179.

Held at Hanover Lanes, Richmond, VA, July 13–17, 1997.

PBA Tour Results

1997 Fall Tour

Date	Event	Winner	Earnings ($)	Runner-Up
Sept 17–21	Oronamin C Japan Cup*	Doug Kent	50,000	Parker Bohn III
Oct 4–8	Ebonite Challenge, Windsor Locks, CT	Norm Duke	21,000	Pete Weber
Oct 13–16	Ebonite Challenge, Rochester, NY	Steve Hoskins	21,000	Rick Steelsmith
Oct 17–22	Mobil 1 Classic	Amleto Monacelli	25,000	Jason Couch
Oct 26–29	Ebonite Challenge, Indianapolis	John Mazza	21,000	Dave D'Entremont
Nov 2–5	Ebonite Challenge, Virginia Beach	Amleto Monacelli	25,000	Steve Hoskins
Nov 6–12	Bayer/Brunswick Touring Players Championship	Steve Hoskins	40,000	Danny Wiseman
Dec 11–14	Merit Mixed Doubles	Tim Criss Carol Gianotti-Block	40,000	Pete Weber C. Dorin-Ballard

1998 Winter Tour

Date	Event	Winner	Earnings ($)	Runner-Up
Jan 20–24	Brentwood Classic	Parker Bohn III	16,000	Tom Baker
Jan 27–31	Long John Silver's Classic	Ricky Ward	16,000	Butch Soper
Feb 1–7	Columbia 300 Open	Roger Bowker	22,000	Butch Soper
Feb 9–14	Peoria Open	David Traber	16,000	W.R. Williams Jr.
Feb 14–21	PBA National Championship	Pete Weber	30,000	Brian Voss
Feb 25–28	STORM Flagship Open	Walter Ray Williams Jr.	19,000	Steve Jaros

1998 Spring Tour

Date	Event	Winner	Earnings ($)	Runner-Up
Apr 5–11	BPAA U.S. Open	Walter Ray Williams Jr.	46,000	Tim Criss
Apr 13–18	Bayer/Brunswick Touring Players Championship	Dennis Horan	40,000	Parker Bohn III
Apr 26–May 2	Tucson Open	Pete Weber	16,000	Brian Himmler
May 5–9	ABC Masters*	Mike Aulby	50,600	Parker Bohn III
May 9–16	Greater Detroit Open	Parker Bohn III	16,000	Doug Kent
May 16–23	Brunswick Johnny Petraglia Open	Brian Voss	28,000	Tim Criss
May 26–30	Greater Harrisburg Open	Parker Bohn III	16,000	Bob Learn Jr.

1998 Summer Tour

Date	Event	Winner	Earnings ($)	Runner-Up
June 6–13	Showboat Invitational	Jason Couch	46,000	A. Monacelli
June 14–20	ACDelco Classic	Steve Hoskins	52,000	Tim Criss
June 26–July 1	PBA Oregon Open	Danny Wiseman	19,000	Sean Swanson
June 27–July 1	PBA Northwest Classic	Tim Criss	16,000	Butch Soper

*Not an official PBA Tour event.

1996–97 Senior Tour (through Aug 30)

Date	Event	Winner	Earnings ($)	Runner-Up
Sept 15–18	St. Petersburg Clearwater Open	Teata Semiz	10,000	Ron Winger
Sept 23–25	Naples PBA Senior Open	Gene Stus	10,000	Ron Winger
Nov 3–7	Senior World Invitational	Dale Eagle	16,000	Barry Asher
Mar 8–12	Greater Albany Senior Open	Pete Couture	9,000	Gary Dickinson
Mar 15–19	Vermont Senior Classic	John Hricsina	8,000	Pete Couture
June 28– July 2	PBA Boise Senior Open	Pete Couture	8,000	Dale Eagle
July 12–16	Seattle Senior Open	Gene Stus	8,000	John Hricsina
July 18–23	Northwest Senior Classic	Gene Stus	8,000	Steve Neff
July 26–Aug 1	Showboat Senior Invitational	Don Helling	22,000	Mike Durbin
Aug 9–15	ABC Senior Masters	Pete Couture	60,000	Ron Garr
Aug 16–20	Glass City Senior Open	Gary Dickinson	9,000	Bob Glass
Aug 22–28	Brunswick Senior Championship	Johnny Petraglia	18,000	Avery LeBlanc

†PWBA Tour Results

1997 Fall Tour

Date	Event	Winner	Earnings ($)	Runner-Up
Aug 17–21	Hammer Players Championship	Marianne DiRupo	16,000	W. Macpherson
Aug 24–28	Lady Ebonite Classic	Nikki Gianulias	11,000	M. DiRupo
Aug 31–Sept 4	Long Island Open	C. Gianotti-Block	11,000	Sandra Jo Odom
Sept 7–11	Columbia 300 Delaware Open	Wendy Macpherson	11,500	C. Gianotti-Block
Sept 14–18	Baltimore Eastern Open	Wendy Macpherson	9,000	C. Dorin-Ballard
Sept 21–25	Three Rivers Open	Carolyn Dorin-Ballard	9,000	D. Miller-Mackie
Sept 28–Oct 2	Track Triton Open	C. Gianotti-Block	9,000	A.M. Duggan
Nov 15–22	Sam's Town Invitational	Kim Adler	17,000	C. Dorin-Ballard
Dec 11–14	Merit Mixed Doubles	Tim Criss	40,000	Pete Weber
		Carol Gianotti-Block		C. Dorin-Ballard

1998 Winter Tour

Date	Event	Winner	Earnings ($)	Runner-Up
Feb 1–5	Lubbock Open	Tish Johnson	9,000	C. Gianotti-Block
Feb 8–12	AMF Rocket City Challenge	Anne Marie Duggan	9,000	C. Gianotti-Block
Feb 15–19	Visionary Bowling Products Classic	Dana Miller-Mackie	11,000	Cathy Dorin
Feb 22–26	Greater Sebring Open	Kendra Cameron	9,000	Kim Canady
Mar 1–5	Greater Orlando Classic	Carolyn Dorin-Ballard	9,000	C. Gianotti Block
Mar 8–12	Atlanta Open	Leanne Barrette	9,000	D. Miller-Mackie

1998 Spring Tour

Date	Event	Winner	Earnings ($)	Runner-Up
May 3–7	Omaha Open	Marianne DiRupo	9,000	C. Gianotti-Block
May 5–11	BPAA U.S. Open	Aleta Sill	40,000	Tammy Turner
May 12–16	WIBC Queens*	Lynda Norry	20,000	Karen Stroud
May 17–21	St. Clair Classic	Dede Davidson	9,000	Aleta Sill

1997 Summer Tour

Date	Event	Winner	Earnings ($)	Runner-Up
July 12–16	Lehigh Valley Classic	Leanne Barrette	9,000	C. Gianotti-Block
July 6–10	Southern Virginia Open	Aleta Sill	9,000	Tammy Turner
July 26–30	Chattanooga Open	Kim Adler	9,000	C. Dorin-Ballard
Aug 2–6	Lady Ebonite Classic	Michelle Feldman	11,000	Kim Adler
Aug 9–13	PWBA Greater Terre Haute Open	Kim Adler	10,000	C. Gianotti-Block
Aug 15–20	Hammer Players Championship	Yvette Smith	16,000	W. Macpherson

†Known as LBPT until 1998. *Not an official LPBT Tour event.

PBA

MONEY LEADERS

Name	Titles	Tournaments	Earnings ($)
Walter Ray Williams Jr.	3	26	322,044
Parker Born III	2	25	273,185
Pete Weber	2	23	252,184
Brain Voss	2	25	199,035
Amleto Monacelli	2	20	185,155

AVERAGE

Name	Games	Pinfall	Average
Walter Ray Williams Jr.	947	210,242	222.00
Pete Weber	867	191,813	221.23
Parker Bohn III	830	182,929	220.39
Amleto Monacelli	768	168,536	219.44
Brian Voss	866	190,003	219.40

Seniors

MONEY LEADERS

Name	Titles	Tournaments	Earnings ($)
Gary Dickinson	3	16	143,140
Larry Laub	3	16	74,805
John Hricsina	1	16	52,465
Gene Stus	1	16	70,335
Pete Couture	1	16	67,425

AVERAGE

Name	Games	Pinfall	Average
Gary Dickinson	674	151,279	224.45
George Pappas	337	75,147	222.99
Earl Anthony	410	91,331	222.76
Pete Couture	693	154,102	222.37
Larry Lamb	666	147,805	221.93

PWBA

MONEY LEADERS

Name	Titles	Tournaments	Earnings ($)
Wendy Macpherson	4	21	165,425
Kim Adler	2	19	142,400
Carolyn Dorin-Ballard	0	21	104,500
Liz Johnson	3	19	95,850
Marianne DiRupo	0	19	92,050

AVERAGE

Name	Games	Pinfall	Average
Wendy Macpherson	915	196,432	214.68
Marianne DiRupo	859	183,036	213.08
Carolyn Dorin-Ballard	911	194,007	212.96
Carol Gianotti-Block	850	180,999	212.94
Liz Johnson	844	178,455	211.44

Men's Majors

BPAA United States Open

Year	Winner	Score	Runner-Up	Site
1942	John Crimmins	265.09–262.33	Joe Norris	Chicago
1943	Connie Schwoegler	not available	Frank Benkovic	Chicago
1944	Ned Day	315.21–298.21	Paul Krumske	Chicago
1945	Buddy Bomar	304.46–296.16	Joe Wilman	Chicago
1946	Joe Wilman	310.27–305.37	Therman Gibson	Chicago
1947	Andy Varipapa	314.16–308.04	Allie Brandt	Chicago
1948	Andy Varipapa	309.23–309.06	Joe Wilman	Chicago
1949	Connie Schwoegler	312.31–307.27	Andy Varipapa	Chicago
1950	Junie McMahon	318.37–307.17	Ralph Smith	Chicago
1951	Dick Hoover	305.29–304.07	Lee Jouglard	Chicago
1952	Junie McMahon	309.29–305.41	Bill Lillard	Chicago
1953	Don Carter	304.17–297.36	Ed Lubanski	Chicago
1954	Don Carter	308.02–307.25	Bill Lillard	Chicago
1955	Steve Nagy	307.17–303.34	Ed Lubanski	Chicago
1956	Bill Lillard	304.30–304.22	Joe Wilman	Chicago
1957	Don Carter	308.49–305.45	Dick Weber	Chicago
1958	Don Carter	311.03–308.09	Buzz Fazio	Minneapolis
1959	Billy Welu	311.48–310.26	Ray Bluth	Buffalo
1960	Harry Smith	312.24–308.12	Bob Chase	Omaha
1961	Bill Tucker	318.49–309.11	Dick Weber	San Bernardino, CA
1962	Dick Weber	299.34–297.38	Roy Lown	Miami Beach
1963	Dick Weber	642–591	Billy Welu	Kansas City, MO
1964	Bob Strampe	714–616	Tommy Tuttle	Dallas
1965	Dick Weber	608–586	Jim St. John	Philadelphia
1966	Dick Weber	684–681	Nelson Burton Jr.	Lansing, MI
1967	Les Schissler	613–610	Pete Tountas	St. Ann, MO
1968	Jim Stefanich	12,401–12,104	Billy Hardwick	Garden City, NY
1969	Billy Hardwick	12,585–11,463	Dick Weber	Miami
1970	Bobby Cooper	12,936–12,307	Billy Hardwick	Northbrook, IL
1971	Mike Limongello	397 (2 games)	Teata Semiz	St. Paul, MN
1972	Don Johnson	233 (1 game)	George Pappas	New York City
1973	Mike McGrath	712 (3 games)	Earl Anthony	New York City
1974	Larry Laub	749 (3 games)	Dave Davis	New York City
1975	Steve Neff	279 (1 game)	Paul Colwell	Grand Prairie, TX
1976	Paul Moser	226 (1 game)	Jim Frazier	Grand Prairie, TX
1977	Johnny Petraglia	279 (1 game)	Bill Spigner	Greensboro, NC
1978	Nelson Burton Jr.	873 (4 games)	Jeff Mattingly	Greensboro, NC
1979	Joe Berardi	445 (2 games)	Earl Anthony	Windsor Locks, CT
1980	Steve Martin	930 (4 games)	Earl Anthony	Windsor Locks, CT
1981	Marshall Holman	684 (3 games)	Mark Roth	Houston
1982	Dave Husted	1011 (4 games)	Gil Sliker	Houston
1983	Gary Dickinson	214 (1 game)	Steve Neff	Oak Lawn, IL
1984	Mark Roth	244 (1 game)	Guppy Troup	Oak Hill, IL
1985	Marshall Holman	233 (1 game)	Wayne Webb	Venice, FL
1986	Steve Cook	467 (2 games)	Frank Ellenburg	Venice, FL
1987	Del Ballard Jr.	525 (2 games)	Pete Weber	Tacoma, WA
1988	Pete Weber	929 (4 games)	Marshall Holman	Atlantic City, NJ
1989	Mike Aulby	429 (2 games)	Jim Pencak	Edmond, OK
1990	Ron Palombi Jr.	269 (1 game)	Amleto Monacelli	Indianapolis
1991	Pete Weber	956 (4 games)	Mark Thayer	Indianapolis
1992	Robert Lawrence	667 (3 games)	Scott Devers	Canandaigua, NY
1993	Del Ballard Jr.	505 (2 games)	Walter Ray Williams Jr.	Canandaigua, NY
1994	Justin Hromek	267 (1 game)	Parker Bohn III	Troy, MI
1995	Dave Husted	266 (1 game)	Paul Koehler	Troy, MI
1996	Dave Husted	730 (3 games)	George Brooks	Indianapolis, IN
1997	no event—tournament rescheduled to April			
1998	Walter Ray Williams Jr.	466 (2 games)	Tim Criss	Fairfield, CT

Note: From 1942 to 1970, the tournament was called the BPAA All-Star. Peterson scoring was used from 1942 through 1962. Under this system, the winner of an individual match game gets one point, plus one point for each 50 pins knocked down. From 1963 through 1967, a three-game championship was held between the two top qualifiers. From 1968 through 1970 total pinfall determined the winner. From 1971 to the present, five qualifiers compete for the championship.

Touring Players Championship

Year	Winner	Score	Runner-Up	Site
1996	Mike Aulby	268 (1 game)	Parker Bohn III	Harmarville, PA
1997	Steve Hoskins	932 (4 games)	Danny Wiseman	Harmarville, PA
1998	Dennis Horan	481 (2 games)	Parker Bohn III	Akron, OH

PBA National Championship

Year	Winner	Score	Runner-Up	Site
1960	Don Carter	6512 (30 games)	Ronnie Gaudern	Memphis
1961	Dave Soutar	5792 (27 games)	Morrie Oppenheim	Cleveland
1962	Carmen Salvino	5369 (25 games)	Don Carter	Philadelphia
1963	Billy Hardwick	13,541 (61 games)	Ray Bluth	Long Island, NY
1964	Bob Strampe	13,979 (61 games)	Ray Bluth	Long Island, NY
1965	Dave Davis	13,895 (61 games)	Jerry McCoy	Detroit
1966	Wayne Zahn	14,006 (61 games)	Nelson Burton Jr.	Long Island, NY
1967	Dave Davis	421 (2 games)	Pete Tountas	New York City
1968	Wayne Zahn	14,182 (60 games)	Nelson Burton Jr.	New York City
1969	Mike McGrath	13,670 (60 games)	Bill Allen	Garden City, NY
1970	Mike McGrath	660 (3 games)	Dave Davis	Garden City, NY
1971	Mike Limongello	911 (4 games)	Dave Davis	Paramus, NJ
1972	Johnny Guenther	12,986 (56 games)	Dick Ritger	Rochester, NY
1973	Earl Anthony	212 (1 game)	Sam Flanagan	Oklahoma City
1974	Earl Anthony	218 (1 game)	Mark Roth	Downey, CA
1975	Earl Anthony	245 (1 game)	Jim Frazier	Downey, CA
1976	Paul Colwell	191 (1 game)	Dave Davis	Seattle
1977	Tommy Hudson	206 (1 game)	Jay Robinson	Seattle
1978	Warren Nelson	453 (2 games)	Joseph Groskind	Reno
1979	Mike Aulby	727 (3 games)	Earl Anthony	Las Vegas
1980	Johnny Petraglia	235 (1 game)	Gary Dickinson	Sterling Heights, MI
1981	Earl Anthony	242 (1 game)	Ernie Schlegel	Toledo, OH
1982	Earl Anthony	233 (1 game)	Charlie Tapp	Toledo, OH
1983	Earl Anthony	210 (1 game)	Mike Durbin	Toledo, OH
1984	Bob Chamberlain	961 (4 games)	Dan Eberl	Toledo, OH
1985	Mike Aulby	476 (2 games)	Steve Cook	Toledo, OH
1986	Tom Crites	190 (1 game)	Mike Aulby	Toledo, OH
1987	Randy Pedersen	759 (3 games)	Amleto Monacelli	Toledo, OH
1988	Brian Voss	246 (1 game)	Todd Thompson	Toledo, OH
1989	Pete Weber	221 (1 game)	Dave Ferraro	Toledo, OH
1990	Jim Pencak	900 (4 games)	Chris Warren	Toledo, OH
1991	Mike Miller	450 (2 games)	Norm Duke	Toledo, OH
1992	Eric Forkel	833 (4 games)	Bob Vespi	Toledo, OH
1993	Ron Palombi Jr.	237 (1 game)	Eugene McCune	Toledo, OH
1994	David Traber	196 (1 game)	Dale Traber	Toledo, OH
1995	Scott Alexander	246 (1 game)	Wayne Webb	Toledo, OH
1996	Butch Soper	442 (2 games)	Walter Ray Williams Jr.	Toledo, OH
1997	Rick Steelsmith	888 (4 games)	Brian Voss	Toledo, OH
1998	Pete Weber	277 (1 game)	David Ozio	Toledo, OH

Note: Totals from 1963–66, 1968–69 and 1972 include bonus pins.

Tournament of Champions

Year	Winner	Score	Runner-Up	Site
1965	Billy Hardwick	484 (2 games)	Dick Weber	Akron, OH
1966	Wayne Zahn	595 (3 games)	Dick Weber	Akron, OH
1967	Jim Stefanich	227 (1 game)	Don Johnson	Akron, OH
1968	Dave Davis	213 (1 game)	Don Johnson	Akron, OH
1969	Jim Godman	266 (1 game)	Jim Stefanich	Akron, OH
1970	Don Johnson	299 (1 game)	Dick Ritger	Akron, OH
1971	Johnny Petraglia	245 (1 game)	Don Johnson	Akron, OH
1972	Mike Durbin	775 (3 games)	Tim Harahan	Akron, OH
1973	Jim Godman	451 (2 games)	Barry Asher	Akron, OH
1974	Earl Anthony	679 (3 games)	Johnny Petraglia	Akron, OH
1975	Dave Davis	448 (2 games)	Barry Asher	Akron, OH
1976	Marshall Holman	441 (2 games)	Billy Hardwick	Akron, OH
1977	Mike Berlin	434 (2 games)	Mike Durbin	Akron, OH
1978	Earl Anthony	237 (1 game)	Teata Semiz	Akron, OH
1979	George Pappas	224 (1 game)	Dick Ritger	Akron, OH
1980	Wayne Webb	750 (3 games)	Gary Dickinson	Akron, OH
1981	Steve Cook	287 (1 game)	Pete Couture	Akron, OH

Tournament of Champions *(Cont.)*

Year	Winner	Score	Runner-Up	Site
1982	Mike Durbin	448 (2 games)	Steve Cook	Akron, OH
1983	Joe Berardi	865 (4 games)	Henry Gonzalez	Akron, OH
1984	Mike Durbin	950 (4 games)	Mike Aulby	Akron, OH
1985	Mark Williams	616 (3 games)	Bob Handley	Akron, OH
1986	Marshall Holman	233 (1 game)	Mark Baker	Akron, OH
1987	Pete Weber	928 (4 games)	Jim Murtishaw	Akron, OH
1988	Mark Williams	237 (1 game)	Tony Westlake	Fairlawn, OH
1989	Del Ballard Jr.	490 (2 games)	Walter Ray Williams Jr.	Fairlawn, OH
1990	Dave Ferraro	226 (1 game)	Tony Westlake	Fairlawn, OH
1991	David Ozio	476 (2 games)	Amleto Monacelli	Fairlawn, OH
1992	Marc McDowell	471 (2 games)	Don Genalo	Fairlawn, OH
1993	George Branham III	227 (1 game)	Parker Bohn III	Fairlawn, OH
1994	Norm Duke	422 (2 games)	Eric Forkel	Fairlawn, OH
1995	Mike Aulby	502 (2 games)	Bob Spaulding	Lake Zurich, IL
1996	Dave D'Entremont	971 (4 games)	Dave Arnold	Lake Zurich, IL
1997	John Gant	446 (2 games)	Mike Aulby	Reno, NV

ABC Masters Tournament

Year	Winner	Scoring Avg	Runner-Up	Site
1951	Lee Jouglard	201.8	Joe Wilman	St. Paul, MN
1952	Willard Taylor	200.32	Andy Varipapa	Milwaukee
1953	Rudy Habetler	200.13	Ed Brosius	Chicago
1954	Eugene Elkins	205.19	W. Taylor	Seattle
1955	Buzz Fazio	204.13	Joe Kristof	Ft. Wayne, IN
1956	Dick Hoover	209.9	Ray Bluth	Rochester, NY
1957	Dick Hoover	216.39	Bill Lillard	Ft. Worth, TX
1958	Tom Hennessy	209.15	Lou Frantz	Syracuse, NY
1959	Ray Bluth	214.26	Billy Golembiewski	St. Louis, MO
1960	Billy Golembiewski	206.13	Steve Nagy	Toledo, OH
1961	Don Carter	211.18	Dick Hoover	Detroit
1962	Billy Golembiewski	223.12	Ron Winger	Des Moines, IA
1963	Harry Smith	219.3	Bobby Meadows	Buffalo
1964	Billy Welu	227	Harry Smith	Oakland, CA
1965	Billy Welu	202.12	Don Ellis	St. Paul, MN
1966	Bob Strampe	219.80	Al Thompson	Rochester, NY
1967	Lou Scalia	216.9	Bill Johnson	Miami Beach
1968	Pete Tountas	220.15	Buzz Fazio	Cincinnati
1969	Jim Chestney	223.2	Barry Asher	Madison, WI
1970	Don Glover	215.10	Bob Strampe	Knoxville, TN
1971	Jim Godman	229.8	Don Johnson	Detroit
1972	Bill Beach	220.27	Jim Godman	Long Beach, CA
1973	Dave Soutar	218.61	Dick Ritger	Syracuse, NY
1974	Paul Colwell	234.17	Steve Neff	Indianapolis
1975	Eddie Ressler	213.51	Sam Flanagan	Dayton, OH
1976	Nelson Burton Jr.	220.79	Steve Carson	Oklahoma City
1977	Earl Anthony	218.21	Jim Godman	Reno
1978	Frank Ellenburg	200.61	Earl Anthony	St. Louis
1979	Doug Myers	202.9	Bill Spigner	Tampa, FL
1980	Neil Burton	206.69	Mark Roth	Louisville
1981	Randy Lightfoot	218.3	Skip Tucker	Memphis
1982	Joe Berardi	207.12	Ted Hannahs	Baltimore
1983	Mike Lastowski	212.65	Pete Weber	Niagara Falls, NY
1984	Earl Anthony	212.5	Gil Sliker	Reno
1985	Steve Wunderlich	210.4	Tommy Kress	Tulsa, OK
1986	Mark Fahy	206.5	Del Ballard Jr.	Las Vegas
1987	Rick Steelsmith	210.7	Brad Snell	Niagara Falls, NY
1988	Del Ballard Jr.	219.1	Keith Smith	Jacksonville, FL
1989	Mike Aulby	218.5	Mike Edwards	Wichita
1990	Chris Warren	231.6	David Ozio	Reno
1991	Doug Kent	226.8	George Branham III	Toledo, OH
1992	Ken Johnson	230.0	Dave D'Entremont	Corpus Christi, TX
1993	Norm Duke	245.68	Patrick Allen	Tulsa, OK
1994	Steve Fehr	213.09	Steve Anderson	Greenacres, FL
1995	Mike Aulby	230.7	Mark Williams	Reno
1996	Ernie Schlegel	221.2	Mike Aulby	Salt Lake City
1997	Jason Queen	225.5	Eric Forkel	Huntsville, AL
1998	Mike Aulby	224.0	Parker Bohn III	Reno, NV

BPAA United States Open

Year	Winner	Score	Runner-Up	Site
1949	Marion Ladewig	113.26–104.26	Catherine Burling	Chicago
1950	Marion Ladewig	151.46–146.06	Stephanie Balogh	Chicago
1951	Marion Ladewig	159.17–148.03	Sylvia Wene	Chicago
1952	Marion Ladewig	154.39–142.05	Shirley Garms	Chicago
1953	Not held			
1954	Marion Ladewig	148.29–143.01	Sylvia Wene	Chicago
1955	Sylvia Wene	142.30–141.11	Sylvia Fanta	Chicago
1955	Anita Cantaline	144.40–144.13	Doris Porter	Chicago
1956	Marion Ladewig	150.16–145.41	Marge Merrick	Chicago
1957	Not held			
1958	Merle Matthews	145.09–143.14	Marion Ladewig	Minneapolis
1959	Marion Ladewig	149.33–143.00	Donna Zimmerman	Buffalo
1960	Sylvia Wene	144.14–143.26	Marion Ladewig	Omaha
1961	Phyllis Notaro	144.13–143.12	Hope Riccilli	San Bernardino, CA
1962	Shirley Garms	138.44–135.49	Joy Abel	Miami Beach
1963	Marion Ladewig	586–578	Bobbie Shaler	Kansas City, MO
1964	LaVerne Carter	683–609	Evelyn Teal	Dallas
1965	Ann Slattery	597–550	Sandy Hooper	Philadelphia
1966	Joy Abel	593–538	Bette Rockwell	Lansing, MI
1967	Gloria Bouvia	578–516	Shirley Garms	St. Ann, MO
1968	Dotty Fothergill	9,000–8,187	Doris Coburn	Garden City, NY
1969	Dotty Fothergill	8,284–8,258	Kayoka Suda	Miami
1970	Mary Baker	8,730–8,465	Judy Cook	Northbrook, IL
1971	Paula Carter	5,660–5,650	June Llewellyn	Kansas City, MO
1972	Lorrie Nichols	5,272–5,189	Mary Baker	Denver
1973	Millie Martorella	5,553–5,294	Patty Costello	Garden City, NY
1974	Patty Costello	219–216	Betty Morris	Irving, TX
1975	Paula Carter	6,500–6,352	Lorrie Nichols	Toledo, OH
1976	Patty Costello	11,341–11,281	Betty Morris	Tulsa, OK
1977	Betty Morris	10,511–10,358	Virginia Norton	Milwaukee
1978	Donna Adamek	236–202	Vesma Grinfelds	Miami
1979	Diana Silva	11,775–11,718	Bev Ortner	Phoenix
1980	Pat Costello	223–199	Shinobu Saitoh	Rockford, IL
1981	Donna Adamek	201–190	Nikki Gianulias	Rockford, IL
1982	Shinobu Saitoh	12,184–12,028	Robin Romeo	Hendersonville, TN
1983	Dana Miller-Mackie	247–200	Aleta Sill	St. Louis
1984	Karen Ellingsworth	236–217	Lorrie Nichols	St. Louis
1985	Pat Mercatani	214–178	Nikki Gianulias	Topeka, KS
1986	Wendy Macpherson	265–179	Lisa Wagner	Topeka, KS
1987	Carol Norman	206–179	Cindy Coburn	Mentor, OH
1988	Lisa Wagner	226–218	Lorrie Nichols	Winston-Salem, NC
1989	Robin Romeo	187–163	Michelle Mullen	Addison, IL
1990	Dana Miller-Mackie	190–189	Tish Johnson	Dearborn Heights, MI
1991	Anne Marie Duggan	196–185	Leanne Barrette	Fountain Valley, CA
1992	Tish Johnson	216–213	Aleta Sill	Fountain Valley, CA
1993	Dede Davidson	213–194	Dana Miller-Mackie	Garland, TX
1994	Aleta Sill	229–170	Anne Marie Duggan	Wichita
1995	Cheryl Daniels	235–180	Tish Johnson	Blaine, MN
1996	Liz Johnson	265–236	Marianne DiRupo	Indianapolis, IN
1997	no event—tournament moved to April			
1998	Aleta Sill	276–151	Tammy Turner	Milford, CT

Note: From 1942 to 1970, the tournament was called the BPAA All-Star. Peterson scoring was used from 1949 through 1962. Under this system, the winner of an individual match game gets one point, plus one point for each 50 pins knocked down. From 1963 through 1967, a three-game championship was held between the two top qualifiers. From 1968 through 1973, 1975–77, 1979 and 1982, total pinfall determined the winner. In the other years, five qualifiers competed in a playoff for the championship, with the final match listed above.

AMF Gold Cup

Year	Winner	Score	Runner-Up	Site
1997	Aleta Sill	221–179	C. Gianotti-Block	Richmond, VA

WIBC Queens

Year	Winner	Score	Runner-Up	Site
1961	Janet Harman	794–776	Eula Touchette	Fort Wayne, IN
1962	Dorothy Wilkinson	799–794	Marion Ladewig	Phoenix
1963	Irene Monterosso	852–803	Georgette DeRosa	Memphis
1964	D. D. Jacobson	740–682	Shirley Garms	Minneapolis
1965	Betty Kuczynski	772–739	LaVerne Carter	Portland, OR
1966	Judy Lee	771–742	Nancy Peterson	New Orleans
1967	Millie Ignizio	840–809	Phyllis Massey	Rochester, NY
1968	Phyllis Massey	884–853	Marian Spencer	San Antonio
1969	Ann Feigel	832–765	Millie Ignizio	San Diego
1970	Millie Ignizio	807–797	Joan Holm	Tulsa, OK
1971	Millie Ignizio	809–778	Katherine Brown	Atlanta
1972	Dotty Fothergill	890–841	Maureen Harris	Kansas City, MO
1973	Dotty Fothergill	804–791	Judy Soutar	Las Vegas
1974	Judy Soutar	939–705	Betty Morris	Houston
1975	Cindy Powell	758–674	Patty Costello	Indianapolis
1976	Pam Buckner	214–178	Shirley Sjostrom	Denver
1977	Dana Stewart	175–167	Vesma Grinfelds	Milwaukee
1978	Loa Boxberger	197–176	Cora Fiebig	Miami
1979	Donna Adamek	216–181	Shinobu Saitoh	Tucson, AZ
1980	Donna Adamek	213–165	Cheryl Robinson	Seattle
1981	Katsuko Sugimoto	166–158	Virginia Norton	Baltimore
1982	Katsuko Sugimoto	160–137	Nikki Gianulias	St. Louis
1983	Aleta Sill	214–188	Dana Miller-Mackie	Las Vegas
1984	Kazue Inahashi	248–222	Aleta Sill	Niagara Falls, NY
1985	Aleta Sill	279–192	Linda Graham	Toledo, OH
1986	Cora Fiebig	223–177	Barbara Thorberg	Orange County, CA
1987	Cathy Almeida	850–817	Lorrie Nichols	Hartford, CT
1988	Wendy Macpherson	213–199	Leanne Barrette	Reno/Carson City, NV
1989	Carol Gianotti	207–177	Sandra Jo Shiery	Bismarck-Mandan, ND
1990	Patty Ann	207–173	Vesma Grinfelds	Tampa, FL
1991	Dede Davidson	231–159	Jeanne Maiden	Cedar Rapids, IA
1992	Cindy Coburn-Carroll	184–170	Dana Miller-Mackie	Lansing, MI
1993	Jan Schmidt	201–163	Pat Costello	Baton Rouge, LA
1994	Anne Marie Duggan	224–177	Wendy Macpherson-Papanos	Salt Lake City
1995	Sandra Postma	226–187	Carolyn Dorin	Tucson, AZ
1996	Lisa Wagner	231–226	Tammy Turner	Buffalo, NY
1997	S.J. Shiery-Odom	209–185	Audry Allen	Reno, NV
1998	Lynda Norry	213–157	Karen Stroud	Davenport, IA

Sam's Town Invitational

Year	Winner	Score	Runner-Up	Site
1984	Aleta Sill	238 (1 game)	Cheryl Daniels	Las Vegas, NV
1985	Patty Costello	236 (1 game)	Robin Romeo	Las Vegas, NV
1986	Aleta Sill	238 (1 game)	Dina Wheeler	Las Vegas, NV
1987	Debbie Bennett	880 (4 games)	Lorrie Nichols	Las Vegas, NV
1988	Donna Adamek	634 (3 games)	Robin Romeo	Las Vegas, NV
1989	Tish Johnson	210 (1 game)	Dede Davidson	Las Vegas, NV
1990	Wendy Macpherson	900 (4 games)	Jeanne Maiden	Las Vegas, NV
1991	Lorrie Nichols	469 (2 games)	Dana Miller-Mackie	Las Vegas, NV
1992	Tish Johnson	279 (1 game)	Robin Romeo	Las Vegas, NV
1993	Robin Romeo	194 (1 game)	Tammy Turner	Las Vegas, NV
1994	Tish Johnson	178 (1 game)	Carol Gianotti	Las Vegas, NV
1995	Michelle Mullen	202 (1 game)	Cheryl Daniels	Las Vegas, NV
1996	C. Gianotti-Block	892 (4 games)	Leanne Barrette	Las Vegas, NV
1997	Kim Adler	953 (4 games)	Wendy Macpherson	Las Vegas, NV

PWBA Championships

1960	Marion Ladewig	1967	Betty Mivalez	1974	Pat Costello
1961	Shirley Garms	1968	Dotty Fothergill	1975	Pam Buckner
1962	Stephanie Balogh	1969	Dotty Fothergill	1976	Patty Costello
1963	Janet Harman	1970	Bobbe North	1977	Vesma Grinfelds
1964	Betty Kuczynski	1971	Patty Costello	1978	Toni Gillard
1965	Helen Duval	1972	Patty Costello	1979	Cindy Coburn
1966	Joy Abel	1973	Betty Morris	1980	Donna Adamek

BWAA Bowler of the Year

1942 ....Johnny Crimmins	1962 ....Don Carter	1980 ....Wayne Webb
1943 ....Ned Day	1963 ....Dick Weber,	1981 ....Earl Anthony
1944 ....Ned Day	Billy Hardwick (PBA)*	1982 ....Earl Anthony
1945 ....Buddy Bomar	1964 ....Billy Hardwick,	1983 ....Earl Anthony
1946 ....Joe Wilman	Bob Strampe (PBA)*	1984 ....Mark Roth
1947 ....Buddy Bomar	1965 ....Dick Weber	1985 ....Mike Aulby
1948 ....Andy Varipapa	1966 ....Wayne Zahn	1986 ....Walter Ray Williams Jr.
1949 ....Connie Schwoegler	1967 ....Dave Davis	1987 ....Marshall Holman
1950 ....Junie McMahon	1968 ....Jim Stefanich	1988 ....Brian Voss
1951 ....Lee Jouglard	1969 ....Billy Hardwick	1989 ....Mike Aulby,
1952 ....Steve Nagy	1970 ....Nelson Burton Jr.	Amleto Monacelli (PBA)*
1953 ....Don Carter	1971 ....Don Johnson	1990 ....Amleto Monacelli
1954 ....Don Carter	1972 ....Don Johnson	1991 ....David Ozio
1955 ....Steve Nagy	1973 ....Don McCune	1992 ....Dave Ferraro
1956 ....Bill Lillard	1974 ....Earl Anthony	1993 ....Walter Ray Williams Jr.
1957 ....Don Carter	1975 ....Earl Anthony	1994 ....Norm Duke
1958 ....Don Carter	1976 ....Earl Anthony	1995 ....Mike Aulby
1959 ....Ed Lubanski	1977 ....Mark Roth	1996 ....Walter Ray Williams Jr.
1960 ....Don Carter	1978 ....Mark Roth	1997 ....Walter Ray Williams Jr.
1961 ....Dick Weber	1979 ....Mark Roth	

*The PBA began selecting a player of the year in 1963. Its selection has been the same as the BWAA's in all but three years.

BWAA Bowler of the Year

1948 ....Val Mikiel	1966 ....Joy Abel	1984 ....Aleta Sill
1949 ....Val Mikiel	1967 ....Millie Martorella	1985 ....Aleta Sill,
1950 ....Marion Ladewig	1968 ....Dotty Fothergill	Patty Costello (PWBA)*
1951 ....Marion Ladewig	1969 ....Dotty Fothergill	1986 ....Lisa Wagner,
1952 ....Marion Ladewig	1970 ....Mary Baker	Jeanne Madden (PWBA)*
1953 ....Marion Ladewig	1971 ....Paula Sperber Carter	1987 ....Betty Morris
1954 ....Marion Ladewig	1972 ....Patty Costello	1988 ....Lisa Wagner
1955 ....Marion Ladewig	1973 ....Judy Soutar	1989 ....Robin Romeo
1956 ....Sylvia Martin	1974 ....Betty Morris	1990 ....Tish Johnson,
1957 ....Anita Cantaline	1975 ....Judy Soutar	Leanne Barrette (PWBA)*
1958 ....Marion Ladewig	1976 ....Patty Costello	1991 ....Leanne Barrette
1959 ....Marion Ladewig	1977 ....Betty Morris	1992 ....Tish Johnson
1960 ....Sylvia Martin	1978 ....Donna Adamek	1993 ....Lisa Wagner
1961 ....Shirley Garms	1979 ....Donna Adamek	1994 ....Anne Marie Duggan
1962 ....Shirley Garms	1980 ....Donna Adamek	1995 ....Tish Johnson
1963 ....Marion Ladewig	1981 ....Donna Adamek	1996 ....Wendy Macpherson
1964 ....LaVerne Carter	1982 ....Nikki Gianulias	1997 ....Wendy Macpherson
1965 ....Betty Kuczynski	1983 ....Lisa Wagner	

*The PWBA began selecting a player of the year in 1983. Its selection has been the same as the BWAA's in all but three years.

Career Leaders

Earnings

MEN

Walter Ray Williams Jr. $2,177,253
Pete Weber $2,075,800
Mike Aulby $1,936,855
Marshall Holman $1,691,194
Brian Voss $1,660,600

WOMEN

Aleta Sill $968,222
Tish Johnson $868,685
Lisa Wagner $756,576
Wendy Macpherson $723,769
Anne Marie Duggan $703,851

Titles

MEN

Earl Anthony 41
Mark Roth 34
Don Johnson 26
Dick Weber 26
Mike Aulby 26

WOMEN

Lisa Wagner 30
Aleta Sill 30
Patty Costello 25
Tish Johnson 22
Donna Adamek 19
Leanne Barrette 19
Nikki Gianulias 19

Note: Men leaders through July 21, 1998; women through August 21, 1998.

Soccer

Sports Illustrated

Vive La France

Zinedine Zidane leads France to its first World Cup

BOB MARTIN

Coup de Grâce

With stingy defense, a balanced attack and the world's finest midfielder, France won one of the best World Cups ever

BY GRANT WAHL

THE FRENCH, AS a rule, have always met soccer with a grand Gallic shrug. Their professional league is only the fifth-best in Europe. Their top players all toil for clubs in Italy and England. Their countrymen invented the World Cup, and yet their national team entered the XVI Coupe du Monde with a history of staggering mediocrity. France had never appeared in a World Cup final, nor had it even *qualified* for the 1990 and '94 tournaments. After the '94 debacle, one French daily had derisively proclaimed, FRANCE QUALIFIES FOR 1998! (it had done so automatically as the host country), and since then the cynics had only multiplied. Driving through Paris on the eve of the Cup, one couldn't help but notice the posters bearing a soccer ball and the typically dour Left Bank slogan: Sport of the Masses, Spasm of Death.

Yet for one glorious July night, at least, Gallic shrugs gave way to Gallic hugs, and the world's best midfielder might have earned himself a Rogaine endorsement. At the gleaming Stade de France in the Paris suburb of Saint-Denis, Les Bleus stunned defending and four-time champion Brazil 3–0 to cap a tournament in which attack-minded play blessedly returned to the world's most popular sport. Zinedine Zidane, France's prematurely balding playmaker, headed in two corner kicks in the first half—the first nonpenalty kick goals in a Cup final since 1986—and midfielder Emmanuel Petit scored in injury time to seal Brazil's most lopsided defeat in 80 World Cup games dating to 1930. To add insult to injury, France played the final 22 minutes with 10 men after Marcel Desailly got a second yellow card.

Few disputed that Les Bleus were the finest team in the tournament, which was one of the best ever, full of splendid games and skillful stars. France scored the most goals of any team (15) and conceded the fewest (2). While they lacked a potent striker—none of France's forwards had more than three goals—they made up for it by sending their skilled defenders forward to score goals when they needed them.

Sport of the masses? Well, there *were*

BOB MARTIN

France's captain Didier Deschamps lifted sport's most coveted trophy.

1.5 million suddenly gung-ho French revelers celebrating their champs on the Champs-Elysées after the final. Spasms of death? We almost had those, too, thanks to the most bizarre series of events ever associated with a World Cup final. Just hours before the game, Ronaldo, Brazil's two-time World Player of the Year, suffered a 30-second-long convulsive fit at the team's hotel. In the bedlam that followed, cries of "He's dead! He's dead!" filled the air, the hotel's manager said later. Reports of the 21-year-old striker's demise were only somewhat exaggerated. After a visit to the emergency room revealed that Ronaldo had no life-threatening infirmities (Brazil's trainer attributed the seizure to "emotional stress"), coach Mario Zagallo inserted him back into the lineup and—surprise!—he played like a man who should have been lying on a gurney at Paris General. "Ronaldo was not fit to play," Zagallo said in a rare moment of candor after the game. "This was a major psychological blow. Everyone was very upset, and so the team played to less than its full potential."

That was a convenient excuse for a team that somnambulated through the final as though it had been chugging *caipirinha*, Brazil's potent national drink, during pregame warmups. It was also a blatant refusal to give props to France, which could have won the game 6–0 had its bumbling forwards, Christophe Dugarry and Stéphane Guivarc'h (he of the baffling apostrophe), not botched shots as wide open as the Arc de Triomphe.

Midfielder Frankie Hejduk (2) was a lone bright spot for the U.S. at France 98.

No World Cup champion has ever owed more to its back line than France did in 1998. Led by the silky tandem of Marcel Desailly and Lilian Thuram, the French defense allowed only one goal during the run of play in its seven Cup matches. And when the front line faltered, French defenders scored all three of the team's goals between the second round and the semis. "It's funny how these things work. I never score, especially not with my left foot," said Thuram, who had both goals in France's 2–1 semifinal victory against Croatia and was the premier defender, if not player, of the tournament.

Of course, Thuram wasn't the only revelation in a Cup with an expanded field of 32 teams. There was Michael Owen, England's Gerber-faced striker, who rocketed past two Argentine defenders to score the tournament's most breathtaking goal. (England eventually lost the second-round battle 3–2 on penalty kicks, in the match of the Cup.)

Owen's debut drew comparisons to that in 1958 of another 18-year-old, a kid by the name of Pelé. There was Dutch forward Dennis Bergkamp, well known for his mortal fear of flying, who mastered the French rails and scored four goals while leading the Dutch to a spot in the semifinals. Finally, there was Croatia's Davor Suker, who didn't even start for his club team Real Madrid, yet won the Golden Boot as the Cup's leading scorer (six goals). The Croatians, playing in their first World Cup, ambushed Germany in the quarters on their way to a stunning third-place finish.

There were low moments, too. Spain, a dark horse pick to win the Cup, hewed to its underachieving past and stumbled back across the Pyrenees after a first-round exit. International referees, instructed by FIFA to eject any player who tackled from behind, waffled between laissez-faire ignorance and Gestapo-worthy crackdowns. (The Denmark–South Africa first-round match had three ejections alone.) Worse yet, the world's best players finally perfected the art of the unmolested pratfall. Chevy

Chase would have been proud of one climactic scene in a quarterfinal match in Marseilles. Argentina's Ariel Ortega faked a fall in the penalty box, only to be accosted by Dutch goalkeeper Edwin van der Sar, who himself crumpled like a paper accordion when the shorter Ortega comically head-butted him with the top of his noggin. The results: Ortega got a red card, van der Sar got pelted with debris from the Argentine fans, and Holland scored the game winner seconds later on a brilliant strike by Bergkamp.

For Americans, though, the most dispiriting part of World Cup '98 was the double-gainer belly flop of the U.S. national team. Clearly the Yanks had improved since their surprising second-round performance in World Cup '94. They had qualified for France with a game to spare, and had followed that with a historic 1–0 upset of Brazil in February and a 3–0 thrashing of Cup-bound Austria in April.

But in retrospect, the Austria victory provided U.S. coach Steve Sampson with a false sense of security, for it gave temporary credence to his desperate last-second overhaul of the American lineup. With only two months remaining before the Cup, Sampson dumped captain John Harkes for mysterious reasons that devolved into a personality conflict, benched veteran defenders Marcelo Balboa and Alexi Lalas and radically resculpted the formation into a 3-6-1. That's three defenders, *six* midfielders and a lone—stranded as it turned out—forward. Even after the U.S. struggled in pre-Cup tune-ups, failing to score in draws against Macedonia and Scotland, Sampson was unwavering in his optimism. "My dream is to get to the third round," he said. "My hope is to get to the second."

In the end, Sampson's hopes and dreams were dashed by the folly of his risks. Three of his starters in the World Cup opener against Germany hadn't even played for the U.S. in the final round of World Cup qualifying, while another had appeared in only a single match. As soon as the opening whistle blew in Paris on June 15, the Germans treated the Americans like so many Beanie Babies to be tossed around the den. Only 20 seconds into the match, Teutonic tough-guy Jens Jeremies flattened U.S. playmaker Claudio Reyna from behind. There was no retaliation—that had been Harkes's role before he was cut—and Germany marched to a laughably easy 2–0 victory.

If the Americans were to have any hope of advancing, they had to beat Iran six days later in Lyons. It was the most politically charged match of the Cup, and the Americans handled it beautifully, exchanging flowers with the Iranians before the game and posing with them for a group photo. Then everything fell apart. The U.S. hit the woodwork three times and dominated the early going but the Iranians played solid defense and focused on the counterattack. Iran's Hamid Estili beat goalkeeper Kasey Keller with a well-placed header late in the first half, and Mehdi Madivikia added another on a countering breakaway in the second. By the time Brian McBride scored the only U.S. goal of the Cup in the 88th minute, it was too late. The Americans would lose 2–1.

Following a spiritless 1–0 loss to Yugoslavia on June 25, the U.S., with one goal for and five against in three losses, finished 32nd out of 32 teams. And without doubt the U.S. featured the Cup's largest collection of whiners and churls. "I blame the coaches for the losses," griped midfielder Tab Ramos, who had made the team only because Sampson had held open a spot until the very last minute while Ramos recovered from knee surgery. By the end of the Cup, Ramos and three other players had announced that they would never again play for Sampson, who made matters easier by resigning.

In late October, U.S. Soccer appeared to be finally ready to replace Sampson with Bruce Arena of Major League Soccer's D.C. United, but not before Arena had firmly established United as the dynasty of American club soccer. After going 24–8 in the regular season, D.C. dispatched Miami and Columbus to advance to the MLS championship game for the third time in the three-year history of the league.

FOR THE RECORD·1997–98

Group Standings

GROUP A

Country	GP	W	L	T	GF	GA	Pts
*Brazil	3	2	1	0	6	3	6
*Norway	3	1	0	2	5	4	5
Morocco	3	1	1	1	5	5	4
Scotland	3	0	2	1	2	6	1

GROUP B

Country	GP	W	L	T	GF	GA	Pts
*Italy	3	2	0	1	7	3	7
*Chile	3	0	0	3	4	4	3
Cameroon	3	0	1	2	3	4	2
Austria	3	0	1	2	2	5	2

GROUP C

Country	GP	W	L	T	GF	GA	Pts
*France	3	3	0	0	9	1	9
*Denmark	3	1	1	1	3	3	4
South Africa	3	0	1	2	3	6	2
Saudi Arabia	3	0	2	1	2	7	1

GROUP D

Country	GP	W	L	T	GF	GA	Pts
*Nigeria	3	2	1	0	5	5	6
*Paraguay	3	1	0	2	3	1	5
Spain	3	1	1	1	8	4	4
Bulgaria	3	0	2	1	1	7	1

GROUP E

Country	GP	W	L	T	GF	GA	Pts
*Netherlands	3	1	0	2	7	2	5
*Mexico	3	1	0	2	7	5	5
Belgium	3	0	0	3	3	3	3
South Korea	3	0	2	1	2	9	1

GROUP F

Country	GP	W	L	T	GF	GA	Pts
*Germany	3	2	0	1	6	2	7
*Yugoslavia	3	2	0	1	4	2	7
Iran	3	1	2	0	2	4	3
United States	3	0	3	0	1	5	0

GROUP G

Country	GP	W	L	T	GF	GA	Pts
*Romania	3	2	0	1	4	2	7
*England	3	2	1	0	5	2	6
Colombia	3	1	2	0	1	3	3
Tunisia	3	0	2	1	1	4	1

GROUP H

Country	GP	W	L	T	GF	GA	Pts
*Argentina	3	3	0	0	7	0	9
*Croatia	3	2	1	0	4	2	6
Jamaica	3	1	2	0	3	9	3
Japan	3	0	3	0	1	4	0

*Advanced to second round.

Note: In group play, teams are awarded three points for a victory, one for a tie. The top two in each group advance to the round of 16.

Group Play Scores

GROUP A

Brazil 2, Scotland 1
Norway 2, Morocco 2
Brazil 3, Morocco 0
Norway 1, Scotland 1
Norway 2, Brazil 1
Morocco 3, Scotland 0

GROUP B

Italy 2, Chile 2
Cameroon 1, Austria 1
Italy 3, Cameroon 0
Chile 1, Austria 1
Italy 2, Austria 1
Chile 1, Cameroon 1

GROUP C

France 3, South Africa 0
Denmark 1, S. Arabia 0
France 4, S. Arabia 0
S. Africa 1, Denmark 1
France 2, Denmark 1
S. Africa 2, S. Arabia 2

GROUP D

Paraguay 0, Bulgaria 0
Nigeria 3, Spain 2
Spain 0, Paraguay 0
Nigeria 1, Bulgaria 0
Spain 6, Bulgaria 1
Paraguay 3, Nigeria 1

GROUP E

Netherlands 0, Belgium 0
Mexico 3, S. Korea 1
Netherlands 5, S. Korea 0
Belgium 2, Mexico 2
Netherlands 2, Mexico 2
Belgium 1, S. Korea 1

GROUP F

Yugoslavia 1, Iran 0
Germany 2, U.S. 0
Germany 2, Yugoslavia 2
Iran 2, U.S. 1
Germany 2 Iran 0
Yugoslavia 1, U.S. 0

GROUP G

Romania 1, Colombia 0
England 2, Tunisia 0
Romania 2, England 1
Colombia 1, Tunisia 0
Romania 1, Tunisia 1
England 2, Colombia 0

GROUP H

Argentina 1, Japan 0
Croatia 3, Jamaica 1
Croatia 1, Japan 0
Argentina 5, Jamaica 0
Argentina 1, Croatia 0
Jamaica 2, Japan 1

WORLD CUP FINAL

Italy
Norway
France
Paraguay
Germany
Mexico
Romania
Croatia

Italy (1–0)
France (0–0) (4–3)
France (1–0) (ot)
France (2–1)
Germany (2–1)
Croatia (3–0)
Croatia (1–0)

France (3–0)

Brazil (3–2)
Brazil (1–1) (4–2)
Netherlands (2–1)

Brazil (4–1)
Denmark (4–1)
Netherlands (2–1)
Argentina (2–2) (4–3)

Brazil
Chile
Nigeria
Denmark
Netherlands
Yugoslavia
Argentina
England

Major League Soccer

Final Standings

WESTERN CONFERENCE

Team	Won	Lost	Pts	GF	GA	SOW
y-D.C. United..24	8	58	74	48		7
x-Columbus....15	17	45	67	56	0	
x-MetroStars...15	17	39	54	63	3	
x-Miami 15	17	35	46	68	5	
Tampa Bay.....12	20	34	46	57	1	
New England ..11	21	29	53	66	2	

EASTERN CONFERENCE

Team	Won	Lost	Pts	GF	GA	SOW
y-Los Angeles..24	8	68	85	44	2	
x-Chicago 20	12	56	62	45	2	
x-Colorado 16	16	44	62	69	2	
x-Dallas 15	17	37	43	59	4	
San Jose 13	19	33	48	60	3	
Kansas City....12	20	32	45	50	2	

Note: Three points for a win. One point for a shootout win. Win and loss columns include shootout wins and losses.

SCORING LEADERS

Player, Team	GP	G	A	Pts
Stern John, Columbus 27	26	5	57	
Cobi Jones, Los Angeles ...24	19	13	51	
Welton, Los Angeles 31	17	11	45	
Raul Diaz Arce, NE 32	18	8	44	
Roy Lassiter, D.C. 31	18	8	44	

GOALS LEADERS

Player, Team	GP	G
Stern John, Columbus.......................27	26	
Cobi Jones, Los Angeles...................24	19	
Roy Lassiter, D.C. United...................31	18	
Raul Diaz Arce, New England.............32	18	
Welton, Los Angeles 31	17	

ASSISTS LEADERS

Player, Team	GP	A
Marco Etcheverry, D.C. United...........29	19	
Mauricio Cienfuegos, Los Angeles.....30	16	
Joe-Max Moore, New England...........21	15	
Eduardo Hurtado, NY/NJ 29	15	

GOALS-AGAINST-AVERAGE LEADERS

Player, Team	GAA
Zach Thornton, Chicago.....................................1.17
Kevin Hartman, Los Angeles...............................1.38
Scott Garlick, D.C...1.43
Mike Ammann, Kansas City 1.56
David Kramer, San Jose......................................1.65

1998 PLAYOFFS

Los Angeles
Dallas
Chicago
Colorado

Los Angeles (2–0)
Chicago (2–0)
Chicago (2–0)

D.C. vs Chicago

D.C. United (2–1)

D.C. United (2–0)
Columbus (2–0)

D.C United
Miami
Columbus
MetroStars

LOS ANGELES, CALIF., OCTOBER 25, 1998
D.C. United vs. Chicago Fire

International Competition

1997–98 U.S. Men's National Team Results

Date	Opponent	Site	Result	U.S. Goals
Nov 2, 1997	Mexico	Mexico City	0–0 T	—
Nov 9	Canada	Burnaby, B.C., Can.	3–0 W	Reyna, Wegerle (2)
Nov 16	El Salvador	Foxboro, MA	4–2 W	McBride (2), Henderson, Preki
Jan 24, 1998	Sweden	Orlando, FL	1–0 W	Wegerle
Feb 1	Cuba	Oakland	3–0 W	Wegerle, Wynalda, Moore
Feb 7	Costa Rica	Oakland	2–1 W	Pope, Preki
Feb 10	Brazil	Los Angeles	1–0 W	Preki
Feb 15	Mexico	Los Angeles	0–1 L	—
Feb 21	Netherlands	Miami	0–2 L	—
Feb 25	Belgium	Brussels	0–2 L	—
Mar 14	Paraguay	San Diego	2–2 T	Deering, Balboa
Apr 22	Austria	Vienna	3–0 W	Hejduk, McBride, Reyna
May 16	Macedonia	San Jose, CA	0–0 T	—
May 24	Kuwait	Portland, OR	2–0 W	Stewart, Ramos
May 30	Scotland	Washington, D.C.	0–0 T	—
June 15	Germany	Paris	0–2 L	—
June 21	Iran	Lyon, France	1–2 L	McBride
June 25	Yugoslavia	Nantes, France	0–1 L	—

Record through Sept 30, 1998: 8-6-4.

1998 U.S. Women's National Team Results

Date	Opponent	Site	Result	U.S. Goals
Jan 18	Sweden	Guangzhou, China	3–0 W	Venturini, Milbrett, Keller
Jan 21	China	Guangzhou, China	0–0 T	—
Jan 24	Norway	Guangzhou, China	3–0 W	Venturini, Hamm, Parlow
Mar 15	Finland	Olhao, Portugal	2–0 W	Akers, Chastain
Mar 17	China	Loule, Portugal	4–1 W	Hamm (3), Lilly
Mar 19	Norway	Lagos, Portugal	1–4 L	Chastain
Mar 21	Sweden	Quarteira, Portugal	3–1 W	Foudy, Chastain, Lilly
April 24	Argentina	Fullerton, CA	8–1 W	Milbrett (3), Akers, Keller (2), Hamm (2)
April 26	Argentina	San Jose, CA	7–0 W	Lilly, Milbrett (2), Akers, Chastain, Foudy, own goal
May 8	Iceland	Indianapolis	6–0 W	Milbrett, Hamm (2), Whalen, Venturini, Keller
May 10	Iceland	Bethlehem, PA	1–0 W	Neaton
May 17	Japan	Tokyo	2–1 W	Keller (2)
May 21	Japan	Kobe, Japan	2–0 W	Lilly, Keller
May 24	Japan	Yokohama, Japan	3–0 W	Chastain, Lilly, Venturini
May 30	New Zealand	Washington, D.C.	5–0 L	Parlow, Keller (2), Fair, Milbrett
June 25	Germany	St. Louis	1–1 T	Parlow
June 28	Germany	Chicago	4–2 W	Lilly, Hamm (3)
July 25	Denmark	Long Island, NY	5–0 W	Milbrett, Akers, Hamm (3)
July 27	China	Long Island, NY	2–0 W	Hamm (2)
Aug 2	Canada	Orlando, FL	4–0 W	Keller (2) Milbrett Foudy
Sept 12	Mexico	Foxboro, MA	9–0 W	Hamm (2), Lilly (2), Milbrett, Macmillan, Fawcett, Venturini, Keller
Sept 18	Russia	Rochester, NY	4–0 W	Milbrett (2), Hamm (2)
Sept 20	Brazil	Richmond, VA	3–0 W	Fawcett, Akers, Keller

Record through Sept 30, 1998: 19-2-2.

International Club Competition

Intercontinental Cup

Competition between winners of European Cup and Libertadores Cup.

TOKYO: DEC 2, 1997

Borussia Dortmund (Ger) ..1 1 —2
Cruzeiro (Brazil) ....0 0 —0

Goals: Zorc (34), Herrlich (85).

Att: 60,000.

Dortmund: Klos, Cesar, Feiersinger, Zorc, Reuter, Moller, Heinrich, Freund, Sousa, Herrlich, Kirovski.
Cruzeiro: Dida, Vitor, Jao Carlos, Goncalves, Elivelton, Fabinho, Cleisson, Palacios, Ricardinho, Bebeto, Donizete.

European Cup-Winners' Cup

Cup winners of countries belonging to UEFA.

STOCKHOLM: MAY 13, 1998

Chelsea (England) ....0 1 —1
VfB Stuttgart (Ger) ....0 0 —0

Goal: Zola (71).

Att: 30,216

Chelsea: De Goey, Petrescu, Leboeuf, Clarke, Poyet (Newton 80), Vialli, Wise, Duberry, Di Matteo, Granvill, Flo (Zola 71).
VfB Stuttgart: Wohlfahrt, Berthold, Yakin, Hagner (Ristic 79), Haber (Georjevic 75), Balakov, Bobic, Schneider (Endress 55), Akpoborie, Soldo, Poschner.

UEFA Cup

Competition between teams other than league champions and cup-winners from UEFA.

PARIS: MAY 6, 1998

Inter Milan (Italy) ....1 2 —3
Lazio (Italy) ....0 0 —0

Goals: Zamorano (5), Zanetti (60), Ronaldo (70).

Att: 45,000

Inter: Pagliuca, Fresi, West, Colonesse, Zanetti, Simeone, Djorkaeff (Moriero 72), Elias, Winter (Cauet 72), Ronaldo, Zamorano (Sartor 74).
Lazio: Marchegiani, Negor, Nesta, Grandoni (Gottardi 55), Favalli, Fuser, Nedved, Jugovic, Venturin (Almeyda 50), Casiraghi, Mancini.

European Cup

League champions of the countries belonging to UEFA (Union of European Football Associations).

AMSTERDAM: MAY 20, 1998

Real Madrid (Spain) ....0 1 —1
Juventus (Italy) ....0 0 —0

Goal: Mijatovic (67).

Att: 47,500.

Real Madrid: Illgner, Panucci, Hierro, Sanchis, Carlos, Karembeu, Redondo, Seedorf, Raul (Amavisca), Mijatovic (Suker 90) Morientes (Jaime 82).
Juventus: Peruzzi, Torricelli, Montero, Iuliano, Pessotto, (Fonseca 71) Di Livio (Tacchinardi 46), Deschamps (Conte 78), Davids, Zidane, Del Piero, Inzaghi.

Libertadores Cup

Competition between champion clubs and runners-up of 10 South American National Associations.

(2ND LEG) GUAYAQUIL, ECUADOR: AUG. 26, 1998

Vasco da Gama (Brazil)..1 1 —2
Barcelona (Ecuador).......0 1 —1

Goals: Luizao (25), Donizete (45), de Avila (79).

(Aggregate: 4–1).

Att: 80,000.

Vasco: Germano, Vagner, Galvao, Odvan, Felipe, Luisinho, Nasa, Juninho, Pedrinho, Donizete, Luizao.

Barcelona: Gomez Montanero, Quisnez, Capurro, George, de Avila, Morlaes, Aires, Asencio, Delgado, Rosero.

1997-98 League Champions—Europe

Country	League Champion	Cup Winner
Albania	Vlaznia Shkoder	Apolonia Fier
Andorra	Charlot Principat	—
Armenia	FK Yerevan	Tsement Ararat
Austria	Sturm Graz	SV Ried
Azerbaijan	Kapaz Ganja	Kapaz Ganja
Belarus	Dinamo Minsk	Lokomotiv Vitebsk
Belgium	Club Bruges	Racing Genk
Bosnia-Herzegovina	Zeljeznicar Sarajevo	
Bulgaria	Litex Lovetch	Levski Sofia
Croatia	Croatia Zagreb	Croatia Zagreb
Cyprus	Anorthosis	Apollon
Czech Republic	Sparta Prague	Jablonec
Denmark	Brøndby	Brøndby
England	Arsenal	Arsenal
Estonia	Flora Tallinn	Flora Tallinn
Faroe Islands	B36 Torshavn*	GI Gotu*
Finland	HJK Helsinki	Haka Valkeakoski
France	Racing Lens	Paris St. Germain
Georgia	Dinamo Tblisi	Dinamo Batumi
Germany	Kaiserslautern	Bayern Munich
Greece	Olympiakos	Panionios
Holland	Ajax	Ajax
Hungary	Ujpest TE	MTK Budapest
Iceland	IBV Vestmannaeyjar	Keflavik
Irish Republic	St. Patrick's Athletic	Cork City
Israel	Beitar Jerusalem	Maccabi Haifa
Italy	Juventus	Lazio
Latvia	Skonto Riga	Skonto Riga
Liechtenstein	no league	Vaduz
Lithuania	Kareda Siauliai	Ekranas Panevezys
Luxembourg	Jeunesse d'Esch	CS Grevenmacher
Macedonia	Sileks Kratovo	Vardar Skopje
Malta	FC Valetta	Hibernians
Moldova	Zimbru Chisinau	Zimbru Chisinau
Northern Ireland	Cliftonville	Glentoran
Norway	Rosenborg*	Valerenga*
Poland	LKS Lódz	Amica Wronki
Portugal	FC Porto	FC Porto
Romania	Steaua Bucharest	Rapid Bucharest
Russia	Spartak Moscow*	Spartak Moscow
San Marino	Folgore	—
Scotland	Glasgow Celtic	Hearts of Midlothian
Slovakia	1FC Kosice	Spartak Trnava
Slovenia	Maribor Branik	Rudar Velenie
Spain	FC Barcelona	FC Barcelona
Sweden	Halmstad*	Helsingborg
Switzerland	Grasshopper Zurich	Lausanne Sports
Turkey	Galatasaray	Besiktas
Ukraine	Dinamo Kiev	Dinamo Kiev
Wales	Barry Town	Bangor City
Yugoslavia	Obilic Belgrade	Partizan Belgrade

Note: Results are from 1998 unless followed by *.

The World Cup

Results

Year	Champion	Score	Runner-Up	Winning Coach
1930	Uruguay	4–2	Argentina	Alberto Supicci
1934	Italy	2–1	Czechoslovakia	Vittorio Pozzo
1938	Italy	4–2	Hungary	Vittorio Pozzo
1950	Uruguay	2–1	Brazil	Juan Lopez
1954	West Germany	3–2	Hungary	Sepp Herberger
1958	Brazil	5–2	Sweden	Vicente Feola
1962	Brazil	3–1	Czechoslovakia	Aymore Moreira
1966	England	4–2	West Germany	Alf Ramsey
1970	Brazil	4–1	Italy	Mario Zagalo
1974	West Germany	2–1	Netherlands	Helmut Schoen
1978	Argentina	3–1	Netherlands	César Menotti
1982	Italy	3–1	West Germany	Enzo Bearzot
1986	Argentina	3–2	West Germany	Carlos Bilardo
1990	West Germany	1–0	Argentina	Franz Beckenbauer
1994	Brazil	0–0 (3–2)	Italy	Carlos Alberto Parreira
1998	France	3–0	Brazil	Aime Jacquet

Alltime World Cup Participation

Of the 62 nations which have taken part in the World Cup Finals, only Brazil has competed in each of the 16 tournaments held to date. West Germany or an undivided Germany (1934, '38, '94 and '98) has played in 15 World Cups.

	Matches	W	T	L	Goals For	Goals Against
Brazil	80	53	14	13	173	78
*Germany	78	45	17	16	162	103
Italy	66	38	16	12	105	62
Argentina	57	29	10	18	100	68
France	41	21	6	14	86	58
England	45	20	13	12	62	42
Yugoslavia	37	17	6	14	60	46
†Russia	34	16	6	12	60	40
Spain	40	16	10	14	61	48
Uruguay	37	15	8	14	61	52
Hungary	32	15	3	14	87	57
Netherlands	31	14	9	8	55	34
Poland	25	13	5	7	39	29
Sweden	37	13	7	17	62	60
Austria	29	12	4	13	42	48
Czechoslovakia	30	11	5	14	44	45
Belgium	32	9	7	16	40	56
Romania	21	8	5	8	30	32
Mexico	37	8	10	19	39	75
Chile	25	7	6	12	31	40
Portugal	9	6	0	3	19	12
Switzerland	22	6	3	13	33	51
Denmark	9	5	1	3	19	13
Croatia	6	4	0	2	9	4
Nigeria	8	4	0	4	13	13
Peru	15	4	3	8	19	31
Paraguay	15	4	6	5	19	27
United States	17	4	1	12	18	38
Scotland	23	4	7	12	25	41
Northern Ireland	13	3	5	5	13	23
Colombia	13	3	2	8	14	23
Cameroon	14	3	6	5	14	25
Bulgaria	25	3	8	14	22	49
Costa Rica	4	2	0	2	4	6
Algeria	6	2	1	3	6	10
East Germany	6	2	2	2	5	5
Saudi Arabia	7	2	1	4	7	13
Norway	8	2	3	3	7	8
Morocco	10	2	4	4	10	13
Wales	5	1	3	1	4	4
Republic of Ireland	9	1	5	3	4	7
Tunisia	6	1	2	3	4	6
North Korea	4	1	1	2	5	9
Cuba	3	1	1	1	5	12
Turkey	3	1	0	2	10	11
Israel	3	1	0	2	1	3
Jamaica	3	1	0	2	3	9
Iran	6	1	1	4	4	12
Honduras	3	0	2	1	2	3
Egypt	4	0	2	2	3	6
Kuwait	3	0	1	2	2	6
Australia	3	0	1	2	0	5
South Korea	14	0	4	10	11	43
Dutch East Indies	1	0	0	1	0	6
Iraq	3	0	0	3	1	4
Canada	3	0	0	3	0	5
United Arab Emirates	3	0	0	3	2	11
New Zealand	3	0	0	3	2	12
Haiti	3	0	0	3	2	14
Zaire	3	0	0	3	0	14
Bolivia	6	0	1	5	1	20
El Salvador	6	0	0	6	1	22
Japan	3	0	0	3	1	4
Greece	3	0	0	3	0	8

*Includes West Germany 1950–90. †Includes USSR 1930–1990.
Note: Matches decided by penalty kicks are shown as drawn games.

World Cup Final Box Scores

URUGUAY 1930

| Uruguay | ....1 | 3 —4 |
| Argentina | ....2 | 0 —2 |

FIRST HALF

Scoring: 1, Uruguay, Dorado (12); 2, Argentina, Peucelle (20); 3, Argentina, Stabile (37).

SECOND HALF

Scoring: 4, Uruguay, Cea (57); 5, Uruguay, Iriarte (68); 6, Uruguay, Castro (89).

Argentina: Botosso, Della Toree, Paternoster, Evaristo, J., Monti, Suarez, Peucelle, Varallo, Stabile, Ferreira, Evaristo, M.

Uruguay: Ballesteros, Nasazzi, Mascheroni, Andrade, Fernandez, Gestido, Dorado, Scarone, Castro, Cea, Iriarte.

Referee: Langenus (Belgium).

FRANCE 1938

| Italy | ....3 | 1 —4 |
| Hungary | ....1 | 1 —2 |

FIRST HALF

Scoring: 1, Italy, Colaussi (5); 2, Hungary, Titkos (7); 3, Italy, Piola (16); 4, Italy, Piola (35).

SECOND HALF

Scoring: 5, Hungary, Sarosi (70); 6, Italy, Colaussi (82).

Italy: Olivieri, Foni, Rava, Serantoni, Andreolo, Locatelli, Biavati, Meazza, Piola, Ferrari, Colaussi.

Hungary: Szabo; Polger, Biro, Szalay, Szucs, Lazar, Sas, Vincze, Sarosi, Zsengeller, Titkos.

Referee: Capdeville (France).

SWITZERLAND 1954

| W Germany | ......2 | 1 —3 |
| Hungary | ....2 | 0 —2 |

FIRST HALF

Scoring: 1, Hungary, Puskas (6); 2, Hungary, Czibor (8); 3, W Germ., Morlock (10); 4, W Germ., Rahn (18).

SECOND HALF

Scoring: 5, W Germ., Rahn (84).

West Germany: Turek; Posipal, Kohlmeyer, Eckel, Liebrich, Mai, Rahn, Morlock, Walter, O., Walter, F., Schaefer.

Hungary: Grosics; Buzansky, Lantos, Bozsik, Lorant, Zakarias, Czibor, Kocsis, Hidegkuti, Puskas, Toth.

Referee: Ling (England).

ITALY 1934

| Italy | ....0 | 1 | 1—2 |
| Czechoslovakia | ..0 | 1 | 0—1 |

SECOND HALF

Scoring: 1, Czech., Puc (70); 2, Italy, Orsi (80).

OVERTIME

Scoring: 3, Italy, Schiavio (95).

Italy: Combi, Monzeglio, Allemandi, Ferraris Monti, Monti, Bertolini, Guaita, Meazza, Schiavio, Ferrari, Orsi.

Czechoslovakia: Planicka, Zenisek, Ctyroky, Kostalek, Cambal, Cambal, Krcil, Junek, Svoboda, Sobotka, Nejedly, Puc.

Referee: Eklind (Sweden).

BRAZIL 1950

| Uruguay | ....0 | 2 —2 |
| Brazil | ....0 | 1 —1 |

SECOND HALF

Scoring: 1, Brazil, Friaca (47); 2, Uruguay, Schiaffino (66); 3, Uruguay, Ghiggia (79).

Uruguay: Maspoli, Gonzales, Tejera, Gambretta, Varela, Andrade, Ghiggia, Perez, Miguez, Schiffiano, Moran.

Brazil: Barbosa, Augusto, Juvenal, Bauer, Banilo, Bigode, Friaca, Zizinho, Ademir, Jair, Chico.

Referee: Reader (England).

SWEDEN 1958

| Brazil | ....2 | 3 —5 |
| Sweden | ....1 | 1 —2 |

FIRST HALF

Scoring:1, Sweden, Liedholm (3); 2, Brazil, Vava (9); 3, Brazil, Vava (32).

SECOND HALF

Scoring: 4, Brazil, Pelé (55); 5, Brazil, Zagalo (68); 6, Sweden Simonsson (80); 7, Brazil, Pelé (90).

Brazil: Glymar, Santos, D., Santos, N., Zito, Bellini, Orlando, Garrincha, Didi, Vava, Pelé, Zagalo.

Sweden: Svensson, Bergmark, Axbom, Boerjesson, Gustavsson, Parling, Hamrin, Gren, Simonsson, Liedholm, Skoglund.

Referee: Guigue (France).

CHILE 1962

| Brazil | ....1 | 2 —3 |
| Czechoslovakia | ....1 | 0 —1 |

FIRST HALF

Scoring: 1, Czech., Masopust (15); 2, Brazil, Amarildo (17).

SECOND HALF

Scoring: 3, Brazil, Zito (68); 4, Brazil, Vava (77).

Brazil: Glymar, Santos, D., Santos, N., Zito, Mauro, Zozimo, Garrincha, Didi, Vava, Amarildo, Zagalo.

Czechoslovakia: Schroiff, Tichy, Novak, Pluskal, Popluhar, Masopust, Pospichal, Scherer, Kvasnak, Kadraba, Jelinek.

Referee: Latychev (USSR).

World Cup Final Box Scores *(Cont.)*

ENGLAND 1966

England............1	1	2—4
W. Germany 1	1	0—2

FIRST HALF

Scoring: 1, W. Germany, Haller (12); 2, England, Hurst (18).

SECOND HALF

Scoring: 3, England, Peters (78); 4, W. Germany, Weber (90).

OVERTIME

Scoring: 5, England, Hurst (101); 6, England, Hurst (120).

England: Banks, Cohen, Wilson, Stiles, Charlton, J., Moore, Ball, Hurst, Hunt, Charlton, R., Peters.

W. Germany: Tilkowski, Hottges, Schmellinger, Beckenbauer, Schulz, Weber, Held, Haller, Seeler, Overath, Emmerich.

Referee: Dienst (Switzerland).

W. GERMANY 1974

W. Germany 2	0 —2
Netherlands.....1	0 —1

FIRST HALF

Scoring: 1, Netherlands, Neeskens, PK (1); 2, W. Germany, Breitner, PK (26); 3, W. Germany, Muller (44).

W. Germany: Maier, Vogts, Beckenbauer, Schwarzenbeck, Breitner, Hoeness, Bonhof, Overath, Grabowski, Muller, Holzenbein.

Netherlands: Jongbloed, Suurbier, Rijsbergen (de Jong), Haan, Krol, Jansen, Neeskens, van Hanagem, Cruyff, Rensenbrink (van der Kerkhof).

Referee: Taylor (England).

ITALY 1982

Italy..................0	3 —3
W. Germany 0	1 —1

SECOND HALF

Scoring: 1, Italy, Rossi (57); 2, Italy, Tardelli (68); 3, Italy, Altobelli (81); 4, Germany, Breitner (83).

Italy: Zoff, Bergomi, Scirea, Collovati, Cabrini, Oriali, Gentile, Tardelli, Conti, Rossi, Graziani (Altobelli, Causio).

W. Germany: Schumacher, Kaltz, Stielike, Foerster, K., Foerster, B., Dremmler (Hrubesch), Breitner, Briegel, Rummenigge (Mueller), Fishcher (Littbrarski).

Referee: Coelho (Brazil).

MEXICO 1986 *(CONT.)*

Argentina: Pumpido, Brown, Cuciuffo, Ruggeri, Olarticoecha, Bastista, Giusti, Burruchaga (Trobbiani 90), Enrique, Maradona, Valdona.

W. Germany: Schumacher, Jakobs, Forster, Eder, Brehme, Matthaus, Berthold, Magath (Hoeness 62), Briegel, Rummenigge, Allofs (Voller 46).

Referee: Filho (Brazil).

MEXICO 1970

Brazil.................1	3 —4
Italy...................1	0 —1

FIRST HALF

Scoring: 1, Brazil, Pelé (18); 2, Italy, Boninsegna (32).

SECOND HALF

Scoring: 3, Brazil, Gerson (65); 4, Brazil, Jairzinho (70); 5, Brazil, Alberto (86).

Brazil: Feliz, Alberto, Brito, Wilson, Piazza, Everaldo, Clodoaldo, Gerson, Jairzinho, Tostao, Pelé, Rivelino.

Italy: Albertosi, Burgnich, Cera, Rosato, Facchetti, Bertini (Juliano), Mazzola, De Sisti, Domenghini, Boninsegna (Rivera), Riva.

Referee: Glockner (E. Germany).

ARGENTINA 1978

Argentina 1	0	2—3
Netherlands 0	1	0—1

FIRST HALF

Scoring: 1, Argentina, Kempes (38).

SECOND HALF

Scoring: 2, Netherlands, Nanninga (81).

OVERTIME

Scoring: 3, Arg., Kempes (104); 4, Arg., Bertoni (114).

Argentina: Fillol, Olguin, Galvan, Passarella, Tarantini, Ardiles (Larrosa), Gallego, Kempes, Bertoni, Luque, Ortiz (Houseman).

Netherlands: Jongbloed, Jansen (Suurbier), Krol, Brandts, Poortvliet, Neeskens, Haan, van der Kerkhoff, W., van der Kerkhoff, R., Rep (Nanninga), Rensenbrink.

Referee: Gonella (Italy).

MEXICO 1986

Argentina 1	2 —3
W. Germany 0	2 —2

FIRST HALF

Scoring: 1, Argentina, Brown (22).

SECOND HALF

Scoring: 2, Arg., Valdano (55); 3, W. Germ., Rummenigge (73); 4, W. Germ., Voller (81); 5, Arg., Burruchaga (83).

ITALY 1990

W. Germany 0	1—1
Argentina 0	0—0

SECOND HALF

Scoring: 1, W. Germany, Brehme, PK (84).

W. Germany: Illgner, Brehme, Kohler, Augenthaler, Buchwald, Berthold (Reuter), Littbarski, Haessler, Mattaeus, Voeller, Klinsmann.

Argentina: Goychoechea, Lorenzo, Serrizuela, Sensini, Ruggeri (Monzon), Simon, Basualdo, Burruchag (Calderon), Maradona, Troglio, Dezottir.

Referee: Coelho (Brazil).

World Cup Final Box Scores *(Cont.)*

UNITED STATES 1994

Italy..................0	0	0—0
Brazil 0	0	0—0

Scoring: None. Shootout goals: Italy—2: Albertini, Evani; Brazil—3: Romario, Branco, Dunga.

Italy: Pagliuca, Benarrivo, Maldini, Baresi, Mussi (Apolloni 35), Albertini, D. Baggio (Evani 95), Berti, Donadoni, Baggio, Massaro.

Brazil: Taffarel, Jorginho (Cafu 21), Branco, Aldair, Santos, Silva, Dunga, Zinho (Viola 106), Mazinho, Bebeto, Romario.

Referee: Sandor Puhl (Hungary).

FRANCE 1998

Brazil 0		0—0
France 2		1—3

FIRST HALF

Scoring: 1, France, Zidane (27); 2, France, Zidane (45).

SECOND HALF

Scoring: 3, France, Petit (90).

Brazil: Taffarel, Cafu, Aldair, Baiano, Carlos, Sampaio (Edmundo 74), Dunga, Rivaldo, Leonardo, (Denilson 46), Bebeto, Ronaldo.

France: Barthez, Lizarazu, Desailly, Thuram, Leboeuf, Djorkaeff (Vieira 75) Deschamps, Zidane, Petit, Karembeu (Boghossian 57), Guivarc'h (Dugarry 66).

Referee: Belqola (Morocco).

Alltime Leaders

GOALS

Player, Nation	Tournaments	Goals	Player, Nation	Tournaments	Goals
Gerd Muller, West Germany	1970, '74	14	Ademir, Brazil	1950	9
Just Fontaine, France	1958	13	Eusebio, Portugal	1966	9
Pelé, Brazil	1958, '62, '66, '70	12	Jairzinho, Brazil	1970, '74	9
Sandor Kocsis, Hungary	1954	11	Paolo Rossi, Italy	1982, '86	9
Teofilo Cubillas, Peru	1970, '78	10	Karl-Heinz Rummenigge,		
Gregorz Lato, Poland	1974, '78, '82	10	W. Germany	1978, '82, '86	9
Helmut Rahn, West Germany	1954, '58	10	Uwe Seeler, West Germany	1958, '62, '66, '70	9
Gary Lineker, England	1986, '90	10	Vava, Brazil	1958, '62	9

LEADING SCORER, CUP BY CUP

Year	Player, Nation	Goals	Year	Player, Nation	Goals
1930	Guillermo Stabile, Argentina	8	1966	Eusebio Ferreira, Portugal	9
1934	Oldrich Nejedly, Czechoslovakia	5	1970	Gerd Mueller, West Germany	10
1938	Leonidas da Silva, Brazil	8	1974	Gregorz Lato, Poland	7
1950	Ademir de Menezes, Brazil	9	1978	Mario Kempes, Argentina	6
1954	Sandor Kocsis, Hungary	11	1982	Paolo Rossi, Italy	6
1958	Just Fontaine, France	13	1986	Gary Lineker, England	6
1962	Florian Albert, Hungary	4	1990	Salvatore Schillaci, Italy	6
	Valentin Ivanov, USSR		1994	Hristo Stoichkov, Bulgaria	6
	Garrincha, Brazil			Oleg Salenko, Russia	
	Drazan Jerkovic, Yugoslavia		1998	Davor Suker, Croatia	6
	Leonel Sanchez, Chile				
	Vava, Brazil				

Most Goals, Individual, One Game

Goals	Player, Nation	Score	Date
5	Oleg Salenko, Russia	Russia–Cameroon, 6–1	6-28-94
4	Leonidas, Brazil	Brazil–Poland, 6–5	6-5-38
4	Ernest Willimowski, Poland	Brazil–Poland, 6–5	6-5-38
4	Gustav Wetterstrim, Sweden	Sweden–Cuba, 8–0	6-12-38
4	Juan Alberto Schiaffino, Uruguay	Uruguay–Bolivia, 8–0	7-2-50
4	Ademir, Brazil	Brazil–Sweden, 7–1	7-9-50
4	Sandor Kocsis, Hungary	Hungary–West Germany, 8–3	6-20-54
4	Just Fontaine, France	France–West Germany, 6–3	6-28-58
4	Eusebio, Portugal	Portugal–North Korea, 5–3	7-23-66
4	Emilio Butragueño, Spain	Spain–Denmark, 5–1	6-18-86

Note: 30 players have scored 31 World Cup hat tricks. Gerd Muller of West Germany is the only man to have two World Cup hat tricks, both in 1970. The last hat tricks were 6-21-98, Gabriel Batistuta (Arg) vs. Jamaica; 6-23-90, Tomas Skuhravy (Czech) vs. Costa Rica; 6-17-90, Michel (Spain) vs. South Korea; and.

Attendance and Goal Scoring, Year by Year

Year	Site	No. of Games	Goals	Goals/Game	Attendance	Avg Att
1930	Uruguay	18	70	3.89	434,500	24,139
1934	Italy	17	70	4.12	395,000	23,235
1938	France	18	84	4.67	483,000	26,833
1950	Brazil	22	88	4.00	1,337,000	60,773
1954	Switzerland	26	140	5.38	943,000	36,269
1958	Sweden	35	126	3.60	868,000	24,800
1962	Chile	32	89	2.78	776,000	24,250
1966	England	32	89	2.78	1,614,677	50,459
1970	Mexico	32	95	2.97	1,673,975	52,312
1974	West Germany	38	97	2.55	1,774,022	46,685
1978	Argentina	38	102	2.68	1,610,215	42,374
1982	Spain	52	146	2.80	1,856,277	35,698
1986	Mexico	52	132	2.54	2,441,731	46,956
1990	Italy	52	115	2.21	2,514,443	48,354
1994	United States	52	140	2.69	3,567,415	68,604
1998	France	64	171	2.67	2,775,400	43,366
Totals		580	1754	3.02	25,064,655	43,215

The United States in the World Cup

URUGUAY 1930: FINAL COMPETITION

Date	Opponent	Result	Scoring
7-13-30	Belgium	3–0 W	US: McGhee 2, Patenaude
7-17-30	Paraguay	3–0 W	US: Patenaude 2, Florie
7-26-30	Argentina	1–6 L	ARG: Monti 2, Scopelli 2, Stabile 2 US: Brown.

ITALY 1934: FINAL COMPETITION

Date	Opponent	Result	Scoring
5-27-34	Italy	1–7 L	US: Donelli ITA: Schiavio 3, Orsi 2, Meazza, Ferrari

BRAZIL 1950: FINAL COMPETITION

Date	Opponent	Result	Scoring
6-25-50	Spain	1–3 L	US: Pariani SPN: Igoa, Basora, Zarra
6-29-50	England	1–0 W	US: Gaetjens.
7-2-50	Chile	2–5 L	US: Wallace, Maca CHL: Robledo, Cremaschi 3, Prieto

ITALY 1990: FINAL COMPETITION

Date	Opponent	Result	Scoring
6-10-90	Czechoslovakia	1–5 L	US: Caligiuri Czech: Skuhravy 2, Hasek, Bilek, Luhovy
6-14-90	Italy	0–1 L	Italy: Giannini
6-19-90	Austria	1–2 L	US: Murray Austria: Rodax, Ogris

UNITED STATES 1994: FINAL COMPETITION

Date	Opponent	Result	Scoring
6-18-94	Switzerland	1–1 T	US: Wynalda Sui: Bregy
6-22-94	Colombia	2–1 W	US: Escobar (own goal), Stewart Colombia: Valencia
6-26-94	Romania	1–0 L	Romania: Petrescu
7-4-94	Brazil	1–0 L	Brazil: Bebeto

FRANCE 1998: FINAL COMPETITION

Date	Opponent	Result	Scoring
6-15-98	Germany	2–0 L	Ger: Möller, Klinsmann
6-21-98	Iran	2–1 L	US: McBride Iran: Estili, Mahdavikia
6-25-98	Yugoslavia	1–0 L	Yugoslavia: Komljenovic

International Competition

European Championship

Official name: the European Football Championship. Held every four years since 1960.

Year	Champion	Score	Runner-up	Year	Champion	Score	Runner-up
1960	USSR	2–1	Yugoslavia	1980	West Germany	2–1	Belgium
1964	Spain	2–1	USSR	1984	France	2–0	Spain
1968	Italy	2–0	Yugoslavia	1988	Holland	2–0	USSR
1972	West Germany	3–0	USSR	1992	Denmark	2–0	Germany
1976	Czechoslovakia*	2–2	West Germany	1996	Germany	2–1	Czech Republic

*Won on penalty kicks.

Under-20 World Championship

Year	Host	Champion	Runner-Up
1977	Tunisia	USSR	Mexico
1979	Japan	Argentina	USSR
1981	Australia	W. Germany	Qatar
1983	Mexico	Brazil	Argentina
1985	USSR	Brazil	Spain
1987	Chile	Yugoslavia	W. Germany
1989	Saudi Arabia	Portugal	Nigeria
1991	Portugal	Portugal	Brazil
1993	Australia	Brazil	Ghana
1995	Qatar	Argentina	Brazil
1997	Malaysia	Argentina	Uruguay

Under-17 World Championship

Year	Champion
1985	Nigeria
1987	USSR
1989	Saudi Arabia
1991	Ghana

Under-17 *(Cont.)*

Year	Champion
1993	Nigeria
1995	Ghana
1997	Brazil

Pan American Games

Year	Champion
1951	Argentina
1955	Argentina
1959	Argentina
1963	Brazil
1967	Mexico
1971	Argentina
1975	Brazil/Mexico (tie)
1979	Brazil
1983	Uruguay
1987	Brazil
1991	United States
1995	Argentina

South American Championship (Copa America)

Year	Champion	Host	Year	Champion	Host
1916	Uruguay	Argentina	1947	Argentina	Ecuador
1917	Uruguay	Uruguay	1949	Brazil	Brazil
1919	Brazil	Brazil	1953	Paraguay	Peru
1920	Uruguay	Chile	1955	Argentina	Chile
1921	Argentina	Argentina	1956	Uruguay	Uruguay
1922	Brazil	Brazil	1957	Argentina	Peru
1923	Uruguay	Uruguay	1958	Argentina	Argentina
1924	Uruguay	Uruguay	1959	Uruguay	Ecuador
1925	Argentina	Argentina	1963	Bolivia	Bolivia
1926	Uruguay	Chile	1967	Uruguay	Uruguay
1927	Argentina	Peru	1975	Peru	Various sites
1929	Argentina	Argentina	1979	Paraguay	Various sites
1935	Uruguay	Peru	1983	Uruguay	Various sites
1937	Argentina	Argentina	1987	Uruguay	Argentina
1939	Peru	Peru	1989	Brazil	Brazil
1941	Argentina	Chile	1990	Brazil	Argentina
1942	Uruguay	Uruguay	1991	Argentina	Chile
1945	Argentina	Chile	1993	Argentina	Ecuador
1946	Argentina	Argentina	1995	Uruguay	Uruguay
			1997	Brazil	Bolivia

Awards

European Footballer of the Year

Year	Player	Club	Year	Player	Club
1956	Stanley Matthews	Blackpool	1973	Johan Cruyff	Barcelona
1957	Alfredo Di Stefano	Real Madrid	1974	Johan Cruyff	Barcelona
1958	Raymond Kopa	Real Madrid	1975	Oleg Blokhin	Dynamo Kiev
1959	Alfredo Di Stefano	Real Madrid	1976	Franz Beckenbauer	Bayern Munich
1960	Luis Suarez	Barcelona	1977	Allan Simonsen	Borussia M'gladbach
1961	Omar Sivori	Juventus	1978	Kevin Keegan	SV Hamburg
1962	Josef Masopust	Dukla Prague	1979	Kevin Keegan	SV Hamburg
1963	Lev Yashin	Moscow Dynamo	1980	Karl-Heinz Rummenigge	Bayern Munich
1964	Denis Law	Manchester United	1981	Karl-Heinz Rummenigge	Bayern Munich
1965	Eusebio	Benfica	1982	Paolo Rossi	Juventus
1966	Bobby Charlton	Manchester United	1983	Michel Platini	Juventus
1967	Florian Albert	Ferencvaros	1984	Michel Platini	Juventus
1968	George Best	Manchester United	1985	Michel Platini	Juventus
1969	Gianni Rivera	AC Milan	1986	Igor Belanov	Dynamo Kiev
1970	Gerd Mueller	Bayern Munich	1987	Ruud Gullit	AC Milan
1971	Johan Cruyff	Ajax	1988	Marco Van Basten	AC Milan
1972	Franz Beckenbauer	Bayern Munich	1989	Marco Van Basten	AC Milan

Awards (Cont.)

European Footballer of the Year (Cont.)

Year	Player	Club	Year	Player	Club
1990	Lothar Matthaeus	Inter Milan	1994	Hristo Stoichkov	Barcelona
1991	Jean-Pierre Papin	Olympique Marseille	1995	George Weah	AC Milan
1992	Marco Van Basten	AC Milan	1996	Matthias Sammer	Borussia Dortmund
1993	Roberto Baggio	Juventus	1997	Ronaldo	Inter Milan

African Footballer of the Year

Year	Player	Nation	Year	Player	Nation
1970	Salif Keita	Mali	1984	ThÇophile Abega	Cameroon
1971	Ibrahim Sunday	Ghana	1985	Mohamed Timoumi	Morocco
1972	Chérif Souleyman	Guinea	1986	Badou Zaki	Morocco
1973	Tshimimu Bwanga	Zaire	1987	Rabah Madjer	Algeria
1974	Paul Moukila	Congo	1988	Kalusha Bwalya	Zambia
1975	Ahmed Faras	Morocco	1989	George Weah	Liberia
1976	Roger Milla	Cameroon	1990	Roger Milla	Cameroon
1977	Dhiab Tarak	Tunisia	1991	Abedi Pele	Ghana
1978	Abdul Razak	Ghana	1992	Abedi Pele	Ghana
1979	Thomas Nkono	Cameroon	1993	Rashidi Yekini	Nigeria
1980	Jean Manga Onguene	Cameroon	1994	George Weah	Liberia
1981	Lakhdar Belloumi	Algeria	1995	George Weah	Liberia
1982	Thomas Nkono	Cameroon	1996	Nwankwo Kanu	Nigeria
1983	Mahmoud Al-Khatib	Egypt	1997	Victor Ikpeba	Nigeria

South American Player of the Year

Year	Player	Team	Year	Player	Team
1971	Tostao	Cruzeiro	1985	Julio Cesar Romero	Fluminense
1972	Teofilo Cubillas	Alianza Lima	1986	Antonio Alzamendi	River Plate
1973	Pelé	Santos	1987	Carlos Valderrama	Deportivo Cali
1974	Elias Figueroa	Internacional	1988	Ruben Paz	Racing Buenos Aires
1975	Elias Figueroa	Internacional	1989	Bebeto	Vasco da Gama
1976	Elias Figueroa	Internacional	1990	Raul Amarilla	Olimpia
1977	Zico	Flamengo	1991	Oscar Ruggeri	Velez Sarsfield
1978	Mario Kempes	Valencia	1992	Rai	São Paulo
1979	Diego Maradona	Argentinos Juniors	1993	Carlos Valderrama	Junior Barranquilla
1980	Diego Maradona	Boca Juniors	1994	Cafu	São Paulo
1981	Zico	Flamengo	1995	Enzo Francescoli	River Plate
1982	Zico	Flamengo	1996	Jose-Luis Chilavert	Velez Sarsfield
1983	Socrates	Corinthians	1997	Marcelo Salas	River Plate
1984	Enzo Francescoli	River Plate			

International Club Competition

Intercontinental Cup

Competition between winners of European Champion Clubs' Cup and Libertadores Cup.

1960...Real Madrid, Spain	1973...Independiente, Argentina	1986...River Plate, Argentina
1961...Penarol, Uruguay	1974...Atletico de Madrid, Spain	1987...Porto, Portugal
1962...Santos, Brazil	1975...No tournament	1988...Nacional, Uruguay
1963...Santos, Brazil	1976...Bayern Munich	1989...Milan, Italy
1964...Inter, Italy	1977...Boca Juniors, Argentina	1990...Milan, Italy
1965...Inter, Italy	1978...No tournament	1991...Red Star Belgrade, Yugos.
1966...Penarol, Uruguay	1979...Olimpia, Paraguay	1992...São Paulo, Brazil
1967...Racing Club, Argentina	1980...Nacional, Uruguay	1993...São Paulo, Brazil
1968...Estudiantes, Argentina	1981...Flamengo, Brazil	1994...Velez Sarsfield, Argentina
1969...Milan, Italy	1982...Penarol, Uruguay	1995...Ajax Amsterdam, Netherlands
1970...Feyenoord, Netherlands	1983...Gremio, Brazil	1996...Juventus, Italy
1971...Nacional, Uruguay	1984...Independiente, Argentina	1997...Borussia Dortmund, Ger.
1972...Ajax, Holland	1985...Juventus, Italy	

Note: Until 1968 a best-of-three-games format decided the winner. After that a two-game/total-goal format was used until Toyota became the sponsor in 1980, moved the game to Tokyo, and switched the format to a one-game championship. The European Cup runner-up substituted for the winner in 1971, 1973, 1974, and 1979.

European Cup

1956...Real Madrid, Spain	1961...Benfica, Portugal	1966...Real Madrid, Spain
1957...Real Madrid, Spain	1962...Benfica, Portugal	1967...Celtic, Scotland
1958...Real Madrid, Spain	1963...AC Milan, Italy	1968...Manchester United, England
1959...Real Madrid, Spain	1964...Inter-Milan, Italy	1969...AC Milan, Italy
1960...Real Madrid, Spain	1965...Inter-Milan, Italy	1970...Feyenoord, Netherlands

European Cup (Cont.)

1971...Ajax Amsterdam, Netherlands
1972...Ajax Amsterdam, Netherlands
1973...Ajax Amsterdam, Netherlands
1974...Bayern Munich, West Germany
1975...Bayern Munich, West Germany
1976...Bayern Munich, West Germany
1977...Liverpool, England

1978...Liverpool, England
1979...Nottingham Forest, England
1980...Nottingham Forest, England
1981...Liverpool, England
1982...Aston Villa, England
1983...SV Hamburg, West Germany
1984...Liverpool, England
1985...Juventus, Italy
1986...Steaua Bucharest, Romania

1987...Porto, Portugal
1988...P.S.V. Eindhoven, Netherlands
1989...AC Milan, Italy
1990...AC Milan, Italy
1991...Red Star Belgrade, Yugoslav.
1992...Barcelona, Spain
1993...Olympique Marseille, France
1994...AC Milan, Italy
1995...Ajax Amsterdam, Netherlands
1996...Juventus, Italy
1997...Borussia Dortmund, Ger.
1998...Real Madrid, Spain

Note: On four occasions the European Cup winner has refused to play in the Intercontinental Cup and has been replaced by the runner-up: Panathinaikos (Greece) in 1971, Juventus (Italy) in 1973, Atletico Madrid (Spain) in 1974, and Malmo (Sweden) in 1979.

Libertadores Cup

Competition between champion clubs and runners-up of 10 South American National Associations.

1960...Penarol, Uruguay
1961...Penarol, Uruguay
1962...Santos, Brazil
1963...Santos, Brazil
1964...Independiente, Argentina
1965...Independiente, Argentina
1966...Penarol, Uruguay
1967...Racing Club, Argentina
1968...Estudiantes, Argentina
1969...Estudiantes, Argentina
1970...Estudiantes, Argentina
1971...Nacional, Uruguay
1972...Independiente, Argentina
1973...Independiente, Argentina

1974...Independiente, Argentina
1975...Independiente, Argentina
1976...Cruzeiro, Brazil
1977...Boca Juniors, Argentina
1978...Boca Juniors, Argentina
1979...Olimpia, Paraguay
1980...Nacional, Uruguay
1981...Flamengo, Brazil
1982...Penarol, Uruguay
1983...Gremio, Brazil
1984...Independiente, Argentina
1985...Argentinos Juniors, Arg
1986...River Plate, Argentina
1987...Penarol, Uruguay

1988...Nacional, Uruguay
1989...Atletico Nacional, Colombia
1990...Olimpia, Paraguay
1991...Colo Colo, Chile
1992...São Paulo, Brazil
1993...São Paulo, Brazil
1994...Velez Sarsfield, Argentina
1995...Gremio, Brazil
1996...River Plate, Argentina
1997...Cruzeiro, Brazil
1998...Vasco da Gama, Brazil

UEFA Cup

Competition between teams other than league champions and cup winners from the Union of European Football Associations.

1958...Barcelona, Spain
1959...No tournament
1960...Barcelona, Spain
1961...AS Roma, Italy
1962...Valencia, Spain
1963...Valencia, Spain
1964...Real Zaragoza, Spain
1965...Ferencvaros, Hungary
1966...Barcelona, Spain
1967...Dynamo Zagreb, Yugoslav.
1968...Leeds United, England
1969...Newcastle United, England
1970...Arsenal, England
1971...Leeds United, England
1972...Tottenham Hotspur, England

1973...Liverpool, England
1974...Feyenoord, Netherlands
1975...Borussia Monchengladbach, West Germany
1976...Liverpool, England
1977...Juventus, Italy
1978...P.S.V. Eindhoven, Netherl.
1979...Borussia Monchengladbach, West Germany
1980...Eintracht Frankfurt, West Germany
1981...Ipswich Town, England
1982...I.F.K. Gothenburg, Sweden
1983...Anderlecht, Belgium
1984...Tottenham Hotspur, England

1985...Real Madrid, Spain
1986...Real Madrid, Spain
1987...I.F.K. Gothenburg, Sweden
1988...Bayer Leverkusen, West Germany
1989...Naples, Italy
1990...Juventus, Italy
1991...Inter-Milan, Italy
1992...Torino, Italy
1993...Juventus, Italy
1994...Internazionale, Italy
1995...Parma, Italy
1996...Bayern Munich, Germany
1997...Schalke 04, Germany
1998...Inter Milan, Italy

European Cup-Winners' Cup

Competition between cup winners of countries belonging to UEFA.

1961...A.C. Fiorentina, Italy
1962...Atletico Madrid, Spain
1963...Tottenham Hotspur, England
1964...Sporting Lisbon, Portugal
1965...West Ham United, England
1966...Borussia Dortmund, West Germany
1967...Bayern Munich, W. Germ.
1968...A.C. Milan, Italy
1969...Slovan Bratislava, Czech.

1970...Manchester City, England
1971...Chelsea, England
1972...Glasgow Rangers, Scotland
1973...A.C. Milan, Italy
1974...Magdeburg, East Germany
1975...Dynamo Kiev, USSR
1976...Anderlecht, Belgium
1977...S.V. Hamburg, W. Germ.
1978...Anderlecht, Belgium
1979...Barcelona, Spain

1980...Valencia, Spain
1981...Dynamo Tbilisi, USSR
1982...Barcelona, Spain
1983...Aberdeen, Scotland
1984...Juventus, Italy
1985...Everton, England
1986...Dynamo Kiev, USSR
1987...Ajax Amsterdam, Netherlands
1988...Mechelen, Belgium
1989...Barcelona, Spain

European Cup-Winners' Cup (Cont.)

1990...Sampdoria, Italy	1993...Parma, Italy	1996...Paris St. Germain, France
1991...Manchester United, England	1994...Arsenal, England	1997...Barcelona, Spain
1992...Werder Bremen, Germany	1995...Real Zaragoza, Spain	1998...Chelsea, England

Major League Soccer

Results

Year	Champion	Score	Runner-up	Regular Season MVP
1996	D.C. United	3–2	Los Angeles	Carlos Valderrama, TB
1997	D.C. United	2–1	Colorado	Preki, Kansas City

A-League

Year	Champion	Score	Runner-Up	Regular Season MVP
1991	San Francisco	1–3, 2–0 (1–0 on penalty kicks)	Albany	Jean Harbor, Maryland
1992	Colorado	1–0	Tampa Bay	Taifour Diane, Colorado
1993	Colorado	3–1 (OT)	Los Angeles	Taifour Diane, Colorado
1994	Montreal	1–0	Colorado	Paulinho, Los Angeles
1995	Seattle	1–2 (SO), 3–0, 2–1 (SO)	Atlanta	Peter Hattrup, Seattle
1996	Seattle	2–0	Rochester	Wolde Harris, Colorado
1997	Milwaukee	2–1 (SO)	Carolina	Doug Miller, Rochester
1998	Rochester	3–1	Minnesota	Mark Baena, Seattle

U.S. Open Cup

Open to all amateur and professional teams in the United States, the annual U.S. Open Cup is the oldest cup competition in the country and among the oldest in the world. The tournament is a single-elimination event running concurrent to the MLS season. The winner advances to the CONCACAF Cup, a tournament of the top club teams from North and Central America.

Year	Champion	Year	Champion
1914	Brooklyn Field Club (NYC)	1943	Brooklyn Hispano SC (NYC)
1915	Bethlehem Steel FC (PA)	1944	Brooklyn Hispano SC (NYC)
1916	Bethlehem Steel FC (PA)	1945	Brookhattan FC (NYC)
1917	Fall River Rovers (MA)	1946	Chicago Viking FC (IL)
1918	Bethlehem Steel FC (PA)	1947	Ponta Delgada SC (Fall River, MA)
1919	Bethlehem Steel FC (PA)	1948	Simpkins-Ford SC (St. Louis)
1920	Ben Miller FC (St. Louis)	1949	Morgan SC (PA)
1921	Robbins Dry Dock FC (Brooklyn)	1950	Simpkins-Ford SC (St. Louis)
1922	Scullin Steel FC (St. Louis)	1951	German Hungarian SC (NYC)
1923	Paterson FC (NJ)	1952	Harmarville SC (PA)
1924	Fall River FC (MA)	1953	Falcons SC (Chicago)
1925	Shawsheen FC (Andover, MA)	1954	New York Americans (NYC)
1926	Bethlehem Steel FC (PA)	1955	Eintracht Sport Club (NYC)
1927	Fall River FC (MA)	1956	Harmarville SC (PA)
1928	New York National FC (NYC)	1957	Kutis SC (St. Louis)
1929	Hakoah All Star SC (NYC)	1958	Los Angeles Kickers (CA)
1930	Fall River FC (MA)	1959	McIlvaine Canvasbacks (Los Angeles)
1931	Fall River FC (MA)		
1932	New Bedford FC (MA)	1960	Ukrainian Nationals (Philadelphia)
1933	Stix, Baer and Fuller FC (St. Louis)	1961	Ukrainian Nationals (Philadelphia)
1934	Stix, Baer and Fuller FC (St. Louis)	1962	New York Hungaria (NYC)
1935	Central Breweries FC (Chicago)	1963	Ukrainian Nationals (Philadelphia)
1936	German-Americans (Philadelphia)	1964	Los Angeles Kickers (CA)
1937	New York American FC (NYC)	1965	New York Hungaria (NYC)
1938	Sparta A and B.A. (Chicago)	1966	Ukrainian Nationals (Philadelphia)
1939	St. Mary's Celtic SC (Brooklyn)	1967	Greek American AA (NYC)
1940	—	1968	Greek American AA (NYC)
1941	Pawtucket FC (RI)	1969	Greek American AA (NYC)
1942	Gallatin SC (PA)	1970	Elizabeth SC (Union, NJ)

Year	Champion
1971	Hota SC (NYC)
1972	Elizabeth SC (Union, NJ)
1973	Maccabee SC (Los Angeles)
1974	Greek American AA (NYC)
1975	Maccabee SC (Los Angeles)
1976	San Francisco AC (CA)
1977	Maccabee SC (Los Angeles)
1978	Maccabee SC (Los Angeles)
1979	Brooklyn Dodgers SC (NYC)
1980	NY Pancyprian-Freedoms (NYC)
1981	Maccabee SC (Los Angeles)
1982	NY Pancyprian-Freedoms (NYC)
1983	NY Pancyprian-Freedoms (NYC)
1984	A.O. Krete (NYC)
1985	Greek American AC (San Francisco)

Year	Champion
1986	Kutis SC (St. Louis)
1987	Club Espana (Washington, D.C.)
1988	Busch SC (St. Louis)
1989	HRC Kickers (St. Petersburg, FL)
1990	AAC Eagles (Chicago)
1991	Brooklyn Italians SC (East NY)
1992	San Jose Oaks (CA)
1993	Club Deportivo Mexico (San Francisco)
1994	Greek American AC (San Francisco)
1995	Richmond Kickers (VA)
1996	Washington D.C. United
1997	Dallas Burn

North American Soccer League

Formed in 1968 by the merger of the National Professional Soccer League and the USA League, both of which had begun operations a year earlier. The NPSL's lone champion was the Oakland Clippers. The USA League, which brought entire teams in from Europe, was won in 1967 by the LA Wolves, who were the English League's Wolverhampton Wanderers.

Year	Champion	Score	Runner-Up	Regular Season MVP
1968	Atlanta	0–0, 3–0	San Diego	John Kowalik, Chi
1969	Kansas City	No game	Atlanta	Cirilio Fernandez, KC
1970	Rochester	3–0,1–3	Washington	Carlos Metidieri, Roch
1971	Dallas	1–2, 4–1, 2–0	Atlanta	Carlos Metidieri, Roch
1972	NY	2–1	St. Louis	Randy Horton, NY
1973	Philadelphia	2–0	Dallas	Warren Archibald, Mia
1974	Los Angeles	4–3*	Miami	Peter Silvester, Balt
1975	Tampa Bay	2–0	Portland	Steve David, Mia
1976	Toronto	3–0	Minnesota	Pelé, NY
1977	NY	2–1	Seattle	Franz Beckenbauer, NY
1978	NY	3–1	Tampa Bay	Mike Flanagan, NE
1979	Vancouver	2–1	Tampa Bay	Johan Cruyff, LA
1980	NY	3–0	Ft. Lauderdale	Roger Davies, Sea
1981	Chicago	1–0*	NY	Giorgio Chinaglia, NY
1982	NY	1–0	Seattle	Peter Ward, Sea
1983	Tulsa	2–0	Toronto	Roberto Cabanas, NY
1984	Chicago	2–1, 3–2	Toronto	Steve Zungul, SJ

*Shootout.

Championship Format: 1968 & 1970: Two games/total goals. 1971 & 1984: Best-of-three series. 1972–1983: One-game championship. Title in 1969 went to the regular-season champion.

Statistical Leaders

SCORING

Year	Player/Team	Pts
1968	John Kowalik, Chi	69
1969	Kaiser Motaung, Atl	36
1970	Kirk Apostolidis, Dall	35
1971	Carlos Metidieri, Roch	46
1972	Randy Horton, NY	22
1973	Kyle Rote, Dall	30
1974	Paul Child, San Jose	36
1975	Steven David, Miami	52
1976	Giorgio Chinaglia, NY	49

Year	Player/Team	Pts
1977	Steven David, LA	58
1978	Giorgio Chinaglia, NY	79
1979	Oscar Fabbiani, Tampa Bay	58
1980	Giorgio Chinaglia, NY	77
1981	Giorgio Chinaglia, NY	74
1982	Giorgio Chinaglia, NY	55
1983	Roberto Cabanas, NY	66
1984	Slavisa Zungul, Golden Bay	50

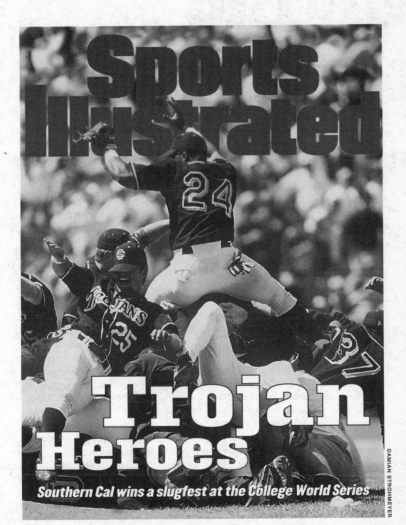

Sports Illustrated

Trojan Heroes

Southern Cal wins a slugfest at the College World Series

DAMIAN STROHMEYER

Alumni Giving

The champions in soccer, hockey and baseball each had a coach seeking to restore glory to his alma mater

BY HANK HERSCH

A check to a scholarship fund, a wing for the new library, a good word placed in an influential ear. The lifeblood of a college is fed by the contributions of its alumni. And by boldly maneuvering in 1997–98, three graduates were able to hand their alma maters that most rare and treasured gift: an NCAA championship trophy.

MEN'S SOCCER

Though he played on three Final Four teams at UCLA from 1972 to '75, midfielder Sigi Schmid was repeatedly denied a championship ring because of the Bruins' shoddy play in goal. So after taking over the program in 1980, Schmid fixed his focus on the pipes, producing a long line of pro-quality keepers—including U.S. national team players David Vanole and Brad Friedel—who would power UCLA to two championships and 14 NCAA tournament appearances in the next 17 years. "I promised myself we would always have solid goalkeeping," said Schmid. "The first player I ever recruited

was a goalkeeper, and we've had solid goalkeeping all the way through."

To develop one star keeper, Schmid believed, you needed to keep two on your roster; top prospects whose interest was in immediate gratification were dissuaded from even applying. "If there's not a good backup," Schmid said, "there's no pressure." Matt Reis, a senior from Mission Viejo, Calif., entered 1997–98 having served as that good backup, first for Chris Snitko, then for Kevin Hartman, each of whom went on to play in Major League Soccer. After appearing in just 15 games his first three years, Reis allowed only 0.64 goals a game as the starter, the fourth lowest average in the nation, to help lead the Bruins to a 22–2 record and their 15th straight postseason berth.

Reis's readiness would be critical for the Bruins in the NCAA semifinals in Richmond, Va., where they faced No. 1–ranked Indiana. The 23–0 Hoosiers were the highest scoring team in the country as well as a painful reminder of Reis's most abject failure. Pressed into duty as a freshman because

Snitko had been red-carded the previous game, Reis was overrun by the Hoosiers in the 1994 semis, 4–1. "Matt is not the same guy he was then," Schmid said, and he was right. The fifth-seeded Bruins upset the Indiana juggernaut 1–0 in triple overtime on freshman forward McKinley Tennyson Jr.'s golden goal. Reis made 11 saves in the game; in the 17 matches prior to it, he had made all of 55.

UCLA had shed the feared Hoosiers to advance to the final against second-ranked, five-time champ Virginia, but the Bruins were by no means in ideal shape. Playmaker Sasha Victorine, defender Kevin Coye and midfielder Pete Vagenas were sidelined by injuries, and a combination of final exams and the 132-minute marathon against Indiana had consumed a lot of players' energy. Then came a sartorial crisis: On the eve of the final, the NCAA demanded that the Bruins' long-sleeve undershirts match their dark-blue uniform jerseys. Thus it was that UCLA associate athletic director Betsy Stephenson played a role in the Bruins' title march: She spent her Saturday night in a third-floor washing room at the Embassy Suites, dyeing 22 white shirts.

To help his team navigate such obstacles, the 44-year-old Schmid scrawled a slogan on the locker room chalkboard before every tournament match: You Gotta Be a Soldier. "Sigi always says you've got to seize the moment," Reis said. "You only get so many chances to make your mark."

Before getting a chance to make his, Reis had his girlfriend, Nicole Odom, paint his toenails yellow, a departure from the blue polish he had used in the semis. But his toe-

SIMON BRUTY

nails were the only thing yellow about Reis in the final. Before a pro-Cavaliers crowd of 20,143, he turned back nine shots, many of them spectacularly. He leaped on two point-blank shots by future MLS forward Brian West, dived to thwart forward Chris Albright and charged off his line and slid, yellow toenails first, to stop midfielder Jason Moore on a breakaway. "We had some great chances," said Virginia coach George Gelnovatch, "but it was like a wall back there."

"Matt's the guy who gets the whole team going," said UCLA junior forward Seth George. "When he's in a zone, we're in a zone. When he made that first huge save, there was no doubt in my mind that we were going to win."

A change of tactics by Schmid after a

DAMIAN STROHMEYER

Got it covered: Turco, the tournament MVP, stopped 28 Eagle shots in the final.

scoreless first half proved equally decisive. Seeing that George, his top scorer, was being bottled up by Cavalier defender Scott Vermillion, Schmid relocated him to the midfield, where he would have more room to operate. On a counterattack in the 80th minute, George took a pass to the left of the penalty area and beat Virginia keeper Brock Yost for the game's first goal. Less than three minutes later George struck again, putting away a rebound of a shot by Tennyson for a 2–0 victory.

For the third time under Schmid, the Bruins had won the national title with a shutout. "We said that it is going to come down to goalkeeping," he said. "And our keeper was better."

MEN'S HOCKEY

Michigan coach Red Berenson is like an overanxious date or a subpar wine. He's always ahead of his time. Only two weeks after Berenson assailed senior goalie Marty Turco for sloppy play and said that the Wolverines hardly deserved to make it into the postseason tournament, his callow team

nipped Boston College 3–2 in overtime for the national title, its second in three years—thanks mainly to a freshman forward and to Turco. "I don't mind having somebody put pressure on me," Turco said. "When I have a bad outing, I look forward to the next one because I know I'm going to do better."

Such forward thinking could be directly traced to Berenson, who in 1962 set a trend by becoming the first U.S. collegian to go straight to the NHL. Just one day after starting for Michigan in the NCAA Final Four, he suited up for the Montreal Canadiens. "Back home in Regina, Saskatchewan, I played for a coach who had been with the Canadiens," he told *The Boston Globe*. "He said, 'Go to school. If you don't make it in the NHL, you weren't supposed to make it. Don't be a hockey bum like me.'"

There has never been the slightest whiff of bum about Berenson: He set a Wolverines scoring record, earned an M.B.A. at Ann Arbor, had 658 points in 17 NHL seasons and was named coach of the year with the St. Louis Blues in 1980–81.

By 1984 the hockey program at his alma mater had fallen on hard times. Recruits were uninterested; attendance was anemic;

the Wolverines had gone 28-44-1 their two previous seasons. But Berenson could still see glorious possibilities in Michigan, and when his son Gordie decided to matriculate, Red came along, too. "To me it wasn't just coaching hockey," Berenson said. "It was coaching Michigan hockey."

Red's sterling credentials as a student, player, coach and trailblazer helped attract prospects, whom he then drove to excel. When Turco and his father, Vince, visited Ann Arbor in 1994, Berenson grilled the goalie on his ability to handle pressure. After Marty had a careless outing in an intrasquad game as a freshman, Berenson benched him. That sort of treatment only steeled Turco, who in the NCAA semifinals later that season would turn back 52 shots in a 4–3 triple overtime loss to Maine. The next season he helped deliver Berenson's first title.

Late in '97–98 the Wolverines dropped three in a row, and Berenson voiced doubts about his inexperienced roster. But the five seniors on his team had the experience of three straight Final Fours, and their unshakable nerves kept the rest of the team calm during the tournament. Especially the steady hand of Turco, who made 19 saves in a 4–0 victory over New Hampshire in the semifinals. Said Craig Button, head scout of the Dallas Stars, who drafted the six-foot, 185-pound Turco, "The biggest thing is that when the game is on the line, he shuts the door."

Energized by a crowd of 18,276 at Boston's FleetCenter for the championship game on April 4, Boston College twice took the lead, but the Wolverines' freshman center Mark Kosick equalized each time. In the first minute of overtime, BC's freshman wing Brian Gionta fired an off-balance wrist shot that Turco kicked aside. Other Eagles would strike the crossbar and a post in OT. Then, with 17:51 gone, Michigan freshman forward Josh Langfeld slipped a shot between the right pad of Boston College goalie Scott Clemmensen and the goalpost to give the Wolverines their ninth national title.

Though he had help from his pipes during overtime, Turco made 28 saves in the final, and when Langfeld beat Clemmensen, the goalie savored a second national title in four

years. As he took off his maize-and-blue gear for the last time, he had feelings his coach knows all too well. "This is a great, great win, but this is also a sad night for me," Turco said. "I mean, it's all over? The best time in my life. Isn't there some way I can get another four-year scholarship to Michigan?"

BASEBALL

In his first trip to the College World Series as USC coach, in 1995, Mike Gillespie tried the hidden-ball trick, which would have worked had the umpire not missed the call. In his most recent trip to Omaha, in 1998, he intentionally walked the winning run to third, and called for a triple steal, both of which ploys worked so well that they propelled the Trojans to an unprecedented 12th national title. As Gillespie put it, "We are aware of what 'the book' says. But sometimes you have to write your own book."

In the annals of USC baseball, Gillespie, 57, holds a special place. As a junior utilityman he scored the lone run in the Trojans victory over Oklahoma State in the 1961 title game; 26 years later, he succeeded the legendary Rod Dedeaux as the Trojans' coach. Gillespie, however, had not been able to increase Southern Cal's title total, and after a 12–10 tournament-opening loss to defending champ LSU in this year's CWS, it seemed unlikely that his fourth-seeded club would be earning much more than a taste of Midwestern hospitality before heading home.

But USC was able to stay alive by upsetting No. 1 Florida 12–10, thanks to an outfielding gem by leftfielder Jeremy Freitas, and to Gillespie's first bold gambit. With Gators on first and second and two outs in the bottom of the 10th, he had star reliever Jack Krawczyk issue an intentional pass to All-America slugger Brad Wilkerson to load the bases, then watched as his stopper went 3 and 2 on the next batter, Casey Smith.

On the next pitch Krawczyk retired Smith on a weak comebacker, and in the top of the 11th Freitas and Rod Perry singled to drive in two runs each for the win. Gillespie's "book" was one most managers would hardly skim, but to hear him tell it, the maneuver was S.O.P. "It wasn't a difficult decision," he said.

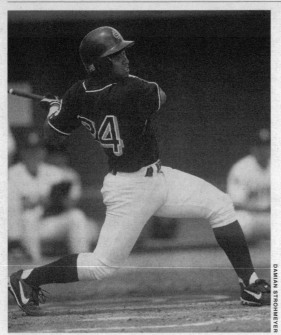

MVP Rachels went 5 for 7 with a homer and seven RBIs in the title game of the CWS.

The 83-year-old Dedeaux was among the record 24,456 spectators at Rosenblatt Stadium on June 6, eager to see if his former program could become the first since 1980 to win the title after losing its tournament opener. The early returns were promising: A pair of dingers by first baseman Robb Gorr off ace Ryan Mills staked the Trojans to an 8–0 lead by the second inning. But no lead was safe in the din of heavy metal at this CWS; the eight teams in the tournament would belt 62 homers, smashing the series mark by 14. "Arenaball," Long Beach State coach Dave Snow derisively called the tater feast.

The Trojans' task was no less dicey after a 7–1 victory over No. 8 Mississippi: They awaited back-to-back showdowns with LSU, which had pounded 14 home runs in its first two games of the Series and was trying to set a record with 11 straight tournament wins. But with a blend of pitching, defense and scrappiness, Southern Cal snuffed the Tigers 5–4 and 8–3. "Put LSU in the Pac-10 and it's just another team," Krawczyk said. "A lot of Eastern schools rely on small stadiums and the bats to win games. They hit home runs and get by without other skills. But when it comes to playing, they're nothing special."

Such tough talk belied the Trojans' recent record; it had been 20 years since they had won a championship. And they would have to defeat a Pac-10 team to win this one. Arizona State had won three of six from the Trojans in their contentious regular-season series, during which Sun Devils coach Pat Murphy accused Gillespie and his players of stealing his team's signs. Gillespie denied the charge. Southern Cal second baseman Wes Rachels said, "At least Coach Murphy said we're good at it."

Arizona State would repeatedly dent Southern Cal's lead, forcing the Trojans to batter back. Clinging to an 11–8 edge in the seventh, USC loaded the bases with two out for Rachels, who was 4 for 4. Gillespie went back to his book.

Noting that ASU reliever Chad Pennington was pitching from a windup, Gillespie called for a steal of home, a tactic he claimed he had employed successfully 15 of 16 times at USC. As Pennington began his delivery, Morgan Ensberg broke for the plate. Ensberg slid feetfirst ahead of Pennington's pitch, which was high. "That steal of home was a great momentum changer," Murphy said. "It was a very big play."

Rachels singled home two more, and USC rolled to a 21–14 triumph that included 39 hits between the two teams, 10 pitchers and a lot of Rachels, who was named the series' most outstanding player. On the 50th anniversary of USC's first championship, Gillespie had swiped another. "We've had all this success and heritage and tradition," said Gillespie. "Among the things I enjoy about it is that we can tack one up and add to it."

FOR THE RECORD·1997–1998

NCAA Team Champions

Fall 1997

Cross-Country

MEN

	Champion	Runner-Up
Division I:	Stanford	Arkansas
Division II:	S Dakota	Central Missouri St
Division III:	N Central	Mount Union

WOMEN

	Champion	Runner-Up
Division I:	Brigham Young	Stanford
Division II:	Adams St	Lewis
Division III:	Cortland St	WI-Eau Claire

Field Hockey

WOMEN

	Champion	Runner-Up
Division I:	N Carolina	Old Dominion
Division II	Bloomsburg	Kutztown
Division III:	William Smith	Cortland St

Football

MEN

	Champion	Runner-Up
Division I-AA:	Youngstown St	McNeese St
Division II:	Northern Colorado	New Haven
Division III:	Mount Union	Lycoming

Soccer

MEN

	Champion	Runner-Up
Division I:	UCLA	Virginia
Division II:	Cal St-Bakersfield	Lynn
Division III:	Wheaton (IL)	College of New Jersey

WOMEN

	Champion	Runner-Up
Division I:	N Carolina	Connecticut
Division II:	Franklin Pierce	West Virginia Wesleyan
Division III:	UC-San Diego	William Smith

Volleyball

WOMEN

	Champion	Runner-Up
Division I:	Stanford	Penn St
Division II:	West Texas A&M	Barry
Division III:	UC-San Diego	Juniata

Water Polo

MEN

Champion	Runner-Up
Pepperdine	Southern Cal

Winter 1997–1998

Basketball

MEN

	Champion	Runner-Up
Division I:	Kentucky	Utah
Division II:	UC-Davis	Kentucky Wesleyan
Division III:	WI-Platteville	Hope

WOMEN

	Champion	Runner-Up
Division I:	Tennessee	Louisiana Tech
Division II:	N Dakota	Emporia St
Division III:	Washington (MO)	Southern Maine

Fencing

Champion	Runner-Up
Penn St	Notre Dame

Gymnastics

MEN

Champion	Runner-Up
California	Iowa

WOMEN

Georgia	Florida

Ice Hockey

MEN

	Champion	Runner-Up
Division I:	Michigan	Boston College
Division II:	AL-Huntsville	Bemidji St
Division III:	Middlebury	WI-Stevens Point

Rifle

Champion	Runner-Up
W Virginia	AK-Fairbanks

Skiing

Champion	Runner-Up
Colorado	Utah

Swimming and Diving

MEN

	Champion	Runner-Up
Division I:	Auburn	Stanford
Division II:	Cal St-Bakersfield	Drury
Division III:	Kenyon	UC-San Diego

WOMEN

	Champion	Runner-Up
Division I:	Stanford	Arizona
Division II:	Drury	Cal St-Bakersfield
Division III:	Kenyon	Denison

Wrestling

MEN

	Champion	Runner-Up
Division I:	Iowa	Oklahoma St
Division II:	N Dakota St	S Dakota St
Division III:	Augsburg	Wartburg

Winter 1997–1998 (Cont.)

Indoor Track and Field

MEN

	Champion	Runner-Up
Division I:	Arkansas	Stanford
Division II:	Abilene Christian	St. Augustine's
Division III:	Lincoln (PA)	Mount Union

WOMEN

	Champion	Runner-Up
Division I:	Texas	Louisiana St
Division II:	Abilene Christian	S Dakota
Division III:	Christopher Newport	Wheaton (MA)

Spring 1998

Baseball

	Champion	Runner-Up
Division I:	Southern Cal	Arizona St
Division II:	Tampa	Kennesaw St
Division III:	Eastern Connecticut St	Cortland St

Golf

MEN

	Champion	Runner-Up
Division I:	UNLV	Clemson
Division II:	Florida Southern	Columbus St
Division III:	Methodist (NC)	Otterbein

WOMEN

	Champion	Runner-Up
Division I:	Arizona St	Florida
Divisions II and III:	Methodist (NC)	Florida Southern

Lacrosse

MEN

	Champion	Runner-Up
Division I:	Princeton	Maryland
Division II:	Adelphi	LIU-C.W. Post
Division III:	Washington (MD)	Nazareth

WOMEN

	Champion	Runner-Up
Divisions I and II:	Maryland	Virginia
Division III:	College of New Jersey	Williams

Rowing

WOMEN

Champion	Runner-Up
Washington	Brown

Softball

	Champion	Runner-Up
Division I:	Fresno St	Arizona
Division II:	California (PA)	Barry
Division III:	WI-Stevens Point	Chapman

Tennis

MEN

	Champion	Runner-Up
Division I:	Stanford	Georgia
Division II:	Lander	Barry
Division III:	UC-Santa Cruz	Williams

Spring 1998 *(Cont.)*

Tennis *(Cont.)*

WOMEN

	Champion	Runner-Up
Division I:	Florida	Duke
Division II:	Lynn	Armstrong Atlantic
Division III:	Skidmore	Kenyon

Outdoor Track and Field

MEN

	Champion	Runner-Up
Division I:	Arkansas	Stanford
Division II:	St. Augustine's	Abilene Christian
Division III:	N Central	Lincoln (PA)

WOMEN

Division I:	Texas	UCLA
Division II:	Abilene Christian	St. Augustine's
Division III:	Christopher Newport	Wheaton (MA)

Volleyball

MEN

Champion	Runner-Up
UCLA	Pepperdine

NCAA Division I Individual Champions

Fall 1997

Cross Country

MEN

Champion	Runner-Up
Mebrahtom Keflezighi, UCLA	Kevin Sullivan, Michigan

WOMEN

Champion	Runner-Up
Carrie Tollefson, Villanova	Amy Skieresz, Arizona

Winter 1997–1998

Fencing

MEN

	Champion	Runner-Up
Sabre	Luke LaValle, Notre Dame	Michael Golia, Pennsylvania
Foil	Ayo Griffin, Yale	Yaron Roth, Pennsylvania
Épée	George Hentea, St. John's (NY)	Eric Tribbett, Stanford

WOMEN

Foil	Felicia Zimmermann, Stanford	Erinn Smart, Columbia-Barnard
Épée	Charlotte Walker, Penn St	Nicole Dygert, St. John's (NY)

Gymnastics

MEN

	Champion	Runner-Up
All-around	Travis Romagnoli, Illinois	Oleg Kosyak, California
Vault	Travis Romagnoli, Illinois	Josh Birckelbaw, California
Parallel bars	Marshall Nelson, Nebraska	Travis Romagnoli, Illinois
Horizontal bar	Todd Bishop, Oklahoma	Travis Romagnoli, Illinois
Floor exercise	Darin Gerlach, Temple	Ron Roeder, Penn St
Pommel horse	Josh Birckelbaw, California	Marshall Nelson, Nebraska
Rings	Dan Fink, Oklahoma	Ron Roeder, Penn St

Winter 1997–1998 *(Cont.)*
Gymnastics *(Cont.)*

WOMEN

	Champion	Runner-Up
All-around	Kim Arnold, Georgia	Karin Lichey, Georgia
Balance beam	Kim Arnold, Georgia	
	Jenni Beathard, Georgia	
	Betsy Hamm, Florida	
Uneven bars	Heidi Moneymaker, UCLA	Nikki Peters, Michigan
Floor exercise	Karin Lichey, Georgia	
	Stella Umeh, UCLA	
Vault	Susan Hines, Florida	
	Larissa Fontaine, Stanford	

Skiing

MEN

	Champion	Runner-Up
Slalom	Izidor Jerman, AK-Anchorage	Stefan Lanziner, New Mexico
Giant slalom	David Viele, Dartmouth	Forest Carey, Middlebury
10-kilometer classical	Thorodd Bakken, Vermont	Frode Kolleruf, Utah
20-kilometer freestyle	Thorodd Bakken, Vermont	Rune Kollerud, Utah

WOMEN

	Champion	Runner-Up
Slalom	Brooke Laundon, Middlebury	Edda Mutter, AK-Anchorage
Giant slalom	Caroline Gedde-Dahl, Colorado	Jennifer Collins, Dartmouth
5-kilometer classical	Line Selnes, Colorado	Kristin Tjelle, Utah
15-kilometer freestyle	Line Selnes, Colorado	Irene Eder, Denver

Wrestling

	Champion	Runner-Up
118 lb	Teague Moore, Oklahoma St	David Morgan, Michigan St
126 lb	Eric Guerrero, Oklahoma St	Eric Jetton, Wisconsin
134 lb	Mark Ironside, Iowa	Michael Lightner, Oklahoma
142 lb	Jeff McGinness, Iowa	Casey Cunningham, Central MI
150 lb	Eric Siebert, Illinois	Chad Kraft, Minnesota
158 lb	Dwight Gardner, Ohio	Hardell Moore, Oklahoma St
167 lb	Joe Williams, Iowa	Brandon Slay, Pennsylvania
177 lb	Mitch Clark, Ohio St	Vertus Jones, West Virginia
190 lb	Tim Hartung, Minnesota	Jason Robison, Edinboro
Heavyweight	Stephen Neal, Cal St-Bakersfield	Trent Hynek, Iowa St

Swimming and Diving

MEN

	Champion	Time	Runner-Up	Time
50-yard freestyle	Brendon Dedekind, Florida St	19.22	Aaron Ciarla, Auburn	19.45
100-yard freestyle	Lars Frolander, SMU	42.12	Neil Walker, Texas	42.83
200-yard freestyle	Ryk Neethling, Arizona	1:34.19	Bela Szabados, USC	1:34.36
500-yard freestyle	Ryk Neethling, Arizona	4:13.42	Tom Malchow, Michigan	4:17.80
1650-yard freestyle	Ryk Neethling, Arizona	14:32.50	Chris Thompson, Michigan	14:46.29
100-yard backstroke	Neil Walker, Texas	46.66	Lenny Krayzelburg, USC	46.90
200-yard backstroke	Tate Blahnik, Stanford	1:41.21	Lenny Krayzelburg, USC	1:41.55
100-yard breaststroke	Jeremy Linn, Tennessee	53.01	Adam Jerger, Auburn	53.31
200-yard breaststroke	Tom Wilkens, Stanford	1:55.02	Blake Holden, Stanford	1:56.90
100-yard butterfly	Lars Frolander, SMU	45.99*	Sabir Muhammad, Stanford	46.18
200-yard butterfly	Matthew Pierce, Stanford	1:43.68	Steven Brown, Stanford	1:44.00
200-yard IM	Tom Wilkens, Stanford	1:45.16	Lionel Moreau, Auburn	1:45.76
400-yard IM	Tom Wilkens, Stanford	3:43.96	Steven Brown, Stanford	3:46.52
	Champion	Pts	Runner-Up	Pts
1-meter diving†	Rio Ramirez, Miami (FL)	630.70	Bryan Gillooly, Miami (FL)	571.95
3-meter diving†	Bryan Gillooly, Miami (FL)	631.40	Rio Ramirez, Miami (FL)	599.15
Platform#	Brent Robert, Alabama	834.45	Paco Rivera, Kentucky	803.90

*Meet record. †Scoring based on 17 dives. #Scoring based on 14 dives.

Winter 1997–1998 *(Cont.)*
Swimming and Diving *(Cont.)*
WOMEN

	Champion	Time	Runner-Up	Time
50-yard freestyle	Catherine Fox, Stanford	22.21	Shannon Hosack, Arizona	22.29
100-yard freestyle	Martina Moravcova, SMU	48.81	Rania Elwani, SMU	49.01
200-yard freestyle	Martina Moravcova, SMU	1:45.11	Shannon Shakespeare, Michigan	1:46.58
500-yard freestyle	Cristina Teuscher, Col-Barnard	4:35.45	Trina Jackson, Arizona	4:38.57
1650-yard freestyle	Trina Jackson, Arizona	15:49.25	Laurie Kline, Arizona	16:02.07
100-yard backstroke	Catherine Fox, Stanford	52.71	Courtney Shealy, Georgia	53.53
200-yard backstroke	Misty Hyman, Stanford	1:53.12	Keegan Walkley, Georgia	1:53.22
100-yard breaststroke	Kristy Kowal, Georgia	59.05	Lindsay Etter, UCLA	1:00.45
200-yard breaststroke	Kristy Kowal, Georgia	2:09.14	Elin Austevoli, Stanford	2:11.04
100-yard butterfly	Misty Hyman, Stanford	51.34*	Richelle Fox, N Carolina	52.69
200-yard butterfly	Misty Hyman, Stanford	1:55.70	Elli Overton, California	1:57.73
200-yard IM	Martina Moravcova, SMU	1:57.37	Elli Overton, California	1:58.38
400-yard IM	Cristina Teuscher, Col-Barnard	4:05.62	Keegan Walkley, Georgia	4:07.53

	Champion	Pts	Runner-Up	Pts
1-meter diving†	Vera Ilyina, Texas	495.70	Jenny Lingamfelter, SMU	457.45
3-meter diving#	Vera Ilyina, Texas	612.60	Laura Wilkinson, Texas	555.75
Platform‡	Kathy Pesek, Tennessee	659.65	Laura Wilkinson, Texas	633.25

*Meet record. †Scoring based on 15 dives. #Scoring based on 17 dives. ‡Scoring based on 12 dives.

Indoor Track and Field
MEN

	Champion	Mark	Runner-Up	Mark
55-meter dash	Ja Warren Hooker, Washington	6.13	Corey Bridges, S Carolina	6.21
55-meter hurdles	Larry Wade, Texas A&M	7.11	Jeremichael Williams, Clemson	7.18
200-meter dash	Shawn Crawford, Clemson	20.69	Milton Campbell, N Carolina	20.79
400-meter dash	Davian Clarke, Miami (FL)	45.86	Brandon Couts, Baylor	45.90
800-meter run	David Krummenacker, GA Tech	1:47.52	Derrick Peterson, Missouri	1:48.71
Mile run	Kevin Sullivan, Michigan	4:03.54	Bryan Berryhill, Colorado St	4:03.56
3,000-meter run	Adam Goucher, Colorado	7:46.03*	Bernard Lagat, Washington St	7:46.45
5,000-meter run	Brad Hauser, Stanford	13:58.50	Sean Kaley, Arkansas	13:58.87
High jump	Kenny Evans, Arkansas	7 ft 6 in	Mark Boswell, Texas	7 ft 5 in
Pole vault	Vesa Rantanen, Minnesota	18 ft 2½ in	Dominic Johnson, Arizona	18 ft 2½ in
Long jump	Bashir Yamini, Iowa	26 ft ¼ in	Maurice Wignall, George Mason	25 ft 6 in
Triple jump	Robert Howard, Arkansas	54 ft 11¼ in	Chris Kwaramba, Idaho	53 ft 5¾ in
Shot put	Brad Snyder, S Carolina	6 ft 4 in	Ralf Kahles, Louisiana St	62 ft 4 in
35-pound wt throw	Libor Charfreitag, SMU	69 ft 8 in	Scott Russell, Kansas	67 ft 6¼ in

WOMEN

	Champion	Mark	Runner-Up	Mark
55-meter dash	Kwajalein Butler, Louisiana St	6.78	Debbie Ferguson, Georgia	6.78
55-meter hurdles	Angie Vaughn, Texas	7.41*	Andria King, Georgia Tech	7.47
200-meter dash	Lakeisha Backus, Texas	23.18	Debbie Ferguson, Georgia	23.22
400-meter dash	Suzann Reid, Texas	52.57	Ryan Tolbert, Vanderbilt	52.79
800-meter run	Hazel Clark, Florida	2:02.53	Julian Reynolds, Georgetown	2:04.75
Mile run	Carmen Douma, Villanova	4:37.74	Angela Graham, Boston College	4:39.62
3,000-meter run	Katie McGregor, Michigan	9:24.68	Jolene Williams, Coastal Carolina	9:25.29
5,000-meter run	Amy Skieresz, Arizona	15:54.48	Marie McMahon, Providence	16:11.77
High jump	Erin Aldrich	6 ft 4 ¼ in	Kajsa Bergquist, SMU	6 ft 3 ¼ in
Pole vault	Melissa Price, Fresno St	13 ft 10 in*	Candy Mason, Kansas	12 ft 7½ in
Long jump	Trecia Smith, Pittsburgh	21 ft 6¼ in	Lacena Golding, Auburn	21 ft 2¾ in
Triple jump	Trecia Smith, Pittsburgh	46 ft 1¼ in	Nicole Gamble, N Carolina	44 ft 6 in
Shot put	Teri Tunks, SMU	60 ft 5¼ in*	Amy Palmer, BYU	56 ft 8¾ in
20-pound wt throw	Lisa Misipeka, S Carolina	70 ft 5¼ in	Renetta Seiler, Kansas St	69 ft 2½ in

*Meet record.

Rifle

	Champion	Pts	Runner-Up	Pts
Smallbore	Karyn Juziuk, Xavier	1169	Jeff Odor, Wyoming	1167
Air rifle	Emily Caruso, Norwich	393†	Dan Jordan, AK-Fairbanks	393

†Caruso had 30 inner 10s to Jordan's 25 to break the tie.

Spring 1998
Golf

MEN

Champion	Score	Runner-Up	Score
James McClean, Minnesota	271	four tied	272

WOMEN

Champion	Score	Runner-Up	Score
Jennifer Rosales, Southern Cal	279	Christina Kuld, Tulsa	282

Outdoor Track and Field

MEN

	Champion	Mark	Runner-Up	Mark
100-meter dash	Leonard Myles-Mills, BYU	10.20 w	Jarmiene Holloway, TCU	10.24 w
200-meter dash	Curtis Perry, Louisiana St	20.40	Daymon Carroll, Florida	20.74
400-meter dash	Jerome Davis, Southern Cal	45.18	Davian Clarke, Miami (FL)	45.28
800-meter run	Khadevis Robinson, Texas Christian	1:46.04	David Krummenacker, Georgia Tech	1:46.40
1,500-meter run	Seneca Lassiter, Arkansas	3:42.34	Gabe Jennings, Stanford	3:42.39
3,000-met. steeple	Matt Kerr, Arkansas	8:36.95	John Mortimer, Michigan	8:40.42
5,000-meter run	Adam Goucher, Colorado	13:31.64	Adbi Abdirahman, Arizona	13:40.61
10,000-meter run	Brad Hausner, Stanford	28:31.30	Brent Hauser, Stanford	28:32.39
110-meter hurdles	Larry Wade, Texas A&M	13.37 w	Terrence Trammell, S Carolina	13.41 w
400-meter hurdles	Angelo Taylor, Georgia Tech	48.14	Omar Brown, Oklahoma	49.38
High jump	Nathan Leeper, Kansas St	7 ft 5¾ in	Jeremy Fischer, Wisconsin	7 ft 4½ in
Pole vault	Toby Stevenson, Stanford	18 ft 2½ in	Borya Celentano, Long Beach	18 ft 2½ in
Long jump	Robert Howard, Arkansas	27 ft 5½.in w	Chris Wright, Nebraska	26 ft 10½ in w
Triple jump	Robert Howard, Arkansas	55 ft 8¼ in	Levar Anderson, Louisiana St	54 ft 0 in
Shot put	Brad Snyder, S Carolina	64 ft 7¾ in	Chima Ugwu, Arizona	63 ft 5¼ in
Discus throw	Casey Malone, Colorado St	200 ft 2 in	Alex Forst, Louisiana St	195 ft 7 in
Hammer throw	Libor Charfreitag, SMU	237 ft 2 in	Bengt Johansson, Southern Cal	236 ft 11 in
Javelin throw	Esko Mikkola, Arizona	268 ft 7 in	Daniel Gustafsson, SMU	251 ft 6 in
Decathlon	Brenden Falconer, Kent	4124 pts	Dominic Johnson, Arizona	4114 pts

WOMEN

	Champion	Mark	Runner-Up	Mark
100-meter dash	Debbie Ferguson, Georgia	10.94 w	Shakedia Jones, UCLA	11.15 w
200-meter dash	Debbie Ferguson, Georgia	22.66	LaTasha Jenkins, Ball St	22.93
400-meter dash	Suziann Reid, Texas	51.22	Yulanda Nelson, Baylor	52.39
800-meter run	Hazel Clark, Florida	2:02.16	Charmaine Howell, S Carolina	2:03.66
1,500-meter run	Carmen Douma, Villanova	4:16.04	Kelly Smith, Colorado	4:16.23
3,000-meter run	Monal Chokshi, Stanford	9:20.18	Courtney Meldrum, BYU	9:22.91
5,000-meter run	Amy Skieresz, Arizona	15:37.77*	Katie McGregor, Michigan	15:50.14
10,000-meter run	Amy Skieresz, Arizona	33:04.12	Angie Kujak, Wisconsin	34:06.76
100-meter hurdles	Angie Vaughn, Texas	12.82 w	Andria King, Georgia Tech	13.17 w
400-meter hurdles	Rosa Jolivet, Texas A&M	55.24	Yvonne Harrison, Illinois	55.87
High jump	Erin Aldrich, Texas	6 ft 4 in	Kajsa Bergqvist, SMU	6 ft 4 in
Pole vault	Bianca Maran, Cal Poly	12 ft 5½ in*	Kim Stewart, Nebraska	12 ft 5½ in
Long jump	Angie Brown, George Mason	21 ft 7½ in w	Trecia Smith, Pittsburgh	21 ft ¾ in w
Triple jump	Trecia Smith, Pittsburgh	45 ft 10½ in	Stacey Bowers, Baylor	44 ft 4¼ in w
Shot put	Tressa Thompson, Nebraska	61 ft 2¼ in*	Teri Tunks, SMU	60 ft 10¾ in
Discus throw	Seilala Sua, UCLA	210 ft 8 in	Suzy Powell, UCLA	192 ft 5 in
Hammer throw	Lisa Misipeka, S Carolina	209 ft 4 in*	Amy Palmer, BYU	208 ft 3 in
Javelin throw	Windy Dean, SMU	184 ft 8 in	Olivia McCoy, Louisiana Tech	176 ft 11 in
Heptathlon	Tiffany Lott, Brigham Young	3652 pts	Tracye Lawyer, Stanford	3452 pts

*Meet record. w=wind-aided.

Tennis

MEN

	Champion	Score	Runner-Up
Singles	Bob Bryan, Stanford	6–3, 6–2	Paul Goldstein, Stanford
Doubles	Bob Bryan & Mike Bryan, Stanford	6–7 (6), 6–2, 6–4	Kelly Gullett & Robert Lindstedt, Pepperdine

WOMEN

	Champion	Score	Runner-Up
Singles	Vanessa Webb, Duke	6–3, 6–4	Ania Bleszynski, Stanford
Doubles	Amanda Augustus & Amy Jensen, California	7–5, 6–3	Dawn Buth & Stephanie Nickitas, Florida

CHAMPIONSHIP RESULTS

Baseball

DIVISION I

Year	Champion	Coach	Score	Runner-Up	Most Outstanding Player
1947	California*	Clint Evans	8–7	Yale	No award
1948	Southern Cal	Sam Barry	9–2	Yale	No award
1949	Texas*	Bibb Falk	10–3	Wake Forest	Charles Teague, Wake Forest, 2B
1950	Texas	Bibb Falk	3–0	Washington St	Ray VanCleef, Rutgers, CF
1951	Oklahoma*	Jack Baer	3–2	Tennnessee	Sidney Hatfield, Tennessee, P-1B
1952	Holy Cross	Jack Barry	8–4	Missouri	James O'Neill, Holy Cross, P
1953	Michigan	Ray Fisher	7–5	Texas	J.L. Smith, Texas, P
1954	Missouri	John (Hi) Simmons	4–1	Rollins	Tom Yewcic, Michigan St, C
1955	Wake Forest	Taylor Sanford	7–6	Western Michigan	Tom Borland, Oklahoma St, P
1956	Minnesota	Dick Siebert	12–1	Arizona	Jerry Thomas, Minnesota, P
1957	California*	George Wolfman	1–0	Penn St	Cal Emery, Penn St, P-1B
1958	Southern Cal	Rod Dedeaux	8–7†	Missouri	Bill Thom, Southern Cal, P
1959	Oklahoma St	Toby Greene	5–3	Arizona	Jim Dobson, Oklahoma St, 3B
1960	Minnesota	Dick Siebert	2–1‡	Southern Cal	John Erickson, Minnesota, 2B
1961	Southern Cal*	Rod Dedeaux	1–0	Oklahoma St	Littleton Fowler, Oklahoma St, P
1962	Michigan	Don Lund	5–4	Santa Clara	Bob Garibaldi, Santa Clara, P
1963	Southern Cal	Rod Dedeaux	5–2	Arizona	Bud Hollowell, Southern Cal, C
1964	Minnesota	Dick Siebert	5–1	Missouri	Joe Ferris, Maine, P
1965	Arizona St	Bobby Winkles	2–1#	Ohio St	Sal Bando, Arizona St, 3B
1966	Ohio St	Marty Karow	8–2	Oklahoma St	Steve Arlin, Ohio St, P
1967	Arizona St	Bobby Winkles	11–2	Houston	Ron Davini, Arizona St, C
1968	Southern Cal*	Rod Dedeaux	4–3	Southern Illinois	Bill Seinsoth, Southern Cal, 1B
1969	Arizona St	Bobby Winkles	10–1	Tulsa	John Dolinsek, Arizona St, LF
1970	Southern Cal	Rod Dedeaux	2–1	Florida St	Gene Ammann, Florida St, P
1971	Southern Cal	Rod Dedeaux	7–2	Southern Illinois	Jerry Tabb, Tulsa, 1B
1972	Southern Cal	Rod Dedeaux	1–0	Arizona St	Russ McQueen, Southern Cal, P
1973	Southern Cal*	Rod Dedeaux	4–3	Arizona St	Dave Winfield, Minnesota, P-OF
1974	Southern Cal	Rod Dedeaux	7–3	Miami (FL)	George Milke, Southern Cal, P
1975	Texas	Cliff Gustafson	5–1	S Carolina	Mickey Reichenbach, Texas, 1B
1976	Arizona	Jerry Kindall	7–1	Eastern Michigan	Steve Powers, Arizona, P-DH
1977	Arizona St	Jim Brock	2–1	S Carolina	Bob Horner, Arizona St, 3B
1978	Southern Cal*	Rod Dedeaux	10–3	Arizona St	Rod Boxberger, Southern Cal, P
1979	Cal St-Fullerton	Augie Garrido	2–1	Arkansas	Tony Hudson, Cal St-Fullerton, P
1980	Arizona	Jerry Kindall	5–3	Hawaii	Terry Francona, Arizona, LF
1981	Arizona St	Jim Brock	7–4	Oklahoma St	Stan Holmes, Arizona St, LF
1982	Miami (FL)*	Ron Fraser	9–3	Wichita St	Dan Smith, Miami (FL), P
1983	Texas*	Cliff Gustafson	4–3	Alabama	Calvin Schiraldi, Texas, P
1984	Cal St-Fullerton	Augie Garrido	3–1	Texas	John Fishel, Cal St-Fullerton, LF
1985	Miami (FL)	Ron Fraser	10–6	Texas	Greg Ellena, Miami (FL), DH
1986	Arizona	Jerry Kindall	10–2	Florida St	Mike Senne, Arizona, LF
1987	Stanford	Mark Marquess	9–5	Oklahoma St	Paul Carey, Stanford, RF
1988	Stanford	Mark Marquess	9–4	Arizona St	Lee Plemel, Stanford, P
1989	Wichita St	Gene Stephenson	5–3	Texas	Greg Brummett, Wichita St, P
1990	Georgia	Steve Webber	2–1	Oklahoma St	Mike Rebhan, Georgia, P
1991	Louisiana St	Skip Bertman	6–3	Wichita St	Gary Hymel, Louisiana St, C
1992	Pepperdine	Andy Lopez	3–2	Cal St-Fullerton	Phil Nevin, Cal St-Fullerton, 3B
1993	Louisiana St	Skip Bertman	8–0	Wichita St	Todd Walker, Louisiana St, 2B
1994	Oklahoma	Larry Cochell	13–5	Georgia Tech	Chip Glass, Oklahoma, CF
1995	Cal St-Fullerton*	Augie Garrido	11–5	Southern Cal	Mark Kotsay, Cal St-Fullerton, CF-P
1996	Louisiana St*	Skip Bertman	9–8	Miami (FL)	Pat Burrell, Miami (FL), 3B
1997	Louisiana St*	Skip Bertman	13–6	Alabama	Brandon Larson, Louisiana St, SS
1998	Southern Cal	Mike Gillespie	21–14	Arizona St	Wes Rachels, Southern Cal, 2B

*Undefeated teams in College World Series play. †12 innings. ‡10 innings. #15 innings.

DIVISION II

Year	Champion	Year	Champion	Year	Champion
1968	Chapman*	1973	UC-Irvine*	1978	Florida Southern
1969	Illinois St*	1974	UC-Irvine	1979	Valdosta St
1970	Cal St-Northridge	1975	Florida Southern	1980	Cal Poly-Pomona*
1971	Florida Southern	1976	Cal Poly-Pomona	1981	Florida Southern*
1972	Florida Southern	1977	UC-Riverside	1982	UC-Riverside*

DIVISION II (Cont.)

Year	Champion	Year	Champion	Year	Champion
1983	Cal Poly-Pomona*	1989	Cal Poly-SLO	1995	Florida Southern*
1984	Cal St-Northridge	1990	Jacksonville St	1996	Kennesaw St*
1985	Florida Southern*	1991	Jacksonville St	1997	Cal St-Chico*
1986	Troy St	1992	Tampa*	1998	Tampa*
1987	Troy St*	1993	Tampa		
1988	Florida Southern*	1994	Central Missouri St		

DIVISION III

Year	Champion	Year	Champion	Year	Champion
1976	Cal St-Stanislaus	1984	Ramapo	1992	William Paterson
1977	Cal St-Stanislaus	1985	WI-Oshkosh	1993	Montclair St
1978	Glassboro St	1986	Marietta	1994	WI-Oshkosh
1979	Glassboro St	1987	Montclair St	1995	La Verne
1980	Ithaca	1988	Ithaca	1996	William Paterson
1981	Marietta	1989	NC Wesleyan	1997	Southern Maine
1982	Eastern Connecticut St	1990	Eastern Connecticut St	1998	Eastern Connecticut St
1983	Marietta	1991	Southern Maine		

*Undefeated teams in final series.

Cross-Country

Men

DIVISION I

Year	Champion	Coach	Pts	Runner-Up	Pts	Individual Champion	Time
1938	Indiana	Earle Hayes	51	Notre Dame	61	Greg Rice, Notre Dame	20:12.9
1939	Michigan St	Lauren Brown	54	Wisconsin	57	Walter Mehl, Wisconsin	20:30.9
1940	Indiana	Earle Hayes	65	Eastern Michigan	68	Gilbert Dodds, Ashland	20:30.2
1941	Rhode Island	Fred Tootell	83	Penn St	110	Fred Wilt, Indiana	20:30.1
1942	Indiana	Earle Hayes	57			Oliver Hunter, Notre Dame	20:18.0
	Penn St	Charles Werner	57				
1943	No meet						
1944	Drake	Bill Easton	25	Notre Dame	64	Fred Feiler, Drake	21:04.2
1945	Drake	Bill Easton	50	Notre Dame	65	Fred Feiler, Drake	21:14.2
1946	Drake	Bill Easton	42	NYU	98	Quentin Brelsford, Ohio Wesleyan	20:22.9
1947	Penn St	Charles Werner	60	Syracuse	72	Jack Milne, N Carolina	20:41.1
1948	Michigan St	Karl Schlademan	41	Wisconsin	69	Robert Black, Rhode Island	19:52.3
1949	Michigan St	Karl Schlademan	59	Syracuse	81	Robert Black, Rhode Island	20:25.7
1950	Penn St	Charles Werner	53	Michigan St	55	Herb Semper Jr, Kansas	20:31.7
1951	Syracuse	Robert Grieve	80	Kansas	118	Herb Semper Jr, Kansas	20:09.5
1952	Michigan St	Karl Schlademan	65	Indiana	68	Charles Capozzoli, Georgetown	19:36.7
1953	Kansas	Bill Easton	70	Indiana	82	Wes Santee, Kansas	19:43.5
1954	Oklahoma St	Ralph Higgins	61	Syracuse	118	Allen Frame, Kansas	19:54.2
1955	Michigan St	Karl Schlademan	46	Kansas	68	Charles Jones, Iowa	19:57.4
1956	Michigan St	Karl Schlademan	28	Kansas	88	Walter McNew, Texas	19:55.7
1957	Notre Dame	Alex Wilson	121	Michigan St	127	Max Truex, Southern Cal	19:12.3
1958	Michigan St	Francis Dittrich	79	Western Michigan	104	Crawford Kennedy, Michigan State	20:07.1
1959	Michigan St	Francis Dittrich	44	Houston	120	Al Lawrence, Houston	20:35.7
1960	Houston	John Morriss	54	Michigan St	80	Al Lawrence, Houston	19:28.2
1961	Oregon St	Sam Bell	68	San Jose St	82	Dale Story, Oregon St	19:46.6
1962	San Jose St	Dean Miller	58	Villanova	69	Tom O'Hara, Loyola (IL)	19:20.3
1963	San Jose St	Dean Miller	53	Oregon	68	Victor Zwolak, Villanova	19:35.0
1964	W Michigan	George Dales	86	Oregon	116	Elmore Banton, Ohio	20:07.5
1965	W Michigan	George Dales	81	Northwestern	114	John Lawson, Kansas	29:24.0
1966	Villanova	James Elliott	79	Kansas St	155	Gerry Lindgren, Washington St	29:01.4
1967	Villanova	James Elliott	91	Air Force	96	Gerry Lindgren, Washington St	30:45.6
1968	Villanova	James Elliott	78	Stanford	100	Michael Ryan, Air Force	29:16.8
1969	UTEP	Wayne Vandenburg	74	Villanova	88	Gerry Lindgren, Washington St	28:59.2
1970	Villanova	James Elliott	85	Oregon	86	Steve Prefontaine, Oregon	28:00.2

Men (Cont.)

DIVISION I (Cont.)

Year	Champion	Coach	Pts	Runner-Up	Pts	Individual Champion	Time
1971	Oregon	Bill Dellinger	83	Washington St	122	Steve Prefontaine, Oregon	29:14.0
1972	Tennessee	Stan Huntsman	134	E Tennessee St	148	Neil Cusack, E Tenn St	28:23.0
1973	Oregon	Bill Dellinger	89	UTEP	157	Steve Prefontaine, Oregon	28:14.0
1974	Oregon	Bill Dellinger	77	Western Kentucky	110	Nick Rose, W Kentucky	29:22.0
1975	UTEP	Ted Banks	88	Washington St	92	Craig Virgin, Illinois	28:23.3
1976	UTEP	Ted Banks	62	Oregon	117	Henry Rono, Washington St	28:06.6
1977	Oregon	Bill Dellinger	100	UTEP	105	Henry Rono, Washington St	28:33.5
1978	UTEP	Ted Banks	56	Oregon	72	Alberto Salazar, Oregon	29:29.7
1979	UTEP	Ted Banks	86	Oregon	93	Henry Rono, Washington St	28:19.6
1980	UTEP	Ted Banks	58	Arkansas	152	Suleiman Nyambui, UTEP	29:04.0
1981	UTEP	Ted Banks	17	Providence	109	Mathews Motshwarateu, UTEP	28:45.6
1982	Wisconsin	Dan McClimon	59	Providence	138	Mark Scrutton, Colorado	30:12.6
1983	Vacated			Wisconsin	164	Zakarie Barie, UTEP	29:20.0
1984	Arkansas	John McDonnell	101	Arizona	111	Ed Eyestone, Brigham Young	29:28.8
1985	Wisconsin	Martin Smith	67	Arkansas	104	Timothy Hacker, Wisconsin	29:17.88
1986	Arkansas	John McDonnell	69	Dartmouth	141	Aaron Ramirez, Arizona	30:27.53
1987	Arkansas	John McDonnell	87	Dartmouth	119	Joe Falcon, Arkansas	29:14.97
1988	Wisconsin	Martin Smith	105	Northern Arizona	160	Robert Kennedy, Indiana	29:20.0
1989	Iowa St	Bill Bergan	54	Oregon	72	John Nuttall, Iowa St	29:30.55
1990	Arkansas	John McDonnell	68	Iowa St	96	Jonah Koech, Iowa St	29:05.0
1991	Arkansas	John McDonnell	52	Iowa St	114	Sean Dollman, Western Ky	30:17.1
1992	Arkansas	John McDonnell	46	Wisconsin	87	Bob Kennedy, Indiana	30:15.3
1993	Arkansas	John McDonnell	31	Brigham Young	153	Josephat Kapkory, Wash St	29:32.4
1994	Iowa St	Bill Bergan	65	Colorado	88	Martin Keino, Arizona	30:08.7
1995	Arkansas	John McDonnell	100	Northern Arizona	142	Godfrey Siamusiye, Arkansas	30:09
1996	Stanford	Vin Lananna	46	Arkansas	74	Godfrey Siamusiye, Arkansas	29:49
1997	Stanford	Vin Lananna	53	Arkansas	56	Mebrahtom Keflezighi, UCLA	28:54

DIVISION II

Year	Champion	Year	Champion	Year	Champion
1958	Northern Illinois	1972	N Dakota St	1986	Edinboro
1959	S Dakota St	1973	S Dakota St	1987	Edinboro
1960	Central St (OH)	1974	SW Missouri St	1988	Edinboro/ Mankato St
1961	Southern Illinois	1975	UC-Irvine	1989	S Dakota St
1962	Central St (OH)	1976	UC-Irvine	1990	Edinboro
1963	Emporia St	1977	Eastern Illinois	1991	MA-Lowell
1964	Kentucky St	1978	Cal Poly-SLO	1992	Adams St
1965	San Diego St	1979	Cal Poly-SLO	1993	Adams St
1966	San Diego St	1980	Humboldt St	1994	Adams St
1967	San Diego St	1981	Millersville	1995	Western St
1968	Eastern Illinois	1982	Eastern Washington	1996	S Dakota St
1969	Eastern Illinois	1983	Cal Poly-Pomona	1997	S Dakota
1970	Eastern Michigan	1984	SE Missouri St		
1971	Cal St-Fullerton	1985	S Dakota St		

DIVISION III

Year	Champion	Year	Champion	Year	Champion
1973	Ashland	1982	N Central	1991	Rochester
1974	Mount Union	1983	Brandeis	1992	N Central
1975	North Central	1984	St. Thomas (MN)	1993	N Central
1976	North Central	1985	Luther	1994	Williams
1977	Occidental	1986	St. Thomas (MN)	1995	Williams
1978	N Central	1987	N Central	1996	WI-La Crosse
1979	N Central	1988	WI-Oshkosh	1997	N Central
1980	Carleton	1989	WI-Oshkosh		
1981	N Central	1990	WI-Oshkosh		

Women

DIVISION I

Year	Champion	Coach	Pts	Runner-Up	Pts	Individual Champion	Time
1981	Virginia	John Vasvary	36	Oregon	83	Betty Springs, N Carolina St	16:19.0
1982	Virginia	Martin Smith	48	Stanford	91	Lesley Welch, Virginia	16:39.7
1983	Oregon	Tom Heinonen	95	Stanford	98	Betty Springs, N Carolina St	16:30.7
1984	Wisconsin	Peter Tegen	63	Stanford	89	Cathy Branta, Wisconsin	16:15.6
1985	Wisconsin	Peter Tegen	58	Iowa St	98	Suzie Tuffey, N Carolina St	16:22.5

Women (Cont.)

DIVISION I (Cont.)

Year	Champion	Coach	Pts	Runner-Up	Pts	Individual Champion	Time
1986	Texas	Terry Crawford	62	Wisconsin	64	Angela Chalmers, N Arizona	16:55.49
1987	Oregon	Tom Heinonen	97	N Carolina St	99	Kimberly Betz, Indiana	16:10.85
1988	Kentucky	Don Weber	75	Oregon	128	Michelle Dekkers, Indiana	16:30.0
1989	Villanova	Marty Stern	99	Kentucky	168	Vicki Huber, Villanova	15:59.86
1990	Villanova	Marty Stern	82	Providence	172	Sonia O'Sullivan, Villanova	16:06.0
1991	Villanova	Marty Stern	85	Arkansas	168	Sonia O'Sullivan, Villanova	16:30.3
1992	Villanova	Marty Stern	123	Arkansas	130	Carole Zajac, Villanova	17:01.9
1993	Villanova	Marty Stern	66	Arkansas	71	Carole Zajac, Villanova	16:40.3
1994	Villanova	John Marshall	75	Michigan	108	Jennifer Rhines, Villanova	16:31.2
1995	Providence	Ray Treacy	88	Colorado	123	Kathy Butler, Wisconsin	16:51
1996	Stanford	Beth Alford-Sullivan	101	Villanova	106	Amy Skieresz, Arizona	17:04
1997	BYU	Patrick Shane	100	Stanford	102	Carrie Tollefson, Villanova	16:58

DIVISION II

Year	Champion	Year	Champion	Year	Champion
1981	S Dakota St	1987	Cal Poly-SLO	1993	Adams St
1982	Cal Poly-SLO	1988	Cal Poly-SLO	1994	Adams St
1983	Cal Poly-SLO	1989	Cal Poly-SLO	1995	Adams St
1984	Cal Poly-SLO	1990	Cal Poly-SLO	1996	Adams St
1985	Cal Poly-SLO	1991	Cal Poly-SLO	1997	Adams St
1986	Cal Poly-SLO	1992	Adams St		

DIVISION III

Year	Champion	Year	Champion	Year	Champion
1981	Central (IA)	1987	St. Thomas (MN)	1992	Cortland St
1982	St. Thomas (MN)		WI-Oshkosh	1993	Cortland St
1983	WI-La Crosse	1988	WI-Oshkosh	1994	Cortland St
1984	St. Thomas (MN)	1989	Cortland St	1995	Cortland St
1985	Franklin & Marshall	1990	Cortland St	1996	WI-Oshkosh
1986	St. Thomas (MN)	1991	WI-Oshkosh	1997	Cortland St

Fencing

Men's and Women's Combined

TEAM CHAMPIONS

Year	Champion	Coach	Pts	Runner-Up	Pts
1990	Penn St	Emmanuil Kaidanov	36	Columbia-Barnard	35
1991	Penn St	Emmanuil Kaidanov	4700	Columbia-Barnard	4200
1992	Columbia-Barnard	George Kolombatovich Aladar Kogler	4150	Penn St	3646
1993	Columbia-Barnard	George Kolumbatovich Aladar Kogler	4525	Penn St	4500
1994	Notre Dame	Michael DeCicco	4350	Penn St	4075
1995	Penn St	Emmanuil Kaidanov	440	St. John's (NY)	413
1996	Penn St	Emmanuil Kaidanov	1500	Notre Dame	1190
1997	Penn St	Emmanuil Kaidanov	1530	Notre Dame	1470
1998	Penn St	Emmanuil Kaidanov	149	Notre Dame	147

Men

TEAM CHAMPIONS

Year	Champion	Coach	Pts	Runner-Up	Pts
1941	Northwestern	Henry Zettleman	28½	Illinois	27
1942	Ohio St	Frank Riebel	34	St. John's (NY)	33½
1943–46	No tournament				
1947	NYU	Martinez Castello	72	Chicago	50½
1948	CCNY	James Montague	30	Navy	28
1949	Army	Servando Velarde	63		
	Rutgers	Donald Cetrulo	63		
1950	Navy	Joseph Fiems	67½	NYU	66½
				Rutgers	66½
1951	Columbia	Servando Velarde	69	Pennsylvania	64
1952	Columbia	Servando Velarde	71	NYU	69
1953	Pennsylvania	Lajos Csiszar	94	Navy	86

Men (Cont.)

TEAM CHAMPIONS (Cont.)

Year	Champion	Coach	Pts	Runner-Up	Pts
1954	Columbia	Irving DeKoff	61		
	NYU	Hugo Castello	61		
1955	Columbia	Irving DeKoff	62	Cornell	57
1956	Illinois	Maxwell Garret	90	Columbia	88
1957	NYU	Hugo Castello	65	Columbia	64
1958	Illinois	Maxwell Garret	47	Columbia	43
1959	Navy	Andre Deladrier	72	NYU	65
1960	NYU	Hugo Castello	65	Navy	57
1961	NYU	Hugo Castello	79	Princeton	68
1962	Navy	Andre Deladrier	76	NYU	74
1963	Columbia	Irving DeKoff	55	Navy	50
1964	Princeton	Stan Sieja	81	NYU	79
1965	Columbia	Irving DeKoff	76	NYU	74
1966	NYU	Hugo Castello	5–0	Army	5–2
1967	NYU	Hugo Castello	72	Pennsylvania	64
1968	Columbia	Louis Bankuti	92	NYU	87
1969	Pennsylvania	Lajos Csiszar	54	Harvard	43
1970	NYU	Hugo Castello	71	Columbia	63
1971	NYU	Hugo Castello	68		
	Columbia	Louis Bankuti	68		
1972	Detroit	Richard Perry	73	NYU	70
1973	NYU	Hugo Castello	76	Pennsylvania	71
1974	NYU	Hugo Castello	92	Wayne St (MI)	87
1975	Wayne St (MI)	Istvan Danosi	89	Cornell	83
1976	NYU	Herbert Cohen	79	Wayne St (MI)	77
1977	Notre Dame	Michael DeCicco	114*	NYU	114
1978	Notre Dame	Michael DeCicco	121	Pennsylvania	110
1979	Wayne St (MI)	Istvan Danosi	119	Notre Dame	108
1980	Wayne St (MI)	Istvan Danosi	111	Pennsylvania	106
				MIT	106
1981	Pennsylvania	Dave Micahnik	113	Wayne St (MI)	111
1982	Wayne St (MI)	Istvan Danosi	85	Clemson	77
1983	Wayne St (MI)	Aladar Kogler	86	Notre Dame	80
1984	Wayne St (MI)	Gil Pezza	69	Penn St	50
1985	Wayne St (MI)	Gil Pezza	141	Notre Dame	140
1986	Notre Dame	Michael DeCicco	151	Columbia	141
1987	Columbia	George Kolombatovich	86	Pennsylvania	78
1988	Columbia	George Kolombatovich Aladar Kogler	90	Notre Dame	83
1989	Columbia	George Kolombatovich Aladar Kogler	88	Penn St	85

*Tie broken by a fence-off. Note: Beginning in 1990, men's and women's combined teams competed for the national championship.

INDIVIDUAL CHAMPIONS

	Foil	Sabre	Épée
1941	Edward McNamara, Northwestern	William Meyer, Dartmouth	G.H. Boland, Illinois
1942	Byron Kreiger, Wayne St (MI)	Andre Deladrier, St. John's (NY)	Ben Burtt, Ohio St
1943–46	No tournament		
1947	Abraham Balk, NYU	Oscar Parsons, Temple	Abraham Balk, NYU
1948	Albert Axelrod, CCNY	James Day, Navy	William Bryan, Navy
1949	Ralph Tedeschi, Rutgers	Alex Treves, Rutgers	Richard C. Bowman, Army
1950	Robert Nielsen, Columbia	Alex Treves, Rutgers	Thomas Stuart, Navy
1951	Robert Nielsen, Columbia	Chamberless Johnston, Princeton	Daniel Chafetz, Columbia
1952	Harold Goldsmith, CCNY	Frank Zimolzak, Navy	James Wallner, NYU
1953	Ed Nober, Brooklyn	Robert Parmacek, Pennsylvania	Jack Tori, Pennsylvania
1954	Robert Goldman, Pennsylvania	Steve Sobel, Columbia	Henry Kolowrat, Princeton
1955	Herman Velasco, Illinois	Barry Pariser, Columbia	Donald Tadrawski, Notre Dame
1956	Ralph DeMarco, Columbia	Gerald Kaufman, Columbia	Kinmont Hoitsma, Princeton
1957	Bruce Davis, Wayne St (MI)	Bernie Balaban, NYU	James Margolis, Columbia
1958	Bruce Davis, Wayne St (MI)	Art Schankin, Illinois	Roland Wommack, Navy
1959	Joe Paletta, Navy	Al Morales, Navy	Roland Wommack, Navy
1960	Gene Glazer, NYU	Mike Desaro, NYU	Gil Eisner, NYU

Men (Cont.)

INDIVIDUAL CHAMPIONS (Cont.)

Foil	Sabre	Épée
1961 ....Herbert Cohen, NYU	Israel Colon, NYU	Jerry Halpern, NYU
1962 ....Herbert Cohen, NYU	Barton Nisonson, Columbia	Thane Hawkins, Navy
1963 ....Jay Lustig, Columbia	Bela Szentivanyi, Wayne St (MI)	Larry Crum, Navy
1964 ....Bill Hicks, Princeton	Craig Bell, Illinois	Paul Pesthy, Rutgers
1965 ....Joe Nalven, Columbia	Howard Goodman, NYU	Paul Pesthy, Rutgers
1966 ....Al Davis, NYU	Paul Apostol, NYU	Bernhardt Hermann, Iowa
1967 ....Mike Gaylor, NYU	Todd Makler, Pennsylvania	George Masin, NYU
1968 ....Gerard Esponda, San Francisco	Todd Makler, Pennsylvania	Don Sieja, Cornell
1969 ....Anthony Kestler, Columbia	Norman Braslow, Penn	James Wetzler, Pennsylvania
1970 ....Walter Krause, NYU	Bruce Soriano, Columbia	John Nadas, Case Reserve
1971 ....Tyrone Simmons, Detroit	Bruce Soriano, Columbia	George Szunyogh, NYU
1972 ....Tyrone Simmons, Detroit	Bruce Soriano, Columbia	Ernesto Fernandez, Penn
1973 ....Brooke Makler, Pennsylvania	Peter Westbrock, NYU	Risto Hurme, NYU
1974 ....Greg Benko, Wayne St (MI)	Steve Danosi, Wayne St (MI)	Risto Hurme, NYU
1975 ....Greg Benko, Wayne St (MI)	Yuri Rabinovich, Wayne St (MI)	Risto Hurme, NYU
1976 ....Greg Benko, Wayne St (MI)	Brian Smith, Columbia	Randy Eggleton, Pennsylvania
1977 ....Pat Gerard, Notre Dame	Mike Sullivan, Notre Dame	Hans Wieselgren, NYU
1978 ....Ernest Simon, Wayne St (MI)	Mike Sullivan, Notre Dame	Bjorne Vaggo, Notre Dame
1979 ....Andrew Bonk, Notre Dame	Yuri Rabinovich, Wayne St (MI)	Carlos Songini, Cleveland St
1980 ....Ernest Simon, Wayne St (MI)	Paul Friedberg, Pennsylvania	Gil Pezza, Wayne St (MI)
1981 ....Ernest Simon, Wayne St (MI)	Paul Friedberg, Pennsylvania	Gil Pezza, Wayne St (MI)
1982 ....Alexander Flom, George Mason	Neil Hick, Wayne St (MI)	Peter Schifrin, San Jose St
1983 ....Demetrios Valsamis, NYU	John Friedberg, N Carolina	Ola Harstrom, Notre Dame
1984 ....Charles Higgs-Coulthard, Notre Dame	Michael Lofton, NYU	Ettore Bianchi, Wayne St (MI)
1985 ....Stephan Chauvel, Wayne St (MI)	Michael Lofton, NYU	Ettore Bianchi, Wayne St (MI)
1986 ....Adam Feldman, Penn St	Michael Lofton, NYU	Chris O'Loughlin, Pennsylvania
1987 ....William Mindel, Columbia	Michael Lofton, NYU	James O'Neill, Harvard
1988 ....Marc Kent, Columbia	Robert Cottingham, Columbia	Jon Normile, Columbia
1989 ....Edward Mufel, Penn St	Peter Cox, Penn St	Jon Normile, Columbia
1990 ....Nick Bravin, Stanford	David Mandell, Columbia	Jubba Beshin, Notre Dame
1991 ....Ben Atkins, Columbia	Vitali Nazlimov, Penn St	Marc Oshima, Columbia
1992 ....Nick Bravin, Stanford	Tom Strzalkowski, Penn St	Harald Bauder, Wayne St
1993 ....Nick Bravin, Stanford	Tom Strzalkowski, Penn St	Ben Atkins, Columbia
1994 ....Kwame van Leeuwen, Harvard	Tom Strzalkowski, Penn St	Harald Winkman, Princeton
1995 ....Sean McClain, Stanford	Paul Palestis, NYU	Mike Gattner, Lawrence
1996 ....Thorstein Becker, Wayne St (MI)	Maxim Pekarev, Princeton	Jeremy Kahn, Duke
1997 ....Cliff Bayer, Pennsylvania	Keith Smart, St. John's (NY)	Alden Clarke, Stanford
1998 ....Ayo Griffin, Yale	Luke LaValle, Notre Dame	George Hentea, St. John's (NY)

Women

TEAM CHAMPIONS

Year	Champion	Coach	Rec	Runner-Up	Rec
1982 ....Wayne St (MI)	Istvan Danosi	7–0	San Jose St	6–1
1983 ....Penn St	Beth Alphin	5–0	Wayne St (MI)	3–2
1984 ....Yale	Henry Harutunian	3–0	Penn St	2–1
1985 ....Yale	Henry Harutunian	3–0	Pennsylvania	2–1
1986 ....Pennsylvania	David Micahnik	3–0	Notre Dame	2–1
1987 ....Notre Dame	Yves Auriol	3–0	Temple	2–1
1988 ....Wayne St (MI)	Gil Pezza	3–0	Notre Dame	2–1
1989 ....Wayne St (MI)	Gil Pezza	3–0	Columbia-Barnard	2–1

Note: Beginning in 1990, men's and women's combined teams competed for the national championship.

INDIVIDUAL CHAMPIONS

Foil	Foil (Cont.)
1982.................Joy Ellingson, San Jose St	1993.................Olga Kalinovskaya, Penn St
1983.................Jana Angelakis, Penn St	1994.................Olga Kalinovskaya, Penn St
1984.................Mary Jane O'Neill, Pennsylvania	1995.................Olga Kalinovskaya, Penn St
1985.................Caitlin Bilodeaux, Columbia-Barnard	1996.................Olga Kalinovskaya, Penn St
1986.................Molly Sullivan, Notre Dame	1997.................Yelena Kalkina, Ohio St
1987.................Caitlin Bilodeaux, Columbia-Barnard	1998.................Felicia Zimmermann, Stanford
1988.................Molly Sullivan, Notre Dame	
1989.................Yasemin Topcu, Wayne St (MI)	**Épée**
1990.................Tzu Moy, Columbia-Barnard	1995.................Tina Loven, St. John's (NY)
1991.................Heidi Piper, Notre Dame	1996.................Nicole Dygert, St. John's (NY)
1992.................Olga Cheryak, Penn St	1997.................Magda Krol, Notre Dame
	1998.................Charlotte Walker, Penn St

Field Hockey

DIVISION I

Year	Champion	Coach	Score	Runner-Up
1981	Connecticut	Diane Wright	4–1	Massachusetts
1982	Old Dominion	Beth Anders	3–2	Connecticut
1983	Old Dominion	Beth Anders	3–1 (3 OT)	Connecticut
1984	Old Dominion	Beth Anders	5–1	Iowa
1985	Connecticut	Diane Wright	3–2	Old Dominion
1986	Iowa	Judith Davidson	2–1 (2 OT)	New Hampshire
1987	Maryland	Sue Tyler	2–1 (OT)	N Carolina
1988	Old Dominion	Beth Anders	2–1	Iowa
1989	N Carolina	Karen Shelton	2–1 (3 OT)*	Old Dominion
1990	Old Dominion	Beth Anders	5–0	N Carolina
1991	Old Dominion	Beth Anders	2–0	N Carolina
1992	Old Dominion	Beth Anders	4–0	Iowa
1993	Maryland	Missy Meharg	2–1 (3 OT)*	N Carolina
1994	James Madison	Christy Morgan	2–1 (3 OT)*	N Carolina
1995	N Carolina	Karen Shelton-Scroggs	5–1	Maryland
1996	N Carolina	Karen Shelton-Scroggs	3–0	Princeton
1997	N Carolina	Karen Shelton	3–2	Old Dominion

*Penalty strokes.

DIVISION II *(DISCONTINUED, THEN RENEWED)*

Year	Champion	Coach	Score	Runner-Up
1981	Pfeiffer	Ellen Briggs	5–3	Bentley
1982	Lock Haven	Sharon E. Taylor	4–1	Bloomsburg
1983	Bloomsburg	Jan Hutchinson	1–0	Lock Haven
1992	Lock Haven	Sharon E. Taylor	3–1	Bloomsburg
1993	Bloomsburg	Jan Hutchinson	2–1 (2 OT)	Lock Haven
1994	Lock Haven	Sharon E. Taylor	2–1	Bloomsburg
1995	Lock Haven	Sharon E. Taylor	1–0	Bloomsburg
1996	Bloomsburg	Jan Hutchinson	1–0	Lock Haven
1997	Bloomsburg	Jan Hutchinson	2–0	Kutztown

DIVISION III

Year	Champion	Year	Champion	Year	Champion
1981	Trenton St	1987	Bloomsburg	1993	Cortland St
1982	Ithaca	1988	Trenton St	1994	Cortland St
1983	Trenton St	1989	Lock Haven	1995	Trenton St
1984	Bloomsburg	1990	Trenton St	1996	College of New Jersey*
1985	Trenton St	1991	Trenton St	1997	William Smith
1986	Salisbury St	1992	William Smith		

*Formerly Trenton St.

Golf

Men

DIVISION I
Results, 1897–1938

Year	Champion	Site	Individual Champion
1897	Yale	Ardsley Casino	Louis Bayard Jr, Princeton
1898	Harvard (spring)		John Reid Jr, Yale
1898	Yale (fall)		James Curtis, Harvard
1899	Harvard		Percy Pyne, Princeton
1900	No tournament		
1901	Harvard	Atlantic City	H. Lindsley, Harvard
1902	Yale (spring)	Garden City	Charles Hitchcock Jr, Yale
1902	Harvard (fall)	Morris County	Chandler Egan, Harvard
1903	Harvard	Garden City	F.O. Reinhart, Princeton
1904	Harvard	Myopia	A.L. White, Harvard
1905	Yale	Garden City	Robert Abbott, Yale
1906	Yale	Garden City	W.E. Clow Jr, Yale
1907	Yale	Nassau	Ellis Knowles, Yale
1908	Yale	Brae Burn	H.H. Wilder, Harvard
1909	Yale	Apawamis	Albert Seckel, Princeton
1910	Yale	Essex County	Robert Hunter, Yale
1911	Yale	Baltusrol	George Stanley, Yale
1912	Yale	Ekwanok	F.C. Davison, Harvard
1913	Yale	Huntingdon Valley	Nathaniel Wheeler, Yale

Men (Cont.)

DIVISION I (Cont.)
Results, 1897–1938 (Cont.)

Year	Champion	Site	Individual Champion
1914	Princeton	Garden City	Edward Allis, Harvard
1915	Yale	Greenwich	Francis Blossom, Yale
1916	Princeton	Oakmont	J.W. Hubbell, Harvard
1917–18	No tournament		
1919	Princeton	Merion	A.L. Walker Jr, Columbia
1920	Princeton	Nassau	Jess Sweetster, Yale
1921	Dartmouth	Greenwich	Simpson Dean, Princeton
1922	Princeton	Garden City	Pollack Boyd, Dartmouth
1923	Princeton	Siwanoy	Dexter Cummings, Yale
1924	Yale	Greenwich	Dexter Cummings, Yale
1925	Yale	Montclair	Fred Lamprecht, Tulane
1926	Yale	Merion	Fred Lamprecht, Tulane
1927	Princeton	Garden City	Watts Gunn, Georgia Tech
1928	Princeton	Apawamis	Maurice McCarthy, Georgetown
1929	Princeton	Hollywood	Tom Aycock, Yale
1930	Princeton	Oakmont	G.T. Dunlap Jr, Princeton
1931	Yale	Olympia Fields	G.T. Dunlap Jr, Princeton
1932	Yale	Hot Springs	J.W. Fischer, Michigan
1933	Yale	Buffalo	Walter Emery, Oklahoma
1934	Michigan	Cleveland	Charles Yates, Georgia Tech
1935	Michigan	Congressional	Ed White, Texas
1936	Yale	North Shore	Charles Kocsis, Michigan
1937	Princeton	Oakmont	Fred Haas Jr, Louisiana St
1938	Stanford	Louisville	John Burke, Georgetown

Results, 1939–1998

Year	Champion	Coach	Score	Runner-Up	Score	Host or Site	Individual Champion
1939	Stanford	Eddie Twiggs	612	Northwestern	614	Wakonda	Vincent D'Antoni, Tulane
				Princeton	614		
1940	Princeton	Walter Bourne	601			Ekwanok	Dixon Brooke, Virginia
	Louisiana St	Mike Donahue	601				
1941	Stanford	Eddie Twiggs	580	Louisiana St	599	Ohio St	Earl Stewart, Louisiana St
1942	Louisiana St	Mike Donahue	590			Notre Dame	Frank Tatum Jr, Stanford
	Stanford	Eddie Twiggs	590				
1943	Yale	William Neale Jr	614	Michigan	618	Olympia Fields	Wallace Ulrich, Carleton
1944	Notre Dame	George Holderith	311	Minnesota	312	Inverness	Louis Lick, Minnesota
1945	Ohio St	Robert Kepler	602	Northwestern	621	Ohio St	John Lorms, Ohio St
1946	Stanford	Eddie Twiggs	619	Michigan	624	Princeton	George Hamer, Georgia
1947	Louisiana St	T. P. Heard	606	Duke	614	Michigan	Dave Barclay, Michigan
1948	San Jose St	Wilbur Hubbard	579	Louisiana St	588	Stanford	Bob Harris, San Jose St
1949	N Texas	Fred Cobb	590	Purdue	600	Iowa St	Harvie Ward, N Carolina
				Texas	600		
1950	N Texas	Fred Cobb	573	Purdue	577	New Mexico	Fred Wampler, Purdue
1951	N Texas	Fred Cobb	588	Ohio St	589	Ohio St	Tom Nieporte, Ohio St
1952	N Texas	Fred Cobb	587	Michigan	593	Purdue	Jim Vickers, Oklahoma
1953	Stanford	Charles Finger	578	N Carolina	580	Broadmoor	Earl Moeller, Oklahoma St
1954	SMU	Graham Ross	572	N Texas	573	Houston, Rice	Hillman Robbins, Memphis St
1955	Louisiana St	Mike Barbato	574	N Texas	583	Tennessee	Joe Campbell, Purdue
1956	Houston	Dave Williams	601	N Texas	602	Ohio St	Rick Jones, Ohio St
				Purdue	602		

Men (Cont.)

DIVISION I (Cont.)
Results, 1939–1998 (Cont.)

Year	Champion	Coach	Score	Runner-Up	Score	Host or Site	Individual Champion
1957 ....Houston	Dave Williams	602	Stanford	603	Broadmoor	Rex Baxter Jr, Houston
1958 ....Houston	Dave Williams	570	Oklahoma St	582	Williams	Phil Rodgers, Houston
1959 ....Houston	Dave Williams	561	Purdue	571	Oregon	Dick Crawford, Houston
1960 ....Houston	Dave Williams	603	Purdue	607	Broadmoor	Dick Crawford, Houston
			Oklahoma St	607		
1961 ....Purdue	Sam Voinoff	584	Arizona St	595	Lafayette	Jack Nicklaus, Ohio St
1962 ....Houston	Dave Williams	588	Oklahoma St	598	Duke	Kermit Zarley, Houston
1963 ....Oklahoma St	Labron Harris	581	Houston	582	Wichita St	R. H. Sikes, Ark
1964 ....Houston	Dave Williams	580	Oklahoma St	587	Broadmoor	Terry Small, San Jose St
1965 ....Houston	Dave Williams	577	Cal St-LA	587	Tennessee	Marty Fleckman, Houston
1966 ....Houston	Dave Williams	582	San Jose St	586	Stanford	Bob Murphy, Florida
1967 ....Houston	Dave Williams	585	Florida	588	Shawnee, PA	Hale Irwin, Colorado
1968 ....Florida	Buster Bishop	1154	Houston	1156	New Mexico St	Grier Jones, Oklahoma St
1969 ....Houston	Dave Williams	1223	Wake Forest	1232	Broadmoor	Bob Clark, Cal St-LA
1970 ....Houston	Dave Williams	1172	Wake Forest	1182	Ohio St	John Mahaffey, Houston
1971 ....Texas	George Hannon	1144	Houston	1151	Arizona	Ben Crenshaw, Texas
1972 ....Texas	George Hannon	1146	Houston	1159	Cape Coral	Ben Crenshaw, Texas Tom Kite, Texas
1973 ....Florida	Buster Bishop	1149	Oklahoma St	1159	Oklahoma St	Ben Crenshaw, Texas
1974 ....Wake Forest	Jess Haddock	1158	Florida	1160	San Diego St	Curtis Strange, Wake Forest
1975 ....Wake Forest	Jess Haddock	1156	Oklahoma St	1189	Ohio St	Jay Haas, Wake Forest
1976 ....Oklahoma St	Mike Holder	1166	Brigham Young	1173	New Mexico	Scott Simpson, Southern Cal
1977 ....Houston	Dave Williams	1197	Oklahoma St	1205	Colgate	Scott Simpson, Southern Cal
1978 ....Oklahoma St	Mike Holder	1140	Georgia	1157	Oregon	David Edwards, Oklahoma St
1979 ....Ohio St	James Brown	1189	Oklahoma St	1191	Wake Forest	Gary Hallberg, Wake Forest
1980 ....Oklahoma St	Mike Holder	1173	Brigham Young	1177	Ohio St	Jay Don Blake, Utah St
1981 ....Brigham Young	Karl Tucker	1161	Oral Roberts	1163	Stanford	Ron Commans, Southern Cal
1982 ....Houston	Dave Williams	1141	Oklahoma St	1151	Pinehurst	Billy Ray Brown, Houston
1983 ....Oklahoma St	Mike Holder	1161	Texas	1168	Fresno St	Jim Carter, Arizona St
1984 ....Houston	Dave Williams	1145	Oklahoma St	1146	Houston	John Inman, N Carolina
1985 ....Houston	Dave Williams	1172	Oklahoma St	1175	Florida	Clark Burroughs, Ohio St
1986 ....Wake Forest	Jess Haddock	1156	Oklahoma St	1160	Wake Forest	Scott Verplank, Oklahoma St
1987 ....Oklahoma St	Mike Holder	1160	Wake Forest	1176	Ohio St	Brian Watts, Oklahoma St
1988 ....UCLA	Eddie Merrins	1176	UTEP	1179	Southern Cal	E.J. Pfister, Oklahoma St
			Oklahoma	1179		
			Oklahoma St	1179		

Men (Cont.)

DIVISION I (Cont.)

Results, 1939–1998 (Cont.)

Year	Champion	Coach	Score	Runner-Up	Score	Host or Site	Individual Champion
1989	Oklahoma	Gregg Grost	1139	Texas	1158	Oklahoma Oklahoma St	Phil Mickelson, Arizona St
1990	Arizona St	Steve Loy	1155	Florida	1157	Florida	Phil Mickelson, Arizona St
1991	Oklahoma St	Mike Holder	1161	N Carolina	1168	San Jose St	Warren Schutte, UNLV
1992	Arizona	Rick LaRose	1129	Arizona St	1136	New Mexico	Phil Mickelson, Arizona St
1993	Florida	Buddy Alexander	1145	Georgia Tech	1146	Kentucky	Todd Demsey, Arizona St
1994	Stanford	Wally Goodwin	1129	Texas	1133	McKinney, TX	Justin Leonard, Texas
1995	Oklahoma St*	Mike Holder	1156	Stanford	1156	Ohio St	Chip Spratlin, Auburn
1996	Arizona St	Randy Lein	1186	UNLV	1189	TN-Chattanooga	Tiger Woods, Stanford
1997	Pepperdine	John Geiberger	1148	Wake Forest	1151	Evanston, Ill.	Charles Warren, Clemson
1998	UNLV	Dwaine Knight	1118	Clemson	1121	Albuquerque	James McLean, Minnesota

*Won sudden death playoff. Notes: Match play, 1897–1964; par-70 tournaments held in 1969, 1973 and 1989; par-71 tournaments held in 1968, 1981 and 1988; all other championships par-72 tournaments. Scores are based on 4 rounds instead of 2 after 1967.

DIVISION II

Year	Champion	Year	Champion	Year	Champion
1963	SW Missouri St	1975	UC-Irvine	1987	Tampa
1964	Southern Illinois	1976	Troy St	1988	Tampa
1965	Middle Tennessee St	1977	Troy St	1989	Columbus St
1966	Cal St-Chico	1978	Columbus St	1990	Florida Southern
1967	Lamar	1979	UC-Davis	1991	Florida Southern
1968	Lamar	1980	Columbus St	1992	Columbus St
1969	Cal St-Northridge	1981	Florida Southern	1993	Abilene Christian
1970	Rollins	1982	Florida Southern	1994	Columbus St
1971	New Orleans	1983	SW Texas St	1995	Florida Southern
1972	New Orleans	1984	Troy St	1996	Florida Southern
1973	Cal St-Northridge	1985	Florida Southern	1997	Columbus St
1974	Cal St-Northridge	1986	Florida Southern	1998	Florida Southern

Note: Par-71 tournaments held in 1967,1970, 1976-78, 1985 and 1988; par-70 tournament held in 1996; and all other championships par-72 tournaments.

DIVISION III

Year	Champion	Year	Champion	Year	Champion
1975	Wooster	1983	Allegheny	1991	Methodist (NC)
1976	Cal St-Stanislaus	1984	Cal St-Stanislaus	1992	Methodist (NC)
1977	Cal St-Stanislaus	1985	Cal St-Stanislaus	1993	UC-San Diego
1978	Cal St-Stanislaus	1986	Cal St-Stanislaus	1994	Methodist (NC)
1979	Cal St-Stanislaus	1987	Cal St-Stanislaus	1995	Methodist (NC)
1980	Cal St-Stanislaus	1988	Cal St-Stanislaus	1996	Methodist (NC)
1981	Cal St-Stanislaus	1989	Cal St-Stanislaus	1997	Methodist (NC)
1982	Rampano	1990	Methodist (NC)	1998	Methodist (NC)

Note: All championships par-72 except for 1986 and 1988, which were par-71; fourth round of 1975 championships canceled as a result of bad weather, first round of 1988 championships canceled as a result of rain.

Women

DIVISION I

Year	Champion	Coach	Score	Runner-Up	Score	Individual Champion
1982	Tulsa	Dale McNamara	1191	Texas Christian	1227	Kathy Baker, Tulsa
1983	Texas Christian	Fred Warren	1193	Tulsa	1196	Penny Hammel, Miami (FL)
1984	Miami (FL)	Lela Cannon	1214	Arizona St	1221	Cindy Schreyer, Georgia
1985	Florida	Mimi Ryan	1218	Tulsa	1233	Danielle Ammaccapane, Arizona St

Golf (Cont.)

Women (Cont.)
DIVISION I (Cont.)

Year	Champion	Coach	Score	Runner-Up	Score	Individual Champion
1986	Florida	Mimi Ryan	1180	Miami (FL)	1188	Page Dunlap, Florida
1987	San Jose St	Mark Gale	1187	Furman	1188	Caroline Keggi, New Mexico
1988	Tulsa	Dale McNamara	1175	Georgia	1182	Melissa McNamara, Tulsa
				Arizona	1182	
1989	San Jose St	Mark Gale	1208	Tulsa	1209	Pat Hurst, San Jose St
1990	Arizona St	Linda Vollstedt	1206	UCLA	1222	Susan Slaughter, Arizona
1991	UCLA*	Jackie Steinmann	1197	San Jose St	1197	Annika Sorenstam, Arizona
1992	San Jose St	Mark Gale	1171	Arizona	1175	Vicki Goetze, Georgia
1993	Arizona St	Linda Vollstedt	1187	Texas	1189	Charlotta Sorenstam, Texas
1994	Arizona St	Linda Vollstedt	1189	Southern Cal	1205	Emilee Klein, Arizona St
1995	Arizona St	Linda Vollstedt	1155	San Jose St	1181	Kristel Mourgue d'Algue, Arizona St
1996	Arizona*	Rick LaRose	1240	San Jose St	1240	Marisa Baena, Arizona
1997	Arizona St	Linda Vollstedt	1178	San Jose St	1180	Heather Bowie, Texas
1998	Arizona St	Linda Vollstedt	1155	Florida	1173	Jennifer Rosales, USC

*Won sudden death playoff. Note: Par-74 tournaments held in 1983 and 1988; par-72 tournament held in 1990; all other championships par-73 tournaments.

DIVISIONS II AND III

Year	Champion	Year	Champion	Year	Champion
1996	Methodist (NC)	1997	Lynn	1998	Methodist (NC)

Gymnastics

Men
TEAM CHAMPIONS

Year	Champion	Coach	Pts	Runner-Up	Pts
1938	Chicago	Dan Hoffer	22	Illinois	18
1939	Illinois	Hartley Price	21	Army	17
1940	Illinois	Hartley Price	20	Navy	17
1941	Illinois	Hartley Price	68.5	Minnesota	52.5
1942	Illinois	Hartley Price	39	Penn St	30
1943–47	No tournament				
1948	Penn St	Gene Wettstone	55	Temple	34.5
1949	Temple	Max Younger	28	Minnesota	18
1950	Illinois	Charley Pond	26	Temple	25
1951	Florida St	Hartley Price	26	Illinois	23.5
				Southern Cal	23.5
1952	Florida St	Hartley Price	89.5	Southern Cal	75
1953	Penn St	Gene Wettstone	91.5	Illinois	68
1954	Penn St	Gene Wettstone	137	Illinois	68
1955	Illinois	Charley Pond	82	Penn St	69
1956	Illinois	Charley Pond	123.5	Penn St	67.5
1957	Penn St	Gene Wettstone	88.5	Illinois	80
1958	Michigan St	George Szypula	79		
	Illinois	Charley Pond	79		
1959	Penn St	Gene Wettstone	152	Illinois	87.5
1960	Penn St	Gene Wettstone	112.5	Southern Cal	65.5
1961	Penn St	Gene Wettstone	88.5	Southern Illinois	80.5
1962	Southern Cal	Jack Beckner	95.5	Southern Illinois	75
1963	Michigan	Newton Loken	129	Southern Illinois	73
1964	Southern Illinois	Bill Meade	84.5	Southern Cal	69.5
1965	Penn St	Gene Wettstone	68.5	Washington	51.5
1966	Southern Illinois	Bill Meade	187.200	California	185.100
1967	Southern Illinois	Bill Meade	189.550	Michigan	187.400
1968	California	Hal Frey	188.250	Southern Illinois	188.150
1969	Iowa	Mike Jacobson	161.175	Penn St	160.450
	Michigan*	Newton Loken		Colorado St	
1970	Michigan	Newton Loken	164.150	Iowa St	164.050
				New Mexico St	
1971	Iowa St	Ed Gagnier	319.075	Southern Illinois	316.650

*Trampoline.

Men (Cont.)
TEAM CHAMPIONS (Cont.)

Year	Champion	Coach	Pts	Runner-Up	Pts
1972	Southern Illinois	Bill Meade	315.925	Iowa St	312.325
1973	Iowa St	Ed Gagnier	325.150	Penn St	323.025
1974	Iowa St	Ed Gagnier	326.100	Arizona St	322.050
1975	California	Hal Frey	437.325	Louisiana St	433.700
1976	Penn St	Gene Wettstone	432.075	Louisiana St	425.125
1977	Indiana St	Roger Counsil	434.475		
	Oklahoma	Paul Ziert	434.475		
1978	Oklahoma	Paul Ziert	439.350	Arizona St	437.075
1979	Nebraska	Francis Allen	448.275	Oklahoma	446.625
1980	Nebraska	Francis Allen	563.300	Iowa St	557.650
1981	Nebraska	Francis Allen	284.600	Oklahoma	281.950
1982	Nebraska	Francis Allen	285.500	UCLA	281.050
1983	Nebraska	Francis Allen	287.800	UCLA	283.900
1984	UCLA	Art Shurlock	287.300	Penn St	281.250
1985	Ohio St	Michael Willson	285.350	Nebraska	284.550
1986	Arizona St	Don Robinson	283.900	Nebraska	283.600
1987	UCLA	Art Shurlock	285.300	Nebraska	284.750
1988	Nebraska	Francis Allen	288.150	Illinois	287.150
1989	Illinois	Yoshi Hayasaki	283.400	Nebraska	282.300
1990	Nebraska	Francis Allen	287.400	Minnesota	287.300
1991	Oklahoma	Greg Buwick	288.025	Penn St	285.500
1992	Stanford	Sadao Hamada	289.575	Nebraska	288.950
1993	Stanford	Sadao Hamada	276.500	Nebraska	275.500
1994	Nebraska	Francis Allen	288.250	Stanford	285.925
1995	Stanford	Sadao Hamada	232.400	Nebraska	231.525
1996	Ohio St	Peter Kormann	232.150	California	231.775
1997	California	Barry Weiner	233.825	Oklahoma	232.725
1998	Caliornia	Barry Weiner	231.200	Iowa	229.675

INDIVIDUAL CHAMPIONS

ALL-AROUND

1938.....Joe Giallombardo, Illinois
1939.....Joe Giallombardo, Illinois
1940.....Joe Giallombardo, Illinois
Paul Fina, Illinois
1941.....Courtney Shanken, Chicago
1942.....Newt Loken, Minnesota
1948.....Ray Sorenson, Penn St
1949.....Joe Kotys, Kent
1950.....Joe Kotys, Kent
1951.....Bill Roetzheim, Florida St
1952.....Jack Beckner, Southern Cal
1953.....Jean Cronstedt, Penn St
1954.....Jean Cronstedt, Penn St
1955.....Karl Schwenzfeier, Penn St
1956.....Don Tonry, Illinois
1957.....Armando Vega, Penn St
1958.....Abie Grossfeld, Illinois
1959.....Armando Vega, Penn St
1960.....Jay Werner, Penn St
1961.....Gregor Weiss, Penn St
1962.....Robert Lynn, Southern Cal
1963.....Gil Larose, Michigan
1964.....Ron Barak, Southern Cal
1965.....Mike Jacobson, Penn St
1966.....Steve Cohen, Penn St
1967.....Steve Cohen, Penn St
1968.....Makoto Sakamoto, USC
1969.....Mauno Nissinen, Wash
1970.....Yoshi Hayasaki, Wash
1971.....Yoshi Hayasaki, Wash
1972.....Steve Hug, Stanford
1973.....Steve Hug, Stanford
Marshall Avener, Penn St

1974.....Steve Hug, Stanford
1975.....Wayne Young, BYU
1976.....Peter Kormann, Southern Conn St
1977.....Kurt Thomas, Indiana St
1978.....Bart Conner, Oklahoma
1979.....Kurt Thomas, Indiana St
1980.....Jim Hartung, Nebraska
1981.....Jim Hartung, Nebraska
1982.....Peter Vidmar, UCLA
1983.....Peter Vidmar, UCLA
1984.....Mitch Gaylord, UCLA
1985.....Wes Suter, Nebraska
1986.....Jon Louis, Stanford
1987.....Tom Schlesinger, Nebraska
1988.....Vacated†
1989.....Patrick Kirsey, Nebraska
1990.....Mike Racanelli, Ohio St
1991.....John Roethlisberger, Minn
1992.....John Roethlisberger, Minn
1993.....John Roethlisberger, Minn
1994.....Dennis Harrison, Nebraska
1995.....Richard Grace, Nebraska
1996.....Blaine Wilson, Ohio St
1997.....Blaine Wilson, Ohio St
1998.....Travis Romagnoli, Illinois

HORIZONTAL BAR

1938.....Bob Sears, Army
1939.....Adam Walters, Temple
1940.....Norm Boardman, Temple
1941.....Newt Loken, Minnesota
1942.....Norm Boardman, Temple
1948.....Joe Calvetti, Illinois
1949.....Bob Stout, Temple

1950.....Joe Kotys, Kent
1951.....Bill Roetzheim, Florida St
1952.....Charles Simms, USC
1953.....Hal Lewis, Navy
1954.....Jean Cronstedt, Penn St
1955.....Carlton Rintz, Michigan St
1956.....Ronnie Amster, Florida St
1957.....Abie Grossfeld, Illinois
1958.....Abie Grossfeld, Illinois
1959.....Stanley Tarshis, Mich St
1960.....Stanley Tarshis, Mich St
1961.....Bruno Klaus, Southern Ill
1962.....Robert Lynn, USC
1963.....Gil Larose, Michigan
1964.....Ron Barak, USC
1965.....Jim Curzi, Michigan St
Mike Jacobsen, Penn St
1966.....Rusty Rock, Cal St-Northridge
1967.....Rich Grigsby, Cal St-Northridge
1968.....Makoto Sakamoto, USC
1969.....Bob Manna, New Mexico
1970.....Yoshi Hayasaki, Wash
1971.....Brent Simmons, Iowa St
1972.....Tom Lindner, Souhern Ill
1973.....Jon Aitken, New Mexico
1974.....Rick Banley, Indiana St
1975.....Rich Larsen, Iowa St
1976.....Tom Beach, California
1977.....John Hart, UCLA
1978.....Mel Cooley, Washington
1979.....Kurt Thomas, Indiana St
1980.....Philip Cahoy, Nebraska

Men (Cont.)

INDIVIDUAL CHAMPIONS (Cont.)

HORIZONTAL BAR (Cont.)

1981.....Philip Cahoy, Nebraska
1982.....Peter Vidmar, UCLA
1983.....Scott Johnson, Nebraska
1984.....Charles Lakes, Illinois
1985.....Dan Hayden, Arizona St
       Wes Suter, Nebraska
1986.....Dan Hayden, Arizona St
1987.....David Moriel, UCLA
1988.....Vacated†
1989.....Vacated†
1990.....Chris Waller, UCLA
1991.....Luis Lopez, New Mexico
1992.....Jair Lynch, Stanford
1993.....Steve McCain, UCLA
1994.....Jim Foody, UCLA
1995.....Rick Kieffer, Nebraska
1996.....Carl Imhauser, Temple
1997.....Marshall Nelson, Nebraska
1998.....Todd Bishop, Oklahoma

PARALLEL BARS

1938.....Erwin Beyer, Chicago
1939.....Bob Sears, Army
1940.....Bob Hanning, Minnesota
1941.....Caton Cobb, Illinois
1942.....Hal Zimmerman, Penn St
1948.....Ray Sorenson, Penn St
1949.....Joe Kotys, Kent
       Mel Stout, Michigan St
1950.....Joe Kotys, Kent
1951.....Jack Beckner, USC
1952.....Jack Beckner, USC
1953.....Jean Cronstedt, Penn St
1954.....Jean Cronstedt, Penn St
1955.....Carlton Rintz, Michigan St
1956.....Armando Vega, Penn St
1957.....Armando Vega, Penn St
1958.....Tad Muzyczko, Mich St
1959.....Armando Vega, Penn St
1960.....Robert Lynn, Southern Cal
1961.....Fred Tijerina, Southern Ill
       Jeff Cardinalli, Springfield
1962.....Robert Lynn, Southern Cal
1963.....Arno Lascari, Michigan
1964.....Ron Barak, Southern Cal
1965.....Jim Curzi, Michigan St
1966.....Jim Curzi, Michigan St
1967.....Makoto Sakamoto, USC
1968.....Makoto Sakamoto, USC
1969.....Ron Rapper, Michigan
1970.....Ron Rapper, Michigan
1971.....Brent Simmons, Iowa St
       Tom Dunn, Penn St
1972.....Dennis Mazur, Iowa St
1973.....Steve Hug, Stanford
1974.....Steve Hug, Stanford
1975.....Yoichi Tomita, Long
       Beach St
1976.....Gene Whelan, Penn St
1977.....Kurt Thomas, Indiana St
1978.....John Corritore, Michigan
1979.....Kurt Thomas, Indiana St
1980.....Philip Cahoy, Nebraska
1981.....Philip Cahoy, Nebraska
       Peter Vidmar, UCLA
       Jim Hartung, Nebraska
1982.....Jim Hartung, Nebraska

1983.....Scott Johnson, Nebraska
1984.....Tim Daggett, UCLA
1985.....Dan Hayden, Arizona St
       Noah Riskin, Ohio St
       Seth Riskin, Ohio St
1986.....Dan Hayden, Arizona St
1987.....Kevin Davis, Nebraska
       Tom Schlesinger, Nebraska
1988.....Kevin Davis, Nebraska
1989.....Vacated†
1990.....Patrick Kirksey, Nebraska
1991.....Scott Keswick, UCLA
       John Roethlisberger, Minn
1992.....Dom Minicucci, Temple
1993.....Jair Lynch, Stanford
1994.....Richard Grace, Nebraska
1995.....Richard Grace, Nebraska
1996.....Jamie Ellis, Stanford
       Blaine Wilson, Ohio St
1997.....Marshall Nelson, Nebraska
1998.....Marshall Nelson, Nebraska

VAULT

1938.....Erwin Beyer, Chicago
1939.....Marv Forman, Illinois
1940.....Earl Shanken, Chicago
1941.....Earl Shanken, Chicago
1942.....Earl Shanken, Chicago
1948.....Jim Peterson, Minnesota
1962.....Bruno Klaus, Southern Ill
1963.....Gil Larose, Michigan
1964.....Sidney Oglesby, Syracuse
1965.....Dan Millman, Berkeley
1966.....Frank Schmitz, S Illinois
1967.....Paul Mayer, S Illinois
1968.....Bruce Colter, Cal St-Los
       Angeles
1969.....Dan Bowles, California
       Jack McCarthy, Illinois
1970.....Doug Boger, Arizona
1971.....Pat Mahoney, Cal St-
       Northridge
1972.....Gary Morava, Southern Ill
1973.....John Crosby, S Conn St
1974.....Greg Goodhue, Oklahoma
1975.....Tom Beach, California
1976.....Sam Shaw, Cal St-
       Fullerton
1977.....Steve Wejmar, Wash
1978.....Ron Galimore, Louisiana St
1979.....Leslie Moore, Oklahoma
1980.....Ron Galimore, Iowa St
1981.....Ron Galimore, Iowa St
1982.....Randall Wickstrom, Cal
       Steve Elliott, Nebraska
1983.....Chris Riegel, Nebraska
       Mark Oates, Oklahoma
1984.....Chris Riegel, Nebraska
1985.....Derrick Cornelius,
       Cortland St
1986.....Chad Fox, New Mexico
1987.....Chad Fox, New Mexico
1988.....Chad Fox, New Mexico
1989.....Chad Fox, New Mexico
1990.....Brad Hayashi, UCLA
1991.....Adam Carton, Penn St
1992.....Jason Hebert, Syracuse
1993.....Steve Wiegel, N Mexico

1994.....Steve McCain, UCLA
1995.....Ian Bachrach, Stanford
1996.....Jay Thornton, Iowa
1997.....Blaine Wilson, Ohio St
1998.....Travis Romagnoli, Illinois

POMMEL HORSE

1938.....Erwin Beyer, Chicago
1939.....Erwin Beyer, Chicago
1940.....Harry Koehnemann, Illinois
1941.....Caton Cobb, Illinois
1942.....Caton Cobb, Illinois
1948.....Steve Greene, Penn St
1949.....Joe Berenato, Temple
1950.....Gene Rabbitt, Syracuse
1951.....Joe Kotys, Kent
1952.....Frank Bare, Illinois
1953.....Carlton Rintz, Michigan St
1954.....Robert Lawrence, Penn St
1955.....Carlton Rintz, Michigan St
1956.....James Brown, Cal St-
       Los Angeles
1957.....John Davis, Illinois
1958.....Bill Buck, Iowa
1959.....Art Shurlock, California
1960.....James Fairchild, California
1961.....James Fairchild, California
1962.....Mike Aufrecht, Illinois
1963.....Russ Mills, Yale
1964.....Russ Mills, Yale
1965.....Bob Elsinger, Springfield
1966.....Gary Hoskins, Cal St-
       Los Angeles
1967.....Keith McCanless, Iowa
1968.....Jack Ryan, Colorado
1969.....Keith McCanless, Iowa
1970.....Russ Hoffman, Iowa St
       John Russo, Wisconsin
1971.....Russ Hoffman, Iowa St
1972.....Russ Hoffman, Iowa St
1973.....Ed Slezak, Indiana St
1974.....Ted Marcy, Stanford
1975.....Ted Marcy, Stanford
1976.....Ted Marcy, Stanford
1977.....Chuck Walter, New Mexico
1978.....Mike Burke, Northern Ill
1979.....Mike Burke, Northern Ill
1980.....David Stoldt, Illinois
1981.....Mark Bergman, California
       Steve Jennings, New Mexico
1982.....Peter Vidmar, UCLA
       Steve Jennings, New Mexico
1983.....Doug Kieso, Northern Ill
1984.....Tim Daggett, UCLA
1985.....Tony Pineda, UCLA
1986.....Curtis Holdsworth, UCLA
1987.....Li Xiao Ping, Cal St-
       Fullerton
1988.....Vacated†
       Mark Sohn, Penn St
1989.....Mark Sohn, Penn St
       Chris Waller, UCLA
1990.....Mark Sohn, Penn St
1991.....Mark Sohn, Penn St
1992.....Che Bowers, Nebraska
1993.....John Roethlisberger, Minn
1994.....Jason Bertram, California
1995.....Drew Durbin, Ohio St

Men (Cont.)
INDIVIDUAL CHAMPIONS (Cont.)

POMMEL HORSE (Cont.)
1996.....Drew Durbin, Ohio St
1997.....Drew Durbin, Ohio St
1998.....Josh Birckelbaw, California

FLOOR EXERCISE
1941.....Lou Fina, Illinois
1953.....Bob Sullivan, Illinois
1954.....Jean Cronstedt, Penn St
1955.....Don Faber, UCLA
1956.....Jamile Ashmore, Florida St
1957.....Norman Marks, Cal St-
     Los Angeles
1958.....Abie Grossfeld, Illinois
1959.....Don Tonry, Illinois
1960.....Ray Hadley, Illinois
1961.....Robert Lynn, Southern Cal
1962.....Robert Lynn, Southern Cal
1963.....Tom Seward, Penn St
     Mike Henderson, Michigan
1964.....Rusty Mitchell, S Illinois
1965.....Frank Schmitz, S Illinois
1966.....Frank Schmitz, S Illinois
1967.....Dave Jacobs, Michigan
1968.....Toby Towson, Michigan St
1969.....Toby Towson, Michigan St
1970.....Tom Proulx, Colorado St
1971.....Stormy Eaton, New Mexico
1972.....Odessa Lovin, Oklahoma
1973.....Odessa Lovin, Oklahoma
1974.....Doug Fitzjarrell, Iowa St
1975.....Kent Brown, Arizona St
1976.....Bob Robbins, Colorado St
1977.....Ron Galimore, Louisiana St

1978.....Curt Austin, Iowa St
1979.....Mike Wilson, Oklahoma
     Bart Conner, Oklahoma
1980.....Steve Elliott, Nebraska
1981.....James Yuhashi, Oregon
1982.....Steve Elliott, Nebraska
1983.....Scott Johnson, Nebraska
     David Branch, Arizona St
     Donnie Hinton, Arizona St
1984.....Kevin Ekburg, Northern Ill
1985.....Wes Suter, Nebraska
1986.....Jerry Burrell, Arizona St
     Brian Ginsberg, UCLA
1987.....Chad Fox, New Mexico
1988.....Chris Wyatt, Temple
1989.....Jody Newman, Arizona St
1990.....Mike Racanelli, Ohio St
1991.....Brad Hayashi, UCLA
1992.....Brian Winkler, Michigan
1993.....Richard Grace, Nebraska
1994.....Mark Booth, Stanford
1995.....Jay Thornton, Iowa
1996.....Ian Bachrach, Stanford
1997.....Jeremy Killen, Oklahoma
1998.....Darin Gerlach, Temple

RINGS
1959.....Armando Vega, Penn St
1960.....Sam Garcia, Southern Cal
1961.....Fred Orlofsky, Southern Ill
1962.....Dale Cooper, Michigan St
1963.....Dale Cooper, Michigan St
1964.....Chris Evans, Arizona St
1965.....Glenn Gailis, Iowa
1966.....Ed Gunny, Michigan St

1967.....Josh Robison, California
1968.....Pat Arnold, Arizona
1969.....Paul Vexler, Penn St
     Ward Maythaler, Iowa St
1970.....Dave Seal, Indiana St
1971.....Charles Ropiequet, S Illinois
1972.....Dave Seal, Indiana St
1973.....Bob Mahorney, Indiana St
1974.....Keith Heaver, Iowa St
1975.....Keith Heaver, Iowa St
1976.....Doug Wood, Iowa St
1977.....Doug Wood, Iowa St
1978.....Scott McEldowney, Oregon
1979.....Kirk Mango, Northern Ill
1980.....Jim Hartung, Nebraska
1981.....Jim Hartung, Nebraska
1982.....Jim Hartung, Nebraska
1983.....Alex Schwartz, UCLA
1984.....Tim Daggett, UCLA
1985.....Mark Diab, Iowa St
1986.....Mark Diab, Iowa St
1987.....Paul O'Neill, Hou. Baptist
1988.....Paul O'Neill, New Mexico
1989.....Vacated†
     Paul O'Neill, New Mexico
1990.....Wayne Cowden, Penn St
1991.....Adam Carton, Penn St
1992.....Scott Keswick, UCLA
1993.....Chris LaMorte, N Mexico
1994.....Chris LaMorte, N Mexico
1995.....Dave Frank, Temple
1996.....Scott McCall, Will. & Mary
     Blaine Wilson, Ohio St
1997.....Blaine Wilson, Ohio St
1998.....Dan Fink, Oklahoma

† Championships won by Miguel Rubio (All Around, 1988; Horizontal Bar, 1988-89) and Alfonso Rodriguez (Pommel Horse, 1988; Rings, 1989; Parallel Bars, 1989) were vacated by action of the NCAA Committee on Infractions.

DIVISION II (DISCONTINUED)

Year	Champion	Coach	Pts	Runner-Up	Pts
1968	Cal St-Northridge	Bill Vincent	179.400	Springfield	178.050
1969	Cal St-Northridge	Bill Vincent	151.800	Southern Connecticut St	145.075
1970	Northwestern Louisiana	Armando Vega	160.250	Southern Connecticut St	159.300
1971	Cal St-Fullerton	Dick Wolfe	158.150	Springfield	156.987
1972	Cal St-Fullerton	Dick Wolfe	160.550	Southern Connecticut St	153.050
1973	Southern Connecticut St	Abe Grossfeld	160.750	Cal St-Northridge	158.700
1974	Cal St-Fullerton	Dick Wolfe	309.800	Southern Connecticut St	309.400
1975	Southern Connecticut St	Abe Grossfeld	411.650	IL-Chicago	398.800
1976	Southern Connecticut St	Abe Grossfeld	419.200	IL-Chicago	388.850
1977	Springfield	Frank Wolcott	395.950	Cal St-Northridge	381.250
1978	IL-Chicago	C. Johnson/A. Gentile	406.850	Cal St-Northridge	400.400
1979	IL-Chicago	Clarence Johnson	418.550	WI-Oshkosh	385.650
1980	WI-Oshkosh	Ken Allen	260.550	Cal St-Chico	256.050
1981	WI-Oshkosh	Ken Allen	209.500	Springfield	201.550
1982	WI-Oshkosh	Ken Allen	216.050	E Stroudsburg	211.200
1983	East Stroudsburg	Bruno Klaus	258.650	WI-Oshkosh	257.850
1984	East Stroudsburg	Bruno Klaus	270.800	Cortland St	246.350

Women
TEAM CHAMPIONS

Year	Champion	Coach	Pts	Runner-Up	Pts
1982	Utah	Greg Marsden	148.60	Cal St-Fullerton	144.10
1983	Utah	Greg Marsden	184.65	Arizona St	183.30
1984	Utah	Greg Marsden	186.05	UCLA	185.55
1985	Utah	Greg Marsden	188.35	Arizona St	186.60
1986	Utah	Greg Marsden	186.95	Arizona St	186.70

Women (Cont.)
TEAM CHAMPIONS (Cont.)

Year	Champion	Coach	Pts	Runner-Up	Pts
1987	Georgia	Suzanne Yoculan	187.90	Utah	187.55
1988	Alabama	Sarah Patterson	190.05	Utah	189.50
1989	Georgia	Suzanne Yoculan	192.65	UCLA	192.60
1990	Utah	Greg Marsden	194.900	Alabama	194.575
1991	Alabama	Sarah Patterson	195.125	Utah	194.375
1992	Utah	Greg Marsden	195.650	Georgia	194.600
1993	Georgia	Suzanne Yoculan	198.000	Alabama	196.825
1994	Utah	Greg Marsden	196.400	Alabama	196.350
1995	Utah	Greg Marsden	196.650	Alabama	196.425
				Michigan	196.425
1996	Alabama	Sarah Patterson	198.025	UCLA	197.475
1997	UCLA	Valorie Kondos	197.150	Arizona St	196.850
1998	Georgia	Suzanne Yoculan	197.725	Florida	196.350

INDIVIDUAL CHAMPIONS

ALL-AROUND
1982.....Sue Stednitz, Utah
1983.....Megan McCunniff, Utah
1984......Megan McCunniff-Marsden, Utah
1985.....Penney Hauschild, Alabama
1986.......Penney Hauschild, Alabama
Jackie Brummer, Arizona St
1987.....Kelly Garrison-Steves, Oklahoma
1988.....Kelly Garrison-Steves, Oklahoma
1989.....Corrinne Wright, Georgia
1990.....Dee Dee Foster, Alabama
1991.....Hope Spivey, Georgia
1992.....Missy Marlowe, Utah
1993.....Jenny Hansen, Kentucky
1994.....Jenny Hansen, Kentucky
1995.....Jenny Hansen, Kentucky
1996.....Meredith Willard, Alabama
1997.....Kim Arnold, Georgia
1998.....Kim Arnold, Georgia

VAULT
1982.....Elaine Alfano, Utah
1983.....Elaine Alfano, Utah
1984.....Megan Marsden, Utah
1985.....Elaine Alfano, Utah
1986.....Kim Neal, Arizona St
Pam Loree, Penn St
1987.....Yumi Mordre, Washington
1988.....Jill Andrews, UCLA
1989.....Kim Hamilton, UCLA
1990.....Michele Bryant, Nebraska
1991.....Anna Basaldva, Arizona
1992.....Tammy Marshall, Mass.
Heather Stepp, Georgia
Kristein Kenoyer, Utah
1993.....Heather Stepp, Georgia
1994.....Jenny Hansen, Kentucky
1995.....Jenny Hansen, Kentucky
1996.....Leah Brown, Georgia
1997.....Susan Hines, Florida
1998.....Susan Hines, Florida

BALANCE BEAM
1982.....Sue Stednitz, Utah
1983.....Julie Goewey, Cal St-Fullerton
1984.....Heidi Anderson, Oregon St
1985.....Lisa Zeis, Arizona St
1986.....Jackie Brummer, Arizona St
1987.....Yumi Mordre, Washington
1988.....Kelly Garrison-Steves, Oklahoma
1989.....Jill Andrews, UCLA
Joy Selig, Oregon St
1990.....Joy Selig, Oregon St
1991.....Missy Marlowe, Utah
1992.....Missy Marlowe, Utah
Dana Dobransky, Alabama
1993.....Dana Dobransky, Alabama
1994.....Jenny Hansen, Kentucky
1995.....Jenny Hansen, Kentucky
1996.....Summer Reid, Utah
1997.....Summer Reid, Utah
Elizabeth Reid, Arizona St
1998.....Larissa Fontaine, Stanford
Susan Hines, Florida

FLOOR EXERCISE
1982.....Mary Ayotte-Law, Oregon St
1983.....Kim Neal, Arizona St
1984.....Maria Anz, Florida
1985.....Lisa Mitzel, Utah
1986.....Lisa Zeis, Arizona St
Penney Hauschild, Alabama
1987.....Kim Hamilton, UCLA
1988.....Kim Hamilton, UCLA
1989.....Corrinne Wright, Georgia
Kim Hamilton, UCLA
1990.....Joy Selig, Oregon St
1991.....Hope Spivey, Georgia
1992.....Missy Marlowe, Utah
1993.....Heather Stepp, Georgia

Tammy Marshall, Mass.
Amy Durham, Oregon St
1994.....Hope Spivey-Sheeley, Georgia
1995.....Jenny Hansen, Kentucky
Stella Umeh, UCLA
Leslie Angeles, Georgia
1996.....Heidi Hornbeek, Arizona
Kim Kelly, Alabama
1997.....Leah Brown, Georgia
1998.....Kim Arnold, Georgia
Jenni Beathard, Georgia
Betsy Hamm, Florida

UNEVEN BARS
1982.....Lisa Shirk, Pittsburgh
1983.....Jeri Cameron, Arizona St
1984.....Jackie Brummer, Arizona St
1985.....Penney Hauschild, Alabama
1986.....Lucy Wener, Georgia
1987.....Lucy Wener, Georgia
1988.....Kelly Garrison-Steves, Oklahoma
1989.....Lucy Wener, Georgia
1990.....Marie Roethlisberger, Minnesota
1991.....Kelly Macy, Georgia
1992.....Missy Marlowe, Utah
1993.....Agina Simpkins, Georgia
Beth Wymer, Michigan
1994.....Sandy Woolsey, Utah
Beth Wymer, Michigan
Lori Strong, Georgia
1995.....Beth Wymer, Michigan
1996.....Stephanie Woods, Alabama
1997.....Jenni Beathard, Georgia
1998.....Karin Lichey, Georgia
Stella Umeh, UCLA

DIVISION II (DISCONTINUED)

Year	Champion	Coach	Pts	Runner-Up	Pts
1982	Cal St-Northridge	Donna Stuart	138.10	Jacksonville St	134.05
1983	Denver	Dan Garcia	174.80	Cal St-Northridge	174.35
1984	Jacksonville St	Robert Dillard	173.40	SE Missouri St	171.45
1985	Jacksonville St	Robert Dillard	176.85	SE Missouri St	173.95
1986	Seattle Pacific	Laurel Tindall	175.80	Jacksonville St	175.15

DIVISION I

Year	Champion	Coach	Score	Runner-Up	Most Outstanding Player
1948	Michigan	Vic Heyliger	8–4	Dartmouth	Joe Riley, Dartmouth, F
1949	Boston Coll.	John Kelley	4–3	Dartmouth	Dick Desmond, Dartmouth, G
1950	Colorado Coll.	Cheddy Thompson	13–4	Boston U	Ralph Bevins, Boston U, G
1951	Michigan	Vic Heyliger	7–1	Brown	Ed Whiston, Brown, G
1952	Michigan	Vic Heyliger	4–1	Colorado Coll.	Kenneth Kinsley, Colorado Coll., G
1953	Michigan	Vic Heyliger	7–3	Minnesota	John Matchefts, Michigan, F
1954	Rensselaer	Ned Harkness	5–4 (OT)	Minnesota	Abbie Moore, Rensselaer, F
1955	Michigan	Vic Heyliger	5–3	Colorado Coll.	Philip Hilton, Colorado Coll., D
1956	Michigan	Vic Heyliger	7–5	Michigan Tech	Lorne Howes, Michigan, G
1957	Colorado Coll.	Thomas Bedecki	13–6	Michigan	Bob McCusker, Colorado Coll., F
1958	Denver	Murray Armstrong	6–2	N Dakota	Murray Massier, Denver, F
1959	N Dakota	Bob May	4–3 (OT)	Michigan St	Reg Morelli, N Dakota, F
1960	Denver	Murray Armstrong	5–3	Michigan Tech	Bob Marquis, Boston U, F
1961	Denver	Murray Armstrong	12–2	St. Lawrence	Barry Urbanski, Boston U, G
1962	Michigan Tech	John MacInnes	7–1	Clarkson	Louis Angotti, Michigan Tech, F
1963	N Dakota	Barney Thorndycraft	6–5	Denver	Al McLean, N Dakota, F
1964	Michigan	Allen Renfrew	6–3	Denver	Bob Gray, Michigan, G
1965	Michigan Tech	John MacInnes	8–2	Boston Coll.	Gary Milroy, Michigan Tech, F
1966	Michigan St	Amo Bessone	6–1	Clarkson	Gaye Cooley, Michigan St, G
1967	Cornell	Ned Harkness	4–1	Boston U	Walt Stanowski, Cornell, D
1968	Denver	Murray Armstrong	4–0	N Dakota	Gerry Powers, Denver, G
1969	Denver	Murray Armstrong	4–3	Cornell	Keith Magnuson, Denver, D
1970	Cornell	Ned Harkness	6–4	Clarkson	Daniel Lodboa, Cornell, D
1971	Boston U	Jack Kelley	4–2	Minnesota	Dan Brady, Boston U, G
1972	Boston U	Jack Kelley	4–0	Cornell	Tim Regan, Boston U, G
1973	Wisconsin	Bob Johnson	4–2	Vacated	Dean Talafous, Wisconsin, F
1974	Minnesota	Herb Brooks	4–2	Michigan Tech	Brad Shelstad, Minnesota, G
1975	Michigan Tech	John MacInnes	6–1	Minnesota	Jim Warden, Michigan Tech, G
1976	Minnesota	Herb Brooks	6–4	Michigan Tech	Tom Vanelli, Minnesota, F
1977	Wisconsin	Bob Johnson	6–5 (OT)	Michigan	Julian Baretta, Wisconsin, G
1978	Boston U	Jack Parker	5–3	Boston Coll.	Jack O'Callahan, Boston U, D
1979	Minnesota	Herb Brooks	4–3	N Dakota	Steve Janaszak, Minnesota, G
1980	N Dakota	John Gasparini	5–2	Northern Michigan	Doug Smail, N Dakota, F
1981	Wisconsin	Bob Johnson	6–3	Minnesota	Marc Behrend, Wisconsin, G
1982	N Dakota	John Gasparini	5–2	Wisconsin	Phil Sykes, N Dakota, F
1983	Wisconsin	Jeff Sauer	6–2	Harvard	Marc Behrend, Wisconsin, G
1984	Bowling Green	Jerry York	5–4 (OT)	MN-Duluth	Gary Kruzich, Bowling Green, G
1985	Rensselaer	Mike Addesa	2–1	Providence	Chris Terreri, Providence, G
1986	Michigan St	Ron Mason	6–5	Harvard	Mike Donnelly, Michigan St, F
1987	N Dakota	John Gasparini	5–3	Michigan St	Tony Hrkac, N Dakota, F
1988	Lake Superior St	Frank Anzalone	4–3 (OT)	St. Lawrence	Bruce Hoffort, Lake Superior St, G
1989	Harvard	Bill Cleary	4–3 (OT)	Minnesota	Ted Donato, Harvard, F
1990	Wisconsin	Jeff Sauer	7–3	Colgate	Chris Tancill, Wisconsin, F
1991	N Michigan	Rick Comley	8–7 (3OT)	Boston U	Scott Beattie, N Michigan, F
1992	Lake Superior St	Jeff Jackson	4–2	Wisconsin	Paul Constantin, Lake Superior St, F
1993	Maine	Shawn Walsh	5–4	Lake Superior St	Jim Montgomery, Maine, F
1994	Lake Superior St	Jeff Jackson	9–1	Boston U	Sean Tallaire, Lake Superior St, F
1995	Boston U	Jack Parker	6–2	Maine	Chris O'Sullivan, Boston U, F
1996	Michigan	Red Berenson	3–2 (OT)	Colorado Coll.	Brendan Morrison, Michigan, F
1997	N Dakota	Dean Blais	6–4	Boston U	Matt Henderson, N Dakota, F
1998	Michigan	Red Berenson	3–2 (OT)	Boston Coll.	Marty Turco, Michigan, G

DIVISION II *(DISCONTINUED, THEN RENEWED)*

Year	Champion	Coach	Score	Runner-Up
1978	Merrimack	Thom Lawler	12–2	Lake Forest
1979	Lowell	Bill Riley Jr	6–4	Mankato St
1980	Mankato St	Don Brose	5–2	Elmira
1981	Lowell	Bill Riley Jr	5–4	Plattsburgh St
1982	Lowell	Bill Riley Jr	6–1	Plattsburgh St
1983	RIT	Brian Mason	4–2	Bemidji St
1984	Bemidji St	R.H. (Bob) Peters	14–4*	Merrimack
1993	Bemidji St	R.H. (Bob) Peters	15–6*	Mercyhurst
1994	Bemidji St	R.H. (Bob) Peters	7–6*	AL-Huntsville
1995	Bemidji St	R.H. (Bob) Peters	11–6*	Mercyhurst
1996	AL-Huntsville	Doug Ross	10–1*	Bemidji St
1997	Bemidji St	R.H. (Bob) Peters	7–4*	AL-Huntsville
1998	AL-Huntsville	Doug Ross	11–4*	Bemidji St

*Two-game, total-goal series.

DIVISION III

Year	Champion	Coach	Score	Runner-Up
1984	Babson	Bob Riley	8–0	Union (NY)
1985	Rochester Inst	Bruce Delventhal	5–1	Bemidji St
1986	Bemidji St	R.H. (Bob) Peters	8–5	Vacated
1987	Vacated			Oswego St
1988	WI-River Falls	Rick Kozuback	7–1, 3–5, 3–0	Elmira
1989	WI-Stevens Point	Mark Mazzoleni	3–3, 3–2	RIT
1990	WI-Stevens Point	Mark Mazzoleni	10–1, 3–6, 1–0	Plattsburgh St
1991	WI-Stevens Point	Mark Mazzoleni	6–2	Mankato St
1992	Plattsburgh St	Bob Emery	7–3	WI-Stevens Point
1993	WI-Stevens Point	Joe Baldarotta	4–3	WI-River Falls
1994	WI-River Falls	Dean Talafous	6–4	WI-Superior
1995	Middlebury	Bill Beaney	1–0	Fredonia St
1996	Middlebury	Bill Beaney	3–2	RIT
1997	Middlebury	Bill Beaney	3–2	WI-Superior
1998	Middlebury	Bill Beaney	2–1	WI-Stevens Point

Lacrosse

Men

DIVISION I

Year	Champion	Coach	Score	Runner-Up
1971	Cornell	Richie Moran	12–6	Maryland
1972	Virginia	Glenn Thiel	13–12	Johns Hopkins
1973	Maryland	Bud Beardmore	10–9 (2 OT)	Johns Hopkins
1974	Johns Hopkins	Bob Scott	17–12	Maryland
1975	Maryland	Bud Beardmore	20–13	Navy
1976	Cornell	Richie Moran	16–13 (OT)	Maryland
1977	Cornell	Richie Moran	16–8	Johns Hopkins
1978	Johns Hopkins	Henry Ciccarone	13–8	Cornell
1979	Johns Hopkins	Henry Ciccarone	15–9	Maryland
1980	Johns Hopkins	Henry Ciccarone	9–8 (2 OT)	Virginia
1981	N Carolina	Willie Scroggs	14–13	Johns Hopkins
1982	N Carolina	Willie Scroggs	7–5	Johns Hopkins
1983	Syracuse	Roy Simmons Jr	17–16	Johns Hopkins
1984	Johns Hopkins	Don Zimmerman	13–10	Syracuse
1985	Johns Hopkins	Don Zimmerman	11–4	Syracuse
1986	N Carolina	Willie Scroggs	10–9 (OT)	Virginia
1987	Johns Hopkins	Don Zimmerman	11–10	Cornell
1988	Syracuse	Roy Simmons Jr	13–8	Cornell
1989	Syracuse	Roy Simmons Jr	13–12	Johns Hopkins
1990	Syracuse	Roy Simmons Jr	21–9	Loyola (MD)
1991	N Carolina	Dave Klarmann	18–13	Towson St
1992	Princeton	Bill Tierney	10–9	Syracuse
1993	Syracuse	Roy Simmons Jr	13–12	N Carolina
1994	Princeton	Bill Tierney	9–8 (OT)	Virginia
1995	Syracuse	Roy Simmons Jr	13–9	Maryland
1996	Princeton	Bill Tierney	13–12 (OT)	Virginia
1997	Princeton	Bill Tierney	19–7	Maryland
1998	Princeton	Bill Tierney	15–5	Maryland

DIVISION II (DISCONTINUED, THEN RENEWED)

Year	Champion	Coach	Score	Runner-Up
1974	Towson St	Carl Runk	18–17 (OT)	Hobart
1975	Cortland St	Chuck Winters	12–11	Hobart
1976	Hobart	Jerry Schmidt	18–9	Adelphi
1977	Hobart	Jerry Schmidt	23–13	Washington (MD)
1978	Roanoke	Paul Griffin	14–13	Hobart
1979	Adelphi	Paul Doherty	17–12	MD-Baltimore County
1980	MD-Baltimore County	Dick Watts	23–14	Adelphi
1981	Adelphi	Paul Doherty	17–14	Loyola (MD)
1993	Adelphi	Kevin Sheehan	11–7	LIU-C.W. Post
1994	Springfield	Keith Bugbee	15–12	New York Tech
1995	Adelphi	Sandy Kapatos	12–10	Springfield
1996	LIU-C.W. Post	Tom Postel	15–10	Adelphi
1997	New York Tech	Jack Kaley	18–11	Adelphi
1998	Adelphi	Sandy Kapatos	18–6	LIU-C.W. Post

Men *(Cont.)*

DIVISION III

Year	Champion	Coach	Score	Runner-Up
1980	Hobart	Dave Urick	11–8	Cortland St
1981	Hobart	Dave Urick	10–8	Cortland St
1982	Hobart	Dave Urick	9–8 (OT)	Washington (MD)
1983	Hobart	Dave Urick	13–9	Roanoke
1984	Hobart	Dave Urick	12–5	Washington (MD)
1985	Hobart	Dave Urick	15–8	Washington (MD)
1986	Hobart	Dave Urick	13–10	Washington (MD)
1987	Hobart	Dave Urick	9–5	Ohio Wesleyan
1988	Hobart	Dave Urick	18–9	Ohio Wesleyan
1989	Hobart	Dave Urick	11–8	Ohio Wesleyan
1990	Hobart	B.J. O'Hara	18–6	Washington (MD)
1991	Hobart	B.J. O'Hara	12–11	Salisbury St
1992	Nazareth (NY)	Scott Nelson	13–12	Hobart
1993	Hobart	B.J. O'Hara	16–10	Ohio Wesleyan
1994	Salisbury St	Jim Berkman	15–9	Hobart
1995	Salisbury St	Jim Berkman	22–13	Nazareth
1996	Nazareth	Scott Nelson	11–10 (OT)	Washington (MD)
1997	Nazareth	Scott Nelson	15–14 (OT)	Washington (MD)
1998	Washington (MD)	John Haus	16–10	Nazareth

Women

DIVISIONS I AND II

Year	Champion	Coach	Score	Runner-Up
1982	Massachusetts	Pamela Hixon	9–6	Trenton St
1983	Delaware	Janet Smith	10–7	Temple
1984	Temple	Tina Sloan Green	6–4	Maryland
1985	New Hampshire	Marisa Didio	6–5	Maryland
1986	Maryland	Sue Tyler	11–10	Penn St
1987	Penn St	Susan Scheetz	7–6	Temple
1988	Temple	Tina Sloan Green	15–7	Penn St
1989	Penn St	Susan Scheetz	7–6	Harvard
1990	Harvard	Carole Kleinfelder	8–7	Maryland
1991	Virginia	Jane Miller	8–6	Maryland
1992	Maryland	Cindy Timchal	11–10	Harvard
1993	Virginia	Jane Miller	8–6 (OT)	Princeton
1994	Princeton	Chris Sailer	10–7	Virginia
1995	Maryland	Cindy Timchal	13–5	Princeton
1996	Maryland	Cindy Timchal	10–5	Virginia
1997	Maryland	Cindy Timchal	8–7	Loyola (MD)
1998	Maryland	Cindy Timchal	11–5	Virginia

DIVISION III

Year	Champion	Score	Runner-Up	Year	Champion	Score	Runner-Up
1985	Trenton St	7–4	Ursinus	1992	Trenton St	5–3	William Smith
1986	Ursinus	12–10	Trenton St	1993	Trenton St	10–9	William Smith
1987	Trenton St	8–7 (OT)	Ursinus	1994	Trenton St	29–11	William Smith
1988	Trenton St	14–11	William Smith	1995	Trenton St	14–13	William Smith
1989	Ursinus	8–6	Trenton St	1996	Trenton St	15–8	Middlebury
1990	Ursinus	7–6	St. Lawrence	1997	Middlebury	14–9	College of NJ*
1991	Trenton St	7–6	Ursinus	1998	Coll. of NJ*	14–9	Williams

*Formerly Trenton St.

Rifle

Men's and Women's Combined

Year	Champion	Coach	Score	Runner-Up	Score	Individual Champions Air Rifle	Smallbore
1980	Tennessee Tech	James Newkirk	6201	W Virginia	6150	Rod Fitz-Randolph, Tennessee Tech	Rod Fitz-Randolph, Tennessee Tech
1981	Tennessee Tech	James Newkirk	6139	W Virginia	6136	John Rost, W Virginia	Kurt Fitz-Randolph, Tennessee Tech
1982	Tennessee Tech	James Newkirk	6138	W Virginia	6136	John Rost, W Virginia	Kurt Fitz-Randolph, Tennessee Tech
1983	W Virginia	Edward Etzel	6166	Tennessee Tech	6148	Ray Slonena, Tennessee Tech	David Johnson, W Virginia
1984	W Virginia	Edward Etzel	6206	E Tennessee St	6142	Pat Spurgin, Murray St	Bob Broughton, W Virginia
1985	Murray St	Elvis Green	6150	W Virginia	6149	Christian Heller, W Virginia	Pat Spurgin, Murray St
1986	W Virginia	Edward Etzel	6229	Murray St	6163	Marianne Wallace, Murray St	Mike Anti, W Virginia
1987	Murray St	Elvis Green	6205	W Virginia	6203	Rob Harbison, TN-Martin	Web Wright, W Virginia
1988	W Virginia	Greg Perrine	6192	Murray St	6183	Deena Wigger, Murray St	Web Wright, W Virginia
1989	W Virginia	Edward Etzel	6234	S Florida	6180	Michelle Scarborough, S Florida	Deb Sinclair, AK-Fairbanks
1990	W Virginia	Marsha Beasley	6205	Navy	6101	Gary Hardy, W Virginia	Michelle Scarborough, S Florida
1991	W Virginia	Marsha Beasley	6171	AK-Fairbanks	6110	Ann Pfiffner, W Virginia	Soma Dutta, UTEP
1992	W Virginia	Marsha Beasley	6214	AK-Fairbanks	6166	Ann Pfiffner, W Virginia	Tim Manges, W Virginia
1993	W Virginia	Marsha Beasley	6179	AK-Fairbanks	6169	Trevor Gathman, W Virginia	Eric Uptagrafft, W Virginia
1994	AK-Fairbanks	Randy Pitney	6194	W Virginia	6187	Nancy Napolski, Kentucky	Cory Brunetti, AK-Fairbanks
1995	W Virginia	Marsha Beasley	6241	Air Force	6187	Benji Belden, Murray St	Oleg Selezner, AK-Fairbanks
1996	W Virginia	Marsha Beasley	6179	Air Force	6168	Trevor Gathman, W Virginia	Joe Johnson, Navy
1997	W Virginia	Marsha Beasley	6223	Kentucky	6175	Marra Hastings, Murray St	Marcos Scrivner, W Virginia
1997	W Virginia	Marsha Beasley	6214	AK-Fairbanks	6175	Emily Caruso, Norwich	Karen Juzinuk, Xavier

Skiing

Men's and Women's Combined

Year	Champion	Coach	Pts	Runner-Up	Pts	Host or Site
1954	Denver	Willy Schaeffler	384.0	Seattle	349.6	NV-Reno
1955	Denver	Willy Schaeffler	567.05	Dartmouth	558.935	Norwich
1956	Denver	Willy Schaeffler	582.01	Dartmouth	541.77	Winter Park
1957	Denver	Willy Schaeffler	577.95	Colorado	545.29	Ogden Snow Basin
1958	Dartmouth	Al Merrill	561.2	Denver	550.6	Dartmouth
1959	Colorado	Bob Beattie	549.4	Denver	543.6	Winter Park
1960	Colorado	Bob Beattie	571.4	Denver	568.6	Bridger Bowl
1961	Denver	Willy Schaeffler	376.19	Middlebury	366.94	Middlebury
1962	Denver	Willy Schaeffler	390.08	Colorado	374.30	Squaw Valley
1963	Denver	Willy Schaeffler	384.6	Colorado	381.6	Solitude
1964	Denver	Willy Schaeffler	370.2	Dartmouth	368.8	Franconia Notch
1965	Denver	Willy Schaeffler	380.5	Utah	378.4	Crystal Mountain
1966	Denver	Willy Schaeffler	381.02	Western Colorado	365.92	Crested Butte
1967	Denver	Willy Schaeffler	376.7	Wyoming	375.9	Sugarloaf Mountain
1968	Wyoming	John Cress	383.9	Denver	376.2	Mount Werner
1969	Denver	Willy Schaeffler	388.6	Dartmouth	372.0	Mount Werner
1970	Denver	Willy Schaeffler	386.6	Dartmouth	378.8	Cannon Mountain
1971	Denver	Peder Pytte	394.7	Colorado	373.1	Terry Peak
1972	Colorado	Bill Marolt	385.3	Denver	380.1	Winter Park
1973	Colorado	Bill Marolt	381.89	Wyoming	377.83	Middlebury

Year	Champion	Coach	Pts	Runner-Up	Pts	Host or Site
1974	Colorado	Bill Marolt	176	Wyoming	162	Jackson Hole
1975	Colorado	Bill Marolt	183	Vermont	115	Fort Lewis
1976	Colorado	Bill Marolt	112			Bates
	Dartmouth	Jim Page	112			
1977	Colorado	Bill Marolt	179	Wyoming	154.5	Winter Park
1978	Colorado	Bill Marolt	152.5	Wyoming	121.5	Cannon Mountain
1979	Colorado	Tim Hinderman	153	Utah	130	Steamboat Springs
1980	Vermont	Chip LaCasse	171	Utah	151	Lake Placid and Stowe
1981	Utah	Pat Miller	183	Vermont	172	Park City
1982	Colorado	Tim Hinderman	461	Vermont	436.5	Lake Placid
1983	Utah	Pat Miller	696	Vermont	650	Bozeman
1984	Utah	Pat Miller	750.5	Vermont	684	New Hampshire
1985	Wyoming	Tim Ameel	764	Utah	744	Bozeman
1986	Utah	Pat Miller	612	Vermont	602	Vermont
1987	Utah	Pat Miller	710	Vermont	627	Anchorage
1988	Utah	Pat Miller	651	Vermont	614	Middlebury
1989	Vermont	Chip LaCasse	672	Utah	668	Jackson Hole
1990	Vermont	Chip LaCasse	671	Utah	571	Vermont
1991	Colorado	Richard Rokos	713	Vermont	682	Park City
1992	Vermont	Chip LaCasse	693.5	New Mexico	642.5	New Hampshire
1993	Utah	Pat Miller	783	Vermont	700.5	Steamboat Springs
1994	Vermont	Chip LaCasse	688	Utah	667	Sugarloaf, ME
1995	Colorado	Richard Rokos	720.5	Utah	711	New Hampshire
1996	Utah	Pat Miller	719	Denver	635.5	Montana St
1997	Utah	Pat Miller	686	Vermont	646.5	Vermont
1998	Colorado	Richard Rokos	654	Utah	651.5	Montana St

Soccer

Men
DIVISION I

Year	Champion	Coach	Score	Runner-Up
1959	St. Louis	Bob Guelker	5–2	Bridgeport
1960	St. Louis	Bob Guelker	3–2	Maryland
1961	West Chester	Mel Lorback	2–0	St. Louis
1962	St. Louis	Bob Guelker	4–3	Maryland
1963	St. Louis	Bob Guelker	3–0	Navy
1964	Navy	F.H. Warner	1–0	Michigan St
1965	St. Louis	Bob Guelker	1–0	Michigan St
1966	San Francisco	Steve Negoesco	5–2	LIU-Brooklyn
1967	Michigan St	Gene Kenney	0–0	Game called
	St. Louis	Harry Keough		due to inclement weather
1968	Maryland	Doyle Royal	2–2 (2 OT)	
	Michigan St	Gene Kenney		
1969	St. Louis	Harry Keough	4–0	San Francisco
1970	St. Louis	Harry Keough	1–0	UCLA
1971	Vacated		3–2	St. Louis
1972	St. Louis	Harry Keough	4–2	UCLA
1973	St. Louis	Harry Keough	2–1 (OT)	UCLA
1974	Howard	Lincoln Phillips	2–1 (4 OT)	St. Louis
1975	San Francisco	Steve Negoesco	4–0	SIU-Edwardsville
1976	San Francisco	Steve Negoesco	1–0	Indiana
1977	Hartwick	Jim Lennox	2–1	San Francisco
1978	Vacated		2–0	Indiana
1979	SIU-Edwardsville	Bob Guelker	3–2	Clemson
1980	San Francisco	Steve Negoesco	4–3 (OT)	Indiana
1981	Connecticut	Joe Morrone	2–1 (OT)	Alabama A&M
1982	Indiana	Jerry Yeagley	2–1 (8 OT)	Duke
1983	Indiana	Jerry Yeagley	1–0 (2 OT)	Columbia
1984	Clemson	I.M. Ibrahim	2–1	Indiana
1985	UCLA	Sigi Schmid	1–0 (8 OT)	American
1986	Duke	John Rennie	1–0	Akron
1987	Clemson	I.M. Ibrahim	2–0	San Diego St
1988	Indiana	Jerry Yeagley	1–0	Howard
1989	Santa Clara	Steve Sampson	1–1 (2 OT)	
	Virginia	Bruce Arena		
1990	UCLA	Sigi Schmid	1–0 (OT)	Rutgers

Men (Cont.)
DIVISION I (Cont.)

Year	Champion	Coach	Score	Runner-Up
1991	Virginia	Bruce Arena	0–0*	Santa Clara
1992	Virginia	Bruce Arena	2–0	San Diego
1993	Virginia	Bruce Arena	2–0	S Carolina
1994	Virginia	Bruce Arena	1–0	Indiana
1995	Wisconsin	Jim Launder	2–0	Duke
1996	St. John's (NY)	Dave Masur	4–1	Florida International
1997	UCLA	Sigi Schmid	2–1	Virginia

*Under a rule passed in 1991, the NCAA determined that when a score is tied after regulation and overtime, and the championship is determined by penalty kicks, the official score will be 0–0.

DIVISION II

Year	Champion	Year	Champion	Year	Champion
1972	SIU-Edwardsville	1981	Tampa	1990	Southern Connecticut St
1973	MO-St. Louis	1982	Florida Int'l	1991	Florida Tech
1974	Adelphi	1983	Seattle Pacific	1992	Southern Connecticut St
1975	Baltimore	1984	Florida Int'l	1993	Seattle Pacific
1976	Loyola (MD)	1985	Seattle Pacific	1994	Tampa
1977	Alabama A&M	1986	Seattle Pacific	1995	Southern Connecticut St
1978	Seattle Pacific	1987	Southern Connecticut St	1996	Grand Canyon
1979	Alabama A&M	1988	Florida Tech	1997	Cal St-Bakersfield
1980	Lock Haven	1989	New Hampshire Col		

DIVISION III

Year	Champion	Year	Champion	Year	Champion
1974	Brockport St	1982	NC-Greensboro	1990	Glassboro St
1975	Babson	1983	NC-Greensboro	1991	UC-San Diego
1976	Brandeis	1984	Wheaton (IL)	1992	Kean
1977	Lock Haven	1985	NC-Greensboro	1993	UC-San Diego
1978	Lock Haven	1986	NC-Greensboro	1994	Bethany (WV)
1979	Babson	1987	NC-Greensboro	1995	Williams
1980	Babson	1988	UC-San Diego	1996	College of New Jersey
1981	Glassboro St	1989	Elizabethtown	1997	Wheaton (IL)

Women
DIVISION I

Year	Champion	Coach	Score	Runner-Up
1982	North Carolina	Anson Dorrance	2–0	Central Florida
1983	North Carolina	Anson Dorrance	4–0	George Mason
1984	North Carolina	Anson Dorrance	2–0	Connecticut
1985	George Mason	Hank Leung	2–0	North Carolina
1986	North Carolina	Anson Dorrance	2–0	Colorado Col
1987	North Carolina	Anson Dorrance	1–0	Massachusetts
1988	North Carolina	Anson Dorrance	4–1	North Carolina St
1989	North Carolina	Anson Dorrance	2–0	Colorado Col
1990	North Carolina	Anson Dorrance	6–0	Connecticut
1991	North Carolina	Anson Dorrance	3–1	Wisconsin
1992	North Carolina	Anson Dorrance	9–1	Duke
1993	North Carolina	Anson Dorrance	6–0	George Mason
1994	North Carolina	Anson Dorrance	5–0	Notre Dame
1995	Notre Dame	Chris Petrucelli	1–0	Portland
1996	North Carolina	Anson Dorrance	1–0	Notre Dame
1997	North Carolina	Anson Dorrance	2–0	Connecticut

DIVISION II

Year	Champion
1988	Cal St-Hayward
1989	Barry
1990	Sonoma St
1991	Cal St-Dominguez Hills
1992	Barry
1993	Barry
1994	Franklin Pierce
1995	Franklin Pierce
1996	Franklin Pierce
1997	Franklin Pierce

DIVISION III

Year	Champion
1986	Rochester
1987	Rochester
1988	William Smith
1989	UC-San Diego
1990	Ithaca
1991	Ithaca
1992	Cortland St
1993	Trenton St
1994	Trenton St
1995	UC-San Diego
1996	UC-San Diego
1997	UC-San Diego

DIVISION I

Year	Champion	Coach	Score	Runner-Up
1982	UCLA*	Sharron Backus	2–0†	Fresno St
1983	Texas A&M	Bob Brock	2–0‡	Cal St-Fullerton
1984	UCLA	Sharron Backus	1–0#	Texas A&M
1985	UCLA	Sharron Backus	2–1**	Nebraska
1986	Cal St-Fullerton*	Judi Garman	3–0	Texas A&M
1987	Texas A&M	Bob Brock	4–1	UCLA
1988	UCLA	Sharron Backus	3–0	Fresno St
1989	UCLA*	Sharron Backus	1–0	Fresno St
1990	UCLA	Sharron Backus	2–0	Fresno St
1991	Arizona	Mike Candrea	5–1	UCLA
1992	UCLA*	Sharron Backus	2–0	Arizona
1993	Arizona	Mike Candrea	1–0	UCLA
1994	Arizona	Mike Candrea	4–0	Cal St-Northridge
1995	Vacated	—		Arizona
1996	Arizona*	Mike Candrea	6–4	Washington
1997	Arizona	Mike Candrea	10–2***	UCLA
1998	Fresno St	Margie Wright	1–0	Arizona

*Undefeated teams in final series. †Eight innings. ‡12 innings. #13 innings. **Nine innings. ***Five innings.

DIVISION II

Year	Champion	Year	Champion	Year	Champion
1982	Sam Houston St	1988	Cal St-Bakersfield	1994	Merrimack
1983	Cal St-Northridge	1989	Cal St-Bakersfield	1995	Kennesaw St
1984	Cal St-Northridge	1990	Cal St-Bakersfield	1996	Kennesaw St
1985	Cal St-Northridge	1991	Augustana (SD)	1997	California (PA)*
1986	SF Austin St	1992	Missouri Southern	1998	California (PA)
1987	Cal St-Northridge	1993	Florida Southern		

DIVISION III

Year	Champion	Year	Champion	Year	Champion
1982	Sam Houston St	1987	Trenton St*	1993	Central (IA)
1982	Eastern Connecticut St*	1988	Central (IA)	1994	Trenton St
1983	Trenton St	1989	Trenton St*	1995	Chapman
1984	Buena Vista*	1990	Eastern Connecticut St	1996	Trenton St*
1985	Eastern Connecticut St	1991	Central (IA)	1997	Simpson*
1986	Eastern Connecticut St	1992	Trenton St	1998	WI-Stevens Point

*Undefeated teams in final series.

Men

DIVISION I

Year	Champion	Coach	Pts	Runner-Up	Pts
1937	Michigan	Matt Mann	75	Ohio St	39
1938	Michigan	Matt Mann	46	Ohio St	45
1939	Michigan	Matt Mann	65	Ohio St	58
1940	Michigan	Matt Mann	45	Yale	42
1941	Michigan	Matt Mann	61	Yale	58
1942	Yale	Robert J. H. Kiphuth	71	Michigan	39
1943	Ohio St	Mike Peppe	81	Michigan	47
1944	Yale	Robert J. H. Kiphuth	39	Michigan	38
1945	Ohio St	Mike Peppe	56	Michigan	48
1946	Ohio St	Mike Peppe	61	Michigan	37
1947	Ohio St	Mike Peppe	66	Michigan	39
1948	Michigan	Matt Mann	44	Ohio St	41
1949	Ohio St	Mike Peppe	49	Iowa	35
1950	Ohio St	Mike Peppe	64	Yale	43
1951	Yale	Robert J. H. Kiphuth	81	Michigan St	60
1952	Ohio St	Mike Peppe	94	Yale	81
1953	Yale	Robert J. H. Kiphuth	96½	Ohio St	73½
1954	Ohio St	Mike Peppe	94	Michigan	67
1955	Ohio St	Mike Peppe	90	Yale	51
				Michigan	51
1956	Ohio St	Mike Peppe	68	Yale	54
1957	Michigan	Gus Stager	69	Yale	61

Men (Cont.)
DIVISION I (Cont.)

Year	Champion	Coach	Pts	Runner-Up	Pts
1958	Michigan	Gus Stager	72	Yale	63
1959	Michigan	Gus Stager	137½	Ohio St	44
1960	Southern Cal	Peter Daland	87	Michigan	73
1961	Michigan	Gus Stager	85	Southern Cal	62
1962	Ohio St	Mike Peppe	92	Southern Cal	46
1963	Southern Cal	Peter Daland	81	Yale	77
1964	Southern Cal	Peter Daland	96	Indiana	91
1965	Southern Cal	Peter Daland	285	Indiana	278½
1966	Southern Cal	Peter Daland	302	Indiana	286
1967	Stanford	Jim Gaughran	275	Southern Cal	260
1968	Indiana	James Counsilman	346	Yale	253
1969	Indiana	James Counsilman	427	Southern Cal	306
1970	Indiana	James Counsilman	332	Southern Cal	235
1971	Indiana	James Counsilman	351	Southern Cal	260
1972	Indiana	James Counsilman	390	Southern Cal	371
1973	Indiana	James Counsilman	358	Tennessee	294
1974	Southern Cal	Peter Daland	339	Indiana	338
1975	Southern Cal	Peter Daland	344	Indiana	274
1976	Southern Cal	Peter Daland	398	Tennessee	237
1977	Southern Cal	Peter Daland	385	Alabama	204
1978	Tennessee	Ray Bussard	307	Auburn	185
1979	California	Nort Thornton	287	Southern Cal	227
1980	California	Nort Thornton	234	Texas	220
1981	Texas	Eddie Reese	259	UCLA	189
1982	UCLA	Ron Ballatore	219	Texas	210
1983	Florida	Randy Reese	238	Southern Meth	227
1984	Florida	Randy Reese	287½	Texas	277
1985	Stanford	Skip Kenney	403½	Florida	302
1986	Stanford	Skip Kenney	404	California	335
1987	Stanford	Skip Kenney	374	Southern Cal	296
1988	Texas	Eddie Reese	424	Southern Cal	369½
1989	Texas	Eddie Reese	475	Stanford	396
1990	Texas	Eddie Reese	506	Southern Cal	423
1991	Texas	Eddie Reese	476	Stanford	420
1992	Stanford	Skip Kenney	632	Texas	356
1993	Stanford	Skip Kenney	520½	Michigan	396
1994	Stanford	Skip Kenney	566½	Texas	445
1995	Michigan	Jon Urbanchek	561	Stanford	475
1996	Texas	Eddie Reese	479	Auburn	443½
1997	Auburn	David Marsh	496½	Stanford	340
1998	Stanford	Skip Kenney	594	Auburn	394½

DIVISION II

Year	Champion	Year	Champion	Year	Champion
1963	SW Missouri St	1975	Cal St-Northridge	1987	Cal St-Bakersfield
1964	Bucknell	1976	Cal St-Chico	1988	Cal St-Bakersfield
1965	San Diego St	1977	Cal St-Northridge	1989	Cal St-Bakersfield
1966	San Diego St	1978	Cal St-Northridge	1990	Cal St-Bakersfield
1967	UC-Santa Barbara	1979	Cal St-Northridge	1991	Cal St-Bakersfield
1968	Long Beach St	1980	Oakland (MI)	1992	Cal St-Bakersfield
1969	UC-Irvine	1981	Cal St-Northridge	1993	Cal St-Bakersfield
1970	UC-Irvine	1982	Cal St-Northridge	1994	Oakland (MI)
1971	UC-Irvine	1983	Cal St-Northridge	1995	Oakland (MI)
1972	Eastern Michigan	1984	Cal St-Northridge	1996	Oakland (MI)
1973	Cal St-Chico	1985	Cal St-Northridge	1997	Oakland (MI)
1974	Cal St-Chico	1986	Cal St-Bakersfield	1998	Cal St-Bakersfield

DIVISION III

Year	Champion	Year	Champion	Year	Champion
1975	Cal St-Chico	1983	Kenyon	1991	Kenyon
1976	St. Lawrence	1984	Kenyon	1992	Kenyon
1977	Johns Hopkins	1985	Kenyon	1993	Kenyon
1978	Johns Hopkins	1986	Kenyon	1994	Kenyon
1979	Johns Hopkins	1987	Kenyon	1995	Kenyon
1980	Kenyon	1988	Kenyon	1996	Kenyon
1981	Kenyon	1989	Kenyon	1997	Kenyon
1982	Kenyon	1990	Kenyon	1998	Kenyon

Women
DIVISION I

Year	Champion	Coach	Pts	Runner-Up	Pts
1982	Florida	Randy Reese	505	Stanford	383
1983	Stanford	George Haines	418½	Florida	389½
1984	Texas	Richard Quick	392	Stanford	324
1985	Texas	Richard Quick	643	Florida	400
1986	Texas	Richard Quick	633	Florida	586
1987	Texas	Richard Quick	648½	Stanford	631½
1988	Texas	Richard Quick	661	Florida	542½
1989	Stanford	Richard Quick	610½	Texas	547
1990	Texas	Mark Schubert	632	Stanford	622½
1991	Texas	Mark Schubert	746	Stanford	653
1992	Stanford	Richard Quick	735½	Texas	651
1993	Stanford	Richard Quick	649½	Florida	421
1994	Stanford	Richard Quick	512	Texas	421
1995	Stanford	Richard Quick	497½	Michigan	478½
1996	Stanford	Richard Quick	478	SMU	397
1997	Southern Cal	Mark Schubert	406	Stanford	395
1998	Stanford	Richard Quick	422	Arizona	378

DIVISION II

Year	Champion	Year	Champion	Year	Champion
1982	Cal St-Northridge	1988	Cal St-Northridge	1994	Oakland (MI)
1983	Clarion	1989	Cal St-Northridge	1995	Air Force
1984	Clarion	1990	Oakland (MI)	1996	Air Force
1985	S Florida	1991	Oakland (MI)	1997	Drury
1986	Clarion	1992	Oakland (MI)	1998	Drury
1987	Cal St-Northridge	1993	Oakland (MI)		

DIVISION III

Year	Champion	Year	Champion	Year	Champion
1982	Williams	1988	Kenyon	1994	Kenyon
1983	Williams	1989	Kenyon	1995	Kenyon
1984	Kenyon	1990	Kenyon	1996	Kenyon
1985	Kenyon	1991	Kenyon	1997	Kenyon
1986	Kenyon	1992	Kenyon	1998	Kenyon
1987	Kenyon	1993	Kenyon		

Tennis

Men
INDIVIDUAL CHAMPIONS 1883-1945

Year	Champion	Year	Champion
1883	Joseph Clark, Harvard (spring)	1904	Robert LeRoy, Columbia
1883	Howard Taylor, Harvard (fall)	1905	E.B. Dewhurst, Pennsylvania
1884	W.P. Knapp, Yale	1906	Robert LeRoy, Columbia
1885	W.P. Knapp, Yale	1907	G. Peabody Gardner Jr, Harvard
1886	G.M. Brinley, Trinity (CT)	1908	Nat Niles, Harvard
1887	P.S. Sears, Harvard	1909	Wallace Johnson, Pennsylvania
1888	P.S. Sears, Harvard	1910	R.A. Holden Jr, Yale
1889	R.P. Huntington Jr, Yale	1911	E.H. Whitney, Harvard
1890	Fred Hovey, Harvard	1912	George Church, Princeton
1891	Fred Hovey, Harvard	1913	Richard Williams II, Harvard
1892	William Larned, Cornell	1914	George Church, Princeton
1893	Malcolm Chace, Brown	1915	Richard Williams II, Harvard
1894	Malcolm Chace, Yale	1916	G. Colket Caner, Harvard
1895	Malcolm Chace, Yale	1917–18	No tournament
1896	Malcolm Whitman, Harvard	1919	Charles Garland, Yale
1897	S.G. Thompson, Princeton	1920	Lascelles Banks, Harvard
1898	Leo Ware, Harvard	1921	Philip Neer, Stanford
1899	Dwight Davis, Harvard	1922	Lucien Williams, Yale
1900	Raymond Little, Princeton	1923	Carl Fischer, Philadelphia Osteo
1901	Fred Alexander, Princeton	1924	Wallace Scott, Washington
1902	William Clothier, Harvard	1925	Edward Chandler, California
1903	E.B. Dewhurst, Pennsylvania	1926	Edward Chandler, California

Men (Cont.)

INDIVIDUAL CHAMPIONS 1883-1945 (Cont.)

Year	Champion	Year	Champion
1927	Wilmer Allison, Texas	1937	Ernest Sutter, Tulane
1928	Julius Seligson, Lehigh	1938	Frank Guernsey, Rice
1929	Berkeley Bell, Texas	1939	Frank Guernsey, Rice
1930	Clifford Sutter, Tulane	1940	Donald McNeil, Kenyon
1931	Keith Gledhill, Stanford	1941	Joseph Hunt, Navy
1932	Clifford Sutter, Tulane	1942	Frederick Schroeder Jr, Stanford
1933	Jack Tidball, UCLA	1943	Pancho Segura, Miami (FL)
1934	Gene Mako, Southern Cal	1944	Pancho Segura, Miami (FL)
1935	Wilbur Hess, Rice	1945	Pancho Segura, Miami (FL)
1936	Ernest Sutter, Tulane		

DIVISION I

Year	Champion	Coach	Pts	Runner-Up	Pts	Individual Champion
1946	Southern Cal	William Moyle	9	William & Mary	6	Robert Falkenburg, Southern Cal
1947	William & Mary	Sharvey G. Umbeck	10	Rice	4	Gardner Larned, William & Mary
1948	William & Mary	Sharvey G. Umbeck	6	San Francisco	5	Harry Likas, San Francisco
1949	San Francisco	Norman Brooks	7	Rollins/Tulane/ Washington	4	Jack Tuero, Tulane
1950	UCLA	William Ackerman	11	California	5	Herbert Flam, UCLA
				Southern Cal	5	
1951	Southern Cal	Louis Wheeler	9	Cincinnati	7	Tony Trabert, Cincinnati
1952	UCLA	J.D. Morgan	11	California	5	Hugh Stewart, Southern Cal
				Southern Cal	5	
1953	UCLA	J.D. Morgan	11	California	6	Hamilton Richardson, Tulane
1954	UCLA	J.D. Morgan	15	Southern Cal	10	Hamilton Richardson, Tulane
1955	Southern Cal	George Toley	12	Texas	7	Jose Aguero, Tulane
1956	UCLA	J.D. Morgan	15	Southern Cal	14	Alejandro Olmedo, Southern Cal
1957	Michigan	William Murphy	10	Tulane	9	Barry MacKay, Michigan
1958	Southern Cal	George Toley	13	Stanford	9	Alejandro Olmedo, Southern Cal
1959	Notre Dame	Thomas Fallon	8			Whitney Reed, San Jose St
	Tulane	Emmet Pare	8			
1960	UCLA	J.D. Morgan	18	Southern Cal	8	Larry Nagler, UCLA
1961	UCLA	J.D. Morgan	17	Southern Cal	16	Allen Fox, UCLA
1962	Southern Cal	George Toley	22	UCLA	12	Rafael Osuna, Southern Cal
1963	Southern Cal	George Toley	27	UCLA	19	Dennis Ralston, Southern Cal
1964	Southern Cal	George Toley	26	UCLA	25	Dennis Ralston, Southern Cal
1965	UCLA	J.D. Morgan	31	Miami (FL)	13	Arthur Ashe, UCLA
1966	Southern Cal	George Toley	27	UCLA	23	Charles Pasarell, UCLA
1967	Southern Cal	George Toley	28	UCLA	23	Bob Lutz, Southern Cal
1968	Southern Cal	George Toley	31	Rice	23	Stan Smith, Southern Cal
1969	Southern Cal	George Toley	35	UCLA	23	Joaquin Loyo-Mayo, Southern Cal
1970	UCLA	Glenn Bassett	26	Trinity (TX)	22	Jeff Borowiak, UCLA
				Rice	22	
1971	UCLA	Glenn Bassett	35	Trinity (TX)	27	Jimmy Connors, UCLA
1972	Trinity (TX)	Clarence Mabry	36	Stanford	30	Dick Stockton, Trinity (TX)
1973	Stanford	Dick Gould	33	Southern Cal	28	Alex Mayer, Stanford
1974	Stanford	Dick Gould	30	Southern Cal	25	John Whitlinger, Stanford
1975	UCLA	Glenn Bassett	27	Miami (FL)	20	Bill Martin, UCLA
1976	Southern Cal	George Toley	21			Bill Scanlon, Trinity (TX)
	UCLA	Glenn Bassett	21			
1977	Stanford	Dick Gould		Trinity (TX)		Matt Mitchell, Stanford
1978	Stanford	Dick Gould		UCLA		John McEnroe, Stanford
1979	UCLA	Glenn Bassett		Trinity (TX)		Kevin Curren, Texas
1980	Stanford	Dick Gould		California		Robert Van't Hof, Southern Cal
1981	Stanford	Dick Gould		UCLA		Tim Mayotte, Stanford
1982	UCLA	Glenn Bassett		Pepperdine		Mike Leach, Michigan
1983	Stanford	Dick Gould		SMU		Greg Holmes, Utah
1984	UCLA	Glenn Bassett		Stanford		Mikael Pernfors, Georgia
1985	Georgia	Dan Magill		UCLA		Mikael Pernfors, Georgia
1986	Stanford	Dick Gould		Pepperdine		Dan Goldie, Stanford
1987	Georgia	Dan Magill		UCLA		Andrew Burrow, Miami (FL)
1988	Stanford	Dick Gould		Louisiana St		Robby Weiss, Pepperdine
1989	Stanford	Dick Gould		Georgia		Donni Leaycraft, Louisiana St
1990	Stanford	Dick Gould		Tennessee		Steve Bryan, Texas
1991	Southern Cal	Dick Leach		Georgia		Jared Palmer, Stanford

Men (Cont.)
DIVISION I (Cont.)

Year	Champion	Coach	Runner-Up	Individual Champion
1992	Stanford	Dick Gould	Notre Dame	Alex O'Brien, Stanford
1993	Southern Cal	Dick Leach	Georgia	Chris Woodruff, Tennessee
1994	Southern Cal	Dick Leach	Stanford	Mark Merklein, Florida
1995	Stanford	Dick Gould	Mississippi	Sargis Sargsian, Arizona St
1996	Stanford	Dick Gould	UCLA	Cecil Mamiit, Southern Cal
1997	Stanford	Dick Gould	Georgia	Luke Smith, UNLV
1998	Stanford	Dick Gould	Georgia	Bob Bryan, Stanford

Note: Prior to 1977, individual wins counted in the team's total points. In 1977, a dual-match single-elimination team championship was initiated, eliminating the point system.

DIVISION II

Year	Champion	Year	Champion	Year	Champion
1963	Cal St-LA	1975	UC-Irvine/San Diego	1987	Chapman
1964	Cal St-LA/S Illinois	1976	Hampton	1988	Chapman
1965	Cal St-LA	1977	UC-Irvine	1989	Hampton
1966	Rollins	1978	SIU-Edwardsville	1990	Cal Poly-SLO
1967	Long Beach St	1979	SIU-Edwardsville	1991	Rollins
1968	Fresno St	1980	SIU-Edwardsville	1992	UC-Davis
1969	Cal St-Northridge	1981	SIU-Edwardsville	1993	Lander (SC)
1970	UC-Irvine	1982	SIU-Edwardsville	1994	Lander (SC)
1971	UC-Irvine	1983	SIU-Edwardsville	1995	Lander (SC)
1972	UC-Irvine/ Rollins	1984	SIU-Edwardsville	1996	Lander (SC)
1973	UC-Irvine	1985	Chapman	1997	Lander (SC)
1974	San Diego	1986	Cal Poly-SLO	1998	Lander (SC)

DIVISION III

Year	Champion	Year	Champion	Year	Champion
1976	Kalamazoo	1983	Redlands	1991	Kalamazoo
1977	Swarthmore	1984	Redlands	1992	Kalamazoo
1978	Kalamazoo	1985	Swarthmore	1993	Kalamazoo
1979	Redlands	1986	Kalamazoo	1994	Washington (MD)
1980	Gustavus Adolphus	1987	Kalamazoo	1995	UC-Santa Cruz
1981	Claremont-M-S	1988	Washington & Lee	1996	UC-Santa Cruz
	Swarthmore	1989	UC-Santa Cruz	1997	Washington (MD)
1982	Gustavus Adolphus	1990	Swarthmore	1998	UC-Santa Cruz

Women
DIVISION I

Year	Champion	Coach	Runner-Up	Individual Champion
1982	Stanford	Frank Brennan	UCLA	Alycia Moulton, Stanford
1983	Southern Cal	Dave Borelli	Trinity (TX)	Beth Herr, Southern Cal
1984	Stanford	Frank Brennan	Southern Cal	Lisa Spain, Georgia
1985	Southern Cal	Dave Borelli	Miami (FL)	Linda Gates, Stanford
1986	Stanford	Frank Brennan	Southern Cal	Patty Fendick, Stanford
1987	Stanford	Frank Brennan	Georgia	Patty Fendick, Stanford
1988	Stanford	Frank Brennan	Florida	Shaun Stafford, Florida
1989	Stanford	Frank Brennan	UCLA	Sandra Birch, Stanford
1990	Stanford	Frank Brennan	Florida	Debbie Graham, Stanford
1991	Stanford	Frank Brennan	UCLA	Sandra Birch, Stanford
1992	Florida	Andy Brandi	Texas	Lisa Raymond, Florida
1993	Texas	Jeff Moore	Stanford	Lisa Raymond, Florida
1994	Georgia	Jeff Wallace	Stanford	Angela Lettiere, Georgia
1995	Texas	Jeff Moore	Florida	Keri Phebus, UCLA
1996	Florida	Andy Brandi	Stanford	Jill Craybas, Florida
1997	Stanford	Frank Brennan	Florida	Lilia Osterloh, Stanford
1998	Florida	Andy Brandi	Duke	Vanessa Webb, Duke

DIVISION II

Year	Champion	Year	Champion	Year	Champion
1982	Cal St-Northridge	1988	SIU-Edwardsville	1994	N Florida
1983	TN-Chattanooga	1989	SIU-Edwardsville	1995	Armstrong St
1984	TN-Chattanooga	1990	UC-Davis	1996	Armstrong St
1985	TN-Chattanooga	1991	Cal Poly-Pomona	1997	Lynn
1986	SIU-Edwardsville	1992	Cal Poly-Pomona	1998	Lynn
1987	SIU-Edwardsville	1993	UC-Davis		

Women (Cont.)
DIVISION III

Year	Champion	Year	Champion	Year	Champion
1982	Occidental	1988	Mary Washington	1994	UC-San Diego
1983	Principia	1989	UC-San Diego	1995	Kenyon
1984	Davidson	1990	Gustavus Adolphus	1996	Emory
1985	UC-San Diego	1991	Mary Washington	1997	Kenyon
1986	Trenton St	1992	Pomona-Pitzer	1998	Kenyon
1987	UC-San Diego	1993	Kenyon		

Indoor Track and Field

Men
DIVISION I

Year	Champion	Coach	Pts	Runner-Up	Pts
1965	Missouri	Tom Botts	14	Oklahoma St	12
1966	Kansas	Bob Timmons	14	Southern Cal	13
1967	Southern Cal	Vern Wolfe	26	Oklahoma	17
1968	Villanova	Jim Elliott	35	Southern Cal	25
1969	Kansas	Bob Timmons	41½	Villanova	33
1970	Kansas	Bob Timmons	27½	Villanova	26
1971	Villanova	Jim Elliott	22	UTEP	19¼
1972	Southern Cal	Vern Wolfe	19	Bowling Green/ Mich St	18
1973	Manhattan	Fred Dwyer	18	Kansas/Kent St/UTEP	12
1974	UTEP	Ted Banks	19	Colorado	18
1975	UTEP	Ted Banks	36	Kansas	17½
1976	UTEP	Ted Banks	23	Villanova	15
1977	Washington St	John Chaplin	25½	UTEP	25
1978	UTEP	Ted Banks	44	Auburn	38
1979	Villanova	Jim Elliott	52	UTEP	51
1980	UTEP	Ted Banks	76	Villanova	42
1981	UTEP	Ted Banks	76	SMU	51
1982	UTEP	John Wedel	67	Arkansas	30
1983	SMU	Ted McLaughlin	43	Villanova	32
1984	Arkansas	John McDonnell	38	Washington St	28
1985	Arkansas	John McDonnell	70	Tennessee	29
1986	Arkansas	John McDonnell	49	Villanova	22
1987	Arkansas	John McDonnell	39	SMU	31
1988	Arkansas	John McDonnell	34	Illinois	29
1989	Arkansas	John McDonnell	34	Florida	31
1990	Arkansas	John McDonnell	44	Texas A&M	36
1991	Arkansas	John McDonnell	34	Georgetown	27
1992	Arkansas	John McDonnell	53	Clemson	46
1993	Arkansas	John McDonnell	66	Clemson	30
1994	Arkansas	John McDonnell	83	UTEP	45
1995	Arkansas	John McDonnell	59	GMU/Tennessee	26
1996	George Mason	John Cook	39	Nebraska	31½
1997	Arkansas	John McDonnell	59	Auburn	27
1998	Arkansas	John McDonnell	56	Stanford	36½

DIVISION II

Year	Champion	Year	Champion	Year	Champion
1985	SE Missouri St	1990	St. Augustine's	1995	St. Augustine's
1986	not held	1991	St. Augustine's	1996	Abilene Christian
1987	St. Augustine's	1992	St. Augustine's	1997	Abilene Christian
1988	Abil. Christian/ St. August.	1993	Abilene Christian	1998	Abilene Christian
1989	St. Augustine's	1994	Abilene Christian		

DIVISION III

Year	Champion	Year	Champion	Year	Champion
1985	St. Thomas (MN)	1990	Lincoln (PA)	1995	Lincoln (PA)
1986	Frostburg St	1991	WI-La Crosse	1996	Lincoln (PA)
1987	WI-La Crosse	1992	WI-La Crosse	1997	WI-La Crosse
1988	WI-La Crosse	1993	WI-La Crosse	1998	Lincoln (PA)
1989	N Central	1994	WI-La Crosse		

Women

DIVISION I

Year	Champion	Coach	Pts	Runner-Up	Pts
1983	Nebraska	Gary Pepin	47	Tennessee	44
1984	Nebraska	Gary Pepin	59	Tennessee	48
1985	Florida St	Gary Winckler	34	Texas	32
1986	Texas	Terry Crawford	31	Southern Cal	26
1987	Louisiana St	Loren Seagrave	49	Tennessee	30
1988	Texas	Terry Crawford	71	Villanova	52
1989	Louisiana St	Pat Henry	61	Villanova	34
1990	Texas	Terry Crawford	50	Wisconsin	26
1991	Louisiana St	Pat Henry	48	Texas	39
1992	Florida	Bev Kearney	50	Stanford	26
1993	Louisiana St	Pat Henry	49	Wisconsin	44
1994	Louisiana St	Pat Henry	48	Alabama	29
1995	Louisiana St	Pat Henry	40	UCLA	37
1996	Louisiana St	Pat Henry	52	Georgia	34
1997	Louisiana St	Pat Henry	49	Texas/ Wisconsin	39
1998	Texas	Bev Kearney	60	Louisiana St	30

DIVISION II

Year	Champion	Year	Champion	Year	Champion
1985	St. Augustine's	1990	Abilene Christian	1995	Abilene Christian
1986	not held	1991	Abilene Christian	1996	Abilene Christian
1987	St. Augustine's	1992	Alabama A&M	1997	Abilene Christian
1988	Abilene Christian	1993	Abilene Christian	1998	Abilene Christian
1989	Abilene Christian	1994	Abilene Christian		

DIVISION III

Year	Champion	Year	Champion	Year	Champion
1985	MA-Boston	1990	Christopher Newport	1995	WI-Oshkosh
1986	MA-Boston	1991	Cortland St	1996	WI-Oshkosh
1987	MA-Boston	1992	Christopher Newport	1997	Christopher Newport
1988	Christopher Newport	1993	Lincoln (PA)	1998	Christopher Newport
1989	Christopher Newport	1994	WI-Oshkosh		

Outdoor Track and Field

Men

DIVISION I

Year	Champion	Coach	Pts	Runner-Up	Pts
1921	Illinois	Harry Gill	20†	Notre Dame	16†
1922	California	Walter Christie	28†	Penn St	19†
1923	Michigan	Stephen Farrell	29†	Mississippi St	16
1924	No meet				
1925	Stanford*	R. L. Templeton	31†		
1926	Southern Cal*	Dean Cromwell	27†		
1927	Illinois*	Harry Gill	35†		
1928	Stanford	R. L. Templeton	72	Ohio St	31
1929	Ohio St	Frank Castleman	50	Washington	42
1930	Southern Cal	Dean Cromwell	55†	Washington	40
1931	Southern Cal	Dean Cromwell	77†	Ohio St	31†
1932	Indiana	Billy Hayes	56	Ohio St	49†
1933	Louisiana St	Bernie Moore	58	Southern Cal	54
1934	Stanford	R. L. Templeton	63	Southern Cal	54†
1935	Southern Cal	Dean Cromwell	74†	Ohio St	40†
1936	Southern Cal	Dean Cromwell	103†	Ohio St	73
1937	Southern Cal	Dean Cromwell	62	Stanford	50
1938	Southern Cal	Dean Cromwell	67†	Stanford	38
1939	Southern Cal	Dean Cromwell	86	Stanford	44†
1940	Southern Cal	Dean Cromwell	47	Stanford	28†
1941	Southern Cal	Dean Cromwell	81†	Indiana	50
1942	Southern Cal	Dean Cromwell	85†	Ohio St	44†
1943	Southern Cal	Dean Cromwell	46	California	39
1944	Illinois	Leo Johnson	79	Notre Dame	43

Men (Cont.)

DIVISION I (Cont.)

Year	Champion	Coach	Pts	Runner-Up	Pts
1945	Navy	E.J. Thomson	62	Illinois	48†
1946	Illinois	Leo Johnson	78	Southern Cal	42†
1947	Illinois	Leo Johnson	59†	Southern Cal	34†
1948	Minnesota	James Kelly	46	Southern Cal	41†
1949	Southern Cal	Jess Hill	55†	UCLA	31
1950	Southern Cal	Jess Hill	49†	Stanford	28
1951	Southern Cal	Jess Mortenson	56	Cornell	40
1952	Southern Cal	Jess Mortenson	66†	San Jose St	24†
1953	Southern Cal	Jess Mortenson	80	Illinois	41
1954	Southern Cal	Jess Mortenson	66†	Illinois	31†
1955	Southern Cal	Jess Mortenson	42	UCLA	34
1956	UCLA	Elvin Drake	55†	Kansas	51
1957	Villanova	James Elliott	47	California	32
1958	Southern Cal	Jess Mortenson	48†	Kansas	40†
1959	Kansas	Bill Easton	73	San Jose St	48
1960	Kansas	Bill Easton	50	Southern Cal	37
1961	Southern Cal	Jess Mortenson	65	Oregon	47
1962	Oregon	William Bowerman	85	Villanova	40†
1963	Southern Cal	Vern Wolfe	61	Stanford	42
1964	Oregon	William Bowerman	70	San Jose St	40
1965	Oregon	William Bowerman	32		
	Southern Cal	Vern Wolfe	32		
1966	UCLA	Jim Bush	81	Brigham Young	33
1967	Southern Cal	Vern Wolfe	86	Oregon	40
1968	Southern Cal	Vern Wolfe	58	Washington St	57
1969	San Jose St	Bud Winter	48	Kansas	45
1970	Brigham Young	Clarence Robison	35		
	Kansas	Bob Timmons	35		
	Oregon	William Bowerman	35		
1971	UCLA	Jim Bush	52	Southern Cal	41
1972	UCLA	Jim Bush	82	Southern Cal	49
1973	UCLA	Jim Bush	56	Oregon	31
1974	Tennessee	Stan Huntsman	60	UCLA	56
1975	UTEP	Ted Banks	55	UCLA	42
1976	Southern Cal	Vern Wolfe	64	UTEP	44
1977	Arizona St	Senon Castillo	64	UTEP	50
1978	UCLA/UTEP	Jim Bush/Ted Banks	50		
1979	UTEP	Ted Banks	64	Villanova	48
1980	UTEP	Ted Banks	69	UCLA	46
1981	UTEP	Ted Banks	70	SMU	57
1982	UTEP	John Wedel	105	Tennessee	94
1983	SMU	Ted McLaughlin	104	Tennessee	102
1984	Oregon	Bill Dellinger	113	Washington St	94½
1985	Arkansas	John McDonnell	61	Washington St	46
1986	SMU	Ted McLaughlin	53	Washington St	52
1987	UCLA	Bob Larsen	81	Texas	28
1988	UCLA	Bob Larsen	82	Texas	41
1989	Louisiana St	Pat Henry	53	Texas A&M	51
1990	Louisiana St	Pat Henry	44	Arkansas	36
1991	Tennessee	Doug Brown	51	Washington St	42
1992	Arkansas	John McDonnell	60	Tennessee	46½
1993	Arkansas	John McDonnell	69	LSU/Ohio St	45
1994	Arkansas	John McDonnell	83	UTEP	45
1995	Arkansas	John McDonnell	61½	UCLA	55
1996	Arkansas	John McDonnell	55	George Mason	40
1997	Arkansas	John McDonnell	55	Texas	42½
1998	Arkansas	John McDonnell	58½	Stanford	51

*Unofficial championship. †Fraction of a point.

Men (Cont.)
DIVISION II

Year	Champion	Year	Champion	Year	Champion
1963	MD-Eastern Shore	1975	Cal St-Northridge	1988	Abilene Christian
1964	Fresno St	1976	UC-Irvine	1989	St. Augustine's
1965	San Diego St	1977	Cal St-Hayward	1990	St. Augustine's
1966	San Diego St	1978	Cal St-LA	1991	St. Augustine's
1967	Long Beach St	1979	Cal Poly-SLO	1992	St. Augustine's
1968	Cal Poly-SLO	1980	Cal Poly-SLO	1993	St. Augustine's
1969	Cal Poly-SLO	1981	Cal Poly-SLO	1994	St. Augustine's
1970	Cal Poly-SLO	1982	Abilene Christian	1995	St. Augustine's
1971	Kentucky St	1983	Abilene Christian	1996	Abilene Christian
1972	Eastern Michigan	1984	Abilene Christian	1997	Abliene Christian
1973	Norfolk St	1985	Abilene Christian	1998	St. Augustine's
1974	Eastern Illinois	1986	Abilene Christian		
	Norfolk St	1987	Abilene Christian		

DIVISION III

Year	Champion	Year	Champion	Year	Champion
1974	Ashland	1983	Glassboro St	1992	WI-La Crosse
1975	Southern-N Orleans	1984	Glassboro St	1993	WI-La Crosse
1976	Southern-N Orleans	1985	Lincoln (PA)	1994	N Central
1977	Southern-N Orleans	1986	Frostburg St	1995	Lincoln (PA)
1978	Occidental	1987	Frostburg St	1996	Lincoln (PA)
1979	Slippery Rock	1988	WI-La Crosse	1997	WI-La Crosse
1980	Glassboro St	1989	N Central	1998	N Central
1981	Glassboro St	1990	Lincoln (PA)		
1982	Glassboro St	1991	WI-La Crosse		

Women
DIVISION I

Year	Champion	Coach	Pts	Runner-Up	Pts
1982	UCLA	Scott Chisam	153	Tennessee	126
1983	UCLA	Scott Chisam	116½	Florida St	108
1984	Florida St	Gary Winckler	145	Tennessee	124
1985	Oregon	Tom Heinonen	52	Florida St/LSU	46
1986	Texas	Terry Crawford	65	Alabama	55
1987	Louisiana St	Loren Seagrave	62	Alabama	53
1988	Louisiana St	Loren Seagrave	61	UCLA	58
1989	Louisiana St	Pat Henry	86	UCLA	47
1990	Louisiana St	Pat Henry	53	UCLA	46
1991	Louisiana St	Pat Henry	78	Texas	67
1992	Louisiana St	Pat Henry	87	Florida	81
1993	Louisiana St	Pat Henry	93	Wisconsin	44
1994	Louisiana St	Pat Henry	86	Texas	43
1995	Louisiana St	Pat Henry	69	UCLA	58
1996	Louisiana St	Pat Henry	81	Texas	52
1997	Louisiana St	Pat Henry	63	Texas	62
1998	Texas	Bev Kearney	60	UCLA	55

DIVISION II

Year	Champion	Year	Champion	Year	Champion
1982	Cal Poly-SLO	1988	Abilene Christian	1994	Alabama A&M
1983	Cal Poly-SLO	1989	Cal Poly-SLO	1995	Abilene Christian
1984	Cal Poly-SLO	1990	Cal Poly-SLO	1996	Abilene Christian
1985	Abilene Christian	1991	Cal Poly-SLO	1997	St. Augustine's
1986	Abilene Christian	1992	Alabama A&M	1998	Abilene Christian
1987	Abilene Christian	1993	Alabama A&M		

DIVISION III

Year	Champion	Year	Champion	Year	Champion
1982	Central (IA)	1988	Chris. Newport	1994	Chris. Newport
1983	WI-La Crosse	1989	Chris. Newport	1995	WI-Oshkosh
1984	WI-La Crosse	1990	WI-Oshkosh	1996	WI-Oshkosh
1985	Cortland St	1991	WI-Oshkosh	1997	WI-Oshkosh
1986	MA-Boston	1992	Chris. Newport	1998	Chris. Newport
1987	Chris. Newport	1993	Lincoln (PA)		

Volleyball

Men

Year	Champion	Coach	Score	Runner-Up	Most Outstanding Player
1970	UCLA	Al Scates	3–0	Long Beach St	Dane Holtzman, UCLA
1971	UCLA	Al Scates	3–0	UC-Santa Barbara	Kirk Kilgore, UCLA
					Tim Bonynge, UC-Santa Barbara
1972	UCLA	Al Scates	3–2	San Diego St	Dick Irvin, UCLA
1973	San Diego St	Jack Henn	3–1	Long Beach St	Duncan McFarland, San Diego St
1974	UCLA	Al Scates	3–2	UC-Santa Barbara	Bob Leonard, UCLA
1975	UCLA	Al Scates	3–1	UC-Santa Barbara	John Bekins, UCLA
1976	UCLA	Al Scates	3–0	Pepperdine	Joe Mika, UCLA
1977	Southern Cal	Ernie Hix	3–1	Ohio St	Celso Kalache, Southern Cal
1978	Pepperdine	Marv Dunphy	3–2	UCLA	Mike Blanchard, Pepperdine
1979	UCLA	Al Scates	3–1	Southern Cal	Sinjin Smith, UCLA
1980	Southern Cal	Ernie Hix	3–1	UCLA	Dusty Dvorak, Southern Cal
1981	UCLA	Al Scates	3–2	Southern Cal	Karch Kiraly, UCLA
1982	UCLA	Al Scates	3–0	Penn St	Karch Kiraly, UCLA
1983	UCLA	Al Scates	3–0	Pepperdine	Ricci Luyties, UCLA
1984	UCLA	Al Scates	3–1	Pepperdine	Ricci Luyties, UCLA
1985	Pepperdine	Marv Dunphy	3–1	Southern Cal	Bob Ctvrtlik, Pepperdine
1986	Pepperdine	Rod Wilde	3–2	Southern Cal	Steve Friedman, Pepperdine
1987	UCLA	Al Scates	3–0	Southern Cal	Ozzie Volstad, UCLA
1988	Southern Cal	Bob Yoder	3–2	UC-Santa Barbara	Jen-Kai Liu, Southern Cal
1989	UCLA	Al Scates	3–1	Stanford	Matt Sonnichsen, UCLA
1990	Southern Cal	Jim McLaughlin	3–1	Long Beach St	Bryan Ivie, Southern Cal
1991	Long Beach St	Ray Ratelle	3–1	Southern Cal	Brent Hilliard, Long Beach St
1992	Pepperdine	Marv Dunphy	3–0	Stanford	Alon Grinberg, Pepperdine
1993	UCLA	Al Scates	3–0	Cal St-Northridge	Mike Sealy/Jeff Nygaard, UCLA
1994	Penn St	Tom Peterson	3–2	UCLA	Ramon Hernandez, Penn St
1995	UCLA	Al Scates	3–0	Penn St	Jeff Nygaard, UCLA
1996	UCLA	Al Scates	3–2	Hawaii	Yuval Katz, Hawaii
1997	Stanford	Ruben Nieves	3–2	UCLA	Mike Lambert, Stanford
1998	UCLA	Al Scates	3–2	Pepperdine	George Roumain, Pepperdine

Women

DIVISION I

Year	Champion	Coach	Score	Runner-Up
1981	Southern Cal	Chuck Erbe	3–2	UCLA
1982	Hawaii	Dave Shoji	3–2	Southern Cal
1983	Hawaii	Dave Shoji	3–0	UCLA
1984	UCLA	Andy Banachowski	3–2	Stanford
1985	Pacific	John Dunning	3–1	Stanford
1986	Pacific	John Dunning	3–0	Nebraska
1987	Hawaii	Dave Shoji	3–1	Stanford
1988	Texas	Mick Haley	3–0	Hawaii
1989	Long Beach St	Brian Gimmillaro	3–0	Nebraska
1990	UCLA	Andy Banachowski	3–0	Pacific
1991	UCLA	Andy Banachowski	3–2	Long Beach St
1992	Stanford	Don Shaw	3–1	UCLA
1993	Long Beach St	Brian Gimmillaro	3–1	Penn St
1994	Stanford	Don Shaw	3–1	UCLA
1995	Nebraska	Terry Pettit	3–1	Texas
1996	Stanford	Don Shaw	3–0	Hawaii
1997	Stanford	Don Shaw	3–2	Penn St

DIVISION II

Year	Champion	Year	Champion	Year	Champion
1981	Cal St-Sacramento	1987	Cal St-Northridge	1993	Northern Michigan
1982	UC-Riverside	1988	Portland St	1994	Northern Michigan
1983	Cal St-Northridge	1989	Cal St-Bakersfield	1995	Barry
1984	Portland St	1990	West Texas A&M	1996	Nebraska-Omaha
1985	Portland St	1991	West Texas A&M	1997	West Texas A&M
1986	UC-Riverside	1992	Portland St		

DIVISION III

Year	Champion	Year	Champion	Year	Champion
1981	UC-San Diego	1987	UC-San Diego	1993	Washington (MO)
1982	La Verne	1988	UC-San Diego	1994	Washington (MO)
1983	Elmhurst	1989	Washington (MO)	1995	Washington (MO)
1984	UC-San Diego	1990	UC-San Diego	1996	Washington (MO)
1985	Elmhurst	1991	Washington (MO)	1997	UC-San Diego
1986	UC-San Diego	1992	Washington (MO)		

Water Polo

Year	Champion	Coach	Score	Runner-Up
1969	UCLA	Bob Horn	5–2	California
1970	UC-Irvine	Ed Newland	7–6 (3 OT)	UCLA
1971	UCLA	Bob Horn	5–3	San Jose St
1972	UCLA	Bob Horn	10–5	UC-Irvine
1973	California	Pete Cutino	8–4	UC-Irvine
1974	California	Pete Cutino	7–6	UC-Irvine
1975	California	Pete Cutino	9–8	UC-Irvine
1976	Stanford	Art Lambert	13–12	UCLA
1977	California	Pete Cutino	8–6	UC-Irvine
1978	Stanford	Dante Dettamanti	7–6 (3 OT)	California
1979	UC-Santa Barbara	Pete Snyder	11–3	UCLA
1980	Stanford	Dante Dettamanti	8–6	California
1981	Stanford	Dante Dettamanti	17–6	Long Beach St
1982	UC-Irvine	Ed Newland	7–4	Stanford
1983	California	Pete Cutino	10–7	Southern Cal
1984	California	Pete Cutino	9–8	Stanford
1985	Stanford	Dante Dettamanti	12–11 (2 OT)	UC-Irvine
1986	Stanford	Dante Dettamanti	9–6	California
1987	California	Pete Cutino	9–8 (OT)	Southern Cal
1988	California	Pete Cutino	14–11	UCLA
1989	UC-Irvine	Ed Newland	9–8	California
1990	California	Steve Heaston	8–7	Stanford
1991	California	Steve Heaston	7–6	UCLA
1992	California	Steve Heaston	12–11	Stanford
1993	Stanford	Dante Dettamanti	11–9	Southern Cal
1994	Stanford	Dante Dettamanti	14–10	Southern Cal
1995	UCLA	Guy Baker	10–8	California
1996	UCLA	Guy Baker	8–7	Southern Cal
1997	Pepperdine	Terry Schroeder	8–7 (OT)	Southern Cal

Wrestling

DIVISION I

Year	Champion	Coach	Pts	Runner-Up	Pts	Most Outstanding Wrestler
1928	Oklahoma St*	E.C. Gallagher				
1929	Oklahoma St	E.C. Gallagher	26	Michigan	18	
1930	Oklahoma St*	E.C. Gallagher	27	Illinois	14	
1931	Oklahoma St*	E.C. Gallagher		Michigan		
1932	Indiana*	W.H. Thom		Oklahoma St		Edwin Belshaw, Indiana
1933	Oklahoma St*	E.C. Gallagher				Allan Kelley, Oklahoma St
	Iowa St*	Hugo Otopalik				Pat Johnson, Harvard
1934	Oklahoma St	E.C. Gallagher	29	Indiana	19	Ben Bishop, Lehigh
1935	Oklahoma St	E.C. Gallagher	36	Oklahoma	18	Ross Flood, Oklahoma St
1936	Oklahoma	Paul Keen	14	Central St (OK)	10	Wayne Martin, Oklahoma
				Oklahoma St	10	
1937	Oklahoma St	E.C. Gallagher	31	Oklahoma	13	Stanley Henson, Oklahoma St
1938	Oklahoma St	E.C. Gallagher	19	Illinois	15	Joe McDaniels, Oklahoma St
1939	Oklahoma St	E.C. Gallagher	33	Lehigh	12	Dale Hanson, Minnesota
1940	Oklahoma St	E.C. Gallagher	24	Indiana	14	Don Nichols, Michigan
1941	Oklahoma St	Art Griffith	37	Michigan St	26	Al Whitehurst, Oklahoma St
1942	Oklahoma St	Art Griffith	31	Michigan St	26	David Arndt, Oklahoma St
1943–45	No tournament					
1946	Oklahoma St	Art Griffith	25	Northern Iowa	24	Gerald Leeman, Northern Iowa
1947	Cornell	Paul Scott	32	Northern Iowa	19	William Koll, Northern Iowa
1948	Oklahoma St	Art Griffith	33	Michigan St	28	William Koll, Northern Iowa
1949	Oklahoma St	Art Griffith	32	Northern Iowa	27	Charles Hetrick, Oklahoma St
1950	Northern Iowa	David McCuskey	30	Purdue	16	Anthony Gizoni, Waynesburg
1951	Oklahoma	Port Robertson	24	Oklahoma St	23	Walter Romanowski, Cornell
1952	Oklahoma	Port Robertson	22	Northern Iowa	21	Tommy Evans, Oklahoma
1953	Penn St	Charles Speidel	21	Oklahoma	15	Frank Bettucci, Cornell
1954	Oklahoma St	Art Griffith	32	Pittsburgh	17	Tommy Evans, Oklahoma
1955	Oklahoma St	Art Griffith	40	Penn St	31	Edward Eichelberger, Lehigh
1956	Oklahoma St	Art Griffith	65	Oklahoma	62	Dan Hodge, Oklahoma
1957	Oklahoma	Port Robertson	73	Pittsburgh	66	Dan Hodge, Oklahoma
1958	Oklahoma St	Myron Roderick	77	Iowa St	62	Dick Delgado, Oklahoma
1959	Oklahoma St	Myron Roderick	73	Iowa St	51	Ron Gray, Iowa St

Wrestling (Cont.)

DIVISION I *(Cont.)*

Year	Champion	Coach	Pts	Runner-Up	Pts	Most Outstanding Wrestler
1960	Oklahoma	Thomas Evans	59	Iowa St	40	Dave Auble, Cornell
1961	Oklahoma St	Myron Roderick	82	Oklahoma	63	E. Gray Simons, Lock Haven
1962	Oklahoma St	Myron Roderick	82	Oklahoma	45	E. Gray Simons, Lock Haven
1963	Oklahoma	Thomas Evans	48	Iowa St	45	Mickey Martin, Oklahoma
1964	Oklahoma St	Myron Roderick	87	Oklahoma	58	Dean Lahr, Colorado
1965	Iowa St	Harold Nichols	87	Oklahoma St	86	Yojiro Uetake, Oklahoma St
1966	Oklahoma St	Myron Roderick	79	Iowa St	70	Yojiro Uetake, Oklahoma St
1967	Michigan St	Grady Peninger	74	Michigan	63	Rich Sanders, Portland St
1968	Oklahoma St	Myron Roderick	81	Iowa St	78	Dwayne Keller, Oklahoma St
1969	Iowa St	Harold Nichols	104	Oklahoma	69	Dan Gable, Iowa St
1970	Iowa St	Harold Nichols	99	Michigan St	84	Larry Owings, Washington
1971	Oklahoma St	Tommy Chesbro	94	Iowa St	66	Darrell Keller, Oklahoma St
1972	Iowa St	Harold Nichols	103	Michigan St	72½	Wade Schalles, Clarion
1973	Iowa St	Harold Nichols	85	Oregon St	72½	Greg Strobel, Oregon St
1974	Oklahoma	Stan Abel	69½	Michigan	67	Floyd Hitchcock, Bloomsburg
1975	Iowa	Gary Kurdelmeier	102	Oklahoma	77	Mike Frick, Lehigh
1976	Iowa	Gary Kurdelmeier	123½	Iowa St	85¾	Chuch Yagla, Iowa
1977	Iowa St	Harold Nichols	95½	Oklahoma St	88¾	Nick Gallo, Hofstra
1978	Iowa	Dan Gable	94½	Iowa St	94	Mark Churella, Michigan
1979	Iowa	Dan Gable	122½	Iowa St	88	Bruce Kinseth, Iowa
1980	Iowa	Dan Gable	110¾	Oklahoma St	87	Howard Harris, Oregon St
1981	Iowa	Dan Gable	129¾	Oklahoma	100¼	Gene Mills, Syracuse
1982	Iowa	Dan Gable	131¾	Iowa St	111	Mark Schultz, Oklahoma
1983	Iowa	Dan Gable	155	Oklahoma St	102	Mike Sheets, Oklahoma St
1984	Iowa	Dan Gable	123¾	Oklahoma St	98	Jim Zalesky, Iowa
1985	Iowa	Dan Gable	145¼	Oklahoma	98½	Barry Davis, Iowa
1986	Iowa	Dan Gable	158	Oklahoma	84¼	Marty Kistler, Iowa
1987	Iowa St	Jim Gibbons	133	Iowa	108	John Smith, Oklahoma St
1988	Arizona St	Bobby Douglas	93	Iowa	85½	Scott Turner, N Carolina St
1989	Oklahoma St	Joe Seay	91¼	Arizona St	70½	Tim Krieger, Iowa St
1990	Oklahoma St	Joe Seay	117¾	Arizona St	104¾	Chris Barnes, Oklahoma St
1991	Iowa	Dan Gable	157	Oklahoma St	108¾	Jeff Prescott, Penn St
1992	Iowa	Dan Gable	149	Oklahoma St	100½	Tom Brands, Iowa
1993	Iowa	Dan Gable	123¾	Penn St	87½	Terry Steiner, Iowa
1994	Oklahoma St	John Smith	94¾	Iowa	76½	Pat Smith, Oklahoma St
1995	Iowa	Dan Gable	134	Oregon St	77½	T.J. Jaworsky, N Carolina
1996	Iowa	Dan Gable	122½	Iowa St	78½	Les Gutches, Oregon St
1997	Iowa	Dan Gable	170	Oklahoma St	113½	Lincoln McIlravy, Iowa
1998	Iowa	Jim Zalesky	115	Minnesota	102	Joe Williams, Iowa

*Unofficial champions.

DIVISION II

Year	Champion	Year	Champion	Year	Champion
1963	Western St (CO)	1975	Northern Iowa	1987	Cal St-Bakersfield
1964	Western St (CO)	1976	Cal St-Bakersfield	1988	N Dakota St
1965	Mankato St	1977	Cal St-Bakersfield	1989	Portland St
1966	Cal Poly-SLO	1978	Northern Iowa	1990	Portland St
1967	Portland St	1979	Cal St-Bakersfield	1991	NE-Omaha
1968	Cal Poly-SLO	1980	Cal St-Bakersfield	1992	Central Oklahoma
1969	Cal Poly-SLO	1981	Cal St-Bakersfield	1993	Central Oklahoma
1970	Cal Poly-SLO	1982	Cal St-Bakersfield	1994	Central Oklahoma
1971	Cal Poly-SLO	1983	Cal St-Bakersfield	1995	Central Oklahoma
1972	Cal Poly-SLO	1984	SIU-Edwardsville	1996	Pittsburgh-Johnstown
1973	Cal Poly-SLO	1985	SIU-Edwardsville	1997	San Francisco St
1974	Cal Poly-SLO	1986	SIU-Edwardsville	1998	N Dakota St

DIVISION III

Year	Champion	Year	Champion	Year	Champion
1974	Wilkes	1983	Brockport St	1992	Brockport
1975	John Carroll	1984	Trenton St	1993	Augsburg
1976	Montclair St	1985	Trenton St	1994	Ithaca
1977	Brockport St	1986	Montclair St	1995	Augsburg
1978	Buffalo	1987	Trenton St	1996	Wartburg
1979	Trenton St	1988	St. Lawrence	1997	Augsburg
1980	Brockport St	1989	Ithaca	1998	Augsburg
1981	Trenton St	1990	Ithaca		
1982	Brockport St	1991	Augsburg		

INDIVIDUAL CHAMPIONSHIP
RECORDS

Swimming

Men

Event	Time	Record Holder	Date
50-yard freestyle	19.14	David Fox, N Carolina St	3-25-93
100-yard freestyle	41.80	Matt Biondi, California	4-4-87
200-yard freestyle	1:33.03	Matt Biondi, California	4-3-87
500-yard freestyle	4:08.75	Tom Dolan, Michigan	3-23-95
1650-yard freestyle	14:29.31	Tom Dolan, Michigan	3-25-95
100-yard backstroke	45.25	Neil Walker, Texas	3-28-97
200-yard backstroke	1:40.64	Jeff Rouse, Stanford	3-28-92
100-yard breaststroke	52.32	Jeremy Linn, Tennessee	3-28-97
200-yard breaststroke	1:53.77	Mike Barrowman, Michigan	3-24-90
100-yard butterfly	45.99	Lars Frolander, SMU	3-28-98
200-yard butterfly	1:41.78	Melvin Stewart, Tennessee	3-30-91
200-yard individual medley	1:43.52	Greg Burgess, Florida	3-25-93
400-yard individual medley	3:38.18	Tom Dolan, Michigan	3-24-95

Women

Event	Time	Record Holder	Date
50-yard freestyle	21.77	Amy Van Dyken, Colorado St	3-18-94
100-yard freestyle	47.61	Jenny Thompson, Stanford	3-21-92
200-yard freestyle	1:43.08	Martina Moravcova, SMU	3-28-97
500-yard freestyle	4:34.39	Janet Evans, Stanford	3-15-90
1650-yard freestyle	15:39.14	Janet Evans, Stanford	3-17-90
100-yard backstroke	53.98	Betsy Mitchell, Texas	3-21-92
200-yard backstroke	1:52.98	Whitney Hedgepeth, Texas	3-21-87
100-yard breaststroke	59.71	Beata Kaszuba, Arizona St	3-17-95
200-yard breaststroke	2:09.71	Beata Kaszuba, Arizona St	3-18-95
100-yard butterfly	51.34	Misty Hyman, Stanford	3-21-98
200-yard butterfly	1:53.42	Summer Sanders, Stanford	3-21-92
200-yard individual medley	1:55.54	Summer Sanders, Stanford	3-20-92
400-yard individual medley	4:02.28	Summer Sanders, Stanford	3-20-92

Indoor Track and Field

Men

Event	Mark	Record Holder	Date
55-meter dash	6.00	Lee McRae, Pittsburgh	3-14-86
55-meter hurdles	7.07	Allen Johnson, N Carolina	3-13-92
200-meter dash	20.36	Obadele Thompson, UTEP	3-8-96
400-meter dash	45.69	Roxbert Martin, Oklahoma	3-8-97
800-meter run	1:45.80	Einars Tupuritis, Wichita St	3-9-96
Mile run	3:55.33	Kevin Sullivan, Michigan	3-11-95
3,000-meter run	7:46.03	Adam Goucher, Colorado	3-14-98
5,000-meter run	13:37.94	Jonah Koech, Iowa St	3-9-90
High jump	7 ft 9¾ in	Hollis Conway, SW Louisiana	3-11-89
Pole vault	19 ft 1½ in	Lawrence Johnson, Tennessee	3-12-94
Long jump	27 ft 10 in	Carl Lewis, Houston	3-13-81
Triple jump	56 ft 9½ in	Keith Connor, SMU	3-13-81
Shot put	69 ft 8½ in	Michael Carter, SMU	3-13-81
		Soren Tallhem, Brigham Young	3-9-85
35-pound weight throw	76 ft 5½ in	Robert Weir, SMU	3-11-83

Women

Event	Mark	Record Holder	Date
55-meter dash	6.56	Gwen Torrence, Georgia	3-14-87
55-meter hurdles	7.41	Michelle Freeman	3-13-92
		Angie Vaughn, Texas	3-14-98
200-meter dash	22.90	Holly Hyche, Indiana St	3-11-94
400-meter dash	51.05	Maicel Malone, Arizona St	3-9-91
800-meter run	2:02.05	Amy Wickus, Wisconsin	3-11-94
Mile run	4:30.63	Suzy Favor, Wisconsin	3-11-89
3,000-meter run	8:54.98	Stephanie Herbst, Wisconsin	3-15-86
5,000-meter run	15:39.75	Amy Skieresz, Arizona	3-7-97
High jump	6 ft 5½ in	Amy Acuff, UCLA	3-11-95
Pole vault	13 ft 10 in	Melissa Price, Fresno St	3-14-98
Long jump	22 ft 1 in	Daphne Saunders, Louisiana St	3-12-94
Triple jump	46 ft 9 in	Suzette Lee, Louisiana St	3-8-97
Shot put	60 ft 5¼ in	Teri Tunks, SMU	3-14-98
20-point weight throw	71 ft 8¾ in	Dawn Ellerbe, S Carolina	3-7-97

Outdoor Track and Field

Men

Event	Mark	Record Holder	Date
100-meter dash	9.92	Ato Bolden, UCLA	6-1-96
200-meter dash	19.87	Lorenzo Daniel, Mississippi St	6-3-88
400-meter dash	44.00	Quincy Watts, Southern Cal	6-6-92
800-meter run	1:44.70	Mark Everett, Florida	6-1-90
1,500-meter run	3:35.30	Sydney Maree, Villanova	6-6-81
3,000-meter steeplechase	8:12.39	Henry Rono, Washington St	6-1-78
5,000-meter run	13:20.63	Sydney Maree, Villanova	6-2-79
10,000-meter run	28:01.30	Suleiman Nyambui, UTEP	6-1-79
110-meter high hurdles	13.22	Greg Foster, UCLA	6-2-78
400-meter intermediate hurdles	47.85	Kevin Young, UCLA	6-3-88
High jump	7 ft 9¾ in	Hollis Conway, SW Louisiana	6-3-89
Pole vault	19 ft 1 in	Lawrence Johnson, Tennessee	5-29-96
Long jump	28 ft	Erick Walder, Arkansas	6-3-93
Triple jump	57 ft 7¾ in	Keith Connor, SMU	6-5-82
Shot put	72 ft 2¼ in	John Godina, UCLA	6-3-95
Discus throw	220 ft	Kamy Keshmiri, Nevada	6-5-92
Hammer throw	265 ft 3 in	Balazs Kiss, Southern Cal	5-31-96
Javelin throw	266 ft 9 in	Todd Riech, Fresno St	6-3-94
Decathlon	8279 pts	Tito Steiner, Brigham Young	6-2/3-81

Women

Event	Mark	Record Holder	Date
100-meter dash	10.78	Dawn Sowell, Louisiana St	6-3-89
200-meter dash	22.04	Dawn Sowell, Louisiana St	6-2-89
400-meter dash	50.18	Pauline Davis, Alabama	6-3-89
800-meter run	1:59.11	Suzy Favor, Wisconsin	6-1-90
1,500-meter run	4:08.26	Suzy Favor, Wisconsin	6-2-90
3,000-meter run	8:47.35	Vicki Huber, Villanova	6-3-88
5,000-meter run	15:37.77	Amy Skieresz, Arizona	6-5-98
10,000-meter run	32:28.57	Sylvia Mosqueda, Cal St-Los Angeles	6-1-88
100-meter hurdles	12.70	Tananjalyn Stanley, Louisiana St	6-3-89
400-meter hurdles	54.54	Ryan Tolbert, Vanderbilt	6-6-97
High jump	6 ft 5 in	Amy Acuff, UCLA	6-3-95
Pole vault	12 ft 5½ in	Bianca Maran, Cal Poly	6-5-98
Long jump	22 ft 9¼ in	Sheila Echols, Louisiana St	6-5-87
Triple jump	46 ft ¾ in	Sheila Hudson, California	6-2-90
Shot put	61 ft 2¼ in	Tressa Thompson, Nebraska	6-4-98
Discus throw	209 ft 10 in	Leslie Deniz, Arizona St	6-4-83
Hammer throw	209 ft 4 in	Lisa Misipeka, S Carolina	6-6-98
Javelin throw	206 ft 9 in	Karin Smith, Cal Poly-SLO	6-4-82
Heptathlon	6527 pts	Diane Guthrie-Gresham, George Mason	6-2/3-95

Olympics

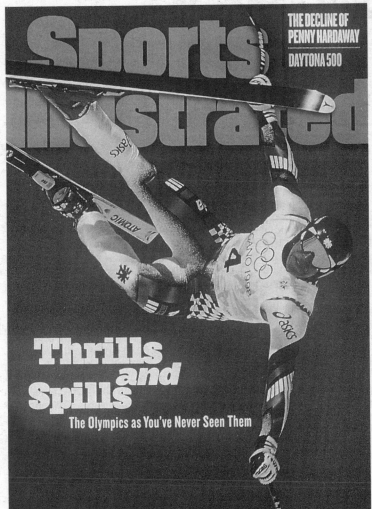

Sports Illustrated

THE DECLINE OF
PENNY HARDAWAY

DAYTONA 500

Thrills and Spills

The Olympics as You've Never Seen Them

CARL YARBROUGH

Winner Games

Despite what you may have seen on TV, Nagano succeeded in staging a friendly, well organized and spirited Olympics

BY MERRELL NODEN

LESS THAN TWO years after the muggy, tawdry, avaricious circus of the Atlanta Olympics—a Games so un-Olympian that International Olympic Committee president Juan Antonio Samaranch refused to bestow upon them his usual perfunctory title of the "best ever"—the Olympic movement desperately needed a triumphant Winter Games in 1998. With future Olympic host cities Sydney, Salt Lake City and Athens looking on nervously, no doubt wondering, What have we gotten ourselves into? a great many Olympic insiders held their breath, waiting to see if Nagano would succeed in staging not just Winter Games but Winner Games.

The omens leading up to the Games were not good. The perpetually robust Japanese economy was actually in trouble, tumbling head-over-heels downhill like a fallen skier and causing concerns that Japan would not be able to meet the Games' $800 million budget. The country's strong environmental lobby had battled Olympic organizers at every turn, forcing them to relocate venues and haggling with the International Ski Federation over the configuration of the downhill ski run. And finally, there was the weather. Never before had the Winter Games been held so far south, and, in a year of globally weird weather, it seemed quite possible the Nagano Games would be snowless.

So there was a feeling of trepidation as the 18th Winter Olympics commenced on Feb. 7. The unusual daylight opening ceremonies seemed oddly stark, its centerpiece being a ritual in which eight wooden pillars were raised in pairs of two to represent the stadium's four gates. U.S. speed skater Eric Flaim, a three-time Olympian, carried the American flag into Minami Stadium. Great Britain's Chris Moon, an anti-landmine activist who had lost his right hand and right leg to one of the devices, carried the Olympic torch into the stadium, and Japanese figure skater Midori Ito lit the Olympic flame.

In marked contrast to the giddy excesses of past ceremonies, the two-hour Nagano

BOB MARTIN

ceremony was simple and solemn. It didn't help that the U.S. appeared to be on the verge of punishing Iraq for rebuffing U.N. weapons inspectors. As he opened the Games, Samaranch called for all nations to follow the example of the ancient Olympics and to refrain from war during the competition "in an effort to bring human tragedies to an end."

Those sentiments might have sounded hopelessly naive, but over the next 16 days the Nagano Games would offer countless examples of the Olympics' capacity to heal and unite humanity. While the couch potato consensus seemed to be that CBS's coverage was lackluster (see sidebar), those who made the long trip to Nagano were bowled over by an avalanche of warmth and hospitality. The people of Nagano, whom initial reports had judged to be lukewarm about hosting these Games, proved to be spectacular hosts. In years to come the Nagano Games will be remembered fondly for the kindness of strangers, demonstrated in acts both grand and humble: a frail old man

Harada redeemed his collapse at Lillehammer with a bronze in Nagano.

crossing a busy street in torrential rain to offer his umbrella; schoolchildren making origami swans for visitors; a grocer racing from his store to give apples to passersby; a cab driver taking his passengers out for drinks on him.

Reuters christened the Nagano Olympics "The Crying Games," but those tears were almost always tears of joy. In every possible way, from the miraculous absence of traffic jams to the smooth flow of press buses, the organization was impeccable. The Japanese heightened the festive mood—and cunningly inspired their next generation of winter Olympians—by busing in thousands of bright-faced schoolchildren who cheered anything that moved. A handwritten sign in the window of a Nagano flower shop summed things up perfectly: WELCOME NAGANO THANK YOU IMPRESSIVE. The only time the Japanese stopped being perfect hosts was when it came time to stomp the competition. The host nation won five gold medals in Nagano, two more than it had won in all previous Winter Games. Especially enthralling were the performances at Hakuba Ski-Jumping Stadium, where as many as 30,000 Japanese fans threw off their customary reserve and whooped like sailors. In the first hour after Japan won the team ski jumping event, the Nagano Olympics Web site received 100,000 hits per minute.

It seemed that every heart in Japan rose and fell with the fortunes of Masahiko (Happy) Harada, who entered these Games as ski jumping's answer to hapless Fred Merkle. Four years ago in Lillehammer, needing only an average jump to clinch the gold medal for his team, Harada had not so much soared as plummeted from the sky, like Icarus, and his team had to settle for the silver. After finishing fifth in the 90-meter jump in Nagano, Harada again seemed destined to be the object of national pity. "What a big burden does God give him," sighed the *Asahi Shimbun* newspaper.

Harada appeared to fumble that big burden once again when he got off a disappointing first jump in the 120-meter event. But on his second jump he threw both caution and his own small body to the wind, soaring into the unmarked snow beyond the 135-meter mark. Eventually the jump was estimated to be 136 meters, good enough for a bronze medal even after the lousy first jump. Interviewed live on Japanese television immediately after the event, Harada broke down in tears and was joined in weepy ecstasy not only by the interviewer but also by an entire nation.

Germany was the big winner in Nagano in the medal tables. Led by Georg Hackl,

SIMON BRUTY

who won his third straight gold medal in the men's single luge, and by Katja Seizinger, who took the women's downhill and the Alpine combined, Germans won 29 medals overall, 12 of them gold. In marquee events, Hermann Maier, a former bricklayer from Austria, survived a spectacular fall in the downhill and went on to win both the Super G and the giant slalom, while Picabo Street of Sun Valley, Idaho, added the Super G gold to the downhill silver she'd won four years earlier (see skiing essay, page 691). In figure skating *(page 703)* 15-year-old Tara Lipinski overtook Michelle Kwan with a brilliant free skate to win the gold, while Ilia Kulik of Russia took the men's title.

Cross-country skiing was dominated by two people, 32-year-old Larissa Lazhutina, an independent-minded Russian who rejected the support of her native federation, and the incomparable Bjørn Dæhlie, who came to Nagano poised to break the alltime Winter Olympics records of five gold medals and 10 overall medals. Lazhutina employed her own full time ski waxer, the striking Russian army colonel Alexander Voronin. "He has the hands of gold," said Lazhutina of Voronin, who, working 20-hour days at a secret location near the Snow Harp course in Hakuba, helped Lazhutina win three golds, a silver and a bronze.

When he was a boy Dæhlie's parents encouraged him to keep up with older skiers by rewarding him with candy. Now 30, Dæhlie is widely considered to be the finest athlete his sport has produced. In Nagano he won the 10-kilometer classical and the 50-kilometer and skied a leg on Norway's gold-medal-winning 4 x 10K relay. In one of the Games' most moving scenes, Dæhlie stuck around to cheer home the last finisher in the 92-man field of the 10-kilometer, Kenya's first Winter Olympian, Philip Boit. "At least one thing I know," said Boit, "I am the best skier in Africa."

Just as proud as the game Boit, but far more successful, were the five women who made up the Canadian curling team, four of whom had given birth in the previous 20 months. After beating Denmark 7–5 to win the first Olympic gold medal in curling, they all wept joyfully on the medal stand. The favored Canadian men lost the gold medal to Switzerland, 9–3.

You didn't have to be much of a purist to feel that many of the newfangled events in Nagano were a bit too X-Games–ish. Then again, without those events, the U.S. would have won three fewer golds. Jonny Moseley of Tiburon, Calif., gave the U.S. the first of its eventual six gold medals, winning the freestyle moguls by executing something called a 360° Mute Grab jump in the final round. The U.S. also won gold medals in the men's and women's aerial competition, with Nikki Stone of Westborough, Mass., taking the women's and Eric

Bergoust of Missoula, Mont., the men's.

"I'm on cloud nine," said Stone, who had overcome a series of back problems and had nearly retired from the sport after failing to qualify for the final at Lillehammer. "I'm walking on sunshine."

So, it seems, was Canadian snowboarder Ross Rebagliati, who after winning the gold medal in giant glalom snowboarding, appeared to give new meaning to the term "half-pipe" by testing positive for marijuana. The IOC board revoked Rebagliati's medal three days after the event but immediately reinstated it following an appeal by the Canadian delegation.

The venerable sport of speed skating saw a technical revolution in Nagano, thanks to so-called clapskates, whose design enables a skater to lift his heel from the skate while the blade remains on the ice. Clapskates allow longer contact with the ice, which means a longer push, which in turn means faster times. Gerard Kewkers, a U.S. coach fretted that "technology [might] take away from the quiet and fine coordination, which is the special beauty of speed skating," and it was impossible to argue that the skates didn't make a difference. In the 10 speed skating events contested in Nagano, surpassing pre-Olympic records became almost routine. When the ice chips settled, there were new world records in half the events and new Olympic marks in the other half. Poor Bart Veldkamp of Belgium broke Johann Olav Koss's mark in the 10,000 meters but still finished outside the medals, in fourth. Ahead of Veldkamp came three Dutch skaters, led by Gianni Romme, whose world record of 13:15.33 hacked more than 15 seconds off Koss's record. Romme also won the 5,000 in a world record 6:22.20 to become one of two double gold medalists in speed skating. The other, his countrywoman Marianne Timmer, took the 1,000 and the 1,500.

Though men's ice hockey has been part of the Olympics since 1920, professional players made their Olympic debut in Nagano. Some 125 NHL players took to the ice, instantly creating a tournament full of Dream Teams and causing NHL commissioner Gary Bettman to salivate every time he opened his mouth. But alas, like the snowboarders, the hockey pros made a mixed impression. There were many thrilling games, topped probably by the Czech Republic's 2–1 upset of Canada in the semis, a game which many ranked among the greatest games ever played. European teams swept the medals, with the Czech Republic beating Russia for the gold medal 1–0 on Petr Svoboda's third-period goal. Czech goalie Dominik Hasek, who moonlights with the Buffalo Sabres, was sensational throughout the tournament, allowing just six goals in six games, with two shutouts.

The U.S. men, who had been favored by many to win the gold, disappointed on the ice and then disgraced themselves in the Olympic Village. In a do-or-die game whose winner would reach the medal round, they never put up much of a fight, losing to the Czechs 4–1. The ugly Ameri-

Canned Goods

Let's face it: For all but a precious few of us, the Winter Olympics are never more than a television experience. We accept it on faith that the Games are taking place somewhere in the real world, nestled cozily in some picture-book Alpine village where everyone is sipping hot chocolate in front of roaring fires. But the closest most of us come to snow is the occasional blizzard of white particles that drifts across our television screens.

As viewed through the CBS window, the Nagano Winter Olympics were an often frustrating, frequently bland, time-delayed hodgepodge of canned features, taped event coverage and live interviews. The storylines seemed disjointed, and there was little suspense, a fact that CBS's Olympics executive producer Rick Gentile blamed on the Games themselves. "This is a bad Olympics," said Gentile. "It's a 32–6 Super Bowl."

If that sounds a mite defensive, recall that CBS paid $375 million for the broadcast rights to the Games—a Winter Olympics record—and though network executives would ultimately declare themselves pleased with the $40 million profit the coverage yielded, one wonders if they were really all that happy with the 16.2 overall TV rating they achieved, the lowest for any Games since 1968.

What went wrong? To be fair, Gentile

Nantz and Co. were overmatched in Nagano.

and his crew faced an unusual set of challenges in covering the Nagano Olympics, not least of which was the 14-hour time difference between Nagano and the East Coast of the U.S. Early on, the network decided that roughly 80% of its coverage would be shown on tape, as part of a "package" that would air during prime time and make heavy use of the roughly 112 feature pieces it had in the can (one of which, Bob Simon's riveting 35-minute feature on Lou Zamperini, who ran the 5,000 meters in the 1936 Summer Games and then found himself in a

cans' abysmal play surprised no one who had gotten a whiff of their arrogance around Nagano. Not only did the Americans seem to spend too much time downing shots rather than slapping them, they also trashed three apartments in the Olympic Village, throwing a fire extinguisher out a window and damaging two others, smashing a hole in a door and breaking furniture. In all, they did an estimated $3,000 worth of damage and then slinked off, the guilty parties never coming forward. Even worse,

in the contempt it showed for the Olympic ideal, was the fact that while committing the vandalism, the U.S. goons woke up a number of speed skaters who were trying to sleep before competition. A bar in Nagano popular with athletes bore the somewhat cryptic name Police 90, which led to the rather obvious but revealing joke: Police 90, USA 0.

It fell to the U.S. women to prove that Americans were capable of both good sportsmanship and good hockey. From the

Japanese prison camp not far from Nagano seven years later, was outstanding).

"We won't pretend to be live when we're not," assured Gentile, and while the network stuck to that, it took considerable heat for waiting almost 24 hours to show skier Picabo Street's gold medal run in the Suger G. Though the event had been delayed by weather, studio host Jim Nantz still could have mentioned the result before signing off and didn't. "She's a big star, and we want to show her entire event to the entire country at the same time," explained Leslie Anne Wade, a CBS spokeswoman. Well, maybe, but by the time CBS got around to showing Street's race, the result had been announced by ESPN, and Street had been interviewed on *CBS This Morning*.

Even more harmful to the goal of building an audience was the weather-related four-day delay of the Games' first marquee event, the men's downhill. Had we American couch potatoes seen Austrian skier Hermann Maier leave terra firma and fly through two snow fences, we would almost certainly have sat up and paid attention. It was also CBS's bad luck that U.S. athletes got off to a very slow start in Nagano, with the first U.S. gold coming on Day 5, and that the U.S. hockey team, whose games were to be carried live, bombed so badly. Weather

forced the postponement of a number of events, and it's hard to generate suspense in the face of uncertainty and frequent rescheduling. Finally, to be bluntly cynical about it, CBS lacked the sleazy, larger-than-Olympic showdown of Nancy and Tonya, which, having built interest for months prior to the 1994 Winter Games, netted NBC a rating of 48.5, third highest ever for a sports event.

Nantz struggled gamely to keep abreast of all the schedule changes, but he seemed stiff. While certainly competent, he never looked comfortable inside CBS's main set on the grounds of Nagano's famed seventh-century Zenkoji temple.

Once when he stepped outside, pigeons landed on him. The folks over at TNT seemed to be having a looser, better time, perhaps because they didn't have the pressure of being the first team.

On the plus side at CBS were Al Trautwig, who did a great job with ski jumping, and Bill Geist, who provided zany features on subjects such as how to eat blowfish. Zanier still and totally out of place was that noted winter sports expert, Kennedy, the former MTV VJ. Finally, there was Jim Rippey, CBS's snowboarding analyst for the Games, who, when he wasn't using obscure terminology—"He's starting to chatter"— gave up all pretense of objectivity by whooping deliriously, "Whoo! Yeah, buddy!"

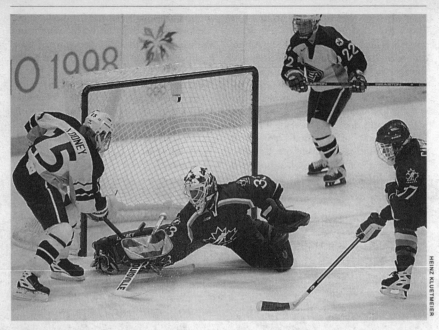

HEINZ KLUETMEIER

The Greatest: with a little help from Ali, Shelly Looney and the U.S. women won gold.

start of the women's tournament, there was little doubt that the competition was a two-team battle between two old nemeses, the U.S. and Canada. On the team bus to the final, the U.S. coaching staff showed the players an inspirational video that showed clips of their own play interspersed with clips from the Muhammad Ali movie *When We Were Kings*. Appearing never to doubt that they, like Ali, were the greatest, the U.S. women beat Canada 3–1.

While this was no Miracle on Ice, like the U.S. men's upset victory over the Soviets in 1980, it was a tremendous advertisement for women's hockey. "People haven't seen our sport; they don't realize it's a real hockey game, they don't expect any body contact," said Sandra Whyte of Harvard, who scored the final U.S. goal. "This is going to cause a big surge in the amount of girls playing."

And there, in a nutshell, is Nagano's greatest legacy—inspiration. The Olympic

spirit felt rejuvenated by these friendly Games, which was fortunate since midsummer brought a flurry of drug scandals. Randy Barnes, the 1996 Olympic shot put champ, and Dennis Mitchell, the 1992 Olympic bronze medalist in the 100-meter dash, were both suspended for doping violations, and swimmer Michelle Smith of Ireland, whose triple gold medal performance in Atlanta had raised many suspicions, was banned for four years for tampering with a drug test. A widespread drug scandal at the Tour de France prompted Samaranch to make some ill-considered remarks about softening IOC doping rules that left other Olympic leaders backpedaling furiously.

The final Games of the 20th century closed on Feb. 22 with a stupendous fireworks display and the thunder of 2,000 drummers. As Samaranch presented the Olympic flag to Salt Lake City mayor Deedee Corradini, the world came away with the feeling that the Olympic movement is strong, inspiring and even necessary, a quadrennial mirror in which we view the best part of ourselves.

1996 Summer Games

TRACK AND FIELD
Men

100 METERS
1. ..Donovan Bailey, Canada — 9.84 WR
2. ..Frankie Fredericks, Namibia — 9.89
3. ..Ato Boldon, Trinidad and Tobago — 9.90

200 METERS
1. ..Michael Johnson, United States — 19.32 WR
2. ..Frankie Fredericks, Namibia — 19.68
3. ..Ato Boldon, Trinidad and Tobago — 19.80

400 METERS
1. ..Michael Johnson, United States — 43.49 OR
2. ..Roger Black, Great Britain — 44.41
3. ..Davis Kamoga, Uganda — 44.53

800 METERS
1. ..Vebjoern Rodal, Norway — 1:42.58 OR
2. ..Hezekiel Sepeng, South Africa — 1:42.74
3. ..Fred Onyancha, Kenya — 1:42.79

1500 METERS
1. ..Noureddine Morceli, Algeria — 3:35.78
2. ..Fermin Cacho, Spain — 3:36.40
3. ..Stephen Kipkorir, Kenya — 3:36.72

5000 METERS
1. ..Venuste Niyongabo, Burundi — 13:07.96
2. ..Paul Bitok, Kenya — 13:08.16
3. ..Khalid Boulami, Morocco — 13:08.37

10,000 METERS
1. ..Haile Gebrselassie, Ethiopia — 27:07.34 OR
2. ..Paul Tergat, Kenya — 27:08.17
3. ..Salah Hissou, Morocco — 27:24.67

MARATHON
1. ..Josia Thugwane, South Africa — 2:12:36
2. ..Bong-Ju Lee, South Korea — 2:12:39
3. ..Eric Wainaina, Kenya — 2:12:44

110-METER HURDLES
1. ..Allen Johnson, United States — 12.95 OR
2. ..Mark Crear, United States — 13.09
3. ..Florian Schwarthoff, Germany — 13.17

400-METER HURDLES
1. ..Derrick Adkins, United States — 47.54
2. ..Samuel Matete, Zambia — 47.78
3. ..Calvin Davis, United States — 47.96

3000-METER STEEPLECHASE
1. ..Joseph Keter, Kenya — 8:07.12
2. ..Moses Kiptanui, Kenya — 8:08.33
3. ..Alessandro Lambruschini, Italy — 8:11.28

4 X 100 METER RELAY
1. ..Canada: Donovan Bailey, Robert Esmie, Glenroy Gilbert, Bruny Surin — 37.69
2. ..United States — 38.05
3. ..Brazil — 38.41

4 X 400 METER RELAY
1. ..United States: Alvin Harrison, Anthuan Maybank, Derek Mills, LaMont Smith — 2:55.99
2. ..Great Britain — 2:56.60
3. ..Jamaica — 2:59.42

20-KILOMETER WALK
1. ..Jefferson Pérez, Ecuador — 1:20:07
2. ..Ilya Markov, Russia — 1:20:16
3. ..Bernardo Segura, Mexico — 1:20:23

50-KILOMETER WALK
1. ..Robert Korzeniowski, Poland — 3:43:30
2. ..Mikhail Shchennikov, Russia — 3:43:46
3. ..Valentin Massana, Spain — 3:44:19

HIGH JUMP
1. ..Charles Austin, United States — 7 ft 10 in OR
2. ..Artur Partyka, Poland — 7 ft 9¼ in
3. ..Steve Smith, Great Britain — 7 ft 8½ in

POLE VAULT
1. ..Jean Galfione, France — 19 ft 5¼ in OR
2. ..Igor Trandenkov, Russia — 19 ft 5¼ in
3. ..Andrei Tivontchik, Germany — 19 ft 5¼ in

LONG JUMP
1. ..Carl Lewis, United States — 27 ft 10¾ in
2. ..James Beckford, Jamaica — 27 ft 2½ in
3. ..Joe Greene, United States — 27 ft ½ in

TRIPLE JUMP
1. ..Kenny Harrison, United States — 59 ft 4¼ in OR
2. ..Jonathan Edwards, Great Britain — 58 ft 8 in
3. ..Yoelvis Quesada, Cuba — 57 ft 2¾ in

SHOT PUT
1. ..Randy Barnes, United States — 70 ft 11 in
2. ..John Godina, United States — 68 ft 2½ in
3. ..Oleksandr Bagach, Ukraine — 68 ft ½ in

DISCUS THROW
1. ..Lars Riedel, Germany — 227 ft 8 in OR
2. ..Vladimir Dubrovshchik, Belarus — 218 ft 6 in
3. ..Vasiliy Kaptyukh, Belarus — 215 ft 10 in

HAMMER THROW
1. ..Balazs Kiss, Hungary — 266 ft 6 in
2. ..Lance Deal, United States — 266 ft 2 in
3. ..Oleksiy Krykun, Ukraine — 262 ft 6 in

JAVELIN
1. ..Jan Zelezny, Czech Republic — 289 ft 3 in
2. ..Steve Backley, Great Britain — 286 ft 10 in
3. ..Seppo Raty, Finland — 285 ft 4 in

DECATHLON
Pts
1. ..Dan O'Brien, United States — 8824 OR
2. ..Frank Busemann, Germany — 8706
3. ..Tomás Dvořák, Czech Republic — 8664

Note: OR=Olympic record. WR=world record. EOR=equals Olympic record. EWR=equals world record.

TRACK AND FIELD *(Cont.)*
Women

100 METERS
1. ..Gail Devers, United States — 10.94
2. ..Merlene Ottey, Jamaica — 10.94
3. ..Gwen Torrence, United States — 10.96

200 METERS
1. ..Marie-José Pérec, France — 22.12
2. ..Merlene Ottey, Jamaica — 22.24
3. ..Mary Onyali, Nigeria — 22.38

400 METERS
1. ..Marie-José Pérec, France — 48.25 OR
2. ..Cathy Freeman, Australia — 48.63
3. ..Falilat Ogunkoya, Nigeria — 49.10

800 METERS
1. ..Svetlana Masterkova, Russia — 1:57.73
2. ..Ana Fidelia Quirot, Cuba — 1:58.11
3. ..Maria Mutola, Mozambique — 1:58.71

1500 METERS
1. ..Svetlana Masterkova, Russia — 4:00.83
2. ..Gabriela Szabo, Russia — 4:01.54
3. ..Theresia Kiesl, Austria — 4:03.02

5000 METERS
1. ..Wang Junxia, China — 14:59.88
2. ..Pauline Konga, Kenya — 15:03.49
3. ..Roberta Brunet, Italy — 15:07.52

10,000 METERS
1. ..Fernanda Ribeiro, Portugal — 31:01.63 OR
2. ..Wang Junxia, China — 31:02.58
3. ..Gete Wami, Ethiopia — 31:06.68

MARATHON
1. ..Fatuma Roba, Ethiopia — 2:26:05
2 ..Valentina Yegorova, Russia — 2:28:05
3. ..Yuko Arimori, Japan — 2:28:39

100-METER HURDLES
1. ..Lyudmila Engqvist, Sweden — 12.58
2. ..Brigita Bukovec, Slovenia — 12.59
3. ..Patricia Girard-Leno, France — 12.65

400-METER HURDLES
1. ..Deon Hemmings, Jamaica — 52.82 OR
2. ..Kim Batten, United States — 53.08
3. ..Tonja Buford-Bailey, United States — 53.22

4 X 100 METER RELAY
1. ..United States: Chryste Gaines — 41.95
   Gail Devers, Inger Miller, Gwen
   Torrence
2. ..Bahamas — 42.14
3. ..Jamaica — 42.24

4 X 400 METER RELAY
1. ..United States: Rochelle Stevens — 3:20.91
   Maicel Malone, Kim Graham,
   Jearl Miles
2. ..Nigeria — 3:21.04
3. ..Germany — 3:21.41

10-KILOMETER WALK
1. ..Elena Nikolayeva, Russia — 41:49 OR
2. ..Elisabetta Perrone, Italy — 42:12
3. ..Wang Yan, China — 42:19

HIGH JUMP
1. ..Stefka Kostadinova, Bulgaria — 6 ft 8¾ in OR
2. ..Niki Bakogianni, Greece — 6 ft 8 in
3. ..Inga Babakova, Ukraine — 6 ft 7 in

LONG JUMP
1. ..Chioma Ajunwa, Nigeria — 23 ft 4½ in
2. ..Fiona May, Italy — 23 ft ½ in
3. ..Jackie Joyner-Kersee, United States — 22 ft 11¾ in

TRIPLE JUMP
1. ..Inessa Kravets, Ukraine — 50 ft 3½ in
2. ..Inna Lasovskaya, Russia — 49 ft 1¾ in
3. ..Sarka Kasparkova, Czech Republic — 49 ft 1¾ in

SHOT PUT
1. ..Astrid Kumbernuss, Germany — 67 ft 5½ in
2. ..Sui Xinmei, China — 65 ft 2¾ in
3. ..Irina Khudorozhkina, Russia — 63 ft 6 in

DISCUS THROW
1. ..Ilke Wyludda, Germany — 228 ft 6 in
2. ..Natalya Sadova, Russia — 218 ft 1 in
3. ..Ellina Zvereva, Belarus — 215 ft 4 in

JAVELIN
1. ..Heli Rantanen, Finland — 222 ft 11 in
2. ..Louise McPaul, Australia — 215 ft
3. ..Trine Hattestad, Norway — 213 ft 2 in

HEPTATHLON
	Pts
1. ..Ghada Shouaa, Syria	6780
2. ..Natasha Sazanovich, Belarus	6563
3. ..Denise Lewis, Great Britain	6489

BADMINTON

Men
SINGLES
1. ..Poul-Erik Hoyer-Larsen, Denmark
2. ..Dong Jiong, China
3. ..Rashid Sidek, Malaysia

DOUBLES
1. ..Rexy Mainaky & Ricky Subagja, Indonesia
2. ..Cheah Soon Kit & Yap Kim Hock, Malaysia
3. ..S. Antonius & Denny Kantono, Indonesia

Women
SINGLES
1. ..Bang Soo Hyun, South Korea
2. ..Mia Audina, Indonesia
3. ..Susi Susanti, Indonesia

DOUBLES
1. ...Ge Fei & Gu Jun, China
2. ..Gil Young Ah & Jang Hye Ock, South Korea
3. ..Qin Yiyuan & Tang Yongshu, China

Note: OR=Olympic record. WR=world record. EOR=equals Olympic record. EWR=equals world record.

BADMINTON (Cont.)

MIXED DOUBLES
1. ....Gil Young Ah & Kim Dong Moon, South Korea
2. ....Park Joo Bong & Ra Kyung Min, South Korea
3. ....Liu Jianjun & Sun Man, China

BASEBALL
1. ....Cuba
2. ....Japan
3. ....United States

CANOE/KAYAK

Men

C-1 FLATWATER 500 METERS
1.	...Martin Doktor, Czech Republic	1:49.93
2.	...Slavomir Knazovicky, Slovakia	1:50.51
3.	...Imre Pulai, Hungary	1:50.75

C-1 FLATWATER 1000 METERS
1.	...Martin Doktor, Czech Republic	3:54.41
2.	...Ivan Klementiev, Latvia	3:54.95
3.	...Gyorgy Zala, Hungary	3:56.36

C-2 FLATWATER 500 METERS
1.	...C. Horváth & G. Kolonics, Hungary	1:40.42
2.	...N. Shuravski & V. Reneischi, Moldova	1:40.45
3.	...G. Andriev & G. Obreja, Romania	1:41.33

C-2 FLATWATER 1000 METERS
1.	...A. Dittmer & G. Kirchbach, Germany	3:31.87
2.	...A. Borsan & M. Glavan, Romania	3:32.29
3.	...C. Horváth & G. Kolonics, Hungary	3:32.51

C-1 WHITEWATER SLALOM
		Pts
1.	...Michal Martikan, Slovakia	151.03
2.	...Lukas Pollert, Czech Republic	151.17
3.	...Patrice Estanguet, France	152.84

C-2 WHITEWATER SLALOM
		Pts
1.	...F. Adisson & W. Forgues, France	158.82
2.	...J. Rohan & M. Simek, Czech Republic	160.16
3.	...A. Ehrenberg & M. Senft, Germany	163.72

K-1 FLATWATER 500 METERS
1.	...Antonio Rossi, Italy	1:37.42
2.	...Knut Holmann, Norway	1:38.33
3.	...Piotr Markiewicz, Poland	1:38.61

K-1 FLATWATER 1000 METERS
1.	...Knut Holmann, Norway	3:25.78
2.	...Beniamino Bonomi, Italy	3:27.07
3.	...Clint Robinson, Australia	3:29.71

Men (Cont.)

K-2 FLATWATER 500 METERS
1.	...K. Bluhm & T. Gutsche, Germany	1:28.69
2.	...B. Bonomi & D. Scarpa, Italy	1:28.72
3.	...D. Collins & A. Trim, Australia	1:29.40

K-2 FLATWATER 1000 METERS
1.	...A. Rossi & D. Scarpa, Italy	3:09.19
2.	...K. Bluhm & T. Gutsche, Germany	3:10.51
3.	...M. Kazanov & A. Dushev, Bulgaria	3:11.20

K-4 FLATWATER 1000 METERS
1.	...Germany	2:51.52
2.	...Hungary	2:53.18
3.	...Russia	2:53.99

K-1 WHITEWATER SLALOM
		Pts
1.	...Oliver Fix, Germany	141.22
2.	...Andraz Vehovar, Slovenia	141.65
3.	...Thomas Becker, Germany	142.79

Women

K-1 FLATWATER 500 METERS
1.	...Rita Kóbán, Hungary	1:47.65
2.	...Caroline Brunet, Canada	1:47.89
3.	...Josefa Idem, Italy	1:48.73

K-2 FLATWATER 500 METERS
1.	...A. Andersson & S. Gunnarsson, Sweden	1:39.32
2.	...R. Portwich & B. Fischer, Germany	1:39.68
3.	...K. Borshert & A. Wood, Australia	1:40.64

K-4 FLATWATER 500 METERS
1.	...Germany	1:31.07
2.	...Switzerland	1:32.70
3.	...Sweden	1:32.91

K-1 WHITEWATER SLALOM
		Pts
1.	...Stepanka Hilgertova, Czech Republic	169.49
2.	...Dana Chladek, United States	169.49
3.	...Myriam Fox-Jerusalmi, France	171.00

BASKETBALL

Men

Final: United States 95, Yugoslavia 69
Lithuania (3rd)
United States: Charles Barkley, Anfernee Hardaway, Grant Hill, Karl Malone, Reggie Miller, Hakeem Olajuwon, Shaquille O'Neal, Scottie Pippen, Mitch Richmond, John Stockton, David Robinson, Gary Payton

Women

Final: United States 111, Brazil 87
Australia (3rd)
United States: Jennifer Azzi, Ruthie Bolton, Teresa Edwards, Lisa Leslie, Rebecca Lobo, Katrina McClain, Nikki McCray, Carla McGhee, Dawn Staley, Katy Steding, Sheryl Swoopes, Venus Lacey

BOXING

LIGHT FLYWEIGHT (106 LB)
1. ....Daniel Petrov, Bulgaria
2. ....Mansueto Velasco, Philippines
3. ....Oleg Kiryukhin, Ukraine
3. ....Rafael Lozano, Spain

FLYWEIGHT (112 LB)
1. ....Maikro Romero, Cuba
2. ....Bolat Zhumadilov, Kazakhstan
3. ....Zoltan Lunka, Germany
3. ....Albert Pakeev, Russia

BANTAMWEIGHT (119 LB)
1. ....István Kovács, Hungary
2. ....Arnaldo Mesa, Cuba
3. ....Vichairachanon Khadpo, Thailand
3. ....Raimkul Malakhbekov, Russia

FEATHERWEIGHT (125 LB)
1. ....Somluck Kamsing, Thailand
2. ....Serafim Todorov, Bulgaria
3. ....Pablo Chacon, Argentina
3. ....Floyd Mayweather, United States

LIGHTWEIGHT (132 LB)
1. ....Hocine Soltani, Algeria
2. ....Tontcho Tontchev, Bulgaria
3. ....Terrance Cauthen, United States
3. ....Leonard Doroftei, Romania

LIGHT WELTERWEIGHT (139 LB)
1. ....Hector Vinent, Cuba
2. ....Oktay Urkal, Germany
3. ....Fathi Missaoui, Tunisia
3. ....Bolat Niyazymbetov, Kazakhstan

WELTERWEIGHT (147 LB)
1. ....Oleg Saitov, Russia
2. ....Juan Hernández, Cuba
3. ....Daniel Santos, Puerto Rico
3. ....Marian Simion, Romania

LIGHT MIDDLEWEIGHT (156 LB)
1. ....David Reid, United States
2. ....Alfredo Duvergel, Cuba
3. ....Ermakhan Ibraimov, Kazakhstan
3. ....Karim Tulaganov, Uzbekistan

MIDDLEWEIGHT (165 LB)
1. ....Ariel Hernández, Cuba
2. ....Malik Beyleroglu, Turkey
3. ....Mohamed Bahari, Algeria
3. ....Rhoshii Wells, United States

LIGHT HEAVYWEIGHT (178 LB)
1. ....Vassili Jirov, Kazakhstan
2. ....Lee Seung Bao, South Korea
3. ....Antonio Tarver, United States
3. ....Thomas Ulrich, Germany

HEAVYWEIGHT (201 LB)
1. ....Félix Sávon, Cuba
2. ....David Defiagbon, Canada
3. ....Nate Jones, United States
3. ....Luan Krasniqi, Germany

SUPERHEAVYWEIGHT (201+ LB)
1. ....Vladimir Klitchko, Ukraine
2. ....Paea Wolfgram, Tonga
3. ....Duncan Dokiwari, Nigeria
3. ....Alexei Lezin, Russia

GYMNASTICS

Men

ALL-AROUND

	Pts
1. ....Li Xiaoshuang, China	58.423
2. ....Alexei Nemov, Russia	58.374
3. ....Vitaly Scherbo, Belarus	58.197

HORIZONTAL BAR

	Pts
1. ....Andreas Wecker, Germany	9.850
2. ....Krasimir Dounev, Bulgaria	9.825
3. ....Vitaly Scherbo, Belarus	9.800
3. ....Fan Bin, China	9.800
3. ....Alexei Nemov, Russia	9.800

PARALLEL BARS

	Pts
1. ....Rustam Sharipov, Ukraine	9.837
2. ....Jair Lynch, United States	9.825
3. ....Vitaly Scherbo, Belarus	9.800

VAULT

	Pts
1. ....Alexei Nemov, Russia	9.787
2. ....Yeo Hong-Chul, South Korea	9.756
3. ....Vitaly Scherbo, Belarus	9.724

POMMEL HORSE

	Pts
1. ....Donghua Li, Switzerland	9.875
2. ....Marius Urzica, Romania	9.825
3. ....Alexei Nemov, Russia	9.787

Women

ALL-AROUND

	Pts
1. ....Lilia Podkopayeva, Ukraine	39.255
2. ....Gina Gogean, Romania	39.075
3. ....Simona Amanar, Romania	39.067
3. ....Lavinia Milosovici, Romania	39.067

VAULT

	Pts
1. ....Simona Amanar, Romania	9.825
2. ....Mo Huilan, China	9.768
3. ....Gina Gogean, Romania	9.750

UNEVEN BARS

	Pts
1. ....Svetlana Chorkina, Russia	9.850
2. ....Bi Wenjing, China	9.837
2. ....Amy Chow, United States	9.837

BALANCE BEAM

	Pts
1. ....Shannon Miller, United States	9.862
2. ....Lilia Podkopayeva, Ukraine	9.825
3. ....Gina Gogean, Romania	9.787

FLOOR EXERCISE

	Pts
1. ....Lilia Podkopayeva, Ukraine	9.887
2. ....Simona Amanar, Romania	9.850
3. ....Dominique Dawes, United States	9.837

GYMNASTICS *(Cont.)*

Men

RINGS

	Pts
1. ....Yuri Chechi, Italy	9.887
2. ....Szilveszter Csollany, Hungary	9.812
2. ....Dan Burinca, Romania	9.812

FLOOR EXERCISE

	Pts
1. ....Ioannis Melissanidis, Greece	9.850
2. ....Li Xiaoshuang, China	9.837
3. ....Alexei Nemov, Russia	9.800

TEAM COMBINED EXERCISES

	Pts
1. ....Russia	576.778
2...........China	575.539
3. ....Ukraine	571.541

Women

TEAM COMBINED EXERCISES

	Pts
1. ....United States: Amanda Borden, Amy Chow, Dominique Dawes, Shannon Miller, Dominique Moceanu, Jaycie Phelps, Kerri Strug	389.225
2. ....Russia	388.404
3. ....Romania	388.246

RHYTHMIC ALL-AROUND

	Pts
1. ....Ekaterina Serebrianskaya, Ukraine	39.683
2. ....Janna Batyrchina, Russia	39.382
3. ....Elena Vitrichenko, Ukraine	39.331

RHYTHMIC TEAM COMBINED EXERCISES

	Pts
1. ....Spain	38.933
2. ....Bulgaria	38.866
3. ....Russia	38.365

SWIMMING

Men

50-METER FREESTYLE

1. ..Aleksandr Popov, Russia	22.13
2. ..Gary Hall Jr, United States	22.26
3. ..Fernando Scherer, Brazil	22.29

100-METER FREESTYLE

1. ..Aleksandr Popov, Russia	48.74
2. ..Gary Hall Jr, United States	48.81
3. ..Gustavo Borges, Brazil	49.02

200-METER FREESTYLE

1. ..Danyon Loader, New Zealand	1:47.63
2. ..Gustavo Borges, Brazil	1:48.08
3. ..Daniel Kowalski, Australia	1:48.25

400-METER FREESTYLE

1. ..Danyon Loader, New Zealand	3:47.97
2. ..Paul Palmer, Great Britain	3:49.00
3. ..Daniel Kowalski, Australia	3:49.39

1500-METER FREESTYLE

1. ..Kieren Perkins, Australia	14:56.40
2. ..Daniel Kowalski, Australia	15:02.43
3. ..Graeme Smith, Great Britain	15:02.48

100-METER BACKSTROKE

1. ..Jeff Rouse, United States	54.10
2. ..Rodolfo Falcon Cabrera, Cuba	54.98
3. ..Neisser Bent, Cuba	55.02

200-METER BACKSTROKE

1. ..Brad Bridgewater, United States	1:58.54
2. ..Tripp Schwenk, United States	1:58.99
3. ..Emanuele Merisi, Italy	1:59.18

100-METER BREASTSTROKE

1. ..Fred DeBurghgraeve, Belgium	1:00.65
2. ..Jeremy Linn, United States	1:00.77
3. ..Mark Warnecke, Germany	1:01.33

200-METER BREASTSTROKE

1. ..Norbert Rózsa, Hungary	2:12.57
2. ..Károly Güttler, Hungary	2:13.03
3. ..Andrei Korneyev, Russia	2:13.17

100-METER BUTTERFLY

1. ..Denis Pankratov, Russia	52.27 WR
2. ..Scott Miller, Australia	52.53
3. ..Vladislav Kulikov, Russia	53.13

200-METER BUTTERFLY

1. ..Denis Pankratov, Russia	1:56.51
2. ..Tom Malchow, United States	1:57.44
3. ..Scott Goodman, Australia	1:57.48

200-METER INDIVIDUAL MEDLEY

1. ..Attila Czene, Hungary	1:59.91 OR
2. ..Jani Sievinen, Finland	2:00.13
3. ..Curtis Myden, Canada	2:01.13

400-METER INDIVIDUAL MEDLEY

1. ..Tom Dolan, United States	4:14.90
2. ..Eric Namesnik, United States	4:15.25
3. ..Curtis Myden, Canada	4:16.28

4 X 100 METER MEDLEY RELAY

1. ..United States: Jeff Rouse, Mark Henderson, Gary Hall Jr., Jeremy Linn	3:34.84 WR
2. ..Russia	3:37.55
3. ..Australia	3:39.56

4 X 100 METER FREESTYLE RELAY

1. ..United States: Jon Olsen, Josh Davis, Bradley Schumacher, Gary Hall Jr.	3:15.41 OR
2. ..Russia	3:17.06
3. ..Germany	3:17.20

4 X 200 METER FREESTYLE RELAY

1. ..United States: Ryan Berube, Joe Hudepohl, Bradley Schumacher, Jon Olsen	7:14.84
2. ..Sweden	7:17.56
3. ..Germany	7:17.71

Note: OR=Olympic record. WR=world record. EOR=equals Olympic record. EWR=equals world record.

SWIMMING (Cont.)
Women

50-METER FREESTYLE
1. ..Amy Van Dyken, United States   24.87
2. ..Le Jingyi, China   24.90
3. ..Sandra Volker, Germany   25.14

100-METER FREESTYLE
1. ..Le Jingyi, China   54.50 OR
2. ..Sandra Volker, Germany   54.88
3. ..Angel Martino, United States   54.93

200-METER FREESTYLE
1. ..Claudia Poll, Costa Rica   1:58.16
2. ..Franziska van Almsick, Germany   1:58.57
3. ..Dagmar Hase, Germany   1:59.56

400-METER FREESTYLE
1. ..Michelle Smith, Ireland   4:07.25
2. ..Dagmar Hase, Germany   4:08.30
3. ..Kirsten Vlieghuis, Netherlands   4:08.70

800-METER FREESTYLE
1. ..Brooke Bennett, United States   8:27.89
2. ..Dagmar Hase, Germany   8:29.91
3. ..Kirsten Vlieghuis, Netherlands   8:30.84

100-METER BACKSTROKE
1. ..Beth Botsford, United States   1:01.19
2. ..Whitney Hedgepeth, United States   1:01.47
3. ..Marianne Kriel, South Africa   1:02.12

200-METER BACKSTROKE
1. ..Krisztina Egerszegi, Hungary   2:07.83
2. ..Whitney Hedgepeth, United States   2:11.98
3. ..Cathleen Rund, Germany   2:12.06

100-METER BREASTSTROKE
1. ..Penelope Heyns, South Africa   1:07.73
2. ..Amanda Beard, United States   1:08.09
3. ..Samantha Riley, Australia   1:09.18

200-METER BREASTSTROKE
1. ..Penelope Heyns, South Africa   2:25.41 OR
2. ..Amanda Beard, United States   2:25.75
3. ..Agnes Kovacs, Hungary   2:26.57

100-METER BUTTERFLY
1. ..Amy Van Dyken, United States   59.13
2. ..Liu Limin, China   59.14
3. ..Angel Martino, United States   59.23

200-METER BUTTERFLY
1. ..Susan O'Neill, Australia   2:07.76
2. ..Petria Thomas, Australia   2:09.82
3. ..Michelle Smith, Ireland   2:09.91

200-METER INDIVIDUAL MEDLEY
1. ..Michelle Smith, Ireland   2:13.93
2. ..Marianne Limpert, Canada   2:14.35
3. ..Lin Li, China   2:14.74

400-METER INDIVIDUAL MEDLEY
1. ..Michelle Smith, Ireland   4:39.18
2. ..Allison Wagner, United States   4:42.03
3. ..Krisztina Egerszegi, Hungary   4:42.53

4 X 100 METER MEDLEY RELAY
1. ..United States: Beth Botsford,   4:02.88
    Amanda Beard, Angel Martino,
    Amy Van Dyken
2. ..Australia   4:05.08
3. ..China   4:07.34

4 X 100 METER FREESTYLE RELAY
1. ..United States: Jenny Thompson,   3:39.29 OR
    Catherine Fox, Angel Martino,
    Amy Van Dyken
2. ..China   3:40.48
3. ..Germany   3:41.48

4 X 200 METER FREESTYLE RELAY
1. ..United States: Trina Jackson,   7:59.87
    Sheila Taormina, Cristina Teuscher,
    Jenny Thompson
2. ..Germany   8:01.55
3. ..Australia   8:05.47

DIVING

Men
SPRINGBOARD

	Pts
1. ....Xiong Ni, China	701.46
2. ....Yu Zhuocheng, China	690.93
3. ....Mark Lenzi, United States	686.49

PLATFORM

	Pts
1. ....Dmitri Sautin, Russia	692.34
2. ....Jan Hempel, Germany	663.27
3. ....Xiao Hailiang, China	658.20

Women
SPRINGBOARD

	Pts
1. ....Fu Mingxia, China	547.68
2. ....Irina Lashko, Russia	512.19
3. ....Annie Pelletier, Canada	509.64

PLATFORM

	Pts
1. ....Fu Mingxia, China	521.58
2. ....Annika Walter, Germany	479.22
3. ....Mary Ellen Clark, United States	472.95

INDIVIDUAL ARCHERY

Men
1. ....Justin Huish, United States
2. ....Magnus Petersson, Sweden
3. ....Oh Kyo Moon, South Korea

Women
1. ....Kim Kyung Wook, South Korea
2. ....He Ying, China
3. ....Olena Sadovnycha, Ukraine

Note: OR=Olympic record. WR=world record. EOR=equals Olympic record. EWR=equals world record.

TEAM ARCHERY

Men

1. ....United States
2. ....South Korea
3. ....Italy

Women

1. ....South Korea
2. ....Germany
3. ....Poland

CYCLING

Men

ROAD RACE

1. ..Pascal Richard, Switzerland	4:53:56
2. ..Rolf Sorensen, Denmark	4:53:56
3. ..Maximilian Sciandri, Great Britain	4:53:58

INDIVIDUAL TIME TRIAL

1. ..Miguel Indurain, Spain	1:04:05
2. ..Abraham Olano, Spain	1:04:17
3. ..Chris Boardman, Great Britain	1:04:36

1 KM TIME TRIAL

1. ..Florian Rousseau, France	1:02.712 OR
2. ..Erin Hartwell, United States	1:02.940
3. ..Takanobu Jumonji, Japan	1:03.261

4000 METER INDIVIDUAL PURSUIT

1. ..Andrea Collinelli, Italy	4:20.893
2. ..Philippe Ermenault, France	4:22.714
3. ..Bradley McGee, Australia	4:26.121

4000 METER TEAM PURSUIT

1. ..France: Christophe Capelle, Philippe Ermenault, Jean-Michel Monin, Francis Moreau, Herve Thuet	4:05.930
2. ..Russia	4:07.730
3. ..Australia	4:07.570

SPRINT

1. ..Jens Fiedler, Germany	10.664
2. ..Marty Nothstein, United States	11.074
3. ..Curt Harnett, Canada	10.947

Men *(Cont.)*

40 KM POINTS RACE

1. ..Silvio Martinello, Italy	37
2. ..Brian Walton, Canada	29
3. ..Stuart O'Grady, Australia	27

Women

ROAD RACE

1. ..Jeannie Longo-Ciprelli, France	2:36:13
2. ..Imelda Chiappa, Italy	2:36.38
3. ..Clara Hughes, Canada	2:36.44

INDIVIDUAL TIME TRIAL

1. ..Zulfiya Zabirova, Russia	36:40
2. ..Jeannie Longo-Ciprelli, France	37:00
3. ..Clara Hughes, Canada	37:13

3000 METER INDIVIDUAL PURSUIT

1. ..Antonella Bellutti, Italy	3:33.595
2. ..Marion Clignet, France	3:38.571
3. ..Judith Arndt, Germany	3:38.744

SPRINT

1. ..Felicia Ballanger, France	11.903
2. ..Michelle Ferris, Australia	12.096
3. ..Ingrid Haringa, Netherlands	12.074

24 KM POINTS RACE

1. ..Nathalie Lancien, France	24
2. ..Ingrid Haringa, Netherlands	23
3. ..Lucy Tyler Sharman, Australia	17

MOUNTAIN BIKING

Men

1. ......Bart Jan Brentjens, Netherlands	2:17:38
2. ......Thomas Frischknecht, Switzerland	2:20:14
3. ......Miguel Martinez, France	2:20:36

Women

1. ......Paola Pezzo, Italy	1:50:51
2. ......Alison Sydor, Canada	1:51:58
3. ......Susan DeMattei, United States	1:52:36

EQUESTRIAN

3-DAY TEAM

1. ......Australia: Wendy Schaeffer, Phillip Dutton, Andrew Hoy, Darien Powers	203.850
2. ......United States	261.100
3. ......New Zealand	268.550

3-DAY INDIVIDUAL

1. ......Blyth Tait, New Zealand	56.80
2. ......Sally Clark, New Zealand	60.40
3. ......Kerry Millikin, United States	73.70

TEAM DRESSAGE

1. ......Germany: Isabell Werth, Monica Theodorescu, Martin Schaudt, Klaus Balkenhol	5553
2. ......The Netherlands	5437
3. ......United States	5309

INDIVIDUAL DRESSAGE

1. ......Isabell Werth, Germany	235.09
2. ......Anky van Grunsven, Netherlands	233.02
3. ......Sven Rothenberger, Netherlands	224.94

TEAM JUMPING

1. ......Germany: Ulrich Kirchoff, Lars Nieberg, Franke Sloothaak, Ludger Beerbaum	1.25
2. ......United States	12.00
3. ......Brazil	17.25

INDIVIDUAL JUMPING

1. ......Ulrich Kirchoff, Germany	1.00
2. ......Willi Melliger, Switzerland	4.00
3. ......Alexandra Ledermann, France	4.00

Note: OR=Olympic record. WR=world record. EOR=equals Olympic record. EWR=equals world record.

FENCING

Men

FOIL
1. ....Alessandro Puccini, Italy
2. ....Lionel Plumenail, France
3. ....Franck Boidin, France

SABRE
1. ....Stanislav Pozdniakov, Russia
2. ....Sergei Sharikov, Russia
3. ....Damien Touya, France

ÉPÉE
1. ....Aleksandr Beketov, Russia
2. ....Ivan Trevejo Perez, Cuba
3. ....Geza Imre, Hungary

TEAM FOIL
1. ....Russia
2. ....Poland
3. ....Cuba

TEAM SABRE
1. ....Russia
2. ....Hungary
3. ....Italy

Men *(Cont.)*

TEAM ÉPÉE
1. ....Italy
2. ....Russia
3. ....France

Women

FOIL
1. ....Laura Badea, Romania
2. ....Valentina Vezzali, Italy
3. ....Giovanna Trillini, Italy

ÉPÉE
1. ....Laura Flessel, France
2. ....Valerie Barlois, France
3. ....Gyöngyi Szalay, Hungary

TEAM FOIL
1. ....Italy
2. ....Romania
3. ....Germany

TEAM ÉPÉE
1. ....France
2. ....Italy
3. ....Russia

FIELD HOCKEY

Men
1. ....The Netherlands
2. ....Spain
3. ....Australia

Women
1. ....Australia
2. ....South Korea
3. ....The Netherlands

TEAM HANDBALL

Men
1. ....Croatia
2. ....Sweden
3. ....Spain

Women
1. ....Denmark
2. ....South Korea
3. ....Hungary

JUDO

Men

EXTRA-LIGHTWEIGHT
1. ....Tadahiro Nomura, Japan
2. ....Girolamo Giovinazzo, Italy
3. ....Dorjpalam Narmandakh, Mongolia
3. ....Richard Trautmann, Germany

HALF-LIGHTWEIGHT
1. ....Udo Quellmalz, Germany
2. ....Yukimasa Nakamura, Japan
3. ....Henrique Guimares, Brazil
3. ....Israel Hernandez Plana, Cuba

LIGHTWEIGHT
1. ....Kenzo Nakamura, Japan
2. ....Kwak Dae Sung, South Korea
3. ....Christophe Gagliano, France
3. ....James Pedro, United States

HALF-MIDDLEWEIGHT
1. ....Djamel Bouras, France
2. ....Toshihiko Koga, Japan
3. ....Cho In Chul, South Korea
3. ....Soso Liparteliani, Georgia

Women

EXTRA-LIGHTWEIGHT
1. ....Kye Sun Hi, North Korea
2. ....Ryoko Tamura, Japan
3. ....Amarilis Savón, Cuba
3. ....Yolanda Soler, Spain

HALF-LIGHTWEIGHT
1. ....Marie-Claire Restoux, France
2. ....Hyun Sook Hee, South Korea
3. ....Noriko Sugawara, Japan
3. ....Legna Verdecia, Cuba

LIGHTWEIGHT
1. ....Driulis González, Cuba
2. ....Jung Sun Yong, South Korea
3. ....Isabel Fernández, Spain
3. ....Marisbel Lomba, Belgium

HALF-MIDDLEWEIGHT
1. ....Yuko Emoto, Japan
2. ....Gella Vandecaveye, Belgium
3. ....Jenny Gal, Netherlands
3. ....Jung Sung Sook, South Korea

JUDO

Men (Cont.)

MIDDLEWEIGHT
1. ....Jeon Ki Young, South Korea
2. ....Armen Bagdasarov, Uzbekistan
3. ....Mark Huizinga, Netherlands
3. ....Marko Spittka, Germany

HALF-HEAVYWEIGHT
1. ....Pawel Nastula, Poland
2. ....Kim Min Soo, South Korea
3. ....Miguel Fernandes, Brazil
3. ....Stéphane Traineau, France

HEAVYWEIGHT
1. ....David Douillet, France
2. ....Ernesto Perez, Spain
3. ....Harry van Barneveld, Belgium
3. ....Frank Möller, Germany

Women (Cont.)

MIDDLEWEIGHT
1. ....Cho Min Sun, South Korea
2. ....Aneta Szczepanska, Poland
3. ....Wang Xianbo, China
3. ....Claudia Zwiers, Netherlands

HALF-HEAVYWEIGHT
1. ....Ulla Werbrouck, Belgium
2. ....Yoko Tanabe, Japan
3. ....Ylenia Scapin, Italy
3. ....Diadenis Luna, Cuba

HEAVYWEIGHT
1. ....Sun Fuming, China
2. ....Estela Rodriguez, Cuba
3. ....Christine Cicot, France
3. ....Johanna Hagn, Germany

MODERN PENTATHLON

1. ....Aleksandr Parygin, Kazakhstan
2. ....Eduard Zenovka, Russia
3. ....Janos Martinek, Hungary

ROWING

Men

SINGLE SCULLS
1.	..Xeno Mueller, Switzerland	6:44.85
2.	..Derek Porter, Canada	6:47.45
3.	..Thomas Lange, Germany	6:47.72

DOUBLE SCULLS
1.	..D. Tizzano & A. Abbagnale, Italy	6:16.98
2.	..K. Undset & S. Stoerseth, Norway	6:18.42
3.	..F. Kowal & S. Barathay, France	6:19.85

LIGHTWEIGHT DOUBLE SCULLS
1.	..M. Gier & M. Gier, Switzerland	6:23.47
2.	..Van Der Linden & Aardewijn, Netherlands	6:26.48
3.	..A. Edwards & B. Hick, Australia	6:26.69

QUADRUPLE SCULLS
1.	..Germany	5:56.93
2.	..United States	5:59.10
3.	..Australia	6:01.65

COXLESS PAIR
1.	..S. Redgrave & M. Pinsent, Great Britain	6:20.09
2.	..D. Weightman & R. Scott, Australia	6:21.02
3.	..M. Andrieux & J. Rolland, France	6:22.15

COXLESS FOUR
1.	..Australia	6:06.37
2.	..France	6:07.03
3.	..Britain	6:07.28

LIGHTWEIGHT COXLESS FOUR
1.	..Denmark	6:09.58
2.	..Canada	6:10.13
3.	..United States	6:12.29

EIGHT-OARS
1.	..The Netherlands	5:42.74
2.	..Germany	5:44.58
3.	..Russia	5:45.77

Women

SINGLE SCULLS
1.	..Ekaterina Khodotovich, Belarus	7:32.21
2.	..Silken Laumann, Canada	7:35.15
3.	..Trine Hansen, Denmark	7:37.20

DOUBLE SCULLS
1.	..M. McBean & K. Heddle, Canada	6:56.84
2.	..Cao Mianying & Zhang Xiuyun, China	6:58.35
3.	..I. Eijs & E. Van Nes, Netherlands	6:58.72

LIGHTWEIGHT DOUBLE SCULLS
1.	..C. Burcica & C. Macoviciuc, Romania	7:12.78
2.	..T. Bell & L. Burns, United States	7:14.65
3.	..R. Joyce & V. Lee, Australia	7:16.56

QUADRUPLE SCULLS
1.	..Germany	6:27.44
2.	..Ukraine	6:30.36
3.	..Canada	6:30.38

COXLESS PAIR
1.	..M. Still & K. Slatter, Australia	7:01.39
2.	..M. Schwen & K. Kraft, United States	7:01.78
3.	..C. Gosse & H. Cortin, France	7:03.82

EIGHT-OARS
1.	..Romania	6:19.73
2.	..Canada	6:24.05
3.	..Belarus	6:24.44

SOCCER

Men
1. ....Nigeria
2. ....Argentina
3. ....Brazil

Women
1. ....United States
2. ....China
3. ....Norway

SOFTBALL

1. ....United States
2. ....China
3. ....Australia

SYNCHRONIZED SWIMMING

1. ....United States
2. ....Canada
3. ....Japan

SHOOTING

Men

RAPID-FIRE PISTOL

	Pts
1......Ralf Schumann, Germany	698
2......Emil Milev, Bulgaria	692.1
3......Vladimir Vokhmianin, Kazakhstan	691.5

FREE PISTOL

	Pts
1......Boris Kokorev, Russia	666.4
2......Igor Basinski, Belarus	662.0
3......Roberto Di Donna, Italy	661.8

AIR PISTOL

	Pts
1......Roberto Di Donna, Italy	684
2......Wang Yifu, China	684
3......Tanu Kiriakov, Bulgaria	683

RUNNING TARGET

	Pts
1......Yang Ling, China	685.8
2......Xiao Jun, China	679.8
3......Miroslav Janus, Czech Republic	678.4

SMALL-BORE RIFLE, THREE-POSITION

	Pts
1......Jean-Pierre Amat, France	1273.9
2......Sergei Beliaev, Kazakhstan	1272.3
3......Wolfram Waibel Jr, Austria	1269.6

SMALL-BORE RIFLE, PRONE

	Pts
1......Christian Klees, Germany	704.8
2......Sergei Beliaev, Kazakhstan	703.3
3......Jozef Gonci, Slovakia	701.9

AIR RIFLE

	Pts
1......Artem Khadzhibekov, Russia	695.7
2......Wolfram Waibel Jr, Austria	695.2
3......Jean-Pierre Amat, France	693.1

TRAP

	Pts
1......Michael Diamond, Australia	149
2......Josh Lakatos, United States	147
3......Lance Bade, United States	147

DOUBLE TRAP

	Pts
1......Russell Mark, Australia	189.0
2......Albano Pera, Italy	183.0
3......Zhang Bing, China	183.0

SKEET

	Pts
1......Ennio Falco, Italy	149.0
2......Miroslaw Rzepkowski, Poland	148.0
3......Andrea Benelli, Italy	147.0

Women

SPORT PISTOL

	Pts
1......Li Duihong, China	687.9
2......Diana Yorgova, Bulgaria	684.8
3......Marina Logvinenko, Russia	684.2

AIR PISTOL

	Pts
1......Olga Klochneva, Russia	490.1
2......Marina Logvinenko, Russia	488.5
3......Maria Grozdeva, Bulgaria	488.5

SMALL-BORE RIFLE, THREE-POSITION

	Pts
1......Aleksandra Ivosev, Yugoslavia	686.1
2......Irina Gerasimenok, Russia	680.1
3......Renata Mauer, Poland	679.8

AIR RIFLE

	Pts
1......Renata Mauer, Poland	497.6
2......Petra Horneber, Germany	497.4
3......Aleksandra Ivosev, Yugoslavia	497.2

DOUBLE TRAP

	Pts
1......Kim Rhode, United States	141.0
2......Susanne Kiermayer, Germany	139.0
3......Deserie Huddleston, Australia	139.0

TABLE TENNIS

Men

SINGLES

1. ....Liu Guoliang, China
2. ....Wang Tao, China
3. ....Joerg Rosskopf, Germany

DOUBLES

1. ....Kong Linghui & Liu Guoliang, China
2. ....Lu Lin & Wang Tao, China
3. ....Lee Chul Seung & Yoo Nam Kyu, South Korea

Women

SINGLES

1. ....Deng Yaping, China
2. ....Chen Jing, Taiwan
3. ....Qiao Hong, China

DOUBLES

1. ....Deng Yaping & Qiao Hong, China
2. ....Liu Wei & Qiao Yunping, China
3. ....Park Hae Jung & Ryu Ji Hae, South Korea

TENNIS

Men

SINGLES

1. ....Andre Agassi, United States
2. ....Sergi Bruguera, Spain
3. ....Leander Paes, India

DOUBLES

1. ....Todd Woodbridge &
   Mark Woodforde, Australia
2. ....Neil Broad &
   Tim Henman, Great Britain
3. ....Marc-Kevin Goellner &
   David Prinosil, Germany

Women

SINGLES

1. ....Lindsay Davenport, United States
2. ....Arantxa Sánchez Vicario, Spain
3. ....Jana Novotna, Czech Republic

DOUBLES

1. ....Gigi Fernandez &
   Mary Joe Fernandez, United States
2. ....Jana Novotna &
   Helena Sukova, Czech Republic
3. ....Conchita Martinez &
   Arantxa Sánchez Vicario, Spain

VOLLEYBALL

Men

1. ....The Netherlands
2. ....Italy
3. ....Yugoslavia

Women

1. ....Cuba
2. ....China
3. ....Brazil

BEACH VOLLEYBALL

Men

1. ....Karch Kiraly & Kent Steffes, United States
2. ....Michael Dodd & M. Whitmarsh, United States
3. ....John Child & Mark Heese, Canada

Women

1. ....S. Pires Tavares & J. Silva Cruz, Brazil
2. ....Monica Rodrigues & A. Samuel Ramos, Brazil
3. ....Natalie Cook & Kerri Ann Pottharst, Australia

WATER POLO

1. ....Spain
2. ....Croatia
3. ....Italy

WEIGHTLIFTING

119 POUNDS

1. ....Halil Mutlu, Turkey — 633 lb OR
2. ....Zhang Xiangsen, China — 616 lb
3. ....Sevdalin Minchev, Bulgaria — 611 lb

130 POUNDS

1. ....Tang Ningsheng, China — 678 lb OR
2. ....Leonidas Sabanis, Greece — 672 lb
3. ....Nikolai Pechalov, Bulgaria — 667 lb

141 POUNDS

1. ....Naim Suleymanoglu, Turkey — 739 lb OR
2. ....Valerios Leonidis, Greece — 733 lb
3. ....Xiao Jiangang, China — 711 lb

154 POUNDS

1. ....Zhan Xugang, China — 787 lb OR
2. ....Kim Myong Nam, North Korea — 761 lb
3. ....Attila Feri, Hungary — 750 lb

167.5 POUNDS

1. ....Pablo Lara, Cuba — 809 lb
2. ....Yoto Yotov, Bulgaria — 794 lb
3. ....Jon Chol, North Korea — 787 lb

183 POUNDS

1. ....Pyrros Dimas, Greece — 864 lb OR
2. ....Marc Huster, Germany — 842 lb
3. ....Andrzej Cofalik, Poland — 820 lb

200.5 POUNDS

1. ....Alexei Petrov, Russia — 886 lb
2. ....Leonidas Kokas, Greece — 860 lb
3. ....Oliver Caruso, Germany — 860 lb

218 POUNDS

1. ....Kakhi Kakhiasvili, Greece — 926 lb OR
2. ....Anatoli Khrapati, Kazakhstan — 904 lb
3. ....Denis Gotfrid, Ukraine — 886 lb

238 POUNDS

1. ....Timur Taimazov, Ukraine — 948 lb
2. ....Sergey Syrtsov, Russia — 926 lb
3. ....Nicu Vlad, Romania — 926 lb

238+ POUNDS

1. ....Andrei Chemerkin, Russia — 1008 lb OR
2. ....Ronny Weller, Germany — 1003 lb
3. ....Stefan Botev, Australia — 992 lb

FREESTYLE WRESTLING

105.5 POUNDS

1. ....Kim Il, North Korea
2. ....Armen Mkrchyan, Armenia
3. ....Alexis Vila, Cuba

114.5 POUNDS

1. ....Valentin Yordanov, Bulgaria
2. ....Namik Abdullayev, Azerbaijan
3. ....Maulen Mamyrov, Kazakhstan

125.5 POUNDS

1. ....Kendall Cross, United States
2. ....Guivi Sissaouri, Canada
3. ....Ri Yong Sam, North Korea

136.5 POUNDS

1. ....Tom Brands, United States
2. ....Jang Jae Sung, South Korea
3. ....Elbrus Tedeyev, Ukraine

Note: OR=Olympic Record. WR=World Record. EOR=Equals Olympic Record. EWR=Equals World Record.

FREESTYLE WRESTLING

149.5 POUNDS

1. Vadim Bogiev, Russia
2. Townsend Saunders, United States
3. Zaza Zazirov, Ukraine

163 POUNDS

1. Buvaysa Saytyev, Russia
2. Park Jang Soon, South Korea
3. Takuya Ota, Japan

180.5 POUNDS

1. Khadzhimurad Magomedov, Russia
2. Yang Hyun Mo, South Korea
3. Amir Reza Khadem Azghadi, Iran

198 POUNDS

1. Rasul Khadem, Iran
2. Makharbek Khadartsev, Russia
3. Eldari Kurtanidze, Georgia

220 POUNDS

1. Kurt Angle, United States
2. Abbas Jadidi, Iran
3. Arawat Sabejew, Germany

286 POUNDS

1. Mahmut Demir, Turkey
2. Alexei Medvedev, Belarus
3. Bruce Baumgartner, United States

GRECO-ROMAN WRESTLING

105.5 POUNDS

1. Sim Kwon Ho, South Korea
2. Aleksandr Pavlov, Belarus
3. Zafar Gouliev, Russia

114.5 POUNDS

1. Armen Nazarian, Armenia
2. Brandon Paulson, United States
3. Andrei Kalashnikov, Ukraine

125.5 POUNDS

1. Yuri Melnichenko, Kazakhstan
2. Dennis Hall, United States
3. Sheng Zetian, China

136.5 POUNDS

1. Wlodzimierz Zawadzki, Poland
2. Juan Luis Maren, Cuba
3. Mahmet Pirim, Turkey

149.5 POUNDS

1. Ryszard Wolny, Poland
2. Ghani Yalouz, France
3. Aleksandr Tretyakov, Russia

163 POUNDS

1. Filberto Azcuy, Cuba
2. Marko Asell, Finland
3. Jozef Tracz, Poland

180.5 POUNDS

1. Hamza Yerlikaya, Turkey
2. Thomas Zander, Germany
3. Valery Tsilent, Belarus

198 POUNDS

1. Vyacheslav Oleynyk, Ukraine
2. Jacek Fafinski, Poland
3. Maik Bullmann, Germany

220 POUNDS

1. Andrzej Wronski, Poland
2. Sergei Lishtvan, Belarus
3. Mikael Ljungberg, Sweden

286 POUNDS

1. Aleksandr Karelin, Russia
2. Matt Ghaffari, United States
3. Sergei Mureiko, Moldova

YACHTING

MEN'S 470

1. Ukraine
2. Great Britain
3. Portugal

MEN'S FINN

1. Mateusz Kusznierewicz, Poland
2. Sebastien Godefroid, Belgium
3. Roy Heiner, Netherlands

MEN'S BOARD

1. Nikolas Kaklamanakis, Greece
2. Carlos Espinola, Argentina
3. Gal Fridman, Israel

WOMEN'S 470

1. Spain
2. Japan
3. Ukraine

WOMEN'S EUROPE

1. Kristine Roug, Denmark
2. Margriet Matthijsse, Netherlands
3. Courtenay Becker-Dey, United States

WOMEN'S BOARD

1. Lee Lai Shan, Hong Kong
2. Barbara Kendall, New Zealnad
3. Alessandra Sensini, Italy

SOLING

1. Germany
2. Russia
3. United States

STAR

1. Torben Grael & Marcelo Ferreira, Brazil
2. Hans Wallen & Bobbie Lohse, Sweden
3. Colin Beashel & David Giles, Australia

TORNADO

1. J. Luis Ballester & Fernando Leon, Spain
2. M. Booth & A. Landenberger, Australia
3. Lars Grael & Kiko Pellicano, Brazil

LASER

1. Robert Scheidt, Brazil
2. Ben Ainslie, Great Britain
3. Peer Moberg, Norway

BIATHLON

Men
10 KILOMETERS
1. ...Ole Einar Bjorndalen, Norway	27:16.2
2. ..Frode Andresen, Norway	28:17.8
3. ..Ville Raikkonen, FInland	28:21.7

20 KILOMETERS
1. ..Halvard Hanevold, Norway	56:16.4
2. ..Pier Alberto Carrara, Italy	56:21.9
3. ..Aleksei Aidarov, Belarus	56:45.5

4 X 7.5 KILOMETER RELAY
1. ....Germany	1:19:43.3
2. ....Norway	1:20:03.4
3. ....Russia	1:20:19.4

Women
7.5 KILOMETERS
1. ...Galina Koukleva, Russia	23:08.0
2. ..Ursula Disl, Germany	23:08.7
3. ..Katrin Apel, Germany	23:32.4

15 KILOMETERS
1. ..Ekaterina Dofovska, Bulgaria	54:52.0
2. ..Elena Petrova, Ukraine	55:09.8
3. ..Ursula Disl, Germany	55:17.9

3 X 7.5 KILOMETER RELAY
1. ....Germany	1:40:13.6
2. ....Russia	1:40:25.2
3. ....Norway	1:40:37.3

BOBSLED

2-MAN BOB
1. ..Pierre Lueders & Dave MacEachern, Canada	3:37.24
1. ..Guenther Huber & Antonio Tartaglia, Italy	3:37.24
3. ..Christoph Langen & Markus Zimmerman, Germany	3:37.89

4-MAN BOB
1. ....Germany II	2:39.41
2. ....Switzerland I	2:40.01
3. ....Britain I	2:40.06
3. ...:......France I	2:40.06

CURLING

Men
1. ....Switzerland
2. ....Canada
3. ....Norway

Women
1. ....Canada
2. ....Denmark
3 ....Sweden

ICE HOCKEY

Men
1. ....Czech Republic
2. ....Russia
3. ....Finland

Women
1. ....United States
2. ....Canada
3. ....Finland

LUGE

Men
SINGLES
1. ..Georg Hackl, Germany	3:18.44
2. ..Armin Zoeggeler, Italy	3:18.94
3. ..Jens Mueller, Germany	3:19.09

DOUBLES
1. ..Stefan Krausse & Jan Behrendt, Germany	1:41.105
1. ..Chris Thorpe & Gordy Sheer, United States	1:41.127
3. ..Mark Grimmette & Brian Martin United States	1:41.217

Women
SINGLES
1. ..Silke Kraushaar, Germany	3:23.779
2....Barbara Niedernhuber, Germany	3:23.781
3....Angelika Neuner, Austria	3:24.253

FIGURE SKATING

Men
1. ....Ilia Kulik, Russia
2. ....Elvis Stojko, Canada
3. ....Philippe Candeloro, France

Women
1. ....Tara Lipinski, United States
2. ....Michelle Kwan, United States
3. ....Lu Chen, China

Pairs
1. ..Oksana Kazakova & Artur Dmitriev, Russia
2. ..Elena Berezhnaya & Anton Sikharulidze, Russia
3. ..Mandy Wötzel & Ingo Steuer, Germany

Ice Dancing
1. ..Pasha Grishuk & Evgeny Platov, Russia
2. ..Anjelika Krylova & Oleg Ovsyannikov, Russia
3. ..Marina Anissina & Gwendal Peizerat, France

SPEED SKATING

Men		Women	
500 METERS		**500 METERS**	
1. ..Hiroyasu Shimizu, Japan	1:11.35*	1. ..Catriona LeMay Doan, Canada	1:16.60*
2. ..Jeremy Wotherspoon, Canada	1:11.84	2. ..Susan Auch, Canada	1:16.93
3. ..Kevin Overland, Canada	1:11.86	3. ..Tomoni Okazaki, Japan	1:17.10
1000 METERS		**1000 METERS**	
1. ..Ids Postma, Netherlands	1:10.64 OR	1. ..Marianne Timmer, Netherlands	1:16.51 OR
2. ..Jan Bos, Netherlands	1:10.71	2. ..Chris Witty, United States	1:16.79
3. ..Hiroyasu Shimizu, Japan	1:11.00	3. ..Catriona LeMay Doan, Canada	1:17.37
1500 METERS		**1500 METERS**	
1. ..Aadne Sondral, Norway	1:47.87 WR	1. ..Marianne Timmer, Netherlands	1:57.58 WR
2. ..Ids Postma, Netherlands	1:48.13	2. ..Gunda Niemann-Stirnemann, Ger	1:58.66
3. ..Rintje Ritsma, Netherlands	1:48.52	3. ..Chris Witty, United States	1:58.97
5000 METERS		**3000 METERS**	
1. ..Gianni Romme, Netherlands	6:22.20 WR	1. ..Gunda Niemann-Stirnemann, Ger	4:07.29 OR
2. ..Rintje Ritsma, Netherlands	6:28.24	2. ..Claudia Pechstein, Germany	4:08.47
3. ..Bart Veldkamp, Belgium	6:28.31	3. ..Anna Friesinger, Germany	4:09.44
10,000 METERS		**5000 METERS**	
1. ..Gianni Romme, Netherlands	13:15.33 WR	1. ..Claudia Pechstein, Germany	6:59.61 WR
2. ..Bob de Jong, Netherlands	13:25.76	2. ..Gunda Niemann-Stirnemann, Ger	6:59.65
3. ..Rintje Ritsma, Netherlands	13:28.19	3. ..Lyudmila Prokasheva, Kazakhstan	7:11.14
500 METERS SHORT TRACK		**500 METERS SHORT TRACK**	
1. ..Takafumi Nishitani, Japan	42.862	1. ..Annie Perreault, Canada	46.568
2. ..An Yulong, China	43.022	2. ..Yang Yang, China	46.627
3. ..Hitoshi Uematsu, Japan	43.713	3. ..Chun Lee Kyung, South Korea	46.335
1000 METERS SHORT TRACK		**1000 METERS SHORT TRACK**	
1. ..Kim Dong Sung, South Korea	1:32.375	1. ..Chun Lee Kyung, South Korea	1:42.776
2. ..Li Jiajun, China	1:32.428	2. ..Yang Yang, China	1:43.343
3. ..Eric Bedard, Canada	1:32.661	3. ..Hye Kyung Won, South Korea	1:43.361
5000-METER SHORT TRACK RELAY		**3000-METER SHORT TRACK RELAY**	
1. ..Canada	7:06.075	1. ..South Korea	4:16.260
2. ..South Korea	7:06.776	2. ..China	4:16.383
3. ..China	7:11.559	3. ..Canada	4:21.205

ALPINE SKIING

Men		Women	
DOWNHILL		**DOWNHILL**	
1. ..Jean-Luc Crétier, France	1:50.11	1. ..Katja Seizinger, Germany	1:28.89
2. ..Lasse Kjus, Norway	1:50.51	2. ..Pernilla Wiberg, Sweden	1:29.18
3. ..Hannes Trinkl, Austria	1:50.63	3. ..Florence Masnada, France	1:29.37
SLALOM		**SLALOM**	
1. ..Hans-Petter Buraas, Norway	1:49.31	1. ..Hilde Gerg, Germany	1:32.40
2. ..Ole Christian Furuseth, Norway	1:50.64	2. ..Deborah Compagnoni, Italy	1:32.46
3. ..Thomas Sykora, Austria	1:50.68	3. ..Zali Steggall, Australia	1:32.67
GIANT SLALOM		**GIANT SLALOM**	
1. ..Hermann Maier, Austria	2:38.51	1. ..Deborah Compagnoni, Italy	2:50.59
2. ..Stefan Eberharter, Austria	2:39.36	2. ..Alexandra Meissnitzer, Austria	2:52.39
3. ..Michael von Grünigen, Switzerland	2:39.69	3. ..Katja Seizinger, Germany	2:52.61
SUPER GIANT SLALOM		**SUPER GIANT SLALOM**	
1. ..Hermann Maier, Austria	1:34.82	1. ..Picabo Street, United States	1:18.02
2. ..Didier Cucher, Switzerland	1:35.43	2. ..Michaela Dorfmeister, Austria	1:18.03
3. ..Hans Knauss, Austria	1:35.43	3. ..Alexandra Meissnitzer, Austria	1:18.09
COMBINED		**COMBINED**	
1. ..Mario Reiter, Austria	3:08.06	1. ..Katja Seizinger, Germany	2:40.74
2. ..Lasse Kjus, Norway	3:08.65	2. ..Martina Ertl, Germany	2:40.92
3. ..Christian Mayer, Austria	3:10.11	3. ..Hilde Gerg, Germany	2:41.50

Note: OR=Olympic Record. WR=World Record. EOR=Equals Olympic Record. EWR=Equals World Record. WB=World Best.
* Final standings based on the combined time of two 500-meter runs. Shimizu set an Olympic record with his second-run time of 35.59 seconds, and LeMay Doan set an Olympic record with her second-run time of 38.21 seconds.

FREESTYLE SKIING

Men	
MOGULS	**Pts**
1. ..Jonny Moseley, United States	26.93
2. ..Janne Lahtela, Finland	26.00
3. ..Sami Mustonen, Finland	25.76

AERIALS	**Pts**
1. ..Eric Bergoust, United States	255.64
2. ..Sebastien Foucras, France	248.79
3. ..Dmitri Dashchinsky, Belarus	240.79

Women	
MOGULS	**Pts**
1. ..Tae Satoya, Japan	25.06
2. ..Tatjana Mittermayer, Germany	24.62
3. ..Kari Traa, Norway	24.09

AERIALS	**Pts**
1. ..Nikki Stone, United States	193.00
2. ..Nannan Xu, China	186.97
3. ..Colette Brand, Switzerland	171.83

NORDIC SKIING

Men

10 KILOMETERS CLASSICAL STYLE	
1. ..Bjørn Dæhlie, Norway	27:24.5
2. ..Markus Gandler, Austria	27:32.5
3. ..Mika Myllylae, Finland	27:40.1

15 KILOMETERS PURSUIT FREESTYLE	
1. ..Thomas Alsgaard, Norway	1:07:01.7
2. ..Bjørn Dæhlie, Norway	1:07:02.8
3. ..Vladimir Smirnov, Kazakhstan	1:07:31.5

30 KILOMETERS CLASSICAL STYLE	
1. ..Mika Myllylae, Finland	1:33:55.8
2. ..Erling Jevne, Norway	1:35:27.1
3. ..Silvio Fauner, Italy	1:36:08.5

50 KILOMETERS FREESTYLE	
1. ..Bjørn Dæhlie, Norway	2:05:08.2
2. ..Niklas Jonsson, Sweden	2:05:16.3
3. ..Christian Hoffmann, Austria	2:06:01.8

4 X 10 KILOMETER RELAY MIXED STYLE	
1................Norway	1:40:55.7
2................Italy	1:40:55.9
3................Finland	1:42:15.5

90-METER HILL SKI JUMPING	**Pts**
1. ..Jani Soininen, Finland	234.5
2. ..Kazuyoshi Funaki, Japan	233.5
3. ..Andreas Widhoelzl, Austria	232.5

120-METER HILL SKI JUMPING	**Pts**
1. ..Kazuyoshi Funaki, Japan	272.3
2. ..Jani Soininen, Finland	260.8
3. ..Masahiko Harada, Japan	258.3

120-METER HILL TEAM SKI JUMPING	**Pts**
1................Japan	933.0
2................Germany	897.4
3................Austria	881.5

INDIVIDUAL COMBINED	**Time behind**
1. ..Bjarte Engen Vik, Norway	—
2. ..Samppa Lajunen, Finland	27.5
3. ..Valery Stoljarov, Russia	28.2

TEAM COMBINED	**Time behind**
1................Norway	—
2................Finland	1:18.9
3................France	1:41.9

Women

5 KILOMETERS CLASSICAL STYLE	
1. ..Larissa Lazhutina, Russia	17:37.9
2. ..Katerina Neumannova, Czech Rep	17:42.7
3. ..Bente Martinsen, Norway	17:49.4

10 KILOMETERS PURSUIT FREESTYLE	
1. ..Larissa Lazhutina, Russia	46:06.9
2. ..Olga Danilova, Russia	46:13.4
3. ..Katerina Neumannova, Czech Rep	46:14.2

15 KILOMETERS CLASSICAL STYLE	
1. ..Olga Danilova, Russia	46:55.04
2. ..Larissa Lazhutina, Russia	47:01.00
3. ..Anita Moen-Guidon, Norway	47:52.06

30 KILOMETERS FREESTYLE	
1. ..Julija Tchepalova, Russia	1:22:01.5
2. ..Stefania Belmondo, Italy	1:22:11.7
3. ..Larissa Lazhutina, Russia	1:23:15.7

4 X 5 KILOMETER RELAY MIXED STYLE	
1. ....Russia	55:13.5
2. ....Norway	55:38.0
3. ....Italy	56:53.3

SNOWBOARDING

Men	
GIANT SLALOM	
1. ..Ross Rebagliati, Canada	2:03.96
2. ..Thomas Prugger, Italy	2:03.98
3. ..Ueli Kestenholz, Switzerland	2:04.08

HALF-PIPE	**Pts**
1. ..Gian Simmen, Switzerland	85.2
2. ..Daniel Franck, Norway	82.4
3. ..Ross Powers, United States	82.1

Women	
GIANT SLALOM	
1. ..Karine Ruby, France	2:17.34
2. ..Heidi Renoth, Germany	2:19.17
3. ..Brigitte Koeck, Austria	2:19.42

HALF-PIPE	**Pts**
1. ..Nicola Thost, Germany	74.6
2. ..Stine Brun Kjeldaas, Norway	74.2
3. ..Shannon Dunn, United States	72.8

Olympic Games Locations and Dates

Summer

	Year	Site	Dates	Competitors Men	Women	Nations	Most Medals	US Medals
I	1896	Athens, Greece	Apr 6–15	311	0	13	Greece (10-19-18—47)	11-6-2—19 (2nd)
II	1900	Paris, France	May 20–Oct 28	1319	11	22	France (29-41-32—102)	20-14-19—53 (2nd)
III	1904	St Louis, United States	July 1–Nov 23	681	6	12	United States (80-86-72—238)	
—	1906	Athens, Greece	Apr 22–May 28	77	7	20	France (15-9-16—40)	12-6-5—23 (4th)
IV	1908	London, Great Britain	Apr 27–Oct 31	1999	36	23	Britain (56-50-39—145)	23-12-12—47 (2nd)
V	1912	Stockholm, Sweden	May 5–July 22	2490	57	28	Sweden (24-24-17—65)	23-19-19—61 (2nd)
VI	1916	Berlin, Germany	Canceled because of war					
VII	1920	Antwerp, Belgium	Apr 20–Sep 12	2543	64	29	United States (41-27-28—96)	
VIII	1924	Paris, France	May 4–July 27	2956	136	44	United States (45-27-27—99)	
IX	1928	Amsterdam, Netherlands	May 17–Aug 12	2724	290	46	United States (22-18-16—56)	
X	1932	Los Angeles, United States	July 30–Aug 14	1281	127	37	United States (41-32-31—104)	
XI	1936	Berlin, Germany	Aug 1–16	3738	328	49	Germany (33-26-30—89)	24-20-12—56 (2nd)
XII	1940	Tokyo, Japan	Canceled because of war					
XIII	1944	London, Great Britain	Canceled because of war					
XIV	1948	London, Great Britain	July 29–Aug 14	3714	385	59	United States (38-27-19—84)	
XV	1952	Helsinki, Finland	July 19–Aug 3	4407	518	69	United States (40-19-17—76)	
XVI	1956	Melbourne, Australia*	Nov 22–Dec 8	2958	384	67	USSR (37-29-32—98)	32-25-17—74 (2nd)
XVII	1960	Rome, Italy	Aug 25–Sep 11	4738	610	83	USSR (43-29-31—103)	34-21-16—71 (2nd)
XVIII	1964	Tokyo, Japan	Oct 10–24	4457	683	93	United States (36-26-28—90)	
XIX	1968	Mexico City, Mexico	Oct 12–27	4750	781	112	United States (45-28-34—107)	
XX	1972	Munich, West Germany	Aug 26–Sep 10	5848	1299	122	USSR (50-27-22—99)	33-31-30—94 (2nd)
XXI	1976	Montreal, Canada	July 17–Aug 1	4834	1251	92†	USSR (49-41-35—125)	34-35-25—94 (3rd)
XXII	1980	Moscow, USSR	July 19–Aug 3	4265	1088	81‡	USSR (80-69-46—195)	Did not compete
XXIII	1984	Los Angeles, United States	July 28–Aug 12	5458	1620	141#	United States (83-61-30—174)	
XXIV	1988	Seoul, South Korea	Sep 17–Oct 2	7105	2476	160	USSR (55-31-46—132)	36-31-27—94 (3rd)
XXV	1992	Barcelona, Spain	July 25–Aug. 9	7555	3008	172	Unified Team (45-38-29—112)	37-34-37—108 (2nd)
XXVI	1996	Atlanta, United States	July 19–Aug 4	6984	3766	197	United States (44-32-25—101)	

*The equestrian events were held in Stockholm, Sweden, June 10–17, 1956.

†This figure includes Cameroon, Egypt, Morocco, and Tunisia, countries that boycotted the 1976 Olympics after some of their athletes had already competed.

‡The U.S. was among 65 countries that did not participate in the 1980 Summer Games in Moscow.

#The USSR, East Germany, and 14 other countries did not participate in the 1984 Summer Games in Los Angeles.

Winter

	Year	Site	Dates	Competitors Men	Women	Nations	Most Medals	US Medals
I	1924	Chamonix, France	Jan 25–Feb 4	281	13	16	Norway (4-7-6—17)	1-2-1—4 (3rd)
II	1928	St Moritz, Switzerland	Feb 11–19	366	27	25	Norway (6-4-5—15)	2-2-2—6 (2nd)
III	1932	Lake Placid, United States	Feb 4–13	277	30	17	United States (6-4-2—12)	
IV	1936	Garmisch-Partenkirchen, Germany	Feb 6–16	680	76	28	Norway (7-5-3—15)	1-0-3—4 (T-5th)
—	1940	Garmisch-Partenkirchen, Germany	Canceled because of war					
—	1944	Cortina d'Ampezzo, Italy	Canceled because of war					
V	1948	St Moritz, Switzerland	Jan 30–Feb 8	636	77	28	Norway (4-3-3—10) Sweden (4-3-3—10) Switzerland (3-4-3—10)	3-4-2—9 (4th)
VI	1952	Oslo, Norway	Feb 14–25	624	108	30	Norway (7-3-6—16)	4-6-1—11 (2nd)
VII	1956	Cortina d'Ampezzo, Italy	Jan 26–Feb 5	687	132	32	USSR (7-3-6—16)	2-3-2—7 (T-4th)
VIII	1960	Squaw Valley, United States	Feb 18–28	502	146	30	USSR (7-5-9—21)	3-4-3—10 (2nd)
IX	1964	Innsbruck, Austria	Jan 29–Feb 9	758	175	36	USSR (11-8-6—25)	1-2-3—6 (7th)
X	1968	Grenoble, France	Feb 6–18	1063	230	37	Norway (6-6-2—14)	1-5-1—7 (T-7th)
XI	1972	Sapporo, Japan	Feb 3–13	927	218	35	USSR (8-5-3—16)	3-2-3—8 (6th)
XII	1976	Innsbruck, Austria	Feb 4–15	1013	248	37	USSR (13-6-8—27)	3-3-4—10 (T-3rd)
XIII	1980	Lake Placid, United States	Feb 13–24	1012	271	37	East Germany (9-7-7—23)	6-4-2—12 (3rd)
XIV	1984	Sarajevo, Yugoslavia	Feb 8–19	1127	283	49	USSR (6-10-9—25)	4-4-0—8 (T-5th)
XV	1988	Calgary, Canada	Feb 13–28	1270	364	57	USSR (11-9-9—29)	2-1-3—6 (T-8th)
XVI	1992	Albertville, France	Feb 8–23	1313	488	65	Germany (10-10-6—26)	5-4-2—11 (6th)
XVII	1994	Lillehammer, Norway	Feb 12–27	1302	542	67	Norway (10-11-5—26)	6-5-2—13 (T-5th)
XVIII	1998	Nagano, Japan	Feb 7–22	2302 total		72	Germany (12-9-8—29)	6-3-4—13 (6th)

Alltime Olympic Medal Winners

Summer

NATIONS

Nation	Gold	Silver	Bronze	Total	Nation	Gold	Silver	Bronze	Total
United States	832	634	553	2019	Australia	86	85	121	292
Soviet Union (1952–88)	395	319	296	1010	Japan	92	89	97	278
Great Britain	169	223	218	610	Romania	63	77	99	239
France	175	179	206	560	Poland	50	67	110	227
Sweden	132	151	174	457	Canada	48	78	90	216
Italy	166	135	144	445	The Netherlands	49	58	81	188
East Germany (1956–88)	159	150	136	445	Bulgaria	43	76	63	182
Hungary	142	129	155	426	Switzerland	46	69	59	174
Germany (1896–1936, 1992–)	124	121	134	379	China	52	63	49	164
					Denmark	38	60	57	155
West Germany (1952–88)	77	104	120	301	Czechoslovakia (1924–92)	49	49	44	142
Finland	99	80	113	292	Belgium	37	49	49	135

Summer *(Cont.)*

INDIVIDUALS — OVERALL

Men					
Athlete, Nation	Sport	G	S	B	Tot
Nikolai Andrianov, USSR	Gym	7	5	3	15
Boris Shakhlin, USSR	Gym	7	4	2	13
Edoardo Mangiarotti, Italy	Fen	6	5	2	13
Takashi Ono, Japan	Gym	5	4	4	13
Paavo Nurmi, Finland	Track	9	3	0	12
Sawao Kato, Japan	Gym	8	3	1	12
Mark Spitz, United States	Swim	9	1	1	11
Matt Biondi, United States	Swim	8	2	1	11
Viktor Chukarin, USSR	Gym	7	3	1	11
Carl Osburn, United States	Shoot	5	4	2	11
Ray Ewry, United States	Track	10	0	0	10
Carl Lewis, United States	Track	9	1	0	10
Aladár Gerevich, Hungary	Fen	7	1	2	10
Akinori Nakayama, Japan	Gym	6	2	2	10
Vitaly Scherbo, UT/Belarus	Gym	6	0	4	10
Aleksandr Dityatin, USSR	Gym	3	6	1	10

Women					
Athlete, Nation	Sport	G	S	B	Tot
Larissa Latynina, USSR	Gym	9	5	4	18
Vera Cáslavská, Czech.	Gym	7	4	0	11
Agnes Keleti, Hungary	Gym	5	3	2	10
Polina Astaknova, USSR	Gym	5	2	3	10
Nadia Comaneci, Romania	Gym	5	3	1	9
Lyudmila Tourischeva, USSR	Gym	4	3	2	9
Kornelia Ender, E Germany	Swim	4	4	0	8
Dawn Fraser, Australia	Swim	4	4	0	8
Shirley Babashoff, United States	Swim	2	6	0	8
Sofia Muratova, USSR	Gym	2	2	4	8
Eight tied with seven.					

INDIVIDUALS — GOLD

Men

Ray Ewry, United States	10	
Paavo Nurmi, Finland	9	
Carl Lewis, United States	9	
Mark Spitz, United States	9	

Sawao Kato, Japan	8
Matt Biondi, United States	8
Nikolai Andrianov, USSR	7
Boris Shakhlin, USSR	7

Viktor Chukarin, USSR	7
Aladár Gerevich, Hungary	7

Women

Larissa Latynina, USSR	9
Vera Cáslavská, Czech	7
Kristin Otto, E Germany	6
Agnes Keleti, Hungary	5
Nadia Comaneci, Romania	5
Polina Astaknova, USSR	5

Krisztina Egerszegi, Hun	5
Jenny Thompson, United States	5
Kornelia Ender, E Germany	4
Dawn Fraser, Australia	4
Lyudmila Tourischeva, USSR	4
Evelyn Ashford, United States	4

Janet Evans, United States	4
Fanny Blankers-Koen, Neth	4
Betty Cuthbert, Australia	4
Pat McCormick, United States	4
Bärbel Eckert Wöckel, E Ger	4
Amy Van Dyken, United States	4

Winter

NATIONS

Nation	Gold	Silver	Bronze	Total	Nation	Gold	Silver	Bronze	Total
Norway	83	85	68	236	East Germany (1956–88)	39	36	35	110
Soviet Union (1956–88)	78	57	59	194	Sweden	36	26	34	96
United States	59	58	40	157	Switzerland	29	31	31	91
Austria	39	53	53	145	Germany (1928–36, '92–)	34	29	25	88
Finland	37	49	48	134	Canada	24	25	29	78

INDIVIDUALS — OVERALL

Men					
Athlete, Nation	Sport	G	S	B	Tot
Bjørn Dæhlie, Norway	N Ski	8	4	0	12
Sixten Jernberg, Sweden	N Ski	4	3	2	9
A. Clas Thunberg, Finland	S Skat	5	1	1	7
Ivar Ballangrud, Norway	S Skat	4	2	1	7
Veikko Hakulinen, Finland	N Ski	3	3	1	7
Eero Mäntyranta, Finland	N Ski	3	2	2	7
Bogdan Musiol, E Ger/Ger	Bob	1	5	1	7

Women					
Athlete, Nation	Sport	G	S	B	Tot
Raisa Smetanina, USSR/UT	N Ski	4	5	1	10
Lyubov Egorova, UT/Russia	N Ski	6	3	0	9
Galina Kulakova, USSR	N Ski	4	2	2	8
Karin (Enke) Kania, E Germany	S Skat	3	4	1	8
Gunda Niemann Stimemann, Ger	S Skat	3	4	1	8
Larissa Lazutina, UT/Russia	N Ski	5	1	1	7
Marja-Liisa Kirvesniemi, Fin	N Ski	3	0	4	7
Andrea Ehrig, E Germany	S Skat	1	5	1	7

INDIVIDUALS — GOLD

Men

Bjørn Dæhlie, Nor	8	
A. Clas Thunberg, Fin	5	
Eric Heiden, U.S.	5	
Sixten Jernberg, Swe	4	
Evgeny Grishin, USSR	4	
J. Olav Koss, Norway	4	

Matti Nykänen, Fin	4
A. Tikhonov, USSR	4
N. Zimyatov, USSR	4
Ivar Ballangrud, Nor	4
Gunde Svan, Swe	4
T. Wassberg, Swe	4

Women

Lyubov Egorova, UT/Russia	6
L. Skoblikova, USSR	6
Larissa Lazutina, UT/Russia	5
Bonnie Blair, U.S.	5

Raisa Smetanina, USSR/UT	4
G. Kulakova, USSR	4
Chun Lee Kyung, Kor	4

TRACK AND FIELD

Men

100 METERS

1896	Thomas Burke, United States	12.0
1900	Frank Jarvis, United States	11.0
1904	Archie Hahn, United States	11.0
1906	Archie Hahn, United States	11.2
1908	Reginald Walker, South Africa	10.8 OR
1912	Ralph Craig, United States	10.8
1920	Charles Paddock, United States	10.8
1924	Harold Abrahams, Great Britain	10.6 OR
1928	Percy Williams, Canada	10.8
1932	Eddie Tolan, United States	10.3 OR
1936	Jesse Owens, United States	10.3
1948	Harrison Dillard, United States	10.3
1952	Lindy Remigino, United States	10.4
1956	Bobby Morrow, United States	10.5
1960	Armin Hary, West Germany	10.2 OR
1964	Bob Hayes, United States	10.0 EWR
1968	Jim Hines, United States	9.95 WR
1972	Valery Borzov, USSR	10.14
1976	Hasely Crawford, Trinidad	10.06
1980	Allan Wells, Great Britain	10.25
1984	Carl Lewis, United States	9.99
1988	Carl Lewis, United States*	9.92 WR
1992	Linford Christie, Great Britain	9.96
1996	Donovan Bailey, Canada	9.84 WR

*Ben Johnson, Canada, disqualified.

200 METERS

1900	John Walter Tewksbury, United States	22.2
1904	Archie Hahn, United States	21.6 OR
1906	Not held	
1908	Robert Kerr, Canada	22.6
1912	Ralph Craig, United States	21.7
1920	Allen Woodring, United States	22.0
1924	Jackson Scholz, United States	21.6
1928	Percy Williams, Canada	21.8
1932	Eddie Tolan, United States	21.2 OR
1936	Jesse Owens, United States	20.7 WR
1948	Mel Patton, United States	21.1
1952	Andrew Stanfield, United States	20.7
1956	Bobby Morrow, United States	20.6 OR
1960	Livio Berruti, Italy	20.5 EWR
1964	Henry Carr, United States	20.3 OR
1968	Tommie Smith, United States	19.83 WR
1972	Valery Borzov, USSR	20.00
1976	Donald Quarrie, Jamaica	20.23
1980	Pietro Mennea, Italy	20.19
1984	Carl Lewis, United States	19.80 OR
1988	Joe DeLoach, United States	19.75 OR
1992	Mike Marsh, United States	20.01
1996	Michael Johnson, United States	19.32 WR

400 METERS

1896	Thomas Burke, United States	54.2
1900	Maxey Long, United States	49.4 OR
1904	Harry Hillman, United States	49.2 OR
1906	Paul Pilgrim, United States	53.2
1908	Wyndham Halswelle, Great Britain	50.0
1912	Charles Reidpath, United States	48.2 OR
1920	Bevil Rudd, South Africa	49.6
1924	Eric Liddell, Great Britain	47.6 OR
1928	Ray Barbuti, United States	47.8
1932	William Carr, United States	46.2 WR

400 METERS *(Cont.)*

1936	Archie Williams, United States	46.5
1948	Arthur Wint, Jamaica	46.2
1952	George Rhoden, Jamaica	45.9
1956	Charles Jenkins, United States	46.7
1960	Otis Davis, United States	44.9 WR
1964	Michael Larrabee, United States	45.1
1968	Lee Evans, United States	43.86 WR
1972	Vincent Matthews, United States	44.66
1976	Alberto Juantorena, Cuba	44.26
1980	Viktor Markin, USSR	44.60
1984	Alonzo Babers, United States	44.27
1988	Steve Lewis, United States	43.87
1992	Quincy Watts, United States	43.50 OR
1996	Michael Johnson, United States	43.49 OR

800 METERS

1896	Edwin Flack, Australia	2:11
1900	Alfred Tysoe, Great Britain	2:01.2
1904	James Lightbody, United States	1:56 OR
1906	Paul Pilgrim, United States	2:01.5
1908	Mel Sheppard, United States	1:52.8 WR
1912	James Meredith, United States	1:51.9 WR
1920	Albert Hill, Great Britain	1:53.4
1924	Douglas Lowe, Great Britain	1:52.4
1928	Douglas Lowe, Great Britain	1:51.8 OR
1932	Thomas Hampson, Great Britain	1:49.8 WR
1936	John Woodruff, United States	1:52.9
1948	Mal Whitfield, United States	1:49.2 OR
1952	Mal Whitfield, United States	1:49.2 EOR
1956	Thomas Courtney, United States	1:47.7 OR
1960	Peter Snell, New Zealand	1:46.3 OR
1964	Peter Snell, New Zealand	1:45.1 OR
1968	Ralph Doubell, Australia	1:44.3 EWR
1972	Dave Wottle, United States	1:45.9
1976	Alberto Juantorena, Cuba	1:43.50 WR
1980	Steve Ovett, Great Britain	1:45.40
1984	Joaquim Cruz, Brazil	1:43.00 OR
1988	Paul Ereng, Kenya	1:43.45
1992	William Tanui, Kenya	1:43.66
1996	Vebjoern Rodal, Norway	1:42.58 OR

1500 METERS

1896	Edwin Flack, Australia	4:33.2
1900	Charles Bennett, Great Britain	4:06.2 WR
1904	James Lightbody, United States	4:05.4 WR
1906	James Lightbody, United States	4:12.0
1908	Mel Sheppard, United States	4:03.4 OR
1912	Arnold Jackson, Great Britain	3:56.8 OR
1920	Albert Hill, Great Britain	4:01.8
1924	Paavo Nurmi, Finland	3:53.6 OR
1928	Harry Larva, Finland	3:53.2 OR
1932	Luigi Beccali, Italy	3:51.2 OR
1936	Jack Lovelock, New Zealand	3:47.8 WR
1948	Henri Eriksson, Sweden	3:49.8
1952	Josef Barthel, Luxemburg	3:45.1 OR
1956	Ron Delany, Ireland	3:41.2 OR
1960	Herb Elliott, Australia	3:35.6 WR
1964	Peter Snell, New Zealand	3:38.1
1968	Kipchoge Keino, Kenya	3:34.9 OR
1972	Pekkha Vasala, Finland	3:36.3
1976	John Walker, New Zealand	3:39.17
1980	Sebastian Coe, Great Britain	3:38.4
1984	Sebastian Coe, Great Britain	3:32.53 OR

Note: OR=Olympic Record. WR=World Record. EOR=Equals Olympic Record. EWR=Equals World Record. WB=World Best.

TRACK AND FIELD (Cont.)
Men (Cont.)

1500 METERS (Cont.)

1988	Peter Rono, Kenya	3:35.96
1992	Fermin Cacho, Spain	3:40.12
1996	Noureddine Morceli, Algeria	3:35.78

5000 METERS

1912	Hannes Kolehmainen, Finland	14:36.6 WR
1920	Joseph Guillemot, France	14:55.6
1924	Paavo Nurmi, Finland	14:31.2 OR
1928	Villie Ritola, Finland	14:38
1932	Lauri Lehtinen, Finland	14:30 OR
1936	Gunnar Hickert, Finland	14:22.2 OR
1948	Gaston Reiff, Belgium	14:17.6 OR
1952	Emil Zatopek, Czechoslovakia	14:06.6 OR
1956	Vladimir Kuts, USSR	13:39.6 OR
1960	Murray Halberg, New Zealand	13:43.4
1964	Bob Schul, United States	13:48.8
1968	Mohamed Gammoudi, Tunisia	14:05.0
1972	Lasse Viren, Finland	13:26.4 OR
1976	Lasse Viren, Finland	13:24.76
1980	Miruts Yifter, Ethiopia	13:21.0
1984	Said Aouita, Morocco	13:05.59 OR
1988	John Ngugi, Kenya	13:11.70
1992	Dieter Baumann, Germany	13:12.52
1996	Venuste Niyongabo, Burundi	13:07.96

10,000 METERS

1912	Hannes Kolehmainen, Finland	31:20.8
1920	Paavo Nurmi, Finland	31:45.8
1924	Vilho (Ville) Ritola, Finland	30:23.2 WR
1928	Paavo Nurmi, Finland	30:18.8 OR
1932	Janusz Kusocinski, Poland	30:11.4 OR
1936	Ilmari Salminen, Finland	30:15.4
1948	Emil Zatopek, Czechoslovakia	29:59.6 OR
1952	Emil Zatopek, Czechoslovakia	29:17.0 OR
1956	Vladimir Kuts, USSR	28:45.6 OR
1960	Pyotr Bolotnikov, USSR	28:32.2 OR
1964	Billy Mills, United States	28:24.4 OR
1968	Naftali Temu, Kenya	29:27.4
1972	Lasse Viren, Finland	27:38.4 WR
1976	Lasse Viren, Finland	27:40.38
1980	Miruts Yifter, Ethiopia	27:42.7
1984	Alberto Cova, Italy	27:47.54
1988	Brahim Boutaib, Morocco	27:21.46 OR
1992	Khalid Skah, Morocco	27:46.70
1996	Haile Gebrselassie, Ethiopia	27:07.34 OR

MARATHON

1896	Spiridon Louis, Greece	2:58:50
1900	Michel Theato, France	2:59:45
1904	Thomas Hicks, United States	3:28:53
1906	William Sherring, Canada	2:51:23.6
1908	John Hayes, United States	2:55:18.4 OR
1912	Kenneth McArthur, South Africa	2:36:54.8
1920	Hannes Kolehmainen, Finland	2:32:35.8 WB
1924	Albin Stenroos, Finland	2:41:22.6
1928	Boughera El Ouafi, France	2:32:57
1932	Juan Zabala, Argentina	2:31:36 OR
1936	Kijung Son, Japan (Korea)	2:29:19.2 OR
1948	Delfo Cabrera, Argentina	2:34:51.6
1952	Emil Zatopek, Czechoslovakia	2:23:03.2 OR
1956	Alain Mimoun O'Kacha, France	2:25:00.0
1960	Abebe Bikila, Ethiopia	2:15:16.2 WB
1964	Abebe Bikila, Ethiopia	2:12:11.2 WB
1968	Mamo Wolde, Ethiopia	2:20:26.4
1972	Frank Shorter, United States	2:12:19.8

MARATHON (Cont.)

1976	Waldemar Cierpinski, East Germany	2:09:55 OR
1980	Waldemar Cierpinski, East Germany	2:11:03.0
1984	Carlos Lopes, Portugal	2:09:21.0 OR
1988	Gelindo Bordin, Italy	2:10:32
1992	Hwang Young-Cho, S Korea	2:13:23
1996	Josia Thugwane, South Africa	2:12:36

Note: Marathon distances: 1896, 1904—40,000 meters; 1900—40,260 meters; 1906—41,860 meters; 1912—40,200 meters; 1920—42,750 meters; 1908 and since 1924—42,195 meters (26 miles, 385 yards).

110-METER HURDLES

1896	Thomas Curtis, United States	17.6
1900	Alvin Kraenzlein, United States	15.4 OR
1904	Frederick Schule, United States	16.0
1906	Robert Leavitt, United States	16.2
1908	Forrest Smithson, United States	15.0 WR
1912	Frederick Kelly, United States	15.1
1920	Earl Thomson, Canada	14.8 WR
1924	Daniel Kinsey, United States	15.0
1928	Sydney Atkinson, South Africa	14.8
1932	George Saling, United States	14.6
1936	Forrest Towns, United States	14.2
1948	William Porter, United States	13.9 OR
1952	Harrison Dillard, United States	13.7 OR
1956	Lee Calhoun, United States	13.5 OR
1960	Lee Calhoun, United States	13.8
1964	Hayes Jones, United States	13.6
1968	Willie Davenport, United States	13.3 OR
1972	Rod Milburn, United States	13.24 EWR
1976	Guy Drut, France	13.30
1980	Thomas Munkelt, East Germany	13.39
1984	Roger Kingdom, United States	13.20 OR
1988	Roger Kingdom, United States	12.98 OR
1992	Mark McKoy, Canada	13.12
1996	Allen Johnson, United States	12.95 OR

400-METER HURDLES

1900	John Walter Tewksbury, United States	57.6
1904	Harry Hillman, United States	53.0
1906	Not held	
1908	Charles Bacon, United States	55.0 WR
1912	Not held	
1920	Frank Loomis, United States	54.0 WR
1924	F. Morgan Taylor, United States	52.6
1928	David Burghley, Great Britain	53.4 OR
1932	Robert Tisdall, Ireland	51.7
1936	Glenn Hardin, United States	52.4
1948	Roy Cochran, United States	51.1 OR
1952	Charles Moore, United States	50.8 OR
1956	Glenn Davis, United States	50.1 EOR
1960	Glenn Davis, United States	49.3 EOR
1964	Rex Cawley, United States	49.6
1968	Dave Hemery, Great Britain	48.12 WR
1972	John Akii-Bua, Uganda	47.82 WR
1976	Edwin Moses, United States	47.64 WR
1980	Volker Beck, East Germany	48.70
1984	Edwin Moses, United States	47.75
1988	Andre Phillips, United States	47.19 OR
1992	Kevin Young, United States	46.78 WR
1996	Derrick Adkins, United States	47.54

TRACK AND FIELD *(Cont.)*
Men *(Cont.)*

3000-METER STEEPLECHASE

1920	Percy Hodge, Great Britain	10:00.4 OR
1924	Vilho (Ville) Ritola, Finland	9:33.6 OR
1928	Toivo Loukola, Finland	9:21.8 WR
1932	Volmari Iso-Hollo, Finland	10:33.4*
1936	Volmari Iso-Hollo, Finland	9:03.8 WR
1948	Thore Sjöstrand, Sweden	9:04.6
1952	Horace Ashenfelter, United States	8:45.4 WR
1956	Chris Brasher, Great Britain	8:41.2 OR
1960	Zdzislaw Krzyszkowiak, Poland	8:34.2 OR
1964	Gaston Roelants, Belgium	8:30.8 OR
1968	Amos Biwott, Kenya	8:51
1972	Kipchoge Keino, Kenya	8:23.6 OR
1976	Anders Gärderud, Sweden	8:08.2 WR
1980	Bronislaw Malinowski, Poland	8:09.7
1984	Julius Korir, Kenya	8:11.8
1988	Julius Kariuki, Kenya	8:05.51 OR
1992	Matthew Birir, Kenya	8:08.84
1996	Joseph Keter, Kenya	8:07.12

*About 3450 meters; extra lap by error.

4 X 100-METER RELAY

1912	Great Britain	42.4 OR
1920	United States	42.2 WR
1924	United States	41.0 EWR
1928	United States	41.0 EWR
1932	United States	40.0 EWR
1936	United States	39.8 WR
1948	United States	40.6
1952	United States	40.1
1956	United States	39.5 WR
1960	West Germany	39.5 EWR
1964	United States	39.0 WR
1968	United States	38.2 WR
1972	United States	38.19 EWR
1976	United States	38.33
1980	USSR	38.26
1984	United States	37.83 WR
1988	USSR	38.19
1992	United States	37.40 WR
1996	Canada	37.69

4 X 400-METER RELAY

1908	United States	3:29.4
1912	United States	3:16.6 WR
1920	Great Britain	3:22.2
1924	United States	3:16.0 WR
1928	United States	3:14.2 WR
1932	United States	3:08.2 WR
1936	Great Britain	3:09.0
1948	United States	3:10.4 WR
1952	Jamaica	3:03.9 WR
1956	United States	3:04.8
1960	United States	3:02.2 WR
1964	United States	3:00.7 WR
1968	United States	2:56.16 WR
1972	Kenya	2:59.8
1976	United States	2:58.65
1980	USSR	3:01.1
1984	United States	2:57.91
1988	United States	2:56.16 EWR
1992	United States	2:55.74 WR
1996	United States	2:55.99

20-KILOMETER WALK

1956	Leonid Spirin, USSR	1:31:27.4
1960	Vladimir Golubnichiy, USSR	1:33:07.2
1964	Kenneth Mathews, Great Britain	1:29:34.0 OR
1968	Vladimir Golubnichiy, USSR	1:33:58.4
1972	Peter Frenkel, East Germany	1:26:42.4 OR
1976	Daniel Bautista, Mexico	1:24:40.6 OR
1980	Maurizio Damilano, Italy	1:23:35.5 OR
1984	Ernesto Canto, Mexico	1:23:13.0 OR
1988	Jozef Pribilinec, Czechoslovakia	1:19:57.0 OR
1992	Daniel Plaza, Spain	1:21:45.0
1996	Jefferson Pérez, Ecuador	1:20:07

50-KILOMETER WALK

1932	Thomas Green, Great Britain	4:50:10
1936	Harold Whitlock, Great Britain	4:30:41.4 OR
1948	John Ljunggren, Sweden	4:41:52
1952	Giuseppe Dordoni, Italy	4:28:07.8 OR
1956	Norman Read, New Zealand	4:30:42.8
1960	Donald Thompson, Great Britain	4:25:30 OR
1964	Abdon Parnich, Italy	4:11:12.4 OR
1968	Christoph Höhne, East Germany	4:20:13.6
1972	Bernd Kannenberg, West Germany	3:56:11.6 OR
1980	Hartwig Gauder, East Germany	3:49:24.0 OR
1984	Raul Gonzalez, Mexico	3:47:26.0 OR
1988	Viacheslav Ivanenko, USSR	3:38:29.0 OR
1992	Andrey Perlov, Unified Team	3:50:13
1996	Robert Korzeniowski, Poland	3:43:30

HIGH JUMP

1896	Ellery Clark, United States	5 ft 11¼ in
1900	Irving Baxter, United States	6 ft 2¾ in OR
1904	Samuel Jones, United States	5 ft 11 in
1906	Cornelius Leahy, Great Britain/Ireland	5 ft 10 in
1908	Harry Porter, United States	6 ft 3 in OR
1912	Alma Richards, United States	6 ft 4 in OR
1920	Richmond Landon, United States	6 ft 4 in OR
1924	Harold Osborn, United States	6 ft 6 in OR
1928	Robert W. King, United States	6 ft 4½ in
1932	Duncan McNaughton, Canada	6 ft 5½ in
1936	Cornelius Johnson, United States	6 ft 8 in OR
1948	John L. Winter, Australia	6 ft 6 in
1952	Walter Davis, United States	6 ft 8½ in OR
1956	Charles Dumas, United States	6 ft 11½ in OR
1960	Robert Shavlakadze, USSR	7 ft 1 in OR
1964	Valery Brumel, USSR	7 ft 1¾ in OR
1968	Dick Fosbury, United States	7 ft 4¼ in OR
1972	Yuri Tarmak, USSR	7 ft 3¾ in
1976	Jacek Wszola, Poland	7 ft 4½ in OR
1980	Gerd Wessig, East Germany	7 ft 8¾ in WR
1984	Dietmar Mögenburg, West Germany	7 ft 8½ in
1988	Gennadiy Avdeyenko, USSR	7 ft 9¾ in OR
1992	Javier Sotomayor, Cuba	7 ft 8 in.
1996	Charles Austin, United States	7 ft 10 in OR

POLE VAULT

1896	William Hoyt, United States	10 ft 10 in
1900	Irving Baxter, United States	10 ft 10 in
1904	Charles Dvorak, United States	11 ft 5¾ in
1906	Fernand Gonder, France	11 ft 5¾ in

Note: OR=Olympic Record. WR=World Record. EOR=Equals Olympic Record. EWR=Equals World Record. WB=World Best.

TRACK AND FIELD (Cont.)
Men (Cont.)

POLE VAULT (Cont.)

1908...	Alfred Gilbert, United States	12 ft 2 in OR
	Edward Cooke Jr, United States	
1912...	Harry Babcock, United States	12 ft 11½ in OR
1920...	Frank Foss, United States	13 ft 5 in WR
1924...	Lee Barnes, United States	12 ft 11½ in
1928...	Sabin Carr, United States	13 ft 9¼ in OR
1932...	William Miller, United States	14 ft 1¾ in OR
1936...	Earle Meadows, United States	14 ft 3¼ in OR
1948...	Guinn Smith, United States	14 ft 1¼ in
1952...	Robert Richards, United States	14 ft 11 in OR
1956...	Robert Richards, United States	14 ft 11½ in OR
1960...	Don Bragg, United States	15 ft 5 in OR
1964...	Fred Hansen, United States	16 ft 8¾ in OR
1968...	Bob Seagren, United States	17 ft 8½ in OR
1972...	Wolfgang Nordwig, East Germany	18 ft ½ in OR
1976...	Tadeusz Slusarski, Poland	18 ft ½ in EOR
1980...	Wladyslaw Kozakiewicz, Poland	18 ft 11½ in WR
1984...	Pierre Quinon, France	18 ft 10¼ in
1988...	Sergei Bubka, USSR	19 ft 4¼ in OR
1992...	Maksim Tarasov, Unified Team	19 ft ¼ in
1996...	Jean Galfione, France	19 ft 5 ¼ in OR

LONG JUMP

1896...	Ellery Clark, United States	20 ft 10 in
1900...	Alvin Kraenzlein, United States	23 ft 6¾ in OR
1904...	Meyer Prinstein, United States	24 ft 1 in OR
1906...	Meyer Prinstein, United States	23 ft 7½ in
1908...	Frank Irons, United States	24 ft 6½ in OR
1912...	Albert Gutterson, United States	24 ft 11¼ in OR
1920...	William Petersson, Sweden	23 ft 5½ in
1924...	DeHart Hubbard, United States	24 ft 5 in
1928...	Edward B. Hamm, United States	25 ft 4½ in OR
1932...	Edward Gordon, United States	25 ft ¾ in
1936...	Jesse Owens, United States	26 ft 5½ in OR
1948...	William Steele, United States	25 ft 8 in
1952...	Jerome Biffle, United States	24 ft 10 in
1956...	Gregory Bell, United States	25 ft 8¼ in
1960...	Ralph Boston, United States	26 ft 7¾ in OR
1964...	Lynn Davies, Great Britain	26 ft 5¾ in
1968...	Bob Beamon, United States	29 ft 2½ in WR
1972...	Randy Williams, United States	27 ft ½ in
1976...	Arnie Robinson, United States	27 ft 4¾ in
1980...	Lutz Dombrowski, East Germany	28 ft ¼ in
1984...	Carl Lewis, United States	28 ft ¼ in
1988...	Carl Lewis, United States	28 ft 7½ in
1992...	Carl Lewis, United States	28 ft 5 ½ in
1996...	Carl Lewis, United States	27 ft 10¾ in

TRIPLE JUMP

1896...	James Connolly, United States	44 ft 11¾ in
1900...	Meyer Prinstein, United States	47 ft 5¾ in OR
1904...	Meyer Prinstein, United States	47 ft 1 in
1906...	Peter O'Connor, Great Britain/Ireland	46 ft 2¼ in
1908...	Timothy Ahearne, Great Britain/Ireland	48 ft 11¼ in OR
1912...	Gustaf Lindblom, Sweden	48 ft 5¼ in
1920...	Vilho Tuulos, Finland	47 ft 7 in
1924...	Anthony Winter, Australia	50 ft 11¼ in WR
1928...	Mikio Oda, Japan	49 ft 11 in
1932...	Chuhei Nambu, Japan	51 ft 7 in WR

TRIPLE JUMP (Cont.)

1936...	Naoto Tajima, Japan	52 ft 6 in WR
1948...	Arne Ahman, Sweden	50 ft 6¼ in
1952...	Adhemar da Silva, Brazil	53 ft 2¾ in WR
1956...	Adhemar da Silva, Brazil	53 ft 7¾ in OR
1960...	Jozef Schmidt, Poland	55 ft 2 in
1964...	Jozef Schmidt, Poland	55 ft 3½ in OR
1968...	Viktor Saneyev, USSR	57 ft ¾ in WR
1972...	Viktor Saneyev, USSR	56 ft 11¾ in
1976...	Viktor Saneyev, USSR	56 ft 8¾ in
1980...	Jaak Uudmae, USSR	56 ft 11¼ in
1984...	Al Joyner, United States	56 ft 7½ in
1988...	Khristo Markov, Bulgaria	57 ft 9½ in OR
1992...	Mike Conley, United States	59 ft 7½ in
1996...	Kenny Harrison, United States	59 ft 4¼ in OR

SHOT PUT

1896...	Robert Garrett, United States	36 ft 9¾ in
1900...	Richard Sheldon, United States	46 ft 3¼ in OR
1904...	Ralph Rose, United States	48 ft 7 in WR
1906...	Martin Sheridan, United States	40 ft 5¼ in
1908...	Ralph Rose, United States	46 ft 7½ in
1912...	Pat McDonald, United States	50 ft 4 in OR
1920...	Ville Porhola, Finland	48 ft 7¼ in
1924...	Clarence Houser, United States	49 ft 2¼ in
1928...	John Kuck, United States	52 ft ¾ in WR
1932...	Leo Sexton, United States	52 ft 6 in OR
1936...	Hans Woellke, Germany	53 ft 1¾ in OR
1948...	Wilbur Thompson, United States	56 ft 2 in OR
1952...	Parry O'Brien, United States	57 ft ½ in OR
1956...	Parry O'Brien, United States	60 ft 11¼ in OR
1960...	William Nieder, United States	64 ft 6¾ in OR
1964...	Dallas Long, United States	66 ft 8½ in OR
1968...	Randy Matson, United States	67 ft 4¾ in
1972...	Wladyslaw Komar, Poland	69 ft 6 in OR
1976...	Udo Beyer, East Germany	69 ft ¾ in
1980...	Vladimir Kiselyov, USSR	70 ft ½ in OR
1984...	Alessandro Andrei, Italy	69 ft 9 in
1988...	Ulf Timmermann, East Germany	73 ft 8¾ in OR
1992...	Mike Stulce, United States	71 ft 2½ in
1996...	Randy Barnes, United States	70 ft 11 in

DISCUS THROW

1896...	Robert Garrett, United States	95 ft 7½ in
1900...	Rudolf Bauer, Hungary	118 ft 3 in OR
1904...	Martin Sheridan, United States	128 ft 10½ in OR
1906...	Martin Sheridan, United States	136 ft
1908...	Martin Sheridan, United States	134 ft 2 in OR
1912...	Armas Taipele, Finland	148 ft 3 in OR
1920...	Elmer Niklander, Finland	146 ft 7 in
1924...	Clarence Houser, United States	151 ft 4 in OR
1928...	Clarence Houser, United States	155 ft 3 in OR
1932...	John Anderson, United States	162 ft 4 in OR
1936...	Ken Carpenter, United States	165 ft 7 in OR
1948...	Adolfo Consolini, Italy	173 ft 2 in OR
1952...	Sim Iness, United States	180 ft 6 in OR
1956...	Al Oerter, United States	184 ft 11 in OR
1960...	Al Oerter, United States	194 ft 2 in OR
1964...	Al Oerter, United States	200 ft 1 in OR
1968...	Al Oerter, United States	212 ft 6 in OR
1972...	Ludvik Danek, Czechoslovakia	211 ft 3 in
1976...	Mac Wilkins, United States	221 ft 5 in OR
1980...	Viktor Rashchupkin, USSR	218 ft 8 in

TRACK AND FIELD *(Cont.)*
Men *(Cont.)*

DISCUS THROW *(Cont.)*

1984...Rolf Dannenberg, West Germany	218 ft 6 in	
1988...Jürgen Schult, East Germany	225 ft 9 in OR	
1992...Romas Ubartas, Lithuania	213 ft 8 in	
1996...Lars Riedel, Germany	227 ft 8 in OR	

HAMMER THROW

1900...John Flanagan, United States	163 ft 1 in
1904...John Flanagan, United States	168 ft 1 in OR
1906...Not held	
1908...John Flanagan, United States	170 ft 4 in OR
1912...Matt McGrath, United States	179 ft 7 in OR
1920...Pat Ryan, United States	173 ft 5 in
1924...Fred Tootell, United States	174 ft 10 in
1928...Patrick O'Callaghan, Ireland	168 ft 7 in
1932...Patrick O'Callaghan, Ireland	176 ft 11 in
1936...Karl Hein, Germany	185 ft 4 in OR
1948...Imre Nemeth, Hungary	183 ft 11 in
1952...Jozsef Csermak, Hungary	197 ft 11 in WR
1956...Harold Connolly, United States	207 ft 3 in OR
1960...Vasily Rudenkov, USSR	220 ft 2 in OR
1964...Romuald Klim, USSR	228 ft 10 in OR
1968...Gyula Zsivotsky, Hungary	240 ft 8 in OR
1972...Anatoli Bondarchuk, USSR	247 ft 8 in OR
1976...Yuri Sedykh, USSR	254 ft 4 in OR
1980...Yuri Sedykh, USSR	268 ft 4 in WR
1984...Juha Tiainen, Finland	256 ft 2 in
1988...Sergei Litvinov, USSR	278 ft 2 in OR
1992...Andrey Abduvaliyev, Unified Team	270 ft 9 in
1996...Balazs Kiss, Hungary	266 ft 6 in

JAVELIN

1908...Erik Lemming, Sweden	179 ft 10 in
1912...Erik Lemming, Sweden	198 ft 11 in WR
1920...Jonni Myyrä, Finland	215 ft 10 in OR
1924...Jonni Myyrä, Finland	206 ft 6 in
1928...Eric Lundkvist, Sweden	218 ft 6 in OR
1932...Matti Jarvinen, Finland	238 ft 6 in OR
1936...Gerhard Stöck, Germany	235 ft 8 in
1948...Kai Rautavaara, Finland	228 ft 10½ in

JAVELIN *(Cont.)*

1952...Cy Young, United States	242 ft 1 in OR
1956...Egil Danielson, Norway	281 ft 2¼ in WR
1960...Viktor Tsibulenko, USSR	277 ft 8 in
1964...Pauli Nevala, Finland	271 ft 2 in
1968...Janis Lusis, USSR	295 ft 7 in OR
1972...Klaus Wolfermann, West Germany	296 ft 10 in OR
1976...Miklos Nemeth, Hungary	310 ft 4 in WR
1980...Dainis Kuta, USSR	299 ft 2⅜ in
1984...Arto Härkönen, Finland	284 ft 8 in
1988...Tapio Korjus, Finland	276 ft 6 in
1992...Jan Zelezny, Czechoslovakia	294 ft 2 in OR
1996...Jan Zelezny, Czech Rep.	289 ft 3 in

DECATHLON

	Pts
1904 ...Thomas Kiely, Ireland	6036
1912 ...Jim Thorpe, United States*	8412 WR
1920 ...Helge Lövland, Norway	6803
1924 ...Harold Osborn, United States	7711 WR
1928 ...Paavo Yrjölä, Finland	8053.29 WR
1932 ...James Bausch, United States	8462 WR
1936 ...Glenn Morris, United States	7900 WR
1948 ...Robert Mathias, United States	7139
1952 ...Robert Mathias, United States	7887 WR
1956 ...Milton Campbell, United States	7937 OR
1960 ...Rafer Johnson, United States	8392 OR
1964 ...Willi Holdorf, West Germany	7887
1968 ...Bill Toomey, United States	8193 OR
1972 ...Nikolai Avilov, USSR	8454 WR
1976 ...Bruce Jenner, United States	8617 WR
1980 ...Daley Thompson, Great Britain	8495
1984 ...Daley Thompson, Great Britain	8798 EWR
1988 ...Christian Schenk, East Germany	8488
1992 ...Robert Zmelik, Czechoslovakia	8611
1996 ...Dan O'Brien, United States	8824 OR

*In 1913, Thorpe was disqualified for having played professional baseball in 1910. His record was restored in 1982.

Women

100 METERS

1928 ....Elizabeth Robinson, United States	12.2 EWR
1932 ....Stella Walsh, Poland	11.9 EWR
1936 ....Helen Stephens, United States	11.5
1948 ....Francina Blankers-Koen, Netherlands	11.9
1952 ....Marjorie Jackson, Australia	11.5 EWR
1956 ....Betty Cuthbert, Australia	11.5 EWR
1960 ....Wilma Rudolph, United States	11.0
1964 ....Wyomia Tyus, United States	11.4
1968 ....Wyomia Tyus, United States	11.0 WR
1972 ....Renate Stecher, East Germany	11.07
1976 ....Annegret Richter, West Germany	11.08
1980 ....Lyudmila Kondratyeva, USSR	11.06
1984 ....Evelyn Ashford, United States	10.97 OR
1988 ....Florence Griffith Joyner, United States	10.54
1992 ....Gail Devers, United States	10.82
1996 ....Gail Devers, United States	10.94

200 METERS

1948 ....Francina Blankers-Koen, Netherlands	24.4
1952 ....Marjorie Jackson, Australia	23.7
1956 ....Betty Cuthbert, Australia	23.4 EOR
1960 ....Wilma Rudolph, United States	24.0
1964 ....Edith McGuire, United States	23.0 OR
1968 ....Irena Szewinska, Poland	22.5 WR
1972 ....Renate Stecher, East Germany	22.40 EWR
1976 ....Bärbel Eckert, East Germany	22.37 OR
1980 ....Bärbel Wöckel (Eckert), East Germany	22.03 OR
1984 ....Valerie Brisco-Hooks, United States	21.81 OR
1988 ....Florence Griffith Joyner, United States	21.34 WR
1992 ....Gwen Torrence, United States	21.81
1996 ....Marie-José Pérec, France	22.12

Note: OR=Olympic Record. WR=World Record. EOR=Equals Olympic Record. EWR=Equals World Record. WB=World Best.

TRACK AND FIELD *(Cont.)*
Women *(Cont.)*

400 METERS

1964	Betty Cuthbert, Australia	52.0 OR
1968	Colette Besson, France	52.0 EOR
1972	Monika Zehrt, East Germany	51.08 OR
1976	Irena Szewinska, Poland	49.29 WR
1980	Marita Koch, East Germany	48.88 OR
1984	Valerie Brisco-Hooks, United States	48.83 OR
1988	Olga Bryzgina, USSR	48.65 OR
1992	Marie-José Pérec, France	48.83
1996	Marie-José Pérec, France	48.25 OR

800 METERS

1928	Lina Radke, Germany	2:16.8 WR
1932	Not held 1932–1956	
1960	Lyudmila Shevtsova, USSR	2:04.3 EWR
1964	Ann Packer, Great Britain	2:01.1 OR
1968	Madeline Manning, United States	2:00.9 OR
1972	Hildegard Falck, West Germany	1:58.55 OR
1976	Tatyana Kazankina, USSR	1:54.94 WR
1980	Nadezhda Olizarenko, USSR	1:53.42 WR
1984	Doina Melinte, Romania	1:57.6
1988	Sigrun Wodars, East Germany	1:56.10
1992	Ellen Van Langen, Netherlands	1:55.54
1996	Svetlana Masterkova, Russia	1:57.73

1500 METERS

1972	Lyudmila Bragina, USSR	4:01.4 WR
1976	Tatyana Kazankina, USSR	4:05.48
1980	Tatyana Kazankina, USSR	3:56.6 OR
1984	Gabriella Dorio, Italy	4:03.25
1988	Paula Ivan, Romania	3:53.96 OR
1992	Hassiba Boulmerka, Algeria	3:55.30
1996	Svetlana Masterkova, Russa	4:00.83

3000 METERS

1984	Maricica Puica, Romania	8:35.96 OR
1988	Tatyana Samolenko, USSR	8:26.53 OR
1992	Elena Romanova, Unified Team	8:46.04

5000 METERS

1996	Wang Junxia, China	14:57.88

10,000 METERS

1988	Olga Bondarenko, USSR	31:05.21 OR
1992	Derartu Tulu, Ethiopia	31:06.02
1996	Fernanda Ribeiro, Portugal	31:01.63 OR

MARATHON

1984	Joan Benoit, United States	2:24:52 OR
1988	Rosa Mota, Portugal	2:25:40
1992	Valentin Yegorova, Unified Team	2:32:41
1996	Fatuma Roba, Ethiopia	2:26:05

80-METER HURDLES

1932	Babe Didrikson, United States	11.7 WR
1936	Trebisonda Valla, Italy	11.7
1948	Francina Blankers-Koen, Netherlands	11.2 OR
1952	Shirley Strickland, Australia	10.9 WR
1956	Shirley Strickland, Australia	10.7 OR
1960	Irina Press, USSR	10.8
1964	Karin Balzer, East Germany	10.5
1968	Maureen Caird, Australia	10.3 OR

100-METER HURDLES

1972	Annelie Ehrhardt, East Germany	12.59 WR
1976	Johanna Schaller, East Germany	12.77
1980	Vera Komisova, USSR	12.56 OR
1984	Benita Fitzgerald-Brown, United States	12.84
1988	Yordanka Donkova, Bulgaria	12.38 OR
1992	Paraskevi Patoulidou, Greece	12.64
1996	Lyudmila Engqvist, Sweden	12.58

400-METER HURDLES

1984	Nawal el Moutawakel, Morocco	54.61 OR
1988	Debra Flintoff-King, Australia	53.17 OR
1992	Sally Gunnell, Great Britain	53.23
1996	Deon Hemmings, Jamaica	52.82 OR

4 X 100-METER RELAY

1928	Canada	48.4 WR
1932	United States	46.9 WR
1936	United States	46.9
1948	Netherlands	47.5
1952	United States	45.9 WR
1956	Australia	44.5 WR
1960	United States	44.5
1964	Poland	43.6
1968	United States	42.8 WR
1972	West Germany	42.81 EWR
1976	East Germany	42.55 OR
1980	East Germany	41.60 WR
1984	United States	41.65
1988	United States	41.98
1992	United States	42.11
1996	United States	41.95

4 X 400-METER RELAY

1972	East Germany	3:23 WR
1976	East Germany	3:19.23 WR
1980	USSR	3:20.02
1984	United States	3:18.29 OR
1988	USSR	3:15.18 WR
1992	Unified Team	3:20.20
1996	United States	3:20.91

10-KILOMETER WALK

1992	Chen Yueling, China	44:32
1996	Elena Nikolayeva, Russia	41:49 OR

HIGH JUMP

1928	Ethel Catherwood, Canada	5 ft 2½ in
1932	Jean Shiley, United States	5 ft 5¼ in WR
1936	Ibolya Csak, Hungary	5 ft 3 in
1948	Alice Coachman, United States	5 ft 6 in
1952	Esther Brand, South Africa	5 ft 5¾ in
1956	Mildred L. McDaniel, United States	5 ft 9¼ in WR
1960	Iolanda Balas, Romania	6 ft ¾ in OR
1964	Iolanda Balas, Romania	6 ft 2¾ in OR
1968	Miloslava Reskova, Czechoslovakia	5 ft 11½ in
1972	Ulrike Meyfarth, West Germany	6 ft 3½ in EWR
1976	Rosemarie Ackermann, East Germany	6 ft 4 in OR

TRACK AND FIELD *(Cont.)*
Women *(Cont.)*

HIGH JUMP *(Cont.)*

1980	Sara Simeoni, Italy	6 ft 5½ in OR
1984	Ulrike Meyfarth, West Germany	6 ft 7½ in OR
1988	Louise Ritter, United States	6 ft 8 in OR
1992	Heike Henkel, Germany	6 ft 7½ in
1996	Stefka Kostadinova, Bulgaria	6 ft 8¾ in OR

LONG JUMP

1948	Olga Gyarmati, Hungary	18 ft 8¼ in
1952	Yvette Williams, New Zealand	20 ft 5¾ in OR
1956	Elzbieta Krzeskinska, Poland	20 ft 10 in EWR
1960	Vyera Krepkina, USSR	20 ft 10¾ in OR
1964	Mary Rand, Great Britain	22 ft 2¼ in WR
1968	Viorica Viscopoleanu, Romania	22 ft 4½ in WR
1972	Heidemarie Rosendahl, West Germany	22 ft 3 in
1976	Angela Voigt, East Germany	22 ft ¾ in
1980	Tatyana Kolpakova, USSR	23 ft 2 in OR
1984	Anisoara Stanciu, Romania	22 ft 10 in
1988	Jackie Joyner-Kersee, United States	24 ft 3½ in OR
1992	Heike Drechsler, Germany	23 ft 5¼ in
1996	Chioma Ajunwa, Nigeria	23 ft 4½ in

TRIPLE JUMP

1996	Inessa Kravets, Ukraine	50 ft 3½ in

SHOT PUT

1948	Micheline Ostermeyer, France	45 ft 1½ in
1952	Galina Zybina, USSR	50 ft 1¾ in WR
1956	Tamara Tyshkevich, USSR	54 ft 5 in OR
1960	Tamara Press, USSR	56 ft 10 in OR
1964	Tamara Press, USSR	59 ft 6¼ in OR
1968	Margitta Gummel, East Germany	64 ft 4 in WR
1972	Nadezhda Chizhova, USSR	69 ft WR
1976	Ivanka Hristova, Bulgaria	69 ft 5¼ in OR
1980	Ilona Slupianek, E Germany	73 ft 6¼ in
1984	Claudia Losch, West Germany	67 ft 2¼ in
1988	Natalya Lisovskaya, USSR	72 ft 11¾ in
1992	Svetlana Kriveleva, Unified Team	69 ft 1¼ in
1996	Astrid Kumbernuss, Germany	67 ft 5½ in

DISCUS THROW

1928	Helena Konopacka, Poland	129 ft 11¾ in WR
1932	Lillian Copeland, United States	133 ft 2 in OR
1936	Gisela Mauermayer, Germany	156 ft 3 in OR
1948	Micheline Ostermeyer, France	137 ft 6 in
1952	Nina Romaschkova, USSR	168 ft 8 in OR

DISCUS THROW *(Cont.)*

1956	Olga Fikotova, Czechoslovakia	176 ft 1 in OR
1960	Nina Ponomaryeva, USSR	180 ft 9 in OR
1964	Tamara Press, USSR	187 ft 10 in OR
1968	Lia Manoliu, Romania	191 ft 2 in OR
1972	Faina Melnik, USSR	218 ft 7 in OR
1976	Evelin Schlaak, East Germany	226 ft 4 in OR
1980	Evelin Jahl (Schlaak), East Germany	229 ft 6 in OR
1984	Ria Stalman, Netherlands	214 ft 5 in
1988	Martina Hellmann, East Germany	237 ft 2 in OR
1992	Maritza Martén, Cuba	229 ft 10 in
1996	Ilke Wyludda, Germany	228 ft 6 in

JAVELIN THROW

1932	Babe Didrikson, United States	143 ft 4 in OR
1936	Tilly Fleischer, Germany	148 ft 3 in OR
1948	Herma Bauma, Austria	149 ft 6 in
1952	Dana Zatopkova, Czechoslovakia	165 ft 7 in
1956	Inese Jaunzeme, USSR	176 ft 8 in
1960	Elvira Ozolina, USSR	183 ft 8 in OR
1964	Mihaela Penes, Romania	198 ft 7 in
1968	Angela Nemeth, Hungary	198 ft
1972	Ruth Fuchs, East Germany	209 ft 7 in OR
1976	Ruth Fuchs, East Germany	216 ft 4 in OR
1980	Maria Colon, Cuba	224 ft 5 in OR
1984	Tessa Sanderson, Great Britain	228 ft 2 in OR
1988	Petra Felke, East Germany	245 ft OR
1992	Silke Renk, Germany	224 ft 2 in
1996	Heli Rantanen, Finland	222 ft 11 in

PENTATHLON

		Pts
1964	Irina Press, USSR	5246 WR
1968	Ingrid Becker, West Germany	5098
1972	Mary Peters, Great Britain	4801 WR*
1976	Siegrun Siegl, East Germany	4745
1980	Nadezhda Tkachenko, USSR	5083 WR

HEPTATHLON

		Pts
1984	Glynis Nunn, Australia	6390 OR
1988	Jackie Joyner-Kersee, United States	7291 WR
1992	Jackie Joyner-Kersee, United States	7044
1996	Ghada Shouaa, Syria	6780

Note: OR=Olympic Record; WR=World Record; EOR=Equals Olympic Record; EWR=Equals World Record; WB=World Best.

BASKETBALL

Men

1936
Final: United States 19, Canada 8
United States: Ralph Bishop, Joe Fortenberry, Carl Knowles, Jack Ragland, Carl Shy, William Wheatley, Francis Johnson, Samuel Balter, John Gibbons, Frank Lubin, Arthur Mollner, Donald Piper, Duane Swanson, Willard Schmidt

1948
Final: United States 65, France 21
United States: Cliff Barker, Don Barksdale, Ralph Beard, Lewis Beck, Vince Boryla, Gordon Carpenter, Alex Groza, Wallace Jones, Bob Kurland, Ray Lumpp, Robert Pitts, Jesse Renick, Bob Robinson, Ken Rollins

1952
Final: United States 36, USSR 25
United States: Charles Hoag, Bill Hougland, Melvin Dean Kelley, Bob Kenney, Clyde Lovellette, Marcus Freiberger, Victor Wayne Glasgow, Frank McCabe, Daniel Pippen, Howard Williams, Ronald Bontemps, Bob Kurland, William Lienhard, John Keller

1956
Final: United States 89, USSR 55
United States: Carl Cain, Bill Hougland, K. C. Jones, Bill Russell, James Walsh, William Evans, Burdette Haldorson, Ron Tomsic, Dick Boushka, Gilbert Ford, Bob Jeangerard, Charles Darling

1960
Final: United States 90, Brazil 63
United States: Jay Arnette, Walt Bellamy, Bob Boozer, Terry Dischinger, Jerry Lucas, Oscar Robertson, Adrian Smith, Burdette Haldorson, Darrall Imhoff, Allen Kelley, Lester Lane, Jerry West

1964
Final: United States 73, USSR 59
United States: Jim Barnes, Bill Bradley, Larry Brown, Joe Caldwell, Mel Counts, Richard Davies, Walt Hazzard, Lucius Jackson, John McCaffrey, Jeff Mullins, Jerry Shipp, George Wilson

1968
Final: United States 65, Yugoslavia 50
United States: John Clawson, Ken Spain, Jo-Jo White, Michael Barrett, Spencer Haywood, Charles Scott, William Hosket, Calvin Fowler, Michael Silliman, Glynn Saulters, James King, Donald Dee

1972
Final: USSR 51, United States 50
United States: Kenneth Davis, Doug Collins, Thomas Henderson, Mike Bantom, Bobby Jones, Dwight Jones, James Forbes, James Brewer, Tom Burleson, Tom McMillen, Kevin Joyce, Ed Ratleff

1976
Final: United States 95, Yugoslavia 74
United States: Phil Ford, Steve Sheppard, Adrian Dantley, Walter Davis, Quinn Buckner, Ernie Grunfeld, Kenny Carr, Scott May, Michel Armstrong, Tom La Garde, Phil Hubbard, Mitch Kupchak

Men

1980
Final: Yugoslavia 86, Italy 77
U.S. participated in boycott.

1984
Final: United States 96, Spain 65
United States: Steve Alford, Leon Wood, Patrick Ewing, Vern Fleming, Alvin Robertson, Michael Jordan, Joe Kleine, Jon Koncak, Wayman Tisdale, Chris Mullin, Sam Perkins, Jeff Turner

1988
Final: USSR 76, Yugoslavia 63
United States (3rd): Mitch Richmond, Charles E. Smith, IV, Vernell Coles, Hersey Hawkins, Jeff Grayer, Charles D. Smith, Willie Anderson, Stacey Augmon, Dan Majerle, Danny Manning, J. R. Reid, David Robinson

1992
Final: United States 117, Croatia 85
United States: David Robinson, Christian Laettner, Patrick Ewing, Larry Bird, Scottie Pippen, Michael Jordan, Clyde Drexler, Karl Malone, John Stockton, Chris Mullin, Charles Barkley, Earvin Johnson

1996
Final: United States 95, Yugoslavia 69
United States: Charles Barkley, Anfernee Hardaway, Grant Hill, Karl Malone, Reggie Miller, Hakeem Olajuwon, Shaquille O'Neal, Scottie Pippen, Mitch Richmond, John Stockton, David Robinson, Gary Payton

Women

1976
Gold, USSR; Silver, United States*
United States: Cindy Brogdon, Susan Rojcewicz, Ann Meyers, Lusia Harris, Nancy Dunkle, Charlotte Lewis, Nancy Lieberman, Gail Marquis, Patricia Roberts, Mary Anne O'Connor, Patricia Head, Julienne Simpson

*In 1976 the women played a round-robin tournament, with the gold medal going to the team with the best record. The USSR won with a 5-0 record, and the USA, with a 3-2 record, was given the silver by virtue of a 95-79 victory over Bulgaria, which was also 3-2.

1980
Final: USSR 104, Bulgaria 73
U.S. participated in boycott.

1984
Final: United States 85, Korea 55
United States: Teresa Edwards, Lea Henry, Lynette Woodard, Anne Donovan, Cathy Boswell, Cheryl Miller, Janice Lawrence, Cindy Noble, Kim Mulkey, Denise Curry, Pamela McGee, Carol Menken-Schaudt

1988
Final: United States 77, Yugoslavia 70
United States: Teresa Edwards, Mary Ethridge, Cynthia Brown, Anne Donovan, Teresa Weatherspoon, Bridgette Gordon, Victoria Bullett, Andrea Lloyd, Katrina McClain, Jennifer Gillom, Cynthia Cooper, Suzanne McConnell

BASKETBALL (Cont.)
Women (Cont.)

1992

Final: Unified Team 76, China 66
United States (3rd): Teresa Edwards, Teresa Weatherspoon, Victoria Bullett, Katrina McClain, Cynthia Cooper, Suzanne McConnell, Daedra Charles, Clarissa Davis, Tammy Jackson, Vickie Orr, Carolyn Jones, Medina Dixon

1996

Final: United States 111, Brazil 87
United States: Jennifer Azzi, Ruthie Bolton, Teresa Edwards, Lisa Leslie, Rebecca Lobo, Katrina McClain, Nikki McCray, Carla McGhee, Dawn Staley, Katy Steding, Sheryl Swoopes, Venus Lacey

BOXING

LIGHT FLYWEIGHT (106 LB)

1968	Francisco Rodriguez, Venezuela
1972	Gyorgy Gedo, Hungary
1976	Jorge Hernandez, Cuba
1980	Shamil Sabyrov, USSR
1984	Paul Gonzalez, United States
1988	Ivailo Hristov, Bulgaria
1992	Rogelio Marcelo, Cuba
1996	Daniel Petrov, Bulgaria

FLYWEIGHT (112 LB)

1904	George Finnegan, United States
1906-1912	Not held
1920	Frank Di Gennara, United States
1924	Fidel LaBarba, United States
1928	Antal Kocsis, Hungary
1932	Istvan Enekes, Hungary
1936	Willi Kaiser, Germany
1948	Pascual Perez, Argentina
1952	Nathan Brooks, United States
1956	Terence Spinks, Great Britain
1960	Gyula Torok, Hungary
1964	Fernando Atzori, Italy
1968	Ricardo Delgado, Mexico
1972	Georgi Kostadinov, Bulgaria
1976	Leo Randolph, United States
1980	Peter Lessov, Bulgaria
1984	Steve McCrory, United States
1988	Kim Kwang Sun, South Korea
1992	Su Choi Chol, North Korea
1996	Maikro Romero, Cuba

BANTAMWEIGHT (119 LB)

1904	Oliver Kirk, United States
1906	Not held
1908	A. Henry Thomas, Great Britain
1912	Not held
1920	Clarence Walker, South Africa
1924	William Smith, South Africa
1928	Vittorio Tamagnini, Italy
1932	Horace Gwynne, Canada
1936	Ulderico Sergo, Italy
1948	Tibor Csik, Hungary
1952	Pentti Hamalainen, Finland
1956	Wolfgang Behrendt, East Germany
1960	Oleg Grigoryev, USSR
1964	Takao Sakurai, Japan
1968	Valery Sokolov, USSR
1972	Orlando Martinez, Cuba
1976	Yong Jo Gu, North Korea
1980	Juan Hernandez, Cuba
1984	Maurizio Stecca, Italy
1988	Kennedy McKinney, United States
1992	Joel Casamayor, Cuba
1996	István Kovács, Hungary

FEATHERWEIGHT (125 LB)

1904	Oliver Kirk, United States
1906	Not held
1908	Richard Gunn, Great Britain
1912	Not held
1920	Paul Fritsch, France
1924	John Fields, United States
1928	Lambertus van Klaveren, Netherlands
1932	Carmelo Robledo, Argentina
1936	Oscar Casanovas, Argentina
1948	Ernesto Formenti, Italy
1952	Jan Zachara, Czechoslovakia
1956	Vladimir Safronov, USSR
1960	Francesco Musso, Italy
1964	Stanislav Stephashkin, USSR
1968	Antonio Roldan, Mexico
1972	Boris Kousnetsov, USSR
1976	Angel Herrera, Cuba
1980	Rudi Fink, East Germany
1984	Meldrick Taylor, United States
1988	Giovanni Parisi, Italy
1992	Andreas Tews, Germany
1996	Somluck Kamsing, Thailand

LIGHTWEIGHT (132 LB)

1904	Harry Spanger, United States
1906	Not held
1908	Frederick Grace, Great Britain
1912	Not held
1920	Samuel Mosberg, United States
1924	Hans Nielsen, Denmark
1928	Carlo Orlandi, Italy
1932	Lawrence Stevens, South Africa
1936	Imre Harangi, Hungary
1948	Gerald Dreyer, South Africa
1952	Aureliano Bolognesi, Italy
1956	Richard McTaggart, Great Britain
1960	Kazimierz Pazdzior, Poland
1964	Jozef Grudzien, Poland
1968	Ronald Harris, United States
1972	Jan Szczepanski, Poland
1976	Howard Davis, United States
1980	Angel Herrera, Cuba
1984	Pernell Whitaker, United States
1988	Andreas Zuelow, East Germany
1992	Oscar De La Hoya, United States
1996	Hocine Soltani, Algeria

LIGHT WELTERWEIGHT (139 LB)

1952	Charles Adkins, United States
1956	Vladimir Yengibaryan, USSR
1960	Bohumil Nemecek, Czechoslovakia
1964	Jerzy Kulej, Poland
1968	Jerzy Kulej, Poland
1972	Ray Seales, United States
1976	Ray Leonard, United States

Summer Games Champions *(Cont.)*

BOXING *(Cont.)*

LIGHT WELTERWEIGHT *(Cont.)*
1980 ....Patrizio Oliva, Italy
1984 ....Jerry Page, United States
1988 ....Viatcheslav Janovski, USSR
1992 ....Hector Vinent, Cuba
1996 ....Hector Vinent, Cuba

WELTERWEIGHT (147 LB)
1904 ....Albert Young, United States
1906-1912 ......Not held
1920 ....Albert Schneider, Canada
1924 ....Jean Delarge, Belgium
1928 ....Edward Morgan, New Zealand
1932 ....Edward Flynn, United States
1936 ....Sten Suvio, Finland
1948 ....Julius Torma, Czechoslovakia
1952 ....Zygmunt Chychla, Poland
1956 ....Nicolae Linca, Romania
1960 ....Giovanni Benvenuti, Italy
1964 ....Marian Kasprzyk, Poland
1968 ....Manfred Wolke, East Germany
1972 ....Emilio Correa, Cuba
1976 ....Jochen Bachfeld, East Germany
1980 ....Andres Aldama, Cuba
1984 ....Mark Breland, United States
1988 ....Robert Wangila, Kenya
1992 ....Michael Carruth, Ireland
1996 ....Oleg Saitov, Russia

LIGHT MIDDLEWEIGHT (156 LB)
1952 ....Laszlo Papp, Hungary
1956 ....Laszlo Papp, Hungary
1960 ....Wilbert McClure, United States
1964 ....Boris Lagutin, USSR
1968 ....Boris Lagutin, USSR
1972 ....Dieter Kottysch, West Germany
1976 ....Jerzy Rybicki, Poland
1980 ....Armando Martinez, Cuba
1984 ....Frank Tate, United States
1988 ....Park Si-Hun, South Korea
1992 ....Juan Lemus, Cuba
1996 ....David Reid, United States

MIDDLEWEIGHT (165 LB)
1904 ....Charles Mayer, United States
1908 ....John Douglas, Great Britain
1912 ....Not held
1920 ....Harry Mallin, Great Britain
1924 ....Harry Mallin, Great Britain
1928 ....Piero Toscani, Italy
1932 ....Carmen Barth, United States
1936 ....Jean Despeaux, France
1948 ....Laszlo Papp, Hungary
1952 ....Floyd Patterson, United States
1956 ....Gennady Schatkov, USSR
1960 ....Edward Crook, United States
1964 ....Valery Popenchenko, USSR
1968 ....Christopher Finnegan, Great Britain
1972 ....Vyacheslav Lemechev, USSR
1976 ....Michael Spinks, United States

MIDDLEWEIGHT *(Cont.)*
1980 ....Jose Gomez, Cuba
1984 ....Shin Joon Sup, South Korea
1988 ....Henry Maske, East Germany
1992 ....Ariel Hernandez, Cuba
1996 ....Ariel Hernandez, Cuba

LIGHT HEAVYWEIGHT (178 LB)
1920 ....Edward Eagan, United States
1924 ....Harry Mitchell, Great Britain
1928 ....Victor Avendano, Argentina
1932 ....David Carstens, South Africa
1936 ....Roger Michelot, France
1948 ....George Hunter, South Africa
1952 ....Norvel Lee, United States
1956 ....James Boyd, United States
1960 ....Cassius Clay, United States
1964 ....Cosimo Pinto, Italy
1968 ....Dan Poznyak, USSR
1972 ....Mate Parlov, Yugoslavia
1976 ....Leon Spinks, United States
1980 ....Slobodan Kacer, Yugoslavia
1984 ....Anton Josipovic, Yugoslavia
1988 ....Andrew Maynard, United States
1992 ....Torsten May, Germany
1996 ....Vassili Jirov, Kazakhstan

HEAVYWEIGHT (OVER 201 LB)
1904 ....Samuel Berger, United States
1906 ....Not held
1908 ....Albert Oldham, Great Britain
1912 ....Not held
1920 ....Ronald Rawson, Great Britain
1924 ....Otto von Porat, Norway
1928 ....Arturo Rodriguez Jurado, Argentina
1932 ....Santiago Lovell, Argentina
1936 ....Herbert Runge, Germany
1948 ....Rafael Inglesias, Argentina
1952 ....H. Edward Sanders, United States
1956 ....T. Peter Rademacher, United States
1960 ....Franco De Piccoli, Italy
1964 ....Joe Frazier, United States
1968 ....George Foreman, United States
1972 ....Teofilo Stevenson, Cuba
1976 ....Teofilo Stevenson, Cuba
1980 ....Teofilo Stevenson, Cuba

HEAVYWEIGHT (201* LB)
1984 ....Henry Tillman, United States
1988 ....Ray Mercer, United States
1992 ....Félix Sávon, Cuba
1996 ....Félix Sávon, Cuba

SUPER HEAVYWEIGHT (UNLIMITED)
1984 ....Tyrell Biggs, United States
1988 ....Lennox Lewis, Canada
1992 ....Roberto Balado, Cuba
1996 ....Vladimir Klitchko, Ukraine

*Until 1984 the heavyweight division was unlimited. With the addition of the super heavyweight division, a limit of 201 pounds was imposed.

SWIMMING
Men
50-METER FREESTYLE
1904 ....Zoltan Halmay, Hungary (50 yds) 28.0
1988 ....Matt Biondi, United States 22.14 WR
1992 ....Aleksandr Popov, Unified Team 22.30
1996 ....Aleksandr Popov, Russia 22.13

SWIMMING *(Cont.)*
Men *(Cont.)*

100-METER FREESTYLE

1896	Alfred Hajos, Hungary	1:22.2 OR
1904	Zoltan Halmay, Hungary (100 yds)	1:02.8
1906	Charles Daniels, United States	1:13.4
1908	Charles Daniels, United States	1:05.6 WR
1912	Duke Kahanamoku, United States	1:03.4
1920	Duke Kahanamoku, United States	1:00.4 WR
1924	John Weissmuller, United States	59.0 OR
1928	John Weissmuller, United States	58.6 OR
1932	Yasuji Miyazaki, Japan	58.2
1936	Ferenc Csik, Hungary	57.6
1948	Wally Ris, United States	57.3 OR
1952	Clarke Scholes, United States	57.4
1956	Jon Henricks, Australia	55.4 OR
1960	John Devitt, Australia	55.2 OR
1964	Don Schollander, United States	53.4 OR
1968	Mike Wenden, Australia	52.2 WR
1972	Mark Spitz, United States	51.22 WR
1976	Jim Montgomery, United States	49.99 WR
1980	Jörg Woithe, East Germany	50.40
1984	Rowdy Gaines, United States	49.80 OR
1988	Matt Biondi, United States	48.63 OR
1992	Aleksandr Popov, Unified Team	49.02
1996	Aleksandr Popov, Russia	48.74

200-METER FREESTYLE

1900	Frederick Lane, Australia	2:25.2 OR
1904	Charles Daniels, United States	2:44.2
1906	Not held 1906-1964	
1968	Michael Wenden, Australia	1:55.2 OR
1972	Mark Spitz, United States	1:52.78 WR
1976	Bruce Furniss, United States	1:50.29 WR
1980	Sergei Kopliakov, USSR	1:49.81 OR
1984	Michael Gross, West Germany	1:47.44 WR
1988	Duncan Armstrong, Australia	1:47.25 WR
1992	Evgueni Sadovyi, Unified Team	1:46.70 OR
1996	Danyon Loader, New Zealand	1:47.63

400-METER FREESTYLE

1896	Paul Neumann, Austria (500 yds)	8:12.6
1904	Charles Daniels, U.S. (440 yds)	6:16.2
1906	Otto Scheff, Austria (440 yds)	6:23.8
1908	Henry Taylor, Great Britain	5:36.8
1912	George Hodgson, Canada	5:24.4
1920	Norman Ross, United States	5:26.8
1924	John Weissmuller, United States	5:04.2 OR
1928	Albert Zorilla, Argentina	5:01.6 OR
1932	Buster Crabbe, United States	4:48.4 OR
1936	Jack Medica, United States	4:44.5 OR
1948	William Smith, United States	4:41.0 OR
1952	Jean Boiteux, France	4:30.7 OR
1956	Murray Rose, Australia	4:27.3 OR
1960	Murray Rose, Australia	4:18.3 OR
1964	Don Schollander, United States	4:12.2 WR
1968	Mike Burton, United States	4:09.0 OR
1972	Brad Cooper, Australia	4:00.27 OR
1976	Brian Goodell, United States	3:51.93 WR
1980	Vladimir Salnikov, USSR	3:51.31 OR
1984	George DiCarlo, United States	3:51.23 OR
1988	Uwe Dassler, East Germany	3:46.95 WR
1992	Evgueni Sadovyi, Unified Team	3:45.00 WR
1996	Danyon Loader, New Zealand	3:47.97

1500-METER FREESTYLE

1908	Henry Taylor, Great Britain	22:48.4 WR
1912	George Hodgson, Canada	22:00.0 WR

1500-METER FREESTYLE *(Cont.)*

1920	Norman Ross, United States	22:23.2
1924	Andrew Charlton, Australia	20:06.6 WR
1928	Arne Borg, Sweden	19:51.8 OR
1932	Kusuo Kitamura, Japan	19:12.4 OR
1936	Noboru Terada, Japan	19:13.7
1948	James McLane, United States	19:18.5
1952	Ford Konno, United States	18:30.3 OR
1956	Murray Rose, Australia	17:58.9
1960	John Konrads, Australia	17:19.6 OR
1964	Robert Windle, Australia	17:01.7 OR
1968	Mike Burton, United States	16:38.9 OR
1972	Mike Burton, United States	15:52.58 OR
1976	Brian Goodell, United States	15:02.40 WR
1980	Vladimir Salnikov, USSR	14:58.27 WR
1984	Michael O'Brien, United States	15:05.20
1988	Vladimir Salnikov, USSR	15:00.40
1992	Kieren Perkins, Australia	14:43.48 WR
1996	Kieren Perkins, Australia	14:56.40

100-METER BACKSTROKE

1904	Walter Brack, Germany (100 yds)	1:16.8
1908	Arno Bieberstein, Germany	1:24.6 WR
1912	Harry Hebner, United States	1:21.2
1920	Warren Kealoha, United States	1:15.2
1924	Warren Kealoha, United States	1:13.2 OR
1928	George Kojac, United States	1:08.2 WR
1932	Masaji Kiyokawa, Japan	1:08.6
1936	Adolph Kiefer, United States	1:05.9 OR
1948	Allen Stack, United States	1:06.4
1952	Yoshi Oyakawa, United States	1:05.4 OR
1956	David Thiele, Australia	1:02.2 OR
1960	David Thiele, Australia	1:01.9 OR
1964	Not held	
1968	Roland Matthes, East Germany	58.7 OR
1972	Roland Matthes, East Germany	56.58 OR
1976	John Naber, United States	55.49 WR
1980	Bengt Baron, Sweden	56.33
1984	Rick Carey, United States	55.79
1988	Daichi Suzuki, Japan	55.05
1992	Mark Tewksbury, Canada	53.98 WR
1996	Jeff Rouse, United States	54.10

200-METER BACKSTROKE

1900	Ernst Hoppenberg, Germany	2:47.0
1904	Not held 1904-1960	
1964	Jed Graef, United States	2:10.3 WR
1968	Roland Matthes, East Germany	2:09.6 OR
1972	Roland Matthes, East Germany	2:02.82 EWR
1976	John Naber, United States	1:59.19 WR
1980	Sandor Wladar, Hungary	2:01.93
1984	Rick Carey, United States	2:00.23
1988	Igor Polianski, USSR	1:59.37
1992	Martin Lopez-Zubero, Spain	1:58.47 OR
1996	Brad Bridgewater, United States	1:58.54

100-METER BREASTSTROKE

1968	Don McKenzie, United States	1:07.7 OR
1972	Nobutaka Taguchi, Japan	1:04.94 WR
1976	John Hencken, United States	1:03.11 WR
1980	Duncan Goodhew, Great Britain	1:03.44
1984	Steve Lundquist, United States	1:01.65 WR
1988	Adrian Moorhouse, Great Britain	1:02.04
1992	Nelson Diebel, United States	1:01.50 OR
1996	Fred DeBurghgraeve, Belgium	1:00.65

Note: OR=Olympic Record. WR=World Record. EOR=Equals Olympic Record. EWR=Equals World Record. WB=World Best.

SWIMMING *(Cont.)*

Men *(Cont.)*

200-METER BREASTSTROKE

1908	Frederick Holman, Great Britain	3:09.2 WR
1912	Walter Bathe, Germany	3:01.8 OR
1920	Haken Malmroth, Sweden	3:04.4
1924	Robert Skelton, United States	2:56.6
1928	Yoshiyuki Tsuruta, Japan	2:48.8 OR
1932	Yoshiyuki Tsuruta, Japan	2:45.4
1936	Tetsuo Hamuro, Japan	2:41.5 OR
1948	Joseph Verdeur, United States	2:39.3 OR
1952	John Davies, Australia	2:34.4 OR
1956	Masura Furukawa, Japan	2:34.7 OR
1960	William Mulliken, United States	2:37.4
1964	Ian O'Brien, Australia	2:27.8 WR
1968	Felipe Munoz, Mexico	2:28.7
1972	John Hencken, United States	2:21.55 WR
1976	David Wilkie, Great Britain	2:15.11 WR
1980	Robertas Zhulpa, USSR	2:15.85
1984	Victor Davis, Canada	2:13.34 WR
1988	Jozsef Szabo, Hungary	2:13.52
1992	Mike Barrowman, United States	2:10.16 WR
1996	Norbert Rózsa, Hungary	2:12.57

100-METER BUTTERFLY

1968	Doug Russell, United States	55.9 OR
1972	Mark Spitz, United States	54.27 WR
1976	Matt Vogel, United States	54.35
1980	Pär Arvidsson, Sweden	54.92
1984	Michael Gross, West Germany	53.08 WR
1988	Anthony Nesty, Suriname	53.00 OR
1992	Pablo Morales, United States	53.32
1996	Denis Pankratov, Russia	52.27 WR

200-METER BUTTERFLY

1956	William Yorzyk, United States	2:19.3 OR
1960	Michael Troy, United States	2:12.8 WR
1964	Kevin Berry, Australia	2:06.6 WR
1968	Carl Robie, United States	2:08.7
1972	Mark Spitz, United States	2:00.70 WR
1976	Mike Bruner, United States	1:59.23 WR
1980	Sergei Fesenko, USSR	1:59.76
1984	Jon Sieben, Australia	1:57.04 WR
1988	Michael Gross, West Germany	1:56.94 OR
1992	Melvin Stewart, United States	1:56.26 OR
1996	Denis Pankratov, Russia	1:56.51

200-METER INDIVIDUAL MEDLEY

1968	Charles Hickcox, United States	2:12.0 OR
1972	Gunnar Larsson, Sweden	2:07.17 WR
1984	Alex Baumann, Canada	2:01.42 WR
1988	Tamas Darnyi, Hungary	2:00.17 WR
1992	Tamas Darnyi, Hungary	2:00.76
1996	Attila Czene, Hungary	1:59.91 OR

400-METER INDIVIDUAL MEDLEY

1964	Richard Roth, United States	4:45.4 WR
1968	Charles Hickcox, United States	4:48.4
1972	Gunnar Larsson, Sweden	4:31.98 OR
1976	Rod Strachan, United States	4:23.68 WR
1980	Aleksandr Sidorenko, USSR	4:22.89 OR
1984	Alex Baumann, Canada	4:17.41 WR
1988	Tamas Darnyi, Hungary	4:14.75 WR
1992	Tamas Darnyi, Hungary	4:14.23 OR
1996	Tom Dolan United States	4:14.90

4 X 100-METER MEDLEY RELAY

1960	United States	4:05.4 WR
1964	United States	3:58.4 WR
1968	United States	3:54.9 WR
1972	United States	3:48.16 WR
1976	United States	3:42.22 WR
1980	Australia	3:45.70
1984	United States	3:39.30 WR
1988	United States	3:36.93 WR
1992	United States	3:36.93 EWR
1996	United States	3:34.84 WR

4 X 100-METER FREESTYLE RELAY

1964	United States	3:32.2 WR
1968	United States	3:31.7 WR
1972	United States	3:26.42 WR
1976-1980	Not held	
1984	United States	3:19.03 WR
1988	United States	3:16.53 WR
1992	United States	3:16.74
1996	United States	3:15.41 OR

4 X 200-METER FREESTYLE RELAY

1906	Hungary (1000 m)	16:52.4
1908	Great Britain	10:55.6
1912	Australia/New Zealand	10:11.6 WR
1920	United States	10:04.4 WR
1924	United States	9:53.4 WR
1928	United States	9:36.2 WR
1932	Japan	8:58.4 WR
1936	Japan	8:51.5 WR
1948	United States	8:46.0 WR
1952	United States	8:31.1 OR
1956	Australia	8:23.6 WR
1960	United States	8:10.2 WR
1964	United States	7:52.1 WR
1968	United States	7:52.33
1972	United States	7:35.78 WR
1976	United States	7:23.22 WR
1980	USSR	7:23.50
1984	United States	7:15.69 WR
1988	United States	7:12.51 WR
1992	Unified Team	7:11.95 WR
1996	United States	7:14.84

Women

50-METER FREESTYLE

1988	Kristin Otto, East Germany	25.49 OR
1992	Yang Wenyi, China	24.79 WR
1996	Amy Van Dyken, United States	24.87

100-METER FREESTYLE

1912	Fanny Durack, Australia	1:22.2
1920	Ethelda Bleibtrey, United States	1:13.6 WR
1924	Ethel Lackie, United States	1:12.4
1928	Albina Osipowich, United States	1:11.0 OR
1932	Helene Madison, United States	1:06.8 OR

100-METER FREESTYLE *(Cont.)*

1936	Hendrika Mastenbroek, Netherlands	1:05.9 OR
1948	Greta Andersen, Denmark	1:06.3
1952	Katalin Szöke, Hungary	1:06.8
1956	Dawn Fraser, Australia	1:02.0 WR
1960	Dawn Fraser, Australia	1:01.2 OR
1964	Dawn Fraser, Australia	59.5 OR
1968	Jan Henne, United States	1:00.0
1972	Sandra Neilson, United States	58.59 OR

SWIMMING *(Cont.)*
Women *(Cont.)*

100-METER FREESTYLE *(Cont.)*

1976	Kornelia Ender, East Germany	55.65 WR
1980	Barbara Krause, East Germany	54.79 WR
1984	Carrie Steinseifer, United States	55.92
	Nancy Hogshead, United States	55.92
1988	Kristin Otto, East Germany	54.93
1992	Zhuang Yong, China	54.64 OR
1996	Le Jingyi, China	54.50 OR

200-METER FREESTYLE

1968	Debbie Meyer, United States	2:10.5 OR
1972	Shane Gould, Australia	2:03.56 WR
1976	Kornelia Ender, East Germany	1:59.26 WR
1980	Barbara Krause, East Germany	1:58.33 OR
1984	Mary Wayte, United States	1:59.23
1988	Heike Friedrich, East Germany	1:57.65 OR
1992	Nicole Haislett, United States	1:57.90
1996	Claudia Poll, Costa Rica	1:58.16

400-METER FREESTYLE

1924	Martha Norelius, United States	6:02.2 OR
1928	Martha Norelius, United States	5:42.8 WR
1932	Helene Madison, United States	5:28.5 WR
1936	Hendrika Mastenbroek, Netherlands	5:26.4 OR
1948	Ann Curtis, United States	5:17.8 OR
1952	Valeria Gyenge, Hungary	5:12.1 OR
1956	Lorraine Crapp, Australia	4:54.6 OR
1960	Chris von Saltza, United States	4:50.6 OR
1964	Virginia Duenkel, United States	4:43.3 OR
1968	Debbie Meyer, United States	4:31.8 OR
1972	Shane Gould, Australia	4:19.44 WR
1976	Petra Thümer, East Germany	4:09.89 WR
1980	Ines Diers, East Germany	4:08.76 WR
1984	Tiffany Cohen, United States	4:07.10 OR
1988	Janet Evans, United States	4:03.85 WR
1992	Dagmar Hase, Germany	4:07.18
1996	Michelle Smith, Ireland	4:07.25

800-METER FREESTYLE

1968	Debbie Meyer, United States	9:24.0 OR
1972	Keena Rothhammer, United States	8:53.68 WR
1976	Petra Thümer, East Germany	8:37.14 WR
1980	Michelle Ford, Australia	8:28.90 OR
1984	Tiffany Cohen, United States	8:24.95 OR
1988	Janet Evans, United States	8:20.20 OR
1992	Janet Evans, United States	8:25.52
1996	Brooke Bennett, United States	8:27.89

100-METER BACKSTROKE

1924	Sybil Bauer, United States	1:23.2 OR
1928	Marie Braun, Netherlands	1:22.0
1932	Eleanor Holm, United States	1:19.4
1936	Dina Senff, Netherlands	1:18.9
1948	Karen Harup, Denmark	1:14.4 OR
1952	Joan Harrison, South Africa	1:14.3
1956	Judy Grinham, Great Britain	1:12.9 OR
1960	Lynn Burke, United States	1:09.3 OR
1964	Cathy Ferguson, United States	1:07.7 WR
1968	Kaye Hall, United States	1:06.2 WR
1972	Melissa Belote, United States	1:05.78 OR
1976	Ulrike Richter, East Germany	1:01.83 OR
1980	Rica Reinisch, East Germany	1:00.86 WR
1984	Theresa Andrews, United States	1:02.55
1988	Kristin Otto, East Germany	1:00.89
1992	Krisztina Egerszegi, Hungary	1:00.68 OR
1996	Beth Botsford, United States	1:01.19

200-METER BACKSTROKE

1968	Pokey Watson, United States	2:24.8 OR
1972	Melissa Belote, United States	2:19.19 WR
1976	Ulrike Richter, East Germany	2:13.43 OR
1980	Rica Reinisch, East Germany	2:11.77 WR
1984	Jolanda De Rover, Netherlands	2:12.38
1988	Krisztina Egerszegi, Hungary	2:09.29 OR
1992	Krisztina Egerszegi, Hungary	2:07.06 OR
1996	Krisztina Egerszegi, Hungary	2:07.83

100-METER BREASTSTROKE

1968	Djurdjica Bjedov, Yugoslavia	1:15.8 OR
1972	Catherine Carr, United States	1:13.58 WR
1976	Hannelore Anke, East Germany	1:11.16
1980	Ute Geweniger, East Germany	1:10.22
1984	Petra Van Staveren, Netherlands	1:09.88 OR
1988	Tania Dangalakova, Bulgaria	1:07.95 OR
1992	Elena Roudkovskaia, Unified Team	1:08.00
1996	Penelope Heyns, South Africa	1:07.73

200-METER BREASTSTROKE

1924	Lucy Morton, Great Britain	3:33.2 OR
1928	Hilde Schrader, Germany	3:12.6
1932	Clare Dennis, Australia	3:06.3 OR
1936	Hideko Maehata, Japan	3:03.6
1948	Petronella Van Vliet, Netherlands	2:57.2
1952	Eva Szekely, Hungary	2:51.7 OR
1956	Ursula Happe, West Germany	2:53.1 OR
1960	Anita Lonsbrough, Great Britain	2:49.5 WR
1964	Galina Prozumenshikova, USSR	2:46.4 OR
1968	Sharon Wichman, United States	2:44.4 OR
1972	Beverly Whitfield, Australia	2:41.71 OR
1976	Marina Koshevaia, USSR	2:33.35 WR
1980	Lina Kaciusyte, USSR	2:29.54 OR
1984	Anne Ottenbrite, Canada	2:30.38
1988	Silke Hoerner, East Germany	2:26.71 WR
1992	Kyoko Iwasaki, Japan	2:26.65 OR
1996	Penelope Heyns, South Africa	2:25.41 OR

100-METER BUTTERFLY

1956	Shelley Mann, United States	1:11.0 OR
1960	Carolyn Schuler, United States	1:09.5 OR
1964	Sharon Stouder, United States	1:04.7 WR
1968	Lynn McClements, Australia	1:05.5
1972	Mayumi Aoki, Japan	1:03.34 WR
1976	Kornelia Ender, East Germany	1:00.13 EWR
1980	Caren Metschuck, East Germany	1:00.42
1984	Mary T. Meagher, United States	59.26
1988	Kristin Otto, East Germany	59.00 OR
1992	Qian Hong, China	58.62 OR
1996	Amy Van Dyken, United States	59.13

200-METER BUTTERFLY

1968	Ada Kok, Netherlands	2:24.7 OR
1972	Karen Moe, United States	2:15.57 WR
1976	Andrea Pollack, East Germany	2:11.41 OR
1980	Ines Geissler, East Germany	2:10.44 OR
1984	Mary T. Meagher, United States	2:06.90 OR
1988	Kathleen Nord, East Germany	2:09.51
1992	Summer Sanders, United States	2:08.67
1996	Susan O'Neill, Australia	2:07.76

200-METER INDIVIDUAL MEDLEY

1968	Claudia Kolb, United States	2:24.7 OR
1972	Shane Gould, Australia	2:23.07 WR
1976	Not held 1976-1980	
1984	Tracy Caulkins, United States	2:12.64 OR

Note: OR=Olympic Record. WR=World Record. EOR=Equals Olympic Record. EWR=Equals World Record. WB=World Best.

SWIMMING (Cont.)
Women (Cont.)

200-METER INDIVIDUAL MEDLEY (Cont.)

1988	Daniela Hunger, East Germany	2:12.59 OR
1992	Lin Li, China	2:11.65 WR
1996	Michelle Smith, Ireland	2:13.93

400-METER INDIVIDUAL MEDLEY

1964	Donna de Varona, United States	5:18.7 OR
1968	Claudia Kolb, United States	5:08.5 OR
1972	Gail Neall, Australia	5:02.97 WR
1976	Ulrike Tauber, East Germany	4:42.77 WR
1980	Petra Schneider, East Germany	4:36.29 WR
1984	Tracy Caulkins, United States	4:39.24
1988	Janet Evans, United States	4:37.76
1992	Krisztina Egerszegi, Hungary	4:36.54
1996	Michelle Smith, Ireland	4:39.18

4 X 100-METER MEDLEY RELAY

1960	United States	4:41.1 WR
1964	United States	4:33.9 WR
1968	United States	4:28.3 OR
1972	United States	4:20.75 WR
1976	East Germany	4:07.95 WR
1980	East Germany	4:06.67 OR
1984	United States	4:08.34
1988	East Germany	4:03.74 OR
1992	United States	4:02.54 WR
1996	United States	4:02.88

4 X 100-METER FREESTYLE RELAY

1912	Great Britain	5:52.8 WR
1920	United States	5:11.6 WR
1924	United States	4:58.8 WR
1928	United States	4:47.6 WR
1932	United States	4:38.0 WR
1936	Netherlands	4:36.0 OR
1948	United States	4:29.2 OR
1952	Hungary	4:24.4 WR
1956	Australia	4:17.1 WR
1960	United States	4:08.9 WR
1964	United States	4:03.8 WR
1968	United States	4:02.5 OR
1972	United States	3:55.19 WR
1976	United States	3:44.82 WR
1980	East Germany	3:42.71 WR
1984	United States	3:43.43
1988	East Germany	3:40.63 OR
1992	United States	3:39.46 WR
1996	United States	3:39.29 OR

4 X 200-METER FREESTYLE RELAY

1996	United States	7:59.87

Note: OR=Olympic Record. WR=World Record. EOR=Equals Olympic Record. EWR=Equals World Record. WB=World Best.

DIVING
Men

SPRINGBOARD

		Pts
1908	Albert Zürner, Germany	85.5
1912	Paul Günther, Germany	79.23
1920	Louis Kuehn, United States	675.40
1924	Albert White, United States	97.46
1928	Pete DesJardins, United States	185.04
1932	Michael Galitzen, United States	161.38
1936	Richard Degener, United States	163.57
1948	Bruce Harlan, United States	163.64
1952	David Browning, United States	205.29
1956	Robert Clotworthy, United States	159.56
1960	Gary Tobian, United States	170.00
1964	Kenneth Sitzberger, United States	159.90
1968	Bernie Wrightson, United States	170.15
1972	Vladimir Vasin, USSR	594.09
1976	Phil Boggs, United States	619.05
1980	Aleksandr Portnov, USSR	905.02
1984	Greg Louganis, United States	754.41
1988	Greg Louganis, United States	730.80
1992	Mark Lenzi, United States	676.53
1996	Xiong Ni, China	701.46

PLATFORM

		Pts
1904	George Sheldon, United States	12.66
1906	Gottlob Walz, Germany	156.0
1908	Hjalmar Johansson, Sweden	83.75
1912	Erik Adlerz, Sweden	73.94
1920	Clarence Pinkston, United States	100.67
1924	Albert White, United States	97.46
1928	Pete DesJardins, United States	98.74
1932	Harold Smith, United States	124.80
1936	Marshall Wayne, United States	113.58
1948	Sammy Lee, United States	130.05
1952	Sammy Lee, United States	156.28
1956	Joaquin Capilla, Mexico	152.44
1960	Robert Webster, United States	165.56
1964	Robert Webster, United States	148.58
1968	Klaus Dibiasi, Italy	164.18
1972	Klaus Dibiasi, Italy	504.12
1976	Klaus Dibiasi, Italy	600.51
1980	Falk Hoffmann, East Germany	835.65
1984	Greg Louganis, United States	710.91
1988	Greg Louganis, United States	638.61
1992	Sun Shuwei, China	677.31
1996	Dmitri Sautin, Russia	692.34

Women
SPRINGBOARD

		Pts
1920	Aileen Riggin, United States	539.90
1924	Elizabeth Becker, United States	474.50
1928	Helen Meany, United States	78.62
1932	Georgia Coleman, United States	87.52
1936	Marjorie Gestring, United States	89.27

		Pts
1948	Victoria Draves, United States	108.74
1952	Patricia McCormick, United States	147.30
1956	Patricia McCormick, United States	142.36
1960	Ingrid Krämer, East Germany	155.81

DIVING *(Cont.)*

Women *(Cont.)*

SPRINGBOARD *(Cont.)*

		Pts
1964	Ingrid Engel Krämer, East Germany	145.00
1968	Sue Gossick, United States	150.77
1972	Micki King, United States	450.03
1976	Jennifer Chandler, United States	506.19
1980	Irina Kalinina, USSR	725.91
1984	Sylvie Bernier, Canada	530.70
1988	Gao Min, China	580.23
1992	Gao Min, China	572.40
1996	Fu Mingxia, China	547.68

PLATFORM

		Pts
1912	Greta Johansson, Sweden	39.90
1920	Stefani Fryland-Clausen, Denmark	34.60
1924	Caroline Smith, United States	33.20

PLATFORM *(Cont.)*

		Pts
1928	Elizabeth B. Pinkston, United States	31.60
1932	Dorothy Poynton, United States	40.26
1936	Dorothy Poynton Hill, United States	33.93
1948	Victoria Draves, United States	68.87
1952	Patricia McCormick, United States	79.37
1956	Patricia McCormick, United States	84.85
1960	Ingrid Krämer, East Germany	91.28
1964	Lesley Bush, United States	99.80
1968	Milena Duchkova, Czechoslovakia	109.59
1972	Ulrika Knape, Sweden	390.00
1976	Elena Vaytsekhovskaya, USSR	406.59
1980	Martina Jäschke, East Germany	596.25
1984	Zhou Jihong, China	435.51
1988	Xu Yanmei, China	445.20
1992	Fu Mingxia, China	461.43
1996	Fu Mingxia, China	521.58

GYMNASTICS

Men

ALL-AROUND

		Pts
1900	Gustave Sandras, France	302
1904	Julius Lenhart, Austria	69.80
1906	Pierre Paysse, France	97
1908	Alberto Braglia, Italy	317.0
1912	Alberto Braglia, Italy	135.0
1920	Giorgio Zampori, Italy	88.35
1924	Leon Stukelj, Yugoslavia	110.340
1928	Georges Miez, Switzerland	247.500
1932	Romeo Neri, Italy	140.625
1936	Alfred Schwarzmann, Germany	113.100
1948	Veikko Huhtanen, Finland	229.70
1952	Viktor Chukarin, USSR	115.70
1956	Viktor Chukarin, USSR	114.25
1960	Boris Shakhlin, USSR	115.95
1964	Yukio Endo, Japan	115.95
1968	Sawao Kato, Japan	115.90
1972	Sawao Kato, Japan	114.65
1976	Nikolai Andrianov, USSR	116.65
1980	Aleksandr Dityatin, USSR	118.65
1984	Koji Gushiken, Japan	118.70
1988	Vladimir Artemov, USSR	119.125
1992	Vitaly Scherbo, Unified Team	59.025
1996	Li Xiaoshuang, China	58.423

HORIZONTAL BAR

		Pts
1896	Hermann Weingärtner, Germany	—
1900	Not held	
1904	Anton Heida, United States	40
1908	Not held 1908–1920	
1924	Leon Stukelj, Yugoslavia	19.73
1928	Georges Miez, Switzerland	19.17
1932	Dallas Bixler, United States	18.33
1936	Aleksanteri Saarvala, Finland	19.367
1948	Josef Stalder, Switzerland	19.85
1952	Jack Günthard, Switzerland	19.55
1956	Takashi Ono, Japan	19.60
1960	Takashi Ono, Japan	19.60
1964	Boris Shakhlin, USSR	19.625
1968	Akinori Nakayama, Japan	19.55
1972	Mitsuo Tsukahara, Japan	19.725

HORIZONTAL BAR *(Cont.)*

		Pts
1976	Mitsuo Tsukahara, Japan	19.675
1980	Stoyan Deltchev, Bulgaria	19.825
1984	Shinji Morisue, Japan	20.00
1988	Vladimir Artemov, USSR	19.90
1992	Trent Dimas, United States	9.875
1996	Andreas Wecker, Germany	9.850

PARALLEL BARS

		Pts
1896	Alfred Flatow, Germany	—
1900	Not held	
1904	George Eyser, United States	44
1908	Not held 1908–1920	
1924	August Güttinger, Switzerland	21.63
1928	Ladislav Vacha, Czechoslovakia	18.83
1932	Romeo Neri, Italy	18.97
1936	Konrad Frey, Germany	19.067
1948	Michael Reusch, Switzerland	19.75
1952	Hans Eugster, Switzerland	19.65
1956	Viktor Chukarin, USSR	19.20
1960	Boris Shakhlin, USSR	19.40
1964	Yukio Endo, Japan	19.675
1968	Akinori Nakayama, Japan	19.475
1972	Sawao Kato, Japan	19.475
1976	Sawao Kato, Japan	19.675
1980	Aleksandr Tkachyov, USSR	19.775
1984	Bart Conner, United States	19.95
1988	Vladimir Artemov, USSR	19.925
1992	Vitaly Scherbo, Unified Team	9.900
1996	Rustan Sharipov, Ukraine	9.837

VAULT

		Pts
1896	Karl Schumann, Germany	—
1900	Not held	
1904	George Eyser, United States	36
1908	Not held 1908–1920	
1924	Frank Kriz, United States	9.98
1928	Eugen Mack, Switzerland	9.58
1932	Savino Guglielmetti, Italy	18.03
1936	Alfred Schwarzmann, Germany	19.20
1948	Paavo Aaltonen, Finland	19.55

GYMNASTICS (Cont.)

Men (Cont.)

VAULT (Cont.)

		Pts
1952	Viktor Chukarin, USSR	19.20
1956	Helmut Bantz, Germany	18.85
1960	Takashi Ono, Japan	19.35
1964	Haruhiro Yamashita, Japan	19.60
1968	Mikhail Voronin, USSR	19.00
1972	Klaus Köste, East Germany	18.85
1976	Nikolai Andrianov, USSR	19.45
1980	Nikolai Andrianov, USSR	19.825
1984	Lou Yun, China	19.95
1988	Lou Yun, China	19.875
1992	Vitaly Scherbo, Unified Team	9.856
1996	Alexei Nemov, Russia	9.787

POMMEL HORSE

		Pts
1896	Louis Zutter, Switzerland	—
1900	Not held	
1904	Anton Heida, United States	42
1908	Not held 1908–1920	
1924	Josef Wilhelm, Switzerland	21.23
1928	Hermann Hänggi, Switzerland	19.75
1932	Istvan Pelle, Hungary	19.07
1936	Konrad Frey, Germany	19.333
1948	Paavo Aaltonen, Finland	19.35
1952	Viktor Chukarin, USSR	19.50
1956	Boris Shakhlin, USSR	19.25
1960	Eugen Ekman, Finland	19.375
1964	Miroslav Cerar, Yugoslavia	19.525
1968	Miroslav Cerar, Yugoslavia	19.325
1972	Viktor Klimenko, USSR	19.125
1976	Zoltan Magyar, Hungary	19.70
1980	Zoltan Magyar, Hungary	19.925
1984	Li Ning, China	19.95
1988	Dmitri Bilozerchev, USSR	19.95
1992	Vitaly Scherbo, Unified Team	9.925
1996	Donghua Li, Switzerland	9.875

RINGS

		Pts
1896	Ioannis Mitropoulos, Greece	—
1900	Not held	
1904	Hermann Glass, United States	45
1908	Not held 1908–1920	
1924	Francesco Martino, Italy	21.553
1928	Leon Stukelj, Yugoslavia	19.25
1932	George Gulack, United States	18.97
1936	Alois Hudec, Czechoslovakia	19.433
1948	Karl Frei, Switzerland	19.80
1952	Grant Shaginyan, USSR	19.75
1956	Albert Azaryan, USSR	19.35
1960	Albert Azaryan, USSR	19.725
1964	Takuji Haytta, Japan	19.475

RINGS (Cont.)

		Pts
1968	Akinori Nakayama, Japan	19.45
1972	Akinori Nakayama, Japan	19.35
1976	Nikolai Andrianov, USSR	19.65
1980	Aleksandr Dityatin, USSR	19.875
1984	Koji Gushiken, Japan	19.85
1988	Holger Behrendt, East Germany	19.925
1992	Vitaly Scherbo, Unified Team	9.937
1996	Yuri Chechi, Italy	9.887

FLOOR EXERCISE

		Pts
1932	Istvan Pelle, Hungary	9.60
1936	Georges Miez, Switzerland	18.666
1948	Ferenc Pataki, Hungary	19.35
1952	K. William Thoresson, Sweden	19.25
1956	Valentin Muratov, USSR	19.20
1960	Nobuyuki Aihara, Japan	19.45
1964	Franco Menichelli, Italy	19.45
1968	Sawao Kato, Japan	19.475
1972	Nikolai Andrianov, USSR	19.175
1976	Nikolai Andrianov, USSR	19.45
1980	Roland Brückner, East Germany	19.75
1984	Li Ning, China	19.925
1988	Sergei Kharkov, USSR	19.925
1992	Li Xiaoshuang, China	9.925
1996	Ioannis Melissanidis, Greece	9.850

TEAM COMBINED EXERCISES

		Pts
1904	Turngemeinde Philadelphia	374.43
1906	Norway	19.00
1908	Sweden	438
1912	Italy	265.75
1920	Italy	359.855
1924	Italy	839.058
1928	Switzerland	1718.625
1932	Italy	541.850
1936	Germany	657.430
1948	Finland	1358.30
1952	USSR	574.40
1956	USSR	568.25
1960	Japan	575.20
1964	Japan	577.95
1968	Japan	575.90
1972	Japan	571.25
1976	Japan	576.85
1980	USSR	598.60
1984	United States	591.40
1988	USSR	593.35
1992	Unified Team	585.45
1996	Russia	576.778

Women

ALL-AROUND

		Pts
1952	Maria Gorokhovskaya, USSR	76.78
1956	Larissa Latynina, USSR	74.933
1960	Larissa Latynina, USSR	77.031
1964	Vera Caslavska, Czechoslovakia	77.564
1968	Vera Caslavska, Czechoslovakia	78.25
1972	Lyudmila Tousischeva, USSR	77.025

		Pts
1976	Nadia Comaneci, Romania	79.275
1980	Yelena Davydova, USSR	79.15
1984	Mary Lou Retton, United States	79.175
1988	Yelena Shushunova, USSR	79.662
1992	Tatiana Gutsu, Unified Team	39.737
1996	Lilia Podkopayeva, Ukraine	39.255

GYMNASTICS *(Cont.)*

Women

VAULT

		Pts
1952	Yekaterina Kalinchuk, USSR	19.20
1956	Larissa Latynina, USSR	18.833
1960	Margarita Nikolayeva, USSR	19.316
1964	Vera Caslavska, Czechoslovakia	19.483
1968	Vera Caslavska, Czechoslovakia	19.775
1972	Karin Janz, East Germany	19.525
1976	Nelli Kim, USSR	19.80
1980	Natalya Shaposhnikova, USSR	19.725
1984	Ecaterina Szabo, Romania	19.875
1988	Svetlana Boginskaya, USSR	19.905
1992	Henrietta Onodi, Hungary	9.925
	Lavinia Milosovici, Romania	9.925
1996	Simona Amanar, Romania	9.825

UNEVEN BARS

		Pts
1952	Margit Korondi, Hungary	19.40
1956	Agnes Keleti, Hungary	18.966
1960	Polina Astakhova, USSR	19.616
1964	Polina Astakhova, USSR	19.332
1968	Vera Caslavska, Czechoslovakia	19.65
1972	Karin Janz, East Germany	19.675
1976	Nadia Comaneci, Romania	20.00
1980	Maxi Gnauck, East Germany	19.875
1984	Ma Yanhong, China	19.95
1988	Daniela Silivas, Romania	20.00
1992	Lu Li, China	10.00
1996	Svetlana Chorkina, Russia	9.850

BALANCE BEAM

		Pts
1952	Nina Bocharova, USSR	19.22
1956	Agnes Keleti, Hungary	18.80
1960	Eva Bosakova, Czechoslovakia	19.283
1964	Vera Caslavska, Czechoslovakia	19.449
1968	Natalya Kuchinskaya, USSR	19.65
1972	Olga Korbut, USSR	19.40
1976	Nadia Comaneci, Romania	19.95
1980	Nadia Comaneci, Romania	19.80
1984	Simona Pauca, Romania	19.80
1988	Daniela Silivas, Romania	19.924
1992	Tatiana Lisenko, Unified Team	9.975
1996	Shannon Miller, United States	9.862

FLOOR EXERCISE

		Pts
1952	Agnes Keleti, Hungary	19.36
1956	Agnes Keleti, Hungary	18.733
1960	Larissa Latynina, USSR	19.583
1964	Larissa Latynina, USSR	19.599
1968	Vera Caslavska, Czechoslovakia	19.675
1972	Olga Korbut, USSR	19.575
1976	Nelli Kim, USSR	19.85
1980	Nadia Comaneci, Romania	19.875
1984	Ecaterina Szabo, Romania	19.975
1988	Daniela Silivas, Romania	19.937
1992	Lavinia Milosovici, Romania	10.00
1996	Lilia Podkopayeva, Ukraine	9.887

TEAM COMBINED EXERCISES

		Pts
1928	The Netherlands	316.75
1932	Not held	
1936	Germany	506.50
1948	Czechoslovakia	445.45
1952	USSR	527.03
1956	USSR	444.800
1960	USSR	382.320
1964	USSR	280.890
1968	USSR	382.85
1972	USSR	380.50
1976	USSR	466.00
1980	USSR	394.90
1984	Romania	392.02
1988	USSR	395.475
1992	Unified Team	395.666
1996	United States	389.225

RHYTHMIC ALL-AROUND

		Pts
1984	Lori Fung, Canada	57.95
1988	Marina Lobach, USSR	60.00
1992	Aleksandra Timoshenko, UTeam	59.037
1996	Ekaterina Serebrianskaya, Ukr	39.683

RHYTHMIC TEAM COMBINED EXERCISES

		Pts
1996	Spain	38.933

SOCCER

Men

1900	Great Britain	1928	Uruguay	1964	Hungary	1988	Soviet Union
1904	Canada	1936	Italy	1968	Hungary	1992	Spain
1908	Great Britain	1948	Sweden	1972	Poland	1996	Nigeria
1912	Great Britain	1952	Hungary	1976	East Germany		
1920	Belgium	1956	Soviet Union	1980	Czechoslovakia		
1924	Uruguay	1960	Yugoslavia	1984	France		

Women

1996	United States

BIATHLON

Men

10 KILOMETERS

1980	....Frank Ullrich, East Germany	32:10.69
1984	....Eirik Kvalfoss, Norway	30:53.8
1988	....Frank-Peter Rötsch, W Germany	25:08.1
1992	....Mark Kirchner, Germany	26:02.3
1994	....Sergei Tchepikov, Russia	28:07.0
1998	....Ole Einar Bjorndalen, Norway	27:16.2

20 KILOMETERS

1960	....Klas Lestander, Sweden	1:33:21.6
1964	....Vladimir Melyanin, Soviet Union	1:20:26.8
1968	....Magnar Solberg, Norway	1:13:45.9
1972	....Magnar Solberg, Norway	1:15:55.5
1976	....Nikolay Kruglov, Soviet Union	1:14:12.26
1980	....Anatoliy Alyabiev, Soviet Union	1:08:16.31
1984	....Peter Angerer, W Germany	1:11:52.7

20 KILOMETERS (Cont.)

1988	....Frank-Peter Rötsch, W Germany	56:33.3
1992	....Evgueni Redkine, Unified Team	57:34.4
1994	....Sergei Tarasov, Russia	57:25.3
1998	....Halvard Hanevold, Norway	56:16.4

4 X 7.5-KILOMETER RELAY

1968	..............Soviet Union	2:13:02.4
1972	..............Soviet Union	1:51:44.92
1976	..............Soviet Union	1:57:55.64
1980	..............Soviet Union	1:34:03.27
1984	..............Soviet Union	1:38:51.7
1988	..............Soviet Union	1:22:30.0
1992	..............Germany	1:24:43.5
1994	..............Germany	1:30:22.1
1998	..............Germany	1:19:43.3

Women

7.5 KILOMETERS

1992	....Antissa Restzova, Unified Team	24:29.2
1994	....Myriam Bedard, Canada	26:08.8
1998	....Galina Koukleva, Russia	23:08.0

15 KILOMETERS

1992	....Antje Misersky, Germany	51:47.2
1994	....Myriam Bedard, Canada	52:06.6
1998	....Ekaterina Dofovska, Bulgaria	54:52.0

3 X 7.5-KILOMETER RELAY

1992	....France	1:15:55.6
1994	....Russia	1:47:19.5
1998	....Germany	1:40:13.6

BOBSLED

4-MAN BOB

1924	....Switzerland (Eduard Scherrer)	5:45.54
1928	....United States	3:20.50
	(William Fiske) (5-man)	
1932	....United States (William Fiske)	7:53.68
1936	....Switzerland (Pierre Musy)	5:19.85
1948	....United States (Francis Tyler)	5:20.10
1952	....Germany (Andreas Ostler)	5:07.84
1956	....Switzerland (Franz Kapus)	5:10.44
1960	...Not held	
1964	....Canada (Victor Emery)	4:14.46
1968	....Italy (Eugenio Monti) (2 runs)	2:17.39
1972	....Switzerland (Jean Wicki)	4:43.07
1976	....East Germany (Meinhard Nehmer)	3:40.43
1980	....East Germany (Meinhard Nehmer)	3:59.92
1984	....East Germany (Wolfgang Hoppe)	3:20.22
1988	....Switzerland (Ekkehard Fasser)	3:47.51
1992	....Austria (Ingo Appelt)	3:53.90
1994	....Germany (Harold Czudaj)	3:27.78
1998	....Germany (Christoph Langen)	2:39.41

Note: Driver in parentheses.

2-MAN BOB

1932	....United States (Hubert Stevens)	8:14.74
1936	....United States (Ivan Brown)	5:29.29
1948	....Switzerland (Felix Endrich)	5:29.20
1952	....Germany (Andreas Ostler)	5:24.54
1956	....Italy (Lamberto Dalla Costa)	5:30.14
1960	...Not held	
1964	....Great Britain (Anthony Nash)	4:21.90
1968	....Italy (Eugenio Monti)	4:41.54
1972	....West Germany	4:57.07
	(Wolfgang Zimmerer)	
1976	....East Germany (Meinhard Nehmer)	3:44.42
1980	....Switzerland (Erich Schärer)	4:09.36
1984	....East Germany (Wolfgang Hoppe)	3:25.56
1988	....USSR (Janis Kipours)	3:53.48
1992	....Switzerland (Gustav Weder)	4:03.26
1994	....Switzerland (Gustav Weder)	3:30.81
1998	....Canada (Pierre Lueders)	3:37.24
	Italy (Guenther Huber)	3:37.24

Note: Driver in parentheses.

CURLING

Men

1998	.....Switzerland, Canada, Norway

Note: Gold, silver, and bronze medals.

Women

1998	.....Canada, Denmark, Sweden

Note: Gold, silver, and bronze medals.

ICE HOCKEY
Men

1920* ....Canada, United States, Czechoslovakia
1924 .....Canada, United States, Great Britain
1928 .....Canada, Sweden, Switzerland
1932 .....Canada, United States, Germany
1936 .....Great Britain, Canada, United States
1948 .....Canada, Czechoslovakia, Switzerland
1952 .....Canada, United States, Sweden
1956 .....USSR, United States, Canada
1960 .....United States, Canada, USSR
1964 .....USSR, Sweden, Czechoslovakia
1968 .....USSR, Czechoslovakia, Canada

1972 ....USSR, United States, Czechoslovakia
1976 .....USSR, Czechoslovakia, West Germany
1980 .....United States, USSR, Sweden
1984 .....USSR, Czechoslovakia, Sweden
1988 .....USSR, Finland, Sweden
1992 .....Unified Team, Canada, Czechoslovakia
1994 .....Sweden, Canada, Finland
1998 .....Czech Republic, Russia, Finland
*Competition held at summer games in Antwerp.
Note: Gold, silver, and bronze medals.

Women

1998 .....United States, Canada, Finland

Note: Gold, silver, and bronze medals.

LUGE
Men

SINGLES			DOUBLES		
1964	Thomas Köhler, East Germany	3:26.77	1964	Austria	1:41.62
1968	Manfred Schmid, Austria	2:52.48	1968	East Germany	1:35.85
1972	Wolfgang Scheidel, W Germany	3:27.58	1972	East Germany	1:28.35
1976	Detlef Guenther, West Germany	3:27.688	1976	East Germany	1:25.604
1980	Bernhard Glass, West Germany	2:54.796	1980	East Germany	1:19.331
1984	Paul Hildgartner, Italy	3:04.258	1984	West Germany	1:23.620
1988	Jens Müller, West Germany	3:05.548	1988	East Germany	1:31.940
1992	Georg Hackl, Germany	3:02.363	1992	Germany	1:32.053
1994	Georg Hackl, Germany	3:21.571	1994	Italy	1:36.720
1998	Georg Hackl, Germany	3:18.44	1998	Germany	1:41.105

Women

SINGLES			SINGLES (Cont.)		
1964	Ortrun Enderlein, Germany	3:24.67	1984	Steffi Martin, East Germany	2:46.570
1968	Erica Lechner, Italy	2:28.66	1988	Steffi Walter (Martin) E Germany	3:03.973
1972	Anna-Maria Müller, East Germany	2:59.18	1992	Doris Neuner, Austria	3:06.696
1976	Margit Schumann, East Germany	2:50.621	1994	Gerda Weissensteiner, Italy	3:15.517
1980	Vera Zozulya, USSR	2:36.537	1998	Silke Kraushaar, Germany	3:23.779

FIGURE SKATING

Men	Women
1908* ....Ulrich Salchow, Sweden	1908* ....Madge Syers, Great Britain
1920† ....Gillis Grafström, Sweden	1920† ....Magda Julin, Sweden
1924 ....Gillis Grafström, Sweden	1924 ....Herma Szabo-Planck, Austria
1928 ....Gillis Grafström, Sweden	1928 ....Sonja Henie, Norway
1932 ....Karl Schäfer, Austria	1932 ....Sonja Henie, Norway
1936 ....Karl Schäfer, Austria	1936 ....Sonja Henie, Norway
1948 ....Dick Button, United States	1948 ....Barbara Ann Scott, Canada
1952 ....Dick Button, United States	1952 ....Jeanette Altwegg, Great Britain
1956 ....Hayes Alan Jenkins, United States	1956 ....Tenley Albright, United States
1960 ....David Jenkins, United States	1960 ....Carol Heiss, United States
1964 ....Manfred Schnelldorfer, West Germany	1964 ....Sjoukje Dijkstra, Netherlands
1968 ....Wolfgang Schwarz, Austria	1968 ....Peggy Fleming, United States
1972 ....Ondrej Nepela, Czechoslovakia	1972 ....Beatrix Schuba, Austria
1976 ....John Curry, Great Britain	1976 ....Dorothy Hamill, United States
1980 ....Robin Cousins, Great Britain	1980 ....Anett Pötzsch, East Germany
1984 ....Scott Hamilton, United States	1984 ....Katarina Witt, East Germany
1988 ....Brian Boitano, United States	1988 ....Katarina Witt, East Germany
1992 ....Victor Petrenko, Unified Team	1992 ....Kristi Yamaguchi, United States
1994 ....Alexei Urmanov, Russia	1994 ....Oksana Baiul, Ukraine
1998 ....Ilia Kulik, Russia	1998 ....Tara Lipinski, United States

*Competition held at summer games in London.
†Competition held at summer games in Antwerp.

FIGURE SKATING (Cont.)
Mixed
PAIRS

1908* ..Anna Hübler & Heinrich Burger, Germany
1920† ..Ludovika & Walter Jakobsson, Finland
1924....Helene Engelmann & Alfred Berger, Austria
1928....Andree Joly & Pierre Brunet, France
1932....Andree Brunet (Joly) & Pierre Brunet, France
1936....Maxi Herber & Ernst Baier, Germany
1948....Micheline Lannoy & Pierre Baugniet, Belgium
1952....Ria Falk and Paul Falk, West Germany
1956....Elisabeth Schwartz & Kurt Oppelt, Austria
1960....Barbara Wagner & Robert Paul, Canada
1964....Lyudmila Beloussova & Oleg Protopopov, USSR
1968....Lyudmila Beloussova & Oleg Protopopov, USSR
1972....Irina Rodnina & Alexei Ulanov, USSR
1976....Irina Rodnina & Aleksandr Zaitsev, USSR
1980....Irina Rodnina & Aleksandr Zaitsev, USSR
1984....Elena Valova & Oleg Vasiliev, USSR
1988....Ekaterina Gordeeva & Sergei Grinkov, USSR
1992....Natalia Michkouteniok & Artour Dmitriev, Unified Team

PAIRS (Cont.)

1994....Ekaterina Gordeeva & Sergei Grinkov, Russia
1998....Oksana Kazakova & Artur Dmitriev, Russia

DANCE

1976....Lyudmila Pakhomova & Aleksandr Gorshkov, USSR
1980....Natalia Linichuk & Gennadi Karponosov, USSR
1984....Jayne Torvill & Christopher Dean, Great Britain
1988....Natalia Bestemianova & Andrei Bukin, USSR
1992....Marina Klimova & Sergei Ponomarenko, Unified Team
1994....Oksana Grishuk and Evgeny Platov, Russia
1998....Pasha Grishuk and Evgeny Platov, Russia

*Competition held at summer games in London.
†Competition held at summer games in Antwerp.

SPEED SKATING
Men

500 METERS

1924....Charles Jewtraw, United States	44.0	
1928....Clas Thunberg, Finland	43.4 OR	
Bernt Evensen, Norway	43.4 OR	
1932....John Shea, United States	43.4 EOR	
1936....Ivar Ballangrud, Norway	43.4 EOR	
1948....Finn Helgesen, Norway	43.1 OR	
1952....Kenneth Henry, United States	43.2	
1956....Yevgeny Grishin, USSR	40.2 EWR	
1960....Yevgeny Grishin, USSR	40.2 EWR	
1964....Terry McDermott, United States	40.1 OR	
1968....Erhard Keller, West Germany	40.3	
1972....Erhard Keller, West Germany	39.44 OR	
1976....Yevgeny Kulikov, USSR	39.17 OR	
1980....Eric Heiden, United States	38.03 OR	
1984....Sergei Fokichev, USSR	38.19	
1988....Uwe-Jens Mey, East Germany	36.45 WR	
1992....Uwe-Jens Mey, East Germany	37.14	
1994....Aleksandr Golubev, Russia	36.33	
1998....Hiroyasu Shimizu, Japan	1:11.35	
second run	35.59 OR	

1000 METERS

1976....Peter Mueller, United States 1:19.32
1980....Eric Heiden, United States 1:15.18 OR
1984....Gaetan Boucher, Canada 1:15.80
1988....Nikolai Gulyaev, USSR 1:13.03 OR
1992....Olaf Zinke, Germany 1:14.85
1994....Dan Jansen, United States 1:12.43 WR
1998....Ids Postma, Netherlands 1:10.64 OR

1500 METERS

1924....Clas Thunberg, Finland 2:20.8
1928....Clas Thunberg, Finland 2:21.1
1932....John Shea, United States 2:57.5
1936....Charles Mathisen, Norway 2:19.2 OR
1948....Sverre Farstad, Norway 2:17.6 OR

1500 METERS (Cont.)

1952....Hjalmar Andersen, Norway	2:20.4	
1956....Yevgeny Grishin, USSR	2:08.6 WR	
Yuri Mikhailov, USSR	2:08.6 WR	
1960....Roald Aas, Norway	2:10.4	
Yevgeny Grishin, USSR	2:10.4	
1964....Ants Anston, USSR	2:10.3	
1968....Cornelis Verkerk, Netherlands	2:03.4 OR	
1972....Ard Schenk, Netherlands	2:02.96 OR	
1976....Jan Egil Storholt, Norway	1:59.38 OR	
1980....Eric Heiden, United States	1:55.44 OR	
1984....Gaetan Boucher, Canada	1:58.36	
1988....Andre Hoffmann, East Germany	1:52.06 WR	
1992....Johann Olav Koss, Norway	1:54.81	
1994....Johann Olav Koss, Norway	1:51.29 WR	
1998....Aadne Sondral, Norway	1:47.87 WR	

5000 METERS

1924....Clas Thunberg, Finland 8:39.0
1928....Ivar Ballangrud, Norway 8:50.5
1932....Irving Jaffee, United States 9:40.8
1936....Ivar Ballangrud, Norway 8:19.6 OR
1948....Reidar Liaklev, Norway 8:29.4
1952....Hjalmar Andersen, Norway 8:10.6 OR
1956....Boris Shilkov, USSR 7:48.7 OR
1960....Viktor Kosichkin, USSR 7:51.3
1964....Knut Johannesen, Norway 7:38.4 OR
1968....Fred Anton Maier, Norway 7:22.4 WR
1972....Ard Schenk, Netherlands 7:23.61
1976....Sten Stensen, Norway 7:24.48
1980....Eric Heiden, United States 7:02.29 OR
1984....Sven Tomas Gustafson, Sweden 7:12.28
1988....Tomas Gustafson, Sweden 6:44.63 WR
1992....Geir Karlstad, Norway 6:59.97
1994....Johann Olav Koss, Norway 6:34.96 WR
1998....Gianni Romme, Netherlands 6:22.20 WR

Note: OR=Olympic Record; WR=World Record; EOR=Equals Olympic Record; EWR=Equals World Record; WB=World Best.

SPEED SKATING *(Cont.)*

Men *(Cont.)*

10,000 METERS			10,000 METERS *(Cont.)*	
1924	Julius Skutnabb, Finland	18:04.8	1968	Johnny Höglin, Sweden	15:23.6 OR
1928	Not held, thawing of ice		1972	Ard Schenk, Netherlands	15:01.35 OR
1932	Irving Jaffee, United States	19:13.6	1976	Piet Kleine, Netherlands	14:50.59 OR
1936	Ivar Ballangrud, Norway	17:24.3 OR	1980	Eric Heiden, United States	14:28.13 WR
1948	Ake Seyffarth, Sweden	17:26.3	1984	Igor Malkov, USSR	14:39.90
1952	Hjalmar Andersen, Norway	16:45.8 OR	1988	Tomas Gustafson, Sweden	13:48.20 WR
1956	Sigvard Ericsson, Sweden	16:35.9 OR	1992	Bart Veldkamp, Netherlands	14:12.12
1960	Knut Johannesen, Norway	15:46.6 WR	1994	Johann Olav Koss, Norway	13:30.55 WR
1964	Jonny Nilsson, Sweden	15:50.1	1998	Gianni Romme, Netherlands	13:15.33 WR

Women

500 METERS			1500 METERS	
1960	Helga Haase, East Germany	45.9	1960	Lydia Skoblikova, USSR	2:25.2 WR
1964	Lydia Skoblikova, USSR	45.0 OR	1964	Lydia Skoblikova, USSR	2:22.6 OR
1968	Lyudmila Titova, USSR	46.1	1968	Kaija Mustonen, Finland	2:22.4 OR
1972	Anne Henning, United States	43.33 OR	1972	Dianne Holum, United States	2:20.85 OR
1976	Sheila Young, United States	42.76 OR	1976	Galina Stepanskaya, USSR	2:16.58 OR
1980	Karin Enke, East Germany	41.78 OR	1980	Anne Borckink, Netherlands	2:10.95 OR
1984	Christa Rothenburger, East Germany	41.02 OR	1984	Karin Enke, East Germany	2:03.42 WR
			1988	Yvonne van Gennip, Netherlands	2:00.68 OR
1988	Bonnie Blair, United States	39.10 WR	1992	Jacqueline Boerner, Germany	2:05.87
1992	Bonnie Blair, United States	40.33	1994	Emese Hunyady, Austria	2:02.19
1994	Bonnie Blair, United States	39.25	1998	Marianne Timmer, Netherlands	1:57.58 WR
1998	Catriona LeMay Doan, Canada	1:16.60			
	second run	38.21 OR	3000 METERS	
			1960	Lydia Skoblikova, USSR	5:14.3
1000 METERS			1964	Lydia Skoblikova, USSR	5:14.9
1960	Klara Guseva, USSR	1:34.1	1968	Johanna Schut, Netherlands	4:56.2 OR
1964	Lydia Skoblikova, USSR	1:33.2 OR	1972	Christina Baas-Kaiser, Netherlands	4:52.14 OR
1968	Carolina Geijssen, Netherlands	1:32.6 OR	1976	Tatiana Averina, USSR	4:45.19 OR
1972	Monika Pflug, West Germany	1:31.40 OR	1980	Bjorg Eva Jensen, Norway	4:32.13 OR
1976	Tatiana Averina, USSR	1:28.43 OR	1984	Andrea Schöne, East Germany	4:24.79 OR
1980	Natalya Petruseva, USSR	1:24.10 OR	1988	Yvonne van Gennip, Netherlands	4:11.94 WR
1984	Karin Enke, East Germany	1:21.61 OR	1992	Gunda Niemann, Germany	4:19.90
1988	Christa Rothenburger, East Germany	1:17.65 WR	1994	Svetlana Bazhanova, Russia	4:17.43
			1998	Gunda Niemann-Stirnemann, Germany	4:07.29 OR
1992	Bonnie Blair, United States	1:21.90			
1994	Bonnie Blair, United States	1:18.74	5000 METERS	
1998	Marianne Timmer, Netherlands	1:16.51 OR	1988	Yvonne van Gennip, Netherlands	7:14.13 WR
			1992	Gunda Niemann, Germany	7:31.57
			1994	Claudia Pechstein, Germany	7:14.37
			1998	Claudia Pechstein, Germany	6:59.61 WR

SHORT TRACK SPEED SKATING

Men

500 METERS		
1994	Chae Ji-Hoon, South Korea	43.54
1998	Takafumi Nishitani, Japan	42.862

1000 METERS		
1992	Kim Ki-Hoon, South Korea	1:30.76
1994	Kim Ki-Hoon, South Korea	1:34.57
1998	Kim Dong Sung, South Korea	1:32.375

5000-METER RELAY	
1992	Korea	7:14.02
1994	Italy	7:11.74
1998	Canada	7:06.075

Women

500 METERS		
1992	Cathy Turner, United States	47.04
1994	Cathy Turner, United States	45.98
1998	Annie Perreault, Canada	46.568

1000 METERS		
1994	Chun Lee Kyung, South Korea	1:36.87
1998	Chun Lee Kyung, South Korea	1:42.776

3000-METER RELAY	
1992	Canada	4:36.62
1994	South Korea	4:26.64
1998	South Korea	4:16.260

ALPINE SKIING

Men

DOWNHILL

1948....Henri Oreiller, France — 2:55.0
1952....Zeno Colo, Italy — 2:30.8
1956....Anton Sailer, Austria — 2:52.2
1960....Jean Vuarnet, France — 2:06.0
1964....Egon Zimmermann, Austria — 2:18.16
1968....Jean-Claude Killy, France — 1:59.85
1972....Bernhard Russi, Switzerland — 1:51.43
1976....Franz Klammer, Austria — 1:45.73
1980....Leonhard Stock, Austria — 1:45.50
1984....Bill Johnson, United States — 1:45.59
1988....Pirmin Zurbriggen, Switzerland — 1:59.63
1992....Patrick Ortlieb, Austria — 1:50.37
1994....Tommy Moe, United States — 1:45.75
1998....Jean-Luc Crétier, France — 1:50.11

SLALOM

1948....Edi Reinalter, Switzerland — 2:10.3
1952....Othmar Schneider, Austria — 2:00.0
1956....Anton Sailer, Austria — 3:14.7
1960....Ernst Hinterseer, Austria — 2:08.9
1964....Josef Stiegler, Austria — 2:11.13
1968....Jean-Claude Killy, France — 1:39.73
1972....Francisco Fernandez — 1:49.27
........Ochoa, Spain
1976....Piero Gros, Italy — 2:03.29
1980....Ingemar Stenmark, Sweden — 1:44.26
1984....Phil Mahre, United States — 1:39.41
1988....Alberto Tomba, Italy — 1:39.47
1992....Finn Christian Jagge, Norway — 1:44.39
1994....Thomas Stangassinger, Austria — 2:02.02
1998....Hans-Petter Buraas, Norway — 1:49.31

GIANT SLALOM

1952....Stein Eriksen, Norway — 2:25.0
1956....Anton Sailer, Austria — 3:00.1
1960....Roger Staub, Switzerland — 1:48.3
1964....Francois Bonlieu, France — 1:46.71
1968....Jean-Claude Killy, France — 3:29.28
1972....Gustav Thöni, Italy — 3:09.62
1976....Heini Hemmi, Switzerland — 3:26.97
1980....Ingemar Stenmark, Sweden — 2:40.74
1984....Max Julen, Switzerland — 2:41.18
1988....Alberto Tomba, Italy — 2:06.37
1992....Alberto Tomba, Italy — 2:06.98
1994....Markus Wasmeier, Germany — 2:52.46
1998....Hermann Maier, Austria — 2:38.51

SUPER GIANT SLALOM

1988....Franck Piccard, France — 1:39.66
1992....Kjetil Andre Aamodt, Norway — 1:13.04
1994....Markus Wasmeier, Germany — 1:32.53
1998....Hermann Maier, Austria — 1:34.82

COMBINED*

		Pts
1936	Franz Pfnür, Germany	99.25
1948	Henri Oreiller, France	3.27
1988	Hubert Strolz, Austria	36.55
1992	Josef Polig, Italy	14.58
1994	Lasse Kjus, Norway	3:17.53
1998	Mario Reiter, Austria	3:08.06

Women

DOWNHILL

1948....Hedy Schlunegger, Switzerland — 2:28.3
1952....Trude Jochum-Beiser, Austria — 1:47.1
1956....Madeleine Berthod, Switzerland — 1:40.7
1960....Heidi Biebl, West Germany — 1:37.6
1964....Christl Haas, Austria — 1:55.39
1968....Olga Pall, Austria — 1:40.87
1972....Marie-Theres Nadig, Switzerland — 1:36.68
1976....Rosi Mittermaier, West Germany — 1:46.16
1980....Annemarie Moser-Pröll, Austria — 1:37.52
1984....Michela Figini, Switzerland — 1:13.36
1988....Marina Kiehl, West Germany — 1:25.86
1992....Kerrin Lee-Gartner, Canada — 1:52.55
1994....Katja Seizinger, Germany — 1:35.93
1998....Katja Seizinger, Germany — 1:28.89

SLALOM

1948....Gretchen Fraser, United States — 1:57.2
1952....Andrea Mead Lawrence, — 2:10.6
........United States
1956....Renee Colliard, Switzerland — 1:52.3
1960....Anne Heggtveigt, Canada — 1:49.6
1964....Christine Goitschel, France — 1:29.86
1968....Marielle Goitschel, France — 1:25.86
1972....Barbara Cochran, United States — 1:31.24
1976....Rosi Mittermaier, West Germany — 1:30.54
1980....Hanni Wenzel, Liechtenstein — 1:25.09
1984....Paoletta Magoni, Italy — 1:36.47
1988....Vreni Schneider, Switzerland — 1:36.69
1992....Petra Kronberger, Austria — 1:32.68
1994....Vreni Schneider, Switzerland — 1:56.01
1998....Hilde Gerg, Germany — 1:32.40

GIANT SLALOM

1952....Andrea Mead Lawrence, U.S. — 2:06.8
1956....Ossi Reichert, West Germany — 1:56.5
1960....Yvonne Rüegg, Switzerland — 1:39.9
1964....Marielle Goitschel, France — 1:52.24
1968....Nancy Greene, Canada — 1:51.97
1972....Marie-Theres Nadig, Switzerland — 1:29.90
1976....Kathy Kreiner, Canada — 1:29.13
1980....Hanni Wenzel, — 2:41.66
........Liechtenstein (2 runs)
1984....Debbie Armstrong, United States — 2:20.98
1988....Vreni Schneider, Switzerland — 2:06.49
1992....Pernilla Wiberg, Sweden — 2:12.74
1994....Deborah Compagnoni, Italy — 2:30.97
1998....Deborah Compagnoni, Italy — 2:50.59

SUPER GIANT SLALOM

1988....Sigrid Wolf, Austria — 1:19.03
1992....Deborah Compagnoni, Italy — 1:21.22
1994....Diann Roffe-Steinrotter, U.S. — 1:22.15
1998....Picabo Street, United States — 1:18.02

COMBINED*

		Pts
1988	Anita Wachter, Austria	29.25
1992	Petra Kronberger, Austria	2.55
1994	Pernilla Wiberg, Sweden	3:05.16
1998	Katja Seizinger, Germany	2:40.74

*Beginning in 1994, scoring was based on time.

FREESTYLE SKIING

Men

MOGULS

		Pts
1992	Edgar Grospiron, France	25.81
1994	Jean-Luc Brassard, Canada	27.24
1998	Jonny Moseley, United States	26.93

AERIALS

		Pts
1994	Andreas Schoenbaechler, Switz	234.67
1998	Eric Bergoust, United States	255.64

Women

MOGULS

		Pts
1992	Donna Weinbrecht, United States	23.69
1994	Stine Lise Hattestad, Norway	25.97
1998	Tae Satoya, Japan	25.06

AERIALS

		Pts
1994	Lina Cherjazova, Uzbekistan	166.84
1998	Nikki Stone, United States	193.00

NORDIC SKIING

Men

10 KILOMETERS CLASSICAL STYLE

1992	Vegard Ulvang, Norway	27:36.0
1994	Bjørn Dæhlie, Norway	24:20.1
1998	Bjørn Dæhlie, Norway	27:24.5

15 KILOMETERS CLASSICAL STYLE

1924	Thorlief Haug, Norway	1:14:31.0*
1928	Johan Gröttumsbraaten, Norway	1:37:01.0†
1932	Sven Utterström, Sweden	1:23:07.0‡
1936	Erik-August Larsson, Sweden	1:14:38.0*
1948	Martin Lundström, Sweden	1:13:50.0*
1952	Hallgeir Brenden, Norway	1:01:34.0*
1956	Hallgeir Brenden, Norway	49:39.0
1960	Haakon Brusveen, Norway	51:55.5
1964	Eero Mantyränta, Finland	50:54.1
1968	Harald Grönningen, Norway	47:54.2
1972	Sven-Ake Lundback, Sweden	45:28.24
1976	Nikolay Bajukov, Unified Team	43:58.47
1980	Thomas Wassberg, Sweden	41:57.63
1984	Gunde Swan, Sweden	41:25.6
1988	Michael Deviatyarov, USSR	41:18.9

*Distance was 18 km; †Distance was 19.7 km;
‡Distance was 18.2 km.

15 KILOMETERS PURSUIT FREESTYLE

1992	Bjørn Dæhlie, Norway	1:05:37.9
1994	Bjørn Dæhlie, Norway	1:00:08.8
1998	Thomas Alsgaard, Norway	1:07:01.7

30 KILOMETERS CLASSICAL STYLE

1956	Veikko Hakulinen, Finland	1:44:06.0
1960	Sixten Jernberg, Sweden	1:51:03.9
1964	Eero Mantyränta, Finland	1:30:50.7
1968	Franco Nones, Italy	1:35:39.2
1972	Viaceslav Vedenine, USSR	1:36:31.2
1976	Sergei Savelyev, USSR	1:30:29.38
1980	Nikolai Simyatov, USSR	1:27:02.80
1984	Nikolai Simyatov, USSR	1:28:56.3
1988	Alexey Prokororov, USSR	1:24:26.3
1992	Vegard Ulvang, Norway	1:22:27.8
1994	Thomas Alsgaard, Norway	1:12:26.4
1998	Mika Myllylae, Finland	1:33:55.8

50 KILOMETERS FREESTYLE

1924	Thorleif Haug, Norway	3:44:32.0
1928	Per Erik Hedlund, Sweden	4:52:03.0
1932	Veli Saarinen, Finland	4:28:00.0
1936	Elis Wiklund, Sweden	3:30:11.0
1948	Nils Karlsson, Sweden	3:47:48.0
1952	Veikko Hakulinen, Finland	3:33:33.0
1956	Sixten Jernberg, Sweden	2:50:27.0
1960	Kalevi Hämäläinen, Finland	2:59:06.3
1964	Sixten Jernberg, Sweden	2:43:52.6

50 KILOMETERS FREESTYLE *(Cont.)*

1968	Olle Ellefsaeter, Norway	2:28:45.8
1972	Paal Tyldrum, Norway	2:43:14.75
1976	Ivar Formo, Norway	2:37:30.50
1980	Nikolai Simyatov, USSR	2:27:24.60
1984	Thomas Wassberg, Sweden	2:15:55.8
1988	Gunde Svan, Sweden	2:04:30.9
1992	Bjørn Dæhlie, Norway	2:03:41.5
1994	Vladimir Smirnov, Kazakhstan	2:07:20.3
1998	Bjørn Dæhlie, Norway	2:05:08.2

4 X 10 KILOMETER RELAY MIXED STYLE

1936	Finland	2:41:33.0
1948	Sweden	2:32:80.0
1952	Finland	2:20:16.0
1956	USSR	2:15:30.0
1960	Finland	2:18:45.6
1964	Sweden	2:18:34.6
1968	Norway	2:08:33.5
1972	USSR	2:04:47.94
1976	Finland	2:07:59.72
1980	USSR	1:57:03.46
1984	Sweden	1:55:06.3
1988	Sweden	1:43:58.6
1992	Norway	1:39:26.0
1994	Italy	1:41:15.0
1998	Norway	1:40:55.7

SKI JUMPING (NORMAL HILL)

		Pts
1964	Veikko Kankkonen, Finland	229.90
1968	Jiri Raska, Czechoslovakia	216.5
1972	Yukio Kasaya, Japan	244.2
1976	Hans-Georg Aschenbach, East Germany	252.0
1980	Toni Innauer, Austria	266.3
1984	Jens Weissflog, East Germany	215.2
1988	Matti Nykänen, Finland	229.1
1992	Ernst Vettori, Austria	222.8
1994	Espen Bredesen, Norway	282.0
1998	Jani Soininen, Finland	234.5

SKI JUMPING (LARGE HILL)

		Pts
1924	Jacob Tullin Thams, Norway	18.960
1928	Alf Andersen, Norway	19.208
1932	Birger Ruud, Norway	228.1
1936	Birger Ruud, Norway	232.0
1948	Petter Hugsted, Norway	228.1
1952	Arnfinn Bergmann, Norway	226.0
1956	Antti Hyvärinen, Finland	227.0
1960	Helmut Recknagel, East Germany	227.2
1964	Toralf Engan, Norway	230.70

NORDIC SKIING (Cont.)
Men (Cont.)

SKI JUMPING (LARGE HILL)

		Pts
1968	Vladimir Beloussov, USSR	231.3
1972	Wojciech Fortuna, Poland	219.9
1976	Karl Schnabl, Austria	234.8
1980	Jouko Tormanen, Finland	271.0
1984	Matti Nykänen, Finland	231.2
1988	Matti Nykänen, Finland	224.0
1992	Toni Nieminen, Finland	239.5
1994	Jens Weissflog, Germany	274.5
1998	Kazuyoshi Funaki, Japan	272.3

TEAM SKI JUMPING

		Pts
1988	Finland	634.4
1992	Finland	644.4
1994	Germany	970.1
1998	Japan	933.0

NORDIC COMBINED

		Pts
1924	Thorleif Haug, Norway	18.906*
1928	Johan Gröttumsbraaten, Norway	17.833*
1932	Johan Gröttumsbraaten, Norway	446.0

NORDIC COMBINED (Cont.)

		Pts
1936	Oddbjörn Hagen, Norway	430.30
1948	Heikki Hasu, Finland	448.80
1952	Simon Slattvik, Norway	451.621
1956	Sverre Stenersen, Norway	455.0
1960	Georg Thoma, West Germany	457.952
1964	Tormod Knutsen, Norway	469.28
1968	Frantz Keller, West Germany	449.04
1972	Ulrich Wehling, East Germany	413.34
1976	Ulrich Wehling, East Germany	423.39
1980	Ulrich Wehling, East Germany	432.20
1984	Tom Sandberg, Norway	422.595
1988	Hippolyt Kempf, Switzerland	432.230
1992	Fabrice Guy, France	426.47
1994	Fred B. Lundberg, Norway	457.970
1998	Bjarte Engen Vik, Norway	41:21.1†

TEAM NORDIC COMBINED

1988	West Germany
1992	Japan
1994	Japan
1998	Norway

* Different scoring system; 1924–1952 distance was 18 km; 1952–present, 15 km.

† Times in the cross country race were not converted into points. According to the Gundersen Method, used since 1988, starting times in the race are staggered in proportion to points earned in the ski jumping segment of the event.

Women

5 KILOMETERS CLASSICAL STYLE

1964	Klaudia Boyarskikh, USSR	17:50.5
1968	Toini Gustafsson, Sweden	16:45.2
1972	Galina Kulakova, USSR	17:00.50
1976	Helena Takalo, Finland	15:48.69
1980	Raisa Smetanina, USSR	15:06.92
1984	Marja-Liisa Hamalainen, Finland	17:04.0
1988	Marjo Matikainen, Finland	15:04.0
1992	Marjut Lukkarinen, Finland	14:13.8
1994	Lyubova Egorova, Russia	14:08.8
1998	Larissa Lazhutina, Russia	17:37.9

10 KILOMETERS CLASSICAL STYLE

1952	Lydia Widemen, Finland	41:40.0
1956	Lyubov Kosyryeva, USSR	38:11.0
1960	Maria Gusakova, USSR	39:46.6
1964	Klaudia Boyarskikh, USSR	40:24.3
1968	Toini Gustafsson, Sweden	36:46.5
1972	Galina Kulakova, USSR	34:17.8
1976	Raisa Smetanina, USSR	30:13.41
1980	Barbara Petzold, East Germany	30:31.54
1984	Marja-Lissa Hamalainen, Finland	31:44.2
1988	Vida Ventsene, USSR	30:08.3

10 KILOMETERS PURSUIT FREESTYLE

1992	Lyubov Egorova, Unified Team	40:07.7
1994	Lyubov Egorova, Russia	41:38.1
1998	Larissa Lazhutina, Russia	46:06.9

15 KILOMETERS CLASSICAL STYLE

1992	Lyubov Egorova, Unified Team	42:20.8
1994	Manuela Di Centa, Italy	39:44.5
1998	Olga Danilova, Russia	46:55.04

20 KILOMETERS FREESTYLE

1984	Marja-Liisa Hamalainen, Finland	1:01:45.0
1988	Tamara Tikhonova, USSR	55:53.6

30 KILOMETERS FREESTYLE

1992	Stefania Belmondo, Italy	1:22:30.1
1994	Manuela Di Centa, Italy	1:25:41.6
1998	Julija Tchepalova, Russia	1:22:01.5

4 X 5-KILOMETER RELAY MIXED STYLE

1956	Finland	1:9:01.0
1960	Sweden	1:4:21.4
1964	USSR	59:20.0
1968	Norway	57:30.0
1972	USSR	48:46.15
1976	USSR	1:07:49.75
1980	East Germany	1:02:11.10
1984	Norway	1:06:49.7
1988	USSR	59:51.1
1992	Unified Team	59:34.8
1994	Russia	57:12.5
1998	Russia	55:13.5

SNOWBOARDING

### Men	### Women

GIANT SLALOM

1998	Ross Rebagliati, Canada	2:03.96

GIANT SLALOM

1998	Karine Ruby, France	2:17.34

HALF-PIPE

		Pts
1998	Gian Simmen, Switzerland	85.2

HALF-PIPE

		Pts
1998	Nicola Thost, Germany	74.6

Track and Field

Sports Illustrated

Chasing History

Marion Jones blisters the 100-meter field at the 1998 Goodwill Games

AL TIELEMANS

Tainted

Drug scandals and public disinterest marred a superb season on the track

BY TIM LAYDEN

IF THE SPORT of track and field were contested in a vacuum where performance was the only barometer of success, it would be a simple matter to call 1998 a spectacular season. World records fell in three men's distance events to the incomparable Haile Gebrselassie of Ethiopia and Hicham El Guerrouj of Morocco, sprint training partners Ato Boldon of Trinidad and Maurice Greene of the United States backed up their ceaseless, entertaining trash talk with dominance on the track, and thrower John Godina was among the world's best in not one but two events. New stars emerged, such as 19-year-old Kenyan 800-meter specialist Japheth Kimutai and 20-year-old Nigerian sprinter Seun Ogunkoya; and old stars, like 30-year-old double Olympic sprint gold medalist Michael Johnson of the United States, and 32-year-old triple jump world-record holder Jonathan Edwards of Great Britain, approached past form, beating back age with vigor.

Above them all, the brilliant Marion Jones of the United States cut a swath across women's sprinting and long jumping like no woman in history, making her attempt at five Olympic gold medals in Sydney in 2000 seem more like a definite possibility than a remote fantasy. In all, it was a year that ignored the built-in quadrennial lull attached to summers when neither an Olympic Games

The respected Mitchell's suspension was a blow to track and field's credibility.

nor a world championships takes place.

Yet track and field in 1998 will not be remembered for its brilliant performances. Instead, the sport continues to fight for its credibility and survival against drug scandals, public disinterest and economic mismanagement. At stake is track and field's future place in the sports marketplace. No longer a competitor to soccer in Europe or football, basketball and baseball in the United States, track and field can become a successful niche sport, like golf and tennis, or a marginal one, like snowboarding and beach volleyball. Or it can fall entirely off the radar screen. Off-track events in 1998 did nothing to foster optimism. The status of the sport is perhaps best illustrated by a questionnaire received by Craig Masback, CEO of USA Track and Field, in which Masback was asked by a potential sponsor "How long has your sport been in the Olympic Games?" Numb, Masback wrote back with no small amount of frustration, "Since 776 B.C."

The year began with corporate shoe giants Nike and Reebok terminating endorsement contracts with many track and field athletes and with USA Track and Field forced to cancel a Grand Prix meet scheduled for Durham, N.C., because of a lack of sponsorship. The venerable Cologne, Germany, Grand Prix was also canceled, proving that track's problems are not limited to the United States. On July 14, El Guerrouj ran a world-record 3:26 1,500 meters at the Golden Gala in Rome, but barely 10,000 spectators witnessed the record in the cavernous, 80,000-seat Olympic Stadium. Major European meets were scarce on U.S. television and even in Europe, available in many countries only on cost-prohibitive pay-per-view.

The worst blow to track's credibility came in late July when U.S. sprinter Dennis Mitchell, a respected three-time Olympian and chair of the athletes' advisory committee, and Randy Barnes, the 1996 Olympic shot put gold medalist, were slapped with drug suspensions by track's international governing body. Mitchell was found in a random drug test to have an abnormally high testosterone ratio, while urinalysis detected in Barnes the presence of androstenedione, a substance banned in track and field but not in baseball, where slugger Mark McGwire admitted using it in his historic home run chase. With Ben Johnson's infamous 1988 Olympic drug bust still fresh in the public's mind, the suspensions of Barnes and Mitchell only served to buttress a stereotype of the track athlete as artificially enhanced.

All of these negatives diverted attention, most tragically, from Jones, the 22-year-old former North Carolina basketball player who is surely among the finest athletes in the world. A little more than a year after Jones—only five months after her final college basketball season—won a world championship in the 100 meters, she ran the 100 in 10.65 seconds. That made her the second-fastest woman in history, behind Florence Griffith Joyner, whose world record is 10.49. In all Jones broke 10.80 nine times and also had the world's fastest time in the 200 meters, 21.62, and the third-best long jump in history, twice going 23', 11¾". She reeled off a 37-event unbeaten streak in the long jump and sprints. "What she's getting ready to do is going to blow everybody's mind," said sprint coach John Smith, a former U.S. Olympian.

It was Smith who coached former UCLA sprinter Boldon to the year's fastest times in both the 100 (9.86 seconds, twice) and 200 meters (19.88). Boldon was pushed all season by Greene, who won the 100 at the Goodwill Games in 9.96.

Gebrselassie reclaimed the 5,000 and 10,000-meter world records that were taken from him by Kenya's Daniel Komen and Paul Tergat late in 1997, running 26:22.75 for the 10,000 on June 1 in Hengelo, Netherlands, and 12:39.36 for the 5,000 12 days later in Helsinki. Godina became the first American in 43 years to win both the shot and the discus at the U.S. nationals and set the stage for a possible Olympic double, which hasn't been done since 1924.

The most stirring moments of the summer came during the two-week made-for-television Goodwill Games on Long Island in late July. Not only did 1996 decathlon gold medalist Dan O'Brien recapture his glory with a victory over rising countryman Chris Huffins, and not only did Johnson anchor the U.S. 4x400-meter relay to a world record, but also Jackie Joyner-Kersee, the grande dame of U.S. women's track and field, reached into the well to win the last heptathlon of her career. She finished in the arms of her husband and coach, Bobby Kersee, the two of them laughing and crying, a lingering image of what the sport has been and can be.

1998 Goodwill Games

Uniondale, New York, July 19–August 2, 1998

Men

100 METERS

1.	Maurice Greene, United States	9.96
2.	Ato Boldon, Trinidad	10.00
3.	Brian Lewis, United States	10.25

200 METERS

1.	Ato Boldon, Trinidad	20.15
2.	Tyree Washington, United States	20.29
3.	Claudinei Da Silva, Brazil	20.81

400 METERS

1.	Michael Johnson, United States	43.76†
2.	Tyree Washington, United States	44.43
3.	Antonio Pettigrew, United States	44.78

800 METERS

1.	Patrick Ndururi, Kenya	1:45.30
2.	Noberto Téllez, Cuba	1:45.92
3.	David Kiptoo, Kenya	1:46.05

MILE

1.	Noureddine Morceli, Algeria	3:53.39
2.	William Tanui, Kenya	3:54.05
3.	Daniel Komen, Kenya	3:54.78

STEEPLECHASE

1.	Bernard Barmasai, Kenya	8:14.26†
2.	John Kosgei, Kenya	8:18.40
3.	Brahim Boulami, Morocco	8:20.00

5000 METERS

1.	Luke Kipkosgei, Kenya	13:20.27
2.	Khalid Boulami, Morocco	13:20.66
3.	Thomas Nyiriki, Kenya	13:23.64

10,000 METERS

1.	Julius Gitahi, Kenya	27:49.26
2.	Simon Maina, Kenya	27:49.65
3.	James Koskei, Kenya	28:51.02

110-METER HURDLES

1.	Mark Crear, United States	13.06†
2.	Allen Johnson, United States	13.10
3.	Reggie Torian, United States	13.16

400-METER HURDLES

1.	Bryan Bronson, United States	47.70†
2.	Angelo Taylor, United States	47.92
3.	Joey Woody, United States	48.59

20-KILOMETER WALK

1.	Ilya Markov, Russia	1:23:29
2.	Daniel Garcia, Mexico	1:25:52
3.	Jefferson Perez, Ecuador	1:29:18

4 X 100 METER RELAY

1.	United States	37.90†
2.	Canada	38.23
3.	Cuba	39.34

4 X 400 METER RELAY

1.	United States	2:54.20 WR
2.	Poland	2:58.00
3.	Jamaica	2:58.33

HIGH JUMP

1.	Javier Sotomayor, Cuba	7 ft 7½ in
2.	Charles Austin, United States	7 ft 7½ in
3.	Brian Brown, United States	7 ft 6 in

POLE VAULT

1.	Jeff Hartwig, United States	19 ft 8 in
2.	Maksim Tarasov, Russia	19 ft ⅛ in
3.	Pat Manson, United States	18 ft 8⅛ in

LONG JUMP

1.	Ivan Pedroso, Cuba	28 ft 7⅛ in
2.	Erick Walder, United States	27 ft 6 in
3.	James Beckford, Jamaica	24 ft 4 in

TRIPLE JUMP

1.	Jonathan Edwards, Great Britain	57 ft 11 in
2.	Yoelbi Quesada, Cuba	56 ft 8 in
3.	Lamark Carter, United States	56 ft 0 in

SHOT PUT

1.	John Godina, United States	70 ft 4 in
2.	C.J. Hunter, United States	68 ft 2 in
3.	Adam Nelson, United States	66 ft 10½ in

DISCUS THROW

1.	Dmitri Shevchenko, Russia	212 ft 8 in
2.	Andy Bloom, United States	209 ft 11 in
3.	John Godina, United States	206 ft 2 in

HAMMER THROW

1.	Vasiliy Sodorenko, Russia	265 ft 4 in
2.	Lance Deal, United States	256 ft 3 in
3.	Ilya Konovalov, Russia	252 ft 11 in

JAVELIN THROW

1.	Marius Corbet, South Africa	290 ft
2.	Steven Backley, Great Britain	284ft 9 in
3.	Konstantinos Gatzioudis, Greece	284 ft 3 in

DECATHLON

1.	Dan O'Brien, United States	8,755 pts.
2.	Chris Huffins, United States	8,576 pts.
3.	Tomas Dvorak, Czech Republic	8,428 pts.

Women

100 METERS

1. ....Marion Jones, United States   10.90†
2. ....Zhanna Pintusevich, Ukraine   11.09
3. ....Inger Miller, United States   11.18

200 METERS

1. ....Marion Jones, United States   21.80†
2. ....Zhanna Pintusevich, Ukraine   22.46
3. ....Beverly McDonald, Jamaica   22.67

400 METERS

1. ....Falilat Ogunkoya, Nigeria   49.89
2. ....Jearl Miles-Clark, United States   50.43
3. ....Sandie Richards, Jamaica   50.98

800 METERS

1. ....Maria Mutola, Mozambique   1:58.83
2. ....Jearl Miles-Clark, United States   1:59:08
3. ....Joetta Clark, United States   2:00.02

MILE

1. ....Svetlana Masterkova, Russia   4:20.39
2. ....Regina Jacobs, United States   4:20.93
3. ....Suzy Hamilton, United States   4:22.93

STEEPLECHASE

1. ....Svetlana Rogova, Russia   9:57.62
2. ....Daniela Petrescu, Romania   9:58.28
3. ....Lesley Lehane, United States   10:08.29

5,000 METERS

1. ....Olga Yegorova, Russia   15:53.05
2. ....Libbie Hickman, United States   15:54.93
3. ....Lyubov Kremlyova, Russia   16:00.20

10,000 METERS

1. ....Tegla Loroupe, Kenya   32:15.44
2. ....Sally Barsosio, Kenya   32:50.16
3. ....Dong Yanmei, China   32:59.85

100-METER HURDLES

1. ....Angela Vaughn, United States   12.72
2. ....Gillian Russell, Jamaica   12.78
3. ....Michelle Freeman, Jamaica   12.85

400-METER HURDLES

1. ....Nezha Bidouhane, Morocco   52.97
2. ....Deon Hemmings, Jamaica   53.09
3. ....Kim Batten, United States   53.52

10-KILOMETER WALK

1. ....TeYelena Nikolayeva, Russia   43:51.97
2. ....Nadezhda Riyashkina, Russia   44:25.99
3. ....Joanne Dow, United States   45:36.92

4 X 100 METER RELAY

1. ....United States   42.06†
2. ....Bahamas   42.19
3. ....Russia   42.62

4 X 400 METER RELAY

1. ....Jamaica   3:20.92
2. ....United States   3:21.03
3. ....Russia   3:21.30

HIGH JUMP

1. ....Tisha Waller, United States   6 ft 5 in
2. ....Yuliya Lyakhova, Russia   6 ft 4 in
2. ....Amy Acuff, United States   6 ft 4 in

POLE VAULT

1. ....Yelena Belyakova, Russia   14 ft 4 in
2. ....Emma George, Australia   14 ft 1¼ in
3. ....Tatyana Gregorieva, Australia   13 ft 9¾ in
3. ....Anzela Balakhonova, Ukraine   13 ft 9¾ in
3. ....Vala Flosadottir, Iceland   13 ft 9¾ in

LONG JUMP

1. ....Shana Williams, United States   22 ft 8 in
2. ....Lyudmila Galkina, Russia   22 ft 5¾ in
3. ....Niki Xanthou, Greece   22 ft 5 in

TRIPLE JUMP

1. ....Sarka Kaspárková, Czech Rep.   48 ft 5¼ in†
2. ....Tatyana Lebedeva, Russia   46 ft 4½ in
3. ....Tiombe Hurd, United States   44 ft 8½ in

SHOT PUT

1 ....Irina Korzhanenko, Russia   65 ft 5 in
2 ....C. Price-Smith, United States   63 ft 10¼ in
3 ....Valentina Fedyushina, Ukraine   62 ft 6½ in

DISCUS THROW

1. ....Natalya Sadova, Russia   215 ft 10 in
2. ....Ilke Wyludda, Germany   209 ft 5 in
3. ....Kristin Kuehl, United States   202 ft 11 in

HAMMER THROW

1 ....Mihaela Melinte, Romania   238 ft 4 in WR
2 ....Olga Kuzenkova, Russia   232 ft 10 in
3. ....Amy Palmer, United States   217 ft 7 in

JAVELIN

1 ....Joanna Stone, Australia   217 ft 5 in
2............Isel Lopez, Cuba   209 ft 1 in
3. ....Sonia Bisset, Cuba   205 ft 6 in

HEPTATHLON

1 ....J. Joyner-Kersee, United States   6,502 pts.
2 ....DeDee Nathan, United States   6,479 pts.
3 ....K. Blair-Labounty, United States   6,465 pts.

†Meet record. WR=world record.

Seattle, June 19–21, 1998

Men

100 METERS

1. ....Tim Harden, Mizuno — 9.88†w
2. ....Brian Lewis, Reebok — 9.98w
3. ....Tim Montgomery, Asics TC — 9.99w

200 METERS

1. ....Gentry Bradley, Nike — 20.47w
2. ....Allen Johnson, unat — 20.54w
3. ....Curtis Perry, Louisiana St — 20.56w

400 METERS

1. ....Jerome Young, St. Augustine's — 44.09
2. ....Tyree Washington, Reebok — 44.38
3. ....Antonio Pettigrew, adidas — 44.40

800 METERS

1. ....Mark Everett, Powerbar Intl. — 1:45.28
2. ....Johnny Gray, Santa Monica TC — 1:45.27
3. ....Trinity Townsend, Ann Arbor TC — 1:45.75

1500 METERS

1. ....Jamey Harris, Reebok — 3:37.99
2. ....Jason Pyrah, unat — 3:38.77
3. ....Paul McMullen, Asics — 3:39.26

STEEPLECHASE

1. ....Pascal Dobert, Nike — 8:33.91
2. ....Tom Nohilly, New Balance — 8:37.56
3. ....John Mortimer, Univ. of Michigan — 8:38.62

5000 METERS

1. ....Marc Davis, Nike — 13:40.62
2. ....Allen Culpepper, adidas — 13:41.13
3. ....Peter Julian, adidas — 13:49.42

10,000 METERS

1. ....Daniel Browne, Army — 29:47.06
2. ....James Menon, Asics — 29:47.58
3. ....Reuben Reina, Asics — 29:47.61

110-METER HURDLES

1. ....Reggie Torian, Asics — 13.03w
2. ....Mark Crear, Reebok — 13.06w
3. ....Dudley Dorvial, Mizuno — 13.30w

400-METER HURDLES

1. ....Bryan Bronson, Nike — 47.03†
2. ....Angelo Taylor, Georgia Tech — 47.90
3. ....Joey Woody, Reebok — 47.97

20-KILOMETER WALK

1. ....Tim Seamann, NYAC — 1:35.07
2. ....Curt Clausen, Shore AC — 1:35.41
3. ....Jonathan Matthews, Reebok — 1:35.58

HIGH JUMP

1. ....Charles Austin, Mizuno — 7ft 6½ in
2. ....Nathan Leeper, Kansas St — 7ft 6½ in
3. ....Hollis Conway, unat — 7ft 4½ in
3. ....Brian Brown, HealthSouth AC — 7ft 4½ in

POLE VAULT

1. ....Jeff Hartwig, Bell Athletics — 19 ft 2¼ in
2. ....Pat Manson, Team US West — 18 ft 10¼ in
3. ....Dean Starkey, Nike — 18 ft 6½ in

LONG JUMP

1. ....Roland McGhee, Nike — 27 ft 2 inw
2. ....Erick Walder, adidas — 27 ft 1¼ inw
3. ....Kevin Dilworth, adidas — 26 ft 6¼ inw

TRIPLE JUMP

1. ....LaMark Carter, Nike — 57 ft 2¾ inw
2. ....Robert Howard, Arkansas — 56 ft 2 inw
3. ....Von Ware, Sheffield Elite — 55 ft 1 inw

SHOT PUT

1. ....John Godina, Reebok–Bruin — 71 ft 2¾ in
2. ...........C.J. Hunter, Nike — 68 ft 4½ in
3. ....Adam Nelson, Dartmouth — 66 ft 9¼ in

DISCUS THROW

1. ....John Godina, Reebok–Bruin — 220 ft 1 in
2. ....Adam Setliff, unat — 217 ft 11 in
3. ....Andrew Bloom, Nike — 217 ft 11 in

HAMMER THROW

1. ....Lance Deal, NYAC — 256 ft 6 in
2. ....Jud Logan, unat — 233 ft 11 in
3. ....Kevin McMahon, Reebok Enc. — 229 ft 6 in

JAVELIN THROW

1. ....Tom Pukstys, adidas — 270 ft 3 in
2. ....Joshua Johnson, Reebok–Bruin — 248 ft 7 in
3. ....Ed Kaminski, unat — 247 ft 6 in

DECATHLON

1. ....Chris Huffins, Mizuno — 8,694 pts.
2. ....Ricky Barber, Gallery Furniture — 8,183 pts.
3. ....Brian Brophy, unat — 8,123 pts.

Women

100 METERS

1. ....Marion Jones, Nike — 10.72†w
2. ....Chryste Gaines, adidas — 10.82w
3. ....Inger Miller, Nike — 11.12w

200 METERS

1. ....Marion Jones, Nike — 22.24
2. ....Zundra Feagin, Asics — 23.04
3. ....Carlette Guidry, adidas — 23.07
3. ....Cheryl Taplin, Vector Sports — 23.07

400 METERS

1. ....Kim Graham, Asics — 50.69
2. ....Rochelle Stevens, Running Start TC — 51.07
3. ....Monique Hennegan, N Carolina — 51.11

800 METERS

1. ....Jearl Miles-Clark, Reebok — 1.58.78
2. ....Joetta Clark, Nike — 1.59.01
3. ....Meredith Valmon, Reebok Enc. — 1.59.29

1500 METERS

1. ....Suzy Hamilton, Nike — 4:05.28
2. ....Amy Wickus, Nike — 4:07.95
3. ....Alisa Harvy, New Balance — 4:08.33

STEEPLECHASE

1. ....Courtney Meldrum, BYU — 10.21.00
2. ....Elizabeth Jackson, BYU — 10.21.20
3. ....Lesley Lehane, Boston AC — 10.25.90

5000 METERS

1. ....Regina Jacobs, Mizuno — 15:32.31
2. ....Libbie Hickman, Nike — 15:39.40
3. ....Amy Rudolph, Reebok — 15:41.31

10,000 METERS

1. ....Lynn Jennings, Nike — 34:09.86
2. ....Jennifer Rhines, adidas — 34:10.31
3. ....Shelly Steely, Asics — 34:11.75

100-METER HURDLES

1. ....Cheryl Dickey, Nike — 12.82
2. ....Angela Vaughn, Texas — 12.88
3. ....Miesha McKelvy, San Diego St — 12.97

400-METER HURDLES

1. ....Kim Batten, Reebok — 53.61
2. ....Michelle Johnson, Tuscon Elite AC — 54.80
3. ....Sandra Glover, unat — 55.11

w=wind aided. †Meet record.

10,000-METER WALK

1. ....Joanne Dow, adidas — 47.06.50
2. ....Michelle Rohl, Moving Comfort — 47.32.70
3. ....Debbi Lawrence, unat — 48.34.40

HIGH JUMP

1. ....Tisha Walker, Nat's Athletic — 6 ft 4½ in
2. ....Amy Acuff, unat — 6 ft 4½ in
3. ....Erin Aldrich, Univ. of Texas — 6 ft 2¾ in

POLE VAULT

1. ....Kellie Suttle, Bell Athletics — 14 ft
2. ....Stacy Dragila, Reebok Racing — 13 ft 5¼ in
3. ....Kimberly Becker, Bell Athletics — 13 ft 5¼ in

LONG JUMP

1. ....Marion Jones, Nike — 23 ft 8 in†w
2. ....Shana Williams, adidas — 22 ft 7¾ inw
3. ....Dawn Burrell, Army–World Class — 22 ft 7¾ inw

TRIPLE JUMP

1. ....Sheila Hudson, unat — 45 ft ¼ inw
2. ....Cynthea Rhodes, Reebok — 44 ft 9¾ in
3. ....Tiombe Hurd, unat — 44 ft 9½ in

SHOT PUT

1. ....Connie Price-Smith, adidas — 61 ft 3 in
2. ....Teri Tunks, SMU — 59 ft 8½ in
3. ....Tressa Thompson, unat — 57 ft 3¾ in

DISCUS THROW

1. ....Seiala Sua, UCLA — 204 ft 2 in
2. ....Kristin Kuehl, unat — 201 ft
3. ....Aretha Hill, Univ. of Washington — 198 ft 5 in

HAMMER THROW

1. ....Windy Dean, SMU — 210 ft 4 in
2. ....Amy Palmer, BYU — 209 ft
3. ....Dawn Ellerbe, NYAC — 208 ft 2 in

JAVELIN THROW

1. ....Nicole Carroll, Asics — 185 ft 7 in
2. ....Windy Dean, SMU — 184 ft 6 in
3. ....Lynda Lipson, Klub Keihas — 183 ft 11 in

HEPTATHLON

1. ....Kelly Blair, Reebok — 6,402 pts.
2. ....Shelia Burrell, unat — 6,294 pts.
3. ....Tiffany Lott, unat — 6,123 pts.

IAAF World Cross-Country Championships

Marrakech, Morocco, March 23, 1998

MEN (12,000 METERS; 7.5 MILES)

1.	Paul Tergat, Kenya	34:01
2.	Paul Koech, Kenya	34:06
3.	Assefa Mezegebu, Ethiopia	34:28

WOMEN (4,000 METERS; 2.5 MILES)

1.	Sonia O'Sullivan, Ireland	12:20
2.	Zohra Ouaziz, Morocco	12:34
3.	Kutre Dulecha, Ethiopia	12:37

Major Marathons

New York City: November 2, 1997

MEN

1.	John Kagwe, Kenya	2:08:12
2.	Joseph Chebet, Kenya	2:09:27
3.	Stefano Baldini, Italy	2:09:31

WOMEN

1.	Franziska Rochat-Moser, Switz.	2:28:43
2.	Colleen de Reuck, South Africa	2:29:11
3.	Franca Fiacconi, Italy	2:30:15

Tokyo: November 30, 1997

WOMEN ONLY

1.	Makiko Ito, Japan	2:27:45
2.	Joyce Chepchumba, Kenya	2:28:02
3.	Jane Salumae, Ethiopia	2:28:23

Fukuoka, Japan: December 7, 1997

MEN ONLY

1.	Josiah Thugwane, South Africa	2:07:28
2.	Toshiyuki Hayata, Japan	2:08:07
3.	Nozomi Saho, Japan	2:08:47

Honolulu: December 14, 1997

MEN

1.	Eric Kimaiyo, Kenya	2:12:17
2.	Jimmy Muindi, Kenya	2:12:50
3.	Thabiso Moqhali, Lesotho	2:13:11

WOMEN

1.	Svetlana Vasilyeva, Russia	2:33:14
2.	Irina Bogacheva, Kyrgyzstan	2:34:01
3.	Jinhong Pan, China	2:35:53

Los Angeles: March 2, 1998

MEN

1.	Zebedayo Bayo, Tanzania	2:11:21
2.	Jonathan Ndambuki, Kenya	2:11:25
3.	Simon Lopuyet, Kenya	2:11:41

WOMEN

1.	Lornah Kiplagat, Kenya	2:34:03
2.	Maura Viceconte, Italy	2:34:13
3.	Hellen Kimaiyo, Kenya	2:35:28

London: April 16, 1998

MEN

1.	Abel Anton, Spain	2:07:57
2.	Abdelkader El Mouaziz, Morocco	2:08:07
3.	Antonio Pinto, Portugal	2:08:13

WOMEN

1.	Catherina McKiernan, Ireland	2:26:26
2.	Liz McColgan, Great Britain	2:26:54
3.	Joyce Chepchumba, Kenya	2:27:22

Rotterdam: April 19, 1998

MEN

1.	Fabian Roncero, Spain	2:07:26
2.	Lee Bong-ju, South Korea	2:07:44
3.	Danilo Goffi, Italy	2:08.33

WOMEN

1.	Tegla Loroupe, Kenya	2:20:47 WR
2.	Junko Asari, Japan	2:26:11
3.	Nadezhda Ilyina, Russia	2:30:08

Boston: April 20, 1998

MEN

1.	Moses Tanui, Kenya	2:07:34
2.	Joseph Chebet, Kenya	2:07:37
3.	Gert Thys, South Africa	2:07:52

WOMEN

1.	Fatuma Roba, Ethiopia	2:23:21
2.	Renata Paradowska, Poland	2:27:17
3.	Anuta Catuna, Romania	2:27:34

WR=world record.

World Records

As of September 3, 1998. World outdoor records are recognized by the International Amateur Athletics Federation (IAAF).

Men

Event	Mark	Record Holder	Date	Site
100 meters	9.84	Donovan Bailey, Canada	7-27-96	Atlanta
200 meters	19.32	Michael Johnson, United States	8-1-96	Atlanta
400 meters	43.29	Butch Reynolds, United States	8-17-88	Zurich
800 meters	1:41.11	Wilson Kipketer, Denmark	8-24-97	Cologne
1,000 meters	2:12.18	Sebastian Coe, Great Britain	7-11-81	Oslo
1,500 meters	3:26.00	Hicham El Guerrouj, Morocco	7-14-98	Rome
Mile	3:44.39	Noureddine Morceli, Algeria	9-5-93	Rieti, Italy
2,000 meters	4:47.88	Noureddine Morceli, Algeria	7-3-95	Paris
3,000 meters	7:20.67	Daniel Komen, Kenya	9-1-96	Rieti, Italy
Steeplechase	7:55.72	Bernard Bermasai	8-24-97	Cologne
5,000 meters	12:39.36	Haile Gebrselassie, Ethiopia	6-13-98	Helsinki
10,000 meters	26:22.75	Haile Gebrselassie, Ethiopia	6-1-98	Hengelo, Netherlands
20,000 meters	56:55.6	Arturo Barrios, Mexico	3-30-91	La Flâche, France
Hour	21,101 meters	Arturo Barrios, Mexico	3-30-91	La Flâche, France
25,000 meters	1:13:55.8	Toshihiko Seko, Japan	3-22-81	Christchurch, New Zealand
30,000 meters	1:29:18.8	Toshihiko Seko, Japan	3-22-81	Christchurch, New Zealand
Marathon	2:06:05	Ronaldo da Costa, Brazil	9-20-98	Berlin
110-meter hurdles	12.91	Colin Jackson, Great Britain	8-20-93	Stuttgart, Germany
400-meter hurdles	46.78	Kevin Young, United States	8-6-92	Barcelona
20-kilometer walk	1:17:25.6	Bernardo Segura, Mexico	5-7-94	Bergen, Norway
30-kilometer walk	2:01:44.1	Maurizio Damilano, Italy	10-3-92	Cuneo, Italy
50-kilometer walk	3:40:58	Andrey Plotnikov, Russia	4-21-96	Sochi
4x100-meter relay	37.40	United States (Mike Marsh, Leroy Burrell, Dennis Mitchell, Carl Lewis)	8-8-92	Barcelona
		United States (Jon Drummond, Andre Cason, Dennis Mitchell, Leroy Burrell)	8-21-93	Stuttgart, Germany
4x200-meter relay	1:18.68	Santa Monica TC (Mike Marsh, Leroy Burrell, Floyd Heard, Carl Lewis)	4-17-94	Walnut, CA
4x400-meter relay	2:54.20	United States (Jerome Young, Antonio Pettigrew, Tyree Washington, Michael Johnson)	7-22-98	New York City
4x800-meter relay	7:03.89	Great Britain (Peter Elliott, Garry Cook, Steve Cram, Sebastian Coe)	8-30-82	London
4x1500-meter relay	14:38.8	West Germany (Thomas Wessinghage, Harald Hudak, Michael Lederer, Karl Fleschen)	8-17-77	Cologne
High jump	8 ft ½ in	Javier Sotomayor, Cuba	7-27-93	Salamanca, Spain
Pole vault	20 ft 1¾ in	Sergei Bubka, Ukraine	7-31-94	Sestriere, Italy
Long jump	29 ft 4½ in	Mike Powell, United States	8-30-91	Tokyo
Triple jump	60 ft ¼ in	Jonathan Edwards, Great Britain	8-7-95	Göteborg, Sweden
Shot put	75 ft 10¼ in	Randy Barnes, United States	5-20-90	Westwood, CA
Discus throw	243 ft 0 in	Jürgen Schult, East Germany	6-6-86	Neubrandenburg, Germany
Hammer throw	284 ft 7 in	Yuri Syedikh, USSR	8-30-86	Stuttgart, Germany
Javelin throw	323 ft 1 in	Jan Zelezny, Czech Republic	5-25-96	Jena, Germany
Decathlon	8891 pts	Dan O'Brien, United States	9-4/5-92	Talence, France

Note: The decathlon consists of 10 events—the 100 meters, long jump, shot put, high jump and 400 meters on the first day; the 110-meter hurdles, discus, pole vault, javelin and 1500 meters on the second.

Women

Event	Mark	Record Holder	Date	Site
100 meters	10.49	Florence Griffith Joyner, United States	7-16-88	Indianapolis
200 meters	21.34	Florence Griffith Joyner, United States	9-29-88	Seoul
400 meters	47.60	Marita Koch, East Germany	10-6-85	Canberra, Australia
800 meters	1:53.28	Jarmila Kratochvílová, Czechoslovakia	7-26-83	Munich
1,000 meters	2:28.98	Svetlana Masterkova, Russia	8-23-96	Brussels
1,500 meters	3:50.46	Qu Yunxia, China	9-11-93	Beijing
Mile	4:12.56	Svetlana Masterkova, Russia	8-14-96	Zurich
2,000 meters	5:25.36	Sonia O'Sullivan, Ireland	7-8-94	Edinburgh
3,000 meters	8:06.11	Wang Junxia, China	9-13-93	Beijing
5,000 meters	14:28.09	Jiang Bo, China	10-23-97	Shanghai
10,000 meters	29:31.78	Wang Junxia, China	9-8-93	Beijing
Hour	18,340 meters	Tegla Loroupe, Kenya	8-8-98	Borgholzhausen, Germany
20,000 meters	1:06:48.8	Izumi Maki, Japan	9-19-93	Amagasaki
25,000 meters	1:29:29.2	Karolina Szabó, Hungary	4-22-88	Budapest
30,000 meters	1:47:05.6	Karolina Szabó, Hungary	4-22-88	Budapest
Marathon	2:20:47	Tegla Loroupe, Kenya	4-19-98	Rotterdam
100-meter hurdles	12.21	Yordanka Donkova, Bulgaria	8-20-88	Stara Zagora, Bulgaria
400-meter hurdles	52.61	Kim Batten, United States	8-11-95	Göteborg, Sweden
5-kilometer walk	20:13.26	Kerry Saxby, Australia	2-25-96	Hobart, Australia
10-kilometer walk	41:04	Yelena Nikolayeva, Russia	4-20-96	Sochi
4x100-meter relay	41.37	East Germany (Silke Gladisch, Sabine Reiger, Ingrid Auerswald, Marlies Göhr)	10-6-85	Canberra, Australia
4x200-meter relay	1:28.15	East Germany (Marlies Göhr, Romy Müller, Bärbel Wöckel, Marita Koch)	8-9-80	Jena, East Germany
4x400-meter relay	3:15.17	USSR (Tatyana Ledovskaya, Olga Nazarova, Maria Pinigina, Olga Bryzgina)	10-1-88	Seoul
4x800-meter relay	7:50.17	USSR (Nadezhda Olizarenko, Lyubov Gurina, Lyudmila Borisova, Irina Podyalovskaya)	8-5-84	Moscow
High jump	6 ft 10¼ in	Stefka Kostadinova, Bulgaria	8-30-87	Rome
Pole vault	15 ft ¾ in	Emma George, Australia	3-21-98	Brisbane, Austrailia
Long jump	24 ft 8¼ in	Galina Chistyakova, USSR	6-11-88	Leningrad
Triple jump	50 ft 10¼ in	Inessa Kravets, Ukraine	8-10-95	Göteborg, Sweden
Shot put	74 ft 3 in	Natalya Lisovskaya, USSR	6-7-87	Moscow
Discus throw	252 ft 0 in	Gabriele Reinsch, East Germany	7-9-88	Neubrandenburg, Germany
Hammer throw	242 ft 1 in	Olga Kuzenkova, Russia	5-15-98	Tolyatti, Russia
Javelin throw	262 ft 5 in	Petra Felke, East Germany	9-9-88	Potsdam, East Germany
Heptathlon	7291 pts	Jackie Joyner-Kersee, U.S.	9-23/24-88	Seoul

Note: The heptathlon consists of 7 events—the 100-meter hurdles, high jump, shot put and 200 meters on the first day; the long jump, javelin and 800 meters on the second.

American Records

As of September 8, 1998. American outdoor records are recognized by USA Track and Field (USATF). WR=world record.

Men

Event	Mark	Record Holder	Date	Site
100 meters	9.85	Leroy Burrell	7-6-94	Lausanne
200 meters	19.32 WR	Michael Johnson	8-1-96	Atlanta
400 meters	43.29 WR	Butch Reynolds	8-17-88	Zurich
800 meters	1:42.60	Johnny Gray	8-28-85	Koblenz, Germany
1,000 meters	2:13.9	Rick Wohlhuter	7-30-74	Oslo
1,500 meters	3:29.77	Sydney Maree	8-25-85	Cologne
Mile	3:47.69	Steve Scott	7-7-82	Oslo
2,000 meters	4:52.44	Jim Spivey	9-15-87	Lausanne
3,000 meters	7:30.84	Bob Kennedy	8-8-98	Monte Carlo
Steeplechase	8:09.17	Henry Marsh	8-28-85	Koblenz, Germany
5,000 meters	12:58.21	Bob Kennedy	8-14-96	Zurich
10,000 meters	27:20.56	Mark Nenow	9-5-86	Brussels
20,000 meters	58:25.0	Bill Rodgers	8-9-77	Boston
Hour	20,547 meters	Bill Rodgers	8-9-77	Boston
25,000 meters	1:14:11.8	Bill Rodgers	2-21-79	Saratoga, CA
30,000 meters	1:31:49	Bill Rodgers	2-21-79	Saratoga, CA
Marathon	2:10:04	Pat Petersen	4-23-89	London
110-meter hurdles	12.92	Roger Kingdom	8-16-89	Zurich
		Allen Johnson	6-23-96	Atlanta
		Allen Johnson	8-23-96	Brussels
400-meter hurdles	46.78 WR	Kevin Young	8-6-92	Barcelona
20-kilometer walk	1:24:26.9	Allen James	5-7-94	Fana, Norway
30-kilometer walk	2:21:40	Herm Nelson	9-7-91	Bellevue, WA
50-kilometer walk	3:59:41.2	Herm Nelson	6-9-96	Seattle
4x100-meter relay	37.40 WR	United States (Mike Marsh, Leroy Burrell, Dennis Mitchell, Carl Lewis)	8-8-92	Barcelona
		United States (Jon Drummond, Andre Cason, Dennis Mitchell, Leroy Burrell)	8-21-93	Stuttgart, Germany
4x200-meter relay	1:18.68 WR	Santa Monica Track Club (Mike Marsh, Leroy Burrell, Floyd Heard, Carl Lewis)	4-17-94	Walnut, CA
4x400-meter relay	2:54.20 WR	United States (Jerome Young, Antonio Pettigrew, Tyree Washington, Michael Johnson)	7-22-98	New York City
4x800-meter relay	7:06.5	Santa Monica Track Club (James Robinson, David Mack, Earl Jones, Johnny Gray)	4-26-86	Walnut, CA
4x1,500-meter relay	14:46.3	National Team (Dan Aldredge, Andy Clifford, Todd Harbour, Tom Duits)	6-24-79	Bourges, France
High jump	7 ft 10½ in	Charles Austin	8-17-91	Zurich
Pole vault	19 ft 8⅜ in	Jeff Hartwig	7-21-98	Uniondale, NY
Long jump	29 ft 4½ in WR	Mike Powell	8-30-91	Tokyo
Triple jump	59 ft 4¼ in	Kenny Harrison	7-27-96	Atlanta
Shot put	75 ft 10¼ in WR	Randy Barnes	5-20-90	Westwood, CA
Discus throw	237 ft 4 in	Ben Plucknett	7-7-81	Stockholm
Hammer throw	270 ft 9 in	Lance Deal	9-7-96	Milan
Javelin throw	285 ft 10 in	Tom Pukstys	5-25-97	Jena, Germany
Decathlon	8891 pts WR	Dan O'Brien	9-4/5-92	Talence, France

Women

Event	Mark	Record Holder	Date	Site
100 meters	10.49 WR	Florence Griffith Joyner	7-16-88	Indianapolis
200 meters	21.34 WR	Florence Griffith Joyner	9-29-88	Seoul
400 meters	48.83	Valerie Brisco-Hooks	8-6-84	Los Angeles
800 meters	1:56.78	Jearl Miles-Clark	8-22-97	Brussels
1,500 meters	3:57.12	Mary Slaney	7-26-83	Stockholm
Mile	4:16.71	Mary Slaney	8-21-85	Zurich
2,000 meters	5:32.7	Mary Slaney	8-3-84	Eugene, OR
3,000 meters	8:25.83	Mary Slaney	9-7-85	Rome
5,000 meters	14:52.49	Regina Jacobs	7-4-98	Brunswick, ME
10,000 meters	31:19.89	Lynn Jennings	8-7-92	Barcelona
Marathon	2:21:21	Joan Samuelson	10-20-85	Chicago
100-meter hurdles	12.46	Gail Devers	8-20-93	Stuttgart, Germany
400-meter hurdles	52.61 WR	Kim Batten	8-11-95	Göteborg, Sweden
5,000-meter walk	20:56.88	Michelle Rohl	4-27-96	Philadelphia
10,000-meter walk	44:41.87	Michelle Rohl	7-26-94	St. Petersburg
4x100-meter relay	41.47	USA National Team (Chryste Gaines, Marion Jones, Inger Miller, Gail Devers)	8-9-97	Athens
4x200-meter relay	1:29.64	Nike International (Tamika Roberts, Inger Miller, Nicole Green, Marion Jones)	4-25-98	Philadelphia
4x400-meter relay	3:15.51	Olympic Team (Denean Howard, Diane Dixon, Valerie Brisco, Florence Griffith Joyner)	10-1-88	Seoul
4x800-meter relay	8:17.09	Athletics West (Sue Addison, Lee Arbogast, Mary Decker, Chris Mullen)	4-24-83	Walnut, CA
High jump	6 ft 8 in	Louise Ritter	7-9-88	Austin, TX
		Louise Ritter	9-30-88	Seoul
Pole vault	14 ft 7 in	Stacy Dragila	5-10-97	Modesto
Long jump	24 ft 7 in	Jackie Joyner-Kersee	5-22-94	New York City
			7-31-94	Sestriere, Italy
Triple jump	47 ft 3½ in	Sheila Hudson	7-8-96	Stockholm
Shot put	66 ft 2½ in	Ramona Pagel	6-25-88	San Diego
Discus throw	216 ft 10 in	Carol Cady	5-31-86	San Jose
Hammer throw	220 ft 1 in	Amy Palmer	4-2-98	Austin, TX
Javelin throw	227 ft 5 in	Kate Schmidt	9-10-77	Fürth, West Germany
Heptathlon	7291 pts WR	Jackie Joyner-Kersee	9-23/24-88	Seoul

World and American Indoor Records

As of September 8, 1998. American indoor records are recognized by USA Track and Field. World Indoor records are recognized by the International Amateur Athletics Federation (IAAF).

Men

Event	Mark	Record Holder	Date	Site
50 meters	5.56	Donovan Bailey, Canadian (W)	2-9-96	Reno
	5.61	James Sanford (A)	2-20-81	San Diego
55 meters*	6.00	Lee McRae (A)	3-14-86	Oklahoma City
60 meters	6.39	Maurice Greene (W, A)	3-1-98	Madrid
200 meters	19.92	Frankie Fredericks, Namibia (W)	2-18-96	Liévin, France
	20.40	Jeff Williams (A)	2-18-96	Liévin, France
400 meters	44.63	Michael Johnson (W, A)	3-4-95	Atlanta
800 meters	1:42.67	Wilson Kipketer, Denmark (W)	3-9-97	Paris
	1:45.00	Johnny Gray (A)	3-8-92	Sindelfingen, Germany
1,000 meters	2:15.26	Noureddine Morceli, Algeria (W)	2-22-92	Birmingham, England
	2:18.19	Ocky Clark (A)	2-12-89	Stuttgart
1,500 meters	3:31.17	Hicham El Guerrouj, Morocco (W)	2-02-97	Stuttgart
	3:38.12	Jeff Atkinson (A)	3-5-89	Budapest
Mile	3:48.45	Hicham El Guerrouj, Morocco (W)	2-12-97	Ghent, Belgium
	3:51.8	Steve Scott (A)	2-20-81	San Diego

Men (Cont.)

Event	Mark	Record Holder	Date	Site
3,000 meters	7:24.90	Daniel Komen, Kenya (W)	2-6-98	Budapest
	7:39.94	Steve Scott (A)	2-10-89	East Rutherford, NJ
5,000 meters	12:51.48	Daniel Komen, Kenya (W)	2-19-98	Stockholm
	13:20.55	Doug Padilla (A)	2-12-82	New York City
50-meter hurdles	6.25	Mark McKoy, Canada (W)	3-5-86	Kobe, Japan
	6.35	Greg Foster (A)	1-27-85	Rosemont, Illinois
	6.35	Greg Foster (A)	1-31-87	Ottawa, Ontario
55-meter hurdles*	6.89	Renaldo Nehemiah (A)	1-20-79	New York City
60-meter hurdles	7.30	Colin Jackson, Great Britain (W)	3-6-94	Sindelfingen, Germany
	7.36	Greg Foster (A)	1-16-87	Los Angeles
5,000-meter walk	18:07.08	Mikhail Shchennikov, Russia (W)	2-14-95	Moscow
	19:18.40	Tim Lewis (A)	3-7-87	Indianapolis
4x200-meter relay	1:22.11	Great Britain (W) (Linford Christie, Darren Braithwaite, Ade Mafe, John Regis)	3-3-91	Glasgow
	1:22.71	National Team (A) (Thomas Jefferson, Raymond Pierre, Antonio McKay Kevin Little)	3-3-91	Glasgow
4x400-meter relay	3:03.05	Germany (W) (Rico Lieder, Jens Carlowitz, Klaus Just, Thomas Schönlebe)	3-10-91	Seville
	3:03.24	National Team (A) (Raymond Pierre, Chip Jenkins, Andrew Valmon, Antonio McKay)	3-10-91	Seville
4x800-meter relay	7:17.8	Soviet Union (W) (Valeriy Taratynov, Stanislav Meshcherskikh, Aleksey Taranov, Viktor Semyashkin)	3-14-71	Sofia
	7:18.23	University of Florida (A) (Dedric Jones, Lewis Lacy, Stephen Adderly, Scott Peters)	3-14-92	Indianapolis
High jump	7 ft 11½ in	Javier Sotomayor, Cuba (W)	3-4-89	Budapest
	7 ft 10½ in	Hollis Conway (A)	3-10-91	Seville
Pole vault	20 ft 2 in	Sergei Bubka, Ukraine (W)	2-21-93	Donetsk, Ukraine
	19 ft 3¾ in	Billy Olsen (A)	1-25-86	Albuquerque
Long jump	28 ft 10¼ in	Carl Lewis (W, A)	1-27-84	New York City
Triple jump	58 ft 6 in	Aliecer Urritia (W)	3-1-97	Sindelfingen, Germany
	58 ft 3¼ in	Mike Conley (A)	2-27-87	New York City
Shot put	74 ft 4¼ in	Randy Barnes (W, A)	1-20-89	Los Angeles
Weight throw	84 ft 10¼ in	Lance Deal (W, A)	3-4-95	Atlanta
Pentathlon	4478 pts	Steve Fritz, United States (W, A)	1-14-95	Lawrence, KS
Heptathlon	6476 pts	Dan O'Brien (W, A)	3-13/14-93	Toronto

*No recognized world record.

Farewell to JJK

The ideal athlete as inspiration has been so beaten up by scandal, greed and lethargy that it is popular to say that a) all athletes are selfish, irresponsible millionaires and b) they always were, minus the millionaire part. It's hip to be cynical.

Then there is Jackie Joyner-Kersee, who on Saturday, August 1, 1998, at a track meet in Edwardsville, Ill., not far from her hometown of East St. Louis, competed for the last time, in a long jump that was largely ceremonial. Her retirement at age 36 ended an 18-year career in which she took part in four Olympics and won three gold medals set the world record in the long jump, and still holds the world record in the heptathlon.

Yet the measure of Joyner-Kersee's greatness came not from a stopwatch or the infernal charts that score the heptathlon. A fuller gauge was the

purity of her efforts, which seemed so often to rise from her soul, and the impact she made on her sport and on women. Her best qualities were on display in her last serious meet, the Goodwill Games heptathlon on July 21 and 22. Far past her prime and only modestly fit, Joyner-Kersee won with a courageous run in the 800 meters, the hep's final event, and one that she has always despised and feared. She cried at the finish, and her ever-present husband-coach, Bobby Kersee, cried even harder. "I can't believe it's over," he said.

It's common in this country to extol the rise of women's sports in the '90s, what with the birth of two pro basketball leagues and U.S. Olympic golds in women's hockey, soccer and softball. For all that, a debt is owed Joyner-Kersee, who helped make it cool for girls to play boys' games and play them hard.

Women

Event	Mark	Record Holder	Date	Site
50 meters	5.96	Irina Privolova, Russia (W)	2-9-95	Madrid
	6.02	Gwen Torrence (A)	2-9-96	Reno, NV
55 meters*	6.56	Gwen Torrence (A)	3-14-87	Oklahoma City
60 meters	6.92	Irina Privalova, Russia (W)	2-11-93	Madrid
	6.92	Irina Privalova, Russia (W)	2-9-95	Madrid
	6.95	Gail Devers (A)	3-12-93	Toronto
	6.95	Marion Jones (A)	3-7-98	Maebashi, Japan
200 meters	21.87	Merlene Ottey, Jamaica (W)	2-13-93	Liévin, France
	22.33	Gwen Torrence (A)	3-2-96	Atlanta
400 meters	49.59	Jarmila Kratochvilová, Czech.(W)	3-7-82	Milan
	50.64	Diane Dixon (A)	3-10-91	Seville
800 meters	1:56.36	Maria Mutola, Mozambique (W)	2-22-98	Liévin, France
	1:58.9	Mary Slaney (A)	2-22-80	San Diego
1,000 meters	2:31.23	Maria Mutola, Mozambique (W)	2-25-96	Stockholm
	2:37.60	Mary Slaney (A)	1-21-89	Portland
1,500 meters	4:00.27	Doina Melinte, Romania (W)	2-9-90	East Rutherford, NJ
	4:00.80	Mary Slaney (A)	2-8-80	New York City
Mile	4:17.14	Doina Melinte, Romania (W)	2-9-90	East Rutherford, NJ
	4:20.5	Mary Slaney (A)	2-19-82	San Diego
3,000 meters	8:33.82	Elly van Hulst, Netherlands (W)	3-4-89	Budapest
	8:40.45	Lynn Jennings (A)	2-23-90	New York City
5,000 meters	15:03.17	Liz McColgan, Scotland (W)	2-22-92	Birmingham, England
	15:22.64	Lynn Jennings (A)	1-7-90	Hanover, NH
50-meter hurdles	6.58	Cornelia Oschkenat, E Germany (W)	2-20-88	Berlin
	6.67	Jackie Joyner-Kersee (A)	2-10-95	Reno, NV
55-meter hurdles*	7.30	Tiffany Lott (A)	2-20-97	Air Force Academy
60-meter hurdles	7.69	Lyudmila Narozhilenko, Russia (W)	2-4-90	Chelyabinsk, Russia
	7.81	Jackie Joyner-Kersee (A)	2-5-89	Fairfax, VA
3,000-meter walk	11:44.00	Yelena Ivanova, CIS (W)	2-7-92	Moscow
	12:20.79	Debbi Lawrence (A)	3-12-93	Toronto
4x200-meter relay	1:32.55	SC Eintracht Hamm, W Gernany (W) (Helga Arendt, Silke-Beate Knoll, Mechthild Kluth, Gisela Kinzel)	2-20-88	Dortmund, W Germany
	1:33.24	National Team (A) (Flirtisha Harris, Chryste Gaines, Terri Dendy, Michele Collins)	2-12-94	Glasgow
4x400-meter relay	3:27.22	Germany (W) (Sandra Seuser, Annett Hesselbarth, Katrin Schreiter, Grit Breuer)	3-10-91	Seville
	3:29.00	National Team (A) (Terri Dendy, Lillie Leatherwood, Jearl Miles, Diane Dixon)	3-10-91	Seville
4x800-meter relay	8:18.71	Russia (W) (Natalya Zaytseva, Olga Kuvnetsova, Yelena Afanasyeva, Yekaterina Podkopayeva)	2-4-94	Moscow
	8:25.50	Villanova (A) (Gina Procaccio, Debbie Grant, Michelle DiMuro, Celeste Halliday)	2-7-87	Gainesville, FL
High jump	6 ft 9½ in	Heike Henkel, Germany (W)	2-8-92	Karlsruhe, Germany
	6 ft 7 in	Tisha Walker (A)	2-28-98	Atlanta
Pole vault	14 ft 11 in	Emma George, Australia (W)	3-26-98	Adelaide, Australia
	14 ft 8¼ in	Stacy Draglia (A)	3-8-98	Sindelfinden, Germany
Long jump	24 ft 2¼ in	Heike Drechsler, E Germany (W)	2-13-88	Vienna
	23 ft 4¾ in	Jackie Joyner-Kersee (A)	3-5-94	Atlanta
Triple jump	49 ft 9 in	Ashia Hansen, Great Britain (W)	2-28-95	Valencia, Spain
	46 ft 8¼ in	Sheila Hudson-Strudwick (A)	3-4-95	Atlanta
Shot put	73 ft 10 in	Helena Fibingerová, Czech. (W)	2-19-77	Jablonec, Czech.
	65 ft ¾ in	Ramona Pagel (A)	2-20-87	Inglewood, CA
Weight throw*	75 ft 2⅛ in	Dawn Ellerbe (W, A)	1-16-98	Laramie, WY
Pentathlon	4991 pts	Irina Byelova, CIS (W)	2-14/15-92	Berlin
	4632 pts	Kym Carter (A)	3-10-95	Barcelona

*No recognized world record.

World Track and Field Championships

Historically, the Olympics have served as the outdoor world championships for track and field. In 1983 the International Amateur Athletic Federation (IAAF) instituted a separate World Championship meet, to be held every 4 years between the Olympics. The first was held in Helsinki in 1983, the second in Rome in 1987, the third in Tokyo in 1991, the fourth in Stuttgart, Germany, in 1993, the fifth in Göteborg, Sweden, in 1995 and the sixth in Athens in 1997. In 1993 the IAAF began to hold the meet on a biennial basis.

Men

100 METERS

1983	Carl Lewis, United States	10.07
1987*	Carl Lewis, United States	9.93 WR
1991	Carl Lewis, United States	9.86 WR
1993	Linford Christie, Great Britain	9.87
1995	Donovan Bailey, Canada	9.97
1997	Maurice Greene, United States	9.86

200 METERS

1983	Calvin Smith, United States	20.14
1987	Calvin Smith United States	20.16
1991	Michael Johnson, United States	20.01
1993	Frank Fredericks, Namibia	19.85
1995	Michael Johnson, United States	19.79
1997	Ato Boldon, Trinidad	20.04

400 METERS

1983	Bert Cameron, Jamaica	45.05
1987	Thomas Schoenlebe, E Germany	44.33
1991	Antonio Pettigrew, United States	44.57
1993	Michael Johnson, United States	43.65
1995	Michael Johnson, United States	43.39
1997	Michael Johnson, United States	44.12

800 METERS

1983	Willi Wulbeck, W Germany	1:43.65
1987	Billy Konchellah, Kenya	1:43.06
1991	Billy Konchellah, Kenya	1:43.99
1993	Paul Ruto, Kenya	1:44.71
1995	Wilson Kipketer, Denmark	1:45.08
1997	Wilson Kipketer, Denmark	1:43.38

1500 METERS

1983	Steve Cram, Great Britain	3:41.59
1987	Abdi Bile, Somalia	3:36.80
1991	Noureddine Morceli, Algeria	3:32.84
1993	Noureddine Morceli, Algeria	3:34.24
1995	Noureddine Morceli, Algeria	3:33.73
1997	Hicham El Guerroj, Morocco	3:35.83

STEEPLECHASE

1983	Patriz Ilg, W Germany	8:15.06
1987	Francesco Panetta, Italy	8:08.57
1991	Moses Kiptanui, Kenya	8:12.59
1993	Moses Kiptanui, Kenya	8:06.36
1995	Moses Kiptanui, Kenya	8:04.16
1997	Wilson Boit Kipketer, Kenya	8:05.84

5000 METERS

1983	Eamonn Coghlan, Ireland	13:28.53
1987	Said Aouita, Morocco	13:26.44
1991	Yobes Ondieki, Kenya	13:14.45
1993	Ismael Kirui, Kenya	13:02.75
1995	Ismael Kirui, Kenya	13:16.77
1997	Daniel Komen, Kenya	13:07.38

10,000 METERS

1983	Alberto Cova, Italy	28:01.04
1987	Paul Kipkoech, Kenya	27:38.63
1991	Moses Tanui, Kenya	27:38.74
1993	Haile Gebrselassie, Ethiopia	27:46.02
1995	Haile Gebrselassie, Ethiopia	27:12.95
1997	Haile Gebrselassie, Ethiopia	27:24.58

MARATHON

1983	Rob de Castella, Australia	2:10:03
1987	Douglas Wakiihuri, Kenya	2:11:48
1991	Hiromi Taniguchi, Japan	2:14:57
1993	Mark Plaatjes, United States	2:13:57
1995	Martín Fiz, Spain	2:11:41
1997	Abel Anton, Spain	2:13:16

110-METER HURDLES

1983	Greg Foster, United States	13.42
1987	Greg Foster, United States	13.21
1991	Greg Foster, United States	13.06
1993	Colin Jackson, Great Britain	12.91 WR
1995	Allen Johnson, United States	13.00
1997	Allen Johnson, United States	12.93

400-METER HURDLES

1983	Edwin Moses, United States	47.50
1987	Edwin Moses, United States	47.46
1991	Samuel Matete, Zambia	47.64
1993	Kevin Young, United States	47.18
1995	Derrick Adkins, United States	47.98
1997	Stéphane Diagana, France	47.70

20-KILOMETER WALK

1983	Ernesto Canto, Mexico	1:20:49
1987	Maurizio Damilano, Italy	1:20:45
1991	Maurizio Damilano, Italy	1:19:37
1993	Valentin Massana, Spain	1:22:31
1995	Michele Didoni, Italy	1:19:59
1997	Daniel Garcia, Mexico	1:21:43

50-KILOMETER WALK

1983	Ronald Weigel, E Germany	3:43:08
1987	Hartwig Gauder, E Germany	3:40:53
1991	Aleksandr Potashov, USSR	3:53:09
1993	Jesus Angel Garcia, Spain	3:41:41
1995	Valentin Kononen, Finland	3:43:42
1997	Robert Korzeniowski, Poland	3:44:46

4 X 100 METER RELAY

1983	United States (Emmit King, Willie Gault, Calvin Smith, Carl Lewis)	37.86
1987	United States (Lee McRae, Lee McNeil, Harvey Glance, Carl Lewis)	37.90
1991	United States (Andre Cason Leroy Burrell, Dennis Mitchell Carl Lewis)	37.50 WR
1993	United States (Jon Drummond, Andre Cason, Dennis Mitchell, Leroy Burrell)	37.48
1995	Canada (Robert Esmie, Glenroy Gilbert, Bruny Surin, Donovan Bailey)	38.31
1997	Canada (Robert Esmie, Glenroy Gilbert, Bruny Surin, Donovan Bailey)	37.86

WR=World record.   *Ben Johnson, Canada, disqualified.

Men (Cont.)

4 X 400 METER RELAY

1983	USSR (Sergei Lovachev, Alecksandr Troschilo, Nikolay Chernyetski, Viktor Markin)	3:00.79
1987	United States (Danny Everett Rod Haley, Antonio McKay, Butch Reynolds)	2:57.29
1991	Great Britain (Roger Black Derek Redmond, John Regis, Kriss Akabusi)	2:57.53
1993	United States (Andrew Valmon, Quincy Watts, Butch Reynolds, Michael Johnson)	2:54.29 WR
1995	United States (Marlon Ramsey, Derek Mills, Butch Reynolds, Michael Johnson)	2:57.32
1997	United States (Jerome Young, Antonio Pettigrew, Chris Jones, Tyree Washington)	2:56.47

HIGH JUMP

1983	Gennadi Avdeyenko, USSR	7 ft 7¼ in
1987	Patrik Sjoberg, Sweden	7 ft 9¾ in
1991	Charles Austin, United States	7 ft 9¾ in
1993	Javier Sotomayor, Cuba	7 ft 10½ in
1995	Troy Kemp, Bahamas	7 ft 9¼ in
1997	Javier Sotomayor	7 ft 9¼ in

POLE VAULT

1983	Sergei Bubka, USSR	18 ft 8¼ in
1987	Sergei Bubka, USSR	19 ft 2¼ in
1991	Sergei Bubka, USSR	19 ft 6¼ in
1993	Sergei Bubka, Ukraine	19 ft 8¼ in
1995	Sergei Bubka, Ukraine	19 ft 5 in
1997	Sergei Bubka, Ukraine	19 ft 8½ in

LONG JUMP

1983	Carl Lewis, United States	28 ft ¾ in
1987	Carl Lewis, United States	28 ft 5¼ in
1991	Mike Powell, U.S.	29 ft 4½ in WR
1993	Mike Powell, United States	28 ft 2¼ in
1995	Ivan Pedroso, Cuba	28 ft 6½ in
1997	Ivan Pedroso, Cuba	27 ft 7½ in

TRIPLE JUMP

1983	Zdzislaw Hoffmann, Poland	57 ft 2 in
1987	Khristo Markov, Bulgaria	58 ft 9 ½ in
1991	Kenny Harrison, United States	58 ft 4 in
1993	Mike Conley, United States	58 ft 7¼ in
1995	Jonathan Edwards, G.B.	60 ft ¼ in WR
1997	Yoelvis Quesada, Cuba	58 ft 6¾ in

SHOT PUT

1983	Edward Sarul, Poland	70 ft 2¼ in
1987	Werner Günthör, Switzerland	72 ft 11¼ in
1991	Werner Günthör, Switzerland	71 ft 1¼ in
1993	Werner Günthör, Switzerland	72 ft 1 in
1995	John Godina, United States	70 ft 5¼ in
1997	John Godina, United States	70 ft 4¼ in

DISCUS THROW

1983	Imrich Bugar, Czech.	222 ft 2 in
1987	Juergen Schult, E Germany	225 ft 6 in
1991	Lars Riedel, Germany	217 ft 2 in
1993	Lars Riedel, Germany	222 ft 2 in
1995	Lars Riedel, Germany	225 ft 7 in
1997	Lars Riedel, Germany	224 ft 10 in

HAMMER THROW

1983	Sergei Litvinov, USSR	271 ft 3 in
1987	Sergei Litvinov, USSR	272 ft 6 in
1991	Yuriy Sedykh, USSR	268 ft
1993	Andrey Abduvaliyev, Tajikistan	267 ft 10 in
1995	Andrey Abduvaliyev, Tajikistan	267 ft 7 in
1997	Heinz Weis, Germany	268 ft 4 in

JAVELIN THROW

1983	Detlef Michel, E Germany	293 ft 7 in
1987	Seppo Räty, Finland	274 ft 1 in
1991	Kimmo Kinnunen, Finland	297 ft 11 in
1993	Jan Zelezny, Czech Republic	282 ft 1 in
1995	Jan Zelezny, Czech Republic	293 ft 11 in
1997	Marius Corbett, South Africa	290 ft 0 in

DECATHLON

1983	Daley Thompson, G Britain	8666 pts
1987	Torsten Voss, E Germany	8680 pts
1991	Dan O'Brien, United States	8812 pts
1993	Dan O'Brien, United States	8817 pts
1995	Dan O'Brien, United States	8695 pts
1997	Tomás Dvorák, Czech Rep.	8837 pts

Women

100 METERS

1983	Marlies Gohr, E Germany	10.97
1987	Silke Gladisch, E Germany	10.90
1991	Katrin Krabbe, Germany	10.99
1993	Gail Devers, United States	10.82
1995	Gwen Torrence, United States	10.85
1997	Marion Jones, United States	10.83

200 METERS

1983	Marita Koch, E Germany	22.13
1987	Silke Gladisch, E Germany	21.74
1991	Katrin Krabbe, Germany	22.09
1993	Merlene Ottey, Jamaica	21.98
1995	Merlene Ottey, Jamaica	22.12
1997	Zhanna Pintusevich, Ukraine	22.32

400 METERS

1983	Jarmila Kratochvilova, Czech.	47.99
1987	Olga Bryzgina, USSR	49.38
1991	Marie-José Pérec, France	49.13
1993	Jearl Miles, United States	49.82
1995	Marie-José Pérec, France	49.28
1997	Cathy Freeman, Australia	49.77

800 METERS

1983	Jarmila Kratochvilova, Czech.	1:54.68
1987	Sigrun Wodars, E Germany	1:55.26
1991	Lilia Nurutdinova, USSR	1:57.50
1993	Maria Mutola, Mozambique	1:55.43
1995	Ana Quirot, Cuba	1:56.11
1997	Ana Quirot, Cuba	1:57.14

WR=World record.　* Contested at 5,000 meters in 1995.

Women (Cont.)

1500 METERS

1983	Mary Slaney, United States	4:00.90
1987	Tatyana Samolenko, USSR	3:58.56
1991	Hassiba Boulmerka, Algeria	4:02.21
1993	Dong Liu, China	4:00.50
1995	Hassiba Boulmerka, Algeria	4:02.42
1997	Carla Sacramento, Portugal	4:04.24

3000 METERS*

1983	Mary Slaney, United States	8:34.62
1987	Tatyana Samolenko, USSR	8:38.73
1991	Tatyana Dorovskikh, USSR	8:35.82
1993	Qu Yunxia, China	8:28.71
1995	Sonia O'Sullivan, Ireland	14:46.47
1997	Gabriela Szabo, Romania	14:57.68

10,000 METERS

1987	Ingrid Kristiansen, Norway	31:05.85
1991	Liz McColgan, Great Britain	31:14.31
1993	Wang Junxia, China	30:49:30
1995	Fernanda Ribeiro, Portugal	31:04.99
1997	Sally Barsosio, Kenya	31:32.92

MARATHON

1983	Grete Waitz, Norway	2:28:09
1987	Rosa Mota, Portugal	2:25:17
1991	Wanda Panfil, Poland	2:29:53
1993	Junko Asari, Japan	2:30:03
1995	Manuela Machado, Portugal	2:25:39*
1997	Hiromi Suzuki, Japan	2:29.48

100-METER HURDLES

1983	Bettine Jahn, E Germany	12.35
1987	Ginka Zagorcheva, Bulgaria	12.34
1991	Lyudmila Narozhilenko, USSR	12.59
1993	Gail Devers, United States	12.46
1995	Gail Devers, United States	12.68
1997	Ludmila Engquist, Sweden	12.50

400-METER HURDLES

1983	Yekaterina Fesenko, USSR	54.14
1987	Sabine Busch, E Germany	53.62
1991	Tatyana Ledovskaya, USSR	53.11
1993	Sally Gunnell, Great Britain	52.74 WR
1995	Kim Batten, United States	52.61
1997	Nezha Bidouane, Morocco	52.97

10-KILOMETER WALK

1987	Irina Strakhova, USSR	44:12
1991	Alina Ivanova, USSR	42:57
1993	Sari Essayah, Finland	42:59
1995	Irina Stankina, Russia	42:13
1997	Annarita Sidoti, Italy	42:56

4 X 100 METER RELAY

1983	East Germany (Silke Gladisch, Marita Koch, Ingrid Auerswald, Marlies Gohr)	41.76
1987	United States (Alice Brown, Diane Williams, Florence Griffith, Pam Marshall)	41.58
1991	Jamaica (Dalia Duhaney, Juliet Cuthbert, Beverley McDonald, Merlene Ottey)	41.94
1993	Russia (Olga Bogoslovskaya, Galina Malchugina, Natalya Voronova, Irina Privalova)	41.49

4 X 100 METER RELAY *(CONT.)*

1995	United States (Celena Mondie-Milner, Carlette Guidry, Chryste Gaines, Gwen Torrence)	42.12
1997	United States (Chryste Gaines, Marion Jones, Inger Miller, Gail Devers)	41.47

4 X 400 METER RELAY

1983	East Germany (Kerstin Walther, Sabine Busch, Marita Koch, Dagmar Rubsam)	3:19.73
1987	E Germany (Dagmar Neubauer, Kirsten Emmelmann, Petra Müller, Sabine Busch)	3:18.63
1991	USSR (Tatyana Ledovskaya, Lyudmila Dzhigalova, Olga Nazarova, Olga Bryzgina)	3:18.43
1993	United States (Gwen Torrence, Maicel Malone, Natasha Kaiser-Brown, Jearl Miles)	3:16.71
1995	United States (Kim Graham, Rochelle Stevens, Camara Jones, Jearl Miles)	3:22.39
1997	Germany (Anke Feller, Uta Rohlander, Anja Rucker, Grit Breuer)	3:20.92

HIGH JUMP

1983	Tamara Bykova, USSR	6 ft 7 in
1987	Stefka Kostadinova, Bulgaria	6 ft 10¼ in
1991	Heike Henkel, Germany	6 ft 8¾ in
1993	Ioamnet Quintero, Cuba	6 ft 6¼ in
1995	Stefka Kostadinova, Bulgaria	6 ft 7 in
1997	Hanne Haugland, Norway	6 ft 6¼ in

LONG JUMP

1983	Heike Daute, E Germany	23 ft 10¼ in
1987	Jackie Joyner-Kersee, U.S.	24 ft 1¾ in
1991	Jackie Joyner-Kersee, U.S.	24 ft ¼ in
1993	Heike Drechsler, Germany	23 ft 4 in
1995	Fiona May, Italy	22 ft 10¾ in w
1997	Lyudmila Galkina, Russia	23 ft 1¾ in

TRIPLE JUMP

1993	Ana Biryukova, Russia	49 ft 6 ¼ in WR
1995	Inessa Kravets, Ukraine	50 ft 10¼ in WR
1997	S. Kasparkova, Czech Rep.	49 ft 10½ in

SHOT PUT

1983	Helena Fibingerova, Czech.	69 ft ¾ in
1987	Natalya Lisovskaya, USSR	69 ft 8¼ in
1991	Zhihong Huang, China	68 ft 4¼ in
1993	Zhihong Huang, China	67 ft 6 in
1995	Astrid Kumbernuss, Germany	69 ft 7½ in
1997	Astrid Kumbernuss, Germany	67 ft 11½ in

DISCUS THROW

1983	Martina Opitz, E Germany	226 ft 2 in
1987	Martina Hellmann, E Germany	235 ft
1991	Tsvetanka Khristova, Bulgaria	233 ft
1993	Olga Burova, Russia	221 ft 1 in
1995	Ellina Zvereva, Belarus	225 ft 2 in
1997	Beatrice Faumuina, New Zeal.	219 ft 3 in

WR=World record. *400 meters short.

World Track and Field Championships *(Cont.)*

Women *(Cont.)*

JAVELIN THROW

1983..............Tiina Lillak, Finland	232 ft 4 in
1987..............Fatima Whitbread, G Britain	251 ft 5 in
1991..............Demei Xu, China	225 ft 8 in
1993..............Trine Hattestad, Finland	227 ft
1995..............Natalya Shikolenko, Belarus	221 ft 8 in
1997..............Trine Hattestad, Norway	225 ft 8 in

HEPTATHLON

1983..............Ramona Neubert, E Germany	6714 pts
1987..............Jackie Joyner-Kersee, U.S.	7128 pts
1991..............Sabine Braun, Germany	6672 pts
1993..............Jackie Joyner-Kersee, U.S.	6837 pts
1995..............Ghada Shouaa, Syria	6651 pts
1997..............Sabine Braun, Germany	6739 pts

Track and Field News Athlete of the Year

Each year (since 1959 for men and since 1974 for women) Track & Field News has chosen the outstanding athlete in the sport.

Men

Year	Athlete	Event
1959	Martin Lauer, West Germany	110-meter hurdles/Decathlon
1960	Rafer Johnson, United States	Decathlon
1961	Ralph Boston, United States	Long jump
1962	Peter Snell, New Zealand	800/1,500 meters
1963	C. K. Yang, Taiwan	Decathlon/Pole vault
1964	Peter Snell, New Zealand	800/1,500 meters
1965	Ron Clarke, Australia	5,000/10,000 meters
1966	Jim Ryun, United States	800/1,500 meters
1967	Jim Ryun, United States	1500 meters
1968	Bob Beamon, United States	Long jump
1969	Bill Toomey, United States	Decathlon
1970	Randy Matson, United States	Shot put
1971	Rod Milburn, United States	110-meter hurdles
1972	Lasse Viren, Finland	5,000/10,000 meters
1973	Ben Jipcho, Kenya	1,500/5,000 meters/Steeplechase
1974	Rick Wohlhuter, United States	800/1,500 meters
1975	John Walker, New Zealand	800/1,500 meters
1976	Alberto Juantorena, Cuba	400/800 meters
1977	Alberto Juantorena, Cuba	400/800 meters
1978	Henry Rono, Kenya	5,000/10,000 meters/Steeplechase
1979	Sebastian Coe, Great Britain	800/1,500 meters
1980	Edwin Moses, United States	400-meter hurdles
1981	Sebastian Coe, Great Britain	800/1500 meters
1982	Carl Lewis, United States	100/200 meters/Long jump
1983	Carl Lewis, United States	100/200 meters/Long jump
1984	Carl Lewis, United States	100/200 meters/Long jump
1985	Said Aouita, Morocco	1,500/5,000 meters
1986	Yuri Syedikh, USSR	Hammer throw
1987	Ben Johnson, Canada	100 meters
1988	Sergei Bubka, USSR	Pole vault
1989	Roger Kingdom, United States	110-meter hurdles
1990	Michael Johnson, United States	200/400 meters
1991	Sergei Bubka, CIS	Pole vault
1992	Kevin Young, United States	400-meter hurdles
1993	Noureddine Morceli, Algeria	1,500/mile/3,000
1994	Noureddine Morceli, Algeria	1,500/mile/3,000/5,000
1995	Haile Gebrselassie, Ethiopia	5,000/10,000
1996	Michael Johnson, United States	200/400 meters
1997	Wilson Kipketer, Denmark	800 meters

Women

Year	Athlete	Event
1974	Irena Szewinska, Poland	100/200/400 meters
1975	Faina Melnik, USSR	Shot put/Discus
1976	Tatyana Kazankina, USSR	800/1,500 meters
1977	Rosemarie Ackermann, East Germany	High jump
1978	Marita Koch, East Germany	100/200/400 meters
1979	Marita Koch, East Germany	100/200/400 meters
1980	Ilona Briesenick, East Germany	Shot put
1981	Evelyn Ashford, United States	100/200 meters
1982	Marita Koch, East Germany	100/200/400 meters
1983	Jarmila Kratochvilova, Czechoslovakia	200/400/800 meters

Women *(Cont.)*

Year	Athlete	Event
1984	Evelyn Ashford, United States	100 meters
1985	Marita Koch, East Germany	100/200/400 meters
1986	Jackie Joyner-Kersee, United States	Long jump/Heptathlon
1987	Jackie Joyner-Kersee, United States	100-meter hurdles/Long jump/Heptathlon
1988	Florence Griffith Joyner, United States	100/200 meters
1989	Ana Quirot, Cuba	400/800 meters
1990	Merlene Ottey, Jamaica	100/200 meters
1991	Heike Henkel, Germany	High jump
1992	Heike Drechsler, Germany	Long Jump
1993	Wang Junxia, China	1,500/3,000/10,000/marathon
1994	Jackie Joyner-Kersee, United States	100-meter hurdles/Long jump/Heptathlon
1995	Sonia O'Sullivan, Ireland	1,500/3,000/5,000
1996	Svetlana Masterkova, Russia	800/1,500
1997	Marion Jones, United States	100/200 meters

Marathon World Record Progression

Men

Record Holder	Time	Date	Site
John Hayes, United States	2:55:18.4	7-24-08	Shepherd's Bush, London
Robert Fowler, United States	2:52:45.4	1-1-09	Yonkers, NY
James Clark, United States	2:46:52.6	2-12-09	New York City
Albert Raines, United States	2:46:04.6	5-8-09	New York City
Frederick Barrett, Great Britain	2:42:31	5-26-09	Shepherd's Bush, London
Harry Green, Great Britain	2:38:16.2	5-12-13	Shepherd's Bush, London
Alexis Ahlgren, Sweden	2:36:06.6	5-31-13	Shepherd's Bush, London
Johannes Kolehmainen, Finland	2:32:35.8	8-22-20	Antwerp, Belgium
Albert Michelsen, United States	2:29:01.8	10-12-25	Port Chester, NY
Fusashige Suzuki, Japan	2:27:49	3-31-35	Tokyo
Yasuo Ikenaka, Japan	2:26:44	4-3-35	Tokyo
Kitei Son, Japan	2:26:42	11-3-35	Tokyo
Yun Bok Suh, Korea	2:25:39	4-19-47	Boston
James Peters, Great Britain	2:20:42.2	6-14-52	Chiswick, England
James Peters, Great Britain	2:18:40.2	6-13-53	Chiswick, England
James Peters, Great Britain	2:18:34.8	10-4-53	Turku, Finland
James Peters, Great Britain	2:17:39.4	6-26-54	Chiswick, England
Sergei Popov, USSR	2:15:17	8-24-58	Stockholm
Abebe Bikila, Ethiopia	2:15:16.2	9-10-60	Rome
Toru Terasawa, Japan	2:15:15.8	2-17-63	Beppu, Japan
Leonard Edelen, United States	2:14:28	6-15-63	Chiswick, England
Basil Heatley, Great Britain	2:13:55	6-13-64	Chiswick, England
Abebe Bikila, Ethiopia	2:12:11.2	6-21-64	Tokyo
Morio Shigematsu, Japan	2:12:00	6-12-65	Chiswick, England
Derek Clayton, Australia	2:09:36.4	12-3-67	Fukuoka, Japan
Derek Clayton, Australia	2:08:33.6	5-30-69	Antwerp, Belgium
Rob de Castella, Australia	2:08:18	12-6-81	Fukuoka, Japan
Steve Jones, Great Britain	2:08:05	10-21-84	Chicago
Carlos Lopes, Portugal	2:07:12	4-20-85	Rotterdam, Netherlands
Belayneh Dinsamo, Ethiopia	2:06:50	4-17-88	Rotterdam, Netherlands

Women

Record Holder	Time	Date	Site
Dale Greig, Great Britain	3:27:45	5-23-64	Ryde, England
Mildred Simpson, New Zealand	3:19:33	7-21-64	Auckland, New Zealand
Maureen Wilton, Canada	3:15:22	5-6-67	Toronto
Anni Pede-Erdkamp, West Germany	3:07:26	9-16-67	Waldniel, West Germany
Caroline Walker, United States	3:02:53	2-28-70	Seaside, OR
Elizabeth Bonner, United States	3:01:42	5-9-71	Philadelphia
Adrienne Beames, Australia	2:46:30	8-31-71	Werribee, Australia
Chantal Langlace, France	2:46:24	10-27-74	Neuf Brisach, France
Jacqueline Hansen, United States	2:43:54.5	12-1-74	Culver City, CA
Liane Winter, West Germany	2:42:24	4-21-75	Boston
Christa Vahlensieck, West Germany	2:40:15.8	5-3-75	Dülmen, West Germany
Jacqueline Hansen, United States	2:38:19	10-12-75	Eugene, OR

Women *(Cont.)*

Record Holder	Time	Date	Site
Chantal Langlace, France	2:35:15.4	5-1-77	Oyarzun, France
Christa Vahlensieck, West Germany	2:34:47.5	9-10-77	West Berlin, West Germany
Grete Waitz, Norway	2:32:29.9	10-22-78	New York City
Grete Waitz, Norway	2:27:32.6	10-21-79	New York City
Grete Waitz, Norway	2:25:41.3	10-26-80	New York City
Grete Waitz, Norway	2:25:29	4-17-83	London
Joan Benoit Samuelson, United States	2:22:43	4-18-83	Boston
Ingrid Kristiansen, Norway	2:21:06	4-21-85	London
Tegla Loroupe, Kenya	2:20:47	4-19-98	Rotterdam, Netherlands

Boston Marathon

The Boston Marathon began in 1897 as a local Patriot's Day event. Run every year but 1918 since then, it has grown into one of the world's premier marathons.

Men

Year	Winner	Time	Year	Winner	Time
1897	John J. McDermott, United States	2:55:10	1948	Gerard Cote, Canada	2:31:02
1898	Ronald J. McDonald, United States	2:42:00	1949	Karl Gosta Leandersson, Sweden	2:31:50
1899	Lawrence J. Brignolia, United States	2:54:38	1950	Kee Yong Ham, Korea	2:32:39
1900	James J. Caffrey, Canada	2:39:44	1951	Shigeki Tanaka, Japan	2:27:45
1901	James J. Caffrey, Canada	2:29:23	1952	Doroteo Flores, Guatemala	2:31:53
1902	Sammy Mellor, United States	2:43:12	1953	Keizo Yamada, Japan	2:18:51
1903	John C. Lorden, United States	2:41:29	1954	Veikko Karvonen, Finland	2:20:39
1904	Michael Spring, United States	2:38:04	1955	Hideo Hamamura, Japan	2:18:22
1905	Fred Lorz, United States	2:38:25	1956	Antti Viskari, Finland	2:14:14
1906	Timothy Ford, United States	2:45:45	1957	John J. Kelley, United States	2:20:05
1907	Tom Longboat, Canada	2:24:24	1958	Franjo Mihalic, Yugoslavia	2:25:54
1908	Thomas Morrissey, United States	2:25:43	1959	Eino Oksanen, Finland	2:22:42
1909	Henri Renaud, United States	2:53:36	1960	Paavo Kotila, Finland	2:20:54
1910	Fred Cameron, Canada	2:28:52	1961	Eino Oksanen, Finland	2:23:39
1911	Clarence H. DeMar, United States	2:21:39	1962	Eino Oksanen, Finland	2:23:48
1912	Mike Ryan, United States	2:21:18	1963	Aurele Vandendriessche, Belgium	2:18:58
1913	Fritz Carlson, United States	2:25:14	1964	Aurele Vandendriessche, Belgium	2:19:59
1914	James Duffy, Canada	2:25:01	1965	Morio Shigematsu, Japan	2:16:33
1915	Edouard Fabre, Canada	2:31:41	1966	Kenji Kimihara, Japan	2:17:11
1916	Arthur Roth, United States	2:27:16	1967	David McKenzie, New Zealand	2:15:45
1917	Bill Kennedy, United States	2:28:37	1968	Amby Burfoot, United States	2:22:17
1918	No race		1969	Yoshiaki Unetani, Japan	2:13:49
1919	Carl Linder, United States	2:29:13	1970	Ron Hill, England	2:10:30
1920	Peter Trivoulidas, Greece	2:29:31	1971	Alvaro Mejia, Colombia	2:18:45
1921	Frank Zuna, United States	2:18:57	1972	Olavi Suomalainen, Finland	2:15:39
1922	Clarence H. DeMar, United States	2:18:10	1973	Jon Anderson, United States	2:16:03
1923	Clarence H. DeMar, United States	2:23:37	1974	Neil Cusack, Ireland	2:13:39
1924	Clarence H. DeMar, United States	2:29:40	1975	Bill Rodgers, United States	2:09:55
1925	Chuck Mellor, United States	2:33:00	1976	Jack Fultz, United States	2:20:19
1926	John C. Miles, Canada	2:25:40	1977	Jerome Drayton, Canada	2:14:46
1927	Clarence H. DeMar, United States	2:40:22	1978	Bill Rodgers, United States	2:10:13
1928	Clarence H. DeMar, United States	2:37:07	1979	Bill Rodgers, United States	2:09:27
1929	John C. Miles, Canada	2:33:08	1980	Bill Rodgers, United States	2:12:11
1930	Clarence H. DeMar, United States	2:34:48	1981	Toshihiko Seko, Japan	2:09:26
1931	James (Hinky) Henigan, United States	2:46:45	1982	Alberto Salazar, United States	2:08:52
1932	Paul de Bruyn, Germany	2:33:36	1983	Gregory A. Meyer, United States	2:09:00
1933	Leslie Pawson, United States	2:31:01	1984	Geoff Smith, England	2:10:34
1934	Dave Komonen, Canada	2:32:53	1985	Geoff Smith, England	2:14:05
1935	John A. Kelley, United States	2:32:07	1986	Rob de Castella, Australia	2:07:51
1936	Ellison M. (Tarzan) Brown, United States	2:33:40	1987	Toshihiko Seko, Japan	2:11:50
1937	Walter Young, Canada	2:33:20	1988	Ibrahim Hussein, Kenya	2:08:43
1938	Leslie Pawson, United States	2:35:34	1989	Abebe Mekonnen, Ethiopia	2:09:06
1939	Ellison M. (Tarzan) Brown, United States	2:28:51	1990	Gelindo Bordin, Italy	2:08:19
1940	Gerard Cote, Canada	2:28:28	1991	Ibrahim Hussein, Kenya	2:11:06
1941	Leslie Pawson, United States	2:30:38	1992	Ibrahim Hussein, Kenya	2:08:14
1942	Bernard Joseph Smith, United States	2:26:51	1993	Cosmas N'Deti, Kenya	2:09:33
1943	Gerard Cote, Canada	2:28:25	1994	Cosmas N'Deti, Kenya	2:07:15
1944	Gerard Cote, Canada	2:31:50	1995	Cosmas N'Deti, Kenya	2:09:22
1945	John A. Kelley, United States	2:30:40	1996	Moses Tanui, Kenya	2:09:16
1946	Stylianos Kyriakides, Greece	2:29:27	1997	Lameck Aguta, Kenya	2:10:34
1947	Yun Bok Suh, Korea	2:25:39	1998	Moses Tanui, Kenya	2:07:34

Boston Marathon (Cont.)

Women

Year	Winner	Time	Year	Winner	Time
1966...Roberta Gibb, United States		3:21:40*	1983...Joan Benoit, United States		2:22:43
1967...Roberta Gibb, United States		3:27:17*	1984...Lorraine Moller, New Zealand		2:29:28
1968...Roberta Gibb, United States		3:30:00*	1985...Lisa Larsen Weidenbach, United States		2:34:06
1969...Sara Mae Berman, United States		3:22:46*	1986...Ingrid Kristiansen, Norway		2:24:55
1970...Sara Mae Berman, United States		3:05:07*	1987...Rosa Mota, Portugal		2:25:21
1971...Sara Mae Berman, United States		3:08:30*	1988...Rosa Mota, Portugal		2:24:30
1972...Nina Kuscsik, United States		3:10:36	1989...Ingrid Kristiansen, Norway		2:24:33
1973...Jacqueline A. Hansen, United States		3:05:59	1990...Rosa Mota, Portugal		2:25:24
1974...Miki Gorman, United States		2:47:11	1991...Wanda Panfil, Poland		2:24:18
1975...Liane Winter, West Germany		2:42:24	1992...Olga Markova, Russia		2:23:43
1976...Kim Merritt, United States		2:47:10	1993...Olga Markova, Russia		2:25:27
1977...Miki Gorman, United States		2:48:33	1994...Uta Pippig, Germany		2:21:45
1978...Gayle Barron, United States		2:44:52	1995...Uta Pippig, Germany		2:25:11
1979...Joan Benoit, United States		2:35:15	1996...Uta Pippig, Germany		2:27:12
1980...Jacqueline Gareau, Canada		2:34:28	1997...Fatuma Roba, Ethiopia		2:26:23
1981...Allison Roe, New Zealand		2:26:46	1998...Fatuma Roba, Ethiopia		2:23:21
1982...Charlotte Teske, West Germany		2:29:33	*Unofficial.		

Note: Over the years the Boston course has varied in length. The distances have been 24 miles, 1232 yards (1897–1923); 26 miles, 209 yards (1924–1926); 26 miles 385 yards (1927–1952); and 25 miles, 958 yards (1953–1956). Since 1957, the course has been certified to be the standard marathon distance of 26 miles, 385 yards.

New York City Marathon

From 1970 through 1975 the New York City Marathon was a small local race run in the city's Central Park. In 1976 it was moved to the streets of New York's five boroughs. It has since become one of the biggest and most prestigious marathons in the world.

Men

Year	Winner	Time	Year	Winner	Time
1970...Gary Muhrcke, United States		2:31:38	1984...Orlando Pizzolato, Italy		2:14:53
1971...Norman Higgins, United States		2:22:54	1985...Orlando Pizzolato, Italy		2:11:34
1972...Sheldon Karlin, United States		2:27:52	1986...Gianni Poli, Italy		2:11:06
1973...Tom Fleming, United States		2:21:54	1987...Ibrahim Hussein, Kenya		2:11:01
1974...Norbert Sander, United States		2:26:30	1988...Steve Jones, Great Britain		2:08:20
1975...Tom Fleming, United States		2:19:27	1989...Juma Ikangaa, Tanzania		2:08:01
1976...Bill Rodgers, United States		2:10:10	1990...Douglas Wakiihuri, Kenya		2:12:39
1977...Bill Rodgers, United States		2:11:28	1991...Salvador Garcia, Mexico		2:09:28
1978...Bill Rodgers, United States		2:12:12	1992...Willie Mtolo, South Africa		2:09:29
1979...Bill Rodgers, United States		2:11:42	1993...Andres Espinosa, Mexico		2:10:04
1980...Alberto Salazar, United States		2:09:41	1994...German Silva, Mexico		2:11:21
1981...Alberto Salazar, United States		2:08:13	1995...German Silva, Mexico		2:11:00
1982...Alberto Salazar, United States		2:09:29	1996...Giacomo Leone, Italy		2:09:54
1983...Rod Dixon, New Zealand		2:08:59	1997...John Kagwe, Kenya		2:08:12

Women

Year	Winner	Time	Year	Winner	Time
1970...No finisher			1984...Grete Waitz, Norway		2:29:30
1971...Beth Bonner, United States		2:55:22	1985...Grete Waitz, Norway		2:28:34
1972...Nina Kuscsik, United States		3:08:41	1986...Grete Waitz, Norway		2:28:06
1973...Nina Kuscsik, United States		2:57:07	1987...Priscilla Welch, Great Britain		2:30:17
1974...Katherine Switzer, United States		3:07:29	1988...Grete Waitz, Norway		2:28:07
1975...Kim Merritt, United States		2:46:14	1989...Ingrid Kristiansen, Norway		2:25:30
1976...Miki Gorman, United States		2:39:11	1990...Wanda Panfiil, Poland		2:30:45
1977...Miki Gorman, United States		2:43:10	1991...Liz McColgan, Scotland		2:27:23
1978...Grete Waitz, Norway		2:32:30	1992...Lisa Ondieki, Australia		2:24:40
1979...Grete Waitz, Norway		2:27:33	1993...Uta Pippig, Germany		2:26:24
1980...Grete Waitz, Norway		2:25:41	1994...Tecla Loroupe, Kenya		2:27:37
1981...Allison Roe, New Zealand		2:25:29	1995...Tecla Loroupe, Kenya		2:28:06
1982...Grete Waitz, Norway		2:27:14	1996...Anuta Catuna, Romania		2:28:18
1983...Grete Waitz, Norway		2:27:00	1997...Franziska Rochat-Moser, Switzerland		2:28:43

World Cross-Country Championships

Conducted by the International Amateur Athletic Federation (IAAF), this meet annually brings together the best runners in the world at every distance from the mile to the marathon to compete in the same cross-country race.

Men

Year	Winner	Winning Team	Year	Winner	Winning Team
1973	Pekka Paivarinta, Finland	Belgium	1986	John Ngugi, Kenya	Kenya
1974	Eric DeBeck, Belgium	Belgium	1987	John Ngugi, Kenya	Kenya
1975	Ian Stewart, Scotland	New Zealand	1988	John Ngugi, Kenya	Kenya
1976	Carlos Lopes, Portugal	England	1989	John Ngugi, Kenya	Kenya
1977	Leon Schots, Belgium	Belgium	1990	Khalid Skah, Morocco	Kenya
1978	John Treacy, Ireland	France	1991	Khalid Skah, Morocco	Kenya
1979	John Treacy, Ireland	England	1992	John Ngugi, Kenya	Kenya
1980	Craig Virgin, United States	England	1993	William Sigei, Kenya	Kenya
1981	Craig Virgin, United States	Ethiopia	1994	William Sigei, Kenya	Kenya
1982	Mohammed Kedir, Ethiopia	Ethiopia	1995	Paul Tergat, Kenya	Kenya
1983	Bekele Debele, Ethiopia	Ethiopia	1996	Paul Tergat, Kenya	Kenya
1984	Carlos Lopes, Portugal	Ethiopia	1997	Paul Tergat, Kenya	Kenya
1985	Carlos Lopes, Portugal	Ethiopia	1998	Paul Tergat, Kenya	Kenya

Women

Year	Winner	Winning Team	Year	Winner	Winning Team
1973	Paola Cacchi, Italy	England	1986	Zola Budd, England	England
1974	Paola Cacchi, Italy	England	1987	Annette Sergent, France	United States
1975	Julie Brown, United States	United States	1988	Ingrid Kristiansen, Norway	USSR
1976	Carmen Valero, Spain	USSR	1989	Annette Sergent, France	USSR
1977	Carmen Valero, Spain	USSR	1990	Lynn Jennings, United States	USSR
1978	Grete Waitz, Norway	Romania	1991	Lynn Jennings, United States	Kenya
1979	Grete Waitz, Norway	United States	1992	Lynn Jennings, United States	Kenya
1980	Grete Waitz, Norway	USSR	1993	Albertina Dias, Portugal	Kenya
1981	Grete Waitz, Norway	USSR	1994	Helen Chepngeno, Kenya	Portugal
1982	Maricica Puica, Romania	USSR	1995	Derartu Tulu, Ethiopia	Kenya
1983	Grete Waitz, Norway	United States	1996	Gete Wami, Ethiopia	Kenya
1984	Maricica Puica, Romania	United States	1997	Derartu Tulu, Ethiopia	Ethiopia
1985	Zola Budd, England	United States	1998	Sonia O'Sullivan, Ireland	Kenya

Notable Achievements

Longest Winning Streaks

MEN

Event	Name and Nationality	Streak	Years
100-meter dash	Bob Hayes, United States	49	1962–64
200-meter dash	Manfred Gemar, Germany	41	1956–60
400-meter run	Michael Johnson, United States	58	1989–97
800-meter run	Mal Whitfield, United States	40	1951–54
1,500-meter run	Josy Barthel, Luxembourg	17	1952
1,500-meter run/mile	Steve Ovett, Great Britain	45	1977–80
Mile	Herb Elliott, Australia	35	1957–60
Steeplechase	Gaston Roelants, Belgium	45	1961–66
5,000-meter run	Emil Zátopek, Czechoslovakia	48	1949–52
10,000-meter run	Emil Zátopek, Czechoslovakia	38	1948–54
Marathon	Frank Shorter, United States	6	1971–73
110-meter hurdles	Jack Davis, United States	44	1952–55
400-meter hurdles	Edwin Moses, United States	107	1977–87
High jump	Ernie Shelton, United States	46	1953–55
Pole vault	Bob Richards, United States	50	1950–52
Long jump	Carl Lewis, United States	65	1981–91
Triple jump	Adhemar da Silva, Brazil	60	1950–56
Shot put	Parry O'Brien, United States	116	1952–56
Discus throw	Ricky Bruch, Sweden	54	1972–73
Hammer throw	Imre Nemeth, Hungary	73	1946–50
Javelin throw	Janis Lusis, USSR	41	1967–70
Decathlon	Bob Mathias, United States	11	1948–56

Longest Winning Streaks *(Cont.)*

WOMEN

Event	Name and Nationality	Streak	Years
100-meter dash	Merlene Ottey, Jamaica	56	1987–91
200-meter dash	Irena Szewinska, Poland	38	1973–75
400-meter run	Irena Szewinska, Poland	36	1973–78
800-meter run	Ana Fidelia Quirot, Cuba	36	1987–90
1,500-meter run	Paula Ivan, Romania	15	1988–91
1,500-meter run/mile	Paula Ivan, Romania	19	1988–90
3,000-meter run	Mary Slaney, United States	10	1982–84
10,000-meter run	Ingrid Kristiansen, Norway	5	1985–87
Marathon	Katrin Dörre, East Germany	10	1982–86
100-meter hurdles	Annelie Ernhardt, East Germany	44	1972–75
400-meter hurdles	Ann-Louise Skoglund, Sweden	18	1981–83
High jump	Iolanda Balas, Romania	140	1956–67
Long jump	Tatyana Shchelkanova, USSR	19	1964–66
Shot put	Nadezhda Chizhova, USSR	57	1969–73
Discus throw	Gisela Mauermeyer, Germany	65	1935–42
Javelin throw	Ruth Fuchs, East Germany	30	1972–73
Multi	Heide Rosendahl, West Germany	15	1969–72

Most Consecutive Years Ranked No. 1 in the World

MEN

No.	Name and Nationality	Event	Years
11	Sergei Bubka, Ukraine	Pole vault	1984–94
9	Viktor Saneyev, USSR	Triple jump	1968–76
8	Bob Richards, United States	Pole vault	1949–56
8	Ralph Boston, United States	Long jump	1960–67

WOMEN

No.	Name and Nationality	Event	Years
9	Iolanda Balas, Romania	High jump	1958–66
8	Ruth Fuchs, East Germany	Javelin throw	1972–79
7	Faina Melnick, USSR	Discus throw	1971–77

Major Barrier Breakers

MEN

Event	Mark	Name and Nationality	Date	Site
sub 10-second 100-meter dash	9.95	Jim Hines, United States	Oct. 14, 1968	Mexico City
sub 20-second 200-meter dash	19.83	Tommie Smith, United States	Oct. 16, 1968	Mexico City
sub 45-second 400-meter run	44.9	Otis Davis, United States	Sept. 6, 1960	Rome
sub 1:45 800-meter run	1:44.3	Peter Snell, New Zealand	Feb. 3, 1962	Christchurch, New Zealand
sub four minute mile	3:59.4	Roger Bannister, Great Britain	May 6, 1954	Oxford
sub 3:50 mile	3:49.4	John Walker, New Zealand	Aug. 12, 1975	Göteborg
sub 13-minute 5,000-meter run	12:58.39	Said Aouita, Morocco	July 22, 1986	Rome
sub 27:00 10,000-meter run	26:58.38	Yobes Ondieki, Kenya	July 10, 1993	Oslo
sub 13-minute 110-meter hurdles	12.93	Renaldo Nehemiah, United States	Aug. 19, 1981	Zurich
sub 50-second 400-meter hurdles	49.5	Glenn Davis, United States	June 29, 1956	Los Angeles
7' high jump	7' ⅝"	Charles Dumas, United States	June 29, 1956	Los Angeles
8' high jump	8'	Javier Sotomayor, Cuba	July 29, 1989	San Juan
60' triple jump	60' ¼"	Jonathan Edwards, Great Britain	Aug. 7, 1995	Göteborg
20' pole vault	20'	Sergei Bubka, USSR	March 15, 1991	San Sebastian, Spain
70' shot put	70' 7¼"	Randy Matson, United States	May 5, 1965	College Station, Texas
200' discus throw	200' 5"	Al Oerter, United States	May 18, 1962	Los Angeles
300' (new) javelin	300' 1"	Steve Backley, Great Britain	Jan. 25, 1992	Auckland, New Zealand

Major Barrier Breakers *(Cont.)*

WOMEN

Event	Mark	Name and Nationality	Date	Site
sub 11-second 100-meter dash	10.88	Marlies Oelsner, East Germany	July 1, 1977	Dresden
sub 22-second 200-meter dash	21.71	Marita Koch, East Germany	June 10, 1979	Karl Marx Stadt
sub 50-second 400-meter run	49.9	Irena Szewinska, Poland	June 22, 1974	Warsaw
sub 2:00 800-meter run	1:59.1	Shin Geum Dan, North Korea	Nov. 12, 1963	Djakarta
sub 4:00 1,500-meter run	3:56.0	Tatyana Kazankina, USSR	June 28, 1976	Podolsk, USSR
sub 4:20 mile	4:17.55	Mary Decker, United States	Feb. 16, 1980	Houston
sub 15:00 5,000-meter run	14:58.89	Ingrid Kristiansen, Norway	June 28, 1984	Oslo
sub 30:00 10,000-meter run	29:31.78	Wang Junxia, China	Sept. 8, 1993	Beijing
sub 2:30 marathon	2:27:33	Grete Waitz, Norway	Oct. 21, 1979	New York City
sub 13-second 100-meter hurdles	12.9	Karin Balzer, East Germany	Sept. 5, 1969	Berlin
6' high jump	6'	Iolanda Balas, Romania	Oct. 18, 1958	Budapest
70' shot put	70' 4½"	Nadyezhda Chizhova, USSR	Sept. 29, 1973	Varna, Bulgaria
200' discus throw	201'	Liesel Westermann, West Germany	Nov. 5, 1967	Sao Paulo
200' javelin throw	201' 4"	Elvira Ozolina, USSR	Aug. 27, 1964	Kiev
first 7,000-point heptathlon	7,148	Jackie Joyner-Kersee, U.S.	July 6–7, 1986	Moscow

Olympic Accomplishments

Oldest Olympic gold medalist—Patrick (Babe) McDonald, United States, 42 years, 26 days, 56-pound weight throw, 1920.

Oldest Olympic medalist—Tebbs Lloyd Johnson, Great Britain, 48 years, 115 days, 1948 (bronze), 50K walk.

Youngest Olympic gold medalist—Barbara Jones, United States, 15 years 123 days, 1952, 4 x 100 relay.

Youngest gold medalist in individual event—Ulrike Meyfarth, West Germany, 16 years, 123 days, 1972, high jump.

World Record Accomplishments*

Most world records equaled or set in a day—6, Jesse Owens, United States, 5/25/35, (9.4 100-yard dash; 26' 8¼" long jump; 20.3 200-meter dash and 220-yard dash; and 22.6 220-yard hurdles and 200-meter hurdles.

Most records in a year—10, Gunder Hägg, Sweden, 1941-42, 1,500 to 5,000 meters.

Most records in a career—35, Sergei Bubka, 1983-94, pole vault indoors and out.

Longest span of record setting—11 years, 20 days, Irena Szewinska, Poland, 1965-76, 200-meter dash.

Youngest person to set a set world record—Carolina Gisolf, Holland, 15 years, 5 days, 1928, high jump , 5' 3¾".

Youngest man to set a world record—John Thomas, United States, 17 years, 355 days, 1959, high jump, 7' 1¼".

Oldest person to set world record—Carlos Lopes, Portugal, 38 years, 59 days, marathon, 2:07:12.

Greatest percentage improvement—6.59, Bob Beamon, United States, 1968, long jump.

Longest lasting record—long jump, 26' 8¼", Jesse Owens, United States, 25 years, 79 days (1935-60).

Highest clearance over head, men—23¾", Franklin Jacobs, United States (5' 8"), 1978.

Highest clearance over head, woman—12¾", Yolanda Henry, United States (5' 6"), 1990.

*Marks sanctioned by the IAAF.

Swimming

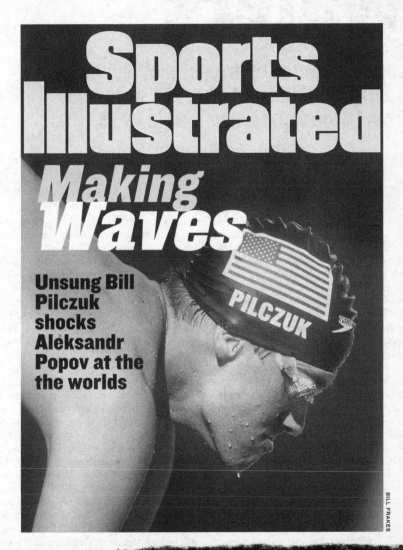

Sports Illustrated

Making Waves

Unsung Bill Pilczuk shocks Aleksandr Popov at the the worlds

PILCZUK

Polluted Waters

Long suspected of drug use, Michelle Smith of Ireland and a host of swimmers from China were suspended in 1998

BY GERRY CALLAHAN

O N AUG. 6, 1998, precisely two years and two days after the curtain came down on the Atlanta Olympics, the nastiest battle of the '96 Summer Games was finally settled. In the war between Michelle Smith and her many accusers in the international swimming community, the final results came back from the lab that day, and the outcome was much different than it was at the Olympics.

At the Georgia Tech Aquatic Center in '96, the controversial Irish swimmer stood defiantly atop the medal stand, denying she had used performance-enhancing drugs. She passed all her urine tests before fleeing an unfriendly Atlanta with three gold medals and a bronze—the first swimming medals ever for Ireland. Smith, 26 at the time, returned to a national celebration in her homeland, but around the globe, the clouds of suspicion never lifted. Her improvement had been too dramatic. She's up to something, whispered her critics. Someday they'll catch her.

Alas, that day came when Smith was sus-

swimming officials ruled she had tampered with a urine sample. A potent concentration of whiskey—which acts as a masking agent—was found in two samples that Smith gave in January '98; FINA concluded that the samples had been manipulated.

For Smith, the punishment serves essentially as a lifetime ban—the 28-year-old redhead will be forced to miss the 2000 Olympics in Sydney and the next world championships, in 2001 in Fukuoka, Japan.

Smith has said she will fight the ban, vowing to take her case to the International Court of Arbitration for Sport in Switzerland. "I firmly believe that there has been a concerted effort on the part of FINA to ensure that I did not swim again and to ensure that by whatever method available to them a ban would be imposed," said Smith.

To her accusers, Smith's ban was met with decidedly mixed feelings. While they were pleased to see her finally get what they believed she had coming to her, they couldn't help but feel it was two years too late. "They've found the whiskey, but she still has the gold at home, said the U.S.'s Alli-

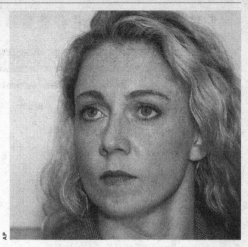

son Wagner, who was second to Smith in the 400 IM at Atlanta. "So it's not quite the same satisfaction."

Smith's downfall marked the second time in '98 that the swimming world scored a victory over suspected cheating. In January, on her way to the world championships in Perth, Australia, Chinese swimmer Yuan Yuan was caught with a thermos filled with 13 vials of human growth hormone. Chinese coach Zhou Zhewen reportedly claimed the substance belonged to him and that he was bringing it into the country for a friend, but to many in the international swimming community it was proof at last that the Chinese were cheating. "More than anything I think I feel sorry for [the Chinese swimmers]," said Jenny Thompson of the U.S. "They're just doing what their coaches tell them." Yuan was suspended for four years and her coach for 15. Four other Chinese swimmers would be suspended for using a steroid-masking diuretic in Perth.

One of the more outspoken critics of performance-enhancing drugs in her sport, Thompson enjoyed an especially satisfying trip to Perth. Although she has five Olympic gold medals, she won each one as part of a relay team. She had never won an individual gold at the Olympics or world championships, often losing to questionable competitors from China. With China busted at last, Thompson captured individual golds in the 100 free and the 100 fly at the worlds, along with two golds and a silver in the relays. The Chinese, who won 12 of the 16 golds at the previous world championships, won six medals, only three gold.

Among those who showed up in '98 and took the sport by storm were sprinter Bill Pilczuk, breaststroker Kurt Grote and backstroker Lenny Krayzelburg, each of whom brought gold back to the U.S. from Perth. Pilczuk pulled off the upset of the year when he won the 50-meter freestyle, defeating Russian legend Aleksandr Popov. Popov had not lost the event in international competition in eight years. "My first reaction was, You've got to be kidding me," said Pilczuk, a 26-year-old New Jersey native.

But the unknown American blasted out of the blocks and never looked back, finishing in a career-best time of 22.29. Popov was second in 22.43. "I was thinking about something else," said the two-time Olympic champ. "I don't remember what that was, but I wasn't concentrating on the race."

Grote, who attends Stanford medical school, won the 200-meter breaststroke at the world championships and followed that with a first-place finish in the 100 at the U.S. nationals and gold medals in both breaststroke events in the Goodwill Games. The San Diego native could be a favorite at the Sydney Olympics.

Krayzelburg will no doubt be right there with him. After capturing two golds in Perth, the 22-year-old from USC nearly set a world record in the 200 meter backstroke at the U.S. championships in August. Krayzelburg, whose family emigrated to Southern California from the Russian city of Odessa when he was 13, settled for the second-fastest time ever. Krayzelburg was as surprised as anyone. "You hear about all these other people who swim fast all the time," he said. "Then all of a sudden, you're one of them."

Or, in the case of Michelle Smith or Yuan Yuan, all of a sudden you're gone.

World Swimming and Diving Championships

Perth, Australia, January 8–18, 1998

Men

50-METER FREESTYLE

1. ....Bill Pilczuk, United States   22.29
2. ....Aleksandr Popov, Russia   22.43
3. ....Michael Klim, Australia   22.47
3. ....Ricardo Busquets, United States   22.47

100-METER FREESTYLE

1. ....Aleksandr Popov, Russia   48.93†
2. ....Michael Klim, Australia   49.20
3. ....Larz Frülander, Sweden   49.53

200-METER FREESTYLE

1. ....Michael Klim, Australia   1:47.41
2. ....Massi Rosolino, Italy   1:48.30
3. ....Pieter van den Hoogenband, Netherlands   1:48.65

400-METER FREESTYLE

1. ....Ian Thorpe, Australia   3:46.29
2. ....Grant Hackett, Australia   3:46.44
3. ....Paul Palmer, Great Britain   3:48.02

1500-METER FREESTYLE

1. ....Grant Hackett, Australia   14:51.70
2. ....Emiliano Brembilla, Italy   15:00.59
3. ....Daniel Kowalski, Australia   15:03.94

100-METER BACKSTROKE

1. ....Lanny Krayzelburg, United States   55.00†
2. ....Mark Versfeld, Canada   55.17
3. ....Stev Theloke, Germany   55.20

200-METER BACKSTROKE

1. ....Lenny Krayzelburg, United States   1:58.84
2. ....Ralf Braun, Germany   1:59.23
3. ....Mark Versfeld, Canada   1:59.39

100-METER BREASTSTROKE

1. ....Frederik Deburghgraeve, Belgium   1:01.34
2. ....Zeng Qiliang, China   1:01.76
3. ....Kurt Grote, United States   1:01.93

200-METER BREASTSTROKE

1. ....Kurt Grote, United States   2:13.40
2. ....Jean-Christophe Sarnin, France   2:13.42
3. ....Norbert Rozsa, Hungary   2:13:59

100-METER BUTTERFLY

1. ....Michael Klim, Australia   52.25†
2. ....Lars Frolander, Sweden   52.79
3. ....Geoff Huegill, Australia   52.90

200-METER BUTTERFLY

1. ....Denys Sylantyev, Ukraine   1:56.61
2. ....Franck Esposito, France   1:56.77
3. ....Tom Malchow, United States   1:57.26

200-METER INDIVIDUAL MEDLEY

1. ....Marcel Wouda, Netherlands   2:01.18
2. ....Xavier Marchand, France   2:01.66
3. ....Ron Karnaugh, United States   2:01:89

400-METER INDIVIDUAL MEDLEY

1. ....Tom Dolan, United States   4:14.95
2. ....Marcel Wouda, Netherlands   4:15.53
3. ....Curtis Myden, Canada   4:16.45

400-METER MEDLEY RELAY

1. ....Australia (Matt Welsh, Phil Rogers, Michael Klim, Chris Fydler)   3:37.98
2. ....United States   3:38.56
3. ....Hungary   3:39.53

400-METER FREESTYLE RELAY

1. ....United States (Bryan Jones, Jon Olsen, Bradley Schumacher, Gary Wayne Jr.)   3:16.69†
2. ....Australia   3:16.97
3. ....Russia   3:18.45

800-METER FREESTYLE RELAY

1. ....Australia (Daniel Kowalski, Grant Hackett, Ian Thorpe, Anthony Rogis)   7:12.48†
2. ....Netherlands   7:16.77
3. ....Great Britain   7:17.33

ONE-METER SPRINGBOARD

1. ....Yu Zhuocheng, China   417.54
2. ....Troy Dumais, United States   415.74
3. ....Holger Schlepps, Germany   398.31

THREE-METER SPRINGBOARD

1. ....Dmitry Sautin, Russia   746.79
2. ....Zhou Yilin, China   694.92
3. ....Vassiliy Lisovskiy, Russia   651.60

10-METER PLATFORM

1. ....Dmitry Sautin, Russia   750.90
2. ....Tian Liang, China   699.30
3. ....Jan Hempel, Germany   624.15

3-METER SYNCHRONIZED

1. ....China (Sun Shuwei, Tian Liang)   313.50
2. ....Australia   308.28
3. ....Great Britain   305.16

10-METER SYNCHRONIZED

1. ....China (Xu Hao, Yu Zhuocheng)   326.34
2. ....Germany   308.01
3. ....Russia   304.02

WATER POLO

1. ....Spain
2. ....Hungary
3. ....Yugoslavia

*American record. †Meet record.

Note: Spain d. Hungary, 6–4; Yugoslavia d. Australia, 8–5.

Women

50-METER FREESTYLE

1. ....Amy Van Dyken, United States   25.15
2. ....Sandra Voelker, Germany   25.32
3. ....Shan Ying, China   25.36

100-METER FREESTYLE

1. ....Jenny Thompson, United States   54.95
2. ....Martina Moravcova, Slovakia   55.09
3. ....Shan Ying, China   55.10

200-METER FREESTYLE

1. ....Claudia Poll, Costa Rica   1:58.90
2. ....Martina Moravcova, Slovakia   1:59.61
3. ....Julia Greville, Australia   2:01.62

400-METER FREESTYLE

1. ....Chen Yan, China   4:06.72
2. ....Brooke Bennett, United States   4:07.07
3. ....Dagmar Hase, Germany   4:08.82

800-METER FREESTYLE

1. ....Brooke Bennett, United States   8.28.71
2. ....Diana Munz, United States   8.29.97
3. ....Kirsten Vlieghuis, Netherlands   8.32.34

100-METER BACKSTROKE

1. ....Lea Maurer, United States   1:01.16
2. ....Mai Nakamura, Japan   1:01.28
3. ....Sandra Volker, Germany   1:10.47

200-METER BACKSTROKE

1. ....Roxanna Maracineanu, France   2:11.26
2. ....Dagmar Hase, Germany   2:11.45
3. ....Mai Nakamura, Japan   2:12.22

100-METER BREASTSTROKE

1. ....Kristy Kowal, United States   1:08.42
2. ....Helen Denman, Australia   1:08.42
3. ....Lauren Van Oosten, Canada   1:08.42

200-METER BREASTSTROKE

1. ....Agnes Kovacs, Hungary   2:25.45†
2. ....Kristy Kowal, United States   2:26.19
3. ....Jenna Street, United States   2:26.50

100-METER BUTTERFLY

1. ....Jenny Thompson, United States   58.46†
2. ....Ayari Aoyama, Japan   58.79
3. ....Petria Thomas, Australia   58.97

200-METER BUTTERFLY

1. ....Susie O'Neill, Australia   2:07.93†
2. ....Petria Thomas, Australia   2:09.08
3. ....Misty Hyman, United States   2:09.98

200-METER INDIVIDUAL MEDLEY

1. ....Wu Yanyan, China   2:10.88
2. ....Chen Yan, China   2:13.66
3. ....Martina Moravcova, Slovakia   2:14.26

400-METER INDIVIDUAL MEDLEY

1. ....Chen Yan, China   4:36.66
2. ....Yana Klochkova, Ukraine   4:38.60
3. ....Yasuko Tajima, Japan   4:39.45

400-METER MEDLEY RELAY

1. ....United States (Kristy Kowal, Lea   4:01.93*
Maurer, Jenny Thompson, Amy
Van Dyken)
2. ....Australia   4:05.12
3. ....Japan   4:06.27

400-METER FREESTYLE RELAY

1. ....United States (Catherine Fox,   3:42.11
Lindsey Farella, Melanie Valerio,
B.J. Bedford)
2. ....Germany   3:43.11
3. ....Australia   3:43.71

800-METER FREESTYLE RELAY

1. ....Germany (Silvia Szalai, Antje   8:01.46
Buschschulte, Janina Goetz,
Franziska Van Almsick)
2. ....United States   8:02.88
3. ....Australia   8:04.19

ONE-METER SPRINGBOARD

1. ....Irina Lashko, Russia   296.07
2. ....Vera Ilyila, Russia   288.06
3. ....Zhang Jing, China   260.31

THREE-METER SPRINGBOARD

1. ....Yulia Pakhalina, Russia   544.62
2. ....Jingjing Guo, China   518.76
3. ....Chantelle Michell, Australia   515.07

10-METER PLATFORM

1. ....Olena Zhupyna, Ukraine   550.41
2. ....Cai Yuyan, China   536.25
3. ....Chen Li, China   519.45

THREE-METER SYNCHRONIZED

1. ....Russia (Irina Lashko, Yulia   282.30
Pakhalina)
2. ....China   276.18
3. ....United States   263.91

10-METER SYNCHRONIZED

1. ....Ukraine (Olena Zhupyna,   278.28
Svitlana Serbina)
2. ....China   276.54
3. ....United States   265.47

WATER POLO

1. ....Italy
2. ....Netherlands
3. ....Australia

Note: Italy d. Netherlands, 7–6; Australia d. Russia, 8–5.

*American record. †Meet record.

Men
Women

U.S. OUTDOOR CHAMPIONSHIPS
Clovis, CA, August 11–15, 1998

	Men	Women
50 free	Bill Pilczuk, Auburn Aquatics, 22.62	Barbara Bedford, Colorado Springs, 25.64
100 free	Jason Lezak, Irvine Nova, 49.93	Jenny Thompson, Stanford Swim, 55.53
200 free	Ugur Taner, Hillenbrand, 1:48.91	Lindsay Benko, Trojan SC, 2:00.67
400 free	Erik Vendt, Ocean St, 3:51.23	Cristina Teuscher, Badger SC, 4:10.80
800 free	Chris Thompson, Club Wolverine, 7:58.26	Diana Munz, Lake Erie Silver, 8:31.74
1500 free	Erik Vendt, Ocean St, 15:10.50	Diana Munz, Lake Erie Silver, 16:16.00
100 back	Lenny Krayzelburg, Trojan SC, 54.64	Barbara Bedford, Colorado Springs, 1:01.11
200 back	Lenny Krayzelburg, Trojan SC, 1:57.38*	Natalie Coughlin, Terrapins, 2:12.03
100 breast	Kurt Grote, Santa Clara, 1:01.60	Kristy Kowal, Athens Bulldogs, 1:08.71†
200 breast	Tom Wilkens, Santa Clara, 2:12.39	Kristy Kowal, Athens Bulldogs, 2:26.27
100 fly	Brock Newman, Swim Atlanta, 53.24	Jenny Thompson, Stanford Swim, 59.74
200 fly	Tom Malchow, Club Wolverine, 1:56.75	Molly Freedman, Curl-Burke, 2:12.02
200 IM	Tom Wilkens, Santa Clara, 2:01.80	Cristina Teuscher, Badger SC, 2:14.18
400 IM	Tom Dolan, Club Wolverine, 4:16.33	Maddy Crippen, Foxcatcher, 4:42.61
400 m relay	Santa Clara, 3:41.96	Hillenbrand, 4:10.33†
400 f relay	Texas Aqua, 3:21.40	Hillenbrand, 3:44.87
800 f relay	Texas Aqua, 7:30.64	Bolles School, 8:12.44

COMMONWEALTH GAMES
Kuala Lumpur, September 7–20, 1998

	Men	Women
50 free	Mark Foster, England, 22.58†	Sue Rolph, England, 25.82
100 free	Michael Klim, Australia, 49.43	Sue Rolph, England, 55.17†
200 free	Ian Thorpe, Australia, 1:46.70†	Susan O'Neill, Australia, 2:00.24
400 free	Ian Thorpe, Australia, 3:44.35	Susan O'Neill, Australia, 4:12.39
1500 free	Grant Hackett, Australia, 14:50.92	Rachel Harris, Australia, 8:42.23
100 back	Mark Versfeld, Canada, 55.52†	Giaan Rooney, Australia, 1:02.43
200 back	Mark Versfeld, Canada, 1:59.67	Katy Sexton, England, 2:13.18
100 breast	Simon Cowley, Australia, 1:02.00	Helen Denman, Australia, 1:08.71
200 breast	Simon Cowley, Australia, 2:13.13	Samantha Riley, Australia, 2:27.30
100 fly	Geoff Huegill, Australia, 52.81	Petria Thomas, Australia, 59.42
200 fly	James Hickman, England, 1:57.11	Susan O'Neill, Australia, 2:06.60†
200 IM	Matthew Dunn, Australia, 2:00.26	Marianne Limpert, Canada, 2:15.05†
400 IM	Trent Steed, Australia, 4:19.89	Joanne Malar, Canada, 4:43.72
400 m relay	Australia, 3:38.52†	Australia, 4:06.36
400 f relay	Australia, 3:17.83	Australia, 3:42.61
800 f relay	Australia, 7:11.86 WR	Australia, 8:13.73†
1-m spgbd	Evan Stewart, Zimbabwe, 384.660	Chantelle Michell, Australia, 271.560
3-m spgbd	Dean Lester Pullar, Australia, 224.520	Erin Bulmer, Canada, 515.880
Platform	Alexandre Despatie, Canada, 195.870	Vyninka Arlow, Australia, 456.480

†Meet record. *American record. WR=world record.

World and American Records Set in 1998

Men

Event	Mark	Record Holder	Date	Site
200 backstroke	1:57.38	Lenny Krayzelburg (A)	8-12-98	Clovis, CA
800 meter free relay	7:11.86	Australia (W) (Ian Thorpe, Daniel Kowalski, Matt Dunn, Michael Klim)	9-20-98	Kuala Lumpur

Women

Event	Mark	Record Holder	Date	Site
100 backstroke	1:00.77	Lea Maurer (A)	1-14-98	Perth, Australia
400 medley relay	4:01.93	United States (A) (Lea Maurer, Kristy Kowal, Jenny Thompson, Amy Van Dyken)	1-16-98	Perth, Australia

World and American Records

MEN
Freestyle

Event	Time	Record Holder	Date	Site
50 meters	21.81	Tom Jager (W, A)	3-24-90	Nashville
100 meters	48.21	Aleksandr Popov, Russia (W)	6-18-94	Monte Carlo
	48.42	Matt Biondi (A)	8-8-88	Austin, TX
200 meters	1:46.69	Giorgio Lamberti, Italy (W)	8-15-89	Bonn
	1:47.72	Matt Biondi (A)	8-8-88	Austin, TX
400 meters	3:43.80	Kieran Perkins, Australia (W)	9-9-94	Rome
	3:48.06	Matt Cetlinski (A)	8-11-88	Austin, TX
800 meters	7:46.00	Kieran Perkins, Australia (W)	8-24-94	Vancouver, B.C.
	7:52.45	Sean Killion (A)	7-27-87	Clovis, CA
1,500 meters	14:41.66	Kieran Perkins, Australia (W)	8-24-94	Vancouver, B.C.
	15:01.51	George DiCarlo (A)	6-30-84	Indianapolis

Backstroke

Event	Time	Record Holder	Date	Site
100 meters	53.86*	Jeff Rouse (W, A)	7-31-92	Barcelona
200 meters	1:56.57	Martin Zubero, Spain (W)	11-23-91	Tuscaloosa, AL
	1:57.38	Lenny Krayzelburg (A)	8-12-98	Clovis, CA

*Set on first leg of relay.

Breaststroke

Event	Time	Record Holder	Date	Site
100 meters	1:00.60	F. Deburghgraeve, Belgium (W)	7-20-96	Atlanta
	1:00.77	Jeremy Linn (A)	7-20-96	Atlanta
200 meters	2:10.16	Mike Barrowman (W,A)	7-29-92	Barcelona

Butterfly

Event	Time	Record Holder	Date	Site
100 meters	52.15	Michael Kilm, Australia (W)	10-9-97	Brisbane, Australia
	52.76	Neil Walker (A)	8-12-97	Fukuoka, Japan
200 meters	1:55.22	Denis Pankratov, Russia (W)	6-14-95	Canet, France
	1:55.69	Melvin Stewart (A)	1-12-91	Perth, Australia

Individual Medley

Event	Time	Record Holder	Date	Site
200 meters	1:59.36	Jani Sievinen, Finland (W)	9-11-94	Rome
	2:00.11	Dave Wharton (A)	8-20-89	Tokyo
400 meters	4:12.30	Tom Dolan (W, A)	9-6-94	Rome

Relays

Event	Time	Record Holder	Date	Site
400 meter medley	3:34.84	United States (W, A) (Jeff Rouse, Jeremy Linn, Mark Henderson, Gary Hall Jr)	7-26-96	Atlanta
400 meter freestyle	3:15.11	United States (W, A) (David Fox, Joe Hudepohl, Jon Olsen, Gary Hall Jr)	8-12-95	Atlanta
800 meter freestyle	7:11.86	Australia (W) (Ian Thorpe, Daniel Kowalski, Matt Dunn, Michael Klim)	9-20-98	Kuala Lumpur
	7:12.51	United States (A) (Troy Dalbey, Matt Cetlinski, Doug Gjertsen, Matt Biondi)	9-21-88	Seoul

WOMEN

Freestyle

Event	Time	Record Holder	Date	Site
50 meters	24.51	Li Jingyi, China (W)	9-11-94	Rome
	24.87	Amy Van Dyken (A)	7-26-96	Atlanta
100 meters	54.01	Li Jingyi, China (W)	9-5-94	Rome
	54.48	Jenny Thompson (A)	3-1-92	Indianapolis
200 meters	1:56.78	Franziska van Almsick, Germany (W)	9-5-94	Rome
	1:57.90	Nicole Haislett (A)	7-27-90	Barcelona
400 meters	4:03.85	Janet Evans (W, A)	9-22-88	Seoul
800 meters	8:16.22	Janet Evans (W, A)	8-20-89	Tokyo
1500 meters	15:52.10	Janet Evans (W, A)	3-26-88	Orlando, FL

Backstroke

Event	Time	Record Holder	Date	Site
100 meters	1:00.16	Cihong He, China (W)	9-10-94	Rome
	1:00.77	Lea Maurer (A)	1-14-98	Perth, Australia
200 meters	2:06.62	Krisztina Egerszegi, Hungary (W)	8-26-91	Athens, Greece
	2:08.60	Betsy Mitchell (A)	6-27-86	Orlando, FL

Breaststroke

Event	Time	Record Holder	Date	Site
100 meters	1:07.02	Penelope Heyns, Russia (W)	7-21-96	Atlanta
	1:08.09	Amanda Beard (A)	7-21-96	Atlanta
200 meters	2:24.76	Rebecca Brown, Australia (W)	3-16-94	Queensland, Aus.
	2:25.35	Anita Nall (A)	3-2-92	Indianapolis

Butterfly

Event	Time	Record Holder	Date	Site
100 meters	57.93	Mary T. Meagher (W, A)	8-13-81	Brown Deer, WI
200 meters	2:05.96	Mary T. Meagher (W, A)	8-13-81	Brown Deer, WI

Individual Medley

Event	Time	Record Holder	Date	Site
200 meters	2:09.72	Yanyan Wu, China (W)	10-17-97	Shanghai
	2:11.91	Summer Sanders (A)	7-30-92	Barcelona
400 meters	4:34.79	Yan Chen, China (W)	10-17-97	Shanghai
	4:37.58	Summer Sanders (A)	7-26-92	Barcelona

Relays

Event	Time	Record Holder	Date	Site
400 meter medley	4:01.67	China (W) (He Cihong, Dai Guohong, Liu Limin, Le Jingyi)	9-10-94	Rome
	4:01.93	United States (A) (Lea Maurer, Kristy Kowal, Jenny Thompson Amy Van Dyken)	1-16-98	Perth, Australia
400 meter freestyle	3:37.91	China (W) (Le Jingyi, Ying Shan, Le Ying, Lu Bin)	9-7-94	Rome
	3:39.29	United States (A) (Angel Martino, Amy Van Dyken, Catherine Fox, Jenny Thompson)	7-22-96	Atlanta
800 meter freestyle	7:55.47	East Germany (W) (Manuela Stellmach, Astrid Strauss, Anke Mohring, Heike Friedrich)	8-18-87	Strasbourg, France
	7:59.87	United States (A) (Trina Jackson, Cristina Teuscher, Sheila Taormina, Jenny Thompson)	7-25-96	Atlanta

Note: Records through Sept. 20, 1998.

Venues: Belgrade, Sept 4–9, 1973; Cali, Colombia, July 18–27, 1975; West Berlin, Aug 20–28, 1978; Guayaquil, Equador, Aug 1–7, 1982; Madrid, Aug 17–22, 1986; Perth, Australia, Jan 7–13, 1991; Rome, Sept 1–11, 1994; Perth, Australia, Jan 8–18, 1998.

MEN

50-meter Freestyle

1986	Tom Jager, United States	22.49‡
1991	Tom Jager, United States	22.16‡
1994	Aleksandr Popov, Russia	22.17
1998	Bill Pilczuk, United States	22.29

100-meter Freestyle

1973	Jim Montgomery, United States	51.70
1975	Andy Coan, United States	51.25
1978	David McCagg, United States	50.24
1982	Jorg Woithe, East Germany	50.18
1986	Matt Biondi, United States	48.94
1991	Matt Biondi, United States	49.18
1994	Aleksandr Popov, Russia	49.12
1998	Aleksandr Popov, Russia	48.93‡

200-meter Freestyle

1973	Jim Montgomery, United States	1:53.02
1975	Tim Shaw, United States	1:52.04‡
1978	Billy Forrester, United States	1:51.02‡
1982	Michael Gross, West Germany	1:49.84
1986	Michael Gross, West Germany	1:47.92
1991	Giorgio Lamberti, Italy	1:47.27‡
1994	Antti Kasvio, Finland	1:47.32
1998	Michael Klim, Australia	1:47.41

400-meter Freestyle

1973	Rick DeMont, United States	3:58.18‡
1975	Tim Shaw, United States	3:54.88‡
1978	Vladimir Salnikov, USSR	3:51.94‡
1982	Vladimir Salnikov, USSR	3:51.30‡
1986	Rainer Henkel, West Germany	3:50.05
1991	Joerg Hoffman, Germany	3:48.04‡
1994	Kieran Perkins, Australia	3:43.80*
1998	Ian Thorpe, Australia	3:46.29

1500-meter Freestyle

1973	Stephen Holland, Australia	15:31.85
1975	Tim Shaw, United States	15:28.92‡
1978	Vladimir Salnikov, USSR	15:03.99‡
1982	Vladimir Salnikov, USSR	15:01.77‡
1986	Rainer Henkel, West Germany	15:05.31
1991	Joerg Hoffman, Germany	14:50.36*
1994	Kieran Perkins, Australia	14:50.52
1998	Grant Hackett, Australia	14:51.70

100-meter Backstroke

1973	Roland Matthes, East Germany	57.47
1975	Roland Matthes, East Germany	58.15
1978	Bob Jackson, United States	56.36‡
1982	Dirk Richter, East Germany	55.95
1986	Igor Polianski, USSR	55.58‡
1991	Jeff Rouse, United States	55.23‡
1994	Martin Lopez Zubero, Spain	55.17‡
1998	Lanny Krayzelburg, United States	55.00‡

200-meter Backstroke

1973	Roland Matthes, East Germany	2:01.87‡
1975	Zoltan Varraszto, Hungary	2:05.05
1978	Jesse Vassallo, United States	2:02.16
1982	Rick Carey, United States	2:00.82‡
1986	Igor Polianski, USSR	1:58.78‡
1991	Martin Zubero, Spain	1:59.52
1994	Vladimir Selkov, Russia	1:57.42‡
1998	Lenny Krayzelburg, United States	1:58.84

100-meter Breaststroke

1973	John Hencken, United States	1:04.02‡
1975	David Wilkie, Great Britain	1:04.26‡
1978	Walter Kusch, West Germany	1:03.56‡
1982	Steve Lundquist, United States	1:02.75‡
1986	Victor Davis, Canada	1:02.71
1991	Norbert Rozsa, Hungary	1:01.45*
1994	Norbert Rozsa, Hungary	1:01.24‡
1998	Frederik Deburghgraeve, Belgium	1:01.34

200-meter Breaststroke

1973	David Wilkie, Great Britain	2:19.28‡
1975	David Wilkie, Great Britain	2:18.23‡
1978	Nick Nevid, United States	2:18.37
1982	Victor Davis, Canada	2:14.77*
1986	Jozsef Szabo, Hungary	2:14.27‡
1991	Mike Barrowman, United States	2:11.23*
1994	Norbert Rozsa, Hungary	2:12.81
1998	Kurt Grote, United States	2:13.40

100-meter Butterfly

1973	Bruce Robertson, Canada	55.69
1975	Greg Jagenburg, United States	55.63
1978	Joe Bottom, United States	54.30
1982	Matt Gribble, United States	53.88‡
1986	Pablo Morales, United States	53.54‡
1991	Anthony Nesty, Suriname	53.29‡
1994	Rafal Szukala, Poland	53.51
1998	Michael Klim, Australia	52.25‡

200-meter Butterfly

1973	Robin Backhaus, United States	2:03.32
1975	Bill Forrester, United States	2:01.95‡
1978	Mike Bruner, United States	1:59.38‡
1982	Michael Gross, East Germany	1:58.85‡
1986	Michael Gross, East Germany	1:56.53‡
1991	Melvin Stewart, United States	1:55.69*
1994	Denis Pankratov, Russia	1:56.54
1998	Denys Sylantyev, Ukraine	1:56.61

200-meter Individual Medley

1973	Gunnar Larsson, Sweden	2:08.36
1975	Andras Hargitay, Hungary	2:07.72
1978	Graham Smith, Canada	2:03.65*
1982	Aleksandr Sidorenko, USSR	2:03.30‡
1986	Tamás Darnyi, Hungary	2:01.57‡
1991	Tamás Darnyi, Hungary	1:59.36*
1994	Jani Sievin, Finland	1:58.16*
1998	Marcel Wouda, Netherlands	2:01.18

400-meter Individual Medley

1973	Andras Hargitay, Hungary	4:31.11
1975	Andras Hargitay, Hungary	4:32.57
1978	Jesse Vassallo, United States	4:20.05*
1982	Ricardo Prado, Brazil	4:19.78*
1986	Tamás Darnyi, Hungary	4:18.98‡
1991	Tamás Darnyi, Hungary	4:12.36*
1994	Tom Dolan, United States	4:12.30*
1998	Tom Dolan, United States	4:14.95

* World record. ‡ Meet record.

MEN *(Cont.)*

400-meter Medley Relay

1973.....United States (Mike Stamm,   3:49.49
      John Hencken, Joe Bottom,
      Jim Montgomery)
1975.....United States (John Murphy,   3:49.00
      Rick Colella, Greg Jagenburg,
      Andy Coan)
1978.....United States (Robert Jackson,   3:44.63
      Nick Nevid, Joe Bottom,
      David McCagg)
1982.....United States (Rick Carey,   3:40.84*
      Steve Lundquist, Matt Gribble,
      Rowdy Gaines)
1986.....United States (Dan Veatch,   3:41.25
      David Lundberg, Pablo Morales,
      Matt Biondi)
1991.....United States (Jeff Rouse,   3:39.66‡
      Eric Wunderlich, Mark Henderson
      Matt Biondi)
1994.....United States (Jeff Rouse, Eric   3:37.74‡
      Wunderlich, Mark Henderson,
      Gary Hall)
1998.....Australia (Matt Welsh, Phil Rogers,   3:37.98
      Robin Backhaus, Rick Klatt,
      Jim Montgomery)

400-meter Freestyle Relay

1973.....United States (Mel Nash,   3:27.18
      Joe Bottom, Jim Montgomery,
      John Murphy)
1975.....United States (Bruce Furniss,   3:24.85
      Jim Montgomery, Andy Coan,
      John Murphy)
1978.....United States (Jack Babashoff,   3:19.74
      Rowdy Gaines, Jim Montgomery,
      David McCagg)
1982.....United States (Chris Cavanaugh,   3:19.26*
      Robin Leamy, David McCagg,
      Rowdy Gaines)
1986.....United States (Tom Jager,   3:19.89
      Mike Heath, Paul Wallace,
      Matt Biondi)
1991.....United States (Tom Jager,   3:17.15‡
      Brent Lang, Doug Gjertsen,
      Matt Biondi)
1994.....United States (Jon Olsen,   3:16.90‡
      Josh Davis, Ugur Taner, Gary Hall)
1998.....United States (Bryan Jones,   3:16.69†
      Jon Olsen, Bradley Schumacher,
      Gary Wayne Jr.)

800-meter Freestyle Relay

1973.....United States (Kurt Krumpholz,   7:33.22*
      Robin Backhaus, Rick Klatt,
      Jim Montgomery)
1975.....West Germany (Klaus Steinbach,   7:39.44
      Werner Lampe, Hans Joachim
      Geisler, Peter Nocke)
1978.....United States (Bruce Furniss,   7:20.82
      Billy Forrester, Bobby Hackett,
      Rowdy Gaines)
1982.....United States (Rich Saeger,   7:21.09
      Jeff Float, Kyle Miller,
      Rowdy Gaines)

1986.....East Germany (Lars Hinneburg,   7:15.91‡
      Thomas Flemming, Dirk Richter,
      Sven Lodziewski)
1991.....Germany (Peter Sitt,   7:13.50‡
      Steffan Zesner, Stefan Pfeiffer,
      Michael Gross)
1994.....Sweden (Christer Waller,   7:17.34
      Tommy Werner, Lars Frolander,
      Anders Holmertz)
1998.....Australia (Daniel Kowalski,   7:12.48†
      Grant Hackett, Ian Thorpe,
      Anthony Rogis)

WOMEN

50-meter Freestyle

1986....Tamara Costache, Romania   25.28*
1991....Zhuang Yong, China   25.47
1994....Le Jingyi, China   24.51*
1998....Amy Van Dyken, United States   25.15

100-meter Freestyle

1973....Kornelia Ender, East Germany   57.54
1975....Kornelia Ender, East Germany   56.50
1978....Barbara Krause, East Germany   55.68‡
1982....Birgit Meineke, East Germany   55.79
1986....Kristin Otto, East Germany   55.05‡
1991....Nicole Haislett, United States   55.17
1994....Le Jingyi, China   54.01*
1998....Jenny Thompson, United States   54.95

200-meter Freestyle

1973.....Keena Rothhammer, United States   2:04.99
1975....Shirley Babashoff, United States   2:02.50
1978....Cynthia Woodhead, United States   1:58.53*
1982....Annemarie Verstappen,   1:59.53‡
      Netherlands
1986....Heike Friedrich, East Germany   1:58.26‡
1991....Hayley Lewis, Australia   2:00.48
1994....Franziska Van Almsick, Germany   1:56.78*
1998....Claudia Poll, Costa Rica   1:58.90

400-meter Freestyle

1973.....Heather Greenwood, United States   4:20.28
1975....Shirley Babashoff, United States   4:22.70
1978....Tracey Wickham, Australia   4:06.28*
1982....Carmela Schmidt, East Germany   4:08.98

* World record; ‡ Meet record.

WOMEN (Cont.)

400-meter Freestyle (Cont.)

1986	Heike Friedrich, East Germany	4:07.45
1991	Janet Evans, United States	4:08.63
1994	Yang Aihua, China	4:09.64
1998	Chen Yan, China	4:06.72

800-meter Freestyle

1973	Novella Calligaris, Italy	8:52.97
1975	Jenny Turrall, Australia	8:44.75‡
1978	Tracey Wickham, Australia	8:24.94‡
1982	Kim Linehan, United States	8:27.48
1986	Astrid Strauss, East Germany	8:28.24
1991	Janet Evans, United States	8:24.05‡
1994	Janet Evans, United States	8:29.85
1998	Brooke Bennett, United States	8.28.71

100-meter Backstroke

1973	Ulrike Richter, East Germany	1:05.42
1975	Ulrike Richter, East Germany	1:03.30‡
1978	Linda Jezek, United States	1:02.55‡
1982	Kristin Otto, East Germany	1:01.30‡
1986	Betsy Mitchell, United States	1:01.74
1991	Krisztina Egerszegi, Hungary	1:01.78
1994	He Cihong, China	1:00.57
1998	Lea Maurer, United States	1:01.16

200-meter Backstroke

1973	Melissa Belote, United States	2:20.52
1975	Birgit Treiber, East Germany	2:15.46*
1978	Linda Jezek, United States	2:11.93*
1982	Cornelia Sirch, East Germany	2:09.91*
1986	Cornelia Sirch, East Germany	2:11.37
1991	Krisztina Egerszegi, Hungary	2:09.15‡
1994	He Cihong, China	2:07.40
1998	Roxana Maracineanu, France	2:11.26

100-meter Breaststroke

1973	Renate Vogel, East Germany	1:13.74
1975	Hannalore Anke, East Germany	1:12.72
1978	Julia Bogdanova, USSR	1:10.31*
1982	Ute Geweniger, East Germany	1:09.14‡
1986	Sylvia Gerasch, East Germany	1:08.11*
1991	Linley Frame, Australia	1:08.81
1994	Samantha Riley, Australia	1:07.96*
1998	Kristy Kowal, United States	1:08.42

200-meter Breaststroke

1973	Renate Vogel, East Germany	2:40.01
1975	Hannalore Anke, East Germany	2:37.25‡
1978	Lina Kachushite, USSR	2:31.42*
1982	Svetlana Varganova, USSR	2:28.82‡
1986	Silke Hoerner, East Germany	2:27.40*
1991	Elena Volkova, USSR	2:29.53
1994	Samantha Riley, Australia	2:26.87‡
1998	Agnes Kovacs, Hungary	2:25.45†

100-meter Butterfly

1973	Kornelia Ender, East Germany	1:02.53
1975	Kornelia Ender, East Germany	1:01.24*
1978	Joan Pennington, United States	1:00.20‡
1982	Mary T. Meagher, United States	59.41‡
1986	Kornelia Gressler, East Germany	59.51
1991	Qian Hong, China	59.68
1994	Liu Limin, China	58.98‡
1998	Jenny Thompson, United States	58.46†

200-meter Butterfly

1973	Rosemarie Kother, East Germany	2:13.76‡
1975	Rosemarie Kother, East Germany	2:15.92
1978	Tracy Caulkins, United States	2:09.87*
1982	Ines Geissler, East Germany	2:08.66‡
1986	Mary T. Meagher, United States	2:08.41‡
1991	Summer Sanders, United States	2:09.24
1994	Liu Limin, China	2:07.25‡
1998	Susie O'Neill, Australia	2:07.93†

200-meter Individual Medley

1973	Andrea Huebner, East Germany	2:20.51
1975	Kathy Heddy, United States	2:19.80
1978	Tracy Caulkins, United States	2:14.07*
1982	Petra Schneider, East Germany	2:11.79
1986	Kristin Otto, East Germany	2:15.56
1991	Li Lin, China	2:13.40
1994	Lu Bin, China	2:12.34‡
1998	Wu Yanyan, China	2:10.88

400-meter Individual Medley

1973	Gudrun Wegner, East Germany	4:57.71
1975	Ulrike Tauber, East Germany	4:52.76‡
1978	Tracy Caulkins, United States	4:40.83*
1982	Petra Schneider, East Germany	4:36.10*
1986	Kathleen Nord, East Germany	4:43.75
1991	Lin Li, China	4:41.45
1994	Dai Guohong, China	4:39.14
1998	Chen Yan, China	4:36.66

400-meter Medley Relay

1973	East Germany (Ulrike Richter, Renate Vogel, Rosemarie Kother, Kornelia Ender)	4:16.84
1975	East Germany (Ulrike Richter, Hannelore Anke, Rosemarie Kother, Kornelia Ender)	4:14.74
1978	United States (Linda Jezek, Tracy Caulkins, Joan Pennington, Cynthia Woodhead)	4:08.21‡
1982	East Germany (Kristin Otto, Ute Gewinger, Ines Geissler, Birgit Meineke)	4:05.8*
1986	East Germany (Kathrin Zimmermann, Sylvia Gerasch, Kornelia Gressler, Kristin Otto)	4:04.82
1991	United States (Janie Wagstaff, Tracey McFarlane, Crissy Ahmann-Leighton, Nicole Haislett)	4:06.51
1994	China (He Cihong, Dai Guohong, Liu Limin, Lu Bin)	4:01.67*
1998	United States (Kristy Kowal, Lea Maurer, Jenny Thompson, Amy Van Dyken)	4:01.93

400-meter Freestyle Relay

1973	East Germany (Kornelia Ender, Andrea Eife, Andrea Huebner, Sylvia Eichner)	3:52.45
1975	East Germany (Kornelia Ender, Barbara Krause, Claudia Hempel, Ute Bruckner)	3:49.37
1978	United States (Tracy Caulkins, Stephanie Elkins, Joan Pennington, Cynthia Woodhead)	3:43.43*

WOMEN *(Cont.)*

400-meter Freestyle Relay *(Cont.)*

1982	East Germany (Birgit Meineke, Susanne Link, Kristin Otto, Caren Metschuk)	3:43.97
1986	East Germany (Kristin Otto, Manuela Stellmach, Sabine Schulze, Heike Friedrich)	3:40.57*
1991	United States (Nicole Haislett, Julie Cooper, Whitney Hedgepeth, Jenny Thompson)	3:43.26
1994	China (Le Jingyi, Ying Shan, Le Ying, Lu Bin)	3:37.91*
1998	United States (Catherine Fox, Lindsey Farella, Melanie Valerio, B.J. Bedford)	3:42.11

800-meter Freestyle Relay

1986	East Germany (Manuela Stellmach, Astrid Strauss, Nadja Bergknecht, Heike Friedrich)	7:59.33*
1991	Germany (Kerstin Kielgass, Manuela Stellmach, Dagmar Hase, Stephanie Ortwig)	8:02.56
1994	China (Le Ying, Yang Alhua, Zhou Guabin, Lu Bin)	7:57.96
1998	Germany (Silvia Szalai, Antje Buschschulte, Janina Goetz, Franziska Van Almsick)	8:02.56

* World record; ‡Meet record.

World Diving Championships

MEN

1-meter Springboard

		Pts
1991	Edwin Jongejans, Netherlands	588.51
1994	Evan Stewart, Zimbabwe	382.14
1998	Yu Zhuocheng, China	417.54

3-meter Springboard

		Pts
1973	Phil Boggs, United States	618.57
1975	Phil Boggs, United States	597.12
1978	Phil Boggs, United States	913.95
1982	Greg Louganis, United States	752.67
1986	Greg Louganis, United States	750.06
1991	Kent Ferguson, United States	650.25
1994	Wu Zhuocheng, China	655.44
1998	Dmitry Sautin, Russia	746.79

Platform

		Pts
1973	Klaus Dibiasi, Italy	559.53
1975	Klaus Dibiasi, Italy	547.98
1978	Greg Louganis, United States	844.11
1982	Greg Louganis, United States	634.26
1986	Greg Louganis, United States	668.58
1991	Sun Shuwei, China	626.79
1994	Dmitry Sautin, Russia	634.71
1998	Dmitry Sautin, Russia	750.90

3-meter Synchronized

		Pts
1998	China (Sun Shuwei, Tian Liang)	313.50

10-meter Synchronized

		Pts
1998	China (Xu Hao, Yu Zhuocheng)	326.34

WOMEN

1-meter Springboard

		Pts
1991	Gao Min, China	478.26
1994	Chen Lixia, China	279.30
1998	Irina Lashko, Russia	296.07

3-meter Springboard

		Pts
1973	Christa Koehler, East Germany	442.17
1975	Irina Kalinina, USSR	489.81
1978	Irina Kalinina, USSR	691.43
1982	Megan Neyer, United States	501.03
1986	Gao Min, China	582.90
1991	Gao Min, China	539.01
1994	Tan Shuping, China	548.49
1998	Yulia Pakhalina, Russia	544.62

Platform

		Pts
1973	Ulrike Knape, Sweden	406.77
1975	Janet Ely, United States	403.89
1978	Irina Kalinina, USSR	412.71
1982	Wendy Wyland, United States	438.79
1986	Chen Lin, China	449.67
1991	Fu Mingxia, China	426.51
1994	Fu Mingxia, China	434.04
1998	Olena Zhupyna, Ukraine	550.41

3-meter Synchronized

		Pts
1998	Russia (Irina Lashko, Yulia Pakhalina)	282.30

10-meter Synchronized

		Pts
1998	Ukraine (Olena Zhupyna, Svitlana Serbina)	278.28

U.S. Olympic Champions

Men

50-METER FREESTYLE

1988....Matt Biondi   22.14*

100-METER FREESTLYE

1906....Charles Daniels   1:13.4
1908....Charles Daniels   1:05.6*
1912....Duke Kahanamoku   1:03.4
1920....Duke Kahanamoku   1:00.4
1924....John Weissmuller   59.0‡
1928....John Weissmuller   58.6‡
1948....Wally Ris   57.3‡
1952....Clarke Scholes   57.4
1964....Don Schollander   53.4‡
1972....Mark Spitz   51.22*
1976....Jim Montgomery   49.99*
1984....Rowdy Gaines   49.80‡
1988....Matt Biondi   48.63‡

200-METER FREESTYLE

1904....Charles Daniels   2:44.2
1906....Not held 1906–1964
1972....Mark Spitz   1:52.78*
1976....Bruce Furniss   1:50.29*

400-METER FREESTYLE

1904....Charles Daniels (440 yds)   6:16.2
1920....Norman Ross   5:26.8
1924....John Weissmuller   5:04.2‡
1932....Buster Crabbe   4:48.4‡
1936....Jack Medica   4:44.5‡
1948....William Smith   4:41.0‡
1964....Don Schollander   4:12.2*
1968....Mike Burton   4:09.0‡
1976....Brian Goodell   3:51.93*
1984....George DiCarlo   3:51.23‡

1500-METER FREESTYLE

1920....Norman Ross   22:23.2
1948....James McLane   19:18.5
1952....Ford Konno   18:30.3‡
1968....Mike Burton   16:38.9‡
1972....Mike Burton   15:52.58‡
1976....Brian Goodell   15:02.40*
1984....Michael O'Brien   15:05.20

100-METER BACKSTROKE

1912....Harry Hebner   1:21.2
1920....Warren Kealoha   1:15.2
1924....Warren Kealoha   1:13.2‡
1928....George Kojac   1:08.2*
1936....Adolph Kiefer   1:05.9‡
1948....Allen Stack   1:06.4
1952....Yoshi Oyakawa   1:05.4‡
1976....John Naber   55.49*
1984....Rick Carey   55.79
1996....Jeff Rouse   54.10

200-METER BACKSTROKE

1964....Jed Graef   2:10.3*
1976....John Naber   1:59.19*
1984....Rick Carey   2:00.23
1996....Brad Bridgewater   1:58.54

100-METER BREASTSTROKE

1968....Donald McKenzie   1:07.7‡
1976....John Hencken   1:03.11*
1984....Steve Lundquist   1:01.65 *
1992....Nelson Diebel   1:01.50‡

200-METER BREASTSTROKE

1924....Robert Skelton   2:56.6
1948....Joseph Verdeur   2:39.3‡
1960....William Mulliken   2:37.4
1972....John Hencken   2:21.55
1992....Mike Barrowman   2:10.16*

100-METER BUTTERFLY

1968....Douglas Russell   55.9‡
1972....Mark Spitz   54.27*
1976....Matt Vogel   54.35
1992....Pablo Morales   53.32

200-METER BUTTERFLY

1956....William Yorzyk   2:19.3‡
1960....Michael Troy   2:12.8*
1968....Carl Robie   2:08.7
1972....Mark Spitz   2:00.70*
1976....Mike Bruner   1:59.23*
1992....Melvin Stewart   1:56.26

200-METER INDIVIDUAL MEDLEY

1968....Charles Hickcox   2:12.0‡

400-METER INDIVIDUAL MEDLEY

1964....Richard Roth   4:45.4*
1968....Charles Hickcox   4:48.4
1976....Rod Strachan   4:23.68*
1996....Tom Dolan   4.:14.90

3-METER SPRINGBOARD DIVING

1920....Louis Kuehn   675.4 points
1924....Albert White   696.4
1928....Pete Desjardins   185.04
1932....Michael Galitzen   161.38
1936....Richard Degener   163.57
1948....Bruce Harlan   163.64
1952....David Browning   205.29
1956....Robert Clotworthy   159.56
1960....Gary Tobian   170.00
1964....Kenneth Sitzberger   159.90
1968....Bernard Wrightson   170.15
1976....Philip Boggs   619.05
1984....Greg Louganis   754.41
1988....Greg Louganis   730.80

PLATFORM DIVING

1904....George Sheldon   12.66 points
1920....Clarence Pinkston   100.67
1924....Albert White   97.46
1928....Pete Desjardins   98.74
1932....Harold Smith   124.80
1936....Marshall Wayne   113.58
1948....Sammy Lee   130.05
1952....Sammy Lee   156.28
1960....Robert Webster   165.56
1964....Robert Webster   148.58
1984....Greg Louganis   576.99
1988....Greg Louganis   638.61

* World record. ‡ Meet (Olympic) record.

Women

50-METER FREESTYLE

1996.....Amy Van Dyken   24.87

100-METER FREESTLYE

1920....Ethelda Bleibtrey	1:13.6*
1924....Ethel Lackie	1:12.4
1928....Albina Osipowich	1:11.0‡
1932....Helene Madison	1:06.8‡
1968....Jan Henne	1:00.0
1972....Sandra Neilson	58.59‡
1984....Carrie Steinseifer	55.92
Nancy Hogshead	55.92

200-METER FREESTYLE

1968....Debbie Meyer	2:10.5‡
1984....Mary Wayte	1:59.23
1992....Nicole Haislett	1:57.90

400-METER FREESTYLE

1924....Martha Norelius	6:02.2‡
1928....Martha Norelius	5:42.8*
1932....Helene Madison	5:28.5*
1948....Ann Curtis	5:17.8‡
1960....Chris von Saltza	4:50.6
1964....Virginia Duenkel	4:43.3‡
1968....Debbie Meyer	4:31.8‡
1984....Tiffany Cohen	4:07.10‡
1988....Janet Evans	4:03.85*

800-METER FREESTYLE

1968....Debbie Meyer	9:24.0‡
1972....Keena Rothhammer	8:53.86*
1984....Tiffany Cohen	8:24.95‡
1988....Janet Evans	8:20.20‡
1992.....Janet Evans	8:25.52
1996.....Brooke Bennett	8:27.89

100-METER BACKSTROKE

1924....Sybil Bauer	1:23.2‡
1932....Eleanor Holm	1:19.4
1960....Lynn Burke	1:09.3‡
1964....Cathy Ferguson	1:07.7*
1968....Kaye Hall	1:06.2*
1972....Melissa Belote	1:05.78‡
1984....Theresa Andrews	1:02.55
1996....Beth Botsford	1:01.19

200-METER BACKSTROKE

1968....Pokey Watson	2:24.8‡
1972....Melissa Belote	2:19.19*

* World record; ‡Meet (Olympic) record.

100-METER BREASTSTROKE

1972....Catherine Carr   1:13.58*

200-METER BREASTSTROKE

1968....Sharon Wichman   2:44.4‡

100-METER BUTTERFLY

1956....Shelley Mann	1:11.0‡
1960....Carolyn Schuler	1:09.5‡
1964....Sharon Stouder	1:04.7*
1984....Mary T. Meagher	59.26
1996....Amy Van Dyken	59.13

200-METER BUTTERFLY

1972....Karen Moe	2:15.57*
1984....Mary T. Meagher	2:06.90‡
1992....Summer Sanders	2:08.67

200-METER INDIVIDUAL MEDLEY

1968....Sharon Wichman	2:44.4‡
1984....Tracy Caulkins	2:12.64‡

400-METER INDIVIDUAL MEDLEY

1964....Donna De Varona	5:18.7‡
1968....Claudia Kolb	5:08.5‡
1984....Tracy Caulkins	4:39.24
1988....Janet Evans	4:37.76

3-METER SPRINGBOARD DIVING

1920....Aileen Riggin	539.9 points
1924....Elizabeth Becker	474.5
1928....Helen Meany	78.62
1932....Georgia Coleman	87.52
1936....Marjorie Gestring	89.27
1948....Victoria Draves	108.74
1952....Patricia McCormick	147.30
1956....Patricia McCormick	142.36
1968....Sue Gossick	150.77
1972....Micki King	450.03
1976....Jennifer Chandler	506.19

PLATFORM DIVING

1924....Caroline Smith	33.2 points
1928....Elizabeth Becker Pinkston	31.6
1932....Dorothy Poynton	40.26
1936....Dorothy Poynton Hill	33.93
1948....Victoria Draves	68.87
1952....Patricia McCormick	79.37
1956....Patricia McCormick	84.85
1964....Lesley Bush	99.80

Notable Achievements

Barrier Breakers

MEN

Event	Barrier	Athlete and Nation	Time	Date
100 Freestyle	1:00	Johnny Weissmuller, United States	58.6	7-9-22
100 Freestyle	:50	James Montgomery, United States	49.99	7-25-76
200 Freestyle	2:00	Don Schollander, United States	1:58.8	7-27-63
200 Freestyle	1:50	Sergei Kopliakov, USSR	1:49.83	4-7-79
400 Freestyle	4:00	Rick DeMont, United States	3:58.18	9-6-73
400 Freestyle	3:50	Vladimir Salnikov, USSR	3:49.57	3-12-82
800 Freestyle	8:00	Vladimir Salnikov, USSR	7:56.49	3-23-79
1500 Freestyle	15:00	Vladimir Salnikov, USSR	14:58.27	7-22-80
100 Backstroke	1:00	Thompson Mann, United States	59.6	10-16-64
200 Backstroke	2:00	John Naber, United States	1:59.19	7-24-76
200 Breaststroke	2:30	Chester Jastremski, United States	2:29.6	8-19-61
100 Butterfly	1:00	Lance Larson, United States	59.0	6-29-60
200 Butterfly	2:00	Roger Pyttel, East Germany	1:59.63	6-3-76

WOMEN

Event	Barrier	Athlete and Nation	Time	Date
100 Freestyle	1:00	Dawn Fraser, Australia	59.9	10-27-62
200 Freestyle	2:00	Kornelia Ender, East Germany	1:59.78	6-2-76
400 Freestyle	4:30	Debbie Meyer, United States	4:29.0	8-18-67
800 Freestyle	10:00	Jane Cederqvist, Sweden	9:55.6	8-17-60
800 Freestyle	9:00	Ann Simmons, United States	8:59.4	9-10-71
1500 Freestyle	20:00	Ilsa Konrads, Australia	19:25.7	1-14-60
	16:00	Janet Evans, United States	15:52.10	3-26-88
200 Backstroke	2:30	Satoko Tanaka, Japan	2:29.6	2-10-63
100 Butterfly	1:00	Christiane Knacke, East Germany	59.78	8-28-77
400 Individual Medley	5:00	Gudrun Wegner, East Germany	4:57.51	9-6-73

Olympic Achievements

MOST INDIVIDUAL GOLDS IN SINGLE OLYMPICS

MEN

No.	Athlete and Nation	Olympic Year	Events
4	Mark Spitz, United States	1972	100, 200 Free; 100, 200 Fly

WOMEN

No.	Athlete and Nation	Olympic Year	Events
4	Kristin Otto, East Germany	1988	50, 100 Free; 100 Back; 100 Fly
3	Debbie Meyer, United States	1968	200, 400, 800 Free
3	Shane Gould, Australia	1972	200, 400 Free; 200 IM
3	Kornelia Ender, East Germany	1976	100, 200 Free; 100 Fly
3	Janet Evans, United States	1988	400, 800 Free; 400 IM
3	Krisztina Egerszegi, Hungary	1992	100, 200 Back; 400 IM
3	Michelle Smith, Ireland	1996	400 Free; 200, 400 IM

Olympic Achievements *(Cont.)*

MOST INDIVIDUAL OLYMPIC GOLD MEDALS, CAREER
MEN

No.	Athlete and Nation	Olympic Years and Events
4	Charles Meldrum Daniels, United States	1904 (220, 440 Free); 1906 (100 Free) 1908 (100 Free)
4	Roland Matthes, East Germany	1968 (100, 200 Back); 1972 (100, 200 Back)
4	Mark Spitz, United States	1972 (100, 200 Free; 100, 200 Fly)

WOMEN

4	Kristin Otto, East Germany	1988 (50 Free; 100 Free, Back and Fly)
4	Janet Evans, United States	1988 (400, 800 Free; 400 IM); 1992 (800 Free)
4	Krisztina Egerszegi, Hungary	1992 (100, 200 Back; 400 IM); 1996 (200 Back)

Most Olympic Gold Medals in a Single Olympics, Men—7, Mark Spitz, United States, 1972: 100, 200 Free; 100, 200 Fly; 4 x 100, 4 x 200 Free Relays; 4 x 100 Medley Relay.

Most Olympic Gold Medals in a Single Olympics, Women—6, Kristin Otto, East Germany, 1988: 50, 100 Free; 100 Back; 100 Fly; 4 x 100 Free Relay; 4 x 100 Medley Relay.

Most Olympic Medals in a Career, Men—11, Matt Biondi, United States: 1984 (one gold), '88 (five gold, one silver, one bronze), '92 (two gold, one silver); 11, Mark Spitz, United States: 1968 (two gold, one silver, one bronze), '72 (seven gold).

Most Olympic Medals in a Career, Women—8, Dawn Fraser, Australia: 1956 (two gold, one silver), '60 (one gold, two silver), '64 (one gold, one silver) 8, Kornelia Ender, East Germany: 1972 (three silver), '76 (four gold, one silver); 8, Shirley Babashoff, United States: 1972 (one gold, two silver); '76 (one gold, four silver).

Winner, Same Event, Three Consecutive Olympics—Dawn Fraser, Australia, 100 Freestyle, 1956, '60, '64; Krisztina Egerszegi, Hungary, 200 Back, 1988, '92, '96.

Youngest Person to Win an Olympic Diving Gold—Marjorie Gestring, United States, 1936, 13 years, 9 months, springboard diving.

Youngest Person to Win an Olympic Swimming Gold—Krisztina Egerszegi, Hungary, 1988, 14 years, one month, 200 backstroke.

Most World Records, Career, Women—42, Ragnhild Hveger, Denmark, 1936–42.

World Record Achievements

Most World Records, Career, Men—32, Arne Borg, Sweden, 1921–29.

Most Freestyle Records Held Concurrently—5, Helene Madison, United States, 1931–33; 5, Shane Gould, Australia, 1972.

Most Consecutive Lowerings of a Record—10, Kornelia Ender, East Germany, 100 Freestyle, 7-13-73 to 7-19-76.

Longest Duration of World Record—19 years, 359 days, 1:04.6 in 100 Free, Willy den Ouden, Netherlands.

Skiing

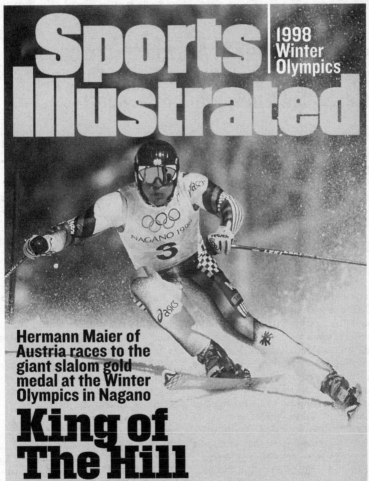

Sports Illustrated

1998 Winter Olympics

Hermann Maier of
Austria races to the
giant slalom gold
medal at the Winter
Olympics in Nagano

King of The Hill

CARL YARBROUGH

The Next Generation

The reckless style of Austria's Hermann Maier typified a season of thrills and spills, and signaled a new era for the sport

BY TIM LAYDEN

IN ONE SEASON, the sport was utterly changed. A former bricklayer from the smallest of Austrian hamlets stretched the limits of bravery by recovering from a frightening, flying crash to win two Olympic gold medals. An aging Italian playboy who also had once expanded the borders in his specialty failed to win a medal at the Games but finished the season with an emotional World Cup slalom victory. They passed on the hill somewhere, Hermann Maier and Alberto Tomba, earmarking 1998 as one of the most memorable years in the recent history of their sport.

Their supporting cast was brilliant as well. America's Picabo Street won a gold medal in Nagano barely 14 months after reconstructive surgery on her left knee and less than two weeks after suffering a concussion in a headfirst fall in Sweden. The sight of Street, tearful and joyous at once, raising her arms to the heavens at the finish of the Super G, was one of the most emotional moments of the Olympic

Games. Street's career was tragically imperiled once again when she broke her left leg and tore the anterior cruciate ligament in her right knee shortly after the Olympics. Her loss is also a huge blow to the U.S. program, which is woefully thin behind her.

Katja Seizinger of Germany became the first woman to repeat as Olympic downhill champion and won the overall World Cup title for the second time in three years. German women swept the top three spots in the World Cup standings but paled in comparison to the Austrian men, who not only swept the top three positions but also had six of the top 10.

Towering over it all was Maier, who replaced Tomba as the brightest star in the ski racing universe. Maier came to the Olympics with a growing legend and 10 World Cup victories on the season. His story was irresistible. A passionate ski racer since early childhood, he had been heartbroken at age 16 by the national ski academy's judgment that he was too small

After winning gold at Nagano, Street suffered another serious injury.

Ingemar Stenmark. He became the first Austrian since Karl Schranz in '70 to win the overall World Cup points title. All of this he accomplished while revolutionizing the speed disciplines of downhill and Super G, and even the fast, technical giant slalom, by skiing a straighter line down the mountain than any other skier has consistently taken. "It's like it's a new era, and he's the beginning," said U.S. 1994 downhill gold medalist Tommy Moe.

The Olympics were to be Maier's grandest stage, and when they were over, his fame would reach worldwide. On the morning of Friday, Feb. 13, after five days of weather-related delays, Maier

and too frail to warrant its further support. Relegated to the minor leagues and supporting himself as a bricklayer and a ski instructor near his hometown of Flachau (pop. 2,500), it appeared his turn on the international stage was finished. At the advanced athletic age of 22, however, after winning regional races for several years, Maier was given an opportunity by the same federation that had scorned him, and so began his spectacular rise to the top of his sport.

In the 1997–98 season, the Hermann-ator, as he came to be called, in honor of another Austrian hero, won five World Cup races in a row, one short of the record shared by Jean-Claude Killy and

shoved himself free of the start house in the downhill on a mountain overlooking the small resort village of Hakuba. Skiing recklessly, as always, he dived far too fast into the steep Alpen Turn near the top of the course and went spectacularly airborne at 65 mph, flying through two rows of safety netting before coming to a stop in deep, soft snow. Miraculously, while creating a highlight clip for the ages, Maier suffered only a bruised shoulder and a sprained knee. Three days later, skiing his signature tight line, he won the Super G by .61 of a second, an enormous margin. By the end of the week he had added a second gold, in the giant slalom, and had jokingly used the German word *unsterblich* to describe

ASSOCIATED PRESS

He took a terrible fall in the giant slalom, on a course that was too fast and too steep for his declining skills. On the final Saturday of the Games, fighting a persistent snowfall in the Shiga Kogen mountains, Tomba struggled through his first slalom run, leaving him far out of medal contention. His Olympic career ended not with gold but with Tomba limping with a sore back into a small shack at the base of the slalom hill and quietly withdrawing from the second run. Three weeks after the Olympics, however, Tomba won the 50th World Cup race of his epic career, a slalom in Crans Montana, Switzerland, before scores of his adoring fans.

Appropriately, the Olympic slalom was won by Hans-Petter

himself. In English it means immortal.

Tomba was once described in similar terms. He took the World Cup by storm in the 1987–88 season, winning nine slalom and giant slalom races with a powerful style in which he seemed to explode through the gates, rather than slash around them. In the Calgary Olympics he won two gold medals. He added a gold and a silver in Albertville and another silver in Lillehammer. Nagano was to be his Olympic farewell, but instead of going out a hero, he left looking beaten and past his prime.

Buraas, a 22-year-old Norwegian with the pocked skin of a teenager still in the throes of puberty and scruffy hair that he dyes a different color for each event. For the slalom at Nagano, he decided to go with flaming pink. Buraas, like Tomba a decade before him, is changing his sport, mastering shorter skis and collapsible gates. "He is," said teammate and slalom silver medal winner Ole Christian Furuseth, "the racer for this moment."

That seemed a perfect title in a year that saw old heroes and old styles pushed aside by new ones.

FOR THE RECORD·1997–1998

World Cup Alpine Racing Season Results

Men

Date	Event	Site	Winner
10-24-97	Parallel Slalom	Tignes, France	Josef Strobl, Austria
10-26-97	Giant Slalom	Tignes, France	Michael von Grünigen, Switz
11-20-97	Giant Slalom	Park City, Utah	Hermann Maier, Austria
11-22-97	Slalom	Park City, Utah	Thomas Stangassinger, Austria
12-4-97	Downhill	Beaver Creek, Colorado	Kristian Ghedina, Italy
12-5-97	Downhill	Beaver Creek, Colorado	Andreas Schifferer, Austria
12-6-97	Super G	Beaver Creek, Colorado	Hermann Maier, Austria
12-14-97	Giant Slalom	Val d'Isère, France	Michael von Grünigen, Switz
12-15-97	Slalom	Sestriere, Italy	Finn Christian Jagge, Norway
12-21-97	Giant Slalom	Alta Badia, Italy	Christian Mayer, Austria
12-29-97	Downhill	Bormio, Italy	Hermann Maier, Austria
12-30-97	Downhill	Bormio, Italy	Andreas Schifferer, Austria
1-3-98	Giant Slalom	Kranjska Gora, Slovenia	Christian Mayer, Austria
1-4-98	Slalom	Kranjska Gora, Slovenia	Thomas Sykora, Austria
1-6-98	Giant Slalom	Saalbach, Austria	Hermann Maier, Austria
1-8-98	Slalom	Schladming, Austria	Alberto Tomba, Italy
1-10-98	Super G	Schladming, Austria	Hermann Maier, Austria
1-11-98	Super G	Schladming, Austria	Hermann Maier, Austria
1-13-98	Giant Slalom	Adelboden, Switzerland	Hermann Maier, Austria
1-16-98	Downhill	Wengen, Switzerland	Hermann Maier, Austria
1-17-98	Downhill	Wengen, Switzerland	Andreas Schifferer, Austria
1-18-98	Slalom	Veysonnaz, Switzerland	Thomas Stangassinger, Austria
1-16/18-98	Combined	Wengen/Veysonnaz, Switzerland	Hermann Maier, Austria
1-23-98	Downhill	Kitzbühel, Austria	Didier Cuche, Switzerland
1-24-98	Downhill	Kitzbühel, Austria	Kristian Ghedina, Italy
1-25-98	Slalom	Kitzbühel, Austria	Thomas Stangassinger, Austria
1-24/25-98	Combined	Kitzbühel, Austria	Kjetil André Aamodt, Norway
1-26-98	Slalom	Kitzbühel, Austria	Thomas Sykora, Austria
1-31-98	Downhill	Garmisch-Partenkirchen, Germany	Andreas Schifferer, Austria
2-1-98	Super G	Garmisch-Partenkirchen, Germany	Hermann Maier, Austria
2-28-98	Giant Slalom	Yong Pyong, Korea	Michael von Grünigen, Switz
3-1-98	Slalom	Yong Pyong, Korea	Ole Kristian Furuseth, Norway
3-8-98	Downhill	Kvitfjell, Norway	Nicolas Burtin, France
3-8-98	Super G	Kvitfjell, Norway	Hans Knauss, Austria
3-13-98	Downhill	Crans-Montana, Switzerland	Josef Strobl, Austria
3-14-98	Giant Slalom	Crans-Montana, Switzerland	Stephan Eberharter, Austria
3-15-98	Slalom	Crans-Montana, Switzerland	Alberto Tomba, Italy

Women

Date	Event	Site	Winner
10-24-97	Parallel Slalom	Tignes, France	Leila Piccard, France
10-25-97	Giant Slalom	Tignes, France	Deborah Compagnoni, Italy
11-21-97	Giant Slalom	Park City, Utah	Deborah Compagnoni, Italy
11-23-97	Slalom	Park City, Utah	Zali Steggall, Australia
11-28-97	Parallel Slalom	Mammoth Mountain, California	Hilde Gerg, Germany
11-29-97	Super G	Mammoth Mountain, California	Katja Seizinger, Germany
12-4-97	Downhill	Lake Louise, Alberta	Katja Seizinger, Germany
12-5-97	Downhill	Lake Louise, Alberta	Katja Seizinger, Germany
12-6-97	Super G	Lake Louise, Alberta	Katja Seizinger, Germany
12-17-97	Downhill	Val d'Isère, France	Katja Seizinger, Germany
12-18-97	Super G	Val d'Isère, France	Katja Seizinger, Germany
12-19-97	Giant Slalom	Val d'Isère, France	Deborah Compagnoni, Italy
12-20-97	Slalom	Val d'Isère, France	Ylva Nowen, Sweden
12-17/20-97	Combined	Val d'Isère, France	Hilde Gerg, Germany
12-27-97	Slalom	Lienz, Austria	Ylva Nowen, Sweden
12-28-97	Slalom	Lienz, Austria	Ylva Nowen, Sweden
1-5-98	Slalom	Bormio, Italy	Ylva Nowen, Sweden
1-6-98	Giant Slalom	Bormio, Italy	Deborah Compagnoni, Italy
1-10-98	Giant Slalom	Bormio, Italy	Martina Ertl, Germany
1-11-98	Slalom	Bormio, Italy	Hilde Gerg, Germany
1-18-98	Downhill	Altenmarkt, Austria	Renate Götschl, Austria
1-18-98	Super G	Altenmarkt, Austria	Martina Ertl, Germany

World Cup Alpine Racing Season Results (Cont.)

Women (Cont.)

Date	Event	Site	Winner
1-22-98	Downhill	Cortina d'Ampezzo, Italy	Isolde Kostner, Italy
1-23-98	Super G	Cortina d'Ampezzo, Italy	Melanie Suchet, France
1-24-98	Super G	Cortina d'Ampezzo, Italy	Katja Seizinger, Germany
1-25-98	Giant Slalom	Cortina d'Ampezzo, Italy	Martina Ertl, Germany
1-28-98	Giant Slalom	Are, Sweden	Martina Ertl, Germany
1-29-98	Slalom	Are, Sweden	Kristina Koznick, United States
1-31-98	Downhill	Are, Sweden	Katja Seizinger, Germany
1-29/31-98	Combined	Are, Sweden	Hilde Gerg, Germany
3-1-98	Slalom	Saalbach, Austria	Martina Ertl, Germany
3-14-98	Slalom	Crans-Montana, Switzerland	Urska Hrovat, Slovenia
3-15-98	Giant Slalom	Crans-Montana, Switzerland	Alexandra Meissnitzer, Austria

World Cup Alpine Racing Final Standings

Men

OVERALL

	Pts
Hermann Maier, Austria	1685
Andreas Schifferer, Austria	1114
Stefan Eberharter, Austria	1030
Kjetil André Aamodt, Norway	901
Hans Knauss, Austria	888
Michael von Grünigen, Switz	746
Josef Strobl, Austria	647
Didier Cuche, Switzerland	627

DOWNHILL

	Pts
Andreas Schifferer, Austria	655
Hermann Maier, Austria	479
Nicolas Burtin, France	469
Didier Cuche, Switzerland	424
Jean-Luc Cretier, France	414
Kristian Ghedina, Italy	412
Stefan Eberharter, Austria	377
Hannes Trinkl, Austria	321

SLALOM

	Pts
Thomas Sykora, Austria	521
Thomas Stangassinger, Aust.	517
Hans-Petter Buraas, Norway	420
Finn Christian Jagge, Norway	345
Kiminobu Kimura, Japan	316
Ole Christian Furuseth, Nor	296
Alberto Tomba, Italy	290
Jure Kosir, Slovenia	257

GIANT SLALOM

	Pts
Hermann Maier, Austria	620
Michael von Grünigen, Switz	560
Christian Mayer, Austria	429
Stefan Eberharter, Austria	388
Hans Knauss, Austria	375
Urs Kälin, Switzerland	277
Steve Locher, Switzerland	246
Rainer Salzgeber, Austria	229

SUPER G

	Pts
Hermann Maier, Austria	400
Hans Knauss, Austria	256
Stefan Eberharter, Austria	220
Patrik Jaerbyn, Sweden	195
Andreas Schifferer, Austria	185
Didier Cuche, Switzerland	163
Luca Cattaneo, Italy	148
Peter Runggaldier, Italy	131

Women

OVERALL

	Pts
Katja Seizinger, Germany	1655
Martina Ertl, Germany	1508
Hilde Gerg, Germany	1391
Deborah Compagnoni, Italy	912
Alexandra Meissnitzer, Austria	884
Ylva Nowen, Sweden	815
Renate Götschl, Austria	787
Isolde Kostner, Italy	695

DOWNHILL

	Pts
Katja Seizinger, Germany	520
Renate Götschl, Austria	392
Isolde Kostner, Italy	292
Melanie Suchet, France	237
Hilde Gerg, Germany	224
Florence Masnada, France	216
Heidi Zurbriggen, Switzerland	185
Alexandra Meissnitzer, Austria	168

SLALOM

	Pts
Ylva Nowen, Sweden	620
Kristina Koznick, United States	560
Hilde Gerg, Germany	451
Urska Hrovat, Slovenia	423
Martina Ertl, Germany	320
Deborah Compagnoni, Italy	304
Trine Putte Bakke, Norway	281
Sabine Egger, Austria	257

GIANT SLALOM

	Pts
Martina Ertl, Germany	591
Deborah Compagnoni, Italy	565
Alexandra Meissnitzer, Austria	445
Sonja Nef, Switzerland	359
Andrine Flemmen, Norway	296
Katja Seizinger, Germany	295
Sophie LeFranc-Duvillard, Fra	252
Leila Piccard, France	224

SUPER G

	Pts
Katja Seizinger, Germany	445
Renate Götschl, Austria	305
Isolde Kostner, Italy	266
Martina Ertl, Germany	259
Melanie Suchet, France	228
Regina Häusl, Germany	204
Hilde Gerg, Germany	197
Heidi Zurbriggen, Switzerland	196

FOR THE RECORD·Year by Year

Event Descriptions

Downhill: A speed event entailing a single run on a course with a minimum vertical drop of 500 meters (800 for Men's World Cup) and very few control gates.
Slalom: A technical event in which times for runs on two courses are totaled to determine the winner. Skiers must make many quick, short turns through a combination of gates (55-75 gates for men, 40-60 for women) over a short course (140-220–meter vertical drop for men, 120-180 for women).
Combined: An event in which scores from designated slalom and downhill races are combined to determine finish order.

Giant Slalom: A faster technical event with fewer, more broadly spaced gates than in the slalom. Times for runs on two courses with vertical drops of 250-400 meters for men and 250-300 meters for women are combined to determine the winner.
Super Giant Slalom: A speed event that is a cross between the downhill and the giant slalom.
Parallel Slalom: A technical event that combines slalom and giant slalom turns.

FIS World Championships

Sites

1931	Mürren, Switzerland
1932	Cortina d'Ampezzo, Italy
1933	Innsbruck, Austria
1934	St Moritz, Switzerland
1935	Mürren, Switzerland
1936	Innsbruck, Austria
1937	Chamonix, France
1938	Engelberg, Switzerland
1939	Zakopane, Poland

Men

DOWNHILL

1931	Walter Prager, Switzerland
1932	Gustav Lantschner, Austria
1933	Walter Prager, Switzerland
1934	David Zogg, Switzerland
1935	Franz Zingerle, Austria
1936	Rudolf Rominger, Switzerland
1937	Émile Allais, France
1938	James Couttet, France
1939	Hans Lantschner, Germany

SLALOM

1931	David Zogg, Switzerland
1932	Friedrich Dauber, Germany
1933	Anton Seelos, Austria
1934	Franz Pfnür, Germany
1935	Anton Seelos, Austria
1936	Rudi Matt, Austria
1937	Émile Allais, France
1938	Rudolf Rominger, Switzerland
1939	Rudolf Rominger, Switzerland

Women

DOWNHILL

1931	Esme Mackinnon, Great Britain
1932	Paola Wiesinger, Italy
1933	Inge Wersin-Lantschner, Austria
1934	Anni Rüegg, Switzerland
1935	Christel Cranz, Germany
1936	Evie Pinching, Great Britain
1937	Christel Cranz, Germany
1938	Lisa Resch, Germany
1939	Christel Cranz, Germany

SLALOM

1931	Esme Mackinnon, Great Britain
1932	Rösli Streiff, Switzerland
1933	Inge Wersin-Lantschner, Austria
1934	Christel Cranz, Germany
1935	Anni Rüegg, Switzerland
1936	Gerda Paumgarten, Austria
1937	Christel Cranz, Germany
1938	Christel Cranz, Germany
1939	Christel Cranz, Germany

FIS World Alpine Ski Championships

Sites

1950	Aspen, Colorado
1954	Are, Sweden
1958	Badgastein, Austria
1962	Chamonix, France
1966	Portillo, Chile
1970	Val Gardena, Italy
1974	St Moritz, Switzerland
1978	Garmisch-Partenkirchen, West Germany
1982	Schladming, Austria
1985	Bormio, Italy
1987	Crans-Montana, Switzerland
1989	Vail, Colorado
1991	Saalbach-Hinterglemm, Austria
1993	Morioka-Shizukuishi, Japan
1996	Sierra Nevada, Spain
1997	Sestriere, Italy

Men
DOWNHILL

1950............Zeno Colo, Italy	1982............Harti Weirather, Austria
1954............Christian Pravda, Austria	1985............Pirmin Zurbriggen, Switzerland
1958............Toni Sailer, Austria	1987............Peter Müller, Switzerland
1962............Karl Schranz, Austria	1989............Hansjörg Tauscher, West Germany
1966............Jean-Claude Killy, France	1991............Franz Heinzer, Switzerland
1970............Bernard Russi, Switzerland	1993............Urs Lehmann, Switzerland
1974............David Zwilling, Austria	1996............Patrick Ortlieb, Austria
1978............Josef Walcher, Austria	1997............Bruno Kernen, Switzerland

SLALOM

1950............Georges Schneider, Switzerland	1982............Ingemar Stenmark, Sweden
1954............Stein Eriksen, Norway	1985............Jonas Nilsson, Sweden
1958............Josl Rieder, Austria	1987............Frank Wörndl, West Germany
1962............Charles Bozon, France	1989............Rudolf Nierlich, Austria
1966............Carlo Senoner, Italy	1991............Marc Girardelli, Luxembourg
1970............Jean-Noël Augert, France	1993............Kjetil André Aamodt, Norway
1974............Gustavo Thoeni, Italy	1996............Alberto Tomba, Italy
1978............Ingemar Stenmark, Sweden	1997............Tom Stiansen, Norway

GIANT SLALOM

1950............Zeno Colo, Italy	1982............Steve Mahre, United States
1954............Stein Eriksen, Norway	1985............Markus Wasmaier, West Germany
1958............Toni Sailer, Austria	1987............Pirmin Zurbriggen, Switzerland
1962............Egon Zimmermann, Austria	1989............Rudolf Nierlich, Austria
1966............Guy Périllat, France	1991............Rudolf Nierlich, Austria
1970............Karl Schranz, Austria	1993............Kjetil André Aamodt, Norway
1974............Gustavo Thoeni, Italy	1996............Alberto Tomba, Italy
1978............Ingemar Stenmark, Sweden	1997............Michael von Grünigen, Switzerland

COMBINED

1982............Michel Vion, France	1991............Stefan Eberharter, Austria
1985............Pirmin Zurbriggen, Switzerland	1993............Lasse Kjus, Norway
1987............Marc Girardelli, Luxembourg	1996............Marc Girardelli, Luxembourg
1989............Marc Girardelli, Luxembourg	1997............Kjetil André Aamodt, Norway

SUPER G

1987............Pirmin Zurbriggen, Switzerland	1993............Cancelled due to weather
1989............Martin Hangl, Switzerland	1996............Atle Skaardal, Norway
1991............Stefan Eberharter, Austria	1997............Atle Skaardal, Norway

Women
DOWNHILL

1950............Trude Beiser-Jochum, Austria	1982............Gerry Sorensen, Canada
1954............Ida Schopfer, Switzerland	1985............Michela Figini, Switzerland
1958............Lucile Wheeler, Canada	1987............Maria Walliser, Switzerland
1962............Christl Haas, Austria	1989............Maria Walliser, Switzerland
1966............Erika Schinegger, Austria	1991............Petra Kronberger, Austria
1970............Annerösli Zryd, Switzerland	1993............Kate Pace, Canada
1974............Annemarie Moser-Pröll, Austria	1996............Picabo Street, United States
1978............Annemarie Moser-Pröll, Austria	1997............Hilary Lindh, United States

SLALOM

1950............Dagmar Rom, Austria	1982............Erika Hess, Switzerland
1954............Trude Klecker, Austria	1985............Perrine Pelen, France
1958............Inger Bjornbakken, Norway	1987............Erika Hess, Switzerland
1962............Marianne Jahn, Austria	1989............Mateja Svet, Yugoslavia
1966............Annie Famose, France	1991............Vreni Schneider, Switzerland
1970............Ingrid Lafforgue, France	1993............Karin Buder, Austria
1974............Hanni Wenzel, Liechtenstein	1996............Pernilla Wiberg, Sweden
1978............Lea Sölkner, Austria	1997............Deborah Compagnoni, Italy

GIANT SLALOM

1950............Dagmar Rom, Austria	1966............Marielle Goitschel, France
1954............Lucienne Schmith-Couttet, France	1970............Betsy Clifford, Canada
1958............Lucile Wheeler, Canada	1974............Fabienne Serrat, France
1962............Marianne Jahn, Austria	1978............Maria Epple, West Germany

Women (Cont.)

GIANT SLALOM (Cont.)

1982 ....Erika Hess, Switzerland	1991 ....Pernilla Wiberg, Sweden
1985 ....Diann Roffe, United States	1993 ....Carole Merle, France
1987 ....Vreni Schneider, Switzerland	1996 ....Deborah Compagnoni, Italy
1989 ....Vreni Schneider, Switzerland	1997 ....Deborah Compagnoni, Italy

COMBINED

1982 ....Erika Hess, Switzerland	1991 ....Chantal Bournissen, Switzerland
1985 ....Erika Hess, Switzerland	1993 ....Miriam Vogt, Germany
1987 ....Erika Hess, Switzerland	1996 ....Pernilla Wiberg, Sweden
1989 ....Tamara McKinney, United States	1997 ....Renate Götschl, Austria

SUPER G

1987 ....Maria Walliser, Switzerland	1993 ....Katja Seizinger, Germany
1989 ....Ulrike Maier, Austria	1996 ....Isolde Kostner, Italy
1991 ....Ulrike Maier, Austria	1997 ....Isolde Kostner, Italy

Note: The 1995 FIS World Alpine Ski Championships were postponed to 1996 due to lack of snow.

World Cup Season Title Holders

Men

OVERALL

1967 ....Jean-Claude Killy, France	1983 ....Phil Mahre, United States
1968 ....Jean-Claude Killy, France	1984 ....Pirmin Zurbriggen, Switzerland
1969 ....Karl Schranz, Austria	1985 ....Marc Girardelli, Luxembourg
1970 ....Karl Schranz, Austria	1986 ....Marc Girardelli, Luxembourg
1971 ....Gustavo Thoeni, Italy	1987 ....Pirmin Zurbriggen, Switzerland
1972 ....Gustavo Thoeni, Italy	1988 ....Pirmin Zurbriggen, Switzerland
1973 ....Gustavo Thoeni, Italy	1989 ....Marc Girardelli, Luxembourg
1974 ....Piero Gros, Italy	1990 ....Pirmin Zurbriggen, Switzerland
1975 ....Gustavo Thoeni, Italy	1991 ....Marc Girardelli, Luxembourg
1976 ....Ingemar Stenmark, Sweden	1992 ....Paul Accola, Switzerland
1977 ....Ingemar Stenmark, Sweden	1993 ....Marc Girardelli, Luxembourg
1978 ....Ingemar Stenmark, Sweden	1994 ....Kjetil André Aamodt, Norway
1979 ....Peter Lüscher, Switzerland	1995 ....Alberto Tomba, Italy
1980 ....Andreas Wenzel, Liechtenstein	1996 ....Lasse Kjus, Norway
1981 ....Phil Mahre, United States	1997 ....Luc Alphand, France
1982 ....Phil Mahre, United States	1998 ....Hermann Maier, Austria

DOWNHILL

1967 ....Jean-Claude Killy, France	1983 ....Franz Klammer, Austria
1968 ....Gerhard Nenning, Austria	1984 ....Urs Raber, Switzerland
1969 ....Karl Schranz, Austria	1985 ....Helmut Höflehner, Austria
1970 ....Karl Schranz, Austria	1986 ....Peter Wirnsberger, Austria
Karl Cordin, Austria	1987 ....Pirmin Zurbriggen, Switzerland
1971 ....Bernhard Russi, Switzerland	1988 ....Pirmin Zurbriggen, Switzerland
1972 ....Bernhard Russi, Switzerland	1989 ....Marc Girardelli, Luxembourg
1973 ....Roland Collumbin, Switzerland	1990 ....Helmut Höflehner, Austria
1974 ....Roland Collumbin, Switzerland	1991 ....Franz Heinzer, Switzerland
1975 ....Franz Klammer, Austria	1992 ....Franz Heinzer, Switzerland
1976 ....Franz Klammer, Austria	1993 ....Franz Heinzer, Switzerland
1977 ....Franz Klammer, Austria	1994 ....Marc Girardelli, Luxembourg
1978 ....Franz Klammer, Austria	1995 ....Luc Alphand, France
1979 ....Peter Müller, Switzerland	1996 ....Luc Alphand, France
1980 ....Peter Müller, Switzerland	1997 ....Luc Alphand, France
1981 ....Harti Weirather, Austria	1998 ....Andreas Schifferer, Austria
1982 ....Steve Podborski, Canada	
Peter Müller, Switzerland	

SLALOM

1967 ....Jean-Claude Killy, France	1970 ....Patrick Russel, France
1968 ....Domeng Giovanoli, Switzerland	Alain Penz, France
1969 ....Jean-Noël Augert, France	1971 ....Jean-Noël Augert, France

Men *(Cont.)*
SLALOM *(Cont.)*

1972 ....Jean-Noël Augert, France	1986 ....Rok Petrovic, Yugoslavia
1973 ....Gustavo Thoeni, Italy	1987 ....Bojan Krizaj, Yugoslavia
1974 ....Gustavo Thoeni, Italy	1988 ....Alberto Tomba, Italy
1975 ....Ingemar Stenmark, Sweden	1989 ....Armin Bittner, West Germany
1976 ....Ingemar Stenmark, Sweden	1990 ....Armin Bittner, West Germany
1977 ....Ingemar Stenmark, Sweden	1991 ....Marc Girardelli, Luxembourg
1978 ....Ingemar Stenmark, Sweden	1992 ....Alberto Tomba, Italy
1979 ....Ingemar Stenmark, Sweden	1993 ....Tomas Fogdof, Sweden
1980 ....Ingemar Stenmark, Sweden	1994 ....Alberto Tomba, Italy
1981 ....Ingemar Stenmark, Sweden	1995 ....Alberto Tomba, Italy
1982 ....Phil Mahre, United States	1996 ....Sebastien Amiez, France
1983 ....Ingemar Stenmark, Sweden	1997 ....Thomas Sykora, Austria
1984 ....Marc Girardelli, Luxembourg	1998 ....Thomas Sykora, Austria
1985 ....Marc Girardelli, Luxembourg	

GIANT SLALOM

1967 ....Jean-Claude Killy, France	1984 ....Ingemar Stenmark, Sweden
1968 ....Jean-Claude Killy, France	Pirmin Zurbriggen, Switzerland
1969 ....Karl Schranz, Austria	1985 ....Marc Girardelli, Luxembourg
1970 ....Gustavo Thoeni, Italy	1986 ....Joël Gaspoz, Switzerland
1971 ....Patrick Russel, France	1987 ....Joël Gaspoz, Switzerland
1972 ....Gustavo Thoeni, Italy	Pirmin Zurbriggen, Switzerland
1973 ....Hans Hinterseer, Austria	1988 ....Alberto Tomba, Italy
1974 ....Piero Gros, Italy	1989 ....Pirmin Zurbriggen, Switzerland
1975 ....Ingemar Stenmark, Sweden	1990 ....Ole-Cristian Furuseth, Norway
1976 ....Ingemar Stenmark, Sweden	Günther Mader, Austria
1977 ....Heini Hemmi, Switzerland	1991 ....Alberto Tomba, Italy
Ingemar Stenmark, Sweden	1992 ....Alberto Tomba, Italy
1978 ....Ingemar Stenmark, Sweden	1993 ....Kjetil André Aamodt, Norway
1979 ....Ingemar Stenmark, Sweden	1994 ....Christian Mayer, Austria
1980 ....Ingemar Stenmark, Sweden	1995 ....Alberto Tomba, Italy
1981 ....Ingemar Stenmark, Sweden	1996 ....Michael von Grünigen, Switzerland
1982 ....Phil Mahre, United States	1997 ....Michael von Grünigen, Switzerland
1983 ....Phil Mahre, United States	1998 ....Hermann Maier, Austria

SUPER G

1986 ....Markus Wasmeier, West Germany	1993 ....Kjetil André Aamodt, Norway
1987 ....Pirmin Zurbriggen, Switzerland	1994 ....Jan Einar Thorsen, Norway
1988 ....Pirmin Zurbriggen, Switzerland	1995 ....Peter Runggaldier, Italy
1989 ....Pirmin Zurbriggen, Switzerland	1996 ....Atle Skaardal, Norway
1990 ....Pirmin Zurbriggen, Switzerland	1997 ....Luc Alphand, France
1991 ....Franz Heinzer, Switzerland	1998 ....Hermann Maier, Austria
1992 ....Paul Accola, Switzerland	

COMBINED

1979 ....Andreas Wenzel, Liechtenstein	1989 ....Marc Girardelli, Luxembourg
1980 ....Andreas Wenzel, Liechtenstein	1990 ....Pirmin Zurbriggen, Switzerland
1981 ....Phil Mahre, United States	1991 ....Marc Girardelli, Luxembourg
1982 ....Phil Mahre, United States	1992 ....Paul Accola, Switzerland
1983 ....Phil Mahre, United States	1993 ....Marc Girardelli, Luxembourg
1984 ....Andreas Wenzel, Liechtenstein	1994 ....Kjetil André Aamodt, Norway
1985 ....Andreas Wenzel, Liechtenstein	1995 ....Marc Girardelli, Luxembourg
1986 ....Markus Wasmeier, West Germany	1996 ....Günther Mader, Austria
1987 ....Pirmin Zurbriggen, Switzerland	1997-98 ....Not awarded
1988 ....Hubert Strolz, Austria	

Women
OVERALL

1967 ....Nancy Greene, Canada	1974 ....Annemarie Moser-Pröll, Austria
1968 ....Nancy Greene, Canada	1975 ....Annemarie Moser-Pröll, Austria
1969 ....Gertrud Gabl, Austria	1976 ....Rosi Mitermaier, West Germany
1970 ....Michèle Jacot, France	1977 ....Lise-Marie Morerod, Switzerland
1971 ....Annemarie Pröll, Austria	1978 ....Hanni Wenzel, Liechtenstein
1972 ....Annemarie Pröll, Austria	1979 ....Annemarie Moser-Pröll, Austria
1973 ....Annemarie Pröll, Austria	1980 ....Hanni Wenzel, Liechtenstein

Women

OVERALL *(Cont.)*

1981 ....Marie-Thérèse Nadig, Switzerland	1990 ....Petra Kronberger, Austria
1982 ....Erika Hess, Switzerland	1991 ....Petra Kronberger, Austria
1983 ....Tamara McKinney, United States	1992 ....Petra Kronberger, Austria
1984 ....Erika Hess, Switzerland	1993 ....Anita Wachter, Austria
1985 ....Michela Figini, Switzerland	1994 ....Vreni Schneider, Switzerland
1986 ....Maria Walliser, Switzerland	1995 ....Vreni Schneider, Switzerland
1987 ....Maria Walliser, Switzerland	1996 ....Katja Seizinger, Germany
1988 ....Michela Figini, Switzerland	1997 ....Pernilla Wiberg, Sweden
1989 ....Vreni Schneider, Switzerland	1998 ....Katja Seizinger, Germany

DOWNHILL

1967 ....Marielle Goitschel, France	1983 ....Doris De Agostini, Switzerland
1968 ....Isabelle Mir, France & Olga Pall, Austria	1984 ....Maria Walliser, Switzerland
1969 ....Wiltrud Drexel, Austria	1985 ....Michela Figini, Switzerland
1970 ....Isabelle Mir, France	1986 ....Maria Walliser, Switzerland
1971 ....Annemarie Pröll, Austria	1987 ....Michela Figini, Switzerland
1972 ....Annemarie Pröll, Austria	1988 ....Michela Figini, Switzerland
1973 ....Annemarie Pröll, Austria	1989 ....Michela Figini, Switzerland
1974 ....Annemarie Moser-Pröll, Austria	1990 ....Katrin Gutensohn-Knopf, Germany
1975 ....Annemarie Moser-Pröll, Austria	1991 ....Chantal Bournissen, Switzerland
1976 ....Brigitte Totschnig, Austria	1992 ....Katja Seizinger, Germany
1977 ....Brigitte Totschnig-Habersatter, Austria	1993 ....Katja Seizinger, Germany
1978 ....Annemarie Moser-Pröll, Austria	1994 ....Katja Seizinger, Germany
1979 ....Annemarie Moser-Pröll, Austria	1995 ....Picabo Street, United States
1980 ....Marie-Thérèse Nadig, Switzerland	1996 ....Picabo Street, United States
1981 ....Marie-Thérèse Nadig, Switzerland	1997 ....Renate Götschl, Austria
1982 ....Marie-Cecile Gros-Gaudenier, France	1998 ....Katja Seizinger, Germany

SLALOM

1967 ....Marielle Goitschel, France	1984 ....Tamara McKinney, United States
1968 ....Marielle Goitschel, France	1985 ....Erika Hess, Switzerland
1969 ....Gertrud Gabl, Austria	1986 ....Roswitha Steiner, Austria
1970 ....Ingrid Lafforgue, France	Erika Hess, Switzerland
1971 ....Britt Lafforgue, France	1987 ....Corrine Schmidhauser, Switzerland
1972 ....Britt Lafforgue, France	1988 ....Roswitha Steiner, Austria
1973 ....Patricia Emonet, France	1989 ....Vreni Schneider, Switzerland
1974 ....Christa Zechmeister, West Germany	1990 ....Vreni Schneider, Switzerland
1975 ....Lise-Marie Morerod, Switzerland	1991 ....Petra Kronberger, Austria
1976 ....Rosi Mittermaier, West Germany	1992 ....Vreni Schneider, Switzerland
1977 ....Lise-Marie Morerod, Switzerland	1993 ....Vreni Schneider, Switzerland
1978 ....Hanni Wenzel, Liechtenstein	1994 ....Vreni Schneider, Switzerland
1979 ....Regina Sackl, Austria	1995 ....Vreni Schneider, Switzerland
1980 ....Perrine Pelen, France	1996 ....Elfi Eder, Austria
1981 ....Erika Hess, Switzerland	1997 ....Pernilla Wiberg, Sweden
1982 ....Erika Hess, Switzerland	1998 ....Ylva Nowen, Sweden
1983 ....Erika Hess, Switzerland	

GIANT SLALOM

1967 ....Nancy Greene, Canada	1984 ....Erika Hess, Switzerland
1968 ....Nancy Greene, Canada	1985 ....Maria Keihl, West Germany
1969 ....Marilyn Cochran, United States	Michela Figini, Switzerland
1970 ....Michèle Jacot, France	1986 ....Vreni Schneider, Switzerland
Françoise Macchi, France	1987 ....Vreni Schneider, Switzerland
1971 ....Annemarie Pröll, Austria	Maria Walliser, Switzerland
1972 ....Annemarie Pröll, Austria	1988 ....Mateja Svet, Yugoslavia
1973 ....Monika Kaserer, Austria	1989 ....Vreni Schneider, Switzerland
1974 ....Hanni Wenzel, Liechtenstein	1990 ....Anita Wachter, Austria
1975 ....Annemarie Moser-Pröll, Austria	1991 ....Vreni Schneider, Switzerland
1976 ....Lise-Marie Morerod, France	1992 ....Carole Merle, France
1977 ....Lise-Marie Morerod, France	1993 ....Carole Merle, France
1978 ....Lise-Marie Morerod, France	1994 ....Anita Wachter, Austria
1979 ....Christa Kinshofer, West Germany	1995 ....Vreni Schneider, Switzerland
1980 ....Hanni Wenzel, Liechtenstein	1996 ....Martina Ertl, Germany
1981 ....Marie-Thérèse Nadig, Switzerland	1997 ....Deborah Compagnoni, Italy
1982 ....Irene Epple, West Germany	1998 ....Martina Ertl, Germany
1983 ....Tamara McKinney, United States	

Women *(Cont.)*

SUPER G

1986	Maria Kiehl, West Germany	1993	Katja Seizinger, Germany
1987	Maria Walliser, Switzerland	1994	Katja Seizinger, Germany
1988	Michela Figini, Switzerland	1995	Katja Seizinger, Germany
1989	Carole Merle, France	1996	Katja Seizinger, Germany
1990	Carole Merle, France	1997	Hilde Gerg, Germany
1991	Carole Merle, France	1998	Katja Seizinger, Germany
1992	Carole Merle, France		

COMBINED

1979	Annemarie Moser-Pröll, Austria	1988	Brigitte Oertli, Switzerland
	Hanni Wenzel, Liechtenstein	1989	Brigitte Oertli, Switzerland
1980	Hanni Wenzel, Liechtenstein	1990	Anita Wachter, Austria
1981	Marie-Thérèse Nadig, Switzerland	1991	Sabine Ginther, Austria
1982	Irene Epple, West Germany	1992	Sabine Ginther, Austria
1983	Hanni Wenzel, Liechtenstein	1993	Anita Wachter, Austria
1984	Erika Hess, Switzerland	1994	Pernilla Wiberg, Sweden
1985	Brigitte Oertli, Switzerland	1995	Pernilla Wiberg, Sweden
1986	Maria Walliser, Switzerland	1996	Anita Wachter, Austria
1987	Brigitte Oertli, Switzerland	1997-98	Not awarded

World Cup Career Victories

Men

DOWNHILL

25	Franz Klammer, Austria
19	Peter Müller, Switzerland
15	Franz Heinzer, Switzerland

SLALOM

40	Ingemar Stenmark, Sweden
35	*Alberto Tomba, Italy
16	*Marc Girardelli, Luxembourg

GIANT SLALOM

46	Ingemar Stenmark, Sweden
15	*Alberto Tomba, Italy
14	*Michael von Grünigen, Switz

SUPER G

10	Pirmin Zurbriggen, Switzerland
7	*Marc Girardelli, Luxembourg
6	Markus Wasmeier, Germany

COMBINED

11	Phil Mahre, United States
	Pirmin Zurbriggen, Switzerland
	*Marc Girardelli, Luxembourg

Women

DOWNHILL

36	Annemarie Moser-Pröll, Austria
17	Michela Figini, Switzerland
16	*Katja Seizinger, Germany

SLALOM

33	Vreni Schneider, Switzerland
21	Erika Hess, Switzerland
15	Perrine Pelen, France

GIANT SLALOM

21	Vreni Schneider, Switzerland
16	Annemarie Moser-Pröll, Austria
15	*Deborah Compagnoni, Italy

SUPER G

16	*Katja Seizinger, Germany
12	Carole Merle, France
3	Maria Kiehl, Germany
	Maria Walliser, Switzerland
	Sigrid Wolf, Austria

COMBINED

8	Hanni Wenzel, Lichtenstein
7	Annemarie Moser-Pröll, Austria
	Brigitte Oertli, Switzerland

*still active

U.S. Olympic Gold Medalists

Men

Year	Winner	Event
1980	Phil Mahre	Combined
1984	Bill Johnson	Downhill
1984	Phil Mahre	Slalom
1994	Tommy Moe	Downhill

Women

Year	Winner	Event
1948	Gretchen Fraser	Slalom
1952	Andrea Mead Lawrence	Slalom
1952	Andrea Mead Lawrence	Giant Slalom
1972	Barbara Ann Cochran	Slalom
1984	Debbie Armstrong	Giant Slalom
1994	Diann Roffe-Steinrotter	Super G
1998	Picabo Street	Super G

Figure Skating

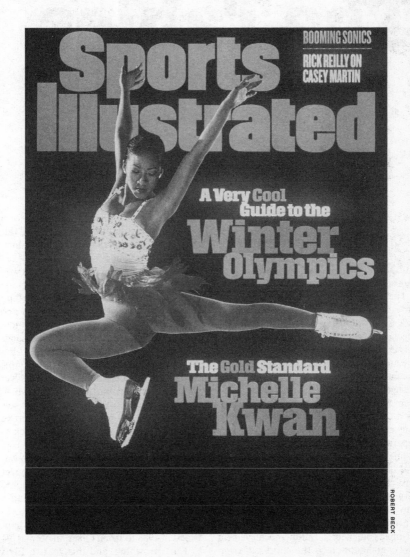

Sports Illustrated

BOOMING SONICS

RICK REILLY ON CASEY MARTIN

A Very Cool Guide to the Winter Olympics

The Gold Standard Michelle Kwan

ROBERT BECK

Tara Turns The Tables

Tara Lipinski surprised favorite Michelle Kwan, and everyone else, at Nagano

BY E.M. SWIFT

EVERYTHING THAT TONYA Harding and her gang of bumbling thugs worked so hard to build in 1994 was torn down in '98 by an Olympic class that exuded decorum and harmony.

The year was tediously seemly. Ice dancing provided the only whiff of controversy, as its judges proved once again that this popular spectator event is less a sport than an exercise in placement memorization. Evgeny Platov and Oksana Grishuk, the whippet-thin eccentric who dyed her hair platinum then changed her name to Pasha so people would stop confusing her with 1994 Olympic champion Oksana Baiul, won every competition they entered, despite the fact that in three separate events leading up to the Nagano Games, Platov fell. Not easy to do in ice dancing. But no matter. If you're the four-time world champions, such gaffes are easily forgiven, and in Nagano this high-energy duo with the fancy footwork became the first ice dancing team to win back-to-back Olympic gold medals. But their achievement was overshadowed by the chorus of complaint which led International Skating Union

president Ottavio Cinquanta to call for a complete overhaul of the judging of this quasi-sport at the peril of its being eliminated from future Games.

The pairs gold medal in Nagano was won by Russia's Artur Dmitriev and Oksana Kazakova, who edged their St. Petersburg training partners, Elena Berezhnaya and Anton Sikharulidze, when Sikharulidze toppled during a routine lift in the last seconds of their long program. For the powerful, dramatic Dmitriev, it was his third Olympic medal, having won both a gold and a silver with his previous partner, Natalia Mishkutienok. Russian or Soviet pairs have now captured the top prize at 10 consecutive Winter Games—a streak that goes back to the Innsbruck Olympics of 1964.

Another streak kept alive at Nagano was of the losing kind: Canada is still 0–forever in men's Olympic titles. The 1998 Games marked the fourth straight Olympiad a Canadian man came in as reigning world champ and left without the gold. It happened in 1988 to Brian Orser, in '92 and '94 to Kurt Browning, and this year to Elvis Stojko. A three-time world champion,

HEINZ KLUETMEIER

came back with a renewed sense of purpose, determined to take her place among the sport's alltime greats. In their only two pre-Olympic meetings, Kwan easily outskated her younger rival, recapturing the U.S. title with two stunning programs that earned her 15 of 18 perfect 6.0s. She both floated *and* soared, exhibiting a combination of athleticism and artistry that no woman had ever matched. Lipinski? By comparison the 4'10", 80-pound hummingbird skated like a precocious child.

It all changed at the Olympics. Kwan, heavily favored, skated with noticeable caution. She made no major mistakes, but what had appeared effortless at the nationals now looked studied and tentative. "She was going for accuracy and consistency," her coach, Frank Carroll, said later. "Her performance was very held in."

Stojko pulled his groin a month before the Olympics, an injury that deprived him of his most potent weapon—a quadruple toe–triple toe combination. In obvious pain, he still landed eight triple jumps in his long program to win the silver medal. The beneficiary of Stojko's misfortune was Russia's Ilia Kulik, a 20-year-old Leonardo DiCaprio look-alike whose apple-cheeked smile melted teenage hearts the world over. But it was Kulik's huge jumps and coltish elegance that made the judges weak in the knees. Kulik's quad toe loop was the centerpiece of the best Olympic performance by a man since Brian Boitano won the gold in 1988. The bronze, in a shocker, was won by France's Philippe Candeloro (he also won the bronze in '94), who bested Todd Eldredge, the five-time U.S. champion. Eldredge will probably turn pro and thus finish his amateur career without an Olympic medal.

Two featherweight Americans made the women's season a memorable one: 17-year-old Michelle Kwan of Torrance, Calif., and 15-year-old Tara Lipinski of Sugar Land, Texas. After Kwan lost both the U.S. and the world championships to Lipinski in '97, she

It was, however, a performance that would have won any other Olympics. But Lipinski, feeling she had nothing to lose, was *out there* during her long program, faster than Kwan and far more energetic. Each triple jump she landed—there were seven in all, including her trademark triple loop–triple loop combination—was followed by a dazzling smile and an up-click in tempo, so that by the time she completed her final illusion spin she was skating with such abandon that she broke into a spontaneous, exultant sprint across the ice. The higher degree of difficulty of Lipinski's program swayed the judges in her favor, six to three, and she became the youngest Winter Olympic individual gold medalist ever, a title formerly held by Sonja Henie.

None of the Olympic champions skated at the world championships in Minneapolis. The worlds have become an anticlimactic appendage to an Olympic year, and this season's edition was especially hollow in view of Lipinski's surprising announcement that she would not defend her Olympic title in 2002 in Salt Lake City. The 15-year-old, in a sign of the times in figure skating, had decided to turn pro.

FOR THE RECORD·1998

World Champions

Minneapolis, March 29–April 5

Women

1........Michelle Kwan, United States
2........Irina Stutskaya, Russia
3........Maria Butyrskaya, Russia

Men

1........Alexei Yagudin, Russia
2........Todd Eldredge, United States
3........Evgeny Plushenko, Russia

Pairs

1........Jenni Meno and Todd Sand, United States
2........Elena Berezhnaya and Anton Sikharvildze, Russia
3........Peggy Schwarz and Mirko Mueller, Germany

Dance

1........Anjelika Krylova and Oleg Ovsyannikov, Russia
2........Marina Anissina and Gwendal Peizer, France
3........Shae-Lynn Bourne and Victor Kraatz, Canada

World Figure Skating Championships Medal Table

Country	Gold	Silver	Bronze	Total
Russia	2	2	2	6
United States	2	1	0	3
France	0	1	0	1
Canada	0	0	1	1
Germany	0	0	1	1

Champions of the United States

Philadelphia, January 4–11

Women

1........Michelle Kwan, Los Angeles FSC
2........Tara Lipinski, Detroit SC
3........Nicole Bobek, Los Angeles FSC

Men

1........Todd Eldredge, Detroit SC
2........Michael Weiss, Washington FSC
3........Scott Davis, Broadmoor SC

Pairs

1........Kyoko Ina and Jason Dungjen,
         SC of New York
2........Shelby Lyons and Brian Wells,
         Broadmoor SC
3........Danielle Hartsell and Steve Hartsell,
         Detriot SC

Dance

1........Elizabeth Punsalan and Jerod Swallow,
         Detroit SC
2........Jessica Joseph and Charles Butler,
         Detroit SC
3........Naomi Lang and Peter Tchernyshev,
         Detroit SC

Skating Terminology*

Basic Skating Terms

Edges: The two sides of the skating blade, on either side of the grooved center. There is an inside edge, on the inner side of the leg; and an outside edge, on the outer side of the leg.

Free Foot, Hip, Knee, Side, Etc.: The foot a skater is not skating on at any one time is the free foot; everything on that side of the body is then called "free." (See also "skating foot.")

Free Skating (Freestyle): A 4- or 5-minute competition program of free-skating components, choreographed to music, with no set elements. Skating moves include jumps, spins, steps and other linking movements.

Skating Foot, Hip, Knee, Side, Etc.: Opposite of the free foot, hip, knee, side, etc. The foot a skater is skating on at any one time is the skating foot; everything on that side of the body is then called "skating."

Toe Picks (Toe Rakes): The teeth at the front of the skate blade, used primarily for certain jumps and spins.

Trace, Tracing: The line left on the ice by the skater's blade.

Jumps

Waltz: A beginner's jump, involving half a revolution in the air, taken from a forward outside edge and landed on the back outside edge of the other foot.

Toe Loop: A one-revolution jump taken off from and landed on the same back outside edge. This jump is similar to the loop jump except that the skater kicks the toe pick of the free leg into the ice upon takeoff, providing added power.

Toe Walley: A jump similar to the toe loop, except that the takeoff is from the inside edge.

Flip: A jump taken off with the toe pick of the free leg from a back inside edge and landed on a back outside edge, with one in-air revolution.

Lutz: A toe jump similar to the flip, taken off with the toe pick of the free leg from a backward outside edge. The skater enters the jump skating in one direction, and concludes the jump skating in the opposite direction. Usually performed in the corners of the rink. Named after inventor Alois Lutz, who first completed the jump in Vienna, 1918.

Salchow: A one-, two- or three-revolution jump. The skater takes off from the back inside edge of one foot and lands backwards on the outside edge of the right foot, the opposite foot from which the skater took off. Named for its originator and first Olympic champion (1908), Sweden's Ulrich Salchow.

Axel: A combination of the waltz and loop jumps, including one-and-a-half revolutions. The only jump begun from a forward outside edge, the axel is landed on the back outside edge of the opposite foot. Named for its inventor, Norway's Axel Paulsen.

Spins

Spin: The rotation of the body in one place on the ice. Various spins are the back, fast or scratch, sit, camel, butterfly and layback.

Camel Spin: A spin with the skater in an arabesque position (the free leg at right angles to the leg on the ice).

Flying Camel Spin: A jump spin ending in the camel-spin position.

Flying Sit Spin: A jump spin in which the skater leaps off the ice, assumes a sitting position at the peak of the jump, lands and spins in a similar sitting position.

Pair Movements/Techniques

Death Spiral: One of the most dramatic moves in figure skating. The man, acting as the center of a circle, holds tightly to the hand of his partner and pulls her around him. The woman, gliding on one foot, achieves a position almost horizontal to the ice.

Lifts: The most spectacular moves in pairs skating. They involve any maneuver in which the man lifts the woman off the ice. The man often holds his partner above his head with one hand.

Throws: The man lifts the woman into the air and throws her away from him. She spins in the air and lands on one foot.

Twist: The man throws the woman into the air. She spins in the air (either a double- or triple-twist), and he catches her at the landing.

*Compiled by the United States Figure Skating Association.

World Champions

Women

1906	Madge Sayers-Cave, Great Britain
1907	Madge Sayers-Cave, Great Britain
1908	Lily Kronberger, Hungary
1909	Lily Kronberger, Hungary
1910	Lily Kronberger, Hungary
1911	Lily Kronberger, Hungary
1912	Opika von Meray Horvath, Hungary
1913	Opika von Meray Horvath, Hungary
1914	Opika von Meray Horvath, Hungary
1915-21	No competition
1922	Herma Plank-Szabo, Austria
1923	Herma Plank-Szabo, Austria
1924	Herma Plank-Szabo, Austria
1925	Herma Jaross-Szabo, Austria
1926	Herma Jaross-Szabo, Austria
1927	Sonja Henie, Norway
1928	Sonja Henie, Norway
1929	Sonja Henie, Norway
1930	Sonja Henie, Norway
1931	Sonja Henie, Norway
1932	Sonja Henie, Norway
1933	Sonja Henie, Norway
1934	Sonja Henie, Norway
1935	Sonja Henie, Norway
1936	Sonja Henie, Norway
1937	Cecilia Colledge, Great Britain
1938	Megan Taylor, Great Britain
1939	Megan Taylor, Great Britain
1940-46	No competition
1947	Barbara Ann Scott, Canada
1948	Barbara Ann Scott, Canada
1949	Alena Vrzanova, Czechoslovakia
1950	Alena Vrzanova, Czechoslovakia
1951	Jeannette Altwegg, Great Britain
1952	Jacqueline duBief, France
1953	Tenley Albright, United States
1954	Gundi Busch, West Germany
1955	Tenley Albright, United States
1956	Carol Heiss, United States
1957	Carol Heiss, United States

Women *(Cont.)*

1958..................Carol Heiss, United States	1979..................Linda Fratianne, United States
1959..................Carol Heiss, United States	1980..................Annett Poetzsch, East Germany
1960..................Carol Heiss, United States	1981..................Denise Biellmann, Switzerland
1961..................No competition	1982..................Elaine Zayak, United States
1962..................Sjoukje Dijkstra, Netherlands	1983..................Rosalynn Sumners, United States
1963..................Sjoukje Dijkstra, Netherlands	1984..................Katarina Witt, East Germany
1964..................Sjoukje Dijkstra, Netherlands	1985..................Katarina Witt, East Germany
1965..................Petra Burka, Canada	1986..................Debi Thomas, United States
1966..................Peggy Fleming, United States	1987..................Katarina Witt, East Germany
1967..................Peggy Fleming, United States	1988..................Katarina Witt, East Germany
1968..................Peggy Fleming, United States	1989..................Midori Ito, Japan
1969..................Gabriele Seyfert, East Germany	1990..................Jill Trenary, United States
1970..................Gabriele Seyfert, East Germany	1991..................Kristi Yamaguchi, United States
1971..................Beatrix Schuba, Austria	1992..................Kristi Yamaguchi, United States
1972..................Beatrix Schuba, Austria	1993..................Oksana Baiul, Ukraine
1973..................Karen Magnussen, Canada	1994..................Yuka Sato, Japan
1974..................Christine Errath, East Germany	1995..................Chen Lu, China
1975..................Dianne DeLeeuw, Netherlands	1996..................Michelle Kwan, United States
1976..................Dorothy Hamill, United States	1997..................Tara Lipinski, United States
1977..................Linda Fratianne, United States	1998..................Michelle Kwan, United States
1978..................Annett Poetzsch, East Germany	

Men

1896..................Gilbert Fuchs, Germany	1951..................Dick Button, United States
1897..................Gustav Hugel, Austria	1952..................Dick Button, United States
1898..................Henning Grenander, Sweden	1953..................Hayes Alan Jenkins, United States
1899..................Gustav Hugel, Austria	1954..................Hayes Alan Jenkins, United States
1900..................Gustav Hugel, Austria	1955..................Hayes Alan Jenkins, United States
1901..................Ulrich Salchow, Sweden	1956..................Hayes Alan Jenkins, United States
1902..................Ulrich Salchow, Sweden	1957..................David W. Jenkins, United States
1903..................Ulrich Salchow, Sweden	1958..................David W. Jenkins, United States
1904..................Ulrich Salchow, Sweden	1959..................David W. Jenkins, United States
1905..................Ulrich Salchow, Sweden	1960..................Alan Giletti, France
1906..................Gilbert Fuchs, Germany	1961..................No competition
1907..................Ulrich Salchow, Sweden	1962..................Donald Jackson, Canada
1908..................Ulrich Salchow, Sweden	1963..................Donald McPherson, Canada
1909..................Ulrich Salchow, Sweden	1964..................Manfred Schneldorfer, W Germany
1910..................Ulrich Salchow, Sweden	1965..................Alain Calmat, France
1911..................Ulrich Salchow, Sweden	1966..................Emmerich Danzer, Austria
1912..................Fritz Kachler, Austria	1967..................Emmerich Danzer, Austria
1913..................Fritz Kachler, Austria	1968..................Emmerich Danzer, Austria
1914..................Gosta Sandhal, Sweden	1969..................Tim Wood, United States
1915-21..............No competition	1970..................Tim Wood, United States
1922..................Gillis Grafstrom, Sweden	1971..................Andrej Nepela, Czechoslovakia
1923..................Fritz Kachler, Austria	1972..................Andrej Nepela, Czechoslovakia
1924..................Gillis Grafstrom, Sweden	1973..................Andrej Nepela, Czechoslovakia
1925..................Willy Bockl, Austria	1974..................Jan Hoffmann, East Germany
1926..................Willy Bockl, Austria	1975..................Sergei Volkov, USSR
1927..................Willy Bockl, Austria	1976..................John Curry, Great Britain
1928..................Willy Bockl, Austria	1977..................Vladimir Kovalev, USSR
1929..................Gillis Grafstrom, Sweden	1978..................Charles Tickner, United States
1930..................Karl Schafer, Austria	1979..................Vladimir Kovalev, USSR
1931..................Karl Schafer, Austria	1980..................Jan Hoffmann, East Germany
1932..................Karl Schafer, Austria	1981..................Scott Hamilton, United States
1933..................Karl Schafer, Austria	1982..................Scott Hamilton, United States
1934..................Karl Schafer, Austria	1983..................Scott Hamilton, United States
1935..................Karl Schafer, Austria	1984..................Scott Hamilton, United States
1936..................Karl Schafer, Austria	1985..................Aleksandr Fadeev, USSR
1937..................Felix Kaspar, Austria	1986..................Brian Boitano, United States
1938..................Felix Kaspar, Austria	1987..................Brian Orser, Canada
1939..................Graham Sharp, Great Britain	1988..................Brian Boitano, United States
1940-46..............No competition	1989..................Kurt Browning, Canada
1947..................Hans Gerschwiler, Switzerland	1990..................Kurt Browning, Canada
1948..................Dick Button, United States	1991..................Kurt Browning, Canada
1949..................Dick Button, United States	1992..................Viktor Petrenko, CIS
1950..................Dick Button, United States	1993..................Kurt Browning, Canada

Men (Cont.)

1994 ....Elvis Stojko, Canada	1997 ....Elvis Stojko, Canada
1995 ....Elvis Stojko, Canada	1998 ....Alexi Yagudin, Russia
1996 ....Todd Eldredge, United States	

Pairs

1908 ....Anna Hubler, Heinrich Burger, Germany
1909 ....Phyllis Johnson, James H. Johnson,
Great Britain
1910 ....Anna Hubler, Heinrich Burger, Germany
1911 ....Ludowika Eilers, Walter Jakobsson,
Germany/Finland
1912 ....Phyllis Johnson, James H. Johnson,
Great Britain
1913 ....Helene Engelmann, Karl Majstrik,
Germany
1914 ....Ludowika Jakobsson-Eilers, Walter
Jakobsson-Eilers, Finland
1915-21 ......No competition
1922 ....Helene Engelmann, Alfred Berger,
Germany
1923 ....Ludowika Jakobsson-Eilers, Walter
Jakobsson-Eilers, Finland
1924 ....Helene Engelmann, Alfred Berger,
Germany
1925 ....Herma Jaross-Szabo, Ludwig Wrede,
Austria
1926 ....Andree Joly, Pierre Brunet, France
1927 ....Herma Jaross-Szabo, Ludwig Wrede,
Austria
1928 ....Andree Joly, Pierre Brunet, France
1929 ....Lilly Scholz, Otto Kaiser, Austria
1930 ....Andree Brunet-Joly, Pierre Brunet-Joly,
France
1931 ....Emilie Rotter, Laszlo Szollas, Hungary
1932 ....Andree Brunet-Joly, Pierre Brunet-Joly,
France
1933 ....Emilie Rotter, Laszlo Szollas, Hungary
1934 ....Emilie Rotter, Laszlo Szollas, Hungary
1935 ....Emilie Rotter, Laszlo Szollas, Hungary
1936 ....Maxi Herber, Ernst Bajer, Germany
1937 ....Maxi Herber, Ernst Bajer, Germany
1938 ....Maxi Herber, Ernst Bajer, Germany
1939 ....Maxi Herber, Ernst Bajer, Germany
1940-46 ......No competition
1947 ....Micheline Lannoy, Pierre Baugniet,
Belgium
1948 ....Micheline Lannoy, Pierre Baugniet,
Belgium
1949 ....Andrea Kekessy, Ede Kiraly, Hungary
1950 ....Karol Kennedy, Peter Kennedy,
United States
1951 ....Ria Baran, Paul Falk, West Germany
1952 ....Ria Baran Falk, Paul Falk, W Germany
1953 ....Jennifer Nicks, John Nicks, Great Britain
1954 ....Frances Dafoe, Norris Bowden, Canada
1955 ....Frances Dafoe, Norris Bowden, Canada
1956 ....Sissy Schwarz, Kurt Oppelt, Austria
1957 ....Barbara Wagner, Robert Paul, Canada
1958 ....Barbara Wagner, Robert Paul, Canada

1959 ....Barbara Wagner, Robert Paul, Canada
1960 ....Barbara Wagner, Robert Paul, Canada
1961 ....No competition
1962 ....Maria Jelinek, Otto Jelinek, Canada
1963 ....Marika Kilius, Hans-Jurgen Baumler,
West Germany
1964 ....Marika Kilius, Hans-Jurgen Baumler,
West Germany
1965 ....Ljudmila Protopopov, Oleg Protopopov,
USSR
1966 ....Ljudmila Protopopov, Oleg Protopopov,
USSR
1967 ....Ljudmila Protopopov, Oleg Protopopov,
USSR
1968 ....Ljudmila Protopopov, Oleg Protopopov,
USSR
1969 ....Irina Rodnina, Alexsei Ulanov, USSR
1970 ....Irina Rodnina, Alexsei Ulanov, USSR
1971 ....Irina Rodnina, Sergei Ulanov, USSR
1972 ....Irina Rodnina, Sergei Ulanov, USSR
1973 ....Irina Rodnina, Aleksandr Zaitsev, USSR
1974 ....Irina Rodnina, Aleksandr Zaitsev, USSR
1975 ....Irina Rodnina, Aleksandr Zaitsev, USSR
1976 ....Irina Rodnina, Aleksandr Zaitsev, USSR
1977 ....Irina Rodnina, Aleksandr Zaitsev, USSR
1978 ....Irina Rodnina, Aleksandr Zaitsev, USSR
1979 ....Tai Babilonia, Randy Gardner,
United States
1980 ....Maria Cherkasova, Sergei Shakhrai,
USSR
1981 ....Irina Vorobieva, Igor Lisovsky, USSR
1982 ....Sabine Baess, Tassilio Thierbach,
East Germany
1983 ....Elena Valova, Oleg Vasiliev, USSR
1984 ....Barbara Underhill, Paul Martini, Canada
1985 ....Elena Valova, Oleg Vasiliev, USSR
1986 ....Ekaterina Gordeeva, Sergei Grinkov, USSR
1987 ....Ekaterina Gordeeva, Sergei Grinkov, USSR
1988 ....Elena Valova, Oleg Vasiliev, USSR
1989 ....Ekaterina Gordeeva, Sergei Grinkov, USSR
1990 ....Ekaterina Gordeeva, Sergei Grinkov, USSR
1991 ....Natalia Mishkutienok, Artur Dmitriev,
USSR
1992 ....Natalia Mishkutienok, Artur Dmitriev, CIS
1993 ....Isabelle Brasseur, Lloyd Eisler, Canada
1994 ....Evgenia Shishkova, Vadim Naumov,
Russia
1995 ....Radka Kovarikova, Rene Novotny,
Czech Republic
1996 ....Marina Eltsova, Andrey Buskhov,
Russia
1997 ....Mandy Wötzel, Ingo Steuer, Germany
1998 ....Jenni Meno and Todd Sand, United States

Dance

1950 ....Lois Waring, Michael McGean,
United States
1951 ....Jean Westwood, Lawrence Demmy,
Great Britain
1952 ....Jean Westwood, Lawrence Demmy,
Great Britain

1953 ....Jean Westwood, Lawrence Demmy,
Great Britain
1954 ....Jean Westwood, Lawrence Demmy,
Great Britain
1955 ....Jean Westwood, Lawrence Demmy,
Great Britain

World Champions (Cont.)

Dance (Cont.)

1956 ....Pamela Wieght, Paul Thomas,
Great Britain
1957 ....June Markham, Courtney Jones,
Great Britain
1958 ....June Markham, Courtney Jones,
Great Britain
1959 ....Doreen D. Denny, Courtney Jones,
Great Britain
1960 ....Doreen D. Denny, Courtney Jones,
Great Britain
1961 ....No competition
1962 ....Eva Romanova, Pavel Roman,
Czechoslovakia
1963 ....Eva Romanova, Pavel Roman,
Czechoslovakia
1964 ....Eva Romanova, Pavel Roman,
Czechoslovakia
1965 ....Eva Romanova, Pavel Roman,
Czechoslovakia
1966 ....Diane Towler, Bernard Ford, Great Britain
1967 ....Diane Towler, Bernard Ford, Great Britain
1968 ....Diane Towler, Bernard Ford, Great Britain
1969 ....Diane Towler, Bernard Ford, Great Britain
1970 ....Ljudmila Pakhomova, Aleksandr
Gorshkov, USSR
1971 ....Ljudmila Pakhomova, Aleksandr
Gorshkov, USSR
1972 ....Ljudmila Pakhomova, Aleksandr
Gorshkov, USSR
1973 ....Ljudmila Pakhomova, Aleksandr
Gorshkov, USSR
1974 ....Ljudmila Pakhomova, Aleksandr
Gorshkov, USSR
1975 ....Irina Moiseeva, Andreij Minenkov, USSR
1976 ....Ljudmila Pakhomova, Aleksandr
Gorshkov, USSR

1977 ....Irina Moiseeva, Andreij Minenkov, USSR
1978 ....Natalia Linichuk, Gennadi Karponosov,
USSR
1979 ....Natalia Linichuk, Gennadi Karponosov,
USSR
1980 ....Krisztina Regoeczy, Andras Sallai,
Hungary
1981 ....Jayne Torvill, Christopher Dean,
Great Britain
1982 ....Jayne Torvill, Christopher Dean,
Great Britain
1983 ....Jayne Torvill, Christopher Dean,
Great Britain
1984 ....Jayne Torvill, Christopher Dean,
Great Britain
1985 ....Natalia Bestemianova, Andrei Bukin, USSR
1986 ....Natalia Bestemianova, Andrei Bukin, USSR
1987 ....Natalia Bestemianova, Andrei Bukin, USSR
1988 ....Natalia Bestemianova, Andrei Bukin, USSR
1989 ....Marina Klimova, Sergei Ponomarenko,
USSR
1990 ....Marina Klimova, Sergei Ponomarenko,
USSR
1991 ....Isabelle Duchesnay, Paul Duchesnay,
France
1992 ....Marina Klimova, Sergei Ponomarenko , CIS
1993 ....Renee Roca, Gorsha Sur, United States
1994 ....Oksana Grishuk, Evgeny Platov, Russia
1995 ....Oksana Grishuk, Evgeny Platov, Russia
1996 ....Oksana Grishuk, Evgeny Platov, Russia
1997 ....Oksana Grishuk, Evgeny Platov, Russia
1998 ....Anjelika Krylova and Oleg Ovsyannikov,
Russia

Champions of the United States

The championships held in 1914, 1918, 1920 and 1921 under the auspices of the International Skating Union of America were open to Canadians, although they were considered to be United States championships. Beginning in 1922, the championships have been held under the auspices of the United States Figure Skating Association.

Women

1914 ....Theresa Weld, SC of Boston
1915-17 ......No competition
1918...........Rosemary S. Beresford, New York SC
1919 ....No competition
1920 ....Theresa Weld, SC of Boston
1921 ....Theresa Weld Blanchard, SC of Boston
1922 ....Theresa Weld Blanchard, SC of Boston
1923 ....Theresa Weld Blanchard, SC of Boston
1924 ....Theresa Weld Blanchard, SC of Boston
1925 ....Beatrix Loughran, New York SC
1926 ....Beatrix Loughran, New York SC
1927 ....Beatrix Loughran, New York SC
1928 ....Maribel Y. Vinson, SC of Boston
1929 ....Maribel Y. Vinson, SC of Boston
1930 ....Maribel Y. Vinson, SC of Boston
1931 ....Maribel Y. Vinson, SC of Boston
1932 ....Maribel Y. Vinson, SC of Boston
1933 ....Maribel Y. Vinson, SC of Boston
1934 ....Suzanne Davis, SC of Boston
1935 ....Maribel Y. Vinson, SC of Boston
1936 ....Maribel Y. Vinson, SC of Boston

1937 ....Maribel Y. Vinson, SC of Boston
1938 ....Joan Tozzer, SC of Boston
1939 ....Joan Tozzer, SC of Boston
1940 ....Joan Tozzer, SC of Boston
1941 ....Jane Vaughn, Philadelphia SC & HS
1942 ....Jane Vaughn Sullivan,
Philadelphia SC & HS
1943...........Gretchen Van Zandt Merrill, SC of Boston
1944...........Gretchen Van Zandt Merrill, SC of Boston
1945...........Gretchen Van Zandt Merrill, SC of Boston
1946...........Gretchen Van Zandt Merrill, SC of Boston
1947...........Gretchen Van Zandt Merrill, SC of Boston
1948...........Gretchen Van Zandt Merrill, SC of Boston
1949 ....Yvonne Claire Sherman, SC of New York
1950 ....Yvonne Claire Sherman, SC of New York
1951 ....Sonya Klopfer, Junior SC of New York
1952 ....Tenley E. Albright, SC of Boston
1953 ....Tenley E. Albright, SC of Boston
1954 ....Tenley E. Albright, SC of Boston
1955 ....Tenley E. Albright, SC of Boston
1956 ....Tenley E. Albright, SC of Boston

Women (Cont.)

1957 ....Carol E. Heiss, SC of New York	1978 ....Linda Fratianne, Los Angeles FSC
1958 ....Carol E. Heiss, SC of New York	1979 ....Linda Fratianne, Los Angeles FSC
1959 ....Carol E. Heiss, SC of New York	1980 ....Linda Fratianne, Los Angeles FSC
1960 ....Carol E. Heiss, SC of New York	1981 ....Elaine Zayak, SC of New York
1961 ....Laurence R. Owen, SC of Boston	1982 ....Rosalynn Sumners, Seattle SC
1962 ....Barbara Roles Pursley, Arctic Blades FSC	1983 ....Rosalynn Sumners, Seattle SC
1963 ....Lorraine G. Hanlon, SC of Boston	1984 ....Rosalynn Sumners, Seattle SC
1964 ....Peggy Fleming, Arctic Blades FSC	1985 ....Tiffany Chin, San Diego FSC
1965 ....Peggy Fleming, Arctic Blades FSC	1986 ....Debi Thomas, Los Angeles FSC
1966 ....Peggy Fleming, City of Colorado Springs	1987 ....Jill Trenary, Broadmoor SC
1967 ....Peggy Fleming, Broadmoor SC	1988 ....Debi Thomas, Los Angeles FSC
1968 ....Peggy Fleming, Broadmoor SC	1989 ....Jill Trenary, Broadmoor SC
1969 ....Janet Lynn, Wagon Wheel FSC	1990 ....Jill Trenary, Broadmoor SC
1970 ....Janet Lynn, Wagon Wheel FSC	1991 ....Tonya Harding, Carousel FSC
1971 ....Janet Lynn, Wagon Wheel FSC	1992 ....Kristi Yamaguchi, St Moritz ISC
1972 ....Janet Lynn, Wagon Wheel FSC	1993 ....Nancy Kerrigan, Colonial FSC
1973 ....Janet Lynn, Wagon Wheel FSC	1994 ....Tonya Harding, Portland FSC
1974 ....Dorothy Hamill, SC of New York	1995 ....Nicole Bobek, Los Angeles FSC
1975 ....Dorothy Hamill, SC of New York	1996 ....Michelle Kwan, Los Angeles FSC
1976 ....Dorothy Hamill, SC of New York	1997 ....Tara Lipinski, Detroit SC
1977 ....Linda Fratianne, Los Angeles FSC	1998 ....Michelle Kwan, Los Angeles FSC

Men

1914 ....Norman M. Scott, WC of Montreal	1958 ....David Jenkins, Broadmoor SC
1915-17 ......No competition	1959 ....David Jenkins, Broadmoor SC
1918 ....Nathaniel W. Niles, SC of Boston	1960 ....David Jenkins, Broadmoor SC
1919 ....No competition	1961 ....Bradley R. Lord, SC of Boston
1920 ....Sherwin C. Badger, SC of Boston	1962 ....Monty Hoyt, Broadmoor SC
1921 ....Sherwin C. Badger, SC of Boston	1963 ....Thomas Litz, Hershey FSC
1922 ....Sherwin C. Badger, SC of Boston	1964 ....Scott Ethan Allen, SC of New York
1923 ....Sherwin C. Badger, SC of Boston	1965 ....Gary C. Visconti, Detroit SC
1924 ....Sherwin C. Badger, SC of Boston	1966 ....Scott Ethan Allen, SC of New York
1925 ....Nathaniel W. Niles, SC of Boston	1967 ....Gary C. Visconti, Detroit SC
1926 ....Chris I. Christenson, Twin City FSC	1968 ....Tim Wood, Detroit SC
1927 ....Nathaniel W. Niles, SC of Boston	1969 ....Tim Wood, Detroit SC
1928 ....Roger F. Turner, SC of Boston	1970 ....Tim Wood, City of Colorado Springs
1929 ....Roger F. Turner, SC of Boston	1971 ....John Misha Petkevich, Great Falls FSC
1930 ....Roger F. Turner, SC of Boston	1972 ....Kenneth Shelley, Arctic Blades FSC
1931 ....Roger F. Turner, SC of Boston	1973 ....Gordon McKellen, Jr, SC of Lake Placid
1932 ....Roger F. Turner, SC of Boston	1974 ....Gordon McKellen, Jr, SC of Lake Placid
1933 ....Roger F. Turner, SC of Boston	1975 ....Gordon McKellen, Jr, SC of Lake Placid
1934 ....Roger F. Turner, SC of Boston	1976 ....Terry Kubicka, Arctic Blades FSC
1935 ....Robin H. Lee, SC of New York	1977 ....Charles Tickner, Denver FSC
1936 ....Robin H. Lee, SC of New York	1978 ....Charles Tickner, Denver FSC
1937 ....Robin H. Lee, SC of New York	1979 ....Charles Tickner, Denver FSC
1938 ....Robin H. Lee, Chicago FSC	1980 ....Charles Tickner, Denver FSC
1939 ....Robin H. Lee, St Paul FSC	1981 ....Scott Hamilton, Philadelphia SC & HS
1940 ....Eugene Turner, Los Angeles FSC	1982 ....Scott Hamilton, Philadelphia SC & HS
1941 ....Eugene Turner, Los Angeles FSC	1983 ....Scott Hamilton, Philadelphia SC & HS
1942 ....Robert Specht, Chicago FSC	1984 ....Scott Hamilton, Philadelphia SC & HS
1943 ....Arthur R. Vaughn, Jr,	1985 ....Brian Boitano, Peninsula FSC
...............Philadelphia SC & HS	1986 ....Brian Boitano, Peninsula FSC
1944-45 .....No competition	1987 ....Brian Boitano, Peninsula FSC
1946 ....Dick Button, Philadelphia SC & HS	1988 ....Brian Boitano, Peninsula FSC
1947 ....Dick Button, Philadelphia SC & HS	1989 ....Christopher Bowman, Los Angeles FSC
1948 ....Dick Button, Philadelphia SC & HS	1990 ....Todd Eldredge, Los Angeles FSC
1949 ....Dick Button, Philadelphia SC & HS	1991 ....Todd Eldredge, Los Angeles FSC
1950 ....Dick Button, SC of Boston	1992 ....Christopher Bowman, Los Angeles FSC
1951 ....Dick Button, SC of Boston	1993 ....Scott Davis, Broadmoor SC
1952 ....Dick Button, SC of Boston	1994 ....Scott Davis, Broadmoor SC
1953 ....Hayes Alan Jenkins, Cleveland SC	1995 ....Todd Eldredge, Detroit SC
1954 ....Hayes Alan Jenkins, Broadmoor SC	1996 ....Rudy Galindo, St Moritz ISC
1955 ....Hayes Alan Jenkins, Broadmoor SC	1997 ....Todd Eldredge, Detroit SC
1956 ....Hayes Alan Jenkins, Broadmoor SC	1998 ....Todd Eldredge, Detroit SC
1957 ....David Jenkins, Broadmoor SC	

Pairs

1914 ......Jeanne Chevalier, Norman M. Scott,
WC of Montreal
1915-17..No competition
1918 ......Theresa Weld, Nathaniel W. Niles,
SC of Boston
1919 ......No competition
1920 ......Theresa Weld, Nathaniel W. Niles,
SC of Boston
1921 ......Theresa Weld Blanchard, Nathaniel W.
Niles, SC of Boston
1922 ......Theresa Weld Blanchard, Nathaniel W.
Niles, SC of Boston
1923 ......Theresa Weld Blanchard, Nathaniel W.
Niles, SC of Boston
1924 ......Theresa Weld Blanchard, Nathaniel W.
Niles, SC of Boston
1925 ......Theresa Weld Blanchard, Nathaniel W.
Niles, SC of Boston
1926 ......Theresa Weld Blanchard, Nathaniel W.
Niles, SC of Boston
1927 ......Theresa Weld Blanchard, Nathaniel W.
Niles, SC of Boston
1928 ......Maribel Y. Vinson, Thornton L. Coolidge,
SC of Boston
1929 ......Maribel Y. Vinson, Thornton L. Coolidge,
SC of Boston
1930 ......Beatrix Loughran, Sherwin C. Badger,
SC of New York
1931 ......Beatrix Loughran, Sherwin C. Badger,
SC of New York
1932 ......Beatrix Loughran, Sherwin C. Badger,
SC of New York
1933 ......Maribel Y. Vinson, George E. B. Hill,
SC of Boston
1934 ......Grace E. Madden, James L. Madden,
SC of Boston
1935 ......Maribel Y. Vinson, George E. B. Hill,
SC of Boston
1936 ......Maribel Y. Vinson, George E. B. Hill,
SC of Boston
1937 ......Maribel Y. Vinson, George E. B. Hill,
SC of Boston
1938 ......Joan Tozzer, M. Bernard Fox, SC of Boston
1939 ......Joan Tozzer, M. Bernard Fox, SC of Boston
1940 ......Joan Tozzer, M. Bernard Fox, SC of Boston
1941 ......Donna Atwood, Eugene Turner, Mercury
FSC/Los Angeles FSC
1942 ......Doris Schubach, Walter Noffke,
Springfield Ice Birds
1943 ......Doris Schubach, Walter Noffke,
Springfield Ice Birds
1944 ......Doris Schubach, Walter Noffke,
Springfield Ice Birds
1945 ......Donna Jeanne Pospisil, Jean-Pierre Brunet,
SC of New York
1946 ......Donna Jeanne Pospisil, Jean-Pierre Brunet,
SC of New York
1947 ......Yvonne Claire Sherman, Robert J.
Swenning, SC of New York
1948 ......Karol Kennedy, Peter Kennedy, Seattle SC
1949 ......Karol Kennedy, Peter Kennedy, Seattle SC
1950 ......Karol Kennedy, Peter Kennedy,
Broadmoor SC
1951 ......Karol Kennedy, Peter Kennedy,
Broadmoor SC
1952 ......Karol Kennedy, Peter Kennedy,
Broadmoor SC

1953 ......Carole Ann Ormaca, Robin Greiner,
SC of Fresno
1954 ......Carole Ann Ormaca, Robin Greiner,
SC of Fresno
1955 ......Carole Ann Ormaca, Robin Greiner,
St Moritz ISC
1956 ......Carole Ann Ormaca, Robin Greiner,
St Moritz ISC
1957 ......Nancy Rouillard Ludington, Ronald
Ludington, Commonwealth FSC/
SC of Boston
1958 ......Nancy Rouillard Ludington, Ronald
Ludington, Commonwealth FSC/
SC of Boston
1959 ......Nancy Rouillard Ludington, Ronald
Ludington, Commonwealth FSC
1960 ......Nancy Rouillard Ludington, Ronald
Ludington, Commonwealth FSC
1961 ......Maribel Y. Owen, Dudley S. Richards,
SC of Boston
1962 ......Dorothyann Nelson, Pieter Kollen,
Village of Lake Placid
1963 ......Judianne Fotheringill, Jerry J. Fotheringill,
Broadmoor SC
1964 ......Judianne Fotheringill, Jerry J. Fotheringill,
Broadmoor SC
1965 ......Vivian Joseph, Ronald Joseph,
Chicago FSC
1966 ......Cynthia Kauffman, Ronald Kauffman,
Seattle SC
1967 ......Cynthia Kauffman, Ronald Kauffman,
Seattle SC
1968 ......Cynthia Kauffman, Ronald Kauffman,
Seattle SC
1969 ......Cynthia Kauffman, Ronald Kauffman,
Seattle SC
1970 ......Jo Jo Starbuck, Kenneth Shelley,
Arctic Blades FSC
1971 ......Jo Jo Starbuck, Kenneth Shelley,
Arctic Blades FSC
1972 ......Jo Jo Starbuck, Kenneth Shelley,
Arctic Blades FSC
1973 ......Melissa Militano, Mark Militano,
SC of New York
1974 ......Melissa Militano, Johnny Johns,
SC of New York/Detroit SC
1975 ......Melissa Militano, Johnny Johns,
SC of New York/Detroit SC
1976 ......Tai Babilonia, Randy Gardner,
Los Angeles FSC
1977 ......Tai Babilonia, Randy Gardner,
Los Angeles FSC
1978 ......Tai Babilonia, Randy Gardner,
Los Angeles FSC/Santa Monica FSC
1979 ......Tai Babilonia, Randy Gardner,
Los Angeles FSC/Santa Monica FSC
1980 ......Tai Babilonia, Randy Gardner,
Los Angeles FSC/Santa Monica FSC
1981 ......Caitlin Carruthers, Peter Carruthers,
SC of Wilmington
1982 ......Caitlin Carruthers, Peter Carruthers,
SC of Wilmington
1983 ......Caitlin Carruthers, Peter Carruthers,
SC of Wilmington
1984 ......Caitlin Carruthers, Peter Carruthers,
SC of Wilmington

Pairs *(Cont.)*

1985 ......Jill Watson, Peter Oppegard,
Los Angeles FSC
1986 ......Gillian Wachsman, Todd Waggoner,
SC of Wilmington
1987 ......Jill Watson, Peter Oppegard,
Los Angeles FSC
1988 ......Jill Watson, Peter Oppegard,
Los Angeles FSC
1989 ......Kristi Yamaguchi, Rudy Galindo, St Mortiz ISC
1990 ......Kristi Yamaguchi, Rudy Galindo, St Mortiz ISC
1991 ......Natasha Kuchiki, Todd Sand,
Los Angeles FSC

1992 ......Calla Urbanski, Rocky Marval,
U of Delaware FSC/SC of New York
1993 ......Calla Urbanski, Rocky Marval,
U of Delaware FSC/SC of New York
1994 ......Jenni Meno, Todd Sand,
Winterhurst FSC/Los Angeles FSC
1995 ......Jenni Meno, Todd Sand,
Winterhurst FSC/Los Angeles FSC
1996 ......Jenni Meno, Todd Sand,
Winterhurst FSC/Los Angeles FSC
1997 ......Kyoko Ina, Jason Dungjen, SC of New York
1998 ......Kyoko Ina, Jason Dungjen, SC of New York

Dance

1914 ......Waltz: Theresa Weld, Nathaniel W. Niles,
SC of Boston
1915-19...No competition
1920 ......Waltz: Theresa Weld, Nathaniel W. Niles,
SC of Boston
Fourteenstep: Gertrude Cheever Porter,
Irving Brokaw, New York SC
1921 ......Waltz and Fourteenstep: Theresa Weld
Blanchard, Nathaniel W. Niles, SC of Boston
1922 ......Waltz: Beatrix Loughran, Edward M.
Howland, New York SC/SC of Boston
Fourteenstep: Theresa Weld Blanchard,
Nathaniel W. Niles, SC of Boston
1923 ......Waltz: Mr. & Mrs. Henry W. Howe,
New York SC
Fourteenstep: Sydney Goode, James B.
Greene, New York SC
1924 ......Waltz: Rosaline Dunn, Frederick Gabel,
New York SC
Fourteenstep: Sydney Goode, James B.
Greene, New York SC
1925 ......Waltz and Fourteenstep: Virginia Slattery,
Ferrier T. Martin, New York SC
1926 ......Waltz: Rosaline Dunn, Joseph K. Savage,
New York SC
Fourteenstep: Sydney Goode, James B.
Greene, New York SC
1927 ......Waltz and Fourteenstep: Rosaline Dunn,
Joseph K. Savage, New York SC
1928 ......Waltz: Rosaline Dunn, Joseph K. Savage,
New York SC
Fourteenstep: Ada Bauman Kelly, George T.
Braakman, New York SC
1929 ......Waltz and Original Dance combined:
Edith C. Secord, Joseph K. Savage,
SC of New York
1930 ......Waltz: Edith C. Secord, Joseph K. Savage,
SC of New York
Original: Clara Rotch Frothingham, George
E. B. Hill, SC of Boston
1931 ......Waltz: Edith C. Secord, Ferrier T. Martin,
SC of New York
Original: Theresa Weld Blanchard, Nathaniel
W. Niles, SC of Boston
1932 ......Waltz: Edith C. Secord, Joseph K. Savage,
SC of New York
Original: Clara Rotch Frothingham, George
E. B. Hill, SC of Boston
1933 ......Waltz: Ilse Twaroschk, Frederick F.
Fleishmann, Brooklyn FSC
Original: Suzanne Davis, Frederick
Goodridge, SC of Boston

1934 ......Waltz: Nettie C. Prantel, Roy Hunt, SC of
New York
Original: Suzanne Davis, Frederick
Goodridge, SC of Boston
1935 ......Waltz: Nettie C. Prantel, Roy Hunt,
SC of New York
1936 ......Marjorie Parker, Joseph K. Savage,
SC of New York
1937 ......Nettie C. Prantel, Harold Hartshorne,
SC of New York
1938 ......Nettie C. Prantel, Harold Hartshorne,
SC of New York
1939 ......Sandy Macdonald, Harold Hartshorne,
SC of New York
1940 ......Sandy Macdonald, Harold Hartshorne,
SC of New York
1941 ......Sandy Macdonald, Harold Hartshorne, SCNY
1942 ......Edith B. Whetstone, Alfred N. Richards, Jr,
Philadelphia SC & HS
1943 .....Marcella May, James Lochead, Jr,
Skate & Ski Club
1944 .....Marcella May, James Lochead, Jr,
Skate & Ski Club
1945 ......Kathe Mehl Williams, Robert J. Swenning,
SC of New York
1946 .....Anne Davies, Carleton C. Hoffner, Jr,
Washington FSC
1947 ......Lois Waring, Walter H. Bainbridge, Jr,
Baltimore FSC/Washigton FSC
1948 ......Lois Waring, Walter H. Bainbridge, Jr,
Baltimore FSC/Washington FSC
1949 ......Lois Waring, Walter H. Bainbridge, Jr,
Baltimore FSC/Washington FSC
1950 ......Lois Waring, Michael McGean, Baltimore FSC
1951 ......Carmel Bodel, Edward L. Bodel,
St Moritz ISC
1952 ......Lois Waring, Michael McGean,
Baltimore FSC
1953 ......Carol Ann Peters, Daniel C. Ryan,
Washington FSC
1954 ......Carmel Bodel, Edward L. Bodel, St Moritz ISC
1955 ......Carmel Bodel, Edward L. Bodel,
St Moritz ISC
1956 ......Joan Zamboni, Roland Junso,
Arctic Blades FSC
1957 ......Sharon McKenzie, Bert Wright,
Los Angeles FSC
1958 ......Andree Anderson, Donald Jacoby, Buffalo SC
1959 ......Andree Anderson Jacoby, Donald Jacoby,
Buffalo SC
1960 ......Margie Ackles, Charles W. Phillips, Jr,
Los Angeles FSC/Arctic Blades FSC

Champions of the United States *(Cont.)*

Dance *(Cont.)*

1961 ......Diane C. Sherbloom, Larry Pierce,
　　　　　Los Angeles FSC/WC of Indianapolis
1962 ......Yvonne N. Littlefield, Peter F. Betts,
　　　　　Arctic Blades FSC/ Paramount, CA
1963 ......Sally Schantz, Stanley Urban,
　　　　　SC of Boston/Buffalo SC
1964 ......Darlene Streich, Charles D. Fetter, Jr,
　　　　　WC of Indianapolis
1965 ......Kristin Fortune, Dennis Sveum,
　　　　　Los Angeles FSC
1966 ......Kristin Fortune, Dennis Sveum,
　　　　　Los Angeles FSC
1967 ......Lorna Dyer, John Carrell, Broadmoor SC
1968 ......Judy Schwomeyer, James Sladky,
　　　　　WC of Indianapolis/Genesee FSC
1969 ......Judy Schwomeyer, James Sladky,
　　　　　WC of Indianapolis/Genesee FSC
1970 ......Judy Schwomeyer, James Sladky,
　　　　　WC of Indianapolis/Genesee FSC
1971 ......Judy Schwomeyer, James Sladky,
　　　　　WC of Indianapolis/Genesee FSC
1972 ......Judy Schwomeyer, James Sladky,
　　　　　WC of Indianapolis/Genesee FSC
1973 ......Mary Karen Campbell, Johnny Johns,
　　　　　Lansing SC/Detroit SC
1974 ......Colleen O'Connor, Jim Millns,
　　　　　Broadmoor SC/City of Colorado Springs
1975 ......Colleen O'Connor, Jim Millns,
　　　　　Broadmoor SC
1976 ......Colleen O'Connor, Jim Millns,
　　　　　Broadmoor SC
1977 ......Judy Genovesi, Kent Weigle,
　　　　　SC of Hartford/Charter Oak FSC
1978 ......Stacey Smith, John Summers,
　　　　　SC of Wilmington

1979 ......Stacey Smith, John Summers,
　　　　　SC of Wilmington
1980 ......Stacey Smith, John Summers,
　　　　　SC of Wilmington
1981 ......Judy Blumberg, Michael Seibert,
　　　　　Broadmoor SC/ISC of Indianapolis
1982 ......Judy Blumberg, Michael Seibert,
　　　　　Broadmoor SC/ISC of Indianapolis
1983 ......Judy Blumberg, Michael Seibert,
　　　　　Pittsburgh FSC
1984 ......Judy Blumberg, Michael Seibert,
　　　　　Pittsburgh FSC
1985 ......Judy Blumberg, Michael Seibert,
　　　　　Pittsburgh FSC
1986 ......Renee Roca, Donald Adair,
　　　　　Genesee FSC/Academy FSC
1987 ......Suzanne Semanick, Scott Gregory,
　　　　　U of Delaware SC
1988 ......Suzanne Semanick, Scott Gregory,
　　　　　U of Delaware SC
1989 ......Susan Wynne, Joseph Druar,
　　　　　Broadmoor SC/Seattle SC
1990 ......Susan Wynne, Joseph Druar,
　　　　　Broadmoor SC/Seattle SC
1991 ......Elizabeth Punsalan, Jerod Swallow,
　　　　　Broadmoor SC
1992 ......April Sargent, Russ Witherby,
　　　　　Ogdensburg FSC/U of Delaware FSC
1993 ......Renee Roca, Gorsha Sur, Broadmoor SC
1994 ......Elizabeth Punsalan, Jerod Swallow,
　　　　　Broadmoor SC/Detroit SC
1995 ......Renee Roca, Gorsha Sur, Broadmoor SC
1996 ......Elizabeth Punsalan, Jerod Swallow, Detroit SC
1997 ......Elizabeth Punsalan, Jerod Swallow, Detroit SC
1998 ......Elizabeth Punsalan, Jerod Swallow, Detroit SC

U.S. Olympic Gold Medalists

Women

1956	Tenley Albright	1976	Dorothy Hamill
1960	Carol Heiss	1992	Kristi Yamaguchi
1968	Peggy Fleming	1998	Tara Lipinski

Men

1948	Richard Button	1960	David W. Jenkins
1952	Richard Button	1984	Scott Hamilton
1956	Hayes Alan Jenkins	1988	Brian Boitano

Special Achievements

Women successfully landing a triple axel in competition:
　Midori Ito, Japan, 1988 free-skating competition at Aichi, Japan.
　Tonya Harding, United States, 1991 U.S. Figure Skating Championship.

Miscellaneous Sports

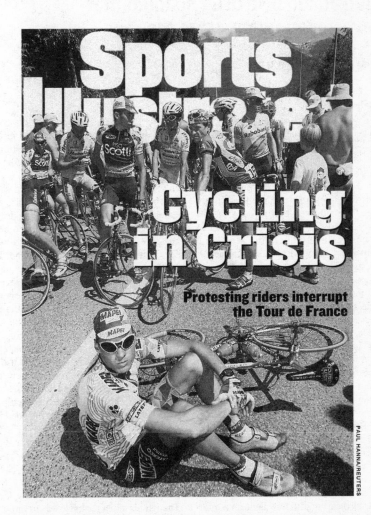

Sports Illustrated

Cycling in Crisis

Protesting riders interrupt
the Tour de France

PAUL HANNA/REUTERS

De-Tour

The 1998 Tour de France was sidetracked by a drug scandal that drove seven teams from the race

BY MERRELL NODEN

N O SPORTING EVENT in the world comes to a more triumphant conclusion than cycling's Tour de France. Having literally toured France in 23 days, climbing the Alps and visiting vineyards from the Loire to the Rhône, the riders sweep into Paris and, before crowds so rapturous you'd think they were hailing a liberating army, they roll up the Champs-Élysées drenched in champagne and sweat, forming a gorgeous cavalcade of bright color.

But the 1998 race was different. This year cycling's great showcase was racked by a drug scandal that drove seven teams from the race, persuaded the gendarmes to search riders' hotel rooms, and impelled riders to stage a misguided protest of police tactics. By the time the 85th edition of the Tour reached the Champs-Élysées on Aug. 2, it had come to resemble something dark and sinister—a perp walk on wheels. As SI's Steve Rushin put it memorably, it was hard to tell the drug peddlers from the drugged pedalers.

For years many have suspected that at its top levels cycling is riddled with drug use, and this year's Tour seemed to confirm that. It also cast a grim new light on a number of past tragedies, including the suspicious deaths of five Dutch cyclists in 1987. "The sport itself is at risk," concluded *VeloNews* in a pained editorial. In the end, this year's Tour raised hard questions about the sport: not just, can it exist, but should it, when so many of the top riders are using dangerous performance-enhancing drugs?

The grim revelations began even before the race did. On July 8, three days before the Tour's scheduled start in Ireland, Willy Voet, a masseur for the Festina team, was stopped by customs officials as he drove into France from Belgium. In Voet's car was a huge quantity of performance-enhancing drugs—anabolic steroids, the blood-thickener EPO and various hormones. Initially Voet tried to fall on his sword for Festina, claiming the substances were for his own use. But that was clearly preposterous given the massive amount of drugs found in the car.

In the week that followed, French police launched an investigation that included thorough searches of riders' rooms. On July 15, Bruno Roussel, the Festina team manager, and Eric Rijckaert, the team doctor, were detained by the French authorities. The following day Roussel's cycling license was suspended by the International Cycling Union. Though his initial response was to throw a fit of Gallic pique, Roussel soon admitted that doping was, in fact, one of the sport's professional hazards. "The object was to optimize performance under strict medical control," said Roussel, who faced charges of buying and transporting drugs. On July 17, Tour officials banished the entire nine-man Festina team, including Richard Virenque, a race favorite.

As suspicions continued to swirl around the

While Pantani (left) celebrated, Dutch official Hendrik Redant was wanted for questioning.

Tour, the cyclists did nothing to convince the public that the problem was small or isolated. On July 29 they staged a protest during the 17th stage, stopping and dismounting their bikes 32 kilometers into the race, then riding the rest of the stage as a group. In a show of empathy, they allowed five members of the TVM team, whose rooms had been raided by French police the day before, to ride together across the finish line. Viewed from outside the peloton, the gesture looked very much like a refusal to acknowledge there was a problem.

After all this, the race itself seemed an afterthought. Marco Pantani, a 28-year-old from Cesenatico, Italy, won, covering the whole dispiriting 3,711.6-kilometer course in 92 hours, 49 minutes and 46 seconds, with Jan Ullrich of Germany second (3:21 behind) and Bobby Julich of the U.S. third (4:08). "I attacked where I could, to put Ullrich in crisis," said Pantani of his stunning ride up the Col du Galibier in cold rain and fog. Pantani's average speed of 39.983 kilometers per hour (24.8 mph) won the fastest Tour in history, though, given the circumstances, one cannot help but cast a suspicious eye on the speedy times.

Unfortunately for Julich, his great ride was lost amid all the bad news. Still he sounded a note of triumph. "All I could think of was how hard I've worked to get here and who I could thank for helping me since I was a snot-nosed 13-year-old punk in Glenwood Springs [Colo.]," said a tearful Julich after the race. "I won't stop now until I either win the Tour de France or I'm too old to ride my bike anymore."

The sad fallout from the '98 Tour didn't end with the race. On Aug. 13, Unipublic, organizers of the Vuelta a España, Spain's three-week, 22-stage race, announced that the 13th stage of the race would not pass through France, as it has in the past. "Team cars and staff members would have to park and wait [in France] with no guarantees against being searched, detained or whatever else happened at the Tour," said Enrique Franco, Unipublic's general director. Shortly after the Tour concluded, the Dutch Rabobank team announced that it would not be competing in this year's Grand Prix Ouest France in Brittany, scheduled for Aug. 30, after race director Jean-Yves Perron told them he could not guarantee that there would not be drug raids by the French police.

So where does cycling go from here? Laying a good deal of responsibility for the sad state of affairs at the feet of Hein Verbruggen, head of the Union Cycliste Internationale (UCI), *VeloNews* called for the establishment of an independent commission "to review the sport from top to bottom." With meetings between riders, doctors and officials scheduled for October '98, it is too early to tell how cycling will respond to this crisis. But it is certain it must act quickly and decisively or face the speedy end of a once great sport.

Archery

National Men's Champions

1879.......Will H. Thompson	1919 ......Dr. Robert Elmer	1961 ......Clayton Sherman
1880 ......L. L. Pedinghaus	1920 ......Dr. Robert Elmer	1962 ......Charles Sandlin
1881 ......F. H. Walworth	1921 ......James Jiles	1963 ......Dave Keaggy Jr.
1882 ......D. H. Nash	1922 ......Dr. Robert Elmer	1964 ......Dave Keaggy Jr.
1883 ......Col. Robert Williams	1923 ......Bill Palmer	1965 ......George Slinzer
1884 ......Col. Robert Williams	1924 ......James Jiles	1966 ......Hardy Ward
1885 ......Col. Robert Williams	1925 ......Dr. Paul Crouch	1967 ......Ray Rogers
1886 ......W. A. Clark	1926 ......Stanley Spencer	1968 ......Hardy Ward
1887 ......W. A. Clark	1927 ......Dr. Paul Crouch	1969 ......Ray Rogers
1888 ......Lewis Maxson	1928 ......Bill Palmer	1970 ......Joe Thornton
1889 ......Lewis Maxson	1929 ......Dr. E. K. Roberts	1971 ......John Williams
1890 ......Lewis Maxson	1930 ......Russ Hoogerhyde	1972 ......Kevin Erlandson
1891 ......Lewis Maxson	1931 ......Russ Hoogerhyde	1973 ......Darrell Pace
1892 ......Lewis Maxson	1932 ......Russ Hoogerhyde	1974 ......Darrell Pace
1893 ......Lewis Maxson	1933 ......Ralph Miller	1975 ......Darrell Pace
1894 ......Lewis Maxson	1934 ......Russ Hoogerhyde	1976 ......Darrell Pace
1895 ......W. B. Robinson	1935 ......Gilman Keasey	1977 ......Rick McKinney
1896 ......Lewis Maxson	1936 ......Gilman Keasey	1978 ......Darrell Pace
1897 ......W. A. Clark	1937 ......Russ Hoogerhyde	1979 ......Rick McKinney
1898 ......Lewis Maxson	1938 ......Pat Chambers	1980 ......Rick McKinney
1899 ......M. C. Howell	1939 ......Pat Chambers	1981 ......Rick McKinney
1900 ......A. R. Clark	1940 ......Russ Hoogerhyde	1982 ......Rick McKinney
1901 ......Will H. Thompson	1941 ......Larry Hughes	1983 ......Rick McKinney
1902 ......Will H. Thompson	1946 ......Wayne Thompson	1984 ......Darrell Pace
1903 ......Will H. Thompson	1947 ......Jack Wilson	1985 ......Rick McKinney
1904 ......George Bryant	1948 ......Larry Hughes	1986 ......Rick McKinney
1905 ......George Bryant	1949 ......Russ Reynolds	1987 ......Rick McKinney
1906 ......Henry Richardson	1950 ......Stan Overby	1988 ......Jay Barrs
1907 ......Henry Richardson	1951 ......Russ Reynolds	1989 ......Ed Eliason
1908 ......Will H. Thompson	1952 ......Robert Larson	1990 ......Ed Eliason
1909 ......George Bryant	1953 ......Bill Glackin	1991 ......Ed Eliason
1910 ......Henry Richardson	1954 ......Robert Rhode	1992 ......Alan Rasor
1911 ......Dr. Robert Elmer	1955 ......Joe Fries	1993 ......Jay Barrs
1912 ......George Bryant	1956 ......Joe Fries	1994 ......Jay Barrs
1913 ......George Bryant	1957 ......Joe Fries	1995 ......Justin Huish
1914 ......Dr. Robert Elmer	1958 ......Robert Bitner	1996 ......Richard (Butch) Johnson
1915 ......Dr. Robert Elmer	1959 ......Wilbert Vetrovsky	1997 ......Richard (Butch) Johnson
1916 ......Dr. Robert Elmer	1960 ......Robert Kadlec	1998 ......Victor Wunderle

National Women's Champions

1879 ......Mrs. S. Brown	1902 ......Mrs. M. C. Howell	1927 ......Mrs. R. Johnson
1880 ......Mrs. T. Davies	1903 ......Mrs. M. C. Howell	1928 ......Beatrice Hodgson
1881 ......Mrs. A. H. Gibbes	1904 ......Mrs. M. C. Howell	1929 ......Audrey Grubbs
1882 ......Mrs. A. H. Gibbes	1905 ......Mrs. M. C. Howell	1930 ......Audrey Grubbs
1883 ......Mrs. M. C. Howell	1906 ......Mrs. E. C. Cook	1931 ......Dorothy Cummings
1884 ......Mrs. H. Hall	1907 ......Mrs. M. C. Howell	1932 ......Ilda Hanchette
1885 ......Mrs. M. C. Howell	1908 ......Harriet Case	1933 ......Madelaine Taylor
1886 ......Mrs. M. C. Howell	1909 ......Harriet Case	1934 ......Desales Mudd
1887 ......Mrs. A. M. Phillips	1910 ......J. V. Sullivan	1935 ......Ruth Hodgert
1888 ......Mrs. A. M. Phillips	1911 ......Mrs. J. S. Taylor	1936 ......Gladys Hammer
1889 ......Mrs. A. M. Phillips	1912 ......Mrs. Witwer Taylor	1937 ......Gladys Hammer
1890 ......Mrs. M. C. Howell	1913 ......Mrs. P. Fletcher	1938 ......Jean Tenney
1891 ......Mrs. M. C. Howell	1914 ......Mrs. B. P. Gray	1939 ......Belvia Carter
1892 ......Mrs. M. C. Howell	1915 ......Cynthia Wesson	1940 ......Ann Weber
1893 ......Mrs. M. C. Howell	1916 ......Cynthia Wesson	1941 ......Ree Dillinger
1894 ......Mrs. Albert Kern	1919 ......Dorothy Smith	1946 ......Ann Weber
1895 ......Mrs. M. C. Howell	1920 ......Cynthia Wesson	1947 ......Ann Weber
1896 ......Mrs. M. C. Howell	1921 ......Mrs. L. C. Smith	1948 ......Jean Lee
1897 ......Mrs. J. S. Baker	1922 ......Dorothy Smith	1949 ......Jean Lee
1898 ......Mrs. M. C. Howell	1923 ......Norma Pierce	1950 ......Jean Lee
1899 ......Mrs. M. C. Howell	1924 ......Dorothy Smith	1951 ......Jean Lee
1900 ......Mrs. M. C. Howell	1925 ......Dorothy Smith	1952 ......Ann Weber
1901 ......Mrs. C. E. Woodruff	1926 ......Dorothy Smith	1953 ......Ann Weber

National Women's Champions (Cont.)

1954 .....Luarette Young	1969 .....Doreen Wilber	1984 .....Ruth Rowe
1955 .....Ann Clark	1970 .....Nancy Myrick	1985 .....Terri Pesho
1956 .....Carole Meinhart	1971 .....Doreen Wilber	1986 .....Debra Ochs
1957 .....Carole Meinhart	1972 .....Ruth Rowe	1987 .....Terry Quinn
1958 .....Carole Meinhart	1973 .....Doreen Wilber	1988 .....Debra Ochs
1959 .....Carole Meinhart	1974 .....Doreen Wilber	1989 .....Debra Ochs
1960 .....Ann Clark	1975 .....Irene Lorensen	1990 .....Denise Parker
1961 .....Victoria Cook	1976 .....Luann Ryon	1991 .....Denise Parker
1962 .....Nancy Vonderheide	1977 .....Luann Ryon	1992 .....Sherry Block
1963 .....Nancy Vonderheide	1978 .....Luann Ryon	1993 .....Denise Parker
1964 .....Victoria Cook	1979 .....Lynette Johnson	1994 .....Judy Adams
1965 .....Nancy Pfeiffer	1980 .....Judi Adams	1995 .....Jessica Carlson
1966 .....Helen Thornton	1981 .....Debra Metzger	1996 .....Janet Dykman
1967 .....Ardelle Mills	1982 .....Luann Ryon	1997 .....Janet Dykman
1968 .....Victoria Cook	1983 .....Nancy Myrick	1998 .....Janet Dykman

Chess

World Champions

FIDE

1866–94 ....Wilhelm Steinitz, Austria	
1894–1921 ....Emanuel Lasker, Germany	
1921–27 ....Jose Capablanca, Cuba	
1927–35 ....Alexander Alekhine, France	
1935–37 ....Max Euwe, Holland	
1937–47 ....Alexander Alekhine, France	
1948–57 ....Mikhail Botvinnik, USSR	
1957–58 ....Vassily Smyslov, USSR	
1958–59 ....Mikhail Botvinnik, USSR	
1960–61 ....Mikhail Tal, USSR	
1961–63 ....Mikhail Botvinnik, USSR	

FIDE (Cont.)

1963–69 ....Tigran Petrosian, USSR
1969–72 ....Boris Spassky, USSR
1972–75 ....Bobby Fischer, United States
1975–85 ....Anatoly Karpov, USSR
1985–93 ....*Garry Kasparov, USSR
1993.........................vacant
1994– ....Anatoly Karpov, Russia

*Kasparov stripped of title by FIDE in 1993.

Professional Chess Association

1993– ....Garry Kasparov

United States Champions

1857–71 ....Paul Morphy	1957–61 ....Bobby Fischer	1987 ....Joel Benjamin
1871–76 ....George Mackenzie	1961–62 ....Larry Evans	Nick DeFirmian
1876–80 ....James Mason	1962–68 ....Bobby Fischer	1988 ....Michael Wilder
1880–89 ....George Mackenzie	1968–69 ....Larry Evans	1989 ....Roman
1889–90 ....Samuel Lipschutz	1969–72 ....Samuel Reshevsky	Dzindzichashvili
1890 ....Jackson Showalter	1972–73 ....Robert Byrne	Stuart Rachels
1890–91 ....Max Judd	1973–74 ....Lubomir Kavale	Yasser Seirawan
1891–92 ....Jackson Showalter	John Grefe	1990 ....Lev Alburt
1892–94 ....Samuel Lipschutz	1974–77 ....Walter Browne	1991 ....Gata Kamski
1894 ....Jackson Showalter	1978–80 ....Lubomir Kavalek	1992 ....Patrick Wolff
1894–95 ....Albert Hodges	1980–81 ....Larry Evans	1993 ....Alex Yermolinsky
1895–97 ....Jackson Showalter	Larry Christiansen	A. Shabalov
1897–1906 ...Harry Pillsbury	Walter Browne	1994 ....Boris Gulko
1906–09 ....Vacant	1981–83 ....Walter Browne	1995 ....Patrick Wolff
1909–36 ....Frank Marshall	Yasser Seirawan	Nick DeFirmian
1936–44 ....Samuel Reshevsky	1983 ....Roman	Alexander Ivanov
1944–46 ....Arnold Denker	Dzindzichashvili	1996 ....Alex Yermolinsky
1946–48 ....Samuel Reshevsky	1983 ....Larry Christiansen	1997 ....Alex Yermolinsky
1948–51 ....Herman Steiner	Walter Browne	1998 ....Alex Yermolinsky
1951–54 ....Larry Evans	1984–85 ....Lev Alburt	
1954–57 ....Arthur Bisguier	1986 ....Yasser Seirawan	

Curling

World Men's Champions

Year	Country, Skip	Year	Country, Skip	Year	Country, Skip
1972	Canada, Crest Melesnuk	1979	Norway, Kristian Soerum	1986	Canada, Ed Luckowich
1973	Sweden, Kjell Oscarius	1980	Canada, Rich Folk	1987	Canada, Russ Howard
1974	U.S., Bud Somerville	1981	Switzerland, Jurg Tanner	1988	Norway, Eigil Ramsfjell
1975	Switzerland, Otto Danieli	1982	Canada, Al Hackner	1989	Canada, Pat Ryan
1976	U.S., Bruce Roberts	1983	Canada, Ed Werenich	1990	Canada, Ed Werenich
1977	Sweden, Ragnar Kamp	1984	Norway, Eigil Ramsfjell	1991	Scotland, David Smith
1978	U.S., Bob Nichols	1985	Canada, Al Hackner	1992	Switzerland, Markus Eggler

Curling *(Cont.)*

World Men's Champions *(Cont.)*

Year	Country, Skip	Year	Country, Skip	Year	Country, Skip
1993	Canada, Russ Howard	1995	Canada, Kerry Burtnyk	1997	Sweden, Peter Lindholm
1994	Canada, Rick Folk	1996	Canada, Jeff Stoughton	1998	Canada, Wayne Middaugh

World Women's Champions

Year	Country, Skip	Year	Country, Skip	Year	Country, Skip
1979	Switzerland, Gaby Casanova	1984	Canada, Connie Lallberte	1992	Sweden, Elisabet Johanssen
1980	Canada, Marj Mitchell	1985	Canada, Linda Moore	1993	Canada, Sandra Peterson
1981	Sweden, Elisabeth Hogstrom	1986	Canada, Marilyn Darte	1994	Canada, Sandra Peterson
1982	Denmark, Marianne Jorgenson	1987	Canada, Pat Sanders	1995	Sweden, Elisabet Gustafson
		1988	Germany, Andrea Schopp	1996	Canada, Marilyn Bodogh
1983	Switzerland, Erika Mueller	1989	Canada, Heather Houston	1997	Canada, Sandra Schmirler
		1990	Norway, Dordi Nordby	1998	Sweden, Elisabet Gustafson
		1991	Norway, Dordi Nordby		

U.S. Men's Champions

Year	Site	Winning Club	Skip
1957	Chicago, IL	Hibbing, MN	Harold Lauber
1958	Milwaukee, WI	Detroit, MI	Douglas Fisk
1959	Green Bay, WI	Hibbing, MN	Fran Kleffman
1960	Chicago, IL	Grafton, ND	Orvil Gilleshammer
1961	Grand Forks, ND	Seattle, WA	Frank Crealock
1962	Detroit, MI	Hibbing, MN	Fran Kleffman
1963	Duluth, MN	Detroit, MI	Mike Slyziuk
1964	Utica, NY	Duluth, MN	Robert Magle Jr.
1965	Seattle, WA	Superior, WI	Bud Somerville
1966	Hibbing, MN	Fargo, ND	Joe Zbacnik
1967	Winchester, MA	Seattle, WA	Bruce Roberts
1968	Madison, WI	Superior, WI	Bud Somerville
1969	Grand Forks, ND	Superior, WI	Bud Somerville
1970	Ardsley, NY	Grafton, ND	Art Tallackson
1971	Duluth, MN	Edmore, ND	Dale Dalziel
1972	Wilmette, IL	Grafton, ND	Robert Labonte
1973	Colorado Springs, CO	Winchester, MA	Charles Reeves
1974	Schenectady, NY	Superior, WI	Bud Somerville
1975	Detroit, MI	Seattle, WA	Ed Risling
1976	Wausau, WI	Hibbing, MN	Bruce Roberts
1977	Northbrook, IL	Hibbing, MN	Bruce Roberts
1978	Utica, NY	Superior, WI	Bob Nichols
1979	Superior, WI	Bemidji, MN	Scott Baird
1980	Bemidji, MN	Hibbing, MN	Paul Pustovar
1981	Fairbanks, AK	Superior, WI	Bob Nichols
1982	Brookline, MA	Madison, WI	Steve Brown
1983	Colorado Springs, CO	Colorado Springs, CO	Don Cooper
1984	Hibbing, MN	Hibbing, MN	Bruce Roberts
1985	Mequon, WI	Wilmette, IL	Tim Wright
1986	Seattle, WA	Madison, WI	Steve Brown
1987	Lake Placid, NY	Seattle, WA	Jim Vukich
1988	St Paul, MN	Seattle, WA	Doug Jones
1989	Detroit, MI	Seattle, WA	Jim Vukich
1990	Superior, WI	Seattle, WA	Doug Jones
1991	Utica, NY	Madison, WI	Steve Brown
1992	Grafton, ND	Seattle, WA	Doug Jones
1993	St Paul, MN	Bemidji, MN	Scott Baird
1994	Duluth, MN	Bemidji, MN	Scott Baird
1995	Appleton, WI	Superior, WI	Tim Somerville
1996	Bemidji, MN	Superior, WI	Tim Somerville
1997	Seattle, WA	Langdon, ND	Craig Disher
1998	Bismarck, SD	Stevens Pt., WI	Paul Pustovar

U.S. Women's Champions

Year	Site	Winning Club	Skip
1977	Wilmette, IL	Hastings, NY	Margaret Smith
1978	Duluth, MN	Wausau, WI	Sandy Robarge
1979	Winchester, MA	Seattle, WA	Nancy Langley
1980	Seattle, WA	Seattle, WA	Sharon Kozal

Curling (Cont.)

U.S. Women's Champions (Cont.)

Year	Site	Winning Club	Skip
1981	Kettle Moraine, WI	Seattle, WA	Nancy Langley
1982	Bowling Green, OH	Oak Park, IL	Ruth Schwenker
1983	Grafton, ND	Seattle, WA	Nancy Langley
1984	Wauwatosa, WI	Duluth, MN	Amy Hatten
1985	Hershey, PA	Fairbanks, AK	Bev Birklid
1986	Chicago, IL	St Paul, MN	Gerri Tilden
1987	St Paul, MN	Seattle, WA	Sharon Good
1988	Darien, CT	Seattle, WA	Nancy Langley
1989	Detroit, MI	Rolla, ND	Jan Lagasse
1990	Superior, WI	Denver, CO	Bev Behnke
1991	Utica, NY	Houston, TX	Maymar Gemmell
1992	Grafton, ND	Madison, WI	Lisa Schoeneberg
1993	St Paul, MN	Denver, CO	Bev Behnke
1994	Duluth, MN	Denver, CO	Bev Behnke
1995	Appleton, WI	Madison, WI	Lisa Schoeneberg
1996	Bemidji, MN	Madison, WI	Lisa Schoeneberg
1997	Seattle, WA	Arlington, WI	Patti Lank
1998	Bismarck, SD	Wilmette, IL	Kari Erickson

Cycling

Professional Road Race World Champions

1927 ....Alfred Binda, Italy
1928 ....George Ronsse, Belgium
1929 ....George Ronsse, Belgium
1930 ....Alfred Binda, Italy
1931 ....Learco Guerra, Italy
1932 ....Alfred Binda, Italy
1933 ....George Speicher, France
1934 ....Karel Kaers, Belgium
1935 ....Jean Aerts, Belgium
1936 ....Antonio Magne, France
1937 ....Elio Meulenberg, Belgium
1938 ....Marcel Kint, Belgium
No competition 1939-45
1946 ....Hans Knecht, Switzerland
1947 ....Theo. Middelkamp, Holland
1948 ....Alberic Schotte, Belgium
1949 ....Henri Van Steenbergen, Belgium
1950 ....Alberic Schotte, Belgium
1951 ....Ferdinand Kubler, Switzerland
1952 ....Heinz Mueller, Germany
1953 ....Fausto Coppi, Italy
1954 ....Louison Bobet, France
1955 ....Stan Ockers, Belgium

1956 ....Rik Van Steenbergen, Belgium
1957 ....Rik Van Steenbergen, Belgium
1958 ....Ercole Baldini, Italy
1959 ....Andre Darrigade, France
1960 ....Rik van Looy, Belgium
1961 ....Rik van Looy, Belgium
1962 ....Jean Stablenski, France
1963 ....Bennoni Beheyt, Belgium
1964 ....Jan Janssen, Holland
1965 ....Tommy Simpson, England
1966 ....Rudi Altig, West Germany
1967 ....Eddy Merckx, Belgium
1968 ....Vittorio Adorni, Italy
1969 ....Harm Ottenbros, Netherlands
1970 ....J.P. Monseré, Belgium
1971 ....Eddy Merckx, Belgium
1972 ....Marino Basso, Italy
1973 ....Felice Gimondi, Italy
1974 ....Eddy Merckx, Belgium
1975 ....Hennie Kuiper, Holland
1976 ....Freddy Maertens, Belgium
1977 ....Francesco Moser, Italy

1978 ....Gerri Knetemann, Holland
1979 ....Jan Raas, Holland
1980 ....Bernard Hinault, France
1981 ....Freddy Maertens, Belgium
1982 ....Giuseppe Saronni, Italy
1983 ....Greg LeMond, United States
1984 ....Claude Criquielion, Belgium
1985 ....Joop Zoetemelk, Holland
1986 ....Moreno Argentin, Italy
1987 ....Stephen Roche, Ireland
1988 ....Maurizio Fondriest, Italy
1989 ....Greg LeMond, United States
1990 ....Rudy Dhaenene, Belgium
1991 ....Gianni Bugno, Italy
1992 ....Gianni Bugno, Italy
1993 ....Lance Armstrong, United States
1994 ....Luc LeBlanc, France
1995 ....Abraham Olano, Spain
1996 ....Johan Museeuw, Belgium
1997 ....Laurent Brochard, France

Tour DuPont Winners

Year	Winner	Time
1989	Dag Otto Lauritzen, Norway	33 hrs, 28 min, 48 sec
1990	Raul Alcala, Mexico	45 hrs, 20 min, 9 sec
1991	Erik Breukink, Holland	48 hrs, 56 min, 53 sec
1992	Greg LeMond, United States	44 hrs, 27 min, 43 sec
1993	Raul Alcala, Mexico	46 hrs, 42 min, 52 sec
1994	Viatcheslav Ekimov, Russia	47 hrs, 14 min, 29 sec
1995	Lance Armstrong, United States	46 hrs, 31 min, 16 sec
1996	Lance Armstrong, United States	48 hrs, 20 min, 5 sec

Note: Race not held since 1996.

Tour de France Winners

Winner	Winner	Time
1903	Maurice Garin, France	94 hrs, 33 min
1904	Henry Cornet, France	96 hrs, 5 min, 56 sec
1905	Louis Trousselier, France	110 hrs, 26 min, 58 sec
1906	Rene Pottier, France	Not available

Tour de France Winners *(Cont.)*

Winner	Winner	Time
1907	Lucien Petit-Breton, France	158 hrs, 54 min, 5 sec
1908	Lucien Petit-Breton, France	Not available
1909	Francois Faber, Luxembourg	157 hrs, 1 min, 22 sec
1910	Octave Lapize, France	162 hrs, 41 min, 30 sec
1911	Gustave Garrigou, France	195 hrs, 37 min
1912	Odile Defraye, Belgium	190 hrs, 30 min, 28 sec
1913	Philippe Thys, Belgium	197 hrs, 54 min
1914	Philippe Thys, Belgium	200 hrs, 28 min, 48 sec
1915–18	No race	
1919	Firmin Lambot, Belgium	231 hrs, 7 min, 15 sec
1920	Philippe Thys, Belgium	228 hrs, 36 min, 13 sec
1921	Leon Scieur, Belgium	221 hrs, 50 min, 26 sec
1922	Firmin Lambot, Belgium	222 hrs, 8 min, 6 sec
1923	Henri Pelissier, France	222 hrs, 15 min, 30 sec
1924	Ottavio Bottechia, Italy	226 hrs, 18 min, 21 sec
1925	Ottavio Bottechia, Italy	219 hrs, 10 min, 18 sec
1926	Lucien Buysse, Belgium	238 hrs, 44 min, 25 sec
1927	Nicolas Frantz, Luxembourg	198 hrs, 16 min, 42 sec
1928	Nicolas Frantz, Luxembourg	192 hrs, 48 min, 58 sec
1929	Maurice Dewaele, Belgium	186 hrs, 39 min, 16 sec
1930	Andre Leducq, France	172 hrs, 12 min, 16 sec
1931	Antonin Magne, France	177 hrs, 10 min, 3 sec
1932	Andre Leducq, France	154 hrs, 12 min, 49 sec
1933	Georges Speicher, France	147 hrs, 51 min, 37 sec
1934	Antonin Magne, France	147 hrs, 13 min, 58 sec
1935	Romain Maes, Belgium	141 hrs, 32 min
1936	Sylvere Maes, Belgium	142 hrs, 47 min, 32 sec
1937	Roger Lapebie, France	138 hrs, 58 min, 31 sec
1938	Gino Bartali, Italy	148 hrs, 29 min, 12 sec
1939	Sylvere Maes, Belgium	132 hrs, 3 min, 17 sec
1940–46	No race	
1947	Jean Robic, France	148 hrs, 11 min, 25 sec
1948	Gino Bartali, Italy	147 hrs, 10 min, 36 sec
1949	Fausto Coppi, Italy	149 hrs, 40 min, 49 sec
1950	Ferdi Kubler, Switzerland	145 hrs, 36 min, 56 sec
1951	Hugo Koblet, Switzerland	142 hrs, 20 min, 14 sec
1952	Fausto Coppi, Italy	151 hrs, 57 min, 20 sec
1953	Louison Bobet, France	129 hrs, 23 min, 25 sec
1954	Louison Bobet, France	140 hrs, 6 min, 5 sec
1955	Louison Bobet, France	130 hrs, 29 min, 26 sec
1956	Roger Walkowiak, France	124 hrs, 1 min, 16 sec
1957	Jacques Anquetil, France	129 hrs, 46 min, 11 sec
1958	Charly Gaul, Luxembourg	116 hrs, 59 min, 5 sec
1959	Federico Bahamontes, Spain	123 hrs, 46 min, 45 sec
1960	Gastone Nencini, Italy	112 hrs, 8 min, 42 sec
1961	Jacques Anquetil, France	122 hrs, 1 min, 33 sec
1962	Jacques Anquetil, France	114 hrs, 31 min, 54 sec
1963	Jacques Anquetil, France	113 hrs, 30 min, 5 sec
1964	Jacques Anquetil, France	127 hrs, 9 min, 44 sec
1965	Felice Gimondi, Italy	116 hrs, 42 min, 6 sec
1966	Lucien Aimar, France	117 hrs, 34 min, 21 sec
1967	Roger Pingeon, France	136 hrs, 53 min, 50 sec
1968	Jan Janssen, Netherlands	133 hrs, 49 min, 32 sec
1969	Eddy Merckx, Belgium	116 hrs, 16 min, 2 sec
1970	Eddy Merckx, Belgium	119 hrs, 31 min, 49 sec
1971	Eddy Merckx, Belgium	96 hrs, 45 min, 14 sec
1972	Eddy Merckx, Belgium	108 hrs, 17 min, 18 sec
1973	Luis Ocana, Spain	122 hrs, 25 min, 34 sec
1974	Eddy Merckx, Belgium	116 hrs, 16 min, 58 sec
1975	Bernard Thevenet, France	114 hrs, 35 min, 31 sec
1976	Lucien Van Impe, Belgium	116 hrs, 22 min, 23 sec
1977	Bernard Thevenet, France	115 hrs, 38 min, 30 sec
1978	Bernard Hinault, France	108 hrs, 18 min
1979	Bernard Hinault, France	103 hrs, 6 min, 50 sec
1980	Joop Zoetemelk, Netherlands	109 hrs, 19 min, 14 sec
1981	Bernard Hinault, France	96 hrs, 19 min, 38 sec
1982	Bernard Hinault, France	92 hrs, 8 min, 46 sec
1983	Laurent Fignon, France	105 hrs, 7 min, 52 sec
1984	Laurent Fignon, France	112 hrs, 3 min, 40 sec
1985	Bernard Hinault, France	113 hrs, 24 min, 23 sec

Tour de France Winners (Cont.)

Winner	Winner	Time
1986	Greg LeMond, United States	110 hrs, 35 min, 19 sec
1987	Stephen Roche, Ireland	115 hrs, 27 min, 42 sec
1988	Pedro Delgado, Spain	84 hrs, 27 min, 53 sec
1989	Greg LeMond, United States	87 hrs, 38 min, 35 sec
1990	Greg LeMond, United States	90 hrs, 43 min, 20 sec
1991	Miguel Induráin, Spain	101 hrs, 1 min, 20 sec
1992	Miguel Induráin, Spain	100 hrs, 49 min, 30 sec
1993	Miguel Induráin, Spain	95 hrs, 57 min, 9 sec
1994	Miguel Induráin, Spain	103 hrs, 38 min, 38 sec
1995	Miguel Induráin, Spain	92 hrs, 44 min, 59 sec
1996	Bjarne Riis, Denmark	95 hrs, 57 min, 16 sec
1997	Jan Ullrich, Germany	100 hrs, 30 min, 35 sec
1998	Marco Pantani, Italy	92 hrs, 49 min, 46 sec

Sled Dog Racing

Iditarod

Year	Winner	Time	Year	Winner	Time
1973	Dick Wilmarth	20 days, 00:49:41	1986	Susan Butcher	11 days, 15:06:00
1974	Carl Huntington	20 days, 15:02:07	1987	Susan Butcher	11 days, 02:05:13
1975	Emmitt Peters	14 days, 14:43:45	1988	Susan Butcher	11 days, 11:41:40
1976	Gerald Riley	18 days, 22:58:17	1989	Joe Runyan	11 days, 05:24:34
1977	Rick Swenson	16 days, 16:27:13	1990	Susan Butcher	11 days, 01:53:23
1978	Dick Mackey	14 days, 18:52:24	1991	Rick Swenson	12 days, 16:34:39
1979	Rick Swenson	15 days, 10:37:47	1992	Martin Buser	10 days, 19:17:15
1980	Joe May	14 days, 07:11:51	1993	Jeff King	10 days, 15:38:15
1981	Rick Swenson	12 days, 08:45:02	1994	Martin Buser	10 days, 13:02:39
1982	Rick Swenson	16 days, 04:40:10	1995	Doug Swingley	9 days, 02:42:19
1983	Dick Mackey	12 days, 14:10:44	1996	Jeff King	9 days, 05:43:13
1984	Dean Osmar	12 days, 15:07:33	1997	Martin Buser	9 days, 08:30:45
1985	Libby Riddles	18 days, 00:20:17	1998	Jeff King	9 days, 05:52:26

Fishing

Saltwater Fishing Records

Species	Weight	Where Caught	Date	Angler
Albacore	88 lb 2 oz	Gran Canaria, Canary Islands	Nov 19, 1977	Siegfried Dickemann
Amberjack, greater	155 lb 10 oz	Challenger Bank, Bermuda	June 24, 1981	Joseph Dawson
Amberjack, Pacific	104 lb	Baja California, Mexico	July 4, 1984	Richard Cresswell
Barracuda, great	85 lb	Christmas Island, Kiribati	April 11, 1992	John W. Helfrich
Barracuda, Mexican	21 lb	Phantom Isle, Costa Rica	Mar 27, 1987	E. Greg Kent
Barracuda, pickhandle	25 lb 5 oz	Scottburgh, Natal, South Africa	July 3, 1996	Demetrios Stamatis
Bass, barred sand	13 lb 3 oz	Huntington Beach, CA	Aug 29, 1988	Robert Halal
Bass, black sea	9 lb 8 oz	Virginia Beach, VA	Jan 9, 1987	Joe Mizelle Jr.
Bass, European	20 lb 11 oz	Stes Maries de la Mer, France	May 6, 1986	Jean Baptiste Bayle
Bass, giant sea	563 lb 8 oz	Anacapa Island, CA	Aug 20, 1968	James D. McAdam Jr.
Bass, redeye	8 lb 12 oz	Apalatchicola River, FL	Jan 28, 1995	Carl W. Davis
Bass, striped	78 lb 8 oz	Atlantic City, NJ	Sep 21, 1982	Albert R. McReynolds
Bluefish	31 lb 12 oz	Hatteras Inlet, NC	Jan 30, 1972	James M. Hussey
Bonefish	19 lb	Zululand, South Africa	May 26, 1962	Brian W. Batchelor
Bonito, Atlantic	18 lb 4 oz	Faial Island, Azores	July 8, 1953	D. G. Higgs
Bonito, Pacific	14 lb 12 oz	Baja California, Mexico	Oct. 12, 1980	Jerome H. Rilling
Cabezon	23 lb	Juan De Fuca Strait, WA	Aug 4, 1990	Wesley Hunter
Cobia	135 lb 9 oz	Shark Bay, Australia	July 9, 1985	Peter W. Goulding
Cod, Atlantic	98 lb 12 oz	Isle of Shoals, NH	June 8, 1969	Alphonse Bielevich
Cod, Pacific	30 lb	Andrew Bay, AK	July 7, 1984	Donald R. Vaughn
Conger	133 lb 4 oz	South Devon, England	June 5, 1995	Vic Evans
Dolphin	87 lb	Papagallo Gulf, Costa Rica	Sep 25, 1976	Manuel Salazar
Drum, black	113 lb 1 oz	Lewes, DE	Sep 15, 1975	Gerald M. Townsend
Drum, red	94 lb 2 oz	Avon, NC	Nov 7, 1984	David Deuel
Eel, American	9 lb 4 oz	Cape May, NJ	Nov 9, 1995	Jeff Pennick
Eel, marbled	36 lb 1 oz	Durban, South Africa	June 10, 1984	Ferdie van Nooten

Saltwater Fishing Records (Cont.)

Species	Weight	Where Caught	Date	Angler
Flounder, southern	20 lb 9 oz	Nassau Sound, FL	Dec 23, 1983	Larenza W. Mungin
Flounder, summer	22 lb 7 oz	Montauk, NY	Sep 15, 1975	Charles Nappi
Grouper, warsaw	436 lb 12 oz	Destin, FL	Dec 22, 1985	Steve Haeusler
Halibut, Atlantic	255 lb 4 oz	Gloucester, MA	July 28, 1989	Sonny Manley
Halibut, California	53 lb 4 oz	Santa Rosa Island, CA	July 7, 1988	Russell J. Harmon
Halibut, Pacific	459 lb	Dutch Harbor, Alaska	June 11, 1996	Jack Tragis
Jack, crevalle	57 lb 5 oz	Barra do Kwanza, Angola	Oct 10, 1992	Cam Nicolson
Jack, horse-eye	24 lb 8 oz	Miami, FL	Dec 20, 1982	Tilo Schnau
Jack, Pacific crevalle	29 lb 8 oz	Playa Zancudo, Costa Rica	Jan 1, 1994	Ronald C. Snody
Jewfish	680 lb	Fernandina Beach, FL	May 20, 1961	Lynn Joyner
Kawakawa	29 lb	Isla Clarion, Mexico	Dec 17, 1986	Ronald Nakamura
Lingcod	69 lb	Langara Island, B.C.	June 16, 1992	Murray M. Romer
Mackerel, cero	17 lb 2 oz	Islamorada, FL	Apr 5, 1986	G. Michael Mills
Mackerel, king	90 lb	Key West, FL	Feb 16, 1976	Norton I. Thomton
Mackerel, narrowbarred	99 lb	Natal, South Africa	Mar 14, 1982	Michael J. Wilkinson
Mackerel, Spanish	13 lb	Ocracoke Inlet, NC	Nov 4, 1987	Robert Cranton
Marlin, Atlantic blue	1402 lb 2 oz	Vitoria, Brazil	Feb 29, 1992	Paulo R. A. Amorim
Marlin, black	1560 lb	Cabo Blanco, Peru	Aug 4, 1953	A. C. Glassell Jr.
Marlin, Pacific blue	1376 lb	Kaaiwi Point, HI	May 31, 1982	J. W. de Beaubien
Marlin, striped	494 lb	Tutukaka, New Zealand	Jan 16, 1986	Bill Boniface
Marlin, white	181 lb 14 oz	Vitoria, Brazil	Dec 8, 1979	Evandro Luiz Caser
Permit	53 lb 4 oz	Lake Worth, FL	Mar 25, 1994	Roy Brooker
Pollock	50 lb	Salstraumen, Norway	Nov 30, 1995	Thor Magnus-Lekang
Pompano, African	50 lb 8 oz	Daytona Beach, FL	Apr 21, 1990	Tom Sargent
Roosterfish	114 lb	La Paz, Mexico	June 1, 1960	Abe Sackheim
Runner, blue	8 lb 7 oz	Port Aransas, TX	Feb 13, 1995	Allen E. Windecker
Runner, rainbow	37 lb 9 oz	Isla Clarion, Mexico	Nov 21, 1991	Tom Pfleger
Sailfish, Atlantic	141 lb 1 oz	Luanda, Angola	Feb 19, 1994	Alfredo de Sousa
Sailfish, Pacific	221 lb	Santa Cruz Island, Ecuador	Feb 12, 1947	C. W. Stewart
Seabass, white	83 lb 12 oz	San Felipe, Mexico	Mar 31, 1953	L. C. Baumgardner
Seatrout, spotted	17 lb 7 oz	Ft. Pierce, FL	May 11, 1995	Craig F. Carson
Shark, bigeye thresher	802 lb	Tutukaka, New Zealand	Feb 8, 1981	Dianne North
Shark, blue	437 lb	Catherine Bay, NSW, Australia	Oct 2, 1976	Peter Hyde
Shark, grter hammrhd	991 lb	Sarasota, FL	May 30, 1982	Allen Ogle
Shark, Greenland	1708 lb 9 oz	Trondheimsfjord, Norway	Oct 18, 1987	Terje Nordtvedt
Shark, porbeagle	507 lb	Caithness, Scotland	Mar 9, 1993	Christopher Bennet
Shark, shortfin mako	1115 lb	Black River, Mauritius	Nov 16, 1988	Patrick Guillanton
Shark, tiger	1780 lb	Cherry Grove, SC	June 14, 1964	Walter Maxwell
Shark, tope	98 lb 8 oz	Santa Monica, CA	Oct 20, 1994	Freed Oakley
Shark, white	2664 lb	Ceduna, Australia	Apr 21, 1959	Alfred Dean
Skipjack, black	26 lb	Baja California, Mexico	Oct 23, 1991	Clifford K. Hamaishi
Snapper, cubera	121 lb 8 oz	Cameron, LA	July 5, 1982	Mike Hebert
Snook	53 lb 10 oz	Parismina Ranch, Costa Rica	Oct 18, 1978	Gilbert Ponzi
Spearfish	90 lb 13 oz	Madeira Island, Portugal	June 2, 1980	Joseph Larkin
Swordfish	1182 lb	Iquique, Chile	May 7, 1953	L. Marron
Tarpon	283 lb 4 oz	Sherbro Island, Sierra Leone	Apr 16, 1991	Yvon Victor Sebag
Tautog	24 lb	Wachapreague, VA	Aug 25, 1987	Gregory Bell
Tilapia	6 lb 5 oz	Lake Arenal, Costa Rica	Feb 10, 1995	Marvin C. Smith
Trevally, bigeye	18 lb 1 oz	Clipperton Island, France	May 12,1990	Rebecca A. Mills
Trevally, giant	145 lb 8 oz	Maui, HI	Mar 28, 1991	Russell Mori
Tuna, Atlantic bigeye	392 lb 6 oz	Puerto Rico, Gran Caneria, Spain	July 25, 1996	Dieter Vogel
Tuna, blackfin	45 lb 8 oz	Key West, FL	May 4, 1996	Sam J. Burnett
Tuna, bluefin	1496 lb	Aulds Cove, Nova Scotia	Oct 26, 1979	Ken Fraser
Tuna, longtail	79 lb 2 oz	Montague Island, NSW, Australia	Apr 12, 1982	Tim Simpson
Tuna, Pacific bigeye	435 lb	Cabo Blanco, Peru	Apr 17, 1957	Russel Lee
Tuna, skipjack	45 lb 4 oz	Baja California, Mexico	Nov 16, 1996	Brian Evans
Tuna, southern bluefin	348 lb 5 oz	Whakatane, New Zealand	Jan 16, 1981	Rex Wood
Tuna, yellowfin	388 lb 12 oz	San Benedicto Is, Mexico	Apr 1, 1977	Curt Wiesenhutter
Tunny, little	35 lb 2 oz	Cape de Garde, Algeria	Dec 14, 1988	Jean Yves Chatard
Wahoo	158 lb 8 oz	Loreto, Baja California, Mexico	June 10, 1996	Keith Winter
Weakfish	19 lb 2 oz	Jones Beach Inlet, NY	Oct 11, 1984	Dennis Rooney
		Delaware Bay, Delaware	May 20, 1989	William E. Thomas
Yellowtail, California	79 lb 4 oz	Baja California, Mexico	July 2, 1991	Robert I. Welker
Yellowtail, southern	114 lb 10 oz	Tauranga, New Zealand	Feb 5, 1984	Mike Godfrey

Freshwater Fishing Records

Species	Weight	Where Caught	Date	Angler
Barramundi	63 lb 2 oz	Queensland, Australia	April 28, 1991	Scott Barnsley
Bass, largemouth	22 lb 4 oz	Montgomery Lake, GA	June 2, 1932	George W. Perry
Bass, rock	3 lb	York River, Ontario	Aug 1, 1974	Peter Gulgin
Bass, smallmouth	10 lb 14 oz	Dale Hollow, TN	April 24, 1969	John T. Gorman
Bass, Suwannee	3 lb 14 oz	Suwannee River, FL	Mar 2, 1985	Ronnie Everett
Bass, white	6 lb 13 oz	Orange, VA	July 31, 1989	Ronald Sprouse
Bass, whiterock	24 lb 3 oz	Leesville Lake, VA	May 12, 1989	David Lambert
Bass, yellow	2 lb 4 oz	Lake Monroe, IN	Mar 27, 1977	Donald L. Stalker
Bluegill	4 lb 12 oz	Ketona Lake, AL	Apr 9, 1950	T. S. Hudson
Bowfin	21 lb 8 oz	Florence, SC	Jan 29, 1980	Robert Harmon
Buffalo, bigmouth	70 lb 5 oz	Bastrop, LA	Apr 21, 1980	Delbert Sisk
Buffalo, black	55 lb 8 oz	Cherokee Lake, TN	May 3, 1984	Edward McLain
Buffalo, smallmouth	68 lb 8 oz	Lake Hamilton, AR	May 16, 1984	Jerry Dolezal
Bullhead, brown	5 lb 11oz	Cedar Creek, FL	Mar 28, 1995	Robert Bengis
Bullhead, yellow	4 lb 4 oz	Mormon Lake, AZ	May 11, 1984	Emily Williams
Burbot	18 lb 11 oz	Angenmanalren, Sweden	Oct 22, 1996	Margit Agren
Carp	75 lb 11 oz	Lac de St Cassien, France	May 21, 1987	Leo van der Gugten
Catfish, blue	111 lb	Tennesee River, AL	July 5, 1996	William P. McKinley
Catfish, channel	58 lb	Santee-Cooper Reservoir, SC	July 7, 1964	W. B. Whaley
Catfish, flathead	91 lb 4 oz	Lake Lewisville, TX	Mar 28, 1982	Mike Rogers
Catfish, white	18 lb 14 oz	Inverness, FL	Sep 21, 1991	Jim Miller
Char, Arctic	32 lb 9 oz	Tree River, Canada	July 30, 1981	Jeffrey Ward
Crappie, white	5 lb 3 oz	Enid Dam, MS	July 31, 1957	Fred L. Bright
Dolly Varden	18 lb 9 oz	Mashutuk River, AK	July 13, 1993	Richard B. Evans
Dorado	51 lb 5 oz	Corrientes, Argentina	Sep 27, 1984	Armando Giudice
Drum, freshwater	54 lb 8 oz	Nickajack Lake, TN	Apr 20, 1972	Benny E. Hull
Gar, alligator	279 lb	Rio Grande River, TX	Dec 2, 1951	Bill Valverde
Gar, Florida	21 lb 3 oz	Boca Raton, FL	June 3, 1981	Jeff Sabol
Gar, longnose	50 lb 5 oz	Trinity River, TX	July 30, 1954	Townsend Miller
Gar, shortnose	5 lb 12 oz	Rend Lake, IL	July 16, 1995	Donna K. Willmert
Gar, spotted	9 lb 12 oz	Lake Mexia, TX	Apr 7, 1994	Rick Rivard
Grayling, Arctic	5 lb 15 oz	Katseyedie River, Northwest Territories	Aug 16, 1967	Jeanne P. Branson
Inconnu	53 lb	Pah River, AK	Aug 20, 1986	Lawrence Hudnall
Kokanee	9 lb 6 oz	Okanagan Lake, Vernon, BC	June 18, 1988	Norm Kuhn
Muskellunge	67 lb 8 oz	Hayward, WI	July 24, 1949	Cal Johnson
Muskellunge, tiger	51 lb 3 oz	Lac Vieux-Desert, WI, MI	July 16, 1919	John Knobla
Peacock, speckled	27 lb	Rio Negro, Brazil	Dec 4,1994	Gerald (Doc) Lawson
Perch, Nile	191 lb 8 oz	Lake Victoria, Kenya	Sep 5, 1991	Andy Davison
Perch, white	4 lb 12 oz	Messalonskee Lake, ME	June 4, 1949	Mrs. Earl Small
Perch, yellow	4 lb 3 oz	Bordentown, NJ	May 1865	C. C. Abbot
Pickerel, chain	9 lb 6 oz	Homerville, GA	Feb 17, 1961	Baxley McQuaig Jr.
Pike, northern	55 lb 1 oz	Lake of Grefeern, West Germany	Oct 16, 1986	Lothar Louis
Redhorse, greater	9 lb 3 oz	Salmon River, Pulaski, NY	May 11, 1985	Jason Wilson
Redhorse, silver	11 lb 7 oz	Plum Creek, WI	May 29, 1985	Neal Long
Salmon, Atlantic	79 lb 2 oz	Tana River, Norway	1928	Henrik Henriksen
Salmon, chinook	97 lb 4 oz	Kenai River, AK	May 17, 1985	Les Anderson
Salmon, chum	35 lb	Edye Pass, Canada	July 11, 1995	Todd A. Johansson
Salmon, coho	33 lb 4 oz	Pulaski, NY	Sep 27, 1989	Jerry Lifton
Salmon, pink	13 lb 1 oz	Ontario, Canada	Sep 23, 1992	Ray Higaki
Salmon, sockeye	15 lb 3 oz	Kenai River, AK	Aug 9, 1987	Stan Roach
Sauger	8 lb 12 oz	Lake Sakakawea, ND	Oct 6, 1971	Mike Fischer
Shad, American	11 lb 4 oz	Connecticut River, MA	May 19, 1986	Bob Thibodo
Sturgeon, white	468 lb	Benicia, CA	July 9, 1983	Joey Pallotta III
Sunfish, green	2 lb 2 oz	Stockton Lake, MO	June 18, 1971	Paul M. Dilley
Sunfish, redbreast	1 lb 12 oz	Suwannee River, FL	May 29, 1984	Alvin Buchanan
Sunfish, redear	5 lb 3 oz	Sacramento, CA	June 27, 1994	Anthony H. White Sr.
Tigerfish, giant	97 lb	Zaire River, Kinshasa, Zaire	July 9, 1988	Raymond Houtmans
Trout, Apache	5 lb 3 oz	Apache Reservation, AZ	May 29, 1991	John Baldwin
Trout, brook	14 lb 8 oz	Nipigon River, Ontario	July 1916	W. J. Cook
Trout, brown	40 lb 4 oz	Heber Springs, AR	May 9, 1992	Howard L. Collins
Trout, bull	32 lb	Lake Pond Oreille, ID	Oct 27, 1949	N. L. Higgins
Trout, cutthroat	41 lb	Pyramid Lake, NV	Dec 1925	J. Skimmerhorn
Trout, golden	11 lb	Cook's Lake, WY	Aug 5, 1948	Charles S. Reed

Freshwater Fishing Records (Cont.)

Species	Weight	Where Caught	Date	Angler
Trout, lake	66 lb 8 oz	Great Bear Lake, Northwest Territories	July 19, 1991	Rodney Harback
Trout, rainbow	42 lb 2 oz	Bell Island, AK	June 22, 1970	David Robert White
Trout, tiger	20 lb 13 oz	Lake Michigan, WI	Aug 12, 1978	Pete M. Friedland
Walleye	25 lb	Old Hickory Lake, TN	Aug 2, 1960	Mabry Harper
Warmouth	2 lb 7 oz	Yellow River, Holt, FL	Oct 19, 1985	Tony D. Dempsey
Whitefish, lake	14 lb 6 oz	Meaford, Ontario	May 21, 1984	Dennis Laycock
Whitefish, mountain	5 lb 8 oz	Elbow River, Calgary, Alberta, Canada	Aug, 1, 1995	Randy G. Woo
Whitefish, broad	9 lb	Tozitna River, AK	July 17, 1989	Al Mathews
Whitefish, round	6 lb	Putahow River, Manitoba	June 14, 1984	Allan J. Ristori
Zander	25 lb 2 oz	Trosa, Sweden	June 12, 1986	Harry Lee Tennison

Greyhound Racing

Annual Greyhound Race of Champions Winners*

Year	Winner (Sex)	Affiliation/Owner	Year	Winner	Affiliation/Owner
1982	DD's Jackie (F)	Wonderland Park/ R.H.Walters Jr.	1988	BB's Old Yellow (M)	Supplemental (Southland)/ Margie Bonita Hyers
1983	Comin' Attraction (F)	Rocky Mt Greyhound Park/ Bob Riggin	1989	Osh Kosh Juliet (F)	Tampa Greyhound Track/ William F. Pollard
1984	Fallon (F)	Tampa Greyhound Track/ E.J. Alderson	1990	Daring Don (M)	Interstate Kennel Club/ Perry Padrta
1985	Lady Delight (F)	Lincoln Greyhound Park/ Julian A. Gay	1991	Mo Kick (M)	Flagler Greyhound Track/ Eric M. Kennon
1986	Ben G Speedboat (M)	Multnomah Kennel Club/ Louis Bennett	1992	Dicky Vallie (M)	Dairyland Greyhound Track/ George Benjamin
1987	ET's Pesky (F)	Supplemental (Flagler)/ Emil Tanis	1993	Mega Morris (M)	Jacksonville Kennel Club/ Ferrell's Kennel

* The Greyhound Race of Champions has not been held since 1993.

Gymnastics

World Champions
MEN
All-Around

Year	Champion and Nation	Year	Champion and Nation
1903	Joseph Martinez, France	1966	Mikhail Voronin, USSR
1905	Marcel Lalue, France	1970	Eizo Kenmotsu, Japan
1907	Joseph Czada, Czechoslovakia	1974	Shigeru Kasamatsu, Japan
1909	Marcos Torres, France	1978	Nikolai Andrianov, USSR
1911	Ferdinand Steiner, Czechoslovakia	1979	Alexander Ditiatin, USSR
1913	Marcos Torres, France	1981	Yuri Korolev, USSR
1922	Peter Sumi, Yug./F. Pechacek, Czech.	1983	Dimitri Bilozertchev, USSR
1926	Peter Sumi, Yugoslavia	1985	Yuri Korolev, USSR
1930	Josip Primozic, Yugoslavia	1987	Dimitri Bilozertchev, USSR
1934	Eugene Mack, Switzerland	1989	Igor Korobchinsky, USSR
1938	Jan Gajdos, Czechoslovakia	1991	Grigori Misutin, CIS
1950	Walter Lehmann, Switzerland	1993	Vitaly Scherbo, Belarus
1954	Valentin Mouratov, USSR / Victor Chukarin, USSR	1994	Ivan Ivankov, Belarus
		1995	Li Xiaoshuang, China
1958	Boris Shaklin, USSR	1997	Ivan Ivankov, Belarus
1962	Yuri Titov, USSR		

Pommel Horse

Year	Champion and Nation	Year	Champion and Nation
1930	Josip Primozic, Yugoslavia	1950	Josef Stalder, Switzerland
1934	Eugene Mack, Switzerland	1954	Grant Chaguinjan, USSR
1938	Michael Reusch, Switzerland	1958	Boris Shaklin, USSR

World Champions (Cont.)

MEN (Cont.)

Pommel Horse (Cont.)

Year	Champion and Nation	Year	Champion and Nation
1962	Miroslav Cerar, Yugoslavia	1987	Zsolt Borkai, Hungary
1966	Miroslav Cerar, Yugoslavia		Dmitri Bilozertchev, USSR
1970	Miroslav Cerar, Yugoslavia	1989	Valentin Moguilny, USSR
1974	Zoltan Magyar, Hungary	1991	Valeri Belenki, USSR
1978	Zoltan Magyar, Hungary	1992	Pae Gil Su, North Korea/ Vitaly
1979	Zoltan Magyar, Hungary		Scherbo, CIS/ Li Jing, China
1981	Michael Mikolai, East Germany	1993	Pae Gil Su, North Korea
	Li Xiaoping, China	1994	Marius Urzica, Romania
1983	Dmitri Bilozertchev, USSR	1995	Li Donghua, Switzerland
1985	Valentin Moguilny, USSR	1996	Pae Gil Su, North Korea
		1997	Valeri Belenki, Germany

Floor Exercise

Year	Champion and Nation	Year	Champion and Nation
1930	Josip Primozic, Yugoslavia	1979	Kurt Thomas, United States
1934	Georges Miesz, Switzerland		Roland Brucker, GDR
1938	Jan Gajdos, Czechoslovakia	1981	Yuri Korolev, USSR/ Li Yuejui, Chi
1950	Josef Stalder, Switzerland	1983	Tong Fei, China
1954	Valentin Mouratov, USSR	1985	Tong Fei, China
	Masao Takemoto, Japan	1987	Lou Yun, China
1958	Masao Takemoto, Japan	1989	Igor Korobchinsky, USSR
1962	Nobuyuki Aihara, Japan	1991	Igor Korobchinsky, USSR
	Yukio Endo, Japan	1993	Grigori Misutin, Ukraine
1966	Akinori Nakayama, Japan	1994	Vitaly Scherbo, Belarus
1970	Akinori Nakayama, Japan	1995	Vitaly Scherbo, Belarus
1974	Shigeru Kasamatsu, Japan	1996	Vitaly Scherbo, Belarus
1978	Kurt Thomas, United States	1997	Alexei Nemov, Russia

Rings

Year	Champion and Nation	Year	Champion and Nation
1930	Emanuel Loffler, Czechoslovakia	1981	Alexander Ditiatin, USSR
1934	Alois Hudec, Czechoslovakia	1983	Dimitri Bilozertchev, USSR
1938	Alois Hudec, Czechoslovakia	1985	Li Ning, China/ Yuri Korolev, USSR
1950	Walter Lehmann, Switzerland	1987	Yuri Korolev, USSR
1954	Albert Azarian, USSR	1989	Andreas Aguilar, West Germany
1958	Albert Azarian, USSR	1991	Grigory Misutin, USSR
1962	Yuri Titov, USSR	1992	Vitaly Scherbo, CIS
1966	Mikhail Voronin, USSR	1993	Yuri Chechi, Italy
1970	Akinori Nakayama, Japan	1994	Yuri Chechi, Italy
1974	N. Andrianov, USSR/ D. Grecu, Rom.	1995	Yuri Chechi, Italy
1978	Nikolai Andrianov, USSR	1996	Yuri Chechi, Italy
1979	Alexander Ditiatin, USSR	1997	Yuri Chechi, Italy

Parallel Bars

Year	Champion and Nation	Year	Champion and Nation
1930	Josip Primozic, Yugoslavia	1983	Vladimir Artemov, USSR
1934	Eugene Mack, Switzerland		Lou Yun, China
1938	Michael Reusch, Switzerland	1985	Sylvio Kroll, East Germany
1950	Hans Eugster, Switzerland		Valentin Moguilny, USSR
1954	Victor Chukarin, USSR	1987	Vladimir Artemov, USSR
1958	Boris Shaklin, USSR	1989	Li Jing, China
1962	Miroslav Cerar, Yugoslavia		Vladimir Artemov, USSR
1966	Sergei Diamidov, USSR	1991	Li Jing, China
1970	Akinori Nakayama, Japan	1992	Li Jin, China
1974	Eizo Kenmotsu, Japan		Alexei Voropaev, CIS
1978	Eizo Kenmotsu, Japan	1993	Vitaly Scherbo, Belarus
1979	Bart Conner, United States	1994	Huang Liping, China
1981	Koji Gushiken, Japan	1995	Vitaly Scherbo, Belarus
	Alexandr Ditiatin, USSR	1996	Rustam Sharipov, Ukraine
		1997	Zhang Jinjing, China

World Champions *(Cont.)*

MEN *(Cont.)*

High Bar

Year	Champion and Nation	Year	Champion and Nation
1930	Istvan Pelle, Hungary	1981	Alexander Takchev, USSR
1934	Ernst Winter, Germany	1983	Dimitri Bilozertchev, USSR
1938	Michael Reusch, Switzerland	1985	Tong Fei, China
1950	Paavo Aaltonen, Finland	1987	Dimitri Bilozertchev, USSR
1954	Valentin Mouratov, USSR	1989	Li Chunyang, China
1958	Boris Shaklin, USSR	1991	Li Chunyang, China/R. Buechner, Germ
1962	Takashi Ono, Japan	1992	Grigori Misutin, CIS
1966	Akinori Nakayama, Japan	1993	Sergei Kharkov, Russia
1970	Eizo Kenmotsu, Japan	1994	Vitaly Scherbo, Belarus
1974	Eberhard Gienger, West Germany	1995	Andreas Wecker, Germany
1978	Shigeru Kasamatsu, Japan	1996	Jesús Carballo, Spain
1979	Kurt Thomas, United States	1997	Jani Tanskanen, Finland

Vault

Year	Champion and Nation	Year	Champion and Nation
1934	Eugene Mack, Switzerland	1983	Arthur Akopian, USSR
1938	Eugene Mack, Switzerland	1985	Yuri Korolev, USSR
1950	Ernst Gebendinger, Switzerland	1987	Lou Yun, China
1954	Leo Sotornik, Czechoslovakia		Sylvio Kroll, East Germany
1958	Yuri Titov, USSR	1989	Joreg Behrend, East Germany
1962	Premysel Krbec, Czechoslovakia	1991	Yoo Ok Youl, South Korea
1966	Haruhiro Yamashita, Japan	1992	Yoo Ok Youl, South Korea
1970	Mitsuo Tsukahara, Japan	1993	Vitaly Scherbo, Belarus
1974	Shigeru Kasamatsu, Japan	1994	Vitaly Scherbo, Belarus
1978	Junichi Shimizu, Japan	1995	G. Misutin, Ukraine/A. Nemov, Russia
1979	Alexander Ditiatin, USSR	1996	Alexei Nemov, Russia
1981	Ralf-Peter Hemmann, East Germany	1997	Sergei Fedorchenko, Kazakhstan

WOMEN

All-Around

Year	Champion and Nation	Year	Champion and Nation
1934	Vlasta Dekanova, Czechoslovakia	1981	Olga Bicherova, USSR
1938	Vlasta Dekanova, Czechoslovakia	1983	Natalia Yurchenko, USSR
1950	Helena Rakoczy, Poland	1985	Elena Shoushounova, USSR
1954	Galina Roudiko, USSR		Oksana Omeliantchik, USSR
1958	Larissa Latynina, USSR	1987	Aurelia Dobre, Romania
1962	Larissa Latynina, USSR	1989	Svetlana Bouguinskaia, USSR
1966	Vera Caslavska, Czechoslovakia	1991	Kim Zmeskal, United States
1970	Ludmilla Tourischeva, USSR	1993	Shannon Miller, United States
1974	Ludmilla Tourischeva, USSR	1994	Shannon Miller, United States
1978	Elena Mukhina, USSR	1995	Lilia Podkopayeva, Ukraine
1979	Nelli Kim, USSR	1997	Svetlana Chorkina, Russia

Floor Exercise

Year	Champion and Nation	Year	Champion and Nation
1950	Helena Rakoczy, Poland	1987	Elena Shoushounova, USSR
1954	Tamara Manina, USSR		Daniela Silivas, Romania
1958	Eva Bosakava, Czechoslovakia	1989	Svetlana Bouguinskaia, USSR
1962	Larissa Latynina, USSR		Daniela Silivas, Romania
1966	Natalia Kuchinskaya, USSR	1991	Cristina Bontas, Romania
1970	Ludmilla Tourischeva, USSR		Oksana Tchusovitina, USSR
1974	Ludmilla Tourischeva, USSR	1992	Kim Zmeskal, United States
1978	Nelli Kim, USSR	1993	Shannon Miller, United States
	Elena Mukhina, USSR	1994	Dina Kochetkova, Russia
1979	Emilia Eberle, Romania	1995	Gina Gogean, Romania
1981	Natalia Ilenko, USSR	1996	Gina Gogean, Romania
1983	Ecaterina Szabo, Romania	1997	Gina Gogean, Romania
1985	Oksana Omeliantchik, USSR		

World Champions (Cont.)
WOMEN (Cont.)

Uneven Bars

Year	Champion and Nation	Year	Champion and Nation
1950	Gertchen Kolar, Austria	1983	Maxi Gnauck, East Germany
	Anna Pettersson, Sweden	1985	Gabriele Fahnrich, East Germany
1954	Agnes Keleti, Hungary	1987	Daniela Silivas, Romania
1958	Larissa Latynina, USSR		Doerte Thuemmler, East Germany
1962	Irina Pervuschina, USSR	1989	Fan Di, China/ Daniela Silivas, Rom
1966	Natalia Kuchinskaya, USSR	1991	Gwang Suk Kim, North Korea
1970	Karin Janz, East Germany	1992	Lavinia Milosivici, Romania
1974	Annelore Zinke, East Germany	1993	Shannon Miller, United States
1978	Marcia Frederick, United States	1994	Luo Li, China
1979	Ma Yanhong, China	1995	Svetlana Chorkina, Russia
	Maxi Gnauck, East Germany	1996	Svetlana Chorkina, Russia
1981	Maxi Gnauck, East Germany	1997	Svetlana Chorkina, Russia

Balance Beam

Year	Champion and Nation	Year	Champion and Nation
1950	Helena Rakoczy, Poland	1985	Daniela Silivas, Romania
1954	Keiko Tanaka, Japan	1987	Aurelia Dobre, Romania
1958	Larissa Latynina, USSR	1989	Daniela Silivas, Romania
1962	Eva Bosakova, Czechoslovakia	1991	Svetlana Boguinskaia, USSR
1966	Natalia Kuchinskaya, USSR	1992	Kim Zmeskal, United States
1970	Erika Zuchold, East Germany	1993	Lavinia Milosovici, Romania
1974	Ludmilla Tourischeva, USSR	1994	Shannon Miller, United States
1978	Nadia Comaneci, Romania	1995	Mo Huilan, China
1979	Vera Cerna, Czechoslovakia	1996	Dina Kochetkova, Russia
1981	Maxi Gnauck, East Germany	1997	Gina Gogean, Romania
1983	Olga Mostepanova, USSR		

Vault

Year	Champion and Nation	Year	Champion and Nation
1950	Helena Rakoczy, Poland	1985	Elena Shoushounova, USSR
1954	T. Manina, USSR/ A. Pettersson, Swe	1987	Elena Shoushounova, USSR
1958	Larissa Latynina, USSR	1989	Olesia Durnik, USSR
1962	Vera Caslavska, Czechoslovakia	1991	Lavinia Milosovici, Romania
1966	Vera Caslavska, Czechoslovakia	1992	Henrietta Onodi, Hungary
1970	Erika Zuchold, East Germany	1993	Elena Piskun, Belarus
1974	Olga Korbut, USSR	1994	Gina Gogean, Romania
1978	Nelli Kim, USSR	1995	L. Podkopayeva, Ukr./S. Amanar, Rom.
1979	Dumitrita Turner, Romania	1996	Gina Gogean, Romania
1981	Maxi Gnauck, East Germany	1997	Simona Amanar, Romania
1983	Boriana Stoyanova, Bulgaria		

National Champions
MEN
All-Around

Year	Champion	Year	Champion	Year	Champion
1963	Art Shurlock	1971	Yoshi Takei	1979	Bart Conner
1964	Rusty Mitchell	1972	Yoshi Takei	1980	Peter Vidmar
1965	Rusty Mitchell	1973	Marshall Avener	1981	Jim Hartung
1966	Rusty Mitchell	1974	John Crosby	1982	Peter Vidmar
1967	Katsuzoki Kanzaki	1975	Tom Beach	1983	Mitch Gaylord
1968	Yoshi Hayasaki		Bart Conner	1984	Mitch Gaylord
1969	Steve Hug	1976	Kurt Thomas	1985	Brian Babcock
1970	Makoto Sakamoto	1977	Kurt Thomas	1986	Tim Daggett
	Mas Watanabe	1978	Kurt Thomas	1987	Scott Johnson

National Champions (Cont.)

MEN (Cont.)

All-Around (Cont.)

Year	Champion	Year	Champion	Year	Champion
1988	Dan Hayden	1992	John Roethlisberger	1996	Blaine Wilson
1989	Tim Ryan	1993	John Roethlisberger	1997	Blaine Wilson
1990	John Roethlisberger	1994	Scott Keswick	1998	Blaine Wilson
1991	Chris Waller	1995	John Roethlisberger		

Floor Exercise

Year	Champion	Year	Champion	Year	Champion
1963	Tom Seward	1974	John Crosby	1988	Mark Oates
1964	Rusty Mitchell	1975	Peter Korman		Charles Lakes
1965	Rusty Mitchell	1977	Ron Galimore	1989	Mike Racanelli
1966	Dan Millman	1978	Kurt Thomas	1990	Bob Stelter
1967	Katsuzoki Kanzaki	1979	Ron Galimore	1991	Mike Racanelli
	Ron Aure	1980	Ron Galimore	1992	Gregg Curtis
1968	Katsuzoki Kanzaki	1981	Jim Hartung	1993	Kerry Huston
1969	Steve Hug	1982	Jim Hartung	1994	Jeremy Killen
	Dave Thor	1983	Mitch Gaylord	1995	Daniel Stover
1970	Makoto Sakamoto	1984	Peter Vidmar	1996	Jay Thornton
1971	John Crosby	1985	Mark Oates	1997	Jason Gatson
1972	Yoshi Takei	1986	Robert Sundstrom	1998	Jason Gatson
1973	John Crosby	1987	John Sweeney		

Pommel Horse

Year	Champion	Year	Champion	Year	Champion
1963	Larry Spiegel	1974	Marshall Avener	1987	Tim Daggett
1964	Sam Bailie	1975	Bart Conner	1988	Kevin Davis
1965	Jack Ryan	1977	Gene Whelan	1989	Kevin Davis
1966	Jack Ryan	1978	Jim Hartung	1990	Patrick Kirksey
1967	Paul Mayer	1979	Bart Conner	1991	Chris Waller
	Dave Doty	1980	Jim Hartung	1992	Chris Waller
1968	Katsuoki Kanzaki	1981	Jim Hartung	1993	Chris Waller
1969	Dave Thor	1982	Jim Hartung	1994	Mihai Begiu
1970	Mas Watanabe	1983	Bart Conner	1995	Mark Sohn
1971	Leonard Caling	1984	Tim Daggett	1996	Josh Stein
1972	Sadao Hamada	1985	Phil Cahoy	1997	John Roethlisberger
1973	Marshall Avener	1986	Phil Cahoy	1998	John Roethlisberger

Rings

Year	Champion	Year	Champion	Year	Champion
1963	Art Shurlock	1974	Tom Weeder	1987	Scott Johnson
1964	Glen Gailis	1975	Tom Beach	1988	Dan Hayden
1965	Glen Gailis	1977	Kurt Thomas	1989	Scott Keswick
1966	Glen Gailis	1978	Mike Silverstein	1990	Scott Keswick
1967	Fred Dennis	1979	Bart Conner	1991	Scott Keswick
	Don Hatch	1980	Jim Hartung	1992	Tim Ryan
1968	Yoshi Hayasaki	1981	Jim Hartung	1993	John Roethlisberger
1969	Fred Dennis	1982	Jim Hartung	1994	Scott Keswick
	Bob Emery		Peter Vidmar	1995	Paul O'Neill
1970	Makoto Sakamoto	1983	Mitch Gaylord	1996	Kip Simons
1971	Yoshi Takei	1984	Jim Hartung	1997	Blaine Wilson
1972	Yoshi Takei	1985	Dan Hayden	1998	Jeff Johnson
1973	Jim Ivicek	1986	Dan Hayden		

Vault

Year	Champion	Year	Champion	Year	Champion
1963	Art Shurlock	1967	Jack Kenan	1971	Gary Morava
1964	Gary Hery		Sid Jensen	1972	Mike Kelley
1965	Brent Williams	1968	Rich Scorza	1973	Gary Morava
1966	Dan Millman	1969	Dave Butzman	1974	John Crosby
		1970	Makoto Sakamoto	1975	Tom Beach

National Champions (Cont.)

MEN (Cont.)

Vault (Cont.)

Year	Champion	Year	Champion	Year	Champion
1977	Ron Galimore	1984	Chris Reigel	1991	Scott Keswick
1978	Jim Hartung	1985	Scott Johnson	1992	Trent Dimas
1979	Ron Galimore		Mark Oates	1993	Bill Roth
1980	Ron Galimore	1986	Scott Wilbanks	1994	Keith Wiley
1981	Ron Galimore	1987	John Sweeney	1995	David St. Pierre
1982	Jim Hartung	1988	John Sweeney/Bill Paul	1996	Blaine Wilson
	Jim Mikus	1989	Bill Roth	1997	Blaine Wilson
1983	Chris Reigel	1990	Lance Ringnald	1998	Brent Klaus

Parallel Bars

Year	Champion	Year	Champion	Year	Champion
1963	Tom Seward	1975	Bart Conner	1986	Tim Daggett
1964	Rusty Mitchell	1977	Kurt Thomas	1987	Scott Johnson
1965	Glen Gailis	1978	Bart Conner	1988	D. Hayden/K. Davis
1966	Ray Hadley	1979	Bart Conner	1989	Conrad Voorsanger
1967	Katsuzoki Kanzaki	1980	Phil Cahoy	1990	Trent Dimas
	Tom Goldsborough		Larry Gerard	1991	Scott Keswick
1968	Yoshi Hayasaki	1981	Bart Conner	1992	Jair Lynch
1969	Steve Hug	1982	Peter Vidmar	1993	Chainey Umphrey
1970	Makoto Sakamoto	1983	Mitch Gaylord	1994	Steve McCain
1971	Brent Simmons	1984	Peter Vidmar	1995	John Roethlisberger
1972	Yoshi Takei		Mitch Gaylord	1996	Jair Lynch
1973	Marshall Avener		Tim Daggett	1997	Blaine Wilson
1974	Jim Ivicek	1985	Tim Daggett	1998	Blaine Wilson

High Bars

Year	Champion	Year	Champion	Year	Champion
1963	Art Shurlock	1975	Tom Beach	1986	D. Hayden/D. Moriel
1964	Glen Gailis	1977	Kurt Thomas	1987	David Moriel
1965	Rusty Mitchell	1978	Kurt Thomas	1988	Dan Hayden
1966	Katsuzoki Kanzaki	1979	Yoichi Tomita	1989	Tim Ryan
1967	Katsuzoki Kanzaki	1980	Jim Hartung	1990	Trent Dimas
	Jerry Fontana	1981	Bart Conner		Lance Ringnald
1968	Yoshi Hayasaki	1982	Mitch Gaylord	1991	Lance Ringnald
1969	Rich Grisby	1983	Mario McCutcheon	1992	Jair Lynch
1970	Makoto Sakamoto	1984	Peter Vidmar	1993	Steve McCain
1971	Yoshi Takei		Tim Daggett	1994	Scott Keswick
1972	Tom Lindner		Mitch Gaylord	1995	John Roethlisberger
1973	John Crosby	1985	Dan Hayden	1996	Bill Roth
1974	Brent Simmons			1997	Douglas Stibel
				1998	Jason Gatson

WOMEN

All-Around

Year	Champion	Year	Champion	Year	Champion
1963	Donna Schanezer	1974	Joan Moore Gnat	1987	Kristie Phillips
1965	Gail Daley	1975	Tammy Manville	1988	Phoebe Mills
1966	Donna Schanezer	1976	Denise Cheshire	1989	Brandy Johnson
1968	Linda Scott	1977	Donna Turnbow	1990	Kim Zmeskal
1969	Joyce Tanac	1978	Kathy Johnson	1991	Kim Zmeskal
	Schroeder	1979	Leslie Pyfer	1992	Kim Zmeskal
1970	Cathy Rigby McCoy	1980	Julianne McNamara	1993	Shannon Miller
1971	Joan Moore Gnat	1981	Tracee Talavera	1994	Dominique Dawes
	Linda Metheny	1982	Tracee Talavera	1995	Dominique Moceanu
	Mulvihill	1983	Dianne Durham	1996	Shannon Miller
1972	Joan Moore Gnat	1984	Mary Lou Retton	1997	Vanessa Adler
	Cathy Rigby McCoy	1985	Sabrina Mar		Kristy Powell
1973	Joan Moore Gnat	1986	Jennifer Sey	1998	Kristen Maloney

National Champions (Cont.)
WOMEN (Cont.)

Vault

Year	Champion	Year	Champion	Year	Champion
1963	Donna Schanezer	1974	Dianne Dunbar	1986	Joyce Wilborn
1965	Gail Daley	1975	Kolleen Casey	1987	Rhonda Faehn
1966	Donna Schanezer	1976	Debbie Wilcox	1988	Rhonda Faehn
1968	Terry Spencer	1977	Lisa Cawthron	1989	Brandy Johnson
1969	Joyce Tanac Schroeder	1978	Rhonda Schwandt Sharon Shapiro	1990	Brandy Johnson
	Cleo Carver	1979	Christa Canary	1991	Kerri Strug
1970	Cathy Rigby McCoy	1980	J. McNamara/B. Kline	1992	Kerri Strug
1971	Joan Moore Gnat	1981	Kim Neal	1993	Dominique Dawes
	Adele Gleaves	1982	Yumi Mordre	1994	Dominique Dawes
1972	Cindy Eastwood	1983	Dianne Durham	1995	Shannon Miller
1973	Roxanne Pierce Mancha	1984	Mary Lou Retton	1996	Dominique Dawes
		1985	Yolanda Mavity	1997	Vanessa Atler
				1998	Dominique Moceanu

Uneven Bars

Year	Champion	Year	Champion	Year	Champion
1963	Donna Schanezer	1974	Diane Dunbar	1987	Melissa Marlowe
1965	Irene Haworth	1975	Leslie Wolfsberger	1988	Chelle Stack
1966	Donna Schanezer	1976	Leslie Wolfsberger	1989	Chelle Stack
1968	Linda Scott	1977	Donna Turnbow	1990	Sandy Woolsey
1969	Joyce Tanac Schroeder	1978	Marcia Frederick	1991	Elisabeth Crandall
	Lisa Nelson	1979	Marcia Frederick	1992	Dominique Dawes
1970	Roxanne Pierce Mancha	1980	Marcia Frederick	1993	Shannon Miller
		1981	Julianne McNamara	1994	Dominique Dawes
1971	Joan Moore Gnat	1982	Marie Roethlisberger	1995	Dominique Dawes
1972	Cathy Rigby McCoy	1983	Julianne McNamara	1996	Dominique Dawes
1973	Roxanne Pierce Mancha	1984	Julianne McNamara	1997	Kristy Powell
		1985	Sabrina Mar	1998	Elise Ray
		1986	Marie Roethlisberger		

Balance Beam

Year	Champion	Year	Champion	Year	Champion
1963	Leissa Krol	1975	Kyle Gayner	1985	Kelly Garrison-Steves
1965	Gail Daley	1976	Carrie Englert	1988	Kelly Garrison-Steves
1966	Irene Haworth	1977	Donna Turnbow	1989	Brandy Johnson
	Linda Scott	1978	Christa Canary	1990	Betty Okino
1968	Linda Scott	1979	Heidi Anderson	1991	Shannon Miller
1969	Lonna Woodward	1980	Kelly Garrison-Steves	1992	K. Strug/K. Zmeskal
1970	Joyce Tanac Schroeder	1981	Tracee Talavera	1993	Dominique Dawes
		1982	Julianne McNamara	1994	Dominique Dawes
1971	Linda Metheny Mulvihill	1983	Dianne Durham	1995	Doni Thompson
		1984	Pam Bileck		Monica Flammer
1972	Kim Chace		Tracee Talavera	1996	Dominique Dawes
1973	Nancy Thies Marshall	1986	Angie Denkins	1997	Kendall Beck
1974	Joan Moore Gnat	1987	Kristie Phillips	1998	Dominique Moceanu

Floor Exercise

Year	Champion	Year	Champion	Year	Champion
1963	Donna Schanezer	1976	Carrie Englert	1988	Phoebe Mills
1965	Gail Daley	1977	Kathy Johnson	1989	Brandy Johnson
1966	Donna Schanezer	1978	Kathy Johnson	1990	Brandy Johnson
1968	Linda Scott	1979	Heidi Anderson	1991	Kim Zmeskal
1970	Cathy Rigby McCoy	1980	Beth Kline		Dominique Dawes
1971	Joan Moore Gnat	1981	Michelle Goodwin	1992	Kim Zmeskal
	Linda Metheny Mulvihill	1982	Amy Koopman	1993	Shannon Miller
		1983	Dianne Durham	1994	Dominique Dawes
1972	Joan Moore Gnat	1984	Mary Lou Retton	1995	Dominique Dawes
1973	Joan Moore Gnat	1985	Sabrina Mar	1996	Dominique Dawes
1974	Joan Moore Gnat	1986	Yolanda Mavity	1997	Lindsay Wing
1975	Kathy Howard	1987	Kristie Phillips	1998	Vanessa Atler

Handball

National Four-Wall Champions
MEN

1919 .....Bill Ranft	1939 .....Joe Platak	1959 .....John Sloan	1979 .....Naty Alvarado
1920 .....Max Gold	1940 .....Joe Platak	1960 .....Jimmy Jacobs	1980 .....Naty Alvarado
1921 .....Carl Haedge	1941 .....Joe Platak	1961 .....John Sloan	1981 .....Fred Lewis
1922 .....Art Shinners	1942 .....Jack Clemente	1962 .....Oscar Obert	1982 .....Naty Alvarado
1923 .....Joe Murray	1943 .....Joe Platak	1963 .....Oscar Obert	1983 .....Naty Alvarado
1924 .....Maynard Laswe	1944 .....Frank Coyle	1964 .....Jimmy Jacobs	1984 .....Naty Alvarado
1925 .....Maynard Laswe	1945 .....Joe Platak	1965 .....Jimmy Jacobs	1985 .....Naty Alvarado
1926 .....Maynard Laswe	1946 .....Angelo Trutio	1966 .....Paul Haber	1986 .....Naty Alvarado
1927 .....George Nelson	1947 .....Gus Lewis	1967 .....Paul Haber	1987 .....Naty Alvarado
1928 .....Joe Griffin	1948 .....Gus Lewis	1968 .....Stuffy Singer	1988 .....Naty Alvarado
1929 .....Al Banuet	1949 .....Vic Hershkowitz	1969 .....Paul Haber	1989 .....Poncho Monreal
1930 .....Al Banuet	1950 .....Ken Schneider	1970 .....Paul Haber	1990 .....Naty Alvarado
1931 .....Al Banuet	1951 .....Walter Plakan	1971 .....Paul Haber	1991 .....John Bike
1932 .....Angelo Trutio	1952 .....Vic Hershkowitz	1972 .....Fred Lewis	1992 .....Octavio Silveyra
1933 .....Sam Atcheson	1953 .....Bob Brady	1973 .....Terry Muck	1993 .....David Chapman
1934 .....Sam Atcheson	1954 .....Vic Hershkowitz	1974 .....Fred Lewis	1994 .....Octavio Silveyra
1935 .....Joe Platak	1955 .....Jimmy Jacobs	1975 .....Fred Lewis	1995 .....David Chapman
1936 .....Joe Platak	1956 .....Jimmy Jacobs	1976 .....Fred Lewis	1996 .....David Chapman
1937 .....Joe Platak	1957 .....Jimmy Jacobs	1977 .....Naty Alvarado	1997 .....Octavio Silveyra
1938 .....Joe Platak	1958 .....John Sloan	1978 .....Fred Lewis	1998 .....David Chapman

WOMEN

1980 .....Rosemary Bellini	1985 .....Peanut Motal	1990 .....Anna Engele	1995 .....Anna Engele
1981 .....Rosemary Bellini	1986 .....Peanut Motal	1991 .....Anna Engele	1996 .....Anna Engele
1982 .....Rosemary Bellini	1987 .....Rosemary Bellini	1992 .....Lisa Fraser	1997 .....Lisa Fraser
1983 .....Diane Harmon	1988 .....Rosemary Bellini	1993 .....Anna Engele	1998 .....Lisa Fraser
1984 .....Rosemary Bellini	1989 .....Anna Engele	1994 .....Anna Engele	

National Three-Wall Champions
MEN

1950 .....Vic Hershkowitz	1963 .....Marty Decatur	1976 .....Lou Russo	1989 .....John Bike
1951 .....Vic Hershkowitz	1964 .....Marty Decatur	1977 .....Fred Lewis	1990 .....Vince Munoz
1952 .....Vic Hershkowitz	1965 .....Carl Obert	1978 .....Fred Lewis	1991 .....John Bike
1953 .....Vic Herskkowitz	1966 .....Marty Decatur	1979 .....Naty Alvarado	1992 .....John Bike
1954 .....Vic Hershkowitz	1967 .....Carl Obert	1980 .....Lou Russo	1993 .....Eric Klarman
1955 .....Vic Hershkowitz	1968 .....Marty Decatur	1981 .....Naty Alvarado	1994 .....David Chapman
1956 .....Vic Hershkowitz	1969 .....Marty Decatur	1982 .....Naty Alvarado	1995 .....David Chapman
1957 .....Vic Hershkowitz	1970 .....Steve August	1983 .....Naty Alvarado	1996 .....Vince Munoz
1958 .....Vic Hershkowitz	1971 .....Lou Russo	1984 .....Naty Alvarado	1997 .....Vince Munoz
1959 .....Jimmy Jacobs	1972 .....Lou Russo	1985 .....Vern Roberts	1998 .....Vince Munoz
1960 .....Jimmy Jacobs	1973 .....Paul Haber	1986 .....Vern Roberts	
1961 .....Jimmy Jacobs	1974 .....Fred Lewis	1987 .....Vern Roberts	
1962 .....Oscar Obert	1975 .....Lou Russo	1988 .....Jon Kendler	

WOMEN

1981 .....Allison Roberts	1986 .....Rosemary Bellini	1991 .....Rosemary Bellini	1996 .....Anna Engele
1982 .....Allison Roberts	1987 .....Rosemary Bellini	1992 .....Anna Engele	1997 .....Allison Roberts
1983 .....Allison Roberts	1988 .....Rosemary Bellini	1993 .....Anna Engele	1998 .....Anna Christoff
1984 .....Rosemary Bellini	1989 .....Rosemary Bellini	1994 .....Anna Engele	
1985 .....Rosemary Bellini	1990 .....Rosemary Bellini	1995 .....Allison Roberts	

World Four-Wall Champions

1984 ....Merv Deckert, Canada	1991 ....Pancho Monreal, United States
1986 ....Vern Roberts, United States	1994 ....David Chapman, United States
1988 ....Naty Alvarado, United States	1997 ....John Bike Jr, United States

Lacrosse

United States Club Lacrosse Association Champions

1960 ......Mt Washington Club	1966 ......Mt Washington Club	1972 ......Carling
1961 ......Baltimore Lacrosse Club	1967 ......Mt Washington Club	1973 ......Long Island Athletic Club
1962 ......Mt Washington Club	1968 ......Long Island Athletic Club	1974 ......Long Island Athletic Club
1963 ......University Club	1969 ......Long Island Athletic Club	1975 ......Mt Washington Club
1964 ......Mt Washington Club	1970 ......Long Island Athletic Club	1976 ......Mt Washington Club
1965 ......Mt Washington Club	1971 ......Long Island Athletic Club	1977 ......Mt Washington Club

United States Club Lacrosse Association Champions (Cont.)

1978	Long Island Athletic Club	1985	LI-Hofstra Lacrosse Club	1992	Maryland Lacrosse Club
1979	Maryland Lacrosse Club	1986	LI-Hofstra Lacrosse Club	1993	Mt Washington Club
1980	Long Island Athletic Club	1987	LI-Hofstra Lacrosse Club	1994	LI-Hofstra Lacrosse Club
1981	Long Island Athletic Club	1988	Maryland Lacrosse Club	1995	Mt Washington Club
1982	Maryland Lacrosse Club	1989	LI-Hofstra Lacrosse Club	1996	LI-Hofstra Lacrosse Club
1983	Maryland Lacrosse Club	1990	Mt Washington Club	1997	LI-Hofstra Lacrosse Club
1984	Maryland Lacrosse Club	1991	Mt Washington Club	1998	LI-Hofstra Lacrosse Club

Little League Baseball

Little League World Series Champions

Year	Champion	Runner-Up	Score	Year	Champion	Runner-Up	Score
1947	Williamsport, PA	Lock Haven, PA	16–7	1973	Tainan City, Taiwan	Tucson, AZ	12–0
1948	Lock Haven, PA	St Petersburg, FL	6–5	1974	Kao-Hsuing, Taiwan	El Cajun, CA	7–2
1949	Hammonton, NJ	Pensacola, FL	5–0	1975	Lakewood, NJ	Tampa, FL	4–3
1950	Houston, TX	Bridgeport, CT	2–1	1976	Tokyo, Japan	Campbell, CA	10–3
1951	Stamford, CT	Austin, TX	3–0	1977	Kao-Hsuing, Taiwan	El Cajun, CA	7–2
1952	Norwalk, CT	Monongahela, PA	4–3	1978	Pin-Tung, Taiwan	Danville, CA	11–1
1953	Birmingham, AL	Schenectady, NY	1–0	1979	Hsien, Taiwan	Campbell, CA	2–1
1954	Schenectady, NY	Colton, CA	7–5	1980	Hua Lian, Taiwan	Tampa, FL	4–3
1955	Morrisville, PA	Merchantville, NJ	4–3	1981	Tai-Chung, Taiwan	Tampa, FL	4–2
1956	Roswell, NM	Merchantville, NJ	3–1	1982	Kirkland, WA	Hsien, Taiwan	6–0
1957	Monterrrey, Mex.	LaMesa, CA	4–0	1983	Marietta, GA	Barahona, D.Rep.	3–1
1958	Monterrey, Mex.	Kankakee, IL	10–1	1984	Seoul, S. Korea	Altamonte Sgs, FL	6–2
1959	Hamtramck, MI	Auburn, CA	12–0	1985	Seoul, S. Korea	Mexicali, Mex.	7–1
1960	Levittown, PA	Ft Worth, TX	5–0	1986	Tainan Park, Taiwan	Tucson, AZ	12–0
1961	El Cajon, CA	El Campo, TX	4–2	1987	Hua Lian, Taiwan	Irvine, CA	21–1
1962	San Jose, CA	Kankakee, IL	3–0	1988	Tai-Chung, Taiwan	Pearl City, HI	10–0
1963	Granada Hills, CA	Stratford, CT	2–1	1989	Trumbull, CT	Kaohsiung, Taiwan	5–2
1964	Staten Island, NY	Monterrey, Mex.	4–0	1990	Taipei, Taiwan	Shippensburg, PA	9–0
1965	Windsor Locks, CT	Stoney Creek, Can.	3–1	1991	Tai-Chung, Taiwan	San Ramon Vly, CA	11–0
1966	Houston, TX	W.New York, NJ	8–2	1992*	Long Beach, CA	Zamboanga, Phil.	6–0
1967	West Tokyo, Japan	Chicago, IL	4–1	1993	Long Beach, CA	David Chiriqui, Pan.	3–2
1968	Osaka, Japan	Richmond, VA	1–0	1994	Maracaibo, Venez.	Northridge, CA	4–3
1969	Taipei, Taiwan	Santa Clara, CA	5–0	1995	Tainan, Taiwan	Sprint, TX	17–3
1970	Wayne, NJ	Campbell, CA	2–0	1996	Kao-Hsuing, Taiwan	Cranston, RI	13–3
1971	Tainan, Taiwan	Gary, IN	12–3	1997	Guadalupe, Mex.	Mission Viejo, CA	5–4
1972	Taipei, Taiwan	Hammond, IN	6–0	1998	Toms River, NJ	Kashima, Japan	12–9

*Long Beach declared a 6–0 winner after the international tournament committee determined that Zamboanga City had used players that were not within its city limits.

Motor Boat Racing

American Power Boat Association Gold Cup Champions

Year	Boat	Driver	Avg MPH	Year	Boat	Driver	Avg MPH
1904	Standard (June)	Carl Riotte	23.160	1918	Miss Detroit II	Gar Wood	51.619
1904	Vingt-et-Un II (Sep)	W. Sharpe Kilmer	24.900	1919	Miss Detroit III	Gar Wood	42.748
1905	Chip I	J. Wainwright	15.000	1920	Miss America I	Gar Wood	62.022
1906	Chip II	J. Wainwright	25.000	1921	Miss America I	Gar Wood	52.825
1907	Chip II	J. Wainwright	23.903	1922	Packard Chriscraft	J. G. Vincent	40.253
1908	Dixie II	E. J. Schroeder	29.938	1923	Packard Chriscraft	Caleb Bragg	43.867
1909	Dixie II	E. J. Schroeder	29.590	1924	Baby Bootlegger	Caleb Bragg	45.302
1910	Dixie III	F. K. Burnham	32.473	1925	Baby Bootlegger	Caleb Bragg	47.240
1911	MIT II	J. H. Hayden	37.000	1926	Greenwich Folly	George Townsend	47.984
1912	P.D.Q. II	A. G. Miles	39.462				
1913	Ankle Deep	Cas Mankowski	42.779	1927	Greenwich Folly	George Townsend	47.662
1914	Baby Speed Demon II	Jim Blackton & Bob Edgren	48.458	1928	No race		
1915	Miss Detroit	Johnny Milot & Jack Beebe	37.656	1929	Imp	Richard Hoyt	48.662
				1930	Hotsy Totsy	Vic Kliesrath	52.673
1916	Miss Minneapolis	Bernard Smith	48.860	1931	Hotsy Totsy	Vic Kliesrath	53.602
1917	Miss Detroit II	Gar Wood	54.410				

American Power Boat Association Gold Cup Champions *(Cont.)*

Year	Boat	Driver	Avg MPH	Year	Boat	Driver	Avg MPH
1932	Delphine IV	Bill Horn	57.775	1969	Miss Budweiser	Bill Sterett	98.504
1933	El Lagarto	George Reis	56.260	1970	Miss Budweiser	Dean Chenoweth	99.562
1934	El Lagarto	George Reis	55.000				
1935	El Lagarto	George Reis	55.056	1971	Miss Madison	Jim McCormick	98.043
1936	Impshi	Kaye Don	45.735	1972	Atlas Van Lines	Bill Muncey	104.277
1937	Notre Dame	Clell Perry	63.675	1973	Miss Budweiser	Dean Chenoweth	99.043
1938	Alagi	Theo Rossi	64.340				
1939	My Sin	Z. G. Simmons, Jr	66.133	1974	Pay 'n Pak	George Henley	104.428
1940	Hotsy Totsy III	Sidney Allen	48.295	1975	Pay 'n Pak	George Henley	108.921
1941	My Sin	Z. G. Simmons, Jr	52.509	1976	Miss U.S.	Tom D'Eath	100.412
1942-45		No race		1977	Atlas Van Lines	Bill Muncey	111.822
1946	Tempo VI	Guy Lombardo	68.132	1978	Atlas Van Lines	Bill Muncey	111.412
1947	Miss Peps V	Danny Foster	57.000	1979	Atlas Van Lines	Bill Muncey	100.765
1948	Miss Great Lakes	Danny Foster	46.845	1980	Miss Budweiser	Dean Chenoweth	106.932
1949	My Sweetie	Bill Cantrell	73.612				
1950	Slo-Mo-Shun V	Ted Jones	78.216	1981	Miss Budweiser	Dean Chenoweth	116.932
1951	Slo-Mo-Shun V	Lou Fageol	90.871				
1952	Slo-Mo-Shun IV	Stan Dollar	79.923	1982	Atlas Van Lines	Chip Hanauer	120.050
1953	Slo-Mo-Shun IV	Joe Taggart & Lou Fageol	99.108	1983	Atlas Van Lines	Chip Hanauer	118.507
				1984	Atlas Van Lines	Chip Hanauer	130.175
1954	Slo-Mo-Shun IV	Joe Taggart & Lou Fageol	92.613	1985	Miller American	Chip Hanauer	120.643
				1986	Miller American	Chip Hanauer	116.523
1955	Gale V	Lee Schoenith	99.552	1987	Miller American	Chip Hanauer	127.620
1956	Miss Thriftaway	Bill Muncey	96.552	1988	Miss Circus Circus	Chip Hanauer & Jim Prevost	123.756
1957	Miss Thriftaway	Bill Muncey	101.787				
1958	Hawaii Kai III	Jack Regas	103.000	1989	Miss Budweiser	Tom D'Eath	131.209
1959	Maverick	Bill Stead	104.481	1990	Miss Budweiser	Tom D'Eath	143.176
1960		No race		1991	Winston Eagle	Mark Tate	137.771
1961	Miss Century 21	Bill Muncey	99.678	1992	Miss Budweiser	Chip Hanauer	136.282
1962	Miss Century 21	Bill Muncey	100.710	1993	Miss Budweiser	Chip Hanauer	141.195
1963	Miss Bardahl	Ron Musson	105.124	1994	Smokin' Joe Camel	Mark Tate	145.260
1964	Miss Bardahl	Ron Musson	103.433	1995	Miss Budweiser	Chip Hanauer	149.160
1965	Miss Bardahl	Ron Musson	103.132	1996	PICO American Dream	Dave Villwock	149.328
1966	Tahoe Miss	Mira Slovak	93.019	1997	Miss Budweiser	Dave Villwock	129.366
1967	Miss Bardahl	Bill Shumacher	101.484	1998	Miss Budweiser	Dave Villwock	140.704
1968	Miss Bardahl	Bill Shumacher	108.173				

Unlimited Hydroplane Racing Association Annual Champion Drivers

Year	Driver	Boat	Wins	Year	Driver	Boat	Wins
1947	Danny Foster	Miss Peps V	6	1973	Mickey Remund	Pay 'n Pack	4
1948	Dan Arena	Such Crust	2	1974	George Henley	Pay 'n Pack	7
1949	Bill Cantrell	My Sweetie	7	1975	Billy Schumacher	Weisfield's	2
1950	Dan Foster	Such Crust/DaphneX	2	1976	Bill Muncey	Atlas Van Lines	5
1951	Chuck Thompson	Miss Pepsi	5	1977	Mickey Remund	Miss Budweiser	3
1952	Chuck Thompson	Miss Pepsi	3	1978	Bill Muncey	Atlas Van Lines	6
1953	Lee Schoenith	Gale II	1	1979	Bill Muncey	Atlas Van Lines	7
1954	Lee Schoenith	Gale V	4	1980	Dean Chenoweth	Miss Budweiser	5
1955	Lee Schoenith	Gale V/Wha Hoppen	1	1981	Dean Chenoweth	Miss Budweiser	6
1956	Russ Schleeh	Shanty I	3	1982	Chip Hanauer	Atlas Van Lines	5
1957	Jack Regas	Hawaii Kai III	5	1983	Chip Hanauer	Atlas Van Lines	5
1958	Mira Slovak	Bardah/Miss Buren	3	1984	Jim Kropfeld	Miss Budweiser	6
1959	Bill Stead	Maverick	5	1985	Chip Hanauer	Miller American	5
1960	Bill Muncey	Miss Thriftway	4	1986	Jim Kropfeld	Miss Budweiser	3
1961	Bill Muncey	Miss Century 21	4	1987	Jim Kropfeld	Miss Budweiser	5
1962	Bill Muncey	Miss Century 21	5	1988	Tom D'Eath	Miss Budweiser	4
1963	Bill Cantrell	Gale V	0	1989	Chip Hanauer	Miss Circus Circus	5
1964	Ron Musson	Miss Bardahl	4	1990	Chip Hanauer	Miss Circus Circus	6
1965	Ron Musson	Miss Bardahl	4	1991	Mark Tate	Winston/Oberto	3
1966	Mira Slovak	Tahoe Miss	4	1992	Chip Hanauer	Miss Budweiser	7
1967	Bill Schumacher	Miss Bardahl	6	1993	Chip Hanauer	Miss Budweiser	7
1968	Bill Schumacher	Miss Bardahl	4	1994	Mark Tate	Smokin' Joe Camel	2
1969	Bill Sterett, Sr	Miss Budweiser	4	1995	Mark Tate	Smokin' Joe Camel	4
1970	Dean Chenoweth	Miss Budweiser	4	1996	Dave Villwock	PICO American Dream	6
1971	Dean Chenoweth	Miss Budweiser	2	1997	Mark Tate	Close Call	1
1972	Bill Muncey	Atlas Van Lines	6				

Unlimited Hydroplane Racing Association Annual Champion Boats

Year	Boat	Owner	Wins	Year	Boat	Owner	Wins
1970	Miss Budweiser	Little-Friedkin	4	1984	Miss Budweiser	Bernie Little	6
1971	Miss Budweiser	Little-Friedkin	2	1985	Miller American	Muncey-Lucero	5
1972	Atlas Van Lines	Joe Schoenith	6	1986	Miss Budweiser	Bernie Little	3
1973	Pay 'n Pak	Dave Heerensperger	4	1987	Miss Budweiser	Bernie Little	5
1974	Pay 'n Pak	Dave Heerensperger	7	1988	Miss Budweiser	Bernie Little	4
1975	Pay 'n Pak	Dave Heerensperger	5	1989	Miss Budweiser	Bernie Little	4
1976	Atlas Van Lines	Bill Muncey	5	1990	Circus Circus	Bill Bennett	6
1977	Miss Budweiser	Bernie Little	3	1991	Miss Budweiser	Bernie Little	4
1978	Atlas Van Lines	Bill Muncey	6	1992	Miss Budweiser	Bernie Little	7
1979	Atlas Van Lines	Bill Muncey	7	1993	Miss Budweiser	Bernie Little	7
1980	Miss Budweiser	Bernie Little	5	1994	Miss Budweiser	Bernie Little	4
1981	Miss Budweiser	Bernie Little	6	1995	Miss Budweiser	Bernie Little	5
1982	Atlas Van Lines	Fran Muncey	5	1996	PICO Amer. Dream	Fred Leland	6
1983	Atlas Van Lines	Muncey-Lucero	3	1997	Miss Budweiser	Bernie Little	5

Polo

United States Open Polo Champions

Year	Champion	Year	Champion	Year	Champion	Year	Champion
1904	Wanderers	1933	Aurora	1960	Oak Brook–C.C.C.	1980	Southern Hills
1905–09	Not contested	1934	Templeton	1961	Milwaukee	1981	Rolex A & K
1910	Ranelagh	1935	Greentree	1962	Santa Barbara	1982	Retama
1911	Not contested	1936	Greentree	1963	Tulsa	1983	Ft. Lauderdale
1912	Cooperstown	1937	Old Westbury	1964	Concar Oak Brook	1984	Retama
1913	Cooperstown	1938	Old Westbury	1965	Oak Brook–Santa Barbara	1985	Carter Ranch
1914	Meadow Brook Magpies	1939	Bostwick Field	1966	Tulsa	1986	Retama II
1915	Not contested	1940	Aknusti	1967	Bunnytyco–Oak Brook	1987	Aloha
1916	Meadow Brook	1941	Gulf Stream	1968	Midland	1988	Les Diables Bleus
1917–18	Not contested	1942–45	Not contested	1969	Tulsa Greenhill	1989	Les Diables Bleus
1919	Meadow Brook	1946	Mexico	1970	Tulsa Greenhill	1990	Les Diables Bleus
1920	Meadow Brook	1947	Old Westbury	1971	Oak Brook	1991	Grant's Farm Manor
1921	Great Neck	1948	Hurricanes	1972	Milwaukee	1992	Hanalei Bay
1922	Argentine	1949	Hurricanes	1973	Oak Brook	1993	Gehache
1923	Meadow Brook	1950	Bostwick	1974	Milwaukee	1994	Aspen
1924	Midwick	1951	Milwaukee	1975	Milwaukee	1995	Outback
1925	Orange County	1952	Beverly Hills	1976	Willow Bend	1996	Outback
1926	Hurricanes	1953	Meadow Brook	1977	Retama	1997	Isla Carroll
1927	Sands Point	1954	C.C.C.–Meadow Brook	1978	Abercrombie & Kent	1998	Esque
1928	Meadow Brook	1955	C.C.C.	1979	Retama		
1929	Hurricanes	1956	Brandywine				
1930	Hurricanes	1957	Detroit				
1931	Santa Paula	1958	Dallas				
1932	Templeton	1959	Circle F				

Top-Ranked Players

The United States Polo Association ranks its registered players from minus 2 to plus 10 goals, with 10 Goal players being the game's best. At present, the USPA recognizes six 10-Goal and nine 9-Goal players:

10-GOAL

Mariano Aguerre (Greenwich)
Michael Azzaro (San Antonio)
Adolfo Cambiaso (Palm Beach)
Guillermo Gracida, Jr (Palm Beach)
Juan Ignacio Merlos (Palm Beach/RoyalPalm)
Sebastian Merlos (Aiken)

9-GOAL

Benjamin Araya (Palm Beach)
Bartolome Castagnola* (Palm Beach)
Gabriel Donoso (Palm Beach)
Carlos Gracida (Palm Beach)
Francisco Hensadon (Myopia)
Tomas Llorente (Palm Beach)
Owen R. Rinehart (Langdon Road)
Ernesto Trotz (Palm Beach)
Christian LaPrida (Palm Beach)

*Players with a handicap of 9T

Rodeo

Professional Rodeo Cowboys Association World Champions

All-Around

1929....Earl Thode	1949....Jim Shoulders	1967....Larry Mahan	1985....Lewis Feild
1930....Clay Carr	1950....Bill Linderman	1968....Larry Mahan	1986....Lewis Feild
1931....John Schneider	1951....Casey Tibbs	1969....Larry Mahan	1987....Lewis Feild
1932....Donald Nesbit	1952....Harry Tompkins	1970....Larry Mahan	1988....Dave Appleton
1933....Clay Carr	1953....Bill Linderman	1971....Phil Lyne	1989....Ty Murray
1934....Leonard Ward	1954....Buck Rutherford	1972....Phil Lyne	1990....Ty Murray
1935....Everett Bowman	1955....Casey Tibbs	1973....Larry Mahan	1991....Ty Murray
1936....John Bowman	1956....Jim Shoulders	1974....Tom Ferguson	1992....Ty Murray
1937....Everett Bowman	1957....Jim Shoulders	1975....Tom Ferguson	1993....Ty Murray
1938....Burel Mulkey	1958....Jim Shoulders	1976....Tom Ferguson	1994....Ty Murray
1939....Paul Carney	1959....Jim Shoulders	1977....Tom Ferguson	1995....Joe Beaver
1940....Fritz Truan	1960....Harry Tompkins	1978....Tom Ferguson	1996....Joe Beaver
1941....Homer Pettigrew	1961....Benny Reynolds	1979....Tom Ferguson	1997....Dan Mortensen
1942....Gerald Roberts	1962....Tom Nesmith	1980....Paul Tierney	
1943....Louis Brooks	1963....Dean Oliver	1981....Jimmie Cooper	
1944....Louis Brooks	1964....Dean Oliver	1982....Chris Lybbert	
1947....Todd Whatley	1965....Dean Oliver	1983....Roy Cooper	
1948....Gerald Roberts	1966....Larry Mahan	1984....Dee Picket	

Saddle Bronc Riding

1929....Earl Thode	1948....Gene Pruett	1965....Shawn Davis	1982....Monty Henson
1930....Clay Carr	1949....Casey Tibbs	1966....Marty Wood	1983....B. Gjermundson
1931....Earl Thode	1950....Bill Linderman	1967....Shawn Davis	1984....B. Gjermundson
1932....Peter Knight	1951....Casey Tibbs	1968....Shawn Davis	1985....B. Gjermundson
1933....Peter Knight	1952....Casey Tibbs	1969....Bill Smith	1986....Bud Munroe
1934....Leonard Ward	1953....Casey Tibbs	1970....Dennis Reiners	1987....Clint Johnson
1935....Peter Knight	1954....Casey Tibbs	1971....Bill Smith	1988....Clint Johnson
1936....Peter Knight	1955....DebCopenhaver	1972....Mel Hyland	1989....Clint Johnson
1937....Burel Mulkey	1956....DebCopenhaver	1973....Bill Smith	1990....Robert Etbauer
1938....Burel Mulkey	1957....Alvin Nelson	1974....John McBeth	1991....Robert Etbauer
1939....Fritz Truan	1958....Marty Wood	1975....Monty Henson	1992....Billy Etbauer
1940....Fritz Truan	1959....Casey Tibbs	1976....Monty Henson	1993....Dan Mortensen
1941....Doff Aber	1960....Enoch Walker	1977....Bobby Berger	1994....Dan Mortensen
1942....Doff Aber	1961....Winston Bruce	1978....Joe Marvel	1995....Dan Mortensen
1943....Louis Brooks	1962....Kenny McLean	1979....Bobby Berger	1996....Billy Etbauer
1944....Louis Brooks	1963....Guy Weeks	1980....Clint Johnson	1997....Dan Mortensen
1947....Carl Olson	1964....Marty Wood	1981....B. Gjermundson	

Bareback Riding

1932....Smoky Snyder	1950....Jim Shoulders	1966....Paul Mayo	1982....Bruce Ford
1933....Nate Waldrum	1951....Casey Tibbs	1967....Clyde Vamvoras	1983....Bruce Ford
1934....Leonard Ward	1952....Harry Tompkins	1968....Clyde Vamvoras	1984....Larry Peabody
1935....Frank Schneider	1953....Eddy Akridge	1969....Gary Tucker	1985....Lewis Feild
1936....Smoky Snyder	1954....Eddy Akridge	1970....Paul Mayo	1986....Lewis Feild
1937....Paul Carney	1955....Eddy Akridge	1971....Joe Alexander	1987....Bruce Ford
1938....Pete Grubb	1956....Jim Shoulders	1972....Joe Alexander	1988....Marvin Garrett
1939....Paul Carney	1957....Jim Shoulders	1973....Joe Alexander	1989....Marvin Garrett
1940....Carl Dossey	1958....Jim Shoulders	1974....Joe Alexander	1990....Chuck Logue
1941....George Mills	1959....Jack Buschbom	1975....Joe Alexander	1991....Clint Corey
1942....Louis Brooks	1960....Jack Buschbom	1976....Joe Alexander	1992....Wayne Herman
1943....Bill Linderman	1961....Eddy Akridge	1977....Joe Alexander	1993....Deb Greenough
1944....Louis Brooks	1962....Ralph Buell	1978....Bruce Ford	1994....Marvin Garrett
1947....Larry Finley	1963....John Hawkins	1979....Bruce Ford	1995....Marvin Garrett
1948....Sonny Tureman	1964....Jim Houston	1980....Bruce Ford	1996....Mark Garrett
1949....Jack Buschbom	1965....Jim Houston	1981....J.C. Trujillo	1997....Eric Mouton

Bull Riding

1929....John Schneider	1932....Smokey Snyder	1936....Smokey Snyder	1941....Dick Griffith
1930....John Schneider	....John Schneider	1937....Smokey Snyder	1942....Dick Griffith
1931....Smokey Snyder	1933....Frank Schneider	1938....Kid Fletcher	1943....Ken Roberts
1932....John Schneider	1934....Frank Schneider	1939....Dick Griffith	1944....Ken Roberts
	1935....Smokey Snyder	1940....Dick Griffith	1947....Wag Blessing

Professional Rodeo Cowboys Association World Champions *(Cont.)*

Bull Riding *(Cont.)*

1948....Harry Tompkins	1961....Ronnie Rossen	1974....Don Gay	1987....Lane Frost
1949....Harry Tompkins	1962....Freckles Brown	1975....Don Gay	1988....Jim Sharp
1950....Harry Tompkins	1963....Bill Kornell	1976....Don Gay	1989....Tuff Hedeman
1951....Jim Shoulders	1964....Bob Wegner	1977....Don Gay	1990....Jim Sharp
1952....Harry Tompkins	1965....Larry Mahan	1978....Don Gay	1991....Tuff Hedeman
1953....Todd Whatley	1966....Ronnie Rossen	1979....Don Gay	1992....Cody Custer
1954....Jim Shoulders	1967....Larry Mahan	1980....Don Gay	1993....Ty Murray
1955....Jim Shoulders	1968....George Paul	1981....Don Gay	1994....Daryl Mills
1956....Jim Shoulders	1969....Doug Brown	1982....Charles Sampson	1995....Jerome Davis
1957....Jim Shoulders	1970....Gary Leffew	1983....Cody Snyder	1996....Terry West
1958....Jim Shoulders	1971....Bill Nelson	1984....Don Gay	1997....Scott Mendes
1959....Jim Shoulders	1972....John Quintana	1985....Ted Nuce	
1960....Harry Tompkins	1973....Bobby Steiner	1986....Tuff Hedeman	

Calf Roping

1929....Everett Bowman	1948....Toots Mansfield	1965....Glen Franklin	1982....Roy Cooper
1930....Jake McClure	1949....Troy Fort	1966....Junior Garrison	1983....Roy Cooper
1931....Herb Meyers	1950....Toots Mansfield	1967....Glen Franklin	1984....Roy Cooper
1932....Richard Merchant	1951....Don McLaughlin	1968....Glen Franklin	1985....Joe Beaver
1933....Bill McFarlane	1952....Don McLaughlin	1969....Dean Oliver	1986....Chris Lybbert
1934....Irby Mundy	1953....Don McLaughlin	1970....Junior Garrison	1987....Joe Beaver
1935....Everett Bowman	1954....Don McLaughlin	1971....Phil Lyne	1988....Joe Beaver
1936....Clyde Burk	1955....Dean Oliver	1972....Phil Lyne	1989....Rabe Rabon
1937....Everett Bowman	1956....Ray Wharton	1973....Ernie Taylor	1990....Troy Pruitt
1938....Burel Mulkey	1957....Don McLaughlin	1974....Tom Ferguson	1991....Fred Whitfield
1939....Toots Mansfield	1958....Dean Oliver	1975....Jeff Copenhaver	1992....Joe Beaver
1940....Toots Mansfield	1959....Jim Bob Altizer	1976....Roy Cooper	1993....Joe Beaver
1941....Toots Mansfield	1960....Dean Oliver	1977....Roy Cooper	1994....Herbert Theriot
1942....Clyde Burk	1961....Dean Oliver	1978....Roy Cooper	1995....Fred Whitfield
1943....Toots Mansfield	1962....Dean Oliver	1979....Paul Tierney	1996....Fred Whitfield
1944....Clyde Burk	1963....Dean Oliver	1980....Roy Cooper	1997....Cody Ohl
1947....Troy Fort	1964....Dean Oliver	1981....Roy Cooper	

Steer Wrestling

1929....Gene Ross	1948....Homer Pettigrew	1965....Harley May	1982....Stan Williamson
1930....Everett Bowman	1949....Bill McGuire	1966....Jack Roddy	1983....Joel Edmondson
1931....Gene Ross	1950....Bill Linderman	1967....Roy Duvall	1984....John W. Jones
1932....Hugh Bennett	1951....Dub Phillips	1968....Jack Roddy	1985....Ote Berry
1933....Everett Bowman	1952....Harley May	1969....Roy Duvall	1986....Steve Duhon
1934....Shorty Ricker	1953....Ross Dollarhide	1970....John W. Jones	1987....Steve Duhon
1935....Everett Bowman	1954....James Bynum	1971....Billy Hale	1988....John W. Jones
1936....Jack Kerschner	1955....Benny Combs	1972....Roy Duvall	1989....John W. Jones
1937....Gene Ross	1956....Harley May	1973....Bob Marshall	1990....Ote Berry
1938....Everett Bowman	1957....Clark McEntire	1974....Tommy Puryear	1991....Ote Berry
1939....Harry Hart	1958....James Bynum	1975....F. Shepperson	1992....Mark Roy
1940....Homer Pettigrew	1959....Harry Charters	1976....Tom Ferguson	1993....Steve Duhon
1941....Hub Whiteman	1960....Bob A. Robinson	1977....Larry Ferguson	1994....Blaine Pederson
1942....Homer Pettigrew	1961....Jim Bynum	1978....Byron Walker	1995....Ote Berry
1943....Homer Pettigrew	1962....Tom Nesmith	1979....Stan Williamson	1996....Chad Bedell
1944....Homer Pettigrew	1963....Jim Bynum	1980....Butch Myers	1997....Brad Gleason
1947....Todd Whatley	1964....C.R. Boucher	1981....Byron Walker	

Team Roping

1929....Charles Maggini	1939....Asbury Schell	1949....Ed Yanez	1959....Jim Rodriguez Jr.
1930....Norman Cowan	1940....Pete Grubb	1950....Buck Sorrels	1960....Jim Rodriguez Jr.
1931....Arthur Beloat	1941....Jim Hudson	1951....Olan Sims	1961....Al Hooper
1932....Ace Gardner	1942....Verne Castro	1952....Asbury Schell	1962....Jim Rodriguez Jr.
1933....Roy Adams	........Vic Castro	1953....Ben Johnson	1963....Les Hirdes
1934....Andy Jauregui	1943....Mark Hull	1954....Eddie Schell	1964....Bill Hamilton
1935....Lawrence Conltk	........Leonard Block	1955....Vern Castro	1965....Jim Rodriguez Jr.
1936....John Rhodes	1944....Murphy Chaney	1956....Dale Smith	1966....Ken Luman
1937....Asbury Schell	1947....Jim Brister	1957....Dale Smith	1967....Joe Glenn
1938....John Rhodes	1948....Joe Glenn	1958....Ted Ashworth	1968....Art Arnold

Team Roping (Cont.)

1969....Jerold Camarillo	1978....Doyle Gellerman	1987....Clay O. Cooper	1995....Bobby Hurley
1970....John Miller	1979....Allen Bach	1988....Jake Barnes	Allen Bach
1971....John Miller	1980....Tee Woolman	1989....Jake Barnes	1996....Steve Purcella
1972....Leo Camarillo	1981....Walt Woodard	1990....Allen Bach	Steve Northcott
1973....Leo Camarillo	1982....Tee Woolman	1991....Bob Harris	1997....Speed Williams
1974....H.P. Evetts	1983....Leo Camarillo	1992....Clay O. Cooper	Rich Skelton
1975....Leo Camarillo	1984....Dee Pickett	1993....Bobby Hurley	
1976....Leo Camarillo	1985....Jake Barnes	1994....Jake Barnes	
1977....Jerold Camarillo	1986....Clay O. Cooper	Clay O. Cooper	

Steer Roping

1929....Charles Maggini	1947....Ike Rude	1965....Sonny Wright	1983....Roy Cooper
1930....Clay Carr	1948....Everett Shaw	1966....Sonny Davis	1984....Guy Allen
1931....Andy Jauregui	1949....Shoat Webster	1967....Jim Bob Altizer	1985....Jim Davis
1932....George Weir	1950....Shoat Webster	1968....Sonny Davis	1986....Jim Davis
1933....John Bowman	1951....Everett Shaw	1969....Walter Arnold	1987....Shaun Burchett
1934....John McEntire	1952....Buddy Neal	1970....Don McLaughlin	1988....Shaun Burchett
1935....Richard Merchant	1953....Ike Rude	1971....Olin Young	1989....Guy Allen
1936....John Bowman	1954....Shoat Webster	1972....Allen Keller	1990....Phil Lyne
1937....Everett Bowman	1955....Shoat Webster	1973....Roy Thompson	1991....Guy Allen
1938....Hugh Bennett	1956....Jim Snively	1974....Olin Young	1992....Guy Allen
1939....Dick Truitt	1957....Clark McEntire	1975....Roy Thompson	1993....Guy Allen
1940....Clay Carr	1958....Clark McEntire	1976....Marvin Cantrell	1994....Guy Allen
1941....Ike Rude	1959....Everett Shaw	1977....Buddy Cockrell	1995....Guy Allen
1942....King Merrit	1960....Don McLaughlin	1978....Sonny Worrell	1996....Guy Allen
1943....Tom Rhodes	1961....Clark McEntire	1979....Gary Good	1997....Guy Allen
1944....Tom Rhodes	1962....Everett Shaw	1980....Guy Allen	
1945....Everett Shaw	1963....Don McLaughlin	1981....Arnold Felts	
1946....Everett Shaw	1964....Sonny Davis	1982....Guy Allen	

Note: In 1945–46 champions were crowned only in Steer Roping.

Rowing

National Collegiate Rowing Champions

MEN'S EIGHT

1985 ....Harvard	1990 ....Wisconsin	1995 ....Brown
1986 ....Wisconsin	1991 ....Pennsylvania	1996 ....Princeton
1987 ....Harvard	1992 ....Harvard	1997 ....Washington
1988 ....Harvard	1993 ....Brown	1998 ....Princeton
1989 ....Harvard	1994 ....Brown	

WOMEN'S EIGHT

1979 ....Yale	1986 ....Wisconsin	1993 ....Princeton
1980 ....California	1987 ....Washington	1994 ....Princeton
1981 ....Washington	1988 ....Washington	1995 ....Princeton
1982 ....Washington	1989 ....Cornell	1996 ....Brown
1983 ....Washington	1990 ....Princeton	1997 ....Washington
1984 ....Washington	1991 ....Boston University	1998 ....Washington
1985 ....Washington	1992 ....Boston University	

Rugby

National Men's Club Championship

Year	Winner	Runner-Up	Year	Winner	Runner-Up
1979	Old Blues (CA)	St Louis Falcons	1989	Old Mission Beach AC	Philly/Whitemarsh
1980	Old Blues (CA)	St. Louis Falcons	1990	Denver Barbos	Old Blues (CA)
1981	Old Blues (CA)	Old Blue (NY)	1991	Old Mission Beach AC	Washington
1982	Old Blues (CA)	Denver Barbos	1992	Old Blues (CA)	Mystic River (MA)
1983	Old Blues (CA)	Dallas Harlequins	1993	Old Mission Beach AC	Milwaukee
1984	Dallas Harlequins	Los Angeles	1994	Old Mission Beach AC	Life College (GA)
1985	Milwaukee	Denver Barbos	1995	Potomac Athletic Club	Old Mission Beach
1986	Old Blues (CA)	Old Blue (NY)	1996	Old Mission Beach AC	Old Blues (CA)
1987	Old Blues (CA)	Pittsburgh	1997	Gentlemen of Aspen	Old Blue (NY)
1988	Old Mission Beach AC	Milwaukee	1998	Gentlemen of Aspen	Old Blue (NY)

Rugby (Cont.)

National Men's Collegiate Championship

Year	Winner	Runner-Up	Year	Winner	Runner-Up
1980	California	Air Force	1990	Air Force	Army
1981	California	Harvard	1991	California	Army
1982	California	Life College	1992	California	Army
1983	California	Air Force	1993	California	Air Force
1984	Harvard	Colorado	1994	California	Navy
1985	California	Maryland	1995	California	Air Force
1986	California	Dartmouth	1996	California	Penn State
1987	San Diego State	Air Force	1997	California	Penn State
1988	California	Dartmouth	1998	California	Stanford
1989	Air Force	Long Beach			

World Cup Championship

Year	Winner	Runner-Up	Year	Winner	Runner-Up
1987	New Zealand	France	1995	South Africa	New Zealand
1991	Australia	England			

Sailing

America's Cup Champions

SCHOONERS AND J-CLASS BOATS

Year	Winner	Skipper	Series	Loser	Skipper
1851	America	Richard Brown			
1870	Magic	Andrew Comstock	1-0	Cambria, Great Britain	J. Tannock
1871	Columbia (2-1)	Nelson Comstock	4-1	Livonia, Great Britain	J. R. Woods
	Sappho (2-0)	Sam Greenwood			
1876	Madeleine	Josephus Williams	2-0	Countess of Dufferin, Canada	J. E. Ellsworth
1881	Mischief	Nathanael Clock	2-0	Atalanta, Canada	Alexander Cuthbert
1885	Puritan	Aubrey Crocker	2-0	Genesta, Great Britain	John Carter
1886	Mayflower	Martin Stone	2-0	Galatea, Great Britain	Dan Bradford
1887	Volunteer	Henry Haff	2-0	Thistle, Great Britain	John Barr
1893	Vigilant	William Hansen	3-0	Valkyrie II, Great Britain	William Granfield
1895	Defender	Henry Haff	3-0	Valkyrie III, Great Britain	William Granfield
1899	Columbia	Charles Barr	3-0	Shamrock I, Great Britain	Archie Hogarth
1901	Columbia	Charles Barr	3-0	Shamrock II, Great Britain	E. A. Sycamore
1903	Reliance	Charles Barr	3-0	Shamrock III, Great Britain	Bob Wringe
1920	Resolute	Charles F. Adams	3-2	Shamrock IV, Great Britain	William Burton
1930	Enterprise	Harold Vanderbilt	4-0	Shamrock V, Great Britain	Ned Heard
1934	Rainbow	Harold Vanderbilt	4-2	Endeavour, Great Britain	T. O. M. Sopwith
1937	Ranger	Harold Vanderbilt	4-0	Endeavour II, Great Britain	T. O. M. Sopwith

12-METER BOATS

Year	Winner	Skipper	Series	Loser	Skipper
1958	Columbia	Briggs Cunningham	4-0	Sceptre, Great Britain	Graham Mann
1962	Weatherly	Bus Mosbacher	4-1	Gretel, Australia	Jock Sturrock
1964	Constellation	Bob Bavier & Eric Ridder	4-0	Sovereign, Australia	Peter Scott
1967	Intrepid	Bus Mosbacher	4-0	Dame Pattie, Australia	Jock Sturrock
1970	Intrepid	Bill Ficker	4-1	Gretel II, Australia	Jim Hardy
1974	Courageous	Ted Hood	4-0	Southern Cross, Australia	John Cuneo
1977	Courageous	Ted Turner	4-0	Australia	Noel Robins
1980	Freedom	Dennis Conner	4-1	Australia	Jim Hardy
1983	Australia II	John Bertrand	4-3	Liberty, United States	Dennis Conner
1987	Stars & Stripes	Dennis Conner	4-0	Kookaburra III, Australia	Iain Murray

60-FOOT CATAMARAN VS 133-FOOT MONOHULL

Year	Winner	Skipper	Series	Loser	Skipper
1988	Stars & Stripes	Dennis Conner	2-0	New Zealand	David Barnes

75-FOOT MONOHULL (IACC)

Year	Winner	Skipper	Series	Loser	Skipper
1992	America[3]	Bill Koch	4-1	Il Moro di Venezia, Italy	Paul Cayard
1995	Black Magic I	Russell Coutts	5-0	Young America, United States	Dennis Conner

Note: Winning entries have been from the United States every year but two; in 1983 an Australian vessel won, and in 1995 a vessel from New Zealand won.

Shooting World Champions

Men

50M FREE RIFLE PRONE

1947 .....O. Sannes, Norway
1949 .....A.C. Jackson,
    United States
1952 .....A.C. Jackson,
    United States
1954 .....G. Boa, Canada
1958 .....M. Nordquist
1962 .....K. Wenk, West Germany
1966 .....D. Boyd, United States
1970 .....M. Fiess, S. Africa
1974 .....K. Bulan, Czech.
1978 .....A. Allan, Great Britain
1982 .....V. Danilshchenko, USSR
1986 .....S. Bereczky, Hungary
1990 .....V. Bochkarev, USSR
1994 .....Venjie Li, China
1998 .....Thomas Tamas, U.S.

AIR RIFLE

1966 .....G. Kümmet, W. Germany
1970 .....G. Kusterman, W. Germ.
1974 .....E. Pedzisz, Poland
1978 .....O. Schlipf, W. Germany
1979 .....K. Hillenbrand
1981 .....F. Bessy, France
1982 .....F. Rettkowski, E. Germ.
1983 .....P. Heberle, France
1985 .....P. Heberle, France
1986 .....H. Riederer, W. Germany
1987 .....K. Ivanov, USSR
1989 .....J. P. Amet, France
1990 .....H. Riederer, W. Germany
1994 .....Boris Polak, Israel
1998 .....Artem Khadjibekov, Russia

MEN'S TRAP

1929 .....De Lumniczer, Hungary
1930 .....M. Arie, United States
1931 .....Kiszkurno, Poland
1933 .....De Lumniczer, Hungary
1934 .....A. Montagh, Hungary
1935 .....R. Sack, W. Germany
1936 .....Kiszkurno, Poland
1937 .....K. Huber, Finland
1938 .....I. Strassburger, Hungary
1939 .....De Lumniczer, Hungary
1947 .....H. Liljedahl, Sweden
1949 .....F. Rocchi, Argentina
1950 .....C. Sala, Italy
1952 .....P.J. Grossi, Argentina
1954 .....C. Merlo, Italy
1958 .....F. Eisenlauer,
    United States
1959 .....H. Badravi, Egypt
1961 .....E. Mattarelli, Italy
1962 .....W. Zimenko, USSR
1965 .....J.E. Lire, Chile
1966 .....K. Jones, United States
1967 .....G. Rennard, Belgium
1969 .....E. Mattarelli, Italy
1970 .....M. Carrega, France
1971 .....M. Carrega, France
1973 .....A. Andrushkin, USSR
1974 .....M. Carrega, France
1975 .....J. Primrose, Canada
1977 .....E. Azkue, Spain
1978 .....E. Vallduvi, Spain
1979 .....M. Carrega, France
1981 .....A. Asanov, USSR
1982 .....L. Giovonnetti, Italy

MEN'S TRAP *(Cont.)*

1983 .....J. Primrose, Canada
1985 .....M. Bednarik, Czech.
1986 .....M. Benarik, Czech.
1987 .....D. Monakov, USSR
1989 .....M. Venturini, Italy
1990 .....J. Damne, E. Germany
1994 .....Dmitriy Monakov, Ukraine
1995 .....Giovanni Pellielo, Italy
1998 .....Giovanni Pellielo, Italy

THREE POSITION RIFLE

1929 .....O. Ericsson, Sweden
1930 .....Petersen, Denmark
1931 .....Amundson, Norway
1933 .....De Lisle, France
1935 .....Leskinnen, Finland
1937 .....Mazoyer, France
1939 .....Steigelmann, Germany
1947 .....I. H. Erben, Sweden
1949 .....P. Janhonen, Finland
1952 .....Kongshaug, Norway
1954 .....A. Bugdanov, USSR
1958 .....Itkis, USSR
1962 .....G. Anderson,
    United States
1966 .....G. Anderson,
    United States
1970 .....Parkhimovitch, USSR
1974 .....L. Wigger, United States
1978 .....E. Svensson, Sweden
1982 .....K. Ivanov, USSR
1986 .....P. Heinz, W. Germany
1990 .....E. C. Lee, S. Korea
1994 .....P. Kurka, Czech Republic
1998 .....Jozef Gonci, Slovakia

Women

THREE POSITION RIFLE

1966 .....M. Thompson,
    United States
1970 .....M. Thompson Murdock,
    United States
1974 .....A. Pelova, Bulgaria
1978 .....W. Oliver, United States
1982 .....M. Helbig, E. Germany
1986 .....V. Letcheva, Bulgaria
1990 .....V. Letcheva, Bulgaria
1994 .....A. Maloukhina, Russia
1998 .....Sonja Pfeilschifter, Germany

AIR RIFLE

1970 .....V. Cherkasque, USSR
1974 .....T. Ratkinova, USSR
1978 .....W. Oliver, United States
1979 .....K. Monez, United States
1981 .....S. Romaristova, USSR
1982 .....S. Lang, W. Germany
1983 .....M. Helbig, E. Germany

AIR RIFLE *(Cont.)*

1985 .....E. Forian, Hungary
1986 .....V. Letcheva, Bulgaria
1987 .....V. Letcheva, Bulgaria
1989 .....V. Letcheva, Bulgaria
1990 .....E. Joc, Hungary
1994 .....Sonja Pfeilschifter, Germany
1998 .....Sonja Pfeilschifter, Germany

SPORT PISTOL

1966 .....N. Rasskazova, USSR
1970 .....N. Stoljarova, USSR
1974 .....N. Stoljarova, USSR
1978 .....K. Dyer, United States
1982 .....P. Balogh, Hungary
1986 .....M. Dobrantcheva, USSR
1990 .....M. Logvinenko, Sov Union
1994 .....Soon Hee Boo, S. Korea
1998 .....Yieqing Cai, China

AIR PISTOL

1970 .....S. Carroll, United States
1974 .....Z. Simonian, USSR
1978 .....K. Hansson, Sweden
1979 .....R. Fox, United States
1981 .....N. Kalinina, USSR
1982 .....M. Dobrantcheva, USSR
1983 .....K. Bodin, Sweden
1985 .....M. Dobrantcheva, USSR
1986 .....A. Völker, E. Germany
1987 .....J. Brajkovic, Yugoslavia
1989 .....N. Salukvadse, USSR
1990 .....Jasna Sekaric, Yugoslavia
1994 .....Jasna Sekaric, IOP
1998 .....Dorisuren Munkhbayar,
    Mongolia

Softball

Men
MAJOR FAST PITCH

1933	J. L. Gill Boosters, Chicago
1934	Ke-Nash-A, Kenosha, WI
1935	Crimson Coaches, Toledo, OH
1936	Kodak Park, Rochester, NY
1937	Briggs Body Team, Detroit
1938	The Pohlers, Cincinnati
1939	Carr's Boosters, Covington, KY
1940	Kodak Park, Rochester, NY
1941	Bendix Brakes, South Bend, IN
1942	Deep Rock Oilers, Tulsa
1943	Hammer Air Field, Fresno
1944	Hammer Air Field, Fresno
1945	Zollner Pistons, Fort Wayne, IN
1946	Zollner Pistons, Fort Wayne, IN
1947	Zollner Pistons, Fort Wayne, IN
1948	Briggs Beautyware, Detroit
1949	Tip Top Tailors, Toronto
1950	Clearwater (FL) Bombers
1951	Dow Chemical, Midland, MI
1952	Briggs Beautyware, Detroit
1953	Briggs Beautyware, Detroit
1954	Clearwater (FL) Bombers
1955	Raybestos Cardinals, Stratford, CT
1956	Clearwater (FL) Bombers
1957	Clearwater (FL) Bombers
1958	Raybestos Cardinals, Stratford, CT
1959	Sealmasters, Aurora, IL
1960	Clearwater (FL) Bombers
1961	Sealmasters, Aurora, IL
1962	Clearwater (FL) Bombers
1963	Clearwater (FL) Bombers
1964	Burch Tool, Detroit
1965	Sealmasters, Aurora, IL
1966	Clearwater (FL) Bombers
1967	Sealmasters, Aurora, IL
1968	Clearwater (FL) Bombers
1969	Raybestos Cardinals, Stratford, CT
1970	Raybestos Cardinals, Stratford, CT
1971	Welty Way, Cedar Rapids, IA
1972	Raybestos Cardinals, Stratford, CT
1973	Clearwater (FL) Bombers
1974	Gianella Bros, Santa Rosa, CA
1975	Rising Sun Hotel, Reading, PA
1976	Raybestos Cardinals, Stratford, CT
1977	Billard Barbell, Reading, PA
1978	Billard Barbell, Reading, PA
1979	McArdle Pontiac/Cadillac, Midland, MI
1980	Peterbilt Western, Seattle
1981	Archer Daniels Midland, Decatur, IL
1982	Peterbilt Western, Seattle
1983	Franklin Cardinals, Stratford, CT
1984	California Kings, Merced, CA
1985	Pay'n Pak, Seattle
1986	Pay'n Pak, Seattle
1987	Pay'n Pak, Seattle
1988	TransAire, Elkhart, IN
1989	Penn Corp, Sioux City, IA
1990	Penn Corp, Sioux City, IA
1991	Guanella Brothers, Rohnert Park, CA
1992	Natl Health Care Disc, Sioux City, IA
1993	Natl Health Care Disc, Sioux City, IA
1994	Decatur Pride, Decatur, IL
1995	Decatur Pride, Decatur, IL
1996	Green Bay All-Car, Green Bay, WI
1997	Green Bay All-Car, Green Bay, WI
1998	Meierhoffer-Fleeman, St. Joseph, MO

SUPER SLOW PITCH

1981	Howard's/Western Steer, Denver, NC
1982	Jerry's Catering, Miami, Fla.
1983	Howard's/Western Steer, Denver, NC
1984	Howard's/Western Steer, Denver, NC
1985	Steele's Sports, Grafton, OH
1986	Steele's Sports, Grafton, OH
1987	Steele's Sports, Grafton, OH
1988	Starpath, Monticello, KY
1989	Ritch's Salvage, Harrisburg, NC
1990	Steele's Silver Bullets, Grafton, OH
1991	Sunbelt/Worth, Centerville, GA
1992	Ritch's Superior, Windsor Locks, CT
1993	Ritch's Superior, Windsor Locks, CT
1994	Bell Corp, Tampa, Fla.
1995	Lighthouse/Worth, Stone Mt., GA
1996	Ritch's Superior, Windsor Locks, CT
1997	Ritch's Superior, Winsor Locks, CT
1998	Lighthouse/Worth, Stone Mt., GA

MAJOR SLOW PITCH

1953	Shields Construction, Newport, KY
1954	Waldneck's Tavern, Cincinnati
1955	Lang Pet Shop, Covington, KY
1956	Gatliff Auto Sales, Newport, KY
1957	Gatliff Auto Sales, Newport, KY
1958	East Side Sports, Detroit
1959	Yorkshire Restaurant, Newport, KY
1960	Hamilton Tailoring, Cincinnati
1961	Hamilton Tailoring, Cincinnati
1962	Skip Hogan A.C., Pittsburgh
1963	Gatliff Auto Sales, Newport, KY
1964	Skip Hogan A.C., Pittsburgh
1965	Skip Hogan A.C., Pittsburgh
1966	Michael's Lounge, Detroit
1967	Jim's Sport Shop, Pittsburgh
1968	County Sports, Levittown, NY
1969	Copper Hearth, Milwaukee
1970	Little Caesar's, Southgate, MI
1971	Pile Drivers, Virginia Beach, VA
1972	Jiffy Club, Louisville, KY
1973	Howard's Furniture, Denver, NC
1974	Howard's Furniture, Denver, NC
1975	Pyramid Cafe, Lakewood, OH
1976	Warren Motors, Jacksonville, FL
1977	Nelson Painting, Oklahoma City
1978	Campbell Carpets, Concord, CA
1979	Nelco Mfg Co, Oklahoma City
1980	Campbell Carpets, Concord, CA
1981	Elite Coating, Gordon, CA
1982	Triangle Sports, Minneapolis
1983	No. 1 Electric & Heating, Gastonia, NC
1984	Lilly Air Systems, Chicago

Softball (Cont.)

Men (Cont.)

MAJOR SLOW PITCH (Cont.)

1985..........Blanton's, Fayetteville, NC	1992..........Vernon's, Jacksonville, FL
1986..........Non-Ferrous Metals, Cleveland	1993..........Back Porch/Destin Roofing, Destin, FL
1987..........Starpath, Monticello, KY	1994..........Riverside RAM/Taylor Bros., Louisville, KY
1988..........Bell Corp/FAF, Tampa, FL	1995..........Riverside/RAM/Taylor/TPS, Louisville, KY
1989..........Ritch's Salvage, Harrisburg, NC	1996..........Bell 2/Robert's/Easton, Orlando, FL
1990..........New Construction, Shelbyville, IN	1997..........Long Haul/TPS, Albertville, Minnesota
1991..........Riverside Paving, Louisville, KY	1998..........Chase Mortgage/Easton, Wilmington, NC

Women
MAJOR FAST PITCH

1933..........Great Northerns, Chicago	1966..........Raybestos Brakettes, Stratford, CT
1934..........Hart Motors, Chicago	1967..........Raybestos Brakettes, Stratford, CT
1935..........Bloomer Girls, Cleveland	1968..........Raybestos Brakettes, Stratford, CT
1936..........Nat'l Screw & Mfg, Cleveland	1969..........Orange (CA) Lionettes
1937..........Nat'l Screw & Mfg, Cleveland	1970..........Orange (CA) Lionettes
1938..........J. J. Krieg's, Alameda, CA	1971..........Raybestos Brakettes, Stratford, CT
1939..........J. J. Krieg's, Alameda, CA	1972..........Raybestos Brakettes, Stratford, CT
1940..........Arizona Ramblers, Phoenix	1973..........Raybestos Brakettes, Stratford, CT
1941..........Higgins Midgets, Tulsa	1974..........Raybestos Brakettes, Stratford, CT
1942..........Jax Maids, New Orleans	1975..........Raybestos Brakettes, Stratford, CT
1943..........Jax Maids, New Orleans	1976..........Raybestos Brakettes, Stratford, CT
1944..........Lind & Pomeroy, Portland, OR	1977..........Raybestos Brakettes, Stratford, CT
1945..........Jax Maids, New Orleans	1978..........Raybestos Brakettes, Stratford, CT
1946..........Jax Maids, New Orleans	1979..........Sun City (AZ) Saints
1947..........Jax Maids, New Orleans	1980..........Raybestos Brakettes, Stratford, CT
1948..........Arizona Ramblers, Phoenix	1981..........Orlando (FL) Rebels
1949..........Arizona Ramblers, Phoenix	1982..........Raybestos Brakettes, Stratford, CT
1950..........Orange (CA) Lionettes	1983..........Raybestos Brakettes, Stratford, CT
1951..........Orange (CA) Lionettes	1984..........Los Angeles Diamonds
1952..........Orange (CA) Lionettes	1985..........Hi-Ho Brakettes, Stratford, CT
1953..........Betsy Ross Rockets, Fresno	1986..........Southern California Invasion, Los Angeles
1954..........Leach Motor Rockets, Fresno	1987..........Orange County Majestics, Anaheim, CA
1955..........Orange (CA) Lionettes	1988..........Hi-Ho Brakettes, Stratford, CT
1956..........Orange (CA) Lionettes	1989..........Whittier (CA) Raiders
1957..........Hacienda Rockets, Fresno	1990..........Raybestos Brakettes, Stratford, CT
1958..........Raybestos Brakettes, Stratford, CT	1991..........Raybestos Brakettes, Stratford, CT
1959..........Raybestos Brakettes, Stratford, CT	1992..........Raybestos Brakettes, Stratford, CT
1960..........Raybestos Brakettes, Stratford, CT	1993..........Redding Rebels, Redding, CA
1961..........Gold Sox, Whittier, CA	1994..........Redding Rebels, Redding, CA
1962..........Orange (CA) Lionettes	1995..........Redding Rebels, Redding, CA
1963..........Raybestos Brakettes, Stratford, CT	1996..........California Commotion, Woodland Hills, CA
1964..........Erv Lind Florists, Portland, OR	1997..........California Commotion, Woodland Hills, CA
1965..........Orange (CA) Lionettes	1998..........California Commotion, Woodland Hills, CA

MAJOR SLOW PITCH

1959..........Pearl Laundry, Richmond, VA	1979..........Bob Hoffman's Dots, Miami
1960..........Carolina Rockets, High Pt, NC	1980..........Howard's Rubi-Otts, Graham, NC
1961..........Dairy Cottage, Covington, KY	1981..........Tifton (GA) Tomboys
1962..........Dana Gardens, Cincinnati	1982..........Richmond (VA) Stompers
1963..........Dana Gardens, Cincinnati	1983..........Spooks, Anoka, MN
1964..........Dana Gardens, Cincinnati	1984..........Spooks, Anoka, MN
1965..........Art's Acres, Omaha	1985..........Key Ford Mustangs, Pensacola, FL
1966..........Dana Gardens, Cincinnati	1986..........Sur-Way Tomboys, Tifton, GA
1967..........Ridge Maintenance, Cleveland	1987..........Key Ford Mustangs, Pensacola, FL
1968..........Escue Pontiac, Cincinnati	1988..........Spooks, Anoka, MN
1969..........Converse Dots, Hialeah, FL	1989..........Canaan's Illusions, Houston
1970..........Rutenschruder Floral, Cincinnati	1990..........Spooks, Anoka, MN
1971..........Gators, Ft Lauderdale, FL	1991..........Kannan's Illusions, San Antonio, TX
1972..........Riverside Ford, Cincinnati	1992..........Universal Plastics, Cookeville, TN
1973..........Sweeney Chevrolet, Cincinnati	1993..........Universal Plastics, Cookeville, TN
1974..........Marks Brothers Dots, Miami	1994..........Universal Plastics, Cookeville, TN
1975..........Marks Brothers Dots, Miami	1995..........Armed Forces, Sacramento, CA
1976..........Sorrento's Pizza, Cincinnati	1996..........Spooks, Anoka, MN
1977..........Fox Valley Lassies, St Charles, IL	1997..........Taylor's Major Slow Pitch, Glendale, MD
1978..........Bob Hoffman's Dots, Miami	1998..........Lakerettes, Conneaut Lake, PA

All-Around World Champions

MEN

1891 .....Joseph F. Donoghue, U.S.	1934 .....Bernt Evensen, Norway	1971 .....Ard Schenk, Netherlands
1893 .....Jaap Eden, Netherlands	1935 .....Michael Staksrud, Nor.	1972 .....Ard Schenk, Netherlands
1895 .....Jaap Eden, Netherlands	1936 .....Ivar Ballangrud, Norway	1973 .....Göran Claeson, Sweden
1896 .....Jaap Eden, Netherlands	1937 .....Michael Staksrud, Nor.	1974 .....Sten Stensen, Norway
1897 .....Jack K. McCulloch, Can.	1938 .....Ivar Ballangrud, Norway	1975 .....Harm Kuipers, Netherlands
1898 .....Peder Ostlund, Norway	1939 .....Birger Wasenius, Finland	1976 .....Piet Kleine, Neth.
1899 .....Peder Ostlund, Norway	1947 .....Lassi Parkkinen, Finland	1977 .....Eric Heiden, U.S.
1900 .....Edvard Engelsaas, Nor.	1948 .....Odd Lundberg, Norway	1978 .....Eric Heiden, U.S.
1901 .....Franz F. Wathan, Finland	1949 .....Kornel Pajor, Hungary	1979 .....Eric Heiden, U.S.
1904 .....Sigurd Mathisen, Norway	1950 .....Hjalmar Andersen, Nor.	1980 .....Hilbert van der Duin, Neth.
1905 .....C. Coen de Koning, Neth.	1951 .....Hjalmar Andersen, Nor.	1981 .....Amund Sjobrand, Norway
1908 .....Oscar Mathisen, Norway	1952 .....Hjalmar Andersen, Nor.	1982 .....Hilbert van der Duin, Neth.
1909 .....Oscar Mathisen, Norway	1953 .....Oleg Goncharenko, USSR	1983 .....Rolf Falk-Larssen, Nor.
1910 .....Nikolai Strunnikov, Russia	1954 .....Boris Shilkov, USSR	1984 .....Oleg Bozhev, USSR
1911 .....Nikolai Strunnikov, Russia	1955 .....Sigvard Ericsson, Swe.	1985 .....Hein Vergeer, Neth.
1912 .....Oscar Mathisen, Norway	1956 .....Oleg Goncharenko, USSR	1986 .....Hein Vergeer, Neth.
1913 .....Oscar Mathisen, Norway	1957 .....Knut Johannesen, Nor.	1987 .....Nikolai Guliaev, USSR
1914 .....Oscar Mathisen, Norway	1958 .....Oleg Goncharenko, USSR	1988 .....Eric Flaim, U.S.
1922 .....Harald Strom, Norway	1959 .....Juhani Järvinen, Finland	1989 .....Leo Visser, Netherlands
1923 .....Klas Thunberg, Finland	1960 .....Boris Stenin, USSR	1990 .....Johann Olav Koss, Nor.
1924 .....Roald Larsen, Norway	1961 .....Henk van der Grift, Neth.	1991 .....Johann Olav Koss, Nor.
1925 .....Klas Thunberg, Finland	1962 .....Viktor Kosichkin, USSR	1992 .....Roberto Sighel, Italy
1926 .....Ivar Ballangrud, Norway	1963 .....Jonny Nilsson, Sweden	1993 .....Falko Zandstra, Neth.
1927 .....Bernt Evensen, Norway	1964 .....Knut Johannesen, Nor.	1994 .....Johann Olav Koss, Nor.
1928 .....Klas Thunberg, Finland	1965 .....Per Ivar Moe, Norway	1995 .....Rintje Ritsma, Neth.
1929 .....Klas Thunberg, Finland	1966 .....Kees Verkerk, Neth.	1996 .....Rintje Ritsma, Neth.
1930 .....Michael Staksrud, Nor.	1967 .....Kees Verkerk, Neth.	1997 .....Ids Postma, Netherlands
1931 .....Klas Thunberg, Finland	1968 .....Fred Anton Maier, Nor.	1998 .....Ids Postma, Netherlands
1932 .....Ivar Ballangrud, Norway	1969 .....Dag Fornaes, Norway	
1933 .....Hans Engnestangen, Nor.	1970 .....Ard Schenk, Netherlands	

WOMEN

1936 .....Kit Klein, U.S.	1962 .....Inga Artamonova, USSR	1982 .....Karin Busch, GDR
1937 .....Laila Schou Nilsen, Nor.	1963 .....Lidia Skoblikova, USSR	1983 .....Andrea Schöne, GDR
1938 .....Laila Schou Nilsen, Nor.	1964 .....Lidia Skoblikova, USSR	1984 .....Karin Enke-Busch, GDR
1939 .....Verné Lesche, Finland	1965 .....Inga Artamonova, USSR	1985 .....Andrea Schöne, GDR
1947 .....Verné Lesche, Finland	1966 .....Valentina Stenina, USSR	1986 .....Karin Kania-Enke, GDR
1948 .....Maria Isakova, USSR	1967 .....Stien Kaiser, Neth.	1987 .....Karin Kania, GDR
1949 .....Maria Isakova, USSR	1968 .....Stien Kaiser, Neth.	1988 .....Karin Kania, GDR
1950 .....Maria Isakova, USSR	1969 .....Lasma Kauniste, USSR	1989 .....Constanze Moser, GDR
1951 .....Eevi Huttunen, Finland	1970 .....Atje Keulen-Deelstra, Neth.	1990 .....Jacqueline Börner, GDR
1952 .....Lidia Selikhova, USSR	1971 .....Nina Statkevich, USSR	1991 .....Gunda Kleemann, Ger.
1953 .....Khalida Shchegoleeva, USSR	1972 .....Atje Keulen-Deelstra, Neth.	1992 .....Gunda Niemann-Kleemann, Germany
1954 .....Lidia Selikhova, USSR	1973 .....Atje Keulen-Deelstra, Neth.	1993 .....Gunda Niemann, Germany
1955 .....Rimma Zhukova, USSR	1974 .....Atje Keulen-Deelstra, Neth.	1994 .....Emese Hunyady, Austria
1956 .....Sofia Kondakova, USSR	1975 .....Karin Kessow, GDR	1995 .....Gunda Niemann, Germany
1957 .....Inga Artamonova, USSR	1976 .....Sylvia Burka, Canada	1996 .....Gunda Niemann, Germany
1958 .....Inga Artamonova, USSR	1977 .....Vera Bryndzej, USSR	1997 .....Gunda Niemann, Germany
1959 .....Tamara Rylova, USSR	1978 .....Tatiana Averina, USSR	1997 .....Gunda Niemann, Germany
1960 .....Valentina Stenina, USSR	1979 .....Beth Heiden, U.S.	1998 .....Gunda Niemann, Germany
1961 .....Valentina Stenina, USSR	1980 .....Natalia Petruseva, USSR	
	1981 .....Natalia Petruseva, USSR	

Squash

National Men's Champions

HARD BALL		HARD BALL (Cont.)		HARD BALL (Cont.)	
Year	Champion	Year	Champion	Year	Champion
1907 ....John A. Miskey		1912 ....Constantine Hutchins		1917 ....Stanley W. Pearson	
1908 ....John A. Miskey		1913 ....Morton L. Newhall		1918–19 ....No tournament	
1909 ....William L. Freeland		1914 ....Constantine Hutchins		1920 ....Charles C. Peabody	
1910 ....John A. Miskey		1915 ....Stanley W. Pearson		1921 ....Stanley W. Pearson	
1911 ....Francis S. White		1916 ....Stanley W. Pearson		1922 ....Stanley W. Pearson	

National Men's Champions (Cont.)

HARD BALL (Cont.)

Year	Champion
1923	Stanley W. Pearson
1924	Gerald Roberts
1925	W. Palmer Dixon
1926	W. Palmer Dixon
1927	Myles Baker
1928	Herbert N. Rawlins Jr.
1929	J. Lawrence Pool
1930	Herbert N. Rawlins Jr.
1931	J. Lawrence Pool
1932	Beckman H. Pool
1933	Beckman H. Pool
1934	Neil J. Sullivan II
1935	Donald Strachan
1936	Germain G. Glidden
1937	Germain G. Glidden
1938	Germain G. Glidden
1939	Donald Strachan
1940	A. Willing Patterson
1941	Charles M. P. Britton
1942	Charles M. P. Britton
1943–45	No tournament
1946	Charles M. P. Britton
1947	Charles M. P. Britton
1948	Stanley W. Pearson Jr.
1949	H. Hunter Lott Jr.
1950	Edward J. Hahn
1951	Edward J. Hahn
1952	Harry B. Conlon
1953	Ernest Howard
1954	G. Diehl Mateer Jr.
1955	Henri R. Salaun
1956	G. Diehl Mateer Jr.

HARD BALL (Cont.)

Year	Champion
1957	Henri R. Salaun
1958	Henri R. Salaun
1959	Benjamin H. Heckscher
1960	G. Diehl Mateer Jr.
1961	Henri R. Salaun
1962	Samuel P. Howe III
1963	Benjamin H. Heckscher
1964	Ralph E. Howe
1965	Stephen T. Vehslage
1966	Victor Niederhoffer
1967	Samuel P. Howe III
1968	Colin Adair
1969	Anil Nayar
1970	Anil Nayar
1971	Colin Adair
1972	Victor Niederhoffer
1973	Victor Niederhoffer
1974	Victor Niederhoffer
1975	Victor Niederhoffer
1976	Peter Briggs
1977	Thomas E. Page
1978	Michael Desaulniers
1979	Mario Sanchez
1980	Michael Desaulniers
1981	Mark Alger
1982	John Nimick
1983	Kenton Jernigan
1984	Kenton Jernigan
1987	Frank J. Stanley IV
1988	Scott Dulmage

HARD BALL (Cont.)

Year	Champion
1989	Rodolfo Rodriquez
1990	Hector Barragan
1991	Hector Barragan
1992	Hector Barragan
1985	Kenton Jernigan
1986	Hugh LaBossier
1993	Hector Barragan
1994	Hector Barragan
1995	W. Keen Butcher
1996	W. Keen Butcher
1997	Rob Hill
1998	Rob Hill

SOFT BALL

Year	Champion
1983	Kenton Jernigan
1984	Kenton Jernigan
1985	Kenton Jernigan
1986	Darius Pandole
1987	Richard Hashim
1988	John Phelan
1989	Will Carlin
1990	Syed Jafry
1991	Hector Barragan
1992	Phil Yarrow
1993	Phil Yarrow
1994	Roberto Rosales
1995	A. Martin Clark
1996	Mohsen Mir
1997	A. Martin Clark
1998	A. Martin Clark

National Women's Champions

HARD BALL

Year	Champion
1928	Eleanora Sears
1929	Margaret Howe
1930	Hazel Wightman
1931	Ruth Banks
1932	Margaret Howe
1933	Susan Noel
1934	Margaret Howe
1935	Margot Lumb
1936	Anne Page
1937	Anne Page
1938	Cecile Bowes
1939	Anne Page
1940	Cecile Bowes
1941	Cecile Bowes
1942–46	No tournament
1947	Anne Page Homer
1948	Cecile Bowes
1949	Janet Morgan
1950	Betty Howe
1951	Jane Austin
1952	Margaret Howe
1953	Margaret Howe
1954	Lois Dilks
1955	Janet Morgan
1956	Betty Howe Constable
1957	Betty Howe Constable
1958	Betty Howe Constable
1959	Betty Howe Constable
1960	Margaret Varner

HARD BALL (Cont.)

Year	Champion
1961	Margaret Varner
1962	Margaret Varner
1963	Margaret Varner
1964	Ann Wetzel
1965	Joyce Davenport
1966	Betty Meade
1967	Betty Meade
1968	Betty Meade
1969	Joyce Davenport
1970	Nina Moyer
1971	Carol Thesieres
1972	Nina Moyer
1973	Gretchen Spruance
1974	Gretchen Spruance
1975	Ginny Akabane
1976	Gretchen Spruance
1977	Gretchen Spruance
1978	Gretchen Spruance
1979	Heather McKay
1980	Barbara Maltby
1981	Barbara Maltby
1982	Alicia McConnell
1983	Alicia McConnell
1984	Alicia McConnell
1985	Alicia McConnell
1986	Alicia McConnell
1987	Alicia McConnell
1988	Alicia McConnell
1986	Alicia McConnell

HARD BALL (Cont.)

Year	Champion
1987	Alicia McConnell
1988	Alicia McConnell
1989	Demer Holleran
1990	Demer Holleran
1991	Demer Holleran
1992	Demer Holleran
1993	Demer Holleran
1994	Demer Holleran

Note: Tournament not held since 1994.

SOFT BALL

Year	Champion
1983	Alicia McConnell
1984	Julie Harris
1985	Sue Clinch
1986	Julie Harris
1987	Diana Staley
1988	Sara Luther
1989	Nancy Gengler
1990	Joyce Maycock
1991	Ellie Pierce
1992	Demer Holleran
1993	Demer Holleran
1994	Demer Holleran
1995	Ellie Pierce
1996	Demer Holleran
1997	Demer Holleran
1998	Latasha Khan

Triathlon

Ironman Championship
MEN

Date	Winner	Time	Site
1978	Gordon Haller	11:46	Waikiki Beach
1979	Tom Warren	11:15:56	Waikiki Beach
1980	Dave Scott	9:24:33	Ala Moana Park
1981	John Howard	9:38:29	Kailua-Kona
1982	Scott Tinley	9:19:41	Kailua-Kona
1982	Dave Scott	9:08:23	Kailua-Kona
1983	Dave Scott	9:05:57	Kailua-Kona
1984	Dave Scott	8:54:20	Kailua-Kona
1985	Scott Tinley	8:50:54	Kailua-Kona
1986	Dave Scott	8:28:37	Kailua-Kona
1987	Dave Scott	8:34:13	Kailua-Kona
1988	Scott Molina	8:31:00	Kailua-Kona
1989	Mark Allen	8:09:15	Kailua-Kona
1990	Mark Allen	8:28:17	Kailua-Kona
1991	Mark Allen	8:18:32	Kailua-Kona
1992	Mark Allen	8:09:09	Kailua-Kona
1993	Mark Allen	8:07:46	Kailua-Kona
1994	Greg Welch	8:20:27	Kailua-Kona
1995	Mark Allen	8:20:34	Kailua-Kona
1996	Luc Van Lierde	8:04:08	Kailua-Kona
1997	Thomas Hellriegel	8:33:01	Kailua-Kona

WOMEN

Date	Winner	Time	Site
1978	No finishers		
1979	Lyn Lemaire	12:55	Waikiki Beach
1980	Robin Beck	11:21:24	Ala Moana Park
1981	Linda Sweeney	12:00:32	Kailua-Kona
1982	Kathleen McCartney	11:09:40	Kailua-Kona
1982	Julie Leach	10:54:08	Kailua-Kona
1983	Sylviane Puntous	10:43:36	Kailua-Kona
1984	Sylviane Puntous	10:25:13	Kailua-Kona
1985	Joanne Ernst	10:25:22	Kailua-Kona
1986	Paula Newby-Fraser	9:49:14	Kailua-Kona
1987	Erin Baker	9:35:25	Kailua-Kona
1988	Paula Newby-Fraser	9:01:01	Kailua-Kona
1989	Paula Newby-Fraser	9:00:56	Kailua-Kona
1990	Erin Baker	9:13:42	Kailua-Kona
1991	Paula Newby-Fraser	9:07:52	Kailua-Kona
1992	Paula Newby-Fraser	8:55:29	Kailua-Kona
1993	Paula Newby-Fraser	8:58:23	Kailua-Kona
1994	Paula Newby-Fraser	9:20:14	Kailua-Kona
1995	Karen Smyers	9:16:46	Kailua-Kona
1996	Paula Newby-Fraser	9:06:49	Kailua-Kona
1997	Heather Fuhr	9:31:43	Kailua-Kona

Note: The Ironman Championship was contested twice in 1982.

Volleyball

World Champions
MEN

Year	Winner	Runnerup	Site
1949	Soviet Union	Czechoslovakia	Prague, Czechoslovakia
1952	Soviet Union	Czechoslovakia	Moscow, Soviet Union
1956	Czechoslovakia	Soviet Union	Paris, France
1960	Soviet Union	Czechoslovakia	Rio de Janeiro, Brazil
1962	Soviet Union	Czechoslovakia	Moscow, Soviet Union
1966	Czechoslovakia	Romania	Prague, Czechoslovakia
1970	East Germany	Bulgaria	Sofia, Bulgaria
1974	Poland	Soviet Union	Mexico City
1978	Soviet Union	Italy	Rome, Italy
1982	Soviet Union	Brazil	Buenos Aires, Argentina
1986	United States	Soviet Union	Paris, France
1990	Italy	Cuba	Rio de Janeiro, Brazil
1994	Italy	Netherlands	Athens, Greece

World Champions (Cont.)
WOMEN

Year	Winner	Runnerup	Site
1952	Soviet Union	Poland	Moscow, Soviet Union
1956	Soviet Union	Romania	Paris, France
1960	Soviet Union	Japan	Rio de Janeiro, Brazil
1962	Japan	Soviet Union	Moscow, Soviet Union
1966	Japan	United States	Prague, Czechoslovakia
1970	Soviet Union	Japan	Sofia, Bulgaria
1974	Japan	Soviet Union	Mexico City
1978	Cuba	Japan	Rome, Italy
1982	China	Peru	Lima, Peru
1986	China	Cuba	Prague, Czechoslovakia
1990	Soviet Union	China	Beijing, China
1994	Cuba	Brazil	Sao Paulo, Brazil

U.S. Men's Open Champions—Gold Division

Year	Champion
1928	Germantown, PA YMCA
1929	Hyde Park YMCA, IL
1930	Hyde Park YMCA, IL
1931	San Antonio, TX YMCA
1932	San Antonio, TX YMCA
1933	Houston, TX YMCA
1934	Houston, TX YMCA
1935	Houston, TX YMCA
1936	Houston, TX YMCA
1937	Duncan YMCA, IL
1938	Houston, TX YMCA
1939	Houston, TX YMCA
1940	Los Angeles AC, CA
1941	North Ave. YMCA, IL
1942	North Ave. YMCA, IL
1943–44	No championships
1945	North Ave. YMCA, IL
1946	Pasadena, CA YMCA
1947	North Ave. YMCA, IL
1948	Hollywood, CA YMCA
1949	Downtown YMCA, CA
1950	Long Beach, CA YMCA
1951	Hollywood, CA YMCA
1952	Hollywood, CA YMCA
1953	Hollywood, CA YMCA
1954	Stockton, CA YMCA
1955	Stockton, CA YMCA
1956	Hollywood, CA YMCA Stars
1957	Hollywood, CA YMCA Stars
1958	Hollywood, CA YMCA Stars
1959	Hollywood, CA YMCA Stars
1960	Westside JCC, CA
1961	Hollywood, CA YMCA
1962	Hollywood, CA YMCA
1963	Hollywood, CA YMCA
1964	Hollywood, CA YMCA Stars
1965	Westside JCC, CA
1966	Sand & Sea Club, CA
1967	Fresno, CA VBC
1968	Westside JCC, Los Angeles, CA
1969	Los Angeles, CA YMCA
1970	Chart House, San Diego
1971	Santa Monica, CA YMCA
1972	Chart House, San Diego
1973	Chuck's Steak, Los Angeles
1974	UC Santa Barbara, CA
1975	Chart House, San Diego
1976	Maliabu, Los Angeles
1977	Chuck's, Santa Barbara
1978	Chuck's, Los Angeles
1979	Nautilus, Long Beach CA
1980	Olympic Club, San Francisco
1981	Nautilus, Long Beach CA
1982	Chuck's, Los Angeles
1983	Nautilus Pacifica, CA
1984	Nautilus Pacifica, CA
1985	Molten/SSI Torrance, CA
1986	Molten, Torrance, CA
1987	Molten, Torrance, CA
1988	Molten, Torrance, CA
1989	Not held
1990	Nike, Carson, CA
1991	Offshore, Woodland Hills, CA
1992	Creole Six Pack, Elmhurst, NY
1993	Asics, Huntington Beach, CA
1994	Asics/Paul Mitchell, Hunt. Beach, CA
1995	Shakter, Belagarad, Ukraine
1996	POL-AM-VBC, Brooklyn, NY
1997	Canuck Stuff VBC, Calgary
1998	T-Town, Tulsa, OK

U.S. Women's Open Champions—Gold Division

Year	Champion
1949	Eagles, Houston
1950	Voit #1, Santa Monica, CA
1951	Eagles, Houston
1952	Voit #1, Santa Monica, CA
1953	Voit #1, Los Angeles
1954	Houstonettes, Houston, TX
1955	Mariners, Santa Monica, CA
1956	Mariners, Santa Monica, CA
1957	Mariners, Santa Monica, CA
1958	Mariners, Santa Monica, CA
1959	Mariners, Santa Monica, CA
1960	Mariners, Santa Monica, CA
1961	Breakers, Long Beach, CA
1962	Shamrocks, Long Beach, CA
1963	Shamrocks, Long Beach, CA
1964	Shamrocks, Long Beach, CA
1965	Shamrocks, Long Beach, CA
1966	Renegades, Los Angeles
1967	Shamrocks, Long Beach, CA
1968	Shamrocks, Long Beach, CA
1969	Shamrocks, Long Beach, CA
1970	Shamrocks, Long Beach, CA
1971	Renegades, Los Angeles
1972	E Pluribus Unum, Houston
1973	E Pluribus Unum, Houston
1974	Renegades, Los Angeles
1975	Adidas, Norwalk, CA
1976	Pasadena, TX

U.S. Women's Open Champions—Gold Division (Cont.)

1977 ....Spoilers, Hermosa, CA	1988 ....Chrysler, Hayward, CA
1978 ....Nick's, Los Angeles	1989 ....Plymouth, Hayward, CA
1979 ....Mavericks, Los Angeles	1990 ....Plymouth, Hayward, CA
1980 ....NAVA, Fountain Valley, CA	1991 ....Fitness, Champaign, IL
1981 ....Utah State, Logan, UT	1992 ....Nick's Kronies, Chicago
1982 ....Monarchs, Hilo, HI	1993 ....Nick's Fishmarket, Chicago
1983 ....Syntex, Stockton, CA	1994 ....Nick's Fishmarket, Chicago
1984 ....Chrysler, Palo Alto, CA	1995 ....Kittleman/Branfield's/Nick's, Chi.
1985 ....Merrill Lynch, Arizona	1996 ....Pure Texas Nuts, Austin, TX
1986 ....Merrill Lynch, Arizona	1997 ....Kittleman/Branfield's/Nick's, Chi.
1987 ....Chrysler, Pleasanton, CA	1998 ....The Exterminators, Barrington, IL

Wrestling

United States National Champions

1983

FREESTYLE	FREESTYLE (Cont.)	GRECO-ROMAN (Cont.)
105.5 ....Rich Salamone	220 ....Greg Gibson	136.5 ....Dan Mello
114.5 ....Joe Gonzales	Hvy ....Bruce Baumgartner	149.5 ....Jim Martinez
125.5 ....Joe Corso	Team ....Sunkist Kids	163 ....James Andre
136.5 ....Rich Dellagatta*	**GRECO-ROMAN**	180.5 ....Steve Goss
149.5 ....Bill Hugent	105.5 ....T. J. Jones	198 ....Steve Fraser*
163 ....Lee Kemp	114.5 ....Mark Fuller	220 ....Dennis Koslowski
180.5 ....Chris Campbell	125.5 ....Rob Hermann	Hvy ....No champion
198 ....Pete Bush		Team ....Minn. Wrestling Club

1984

FREESTYLE	FREESTYLE (Cont.)	GRECO-ROMAN (Cont.)
105.5 ....Rich Salamone	220 ....Harold Smith	149.5 ....Jim Martinez*
114.5 ....Charlie Heard	Hvy ....Bruce Baumgartner	163 ....John Matthews
125.5 ....Joe Corso	Team ....Sunkist Kids	180.5 ....Tom Press
136.5 ....Rich Dellagatta*	**GRECO-ROMAN**	198 ....Mike Houck
149.5 ....Andre Metzger	105.5 ....T. J. Jones	220 ....No champion
163 ....Dave Schultz*	114.5 ....Mark Fuller	Hvy ....No champion
180.5 ....Mark Schultz	136.5 ....Dan Mello	Team ....Adirondack 3-Style, WA
198 ....Steve Fraser		

1985

FREESTYLE	FREESTYLE (Cont.)	GRECO-ROMAN (Cont.)
105.5 ....Tim Vanni	220 ....Greg Gibson	136.5 ....Buddy Lee
114.5 ....Jim Martin	286 ....Bruce Baumgartner	149.5 ....Jim Martinez
125.5 ....Charlie Heard	Team ....Sunkist Kids	163 ....David Butler
136.5 ....Darryl Burley	**GRECO-ROMAN**	180.5 ....Chris Catallo
149.5 ....Bill Nugent*	105.5 ....T. J. Jones	198 ....Mike Houck
163 ....Kenny Monday	114.5 ....Mark Fuller	220 ....Greg Gibson
180.5 ....Mike Sheets	125.5 ....Eric Seward*	286 ....Dennis Koslowski
198 ....Mark Schultz		Team .......U.S. Marine Corps

1986

FREESTYLE	FREESTYLE (Cont.)	GRECO-ROMAN (Cont.)
105.5 ....Rich Salamone	286 ....Bruce Baumgartner	136.5 ....Frank Famiano
114.5 ....Joe Gonzales	Team ....Sunkist Kids (Div. I)	149.5 ....Jim Martinez
125.5 ....Kevin Darkus	Hawkeye Wrestling	163 ....David Butler*
136.5 ....John Smith	Club (Div. II)	180.5 ....Darryl Gholar
149.5 ....Andre Metzger*	**GRECO-ROMAN**	198 ....Derrick Waldroup
163 ....Dave Schultz	105.5 ....Eric Wetzel	220 ....Dennis Koslowski
180.5 ....Mark Schultz	114.5 ....Shawn Sheldon	286 ....Duane Koslowski
198 ....Jim Scherr	125.5 ....Anthony Amado	Team .......U.S. Marine Corps (Div. I)
220 ....Dan Severn		U.S. Navy (Div. II)

1987

FREESTYLE	FREESTYLE (Cont.)	FREESTYLE (Cont.)
105.5 ....Takashi Irie	149.5 ....Andre Metzger	220 ....Bill Scherr
114.5 ....Mitsuru Sato	163 ....Dave Schultz*	286 ....Bruce Baumgartner
125.5 ....Barry Davis	180.5 ....Mark Schultz	Team ....Sunkist Kids (Div. I)
136.5 ....Takumi Adachi	198 ....Jim Scherr	Team Foxcatcher (Div. II)

United States National Champions *(Cont.)*

1987 *(Cont.)*

GRECO-ROMAN

105.5	Eric Wetzel
114.5	Shawn Sheldon
125.5	Eric Seward
136.5	Frank Famiano

GRECO-ROMAN *(Cont.)*

149.5	Jim Martinez
163	David Butler
180.5	Chris Catallo
198	Derrick Waldroup*

GRECO-ROMAN *(Cont.)*

220	Dennis Koslowski
286	Duane Koslowski
Team	U.S. Marine Corp (Div. I)
	U.S. Army (Div. II)

1988

FREESTYLE

105.5	Tim Vanni
114.5	Joe Gonzales
125.5	Kevin Darkus
136.5	John Smith*
149.5	Nate Carr
163	Kenny Monday
180.5	Dave Schultz
198	Melvin Douglas III
220	Bill Scherr

FREESTYLE *(Cont.)*

286	Bruce Baumgartner
Team	Sunkist Kids (Div. I)
	Team Foxcatcher (Div. II)

GRECO-ROMAN

105.5	T. J. Jones
114.5	Shawn Sheldon
125.5	Gogi Parseghian*
136.5	Dalen Wasmund

GRECO-ROMAN *(Cont.)*

149.5	Craig Pollard
163	Tony Thomas
180.5	Darryl Gholar
198	Mike Carolan
220	Dennis Koslowski
286	Duane Koslowski
Team	U.S. Marine Corps (Div. I)
	Sunkist Kids (Div. II)

1989

FREESTYLE

105.5	Tim Vanni
114.5	Zeke Jones
125.5	Brad Penrith
136.5	John Smith
149.5	Nate Carr
163	Rob Koll
180.5	Rico Chiapparelli
198	Jim Scherr*
220	Bill Scherr

FREESTYLE *(Cont.)*

286	Bruce Baumgartner
Team	Sunkist Kids (Div. I)
	Team Foxcatcher (Div. II)

GRECO-ROMAN

105.5	Lew Dorrance
114.5	Mark Fuller
125.5	Gogi Parseghian
136.5	Isaac Anderson

GRECO-ROMAN *(Cont.)*

149.5	Andy Seras*
163	David Butler
180.5	John Morgan
198	Michial Foy
220	Steve Lawson
286	Craig Pittman
Team	U.S. Marine Corps (Div. I)
	Jets USA (Div. II)

1990

FREESTYLE

105.5	Rob Eiter
114.5	Zeke Jones
125.5	Joe Melchiore
136.5	John Smith
149.5	Nate Carr
163	Rob Koll
180.5	Royce Alger
198	Chris Campbell*
220	Bill Scherr

FREESTYLE *(Cont.)*

286	Bruce Baumgartner
Team	Sunkist Kids (Div. I)
	Team Foxcatcher (Div. II)

GRECO-ROMAN

105.5	Lew Dorrance
114.5	Sam Henson
125.5	Mark Pustelnik
136.5	Isaac Anderson

GRECO-ROMAN *(Cont.)*

149.5	Andy Seras
163	David Butler
180.5	Derrick Waldroup
198	Randy Couture*
220	Chris Tironi
286	Matt Ghaffari
Team	Jets USA (Div. I)
	California Jets (Div. II)

1991

FREESTYLE

105.5	Tim Vanni
114.5	Zeke Jones
125.5	Brad Penrith
136.5	John Smith*
149.5	Townsend Saunders
163	Kenny Monday
180.5	Kevin Jackson
198	Chris Campbell

FREESTYLE *(Cont.)*

220	Mark Coleman
286	Bruce Baumgartner
Team	Sunkist Kids (Div. I)
	Jets USA (Div. II)

GRECO-ROMAN

105.5	Eric Wetzel
114.5	Shawn Sheldon
125.5	Frank Famiano

GRECO-ROMAN *(Cont.)*

136.5	Buddy Lee
149.5	Andy Seras
163	Gordy Morgan
180.5	John Morgan*
198	Michial Foy
220	Dennis Koslowski
286	Craig Pittman
Team	Jets USA (Div. I)
	Sunkist Kids (Div. II)

1992

FREESTYLE

105.5	Rob Eiter
114.5	Jack Griffin
125.5	Kendall Cross*
136.5	John Fisher
149.5	Matt Demaray
163	Greg Elinsky
180.5	Royce Alger
198	Dan Chaid
220	Bill Scherr

FREESTYLE *(Cont.)*

286	Bruce Baumgartner
Team	Sunkist Kids (Div. I)
	Team Foxcatcher (Div. II)

GRECO-ROMAN

105.5	Eric Wetzel
114.5	Mark Fuller
125.5	Dennis Hall
136.5	Buddy Lee*

GRECO-ROMAN *(Cont.)*

149.5	Rodney Smith
163	Travis West
180.5	John Morgan
198	Michial Foy
220	Dennis Koslowski
286	Matt Ghaffari
Team	NY Athletic Club (Div. I)
	Sunkist Kids (Div. II)

*Outstanding wrestler.

United States National Champions *(Cont.)*

1993

FREESTYLE		FREESTYLE *(Cont.)*		GRECO-ROMAN *(Cont.)*	
105.5	Rob Eiter	286	Bruce Baumgartner	149.5	Andy Seras
114.5	Zeke Jones	Team	Sunkist Kids (Div. I)	163	Gordy Morgan
125.5	Brad Penrith		Team Foxcatcher (Div. II)	180.5	Dan Henderson
136.5	Tom Brands			198	Randy Couture
149.5	Matt Demaray	**GRECO-ROMAN**		220	James Johnson
163	Dave Schultz*	105.5	Eric Wetzel	286	Matt Ghaffari
180.5	Kevin Jackson	114.5	Shawn Sheldon	Team	NY Athletic Club (Div. I)
198	Melvin Douglas	125.5	Dennis Hall*		Sunkist Kids (Div. II)
220	Kirk Trost	136.5	Shon Lewis		

1994

FREESTYLE		FREESTYLE *(Cont.)*		GRECO-ROMAN *(Cont.)*	
105.5	Tim Vanni	286	Bruce Baumgartner*	149.5	Andy Seras*
114.5	Zeke Jones	Team	Sunkist Kids (Div. I)	163	Gordy Morgan
125.5	Terry Brands		Team Foxcatcher (Div. II)	180.5	Dan Henderson
136.5	Tom Brands	**GRECO-ROMAN**		198	Derrick Waldroup
149.5	Matt Demaray	105.5	Isaac Ramaswamy	220	James Johnson
163	Dave Schultz	114.5	Shawn Sheldon	286	Matt Ghaffari
180.5	Royce Alger	125.5	Dennis Hall	Team	Armed Forces (Div. I)
198	Melvin Douglas	136.5	Shon Lewis		NY Athletic Club (Div. II)
220	Mark Kerr				

1995

FREESTYLE		FREESTYLE *(Cont.)*		GRECO-ROMAN *(Cont.)*	
105.5	Rob Eiter	286	Bruce Baumgartner	149.5	Heath Sims
114.5	Lou Rosselli	Team	Sunkist Kids (Div. I)	163	Matt Lindland
125.5	Kendall Cross*		Team Foxcatcher (Div. II)	180.5	Marty Morgan
136.5	Tom Brands	**GRECO-ROMAN**		198	Michial Foy
149.5	Matt Demaray	105.5	Isaac Ramaswamy	220	James Johnson
163	Dave Schultz	114.5	Shawn Sheldon	286	Rulon Gardner
180.5	Kevin Jackson	125.5	Dennis Hall*	Team	Armed Forces (Div. I)
198	Melvin Douglas	136.5	Van Fronhofer		Sunkist Kids (Div. II)
220	Kurt Angle				

1996

FREESTYLE		FREESTYLE *(Cont.)*		GRECO-ROMAN *(Cont.)*	
105.5	Rob Eiter	286	Bruce Baumgartner	149.5	Rodney Smith
114.5	Lou Rosselli	Team	Sunkist Kids (Div. I)	163	Keith Sieracki
125.5	Kendall Cross		NY Athletic Club (Div. II)	180.5	Marty Morgan
136.5	Tom Brands	**GRECO-ROMAN**		198	Michial Foy
149.5	Townsend Saunders	105.5	Mujaahid Maynard	220	John Oostendrop
163	Kenny Monday	114.5	Shawn Sheldon	286	Matt Ghaffari
180.5	Les Gutches*	125.5	Dennis Hall*	Team	Armed Forces (Div. I)
198	Melvin Douglas	136.5	Shon Lewis		Sunkist Kids (Div. II)
220	Kurt Angle				

1997

FREESTYLE		FREESTYLE *(Cont.)*		GRECO-ROMAN *(Cont.)*	
110	Kanamti Soloman	275.5	Tom Erikson	138.75	Kevin Bracken
119	Zeke Jones	Team	Sunkist Kids (Div. I)	152	Chris Saba
127.75	Terry Brands		NY Athletic Club (Div. II)	167.5	Miguel Spencer
138.75	Carl Kolat	**GRECO-ROMAN**		187.25	Dan Henderson
152	Lincoln McIlravy*	110	Mark Yanagihara	213.75	Randy Couture*
167.5	Dan St. John	119	Broderick Lee	275.5	Rulon Gardiner
187.25	Les Gutches	127.75	Dennis Hall	Team	Armed Forces (Div. I)
213.75	Melvin Douglas				NY Athletic Club (Div. II)

1998

FREESTYLE		FREESTYLE *(Cont.)*		GRECO-ROMAN *(Cont.)*	
119	Sam Henson	286	Tolly Thompson	152	Chris Saba
127.75	Tony Purler	Team	Sunkist Kids (Div. I)	167.5	Matt Lindland
138.75	Shawn Charles		NY Athletic Club (Div. II)	187.25	Dan Niebuhr*
152	Lincoln McIlravy	**GRECO-ROMAN**		213.75	Jason Klohs
167.5	Steve Marianetti	119	Shawn Sheldon	286	Matt Ghaffari
187.25	Les Gutches*	127.75	Dennis Hall	Team	Armed Forces (Div. I)
213.75	Melvin Douglas	138.75	Shon Lewis		Sunkist Kids (Div. II)

*Outstanding wrestler.

The Sports Market

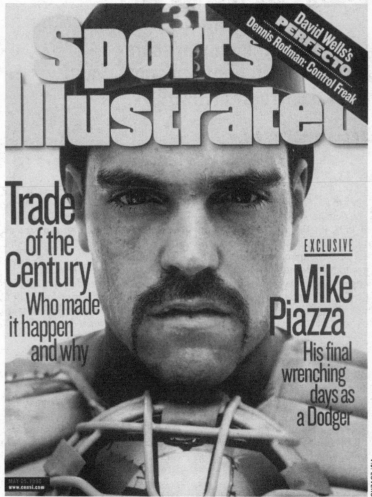

Bear Market

Despite wild spending in some quarters, the business of sport underwent a general correction in 1998

BY KELLI ANDERSON

I F THERE'S ONE thing we've learned from the sports business during 1998, it's that there's no accounting for ... accounting. Marlins owner Wayne Huizenga spent a fortune assembling a world championship baseball team, then stripped that team of its stars and put it on the block because it was costing him too much money. TV ratings have plunged for pro sports leagues across the board, yet the NBA, the NFL and the NHL all convinced networks and cable companies to pony up at least twice as much money for new TV contracts. And that lockout in the $1.7 billion-a-year business known as the NBA? The owners say they are losing money, while the players, assessing the same balance sheet, beg to differ.

We also learned that there's no accounting for attendance. The biggest draw in baseball, after home run hero Mark McGwire and his main competitor Sammy Sosa, was Beanie Baby giveaway nights. And get this: The worst team in the WNBA—make that one of the worst teams in the history of professional sports—the 3–27 Washington Mystics, drew the biggest crowds in the league, 15,910 per home game, an average that more than a few NBA teams would be proud of.

Alas, conventional wisdom—and conventional accounting—did occasionally prevail in 1998. The captains of the $8 billion athletic shoe industry, for instance, recognized red ink when they saw it, and acted accordingly. Nike reported a $67.7 million first-quarter loss, its first such loss in 13 years. Reebok, Fila and Converse also took first-quarter nosedives as fickle consumers started spurning athletic shoes in favor of so-called "brown shoes" like Doc Martens and Timberlands. As a result, some star athletes with expensive endorsement contracts were cut loose. When Shaquille O'Neal's five-year, $15 million Reebok deal expired in the summer of '98, it wasn't renewed. Reebok also dumped Dallas Cowboys running back Emmitt Smith and Milwaukee Bucks forward Glenn Robinson while slashing its endorse-

Catch and release: After bagging a World Series title, Huizenga let the Marlins go.

ment roster from 960 to 260. Converse said bye-bye to "Grandmama" Larry Johnson, and Nike told 24 NBA players that their deals will switch from guaranteed money to performance-based payments next year.

Indeed, the only athlete who could be counted on to sell shoes properly was Michael Jordan. But then, what can't that guy sell? In its June 22 issue, *Fortune* magazine estimated that Jordan's economic impact on the U.S. since joining the NBA in 1984—the total sales of stuff he endorses plus NBA merchandise, the rise in TV and advertising revenues and the increased game attendance—was $10 billion, roughly the wallop delivered by the state of Vermont.

If and when he retires from the marketing whirl, Jordan will be a tough act to follow. Even Tiger Woods, the man who was supposed to be his heir, both in surpassing athletic performance and marketing clout, so far hasn't proved to be such a great pitchman for Nike, which in 1996

gave the golfer a reported $40 million for five years. This year the Woods clothing line, featuring bowling-shoe style spikes priced as high as $225 and mildly nonconformist shirts that went for $75—economically out of reach for those to whom they most appealed, young kids—got marked for early closeout on pro-shop shelves across the country. Said one Nevada retailer of the line, "It just plain flat was a total disaster."

It wouldn't be the only disaster with a golfer's name attached to it. Though it was a great year for the PGA Tour, which offered record purses, and for golf-course construction, which boomed in the U.S., many equipment companies were slammed by the economic crisis in Asia, a lack of product innovation, and El Niño, which soaked courses from California to Florida during the winter. In the span of one week in July, Fred Couples's Lynx Golf, Inc. filed for bankruptcy, Jack Nicklaus's company announced major losses, and Arnold Palmer Golf Co. laid off 89 employees. Callaway, the company that introduced the Big Bertha driver seven years ago but hasn't

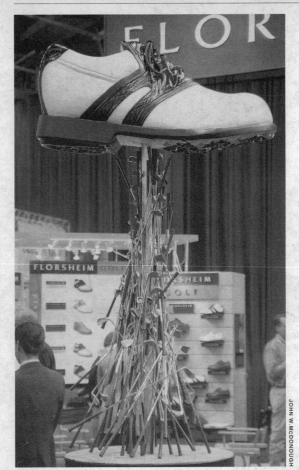

JOHN W. McDONOUGH

No shoo-in: sales of golf
equipment, once a sure
thing, plummeted in '98.

domain. When the NFL demanded that Coca-Cola up its sponsorship from $15 million a year to $36 million, Coke opted for a diet $4 million package instead.

This sort of sane rethinking of the vast amounts of money corporations pour into sports did not extend into the electronic media. According to *U.S. News and World Report*, the TV ratings for pro sports leagues have swooned in the last 10 years: Baseball ratings are down 30%, the NBA 14% and the NFL 22%. Yet the NBA, the NFL and the NHL all inked monstrous new TV deals in 1997–98. Most baffling was the megadeal Disney struck to televise pro hockey, a sport that viewers, through increasing indifference, have deemed all but unwatchable. According to a survey conducted for SI in the spring of 1998, the NHL ranks sixth in fan interest,

topped it since going public to much fanfare in 1992, lost 30% of its value in one day. As a result, the endorsement market was relatively dry for prospective pros like '97 U.S. Amateur champ Matt Kuchar, who decided, perhaps as a consequence, to stay at Georgia Tech for another year.

The sponsorship market underwent a few corrections as well. Longtime Olympics sponsor IBM, which spent a reported $100 million on the Nagano Olympics, said no to Olympic sponsorship beyond the Sydney Games after Olympic officials demanded more money while seeking a more profitable sponsorship for the Games' internet services—once IBM's

behind auto racing and golf. That lowly status was supported by Fox's regular-season ratings, which shrank from 1.9 to 1.4 last year, and ESPN's playoff ratings, which plunged from 1.7 to 1.2. Yet Disney, desperate for programming, pitched an astonishing $600 million bid to show games on ABC, ESPN and ESPN2 for five years starting in 1999. That's $120 million a year, considerably more than the $45 million average Fox and ESPN are currently paying.

Until that deal was negotiated in August '98, it was hard to imagine anything dwarfing, in relative shock value, the TV lucre coming to the NBA and NFL. The NBA's contract with NBC and Turner, scheduled to start this season—lockout or not—is worth $2.6 billion over four years, which represents a 136% increase over the $1.1 billion total of the previous deal. The NFL's new eight-year deals with ABC, CBS, ESPN and Fox are worth $2.2 billion a year, twice the value of the old contracts.

That's a $17.6 billion total, more money than it would take to buy all 30 current NFL teams at *twice* the record price of $250 million that Red McCombs paid for the Minnesota Vikings in '98. One could even throw in the new Cleveland Browns franchise—which was expected to be awarded in September '98 for somewhere between $500 million and $1 billion—and still be under TV's NFL tab. This fact wasn't lost on the chief thinkers at Turner and NBC, the only major TV players to be left out of the NFL deal. The two companies announced a plan to create their own made-for-television league, to launch in the summer of 2000. As currently imagined, the league would include 10 to 12 franchises, run a 10-week regular season, feature mikes and cameras in the huddles and locker rooms and draw players from a pool of former

Now with Carolina, Gilbert (94) is the highest-paid defensive player ever.

collegians who have a regional following.

Organizers of the proposed league say they don't plan to compete with the NFL for players—salaries would top out at $100,000—so they will be spared the obscene contracts of players such as the Carolina Panthers' Sean Gilbert, who sat out all of 1997 after five inconsistent seasons yet became, in the wake of January's TV windfall, the highest-paid defensive player in NFL history, with a seven-year, $46.5 million deal.

Such absurd overpayment is usually the province of the NBA, but this off-season everything contractual was put on hold as owners and players clashed over the salary cap and its various loopholes. Owners, who foresee financial doom in the collective bargaining agreement that was signed in September '95, were especially eager to dispense with the Larry Bird exception, which allows teams to re-sign their own free agents for any amount, regardless of cap space—and which explains the $100 million–plus deals of players such as Miami's Alonzo Mourning and Washington's Juwan Howard. Owners also wanted to restructure the rookie salary scale, which allows first-round draft picks to become free agents after three years. The players, whose aver-

JOHN BEIVER

What effect will Fedorov's arbitration hearing have on future NHL contracts?

age salary is $2.6 million a year, want to leave the agreement alone. As the two parties quibbled into September '98 over the issue of paying players during the lockout, hope for an on-time start to the '98–99 season faded.

Of course, baseball proved this year that a sport can rebound from profound labor troubles. After experiencing widespread disaffection in the wake of the '94 strike, fans started to stream back to ballparks in 1998. But baseball's 10% overall attendance hike may have owed more to the national craze for Beanie Babies—a $5, seven-inch beanbag animal that comes in about 150 varieties—than to great performances by pitchers like Kerry Wood and Greg Maddux and sluggers like McGwire, Sosa and Ken Griffey Jr. Beanie Babies were given out at some two dozen baseball games, and their draw was impressive. When David Wells pitched in Yankee Stadium on May 12, no Beanie Babies were offered, and just 16,606 people turned out. When Wells pitched on May 17, however, Valentino the Beanie Baby Bear was being handed out, which is why 49,820 people can say they were witness to the first Yankee perfect game since Don Larsen's in 1956.

All things warm and fuzzy aside, there was much to disparage in baseball. There was, of course, Huizenga's infamous fire sale, in which he sold or traded nearly every starter so he could unload the franchise. Meanwhile, Rupert Murdoch's News Corp., the parent company of Fox, gobbled up the Dodgers for $350 million, the highest sale price—by $100 million—ever for a baseball team. That acquisition, and the fact that Dodger Mike Piazza turned down a record $80 million, six-year contract extension, begat the colossal swap of Piazza and Todd Zeile to the Marlins for Gary Sheffield, Charles Johnson, Bobby Bonilla, Jim Eisenreich and Manuel Barrios. (Piazza and Zeile would be moved again, to the Mets and Rangers, respectively.) It was by most measures the biggest trade in baseball history, involving $108.1 million in contracts and four All-Stars. But what could prove to be the most earthshaking precedent in the deal was the fact that the entire transaction was orchestrated by corporate suits. Not a single manager or general manager was involved. "I'd like to think that was a one-time occurrence," said Dodgers G.M. Fred Claire.

Another precedent that set off alarms in the sport was the contract signed by J.D. Drew, a 22-year-old centerfielder who had turned down the Phillies' incentive-laden $6 million offer last year after being drafted second. The Cardinals drafted Drew fifth this year and agreed, after much haggling, to give him a guaranteed $7 million over four years, the largest deal ever for a ballplayer signed by the team that drafted him. The deal, which Cardinal Brian Jordan called outrageous, gave Drew more guaranteed money than all but seven of the 25 big league Cardinals and was sure to affect the pay scale of future free agents and draft picks.

Hockey had a much more high-profile holdout in the Red Wings' Sergei Fedorov, who denied Detroit his services for 59 games and signed an offer sheet from Carolina in February. The offer sheet, which Detroit had the option of matching, included $38 million for six years, plus an extra $12 million bonus should the Hurricanes make it to the third round of the playoffs. In arbitration hearings the NHL claimed this put an unfair burden on Detroit because the Red Wings were very likely to advance beyond the second round, while Carolina had almost no hope of doing so. An arbitrator ruled against the league, Detroit matched the offer and eventually won the Stanley Cup. But observers worried: Would such a ruling encourage future teams faced with paying huge bonuses to tank?

Seven- and eight-figure bonuses were far from the ken of the organizers of the American Basketball League, which appeared to be foundering as it entered its third season. Although the league moved forward by adding two new franchises, in Nashville and Chicago, it had to make a temporary 10% staff-wide pay cut in midsummer and suffered some heavy blows at the end of August: During the week in which the rival WNBA was conducting its championship series, the ABL closed its one-year-old Long Beach franchise and lost founding superstar point guard Dawn Staley to the WNBA.

For anyone who wants the largest possible forum for her skills, it's hard to argue with the marketing and exposure machine that the WNBA, under the control of the NBA, has unsurprisingly turned out to be. Though TV ratings were down from last summer, season-ticket sales increased by 72%, and overall attendance rose 12% to over 10,000 frenzied souls a game. But with few players able to live year-round off their salaries (the league's median salary was $25,000) and many unsatisfied with the limited health benefits, there was talk among players of forming a union. "A union is inevitable," said league president Val Ackerman. "But that's part of being a major league sport."

Money demands on a young league like the WNBA may derail the enterprise or may inspire creativity, as we saw elsewhere in sports this year. Indeed, it is to sports' demand for bigger and bigger sums of money from television that we owe, for better or worse, the recent advent of virtual advertising, a technology that superimposes computer-generated ads, visible only to TV viewers, onto playing fields and stadium fences. Where a spectator present at an auto race sees a grassy infield, a viewer at home might see a big Pennzoil ad, as was the case at the Brickyard 400 in early August '98. Because a virtual ad might stay in place throughout half an inning of baseball action, it offers better exposure than a 30-second spot that viewers can channel surf through. The potential for conflict of interest is huge—What if a team sells Miller Beer a billboard space that the network superimposes with a virtual ad for Bud Light?—which is why virtual ads have already been banned from the Olympic Games in Sydney. But virtual advertising, or something like it, will be with us as long as media companies and corporations agree to keep feeding the maw of professional sports. And they will, even though the sports marketplace differs from sports in at least one important respect: In the sports marketplace it is sometimes hard to distinguish the winners from the losers.

Baseball Directory

Major League Baseball

Address: 350 Park Avenue
             New York, NY 10022
Telephone: (212) 339-7800
Chairman of the Executive Council: Bud Selig
President: Paul Beeston
Executive Director, Public Relations: Richard Levin

Major League Baseball Players Association

Address: 12 East 49th Street, 24th Floor
             New York, NY 10017
Telephone: (212) 826-0808
Executive Director: Donald Fehr
Director of Marketing: Judy Heeter
Director of Licensing: Richard Weiss

American League

American League Office

Address: 350 Park Avenue
             New York, NY 10022
Telephone: (212) 339-7600
President: Dr. Gene Budig
VP of Media Affairs and Administration: Phyllis Merhige

Baltimore Orioles

Address: Oriole Park at Camden Yards
             333 W Camden Street
             Baltimore, MD 21201
Telephone: (410) 685-9800
Stadium (Capacity): Camden Yards (48,262)
Managing Partner and Owner: Peter G. Angelos
Vice Chairmen: Thomas Clancy and Joseph Foss
Manager: Ray Miller
Director of Public Relations: John Maroon

Boston Red Sox

Address: 4 Yawkey Way
             Fenway Park
             Boston, MA 02215
Telephone: (617) 267-9440
Stadium (Capacity): Fenway Park (33,871)
Majority Owner and CEO: John Harrington
Executive VP and GM: Daniel F. Duquette
Manager: Jimy Williams
Vice President, Public Affairs: Dick Bresciani

California Angels

Address: P.O. Box 2000/Anaheim Stadium
             Anaheim, CA 92803
Telephone: (714) 940-2000
Stadium (Capacity): Edison International Field of
Anaheim (45,000)
Owners: Gene Autry and Walt Disney Company
General Manager: Bill Bavasi
Manager: Terry Collins
Director of Communications: Tim Mead

Chicago White Sox

Address: Comiskey Park
             333 West 35th Street
             Chicago, IL 60616
Telephone: (312) 674-1000
Stadium (Capacity): Comiskey Park (44,321)
Chairman: Jerry Reinsdorf
General Manager: Ron Schueler
Manager: Jerry Manuel
Director of Publc Relations: Scott Reifert

Cleveland Indians

Address: Jacobs Field
             2401 Ontario Street
             Cleveland, OH 44115-4003
Telephone: (216) 420-4200
Stadium (Capacity): Jacobs Field (43,368)
Chairman of the Board and CEO: Richard Jacobs
Executive VP and General Manager: John Hart
Manager: Mike Hargrove
Vice President, Public Relations: Bob DiBiasio

Detroit Tigers

Address: 2121 Trumbull Ave.
             Tiger Stadium
             Detroit, MI 48216
Telephone: (313) 962-4000
Stadium (Capacity): Tiger Stadium (46,945)
Owner: Mike Ilitch
Chief Executive Officer and President: John McHale
Interim Manager: Larry Parrish
Director of Public Relations: Tyler Barnes

Kansas City Royals

Address: P.O. Box 419969
             Kansas City, MO 64141
Telephone: (816) 921-8000
Stadium (Capacity): Kauffman Stadium (40,625)
Chairman of the Board and CEO: David D. Glass
General Manager: Herk Robinson
Manager: Tony Muser
Vice President, Communications: Mike Levy

Milwaukee Brewers

Address: P.O. Box 3099
             Milwaukee, WI 53201-3099
Telephone: (414) 933-4114
Stadium (Capacity): Milwaukee County Stadium (53,192)
President and CEO: Wendy Selig-Prieb
Senior VP, Baseball Operations: Sal Bando
Manager: Phil Garner
Media Relations: Jon Greenberg

Minnesota Twins

Address: 34 Kirby Puckett Place
             Minneapolis, MN 55415
Telephone: (612) 375-1366
Stadium (Capacity): Hubert H. Humphrey
Metrodome (48,678)
Owner: Carl Pohlad
General Manager: Terry Ryan
Manager: Tom Kelly
Manager of Media Relations: Sean Harlin

New York Yankees

Address: Yankee Stadium
             Bronx, NY 10451
Telephone: (718) 293-4300
Stadium (Capacity): Yankee Stadium (57,545)
Principal Owner: George Steinbrenner
Vice President and Executive Consul: Lonn Trost
General Manager: Brian Cashman
Manager: Joe Torre
Director of Media Relations: Rick Cerone

Oakland Athletics

Address: 7677 Oakport St., 2nd floor
             Oakland, CA 94621
Telephone: (510) 638-4900
Stadium (Capacity): Oakland-Alameda County
Coliseum (43,662)
Owners: Steve Schott and Ken Hofmann
President: Sandy Alderson
General Manager: Billy Beane
Baseball Information Manager: Mike Selleck

American League (Cont.)

Seattle Mariners
Address: P.O. Box 4100
             Seattle, WA 98104
Telephone: (206) 346-4000
Stadium (Capacity): The Kingdome (59,166)
Chairman: John Ellis
General Manager: Woody Woodward
Manager: Lou Piniella
Director of Public Relations: Dave Aust

Tampa Bay Devil Rays
Address: One Tropicana Drive
             St. Petersburg, FL 33705
Telephone: (813) 825-3137
Stadium (Capacity): Tropicana Field (45,369)
Managing General Partner and CEO: Vincent Naimoli
Senior VP and General Manager: Chuck Lamar
Manager: Larry Rothschild
Vice President, Public Relations: Rick Vaughn

Texas Rangers
Address: P.O. Box 90111
             Arlington, TX 76004
Telephone: (817) 273-5222
Stadium (Capacity): The Ballpark in Arlington (49,166)
Owner: Thomas O. Hicks
General Manager: Doug Melvin
Manager: Johnny Oates
Vice President, Public Relations: John Blake

Toronto Blue Jays
Address: SkyDome
             1 Blue Jays Way, Suite 3200
             Toronto, Ontario, Canada M5V 1J1
Telephone: (416) 341-1000
Stadium (Capacity): SkyDome (50,516)
Chairman and Chief Executive: Sam Pollock
Executive VP of Baseball Operations: Gord Ash
Manager: Tim Johnson
Vice president, Media Relations: Howard Starkman

National League

National League Office
Address: 350 Park Avenue
             New York, NY 10022
Telephone: (212) 339-7700
President: Leonard Coleman
Director of Public Relations: Ricky Clemons

Arizona Diamondbacks
Address: 401 East Jefferson Street
             Phoenix, AZ 85004
Telephone: (602) 462-6500
Stadium (Capacity): Bank One Ballpark (49,000)
Managing General Partner: Jerry Colangelo
General Manager: Joe Garagiola Jr.
Manager: Buck Showalter
Director of Public Relations: Mike Swanson

Atlanta Braves
Address: P.O. Box 4064
             Atlanta, GA 30302
Telephone: (404) 522-7630
Stadium (Capacity): Turner Field (48,885)
Owner: Ted Turner
General Manager: John Schuerholz
Manager: Bobby Cox
Director of Public Relations: Jim Schultz

Chicago Cubs
Address: Wrigley Field
             1060 West Addison
             Chicago, IL 60613
Telephone: (773) 404-2827
Stadium (Capacity): Wrigley Field (38,884)
President and CEO: Andrew B. MacPhail
Executive VP of Business Operations: Mark McGuire
General Manager: Ed Lynch
Manager: Jim Riggleman
Director of Media Relations: Sharon Panozzo

Cincinnati Reds
Address: 100 Cinergy Field
             Cincinnati, OH 45202
Telephone: (513) 421-4510
Stadium (Capacity): Cinergy Field (52,953)
General Partner: Marge Schott
General Manager: James G. Bowden
Managing Executive: John L. Allen
Manager: Jack McKeon
Director of Media Relations: Rob Butcher

Colorado Rockies
Address: 2001 Blake Street
             Denver, CO 80205
Telephone: (303) 292-0200
Stadium (Capacity): Coors Field (50,381)
Chairman, President and CEO: Jerry McMorris
Senior VP of Business Operations: Keli McGregor
General Manager and Executive VP: Bob Gebhard
Manager: Don Baylor
Director of Public Relations: Jay Alves

Florida Marlins
Address: 2267 N.W. 199th Street
             Miami, FL 33056
Telephone: (305) 626-7400
Stadium (Capacity): Pro Player Stadium (42,531)
Owner: H. Wayne Huizenga
General Manager: Dave Dombrowski
Manager: Jim Leyland
Director of Baseball Information and Publicity: Ron Colangelo

Houston Astros
Address: P.O. Box 288
             Houston, TX 77001
Telephone: (713) 799-9500
Stadium (Capacity): Astrodome (54,313)
Chairman: Drayton McLane
General Manager: Gerry Hunsicker
Manager: Larry Dierker
Director of Media Relations: Rob Matwick

Los Angeles Dodgers
Address: 1000 Elysian Park Avenue
             Los Angeles, CA 90012-1199
Telephone: (213) 224-1500
Stadium (Capacity): Dodger Stadium (56,000)
President: Bob Graziano
General Manager: Kevin Malone
Manager: Glen Hoffman
Director of Publicity: Derrick Hall

Montreal Expos
Address: P.O. Box 500
             Station M
             Montreal
             Quebec, Canada H1V 3P2
Telephone: (514) 253-3434

National League *(Cont.)*

Montreal Expos *(Cont.)*
Stadium (Capacity): Olympic Stadium (46,500)
President: Claude Brochu
Vice President and General Manager: Jim Beattie
Manager: Felipe Alou
Director, Media Relations: Peter Loyello

New York Mets
Address: Shea Stadium
123-01 Roosevelt Ave.
Flushing, NY 11368
Telephone: (718) 507-6387
Stadium (Capacity): Shea Stadium (55,775)
Chairman: Nelson Doubleday
President and Chief Executive Officer: Fred Wilpon
Senior VP and General Manager: Steve Phillips
Manager: Bobby Valentine
Director of Media Relations: Jay Horwitz

Philadelphia Phillies
Address: P.O. Box 7575
Philadelphia, PA 19101-7575
Telephone: (215) 463-6000
Stadium (Capacity): Veterans Stadium (62,409)
Chairman: Bill Giles
President: David T. Montgomery
General Manager: Ed Wade
Manager: Terry Francona
Vice President, Public Relations: Larry Shenk

Pittsburgh Pirates
Address: P.O. Box 7000
Pittsburgh, PA 15212
Telephone: (412) 323-5000
Stadium (Capacity): Three Rivers Stadium (47,972)
CEO and Managing General Partner: Kevin McClatchy

Pittsburgh Pirates *(Cont.)*
General Manager: Cam Bonifay
Manager: Gene Lamont
Director of Media Relations: Jim Trdinich

St. Louis Cardinals
Address: Busch Stadium
250 Stadium Plaza
St. Louis, MO 63102
Telephone: (314) 421-3060
Stadium (Capacity): Busch Stadium (49,676)
President and CEO: Mark Lamping
General Manager: Walt Jocketty
Manager: Tony LaRussa
Director of Media Relations: Brian Bartow

San Diego Padres
Address: P.O. Box 122000
San Diego, CA 92112
Telephone: (619) 283-4494
Stadium (Capacity): Qualcomm Stadium (56,975)
Chairman: John Moores
General Manager: Kevin Towers
Manager: Bruce Bochy
Director of Media Relations: Glenn Geffner

San Francisco Giants
Address: 3Com Park
San Francisco, CA 94124
Telephone: (415) 468-3700
Stadium (Capacity): 3Com Park (63,000)
President/Managing General Partner: Peter Magowan
General Manager: Brian Sabean
Manager: Dusty Baker
Vice President, Communications: Bob Rose

Pro Football Directory

National Football League
Address: 280 Park Avenue
New York, NY 10017
Telephone: (212) 450-2000
Commissioner: Paul Tagliabue

NFL Players Association
Address: 2021 L Street, N.W.
Washington, D.C. 20036
Telephone: (202) 463-2200
Executive Director: Gene Upshaw
Director, Public Relations: Frank Woschitz

National Conference

Arizona Cardinals
Address: P.O. Box 888
Phoenix, AZ 85001
Telephone: (602) 379-0101
Stadium (Capacity): Sun Devil Stadium (73,377)
President and Owner: Bill Bidwill
Vice President: Larry Wilson
General Manager: Michael Bidwill
Head Coach: Vince Tobin
Director of Public Relations: Paul Jensen

Atlanta Falcons
Address: 1 Falcon Place
Suwanee, GA 30024
Telephone: (770) 945-1111
Stadium (Capacity): Georgia Dome (71,228)
President: Taylor W. Smith
Director of Player Personnel: Ron Hill
Coach: Dan Reeves
Publicity Director: Charlie Taylor

Carolina Panthers
Address: Ericsson Stadium
800 South Mint St.
Charlotte, NC 28202
Telephone: (704) 358-7000
Stadium (Capacity): Ericsson Stadium (73,248)
Founder and Owner: Jerry Richardson
President: Mark Richardson
Coach: Dom Capers
Director of Communications: Charlie Dayton

Chicago Bears
Address: 1000 Football Drive
Lake Forest, IL 60045
Telephone: (847) 295-6600
Stadium (Capacity): Soldier Field (66,946)
President: Michael McCaskey
Coach: Dave Wannstedt
Director of Public Relations: Bryan Harlan

National Conference *(Cont.)*

Dallas Cowboys
Address: One Cowboys Parkway
            Irving, TX 75063
Telephone: (972) 556-9900
Stadium (Capacity): Texas Stadium (65,921)
Owner, President and General Manager: Jerry Jones
Coach: Chan Gailey
Public Relations Director: Rich Dalrymple

Detroit Lions
Address: 1200 Featherstone Road
            Pontiac, MI 48342
Telephone: (248) 335-4131
Stadium (Capacity): Pontiac Silverdome (80,311)
Chairman and President: William Clay Ford
Executive Vice President and CEO: Chuck Schmidt
Vice Chairman: William Clayford
Coach: Bobby Ross
Director of Media Relations: Mike Murray

Green Bay Packers
Address: 1265 Lombardi Avenue
            Green Bay, WI 54304
Telephone: (920) 496-5700
Stadium (Capacity): Lambeau Field (60,790)
President: Bob Harlan
General Manager: Ron Wolf
Coach: Mike Holmgren
Public Relations Director: Lee Remmel

Minnesota Vikings
Address: 9520 Viking Drive
            Eden Prairie, MN 55344
Telephone: (612) 828-6500
Stadium (Capacity): HHH Metrodome (64,000)
Owner: Red McCombs
President: Roger L. Headrick
Coach: Dennis Green
Public Relations Director: Bob Hagan

New Orleans Saints
Address: 5800 Airline Highway
            Metairie, LA 70003
Telephone: (504) 733-0255
Stadium (Capacity): Louisiana Superdome (69,049)
Owner: Tom Benson
President, General Manager and CEO: Bill Kuharich
Head Coach: Mike Ditka
Director of Media Relations: Greg Bensel

New York Giants
Address: Giants Stadium
            East Rutherford, NJ 07073
Telephone: (201) 935-8111
Stadium (Capacity): Giants Stadium (79,469)
President and co-CEO: Wellington T. Mara
Chairman and co-CEO: Preston Robert Tisch
Senior VP and General Manager: Ernie Accorsi
Coach: Jim Fassel
Vice President of Communications: Pat Hanlon

Philadelphia Eagles
Address: Veterans Stadium
            3501 South Broad Street
            Philadelphia, PA 19148
Telephone: (215) 463-2500
Stadium (Capacity): Veterans Stadium (65,352)
Owner: Jeffrey Lurie
Executive Vice President: Joe Banner
Director of Football Operations: Tom Modrak
Coach: Ray Rhodes
Director of Public Relations: Ron Howard

St. Louis Rams
Address: One Rams Way
            St. Louis, MO 63045
Telephone: (314) 982-7267
Stadium (Capacity): Trans World Dome (66,000)
Owner and Chairman: Georgia Frontiere
Vice Chairman and Owner: Stan Kroenke
President: John Shaw
Coach: Dick Vermeil
Director of Public Relations: Rick Smith

San Francisco 49ers
Address: 4949 Centennial Boulevard
            Santa Clara, CA 95054
Telephone: (408) 562-4949
Stadium (Capacity): 3Com Park (70,207)
Owner: Edward J. DeBartolo Corporation
Edward J. DeBartolo Jr., Denise DeBartolo-York
General Manager: Dwight Clark
Coach: Steve Mariucci
Public Relations Director: Rodney Knox

Tampa Bay Buccaneers
Address: One Buccaneer Place
            Tampa, FL 33607
Telephone: (813) 870-2700
Stadium (Capacity): Raymond James Stadium
  (75,000)
Owner: Malcolm Glazer
General Manager: Rich McKay
Coach: Tony Dungy
Director of Communications: Reggie Roberts

Washington Redskins
Address: 21300 Redskin Park Drive
            Ashburn, VA 20147
Telephone: (703) 478-8900
Stadium (Capacity): Jack Kent Cooke Stadium
  (80,116)
President: John Kent Cooke, Sr.
General Manager: Charley Casserly
Coach: Norv Turner
Director of Public Relations: Mike McCall

American Conference

Buffalo Bills
Address: One Bills Drive
            Orchard Park, NY 14127
Telephone: (716) 648-1800
Stadium (Capacity): Rich Stadium (80,024)
President: Ralph C. Wilson Jr.
Executive VP and General Manager: John Butler
Coach: Wade Phillips
Director of Media Relations: Scott Berchtold

Baltimore Ravens
Address: 11001 Owings Mills Blvd.
            Owings Mills, MD 21117
Telephone: (410) 654-6200
Stadium (Capacity): New NFL Stadium at Camden
Yards (69,354)
President: Art Modell
Coach: Ted Marchibroda
VP and Director of Public Relations: Kevin Byrne

American Conference *(Cont.)*

Cincinnati Bengals

Address: One Bengals Drive
                Cincinnati, OH 45204
Telephone: (513) 621-3550
Stadium (Capacity): Cinergy Field (60,398)
President and General Manager: Mike Brown
Vice President: John Sawyer
Coach: Bruce Coslet
Director of Public Relations: Jack Brennan

Denver Broncos

Address: 13655 Broncos Parkway
                Englewood, CO 80112
Telephone: (303) 649-9000
Stadium (Capacity): Mile High Stadium (76,078)
President and Chief Executive Officer: Pat Bowlen
General Manager: John Beake
Coach: Mike Shanahan
Director of Media Relations: Jim Saccomano

Indianapolis Colts

Address: P.O. Box 535000
                Indianapolis, IN 46253
Telephone: (317) 297-2658
Stadium (Capacity): RCA Dome (60,272)
Owner and Chief Executive Officer: Jim Irsay
President: Bill Polian
Vice Chairman and COO: Michael Schernoff
Coach: Jim Mora
Public Relations Director: Craig Kelley

Jacksonville Jaguars

Address: One Alltel Stadium Place
                Jacksonville, FL 32202
Telephone: (904) 633-6000
Stadium (Capacity): Alltel Stadium (73,000)
Owner: J. Wayne Weaver
Vice President and CFO: Bill Prescott
Senior VP of Football Operations: Michael Huyghue
Coach: Tom Coughlin
Executive Director of Communications: Dan Edwards

Kansas City Chiefs

Address: One Arrowhead Drive
                Kansas City, MO 64129
Telephone: (816) 924-9300
Stadium (Capacity): Arrowhead Stadium (79,101)
Founder: Lamar Hunt
CEO, President and General Manager: Carl Peterson
Coach: Marty Schottenheimer
Public Relations Director: Bob Moore

Miami Dolphins

Address: 7500 S.W. 30th Street
                Davie, FL 33314
Telephone: (954) 452-7000
Stadium (Capacity): Pro Player Stadium (75,192)
Chairman of the Board/Owner: H. Wayne Huizenga
President and COO: Eddie J. Jones
General Manager and Head Coach: Jimmy Johnson
Senior VP Media Relations: Harvey Greene

New England Patriots

Address: Foxboro Stadium
                60 Washington St.
                Foxboro, MA 02035
Telephone: (508) 543-8200
Stadium (Capacity): Foxboro Stadium (60,292)
President and Chief Executive Officer: Robert K. Kraft

New England Patriots *(Cont.)*

VP Owners Representative: Jonathan Kraft
VP Business Operations: Andy Wasynczuk
Coach: Pete Carroll
VP of Public and Community Relations: Donald Lowery

New York Jets

Address: 1000 Fulton Avenue
                Hempstead, NY 11550
Telephone: (516) 560-8100
Stadium (Capacity): Giants Stadium (78,739)
Chairman of the Board: Leon Hess
Director of Player Personnel: Dick Haley
Coach: Bill Parcells
Director of Public Relations: Frank Ramos

Oakland Raiders

Address: 1220 Harbor Bay Parkway
                Alameda, CA 94502
Telephone: (510) 864-5000
Stadium (Capacity): Oakland-Alameda County
  Coliseum (62,500)
President of the General Partner: Al Davis
Coach: Jon Gruden
Executive Assistant: Al LoCasale
Director of Public Relations: Mike Taylor

Pittsburgh Steelers

Address: Three Rivers Stadium
                300 Stadium Circle
                Pittsburgh, PA 15212
Telephone: (412) 323-1200
Stadium (Capacity): Three Rivers Stadium (59,600)
President: Dan Rooney
Director of Football Operations: Tom Donahoe
Coach: Bill Cowher
Director of Communications: Ron Wahl

San Diego Chargers

Address: Qualcomm Stadium
                4020 Murphy Canyon Road
                San Diego, CA 92123
Telephone: (619) 874-4500
Stadium (Capacity): Qualcomm Stadium (71,400)
Chairman of the Board and President:
  Alex G. Spanos
General Manager: Bobby Beathard
Coach: Kevin Gilbride
Director of Public Relations: Bill Johnston

Seattle Seahawks

Address: 11220 N.E. 53rd Street
                Kirkland, WA 98033
Telephone: (425) 827-9777
Stadium (Capacity): The Kingdome (66,400)
Owner: Paul Allen
President: Bob Whitsitt
Coach: Dennis Erickson
VP of Administration and Communications: Gary Wright
Director of Public Relations: Dave Pearson

Tennessee Oilers

Address: 7640 Highway S
                Nashville, TN 37221
Telephone: 615-673-1503
Stadium (Capacity): Memphis Liberty Bowl (63,320)
President: K.S. (Bud) Adams Jr.
General Manager: Floyd Reese
Coach: Jeff Fisher
Director of Media Relations: Tony Wyllie

Other Leagues

Canadian Football League
Address: 110 Eglinton Avenue West, 5th floor
            Toronto, Ontario M4A1A3, Canada
Telephone: (416) 322-9650
Commissioner: John Tory
Chief Operating Officer: Jeff Giles
Communications Manager: Jim Neish

NFL EUROPE
Address: 280 Park Avenue
            New York, NY 10017
Telephone: (212) 450-2000
President: Oliver Luck (Frankfurt)
Chief Operating Officer: Ken Saunders (London)
Director of Communications: David Tossel

Pro Basketball Directory

National Basketball Association
Address: 645 Fifth Avenue
            New York, NY 10022
Telephone: (212) 826-7000
Commissioner: David Stern
Deputy Commissioner: Russell Granik
VP and GM, Communications Group: Brian McIntyre

National Basketball Association Players Association
Address: 1700 Broadway
            Suite 1400
            New York, NY 10019
Telephone: (212) 655-0880
Executive Director: William Hunter

Atlanta Hawks
Address: One CNN Center, South Tower
            Suite 405
            Atlanta, GA 30303
Telephone: (404) 827-3800
Arena (Capacity): The Georgia Dome (34,821)
Owner: Ted Turner
President: Stan Kasten
General Manager: Pete Babcock
Coach: Lenny Wilkens
Director of Media Relations: Arthur Triche

Boston Celtics
Address: 151 Merrimac Street
            Boston, MA 02114
Telephone: (617) 523-6050
Arena (Capacity): FleetCenter (18,624)
Owner and Chairman of the Board: Paul Gaston
President and Head Coach: Rick Pitino
General Manager: Chris Wallace
Director of Media Relations: R. Jeffrey Twiss

Charlotte Hornets
Address: 100 Hive Drive
            Charlotte, NC 28217
Telephone: (704) 357-0252
Arena (Capacity): Charlotte Coliseum (24,042)
Owner: George Shinn
Coach: Dave Cowens
VP of Public Relations: Harold Kaufman

Chicago Bulls
Address: 1901 W. Madison Street
            Chicago, IL 60612
Telephone: (312) 455-4000
Arena (Capacity): United Center (21,711)
Chairman: Jerry Reinsdorf
GM and VP of Basketball Operations: Jerry Krause
Coach: TBA
Senior Director of Media Services: Tim Hallam

Cleveland Cavaliers
Address: One Center Court
            Cleveland, OH 44115
Telephone: (216) 420-2000
Arena (Capacity): Gund Arena (20,562)
Chairman: Gordon Gund
President and COO, Team Division: Wayne Embry
Coach: Mike Fratello
Director of Media Relations: Bob Zink

Dallas Mavericks
Address: Reunion Arena
            777 Sports Street
            Dallas, TX 75207
Telephone: (214) 748-1808
Arena (Capacity): Reunion Arena (18,042)
Owners: Ross Perot Jr.
Director of Player Personnel: Keith Grant
General Manager and Head Coach: Don Nelson
VP of Communications: Kevin Sullivan

Denver Nuggets
Address: McNichols Sports Arena
            1635 Clay Street
            Denver, CO 80204
Telephone: (303) 893-6700
Arena (Capacity): McNichols Sports Arena (17,171)
Owners: Ascent Entertainment Group
General Manager: Dan Issel
Coach: TBA
Media Relations Director: Tommy Sheppard

Detroit Pistons
Address: The Palace of Auburn Hills
            Two Championship Drive
            Auburn Hills, MI 48326
Telephone: (248) 377-0100
Arena (Capacity): The Palace of Auburn Hills (22,076)
Owner: William M. Davidson
VP of Basketball Operations: Rick Sund
Coach: Alvin Gentry
VP of Public Relations: Matt Dobek

Golden State Warriors
Address: 1011 Broadway, 20th floor
            Oakland, CA 94607-4019
Telephone: (510) 986-2200
Arena (Capacity): The New Arena in Oakland (19,200)
Owner and CEO: Christopher Cohan
General Manager: Garry St. Jean
Coach: P.J. Carlesimo
Director of Public Relations: Raymond Ridder

Houston Rockets

Address: The Summit
            Two Greenway Plaza, Suite 400
            Houston, TX 77046
Telephone: (713) 627-3865
Arena (Capacity): The Summit (16,285)
Owner: Leslie Alexander
Chief Operating Officer: Ken Harman
Sr. Executive VP of Business Operations: John Thomas
Sr. Executive VP of Basketball Affairs: Robert Barr
Executive VP of Basketball Affairs: Carroll Dawson
Coach: Rudy Tomjanovich
Manager of Media Services: Tim Frank

Indiana Pacers

Address: 300 E. Market Street
            Indianapolis, IN 46204
Telephone: (317) 263-2100
Arena (Capacity): Market Square Arena (16,530)
Owners: Melvin Simon and Herbert Simon
General Manager: David Kahn
President: Donnie Walsh
Executive VP and Head Coach: Larry Bird
Media Relations Director: David Benner

Los Angeles Clippers

Address: L.A. Memorial Sports Arena
            3939 S. Figueroa Street
            Los Angeles, CA 90037
Telephone: (213) 748-8000
Arena (Capacity): L.A. Memorial Sports Arena (16,021)
Owner: Donald T. Sterling
Vice President of Basketball Operations: Elgin Baylor
Coach: TBA
Vice President of Communications: Joe Safety

Los Angeles Lakers

Address: Great Western Forum
            3900 West Manchester Boulevard
            Inglewood, CA 90306
Telephone: (310) 419-3100
Arena (Capacity): The Great Western Forum (17,505)
Owner: Dr. Jerry Buss
Vice President of Basketball Operations: Jerry West
General Manager: Mitch Kupchak
Coach: Del Harris
Director of Public Relations: John Black

Miami Heat

Address: Sun Trust International Center
            One SE 3rd Ave., Suite 2300
            Miami, FL 33131
Telephone: (305) 577-4328
Arena (Capacity): Miami Arena (15,200)
Managing General Partner: Mickey Arison
Executive VP of Business Operations: Pauline Winick
President and Coach: Pat Riley
General Manager: Randy Pfund
President of Business Operations: Jay Cross
Director of Sports Media Relations: Tim Donovan

Milwaukee Bucks

Address: The Bradley Center
            1001 N. Fourth Street
            Milwaukee, WI 53203
Telephone: (414) 227-0500
Arena (Capacity): The Bradley Center (18,717)
Owner: Herb Kohl
General Manager: Bob Weinhauer
Coach: TBA
Public Relations Director: Bill King II

Minnesota Timberwolves

Address: 600 First Avenue North
            Minneapolis, MN 55403
Telephone: (612) 673-1602
Arena (Capacity): Target Center (19,006)
Owner: Glen Taylor
VP of Basketball Operations: Kevin McHale
General Manager and Coach: Phil (Flip) Saunders
Manager of PR and Communications: Kent Wipf

New Jersey Nets

Address: Nets Champion Center
            390 Murray Hill Parkway
            East Rutherford, NJ 07073
Telephone: (201) 935-8888
Arena (Capacity): Continental Airlines Arena (20,049)
Co-Chairman of the Board and CEO: Finn Wentworth
Co-Chairman of the Board: Lewis Katz
Vice Chairman: David Gerstein
President and COO: Michael Rowe
VP of Basketball Operations and Coach: John Calipari
Director of Public Relations: John Mertz

New York Knickerbockers

Address: Madison Square Garden
            Two Pennsylvania Plaza
            New York, NY 10121
Telephone: (212) 465-5867
Arena (Capacity): Madison Square Garden (19,763)
Owner: ITT/Sheraton and Cablevision
President: David W. Checketts
President and General Manager: Ernie Grunfeld
Coach: Jeff Van Gundy
Vice President of Public Relations: Chris Weiller

Orlando Magic

Address: P.O. Box 76
            Orlando, FL 32802
Telephone: (407) 649-3200
Arena (Capacity): Orlando Arena (17,248)
Owner: Rich DeVos
Senior Executive Vice President: Pat Williams
General Manager: John Gabriel
Coach: Chuck Daly
Senior Director of Communications: Alex Martins

Philadelphia 76ers

Address: First Union Center
            3601 South Broad Street
            Philadelphia, PA 19148
Telephone: (215) 339-7600
Arena (Capacity): CoreStates Center (20,444)
Owner and President: Pat Croce
Head Coach and Vice President of Basketball
  Operations: Larry Brown
General Manager: Billy King
Manager of Media Relations: Bill Bonsiewicz

Phoenix Suns

Address: P.O. Box 1369
            Phoenix, AZ 85001
Telephone: (602) 379-7867
Arena (Capacity): America West Arena (19,023)
Owner: Jerry Colangelo
Coach: Danny Ainge
Media Relations Director: Julie Fie

Portland Trail Blazers

Address: One Center Court
            Suite 200
            Portland, OR 97227
Telephone: (503) 234-9291
Arena (Capacity): Rose Garden Arena (21,401)
Chairman of the Board: Paul Allen

Portland Trail Blazers *(Cont.)*
President and General Manager: Bob Whitsitt
Coach: Mike Dunleavy
Director of Sports Communication: John Christiansen

Sacramento Kings
Address: One Sports Parkway
             Sacramento, CA 95834
Telephone: (916) 928-0000
Arena (Capacity): ARCO Arena (17,317)
Managing General Partner: Jim Thomas
Vice President of Basketball Operations: Geoff Petrie
Coach: TBA
Director of Media Relations: Troy Hanson

San Antonio Spurs
Address: Alamodome
             100 Montana
             San Antonio, TX 78203
Telephone: (210) 554-7787
Arena (Capacity): Alamodome (34,215)
Chairman: Peter Holt
Head Coach and General Manager: Gregg Popovich
Director of Media Services: Tom James

Seattle SuperSonics
Address: 190 Queen Anne Avenue North
             Suite 200
             Seattle, WA 98109
Telephone: (206) 281-5847
Arena (Capacity): KeyArena (17,100)
Owner: Barry Ackerley
President and General Manager: Wally Walker
Coach: Paul Westphal
Director of Media Relations: Cheri Hanson

Toronto Raptors
Address: 20 Bay Street, Suite 1702
             Toronto, Ontario, Canada M5J 2N8
Telephone: (416) 214-2255
Arena (Capacity): SkyDome (20,125)
Owner: Maple Leaf Sports and Entertainment, Ltd.
VP and General Manager: Glen Grunwald
Coach: Butch Carter
Coordinator of Communications: Matt Akler

Utah Jazz
Address: 301 West So. Temple
             Salt Lake City, UT 84101
Telephone: (801) 575-7800
Arena (Capacity): Delta Center (19,911)
Owner: Larry H. Miller

Utah Jazz *(Cont.)*
General Manager: R. Tim Howells
Coach: Jerry Sloan
Director of Media Relations: Kim Turner

Vancouver Grizzlies
Address: General Motors Place
             800 Griffiths Way
             Vancouver, B.C., Canada V6B 6G1
Telephone: (604) 899-4666
Arena (Capacity): General Motors Place (19,193)
Owner: Orca Bay Sports and Entertainment
General Manager: Stu Jackson
Coach: Brian Hill
Director of Media Relations: Steve Frost

Washington Wizards
Address: One Harry S. Truman Drive
             Landover, MD 20785
Telephone: (202) 661-5000
Arena (Capacity): USAir Arena (18,756)
Owner: Abe Pollin
General Manager and Vice President: Wes Unseld
Coach: Bernie Bickerstaff
Director of Public Relations: Maureen Lewis

Other Leagues

Continental Basketball Association
Address: Two Arizona Center
             400 North 5th Street, Suite 1425
             Phoenix, AZ 85004
Telephone: (602) 254-6677
Commissioner: Gary Hunter
VP of Basketball Operations: Wade Morehead

American Basketball League
Address: 1900 Embarcadero Road, Suite 110
             Palo Alto, CA 94303
Telephone: (650) 856-3225
Chief Executive Officer: Gary Cavalli
Director of Media Relations: Dean Jutilla

Women's National Basketball Association
Address: 645 Fifth Avenue
             New York, NY 10022
Telephone: (212) 688-9622
President: Valerie B. Ackerman
Director of Communications: Mark Pray

Hockey Directory

National Hockey League
Address: 1251 Avenue of the Americas
             47th floor
             New York, NY 10020-1198
Telephone: (212) 789-2000
Commissioner: Gary Bettman
Senior VP and Chief Operating Officer: Steven Solomon
Senior VP and Dir. of Hockey Operations: Colin Cambell
Vice President, Public Relations: Arthur Pincus

National Hockey League Players Association
Address: 777 Bay Street, Suite 2400
             Toronto, Ontario, Canada M5G 2C8
Telephone: (416) 408-4040
Executive Director: Bob Goodenow

Mighty Ducks of Anaheim
Address: Arrowhead Pond of Anaheim
             2695 Katella Avenue
             Anaheim, CA 92806
Telephone: (714) 940-2900
Arena (Capacity): Arrowhead Pond of Anaheim (17,174)
Chairman and Governor: Tony Tavares
President and General Manager: Pierre Gauthier
Coach: Craig Hartsburg
Manager of Communications: Rob Scichili

Boston Bruins
Address: One FleetCenter, Suite 250
             Boston, MA 02114-1303
Telephone: (617) 624-1900
Arena (Capacity): FleetCenter (17,565)

Boston Bruins *(Cont.)*
Owner and Governor: Jeremy M. Jacobs
Alternative Governor, President and General
 Manager: Harry Sinden
Coach: Pat Burns
Director of Media Relations: Heidi Holland

Buffalo Sabres
Address: Marine Midland Arena
             One Seymour H. Knox III Plaza
             Buffalo, NY 14203
Telephone: (716) 855-4100
Arena (Capacity): Marine Midland Arena (18,595)
Chairman of the Board: John J. Rigas
CEO: Tim J. Rigas
General Manager: Darcy Regier
Coach: Lindy Ruff
Director of Communications: Michael Gilbert

Calgary Flames
Address: Canadian Airlines Saddledome
             555 Saddledome Rise, SE
             Calgary, Alberta T2G 2W1
Telephone: (403) 777-2177
Arena (Capacity): Canadian Airlines Saddledome
 (17,104)
Owners: Grant A. Bartlett, Harley N. Hotchkiss, N.
 Murray Edwards, Ronald V. Joyce, Alvin G. Libin,
 Allan P. Markin, J.R. McCaig, Byron J. Seaman,
 Daryl K. Seaman
President: Ron Bremner
General Manager: Al Coates
Director of Hockey Operations: Al MacNeil
Coach: Brian Sutter
Director of Communications: Peter Hanlon

Carolina Hurricanes
Address: 5000 Aerial Center, Suite 100
             Morrisville, NC 27560
Telephone: (919) 467-7825
Arena (Capacity): Greensboro Coliseum Complex
 (21,500)
Owner: KTR Hockey Ltd. Partnership
President and General Manager: Jim Rutherford
Assistant General Manager: Terry McDonnell
Coach: Paul Maurice
Director of Public Relations: Chris Brown

Chicago Blackhawks
Address: United Center
             1901 W. Madison Street
             Chicago, IL 60612
Telephone: (312) 455-7000
Arena (Capacity): United Center (20,500)
President: William W. Wirtz
Senior Vice President: Robert Pulford
General Manager: Bob Murray
Coach: Dirk Graham
Public Relations Director: Jim DeMaria

Colorado Avalanche
Address: McNichols Sports Arena
             1635 Clay Street
             Denver, CO 80204
Telephone: (303) 893-6700
Arena (Capacity): McNichols Sports Arena (16,061)
Owner: Ascent Entertainment Group
President and General Manager: Pierre Lacroix
Coach: Bob Hartley
Director of Media Relations and Team Services:
 Jean Martineau

Dallas Stars
Address: 211 Cowboys Parkway
             Irving, TX 75063
Telephone: (972) 868-2890
Arena (Capacity): Reunion Arena (16,928)
Owner: Thomas O. Hicks
General Manager: Bob Gainey
Coach: Ken Hitchcock
Director of Public Relations: Larry Kelly

Detroit Red Wings
Address: Joe Louis Sports Arena
             600 Civic Center Drive
             Detroit, MI 48226
Telephone: (313) 396-7544
Arena (Capacity): Joe Louis Sports Arena (19,983)
Senior Vice President: Jim Devellano
Head Coach: Scott Bowman
General Manager: Ken Holland
Director of Media Relations: John Hahn

Edmonton Oilers
Address: 11230 110th Street, 2nd floor
             Edmonton, Alberta T5G 3G8
Telephone: (403) 414-4000
Arena (Capacity): Edmonton Coliseum (17,099)
Owner: Edmonton Investor Group
Governor: Jim Hole
Alt. Governor, President and GM: Glen Sather
Coach: Ron Low
VP of Public Relations: Bill Tuele

Florida Panthers
Address: 100 Northeast Third Avenue, 2nd floor
             Fort Lauderdale, FL 33301
Telephone: (954) 835-7000
Arena (Capacity): Miami Arena (14,703)
Owner: H. Wayne Huizenga
General Manager: Bryan Murray
Coach: Doug MacLean
Director of Media Relations: Mike Hanson

Los Angeles Kings
Address: The Great Western Forum
             3900 West Manchester Boulevard
             P.O. Box 17013
             Inglewood, CA 90308
Telephone: (310) 419-3160
Arena (Capacity): The Great Western Forum (16,005)
President: Tim Leiweke
General Manager: Dave Taylor
Coach: Larry Robinson
Media Relations Director: Mike Altieri

Montreal Canadiens
Address: Molson Centre
             1260 de la Gauchetiere West
             Montreal, Quebec H3B 5E8
Telephone: (514) 932-2582
Arena (Capacity): Molson Centre (21,000)
Chairman, Pres., and Governor: Ronald Corey
General Manager: Regean Houle
Coach: Alain Vigneault
Director of Communications: Donald Beauchamp

New Jersey Devils
Address: Continental Airlines Arena, PO Box 504
             East Rutherford, NJ 07073
Telephone: (201) 935-6050
Arena (Capacity): Continental Airlines Arena (19,040)
Chairman: John J. McMullen
President and General Manager: Lou Lamoriello
Coach: Robbie Ftorek
Director of Public Relations: Kevin Deffart

New York Islanders
Address: Nassau Veterans Memorial Coliseum
                Uniondale, NY 11553
Telephone: (516) 794-4100
Arena (Capacity): Nassau Veterans Memorial
  Coliseum (16,297)
Co-Chairmen: Steven M. Gluckstern, Howard T.
  Milstein and Edward Milstein
General Manager and Coach: Mike Milbury
Media Relations Director: Chris Botta

New York Rangers
Address: Madison Square Garden
                2 Pennsylvania Plaza
                New York, NY 10121
Telephone: (212) 465-6000
Arena (Capacity): Madison Square Garden (18,200)
Owner: Cablevision
President and General Manager: Neil Smith
Coach: John Muckler
Director of Communications: John Rosasco

Ottawa Senators
Address: The Corel Center
                1000 Palladium Drive
                Kanata, Ontario K2V 1A5
Telephone: (613) 599-0250
Arena (Capacity): The Corel Centre (18,500)
Founder: Bruce M. Firestone
Chairman and Governor: Rod Bryden
President and Chief Executive Officer: Roy Mlakar
General Manager: Rick Dudley
Coach: Jacques Martin
Director of Media Relations: Morgan Quarry

Philadelphia Flyers
Address: First Union Center
                3601 South Broad Street
                Philadelphia, PA 19148
Telephone: (215) 465-4500
Arena (Capacity): CoreStates Center (19,600)
Majority Owner: Comcast Spectacor
Chairman: Ed Snider
President and General Manager: Bob Clarke
Coach: Roger Neilson
Director of Public Relations: Zack Hill

Phoenix Coyotes
Address: Cellular One Ice Den
                9375 East Belle Road
                Scottsdale, AZ 85264
Telephone: (602) 473-5600
Arena (Capacity): America West Arena (16,210)
Chief Executive Officer and Governor: Richard Burke
Owner, CEO and Governor: Richard Burke
GM and Alternate Governor: Bobby Smith
Coach: Jim Schoenfeld
Director of Media and Player Relations: Richard Nairn

Pittsburgh Penguins
Address: Civic Arena
                66 Mario Lemieux Place
                Pittsburgh, PA 15219
Telephone: (412) 642-1300
Arena (Capacity): Civic Arena (16,958)
Owners: Howard Baldwin and Roger Marino
General Manager: Craig Patrick
Coach: Kevin Constantine
Director of Media Relations: Steve Bovino

St. Louis Blues
Address: Kiel Center
                1401 Clark Avenue
                St. Louis, MO 63103
Telephone: (314) 622-2500
Arena (Capacity): Kiel Center (19,260)
President and Chief Executive Officer: Mark Sauer
Coach: Joel Quenneville
General Manager and Coach: Larry Pleau
Director of Public Relations: Jeff Trammel

San Jose Sharks
Address: San Jose Arena
                525 West Santa Clara Street
                San Jose, CA 95113
Telephone: (408) 287-7070
Arena (Capacity): San Jose Arena (17,483)
Owners: George and Gordon Gund
Executive VP and General Manager: Dean Lombardi
Coach: Darryl Sutter
Director of Media Relations: Ken Arnold

Tampa Bay Lightning
Address: 401 Channelside Drive
                Tampa, FL 33602
Telephone: (813) 229-2658
Arena (Capacity): Ice Palace (19,758)
Owner: Arthur L. Williams
President, CEO and Governor: Billy McGehee
General Manager and Alt. Governor: Phil Esposito
Coach: Jacques Demers
Director of Media Relations: Jay Preble

Toronto Maple Leafs
Address: Maple Leaf Gardens
                60 Carlton Street
                Toronto, Ontario M5B 1L1
Telephone: (416) 977-1641
Arena (Capacity): Maple Leaf Gardens (15,726)
Chairman of the Board: Steve A. Stavro
President and General Manager: Ken Dryden
Associate General Manager: Mike Smith
Coach: Pat Quinn
Manager of Media Relations: Pat Park

Vancouver Canucks
Address: General Motors Place
                800 Griffiths Way
                Vancouver, B.C. V6B 6G1
Telephone: (604) 899-4600
Arena (Capacity): General Motors Place (18,422)
Chairman and Governor: John E. McCaw Jr.
Deputy Chairman, Orca Bay Sports and
  Entertainment: Stanley McCammon
President, CEO and Alternate Governor: Stephen T.
  Bellringer
General Manager: Brian Burke
Coach: Mike Keenan
Assistant of Media Relations: Chris Brunwell

Washington Capitals
Address: MCI Center
                601 F Street, NW
                Washington, D.C. 20004
Telephone: (202) 628-3200
Arena (Capacity): MCI Center (19,740)
President and Governor: Richard M. Patrick
Chairman of the Board: Abe Pollin
VP and General Manager: George McPhee
Coach: Ron Wilson
Senior VP of Communications: Matt Williams

NATIONAL COLLEGIATE ATHLETIC ASSOCIATION (NCAA)
Address: 6201 College Boulevard
             Overland Park, KS 66211
Telephone: (913) 339-1906
President: Cedric Dempsey
Director of Public Relations: Wallace I. Renfro

ATLANTIC COAST CONFERENCE
Address: P.O. Drawer ACC
             Greensboro, NC 27417-6724
Telephone: (910) 854-8787
Commissioner: John Swofford
Director of Media Relations: Brian Morrison

Clemson University
Address: Clemson, SC 29633
Nickname: Tigers
Telephone: (864) 656-2114
Football Stadium (Capacity): Clemson Memorial
  Stadium (81,474)
Basketball Arena (Capacity): Littlejohn Coliseum (11,020)
President: Deno Curris
Athletic Director: Bobby Robinson
Football Coach: Tommy West
Basketball Coach: Larry Shyatt
Sports Information Director: Tim Bourret

Duke University
Address: Durham, NC 27708
Nickname: Blue Devils
Telephone: (919) 684-2633
Football Stadium (Capacity): Wallace Wade Stadium
  (33,941)
Basketball Arena (Capacity): Cameron Indoor
  Stadium (9,314)
President: Nan Keohane
Athletic Director: Joe Alleva
Football Coach: Fred Goldsmith
Basketball Coach: Mike Krzyzewski
Sports Information Director: Mike Cragg

Florida State University
Address: P.O. Box 2195
             Tallahassee, FL 32316
Nickname: Seminoles
Telephone: (850) 644-1403
Football Stadium (Capacity): Doak S. Campbell
  Stadium (80,000)
Basketball Arena (Capacity): Leon County Civic
  Center (12,200)
President: Sandy D'Alemberte
Athletic Director: Dave Hart
Football Coach: Bobby Bowden
Basketball Coach: Steve Robinson
Sports Information Director: Rob Wilson

Georgia Tech
Address: 150 Bobby Dodd Way
             Atlanta, GA 30332
Nickname: Yellow Jackets
Telephone: (404) 894-5445
Football Stadium (Capacity): Bobby Dodd
  Stadium at Grant Field (46,000)
Basketball Arena (Capacity): Alexander Memorial
  Coliseum at McDonald's Center (10,000)
President: G. Wayne Clough
Athletic Director: David Braine
Football Coach: George O'Leary
Basketball Coach: Bobby Cremins
Director of Communications: Mike Finn

University of Maryland
Address: P.O. Box 295
             College Park, MD 20742
Nickname: Terrapins
Telephone: (301) 314-7064
Football Stadium (Capacity): Byrd Stadium (48,055)
Basketball Arena (Capacity): Cole Fieldhouse
  (14,500)
President: Dr. C.D. Mote, Jr.
Athletic Director: Deborah A. Yow
Football Coach: Ron Vanderlinden
Basketball Coach: Gary Williams
Sports Information Director: David Haglund

University of North Carolina
Address: P.O. Box 2126
             Chapel Hill, NC 27515
Nickname: Tar Heels
Telephone: (919) 962-2123
Football Stadium (Capacity): Kenan Memorial
  Stadium (60,000)
Basketball Arena (Capacity): Dean E. Smith Center
  (21,572)
Chancellor: Dr. Michael Hooker
Athletic Director: Dick Baddour
Football Coach: Carl Torbush
Men's Basketball Coach: Bill Guthridge
Women's Basketball Coach: Sylvia Hatchell
Sports Information Director: Rick Brewer

North Carolina State University
Address: Box 8501
             Raleigh, NC 27695
Nickname: Wolfpack
Telephone: (919) 515-2102
Football Stadium (Capacity): Carter-Finley Stadium
  (51,500)
Basketball Arena (Capacity): Reynolds Coliseum
  (12,400)
Chancellor: Dr. Marye Anne Fox
Athletic Director: Les Robinson
Football Coach: Mike O'Cain
Basketball Coach: Herb Sendex
Sports Information Director: TBA

University of Virginia
Address: P.O. Box 3785
             Charlottesville, VA 22903
Nickname: Cavaliers
Telephone: (804) 982-5500
Football Stadium (Capacity): Scott Stadium (42,000)
Basketball Arena (Capacity): University Hall (8,500)
President: John Casteen III
Athletic Director: Terry Holland
Football Coach: George Welsh
Men's Basketball Coach: Pete Gillen
Women's Basketball Coach: Debbie Ryan
Sports Information Director: Rich Murray

Wake Forest University
Address: P.O. Box 7426
             Winston-Salem, NC 27109
Nickname: Demon Deacons
Telephone: (910) 759-5640
Football Stadium (Capacity): Groves Stadium (31,500)
Basketball Arena (Capacity): Lawrence Joel
  Memorial Coliseum (14,407)
President: Dr. Thomas K. Hearn Jr.
Athletic Director: Ron Wellman
Football Coach: Jim Caldwell
Basketball Coach: Dave Odom
Sports Information Director: John Justus

College Sports Directory (Cont.)

BIG EAST CONFERENCE
Address: 56 Exchange Terrace, 5th floor
            Providence, RI 02903
Telephone: (401) 272-9108
Commissioner: Michael A. Tranghese
Associate Commissioner for Public Relations: John Paquette

Boston College
Address: Chestnut Hill, MA 02467
Nickname: Eagles
Telephone: (617) 552-3004
Football Stadium (Capacity): Alumni Stadium (44,500)
Basketball Arena (Capacity): Silvio O. Conte Forum (8,606)
President: Rev. William P. Leahy, S.J.
Athletic Director: Jene DeFillippo
Football Coach: Tom O'Brien
Basketball Coach: Al Skinner
Sports Information Director: Chris Cameron

University of Connecticut
Address: 2095 Hillside Road
            Storrs, CT 06269-3078
Nickname: Huskies
Telephone: (860) 486-3531
Football Stadium (Capacity): Memorial Stadium (16,200)
Basketball Arena (Capacity): Gampel Pavilion (10,027)
President: Philip E. Austin
Athletic Director: Lew Perkins
Football Coach: Skip Holtz
Men's Basketball Coach: Jim Calhoun
Women's Basketball Coach: Geno Auriemma
Sports Information Director: Tim Tolokan
Note: Division I-AA football.

Georgetown University
Address: McDonough Arena
            Box 571124
            Washington, DC 20057-1121
Nickname: Hoyas
Telephone: (202) 687-2435
Football Stadium (Capacity): Kehoe Field (2,400)
Basketball Arena (Capacity): MCI Center (26,000)
President: Rev. Leo J. O'Donovan S.J.
Senior Athletic Director: Francis X. Rienzo
Athletic Director: Joseph Lang
Football Coach: Robert Benson
Basketball Coach: John Thompson
Sports Information Director: Bill Shapland (Men's basketball), Bill Hurd
Note: Division I-AA football.

University of Miami
Address: One Hurricane Drive
            Coral Gables, FL 33146
Nickname: Hurricanes
Telephone: (305) 284-3244
Football Stadium (Capacity): Orange Bowl (72,319)
Basketball Arena (Capacity): Miami Arena (15,508)
President: Edward T. Foote II
Athletic Director: Paul Dee
Football Coach: Butch Davis
Basketball Coach: Leonard Hamilton
Sports Information Director: Bob Burda

University of Pittsburgh
Address: Dept. of Athletics
            P.O. Box 7436
            Pittsburgh, PA 15213-0436
Nickname: Panthers
Telephone: (412) 648-8240
Football Stadium (Capacity): Pitt Stadium (56,150)
Basketball Arena (Capacity): Fitzgerald Field House (6,798), Pittsburgh Civic Arena (17,159)
Chancellor: Mark A. Nordenberg
Athletic Director: Steven Pederson
Football Coach: Walt Harris
Basketball Coach: Ralph Willard
Sports Information Director: E.J. Borghetti

Providence College
Address: River Avenue
            Providence, RI 02918
Nickname: Friars
Telephone: (401) 865-2265
Basketball Arena (Capacity): Providence Civic Center (13,410)
President: Rev. Philip A. Smith, O.P.
Assistant VP for Athletics: John Marinatto
Basketball Coach: Tim Welsh
Sports Information Director: Tim Connor
Note: No football program.

Rutgers University
Address: 83 Rockefeller Road
            P.O. Box 1149
            Piscataway, NJ 08854-8053
Nickname: Scarlet Knights
Telephone: (732) 445-4200
Football Stadium (Capacity): Rutgers Stadium (42,000)
Basketball Arena (Capacity): Louis Brown Athletic Center (8,500)
President: Dr. Francis L. Lawrence
Athletic Director: Bob Mulcahy III
Football Coach: Terry Shea
Basketball Coach: Kevin Bannon
Sports Information Director: John Wooding

St. John's University
Address: 8000 Utopia Parkway
            Jamaica, NY 11439
Nickname: Red Storm
Telephone: (718) 990-6367
Football Stadium (Capacity): St. John's Stadium (3,000)
Basketball Arena (Capacity): Alumni Hall (6,008), Madison Square Garden (19,876)
President: Rev. Donald J. Harrington, C.M.
Athletic Director: Edward J. Manetta Jr.
Football Coach: Bob Ricca
Basketball Coach: Mike Jarvis
Sports Information Director: Dominic Scianna
Note: Division I-AA football.

Seton Hall University
Address: 400 South Orange Avenue
            South Orange, NJ 07079
Nickname: Pirates
Telephone: (973) 761-9497
Basketball Arena (Capacity): Walsh Auditorium (3,200), The Meadowlands (20,029)
President: Monsignor Robert T. Sheeran
Athletic Director: Jeff Fogelson
Basketball Coach: Tommy Amaker
Sports Information Director: TBA
Note: No football program.

Syracuse University

Address: Manley Field House
           Syracuse, NY 13244-5020
Nickname: Orangemen
Telephone: (315) 443-2608
Football Stadium (Capacity): Carrier Dome (49,550)
Basketball Arena (Capacity): Carrier Dome (33,000)
Chancellor: Dr. Kenneth Shaw
Athletic Director: Jake Crouthamel
Football Coach: Paul Pasqualoni
Basketball Coach: Jim Boeheim
Sports Information Director: Sue Cornelius Edson

Temple University

Address: Vivacqua Hall, 4th Floor
           1700 North Broad Street
           Philadelphia, PA 19121-0842
Nickname: Owls
Telephone: (215) 204-7445
Football Stadium (Capacity): Veterans Stadium (66,592)
Basketball Arena (Capacity): Apollo of Temple (10,224)
President: Peter J. Liacouras
Athletic Director: Dave O'Brien
Football Coach: Bobby Wallace
Basketball Coach: John Chaney
Sports Information Director: Brian Kirschner
Note: Plays football in Big East, basketball in Atlantic 10 Conference.

Villanova University

Address: 800 Lancaster Avenue
           Villanova, PA 19085
Nickname: Wildcats
Telephone: (610) 519-4110
Football Stadium (Capacity): Villanova Stadium (12,000)
Basketball Arena (Capacity): The Pavilion (6,500),
  CoreStates Spectrum (18,060), CoreStates Center
  (20,000)
President: Rev. Edmund Dobbin, O.S.A.
Athletic Director: Tim Hofferth
Football Coach: Andy Talley
Basketball Coach: Steve Lappas
Sports Information Director: Dean Kenefick
Note: Division I-AA football.

Virginia Tech

Address: Jamerson Athletic Center
           Blacksburg, VA 24061
Nickname: Hokies
Telephone: (540) 231-6726
Football Stadium (Capacity): Lane Stadium/Worsham
  Field (50,000)
Basketball Arena (Capacity): Cassell Coliseum (9,971)
President: Dr. Paul Torgersen
Athletic Director: Jim Weaver
Football Coach: Frank Beamer
Basketball Coach: Bobby Hussey
Sports Information Director: Dave Smith
Note: Plays football in Big East, basketball in Atlantic 10.

West Virginia University

Address: P.O. Box 0877
           Morgantown, WV 26507-0877
Nickname: Mountaineers
Telephone: (304) 293-2821
Football Stadium (Capacity): Mountaineer Field (63,500)
Basketball Arena (Capacity): WVU Coliseum (14,000)
President: David Hardesty
Athletic Director: Ed Pastilong
Football Coach: Don Nehlen
Basketball Coach: Gale Catlett
Sports Information Director: Shelley Poe

BIG TEN CONFERENCE

Address: 1500 West Higgins Road
           Park Ridge, IL 60068
Telephone: (847) 696-1010
Commissioner: James E. Delany
Assistant Commissioner: Mark Rudner

University of Illinois

Address: 1700 S 4th Street
           Champaign, IL 61820
Nickname: Fighting Illini
Telephone: (217) 333-1390
Football Stadium (Capacity): Memorial Stadium (70,904)
Basketball Arena (Capacity): Assembly Hall (16,450)
President: James Stukel
Athletic Director: Ronald Guenther
Football Coach: Ron Turner
Men's Basketball Coach: Lon Kruger
Women's Basketball Coach: Theresa Grentz
Sports Information Director: Dave Johnson

Indiana University

Address: Assembly Hall
           1001 E. 17th Street
           Bloomington, IN 47408-1590
Nickname: Hoosiers
Telephone: (812) 855-2421
Football Stadium (Capacity): Memorial
  Stadium (52,354)
Basketball Arena (Capacity): Assembly Hall (17,357)
President: Myles Brand
Athletic Director: Clarence Doninger
Football Coach: Cam Cameron
Basketball Coach: Bob Knight
Sports Information Director: Kit Klingelhoffer

University of Iowa

Address: 157 Carver-Hawkeye Arena
           Iowa City, IA 52242
Nickname: Hawkeyes
Telephone: (319) 335-9411
Football Stadium (Capacity): Kinnick Stadium (70,397)
Basketball Arena (Capacity): Carver-Hawkeye
  Arena (15,500)
President: Mary Sue Coleman
Athletic Director: Robert Bowlsby
Football Coach: Hayden Fry
Men's Basketball Coach: Tom Davis
Women's Basketball Coach: Angie Lee
Sports Information Director: Phil Haddy (Men's),
  Derick Hackett (Women's)

University of Michigan

Address: 1000 S. State Street
           Ann Arbor, MI 48109
Nickname: Wolverines
Telephone: (313) 763-4423
Football Stadium (Capacity): Michigan
  Stadium (102,501)
Basketball Arena (Capacity): Crisler Arena (13,562)
President: Tom Goss
Athletic Director: Dr. Joseph Roberson
Football Coach: Lloyd Carr
Basketball Coach: Brian Ellerbe
Sports Information Director: Bruce Madej

Michigan State University

Address: 401 Olds Hall
East Lansing, MI 48824
Nickname: Spartans
Telephone: (517) 355-2271
Football Stadium (Capacity): Spartan Stadium (72,027)
Basketball Arena (Capacity): Jack Breslin Student
Events Center (15,138)
President: M. Peter McPherson
Athletic Director: Merritt J. Norvell Jr., Ph.D.
Football Coach: Nick Saban
Basketball Coach: Tom Izzo
Sports Information Director: John Lewandowski

University of Minnesota

Address: 208 Bierman Athletic Building
Minneapolis, MN 55455
Nickname: Golden Gophers
Telephone: (612) 625-4090
Football Stadium (Capacity): Hubert H. Humphrey
Metrodome (63,669)
Basketball Arena (Capacity): Williams Arena (14,625)
President: Mark Yudof
Athletic Director: Dr. Mark Dienhart
Football Coach: Len Mason
Basketball Coach: Clem Haskins
Sports Information Director: Marc Ryan

Northwestern University

Address: 1501 Central Street
Evanston, IL 60208
Nickname: Wildcats
Telephone: (847) 491-3205
Football Stadium (Capacity): Ryan Field (49,256)
Basketball Arena (Capacity): Welsh-Ryan Arena (8,117)
President: Henry S. Bienen
Athletic Director: Rick Taylor
Football Coach: Gary Barnett
Basketball Coach: Kevin O'Neill
Director of Media Services: Brad Hurlbut

Ohio State University

Address: 410 Woody Hayes Drive
St. John Arena, Room 124
Columbus, OH 43210
Nickname: Buckeyes
Telephone: (614) 292-6861
Football Stadium (Capacity): Ohio Stadium (91,470)
Basketball Arena (Capacity): Jerome Schottein
Center (19,000)
President: William Kirwin
Athletic Director: Andy Geiger
Football Coach: John Cooper
Basketball Coach: Jim O'Brian
Sports Information Director: Gerry Emig

Penn State University

Address: 101 D Bryce Jordan Center
University Park, PA 16802
Nickname: Nittany Lions
Telephone: (814) 865-1757
Football Stadium (Capacity): Beaver Stadium (93,967)
Basketball Arena (Capacity): Bryce Jordan Center
(15,000)
President: Dr. Graham Spanier
Athletic Director: Tim Curley
Football Coach: Joe Paterno
Men's Basketball Coach: Jerry Dunn
Women's Basketball Coach: Rene Portland
Sports Information Director: Jeff Nelson

Purdue University

Address: Mackey Arena, Room 15
West Lafayette, IN 47907
Nickname: Boilermakers
Telephone: (765) 494-3200
Football Stadium (Capacity): Ross-Ade Stadium
(67,861)
Basketball Arena (Capacity): Mackey Arena (14,123)
President: Dr. Steven C. Beering
Athletic Director: Morgan Burke
Football Coach: Joe Tiller
Basketball Coach: Gene Keady
Sports Information Director: Jim Vruggink

University of Wisconsin

Address: 1440 Monroe Street
Madison, WI 53711
Nickname: Badgers
Telephone: (608) 262-1811
Football Stadium (Capacity): Camp Randall
Stadium (76,129)
Basketball Arena (Capacity): Kohl Center (16,500)
Chancellor: David Ward
Athletic Director: Pat Richter
Football Coach: Barry Alvarez
Basketball Coach: Dick Bennett
Sports Information Director: Steve Malchow

BIG TWELVE CONFERENCE

Address: 2201 Stemmons Freeway, 28th floor
Dallas, TX 75207-2805
Telephone: (214) 742-1212
Interim Commissioner: Dave Martin
Director of Media Relations: Bo Carter

Baylor University

Address: 150 Bear Run
Waco, TX 76711
Nickname: Bears
Telephone: (254) 710-2743
Football Stadium (Capacity): Floyd Casey
Stadium (50,000)
Basketball Arena (Capacity): Ferrell Center (10,078)
President: Robert Sloan
Athletic Director: Tom Stanton
Football Coach: Dave Roberts
Basketball Coach: Harry Miller
Sports Information Directors: Brian McCallum, Julie
Bennett and Jason Archinal

University of Colorado

Address: Campus Box 357
Boulder, CO 80309
Nickname: Buffaloes
Telephone: (303) 492-5626
Football Stadium (Capacity): Folsom Field (51,808)
Basketball Arena (Capacity): Coors Event
Center (11,198)
President: John Buechner
Athletic Director: Dick Tharpe
Football Coach: Rick Neuheisel
Men's Basketball Coach: Ricardo Patton
Women's Basketball Coach: Ceal Barry
Sports Information Director: David Plati

Iowa State University
Address: 1800 S. Fourth Street
Jacobson Building
Ames, IA 50011
Nickname: Cyclones
Telephone: (515) 294-3372
Football Stadium (Capacity): Cyclone Stadium-Jack Trice Field (43,000)
Basketball Arena (Capacity): Jack Trice Stadium (14,020)
President: Dr. Martin C. Jischke
Athletic Director: Gene Smith
Football Coach: Dan McCarney
Basketball Coach: Larry Eustachy
Sports Information Director: Tom Kroeschell

University of Kansas
Address: Allen Field House, Room 104
Lawrence, KS 66045
Nickname: Jayhawks
Telephone: (913) 864-3417
Football Stadium (Capacity): Memorial Stadium (50,250)
Basketball Arena (Capacity): Allen Field House (16,300)
Chancellor: Robert Hemenway
Athletic Director: Dr. Bob Fredrick
Football Coach: Terry Allen
Men's Basketball Coach: Roy Williams
Women's Basketball Coach: Marian Washington
Sports Information Director: Doug Vance

Kansas State University
Address: 1800 College Ave., Suite 144
Manhattan, KS 66502
Nickname: Wildcats
Telephone: (913) 532-6735
Football Stadium (Capacity): KSU Stadium-Wagner Field (42,000)
Basketball Arena (Capacity): Bramlage Coliseum (13,500)
President: Dr. Jon Wefald
Athletic Director: Max Urick
Football Coach: Bill Snyder
Basketball Coach: Tom Asbury
Sports Information Director: Kent Brown

University of Missouri
Address: P.O. Box 677
Columbia, MO 65205
Nickname: Tigers
Telephone: (573) 882-3241
Football Stadium (Capacity): Faurot Field/Memorial Stadium (62,000)
Basketball Arena (Capacity): Hearnes Center (13,300)
Chancellor: Dr. Richard Wallace
Athletic Director: Michael F. Alden
Football Coach: Larry Smith
Basketball Coach: Norm Stewart
Sports Information Director: Bob Brendel

University of Nebraska
Address: 116 South Stadium
Lincoln, NE 68588
Nickname: Cornhuskers
Telephone: (402) 472-2263
Football Stadium (Capacity): Memorial Stadium (72,700)
Basketball Arena (Capacity): Bob Devaney Sports Center (14,302)
President: L. Dennis Smith
Athletic Director: Bill Byrne
Football Coach: Frank Solich
Basketball Coach: Danny Nee
Sports Information Director: Chris Anderson

University of Oklahoma
Address: 180 W. Brooks, Room 235
Norman, OK 73019
Nickname: Sooners
Telephone: (405) 325-8231
Football Stadium (Capacity): Memorial Stadium/Owen Field (75,004)
Basketball Arena (Capacity): Lloyd Noble Center (11,100)
President: David Boren
Athletic Director: Joe Castiglione
Football Coach: John Blake
Basketball Coach: Kelvin Sampson
Sports Information Director: Mike Prusinski

Oklahoma State University
Address: 202 Gallagher-Iba Arena
Stillwater, OK 74078
Nickname: Cowboys
Telephone: (405) 744-5749
Football Stadium (Capacity): Lewis Field (50,614)
Basketball Arena (Capacity): Gallagher-Iba Arena (6,381)
President: Dr. James Halligan
Athletic Director: Terry Don Phillips
Football Coach: Bob Simmons
Basketball Coach: Eddie Sutton
Sports Information Director: Steve Buzzard

University of Texas
Address: P.O. Box 7399
Austin, TX 78713
Nickname: Longhorns
Telephone: (512) 471-7437
Football Stadium (Capacity): Darrell K. Royal/Texas Memorial Stadium (80,216)
Basketball Arena (Capacity): Erwin Special Events Center (16,231)
Chancellor: Dr. William Cunningham
Athletic Director: DeLoss Dodds
Football Coach: Mack Brown
Basketball Coach: Rick Barnes
Sports Information Director: John Bianco

Texas A&M University
Address: John Koldus Building, Room 222
College Station, TX 77843-1228
Nickname: Aggies
Telephone: (409) 845-3218
Football Stadium (Capacity): Kyle Field (58,000)
Basketball Arena (Capacity): Reed Arena (12,500)
President: Dr. Ray Bowen
Athletic Director: Wally Groff
Football Coach: R.C. Slocum
Basketball Coach: Melvin Watkins
Sports Information Director: Alan Cannon

Texas Tech University

Address: Box 43021
Lubbock, TX 79409
Nickname: Red Raiders
Telephone: (806) 742-2770
Football Stadium (Capacity): Jones Stadium (50,500)
Basketball Arena (Capacity): Lubbock Municipal
Coliseum (8,174)
President: Donald Harragan
Athletic Director: Gerald Myers
Football Coach: Spike Dykes
Men's Basketball Coach: James Dickey
Women's Basketball Coach: Marsha Sharp
Sports Information Director: Richard Kilwien

BIG WEST CONFERENCE

Address: 2 Corporate Park, Suite 206
Irvine, CA 92606
Telephone: (714) 261-2525
Commissioner: Dennis Farrell
Publicity Director: Mike Daniels

Boise State University

Address: 1910 University Drive
Boise, ID 83725
Nickname: Broncos
Telephone: (208) 385-1981
Football Stadium (Capacity) Lyle Smith Field (30,000)
Basketball Arena (Capacity): BSU Pavilion (13,000)
President: Dr. Charles Ruch
Athletic Director: Gene Bleymaier
Football Coach: Dirk Coetter
Basketball Coach: Rod Jensen
Sports Information Director: Max Corbet

Cal Poly San Luis Obispo

Address: One Grand Avenue
San Luis Obispo, CA 93407
Nickname: Mustangs
Telephone: (805) 756-2923
Football Stadium (Capacity): Mustang Stadium (8,500)
Basketball Arena (Capacity): Mott Gym (3,500)
President: Dr. Warren J. Baker
Athletic Director: John McCutcheon
Football Coach: Larry Welsh
Basketball Coach: Jeff Schneider
Sports Information Director: Jason Sullivan

University of California–Irvine

Address: Intercollegiate Athletics, Crawford Hall
Irvine, CA 92697
Nickname: Anteaters
Telephone: (714) 824-5814
Basketball Arena (Capacity): Bren Event Center (5,000)
Chancellor: Ralph Cicerone
Athletic Director: Dan Guerrero
Basketball Coach: Pat Douglass
Sports Information Director: Bob Olson
Note: No football program.

University of California–Santa Barbara

Address: Department of Athletics
1000 Robertson Gymnasium
Santa Barbara, CA 93106-7211
Nickname: Gauchos
Telephone: (805) 893-3428
Basketball Arena (Capacity): Thunderdome (6,000)
Chancellor: Henry Yang
Athletic Director: Gary Cunningham
Basketball Coach: Bob Williams
Sports Information Director: Bill Mahoney
Note: No football program.

California State University–Fullerton

Address: 800 North State College Boulevard
P.O. Box 6810
Fullerton, CA 92834-6810
Nickname: Titans
Telephone: (714) 278-3970
Basketball Arena (Capacity): Titan Gym (3,500)
President: Dr. Milton A. Gordon
Athletic Director: John Easterbrook
Basketball Coach: Bob Hawking
Sports Information Director: Mel Franks
Note: No football program.

University of Idaho

Address: Kibbie Activities Center
Moscow, ID 83844-2302
Nickname: Vandals
Telephone: (208) 885-0211
Football Stadium (Capacity): Kibbie Dome (16,000)
Basketball Arena (Capacity): Kibbie Dome (10,000)
President: Dr. Robert Hoover
Athletic Director: Mike Bohn
Football Coach: Chris Tormey
Basketball Coach: David Farrar
Sports Information Director: Becky Paull

Long Beach State University

Address: 1250 Bellflower Boulevard
Long Beach, CA 90840
Nickname: 49ers
Telephone: (562) 985-8569
Basketball Arena (Capacity): The Pyramid (5,000)
President: Dr. Robert C. Maxson
Athletic Director: Bill Shumard
Basketball Coach: Wayne Morgan
Sports Information Director: Steve Janisch
Note: No football program.

University of Nevada–Reno

Address: Lawlor Annex, MS232
Athletic Department Room 232
Reno, NV 89557-0110
Nickname: Wolf Pack
Telephone: (702) 784-4600
Football Stadium (Capacity): Mackay Stadium
(31,545)
Basketball Arena (Capacity): Lawlor Event Center
(11,200)
President: Joe Crowley
Athletic Director: Chris Ault
Football Coach: Jeff Tisdel
Basketball Coach: Pat Foster
Sports Information Director: Paul Stuart

New Mexico State University

Address: Department of Athletics, MSC 3145
P.O. Box 30001
Las Cruces, NM 88003
Nickname: Aggies
Telephone: (505) 646-4126
Football Stadium (Capacity): Aggie Memorial
Stadium (30,343)
Basketball Arena (Capacity): Pan American
Center (13,071)
President: Dr. William Conroy
Athletic Director: Jim Paul
Football Coach: Tony Samuel
Basketball Coach: Lou Henson
Sports Information Director: TBA

University of North Texas
Address: P.O. Box 311397
              Denton, TX 76203-1397
Nickname: Eagles, Mean Green
Telephone: (940) 565-2664
Football Stadium (Capacity): Fouts Field (30,500)
Basketball Arena (Capacity): Super Pit (10,032)
President: Dr. Alfred F. Hurley
Athletic Director: Craig Helwig
Football Coach: Darrell Dickey
Basketball Coach: Vic Trilly
Sports Information Director: Sean Johnson

University of the Pacific
Address: 3601 Pacific Avenue
              Stockton, CA 95211
Nickname: Tigers
Telephone: (209) 946-2472
Football Stadium (Capacity): Amos Alonzo Stagg
  Memorial Stadium (30,000)
Basketball Arena (Capacity): Alex G. Spanos
  Center (6,150)
President: Dr. Donald DeRosa
Athletic Director: Michael McNeely
Basketball Coach: Bob Thomason
Sports Information Director: Mike Millerick
Note: No football program.

Utah State University
Address: 7400 Old Main Hill
              Logan, UT 84322-7400
Nickname: Aggies
Telephone: (801) 797-1850
Football Stadium (Capacity): Romney Stadium
  (30,000)
Basketball Arena (Capacity): The Smith
  Spectrum (11,000)
President: Dr. George H. Emert
Athletic Director: Bruce Vand De Velde
Football Coach: Dave Arslanian
Basketball Coach: Stew Morrill
Sports Information Director: Mike Strauss

CONFERENCE USA
Address: 35 East Wacker Drive, Suite 650
              Chicago, IL 60601
Telephone: (312) 553-0483
Comissioner: Michael Slive
Media Relations Director: Brian Teter

University of Alabama-Birmingham
Address: Bartow Arena
              617 13th Street South
              Birmingham, AL 35294
Nickname: Blazers
Telephone: (205) 934-7252
Football Stadium (Capacity): Legion Field (83,091)
Basketball Arena (Capacity): Bartow Arena (8,500)
President: Dr. Ann Reynolds
Athletic Director: Gene Bartow
Football Coach: Watson Brown
Basketball Coach: Murray Bartow
Sports Information Director: Grant Shingleton

University of Cincinnati
Address: 309 Lawrence Hall
              Cincinnati, OH 45221-0021
Nickname: Bearcats
Telephone: (513) 556-5191
Football Stadium (Capacity): Nippert Stadium (35,000)
Basketball Arena (Capacity): Myrl Shoemaker
  Center (13,176)
President: Dr. Joseph A. Steger
Athletic Director: Bob Goin
Football Coach: Rick Minter
Basketball Coach: Bob Huggins
Sports Information Director: Tom Hathaway

DePaul University
Address: 1011 West Belden Avenue
              Chicago, IL 60614
Nickname: Blue Demons
Telephone: (773) 325-7526
Basketball Arena (Capacity): Rosemont
  Horizon (17,500)
President: Rev. John P. Minogue, C.M.
Athletic Director: Bill Bradshaw
Basketball Coach: Pat Kennedy
Sports Information Director: John Lanctot
Note: No football program.

University of Houston
Address: 3100 Cullen Boulevard
              Houston, TX 77204
Nickname: Cougars
Telephone: (713) 743-9370
Football Stadium (Capacity): Astrodome (65,000)
Basketball Arena (Capacity): Robertson Stadium
  (20,000), Hofheinz Pavilion (8,479)
Chancellor and President: Dr. Arthur Smith
Athletic Director: Chet Gladchuk
Football Coach: Kim Helton
Basketball Coach: Clyde Drexler
Sports Information Director: Donna Turner

University of Louisville
Address: Louisville, KY 40292
Nickname: Cardinals
Telephone: (502) 852-5732
Football Stadium (Capacity): Papa John's Cardinal
  Stadium (42,000)
Basketball Arena (Capacity): Freedom Hall (19,000)
President: Dr. John Schumaker
Athletic Director: Tom Jurich
Football Coach: John L. Smith
Basketball Coach: Denny Crum
Sports Information Director: Kenny Klein

Marquette University
Address: P.O. Box 1881
              Milwaukee, WI 53201-1881
Nickname: Golden Eagles
Telephone: (414) 288-7447
Basketball Arena (Capacity): Bradley Center (19,150)
President: Rev. Robert W. Wild, S.J.
Athletic Director: Bill Cords
Basketball Coach: Mike Deane
Sports Information Director: Kathleen Hohl
Note: No football program.

University of Memphis

Address: 570 Normal, Room 205
             Memphis, TN 38152
Nickname: Tigers
Telephone: (901) 678-2337
Football Stadium (Capacity): Liberty Bowl Memorial
  Stadium/Rex Dockery Field (62,380)
Basketball Arena (Capacity): The Pyramid (20,142)
President: Dr. V. Lane Rawlins
Athletic Director: R.C. Johnson
Football Coach: Rip Scherer
Basketball Coach: Tic Price
Sports Information Director: Bob Winn

University of North Carolina–Charlotte

Address: 9201 University City Boulevard
             UNC-Charlotte
             Student Activity Center
             Charlotte, NC 28223-0001
Nickname: 49ers
Telephone: (704) 547-4937
Basketball Arena (Capacity): Dale F. Halton
  Arena (9,100)
Chancellor: James H. Woodward
Athletic Director: Judy W. Rose
Basketball Coach: Bobby Lute
Sports Information Director: Tom Whitestone
Note: No football program.

Saint Louis University

Address: 221 North Grand Boulevard, Room 38
             St. Louis, MO 63103-2097
Nickname: Billikens
Telephone: (314) 977-3462
Basketball Arena (Capacity): Kiel Center (20,000)
President: Fr. Lawrence Biondi, S.J.
Athletic Director: Doug Woolard
Basketball Coach: Charlie Spoonhour
Sports Information Director: Doug McIlhagga
Note: No football program.

University of South Florida

Address: 4202 East Fowler Ave., PED 214
             Tampa, FL 33620
Nickname: Bulls
Telephone: (813) 974-2125
Football Stadium (Capacity): Tampa Stadium
  (46,500)
Basketball Arena (Capacity): Sun Dome (10,411)
President: Betty Castor
Athletic Director: Paul Griffin
Football Coach: Jim Leavitt
Basketball Coach: Seth Greenberg
Sports Information Director: John Gerdes
Note: The football program began with the 1997 season.

University of Southern Mississippi

Address: P.O. Box 5161
             Hattiesburg, MS 39406
Nickname: Golden Eagles
Telephone: (601) 266-4503
Football Stadium (Capacity): M.M. Roberts
  Stadium (33,000)
Basketball Arena (Capacity): Reed Green
  Coliseum (8,095)
President: Dr. Horace Fleming
Athletic Director: H.C. Bill McLellan
Football Coach: Jeff Bower
Basketball Coach: James Green
Sports Information Director: Regiel Napier

Tulane University

Address: James Wilson Jr. Center for
             Intercollegiate Athletics
             New Orleans, LA 70118
Nickname: Green Wave
Telephone: (504) 865-5501
Football Stadium (Capacity): Louisiana Superdome
  (69,767)
Basketball Arena (Capacity): Fogelman Arena (3,600)
President: Scott Cowen
Athletic Director: Sandy Barbour
Football Coach: Tommy Bowden
Basketball Coach: Perry Clark
Sports Information Director: Scott Stricklin

IVY LEAGUE

Address: 330 Alexander Street, Princeton, NJ 08544
Telephone: (609) 258-6426
Executive Director: Jeff Orleans
Publicity Director: Chuck Yrigoyen

Brown University

Address: 235 Hope Street, Providence, RI 02912
Nickname: Bears
Telephone: (401) 863-2211
Football Stadium (Capacity): Brown Stadium (20,000)
Basketball Arena (Capacity): Paul Bailey Pizzitola
  Memorial Sports Center (3,100)
President: E. Gordon Gee
Athletic Director: David Roach
Football Coach: Phil Estes
Basketball Coach: Franklin Dobbs
Sports Information Director: Christopher Humm

Columbia University

Address: Dodge Physical Fitness Center
             New York, NY 10027
Nickname: Lions
Telephone: (212) 854-2534
Football Stadium (Capacity): Lawrence A. Wien
  Stadium at Baker Field (17,000)
Basketball Arena (Capacity): Levien Gymnasium (3,400)
President: Dr. George Rupp
Athletic Director: Dr. John Reeves
Football Coach: Ray Tellier
Basketball Coach: Armond Hill
Director of Athletic Communications: Brian Bodine

Cornell University

Address: Teagle Hall, Campus Road
             Ithaca, NY 14853-6701
Nickname: Big Red
Telephone: (607) 255-5220
Football Stadium (Capacity): Schoellkopf Field (25,597)
Basketball Arena (Capacity): Newman Arena (4,473)
President: Hunter R. Rawlings III
Athletic Director: Charles Moore
Football Coach: Pete Mangurian
Basketball Coach: Scott Thompson
Sports Information Director: Patrick Gillespie

Dartmouth College

Address: 6083 Alumni Gym
             Hanover, NH 03755-3512
Nickname: Big Green
Telephone: (603) 646-2465
Football Stadium (Capacity): Memorial Field (20,416)
Basketball Arena (Capacity): Leede Arena (2,100)
President: James Wright
Athletic Director: Richard G. Jaeger
Football Coach: John Lyons
Basketball Coach: Dave Faucher
Sports Information Director: Kathy Slattery

Harvard University

Address: 65 North Harvard St.
            Murr Center
            Boston, MA 02163
Nickname: Crimson
Telephone: (617) 495-2206
Football Stadium (Capacity): Harvard Stadium (30,898)
Basketball Arena (Capacity): Lavietes Pavilion (2,198)
President: Neil L. Rudenstine
Athletic Director: William J. Cleary Jr.
Football Coach: Tim Murphy
Basketball Coach: Frank Sullivan
Sports Information Director: John Veneziano

University of Pennsylvania

Address: Weightman Hall South
            235 South 33rd Street
            Philadelphia, PA 19104-6322
Nickname: Quakers
Telephone: (215) 898-6128
Football Stadium (Capacity): Franklin Field (52,593)
Basketball Arena (Capacity): The Palestra (8,700)
President: Dr. Judith Rodin
Athletic Director: Steven Bilsky
Football Coach: Al Bagnoli
Basketball Coach: Fran Dunphy
Director, Athletic Communications: Shaun May

Princeton University

Address: P.O. Box 71
            Jadwin Gym
            Princeton, NJ 08544
Nickname: Tigers
Telephone: (609) 258-3568
Football Stadium (Capacity): Princeton Stadium (30,000),
Basketball Arena (Capacity): Jadwin Gym (7,230)
President: Harold Shapiro
Athletic Director: Gary D. Walters
Football Coach: Steve Tosches
Basketball Coach: Bill Carmody
Sports Information Director: Jerry Price

Yale University

Address: Box 208216
            New Haven, CT 06520
Nickname: Bulldogs, Elis
Telephone: (203) 432-1456
Football Stadium (Capacity): Yale Bowl (64,269)
Basketball Arena (Capacity): John J. Lee Amphitheater (3,100)
President: Richard C. Levin
Athletic Director: Tom Beckett
Football Coach: Jack Siedlecki
Basketball Coach: Dick Kuchen
Sports Information Director: Steve Conn

MID-AMERICAN CONFERENCE

Address: Four Seagate, Suite 102
            Toledo, OH 43604
Telephone: (419) 249-7177
Commissioner: Jerry Ippoliti
Director of Communications: Gary Richter

Ball State University

Address: 2000 University Avenue
            Muncie, IN 47306
Nickname: Cardinals
Telephone: (765) 285-8225
Football Stadium (Capacity): Ball State University Stadium (21,581)
Basketball Arena (Capacity): University Arena (11,500)
President: Dr. John E. Worthen
Athletic Director: Andrea Seger
Football Coach: Bill Lynch
Basketball Coach: Ray McCallum
Athletic Communications Director: Joe Hernandez

Bowling Green University

Address: Perry Stadium East
            Bowling Green, OH 43403
Nickname: Falcons
Telephone: (419) 372-2401
Football Stadium (Capacity): Doyt L. Perry Stadium (30,599)
Basketball Arena (Capacity): Anderson Arena (5,000)
President: Dr. Sidney A. Ribeau
Athletic Director: Ron Zwierlein
Football Coach: Gary Blackney
Basketball Coach: Dan Dakich
Sports Information Director: Steve Barr

Central Michigan University

Address: West Hall
            Mount Pleasant, MI 48859
Nickname: Chippewas
Telephone: (517) 774-3277
Football Stadium (Capacity): Kelly/Shorts Stadium (30,086)
Basketball Arena (Capacity): Rose Arena (5,200)
President: Leonard Plachta
Athletic Director: Herb Deromedi
Football Coach: Dick Flynn
Basketball Coach: Jay Smith
Sports Information Director: Fred Stabley, Jr.

Eastern Michigan University

Address: 371 Convocation Center
            Ypsilanti, MI 48197
Nickname: Eagles
Telephone: (313) 487-0317
Football Stadium (Capacity): Rynearson Stadium (30,200)
Basketball Arena (Capacity): Convocation Center (8,857)
President: Dr. William Shelton
Interim Athletic Director: Carol Houston
Football Coach: Rick Rasnick
Basketball Coach: Milton Barnes
Sports Information Director: Jim Streeter

Kent State University

Address: P.O. Box 5190
            Kent, OH 44242
Nickname: Golden Flashes
Telephone: (330) 672-2110
Football Stadium (Capacity): Dix Stadium (30,520)
Basketball Arena (Capacity): Memorial Athletic and Convocation Center (6,327)
President: Dr. Carol A. Cartwright
Athletic Director: Laing Kennedy
Football Coach: Dan Pees
Basketball Coach: Gary Waters
Sports Information Director: Dale Gallagher

College Sports Directory (Cont.)

Miami University
Address: Millett Hall
             Oxford, OH 45056
Nickname: Red Hawks
Telephone: (513) 529-3113
Football Stadium (Capacity): Yager Stadium (30,012)
Basketball Arena (Capacity): Millett Hall (9,200)
President: Dr. James Garland
Athletic Director: Joel Maturi
Football Coach: Randy Walker
Basketball Coach: Charlie Coles
Sports Information Director: Mike Wolf

Ohio University
Address: P.O. Box 689
             Convocation Center
             Athens, OH 45701-2979
Nickname: Bobcats
Telephone: (740) 593-1174
Football Stadium (Capacity): Don Peden
  Stadium (20,000)
Basketball Arena (Capacity): Convocation
  Center (13,000)
President: Dr. Robert Glidden
Athletic Director: Thomas Boeh
Football Coach: Jim Grobe
Basketball Coach: Larry Hunter
Director of Sports Media Services: George Mauzy

University of Toledo
Address: 2801 W. Bancroft St.
             Toledo, OH 43606
Nickname: Rockets
Telephone: (419) 530-3790
Football Stadium (Capacity): Glass Bowl (26,248)
Basketball Arena (Capacity): Savage Hall (9,000)
President: Dr. Frank E. Horton
Athletic Director: Pete Liske
Football Coach: Gary Pinkel
Basketball Coach: Stan Joplin
Sports Information Director: Paul Helgren

Western Michigan University
Address: Kalamazoo, MI 49008
Nickname: Broncos
Telephone: (616) 387-4138
Football Stadium (Capacity): Waldo Stadium (30,200)
Basketball Arena (Capacity): University Arena (5,800)
President: Dr. Elson Floyd
Athletic Director: Kathy Beauregard
Football Coach: Gary Darnell
Basketball Coach: Bob Donewald
Sports Information Director: John Beatty

PACIFIC-10 CONFERENCE
Address: 800 S. Broadway, Suite 400
             Walnut Creek, CA 94596
Telephone: (510) 932-4411
Commissioner: Thomas C. Hansen
Publicity Director: Jim Muldoon

University of Arizona
Address: 106 McHale Center
             Tuscon, AZ 85721
Nickname: Wildcats
Telephone: (520) 621-4163
Football Stadium (Capacity): Arizona Stadium (57,803)
Basketball Arena (Capacity): McHale Center (14,489)
President: Dr. Peter Likins
Athletic Director: Jim Livengood
Football Coach: Dick Tomey
Basketball Coach: Lute Olson
Sports Information Director: Tom Duddleston

Arizona State University
Address: ICA Building, Room 105
             Tempe, AZ 85287-2505
Nickname: Sun Devils
Telephone: (602) 965-6592
Football Stadium (Capacity): Sun Devil Stadium (73,656)
Basketball Arena (Capacity): Wells Fargo Arena
  (14,198)
President: Lattie Coor
Athletic Director: Dr. Kevin White
Football Coach: Bruce Snyder
Basketball Coach: Rob Evans
Sports Information Director: Mark Brand

University of California at Berkeley
Address: 210 Memorial Stadium
             Berkeley, CA 94720
Nickname: Golden Bears
Telephone: (510) 642-5363
Football Stadium (Capacity): Memorial Stadium (75,028)
Basketball Arena (Capacity): The New Arena in
  Oakland (19,200)
Chancellor: Robert Berdahl
Athletic Director: John Kasser
Football Coach: Tom Holmoe
Basketball Coach: Ben Braun
Sports Information Director: Kevin Reneau

University of California at Los Angeles
Address: P.O. Box 24044
             Los Angeles, CA 90024-0044
Nickname: Bruins
Telephone: (310) 206-6831
Football Stadium (Capacity): Rose Bowl (102,083)
Basketball Arena (Capacity): Pauley Pavilion (12,819)
Chancellor: Albert Carnesale
Athletic Director: Peter T. Dalis
Football Coach: Bob Toledo
Basketball Coach: Steve Lavin
Sports Information Director: Marc Dellins

University of Oregon
Address: Len Casanova Athletic Center
             2727 Leo Harris Parkway
             Eugene, OR 97401
Nickname: Ducks
Telephone: (541) 346-5488
Football Stadium (Capacity): Autzen Stadium (41,698)
Basketball Arena (Capacity): McArthur Court (9,738)
President: David Frohnmayer
Athletic Director: Bill Moos
Football Coach: Mike Bellotti
Basketball Coach: Ernie Kent
Director of Media Services: David Williford

Oregon State University
Address: Gill Coliseum
             Corvallis, OR 97331
Nickname: Beavers
Telephone: (541) 737-3720
Football Stadium (Capacity): Parker Stadium (35,362)
Basketball Arena (Capacity): Gill Coliseum (10,400)
President: Dr. Paul Risser
Athletic Director: Mitch Barnhart
Football Coach: Mike Riley
Basketball Coach: Eddie Payne
Sports Information Director: Hal Cowan

College Sports Directory *(Cont.)*

University of Southern California
Address: Los Angeles, CA 90089-0602
Nickname: Trojans
Telephone: (213) 740-8480
Football Stadium (Capacity): Los Angeles Memorial Coliseum (92,000)
Basketball Arena (Capacity): Los Angeles Sports Arena (15,509)
President: Dr. Steven Sample
Athletic Director: Mike Garrett
Football Coach: Paul Hackett
Basketball Coach: Henry Bibby
Sports Information Director: Tim Tessalone

Stanford University
Address: Arrillaga Family Sports Center Stanford, CA 94305
Nickname: Cardinal
Telephone: (650) 723-4418
Football Stadium (Capacity): Stanford Stadium (85,500)
Basketball Arena (Capacity): Maples Pavilion (7,391)
President: Dr. Gerhard Casper
Athletic Director: Dr. Ted Leland
Football Coach: Tyrone Willingham
Men's Basketball Coach: Mike Montgomery
Women's Basketball Coach: Tara Van Derveer
Sports Information Director: Gary Migdol

University of Washington
Address: UW Media Relations Graves Building, Box 354070 Seattle, WA 98195-4070
Nickname: Huskies
Telephone: (206) 543-2230
Football Stadium (Capacity): Husky Stadium (72,500)
Basketball Arena (Capacity): Hec Edmundson Pavilion (8,000)
President: Richard L. McCormick
Athletic Director: Barbara Hedges
Football Coach: Jim Lambright
Basketball Coach: Bob Bender
Sports Information Director: Jim Daves

Washington State University
Address: P.O. Box 641602 Pullman, WA 99164-1602
Nickname: Cougars
Telephone: (509) 535-2684
Football Stadium (Capacity): Martin Stadium (37,600)
Basketball Arena (Capacity): Friel Court (12,058)
President: Samuel H. Smith
Athletic Director: Rick Dickson
Football Coach: Mike Price
Basketball Coach: Kevin Eastman
Sports Information Director: Rod Commons

SOUTHEASTERN CONFERENCE
Address: 2201 Civic Center Boulevard Birmingham, AL 35203
Telephone: (205) 458-3000
Commissioner: Roy Kramer
Publicity Director: Charles Bloom

University of Alabama
Address: P.O. Box 870391 323 Paul Bryant Drive Tuscaloosa, AL 35487
Nickname: Crimson Tide
Telephone: (205) 348-6084
Football Stadium (Capacity): Bryant-Denny Stadium (83,818)
Basketball Arena (Capacity): Coleman Coliseum (15,043)
President: Dr. Andrew Sorensen
Athletic Director: Bob Bockrath
Football Coach: Mike DuBose
Men's Basketball Coach: Mark Gottfried
Women's Basketball Coach: Rick Moody
Sports Information Director: Larry White

University of Arkansas
Address: Broyles Athletic Center Fayetteville, AR 72701
Nickname: Razorbacks
Telephone: (501) 575-2751
Football Stadium (Capacity): Razorback Stadium (50,000); War Memorial Stadium (53,727)
Basketball Arena (Capacity): Bud Walton Arena (19,500)
Chancellor: Dr. John White
Athletic Director: Frank Broyles
Football Coach: Nutt Houston
Basketball Coach: Nolan Richardson
Sports Information Director: Rick Schaeffer

Auburn University
Address: P.O. Box 351 Auburn, AL 36831-0351
Nickname: Tigers
Telephone: (334) 844-9800
Football Stadium (Capacity): Jordan Hare Stadium (85,214)
Basketball Arena (Capacity): Beard-Eaves Memorial Coliseum (13,500)
President: Dr. William V. Muse
Athletic Director: David Housel
Football Coach: Terry Bowden
Men's Basketball Coach: Cliff Ellis
Women's Basketball Coach: Joe Ciampi
Sports Information Director: Kent Partridge

University of Florida
Address: P.O. Box 14485 Gainesville, FL 32604
Nickname: Gators
Telephone: (352) 375-4683
Football Stadium (Capacity): Ben Hill Griffin Stadium at Florida Field (83,000)
Basketball Arena (Capacity): Stephen C. O'Connell Center (12,000)
President: Dr. John Lombardi
Athletic Director: Jeremy Foley
Football Coach: Steve Spurrier
Men's Basketball Coach: Billy Donovan
Women's Basketball Coach: Carol Ross
Sports Information Director: John Humenik

University of Georgia

Address: P.O. Box 1472
Athens, GA 30603-1472
Nickname: Bulldogs
Telephone: (706) 542-1621
Football Stadium (Capacity): Sanford Stadium (86,117)
Basketball Arena (Capacity): Stegman Coliseum (10,523)
President: Dr. Michael F. Adams
Athletic Director: Vince Dooley
Football Coach: Jim Donnan
Men's Basketball Coach: Ron Jirsa
Women's Basketball Coach: Andy Landers
Sports Information Director: Claude Felton

University of Kentucky

Address: 23 Memorial Coliseum
Lexington, KY 40506-0019
Nickname: Wildcats
Telephone: (606) 257-3838
Football Stadium (Capacity): Commonwealth Stadium (57,800)
Basketball Arena (Capacity): Rupp Arena (24,000)
President: Dr. Charles Wethington Jr.
Athletic Director: C. M. Newton
Football Coach: Hal Mumme
Basketball Coach: Orlando (Tubby) Smith
Sports Information Director: Rena Vicini

Louisiana State University

Address: P.O. Box 25095
Baton Rouge, LA 70894
Nickname: Fighting Tigers
Telephone: (504) 388-8226
Football Stadium (Capacity): Tiger Stadium (79,940)
Basketball Arena (Capacity): Pete Maravich Assembly Center (14,164)
Chancellor: Dr. William Jenkins
Athletic Director: Joe Dean
Football Coach: Gerry DiNardo
Men's Basketball Coach: John Brady
Women's Basketball Coach: Sue Gunther
Sports Information Director: Herb Vincent

University of Mississippi

Address: P.O. Box 217
University, MS 38677
Nickname: Rebels
Telephone: (601) 232-7522
Football Stadium (Capacity): Vaught-Hemingway Stadium/Hollingsworth Field (50,577)
Basketball Arena (Capacity): C.M. (Tad) Smith Coliseum (8,135)
Chancellor: Dr. Robert C. Khayat
Athletic Director: John Schafer
Football Coach: Tommy Tuberville
Basketball Coach: Rod Barnes
Sports Information Director: Langston Rogers

Mississippi State University

Address: P.O. Drawer 5308
Mississippi St., MS 39762
Nickname: Bulldogs
Telephone: (601) 325-2703
Football Stadium (Capacity): Scott Field (40,656)
Basketball Arena (Capacity): Humphrey Coliseum (10,000)
President: Malcolm Portera
Athletic Director: Larry Templeton
Football Coach: Jackie Sherrill
Basketball Coach: Rick Stansbury
Sports Information Director: Mike Nemeth

University of South Carolina

Address: Rex Enright Athletic Center
1300 Rosewood Drive
Columbia, SC 29208
Nickname: Gamecocks
Telephone: (803) 777-5204
Football Stadium (Capacity): Williams-Brice Stadium (80,250)
Basketball Arena (Capacity): Frank McGuire Arena (12,401)
President: Dr. John Palms
Athletic Director: Dr. Mike McGee
Football Coach: Brad Scott
Basketball Coach: Eddie Fogler
Sports Information Director: Kerry Tharp

University of Tennessee

Address: P.O. Box 15016
Knoxville, TN 37901
Nickname: Volunteers
Telephone: (423) 974-1212
Football Stadium (Capacity): Neyland Stadium (102,854)
Basketball Arena (Capacity): Thompson-Boling Arena and Assembly Center (24,535)
President: Dr. Joseph E. Johnson
Athletic Director: Doug Dickey
Football Coach: Phillip Fulmer
Men's Basketball Coach: Jerry Green
Women's Basketball Coach: Pat Summitt
Sports Information Directors: Bud Ford (Men's), Debby Jennings (Women's)

Vanderbilt University

Address: P.O. Box 120158
Nashville, TN 37212
Nickname: Commodores
Telephone: (615) 322-4121
Football Stadium (Capacity): Vanderbilt Stadium (41,448)
Basketball Arena (Capacity): Memorial Gym (15,311)
Chancellor: Joe B. Wyatt
Athletic Director: Todd Turner
Football Coach: Woody Widenhofer
Men's Basketball Coach: Jan Van Breda Kolff
Women's Basketball Coach: Jen Foster
Sports Information Director: Rod Williamson

WESTERN ATHLETIC CONFERENCE

Address: 9250 East Costilla Avenue, Suite 300
Englewood, CO 80112
Telephone: (303) 799-9221
Commissioner: Karl Benson
Publicity Director: Jeff Hurd

Air Force

Address: 2169 Field House Drive
USAF Academy, CO 80840-9500
Nickname: Falcons
Telephone: (719) 333-2313
Football Stadium (Capacity): Falcon Stadium (52,480)
Basketball Arena (Capacity): Clune Arena (6,002)
President: Lt. Gen. Tad Oelstrom
Athletic Director: Col. Randall W. Spetman
Football Coach: Fisher DeBerry
Basketball Coach: Reggie Minton
Sports Information Director: David Kellogg

Brigham Young University

Address: 30 Smith Field House
               Provo, UT 84602
Nickname: Cougars
Telephone: (801) 378-4911
Football Stadium (Capacity): Cougar Stadium (65,000)
Basketball Arena (Capacity): Marriott Center (23,000)
President: Merrill J. Bateman
Athletic Director: Rondo Fehlberg
Football Coach: LaVell Edwards
Basketball Coach: Steve Cleveland
Sports Information Directors: Brian Dangerfield and
  Brett Pyne

Colorado State University

Address: Moby Arena
               Fort Collins, CO 80523
Nickname: Rams
Telephone: (970) 491-5300
Football Stadium (Capacity): Hughes Stadium (30,000)
Basketball Arena (Capacity): Moby Arena (9,001)
President: Dr. Albert C. Yates
Athletic Director: Tim Weiser
Football Coach: Sonny Lubick
Basketball Coach: Ritchie McKay
Sports Information Director: Gary Ozello

Fresno State University

Address: 5305 N. Campus Drive, Room 153
               Fresno, CA 93740-8020
Nickname: Bulldogs
Telephone: (209) 278-2643
Football Stadium (Capacity): Bulldog
  Stadium (41,031)
Basketball Arena (Capacity): Selland Arena (10,132)
President: Dr. John Welty
Athletic Director: Dr. Al Bohl
Football Coach: Pat Hill
Basketball Coach: Jerry Tarkanian
Sports Information Director: Rose Pietrzak

University of Hawaii

Address: 1337 Lower Campus Road
               Honolulu, HI 96822-2370
Nickname: Rainbow Warriors
Telephone: (808) 956-7523
Football Stadium (Capacity): Aloha Stadium (50,000)
Basketball Arena (Capacity): Stan Sheriff Center
  (10,225)
President: Dr. Kenneth Mortimer
Athletic Director: Hugh Yoshida
Football Coach: Fred von Appen
Basketball Coach: Riley Wallace
Sports Information Director: Lois Manin

University of Nevada at Las Vegas

Address: 4505 Maryland Parkway
               Las Vegas, NV 89154-0004
Nickname: Rebels
Telephone: (702) 895-3207
Football Stadium (Capacity): Sam Boyd
  Stadium (32,000)
Basketball Arena (Capacity): Thomas and Mack
  Center (18,500)
President: Dr. Carol C. Harter
Athletic Director: Charles Cavagnaro
Football Coach: Jeff Horton
Basketball Coach: Bill Bayno
Sports Information Director: Jim Gemma

University of New Mexico

Address: UNM South Complex
               Albuquerque, NM 87131-0041
Nickname: Lobos
Telephone: (505) 277-6375
Football Stadium (Capacity): University Stadium (30,646)
Basketball Arena (Capacity): University Arena—The
  Pit (18,018)
Interim President: Dr. William Gordon
Athletic Director: Rudy Davalos
Football Coach: Rocky Long
Basketball Coach: Dave Bliss
Sports Information Director: Greg Remington

Rice University

Address: 6100 Main, MS548
               Houston, TX 77005-1892
Nickname: Owls
Telephone: (713) 527-4034
Football Stadium (Capacity): Rice Stadium (70,000)
Basketball Arena (Capacity): Autry Court (5,000)
President: Malcolm Gillis
Athletic Director: Bobby May
Football Coach: Ken Hatfield
Basketball Coach: Willis Wilson
Sports Information Director: Bill Cousins

San Diego State University

Address: San Diego, CA 92182-4309
Nickname: Aztecs
Telephone: (619) 594-5547
Football Stadium (Capacity): Qualcomm
  Stadium (71,400)
Basketball Arena (Capacity): Cox Arena (12,414)
President: Dr. Stephen Weber
Athletic Director: Rick Bay
Football Coach: Ted Tollner
Basketball Coach: Fred Trenkle
Sports Information Director: John Rosenthal

San Jose State University

Address: One Washington Square
               San Jose, CA 95192-0062
Nickname: Spartans
Telephone: (408) 924-1217
Football Stadium (Capacity): Spartan Stadium
  (30,478)
Basketball Arena (Capacity): Event Center (5,000)
President: Dr. Robert L. Caret
Athletic Director: Chuck Bell
Football Coach: Dave Baldwin
Basketball Coach: Phil Johnson
Sports Information Director: Lawrence Fan

Southern Methodist University

Address: SMU Box 216
               Dallas, TX 75275
Nickname: Mustangs
Telephone: (214) 768-2883
Football Stadium (Capacity): Cotton Bowl (68,252)
Basketball Arena (Capacity): Moody Coliseum (8,998)
President: R. Gerald Turner
Athletic Director: Jim Copeland
Football Coach: Mike Cavan
Basketball Coach: Mike Dement
Sports Information Director: Jon Jackson

University of Texas at El Paso
Address: 201 Baltimore
             El Paso, TX 79968
Nickname: Miners
Telephone: (915) 747-5330
Football Stadium (Capacity): Sun Bowl (52,000)
Basketball Arena (Capacity): Special Events
Center (12,222)
President: Dr. Diana Natalicio
Athletic Director: Bob Stull
Football Coach: Charlie Bailey
Basketball Coach: Don Haskins
Sports Information Director: Chris Burkhalter

Texas Christian University
Address: Box 297600
             Fort Worth, TX 76129
Nickname: Horned Frogs
Telephone: (817) 921-7969
Football Stadium (Capacity): Amon G. Carter
Stadium (46,000)
Basketball Arena (Capacity): Daniel-Meyer
Coliseum (7,166)
Chancellor: Dr. William E. Tucker
Athletic Director: Frank Windegger
Football Coach: Pat Sullivan
Basketball Coach: Billy Tubbs
Sports Information Director: Glen Stone

University of Tulsa
Address: 600 S. College
             Tulsa, OK 74104-3189
Nickname: Golden Hurricane
Telephone: (918) 631-2395
Football Stadium (Capacity): Skelly Stadium (40,385)
Basketball Arena (Capacity): Donald W. Reynolds
Center (8,300)
President: Robert Lawless
Athletic Director: Judy MacLeod
Football Coach: Dave Rader
Basketball Coach: Bill Self
Sports Information Director: Don Tomkalski

University of Utah
Address: 1825 E. South Campus Drive, Front
             Salt Lake City, UT 84112-0900
Nickname: Utes
Telephone: (801) 581-8171
Football Stadium (Capacity): Rice-Eccles Stadium
(46,500)
Basketball Arena (Capacity): Jon M. Huntsman
Center (15,000)
President: Dr. Bernie Machen
Athletic Director: Dr. Chris Hill
Football Coach: Ron McBride
Basketball Coach: Rick Majerus
Sports Information Director: Liz Abel

University of Wyoming
Address: P.O. Box 3414
             Laramie, WY 82071-3414
Nickname: Cowboys
Telephone: (307) 766-2256
Football Stadium (Capacity): War Memorial Stadium
(33,500)
Basketball Arena (Capacity): Arena-Auditorium (15,028)
President: Dr. Philip Dubois
Athletic Director: Lee Moon
Football Coach: Dana Dimel
Basketball Coach: Steve McClain
Sports Information Director: Kevin McKinney

INDEPENDENTS
Army
Address: Howard Road Building 639
             West Point, NY 10996
Nickname: Cadets/Black Knights
Telephone: (914) 938-3303
Football Stadium (Capacity): Michie Stadium (39,929)
Basketball Arena (Capacity): Christl Arena (5,043)
Superintendent: Lt. Gen. Daniel W. Christman
Athletic Director: Al Vanderbush
Football Coach: Bob Sutton
Basketball Coach: Pat Harris
Sports Information Director: Bob Beretta
Note: Plays football in Conference USA, basketball in Patriot League.

East Carolina University
Address: Greenville, NC 27858-4353
Nickname: Pirates
Telephone: (919) 328-4600
Football Stadium (Capacity): Dowdy-Ficklen
Stadium (43,000)
Basketball Arena (Capacity): Williams Arena (7,500)
Chancellor: Dr. Richard R. Eakin
Athletic Director: Michael A. Hamrick
Football Coach: Steve Logan
Basketball Coach: Joe Dooley
Sports Information Director: Norm Reilly

Navy
Address: 566 Brownson Road, Ricketts Hall
             Annapolis, MD 21402
Nickname: Midshipmen
Telephone: (410) 293-2340
Football Stadium (Capacity): Navy-Marine Corps
Memorial Stadium (30,000)
Basketball Arena (Capacity): Alumni Hall (5,700)
Superintendent: John Ryan, USN
Athletic Director: Jack Lengyel
Football Coach: Charlie Weatherby
Basketball Coach: Don DeVoe
Sports Information Director: Scott Strasemeier
Note: Plays football as independent, basketball in Patriot League.

University of Notre Dame
Address: Joyce Center
             Notre Dame, IN 46556
Nickname: Fighting Irish
Telephone: (219) 631-6107
Football Stadium (Capacity): Notre Dame
Stadium (80,225)
Basketball Arena (Capacity): Joyce Athletic and
Convocation Center (11,418)
President: Rev. Edward A. Malloy, CSC
Athletic Director: Michael Wadsworth
Football Coach: Bob Davie
Men's Basketball Coach: John MacLeod
Women's Basketball Coach: Muffet McGraw
Sports Information Director: John Heisler

Olympic Sports Directory

United States Olympic Committee
Address: Olympic House
                1 Olympic Plaza
                Colorado Springs, CO 80909
Telephone: (719) 632-5551
Executive Director: Dick Schultz
Assistant Executive Director for Media and Public
  Affairs: Mike Moran

U.S. Olympic Training Centers
Address: 1 Olympic Plaza
                Colorado Springs, CO 80909
Telephone: (719) 578-4500 extension-5500
Director: Benita Fitzgerald Mosley

Address: 421 Old Military Road
                Lake Placid, NY 12946
Telephone: (518) 523-2600
Director: Jack Favro

U.S. Olympic Training Centers (Cont.)
Address: 2800 Olympic Parkway
                Chula Vista, CA 91915
Telephone: (619) 656-1500
Director: Patrice Milkovich

International Olympic Committee
Address: Chateau de Vidy
                CH-1007 Lausanne, Switzerland
Telephone: 41-21-621-6111
President: Juan Antonio Samaranch
Director General: Francois Carrard
Public Information Contact: Fekrou Kidane

Sydney Olympic Organizing Committee
Address: GPO Box 2000
                Sydney, NSW 2001, Australia
Telephone: 61-29-297-2000
President: Hon. Michael Knight, MP
GM of Media: Milton Cockburn
(XXVIIth Summer Games; Sept. 15–Oct. 1, 2000)

U.S. Olympic Organizations

National Archery Association (NAA)
Address: 1 Olympic Plaza
                Colorado Springs, CO 80909
Telephone: (719) 578-4576
President: Jane Johnson
Executive Director: George Greenway
Media Relations: Bill Kellick

USA Badminton
Address: 1 Olympic Plaza
                Colorado Springs, CO 80909
Telephone: (719) 578-4808
President: Steve Kearney
Executive Director: Holly Martin
Media Contact: Chris Trenholme

USA Baseball
Address: Hi Corbett Field
                3400 East Camino Campestre
                Tucson, AZ 85716
Telephone: (520) 327-9700
President: Neil Lantz
Executive Director: Daniel F. O'Brien
Media Relations Director: George Doig

USA Basketball
Address: 5465 Mark Dabling Blvd.
                Colorado Springs, CO 80918
Telephone: (719) 590-4800
President: Russ Granik
Executive Director: Warren Brown
Assistant Executive Director for Public Relations:
  Craig Miller

U.S. Biathlon Association (USBA)
Address: 29 Ethan Allen Avenue
                Colchester, VT 05446
Telephone: 1 (800) 242-8456
President: Lyle Nelson
Executive Director: Stephen R. Sands
Media Contat: Mary Grace

U.S. Bobsled and Skeleton Federation
Address: P.O. Box 828
                Lake Placid, NY 12946
Telephone: (518) 523-1842
President: Jim Morris
Executive Director: Matt Roy
Communications Director: Becky Metanic

USA Bowling
Address: 5301 South 76th Street
                Greendale, WI 53129
Telephone: (414) 421-9008
President: Elaine Hagin
Executive Director: Gerald Koenig
Communications Directors: Mark Miller and Marc
Whitney

USA Boxing, Inc.
Address: 1 Olympic Plaza
                Colorado Springs, CO 80909
Telephone: (719) 578-4506
President: Gary Toney
Executive Director: Chris Campbell
Director of PR and Media: Shilpa Bakre

U.S. Canoe and Kayak Team
Address: P.O. Box 789
                Lake Placid, NY 12946
Telephone: (518) 523-1855
Chairman of the Board: Helen Collins
Executive Director: Terry Kent
Director of Communications: Lisa Fish

USA Cycling
Address: 1 Olympic Plaza
                Colorado Springs, CO 80909
Telephone: (719) 578-4581
President: Mike Plant
Executive Director and Chief Executive Officer:
  Lisa Voight
Director of Communications: Richard Wanninger

United States Diving, Inc. (USD)
Address: Pan American Plaza, Suite 430
                201 South Capitol Avenue
                Indianapolis, IN 46225
Telephone: (317) 237-5252
President: Steve McFarland
Executive Director: Todd Smith
Director of Communications: Seth Pederson

U.S. Equestrian Team (USET)
Address: Pottersville Rd.
            Gladstone, NJ 07934
Telephone: (908) 234-0155
Executive Director: Robert C. Standish
Director of Public Relations: Marty Bauman

U.S. Fencing Association (USFA)
Address: 1 Olympic Plaza
            Colorado Springs, CO 80909
Telephone: (719) 578-4511
President: Don Alperstein
Executive Director: Michael Massik
Media Relations Director: Colleen Walker-Mar

U.S. Field Hockey Association (USFHA)
Address: 1 Olympic Plaza
            Colorado Springs, CO 80909-5773
Telephone: (719) 578-4567
President: Jenepher Shillingford
Executive Director: Jane Betts
Director of Public Relations: Howard Thomas

U.S. Figure Skating Association (USFSA)
Address: 20 First Street
            Colorado Springs, CO 80906
Telephone: (719) 635-5200
President: James Disbrow
Executive Director: John LeFevre
Director of Development: Kristin Matta
Communications Coordinator: Bob Dunlop

USA Gymnastics
Address: Pan American Plaza, Suite 300
            201 South Capitol Avenue
            Indianapolis, IN 46225
Telephone: (317) 237-5050
Chairman of the Board: Sandy Knapp
President: Robert Colarossi
Director of Public Relations: Craig Bohnert

USA Hockey
Address: 1775 Bob Johnson Drive
            Colorado Springs, CO 80906
Telephone: (719) 576-8724
President: Walter L. Bush, Jr.
Executive Director: David Ogrean
Director of Public Relations and Media: Darryl Seibel

United States Judo, Inc. (USJ)
Address: 1 Olympic Plaza
            Colorado Springs, CO 80909
Telephone: (719) 578-4730
President: Yoshihiro Uchida
Director of Marketing: Chris Cordes

U.S. Luge Association (USLA)
Address: 35 Church Street
            Lake Placid, NY 12946
Telephone: (518) 523-2071
President: Doug Bateman
Executive Director: Ron Rossi
Public Relations Manager: Sandy Caligiore

U.S. Modern Pentathlon Association (USMPA)
Address: 7330 San Pedro, Box 10
            San Antonio, TX 78216
Telephone: (210) 528-2999
President: Dr. Risto Hurme
Interim Executive Director: Rob Stull

U.S. Racquetball Association
Address: 1685 West Uintah
            Colorado Springs, CO 80904
Telephone: (719) 635-5396
President: Otto Dietrich
Executive Director: Luke St. Onge
Public Relations Director: Linda Mojer

USA Roller Skating
Address: 4730 South Street
            P.O. Box 6579
            Lincoln, NE 68506
Telephone: (402) 483-7551
President: Betty Ann Danna
Executive Director: George H. Pickard
Sports Information Director: Jean Stanek

U.S. Rowing
Address: Pan American Plaza, Suite 400
            201 South Capitol Avenue
            Indianapolis, IN 46225
Telephone: (317) 237-5656
President: Dave Vogel
Executive Director: Frank J. Coyle
Press Contact: Brett Johnson

U.S. Sailing Association
Address: P.O. Box 1260
            Portsmouth, RI 02871
Telephone: (401) 683-0800
President: James P. Muldoon
Executive Director: Terry Harper
Communications Coordinator: Susan Cook
Olympic Yachting Director: Jonathan R. Harley

USA Shooting
Address: 1 Olympic Plaza
            Colorado Springs, CO 80909
Telephone: (719) 578-4670
President of the Board: Stevan B. Richards
Executive Director: Robert L. Jursnick
Director of Public Relations: Bob Groate

U.S. Ski and Snowboard Association
Address: P.O. Box 100
            Park City, UT 84060
Telephone: (435) 649-9090
Chairman: Jim McCarthy
President and CEO: Bill Marolt
Vice President of Communications and Media:
  Tom Kelly
Media Services Coordinator: Deborah Engen

U.S. Soccer Federation (USSF)
Address: 1801-1811 South Prairie Avenue
            Chicago, IL 60616
Telephone: (312) 808-1300
President: Robert Contiguglia
Executive Director: Hank Steinbrecher
Director of Communications: James Trecker

Amateur Softball Association (ASA)
Address: 2801 N.E. 50th Street
            Oklahoma City, OK 73111
Telephone: (405) 424-5266
President: Bill Humphrey
Executive Director: Ron Radigonda
Director of Communications: Ron Babb

U.S. Speed Skating
Address: P.O. Box 450639
            Westlake OH 44145
Telephone: (440) 899-0128
President: Bill Cushman
Executive Director: Katie Marquard
Public Relations Director: Kathleen Lynn
Publicity telephone: (719) 578-4543

U.S. Swimming, Inc. (USS)
Address: 1 Olympic Plaza
            Colorado Springs, CO 80909
Telephone: (719) 578-4578
President: Carol Zaleski
Executive Director: Chuck Wielgus
Communications Director: Charlie Snyder

U.S. Synchronized Swimming, Inc. (USSS)
Address: Pan American Plaza, Suite 901
            201 South Capitol Avenue
            Indianapolis, IN 46225
Telephone: (317) 237-5700
President: Laurette Longmire
Executive Director: Debbie Hesse
Media Relations: Brian Eaton

U.S. Table Tennis Association (USTTA)
Address: 1 Olympic Plaza
            Colorado Springs, CO 80909
Telephone: (719) 578-4583
Executive Director: Paul Montville
President: Jim Mcqueen
Executive Director: Kevin Carlon
Communications Director: TBA

U.S. Taekwondo Union (USTU)
Address: 1 Olympic Plaza, Suite 405
            Colorado Springs, CO 80909
Telephone: (719) 578-4632
President: Sang Lee
Executive Director: R. Jay Warwick

USA Team Handball
Address: 1903 Powers Ferry Road, Suite 230
            Atlanta, GA 30339
Telephone: (770) 956-7660
President: Dennis Berkholtz
Executive Director: TBA

U.S. Tennis Association
Address: 70 West Red Oak Lane
            White Plains, NY 10604
Telephone: (914) 696-7000
President: Dr. Harry Marmion
Executive Director: Richard D. Ferman
Director of Communications: Page Crosland

USA Track & Field (formerly TAC)
Address: P.O. Box 120
            Indianapolis, IN 46206-0120
Telephone: (317) 261-0500
President: Patricia F. Rico
Chief Executive Officer: Craig A. Masback
Media Information Officer: Pete Cava

U.S. Volleyball Association (USVBA)
Address: 3595 East Fountain Boulevard, Suite I-2
            Colorado Springs, CO 80910-1740
Telephone: (719) 637-8300
President: Rebecca Howard
Executive Director: Kerry Klostermann
Director of Marketing and Communications: Lorene
  Graves

United States Water Polo (USWP)
Address: 1685 West Uintah
            Colorado Springs, CO 80904
Telephone: (719) 634-0699
President: Brett Bernard
Executive Director: Bruce J. Wigo
Scoreboard Editor: Kyle Utsumi

USA Weightlifting
Address: 1 Olympic Plaza
            Colorado Springs, CO 80909
Telephone: (719) 578-4508
President: Brian Derwin
Executive Director and Media Contact: Jim Fox

USA Wrestling
Address: 6155 Lehman Drive
            Colorado Springs, CO 80918
Telephone: (719) 598-8181
President: Bruce Baumgartner
Executive Director: Jim Scherr
Director of Communications: Gary Abbott

Affiliated Sports Organizations

Amateur Athletic Union (AAU)
Address: Walt Disney World Resort
P.O. Box 10000
Lake Buena Vista, FL 32830-1000
Telephone: (407) 934-7220
President: Bobby Dodd
Public Relations: John Hodges

U.S. Curling Association (USCA)
Address: 1100 CenterPoint Drive
P.O. Box 866
Stevens Point, WI 54481
Telephone: (715) 344-1199
President: D. Clark Higgins
Executive Director: David Garber
Communications Manager: Rick Patzke

USA Karate Federation
Address: 1300 Kenmore Boulevard
Akron, OH 44314
Telephone: (330) 753-3114
President: George Anderson

U.S. Orienteering Federation
Address: P.O. Box 1444
Forest Park, GA 30298
Telephone: (404) 363-2110
President: Gary Kraght
Executive Director: Robin Shannonhouse
Director, Marketing and Public Relations: John Nash
Publicity telephone: (207) 439-7096

U.S. Squash Racquets Association
Address: 23 Cynwyd Road
P.O. Box 1216
Bala Cynwyd, PA 19004
Telephone: (610) 667-4006
President: Taylor Quick
Executive Director: Craig Brand

USA Trampoline and Tumbling
Address: 400 West Broadway, Suite 207
or P.O. Box 306
Brownfield, TX 79316-0306
Telephone: (806) 637-8670
President: Paul Parilla
Executive Director: Ann Sims

USA Triathlon
Address: 3595 East Fountain Boulevard, Suite F-1
Colorado Springs, CO 80910
Telephone: (719) 597-9090
President: Jonathan Grinder
Executive Director: Steve Locke
Media Relations Coordinator: Mike McCarley

Underwater Society of America
Address: P.O. Box 628
Daly City, CA 94017
Telephone: (650) 583-8492
President and Public Relations Manager: Carol Rose

USA Waterski
Address: 799 Overlook Drive, S.E.
Winter Haven, FL 33884
Telephone: (941) 324-4341
President: Sherm Schrast
Executive Director: Steve McDermeit
Public Relations Manager: Greg Nixon

Miscellaneous Sports Directory

Championship Auto Racing Teams (CART)
Address: 755 West Big Beaver Road, Suite 800
Troy, MI 48084
Telephone: (248) 362-8800
President and CEO: Andrew Craig
Director of Publicity: Ron Richards

Indy Racing League
Address: 4565 West 16th Street
Indianapolis, IN 46222
Telephone: (317) 484-6526
President and Founder: Tony George
Executive Director: Leo Mehl
Public Relations Manager: Lisa Summers

Professional Sports Car Racing, Inc.
Address: 3502 Henderson Boulevard
Tampa, FL 33609
Telephone: (813) 877-4672
President: Michael Gue
Communications Director: Bob Holland

National Association for Stock Car Auto Racing (NASCAR)
Address: 1801 W International Speedway Blvd.
Daytona Beach, FL 32120
Telephone: (904) 253-0611
President: Bill France Jr.
Director of Communications Worldwide: John Griffin

National Hot Rod Association
Address: 2035 East Financial Way
Glendora, CA 91741
Telephone: (626) 914-4761
President: Dallas Gardner
Director of Communications: Denny Darnell

Bowling, Inc.
Address: 5301 South 76th Street
Greendale, WI 53129-1191
Telephone: (414) 421-0900
President: David Patrick
Public Relations Manager: Bryan Lemonds
Women's International Bowling Congress President: Joyce Deitch
American Bowling Congress President: Roger Dalkin

Professional Women's Bowling Association

Address: 7171 Cherryvale Boulevard
            Rockford, IL 61112
Telephone: (815) 332-5756
Tournament Director: Rick Ramsey
Media Director: Dan Leary

Professional Bowlers Association

Address: P.O. Box 5118
            1720 Merriman Road
            Akron, OH 44334-0118
Telephone: (330) 836-5568
Commissioner: Mark Gerberich
Public Relations Director: Dave Schroeder

U.S. Chess Federation

Address: 3054 NYS Route 9 W
            New Windsor, NY 12553
Telephone: (914) 562-8350
Executive Director: Michael Zaballo
Associate Director: Eric Johnson

International Game Fish Association

Address: 300 Golf Stream Way
            Dania, FL 33004
Telephone: (954) 927-2628
President: Mike Leech

Ladies Professional Golf Association

Address: 100 International Golf Drive
            Daytona Beach, FL 32124
Telephone: (904) 274-6200
Commissioner: Jim Ritts
Director of Communications: Leslie King

PGA Tour

Address: 112 PGA Tour Boulevard
            Ponte Vedra Beach, FL 32082
Telephone: (904) 285-3700
Commissioner: Timothy W. Finchem
Senior Vice President of Communications:
  Bob Combs

Professional Golfers' Association of America

Address: 100 Avenue of the Champions
            Box 109601
            Palm Beach Gardens, FL 33410-9601
Telephone: (561) 624-8400
President: Ken Lindsay
Director of Public Relations: Julius Mason

United States Golf Association

Address: P.O. Box 708, Golf House
            Liberty Corner Road
            Far Hills, NJ 07931-0708
Telephone: (908) 234-2300
President: F. Morgan Taylor
Director of Communications: Marty Parkes

American Greyhound Track Operators Association

Address: P.O. Box 100279
            Birmingham, AL 35210
Telephone: (205) 838-1574
President: Roy Berger
Secretary and Managing Coordinator: Stan Flint

U.S. Handball Association

Address: 2333 North Tucson Boulevard
            Tucson, AZ 85716
Telephone: (520) 795-0434
Executive Director: Vern Roberts
Director of Public Relations: Ron Carpenter

Breeders' Cup Limited

Address: 2525 Harrodsburg Road
            Lexington, KY 40504
Telephone: (606) 223-5444
President: D. G. Van Clief Jr.
Media Relations Directors: Dan Metzger and James
  Gluckson

The Jockeys' Guild, Inc.

Address: 250 West Main Street, Suite 1820
            Lexington, KY 40507
Telephone: (606) 259-3211
President: Gary Stevens
National Manager and Secretary: John Giovanni

Thoroughbred Racing Associations of America

Address: 420 Fair Hill Drive, Suite 1
            Elkton, MD 21921
Telephone: (410) 392-9200
President: Harold G. Handel

Thoroughbred Racing Communications, Inc.

Address: 40 East 52nd Street
            New York, NY 10022
Telephone: (212) 371-5910
Executive Director: Tom Merritt
Director of Media Relations and Development:
  Bob Curran

United States Trotting Association

Address: 750 Michigan Avenue
            Columbus, OH 43215
Telephone: (614) 224-2291
President: Corwin Nixon
Director of Publicity: John Pawlak

Iditarod Trail Committee

Address: P.O. Box 870800
            Wasilla, AK 99687
Telephone: (907) 376-5155
Executive Director: Stan Hooley
Race Director: Joanne Potts

U.S. Lacrosse

Address: 113 W University Parkway
            Baltimore, MD 21210
Telephone: (410) 235-6882
Executive Director: Steven B. Stenersen

Little League Baseball, Inc.

Address: P.O. Box 3485
            Williamsport, PA 17701
Telephone: (717) 326-1921
President: Stephen Keener
Communications Director: Dennis Sullivan

U.S. Polo Association

Address: 4059 Iron Works Parkway
             Lexington, KY 40511
Telephone: (606) 255-0593
Executive Director: George Alexander Jr.
Media Contact: Merle Jenkins

American Powerboating Association

Address: P.O. Box 377
             Eastpointe, MI 48021
Telephone: (810) 773-9700
Executive Administrator: Gloria Urbin

Professional Rodeo Cowboys Association

Address: 101 Pro Rodeo Drive
             Colorado Springs, CO 80919
Telephone: (719) 593-8840
Commissioner: Steve Hatchell
Director of Communications: Steve Fleming

U.S.A. Rugby Football Union

Address: 3595 East Fountain Boulevard
             Colorado Springs, CO 80910
Telephone: (719) 637-1022
President: Anne Barry
Communications and Membership: Mia Shapiro

The United Systems of Independent Soccer Leagues

Address: 14497 North Dale Mabry Highway,
             Suite 201
             Tampa, FL 33618
Telephone: (813) 963-3909
Commissioner: Francisco Marcos
Media Relations Contacts: Bryan Chenault and Chad Harmon

Major League Soccer

Address: 110 East 42nd Street, Suite 1000
             New York, NY 10017
Telephone: (212) 687-1400
Commissioner: Doug Logan
Director of Communications: Dan Courtemanche

National Professional Soccer League

Address: 115 Dewalt Avenue NW, 5th floor
             Canton, OH 44702
Telephone: (330) 455-4625
Commissioner: Steve Paxos
Director of Media Relations: Bob Young

Association of Tennis Professionals Tour

Address: 201 ATP Tour Boulevard
             Ponte Vedra Beach, FL 32082
Telephone: (904) 285-8000
Chief Executive Officer: Mark Miles
Vice President of Communications: Fran Michaelman

COREL WTA Tour (Women's Tennis)

Address: 1266 East Main Street, 4th floor
             Stamford, CT 06902-3546
Telephone: (203) 978-1740; (813) 895-5000
Chief Executive Officer: Bart McGuire
Director of Communications: Joe Favorito

Association of Volleyball Professionals

Address: 330 Washington Blvd., Suite 600
             Marina Del Rey, CA 90292
Telephone: (310) 577-0775
Chief Executive Officer: Harry Usher
Vice President of Sales and Marketing:
 Tom Yamaguchi

MINOR LEAGUES

Baseball (AAA)

National Association of Professional Baseball Leagues

Address: 201 Bayshore Drive S.E.
             St. Petersburg, FL 33701
Telephone: (727) 822-6937
President: Mike Moore
Director of Media Relations: Jim Ferguson

International League

Address: 55 South High Street, Suite 202
             Dublin, OH 43017
Telephone: (614) 791-9300
President: Randy Mobley

Pacific Coast League

Address: 1631 Mesa Avenue
             Colorado Springs, CO 80906
Telephone: (719) 636-3399
President: Branch Rickey

Mexican League

Address: Angela Pola #16
             Col. Periodista, C.P. 11220
             Mexico D.F.
Telephone: 011-525-577-10-07
President: Pedro Cisneros

Hockey

American Hockey League

Address: 425 Union Street
             West Springfield, MA 01089
Telephone: (413) 781-2030
President: David Andrews
Senior Vice President of Hockey Operations:
 Gordon Anziano
Manager of Communications and PR: Brent Maurer

International Hockey League

Address: 1577 North Woodward Ave., Suite 212
             Bloomfield Hills, MI 48304
Telephone: (248) 258-0580
President: Douglas Moss
Director of Communications: Jim Anderson

Hall of Fame Directory

National Baseball Hall of Fame and Museum
Address: P.O. Box 590/25 Main Street
        Cooperstown, NY 13326
Telephone: (607) 547-7200
President: Donald C. Marr Jr.
Vice President: Frank Simio
Executive Director, Communications and Education:
 Jeff Idelson

Naismith Memorial Basketball Hall of Fame
Address: 1150 West Columbus Avenue
        Springfield, MA 01101
Telephone: (413) 781-6500
President: Joseph O'Brien
Director of Public Relations: Robin Deutsch

National Bowling Hall of Fame and Museum
Address: 111 Stadium Plaza
        St. Louis, MO 63102
Telephone: (314) 231-6340
Executive Director: Gerald Baltz
Communications Director: Jim Baer

National Boxing Hall of Fame
Address: 1 Hall of Fame Drive
        Canastota, NY 13032
Telephone: (315) 697-7095
President: Donald Ackerman
Executive Director: Edward Brophy

Professional Football Hall of Fame
Address: 2121 George Halas Drive NW
        Canton, OH 44708
Telephone: (330) 456-8207
Executive Director: John Bankert
Vice President of Public Relations: Joe Horrigan

LPGA Hall of Fame
Address: 100 International Golf Drive
        Daytona Beach, FL 32124
Telephone: (904) 274-6200
Commissioner: Jim Ritts
Communications Director: Leslie King

Hockey Hall of Fame
Address: 30 Young Street BCE Place
        Toronto, Ontario Canada M5E 1X8
Telephone: (416) 360-7735
Chairman: William Hay
President: Jeff Denomme
VP of Marketing and Communications: Bryan Black
VP of Finance and Operations: Jeff Denomme

National Museum of Racing and Hall of Fame
Address: 191 Union Avenue
        Saratoga Springs, NY 12866
Telephone: (518) 584-0400
Executive Director: Peter Hammell
Assistant Director: Catherine Maguire
Communications Officer: Richard Hamilton

National Soccer Hall of Fame
Address: 5-11 Ford Avenue
        Oneonta, NY 13820
Telephone: (607) 432-3351
Executive Director: Will Lunn

International Swimming Hall of Fame
Address: 1 Hall of Fame Drive
        Fort Lauderdale, FL 33316
Telephone: (954) 462-6536
President: Dr. Samuel J. Freas
Director of Public Relations: Holly Heil

International Tennis Hall of Fame
Address: 194 Bellevue Avenue
        Newport, RI 02840
Telephone: (401) 849-3990
Executive Vice President and Chief Operating
 Officer: Mark Stenning
Marketing Manager: Michael Bridges

National Track & Field Hall of Fame
Address: 1 RCA Dome, Suite 140
        Indianapolis, IN 46225
Telephone: (317) 261-0500
Chief Executive Officer: Craig Masback
Director of Media Relations: Pete Cava

Awards

DECEMBER 22, 1997

Sports Illustrated

Sportsman of the Year Dean Smith

BRIAN LANKER

FOR THE RECORD · Year by Year

Athlete Awards

Sports Illustrated Sportsman of the Year

1954 ....Roger Bannister, Track and Field	1981 ....Sugar Ray Leonard, Boxing
1955 ....Johnny Podres, Baseball	1982 ....Wayne Gretzky, Hockey
1956 ....Bobby Morrow, Track and Field	1983 ....Mary Decker, Track and Field
1957 ....Stan Musial, Baseball	1984 ....Mary Lou Retton, Gymnastics
1958 ....Rafer Johnson, Track and Field		Edwin Moses, Track and Field
1959 ....Ingemar Johansson, Boxing	1985 ....Kareem Abdul-Jabbar, Pro
1960 ....Arnold Palmer, Golf		Basketball
1961 ....Jerry Lucas, Basketball	1986 ....Joe Paterno, Football
1962 ....Terry Baker, Football	1987 ....Athletes Who Care:
1963 ....Pete Rozelle, Pro Football		Bob Bourne, Hockey
1964 ....Ken Venturi, Golf		Kip Keino, Track and Field
1965 ....Sandy Koufax, Baseball		Judi Brown King, Track and Field
1966 ....Jim Ryun, Track and Field		Dale Murphy, Baseball
1967 ....Carl Yastrzemski, Baseball		Chip Rives, Football
1968 ....Bill Russell, Pro Basketball		Patty Sheehan, Golf
1969 ....Tom Seaver, Baseball		Rory Sparrow, Pro Basketball
1970 ....Bobby Orr, Hockey		Reggie Williams, Pro Football
1971 ....Lee Trevino, Golf	1988 ....Orel Hershiser, Baseball
1972 ....Billie Jean King, Tennis	1989 ....Greg LeMond, Cycling
	John Wooden, Basketball	1990 ....Joe Montana, Pro Football
1973 ....Jackie Stewart, Auto Racing	1991 ....Michael Jordan, Pro Basketball
1974 ....Muhammad Ali, Boxing	1992 ....Arthur Ashe, Tennis
1975 ....Pete Rose, Baseball	1993 ....Don Shula, Pro Football
1976 ....Chris Evert, Tennis	1994 ....Bonnie Blair, Speed Skating
1977 ....Steve Cauthen, Horse Racing		Johann Olav Koss, Speed Skating
1978 ....Jack Nicklaus, Golf	1995 ....Cal Ripken Jr, Baseball
1979 ....Terry Bradshaw, Pro Football	1996 ....Tiger Woods, Golf
	Willie Stargell, Baseball	1997 ....Dean Smith, College Basketball
1980 .......................U.S. Olympic Hockey Team		Coach

Associated Press Athletes of the Year

	MEN	WOMEN
1931	.........................Pepper Martin, Baseball	Helene Madison, Swimming
1932	.........................Gene Sarazen, Golf	Babe Didrikson, Track and Field
1933	.........................Carl Hubbell, Baseball	Helen Jacobs, Tennis
1934	.........................Dizzy Dean, Baseball	Virginia Van Wie, Golf
1935	.........................Joe Louis, Boxing	Helen Wills Moody, Tennis
1936	.........................Jesse Owens, Track and Field	Helen Stephens, Track and Field
1937	.........................Don Budge, Tennis	Katherine Rawls, Swimming
1938	.........................Don Budge, Tennis	Patty Berg, Golf
1939	.........................Nile Kinnick, Football	Alice Marble, Tennis
1940	.........................Tom Harmon, Football	Alice Marble, Tennis
1941	.........................Joe DiMaggio, Baseball	Betty Hicks Newell, Golf
1942	.........................Frank Sinkwich, Football	Gloria Callen, Swimming
1943	.........................Gunder Haegg, Track and Field	Patty Berg, Golf
1944	.........................Byron Nelson, Golf	Ann Curtis, Swimming
1945	.........................Bryon Nelson, Golf	Babe Didrikson Zaharias, Golf
1946	.........................Glenn Davis, Football	Babe Didrikson Zaharias, Golf
1947	.........................Johnny Lujack, Football	Babe Didrikson Zaharias, Golf
1948	.........................Lou Boudreau, Baseball	Fanny Blankers-Koen, Track and Field
1949	.........................Leon Hart, Football	Marlene Bauer, Golf
1950	.........................Jim Konstanty, Baseball	Babe Didrikson Zaharias, Golf
1951	.........................Dick Kazmaier, Football	Maureen Connolly, Tennis
1952	.........................Bob Mathias, Track and Field	Maureen Connolly, Tennis
1953	.........................Ben Hogan, Golf	Maureen Connolly, Tennis
1954	.........................Willie Mays, Baseball	Babe Didrikson Zaharias, Golf
1955	.........................Hopalong Cassidy, Football	Patty Berg, Golf
1956	.........................Mickey Mantle, Baseball	Pat McCormick, Diving
1957	.........................Ted Williams, Baseball	Althea Gibson, Tennis
1958	.........................Herb Elliott, Track and Field	Althea Gibson, Tennis
1959	.........................Ingemar Johansson, Boxing	Maria Bueno, Tennis
1960	.........................Rafer Johnson, Track and Field	Wilma Rudolph, Track and Field
1961	.........................Roger Maris, Baseball	Wilma Rudolph, Track and Field
1962	.........................Maury Wills, Baseball	Dawn Fraser, Swimming
1963	.........................Sandy Koufax, Baseball	Mickey Wright, Golf
1964	.........................Don Schollander, Swimming	Mickey Wright, Golf

Associated Press Athletes of the Year (Cont.)

	MEN	WOMEN
1965	Sandy Koufax, Baseball	Kathy Whitworth, Golf
1966	Frank Robinson, Baseball	Kathy Whitworth, Golf
1967	Carl Yastrzemski, Baseball	Billie Jean King, Tennis
1968	Denny McLain, Baseball	Peggy Fleming, Skating
1969	Tom Seaver, Baseball	Debbie Meyer, Swimming
1970	George Blanda, Pro Football	Chi Cheng, Track and Field
1971	Lee Trevino, Golf	Evonne Goolagong, Tennis
1972	Mark Spitz, Swimming	Olga Korbut, Gymnastics
1973	O.J. Simpson, Pro Football	Billie Jean King, Tennis
1974	Muhammad Ali, Boxing	Chris Evert, Tennis
1975	Fred Lynn, Baseball	Chris Evert, Tennis
1976	Bruce Jenner, Track and Field	Nadia Comaneci, Gymnastics
1977	Steve Cauthen, Horse Racing	Chris Evert, Tennis
1978	Ron Guidry, Baseball	Nancy Lopez, Golf
1979	Willie Stargell, Baseball	Tracy Austin, Tennis
1980	U.S. Olympic Hockey Team	Chris Evert Lloyd, Tennis
1981	John McEnroe, Tennis	Tracy Austin, Tennis
1982	Wayne Gretzky, Hockey	Mary Decker, Track and Field
1983	Carl Lewis, Track and Field	Martina Navratilova, Tennis
1984	Carl Lewis, Track and Field	Mary Lou Retton, Gymnastics
1985	Dwight Gooden, Baseball	Nancy Lopez, Golf
1986	Larry Bird, Pro Basketball	Martina Navratilova, Tennis
1987	Ben Johnson, Track and Field	Jackie Joyner-Kersee, Track and Field
1988	Orel Hershiser, Baseball	Florence Griffith Joyner, Track and Field
1989	Joe Montana, Pro Football	Steffi Graf, Tennis
1990	Joe Montana, Pro Football	Beth Daniel, Golf
1991	Michael Jordan, Pro Basketball	Monica Seles, Tennis
1992	Michael Jordan, Pro Basketball	Monica Seles, Tennis
1993	Michael Jordan, Pro Basketball	Sheryl Swoopes, Basketball
1994	George Foreman, Boxing	Bonnie Blair, Speed Skating
1995	Cal Ripken Jr., Baseball	Rebecca Lobo, Basketball
1996	Michael Johnson, Track and Field	Amy Van Dyken, Swimming
1997	Tiger Woods, Golf	Martina Hingis, Tennis

James E. Sullivan Award

Presented annually by the AAU to the athlete who "by his or her performance, example and influence as an amateur, has done the most during the year to advance the cause of sportsmanship."

1930	Bobby Jones, Golf	1962	Jim Beatty, Track and Field
1931	Barney Berlinger, Track and Field	1963	John Pennel, Track and Field
1932	Jim Bausch, Track and Field	1964	Don Schollander, Swimming
1933	Glenn Cunningham, Track and Field	1965	Bill Bradley, Basketball
1934	Bill Bonthron, Track and Field	1966	Jim Ryun, Track and Field
1935	Lawson Little, Golf	1967	Randy Matson, Track and Field
1936	Glenn Morris, Track and Field	1968	Debbie Meyer, Swimming
1937	Don Budge, Tennis	1969	Bill Toomey, Track and Field
1938	Don Lash, Track and Field	1970	John Kinsella, Swimming
1939	Joe Burk, Rowing	1971	Mark Spitz, Swimming
1940	Greg Rice, Track and Field	1972	Frank Shorter, Track and Field
1941	Leslie MacMitchell, Track and Field	1973	Bill Walton, Basketball
1942	Cornelius Warmerdam, Track	1974	Rich Wohlhuter, Track and Field
1943	Gilbert Dodds, Track and Field	1975	Tim Shaw, Swimming
1944	Ann Curtis, Swimming	1976	Bruce Jenner, Track and Field
1945	Doc Blanchard, Football	1977	John Naber, Swimming
1946	Arnold Tucker, Football	1978	Tracy Caulkins, Swimming
1947	John B. Kelly Jr, Rowing	1979	Kurt Thomas, Gymnastics
1948	Bob Mathias, Track and Field	1980	Eric Heiden, Speed Skating
1949	Dick Button, Skating	1981	Carl Lewis, Track and Field
1950	Fred Wilt, Track and Field	1982	Mary Decker, Track and Field
1951	Bob Richards, Track and Field	1983	Edwin Moses, Track and Field
1952	Horace Ashenfelter, Track and Field	1984	Greg Louganis, Diving
1953	Sammy Lee, Diving	1985	Joan B. Samuelson, Track and Field
1954	Mal Whitfield, Track and Field	1986	Jackie Joyner-Kersee, Track and Field
1955	Harrison Dillard, Track and Field	1987	Jim Abbott, Baseball
1956	Pat McCormick, Diving	1988	Florence Griffith Joyner, Track
1957	Bobby Morrow, Track and Field	1989	Janet Evans, Swimming
1958	Glenn Davis, Track and Field	1990	John Smith, Wrestling
1959	Parry O'Brien, Track and Field	1991	Mike Powell, Track and Field
1960	Rafer Johnson, Track and Field	1992	Bonnie Blair, Speed Skating
1961	Wilma Rudolph, Track and Field	1993	Charlie Ward, Football, Basketball

James E. Sullivan Award (Cont.)

1994	Dan Jansen, Speed Skating	1996	Michael Johnson, Track and Field
1995	Bruce Baumgartner, Wrestling	1997	Peyton Manning, Football

The Sporting News Man of the Year

1968	Denny McLain, Baseball	1984	Peter Ueberroth, LA Olympics
1969	Tom Seaver, Baseball	1985	Pete Rose, Baseball
1970	John Wooden, Basketball	1986	Larry Bird, Pro Basketball
1971	Lee Trevino, Golf	1987	No award
1972	Charles O. Finley, Baseball	1988	Jackie Joyner-Kersee, Track and Field
1973	O.J. Simpson, Pro Football	1989	Joe Montana, Pro Football
1974	Lou Brock, Baseball	1990	Nolan Ryan, Baseball
1975	Archie Griffin, Football	1991	Michael Jordan, Pro Basketball
1976	Larry O'Brien, Pro Basketball	1992	Mike Krzyzewski, Basketball
1977	Steve Cauthen, Horse Racing	1993	Pat Gillick and Cito Gaston, Baseball
1978	Ron Guidry, Baseball		
1979	Willie Stargell, Baseball	1994	Emmitt Smith, Pro Football
1980	George Brett, Baseball	1995	Cal Ripken Jr, Baseball
1981	Wayne Gretzky, Hockey	1996	Joe Torre, Baseball
1982	Whitey Herzog, Baseball	1997	Michael Jordan, Basketball
1983	Bowie Kuhn, Baseball		

United Press International Male and Female Athlete of the Year

	MEN	WOMEN
1974	Muhammad Ali, Boxing	Irena Szewinska, Track and Field
1975	Joao Oliveira, Track and Field	Nadia Comaneci, Gymnastics
1976	Alberto Juantorena, Track and Field	Nadia Comaneci, Gymnastics
1977	Alberto Juantorena, Track and Field	Rosie Ackermann, Track and Field
1978	Henry Rono, Track and Field	Tracy Caulkins, Swimming
1979	Sebastian Coe, Track and Field	Marita Koch, Track and Field
1980	Eric Heiden, Speed Skating	Hanni Wenzel, Alpine Skiing
1981	Sebastian Coe, Track and Field	Chris Evert Lloyd, Tennis
1982	Daley Thompson, Track and Field	Marita Koch, Track and Field
1983	Carl Lewis, Track and Field	Jarmila Kratochvilova, Track and Field
1984	Carl Lewis, Track and Field	Martina Navratilova, Tennis
1985	Steve Cram, Track and Field	Mary Decker Slaney, Track and Field
1986	Diego Maradona, Soccer	Heike Drechsler, Track and Field
1987	Ben Johnson, Track and Field	Steffi Graf, Tennis
1988	Matt Biondi, Swimming	Florence Griffith Joyner, Track and Field
1989	Boris Becker, Tennis	Steffi Graf, Tennis
1990	Stefan Edberg, Tennis	Merlene Ottey, Track and Field
1991	Michael Jordan, Pro Basketball	Monica Seles, Tennis
1992	Mario Lemieux, Hockey	Monica Seles, Tennis
1993	Michael Jordan, Pro Basketball	Steffi Graf, Tennis
1994	Nick Price, Golf	Bonnie Blair, Speed Skating
1995	Cal Ripken Jr, Baseball	Steffi Graf, Tennis
1996	Award not given	Award not given
1997	Award not given	Award not given

Dial Award

Presented annually by the Dial Corporation to the male and female national high school athlete/scholar of the year.

	BOYS	GIRLS
1979	Herschel Walker, Football	No award
1980	Bill Fralic, Football	Carol Lewis, Track and Field
1981	Kevin Willhite, Football	Cheryl Miller, Basketball
1982	Mike Smith, Basketball	Elaine Zayak, Skating
1983	Chris Spielman, Football	Melanie Buddemeyer, Swimming
1984	Hart Lee Dykes, Football	Nora Lewis, Basketball
1985	Jeff George, Football	Gea Johnson, Track and Field
1986	Scott Schaffner, Football	Mya Johnson, Track and Field
1987	Todd Marinovich, Football	Kristi Overton, Water Skiing
1988	Carlton Gray, Football	Courtney Cox, Basketball
1989	Robert Smith, Football	Lisa Leslie, Basketball
1990	Derrick Brooks, Football	Vicki Goetze, Golf
1991	Jeff Buckey, Football, Track and Field	Katie Smith, Basketball, Volleyball, Track
1992	Jacque Vaughn, Basketball	Amanda White, Track and Field, Swimming
1993	Tiger Woods, Golf	Kristin Folkl, Basketball
1994	Taymon Domzalski, Basketball	Shannon Miller, Gymnastics
1995	Brent Abernathy, Baseball	Shea Ralph, Basketball
1996	Grant Irons, Football	Grace Park, Golf
1997	Ronald Curry, Football	Michelle Kwan, Figure Skating

Profiles

OCTOBER 27, 1997 Sports Illustrated

COACH
Larry Bird

P Pacers

HEINZ KLUETMEIER

Henry Aaron (b. 2-5-34): Baseball OF. "Hammerin' Hank." Alltime leader in HR (755) and RBI (2,297); third in hits (3,771). 1957 MVP. Led league in HR and RBI 4 times each, runs scored 3 times, hits and batting average 2 times. No. 44, he had 44 homers 4 times. Had 40+ HR 8 times; 100+ RBI 11 times; .300+ average 14 times. 24-time All-Star. Career span 1954–76; jersey number retired by Atlanta and Milwaukee.

Kareem Abdul-Jabbar (b. 4-16-47): Born Lew Alcindor. Basketball C. Alltime leader points scored (38,387), field goals attempted (28,307), field goals made (15,837); second alltime blocked shots (3,189); third alltime rebounds (17,440). Won 6 MVP awards (1971–72, 1974, 1976–77, 1980). Career scoring average was 24.6, rebounding average 11.2. 10-time All-Star, All-Defensive team 5 times. 1970 Rookie of the Year. Played on 6 championship teams; was playoff MVP in 1971, 1985. Career span 1969–88 with Milwaukee, Los Angeles. Also played on 3 NCAA championship teams with UCLA; tournament MVP 1967–69; Player of the Year 2 times.

Affirmed (b. 2-21-75): Thoroughbred race horse. Triple Crown winner in 1978 with jockey Steve Cauthen aboard. Trained by Laz Barrera.

Troy Aikman (b. 11-21-66): Football QB. MVP of Super Bowl XXVII, in which he completed 22 of 30 passes for 273 yards and four TDs with no interceptions. Led Cowboys to victory in Super Bowls XXVIII and XXX. Career span since 1989 with Dallas Cowboys.

Tenley Albright (b. 7-18-35): Figure skater. Gold medalist at 1956 Olympics, silver medalist at 1952 Olympics. World champion 2 times (1953, 1955) and U.S. champion 5 consecutive years (1952–56).

Grover Cleveland Alexander (b. 2-26-1887, d. 11-4-50): Baseball RHP. Tied for third alltime most wins (373), second most shutouts (90). Won 30+ games 3 times, 20+ games 6 other times. Set rookie record with 28 wins in 1911. Career span 1911–30 with Philadelphia (NL), Chicago (NL), St. Louis (NL).

Vasili Alexeyev (b. 1942): Soviet weightlifter. Gold medalist at 2 consecutive Olympics in 1972, 1976. World champion 8 times.

Muhammad Ali (b. 1-17-42): Born Cassius Clay. Boxer. Heavyweight champion 3 times (1964–67, 1974–78, 1978–79). Stripped of title in 1967 because he refused to serve in the Vietnam War. Career record 56–5 with 37 KOs. Defended title 19 times. Also light heavyweight gold medalist at 1960 Olympics.

Phog Allen (b. 11-18-1885, d. 9-16-74): College baskeball coach. Fifth alltime most wins (746); .739 career winning percentage. Won 1952 NCAA championship. Most of career, 1920–56, with Kansas.

Bobby Allison (b. 12-3-37): Auto racer. Third all-time in NASCAR victories (84) at the time of his retirement. Won Daytona 500 3 times (1978, 1982, 1988). Also NASCAR champion in 1983.

Naty Alvarado (b. 7-25-55): Mexican-born handball player. "El Gato (The Cat)." Won a record 11 U.S. pro four-wall handball titles starting in 1977.

Lance Alworth (b. 8-3-40): Football WR. "Bambi" led AFL in receiving in 1966, '68 and '69. 200+ yards in a game 5 times in career, a record. Gained 100+ yards in game 41 times. In 1965 gained 1,602 yards receiving.

Career span 1962–70 with San Diego and 1971–72 with Dallas. Elected to Pro Football Hall of Fame 1978.

Sparky Anderson (b. 2-22-34): Baseball manager. Only manager to win World Series in both leagues (Cincinnati, 1975–76; Detroit, 1984); only manager to win 100 games in both leagues.

Willie Anderson (b. 1880, d. 1910): Scottish golfer. Won U.S. Open 4 times (1901 and an unmatched three straight, 1903–05). Also won 4 Western Opens between 1902 and 1909.

Mario Andretti (b. 2-28-40): Auto racer. The only driver in history to win Daytona 500 (1967), Indy 500 (1969) and Formula One world championship (1978). Second alltime in CART victories (52) as of retirement in Oct. 1994. Also 12 career Formula One victories. USAC/CART champion 4 times (consecutively 1965–66, 1969, 1984).

Earl Anthony (b. 4-27-38): Bowler. Won PBA National Championship 6 times, more than any other bowler (consecutively 1973–75, 1981–83) and Tournament of Champions 2 times (1974, 1978). First bowler to top $1 million in career earnings. Bowler of the Year 6 times (consecutively 1974–76, 1981–83). Has won 41 career PBA titles since 1970.

Said Aouita (b. 11-2-60): Track and field. Moroccan set world records in 2,000 meters (4:50.81 in 1987), and 5,000 meters (12:58.39 in 1987). 1984 Olympic champion in 5,000; 1988 Olympic third place in 800.

Al Arbour (b. 11-1-32): Hockey D-coach. Led NY Islanders to 4 consecutive Stanley Cup championships (1980–83). Also played on 3 Stanley Cup champions: Detroit, Chicago and Toronto, from 1953 to 1971.

Eddie Arcaro (b. 2-19-16, d. 11-14-97): Horse racing jockey. The only jockey to win the Triple Crown 2 times (aboard Whirlaway in 1941, Citation in 1948). Rode Preakness Stakes winner (1941, 1948, consecutively 1950–51, 1955, 1957) and Belmont Stakes winner (consecutively 1941–42, 1945, 1948, 1952, 1955) 6 times each and Kentucky Derby winner 5 times (1938, 1941, 1945, 1948, 1952). 4,779 career wins.

Nate Archibald (b. 9-2-48): Basketball player. "Tiny" only by NBA standards at 6' 1", 160 pounds. Drafted by Cincinnati in 1970. Led NBA in scoring (34.0) and assists (11.4) in 1972–73. First team, all-NBA in 1973, '75 and '76. MVP of NBA All Star game in 1981. Retired in 1984.

Alexis Arguello (b. 4-19-52): Nicaraguan boxer. Won world titles in three weight classes, featherweight, super featherweight and lightweight. Won first title, WBA featherweight, on 11-23-74 when he KO'd Ruben Olivares in 13. Career record: 88 bouts; won 64 by KO, 16 by decision; lost eight.

Henry Armstrong (b. 12-12-12, d. 10-24-88): Boxer. Champion in 3 different weight classes: featherweight (1937–relinquished 1938), welterweight (1938–40) and lightweight (1938–39). Career record 145-20-9 with 98 KOs (27 consecutively, 1937–38) from 1931 to 1945.

Arthur Ashe (b. 7-10-43, d. 2-6-93): Tennis player. First black man to win U.S. Open (1968, as an amateur), Australian Open (1970) and Wimbledon singles titles (1975). 33 career tournament victories. Member of Davis Cup team 1963–78; captain 1980–85.

Assault (b. 1943, d. 1971): Thoroughbred race horse. Horse of the Year for 1946; won Triple Crown that year.

Won Kentucky Derby by 8 lengths; Preakness by a neck over Lord Boswell; and the Belmont by 3 lengths from Natchez. Trained by Max Hirsch.

Red Auerbach (b. 9-20-17): Basketball coach-executive. 938 career wins. Coached Boston from 1946 to 1965, winning 9 championships, 8 consecutively. Had .662 career winning percentage, with 50+ wins 8 consecutive seasons. Also won 7 championships as general manager.

Hobey Baker (b. 1-15-1892, d. 12-21-18): Sportsman. Member of both college football and hockey Halls of Fame. College hockey and football star at Princeton, 1911–14. Fighter pilot in World War I, died in plane crash. College hockey Player of the Year award named in his honor.

Seve Ballesteros (b. 4-9-57): Spanish golfer. Notorious scrambler. Won British Opens in 1979, '84 and '88. Won Masters in 1980 and '83.

Ernie Banks (b. 1-31-31): Baseball SS-1B. "Mr. Cub." Won 2 consecutive MVP awards, in 1958–59. 512 career HR. League leader in HR, RBI 2 times each; career batting average of .274; 40+ HR 5 times; 100+ RBI 8 times. Most HR by a shortstop with 47 in 1958. Career span 1953–71 with Chicago.

Roger Bannister (b. 3-23-29): Track and field. British runner broke the 4-minute mile barrier, running 3:59.4 on May 6, 1954.

Red Barber (b. 2-17-08, d. 10-22-92): Sportscaster. TV-radio baseball announcer was the voice of Cincinnati, Brooklyn and NY Yankees. His expressions, such as "sitting in the catbird seat," "pea patch" and "rhubarb" captivated audiences from 1934 to 1966.

Charles Barkley (b. 2-20-63): Basketball F. All-Rookie team, 1985. Led NBA in rebounding, 1987. Averaged 20+ points in seven of 8 seasons with Philadelphia. 1992 Olympic team leading scorer. Traded to Phoenix before 1992–93 season, then to Houston before '96–97 season. League MVP for 1992–93 season.

Rick Barry (b. 3-28-44): Basketball F. Only player in history to win scoring titles in NBA (San Francisco, 1967) and ABA (Oakland, 1969). Second alltime highest free throw percentage (.900). Career scoring average 23.2. Led league in free throw percentage 6 times, steals and scoring 1 time each. Averaged 30+ points 2 times, 20+ points 6 other times. 5-time All-Star. 1975 playoff MVP with Golden State. 1966 Rookie of the Year. Career span 1967–79.

Carmen Basilio (b. 4-2-27): Boxer. Won titles in two weight classes, welter and middle. Won world welter title by TKO of Tony DeMarco in 12 rounds on 6-10-55. Won and then lost middleweight title in two 15-round fights with Ray Robinson. Made three unsuccessful bids to regain middle title. *The Ring* Fighter of the Year for 1957. Career record: 78 bouts; won 26 by KO and 29 by decision; drew 7; lost 16, two by KO.

Sammy Baugh (b. 3-17-14): Football QB-P. Led league in passing 6 times and punting 4 times, a record. Also holds record for highest career punting average (45.1) and highest season average (51.0 in 1940). Career span 1937–52 with Washington. Also All-America with Texas Christian 3 consecutive seasons.

Elgin Baylor (b. 9-16-34): Basketball F. Third alltime highest scoring average (27.4), scored 23,149 points. Averaged 30+ points 3 consecutive seasons, 20+ points 8 other times. 10-time All-Star. 1959 Rookie of the Year. Played in 8 finals without winning championship. Career span 1958–71 with Los Angeles. Also 1958 MVP in NCAA tournament with Seattle.

Bob Beamon (b. 8-29-46): Track and field. Gold medalist in long jump at 1968 Olympics with world record jump of 29' 2½" that stood until 1991.

Franz Beckenbauer (b. 1945): West German soccer player. Captain of 1974 World Cup champions and coach of 1990 champions. Also played for NY Cosmos from 1977 to 1980.

Boris Becker (b. 11-22-67): German tennis player. The youngest male player to win a Wimbledon singles title at age 17 in 1985. Won 3 Wimbledon titles (consecutively 1985–86, 1989), 1 U.S. Open (1989) and 1 Australian Open title (1991). Led West Germany to 2 consecutive Davis Cup victories (1988–89).

Chuck Bednarik (b. 5-1-25): Football C-LB. Last of the great two-way players, was named All-Pro at both center and linebacker. Missed only 3 games in 14 seasons with Philadelphia from 1949–62. Also All-America 2 times at Pennsylvania.

Clair Bee (b. 3-2-1896, d. 5-20-83): Basketball coach. Originated 1-3-1 defense, helped develop three-second rule, 24-second clock. Won 82.7 percent of games as coach for Rider College and Long Island University. Coach, Baltimore Bullets, 1952–54. Author, 23-volume Chip Hilton series for children, 21 nonfiction sports books.

Jean Beliveau (b. 8-31-31): Hockey C. Won MVP award 2 times (1956, 1964), playoff MVP in 1965. Led league in assists 3 times, goals 2 times and points 1 time. 507 career goals, 712 assists. All-Star 6 times. Played on 10 Stanley Cup champions with Montreal from 1950 to 1971.

Bert Bell (b. 2-25-1895, d. 10-11-59): Football executive. Second NFL commissioner (1946–59). Also owner of Philadelphia (1933–40) and Pittsburgh (1941–46). Proposed the first college draft in 1936.

James (Cool Papa) Bell (b. 5-17-03, d. 3-7-91): Baseball OF. Legendary foot speed—according to Satchel Paige could flip light switch and be in bed before room was dark. Hit .392 in games against white major leaguers. Career span 1922–46 with many teams of the Negro Leagues, including the Pittsburgh Crawfords and the Homestead Grays. Inducted in the Hall of Fame in 1974.

Lyudmila Belousova/Oleg Protopov (no dates of birth available): Soviet figure skaters. Won Olympic gold medal in pairs competition in 1964 and 1968. Won four consecutive World and European championships (1965–68) and eight consecutive Soviet titles (1961–68).

Deane Beman (b. 4-22-38): Commissioner of the PGA Tour 1974–94. Won British Amateur title in 1959 and U.S. Amateur titles in 1960 and 1963.

Johnny Bench (b. 12-7-47): Baseball C. MVP in 1970, 1972; World Series MVP in 1976; Rookie of the Year in 1968. 389 career HR. League leader in HR 2 times, RBI 3 times. Career span 1967–83 with Cincinnati. Elected to Hall of Fame in 1989.

Patty Berg (b. 2-13-18): Golfer. Alltime women's leader in major championships (16), third alltime in career wins (57). Won Titleholders Championship and Western Open 7 times each, the most of any golfer. Also won U.S. Women's Amateur (1938) and U.S. Women's Open (1946).

Yogi Berra (b. 5-12-25): Baseball C. Played on 10 World Series winners. Alltime Series leader in games, at bats, hits and doubles. MVP in 1951 and consecutively 1954–55. 358 career HR. Career span 1946–63, '65. Also managed pennant-winning Yankees (1964) and Mets (1973).

Jay Berwanger (b. 3-19-14): College football RB. Won the first Heisman Trophy and named All-America with Chicago in 1935.

Raymond Berry (b. 2-27-33): Football E. Led NFL in receiving 1958–60. In 13-season career, caught 631 passes, 68 for TDs. Career span 1955–67, all with Baltimore Colts. Later coached New England Patriots from 1984–89 with 51–41 record.

George Best (b. 5-22-46): Northern Ireland soccer player. Led Manchester United to European Cup title in 1968. Named England's and Europe's Player of the Year in 1968. Played in North American Soccer League for Los Angeles (1976–78), Fort Lauderdale (1978–79) and San Jose (1980–81). Frequent troubles with alcohol and gambling shadowed career.

Abebe Bikila (b. 8-7-32, d. 10-25-73): Track and field. Ethiopian barefoot runner won consecutive gold medals in the marathon at Olympics, in 1960 and 1964.

Fred Biletnikoff (b. 2-23-43): Football WR. In 14 pro seasons caught 589 passes for 8,974 yards and 76 TDs. In 1971 led NFL receivers with 61 catches; in '72 led AFC with 58. Career span 1965–78, all with Raiders. Elected to Pro Football Hall of Fame in 1988.

Dmitri Bilozerchev (b. 12-22-66): Soviet gymnast. Won 3 gold medals at 1988 Olympics. Made comeback after shattering his left leg into 44 pieces in 1985. Two-time world champion (1983, 1987). At 16, became youngest to win all-around world championship title in 1983.

Dave Bing (b. 11-24-43): Basketball G. Averaged 24.8 points a game in four years at Syracuse. NBA Rookie of Year in 1967. Led NBA in scoring (27.1) in 1968. MVP NBA All Star game in 1976. In 12-year career from 1967–78, most of it with Detroit Pistons, averaged 20.3 points.

Matt Biondi (b. 10-8-65): Swimmer. Winner of 5 gold medals, 1 silver medal and 1 bronze medal at 1988 Olympics. Won one gold and one silver at 1992 Olympics.

Larry Bird (b. 12-7-56): Basketball F. Won 3 consecutive MVP awards (1984–86) and 2 playoff MVP awards (1984, 1986). Also Rookie of the Year (1980) and All-Star 9 consecutive seasons. Led league in free throw percentage 4 times. Averaged 20+ points 10 times. Career span 1979–1992 with Boston. Named College Player of the Year in 1979 with Indiana State. 1997–98 NBA Coach of the Year in first year as coach of Indiana Pacers.

Bonnie Blair (b. 3-18-64): Speed skater. Won gold medal in 500 meters and bronze medal in 1,000 meters at 1988 Olympics and gold medals in both events in 1992 and '94. Also 1989 World Sprint champion. Winner of 1992 Sullivan Award. *Sports Illustrated* Sportswoman of the Year, 1994.

Toe Blake (b. 8-21-12, d. 5-17-95): Hockey LW and coach. Second alltime highest winning percentage (.634) and fifth in wins (500). Led Montreal to 8 Stanley Cup championships from 1955 to 1968 (consecutively 1956–60, 1965–66, 1968). Also MVP and scoring leader in 1939. Played on 2 Stanley Cup champions with Montreal from 1932 to 1948.

Doc Blanchard (b. 12-11-24): College football FB. "Mr. Inside." Teamed with Glenn Davis to lead Army to 3 consecutive undefeated seasons (1944–46) and 2 consecutive national championships (1944–45). Won Heisman Trophy and Sullivan Award in 1945. Also All-America 3 times.

George Blanda (b. 9-17-27): Football QB-K. Alltime leader in seasons played (26), games played (340), points scored (2,002) and points after touchdown (943); kicked 335 field goals. Also passed for 26,920 career yards and 236 touchdowns. Tied record with 7 touchdown passes on Nov. 19, 1961. Player of the Year 2 times (1961, 1970). Retired at age 48, the oldest to ever play. Career span 1949–75 with Chicago, Houston, Oakland.

Fanny Blankers-Koen (b. 4-26-18): Track and field. Dutch athlete won four gold medals at 1948 Olympics, in 100-meters; 200 meters; 80-meter hurdles; and 400-meter relay. Versatile, she also set world records in high jump (5' 7 ¼" in 1943), long jump (20' 6" in 1943) and pentathlon (4,692 points in 1951).

Wade Boggs (b. 6-15-58): Baseball 3B. Won 5 batting titles (1983, consecutively 1985–88); has had .350+ average 5 times, 200+ hits 7 times. Won World Series with 1996 Yankees. Career span 1982–92 with Boston, 1993–97 with New York Yankees, 1998– with Tampa Bay.

Nick Bolletieri (b. 7-31-31): Tennis coach. Since 1976, has run Nick Bolletieri Tennis Academy in Bradenton, Fla. Former residents of the academy include Andre Agassi, Monica Seles and Jim Courier.

Barry Bonds (b. 7-24-64): Baseball OF. One of two players—the other is Jose Canseco—to top 40 homers (42) and 40 steals (40) in same season (1996). Three-time National League MVP (1990, '92, '93); Career span 1986 to '92, with Pirates; 1993– with Giants.

Bjorn Borg (b. 6-6-56): Swedish tennis player. Second alltime in Grand Slam singles titles (11—tied with Rod Laver). Set modern record by winning 5 consecutive Wimbledon titles (1976–80). Won 6 French Open titles (consecutively 1974–75, 1978–81). Reached U.S. Open final 4 times, but title eluded him. 65 career tournament victories. Led Sweden to Davis Cup win in 1975.

Julius Boros (b. 3-3-20): Golfer. Won U.S. Opens in 1952 at Northwood CC in Dallas and in 1963 at The Country Club in Brookline, Mass. Also won 1968 PGA Championship at Pecan Valley CC, San Antonio, when 48 years old, making him oldest winner of a major ever. Led PGA money list in 1952 and '55.

Mike Bossy (b. 1-22-57): Hockey RW. In 1978 set NHL rookie scoring record of 54 goals, broken in 1993. Scored 50 or more each of first nine seasons, totaling 573 goals and 1,126 points in 10 seasons (1977–78 through 1986–87) with New York Islanders. Elected to Hall of Fame in 1991.

Ralph Boston (b. 5-9-39): Track and field. Long jumper won medals at 3 consecutive Olympics: gold in 1960, silver in 1964, bronze in 1968.

Ray Bourque (b. 12-28-60): Hockey D. Won Norris Trophy as NHL's top defenseman five times. Career span since1979 with Boston Bruins.

Scotty Bowman (b. 9-18-33): Hockey coach. Ended 1997–98 season as alltime leader in regular season wins (1,057) and in regular season winning percentage (.658). Also alltime leader in playoff wins (194). Has won 8 Stanley Cups; coached Montreal, St. Louis,

Buffalo, and Detroit. Won Jack Adams Award, Coach of the Year, 1976–77.

Bill Bradley (b. 7-28-43): Basketball F. Played on 2 NBA championship teams with New York from 1967 to 1977. Player of the Year and NCAA tournament MVP in 1965 with Princeton; All-America 3 times; Sullivan Award winner in 1965. Rhodes scholar. U.S. Senator (D-NJ) 1979–96.

Terry Bradshaw (b. 9-2-48): Football QB. Played on 4 Super Bowl champions (consecutively 1974–75, 1978–79); named Super Bowl MVP 2 consecutive seasons (1978–79). 212 career touchdown passes; 27,989 yards passing. Player of the Year in 1978. Career span 1970–83 with Pittsburgh.

George Brett (b. 5-15-53): Baseball 3B-1B. MVP in 1980 with .390 batting average; 3 batting titles, in 1976, 1980, 1990; and .300+ average 11 times. Led league in hits and triples 3 times. Reached 3,000-hit mark in 1992. Career span 1973–93, with Kansas City. Career totals: 3,153 hits; 317 HR; 1,595 RBIs; batting average .305.

Bret Hanover (b. 1962, d. 1993): Horse. Son of Adios. Won 62 of 68 harness races and earned $922,616. Undefeated as two-year-old. From total of 1,694 foals, he sired winners of $61 million and 511 horses which have recorded sub-2:00 performances.

Lou Brock (b. 6-18-39): Baseball OF. Second alltime most stolen bases (938); second most season steals in modern era (118). Led league in steals 8 times, with 50+ steals 12 consecutive seasons. Alltime World Series leader in steals (14—tied with Eddie Collins); hit .391 in World Series play. 3,023 career hits. Career span 1961–64 Chicago (NL), 1964–79 St. Louis.

Jim Brown (b. 2-17-36): Football FB. 126 career touchdowns; fourth in yards rushing (12,312). Led league in rushing a record 8 times. His 5.2 yards per carry average is the best ever. Player of the Year 4 times (consecutively 1957–58, 1963, 1965) and Rookie of the Year in 1957. Rushed for 1,000+ yards in 7 seasons, 200+ yards in 4 games, 100+ yards in 54 other games. Career span 1957–65 with Cleveland; never missed a game. Also All-America with Syracuse.

Paul Brown (b. 9-7-08, d. 8-5-91): Football coach. Led Cleveland to 10 consecutive championship games. Won 4 consecutive AAFC titles (1946–49) and 3 NFL titles (1950, consecutively 1954–55). Coached Cleveland from 1946 to 1962; became first coach of Cincinnati, 1968–75, and then general manager. Career coaching record 222-113-9. Also won national championship with Ohio State in 1942.

Avery Brundage (b. 9-28-1887, d. 5-5-75): Amateur sports executive. President of International Olympic Committee 1952–72. Served as president of U.S. Olympic Committee 1929–53. Also president of Amateur Athletic Union 1928–35. Member of 1912 U.S. Olympic track and field team.

Paul (Bear) Bryant (b. 9-11-13, d. 1-26-83): College football coach. Alltime Division I-A leader in wins (323). Won 6 national championships (1961, consecutively 1964–65, 1973, consecutively 1978–79) with Alabama. Career record 323–85–17, including 4 undefeated seasons. Also won 15 bowl games. Career span 1945–82 with Maryland, Kentucky, Texas A&M, Alabama.

Sergei Bubka (b. 12-4-63): Track and field. Ukrainian pole vaulter was gold medalist at 1988 Olympics. Only five-time world outdoor champion in any event (1983, 1987, 1991, 1993, 1995). First man to vault 20 feet, set

world indoor record of 20' 2" on 2-21-93 and world outdoor record of 20' 1½", set on 9-20-92.

Buck Buchanan (b. 9-10-40): Football DT. Career span 1963–75 with Kansas City Chiefs. Elected to Pro Football Hall of Fame 1990.

Don Budge (b. 6-13-15): Tennis player. First player to achieve the Grand Slam, in 1938. Won 2 consecutive Wimbledon and U.S. singles titles (1937–38), 1 French and 1 Australian title (1938).

Dick Butkus (b. 12-9-42): Football LB. Recovered 25 opponents' fumbles, third most in history. Selected for Pro Bowl 8 times. Career span 1965–73 with Chicago. Also All-America 2 times with Illinois. Award recognizing the outstanding college linebacker named in his honor.

Dick Button (b. 7-18-29): Figure skater. Gold medalist at 2 consecutive Olympics in 1948, 1952. World champion 5 consecutive years (1948–52) and U.S. champion 7 consecutive years (1946–52). Sullivan Award winner in 1949.

Walter Byers (b. 3-13-22): Amateur sports executive. First executive director of NCAA, served from 1952 to 1987.

Frank Calder (b. 11-17-1877, d. 2-4-43): Hockey executive. First commissioner of NHL, served from 1917 to 1943. Rookie of the Year award named in his honor.

Walter Camp (b. 4-7-1859, d. 3-14-25): Football pioneer. Played for Yale in its first football game vs. Harvard on Nov. 17, 1876. Proposed rules such as 11 men per side, scrimmage line, center snap, yards and downs. Founded the All-America selections in 1889.

Roy Campanella (b. 11-19-21; d. 6-26-93): Baseball C. Career span 1948–57, ended when paralyzed in car crash. MVP in 1951, 1953, 1955. Played on 5 pennant winners; 1955 World Series winner with Brooklyn Dodgers.

Earl Campbell (b. 3-29-55): Football RB. 9,407 career rushing yards; fourth alltime in season yards rushing (1,934 in 1980); 19 TDs rushing in 1979. Led league in rushing 3 consecutive seasons. Rushed for 1,000+ yards in 5 seasons. Scored 74 career touchdowns. Player of the Year 2 consecutive seasons (1978–79). Rookie of the Year in 1978. Career span 1978–85 with Houston, New Orleans. Won Heisman Trophy with Texas in 1977.

John Campbell (b. 4-8-55): Canadian harness racing driver. Alltime leading money winner with over $100 million in earnings. Leading money winner each year 1986–90.

Billy Cannon (b. 2-8-37): Football RB. Led Louisiana State to national championship in 1958 and won Heisman Trophy in 1959. Signed contract in both NFL (Los Angeles) and AFL (Houston). Houston won lawsuit for his services. Played in 6 AFL championship games with Houston, Oakland, Kansas City. Career span 1960–70. Served three-year jail term for 1983 conviction on counterfeiting charges.

Jose Canseco (b. 7-2-64): Baseball OF. One of two players—the other is Barry Bonds—to top 40 homers (42) and 40 steals (40) in same season (1988). AL MVP in 1988, when he also batted .307 with 124 RBIs. Career span 1985–1992 and 1997 with Oakland; 1993–94 with Texas; 1995–96 with Boston, 1998– with Toronto.

Harry Caray (b. 3-1-17, d. 2-18-98): Sportscaster. TV-radio baseball announcer 1945–97 with St. Louis (NL),

Oakland, Chicago (AL) and Chicago (NL). Achieved celebrity status on Cubs' superstation WGN by singing "Take Me Out to the Ballgame" with Wrigley Field fans.

Rod Carew (b. 10-1-45): Baseball 2B-1B. Won 7 batting titles (1969, consecutively 1972–75, 1977–78). Had .328 career average, 3,053 career hits, and .300+ average 15 times. 1977 MVP; 1967 Rookie of the Year. Career span 1967–85; jersey number (29) retired by Minnesota and California.

Steve Carlton (b. 12-22-44): Baseball LHP. Second alltime most strikeouts (4,136). 4 Cy Young awards (1972, 1977, 1980, 1982). 329 career wins; won 20+ games 6 times. League leader in wins 4 times, innings pitched and strikeouts 5 times each. Struck out 19 batters in one game in 1969. Career span 1965–88 with St. Louis, Philadelphia and four other teams in last two years.

JoAnne Carner (b. 4-21-39): Golfer. Won 42 titles, including U.S. Women's Opens in 1971 and '76 and du Maurier Classic in 1975 and '78. LPGA top earner in 1974 and 1982–83. LPGA Player of the Year in 1974 and 1981–82. Won five Vare Trophies (1974–75 and 1981–83).

Joe Carr (b. 10-22-1880; d. 5-20-39): Football administrator. Instrumental in forming American Professional Football Association in 1920. President of AAFA from 1922 to '39.

Don Carter (b. 7-29-26): Bowler. Won All-Star Tournament 4 times (1952, 1954, 1956, 1958) and PBA National Championship in 1960. Voted Bowler of the Year 6 times (consecutively 1953–54, 1957–58, 1960, 1962).

Alexander Cartwright (b. 4-17-1820, d. 7-12-1892): Baseball pioneer. Credited with setting the basic rules of baseball: bases 90 feet apart, 9 men per side, 3 strikes per out and 3 outs per inning. On June 19, 1846, in what is often cited as the first baseball game, his New York Knickerbockers lost to the New York Nine 23–1 at Elysian Fields in Hoboken, NJ.

Billy Casper (b. 6-24-31): Golfer. Famed putter. Won 51 PGA tournaments. PGA Player of Year in both 1966 and '70. Won Vardon Trophy in 1960, '63, '64, '65 and '68. Won the U.S. Open twice, in 1959 at Winged Foot in Mamaroneck, New York, and in 1966 in 18-hole playoff over Arnold Palmer at Olympic Club, San Francisco. Beat Gene Littler in 18 hole playoff to win 1970 Masters.

Tracy Caulkins (b. 1-11-63): Swimmer. Won 3 gold medals at 1984 Olympics. Won 48 U.S. national titles, more than any other swimmer, from 1978 to 1984. Also won Sullivan Award in 1978.

Steve Cauthen (b. 5-1-60): Jockey. In 1978 became youngest jockey to win Triple Crown, aboard Affirmed. First jockey to top $6 million in season earnings (1977). *Sports Illustrated* Sportsman of Year for 1977. Moved to England in 1979; rode Epsom Derby winners Slip Anchor (1985) and Reference Point (1987).

Evonne Goolagong Cawley (b. 7-31-51): Tennis. Won 4 Australian Open titles from 1974 through '77; won '71 French Open; Wimbledon in 1971 and '80. Runnerup four straight years at U.S. Open (1973–76), which she never won.

Bill Chadwick (b. 10-10-15): Hockey referee. Spent 16 years as a referee despite vision in only one eye. Developed hand signals to signify penalties. Also former television announcer for the New York Rangers.

Wilt Chamberlain (b. 8-21-36): Basketball C. Alltime leader in rebounds (23,924) and rebounding average (22.9). Alltime season leader in points scored (4,029 in 1962), scoring average (50.4 in 1962), rebounding average (27.2 in 1961) and field goal percentage (.727 in 1973). Alltime single-game most points scored (100 in 1962) and most rebounds (55 in 1960). Second alltime most points scored (31,419) and most field goals made (12,681). 4 MVP awards (1960, consecutively 1966–68); playoff MVP in 1972 and 1960 Rookie of the Year. 7-time All-Star. 30.1 career scoring average. Career span 1959–72 with Philadelphia, Los Angeles. College Player of the Year in 1957 at Kansas.

Colin Chapman (b. 1928, d. 12-16-83): Auto racing engineer. Founded Lotus race and street cars, designing the first Lotus racer in 1948. Introduced the monocoque design for Formula One cars in 1962 and ground effects in 1978.

Julio Cesar Chavez (b. 7-12-62): Boxer. Career record through 6-22-98: 100-2-2. Held titles as junior welterweight, lightweight and super featherweight.

Gerry Cheevers (b. 12-7-40): Hockey goalie. Goaltender for Stanley Cup-winning Boston Bruins teams of 1970 and '72. In 12 seasons with Boston had 230-94-74 record with a goals against average of 2.89. Also coached Bruins from 1980–84, with 204-126-46 record. Elected to Hall of Fame 1985.

Citation (b. 4-11-45, d. 8-8-70): Thoroughbred race horse. Triple Crown winner in 1948 with jockey Eddie Arcaro aboard. Trained by Ben A. Jones.

King Clancy (b. 2-25-03, d. 11-6-86): Hockey D. Four-time All-Star. Coach, Montreal Maroons, Toronto. Also referee. Trophy named in his honor, recognizing leadership qualities and contribution to community.

Jim Clark (b. 3-4-36, d. 4-7-68): Scottish auto racer. Twenty-five career Formula 1 victories. Formula 1 champion 2 times (1963, 1965). Won Indy 500 in 1965. Named Indy 500 Rookie of the Year in 1963. Killed during competition in 1968 at age 32.

Bobby Clarke (b. 8-13-49): Hockey C. Won MVP award 3 times (1973, consecutively 1975–76). 358 career goals, 852 assists. Scored 100+ points 3 times. Played on 2 consecutive Stanley Cup champions (1974–75) with Philadelphia. Career span 1969 to 1984. Also general manager with Philadelphia 1984–90, Minnesota 1991–92, Florida 1993–94, and Philadelphia since 1994.

Roger Clemens (b. 8-4-62): Baseball RHP. Has struck out a record 20 batters in one game on two occasions. Won 4 Cy Young Awards (1986–87, '91, '97), most by an AL pitcher. Also 1986 MVP. League leader in ERA 5 times, wins and strikeouts 3 times each. Won Triple Crown of pitching in 1997 with 21 wins, 292 strikeouts and 2.05 ERA. Career span 1984–96 with Boston, 1997– with Toronto.

Roberto Clemente (b. 8-18-34, d. 12-31-72): Baseball OF. Killed in plane crash while still an active player. Had 3,000 career hits and .317 career average. 4 batting titles; .300+ average 13 times. 1966 MVP; 1971 World Series MVP. 12 consecutive Gold Gloves; led league in assists 5 times. Career span 1955–72 with Pittsburgh.

Ty Cobb (b. 12-18-1886, d. 7-17-61): Baseball OF. Alltime leader in batting average (.366) and runs scored (2,245); second most hits (4,191); fourth most stolen bases (892). 1911 MVP and 1909 Triple Crown winner. 12 batting titles. Had .400+ average 3 times, .350+ average 13 other times; 200+ hits 9 times. Led league in hits 7 times, steals 6 times and runs scored 5 times. Career span 1905–28 with Detroit.

Mickey Cochrane (b. 4-6-03, d. 6-28-62): Baseball C. Alltime highest career batting average among catchers (.320). MVP in 1928, 1934. Had .300+ average 8 times. Career span 1925–37 with Philadelphia, Detroit.

Sebastian Coe (b. 9-29-56): Track and field. British runner was gold medalist in 1,500 meters and silver medalist in 800 meters at 2 consecutive Olympics in 1980, 1984. Set world record in 800 meters (1:41.73 in 1981) and 1,000 meters (2:12.18 in 1981). Served in Parliament after his running career.

Eddie Collins (b. 5-2-1887, d. 3-25-51): Baseball 2B. Alltime leader among 2nd basemen in games, chances and assists; led league in fielding 9 times. 3,311 career hits; .333 career average; .330+ average 12 times. 743 career stolen bases; alltime most World Series steals (14—tied high with Lou Brock); alltime leader in single-game steals (6, twice). 1914 MVP. Career span 1906–30 with Philadelphia, Chicago.

Nadia Comaneci (b. 11-12-61): Romanian gymnast. First ever to score a perfect 10 at Olympics (on uneven parallel bars in 1976). Won 3 gold, 2 silver and 1 bronze medal at 1976 Olympics. Also won 2 gold and 2 silver medals at 1980 Olympics.

Dennis Conner (b. 9-16-42): Sailing. Captain of America's Cup winner 3 times (1980, '87, '88).

Maureen Connolly (b. 9-17-34, d. 6-21-69): Tennis player. "Little Mo" first woman to achieve the Grand Slam, in 1953. Won the U.S. singles title in 1951 at age 16. Thereafter lost only 4 matches before retiring in 1954 because of a broken leg caused by a riding accident. Was never beaten in singles at Wimbledon, winning 3 consecutive titles (1952–54). Won 3 consecutive U.S. singles titles (1951–53) and 2 consecutive French titles (1953–54). Also won 1 Australian title (1953).

Jimmy Connors (b. 9-2-52): Tennis player. Alltime men's leader in tournament victories (109). Held men's #1 ranking a record 160 consecutive weeks, July 29, 1974 through Aug. 16, 1977. Won 5 U.S. Open singles titles on 3 different surfaces (grass 1974, clay 1976, hard 1978, consecutively 1982–83). Won 2 Wimbledon singles titles (1974, 1982) further apart than anyone since Bill Tilden. Also won 1974 Australian Open title. Reached Grand Slam final 7 other times.

Jim Corbett (b. 9-1-1866; d. 2-18-33): Boxer. "Gentleman Jim." Invented jab. Fight with Australian Peter Jackson on 5-21-1891 ruled no contest when neither could continue into 62nd round. Won heavyweight title on 9-7-1892 with a KO of John Sullivan in 21 rounds; it was first heavyweight title fight using gloves. Lost title when KO'd by Bob Fitzsimmons in 14 on 3-17-1897, then lost two bids to regain it against Jim Jeffries. Career record: 19 fights; won 7 by KO and 4 by decision; drew 2; lost 4; 2 no decision.

Angel Cordero (b. 11-8-42): Jockey. Through June 1996, third alltime in wins (7,057) and earnings ($164,561,227). Led yearly earnings three times, in 1976 and 1982–83, winning Eclipse Awards in the last two years.

Howard Cosell (b. 3-25-18, d. 4-23-95): Sportscaster. Lawyer turned TV-radio sports commentator in 1953. Best known for his work on "Monday Night Football." His nasal voice and "tell it like it is" approach made him a controversial figure.

James (Doc) Counsilman (b. 12-28-20): Swimming coach. Coached Indiana from 1957 to 1990. Won 6 consecutive NCAA championships (1968–73). Career record 287–36–1. Coached U.S. men's team at Olympics in 1964, 1976. Also oldest person to swim English Channel (58 in 1979).

Count Fleet (b. 3-24-40, d. 12-3-73): Thoroughbred race horse. Triple Crown winner in 1943 with jockey Johnny Longden aboard. Trained by Don Cameron.

Yvan Cournoyer (b. 11-22-43): Hockey RW. "The Roadrunner" had 428 goals and 435 assists during his 15 season career with the Montreal Canadiens. Had 25 or more goals in 12 straight seasons. Played on 10 Stanley Cup championship teams. Elected to Hall of Fame in 1982.

Margaret Smith Court (b. 7-16-42): Australian tennis player. Alltime leader in Grand Slam singles titles (24) and total Grand Slam titles (62). Achieved Grand Slam in 1970 and mixed doubles Grand Slam in 1963 with Ken Fletcher. Won 11 Australian singles titles (consecutively 1960–66, 1969–71, 1973), 5 French titles (1962, 1964, consecutively 1969–70, 1973), 5 U.S. titles (1962, 1965, consecutively 1969–70, 1973) and 3 Wimbledon titles (1963, 1965, 1970). Also won 19 Grand Slam doubles titles and 19 mixed doubles titles.

Bob Cousy (b. 8-9-28): Basketball G. Finished career with 6,955 assists; in 1958 had 28 assists in a single game. League leader in assists 8 consecutive seasons. Averaged 18+ points and named to All-Star team 10 consecutive seasons. 1957 MVP. Played on 6 championship teams with Boston from 1950 to 1969. Also played on NCAA championship team in 1947 with Holy Cross.

Dave Cowens (b. 10-25-48): Basketball C. After college career at Florida State, NBA co-Rookie of Year in 1971. NBA MVP for 1973. All-Star game MVP in 1973. Career span 1970–71 through 1982–83, all but the last year with the Boston Celtics. Coach of Charlotte Hornets 1996–. Elected to Hall of Fame in 1991.

Ben Crenshaw (b. 1-11-52): Golfer. Legendary putter. Won Masters in 1984 and 1995.

Larry Csonka (b. 12-25-46): Football RB. In 11 seasons rushed 1,891 times for 8,081 yards (4.3 per carry) and 64 TDs. MVP of Super Bowl VIII, when he rushed 33 times for a then Super Bowl record 145 yards in Miami's 24–7 defeat of Minnesota. Career span 1968–74, 1979 with Miami Dolphins; 1976–78 with New York Giants. Elected to Hall of Fame in 1987.

Billy Cunningham (b. 6-3-43): Basketball player and coach. Averaged 24.8 points a game at North Carolina. In nine seasons (1965–66 through 1975–76) with Philadelphia 76ers, averaged 20.8 points per game. All NBA first team 1969, '70 and '71. In 8 seasons as Sixers coach went 454–196 in regular season, 66–39 in playoffs and won NBA title in 1983. Elected to Hall of Fame in 1985.

Chuck Daly (b. 7-20-30): Basketball coach. Won 2 consecutive championships with Detroit (1989–90). Won 50+ games 4 consecutive seasons. Coach of 1992 Olympic team. Career span as pro coach 1983–92 with Pistons; 1992–94 with New Jersey; 1997– with Orlando.

Damascus (b. 1964, d. 1995): Thoroughbred race horse. After finishing 3rd in 1967 Kentucky Derby, won the Preakness, the Belmont, the Dwyer, the American Derby, the Travers, the Woodward and others—12 of 16 starts. Unanimous Horse of the Year in 1967.

Stanley Dancer (b. 7-25-27): Harness racing driver. Only driver to win the Trotting Triple Crown 2 times (Nevele Pride in 1968, Super Bowl in 1972). Also won Pacing Triple Crown driving Most Happy Fella in 1970. Won The Hambletonian 4 times (1968, 1972, 1975, 1983). Driver of the Year in 1968. ·

Tamas Darnyi (b. 6-3-67): Hungarian swimmer. Gold medalist in 200-meter and 400-meter individual medleys at 1988 and 1992 Olympics. Also won both events at World Championships in 1986 and 1991. Set world records in these events at 1991 Championships (1:59.36 and 4:12.36).

Al Davis (b. 7-4-29): Football executive. Owner and general manager of Oakland-LA Raiders since 1963. Built winningest franchise in sports history (332-221-11—a .598 winning percentage entering the 1998 season). Team has won 3 Super Bowl championships (1976, 1980, 1983). Also served as AFL commissioner in 1966, helped negotiate AFL–NFL merger.

Ernie Davis (b. 12-14-39, d. 5-18-63): Football RB. Won Heisman Trophy in 1961, the first black man to win the award. All-America 3 times at Syracuse. First selection in 1962 NFL draft, but became fatally ill with leukemia and never played professionally.

Glenn Davis (b. 12-26-24): College football HB. "Mr. Outside." Teamed with Doc Blanchard to lead Army to 3 consecutive undefeated seasons (1944–46) and 2 consecutive national championships (1944–45). Won Heisman Trophy in 1946. Also named All-America 3 times.

John Davis (b. 1-12-21, d. 7-13-84): Weightlifter. Gold medalist at 2 consecutive Olympics, 1948, 1952. World champion 6 times.

Pete Dawkins (b. 3-8-38): Football RB. Starred at Army 1956–58. Won Heisman Trophy 1958. Was first captain of cadets, class president, top 5 percent of class academically, and football team captain; first man to do all four at West Point. Did not play pro football. Attended Oxford on Rhodes scholarship, won two Bronze Stars in Vietnam, rose to brigadier general before leaving Army to become investment banker. Made unsuccessful run for Senate from New Jersey in 1988.

Len Dawson (b. 6-20-35): Football QB. Completed 2,136 of 3,741 pass attempts with 239 TDs. In Super Bowl I threw for one TD in 35–10 loss to Green Bay. MVP of Super Bowl IV. Career span 1957–75, the last 13 seasons with Kansas City Chiefs. Elected to Hall of Fame in 1987.

Dizzy Dean (b. 1-16-11, d. 7-17-74): Baseball RHP. 1934 MVP with 30 wins. League leader in strikeouts, complete games 4 times each. 150 career wins. Arm trouble shortened career after 134 wins by age 26. Career span 1930–41 and 1947 with St. Louis and Chicago Cubs.

Dave DeBusschere (b. 10-16-40): Basketball F. NBA First Team Defense six straight seasons, 1969–74. Member of NBA champion New York Knicks in 1970 and '73. Career span 1962–63 through middle of 1968–69 season with Detroit Pistons; through 1973–74 with Knicks. Youngest coach (24) in NBA history. Elected to NBA Hall of Fame in 1982.

Pierre de Coubertin (b. 1-1-1863, d. 9-2-37): Frenchman called the father of the Modern Olympics. President of International Olympic Committee from 1896 to 1925.

Jack Dempsey (b. 6-24-1895, d. 5-31-83): Boxer. Heavyweight champion (1919–26), lost title to Gene Tunney and rematch in the famous "long count" bout in 1927. Career record 62-6-10 with 49 KOs from 1914 to 1928.

Gail Devers (b. 11-19-66): Track and field sprinter/hurdler. Won 100 at 1992 and '96 Olympics; leading 100 hurdles in '92 when she tripped over final hurdle and finished fifth. Successfully completed 100m/100h double at 1993 World Championships, winning 100 in 10.82 and 100 hurdles in American record 12.46. Also won '93 world indoor title in 60 (6.95). Battled Graves Disease.

Klaus Dibiasi (b. 10-6-47): Italian diver. Gold medalist in platform at 3 consecutive Olympics (1968, 1972, 1976) and silver medalist at 1964 Olympics.

Eric Dickerson (b. 9-2-60): Football RB. Alltime season leader in yards rushing (2,105 in 1984), third alltime most career yards rushing (13,259). Rushed for 1,000+ yards in 7 consecutive seasons; 100+ yards in 61 games, including 12 times in 1984. Led league in rushing 4 times. Rookie of the Year in 1983. Career span 1983–93 with Los Angeles Rams, Indianapolis, L.A. Raiders and Atlanta Falcons.

Bill Dickey (b. 6-6-07 d. 11-12-93): Baseball C. Lifetime average .313. Hit 202 career home runs. Played on 11 AL All-Star teams. In eight World Series, hit five homers and 24 RBIs. Career span 1928–43 and 1946, all with the New York Yankees. Inducted to Hall of Fame 1954.

Harrison Dillard (b. 7-8-23): Track and field. Only man to win Olympic gold medal in sprint (100 meters in 1948) and hurdles (110 meters in 1952). Sullivan Award winner in 1955.

Joe DiMaggio (b. 11-25-14): Baseball OF. Voted baseball's greatest living player. Record 56-game hitting streak in 1941. MVP in 1939, 1941, 1947. Had .325 career batting average; .300+ average 11 times; 100+ RBI 9 times. League leader in batting average, HR, and RBI 2 times each. Played on 10 World Series winners with NY Yankees. Career span 1936–51.

Mike Ditka (b. 10-18-39): Football TE-Coach. NFL Rookie of the Year in 1961. Named to Pro Bowl five times. Made 427 catches for 5,812 yards and 43 TDs. Career span 1961 to '72 with Bears, Eagles and Cowboys. Coach of Bears from 1982–92 with 112–68 overall record. Coach of Bears team that won Super Bowl XX, 46–10 over New England. Coach of New Orleans 1997–. Elected to Hall of Fame 1988.

Tony Dorsett (b. 4-7-54): Football RB. Third alltime in yards rushing (12,739), fourth in attempts (2,936). Rushed for 1,000+ yards in 8 seasons. Set record for longest run from scrimmage with 99-yard touchdown run on Jan. 3, 1983. Scored 91 career touchdowns. Named Rookie of the Year in 1977. Career span 1977–88 with Dallas, Denver. Also won Heisman Trophy in 1976, leading Pittsburgh to national championship. Alltime NCAA leader in yards rushing and only man to break 6,000-yard barrier (6,082).

Abner Doubleday (b. 6-26-1819, d. 1-26-1893): Civil War hero incorrectly credited as the inventor of baseball in Cooperstown, NY, in 1839.

Clyde Drexler (b. 6-22-62): Basketball G. Nicknamed "The Glide" for his smooth play. Member of U.S. "Dream Team" that won 1992 Olympic gold medal. Career span 1984–1994 with Portland Trail Blazers and 1995–98 with Houston Rockets, with whom he won his first NBA title in 1995.

Ken Dryden (b. 8-8-47): Hockey G. Goaltender of the Year 5 times (1973, consecutively 1976–79). Playoff MVP as a rookie in 1971, maintained rookie status and named Rookie of the Year in 1972. Led league in goals against average 5 times. Career record 258-57-74, including 46 shutouts. Career 2.24 goals against average is the modern record. 4 playoff shutouts in 1977. Played on 6 Stanley Cup champions with Montreal from 1970 to 1979.

Don Drysdale (b. 7-23-36, d. 7-3-93): Baseball RHP. Led NL three times in strikeouts (1959, '60, '62) and once in wins (1962). Won 1962 Cy Young Award with 25–9 mark. In 1968 pitched six straight shutouts en route to major league record—broken in 1988 by Orel Hershiser—of 58 consecutive scoreless innings. Career record of 209-166, with 2,484 K's and ERA of 2.95. Career span 1956–69, all with Dodgers. Inducted into Hall of Fame 1984.

Roberto Duran (b. 6-16-51): Panamanian boxer. Champion in 3 different weight classes: lightweight (1972–79), welterweight (1980, lost rematch to Sugar Ray Leonard in famous "no más" bout) and junior middleweight (1983–84).

Leo Durocher (b. 7-27-05, d. 10-7-91): Baseball manager. "Leo the Lip." Said "Nice guys finish last." Managed 3 pennant winners and 1954 World Series winner. Won 2,008 games in 24 years. Led Brooklyn 1939–48; New York 1948–55; Chicago 1966–72; and Houston 1972–73.

Eddie Eagan (b. 4-26-1898, d. 6-14-67): Only American athlete to win gold medal at Summer and Winter Olympic Games (boxing 1920, bobsled 1932).

Alan Eagleson (b. 4-24-33): Hockey labor leader. Founder of NHL Players' Association and its executive director from 1967–92. Pleaded guilty on 1-6-98 to three counts of fraud and theft involving players' insurance premiums; served six months with a 18-month jail sentence. Resigned from Hall of Fame 3-25-98.

Dale Earnhardt (b. 4-29-52): Auto racer. NASCAR champion 7 times (1980, 1986–87, 1990–91, 1993–94). 70 career NASCAR victories through 6-22-98.

Stefan Edberg (b. 1-19-66): Swedish tennis player. Won 2 Wimbledon singles titles (1988, 1990), 2 Australian Open titles (1985, 1987) and 2 U.S. Open titles (1991, 1992). Led Sweden to 3 Davis Cup victories (consecutively 1984–85, 1987).

Gertrude Ederle (b. 10-23-06): Swimmer. First woman to swim the English Channel, in 1926. Swam 21 miles from France to England in 14:39. Also won 3 medals at the 1924 Olympics.

Herb Elliott (b. 2-25-38): Track and field. Australian runner was gold medalist in 1960 Olympic 1,500 meters in world record 3:35.6. Also set world mile record of 3:54.5 in 1958. Undefeated at 1500 meters/mile in international competition. Retired at 22.

John Elway (b. 6-28-60): Football QB. First player taken in 1983 NFL draft. Topped 3,000 yards passing every season from 1985–91. Through '97 season had thrown for 48,669 yards, 278 TDs. Famous for last-minute drives. Won Super Bowl XXXII after three previous Super Bowl losses. Career span since 1983 with Denver Broncos.

Roy Emerson (b. 11-3-36): Australian tennis player. Alltime men's leader in Grand Slam singles titles (12). Won 6 Australian titles, 5 consecutively (1961, 1963–67), 2 consecutive Wimbledon titles (1964–65), 2 U.S. titles (1961, 1964) and 2 French titles (1963, 1967). Also won 13 Grand Slam doubles titles.

Kornelia Ender (b. 10-25-58): East German swimmer. Won 4 gold medals at 1976 Olympics and 3 silver medals at 1972 Olympics.

Julius Erving (b. 2-22-50): "Dr. J." Basketball F. Third alltime most points scored for combined ABA and NBA career (30,026). 24.2 scoring average. Averaged 20+ points 14 consecutive seasons. 4 MVP awards, consecutively 1974–76, 1981; playoff MVP 1974, 1976. All-Star 9 times. Led league in scoring 3 times. Played on 3 championship teams, with New York (ABA) and Philadelphia (NBA). Career span 1971 to 1986. Executive VP of Orlando 1997–. Elected to Hall of Fame in 1993.

Phil Esposito (b. 2-20-42): Hockey C. "Espo." First to break the 100-point barrier (126 in 1969). 1,590 career points, 717 goals, and 873 assists. Led league in goals 6 consecutive seasons, points 5 times and assists 3 times. Won MVP award 2 times (1969, 1974). Scored 30+ goals 13 consecutive seasons and 100+ points 6 times. All-Star 6 times. Career span 1963–81 with Chicago, Boston, NY Rangers. General manager of NY Rangers from 1986–89. Currently GM of Tampa Bay.

Tony Esposito (b. 4-23-43): Hockey goalie. Brother of Phil. A five-time All Star during 16-season NHL career, almost all of it with the Chicago Blackhawks. In 886 games gave up 2,563 goals, an average of 2.92 per game. Won or shared Vezina Trophy three times. Elected to Hall of Fame in 1988.

Janet Evans (b. 8-28-71): Swimmer. Competed in 1988, '92 and '96 Olympics, winning 3 gold medals in '88 and 1 in '92. Set world record in 400-meter freestyle (4:03.85 in 1988), 800-meter freestyle (8:16.22 in 1989) and 1,500-meter freestyle (15:52.10 in 1988). Sullivan Award winner in 1989.

Lee Evans (b. 2-25-47): Track and field. Gold medalist in 400 meters at 1968 Olympics with world record time of 43.86 that stood until 1988.

Chris Evert (b. 12-21-54): Also Chris Evert Lloyd. Tennis player. Second alltime in tournament victories (157). Tied for fourth alltime in women's Grand Slam singles titles (18). Won at least 1 Grand Slam singles title every year from 1974 to '86. Won 7 French Open titles (1974–75, 1979–80, 1983, 1985–86), 6 U.S. Open titles (1975–77, 1978, 1980, 1982), 3 Wimbledon titles (1974, 1976, 1981) and 2 Australian Open titles (1982, 1984). Reached Grand Slam finals 16 other times. Reached semifinals at 52 of her last 56 Grand Slams.

Weeb Ewbank (b. 5-6-07): Football coach. Only coach to win titles in both the NFL and AFL. Coached Baltimore Colts to classic overtime defeat of New York Giants in 1958 and New York Jets to their stunning 16–7 win over Baltimore in Super Bowl III. Career record of 134-130-7. Career span 1954–62 with Colts and 1963–73 with Jets. Elected to Hall of Fame in 1978.

Patrick Ewing (b. 8-5-62): Basketball C. 1986 Rookie of the Year with New York. 20+ points average in all 12 seasons with Knicks. All-NBA first team 1990. Played on 3 NCAA final teams with Georgetown (1982, 1984–85); tournament MVP in 1984. All-America 3 times.

Nick Faldo (b. 7-18-57): British golfer. Three-time winner of Masters (1989–90, consecutively, 1996) and British Open 3 times (1987, 1990, 1992).

Juan Manuel Fangio (b. 6-24-11, d. 7-17-95): Argentine auto racer. 24 Formula 1 victories in just 51 starts. Formula 1 champion 5 times, the most of any driver (1951, consecutively 1954–57). Retired in 1958.

Bob Feller (b. 11-3-18): Baseball RHP. League leader in wins 6 times, strikeouts 7 times, innings pitched 5 times. Pitched 3 no-hitters and 12 one-hitters. 266 career wins; 2,581 career strikeouts. Won 20+ games 6 times. Served 4 years in military during career. Career span 1936–41, 1945–56 with Cleveland.

Tom Ferguson (b. 12-20-50): Rodeo. First to top $1 million in career earnings. All-Around champion 6 consecutive years (1974–79).

Enzo Ferrari (b. 2-8-1898, d. 8-14-88): Auto racing engineer. Team owner since 1929, he built first Ferrari race car in Italy in 1947 and continued to preside over Ferrari race and street cars until his death. In 68 years of competition, Ferrari's cars have won over 5,000 races.

Mark Fidrych (b. 8-14-54): Baseball RHP. "The Bird." Rookie of the Year in 1976 with Detroit. Had 19–9 record with league-best 2.39 ERA and 24 complete games. Habit of talking to the ball on the mound made him a cult hero. Arm injuries curtailed career.

Cecil Fielder (b. 9-21-63): Baseball 1B. Hit 51 HR in 1990. Has led the major leagues in HR twice and RBI 3 consecutive seasons (1990–92) after spending 1989 season in Japanese league. Career span since 1985 with Toronto, Detroit, NY Yankees and Anaheim.

Herve Filion (b. 2-1-40): Harness racing driver. Alltime leader in career wins (more than 13,000). Driver of the Year 10 times, more than any other driver (consecutively 1969–74, 1978, 1981, 1989).

Rollie Fingers (b. 8-25-46): Baseball RHP. Fourth alltime in relief wins (107); 341 career saves; 944 appearances. 1981 Cy Young and MVP winner; 1974 World Series MVP. Alltime leader in saves (6). Career span 1968–85 with Oakland, San Diego, Milwaukee.

Bobby Fischer (b. 3-9-43): Chess. World champion from 1972 to 1975, the only American to hold title. Never played competitive chess during his reign. Forfeited title to Anatoly Karpov by refusing to play him.

Carlton Fisk (b. 12-26-47): Baseball C. Alltime HR leader among catchers (352) and second in games caught (2,226). 376 career HR, including a record 75 after age 40. Rookie of the Year in 1972 and All-Star 11 times. Hit dramatic 12th-inning HR to win Game 6 of 1975 World Series. Career span 1969–93 with Boston, Chicago (AL).

Emerson Fittipaldi (b. 12-12-46): Brazilian auto racer. Won Indy 500 in 1989 and '93. Won CART championship in 1989. Formula 1 champion 2 times (1972, 1974).

James Fitzsimmons (b. 7-23-1874, d. 3-11-66): Horse racing trainer. "Sunny Jim." Trained Triple Crown winner 2 times (Gallant Fox in 1930, Omaha in 1935). Trained Belmont Stakes winner 6 times (1930, 1932, consecutively 1935–36, 1939, 1955), Preakness Stakes winner 4 times (1930, 1935, 1955, 1957) and Kentucky Derby winner 3 times (1930, 1935, 1939).

Peggy Fleming (b. 7-27-48): Figure skater. Olympic champion 1968. World champion (1966–68) and U.S. champion (1964–68).

Curt Flood (b. 1-18-38, d. 1-20-97): Baseball OF. Won 7 consecutive Gold Gloves from 1963 to 1969. Career batting average of .293. Refused to be traded after 1969 season, challenging baseball's reserve clause. Supreme Court rejected his plea, but baseball was eventually forced to adopt free agency system. Career span 1956–69 with St. Louis.

Whitey Ford (b. 10-21-26): Baseball LHP. Alltime World Series leader in wins, losses, games started, innings pitched, hits allowed, walks and strikeouts. 236 career wins, 2.75 ERA. Alltime leader career winning percentage (.690—tied with Dave Foutz). Led league in wins and winning percentage 3 times each; ERA, shutouts, innings pitched 2 times each. 1961 Cy Young winner and World Series MVP. Career span 1950, 1953–67 with New York Yankees.

Forego (b. 1970, d. 8-27-97): Thoroughbred race horse. Horse of the Year in 1974 (won 8 of 13 starts); '75 (won 6 of 9); and '76 (won 6 of 8). Finished fourth in 1973 Kentucky Derby. Over six years won 34 of 57 starts and $1,938,957.

George Foreman (b. 1-22-48): Boxer. Heavyweight champion (1973–74). Retired in 1977, but returned to the ring in 1987. Lost 12-round decision to champion Evander Holyfield in 1991. Retired after losing to Tommy Morrison 6-7-93; returned again in 1994 at age 45 to KO Michael Moorer for heavyweight title. Also heavyweight gold medalist at 1968 Olympics.

Dick Fosbury (b. 3-6-47): Track and field. Gold medalist in high jump at 1968 Olympics. Introduced back-to-the-bar style of high jumping, called the "Fosbury Flop."

Jimmie Foxx (b. 10-22-07, d. 7-21-67): Baseball 1B. Won 3 MVP awards, consecutively 1932–33, 1938. Fourth alltime highest slugging average (.609), with 534 career HR; hit 30+ HR 12 consecutive seasons, 100+ RBI 13 consecutive seasons. Won Triple Crown in 1933. Led league in HR 4 times, batting average 2 times. Career span 1925–45 with Philadelphia, Boston.

A.J. Foyt (b. 1-16-35): Auto racer. Alltime leader in Indy Car victories (67). Won Indy 500 4 times (1961, 1964, 1967, 1977), Daytona 500 1 time (1972), 24 Hours of Daytona 2 times (1983, 1985) and 24 Hours of LeMans 1 time (1967). USAC champion 7 times, more than any other driver (consecutively 1960–61, 1963–64, 1967, 1975, 1979).

William H.G. France (b. 9-26-09, d. 6-7-92): Auto racing executive. Founder of NASCAR and president from 1948 to 1972, succeeded by his son Bill Jr. Builder of Daytona and Talladega speedways.

Dawn Fraser (b. 9-4-37): Australian swimmer. First swimmer to win gold medal in same event at 3 consecutive Olympics (100-meter freestyle in 1956, 1960, 1964). First woman to break the 1-minute barrier at 100 meters (59.9 in 1962).

Joe Frazier (b. 1-12-44): Boxer. "Smokin' Joe." Heavyweight champion (1970–73). Best known for his 3 epic bouts with Muhammad Ali. Career record 32-4-1 with 27 KOs from 1965 to 1976. Also heavyweight gold medalist at 1964 Olympics.

Walt Frazier (b. 3-29-45): Basketball G. Point guard on championship Knick teams of 1970 and '73. First team All Star in 1970, '72, '74 and '75. First team All Defense every year from 1969–1975. Averaged 18.9 points per game in 13-season NBA career. Elected to Hall of Fame in 1986.

Frankie Frisch (b. 9-9-1898, d. 3-12-73): Baseball IF. "The Fordham Flash." Led NL in hits in 1923 (223). Hit over .300 13 seasons. Scored 100+ runs 7 times. Drove in 100+ runs three times. Career .316 batting average. Career span 1919–26 with New York Giants and 1927–37 with St. Louis Cardinals "Gashouse Gang." NL MVP in 1931. Elected to Hall of Fame in 1947.

Dan Gable (b. 10-25-48): Wrestler. Gold medalist in 149–pound division at 1972 Olympics. Also NCAA champion 2 times (in 1968 at 130 pounds, in 1969 at 137 pounds). Coached Iowa to NCAA championship 15 times (consecutively 1978–86, 1991–93 and 1995–97).

Clarence Gaines (b. 5-21-23): College basketball coach. "Bighouse." Retired after 1992–93 season with 828 career wins in 46 seasons at Division II Winston-Salem State since 1947.

John Galbreath (b. 8-10-1897, d. 7-20-88): Horse racing owner. Owner of Darby Dan Farms from 1935 until his death and of baseball's Pittsburgh Pirates from 1946 to 1985. Only man to breed and own winners of both the Kentucky Derby (Chateaugay in 1963 and Proud Clarion in 1967) and the Epsom Derby (Roberto in 1972).

Gallant Fox (b. 3-23-27, d. 11-13-54): Thoroughbred race horse. Triple Crown winner in 1930 with jockey Earle Sande aboard. Trained by James Fitzsimmons. The only Triple Crown winner to sire another Triple Crown winner (Omaha in 1935).

Don Garlits (b. 1-14-32): Auto racer. "Big Daddy." Has won 35 National Hot Rod Association top fuel events. Won 3 NHRA top fuel points titles (1975, 1985–86). First top fuel driver to surpass 190 mph (1963), 200 mph (1964), 240 mph (1973), 250 mph (1975) and 270 mph (1986). Credited with developing rear engine dragster.

Lou Gehrig (b. 6-19-03, d. 6-2-41): Baseball 1B. "The Iron Horse." Second alltime in consecutive games played (2,130), leader in grand slam HR (23), third in RBI (1,995) and slugging average (.632). MVP in 1927, 1936; won Triple Crown in 1934. .340 career average; 493 career HR. 100+ RBI 13 consecutive seasons. Led league in RBI 5 times and HR 3 times. Played on 7 World Series winners with New York Yankees. Died of disease since named for him. Career span 1923–39.

Bernie Geoffrion (b. 2-16-31): Hockey RW. "Boom Boom" for his powerful slapshot. Won Hart Memorial Trophy for 1960–61. Scored 393 goals and 429 assists in 16 seasons (1950–51 through 1967–68), the first 14 with the Montreal Canadiens, the final two with the New York Rangers. Elected to Hall of Fame 1972.

Eddie Giacomin (b. 6-6-39): Hockey goalie. "Fast Eddie" led NHL goalies in games won for three straight seasons. Shared Vezina Trophy for 1970–71. In 610 games gave up 1,675 goals, a goals against average of 2.82. Career span 1965–75 with the New York Rangers and 1975–78 with Detroit Red Wings.

Althea Gibson (b. 8-25-27): Tennis player. Won 2 consecutive Wimbledon and U.S. singles titles (1957–58), the first black player to win these tournaments. Also won 1 French title (1956).

Bob Gibson (b. 11-9-35): Baseball RHP. 1968 Cy Young and MVP award winner with modern National League best ERA (1.12) and second most shutouts (13). Also 1970 Cy Young award winner. Record holder for most strikeouts in a World Series game (17); Series MVP in 1964, 1967. Won 20+ games 5 times. 251 career wins; 3,117 strikeouts. Pitched no-hitter in 1971. Career span 1959–75 with St. Louis.

Josh Gibson (b. 12-21-11, d. 1-20-47): Baseball C in Negro leagues. "The Black Babe Ruth." Couldn't play in major leagues because of skin color. Credited with 950 HR (75 in 1931, 69 in 1934) and .350 batting

average. Had .400+ average 2 times. Career span 1930–46 with Homestead Grays, Pittsburgh Crawfords.

Kirk Gibson (b. 5-28-57): Baseball OF. Played on 2 World Series champions (Detroit in 1984 and Los Angeles in 1988). Hit dramatic pinch-hit HR in 9th inning to win Game 1 of 1988 series. MVP in 1988. Career span 1979–94 with Detroit, LA, KC, Pitt. Also starred in baseball and football at Michigan State.

Frank Gifford (b. 8-16-30): Football RB. NFL Player of Year in 1956 when he rushed for 819 yards and caught 51 passes. Played in seven Pro Bowls. Retired for one season after ferocious hit by Chuck Bednarik. Career span 1952–60 and 1962–64, all with New York Giants. Elected to Hall of Fame in 1977.

Rod Gilbert (b. 7-1-41): Hockey RW. Played 16 seasons, all with the New York Rangers (1960–61 through 1977–78), and had 406 goals and 615 assists. Elected to Hall of Fame 1982.

Sid Gillman (b. 10-26-11): Football coach. Developed wide-open, pass-oriented style of offense, introduced techniques for situational player substitutions and the study of game films. Won one division title with Los Angeles Rams and five division titles and one AFL championship (1963) with Los Angeles/San Diego Chargers. Career span 1955–59 Los Angeles Rams; 1960 Los Angeles Chargers; 1961–69 San Diego; 1973–74 Houston. Lifetime record 124-101-7. Also general manager in San Diego and Houston.

Pancho Gonzales (b. 5-9-28, d. 7-3-95): Tennis player. Won 2 consecutive U.S. singles titles (1948–49). In 1969, at age 41, beat Charlie Pasarell 22–24, 1–6, 16–14, 6–3, 11–9 in longest Wimbledon match ever (5:12).

Shane Gould (b. 11-23-56): Australian swimmer. Won 3 gold medals, 1 silver and 1 bronze at 1972 Olympics. Set 11 world records over 23-month period beginning in 1971. Held world record in 5 freestyle distances ranging from 100 meters to 1,500 meters in late 1971 and 1972. Retired at age 16.

Steffi Graf (b. 6-14-69): German tennis player. Achieved the Grand Slam in 1988. Has won 4 Australian Open singles titles (1988–90, '94), 7 Wimbledon titles (1988–89, 1991–93, '95–96), 5 French Open titles (1987–88, '93 and '95–96) and 5 U.S. Open titles (1988–89, '93 and '95–96). Held the No. 1 ranking a record 186 weeks; Aug. 17, 1987 through March 10, 1991. Gold medalist at 1988 Olympics. Second in alltime Grand Slam singles titles (21).

Otto Graham (b. 12-6-21): Football QB. Led Cleveland to 10 championship games in his 10-year career. Played on 4 consecutive AAFC champions (1946–49) and 3 NFL champions (1950, consecutively 1954–55). Combined league totals: 23,584 yards passing, 174 touchdown passes. Player of the Year 2 times (1953, 1955). Led league in passing 6 times. Career span 1946–55.

Red Grange (b. 6-13-03, d. 1-28-91): Football HB. "The Galloping Ghost." All-America 3 consecutive seasons with Illinois (1923–25), scoring 31 touchdowns in 20–game collegiate career. Signed by George Halas of Chicago in 1925, attracted sellout crowds across the country. Established the first AFL with manager C.C. Pyle in 1926, but league folded after 1 year. Career span 1925–34 with Chicago, New York.

Rocky Graziano (b. 6-7-22, d. 5-22-90): Boxer. Middleweight champion from 1947 to 1948. Career record 67–13. Endured 3 brutal title fights against Tony

Zale, with Zale winning by KO in 1946 and 1948, and Graziano winning by KO in 1947.

Hank Greenberg (b. 1-1-11, d. 9-4-86): Baseball 1B. 331 career HR (58 in 1938). MVP in 1935, 1940. League leader in HR and RBI 4 times each. Fifth alltime highest slugging average (.605). 100+ RBI 7 times. Career span 1933-41, 1945-47 with Detroit, Pittsburgh.

Joe Greene (b. 9-24-46): Football DT. "Mean Joe." Anchored Pittsburgh's famed "Steel Curtain" defense. Selected for Pro Bowl 10 times. Played on 4 Super Bowl champions (consecutively 1974-75, 1978-79). Career span 1969 to 1981.

Forrest Gregg (b. 10-18-33): Football OT/G. Played in then-record 188 straight games from 1956 through 1971. Named all-NFL eight straight years starting in 1960. Career span 1956–71, most of it with Green Bay Packers. Played on winning Packer team in first two Super Bowls. Inducted into Hall of Fame in 1977.

Wayne Gretzky (b. 1-26-61): Hockey C. "The Great One." Most dominant player in history. Alltime scoring leader in points (2,795), assists (1,910), and goals (885). Alltime single-season scoring leader in points (215 in 1986), goals (92 in 1982) and assists (163 in 1986). Has won MVP award 9 times, more than any other player (consecutively 1980-87, 1989). Led league in assists 16 times, scoring 11 times, goals 5 times. Scored 200+ points 4 times, 100+ points 10 other times; 70+ goals 4 consecutive seasons, 50+ goals 5 other times; 100+ assists 11 consecutive seasons. Playoff MVP 2 times (1985, 1988). Played on 4 Stanley Cup champions with Edmonton from 1978 to 1988. Traded to Los Angeles on Aug. 9, 1988, then to St. Louis Feb. 1996. Moved as a free agent to NY Rangers before 1996–97 season.

Bob Griese (b. 2-3-45): Football QB. Career span 1967–80 with Miami Dolphins. Played in three straight Super Bowls, 1971–73. Quarterback of 1972 Dolphin team that went 17–0. Won Super Bowl VII and VIII. In 14 seasons completed 1,926 passes for 25,092 yards and 192 TDs. Elected to Hall of Fame in 1990.

Archie Griffin (b. 8-21-54): College football RB. Only player to win the Heisman Trophy 2 times (consecutively 1974-75), with Ohio State. Fourth alltime NCAA most yards rushing (5,177), his 6.13 yards per carry is the collegiate record. Professional career span 1976-83 with Cincinnati; totaled 2,808 yards rushing and 192 receptions.

Lefty Grove (b. 3-6-00, d. 5-22-75): Baseball LHP. 300 career wins and fourth alltime highest winning percentage (.680). League leader in ERA 9 times, strikeouts 7 consecutive seasons. Won 20+ games 8 times. 1931 MVP. Career span 1925-41 with Philadelphia, Boston.

Tony Gwynn (b. 5-9-60): Baseball OF. 8 batting titles (1984, consecutively 1987–89, 1994–97). League leader in hits 6 times, with .300+ average 15 times, 200+ hits 5 times. Career span since 1982 with San Diego.

Walter Hagen (b. 12-21-1892, d. 10-5-69): Golfer. Third alltime leader in major championships (11). Won PGA Championship 5 times (1921, consecutively 1924-27), British Open 4 times (1922, 1924, consecutively 1928-29) and U.S. Open 2 times (1914, 1919). Won 40 career tournaments.

Marvin Hagler (b. 5-23-54): Boxer. "Marvelous." Middleweight champion (1980-87). Career record 62-3-2 with 52 KOs from 1973 to 1987. Defended title 13 times.

George Halas (b. 2-2-1895, d. 10-31-83): Football owner and coach. "Papa Bear." Alltime leader in seasons coaching (40) and second in wins (324). Career record 324-151-31 intermittently from 1920 to 1967. Remained as owner until his death. Chicago won a record 7 NFL championships during his tenure.

Glenn Hall (b. 10-3-31): Hockey goalie. "Mr. Goalie" was an All-Star goalie in 11 of his 18 seasons. Set record for consecutive games by a goaltender, with 502, and ended career with goals against average of 2.51. Won or shared Vezina Trophy three times. Career span 1952–53 through 1970–71.

Arthur B. (Bull) Hancock (b. 1-24-10, d. 9-14-72): Horse racing owner. Owner of Claiborne Farm and arguably the greatest breeder in history. For 15 straight years, from 1955 to 1969, a Claiborne stallion led the sire list. Foaled at Claiborne Farm were 4 Horses of the Year (Kelso, Round Table, Bold Ruler and Nashua).

Tom Harmon (b. 9-28-19, d. 3-17-90): Football RB. Won Heisman Trophy in 1940 with Michigan. Triple-threat back led nation in scoring and named All-America 2 consecutive seasons (1939-40). Awarded Silver Star and Purple Heart in World War II. Played in NFL with Los Angeles (1946-47).

Franco Harris (b. 3-7-50): Football RB. Rushed for 12,120 yards and 91 touchdowns. Gained 1,000+ yards in 8 seasons, 100+ yards in 47 games. Scored 100 career touchdowns. Selected for Pro Bowl 9 times. Rookie of the Year in 1972. Played on 4 Super Bowl champions (consecutively 1974–75, 1978–79) with Pittsburgh. Super Bowl MVP in 1974. Holds Super Bowl record for most rushing yards (354). Made the "Immaculate Reception" to win 1972 playoff game against Oakland. Career span 1972–83 with Pittsburgh. Elected to the Hall of Fame in 1990.

Leon Hart (b. 11-2-28): Football DE. Won Heisman Trophy in 1949, the last lineman to win the award. Played on 3 national champions with Notre Dame (consecutively 1946–47, 1949) and the Irish went undefeated during his 4 years (36-0-2). Also played on 3 NFL champions with Detroit. Career span 1950-57.

Bill Hartack (b. 12-9-32): Horse racing jockey. Rode Kentucky Derby winner 5 times (1957, 1960, 1962, 1964, 1969), Preakness Stakes winner 3 times (1956, 1964, 1969) and Belmont Stakes winner 1 time (1960).

Doug Harvey (b. 12-19-24, d. 12-26-90): Hockey D. Defensive Player of the Year 7 times (consecutively 1954-57, 1959-61). Led league in assists in 1954. All-Star 10 times. Played on 6 Stanley Cup champions with Montreal from 1947 to 1968.

Billy Haughton (b. 11-2-23, d. 7-15-86): Harness racing driver. Won the Pacing Triple Crown driving Rum Customer in 1968. Won The Hambletonian 4 times (1974, consecutively 1976-77, 1980).

John Havlicek (b. 4-8-40): Basketball F/G. Member of Ohio State team that won 1960 NCAA title. "Hondo" averaged 20.8 points per game over 16-season NBA career, all with Boston. First team NBA All Star in 1971, '72, '73 and '74. Member of eight Celtic teams that won NBA title. Playoff MVP 1974. Elected to Hall of Fame in 1983.

Elvin Hayes (b. 11-17-45): Basketball C. 1968 *Sporting News* College Player of Year as Houston senior. Averaged 21.0 points per game over 16-season NBA career. Led NBA in scoring (28.4) in 1969 and in rebounding in 1970 (16.9 per game) and '74

(18.1). First team All NBA in 1975, '77 and '79. Elected to Hall of Fame in 1989.

Woody Hayes (b. 2-14-13, d. 3-12-87): College football coach. Won national championship 3 times (1954, 1957, 1968) and Rose Bowl 4 times. Career record 238-72-10, including 4 undefeated seasons, with Ohio State from 1951 to 1978. Forced to resign after striking an opposing player during 1978 Gator Bowl.

Marques Haynes (b. 10-3-26): Basketball G. Known as "The World's Greatest Dribbler." Beginning in 1946 barnstormed more than 4 million miles throughout 97 countries for the Harlem Globetrotters, Harlem Magicians, Meadowlark Lemon's Bucketeers, Harlem Wizards.

Thomas Hearns (b. 10-18-58): Boxer. "Hit Man." Champion in 5 different weight classes: junior middleweight, light heavyweight, middleweight, super middleweight, and light heavyweight.

Eric Heiden (b. 6-14-58): Speed skater. Won 5 gold medals at 1980 Olympics. World champion 3 consecutive years (1977-79). Also won Sullivan Award in 1980.

Carol Heiss (b. 1-20-40): Figure skater. Gold medalist at 1960 Olympics, silver medalist at 1956 Olympics. World champion 5 consecutive years (1956-60) and U.S. champion 4 consecutive years (1957-60). Married 1956 gold medalist Hayes Jenkins.

Rickey Henderson (b. 12-25-57): Baseball OF. Alltime career stolen base leader (1,231 through 1997); modern season stolen base record holder in 1982 (130). Led league in steals 11 times. 1990 MVP. Alltime most HR leading off game. Career span since 1979 with Oakland, NY Yankees, Toronto and San Diego.

Sonja Henie (b. 4-8-12, d. 10-12-69): Norwegian figure skater. Gold medalist at 3 consecutive Olympics (1928, 1932, 1936). World champion 10 consecutive years (1927-36).

Orel Hershiser (b. 9-16-58): Baseball RHP. Alltime leader most consecutive scoreless innings pitched (59 in 1988). Cy Young Award winner in 1988 and World Series MVP. Career span 1983-94, Los Angeles; 1995-97, Cleveland; 1998- San Francisco.

Foster Hewitt (b. 11-21-02, d. 4-22-85): Hockey sportscaster. In 1923, aired one of hockey's first radio broadcasts. Became the voice of hockey in Canada on radio and later television. Famous for the phrase, "He shoots ... he scores!"

Tommy Hitchcock (b. 2-11-00, d. 4-19-44): Polo. 10-goal rating 18 times in his 19-year career from 1922 to 1940. Killed in plane crash in World War II.

Lew Hoad (b. 11-23-34): Australian tennis player. Won 2 consecutive Wimbledon singles titles (1956-57). Also won French title and Australian title in 1956, but failed to achieve the Grand Slam when defeated at Forest Hills by countryman Ken Rosewall.

Ben Hogan (b. 8-13-12, d. 7-25-97): Golfer. Third alltime in career wins (63). Won U.S. Open 4 times (1948, consecutively 1950-51, 1953), the Masters (1951, 1953) and PGA Championship (1946, 1948) 2 times each and British Open once (1953). PGA Player of the Year 4 times (1948, consecutively 1950-51, 1953).

Marshall Holman (b. 9-29-54): Bowler. Won 21 PBA titles between 1975 and 1988. Had leading average in 1987 (213.54) and was named PBA Bowler of the Year.

Nat Holman (b. 10-18-1896, d. 2-12-95): College basketball coach. Only coach in history to win NCAA

and NIT championships in same season in 1950 with CCNY. 423 career wins, a .689 winning percentage.

Larry Holmes (b. 11-3-49): Boxer. Heavyweight champion (1978-85). Career record 53-3 with 37 KOs from 1973 to 1991. Defended title 21 times. Fought periodically after 1991, never for title.

Lou Holtz (b. 1-6-37): Football coach. Coached Notre Dame to national championship in 1988 with 12-0 record and a 34-21 win over West Virginia in Fiesta Bowl. Retired after 1996 season with a 216-95-7 career record. 10-8-2 career record in bowl games. Career span 1969-71 at William & Mary (13-20); 1972-75 at N.C. State (33-12-3); 1977-83 at Arkansas (60-21-2); 1984-85 at Minnesota (10-12); and 1986-96 at Notre Dame (100-30-2).

Evander Holyfield (b. 10-19-62): Boxer. Won heavyweight crown Oct. 25, 1990 when he beat James (Buster) Douglas in Las Vegas. Lost title to Riddick Bowe in Las Vegas on 11-13-92, regained it from Bowe one year later, then lost to Michael Moorer on 4-22-94. Defeated Mike Tyson for WBA crown on 11-9-96 to join Muhammad Ali as the only men to win the heavyweight title three times. Won rematch on 6-28-97 when Tyson was disqualified for biting Holyfield's ears.

Red Holzman (b. 8-10-20): Basketball coach. Led New York Knicks to NBA title in 1970 and '73. NBA Coach of the Year in 1970. Member of Rochester team that won NBA title in both 1946 (in NBL) and '51. After two-year coaching stints with Milwaukee and St. Louis, coached New York Knicks from 1968-82. Elected to Hall of Fame in 1985.

Harry Hopman (b. 8-12-06, d. 12-27-85): Australian tennis player. As nonplaying captain, led Australia to 15 Davis Cup titles between 1950 and 1969. Mentor to Lew Hoad, Ken Rosewall, Rod Laver and John Newcombe.

Willie Hoppe (b. 10-11-1887, d. 2-1-59): Billiards. Won 51 world championship matches from 1904 to 1952.

Rogers Hornsby (b. 4-27-1896, d. 1-5-63): Baseball 2B. Second all-time highest career batting average (.358) and 7 batting titles, including .424 average in 1924. 200+ hits 7 times; .400+ average 3 times and .300+ average 12 other times. Led league in slugging average 9 times. Triple Crown winner in 1922, 1925; MVP award winner in 1925, 1929. Career span 1915-37 with St. Louis (NL), New York (NL), Boston, Chicago (NL).

Paul Hornung (b. 12-23-35): Football RB-K. Led league in scoring 3 consecutive seasons, including a record 176 points in 1960 (15 touchdowns, 15 field goals, 41 extra points). Player of the Year in 1961. Career span 1957-66 with Green Bay. Suspended for 1963 season by Pete Rozelle for gambling. Also won Heisman Trophy in 1956 with Notre Dame.

Gordie Howe (b. 3-31-28): Hockey RW. Second alltime in goals (801), first in years played (26) and games (1,767). Finished career with 1,850 points and 1,049 assists. Won MVP award 6 times (consecutively 1952-53, 1957-58, 1960, 1963). Led league in scoring 6 times, goals 5 times and assists 3 times. Scored 40+ goals 5 times, 30+ goals 13 other times, 100+ points 3 times. All-Star 12 times. Played on 4 Stanley Cup champions with Detroit from 1946 to 1971. Teamed with sons Mark and Marty in the WHA with Houston and New England from 1973 to 1979, in NHL with Hartford in 1980.

Carl Hubbell (b. 6-22-03, d. 11-21-88): Baseball LHP. 253 career wins. MVP in 1933, 1936. League leader in wins and ERA 3 times each. Won 24 consecutive games from 1936 to 1937. Struck out Ruth, Gehrig, Foxx, Simmons and Cronin consecutively in 1934 All-Star game. Pitched no-hitter in 1929. Career span 1928–43 with New York.

Sam Huff (b. 10-4-34): Football LB. Made 30 interceptions. Career span 1956–69 with New York Giants and Washington Redskins. Elected to Hall of Fame in 1982.

Bobby Hull (b. 1-3-39): Hockey LW. "The Golden Jet." Led league in goals 7 times and points 3 times. 610 career goals. Scored 50+ goals 5 times, 30+ goals 8 other times. Won MVP award 2 consecutive seasons (1965–66). Son Brett won MVP award in 1991, the only father and son to be so honored. All-Star 10 times. Career span 1957–72 with Chicago, 1973–80 with Winnipeg of WHA.

Brett Hull (b. 8-9-64): Hockey RW. Son of Bobby Hull. Won Hart Memorial Trophy for 1990–91 season. Career span 1986–87 with Calgary Flames; since 1987 with St. Louis Blues.

Jim (Catfish) Hunter (b. 4-8-46): Baseball RHP. 1974 Cy Young award winner. Won 20+ games 5 consecutive seasons. Led league in wins and winning percentage 2 times each, ERA 1 time. 250+ innings pitched 8 times. Pitched perfect game in 1968. Member of 5 World Series champions for Oakland and New York Yankees. Career span 1965–79.

Don Hutson (b. 1-31-13, d. 6-26-97): Football WR. Third alltime in touchdown receptions (99). Led league in pass receptions 8 times, receiving yards 7 times and scoring 5 consecutive seasons. Caught at least 1 pass in 95 consecutive games. Player of the Year 2 consecutive seasons (1941–42). Career span 1935–45 with Green Bay.

Hank Iba (b. 8-6-04; d. 1-15-93): College basketball coach. Coached Oklahoma A&M (which became Oklahoma State) from 1934 to 1970. Team won NCAA titles in 1945 and '46. 767 career wins is third alltime behind Dean Smith and Adolph Rupp.

Jackie Ickx (b. 1-1-45): Belgian auto racer. Won the 24 Hours of LeMans a record six times (1969, consecutively 1975–77, 1981–82) before retiring in 1985.

Punch Imlach (b. 3-15-18, d. 12-1-87): Hockey coach. 467 wins. With Toronto from 1958 to 1969. Won 4 Stanley Cup championships (consecutively 1962–64, 1967).

Bo Jackson (b. 11-30-62): Baseball OF and Football RB. Only person in history to be named to baseball All-Star game and football Pro Bowl game. 1985 Heisman Trophy winner at Auburn. First pick in 1986 NFL draft by Tampa Bay, but opted to play baseball at Kansas City. 1989 All-Star game MVP. Signed with football's LA Raiders in 1988. Sustained football injury in 1990, released from baseball contract by KC, signed by Chicago (AL) and returned from injury in early September 1991, but comeback failed at first. Had hip replacement surgery and hit homer in first at bat afterwards. Retired 1994.

Joe Jackson (b. 7-16-1889, d. 12-5-51): Baseball OF. "Shoeless Joe." Third alltime highest career batting average (.356), with .300+ average 11 times. One of the "8 men out" banned from baseball for throwing 1919 World Series. Career span 1908–20 with Cleveland, Chicago.

Reggie Jackson (b. 5-18-46): Baseball OF. "Mr. October." Alltime leader in World Series slugging average (.755). 1977 Series MVP, hit 3 HR in final game on 3 consecutive pitches. 563 career HR total is sixth best alltime. Led league in HR 4 times. 1973 MVP. Alltime strikeout leader (2,597). In a 12-year period played on 10 first-place teams, 5 World Series winners. Career span 1967–87 with Oakland, New York, California. Inducted into baseball Hall of Fame in 1993.

Bruce Jenner (b. 10-28-49): Track and Field. Set then-world decathlon record (8,634) in winning gold medal at 1976 Olympics. Sullivan Award winner in 1976.

John Henry (b. 1975): Thoroughbred race horse. Sold as yearling for $1,100, the gelding was Horse of the Year in 1981 and in 1984 and retired with then-record $6,597,947 in winnings.

Ben Johnson (b. 12-30-61): Track and field. Canadian sprinter set world record in 100 meters (9.83 in 1987). Won event at 1988 Olympics in 9.79, but gold medal revoked for failing drug test. Both world records revoked for steroid usage. Suspended for life after testing positive for elevated testosterone level at an indoor meet in Montreal on 1-17-93.

Earvin (Magic) Johnson (b. 8-14-59): Basketball G. Retired Nov. 7, 1991 after being diagnosed with HIV, the virus that causes AIDS. Returned to Lakers Feb '96 at age 36. Finished career second alltime in assists (10,141); alltime playoff leader in assists (2,346) and steals (358). MVP award 3 times (1987, consecutively 1989–90) and playoff MVP in 1980, '82 and '87. Played on 5 championship teams with Los Angeles since 1979. All-Star 8 consecutive seasons. League leader in assists 4 times, steals 2 times, free throw percentage once. Also won NCAA championship and named tournament MVP in 1979 with Michigan State.

Jack Johnson (b. 3-31-1878, d. 6-10-46): Boxer. First black heavyweight champion (1908-15). Career record 78-8-12 with 45 KOs from 1897 to 1928.

Jimmy Johnson (b. 7-16-43): Football coach. Led the Cowboys from 1–15 in 1989, his first season in Dallas, to a 52–17 win over the Buffalo Bills in the Super Bowl XXVII just four seasons later. Also coached Super Bowl XXVIII champion Cowboys before resigning because of a dispute with owner Jerry Jones. Head coach at Oklahoma State from 1979–83 and Univ. of Miami 1984–88 with career collegiate record of 81-34-3. Johnson's Hurricanes won national championship in 1987. Succeeded Don Shula as Miami Dolphins coach, Jan. '96.

Michael Johnson (b. 9-13-67): Track and field sprinter. First man to win gold medals in both the 200 and 400 at the Olympics (1996). Broke 17-year-old 200-meter world record (from 19.72 to 19.66) in '96 U.S. Olympic trials, then further lowered mark to 19.32 at Atlanta. Won 200 at 1991 World Championships, 400 at '93 worlds and both events at the '95 worlds. Anchored U.S. 4x400 team at 1993 World Championship to world record of 2:54.29 with fastest ever relay carry of 42.97.

Walter Johnson (b. 11-6-1887, d. 12-10-46): Baseball RHP. "Big Train." Alltime leader in shutouts (110), second in wins (416), fourth in losses (279) and third in innings pitched (5,914). His 2.17 career ERA and 3,509 career strikeouts are seventh best alltime. MVP in 1913, 1924. Won 20+ games 12 times. League leader in strikeouts 12 times, ERA 5 times, wins 6 times. Pitched no-hitter in 1920. Career span 1907–27 with Washington.

Ben A. Jones (b. 12-31-1882, d. 6-13-61): Horse racing trainer. Trained Triple Crown winner (Whirlaway in 1941). Trained Kentucky Derby winner 6 times, more than any other trainer (1938, 1941, 1944, consecutively 1948-49, 1952), Preakness Stakes winner 2 times (1941, 1944) and Belmont Stakes winner 1 time (1941).

Bobby Jones (b. 3-17-02, d. 12-18-71): Golfer. Achieved golf's only recognized Grand Slam in 1930. Second alltime in major championships (13). Won U.S. Amateur 5 times, more than any golfer (consecutively 1924-25, 1927-28, 1930), U.S. Open 4 times (1923, 1926, consecutively 1929-30), British Open 3 times (consecutively 1926-27, 1930) and British Amateur (1930). Also designed Augusta National course, site of the Masters, and founded the tournament. Winner of Sullivan Award in 1930.

K.C. Jones (b. 5-25-32): Basketball G-coach. Member of 8 straight NBA-championship Boston Celtic teams in his nine season career from 1958–59 through 1966–67. Averaged 7.4 points and 4.3 assists per game. Coached Celtics from 1983–84 through 1987–88, with 308–102 regular season record and 65–37 playoff record with NBA titles in 1984 and '86.

Robert Trent Jones (b. 6-20-06): English-born golf course architect designed or remodelled over 400 courses, including Baltusrol, Hazeltine, Oak Hill and Winged Foot. In the mid-60s five straight U.S. Opens were played on courses designed or remodeled by Jones.

Sam Jones (b. 6-24-33): Basketball G. Played 12 seasons with Boston Celtics (1958–69) and made the playoffs every year, winning NBA title every year from 1959–66 plus 1968 and '69. Averaged 17.7 points per game for career. Elected to Hall of Fame in 1983.

Michael Jordan (b. 2-17-63): Basketball G. "Air." After 1997–98 season, alltime highest regular season scoring average (31.5) and most points scored in a playoff game (63 in 1986). Led Bulls to record 72 wins in 1995–96. Led league in scoring a record 10 seasons, steals 3 times. MVP in 1988, 1991–92,'96 and '98; Finals MVP in 1991–93 and 1996–98; Rookie of the Year in 1985. All-Star team 6 consecutive seasons, All-Defensive team 5 consecutive seasons. Career span 1984–93, 1995– with Chicago. Announced retirement on 10-6-93, returned in March 1995. Also College Player of the Year in 1984. Played on NCAA championship team with North Carolina in 1982. Member of gold medal-winning 1984 and '92 Olympic teams.

Florence Griffith Joyner (b. 12-21-59): Track and field. Won 3 gold medals (100 meters, 200 meters, 4x100-meter relay) at 1988 Olympics; Set world record in 100 (10.49) in 1988 and in 200 (21.34) at the 1988 Olympics. Sullivan Award winner in 1988.

Jackie Joyner-Kersee (b. 3-3-62): Track and field. Gold medalist in heptathlon and long jump at 1988 Olympics and in the former at the 1992 Olympics. Set heptathlon world record (7,291 points) at 1988 Olympics. Also won silver medal in heptathlon at 1984 Olympics and bronze in long jump at 1992 and '96 Olympics. Sullivan Award winner in 1986.

Alberto Juantorena (b. 3-12-51): Track and field. Cuban was gold medalist in 400 meters and 800 meters at 1976 Olympics.

Wang Junxia (b. 1963): Chinese distance runner. Broke four existing world records over six days in Sept. 1993. Broke 10,000 (29:31.78) on 9-8; ran 1500 in

3:51.92 in finishing second to countrywoman Qu Yunxia's world record of 3:50.46 on 9-11; ran 3,000 record of 8:12.19 in heats on 9-12 and lowered it to 8:06.11 on 9-13. Won gold in 5,000 and silver in 10,000 at 1996 Olympics.

Sonny Jurgensen (b. 8-23-34): Football QB. In 18 seasons completed 2,433 of 4,262 pass attempts for 32,224 yards and 255 TDs. Led NFL in passing both 1967 and '69. Career span 1957–1974 with Philadelphia Eagles and Washington Redskins. Elected to Hall of Fame in 1983.

Duke Kahanamoku (b. 8-24-1890, d. 1-22-68): Swimmer. Won a total of 5 medals (3 gold and 2 silver) at 3 Olympics in 1912, 1920, 1924. Introduced the crawl stroke to America. Surfing pioneer and water polo player. Later sheriff of Honolulu.

Al Kaline (b. 12-19-34): Baseball OF. 3,007 career hits and 399 career HR. As a 20-year-old in 1955, became youngest player to win batting title, with .340 average. Had .300+ average 9 times. Played in 18 All-Star games. Career span 1953–74 with Detroit.

Anatoly Karpov (b. 5-23-61): Soviet chess player. First world champion to receive title by default, in 1975, when Bobby Fischer chose not to defend his crown. Champion until 1985 when beaten by Garry Kasparov. Recognized by FIDE as champion in 1994.

Garry Kasparov (b. 4-13-63): Born Harry Weinstein. Chess player. World champion from 1985 to 1993 when stripped of title by FIDE. Won six-game series against IBM computer, Deep Blue, in 1996. Lost to Deep Blue in 1997.

Kip Keino (b. 1-17-40): Track and field. Kenyan was gold medalist in 1,500 meters at 1968 Olympics and in steeplechase at 1972 Olympics.

Jim Kelly (b. 2-14-60): Football QB. Led NFL in passing in 1990 (219 of 346 for 2,829 yards and 24 TDs). Led AFC in passing in 1991. In 11 seasons completed 2,874 of 4,779 attempts for 35,467 yards and 237 TDs. Career span 1983–85 with New Jersey Generals (USFL), 1986-96 with Buffalo Bills. Led Bills to four straight Super Bowls, all losses.

Kelso (b. 1957, d. 1983): Thoroughbred race horse. Gelding was Horse of the Year 5 straight years (1960-64). Finished in the money in 53 of 63 races. Career earnings $1,977,896.

Harmon Killebrew (b. 6-29-36): Baseball 3B-1B. 573 career HR total is fifth most alltime. 100+ RBI 9 times, 40+ HR 8 times. League leader in HR 6 times and RBI 4 times. 1969 MVP. 100+ walks and strikeouts 7 times each. Career span 1954-75 with Washington, Minnesota.

Jean Claude Killy (b. 8-30-43): French skier. Won 3 gold medals at 1968 Olympics. World Cup overall champion 2 consecutive years (1967-68).

Ralph Kiner (b. 10-27-22): Baseball OF. Second to Babe Ruth in alltime HR frequency (7.1 HR every 100 at bats). 369 career HR. Led league in HR 7 consecutive seasons, with 50+ HR 2 times; 100+ RBI and runs scored in same season 6 times; 100+ walks 6 times. Career span 1946–55 with Pittsburgh, Chicago (NL), and Cleveland.

Billie Jean King (b. 11-22-43): Tennis player. Won a record 20 Wimbledon titles, including 6 singles titles (consecutively 1966-68, 1972-73, 1975). Won 4 U.S. singles titles (1967, consecutively 1971-72, 1974), and singles titles at Australian Open (1968) and French

Open (1972). Won 27 Grand Slam doubles titles—total of 39 Grand Slam titles is third alltime. Helped found the women's pro tour in 1970, serving as president of the Women's Tennis Association 2 times. Helped form Team Tennis.

Nile Kinnick (b. 7-9-18, d. 6-2-43): College football RB. Won the Heisman Trophy in 1939 with Iowa. Premier runner, passer and punter was killed in plane crash during routine Navy training flight. Stadium in Iowa City named in his honor.

Tom Kite (b. 12-9-49): Golfer. Second alltime PGA money leader. Led PGA in scoring average in 1981 (69.80) and '82 (70.21). PGA Player of Year in 1989, when he won a then-record $1,395,278. Shook reputation for failing to win the big ones by winning 1992 U.S. Open at windy Pebble Beach.

Franz Klammer (b. 12-3-54): Austrian alpine skier. Greatest downhiller ever. Gold medalist in downhill at 1976 Olympics. Also won four World Cup downhill titles (1975–78).

Bob Knight (b. 10-25-40): College basketball coach. Won 3 NCAA championships with Indiana in 1976, 1981, 1987. Coached U.S. Olympic team to gold medal in 1984. 720 career wins and .727 career winning percentage entering 1998–99 season. Career span since 1966 with Army, Indiana.

Olga Korbut (b. 5-16-55): Soviet gymnast. First ever to complete backward somersault on balance beam. Won 3 gold medals at 1972 Olympics.

Sandy Koufax (b. 12-30-35): Baseball LHP. Cy Young Award winner 3 times (1963, consecutively 1965-66); and MVP in 1963; World Series MVP in 1963, 1965. Pitched 1 perfect game, 3 no-hitters. League leader in ERA 5 consecutive seasons, strikeouts 4 times. Won 25+ games 3 times. Career record 165-87, with 2.76 ERA. Career span 1955-66 with Brooklyn/Los Angeles.

Jack Kramer (b. 8-1-21): Tennis player. Won 2 consecutive U.S. singles titles (1946-47) and 1 Wimbledon title (1947). Also won 6 Grand Slam doubles titles. Served as executive director of Association of Tennis Professionals from 1972 to 1975.

Ingrid Kristiansen (b. 3-21-56): Track and field. Norwegian runner is only person—male or female—to hold world records in 5,000 meters (14:37.33 set in 1986), 10,000 meters (30:13.74 set in 1986) and marathon (2:21:06 set in 1985, a record that still stands). Also won Boston Marathon 2 times (1986, 1989) and New York City Marathon once (1989).

Bob Kurland (b. 12-23-24): College basketball player. 6' 10¼" center on Oklahoma A&M teams that won NCAA titles in 1945 and '46. Consensus All America and NCAA tournament MVP in both 1945 and '46. Led nation in scoring in '46. His habit of swatting shots off rim led to creation of goaltending rule in 1945. Won gold medals in both 1948 and '52 Olympics. Turned down lucrative pro offers, playing instead for Phillips 66 Oilers AAU team.

Rene Lacoste (b. 7-2-05, d. 10-12-96): French tennis player. "The Crocodile." One of France's "Four Musketeers" of the 1920s. Won 3 French singles titles (1925, 1927, 1929), 2 consecutive U.S. titles (1926–27) and 2 Wimbledon titles (1925, 1928). Also designed casual shirt with embroidered crocodile that bears his name.

Marion Ladewig (b. 10-30-14): Bowler. Won All-Star Tournament 8 times (consecutively 1949–52, 1954, 1956, 1959, 1963) and WPBA National Championship

once (1960). Also voted Bowler of the Year 9 times (consecutively 1950–54, 1957–59, 1963).

Guy Lafleur (b. 9-20-51): Hockey RW. Won MVP award 2 consecutive seasons (1977–78), playoff MVP in 1977. Scored 50+ goals and 100+ points 6 consecutive seasons. Led league in points scored 3 consecutive seasons, goals and assists 1 time each. 560 career goals, 793 assists. Played on 5 Stanley Cup champions with Montreal from 1971 to 1985.

Curly Lambeau (b. 4-9-1898; d. 6-1-65): Football QB and coach. Quarterback for Packers team in early 20's. Record of 212-106-21 in his 29 seasons (1921–49) as Packer coach, winning three NFL titles in 1929–31.

Jack Lambert (b. 7-8-52): Football LB. Anchored Pittsburgh's famed "Steel Curtain" defense. Selected for Pro Bowl 9 times. Played on 4 Super Bowl champions (consecutively 1974–75, 1978–79) with Pittsburgh from 1974 to 1984.

Jake LaMotta (b. 7-10-21): Boxer. "The Bronx Bull." Subject of *Raging Bull*, movie by Martin Scorsese, starring Robert DeNiro. Won middleweight title by knocking out Marcel Cerdan in 10 on 6-16-49. Lost title to Ray Robinson, who KO'd him in 13 on 2-13-51. Career record: 106 bouts; won 30 by KO and 53 by decision; drew 4; and lost 19, 4 by KO.

Kenesaw Mountain Landis (b. 11-20-1866, d. 11-25-44): Baseball's first and most powerful commissioner from 1920 to 1944. By banning the 8 "Black Sox" involved in the fixing of the 1919 World Series, he restored public confidence in the integrity of baseball.

Tom Landry (b. 9-11-24): Football coach. Third alltime in wins (270). The first coach in Dallas history, from 1960 to 1988. Led team to 13 division titles, 7 championship games and 5 Super Bowls. Won 2 Super Bowl championships (1971, 1977). Career record 270-178-6.

Dick (Night Train) Lane (b. 4-16-28): Football DB. Third alltime in interceptions (68) and second in interception yardage (1,207). Set record with 14 interceptions as a rookie in 1952. Career span 1952–65 with Los Angeles, Chicago Cardinals, Detroit.

Joe Lapchick (b. 4-12-00, d. 8-10-70): Basketball C-coach. One of the first big men in basketball, member of New York's Original Celtics. Coached St. John's (1936–47, 1956–65) winning four NIT Tournaments. Coached New York Knicks, 1947–56.

Steve Largent (b. 9-28-54): Football WR. Third alltime in pass receptions (819), second in TD receptions (100). 177 consecutive games with reception, 10 seasons with 50+ receptions and 8 seasons with 1,000+ yards receiving. Career span 1976–89 with Seattle.

Don Larsen (b. 8-7-29): Baseball RHP. Pitched only perfect game in World Series history for the NY Yankees on Oct. 8, 1956, beating the Dodgers 2–0; named World Series MVP. Career span 1953–67 for many teams.

Tommy Lasorda (b. 9-22-27): Baseball manager. Spent nearly his entire minor and major league career in Dodgers organization as a pitcher, coach and manager. Managed Dodgers since 1977, winning 4 pennants and 2 World Series (1981, 1988). Retired July 1996, citing health concerns. Only three men managed one baseball team longer.

Rod Laver (b. 8-9-38): Australian tennis player. "Rocket." Only player to achieve the Grand Slam twice (as an amateur in 1962 and as a pro in 1969). Second alltime in men's Grand Slam singles titles (11—tied with Bjorn Borg). Won 4 Wimbledon titles (consecutively 1961-62, 1968-69), 3 Australian titles (1960, 1962, 1969), 2 U.S. titles (1962, 69) and 2 French titles (1962, 1969). Also won 8 Grand Slam doubles titles. First player to earn $1 million in prize money. 47 career tournament victories. Member of undefeated Australian Davis Cup team from 1959 to 1962.

Andrea Mead Lawrence (b. 4-19-32): Skier. Gold medalist in slalom and giant slalom at 1952 Olympics.

Bobby Layne (b. 12-19-26; d. 12-1-86): Football QB. Led Detroit Lions to NFL championships in both 1952 and '53. In 1952 led NFL in every passing category. Career span 1948–62, most with the Detroit Lions. Elected to Hall of Fame in 1967.

Sammy Lee (b. 8-1-20): Diver. Gold medalist at 2 consecutive Olympics (highboard in 1948, 1952); bronze medalist in springboard at 1948 Olympics. Won the 1953 Sullivan Award. Also 1960 U.S. Olympic diving coach.

Jacques Lemaire (b. 9-7-45): Hockey C-Coach. As center for Montreal Canadiens from 1967–68 through 1978–79 was part of eight Stanley Cup winning teams. Over 12 seasons, all with Montreal, scored 366 goals and had 469 assists. Elected to Hall of Fame in 1984. Coached Canadiens 1983-85 and N.J. Devils 1993–98.

Mario Lemieux (b. 10-5-65): Hockey C. Won MVP award in 1988, '93, '96. Playoff MVP in 1991. Led league in most points 5 seasons and goals scored 3 seasons, assists 1 season. Scored 40+ goals and 100+ points 6 consecutive seasons, including 85 goals and 199 points in 1989. Rookie of the Year in 1985. Won 1992–93 scoring title despite sitting out six weeks to receive treatment for Hodgkin's disease, a form of cancer. Sat out 1994–95 season, returned in '95–96 to lead league in scoring and become second fastest player to score 500 career goals. Career span 1984–94, 1995–97 with Pittsburgh.

Greg LeMond (b. 6-26-61): Cyclist. Only American to win Tour de France; won event 3 times (1986, consecutively 1989–90). Recovered from hunting accident to win in 1989.

Ivan Lendl (b. 3-7-60): Tennis player. Second alltime men's most career tournament victories (94). Won 3 consecutive U.S. Open singles titles (1985–87) and 3 French Open titles (1984, consecutively 1985–86). Also won 2 consecutive Australian Open titles (1989–90). Reached Grand Slam final 9 other times.

Suzanne Lenglen (b. 5-24-1899, d. 7-4-38): French tennis player. Lost only 1 match from 1919 to her retirement in 1926. Won 6 Wimbledon singles and doubles titles (consecutively 1919–23, 1925). Won 6 French singles and doubles titles (consecutively 1920–23, 1925–26).

Sugar Ray Leonard (b. 5-17-56): Boxer. Champion in 5 different weight classes: welterweight, junior middleweight, middleweight, light heavyweight and super middleweight. Career record 36-3-1 with 25 KOs from 1977 to 1997, including comeback loss to Hector Camacho at the age of 41. Also light welterweight gold medalist at 1976 Olympics.

Carl Lewis (b. 7-1-61): Track and field. Held world record for 100 meters 9.86; set on 8-25-91 at World Championships in Tokyo. Duplicated Jesse Owens's feat by winning 4 gold medals at 1984 Olympics (100 and

200 meters, 4x100-meter relay and long jump). Also won 2 gold medals (100 meters, long jump) and 1 silver (200 meters) at 1988 Olympics and two gold medals (long jump, 4x100 relay) at 1992 Olympics. Sullivan Award winner in 1981. Won 1996 Olympic long jump gold at age 35, giving him nine career gold medals and making him just the second track and field athlete (along with Al Oerter) to win four golds in a single event.

Nancy Lieberman (b. 7-1-58): Basketball G. Three-time All-America at Old Dominion. Player of the Year (1979, 1980). Olympian, 1976, and selected for 1980 team, but quit because of Moscow boycott. Promoter of women's basketball, played in WPBL, WABA. First woman to play basketball in a men's professional league (USBL), in 1986. Joined WNBA in 1997.

Bob Lilly (b. 7-26-39): Football DT. Dallas Cowboys' first ever draft pick, first Pro Bowl player and first all-NFL choice. Made all-NFL eight times. Career span 1961–74, all with Cowboys. Elected to Hall of Fame in 1980.

Sonny Liston (b. 5-8-32, d. 12-30-70): Boxer. Heavyweight champion from 1962 to 1964. Won title by KO of Floyd Patterson on 9-25-62. Lost title when TKO'd by Cassius Clay (Muhammad Ali) on 2-25-64 and then lost rematch on 5-25-65 when KO'd in first round. Career record: 54 fights; won 39 by KO and 11 by decision; lost 4, three by KO.

Vince Lombardi (b. 6-11-13, d. 9-3-70): Football coach. Second highest alltime winning percentage (.740). Career record 105-35-6. Won 5 NFL championships and 2 consecutive Super Bowl titles with Green Bay from 1959 to 1967. Coached Washington in 1969. Super Bowl trophy named in his honor.

Johnny Longden (b. 2-14-07): Horse racing jockey. Rode Triple Crown winner Count Fleet in 1943. 6,032 wins.

Nancy Lopez (b. 1-6-57): Golfer. LPGA Player of the Year 4 times (consecutively 1978-79, 1985, 1988). Winner of LPGA Championship 3 times (1978, 1985, 1989). Member of the LPGA Hall of Fame.

Greg Louganis (b. 1-29-60): Diver. Gold medalist in platform and springboard at 2 consecutive Olympics in 1984, 1988. World champion 5 times (platform in 1978, 1982, 1986; springboard in 1982, 1986). Also Sullivan Award winner in 1984.

Joe Louis (b. 5-13-14, d. 4-12-81): Boxer. "The Brown Bomber." Longest title reign of any heavyweight champion (11 years, 9 months) from June 1937 through March 1949. Career record 63-3 with 49 KOs from 1934 to 1951. Defended title 25 times.

Jerry Lucas (b. 3-30-40): Basketball F. Star at Ohio State. *Sporting News* College Player of Year in both 1961 and '62. In 1960 member of both NCAA championship team and gold-medal winning U.S. Olympic team. Averaged over 20 points and 20 rebounds a game for college career. NBA Rookie of Year in 1964. In 11 NBA seasons averaged 17 points a game. Elected to Hall of Fame in 1979.

Sid Luckman (b. 11-21-16, d. 7-5-98): Football QB. Played on 4 NFL champions (consecutively 1940–41, 1943, 1946) with Chicago. Player of the Year in 1943. Tied record with 7 touchdown passes on Nov. 14, 1943. All-Pro 6 times. 137 career touchdown passes. Career span 1939–50. Also All-America with Columbia.

Jon Lugbill (b. 5-27-61): White water canoe racer. Won 5 world singles titles from 1979 to 1989.

Hank Luisetti (b. 6-16-16): Basketball F. The first player to use the one-handed shot. All-America at Stanford 3 consecutive years from 1936–38.

D. Wayne Lukas (b. 9-2-35): Horse racing trainer. Former college basketball coach and quarter horse trainer takes mass production approach with stables at most major tracks around country. Trained two Horses of the Year, Lady's Secret in 1986 and Criminal Type in 1990. Won 1988 Kentucky Derby with a filly, Winning Colors. Won 1994 Preakness and Belmont with Tabasco Cat. Won all three Triple Crown races in 1995, with Thunder Gulch (Kentucky Derby and Belmont) and Timber County (Preakness). Six-race Triple Crown winning streak ended at '96 Preakness.

Connie Mack (b. 2-22-1862, d. 2-8-56): Born Cornelius McGillicuddy. Baseball manager. Managed Philadelphia for 50 years (1901–50) until age 87. All-time leader in games (7,755), wins (3,731) and losses (3,948). Won 9 pennants and 5 World Series (1910–11, 1913, 1929–30).

Greg Maddux (b. 4-14-66): Baseball P. Won unprecedented fourth consecutive Cy Young Award in 1995, when he was 19–2 with a 1.63 ERA and led the Atlanta Braves to their first World Series title. Career span 1986–92 Chicago (NL), 1993– Atlanta.

Larry Mahan (b. 11-21-43): Rodeo. All-Around champion 6 times (consecutively 1966–70, 1973).

Frank Mahovlich (b. 1-10-38): Hockey LW. Winner of Calder Trophy for top rookie for 1957–58 season. In 18 NHL seasons with Toronto Maple Leafs, Detroit Red Wings and Montreal Canadiens, had 533 goals and 570 assists. Played for six Stanley Cup winners. Elected to Hall of Fame 1981.

Phil Mahre (b. 5-10-57): Skier. Gold medalist in slalom at 1984 Olympics (twin brother Steve won silver medal). World Cup champion 3 consecutive years (1981–83).

Joe Malone (b. 2-28-1890, d. 5-15-69): Hockey F. "Phantom Joe." Led the NHL in its first season, 1917–18, with 44 goals in 20 games with Montreal. Led league in scoring 2 times (1918, 1920). Holds NHL record with most goals scored, single game (7) in 1920.

Karl Malone (b. 7-24-63): Basketball F. "The Mailman." Eight-time first-team All-Star. All-Star MVP, 1989, 1993 (shared with John Stockton). All-Rookie team, 1986. League MVP in 1997 when he led Jazz to NBA Finals. Member of 1992 and '96 Olympic teams. Career span since 1985 with Utah.

Moses Malone (b. 3-23-55): Basketball C. Alltime leader free throws made (8,531), fifth in rebounds (16,212) and third in points scored (27,409). 3 MVP awards in 1979, consecutively 1982–83; playoff MVP in 1983. 4-time All-Star. Led league in rebounding 6 times, 5 consecutively. Career span 1976–95 with Houston, Philadelphia, Washington, Atlanta, Milwaukee, San Antonio.

Man o' War (b. 1917, d. 1947): Thoroughbred race horse. Won 20 of 21 races 1919–20. Only loss was in 1919 in Sanford Stakes to Upset. Passed up Derby but won both Preakness and Belmont. Winner of $249,465. Sire of War Admiral, 1937 Triple Crown winner.

Mickey Mantle (b. 10-20-31, d. 8-13-95): Baseball OF. Won 3 MVP awards, consecutively 1956–57 and 1962; won Triple Crown in 1956. 536 career HR. Greatest switch hitter in history. Played in 20 All-Star games. Alltime World Series leader in HR (18), RBI (40)

and runs scored (42). No. 7 was a member of 7 World Series winners with NY Yankees. Career span 1951–68.

Diego Maradona (b. 10-30-60): Argentine soccer player. Led Argentina to 1986 World Cup victory and to 1990 World Cup finals. Led Naples to Italian League titles (1987, 1990), Italian Cup (1987) and to European Champions' Cup title (1989). Throughout 1980s often acknowledged as best player in the world. Tested positive for cocaine and suspended by FIFA and Italian Soccer Federation for 15 months in March 1991. Failed drug test in 1994 World Cup and suspended before second round.

Pete Maravich (b. 6-22-47, d. 1-5-88): Basketball G. "Pistol Pete." Alltime NCAA leader in points scored (3,667), scoring average (44.2) and games scoring 50+ points (28, including then Division I record 69 points in 1970). Alltime season leader in points scored (1,381) and scoring average (44.5) in 1970. College Player of the Year in 1970. NCAA scoring leader and All-America 3 consecutive seasons from 1968 to 1970 with Louisiana State. Also led NBA in scoring in 1977. Averaged 20+ points 8 times. All-Star 2 times. Career span 1970–79 with Atlanta, New Orleans/Utah, Boston.

Gino Marchetti (b. 1-2-27): Football DE. Played in Pro Bowl every year from 1955 to '65, except 1958 when he broke right ankle tackling Frank Gifford in Colts' 23–17 win over the Giants. Career span 1952–66, almost all with Baltimore Colts. Inducted into Hall of Fame in 1972.

Rocky Marciano (b. 9-1-23, d. 8-31-69): Boxer. Heavyweight champion (1952–56). Career record 49–0 with 43 KOs from 1947 to 1956. Only heavyweight to retire as undefeated champion.

Juan Marichal (b. 10-24-37): Baseball RHP. 243 career wins, 2.89 career ERA. Won 20+ games 6 times; 250+ innings pitched 8 times; 200+ strikeouts 6 times. Pitched no-hitter in 1963. Career span 1960–75, mostly with San Francisco.

Dan Marino (b. 9-15-61): Football QB. Set alltime season record for yards passing (5,084) and touchdown passes (48) in 1984. Has passed for 4,000+ yards 5 other seasons. Player of the Year in 1984. Career totals through 1997–98 season: 55,416 yards passing, 385 touchdown passes, first alltime in both categories. Career span since 1983 with Miami.

Roger Maris (b. 9-10-34, d. 12-14-85): Baseball OF. Broke Babe Ruth's alltime season HR record with 61 in 1961. Won consecutive MVP awards and led league in RBI 1960–61. Career span 1957–68 with Kansas City, New York (AL), St. Louis.

Billy Martin (b. 5-16-28, d. 12-25-89): Baseball 2B-manager. Volatile manager was hired and fired by Minnesota, Detroit, Texas, New York Yankees (5 times!) and Oakland from 1969 to 1988. Won World Series with Yankees as manager in 1977 and as player 4 times.

Eddie Mathews (b. 10-13-31): Baseball 3B. 512 career HR and 30+ HR 9 consecutive seasons. League leader in HR 2 times, walks 4 times. Career span 1952–68 with Milwaukee.

Christy Mathewson (b. 8-12-1880, d. 10-7-25): Baseball RHP. Third alltime most wins (373, tied with Grover Alexander) and shutouts (79); career ERA 2.13. Led league in wins 5 times; won 30+ games 4 times and 20+ games 9 other times. Led league in ERA and strikeouts 5 times each. 300+ innings pitched 11 times. Pitched 2 no-hitters. Pitched 3 shutouts in 1905 World Series. Career span 1900–16 with New York. Played one game for Cincinnati in 1916.

Bob Mathias (b. 11-17-30): Track and field. At age 17, youngest to win gold medal in decathlon at 1948 Olympics. First decathlete to win gold medal at consecutive Olympics (1948, 1952). Also won Sullivan Award in 1948.

Ollie Matson (b. 5-1-30): Football RB. Versatile runner totalled 12,884 combined yards rushing, receiving and kick returning. Scored 73 career touchdowns, including a 105-yard kickoff return on Oct. 14, 1956, the second longest ever. Career span 1952–66 with Chicago Cardinals, Los Angeles, Detroit, Philadelphia. Also won bronze medal in 400-meters at 1952 Olympics.

Roland Matthes (b. 11-17-50): German swimmer. Gold medalist in 100-meter and 200-meter backstroke at 2 consecutive Olympics (1968, 1972). Set 16 world records from 1967 to 1973.

Don Maynard (b. 1-25-37): Football WR. Retired in 1973 as the NFL's alltime leading receiver. In 15 seasons, 10 with the New York Jets, caught 633 passes for 11,834 yards and 88 TDs. Averaged 18.7 yards per catch for career. In 1967 and '68 led AFL with average of 20.2 and 22.8 yards per catch. Elected to Hall of Fame in 1987.

Willie Mays (b. 5-6-31): Baseball OF. "Say Hey Kid." MVP in 1954, 1965; Rookie of the Year in 1951. Third alltime most HR (660), with 50+ HR 2 times, 30+ HR 9 other times. Led league in HR 4 times. 100+ RBI 10 times; 100+ runs scored 12 consecutive seasons. 3,283 career hits. Led league in stolen bases 4 consecutive seasons. 30 HR and 30 steals in same season 2 times and first man in history to hit 300+ HR and steal 300+ bases. Won 11 consecutive Gold Gloves; set record for career putouts by an outfielder and league record for total chances. His catch in the 1954 World Series off the bat of Vic Wertz called the greatest ever. Career span 1951–73 with New York and San Francisco Giants, New York Mets.

Bill Mazeroski (b. 9-5-36): Baseball 2B. Hit dramatic 9th-inning home run in Game 7 to win 1960 World Series, first of only two Series to end on a home run. Also a great fielder, won Gold Glove 8 times. Led league in assists 9 times, double plays 8 times and putouts 5 times.

Joe McCarthy (b. 4-21-1887, d. 1-3-78): Baseball manager. Alltime highest winning percentage among managers for regular season (.615) and World Series (.763). First manager to win pennants in both leagues (Chicago (NL), 1929, New York (AL), 1932). From 1926 to 1950 his teams won 7 World Series and 9 pennants.

Mark McCormack (b. 11-6-30): Sports marketing agent. Founded International Management Group in 1962. Also author of best-selling business advice books.

Pat McCormick (b. 5-12-30): Diver. Gold medalist in platform and springboard at 2 consecutive Olympics (1952, 1956). Also won Sullivan Award in 1956.

Willie McCovey (b. 1-10-38): Baseball 1B. Led NL in homers three times (1963, '68, '69) and in RBIs twice (1968–69). 521 career homers. .270 career batting average. Hit 18 grand slams. Rookie of Year 1959. NL MVP in 1969. Career span 1959–73 and 1977–80 with San Francisco Giants, 1974–76 with San Diego Padres and 1976 with Oakland A's. Elected to Hall of Fame in 1986.

John McEnroe (b. 2-26-59): Tennis player. Won 4 U.S. Open singles titles (consecutively 1979–81, 1984) and 3 Wimbledon titles (1981, consecutively 1983–84).

Also won 8 Grand Slam doubles titles. Third alltime men's most career tournament victories (77). Led U.S. to 5 Davis Cup victories (1978–79, 1981–82, 1992).

John McGraw (b. 4-7-1873, d. 2-25-34): Baseball manager. Second alltime most games (4,801) and wins (2,784). Guided New York Giants to 3 World Series titles and 10 pennants from 1902 to 1932.

Denny McLain (b. 3-29-44): Baseball RHP. Last pitcher to win 30+ games in a season (Detroit, 1968); won 20+ games 2 other times. Won 2 consecutive Cy Young Awards (1968–69). Led league in innings pitched 2 times. Served 2½-year jail term for 1985 conviction of extortion, racketeering and drug possession. Re-entered prison in 1997 on fraud conviction. Career span 1963–72.

Mary T. Meagher (b. 10-27-64): Swimmer. "Madame Butterfly." Won 3 gold medals at 1984 Olympics (100-meter butterfly, 200-meter butterfly and 400-medley relay). In 1981 set world records in 100-meter butterfly (57.93) and 200-meter butterfly (2:05.96).

Rick Mears (b. 12-3-51): Auto racer. Has won Indy 500 4 times (1979, 1984, 1988, 1991) and been CART champion 3 times (1979, consecutively 1981-82). Named Indy 500 Rookie of the Year in 1978.

Mark Messier (b. 1-18-61): Hockey C. Two-time Hart Trophy (MVP) winnner; won Stanley Cups with Edmonton (1984, '85, '87, '88 and '90) and NY Rangers (1994). Among top five alltime in points, top ten in goals, assists. Career span 1979–91 Edmonton, 1991–96 NY Rangers, 1997– Vancouver.

Cary Middlecoff (b. 1-6-21): Golfer. Also a dentist. Won 40 PGA tournaments, including 1955 Masters and U.S. Opens in 1949 and '56. Won 1956 Vardon Trophy.

George Mikan (b. 6-18-24): Basketball C. Averaged 20+ points per game and named to All-Star team 6 consecutive seasons. Led league in scoring 3 times, rebounding 1 time. Played on 5 championship teams in 6 years (1949–54) with Minneapolis. Also played on 1945 NIT championship team with DePaul. All-America 3 times. Served as ABA Commissioner from 1968 to 1969.

Stan Mikita (b. 5-20-40): Hockey C. Won MVP award 2 consecutive seasons (1967–68). 926 career assists, 1,467 career points. Led league in assists 4 consecutive seasons and points 4 times. 541 career goals. All-Star 6 times. Career span 1958–80 with Chicago.

Del Miller (b. 7-5-13; d. 8-19-96): Harness racing driver. Raced in 8 decades, beginning in 1929, the longest career of any athlete. Won The Hambletonian in 1950.

Marvin Miller (b. 4-14-17): Labor negotiator. Union chief of Major League Baseball Players Association from 1966 to 1984. Led strikes in 1972 and 1981. Negotiated 5 labor contracts with owners that increased minimum salary and pension fund, allowed for agents and arbitration, and brought about the end of the reserve clause and the beginning of free agency.

Art Monk (b. 12-5-57): Football WR. Second alltime in pass receptions (940 for 12,721 and 68 TDs through end of 1995–96 season). 106 catches in 1984 was then NFL single season record. Career span 1980–93 with Redskins, 1993–95 with New York Jets, 1995 with Eagles.

Earl Monroe (b. 11-21-44): Basketball G. "The Pearl" played 13 seasons (1968–80) with the Baltimore Bullets and New York Knicks. NBA Rookie of Year in

1968. Member of 1973 NBA championship Knicks team. Averaged 18.8 points a game. Elected to Hall of Fame 1989.

Joe Montana (b. 6-11-56): Football QB. Second alltime highest-rated passer (92.3); third in completions (3,409); retired with 40,551 passing yards and 273 touchdown passes. Won 4 Super Bowl championships (1981, 1984, consecutively 1988–89) with San Francisco. Named Super Bowl MVP 3 times (1981, 1984, 1989). Player of the Year in 1989. Also led Notre Dame to national championship in 1977. Career span 1979–92 with San Francisco, 1993–94 Kansas City.

Carlos Monzon (b. 8-7-42, d. 1-8-95): Argentine boxer. Longest title reign of any middleweight champion (6 years, 9 months) from Nov. 1970 through Aug. 1977. Career record 89-3-9 with 61 KOs from 1963 to 1977. Won 82 consecutive bouts from 1964 to 1977. Defended title 14 times. Retired as champion.

Helen Wills Moody (b. 10-6-05, d. 1-1-98): Tennis player. Third alltime most women's Grand Slam singles titles (19). Her 8 Wimbledon titles are second most alltime (consecutively 1927–30, 1932–33, 1935, 1938). Won 7 U.S. titles (consecutively 1923–25, 1927–29, 1931) and 4 French titles (consecutively 1928–30,. 1932). Also won 12 Grand Slam doubles titles.

Archie Moore (b. 12-13-16): Boxer. Longest title reign of any light heavyweight champion (9 years, 1 month) from Dec. 1952 through Feb. 1962. Career record 199-26-8 with an alltime record 145 KOs from 1935 to 1965. Retired at age 52.

Davey Moore (b. 11-1-33; d. 3-23-63): Boxer. Won featherweight title by KO of Kid Bassey in 13 on 3-18-59. Five successful defenses of title, before losing it on 3-21-63 to Sugar Ramos who KO'd him in 10. Died two days after fight of brain damage suffered during fight. Career record: 67 bouts; won 30 by KO, 28 by decision, 1 because of foul; drew 1; lost 7, two by KO.

Noureddine Morceli (b. 2-20-70). Algerian track and field middle distance runner. Set world record for mile (3:44.39) in Rieti, Italy, on 9-5-93. Set world record for 1,500 (3:28.86) on 9-5-92. World champion at 1,500 in both 1991 and '93. Finished a shocking seventh at 1992 Olympics, but won gold medal in '96 at Atlanta. Only man ever to rank first in the world at 1,500/mile four straight years (1990–93).

Joe Morgan (b. 9-19-43): Baseball 2B. Won 2 consecutive MVP awards in 1975-76. Third alltime most walks (1,865). 689 stolen bases. Led league in walks 4 times. 100+ walks and runs scored 8 times each; 40+ stolen bases 9 times. Won 5 Gold Gloves. Second alltime most games played by 2nd baseman (2,527). Career span 1963–84 with Houston, Cincinnati.

Willie Mosconi (b. 6-27-13; d. 9-16-93): Pocket billiards player. Won world title a record 15 straight times between 1941 and 1957. Once pocketed 526 balls without a miss.

Edwin Moses (b. 8-31-55): Track and field. Gold medalist in 400-meter hurdles at 2 Olympics, in 1976, 1984 (U.S. boycotted 1980 Games); bronze medalist at 1988 Olympics. Set four world records in 400-meter hurdles (best of 47.02 set on 8-31-83). Won 122 consecutive races from 1977 to 1987. Won Sullivan Award in 1983.

Marion Motley (b. 6-5-20): Football FB. All-time AAFC leader in yards rushing (3,024). Also led NFL in rushing once. Combined league totals: 4,712 yards

rushing, 39 touchdowns. Played with four consecutive AAFC champions (1946–49) and one NFL champion (1950). With Cleveland 1946–1953.

Shirley Muldowney (b. 6-19-40): Drag racer. First woman to win the Top Fuel championship, which she won 3 times (1977, 1980, 1982).

Anthony Munoz (b. 8-19-58): Football OT. Probably the greatest tackle ever. Made Pro Bowl a record-tying 11 times. Career span 1980–92 with the Cincinnati Bengals. Elected to Hall of Fame 1998.

Isaac Murphy (b. 4-16-1861, d. 2-12-1896): Horse racing jockey. Top jockey of his era, Murphy, who was black, won 3 Kentucky Derbys (aboard Buchanan in 1884, Riley in 1890 and Kingman in 1891).

Eddie Murray (b. 2-24-56): Baseball 1B. 100+ RBIs 6 seasons and 30+ HRs five seasons. Retired with 3,255 hits, 504 HRs and 1,917 RBI. Alltime leader in RBI by switch hitter. Career span 1977–88, '96 with Baltimore Orioles; 1989–91, '97 with Los Angeles; 1992–93 with New York Mets, 1994–96 with Cleveland; 1997 with Anaheim.

Jim Murray (b. 12-29-19): Sportswriter. Won Pulitzer Prize in 1990. Named Sportswriter of the Year 14 times. Columnist for *Los Angeles Times* since 1961.

Ty Murray (b. 10-11-69): Rodeo cowboy. All-Around world champion, 1989–94. Set single-season earnings record, 1990 ($213,771). Rookie of the Year, 1988. At 20 in 1989, became youngest man ever to win national all-around title.

Stan Musial (b. 11-21-20): Baseball OF-1B. "Stan the Man." Had .331 career batting average and 475 career HR. MVP award winner 1943, 1946, 1948. Fourth alltime in hits (3,630) and third in doubles (725). Won 7 batting titles. Led league in hits 6 times, slugging average 5 times, doubles 8 times. Had .300+ batting average 17 times, 200+ hits 6 times, 100+ RBI 10 times, and 100+ runs scored 11 times. 24-time All-Star. Career span 1941-63 with St. Louis.

John Naber (b. 1-20-56): Swimmer. Won 4 gold medals and 1 silver medal at 1976 Olympics. Sullivan Award winner in 1977.

Bronko Nagurski (b. 11-3-08, d. 1-7-90): Football FB. Punishing runner played on 3 NFL champions (1932, '33, 1943) with Bears. 2,778 career yards, 1930–37 and 1943 with Chicago.

James Naismith (b. 11-6-1861, d. 11-28-39): Invented basketball in 1891 while an instructor at YMCA Training School in Springfield, Mass. Refined the game while a professor at Kansas from 1898 to 1937. Hall of Fame is named for him.

Joe Namath (b. 5-31-43): Football QB. "Broadway Joe." Super Bowl MVP in 1968 after he guaranteed victory for AFL. 173 career touchdown passes. Led league in yards passing 3 times, including 4,007 yards in 1967. Player of the Year in 1968, Rookie of the Year in 1965. Career span 1965–77 with NY Jets, LA Rams.

Ilie Nastase (b. 7-19-46): Romanian tennis player. "Nasty" for his unruly deportment on court. Beat Arthur Ashe to win 1972 U.S. Open title. Won 1973 French Open. Twice Wimbledon runnerup (to Stan Smith in 1972 and Bjorn Borg in '76).

Martina Navratilova (b. 10-18-56): Tennis player. Fourth alltime most women's Grand Slam singles titles (18—tied with Chris Evert). Won a record 9 Wimbledon titles, including 6 consecutively (1978–79, 1982–87, '90). Won 4 U.S. Open titles (consecutively 1983–84, 1986–87), 3 Australian Open titles (1981, '83, '85) and 2 French Open titles (1982, '84). Reached Grand Slam final 13 other times. Also won 38 Grand Slam doubles titles. Her total of 56 Grand Slam titles is second alltime to Margaret Court's. Set mark for longest winning streak with 74 matches in 1984. Also won the doubles Grand Slam in 1984 with Pam Shriver. Won 109 consecutive matches with Shriver from 1983–85. Retired after 1994 season.

Byron Nelson (b. 2-14-12): Golfer. Won the Masters (1937, 1942) and PGA Championship (1940, 1945) 2 times each and U.S. Open once (1939). Won 52 career tournaments, including 11 consecutively in 1945.

Ernie Nevers (b. 6-11-03, d. 5-3-76): Football FB. Set alltime pro single game record for points scored (40) and touchdowns (6) on Nov. 28, 1929. Career span 1926-31 with Duluth, Chicago. Also a pitcher with St. Louis, surrendered 2 of Babe Ruth's 60 HR in 1927. All-America at Stanford, earned 11 letters in 4 sports.

John Newcombe (b. 5-23-44): Australian tennis player. Won 3 Wimbledon singles titles (1967, consecutively 1970–71), 2 U.S. titles (1967, 1973) and 2 Australian Open titles (1973, 1975). Also won 17 Grand Slam doubles titles.

Pete Newell (b. 8-31-15): College basketball coach. Despite coaching only 13 seasons, 1947 through 1960, was first coach to win NIT, NCAA and Olympic crowns. Led Univ. of San Francisco to 1949 NIT title, Cal to 1959 NCAA title, and the 1960 U.S. Olympic basketball team that included Jerry Lucas, Oscar Robertson and Jerry West to gold medal. Overall collegiate coaching record of 234–123.

Jack Nicklaus (b. 1-21-40): Golfer. "The Golden Bear." Alltime leader in major championships (20). Second alltime in career wins (70). Won Masters 6 times, more than any golfer (1963, consecutively 1965-66, '72, '75, '86—at age 46, the oldest player to win event), PGA Championship 5 times (1963, '71, '73, '75, '80), U.S. Open 4 times (1962, '67, '72, '80), British Open 3 times (1966, '70, '78) and U.S. Amateur 2 times (1959, '61). PGA Player of the Year 5 times (1967, consecutively 1972–73, 1975–76). Also NCAA champion with Ohio State in 1961.

Ray Nitschke (b. 12-29-36): Football LB. Defensive signal caller for the great Packer teams of the '60s. Voted Packer MVP by teammates after 1967 season. MVP of the 1962 NFL title game. Career span 1958–72 with Green Bay Packers.

Greg Norman (b. 2-10-55): Golfer. "The Shark" led PGA in winnings in 1986, '90, '95–96. Won Vardon Trophy twice, 1989–90. Won two British Opens (1986,'93) but is almost as famous for his heartbreaking misses. Beaten at the 1986 PGA when Bob Tway holed out a sand shot and '87 Masters when Larry Mize chipped in from a downhill lie. Blew a six-stroke, third-round lead to lose to Nick Faldo by five shots at 1996 Masters. PGA Player of the Year twice 1996.

James D. Norris (b. 11-6-06, d. 2-25-66): Hockey executive. Owner of Detroit from 1933 to 1943 and Chicago from 1946 to 1966. Teams won 4 Stanley Cup championships (consecutively 1936–37, 1943, 1961). Defensive Player of the Year award named in his honor. Also a boxing promoter, operated International Boxing Club from 1949 to 1958.

Paavo Nurmi (b. 6-13-1897, d. 10-2-73): Track and field. Finnish middle- and long-distance runner won a total of 9 gold medals at 3 Olympics in 1920, 1924, 1928.

Matti Nykänen (b. 7-17-63): Finnish ski jumper. Three-time Olympic gold medalist. Won 90-meter jump (1984, 1988) and 70-meter jump (1988). World champion on 90-meter jump in 1982. Won four World Cups (1983, 1985, 1986, 1988).

Dan O'Brien (b. 7-18-66): Track and field decathlete. Won world decathlon title in 1991, '93 and '95. Set world decathlon record of 8,891 in Talence, France, on 9-4/5-92. Heavily favored to win 1992 Olympic decathlon but missed making U.S. team when he no-heighted in pole vault at U.S. Olympic Trials. Won gold medal at 1996 Olympics in Atlanta.

Parry O'Brien (b. 1-28-32): Track and field. Shot putter who revolutionized the event with his "glide" technique and won Olympic gold medals in 1952 and 1956, silver in 1960. Set 10 world records from 1953 to 1959, topped by a put of 63' 4" in 1959. Sullivan Award winner in 1959.

Al Oerter (b. 8-19-36): Track and field. Gold medalist in discus at 4 consecutive Olympics (1956, 1960, 1964, 1968), setting Olympic record each time. First to break the 200-foot barrier, throwing 200' 5" in 1962.

Sadaharu Oh (b. 5-20-40): Baseball 1B in Japanese league. 868 career HR in 22 seasons for the Tokyo Giants. Led league in HR 15 times, RBI 13 times, batting 5 times and runs 13 consecutive seasons. Awarded MVP 9 times; won 2 consecutive Triple Crowns and 9 Gold Gloves.

Hakeem Olajuwon (b. 1-21-63): Basketball C. From Nigeria. Led NCAA in field goal percentage, rebounding and blocked shots in 1984 at Houston. Alltime NBA career leader in blocked shots (3,459 through 1997–98). All-NBA First Team 1987–89, '93–94. League MVP in 1994 as he led Houston to NBA title (repeated in '95). Career span since 1985 with the Rockets. Member of 1996 U.S. Olympic team.

Merlin Olsen (b. 9-15-40): Fooball DT. Part of LA Rams "Fearsome Foursome" defensive line. Named to Pro Bowl 14 straight times. Career span 1962–76, all with LA Rams. Elected to Hall of Fame 1982.

Omaha (b. 1932, d. 1959): Thoroughbred race horse. In 1935 third horse to win Triple Crown. Won Kentucky Derby by 1½ lengths over Roman Soldier; Preakness by 6 over Firethorn; and the Belmont by 1½ from Firethorn. Trained by Sunny Jim Fitzsimmons.

Shaquille O'Neal (b. 3-6-72): Basketball C. Led NCAA in blocked shots in 1992, with 5.23 a game; averaged 4.58 over his 90-game, three-year career. Top pick of Orlando Magic in 1992 NBA draft. Almost unanimous NBA Rookie of the Year 1993. Averaged 23.4 points, 13.9 rebounds and 3.5 blocked shots in first NBA season. Led league in scoring with 29.3 average in 1994–95. Member of 1996 U.S. Olympic team. Moved to LA Lakers as free agent in July 1996.

Bobby Orr (b. 3-20-48): Hockey D. Defensive Player of the Year more than any other player, 8 consecutive seasons (1968-75). Won MVP award 3 consecutive seasons (1970-72), playoff MVP 2 times (1970, 1972). Also Rookie of the Year in 1967. Led league in assists 5 times and scoring 2 times. Career span 1966–77 with Boston.

Mel Ott (b. 3-2-09, d. 11-21-58): Baseball OF. 511 career HR, 1,861 RBI, .304 batting average. League leader in HR and walks 6 times each. 100+ RBI 9 times and 100+ walks 10 times. Career span 1926–47 with New York Giants.

Jim Otto (b. 1-5-38): Football C. Number 00 started every game (308) in his 15-year career (1960–74) with the Oakland Raiders. Inducted to Hall of Fame in 1980.

Kristin Otto (b. 1966): German swimmer. Won 6 gold medals for East Germany at 1988 Olympics.

Jesse Owens (b. 9-12-13, d. 3-31-80): Track and field. Gold medalist in 4 events (100 meters and 200 meters; 4x100-meter relay and long jump) at 1936 Olympics. At the 1935 Big 10 championship set or equaled 4 world record in 70 minutes, including 100 yards, long jump, 220-yard low hurdles and 220 dash.

Alan Page (b. 8-7-45): Football DT. First defensive player to be named NFL Player of the Year, in 1972. Career span 1967–78 with Minnesota Vikings and 1978–81 with Chicago Bears. Now sits on Minnesota Supreme Court.

Satchel Paige (b. 7-7-06, d. 6-8-82): Baseball RHP. Alltime greatest black pitcher, didn't pitch in major leagues until 1948 at age 42 with Cleveland. Oldest pitcher in major league history at age 59 with Kansas City in 1965. Pitched in the Negro leagues from 1926 to 1950 with Birmingham Black Barons, Pittsburgh Crawfords and Kansas City Monarchs. Estimated career record is 2,000 wins, 250 shutouts, 30,000 strikeouts, 45 no-hitters. Said "Don't look back. Something may be gaining on you."

Arnold Palmer (b. 9-10-29): Golfer. Fourth alltime in career wins (60). Won the Masters 4 times (1958, 1960, 1962, 1964), British Open 2 consecutive years (1961–62) and U.S. Open (1960) and U.S. Amateur (1954) once each. PGA Player of the Year 2 times (1960, 1962). The first golfer to surpass $1 million in career earnings. Also won Seniors Championship 2 times (1980, 1984) and U.S. Senior Open once (1981).

Jim Palmer (b. 10-15-45): Baseball RHP. 268 career wins, 2.86 ERA. Won 3 Cy Young Awards (1973, consecutively 1975–76). Won 20+ games 8 times. Led league in wins 3 times, innings pitched 4 times, ERA 2 times. Never allowed a grand slam HR. Pitched on 6 World Series teams with Baltimore, including shutout at age 20. Pitched no-hitter in 1969. Career span 1965–84.

Bernie Parent (b. 4-3-45): Hockey G. Alltime leader for wins in a season (47 in 1974). Goaltender of the Year, playoff MVP, league leader in wins, goals against average and shutouts 2 consecutive seasons (1974–75). Career record 270-197-121, including 55 shutouts. Career 2.55 goals against average. Tied record of 4 playoff shutouts in 1975. Played on 2 consecutive Stanley Cup champions (1974–75). Career span 1965–79 with Philadelphia.

Brad Park (b. 7-6-48): Hockey D. Seven-time All Star. In 17 seasons with the New York Rangers, Boston Bruins and Detroit Red Wings (1968–69 through 1984–85) scored 213 goals and had 683 assists. Elected to Hall of Fame 1988.

Jim Parker (b. 4-3-34): Football T/G. Winner of 1956 Outland Trophy as Ohio State senior. Blocked for Johnny Unitas. All-NFL four times at guard, four times at tackle. Career span 1957–67, all with Baltimore Colts. Inducted to Hall of Fame in 1973.

Joe Paterno (b. 12-21-26): College football coach. Fourth alltime in wins in Division I-A (298 through 1997—the most of any active coach at that level). Has won 2 national championships (1982, 1986) with Penn State since 1966. Career record 298-77-3, including 5 undefeated seasons. Has also won 18 bowl games.

Lester Patrick (b. 12-30-1883, d. 6-1-60): Hockey coach. Led NY Rangers to three Stanley Cup championships (1928, 1933, 1940). Originated the NHL's farm system and developed playoff format.

Floyd Patterson (b. 1-4-35): Boxer. Heavyweight champion 2 times (1956-59, 1960-62). First heavyweight to regain title, in rematch with Ingemar Johansson. Career record 55-8-1 with 40 KOs from 1952 to 1972. Also middleweight gold medalist at 1952 Olympics.

Walter Payton (b. 7-25-54): Football RB. Alltime leader in yards rushing (16,726), rushing attempts (3,838), seasons gaining 1,000+ yards rushing (10); and second in rushing touchdowns (110). 125 career touchdowns. Rushed for a record 275 yards on Nov. 20, 1977. Selected for Pro Bowl 9 times. Player of the Year 2 times (1977, 1985). Led league in rushing 5 consecutive seasons. Career span 1975–87 with Chicago.

Pele (b. 10-23-40): Born Edson Arantes do Nascimento. Brazilian soccer player. Soccer's great ambassador. Played on 3 World Cup winners with Brazil (1958, 1962, 1970). Helped promote soccer in U.S. by playing with NY Cosmos from 1975 to 1977. Scored 1,281 goals in 22 years.

Willie Pep (b. 9-19-22): Boxer. Featherweight champion 2 times (1942-48, 1949-50). Lost title to Sandy Saddler, won it back in rematch, then lost it to Saddler again. Career record 230-11-1 with 65 KOs from 1940 to 1966. Won 73 consecutive bouts from 1940 to 1943. Defended title 9 times.

Gil Perreault (b. 11-13-50): Hockey C. Won Calder Trophy as NHL's top rookie for 1970–71 season. Played 17 seasons (1970–71 through 1986–87), all with Buffalo Sabres. Scored 512 goals and had 814 assists in career. Elected to Hall of Fame in 1990.

Fred Perry (b. 5-18-09, d. 2-2-95): British tennis player. Won 3 consecutive Wimbledon singles titles (1934–36), the last British man to win the tournament. Also won 3 U.S. titles (consecutively 1933–34, 1936), 1 French title (1935) and 1 Australian title (1934).

Gaylord Perry (b. 9-15-38): Baseball RHP. Only pitcher to win Cy Young Award in both leagues (Cleveland 1972, San Diego 1978). 314 career wins, 3,534 strikeouts. 20+ wins 5 times; 200+ strikeouts 8 times; 250+ innings pitched 12 times. Pitched no-hitter in 1968. Admitted to throwing a spitter. Career span 1962-83 with San Francisco, Cleveland, San Diego.

Bob Pettit (b. 12-12-32): Basketball F. First player in history to break 20,000-point barrier (20,880 career points scored). 26.4 career scoring average; 16.2 rebound avg. MVP in 1956, 1959; Rookie of the Year in 1955. All-Star 10 consecutive seasons. Led league in scoring 2 times, rebounding 1 time. Career span 1954–64 with St. Louis.

Richard Petty (b. 7-2-37): Auto racer. Alltime leader in NASCAR victories (200). Daytona 500 winner (1964, 1966, 1971, consecutively 1973-74, 1979, 1981) and NASCAR champion (1964, 1967, consecutively 1971–72, 1974–75, 1979) 7 times each, the most of any driver. First stock car racer to reach $1 million in earnings. Son of Lee Petty, 3-time NASCAR champion (1954, consecutively 1958–59). Retired after 1992 season.

Laffit Pincay Jr. (b. 12-29-46): Jockey. Second only to Bill Shoemaker in wins. Among the top money-winners of all time, approaching $200,000,000 in career earnings. Won 5 Eclipse Awards as outstanding jockey. Rode 3 Kentucky Derby winners; 2 Preakness winners; and 1 Belmont winner.

Jacques Plante (b. 1-17-29, d. 2-27-86): Hockey G. First goalie to wear a mask. Second alltime in wins (434) and second lowest modern goals against average (2.38). Goaltender of the Year 7 times, more than any other goalie (consecutively 1955-59, 1961, 1968). Won MVP award in 1961. Led league in goals against average 8 times, wins 6 times and shutouts 4 times. Was on 6 Stanley Cup champions with Montreal from 1952 to 1962 and played for 4 other teams until retirement in 1972.

Gary Player (b. 11-1-35): South African golfer. Won the Masters (1961, 1974, 1978) and British Open (1959, 1968, 1974) 3 times each, PGA Championship 2 times (1962, 1972) and U.S. Open (1965). Also won Seniors Championship 3 times (1986, 1988, 1990) and U.S. Senior Open 2 consecutive years (1987–88).

Sam Pollock (b. 12-15-25): Hockey executive. As general manager of Montreal from 1964 to 1978 won 9 Stanley Cup championships (1965–66, 1968–69, 1971, 1973, 1976–78).

Denis Potvin (b. 10-29-53): Hockey D. Seven-time All Star during 15-season career (1973–74 through 1987–88), all with New York Islanders. Won Calder Trophy for 1973–74 season. Won Norris Trophy three times. Captained Islanders to four Stanley Cup championships. Elected to Hall of Fame in 1991.

Mike Powell (b. 11-10-63): Track and field. Long jumper broke Bob Beamon's 23-year-old world record at 1991 World Championships in Tokyo with a jump of 29' 4½". Won silver in 1992 Olympics.

Annemarie Moser-Pröll (b. 3-27-53): Austrian skier. Gold medalist in downhill at 1980 Olympics. World Cup overall champion 6 times, more than any other skier (consecutively 1971–75, 1979).

Alain Prost (b. 2-24-55): French auto racer. Alltime leader in Formula 1 victories (51). Formula 1 champion 4 times (consecutively 1985–86, 1989, 1993).

Jack Ramsay (b. 2-21-25): Basketball coach. Coached 11 seasons at St. Joseph's University, with 234–72 record. Overall record of 864–783 as NBA coach. Coach of NBA champion 1977 Portland Trail Blazers. Elected to Hall of Fame 1992.

Jean Ratelle (b. 10-3-40): Hockey C. In 21-season career (1960–61 through 1980–81) with the New York Rangers and Boston Bruins, scored 491 goals and had 776 assists. Twice won Lady Byng Trophy. Elected to Hall of Fame in 1985.

Willis Reed (b. 6-25-42): Basketball C. Played 10 seasons (1965–74), all with the New York Knicks. Career average of 18.7 points a game. NBA Rookie of Year in 1965. Playoff MVP of both Knick championship teams, in 1970 and '73. NBA MVP in 1970. Elected to Hall of Fame in 1981.

Harold Henry (Pee Wee) Reese (b. 7-23-18): Baseball SS. Played for 7 pennant-winning Dodger teams. Led NL in runs scored in 1949, with 132. Elected to Hall of Fame in 1984.

Mary Lou Retton (b. 1-24-68): Gymnast. Won 1 gold, 1 silver and 2 bronze medals at 1984 Olympics.

Grantland Rice (b. 11-1-1880, d. 7-13-54): Sportswriter. Legendary figure during sport's Golden Age of the 1920s. Wrote "When the Last Great Scorer comes / To mark against your name, / He'll write not 'won' or 'lost' / But how you played the game." Also named the 1924-25 Notre Dame backfield the "Four Horsemen."

Jerry Rice (b. 10-13-62): Football WR. Entering 1998 season, alltime leader in touchdowns (166), touchdown receptions (155) and in consecutive games with a TD reception (13 in 1988). Player of the Year in 1987 and led league in scoring (138 points on 23 touchdowns). Super Bowl MVP in 1989 with record 215 receiving yards on 11 catches. Also set Super Bowl record with 3 touchdown receptions in 1990 and in 1995. Career span since 1985 with San Francisco 49ers.

Henri Richard (b. 2-29-36): Hockey C. "The Pocket Rocket." Won 11 Stanley Cup championships with Montreal. Four-time All-Star. Career span 1955–1975.

Maurice Richard (b. 8-4-21): Hockey RW. "The Rocket." First player ever to score 50 goals in a season, in 1945. Led league in goals 5 times. 544 career goals. Won MVP award in 1947. All-Star 8 times. Tied playoff game record for most goals (5 on March 23, 1944). Won 8 Stanley Cup championships with Montreal 1942–1959.

Bob Richards (b. 2-2-26): Track and field. The only pole vaulter to win gold medal at 2 consecutive Olympics (1952, 1956). Also won Sullivan Award in 1951.

Branch Rickey (b. 12-20-1881, d. 12-9-65): Baseball executive. Integrated major league baseball in 1947 by signing Jackie Robinson to contract with Brooklyn Dodgers. Conceived minor league farm system in 1919 at St. Louis; instituted batting cage and sliding pit.

Pat Riley (b. 3-20-45): Basketball coach. Going into 1998–99 season most playoff wins (147). Coached Los Angeles to 4 championships, 2 consecutively, from 1981 to 1989. 60+ wins 7 times (4 times consecutively), 50+ wins 4 other times. Coach of the Year in 1990, '93 and '97. Led New York Knicks to NBA Finals in 1994, then left three weeks later to become coach and part owner of Miami Heat.

Cal Ripken Jr (b. 8-24-60): Baseball SS-3B. Broke Lou Gehrig's record for most consecutive games played (2,131) on Sept. 5, 1995; streak intact through 1997. Set record for consecutive errorless games by a shortstop (95 in 1990). MVP in 1983 and '91. Rookie of the Year in 1982. Hit 20+ HRs in 10 consecutive seasons; 13-time All-Star.

Glenn (Fireball) Roberts (b. 1-20-31, d. 7-2-64): Auto racer. Won 34 NASCAR races. Died as a result of fiery accident in World 600 at Charlotte Motor Speedway in May 1964. At time of his death had won more major races than any other driver in NASCAR history.

Oscar Robertson (b. 11-24-38): Basketball G. "The Big O." 9,887 career assists; 26,710 points, 25.7 ppg. MVP in 1964, All-Star 9 consecutive seasons and 1961 Rookie of the Year. Led league in assists 6 times, free throw percentage 2 times. Averaged 30+ points 6 times in 7 seasons, 20+ points 4 other times. Only player in history to average a season triple-double (1961). Career span 1960-72 with Cincinnati, Milwaukee. Also College Player of the Year, All-America and NCAA scoring leader 3 consecutive seasons from 1958 to 1960 with Cincinnati. Third all-time NCAA highest scoring average (33.8); seventh most points scored (2,973).

Brooks Robinson (b. 5-18-37): Baseball 3B. Alltime leader in assists, putouts, double plays and fielding average among 3rd baseman. Won 16 consecutive Gold Gloves. Led league in fielding average a record 11 times. MVP in 1964—led league in RBI—and MVP in 1970 World Series. Career span 1955–77 with Baltimore.

David Robinson (b. 8-6-65): Basketball C. *Sporting News* Player of the Year in 1987. Led college players in

1986 in both rebounding (13.0) and blocked shots (5.91). 1990 NBA Rookie of the Year. Led NBA in rebounding 1991 (13.0), in scoring 1994 (29.8) and in blocked shots in 1992, when he was named Defensive Player of the Year. Named NBA MVP in 1995. Member of 1988, '92 and '96 Olympic teams. Career span since 1989 with San Antonio.

Eddie Robinson (b. 2-13-19): College football coach. Retired with alltime college record 408 career wins through 1941–97 at Division I-AA Grambling State.

Frank Robinson (b. 8-31-35): Baseball OF-manager. Only player to win MVP awards in both leagues (Cincinnati, 1961, Baltimore, 1966). Won Triple Crown and World Series MVP in 1966. Fourth alltime most HR (586). 30+ HR 11 times; 100+ RBI 6 times; 100+ runs scored 8 times (led league 3 times). Had .300+ batting average 9 times. Became first black manager in major leagues, with Cleveland in 1975. Career span as player 1956-76. Career span as manager 1975–77 with Cleveland; 1981–84 with San Francisco; 1988–91 with Baltimore.

Jackie Robinson (b. 1-13-19, d. 10-24-72): Baseball 2B. Broke the color barrier as first black player in major leagues in 1947 with Brooklyn Dodgers. 1947 Rookie of the Year; 1949 MVP with .342 batting average to lead league. Had .311 career batting average. Led league in stolen bases 2 times; stole home 19 times. Played on 6 pennant winners in 10 years with Brooklyn. Elected to Hall of Fame in 1962.

Larry Robinson (b. 6-2-51): Hockey D. Twice won Norris Trophy as NHL's top defenseman. Career span 1972–73 through 1991–92, all but the last three with the Montreal Canadiens. Member of six Montreal teams that won Stanley Cup. Awarded Conn Smythe Trophy as MVP of 1978 Stanley Cup.

Sugar Ray Robinson (b. 5-3-21, d. 4-12-89): Born Walker Smith, Jr. Boxer. Called best pound-for-pound boxer ever. Welterweight champ (1946–51) and middleweight champ 5 times. Career record: 174-19-6 with 109 KOs from 1940–65. Won 91 consecutive bouts from 1943–51. 15 losses came after age 35.

Knute Rockne (b. 3-4-1888, d. 3-31-31): College football coach. Won national championship 3 times (1924, consecutively 1929-30). Alltime highest winning percentage (.881). Career record 105-12-5, including 5 undefeated seasons, with Notre Dame from 1918 to 1930.

Bill Rodgers (b. 12-23-47): Track and field. Won the Boston and New York City marathons 4 times each between 1975 and 1980.

Dennis Rodman (b. 5-13-61): Basketball F. NBA Defensive Player of the Year 1990, '91. First player to win seven consecutive rebounding titles; won NBA titles with Detroit 1989 and '90 and Chicago 1996-98. Career span 1986–93 with Detroit, '93–95 with San Antonio and '95– Chicago.

Chi Chi Rodriguez (b. 10-23-35): Golfer. Led senior money list for 1987 ($509,145). Won 8 events during PGA career that began in 1960.

Art Rooney (b. 1-27-01; d. 8-25-88): Owner of Pittsburgh Steelers. Bought team in 1933 and ran it until his death in 1988. Elected to Hall of Fame in 1964.

Murray Rose (b. 1-6-39) Australian swimmer. Won 3 gold medals (including 400- and 1500-meter freestyle) at 1956 Olympics. Also won 1 gold, 1 silver and 1 bronze medal at 1960 Olympics.

Pete Rose (b. 4-14-41): Baseball OF-IF. "Charlie Hustle." Alltime leader in hits (4,256), games played

(3,562) and at bats (14,053); second in doubles (746); fourth in runs scored (2,165). Had .303 career average and won 3 batting titles. Averaged .300+ 15 times, 200+ hits and 100+ runs scored each 10 times. Led league in hits 7 times, runs scored 4 times, doubles 5 times. 1963 Rookie of the Year; 1973 MVP; 1975 World Series MVP. Had 44-game hitting streak in 1978. Played in 17 All-Star games, starting at 5 different positions. Career span 1963–86 with Cincinnati, Philadelphia. Manager of Cincinnati from 1984 to 1989. Banned from baseball for life by Commissioner Bart Giamatti in 1989 for betting activities. Served 5-month jail term for tax evasion in 1990. Ineligible for Hall of Fame.

Ken Rosewall (b. 11-2-34): Australian tennis player. Won Grand Slam singles titles at ages 18 and 35. Won 4 Australian titles (1953, 1955, consecutively 1971–72), 2 French titles (1953, 1968) and 2 U.S. titles (1956, 1970). Reached 4 Wimbledon finals, but title eluded him.

Art Ross (b. 1-13-1886, d. 8-5-64): Hockey D-coach. Improved design of puck and goal net. Manager-coach of Boston, 1924-45, won Stanley Cup, 1938-39. The Art Ross Trophy is awarded to the NHL scoring champion.

Donald Ross (b. 1873, d. 4-26-48): Scottish-born golf course architect. Trained at St. Andrews under Old Tom Morris. Designed over 500 courses, including Pinehurst No. 2 course and Oakland Hills.

Patrick Roy (b. 10-5-65): Hockey G. Won Vezina Trophy three times. Won Conn Smythe Trophy twice (1986, '93). Career span 1984–95 Montreal, '95–Colorado. Traded to Colorado by Montreal in Dec. '95, won '96 Stanley Cup with Avalanche. Second-youngest goalie to reach 300 career wins.

Pete Rozelle (b. 3-1-26, d. 12-6-96): Football executive. Fourth NFL commissioner, served from 1960 to 1989. During his term, league expanded from 12 to 28 teams. Created Super Bowl in 1966 and negotiated merger with AFL. Devised plan for revenue sharing of lucrative TV monies among owners. Presided during players' strikes of 1982, 1987.

Wilma Rudolph (b. 6-23-40, d. 11-12-94): Track and field. Gold medalist in 3 events (100-, 200- and 4x100-meter relay) at 1960 Olympics. Also won Sullivan Award in 1961.

Adolph Rupp (b. 9-2-01, d. 12-10-77): College basketball coach. Second alltime in NCAA wins (876) and third highest winning percentage (.822). Won 4 NCAA championships: consecutively 1948–49, 1951, 1958. Career span 1930–72 with Kentucky.

Amos Rusie (b. 5-3-1871, d. 12-6-42): Baseball RHP. Fastball was so intimidating that in 1893 the pitching mound was moved back 5' 6" to its present distance of 60' 6." Led league in strikeouts and walks 5 times each. Career record 246–174, 3.07 ERA with New York (NL) from 1889–1901.

Bill Russell (b. 2-12-34): Basketball C. Won MVP award 5 times (1958, consecutively 1961-63, 1965). Played on 11 championship teams, 8 consecutively, with Boston (1957, 1959–66, 1968–69). Player-coach 1968–69 (league's first black coach). Second alltime most rebounds (21,620) and second highest rebounding average (22.5); second most rebounds in a game (51 in 1960). Led league in rebounding 4 times. Also played on 2 consecutive NCAA championship teams with San Francisco in 1955-56; tournament MVP in 1955. Member of gold medal-winning 1956 Olympic team.

Babe Ruth (b. 2-6-1895, d. 8-16-48): Born George Herman Ruth. Baseball P-OF. Most dominant player in history. Alltime leader in slugging average (.690), HR frequency (8.5 HR every 100 at bats) and walks (2,056); second alltime most HR (714), RBI (2,211) and runs scored (2,174). Holds season record highest slugging average (.847 in 1920). 1923 MVP. Had .342 career batting average and 2,873 hits. 60 HR in 1927, 50+ HR 3 other times and 40+ HR 7 other times; 100+ RBI and 100+ walks 13 times each; 100+ runs scored 12 times. Second alltime most World Series HR (15), including his "called shot" off Charlie Root in 1932. Began career as a pitcher for Boston Red Sox: 94 career wins and 2.28 ERA. Won 20+ games 2 times; ERA leader in 1916. Played on 10 pennant winners, 7 World Series winners (3 with Boston, 4 with New York). Sold to Yankees in 1920 (Boston hasn't won World Series since). Career span 1914–35.

Nolan Ryan (b. 1-31-47): Baseball RHP. Pitched record 7th no-hitter on May 1, 1991. Alltime leader in strikeouts (5,714), walks (2,795). League leader in strikeouts 11 times, walks 8 times, shutouts 3 times, ERA 2 times. 300+ strikeouts 6 times, including season record of 383 in 1973. 324 career wins. Career span 1966–93 with New York (NL), California, Houston, Texas.

Jim Ryun (b. 4-29-47): Track and field. Youngest ever to run under four minutes for the mile (3:59.0 at 17 years, 37 days). Set two world records in mile (3:51.3 in 1966 and 3:51.1 in 1967) and one in 1,500 (3:33.1 in 1967). Plagued by bad luck at Olympics; won silver medal in 1968 1,500 meters despite mononucleosis; was bumped and fell in 1972. Won Sullivan Award in 1967.

Toni Sailer (b. 11-17-35): Austrian skier. Won gold medals in 1956 Olympics in slalom, giant slalom and downhill, the first skier to accomplish the feat.

Juan Antonio Samaranch (b. 7-17-20): Amateur sports executive. Since 1980, Spaniard has served as president of International Olympic Committee.

Joan Benoit Samuelson (b. 5-16-57): Track and field. Gold medalist in first ever women's Olympic marathon (1984). Won Boston Marathon 2 times (1979, 1983). Sullivan Award winner in 1985.

Barry Sanders (b. 7-16-68): Football RB. Alltime NCAA season leader in yards rushing (2,628 in 1988). Won Heisman Trophy in 1988 at Oklahoma State. Entered NFL in 1989 with Detroit and named Rookie of the Year. Gained 1,000+ yards rushing in each of his first 9 seasons. Ended 1997-98 season second alltime career rushing yards (13,778). Third player to rush for over 2,000 yards (2,053 in 1997). Led league in rushing in 1990, '94 and 1996–97.

Gene Sarazen (b. 2-27-02): Golfer. Won PGA Championship 3 times (consecutively 1922-23, 1933), U.S. Open 2 times (1922, 1932), British Open once (1932) and the Masters once (1935). His win at the Masters included golf's most famous shot, a double eagle on the 15th hole of the final round to tie Craig Wood (Sarazen then won the playoff). Won 38 career tournaments. Also won Seniors Championship 2 times (1954, 1958). Pioneered the sand wedge in 1930.

Glen Sather (b. 9-2-43): Hockey coach and general manager. As coach, third alltime highest winning percentage (.616). 464 regular season wins. Led Edmonton to 4 Stanley Cup championships (consecutively 1984–85, 1987–88) from 1979 to 1989 and 1993–94. Also played for 6 teams from 1966 to 1976.

Terry Sawchuk (b. 12-28-29): Hockey G. Alltime leader in wins (447) and shutouts (103). Career 2.52 goals against average. Goaltender of the Year 4 times

(consecutively 1951–52, 1954, 1964). Led league in wins and shutouts 3 times and goals against average 2 times. Rookie of the Year in 1950. Tied record of 4 playoff shutouts in 1952. Played on 4 Stanley Cup champions with Detroit and Toronto from 1949 to 1969.

Gale Sayers (b. 5-30-43): Football RB. Alltime leader in kickoff return average (30.6). Scored 56 career touchdowns, including a rookie record 22 in 1965. Led league in rushing and gained 1,000+ yards rushing 2 times. Averaged 5 yards per carry. Rookie of the Year in 1965. Tied record with 6 rushing touchdowns on Dec. 12, 1965. Career span 1965–71 with Chicago cut short due to knee injury. Also All-America 2 times with Kansas.

Dolph Schayes (b. 5-19-28): Basketball player. College star at NYU. In 1960 became first NBA player to reach 15,000 career points. Also first NBA player to play in 1,000 games. Led NBA in free throw percentage three times, and averaged .843 for his career. Over stretch of 10 years played in 706 consecutive games. Elected to Hall of Fame 1972.

Bo Schembechler (b. 4-1-29): Football coach. In 21 seasons at Michigan from 1969–89, had a 194-48-5 record. Overall college coaching record 234-65-8.

Mike Schmidt (b. 9-27-49): Baseball 3B. Won 3 MVP awards (1980, '81, '86). 548 career HR, seventh alltime. Led league in HR 8 times, slugging average 5 times and RBI, walks and strikeouts 4 times each. 40+ HR 3 times, 30+ HR 10 other times; 100+ RBI 9 times, 100+ runs scored 7 times, 100+ strikeouts 12 times and third alltime most strikeouts (1,883). 100+ walks 7 times. Won 10 Gold Gloves. Career span 1972–89 with Philadelphia. Elected to the Hall of Fame in 1995.

Don Schollander (b. 4-30-46): Swimmer. Won 4 gold medals (including 100- and 400-meter freestyle) at 1964 Olympics; won 1 gold and 1 silver medal at 1968 Olympics. Also won Sullivan Award in 1964.

Dick Schultz (b. 9-5-29): Amateur sports executive. Second executive director of the NCAA, served from 1987 to '93. Also served as athletic director at Cornell (1976–81) and Virginia (1981–87).

Seattle Slew (b. 1974): Thoroughbred race horse. Horse of the Year for 1977, when he won the Triple Crown, winning the Kentucky Derby by 1¾ lengths; the Preakness by 1½; and the Belmont by 4. In three-year career from 1976–78, won 14 of 17 starts.

Tom Seaver (b. 11-17-44): Baseball RHP. "Tom Terrific." 311 career wins. 2.86 ERA. Cy Young Award winner 3 times (1969, 1973, 1975) and Rookie of the Year 1967. Fourth alltime most strikeouts (3,640). Led league in strikeouts 5 times, winning percentage 4 times and wins and ERA 3 times each. Won 20+ games 5 times; 200+ strikeouts 10 times. Struck out 19 batters in 1 game in 1970, including the final 10 in succession. Pitched no-hitter in 1978. Career span 1967–86 with New York Mets, Cincinnati, Chicago White Sox, Boston.

Secretariat (b. 3-30-70, d. 10-4-89): Thoroughbred race horse. Triple Crown winner in 1973 with jockey Ron Turcotte aboard. Trained by Lucien Laurin.

Monica Seles (b. 12-2-73): Tennis player. Has won 3 consecutive French Open singles titles (1990-92), 4 Australian Open titles (1991-93, '96) and 2 U.S. Open titles (1991-92). Seles' 1993 season ended on 4-30 when she was stabbed in the back by Gunther Parche while seated during a changeover in a tournament in Hamburg, Germany; also missed 1994 season. Returned to tennis in 1995, reached U.S. Open final.

Bill Sharman (b. 5-25-26): Basketball G. First team All Star four straight years 1956–59. Led NBA in free throw percentage every year from 1953–57, and in 1959 and '61. All Star Game MVP in 1955. NBA Coach of the Year in 1972, when his Lakers won NBA title. Elected to Hall of Fame in 1974.

Wilbur Shaw (b. 10-31-02, d. 10-30-54): Auto racer. Won Indy 500 3 times in 4 years (1937, consecutively 1939–40). AAA champion 2 times (1937, 1939). Also pioneered the use of the crash helmet after suffering skull fracture in 1923 crash.

Patty Sheehan (b. 10-27-57): Golfer. Won back-to-back LPGA championships, 1983–84. Won 1992 and '94 U.S. Women's Opens, '93 LPGA title. 1983 LPGA Player of Year. Vare Trophy winner in 1984. Through '96 season, 35 career wins on LPGA tour; fourth alltime in earnings, with $5,121,437.01.

Fred Shero (b. 10-23-25, d. 11-24-90): Hockey coach. Fourth alltime highest winning percentage (.612, regular season). Led Philadelphia to 2 Stanley Cup championships (1974–75). Also coached NY Rangers. Played defense for NY Rangers, 1947–50.

Bill Shoemaker (b. 8-19-31): Horse racing jockey. Alltime leader in wins (8,833). Rode Belmont Stakes winner 5 times (1957, 1959, 1962, 1967, 1975), Kentucky Derby winner 4 times (1955, 1959, 1965, 1986—at age 54, the oldest jockey to win Derby) and Preakness Stakes winner 2 times (1963, 1967). Also won Eclipse Award in 1981.

Eddie Shore (b. 11-25-02, d. 3-16-85): Hockey D. Won MVP award 4 times (1933, consecutively 1935–36, 1938). All-Star 7 times. Played on 2 Stanley Cup champions with Boston from 1926 to 1940.

Frank Shorter (b. 10-31-47): Track and field. Gold medalist in marathon at 1972 Olympics, the first American to win the event since 1908. Olympic silver medalist in 1976 marathon. Sullivan Award winner in 1972.

Jim Shoulders (b. 5-13-28): Rodeo. Sixteen career titles. All-Around champion 5 times (1949, consecutively 1956–59).

Don Shula (b. 1-4-30): Football coach. Alltime leader in wins (347). Won 2 consecutive Super Bowl championships (1972–73) with Miami, including NFL's only undefeated season in 1972. Also reached Super Bowl 4 other times. Career span 1963–70 with Baltimore, 1970–95 Miami.

Al Simmons (b. 5-22-02; d. 5-26-56): Baseball OF. "Bucketfoot Al" for hitting stance. Named AL MVP for 1929, when he led league with 157 RBIs. Led league in batting average in 1930 (.381) and '31 (.390). Lifetime average of .334 with 307 homers. Career span 1924–44 with a variety of teams, but mostly Philadelphia A's. Elected to Hall of Fame in 1953.

O.J. Simpson (b. 7-9-47): Given name Orenthal James. Football RB. 11,236 career yards rushing. Gained 1,000+ yards rushing 5 consecutive seasons, including then-record 2,003 yards in 1973. Player of the Year 3 times (consecutively 1972–73, 1975). Led league in rushing 4 times. Gained 200+ yards rushing in a game a record 6 times, including 273 yards on Nov. 25, 1976. Scored 61 career touchdowns, including 23 in 1975. Also won Heisman Trophy with USC in 1968.

Sir Barton (b. 1916, d. 1937): Thoroughbred race horse. In 1919, before they were linked as the Triple Crown, became first horse to win the Kentucky Derby,

the Preakness and the Belmont Stakes. Won 8 of 13 starts as 3-year-old.

George Sisler (b. 3-24-1893, d. 3-26-73): Baseball 1B. Alltime most hits in a season (257 in 1920). League leader in hits 2 times, with 200+ hits 6 times. Won 2 batting titles, including .420 average in 1922; averaged .400+ 2 times and .300+ 11 other times. Had 2,812 career hits and .340 average. Career span 1915-30 with St. Louis.

Mary Decker Slaney (b. 8-4-58): Track and field. American record holder in 5 events ranging from 800 to 3,000 meters. Won 1,500 and 3,000 meters at World Championships in 1983. Lost chance for medal at 1984 Olympics when she tripped and fell after contact with Zola Budd. Won Sullivan Award in 1982. Competed in 1996 Olympics at age 37.

Dean Smith (b. 2-28-31): College basketball coach. Alltime leader in wins (879); fifth alltime highest winning percentage (.776). Alltime most NCAA tournament appearances (27), reached Final Four 11 times. Won NCAA championship in 1982 and '93. Coached 1976 Olympic team to gold medal. Career span 1962–97 with North Carolina. 1997 *Sports Illustrated* Sportsman of the Year.

Emmitt Smith (b. 5-15-69): Football RB. Led NFL in rushing in 1991 (1,563 yards), '92 (1,713 and 18 TDs), and '95 (1,773). Record 25 TDs in 1995. Rushed for 108 yards in 52–17 Cowboys win over Bills in Super Bowl XXVII. Rushed for 132 yards and named MVP of Super Bowl XXVIII, a 30–13 Dallas victory over Buffalo. Career span since 1990 with Cowboys.

Ozzie Smith (b. 12-26-54): Baseball SS. "The Wizard of Oz." May be the best defensive shortstop in history. Holds alltime record for most assists in a season among shortstops (621 in 1980). Career double-play and assist leader among shortstops. 14-time All-Star. Won 13 consecutive Gold Gloves. Career span 1978–96 with San Diego, St. Louis.

Red Smith (b. 9-25-05, d. 1-15-82): Sportswriter. Won Pulitzer Prize in 1976. After Grantland Rice, the most widely syndicated sports columnist. His literate essays appeared in the *NY Herald Tribune* from 1945 to 1971 and the *NY Times* from 1971 to 1982.

Stan Smith (b. 12-14-46): Tennis. Won 39 tournaments in career, including 1972 Wimbledon in 5 sets over Ilie Nastase. Won 1971 U.S. Open over Jan Kodes and amateur version of U.S. Open in 1969. 1970 won inaugural Grand Prix Masters. Inducted to Tennis Hall of Fame in 1987.

Tommie Smith (b. 6-5-44): Track and field. Sprinter won 1968 Olympic 200 meters in world record of 19.83, then was expelled from Olympic Village, along with bronze medalist John Carlos, for raising black-gloved fist and bowing head during playing of national anthem to protest racism in U.S.

Conn Smythe (b. 2-1-1895, d. 11-18-80): Hockey executive. As general manager with Toronto from 1929 to 1961 won 7 Stanley Cup championships (1932, 1942, 1945, consecutively 1947–49, 1951). Award for playoff MVP named in his honor.

Sam Snead (b. 5-27-12): Golfer. Alltime leader in career wins (81). Won the Masters (1949, 1952, 1954) and PGA Championship (1942, 1949, 1951) 3 times each and British Open (1946). Runner-up at U.S. Open 4 times, but title eluded him. PGA Player of the Year in 1949. Won Seniors Championship 6 times, more than any golfer (1964–65, 1967, 1970, 1972–73).

Peter Snell (b. 12-17-38): Track and field. New Zealand runner was gold medalist in 800 meters at 2 consecutive Olympics in 1960, 1964. Also gold medalist in 1,500 meters at 1964 Olympics. Twice broke world mile record; broke world 800 record once.

Duke Snider (b. 9-19-26): Baseball OF. Career .295 average, 407 HR and 1,333 RBIs. Hit 40+ HR 5 consecutive seasons and 100+ RBIs 6 times. Also led league in runs scored 3 consecutive seasons. Played on 6 pennant winners with the Brooklyn Dodgers. World Series total of 11 HR and 26 RBIs are NL best. Career span from 1947–64.

Javier Sotomayor (b. 10-13-67): Track and field. Cuban high jumper broke the 8-foot barrier with world record jump of 8' 0" in 1989. Set current record of 8' ½" in 7-27-93 in Salamanca, Spain.

Warren Spahn (b. 4-23-21): Baseball LHP. Alltime leader in games won for a lefthander (363): 20+ wins 13 times. League leader in wins 8 times (5 seasons consecutively), complete games 9 times (7 seasons consecutively), strikeouts 4 consecutive seasons, innings pitched 4 times and ERA 3 times. 1957 Cy Young award. 63 career shutouts. Pitched 2 no-hitters after age 39. Career span 1942–65, all but last year with Boston Braves, Milwaukee.

Tris Speaker (b. 4-4-1888, d. 12-8-58): Baseball OF. Alltime leader in doubles (792), fifth in hits (3,514) and fifth in batting average (.345). 1 batting title (.386 in 1916), but .375+ average 6 times and .300+ average 12 other times. League leader in doubles 8 times, hits 2 times and HR and RBI 1 time each. 200+ hits 4 times, 40+ doubles 10 times and 100+ runs scored 7 times. MVP in 1912. Career span 1907–28 with Boston, Cleveland.

Michael Spinks (b. 7-13-56): Boxer. 1976 Olympic middleweight champion. Brother Leon was heavyweight champ. Won world light heavyweight title on 7-18-81. Defended it 5 times and consolidated light heavy titles with decision over Dwight Braxton on 3-18-83. Defended four more times. Won heavyweight title on 9-22-85 in decision over Larry Holmes. Lost title to Mike Tyson in 91 seconds on 6-27-88.

Mark Spitz (b. 2-10-50): Swimmer. Won a record 7 gold medals (2 in freestyle, 2 in butterfly, 3 in relays) at 1972 Olympics, setting world record in each event. Also won 2 gold medals and 1 silver and 1 bronze medal at 1968 Olympics. Sullivan Award winner in 1971.

Amos Alonzo Stagg (b. 8-16-1862, d. 3-17-65): College football coach. Third alltime in wins (314). Won national championship with Chicago in 1905. Coach of the Year with Pacific in 1943 at age 81. Career record 314-199-35, including 5 undefeated seasons, from 1892 to 1946. Only person elected to both college football and basketball Halls of Fame. Played in the first basketball game in 1891.

Willie Stargell (b. 3-6-40): Baseball OF/1B. "Pops" achieved a 1979 MVP triple crown, winning NL regular season, playoff and World Series MVP awards. Led NL in homers in 1971 and '73. Hit 475 career homers. Drove in 1,540 runs. Had .282 career batting average. Played all 21 seasons with the Pirates. Elected to Hall of Fame in 1988.

Bart Starr (b. 1-9-34): Football QB. Played on 3 NFL champions (consecutively 1961–62, 1965) and first two Super Bowl champions (1966–67) with Green Bay. Also named MVP of first two Super Bowls. Player of the Year in 1966. Led league in passing 3 times. Also coached Green Bay to 53-77-3 record from 1975 to 1983.

Roger Staubach (b. 2-5-42): Football QB. Won Heisman Trophy with Navy as a junior in 1963. Served 4-year military obligation before turning pro. Led Dallas to 6 NFC Championships, 4 Super Bowls and 2 Super Bowl titles (1971, 1977). Player of the Year and Super Bowl MVP in 1971. Also led league in passing 4 times. Career span 1969–79.

Jan Stenerud (b. 11-26-42): Football K. Third on NFL scoring list, with 1,699 points. Converted 373 field goals in 558 attempts. Career span 1967–79 with Kansas City Chiefs, 1980–83 with Green Bay Packers and 1984–85 with Minnesota Vikings. First pure kicker inducted to Hall of Fame, 1991.

Casey Stengel (b. 7-30-1890, d. 9-29-75): Baseball manager. "The Ol' Perfesser." Managed New York Yankees to 10 pennants and 7 World Series titles (5 consecutively) in 12 years from 1949 to 1960. Alltime leader in World Series games (63), wins (37) and losses (26). Platoon system was his trademark strategy, Stengelese his trademark language ("You could look it up"). Managed New York Mets from 1962 to 1965. Jersey number (37) retired by Yankees and Mets.

Ingemar Stenmark (b. 3-18-56): Swedish skier. Gold medalist in slalom and giant slalom at 1980 Olympics. World Cup overall champion 3 consecutive years (1976–78).

Woody Stephens (b. 9-1-13): Horse racing trainer. Trained 2 Kentucky Derby winners (Cannonade, who won the 100th Derby in 1974 and Swale in 1984) and 5 straight Belmont winners from 1982-86, starting with 1982 Horse of the Year Conquistador Cielo.

David Stern (b. 9-22-42): Fourth NBA commissioner. Served since 1984. Oversaw unprecedented growth of league. Owners rewarded him with 5-year, $40-million contract extension in 1996.

Jackie Stewart (b. 6-11-39): Scottish auto racer. Fourth alltime in Formula 1 victories (27); Formula 1 champion 3 times (1969, 1971, 1973). Also Indy 500 Rookie of the Year in 1966. Retired in 1973.

John Stockton (b. 3-26-62): Basketball G. Alltime leader in assists (12,713) and steals (2,620). Set single-season assist record of 1,164 in 1990–91. Led NBA in assists a record nine consecutive times, 1988–96. Nine-time All-Star, consecutively 1989–97. Co-MVP (with Karl Malone) of 1993 All-Star Game. Member of 1992 and '96 Olympic teams. Career span since 1984 with Utah.

John L. Sullivan (b. 10-15-1858, d. 2-2-18): Boxer. Last bareknuckle champion. Heavyweight title holder (1882–92), lost to Jim Corbett. Career record 38-1-3 with 33 KOs from 1878 to 1892.

Paul Tagliabue (b. 11-24-40): Football executive. Fifth NFL commissioner, has served since 1989.

Anatoli Tarasov (b. 1918): Hockey coach. Orchestrated Soviet Union's emergence as a hockey power. Won 9 consecutive world amateur championships (1963–71) and 3 Olympic gold medals in 1964, 1968, 1972.

Fran Tarkenton (b. 2-3-40): Football QB. Hall of Fame QB retired with 342 touchdown passes, 47,003 yards passing, 6,467 pass attempts and 3,686 pass completions. Player of the Year in 1975. Career span 1961–78 with Minnesota, NY Giants.

Lawrence Taylor (b. 2-4-59): Football LB. Revolutionized the linebacker position. Ended 1993 season as the alltime leader in sacks. Also named to

Pro Bowl a record 10 consecutive seasons. Player of the Year in 1986. Has played on 2 Super Bowl champions with New York Giants (1986, 1990). Career span 1981–93 with Giants.

Isiah Thomas (b. 4-30-61): Basketball G. Member of Indiana University team that won 1981 NCAA title. Point guard for Detroit Pistons 1982–94. All-NBA First Team 1984, '85 and '86. NBA All Star Game MVP both 1984 and '86. Led NBA in assists (13.9) in 1984–85. Fourth alltime in assists (9,061). Member of Pistons team that won NBA title in both 1989 and '90. GM of Toronto Raptors 1995–97.

Thurman Thomas (b. 5-15-66): Football RB. Led AFC in rushing both 1990 (1,297 yards) and '91 (1,407). Career span since 1988 with Buffalo Bills.

Daley Thompson (b. 7-30-58): Track and field. British decathlete was gold medalist at 2 consecutive Olympics in 1980, 1984. At 1984 Olympics set world record (8,847 points) that lasted eight years.

John Thompson (b. 9-2-41): College basketball coach. Head coach at Georgetown (1973–), where he coached Patrick Ewing, Alonzo Mourning and Dikembe Mutombo. Won NCAA title in 1984, runnerup in 1982 and '85.

Bobby Thomson (b. 10-25-23): Baseball OF. Hit dramatic 9th-inning playoff home run to win NL pennant for New York Giants on Oct. 3, 1951. The Giants came from 13½ games behind the Brooklyn Dodgers on Aug. 11 to win the pennant on Thomson's 3-run homer off Ralph Branca in the final game of the 3-game playoff.

Jim Thorpe (b. 5-28-1888, d. 3-28-53): Sportsman. Gold medalist in decathlon and pentathlon at 1912 Olympics. Played pro baseball with New York (NL) and Cincinnati 1913–19, and pro football with several teams 1919–26. Also All-America 2 times with Carlisle.

Dick Tiger (b. 8-14-29; d. 12-14-71): Nigerian boxer. Born Richard Ihetu. Won middleweight title by decision over Gene Fullmer on 10-23-62. Lost middle title to Joey Giardello on 12-7-63, then regained it from Giardello on 10-21-65. Won world light heavyweight title by decision over Jose Torres on 12-16-66, then lost it when KO'd by Bob Foster in 4 on 5-24-68. *The Ring* Fighter of the Year for 1962 and '65. Career record: 61-17-3. Elected to Boxing Hall of Fame 1974.

Bill Tilden (b. 2-10-1893, d. 6-5-53): Tennis player. "Big Bill." Won 7 U.S. singles titles, 6 consecutively (1920–25, 1929) and 3 Wimbledon titles (consecutively 1920–21, 1930). Also won 6 Grand Slam doubles titles. Led U.S. to 7 consecutive Davis Cup victories (1920-26).

Ted Tinling (b. 6-23-10, d. 5-23-90): British tennis couturier. The premier source on women's tennis from Suzanne Lenglen to Steffi Graf. Also designed tennis clothes, most notably the frilled lace panties worn by Gorgeous Gussy Moran at Wimbledon in 1949.

Y.A. Tittle (b. 10-24-26): Football QB. Threw 33 TD passes in 1962 and in '63 led league in passing, completing 221 of 367 attempts for 3,145 yards and 36 TDs. Career span 1948–64, mostly with San Francisco 49ers and New York Giants. Inducted into Hall of Fame 1971.

Jayne Torvill/Christopher Dean (b. 10-7-57/ b. 7-27-58): British figure skaters. Won 4 consecutive ice dancing world championships (1981–84) and Olympic ice dancing gold medal (1984). Won world professional championships in 1985. Won Olympic ice dancing bronze in 1994.

Vladislav Tretiak (b. 4-25-52): Hockey G. Led Soviet Union to 3 gold medals at Olympics in 1972, 1976, 1984. Played on 13 world amateur champions from 1970 to 1984.

Lee Trevino (b. 12-1-39): Golfer. Won U.S. Open (1968, 1971), British Open (consecutively 1971-72) and PGA Championship (1974, 1984) 2 times each. PGA Player of the Year in 1971. Also won U.S. Senior Open in 1990. First Senior $1 million season.

Emlen Tunnell (b. 3-29-25, d. 7-23-75): Football S. Alltime leader in interception yardage (1,282) and second in interceptions (79). All-Pro 9 times. Career span 1948–61 with New York Giants and Green Bay.

Gene Tunney (b. 5-25-1897, d. 11-7-78): Boxer. Heavyweight champion (1926-28). Defeated Jack Dempsey 2 times, including famous "long count" bout. Career record 65-2-1 with 43 KOs from 1915 to 1928. Retired as champion.

Ted Turner (b. 11-19-38): Sportsman. Skipper who successfully defended the America's Cup in 1977. Also owner of the Atlanta Braves since 1976 and Hawks since 1977. Founded the Goodwill Games in 1986.

Mike Tyson (b. 6-30-66): Boxer. Youngest heavyweight champion at 19 years old in 1986. Held title until knocked out by James (Buster) Douglas in Tokyo on Feb. 10, 1990. Career record as of 6-28-97 44–3 with 37 KOs since 1985. Convicted of rape in 1992, released from prison in 1995. Lost WBA title to Evander Holyfield on 11-9-96. In one of boxing's more bizarre episodes, disqualified from rematch on 6-28-97 for biting Holyfield's ears.

Johnny Unitas (b. 5-7-33): Football QB. 47 consecutive games throwing touchdown pass (1956–60); 290 career touchdown passes; 40,239 career passing yards. Led league in touchdown passes 4 consecutive seasons. Player of the Year 3 times (1959, 1964, 1967). Career span 1956–72 with Baltimore, San Diego.

Al Unser Sr. (b. 5-29-39): Auto racer. Won Indy 500 4 times (1970, 71, '78, '87). Retired with 39 career CART victories. USAC/CART champion 3 times (1970, 1983, 1985). Brother of Bobby.

Bobby Unser (b. 2-20-34): Auto racer. Won Indy 500 3 times (1968, 1975, 1981). Retired with 35 career victories. USAC champion 2 times (1968, 1974). Brother of Al Sr.

Harold S. Vanderbilt (b. 7-6-1884, d. 7-4-70): Sailor. Owner and skipper who successfully defended the America's Cup 3 consecutive times (1930, 1934, 1937).

Glenna Collett Vare (b. 6-20-03, d. 2-2-89): Golfer. Won U.S. Women's Amateur 6 times, more than any golfer (1922, 1925, consecutively 1928–30, 1935).

Bill Veeck (b. 2-9-14, d. 1-2-86): Baseball owner. From 1946 to 1980, owned ballclubs in Cleveland, St. Louis (AL), Chicago (AL). In 1948, Cleveland became baseball's first team to draw 2 million in attendance. That year Veeck integrated AL by signing Larry Doby and then Satchel Paige. A brilliant promoter, Veeck sent midget Eddie Gaedel up to bat for St. Louis in 1951. Brought exploding scoreboard to stadiums and put players' names on uniforms.

Guillermo Vilas (b. 8-17-52): Tennis. Argentine won 50 straight matches in 1977. In '77 won French Open, where he beat Brian Gottfried, and the U.S. Open, where he beat Jimmy Connors. Also won Australian Open twice, 1978–79.

Lasse Viren (b. 7-22-49): Track and field. Finnish runner was gold medalist in 5,000 and 10,000 meters at 2 consecutive Olympics (1972, 1976).

Virginia Wade (b. 7-10-45): Tennis. Beloved in Britain, Wade won three major titles, most notably Wimbledon in 1977, its centenary year, where she triumphed over Betty Stove. Also won 1968 U.S. Open, '72 Australian Open, and doubles titles in 1973 at the Australian, French and U.S. Opens, all with Margaret Smith Court.

Honus Wagner (b. 2-24-1874, d. 12-6-55): Baseball SS. Had .327 career batting average, 3,415 hits and 8 batting titles. Averaged .300+ 15 consecutive seasons. Led league in RBI 4 times, with 100+ RBI 9 times. Third alltime in triples (252) and league leader in doubles 8 times. 703 career stolen bases, league leader in steals 5 times. Career span 1897–1917 with Pittsburgh.

Grete Waitz (b. 10-1-53): Track and field. Norwegian runner has won New York City Marathon a record 9 times (consecutively 1978–80, 1982–86, 1988). Won the women's marathon at the 1983 World Championship.

Jersey Joe Walcott (b. 10-31-14, d. 2-25-94): Boxer. Heavyweight champion from 1951 to 1952. Won title at age 37 on fifth attempt before surrendering it to Rocky Marciano. Later became sheriff of Camden, NJ.

Doak Walker (b. 1-1-27): Football HB. Led league in scoring 2 times, his first and final seasons. All-Pro 5 times. Played on 2 consecutive NFL champions (1952-53) with Detroit. Career span 1950 to 1955. Also won Heisman Trophy as a junior in 1948. All-America 3 consecutive seasons with SMU.

Herschel Walker (b. 3-3-62): Football RB. Won Heisman Trophy in 1982 with Georgia. Turned pro by entering USFL with New Jersey. Gained 7,000+ rushing yards and scored 61 touchdowns in 3 seasons before league folded. Entered NFL in 1986 with Dallas and led league in rushing yards (1,514 in 1988).

Bill Walsh (b. 11-30-31): Football coach. Led San Francisco to four Super Bowl wins, after the 1981, '84, '88 and '89 seasons. Career record with 49ers 102-63-1. Developed short-passing game. Returned to Stanford University for 1992 season.

Bill Walton (b. 11-5-52): Basketball C. College Player of the Year 3 consecutive seasons (1972–74). Played on 2 consecutive NCAA championship teams (1972–73) with UCLA; tournament MVP twice (1972–73). Sullivan Award winner in 1973. NBA MVP in 1978, playoff MVP in 1977. Led league in rebounding and blocks in 1977. Career span 1974–86 with Portland, San Diego, Boston.

War Admiral (b. 1934, d. 1959): Thoroughbred race horse. A son of Man o' War, won Triple Crown and Horse of the Year honors in 1937.

Paul Warfield (b. 11-28-42): Football WR. Caught 427 passes for 8,565 yards and 85 TDs. Played on two Super Bowl-winning Miami Dolphins teams. Career span 1964–77, all with Cleveland Browns except for 1970–74 with Miami Dolphins. Inducted to Hall of Fame 1983.

Glenn (Pop) Warner (b. 4-5-1871, d. 9-7-54): College football coach. Second alltime in wins (319). Won 3 national championships with Pittsburgh (1916, 1918) and Stanford (1926). Career record 319-106-32 with 6 teams from 1896 to 1938.

Tom Watson (b. 9-4-49): Golfer. Winner of British Open 5 times (1975, 1977, 1980, consecutively 1982-83), the Masters 2 times (1977, 1981) and U.S. Open once (1982). PGA Player of the Year 6 times, more than any golfer (consecutively 1977–80, 1982, 1984).

Dick Weber (b. 12-23-29): Bowler. Won All-Star Tournament 4 times (consecutively 1962–63, 1965–66). Voted Bowler of the Year 3 times (1961, 1963, 1965). Won 31 career PBA titles.

Johnny Weismuller (b. 6-2-04, d. 1-21-84): Swimmer. Won 3 gold medals (including 100- and 400-meter freestyle) at 1924 Olympics and 2 gold medals at 1928 Olympics. Also played Tarzan in the movies.

Jerry West (b. 5-28-38): Basketball G. 10 time All-Star; All-Defensive Team 4 times; 1969 playoff MVP. Led league in assists and scoring 1 time each. Career span 1960–72 with Los Angeles. Currently executive vice president of Lakers. Also NCAA tournament MVP in 1959. All-America 2 times with West Virginia. Played on 1960 gold medal-winning Olympic team.

Whirlaway (b. 4-2-38, d. 4-6-53): Thoroughbred race horse. Triple Crown winner in 1941 with jockey Eddie Arcaro aboard. Trained by Ben A. Jones.

Byron (Whizzer) White (b. 6-8-17): Football RB. Led NFL in rushing 2 times (Pittsburgh in 1938, Detroit in 1940). Led NCAA in scoring and rushing with Colorado in 1937; named All-America. Supreme Court justice 1962–93.

Reggie White (b. 12-19-62): Football DE. Fearsome pass rusher. Winner in new era of free agency, signed with Green Bay in 1993 for $17 million over four years. Career span: 1984 with Memphis Showboats, 1985–92 with Philadelphia, since 1993 with Packers. Member of Green Bay 1997 Super Bowl championship team.

Charles Whittingham (b. 4-13-13): Thoroughbred race horse trainer. "Bald Eagle" after losing hair to tropical disease in World War II. In 1986 became the oldest trainer to win Kentucky Derby, with Ferdinand. Led yearly earnings list for trainers from 1970–73 consecutively; in 1975; and in 1981–82 consecutively. Won three Eclipse Awards and trained two Horses of the Year (Ack Ack in 1971 and Ferdinand in 1987).

Kathy Whitworth (b. 9-27-39): Golfer. Alltime LPGA leader with 88 tour victories, including six majors. Won LPGA Championship in 1967, '71 and '75. Won 1977 Dinah Shore. Won Titleholders Championship (extinct major) in 1965 and '66. Won Western Open (extinct major) in 1967. Won Vare Trophy every year from 1965–72, except 1968. LPGA Player of Year from 1966–69 and 1971–73.

Hoyt Wilhelm (b. 7-26-23): Baseball RHP. Hall of Famer. Threw knuckleball until age 48. Alltime pitching leader in games (1,070). Career record: 143-122, 2.52 ERA, 227 saves. Hit home run in his first at bat (never hit another) and pitched no-hitter in 1958. Career span with 9 teams from 1952–72.

Bud Wilkinson (b. 4-23-15 d. 2-9-94): Football coach. Alltime NCAA leader in consecutive wins (47, 1953–57). Won 3 national championships (1950, consecutively 1955–56) with Oklahoma, where he coached from 1947 to 1963. Won Orange Bowl 4 times and Sugar Bowl 2 times. Career record 145-29-4, including 4 undefeated seasons. Also coached with St. Louis of NFL in 1978–79.

Billy Williams (b. 6-15-38): Baseball OF. "Sweet Swinging." NL Rookie of the Year for 1961. Hit 426 career home runs. Drove in 1,475 runs. Lifetime average of .290. Named to six NL All Star teams. Career span 1959–74 with Chicago Cubs, 1975–76 with Oakland A's. Elected to Hall of Fame in 1987.

Ted Williams (b. 8-30-18): Baseball OF. "The Splendid Splinter." Last player to hit .400 (.406 in 1941). MVP in 1946, 1949 and Triple Crown winner in 1942, 1947. Sixth alltime highest batting average (.344), second most walks (2,019) and second highest slugging average (.634). 521 career HR, 1,839 career RBIs. League leader in batting average and runs scored 6 times each, RBI and HR 4 times each, walks 8 times and doubles 2 times. Had .300+ average 15 consecutive seasons; 100+ RBI and runs scored 9 times each; 30+ HR 8 times; and 100+ walks 11 times. Lost nearly 5 seasons to military service. Career span 1939–42 and 1946–60 with Boston.

Hack Wilson (b. 4-26-00; d. 11-23-48): Baseball OF. Stood 5' 6" but weighed 210. Had five incredible seasons 1926–30. Best was 1930 when he hit .356, scored 146 runs, hit a NL record 56 homers and drove in 190, which is still the major league record. Career span 1923–34 with several teams. Elected to Hall of Fame in 1979.

Dave Winfield (b. 10-3-51): Baseball OF. Drafted out of Univ. of Minnesota for both pro basketball and football. Led NL in RBIs in 1979 (118). In 1992, first 40-year-old to get 100+ RBIs, with 108. Hit clutch double to win 1992 World Series. Got 3,000th hit, off Dennis Eckersley, on 9-16-93. Career span 1973–80 with San Diego; 1981–90 with Yankees; 1990–91 with California; 1992 with Toronto; 1993–94 with Minnesota; and 1995 with Cleveland.

Major W.C. Wingfield (b. 10-16-1833, d. 4-18-12): British tennis pioneer. Credited with inventing the game of tennis, which he called "Sphairistike" or "sticky" and patented in February 1874.

Colonel Matt Winn (b. 6-30-1861, d. 10-6-49): As general manager of Churchill Downs from 1904 until his death, elevated the Kentucky Derby into the premier race in the country.

Katarina Witt (b. 12-3-65): East German figure skater. Gold medalist at 2 consecutive Olympics in 1984, 1988. Also world champion 4 times (consecutively 1984–85, 1987–88).

John Wooden (b. 10-14-10): College basketball coach. First member of basketball Hall of Fame as coach and player. Coached UCLA to 10 NCAA championships in 12 years (consecutively 1964–65, 1967–73, 1975). Alltime winning streak 88 games (1971–74). 664 career wins and fourth alltime highest winning percentage (.804). Career span 1949–75 with UCLA. 1932 College Player of the Year at Purdue.

Tiger Woods (b. 12-30-75): Golfer. After winning three consecutive U.S. Junior Amateur titles (1991–93), followed by three consecutive U.S. Amateur titles (1994–96), took the PGA tour by storm, winning six of his first 21 tournaments, including the 1997 Masters. There he was the youngest winner ever, scoring a record low 270, and winning by the widest margin in tournament history, 12 strokes. 1996 *Sports Illustrated* Sportsman of the Year.

Mickey Wright (b. 2-14-35): Golfer. Second alltime in career wins (82) and major championships (13—tied with Louise Suggs). Won U.S. Open 4 times (consecutively 1958-59, 1961, 1964), LPGA Championship 4 times (1958, consecutively 1960–61, 1963), Western Open 3 times (consecutively 1962–63, 1966).

Cale Yarborough (b. 3-27-40): Auto racer. Won Daytona 500 4 times (1968, 1977, consecutively 1983-84). Fifth alltime in NASCAR victories (83). Also NASCAR champion 3 consecutive years (1976–78).

Carl Yastrzemski (b. 8-22-39): Baseball OF. "Yaz." 3,419 career hits, 452 HR. 1967 MVP and Triple Crown winner. 3 batting titles, including .301 in 1968, the lowest ever to win. Second alltime in games played (3,308) and fourth in walks (1,845). Career span 1961–83 with Boston.

Cy Young (b. 3-29-1867, d. 11-4-55): Baseball RHP. Alltime leader in wins (511), losses (315), innings pitched (7,354.2) and complete games (749); fourth in shutouts (76). Had 2.63 career ERA. Pitched 3 no-hitters, including a perfect game in 1904. Pitching award named in his honor. Career span 1890–1911 with Cleveland, Boston.

Robin Yount (b. 9-16-55): Baseball OF/SS. Became Brewers shortstop at 18. Landslide winner of 1982 AL MVP when he hit .331 with 29 homers. Hit .414 in Brewers' 1982 Series loss to Cardinals. 3,142 hits. Shoulder injury made Yount move to outfield in 1984. Career span 1974–93, all with the Brewers.

Steve Yzerman (b. 5-9-65): Hockey C. Won Stanley Cup consecutively 1997–98 as Red Wings swept both series. Won Conn Smythe trophy 1998. Scored 100+ points six consecutive seasons (1987–88 through 1992–93). Career span since 1983 with Detroit.

Babe Didrikson Zaharias (b. 6-26-14, d. 9-27-56): Sportswoman. Gold medalist in 80-meter hurdles and javelin throw at 1932 Olympics; also won silver medal in high jump (her gold medal jump was disallowed for using the then-illegal western roll). Became a golfer in 1935 and won 12 major titles, including U.S. Open 3 times (1948, 1950, 1954—a year after cancer surgery). Also helped found the LPGA in 1949.

Tony Zale (b. 5-29-13, d. 3-20-97): Boxer. Born Anthony Zaleski. "The Man of Steel." Won vacant middleweight title by decision over Georgie Abrams on 11-28-41. Lost title to Billy Conn on 2-13-42. Spent almost 4 years in Navy. Retained title with KO of Rocky Graziano in 6 on 9-27-46; lost it to Graziano by KO in 6 on 7-17-47; and reclaimed it by KOing Graziano in 3 on 6-10-48. Lost title to Marcel Cerdan, (KO 12) on 9-21-48. Career record: 88 bouts; won 46 by KO and 24 by decision; drew 2; lost 16, 4 by KO. Elected to Boxing Hall of Fame 1958.

Emil Zatopek (b. 9-19-22): Track and field. Czechoslovakian runner became only athlete to win gold medal in 5,000 and 10,000 meters and marathon, at 1952 Olympics. Also gold medalist in 10,000 meters at 1948 Olympics.

Obituaries

Obituaries

Frederick Alderman, 93, runner. Alderman won both the 100- and 220-yard dashes in the 1927 NCAA championships for Michigan State. In the 1928 Olympics in Amsterdam, he ran on the U.S. 400-meter relay team, helping the Americans win a gold medal while they set a world record. As the United States' oldest surviving Olympic track and field gold medalist, Alderman carried the torch just outside Porterdale, GA, for the 1996 Atlanta Games. In Social Circle, GA, of congestive heart failure, September 20.

Lionel Aldridge, 56, football player. As a defensive end, Aldridge played with the Green Bay Packers from 1963 to '71, winning three NFL titles and the first two Super Bowls. He also played for the San Diego Chargers in 1972 and '73. He worked for some time in sports broadcasting before psychiatric problems left him homeless. After settling in Milwaukee, he found treatment and became an advocate for others who suffer from mental illnesses. In Shorewood, WI, of natural causes, February 12.

Elia Maria Gonzalez Alvarez, 93, tennis player. Best known as Lili Alvarez, she won her first international title only one year after she began to play tennis at age 11. Through the 1920s she dominated Spanish tennis; she made her way to three consecutive Wimbledon finals in 1926 to '28 and won the 1929 French Open doubles title with Kea Baumann of the Netherlands. After she retired from sports in 1942 she wrote several books of essays and poems. In Madrid, of natural causes, July 8.

Eddie Arcaro, 81, jockey. Known as the "Master," Arcaro is still revered as the consummate jockey. *SI's* William Nack writes:

"Between 1938 and '61, from the afternoon when he won his first Kentucky Derby, on Lawrin, to that autumn day when he hung up his tack for the last time, Arcaro came to be known as more than merely the ablest, most resourceful rider to sit on a thoroughbred. Indeed, his name became a synonym for *jockey*, his career an enduring lesson in the art and craft of race riding. Many of the sport's old-timers still see him as the standard of excellence.

"In his 31 years in the saddle, beginning in 1931, Arcaro won 4,779 races on 24,092 mounts and more than $30 million in purses, but he's not remembered for his numbers. Though Bill Shoemaker won almost twice as many races (8,833) as Arcaro, and Laffit Pincay Jr. more than six times as much money ($190,089,776), no jockey ever dominated the sport at its highest levels as Arcaro did. He's the only rider to win two Triple Crowns, on Whirlaway in '41 and Citation in '48, and his 17 victories in Triple Crown events—five Derbys, six Preaknesses and six Belmonts—is a record that is unlikely to be broken. Whirly and Big Cy aside, a list of Arcaro's celebrated mounts reads like a *Burke's Peerage* of horses: Kelso, Nashua, Assault, Bold Ruler, Native Dancer, Sword Dancer and Busher.

"The horseplayers called him Steady Eddie and Heady Eddie and bet him with both fists. He was a strong finisher, with sure and sensitive hands, but it was his keen sense of pace and his riding savvy that set him apart. He was simply smarter than everybody else on the track. On the day of the historic 1955 match race between Derby winner Swaps and Preakness and Belmont champion Nashua, Arcaro had bettors at Washington Park in Chicago scratching their heads when he climbed on a cheap claimer named Mighty Moment in the fourth race. What was the great Arcaro doing on that plug? They soon learned. All the way around the track, on his way to finishing sixth, Arcaro was looking down and studying the muddy course, scouting it for Nashua in the seventh.

"In that race Swaps, Shoemaker up, figured to go to the lead, and Arcaro knew that match races are won on the front end. So, waiting in the gate for the start, he began hollering and thrashing Nashua with his whip; as the gates popped open, the wide-eyed bay burst to the lead. Arcaro then herded Nashua into Swaps on the first turn, forcing Shoemaker's horse to the deeper going on the outside, and won the race right there. Nashua led a tiring Swaps by six at the wire.

"Heady Eddie. There was only one."

In Miami, of liver cancer, November 14, 1997.

Cliff Barker, 77, basketball player. After serving in World War II, Barker attended the University of Kentucky, where as a forward with the "Fabulous Five" he won NCAA titles in 1948 and '49. In the summer between the two championship seasons, coach Adolph Rupp, Barker and the rest of the Wildcat starters teamed with players from the Phillips 66 Oilers of the Amateur Athletic Union to win the Olympic gold medal in London. After graduating in 1949, Barker played in the NBA for three seasons with the Indianapolis Olympians, a team he co-owned with three of his former Kentucky teammates. He also coached the team through its first season and a half. In Satsuma, FL, undisclosed causes , March 17.

Mark Belanger, 54, baseball player. A shortstop for the Baltimore Orioles from 1965 to '81, Belanger was a mediocre hitter—with a career batting average of .228—but a first-rate fielder, winning the Gold Glove eight times, in 1969, 1971 and 1973–78. He believed that his quickness and range on the field came out of his skill at basketball, which in high school he thought he played better than baseball. He played one season with the Los Angeles Dodgers as a free agent in 1982, then retired from the game to work for the Major League Baseball Players Association. In New York, of cancer, October 6.

Aaron Brown, 53, football player. As a starting defensive end, Brown won Super Bowl IV in 1970 with the Kansas City Chiefs. The Chiefs drafted him out of the University of Minnesota in the first round in 1966, and he played with Kansas City through 1972 and with the Green Bay Packers in 1973 and '74. In Houston, of injuries from being struck by a car, November 15, 1997.

George Cafego, 82, football player and coach. Better known for coaching punters and kickers, George (Bad News) Cafego first made his mark in football as a two-time All-American tailback and safety at Tennessee in 1938 and in 1939, when the Volunteers shut out all of their regular-season opponents. He later coached tailbacks and defensive backs at Tennessee, Furman, Wyoming and Arkansas and worked with such kickers and punters as Fuad Reveiz and Craig Colquitt. After retiring in 1984 he consulted NFL teams on their kicking problems. He was inducted into the College Football Hall of Fame in 1969. In Knoxville, of natural causes, February 9.

Harry Caray, 77, broadcaster. Born Harry Christopher Carabina, Harry Caray grew up an orphan in St. Louis, where in 1945 he began his broadcasting career calling games for the Cardinals. In that first of 25 years with the Cardinals he often exclaimed, "Holy Cow!" in lieu of expressing himself more profanely; the expression later became the signature of Yankees broadcaster Phil Rizzuto. In Chicago, where he called games for the White Sox (from 1971–81) and the Cubs, his flamboyant persona took on mythic proportions. This would have been his 54th season, in which he anticipated working with Chip Caray, one of his 15 grandchildren. Caray was inducted into the baseball Hall of Fame in 1989.

SI's Leigh Montville writes:

"The time was five o'clock in the morning. The bars had closed in Chicago. There was no more beer. This seemed to be a great injustice.

"The two sportswriters from Boston and New York— O.K., I was the one from Boston—stepped onto Rush Street, resigned to their fate, ready for the sad walk back to their hotel. A small miracle occurred. Harry Caray appeared.

"Caray, the longtime Chicago Cubs announcer and Windy City baseball institution who died on February 18 at age 77 (or something reasonably close to it; Harry was always coy about his age), was surrounded by a group of 15, maybe 20 people who were acolytes, fans, hangers-on, bystanders. He moved down the street as if he were the Pope on a late-night mission to save late-night souls. He talked in that loud and emphatic way of his, and the acolytes talked back. There was a glow about the entire group.

" 'Harry,' said the New York sportswriter, 'is there any place where we can get another beer?'

" 'No problem,' Harry boomed. 'Follow me.'

"We became part of the group. People joined. People left. We were Harry's happy late-night congregation. Cabdrivers honked their horns at Harry, at us. People waved and shouted. Harry shouted back. We arrived at a bar on Rush, a few blocks from where we started. Harry rapped on the window. The place was obviously closed: waiters and waitresses mopping the floor, stools on top of the bar. The owner came to the window to see the source of the rapping. His face lit up like a Budweiser sign.

" 'Howyadoin'!' Harry shouted through the plate glass. 'Any chance of getting a beer here?'

"The owner's smile grew larger. He hurried with the locks. He motioned for a waitress to take some stools off the bar. He opened the door as if this were his first day of business. Harry pushed the two sportswriters inside.

" 'Have a good time,' Harry said. 'See you tomorrow.' And he left. With the acolytes. With the fans. With the excitement.

"The owner's smile disappeared. He took the two sportswriters to the bar, opened two beers and returned to work without saying a word. The two sportswriters drank their beers in silence as the waiters and waitresses continued to mop and the room filled with the smell of disinfectant. Five minutes later, beers unfinished, the sportswriters quietly left, nodding to the owner on the way out.

"The feeling was a bit like the feeling now—Harry Caray, dead on February 18. The night was not as much fun anymore. The brass band had moved along to someplace else."

In Rancho Mirage, CA, after heart malfunction, on February 18.

Al Ciraldo, 76, broadcaster. The voice of Georgia Tech football, Ciraldo made "toe meets leather," his trademark line before kickoffs. He began his broadcasting career in 1949 as a play-by-play announcer for University of Georgia basketball games. From 1954, when he called his first Georgia Tech football game, to 1993, Ciraldo broadcasted 416 football games and 1030 basketball games. After the 1992–93 season he hosted pre-game, halftime and post-game shows. In Atlanta, of complications from congestive heart failure, November 7, 1997.

Lisa Coole, 23, swimmer. The most decorated swimmer at the University of Georgia, Coole was a 19-time All-American and won two NCAA titles, in the 100-meter butterfly in 1996 and in the 200 freestyle relay in 1995. In 1997, her senior year, she was named NCAA Woman of the Year, and in January she received NCAA Today's Top VIII Award, an honor given to graduated seniors for their athletic, academic and leadership achievements. She had recently completed her first year in the College of Veterinary Medicine at the University of Illinois. In Champaign, IL, from injuries sustained in a car accident, May 16.

Roy Evans, 88, table tennis executive. As the president of the International Table Tennis Federation, Evans was instrumental in the "ping-pong diplomacy" between China and the United States. In Beijing in 1971, he met President Chou En-lai, who wanted China to reenter international table tennis competition. Following a suggestion by Evans, China invited several teams, including those of the United States, Britain, Canada, Colombia and Nigeria, to visit the country after that year's championships in Japan. On April 14, 1971, at a reception for the table tennis teams in the Great Hall of the People, Chou, referring to the relations between the United States and China, said, "These have been cut off for a long time. Now, with your acceptance of our invitation, you have opened a new page in the relations of the Chinese and American peoples." On the same day, President Nixon announced that trade and traveling restrictions between the two nations would be relaxed. Evans served as general secretary of the Table Tennis Federation from 1951 to '67, and then served as president for 20 years. In Cardiff, Wales, of natural causes, May 18.

Tim Flock, 73, auto racer. The NASCAR Winston Cup champion in 1952 and '55 and winner of 40 races, Flock was named one of the top 50 drivers of NASCAR's first 50 years. The youngest of a colorful trio of brothers, he drove with a monkey, Jocko Flocko, as a passenger in eight races in 1953. He was inducted into the International Motor Sports Hall of Fame in 1991. In Charlotte, NC, from liver and throat cancers, March 31.

Lawrence Gable, 48, basketball player. After he graduated from high school 31 years ago, Gable joined the Harlem Wizards, a Globetrotters-style basketball team that played against amateur teams at schools, at camps and for charity. He later left the team to earn an art degree at Morehouse College in Atlanta, but joined the team again six years ago. He also served as recreation coordinator for the Frederick Douglass Center–Children's AIDS Society in New York City. He collapsed during a performance at Dwight D. Eisenhower, an elementary school in Freehold, NJ. In Freehold, NJ, of a heart attack, June 8.

Pete Griffin, 81, football and track coach. As the track coach at Florida A&M, Griffin trained Bob Hayes, who won the 1964 Olympic title in the 100 with a world record–tying time of 10.0. Griffin played center on Florida A&M's undefeated and unscored-upon football team during the 1938 regular season. From 1944 to '70 Griffin worked as an assistant football coach as well as head track coach at Florida A&M. In 1970 he served as head coach of the football team, and in 1973 he returned as assistant coach until he retired in 1976. In Tallahassee, after a long illness, May 13.

Sam Hairston, 77, baseball player. Hairston, the first African American to play for the Chicago White Sox, spent 48 seasons with the organization as a player, coach and scout. He began his professional baseball career in 1945 as a catcher for the Cincinnati-Indianapolis Clowns of the Negro American League. In 1950 he won the league's Triple Crown, batting .424 with 71 RBIs and 17 home runs. He signed with the White Sox in 1950 and debuted with the team on July 21, 1951, in the first of only four games in the major leagues. He spent the last 12 seasons as a coach for the Birmingham Barons of the Southern League. In Birmingham, undisclosed causes, October 31, 1997.

Mary Fendrich Hulman, 93, auto racing chairwoman. After her husband, Indianapolis Motor Speedway owner Tony Hulman, died in 1977, Fendrich Hulman took over as the Speedway chairwoman of the board and for nearly 20 years gave the command, "Gentlemen, start your engines," at the Indianapolis 500. She gave the command for the last time at the NASCAR Brickyard 400 in 1996 and in 1997 relinquished the responsibility to her daughter, Mary Hulman George, the mother of Indy Racing League founder Tony George. Fendrich. In Indianapolis, of emphysema, April 10.

Anna May Hutchison, 73, pitcher. Hutchison began her pro baseball career with the Racine (WI) Belles of the All-American Girls' Baseball League in 1944 as a catcher, and in the next season became a pitcher for the team. In the 1946–47 season she mastered the side-arm delivery and won 53 games. After retiring from baseball she graduated from the University of Wisconsin-Parkside and taught elementary school. She appeared in the 1992 movie *A League of Their Own*, which celebrated the women who played in the short-lived women's pro baseball league. In Louisville, KY, of undisclosed causes, January 31.

Buddy Jeannette, 80, basketball player. Over the course of his 10-season professional career Harry Edward Jeannette played in three leagues: the National Basketball League, the American Basketball League and the Basketball Association of America, the forerunner of the NBA. He played on several championship-winning teams, including the Detroit Eagles, the Sheboygan (WI) Redskins and the Fort Wayne (IN) Pistons; and as a player-coach he led the Baltimore Bullets to the BAA title in 1947–48. He was inducted into the Hall of Fame in 1994. In Nashua, NH, of complications from a stroke, March 11.

Curtis Jones, 55, football coach. As University of Missouri defensive line coach, Jones and his son, Corby (now the starting quarterback for the Detroit Lions), helped lead the team to its first winning record (7–4) in 14 years. Jones began coaching at Missouri in 1993. In Columbia, MO, of a heart attack, July 26.

Florence Griffith Joyner, 38, sprinter. The fastest woman in the world, Griffith Joyner holds world records in the 100- and 200-meters which have stood for more than ten years. In 1988 in Seoul she won

Olympic gold in both of those events and won an additional gold medal in the 100-meter relay. She retired from racing in 1989.

SI's Tim Layden writes:

"Close your eyes and speak her stage name: Flo-Jo. An image forms in the mind. She's running impossibly fast, drawing clear from other in the race while wearing a uniform that's the child of Nike and Victoria's Secret. Her long nails rake the air in abrupt, efficient strokes, and her raven hair trails behind her. At the finish, an expressionless face suddenly beams. It's a picture of speed and beauty and joy, and, once witnessed, it's unforgettable.

"Florence Griffith Joyner was not alone among athletes in burning herself into the public memory. Jordan, Tiger, Big Mac. The list grows. But Flo-Jo was alone in her sport. When she died in her sleep early Monday morning of an apparent heart seizure at age 38, she left a legacy not just of decade-old world records but also of a personal and athletic style that mixed with a savvy business acumen to propel her far beyond the arena in which she compete. Track and field is fighting for survival precisely for the lack of electric stars like Flo-Jo, who even at the time of her death, 10 years past her prime, remained in possession of her milk mustache.

"In the summer of 1988 Griffith Joyner (who was married to triple jumper Al Joyner and was the sister-in-law of Jackie Joyner-Kersee) exploded from the workaday sprinter who had won the silver medal in the 200 meters at the boycott-thinned 1984 Olympics into the fastest woman in history. She ran the 100 in 10.49 seconds in a heat at that year's U.S. Olympic Trials, a world record that wasn't approached until this September, when Marion Jones ran 10.65. Flo-Jo won three gold medals at the '88 Games and set a world record of 21.34 in the 200. Jones, the second-fastest woman ever, ran 21.62 this year, still far off the mark. 'She was just on another level,' says '84 Olympic 100 champion Evelyn Ashford, who was second to Flo-Jo in '88.

"It wasn't simply the speed with which Flo-Jo rose to greatness that formed her legend but also the style. She wore one-legged unitards and lace attachments when other women were still wearing shorts. She wore makeup and grew spectacularly long nails. She melded athleticism and glamour like no other woman. Sprint coach and former U.S. Olympian John Smith saw Flo-Jo run in the spring of 1988 and was stunned by her progress and her appearance. 'Florence—we all called her Florence then—was always a hard worker and she had good form,' says Smith, 'but that year she had the outfits and the nails and hte name, and she was in the best shape of her life. Suddenly, she just had everything figured out. It was beautiful to watch.' ...

"Florence Griffith Joyner died young, leaving a seven-year-old daughter and a husband whose own mother died at 37. She ran fast and beautifully, and it's best now to remember only that, to let the whispers fall silent."

In Mission Viejo, CA, of an apparent heart attack, September 21.

Buck Leonard, 90, baseball player. Walter Fenner Leonard began his professional baseball career with the Rocky Mount (NC) Black Swans in 1925. From 1933 to '50 he played first base for the Brooklyn Royal Giants and the Homestead Grays of the Negro Leagues. A left-handed slugger, he and catcher Josh Gibson led the Grays to nine consecutive Negro League titles from 1937–45. Known as the Babe

Ruth and Lou Gehrig of black baseball, Gibson and Leonard batted 3–4, just as their major league counterparts did. In 1942 Washington Senators owner Clark Griffith considered signing Leonard, but failed to follow through; and after Jackie Robinson joined the major leagues in 1947, Cleveland Indians owner Bill Veeck approached Leonard about joining the team, but he declined, believing he was too old for the majors. He did, however, play five seasons in the Mexican Leagues until he finally retired from baseball, in 1955 at the age of 48. Leonard later worked to establish a museum in Kansas City to commemorate the Negro League. He was inducted into the Hall of Fame in 1972. In Rocky Mount, NC, of complications from a stroke suffered more than ten years ago, November 27, 1997.

Sid Luckman, 81, football player. Chicago Bears owner George Halas traded two players and a draft choice to Pittsburgh in 1939 to acquire Luckman, an All-American swing-wing tailback at Columbia. Halas offered Luckman $5,000, the highest salary paid by the Bears at that time, and then converted him into football's first nationally acclaimed T-formation quarterback.

SI's Paul Zimmerman writes:

"When Sid Luckman died … the last originator of the oldest offensive formation still in use was gone. The T with a man in motion was the brain work of a coaching triumvirate of George Halas, Clark Shaughnessy and Ralph Jones, and Luckman, a 22-year-old Chicago Bears rookie out of Columbia, was the man chosen to implement it on the field. That was in 1939, and the basic set remains.

" 'I'd been a single-wing tailback,' Luckman said when I visited him at his Fort Lauderdale suburban apartment in May. 'You're set deep, the ball comes to you, and you either pass, run or spin. When I came to the Bears, we worked for hours on my spinning, on hiding the ball, only this time it was as a T quarterback. They brought in the old Bears quarterback, Carl Brumbaugh, to work with me. We spent endless time just going over my footwork, faking, spinning, setting up as fast as I could, running to my left and throwing right, days and days of it.'

"Luckman seemed frail as we talked. All the charm that I remembered from the dozen or so times I had interviewed him through the years was there, but he'd occasionally stop to gather himself, to get things just right. Seated with him at a table heaped with charts and memorabilia and the scrapbooks of a lifetime in the game, I felt as if I were listening to Orville Wright describing the origins of the flying machine.

" 'Ralph Jones had coached the T with the Bears in the early 1930s,' Luckman said, 'but it was the old T, with everyone bunched in there. Shaughnessy was coaching at the University of Chicago, and they were about to drop football, so he spent a lot of time with us. I'd be up in Shaughnessy's room every night in training camp, going over every aspect of the thing. The whole idea was to spread the field and give the defense more area to cover.

" 'We had an 11 o'clock curfew, and Halas would drop by around 1 a.m. and say, "That's enough, Sid. Go to bed." '

"The system was still experimental in 1939, and Luckman was a backup tailback in the Bears' basic offense, the single wing. But on Oct. 22, with Chicago trailing the New York Giants 16–0 at the Polo Grounds, Halas told Luckman, 'Get in at quarterback and run the T.'

" 'Bob MacLeod, our right halfback, went in motion

and ran straight down the field on a stop-and-go,' Luckman said. 'I was so nervous I threw a duck, end over end. The defensive back had the interception, but MacLeod took the ball away from him and went all the way. Then I threw a little swing pass to Bob Swisher, and he shook a couple of tackles and went 60 yards for another score. We lost the game 16–13, and we used the T off and on for the rest of the season, but no one made a big thing about it.'

"The T explosion came one year later. While the Bears were using the formation to go 8–3 on the way to the NFL Championship Game, in which they would annihilate the Washington Redskins 73–0, Shaughnessy, who had moved on to coach Stanford, was dazzling the college world with the T. Stanford went 9–0, then beat Nebraska 21–13 in the Rose Bowl. The rush was on. 'I went back to Columbia to help Lou Little put in the T,' Luckman said. 'I went to Holy Cross, to Army when Red Blaik called me, to Notre Dame to work with Johnny Lujack and George Ratterman.'

"The Bears won four NFL titles in the 1940s, and other teams gradually switched to the new formation. Luckman, who in 10 games in 1943 threw 28 touchdown passes en route to winning league MVP honors, was the first T master, a gifted passer, long and short, a skilled faker and ball handler. He was there when it all began."

In North Miami Beach, Fla, of a heart attack, July 5.

Earl Manigault, 53, basketball player. Kareem Abdul-Jabbar called him "the best player his size in the history of New York City," but Earl (the Goat) Manigault never brought his talents to the national or professional ranks. In the 1960s, on the courts at 98th Street—which became known as "Goat Park"—he established his legend with such stunts as leaping to place a quarter on top of the backboard and reverse-dunking the ball 36 consecutive times to win a bet. While such dazzling moves made their way from the playground to the NBA, Manigault did not; crippled with a heroin addiction, he was released from a 1971 tryout with the ABA's Utah Stars and twice served time in prison. He later overcame his addiction and returned to Harlem as a community activist, working in a neighborhood recreation and counseling center for teens and coaching the Wadleigh High School basketball team, which won this year's city championship. In New York, of congestive heart failure, May 15.

Russ Meyer, 74, pitcher. Meyer's professional career began in 1942, and from 1946 to '59 he pitched in the majors with the Chicago Cubs, Philadelphia Phillies, Brooklyn Dodgers, Cincinnati Reds, Boston Red Sox and Kansas City Athletics. He pitched in three World Series, with the Phillies in 1950 and the Dodgers in 1953 and '55. He spent 12 years with the New York Yankees organization and in 1992 served as the team's bench coach. In Oglesby, IL, of congestive heart failure after a long illness, November 16, 1997.

Marshall Davis Miles, 92, boxing manager. Miles met and befriended Joe Louis when the heavyweight champion was a young fighter. Never a boxer himself, he took charge of Louis's career after the fighter's manager John Roxborough was imprisoned in 1946. The partnership lasted until Louis retired his title in 1949. In Buffalo, NY, after a long illness, December 4, 1997.

Glenn Montgomery, 31, football player. A defensive lineman for the Houston Oilers from 1989 to '95, Montgomery was diagnosed with the neuromuscular illness known as "Lou Gehrig's disease" in 1996, the same year he was traded from the Oilers to the Seattle Seahawks. In Dallas, from amyotrophic lateral sclerosis, June 28.

Helen Wills Moody, 92, tennis player. Moody's record eight Wimbledon singles titles stood for 52 years, until Martina Navratilova won her ninth in 1990. Although she never took a lesson, she won 31 titles from 1923 to '38. She also won an Olympic gold medal in Paris in 1924 and went 18–2 in Wightman Cup singles matches. She was inducted into the International Tennis Hall of Fame in 1959.

SI writes:

"Long before Martina Hingis astounded the tennis world with her precocity, there was Helen Wills Moody. Long before Steffi Graf overpowered opponents with a mighty forehand, there was Helen Wills Moody. Long before Billie Jean King, Chris Evert or Martina Navratilova dominated their sport with distinctive shotmaking and distinctive personalities, there was Helen Wills Moody. A giant of America's Golden Age of Sports, the female counterpart to Ruth, Dempsey and Grange, the woman known as Little Miss Poker Face and Queen Helen died on January 1 at a convalescent hospital in Carmel, Calif.

"Like many female tennis champions, Wills Moody was a progidy. Growing up in California, she learned the game by watching players at the Berkeley Tennis Club. At age 15, two years after she began playing, she won the girls' national 18-and-under title, and two years later she became the youngest U.S. women's singles champion. She never had a formal lesson and certainly never adopted the conditioning regimen of modern-day players. But from '23, when she won the first of her seven U.S. crowns, until '38, when she won the last of her eight Wimbledon titles, she was almost unbeatable, a force of nature, particularly from the forehand side, who rarely changed expressions or showed an opponent mercy. She once had a streak of 180 matches in elite competition during which she didn't lose a set. 'Her footwork didn't have to be great,' said tennis great Don Budge, 'because she controlled play by hitting the ball so hard.'

"Wills Moody had a certain icy elegance that predated Evert's. Generations of female players wore white eyeshades because Wills Moody did. She was an artist whose drawings and paintings were exhibited in the U.S. and abroad and, as Navratilova later did, she wrote a mystery novel, *Death Serves an Ace*.

"After her retirement Wills Moody stayed out of the headlines, surfacing only occasionally to reveal that she had remained a fan of tennis and had a special fondness for Navratilova, whose ninth Wimbledon singles title in 1990 broke Wills Moody's record. But Wills Moody's Garbo-like mystique was not the reason she will remain an almost mythic sports figure—for that, credit her extraordinary tennis game."

In Carmel, CA, of natural causes, January 1.

Francis T. Murray, 82, football player. An All-American in football and basketball at the University of Pennsylvania, Francis (Franny) Murray also played two seasons with the Philadelphia Eagles. He later served as Pennsylvania's athletic director. He was the last surviving member of the Quakers' "Destiny Backfield," which also featured Lew Elverson, Bill Kurlish and Eddie Warwick. In 1936 he averaged 67 yards per punt, including an 80-yarder. In a win over Michigan that year, Murray called the signals, blocked and punted, dropping the ball inside the Wolverines' 12-yard line six times. He also scored two touchdowns,

passed for one, kicked three extra points and intercepted four passes in the 27–7 victory. In Boca Raton, FL, of complications from a stroke he suffered four years ago, June 28.

Jim Murray, 78, sportswriter. After writing for *Time* from 1948 to '59 and *Sports Illustrated* from 1953 to '61, Murray joined the staff of the *Los Angeles Times* in 1961. Rich with humor and insight, his columns, which appeared three times a week on the front page of the sports section, transformed the art of sportswriting. He was one of only four sportswriters to win the Pulitzer.

SI 's Rick Reilly writes:

"I once asked Jim Murray if he kept a few extra columns in the bank for days when he had the flu or a tee time or an incurably blank computer screen. 'Of course not! he yowled. 'What if I die one ahead?'

"On Sunday, August 16, Jim Murray, the greatest sportswriter who ever lived, kissed his gorgeous wife, started to put on his pajamas, said, 'Linda, something's wrong,' and collapsed. The doctor was there in five minutes, but it was too late. Jim had died of a heart attack. He was 78.

"He got his wish, though. He didn't have any columns saved up. Too bad. We could use a few laughs right now.

"Murray on huge Boog Powell: 'They're going to make an umbrella stand out of his foot.'

"On how they ought to begin the Indianapolis 500: 'Gentlemen, start your coffins.'

"On baseball: 'Willie Mays's glove is where triples go to die.'

"On Roger Staubach: 'Square as a piece of fudge.'

"On Elgin Baylor: 'Unstoppable as a woman's tears.'

"Murray could write anything; sports just happened to get lucky.... He wrote the nation's best sports column for 37 delicious years at the *Los Angeles Times*, but, come to think of it, the column was about sports sort of the way *Citizen Kane* was about sleds....

"Murray never went on *The Sports Reporters*, never had his own radio show, never even liked his picture to be in the paper. But he had more impact than any sportswriter since Grantland Rice. The 10-shot cut rule in golf was Murray's idea. It was Murray who shamed the Masters into finally allowing Lee Elder to play, in 1975. ('Wouldn't it be nice to have a black American at Augusta in something other than a coverall?' Murray wrote.)

"One time, at a U.S. Open, Arnold Palmer found himself in a ditch. He was trying to figure out what shot to play when he looked up and saw Murray. 'What would Hogan do in a situation like this?' Palmer asked. Murray looked down and said, 'Hogan wouldn't *be* in a situation like that.'

"It wasn't all laughs, yet through the heartache, illness and sorrow, Murray wrote on. His son Ricky died of a drug overdose, and Jim blamed himself in part. The love of his youth—his first wife, Gerry—died of cancer 14 years ago, and I thought Jim would never turn the lights up in his house again, until Linda came along. His eyes had this annoying habit of going out on him. He dictated the column blind for six months and was still better than anybody in the country.

"America tried to tell him. He won a Pulitzer. He's in the Baseball Hall of Fame. He was named National Sportswriter of the Year for 12 straight years, 14 in all. There was a little dinner honoring him a few years back. Nothing special. Kirk Douglas showed up. Dinah Shore. Barron Hilton. Some couple came in to hand Murray the Richstone Man of the Year community service award: President and Mrs. Reagan. Yet Murray was so humble that when you left him—even if you were the third-string volleyball writer in Modesto—you couldn't remember which of you was the legend.

"Finest man I ever knew.

"Lately, I was waiting for Jim to retire and hoping like hell he wouldn't. 'Writing a column is like riding a tiger,' he used to say. 'You'd like to get off, but you have no idea how.'

"Rotten luck. He finally found a way."

In Brentwood, CA, of a heart attack, August 16.

Ray Nitschke, 61, football player. With the Green Bay Packers from 1958 to '72, Nitschke set the standard of toughness at his position, middle linebacker. He was recently named the fourth-best player in the team's history, behind receiver Don Hutson, current quarterback Brett Favre and former quarterback Bart Starr, who played with Nitschke on Vince Lombardi's NFL title– and Super Bowl–winning teams. Nitschke made his home in Green Bay and after retiring often attended Packers practices and road games. He was inducted into the Hall of Fame in 1978.

SI 's Paul Zimmerman writes:

"The NFL of the 1960s seemed peopled by mythic and muddy behemoths, most formidable among them its middle linebackers, who were tough enough to jam the straight-ahead run and agile enough to range from sideline to sideline. Their names were Ray Nitschke, Dick Butkus, Chuck Bednarik, Joe Schmidt and Tommy Nobis. The best of them, some said, was the Green Bay Packers' Nitschke, who died of a heart attack on March 8 at age 61.

"Balding, almost toothless, playing in a seemingly perpetual rage, Nitschke would have been a caricature of the maniacal middleman except for how well he performed from 1958 until '72. He ran the defense for all of Vince Lombardi's five championship teams. If the power sweep epitomized the Packers' offense, it was Nitschke's traffic-cop command and surprising athleticism—he had 25 interceptions in his 15 seasons—that defined their take-no-prisoners defense.

"After his retirement, Nitschke made his home in (where else?) Green Bay. But he did have a part-time career as a celebrity pitchman, his tough-guy looks and gentle demeanor offering a combination irresistible to Madison Avenue. What the general public never saw was his annual performance at the Pro Football Hall of Fame, where Nitschke spoke of the game he loved. The stage was the annual preinduction luncheon, where all the members (Nitschke made the Hall in 1978) are invited to deliver a short speech. Nitschke would get to his feet almost painfully—he moved in a kind of rolling, limping walk from the years of wear and tear on his knees—adjust his glasses and, in a deep rumble, impart his feelings about the fame that had taken this third-round draft pick from Illinois to the top of the sports world. When it was over, more than a few listeners were left staring at their plates, moved by the emotion shown by this hard, and soft, man."

In Venice, FL, of a heart attack, March 8.

Harry Ornest, 75, owner. Ornest owned the St. Louis Blues from 1983 to '86 and the Toronto Argonauts of the Canadian Football League from 1988 to '91. He also founded the Class AAA minor league baseball team, the Vancouver Canadians, in 1978; and, as its largest shareholder, he served as the deputy managing director of the Hollywood Park racetrack. In Los Angeles, after a brief illness, July 21.

Willie Pastrano, 62, boxer. Willie (the Wisp) Pastrano fought 77 times before he won the light-heavyweight title from Harold Johnson in 1963 and lost the title two years later to Jose Torres. He retired with a record of 63-13-8, with 14 knockouts. As an amateur, Muhammad Ali learned from Pastrano how to dance in the ring. Ali admired Pastrano's footwork so much, in fact, that he once waited two hours to spar with him in Louisville. In New Orleans, from liver cancer, December 6.

Gabe Paul Sr., 88, baseball executive. Paul helped to put together pennant-winning teams for the Cincinnati Reds and the New York Yankees and twice won executive-of-the-year awards. From 1951 to '61 he served as vice president and general manager of the Reds. The Reds won the National League pennant in 1961 and lost to the Yankees in the World Series, but by that time Paul had joined the Cleveland Indians organization. In 1973 he joined the Yankees as president of the organization, and in 1976 the Yankees took the American League pennant—to lose to the Reds in the World Series. After the Yankees won the World Series in the following year Paul returned to the Indians. In Tampa, FL, after a long illness, April 26.

Elijah Pitts, 60, football player and coach. A running back, Pitts played for the Green Bay Packers from 1961 to '69 and again in '71. In the Packers' Super Bowl I victory over the Kansas City Chiefs he scored two touchdowns. After he retired from playing, he became an assistant coach for the Los Angeles Rams, the Buffalo Bills and the Houston Oilers and the Hamilton Tiger-Cats of the Canadian Football League from 1974 to '84. In 1992 he became the assistant head coach of the Bills, with whom he returned to the Super Bowl four times. He was on medical leave from the Bills since he was diagnosed with cancer in October 1997. In Buffalo, NY, of abdominal cancer, July 10.

Dan Quisenberry, 45, pitcher. With his submarine pitching style, Quisenberry helped the Kansas City Royals win two American League pennants and the 1985 World Series. In 12 seasons with the Royals, St. Louis Cardinals and San Francisco Giants, he went 56–46 with a 2.76 ERA and 244 saves. He led the American League in saves five times, and with 45 in 1983 set a major league record. In Leawood, KS, of a brain tumor, September 30.

Joe Shear, 54, auto racer. As a 13-year-old Shear built his first racing car, and through his career he won more than 350 stock-car races. Although he was diagnosed with cancer in January 1995, he continued to compete, winning 17 of his final 46 races. In his last race, the Winston Short Track Nationals in Rockford, IL, he lost both front fenders but won the title. In Beloit, WI, of cancer, March 9.

Rankin M. Smith, 72, owner. Smith founded the Atlanta Falcons in 1965 and led the drive to build the Georgia Dome, which hosted Super Bowl XXVIII and will do so again in 2000. In Atlanta, of heart failure, October 25, 1997.

Woody Stephens, 84, horse trainer. Despite his dependency on an oxygen tank after he had heart bypass surgery in 1990, Stephens continued to train horses until September of last year. In his 61 years of training horses he won the Kentucky Derby twice (with Cannonade in 1974 and Swale in 1984), the Preakness (with Blue Man in 1952) and the Belmont Stakes an unmatched five consecutive times. He began his career in thoroughbred racing as a 13-year-old, breaking in yearlings, but by his late teens had to abandon competitive riding because he had grown too large. Although he was inducted into the Hall of Fame in 1976 and won the 1983 Eclipse Award as trainer of the year, he always regretted that he could not have been more successful as a jockey.

SI 's William Nack writes:

"The stately old pleasure dome on Long Island had never witnessed a spectacle quite like it. Moments after an 8–1 shot named Danzig Connection swept to victory in the 1986 Belmont Stakes, the colt's 72-year-old trainer, Woody Stephens, floated, on mounting waves of sound, toward the winner's circle at Belmont Park. Stephens had just won an unprecedented fifth straight Belmont, and as he made his way past the blue bloods in the box seats, you could hear the tribute building among the blue collars in the grandstand below, a murmur and then a chant rising louder and louder: 'Wood-*dee!* Wood-*dee!*' Of all the cherished memories from more than 30 years at Belmont, my warmest is of that June afternoon, of the inimitable Woody moving with that swagger through the crowds. Woodford Cefis Stephens had earned the ultimate benediction—the unequivocal adulation of the New York player.

"Stephens, 84, died on August 22 of complications stemming from chronic emphysema, and horse racing thus lost one of its most beloved and colorful characters. After leaving a hard-scrabble boyhood in the hills of eastern Kentucky, he rose to become one of America's preeminent horsemen, an artful raconteur, horse whisperer and Hall of Famer who spun tales of his life as magically as he conditioned horses to run hard and long. He trained two Kentucky Derby winners, Cannonade (1974) and Swale ('84), and some of the finest horses ever to race in the U.S.: Traffic Judge, Bald Eagle, Never Bend, Smart Angle, Conquistador Cielo and Devil's Bag among them.

"Eleven years after his triumphant moment, Woody was back at Belmont for the 1997 Stakes, holding court in the stable area, sniffing oxygen from a tank, paying the price for a lifetime of unfiltered cigarettes. But he was still crowing. 'That record will stand long after I've said good night,' he said. Right again. Good night, Woody. And thanks."

In Miami Lakes, Fla., of complications from chronic emphysema, August 22.

Elmer Valo, 78, baseball player. An outfielder who played for eight teams in 20 seasons (1940–43, '46–61) in the major leagues, Valo once memorably crashed through the right-field wall and into the seats to prevent a Yogi Berra home run. In later years he scouted for the Philadelphia Phillies and worked as a spring training instructor. In Palmerton, PA, after a stroke, July 19.

Doak Walker, 71, football player. Walker played running back, wide receiver, quarterback and defensive back at Southern Methodist, where he was a three-time All-American and the school's only Heisman Trophy winner. In a 1947 game against Texas Christian, with the Mustangs trailing 19–13 with 1:40 to play, Walker returned a kickoff 75 yards to set up his touchdown reception that preserved SMU's undefeated season. In six seasons in the NFL with the Lions, Walker was All-Pro four times and helped Detroit win two NFL championships. In the 1953 NFL Championship game, Walker scored a touchdown and kicked one field goal and two extra points in the Lions' 17–16 victory over the Cleveland Browns. He was

elected to both College and Pro Football Halls of Fame, and an award that bears his name honors the nation's top college running back. In Steamboat Springs, CO, of complications from paralysis suffered during a January skiing accident, September 27.

Todd Witsken, 34, tennis player. A doubles specialist, Witsken won 11 doubles titles, including the 1988 Italian Open and 1989 Stockholm Open. He never won a singles title, but notably defeated Jimmy Connors in the third round of the 1986 U.S. Open. He served as the director of the Indianapolis Tennis Center after he retired from the ATP Tour in 1993. In Zionsville, IN, of brain cancer, May 25.

John Wyatt Jr., 63, pitcher. Wyatt began his pitching career in the Negro Leagues, then in 1961 joined the Kansas City Athletics. He also played for the Boston Red Sox, for whom he pitched a win against St. Louis in the sixth game of the 1967 World Series. He ended his major league career in 1969 with the Athletics, by then in Oakland. In Omaha, of a heart attack, April 6.

1999 Major Events

JANUARY

Major College Bowl Games	Jan. 1 & 2
NFL Wild Card Weekend	Jan. 2 & 3
Fiesta Bowl/National Championship	Jan 4
NFL Divisional Playoffs	Jan. 9 & 10
NFL Conference Championships	Jan. 17
Australian Open	Jan. 18–25
NHL All-Star Game	Jan. 24
Super Bowl XXXIII	Jan. 31

FEBRUARY

Millrose Games	Feb. 5
AFC-NFC Pro Bowl	Feb. 7
NBA All-Star Game	Feb. 7
U.S. Figure Skating Championships	Feb. 7–14
Daytona 500	Feb. 14
PBA National Championship	Feb 21–27

MARCH

World Indoor Track and Field Champ.	March 5–7
Major League Soccer Season Begins	March 20
World Figure Skating Championships	March 21–28
The Players Championship	March 25–28
NCAA Final Four	March 27–29

APRIL

Baseball Opening Day	April 5
Masters Tournament	April 8–11
Boston Marathon	April 19
Stanley Cup Playoffs Begin	April 21

MAY

Kentucky Derby	May 1
Preakness	May 15
French Open Tennis	May 24–30
Indianapolis 500	May 30

JUNE

NBA Finals Begin	June 2
Belmont Stakes	June 5
U.S. Open Golf	June 17–20
Stanley Cup Finals Begin	June 19
Women's World Cup	June 21
Wimbeldon Tennis	June 21–27

JULY

Baseball All-Star Game	July 13
British Open Golf	July 15–18
Pan American Games	July 24–30

AUGUST

PGA Championship	Aug. 12–15
World Track and Field Championships	Aug. 20–29
College Football Season Begins	Aug. 28
U.S. Open Tennis	Aug. 30–Sept. 5

SEPTEMBER

NFL Season Begins	Sept. 12

OCTOBER

NHL Season Begins	Oct. 7
World Series	Oct. 16
MLS Cup '99	Oct. 24

NOVEMBER

NBA Regular Season Begins	Nov. 2
Breeders' Cup	Nov. 6
New York Marathon	Nov. 7
Chase Championships	Nov. 15–21
ATP World Tour Championships	Nov. 15–21

DECEMBER

Heisman Trophy Presentation	Dec. 11
Major College Bowl Games Begin	Dec. 18